Handbook of International Documentation and Information

Volume 13

World Guide
to
Scientific Associations
and
Learned Societies

7th Edition

K·G·Saur München 1998

Editor / Redaktion:

Michael Zils

Adresse:
K.G. Saur Verlag, Luppenstraße 1b, D-04177 Leipzig
Tel. +49 341 4869911, Fax +49 341 4869913

Die Deutsche Bibliothek – CIP-Einheitsaufnahme

World guide to scientific associations and learned societies /
[ed.: Michael Zils]. – 7. ed. – München : Saur, 1998
(Handbook of international documentation and information ; Vol. 13)
ISBN 3–598–20581–3

Printed on acid-free paper

Data preparation and automatic data processing
by Microcomposition, München

Printed and Bound: Strauss Offsetdruck, Mörlenbach

ISBN 3–598–20581–3
ISSN 0939–1959

Foreword

The new seventh edition of the «World Guide to Scientific Associations and Learned Societies» provides description of some 17,100 associations and societies from the fields of science, culture and technology.

The work is arranged alphabetically by name within an A – Z of countries (following English spelling). The seventh edition also contains an Alphabetical Index of Association Names, a Subject Index, and a Publications Index. The manuscript was revised with the help of an internationally sent questionnaire, as well as a wide range of national and international source works. Besides corrections and deletions, the new edition also lists more than 1,400 new associations and societies.

Each entry contains the following information (as far as data was available): association name, address, telephone, telefax, year of foundation, number of members, president, general secretary, area of activity and details on periodical publications. The editorial deadline was the 31st October 1997. New entries and amendments which reached us after this date could unfortunately not be included in the seventh edition.

The use of electronic media in the production of the work means that we are able to offer address collections for all subject groups. Please contact us if you are interested in this offer.

We would like to thank all associations and societies for their friendly cooperation. Please let us know of any necessary amendments of further societies which should be included in the World Guide to Scientific Associations and Learned Societies. Your information helps to improve still further upon the accuracy and reliability of this reference work.

November 1997   The Editorial

Vorwort

Die vorliegende 7. Ausgabe des «Internationalen Verzeichnisses wissenschaftlicher Verbände und Gesellschaften» enthält ca. 17.100 Verbände und Gesellschaften aus den Bereichen Wissenschaft, Kultur und Technik.

Das Werk ist nach dem englischen Länderalphabet und innerhalb der Länder namensalphabetisch geordnet. Außerdem enthält die 7. Ausgabe ein alphabetisches Verzeichnis aller Verbandsnamen, ein Register nach Fachgebieten und ein Register der periodischen Publikationen. Die Manuskript-Bearbeitung erfolgte anhand eines weltweiten Fragebogenversands sowie zahlreicher internationaler und nationaler Quellenwerke. Außer den daraus resultierenden Korrekturen und Löschungen wurden mehr als 1.400 neue Verbände und Gesellschaften erstmals aufgenommen.

Die Einzeleinträge enthalten – sofern bekannt – folgende Detailinformation: Verbandsname, Adresse, Telefon, Telefax, Gründungsjahr, Mitgliederzahl, Präsident, Generalsekretär, Tätigkeitsgebiete und periodische Publikationen mit Hinweisen auf die Erscheinungsweise. Redaktionsschluß war der 31. Oktober 1997. Neueintragungen und Änderungen, die uns nach diesem Datum erreichten, konnten für die vorliegende 7. Ausgabe leider nicht mehr berücksichtigt werden.

Die elektronische Speicherung der Daten ermöglicht es uns, Adressenkollektionen aller Fachgruppen anzubieten. Bei Interesse bitten wir um Ihre Kontaktaufnahme.

Wir danken allen Verbänden und Gesellschaften für Ihre freundliche Unterstützung unserer redaktionellen Arbeit. Bitte machen Sie uns auf Fehler oder fehlende Verbände aufmerksam. Ihre entsprechenden Hinweise tragen dazu bei, die Genauigkeit und Zuverlässigkeit dieses Nachschlagewerks noch zu erhöhen.

November 1997   Die Redaktion

Contents

Inhaltsverzeichnis

Contents / Inhaltsverzeichnis

Contents / Inhaltsverzeichnis

Contents / Inhaltsverzeichnis

INDEX

REGISTER

Areas of Specialization Abbreviations

Acoustics	Acoustics	Ecology	Ecology
Adult Educ	Adult Education	Econ	Economics
Advert	Advertising	Educ	Education
Aero	Aeronautics, Aviation, Space Technology	Educ Handic	Education of the Handicapped
Agri	Agriculture	Electric Eng	Electrical Engineering
Air Cond	Air Conditioning	Electrochem	Electrochemistry
Anat	Anatomy	Electronic Eng	Electronic Engineering
Anesthetics	Anesthetics	Endocrinology	Endocrinology
Animal Husb	Animal Husbandry	Energy	Energy
Anthro	Anthropology	Eng	Engineering
Antique	Antiquities	Entomology	Entomology
Archeol	Archeology	Ethnology	Ethnology
Archit	Architecture	Family Plan	Family Planning
Archives	Archives	Finance	Finance
Arts	Arts	Fine Arts	Fine Arts
Astronomy	Astronomy	Fisheries	Fisheries
Astrophys	Astrophysics	Folklore	Folklore
Auto Eng	Automotive Engineering	Food	Food
Behav Sci	Behavioral Sciences	Forensic Med	Forensic Medicine
Bio	Biology	Forestry	Forestry
Biochem	Biochemistry	Futurology	Futurology
Biophys	Biophysics	Gastroenter	Gastroenterology
Botany	Botany	Genealogy	Genealogy, Heraldry
Botany, Specific	Botany, Specific	Genetics	Genetics
Business Admin	Business Administration, Management	Geography	Geography
		Geology	Geology
Cardiol	Cardiology	Geomorph	Geomorphology
Cart	Cartography	Geophys	Geophysics
Cell Biol & Cancer Res	Cell Biology, Cancer Research	Geriatrics	Geriatrics
		Graphic & Dec Arts, Design	Graphic and Decorative Arts, Design
Chem	Chemistry		
Cinema	Cinematography	Graphology	Graphology
Civil Eng	Civil Engineering	Gynecology	Gynecology
Coffee, Tea, Cocoa	Coffee, Tea, Cocoa	Hematology	Hematology
Comm	Communications	Hist	History
Comm Sci	Communication Science	Home Econ	Home Economics
Commerce	Commerce	Homeopathy	Homeopathy
Computer & Info Sci	Computer and Information Science, Data Processing	Hort	Horticulture
		Humanities	Humanities, general
		Hydrology	Hydrology
Criminology	Criminology	Hygiene	Hygiene
Crop Husb	Crop Husbandry	Immunology	Immunology
Cultur Hist	Cultural History, History of Civilization	Insurance	Insurance
		Intern Med	Internal Medicine
Cybernetics	Cybernetics	Int'l Relat	International Relations
Dairy Sci	Dairy Science	Journalism	Journalism
Dent	Dentistry	Law	Law
Depth Psych	Depth Psychology	Libraries & Bk Sci	Librarianship and Book Science
Derm	Dermatology		
Develop Areas	Developing Areas	Ling	Linguistics
Diabetes	Diabetes	Lit	Literature
Doc	Documentation	Logic	Logic

Logopedy	Logopedy	Prom Peace	Promotion of Peace
Mach Eng	Machine Engineering	Psych	Psychology
Marketing	Marketing	Psychiatry	Psychiatry
Mass Media	Mass Media	Psychoan	Psychoanalysis
Materials Sci	Materials Science	Public Admin	Public Administration
Math	Mathematics	Public Health	Public Health
Med	Medicine	Pulmon Dis	Pulmonary Disease
Metallurgy	Metallurgy	Radiology	Radiology
Microbio	Microbiology	Rehabil	Rehabilitation
Military Sci	Military Science	Rel & Theol	Religions and Theology
Mineralogy	Mineralogy	Rheuma	Rheumatology
Mining	Mining	Safety	Safety and Protection,
Music	Musicology		Safety Engineering
Nat Res	Natural Resources	Sci	Science, general
Nat Sci	Natural Sciences, general	Soc Sci	Social Sciences
Navig	Navigation	Socialism	Socialism
Neurology	Neurology	Sociology	Sociology
Nucl Med	Nuclear Medicine	Speleology	Speleology
Nucl Res	Nuclear Research	Sports	Sports
Numismatics	Numismatics	Standards	Standardization
Nutrition	Nutrition	Stats	Statistics
Oceanography	Oceanography, Marine	Stomatology	Stomatology
	Sciences	Surgery	Surgery
Ophthal	Ophthalmology	Surveying	Surveying, Photogram-
Optics	Optics		metry
Ornithology	Ornithology	Textiles	Textiles
Orthopedics	Orthopedics	Therapeutics	Therapeutics
Otorhinolaryngology	Otorhinolaryngology	Tobacco	Tobacco
Paleontology	Paleontology	Toxicology	Toxicology
Parapsych	Parapsychology	Transport	Transport and Traffic
Pathology	Pathology	Traumatology	Traumatology
Pediatrics	Pediatrics	Travel	Travel and Tourism
Perf Arts	Performing Arts, Theater	Trop Med	Tropical Medicine
Petrochem	Petrochemistry	Urban Plan	Urban and Regional
Pharmacol	Pharmacology		Planning
Philos	Philosophy	Urology	Urology
Photo	Photography	Venereology	Venereology
Physical Therapy	Physical Therapy	Vet Med	Veterinary Medicine
Physics	Physics	Water Res	Water Resources
Physiology	Physiology	Wines	Wines and Wine Making
Poli Sci	Political Science	X-Ray Tech	X-Ray Technology
Preserv Hist	Preservation of Historical	Zoology	Zoology
Monuments	Monuments, Restoration		

Abkürzungsverzeichnis der Fachgebiete

Acoustics	Akustik	Econ	Wirtschaft
Adult Educ	Erwachsenenbildung	Educ	Erziehung und Ausbildung
Advert	Werbung	Educ Handic	Behindertenpädagogik
Aero	Luftfahrt, Raumfahrt-	Electric Eng	Elektrotechnik
	technik	Electrochem	Elektrochemie
Agri	Landwirtschaft	Electronic Eng	Elektronik
Air Cond	Klimatechnik	Endocrinology	Endokrinologie
Anat	Anatomie	Energy	Energiewesen
Anesthetics	Anästhesiologie	Eng	Ingenieurwesen
Animal Husb	Tierzüchtung	Entomology	Insektenkunde
Anthro	Anthropologie	Ethnology	Völkerkunde
Antique	Antiquitäten	Family Plan	Familienplanung
Archeol	Archäologie	Finance	Finanzen
Archit	Architektur	Fine Arts	Malerei, Bildhauerei
Archives	Archivwesen	Fisheries	Fischerei
Arts	Kunst	Folklore	Volkskunde
Astronomy	Astronomie	Food	Nahrungsmittel
Astrophys	Astrophysik	Forensic Med	Gerichtsmedizin
Auto Eng	Kraftfahrzeugbau	Forestry	Forstwirtschaft
Behav Sci	Verhaltensforschung	Futurology	Futurologie
Bio	Biologie	Gastroenter	Gastroenterologie
Biochem	Biochemie	Genealogy	Genealogie, Heraldik
Biophys	Biophysik	Genetics	Genetik
Botany	Botanik	Geography	Geographie
Botany, Specific	Botanik, Systematische	Geology	Geologie
Business Admin	Unternehmensführung,	Geomorph	Geomorphologie
	Betriebswirtschaft	Geophys	Geophysik
Cardiol	Kardiologie	Geriatrics	Geriatrie
Cart	Kartographie	Graphic & Dec Arts,	Graphische und
Cell Biol & Cancer	Zellbiologie, Krebsfor-	Design	Dekorative Künste,
Res	schung		Design
Chem	Chemie	Graphology	Graphologie
Cinema	Filmkunst	Gynecology	Gynäkologie
Civil Eng	Bautechnik	Hematology	Hämatologie
Coffee, Tea, Cocoa	Kaffee, Tee, Kakao	Hist	Geschichte
Comm	Nachrichtentechnik	Home Econ	Hauswirtschaft
Comm Sci	Kommunikationswissen-	Homeopathy	Homöopathie
	schaft	Hort	Gartenbau
Commerce	Handel	Humanities	Geisteswissenschaften,
Computer & Info	Informatik, Datenverarbei-		allgemeine
Sci	tung	Hydrology	Hydrologie
Criminology	Kriminologie	Hygiene	Hygiene
Crop Husb	Nutzpflanzenzüchtung	Immunology	Immunologie
Cultur Hist	Kulturgeschichte	Insurance	Versicherung
Cybernetics	Kybernetik	Intern Med	Innere Medizin
Dairy Sci	Milchwirtschaft	Int'l Relat	Internationale
Dent	Zahnheilkunde		Beziehungen
Depth Psych	Tiefenpsychologie	Journalism	Publizistik
Derm	Dermatologie	Law	Recht
Develop Areas	Entwicklungshilfe	Libraries & Bk Sci	Bibliotheks- und
Diabetes	Diabetes		Buchwesen
Doc	Dokumentation	Ling	Linguistik
Ecology	Ökologie	Lit	Literatur

Logic	Logik	Prom Peace	Friedensforschung
Logopedy	Logopädie	Psych	Psychologie
Mach Eng	Maschinenbau	Psychiatry	Psychiatrie
Marketing	Marktforschung	Psychoan	Psychoanalyse
Mass Media	Massenmedien	Public Admin	Verwaltung
Materials Sci	Werkstoffkunde	Public Health	Gesundheitswesen
Math	Mathematik	Pulmon Dis	Pulmologie
Med	Medizin	Radiology	Radiologie
Metallurgy	Metallurgie	Rehabil	Rehabilitation
Microbio	Mikrobiologie	Rel & Theol	Religionsphilosophie,
Military Sci	Militärwissenschaft		Theologie
Mineralogy	Mineralogie	Rheuma	Rheumatologie
Mining	Bergbau	Safety	Unfallverhütung,
Music	Musikwissenschaft		Sicherheitstechnik
Nat Res	Rohstoffe	Sci	Wissenschaft, allgemeine
Nat Sci	Naturwissenschaften,	Soc Sci	Sozialwissenschaften
	allgemeine	Socialism	Sozialismus
Navig	Navigation	Sociology	Soziologie
Neurology	Neurologie	Speleology	Höhlenkunde
Nucl Med	Nuklearmedizin	Sports	Sport
Nucl Res	Kernforschung	Standards	Normung
Numismatics	Numismatik	Stats	Statistik
Nutrition	Ernährung	Stomatology	Stomatologie
Oceanography	Meereskunde	Surgery	Chirurgie
Ophthal	Augenheilkunde	Surveying	Landvermessung,
Optics	Optik		Photogrammetrie
Ornithology	Ornithologie	Textiles	Textilien
Orthopedics	Orthopädie	Therapeutics	Therapeutik
Otorhinolaryngology	Hals-Nasen-	Tobacco	Tabak
	Ohrenheilkunde	Toxicology	Toxikologie
Paleontology	Paläontologie	Transport	Verkehrswesen
Parapsych	Parapsychologie	Traumatology	Traumatologie
Pathology	Pathologie	Travel	Reisen und Tourismus
Pediatrics	Pädiatrie	Trop Med	Tropenmedizin
Perf Arts	Darstellende Künste,	Urban Plan	Stadt- und Regional-
	Theater		planung
Petrochem	Petrochemie	Urology	Urologie
Pharmacol	Pharmakologie	Venereology	Venerologie
Philos	Philosophie	Vet Med	Veterinärmedizin
Photo	Photographie	Water Res	Wasserversorung
Physical Therapy	Physiotherapie	Wines	Wein und Weinbau
Physics	Physik	X-Ray Tech	Roentgenologie
Physiology	Physiologie	Zoology	Zoologie
Poli Sci	Politologie		
Preserv Hist	Denkmalschutz,		
Monuments	Restaurierung		

World Guide
to Scientific Associations
and Learned Societies

Internationales Verzeichnis
wissenschaftlicher Verbände
und Gesellschaften

Afghanistan

Afghanistan Academy of Sciences, Sher Alikhan St, Kabul
T: (93) 20350
Founded: 1979
Focus: Sci
Periodical
Pashtu Quarterly (quarterly) 00001

Albania

Academy of Sciences, Rruga Myslym Shyri 7, Tirana
T: (042) 6049
Founded: 1972; Members: 29
Pres: Shaban Demiraj; Gen Secr: Emin Riza
Focus: Sci
Periodicals
Ceshtje te folklorit shqiptar: Problems of the Albanian Folklore (irregularly)
Ceshtje te gramatikes se shqipes se sotme: Problems of the Grammar of the Modern Albanian (irregularly)
Dialektologjia Shqiptare: Albanian Dialectology (irregularly)
Ethnographie Albanaise (irregularly)
Etnografia Shqiptare (irregularly)
Gjuha jone (quarterly)
Iliria: Illyria (semi-annually)
Informatika dhe Matematika Llogaritese: Informatics and Computer Nathematics (irregularly)
Kerkime dhe Studime Hidraulike: Hydraulic Studies (irregularly)
Kultura Popullore: Folk Culture (semi-annually)
Punime te Institutit te Fizikes Berthamore: Studies of the Institute of Nuclear Physics (irregularly)
Studia Albanica (semi-annually)
Studime Filologjike: Philological Studies (quarterly)
Studime Gjeografike: Geographic Studies (irregularly)
Studime Historike: Historical Studies (quarterly)
Studime Meteorologjike e Hidrologjike: Meteorological and Hydrological Studies (irregularly)
Studime per Letersine Shqiptare: Studies on Albanian Literature (irregularly)
Vjetar i Punimeve Shkencore te Qendres se Kerkimeve Biologjike: Yearbook of the Biological Research Centre (irregularly) 00002

Lidhja e Shkrimtareve dhe e Artisteve te Shqiperise, Z. Baboci 37, Tirana
Founded: 1957; Members: 1750
Pres: Dritero Agolli
Focus: Lit
Periodicals
Drita: Journal (weekly)
Les Lettres Albanaises (quarterly) . . . 00003

PEN Centre of Albania, c/o Lidhja e Shkrimtareve dhe e Artisteve te Shqiperise, Z. Baboci 37, Tirana
Pres: Besnik Mustafaj; Gen Secr: Piro Misho
Focus: Lit 00004

Shoqata e Gjeologeve te Shqiperise / Geologists' Association of Albania, Bloku Vasil Shanto, Tirana
T: (042) 26597
Founded: 1989; Members: 450
Pres: Aleksander Cina; Gen Secr: Ilir Alliu
Focus: Geology 00005

Algeria

El-Djazairia El-Mossilia, 1 Rue Hamitouche, Alger
Founded: 1930; Members: 452
Pres: Ali Benmerabet; Gen Secr: Abdel-Hadi Meraoubi
Focus: Cultur Hist 00006

Organisme National de la Recherche Scientifique, Rte de Dély Ibrahim, Ben Aknoun, Alger
Focus: Sci 00007

Société Archéologique du Département de Constantine, c/o Musée Gustave Mercier, Constantine
Founded: 1852; Members: 250
Pres: Dr. Baghli
Focus: Archeol
Periodical
Recueil des Notices et Mémoires . . . 00008

Société Historique Algérienne, c/o Faculté des Lettres, Université, Alger
Founded: 1963; Members: 600
Focus: Hist 00009

Union Médicale Algérienne, 3 Blvd Zirout Yousef, Alger
Focus: Med
Periodical
Algérie Médicale 00010

Unité de Recherches sur les Resources Biologiques Terrestres (CRBT), 2 Rue Didouche Mourad, Alger
T: (02) 642705; Fax: 642705
Founded: 1974; Members: 22
Pres: D. Nedjrachie
Focus: Bio; Ecology
Periodical
Biocenoses (annually) 00011

Andorra

Associació Cultural i Artística Els Esquirols, Sala Parroquial, Plaça de l'Església, La Massana
Focus: Cultur Hist; Arts 00012

Associació per la Defensa de la Natura, Apartat de Correus Espanyols 96, Andorra la Vella
T: 843248; Fax: 843868
Founded: 1986; Members: 250
Pres: Esther Bartumev; Gen Secr: Wiebke Berger
Focus: Ecology 00013

Cercle de les Arts i de les Lletres, Av Carlemany 24, Escaldes-Engordany
T: 21233
Founded: 1968
Pres: Joan Burgués Martisella
Focus: Arts; Lit 00014

Comitè Andorrà de Ciències Històriques, Apartat de Correus 113, Andorra la Vella
T: 24077
Founded: 1979; Members: 32
Pres: Lidia Armengol Vila; Gen Secr: Xavier Llovera Massana
Focus: Hist
Periodical
Butlletí Andorrà de Ciències Històriques . 00015

International Council of Museums, Andorran National Committee, c/o Patrimoni Cultural d'Andorra, Carretera de Bixessarri s/n, Aixovall
T: 844141; Fax: 844343
Founded: 1988
Pres: Marta Planas de la Maza; Gen Secr: Angels Ruf Riba
Focus: Arts 00016

Societat Andorrana de Ciències, Carrer Princep Benlloch 30, Andorra la Vella
T: 852383; Fax: 852383
Founded: 1983
Pres: J. Vilanova
Focus: Sci 00017

Angola

União dos Escritores Angolanos, CP 2767-C, Luanda
T: (02) 322155
Founded: 1975; Members: 75
Gen Secr: Luandino Vieira
Focus: Lit
Periodical
Lavra & Oficina (monthly) 00018

Antigua and Barbuda

Library Association of Antigua and Barbuda, c/o Economic Affairs Secretariat, Organization of Eastern Caribbean States, POB 822, Saint John's
T: 4623500; Fax: 4621537
Founded: 1983; Members: 40
Pres: Molivar Spencer; Gen Secr: Tracy Samuel
Focus: Libraries & Bk Sci 00019

Argentina

Academia Argentina de Cirugía, Marcelo T. de Alvear 2415, 1122 Buenos Aires
T: (01) 9253649
Founded: 1911
Pres: Vicente Gutierrez; Gen Secr: Jorge Sivori
Focus: Surgery 00020

Academia Argentina de Letras, Sánchez de Bustamante 2663, 1425 Buenos Aires
T: (01) 8023814; Fax: 8028390
Founded: 1931
Pres: Raúl H. Castagnino; Gen Secr: Rodolfo Modern
Focus: Lit
Periodical
Boletín (quarterly) 00021

Academia de Ciencias Médicas, CC 130, 5000 Córdoba
T: (051) 690051
Founded: 1975; Members: 350
Pres: Dr. Remo Bergoglio; Gen Secr: Jesús R. Giraudo
Focus: Med 00022

Academia Nacional de Agronomía y Veterinaría, Av Alvear 1711, 1014 Buenos Aires
T: (01) 8124168, 8154616; Fax: 8124168, 8154616
Founded: 1909; Members: 87
Pres: Dr. Norberto Ras; Gen Secr: Dr. Alberto Cano
Focus: Agri; Vet Med
Periodical
Anales (annually) 00023

Academia Nacional de Bellas Artes, Sánchez de Bustamante 2663, 1425 Buenos Aires
T: (01) 8022469
Founded: 1936; Members: 60
Pres: Alfredo C. Casares; Gen Secr: Ary Brizzi
Focus: Arts 00024

Academia Nacional de Ciencias de Buenos Aires, Av Alvear 1711, 1014 Buenos Aires
T: (01) 413066
Founded: 1935; Members: 35
Pres: Oscar A. Quihillalt; Gen Secr: Dr. Amalia de Bórmida
Focus: Sci 00025

Academia Nacional de Ciencias de Córdoba, Av Velez Sarsfield 229, Casilla de Correo 36, 5000 Córdoba
T: (051) 229687; Fax: 244092
Founded: 1869; Members: 35
Pres: Dr. Alberto P. Maiztegui; Gen Secr: Dr. Alfredo Cocucci
Focus: Nat Sci
Periodicals
Actas (irregularly)
Boletín (irregularly)
Miscelanea (irregularly) 00026

Academia Nacional de Ciencias Económicas, Av Alvear 1790, 1014 Buenos Aires
T: (01) 8132344; Fax: 8132078
Founded: 1914; Members: 35
Pres: Dr. Enrique J. Reig; Gen Secr: Dr. Luis García Martínez
Focus: Econ
Periodical
Anales 00027

Academia Nacional de Ciencias Exactas, Físicas y Naturales (ANCEFN) / National Academy of Exact, Physical and Natural Sciences, Av Alvear 1711, 1014 Buenos Aires
T: (01) 8112998; Fax: 8116951
Founded: 1874; Members: 122
Pres: Dr. Mario A.J. Mariscotti; Gen Secr: Dr. H. Fanchiotti
Focus: Math; Physics; Nat Sci
Periodical
Anales (annually) 00028

Academia Nacional de Ciencias Morales y Políticas, Av Alvear 1711, 1014 Buenos Aires
T: (01) 8112049
Founded: 1938; Members: 35
Pres: Dr. Jorge A. Aja Espil; Gen Secr: Carlos A. Sánchez Sañudo
Focus: Philos; Poli Sci 00029

Academia Nacional de Derecho y Ciencias Sociales, Av Alvear 1711, 1014 Buenos Aires
T: (01) 8213522
Founded: 1874; Members: 25
Pres: Dr. Segundo Linares Quintana
Focus: Law; Sociology
Periodical
Anales 00030

Academia Nacional de Derecho y Ciencias Sociales (Córdoba), Artigas 74, 5000 Córdoba
T: (051) 214929; Fax: 214929
Founded: 1941; Members: 112
Pres: Dr. Luis Moisset de Espanés; Gen Secr: Dr. Ricardo Haro
Focus: Law; Sociology
Periodicals
Anales
Ediciones Academia 00031

Academia Nacional de Geografía, Av Alvear 1711, 1014 Buenos Aires
T: (01) 413066
Founded: 1956; Members: 30
Pres: Lorenzo Dagnino Pastore; Gen Secr: Aristides Incarnato
Focus: Geography
Periodical
Anales 00032

Academia Nacional de la Historia, Balcarce 139, 1064 Buenos Aires
T: (01) 3434416; E-Mail: postmaster@anh.edu.ar; Fax: 3314633
Members: 40
Pres: Víctor Tau Anzoátegui; Gen Secr: Miguel Angel de Marco
Focus: Hist
Periodicals
Boletín (annually)
Investigaciones y Ensayos (semi-annually) 00033

Academia Nacional de Medicina, Las Heras 3092, 1425 Buenos Aires
T: (01) 8056890; Fax: 8066638
Founded: 1822; Members: 35
Pres: Andres O.M. Stoppani; Gen Secr: Mario A. Copello
Focus: Med
Periodical
Boletín (semi-annually) 00034

Asociación Archivística Argentina, Leandro N. Alem 250, Buenos Aires
T: (01) 335531
Founded: 1968; Members: 160
Pres: Luis F. Piazzali; Gen Secr: Dr. Augusto Fernández Pinto
Focus: Archives
Periodical
Boletín 00035

Asociación Argentina Amigos de la Astronomía (A.A.A.A.), CC 369, Correo Central, 1000 Buenos Aires
T: (01) 883366; Fax: 883366
Founded: 1929; Members: 1000
Pres: Gloria Roitman
Focus: Astronomy
Periodical
Revista Astronómica 00036

Asociación Argentina de Astronomía, c/o Observatorio Astronómico, 1900 La Plata
T: (021) 27308
Founded: 1958; Members: 120
Pres: Raúl Colomb; Gen Secr: Hugo Levato
Focus: Astronomy
Periodical
Boletín (annually) 00037

Asociación Argentina de Bibliotecas y Centros de Información Científicos y Técnicos, Santa Fé 1145, 1059 Buenos Aires
T: (01) 3938406
Founded: 1937; Members: 84
Pres: Abilio Bassets; Gen Secr: Ernesto G. Gietz
Focus: Libraries & Bk Sci 00038

Asociación Argentina de Biología y Medicina Nuclear, Santa Fé 1145, 1059 Buenos Aires
T: (01) 3935682
Founded: 1963; Members: 190
Pres: Dr. Juan J. O'Farrell; Gen Secr: Dr. Carlos Cañellas
Focus: Bio; Nucl Med 00039

Asociación Argentina de Ciencias Naturales, Av Angel Gallardo 470, 1405 Buenos Aires
T: (01) 9828370; E-Mail: physis@muanbe.gov.ar; Fax: 9824494
Founded: 1912; Members: 500
Pres: Juan Carlos Giacchi; Gen Secr: Cristina Marinone
Focus: Nat Sci
Periodical
Revista Physis (semi-annually) 00040

Asociación Argentina de Cirugía, Marcelo T. de Alvear 2415, 1122 Buenos Aires
T: (01) 822905; Fax: 8226458
Founded: 1930; Members: 4000
Pres: Frutos Enrique Ortiz; Gen Secr: Martín Mihura
Focus: Surgery
Periodicals
Anuario
Boletín
Revista Argentina de Cirugía (8 times annually) 00041

Asociación Argentina de Ecología, CC 1025, Correo Central, 5000 Córdoba
T: (051) 22284 ext 49
Founded: 1972; Members: 600
Pres: Dr. Raúl A. Montenegro
Focus: Ecology
Periodical
Bulletin (3 times annually) 00042

Asociación Argentina de Estudios Americanos, Maipú 672, 1424 Buenos Aires
T: (01) 3924971
Focus: Ethnology 00043

Asociación Argentina de Farmacia y Bioquímica Industrial, Uruguay 469, 1015 Buenos Aires
T: (01) 3730462, 3738900; E-Mail: safybi@mortero.satlink.net; Fax: 3727389
Founded: 1952; Members: 1600
Pres: Dr. Carlos Jacobi; Gen Secr: Dr. Raúl Alberto Revilla
Focus: Pharmacol; Biochem 00044

Asociación Argentina de Geofísicos y Geodestas / Argentine Association of Geophysicists and Geodesists, CC 106, 1428 Buenos Aires
Founded: 1959
Pres: Dr. María L. Altinger; Gen Secr: Dr. María C. Pomposiello
Focus: Surveying; Geology
Periodicals
Boletín (3 times annually)
Geoacta (bi-annually) 00045

Asociación Argentina de la Ciencia del Suelo, J.R. de Velasco 847, 1414 Buenos Aires
T: (01) 7718968; E-Mail: radio@ferlav.agro.uba.ar; Fax: 5221687, 5228395
Founded: 1958; Members: 800
Pres: G. Moscatlli; Gen Secr: R. Alvarez
Focus: Agri
Periodicals
Boletín (3 times annually)
Ciencia del Suelo (semi-annually) . . . 00046

Asociación Argentina de Micología, c/o Dept de Microbiología, Facultad de Medicina, Universidad de Buenos Aires, Paraguay 2155, 1121 Buenos Aires
T: (01) 9627274; Fax: 9625404
Founded: 1960; Members: 150
Pres: Dr. Ana M. Robles; Gen Secr: Dr. Alicia Arechavala
Focus: Botany, Specific
Periodical
Revista (3 times annually) 00047

Asociación Argentina de Ortopedía y Traumatología, Vicente López 1878, 1128 Buenos Aires
T: (01) 8012320; Fax: 8017703
Founded: 1936; Members: 2138
Pres: Dr. Alberto Cáneva; Gen Secr: Dr. Carlos Tello
Focus: Orthopedics; Traumatology

Periodical
Revista de la Asociación de Ortopedía y Traumatología (bi-monthly) *00048*

Asociación Argentina del Frío, Av Mayo 1123, 1085 Buenos Aires
T: (01) 387544
Founded: 1932; Members: 178
Pres: Roberto Segura; Gen Secr: Roberto Aguilo
Focus: Eng; Air Cond
Periodical
Clima (monthly) *00049*

Asociación Argentina para el Progreso de las Ciencias, Av Alvear 1711, 1014 Buenos Aires
T: (01) 8112998; Fax: 8116951
Founded: 1933; Members: 215
Pres: Dr. Eduardo Hernán Charreau; Gen Secr: Dr. Augusto F. García
Focus: Nat Sci
Periodical
Ciencia e Investigación *00050*

Asociación Bernardino Rivadavia, Av Colón 31, 8000 Bahía Blanca
T: (091) 27492
Founded: 1882
Pres: Prof. Raúl Oscar Gouarnalusse; Gen Secr: María Luisa Gastaminza
Focus: Libraries & Bk Sci
Periodical
Boletín Informativo (quarterly) *00051*

Asociación Bioquímica Argentina, Venezuela 1823, 1096 Buenos Aires
T: (01) 382907
Founded: 1934
Focus: Biochem *00052*

Asociación de Bibliotecarios Graduados de la República Argentina (ABGRA), Corrientes 1642, 1042 Buenos Aires
T: (01) 3824821
Founded: 1953; Members: 1000
Pres: Roberto Jorge Servidio; Gen Secr: Claudia Rodriguez
Focus: Libraries & Bk Sci
Periodicals
Bibliotecologia y Documentación
Boletín Informativo
Trabajos de Congresos (irregularly) . . . *00053*

Asociación Electrotécnica Argentina, Posadas 1659, 1112 Buenos Aires
T: (01) 8043454
Founded: 1913; Members: 2000
Pres: Ernesto H. Rodil
Focus: Electric Eng
Periodical
Revista Electrotécnica *00054*

Asociación Geológica Argentina / Argentinian Geological Association, Maipú 645, 1006 Buenos Aires
T: (01) 3222820
Founded: 1945; Members: 1750
Pres: Dr. A.C. Riccardi; Gen Secr: P. Alvarez
Focus: Geology
Periodical
Revista de la Asociación Geológica Argentina: RAGA (quarterly) *00055*

Asociación Latinoamericana de Centros de Educación (ALCECOOP) / Latin American Association of Cooperative Centres of Education, Laprida 1062, Casilla 135, 2000 Rosario
T: (041) 48106; Fax: 245832
Founded: 1989
Focus: Educ *00056*

Asociación Médica Argentina, Santa Fé 1171, 1059 Buenos Aires
T: (01) 411633
Founded: 1891
Pres: Juan Carlos Fernandez; Gen Secr: Laura Astarloa
Focus: Med
Periodical
Revista *00057*

Asociación Odontológica Argentina, Junín 959, 1113 Buenos Aires
T: (01) 9616141
Founded: 1896; Members: 7500
Pres: Juan Carlos Fernández; Gen Secr: Eugenio L. Henry
Focus: Dent
Periodical
Revista (quarterly) *00058*

Asociación Paleontológica Argentina (APA), Maipú 645, 1006 Buenos Aires
T: (01) 3222820; Fax: 3267463
Founded: 1955; Members: 500
Pres: Dr. Miguel Manceñido; Gen Secr: Sara Parma
Focus: Paleontology
Periodical
Ameghiniana (quarterly) *00059*

Asociación para la Lucha contra la Parálisis Infantil, Salguero 1639, 1425 Buenos Aires
T: (01) 841034
Founded: 1943; Members: 30
Pres: Verónica S.M. de Busto
Focus: Pediatrics *00060*

Asociación Química Argentina, Sánchez de Bustamente 1749, 1425 Buenos Aires
T: (01) 8224886; E-Mail: info@aqa.org.ar; Fax: 8224886
Founded: 1912; Members: 2000
Pres: Dr. Marcelo J. Vernengo; Gen Secr: Dr. Eduardo Castro
Focus: Chem
Periodicals
Anales (bi-monthly)
Boletín (5 times annually)
Industria y Química (5 times annually) . *00061*

Centro Argentino de Espeleología, Av de Mayo 651, 1428 Buenos Aires
T: (01) 3316798
Founded: 1970; Members: 60
Pres: Julio Goyén Aguado; Gen Secr: Roberto Oscar Bermejo
Focus: Geology *00062*

Centro Argentino de Información Científica y Tecnológica (CAICYT), Moreno 431-433, 1091 Buenos Aires
T: (01) 305749
Focus: Eng; Sci; Doc *00063*

Centro Argentino de Ingenieros (CAI) / Argentine Centre of Engineering, Cerrito 1250, 1010 Buenos Aires
T: (01) 8114961; Fax: 8120475
Founded: 1895; Members: 10231
Pres: Oscar A. Bouzo
Focus: Eng
Periodical
CAI Informa (3 times annually) *00064*

Colegio de Abogados de la Ciudad de Buenos Aires, Montevideo 640, 1019 Buenos Aires
T: (01) 3712690; Fax: 3712690
Founded: 1913; Members: 1600
Pres: Dr. Oscar Alvarado Uriburu; Gen Secr: Dr. Uriel F. O'Farrell
Focus: Law
Periodical
Revista (semi-annually) *00065*

Comisión Nacional de Energía Atómica, Av del Libertador 8250, 1429 Buenos Aires
T: (01) 7041000; Fax: 7032645
Founded: 1950
Pres: Dr. Manuel Angel Mondino
Focus: Nucl Res
Periodical
Informes *00066*

Comisión Nacional de Investigaciones Espaciales (CNIE) / National Commission for Space Research, Dorrego 4018, 1425 Buenos Aires
T: (01) 7725474
Founded: 1960
Pres: Genaro Mario Sciola
Focus: Aero; Nat Res *00067*

Comisión Nacional de Museos y de Monumentos y Lugares Históricos, Av de Mayo 556, 1084 Buenos Aires
T: (01) 3316151
Founded: 1938
Pres: Jorge Enrique Hardoy; Gen Secr: Matilde I. Orueta
Focus: Preserv Hist Monuments; Arts
Periodical
Boletín *00068*

Comisión Nacional Protectora de Bibliotecas Populares / National Commission for the Protection of Public Libraries, Ayacucho 1578, 1112 Buenos Aires
T: (01) 8036545
Founded: 1870
Pres: Prof. Daniel R. Rios; Gen Secr: Prof. Ana T. Dobra
Focus: Econ
Periodical
Boletín *00069*

Comisión Panamericana de Normas Técnicas (COPANT) / Pan American Standards Commission, Lima 629, 1073 Buenos Aires
T: (01) 375123; E-Mail: COPANTEC
Founded: 1961; Members: 21
Focus: Standards
Periodical
Noticias COPANT: Catalogue of Standards (quarterly) *00070*

Consejo Nacional de Investigaciones Científicas y Técnicas (CONICET) / National Council of Scientific and Technical Research, Rivadavia 1917, 1033 Buenos Aires
T: (01) 9537230; Fax: 9534345
Founded: 1958; Members: 8100
Pres: Carlos Cavotti
Focus: Eng; Sci
Periodical
Boletín SECYT-CONICET (monthly) . . . *00071*

Departamento de Estudios Etnográficos y Coloniales / Dept of Ethnographical and Colonial Studies, Calle 25 de Mayo 1470, 3000 Santa Fé
T: (042) 595857; Fax: 595857
Founded: 1940
Pres: Luis Maria Calvo; Gen Secr: Prof. Maria A.V. de Fabbroni
Focus: Ethnology
Periodical
America (annually) *00072*

Federación Argentina de Asociaciones de Anestesiología, J.F. Aranguren 1323, 1405 Buenos Aires
T: (01) 4312463; Fax: 4312463
Founded: 1970; Members: 1113
Pres: Dr. Alfredo Pairetti
Focus: Anesthetics
Periodicals
Boletín Informativo
Revista Argentina de Anestesiología . . *00073*

Federación Lanera Argentina (FLA), Av Paseo Colón 823, 1063 Buenos Aires
T: (01) 3007661; Fax: 3616517
Founded: 1929; Members: 86
Focus: Marketing; Textiles
Periodicals
Boletín Lanero (daily)
Informe Mensual Estadístico (monthly) . . *00074*

Fondo Nacional de las Artes / National Arts Foundation, Alsina 673, 1087 Buenos Aires
T: (01) 3431591
Founded: 1958
Pres: Amalia Lagroze de Fortabat
Focus: Arts
Periodicals
Anuario del Teatro Argentino
Bibliografía Argentina de Artes y Letras (quarterly)
Informativo (monthly) *00075*

Fundación Miguel Lillo, Miguel Lillo 251, 4000 San Miguel de Tucumán
T: (081) 330868; Fax: 330868
Founded: 1931
Focus: Botany; Geology; Zoology
Periodicals
Acta Geologica Lilloana (irregularly)
Acta Zoologica Lilloana (irregularly)
Genera et Species Animalium Argentinorum (irregularly)
Genera et Species Plantarum Argentinorum (irregularly)
Lilloa (irregularly) *00076*

Grupo Argentino del Color, 1650 San Martín, CC 157
T: (01) 7544141; Fax: 7542102
Founded: 1979
Pres: José Luis Caivano; Gen Secr: Antonio Alvarez
Focus: Chem *00077*

Grupo Latinoamericano de R.I.L.E.M. (GLAR), Av L. N. Alem 1067, 1001 Buenos Aires
T: (01) 3133013
Founded: 1963; Members: 61
Focus: Civil Eng; Materials Sci
Periodical
GLARILEM Informations (3-4 times annually) *00078*

Instituto Bonaerense de Numismática y Antigüedades, San Martín 336, 1004 Buenos Aires
T: (01) 492659
Founded: 1872; Members: 107
Pres: Humberto F. Burzio
Focus: Numismatics; Antique
Periodical
Boletín *00079*

Junta de Historia Eclesiástica Argentina, Reconquista 269, 1003 Buenos Aires
T: (01) 3316239
Founded: 1942; Members: 100
Pres: Prof. Carlos M. Gelly y Obes; Gen Secr: Alberto S.J. de Paula
Focus: Rel & Theol
Periodicals
Boletín
Revista Archivum (annually) *00080*

Liga Argentina contra la Tuberculosis (LALAT), Santa Fé 4292, 1425 Buenos Aires
T: (01) 7742811
Founded: 1901
Pres: Dr. Rodolfo Cucchiani Acevedo; Gen Secr: Dr. Germán Quintela Novoa
Focus: Pulmon Dis
Periodicals
Doble Cruz (semi-annually)
Revista Argentina del Toiax (quarterly) . *00081*

PEN Club Argentino, Rivadavia 4060, 1205 Buenos Aires
Founded: 1930; Members: 100
Pres: Miguel A. Olivera
Focus: Lit
Periodical
Boletín *00082*

Sociedad Argentina de Alergia e Inmunopatología (SAAI), Santa Fé 1171, 1059 Buenos Aires
T: (01) 411633; Fax: 7847285
Founded: 1940; Members: 84
Pres: Dr. Zelma Coronel
Focus: Immunology
Periodicals
An Up-to-Date in Pollenosis and Drug Allergy (annually)
Clinical Reports of Allergy and Immunology (monthly)
Monographs of Allergy and Clinical Immunoloogy (annually) *00083*

Sociedad Argentina de Antropología, Moreno 350, 1091 Buenos Aires
Founded: 1936; Members: 255
Pres: M.M. Podestá; Gen Secr: G. Guraieb
Focus: Anthro
Periodical
Relaciones (annually) *00084*

Sociedad Argentina de Autores y Compositores de Música (SADAIC), Lavalle 1547, 1048 Buenos Aires
T: (01) 3798600; Fax: 111985
Founded: 1936; Members: 25000
Pres: Ariel Ramirez; Gen Secr: Cesar Isella
Focus: Music; Lit
Periodical
Catálogos Bibliográficos *00085*

Sociedad Argentina de Biología, Vuelta de Obligado 2490, 1428 Buenos Aires
T: (01) 7832869
Founded: 1920; Members: 180
Pres: Dr. José Rimo Barañao; Gen Secr: Dr. Juan Carlos Calvo
Focus: Bio
Periodical
Revista (semi-annually) *00086*

Sociedad Argentina de Botánica, c/o Museu Argentino de Ciencias Natur., Av A. Gallardo 470, 1405 Buenos Aires
Founded: 1945
Focus: Botany
Periodical
Boletín (annually) *00087*

Sociedad Argentina de Ciencias Fisiológicas (SACF) / Argentine Society of Physiological Sciences, Solís 453, 1078 Buenos Aires
T: (01) 3831110; Fax: 3810323
Founded: 1950; Members: 150
Pres: Prof. Dr. Pedro Aramendía; Gen Secr: Dr. Ricardo A. Quinteiro
Focus: Physiology *00088*

Sociedad Argentina de Ciencias Neurológicas, Psiquiátricas y Neuroquirúrgicas, Santa Fé 1171, 1059 Buenos Aires
T: (01) 411633
Founded: 1920; Members: 400
Pres: Prof. Dr. Diego Brage; Gen Secr: Prof. Dr. Carlos Márquez
Focus: Surgery; Neurology; Psychiatry
Periodical
Revista (monthly) *00089*

Sociedad Argentina de Endocrinología y Metabolismo / Argentine Society of Endocrinology and Metabolism, Viamonte 2506, 1056 Buenos Aires
T: (01) 9637166; Fax: 9615106
Founded: 1941; Members: 500
Pres: Dr. Mario Pisarev; Gen Secr: Dr. Alicia Gaura
Focus: Endocrinology
Periodical
Revista Argentina de Endocrinologia y Metabolismo (quarterly) *00090*

Sociedad Argentina de Estudios Geográficos / Argentine Society of Geographical Studies, Rodriguez Peña 158, 1020 Buenos Aires
T: (01) 402076; Fax: 3823305
Founded: 1922; Members: 4000
Pres: Dr. Susana I. Curto de Casas; Gen Secr: A.S. Conte
Focus: Geography
Periodical
Boletín (annually) *00091*

Sociedad Argentina de Farmacología y Terapéutica, Santa Fé 1171, 1059 Buenos Aires
T: (01) 411633
Founded: 1929; Members: 100
Pres: Prof. Dr. Manuel Litter; Gen Secr: Dr. José A.L. Chiesa
Focus: Pharmacol; Therapeutics *00092*

Sociedad Argentina de Fisiología Vegetal, c/o Departamento de Agronomía, U.N.S., 8000 Bahía Blanca
T: (091) 34775; Fax: 21942
Founded: 1958; Members: 260
Pres: Dr. Gustavo A. Orioli; Gen Secr: Dr. Luis F. Hernandez
Focus: Botany *00093*

Sociedad Argentina de Gastroenterología, Santa Fé 1171, 1059 Buenos Aires
T: (01) 411633
Founded: 1927; Members: 900
Pres: Dr. Erman E. Crosetti; Gen Secr: Dr. Leonardo Pinchuk
Focus: Gastroenter
Periodical
Acta Gastroenterológica Latinoamericana . *00094*

Sociedad Argentina de Gerontología y Geriatría, French 2657, 1425 Buenos Aires
T: (01) 8057051; Fax: 5660369
Founded: 1950; Members: 1500
Pres: Prof. Dr. Ernesto F. Chalita; Gen Secr: Dr. Isidoro Fainstein
Focus: Geriatrics
Periodical
Sinopsis de Geriatría (quarterly) *00095*

Sociedad Argentina de Hematología (SAH), Av Angel Gallardo 899, 1405 Buenos Aires
Founded: 1948; Members: 350
Pres: Dr. Guillermo Carlos Vilaseca; Gen Secr: Dr. Eduardo Dibar
Focus: Hematology 00096

Sociedad Argentina de Investigación Clínica, c/o Instituto de Investigaciones Médicas, U.B.A., Donato Alvarez 3150, 1427 Buenos Aires
T: (01) 5732619; Fax: 5732619
Founded: 1960; Members: 500
Pres: Basilio A. Kotsias; Gen Secr: Adriana Fraga
Focus: Med; Surgery
Periodical
Medicina (annually) 00097

Sociedad Argentina de Leprología, CC 2899, 1000 Buenos Aires
T: (01) 831815
Founded: 1954
Gen Secr: J.C. Gatti
Focus: Derm
Periodical
Leprología (2-3 times annually) 00098

Sociedad Argentina de Oftalmología, Santa Fé 1171, 1059 Buenos Aires
T: (01) 2410392
Founded: 1920; Members: 2000
Pres: Dr. Roberto Sampoalesi; Gen Secr: Dr. José A. Badia
Focus: Ophthal
Periodical
Archivos de Oftalmología de Buenos Aires (monthly) 00099

Sociedad Argentina de Patología, Santa Fé 1171, 1059 Buenos Aires
T: (01) 411633
Founded: 1933; Members: 220
Pres: Dr. Alberto Sundblad; Gen Secr: Dr. Mabel Pomar de Gil
Focus: Pathology
Periodical
Archivos 00100

Sociedad Argentina de Pediatría, Coronel Díaz 1971, 1425 Buenos Aires
T: (01) 8242063
Founded: 1911; Members: 7500
Pres: Dr. Carlos A. Gianantonio; Gen Secr: Dr. María Luisa Ageitos
Focus: Pediatrics
Periodical
Archivos Argentinos de Pediatría (bi-monthly) 00101

Sociedad Argentina de Psicología, Callao 435, 1022 Buenos Aires
T: (01) 4323760
Founded: 1930
Pres: Juan Cuatrecasas
Focus: Psych 00102

Sociedad Argentina de Sociología, Trejo 241, 5000 Córdoba
T: (051) 45901
Founded: 1950
Pres: Prof. Alfredo Poviña; Gen Secr: Prof. Odorico Pires Pinto
Focus: Sociology 00103

Sociedad Central de Arquitectos, Montevideo 938, 1019 Buenos Aires
T: (01) 422375; Fax: 8136629
Founded: 1886; Members: 8500
Pres: Julio Keselman; Gen Secr: Guillermo Marenco
Focus: Archit 00104

Sociedad Científica Argentina, Santa Fé 1145, 1059 Buenos Aires
T: (01) 3938406
Founded: 1872; Members: 954
Pres: Arturo Otaño Sahores
Focus: Sci 00105

Sociedad de Cirugía de Buenos Aires, Santa Fé 1171, 1059 Buenos Aires
T: (01) 440664
Pres: Ivan Goñi Moreno; Gen Secr: Guillermo I. Belleville
Focus: Surgery 00106

Sociedad de Medicina Legal y Toxicologia, Sarmiento 1271, 1041 Buenos Aires
Founded: 1929; Members: 110
Pres: Dr. José Belbey; Gen Secr: Dr. Alfredo G. Ferrer Zanchi
Focus: Med; Toxicology 00107

Sociedad de Psicología Médica, Psicoanálisis y Medicina Psicosomática, Santa Fé 1171, 1059 Buenos Aires
T: (01) 8142182
Founded: 1939; Members: 80
Pres: Dr. José Cukier; Gen Secr: Dr. A. Stisman
Focus: Psychiatry; Psych 00108

Sociedad Entomológica Argentina (SEA) / Argentine Entomological Society, c/o Museo de la Plata, Paseo del Bosque s/n, 1900 La Plata
T: (021) 39125; Fax: 257527
Founded: 1925; Members: 380
Pres: Dr. Norma B. Diaz; Gen Secr: Dr. Amalia A. Lanteri
Focus: Entomology
Periodical
Revista de la Sociedad Entomológica Argentina (annually) 00109

Sociedad General de Autores de la Argentina, J.A. Pacheco de Melo 1820, 1126 Buenos Aires
T: (01) 421227
Founded: 1910; Members: 2000
Pres: Roberto A. Talice; Gen Secr: Emilio Villalba Welsh
Focus: Lit
Periodical
Boletín (quarterly) 00110

Sociedad Rural Argentina, Florida 460, 1005 Buenos Aires
T: (01) 3220468
Founded: 1866; Members: 10000
Pres: Enrique C. Crotto
Focus: Agri; Vet Med 00111

Unión Matemática Argentina, FAMDF, Ciudad Universitaria, 5000 Cordoba
T: (051) 690330; Fax: 695101
Founded: 1936; Members: 600
Pres: Dr. Juan Tirao; Gen Secr: Dr. Jorge A. Vargas
Focus: Math
Periodical
Revista de la Unión Matemática Argentina 00112

Armenia

Armenian National Academy of Sciences, Pr Marshala Bagramyana 24, 375019 Yerevan
T: (02) 527031
Founded: 1943; Members: 101
Focus: Sci
Periodicals
Astrofizika: Astrophysics
Biologicheskii Zhurnal Armenii: Biological Journal of Armenia
Doklady: Report
Istoriko-Filologicheskii Zhurnal: Historical and Philological Journal
Izvestiya: Bulletin
Khimicheskii Zhurnal Armenii: Chemical Journal of Armenia
Neirokhimiya: Neurochemistry
Soobshcheniya Byurakanskoi Observatorii: Report of the Byurakan Astrophysical Observatory
Vestnik Obshchestvennykh Nauk: Herald of Social Sciences
Zhurnal Experimentalnoi i Klinicheskoi Medisiny: Journal of Experimental and Clinical Medicine 00113

Yerevan Academy of National Economy, Ul Abovyana 52, 375025 Yerevan
T: (02) 560413
Members: 1975
Focus: Econ
Periodical
Economics 00114

Australia

Academy of the Social Sciences in Australia (ASSA), GPOB 1956, Canberra, ACT 2601
Founded: 1971; Members: 174
Pres: P. Bourke; Gen Secr: Dr. J. Jupp
Focus: Sociology
Periodicals
Newsletter (quarterly)
Report (annually) 00115

Accounting Association of Australia and New Zealand (A.A.A.N.Z.), 170 Queen St, Melbourne, Vic 3000
T: (03) 96420227; E-Mail: effiem@clyde.its.unimelb.edu.au; Fax: 96420227
Founded: 1960; Members: 1100
Pres: Prof. Donald Stokes; Gen Secr: Prof. Roger Willett
Focus: Business Admin; Finance
Periodical
Accounting and Finance (semi-annually) . 00116

Agriculture and Resource Management Council of Australia and New Zealand, c/o Dept of Primary Industries and Energy, Barton, Canberra, ACT 2600
T: (06) 2725216; Fax: 2724772
Founded: 1992
Gen Secr: J.W. Graham
Focus: Agri
Periodicals
Newsletter (quarterly)
Report (annually) 00117

Anthropological Society of New South Wales, c/o Anthropology Dept, University of Sydney, Sydney, NSW 2006
Fax: (02) 93515489
Founded: 1928; Members: 170
Pres: Prof. Michael Allen; Gen Secr: P.J.F. Newton
Focus: Anthro
Periodical
The Australian Journal of Anthropology (3 times annually) 00118

Appita, 255 Drummond St, Ste 47, Carlton, Vic 3053
T: (03) 93472377; E-Mail: appita@isp.com.au; Fax: 93481206
Founded: 1946; Members: 1550
Gen Secr: Peter Brown
Focus: Materials Sci
Periodical
Appita Journal (bi-monthly) 00119

Archaeological and Anthropological Society of Victoria, POB 328C, Melbourne, Vic 3001
Founded: 1934
Focus: Anthro; Archeol
Periodical
Artefact (annually) 00120

Arts Council of Australia, 80 George St, The Rocks, Sydney, NSW 2000
Founded: 1946; Members: 20000
Focus: Arts 00121

Asia Pacific Food Analysis Network (APFAN), c/o Div of Botany and Zoology, Australian National University, Canberra, ACT 0200
T: (06) 2490775; E-Mail: howard.bradbury@anu.edu.au; Fax: 2495573
Founded: 1989; Members: 350
Pres: Dr. J. Howard Bradbury
Focus: Food 00122

Asian and Pacific Association for Social Work Education (APASWE), c/o Dept of Social Work, La Trobe University, Bundoora 3083
T: (03) 4792570 ext 2854; Fax: 4785814
Founded: 1974
Focus: Soc Sci; Educ
Periodical
APASWE Newsletter 00123

Asian-Australasian Society of Neurological Surgeons, 201 Wickham Terrace, Brisbane 4001
T: (07) 8393393
Founded: 1964; Members: 18
Focus: Neurology; Surgery 00124

Asian Coordinating Group for Chemistry (ACGC), GPOB 2905, Darwin, NT 0801
T: (08) 89995438; E-Mail: bun@dme.nt.gov.au; Fax: 89996527
Founded: 1984
Pres: Dr. B.N. Noller; Gen Secr: Prof. J. Webb
Focus: Chem 00125

Asian Network for Analytical and Inorganic Chemistry (ANAIC), c/o School of Mathematical and Physical Sciences, Murdoch University, Perth 6150
T: (09) 3322211, 3322152; Fax: 3322507
Founded: 1984; Members: 18
Focus: Chem
Periodical
Network News 00126

Asian Pacific Confederation of Chemical Engineering (APCChE), c/o Institution of Engineers in Australia, 11 National Circuit, Barton 2600
T: (06) 706555; Fax: 2731488
Founded: 1975
Focus: Eng
Periodical
APCChE Newsletter 00127

Asian-Pacific Corrosion Control Organization (APCC), Science Centre, 35-43 Clarence St, Sydney 2000
T: (02) 2659177
Focus: Metallurgy 00128

Asian Pacific Federation of Clinical Biochemistry (APFCB), c/o Clinical Chemistry Div, Institute of Medical and Veterinary Science, POB 14, Rundle Mall Post Office, Adelaide 5000
T: (08) 2287563; Fax: 2287538
Founded: 1982
Focus: Chem
Periodical
APFCB News (semi-annually) 00129

Asian Pan-Pacific Society for Paediatric Gastroenterology and Nutrition (APPSGAN), c/o Health Dept of Western Australia, 189 Royal St, East Perth 6004
T: (09) 2222491; Fax: 2222481
Founded: 1976
Focus: Nutrition; Pediatrics; Gastroenter . 00130

Asian Securities Analysts Federation, Australia Sq, 2000 Sydney, POB H99
T: (02) 92476027; E-Mail: lizcart@asaf.org.au; Fax: 92516283
Founded: 1978; Members: 12
Gen Secr: Elizabeth Cartwright
Focus: Poli Sci 00131

Association of Australasian and Pacific Area Police Medical Officers, c/o Office of Forensic Medicine, POB 2763, Melbourne, 3000
T: (03) 6671657; Fax: 6671709
Focus: Forensic Med 00132

Astronomical Society of Australia (ASA), c/o School of Physics, University of Sydney, Sydney, NSW 2006
T: (02) 93513184; E-Mail: j.obyrne@physics.usyd.edu.au; Fax: 93517726
Founded: 1966; Members: 350
Pres: Dr. R.W. Clay; Gen Secr: Dr. M.L. Duldig; Dr. J.W. O'Byrne
Focus: Astronomy; Astrophys
Periodical
Proceedings (3 times annually) 00133

Astronomical Society of Queensland, 14 Suelin St, Boondall, Qld 4034
Founded: 1927
Focus: Astronomy 00134

Astronomical Society of South Australia, GPOB 199, Adelaide, SA 5001
T: (08) 83381231
Founded: 1892; Members: 350
Pres: P. Rogers; Gen Secr: P.A. Ellin
Focus: Astronomy
Periodicals
Astronomical Data (annually)
Bulletin (monthly) 00135

Astronomical Society of Tasmania, POB 1654, Hobart, Tas 7001
T: (03) 63447100; E-Mail: peter@vision.net.au
Founded: 1934; Members: 93
Pres: R. Coghlan; Gen Secr: M. Mulcahy
Focus: Astronomy
Periodical
Bulletin (bi-monthly) 00136

Astronomical Society of Victoria (ASV), GPOB 1059J, Melbourne, Vic 3001
T: (03) 98887130
Founded: 1922; Members: 800
Pres: Perry Vlahos; Gen Secr: Roger Davis
Focus: Astronomy
Periodicals
ASV Newsletter (bi-monthly)
ASV Yearbook (annually) 00137

Australasian and Pacific Society for Eighteenth-Century Studies, c/o Dept of English, Monash University, Clayton, Vic 3168
Founded: 1970; Members: 80
Pres: Prof. C. Probyn
Focus: Hist
Periodical
Australian Journal of Dairy Technology . 00138

Australasian Association for the History, Philosophy and Social Studies of Science (AAHPSSS), c/o History Dept, University, Sydney, NSW 2006
T: (02) 6923610
Founded: 1967; Members: 150
Focus: Hist; Philos; Sociology 00139

Australasian Association of Clinical Biochemists, POB 278, Mount Lawley, WA 6929
T: (09) 3705224; Fax: 3704409
Founded: 1961; Members: 1400
Pres: D.C. Sampson; Gen Secr: J. Galligan
Focus: Biochem
Periodical
The Australian Quarterly (quarterly) . . . 00140

Australasian Association of Philosophy (AAP), c/o Dept of Philosophy, La Trobe University, Melbourne, Vic 3083
T: (03) 94792439; E-Mail: phiajp@lure.latrobe.edu.au; Fax: 94793639
Founded: 1923; Members: 400
Pres: John Bishop; Gen Secr: G. Marshall
Focus: Philos
Periodical
Australasian Journal of Philosophy (quarterly) 00141

Australasian Ceramic Society, c/o ANSTO, PMB 1, Menai, NSW 2234
T: (02) 7173477; Fax: 5437179
Founded: 1961; Members: 550
Pres: R. Stead; Gen Secr: Dr. D.S. Pereira
Focus: Materials Sci
Periodical
Journal (semi-annually) 00142

The Australasian College of Dermatologists, 136 Pittwater Rd, Gladesville, NSW 2111
T: (02) 98796177; Fax: 98161174
Founded: 1966; Members: 260
Pres: Dr. W. Land; Gen Secr: Dr. D. Wong
Focus: Derm
Periodical
The Australasian Journal of Dermatology (quarterly) 00143

Australasian College of Physical Scientists and Engineers in Medicine, c/o Dept of Physical Sciences, Peter MacCallum Cancer Institute, Saint Andrews Pl, East Melbourne, Vic 3002
T: (03) 96561253; E-Mail: jcoles@petermac.unimelb.edu.au; Fax: 96504870
Founded: 1977; Members: 370
Pres: R.D. Jones; Gen Secr: Dr. J.R. Coles
Focus: Med 00144

Australasian College of Sexual Health Physicians, c/o Sydney Sexual Health Centre, Sydney Hospital, POB 1614, Sydney, NSW 2001
T: (02) 93827457; Fax: 93827475
Founded: 1988
Pres: Dr. Ian Denham; Gen Secr: Dr. K. Brown
Focus: Venereology
Periodical
Venereology 00145

Australasian Corrosion Association (A.C.A.), c/o Corrosion Prevention Center, POB 23400, Mount Waverley, Vic 3149
T: 398095266; E-Mail: corrprev@internex.net.au; Fax: 398095344

Founded: 1955; Members: 1200
Pres: John Brislow; Gen Secr: Sally Nugent
Focus: Metallurgy
Periodicals
ACA Conference Proceedings (annually)
Corrosion & Materials (bi-monthly) . . 00146

Australasian Institute of Mining and Metallurgy, 31 Pelham St, Carlton, Vic 3053
T: (03) 96623166; Fax: 96623662
Founded: 1893; Members: 8500
Pres: John Ralph; Gen Secr: J.M. Webber
Focus: Mining; Metallurgy . . . 00147

Australasian Pharmaceutical Science Association (APSA), c/o Dept of Pharmacy, University of Sydney, Sydney, NSW 2007
T: (02) 93512320; Fax: 93512320
Founded: 1960; Members: 150
Pres: Prof. K.F. Brown; Gen Secr: Prof. C. Armour
Focus: Pharmacol
Periodical
Newsletter (2-4 times annually) 00148

Australasian Plant Pathology Society (APPS), 32 Range St, Toowoomba, Qld 4350
T: (076) 325654; E-Mail: dodmanb@tmba.design.net.au; Fax: 325685
Founded: 1969; Members: 430
Pres: Dr. J.F. Brown; Gen Secr: Dr. H. Ogle
Focus: Botany 00149

Australasian Political Studies Association (APSA), c/o Faculty of Arts, University of New England, Armidale, 2351
T: (02) 67733407; E-Mail: tmoore2@metz.une.edu.au; Fax: 67733317
Founded: 1952
Pres: Andrew Parkin; Gen Secr: Tod Moore
Focus: Poli Sci
Periodicals
APSA Newsletter (5 times annually)
Australian Journal of Political Sciences (semi-annually) 00150

Australia Council, 181 Lawson St, Redfern, NWS 2016
T: (02) 99509000; Fax: 99509111
Founded: 1968
Pres: Hilary McPhee
Focus: Arts 00151

Australian Academy of Science (AAS), GPOB 783, Canberra, ACT 2601
T: (02) 62475777; E-Mail: eb@science.org.au; Fax: 62574620
Founded: 1954; Members: 305
Pres: Sir Gustav Wossal; Gen Secr: P. Vallee
Focus: Sci
Periodicals
Historical Records of Australian Science (annually)
Newsletter (quarterly)
Yearbook (annually) 00152

Australian Academy of Technological Sciences and Engineering, Ian McLennan House, 197 Royal Parade, Parkville, Vic 3052
T: (03) 93470622; Fax: 93478237
Founded: 1976; Members: 541
Pres: Sir Arvi Parbo; Gen Secr: Prof. F.P. Larkins
Focus: Eng
Periodicals
Annual Report (annually)
Focus Newsletter
Handbook
Symposia Series 00153

Australian Academy of the Humanities (A.A.H.), GPOB 93, Canberra, ACT 2601
T: (06) 2487744; E-Mail: yvonne.gentry@anv.edu.au; Fax: 2486287
Founded: 1969; Members: 292
Pres: Prof. Margaret Clunies Ross; Gen Secr: Prof. Paul Weaver
Focus: Humanities
Periodicals
Proceedings (annually)
Symposium (quarterly) 00154

Australian Acoustical Society (A.A.S.), Private Bag 1, Darlinghurst, NSW 2010
T: (02) 93316920; Fax: 93317296
Founded: 1971; Members: 410
Pres: C.G. Don; Gen Secr: D.J. Watkins
Focus: Acoustics
Periodical
Acoustics Australia (3 times annually) . . 00155

Australian Agricultural and Resource Economics Society (A.A.E.S.), c/o Australian National University, LPO Box A321, Canberra, ACT 2601
T: (06) 2492226; E-Mail: journal.ajare@anu.edu.au; Fax: 2492226
Founded: 1957; Members: 550
Pres: Dr. L. Paul O'Mara; Gen Secr: Peter N. Daniel
Focus: Agri; Ecology
Periodical
Australian Journal of Agricultural and Resource Economics (quarterly) . . . 00156

The Australian Agricultural Council, c/o Commonwealth Dept of Primary Industries and Energy, Canberra, ACT 2600
Founded: 1934; Members: 9
Focus: Agri 00157

Australian and New Zealand Association for Medieval and Renaissance Studies, c/o Dept of English, Sydney University, Sydney, NSW 2006
Founded: 1968; Members: 300
Gen Secr: D.P. Speed
Focus: Hist; Lit
Periodical
Parergon (annually) 00158

Australian and New Zealand Association for the Advancement of Science (ANZAAS), POB 2816, Canberra, ACT 2601
Founded: 1886; Members: 1000
Gen Secr: Don Tier
Focus: Sci 00159

Australian and New Zealand Society of Nuclear Medicine, c/o Science Centre, Private Bag 1, Darlinghurst, NSW 2010
T: (02) 3316920
Founded: 1969; Members: 500
Pres: A. Van der Schaaf; Gen Secr: J.G. Chan
Focus: Nucl Med
Periodical
Newsletter of the Australian and New Zealand Society of Nuclear Medicine (quarterly) . 00160

Australian and New Zealand Solar Energy Society, POB 1140, Maroubra, NSW 2035
T: (02) 93110003; E-Mail: anzses@keystone.arch.unsw.edu.au; Fax: 93110004
Founded: 1962; Members: 985
Pres: T.R. Lee; Gen Secr: Dr. A. Sproul
Focus: Energy
Periodical
Solar Progress 00161

Australian Association for the Study of Religions (AASR), 87 Cavendish St, Stanmore, NSW 2048
T: (02) 95576030
Founded: 1975; Members: 320
Pres: Dr. Trevor Jordan; Gen Secr: Tricia Blomberry
Focus: Rel & Theol; Hist
Periodical
Australian Religion Studies Review (semi-annually) 00162

Australian Association of Adult and Community Education, POB 308, Jamison Centre, ACT 2614
T: (06) 2517933; Fax: 2517935
Founded: 1961; Members: 700
Pres: Dr. Jim Saleeba; Gen Secr: Alastair Crombie
Focus: Adult Educ 00163

Australian Association of Neurologists (A.A.N.), 145 Macquairie St, Sydney, NSW 2000
T: (02) 92565443; E-Mail: aboyce@giga.net.au; Fax: 92523310
Founded: 1950; Members: 400
Pres: Dr. R.J. Burns; Gen Secr: Alice Boyce
Focus: Neurology
Periodical
Clinical Neuroscience (quarterly) 00164

Australian Association of Occupational Therapists (A.A.O.T.), 97 Grange Rd, Alphington, Vic 3078
Founded: 1945; Members: 7
Focus: Therapeutics
Periodical
Australian Occupational Therapy Journal (quarterly) 00165

Australian Association of Social Workers, POB 1059, North Richmond, Vic 3121
T: 416960, 414797
Founded: 1946
Focus: Sociology 00166

Australian Bar Association, Level 5, Inns of Court, 107 North Quay, Brisbane, Qld 4000
T: (07) 32362477; Fax: 32361180
Founded: 1962; Members: 5000
Pres: Chris Pullin
Focus: Law 00167

Australian Biochemical Society, c/o Dr. R.J. Porra, C.S.I.R.O.-Div of Plant Industry, GPOB 1600, Canberra, ACT 2601
T: (06) 465465; Fax: 473785
Founded: 1955; Members: 1000
Focus: Biochem
Periodical
Proceedings (annually) 00168

Australian Bird Study Association, GPOB A313, Sydney South, NSW 1235
T: (02) 96051426; Fax: 92517231
Founded: 1960; Members: 510
Pres: Alan Leishman
Focus: Ornithology
Periodical
Corella (quarterly) 00169

Australian Cancer Society, 500 George St, Sydney, NSW 2000
Founded: 1961
Focus: Cell Biol & Cancer Res
Periodical
Cancer Forum (3 times annually) . . . 00170

Australian Clay Minerals Society (ACMS), c/o C.S.I.R.O.-Div of Soils, GPOB 639, Canberra, ACT 2601
Founded: 1962; Members: 47
Focus: Mineralogy

Periodical
Proceedings National Conference 00171

Australian College of Education, 42 Geils Court, Deakin, ACT 2600
T: (06) 2811677
Founded: 1959; Members: 6000
Gen Secr: Beverley J. Pope
Focus: Educ
Periodicals
ACE News (quarterly)
Unicorn (quarterly) 00172

The Australian College of Obstetricians and Gynaecologists (A.C.O.G.), 8 La Trobe St, Melbourne, Vic 3000
T: (03) 3470231
Founded: 1978; Members: 870
Focus: Gynecology 00173

Australian College of Paediatrics (A.C.P.), POB 30, Parkville, Vic 3052
T: (03) 93474310; E-Mail: acp@cryptic.rch.unimelb.edu.au; Fax: 93472120
Founded: 1956; Members: 1000
Pres: Prof. P.D. Phelan; Gen Secr: Dr. T.D. Bohane
Focus: Pediatrics
Periodical
Journal of Paeditrics and Child Health (bi-monthly) 00174

Australian Committee of Directors of Principals (ACDP), Churchill House, 218 Northbourne Av, Braddon, ACT 2601
T: (062) 478880; E-Mail: ACOMDAP; Fax: 573079
Founded: 1983; Members: 40
Focus: Educ
Periodical
Newsletter (4-5 times annually) 00175

Australian Conservation Foundation, 340 Gore St, Fitzroy, Vic 3065
T: (03) 4161166; Fax: 4160767
Founded: 1965; Members: 90000
Pres: Prof. David Yencken; Gen Secr: Patricia J. Caswell
Focus: Nat Res; Ecology
Periodicals
Habitat Australia
Newsletter 00176

Australian Council for Educational Research (ACER), 19 Prospect Hill Rd, Private Bag 55, Camberwell, Vic 3124
T: (03) 92775500
Founded: 1930; Members: 25
Gen Secr: Prof. Barry McGaw
Focus: Educ
Periodicals
Australian Education Index (quarterly)
Australian Education Review (irregularly)
Australian Journal of Education (3 times annually)
Bibliography of Educational Theses in Australia (annually)
Newsletter (3 times annually) 00177

The Australian Council for Health, Physical Education and Recreation (ACHPER), POB 304, Hindmarsh, SA 5007
T: (08) 83403388; E-Mail: achper@camtech.net.au; Fax: 83403399
Founded: 1952; Members: 3500
Pres: L. Embrey; Gen Secr: J. Emmel
Focus: Public Health; Sports
Periodicals
ACHPER Active & Healthy Magazine (quarterly)
ACHPER Healthy Lifestyles Journal (quarterly)
Australian Journal of Science and Medicine in Sport (quarterly) 00178

Australian Council of National Trusts, POB 1002, Civic Square, ACT 2608
T: (06) 2476766; Fax: 2491395
Founded: 1965; Members: 75000
Gen Secr: Alan Graham
Focus: Ecology; Preserv Hist Monuments
Periodical
Heritage Australia 00179

Australian Dental Association, Northern Territory Branch, POB 4496, Darwin, NT 5794
Focus: Dent 00180

Australian Dental Association, Queensland Branch, 61 Brookes St, Bowen Hills, Qld 4006
T: (07) 2529866; Fax: 2524488
Focus: Dent 00181

Australian Dental Association, South Australian Branch, POB 858, Unley, SA 5061
T: (08) 82728111
Focus: Dent 00182

Australian Dental Association, Tasmania Branch, 130 Main Rd, New Town, Tas 7008
T: (002) 295917
Focus: Dent 00183

Australian Dental Association, Victorian Branch, POB 434, Toorak, Vic 3142
T: (03) 98268318; E-Mail: adavbinfo@adavb.com.au; Fax: 98241095
Founded: 1928; Members: 1950
Pres: Dr. John Matthews; Gen Secr: Garry Pearson
Focus: Dent 00184

Australian Dental Association, Western Australia Branch, 14 Altona St, West Perth, WA 6005
T: (09) 3217880
Focus: Dent 00185

The Australian Entomological Society, c/o Plant Research Institute, Swan St, Burnley, Vic 3121
Fax: (03) 8195653
Founded: 1965; Members: 769
Focus: Entomology
Periodicals
Journal of the Australian Entomological Society (annually)
Myrmecia (quarterly) 00186

Australian Fabian Society, GPOB 2707X, Melbourne, Vic 3001
Focus: Socialism; Poli Sci
Periodical
Fabian Pamphlets 00187

Australian Federation for Medical and Biological Engineering, c/o Dept of Electrical Engineering, University of Melbourne, Parkville, Vic 3052
T: 3416686
Founded: 1959
Focus: Eng; Med; Bio 00188

Australian Geological Survey Organisation (AGSO), GPOB 378, Canberra, ACT 2601
T: (06) 2499111; Fax: 2499999
Founded: 1946
Gen Secr: Neil Williams
Focus: Geology
Periodical
Bulletin 00189

Australian Geomechanics Society, c/o The Institution of Engineers, Australia, 11 National Circuit, Barton, ACT 2600
T: (062) 2706555; E-Mail: Valerie_J_Lee@ieaust.org.au; Fax: 2731488
Founded: 1970; Members: 870
Pres: Dr. A.B. Phillips; Gen Secr: V. Lee
Focus: Mining; Geology
Periodical
Australian Geomechanics (semi-annually) . 00190

Australian Institute of Aboriginal and Torres Strait Islander Studies, GPOB 553, Canberra, ACT 2601
Founded: 1961
Pres: Dr. William Jonas
Focus: Ethnology
Periodicals
Australian Aboriginal Studies
Bibliographies
Manuals
Newsletter (semi-annually)
Regional and Research Studies 00191

Australian Institute of Agricultural Science, 91 Rathdowne St, Carlton, Vic 3053
T: (03) 96621077; Fax: 96622727
Founded: 1935; Members: 2500
Gen Secr: Simon L. Field
Focus: Agri
Periodical
Agricultural Science (quarterly) 00192

Australian Institute of Archaeology, Level 2, Centreway Arcade, 259 Collins St, Melbourne, Vic 3000
T: (03) 96503477; Fax: 96542774
Founded: 1946; Members: 500
Pres: J.A. Tibble
Focus: Archeol
Periodical
Buried History (quarterly) 00193

Australian Institute of Credit Management, POB 558, Artarmon, NSW 2064
Founded: 1967; Members: 3000
Pres: W.L. Duncan; Gen Secr: L.J. Wilson
Focus: Finance
Periodical
Credit Review (bi-monthly) 00194

Australian Institute of Criminology, GPOB 2994, Canberra, ACT 2601
T: (06) 2740200; Fax: 2740201
Founded: 1973
Gen Secr: Dr. Grant Wardlaw
Focus: Criminology
Periodicals
Australian Criminology Information Bulletin (semi-annually)
Criminology Australia (quarterly) 00195

Australian Institute of Energy, POB 230, Wahroonga, NSW 2076
T: (02) 94491800; E-Mail: nie@tpgi.com.au; Fax: 99839665
Founded: 1978; Members: 1500
Pres: Frederick Phillips; Gen Secr: Colin Paulson
Focus: Energy
Periodical
News Journal (bi-monthly) 00196

Australian Institute of Food Science and Technology Inc., POB 1493, North Sydney, NSW 2059
T: (02) 99594499; E-Mail: Foodaust@foodaust.com.au; Fax: 99544327
Founded: 1949; Members: 2200
Pres: Richard Mason; Gen Secr: Robert Hamilton
Focus: Eng; Food

Periodical
Food Australia (monthly) 00197

Australian Institute of Industrial Psychology, 33-35 Bligh St, Sydney, NSW 2000
T: (02) 2325063
Founded: 1927
Focus: Psych 00198

Australian Institute of International Affairs (A.I.I.A.), 32 Thesiger Court, Deakin, ACT 2600
T: (06) 2822133; E-Mail: ceo@aiia.asn.au; Fax: 2852334
Founded: 1933; Members: 2000
Pres: R.H. Searby; Gen Secr: C.M. Jackman
Focus: Int'l Relat
Periodical
Australian Journal of International Relations (3 times annually) 00199

Australian Institute of Management, 181 Fitzroy St, Saint Kilda, Vic 3182
T: (03) 5348181; Fax: 5345050
Founded: 1941; Members: 25500
Pres: Bernard T. Cronin
Focus: Business Admin 00200

Australian Institute of Marine Science, PMB 3, Townsville, Qld 4810
T: (077) 534211; E-Mail: postmaster@aims.gov.au; Fax: 725852
Founded: 1972; Members: 160
Pres: Dr. R. Reichelt
Focus: Oceanography
Periodical
Annual Report: Annual Research Plan . 00201

Australian Institute of Mining and Metallurgy (AIMM), 31 Pelham St, Carlton, Vic 3053
T: (03) 96623166; E-Mail: marketing@ausimm.com.au; Fax: 96623662
Founded: 1893; Members: 8400
Pres: Michael Buckenham; Gen Secr: J.M. Webber
Focus: Mining; Metallurgy
Periodicals
The Ausimm Bulletin (8 times annually)
The Ausimm Proceedings (semi-annually) 00202

Australian Institute of Navigation (A.I.N.), GPOB 2250, Sydney, NSW 1043
T: (02) 92646413; Fax: 92671682
Founded: 1949; Members: 600
Gen Secr: K.L. Duncan
Focus: Navig 00203

Australian Institute of Nuclear Science and Engineering (AINSE), PMB 1, Menai, NSW 2234
T: (02) 97173376; Fax: 97179268
Founded: 1958
Gen Secr: Dr. R. Gammon
Focus: Nucl Res
Periodical
AINSE Annual Report (annually) 00204

Australian Institute of Physics (AIP), 1/21 Vale St, North Melbourne, Vic 3051
T: (03) 3266669; Fax: 3282670
Founded: 1963; Members: 2500
Pres: Prof. R. MacDonald; Gen Secr: Moira Welch
Focus: Physics 00205

Australian Institute of Quantity Surveyors, POB 301, Deakin West, ACT 2600
T: (06) 2822222; Fax: 2852427
Founded: 1971; Members: 2000
Pres: Prof. Dennis Lenard; Gen Secr: Terry Sanders
Focus: Surveying
Periodical
The Building Economist (quarterly) . . . 00206

Australian Institute of Radiography (A.I.R.), 212 Clarendon St, East Melbourne, Vic 3002
T: (03) 4193336
Founded: 1950; Members: 2300
Focus: Radiology
Periodical
The Radiographer (quarterly) 00207

Australian Institute of Urban Studies (AIUS), POB 809, Canberra, ACT 2601
Founded: 1966; Members: 750
Focus: Urban Plan
Periodicals
Australian Institute of Urban Studies (annually)
Australian Urban Studies (quarterly) . . 00208

Australian Institute of Valuers and Land Economists, 6 Campion St, Deakin, ACT 2600
T: (06) 2822411; Fax: 2852194
Founded: 1926; Members: 7000
Pres: Gregory Clarke; Gen Secr: Brian Nye
Focus: Finance
Periodical
The Valuer and Land Economist (quarterly) 00209

Australian Library and Information Association, POB E441, Kingston, ACT 2604
T: (06) 2851877; Fax: 2822249
Founded: 1936; Members: 9500
Pres: Kerry Smith; Gen Secr: Virginia Walsh
Focus: Libraries & Bk Sci
Periodicals
Australian Academic Research Libraries (quarterly)
Australian Library Journal (quarterly)
Australian Special Libraries News (quarterly)
Cataloguing Australia (quarterly)
Incite (monthly)
Orana (quarterly) 00210

Australian Mammal Society, c/o Dept of Tropical Environment Studies and Geography, James Cook University, Townsville, Qld 4811
Founded: 1959; Members: 560
Pres: Prof. Helene Marsh; Gen Secr: Dr. P. Corkeron
Focus: Zoology
Periodical
Australian Mammalogy (semi-annually) . . 00211

The Australian Mathematical Society (A.M.S.), c/o Dept of Mathematics, University of Tasmania, GPOB 252-37, Hobart, Tas 7001
T: (03) 62262442; E-Mail: elliott@hilbert.maths.utas.edu.au; Fax: 62262867
Founded: 1956; Members: 900
Pres: Prof. A.J. van der Poorten; Gen Secr: Prof. D. Elliott
Focus: Math
Periodicals
Bulletin (semi-annually)
Gazette (bi-monthly)
Journal: Series A (semi-annually)
Journal: Series B (annually) 00212

Australian Mathematics Trust (AMT), c/o University of Canberra, POB 1, Belconnen, ACT 2616
T: (02) 62012440
Founded: 1978
Pres: P.J. Taylor; Gen Secr: S. Bakker
Focus: Math
Periodicals
Australian Mathematics Competition for the Westpac Awards: Solutions and Statistics (annually)
Math Competitions: The Australian Scene (annually)
Mathematics Competitions: Journal of the World Federation of National Mathematics Competition (semi-annually) 00213

Australian Medical Association (AMA), 42 Macquarie St, Barton, ACT 2600
T: (06) 2705400; E-Mail: ama@com.au; Fax: 2705499
Founded: 1962; Members: 25000
Gen Secr: Bill Coote
Focus: Med
Periodicals
Australian Medicine
Medical Journal of Australia 00214

Australian National Committee on Large Dams (ANCOLD), c/o Queensland Water Resources Commission, GPOB 2454, Brisbane, Qld 4001
T: (07) 2247281
Founded: 1960; Members: 112
Focus: Civil Eng
Periodical
ANCOLD Bulletin (3 times annually) . . 00215

Australian Nuclear Science and Technology Organisation (ANSTO), Private Mail Bag 1, Menai, NSW 2234
T: (02) 97173111; E-Mail: webmaster@ansto.gov.au; Fax: 97175097
Founded: 1955
Pres: Prof. Helen Garnett
Focus: Nucl Res
Periodical
Annual Report (annually) 00216

Australian Numismatic Society (ANS), Royal Exchange, POB R4, Sydney, NSW 1225
T: (02) 94517896; E-Mail: Rod.Sell@Hlos.com.au; Fax: 94516171
Founded: 1913; Members: 200
Pres: T.E. Hanley; Gen Secr: T.E. Sell
Focus: Numismatics
Periodical
Report (quarterly) 00217

Australian Optometrical Association, POB 185, Carlton South, Vic 3053
T: (03) 96636833
Founded: 1918; Members: 2000
Pres: Colin Waldron; Gen Secr: Joseph Chakman
Focus: Optics
Periodicals
Australian Optometry (monthly)
Clinical & Experimental Optometry (bi-monthly) 00218

Australian Orthopaedic Association, 229 Macquarie St, Sydney, NSW 2000
T: (02) 2333018; Fax: 2218301
Founded: 1936
Focus: Orthopedics 00219

Australian Petroleum Exploration Association (APEA), 60 Margaret St, Sydney, NSW 2000
T: (02) 276718
Founded: 1959; Members: 219
Focus: Mining
Periodical
APEA Journal (semi-annually) 00220

Australian Physiological and Pharmacological Society, c/o Dept of Physiology, Monash University, Clayton, Vic 3168
T: (03) 99052507; E-Mail: tony.luff@med.monash.edu.au; Fax: 99052547
Founded: 1960; Members: 550
Pres: Prof. J.A. Young; Gen Secr: Prof. A.R. Luff
Focus: Physiology; Pharmacol
Periodical
Proceedings (semi-annually) 00221

Australian Physiotherapy Association, POB 119, Concord, NSW 2137
Founded: 1905; Members: 2700
Pres: Kingsley Gibson; Gen Secr: Mark Brown
Focus: Therapeutics
Periodical
NSW Physiotherapy Bulletin (monthly) . . 00222

Australian Postgraduate Federation in Medicine, 22 Lascelles Av, Camperdown, VIC 3147
T: (03) 2408671
Founded: 1962; Members: 40
Focus: Med; Adult Educ 00223

The Australian Psychological Society, 1 Grattan St, Carlton, Vic 3053
T: (03) 96636166; Fax: 96636177
Founded: 1966; Members: 12000
Pres: B.J. Clowe; Gen Secr: Dr. A.F. Garton
Focus: Psych
Periodicals
Australian Journal of Psychology (3 times annually)
Australian Psychologist (3 times annually)
In-Psych: The Bulletin of the Australian Psychological Society (bi-monthly) . . . 00224

Australian Remedial Education Association (AREA), GPOB 334, Camberwell, Vic 3124
T: 821659
Founded: 1964; Members: 560
Focus: Educ 00225

Australian Research Council, c/o Dept of Employment, Education, Training and Youth Affairs, 64 Northbourne Av, Canberra, ACT 2601
T: (06) 2409837; Fax: 2409869
Founded: 1965
Pres: Prof. M.H. Brennan
Focus: Educ 00226

Australian Robot Association, GPOB 1527, Sydney, NSW 2001
T: (02) 99594632; Fax: 99594632
Founded: 1981
Pres: Prof. Malcolm Good; Gen Secr: Michael Kassler
Focus: Eng
Periodical
Newsletter 00227

Australian Science Teachers Association (A.S.T.A.), 15 Sussex St, Warradale, SA 5046
T: 2966472
Founded: 1950; Members: 4000
Focus: Sci; Educ 00228

Australian Society for Fish Biology, c/o Marine Science Laboratories, POB 114, Queenscliff, Vic 3225
T: (03) 52580111; E-Mail: K.hall@msl.02.au; Fax: 52580270
Founded: 1971; Members: 530
Pres: Dr. P. Young; Gen Secr: C. Bulman
Focus: Zoology
Periodical
Newsletter (semi-annually) 00229

Australian Society for Limnology, c/o Museum of Victoria, 71 Victoria Crescent, Abbotsford, Vic 3067
T: (03) 92840218; E-Mail: rmarch@pioneer.mov.vic.gov.au; Fax: 94160475
Founded: 1961; Members: 570
Pres: Dr. Max Finlayson; Gen Secr: Dr. Richard Marchant
Focus: Bio
Periodicals
Newsletter (quarterly)
Special Publications (irregularly) 00230

Australian Society for Medical Research, 145 Maquarie St, Sydney, NSW 2000
T: (02) 92565450; E-Mail: asmr@world.net; Fax: 92520294
Founded: 1961; Members: 1135
Pres: Dr. K. Scott; Gen Secr: Dr. Judy Halliday
Focus: Med
Periodical
Proceedings (annually) 00231

Australian Society for Microbiology (A.S.M.), Unit 23, 20 Commercial Rd, Melbourne, Vic 3004
T: (03) 98678699; Fax: 98678722
Founded: 1959; Members: 3200
Pres: Dr. D. Groot Obbink; Gen Secr: Dr. J. Lanser
Focus: Microbio 00232

Australian Society for Operations Research (ASOR), GPOB 2021S, Melbourne, Vic 3001
Founded: 1972; Members: 500
Focus: Computer & Info Sci
Periodical
ASOR Bulletin (semi-annually) 00233

Australian Society for Parasitology, c/o ACTS, GPOB 2200, Canberra, ACT 2601
T: (06) 2573299; Fax: 2573256
Founded: 1964; Members: 450
Focus: Immunology
Periodical
International Journal for Parasitology . . 00234

Australian Society for Reproductive Biology, c/o Dept of Biology Science, University of Newcastle, Newcastle, NSW 2308
T: (049) 685511
Founded: 1969
Focus: Bio 00235

Australian Society of Anaesthesists (ASA), POB 345, Paddington, NSW 2021
T: 3313211
Founded: 1934; Members: 1500
Focus: Anesthetics
Periodical
Anaesthesia and Intensive Care (quarterly) 00236

Australian Society of Authors (A.S.A.), POB 1566, Strawberry Hills, NSW 2012
T: (02) 93180877; E-Mail: asauthors@peg.pegasus.oz.au; Fax: 93180530
Founded: 1963; Members: 2800
Gen Secr: Lynne Spender
Focus: Lit
Periodicals
A-Z of Authorship
The Australian Author (quarterly)
Australian Book Contracts 00237

Australian Society of Clinical Hypnotherapists, POB 471, Eastwood, NSW 2122
T: (02) 8742776; Fax: 8047149
Founded: 1974; Members: 400
Pres: Robert Carlon; Gen Secr: E. Carmen
Focus: Therapeutics 00238

Australian Society of Cosmetic Chemists, POB 301, Kingsgrove, NSW 2208
Founded: 1964
Focus: Chem
Periodical
Cosmetic Science in Australia (quarterly) 00239

Australian Society of Endodontology (A.S.E.), 188 North Terrace, Adelaide, SA 5000
T: (08) 82214243; Fax: 84100709
Founded: 1967; Members: 800
Pres: Dr. M. Wotzke; Gen Secr: Dr. A. Papaleorriou
Focus: Dent 00240

Australian Society of Herpetologists Inc., c/o John Wombey, C.S.I.R.O. Div of Wildlife and Ecology, POB 84, Lyneham, ACT 2602
E-Mail: J.Wombey@dwe.csiro.au
Founded: 1964; Members: 260
Gen Secr: John Wombey
Focus: Zoology
Periodical
Newsletter (semi-annually) 00241

Australian Society of Indexers (AusSI), POB R598, Royal Exchange NSW 1225
T: (03) 95716341; E-Mail: mindexer@interconnect.com.au; Fax: 95716341
Founded: 1976; Members: 220
Pres: Alan Walker; Gen Secr: Lorraine Doyle
Focus: Libraries & Bk Sci
Periodicals
Indexers Available (annually)
Newsletter (monthly) 00242

Australian Society of Orthodontists, 167 Saint George Terrace, Perth, WA 6000
Founded: 1927
Focus: Dent 00243

Australian Society of Plant Physiologists (A.S.P.P.), c/o Dr. I.F. Wardlaw, C.S.I.R.O. Div of Plant Industry, GPOB 1600, Canberra, ACT 2601
T: (06) 465838
Founded: 1958; Members: 641
Focus: Botany 00244

Australian Society of Prosthodontists (A.S.P.), c/o School of Dental Science, 711 Elizabeth St, Melbourne, WA 3000
T: (03) 3474222
Founded: 1961; Members: 250
Focus: Dent 00245

Australian Society of Soil Science (ASSSI), c/o C.S.I.R.O. Cunningham Laboratory, 306 Carmidy Rd, Saint Lucia, QND 4061
T: (01) 37700209
Founded: 1956; Members: 104
Focus: Agri 00246

Australian Sociological Association, c/o School of Social Inquiry, Deakin University, 662 Blackburn Rd, Clayton, Vic 3168
Founded: 1963; Members: 550
Pres: Prof. Bryan S. Turner; Gen Secr: Dr. Marilyn Poole
Focus: Sociology 00247

Australian Veterinary Association (AVA), 134-136 Hampden Rd, POB 371, Artarmon, NSW 2064
T: 4112733
Founded: 1921; Members: 4000
Pres: W. Scanlon; Gen Secr: B. Horsfield
Focus: Vet Med
Periodicals
Australian Advances in Veterinary Science (annually)
Australian Veterinary Journal (monthly)
AVA Yearbook (annually) 00248

Australian Vice-Chancellors' Committee, GPOB 1142, Canberra, ACT 2601
Founded: 1920; Members: 37
Pres: Prof. F. Gale; Gen Secr: Stuart Anthony Hamilton
Focus: Educ
Periodicals
Information Summaries (irregularly)
Occasional Papers
Univation (3 times annually) 00249

Australian Wool Corporation, Wool House, 369 Royal Parade, Parkville, Vic 3052
Fax: (03) 3419273
Founded: 1936
Focus: Textiles
Periodical
Annual Report (annually) 00250

Australian Zinc Development Association, 95 Collins St, Melbourne, Vic 3000
Focus: Metallurgy 00251

Bibliographical Society of Australia and New Zealand, c/o Margaret Dent, National Library of Australia, Canberra, ACT 2600
Founded: 1969; Members: 248
Pres: W.D. Thorn
Focus: Libraries & Bk Sci
Periodicals
Broadsheet (3-4 times annually)
Bulletin (quarterly) 00252

Bio-Rhythm Research and Information Centre, 22 Mungala St, Rochdale, Brisbane, Qld 4123
T: (07) 3414928
Founded: 1954
Focus: Bio
Periodical
The Basic Biorhythm Story 00253

Bird Observers Club of Australia (B.O.C.), 183 Springvale Rd, Nunawading, Vic 3131
T: (03) 98775342
Founded: 1905; Members: 4000
Focus: Ornithology
Periodicals
The Australian Bird Watcher (quarterly)
The Bird Observer (monthly) 00254

Botany 2000-Asia, c/o Dept of Conservation and Land Management, Western Australian Herbarium, George St, Kensington
T: (09) 3670515; Fax: 3670515
Founded: 1989
Focus: Botany 00255

The Cardiac Society of Australia and New Zealand, 145 Macquarie St, Sydney, NSW 2000
T: (02) 274461; Fax: 231320
Founded: 1951; Members: 1100
Focus: Cardiol 00256

Chartered Institute of Transport in Australia, Queen Victoria Bldgs, POB Q398, Queen Victoria P.O., Sydney, NSW 1230
T: (02) 92646413; Fax: 92671682
Founded: 1935; Members: 2500
Gen Secr: K.L. Duncan
Focus: Transport
Periodicals
Australian Transport Review (annually)
CITIA News (bi-monthly) 00257

Clean Air Society of Australia and New Zealand, POB 191, Eastwood, NSW 2122
T: 20557
Founded: 1966
Focus: Ecology 00258

Commission for the Conservation of Antarctic Marine Living Resources (CCAMLR), 25 Old Wharf, Hobart 7000
T: (02) 310366; Fax: 232714
Founded: 1982; Members: 20
Focus: Ecology
Periodicals
CCAMLR Newsletter (semi-annually)
CCAMLR Statistical Bulletin 00259

Committee for Economic Development of Australia (CEDA), CEDA House, 123 Lonsdale St, Melbourne, Vic 3000
T: (03) 96623544; Fax: 96637271
Founded: 1960; Members: 965
Pres: Dr. W.W.J. Uhlenbruch; Gen Secr: Dr. J.P. Nieuwenhuysen
Focus: Econ
Periodicals
PEN: Public Economic Newsletter (annually)
PIPS: Public Information Paper (annually) 00260

Commonwealth Institute of Valuers, 119 York St, Sydney
Founded: 1926; Members: 5 000
Focus: Finance
Periodical
The Valuer (quarterly) 00261

Commonwealth Scientific and Industrial Research Organisation (C.S.I.R.O.), POB 53, Parkville, Vic 3052
T: (03) 6627111; Fax: 6627196
Founded: 1926; Members: 7000
Pres: Prof. A. Clarke; Gen Secr: Malcolm McIntosh
Focus: Sci; Eng

Periodicals
Australian Forest Research (quarterly)
Australian Journal of Agricultural Research (bi-monthly)
Australian Journal of Biological Sciences (bi-monthly)
Australian Journal of Botany (bi-monthly)
Australian Journal of Chemistry (monthly)
Australian Journal of Experimental Agriculture and Animal Husbandry (quarterly)
Australian Journal of Marine and Freshwater Research (bi-monthly)
Australian Journal of Physics (bi-monthly)
Australian Journal of Plant Physiology (bi-monthly)
Australian Journal of Soil Research (quarterly)
Australian Journal of Zoology (bi-monthly)
Australian Wildlife Research
Brunonia (semi-annually)
Food Research Quarterly (quarterly) . . 00262

The Contact Lens Society of Australia (C.L.S.A.), 818 Australia Sq Tower, 264 George St, Sydney, NSW 2000
T: (02) 9273997; Fax: 92513311
Founded: 1962; Members: 650
Pres: N. Brandon; Gen Secr: Kenneth W. Bell
Focus: Ophthal 00263

Council for International Congresses of Entomology, c/o Div of Entomology, C.S.I.R.O., GPOB 1700, Canberra, ACT 2601
Members: 23
Focus: Entomology 00264

Council of Adult Education, 256 Flinders St, Melbourne, Vic 3000
T: (03) 96520611; Fax: 96546759
Founded: 1947
Pres: Brian Weeks; Gen Secr: Graham Stevenson
Focus: Adult Educ
Periodical
Groupe Affairs (3 times annually) . . 00265

Defence Science and Technolohy Organisation, Anzac Park West Offices, Constitution Av, Canberra, ACT 2600
T: (06) 2666661; Fax: 2666320
Focus: Military Sci 00266

Dietitians Association of Australia (D.A.A.), 1-8 Phipps Close Deakin, Canberra, ACT 2600
T: (06) 2829555; E-Mail: daacanb@hcn.net.au; Fax: 2829888
Founded: 1983; Members: 1900
Focus: Nutrition
Periodicals
Australian Journal of Nutritrion & Dietetics Newsletter 00267

Eastern Dredging Association (EADA), GPOB 1818, Brisbane 4001
Founded: 1982
Focus: Civil Eng 00268

Ecological Society of Australia (E.S.A.), POB 1564, Canberra, ACT 2601
Founded: 1960; Members: 1000
Pres: Prof. J.B. Kirkpatrick; Gen Secr: Dr. J. Whinam
Focus: Ecology
Periodical
Australian Journal of Ecology (quarterly) . 00269

Endocrine Society of Australia (ESA), c/o Institute of Reproduction and Development, Monash University, Clayton, Vic 3168
T: (03) 95503571; E-Mail: gail.risbridge@med.monash.edu.au; Fax: 95503584
Founded: 1958; Members: 500
Pres: Prof. Duncan J. Topliss; Gen Secr: Dr. Gail P. Risbridger
Focus: Endocrinology
Periodical
Proceedings (annually) 00270

English Association – Sydney Branch, c/o Dept of English, University of Sydney, Sydney, NSW 2006
Founded: 1923; Members: 170
Pres: Prof. Elizabeth Webby; Gen Secr: C.A. Lee
Focus: Ling
Periodical
Southerly (quarterly) 00271

Entomological Society of New South Wales, c/o Dept of Entomology, The Australian Museum, 6-8 College St, Sydney, NSW 2001
Founded: 1952; Members: 194
Pres: G.R. Brown; Gen Secr: M.J. Fletcher
Focus: Entomology
Periodical
General and Applied Entomology (annually)
. . . . 00272

Entomological Society of Queensland, c/o Entomology Dept, University of Queensland, Brisbane, Qld 4072
Founded: 1923; Members: 300
Pres: Dr. D. Yeates; Gen Secr: Dr. L.E. Muir
Focus: Entomology
Periodicals
Australian Entomologist (quarterly)
News Bulletin (10 times annually) . . . 00273

Ergonomics Society of Australia, c/o Prof. R.A. Williams, University of Melbourne, Parkville, Vic 3052
T: (03) 3445311; Fax: 3473986
Founded: 1925; Members: 3200
Pres: B. Fraser; Gen Secr: P. Abelson
Focus: Orthopedics

Periodical
Conference Proceedings (annually) . . . 00274

Federation of Australian Scientific and Technological Societies, POB 218, Deakin West, ACT 2601
T: (06) 2822026; Fax: 2822953
Founded: 1985; Members: 60
Pres: Dr. Joe Baker; Gen Secr: T. Gascoigne
Focus: Sci; Eng 00275

Fellowship of Australian Writers, POB 488, Rezelle, NSW 2039
Founded: 1928; Members: 3500
Pres: Beverley Earnshaw; Gen Secr: Alan Russell
Focus: Lit
Periodical
Bulletin (bi-monthly) 00276

Field Naturalists Club of Victoria (F.N.C.V.), c/o National Herbarium, Locked Bag 3, PO, Blackburn, Vic 3130
Founded: 1880; Members: 900
Pres: Prof. Robert Wallis
Focus: Hist; Nat Sci; Ecology
Periodical
The Victorian Naturalist (bi-monthly) . . 00277

The Field Naturalists' Society of South Australia (FNSSA), GPOB 1594, Adelaide, SA 5001
Founded: 1883; Members: 380
Focus: Hist; Nat Sci; Ecology
Periodical
The South Australian Naturalist (quarterly) 00278

Food Technology Association of New South Wales, 60 York St, Sydney, NSW 2000
T: (02) 2900700
Founded: 1946
Focus: Eng; Nutrition 00279

Food Technology Association of Queensland, 375 Wickham Terrace, Brisbane, Qld 4000
Founded: 1947
Focus: Nutrition 00280

Food Technology Association of Tasmania, 191 Liverpool St, Hobart, Tas 7000
T: (002) 345933
Founded: 1952
Focus: Nutrition 00281

Food Technology Association of Western Australia, 212-220 Adelaide Terrace, POB 6209, Perth, WA 6000
Founded: 1954
Focus: Eng; Nutrition 00282

Geographical Society of New South Wales, POB 602, Gladesville, NSW 2111
T: (02) 8173647
Founded: 1927; Members: 500
Gen Secr: J. Dodson
Focus: Geography
Periodical
Australian Geographer (semi-annually) . . 00283

Geological Society of Australia, 301 George St, Sydney, NSW 2000
T: (02) 92902194; E-Mail: misha@sa.org.au; Fax: 92902198
Founded: 1953; Members: 3200
Pres: Dr. David Denham; Gen Secr: Misha Frankel
Focus: Geology
Periodicals
The Australian Geologist (quarterly)
Australian Journal of Earth Sciences (bi-monthly)
Meeting Abstracts (irregularly) 00284

Geological Survey of New South Wales, c/o Dept of Mineral Resources, POB 536, Saint Leonards
T: (02) 99018300; Fax: 99018256
Founded: 1874
Gen Secr: J.N. Cramsie
Focus: Geology
Periodicals
Bulletin
Geological Maps and Notes
Geological Memoirs
Metallogenic Maps and Notes
Mineral Industry
Mineral Resources
Palaeontological Memoirs
Quarterly Notes (quarterly)
Records 00285

Geological Survey of Victoria, c/o Dept of Natural Resources and Environment, POB 2145 MDC, Fitzroy, Vic 3065
T: (03) 94127802; Fax: 94127803
Founded: 1852
Gen Secr: Tom Dickson
Focus: Geology 00286

Gosford District Historical Research and Heritage Association, 230 Scenic Rd, Killcare Heights, Hardy's Bay, NSW 2256
Focus: Hist 00287

Horological Guild of Australasia, 228 Pitt St, Sydney, NSW 2000
T: (02) 9828561
Founded: 1951
Focus: Eng 00288

IDP Education Australia, GPOB 2006, Canberra, ACT 2601
T: (06) 2858222; Fax: 2853036
Founded: 1969; Members: 3000
Pres: Dr. D.G. Blight; Gen Secr: W.L. Streat
Focus: Educ
Periodicals
Journal of Electrical and Electronics Engineering Monitor (monthly)
Proceedings of the I.R.E.E. (quarterly) . 00289

Indo-Pacific Prehistory Association (IPPA), c/o Dept of Archaeology and Anthropology, Faculty of Arts, Australian National University, Canberra, ACT 0200
T: (06) 2494395; Fax: 2492711
Founded: 1929; Members: 250
Gen Secr: Dr. P. Bellwood
Focus: Anthro; Hist; Archeol
Periodical
Bulletin (annually) 00290

Institute of Materials Handling, 79 Buckhurst St, South Melbourne, Vic 3205
T: (03) 6991333
Founded: 1953
Focus: Materials Sci 00291

Institute of Mental Health Research and Postgraduate Training, 35 Poplar Rd, Parkville, Vic 3052
Founded: 1955
Focus: Psychiatry
Periodical
Statistical Bulletin (annually) 00292

Institute of Metals and Materials Australasia, 205/21 Bedford St, North Melbourne, Vic 3051
T: (03) 93267266; E-Mail: imma@immanet.asn.au; Fax: 93267272
Founded: 1946; Members: 1500
Gen Secr: Dr. I.J. McKee
Focus: Metallurgy
Periodicals
Materials Australia (bi-monthly)
Materials Forum (annually) 00293

Institute of Municipal Management (IMM), 49-51 Stead St, South Melbourne, Vic 3205
T: (03) 96459044; E-Mail: bbeattie@imm.org.au; Fax: 96901377
Founded: 1936; Members: 2700
Gen Secr: Barrie Beattie
Focus: Public Admin
Periodical
Local Government Management (bi-monthly)
. . . . 00294

Institute of Photographic Technology, GPOB 5385BB, Melbourne, Vic 3001
Founded: 1945
Focus: Eng; Photo 00295

Institute of Public Affairs (IPA), 128-136 Jolimont Rd, Jolimont, Vic 3002
T: (03) 654-7499; Fax: 6507627
Founded: 1943; Members: 4050
Pres: George Littlewood; Gen Secr: Mike Nahan
Focus: Econ; Business Admin
Periodicals
IPA Facts (quarterly)
IPA Review (quarterly)
Policy Issues 00296

Institute of Transport, 22 Karne St, Beverly Hills, NSW 2209
Founded: 1919
Focus: Transport 00297

Institution of Engineers – Australia, 11 National Circuit, Barton, ACT 2600
T: (06) 2706555; E-Mail: contact_cust_service@aust.org.au; Fax: 2731488
Founded: 1919; Members: 65000
Pres: Barry Grear; Gen Secr: John Webster
Focus: Eng
Periodicals
Australian Geomechanics News (semi-annually)
Chemical Engineering in Australia (quarterly)
Civil Engineering Transactions (quarterly)
Conference Volumes (monthly)
Engineers Australia (monthly)
General Engineering Transactions (annually)
Journal of Electrical & Electronics Engineering in Australia (annually)
Mechanical Engineering Transactions (annually)
. . . . 00298

Institution of Surveyors – Australia, 27-29 Napier Close, Deakin, Canberra, ACT 2600
T: (06) 2822282; E-Mail: institution_of_surveyor@icaust.org.au; Fax: 2822576
Founded: 1952; Members: 3500
Pres: I.H. Marshall; Gen Secr: J.D. Crickmore
Focus: Eng 00299

Inter-Union Commission on Frequency Allocations for Radio Astronomy and Space Science, c/o Dr. B.J. Robinson, C.S.I.R.O., POB 76, Epping, NSW 2121
T: (02) 8680222; Fax: 8680457
Founded: 1950
Focus: Astronomy; Comm 00300

International Association of Environmental Mutagen Societies, c/o Dept of Haematology, Flinders University, Adelaide, SA 5042
T: (08) 2044431; Fax: 2045450
Founded: 1973; Members: 2500
Focus: Bio 00301

International Association of Trichologists (IAT), 185 Elizabeth St, Ste 919, Sydney, NSW 2000
T: (2) 92671384; Fax: 82968450
Founded: 1973; Members: 100
Pres: Foster Tomkies; Gen Secr: David Salinger
Focus: Med; Immunology 00302

International Commission for Uniform Methods of Sugar Analysis, c/o CSR Ltd., Central Laborarory, 37-41 Waterloo Rd, NSW 2113 North Ryde
T: (02) 98591905; Fax: 98591900
Founded: 1897; Members: 250
Pres: Dr. Murray R. Player; Gen Secr: R. McCowage
Focus: Food 00303

Law Council of Australia, 19 Torrens St, Braddon, ACT 2612
T: (06) 2473788; Fax: 2480639
Founded: 1933; Members: 31000
Pres: Bret Walker; Gen Secr: Peter G. Levy
Focus: Law
Periodical
Australian Lawyer (monthly) 00304

Law Society of New South Wales, 170 Phillip St, Sydney, NSW 2000
T: (02) 99260333; Fax: 2315809
Founded: 1884; Members: 13200
Gen Secr: M. Richardson
Focus: Law
Periodicals
Caveat (11 times annually)
Law Society Journal (11 times annually) 00305

Linnean Society of New South Wales, 6-24 Cliff St, POB 457, Milsons Point, NSW 2061
T: 94843616
Founded: 1884; Members: 200
Pres: Dr. Alex Ritchie; Gen Secr: Barbara Stoddard
Focus: Hist; Nat Sci 00306

Malacological Society of Australia, c/o Dept of Malacology, Australian Museum, 6-8 College St, Sydney, NSW 2000
T: (02) 92306275; Fax: 93206050
Founded: 1955; Members: 400
Pres: Dr. W. Ponder; Gen Secr: A. Miller
Focus: Zoology
Periodicals
Australian Shell News (quarterly)
Journal (annually) 00307

Mapping Sciences Institute Australia, GPOB 1817, Brisbane, Qld 4001
Founded: 1953; Members: 1330
Gen Secr: K.H. Smith
Focus: Cart
Periodicals
Australian Geographical Studies (annually)
Newsletter (semi-annually) 00308

Medical Society of Victoria, 293 Royal Parade, Parkville, Vic 3052
T: 3478722
Founded: 1852
Focus: Med 00309

Medico Legal Society of New South Wales, POB 121, Saint Leonards, NSW 2065
T: 4398822
Founded: 1947
Focus: Law
Periodical
Proceedings 00310

Museums Association of Australia, 24 Queens Parade, North Fitzroy, Vic 3001
T: (03) 94863399; E-Mail: MANat@access.net.au; Fax: 94863788
Founded: 1937; Members: 2200
Pres: Dr. Sue-Anne Wallace
Focus: Arts
Periodicals
Museum National (quarterly)
Museums Australia (annually) 00311

Musicological Society of Australia, GPOB 2404, Canberra, ACT 2601
Founded: 1963; Members: 300
Pres: Shirley Trembath; Gen Secr: Anne-Marie Forbes
Focus: Music
Periodicals
Musicology Australia (annually)
Newsletter (3 times annually) 00312

National Health and Medical Research Council, GPOB 9848, Canberra, ACT 2601
T: (06) 2891555 k703) 2897802
Founded: 1936; Members: 28
Gen Secr: D. Ariotti
Focus: Public Health; Med
Periodicals
Council Session Reports
Medical Research Projects (annually) . . 00313

Native Plants Preservation Society of Victoria, 3 Denham Pl, Toorak, Vic 3142
Founded: 1952
Focus: Ecology 00314

Natural Resources Conservation League of Victoria (N.R.C.L.), 593 Springvale Rd, Springvale South, Vic 3172
T: (03) 95469744; Fax: 95478791
Founded: 1944; Members: 4400
Pres: Pamela Manning; Gen Secr: Dr. Peter Yau
Focus: Ecology
Periodical
Trees and Natural Resources (quarterly) . 00315

North Queensland Naturalists Club (N.Q.N.C.), POB 991, Cairns, Qld 4870
Founded: 1932; Members: 100
Focus: Hist; Nat Sci; Ecology 00316

Oaks Historical Society, Strathmore Rd, The Oaks, NSW 2570
T: (046) 571366
Focus: Hist 00317

Opticians and Optometrists Association of New South Wales, 235 Elizabeth St, Sydney, NSW 2000
T: (02) 265284
Founded: 1926
Focus: Optics; Ophthal 00318

Paediatric Society of Victoria, c/o Royal Children's Hospital, Flemington Rd, Parkville, Vic 3052
T: 3475522
Founded: 1906
Focus: Pediatrics 00319

PEN International (Sydney Centre), POB 153, Woollahra, NSW 2025
T: 325668
Founded: 1926; Members: 160
Pres: Stella Wilkes
Focus: Lit
Periodical
Newsletter (quarterly) 00320

Plant Protection Society of Western Australia, POB 190, Victoria Park, WA 6100
T: (09) 3683333; Fax: 3681205
Founded: 1976; Members: 97
Focus: Ecology
Periodical
Proceedings (irregularly) 00321

Queensland Institute for Educational Research, c/o Faculty of Education, University of Queensland, Saint Lucia, Qld 4067
T: 3706969
Founded: 1930
Focus: Educ 00322

The Queensland Naturalists' Club (Q.N.C.), GPOB 1220, Brisbane, Qld 4001
T: (07) 3722028
Founded: 1906; Members: 440
Focus: Hist; Nat Sci; Ecology
Periodical
The Queensland Naturalist (bi-annually) . 00323

The Royal Aeronautical Society (Australian Division), POB 573, Mascot, NSW 2020
Founded: 1927; Members: 600
Pres: J. Faulkner; Gen Secr: R.D. Barkla
Focus: Aero 00324

Royal Agricultural and Horticultural Society of South Australia, Royal Showground, Wayville, SA 5034
T: (08) 82105211; Fax: 82121944
Founded: 1839; Members: 6000
Pres: J. Duncan; Gen Secr: Gary Campbell
Focus: Hort; Agri 00325

Royal Agricultural Society of Tasmania, Rothmans Bldg, Royal Showgrounds, Glenorchy, Tas 7010
T: 726812
Founded: 1862
Focus: Agri 00326

The Royal Agricultural Society of Western Australia, POB 135, Claremont, WA 6010
T: 311933
Founded: 1829; Members: 3600
Focus: Agri 00327

Royal Art Society of New South Wales, 25-27 Walker St, North Sydney, NSW 2060
Founded: 1880; Members: 640
Pres: Ron Stannard; Gen Secr: Marjorie McLachlan
Focus: Arts
Periodical
Newsletter (monthly) 00328

Royal Australasian College of Dental Surgeons, 64 Castlereagh St, Sydney, NSW 2000
T: (02) 2323800; E-Mail: registrar@racds.org; Fax: 2218108
Founded: 1965; Members: 1070
Pres: S.C. Warneke; Gen Secr: K.H. Wendon
Focus: Surgery
Periodical
Annals (annually) 00329

The Royal Australasian College of Physicians (RACP), 145 Macquarie St, Sydney, NSW 2000
T: (02) 92565444; Fax: 92523310
Founded: 1938; Members: 5915
Pres: Prof. R. Smallwood; Gen Secr: D.W. Swinbourne
Focus: Med
Periodical
Australian and New Zealand Journal of Medicine (bi-monthly) 00330

The Royal Australasian College of Radiologists, 51 Druitt St, Sydney, NSW 2000
T: (02) 92643555; Fax: 92647799
Founded: 1935; Members: 2211
Pres: Dr. Turab Chakera; Gen Secr: Dr. Luke Baker
Focus: Radiology
Periodical
Australasian Radiology (quarterly) . . . 00331

Royal Australasian College of Surgeons (R.A.C.S.), Spring St, Melbourne, Vic 3000
T: (03) 92491200; Fax: 92491219
Founded: 1927; Members: 4600
Gen Secr: P.H. Carter
Focus: Surgery
Periodical
Australian and New Zealand Journal of Surgery (monthly) 00332

Royal Australasian Ornithologists Union (R.A.O.U.), 415 Riversdale Rd, Hawthorn East, Vic 3123
T: (03) 98822622; Fax: 98822677
Founded: 1901; Members: 5000
Pres: Prof. B. Snape; Gen Secr: B. Wilson
Focus: Ornithology 00333

Royal Australian and New-Zealand College of Psychiatrists (R.A.N.Z.C.P.), Maudsley House, 390 La Trobe St, Melbourne, Vic 3000
T: (03) 96400646; Fax: 96425652
Founded: 1963; Members: 2075
Pres: Prof. George Lipton; Gen Secr: Dr. Michael Epstein
Focus: Psychiatry 00334

Royal Australian Chemical Institute (R.A.C.I.), 1/21 Vale St, North Melbourne, Vic 3051
T: (03) 93282033; Fax: 93282670
Founded: 1917; Members: 9500
Gen Secr: Dr. S. Cumming
Focus: Chem 00335

Royal Australian College of Ophthalmologists, 27 Commonwealth St, Sydney, NSW 2010
T: (02) 92677006; E-Mail: racosec@medeserv.cem.au; Fax: 92676534
Founded: 1969; Members: 976
Pres: Dr. Frank Martin; Gen Secr: Dr. Stephen Cains
Focus: Ophthal
Periodical
Australian and New Zealand Journal of Ophthalmology (quarterly) 00336

Royal Australian Historical Society, History House, 133 Macquarie St, Sydney, NSW 2000
T: (02) 92478001; Fax: 92477854
Founded: 1901; Members: 2000
Gen Secr: Ralph Derbidge
Focus: Hist
Periodicals
History Magazine (quarterly)
Journal (bi-monthly) 00337

Royal Australian Planning Institute (RAPI), 615 Burwood Rd, Hawthorn, Vic 3122
T: (03) 98190728; E-Mail: rapinat@creative.access.com.au; Fax: 98190676
Founded: 1951; Members: 3300
Pres: Barrie Melotte; Gen Secr: Richard Head
Focus: Urban Plan
Periodical
Australian Planner (quarterly) 00338

Royal College of Nursing – Australia, 1 Napier Close, Deakin, ACT 2600
T: (06) 2825633; Fax: 2823565
Founded: 1949; Members: 5000
Gen Secr: Elizabeth C. Percival
Focus: Med 00339

Royal College of Pathologists of Australasia, Durham Hall, 207 Albion St, Surrey Hills, NSW 2010
Founded: 1956; Members: 1500
Pres: Dr. E. Raik; Gen Secr: Dr. C. McLeod
Focus: Pathology
Periodical
Pathology 00340

Royal Geographical Society of Queensland (R.G.S.A.), 112 Brookes St, Fortitude Valley, Qld 4006
T: (07) 32523856; Fax: 32524986
Founded: 1885; Members: 580
Pres: John Holmes; Gen Secr: Keith Smith
Focus: Geography 00341

The Royal Historical Society of Queensland (R.H.S.Q.), Commissariat Stores, 115 William St, POB 12057, Brisbane North Quay, Qld 4002
T: (07) 32214198; Fax: 32214198
Founded: 1913; Members: 600
Pres: Dr. M.D. White; Gen Secr: Kirstie Moar
Focus: Hist
Periodicals
Journal of The Royal Historical Society of Queensland (quarterly)
The Royal Historical Society of Queensland Bulletin (monthly) 00342

Royal Historical Society of Victoria (RHSV), Royal Mint, 280 William St, Melbourne, Vic 3000
T: (03) 96701219; Fax: 96701241
Founded: 1909; Members: 1600
Pres: Prof. Weston Bate; Gen Secr: Kevin Gates
Focus: Hist
Periodicals
History News (monthly)
Journal (quarterly) 00343

Royal Horticultural Society of New South Wales, GPOB 4728, Sydney, NSW 2001
Founded: 1862; Members: 510
Focus: Hort 00344

Royal Melbourne Institute of Technology, GPOB 2476V, Melbourne, Vic 3001
Focus: Eng 00345

Royal Queensland Art Society, GPOB 1602, Brisbane, Qld 4001
T: (07) 98313455
Founded: 1887; Members: 850
Gen Secr: Karen Kane
Focus: Arts 00346

Royal Society of New South Wales, 134 Herring Rd, POB 1525, North Ryde, NSW 2113
T: (02) 98874448
Founded: 1821; Members: 305
Pres: Dr. E.C. Potter; Gen Secr: Dr. P.R. Evans
Focus: Sci
Periodicals
Bulletin (monthly)
Journal (semi-annually)
Journal and Proceedings (semi-annually) . 00347

Royal Society of Queensland, POB 21, Saint Lucia, Qld 4067
T: (07) 38407708; Fax: 38461226
Founded: 1884; Members: 250
Pres: Dr. John Jell; Gen Secr: Ray Harty
Focus: Sci
Periodicals
Newsletter (quarterly)
Proceedings (annually)
Symposia (annually) 00348

Royal Society of South Australia, c/o South Australian Museum, North Terrace, Adelaide, SA 5000
T: (08) 82235360
Founded: 1853; Members: 300
Pres: Dr. Tom C.R. White; Gen Secr: Dr. Ole W. Wiebkin
Focus: Sci
Periodicals
Regional Natural Histories (irregularly)
Transactions (semi-annually) 00349

Royal Society of Tasmania, GPOB 1166M, Hobart, Tas 7001
T: (03) 62350777; Fax: 62347139
Founded: 1843; Members: 480
Gen Secr: Dr. M.R. Banks
Focus: Sci
Periodical
Papers and Proceedings of the Royal Society of Tasmania (annually) 00350

Royal Society of Victoria, 9 Victoria St, Melbourne, Vic 3000
T: (03) 96635259; E-Mail: rsvinc@vicnet.net.au; Fax: 96632301
Founded: 1854; Members: 650
Pres: Prof. H.H. Bolotin; Gen Secr: I. Endersby
Focus: Sci
Periodical
Proceedings (semi-annually) 00351

Royal Society of Western Australia, c/o Western Australian Museum, Francis St, Perth, WA 6000
Fax: (09) 3104929
Founded: 1913; Members: 350
Pres: Dr. S. Hopper
Focus: Sci
Periodical
Journal of the Royal Society of Western Australia (quarterly) 00352

Royal South Australian Society of Arts, 122 Kintore Av, Adelaide, SA 5000
T: (08) 2234704
Founded: 1856; Members: 702
Pres: Andrew Steiner; Gen Secr: Paul Griscti
Focus: Arts
Periodical
Kalori (quarterly) 00353

Royal Western Australian Historical Society, Stirling House, 49 Broadway, Nedlands, WA 6009
T: (09) 3863841; Fax: 3863309
Founded: 1926; Members: 1000
Gen Secr: K. Carman-Browns
Focus: Hist
Periodicals
Early Days (annually)
Newsletter (monthly) 00354

Royal Zoological Society of New South Wales, POB 20, Mosman, NSW 2088
T: (02) 99697336; Fax: 99697336
Founded: 1879; Members: 1500
Pres: Christopher Dickman; Gen Secr: Lyndall Dawson
Focus: Zoology
Periodical
Australian Zoologist (quarterly) 00355

Royal Zoological Society of South Australia, c/o Adelaide Zoo, Frome Rd, Adelaide, SA 5000
T: (08) 82673255; Fax: 82390637
Founded: 1878; Members: 5270
Pres: Prof. M. Tyler; Gen Secr: D. Langdon
Focus: Zoology
Periodicals
Annual Report (annually)
Zoo Times (quarterly) 00356

Safe Water Association of New South Wales, George St, GPOB 369, Sydney, NSW 2001
Focus: Water Res
Periodical
The Australian Fluoridation News (bi-monthly)
. . . . *00357*

School Library Association of the Northern Territory (SLANT), POB 3162, Darwin, NT 0801
Members: 90
Focus: Libraries & Bk Sci *00358*

Science Teachers Association of Queensland (S.T.A.Q.), POB 84, Spring Hill, Qld 4000
Founded: 1945; Members: 530
Focus: Sci; Educ *00359*

Science Teachers' Association of Victoria, 191 Royal Parade, Parkville, Vic 3052
T: 3472537
Founded: 1943
Focus: Sci; Educ *00360*

Society for Social Responsibility in Science (A.C.T.) (SSRS), POB 48, Canberra, ACT 2601
T: (06) 465682
Founded: 1970; Members: 150
Focus: Sociology *00361*

Society of Australian Genealogists, Richmond Villa, 120 Kent St, Sydney, NSW 2000
T: (02) 2473953
Founded: 1932; Members: 7500
Pres: E.C. Best; Gen Secr: H.E. Garnsey
Focus: Genealogy
Periodical
Descent (quarterly) *00362*

Society of Leather Technologists and Chemists, c/o Austral Finishes Pty Ltd, 19 Wilson St, Botany, NSW 2019
Founded: 1897; Members: 71
Focus: Eng; Chem *00363*

Sociological Association of Australia and New Zealand, c/o Dept of Social Sciences, Mitchell College of Advanced Education, Bathurst, NSW 2795
Founded: 1963; Members: 600
Focus: Sociology
Periodical
The Australian and New Zealand Journal of Sociology (3 times annually) *00364*

South Australian Ornithological Association (S.A.O.A.), c/o South Australian Museum, North Terrace, Adelaide, SA 5000
T: (08) 82787866; Fax: 82787866
Founded: 1899; Members: 500
Pres: Dr. David Robertson; Gen Secr: Dr. Josie Pyle
Focus: Ornithology
Periodicals
Newsletter (quarterly)
The South Australian Ornithologist (semi-annually)
. . . . *00365*

South Australian Science Teachers Association, 163a Greenhill Rd, Parkside, SA 5063
Founded: 1941; Members: 850
Focus: Sci; Educ
Periodical
Sasta Journal (3 times annually) . . . *00366*

Statistical Society of Australia (S.S.A.), GPOB 573, Canberra, ACT 2601
Founded: 1959; Members: 900
Pres: H. MacGillivray; Gen Secr: N. Weber
Focus: Stats
Periodicals
Australian Journal of Statistics (3 times annually)
Newsletter (quarterly) *00367*

Sydney University Chemical Engineering Association (S.U.C.E.A.), c/o Dept of Chemical Engineering, University of Sydney, Sydney, NSW 2006
T: (02) 6608455
Members: 500
Focus: Chem; Eng *00368*

Sydney University Chemical Society, c/o School of Chemistry, University, Sydney, NSW 2006
T: (02) 6922732; Fax: 6923329
Founded: 1929
Focus: Chem *00369*

Sydney University Medical Society, D06 Blackburn Bldg, University of Sydney, NSW 2006
T: (02) 93512482; E-Mail: medsoc@usyd.edu.au; Fax: 93516197
Founded: 1886
Focus: Med *00370*

Sydney University Psychological Society, c/o Psychology Dept, University, Sydney, NSW 2006
T: (02) 6600522
Founded: 1929
Focus: Psych *00371*

Sydney University Veterinary Society, c/o Faculty of Veterinary Science, University, Sydney, NSW 2006
Focus: Vet Med *00372*

Tasmanian Geological Survey, c/o Mineral Resources Tasmania, POB 56, Rosny, Tas 7018
T: (03) 62338333; Fax: 62338338
Founded: 1860
Pres: Dr. A.V. Brown
Focus: Geology; Geophys
Periodicals
Explanatory Report
Geological Survey Bulletin
Geological Survey Paper
Technical Report *00373*

Tasmanian Historical Research Association, POB 441, Sandy Bay, Tas 7005
Founded: 1951; Members: 400
Pres: Dr. Stefan Petrow; Gen Secr: J.E. Scrivener
Focus: Hist
Periodical
Papers and Proceedings (quarterly) . . . *00374*

Tasmanian University Agricultural Science Society, c/o Agricultural Faculty, University of Tasmania, GPOB 252, Hobart, Tas 7001
T: (002) 230561
Founded: 1962; Members: 45
Focus: Agri *00375*

Telecommunication Society of Australia (T.S.A.), GPOB 4050, Melbourne, Vic 3001
T: (03) 6307650
Founded: 1874; Members: 6000
Focus: Electric Eng *00376*

The Tropical Grassland Society of Australia Inc., 306 Carmody Rd, Saint Lucia, Qld 4067
T: (07) 33770209; E-Mail: tgs@tag.csiro.au; Fax: 33713946
Founded: 1963; Members: 650
Pres: Dr. C.P. Miller; Gen Secr: John Hodgkinson
Focus: Agri
Periodical
Tropical Grasslands (quarterly) *00377*

University Geographical Society, c/o Dept of Geography, University of Western Australia, Nedlands, WA 6009
T: (09) 3802698
Founded: 1964; Members: 140
Focus: Geography
Periodicals
Australind (irregularly)
Real World *00378*

University of New South Wales Chemical Engineering Association, c/o University of New South Wales, POB 1, Kensington, NSW 2033
T: 6630351
Founded: 1962
Focus: Eng *00379*

Victorian Artists' Society, 430 Albert St, East Melbourne, Vic 3002
T: (03) 96621484; Fax: 96622343
Founded: 1870; Members: 1000
Pres: Kathlyn Ballard; Gen Secr: Beverley Snelling
Focus: Arts
Periodicals
Annual Report (annually)
News Letter *00380*

Victorian Public Interest Research Group, 47 Charles St, Fitzroy, Vic 3065
Focus: Econ *00381*

Water Authorities Association of Victoria, 468 Saint Kilda Rd, Melbourne, Vic 3004
T: (03) 2675266
Founded: 1988
Focus: Civil Eng *00382*

Water Research Foundation of Australia, c/o Centre for Resource and Environmental Studies, Australian National University, Canberra, ACT 0200
T: (06) 2490651; Fax: 2490757
Founded: 1956; Members: 600
Gen Secr: D.J. Beale
Focus: Water Res *00383*

Weed Science Society of New South Wales, POB K287, Haymarket, NSW 2000
T: 6310655
Founded: 1966; Members: 125
Focus: Botany *00384*

Weed Science Society of South Australia, c/o Ian Clunies Ross Centre, Australian Mineral Foundation, Conyngham St, Glenside, SA 5065
T: (085) 797821
Founded: 1970; Members: 50
Focus: Botany
Periodical
Newsletter (9 times annually) *00385*

Western Australian Mental Health Association, 311-313 Hay St, Subiaco, WA 6008
T: 811986
Founded: 1960; Members: 300
Focus: Psychiatry *00386*

The Western Australian Naturalists' Club, POB 156, Nedlands, WA 6909
Founded: 1924; Members: 545
Pres: Alan Notley; Gen Secr: Gordon Elliott
Focus: Hist; Nat Sci; Ecology
Periodical
Western Australian Naturalist (semi-annually)
. . . . *00387*

Western Australian Shell Club (W.A.S.C.), c/o W.A. Museum, Francis St, Perth, WA 6000
T: (09) 2714639
Founded: 1965; Members: 94
Focus: Ecology
Periodical
W.A. Shell Collector (quarterly) *00388*

Wildlife Conservation Society, Ettamogah Sanctuary, Hume Hwy, Lavington, NSW 2641
T: 251473
Founded: 1967
Focus: Ecology *00389*

Wildlife Preservation Society of Australia (W.L.P.S. of A.), POB 3428, Sydney, NSW 2001
Founded: 1909; Members: 500
Pres: Vincent Serventy; Gen Secr: Sandy Johnson
Focus: Ecology
Periodical
Australian Wildlife Newsletter (quarterly) . *00390*

Zoological Board of Victoria, POB 74, Parkville, Vic 3052
T: (03) 92859300; Fax: 92859330
Founded: 1937; Members: 9
Pres: D.K. Hayward; Gen Secr: C.R. Larcombe
Focus: Zoology *00391*

Austria

Adalbert Stifter-Gesellschaft (A.St.G.), c/o Historisches Museum, Karlspl, 1040 Wien
T: (01) 505874784031; Fax: 50587477201
Founded: 1918; Members: 150
Pres: Dr. Günter Büriegl; Gen Secr: Dr. Ursula Storch
Focus: Lit *00392*

Ärztekammer für Kärnten, Bahnhofstr 22, 9020 Klagenfurt
T: (0463) 514222
Focus: Med
Periodical
Mitteilungen der Ärztekammer für Kärnten (monthly) *00393*

Ärztekammer für Niederösterreich, Wipplingerstr 2, 1010 Wien
T: (01) 633611
Focus: Med *00394*

Ärztekammer für Wien, Weihburggasse 10-12, 1010 Wien
T: (01) 51501223; Fax: 51501289
Focus: Med
Periodical
Wiener Arzt (11 times annually) *00395*

Akademie der bildenden Künste in Wien, Schillerpl 3, 1010 Wien
T: (01) 58816
Focus: Arts *00396*

Akademie für Allgemeinmedizin, Universitätspl 4, 8010 Graz
T: (031581) 323
Founded: 1978
Focus: Med *00397*

Akademie für Sozialarbeit der Stadt Wien, Freytaggasse 32, 1210 Wien
T: (01) 2717251; Fax: 27053634
Founded: 1918
Focus: Soc Sci *00398*

Akademische Arbeitsgemeinschaft für Volkskunde, Hanuschgasse 3, 1010 Wien
T: (01) 5123837
Founded: 1967; Members: 80
Pres: Prof. Dr. Hermann Steininger
Focus: Ethnology; Folklore *00399*

Anthropologische Gesellschaft in Wien (AGW), Burgring 7, 1014 Wien, Postfach 417
Founded: 1870; Members: 335
Pres: Prof. Dr. Karl Wernhart; Gen Secr: Dr. Herbert Kritscher
Focus: Anthro; Ethnology; Hist
Periodicals
Anthropologische Forschungen (irregularly)
Mitteilungen der Anthropologischen Gesellschaft in Wien (annually)
Prähistorische Forschungen (irregularly)
Völkerkundliche Veröffentlichungen (irregularly)
Volkskundliche Veröffentlichungen (irregularly)
. . . . *00400*

Anton Bruckner Institut Linz, Untere Donaulände 7, 4010 Linz
T: (0732) 7612268; (0222) 5131396; Fax: 5133851
Founded: 1978; Members: 6
Pres: Prof. Dr. Othmar Wessely; Gen Secr: Dr. Elisabeth Maier
Focus: Music
Periodical
Bruckner-Jahrbuch (irregularly) *00401*

Arbeitsgemeinschaft audiovisueller Archive Österreichs (AGAVA), Theodor-Körner-Str 38, 8020 Graz
T: (0316) 685877; Fax: 68587738
Founded: 1976; Members: 71
Pres: Prof. Dr. Gerhard Jagschitz; Gen Secr: Dr. Brigitte Schaffer
Focus: Archives
Periodical
Das audiovisuelle Archiv (semi-annually) . *00402*

Arbeitsgemeinschaft der Musikerzieher Österreichs (AGMÖ), c/o Bundesgymnasium Wien 3, Josef Gall-Gasse 2, 1020 Wien
T: (01) 7293025; Fax: 7266698
Founded: 1947; Members: 2285
Pres: Dr. Wolf Peschl; Gen Secr: Richard Klinghofer
Focus: Music; Educ
Periodical
Musikerziehung: Zeitschrift der Musikerzieher Österreichs (5 times annually) *00403*

Arbeitsgemeinschaft für Deutschdidaktik, c/o Institut für Germanistik, Universität für Bildungswissenschaften, Universitätsstr 65-67, 9022 Klagenfurt
T: (0463) 2700458; E-Mail: werner.wintersteiner@uni-klu.ac.at; Fax: 27006110
Founded: 1976
Pres: Werner Wintersteiner; Gen Secr: Eva Rastner
Focus: Educ; Ling; Lit
Periodical
Informationen zur Deutschdidaktik (quarterly)
. . . . *00404*

Arbeitsgemeinschaft für klinische Ernährung (AKE) / Austrian Society for Parenteral and Enteral Nutrition, P. O. Box 53, 1097 Wien
Focus: Nutrition *00405*

Arbeitsgemeinschaft für Präventivpsychologie, Stadiongasse 6-8, 1010 Wien
T: (01) 4055204; Fax: 406448618
Founded: 1980; Members: 450
Pres: Dr. Christian Konrad; Gen Secr: Dr. Anneliese Fuchs
Focus: Psych
Periodical
APP-Info: Vereinszeitschrift der Arge für Präventivpsychologie (quarterly) *00406*

Arbeitsgemeinschaft für Psychotechnik in Österreich (APÖ), Vegagasse 4, 1190 Wien
T: (01) 341130
Founded: 1926; Members: 30
Pres: Dr.Guido Hackl; Gen Secr: Dr. Hans Grümm
Focus: Psych
Periodical
Mensch und Arbeit (bi-monthly) *00407*

Arbeitsgemeinschaft für Wissenschaft und Politik, Innrain 52, 6020 Innsbruck
Fax: (0512) 5072897
Founded: 1971; Members: 50
Pres: Prof. Dr. Hans Köchler
Focus: Sci; Poli Sci *00408*

Arbeitsgemeinschaft Österreichischer Entomologen (AÖG), Ludo-Hartmann-Pl 7, 1160 Wien
T: (01) 4030338
Founded: 1949; Members: 250
Focus: Entomology
Periodical
Zeitschrift der Arbeitsgemeinschaft Österreichischer Entomologen (quarterly) *00409*

Arbeitsgemeinschaft Personenzentrierte Psychotherapie und Gesprächsführung, Postfach 524, 1171 Wien
T: (01) 4095573; Fax: 4095573
Focus: Psych; Therapeutics *00410*

Arbeitsgemeinschaft zur Erforschung der Ärztlichen Allgemeinpraxis, c/o Niederösterreichisches Institut für Allgemeinmedizin, 3595 Brunn
T: (02989) 2249; Fax: 224918
Focus: Med *00411*

Arbeitskreis der Wiener Altgermanisten, c/o Institut für Germanistik, Universität, Universitätsstr 7, 1010 Wien
T: (01) 43002389
Founded: 1959; Members: 188
Focus: Ling; Lit *00412*

Arbeitskreis der Wiener Skandinavisten, c/o Abteilung Skandinavistik, Institut für Germanistik, Universität Wien, Dr. Karl-Lueger-Ring 1, 1010 Wien
T: (01) 401032673
Founded: 1976; Members: 32
Pres: Prof. Dr. Sven Hakon Rossel
Focus: Ling; Lit *00413*

Arbeitskreis für neue Methoden in der Regionalforschung (AMR), Gustav-Tschermak-Gasse 36, 1190 Wien
T: (01) 6387470
Founded: 1971; Members: 80
Focus: Urban Plan *00414*

Arbeitskreis für Tibetische und Buddhistische Studien, Maria-Theresien-Str 3, 1090 Wien
T: (01) 347493
Founded: 1977; Members: 20
Focus: Ethnology; Rel & Theol
Periodical
Wiener Studien zur Tibetologie und Buddhismuskunde *00415*

Archaeoloische Gesellschaft Steiermark (AGST), Plüddemanngasse 95a, 8010 Graz
Founded: 1979; Members: 220
Pres: Dr. Manfred Hainzmann; Dr. Diether Kramer; Dr. Erwin Pochmarski
Focus: Archeol

Periodicals
Mitteilungen der Archäologischen Gesellschaft Steiermark (irregularly)
Nachrichtenblatt AGST (semi-annually) . . 00416

Arthur Schnitzler-Institut, Herrengasse 5, 1010 Wien
T: (01) 5338159; Fax: 5334067
Founded: 1974
Focus: Lit 00417

Asian Regional Cooperative Project on Food Irradiation (RPFI), c/o FAO/IAEA Div of Nuclear Techniques in Food and Agriculture, Food Preservation Section, Postfach 100, 1400 Wien
T: (01) 20600; Fax: 20607
Founded: 1980; Members: 13
Focus: Food 00418

Association Internationale du Théâtre pour l'Enfance et la Jeunesse, Burggasse 28-32, 1070 Wien
T: (01) 523172940; Fax: 523172990
Founded: 1965; Members: 65
Pres: Michael Fitzgerald; Gen Secr: Ulli Plichta
Focus: Perf Arts 00419

Austria Esperantista Federacio, Fünfhausgasse 16, 1150 Wien
T: (01) 8934196
Founded: 1935; Members: 500
Pres: Prof. Dr. Hans Michael Maitzen; Gen Secr: Leopold Patek
Focus: Ling
Periodical
Austria-Esperanto-Revuo (quarterly) . . . 00420

Austrotransplant – Österreichische Gesellschaft für Transplantation, Transfusion und Genetik, c/o Institut für Blutgruppenserologie, Spitalgasse 4, 1090 Wien
Founded: 1970; Members: 102
Focus: Genetics; Surgery 00421

Autorenkreis Linz, c/o Margret Czerni, Schubertstr 7, 4020 Linz
Focus: Lit 00422

Berufsverband freiberuflich tätiger Tierärzte Österreichs (BFÖ), c/o Dr. Beatrix Neumayer, 5741 Neukirchen 381
T: (03682) 22937; Fax: 22937
Founded: 1958; Members: 250
Pres: Dr. Ernst von Gimborn
Focus: Vet Med
Periodical
Der Österreichische Freiberufstierarzt (quarterly) 00423

Berufsverband Österreichischer Psychologen (B.Ö.P.), Salzgries 10, 1010 Wien
T: (01) 5335265
Founded: 1953; Members: 823
Focus: Psych
Periodical
Psychologie in Österreich (bi-monthly) . . 00424

Bundeskammer der Tierärzte Österreichs, Biberstr 22, 1010 Wien
T: (01) 5121766; Fax: 5121470
Founded: 1948; Members: 2000
Pres: Dr. Franz Josef Jäger; Gen Secr: Dr. Richard Elhenicky
Focus: Vet Med
Periodical
Vet-Journal: Zeitschrift der Österr. Tierärztinnen und Tierärzte (11 times annually) . . . 00425

Chemisch-Physikalische Gesellschaft in Wien, Strudlhofgasse 4, 1090 Wien
T: (01) 342630
Founded: 1869; Members: 260
Pres: Prof. P. Weinzierl; Gen Secr: F. Vesely
Focus: Chem; Physics
Periodical
Bulletin (semi-annually) 00426

Commission Internationale de l'Eclairage (CIE) / International Commission on Illumination, Kegelgasse 27, 1030 Wien
T: (01) 71431870; E-Mail: ciecb@ping.at; Fax: 713083818
Founded: 1901
Pres: Dr. S. Hsia; Gen Secr: C. Hermann
Focus: Eng
Periodical
CIE (quarterly) 00427

Commission Internationale d'Histoire du Sel (CIHS), c/o Universität, Innrain 52, 6020 Innsbruck
T: (0512) 5078058; E-Mail: rudi.palme@uibk.ac.at; Fax: 507-2831
Founded: 1988; Members: 142
Pres: Prof. Jean-Claude Hocquet; Gen Secr: Prof. Dr. Rudolf Palme
Focus: Cultur Hist 00428

Deutscher Rechtshistorikertag, c/o Institut für Österreichische Rechtsgeschichte, Universitätspl 3, 8010 Graz
Focus: Law; Hist 00429

Diplomatische Akademie Wien / Diplomatic Academy of Vienna, Favoritenstr 15, 1040 Wien
T: (01) 5042265
Founded: 1964
Focus: Poli Sci
Periodical
Jahrbuch (annually) 00430

Dokumentationsarchiv des österreichischen Widerstandes, Wipplingerstr 8, 1010 Wien
T: (01) 53436739
Founded: 1963; Members: 203
Focus: Hist
Periodicals
Jahrbuch (annually)
Mitteilungen des Dokumentationsarchives des österreichischen Widerstandes 00431

Dokumentationsstelle für neuere österreichische Literatur, Seidengasse 13, 1070 Wien
T: (01) 5262044; E-Mail: ep@lithaus.at; Fax: 526204430
Founded: 1966
Focus: Lit
Periodical
Zirkular (quarterly) 00432

Eranos Vindobonensis, c/o Institut für Klassische Philologie, Universität, Dr.-Karl-Lueger-Ring 1, 1010 Wien
T: (01) 401032719; E-Mail: Kurt.smolak@univie.ac.at; Fax: 4034848
Founded: 1885; Members: 91
Pres: wechselt jährlich; Gen Secr: Dr. Paul Raimund Lorenz
Focus: Ling; Lit; Archeol; Hist 00433

Europäisches Universitätszentrum für Friedensstudien (EPU), 7461 Burg Schlaining
T: (03355) 2498; Fax: 2381
Founded: 1987
Pres: Dr. Gerald Mader
Focus: Prom Peace 00434

Europäisches Zentrum für Wohlfahrtspolitik und Sozialforschung, Berggasse 17, 1090 Wien
T: (01) 31945050; E-Mail: ec@euro.centre.org; Fax: 319450519
Founded: 1974
Gen Secr: Prof. Dr. B. Marin
Focus: Poli Sci; Sociology; Econ
Periodicals
Eurosocial Reports
Newsletter/Bulletin d'Information/Nachrichten (quarterly) 00435

European Architectural Endoscopy Association (EAEA), c/o Technische Universität Wien, Karlspl 13, 1040 Wien
T: (01) 588013382; Fax: 588013382
Focus: Archit 00436

European Association for Catholic Adult Education, Kapuzinerstr 84, 4020 Linz
T: (0732) 274441 ext 238
Founded: 1963
Focus: Adult Educ
Periodical
FEECA Bulletin (semi-annually) 00437

European Bone Marrow Transplant Group (EBMT), Interconvention, Austria Centre, 1450 Wien
Focus: Surgery 00438

European Centre for Social Welfare Policy and Research (ECSWPR), Berggasse 17, 1090 Wien
Fax: (01) 314505
Founded: 1974
Focus: Soc Sci
Periodicals
Eurosocial Bulletin (quarterly)
Journal für Sozialforschung (quarterly)
Sovetskaya Tyurkologiya: Soviet Turkology 00439

European Cooperation in Social Science Information and Documentation (ECSSID), c/o Vienna Centre, Grünangergasse 2, Postfach 974, 1010 Wien
T: (01) 5124333; Fax: 5125366
Focus: Soc Sci
Periodical
ECSSID Bulletin 00440

European Coordination Centre for Research and Documentation in Social Sciences, c/o Vienna Centre, Grünangergasse 2, 1010 Wien
T: (01) 5124333; Fax: 512536616
Founded: 1963
Focus: Soc Sci
Periodical
Vienna Centre Newsletter (3 times annually) 00441

Evangelische Akademie in Wien, Schwarzspanierstr 13, Postfach 15, 1096 Wien
T: (01) 4080695; Fax: 408069533
Founded: 1955
Gen Secr: Dr. Thomas Krobath
Focus: Rel & Theol; Adult Educ . . . 00442

Föderation der Internationalen Donausymposia über Diabetes mellitus, c/o Klinik für Innere Medizin III, Währinger Gürtel 18-20, 1090 Wien
Focus: Diabetes 00443

Forschungsgemeinschaft für Erkrankungen des Bewegungsapparates, Hochstr 31, 1238 Wien
T: (01) 881371
Founded: 1966
Focus: Orthopedics 00444

Forschungsgesellschaft für das Verkehrs- und Straßenwesen im ÖIAV (FVS), Eschenbachgasse 9, 1010 Wien
T: (01) 587353631; Fax: 58735365
Founded: 1950; Members: 964
Focus: Transport; Civil Eng
Periodical
Schriftenreihe der FVS (irregularly) . . . 00445

Forschungsgesellschaft für Psycho-Elektronik und Kybernetik, Sechskrügelgasse 2, 1030 Wien
T: (01) 71247383
Founded: 1971; Members: 127
Focus: Electronic Eng; Cybernetics
Periodical
Psychotronics (irregularly) 00446

Forschungsgesellschaft für Wohnen, Bauen und Planen (FGW), Löwengasse 47, 1030 Wien
T: (01) 7126251; E-Mail: fgw@cso.at; Fax: 712625121
Founded: 1956; Members: 300
Pres: Dr. Wolfgang Ulrich; Gen Secr: Wolfgang Amonn
Focus: Civil Eng
Periodical
Wohnbauforschung in Österreich (WBFÖ) (bi-monthly) 00447

Franz Schmidt-Gesellschaft, c/o Musikverein, Bösendorferstr 12, 1010 Wien
T: (02) 505172171
Founded: 1951; Members: 160
Pres: Prof. Albert Moser; Gen Secr: Dr. Carmen Ottner
Focus: Music
Periodical
Studien zu Franz Schmidt (annually) . . 00448

Freiheitliche Akademie, Kärntner Str 28, 1010 Wien
T: (01) 51294520
Founded: 1867; Members: 7
Focus: Educ 00449

Friedrich Hebbel-Gesellschaft, Frauengasse 14, 1170 Wien
T: (01) 4893432; 3109876; Fax: 4893683
Founded: 1957; Members: 184
Pres: Ida Koller-Andorf; Gen Secr: Elfriede Benesch
Focus: Lit 00450

Gemeinnütziger Verein zur Durchführung von Lehr- und Forschungsaufgaben an der Wirtschaftsuniversität Wien, Augasse 2-6, 1090 Wien
T: (01) 340525693
Founded: 1987
Focus: Econ 00451

Geschichtsverein für Kärnten, Museumgasse 2, 9020 Klagenfurt
T: (0463) 53630573; Fax: 53630540
Founded: 1844; Members: 2233
Pres: Dr. Claudia Fräss-Ehrfeld; Gen Secr: Prof. Dr. Gernot Piccottini
Focus: Hist
Periodical
Carinthia I: Zeitschrift für geschichtliche Landeskunde von Kärnten (annually) . . 00452

Gesellschaft der Ärzte in Vorarlberg, Schulgasse 17, 6850 Dornbirn
Founded: 1951; Members: 452
Focus: Med 00453

Gesellschaft der Ärzte in Wien, Frankgasse 8, Postfach 147, 1096 Wien
T: (01) 4054777; E-Mail: info@billrothhaus.at; Fax: 4023090
Founded: 1837; Members: 1752
Focus: Med
Periodical
Wiener Klinische Wochenschrift (bi-weekly) 00454

Gesellschaft der Chirurgen in Wien, c/o Neues Allgemeines Krankenhaus, 1090 Wien
T: (01) 404002243; Fax: 404004004
Founded: 1935; Members: 137
Focus: Surgery 00455

Gesellschaft der Freunde der Biologischen Station Wilhelminenberg, Savoyenstr 1, 1160 Wien
Founded: 1957; Members: 790
Focus: Bio 00456

Gesellschaft der Freunde der Neuen Galerie, Sackgasse 16, 8010 Graz
T: (0316) 829155, 829186; E-Mail: neue-galerie-graz@sime.com; Fax: 815401
Founded: 1946; Members: 100
Pres: Dr. Michael Mayer-Rieckh; Gen Secr: Dr. Werner Fenz
Focus: Arts 00457

Gesellschaft der Freunde des Kunsthistorischen Institutes der Karl-Franzens-Universität in Graz, Universitätspl 3, 8010 Graz
T: (0316) 3802395
Founded: 1964; Members: 114
Focus: Arts 00458

Gesellschaft der Geologie- und Bergbaustudenten in Österreich, c/o Institut für Geologie, Universität, Universitätsstr 7, 1010 Wien
T: (01) 43002518
Founded: 1948; Members: 329
Focus: Geology; Mining 00459

Gesellschaft der Kunstfreunde, Neudeggergasse 8, 1080 Wien
T: (01) 423125
Focus: Arts 00460

Gesellschaft der Musikfreunde in Wien (GdM), Bösendorferstr 12, 1010 Wien
T: (01) 5058681; Fax: 5059409
Founded: 1812; Members: 10000
Pres: Prof. Dr. Horst Haschek; Gen Secr: Dr. Thomas Angyan
Focus: Music
Periodical
Musikfreunde (8 times annually) 00461

Gesellschaft für Arbeitsrecht und Sozialrecht, c/o Institut für Arbeitsrecht und Sozialrecht, Auhof, 4040 Linz
Founded: 1965
Focus: Law 00462

Gesellschaft für biologische und psychosomatische Medizin, Peterspl 4, 1010 Wien
Focus: Psychiatry; Neurology 00463

Gesellschaft für Chemiewirtschaft, Salesianergasse 208, 1030 Wien
T: (01) 725611360
Founded: 1949; Members: 251
Focus: Chem; Econ 00464

Gesellschaft für das Recht der Ostkirchen, c/o Institut für Kirchenrecht, Freyung 6, 1010 Wien
T: (01) 5333861; Fax: 5351019
Founded: 1971; Members: 200
Focus: Law; Rel & Theol
Periodical
Kanon: Jahrbuch der Gesellschaft für das Recht der Ostkirchen 00465

Gesellschaft für die Geschichte des Protestantismus in Österreich (GPrÖ), c/o Evangelisch-theologische Fakultät, Universität, Rooseveltpl 10, 1090 Wien
T: (01) 40659810; Fax: 406598144
Founded: 1880; Members: 300
Pres: Prof. Dr. Gustav Reingrabner; Gen Secr: Prof. Dr. Karl Schwarz
Focus: Hist; Rel & Theol
Periodical
Jahrbuch für die Geschichte des Protestantismus Oesterreich 00466

Gesellschaft für Ganzheitsforschung (G.f.G.), c/o Wirtschaftsuniversität Wien, Augasse 2-6, 1090 Wien
T: (01) 313364531; Fax: 31336727
Founded: 1956; Members: 120
Pres: Prof. Dr. J. Hanns Pichler; Gen Secr: Dr. Hubert Verhonig
Focus: Philos; Sociology; Econ
Periodical
Zeitschrift für Ganzheitsforschung (quarterly) 00467

Gesellschaft für Geschichte der Neuzeit, c/o Prof. Dr. Fritz Fellner, Ignaz-Rieder-Kai 19, 5020 Salzburg
T: (0662) 80444757
Founded: 1981; Members: 67
Focus: Hist 00468

Gesellschaft für Innere Medizin in Wien, Garnisongasse 13, 1090 Wien
Founded: 1902; Members: 375
Focus: Intern Med 00469

Gesellschaft für Input-Output-Analyse, Postfach 108, 1033 Wien
T: (01) 224430210; Fax: 30210
Founded: 1988; Members: 288
Pres: Dr. Jiri Skolka; Gen Secr: Dr. Norbert Rainer
Focus: Computer & Info Sci
Periodical
Economic Systems Research (quarterly) . 00470

Gesellschaft für Klassische Philologie in Innsbruck, c/o Institut für Klassische Philologie, Neue Universität, Innrain 52, 6020 Innsbruck
Founded: 1958; Members: 200
Pres: Lav Šubarić; Gen Secr: Anna Christoph
Focus: Ling; Lit
Periodical
Acta Philologica Aenipotana 00471

Gesellschaft für Kulturpsychologie, Schwesternweg 9, 5020 Salzburg
T: (0662) 80445111
Founded: 1987; Members: 26
Focus: Psych 00472

Gesellschaft für Logotherapie und Existenzanalyse, Eduard-Sueß-Gasse 10, 1150 Wien
T: (01) 9859566; Fax: 9824845
Founded: 1984; Members: 800
Pres: Dr. A. Längle; Gen Secr: Dr. Liselotte Tutsch
Focus: Therapeutics
Periodical
Existenzanalyse (3 times annually) . . . 00473

Gesellschaft für Manuelle Lymphdrainage nach Dr. Vodder, Alleestr 30, 6344 Walchsee
T: (05374) 52450; Fax: 52454
Founded: 1973; Members: 800
Focus: Cell Biol & Cancer Res 00474

Gesellschaft für österreichische Kulturgeschichte, Haydngasse 1, 7000 Eisenstadt
Founded: 1968
Focus: Hist
Periodical
Jahrbuch für österreichische Kulturgeschichte (annually) 00475

Gesellschaft für Ost- und Südostkunde / Association for Eastern and Southeastern European Studies, Wienerstr 131, 4024 Linz
T: (0732) 273380
Founded: 1955; Members: 90
Focus: Ethnology
Periodicals
Das Kleine Ostpanorama (quarterly)
Ostpanorama-Sonderausgabe (annually) . 00476

Gesellschaft für Phänomenologie und Kritische Anthropologie, c/o Prof. Dr. Benedikt, Chimanistr 27, 1190 Wien
Focus: Anthro 00477

Gesellschaft für Photographie und Geschichte, c/o Institut für Zeitgeschichte, Universität, Rotenhausgasse 6, 1090 Wien
T: (01) 426280
Founded: 1988
Focus: Photo; Hist
Periodical
Photographie und Gesellschaft (quarterly) 00478

Gesellschaft für politische Aufklärung, c/o Institut für Höhere Studien und wissenschaftliche Forschung, Stumpergasse 56, 1060 Wien
T: (01) 59991172; Fax: 5970635
Founded: 1982; Members: 24
Focus: Poli Sci
Periodical
Informationen der Gesellschaft für politische Aufklärung (quarterly) 00479

Gesellschaft für Salzburger Landeskunde (GSLK), Michael-Pacher-Str 40, 5020 Salzburg
T: (0662) 80424664
Founded: 1860; Members: 1513
Focus: Hist
Periodical
Mitteilungen (annually) 00480

Gesellschaft für Soziologie an der Universität Graz, Universitätsstr 15, 8010 Graz
T: (0316) 3803540; Fax: 3809515
Founded: 1951; Members: 160
Pres: jährlich wechselnd
Focus: Sociology 00481

Gesellschaft für Strategische Unternehmensführung, c/o Institut für Unternehmensführung, Universität, Rennweg 25, 6020 Innsbruck
T: (0512) 57700111; Fax: 57700117
Founded: 1982; Members: 80
Focus: Business Admin
Periodical
Informationsdienst 00482

Gesellschaft für vergleichende Felsbildforschung (GE.FE.BI.), Geidorfgürtel 40, 8010 Graz
T: (0316) 329845
Founded: 1977; Members: 42
Focus: Arts
Periodical
Jahrbuch (annually) 00483

Gesellschaft für vergleichende Kunstforschung, c/o Institut für Kunstgeschichte, Universitätsstr 7, 1010 Wien
T: (01) 43002509; Fax: 4028510
Founded: 1934; Members: 300
Gen Secr: Prof. Dr. Walter Krause
Focus: Arts
Periodical
Mitteilungen der Gesellschaft für vergleichende Kunstforschung (3 times annually) . . . 00484

Gesellschaft österreichischer Chemiker (VÖCH), Nibelungengasse 11, 1010 Wien
Founded: 1897; Members: 5500
Pres: Prof. Alfred Schmidt; Gen Secr: Dr. Frank A. Battig
Focus: Chem
Periodical
Monatshefte für Chemie (monthly) . . . 00485

Gesellschaft zum Studium und zur Erneuerung der Struktur der Rechtsordnung, c/o o. Univ.-Prof. DDr. Dr. h.c. Robert Walter, Schottenbastei 10-16, 1010 Wien
T: (01) 401033112; Fax: 5334099
Founded: 1970; Members: 89
Pres: Prof. Dr. Dr. Robert Walter
Focus: Law 00486

Gesellschaft zur Erforschung slawischer Sprachen und Kulturen, Heinrichstr 26, 8010 Graz
Founded: 1973
Focus: Ethnology; Ling 00487

Gesellschaft zur Errichtung der Akademie für Allgemeinmedizin, Universitätspl 4, 8010 Graz
T: (0316) 31581323
Founded: 1978
Focus: Med 00488

Gesellschaft zur Förderung des industriellen Pflanzenbaus, Getreidemarkt 9, 1060 Wien
Founded: 1964
Focus: Agri 00489

Gesellschaft zur Förderung Slawistischer Studien, Teschnergasse 4, 1180 Wien
T: (01) 401032941
Founded: 1983
Focus: Ling; Lit
Periodical
Wiener Slawistischer Almanach (WSA) (semi-annually) 00490

Gesellschaft zur Förderung von Nordamerika-Studien an der Universität Wien, Lammgasse 8, 1080 Wien
T: (01) 438679
Founded: 1985; Members: 20
Focus: Ethnology 00491

Gesellschaft zur Herausgabe von Denkmälern der Tonkunst in Österreich, c/o Institut für Musikwissenschaft, Universitätsstr 7, 1010 Wien
T: (01) 401032629; Fax: 4020533
Founded: 1893; Members: 230
Focus: Music
Periodicals
Studien zur Musikwissenschaft
Wiener Beiträge zur Musikwissenschaft . 00492

Gregor Mendel-Gesellschaft Wien, c/o Institut für Pflanzenbau und Pflanzenzüchtung, Gregor-Mendel-Str 33, 1180 Wien
T: (01) 342500
Founded: 1972
Focus: Genetics 00493

Grillparzer-Gesellschaft, Gumpendorfer Str 15, 1060 Wien
T: (01) 5861090; Fax: 5868217
Founded: 1890; Members: 200
Pres: Dr. Leopold O. Knobloch; Gen Secr: Dr. Martina Schmidt
Focus: Lit
Periodical
Grillparzer-Jahrbuch (bi-annually) 00494

Haus des Meeres Vivarium Wien, Fritz-Grünbaum-Pl 1, 1060 Wien
T: (01) 5871417; Fax: 5860617
Founded: 1957; Members: 30
Pres: Prof. Dr. Jörg Ott
Focus: Bio; Oceanography 00495

Heraldisch-Genealogische Gesellschaft Adler, 1014 Wien, Postfach 25
Founded: 1870; Members: 850
Pres: Dr. Georg Johannes Kugler; Gen Secr: Dr. Andreas Cornaro
Focus: Genealogy
Periodical
Adler: Zeitschrift für Genealogie und Heraldik (quarterly) 00496

Historische Landeskommission für Steiermark, Karmeliterpl 3, 8010 Graz
T: (0316) 8773015; Fax: 8775504
Founded: 1892; Members: 31
Pres: Waltraud Klasnic; Gen Secr: Prof. Dr. Othmar Pickl
Focus: Hist
Periodical
Forschungen zur geschichtlichen Landeskunde der Steiermark 00497

Historischer Verein für Steiermark, Hamerlinggasse 3, 8010 Graz
T: (0316) 8772366
Founded: 1850; Members: 1400
Focus: Hist
Periodicals
Blätter für Heimatkunde (quarterly)
Zeitschrift des Historischen Vereins für Steiermark (annually) 00498

IMZ International Music Centre, Speisinger Str 121-127, 1230 Wien
T: (01) 8890315; E-Mail: imz@magnet.at; Fax: 889031577
Founded: 1961; Members: 250
Pres: Avril MacRory; Gen Secr: Dr. Franz Patay
Focus: Music
Periodical
Music in the Media: IMZ-Bulletin (bi-monthly) 00499

Innsbrucker Arbeitskreis für Psychoanalyse, Psychoanalytisches Forschungs- und Ausbildungsinstitut, Collingasse 7, 6020 Innsbruck
T: (05222) 582827, 577905
Founded: 1976; Members: 26
Focus: Psychoan 00500

Innsbrucker Germanistische Arbeitsgemeinschaft (IGA), c/o Institut für Germanistik, Innrain 52, 6020 Innsbruck
T: (0512) 7243453
Members: 20
Focus: Ling; Lit 00501

Innsbrucker Gesellschaft zur Pflege der Geisteswissenschaften (IGG), Innrain 52, 6020 Innsbruck
T: (0512) 5073535
Founded: 1949; Members: 80
Focus: Humanities
Periodical
Innsbrucker Beiträge zur Kulturwissenschaft (irregularly) 00502

Innsbrucker Sprachwissenschaftliche Gesellschaft (ISG), Innrain 52, 6020 Innsbruck
T: (0512) 5074066; E-Mail: Barbara.Stefan@uibk.ac.at; Fax: 5072837
Founded: 1970; Members: 90
Pres: Dr. Barbara Stefan; Gen Secr: Marialuise Haslinger
Focus: Ling 00503

Institut für Grenzgebiete der Wissenschaft (IGW), Maximilianstr 8, Postfach 8, 6010 Innsbruck
T: (0512) 574772; E-Mail: IGW@uibk.ac.at; Fax: 586463
Founded: 1980; Members: 370
Pres: Prof. Dr. Dr. P. Andreas Resch
Focus: Sci
Periodicals
Ethica: Wissenschaft und Verantwortung (quarterly)
Grenzgebiete der Wissenschaft (quarterly) 00504

Institut für Österreichische Musikdokumentation (IÖM), Augustinerstr 1, 1010 Wien
T: (01) 5335087; Fax: 53410310
Founded: 1972; Members: 8
Focus: Music 00505

Institut für Österreichkunde, Hanuschgasse 3, 1010 Wien
T: (01) 5127932
Founded: 1957; Members: 700
Pres: Prof. Dr. Ernst Bruckmüller; Gen Secr: Prof. Hermann Möcker
Focus: Hist; Poli Sci; Lit; Ling; Geography; Econ
Periodical
Österreich in Geschichte und Literatur (mit Geographie) (bi-monthly) 00506

Institut für Sozialdienste, gemeinnützige GmbH, Schedlerstr 10, 6900 Bregenz
T: (05574) 451870; E-Mail: ifs@ifs.vd.at; Fax: 4518721
Founded: 1962; Members: 43
Pres: Dr. Anton Flixi; Gen Secr: Dr. Stefan Allgäver
Focus: Soc Sci
Periodical
IfS-Information (quarterly) 00507

Institut für Soziales Design – Entwicklung und Forschung (ISD), Grenzackerstr 7-11, 1100 Wien
T: (01) 6030772
Founded: 1975; Members: 20
Focus: Graphic & Dec Arts, Design . . 00508

Institut für Wissenschaft und Kunst (IWK), Berggasse 17, 1090 Wien
T: (01) 3174342
Founded: 1946; Members: 800
Pres: Dr. Helga Konrad; Gen Secr: Dr. Helga Kaschl
Focus: Sci; Arts
Periodical
Mitteilungen (quarterly) 00509

International Association of Schools of Social Work (IASSW), Palais Palfy, Josefpl 6, 1010 Wien
T: (01) 5134297; Fax: 5138468
Founded: 1929; Members: 500
Focus: Adult Educ; Sociology
Periodicals
International Social Work (quarterly)
Newsletter (3 times annually) 00510

International Atomic Energy Agency (IAEA), c/o Vienna International Centre, Wagramerstr 5, Postfach 100, 1400 Wien
T: (01) 20600; E-Mail: official.mail@iaea.org; Fax: 20607
Founded: 1957; Members: 124
Gen Secr: Dr. Hans Blix
Focus: Energy; Nucl Res
Periodicals
IAEA Bulletin (quarterly)
IAEA Newsbrief (quarterly)
Meetings on Atomic Energy (quarterly) . 00511

International Council on Social Welfare (ICSW), Koestlergasse 1, 1060 Wien
Fax: (01) 5879951
Founded: 1928
Focus: Soc Sci
Periodical
ICSW-Information 00512

International Federation of Automatic Control (IFAC), Schlosspl 12, 2361 Laxenburg
T: (02236) 71447; Fax: 72859
Founded: 1957; Members: 44
Focus: Eng
Periodicals
Automatica (bi-monthly)
Newsletter (bi-monthly) 00513

International Institute for Applied Systems Analysis (IIASA), Schlosspl 1, 2361 Laxenburg
T: (02236) 807; E-Mail: info@iiasa.ac.at; Fax: 71313
Founded: 1972
Focus: Ecology; Econ; Eng
Periodical
Options (quarterly) 00514

International Law Association, Österreichischer Zweigverein, Rotenturmstr 13, 1010 Wien
Founded: 1947
Focus: Law 00515

International Society of Soil Science, c/o Universität für Bodenkultur, Gregor-Mendel-Str 33, 1180 Wien
T: (01) 3106026; Fax: 3106027
Founded: 1924; Members: 7500
Pres: Prof. A. Ruellan; Gen Secr: Prof. W.E.H. Blum
Focus: Agri
Periodical
Bulletin (semi-annually) 00516

Internationale Albrechtsberger-Gesellschaft, Rathaus, 3400 Klosteneuburg
T: (02243) 6795222
Founded: 1962; Members: 70
Focus: Music 00517

Internationale Bruckner-Gesellschaft, Rathauspl 3, 1010 Wien
T: (01) 427140
Focus: Music
Periodical
Mitteilungsblatt der IBG (semi-annually) . 00518

Internationale Chopin-Gesellschaft in Wien, Biberstr 4, 1010 Wien
T: (01) 5122374; Fax: 512646375
Founded: 1952; Members: 240
Pres: Dr. Theodor Kanitzer
Focus: Music
Periodical
Wiener Chopin-Blätter (2-3 times annually) 00519

Internationale Coronelli-Gesellschaft für Globen- und Instrumentenkunde, Dominikanerbastei 21, 1010 Wien
T: (01) 5333285; Fax: 5320824
Founded: 1952; Members: 280
Pres: Prof. Rudolf Schmidt; Gen Secr: Dr. Johannes Dörflinger
Focus: Cart
Periodical
Der Globusfreund (irregularly) 00520

Internationale Franz Lehár-Gesellschaft, Neulerchenfelderstr 3-7, 1160 Wien
Founded: 1949
Gen Secr: Prof. Eduard Macku
Focus: Music 00521

Internationale Gesellschaft für Getreidewissenschaft und -technologie / International Association for Cereal Science and Technology, Wienerstr 22, Postfach 77, 2320 Schwechat
T: 777202; Fax: 777204
Founded: 1955; Members: 33
Focus: Biochem
Periodical
Newsletter (quarterly) 00522

Internationale Gesellschaft für Ingenieurpädagogik, c/o Universität für Bildungswissenschaften, Universitätsstr 65-67, 9022 Klagenfurt
T: (0463) 2700371; E-Mail: utmp@uni.klu.ac.at; Fax: 2700292
Founded: 1972; Members: 300
Pres: Prof. Dr. Adolf Melezinek; Gen Secr: Dr. Hartmut Weidner
Focus: Eng; Educ
Periodical
IGIP-Report (3 times annually) 00523

Internationale Gesellschaft für Jazzforschung (IGJ), c/o Institut für Jazzforschung, Hochschule für Musik und darstellende Kunst, Leonhardstr 15, 8010 Graz
T: (0316) 3891221
Founded: 1969; Members: 286
Focus: Music
Periodicals
Beiträge zur Jazzforschung: Studies in Jazz Research (irregularly)
Jazzforschung: Jazz Research (annually) . 00524

Internationale Gesellschaft zur Erforschung und Förderung der Blasmusik (IGEB) / International Society for the Promotion and Investigation of Band Music, Leonhardstr 15, 8010 Graz
T: (0316) 3891123
Founded: 1974
Focus: Music
Periodicals
Alta Musica: Jahrbücher (annually)
Mitteilungsblatt (3 times annually) . . . 00525

Internationale Gustav Mahler Gesellschaft (IGMG), Wiedner Gürtel 6, 1040 Wien
T: (01) 5057330
Founded: 1955; Members: 450
Pres: Dr. Rainer Bischof; Gen Secr: Emmy Hauswirth
Focus: Music
Periodical
Nachrichten zur Mahler-Forschung: News about Mahler Research (semi-annually) 00526

Internationale Hugo Wolf-Gesellschaft, Latschkagasse 4, 1090 Wien
T: (01) 3101388
Founded: 1956; Members: 35
Focus: Music 00527

Internationale Lenau-Gesellschaft e.V., Rathaus, Josef-Wolfik-Str 1, 2000 Stockerau
T: (02266) 69510/12
Founded: 1894

Pres: Leopold Richentzky; Gen Secr: Dr. Gustav Fischer
Focus: Lit 00528

Internationale Nestroy-Gesellschaft, Gentzgasse 10/3/2, 1180 Wien
T: (01) 4707067; Fax: 4707067
Founded: 1973; Members: 245
Pres: Prof. Dr. Heinrich Kraus; Gen Secr: Karl Zimmel
Focus: Perf Arts; Lit
Periodical
Nestroyana: Blätter der Internationalen Nestroy-Gesellschaft (semi-annually) 00529

Internationale Paracelsus-Gesellschaft (IPG), Ignaz-Harrer-Str 79, 5020 Salzburg
Founded: 1950; Members: 342
Pres: Prof. Dr. Gerhart Harrer; Gen Secr: Gertraud Weiss
Focus: Med; Philos; Rel & Theol
Periodicals
Paracelsusbrief: Mitteilungsblatt (irregularly)
Salzburger Beiträge zur Paracelsusforschung 00530

Internationale Schönberg-Gesellschaft, Bernhardgasse 6, 2340 Mödling
T: (02236) 42223
Founded: 1972
Focus: Music
Periodical
Mitteilungen (semi-annually) 00531

Internationale Sportwissenschaftliche Gesellschaft Graz, Prenterweg 28, 8045 Graz-Weinitzen
T: (03132) 2463; Fax: 4467
Founded: 1959; Members: 350
Pres: Prof. Dr. Heinz Recla; Gen Secr: Peter Chen
Focus: Sports 00532

Internationale Tagung der Historikerinnen und Historiker der Arbeiterinnen- und Arbeiterbewegung (ITH), Altes Rathaus, Wipplingerstr 8, 1010 Wien
T: (01) 5343601776; E-Mail: docarch@email.adis.at; Fax: 534369901771
Founded: 1964; Members: 120
Pres: Prof. Dr. Helmut Konrad; Gen Secr: Christine Schindler
Focus: Hist; Socialism
Periodical
Rundbrief/Newsletter 00533

Internationale Vereinigung für Selbstmordprophylaxe (IASP) / International Association for Suicide Prevention, c/o Institut für medizinische Psychology, Severingasse 9, 1090 Wien
T: (01) 408356824; Fax: 408356812
Founded: 1960; Members: 300
Focus: Psych; Psychiatry
Periodical
Crisis: Journal of Crisis Intervention and Suicide Prevention (quarterly) 00534

Internationaler Verband Forstlicher Forschungsanstalten / Union Internationale des Instituts de Recherche Forestières / International Union of Forestry Research Organisations, Schönbrunn, Tirolergarten, 1131 Wien
T: (01) 8770151; Fax: 829355
Founded: 1891; Members: 15000
Focus: Forestry
Periodical
IUFRO-NEWS (quarterly) 00535

Internationales Forschungszentrum für Grundfragen der Wissenschaften, Mönchsberg 2a, 5020 Salzburg
T: (0662) 842521; Fax: 84252118
Founded: 1961; Members: 24
Focus: Sci
Periodicals
Erkenntnis
Journal of Symbolic Logic
Kairos
Synthese
Zeitgeschichte 00536

Internationales Institut für den Frieden / International Institute for Peace, c/o Dr. Peter Stania, Möllwaldpl 5, 1040 Wien
T: (01) 5046437; E-Mail: paxinstitu vienna; Fax: 5053236
Founded: 1957
Focus: Poli Sci; Soc Sci; Nat Sci
Periodicals
IIP Monitor (irregularly)
Peace in the Sciences: Occasional Papers (quarterly) 00537

Internationales Institut für Jugendliteratur und Leseforschung, Mayerhofgasse 6, 1040 Wien
T: (01) 5050359; E-Mail: kidlit@netway.at; Fax: 505035917
Founded: 1965; Members: 500
Pres: Dr. Hilde Hawlicek; Gen Secr: Karin Sollat
Focus: Lit
Periodical
1000 + 1 Buch (bi-monthly) 00538

Joanneum-Verein, Raubergasse 10, 8010 Graz
T: (0316) 8772461
Founded: 1819; Members: 415
Focus: Arts 00539

Johann-Joseph-Fux-Gesellschaft, c/o Institut für Musikethnologie, Hochschule für Musik und darstellende Kunst, Leonhardstr 15, 8010 Graz
T: (0316) 3891122
Founded: 1955; Members: 75
Focus: Lit
Periodical
Jahresgabe der Johann-Joseph-Fux-Gesellschaft (annually) 00540

Johann Strauß-Gesellschaft Wien, Kleeblattgasse 9/9, 1010 Wien
T: (01) 5339194
Founded: 1936; Members: 300
Pres: Prof. Franz Mailer; Gen Secr: Hannelore Mohl
Focus: Music
Periodical
Wiener Bonbons: Zeitschrift der Wiener Johann Strauß-Gesellschaft für Musiker und Musikfreunde (quarterly) 00541

Kärntner Juristische Gesellschaft (KJG), Dobernigstr 2, 9010 Klagenfurt
T: (0463) 5840288
Founded: 1950; Members: 480
Focus: Law 00542

Klagenfurter Sprachwissenschaftliche Gesellschaft, Universitätsstr 67, 9020 Klagenfurt
T: (0463) 2700347; Fax: 2700100
Founded: 1977; Members: 40
Focus: Ling
Periodical
Klagenfurter Beiträge zur Sprachwissenschaft (annually) 00543

Kommission für Neuere Geschichte Österreichs, c/o Institut für Geschichte, Universität Salzburg, Rudolfskai 42, 5020 Salzburg
T: (0662) 80444776; E-Mail: franz.adlgasser@sbg.ac.at; Fax: 8044413
Founded: 1902; Members: 25
Pres: Prof. Dr. Fritz Fellner; Gen Secr: Dr. Franz Adlgasser
Focus: Hist 00544

Kontext - Institut für Kommunikations- und Textanalysen, Margaretenpl 4, 1050 Wien
T: (01) 5457764
Founded: 1988; Members: 20
Focus: Comm Sci; Ling 00545

Krahuletz-Gesellschaft, c/o Krahuletz-Museum, 3730 Eggenburg
Founded: 1899
Focus: Arts 00546

Künstlerhaus - Gesellschaft Bildender Künstler Österreichs, Karlspl 5, 1010 Wien
T: (01) 5879663; Fax: 5878736
Founded: 1861; Members: 460
Pres: Peter Kodera
Focus: Arts 00547

Kulturgeschichtliche Gesellschaft am Landesmuseum Joanneum, Neutorgasse 45, 8010 Graz
T: (0316) 80174780
Founded: 1948
Focus: Hist 00548

Kunsthistorische Gesellschaft, c/o Institut für Kunstgeschichte, Universitätsstr 7, 1010 Wien
T: (01) 401032617
Founded: 1956; Members: 152
Pres: Prof. Dr. Gerhard Schmidt
Focus: Hist; Arts 00549

Kunsthistorische Gesellschaft an der Universität Graz, c/o Kunsthistorisches Institut, Universität, 8010 Graz
Founded: 1959; Members: 43
Focus: Hist; Arts 00550

Kuratorium für Verkehrssicherheit, Ölzeltgasse 3, 1030 Wien
T: (01) 717700; Fax: 717709
Founded: 1959
Pres: Josef Svoboda; Gen Secr: Franz M. Bogner
Focus: Transport 00551

Landesverein für Höhlenkunde in Wien und Niederösterreich, Obere Donaustr 97, 1020 Wien
Founded: 1937
Focus: Speleology
Periodical
Die Höhle 00552

Ludwig Boltzmann-Gesellschaft, Österreichische Vereinigung zur Förderung der wissenschaftlichen Forschung (LBG), Hofburg, Postfach 33, 1014 Wien
T: (01) 5338024, 5336082
Founded: 1960; Members: 126
Focus: Med; Nat Sci; Eng; Agri; Forestry 00553

Mathematisch-Physikalische Gesellschaft in Innsbruck, Technikerstr 25, 6020 Innsbruck
Fax: (0512) 5072920
Founded: 1936; Members: 130
Focus: Math; Physics 00554

Mediacult - Internationales Forschungsinstitut für Medien, Kommunikation und kulturelle Entwicklung, Schönburgstr 27, 1040 Wien
T: (01) 5041316; E-Mail: Mediacul@ping.at; Fax: 50413164
Founded: 1969; Members: 64
Pres: Peter Etzkorn; Gen Secr: Alfred Smudits
Focus: Music; Perf Arts; Sociology; Mass Media; Comm Sci
Periodical
Mediacult Newsletter (semi-annually) . . 00555

Medizinische Gesellschaft für Oberösterreich, Dinghoferstr 4, 4020 Linz
T: (0732) 77837164; Fax: 77837158
Founded: 1946; Members: 2686
Focus: Med 00556

Mikrographische Gesellschaft, Aßmayergasse 11, 1120 Wien
T: (01) 8138446; Fax: 8138446
Founded: 1910; Members: 80
Pres: Prof. Erich Steiner; Gen Secr: Friedrich Posch
Focus: Eng
Periodical
Informationsblatt (3 times annually) . . . 00557

Montanhistorischer Verein für Österreich, Peter-Tunner-Str 15, Postfach 1, 8704 Leoben-Donawitz
T: (03842) 40702377
Founded: 1976; Members: 750
Focus: Mining; Hist
Periodical
Leobener Grüne Hefte, Neue Folge (annually) 00558

Musealverein in Hallstatt, c/o Museum, 4830 Hallstatt
T: (06134) 8280; Fax: 8280
Founded: 1884; Members: 280
Pres: rudolf Gamsjäger
Focus: Arts 00559

Museums-Verein Stillfried, 2262 Stillfried
Founded: 1914; Members: 120
Focus: Arts 00560

Nationalökonomische Gesellschaft (NÖG) / Austrian Economic Association, c/o Institut für Volkswirtschaftslehre, Technische Universität, Karlspl 13, 1040 Wien
Founded: 1917; Members: 280
Focus: Econ
Periodical
Empirica - Austrian Economic Papers (semi-annually) 00561

Naturwissenschaftlich-Medizinische Vereinigung in Salzburg, Schopperstr 13, 5020 Salzburg
T: (0662) 510204
Founded: 1974; Members: 78
Focus: Med
Periodical
Berichte der naturwissenschaftlich-medizinischen Vereinigung Salzburg 00562

Naturwissenschaftlich-medizinischer Verein in Innsbruck, Technikerstr 25, 6020 Innsbruck
T: (0512) 5076142; 5076143; E-Mail: Erwin.meyer@uibk.ac.at; Fax: 5072930
Founded: 1870; Members: 300
Pres: jährliche Neuwahl; Gen Secr: Prof. Dr. Wolfgang Schedl
Focus: Med; Nat Sci
Periodical
Berichte Naturwissenschaftlich-medizinischer Verein in Innsbruck (annually) 00563

Naturwissenschaftlicher Verein für Kärnten, Museumgasse 2, 9020 Klagenfurt
T: (04222) 53630574
Founded: 1848; Members: 1300
Pres: Dr. Hans Sampl
Focus: Nat Sci
Periodicals
Carinthia II: Naturwissenschaftliche Beiträge zur Heimatkunde Kärntens (annually)
Karinthin (semi-annually) 00564

Naturwissenschaftlicher Verein für Steiermark, c/o Universitätsbibliothek, Universitätspl 3, 8010 Graz
T: (0316) 3805540; E-Mail: karl.ettinger@kfunigraz.ac.at; Fax: 3809865
Founded: 1862; Members: 440
Pres: Prof. Dr. Georg Hoinkes; Gen Secr: Dr. Karl Ettinger; Dr. Aberra Mogessie
Focus: Nat Sci
Periodical
Mitteilungen des Naturwissenschaftlichen Vereins für Steiermark (annually) 00565

Niederösterreichisches Bildungs- und Heimatwerk, Arbeitsgemeinschaft für Volkskunde, Strauchgasse 3, 1010 Wien
Founded: 1960
Focus: Ethnology 00566

Oberösterreichischer Musealverein, Landstr 31, 4020 Linz
T: (0732) 770218
Founded: 1833; Members: 1200
Pres: Dr. Georg Heilingsetzer
Focus: Arts
Periodicals
Beiträge zur Landeskunde von Oberösterreich: I. Historische Reihe
Beiträge zur Landeskunde von Oberösterreich: II. Naturwissenschaftliche Reihe
Jahrbuch: Teil I Abhandlungen, Teil II Berichte
Mitteilungen (quarterly)
Schriftenreihe 00567

Ökosoziales Forum, Franz-Josefs-Kai 13, 1010 Wien
T: (01) 5330797; Fax: 533079790
Founded: 1969
Focus: Ecology
Periodical
Agrarische Rundschau (bi-monthly) . . . 00568

Österreichische Ärztegesellschaft für Psychotherapie, Mariannengasse 10, 1090 Wien
Founded: 1950; Members: 30
Pres: Prof. V.E. Frankl
Focus: Therapeutics; Psych 00569

Österreichische Ärztegesellschaft zur Bekämpfung der cystischen Fibrose, c/o Universitäts-Kinderklinik, Währinger Gürtel 18-20, 1090 Wien
T: (01) 48993232
Founded: 1968; Members: 30
Focus: Cell Biol & Cancer Res 00570

Österreichische Ärztekammer (ÖÄK), Weihburggasse 10-12, Postfach 213, 1010 Wien
T: (01) 514060; Fax: 5140642
Founded: 1950; Members: 29000
Focus: Med
Periodicals
medizin populär: Patienteninformation der Österreichischen Ärztekammer (10 times annually)
Österreichische Ärztezeitung: Organ der Österreichischen Ärztekammer (bi-weekly) 00571

Österreichische ärztliche Gesellschaft für medizinisches und technisches Ozon, c/o Prof. Dr. Ottokar Rokitansky, Walfischgasse 14, 1010 Wien
T: (01) 5131948; Fax: 5131948
Focus: Therapeutics 00572

Österreichische Akademie der Wissenschaften (ÖAW), Dr.-Ignaz-Seipel-Pl 2, 1010 Wien
T: (01) 51581; Fax: 5139541
Founded: 1847; Members: 479
Pres: Prof. Dr. Werner Welzig; Gen Secr: Prof. Dr. Herbert Mang
Focus: Sci
Periodicals
Anzeiger der mathematisch-naturwissenschaftlichen Klasse (annually)
Anzeiger der philosophisch-historischen Klasse (annually)
Jahrbuch der österreichischen Byzantinistik (annually)
Römische Historische Mitteilungen (annually)
Sitzungsbericht I und II (annually)
Sprachkunst: Beiträge zur Literaturwissenschaft (annually)
Wiener Slavistisches Jahrbuch (annually)
Wiener Studien: Zeitschrift für Klassische Philologie und Patristik (annually)
Wiener Zeitschrift für die Kunde Südasiens und Archiv für indische Philosophie (annually)
Zeitschrift des Instituts für Demographie: Demographische Informationen 00573

Österreichische Arbeitsgemeinschaft für morphologische und funktionelle Atheroskleroseforschung, Schwarzspanierstr 17, 1090 Wien
T: (01) 431526395
Founded: 1975; Members: 125
Focus: Physiology; Pathology 00574

Österreichische Arbeitsgemeinschaft für Neuropsychiatrie und Psychologie des Kindes- und Jugendalters und verwandter Berufe (ÖANP), Währinger Gürtel 18-20, 1090 Wien
T: (01) 48003012
Founded: 1973; Members: 400
Focus: Psychiatry; Psych 00575

Österreichische Arbeitsgemeinschaft für Rehabilitation / Dachorganisation der österreichischen Behindertenverbände, Stubenring 2-4, 1010 Wien
T: (01) 5131533; Fax: 5131533150
Founded: 1950
Pres: Dr. Klaus Voget; Gen Secr: Heinz Schneider
Focus: Rehabil
Periodical
Monatsbericht: Sozialpolitische Rundschau (monthly) 00576

Österreichische Arbeitsgemeinschaft für Volksgesundheit (ÖAV), Stubenring 6, 1010 Wien
T: (01) 529661
Founded: 1947; Members: 110
Focus: Public Health
Periodical
ÖAV-Informationen (quarterly) 00577

Österreichische Arbeitskreise für Tiefenpsychologie (ÖAKT), c/o Psychologisches Institut, Universität, Akademiestr 20, 5020 Salzburg
T: (0662) 33501305
Founded: 1947; Members: 66
Focus: Psych 00578

Österreichische Bankwissenschaftliche Gesellschaft (BWG), Wallnerstr 3, 1010 Wien
T: (01) 5335050; Fax: 53127247
Founded: 1952; Members: ca. 300
Pres: Dr. Klaus Liebscher; Gen Secr: Otto Lucius
Focus: Finance

Periodicals
Bank-Archiv (monthly)
Bankwissenschaftliche Schriftenreihe (irregularly)
Diskussionsreihe Bank + Börse (irregularly)
. . . . 00579

Österreichische Bibelgesellschaft, Breite
Gasse 8, 1070 Wien
T: (01) 5238240
Focus: Rel & Theol 00580

Österreichische Biochemische Gesellschaft,
c/o Institut für Molekularbiologie, Billrothstr 11,
5020 Salzburg
T: (0662) 6396122; Fax: 6396129
Founded: 1954; Members: 825
Pres: Prof. Dr. G. Kreil; Gen Secr: Dr. M.
Gimona
Focus: Biochem 00581

**Österreichische Biophysikalische
Gesellschaft**, c/o Institut für allgemeine und
experimentelle Pathologie, Währinger Str 13, 1090
Wien
T: (01) 431526333
Founded: 1961; Members: 150
Focus: Biophys 00582

**Österreichische Bodenkundliche Gesellschaft
(ÖBG)**, c/o Universität für Bodenkultur, Gregor-
Mendel-Str 33, 1180 Wien
T: (01) 476540
Founded: 1954; Members: 269
Focus: Geology
Periodical
Mitteilungen der Österreichischen Bodenkundlichen
Gesellschaft (semi-annually) 00583

Österreichische Byzantinische Gesellschaft,
Postgasse 7-9, 1010 Wien
T: (01) 5120217; E-Mail: Byzneo@univie.ac.at;
Fax: 5127023
Founded: 1946; Members: 150
Pres: Prof. Dr. Johannes Koder
Focus: Hist; Cultur Hist
Periodical
Mitteilungen aus der österreichischen Byzantinistik
und Neogräzistik (annually) 00584

**Österreichische Computer-Gesellschaft
(OCG)**, Wollzeile 1, 1010 Wien
T: (01) 5120235; Fax: 5120235
Founded: 1975; Members: 1000
Focus: Computer & Info Sci
Periodicals
ocg-Kommunikativ (bi-monthly)
ocg-Schriftenreihe (irregularly) 00585

Österreichische Dentistenkammer (ÖDK),
Kohlmarkt 11, 1010 Wien
T: (01) 5337064; Fax: 5350758
Founded: 1949; Members: 388
Focus: Dent
Periodical
Österreichische Zahnärzte-Zeitung (monthly) 00586

Österreichische Diabetikervereinigung, Obere
Augartenstr 26-28, 1020 Wien
T: (01) 3323217; Fax: 3326828
Founded: 1978; Members: 4400
Focus: Diabetes
Periodical
Mein Leben (quarterly) 00587

Österreichische Entomologische Gesellschaft,
c/o Institut für Naturschutz und Landschaftspflege,
Heinrichstr 5, 8010 Graz
T: (0316) 36068; Fax: 360685
Founded: 1975; Members: 121
Focus: Entomology 00588

**Österreichische Ethnologische Gesellschaft
(ÖEG)**, c/o Museum für Völkerkunde, Neue
Hofburg, Heldenpl, 1014 Wien
T: (01) 53430519; Fax: 5355320
Founded: 1957; Members: 221
Pres: Dr. Ferdinand Anders
Focus: Ethnology
Periodical
Wiener Völkerkundliche Mitteilungen (WVM)
(annually) 00589

**Österreichische Ethnomedizinische
Gesellschaft**, c/o Institut für Geschichte der
Medizin, Währingerstr 25, 1090 Wien
T: (01) 408778041; Fax: 4083894
Founded: 1978; Members: 91
Pres: Prof. Dr. Karl R. Wernhart
Focus: Ethnology; Med 00590

Österreichische Exlibris-Gesellschaft,
c/o Gertrud Slattner, Ferdinandstr 14, 1020 Wien
T: (01) 2615213
Founded: 1903; Members: 239
Focus: Lit
Periodical
Mitteilungen der Österreichischen Exlibris-
Gesellschaft (3 times annually) 00591

Österreichische Forschungsgemeinschaft,
Berggasse 25, 1090 Wien
T: (01) 3195770; Fax: 319577020
Focus: Sci 00592

Österreichische Gartenbau-Gesellschaft,
Parkring 12, 1010 Wien
T: (01) 5128416, 5128808; E-Mail: oegg@
oegg.or.at; Fax: 512841617
Founded: 1837; Members: 4500
Pres: Dr. Gerhard Wirth; Gen Secr: Monika
Urbancic
Focus: Hort

Periodical
Garten (11 times annually) 00593

Österreichische Geodätische Kommission,
c/o Bundesamt für Eich- und Vermessungswesen,
Schiffamtsgasse 1-3, 1025 Wien
T: (01) 211763201; Fax: 2161062
Founded: 1863; Members: 20
Pres: Prof. Dr. H. Sünkel; Gen Secr: Dr. E.
Erker
Focus: Surveying
Periodical
Geodätische Arbeiten Österreichs für die
Internationale Erdmessung (irregularly) . 00594

**Österreichische Geographische Gesellschaft
(ÖGG)**, Karl-Schweighofer-Gasse 3, 1071 Wien
T: (01) 5237974; Fax: 5237974
Founded: 1856; Members: 1317
Pres: Prof. Dr. Ingrid Kretschmer; Gen Secr:
andreas Riedl
Focus: Geography
Periodical
Mitteilungen der Österreichischen Geographischen
Gesellschaft (annually) 00595

**Österreichische Geographische Gesellschaft,
Zweigverein Innsbruck**, Innrain 52, 6020
Innsbruck
T: (0512) 5073112, 5073101; Fax: 5073132
Founded: 1971; Members: 420
Focus: Geography
Periodical
Jahresbericht 00596

**Österreichische Geologische Gesellschaft
(ÖGG)**, c/o Geologische Bundesanstalt,
Rasumofskygasse 23, 1031 Wien
T: (01) 712567454; E-Mail: oegg@cc.geolba.ac.at;
Fax: 712567456
Founded: 1907; Members: 750
Pres: Prof. Dr. Eckard Wallbrecher; Gen Secr:
Thomas Hofmann
Focus: Geology
Periodical
Mitteilungen der Österreichischen Geologischen
Gesellschaft (annually) 00597

Österreichische Gesellschaft der Tierärzte,
Josef-Baumanngasse 1, 1210 Wien
T: (01) 25077; E-Mail: Sabine.schaefer@vv-
wien.ac.at; Fax: 250771090
Founded: 1919; Members: 1200
Pres: Prof. Dr. A. Holzmann; Gen Secr: Dr. S.
Schäfer
Focus: Vet Med
Periodical
Wiener Tierärztliche Monatsschrift (monthly) 00598

**Österreichische Gesellschaft für ärztliche
Hypnose und autogenes Training**,
Pyrkergasse 23, 1190 Wien
T: (01) 362366
Founded: 1969; Members: 170
Focus: Psych 00599

**Österreichische Gesellschaft für Agrar- und
Umweltrecht**, c/o Institut für Wirtschaft, Politik
und Recht, Universität für Bodenkultur, Gregor-
Mendel-Str 33, 1180 Wien
T: (01) 47654; Fax: 3105175
Founded: 1967; Members: 127
Focus: Law
Periodical
Agrarische Rundschau (bi-monthly) . . . 00600

**Österreichische Gesellschaft für Akupunktur
und Aurikulotherapie**, c/o Kaiserin-Elisabeth-
Spital, Huglgasse 1-3, 1150 Wien
T: (01) 981045758; Fax: 981045759
Founded: 1954; Members: 2000
Focus: Anesthetics; Med; Physical Therapy
Periodical
Deutsche Zeitschrift für Akupunktur (bi-monthly)
. . . . 00601

**Österreichische Gesellschaft für
Allgemeinmedizin (ÖGAM)**, Bahnhofstr 22, 9020
Klagenfurt
T: (0463) 55449
Focus: Med 00602

**Österreichische Gesellschaft für
Amerikastudien** / Austrian Association for
American Studies, Akademiestr 24c, 5020
Salzburg
E-Mail: arno.heller@funigraz.ac.at; Fax: (0316)
3809768
Founded: 1970; Members: 108
Pres: Arno Heller; Gen Secr: Elisabeth Kraus
Focus: Lit; Hist; Cultur Hist; Cinema; Mass Media
. . . . 00603

**Österreichische Gesellschaft für
Anästhesiologie, Reanimation und
Intensivmedizin**, Johann-Nepomuk-Vogl-Pl 1,
1180 Wien
T: (01) 4064810; Fax: 4064811
Founded: 1951; Members: 1025
Pres: Prof. M. Zimpfer; Gen Secr: Prof. W.
Mauritz
Focus: Anesthetics; Med
Periodical
Der Anaesthesist 00604

**Österreichische Gesellschaft für Analytische
Chemie**, c/o Prof. Dr. M. Grasserbauer, Institut
für Analytische Chemie, Technische Universität
Wien, Getreidemarkt 9, 1060 Wien
T: (01) 588014847; Fax: 5867813

Founded: 1948; Members: 400
Pres: Prof. Dr. M. Grasserbauer; Gen Secr: Prof.
Dr. G. Stingeder
Focus: Chem 00605

**Österreichische Gesellschaft für angewandte
Fremdenverkehrswissenschaft (ÖGFW)**,
Türkenschanzstr 18, 1018 Wien
T: (01) 346656
Focus: Econ 00606

**Österreichische Gesellschaft für angewandte
Zytologie**, Roseggerweg 48, 8036 Graz
T: (0316) 3852567
Founded: 1964; Members: 324
Pres: Prof. Dr. H. P. Dinges; Gen Secr: Prof.
Dr. Gerhard Breitenecker
Focus: Cell Biol & Cancer Res; Physiology
Periodical
Acta Cytologica (bi-monthly) 00607

Österreichische Gesellschaft für Angiologie,
c/o 1. Medizinische Universitätsklinik, Lazarettgasse
14, 1090 Wien
Founded: 1966; Members: 350
Focus: Med 00608

**Österreichische Gesellschaft für
Arbeitsmedizin**, c/o Arbeitsmedizinisches
Zentrum, 6060 Hall in Tirol
T: (05223) 57304; Fax: 5730410
Founded: 1954; Members: 430
Pres: Prof. Dr. Egmont Baumgartner
Focus: Med; Hygiene 00609

**Österreichische Gesellschaft für Arbeitsrecht
und Sozialrecht**, c/o Institut für Arbeitsrecht und
Sozialrecht, Universität, 4040 Linz-Auhof
T: (0732) 2468255
Founded: 1965; Members: 86
Focus: Law 00610

**Österreichische Gesellschaft für Archäologie
(ÖGA)**, c/o Institut für Alte Geschichte,
Altertumskunde und Epigraphik, Universität Wien,
Dr.-Karl-Lueger-Ring 1, 1010 Wien
T: (01) 401032200; Fax: 401032118
Founded: 1972; Members: 190
Pres: Prof. Dr. Ekkehard Weber
Focus: Archeol
Periodical
Römisches Österreich (annually) 00611

Österreichische Gesellschaft für Architektur,
Liechtensteinstr 46a, 1090 Wien
T: (01) 3197715; E-Mail: oegfa@aaf.or.at;
Fax: 3197715
Founded: 1965; Members: ca. 500
Pres: Irmgard Frank; Gen Secr: Sabine
Bartschieser
Focus: Archit
Periodicals
UmBau (annually)
UmSicht (2-3 times annually) 00612

**Österreichische Gesellschaft für Artificial
Intelligence**, 1014 Wien, Postfach 177
T: (01) 53532810; E-Mail: oegai@ai.univie.ac.at;
Fax: 5040532
Founded: 1981; Members: 240
Pres: Dr. Silvia Miksch
Focus: Electronic Eng
Periodical
ÖGAI Journal (quarterly) 00613

**Österreichische Gesellschaft für
Aussenpolitik und Internationale
Beziehungen**, Hofburg, Schweizer Hof,
Brunnenstiege, 1010 Wien
T: (01) 5354627; 535P107; Fax: 5354627
Founded: 1958; Members: 500
Pres: Dr. Wolfgang Schellenberg
Focus: Poli Sci
Periodical
Österreichisches Jahrbuch für Internationale Politik
(annually) 00614

**Österreichische Gesellschaft für Autogenes
Training und allgemeine Psychotherapie**,
Schelleingasse 8, 1040 Wien
T: (01) 5054454
Founded: 1969; Members: 680
Focus: Psychoan; Therapeutics 00615

**Österreichische Gesellschaft für Balneologie
und medizinische Klimatologie**, c/o Institut
für medizinische Physiologie, Universität Wien,
Schwarzspanierstr 17, 1090 Wien
Founded: 1956; Members: 136
Pres: Dr. W. Marktl
Focus: Physiology
Periodical
Zeitschrift für Physikalische Medizin, Balneologie
und Medizinische Klimatologie 00616

**Österreichische Gesellschaft für
Biomedizinische Technik**, c/o Technische
Universität, Gusshausstr 27-29, 1040 Wien
T: (01) 588013842; Fax: 5052666
Founded: 1975; Members: 202
Focus: Med 00617

**Österreichische Gesellschaft für Bionome
Psychotherapie**, Pyrkergasse 23, 1190 Wien
Founded: 1978
Focus: Psych; Therapeutics 00618

**Österreichische Gesellschaft für China-
Forschung (ÖGCF)**, Wickenburggasse 4, 1080
Wien
T: (01) 4069793; Fax: 4069794
Founded: 1971

Pres: Walter Strutzenberger; Gen Secr: Prof. Gerd
Kaminski
Focus: Sociology; Nat Sci
Periodical
China-Report (quarterly) 00619

Österreichische Gesellschaft für Chirurgie,
Frankgasse 8, Postfach 80, 1096 Wien
T: (01) 4087920; Fax: 4081328
Founded: 1958; Members: 1430
Pres: Dr. Franz Stöger; Gen Secr: Prof. Dr. Karl
Dinstl
Focus: Surgery
Periodicals
Acta Chirurgica Austriaca (bi-monthly)
Mitteilungen der Österreichischen Gesellschaft für
Chirurgie mit den assoziierten Fachgesellschaften
(quarterly) 00620

**Österreichische Gesellschaft für Chirurgische
Forschung**, c/o Zentrum für Biomedizinische
Forschung, Allgemeines Krankenhaus, Währinger
Gürtel 18-20, 1090 Wien
T: (01) 404005221; Fax: 404005229
Founded: 1976; Members: 240
Focus: Surgery
Periodical
Wissenschaftlicher Bericht des jährlich
abgehaltenen Seminars (annually) . . . 00621

**Österreichische Gesellschaft für Christliche
Kunst**, Stephanspl 3, 1010 Wien
Founded: 1909; Members: 133
Pres: Dr. Alfred Sammer
Focus: Arts 00622

**Österreichische Gesellschaft für Denkmal-
und Ortsbildpflege**, Künstlerhaus, Karlspl 5,
1010 Wien
T: (01) 5879663
Founded: 1947; Members: 670
Focus: Preserv Hist Monuments
Periodicals
Steine Sprechen (quarterly)
Steinschlag (quarterly) 00623

**Österreichische Gesellschaft für
Dermatologie und Venerologie**,
c/o Fachbereich Dermatologie, Muellner Hauptstr
48, 5020 Salzburg
Pres: Prof. Dr. H. Hintner; Gen Secr: Dr. J.
Auböck
Focus: Derm 00624

**Österreichische Gesellschaft für
Dokumentation und Information (ÖGDI)**,
Heinestr 38, 1021 Wien
T: (01) 267535
Founded: 1951; Members: 180
Pres: H. Jobst
Focus: Doc; Computer & Info Sci
Periodical
Fakten, Daten, Zitate: Das Informationsangebot für
Wissenschaft & Wirtschaft (quarterly) . . 00625

**Österreichische Gesellschaft für
Elektroencephalographie und klinische
Neurophysiologie**, c/o Universitätsklinik für
Neurologie, Anichstr 35, 6020 Innsbruck
Founded: 1953; Members: 350
Focus: Physiology
Periodical
EEG/EMG 00626

**Österreichische Gesellschaft für
Elektronenmikroskopie**, c/o Zentrum für
Elektronenmikroskopie Graz, Steyrergasse 17, 8010
Graz
T: (0316) 825363; Fax: 811596
Founded: 1965; Members: 238
Focus: Optics 00627

**Österreichische Gesellschaft für
Erdölwissenschaften (ÖGEW)**, Erdbergstr 72,
1031 Wien
T: (01) 7132348
Founded: 1960; Members: 500
Pres: Prof. Dr. H. Schindlbauer
Focus: Geology
Periodical
Erdöl Erdgas Kohle (monthly) 00628

**Österreichische Gesellschaft für
Ernährungsforschung (ÖGE)**, Zaunergasse 1-3,
Postfach 74, 1037 Wien
T: (01) 7147193; Fax: 7186146
Founded: 1950; Members: 850
Pres: Prof. Dr. Werner Pfannhauser
Focus: Food
Periodical
ernährung-nutrition (11 times annually) . 00629

**Österreichische Gesellschaft für
Filmwissenschaft, Kommunikations- und
Medienforschung (ÖGFKM)**, Rauhensteingasse
5, 1010 Wien
T: (01) 5129936; Fax: 5135330
Founded: 1952; Members: 200
Pres: Prof. Dr. Giselher Guttmann; Gen Secr: Dr.
Josef Schuchnig
Focus: Cinema; Comm Sci
Periodicals
Film/Video Manual (3 times annually)
Filmkunst (quarterly)
Mitteilungen der ÖGFKM (8-10 times annually)
. . . . 00630

**Österreichische Gesellschaft für
Friedensforschung**, Landstrasser Hauptstr 24,
1030 Wien
Focus: Poli Sci; Prom Peace 00631

Österreichische Gesellschaft für Gastroenterologie und Hepatologie (ÖGGH), c/o Universitätsklinik für Innere Medizin IV, Währinger Gürtel 18-20, 1090 Wien
T: (01) 404004744; Fax: 404004735
Founded: 1968; Members: 633
Focus: Gastroenter
Periodical
Zeitschrift für Gastroenterologie 00632

Österreichische Gesellschaft für Gefässchirurgie, c/o Landeskrankenanstalten Salzburg, Müllner Hauptstr 48, 5020 Salzburg
Focus: Surgery 00633

Österreichische Gesellschaft für Geriatrie und Gerontologie, c/o Krankenhaus der Barmherzigen Brüder, Medizinische Abteilung, Grosse Mohrengasse 9, 1020 Wien
T: (01) 21121395
Founded: 1955; Members: 200
Pres: Prof. Dr. R. Willvonseder; Gen Secr: Prof. Dr. Monika Skalicky
Focus: Geriatrics
Periodicals
Aktuelle Gerontologie (monthly)
Scriptum Geriatricum (annually) 00634

Österreichische Gesellschaft für gerichtliche Medizin, Sensengasse 2, 1090 Wien
T: (01) 4024051; Fax: 4052726
Founded: 1965; Members: 64
Pres: Prof. Dr. Georg Bauer; Gen Secr: Dr. Wolfgang Denk
Focus: Forensic Med
Periodical
Beiträge zur Gerichtlichen Medizin (annually) 00635

Österreichische Gesellschaft für Geschichte der Pharmazie, Spitalgasse 31, 1090 Wien
T: (01) 5580555
Founded: 1950; Members: 146
Focus: Hist; Pharmacol 00636

Österreichische Gesellschaft für Gesetzgebungslehre (ÖGGL), c/o Institut für Verfassungs- und Verwaltungsrecht, Kapitelgasse 5-7, 5020 Salzburg
T: (0662) 80443630; Fax: 8044303
Founded: 1982; Members: 150
Focus: Law 00637

Österreichische Gesellschaft für Gruppendynamik und Organisationsberatung, c/o Institut für Philosophie, Universität, Universitätsstr 67, 9022 Klagenfurt
T: (0463) 37509
Founded: 1973; Members: 80
Focus: Philos 00638

Österreichische Gesellschaft für Gynäkologie und Geburtshilfe, Spitalgasse 23, 1090 Wien
T: (01) 404002915; Fax: 404002911
Founded: 1980; Members: 398
Focus: Gynecology 00639

Österreichische Gesellschaft für Hals-, Nasen- und Ohrenheilkunde, Kopf- und Halschirurgie, c/o Universitäts-HNO-Klinik, Währinger Gürtel 18-20, 1090 Wien
T: (01) 404003350; Fax: 404003350
Founded: 1892; Members: 626
Pres: Prof. Dr. W.F. Thumfahrt; Gen Secr: Prof. Dr. K. Albegger
Focus: Otorhinolaryngology; Surgery
Periodical
Laryngologie, Rhinologie, Otologie (monthly) 00640

Österreichische Gesellschaft für Hochschuldidaktik, Strozzigasse 2, 1080 Wien
Fax: (01) 425618248
Founded: 1977; Members: 150
Focus: Educ
Periodical
Zeitschrift für Hochschuldidaktik: Beiträge zu Studium, Wissenschaft und Beruf . . . 00641

Österreichische Gesellschaft für Holzforschung (ÖGH), Arsenal, Franz-Grill-Str 7, 1031 Wien
T: (01) 79826230; E-Mail: ohfi@adis.at; Fax: 798262350
Founded: 1947; Members: 180
Pres: Helmuth Neuner; Gen Secr: Wolfgang Winter
Focus: Forestry
Periodical
Holzforschung und Holzverwertung: Mitteilungen (bi-monthly) 00642

Österreichische Gesellschaft für Humanökologie, Karlspl 13, 1040 Wien
T: (01) 653785799
Founded: 1976
Focus: Ecology 00643

Österreichische Gesellschaft für Hygiene, Mikrobiologie und Präventivmedizin (ÖGHMP), Kinderspitalgasse 15, 1095 Wien
T: (01) 40490; Fax: 40490
Founded: 1925; Members: 430
Pres: Prof. Dr. Dr. Ernst Brandl; Gen Secr: Prof. Dr. Gerold Stanek
Focus: Hygiene; Med; Microbio 00644

Österreichische Gesellschaft für Industrielle Strahltechnik (ÖGIST), Costenoblegasse 2, 1130 Wien
T: (01) 588013869
Founded: 1979; Members: 6
Focus: Radiology
Periodical
Mitteilungen der ÖGIST 00645

Österreichische Gesellschaft für Informatik (ÖGI), Altenbergerstr 69, 4040 Linz
T: (0732) 24689238
Founded: 1975; Members: 200
Focus: Computer & Info Sci 00646

Österreichische Gesellschaft für Innere Medizin, c/o Allgemeines Krankenhaus, Währinger Gürtel 18-20, 1090 Wien
Founded: 1886; Members: 400
Pres: Prof. Dr. A. Gangl
Focus: Intern Med
Periodical
Wiener Zeitschrift für Innere Medizin . . 00647

Österreichische Gesellschaft für internistische Intensivmedizin, c/o Intensivstation, Klinik für Innere Medizin IV, Währinger Gürtel 18-20, 1090 Wien
Founded: 1970; Members: 290
Focus: Intern Med 00648

Österreichische Gesellschaft für Kinder- und Jugendheilkunde, c/o G. von Preyer'sches Kinderspital, Schrankenberggasse 31, 1100 Wien
T: (01) 60113201; Fax: 60113311
Founded: 1962; Members: 805
Pres: Prof. Dr. Walter Stögmann; Gen Secr: Dr. Franz Paky
Focus: Pediatrics
Periodical
Pädiatrie und Pädologie 00649

Österreichische Gesellschaft für Kinderchirurgie, c/o Universitätsklinik für Kinderchirurgie, Auenbruggerpl 34, 8036 Graz
Founded: 1966; Members: 70
Focus: Surgery 00650

Österreichische Gesellschaft für Kinderphilosophie (KiPHi), Schmiedgasse 12, 8010 Graz
Fax: (0316) 811513
Founded: 1985
Focus: Philos
Periodical
Info Kinderphilosophie (quarterly) 00651

Österreichische Gesellschaft für Kirchenrecht, c/o Institut für Kirchenrecht, Freyung 6, 1010 Wien
T: (01) 5339861; Fax: 5351019
Founded: 1949; Members: 225
Focus: Law; Rel & Theol
Periodical
Österreichisches Archiv für Kirchenrecht (quarterly) 00652

Österreichische Gesellschaft für Klinische Chemie (ÖGKC), Währingerstr 10, 1090 Wien
T: (01) 4252649
Founded: 1968; Members: 500
Pres: Prof. Dr. P.M. Bayen; Gen Secr: Dr. W. Hübl
Focus: Chem
Periodical
Berichte der ÖGKC 00653

Österreichische Gesellschaft für Klinische Neurophysiologie, c/o Institut für Neurophysiologie, Universität Wien, Währingerstr 17, 1090 Wien
Founded: 1953
Focus: Neurology; Physiology
Periodical
EEG/EMG (quarterly) 00654

Österreichische Gesellschaft für Kommunikationsfragen (ÖKG) / Austrian Society for Communication, c/o Institut für Publizistik und Kommunikationswissenschaft, Universität Salzburg, Rudolfskai 42, 5020 Salzburg
T: (0662) 80444150; Fax: 80444190
Founded: 1976; Members: 480
Gen Secr: Dr. Rudolf Renger
Focus: Comm Sci; Journalism
Periodical
Medien-Journal (quarterly) 00655

Österreichische Gesellschaft für Laboratoriumsmedizin, Franz-Josefs-Kai 65, 1010 Wien
T: (01) 349130
Founded: 1973; Members: 72
Focus: Med 00656

Österreichische Gesellschaft für Literatur, Herrengasse 5, 1010 Wien
T: (01) 5338159; Fax: 5334067
Founded: 1961
Pres: Marianne Gruber
Focus: Lit 00657

Österreichische Gesellschaft für Logopädie, Phoniatrie und Pädoaudiologie, c/o Univ. HNO-Klinik Wien, Klinische Abteilung Phoniatrie-Logopädie, Währingergürtel 18-20, 1090 Wien
T: (01) 404003317
Founded: 1951; Members: 150-200
Focus: Logopedy; Otorhinolaryngology . . 00658

Österreichische Gesellschaft für Lungenerkrankungen und Tuberkulose, c/o Wiener Medizinische Akademie, Alserstr 4, 1090 Wien
T: (01) 405138321; E-Mail: medacad@via.at; Fax: 405138323
Founded: 1950; Members: 550
Pres: Dr. Kurt Aigner; Gen Secr: Dr. M. Neumann
Focus: Pulmon Dis
Periodical
Jahresberichte der wissenschaftlichen Veranstaltungen 00659

Österreichische Gesellschaft für Medizinsoziologie (ÖGMS), Stumpergasse 56, 1060 Wien
T: (01) 59991243; Fax: 5971871
Founded: 1978; Members: 15
Focus: Med; Sociology 00660

Österreichische Gesellschaft für Meteorologie, Hohe Warte 38, 1190 Wien
T: (01) 36026; Fax: 3691233
Founded: 1865; Members: 230
Pres: Prof. Dr. Helmut Pichler; Gen Secr: Dr. E. Dreiseitl
Focus: Geophys
Periodicals
Meteorologische Zeitschrift (bi-monthly)
Wetter und Leben: Zeitschrift für Angewandte Meteorologie (quarterly) 00661

Österreichische Gesellschaft für Mikrochemie und analytische Chemie (ÖGMAC), c/o Institut für analytische Chemie und Mikrochemie, Technischen Universität, Getreidemarkt 9, 1060 Wien
T: (01) 4322258801, 48474940
Founded: 1946; Members: 220
Focus: Chem 00662

Österreichische Gesellschaft für Musik (ÖGfM), Hanuschgasse 3, 1010 Wien
T: (01) 5123143; Fax: 5124299
Founded: 1963; Members: 1000
Pres: Prof. Gerhard Wimberger; Gen Secr: Dr. Harald Goertz
Focus: Music
Periodical
Beiträge (irregularly) 00663

Österreichische Gesellschaft für Nephrologie, c/o Krankenhaus der Elisabethinen, 4020 Linz
T: (0732) 278021
Focus: Med; Geriatrics
Periodical
Nephrologische Nachrichten (quarterly) . . 00664

Österreichische Gesellschaft für Neugriechische Studien, c/o Institut für Byzantinistik und Neogräzistik, Postgasse 7, 1010 Wien
T: (01) 5120217; E-Mail: maria.stassinopoulou@univie.ac.at; Fax: 5127023
Founded: 1988; Members: 48
Pres: Dr. Maria Stassinopoulou; Gen Secr: Prof. Dr. Max D. Peyfuss
Focus: Ling; Lit 00665

Österreichische Gesellschaft für Neurochirurgie, Währinger Gürtel 18-20, 1090 Wien
Fax: (01) 404004566
Founded: 1961; Members: 85
Focus: Surgery 00666

Österreichische Gesellschaft für Neurologie und Psychiatrie, c/o NKH Maria Theresien Schlössel, Hofzeile 18-20, 1190 Wien
T: (01) 3683455330; E-Mail: oegnp@ins.at; Fax: 3694400
Founded: 1957; Members: 550
Pres: Prof. Dr. E. Deisenhammer; Gen Secr: Prof. Dr. H. Binder; Prof. Dr. P. König
Focus: Psychiatry; Neurology
Periodical
Neuropsychiatrie (quarterly) 00667

Österreichische Gesellschaft für Neuropathologie, c/o Neurologisches Institut, Universität, Schwarzspanierstr 17, 1090 Wien
T: (01) 84163431
Founded: 1964; Members: 48
Focus: Pathology
Periodical
Current Topics in Neuropathology (annually) 00668

Österreichische Gesellschaft für Operations Research (ÖGOR), Argentinierstr 8, 1040 Wien
T: (0316) 3803490; 3803491; 3803492; E-Mail: Ulrike.Leopold@kfunigraz.ac.at; Fax: 3809560
Founded: 1978; Members: ca. 200
Pres: Prof. Dr. Ulrike Leopold; Gen Secr: Prof. Dr. Werner Jammernegg
Focus: Business Admin; Math
Periodical
ÖGOR-Nachrichten: Central European Journal of Operations Research and Economics (quarterly) 00669

Österreichische Gesellschaft für Orthopädie und Orthopädische Chirurgie, c/o Orthopädische Universitätsklinik, Garnisongasse 13, 1090 Wien
Founded: 1948; Members: 276
Focus: Orthopedics; Surgery 00670

Österreichische Gesellschaft für Parapsychologie und Grenzbereiche der Wissenschaften, c/o Technische Universität Wien, Gußhausstr 27, 1040 Wien
T: (01) 4058335; E-Mail: peter.mulacz@blackbox.at
Founded: 1927; Members: 190
Pres: Prof. Dr. Manfred Kremser; Gen Secr: W. Peter Mulacz
Focus: Parapsych 00671

Österreichische Gesellschaft für Pathologie, c/o Pathologisch-anatomisches Institut, Universität, Währinger Gürtel 18-20, 1090 Wien
T: (01) 404003651; Fax: 423402
Founded: 1921; Members: 250
Focus: Pathology 00672

Österreichische Gesellschaft für Perinatale Medizin, c/o Universitäts-Frauenklinik, Spitalgasse 23, 1090 Wien
T: (01) 404002915; Fax: 404002911
Founded: 1972; Members: 350
Focus: Gynecology 00673

Österreichische Gesellschaft für Philosophie, c/o DDR. Winfried Löffler, Universitätsstr 4, 6020 Innsbruck
T: (0512) 5078525; E-Mail: winfried loeffler@uibk.ac.at
Founded: 1985; Members: 140
Pres: Prof. Edmund Runggaldier; Gen Secr: Dr. Winfried Löffler
Focus: Philos
Periodical
Philosophie-Österreich (semi-annually) . . 00674

Österreichische Gesellschaft für Physikalische Medizin und Rehabilitation, c/o Institut für Physikalische Medizin, Hanuschkrankenhaus, Heinrich-Collin-Str 30, 1140 Wien
T: (01) 9149701; Fax: 9149264
Founded: 1951; Members: 180
Pres: Dr. O. Rathkolb; Gen Secr: Dr. K. Ammer
Focus: Rehabil; Physiology; Physical Therapy
Periodical
Österreichische Zeitschrift für Physikalische Medizin und Rehabilitation 00675

Österreichische Gesellschaft für Politikwissenschaft, Stumpergasse 56, 1060 Wien
T: (01) 59991166; E-Mail: hafner@ihssv.wsr.ac.at; Fax: 59991171
Founded: 1972; Members: 490
Pres: Dr. Sonja Puntscher-Riekmann; Gen Secr: Dr. Josef Melchior
Focus: Poli Sci
Periodicals
ÖGPW-Rundbrief (quarterly)
Österreichische Zeitschrift für Politikwissenschaft; ÖZP (quarterly) 00676

Österreichische Gesellschaft für Psychische Hygiene, c/o Psychiatrische Universitätsklinik, Lazarettgasse 14, 1090 Wien
T: (01) 48003567
Founded: 1948; Members: 85
Focus: Hygiene
Periodical
Wiener Zeitschrift für Nervenheilkunde . . 00677

Österreichische Gesellschaft für Raumplanung, Karlspl 13, 1040 Wien
T: (01) 588013380
Founded: 1954; Members: 1000
Pres: Prof. Dr. Klaus Semsroth
Focus: Urban Plan
Periodical
Schriftenreihe 00678

Österreichische Gesellschaft für Rechtsvergleichung (ÖGfRV), c/o Institut für Rechtsvergleichung, Universität, Schottenbastei 10-16, 1010 Wien
T: (01) 401033240
Founded: 1959; Members: 183
Focus: Law
Periodicals
Wiener Rechtswissenschaftliche Studien
Zeitschrift für Rechtsvergleichung, Internationales Privatrecht und Europarecht 00679

Österreichische Gesellschaft für Religionswissenschaft, Hans-Pfitzner-Str 5, 5020 Salzburg
Founded: 1962
Focus: Rel & Theol 00680

Österreichische Gesellschaft für Schweisstechnik, Arsenal, 1030 Wien
T: (01) 782168
Founded: 1947
Focus: Eng
Periodical
Schweisstechnik (monthly) 00681

Österreichische Gesellschaft für Semiotik (ÖGS), c/o Institut für Romanistik, Universität, Schlickgasse 4, 1090 Wien
T: (01) 316146
Founded: 1976; Members: 174
Focus: Ling
Periodicals
Angewandte Semiotik
Semiotische Berichte: Zeitschrift für Semiotik 00682

Österreichische Gesellschaft für Soziologie (ÖGS), c/o Institut für Soziologie, Betriebswirtschaftliches Zentrum, Brünnerstr 72, 1210 Wien
T: (01) 29128542; Fax: 29128544
Founded: 1950
Pres: Prof. Dr. Franz Traxler
Focus: Sociology
Periodical
Österreichische Zeitschrift für Soziologie (quarterly) 00683

Österreichische Gesellschaft für Sprachheilpädagogik, Erlachgasse 91, 1100 Wien
T: (01) 6033796
Founded: 1969; Members: 1500
Focus: Educ; Rehabil; Educ Handic
Periodical
Der Sprachheilpädagoge (quarterly) . . . 00684

Österreichische Gesellschaft für Statistik (ÖGS), Hintere Zollamtstr 2b, Postfach 90, 1033 Wien
T: (01) 71128
Founded: 1951; Members: 450
Focus: Computer & Info Sci; Stats
Periodical
Österreichische Zeitschrift für Statistik und Informatik (quarterly) 00685

Österreichische Gesellschaft für Strassenwesen (ÖGS), Marxergasse 10, 1030 Wien
T: (01) 736296
Founded: 1950; Members: 120
Focus: Transport
Periodical
Die Straße im Scheinwetter: Monatsberichte (monthly) 00686

Österreichische Gesellschaft für Tropenmedizin und Parasitologie, Kinderspitalgasse 15, 1095 Wien
T: (01) 40490
Founded: 1967; Members: 200
Focus: Trop Med
Periodical
Mitteilungen (annually) 00687

Österreichische Gesellschaft für Unfallchirurgie (ÖGfU), Donaueschingenstr 13, 1200 Wien
T: (01) 33110
Founded: 1965; Members: 900
Pres: Dr. H. Hackstock; Gen Secr: Dr. W. Buchinger
Focus: Surgery
Periodical
Kongreßberichte: Hefte zur Unfallkunde (annually) 00688

Österreichische Gesellschaft für Unternehmensgeschichte, Augasse 2-6, 1090 Wien
T: (01) 2536004711
Members: 120
Focus: Hist; Econ 00689

Österreichische Gesellschaft für Ur- und Frühgeschichte, c/o Institut für Ur- und Frühgeschichte, Franz-Klein-Gasse 1, 1190 Wien
T: (01) 31352373; Fax: 31352350
Founded: 1950; Members: 1050
Gen Secr: Alexandra Krenn-Leer
Focus: Hist
Periodical
Archäologie Österreichs (semi-annually) . 00690

Österreichische Gesellschaft für Urologie, c/o Urologische Universitätsklinik, Währinger Gürtel 16-18, 1090 Wien
Founded: 1947; Members: 338
Pres: Prof. Dr. H. Madersbacher
Focus: Urology 00691

Österreichische Gesellschaft für Vakuumtechnik, c/o Institut für Allgemeine Physik, Karlspl 13, 1040 Wien
Founded: 1969; Members: 170
Focus: Eng 00692

Österreichische Gesellschaft für Vermessung und Geoinformation, Schiffamtsgasse 1-3, 1025 Wien
T: (01) 211763603; Fax: 2167551
Founded: 1903; Members: 690
Pres: August Hochwartner; Gen Secr: Gert Steinkellner
Focus: Surveying
Periodical
Österreichische Zeitschrift für Vermessung und Geoinformation (VGI) (quarterly) 00693

Österreichische Gesellschaft für Versicherungsfachwissen, Schwarzenbergpl 7, 1030 Wien
T: (01) 7132135; Fax: 7132262
Pres: Dr. Franz Vogler; Gen Secr: Katharina Trampisch
Focus: Insurance
Periodical
Die Versicherungsrundschau (monthly) . . 00694

Österreichische Gesellschaft für Vogelkunde (ÖGV), c/o Naturhistorisches Museum, Burgring 7, Postfach 417, 1014 Wien
T: (01) 934651; Fax: 935254
Founded: 1953; Members: 1400
Focus: Ornithology
Periodical
Egretta: Vogelkundliche Nachrichten aus Österreich (semi-annually) 00695

Österreichische Gesellschaft für Warenkunde und Technologie (ÖGWT), c/o Institut für Technologie und Warenwirtschaftslehre, Wirtschaftsuniversität, Augasse 2-6, 1090 Wien
T: (01) 313364806; Fax: 31336706
Founded: 1957; Members: 83
Focus: Business Admin; Eng
Periodicals
Bioware: Zeitschrift für Biologie und Warenlehre (3 times annually)
Forum Ware: Die Ware und ihre Bedeutung für Mensch, Wirtschaft und Natur (quarterly) 00696

Österreichische Gesellschaft für Weltraumforschung, Postfach 67, 6020 Innsbruck
Founded: 1952
Focus: Astronomy 00697

Österreichische Gesellschaft für Wirtschaftspolitik, Franz-Klein-Gasse 1, 1190 Wien
Founded: 1947
Focus: Poli Sci 00698

Österreichische Gesellschaft für Wirtschaftsraumforschung (ÖGW), c/o Institut für Wirtschafts- und Sozialgeographie, Augasse 2-6, 1090 Wien
T: (01) 3692099; E-Mail: hofmayer@wu-wien.ac.at; Fax: 369299918
Founded: 1962; Members: 90
Pres: Prof. Dr. Klaus Arnold; Gen Secr: Dr. Friedrich Benesch
Focus: Econ; Geography
Periodicals
Wiener Geographische Schriften (irregularly)
Wirtschaftsgeographische Studien (annually) 00699

Österreichische Gesellschaft für Wirtschaftssoziologie, c/o Wirtschaftsuniversität, Augasse 2-6, 1090 Wien
T: (01) 340525742
Founded: 1973; Members: 25
Focus: Sociology
Periodical
Studien zur Soziologie (irregularly) . . . 00700

Österreichische Gesellschaft für Wissenschaftsgeschichte, Postgasse 7-9, 1010 Wien
Founded: 1980; Members: 200
Focus: Hist; Nat Sci
Periodical
Mitteilungen (quarterly) 00701

Österreichische Gesellschaft für Zahn-, Mund- und Kieferheilkunde, c/o Bundesfachgruppe für Zahn-, Mund- und Kieferheilkunde der Österreichischen Ärztekammer, Weihburggasse 10-12, 1010 Wien
T: (01) 5125126; Fax: 512512667
Founded: 1861; Members: 1960
Pres: Prof. Dr. Rudolf Slavicek; Gen Secr: Prof. Wilhelm O. Ambros
Focus: Dent; Stomatology
Periodical
Zeitschrift für Stomatologie (10 times annually) 00702

Österreichische Gesellschaft für Zeitgeschichte, Rotenhausgasse 6, 1090 Wien
Founded: 1960; Members: 10
Focus: Hist
Periodicals
Jahrbuch für Zeitgeschichte (annually)
Materialien zur Zeitgeschichte (irregularly)
Veröffentlichungen zur Zeitgeschichte (irregularly) 00703

Österreichische Gesellschaft und Institut für Umweltschutz, Umwelttechnologie und Umweltwissenschaften, Marc-Aurel-Str 5, 1010 Wien
T: (01) 634124
Focus: Ecology; Eng; Nat Sci 00704

Österreichische Gesellschaft zum Studium der Sterilität und Fertilität, c/o 1. Universitäts-Frauenklinik, Spitalgasse 23, 1090 Wien
T: (01) 404002851
Founded: 1956; Members: 114
Pres: Prof. Dr. G. Tscherne; Gen Secr: Prof. Dr. J.C. Huber
Focus: Gynecology 00705

Österreichische Gesellschaft zur Bekämpfung der Cystischen Fibrose, c/o Universitäts-Kinderklinik, Währinger Gürtel 18-20, 1090 Wien
Founded: 1968
Focus: Physiology; Pathology 00706

Österreichische Gesellschaft zur Erforschung des 18. Jahrhunderts, c/o Institut für Geschichte, Universität, Dr.-Karl-Lueger-Ring 1, 1010 Wien
T: (01) 43002280
Members: 140
Focus: Hist 00707

Österreichische Gesellschaft zur Föderung von Umweltschutz und Energieforschung (ÖGEFUE), Obere Weissgerberstr 16, 1030 Wien
T: (01) 7358234
Founded: 1973; Members: 3500
Focus: Ecology; Energy
Periodical
Umwelt-Report (quarterly) 00708

Österreichische Gesellschaft zur Förderung medizin-meteorologischer Forschung in Österreich, Hohe Warte 38, 1190 Wien
T: (01) 364453
Members: 180
Focus: Med 00709

Österreichische Hämophilie-Gesellschaft (ÖHG) / Austrian Hemophilia Society, Obere Augartenstr. 26-29, 1020 Wien
T: (01) 3303257
Founded: 1965; Members: 700
Focus: Hematology
Periodical
Mitgliederzeitschrift der Österreichischen Hämophilie Gesellschaft (irregularly) 00710

Österreichische Himalaya-Gesellschaft (ÖHG), Prinz-Eugen-Str 12, 1040 Wien
T: (01) 6540553
Focus: Geology 00711

Österreichische Humanistische Gesellschaft für die Steiermark, c/o Institut für Römisches Recht, Universitätsstr 15, 8010 Graz
T: (0316) 3803271; E-Mail: gerhard.thuer@kfunigraz.ac.at
Founded: 1946; Members: 350
Pres: Prof. Dr. Gerhard Thür; Gen Secr: Dr. Erwin Pochmarski
Focus: Humanities 00712

Österreichische Kardiologische Gesellschaft, c/o Universitätsklinik für Innere Med. II /Abteilung Kardiologie, Währinger Gürtel 18-20, 1090 Wien
T: (01) 404004357; E-Mail: dbuck@mail.kard.akh-wien.ac.at; Fax: 4081148
Founded: 1968; Members: ca. 950
Pres: Prof. Dr. M. Deutsch; Gen Secr: Prof. Dr. J. Tilczoch
Focus: Cardiol
Periodical
Acta medica austriaca (bi-monthly) . . . 00713

Österreichische Krebshilfe – Österreichische Krebsgesellschaft, Spitalgasse 19, 1090 Wien
T: (01) 426363, 425139; Fax: 425139
Founded: 1910; Members: 1500
Focus: Cell Biol & Cancer Res
Periodical
Onkologie (annually) 00714

Österreichische Krebshilfe Steiermark, Plüddemanngasse 51, 8010 Graz
T: (0316) 4744330; E-Mail: oe_krebshilfe@mail.styria.com; Fax: 47443310
Founded: 1974; Members: 200
Pres: Prof. Dr. Peter Steindorfer; Gen Secr: Scherer Christian
Focus: Cell Biol & Cancer Res 00715

Österreichische Kulturgemeinschaft, Gunoldstr 14, 1019 Wien
T: (01) 365168
Focus: Ethnology 00716

Österreichische Ludwig-Wittgenstein-Gesellschaft, 2880 Kirchberg
T: (02641) 2280
Focus: Philos 00717

Österreichische Mathematische Gesellschaft (ÖMG) / TU wien 118/2, c/o TU Wien, Wiedner Hauptstr 8-10, 1040 Wien
T: (01) 588015454; E-Mail: friedrich.urbanek@tuwien.ac.at
Founded: 1903; Members: 1200
Pres: Prof. Dr. G. Helmberg
Focus: Math
Periodical
International Mathematical News (3 times annually) 00718

Österreichische medizinische Gesellschaft für Neuraltherapie nach Huneke-Regulationsforschung (ÖNR), Wastiangasse 7, 8010 Graz
T: (05354) 2120; Fax: 472575
Founded: 1971; Members: 715
Focus: Therapeutics
Periodical
Ganzheitsmedizin: Zeitschrift für Regulationsmedizin (quarterly) 00719

Österreichische Mineralogische Gesellschaft (ÖMG), c/o Naturhistorisches Museum, Burgring 7, Postfach 417, 1014 Wien
T: (01) 52177567; Fax: 52177264
Founded: 1901; Members: 333
Pres: Prof. Dr. Ekkehart Tillmanns; Gen Secr: Dr. Vera M. F. Hammer
Focus: Mineralogy
Periodical
Mitteilungen der ÖMG (annually) 00720

Österreichische Multiple Sklerosis Gesellschaft, Währinger Gürtel 18-20, 1090 Wien
Fax: (01) 404003141
Focus: Neurology
Periodical
Neue Horizonte (quarterly) 00721

Österreichische Mykologische Gesellschaft (ÖMG), c/o Institut für Botanik, Universität, Rennweg 14, 1030 Wien
T: (01) 79794; E-Mail: irmgard.greilhuber@univie.ac.at; Fax: 79794131
Founded: 1919; Members: 300
Pres: Prof. Dr. Meinhard Moser; Gen Secr: Dr. Irmgard Krisai-Greilhuber
Focus: Botany
Periodical
Österreichische Zeitschrift für Pilzkunde (annually) 00722

Österreichische Numismatische Gesellschaft (ÖNG), Burgring 5, 1010 Wien
T: (01) 52524383; Fax: 52524501
Founded: 1870; Members: 400
Pres: Helmut Hirschberg; Gen Secr: Dr. Karl Schulz
Focus: Numismatics
Periodicals
Mitteilungen der Österreichischen Numismatischen Gesellschaft (bi-monthly)
Numismatische Zeitschrift (irregularly) . . 00723

Österreichische Ophthalmologische Gesellschaft (ÖOG), Schlösselgasse 9, 1080 Wien
T: (01) 4028540; Fax: 4027935
Founded: 1955; Members: 650
Pres: Prof. Dr. Gnad; Gen Secr: Dr. Drobec
Focus: Ophthal
Periodical
Spektrum der Augenheilkunde (bi-monthly) 00724

Österreichische Orchideen-Gesellschaft, Postfach 300, 1222 Wien
T: (01) 5128416
Focus: Botany
Periodical
Der Orchideenkurier (quarterly) 00725

Österreichische Orient-Gesellschaft Hammer-Purgstall, Dominikanerbastei 6, 1010 Wien
T: (01) 5128936; Fax: 512893617
Members: 163
Focus: Ethnology; Ling 00726

Österreichische Pädagogische Gesellschaft, c/o Institut für Erziehungswissenschaften, Garnisongasse 3, Postfach 26, 1096 Wien
T: (01) 4066171DW14; Fax: 4066171DW31
Founded: 1966; Members: 300
Pres: Dr. Josef Kurzreiter; Gen Secr: Prof. Dr. Dr. Nikolaus Severinski
Focus: Educ 00727

Österreichische Paläontologische Gesellschaft (ÖPG), Althanstr 14, 1090 Wien
T: (01) 313369724; E-Mail: dann@pal.univie.ac.at; Fax: 31336784
Founded: 1966; Members: 165
Focus: Paleontology 00728

Österreichische Pharmazeutische Gesellschaft (ÖPhG), c/o Institut für Pharmakognosie, Pharmaziezentrum, Althaustr 14, 1090 Wien
T: (01) 313368073; E-Mail: Gottfried.reznicek@univie.ac.at; Fax: 31336772
Founded: 1979; Members: 950
Pres: Prof. Dr. W. Kubelka; Gen Secr: Dr. G. Reznicek
Focus: Pharmacol
Periodical
Scientia Pharmaceutica (quarterly) . . . 00729

Österreichische Physikalische Gesellschaft (ÖPG), c/o Prof. Dr. R. Dobrozemsky, Österreichisches Forschungszentrum, 2444 Seibersdorf
T: (02254) 803137
Founded: 1950; Members: 870
Pres: H. List; Gen Secr: Prof. Dr. R. Dobrozemsky
Focus: Physics 00730

Österreichische Physiologische Gesellschaft, Schwarzspanierstr 17, 1090 Wien
T: (01) 40480239; Fax: 4028822
Founded: 1974; Members: 83
Focus: Physiology 00731

Österreichische Raumordnungskonferenz (ÖROK) / Austrian Conference on Regional Planning, Annagasse 5, 1010 Wien
T: (01) 5134888; Fax: 5134890
Founded: 1971
Focus: Urban Plan
Periodical
ÖROK-Schriftenreihe (irregularly) 00732

Österreichische Rektorenkonferenz (ÖRK), Liechtensteinstr 22, 1090 Wien
T: (01) 31056560; Fax: 31056522
Founded: 1911; Members: 36
Pres: Prof. Dr. Peter Skalicky; Gen Secr: Dr. Andrea Henzl
Focus: Educ 00733

Österreichische Röntgengesellschaft – Gesellschaft für medizinische Radiologie und Nuklearmedizin, Rotenhausgasse 6, 1090 Wien
T: (01) 435222
Founded: 1946; Members: 600
Gen Secr: Dr. G. Mostbeck
Focus: Radiology; X-Ray Tech; Nucl Med
Periodical
ÖRG-Mitteilungen 00734

Österreichische Sportwissenschaftliche Gesellschaft, c/o Institut für Sportwissenschaften, Akademiestr 26, 5020 Salzburg
T: (0662) 80444857
Members: 140
Focus: Sports 00735

Österreichische Statistische Gesellschaft, 1033 Wien, Postfach 90
Founded: 1951; Members: 500
Focus: Stats
Periodical
Österreichische Zeitschrift für Statistika und Informatik (quarterly) 00736

Österreichische Studiengesellschaft für Kinderpsychoanalyse, Konstanze-Weber-Gasse 45, 5020 Salzburg
T: (0662) 845138
Founded: 1976; Members: 15
Focus: Psychoan
Periodical
Studien zur Kinderpsychoanalyse (annually) 00737

Österreichische Studiengesellschaft für Kybernetik (ÖSGK), Schottengasse 3, 1010 Wien
T: (01) 53532810; Fax: 5320652
Founded: 1969; Members: 676
Pres: Prof. Dr. Robert Trappl
Focus: Cybernetics
Periodicals
Berichte: Reports (bi-monthly)
Cybernetics and Systems: An International Journal (quarterly) 00738

Österreichische Tribologische Gesellschaft (ÖTG) / Wissenschaftlicher Verein – Arbeitsgemeinschaft für Reibungs- und Verschleissfragen / Austrian Society of Tribology, Gußhausstr 27-29, 1040 Wien
T: (01) 5053400; Fax: 5053400
Founded: 1976; Members: 36
Focus: Eng; Physics; Chem; Econ . . . 00739

Österreichische Vereinigung der Zellstoff- und Papierchemiker und -techniker (ÖZEPA), Gumpendorfer Str 6, 1060 Wien
T: (01) 58886207; Fax: 58886222
Members: 282
Focus: Chem; Eng 00740

Österreichische Vereinigung für politische Wissenschaften, Judenpl 11, 1014 Wien
Founded: 1951
Focus: Poli Sci 00741

Österreichische Verkehrswissenschaftliche Gesellschaft (ÖVG), Elisabethstr 9, 1010 Wien
T: (01) 5879727
Founded: 1926; Members: 940
Focus: Transport
Periodicals
ÖVG-Spezial
Verkehrsannalen 00742

Österreichische Verwaltungswissenschaftliche Gesellschaft, Tuchlauben 13, 1010 Wien
T: (01) 53437122; E-Mail: sbt-p@ra-schoebate.co.at; Fax: 53437107
Founded: 1948; Members: ca. 100
Pres: Prof. Dr. Ludwig Adamorich; Gen Secr: Prof. Dr.Dr. Walter Barfuß
Focus: Business Admin 00743

Österreichische Werbewissenschaftliche Gesellschaft, Augasse 2-6, 1090 Wien
T: (01) 313364617
Founded: 1955; Members: 1500
Focus: Advert
Periodical
Werbeforschung & Praxis (5 times annually) 00744

Österreichische wissenschaftliche Gesellschaft für Prophylaktische Medizin und Sozialhygiene, Berggasse 4, 1090 Wien
T: (01) 343685
Founded: 1954; Members: 180
Focus: Med; Hygiene
Periodical
Sozialmedizinische Schriftenreihe 00745

Österreichischer Alpenverein, Wissenschaftlicher Unterausschuss (ÖAV), Wilhelm-Greil-Str 15, 6010 Innsbruck
T: (0512) 23171
Founded: 1862; Members: 4
Focus: Geology 00746

Österreichischer Arbeitskreis für Gruppentherapie und Gruppendynamik (ÖAGG), Heiligenstädter Str 7, 1190 Wien
T: (01) 3117062
Founded: 1959; Members: 938
Focus: Therapeutics
Periodicals
Feedback (semi-annually)
Gruppenpsychotherapie und Gruppendynamik (quarterly) 00747

Österreichischer Arbeitskreis für Soziologie des Sports und der Leibeserziehung / Austrian Committee for Sociology of Sport, c/o Prof. Dr. Roland Bässler, Auf der Schmelz 6, 1150 Wien
T: (01) 9822661112; Fax: 9822661131
Founded: 1969; Members: 20
Focus: Sociology; Sports
Periodical
Sportsoziologie: Informationsschrift des Österreichischen Arbeitskreises für Soziologie des Sports und der Leibeserziehung (irregularly) 00748

Österreichischer Arbeitskreis für Stadtgeschichtsforschung, Römerstr 14, Postfach 320, 4010 Linz
T: (0732) 781064; Fax: 7810644
Founded: 1969; Members: 104
Pres: Dr. Fritz Mayrhofer; Gen Secr: Dr. Anneliese Schweiger
Focus: Hist
Periodicals
Arbeitsbehelfe
Pro Civitate Austriae 00749

Österreichischer Arbeitsring / ÖAR, Hollenbach 59, 3830 Waidhofen/Thaya
Focus: Arts 00750

Österreichischer Arbeitsring für Lärmbekämpfung (ÖAL), Wexstr 19-23, 1200 Wien
T: (01) 33126400; 33126411; Fax: 3305925
Founded: 1958
Focus: Ecology
Periodical
ÖAL-Richtlinien (irregularly) 00751

Österreichischer Astronomischer Verein (AV), Hasenwartgasse 32, 1238 Wien
T: (01) 8893541; E-Mail: astbuero@astronomisches-buero-wien.or.at; Fax: 8893541
Founded: 1924; Members: 1500
Pres: Johann Albrecht; Gen Secr: Prof. Hermann Mucke
Focus: Astronomy
Periodical
Österreichischer Himmelskalender (annually) 00752

Österreichischer Burgenlandbund, Arbeitsgemeinschaft für Burgenländische Geschichte und Persönlichkeiten-Deutschtum in Ungarn, c/o Dr. Emmerich Karl Horvath, Gartengasse 12, 7000 Eisenstadt
T: (02682) 2893
Founded: 1958; Members: 8
Focus: Hist 00753

Österreichischer Burgenverein / Verein zur Erhaltung Historischer Bauten, Gonzagagasse 9, 1010 Wien
T: (01) 5358191; Fax: 5358196
Founded: 1955; Members: 700
Focus: Hist
Periodical
ARX: Burgen und Schlösser in Bayern, Österreich und Südtirol (semi-annually) 00754

Österreichischer Fachverband für Volkskunde (ÖFVK), Hans-Sachs-Gasse 3, 8010 Graz
Founded: 1958; Members: 100
Focus: Ethnology 00755

Österreichischer Fernschulverband, Margaretenstr 65, 1050 Wien
T: (01) 5879650
Focus: Educ 00756

Österreichischer Ingenieur- und Architektenverein (ÖIAV), Eschenbachgasse 9, 1010 Wien
T: (01) 5873536
Founded: 1848; Members: 7000
Pres: Karl Rabus; Gen Secr: Friedrich Smola
Focus: Archit
Periodical
Österreichische Ingenieur- und Architekten-Zeitschrift (monthly) 00757

Österreichischer Juristentag, Postfach 3, 1016 Wien
T: (01) 5261100
Founded: 1960; Members: 1500
Focus: Law
Periodical
Verhandlungen des Österreichischen Juristentages 00758

Österreichischer Komponistenbund, Baumannstr 8-10, 1030 Wien
T: (01) 7147233; Fax: 7147233
Founded: 1913; Members: 414
Pres: Prof. Heinrich Gattermeyer; Gen Secr: Bärbel Beiernienstedt
Focus: Music 00759

Österreichischer Kunsthistorikerverband, c/o Bundesdenkmalamt, Hofburg, 1010 Wien
T: (01) 5353964
Members: 450
Focus: Arts; Hist 00760

Österreichischer Museumsbund, Burgring 5, 1010 Wien
T: (01) 52524350; Fax: 52524352
Focus: Arts 00761

Österreichischer Naturschutzbund (ÖNB), Arenbergstr 10, 5020 Salzburg
T: (0662) 75492
Founded: 1913; Members: 60000
Focus: Ecology
Periodicals
Natur und Land (quarterly)
ÖNB-Kurier (quarterly)
Steirischer Naturschutzbrief (quarterly)
Wiener Naturschutznachrichten (quarterly) 00762

Österreichischer PEN-Club, Bankgasse 8, 1010 Wien
T: (01) 5334459; Fax: 5328749
Founded: 1922
Focus: Lit
Periodical
PEN-Nachrichten (semi-annually) 00763

Österreichischer Schriftstellerverband, Kettenbrückengasse 11, 1050 Wien
T: (01) 564151
Focus: Lit
Periodical
Literarisches Österreich (quarterly) . . . 00764

Österreichischer Sportlehrerverband (ÖSLV), Prinz Eugen-Str 12, Haus des Sports, 1040 Wien
Focus: Sports
Periodical
Informationsblatt des ÖSLV (quarterly) . . 00765

Österreichischer Stahlbauverband, Larochegasse 28, 1130 Wien
T: (01) 8776170; Fax: 8774836
Focus: Civil Eng
Periodicals
Stahlbau-Rundschau (semi-annually)
Stahlbau-Rundschau-Mitteilungen (bi-monthly) 00766

Österreichischer Verband für Elektrotechnik (ÖVE) / Austrian Electrotechnical Association, Eschenbachgasse 9, 1010 Wien
T: (01) 58763730; Fax: 567408
Focus: Electric Eng
Periodical
e & i Elektrotechnik und Informationstechnik (monthly) 00767

Österreichischer Verband für Strahlenschutz (ÖVS), c/o Forschungszentrum Seibersdorf, 2444 Seibersdorf
T: (02254) 7802500; Fax: 74060
Founded: 1966; Members: 307
Focus: Ecology; Radiology
Periodicals
Mitteilungsblatt des ÖVS (quarterly)
Tagungsberichte 00768

Österreichischer Verein für Individualpsychologie, Fasangartengasse 45, 1130 Wien
Founded: 1912; Members: 250
Pres: Prof. Dr. Max Friedrich; Gen Secr: Dr. Roswitha Donner
Focus: Psych
Periodical
Zeitschrift für Individualpsychologie (quarterly) 00769

Österreichisches College: Collegegemeinschaft Wien, c/o Institut für Philosophie, Universitätsstr 7, 1010 Wien
T: (01) 43002402
Founded: 1945; Members: 52
Focus: Educ 00770

Österreichisches Forschungsinstitut für Sparkassenwesen, Grimmelshausengasse 1, 1030 Wien
T: (01) 71169290
Founded: 1951; Members: 140
Focus: Finance 00771

Österreichisches Giesserei-Institut, Verein für Praktische Giessereiforschung (ÖGI), Parkstr 21, 8700 Leoben
T: (03842) 431010, 430720; Fax: 4310116
Founded: 1952; Members: 124
Focus: Metallurgy
Periodical
Gießerei-Rundschau (monthly) 00772

Österreichisches Institut für Bibliographie, Rathauspl 4, 1010 Wien
Founded: 1949
Focus: Libraries & Bk Sci 00773

Österreichisches Institut für Wirtschaftsforschung, Arsenal, Postfach 91, 1103 Wien
T: (01) 7826010; Fax: 789386
Focus: Econ
Periodicals
Empirica: Austrian Economic Papers (2-4 times annually)
Monatsberichte des Österreichischen Institutes für Wirtschaftsforschung (monthly) 00774

Österreichisches Lateinamerika-Institut, Schlickgasse 1, 1090 Wien
T: (01) 3107465
Founded: 1965; Members: 1500
Focus: Ethnology; Develop Areas; Poli Sci; Sociology 00775

Österreichisches Normungsinstitut (ON), Heinestr 38, Postfach 130, 1021 Wien
T: (01) 267535; E-Mail: austria norm; Fax: 267552
Founded: 1920; Members: 460
Focus: Standards
Periodical
ÖNORM: Fachzeitschrift des ON Österreichisches Normungsinstitut (monthly) 00776

Österreichisches Ost- und Südosteuropa-Institut / Austrian Institute of East and South-East European Studies, Josefspl 6, 1010 Wien
T: (01) 5121895; Fax: 512189553
Founded: 1958
Pres: Prof. Dr. Arnold Suppan; Gen Secr: Dr. Waltraud Heindl
Focus: Hist; Geography; Cultur Hist; Educ; Law; Poli Sci
Periodicals
Österreichische Osthefte (quarterly)
Ost-Dokumentation Bildungs-, Wissenschafts- und Kulturpolitik (quarterly) 00777

Österreichisches Produktivitäts- und Wirtschaftlichkeits-Zentrum (ÖPWZ), Rockhgasse 6, 1014 Wien
T: (01) 5338636; Fax: 533863636
Founded: 1950; Members: 7
Focus: Business Admin 00778

Österreichisches Studienzentrum für Frieden und Konfliktforschung, 7461 Burg Schlaining
T: (03355) 2498; Fax: 2662
Founded: 1983
Pres: Dr. Gerald Mader
Focus: Prom Peace 00779

Orientalische Gesellschaft (OG), Universitätsstr 7, 1010 Wien
T: (01) 43002593; Fax: 4020533
Founded: 1952; Members: 71
Pres: Prof. Dr. Hermann Hunger; Gen Secr: Prof. Dr. Arne A. Ambros
Focus: Ling; Ethnology 00780

Philosophische Gesellschaft an der Universität Graz, c/o Philosophisches Institut, Heinrichstr 26, 8010 Graz
Focus: Philos 00781

Philosophische Gesellschaft in Salzburg, c/o Institut für Philosophie, Franziskanergasse 1, 5020 Salzburg
T: (0662) 80444070
Founded: 1966; Members: 91
Focus: Philos 00782

Philosophische Gesellschaft Innsbruck, c/o Institut für Philosophie, Innrain 20, 6020 Innsbruck
T: (0512) 5074030; 5074031; Fax: 5072891
Founded: 1974; Members: 100
Pres: Prof. Dr. Reinhard Kleinknecht; Gen Secr: Prof. Dr. Rainer Thurnher
Focus: Philos 00783

Philosophische Gesellschaft Klagenfurt, c/o Universität für Bildungswissenschaften, Universitätsstr 67, 9020 Klagenfurt
T: (04222) 23730504
Founded: 1973; Members: 65
Focus: Philos 00784

Philosophische Gesellschaft Wien, c/o Institut für Philosophie, Universitätsstr 7, 1010 Wien
T: (01) 43002402, 401032402
Founded: 1954; Members: 100
Pres: Prof. Dr. Hans-Dieter Klein
Focus: Philos 00785

Pro Austria / Gesellschaft zur Erforschung und Förderung der österreichischen Bundesstaatsidee und des österreichischen Nationalbewusstseins, Josefspl 1, 1010 Wien
T: (01) 521684245
Founded: 1969
Focus: Ethnology 00786

Rudolf Kassner-Gesellschaft, c/o Prof. Dr. Viktor Suchy, Schanzstr 33, 1140 Wien
T: (01) 9820394
Founded: 1961; Members: 19
Focus: Lit 00787

Salzburger Ärztegesellschaft, c/o Landeskrankenanstalten, Müllner Hauptstr 48, 5020 Salzburg
T: (0662) 44824427; Fax: 44824427
Founded: 1849 (1964); Members: 800
Pres: Prof. Dr. Alfred Aigner; Gen Secr: Dr. Josef Koller
Focus: Med 00788

Salzburger Arbeitskreis für Psychoanalyse, Getreidegasse 16, 5020 Salzburg
T: (0662) 842205
Members: 32
Focus: Psychoan 00789

Salzburger Institut für juristische Information und Fortbildung (SIJIF), Künstlerhausgasse 4, 5020 Salzburg
T: (0662) 843663; Fax: 847986
Founded: 1976
Focus: Law 00790

Salzburger Juristische Gesellschaft, Churfürststr 1, 5020 Salzburg
T: (0662) 80443510; 80443519; Fax: 8044132
Founded: 1970; Members: 167
Pres: Prof. Dr. Rolf Ostheim; Gen Secr: Prof. Dr. Wolfgang Schuhmacher
Focus: Law 00791

Salzburger Kulturvereinigung (SKV), Waagpl 1a, 5010 Salzburg
T: (0662) 845346; Fax: 842665
Founded: 1947; Members: 10250
Pres: Dr. Hans Katschthaler; Gen Secr: Dr. Heinz Klier
Focus: Ethnology 00792

SIGMA – Salzburger Gesellschaft für Semiologie, c/o Dr. Sigrid Schmid, Institut für Germanistik, Akademiestr 20, 5020 Salzburg
T: (0662) 80444358; Fax: 8044612
Founded: 1986; Members: 21
Focus: Ethnology; Lit; Hist 00793

Sigmund Freud-Gesellschaft, Berggasse 19, 1090 Wien
T: (01) 3191596; E-Mail: freud-museum@tø.or.at; Fax: 3170279
Founded: 1968; Members: 1100
Pres: Dr. Harald Leupold-Löwenthal; Gen Secr: Inge Scholz-Strasser
Focus: Psych; Psychoan
Periodical
Newsletter der Sigmund Freud-Gesellschaft (quarterly) 00794

Societas Linguistica Europaea, Universitätsstr 7, 1010 Wien
T: (01) 401032655
Founded: 1966; Members: 1100
Pres: Prof. Dr. Jan Svartvik; Gen Secr: Prof. Dr. Dieter Kastovsky
Focus: Ling
Periodicals
Folia Linguistica
Folia Linguistica Historica 00795

Sonnblick-Verein, Hohe Warte 38, 1190 Wien
T: (01) 360262701; E-Mail: Otto.motschka@zamg.ac.at; Fax: 360262720
Founded: 1892; Members: 350
Pres: Dr. H. Kienzl; Gen Secr: Dr. Otto Motschka
Focus: Geophys
Periodical
Jahresbericht (irregularly) 00796

Sozialwissenschaftliche Arbeitsgemeinschaft (SWA), Johannesgasse 4, 1010 Wien
T: (01) 524850
Founded: 1953
Focus: Sociology 00797

Sozialwissenschaftliche Studiengesellschaft (SWS), Maria-Theresien-Str 9, 1090 Wien
T: (01) 3173127; Fax: 3102238
Founded: 1960; Members: 40
Focus: Sociology
Periodical
SWS-Rundschau (quarterly) 00798

Steirische Gesellschaft für Psychologie, c/o Prof. Dr. Helmuth P. Huber, Universitätspl 2, 8010 Graz
T: (0316) 3805113
Founded: 1980; Members: 183
Focus: Psych 00799

SYNEMA – Gesellschaft für Film und Medien, Neubaugasse 36, 1070 Wien
T: (01) 5233797; Fax: 5233797
Founded: 1981; Members: 60
Pres: Dr. Georg Haberl; Gen Secr: Prof. Gottfried Schlemmer
Focus: Cinema; Mass Media
Periodical
Kinoschriften 00800

Technisch-Wissenschaftlicher Verein Bergmännischer Verband Österreichs (BVÖ), c/o Montanuniversität, Franz-Josef-Str 18, 8700 Leoben
T: (03842) 45279; Fax: 402530
Founded: 1950; Members: 853
Focus: Mining
Periodical
Berg- und Hüttenmännische Monatshefte (bi-monthly) 00801

Technisch-wissenschaftlicher Verein Eisenhütte Österreich, c/o Institut für Eisenhüttenkunde, Montanuniversität, 8700 Leoben
T: (03842) 45189; Fax: 46852
Founded: 1925; Members: 1097
Focus: Metallurgy
Periodical
Berg- und Hüttenmännische Monatshefte (bi-monthly) 00802

Theresianische Akademie, Favoritenstr 15, 1040 Wien
T: (01) 50515710/70, 5046004
Focus: Educ; Hist 00803

Tiroler Gesellschaft zur Förderung der Alterswisschaft und des Seniorenstudiums an der Universität Innsbruck, Josef-Hirn-Str 7, 6020 Innsbruck
T: (05222) 20750
Founded: 1981; Members: 228
Focus: Geriatrics 00804

Tiroler Juristische Gesellschaft, c/o Universität, Innrain 80, 6020 Innsbruck
T: (05222) 5072561
Founded: 1968; Members: 218
Focus: Law 00805

Verband der Akademikerinnen Österreichs (VAÖ), Reitschulgasse 2, 1010 Wien
T: (01) 5339080
Founded: 1922; Members: 650
Pres: Ingrid Fleischmann; Gen Secr: Dr. Gabriele Huber
Focus: Sci
Periodical
VAÖ Mitteilungen (quarterly) 00806

Verband der diplomierten Physiotherapeuten Österreichs, Gießergasse 6, 1090 Wien
T: (01) 4087577
Founded: 1962; Members: 2000
Focus: Physical Therapy
Periodical
Physiotherapie (quarterly) 00807

Verband der Geistig Schaffenden Österreichs, Kärntnerstr 51, 1010 Wien
T: (01) 525865, 5125865
Focus: Music; Arts
Periodical
Der Geistig Schaffende (quarterly) . . . 00808

Verband der Marktforscher Österreichs (VMÖ), Postfach 182, 1013 Wien
T: (01) 63391102
Founded: 1963; Members: 150
Focus: Marketing 00809

Verband der Österreicher zur Wahrung der Geschichte Österreichs, Huttengasse 8, 1014 Wien
T: (01) 9247102
Founded: 1964; Members: 433
Focus: Hist 00810

Verband der österreichischen Neuphilologen (VÖN), Universitätsstr 6, 1090 Wien
Fax: (01) 4038384
Founded: 1955
Focus: Ling; Lit
Periodical
Moderne Sprachen (quarterly) 00811

Verband der Russischlehrer Österreichs (VRÖ), Josefspl 6, 1010 Wien
Focus: Educ; Ling
Periodical
Mitteilungen für Lehrer slawischer Fremdsprachen (semi-annually) 00812

Verband der wissenschaftlichen Gesellschaften Österreichs (VWGÖ), Lindengasse 37, 1070 Wien
T: (01) 934756
Founded: 1949; Members: 321
Focus: Sci 00813

Verband für medizinischen Strahlenschutz in Österreich (VMSÖ), Embelgasse 52, 1050 Wien
T: (01) 555332
Founded: 1974; Members: 500
Focus: Radiology
Periodical
Informationsblatt (1-2 times annually) . . 00814

Verband niederösterreichischer Volkshochschulen, Zelinkagasse 2, 1010 Wien
T: (01) 5335379, 5355605
Focus: Adult Educ 00815

Verband österreichischer Archivare (VÖA), Postfach 164, 1014 Wien
T: (01) 932740
Founded: 1967; Members: 300
Focus: Archives
Periodical
Scrinium-Zeitschrift (semi-annually) . . . 00816

Verband Österreichischer Bildungswerke, Heinrichgasse 4, 1010 Wien
T: (01) 636547
Focus: Educ 00817

Verband Österreichischer Historiker und Geschichtsvereine, c/o Österreichisches Staatsarchiv, Nottendorfer Gasse 2, 1030 Wien
T: (01) 79540100; Fax: 79540109
Founded: 1949; Members: 133
Pres: Dr. Alfred Ogris; Gen Secr: Dr. Erwin A. Schmidl
Focus: Hist 00818

Verband Österreichischer Höhlenforscher, Obere Donaustr 97/1/61, 1020 Wien
Founded: 1949; Members: 21 Vereine; 16 Schauhöhlenbetriebe
Pres: Heinz Ilming; Gen Secr: Günter Stummer
Focus: Speleology
Periodicals
Die Höhle: Zeitschrift für Karst- und Höhlenkunde (quarterly)
Wissenschaftliche Beihefte zur Zeitschrift Die Höhle (irregularly) 00819

Verband Österreichischer Kurärzte, Josefspl 6, 1010 Wien
T: (01) 5121904
Focus: Med 00820

Verband Österreichischer Privat-Museen, 4654 Bad Winsbach-Neydharting
Founded: 1950; Members: 156
Focus: Arts
Periodical
Die Österreichische Kunstforschung (irregularly) 00821

Verband Österreichischer Sportärzte, Auf der Schmelz 6, 1150 Wien
T: (01) 9822661174
Founded: 1950; Members: 714
Focus: Med 00822

Verband Österreichischer Volksbüchereien und Volksbibliothekare, Lange Gasse 37, 1080 Wien
T: (01) 439722
Founded: 1948; Members: 780
Focus: Libraries & Bk Sci 00823

Verband Österreichischer Volkshochschulen, Rudolfspl 8, 1010 Wien
T: (01) 630245
Focus: Adult Educ
Periodical
Die Österreichische Volkshochschule (quarterly) 00824

Verband Österreichischer Wirtschaftsakademiker (VÖWA), Teinfaltstr 1, 1010 Wien
T: (01) 5336876; Fax: 5327669
Founded: 1927; Members: 1900
Focus: Econ
Periodical
Wirtschaftskurier (bi-monthly) 00825

Verein der Freunde der im Mittelalter von Österreich aus besiedelten Sprachinseln, Semperstr 29, 1180 Wien
T: (01) 4796083
Founded: 1972; Members: 210
Focus: Ling
Periodical
Beiträge zur Sprachinselforschung (annually) 00826

Verein der Freunde des Radwerkes IV in Vordernberg, Peter-Tunner-Str 2, 8794 Vordernberg
T: (03849) 283
Founded: 1956; Members: 120
Focus: Hist 00827

Verein der Mundartfreunde Österreichs, Postgasse 7-9, 1010 Wien
Members: 150
Focus: Lit
Periodical
Mitteilungen der Mundartfreunde Österreichs (irregularly) 00828

Verein der Museumsfreunde in Wien, Praterstr 30, 1020 Wien
T: (01) 269371; Fax: 214890004
Founded: 1911; Members: 2900
Focus: Arts
Periodical
Mitteilungen des Vereins der Museumsfreunde in Wien (10 times annually) 00829

Verein Forschung für die graphischen Medien (VFG), Leyserstr 6, 1140 Wien
T: (01) 9823914121; E-Mail: hgblva@graphix.htl-tex.ac.at; Fax: 9821710
Founded: 1966; Members: 88
Focus: Eng 00830

Verein Freunde der Völkerkunde, c/o Museum für Völkerkunde, Neue Hofburg, 1014 Wien
T: (01) 52177; Fax: 5355320
Founded: 1933; Members: 185
Focus: Ethnology
Periodical
Archiv für Völkerkunde (annually) . . . 00831

Verein für Geschichte der Arbeiterbewegung, Rechte Wienzeile 97, 1050 Wien
T: (01) 5467870; Fax: 5463097
Founded: 1959; Members: 382
Focus: Hist; Sociology; Socialism
Periodical
Archiv: Mitteilungsblatt (quarterly) 00832

Verein für Geschichte der Stadt Wien (VGStW), c/o Wiener Stadt- und Landesarchiv, Rathaus, 1082 Wien
T: (01) 400084815
Founded: 1853; Members: 1575
Pres: Prof. Dr. Felix Czeike; Gen Secr: Dr. Karl Fischer
Focus: Hist
Periodicals
Forschungen und Beiträge zur Wiener Stadtgeschichte (irregularly)
Jahrbuch des Vereins für Geschichte der Stadt Wien (annually)
Wiener Geschichtsblätter (quarterly) . . . 00833

Verein für Landeskunde von Niederösterreich, Alserbachstr 41, 1090 Wien
T: (01) 531106255
Founded: 1864; Members: 1300
Pres: Prof. Dr. Hermann Riepl; Gen Secr: Willibald Rosner
Focus: Hist
Periodicals
Jahrbuch für Landeskunde von Niederösterreich (annually)
Unsere Heimat (quarterly) 00834

Verein für Psychiatrie und Neurologie, c/o Neurologische Universitätsklinik, Währinger Gürtel 18-20, 1090 Wien
Founded: 1868; Members: 400
Pres: Prof. Dr. B. Mamoli
Focus: Psychiatry; Neurology 00835

Verein für Sozial- und Wirtschaftspolitik, Ebendorferstr 6, 1010 Wien
T: (01) 422674; Fax: 4023777
Founded: 1953; Members: 283
Focus: Poli Sci
Periodical
Gesellschaft und Politik (quarterly) . . . 00836

Verein für Volkskunde in Wien, Laudongasse 15-19, 1080 Wien
T: (01) 4068905; E-Mail: volkskundemuseum.wien@netway.at; Fax: 4085342
Founded: 1894; Members: 900
Pres: Dr. Klaus Beitl; Gen Secr: Dr. Franz Grieshofer; Dr. Margot Schindler
Focus: Ethnology
Periodicals
Oesterreichische Zeitschrift für Volkskunde (quarterly)
Volkskunde in Österreich: Nachrichtenblatt des Vereins für Volkskunde (10 times annually) 00837

Verein Montandenkmal Altböckstein, Postfach 78, 8700 Leoben
Founded: 1979; Members: 120
Pres: Eva Sika
Focus: Preserv Hist Monuments
Periodicals
Böcksteiner Montana
Jahresberichte (irregularly) 00838

Verein Muttersprache, Postfach 27, 2103 Lang-Enzersdorf
T: (02244) 30542; Fax: 30542
Founded: 1949; Members: 1450
Pres: Stefan Micko; Gen Secr: Ursula Mader
Focus: Ling
Periodicals
Schriftenreihe Wissenschaft (irregularly)
Wiener Sprachblätter (quarterly) 00839

Verein Österreichischer Lebensmittel- und Biotechnologen (V.Ö.L.B.), c/o Institut für Lebensmitteltechnologie, Muthgasse 18, 1190 Wien
Founded: 1968; Members: 450
Pres: Prof. Dr. Josef Weiss; Gen Secr: Karl Vogl
Focus: Food; Eng 00840

Verein österreichischer Ledertechniker (VÖLT), Rosensteingasse 79, 1170 Wien
T: (01) 461480; Fax: 454068
Founded: 1950; Members: 250
Focus: Eng 00841

Verein Österreichischer Textilchemiker und Coloristen (VÖTC), Postfach 2, 6850 Dornbirn
Focus: Chem 00842

Verein Tiroler Landesmuseum Ferdinandeum, Museumstr 15, 6020 Innsbruck
T: (0512) 59489; Fax: 5948988
Founded: 1823; Members: 3500
Pres: Prof. Dr. Josef Riedmann; Gen Secr: Dr. Gert Ammann
Focus: Arts; Archeol; Hist; Nat Sci
Periodical
Veröffentlichungen des Tiroler Landesmuseums Ferdinandeum (annually) 00843

Verein Wiener Frauenverlag, Lange Gasse 51, 1080 Wien
T: (01) 4390412
Founded: 1980; Members: 42
Focus: Lit 00844

Verein zur Förderung des physikalischen und chemischen Unterrichts, c/o Institut für theoretische Physik, Strudlhofgasse 4, 1090 Wien
T: (01) 313673415; Fax: 3172220
Founded: 1895; Members: 1160
Focus: Chem; Educ; Physics
Periodical
Plus Lucis (quarterly) 00845

Verein zur Verbreitung naturwissenschaftlicher Kenntnisse, Althanstr 14, 1091 Wien
Founded: 1860
Focus: Nat Sci
Periodical
Schriften (annually) 00846

Vereinigung bildender Künstler (Wiener Secession), Friedrichstr 12, 1010 Wien
Fax: (01) 587530734
Founded: 1897; Members: 209
Focus: Arts 00847

Vereinigung Burgenländischer Geographen, 7442 Lockenhaus
T: (02616) 3374; Fax: 33744
Founded: 1975; Members: 620
Pres: Emmerich Gager
Focus: Geography
Periodical
Geographisches Jahrbuch Burgenland (annually) 00848

Vereinigung der Humanistischen Gesellschaften Österreichs, c/o Institut für Klassische Philologie, Universität, Universitätspl 3, 8010 Graz
Focus: Philos 00849

Vereinigung der kooperativen Forschungsinstitute der Österreichischen Wirtschaft, Eschenbachgasse 11, 1010 Wien
T: (01) 587363323; Fax: 5870192
Founded: 1954; Members: 31
Pres: Prof. Dr. Theo Gumpelmayer; Gen Secr: Dr. Johann Jäger
Focus: Econ
Periodical
ACR-Info (3-4 times annually) 00850

Vereinigung für Angewandte Lagerstättenforschung, c/o Montanuniversität, Franz-Josef-Str 19, 8700 Leoben
Founded: 1975
Focus: Geology 00851

Vereinigung für Hydrogeologische Forschungen in Graz, Rechbauerstr 12, 8010 Graz
T: (0316) 8020373
Founded: 1962; Members: 300
Focus: Geology
Periodical
Steirische Beiträge zur Hydrogeologie . . 00852

Vereinigung für wissenschaftliche Grundlagenforschung, Heinrichstr 26, 8010 Graz
Founded: 1964; Members: 39
Focus: Sci; Philos 00853

Vereinigung Österreichischer Ärzte (VÖÄ), Weihburggasse 10-12, 1010 Wien
T: (01) 527958
Founded: 1945; Members: 1800
Focus: Med
Periodical
Der Österreichische Arzt (bi-monthly)   . . 00854

Vereinigung Österreichischer Bibliothekarinnen und Bibliothekare (VÖBB), Innrain 50, 6010 Innsbruck
T: (0512) 5072425; Fax: 5072864
Founded: 1896; Members: 1020
Pres: Dr. Walter Neuhauser
Focus: Libraries & Bk Sci
Periodical
BIBLOS: Mitteilungen der Vereinigung Österreichischer Bibliothekarinnen und Bibliothekare   00855

Volkswirtschaftliche Gesellschaft Österreich / Verband für Bildungswesen, Bauernmarkt 21, 1010 Wien
T: (01) 5351185
Focus: Econ
Periodical
Wirtschaft in der Praxis (5-8 times annually)
. . . . 00856

Volkswirtschaftliche Gesellschaft Wien, Fischhof 3, 1010 Wien
T: (01) 5330871; Fax: 5330688
Founded: 1958
Pres: Michael Stermann; Gen Secr: Dr. Wolfgang Steffanides
Focus: Econ
Periodical
Die Aussprache (quarterly)   00857

Vorarlberger Landesmuseumsverein (VLMV), Flüherstr 4, 6900 Bregenz
T: (05574) 65484
Founded: 1857; Members: 1200
Pres: Dr. Edwin Oberhauser; Gen Secr: Dr. Walter Krieg
Focus: Hist; Sci
Periodical
Jahrbuch des Vorarlberger Landesmuseumsvereins (annually)   00858

Waldviertler Heimatbund, Wissenschaftliche Sektion, Postfach 100, 3580 Horn
T: (02982) 3991
Founded: 1951; Members: 1100
Pres: Prof. Dr. Erich Rabl
Focus: Hist
Periodical
Das Waldviertel: Zeitschrift für Heimat- und Regionalkunde des Waldviertels und der Wachau (quarterly)   00859

Wiener Arbeitskreis für Psychoanalyse, Postfach 76, 1000 Wien
T: (01) 7153957
Founded: 1947; Members: 23
Focus: Psychoan   00860

Wiener Beethoven-Gesellschaft (WBG), Probusgasse 6, 1190 Wien
T: (01) 3188215
Founded: 1954; Members: 320
Pres: Prof. Alexander Jenner; Gen Secr: Walther Brauneis
Focus: Music
Periodical
Mitteilungsblatt der Wiener Beethoven-Gesellschaft (quarterly)   00861

Wiener Bibliophilen-Gesellschaft (WBG), c/o Walter R. Schaden, Sonnenfelsgasse 4, 1010 Wien
T: (01) 5138289; Fax: 5126028
Founded: 1912; Members: 220
Pres: Dr. Peter Leisching; Gen Secr: Andrea Kourgli
Focus: Libraries & Bk Sci   00862

Wiener Gesellschaft für Innere Medizin, Währinger Gürtel 18-20, 1090 Wien
T: (01) 404004409; Fax: 4026930
Members: 223
Focus: Intern Med   00863

Wiener Gesellschaft für Theaterforschung, c/o Institut für Theaterwissenschaft, Hofburg, Battmyanystiege, 1010 Wien
T: (01) 5350599; Fax: 5350590
Founded: 1944; Members: 100
Pres: Prof. Wolfgang Greisenegger; Gen Secr: Otto G. Schindler
Focus: Perf Arts
Periodicals
Quellen zur Theatergeschichte (irregularly)
Theater in Österreich: Verzeichnis der Inszenierungen (theadok) (annually)   . . 00864

Wiener Goethe-Verein, Stallburggasse 2, 1010 Wien
T: (01) 401032542
Founded: 1878; Members: 300
Pres: Prof. Dr. Herbert Zeman
Focus: Lit
Periodical
Jahrbuch des Wiener Goethe-Vereins (annually)
. . . . 00865

Wiener Humanistische Gesellschaft, c/o Institut für Klassische Philologie, Universität, Dr. Karl-Lueger-Ring 1, 1010 Wien

T: (01) 401032719; E-Mail: kurt.smolak@ univie.ac.at; Fax: 4034848
Founded: 1946; Members: 600
Pres: Prof. Dr. Heinrich Stremitzer; Prof. Dr. Kurt Smolak; Gen Secr: Margit Kamptner
Focus: Ling; Lit; Hist
Periodical
Wiener Humanistische Blätter (annually)   . 00866

Wiener Institut für Entwicklungsfragen und Zusammenarbeit / Vienna Institute for Development and Cooperation, Weyrgasse 5, 1030 Wien
T: (01) 7133594; E-Mail: vidc@magnet.at; Fax: 713359473
Founded: 1962
Pres: Dr. Franz Vranitzky; Gen Secr: Dr. Erich Andrlik
Focus: Econ; Develop Areas; Poli Sci; Int'l Relat
Periodical
Report Series (irregularly)   00867

Wiener Institut für Internationale Wirtschaftsvergleiche, Postfach 87, 1103 Wien
T: (01) 7826010; Fax: 787120
Founded: 1972
Focus: Econ
Periodicals
Comecon Data
East-West European Economic Interaction/Workshop Papers
Forschungsberichte: Reprint-Serie
Studien über Wirtschafts- und Systemvergleiche
. . . . 00868

Wiener Juristische Gesellschaft (WJG), Tuchlauben 13, 1010 Wien
T: (01) 534370; Fax: 5332521
Founded: 1867; Members: 600
Pres: Prof. Dr. Walter Barfuß
Focus: Law   00869

Wiener Katholische Akademie, Ebendorferstr 8, 1010 Wien
T: (01) 4023917
Founded: 1945; Members: 160
Pres: Erzbischof Dr. P.C. Schönborn; Gen Secr: Dr. E. Maier
Focus: Bio; Neurology   00870

Wiener Konzerthausgesellschaft, Lothringerstr 20, 1030 Wien
T: (01) 71246860; E-Mail: mail@konzerthaus.at; Fax: 7131709
Founded: 1913; Members: 4000
Pres: Dr. Harald Sturminger; Gen Secr: Christoph Lieben-Seutter
Focus: Music
Periodical
Konzerthaus-Nachrichten (8 times annually)   00871

Wiener Kulturkreis, Prinz-Eugen-Str 3, 1030 Wien
T: (01) 784350
Founded: 1947; Members: 750
Focus: Arts; Sci   00872

Wiener Medizinische Akademie für Ärztliche Fortbildung und Forschung, c/o Allgemeines Krankenhaus, Alserstr 4, 1090 Wien
T: (01) 40513830; Fax: 405138323
Founded: 1896; Members: 320
Pres: Prof. Dr. R. Kotz
Focus: Med; Adult Educ   00873

Wiener Psychoanalytische Vereinigung, Gonzagagasse 11, 1010 Wien
T: (01) 5330767; Fax: 5330767
Founded: 1910; Members: 68
Focus: Psychoan
Periodical
Bulletin der Wiener Psychoanalytischen Vereinigung (semi-annually)   00874

Wiener Rechtsgeschichtliche Gesellschaft, Schottenbastei 10-16, 1010 Wien
T: (01) 43003260
Founded: 1975; Members: 486
Focus: Law   00875

Wiener Schubertbund, Lothringerstr 20, 1030 Wien
T: (01) 732429
Focus: Music   00876

Wiener Secession, Friedrichstr 12, 1010 Wien
Founded: 1897; Members: 150
Pres: Werner Würtinger
Focus: Arts   00877

Wiener Sprachgesellschaft (WSG), c/o Institut für Sprachwissenschaft, Universität Wien, Dr.-Karl-Lueger-Ring 1, 1010 Wien
T: (01) 4039080
Founded: 1947; Members: 200
Pres: Prof. W.U. Dressler; Gen Secr: Dr. H.C. Luschutzky
Focus: Ling
Periodical
Die Sprache: Zeitschrift für Sprachwissenschaft (semi-annually)   00878

Wissenschaftliche Ärztegesellschaft Innsbruck, c/o Landeskrankenhaus, Anichstr 35, 6020 Innsbruck
T: (0512) 28711900
Founded: 1894; Members: 900
Focus: Med   00879

Wissenschaftliche Arbeitsgemeinschaft für Leibeserziehung und Sportmedizin in Innsbruck, Fürstenweg 185, 6020 Innsbruck
T: (0522) 5076530
Founded: 1969; Members: 24
Focus: Med; Sports   00880

Wissenschaftliche Gesellschaft der Ärzte in der Steiermark, Auenbruggerpl 25, 8036 Graz
T: (0316) 382653; Fax: 3853062
Founded: 1863; Members: 1500
Focus: Med
Periodical
Abstracts über die wissenschaftlichen Sitzungen
. . . . 00881

Wissenschaftliche Gesellschaft für Sport und Leibeserziehung am Institut für Sportwissenschaften der Universität Salzburg, Akademiestr 26, 5020 Salzburg
T: (0662) 44511252
Founded: 1970; Members: 50
Focus: Sports
Periodical
Salzburger Beiträge zum Sport unserer Zeit
. . . . 00882

Zentralvereinigung der Architekten Österreichs, Salvatorgasse 10, 1010 Wien
T: (01) 5334429
Founded: 1907; Members: 700
Pres: Prof. Eugen Wörle
Focus: Archit   00883

Zoologisch-Botanische Gesellschaft in Österreich, Althanstr 14, Postfach 287, 1091 Wien
T: (01) 314510
Founded: 1851; Members: 540
Pres: Prof. Dr. Walter Fiedler; Gen Secr: Dr. Wolfgang Punz
Focus: Botany; Zoology
Periodicals
Abhandlungen der Zoologisch-Botanischen Gesellschaft (irregularly)
Koleopterologische Rundschau (annually)
Verhandlungen der Zoologisch-Botanischen Gesellschaft (annually)   00884

Azerbaijan

Azerbaijan Academy of Sciences, Isteglal 10, 370601 Baku
Members: 39
Pres: E.Y. Salaev; Gen Secr: A.A.K. Nadirov
Focus: Sci
Periodicals
Azerbaidzhanskii Khimicheskii Zhurnal: Azerbaijan Chemical Journal
Doklady: Report
Izvestiya: Bulletin
Sibirskii Vestnik Selskokhozyaistvennoi Nauki: Siberian Agricultural Science Journal
Tsirkulyar Shemakhinskoi Astrofizicheskoi Observatorii: Newsletter of the Shemakha Astrophysics Observatory   00885

Azerbaijan Biochemical Society, Isteglal 10, 370601 Baku
Pres: A.A. Gasanov
Focus: Biochem   00886

Azerbaijan Genetics and Selection Society, Isteglal 10, 370601 Baku
Pres: I.K. Abdullaev
Focus: Genetics   00887

Azerbaijan Mathematics Society, Isteglal 10, 370601 Baku
Pres: M.A. Dzhavadov
Focus: Math   00888

Azerbaijan Physical Society, Pr Narimanova 33, 370143 Baku
Pres: G.M. Abdullaev
Focus: Physics   00889

Geographical Society of Azerbaijan, Isteglal 10, 370601 Baku
Pres: Prof. K.K. Gyul
Focus: Geography   00890

Helminthological Society, Isteglal 10, 370601 Baku
Pres: S.M. Asadov
Focus: Nat Sci   00891

Mineralogical Society, Isteglal 10, 370601 Baku
Pres: M.A. Kashkal
Focus: Mineralogy   00892

Palaeontological Society, Isteglal 10, 370601 Baku
Pres: K.A. Alizade
Focus: Paleontology   00893

Society of Physiologists and Pharmacologists, Isteglal 10, 370601 Baku
Pres: G.G. Gasanov
Focus: Physiology; Pharmacol   00894

Society of Soil Scientists, Isteglal 10, 370601 Baku
Pres: D.M. Guseinov
Focus: Agri   00895

Yeni Musiqi / Society for Contemorary Music, Haqverdiyev kuchesi 3a-32, Baku 370141
T: (012) 390670, 983446; Fax: 387601, 981330
Pres: Jahangir (vice) Selimkhanov
Focus: Music   00896

Bahamas

Bahamas Historical Society, POB SS 6833, Nassau
Founded: 1959; Members: 400
Pres: Dr. Gail Saunders; Gen Secr: J.L. Johnson
Focus: Hist
Periodical
Journal (annually)   00897

Bahamas National Trust, POB N4105, Nassau
T: 3931317; Fax: 3934978
Founded: 1958; Members: 3000
Gen Secr: Gary E. Larson
Focus: Ecology
Periodicals
The Bahamas Naturalist (semi-annually)
Currents (bi-monthly)   00898

Bahrain

Bahrain Arts Society, POB 26264, Manama
T: 590551; Fax: 594211
Founded: 1983; Members: 184
Pres: Ali Al-Mahmeed
Focus: Arts   00899

Bahrain Bar Society, POB 5025, Manama
T: 720566; Fax: 721219
Founded: 1977; Members: 65
Pres: Ali Abdulla Alayoobi
Focus: Law   00900

Bahrain Centre for Studies and Research, POB 496, Manama
T: 754757; Fax: 754678
Founded: 1981
Gen Secr: Dr. Hamad Al-Sulayti
Focus: Sci   00901

Bahrain Computer Society, POB 26089, Manama
T: 245366
Founded: 1981; Members: 114
Pres: Mohammed Ahmed Al-Amer
Focus: Computer & Info Sci   00902

Bahrain Contemporary Art Association, POB 26232, Manama
T: 728046
Founded: 1970; Members: 60
Pres: Abdul Karim Al-Orrayed
Focus: Arts   00903

Bahrain Historical and Archaeological Society, POB 5087, Manama
T: 727895
Founded: 1953; Members: 143
Pres: Dr. Essa Amin; Gen Secr: Dr. Khalid Khalifa Al-Khalifa
Focus: Hist; Archeol   00904

Bahrain Medical Society, POB 26136, Manama
T: 742666; Fax: 715559
Founded: 1972; Members: 365
Pres: Dr. Ali J. Al-Aradi; Gen Secr: Dr. Ahmed J. Jamal
Focus: Med
Periodical
Journal of the Bahrain Medical Society (3 times annually)   00905

Bahrain Society of Engineers, POB 835, Manama
T: 727100; Fax: 729819
Founded: 1972; Members: 950
Pres: Abdulla M. Juma; Gen Secr: Saeed A. Asbool
Focus: Eng
Periodical
Al-Mohandes (quarterly)   00906

Bahrain Society of Sociologists, POB 26488, Manama
T: 727483
Founded: 1979; Members: 65
Pres: Dr. Ahmed Al-Sharyan; Gen Secr: Ebrahim Alalawi
Focus: Sociology   00907

Bahrain Writers and Literators Association, POB 1010, Manama
Founded: 1969; Members: 40
Pres: Ali Al-Shargawi; Gen Secr: Fareed Ramadan
Focus: Lit   00908

The Islamic Association, POB 22484, Muharraq
T: 671788; Fax: 676718
Founded: 1979; Members: 110
Pres: Abdulrahman E. Abdul Salam
Focus: Rel & Theol   00909

Bangladesh

Asiatic Society of Bangladesh, 5 Old Secretariat Rd, Dhaka
T: (02) 9560500
Founded: 1952
Pres: Prof. Akmal Hussain
Focus: Anthro 00910

Association of Universities of Bangladesh, 28 Shyamolee, Dhaka 7
Gen Secr: M.K. Hussain Sirkar
Focus: Educ 00911

Bangla Academy, Burdwan House, Dhaka 2
Founded: 1972
Gen Secr: Dr. A.H. Siddiqui
Focus: Sci
Periodicals
Dhan Shaliker Desh (monthly)
Journal (semi-annually)
Research Journal
Science Journal (quarterly) 00912

Bangladesh Academy of Sciences, 3/8 Asad Av, Mohammadpur, Dhaka 7
T: (02) 310425
Founded: 1973; Members: 42
Pres: Dr. S.D. Chaudhuri; Gen Secr: Prof. Aminul Islam
Focus: Sci 00913

Bangladesh Atomic Energy Commission, POB 158, Dhaka
T: (02) 502600
Founded: 1973
Gen Secr: Dr. M.A. Manna
Focus: Energy
Periodical
Nuclear Science & Applications (semi-annually)
. . . . 00914

Bangladesh Council of Scientific and Industrial Research, Mirpur Rd, Dhanmondi, Dhaka 5
T: (02) 505686
Founded: 1955
Pres: Prof. Dr. S.S.M.A. Khorasani; Gen Secr: K.C. Sikdar
Focus: Sci; Eng 00915

Bangladesh Economic Association, c/o Economics Dept, Dhaka University, Dhaka
Founded: 1958
Pres: Dr. Mazharul Huq; Gen Secr: Dr. S.R. Bose
Focus: Econ 00916

Bangladesh Medical Association, BMA House, 15/2 Topkhana Rd, Dhaka
Founded: 1971; Members: 10000
Pres: Dr. M.A. Majed; Gen Secr: Dr. Gari Abdul Hoque
Focus: Med 00917

Institution of Engineers - Bangladesh, Ramna, Dhaka
Founded: 1948; Members: 6000
Pres: S.M. Al-Husainy; Gen Secr: Abdul Quassem
Focus: Eng 00918

Library Association of Bangladesh, c/o Library Training Institute, Bangladesh Public Library Bldg, Shahbagh, Ramna, Dhaka
T: (02) 504269
Founded: 1956
Pres: A.K.M. Abdun Nur; Gen Secr: M. Shamsul Islam Kahn
Focus: Libraries & Bk Sci
Periodical
The Eastern Librarian (quarterly) 00919

Society of Arts, Literature and Welfare, Society Park, K.C. Dey Rd, Chittagong
Founded: 1942; Members: 500
Gen Secr: Nesar Ahmed Chowdhury
Focus: Arts; Lit 00920

Zoological Society of Bangladesh, c/o Dept of Zoology, Dhaka University, Dhaka 1000
T: (02) 505505
Founded: 1972; Members: 650
Pres: Dr. Mahmud-Ul Ameen; Gen Secr: Dr. Rezaur Rahman
Focus: Zoology
Periodical
Bangladesh Journal of Zoology (semi-annually)
. . . . 00921

Barbados

Barbados Association of Medical Practitioners, c/o Queen Elizabeth Hospital, Martindales Rd, Saint Michael
Founded: 1973; Members: 125
Pres: Prof. E.R. Walrond; Gen Secr: Dr. G. Dixit
Focus: Med
Periodical
Newsletter (quarterly) 00922

Barbados Museum and Historical Society (BMHS), Saint Ann's Garrison
T: 4270201; Fax: 4295946
Founded: 1933; Members: 900
Pres: Dr. T. Carmichael; Gen Secr: H. Alissandra Cummins
Focus: Hist; Arts; Geology; Zoology; Archeol
Periodicals
Journal of BMHS (annually)
Newsletter (quarterly) 00923

Barbados Pharmaceutical Society, POB 820E, Saint Michael
Founded: 1948; Members: 155
Pres: Delores Morris; Gen Secr: George Alleyne
Focus: Pharmacol 00924

Caribbean Conservation Association (CCA), Savannah Lodge, Garrison, Saint Michael
T: 4265373; Fax: 4298483
Founded: 1967; Members: 509
Pres: Cecil Jacobs; Gen Secr: Glenda Medina
Focus: Ecology; Cultur Hist
Periodical
Caribbean Conservation News (quarterly) 00925

Library Association of Barbados, POB 827E, Bridgetown
Founded: 1968; Members: 60
Pres: Shirley Yearwood; Gen Secr: Hazelyn Devonish
Focus: Libraries & Bk Sci
Periodicals
Bulletin (annually)
Update: A Newsletter (irregularly) . . . 00926

Belarus

Academy of Agricultural Sciences of the Republic of Belarus, Vul Knorina 1, 220049 Minsk
T: (017) 2660617; Fax: 2688083
Founded: 1840; Members: 43
Pres: Vitaly S. Antonyuk; Gen Secr: Vladimir A. Shcherbakov
Focus: Agri 00927

Academy of Sciences of Belarus, Pr. Skaryny 66, 220072 Minsk
T: (017) 2684801; Fax: 2393163
Founded: 1929; Members: 179
Pres: Leonid M Sushchenya; Gen Secr: Andrei M. Goncharenko
Focus: Sci
Periodicals
Differentsialnye Uravneniya: Differential Equations (monthly)
Doklady: Report
Inzhenerno-Fizicheskii Zhurnal: Engineerring Physics Journal
Trenie i Iznos: Friction and Wear (bi-monthly)
Vestsi: Bulletin
Zhurnal Prikladnoi Spektroskopii: Journal of Applied Spectroscopy 00928

Belgium

Académie Européenne des Ecrivains Publics (AEP) / European Academy of Public Writers, 1-13 Rue Defacqz, 1050 Bruxelles
T: (02) 5380473
Focus: Lit 00929

Académie Royale d'Archéologie de Belgique, c/o Musées Royaux d'Art et d'Histoire, 10 Parc du Cinquantenaire, 1000 Bruxelles
Founded: 1842; Members: 100
Pres: Maurice Colaert; Gen Secr: Claire Dumortier
Focus: Archeol
Periodical
Revue Belge d'Archéologie et d'Histoire de l'Art (annually) 00930

Académie Royale de Langue et de Littérature Françaises, 1 Rue Ducale, 1000 Bruxelles
T: (02) 5502277; Fax: 5502275
Founded: 1920; Members: 40
Pres: Raymond Trousson; Gen Secr: André Coosse
Focus: Ling; Lit
Periodicals
Annuaire (annually)
Bulletin 00931

Académie Royale de Médecine de Belgique (ARMB), 1 Rue Ducale, 1000 Bruxelles
T: (02) 5502255; Fax: 5502265
Founded: 1841; Members: 320
Gen Secr: Prof. A. de Scoville
Focus: Med
Periodical
Bulletin et Mémoires de l'Académie Royale de Médecine de Belgique (monthly) 00932

Académie Royale des Sciences, des Lettres et des Beaux-Arts de Belgique, 1 Rue Ducale, 1000 Bruxelles
T: (02) 5502211; Fax: 5502205
Founded: 1772; Members: 300
Pres: Serge Vandenam; Gen Secr: P. Roberts-Jones
Focus: Arts; Lit; Sci
Periodicals
Annuaire de l'Académie (annually)
Bulletin de la Classe des Beaux-Arts (semi-annually)
Bulletin de la Classe des Lettres (semi-annually)
Bulletin de la Classe des Sciences (semi-annually)
Mémoires de la Classe des Beaux-Arts (irregularly)
Mémoires de la Classe des Lettres (irregularly)
Mémoires de la Classe des Sciences (irregularly)
. . . . 00933

Académie Royale des Sciences d'Outre-Mer, 1 Rue Defacqz, 1050 Bruxelles
T: (02) 5380211; Fax: 5392353
Founded: 1928; Members: 267
Gen Secr: Prof. J.-J. Symoens
Focus: Poli Sci; Med; Nat Sci
Periodical
Bulletin des Sciences (quarterly) 00934

Alliance Agricole Belge, 23-25 Rue de la Science, 1040 Bruxelles
T: (02) 2307295; Fax: 2304251
Founded: 1930; Members: 20000
Pres: L. Mathy; Gen Secr: J. Havet
Focus: Agri 00935

Alzheimer Europe (AE), c/o ECAS, 98 Rue du Trône, 1050 Bruxelles
T: (02) 5124444; Fax: 5126673
Founded: 1990
Focus: Med
Periodical
Alzheimer Europe Annual Newsletter (annually)
. . . . 00936

Architects Council of Europe (ACE), 207 Av Louise, 1050 Bruxelles
T: (02) 6450905, 6450982; E-Mail: ace.cae@skynet.be; Fax: 6450964
Founded: 1990; Members: 21
Gen Secr: Alain Sagne
Focus: Archit 00937

Archives et Bibliothèques de Belgique / Archief- en Biblioteekwezen in Belgie, 4 Blvd de l'Empereur, 1000 Bruxelles
T: (02) 5195351
Founded: 1907
Pres: F. Daelemans; Gen Secr: W. de Vos
Focus: Libraries & Bk Sci; Archives
Periodical
Archives et Bibliothèques de Belgique: Archief- en Bibliotheekwezen in Belgie (annually) . . 00938

ASM International-European Council, 19 Rue de l'Orme, 1040 Bruxelles
T: (02) 7331264, 7341240; Fax: 7346702
Founded: 1985
Focus: Eng 00939

Asocio por la Enkonduko de Nova Biologia Nomenklaturo / Vereniging voor het Invoeren van Nieuwe Biologische Nomenklatuur / Association for the Introduction of New Biological Nomenclature, Hertendreef 12, 2920 Kalmthout
T: (03) 6669949
Founded: 1971
Pres: Luk van Nassauw; Gen Secr: W.M.A. de Smet
Focus: Standards; Bio 00940

Association Actuarielle Internationale (AAI), c/o CGER, 48 Rue du Fossé-aux-Loups, 1000 Bruxelles
T: (02) 2136976; Fax: 2136799
Founded: 1895
Focus: Insurance
Periodicals
ASTIN Bulletin (semi-annually)
Bulletin AAI (semi-annually)
Index AAI (annually) 00941

Association Belge de Documentation (ABD), 119 Blvd L. Schmidt-laan, 1040 Bruxelles
Founded: 1947; Members: 240
Pres: Jean-Louis Janssens; Gen Secr: Philippe Laurent
Focus: Doc
Periodicals
ABD Flash (monthly)
Cahiers de la Documentation (quarterly) . 00942

Association Belge de Droit Rural (A.B.D.R.-B.V.A.R.) / Belgische Vereniging voor Agrarisch Recht, c/o Vlaamse Landmaatschappij, 72 Av de la Toison d'Or, 1060 Bruxelles
T: (02) 5437208; Fax: 5437399
Founded: 1961; Members: 455
Pres: R. de Meyer; Gen Secr: M. Heyerick
Focus: Law
Periodical
Revue de Droit Rural: Tijdschrift voor Agrarisch Recht (quarterly) 00943

Association Belge de Photographie et de Cinématographie (ABPC), 57 Rue Claessens, 1020 Bruxelles
Founded: 1874; Members: 130
Pres: J. Peeters
Focus: Cinema; Photo
Periodical
Informations (monthly) 00944

Association Belge de Radioprotection / Belgische Vereniging voor Stralingsbescherming, 14 Rue Juliette Wytsman, 1050 Bruxelles
E-Mail: 106237.1335@compuserve.com; Fax: (02) 6606322
Founded: 1963; Members: 260
Pres: Dr. C. Thielemans; Gen Secr: J. Czerwiec-Pote
Focus: Radiology
Periodical
Annales: Annalen (quarterly) 00945

Association Belge de Santé Publique, c/o National Institute of Hygiene and Epidemiology, 14 Rue Juliette Weytsman, 1050 Bruxelles
Founded: 1938; Members: 160
Pres: Prof. Dr. H. van Van Oyen
Focus: Hygiene; Public Health 00946

Association Belge des Analystes Financiers, c/o Générale de Banque, 3 Montagne du Parc, 1000 Bruxelles
T: (02) 5163564; Fax: 5163763
Founded: 1959; Members: 424
Focus: Finance 00947

Association Belge d'Hygiène et de Médecine Sociale, c/o National Institute of Hygiene and Epidemiology, 14 Rue Juliette Weytsman, 1050 Bruxelles
Founded: 1938; Members: 160
Pres: Prof. Dr. H. van Oyen; Gen Secr: Dr. V. van Casteren
Focus: Hygiene; Public Health 00948

Association de l'Europe Occidentale pour la Psychologie Aéronautique, 35 Rue Cardinal Mercier, 1000 Bruxelles
T: (02) 5119060
Founded: 1956; Members: 100
Focus: Psych 00949

Association des Diplomés en Histoire de l'Art et Archéologie de l'Université Catholique de Louvain, c/o Collège Erasme, 1 Pl Blaise Pascal, 1348 Louvain-la-Neuve
T: (010) 474880; E-Mail: hackens@axka.ucl.ac.be; Fax: 472579
Founded: 1965; Members: 250
Focus: Archeol; Hist; Arts; Cultur Hist
Periodical
Revue des Archéologues et Historiens d'Art de Louvain (annually) 00950

Association des Ecrivains Belges de Langue Française (A.E.B.), 150 Chaussée de Wavre, 1050 Bruxelles
T: (02) 5122968
Founded: 1902; Members: 500
Pres: France Bastia; Gen Secr: Emile Kesteman
Focus: Lit
Periodical
Nos Lettres (monthly) 00951

Association des Enseignants F. Matthias Alexander Technique de Belgique, 4 Rue des Fonds, 1380 Lasne
T: (02) 6333059; Fax: 6333059
Founded: 1983
Gen Secr: Christel Bobine
Focus: Educ 00952

Association des Sociétés Scientifiques Médicales Belges, 138a Av Circulaire, 1180 Bruxelles
T: (02) 3745158; Fax: 3749628
Founded: 1945; Members: 4000
Pres: Dr. G. Stalpaert
Focus: Med 00953

Association d'Instituts Européens de Conjoncture Economique (AIECE) / Association of European Conjuncture Institutes, 3 Pl Montesquieu, BP 4, 1348 Louvain-la-Neuve
T: (010) 474152
Founded: 1957; Members: 36
Focus: Econ
Periodical
Report (semi-annually) 00954

Association Européenne Camac / European Camac Association, c/o UCL, FYAM, 2 Chemin du Cyclotron, 1348 Louvain-la-Neuve
T: (010) 4363244
Founded: 1975; Members: 354
Focus: Eng
Periodical
ECA Newsletter (3 times annually) . . . 00955

Association Européenne de l'Ethnie Française (AEEF), 22 Rue Henri Vieuxtemps, 1070 Bruxelles
Founded: 1959
Focus: Ethnology
Periodical
L'Ethnie Française d'Europe (quarterly) . 00956

Association Européenne des Barreaux des Courts Suprêmes, Bergstr 16, 1851 Grimbergen
Founded: 1990
Focus: Law 00957

Association Européenne des Centres de Lutte contre les Poisons (A.E.C.A.P.) / European Association of Poisons Control Centres, 1 Rue Joseph Stallaert, 1060 Bruxelles
T: (02) 3451818, 3457473; Fax: 3475860
Founded: 1966; Members: 177
Focus: Toxicology
Periodicals
Bulletin de Médecine Légale et de Toxicologie Médicale
European Journal of Toxicology
Newsletter (quarterly)
Reports of Meetings 00958

Association Européenne des Centres Nationaux de Productivité / European Association of National Productivitn Centres, 60 Rue de la Concorde, 1050 Bruxelles
T: (02) 5117100
Founded: 1966; Members: 17
Focus: Econ
Periodicals
EPI (quarterly)
Europroductivity (monthly) 00959

Association Européenne des Institutions d'Aménagement Rural, c/o Vlaamse Landmaatschappij, 72 Av de la Toison d'Or, 1060 Bruxelles
T: (02) 5437397; Fax: 5437399
Founded: 1965
Pres: R. Albrecht; Gen Secr: M. Dubois
Focus: Urban Plan *00960*

Association Européenne pour le Droit Bancaire et Financier (AEDBF), 103 Blvd Auguste Reyers, 1040 Bruxelles
T: (02) 7364057
Founded: 1990
Focus: Law *00961*

Association for European Training for Employees in Technology, 38 Rue Fossé-aux-Loups, 1000 Bruxelles
T: (02) 2182865; Fax: 2182836
Founded: 1986
Gen Secr: Antonio Miniutti
Focus: Educ; Eng *00962*

Association for Teacher Education in Europe (ATEE), 60 Rue de la Concorde, 1050 Bruxelles
T: (02) 5409781; E-Mail: isabel.garcia.tinto@inßboard.be; Fax: 5341172
Founded: 1976; Members: 600
Pres: Dr. Mireia Montané; Gen Secr: Isabel Garcia Tintó
Focus: Educ
Periodicals
ATEE News (3 times annually)
European Journal of Teacher Education (3 times annually) *00963*

Association Internationale de Cybernétique (AIC) / International Association for Cybernetics, Palais des Expositions, Pl André Rijckmans, 5000 Namur
T: (081) 735209; Fax: 742945
Founded: 1957; Members: 200
Focus: Cybernetics
Periodicals
Cybernetica (quarterly)
Proceedings of International Congresses on Cybernetics (every 3 years) *00964*

Association Internationale de Droit Economique (AIDE), c/o CRIDE, UCL, 3 Pl Montesquieu, 1348 Louvain-la-Neuve
Founded: 1982
Focus: Law *00965*

Association Internationale des Ecoles Supérieures d'Education Physique (AIESEP), c/o Institut Supérieur d'Education Physique, Université, 21 Sart-Tilman, 4000 Liège
Fax: (041) 562901
Founded: 1962
Focus: Sports
Periodical
Proceedings of AIESEP (annually) . . . *00966*

Association Internationale des Etudes Coptes, c/o Institut Orientaliste, Collège Erasme, 1348 Louvain-la-Neuve
T: (010) 473199
Focus: Rel & Theol *00967*

Association Internationale des Juristes Démocrates (AIJD) / International Association of Democratic Lawyers, 263 Av Albert, 1180 Bruxelles
T: (02) 3451471
Founded: 1946
Focus: Law
Periodical
International Review of Contemporary Law (semi-annually) *00968*

Association Internationale des Laboratoires Textiles Lainiers, 19 Rue du Luxembourg, 1000 Bruxelles
T: (02) 5130620; Fax: 5140665
Founded: 1969; Members: 120
Pres: Yves Graux; Gen Secr: Dimitri Orekhoff
Focus: Textiles *00969*

Association Internationale des Mathématiques et Calculateurs en Simulation (IMACS) / International Association for Mathematics and Computers in Simulation, c/o Institut Montefiore, Bât. B28 Sart-Tilman, 4000 Liège
T: (041) 563710
Founded: 1955; Members: 1250
Focus: Math; Computer & Info Sci
Periodical
Mathematics and Computer in Simulation: Applied Numerical Mathematics (bi-monthly) . . . *00970*

Association Internationale des Métiers et Enseignements d'Art (AIMEA), 32 Av J.G. van Goolen, 1200 Bruxelles
T: (02) 7703706
Founded: 1938
Focus: Arts; Educ *00971*

Association Internationale pour la Coopération et le Développement en Afrique Australe (ACODA), Schoonzichtlaan 46, 3009 Winksele
Founded: 1990
Focus: Develop Areas *00972*

Association Internationale pour le Progrès Social (AIPS), 7 Sq Wiser, 1040 Bruxelles
T: (02) 2310662
Founded: 1925
Focus: Sociology
Periodical
Bulletin d'Information *00973*

Association Internationale pour l'Utilisation des Langues Régionales à l'Ecole (SCOLARE), 9 Rue du Beau-Mur, 4030 Liège
T: (041) 415072
Focus: Ling *00974*

Association Laïque pour l'Education et la Formation Professionnelle des Adolescents en Europe (ALEFPA-Europe), 117 Av Sainte-Anne, 1640 Bruxelles
T: (02) 3581165
Founded: 1987
Focus: Adult Educ *00975*

Association Médicale Européenne, 34 Blvd Général Jacques, 1050 Bruxelles
Founded: 1991
Focus: Med *00976*

Association Mondiale des Sciences de l'Education (A.M.S.E.) / World Association for Educational Research, Henri Dunantlaan 1, 9000 Gent
T: (09) 2646378; E-Mail: vivence.henderickx@rug.ac.be; Fax: 2646490
Founded: 1953; Members: 310
Pres: Prof. Dr. Y. Iram; Gen Secr: Prof. Dr. M.-L. van Herreweghe
Focus: Educ
Periodical
Communicationes (semi-annually) *00977*

Association Nationale pour la Protection contre l'Incendie et l'Intrusion (ANPI), Parc Scientifique Fleming, 1348 Louvain-La-Neuve
T: (010) 475211; E-Mail: info@anpi-nvbb.be; Fax: 475270
Founded: 1957
Pres: Alain Georges
Focus: Safety
Periodicals
ANPI magazine (quarterly)
NVBB magazine (quarterly) *00978*

Association of Belgian Actuaries (ABA), c/o IMT, Consulting Actuaries, Mgr. Van Waeyenberghlaan 32, 3000 Leuven
T: (016) 298907; Fax: 298939
Founded: 1996
Pres: Eddy van den Bovie; Gen Secr: Ann Verlinden
Focus: Insurance *00979*

Association pour la Promotion des Publications Scientifiques (A.P.P.S.), 26 Av de l'Amarante, 1020 Bruxelles
T: (02) 2682933; Fax: 2682514
Founded: 1981; Members: 100
Pres: Dr. Jean C. Baudet
Focus: Libraries & Bk Sci
Periodical
Ingénieur et Industrie (10 times annually) *00980*

Association pour les Etudes et Recherches de Zoologie Appliquée et de Phytopathologie (A.E.R.Z.A.P.) / Vereniging voor Studie en Onderzoek over Fytopathologie en Toegepaste Zoologie, c/o Royal Research Station of Gorsem, Brede Akker 3, 3800 Sint-Truiden
T: (011) 682019; E-Mail: gorsem@tornado.be; Fax: 674318
Founded: 1944; Members: 155
Focus: Pathology; Zoology
Periodical
Parasitica (quarterly) *00981*

Association pour l'Etude et l'Evaluation Epidémiologiques des Désastres dans les Pays en Voie de Développement, 30 Clos Chapelle-aux-Champs, EPID 3034, 1200 Bruxelles
T: (02) 7643823; E-Mail: sapir@epid.ucl.ac.be; Fax: 7643441
Founded: 1973
Gen Secr: Fabienne Keymeulen
Focus: Develop Areas; Trop Med; Public Health *00982*

Association pour l'Etude Taxonomique de la Flore d'Afrique Tropicale (AETFAT), 136 Rue de la Hulpe, 1331 Rosières
T: (02) 6532457, 6490030
Founded: 1951; Members: 704
Focus: Botany *00983*

Association Professionnelle Belge des Pédiatres, 20 Av de la Couronne, 1050 Bruxelles
T: (02) 6492147
Founded: 1954; Members: 365
Focus: Pediatrics *00984*

Association Professionnelle des Bibliothécaires et Documentalistes (APBD), 7 Rue des Marronniers, 5651 Thy-le-Château
T: (071) 614335; Fax: 611634
Founded: 1975; Members: 300
Pres: Jean-Claude Trefois; Gen Secr: Angélique Mattioli
Focus: Libraries & Bk Sci; Doc
Periodical
Bloc-Notes (10 times annually) *00985*

Association Royale des Actuaires Belges (ARAB) / Koninklijke Vereniging der Belgische Actuarissen, 48 Rue du Fossé-aux-Loups, 1000 Bruxelles
T: (02) 2184490
Founded: 1895; Members: 461
Focus: Insurance
Periodical
Bulletin (annually) *00986*

Association Royale des Demeures Historiques de Belgique, 24 Rue Vergote, 1200 Bruxelles
T: (02) 7350965; Fax: 7359912
Founded: 1934; Members: 2000
Pres: Prince Alexandre de Merode
Focus: Preserv Hist Monuments
Periodical
La Maison d'Hier et d'Aujourd'hui (quarterly) *00987*

Aviation Research and Development Institute (ARDI), 50 Rue P. Van Obberghen, 1140 Bruxelles
Founded: 1989
Focus: Aero *00988*

Belgisch Instituut voor Arbeidsverhoudingen, c/o Collegium Falconis, Tiensestr 41, 3000 Leuven
Focus: Law *00989*

Belgische Vereniging voor Aardrijkskundige Studies / Société Belge d'Etudes Géographiques, W. de Croylaan 42, 3001 Heverlee
T: (016) 322427; Fax: 322980
Founded: 1931; Members: 400
Pres: Y. Verhasselt; Gen Secr: H. van der Haegen
Focus: Geography
Periodical
Tijdschrift: Bulletin (semi-annually) . . . *00990*

Belgische Vereniging voor Tropische Geneeskunde / Société Belge de Médecine Tropicale, Nationalestr 155, 2000 Antwerpen
T: (03) 2476240; E-Mail: bgryseels@itg.be; Fax: 2481133
Founded: 1920; Members: 540
Gen Secr: Prof. B. Gryseels
Focus: Trop Med
Periodical
Tropical Medicine and International Health (monthly) *00991*

Belgische Wetenschappelijke Vereniging voor Neurochirurgie, Bisschopsdreef 53, 8000 Brugge
Founded: 1977; Members: 50
Focus: Surgery; Neurology *00992*

Benelux Association of Energy Economists (BAEE), 39 Rue de la Régence, 1000 Bruxelles
T: (02) 5193823; Fax: 5134206
Founded: 1984
Focus: Energy *00993*

Benelux Phlebology Society, 180 Av du Roi Albert, 1080 Bruxelles
Founded: 1961
Focus: Med *00994*

Biotechnology Research for Innovation, Development and Growth in Europe (BRIDGE), 200 Rue de la Loi, 1049 Bruxelles
T: (02) 2354044; Fax: 2350145
Founded: 1989
Focus: Eng *00995*

Bisnuth Institute, Borgtstr 301, 1850 Grimbergen
T: (02) 2524747; E-Mail: palmieri@skynet.be; Fax: 2522775
Founded: 1972
Gen Secr: Yves Palmieri
Focus: Mineralogy *00996*

Board of Governors of the European Schools, 200 Rue de la Loi, 1049 Bruxelles
T: (02) 2351111; Fax: 2301930
Founded: 1957; Members: 12
Focus: Educ
Periodical
Pedagogical Bulletin (quarterly) *00997*

Branche Belge de la Société de Chimie Industrielle, 3 Rue Ravenstein, 1000 Bruxelles
Fax: (02) 5145735
Focus: Chem *00998*

Bureau International d'Audiophonologie / International Office for Audiophonology, 29 Rue J. B. Vandercammen, 1160 Bruxelles
T: (02) 6731036
Founded: 1964; Members: 269
Focus: Med; Ling
Periodical
Rapport Annuel: Recommandations (annually) *00999*

Bureau International de la Récupération et du Recyclage (BIR), 24 Rue du Lombard, 1000 Bruxelles
T: (02) 5142180; E-Mail: bir.sec@skynet.be; Fax: 5141226
Founded: 1948; Members: 585
Pres: Anthony P. Bird; Gen Secr: Francis Veys
Focus: Ecology *01000*

Bureau International Technique de l'ABS (BIT), 4 Av E. Van Nieuwenhuyse, 1160 Bruxelles
T: (02) 6767247; Fax: 6767301
Founded: 1974; Members: 7
Gen Secr: D. Thomas
Focus: Eng *01001*

Bureau International Technique des Polyesters Insaturés, 4 Av E. Van Nieuwenhuyse, 1160 Bruxelles
T: (02) 6767247; Fax: 6767301
Founded: 1969; Members: 14
Gen Secr: D. Thomas
Focus: Eng *01002*

Bureau International Technique du Spathfluor, 4 Av E. Van Nieuwenhuyse, 1160 Bruxelles
T: (02) 6767211; Fax: 6767300
Founded: 1974
Focus: Eng *01003*

Cadmium Pigments Association, c/o CEFIC, 4 Av E. Van Nieuwenhuyse, 1160 Bruxelles
T: (02) 6767211; Fax: 6767301
Focus: Metallurgy *01004*

CENELEC, 35 Rue de Stassaert, 1050 Bruxelles
T: (02) 5196871; E-Mail: cenelec@cenclcbel.be; Fax: 5196919
Members: 18
Pres: H. Wanda; Gen Secr: Stephen P.A. Marriott
Focus: Standards
Periodical
CEN/CENELEC/ETSI Bulletin *01005*

Central Bureau for Nuclear Measurements (CBNM), Steenweg naar Retie, 2440 Geel
T: (014) 571211; Fax: 584273
Founded: 1960
Focus: Nucl Res *01006*

Centre Belge pour la Gestion de la Qualité, F. Williotstr 9, 2600 Berchem
T: (03) 2804700; Fax: 2804719
Founded: 1973; Members: 1900
Pres: C.M. Horrez; Gen Secr: B. Vanbriel
Focus: Materials Sci *01007*

Centre Européen des Silicones (CES), 4 Av E. Van Nieuwenhuyse, 1160 Bruxelles
T: (02) 6767211; Fax: 6767301
Founded: 1968; Members: 9
Gen Secr: D. Thomas
Focus: Chem *01008*

Centre Européen pour l'Etude de l'Argumentation (CEAA), c/o Institut de Philosophie, 143 Av A. Buyl, 1050 Bruxelles
T: (02) 6422628
Focus: Philos *01009*

Centre for Research on European Women (CREW), 21 Rue de la Tourelle, 1040 Bruxelles
T: (02) 2305158; Fax: 2306230
Founded: 1980
Focus: Soc Sci
Periodical
CREW Report (monthly) *01010*

Centre for Research on the Epidemiology of Disasters (CRED), c/o Ecole de Santé Publique, 30 Clos Chapelle-aux-Champs, EPID 3034, 1200 Bruxelles
T: (02) 7643823; E-Mail: sapir@epid.ucl.ac.be; Fax: 7643441
Founded: 1973
Gen Secr: Fabienne Keymeulen
Focus: Med *01011*

Centre International de Documentation Marguerite Yourcenar (CIDMY), c/o Archives de Bruxelles, 65 Rue des Tanneurs, 1000 Bruxelles
T: (02) 5027475; Fax: 5027475
Founded: 1989
Focus: Sci *01012*

Centre International de Liaison des Ecoles de Cinéma et de Télévision (CILECT), 8 Rue Thérésienne, 1000 Bruxelles
T: (02) 5119839; E-Mail: hverh.cilect@skynet.be; Fax: 5110035
Founded: 1955; Members: 102
Pres: Gustavo Montiel; Gen Secr: Henry Verhasselt
Focus: Educ; Cinema
Periodical
CILECT Newsletter (quarterly) *01013*

Centre International de Recherches et d'Information sur l'Economie Publique, Sociale et Coopérative (CIRIEC), c/o Université de Liège, Sart-Tilman, Bâtiment B33, 4000 Liège
T: (04) 3662746; E-Mail: ciriec@ulg.ac.be; Fax: 3662958
Founded: 1947; Members: 13
Pres: Dr. Fritz Gautier; Gen Secr: Prof. Dr. Bernard Thiry
Focus: Econ
Periodical
Annals of Public and Cooperative Economics (quarterly) *01014*

Centre International de Recherches Glyptographiques (CIRG), 13 Rue Mathias de la Bruyère, 1440 Braine-le-Château
T: (02) 3660529
Founded: 1981
Focus: Hist *01015*

Centre International des Langues, Littératures et Traditions d'Afrique au Service du Développement (CILTADE), 30 Av des Clos, 1348 Louvain-la-Neuve
T: (010) 450665
Founded: 1986
Focus: Ling; Lit; Hist 01016

Centre International d'Etude de la Peinture Médiévale des Bassins de l'Escaut et de la Meuse / International Centre for the Study of Medieval Painting in the Schelde and the Meuse Valleys, 1 Parc du Cinquantenaire, 1000 Bruxelles
T: (02) 7396866; E-Mail: mund@kikirpa.be; Fax: 7320105
Founded: 1950; Members: 15
Pres: H. Pauwels
Focus: Fine Arts
Periodicals
Contributions à l'Etude des Primitifs Flamands (annually)
Corpus de la Peinture des Anciens Pays-Bas Méridionaux au 15e Siècle
Répertoire des Peintures Flamandes du 15e Siècle 01017

Centre International d'Etudes de la Formation Religieuse / International Centre for Studies in Religious Education, 184-186 Rue Washington, 1050 Bruxelles
T: (02) 3441882; Fax: 3465745
Founded: 1935; Members: 7
Focus: Educ; Rel & Theol
Periodicals
Lumen Vitae: International Review of Religious Education (quarterly)
Lumen Vitae: Revue Internationale de la Formation Religieuse (quarterly) 01018

Centre International d'Etudes, de Recherche et d'Action pour le Développemnt (CINTERAD), 186 Blvd Louis Schmidt, 1050 Bruxelles
Founded: Gbossa, Lambert; Members: 13
Focus: Develop Areas 01019

Centre International d'Etudes du Lindane (CIEL), 4 Av E. Van Nieuwenhuyse, 1160 Bruxelles
T: (02) 6767241; Fax: 6767301
Founded: 1969
Focus: Chem 01020

Centre of Promotion of Catholic Education in Europe / Centre de Promotion de l'Enseignement Catholique en Europe, 42 Rue de l'Industrie, 1040 Bruxelles
T: (02) 5117501; Fax: 5145989
Founded: 1984
Focus: Educ 01021

Centre pour l'Etude des Problèmes du Monde Musulman Contemporain / Study Centre for Problems of the Contemporary Muslim World, 44 Av Jeanne, 1050 Bruxelles
T: (02) 6423359
Founded: 1958
Gen Secr: Destrée. A.
Focus: Rel & Theol; Anthro
Periodical
Le Monde Muselman Contemporain-Initiations 01022

Cercle Archéologique de Mons (CAM), c/o Maison Losseau, 37 Rue de Nimy, 7000 Mons
T: (065) 331765
Founded: 1856; Members: 350
Focus: Archeol 01023

Cercle Benelux d'Histoire de la Pharmacie, Romeinselaan 6, 8500 Kortrijk
T: (056) 225499
Founded: 1950
Focus: Pharmacol; Hist 01024

Cercle d'Etudes Numismatiques (CEN), 4 Blvd de l'Empereur, 1000 Bruxelles
T: (02) 5136180
Founded: 1964; Members: 465
Focus: Numismatics
Periodical
Traveaux 01025

Chambre Belge des Pédicures Médicaux (CBPM), 5 Av des Cormorans, 1150 Bruxelles
T: (02) 7713864
Founded: 1939; Members: 200
Focus: Orthopedics 01026

Chambre Belge des Traducteurs, Interprètes et Philologues (CBTIF), c/o M. Lepeer, 110 Av de Heyn, 1090 Bruxelles
Founded: 1955; Members: 250
Focus: Ling; Lit 01027

China-Europe Management Institute (CEMI), c/o EFMD, 40 Rue Washington, 1050 Bruxelles
T: (02) 6480385; Fax: 8418412
Founded: 1989
Focus: Business Admin 01028

Coimbra Group, c/o UCL, 15 Av de l'Assomption, 1200 Bruxelles
T: (02) 7642209; Fax: 7642299
Founded: 1985; Members: 30
Focus: Educ 01029

College of Europe, Dyver 10-11, 8000 Brugge
T: (050) 335334; Fax: 343158
Founded: 1949
Pres: Otto von der Gablentz
Focus: Educ
Periodical
Information (annually) 01030

Comité d'Associations Européennes de Médecins Catholiques (CAEMC), 38 Rue des Deux-Eglises, 1040 Bruxelles
Focus: Med 01031

Comité de Liaison des Architectes de l'Europe Unie, 158 Rue de Livourne, 1050 Bruxelles
Founded: 1959
Focus: Archit 01032

Comité des Cancérologues de la Communauté Européenne, 75 Av Hippocrate, BP 7550, 1200 Bruxelles
T: (02) 7623292; Fax: 7645322
Focus: Cell Biol & Cancer Res 01033

Comité d'Etude de la Corrosion et de la Protection des Canalisations (CEOCOR), c/o Institut de Chimie et Métallurgie, 2 Rue Armand Stevart, 4000 Liège
T: (041) 520180
Founded: 1963; Members: 120
Focus: Materials Sci; Metallurgy 01034

Comité d'Etude des Producteurs de Charbon d'Europe Occidentale (CEPCEO), 168 Av de Tervueren, 1150 Bruxelles
T: (02) 7719974
Founded: 1953
Focus: Mining
Periodical
CEPCEO Report 01035

Comité Economique et Social des Communautés Européennes (CES) / Economic and Social Committee of the European Communities, 2 Rue Ravenstein, 1000 Bruxelles
T: (02) 5199011; Fax: 5134893
Members: 189
Focus: Econ; Sociology
Periodical
CES Bulletin (quarterly) 01036

Comité Européen de Recherche et de Développement (CERD), 200 Rue de la Loi, 1040 Bruxelles
T: (02) 2351111 ext 3774
Founded: 1973
Focus: Econ 01037

Comité International de Médecine Militaire / International Committee of Military Medicine, c/o Hôpital Militaire, 79 Rue Saint-Laurent, 4000 Liège
T: (04) 2222183; Fax: 2222150
Founded: 1921; Members: 90
Pres: Lu Zengqi; Gen Secr: Dr. M. Cools
Focus: Med
Periodical
Revue Internationale des Services de Santé des Forces Armées: International Review of the Armed Forces Medical Services (quarterly) 01038

Comité International de Recherche et d'Etude de Facteurs de l'Ambiance (CIFA), 27 Drève des Wégélias, 1170 Bruxelles
T: (02) 6490030
Focus: Ecology 01039

Comité National Belge de l'Organisation Scientifique (CNBOS), 93 Rue de Stassart, 1050 Bruxelles
T: (02) 5112844
Founded: 1926
Focus: Metallurgy 01040

Comité National pour l'Etude et la Prévention de l'Alcoolisme et des Autres Toxicomanies (CNA), 78 Rue du Rempart-des-Moines, 1000 Bruxelles
T: (02) 5111188
Founded: 1949; Members: 21
Focus: Sociology 01041

Commission Belge de Bibliographie, 4 Blvd de l'Empereur, 1000 Bruxelles
T: (02) 80510464; E-Mail: chriverb@skynet.be; Fax: 80510465
Founded: 1951; Members: 68
Pres: C.F. Verbeke
Focus: Libraries & Bk Sci
Periodical
Bibliographica Belgica 01042

Commission of the European Communities Liaison Committee of Historians / Groupe de Liaison des Historiens près la Commission des Communautés Européennes, c/o Unité d'Histoire Contemporaine, Collège Erasme, UCL, 1 Pl Blaise Pascal, 1348 Louvain-la-Neuve
Founded: 1982
Focus: Hist
Periodical
Lettre d'Information des Historiens de l'Europe Contemporaine 01043

Commission Royale d'Histoire, Palais des Académies, 1 Rue Ducale, 1000 Bruxelles
Founded: 1834
Pres: J.J. Hoebancx; Gen Secr: W. Prevenier
Focus: Hist 01044

Committee on Higher Education in the European Community (CHEEC), c/o HEURAS, 60 Rue de la Concorde, 1050 Bruxelles
T: (02) 5143340; Fax: 5141172
Focus: Educ 01045

Committee on the Challenges of Modern Society (CCMS), c/o North Atlantic Treaty Organization, 1110 Bruxelles
T: (02) 7074850; Fax: 7074232
Founded: 1969; Members: 16
Focus: Ecology; Sci 01046

Common Office for European Training / Office Commun de Formation Européenne, 43-45 Rue Notre-Dame, 7000 Mons
T: (065) 364259; Fax: 317443
Founded: 1986
Focus: Educ 01047

Community Network for European Education and Training (COMNET), 6 Quai Banning, 4000 Liège
T: (041) 528085; Fax: 534097
Founded: 1988; Members: 90
Focus: Educ
Periodical
COMNET Newsletter 01048

Comparative Education Society in Europe (CESE), 60 Rue de la Concorde, 1050 Bruxelles
T: (02) 5143340; Fax: 5141172
Founded: 1961
Focus: Educ
Periodical
CESE Newsletter 01049

Concorde / Centre for Organisations and Networks Cooperating in Research and Development of Education, 60 Rue de la Concorde, 1050 Bruxelles
T: (02) 5409740; Fax: 5141172
Founded: 1994; Members: 50
Gen Secr: Carmen du Bois
Focus: Educ 01050

Confédération d'Associations d'Ecoles Indépendantes de la Communauté Européenne (CADEICA), 15 Av Montana, 1180 Bruxelles
Founded: 1989
Focus: Educ 01051

Confédération Européenne des Syndicats Nationaux et Associations Professionnelles de Pédiatres, 20 Av de la Couronne, 1050 Bruxelles
T: (02) 6492147
Founded: 1959
Focus: Pediatrics 01052

Confederation of European Specialists in Paediatrics (CESP), 20 Av de la Couronne, 1050 Bruxelles
T: (02) 6492147; E-Mail: 616052; Fax: 6492690
Founded: 1959
Focus: Pediatrics 01053

Conférence des Recteurs des Universités Belges, 5 Rue d'Egmont, 1050 Bruxelles
T: (02) 5049211; Fax: 5140006
Founded: 1973
Focus: Sci 01054

Conférence Diplomatique de Droit Maritime International, c/o Ministère des Affaires Etrangères et du Commerce Extérieur, 2 Rue Quatre Bras, 1000 Bruxelles
T: (02) 5136240
Founded: 1905
Focus: Law 01055

Conférence Internationale Permanente de Directeurs d'Instituts Universitaires pour la Formation de Traducteurs et d'Interprètes (CIUTI), Schildersstr 41, 2000 Antwerpen
T: (03) 2389832
Founded: 1961; Members: 17
Focus: Educ; Ling 01056

Conferentie voor Regionale Ontwikkeling in Noord-West-Europa / Conférence des Regions de l'Europe du Nord-Ouest / Conference of Regions of North-West-Europe, Postbus 107, 8000 Brugge
Founded: 1955; Members: 5
Pres: Angus MacMillan; Gen Secr: Prof. Dr. I.B.F. Kormoss
Focus: Urban Plan
Periodical
Proceedings of Seminars Organized (irregularly) 01057

Conseil Consultatif Economique et Social de l'Union Economique Benelux (CCES), 21 Av de la Joyeuse Entrée, 1040 Bruxelles
T: (02) 2338904
Founded: 1960
Focus: Econ; Sociology
Periodical
Report of Council Meetings 01058

Conseil des Recteurs des Institutions Universitaires Francophones de Belgique, 5 Rue d'Egmont, 1000 Bruxelles
T: (02) 5049300; Fax: 5140006
Focus: Educ 01059

Conseil Interuniversitaire de la Communauté Française, 5 Rue d'Egmont, 1050 Bruxelles
T: (02) 5049211; Fax: 5049292
Founded: 1980
Gen Secr: Etienne Loeckx
Focus: Adult Educ 01060

Conseil National de l'Ordre des Médecins, 32 Pl de Jamblinne de Meux, 1040 Bruxelles
T: (02) 7368291
Founded: 1947
Focus: Med
Periodical
Bulletin du Conseil National: Tijdschrift Nationale Raad (quarterly) 01061

Conseil Supérieur de Statistique (C.S.S.), 44 Rue de Louvain, 1000 Bruxelles
T: (02) 5486211; Fax: 5486367
Founded: 1841; Members: 36
Pres: M. Despontin; Gen Secr: G. Dupont
Focus: Stats 01062

Cooperation for Open Systems Interconnection Networking in Europe (COSINE), c/o CEC, 200 Rue de la Loi, 1049 Bruxelles
T: (02) 2362075; Fax: 2353821
Founded: 1985; Members: 19
Focus: Computer & Info Sci 01063

Coordinating European Council for the Development of Performance Tests for Transport Fuels, Lubricants and other Fluids, 1 Pl Madou, 1210 Bruxelles
T: (02) 2261930; E-Mail: cepalmer@compuserve.com; Fax: 2261939
Founded: 1963; Members: 1500
Gen Secr: Francis Palmer
Focus: Chem 01064

Coordination et Promotion de l'Enseignement de la Réligion dans les Ecoles Européennes (COOPERE), c/o COMECE, 42 Rue Stévin, 1000 Bruxelles
T: (02) 2307316; Fax: 2303334
Founded: 1989; Members: 8
Pres: Paul Collowald; Gen Secr: Cathérine Roba
Focus: Rel & Theol; Educ 01065

C.R.I.F., Technologiepark 9, 9052 Zwijnaarde
T: (09) 2645689; Fax: 2645848
Founded: 1929; Members: 200
Focus: Metallurgy 01066

Dedicated Road Infrastructure for Vehicle Safety in Europe (DRIVE), 200 Rue de la Loi, 1049 Bruxelles
T: (02) 2363449; Fax: 2362391
Founded: 1988; Members: 17
Focus: Transport 01067

Dentist's Liaison Committee for the EEC, 1 Rue Newton, 1000 Bruxelles
T: (02) 7325407; Fax: 7325407
Focus: Pathology 01068

Euratom Scientific and Technical Committee, c/o CEC, 200 Rue de la Loi, 1049 Bruxelles
T: (02) 2354494; Fax: 2350150
Focus: Nucl Res 01069

Eureka, 19h Av des Arts, 1040 Bruxelles
T: (02) 2292240; Fax: 2187906
Founded: 1985; Members: 25
Gen Secr: Pol van den Bergen
Focus: Sci 01070

Euro-China Research Association in Management (ECRAM), c/o EFMD, 40 Rue Washington, 1050 Bruxelles
T: (02) 6480385; Fax: 6460768
Focus: Business Admin 01071

Euro-China Research Centre for Business Cooperation (ECRCBC), 3 Av d'Uccle, 1190 Bruxelles
T: (02) 3445907; Fax: 3473096
Founded: 1990
Focus: Business Admin 01072

Euro Chlor, c/o CEFIC, 4 Av E. Van Nieuwenhuyse, 1160 Bruxelles
T: (02) 6767211; E-Mail: eurochlor@cefic.be; Fax: 6767241
Members: 45
Gen Secr: Gilliatt; Dr. Barrie S.
Focus: Chem 01073

eurogas, 4 Av Palmerston, 1000 Bruxelles
T: (02) 2371111; E-Mail: eurogas@arcadis.be; Fax: 2306291
Founded: 1990
Focus: Econ 01074

Europa Esperanto-Centro (EEC), Pr. Leopoldstr 51, 8310 Brugge
T: (030) 354935
Founded: 1977
Focus: Ling 01075

Europe 2000, Ochtmachtlaan 10, 1040 Bruxelles
T: (02) 6427641; Fax: 6427636
Founded: 1989; Members: 550
Pres: Dr. R.A. Gonsalves; Gen Secr: T. Sleeswijk Visser
Focus: Law 01076

European Academy for Film and Television / Académie Européenne du Cinéma et de la Télévision, 69 Rue Verte, 1210 Bruxelles
T: (02) 2186607; Fax: 2175572
Founded: 1990; Members: 18
Gen Secr: Dimitri Balachoff
Focus: Mass Media; Cinema 01077

European Accounting Association (EAA) / Association Européenne de Comptabilité, c/o EIASM, 13 Rue d'Egmont, 1000 Bruxelles
T: (02) 5119111; E-Mail: eaa@eiasm.be; Fax: 5121929
Founded: 1977
Pres: Prof. A. Wagenhofer
Focus: Business Admin
Periodical
The European Accounting Review . . . 01078

European Alliance for Safe Meat, 64 Rue Franz Merjay, 1060 Bruxelles
T: (02) 5390231; Fax: 5390280
Founded: 1991
Focus: Food 01079

European Anthropological Association, c/o Laboratorium Antropogenetika, Pleinlaan 2, 1080 Bruxelles
T: (02) 6293426; E-Mail: rhauspie@vnet3.vub.ac.be; Fax: 6293408
Founded: 1975; Members: 800
Pres: Prof. Charles Susanne; Gen Secr: Dr. Roland Hauspie
Focus: Anthro
Periodicals
International Journal of Anthropology
Newsletter 01080

European Association against Fibre Pollution (EAFP) / Association Européenne pour la Réduction de la Pollution due aux Fibres, 119 Blvd Louis Schmidt, 1040 Bruxelles
Founded: 1988
Focus: Ecology 01081

European Association against Pigmentary Dystrophy and its Syndromes / Association Européenne contre la Lutte contre la Rétinite Pigmentaire et ses Syndromes, 3 Blvd de la Cambre, 1050 Bruxelles
T: (02) 6402504; Fax: 6402504
Founded: 1985
Focus: Derm 01082

European Association for Audiovisual Media Education / Association Européenne pour l'Education aux Médias Audiovisuels, 162 Rue du Midi, 1000 Bruxelles
T: (02) 5020643
Founded: 1989
Focus: Educ
Periodical
AEEMA Newsletter (bi-monthly) 01083

European Association for Burgundy Studies (EABS), c/o Facultés Universitaires Saint-Louis, 43 Blvd du Jardin Botanique, 1000 Bruxelles
T: (02) 2117811; Fax: 2117997
Gen Secr: Prof. Jean-Marie Cauchies
Focus: Cultur Hist 01084

European Association for Country Planning Institutions / Association Européenne des Institutions d'Aménagement Rural, 72 Av de la Toison d'Or, 1060 Bruxelles
T: (02) 5388160
Founded: 1965; Members: 16
Focus: Urban Plan 01085

European Association for Health Information and Libraries (EAHIL) / Association Européenne pour l'Information et les Bibliothèques de Santé, 60 Rue de la Concorde, 1050 Bruxelles
T: (02) 5118063; E-Mail: rosellyne.hoet@infoboard.be; Fax: 5118063
Founded: 1987
Pres: Elisabeth Husem; Gen Secr: Tony McSean
Focus: Libraries & Bk Sci; Computer & Info Sci
Periodical
Newsletter to European Health Librarians (quarterly) 01086

European Association for Information on Local Development / Association Européenne pour l'Information sur le Développement Local, 34 Rue Breydel, 1040 Bruxelles
T: (02) 2305234; Fax: 2303482
Focus: Develop Areas 01087

European Association for Research in Industrial Economics (EARIE) / Association Européenne de la Recherche en Economie Industrielle, c/o EIASM, 13 Rue d'Egmont, 1000 Bruxelles
T: (02) 5119116; E-Mail: earie@eiasn.be; Fax: 5121929
Founded: 1974; Members: 400
Pres: Prof. Paul Geroski
Focus: Business Admin 01088

European Association for Research into Adapted Physical Activity / Association Européenne de Recherche en Avtivité Adaptée, c/o Institut Supérieur d'Education Physique, Université Libre de Bruxelles, 28 Av Paul Héger, 1050 Bruxelles
Founded: 1987
Focus: Sports 01089

European Association for Textile Polyolefins (EATP) / Association Européenne des Polyoléfines Textiles, 4 Av E. Van Nieuwenhuyse, 1160 Bruxelles
T: (02) 6767472; Fax: 6767474
Founded: 1971; Members: 70
Pres: Berry Wiersum; Gen Secr: J.P. Peckstadt
Focus: Textiles 01090

European Association for the Promotion of Poetry, Blijde Inkomststr 9, 3000 Leuven
T: (016) 235351; Fax: 234949
Founded: 1979
Focus: Lit
Periodical
PI (European Poetry Quarterly) (quarterly) 01091

European Association for the Promotion of the Hand Hygiene / Association Européenne pour la Promotion de l'Hygiène des Mains, 46 Rue Lieutenant Liedel, 1070 Bruxelles
T: (02) 5212099
Founded: 1983; Members: 24
Focus: Hygiene 01092

European Association for the Study of Safety Problems in the Production and Use of Propellant Powders (EASSP) / Association Européenne pour l'Etude des Problèmes de Sécurité dans la Fabrication et l'Emploi des Poudres Propulsives, 4 Av E. Van Nieuwenhuyse, 1160 Bruxelles
T: (02) 6767211
Founded: 1977
Focus: Eng 01093

European Association for the Teaching of Legal Theory (EATLT) / Association Européenne pour l'Enseignement de la Théorie du Droit, c/o Facultés Universitaires Saint-Louis, 43 Blvd du Jardin Botanique, 1000 Bruxelles
T: (02) 2117811
Focus: Law; Educ 01094

European Association of Agricultural Economists (EAAE) / Association Européenne d'Economistes Agricoles, 82 Rue de Trèves, 1040 Bruxelles
Founded: 1975; Members: 1000
Focus: Agri
Periodical
EAAE Newsletter 01095

European Association of Architectural Education / Association Européenne pour l'Enseignement de l'Architecture, c/o Unité Architecture, Université Catholique de Louvain, 1 Pl du Levant, 1348 Louvain-la-Neuve
T: (010) 451558; Fax: 452809
Founded: 1975; Members: 120
Pres: Pierre von Heiss; Gen Secr: Nicole Mouzon
Focus: Educ; Archit
Periodicals
EAAE News Sheet (3 times annually)
STOA (semi-annually) 01096

European Association of Centers of Medical Ethics / Association Européenne des Centres d'Ethique Médicale, 5 Promenade de l'Alma, BP 4534, 1200 Bruxelles
T: (02) 7620297
Founded: 1985
Focus: Philos 01097

European Association of Classification Societies (EurACS), c/o Germanischer Lloyd, Victor Govaerslaan 16, 2060 Antwerpen
T: (031) 6460416; Fax: 6460064
Founded: 1979
Focus: Standards
Periodical
EurACs 01098

European Association of Education and Research in Public Relations (CERP-EDUCATION), c/o Hibo, Sint Pietersnieuwstr 160, 9000 Gent
T: (091) 250092; Fax: 330949
Members: 89
Focus: Educ 01099

European Association of Experimental Social Psychology / Association Européenne de Psychologie Sociale Expérimentale, c/o Faculté de Psychologie, Université de Louvain, 20 Voie du Roman Pays, 1348 Louvain-la-Neuve
T: (010) 474036; Fax: 472999
Founded: 1964; Members: 348
Focus: Psych
Periodical
European Journal of Social Psychology . 01100

European Association of Hearing Aid Audiologists / Association Européenne des Audioprothésistes, 16 Av Général Jourdan, 6220 Fleurus
Founded: 1968
Focus: Otorhinolaryngology 01101

European Association of Historical Associations, c/o Faculté de Philosophie et Lettres, Université Catholique de Louvain, 1348 Louvain-la-Neuve
Focus: Hist 01102

European Association of Metals / Association Européenne des Métaux, 12 Av de Broqueville, 1150 Bruxelles
T: (02) 7756311; Fax: 7790523
Founded: 1957; Members: 21
Gen Secr: Jacques Spaas
Focus: Metallurgy 01103

European Association of Podologists / Association Européenne des Podologues, 5 Av des Cormorans, 1150 Bruxelles
T: (02) 7713864
Focus: Med 01104

European Association of Radiology (EAR), c/o Dept of Radiology, University Hospital, Herestr 49, 3000 Leuven
T: (016) 213771; Fax: 213769
Founded: 1962; Members: 100
Gen Secr: Prof. Dr. Albert Baert
Focus: Radiology
Periodical
Newsletter 01105

European Association of Users of Satellites in Training and Education Programmes (EUROSTEP), c/o OXFAM Solidarity of Belgium, 39 Rue du Conseil, 1050 Bruxelles
T: (02) 5129990
Founded: 1964
Gen Secr: S. Declercq
Focus: Educ 01106

European Association of Veterinary Anatomists, c/o Faculty of Veterinary Medicine, Salisburylaan 133, 9820 Merelbeke
T: (09) 2647712; E-Mail: henri.lauwers@rug.ac.be; Fax: 2647790
Founded: 1964; Members: 270
Pres: Prof. Dr. Henri Lauwers; Gen Secr: Prof. Dr. Ignacio Salazar
Focus: Vet Med
Periodical
Anatomia, Histologia, Embryologia: Journal of Veterinary Medicine (4-6 times annually) . 01107

European Association on Catalysis / Association Européenne de Catalyse, c/o Dept de Chimie, Laboratoire de Catalyse, Faculté Universitaire de Namur, 61 Rue de Bruxelles, 5000 Namur
T: (081) 724554; Fax: 230391
Founded: 1980
Focus: Chem 01108

European Bitumen Association (EUROBITUME), c/o Centre d'Information du Bitume, 351 Blvd Emile Bockstael, 1020 Bruxelles
T: (02) 4782589
Founded: 1969
Focus: Materials Sci 01109

European Brain Injury Society (EBIS) / Association Européenne d'Etude des Traumatisés Crâniens et de leur Réinsertion, 17 Rue de Londres, 1050 Bruxelles
Founded: 1990
Focus: Neurology 01110

European Bureau for Conservation and Development (EBCD), 9 Rue de la Science, 1040 Bruxelles
T: (02) 2303070; Fax: 2308272
Founded: 1989
Focus: Ecology 01111

European Bureau of Lesser-Used Languages / Bureau Européen des Langues moins Répandues, 49 Rue Saint-Josse, 1210 Bruxelles
T: (02) 2182590; E-Mail: pub00341@innet.be; Fax: 2181974
Founded: 1982
Pres: Allan Wynne Jones; Gen Secr: D. O'Riagain
Focus: Ling 01112

European Burns Association (EBA), c/o Akademisch Ziekenhius Sint-Pieter, Katholiek Universiteit, 3000 Leuven
Focus: Derm 01113

European Business Ethics Network (EBEN), c/o EFMD, 40 Rue Washington, 1050 Bruxelles
T: (02) 6480385; Fax: 6460768
Founded: 1987; Members: 227
Focus: Philos 01114

European Cancer Prevention Organizazion / ECP, 1307 Chaussée de Waterloo, 1180 Bruxelles
Founded: 1981; Members: 120
Focus: Cell Biol & Cancer Res 01115

European Capitals Universities Network (UNICA), c/o International Relations Department, 28 Av Franklin Roosevelt, 1050 Bruxelles
T: (02) 6503152; E-Mail: unica@unica.ulb.ac.be; Fax: 6504243
Founded: 1990; Members: 24
Pres: Pierre Ducrey; Gen Secr: Chantal Zoller
Focus: Educ 01116

European Carbon Black Centre, 73 Av du Karreveld, 1180 Bruxelles
Founded: 1966
Focus: Energy 01117

European Centre for Ecotoxicology and Toxicology of Chemicals (ECETOC), 4 Av E. Van Nieuwenhuyse, 1160 Bruxelles
T: (02) 6753600; Fax: 6753625
Founded: 1978; Members: 53
Pres: J.J. van de Berg; Gen Secr: Dr. F.M. Carpanini
Focus: Ecology; Toxicology 01118

European Centre for Ethnolinguistic Cartography, 13 Rue Lenoir, 1090 Bruxelles
T: (02) 4285614; Fax: 4285614
Founded: 1986
Pres: Prof. Dr. Colin Williams; Gen Secr: Dr. Y.J.D. Peeters
Focus: Cart; Ling 01119

European Centre for Geodynamics and Seismology (ECGS), c/o Observatoire Royal, 3 Av Circulaire, 1180 Bruxelles
T: (02) 3730211; E-Mail: ducarme@oma.be; Fax: 3749822
Founded: 1988; Members: 9
Pres: J. Flick; Gen Secr: Dr. B. Ducarme
Focus: Geology 01120

European Centre for Plastics in the Environment, c/o APME, 4 Av Van Nieuwenhuyse, 1160 Bruxelles
T: (02) 6767211; Fax: 6767300
Focus: Ecology 01121

European Centre for Strategic Management of Universities (ESMU), 14 Rue Montoyer, 1040 Bruxelles
T: (02) 5138622; Fax: 5125743
Founded: 1986
Focus: Public Admin 01122

European Centre of Ophthalmology, 32 Rue du Méridien, 1030 Bruxelles
Founded: 1990
Focus: Ophthal 01123

European Centre of Studies on Linear Alkylbenzene, c/o ECOSOL, 4 Av E. Van Nieuwenhuyse, 1160 Bruxelles
T: (02) 6767246; Fax: 6767301
Founded: 1986
Gen Secr: Christian Jassogne
Focus: Chem 01124

European Chlorinated Solvents Association, 4 Av E. Van Nieuwenhuyse, 1160 Bruxelles
T: (02) 6767211; Fax: 6767301
Focus: Chem 01125

European Coil Coating Association (ECCA), 47 Rue Montoyer, 1040 Bruxelles
T: (02) 5136052; Fax: 5114361
Founded: 1967
Focus: Metallurgy 01126

European Committee for Catholic Education, 42 Rue de l'Industrie, 1040 Bruxelles
T: (02) 5118232; Fax: 5145989
Founded: 1974
Focus: Educ 01127

European Committee for Electrotechnical Standardization, 35 Rue de Stassart, 1050 Bruxelles
T: (02) 5196871; Fax: 5196919
Founded: 1973; Members: 14
Gen Secr: Stephen Marriott
Focus: Standards 01128

European Committee for Interoperable Systems (ECIS), c/o Bates & Wacker, 9 Rue du Moniteur, 1000 Bruxelles
T: (02) 2190305; Fax: 2193215
Founded: 1989
Focus: Computer & Info Sci 01129

European Committee for Iron and Steel Standardization (ECISS), c/o CEN, 36 Rue de Stassart, 1050 Bruxelles
T: (02) 5196811; Fax: 5196819
Focus: Standards 01130

European Committee for Treatment and Research in Multiple Sclerosis, c/o Belgisch Centrum voor Multiple Sclerosis, Vanheylenstr 16, 1910 Melsbroek
T: (02) 7518030
Focus: Med 01131

European Committee of Organic Surfactants and their Intermediates, 4 Av E. Van Nieuwenhuyse, 1160 Bruxelles
T: (02) 6767246; Fax: 6767301
Founded: 1974
Gen Secr: Christian Jassogne
Focus: Chem 01132

European Committee on Computational Methods in Applied Sciences (ECCOMAS), c/o VUB, Triomflaan 43, 1160 Bruxelles
T: (02) 6412878; Fax: 6412880
Focus: Computer & Info Sci 01133

European Community Biologists Association (ECBA), 175 Rue des Brasseurs, 5000 Namur
T: (081) 241133; Fax: 241164
Founded: 1975; Members: 17
Focus: Bio 01134

European Community Network of the National Academic Recognition Information Centres (NARIC), c/o Erasmus Bureau, 70 Rue Montoyer, 1040 Bruxelles
T: (02) 2330111; Fax: 2330150
Founded: 1984; Members: 20
Focus: Sci 01135

European Community University Professors in Ophthalmology (EUPO), c/o UZ Gent, De Pintelaan 185, 9000 Gent
T: (091) 402319; Fax: 404963
Founded: 1988; Members: 196
Focus: Ophthal 01136

European Confederation for EC Agricultural Engineers, c/o CEPFAR, 23-25 Rue de la Science, 1040 Bruxelles
T: (02) 2303445; E-Mail: sylvia.Oreifig@agr.kuleuven.ac.be; Fax: 2311845
Founded: 1987
Gen Secr: Sylvia Oreifig
Focus: Eng; Agri 01137

European Consumer Law Group (ECLG), c/o Faculté de Droit, UCL, 2 Pl Montesquieu, 1348 Louvain-la-Neuve
Founded: 1977; Members: 25
Focus: Law 01138

European Control Data Users Group (ECODU), c/o Rekenzentrum, Limburgs Universitaire Centrum, Universitaire Campus, 3590 Diepenbeek
T: (011) 286111
Founded: 1965
Focus: Computer & Info Sci 01139

European Convention for Constructional Steelwork (ECCS), 32-36 Av des Ombrages, 1200 Bruxelles
T: (02) 7620429; E-Mail: eccs@steelconstruct.com; Fax: 7620935
Founded: 1955
Gen Secr: R.V. Salkin
Focus: Civil Eng 01140

European Cooperation in the Field of Scientific and Technical Research, c/o Council of the European Communities, 170 Rue de la Loi, 1049 Bruxelles
T: (02) 2346111; Fax: 2347381
Founded: 1970; Members: 24
Focus: Sci; Eng 01141

European Council for Rural Law, c/o Vlaamse Landmaatschappij, 72 Av de la Toison d'Or, 1060 Bruxelles
T: (02) 5437208; Fax: 5437399
Founded: 1957
Pres: A. Lennon; Gen Secr: Marc Heyerick
Focus: Law 01142

European Council of Integrated Medicine (ECIM), 71 Rue des Echevins, 1050 Bruxelles
T: (02) 6483480
Focus: Med 01143

European Crop Protection Association (ECPA), 79a Av Albert Lancaster, 1180 Bruxelles
T: (02) 3756860; Fax: 3752793
Members: 30
Focus: Crop Husb 01144

European Down's Syndrome Association (EDSA), 41 Rue Victor Close, 4800 Verviers
T: (087) 223355; E-Mail: edsa-apem@fornado.be; Fax: 220716
Founded: 1987; Members: 50
Gen Secr: Richard Bonjean
Focus: Psych; Educ; Med 01145

European Economic Association (EEA), Naamsestr 69, 3000 Leuven
T: (016) 326911; Fax: 326910
Founded: 1985; Members: 1693
Pres: Prof. Reinhard Selten; Gen Secr: Prof. Anton Barten
Focus: Econ 01146

European Economic Research and Advisory Consortium (ERECO), 48 Rue du Cardinal, 1040 Bruxelles
T: (02) 2302212; Fax: 2306499
Founded: 1990
Focus: Econ 01147

European Educational Association for News Distribution, 20 Allée des Bouleaux, 6280 Gerpinnes
T: (071) 216153; Fax: 217713
Founded: 1971
Focus: Educ 01148

European Environment Agency (EEA), c/o CEC, Directorate General XI, 200 Rue de la Loi, 1049 Bruxelles
T: (02) 2351111; Fax: 2350138
Founded: 1990
Focus: Ecology 01149

European Environment Information and Observation Network, c/o CEC, Diretorate-General XI, 200 Rue de la Loi, 1049 Bruxelles
T: (02) 2968814; Fax: 2969562
Founded: 1990
Focus: Ecology 01150

European Environmental Bureau (EEB), 22-26 Rue de la Victoire, 1060 Bruxelles
T: (02) 5390037; Fax: 5390921
Founded: 1974; Members: 130
Gen Secr: John Hontelez
Focus: Ecology 01151

European Extruded Polystyrene Insulation Board Association (EXIBA), 4 Av E. Van Nieuwenhuyse, 1160 Bruxelles
T: (02) 6767247; Fax: 6767301
Founded: 1987; Members: 9
Gen Secr: D. Thomas
Focus: Materials Sci 01152

European Family Therapy Association (EFTA), 1 Rue Defacqz, 1050 Bruxelles
T: (02) 6401372
Focus: Therapeutics 01153

European Federation for the Education of Children of Occupational Travellers (EFECOT), 42 Rue de l'Industrie, 1040 Bruxelles
T: (02) 5118232; Fax: 5145989
Founded: 1988
Focus: Educ 01154

European Federation of Animal Health, 1 Rue Defacqz, 1000 Bruxelles
T: (02) 5437560; E-Mail: fedesa@fedesa.be; Fax: 5370049
Founded: 1987; Members: 35
Pres: Dr. R. Harsboom; Gen Secr: Dr. J. Vanhemelrijk
Focus: Vet Med
Periodical
Animal Health Focus (3 times annually) . 01155

European Federation of Child Neurology Societies (EFCNS), c/o Service de Neurologie Pédiatrique, UCL-Cliniques Universitaires Saint-Luc, 10 Av Hippocrate, 1200 Bruxelles
T: (02) 7641303; Fax: 7645231
Founded: 1970
Focus: Neurology 01156

European Federation of Energy Management Associations (EFEM), c/o Energik, Brouwersvliet 15, 2000 Antwerpen
T: (03) 2311660
Founded: 1986
Focus: Business Admin 01157

European Finance Association, 13 Rue d'Egmont, 1000 Bruxelles
T: (02) 5119116; E-Mail: efa@eiasm.be; Fax: 5121929
Pres: Prof. Dag Michalsen
Focus: Educ; Finance
Periodical
Newsletter (semi-annually) 01158

European International Business Academy, c/o EIASM, 13 Rue d'Egmont, 1000 Bruxelles
T: (02) 5119116; E-Mail: eiba@eiasm.be; Fax: 5121929
Founded: 1974; Members: 300
Pres: Prof. Klaus Macharzina
Focus: Adult Educ
Periodical
Newsletter (semi-annually) 01159

European Power Electronics and Drives Association, 2 Blvd de la Plaine, 1050 Bruxelles
T: (02) 6412819
Founded: 1989; Members: 300
Focus: Electronic Eng
Periodical
EPE Journal (quarterly) 01160

European Society for Radiation Biology, c/o Dept de Pathologie, Hôpital Universitaire, 4000 Liège
Founded: 1959
Focus: Bio; Radiology
Periodical
International Journal of Radiation Biology 01161

European Society of Nematologists, c/o Centrum Landbk. Onderzoek, Burg. Van Gansberghelaan 96, 9820 Merkelbeke
T: (09) 2720271; E-Mail: m.moens@clo.fgov.be; Fax: 2720215
Founded: 1955; Members: 510
Pres: Dr. D.L. Trudgill; Gen Secr: Dr. M. Moens
Focus: Zoology 01162

European Technical Association for Protective Coatings (E.T.A.P.C.), Korenstr 6-8, 2170 Merksem
T: (03) 6463373; Fax: 6454905
Founded: 1972
Pres: W. Viaene; Gen Secr: K. Mertes
Focus: Materials Sci 01163

European Trade Union Institute (ETUI), 155 Blvd Emile Jacqmain, 1210 Bruxelles
T: (02) 2240470; E-Mail: etui@etuc.org; Fax: 2240502
Founded: 1978
Focus: Socialism; Sociology; Econ; Poli Sci
Periodicals
ETUI Documentation Centre Bulletin (quarterly)
ETUI INFOletter (irregularly)
Transfer (quarterly) 01164

EURYDICE / Education Information Network Europe, 15 Rue d'Arlon, 1050 Bruxelles
T: (02) 2383011; E-Mail: EURYDICE.UEE@infoboard.be; Fax: 2306562
Founded: 1980; Members: 25
Gen Secr: Luce Pépin
Focus: Educ
Periodical
EURYDICE Info (2-3 times annually) . . 01165

Fédération Belge d'Education Physique (FBEP), c/o Free-University, 1050 Bruxelles
T: (02) 3581446
Founded: 1923; Members: 3000
Focus: Sports 01166

Fédération Belge des Chambres Syndicales de Médecins (FBCSM), 15 Rue du Château, 1420 Braine l'Allend
T: 3843930
Founded: 1963; Members: 4000
Focus: Med 01167

Fédération de l'Enseignement Secondaire Catholique, 1 Rue Guimard, 1040 Bruxelles
T: (02) 5070759; Fax: 5070746
Members: 307
Gen Secr: Etienne Florkin
Focus: Educ 01168

Fédération Européenne de Médecine Physique et Réadaption / European Federation for Physical Medicine and Rehabilitation, c/o Kliniek voor Fysiotherapie en Orthopedie, De Pintelaan 185, 9000 Gent
T: (09) 2402234; Fax: 2404975
Founded: 1963
Focus: Med; Physical Therapy; Rehabil
Periodicals
Europa Medicophysica
European Journal of Physical Medicine and Rehabilitation (bi-monthly) 01169

Fédération Internationale des Instituts de Recherches Socio-Religieuses (FERES), 5 Av Sainte-Gertrude, 1348 Louvain-la-Neuve
T: (010) 450822
Founded: 1958; Members: 38
Focus: Sociology; Rel & Theol
Periodical
Social Compass: International Review of Sociology of Religion (quarterly) 01170

Federation of Veterinarians of Europe, 41 Av Fonsny, 1060 Bruxelles
T: (02) 25382963; Fax: 5372828
Founded: 1961
Focus: Vet Med 01171

Fédération Royale des Sociétés d'Architectes de Belgique (FAB), 537 Blvd de Smet de Naeyer, 1020 Bruxelles
Members: 16
Gen Secr: E. Draps
Focus: Archit 01172

Fondation Archéologique / Archaeological Foundation, c/o Université Libre de Bruxelles, 50 Av Franklin Roosevelt, 1050 Bruxelles
T: (02) 6502421; Fax: 6502450
Founded: 1930
Focus: Archeol
Periodical
Culture et Cité 01173

Fondation Egyptologique Reine Elisabeth, 10 Parc du Cinquantenaire, 1040 Bruxelles
T: (02) 7417364
Founded: 1923; Members: 650
Pres: Comte d' Arschot
Focus: Anthro; Ethnology; Archeol
Periodicals
Bibliographie Papyrologique (bi-monthly)
Chronique d'Egypte (semi-annually) . . . 01174

Fondation Fernand Lazard, 11 Rue d'Egmont, 1050 Bruxelles
Founded: 1949
Focus: Educ 01175

Geologica Belgica, 13 Rue Jenner, 1000 Bruxelles
T: (02) 6270410; Fax: 6477359
Founded: 1887; Members: 650
Pres: J. Verniers; Gen Secr: M. Dusar
Focus: Geology 01176

Groupe Belge d'Etude de l'Arriération Mentale, 66 Rue de la Limite, 1030 Bruxelles
Focus: Educ Handic
Periodical
Proceedings (irregularly) 01177

Groupement Belge des Omnipraticiens (GBO), 76 Rue du Tabellion, 1050 Bruxelles
T: (02) 5387365; Fax: 5385105
Founded: 1968
Pres: Dr. Philippe Vandermeeren; Gen Secr: Jean Michael Melis
Focus: Med
Periodical
GBO (10 times annually) 01178

Groupement des Unions Professionnelles Belges de Médecins Spécialistes (GBS), 20 Av de la Couronne, 1050 Bruxelles
T: (02) 6492147; Fax: 6492690
Members: 21
Focus: Med
Periodical
Le Médecin Spécialiste (10 times annually) 01179

Groupement International pour la Recherche Scientifique en Odontologie et en Stomatologie (GIRSO), 322 Rue Haute, 1000 Bruxelles
T: (02) 5380000
Founded: 1956; Members: 200
Focus: Dent; Stomatology 01180

Groupement International pour la Recherche Scientifique en Stomatologie et Odontologie (GIRSO), 19 Av Jeanne, 1050 Bruxelles
T: (02) 6482481
Founded: 1956; Members: 200
Focus: Stomatology; Dent
Periodical
Bulletin du GIRSO (quarterly) 01181

Icon / Association on Marginal Literature and Art, Lobergenbos 27, 3200 Leuven
Focus: Lit; Arts
Periodical
Cahier (annually) 01182

INBEL, Institut Belge d'Information et de Documentation, 155 Rue de la Loi, 1040 Bruxelles
T: (02) 2874111; Fax: 2874100
Founded: 1962
Focus: Doc
Periodical
FAITS/FEITEN (weekly) 01183

Institut Archéologique du Luxembourg (IAL), 13 Rue des Martyrs, 6700 Arlon
T: (063) 221236
Founded: 1847; Members: 800
Pres: Roger Petit; Gen Secr: Louis Lefebvre
Focus: Archeol; Hist; Folklore; Genealogy; Arts; Numismatics
Periodicals
Annales de l'Institut Archéologique du Luxembourg (annually)
Bulletin (semi-annually) 01184

Institut Archéologique Liégeois (IAL), c/o Musée Curtius, 13 Quai de Maastricht, 4000 Liège
Founded: 1850; Members: 450
Pres: Jean-Louis Kupper; Gen Secr: B. Dumont
Focus: Archeol; Hist
Periodical
Bulletin de l'Institut Archéologique Liègeois (annually) 01185

Institut Belge de Droit Comparé, 14 Rue Bosquet, 1060 Bruxelles
T: (02) 5380618
Founded: 1907; Members: 400
Pres: M. Vauthier; Gen Secr: Paul Landrien
Focus: Law
Periodical
La Revue de Droit International et de Droit Comparé (quarterly) 01186

Institut Belge de la Soudure (IBS), 21 Rue des Drapiers, 1050 Bruxelles
T: (02) 5122892; Fax: 5127457
Founded: 1942; Members: 315
Focus: Eng
Periodical
Revue de la Soudure-Lastijdschrift (quarterly) 01187

Institut Belge de Normalisation (IBN), 29 Av de la Brabançonne, 1040 Bruxelles
T: (02) 7349205; Fax: 7334264
Founded: 1946; Members: 962
Gen Secr: P. Croon
Focus: Standards
Periodical
Revue IBN (10 times annually) 01188

Institut Belge de Régulation et d'Automatisme (IBRA), 3 Rue Ravenstein, 1000 Bruxelles
T: (02) 5117004; Fax: 5117004
Founded: 1955; Members: 500
Focus: Eng
Periodicals
Automatique (3 times annually)
Journal A.: Benelux Quarterly Journal on Automatic Control 01189

Institut Belge des Hautes Etudes Chinoises, c/o Musées Royaux d'Art et d'Histoire, 10 Parc du Cinquantenaire, 1000 Bruxelles
T: (02) 7417355, 7417342, 7417377; Fax: 7337735
Founded: 1929; Members: 400
Pres: P. Willockx
Focus: Ling; Philos; Hist; Rel & Theol; Arts; Archeol
Periodical
Mélanges Chinois et Bouddhiques (irregularly) 01190

Institut Belge des Sciences Administratives (I.B.S.A.), Bewindstr 15, 1000 Bruxelles
Founded: 1936; Members: 150
Pres: W. Lambrechts
Focus: Business Admin
Periodical
Administration Publique (monthly) 01191

Institut Européen d'Ecologie et de Cancérologie, 24bis Rue des Fripiers, 1000 Bruxelles
T: (02) 2190830
Founded: 1965
Focus: Ecology; Cell Biol & Cancer Res
Periodical
Medicine-Biology-Environment (semi-annually) 01192

Institut Européen des Armes de Chasse et de Sport, 3 Rue Charles Morren, 4000 Liège
T: (041) 533986, 713778; Fax: 533989
Founded: 1977; Members: 8
Focus: Eng 01193

Institut Européen Interuniversitaire de l'Action Sociale (IEIAS), 179 Rue du Debarcadère, 6001 Marcinelle
T: (071) 447211; Fax: 471104
Founded: 1970
Pres: Joseph Gillain; Gen Secr: Serge Mayence
Focus: Sociology; Soc Sci; Geriatrics . . 01194

Institut Géographique National, 13 Abbaye de la Cambre, 1050 Bruxelles
T: (02) 6486480; Fax: 6462542
Founded: 1831; Members: 450
Gen Secr: J. de Smet
Focus: Geography 01195

Institut Historique Belge de Rome (I.H.B.R.), 3 Av du Derby, 1050 Bruxelles
T: (02) 6492381
Founded: 1902
Focus: Hist 01196

Institut International de Recherches Betteravières (I.I.R.B.) / International Institute for Sugar Beeb Research, 47 Rue Montoyer, 1000 Bruxelles
T: (02) 5091530/33; E-Mail: iirb@areadis.be; Fax: 5126506
Founded: 1932; Members: 600
Pres: H.R. Dvas; Gen Secr: R. Beckers
Focus: Agri
Periodical
Proceedings (annually) 01197

Institut International des Sciences Administratives (IISA) / International Institute of Administrative Sciences, 1 Rue Defacqz, 1050 Bruxelles
T: (02) 5389165; E-Mail: INTERADMIN; Fax: 5379702
Founded: 1930; Members: 48
Focus: Public Admin
Periodicals
Infoadmin (annually)
International Review of Administrative Sciences (quarterly) 01198

Institut National de Cinématographie Scientifique de Belgique, 29 Rue Vautier, 1000 Bruxelles
T: (02) 6274225
Pres: Prof. G. Thines; Gen Secr: A. Quintart
Focus: Cinema 01199

Institut Royal Belge du Pétrole (IBP), 4 Rue de la Science, 1040 Bruxelles
T: (02) 5728767; Fax: 4480825
Founded: 1937; Members: 612
Focus: Materials Sci
Periodical
Annales/Annalen (quarterly) 01200

Institut Royal des Relations Internationales (IRRI), 65 Rue Belliard, 1040 Bruxelles
T: (02) 2302230; Fax: 2305230
Founded: 1947; Members: 1200
Pres: Vicomte E. Davignon; Gen Secr: M.T. Bockstaele
Focus: Poli Sci; Law; Econ
Periodical
Studia Diplomatica (bi-monthly) 01201

International Committee of Dialectologists, c/o Centre International de Dialectologie Générale, Université Catholique, Ravenstr 46, 3000 Leuven
Focus: Ling 01202

International Council of Onomastic Sciences (ICOS), c/o International Centre of Onomastics, Blijde Inkomststr 21, 3000 Leuven
T: (016) 324819; Fax: 324767
Founded: 1949; Members: 200
Gen Secr: Prof. Dr. R. Rentenaar
Focus: Ling
Periodical
Onoma 01203

International Diabetes Federation (IDF), 40 Rue Washington, 1050 Bruxelles
T: (02) 6474414; Fax: 6408565
Founded: 1949; Members: 1675
Focus: Diabetes
Periodicals
IDF Bulletin (3 times annually)
IDF Newsletter (3 times annually) . . . 01204

International Educational and Cultural Association (ITECA), Merellaan 10, 1150 Bruxelles
T: (02) 6738437
Focus: Educ 01205

International Institute for Organizational and Social Development (I.O.D.), Predikherenberg 55, 3010 Leuven
T: (016) 251671; E-Mail: iod@glo.be; Fax: 251680
Founded: 1970; Members: 6
Gen Secr: Thérèse vanden Bempt
Focus: Business Admin 01206

International Institute of Cellular and Molecular Pathology, 75 Av Hippocrate, 1200 Bruxelles
T: (02) 7647550; Fax: 7647573
Founded: 1974; Members: 200
Pres: Prof. Dr. T. Boon; Gen Secr: P. Penninckx
Focus: Pathology
Periodical
Scientific Report (annually) 01207

International Iron and Steel Institute, 120 Rue Colonel Bourg, 1140 Bruxelles
T: (02) 7028900; Fax: 7028899
Founded: 1967; Members: 175
Gen Secr: L.J. Holschuh
Focus: Metallurgy
Periodicals
Bulletin
Conference Proceedings
Statistical and Economic Reports
Technical Surveys
World Steel in Figures 01208

International League of Societies for Persons with Mental Handicap, 248 Av Louise, 1050 Bruxelles
T: (02) 6476180; Fax: 6472969
Founded: 1960; Members: 149
Focus: Rehabil
Periodical
News of the International League (semi-annually) 01209

International PEN Club, Flemish Centre, Luchtlaan 4, 1710 Dilbeek
Gen Secr: Willem M. Roggeman
Focus: Lit
Periodical
PEN-Tijdingen (quarterly) 01210

International PEN Club, French Speaking Branch, 10 Av des Cerfs, 1950 Kraainem
T: (02) 7314847; Fax: 7314847
Founded: 1922; Members: 370
Pres: Georges Sion; Gen Secr: Huguette de Broqueville
Focus: Lit 01211

International Rhinologic Society (IRS), c/o ENT Dept A.Z-V.U.B., Laarbeeklaan 101, 1090 Bruxelles
T: (02) 4776422; Fax: 4776423
Founded: 1965; Members: 5000
Gen Secr: P.A.R. Clement
Focus: Otorhinolaryngology
Periodicals
Journal (quarterly)
Journal of Rhinology (annually) 01212

International Secretariat for University Study of Education, Baertsoenkaai 3, 9000 Gent
Focus: Educ 01213

International Union for the Scientific Study of Population, 34 Rue des Augustins, 4000 Liège
T: (041) 224080; Fax: 223847
Founded: 1928; Members: 1900
Focus: Sociology
Periodical
UIESP Newsletter 01214

Internationale de l'Education / Education International, 155 Blvd E. Jacqmain, 1210 Bruxelles
T: (02) 2240611; Fax: 2240606
Founded: 1951 (1993)
Gen Secr: Fred van Leeuwen
Focus: Educ 01215

Koninklijk Aardrijkskundig Genootschap van Antwerpen, Frankrijklei 64, 2000 Antwerpen
Founded: 1876; Members: 455
Pres: René della Faille de Waerloos; Gen Secr: P. Vincentelli
Focus: Geography 01216

Koninklijk Sterrenkundige Genootschap van Antwerpen, Boerhaavestr 94, 2008 Antwerpen
Founded: 1905; Members: 230
Pres: Willy de Kort; Gen Secr: Baron R. de Terwangne
Focus: Astronomy 01217

Koninklijke Academie en Nationaal Hoger Instituut voor Schone Kunsten (KASKA-NHISKA), Mutsaertstr 31, 2000 Antwerpen
T: (03) 2314186, 2324161, 2335619
Founded: 1663; Members: 87
Focus: Arts 01218

Koninklijke Academie voor Geneeskunde van België, Hertogsstr 1, 1000 Bruxelles
Founded: 1938; Members: 162
Pres: Prof. Dr. P. de Schouwer; Gen Secr: Prof. Dr. M. Bogaert
Focus: Med
Periodical
Verhandelingen (bi-monthly) 01219

Koninklijke Academie voor Nederlandse Taal- en Letterkunde (KANTL), Koningstr 18, 9000 Gent
T: (09) 2659340; Fax: 2659349
Founded: 1886; Members: 30
Gen Secr: Prof. Dr. Georges de Schutter
Focus: Ling; Lit
Periodical
Verslagen en Mededelingen (2-3 times annually) 01220

Koninklijke Academie voor Wetenschappen, Letteren en Schone Kunsten van België, Hertogsstr 1, 1000 Bruxelles
T: (02) 5112623; Fax: 5110143
Founded: 1938; Members: 289
Pres: J. Ijsewijn; Gen Secr: G. Verbeke
Focus: Fine Arts; Law; Philos; Humanities; Hist; Rel & Theol; Music; Nat Sci; Eng; Ling; Lit
Periodicals
Academiae Analecta: Mededelingen van de K.A.W.L.S.K. Klasse der Letteren (irregularly)
Academiae Analecta: Mededelingen van de K.A.W.L.S.K. Klasse der Schone Kunsten (irregularly)
Academiae Analecta: Mededelingen van de K.A.W.L.S.K. Klasse der Wetenschappen (irregularly)
Jaarboek (annually) 01221

Koninklijke Belgische Vereniging voor Dermatologie en Venerologie / Société Royale Belge de Dermatologie et de Vénérologie, c/o Dr. J. De Weert, Vrijheidslaan 20, 9000 Gent
T: (09) 2402287; Fax: 2404996
Founded: 1901; Members: 517
Pres: Prof. D. Roseeuw; Gen Secr: Dr. J. de Weert
Focus: Derm; Venereology 01222

Koninklijke Maatschappij voor Dierkunde van Antwerpen / Royal Zoological Society of Antwerp, Koningin Astridplein 26, 2018 Antwerpen
T: (03) 2024540; Fax: 2024547
Founded: 1843; Members: 19300
Gen Secr: F.J. Daman
Focus: Zoology
Periodical
Zoo (quarterly) 01223

Koninklijke Vereniging voor Natuur- en Stedeschoon, Koningin Astridplein 24, 2018 Antwerpen
T: (03) 2323531; Fax: 2323531
Founded: 1910; Members: 1250
Pres: Rutger Steenmeijer; Gen Secr: Hélène Lacor
Focus: Ecology; Urban Plan
Periodical
Natuur- en Stedeschoon (bi-monthly) . . 01224

Koninklijke Vereniging voor Vogel- en Natuurstudie de Wielewaal, Graatakker 11, 2300 Turnhout
T: (014) 412252; Fax: 439651
Founded: 1933; Members: 10000
Pres: Luc Meul; Gen Secr: Luc van Gompel
Focus: Ornithology
Periodicals
Oriolus (quarterly)
Wielewaal (bi-monthly) 01225

Koninklijke Vlaamse Chemische Vereniging, Coupure Rechts, 9000 Gent
T: (09) 2233373; Fax: 2233455
Founded: 1939; Members: 1500
Pres: Dr. J. Engelmann
Focus: Chem 01226

Koninklijke Vlaamse Ingenieursvereniging, Desguinlei 214, 2018 Antwerpen
T: (03) 2160996; Fax: 2160689
Founded: 1928; Members: 11900
Pres: M. Naze; Gen Secr: L. Monserez
Focus: Eng 01227

Ligue Belge contre l'Epilepsie, 135 Av Albert, 1190 Bruxelles
T: (02) 3443263; Fax: 3461193
Founded: 1955
Focus: Pathology 01228

Les Naturalistes Belges, 29 Rue Vautier, 1000 Bruxelles
Founded: 1918; Members: 1000
Pres: Alain Quintart
Focus: Nat Sci
Periodical
Bulletin (quarterly) 01229

Oeuvre Belge du Cancer (OBC), 217 Rue Royale, 1210 Bruxelles
T: (02) 2258211; Fax: 2258290
Founded: 1950
Focus: Cell Biol & Cancer Res 01230

Office Généalogique et Héraldique de Belgique, 93 Av Charles Thielemans, 1150 Bruxelles
T: (02) 7725027
Founded: 1942
Focus: Genealogy
Periodicals
Le Héraut (quarterly)
Le Parchemin (bi-monthly)
Le Recueil Généalogique et Héraldique de Belgique (annually) 01231

Office International de l'Enseignement Catholique (OIEC), 60 Rue des Eburons, 1040 Bruxelles
T: (02) 2307252
Founded: 1952; Members: 84
Focus: Educ; Rel & Theol
Periodical
Bulletin de l'OIEC (bi-monthly) 01232

Ordre des Architectes / Orde van Architecten, Livornostr 160, 1050 Bruxelles
T: (02) 6470669; Fax: 6463818
Founded: 1963; Members: 8000
Focus: Archit 01233

Politologisch Instituut, Van Evenstr 2b, 3000 Leuven
T: (016) 323254; Fax: 323088
Founded: 1958; Members: 600
Pres: Wilfried Dewachter
Focus: Poli Sci 01234

Ruusbroecgenootschap, Prinsstr 13, 2000 Antwerpen
T: (03) 2204367; Fax: 2204420
Founded: 1925; Members: 7
Pres: Dr. G. de Baere
Focus: Rel & Theol
Periodical
Ons Geestelijk Erf (quarterly) 01235

Societas Logopedica Latina, 69 Rue de Bruxelles, 3000 Leuven
Founded: 1967; Members: 300
Focus: Logopedy 01236

Société Archéologique de Namur, Hôtel de Gaiffier d'Hestroy, 24 Rue de Fer, 5000 Namur
T: (081) 224362; Fax: 224362
Founded: 1845; Members: 430
Pres: Cécile Douxechamps-Lefevre; Gen Secr: Jacques Toussaint
Focus: Archeol; Hist
Periodical
Annales de la Société Archéologique de Namur (ASAN) (annually) 01237

Société Astronomique de Liège (SAL), c/o Institut d'Astrophysique, 5 Av de Cointe, 4000 Liège
T: (04) 2533590
Founded: 1938; Members: 800
Pres: A. Lausberg; Gen Secr: L. Pauquay
Focus: Astronomy
Periodical
Le Ciel (monthly) 01238

Société Belge d'Allergologie et d'immunologie Clinique, c/o Academic Hospital, De Pintelaan 185, 9000 Gent
Founded: 1946; Members: 250
Focus: Immunology 01239

Société Belge d'Anesthésie et de Réanimation / Belgische Vereniging voor Anesthesie en Reanimatie / Belgian Society of Anaesthesia and Resuscitation, c/o Dept of Anesthesiology, University Hospital, De Pintelaan 185, 9000 Gent
T: (09) 2403281; Fax: 2404987
Founded: 1963; Members: 705
Pres: Prof. Dr. A. d' Hollander; Gen Secr: Prof. Dr. G. Rolly
Focus: Anesthetics
Periodical
Acta Anaesthesiologica Belgica (quarterly) 01240

Société Belge de Biochimie et de Biologie Moléculaire, 75 Av Hippocrate, 1200 Bruxelles
T: (02) 7647451; Fax: 7647573
Founded: 1951; Members: 1050
Gen Secr: Philippe Hoet
Focus: Biochem; Biophys 01241

Société Belge de Cardiologie, 43 Rue des Champs-Elysées, 1050 Bruxelles
Fax: (02) 4776381
Focus: Cardiol
Periodicals
Acta Cardiologica Belgica (bi-monthly)
News Bulletin (semi-annually) 01242

Société Belge de Géologie (SBG), 13 Rue Jenner, 1000 Bruxelles
T: (02) 6270410; Fax: 6477359
Founded: 1887; Members: 430
Pres: Léon Dejonghe; Gen Secr: Vos. W. de
Focus: Geology
Periodical
Géologie (annually) 01243

Société Belge de Médecine Tropicale, Nationalestr 155, 2000 Antwerpen
Founded: 1920; Members: 545
Gen Secr: Prof. Dr. B. Gryseels
Focus: Trop Med 01244

Société Belge de Microscopie Electronique (SBME), c/o CRM, 69 Rue du Val-Benot, 4000 Liège
T: (041) 527050
Founded: 1966; Members: 160
Focus: Electronic Eng 01245

Société Belge de Musicologie, 30 Rue de la Régence, 1000 Bruxelles
E-Mail: vanhulst@ulb.ac.be
Founded: 1946; Members: 300
Pres: R. Wangermee; Gen Secr: H. Vanhulst
Focus: Music
Periodical
Revue Belge de Musicology (annually) . 01246

Société Belge de Pédiatrie, 20 Av de la Couronne, 1050 Bruxelles
T: (02) 6492147
Founded: 1926; Members: 650
Gen Secr: Prof. J. Ramet
Focus: Pediatrics 01247

Société Belge de Philosophie, c/o Institut de Philosophie, 143 Av Adolphe Buyl, 1050 Bruxelles
Fax: (02) 6503647
Founded: 1920; Members: 100
Focus: Philos 01248

Société Belge de Photogrammétrie, de Télédétection et de Cartographie, C.A.E.-Tour Finances, 50 Blvd du Jardin Botanique, 1010 Bruxelles
Founded: 1931; Members: 163
Pres: R. Thonnard; Gen Secr: José Van Hemelrijck
Focus: Surveying; Cart
Periodical
Bulletin (quarterly) 01249

Société Belge de Physique (S.B.P.) / Belgische Natuurkundige Vereniging / Belgian Physical Society, c/o Belgisch Instituut voor Ruimte-Aéronomie, 3 Av Circulaire, 1180 Bruxelles
Founded: 1929; Members: 470
Gen Secr: Dr. Johan Ingels
Focus: Physics
Periodicals
Physicalia Info (bi-monthly)
Physicalia Magazine (quarterly) 01250

Société Belge de Psychologie (SBP), Dieweg 47, 1180 Bruxelles
T: (02) 3742896
Founded: 1946; Members: 450
Focus: Psych 01251

Société Belge de Vacuologie et de Vacuotechnique, 30 Av de la Renaissance, 1040 Bruxelles
Founded: 1963; Members: 62
Focus: Physics; Eng 01252

Société Belge d'Ergologie (SBE), 46 Av Michel Ange, 1040 Bruxelles
T: (02) 7330952
Founded: 1935; Members: 2000
Focus: Eng 01253

Société Belge des Auteurs, Compositeurs et Editeurs (SABAM), 75-77 Rue d'Arlon, 1040 Bruxelles
T: (02) 2302660; Fax: 2311800
Founded: 1922; Members: 11000
Pres: Vic Legley
Focus: Lit; Music
Periodical
Bulletin (3 times annually) 01254

Société Belge des Urbanistes et Architectes Modernistes, 366 Av Brugmann, 1180 Bruxelles
E-Mail: BIBREG.Bru
Founded: 1919
Gen Secr: L. Obizinski
Focus: Archit; Urban Plan 01255

Société Belge d'Etudes Byzantines, 4 Blvd de l'Empereur, 1000 Bruxelles
Founded: 1956; Members: 75
Pres: Edmond Voordeckers; Gen Secr: José Declerck
Focus: Hist
Periodical
Byzantion: Revue Internationale des Etudes Byzantines (semi-annually) 01256

Société Belge d'Histoire des Hôpitaux, c/o Archives de l'Assistance Publique, 298a Rue Haute, 1000 Bruxelles
Founded: 1963
Focus: Hist 01257

Société Belge d'Ophthalmologie, Section Francophone, c/o Hôpital Saint-Luc, 10 Av Hippocrate, 1200 Bruxelles
Founded: 1896; Members: 550
Pres: Prof. J.M. Lemagne
Focus: Ophthal
Periodical
Bulletin (quarterly) 01258

Société Beneluxienne de Métallurgie, 43 Rue des Champs-Elysees, 1050 Bruxelles
Focus: Metallurgy 01259

Société Centrale d'Architecture de Belgique (S.C.A.B.), 3 Rue Ravenstein, 1000 Bruxelles
T: (02) 5113492
Founded: 1872; Members: 180
Pres: Jean-Pierre Sainte-Nois; Gen Secr: Ghislain Ladrière
Focus: Archit
Periodical
Bulletin Mensuel (monthly) 01260

Société de Langue et de Littérature Wallonnes, c/o Université de Liège, 7 Pl du XX Août, 4000 Liège
T: (086) 344432
Founded: 1856; Members: 400
Pres: Emile Giuiard; Gen Secr: Victor George
Focus: Ling; Lit
Periodicals
Dialectes de Wallonie (annually)
Wallonnes 01261

Société d'Ergonomie de Langue Française, c/o ERGODIN, 64 Rue d'Ophem, 1000 Bruxelles
T: (02) 2181667
Founded: 1963; Members: 378
Pres: Francis Six; Gen Secr: Dina Notte
Focus: Physiology; Eng; Psych; Soc Sci 01262

Société des Bollandistes, 24 Blvd Saint-Michel, 1040 Bruxelles
E-Mail: socboll@lib.kbr.be; Fax: (02) 7393332
Founded: 1630; Members: 8
Pres: Joseph van der Straeten; Gen Secr: Bernard Joassart
Focus: Hist; Rel & Theol
Periodical
Analecta Bollandiana (semi-annually) . . 01263

Société des Physiciens des Hôpitaux d'Expression Française, c/o Service de Radiothérapie, Hôpital de Bavière, 66 Blvd de la Constitution, 4020 Liège
Focus: Physiology 01264

Société d'Etudes Latines de Bruxelles, 6 Rue du Palais Saint-Jacques, 7500 Tournai
T: (069) 214713; Fax: 214713
Founded: 1937; Members: 750
Pres: C. Deroux; Gen Secr: J. Dumortier-Bibauw
Focus: Ling; Hist; Archeol
Periodical
Latomus: Revue d'Etudes Latines . . . 01265

Société Européenne pour la Formation des Ingénieurs / European Society for Engineering Education, 60 Rue de la Concorde, 1050 Bruxelles
T: (02) 5409770; E-Mail: françoise.côme@infoboard.be; Fax: 5409715
Founded: 1973; Members: 500
Pres: Dr. Walter Schaufelberger; Gen Secr: Françoise Côme
Focus: Educ; Eng
Periodicals
European Journal of Engineering Education (quarterly)
SEFI-News (bi-monthly) 01266

Société Géologique de Belgique (S.G.B.), c/o Université, Sart-Tilman, Bâtiment 12, 4000 Liège
T: (041) 3655395; Fax: 43665722
Founded: 1874; Members: 458
Pres: Michel Vanquestaine; Gen Secr: Muriel Demaret
Focus: Geology
Periodical
Annales (semi-annually) 01267

Société Internationale de Chirurgie Orthopédique et de Traumatologie (SICOT), 40 Rue Washington, 1050 Bruxelles
T: (02) 6486823; Fax: 6498601
Founded: 1929; Members: 2496
Focus: Surgery; Traumatology
Periodical
International Orthopaedics (bi-monthly) . . 01268

Société Internationale de Droit Pénal Militaire et de Droit de la Guerre, c/o Auditorat Général près de la Cour Militaire, Palais de Justice, 1000 Bruxelles
Fax: (02) 5086085
Founded: 1956
Focus: Law
Periodical
The Military Law and Law of War Review (annually) 01269

Société Internationale pour la Recherche sur les Maladies de Civilisation et sur l'Environnement (SIRMCE) / International Society for Research on Civilization Diseases and on Environment, 20 Sq Larousse, 1060 Bruxelles
T: (02) 3430461
Founded: 1973; Members: 700
Focus: Med; Ecology; Public Health
Periodical
Congress Proceedings 01270

Société Internationale pour l'Etude de la Philosophie Médiévale (S.I.E.P.M.), c/o Collège Mercier, 14 Pl du Cardinal Mercier, 1348 Louvain-la-Neuve
T: (010) 474807; E-Mail: danhier@sofi.ucl.ac.be; Fax: 478285
Founded: 1959; Members: 523
Pres: Albert Zimmermann; Gen Secr: Jacqueline Hamesse
Focus: Philos
Periodical
Bulletin de Philosophie Médievale (annually) 01271

Société Mathématique de Belgique, ULB Campus Plaine, Blvd du Triomphe, BP 218/01, 1050 Bruxelles
Founded: 1921; Members: 500
Gen Secr: Jules Leroy
Focus: Math
Periodical
Bulletin (quarterly) 01272

Société Nationale de Laiterie, 95-99 Rue Froissart, 1040 Bruxelles
T: (02) 2381611; Fax: 2306503
Founded: 1903
Pres: R. Desmedt; Gen Secr: E. Dobbelaere
Focus: Dairy Sci 01273

Société Philosophique de Bruxelles, 79 Blvd Mettewie, BP 19, 1080 Bruxelles
T: (02) 4663345
Founded: 1980; Members: 30
Pres: J. Sojcher; Gen Secr: G. Hottois
Focus: Med 01274

Société Philosophique de Louvain, c/o Institut Supérieur de Philosophie, Collège Thomas More, 1 Chemin d'Aristote, 1348 Louvain-la-Neuve
T: (010) 474613
Founded: 1888; Members: 225
Pres: Ghislaine Florival; Gen Secr: J. Etienne
Focus: Philos 01275

Société Royale Belge d'Anthropologie et de Préhistoire, 29 Rue Vautier, 1000 Bruxelles
T: (02) 6274385; Fax: 6274113
Founded: 1882; Members: 135
Pres: Rosine Orban; Gen Secr: Anne Hauzeur
Focus: Anthro; Hist; Archeol
Periodicals
Anthropologie et Préhistoire (annually)
Hominid Remains: An Up-date (irregularly) 01276

Société Royale Belge d'Astronomie, de Météorologie et de Physique du Globe, 3 Av Circulaire, 1180 Bruxelles
T: (02) 3730253; Fax: 3749822
Founded: 1895; Members: 750
Pres: Léo Houziaux; Gen Secr: T. Camelbeeck
Focus: Astronomy; Geophys
Periodical
Ciel et Terre (bi-monthly) 01277

Société Royale Belge de Chirurgie / Royal Belgian Society of Surgery, 138a Av Circulaire, 1180 Bruxelles
Founded: 1893; Members: 1000
Focus: Surgery
Periodical
Acta Chirurgica Belgica (bi-monthly) . . 01278

Société Royale Belge de Géographie (SRBG), c/o Institut de Géographie, Campus de la Plaine ULB, Blvd du Triomphe, CP 246, 1050 Bruxelles
T: (02) 6505073; Fax: 6505092
Founded: 1876; Members: 400
Pres: H. Nicolai; Gen Secr: J.-M. Decroly
Focus: Geography
Periodical
Revue Belge de Géographie (irregularly) 01279

Société Royale Belge de Gynécologie et d'Obstétrique, 309 Av Molière, 1060 Bruxelles
Founded: 1889
Focus: Gynecology 01280

Société Royale Belge de Médecine Physique et de Réhabilitation, 37 Blvd Louis Smidt, 1040 Bruxelles
Founded: 1937; Members: 262
Focus: Rehabil; Physiology 01281

Société Royale Belge de Rheumatologie, 33 Rue du Saphir, 1040 Bruxelles
T: (02) 7369439
Founded: 1926; Members: 250
Focus: Rheuma 01282

Société Royale Belge de Stomatologie et Chirurgie Maxillo-Faciale, c/o Dr. M. van Kerkhove, Koning Albertlaan 157, 9000 Gent
T: (09) 2223156; Fax: 2216918
Founded: 1900; Members: 215
Pres: Dr. C. Borghgraef; Gen Secr: Dr. M. van Kerkhove
Focus: Stomatology; Surgery 01283

Société Royale Belge d'Entomologie, 29 Rue Vautier, 1000 Bruxelles
T: (02) 6274296; E-Mail: GCOULON@KBINIRSNB.BE; Fax: 6274132
Founded: 1855; Members: 250
Gen Secr: G. Coulon
Focus: Entomology
Periodicals
Bulletin et Annales
Catalogue des Coléoptères de Belgique
Mémoires 01284

Société Royale Belge des Electriciens (SRBE), 2 Blvd de la Plaine, 1050 Bruxelles
T: (02) 6292819; E-Mail: srbe-kbve@etcc2.vub.ac.be; Fax: 6293620
Founded: 1884; Members: 1600
Pres: X. van Merris
Focus: Electric Eng
Periodical
Revue E Tijdschrift (quarterly) 01285

Société Royale Belge des Ingénieurs et Industriels, 3 Rue Ravenstein, 1000 Bruxelles
T: (02) 5115856; Fax: 5145795
Founded: 1885; Members: 2000
Pres: Pierre Klees
Focus: Eng 01286

Société Royale d'Archéologie de Bruxelles, 185 Av Winston Churchill, 1180 Bruxelles
T: (02) 3444620
Founded: 1887; Members: 450
Pres: P.P. Bonenfanti; Gen Secr: A. Vanrie
Focus: Archeol
Periodicals
Annales
Bulletin 01287

Société Royale de Chimie, ULB Campus Plaine, Blvd du Triomphe, CP 206/4, 1050 Bruxelles
T: (02) 6505208; Fax: 6505184
Founded: 1887; Members: 1000
Pres: Dr. A. Scarso; Gen Secr: Prof. R. Fuks
Focus: Chem
Periodicals
Bulletin (monthly)
Chimie Nouvelle (quarterly) 01288

Société Royale de Médecine Mentale de Belgique, 6 Rue Jean Paquot, 1050 Bruxelles
T: (02) 6482110
Founded: 1869; Members: 179
Focus: Psychiatry
Periodical
Acta Psychiatrica Belgica (bi-monthly) . . 01289

Société Royale de Numismatique de Belgique, c/o Musée de la Banque Nationale, Blvd de Berlaimont, 1000 Bruxelles
Founded: 1841; Members: 277
Pres: Hubert Frère; Gen Secr: F. de Callatay
Focus: Numismatics 01290

Société Royale d'Economie Politique de Belgique, c/o CIFOP, 1b Av Général Michel, 6000 Charleroi
T: (071) 327394; Fax: 328676
Founded: 1855; Members: 400
Pres: René Lamy; Gen Secr: Albert Schleiper
Focus: Poli Sci
Periodical
Comptes Rendus des Travaux (5-6 times annually) 01291

Société Royale des Amis du Musée Royal de l'Armée et d'Histoire Militaire, c/o Musée Royal de l'Armée, 3 Parc du Cinquantenaire, 1000 Bruxelles
T: (02) 7334493/28; Fax: 7422369
Founded: 1925; Members: 550
Pres: François Crepain; Gen Secr: Michel Jaupart
Focus: Military Sci; Hist 01292

Société Royale des Beaux-Arts, 25 Av J. Lambeaux, 1000 Bruxelles
Founded: 1893
Pres: Baron Albert Houtart; Gen Secr: P.P. Hamesse
Focus: Arts 01293

Société Royale des Bibliophiles et Iconophiles de Belgique, 4 Blvd de l'Empereur, 1000 Bruxelles
Founded: 1910; Members: 150
Focus: Libraries & Bk Sci
Periodical
Le Livre et l'Estampe (semi-annually) . . 01294

Société Royale des Sciences de Liège, 12 Grande Traverse, Sart Tilman, Bâtiment B37, 4000 Liège 1
Founded: 1835; Members: 220
Gen Secr: Prof. J. Godeaux
Focus: Sci
Periodical
Bulletin (bi-monthly) 01295

Société Royale des Sciences Médicales et Naturelles de Bruxelles, 115 Blvd de Waterloo, 1000 Bruxelles
Founded: 1822; Members: 150
Focus: Med; Nat Sci 01296

Société Royale Zoologique de Belgique / Koninklijke Belgische Vereniging voor Dierkunde, 50 Av F.D. Roosevelt, 1050 Bruxelles
T: (02) 6502054
Founded: 1863; Members: 400
Pres: J. Hulselmans; Gen Secr: F. de Vree
Focus: Zoology
Periodical
Belgian Journal of Zoology (semi-annually) 01297

Société Scientifique de Bruxelles, 61 Rue de Bruxelles, 5000 Namur
T: (081) 230391; E-Mail: charles.courtroy@fundp.ac.be; Fax: 724502
Founded: 1875; Members: 200
Pres: X. de Hemptinne; Gen Secr: C. Courtoy
Focus: Sci
Periodical
Revue des Questions Scientifiques . . . 01298

Société Technique et Chimique de Sucrerie de Belgique, 182 Av de Tervueren, 1150 Bruxelles
T: (02) 7710130
Founded: 1931; Members: 170
Focus: Eng; Chem 01299

Tantalum-Niobium International Study Center, 40 Rue Washington, 1050 Bruxelles
T: (02) 6495158; Fax: 6496447
Founded: 1974; Members: 50
Gen Secr: J.A. Wickens
Focus: Eng; Metallurgy
Periodical
Bulletin (quarterly) 01300

top E – European Consulting Engineering Network, 124 Av Louise, 1050 Bruxelles
T: (02) 6441109; E-Mail: topebh@compuserve.com; Fax: 6409256
Founded: 1990; Members: 1200
Pres: M. Goblet; Gen Secr: P. Fusager
Focus: Eng 01301

Union Académique Internationale (UAI) / International Union of Academies, 1 Rue Ducale, 1000 Bruxelles
T: (02) 5502200; Fax: 5502205
Founded: 1919; Members: 40
Pres: Aurelio Roncaglia; Gen Secr: P. Roberts-Jones
Focus: Sci
Periodical
Compte Rendu des Sessions (annually) . 01302

Union Belge des Géomètres-Experts Immobiliers (UBG) / Belgische Unie van Landmeters en Meetkundigen-Schatters van Onroerende Goederen, 76 Rue du Nord, 1000 Bruxelles
T: (02) 2180713; Fax: 2193147
Founded: 1946; Members: 700
Focus: Surveying; Civil Eng
Periodical
Landmeter Expert Vastgoed (10 times annually) 01303

Union Belge des Journalistes et Ecrivains du Tourisme (U.B.J.E.T.) / Belgische Vereniging van Toeristische Schrijvers en Journalisten, Vlierkenstr 147, 1800 Vilvoorde
T: (02) 2516125
Founded: 1951; Members: 151
Focus: Lit
Periodicals
Nieuws (quarterly)
Nouvelles (quarterly) 01304

Union des Associations d'Assistants Sociaux Francophones (U.F.A.S.), 3c Rue de la Vièrge Noire, 1000 Bruxelles
Members: 3000
Focus: Sociology 01305

Union Européenne des Médecins Spécialistes (UEMS), 20 Av de la Couronne, 1050 Bruxelles
T: (02) 6495164; Fax: 6403730
Founded: 1958
Focus: Med 01306

Union Internationale des Sciences Préhistoriques et Protohistoriques (UISPP), c/o Département d'Archéologie et d'Histoire Ancienne de l'Europe, Université de Gent, Blandijnberg 2, 9000 Gent
T: (09) 2644111; E-Mail: uispp@ping.be; Fax: 2644173
Founded: 1931
Gen Secr: Prof. Dr. J. Bourgeois
Focus: Hist; Archeol 01307

Union Professionnelle Belge des Médécins Ophthalmologistes (UPBMO), 20 Av de la Couronne, 1050 Bruxelles
T: (02) 6492147; Fax: 6492690
Founded: 1928; Members: 417
Pres: Dr. Christian Devuyst; Gen Secr: Dr. Yves Kastelyn
Focus: Ophthal 01308

Union Radio-Scientifique Internationale (URSI), c/o INTEC, Sint Pietersnieuwstr 41, 9000 Gent
T: (09) 2643320; E-Mail: helev@intec.rug.ac.be; Fax: 2644288
Founded: 1913; Members: 45
Pres: Prof. T.B.A. Senior; Gen Secr: I. Helev
Focus: Electric Eng; Computer & Info Sci; Comm
Periodicals
Modern Radio Science (3 times annually)
Proceedings of General Assemblies (3 times annually)
The Radio Science Bulletin (quarterly)
Review of Radio Science (3 times annually)
. . . . 01309

Union Royale Belge pour les Pays d'Outre-Mer, 22 Rue de Stassart, 1050 Bruxelles
Founded: 1912; Members: 28
Pres: Pierre André
Focus: Geography 01310

Union Scientifique Continentale du Verre (U.S.C.V.), 10 Blvd Defontaine, 6000 Charleroi
T: (071) 310041; Fax: 334480
Founded: 1950; Members: 111
Focus: Materials Sci 01311

Union Syndicale Vétérinaire Belge (USVB), 41 Av Fonsny, 1060 Bruxelles
T: (02) 5381754
Founded: 1934; Members: 1220
Focus: Vet Med 01312

Vereniging der Antwerpsche Bibliophielen, c/o Museum Plantin-Moretus, Vrijdagmarkt 22, 2000 Antwerpen
T: (03) 2330294; Fax: 2262516
Founded: 1877
Focus: Libraries & Bk Sci
Periodical
De Gulden Passer 01313

Vereniging Leraars Aardrijkskunde, De Croylaan 42, 3001 Heverlee
Founded: 1977; Members: 1169
Focus: Educ; Geography
Periodical
De Aardrijkskunde (quarterly) 01314

Vereniging van Religieus-Wetenschappelijke Bibliothecarissen (V.R.B.), Minderbroederstr 5, 3800 Sint Truiden
Founded: 1965; Members: 65
Pres: E. d' Hondt; Gen Secr: Kris Van de Casteele
Focus: Libraries & Bk Sci
Periodical
V.R.B.-Informatie (quarterly) 01315

Vlaams Kinesitherapeuten Verbond (VKV), Boeschepestr 70, 8970 Poperinge
T: 333186
Founded: 1963; Members: 3200
Focus: Therapeutics 01316

Vlaamse Chemische Vereniging (VCV), Krijgslaan 281, 9000 Gent
T: (091) 225715 ext 2827
Founded: 1939; Members: 1800
Focus: Chem
Periodicals
Bulletin des Sociétés Chimiques Belges (monthly)
Chemie Magazine (monthly) 01317

Vlaamse Interuniversitaire Raad / Flemish Interuniversity Council, 5 Rue d'Egmont, 1050 Bruxelles
T: (02) 5129110; Fax: 5122996
Founded: 1976
Gen Secr: Jef Van der Perre
Focus: Adult Educ 01318

Vlaamse Museumvereniging / Flemish Museums Association, c/o A. Stroorants, Stedelijke Musea, Nijverheidsstr 1, 9200 Dendermonde
Founded: 1968; Members: 295
Pres: F. van Noten
Focus: Arts
Periodicals
Museumbrief (3 times annually)
Museumleven (annually) 01319

Vlaamse Vereniging voor Familiekunde, Van Heybeeckstr 3, 2170 Merksen
T: (03) 6469988; Fax: 6444620
Founded: 1964; Members: 3000
Focus: Genealogy
Periodical
Vlaamse Stam: Tijdschrift voor Familiegeschiedenis (monthly) 01320

Von Karman Institute for Fluid Dynamics / Postgraduate Teaching and Research Organization, 72 Chaussée de Waterloo, 1640 Rhode-Saint-Genese
T: (02) 3599611; Fax: 3599600
Founded: 1956; Members: 80
Gen Secr: John F. Wendt
Focus: Aero
Periodicals
Lecture Series Notes
Technical Notes 01321

Belize

Belize Library Association, c/o Central Library, Bliss Institute, POB 287 POB 287, Belize City
T: 7267
Founded: 1976; Members: 50
Pres: H.W. Young; Gen Secr: R.T. Hulse
Focus: Libraries & Bk Sci 01322

Benin

African Geographers' Association, BP 7060, Cotonou
T: 331917; Fax: 331981
Founded: 1981; Members: 45
Focus: Geography 01323

African Union for the Management of Development Banks (UAMDB), BP 2045, Cotonou
Focus: Finance 01324

Association des Pédiatres d'Afrique Noire Francophone (APANF), BP 523, Cotonou
Founded: 1981
Focus: Pediatrics 01325

Bermuda

Amalgamated Bermuda Union of Teachers, POB 726, Hamilton
Founded: 1963
Focus: Educ 01326

Astronomical Society of Bermuda, POB 1054, Hamilton 5
Pres: Morley E.B. Nash; Gen Secr: C. McGonagle
Focus: Astronomy
Periodicals
Bermuda Sky Watch
Cosmos 01327

Bermuda Audubon Society, POB 1328, Hamilton 5
T: 2972623
Founded: 1960; Members: 300
Pres: Jeremy Madeiros
Focus: Ecology; Educ
Periodical
Newsletter (4-6 times annually) 01328

Bermuda Historical Society, 13 Queen St, Hamilton 11
T: 2952487
Founded: 1895; Members: 130
Pres: Andrew Bermingham
Focus: Hist 01329

Bermuda Medical Society, POB 1023, Hamilton
Founded: 1970; Members: 70
Pres: Dr. Ian C. Fulton; Gen Secr: Dr. Shane Marshall
Focus: Med 01330

Bermuda National Trust, POB 61, Hamilton
T: 2366483; Fax: 2360617
Founded: 1970; Members: 4000
Pres: David L. White; Gen Secr: Amanda Outerbridge
Focus: Humanities
Periodical
Newsletter (quarterly) 01331

Bermuda Society of Arts, West Gallery, City Hall, POB 1202, Hamilton 5
Founded: 1956; Members: 625
Pres: Elmer Midgett; Gen Secr: Jamie Carlington
Focus: Arts 01332

Bermuda Technical Society, POB 2420, Hamilton
T: 2362730; Fax: 2955077
Members: 60
Pres: Dr. M. Brewer; Gen Secr: V. Fishington
Focus: Eng 01333

Saint George's Historical Society, Corner Duke of Kent St and Featherbed Alley, POB 279, Saint George's
Members: 186
Pres: Ann Spurling
Focus: Hist 01334

Bolivia

Academia Boliviana, Casilla 4145, La Paz
Founded: 1927; Members: 26
Pres: Juan Quirós; Gen Secr: Carlos Castañon Barrientos
Focus: Sci
Periodical
Revista 01335

Academia Nacional de Ciencias de Bolivia, Av 16 de Julio 1732, Casilla 5829, La Paz
T: (02) 363990; Fax: 379681
Founded: 1960; Members: 42
Pres: Dr. Carlos Aguirre Bastos; Gen Secr: Ismael Montes de Oca
Focus: Sci
Periodicals
Boletín Informativo (monthly)
Publicaciones (irregularly)
Revista (semi-annually) 01336

Academia Nacional de la Historia, Av Abel Iturralde 205, La Paz
Founded: 1929; Members: 18
Pres: Dr. David Alvestegui; Gen Secr: Dr. Humberto Vázquez-Machicado
Focus: Hist 01337

Asociación de Ingenieros y Geólogos de Yacimientos Petrolíferos Fiscales Bolivianos (AIGYPFB), Casilla 401, La Paz
Founded: 1959; Members: 210
Pres: Juan Carrasco
Focus: Geology; Energy 01338

Ateneo de Medicina de Sucre, Sucre
Pres: Dr. Agustín Benávides; Gen Secr: Dr. Romelio A. Subieta
Focus: Med 01339

Círculo de Bellas Artes, Plaza Teatro, La Paz
Founded: 1912
Pres: Ernesto Peñaranda
Focus: Arts 01340

Colegio de Arquitectos de Bolivia, Casilla 11876, La Paz
T: (02) 391568; Fax: 391568
Founded: 1940; Members: 2500
Pres: F. Cavero M.; Gen Secr: Juan C. Barrientos M.
Focus: Archit 01341

PEN Club de Bolivia-Centro Internacional de Escritores, Goitia 17, Casilla 149, La Paz
Founded: 1931; Members: 47
Gen Secr: Yolanda Bedregal de Cónitzer
Focus: Lit 01342

Sociedad de Estudios Geográficos e Históricos, Plaza 24 de Setiembre, Santa Cruz de la Sierra
Founded: 1903
Pres: Dr. Hernando Sanabria Fernández; Gen Secr: Plácido Molina B.
Focus: Geography; Hist 01343

Sociedad de Pediatría de Cochabamba, Casilla 1429, Cochabamba
Founded: 1945; Members: 14
Pres: Dr. Julio Corrales Badani; Gen Secr: Dr. Moises Sejas
Focus: Pediatrics 01344

Sociedad Geográfica de La Paz, Plaza Abaroa 13, Casilla 1487, La Paz
Founded: 1889; Members: 580
Pres: Dr. Gregorio Loza Balsa
Focus: Geography 01345

Sociedad Geográfica y de Historia Potosí, Casa Real de Moneda, Casilla de Correo 39, Potosí
Founded: 1905; Members: 20
Pres: Luis Alfonso Fernández; Gen Secr: Prof. Eduardo Araujo Villegas
Focus: Geography; Hist 01346

Sociedad Geográfica y de Historia Sucre, Plaza 25 de Mayo, Sucre
Founded: 1887; Members: 8
Pres: Dr. Joaquín Gantier V.
Focus: Geography 01347

Sociedad Geológica Boliviana, Reyes Ortiz 1673, Casilla 2729, La Paz
Founded: 1961
Pres: L. Riuz G.
Focus: Geology 01348

Sociedad Rural Boliviana, Casilla 786, La Paz
Founded: 1934; Members: 30
Pres: José Luis Aramayo V.
Focus: Agri
Periodicals
IFAP News
Universitas 01349

Bosnia and Hercegovina

Društvo Bibliotekara BiH, Obala V. Stepe 42, 71000 Sarajevo
T: (071) 283245
Founded: 1949 Cukac, Neda
Gen Secr: Miodrag Rakic
Focus: Libraries & Bk Sci 01350

Društvo Istoričara BiH, c/o Filozofski Fakultet, Račkog 1, 71000 Sarajevo
Focus: Hist 01351

Društvo Ljekara BiH, Maršala Tita 7, 71000 Sarajevo
Focus: Med 01352

Društvo Matematičara, Fizičara i Astronoma BiH, c/o Prirodnomatematički Fakultet, Vojvode Putnika 43, 71000 Sarajevo
Focus: Math; Physics; Astronomy . . . 01353

Geografsko Društvo BiH, c/o Prirodno-Matematički Fakultet, Vojvode Putnika 43a, 71000 Sarajevo
Founded: 1947; Members: 1541
Pres: Dr. Miloš Bjelovitič; Gen Secr: Dr. K. Papič
Focus: Geography 01354

Muzička Omladina BiH, c/o Muzička Akademija, 71000 Sarajevo
T: (071) 25007
Founded: 1958; Members: 40000
Pres: Krešimir Božič; Gen Secr: Borislav Čurič
Focus: Music 01355

Pedagoško Društvo BiH, Djure Djakovica 5, 71000 Sarajevo
Focus: Educ 01356

Savez za Esperanto BiH, Vase Pelagiča 8, 71000 Sarajevo
T: (071) 37043
Founded: 1949; Members: 12000
Focus: Ling 01357

Savez Zdravstvenih Radnika BiH, Moše Pijade 25, 71000 Sarajevo
Gen Secr: Nevenka Kovačevič
Focus: Med 01358

Udruženje Književnih Prevodilaca BiH, Veljka Cubriloviča 5, 71000 Sarajevo
Focus: Ling 01359

Udruženje Književnika BiH, Preradovičeva 3, 71000 Sarajevo
T: (071) 516400
Founded: 1945; Members: 225
Pres: A. Sidran
Focus: Lit 01360

Udruženje Kompozitora BiH, Radičeva 15, 71000 Sarajevo
Focus: Music 01361

Udruženje Muzičkih Umjetnika BiH, Sv Markovicá 1, 71000 Sarajevo
Focus: Music 01362

Botswana

Botswana Library Association, POB 1310, Gaborone
T: 351151
Founded: 1978; Members: 50
Pres: Dr. A.P.N. Thapisa; Gen Secr: F.M. Lamusse
Focus: Libraries & Bk Sci 01363

Botswana Society, POB 71, Gaborone
T: 351500; Fax: 359321
Founded: 1968; Members: 450
Pres: Gobe W. Matenge; Gen Secr: D. Dambe
Focus: Sci
Periodical
Botswana Notes and Records (annually) . 01364

Brazil

Academia Alagoana de Letras, 57000 Maceió, AL
Focus: Lit 01365

Academia Amazonense de Letras, Rua Ramos Ferreira 1009, 69000 Manaus, AM
Founded: 1918; Members: 40
Pres: Djalma Batista
Focus: Lit
Periodical
Revista 01366

Academia Brasileira de Ciência da Administração / Brazilian Academy of Administration, Praia de Botafogo 190, 22253-900 Rio de Janeiro, RJ
Founded: 1973; Members: 40
Pres: Jorge Oscar de Mello Flores; Gen Secr: Fanny Tchaikowski
Focus: Public Admin 01367

Academia Brasileira de Ciências / Brazilian Academy of Sciences, Rua Anfilófio de Carvalho 29, 20030-060 Rio de Janeiro, RJ
T: (021) 2204794; Fax: 2404695
Founded: 1916; Members: 443
Pres: Prof. Eduardo Moacyr Krieger; Gen Secr: Affonso Augusto Guidão Gomes
Focus: Sci
Periodicals
Anais da Academia Brasileira de Ciências (quarterly)
Revista Brasileira de Biologia (quarterly) . 01368

Academia Brasileira de Letras, Av Presidente Wilson 203, 20030 Rio de Janeiro, RJ
Founded: 1897
Gen Secr: Abgar Renault
Focus: Lit
Periodical
Revista 01369

Academia Cachoeirense de Letras, Prāca J. Monteiro 105, 29300 Cachoeira de Itapemerim, ES
Founded: 1962; Members: 40
Pres: Evandro Moreira
Focus: Lit 01370

Academia Campinense de Letras, Rua Marechal Deodoro 525, 13100 Campinas, SP
Focus: Lit
Periodical
Publicações (irregularly) 01371

Academia Catarinense de Letras, Rua Vidal Ramos, Edificio José Daux, 88000 Florianópolis, SC
Founded: 1920; Members: 60
Pres: Theobaldo Costa Jamundá
Focus: Lit
Periodical
Revista 01372

Academia Cearense de Letras, Palácio Senador Alencar, Rua São Paulo 51, 60030 Fortaleza, CE
Founded: 1894; Members: 61
Pres: Claudio Martins; Gen Secr: I. de Santiago Espindola
Focus: Lit
Periodical
Revista 01373

Academia de Letras, 58000 João Pessoa, PB
Focus: Lit 01374

Academia de Letras da Bahia, Av Joana Angélica 198, Nazaré, 40050 Salvador, BA
T: (071) 2437614
Founded: 1917; Members: 59
Pres: Claudio Veiga
Focus: Lit
Periodical
Revista 01375

Academia de Letras de Piauí, 64000 Teresina, PI
Focus: Lit
Periodical
Revista 01376

Academia de Letras e Artes do Planalto / Planalto Academy of Arts and Letters, Rua do Santíssimo Sacramento 32, 72800-000 Luziânia, GO
T: (061) 6211184
Founded: 1976; Members: 30
Pres: Terezinha de Jesus Roriz Machado
Focus: Arts; Lit 01377

Academia de Medicina de São Paulo, Rua Teodoro Sampaio 115, 05405 São Paulo, SP
T: (011) 8539677
Founded: 1895
Pres: Prof. Raul Marino Junior; Gen Secr: Prof. Claudio Cohen
Focus: Med 01378

Academia Matogrossense de Letras, Rua 13 de Junho 173, 78000 Cuiabá, MT
Founded: 1921
Focus: Lit
Periodical
Revista 01379

Academia Mineira de Letras, Rua da Bahia 1466, 30160 Belo Horizonte, MG
Pres: V. Moreira
Focus: Lit 01380

Academia Nacional de Farmacia, Rua dos Andradas 96, 20000 Rio de Janeiro, RJ
Founded: 1937
Focus: Pharmacol
Periodical
Boletim 01381

Academia Nacional de Medicina, Av General Justo 365, CP 459, 20021-130 Rio de Janeiro, RJ
T: (021) 2621732; Fax: 2408673
Founded: 1829; Members: 100
Pres: Rubem David Azulay; Gen Secr: Jarbas A. Porto
Focus: Med
Periodical
Boletim 01382

Academia Paraibana de Letras, Rua Duque de Caxias 25, CP 334, 58000 João Pessoa, PB
Founded: 1941; Members: 40
Pres: Afonso Pereira da Silva
Focus: Lit
Periodicals
Boletim Informativo
Discursos e Ensaios
Revista 01383

Academia Paulista de Letras (APL), Largo do Arouche 312, 01219 São Paulo, SP
T: (011) 2207222
Founded: 1909; Members: 40
Pres: Antônio Soares Amôra
Focus: Lit
Periodical
Revista No. 107 01384

Academia Pernambucana de Letras, Av Rui Barbosa 1596, Graças, 52050-000 Recife, PE
Fax: (081) 2682211
Founded: 1901; Members: 40
Pres: Luiz de Magalhaes Melo
Focus: Lit
Periodical
Revista 01385

Academia Piauiense de Letras, 64001-490 Teresina, PI
Pres: Manoel Paulo Nunes
Focus: Humanities
Periodical
Revista (semi-annually) 01386

Academia Riograndense de Letras, Rua Cândido Silveira 43, 90000 Pôrto Alegre, RS
Focus: Lit
Periodical
Revista 01387

Asociación Interamericana de Ingenieria Sanitaria y Ambiental / Inter-American Association of Sanitary and Environmental Engineering, Rua Nicolau Gagliard 354, 05429 Saõ Paulo, SP
T: (011) 2124080; Fax: 8142441
Founded: 1946; Members: 10000
Focus: Eng
Periodicals
Desafio (quarterly)
Ingenieria Sanitaria (quarterly) 01388

Asociación Latinoamericana de Escuelas de Trabajo Social (ALAETS) / Latin American Association of Schools of Social Work, c/o Dep de Servicio Social, Universidade Federal do Maranho, 65000 Saõ Luís, MA
Founded: 1965
Focus: Soc Sci; Educ 01389

Asociación Latinoamericana de Paleobotánica y Palinología (ALPP) / Latin American Association of Paleobotany and Palynology, c/o Instituto de Geociencias, Universidade Federal do RGS, CP 15001, Porto Alegre, RS
Founded: 1972
Focus: Paleontology; Botany
Periodical
Boletín de la Asociación Latinoamericana de Paleobotánicy y Palinología (semi-annually) 01390

Asociación Latinoamericana para la Producción Animal (ALPA) / Latin American Association for Animal Production, Av Benito Goncalves 7712, CP 776, 90001 Porto Alegre, RS
T: (0512) 365011; Fax: 272295
Founded: 1966; Members: 23
Focus: Animal Husb 01391

Associação Bahiana de Medicina, Av 7 de Setembro 48, 40000 Salvador, BA
Founded: 1894
Pres: Dr. José Silveira
Focus: Med 01392

Associação Brasileira de Educadores Lassalistas, Av José Pereira Lopes 252, CP 352, 13560 São Carlos, SP
T: (0162) 710121; Fax: 717100
Focus: Educ 01393

Associação Brasileira de Engenharia Sanitária e Ambiental (ABES), Av Beira Mar 216, 20021-060 Rio de Janeiro, RJ
T: (021) 2103221; E-Mail: ABESRIO;
Fax: 2626838
Founded: 1966; Members: 8000
Focus: Ecology
Periodicals
Catálogo Brasileiro de Engenharia Sanitária e Ambiental – CABES (annually)
Jornal de ABES (monthly)
Revista Bio (quarterly) 01394

Associação Brasileira de Escolas Superiores Católicas (ABESC), SGAN, Quadra 916, Módulo B, 70790-160 Brasília, DF
Focus: Educ 01395

Associação Brasileira de Farmacêuticos, Rua Andradas 96, 20051 Rio de Janeiro
T: (021) 2630791
Founded: 1916; Members: 2000
Pres: Salvador Alves Pereira; Gen Secr: Nuno Alvares Pereira
Focus: Pharmacol
Periodical
Revista Brasileira de Farmacia 01396

Associação Brasileira de Imprensa, Rua Araujo Porto Alegre 71, 20000 Rio de Janairo, RJ
Focus: Libraries & Bk Sci 01397

Associação Brasileira de Mecânica dos Solos e Engenharia Geotécnica (ABMS), CP 0141, 01000 São Paulo, SP
T: (011) 2687325; E-Mail: abms@ipt.br;
Fax: 2687325
Founded: 1950; Members: 950
Pres: Prof. Willy Alvarenga Lacerda; Gen Secr: Luiz Guilherme F.S. de Mello
Focus: Eng
Periodical
Solos e Rochas (quarterly) 01398

Associação Brasileira de Metalurgia e Materiais, Rua Antônio Comparato 218, 04605-030 São Paulo, SP
Founded: 1944; Members: 5500
Pres: Sylvio N. Coutinho
Focus: Metallurgy; Materials Sci 01399

Associação Brasileira de Odontologia, Av 13 de Maio 13, Rio de Janeiro, RJ
Founded: 1937; Members: 1500
Pres: Dr. Mário Araújo
Focus: Dent
Periodical
Revista Brasileira de Odontologia (monthly) 01400

Associação Brasileira de Química, Rua Alcindo Guanabara 24, 20031-130 Rio de Janeiro, RJ
T: (021) 2621837; Fax: 2626044
Founded: 1922; Members: 3000
Pres: Eduardo McMannis Torres
Focus: Chem 01401

Associação Católica Interamericana de Filosofía, Rua Marquês de São Vicente 293, 22451 Rio de Janeiro, FJ
T: (021) 2744596
Founded: 1972
Focus: Philos 01402

Associação de Educação Católica do Brasil, SCS Q3, Bloco A, 79, Edif João Paulo II, 70300 Brasília, DF
Founded: 1945; Members: 1750
Pres: P. Agustín Castejón
Focus: Educ
Periodical
Revista de Educação AEC 01403

Associação de Engenharia Química, Conjunto das Químicas, Bloco 19, Cidade Universitária, São Paulo, SP
Founded: 1944; Members: 500
Pres: Aldo Tonso; Gen Secr: Udo Hupfeld
Focus: Eng 01404

Associação de Ensino, Rua Hygino Muzzi Filho 1001, CP 554, 17525-902 Marília, SP
T: (014) 4338088; E-Mail: Proaco@Unimar.br;
Fax: 4338691
Founded: 1956; Members: 4
Pres: Márcio Mesquita Serva; Gen Secr: José Francisco de Almeida Pimentel
Focus: Educ 01405

Associação de Ensino e Cultura Urubupungá, Av Cel. Jonas Alves de Mello 1660, CP 126, 15370 Pereira Barreto, SP
T: 2044
Focus: Educ 01406

Associação de Geografia Teorética, CP 178, 13500-230 Rio Claro, SP
T: (019) 5249622; Fax: 5249622
Founded: 1971; Members: 400
Pres: Lucia Helena de Oliveira Gerardi
Focus: Geography
Periodicals
Boletim de Geografia Teorética (semi-annually)
Geografia (semi-annually) 01407

Associação dos Advogados, Largo de São Francisco 34, 01005 São Paulo, SP
T: (011) 2588355
Focus: Law 01408

Associação dos Arquivistas Brasileiros, Rua da Candelária 9, 20091-020 Rio de Janeiro, RJ
T: (021) 2337142; Fax: 2337142
Founded: 1971; Members: 2050
Pres: Lia Temporal Malcher; Gen Secr: Laura Regina Xavier
Focus: Archives 01409

Associação Educacional Presidente Kennedy, Rua Barão de Maurá 600, 07000 Guarulhos, SP
T: 2095681
Focus: Educ 01410

Associação Internacional de Críticos de Arte, Rua Visconde de Piraja 228, App 802, 20000 Rio de Janeiro, RJ
Focus: Arts 01411

Associação Internacional de Lunologia, CP 322, 01000 São Paulo, SP
Founded: 1969
Focus: Astronomy 01412

Associação Itaquerense de Ensino, Rua Carolina Fonseca 548, 08200 Itaquera, SP
T: 2976065
Focus: Educ 01413

Associação Médica Brasileira, Rua São Carlos do Prinhal 324, CP 8904, 01333 São Paulo, SP
T: (011) 2893511
Founded: 1951; Members: 35000
Pres: Dr. Pedro Kassab
Focus: Med
Periodicals
Journal da Associação Médica Brasileira (monthly)
Revista da Associação Médica Brasileira (quarterly) 01414

Associação Panamericana de Medicina Social / Pan American Association of Social Medicine, Moura 81, Tijuca, Rio de Janeiro, RJ
Focus: Med 01415

Associação Paulista de Bibliotecários (APB), Rua Maestro Cardim 94, Liberdade, 01323-000 São Paulo
T: (011) 2853831; Fax: 2853831
Founded: 1938; Members: 1500
Focus: Libraries & Bk Sci
Periodical
Palavra Chave: Key Word (irregularly) . 01416

Associação Paulista de Medicina, Av Brigadeiro Luíz Antônio 278, CP 2103, 01000 São Paulo, SP
T: (011) 2323141; E-Mail: apm@apm.org.br;
Fax: 6077979
Founded: 1930; Members: 25000
Pres: Dr. Eleuses Vieira de Paiva; Gen Secr: Dr. Antonio José Gonçalves
Focus: Med
Periodicals
Diagnóstico e Tratamento (bi-monthly)
Jornal da Associação Paulista de Medicina (monthly)
Revista Paulista de Medicina (bi-monthly) 01417

Associação Pernambucana de Bibliotecarios, Rua das Fronteiras 255, 50000 Recife, PE
Focus: Libraries & Bk Sci 01418

Associação Prudentina de Educação e Cultura, Rua José Bongiovani 700, 19100 Presidente Prudente
Focus: Educ; Physical Therapy; Hygiene; Vet Med; Business Admin 01419

Associação Rio-Grandense de Bibliotecarios (ARB), CP 2344, 90020-122 Pôrto Alegre, RS
T: (051) 2258194
Founded: 1951; Members: 500
Focus: Libraries & Bk Sci 01420

Associação Tibirica de Educação, Largo São Bento, 01029 São Paulo, SP
T: (011) 2273377
Focus: Educ 01421

Associação Universitaria Santa Ursula, Rua Fernando Ferrari 75, 20000 Rio de Janeiro, RJ
Focus: Educ 01422

Association of Amazonian Universities, CP 558, 66017-970 Belém, Pará
T: (091) 2243641; E-Mail: unamaz@amazon.com.br; Fax: 2242055
Founded: 1987; Members: 73
Pres: Dr. José Seixas Lourenço
Focus: Educ 01423

Association of Latin American Lawyers for the Defense of Human Rights, Av São Luiz 131, 01046 São Paulo, SP
Founded: 1979
Focus: Law 01424

Centro Acadêmico Hugo Simas, Rua Marechal Floriano Peixoto 524, 80000 Curitiba, PI
Focus: Sci 01425

Centro Brasileiro de Estudos, Rua Sacramento 108, 13100 Campinas, SP
Focus: Sci 01426

Centro Brasileiro de Pesquisas Fisicas, Rua Xavier Sigaud 150, 22290 Rio de Janeiro, RJ
T: (021) 5410337; Fax: 5412047
Founded: 1949
Gen Secr: Amós Troper
Focus: Physics 01427

Centro Cultural de Botucatu, Rua Cesário Alvim 296, 18600 Botucatu, SP
Focus: Sci 01428

Centro de Análise Conjuntura Econômica / Centre for Analysis of Economic Affairs, Av Gomes Freire 647, 20231 Rio de Janeiro, RJ
Focus: Econ 01429

Centro de Aperfeiçoamento e Especialização Médica, Rua Sacadura Cabral 178, 20000 Rio de Janeiro, RJ
Focus: Metallurgy 01430

Centro de Biomédica de Campina Grande, 58100 Campina Grande, PB
Focus: Bio; Med 01431

Centro de Ciências, Letras e Artes, Rua Bernardino de Campos 989, 13100 Campinas, SP
Focus: Lit 01432

Centro de Estudos de Demografía Histórica de América Latina, c/o Faculdade de Filosofía, Letras e Ciencias Humanas, Universidade de São Paulo, CP 8105, 05508-900 São Paulo
T: (011) 8183745; E-Mail: CEDHAL@org.usp.br;
Fax: 8155273
Founded: 1986
Gen Secr: Dr. Eni de Mesquita Samara
Focus: Hist
Periodicals
Estudios CEDHAL (semi-annually)
Populações – Boletim do CEDHAL (semi-annually) 01433

Centro de Estudos e Pesquisas em Administração, Av João Pessoa 52, 90000 Porto Alegre
T: (0512) 243837
Founded: 1959
Focus: Public Admin 01434

Centro de Pesquisa Agropecuária do Trópico-Árido (CPATSA), BR-428, Km 152, s/n, Zona Rural, Apdo 23, 56300-000 Petrolina, PE
T: (081) 8621711; Fax: 8621744
Founded: 1975
Focus: Agri
Periodicals
Annual Research Report (irregularly)
Research Bulletin (irregularly)
Technical Bulletin (irregularly)
Technical Information (irregularly) 01435

Centro de Pesquisa Agropecuária do Trópico Umido (CPATU), Travessa Dr. Eneas Pinheiro, Bairro do Marco, CP 48, 66000 Belém
Focus: Agri
Periodicals
Boletim de Pesquisa
Circular Técnica
Documentos
Relatório Décimo Anual CPATU 01436

Centro de Pesquisa Agropecuária dos Cerrados (CPAC) / Center for Agricultural Research for the Brazilian Savannahs, Estrada Brasilia-Fortaleza Km 18, CP 08223, 73301-970 Planaltina, DF
T: (061) 3891171; Fax: 3892953
Focus: Agri
Periodicals
Anual do Centro de Pesquisa Agropecuária dos Cerrados (annually)
Boletim de Pesquisa (irregularly)
Circular Técnica (irregularly)
Comunicado Técnico (irregularly)
Documentos (irregularly)
Pesquisa em Andamento (irregularly) . . 01437

Centro de Pesquisas de Geografia do Brasil, Largo de São Francisco, 20000 Rio de Janeiro, RJ
Focus: Geography 01438

Centro de Pesquisas Folclóricas, c/o Escola de Música, Rua do Passeio 98, 20021 Rio de Janeiro, RJ
Focus: Ethnology
Periodical
Revista Brasileira de Música 01439

Centro Latino Americano de Física (CLAF) / Latin American Centre for Physics, Av Venceslau Braz 71, 22290-970 Rio de Janeiro, RJ
T: (021) 2955096, 2955145; E-Mail: CELAFI; Fax: 5412047
Founded: 1962
Focus: Physics
Periodical
Noticia (quarterly) 01440

Centro Nacional de Informação Científica em Microbiologia, Av Pasteur 250, 20000 Rio de Janeiro, RJ
Focus: Microbio 01441

Centro Nacional de Pesquisa de Arroz e Feijão (EMBRAPA), Rodovia GYN 10, km 12, CP 179, 74001-970 Goiânia, GO
Fax: (062) 2613880
Focus: Agri; Food
Periodicals
Série Documentos (irregularly)
Série Técnica (irregularly) 01442

Centro Nacional de Pesquisa de Mandioca e Fruticultura (EMBRAPA), Rua Lauro Passos, CP 007, 44380 Cruz das Almas, BA
T: 7212120
Focus: Agri; Food
Periodicals
Boletim Agrometeorológico (annually)
Boletim de Pesquisa (irregularly)
Boletim Informativo (monthly)
Circular Técnica (irregularly)
Comunicado Técnico (irregularly)
Documentos (irregularly)
Pesquisa em Andamento (irregularly)
Relatório Técnico Anual (annually)
Revista Brasileira de Mandioca (bi-monthly) 01443

Centro Nacional de Pesquisa de Milho e Sorgo, CP 151, 35701-970 Sete Lagoas, MG
T: (031) 9215644; Fax: 9219252
Founded: 1974
Focus: Agri
Periodicals
Circular Técnica
Documentos
Relatório 01444

Centro Nacional de Pesquisa de Seringueira (EMBRAPA), Rodovia AM 10, km 30, CP 319, 69000 Manaus, AM
T: (092) 2341417
Focus: Sci
Periodicals
Boletim de Pesquisa
Circular Técnica
Resumos Informativos
Série Documento 01445

Centro Nacional de Pesquisa de Soja (EMBRAPA), Rodovia Celso Garcia Cid, Km 375, CP 1061, 86100 Londrina
Focus: Food; Agri 01446

Centro Nacional de Pesquisa do Algodão (EMBRAPA), CP 174, 58100 Campina Grande, PB
Focus: Agri 01447

Centro Regional de Pesquisas Educacionais do Sul, Av Oswaldo Aranha 271, CP 2872, 90000 Porto Alegre, RS
Focus: Educ 01448

Comissão Brasileira de Documentâcão Agricola (CBDA), c/o Ministério da Agricultura, Anexo I, Bloco H, Ala Oeste, Esplanada dos Ministérios, CP 102432, 70043 Brasília, DF
T: (061) 2251101
Focus: Doc
Periodical
Agricolas (quarterly) 01449

Comissão Nacional de Energia Nuclear (CNEN), Rua General Severiano 90, Botafogo, 22294-900 Rio de Janeiro, RJ
T: (021) 295-9596
Founded: 1956
Pres: José M. Esteves dos Santos
Focus: Energy 01450

Comissão Nacional de Folclore, Av Marechal Floriano 196, 20080-002 Rio de Janeiro, RJ
T: (021) 5162458; Fax: 5162458
Founded: 1947; Members: 6
Pres: Atico Vilas Boas da Mota; Gen Secr: Paulo de Carvalho-Neto
Focus: Ethnology; Folklore
Periodical
Boletim da Comissão Nacional de Folclore (quarterly) 01451

Confederación Panamericana de Medicina Deportiva (COPAMADE), Rua Felipe Becker 95, 91330 Porto Alegre, R.S.
T: (0512) 348083
Founded: 1975; Members: 27
Focus: Med 01452

Conselho de Reitores das Universidades Brasileiras, SEUP/Norte, Quadra 516, Conj D, Lote 09, 70770-535 Brasília, DF
T: (061) 2722960; Fax: 2744621
Founded: 1966; Members: 114
Pres: José Martins Filho; Gen Secr: Maria Helena Alves Garcia
Focus: Educ
Periodical
Planejamento (monthly) 01453

Conselho Federal de Biblioteconomia, 712/713, Bloco A, Ent 31, Sobreloja, Sala 2, 70760 Brasília, DF
T: (061) 2736668
Founded: 1966
Pres: Maria Lucia Almeida
Focus: Libraries & Bk Sci 01454

Conselho Nacional de Desenvolvimento Científico e Tecnológico / National Council of Scientific and Technological Development, Av W-3 Norte, Quadra 507, Bl B, 70740-905 Brasília, DF
T: (061) 3489400
Founded: 1951
Pres: José Galizia Tundisi
Focus: Eng
Periodical
Revista Brasileira de Tecnologia (bi-monthly) 01455

Conselho Nacional de Educação, SGAS 607, Lote 50, 70200-670 Brasília, DF
T: (061) 2440387; Fax: 2448374
Members: 24
Pres: Hésio Cordeiro
Focus: Educ 01456

Conselho Nacional Serviço Social, Imprensa 16, 20000 Rio de Janeiro, RJ
Focus: Sociology 01457

Coordenação de Folclore e Cultura Popular, Rua do Catete 179, 22220-000 Rio de Janeiro, RJ
T: (021) 2850441
Focus: Ethnology
Periodicals
Bibliografia Folclórica
Cuadernos de Folclore
Documentário Sonoro
Série Encontros e Estudos
Série Referência 01458

Federação Brasileira de Associaeões de Bibliotecários (FEBAB), Rua Avanhandava 40, 01306 São Paulo
T: (011) 2579979
Founded: 1959; Members: 27
Pres: J.C. Gomes Ribeiro; Gen Secr: W. Rosa
Focus: Libraries & Bk Sci
Periodicals
Jornal da Febab (irregularly)
Revista Brasileira de Biblioteconomia e Documentação (semi-annually) 01459

Fundação Getulio Vargas (FGV), Praia de Botafogo 190, 22253-900 Rio de Janeiro, RJ
T: (021) 5369100; E-Mail: flores@fgv.br; Fax: 5536372
Founded: 1944; Members: 1440
Pres: Prof. Jorge Oscar Mello Flores
Focus: Sci
Periodicals
Correio da Unesco (monthly)
Finanças e Desenvolvimento (quarterly)
Revista Brasileira de Economia (quarterly)
Revista de Administraçao de Empresas (bi-monthly)
Revista de Administração Pública (quarterly) 01460

Fundação Joaquim Nabuco (FUNDAJ) / Joaquim Nabuco Foundation, Av 17 de Agosto 2187, Casa Forte, 52061-540 Recife, PE
T: (081) 4415500; Fax: 4415600
Founded: 1949; Members: 520
Pres: Fernando de Mello Freyre
Focus: Anthro; Econ; Sociology; Educ; Hist
Periodicals
Cadernos de Estudos Sociais (semi-annually)
Revista Ciência e Trópico (semi-annually) 01461

Instituto Arqueológico, Histórico e Geográfico Pernambucano, Rua do Hospicio 130, 50000 Recife, PE
Founded: 1862; Members: 180
Pres: José Antonio Gonsalves de Melo
Focus: Hist; Geography; Archeol 01462

Instituto Brasileiro de Economia / Brazilian Institute of Economics, c/o Getúlio Vergas Foundation, CP 62-591, 22250 Rio de Janeiro, RJ
Founded: 1951
Pres: Salazar P. Brandão
Focus: Econ
Periodicals
Agroanalysis (monthly)
National Accounts (annually)
Revista Brasileira de Economia (quarterly)
Revista Conjuntura Economia (monthly) . 01463

Instituto Brasileiro de Educâcão, Cíencia e Cultura (IBECC), Av Marechal Floriano 196, 20080 Rio de Janeiro, RJ
T: (021) 5162458; Fax: 5162458
Founded: 1946; Members: 60
Pres: José Pelucio Ferreira; Gen Secr: Joaquim Caetano Gentil Neto
Focus: Educ; Sci; Cultur Hist
Periodical
Correio do IBECC (semi-annually) . . . 01464

Instituto Brasileiro de Relações Internacionais, Praia de Botafogo 186, 22250 Rio de Janeiro, RJ
Founded: 1954
Gen Secr: V. de Paiva Leite
Focus: Poli Sci 01465

Instituto de Botânica / Botanical Institute, Av Miguel Estefano 3687, CP 4005, 01000 São Paulo, SP
T: (011) 2753322; Fax: 5773678
Founded: 1938; Members: 81
Focus: Botany
Periodicals
Boletin do Instituto de Botánica (irregularly)
Hoehnea (irregularly)
Monographs (irregularly) 01466

Instituto de Engenharia de São Paulo, Palacio Mauá, 01000 São Paulo, SP
Founded: 1917; Members: 10000
Pres: Luiz Alfredo Falcão Bauer
Focus: Eng 01467

Instituto de Planejamento de Pernambuco, Rua Gervásio Pires 399, Boa Vista, 50000 Recife, PE
T: (081) 2315005; Fax: 2313379
Founded: 1952; Members: 226
Focus: Agri; Ecology; Econ; Sociology
Periodicals
Desempenho da Economia de Pernambuco (annually)
Revista Pernambucana de Desenvolvimento (semi-annually)
Sondagem Conjuntural (quarterly) . . . 01468

Instituto do Ceará, Rua Barão do Rio Branco 1594, 60025-061 Fortaleza, CE
Founded: 1887; Members: 40
Pres: Prof. Paulo Ayrton Araujo; Gen Secr: Prof. José Liberal de Castro
Focus: Hist; Geography; Anthro
Periodical
Revista do Instituto do Ceará (annually) 01469

Instituto dos Advogados Brasileiros, Av Marechal Câmera 210, 20020-080 Rio de Janeiro, RJ
Founded: 1843; Members: 1141
Pres: Ricardo César Pereira Lira
Focus: Law 01470

Instituto Genealógico Brasileiro, Rua Dr. Zuquim 1525, 01000 São Paulo, SP
Pres: Salvador de Moya; Gen Secr: Dr. Jorge Bueno de Miranda
Focus: Genealogy 01471

Instituto Geográfico e Histórico da Bahia (I.G.H.B.), Av 7 de Setembro 94A, 40060-001 Salvador, BA
T: (071) 3222453; Fax: 3214787
Founded: 1894; Members: 300
Pres: Prof. Consuelo Pondé de Sena; Gen Secr: Dr. L. de Andrade Lima
Focus: Geography; Hist
Periodical
Revista do I.G.H.B. (irregularly) 01472

Instituto Geográfico e Histórico do Amazonas, Rua B. Ramos 117, 69000 Manaus, AM
T: (092) 2327077
Founded: 1917; Members: 120
Pres: Dr. Roberto dos Santos Pereira Braga; Gen Secr: Dr. José Roberto Tadros
Focus: Geography; Hist 01473

Instituto Histórico de Alagoas, Rua J. Pessoa 382, 57000 Maceío, AL
Founded: 1869; Members: 40
Pres: Dr. José Lages Filho; Gen Secr: Dr. Abelardo Duarte
Focus: Hist 01474

Instituto Histórico e Geográfico Brasileiro, Av A. Severo 8, 20021 Rio de Janeiro, RJ
Fax: (021) 2524430
Founded: 1838
Pres: Vicente Tapajós; Gen Secr: Prof. Guilherme de Andréa Frota
Focus: Geography; Hist
Periodical
Revista (quarterly) 01475

Instituto Histórico e Geográfico de Goiás, Rua 82, No 455, S Sul, 74000 Goiânia, GO
T: (062) 2244622
Founded: 1933; Members: 60
Gen Secr: Dr. C. Natal e Silva
Focus: Geography; Hist 01476

Instituto Histórico e Geográfico de Santa Catarina (IHGSC), Praca XV de Novembro, Palácio Cruz e Sousa, CP 1582, 88000 Florianópolis
T: (048) 2213502; Fax: 2225111
Founded: 1896; Members: 100
Pres: Prof. Dr. Osvaldo Ferreira de Melo; Gen Secr: Prof. Lelia Pereira da Silva Nunes
Focus: Geography; Hist
Periodical
Revista do IHGSC (annually) 01477

Instituto Histórico e Geográfico de Santos, Av Concelheiro Nébias 689, Boqueirão, 11100 Santos, SP
Focus: Hist; Geography 01478

Instituto Histórico e Geográfico de São Paulo, Rua Benjamin Constant 158, 01005-000 São Paulo, SP
Founded: 1894
Pres: H. Donato; Gen Secr: Mario Savelli
Focus: Geography; Hist
Periodical
Revista (annually) 01479

Instituto Histórico e Geográfico de Sergipe, Rua de Itabaianinha 41, 49000 Aracajú, SE
Founded: 1912
Pres: Prof. Maria Thetis Nuens
Focus: Geography; Hist 01480

Instituto Histórico e Geográfico do Espírito Santo, Av República 374, 29020-620 Vitória
Founded: 1916
Pres: Prof. Renato Pacheco
Focus: Hist; Geography
Periodical
Acta Oncologica Brasileira (quarterly) . . 01481

Instituto Histórico e Geográfico do Maranhão, Rua Santa Rita 230, 65000 São Luís, MA
Founded: 1925
Pres: Dr. José Ribamar Seguins; Gen Secr: Dr. F. Marialva Montalverne Frota
Focus: Geography; Hist
Periodical
Revista 01482

Instituto Histórico e Geográfico do Pará, Rua d'Aveiro-Cidade Irmã 62, CP 547, 66000 Belém, PA
Founded: 1900
Pres: Dr. José Rodrigues da Silveira Neito; Gen Secr: Dr. A. de Oliveira Mello
Focus: Geography; Hist
Periodical
Leusla (irregularly) 01483

Instituto Histórico e Geográfico do Rio Grande do Norte, Rua da Conceição 622, 59000 Natal
Founded: 1902
Pres: Dr. Enélio Lima Petrovich
Focus: Geography; Hist
Periodical
Revista do I.H.G./R.N. (annually) 01484

Instituto Histórico e Geográfico do Rio Grande do Sul, Rua Riachuelo 1317, 90010-271 Porto Alegre, RS
T: (051) 2243760; Fax: 2243760
Founded: 1920; Members: 30
Pres: Dr. Sérgio da Costa Franco; Gen Secr: Prof. Raphael Copstein
Focus: Geography; Hist
Periodical
Revista do Instituto Histórico e Geográfico do Rio Grande do Sul (annually) 01485

Instituto Histórico e Geográfico Paraíbano, Rua Barão do Abiaí 64, CP 37, 58000 João Pessoa, PB
Founded: 1905; Members: 70
Pres: J. de Britto Pereira
Focus: Geography; Hist 01486

Instituto Histórico, Geográfico e Etnográfico Paranaense, Rua J. Loureiro 43, 80000 Curitiba, Pl
Founded: 1900
Pres: Luiz Carlos Pereira Tourinho
Focus: Ethnology; Geography; Hist . . . 01487

Instituto Nacional de Estudos e Pesquisas Educacionais / National Institute for Educational Research, CP 04366, 70300 Brasília, DF
Focus: Educ 01488

Instituto Nacional de Pesquisas da Amazonia, Rua André Araújo 1756, CP 478, 69083-970 Manaus, AM
T: (092) 6423377; E-Mail: ozorio@cr-am.rnp.br; Fax: 6433095
Founded: 1954; Members: 802
Pres: Ozorio José de Menezes Fonseco
Focus: Ecology; Botany; Bio; Forestry; Chem; Nutrition; Eng; Med

Periodical
Acta Amazonica (bi-monthly) 01489

Instituto Nacional de Pesquisas Hidroviarias, Rua General Gurjão 166, 20000 Rio de Janeiro, RJ
Focus: Water Res 01490

Instituto Nacional de Tecnologia (INT) / National Institute of Technology, Av Venezuela 82, 20081 Rio de Janeiro, RJ
T: (021) 2231320
Founded: 1921
Focus: Chem; Eng
Periodicals
Corrosão & Protecão Boletim Informativo (bi-monthly)
Informativo INT (quarterly) 01491

Instituto Nacional do Cancer, Praça Cruz Vermelha 23, 20000 Rio de Janeiro, RJ
Focus: Cell Biol & Cancer Res 01492

Instituto Nacional do Livro, Av W/3 Sul, Entre Quadras 506, 70000 Brasília, DF
Focus: Libraries & Bk Sci 01493

Instituto Nacional do Livro, Rua Pedro Lessa 36, 20000 Rio de Janeiro, RJ
Focus: Libraries & Bk Sci 01494

Instituto Nami Jafet para o Progreso da Ciência e Cultura, Rua Agostinho Gomes 1455, São Paulo, SP
Founded: 1961
Focus: Sci; Cultur Hist 01495

International Communication Agency (ICA), Av Paulista 2439, 01000 São Paulo, SP
Focus: Lit 01496

International Mathematical Union (IMU), c/o IMPA, Estrada D. Castouna 110, 22460 Rio de Janeiro, RJ
T: (021) 2949032; Fax: 5124112
Founded: 1952; Members: 55
Focus: Math
Periodical
IMU Bulletin 01497

International Seaweed Association (ISA), c/o Eurico C. Oliveira, Instituto de Biociências, USP, CP 11461, 05422-970 São Paulo, SP
T: (011) 8187630; Fax: 8187547
Founded: 1977; Members: 750
Pres: Mark A. Ragan; Gen Secr: Eurico C. Oliveira
Focus: Botany; Bio
Periodical
Proceedings 01498

Latin American Centre for Physics, Av Wenceslau Bráz 71, 22290 Rio de Janeiro, RJ
T: (021) 2955096
Founded: 1962; Members: 13
Focus: Physics
Periodical
Noticia 01499

Organização Guarão de Ensino, Av Pedro de Toledo, 12500 Guaratinguetá, SP
T: 224416
Focus: Educ 01500

PEN Clube do Brasil - Associação Universal de Escritores, Praia do Flamengo 172, 20000 Rio de Janeiro, RJ
Founded: 1936; Members: 106
Pres: Prof. Marcos Almir Madeira
Focus: Lit
Periodical
Boletim 01501

Secção de Farmacia Galénica, c/o Universidade do Paraná, 80000 Curitiba, PI
Founded: 1960
Focus: Pharmacol 01502

Secretaria do Patrimônio Histórico e Artístico Nacional Nacional (SPHAN), Rua da Imprensa 16, 20000 Rio de Janeiro
Founded: 1937
Focus: Hist; Arts
Periodical
Revista do Patrimônio Histórico e Artístico Nacional (annually) 01503

Sociedade Botânica do Brasil, CP 09888, 70302 Brasília, DF
Founded: 1950; Members: 2800
Pres: Eliana Nogueira
Focus: Botany 01504

Sociedade Brasileira de Autores Teatrais, Rua da Quitanda 194, 20091-000 Rio de Janeiro
T: (021) 2539383; Fax: 2832544
Founded: 1917; Members: 9700
Pres: Renato José Pécora; Gen Secr: Neide Silva de Barros
Focus: Perf Arts
Periodical
Revista de Teatro (quarterly) 01505

Sociedade Brasileira de Belas Artes, Rua Araújo Pôrto Alegre 70, 20000 Rio de Janeiro, RJ
Focus: Arts 01506

Sociedade Brasileira de Cartografia, Av Presidente Wilson 210, 20030-210 Rio de Janeiro, RJ
Founded: 1958; Members: 1500
Pres: Fernando Coutinho de Araujo Amdadeo
Focus: Cart 01507

Sociedade Brasileira de Cultura, Alameda Eduardo Prado 705, 01218 São Paulo, SP
Focus: Cultur Hist
Periodicals
Convivium: Revista de Investigação e Cultura (semi-annually)
Política e Estratégia: Revista de Politica Internacional e Assuntos Militares . . . 01508

Sociedade Brasileira de Dermatologia (SBD) / Brazilian Society of Dermatology, CP 389, 20001-970 Rio de Janeiro, RJ
T: (021) 2536747
Founded: 1912; Members: 2100
Gen Secr: Dr. Marcia Ramos e Silva
Focus: Derm
Periodical
Anais Brasileiros de Dermatologia (bi-monthly) 01509

Sociedade Brasileira de Entomologia (SBE), CP 9063, 01065-970 São Paulo, SP
T: (011) 2743455; E-Mail: gnaspini@usp.br
Founded: 1937; Members: 500
Pres: Carlos Ribeiro Vilela; Gen Secr: Pedro Gnaspini-Netto
Focus: Entomology
Periodical
Revista Brasileira de Entomologia (quarterly) 01510

Sociedade Brasileira de Filosofia, Praça da República 54, 20000 Rio de Janeiro, RJ
Founded: 1927; Members: 105
Pres: Dr. Herbert Canabarro Reichardt
Focus: Philos 01511

Sociedade Brasileira de Genética / Brazilian Genetics Society, c/o Departamento de Genética, Faculdade de Medicina, USP, 14049 Ribeirão Preto
T: (016) 6331610
Founded: 1955; Members: 2000
Focus: Genetics
Periodical
Revista Brasileira de Genética: Brazilian Journal of Genetics (quarterly) 01512

Sociedade Brasileira de Geografia, Prâca da República 54, 20000 Rio de Janeiro, RJ
Founded: 1883; Members: 284
Pres: Prof. J. de Castro Pires Ferreira
Focus: Geography 01513

Sociedade Brasileira de Geologia, c/o Instituto de Geociências, USP, CP 20897, 01498 São Paulo, SP
T: (011) 2126166
Founded: 1945; Members: 4000
Focus: Geology
Periodicals
Revista Brasileira de Geociências (quarterly)
Revista Ciências da Terra (bi-monthly) . 01514

Sociedade Brasileira de Instrução, Rua da Matriz 82, 22260-100 Botafogo, RJ
T: (021) 2867146
Focus: Sociology; Poli Sci
Periodicals
Caderno de Conjuntura (irregularly)
DADOS (3 times annually)
Indice de Ciências Sociais (semi-annually)
Série Estudos (irregularly) 01515

Sociedade Brasileira de Microbiologia, Av Pasteur 250, 20000 Rio de Janeiro, RJ
Founded: 1956
Focus: Microbio 01516

Sociedade Brasileira de Romanistas, Av Rio Branco 123, 20000 Rio de Janeiro, RJ
Focus: Ling 01517

Sociedade Brasileira para o Progresso da Ciência, Rua Maria Antonia 294, 01222-010 São Paulo
T: (011) 2592766; Fax: 6061002
Founded: 1948; Members: 30020
Pres: Sérgio H. Ferreira; Gen Secr: Ademar Freire Maia
Focus: Sci 01518

Sociedade Cientifica de São Paulo, CP 2679, São Paulo, SP
Founded: 1939
Pres: Dr. G.F. de Almeida
Focus: Sci 01519

Sociedade Civil de Educação São Marcos, Av Nazaré 900, 04262 São Paulo, SP
T: (011) 2745711
Focus: Educ 01520

Sociedade de Biologia do Brasil, CP 1587, 20000 Rio de Janeiro, RJ
Founded: 1947
Focus: Bio 01521

Sociedade de Biologia do Rio Grande do Sul, Av Candido de Godoy 112, 90000 Pôrto Alegre, RS
Focus: Bio 01522

Sociedade de Cultura e Educação do Litoral Sul, Rua São Francisco Xavier 165, 11900 Registro, SP
T: 22360
Focus: Educ 01523

Sociedade de Engenharia do Rio Grande do Sul (SERGS), Travessa Eng. Acilino Carvalho 33, 90000 Pôrto Alegre, RS
T: (0512) 246133
Founded: 1930; Members: 3660
Focus: Eng 01524

Sociedade de Ensino Piratininga, Av Angélica 381, 01277 São Paulo, SP
T: (011) 666628
Focus: Educ 01525

Sociedade de Farmácia e Química de São Paulo, Av Brigadeiro Luiz Antonio 393, 01317 São Paulo, SP
Founded: 1924; Members: 300
Focus: Bio; Chem; Pharmacol
Periodical
Anais de Farmácia e Química (annually) 01526

Sociedade de Medicina de Alagoas, Rua Barão de Anadia 5, CP 57025, 57000 Maceió, AL
T: (082) 2233463; Fax: 2233463
Founded: 1917; Members: 1200
Pres: Dr. Sergio Toledo Barbosa
Focus: Med 01527

Sociedade de Pediatria da Bahia, Av Joanna Angélica 75, 40000 Salvador, BA
Members: 43
Focus: Pediatrics 01528

Sociedade Geográfica Brasileira (SGB), Rua 24 de Maio 104, 01041 São Paulo, SP
T: (011) 327802
Founded: 1948
Focus: Geography 01529

Sociedade Nacional de Agricultura, Av General Justo 171, CP 1245, 20021-130 Rio de Janeiro
T: (021) 5330088, 2624223; Fax: 2404189
Founded: 1897
Pres: Octavio Mello Alvarenga; Gen Secr: Elvo Santoro
Focus: Agri
Periodical
A Lavoura (3 times annually) 01530

Sociedade Paranaense de Matemática, CP 1261, 80001-970 Curitiba, PR
Founded: 1953
Focus: Math
Periodical
Boletim da Sociedade Paranaense de Matemática (semi-annually) 01531

Sociedade Propagadora Esdeva, Rua Halfeld 1179, 36100 Juiz de Fora, MG
Focus: Sci 01532

Sociedade Visconde de São Leopoldo, Rua Carvalho de Mendonça 140, 11100 Santos, SP
T: 345187
Focus: Sci 01533

Unidade de Pesquisa de Ambito Estadual em Barreiras (EMBRAPA), Rodovia Barreiras, São Desiderio, Km 15, 47800 Barreiras, BA
Focus: Sci 01534

Unidade de Pesquisa de Ambito Estadual em Campos (EMBRAPA), Av Francisco Lamego 134, 28100 Campos, RJ
Focus: Sci 01535

Unidade de Pesquisa de Ambito Estadual em Corumba (EMBRAPA), Rua Antonio Maria 786, 79300 Corumba, MT
Focus: Sci 01536

Unidade de Pesquisa de Ambito Estadual em Dourados (EMBRAPA), Rua Joachim Teixeira Alves 2190, 79800 Dourados, MT
Focus: Sci 01537

Unidade de Pesquisa de Ambito Estadual em Itaguai (EMBRAPA), Antiga Rodoviario São Paulo, Km 47, 26000 Nova Iguaçu, RJ
Focus: Sci 01538

Unidade de Pesquisa de Ambito Estadual em Itapirema (EMBRAPA), 55900 Goiânia, GO
Focus: Sci 01539

Unidade de Pesquisa de Ambito Estadual em Manaus (EMBRAPA), Rodovia Torquato Tapajos, Km 30, CP 455, 69000 Manaus, AM
Focus: Sci 01540

Unidade de Pesquisa de Ambito Estadual em Ponta Grossa (EMBRAPA), Av Presidente Kennedy, Rodovia do Café, Km 104, 84100 Ponta Grossa
Focus: Sci
Periodicals
Boletim Técnico
Circular
Informe da Pesquisa
Relatório de Atividades
Relatório Técnico 01541

Unidade de Pesquisa de Ambito Estadual em Porto Velho (EMBRAPA), c/o Laboratorio de Solos, 78900 Porto Velho, RO
Focus: Sci 01542

Unidade de Pesquisa de Ambito Estadual em Teresina (EMBRAPA), Av Perimetral 5650, 64000 Teresina, PI
T: 2620
Focus: Sci 01543

Bulgaria

Academy of Agricultural Sciences, Bul Dragan Cankov 6, Sofia
Founded: 1961; Members: 30
Focus: Agri 01544

Balkanmedia Association, Luibotran 96, 1407 Sofia
T: (02) 814256; Fax: 871698
Founded: 1990
Pres: R. Milev
Focus: Mass Media
Periodical
Balkanmedia 01545

Bulgarian Academy of Sciences, 15 Noemvri 1, 1040 Sofia
T: (02) 84141; Fax: 880448
Founded: 1869; Members: 164
Pres: Prof. Dr. Ivan Yukhnovski; Gen Secr: Prof. Naum Yakimov
Focus: Sci 01546

Bulgarian Association of Criminology, Vitosha 2, 1000 Sofia
T: (02) 874751
Founded: 1986
Focus: Criminology 01547

Bulgarian Association of International Law, G. Benkovski 3, 1000 Sofia
T: (02) 871548
Founded: 1962; Members: 50
Pres: A. Jankov; Gen Secr: Dr. M. Ganev
Focus: Law 01548

Bulgarian Association of Penal Law, Vazov 42, 1000 Sofia
T: (02) 882647
Founded: 1961; Members: 70
Pres: Prof. D. Mikhailov
Focus: Law 01549

Bulgarian Astronautical Society, Gurgulyat 1, 1463 Sofia
T: (02) 514077
Founded: 1957; Members: 100
Gen Secr: I. Ivanov
Focus: Aero 01550

Bulgarian Biochemical and Biophysical Society, c/o Institute of Molecular Biology, Bulgarian Academy of Sciences, Acad. G. Bonchev Str Bl 21, Sofia 1113
Members: 250
Focus: Biochem; Biophys 01551

Bulgarian Botanical Society, Acad. B. Bonchev Bl 23, 1113 Sofia
T: (02) 720685; Fax: 758140
Founded: 1923; Members: 150
Pres: Dr. S. Kozhuharov; Gen Secr: M. Anchev
Focus: Botany 01552

Bulgarian Dermatological Society (BDD), Bul G. Sofiisky 1, 1431 Sofia
Founded: 1920; Members: 40
Focus: Derm
Periodical
Dermatologia i Venerologia (quarterly) . . 01553

Bulgarian Geographical Society, Tsar Osvoboditel 15, 1000 Sofia
T: (02) 464310; Fax: 446487
Founded: 1918
Pres: Prof. P.V. Petrov; Gen Secr: L. Tsankova
Focus: Geography 01554

Bulgarian Geological Society (BGS), Moskovska 6, POB 228, 1000 Sofia
T: (02) 872450; Fax: 884979
Founded: 1925; Members: 460
Pres: N. Zidarov; Gen Secr: A. Chatalov
Focus: Geology
Periodical
Review of the Bulgarian Geological Society (3 times annually) 01555

The Bulgarian Gynecological and Obstetrical Society, Zdrave 2, 1431 Sofia
T: (02) 521026
Founded: 1961; Members: 600
Focus: Gynecology
Periodicals
Akuserstvo i Ginekologija (bi-monthly)
Problems of Obstetrics and Gynecology (annually) 01556

Bulgarian Historical Society, Pirotska 5, 1000 Sofia
T: (02) 891689
Founded: 1901
Pres: D. Kosev; Gen Secr: Prof. S. Trifonov
Focus: Hist 01557

Bulgarian Nutrition Society, c/o Institute of Gastroentereology and Nutrition, D. Nesterov Str 5, 1431 Sofia
Focus: Food 01558

Bulgarian Philologists' Society, Moskovska 13, 1000 Sofia
T: (02) 803311
Founded: 1977
Pres: Prof. S. Hadzhikosev
Focus: Ling; Lit 01559

Bulgarian Philosophical Society, Lege 5, 1000 Sofia
T: (02) 884035
Founded: 1968
Pres: Kiril Vasilev; Gen Secr: A. Cholakov
Focus: Philos 01560

Bulgarian Psychological Association, Liulin Planina 14, POB 1333, 1606 Sofia
T: (02) 541295
Founded: 1968
Pres: Prof. E. Gerganov
Focus: Psych
Periodical
Balgarsko Spisanie po Psikhologija (bi-monthly)
. . . . 01561

Bulgarian Scientific Pharmaceutical Association, Dunav 2, Sofia
Focus: Pharmacol
Periodical
Farmacija (bi-monthly) 01562

Bulgarian Society for Microbiology, Tolbukhin 18, Sofia
Focus: Microbio 01563

Bulgarian Society of Anaesthesiology and Resuscitation, Bul G. Sofiisky 1, Sofia
Members: 200
Focus: Anesthetics 01564

Bulgarian Society of Cardiology, Mico Papo 65, 1309 Sofia
Members: 70
Focus: Cardiol; Rheuma 01565

Bulgarian Society of Electroencephalography, Electromyography and Clinical Neurophysiology, c/o First Neurological Clinic, Medical Academy, G. Sofiliski Bul 1, 1431 Sofia
Members: 20
Focus: Physiology; Neurology 01566

Bulgarian Society of Natural History, D. Zankov 8, 1164 Sofia
T: (02) 666594
Founded: 1896; Members: 1000
Pres: Prof. D. Vodenicharov; Gen Secr: A. Dimitrov
Focus: Nat Sci 01567

Bulgarian Society of Neuroscience, Zdrave 2, 1431 Sofia
T: (02) 518783
Founded: 1987
Pres: Prof. C. Khristozov; Gen Secr: Prof. V. Ovcharov
Focus: Neurology 01568

Bulgarian Society of Neurosurgery (BSN), Bul G. Sofiisky 1, 1431 Sofia
T: (02) 5321316
Founded: 1975; Members: 83
Focus: Surgery
Periodical
Journal of Neurology, Psychiatry and Neurosurgery (bi-monthly) 01569

Bulgarian Society of Parasitology, Acad. G. Bonchev Bl 25, 1113 Sofia
Founded: 1965
Pres: I. Vasilev
Focus: Med 01570

Bulgarian Society of Physiological Sciences, c/o Dept of Physiology, Medical Academy, 1431 Sofia
Focus: Physiology 01571

Bulgarian Society of Sports Medicine and Kinesitherapy, c/o Dept of Sports Medicine, National Sports Academy, Gurgulyat 1, 1000 Sofia
T: (02) 894145
Founded: 1953; Members: 300
Pres: Prof. Dr. S. Savov; Gen Secr: Dr. Todor Toborov
Focus: Med; Therapeutics 01572

Bulgarian Sociological Society, Lege 5, 1000 Sofia
T: (02) 884035; Fax: 467884
Founded: 1959
Pres: Prof. Dr. Petar-Emil Mitev; Gen Secr: Ivan Velev
Focus: Sociology 01573

Bulgarian Soil Society, Shosé Bankya 7, POB 1369, 1080 Sofia
T: (02) 242257
Founded: 1959; Members: 200
Pres: Prof. T. Boyadzhiev; Gen Secr: Prof. Dr. R. Dilkova
Focus: Agri 01574

Bulgarian Translators' Union, Graf Ignatiev 16, POB 161, 1000 Sofia
T: (02) 9810960
Founded: 1974
Pres: G. Savov
Focus: Ling
Periodical
News Bulletin 01575

Bulgarian Union of Public Libraries, Ul Alabin 31, Sofia
Focus: Libraries & Bk Sci 01576

Carpathian Balkan Geological Association (CBGA), c/o University of Sofia, 1504 Sofia
Focus: Geology 01577

Central Council of Scientific and Technical Unions, Ravovski 108, 1000 Sofia
T: (02) 898379
Founded: 1949
Focus: Sci; Eng 01578

Federation of Scientific and Technical Unions in Bulgaria, G. Rakovski 108, 1000 Sofia
T: (02) 898379; Fax: 879360
Founded: 1893
Pres: Prof. N. Vasilev
Focus: Sci; Eng 01579

Scientific and Technical Union of Civil Engineering, G. Rakovski 108, 1000 Sofia
T: (02) 884678; Fax: 879360
Founded: 1965
Pres: Dr. I. Nikolov; Gen Secr: M. Ruseva
Focus: Civil Eng 01580

Scientific and Technical Union of Energetics, G. Rakovski 108, 1000 Sofia
T: (02) 884158; Fax: 879360
Founded: 1965
Pres: Prof. L. Petranchin; Gen Secr: D. Tomov
Focus: Eng; Electric Eng; Comm
Periodical
Energetika 01581

Scientific and Technical Union of Forest Engineering, G. Rakovski 108, 1000 Sofia
T: (02) 883683; Fax: 879360
Founded: 1965
Pres: V. Karamfolov; Gen Secr: S. Savov
Focus: Forestry
Periodical
Darvoobrabotvasta i mebelna Promislenost 01582

Scientific and Technical Union of Mechanical Engineering, G. Rakovski 108, 1000 Sofia
T: (02) 877290; Fax: 879360
Founded: 1965
Pres: Prof. A. Skordev; Gen Secr: D. Damjanov
Focus: Eng 01583

Scientific and Technical Union of Mining, Geology and Metallurgy, G. Rakovski 108, 1000 Sofia
T: (02) 875727; Fax: 879360
Founded: 1965
Gen Secr: Prof. V. Genevski, V. Stoyanov
Focus: Mining; Geology; Metallurgy
Periodicals
Metalurgija
Rudodobiv
Vaglista 01584

Scientific and Technical Union of Specialists in Agriculture, Rakovski 108, 1000 Sofia
T: (02) 876513; Fax: 879360
Founded: 1965
Pres: Prof. Nikola Tomov
Focus: Agri 01585

Scientific and Technical Union of Textiles, Clothing and Leather, G. Rakovski 108, 1000 Sofia
T: (02) 881641; Fax: 879360
Founded: 1965
Pres: Prof. E. Kantchev; Gen Secr: I. Mechev
Focus: Textiles 01586

Scientific and Technical Union of the Food Industry, G. Rakovski 108, 1000 Sofia
T: (02) 874744; Fax: 879360
Founded: 1965
Pres: K. Klyamov; Gen Secr: V. Furnadzhiev
Focus: Eng; Food 01587

Scientific and Technical Union of Transport, G. Rakovski 108, 1000 Sofia
T: (02) 872371; Fax: 879360
Founded: 1965
Pres: S. Kotov; Gen Secr: S. Sapundzhiev
Focus: Transport 01588

Scientific and Technical Union of Water Works, G. Rakovski 108, 1000 Sofia
T: (02) 885303; Fax: 879360
Founded: 1965
Pres: Prof. E. Monev; Gen Secr: M. Sjarova
Focus: Civil Eng 01589

Society of Aesthetes and Art and Literary Critics, Patriarh Evtimij 48, 1000 Sofia
Founded: 1970
Pres: Prof. A. Stojkov; Gen Secr: Prof. K. Goranov
Focus: Philos; Arts; Lit 01590

Union of Architects in Bulgaria, Krakra 11, 1504 Sofia
T: (02) 442673; Fax: 465132
Founded: 1965; Members: 4000
Pres: Prof. E. Tsvetkov
Focus: Archit
Periodical
Architecture and Society 01591

Union of Bulgarian Artists, Shipka 6, 1504 Sofia
T: (02) 446115; Fax: 463129
Founded: 1893
Pres: L. Zidarov
Focus: Arts 01592

Union of Bulgarian Composers, Ivan Vazov 2, 1000 Sofia
T: (02) 881560; Fax: 874378
Founded: 1947; Members: 207
Pres: Prof. L. Nikolov
Focus: Music 01593

Union of Bulgarian Film Makers, Exarkh Josif 37, 1000 Sofia
T: (02) 878956; Fax: 879530
Founded: 1934; Members: 900
Pres: K.H. Totev
Focus: Cinema
Periodicals
Filmovi Novini
Kinoizkustvo 01594

Union of Bulgarian Mathematicians, Acad. G. Bonchev Bl 8, 1113 Sofia
T: (02) 738076; Fax: 721089
Founded: 1977; Members: 8000
Pres: Dr. C. Lozanov; Gen Secr: S. Grozdev
Focus: Math
Periodical
Mathematics and Mathematical Education (annually) 01595

Union of Bulgarian Writers, Angel Kanchev 5, 1000 Sofia
T: (02) 874757
Founded: 1913; Members: 483
Pres: N. Haitov
Focus: Lit 01596

Union of Chemists in Bulgaria, G. Rakovski 108, 1000 Sofia
T: (02) 875812; Fax: 879360
Founded: 1901
Pres: G. Bliznakov; Gen Secr: S. Dzalev
Focus: Chem 01597

Union of Economists, G. Rakovski 108, 1000 Sofia
Fax: (02) 781847
Founded: 1968
Pres: R. Georgiev; Gen Secr: I. Popov
Focus: Econ
Periodical
Bjuletin 01598

Union of Electronic and Electrical Engineering and Communications, G. Rakovski 108, 1000 Sofia
T: (02) 879967; Fax: 879360
Founded: 1965
Pres: D. Michev
Focus: Energy; Electric Eng 01599

Union of Numismatic Societies, Pirotska 5, 1000 Sofia
T: (02) 877184
Founded: 1964; Members: 850
Pres: Prof. Dr. Yordanka Yurukova; Gen Secr: Dr. L. Bojlov
Focus: Ling
Periodical
Revue Numismatica (quarterly) 01600

Union of Physicists in Bulgaria, J. Bourchier 5, 1126 Sofia
T: (02) 627660
Founded: 1990
Pres: Prof. I. Lalov; Gen Secr: Prof. M. Veleva
Focus: Physics 01601

Union of Scientific Medical Societies in Bulgaria, Serdica 2, 1000 Sofia
T: (02) 883111; Fax: 876266
Founded: 1968; Members: 60
Pres: Prof. N. Nachev; Gen Secr: Prof. Dr. V. Vasilev
Focus: Med
Periodical
Information Bulletin (quarterly) 01602

Union of Scientists in Bulgaria, Oborishte 35, 1504 Sofia
T: (02) 441157; Fax: 441590
Founded: 1944; Members: 9367
Pres: Prof. I. Matev; Gen Secr: Prof. K. Gabrovski
Focus: Sci
Periodicals
Medical Archives (quarterly)
Scientific Life (bi-monthly) 01603

Union of Surveyors and Land Managers, G.Rakovski 108, 1000 Sofia
T: (02) 898379; Fax: 879360
Founded: 1937
Pres: Prof. Dr. G. Milev; Gen Secr: S. Bogdanov
Focus: Surveying 01604

Burkina Faso

Organisation de Coordination et de Coopération pour la Lutte contre les Grandes Endémies (OCCGE), 01 BP 153, Bobo-Dioulasso
T: 970101; Fax: 970099
Founded: 1966
Gen Secr: A.A. Rhaly
Focus: Med 01605

Cameroon

Association des Institutions d'Enseignement Théologique en Afrique Centrale (ASTHEOL-CENTRAL), c/o Faculté de Théologie Protestante, BP 4011, Yaoundé
Focus: Rel & Theol; Educ 01606

Association Oecuménique des Théologiens Africains (AOTA), BP 1539, Yaoundé
Focus: Rel & Theol 01607

Canada

Académie des Lettres du Québec, 5724 Chemin de la Côte Saint-Antoine, Montréal, Qué. H4A 1R9
T: (514) 488-5883; Fax: (514) 488-5883
Founded: 1944; Members: 36
Pres: Jean-Guy Pilon
Focus: Ling; Lit
Periodical
Les Cahiers de l'Académie (irregularly) . 01608

Academy of Canadian Cinema and Television, 158 Pearl St, Toronto, Ont. M5H 1L3
T: (416) 591-2040; Fax: (416) 591-2157
Founded: 1979; Members: 2500
Pres: Ann Medina
Focus: Cinema; Mass Media
Periodical
Infocus (3-4 times annually) 01609

Academy of Medicine-Ottawa, 1867 Alta Vista Dr, POB 8223, Ottawa, Ont. K1G 3H7
T: (613) 733-2604; Fax: (613) 731-1779
Founded: 1931; Members: 600
Pres: Dr. Byron Lemmex; Gen Secr: Gayle Desserud
Focus: Med
Periodical
Bulletin (quarterly) 01610

Academy of Medicine-Toronto, 704 Spadina Rd, POB 549, Station P, Toronto, Ont. M5S 2T1
T: (416) 465-2800
Founded: 1907; Members: 2800
Pres: Dr. John H. Fowler; Gen Secr: Dr. D.J. McKnight
Focus: Med
Periodical
Bulletin 01611

Academy of Psychology, POB 4251, Ottawa, Ont. K1S 5B3
T: (613) 235-2529
Gen Secr: Gilles Hubert
Focus: Psych 01612

Adlerian Psychological Association of British Columbia, 1193 Kingsway, Vancouver, B.C. V5V 3C9
T: (604) 874-4614; E-Mail: adler@mindlink.bc.ca; Fax: (604) 874-4634
Founded: 1973; Members: 350
Gen Secr: Joan McMahon
Focus: Psych
Periodicals
Newsletter
Quarterly (quarterly) 01613

Administrative Sciences Association of Canada, c/o Département des Sciences Administratives, CP 6192, Succ A, Montréal, Qué. H3C 4R2
T: (514) 987-3697; Fax: (514) 987-3343
Founded: 1982; Members: 800
Pres: P. Andiappan; Gen Secr: I. Lepine
Focus: Public Admin
Periodicals
Canadian Journal of Administrative Sciences (quarterly)
Newsletter (quarterly)
Proceedings (annually) 01614

African Literature Association (ALA), c/o Dept of Modern Languages and Comparative Studies, University of Alberta, Edmonton, Alta. T6G 2E6
T: (403) 492-4926
Founded: 1974; Members: 500
Gen Secr: Dr. Stephen Arnold
Focus: Lit
Periodicals
ALA Bulletin (quarterly)
Annual Selected Conference Paper . . . 01615

African Studies Committee, c/o Dept of Political Science, Carleton University, Ottawa, Ont. K1S 5B6
T: (613) 788-2777
Gen Secr: Chris Brown
Focus: Ethnology 01616

Agricultural Institute of Canada / Institut Agricole du Canada, 141 Laurier Av W, Ottawa, Ont. K1P 5J3
T: (613) 232-9459; Fax: (613) 594-5190
Founded: 1920; Members: 18
Gen Secr: Roy Carver
Focus: Agri
Periodicals
Canadian Journal of Animal Science
Canadian Journal of Plant Science
Canadian Journal of Soil Science . . . 01617

Alberta Association of College Librarians, c/o Learning Resources Centre, Grant MacEwan Community College, 10700 104 Av, Edmonton, Alta. T5J 4S2
T: (403) 497-5894; Fax: (403) 497-5895
Members: 75
Gen Secr: Patricia Lloyd
Focus: Libraries & Bk Sci 01618

Alberta Association of Library Technicians, POB 700, Edmonton, Alta. T5J 2L4
T: (403) 422-8243
Founded: 1974; Members: 293
Pres: Kim Varey
Focus: Libraries & Bk Sci 01619

Alberta Association of Medical Radiation Technologists, 2210 39 St N, Lethbridge, Alta. T1H 5J2
T: (403) 320-9729; Fax: (403) 320-1728
Founded: 1963; Members: 1470
Focus: Radiology 01620

Alberta Association of Registered Occupational Therapists, 301 Whitemud Business Park, 4245 975 St, Edmonton, Alta. T6E 5Y7
T: (403) 436-8381; Fax: (403) 437-3145
Founded: 1952; Members: 664
Gen Secr: Lorna Reimer
Focus: Therapeutics
Periodical
AAROT Newsletter (10 times annually) . 01621

Alberta Association of Rehabilitation Centres, 2725 12 St NE, POB 105, Calgary, Alta. T2E 7J2
T: (403) 250-9495; Fax: (403) 291-9864
Founded: 1972; Members: 25
Pres: Rita Thompson; Gen Secr: Gail Roberson
Focus: Rehabil 01622

Alberta Association on Gerontology, 1070 McDougall Rd NE, Calgary, Alta. T2E 7Z2
T: (403) 267-2930; Fax: (403) 267-2797
Founded: 1980
Pres: Ruth R. Wolfe; Gen Secr: Jean Welsh
Focus: Geriatrics 01623

Alberta Construction Association, 10949 120 St, Edmonton, Alta. T5H 3R2
T: (403) 455-1122; Fax: (403) 451-2152
Founded: 1958; Members: 1109
Gen Secr: M. Ellis
Focus: Civil Eng
Periodicals
Alberta Construction (bi-monthly)
Membership Roster (annually) 01624

Alberta Dental Assistants Association, 10335 178 St, Edmonton, Alta. T5S 1R5
T: (403) 486-2526; Fax: (403) 486-2728
Founded: 1956; Members: 3400
Gen Secr: Melanie Bachand
Focus: Dent 01625

Alberta Dental Association, 8230 105 St, Ste 101, Edmonton, Alta. T6E 5H9
T: (403) 432-1012; Fax: (403) 433-4864
Members: 1300
Gen Secr: Gordon Thompson
Focus: Dent 01626

Alberta Educational Communications Corporation, 3720 76 Av, Edmonton, Alta. T6B 2N9
T: (403) 440-7777; Fax: (403) 440-8899
Founded: 1973
Gen Secr: Malcolm Knox
Focus: Educ; Comm 01627

Alberta Family History Society, POB 30270, Station B, Calgary, Alta. T2M 4P1
Founded: 1980; Members: 300
Pres: Noreen Chambers
Focus: Hist 01628

Alberta Genealogical Society, 116 Prince of Wales Armouries Heritage Centre, 10440 108 Av, Edmonton, Alta. T5H 3Z9
T: (403) 424-4929; Fax: (403) 423-8980
Founded: 1973; Members: 800
Pres: Margo Moffat
Focus: Genealogy
Periodical
Relatively Speaking (quarterly) 01629

Alberta Government Civil Lawyers Association, 9833 109 St, Edmonton, Alta. T5K 2E8
T: (403) 498-3311; Fax: (403) 425-0307
Founded: 1976; Members: 100
Pres: Herb Schlotter
Focus: Law 01630

Alberta Health Record Association, POB 1752, Edmonton, Alta. T5J 2P1
T: (403) 413-7239
Founded: 1961; Members: 500
Gen Secr: Vera Horobec
Focus: Public Health 01631

Alberta Institute of Agrologists, POB 5097, Airdrie, Alta. T4B 2B2
T: (403) 948-1231; E-Mail: P.Ag@aia.ab.ca;
Fax: (403) 948-3141
Pres: Roger Lore
Focus: Agri 01632

Alberta Lung Association, POB 4500, Edmonton, Alta. T6E 6K2
T: (403) 492-0354
Founded: 1939
Gen Secr: Gary Lathan
Focus: Pulmon Dis 01633

Alberta Medical Association, 12230 106 Av NW, Edmonton, Alta. T5N 3Z1
T: (403) 482-2626; E-Mail: ama_mail@amda.ab.ca;
Fax: (403) 482-5445
Members: 4400
Gen Secr: Dr.Robert A. Burns
Focus: Med 01634

Alberta Museums Association, 9829 103 St, Edmonton, Alta. T5J 0X9
T: (403) 424-2626; E-Mail: can-ama@immedia.ca;
Fax: (403) 425-1679
Founded: 1971; Members: 488
Gen Secr: Adriana A. Davies
Focus: Archives 01635

Alberta Psychiatric Association, c/o Holy Cross Hospital, Calgary, Alta. T5J 2J7
T: (403) 247-9507
Pres: Dr. Ron Aldons
Focus: Psychiatry 01636

Alberta Public Health Association, 11715 101 St, Peace River, Alta. T8S 1L8
T: (403) 624-7120; Fax: (403) 624-7122
Founded: 1943; Members: 300
Pres: H. Campsall
Focus: Public Health 01637

Alberta Registered Dietitians Association, 18104 102 Av, Edmonton, Alta. T5S 1S7
T: (403) 448-0059; Fax: (403) 489-7759
Founded: 1959; Members: 460
Gen Secr: L. Cannataro
Focus: Nutrition 01638

Alberta Registered Music Teachers' Association, 8728 93 Av, Edmonton, Alb. T6C 1T8
T: (403) 468-5509
Focus: Educ; Music 01639

Alberta Safety Council, 10526 Jasper Av, Ste 201, Edmonton, Alta. T5J 1Z7
T: (403) 428-7555; Fax: (403) 428-7557
Founded: 1946; Members: 204
Gen Secr: Eya Zariwny
Focus: Safety 01640

Alberta Science Centre Society, POB 2100, Station M, Calgary, Alta. T2P 4H5
T: (403) 221-3700; E-Mail: discover@calgaryscience.ca; Fax: (403) 237-0186
Members: 2000
Pres: S. Haddon; Gen Secr: L. Kwinter
Focus: Sci 01641

Alberta Society of Professional Biologists, 4246 97 St, Edmonton, Alta. T6E 5Z9
T: (403) 434-5765; E-Mail: aspb@ccinet.ab.ca;
Fax: (403) 435-7503
Founded: 1973; Members: 300
Gen Secr: Bonnie Holtby
Focus: Bio 01642

Alberta Speleological Society, POB 22324, Calgary, Alta. T2P 4J1
T: (403) 245-8823
Founded: 1968; Members: 50
Pres: Taco Van Ieperen; Gen Secr: Ian Drummond
Focus: Speleology 01643

Alberta Sulphur Research, c/o Chemistry Dept, University of Calgary, 2500 University Dr NW, Calgary, Alta. T2N 1N4
T: (403) 220-5372; E-Mail: asrinfo@acs.ucalgary.ca;
Fax: (403) 284-2054
Founded: 1964; Members: 35
Gen Secr: Peter Clarke
Focus: Chem; Nat Res
Periodical
Bulletin (quarterly) 01644

Alberta Teachers' Association, 11010 142 St, Edmonton, Alta. T5N 2R1
T: (403) 453-2411; Fax: (403) 455-6481
Founded: 1918; Members: 39000
Gen Secr: Dr. Julius Buski
Focus: Educ
Periodicals
The ATA Magazine (quarterly)
The ATA News (bi-weekly) 01645

Alberta Veterinary Medical Association, 8615 149 St, Edmonton, Alta. T5R 1B3
T: (403) 489-5007; Fax: (403) 484-8311
Founded: 1905; Members: 820
Pres: Dr. Brent Jackson
Focus: Vet Med
Periodical
Newsletter 01646

Alcuin Society, POB 3216, Vancouver, B.C. V6B 3X8
T: (604) 872-2326; Fax: (604) 872-4235
Founded: 1965; Members: 230
Gen Secr: Doreen E. Eddy
Focus: Educ; Libraries & Bk Sci . . . 01647

Allergy Asthma Information Association, 30 Eglinton Av W, Mississauga, Ont. L5R 3E7
T: (905) 712-2242; Fax: (905) 712-2245
Founded: 1964; Members: 5925
Gen Secr: Susan Daglish
Focus: Derm 01648

Allergy Foundation of Canada, POB 1904, Saskatoon, Sask. S7K 3S5
T: (306) 373-7591; E-Mail: swoynars@eagle.wbm.ca
Founded: 1974; Members: 400
Pres: Sandy Woynarski
Focus: Derm
Periodical
Allergy Alert (quarterly) 01649

Allied Arts Council of Spruce Grove, POB 3511, Spruce Grove, Alta. T7X 3A9
T: (403) 962-0664
Founded: 1980; Members: 40
Pres: Rick LeBlanc
Focus: Arts 01650

Alzheimer Society of Canada, 1320 Yonge St, Toronto, Ont. M4T 1X2
T: (416) 925-3552; Fax: (416) 925-1649
Founded: 1977; Members: 12000
Gen Secr: Stephen E. Rudin
Focus: Geriatrics
Periodicals
Alzheimer Report (quarterly)
Newsletter 01651

American Civil War Historical Re-Enactment Society, 7 Norcross Rd, Downsview, Ont. M3H 2R3
T: (416) 638-9837
Gen Secr: Daryn Tucker
Focus: Hist 01652

American Historical Society of Germans from Russia, 2940 Toronto Cr, Calgary, Alta. T2N 3W5
T: (403) 284-0654
Gen Secr: Martha Nielsen
Focus: Hist 01653

American Society for Information Science – Western Canada Chapter, c/o University of Lethbridge Library, 4401 University Dr, Lethbridge, Alta. T1K 3M4
T: (403) 329-2008; Fax: (403) 329-2022
Pres: Leona Jacobs
Focus: Computer & Info Sci 01654

American Society of Heating, Refrigerating and Air Conditioning Engineers – Toronto Chapter, 5045 Orbitor Dr, Mississauga, Ont. L4W 4Y4
T: (905) 602-4714; Fax: (905) 602-1197
Members: 260
Pres: D. Tayor
Focus: Eng 01655

Amherst Township Historical Society, c/o Cumberland County Museum, 150 Church St, Amherst, N.S. B4H 3C3
T: (902) 667-2561; Fax: (902) 667-2561
Founded: 1973; Members: 150
Pres: Kim M. Gorveatt
Focus: Hist 01656

Amyotrophic Lateral Sclerosis Society of Canada / Société Canadienne de la Sclérose Laterale Amyotrophique, 6 Adelaide St E, Toronto, Ont. M5C 1H6
T: (416) 362-0269; E-Mail: alssoc@inforamp.net;
Fax: (416) 362-0414
Founded: 1977; Members: 1589
Pres: W. Brian Smith; Gen Secr: G. Dewar
Focus: Neurology
Periodicals
ALS News (quarterly)
Info ALS (annually) 01657

Anthroposophical Society in Canada, 81 Lawton Blvd, Toronto, Ont. M4V 1Z6
T: (416) 481-2886
Founded: 1953; Members: 450
Pres: George Wilson
Focus: Philos 01658

Aplastic Anemia Association of Canada, 22 Aikenhead Rd, Etobicoke, Ont. M9R 2Z3
T: (416) 235-0468; Fax: (416) 576-7400
Members: 450
Pres: Don McIntyre
Focus: Med 01659

Architectural Intitute of British Columbia, 131 Water St, Vancouver, B.C. V6B 4M3
T: (604) 683-8588; E-Mail: aibc@aibc.ba.ca;
Fax: (604) 683-8568
Founded: 1914; Members: 1300
Pres: B. Maples; Gen Secr: Cheryl Williams
Focus: Archit 01660

Archives Association of British Columbia (AABC), c/o POB 78530, RPO University, Vancouver, B.C. V6T 1Z4
Founded: 1990; Members: 300
Pres: Joni Mitchell
Focus: Archives 01661

Archives Association of Ontario (AAO), POB 46009, Station College Park, Toronto, Ont. M5B 2L8
T: (416) 792-1173; Fax: (416) 792-2530
Founded: 1993; Members: 650
Pres: Stephen Posner; Gen Secr: Barbara Schon
Focus: Archives
Periodicals
Newsletter
Off the Record (bi-monthly) 01662

Archives Council of Prince Edward Island, c/o Public Archives, POB 1000, Charlottetown, P.E.I. C1A 7M4
T: (902) 368-4351; Fax: (902) 368-5544
Founded: 1987; Members: 9
Pres: Marilyn Bell
Focus: Archives 01663

Archives Society of Alberta, POB 21080, RPO Dominion, Calgary, Alta. T2P 4H5
Founded: 1993; Members: 246
Pres: Bryan Corbett
Focus: Archives 01664

Arctic Institute of North America (AINA), c/o University of Calgary, 2500 University Dr NW, Calgary, Alta. T2N 1N4
T: (403) 220-7515; Fax: (403) 282-4609
Founded: 1945; Members: 2000
Gen Secr: Michael P. Robinson
Focus: Geography
Periodicals
Information North (monthly)
Journal Arctic (quarterly) 01665

Arthritis Society, 250 Bloor St E, Toronto, Ont. M4W 3P2
T: (416) 967-1414; Fax: (416) 967-7171
Founded: 1948
Pres: Denis Morrice
Focus: Med 01666

Association Canadienne d'Education de Langue Française (ACELF), 268 Rue Marie de l'Incarnation, Québec, Qué. G1N 3G4
T: (418) 681-4661; E-Mail: informat@acelf.ca;
Fax: (418) 681-3389
Founded: 1947; Members: 613
Pres: Louis-Gabriel Bordeleau
Focus: Educ; Ling
Periodical
Revue de l'ACELF 01667

Association Canadienne-Française pour l'Avancement des Sciences, 425 Rue de la Gauchetière Est, Montréal, Qué. H2L 2M7
T: (514) 849-0045; Fax: (514) 849-5558
Founded: 1923; Members: 8040
Pres: Jennifer Stoddart; Gen Secr: Germain Godbout
Focus: Nat Sci
Periodical
Annales (annually) 01668

Association de la Paralysie Cérébrale du Québec, 4810 Rue de Rouen, Montréal, Qué. H1V 3T4
T: (514) 257-4341; Fax: (514) 257-4349
Founded: 1949; Members: 3700
Gen Secr: Hélène Tremblay
Focus: Neurology 01669

Association de Psychologie du Travail de Langue Française, c/o Dept des Relations Industrielles, Université Laval, Québec, Qué. G1K 7P4
T: (418) 656-2131 poste 2794; Fax: (418) 656-7688
Founded: 1987
Pres: Prof. Alain Larocque
Focus: Psych 01670

Association des Allergologues et Immunologues du Québec, 2 Complexe Desjardins, Ste 3000, Montréal, Qué. H5B 1G8
T: (514) 350-5101
Pres: John Weisnagel; Gen Secr: André Caron
Focus: Derm; Immunology 01671

Association des Bibliothécaires du Québec, 525 Mount Pleasant, Westmount, Qué. H3Y 3H6
T: (514) 935-6357
Founded: 1932; Members: 200
Gen Secr: Marie Eberlin
Focus: Libraries & Bk Sci 01672

Association des Biologistes du Québec (ABQ), 1208 Rue Beaubien Est, Montréal, Qué. H2S 1T7
T: (514) 279-7115
Founded: 1973; Members: 600
Pres: Robert Hamelin
Focus: Bio
Periodical
In Vivo (5 times annually) 01673

Association des Chirurgiens Généraux du Québec, 2 Complexe Desjardins, CP 216, Succ Desjardins, Montréal, Qué. H5B 1G8
T: (514) 350-5107; Fax: (514) 350-5157
Founded: 1965; Members: 610
Pres: Michel Talbot; Gen Secr: Grégoire Bégin
Focus: Surgery 01674

Association des Collèges Privés du Québec, 1940 Blvd Henri Bourassa Est, Montréal, Qué. H2B 1S2
T: (514) 381-8891; Fax: (514) 381-4086
Founded: 1968; Members: 26
Pres: Benoit Lauzière; Gen Secr: Jacques N. Tremblay
Focus: Educ 01675

Association des Diplômés de Polytechnique, CP 6079, Succ Centre-Ville, Montréal, Qué. H3C 3A7
T: (514) 344-4764; E-Mail: ado@courrier.polymtl.ca;
Fax: (514) 340-4472
Founded: 1910; Members: 17000
Gen Secr: Danielle Rose
Focus: Eng
Periodical
Journal d'Ingénieur (bi-monthly) 01676

Association des Enseignantes et des Enseignants Franco-Ontariens, 681 Belfast Rd, Ottawa, Ont. K1G 0Z4
T: (613) 244-2336; Fax: (613) 563-7718
Founded: 1939; Members: 6607
Gen Secr: Guy Matte
Focus: Educ 01677

Association des Enseignantes et des Enseignants Francophones du Nouveau-Brunswick, POB 712, Fredericton, N.B. E3B 5B4
T: (506) 452-8921; Fax: (506) 453-9795
Founded: 1970; Members: 2700
Gen Secr: Ronald LeBreton
Focus: Educ 01678

Association des Ingénieurs-Conseils du Québec, 2050 Rue Mansfield, Montréal, Qué. H3A 1Y9
T: (514) 288-2032; Fax: (514) 288-2306
Founded: 1974
Gen Secr: Johanne Desrochers
Focus: Eng 01679

Association des Institutions de Niveaux Préscolaire et Elémentaire du Québec, 1940 Blvd Henri-Bourassa Est, Montréal, Qué. H2B 1S2
T: (514) 381-8891; Fax: (514) 381-8126
Founded: 1970; Members: 45
Pres: Jacques About
Focus: Educ 01680

Association des Institutions d'Enseignement Secondaire, 1940 Blvd Henri-Bourassa Est, Montréal, Qué. H2B 1S2
T: (514) 381-8891; E-Mail: cadre@cam.org; Fax: (514) 381-4086
Founded: 1968; Members: 96
Gen Secr: Micheline Lavallée
Focus: Educ 01681

Association des Médecins de Langue Française du Canada, 8355 Blvd Saint-Laurent, Montréal, Qué. H2P 2Z6
T: (514) 388-2228; Fax: (514) 388-5335
Founded: 1902; Members: 5000
Gen Secr: André de Sève
Focus: Med 01682

Association des Médecins du Travail du Québec, 1100 Av Beaumont, Mount Royal, Qué. H3P 3E5
T: (514) 344-1662; Fax: (514) 737-6431
Members: 250
Pres: Alain Gagnon; Gen Secr: Jocelyne Lessard
Focus: Hygiene
Periodical
Bulletin (quarterly) 01683

Association des Microbiologistes du Québec, 1208 Rue Beaubien Est, Montréal, Qué. H2S 1T7
T: (514) 279-7115; Fax: (514) 279-7115
Pres: Pierre Ward
Focus: Microbio 01684

Association des Physiâtres du Québec, 2 Complexe Desjardins, Ste 3000, Montréal, Qué. H5B 1G8
T: (514) 350-5119; Fax: (514) 350-5100
Pres: Marcel Morand; Gen Secr: Denis Raymond
Focus: Psychiatry 01685

Association des Professeurs de Français de la Saskatchewan / Saskatchewan Association of Teachers of French, 619 Highlands Cresc, Saskatoon, Sask. S7H 4Y3
T: (306) 373-6350
Founded: 1967; Members: 239
Pres: Raymond Anderson
Focus: Educ; Ling 01686

Association des Professeurs de Français des Universités et Collèges Canadiens, c/o Dept of Modern Languages, King's College, London, Ont. N6A 2M3
E-Mail: apfucc@julian.uwo.ca
Founded: 1958; Members: 400
Pres: Anthony Purdy
Focus: Educ; Ling 01687

Association des Professeurs de l'Ecole Polytechnique de Montréal, CP 6079, Succ Centre-Ville, Montréal, Qué. H3C 3A7
T: (514) 340-4979
Members: 190
Pres: Louis Lefebvre
Focus: Educ; Eng 01688

Association des Psycho-Educateurs du Québec, 426 Rue Fleury Ouest, Montréal, Qué. H3L 1V7
T: (514) 385-0341; Fax: (514) 385-0527
Pres: Claude Pariseau
Focus: Educ; Psych 01689

Association des Psychologues du Québec, 1150 Blvd Saint-Joseph Est, Montréal, Qué. H2J 1L5
T: (514) 528-7498; Fax: (514) 528-6020
Founded: 1989; Members: 400
Pres: Daniel-Laurent Frégeau
Focus: Psych 01690

Association des Spécialistes en Chirurgie Plastique et Esthétique du Québec, 2 Complexe Desjardins, Ste 3000, Montréal, Qué. H5B 1G8
T: (514) 350-5109
Pres: Louise Duranceau; Gen Secr: Raymonde Dionne
Focus: Surgery 01691

Association des Urologues du Québec, 2 Complexe Desjardins, Ste 3000, Montréal, Qué. H5B 1G8
T: (514) 350-5131
Founded: 1961
Pres: Claude Trudel
Focus: Urology 01692

Association Diabète Québec, 5635 Rue Sherbrooke Est, Montréal, Qué. H1N 1A2
T: (514) 259-3422; Fax: (514) 259-9286
Pres: Serge Langlois
Focus: Diabetes 01693

Association for Canadian Educational Resources, 3665 Flamewood Dr, Mississauga, Ont. L4Y 3P5
T: (905) 275-7685; E-Mail: acercass@astral.magic.ca; Fax: (905) 275-9420
Founded: 1991; Members: 50
Pres: Alice Casselman; Gen Secr: Judy Smith
Focus: Educ 01694

Association for Canadian Studies (ACS) / Association d'Etudes Canadiennes, CP 8888, Succ Centre-Ville, Montréal, Qué. H3C 3P8
T: (514) 987-7784; E-Mail: acs-aec@uqam.ca; Fax: (514) 987-8210
Founded: 1973 Dickinson, John; Members: 750
Gen Secr: Vincent Masciotra
Focus: Hist; Sociology
Periodicals
ACS Newsletter/Bulletin de l'AEC (quarterly)
Canadian Issues (annually) 01695

Association for Media and Technology in Education, 3-1750 The Queensway, Etobicoke, Ont. M9C 5H5
T: (604) 323-5627; Fax: (604) 323-5577
Founded: 1970; Members: 400
Pres: Dr. Katy Campbell; Gen Secr: Mary Anne Epp
Focus: Mass Media; Educ
Periodical
Media Message (quarterly) 01696

Association for the Study of Canadian Radio and Television / Association pour les Etudes sur la Radio-Télévision Canadienne, 1455 Blvd de Maisonneuve Ouest, Montréal, Qué. H3G 1M8
T: (514) 848-2385; Fax: (514) 848-4501
Founded: 1978; Members: 200
Pres: Prof. Howard Fink
Focus: Mass Media 01697

Association Française des Conseils Scolaires de l'Ontario, 435 Saint Laurent Blvd, Ottawa, Ont. K1K 2Z8
T: (613) 745-3195; Fax: (613) 745-4772
Founded: 1944; Members: 800
Gen Secr: J. Ladouceur
Focus: Educ
Periodicals
Cahier des Actualités (semi-annually)
Infoscolaire (monthly) 01698

Association Francophone Internationale des Directeurs d'Etablissements Scolaires (AFIDES) / International Association of French-Speaking Directors of Educational Institutions, 500 Blvd Crémazie Est, Montréal, Qué. H2P 1E7
T: (514) 383-7335; E-Mail: afides@grics.qc.ca; Fax: (514) 384-2139
Founded: 1983; Members: 4000
Gen Secr: Richard Charron
Focus: Educ
Periodical
La Revue des Echanges (quarterly) . . 01699

Association Mathématique du Québec, CP 9, Succ Rosemont, Montréal, Qué. H1X 3B6
T: (514) 735-1273; Fax: (514) 342-0693
Founded: 1958; Members: 900
Gen Secr: Jean-Denis Groleau
Focus: Math
Periodical
Bulletin de l'AMQ (quarterly) 01700

Association Médicale du Québec / Quebec Medical Association, 1000 Rue de la Gauchetière Ouest, Ste 660, Montréal, Qué. H3B 4W5
T: (514) 866-0660; Fax: (514) 866-0670
Founded: 1929; Members: 6500
Gen Secr: Gilles Bellefeuille
Focus: Med 01701

Association Museums New Brunswick / Association des Musées du Nouveau-Brunswick, 503 Queen St, POB 116, Station A, Fredericton, N.B. E3B 4Y2
T: (506) 452-2908; E-Mail: muse@nbet.nb.ca
Founded: 1974; Members: 147
Focus: Archives 01702

Association of British Columbia Teachers of English as an Additional Language, 4664 Lougheed Hwy, Burnaby, B.C. V5C 5T5
T: (604) 294-8325; E-Mail: bcteal@unixg.ubc.ca; Fax: (604) 294-8355
Founded: 1967; Members: 1000
Pres: Christine Stechishin
Focus: Educ; Ling 01703

Association of Canadian Archivists (ACA), POB 2596, Station D, Ottawa, Ont. K1P 5W6
T: (613) 443-0251; E-Mail: ltardif@magmacom.com; Fax: (613) 443-0261
Founded: 1975; Members: 730
Pres: Terry Thompson; Gen Secr: Patrick Burden
Focus: Archives
Periodicals
ACA Bulletin (bi-monthly)
Archivaria (bi-annually) 01704

Association of Canadian Bible Colleges, POB 4311, Three Hills, Alta. T0M 2N0
T: (403) 443-5511; Fax: (403) 443-5540
Members: 43
Pres: Dr. Larry McKinney; Gen Secr: Peter Doell
Focus: Rel & Theol 01705

Association of Canadian College and University Teachers of English, c/o Dept of English, Dalhousie University, Halifax, N.S. B3H 3J5
T: (902) 494-2974; E-Mail: accute@is.dal.ca
Pres: Marjorie Stone; Gen Secr: David McNeil
Focus: Educ; Ling 01706

Association of Canadian Community Colleges / Association des Collèges Communautaires du Canada, 1223 Michael St N, Ste 200, Ottawa, Ont. K1J 7T2
T: (613) 746-2222; Fax: (613) 746-6721
Founded: 1972; Members: 160
Pres: Tom Norton
Focus: Educ
Periodicals
Bulletin (monthly)
College Canada
Communiqué (quarterly)
Newsletter 01707

Association of Canadian Faculties of Dentistry / Association des Facultés Dentaires du Canada, 1815 Alta Vista Dr, Ste 109, Ottawa, Ont. K1G 3Y6
T: (613) 738-7732; Fax: (613) 738-2107
Founded: 1967; Members: 450
Gen Secr: Lorraine Emmerson
Focus: Dent 01708

Association of Canadian Map Libraries and Archives (ACMLA), c/o Visual and Sound Archives, National Archives of Canada, 344 Wellington St, Ottawa, Ont. K1A 0N3
T: (613) 996-6009; Fax: (613) 995-6575
Founded: 1967; Members: 260
Pres: A. Wood
Focus: Libraries & Bk Sci; Cart 01709

Association of Canadian Medical Colleges / Association des Facultés de Médecine du Canada, 774 Echo Dr, Ottawa, Ont. K1S 5P2
T: (613) 730-0687; E-Mail: acma@rcpsc.edu; Fax: (613) 730-1196
Founded: 1943; Members: 16
Pres: Dr. Arnold Aberman; Gen Secr: Dr. David Hawkins
Focus: Med
Periodical
Forum (bi-monthly) 01710

Association of Canadian Universities for Northern Studies / Association Universitaire Canadienne d'Etudes Nordiques, 17 York St, Ste 405, Ottawa, Ont. K1N 9J6
T: (613) 562-0515; Fax: (613) 562-0533
Founded: 1977; Members: 35
Pres: Dr. Roger H. King
Focus: Hist; Sociology; Lit
Periodical
Northline/Point Nord (quarterly) 01711

Association of Canadian University Planning Programs, c/o Dept of City Planning, University of Manitoba, Winnipeg, Man. R3T 2N2
T: (204) 474-8761; Fax: (204) 275-7198
Founded: 1978; Members: 16
Pres: Dr. Christine McKee
Focus: Urban Plan 01712

Association of Concern for Ultimate Reality and Meaning, 15 Saint Mary St, Ste 209, Toronto, Ont. M4Y 2R5
T: (416) 922-2476; Fax: (416) 922-2898
Founded: 1976; Members: 25
Gen Secr: Prof. Tibor Horvath
Focus: Philos
Periodical
Ultimate Reality and Meaning 01713

Association of Deans of Pharmacy of Canada / Association des Doyens de Pharmacie du Canada, c/o Faculty of Pharmacy, University of Montréal, Montréal, Qué. H3C 3J7
T: (514) 343-6440; E-Mail: goyerr@ere.umontreal.ca; Fax: (514) 343-7377
Founded: 1965; Members: 9
Pres: Robert Goyer
Focus: Pharmacol 01714

Association of Directors of Journalism Programs in Canadian Universities / Association des Directeurs et Coordonnateurs des Programmes de Journalisme des Universités Canadienne, c/o School of Journalism and Communication, Carleton University, Ottawa, Ont. K1S 5B6
T: (613) 520-7404; Fax: (613) 520-6690
Founded: 1982; Members: 9
Focus: Journalism 01715

Association of Educators of Gifted, Talented and Creative Children, c/o British Columbia Teacher's Federation, 550 Sixth Av W, Ste 100, Vancouver, B.C. V5Z 4P2
T: (604) 871-1848; Fax: (604) 871-2291
Founded: 1979; Members: 430
Focus: Educ 01716

Association of Exploration Geochemists, POB 26099, Nepean, Ont. K2H 9R0
T: (613) 828-0199; Fax: (613) 828-9288
Founded: 1970; Members: 1000
Pres: William B. Coker
Focus: Geology 01717

Association of Faculties of Pharmacy of Canada / Association des Facultés de Pharmacie du Canada, 425 Adelaide St, Sakatoon, Sask. S7J 0H9
T: (306) 653-3513; Fax: (306) 665-1916
Founded: 1969; Members: 154
Gen Secr: Kenneth A. Ready
Focus: Pharmacol 01718

Association of Manitoba Museums (AMM), 167 Lombard Av, Ste 422, Winnipeg, Man. R3B 0T6
T: (204) 947-1782; Fax: (204) 942-1555
Founded: 1972; Members: 250
Focus: Arts
Periodicals
AMM Newsletter (bi-monthly)
Dawson & Hind (3 times annually) . . . 01719

Association of Occupational Therapists of Manitoba, 425 Elgin Av, Ste 114, Winnipeg, Man. R3A 1P2
T: (204) 957-1214; Fax: (204) 942-7828
Founded: 1971; Members: 178
Gen Secr: Sharon Kathleen Eadie
Focus: Therapeutics 01720

Association of Parliamentary Librarians in Canada (APLIC) / Association des Bibliothécaires Parlementaires du Canada, c/o Library of Parliament, 111 Wellington St, Ottawa, Ont. K1A 0A9
T: (613) 996-4934; Fax: (613) 996-7092
Founded: 1975
Focus: Libraries & Bk Sci
Periodical
APLIC Bulletin: Bulletin ABPAC (semi-annually) 01721

Association of Psychologists of Nova Scotia, POB 594, Station M, Halifax, N.S. B3H 2R7
T: (902) 422-9183; Fax: (902) 422-9183
Founded: 1965; Members: 210
Focus: Psych 01722

Association of Registrars of the Universities and Colleges of Canada / Association des Régistraires des Universités et Collèges du Canada, c/o Bishop's University, Lennoxville, Qué. J1M 1Z7
T: (819) 822-9675; E-Mail: amontgom@admin.ubishops.ca; Fax: (819) 822-9616
Founded: 1964; Members: 200
Focus: Educ 01723

Association of Small Public Libraries of Ontario, c/o Saint Marys Public Library, 15 Church St N, Saint Marys, Ont. N4X 1B4
T: (519) 284-3346; Fax: (519) 284-2630
Founded: 1981
Focus: Libraries & Bk Sci 01724

Association of Universities and Colleges of Canada, 350 Albert St, Ste 600, Ottawa, Ont. K1R 1B1
T: (613) 563-1236; Fax: (613) 563-9745
Founded: 1911; Members: 89
Focus: Sci
Periodical
University Affairs (10 times annually) . . 01725

Association of University Forestry Schools of Canada / Association de Ecoles Forestières Universitaires du Canada, c/o Faculté de Foresterie et de Géomatique, Université Laval, CP 2208, Succ Terminus, Sainte-Foy, Qué. G1K 7P4
T: (418) 656-2116; Fax: (418) 656-3177
Founded: 1973
Gen Secr: Prof. Claude Godbout
Focus: Forestry 01726

Association of University of New Brunswick Teachers, POB 4400, Station A, Fredericton, N.B. E3B 5A3
T: (506) 453-4661; Fax: (506) 453-3514
Pres: Dr. Jack Vanderlinde
Focus: Educ 01727

Association of Workers' Compensation Boards of Canada / Association des Commissions des Accidents du Travail du Canada, 10665 Jasper Av, Ste 1350, Edmonton, Alta. T5J 3S9
T: (403) 425-5462; Fax: (403) 427-2385
Founded: 1919
Gen Secr: John Wisocky
Focus: Safety 01728

Association Paritaire de Prévention pour la Santé et la Securité du Travail, 7450 Blvd Les Galeries d'Anjou, Ste 460, Anjou, Qué. H1M 3M3
T: (514) 355-6190; Fax: (514) 355-7861
Founded: 1985
Focus: Safety; Public Health 01729

Association pour l'Avancement des Sciences et des Techniques de la Documentation (ASTED), 3414 Av du Parc, Ste 202, Montréal, Qué. H2X 2H5
T: (514) 281-5012; E-Mail: info@asted.org; Fax: (514) 281-8219
Founded: 1973; Members: 900
Pres: Joanne Cournoyer
Focus: Doc
Periodical
Documentation et Bibliothèques (quarterly) 01730

Association Professionnelle des Gégraphes du Québec, 182 Rue des Marguerites, Saint-Rédempteur-de-Lévis, Qué. G6K 1H3
T: (418) 836-5288
Founded: 1962; Members: 162
Focus: Geography 01731

Association Pulmonaire du Québec / Québec Lung Association, 4837 Rue Boyer, Ste 100, Montréal, Qué. H2J 3E6
T: (514) 252-7070; Fax: (514) 596-1883
Founded: 1938; Members: 300
Gen Secr: Claude Robitaille
Focus: Pulmon Dis 01732

Association Québécoise des Archivistes Médicales, 4357 Pl Viger, Rock-Forest, Qué. J1N 1Y9
T: (819) 567-6935; Fax: (819) 823-0799
Founded: 1959; Members: 1051
Focus: Archives 01733

Association Québécoise des Techniques de l'Eau, 911 Rue Jean-Talon Est, Ste 220, Montréal, Qué. H2R 1V5
T: (514) 270-7110; E-Mail: assqenv@login.net; Fax: (514) 270-7154
Founded: 1962; Members: 1500
Gen Secr: Eric Bouchard
Focus: Water Res
Periodicals
Effluent (10 times annually)
Sciences et Techniques de l'Eau (quarterly) 01734

Asthma Society of Canada, 130 Bridgeland Av, Ste 425, Toronto, Ont. M6A 1Z4
T: (416) 787-4050; Fax: (416) 787-5807
Focus: Rheuma 01735

Atlantic Planning Institute, POB 2012, RPO Central, Halifax, N.S. B3J 2Z1
T: (506) 577-4391; E-Mail: ncollins@fox.nstn.ca
Members: 270
Focus: Urban Plan
Periodical
The Atlantic Planners Pen (quarterly) . . 01736

Atlantic Provinces Council on the Sciences / Conseil des Provinces Atlantiques pour les Sciences, c/o Science Dept, Memorial University of Newfoundland, POB 4200, Sain John's, Nfld. A1B 3X7
T: (709) 737-8918; Fax: (709) 737-4569
Founded: 1962
Focus: Sci 01737

Atlantic Provinces Library Association (APLA), c/o School of Library and Information Studies, Dalhousie University, 6225 University Av, Halifax, N.S. B3H 4H8
T: (902) 494-3656; Fax: (902) 494-2319
Founded: 1957
Pres: Susan Libby
Focus: Libraries & Bk Sci
Periodical
APLA Bulletin (bi-monthly) 01738

Atlantic Region Education Association, 236 Saint George St, POB 5100, Moncton, N.B. E1C 8R2
T: (506) 857-2204
Focus: Educ 01739

Bibliographical Society of Canada / Société Bibliographique du Canada, POB 575, Station P, Toronto, Ont. M5S 2T1
E-Mail: dondertman@library.utoronto.ca
Founded: 1946; Members: 500
Pres: Thomas Vincent; Gen Secr: Anne Dondertman
Focus: Libraries & Bk Sci
Periodicals
Bulletin (semi-annually)
Papers/Cahiers (annually) 01740

Biophysical Society of Canada, c/o Institute of Biodiagnostics, National Research Council, 435 Ellice Av, Winnipeg, Man. R3B 1Y6
T: (204) 984-5146; Fax: (204) 984-6978
Founded: 1985; Members: 80
Gen Secr: Dr. Roxanne Deslauriers
Focus: Biophys 01741

Brewing and Malting Barley Research Institute, 167 Lombard Av, Ste 206, Winnipeg, Man. R3B 0T6
T: (204) 942-1407; Fax: (204) 947-5960
Founded: 1948
Gen Secr: Dr. N.T. Kendall
Focus: Nutrition 01742

British Columbia Art Therapy Association, 1002 Redcap St, Duncan, B.C. V9L 1M3
T: (604) 251-3809
Founded: 1978
Focus: Arts; Therapeutics 01743

British Columbia Association of Podiatrists (BCAP), 2309 41 Av W, Ste 203, Vancouver, B.C. V6M 2A3
T: (604) 261-2265; Fax: (604) 737-1146
Founded: 1968
Pres: Dr. J. Wong-Sing
Focus: Orthopedics
Periodical
BCAP Newsletter (quarterly) 01744

British Columbia Association of Speech, Language Pathologists and Audiologists, 9912 Lougheed Hwy, Burnaby, B.C. V3G 1N3
T: (604) 420-2222; Fax: (604) 420-9559
Founded: 1957; Members: 243
Focus: Logopedy 01745

British Columbia Cancer Foundation, 601 10 Av W, Vancouver, B.C. V5Z 1L3
T: (604) 877-6010; Fax: (604) 872-4596
Founded: 1935; Members: 150
Focus: Cell Biol & Cancer Res
Periodical
Cancer Research News (quarterly) . . . 01746

British Columbia Drama Association, 1005 Broad St Ste 307, Victoria, B.C. V8W 2A1
T: (250) 381-2443; Fax: (250) 381-4419
Founded: 1933; Members: 3000
Gen Secr: Jim Harding
Focus: Perf Arts 01747

British Columbia Genealogical Society, Lansdowne Mall, POB 88054, Richmond, B.C. V6X 3T6
T: (604) 988-6075
Founded: 1971
Pres: Peter S.N. Claydon
Focus: Genealogy
Periodicals
British Columbia Generalogist (quarterly)
Newsletter (bi-monthly) 01748

British Columbia Historical Federation, POB 746, Grand Forks, B.C. V0H 1H0
T: (250) 442-3865
Founded: 1922; Members: 1932
Pres: Alice Glanville
Focus: Hist 01749

British Columbia Library Association, 6545 Bonsor Av, Ste 110, Burnaby, B.C. V5H 1H3
T: (604) 430-9633; E-Mail: bcla@unixg.ubc.ca; Fax: (604) 430-8595
Founded: 1911; Members: 900
Pres: Ron Clancy
Focus: Libraries & Bk Sci 01750

British Columbia Medical Association, 1665 Broadway W, Ste 115, Vancouver, B.C. V6J 5A4
T: (604) 736-5551; Fax: (604) 733-7317
Founded: 1900; Members: 6921
Pres: Dr. Derryck Smith; Gen Secr: Dr. Norman D. Finlayson
Focus: Med 01751

British Columbia Museums Association, 514 Government St, Victoria, B.C. V8V 4X4
T: (250) 387-3315; Fax: (250) 387-1251
Founded: 1957; Members: 500
Gen Secr: Gregory Evans
Focus: Archives
Periodical
Museum Round-up (monthly) 01752

British Columbia Parkinsons's Disease Association, 411 Dunsmuir St, Vancouver, B.C. V6B 1X4
T: (604) 662-3240; Fax: (604) 662-3241
Members: 85
Gen Secr: L. Raphael
Focus: Intern Med 01753

British Columbia Pharmacy Association, 3751 Shell Rd, Ste 150, Richmond, B.C. V6X 2W2
T: (604) 279-2053; Fax: (604) 279-2065
Founded: 1968; Members: 1675
Gen Secr: Frank Merlin Archer
Focus: Pharmacol
Periodical
In Pharmation: B.C. Pharmacist (bi-monthly) 01754

British Columbia Public Health Association, 2182 12 St W, Ste 101, Vancouver, B.C. V6K 2N4
T: (604) 731-4970; Fax: (604) 731-5965
Focus: Public Health 01755

British Columbia Society of Occupational Therapists (B.C.S.O.T.), 1755 W Broadway Av, Ste 402, Vancouver, B.C. V6J 4S5
T: (604) 736-5645; E-Mail: bcsot@unixg.ubc.ca; Fax: (604) 736-5606
Founded: 1945; Members: 622
Gen Secr: Margot Kiss
Focus: Therapeutics
Periodical
OT Line (monthly) 01756

British Columbia Society of Respiratory Therapists, POB 4760, Vancouver, B.C. V6B 4A4
T: (604) 623-2227
Members: 370
Pres: Dave Sheets
Focus: Therapeutics 01757

British Columbia Teacher-Librarians' Association, c/o British Columbia Teachers' Federation, 550 Sixth Av W, Ste 100, Vancouver, B.C. V5Z 4P2
T: (604) 871-1848; Fax: (604) 871-2291
Members: 925
Pres: Patricia Finlay
Focus: Libraries & Bk Sci 01758

British Columbia Teachers' Federation, 550 Sixth Av W, Ste 100, Vancouver, B.C. V5Z 4P2
T: (604) 871-2283; Fax: (604) 871-2294
Founded: 1916; Members: 41358
Gen Secr: Elsie McMurphy
Focus: Educ 01759

British Columbia Transplant Society, 555 W 12 Av, East Tower, Vancouver, B.C. V5Z 3X7
T: (604) 877-2100; Fax: (604) 877-2111
Founded: 1985
Gen Secr: Bill Barrable
Focus: Surgery 01760

Broadcast Educators Association of Canada, 741 Colborne St, Brantford, Ont. N3S 3R9
T: (519) 753-1058; E-Mail: bradfoj@operatns.mohawkc.on.ca
Founded: 1977; Members: 184
Pres: Jane Bonisteel; Gen Secr: John Bradford
Focus: Educ 01761

Broadcast Research Council of Canada, 2 Bloor St W, Ste 100, Toronto, Ont. M4W 3E2
Fax: (416) 929-2529
Founded: 1965; Members: 190
Focus: Mass Media 01762

Brodie Club, 2 S FRont St, Ste 1107, Belleville, Ont. K8N 5K7
Founded: 1922; Members: 30
Focus: Anthro 01763

Bruce Law Association, 215 Cayley St, POB 818, Walkerton, Ont. N0G 2V0
T: (519) 881-2384
Focus: Law 01764

Calgary Zoological Society, POB 3036, Station B, Calgary, Alta. T2M 4R8
T: (403) 265-9300; Fax: (403) 237-7582
Focus: Zoology 01765

Canada Safety Council / Conseil Canadien de la Sécurité, 1020 Thomas Spratt Pl, Ottawa, Ont. K1G 5L5
T: (613) 739-1535; Fax: (613) 739-1566
Founded: 1968; Members: 500
Pres: Emile-J. Thérien
Focus: Safety
Periodicals
Council Update (monthly)
Living Safety (quarterly)
News Brake (monthly)
Public Focus (monthly)
Safety Canada (bi-monthly)
Safetylines (monthly) 01766

Canadian Academic Accounting Association, c/o Faculty of Management, University of Toronto, 120 King St W, Ste 850, POB 176, Hamilton, Ont. L8N 3C3
T: (905) 525-1884; Fax: (905) 525-3046
Founded: 1976; Members: 715
Focus: Business Admin
Periodicals
Canadian Accounting Education and Research News (quarterly)
Contemporary Accounting Research (bi-annually) 01767

Canadian Academy International, 1789 Lamothe St, Sudbury, Ont. P3A 2J9
Fax: (705) 524-2979
Founded: 1989
Pres: John H. Ovens; Gen Secr: Leo D. Leclair
Focus: Sci 01768

Canadian Academy of Child Psychiatry, POB 130, Nobleton, Ont. L0G 1N0
T: (905) 859-4420; Fax: (905) 830-5972
Founded: 1981; Members: 323
Gen Secr: Dr. Jennifer H. Steadman
Focus: Psychiatry 01769

Canadian Academy of Engineering, 130 Albert St, Ste 1414, Ottawa, K1P 5G4
T: (613) 235-9056; Fax: (613) 230-5759
Founded: 1987; Members: 250
Pres: Dr. Angus Broneau; Gen Secr: Dr. Léopold M. Nadeau
Focus: Eng
Periodical
Newsbrief (quarterly) 01770

Canadian Academy of Facial Plastic and Reconstructive Surgery, 600 University Av, Ste 401, Toronto, Ont. M5G 1X5
T: (905) 569-6965
Founded: 1981
Focus: Surgery 01771

Canadian Academy of Oral Pathology, c/o Dept of Oral Pathology, University of Western Ontario, London, Ont. N6A 5C1
T: (519) 679-2111; Fax: (519) 661-3370
Pres: Dr. T.D. Dailey
Focus: Otorhinolaryngology; Pathology . . 01772

Canadian Academy of Oral Radiology, c/o Faculty of Dentistry, University of Toronto, 124 Edward St, Toronto, Ont. M5G 1G6
T: (416) 979-4932 ext 4365; Fax: (416) 979-4936
Members: 40
Pres: Dr.P.A. Sikorski
Focus: Radiology; Otorhinolaryngology . . 01773

Canadian Academy of Periondontology, 1815 Alta Vista Dr, Ste 103, Ottawa, Ont. K1G 3Y6
T: (613) 523-3876; Fax: (613) 523-1968
Founded: 1968; Members: 300
Pres: Dr. Marlene Mader
Focus: Dent 01774

Canadian Academy of Psychiatry and the Law, 302 The East Mall, Ste 400, Toronto, Ont. M9B 6C7
T: (416) 236-5600; Fax: (416) 236-5603
Members: 80
Gen Secr: Dr. Graham Glancy
Focus: Psychiatry; Law 01775

Canadian Academy of Recording Arts and Sciences, 124 Merton St, Toronto, Ont. M4S 2Z2
T: (416) 485-3135; Fax: (416) 485-4978
Founded: 1975; Members: 1450
Gen Secr: Daisy C. Falle
Focus: Music
Periodical
Newsletter (bi-monthly) 01776

Canadian Academy of Sport Medicine / Académie Canadienne de Medécine Sportive, 1600 James Naismith Dr, Gloucester, Ont. K1B 5N4
T: (613) 748-5851; Fax: (613) 748-5850
Founded: 1970; Members: 500
Pres: Dr. Nicholas Montadi
Focus: Physical Therapy 01777

Canadian Academy of the History of Pharmacy / Académie Canadienne d'Histoire de la Pharmacie, c/o Faculty of Pharmacy, University of Toronto, 33 Russell St, Toronto, Ont. M5S 2S2
T: (416) 978-2889; Fax: (416) 978-8511
Founded: 1955; Members: 195
Gen Secr: Dr. Ernst W. Stieb
Focus: Pharmacol 01778

Canadian Academy of Urological Surgeons, 2075 Bayview Av, Ste 1039A, Toronto, Ont. M4W 3M5
Gen Secr: S. Herschorn
Focus: Surgery; Urology 01779

Canadian Acoustical Association / Association Canadienne d'Acoustique, 41 Watson Av, Toronto, Ont. M6S 4C9
T: (905) 762-6093; Fax: (905) 670-1698
Founded: 1977; Members: 480
Focus: Acoustics
Periodical
Canadian Acoustics/Acoustique Canadienne (quarterly) 01780

Canadian Advanced Technology Association, 388 Albert St, Ottawa, Ont. K1P 5H9
T: (613) 236-6550; E-Mail: info@cata.ca; Fax: (613) 236-8189
Founded: 1978; Members: 26
Pres: John Reid
Focus: Eng 01781

Canadian Advertising Research Foundation (CARF) / Fondation Canadienne de Recherche en Publicité, 175 Bloor St E, South Tower, Ste 307, Toronto, Ont. M4W 3R8
T: (416) 964-3832; Fax: (416) 964-0771
Founded: 1949; Members: 118
Focus: Advert
Periodical
CARF Newsletter 01782

Canadian Aeronautics and Space Institute / Institut Aéronautique et Spatial du Canada, 130 Slater St, Ste 818, Ottawa, Ont. K1P 6E2
T: (613) 234-0191; E-Mail: ab144@freenet.carleton.ca; Fax: (613) 234-9039
Founded: 1954; Members: 1835
Gen Secr: Ian M. Ross
Focus: Aero
Periodical
Canadian Aeronautics and Space Journal (quarterly) 01783

Canadian Agricultural Economics and Farm Management Society, 151 Slater St, Suite 907, Ottawa, Ont. K1P 5H4
T: (613) 232-9459; Fax: (613) 594-5190
Founded: 1952; Members: 500
Gen Secr: Jeff Corman
Focus: Agri
Periodical
Canadian Journal of Agricultural Economics (quarterly) 01784

Canadian Alarm and Security Association (CANASA) / Association Canadienne de l'Alarme et de la Securité, 610 Alden Rd, Ste 201, Markham, Ont. L3R 9Z1
T: (905) 513-0622; E-Mail: staff@canasa.org; Fax: (905) 513-0624
Founded: 1977; Members: 260
Gen Secr: Shayla Gunter
Focus: Safety
Periodical
CANASA Newsletter (2-3 times annually) 01785

Canadian Anaesthetists' Society / Société Canadienne des Anesthésistes, 1 Eglinton Av E, Ste 208, Toronto, Ont. M4P 3A1
T: (416) 480-0602; E-Mail: cas@multinet.org; Fax: (416) 480-0320
Founded: 1943; Members: 2250
Pres: Dr. Pierre Limoges
Focus: Anesthetics 01786

Canadian Anthropology Society, c/o Dept of Sociology and Anthropology, Concordia University, 1455 Blvd de Maisonneuve Ouest, Montréal Qué. H3G 1M8
Gen Secr: Linda Oren
Focus: Anthro 01787

Canadian Archaeological Association, 3170 Tillicum Rd, Space 162, Victoria, B.C. V9A 7H7
T: (250) 478-1147; Fax: (205) 388-7373
Founded: 1968; Members: 450
Gen Secr: Bjorn O. Simonsen
Focus: Archeol

Periodical
Canadian Journal of Archaeology . . . 01788

Canadian Art Museums Directors Organization / Organisation des Directeurs des Musées d'Art Canadiens, c/o Nickle Arts Museum, University of Calgary, 2500 University Dr NW, Calgary, Alta. T2N 1N4
E-Mail: nickle@acs.ucalgary.ca
Founded: 1964; Members: 55
Pres: Ann Davis
Focus: Arts 01789

Canadian Association for Adult Education, 29 Prince Arthur Av, Toronto, Ont. M5R 1B2
T: (416) 964-0559; Fax: (416) 964-9226
Founded: 1935; Members: 1000
Pres: Teresa MacNeil; Gen Secr: Ian Morrison
Focus: Adult Educ
Periodicals
Learning (quarterly)
Resources Kit (bi-monthly) 01790

Canadian Association for American Studies (CAAS), c/o Dept of English, University of Guelph, MacKinnon Bldg, Guelph, Ont. N1G 2W1
T: (519) 824-4120; Fax: (519) 766-0844
Founded: 1964; Members: 700
Pres: Christine Bold
Focus: Hist
Periodicals
Canadian Review of American Studies (quarterly)
Newsletter (semi-annually) 01791

Canadian Association for Anatomy, Neurobiology and Cell Biology, c/o Dept of Anatomy, University of Manitoba, 730 William Av, Winnipeg, Man. R3E 0W3
T: (204) 789-3796; E-Mail: bruni@bldghsc.lanl.umanitoba.ca; Fax: (204) 772-0622
Founded: 1956
Pres: Peter Haase
Focus: Anat; Bio; Cell Biol & Cancer Res
Periodical
Newsletter (annually) 01792

Canadian Association for Clinical Microbiology and Infectious Diseases, 20045 Montée Sainte-Marie, Montréal, Qué. H9X 3R5
T: (514) 457-2070; Fax: (514) 457-6346
Founded: 1980; Members: 400
Focus: Microbio; Med 01793

Canadian Association for Corporate Growth, c/o ABN AMRO Bank Canada, POB 114, Station Toronto Dominion, Toronto, Ont. M5K 1G8
T: (416) 365-2932; Fax: (416) 367-1485
Founded: 1973
Pres: Barbara Corder
Focus: Econ 01794

Canadian Association for Dental Research / Association Canadienne de Recherches Dentaires, c/o Faculty of Dentistry, University of Alberta, 46 University Campus NW, Rm 3036, Edmonton, Alta. T6G 2N8
T: (403) 492-3631; Fax: (403) 491-1624
Founded: 1976; Members: 325
Focus: Dent 01795

Canadian Association for Distance Education, 1 Stewart St, Ste 205, Ottawa, Ont. K1N 6H7
T: (613) 230-3630; E-Mail: csse@acadvm1.uottawa.ca; Fax: (613) 230-2746
Founded: 1984
Pres: Barbara Spronk
Focus: Educ 01796

Canadian Association for Health, Physical Education, Recreation and Dance, 1600 Naismith Dr, Ste 809, Gloucester, Ont. K1B 5N4
T: (613) 748-5622; Fax: (613) 748-5737
Founded: 1933; Members: 2500
Focus: Public Health; Sports 01797

Canadian Association for Information Science / Association Canadienne des Sciences de l'Information, c/o FIS, University of Toronto, 140 Saint George St, Toronto, Ont. M5S 1A1
T: (416) 978-8876; Fax: (416) 971-1399
Founded: 1974; Members: 600
Focus: Computer & Info Sci
Periodicals
CAIS Newsletter: Nouvelles ACSI (quarterly)
Canadian Journal of Information Science: Revue canadienne des sciences de l'information (annually)
Proceedings of the Annual Conference: Procesverbaux de la conférence (annually) 01798

Canadian Association for Irish Studies, c/o Dept of English, Trent University, Peterborough, Ont. K9J 7B8
T: (705) 748-1206
Founded: 1956; Members: 400
Pres: Finn Gallagher
Focus: Ethnology
Periodical
Canadian Journal of Irish Studies (semi-annually) 01799

Canadian Association for Laboratory Animal Science / Association Canadienne pour la Technologie des Animaux de Laboratoire, c/o Biosciences Animal Service, University of Alberta, CW 401 Biological Science Bldg, Edmonton, Alta. T6G 2E9
T: (403) 492-5193; Fax: (403) 492-7257
Founded: 1962; Members: 500
Focus: Vet Med
Periodical
Newsletter (bi-monthly) 01800

Canadian Association for Music Therapy, c/o Wilfrid Laurier University, 75 University Av W, Waterloo, Ont. N2L 3C5
T: (519) 884-1970 ext 6828; Fax: (519) 884-8853
Founded: 1974; Members: 350
Pres: Dr. Johanne Brodeur
Focus: Music; Therapeutics 01801

Canadian Association for Pastoral Practice and Education, 47 Queen's Park Cres, Toronto, Ont. M5C 2C3
T: (416) 977-3700; E-Mail: jkraus@enterprise.ca; Fax: (416) 978-7821
Founded: 1965
Gen Secr: Jan K. Kraus
Focus: Educ; Rel & Theol 01802

Canadian Association for Production and Inventory Control, 3 Church St, Ste 604, Toronto, Ont. M5E 1M2
T: (416) 364-5007; Fax: (416) 862-0315
Founded: 1962
Focus: Materials Sci 01803

Canadian Association for Scottish Studies / Société des Etudes Ecossaises, c/o Dept of History, University of Guelph, Guelph, Ont. N1G 2W1
T: (519) 824-4120 ext 3888
Founded: 1971; Members: 217
Focus: Ethnology 01804

Canadian Association for the Advancement of Netherlandic Studies / Association Canadienne pour l'Avancement des Etudes Néerlandaises, c/o Dept of Classics, Acadia University, Wolfville, N.S. B0P 1X0
T: (902) 542-2200 ext 1267; Fax: (902) 542-4727
Founded: 1971; Members: 300
Pres: Beert Verstraete
Focus: Ling; Lit; Cultur Hist; Sociology; Poli Sci
Periodical
Canadian Journal of Netherlandic Studies (semi-annually) 01805

Canadian Association for the Social Studies, c/o RC School Board of Saint John's Belvedere, Bonaventure Av, Saint John's, N.F. A1C 3Z4
T: (709) 753-8530; Fax: (709) 753-8407
Focus: Sociology 01806

Canadian Association for the Study of Adult Education, 515 W Hastings St, Vancouver, B.C. V6B 5K3
T: (604) 291-5070
Focus: Adult Educ 01807

Canadian Association for University Continuing Education / Association pour l'Education Permanente dans les Universités du Canada, 350 Albert St, Ste 320, Ottawa, Ont. K1R 1B1
T: (613) 563-1236; E-Mail: kclements@aucc.ca; Fax: (613) 563-7739
Founded: 1974; Members: 74
Focus: Educ 01808

Canadian Association of African Studies / Association Canadienne des Etudes Africaines, 855 Rue Sherbrooke Ouest, Montréal, Qué. H3A 2T7
T: (514) 398-4800; Fax: (514) 398-1770
Founded: 1971; Members: 300
Gen Secr: Prof. Frank Kanz
Focus: Ethnology
Periodicals
Canadian Journal of African Studies (3 times annually)
Newsletter (semi-annually) 01809

Canadian Association of Business Education Teachers, c/o Halton Board of Education, 2050 Guelph Line, POB 5005, Burlington, Ont. L7R 3Z2
T: (905) 335-3663; Fax: (905) 335-9802
Founded: 1967
Pres: Al Renner
Focus: Educ 01810

Canadian Association of Foundations of Education / Association Canadienne pour l'Etude des Fondements de l'Education, c/o Dept of Educational Studies, University of British Columbia, 2125 Main Mall, Vancouver, B.C. V6T 1Z4
T: (604) 822-5295; E-Mail: donald.fisher@ubc.ca; Fax: (604) 822-4244
Founded: 1971; Members: 190
Pres: Dr. Donald Fisher
Focus: Educ 01811

Canadian Association of Future Studies, CP 40, Succ Victoria, Montréal, Qué. H3Z 3V4
T: (514) 487-9154; Fax: (514) 481-0180
Founded: 1976; Members: 300
Focus: Futurology
Periodical
Futures Canada (quarterly) 01812

Canadian Association of Gastroenterology / Association Canadienne de Gastroentérologie, c/o Dept of GI Research, University of Calgary, 3330 Hospital Dr NW, Calgary, Alta. T2N 4N1
T: (403) 220-4539; Fax: (403) 283-3028
Founded: 1961; Members: 254
Focus: Gastroenter 01813

Canadian Association of Geographers (CAG) / Association Canadienne des Géographes, c/o McGill University, Burnside Hall, 805 Rue Sherbrooke Ouest, Montréal, Qué. H3A 2K6
T: (514) 398-4946; Fax: (514) 398-7437
Founded: 1951; Members: 2050
Pres: Dr. John C. Everitt; Gen Secr: Dr. Mark Rosenberg
Focus: Geography
Periodicals
The Canadian Geographer (quarterly)
The Directory (annually)
The Operational Geographer (quarterly) . 01814

Canadian Association of Independent Schools, POB 1502, Saint Catherines, Ont. L2R 7J9
T: (905) 688-4866; E-Mail: cais@ridley.on.ca; Fax: (905) 688-5778
Founded: 1979
Focus: Educ 01815

Canadian Association of Law Libraries (CALL), 190 Railway St, POB 1570, Kingston, Ont. K7L 5C8
T: (613) 531-9338; E-Mail: call@adan.kingston.net
Founded: 1961; Members: 480
Gen Secr: Elizabeth Hooper
Focus: Libraries & Bk Sci
Periodical
CALL Newsletter (5 times annually) . . 01816

Canadian Association of Law Teachers, c/o Canadian Bar Association, 50 O'Connor St, Ste 902, Ottawa, Ont. K1P 6L2
Members: 700
Pres: Dr. Anne Stalker
Focus: Law; Educ 01817

Canadian Association of Marketing Research Organizations, 191 The West Mall, Ste 1105, Etobicoke, Ont. M9C 5K8
T: (416) 620-7420; E-Mail: bbandc@enterprise.ca; Fax: (416) 620-5392
Founded: 1975; Members: 22
Gen Secr: Dave Stark
Focus: Marketing 01818

Canadian Association of Music Libraries, Archives and Documentation Centres (CAML), c/o National Library, Music Division, 395 Wellington St, Ottawa, Ont. K1A 0N4
T: (613) 996-2300; E-Mail: stm@psb.nlc-bnc.ca; Fax: (613) 952-2895
Founded: 1973; Members: 132
Focus: Libraries & Bk Sci; Music
Periodical
Newsletter (3 times annually) 01819

Canadian Association of Optometrists / Association Canadienne des Optométristes, 234 Argyle Av, Ottawa, Ont. K2P 1B9
T: (613) 235-7924; Fax: (613) 235-2025
Founded: 1948; Members: 2800
Focus: Ophthal
Periodical
The Canadian Journal of Optometry (quarterly) 01820

Canadian Association of Paediatric Surgeons / Association de la Chirurgie Infantile Canadienne, c/o Regina General Hospital, 1440 14 Av, Regina, Sask. S4P 0W5
T: (306) 359-4542; Fax: (306) 359-4723
Founded: 1968; Members: 60
Focus: Pediatrics; Surgery 01821

Canadian Association of Pathologists / Association Canadienne des Pathologistes, c/o Toronto General Hospital, 200 Elizabeth St, Toronto, Ont. M5G 2C4
T: (416) 340-3008; Fax: (416) 340-4706
Founded: 1949; Members: 650
Focus: Pathology 01822

Canadian Association of Physical Medicine and Rehabilitation / Association Canadienne de Médecine Physique et de Réadaptation, 774 Echo Dr, Ottawa, Ont. K1S 5N8
T: (613) 730-6240; Fax: (613) 730-1116
Founded: 1962; Members: 230
Focus: Physical Therapy
Periodical
Newsletter (quarterly) 01823

Canadian Association of Physicists / Association Canadienne des Physiciens et Physiciennes, 150 Louis Pasteur Av, Ste 112, Ottawa, Ont. K1N 6NS
T: (613) 562-5614; E-Mail: cap@physics.uottawa.ca; Fax: (613) 562-5615
Founded: 1945; Members: 2100
Pres: Dr. Paul Vincett; Gen Secr: Francine M. Ford
Focus: Physics
Periodical
Physics in Canada (bi-monthly) 01824

Canadian Association of Radiologists / Association Canadienne des Radiologistes, 5101 Rue Buchan, Ste 510, Montréal, Qué. H4P 2R9
T: (514) 738-3111; Fax: (514) 738-5199
Founded: 1937; Members: 1700
Focus: Nucl Med 01825

Canadian Association of Research Libraries / Association des Bibliothèques de Recherche du Canada, c/o University of Ottawa, Morisset Hall, 65 University St, Rm 602, Ottawa, Ont. K1N 9A5
T: (613) 562-5800 ext 3652; Fax: (613) 562-5195
Founded: 1976
Pres: C. Presser
Focus: Libraries & Bk Sci 01826

Canadian Association of Special Libraries and Information Services, 3 Greystone Walk, Ste 29, Scarborough, Ont. M1K 5J4
T: (403) 261-1263
Founded: 1969; Members: 1200
Pres: Mary-L. Brennan
Focus: Libraries & Bk Sci
Periodical
Newsletter 01827

Canadian Association of University Schools of Nursing (CAUSN) / Association Canadienne des Ecoles Universitaires de Nursing, 350 Albert St, Ste 325, Ottawa, Ont. K1R 1B1
T: (613) 563-1236 ext 280; Fax: (613) 563-7739
Founded: 1942
Focus: Educ; Med
Periodicals
The Canadian Journal of Nursing (quarterly)
CAUSN Newsletter (quarterly) 01828

Canadian Association of University Schools of Rehabilitation / Association Canadienne des Ecoles Universitaires de Réadaptation, c/o School of Physical and Occupational Therapy, McGill University, 3654 Drummond St, Montréal, Qué. H3G 1Y5
T: (514) 398-4500; Fax: (514) 398-6360
Founded: 1965
Focus: Educ; Rehabil 01829

Canadian Association of University Teachers / Association Canadienne des Professeurs d'Université, 2675 Queensview Dr, Ottawa, Ont. K2B 8K2
T: (613) 820-2270; E-Mail: acppu@caut.ca; Fax: (613) 820-7244
Founded: 1951; Members: 362
Gen Secr: Dr. Donald C. Savage
Focus: Educ 01830

Canadian Association of University Teachers of German / Association des Professeurs d'Allemand des Universités Canadiennes, c/o Dept of Germanic and Slavic Languages, University of Regina, Regina, Sask. S4S 0A2
E-Mail: dietrick@uwinnipeg.ca
Founded: 1961; Members: 300
Pres: L. Dietrick
Focus: Educ; Ling
Periodical
Seminar (quarterly) 01831

Canadian Association on Water Quality, c/o Environmental Technology Centre, 3439 River Rd S, Gloucester, Ont. K1A 0H3
T: (613) 990-9849; Fax: (613) 990-9855
Founded: 1966; Members: 163
Focus: Water Res 01832

Canadian Astronomical Society / Société Canadienne d'Astronomie, c/o Dépt de Physique, Université de Montréal, Montréal, Qué. H3C 3J7
T: (514) 343-2364; E-Mail: casca@astro.umontreal.ca; Fax: (514) 343-2071
Founded: 1971; Members: 360
Focus: Astronomy 01833

Canadian Athletic Therapists Association / Association Canadienne des Thérapeutes du Sport, 1600 James Naismith Dr, Ste 507, Gloucester, Ont. K1B 5N4
T: (613) 748-5876; Fax: (613) 748-5850
Founded: 1965; Members: 500
Pres: Dale Butterwick
Focus: Physical Therapy
Periodical
Journal of the Canadian Athletic Therapists (quarterly) 01834

Canadian Authors Association, 27 Doxsee Av N, Campbellford, Ont. K0L 1L0
T: (705) 653-0323; Fax: (705) 653-0593
Founded: 1921; Members: 950
Pres: Cora Taylor
Focus: Lit
Periodical
Canadian Author & Bookman (quarterly) . 01835

Canadian Aviation Historical Society (C.A.H.S.), POB 224, Station A, North York, Ont. M2N 5S8
Founded: 1963; Members: 1300
Pres: Jack Gow; Gen Secr: Ed Rice
Focus: Aero; Hist
Periodical
C.A.H.S. Journal (quarterly) 01836

Canadian Bar Association (CBA/ABC) / Association du Barreau Canadien, 50 O'Connor St, Ste 902, Ottawa, Ont. K1P 6L2
T: (613) 237-2925; E-Mail: info@cba.org; Fax: (613) 237-0185
Founded: 1921; Members: 36000
Pres: Gordon Proudfoot
Focus: Law
Periodicals
Canadian Bar Review (quarterly)
National (monthly) 01837

Canadian Botanical Association (CBA) / Association Botanique du Canada, c/o Dept of Botany, University of Guelph, 50 Stone Rd E, Ste 158, Guelph, Ont. N1G 2W1
T: (519) 824-4120 ext 2745; Fax: (519) 767-1991
Founded: 1965; Members: 300
Focus: Botany

Periodical
CBA/ABC Bulletin (quarterly) *01838*

Canadian Bureau for International Education / Bureau Canadien de l'Education Internationale, 220 Laurier Av W, Ste 1100, Ottawa, Ont. K1P 5Z9
T: (613) 237-4820; E-Mail: jfox@cbic.ca;
Fax: (613) 237-1073
Founded: 1966; Members: 120
Pres: James W. Fox
Focus: Educ
Periodicals
Annual Report (annually)
International Education Magazine (bi-monthly)
. . . . *01839*

Canadian Bureau for the Advancement of Music / Bureau Canadien pour l'Avancement de Musique, Exhibition Pl, Toronto, Ont. M6K 3C3
T: (416) 260-6451
Founded: 1917 k7156= 160
Focus: Music *01840*

Canadian Cancer Society / Société Canadienne du Cancer, 10 Alcorn Av, Ste 200, Toronto, Ont. M4V 3B1
T: (416) 961-7223; Fax: (416) 961-4189
Founded: 1938
Pres: Dr. Ronald J. Potter; Gen Secr: Maaike Asselbergs
Focus: Cell Biol & Cancer Res
Periodical
Progress Against Cancer (quarterly) . . *01841*

Canadian Canon Law Society / Société Canadienne de Droit Canonique, 223 Main St, Ottawa, Ont. K1S 1C4
T: (613) 236-1393 ext 2215; Fax: (613) 236-5278
Founded: 1966; Members: 425
Focus: Rel & Theol; Law
Periodical
Newsletter/Bulletin de Nouvelles (semi-annually)
. . . . *01842*

Canadian Cardiovascular Society / Société Canadienne de Cardiologie, 360 Victoria Av, Rm 401, Westmount, Qué. H3Z 2N4
T: (514) 482-3407; Fax: (514) 482-6574
Founded: 1962; Members: 930
Focus: Cardiol *01843*

Canadian Cartographic Association / Association Canadienne de Cartographie, c/o Geography Dept, University of Calgary, 2500 University Dr NW, Calgary, Alta. T2N 1N4
T: (403) 278-5069; E-Mail: mkrieger@acs.ucalgary.ca; Fax: (403) 282-6561
Founded: 1975; Members: 400
Focus: Cart
Periodical
Cartographica (quarterly) *01844*

Canadian Catholic Historical Association (English Section), 1155 Yonge St, Toronto, Ont. M4T 1W2
T: (416) 934-3400 ext 504; Fax: (416) 934-3444
Founded: 1933; Members: 320
Gen Secr: Edward Jackman
Focus: Hist; Rel & Theol *01845*

Canadian Celtic Arts Association, c/o Saint Michael's College, University of Toronto, 81 Saint Mary St, Toronto, Ont. M5S 1J4
T: (416) 926-7145; Fax: (416) 926-7276
Founded: 1977; Members: 200
Gen Secr: Jean Talman
Focus: Arts *01846*

Canadian Centre for Architecture, 1920 Rue Baile, Montréal, Qué. H3H 2S6
T: (514) 939-7000; E-Mail: ref@cca.qc.ca;
Fax: (514) 936-7029)
Founded: 1979; Members: 1800
Focus: Archit *01847*

Canadian Ceramic Society, 2175 Sheppard Av E, Ste 310, North York, Ont. M2J 1W8
T: (416) 491-2886; E-Mail: taylor@interlog.com;
Fax: (416) 491-1670
Founded: 1901; Members: 420
Pres: Al Matthews
Focus: Materials Sci
Periodical
Canadian Ceramics (quarterly) *01848*

Canadian Children's Book Centre, 35 Spadina Rd, Toronto, Ont. M5R 2S9
T: (416) 975-0010; E-Mail: ccbc@lglobal.com;
Fax: (416) 975-1839
Founded: 1976; Members: 1200
Gen Secr: Charlotte Teeple
Focus: Libraries & Bk Sci
Periodical
Children's Book News (quarterly) *01849*

Canadian Chiropractic Association / Association Chiropratique Canadienne, 1396 Ellington Av W, Toronto, Ont. M6C 2E4
T: (416) 718-5656; Fax: (416) 781-7344
Founded: 1943; Members: 3450
Focus: Surgery
Periodical
Journal of the CCA (quarterly) *01850*

Canadian Chiropractic Historial Association, 101 McRae Dr, Toronto, Ont. M4G 1S6
T: (416) 482-2340
Pres: Dr. H. Lee
Focus: Surgery; Hist *01851*

Canadian Coalition for Nuclear Responsibility / Regroupement pour la Surveillance du Nucléaire, CP 236, Succ Snowdon, Montréal, Qué. H3X 3T4
T: (514) 489-5118; Fax: (514) 489-5118
Founded: 1975
Focus: Nucl Res *01852*

Canadian College of Medical Geneticists, 774 Echo Dr, Ottawa, Ont. K1S 5N8
T: (613) 730-6250; E-Mail: ccmg@rcpsc.edu;
Fax: (613) 730-1116
Founded: 1975; Members: 145
Gen Secr: Dr. Alessandra Duncan
Focus: Genetics; Med *01853*

Canadian College of Teachers / Collège Canadien des Enseignants, 201A Sherwood Dr, POB 57157, RPO Eastgate, Sherwood Park, Alta. T8A 5L7
T: (403) 922-6668; Fax: (403) 922-2885
Founded: 1958; Members: 1200
Gen Secr: Ronald E. Johnston
Focus: Educ *01854*

Canadian Committee of Byzantinists, c/o University of Waterloo, 200 University Av W, Waterloo, Ont. N2L 3G1
T: (519) 885-1211 ext 3565; E-Mail: dsahas@uwaterloo.waterloo.ca; Fax: (519) 746-3097
Members: 30
Focus: Cultur Hist *01855*

Canadian Conference of the Arts / Conférence Canadienne des Arts, 189 Laurier Av W, Ottawa, Ont. K1N 6P1
T: (613) 238-3561; E-Mail: ccarts@globalx.net;
Fax: (613) 238-4849
Founded: 1945; Members: 1200
Pres: Mireille Gagné
Focus: Arts *01856*

Canadian Construction Association / Association Canadienne de la Construction, 85 Albert St, Ottawa, Ont. K1P 6A4
T: (613) 236-9455; Fax: (613) 236-9526
Founded: 1914; Members: 25000
Focus: Civil Eng
Periodical
Construction (bi-monthly) *01857*

Canadian Council for European Affairs / Conseil Canadien des Affaires Européennes, c/o Dept of Political Studies, University of Saskatchewan, Saskatoon, Sask. S7N 0W0
T: (306) 966-5231; Fax: (306) 966-8839
Founded: 1980
Pres: Eldon P. Black; Gen Secr: Prof. Hans J. Michelmann
Focus: Int'l Relat
Periodical
Journal of European Integration *01858*

Canadian Council of Library Schools / Conseil Canadien des Ecoles de Bibliothéconomie, c/o Ecole de Bibliothéconomie et des Sciences de l'Information, CP 6128, Succ A, Montréal, Qué. H3C 3J7
T: (514) 343-7400; Fax: (514) 343-5753
Founded: 1972
Focus: Libraries & Bk Sci *01859*

Canadian Council of Professional Engineers, 116 Albert St, Ste 401, Ottawa, Ont. K1P 5G3
T: (613) 232-2474; Fax: (613) 230-5759
Founded: 1936; Members: 151000
Pres: Daniel Verreault
Focus: Eng *01860*

Canadian Council of Teachers of English Language Arts (CCTELA), c/o Association Management Centre, POB 4143, Station C, Calgary, Alta. T2R 5M9
T: (204) 474-8564; Fax: (204) 275-5962
Founded: 1967; Members: 1200
Focus: Educ; Ling
Periodicals
CCTELA Newsletter (quarterly)
English Quarterly (quarterly) *01861*

Canadian Council of University Biology Chairs / Conseil Universitaire des Directeurs de Biologie du Canada, c/o Dept of Botany, University of Guelph, Axelrod Bldg, Guelph, Ont. N1G 2W1
T: (519) 824-4120 ext 6000; E-Mail: lperterso@uoguelph.ca; Fax: (519) 767-1991
Focus: Bio *01862*

Canadian Council of University Physical Education and Kinesiology Administrators, c/o Dept of Physical Education and Recreation, McGill University, Montréal, Qué. H2W 1S4
T: (514) 398-4185; Fax: (514) 398-4186
Focus: Sports *01863*

Canadian Council on Social Development / Conseil Canadien de Développement Social, 441 MacLaren St, Ottawa, Ont. K2P 2H3
T: (613) 236-8977; E-Mail: council@achilles.net;
Fax: (613) 236-2750
Founded: 1920; Members: 900
Focus: Sociology *01864*

Canadian Country Music Association, 3800 Steeles Av W, Ste 127, Woodbridge, Ont. L4L 4G9
T: (905) 850-1144; Fax: (905) 856-1633
Founded: 1976; Members: 1730
Focus: Music *01865*

Canadian Criminal Justice Association / Association Canadienne de Justice Pénale, 383 Parkdale Av, Ste 304, Ottawa, Ont. K1Y 4R4
T: (613) 725-3715; E-Mail: ccja@istar.ca;
Fax: (613) 725-3720
Founded: 1919; Members: 1000
Focus: Criminology
Periodicals
Canadian Journal of Criminology: Revue canadienne de criminologie (quarterly)
Directory Services for Victims of Crime: Répertoire Services aux victimes d'actes criminels (annually)
Justice Directory of Services: Répertoire des services (annually)
Justice Report: Actualités-Justice (quarterly) *01866*

Canadian Dental Association / Association Dentaire Canadienne, 1815 Alta Vista Dr, Ottawa, Ont. K1G 3Y6
T: (613) 523-1770; Fax: (613) 523-7736
Founded: 1902; Members: 11436
Gen Secr: Jardine Neilson
Focus: Dent
Periodical
Canadian Dental Association Journal (monthly)
. . . . *01867*

Canadian Dermatology Association / Association Canadienne de Dermatologie, 774 Echo Dr, Ste 521, Ottawa, Ont. K1S 5N8
T: (613) 730-6262; Fax: (613) 730-1116
Members: 400
Focus: Derm *01868*

Canadian Diabetes Association, 15 Toronto St, Ste 800, Toronto, Ont. M5C 2E3
T: (416) 363-3373; E-Mail: info@cda-nat.org;
Fax: (416) 363-3393
Founded: 1953; Members: 50000
Gen Secr: Jim O'Brien
Focus: Cardiol *01869*

Canadian Dietetic Association / Association Canadienne des Diététistes, 480 University Av, Ste 601, Toronto, Ont. M5G 1V2
T: (416) 596-0857; Fax: (416) 596-0603
Founded: 1935; Members: 3509
Focus: Nutrition *01870*

Canadian Drilling Association, 222 McIntyre St W, Ste 306, North Bay, Ont. P1B 2Y8
T: (705) 476-6992; Fax: (705) 476-9494
Founded: 1938
Focus: Eng *01871*

Canadian Economics Association, c/o Dept of Economics, University of Toronto, 150 Saint George St, Toronto, Ont. M5S 3G7
T: (416) 978-6295; E-Mail: cea@qed.econ.queensu.ca; Fax: (416) 978-6713
Founded: 1967
Gen Secr: Prof. Michael Denny
Focus: Econ
Periodical
Canadian Journal of Economics *01872*

Canadian Education Association (CEA/ACE) / Association Canadienne d'Education, 252 Bloor St W, Ste 8-200, Toronto, Ont. M5S 1V5
T: (416) 924-7721; E-Mail: acea@hookup.net;
Fax: (416) 924-3188
Founded: 1891; Members: 780
Gen Secr: Penny Milton
Focus: Educ
Periodicals
CEA Handbook
CEA Newsletter: Nouvelles
Education Canada (quarterly) *01873*

Canadian Electricity Association / Association Canadienne de l'Electricité, 1 Westmount Sq, Ste 1600, Montréal, Qué. H3Z 2P9
T: (514) 937-6181; Fax: (514) 937-6498
Founded: 1891; Members: 2380
Pres: Hans R. Konow; Gen Secr: I. Murray Phillips
Focus: Electric Eng
Periodicals
Bulletin
Research Reports *01874*

Canadian Energy Research Institute, 3512 33 St NW, Ste 150, Calgary, Alta. T2L 2A6
T: (403) 282-1231; E-Mail: cdneri@acs.ucalgary.ca;
Fax: (403) 284-4181
Founded: 1975
Gen Secr: R.J. Buchanan
Focus: Energy *01875*

Canadian Esperanto Youth / Jeunesse Espérantiste Canadienne, POB 2159, Sidney, B.C. V8L 3S6
T: (250) 474-3137; E-Mail: phopkins@sol.uvic.ca
Founded: 1976
Focus: Ling *01876*

Canadian Ethnic Studies Association (CESA) / Société Canadienne d'Etudes Ethniques, c/o Centre d'Etudes Ethniques, Université de Montréal, CP 6128, Succ Centre-Ville, Montréal, Qué. H3C 3J7
Founded: 1977; Members: 1300
Focus: Ethnology
Periodicals
Canadian Ethnic Studies
CESA Bulletin (quarterly)
Proceedings (semi-annually) *01877*

Canadian Federation for the Humanities (CFH) / Fédération Canadienne des Etudes Humaines, 151 Slater St, Ste 407, Ottawa, Ont. K1P 5H3
T: (613) 236-4686; E-Mail: cfhxt@acadvm1.uottawa.ca; Fax: (613) 236-4853
Founded: 1943; Members: 8000
Focus: Humanities
Periodical
Bulletin (semi-annually) *01878*

Canadian Federation of Biological Societies (CFBS) / Fédération Canadienne des Sociétés de Biologie, 1750 Courtwood Cresc, Ste 104, Ottawa, Ont. K2C 2B5
T: (613) 225-8889; E-Mail: cfbs@hpb.hwc.ca;
Fax: (613) 225-9621
Founded: 1957; Members: 5000
Focus: Bio
Periodicals
CFBS Newsletter (semi-annually)
Programme & Proceedings (annually) . . *01879*

Canadian Federation of University Women / Fédération Canadienne des Femmes Diplômées des Universités, 297 Dupuis St, Ste 308, Ottawa, Ont. K1L 7H8
T: (613) 747-7339; Fax: (613) 747-8358
Founded: 1919; Members: 12500
Focus: Educ *01880*

Canadian Fertility and Andrology Society / Société Canadienne de Fertilité et d'Andrologie, 2065 Alexandre Desève, Ste 409, Montréal, Qué. H2L 2W5
T: (514) 524-9009; Fax: (514) 524-2163
Founded: 1954; Members: 250
Focus: Venereology *01881*

Canadian Fertilizer Institute / Institut Canadien des Engrais, 222 Queen St, Ste 1540, Ottawa, Ont. K1P 5V9
T: (613) 230-2600; Fax: (613) 230-5142
Founded: 1958
Focus: Agri *01882*

Canadian Film Institute / Institut Canadien du Film, 2 Daly Av, Ottawa, Ont. K1N 6E2
T: (613) 232-8769; Fax: (613) 232-6727
Founded: 1935
Pres: Serge Losique
Focus: Cinema
Periodical
The Guide to Film, Television and Communications Courses in Canada (bi-annually)
. . . . *01883*

Canadian Fire Safety Association / Association Canadienne de Sécurité Incendie, 2175 Sheppard Av E, Ste 310, North York, Ont. M2J 1W8
T: (416) 492-9417; E-Mail: taylor@interlog.com;
Fax: (416) 491-1670
Founded: 1971; Members: 500
Focus: Safety *01884*

Canadian Folk Arts Council / Conseil Canadien des Arts Populaires, 263 Adelaide St W, Toronto, Ont. M5H 1Y2
T: (416) 977-7456
Founded: 1964; Members: 130
Focus: Folklore; Arts *01885*

Canadian Forestry Association, 185 Somerset St W, Ste 203, Ottawa, Ont. K2P 0J2
T: (613) 232-1815; Fax: (613) 232-4210
Founded: 1900; Members: 35000
Gen Secr: Glen Blouin
Focus: Forestry
Periodical
What They Say About Forestry on the Hill (bi-monthly) *01886*

Canadian Foundation for Economic Education / Fondation Canadienne d'Education Economique, 2 Saint Clair Av W, Ste 501, Toronto, Ont. M4V 1L5
T: (416) 968-2236; Fax: (416) 968-0488
Founded: 1974; Members: 2000
Focus: Econ; Educ *01887*

Canadian Foundation for the Study of Infant Deaths, 586 Eglinton Av E, Ste 308, Toronto, Ont. M4P 1P2
T: (416) 488-3260; E-Mail: sidscanada@oinforamp.net; Fax: (416) 488-3864
Founded: 1973; Members: 200
Gen Secr: Beverley DeBruyn
Focus: Pediatrics *01888*

Canadian Gas Association / Association Canadienne du Gaz, 243 Consumers Rd, Ste 1200, North York, Ont. M2J 5E3
T: (416) 498-1994; E-Mail: cga@cga.ca;
Fax: (416) 498-7465
Founded: 1907; Members: 650
Focus: Energy
Periodical
CGA News (monthly) *01889*

Canadian Gemmological Association, 1767 Avenue Rd, Toronto, Ont. M5M 3Y8
T: (416) 785-0962; Fax: (416) 785-9043
Founded: 1958; Members: 400
Pres: Zia Hasan
Focus: Mineralogy
Periodical
Canadian Gemmologist (quarterly) . . . *01890*

Canadian General Standards Board, 222 Queen St, Ste 1402, Ottawa, Ont. K1A 1G6
T: (613) 941-8709; Fax: (613) 941-8706
Focus: Standards 01891

Canadian Geoscience Council / Conseil Géoscientifique Canadien, c/o Dept of Earth Sciences, University of Waterloo, 200 University Av W, Waterloo, Ont. N2L 3G1
T: (519) 855-1211 ext 3029; E-Mail: avmorgan@sciborg.uwaterloo.ca; Fax: (519) 746-0183
Founded: 1972
Gen Secr: Alan V. Morgan
Focus: Geology 01892

Canadian Geotechnical Society / Société Canadienne Géotechnique, 170 Attwell Dr, Ste 501, Etobicoke, Ont. M9W 6A3
T: (514) 674-0366; Fax: (514) 674-9507
Founded: 1972; Members: 1254
Focus: Eng 01893

Canadian Group Psychotherapy Association / Association Canadienne de Psychothérapie de Groupe, 11 Millstone Cresc, Whitby, Ont. L1R 1T4
T: (905) 666-0555; Fax: (905) 666-0000
Founded: 1980; Members: 225
Focus: Therapeutics; Psych 01894

Canadian Health Libraries Association / Association des Bibliothèques de la Santé du Canada, POB 94038, Toronto, Ont. M4N 3R1
T: (416) 485-0377; Fax: (416) 485-0377
Founded: 1976; Members: 325
Focus: Libraries & Bk Sci; Public Health 01895

Canadian Hearing Society, 271 Spadina Rd, Toronto, Ont. M5R 2V3
T: (416) 964-9595; E-Mail: info@chs.ca; Fax: (416) 928-2525
Founded: 1979
Gen Secr: David A. Allen
Focus: Logopedy 01896

Canadian Hematology Society / Société Canadienne d'Hématologie, c/o Ottawa General Hospital, 501 Smyth Rd, Ottawa, Ont. K1H 8L6
T: (613) 737-8178; Fax: (613) 737-8141
Founded: 1971; Members: 200
Focus: Hematology 01897

Canadian Historical Association, 395 Wellington St, Ottawa, Ont. K1A 0N3
T: (613) 233-7885; E-Mail: 74143.1061@compuserve.com; Fax: (613) 567-3110
Founded: 1922; Members: 1800
Gen Secr: Joanne Mineault
Focus: Hist
Periodicals
Canada's Ethnic Groups Series
Historical Booklets (semi-annually)
Historical Papers (annually) 01898

Canadian Image Processing and Pattern Recognition Society, Campus de l'Université de Montréal, 2900 Blvd Edouard-Montpetit, Montréal, Qué. H3C 3AQ7
Founded: 1984; Members: 200
Focus: Computer & Info Sci 01899

Canadian Industrial Arts Association, c/o Faculty of Education, University of New Brunswick, Fredericton, N.B. E3B 6E3
T: (506) 453-3508; Fax: (506) 453-3569
Founded: 1965; Members: 250
Pres: Alfred T. Steeves
Focus: Arts 01900

Canadian Institute for Environmental Law and Policy / Institut Canadien du Droit et de la Politique de l'Environnement, 517 College St, Ste 400, Toronto, Ont. M6G 4A2
T: (416) 923-3529; E-Mail: cielap@web.net; Fax: (416) 923-5949
Founded: 1970; Members: 800
Gen Secr: Anne Mitchell
Focus: Law; Poli Sci 01901

Canadian Institute for Historical Microreproductions / Institut Canadien de Microréproductions Historiques, POB 2428, Station D, Ottawa, Ont. K1P 5W5
T: (613) 235-2628; E-Mail: cihmicmh@nlo.nlc.bnc.ca; Fax: (613) 235-9752
Founded: 1978
Focus: Doc 01902

Canadian Institute for Organization Management, 55 Metcalfe St, Ste 1160, Ottawa, Ont. K1P 6N4
T: (613) 238-4000; Fax: (613) 238-7643
Founded: 1946
Gen Secr: Roger Stanion
Focus: Business Admin 01903

Canadian Institute for the Administration of Justice, c/o Faculté de Droit, Université de Montréal, CP 6128, Succ Centre-Ville, Montréal, Qué. H3C 3J7
T: (514) 343-6157; E-Mail: ciajumontreal.ca; Fax: (514) 343-6296
Founded: 1974
Gen Secr: Christine Robertson
Focus: Law 01904

Canadian Institute of Chartered Accountants, 277 Wellington St W, Toronto, Ont. M5V 3H2
T: (416) 977-3222; Fax: (416) 977-8585
Founded: 1902; Members: 50565
Pres: Michael Rayner
Focus: Business Admin
Periodicals
CA Magazine (monthly)
Members Directory (bi-annually) 01905

Canadian Institute of Child Health / Institut Canadien de la Santé Infantile, 885 Meadowlands Dr E, Ottawa, Ont. K2C 3N2
T: (613) 224-4144; E-Mail: cich@igs.net; Fax: (613) 224-4145
Founded: 1977
Gen Secr: Denise Avard
Focus: Pediatrics
Periodical
Child Health (quarterly) 01906

Canadian Institute of Financial Planning, 151 Yonge St, Ste 503, Toronto, Ont. M5C 2W7
T: (416) 865-1237; Fax: (416) 861-9937
Focus: Finance 01907

Canadian Institute of Food Science and Technology (CIFST) / Institut Canadien de Science et Technologie Alimentaires, 191 The West Mall, Ste 1105, Etobicoke, Ont. M9C 5K8
T: (416) 626-3140; Fax: (416) 620-5392
Founded: 1951; Members: 1800
Focus: Food
Periodical
CIFST Journal (5 times annually) . . . 01908

Canadian Institute of Forestry / Institut Forestier du Canada, 151 Slater St, Ste 606, Ottawa, Ont. K1P 5H3
T: (613) 234-2242; E-Mail: cif@cif-ifc.org; Fax: (613) 234-6181
Founded: 1908; Members: 2400
Gen Secr: Roxanne Comeau
Focus: Forestry
Periodical
The Forestry Chronicle (bi-monthly) . . . 01909

Canadian Institute of Hypnotism / Institut Canadienne d'Hypnotisme, 110 Rue Greystone, Montréal, Qué. H9R 5T6
T: (514) 426-1010; Fax: (514) 426-4680
Founded: 1953; Members: 401
Gen Secr: Maurice Kershaw
Focus: Psychoan 01910

Canadian Institute of International Affairs, 5 Devonshire Pl, Toronto, Ont. M5S 2C8
T: (416) 979-1851; Fax: (416) 979-8575
Founded: 1928; Members: 2100
Pres: Alan Sullivan; Gen Secr: Peter White
Focus: Poli Sci
Periodicals
Behind the Headlines (bi-monthly)
Etudes Internationales (quarterly)
International Journal (quarterly) 01911

Canadian Institute of Management / Institut Canadien de Gestion, 2175 Sheppard Av E, Ste 110, North York, Ont. M2J 1W8
T: (416) 493-0155; Fax: (416) 491-1670
Founded: 1942; Members: 3500
Gen Secr: Joan L. Milne
Focus: Business Admin
Periodical
Canadian Manager Magazine 01912

Canadian Institute of Mining, Metallurgy and Petroleum, 3400 de Maisonneuve Blvd W, Ste 1210, Montréal, Qué. H3Z 3B8
T: (514) 939-2710; Fax: (514) 935-2714
Founded: 1898; Members: 12760
Gen Secr: Y. Jacques
Focus: Mining; Metallurgy
Periodicals
Bulletin (monthly)
Directory (annually)
Journal of Canadian Petroleum Technology (bi-monthly) 01913

Canadian Institute of Planners / Institut Canadien des Urbanistes, 541 Sussex Dr, Ottawa, Ont. K1N 6Z6
Founded: 1919; Members: 4400
Pres: Barbara Dembek; Gen Secr: Rachael Corbett
Focus: Urban Plan
Periodical
Plan Canada (10 times annually) . . . 01914

Canadian Institute of Stress, 1235 Bay St, Ste 500, Toronto, Ont. M5R 3K4
T: (416) 961-8575; Fax: (416) 237-1828
Focus: Public Health 01915

Canadian Institute of Treated Wood / Institut Canadien des Bois Traités, 2430 Don Reid Dr, Ste 200, Ottawa, Ont. K1H 8P5
T: (613) 737-4337; Fax: (613) 247-0540
Founded: 1955; Members: 40
Focus: Forestry; Ecology 01916

Canadian Institute of Ukrainian Studies, c/o 352 Athabasca Hall, University of Alberta, 26 University Campus NW, Edmonton, Alta. T6G 2E8
T: (403) 492-2972; Fax: (403) 492-4967
Founded: 1976
Gen Secr: Dr. Zenon Kohut
Focus: Ethnology
Periodical
Journal of Ukrainian Studies 01917

Canadian Law and Society Association, 318 Osgoode, 4700 Keele St, Toronto, Ont. M3G 1P3
T: (416) 736-5037; E-Mail: fzemans@yorku.ca; Fax: (416) 736-5615
Founded: 1985; Members: 300
Pres: Wes Pue
Focus: Law; Sociology 01918

Canadian Library Association (CLA), 200 Elgin St, Ste 602, Ottawa, Ont. K2P 1L5
T: (613) 232-9625; E-Mail: ai077@freenet.carleton.ca; Fax: (613) 563-9895
Founded: 1946; Members: 3800
Pres: Karen Harrison; Gen Secr: Karen Adams
Focus: Libraries & Bk Sci
Periodicals
Canadian Library Journal (bi-monthly)
Canadian Materials
Feliciter (monthly) 01919

Canadian Linguistic Association (CLA) / Association Canadienne de Linguistique, c/o Dept of Linguistics, Memorial University, Saint John's, Nfld. A1B 3X9
T: (709) 737-8134; Fax: (709) 737-4000
Founded: 1954; Members: 750
Gen Secr: James Black
Focus: Ling
Periodical
The Canadian Journal of Linguistics (semi-annually) 01920

Canadian Lung Association (CLA), 1900 City Park Dr, Ste 508, Gloucester, Ont. K1J 1A3
T: (613) 747-6776; Fax: (613) 747-7430
Founded: 1900
Gen Secr: Margo Craig Garrison
Focus: Pulmon Dis
Periodical
Canadian Lung Association Bulletin (3 times annually) 01921

Canadian Maritime Law Association / Association Canadienne de Droit Maritime, 360 Rue Saint-Jacques, Ste 2000, Montréal, Qué. H2Y 1P5
T: (514) 849-4161; Fax: (514) 849-4167
Founded: 1951; Members: 311
Focus: Law 01922

Canadian Mathematical Society / Société Mathématique du Canada, 577 King Edward St, Ste 109, POB 415, Station A, Ottawa, Ont. K1N 6N5
T: (613) 562-5702; E-Mail: exsmc@acadvm1.uottawa.ca; Fax: (613) 565-1539
Founded: 1945; Members: 1237
Gen Secr: Dr. Graham P. Wright
Focus: Math
Periodicals
Applied Mathematics Notes (quarterly)
Canadian Mathematical Bulletin (quarterly) 01923

Canadian Medical and Biological Engineering Society / Société Canadienne de Génie Biomédical, Rm 393, Bldg M55, National Research Council of Canada, 1500 Montréal Rd, Ottawa, Ont. K1A 0R8
T: (613) 993-1686; Fax: (613) 954-2216
Founded: 1965; Members: 350
Focus: Med; Bio; Eng 01924

Canadian Medical Association / Association Médicale Canadienne, 1867 Alta Vista Dr, Ottawa, Ont. K1G 3Y6
T: (613) 731-9331; Fax: (613) 731-9013
Founded: 1867; Members: 42000
Pres: Dr. Judith Kazimirski; Gen Secr: Léo-Paul Landry
Focus: Med
Periodicals
Canadian Journal of Surgery: Journal canadien de chirurgie (bi-weekly)
CMA Journal: Journal de l'Association médicale canadienne (bi-monthly)
Net Worth: Valeurs nettes (monthly) . . 01925

Canadian Meteorological and Oceanographic Society / Société Canadienne de Météorologie et d'Océanographie, 151 Slater St, Ste 903, Ottawa, Ont. K1P 5H3
T: (613) 990-0300; E-Mail: cmos@ottmed.meds.dfo.ca; Fax: (613) 990-5510
Founded: 1967; Members: 920
Pres: Dr. Michel Beland; Gen Secr: Dr. Neil J. Campbell
Focus: Oceanography; Geophys
Periodicals
Atmosphere-Ocean (quarterly)
Chinook (quarterly)
Climatological Bulletin (tri-annually) . . . 01926

Canadian Museums Association (CMA) / Association des Musées Canadiens, 280 Metcalfe St, Ste 400, Ottawa, Ont. K2P 1R7
T: (613) 567-0099; Fax: (613) 233-5438
Founded: 1947; Members: 2500
Gen Secr: John G. McAvity
Focus: Arts
Periodicals
Muse (quarterly)
Museogramme (monthly) 01927

Canadian Music Centre / Centre de Musique Canadienne, 20 Saint Joseph St, Toronto, Ont. M4Y 1J9
T: (416) 961-6601; E-Mail: cmc@interlog.com; Fax: (416) 961-7198
Founded: 1959; Members: 675
Gen Secr: Simone Auger
Focus: Music
Periodical
Acquisitions (annually) 01928

Canadian Natural Health Association, 439 Wellington St W, Ste 5, Toronto, Ont. M5V 1E7
T: (416) 977-2642; Fax: (416) 977-1536
Founded: 1960; Members: 765
Gen Secr: Hélène Roussel
Focus: Public Health 01929

Canadian Nautical Research Society, 151A Second Av, POB 21076, Ottawa, Ont. K1S 5N1
T: (709) 737-8424; E-Mail: lfisher@kean.ucs.mun.ca; Fax: (709) 737-4569
Founded: 1982; Members: 271
Pres: Faye Kert; Gen Secr: Lewis Fischer
Focus: Navig
Periodicals
Argonauta (quarterly)
Canadian Maritime Bibliography (annually) 01930

Canadian Neurological Society / Société Canadienne de Neurologie, 906 12 Av, Ste 810, Calgary, Alta. T2R 1K7
T: (403) 229-9544; Fax: (403) 229-1661
Founded: 1948; Members: 500
Pres: Dr. O. Suchowersky
Focus: Neurology 01931

Canadian Nuclear Association / Association Nucléaire Canadienne, 144 Front St W, Ste 475, Toronto, Ont. M5J 2L7
T: (416) 977-6152; Fax: (416) 979-8356
Founded: 1960; Members: 112
Pres: Jack Richman
Focus: Nucl Res
Periodicals
Bulletin of the Canadian Nuclear Society (bi-monthly)
CNA Annual International Conference Proceedings (annually)
Nuclear Canada (9 times annually)
Nuclear Canada Yearbook (annually) . . 01932

Canadian Numismatic Association, POB 226, Barrie, Ont. L4M 4T2
T: (705) 737-0845; Fax: (705) 737-0293
Founded: 1950; Members: 1900
Pres: Yvon Marquis
Focus: Numismatics
Periodical
The Canadian Numismatic Journal (monthly) 01933

Canadian Operational Research Society (CORS), POB 2225, Station D, Ottawa, Ont. K1P 5W4
T: (613) 992-4079
Founded: 1958; Members: 760
Gen Secr: Dr. Sia Kahkeshan
Focus: Business Admin
Periodicals
Bulletin (9 times annually)
Infor (quarterly) 01934

Canadian Ophthalmological Society, 1525 Carling Av, Ste 610, Ottawa, Ont. K1Z 8R9
T: (613) 729-6779; Fax: (613) 729-7209
Founded: 1937; Members: 863
Gen Secr: Hubert Drouin
Focus: Ophthal 01935

Canadian Oral History Association / Société Canadienne d'Histoire Orale, POB 2064, Station D, Ottawa, Ont. K1P 5W3
T: (613) 996-6996; Fax: (613) 995-6575
Founded: 1974; Members: 103
Focus: Hist 01936

Canadian Orthoptic Society, c/o I.W.K. Children's Hospital, Orthoptic Clinic, 5850 University Av, POB 3070, Halifax, N.S. B3J 3G9
T: (902) 428-8021; Fax: (902) 428-3207
Founded: 1967; Members: 120
Pres: Brenda Hum-Boutilier
Focus: Ophthal 01937

Canadian Osteogenesis Imperfecta Society, 128 Thornhill Cres, Chatham, Ont. N7L 4M3
Members: 350
Gen Secr: Mary Lou Kearney
Focus: Med; Pathology 01938

Canadian Osteopathic Aid Society / Sociètè Canadienne d'Assistance Ostéopathique, 575 Waterloo St, London, Ont. N6B 2R2
T: (519) 439-5521
Founded: 1960; Members: 160
Focus: Med; Pathology 01939

Canadian Osteopathic Association / Société Canadienne Ostéopathique, 575 Waterloo St, London, Ont. N6B 2R2
Founded: 1926; Members: 24
Gen Secr: Marguerite Torney
Focus: Med; Pathology 01940

Canadian Paediatric Society / Société Canadienne de Pédiatrie, c/o Children's Hospital of Eastern Ontario, 401 Smyth Rd, Ottawa, Ont. K1H 8L1
T: (613) 737-2728; Fax: (613) 737-2794
Founded: 1951; Members: 1800
Pres: Dr. Pierre Beaudry
Focus: Pediatrics
Periodical
News Bulletin (bi-monthly) 01941

Canadian Paraplegic Association / Association Canadienne des Paraplégiques, 1101 Prince of Wales Dr, Ste 320, Ottawa, Ont. K2C 3W7
T: (613) 723-1033; E-Mail: eboyd@cyberplus.ca; Fax: (613) 723-1060
Founded: 1945; Members: 4000
Pres: Marie Trudeau
Focus: Pathology; Med 01942

Canadian Peace Research and Education Association / Association Canadienne de Recherhe et d'Education pour la Paix, c/o Dept of Political Science, Brandon University, 270 18 St, Brandon, Man. R7A 6A9
T: (204) 789-7485
Founded: 1966
Focus: Prom Peace; Educ
Periodical
Peace Research 01943

Canadian Petroleum Law Foundation, c/o Canadian Occidental Petroleum Ltd, 635 Eighth Av SW, Ste 1500, Calgary, Alta. T2P 3Z1
T: (403) 234-6700; Fax: (403) 234-6971
Founded: 1963; Members: 203
Focus: Law 01944

Canadian Pharmaceutical Association (CPhA) / Association Pharmaceutique Canadienne, 1785 Alta Vista Dr, Ottawa, Ont. K1G 3Y6
T: (613) 523-7877; Fax: (613) 523-0445
Founded: 1907; Members: 10000
Gen Secr: Leroy C. Fevang
Focus: Pharmacol
Periodical
Canadian Pharmaceutical Journal (monthly) 01945

Canadian Philosophical Association (CPA) / Association Canadienne de Philosophie, c/o Dept of Philosophy, UQAM, 400 Rue Sainte-Catherine Est, Montrél, Qué. H2X 3J8
T: (514) 987-3253; Fax: (514) 987-8721
Founded: 1962; Members: 1400
Pres: Josiane Boulad Ayoub
Focus: Philos
Periodicals
Bulletin (semi-annually)
Dialogue (quarterly) 01946

Canadian Physiological Society / Société Canadienne de Physiologie, c/o Dept of Physiology, University of Alberta, Medical Sciences Bldg, Edmonton, Alta. T6G 2H7
T: (403) 492-2620; E-Mail: cheese@dean.med.ualberta.ca; Fax: (403) 492-8915
Founded: 1935; Members: 530
Gen Secr: C.I. Cheeseman
Focus: Physiology
Periodical
Physiology Canada (quarterly) 01947

Canadian Phytopathological Society / Société Canadienne de Phytopathologie, c/o MAPAQ Centre de Recherche, POB 455, Les Buissons, Qué. G0H 1H0
T: (418) 567-2235; Fax: (418) 567-8791
Founded: 1929; Members: 508
Gen Secr: Dr. B. Otrysko
Focus: Botany
Periodical
Canadian Journal of Plant Pathology (quarterly) 01948

Canadian Polish Research Institute, 288 Roncesvalles Av, Toronto, Ont. M6R 2M4
T: (416) 535-6233
Founded: 1951; Members: 24
Gen Secr: Rudolph Kolger
Focus: Hist; Sociology
Periodical
Studies (annually) 01949

Canadian Political Science Association / Association Canadienne de Science Politique, 1 Stewart St, Ste 205, Ottawa, Ont. K1N 6H7
T: (613) 564-4026; E-Mail: cpsa@csse.ca; Fax: (613) 230-2746
Founded: 1913; Members: 3100
Gen Secr: Michelle Hopkins
Focus: Poli Sci
Periodicals
The Bulletin: Le Bulletin
The Canadian Journal of Political Science: Revue canadienne de science politique 01950

Canadian Psoriasis Foundation, 1306 Wellington St, Ste 500A, Ottawa, Ont. K1Y 3B2
T: (613) 728-4000; Fax: (613) 728-8913
Founded: 1983; Members: 1150
Pres: Raymond L. du Plessis
Focus: Derm
Periodical
Canadian Psoriasis Foundation Newsletter (quarterly) 01951

Canadian Psychiatric Association / Association des Psychiatres du Canada, 237 Argyle Av, Ste 200, Ottawa, Ont. K2P 1B8
T: (613) 234-2815 ext 26; E-Mail: cpa@medical.org; Fax: (613) 234-9857
Founded: 1951; Members: 2300
Gen Secr: Alex Saunders
Focus: Psychiatry
Periodical
The Canadian Journal of Psychiatry (8 times annually) 01952

Canadian Psychiatric Research Foundation, 60 Bloor St W, Ste 307, Toronto, Ont. M4W 3B8
T: (416) 975-9891
Founded: 1980
Gen Secr: Ron Rea
Focus: Psychiatry 01953

Canadian Psychoanalytic Society / Société Canadienne de Psychoanalyse, 7000 Ch Côte des Neiges, Montréal, Qué. H3S 2C1
T: (514) 738-6393; E-Mail: psyanal@aei.ca
Founded: 1952; Members: 370
Gen Secr: Nadia Gargour
Focus: Psychoan 01954

Canadian Psychological Association / Société Canadienne de Psychologie, 151 Slater St, Ste 205, Ottawa, Ont. K1P 5H3
T: (613) 237-2144; E-Mail: cpa@psychologyassoc.ca; Fax: (613) 237-1674
Founded: 1939; Members: 4000
Pres: Dr. David R. Evans; Gen Secr: Dr. John C. Service
Focus: Psych
Periodicals
Canadian Journal of Behavioural Sience (quarterly)
Canadian Journal of Psychology (quarterly)
Canadian Psychology (quarterly)
Highlights (quarterly) 01955

Canadian Public Health Association, 1565 Carling Av, Ste 400, Ottawa, Ont. K1Z 8R1
T: (613) 725-3769; Fax: (613) 725-9826
Founded: 1912; Members: 3500
Pres: Dr. John Hastings; Gen Secr: Gerald H. Dafoe
Focus: Public Health
Periodical
Canadian Journal of Public Health (bi-monthly) 01956

Canadian Public Relations Society / Société Canadienne des Relations Publiques,, 220 Laurier Av W, Ste 720, Ottawa, Ont. K1P 5Z9
T: (613) 232-1222; Fax: (613) 232-0565
Founded: 1948; Members: 1500
Focus: Advert 01957

Canadian Quaternary Association / Association Canadienne pour l'Etude du Quaternaire, c/o NBDNR Geological Survey, POB 6000, Fredericton, N.B. E3B 5H1
T: (506) 453-7947; Fax: (506) 444-4176
Founded: 1979
Gen Secr: T. Pronk
Focus: Geology; Geography; Bio; Archeol
Periodicals
CANQA Newsletter/Bulletin (semi-annually)
Géographie Physique et Quaternaire (3 times annually) 01958

Canadian Railroad Historical Association / Association Canadienne d'Histoire Ferroviaire, 120 Rue Saint-Pierre, Saint Constant, Qué. J5A 2G9
T: (514) 632-2410
Founded: 1932; Members: 1100
Focus: Hist; Cultur Hist 01959

Canadian Research Institute for the Advancement of Women, 151 Slater St, Ste 408, Ottawa, Ont. K1P 5H3
T: (613) 563-0681; E-Mail: criaw@worldlink.ca
Founded: 1976; Members: 1235
Focus: Sociology 01960

Canadian Research Management Association / Association Canadienne de la Gestion de la Recherche, 130 Albert St, Ste 1004, Ottawa, Ont. K1P 5G4
T: (613) 567-9049; Fax: (613) 567-4562
Founded: 1963; Members: 240
Focus: Business Admin 01961

Canadian Rodeo Historical Association, 2116 27 Av NE, Ste 233, Calgary, Alta. T2E 7A6
T: (403) 250-1741
Focus: Cultur Hist 01962

Canadian Schizophrenia Foundation, 16 Florence Av, North York, Ont. M2N 1E9
T: (416) 733-2117; Fax: (416) 733-2352
Founded: 1969; Members: 1000
Gen Secr: Steven Carter
Focus: Psychiatry
Periodicals
Health & Nutrition Update (quarterly)
The Journal of Orthomolecular Medicine (quarterly) 01963

Canadian Science and Technology Historical Association, 758 Holt Cres, Ottawa, Ont. K1G 2Y7
T: (613) 733-3188; E-Mail: ae267@freenet.carleton.ca
Founded: 1980; Members: 150
Pres: Marianne Ainley
Focus: Eng; Cultur Hist
Periodical
Scientia Canadensis (semi-annually) . . . 01964

Canadian Sheet Steel Building Institute / Institut Canadien de la Tôle d'Acier pour le Bâtiment, 652 Bishop St N, Ste 2A, Cambridge, Ont. N3H 4V6
T: (519) 650-1285; Fax: (519) 650-8081
Founded: 1961; Members: 32
Gen Secr: Steven R. Fox
Focus: Civil Eng 01965

Canadian Sickle Cell Society / Société de l'Anémie Falciforme du Canada, 6999 Côte des Neiges, Ste 33, Montréal, Qué., H3S 2B8
T: (514) 735-5109
Founded: 1978; Members: 978
Focus: Hematology 01966

Canadian Society for Civil Engineering / Société Canadienne de Génie Civil, 2155 Rue Guy, Ste 840, Montréal, Qué. H3H 2R9
T: (514) 933-2634; E-Mail: csc@musica.mcgill.ca; Fax: (514) 933-3504
Founded: 1972; Members: 5000
Focus: Civil Eng
Periodical
The Canadian Journal of Civil Engineering (quarterly) 01967

Canadian Society for Clinical Investigation / Société Canadienne de Recherches Cliniques, 774 Echo Dr, Ottawa, Ont. K1S 5N8
T: (613) 730-6240; Fax: (613) 730-8194
Founded: 1951; Members: 800
Pres: Dr. Paul M. Walker
Focus: Med 01968

Canadian Society for Color in Art, Industry and Science, NRC Institute for National Measurement Standards Bldg, M36 Rm 1119, Ottawa, Ont. K1A 0R6
T: (613) 993-9347; Fax: (613) 952-1394
Founded: 1972; Members: 126
Focus: Chem 01969

Canadian Society for Computational Studies of Intelligence / Société Canadienne pour l'Etude d'Intelligence par Ordinateur, c/o Dept of Computer Science, University of Ottawa, Ottawa, Ont. K1N 6B5
T: (613) 564-5069; Fax: (613) 564-9486
Founded: 1973; Members: 500
Focus: Computer & Info Sci 01970

Canadian Society for Education through Art / Société Canadienne d'Education par l'Art, 675 Samuel de Champlain, Boucherville, Qué. J4B 6C4
T: (514) 655-2435; Fax: (514) 655-4379
Founded: 1955; Members: 350
Focus: Educ
Periodicals
Canadian Review of Art Education Research
The Journal
Newsletter 01971

Canadian Society for Eighteenth-Century Studies, c/o Dept of English, Wilfred Laurier University, Waterloo, Ont. N2L 3C5
T: (519) 884-0710 ext 3581; Fax: (519) 884-8854
Founded: 1969; Members: 219
Pres: Peter Sabor
Focus: Hist 01972

Canadian Society for Endocrinology and Metabolism / Société Canadienne d'Endocrinologie et Métabolisme, c/o Montréal Children's Hospital, 2300 Tupper St, Montréal, Qué. H3H 1P3
T: (514) 934-4400; Fax: (514) 934-4494
Founded: 1972; Members: 290
Focus: Endocrinology 01973

Canadian Society for Engineering Management, c/o Base Service Canada Inc., 250 Consumers Rd, Ste 301, North York, M2J 4V6
T: (416) 494-1440; E-Mail: base@onramp.ca; Fax: (416) 495-8723
Founded: 1981; Members: 300
Focus: Business Admin; Eng 01974

Canadian Society for Horticultural Science / Société Canadienne de Science Horticole, c/o Plant Science Dept, McGill University, McDonald Campus, Montréal, Qué. H9X 1C0
T: (514) 398-7756; E-Mail: Wees@agradm.lan.mcgill.ca; Fax: (514) 398-7955
Founded: 1956; Members: 28ß
Focus: Hort 01975

Canadian Society for International Health / Société Canadienne de la Santé Internationale, 170 Laurier Av W, Ste 902, Ottawa, Ont. K1P 5V5
T: (613) 230-2654; E-Mail: csih@fox.nstn.ca; Fax: (613) 230-8401
Founded: 1977; Members: 850
Focus: Public Health
Periodical
Synergy: Newsletter (quarterly) 01976

Canadian Society for Italian Studies / Société Canadienne pour les Etudes Italiennes, c/o Dept of Italian, Saint Jerome's College, University of Waterloo, Waterloo, Ont. N2L 3G3
Founded: 1972; Members: 250
Gen Secr: Gabriele Niccoli
Focus: Hist
Periodical
Quaderni d'italianistica (semi-annually) . . 01977

Canadian Society for Mechanical Engineering (CSME) / Société Canadienne de Génie Mécanique, 130 Slater St, Ste 405A, Ottawa, Ont. K1P 6E2
T: (613) 232-8811; E-Mail: csocme@istar.ca; Fax: (613) 230-9607
Founded: 1887; Members: 2200
Focus: Eng
Periodical
CSME Transactions 01978

Canadian Society for Nondestructive Testing, 966 Pantera Dr, Ste 7, Mississauga, Ont. L4W 2S1
T: (905) 238-4846; Fax: (905) 238-0689
Founded: 1964; Members: 1160
Gen Secr: Angie Giglio
Focus: Materials Sci 01979

Canadian Society for Nutritional Sciences, c/o Dept of Home Economics, Mount Saint Vincent University, 166 Bedford Hwy, Halifax, N.S. B3M 2J6
T: (902) 443-4450 ext 248
Founded: 1957; Members: 330
Gen Secr: Dr. Theresa Glanville
Focus: Nutrition
Periodical
Nutrition Forum (semi-annually) 01980

Canadian Society for Psychomotor Learning and Sport Psychology, c/o Faculty of Kinesiology, University of Calgary, Calgary, Alta. T2N 1N4
T: (403) 220-3428; Fax: (403) 289-9117
Founded: 1970; Members: 200
Pres: Dr. J. Deakin; Gen Secr: Dr. T. Gabriele
Focus: Psych 01981

Canadian Society for the History and Philosophy of Science, c/o Dept of History, Simon Fraser University, Burnaby, B.C. V5A 1S6
T: (604) 291-3521; E-Mail: hgay@sfu.ca; Fax: (604) 291-5837
Founded: 1959; Members: 120
Pres: Maurice Gagnon
Focus: Cultur Hist; Philos 01982

Canadian Society for the Study of Education (CSSE) / Société Canadienne pour l'Etude de l'Education, 1 Stewart St, Ste 205, Ottawa, Ont. K1N 6H7
T: (613) 230-3532; E-Mail: csse@acadvm1.uottawa.ca; Fax: (613) 230-2746
Founded: 1972; Members: 1000
Pres: Phil Nagy; Gen Secr: Tim Howard
Focus: Educ
Periodicals
Canadian Journal of Education: Revue canadienne de l'éducation (quarterly)
CSSE News: Nouvelles SCEE (8 times annually) 01983

Canadian Society for the Study of Higher Education / Société Canadienne pour l'Etude de l'Enseignement Supérieur, 350 Albert St, Ste 320, Ottawa, Ont. K1R 1B1
T: (613) 563-1236; E-Mail: kclements@aucc.ca; Fax: (613) 563-7739
Founded: 1970; Members: 535
Focus: Educ
Periodical
Canadian Journal of Higher Education (3 times annually) 01984

Canadian Society for the Weizmann Institute of Science, 45 Sheppard Av E, Ste 218, North York, Ont. M2N 5W9
T: (416) 733-9220; Fax: (416) 733-9430
Founded: 1965
Focus: Sci 01985

Canadian Society of Agricultural Engineering / Société Canadienne de Génie Rural, POB 381, RPO University, Saskatoon, Sask. S7N 4J8
T: (306) 966-5335; E-Mail: norum@sask.usask.ca; Fax: (306) 966-5334
Founded: 1958; Members: 818
Gen Secr: D.I. Norum
Focus: Agri
Periodical
Canadian Agricultural Engineering Journal (semi-annually) 01986

Canadian Society of Agronomy / Société Canadienne d'Agronomie, 151 Slater St, Ste 907, Ottawa, Ont. K1P 5H4
T: (613) 232-9459; Fax: (613) 594-5190
Founded: 1954; Members: 300
Focus: Agri 01987

Canadian Society of Animal Science (CSAS), 151 Slater St, Ste 907, Ottawa, Ont. K1P 5H4
T: (613) 232-9459; Fax: (613) 594-5190
Founded: 1951; Members: 600
Pres: Valerie Stevens; Gen Secr: Dr. Roland Rotter
Focus: Zoology
Periodicals
Canadian Journal of Animal Science (quarterly)
CSAS Newsletter (quarterly) 01988

Canadian Society of Biblical Studies / Société Canadienne des Etudes Bibliques, c/o Dept of Religious Studies, Memorial University, POB 4200, Station C, Saint John's, Nfld. A1C 5S7
T: (709) 737-8166; Fax: (709) 737-4569
Founded: 1933; Members: 283
Gen Secr: Prof. David J. Hawkin
Focus: Rel & Theol
Periodicals
Society Bulletin (annually)
Ugaritic Newsletter (annually) 01989

Canadian Society of Cardiology Technologists, 201 Portage Av, Ste 2200, Winnipeg, Man. R3B 3L3
Founded: 1970; Members: 875
Pres: Ruth Scott
Focus: Cardiol 01990

Canadian Society of Children's Authors, Illustrators and Performers (CANSCAIP) / Société Canadienne des Auteurs, Illustrateurs et Artistes pour Enfants, 35 Spadina Rd, Toronto, Ont. M5R 2S9
T: (416) 515-1559; E-Mail: canscaip@interlog.com; Fax: (416) 515-7022
Founded: 1977; Members: 1160
Focus: Graphic & Dec Arts, Design; Perf Arts; Lit
Periodical
CANSCAIP News (quarterly) 01991

Canadian Society of Cinematographers, 235 Carlow Av, Ste 602, Toronto, Ont. M4M 2S1
T: (416) 966-6710
Founded: 1959; Members: 400
Gen Secr: Jennifer Hietala
Focus: Cinema 01992

Canadian Society of Clinical Neurophysiologists, POB 4220, Station C, Calgary, Alta. T2T 5N1
T: (403) 229-9544; Fax: (403) 229-1661
Members: 200
Focus: Neurology 01993

Canadian Society of Cytology, c/o Dept of Pathology, H.S.C., 820 Sherbrook St, Winnipeg, Man. R3A 1R9
T: (204) 787-1657; Fax: (204) 787-4942
Members: 380
Gen Secr: Dr. M.A. Auger
Focus: Cell Biol & Cancer Res
Periodical
Canadian Society of Cytology Bulletin (quarterly) 01994

Canadian Society of Environmental Biologists, POB 962, Station F, Toronto, Ont. M4Y 2N9
T: (705) 743-5780; E-Mail: gleering@trentu.ca; Fax: (705) 743-9592
Founded: 1943; Members: 500
Pres: Sean Sharpe; Gen Secr: Gerry Leering
Focus: Bio; Ecology 01995

Canadian Society of Landscape Architects (CSLA) / Association des Architectes Paysagistes du Canada, Site 5, RR 1, Box 7, Okotoks, Alta. T0L 1T0
T: (403) 938-2476; E-Mail: csla@agt.net; Fax: (403) 938-2476
Founded: 1934; Members: 1300
Focus: Archit
Periodicals
CSLA Bulletin (bi-monthly)
Landscape Architectural Review (5 times annually) 01996

Canadian Society of Microbiologists (CSM) / Société Canadienne des Microbiologistes, 1200 Prince of Wales Dr E, Ottawa, Ont. K2C 1M9
T: (613) 723-7233; Fax: (613) 723-8792
Founded: 1958; Members: 667
Pres: T. Trust; Gen Secr: Lynn Anderson
Focus: Microbio
Periodicals
CSM Newsletter (3 times annually)
Programme & Abstracts (annually) . . . 01997

Canadian Society of Orthopaedic Technologists / Société Canadienne des Technologistes en Orthopédie, 4433 Sheppard Av E, Ste 200, Agincourt, Ont. M1S 1V3
T: (416) 292-0687; E-Mail: cinascot@idirect.com; Fax: (416) 292-1038
Founded: 1972; Members: 350
Focus: Orthopedics
Periodicals
BodyCast (quarterly)
NewsCast (quarterly) 01998

Canadian Society of Otolaryngology, Head and Neck Surgery, 55 MacGregor Av, Toronto, Ont. M6S 2A1
T: (519) 439-1850; Fax: (519) 672-4602
Members: 640
Pres: Dr. Murray Morrison; Gen Secr: Donna Humphrey
Focus: Otorhinolaryngology; Surgery
Periodical
Journal of Otolaryngology (bi-monthly) . . 01999

Canadian Society of Painters in Watercolour, 258 Wallace Av, Ste 102, Toronto, Ont. M6P 3M9
T: (416) 533-5100
Founded: 1926; Members: 260
Focus: Fine Arts
Periodical
Newsletter (3 times annually) 02000

Canadian Society of Petroleum Geologists, 206 Seventh Av SW, Ste 505, Calgary, Alta. T2P 0W7
T: (403) 264-5610; E-Mail: cspg@cspg.org; Fax: (403) 264-5898
Founded: 1928; Members: 3200
Pres: Gerry Reinson
Focus: Geology
Periodical
Bulletin of Canadian Petroleum Geology (quarterly) 02001

Canadian Society of Plant Physiologists / Société Canadienne de Physiologie Végétale, c/o Dept of Biological Sciences, University of Alberta, Edmonton, Alta. T6G 2E9
T: (613) 492-5463; Fax: (613) 492-9234
Founded: 1958; Members: 592
Pres: Dr. Ronald Poole
Focus: Botany 02002

Canadian Society of Plastic Surgeons, 30 Blvd Saint-Joseph Est, Ste 520, Montréal, Qué. H2T 1G9
T: (514) 843-5415; Fax: (514) 843-5415
Founded: 1947; Members: 400
Pres: Dr. Carolyn Kerrigan
Focus: Surgery 02003

Canadian Society of Safety Engineering, 330 Bay St, Ste 602, Toronto, Ont. M5H 2S8
T: (416) 368-2230; Fax: (416) 368-8429
Founded: 1972; Members: 2155
Focus: Safety 02004

Canadian Society of Soil Science / Société Canadienne de la Science du Sol, POB 21018, RPO West End, Brandon, Man. R7B 3W8
T: (204) 725-4336; Fax: (204) 725-0624
Founded: 1955; Members: 450
Pres: Al Fedkenheuer
Focus: Agri 02005

Canadian Society of Zoologists, c/o Dépt d'Océanographie, Université du Québec, 600 Allée des Ursulines, Québec, Qué. G5L 3A1
T: (418) 724-1704; Fax: (418) 724-1842
Founded: 1961; Members: 671
Pres: Dr. Andrew Spencer
Focus: Zoology 02006

Canadian Sociology and Anthropology Association / Société Canadienne de Sociologie et d'Anthropologie, 1455 Blvd de Maisonneuve Ouest, Ste N-317-1, Montréal, Qué. H3G 1M8
T: (514) 848-8780; E-Mail: csaa@vox2.concordia.ca; Fax: (514) 848-4539
Founded: 1966; Members: 1700
Focus: Anthro; Sociology
Periodical
Canadian Review of Sociology and Anthropology 02007

Canadian Speech Communicators Association, c/o Lethbridge Community College, 3000 S College Dr, Lethbridge, Alta. T1K 1L6
T: (403) 320-3344; Fax: (403) 320-1461
Gen Secr: Yvonne Holm
Focus: Logopedy
Periodical
Human Communication 02008

Canadian Spice Association, c/o Halford-Lewis Ltd, 465 Saint Jean St, Ste 606, Montréal, Qué. H2Y 2R6
T: (514) 842-7857; Fax: (514) 842-6312
Founded: 1942; Members: 59
Focus: Food 02009

Canadian Standards Association / Association Canadienne de Normalisation, 178 Rexdale Blvd, Etobicoke, Ont. M9W 1R3
T: (416) 747-4007; Fax: (416) 747-2475
Founded: 1919; Members: 7000
Focus: Standards
Periodicals
CSA + Le Consommateur (quarterly)
CSA + The Consumer (quarterly)
Information Update
Standards Canada (quarterly) 02010

Canadian Steel Environmental Association, 50 O'Connor St, Ste 1425, Ottawa, Ont. K1P 6L2
T: (613) 238-6049; Fax: (613) 238-1832
Founded: 1974
Pres: A. Schuldt
Focus: Metallurgy 02011

Canadian Steel Industry Research Association / Association pour la Recherche dans l'Industrie Sidérurgique Canadienne, 50 O'Connor St, Ste 1425, Ottawa, Ont. K1P 6L2
T: (613) 238-6049; Fax: (613) 238-1832
Founded: 1978
Focus: Metallurgy 02012

Canadian Teachers' Federation / Fédération Canadienne des Enseignantes et Enseignants, 110 Argyle Av, Ottawa, Ont. K2P 1B4
T: (613) 232-1505; E-Mail: info@ctf-fce.ca; Fax: (613) 232-1886
Founded: 1920; Members: 13
Focus: Educ 02013

Canadian Technion Society / Société Canadienne Technion, 970 Lawrence Av W, Ste 206, Toronto, Ont. M6A 3B6
T: (416) 789-4545; Fax: (416) 789-0255
Founded: 1945; Members: 5000
Focus: Eng 02014

Canadian Theatre Critics Association / Association des Critiques de Théâtre du Canada, 181 University Av, Ste 2100, Toronto, Ont. M5H 3M7
T: (416) 367-8896; Fax: (416) 367-5992
Founded: 1979; Members: 65
Focus: Journalism; Perf Arts 02015

Canadian Thoracic Society (CTS), c/o Canadian Lung Association, 1900 City Park Dr, Ste 508, Gloucester, Ont. K1J 1A3
T: (613) 747-6776; Fax: (613) 747-7430
Founded: 1958; Members: 300
Gen Secr: Michelle Gaudreau
Focus: Pulmon Dis 02016

Canadian University and College Conference Officers Association, c/o Ryerson Polytechnic University, 160 Mutual St, Toronto, Ont. M5B 2M2
T: (416) 979-5284; Fax: (416) 979-5212
Members: 60
Focus: Educ 02017

Canadian University and College Counselling Association, c/o Centre for Student Development, McMaster University, 409 Hamilton Hall, Hamilton, Ont. L8S 4K1
T: (905) 525-9140 ext 24711; E-Mail: nifakis@mcmaster.ca; Fax: (905) 529-8972
Founded: 1963
Focus: Public Admin; Educ 02018

Canadian University Music Society / Société de Musique des Universités Canadiennes, c/o Faculty of Music, Wilfried Laurier University, Waterloo, Ont. N2L 3C5
T: (519) 253-4232; Fax: (519) 973-7050
Founded: 1979; Members: 360
Focus: Music
Periodical
Canadian University Music Review: Revue de musique des universités canadiennes (bi-annually) 02019

Canadian Urban Transit Association / Association Canadienne du Transport Urbain, 55 York St, Ste 901, Toronto, Ont. M5J 1R7
T: (416) 365-9800; Fax: (416) 365-1295
Founded: 1904; Members: 225
Focus: Transport
Periodicals
Annual Report (annually)
Transit Fact Book & Membership Directory (annually)
Transit Topics (monthly) 02020

Canadian Urological Association, c/o Health Science Centre, 820 Sherbrook St, Rm GE446, Winnipeg, Man. R3A 1R9
T: (204) 787-3677; Fax: (204) 787-3040
Founded: 1945; Members: 600
Focus: Urology 02021

Canadian Veterinary Medical Association / Association Canadienne des Vétérinaires, 339 Booth St, Ottawa, Ont. K1R 7K1
T: (613) 236-1162; Fax: (613) 236-9681
Founded: 1948; Members: 3700
Focus: Vet Med
Periodicals
Canadian Journal of Comparative Medicine (quarterly)
Canadian Veterinary Journal (monthly) . 02022

Canadian Water Quality Association / Association Canadienne pour la Qualité de l'Eau, 151 Frobisher Dr, Ste 201A, Waterloo, Ont. N2V 2C9
T: (519) 885-3854; Fax: (519) 747-9124
Founded: 1960; Members: 205
Gen Secr: Lou J. Smith
Focus: Water Res; Ecology 02023

Canadian Welding Bureau / Bureau Canadien de Soudage, 7250 W Credit Av, Mississauga, Ont. L5N 5N1
T: (905) 542-1312; Fax: (905) 542-1318
Founded: 1947; Members: 2700
Focus: Standards 02024

Canadian Wind Energy Association / Association Canadienne d'Energie Ecolienne, 3553 31 St NW, Ste 100, Calgary, Alta. T2L 2K7
T: (403) 289-7713; E-Mail: canwea@aol.com; Fax: (403) 282-1238
Founded: 1984; Members: 250
Gen Secr: Cindy Bourns
Focus: Energy
Periodical
CWEA Newsletter (annually) 02025

Canadian Writers' Foundation, 124 Clarendon Av, Ottawa, Ont. K1Y 0R3
T: (613) 728-0602
Gen Secr: Marianne Neily
Focus: Lit 02026

Cancer Research Society / Société de Recherche sur le Cancer, 1 Pl Ville Marie, Ste 2332, Montréal, Qué. H3B 3M5
T: (514) 861-9227; Fax: (514) 861-9220
Founded: 1945; Members: 3000
Focus: Cell Biol & Cancer Res
Periodical
The Recorder (bi-annually) 02027

Cardiology Technologists Association of British Columbia, POB 76722, RPO Collingwood, Vancouver, B.C. V5R 6A8
Founded: 1975; Members: 439
Pres: R. Payne
Focus: Cardiol 02028

Cardiology Technologists Association of Ontario, 6o N Centre Rd, POB 27022, London, Ont. N5X 3W0
T: (519) 858-9868
Members: 500
Pres: Euretha Hayde
Focus: Cardiol
Periodical
Heartbeat (semi-annually) 02029

Catholic Public Schools Society, 2935 Hwy 16 W, Prince George, B.C. V2N 3Z2
T: (250) 964-4424
Pres: Ted West
Focus: Educ 02030

Centrale de l'Enseignement du Québec (CEQ), 9405 Rue Sherbrooke Est, Montréal, Qué. H1L 6P3
T: (514) 356-8888; E-Mail: info@ceq.qc.ca; Fax: (514) 356-9999
Founded: 1946; Members: 115000
Pres: Lorraine Pagé
Focus: Educ
Periodical
Nouvelles CEQ (bi-monthly) 02031

Centre d'Animation, de Développement et de Recherche en Education, 1940 Blvd Henri Bourassa Est, Montréal, Qué. H2B 1S2
T: (514) 381-8891; E-Mail: cadre@cam.org; Fax: (514) 381-4086
Founded: 1968
Focus: Educ
Periodical
Prospectives (3 times annually) 02032

Centre for Bioethics, c/o University of Toronto, 88 College St, Toronto, Ont. M5G 1L4
T: (416) 978-2709; Fax: (416) 978-1911
Founded: 1976
Focus: Med
Periodicals
Journal of Palliative Care (quarterly)
Synapse: A Canadian News Service for Biomedical Ethics (quarterly)
Synapse: Un service canadien d'information en éthique biomédicale (quarterly) 02033

Centre for Engineering Research, c/o Edmonton Research Park, 200 Karl Clark Rd, Edmonton, Alta. T6N 1E2
T: (403) 450-3300; E-Mail: cfer@cfer.ualberta.ca; Fax: (403) 450-3700
Founded: 1983; Members: 14
Pres: Touraj Nasseri
Focus: Eng 02034

Centre for Research on Latin America and the Caribbean (CERLAC), c/o York University, 240 York Lanes, 4700 Keele St, North York, Ont. M3J 1P3
T: (416) 736-5237; E-Mail: cerlac@yorku.ca
Founded: 1978; Members: 112
Gen Secr: Prof. Patrick Taylor
Focus: Soc Sci; Poli Sci; Econ 02035

Centre Franco-Ontarien de Resources Pédagogiques, 290 Dupuis St, Vanier, Ont. K1L 1A2
T: (613) 747-8000; Fax: (613) 747-2808
Founded: 1974
Gen Secr: Bernadette LaRochelle
Focus: Educ 02036

Ceramics and Stone Accident Prevention Association, c/o IAPA District 4 Office, 1090 Don Mills Rd, Ste 405, North York, Ont. M3C 3R6
T: (416) 449-5755
Members: 625
Gen Secr: Lori Chambers
Focus: Safety 02037

Cercles des Jeunes Naturalistes (CJN), c/o Jardin Botanique de Montréal, 4101 Rue Sherbrooke Est, Ste 4101, Montréal, Qué. H1X 2B2
T: (514) 252-3023; Fax: (514) 252-3023
Founded: 1931; Members: 3000
Gen Secr: Claude Ouellet
Focus: Nat Sci
Periodicals
Feuillets du Naturaliste
Tracts CJN 02038

Cerebral Palsy Association in Alberta, 5940 MacLeod Trail S, Ste 106, Calgary, Alta. T2H 2G4
T: (403) 253-5955; E-Mail: cpaa@agt.net; Fax: (403) 258-0812
Members: 725
Gen Secr: 1976
Focus: Neurology
Periodical
CP Reporter (quarterly) 02039

Cerebral Palsy Association of British Columbia, 4423 Boundary Rd, Vancouver, B.C. V5R 2N3
T: (604) 431-3833; Fax: (604) 431-3822
Founded: 1954
Pres: Susan Eisenberger
Focus: Neurology 02040

Cerebral Palsy Association of Manitoba, 825 Sherbrooke St, Winnipeg, Man. R3A 1M5
T: (204) 774-9427; Fax: (204) 786-0860
Gen Secr: Laura Schnellert
Focus: Neurology 02041

Champlain Society (CS), POB 592, Station R, Toronto, Ont. M4G 4E1
T: (416) 482-9635; Fax: (416) 482-9341
Founded: 1905; Members: 850
Pres: Ian Wilson
Focus: Hist 02042

Charles H. Ivey Foundation, 201 Consumers Rd, Ste 105, Willowdale, Ont. M2J 4G8
T: (416) 498-1555
Founded: 1957; Members: 10
Gen Secr: Mary D. Megson
Focus: Sci 02043

Chemical Industries Accident Prevention Association, c/o IAPA District 4 Office, 1090 Don Mills Rd, Ste 405, North York, Ont. M3C 3R6
T: (416) 449-5755
Gen Secr: Lori Chambers
Focus: Safety; Chem 02044

Chemical Institute of Canada, 130 Slater St, Ste 550, Ottawa, Ont. K1P 6E2
T: (613) 232-6252; E-Mail: cscxt@acadvm1.uottawa.ca; Fax: (613) 232-5862
Founded: 1945; Members: 6000
Pres: J.R. Grace; Gen Secr: Dr. Anne E. Alper

Focus: Chem
Periodicals
Canadian Chemical News (11 times annually)
The Canadian Journal of Chemical Engineering (bi-monthly) 02045

Children's Oncology Care of Ontario, 26 Gerrard St E, Toronto, Ont. M5B 1G3
T: (416) 977-0458; Fax: (416) 977-8807
Founded: 1981; Members: 120
Pres: Betsy Wright
Focus: Cell Biol & Cancer Res; Pediatrics 02046

Children's Rehabilitation and Cerebral Palsy Association, c/o Neurological Centre, 2805 Kingsway, Vancouver, B.C. V5R 5H9
T: (604) 451-5511; Fax: (604) 451-5651
Founded: 1945; Members: 140
Gen Secr: D.A. Ewen
Focus: Neurology; Pediatrics; Rehabil . . 02047

Church Library Association of Ontario, 13 Tallwood Dr, West Montrose, Ont. N0B 2V0
T: (519) 669-4789
Founded: 1969; Members: 200
Pres: Elsie Riva
Focus: Libraries & Bk Sci 02048

Cinémathèque Québécoise, 335 Blvd de Maisonneuve Est, Montréal, Qué. H2X 1K1
T: (514) 842-9763; Fax: (514) 842-1816
Founded: 1963; Members: 500
Focus: Cinema
Periodical
La Revue de la Cinémathèque (5 times annually) 02049

Clinical Research Society of Toronto, 112 College St, Toronto, Ont. M5G 1L6
T: (416) 978-7150
Pres: Jennifer Dorrington
Focus: Med 02050

College of Dental Surgeons of British Columbia, 1765 Eighth Av W, Ste 500, Vancouver, B.C. V6J 5C6
T: (604) 736-3621; Fax: (604) 734-9448
Founded: 1908; Members: 6500
Focus: Dent 02051

College of Dental Surgeons of Saskatchewan, 728 Spadina Cesc E, Ste 202, Saskatoon, Sask. S7K 4H7
T: (306) 244-5072; Fax: (306) 244-2476
Founded: 1906; Members: 375
Gen Secr: Dr. G.H. Peacock
Focus: Dent 02052

College of Family Physicians of Canada / Collège des Médecins de Famille du Canada, 2630 Skymark Av, Mississauga, Ont. L4W 5A4
T: (905) 629-0900; Fax: (905) 629-0893
Founded: 1954; Members: 13700
Pres: Dr. Cheri Bethune
Focus: Med
Periodicals
Canadian Family Physician (monthly)
Family Medicine Research Update (semi-annually) 02053

College of Physicians and Surgeons of Alberta, 10180 101 St, Ste 900, Edmonton, Ata. T5J 4P8
T: (403) 423-4764; Fax: (403) 420-0651
Members: 4700
Focus: Physiology; Surgery 02054

College of Physicians and Surgeons of British Columbia, 1807 Tenth Av W, Vancouver, B.C. V6J 2A9
T: (604) 733-7758; Fax: (604) 733-3503
Founded: 1886; Members: 6800
Focus: Physiology; Surgery 02055

College of Physicians and Surgeons of Manitoba, 494 Saint James St, Winnipeg, Man. R3G 3J4
T: (204) 774-4344; Fax: (204) 774-0750
Founded: 1871; Members: 2191
Focus: Physiology; Surgery 02056

College of Physicians and Surgeons of New Brunswick, 1 Hampton Rd, POB 628, Rothesay, N.B. E2E 5A7
T: (506) 658-0959; E-Mail: cpsnb@nbnet.nb.ca; Fax: (506) 849-5069
Members: 1228
Gen Secr: Ed Schollenberg
Focus: Med; Surgery 02057

College of Physicians and Surgeons of Ontario, 80 College St, Toronto, Ont. M5G 2E2
T: (416) 967-2600
Founded: 1866
Gen Secr: Dr. Michael E. 26000 Dixon
Focus: Physiology; Surgery 02058

College of Physicians and Surgeons of Saskatchewan, 211 Fourth Av S, Saskatoon, Sask. S7K 1N1
T: (306) 244-7355; Fax: (306) 244-0090
Founded: 1905; Members: 1500
Gen Secr: Jeannette Heinen
Focus: Physiology; Surgery 02059

College of Psychologists of New Brunswick / Collège des Psychologues du Nouveau-Brunswick, 403 Regent St, Ste 211, Fredericton, N.B. E3B 3X6
T: (506) 459-1994; Fax: (506) 459-3608
Founded: 1965; Members: 150
Focus: Physiology 02060

Committee on Atlantic Studies (CAS), c/o Dept of Political Science, Carleton University, Colonel By Dr, Ottawa Ont. K1S 5B6
T: (613) 288-2780
Founded: 1964; Members: 50
Gen Secr: Prof. Robert J. Jackson
Focus: Poli Sci 02061

Commonwealth Association for Education in Journalism and Communication (CAEJC), c/o Faculty of Law, University of Western Ontario, 1151 Richmond St, London, Ont. N6A 3K7
T: (519) 661-3348; E-Mail: caejc@julian.uwo.ca; Fax: (519) 661-3790
Founded: 1985; Members: 600
Gen Secr: Prof. Robert Martin
Focus: Comm Sci; Educ
Periodical
CAEJC Newsletter (annually) 02062

Commonwealth Association of Museums (CAM), c/o Glenbow Museum, 130 Ninth Av SE, Calgary, Alta. T2G 0P3
T: (403) 264-8300; Fax: (403) 265-9769
Founded: 1974; Members: 100
Pres: S. Gorakshkov; Gen Secr: Dianna Thompson
Focus: Arts
Periodical
CAM Newsletter 02063

Commonwealth of Learning (COL), Pacific Centre, 777 Dunsmuir St, Ste 1700, POB 10428, Vancouver, B.C. V7Y 1K4
T: (604) 775-8200; E-Mail: info@col.org; Fax: (604) 775-8210
Founded: 1988; Members: 53
Pres: Prof. Gajaraj Dhanarajan
Focus: Educ 02064

Community Planning Association of Alberta, 238 90 Av SE, Ste 304, Calgary, Alta. T2J 6P6
T: (403) 291-3505
Founded: 1946
Gen Secr: Lynne Friesen
Focus: Urban Plan 02065

Community Planning Association of Canada, 2837 Dewdney, Regina, Sask. S4T 0X8
T: (306) 525-0141
Founded: 1949; Members: 228
Focus: Urban Plan 02066

Computer Communications Institute, 98 Pechlam Av, North York, Ont. M2R 2T5
T: (416) 222-3145
Focus: Computer & Info Sci 02067

Confederation of Alberta Faculty Associations, c/o University of Alberta, 115 Assiniboia Hall, Edmonton, Alta. T6G 2E7
T: (403) 492-5630; Fax: (403) 492-6145
Founded: 1971; Members: 3515
Pres: James Marino
Focus: Sci 02068

Conference Board of Canada, 255 Smyth Rd, Ottawa, Ont. K1N 6C3
T: (613) 526-3280; Fax: (613) 526-4857
Founded: 1954; Members: 800
Pres: James R. Nininger
Focus: Econ; Business Admin 02069

Conference of Defence Associations Institute / Institut du Congrès des Associations de la Défense, 100 Gloucester St, Ste 500, Ottawa, Ont. K2P 0A4
T: (613) 563-1387; E-Mail: cdai@magi.com; Fax: (613) 235-0784
Founded: 1987; Members: 790
Pres: B. Shapiro; Gen Secr: D.E. Code
Focus: Military Sci 02070

Congregational Libraries Association of British Columbia, 2695 33 Av W, Vancouver, B.C. V6N 2E8
T: (604) 266-1858
Founded: 1971; Members: 135
Pres: Doreen Holden
Focus: Libraries & Bk Sci 02071

Conservation Council of New Brunswick / Conseil de la Conservation du Nouveau-Brunswick, 180 Saint John St, Fredericton, N.B. E3B 4A9
T: (506) 458-8747; E-Mail: ccnb@web.apc.org; Fax: (506) 458-1047
Founded: 1969; Members: 550
Gen Secr: David Coon
Focus: Preserv Hist Monuments
Periodical
Eco Allert (bi-monthly) 02072

Conservation Council of Ontario, 489 College St, Ste 506, Toronto, Ont. M6G 1A5
T: (416) 969-9637; E-Mail: cco@web.apc.org; Fax: (416) 960-8053
Founded: 1952; Members: 83
Pres: Dr. Kenneth H. MacKay
Focus: Preserv Hist Monuments
Periodicals
Ontario Conservation News (11 times annually)
Worldwatch Papers 02073

Construction Safety Association of Ontaria, 74 Victoria St, Toronto, Ont. M5C 2A5
T: (416) 366-1501; Fax: (416) 366-0232
Founded: 1929; Members: 35000
Gen Secr: Cyrelle Shoub
Focus: Safety
Periodical
The Counsellor (monthly) 02074

Council of Canadian Law Deans / Conseil des Doyens et des Doyennes des Facultes de Droit du Canada, c/o Faculty of Law, University of Ottawa, 57 Louis Pasteur, POB 415, Station A, Ottawa, Ont. K1N 6N5
T: (613) 562-5889; Fax: (613) 562-5121
Focus: Law 02075

Council of Canadian University Chemistry Chairmen, Dept of Chemistry, University of Manitoba, Winnipeg, Man. R3T 2N2
T: (204) 474-9321; Fax: (204) 275-0905
Founded: 1970
Focus: Chem 02076

Council of Ontario Universities / Conseil des Universités de l'Ontario, 444 Yonge St, Ste 203, Toronto, Ont. M5B 2H4
T: (416) 979-2165; Fax: (416) 979-8635
Founded: 1961; Members: 20
Focus: Sci 02077

Council of Prairie and Pacific University Libraries, c/o University of Calgary Library, 2500 University Dr NW, Calgary, Alta. T2N 1N4
T: (403) 249-8626; E-Mail: hafry@acs.ucalgary.ca; Fax: (403) 246-6976
Founded: 1991; Members: 13
Pres: Williams Maes; Gen Secr: Hazel Fry
Focus: Libraries & Bk Sci 02078

Council of Western Canadian University Presidents, c/o University of Regina, 3737 Wascana Pkwy, Ste 100, Regina, Sask. S4S 0A2
T: (306) 585-4382; Fax: (306) 585-5200
Members: 21
Pres: Donald O. Wells
Focus: Educ 02079

Council on Homosexuality and Religion / Conseil de l'Homosexualité et la Religion, POB 1912, Winnipeg, Man. R3C 3R2
T: (204) 474-0212; Fax: (204) 478-1160
Founded: 1976; Members: 61
Pres: A.E. Millward
Focus: Rel & Theol 02080

County of York Law Association, 361 University Av, Toronto, Ont. M5G 1T3
T: (416) 327-5700; E-Mail: matthea@gov.on.ca; Fax: (416) 947-9148
Founded: 1885; Members: 4200
Focus: Law 02081

Cumberland County Family Planning Association, 16 Church St, POB 661, Amherst, N.S. B4H 4B8
T: (902) 667-7500
Founded: 1981; Members: 44
Focus: Family Plan 02082

Dental Association of Prince Edward Island, 184 Belvedere Av, Charlottetown, P.E.I. C1A 2Z1
T: (902) 566-5199; Fax: (902) 892-4470
Members: 43
Focus: Dent 02083

Denturist Association of Canada, POB 46114, RPO Westdale, Winnipeg, Man. R3R 3S3
T: (204) 897-1087; Fax: (204) 895-9595
Founded: 1971; Members: 1150
Pres: Austin J. Carbone
Focus: Dent 02084

Donner Canadian Foundation / Fondation Canadienne Donner, 212 King St W, Ste 402, Toronto, Ont. M5H 1K5
T: (416) 593-5125
Founded: 1950
Pres: D. Gaffney Cross
Focus: Sci 02085

Economics Society of Northern Alberta, POB 1434, Main Station, Edmonton, Alta. T5J 2N5
T: (403) 467-8405; Fax: (403) 467-8405
Founded: 1975; Members: 180
Focus: Econ 02086

Electric Vehicle Association of Canada (EVAC), 21 Concourse Gate, Ste 11, Nepean, Ont. K2E 7S4
T: (613) 723-3127; Fax: (613) 723-8275
Founded: 1978; Members: 30
Gen Secr: Tom Lewinson
Focus: Auto Eng
Periodical
EVAC Newsletter (bi-monthly) 02087

Energy Probe Research Foundation, 225 Brunswick Av, Toronto, Ont. M5S 2M6
T: (416) 964-9223; Fax: (416) 964-8239
Founded: 1980; Members: 50000
Pres: Patricia Adams
Focus: Energy 02088

Engineering Institute of Canada, 1980 Ogilvie Rd, POB 27078, RPO Gloucester Center, Gloucester, Ont. K1J 9L9
T: (613) 742-5185; E-Mail: eic@nrc.ca; Fax: (613) 742-5189
Founded: 1887
Pres: John Plant; Gen Secr: Michael Bozozuk
Focus: Eng
Periodicals
Canadian Electrical and Computer Engineering Journal (quarterly)
Canadian Geotechnical Journal (quarterly)
Canadian Journal of Civil Engineering (monthly)
Transactions of the Canadian Society for Mechanical Engineering (quarterly) . . . 02089

Entomological Society of British Columbia, c/o Ministry of Forests, Seed Pest Management, 7380 Puckle Rd, Saanichton, B.C. V8M 1W4
T: (250) 652-6593; E-Mail: rgbennet@mfor01.for.gov.bc.ca; Fax: (250) 652-4204
Founded: 1903; Members: 230
Focus: Entomology
Periodicals
Economic Entomology (annually)
General Entomology (annually)
Systematic Entomology (annually) . . . 02090

Entomological Society of Canada / Société d'Entomologie du Canada, 393 Winston Av, Ottawa, Ont. K2A 1Y8
T: (613) 725-2619; Fax: (613) 725-9349
Founded: 1863; Members: 678
Pres: Hugh Danks; Gen Secr: A. Devine
Focus: Entomology
Periodicals
Bulletin (quarterly)
Canadian Entomologist (monthly)
Memoirs (irregularly) 02091

Entomological Society of Manitoba, c/o Agriculture Canada Research Station, 195 Dafoe Rd, Winnipeg, Man. R3T 2M9
T: (204) 983-1452; Fax: (204) 983-4604
Founded: 1944; Members: 150
Gen Secr: B. Timlick
Focus: Entomology
Periodical
Proceedings of the Society (annually) . . 02092

Entomological Society of Ontario, 1219 Queen St E, POB 490, Sault Sainte-Marie, Ont. P6A 5M7
T: (519) 824-4120 ext 2479
Founded: 1873; Members: 253
Gen Secr: Barry Lyons
Focus: Entomology
Periodical
Proceedings of the Entomological Society of Ontario (annually) 02093

Entomological Society of Saskatchewan, c/o Agriculture Canada Research Station, 107 Science Pl, Saskatoon, Sask. S7N 0X2
T: (306) 975-7014
Founded: 1952; Members: 44
Gen Secr: O. Offert
Focus: Entomology
Periodicals
Annual Proceedings
Newsletter (irregularly) 02094

Epilepsy Canada, 1470 Rue Peet, Ste 745, Montréal, Qué. H3A 1T1
T: (514) 845-7855; E-Mail: epilepsy@generation.net; Fax: (514) 845-7866
Founded: 1966; Members: 6000
Pres: Dr. M. Riley-Reidy; Gen Secr: Denise Crépin
Focus: Pathology 02095

Fédération des Affaires Sociales / Social Affairs Federation, 1601 Av de Lorimier, Montréal, Qué. H2K 4M5
T: (514) 598-2210; Fax: (514) 598-2223
Members: 94675
Focus: Soc Sci; Sociology 02096

Fédération des Commissions Scolaires du Québec, 1001 Av Bégon, CP 490, Sainte Foy, Qué. G1V 4C7
T: (418) 651-3220; Fax: (418) 651-2574
Members: 137
Pres: Diane Drouin
Focus: Educ; Public Admin 02097

Fédération du Québec pour le Planning des Naissances / Quebec Family Planning Federation, 4428 Blvd Saint-Laurent, Ste 302, Montréal, Qué. H2W 1Z5
T: (514) 844-3721; Fax: (514) 844-8736
Founded: 1972
Focus: Family Plan 02098

Fédération Nationale des Enseignants et des Enseignantes du Québec, 1601 Rue de Lorimier, Montréal, Qué. H2K 4M5
T: (514) 598-2241; Fax: (514) 598-2190
Founded: 1969; Members: 17500
Gen Secr: Jean Salman
Focus: Educ 02099

Federation of English Speaking Catholic Teachers, 1400 Rue Sauvé Ouest, Ste 279, Montréal, Qué. H4N 1C5
T: (514) 956-8072
Founded: 1943
Gen Secr: Leo Fernandes
Focus: Educ 02100

Federation of Independent School Associations of British Columbia, 150 Robson St, Vancouver, B.C. V6B 2A7
T: (604) 684-6023; Fax: (604) 684-3163
Founded: 1966; Members: 204
Gen Secr: Fred Herfst
Focus: Educ 02101

Federation of Independent Schools in Canada, 9125 50 St, Edmonton, Alta. T6B 2H3
T: (403) 469-9868
Founded: 1980
Gen Secr: Gary Duthler
Focus: Educ 02102

Federation of Medical Women of Canada / Fédération des Femmes Médecins du Canada, 1815 Alta Vista Dr, Ste 107, Ottawa, Ont. K1G 3Y6
T: (613) 731-1026; Fax: (613) 731-8748
Founded: 1924; Members: 1670
Focus: Med 02103

Federation of New Brunswick Faculty Associations / Fédération des Associations de Professeurs d'Université du Nouveau-Brunswick, 65 Brunswick St, Ste 297, Fredericton, N.B. E3B 1G5
T: (506) 458-8977; Fax: (506) 458-5620
Founded: 1969; Members: 1106
Gen Secr: Desmond A. Morley
Focus: Sci 02104

Federation of Women Teachers' Associations of Ontario, 1260 Bay St, Toronto, Ont. M5R 2B8
T: (416) 964-1232; Fax: (416) 964-0512
Founded: 1918; Members: 41078
Focus: Educ 02105

Fédération Québécoise des Directeurs et Directrices d'Etablissements d'Enseignement, 7855 Blvd Louis-H. Lafontaine, Ste 100, Anjou, Qué. H1K 4E4
T: (514) 353-7511; Fax: (514) 353-2064
Founded: 1961; Members: 3876
Pres: Guy Lessard
Focus: Educ; Public Admin
Periodical
Information (5 times annually) 02106

Fire Prevention Canada Association / Association Canadienne de Prévention des Incendies, 2425 Don Reid Dr, Ste 1, Ottawa, Ont. K1H 1H4
T: (613) 736-8131; Fax: (613) 736-0684
Founded: 1956; Members: 1000
Gen Secr: Marcel Ethier
Focus: Safety 02107

Fondation J. Armand Bombardier / J. Armand Bombardier Foundation, 1000 Rue J.A. Bombardier, CP 370, Valcourt, Qué. J0E 2L0
T: (514) 532-2258; Fax: (514) 532-5499
Founded: 1965
Gen Secr: France Bissonnette
Focus: Sci 02108

Fondation Lionel Groulx, 261 Av Bloomfield, Outremont, Qué. H2V 3R6
T: (514) 271-4759; Fax: (514) 6369
Founded: 1956
Gen Secr: Jean-Marc Leger
Focus: Sci 02109

Food Products Accident Prevention Association, c/o IAPA District 2 Office, 73 Water St N, Cambridge, Ont. N1R 7L6
T: (519) 624-4272; Fax: (519) 624-5200
Gen Secr: Marie Peaker
Focus: Safety; Food 02110

Fraser Institute, 626 Bute St, Vancouver B.C. V6E 3M1
T: (604) 688-0221; E-Mail: info@fraserinstitute.ca; Fax: (604) 688-8539
Founded: 1974; Members: 2700
Gen Secr: Dr. Michael A. Walker
Focus: Sci
Periodicals
Fraser Forum (monthly)
On Balance (monthly) 02111

Gairdner Foundation, 255 Yorkland Blvd, Ste 220, Willowdale, Ont. M2J 1S3
T: (416) 493-3101; Fax: (416) 493-8158
Founded: 1957
Gen Secr: Sally-Anne Hrica
Focus: Sci 02112

Genealogical Association of Nova Scotia, POB 641, Halifax, N.S. B3J 2T3
E-Mail: ab018@ccn.dal.ca
Founded: 1982; Members: 1200
Pres: Vernon Spurr
Focus: Genealogy
Periodical
The Nova Scotia Genealogist (3 times annually) 02113

Genealogical Institute of the Maritimes, POB 3142, South Postal Station, Halifax, N.S. B3J 3H5
T: (902) 424-6065
Founded: 1983; Members: 97
Pres: L. Yorke; Gen Secr: Virginia Clark
Focus: Genealogy
Periodical
Annual Report (annually) 02114

Genetics Society of Canada / Société de Génétique du Canada, 151 Slater St, Ste 907, Ottawa, Ont. K1P 5H4
T: (613) 232-9459; Fax: (613) 594-5190
Founded: 1956; Members: 392
Pres: Phyllis McAlpine; Gen Secr: Joanne Lechuk
Focus: Genetics
Periodical
Bulletin (quarterly) 02115

Geological Association of Canada / Association Géologique du Canada, c/o Dept of Earth Sciences, Memorial University of Newfoundland, 240 Prince Philip Dr, Saint John's, Nfld. A1B 3X5
T: (709) 737-8394; E-Mail: gac@sparky2.esd.mun.ca; Fax: (709) 737-2532
Founded: 1947; Members: 2600
Gen Secr: R.N. Hiscott
Focus: Geology
Periodical
Geoscience Canada (quarterly) 02116

Gerontology Association of Nova Scotia, POB 817, Dartmouth, N.S. B2Y 3Z3
T: (902) 464-8212; Fax: (902) 464-8220
Focus: Geriatrics 02117

Grain, Feed and Fertilizer Accident Prevention Association, c/o IAPA District 1 Office, 1020 Hargrieve Rd, Unit M, London, Ont. N6E 1P5
T: (519) 686-9698; Fax: (519) 686-9125
Gen Secr: C.J. George
Focus: Safety; Nutrition 02118

Hamber Foundation, 1055 Dunsmuir St, POB 49390, Station Bentall Centre, Vancouver, B.C. V7X 1P3
Founded: 1964
Focus: Sci 02119

Health Libraries Association of British Columbia (HLABC), c/o British Columbia Agency, 600 Tenth Av W, Vancouver, B.C. V5Z 4E6
T: (604) 877-6000 ext 2692; E-Mail: bccalib@wimsey.com; Fax: (604) 872-4596
Founded: 1980
Focus: Libraries & Bk Sci; Public Health
Periodical
HLABC Forum (quarterly) 02120

Heart and Stroke Foundation of Alberta, 1825 Park Rd SE, Calgary, Alta. T2G 3Y6
T: (403) 264-5549; Fax: (403) 237-0803
Founded: 1957
Gen Secr: John L. Paquet
Focus: Cardiol 02121

Heraldry Society of Canada / Société Héraldique du Canada, POB 8182, Station T, Gloucester, Ont. K1G 3H9
T: (613) 231-0867; E-Mail: hsc@bsc.ca
Founded: 1966; Members: 600
Pres: Jean Matheson; Gen Secr: Howard Heck
Focus: Genealogy
Periodical
Heraldry in Canada (5 times annually) . 02122

Historical Society of Alberta, POB 4035, Station C, Calgary, Alta. T2T 5M9
T: (403) 261-3662; Fax: (403) 269-6029
Founded: 1907; Members: 1300
Pres: Kathryn Ivany
Focus: Hist 02123

Historical Society of Mecklenburg Upper Canada, POB 193, Station K, Toronto, Ont. M4P 2G5
T: (416) 759-8897
Founded: 1972
Pres: Rolf A. Piro
Focus: Hist 02124

Historical Society of the Gatineau, POB 485, Chelsea, Qué. J0X 1N0
T: (819) 827-4432; Fax: (819) 827-5380
Founded: 1962; Members: 300
Pres: J. Carol Martin
Focus: Hist
Periodical
Up the Gatineau! (annually) 02125

Human Factors Association of Canada / Association Canadienne d'Ergonomie, 6519B Mississauga Rd, Mississauga, Ont. L5N 1A6
T: (416) 567-7193; Fax: (416) 567-7191
Founded: 1968; Members: 600
Gen Secr: Peter Fletcher
Focus: Physiology; Eng; Psych
Periodicals
Annual Conference Proceedings (annually)
Communiqué (bi-monthly) 02126

Huntington Society of Canada / Société Huntington du Canada, 13 Water St N, POB 1269, Cambridge, Ont. N1R 7G6
T: (519) 622-1002; Fax: (519) 622-7370
Founded: 1973; Members: 7050
Gen Secr: Ralph M. Walker
Focus: Geography 02127

ICOM Museums Canada, 280 Metcalfe St, Ste 400, Ottawa, Ont. K2P 1R7
T: (613) 567-0099; Fax: (613) 233-5438
Founded: 1946; Members: 325
Pres: Michel Côté
Focus: Arts 02128

Independent Schools Association of British Columbia, c/o Glenlyon Norfolk School, 801 Bank St, Victoria, B.C. V8S 4A8
T: (604) 596-2621
Founded: 1930
Pres: David Brooks
Focus: Educ 02129

Indexing and Abstracting Society of Canada (IASC) / Société Canadienne pour l'Analyse des Documents, POB 744, Station F, Toronto, Ont. M4Y 2N6
T: (416) 496-5025; Fax: (416) 496-5068
Founded: 1977; Members: 136
Focus: Libraries & Bk Sci; Standards
Periodical
IASC Bulletin: Bulletin de la SCAD (quarterly) 02130

Industrial Accident Prevention Association, 250 Yonge St, Toronto, Ont. M5B 2N4
T: (416) 506-8888; Fax: (416) 506-8880
Founded: 1917; Members: 103000
Gen Secr: Maureen C. Shaw
Focus: Metallurgy
Periodical
Accident Prevention (10 times annually) . 02131

Information Resource Management Association of Canada (IRMAC), POB 5639, Station A, Toronto, Ont. M5W 1N8
E-Mail: irmac@io.org
Founded: 1971; Members: 250
Focus: Computer & Info Sci 02132

Institut Canadien d'Education des Adultes, 5225 Rue Berri, Ste 300, Montréal, Qué. H2J 2S4
T: (514) 948-2044; Fax: (514) 948-2040
Founded: 1956
Focus: Adult Educ 02133

Institut d'Histoire de l'Amérique Française, 261 Av Bloomfield, Montréal, Qué. H2V 3R6
T: (514) 278-2232; Fax: (514) 271-6369
Founded: 1947; Members: 1000
Pres: Micheline Dumont
Focus: Hist
Periodical
Revue d'Histoire de l'Amérique Française (quarterly) 02134

Institut Militaire de Québec, CP 843, Haute-Ville, Québec, Qué. G1R 4S7
T: (418) 694-3667
Founded: 1928; Members: 250
Focus: Military Sci 02135

Institute for Aerospace Studies, c/o University of Toronto, 4925 Dufferin St, North York, Ont. M3H 5T6
T: (416) 667-7701; E-Mail: info@utias.utoronto.ca; Fax: (416) 667-7799
Founded: 1949; Members: 68
Gen Secr: Dr. A.A. Haasz
Focus: Aero
Periodicals
UTIAS Annual Report (annually)
UTIAS Reports (irregularly)
UTIAS Reviews (irregularly)
UTIAS Technical Notes (irregularly) . . . 02136

Institute for Canadian Studies (ICS), 298 Garry St, Winnipeg, Man. R3C 1H3
T: (204) 925-8781; E-Mail: lisashaw@instcanstudies.mb.ca; Fax: (204) 943-2261
Founded: 1992
Gen Secr: W.H. Loewen
Focus: Econ; Sociology; Poli Sci; Law . 02137

Institute for Research on Public Policy / Institut de Recherches Politiques, 1470 Rue Peel, Ste 200, Montréal, Qué. H3A 1T1
T: (514) 985-2461; Fax: (514) 985-2559
Founded: 1972; Members: 71
Focus: Poli Sci
Periodicals
The Institute
Policy Options (bi-monthly) 02138

Institute of Canadian Advertising, 2300 Yonge St, Ste 500, POB 2350, Toronto, Ont. M4P 1E4
T: (416) 482-1396; E-Mail: ica@goodmedia.com; Fax: (416) 481-1856
Founded: 1905; Members: 64
Focus: Advert 02139

Institute of Chartered Accountants of Ontario / Institut des Comptables Agréés de l'Ontario, 69 E Bloor St E, Toronto, Ont. M4W 1B3
T: (416) 962-1841; E-Mail: exaf@icao.on.ca; Fax: (416) 962-8900
Founded: 1879; Members: 26000
Focus: Finance
Periodical
Check Mark 02140

Institute of Electrical and Electronics Engineers Canada, 86 Main St, POB 830, Dundas, Ont. L9H 2R1
T: (905) 628-9554; E-Mail: member.service@ieee.ca; Fax: (905) 628-9554
Founded: 1884
Focus: Electric Eng
Periodical
Canadian Electrical Engineering Journal (quarterly) 02141

Institute of Public Administration of Canada (IPAC) / Institut d'Administration Publique du Canada, 150 Eglinton Av, Ste 305, Toronto, Ont. M4P 1E8
T: (416) 923-3666; Fax: (416) 923-3667
Founded: 1947; Members: 3500
Gen Secr: Joseph M. Galimberti
Focus: Public Admin
Periodical
IPAC Bulletin (bi-monthly) 02142

Institute of Textile Science, 1 Rue Pacifique, Sainte-Anne-de-Bellevue, Qué. H9X 1C5
T: (514) 457-2347
Founded: 1956; Members: 180
Gen Secr: Carmen Morosan
Focus: Textiles
Periodical
Canadian Textile Journal (monthly) . . . 02143

Insurers' Advisory Organization (IAO), 18 King St E, Ste 700, Toronto, Ont. M5C 1C4
T: (416) 368-1801; Fax: (416) 368-0333
Founded: 1883; Members: 65
Focus: Insurance
Periodicals
The IAO Inspector (quarterly)
The Quarterly Report (quarterly) 02144

Inter-American Commercial Arbitration Commission (Canadian Section) / Commission Interaméricaine d'Arbitrage Commercial (Section Canadienne), c/o Canadian Arbitration Centre and Amicable Composition Centre, Faculty of Law, University of Ottawa, POB 450, Station A, Ottawa, Ont. K1N 6N5
T: (613) 564-5939; Fax: (613) 564-9800
Founded: 1934; Members: 50
Focus: Law 02145

International Agricultural Exchange Association, 7710 Fifth St SE, Ste 105, Calgary, Alta. T2H 2L9
T: (403) 255-7799
Founded: 1963; Members: 5000
Gen Secr: Debbie Kletzel
Focus: Agri 02146

International Association of Geochemistry and Cosmochemistry, c/o AECL Research, Station 40, Pinawa, Man. R0E 1L0
T: (204) 753-2311 ext 2207; E-Mail: gascoynem@aecl.ca; Fax: (204) 753-2703
Founded: 1967; Members: 640
Gen Secr: Dr. Mel Gascoyne
Focus: Chem; Geology 02147

International Association of Master Penmen and Teachers of Handwriting (IAMPTH), 34 Broadway Av, Ottawa, Ont. K1S 2V6
T: (613) 232-3014
Founded: 1950; Members: 200
Gen Secr: Fred D. Richardson
Focus: Educ
Periodical
Penmens News Letter (bi-monthly) . . . 02148

International Association of Music Libraries, Archives and Documentation Centres, c/o Carleton University Library, 1125 Colonel By Dr, Ottawa, KIS 5B6
T: (613) 5202600 Ext.8150; Fax: (613) 5203583
Founded: 1951; Members: 2000
Focus: Libraries & Bk Sci; Music; Archives; Doc 02149

International Congress of University Adult Education (ICUAE), c/o Dept of Extension and Summer Session, University of New Brunswick, POB 4400, Station A, Fredericton, N.B. E3B 5A3
T: (506) 453-4646; E-Mail: morris@unb.ca; Fax: (506) 453-3572
Founded: 1960; Members: 175
Gen Secr: Dr. John F. Morris
Focus: Adult Educ
Periodical
International Journal of University Adult Education (3 times annually) 02150

International Council for Adult Education / Conseil International d'Education des Adultes, 720 Bathurst Av, Ste 500, Toronto, Ont. M5S 2R4
T: (416) 588-1211; E-Mail: icae@web.apc.org; Fax: (416) 588-5725
Founded: 1973
Pres: Lalita Ramdas; Gen Secr: Raymond Desrochers
Focus: Adult Educ
Periodical
News from the Secretariat (quarterly) . . 02151

International Development Education Resource Association (IDERA), 2678 Broadway Av W, Ste 200, Vancouver, B.C. V6K 2G3
T: (604) 732-1496; E-Mail: idera@web.apc.org
Founded: 1974; Members: 65
Gen Secr: Stuart Black
Focus: Educ
Periodicals
IDERA Newsletter
Press Relief 02152

International Development Research Centre / Centre de Recherches pour le Développement International, 250 Albert St, POB 8500, Ottawa, Ont. K1G 3H9
T: (613) 236-6163; E-Mail: info@idrc.ca (613) 563-0815
Founded: 1970
Focus: Food; Agri; Nutrition; Public Health; Soc Sci; Computer & Info Sci
Periodicals
Annual Report (annually)
Busqueda (annually)
Quête d'avenirs (annually)
Searching (annually) 02153

International Federation of Health Records Organizations, 2709 Victoria Dr, Ste 303, Vancouver, B.C. V5N 5T6
T: (604) 877-3004; E-Mail: vicki_tichbourne@chara-svh.hosp.gov.bc.ca; Fax: (604) 876-6729
Members: 20
Pres: Vicki Tichbourne
Focus: Public Health
Periodical
Newsletter 02154

International Federation on Ageing, 380 Rue Saint-Antoine Ouest, Ste 3200, Montréal, Qué. H2Y 3X7
T: (514) 287-9679; E-Mail: ifa@citenet.net; Fax: (514) 987-1567
Founded: 1973
Gen Secr: Nigel Martin
Focus: Geriatrics 02155

International Phototherapy Association, c/o Photo Therapy Centre, 1300 Richards St, Ste 205, Vancouver, B.C. V6B 3G6
T: (604) 689-9709; Fax: (604) 689-9709
Pres: Judy Weiser
Focus: Photo; Therapeutics 02156

International Society for Biomedical Research on Alcoholism, 33 Russell St, Toronto, Ont. M5S 2S1
T: (416) 978-6374
Founded: 1980
Gen Secr: Dr. Yedy Israel
Focus: Med 02157

International Society for Research in Palmistry, 351 Victoria Av, Westmount, Qué. H3Z 2N1
T: (514) 488-2292; Fax: (514) 488-3822
Gen Secr: Ghanshyam Singh
Focus: Parapsych 02158

International Society of Electrophysiological Kinesiology (ISEK), Dept of Psychology, Concordia University, 7141 Sherbrooke St W, Montréal, Qué. H4B 1R6
T: (514) 848-2231; Fax: (514) 848-4545
Founded: 1965; Members: 500
Pres: Dr. H.W. Ladd
Focus: Physiology
Periodical
Society Newsletter (quarterly) 02159

International Theatre Institute - Canadian Centre, c/o Acadia University, POB 1441, Wolfville, N.S. B0P 1X0
T: (902) 542-1932; Fax: (902) 542-1526
Founded: 1979; Members: 250
Gen Secr: Andria Hill
Focus: Perf Arts 02160

International Union of Food Science and Technology (IUFoST), 3110 Seneca Dr, Oakville, L6L 1B2
T: (905) 8273492; E-Mail: infost@inforamp.net; Fax: (905) 8279213
Founded: 1970; Members: 50 countries
Pres: Prof. Peter A. Biacs; Gen Secr: J.P. Meyers
Focus: Food 02161

Jane Austen Society of North America, 200 Kingsmount Blvd, Sudbury, Ont. P3E 1K9
T: (705) 670-1357
Founded: 1979; Members: 3295
Focus: Lit
Periodical
Persuasions (annually) 02162

Juvenile Diabetes Foundation Canada, 89 Granton Dr, Richmond Hill, Ont. L4B 2N5
T: (905) 889-4171; Fax: (905) 889-4209
Founded: 1974
Pres: Terry A. Jackson; Gen Secr: Tim Feher
Focus: Diabetes 02163

Lapidary, Rock and Mineral Society of British Columbia, 8172 Lawrence Ln, Mission, B.C. V2V 6R7
T: (604) 826-5312
Pres: Doug Dixon
Focus: Mineralogy 02164

Laubach Literacy Canada, 70 Crown St, Ste 225, Saint John, N.B. E2L 2X6
T: (506) 634-1980; Fax: (506) 634-0944
Founded: 1981; Members: 11000
Pres: James B. Morrow
Focus: Lit 02165

Law Foundation of Nova Scotia, POB 325, Halifax, N.S. B3J 2N7
T: (902) 422-8335; Fax: (902) 492-0424
Founded: 1976; Members: 9
Gen Secr: Mary Helleiner
Focus: Law 02166

Law Society of Manitoba, 219 Kennedy St, Winnipeg, Man. R3C 1S8
T: (204) 942-5571; Fax: (204) 956-0624
Founded: 1877; Members: 1659
Gen Secr: Deborah J. McCowley
Focus: Law
Periodical
Law Society of Manitoba Communiqué (10 times annually) 02167

Law Society of Newfoundland, POB 1028, Station C, Saint John's, Nfld. A1C 5M3
T: (709) 722-4740; Fax: (709) 722-8902
Founded: 1834
Gen Secr: Peter G. Ringrose
Focus: Law 02168

Law Society of Saskatchewan, 2500 Victoria Av, Ste 1100, Regina, Sask. S4P 3X2
T: (306) 569-8242; Fax: (306) 352-2989
Founded: 1907
Gen Secr: A. Kirsten Logan
Focus: Law
Periodicals
Journal (3 times annually)
This Week's Law (monthly) 02169

Law Society of the Northwest Territories, POB 1298, Yellowknife, N.W.T. X1A 2N9
T: (403) 873-3828; Fax: (403) 873-6344
Founded: 1978; Members: 313
Gen Secr: Becky McCaffrey
Focus: Law 02170

Law Society of Upper Canada, Osgoode Hall, 130 Queen St W, Toronto, Ont. M5H 2N6
T: (416) 947-3300; Fax: (416) 947-5967
Founded: 1797; Members: 26500
Gen Secr: Richard F. Tinsley
Focus: Law
Periodicals
Communiqué (quarterly)
Gazette 02171

League of Canadian Poets, 54 Wolseley St, Toronto, Ont. M5T 1A5
T: (416) 504-1657; E-Mail: league@io.org; Fax: (416) 703-0059
Founded: 1966; Members: 400
Gen Secr: Edita Petrauskaite
Focus: Lit
Periodical
Newsletter (bi-monthly) 02172

Learning Disabilities Association of Canada, 323 Chapel St, Ste 200, Ottawa, Ont. K1N 7Z2
T: (613) 238-5721; Fax: (613) 235-5391
Founded: 1971; Members: 10000
Focus: Educ
Periodical
National (quarterly) 02173

Library Association of Alberta (LAA), 80 Baker Cres, Calgary, Alta. T2L 1R4
T: (403) 284-5818; E-Mail: laa@freenet.calgary.ab.ca; Fax: (403) 282-6646
Founded: 1939; Members: 650
Pres: Peg Hofmann
Focus: Libraries & Bk Sci
Periodical
Letter of the LAA (bi-monthly) 02174

Ligue de Sécurite du Québec / Quebec Safety League, 2536 Rue Lapierre, Lasalle, Qué. H8N 2W9
T: (514) 595-9110; Fax: (514) 595-3398
Founded: 1923; Members: 210
Focus: Safety
Periodical
Famille Avertie (quarterly) 02175

Lung Association of Nova Scotia, 17 Alma Cres, Halifax, N.S. B3N 3E6
T: (902) 443-8141; E-Mail: info@ns.lung.ca; Fax: (902) 445-2573
Gen Secr: Bill VanGorder
Focus: Pulmon Dis 02176

Manitoba Archaeological Society, POB 1171, Winnipeg, Man. R3C 2Y4
T: (204) 942-7243; Fax: (204) 942-3749
Founded: 1961; Members: 225
Pres: A.P. Buchner
Focus: Archeol
Periodical
Manitoba Archaeological Quarterly (quarterly) 02177

Manitoba Arts Council, 93 Lombard Av, Ste 525, Winnipeg, Man. R3B 3B1
T: (204) 945-2237; Fax: (204) 945-5925
Gen Secr: Victor J. Enns
Focus: Arts 02178

Manitoba Association for Art Education, 191 Harcourt St, Winnipeg, Man. R3J 3H2
T: (204) 888-7961
Focus: Arts; Educ 02179

Manitoba Association for the Promotion of Ancestral Languages, 1574 Main St, Winnipeg, Man. R2W 5J8
T: (204) 338-7951; Fax: (204) 334-8277
Founded: 1983; Members: 15
Pres: Laura Shabaga
Focus: Ling
Periodical
Manitoba Heritage Review (semi-annually) 02180

Manitoba Association of Library Technicians, POB 1872, Winnipeg, Man. R3C 3R1
T: (204) 945-3360
Founded: 1971; Members: 76
Pres: Kris Rytter
Focus: Libraries & Bk Sci 02181

Manitoba Association of Medical Radiation Technologists, 819 Sargent Av, Ste 215, Winnipeg, Man. R3E 0B9
Pres: Sheila Boutcher
Focus: Nucl Med; Radiology 02182

Manitoba Association of School Trustees, 191 Provencher Blvd, Winnipeg, Man. R2H 0G4
T: (204) 233-1595; Fax: (204) 231-1356
Founded: 1965
Gen Secr: Dr. J.B. MacNeil
Focus: Educ
Periodicals
MAST (semi-annually)
Newsletter (10 times annually) 02183

Manitoba Association on Gerontology, POB 1833, Winnipeg, Man. R3C 3R1
T: (204) 783-8389
Founded: 1980; Members: 90
Pres: Patti Chiapetta
Focus: Geriatrics 02184

Manitoba Cancer Treatment and Research Foundation, 100 Olivia St, Winnipeg, Man. R3E 0V9
T: (204) 787-2136; Fax: (204) 783-6875
Gen Secr: Donna Pacholok
Focus: Cell Biol & Cancer Res 02185

Manitoba Dental Association, 698 Corydon Av, Ste 103, Winnipeg, Man. R3M 0X9
T: (204) 453-0055; Fax: (204) 453-0108
Founded: 1883; Members: 540
Gen Secr: Dr. M.A. Lasko
Focus: Dent 02186

Manitoba Genealogical Society, POB 2066, Winnipeg, Man. R3C 3R4
T: (204) 944-1153
Founded: 1976; Members: 804
Gen Secr: Louisa Shermerhorn
Focus: Genealogy
Periodicals
Generations (quarterly)
Newsletter (quarterly) 02187

Manitoba Health Libraries Association, c/o Medical Library, University of Manitoba, 770 Bannatyne Av, Winnipeg, Man. R3E 0W3
T: (204) 237-2808; E-Mail: poluha@bldghsc.lan.umanitoba.ca; Fax: (204) 235-3339
Founded: 1979; Members: 48
Pres: David Colborne
Focus: Libraries & Bk Sci; Public Health 02188

Manitoba Health Record Association, POB 1544, Winnipeg, Man. R3C 2Z4
T: (204) 235-3188; Fax: (204) 235-3126
Members: 160
Pres: Lorna Pankratz
Focus: Public Health 02189

Manitoba Historical Society, 167 Lombard Av, Ste 470, Winnipeg, Man. R3B 0T6
T: (204) 947-0559
Founded: 1879; Members: 653
Gen Secr: Celine M. Kean
Focus: Hist 02190

Manitoba Indian Education Association, 352 Donald St, Ste 305, Winnipeg, Man. R3B 2H8
T: (204) 947-0421; Fax: (204) 942-3067
Focus: Educ 02191

Manitoba Institute of Agrologists, 16 Lowell Pl, Winnipeg, Man. R3T 4H8
T: (204) 275-3721; E-Mail: murphy@mia.ca; Fax: (204) 261-6565
Founded: 1950; Members: 760
Gen Secr: Lee Anne Murphy
Focus: Agri 02192

Manitoba Library Association, 100 Arthur St, Ste 208, Winnipeg, Man. R3B 1H3
T: (204) 943-4567; Fax: (204) 942-1555
Founded: 1936; Members: 270
Pres: Karen Hunt
Focus: Libraries & Bk Sci 02193

Manitoba Library Trustee Association, POB 1168, Gimli, Man. R0C 1B0
T: (204) 642-8860
Founded: 1970
Pres: Shirley Bergen
Focus: Libraries & Bk Sci 02194

Manitoba Lung Association, 629 McDermot Av, Winnipeg, Man. R3A 1P6
T: (204) 774-5501; Fax: (204) 772-5083
Members: 51000
Gen Secr: Arlene Gibson
Focus: Pulmon Dis 02195

Manitoba Medical Association, 125 Sherbrook St, Winnipeg, Man. R3C 2B5
T: (204) 786-7565; Fax: (204) 775-9696
Founded: 1908; Members: 2117
Gen Secr: John A. Laplume
Focus: Med 02196

Manitoba Naturalists Society (MNS), 63 Albert St, Ste 401, Winnipeg, Man. R3B 1G4
T: (204) 943-9029; Fax: (204) 943-9029
Founded: 1920; Members: 1350
Pres: Ron Clay; Gen Secr: Herta Gudauskas
Focus: Nat Sci
Periodical
Bulletin (monthly) 02197

Manitoba Safety Council, 213 Notre Dame Av, Ste 700, Winnipeg, Man. R3B 1N3
T: (204) 949-1085; Fax: (204) 956-2897
Founded: 1920; Members: 204
Gen Secr: Rita L. Roeland
Focus: Safety 02198

Manitoba School Library Association, c/o Manitoba Teachers Society, 191 Harcourt St, Winnipeg, Man. R3J 3H2
T: (204) 888-7961; Fax: (204) 831-0872
Members: 210
Pres: B. Poustie
Focus: Libraries & Bk Sci 02199

Manitoba Society of Occupational Therapists (MSOT), 425 Elgin Av, Ste 1114, Winnipeg, Man. R3A 1P2
T: (204) 957-1214; Fax: (204) 942-7828
Founded: 1963; Members: 186
Pres: Heather Colquehoun
Focus: Therapeutics
Periodical
Update (10 times annually) 02200

Manitoba Speech and Hearing Association, 285 Pembina Hwy, Ste 321, Winnipeg, Man. R3L 2E1
T: (204) 453-4539; Fax: (204) 477-1881
Founded: 1961; Members: 265
Pres: Kelly Lukaszewski; Gen Secr: Tammy Johannson
Focus: Logopedy
Periodical
Hearsay (5 times annually) 02201

Manitoba Teachers' Society, 191 Harcourt St, Winnipeg, Man. R3J 3H2
T: (204) 888-7961; Fax: (204) 831-0877
Founded: 1919; Members: 13060
Gen Secr: Jean Gisiger
Focus: Educ 02202

Manitoba Veterinary Medicine Association, 2989 Pembina Hwy, Ste 203, Winnipeg, Man. R3T 2N5
T: (204) 269-0625; Fax: (204) 269-1129
Founded: 1890; Members: 225
Pres: Dr. Ron Mentz
Focus: Vet Med 02203

Medical Council of Canada / Conseil Médical du Canada, 2283 Saint Laurent Blvd, Ste 300, POB 8234, Station T, Ottawa, Ont. K1G 3H7
T: (613) 521-8787; Fax: (613) 521-9417
Founded: 1912; Members: 39
Focus: Med 02204

Medical Society of Nova Scotia, City of Lakes Business Park, 5 Spectacle Lake Dr, Dartmouth, N.S. B3B 1X7
T: (902) 468-1866; Fax: (902) 468-6578
Founded: 1861; Members: 1900
Gen Secr: Richard Dyke
Focus: Med 02205

Medical Society of Prince Edward Island, 559 N River Rd, Charlottetown, P.E.I. C1A 1J7
T: (902) 368-7303; Fax: (902) 566-3934
Founded: 1855; Members: 170
Gen Secr: Marilyn Lowther
Focus: Med 02206

Micmac Association for Cultural Studies, POB 961, Sydney, N.S. B1P 6J4
T: (902) 567-1752; Fax: (902) 564-2137
Founded: 1974; Members: 6000
Focus: Arts; Cultur Hist 02207

Microscopical Society of Canada, c/o Dept of Pathology, McMaster University, 1200 Main St W, Hamilton, Ont. L8N 3Z5
T: (905) 525-9140 ext 22496; Fax: (905) 577-0198
Founded: 1973; Members: 650
Focus: Optics 02208

Migraine Association of Canada, 365 Bloor St E, Ste 1902, Toronto, Ont. M4W 3L4
T: (416) 920-4916; Fax: (416) 920-3677
Founded: 1974; Members: 6500
Gen Secr: Anne Kerr
Focus: Sociology
Periodical
Migraine Report (quarterly) 02209

Mineralogical Association of Canada, 1460 Merivale Rd, POB 78087, RPO Merivale, Ottawa, Ont. K2E 1B1
T: (613) 226-4651; Fax: (613) 226-4651
Founded: 1957; Members: 1776
Focus: Mineralogy; Petrochem
Periodicals
The Canadian Mineralogist (quarterly)
Newsletter (semi-annually) 02210

Mining Association of British Columbia, 840 W Hastings St, Vancouver, B.C. V6E 1C8
T: (604) 681-4321; E-Mail: infodata@info-mine.com; Fax: (604) 681-5305
Founded: 1921; Members: 54
Pres: Gary K. Livingstone
Focus: Mining 02211

Mining Association of Manitoba, 305 Broadway Av, Ste 700, Winnipeg, Man. R3C 3J7
T: (204) 942-2789; Fax: (204) 943-4371
Founded: 1940; Members: 17
Gen Secr: Ed Huebert
Focus: Mining 02212

Mining Society of Nova Scotia, 88 Leeside Dr, Sydney, N.S. B1R 1S6
T: (902) 567-2147; Fax: (902) 567-2147
Founded: 1887; Members: 250
Gen Secr: George Sigut
Focus: Mining 02213

Multicultural History Society of Ontario, 43 Queen's Park Cres E, Toronto, Ont. M5S 2C3
T: (416) 979-2973; Fax: (416) 979-7947
Founded: 1976; Members: 155
Focus: Hist 02214

Multiple Dwelling Standards Association, 163 Beechwood Av, North York, Ont. M2L 1J9
T: (416) 449-7700
Founded: 1970
Pres: Jan Schwartz
Focus: Standards 02215

Museums Association of Saskatchewan, 1808 Smith St, Regina, Sask. S4P 2N4
T: (306) 780-9279; E-Mail: can-mas@immedia.ca; Fax: (306) 359-6758
Founded: 1967; Members: 890
Gen Secr: Gayl Hipperson
Focus: Archives

Periodical
Liaison: Saskatchewan's Heritage Review (quarterly) 02216

Myasthenia Gravis Foundation of British Columbia, 2805 Kingsway Av, Vancouver, B.C. V5R 5H9
T: (604) 451-5511; Fax: (604) 451-5651
Founded: 1955; Members: 135
Focus: Neurology 02217

National Association for Photographic Art / Association Nationale d'Art Photographique, 31858 Hopedale Av, Clearbrook, B.C. V2T 2G7
T: (604) 855-4848; Fax: (604) 859-6288
Founded: 1969; Members: 1235
Focus: Photo 02218

National Association of Women and the Law, 1 Nicholas St, Ste 604, Ottawa, Ont. K1N 7B7
T: (613) 241-7570; Fax: (613) 241-4657
Founded: 1974; Members: 1000
Gen Secr: Cheryl Boon
Focus: Law 02219

National Dental Examining Board of Canada, 100 Bronson Av, Ste 203, Ottawa, Ont. K1R 6G8
T: (613) 236-5912; Fax: (613) 236-8386
Gen Secr: Dr. Jack D. Gerrow
Focus: Dent 02220

Natural History Society of Prince Edward Island, POB 2346, Charlottetown, P.E.I. C1A 1Y6
T: (902) 894-9297
Founded: 1969; Members: 222
Pres: Ray Cooke
Focus: Nat Sci
Periodical
Island Naturalist (5-6 times annually) . . 02221

New Brunswick Association of Pathologists, c/o Dept of Laboratory Medicine, Saint John Regional Hospital, POB 2100, Saint John, N.B. E2L 4L2
T: (506) 648-6501
Members: 18
Pres: John S. Mackay
Focus: Pathology 02222

New Brunswick Dental Society, 520 King St, Ste 820, POB 488, Station A, Fredericton, N.B. E3B 4Z9
T: (506) 452-8575; Fax: (506) 452-1872
Founded: 1890; Members: 220
Focus: Dent 02223

New Brunswick Denturists Association, POB 954, Saint John, N.B. E0J 2B0
T: (506) 450-4900
Founded: 1973; Members: 40
Gen Secr: William D. Buxton
Focus: Dent 02224

New Brunswick Genealogical Society, POB 3235, Station B, Fredericton, N.B. E3A 5G9
Founded: 1979; Members: 1000
Pres: Joan Pearce
Focus: Genealogy 02225

New Brunswick Gerontology Association, RR 4, Hampton, N.B. E0G 1Z0
T: (506) 832-5595; Fax: (506) 832-7674
Pres: Judy Paquet
Focus: Geriatrics 02226

New Brunswick Health Record Association, c/o Moncton Hospital, 135 MacBeath Av, Moncton, N.B. E1C 6Z8
T: (506) 857-5111
Founded: 1963; Members: 35
Pres: Claire Esson
Focus: Public Health 02227

New Brunswick Historical Society, 120 Union St, Saint John, N.B. E2L 1A3
T: (506) 672-4056
Founded: 1874; Members: 208
Gen Secr: Carolyn Johnson
Focus: Hist 02228

New Brunswick Institute of Agrologists / Institut des Agronomes du Nouveau-Brunswick, POB 3479, Postal Station B, Fredericton, N.B. E3A 5H2
T: (506) 453-2717; E-Mail: estabrookse@em.agr.ca
Founded: 1960; Members: 200
Focus: Agri
Periodical
Newsletter (quarterly) 02229

New Brunswick Lung Association / Association Pulmonaire du Nouveau-Brunswick, 65 Brunswick St, Ste 257, Fredericton, N.B. E3B 1G5
T: (506) 455-8961; Fax: (506) 462-0939
Gen Secr: Ken Maybee
Focus: Pulmon Dis 02230

New Brunswick Medical Society / Société Médicale du Nouveau-Brunswick, 176 York St, Fredericton, N.B. E3B 3N7
T: (506) 458-8860; Fax: (506) 458-9853
Founded: 1867; Members: 1160
Focus: Med 02231

New Brunswick Psychiatric Association, POB 3220, Station B, Saint John, N.B. E2M 4H7
T: (506) 672-7871; Fax: (506) 635-1614
Founded: 1957; Members: 45
Gen Secr: Jeanette Logan
Focus: Psychiatry 02232

New Brunswick Safety Council / Conseil de Securité du Nouveau-Brunswick, 440 Wilsey Rd, Ste 204, Fredericton, N.B. E3B 7G5
T: (506) 458-8034; Fax: (506) 444-0177
Founded: 1967; Members: 200
Pres: Ron Carr
Focus: Safety 02233

New Brunswick School Supervisor's Association, c/o School District 15, 1077 Saint George Blvd, POB 1058, Moncton, N.B. E2A 4H8
T: (506) 547-2777; Fax: (506) 547-2783
Founded: 1967; Members: 73
Pres: Kathy Baldwin
Focus: Educ 02234

New Brunswick Teachers' Association, POB 752, Fredericton, N.B. E3B 5R6
T: (506) 452-8921; Fax: (506) 453-9795
Founded: 1902; Members: 8777
Focus: Educ 02235

New Brunswick Veterinary Medical Association, POB 1065, Moncton, N.B. E1C 8P2
T: (506) 851-7654; Fax: (506) 851-2524
Founded: 1919; Members: 147
Gen Secr: Dr. R. Pattie
Focus: Vet Med 02236

Newfoundland and Labrador Association of Occupational Therapists, POB 5423, Saint John's, Nfld. A1C 5W2
T: (709) 738-2434
Founded: 1970; Members: 72
Focus: Therapeutics 02237

Newfoundland and Labrador Veterinary Medical Association, POB 818, Mount Pearl, Nfld. A1N 3C8
T: (709) 576-2131; Fax: (709) 576-6046
Members: 36
Pres: Darya Campbell; Gen Secr: Helene Van Doninck
Focus: Vet Med 02238

Newfoundland Association of Medical Radiation Technologists, 3 Sandhurst Pl, POB 2794, Paradise, Nfld. A1L 1E9
T: (709) 782-2107
Members: 300
Focus: Radiology; Nucl Med 02239

Newfoundland Dietetic Association, POB 1756, Station C, Saint John's, Nfld. A1C 5P5
T: (709) 729-4424; Fax: (709) 729-5824
Founded: 1957; Members: 106
Focus: Nutrition 02240

Newfoundland Historical Society, Colonial Bldg, Rm 15, Saint John's, Nfld. A1C 2C9
T: (709) 722-3191; Fax: (709) 729-0578
Founded: 1881; Members: 200
Focus: Hist 02241

Newfoundland Lung Association, 292 LeMarchant Rd, POB 5250, Station C, Saint John's, Nfld. A1C 5W1
T: (709) 726-4664; Fax: (709) 726-2550
Founded: 1944; Members: 10000
Focus: Pulmon Dis 02242

Newfoundland Medical Board, 139 Water St, Ste 6, Saint John's, Nfld. A1C 1B2
T: (709) 726-8546; Fax: (709) 726-4725
Founded: 1893; Members: 12
Focus: Med 02243

Northwest Territories Law Foundation, POB 2594, Yellowknife, N.W.T. X1A 2P9
T: (403) 873-8275; Fax: (403) 873-6064
Founded: 1981
Gen Secr: Wendy Carter
Focus: Law 02244

Northwest Territories Library Association, POB 2276, Yellowknife, N.W.T. X1A 2P7
T: (403) 920-8617; Fax: (403) 873-0368
Pres: Susan Baer
Focus: Libraries & Bk Sci 02245

Northwest Territories Teachers' Association, 5018 48 St, POB 2340, Yellowknife, N.W.T. X1A 2P7
T: (403) 873-8501; Fax: (403) 873-2366
Founded: 1953; Members: 1077
Gen Secr: Blake W. Lyons
Focus: Educ 02246

Nova Scotia Association of Optometrists, Camp 83, Caribou Wilds, RR 4, Lower Sackville, N.S. B4C 3B1
T: (902) 835-9318; Fax: (902) 928-0933
Members: 59
Pres: Dr. Ray Wagg; Gen Secr: Dr. Carl Davis
Focus: Ophthal; Optics
Periodical
Newsletter (quarterly) 02247

Nova Scotia Barristers' Society, 1645 Granville St, Ste 1101, Halifax, N.S. B3J 1X3
T: (902) 422-1491; Fax: (902) 429-4869
Founded: 1857; Members: 2451
Focus: Law
Periodical
Nova Scotia Law News (bi-monthly) . . 02248

Nova Scotia Chiropractic Association, POB 1041, Port Hawkesbury, N.S. B0E 2V0
T: (902) 625-0005; Fax: (902) 625-1441
Founded: 1953; Members: 31
Focus: Orthopedics 02249

Nova Scotia Confederation of University Faculty Associations, 1646 Barrington St, Ste 404, Halifax, N.S. B3J 2A3
T: (902) 422-1204
Founded: 1975; Members: 1709
Gen Secr: John D'Orsay
Focus: Sci 02250

Nova Scotia Dental Association, 5991 Spring Garden Rd, Ste 604, Halifax, N.S. B3H 1Y6
T: (902) 420-0088; Fax: (902) 423-6537
Founded: 1891; Members: 515
Focus: Dent
Periodical
Nova Scotia Dentist (bi-monthly) 02251

Nova Scotia Dietetic Association, POB 36104, RPO Garden, Halifax, N.S. B3J 3S9
T: (902) 835-9706
Founded: 1958; Members: 314
Pres: Kimberlee A. Mitchell
Focus: Nutrition 02252

Nova Scotia Institute of Agrologists, c/o Nova Scotia Agricultural College, POB 550, Truro, N.S. B2N 5E3
T: (902) 893-6520; E-Mail: NSIA_info@nsac.ns.ca; Fax: (902) 893-6393
Founded: 1953; Members: 300
Focus: Agri 02253

Nova Scotia Library Association, c/o Nova Scotia Provincial Library, 3770 Kempt Rd, Halifax, N.S. B3K 4X8
T: (902) 424-2478; Fax: (902) 424-0633
Founded: 1973; Members: 200
Pres: Frances Newman
Focus: Libraries & Bk Sci
Periodical
Newsletter (quarterly) 02254

Nova Scotia Mineral and Gem Society, 9 Loon Terrace, Bedford, N.S. B4A 3X9
T: (902) 835-6869
Pres: William Plavac
Focus: Mineralogy 02255

Nova Scotia Pharmaceutical Society, 1526 Dresden Row, POB 3363, Halifax, N.S. B3J 3J1
Founded: 1876
Gen Secr: Susan Wedlake
Focus: Pharmacol 02256

Nova Scotia Safety Council, Bloomfield Centre, 2786 Agricola St, Ste 207, Halifax, N.S. B3K 4E1
T: (902) 454-9621; Fax: (902) 454-6027
Founded: 1958; Members: 150
Gen Secr: Lloyd A. Mitchell
Focus: Safety 02257

Nova Scotia School Boards Association, POB 605, Station M, Halifax, N.S. B3J 2R7
T: (902) 420-9191; E-Mail: nssba@fax.stna.ca; Fax: (902) 429-7405
Founded: 1954; Members: 22
Focus: Educ; Public Admin
Periodical
Newsletter (10 times annually) 02258

Nova Scotia Society of Medical Radiation Technologists, 301 Basinview Dr, Bedford, N.S. B4A 3B8
T: (902) 428-8210; Fax: (902) 428-8853
Founded: 1963; Members: 425
Gen Secr: Marlene Warren
Focus: Radiology; Nucl Med 02259

Nova Scotia Society of Occupational Therapists, POB 3381, Station South, Halifax, N.S. B3J 3J1
T: (902) 492-3620
Founded: 1951; Members: 60
Pres: Brenda Baxendale
Focus: Therapeutics
Periodical
Info (quarterly) 02260

Nova Scotia Teachers Union, 3106 Dutch Village Rd, Armdale, N.S. B3L 4L7
T: (902) 477-5621; Fax: (902) 477-3517
Founded: 1895; Members: 11371
Gen Secr: Ronald Morrison
Focus: Educ 02261

Nova Scotia Veterinary Medical Association, 15 Cobequid Rd, Lower Sackville, N.S. B4C 2M9
T: (902) 865-1876; Fax: (902) 865-3759
Founded: 1913; Members: 150
Focus: Vet Med 02262

Nova Scotian Institute of Science (NSIS), c/o Science Services University Library, Dalhousie University, 6225 University Av, Halifax, N.S. B4H 4H8
T: (902) 494-2384; Fax: (902) 494-2062
Founded: 1862; Members: 420
Pres: R.P. Gupta
Focus: Sci
Periodical
Proceedings (quarterly) 02263

Occupational Hygiene Association of Ontario, 65198 Mississauga Rd, Mississauga, Ont. L5N 1A6
T: (905) 567-7196; Fax: (905) 567-7191
Founded: 1984; Members: 550
Focus: Hygiene 02264

Ontario Archaeological Society, 126 Willowdale Av, North York, Ont. M2N 4Y2
T: (416) 730-0797; E-Mail: oas.io.org; Fax: (416) 730-0797
Founded: 1950; Members: 700
Pres: Henry Van Lieshout; Gen Secr: Ellen Blaubergs
Focus: Archeol; Anthro
Periodicals
Arch Notes (bi-monthly)
Ontario Archaeology (semi-annually) . . . 02265

Ontario Association for Curriculum Development, POB 931, Station B, London, Ont. N6A 5K1
T: (519) 438-8390; Fax: (519) 679-6855
Founded: 1950; Members: 940
Gen Secr: Jack D. Little
Focus: Educ
Periodical
Conference Report (annually) 02266

Ontario Association of Architects, 111 Moatfield Dr, North York, Ont. M3B 3L6
T: (416) 449-6898; Fax: (416) 449-5756
Founded: 1889; Members: 3500
Pres: Anthony J. Griffiths; Gen Secr: Phyllis Clasby
Focus: Archit 02267

Ontario Association of Library Technicians, 1500 Upper Middle Rd W, POB 76010, Oakville, Ont. L6M 3H5
Founded: 1973; Members: 474
Focus: Libraries & Bk Sci 02268

Ontario Black History Society, c/o Ontario Heritage Centre, 10 Adelaide St E, Ste 202, Toronto, Ont. M5C 1J3
T: (416) 867-9420; Fax: (416) 867-8691
Founded: 1978; Members: 365
Focus: Hist 02269

Ontario Cancer Institute, c/o Princess Margaret Hospital, 500 Sherbourne St, Toronto, Ont. M4X 1K9
T: (416) 926-4482; Fax: (416) 926-6566
Founded: 1943
Focus: Cell Biol & Cancer Res 02270

Ontario Chiropractic Association (OCA), 5160 Explorer Dr, Ste 30, Mississauga, Ont. L4W 4T7
T: (905) 629-8211; Fax: (905) 629-8214
Founded: 1929; Members: 1500
Gen Secr: Peter Waite
Focus: Orthopedics
Periodical
OCA News (bi-monthly) 02271

Ontario Co-operative Education Association, 939 Progress Av, Scarborough, Ont. M1G 3T8
T: (416) 396-6329; E-Mail: bmisener@interhop.net; Fax: (416) 396-6739
Founded: 1976; Members: 800
Pres: Judi Misener
Focus: Educ 02272

Ontario College of Pharmacists, 31 Governers Rd, Toronto, Ont. M4W 2E9
T: (416) 962-4861; Fax: (416) 962-1619
Focus: Pharmacol 02273

Ontario Council for Leadership in Educational Administration, 252 Bloor St W, Ste 115, Toronto, Ont. M5S 1V5
T: (416) 944-2652; Fax: (416) 944-3822
Founded: 1973
Gen Secr: Peter E. Angelini
Focus: Educ 02274

Ontario Council of University Libraries, c/o University of Ottawa, 65 University, Ottawa, Ont. K1N 9A5
T: (613) 562-5883; Fax: (613) 562-5195
Founded: 1974; Members: 20
Focus: Libraries & Bk Sci 02275

Ontario Dental Association, 4 New St, Toronto, Ont. M5R 1P6
T: (416) 922-3900; Fax: (416) 922-9005
Members: 4380
Gen Secr: J.C. Gillies
Focus: Dent
Periodical
Ontario Dentist (monthly) 02276

Ontario Educational Research Council, 252 Bloor St W, Ste 8-200, Toronto, Ont. M5S 1V6
T: (416) 924-6982; Fax: (416) 924-3188
Founded: 1959; Members: 160
Focus: Econ 02277

Ontario Electric Railway Historical Association, POB 578, Milton, Ont. L9T 5A2
T: (519) 856-9802
Founded: 1953; Members: 250
Focus: Cultur Hist 02278

Ontario Federation of Independent Schools, 2199 Regency Terrace, Ottawa, Ont. K2C 1H2
T: (905) 596-4013; Fax: (905) 596-4971
Founded: 1974; Members: 655
Gen Secr: Elaine Hopkins
Focus: Educ 02279

Ontario Genealogical Society, 40 Orchard View Blvd, Ste 102, Toronto, Ont. M4R 1B9
T: (416) 489-0734; Fax: (416) 489-9803
Founded: 1961; Members: 6900
Gen Secr: Edna Hudson
Focus: Genealogy

Periodicals
Families (quarterly)
Newsleaf (quarterly) *02280*

Ontario Gerontology Association, 7777 Keele St, Concord, Ont. L4K 1Y7
T: (905) 660-1056; Fax: (905) 660-7450
Founded: 1982; Members: 300
Pres: Dorothy Klein
Focus: Geriatrics
Periodical
Newsletter (bi-monthly) *02281*

Ontario Historical Society, 34 Parkview Av, North York, Ont. M2N 3Y2
T: (416) 226-9011; Fax: (416) 226-2740
Founded: 1888; Members: 2900
Gen Secr: Dorothy Duncan
Focus: Hist
Periodicals
Approaching Ontario's Past (irregularly)
Bulletin (quarterly)
Ontario History *02282*

Ontario Institute of Agrologists, 1 Stone Rd W, Guelph, Ont. N1G 4Y2
T: (519) 826-4226; E-Mail: oia@freespace.net; Fax: (519) 826-4228
Founded: 1960; Members: 1250
Gen Secr: Ruth Friendship-Keller
Focus: Agri *02283*

Ontario Library Association, 100 Lombard St, Ste 303, Toronto, Ont. M5C 1M3
T: (416) 336-3388; E-Mail: jgilbert@interlog.com; Fax: (416) 941-9581
Founded: 1900; Members: 4000
Pres: Jane Horrocks
Focus: Libraries & Bk Sci *02284*

Ontario Lung Association, 573 King St E, Ste 201, Toronto, Ont. M5A 4L3
T: (416) 864-9911; Fax: (416) 864-9916
Founded: 1945; Members: 850
Focus: Pulmon Dis
Periodicals
Lung Line (3 times annually)
Ontario Respiratory Care Society Update (3 times annually)
Ontario Thoracic Reviews (semi-annually) *02285*

Ontario Museum Association (OMA), 50 Baldwin St, Toronto, Ont. M5T 1L4
T: (416) 348-8672; E-Mail: can-oma@immedia.co; Fax: (416) 348-0438
Founded: 1972; Members: 850
Gen Secr: Dr. Barbara Efrat
Focus: Arts *02286*

Ontario Podiatry Association, 2 Sheppard Av E, Ste 900, North York, Ont. M2M 5Y7
T: (416) 927-9111; Fax: (416) 733-2491
Founded: 1944; Members: 61
Gen Secr: Gloria Patterson
Focus: Orthopedics *02287*

Ontario Psychogeriatric Association, 2175 Sheppard Av E, Ste 110, North York, Ont. M2J 1W8
T: (416) 491-3556; Fax: (416) 491-1670
Founded: 1974; Members: 600
Focus: Geriatrics
Periodicals
Newsletter (5 times annually)
Proceeding (annually) *02288*

Ontario Public Interest Research Group, 455 Spadina Av, Ste 201, Toronto, Ont. M5S 2G8
T: (416) 978-7770; E-Mail: opirg@web.net
Focus: Sociology *02289*

Ontario Public School Boards Association, 439 University Av, Toronto, Ont. M5G 1Y8
T: (416) 340-2540; E-Mail: admin@opsba.org; Fax: (416) 340-7571
Gen Secr: Mike Benson
Focus: Educ *02290*

Ontario Public School Teachers' Federation, 5160 Orbitor Dr, Mississauga, Ont. L4W 5H2
T: (905) 238-0200; Fax: (905) 238-0201
Founded: 1921; Members: 32000
Focus: Educ *02291*

Ontario Registered Music Teachers Association, POB 635, Timmins, Ont. P4N 7G2
T: (705) 267-1224
Focus: Educ; Music *02292*

Ontario School Counsellors' Association, 19 Treadgold Crescent, North York, Ont. M3A 1X1
T: (416) 449-9321; E-Mail: mauthom@enorea.on.ca
Founded: 1000; Members: 900
Focus: Educ
Periodical
Ontario School Counsellor Association Reports (quarterly) *02293*

Ontario Secondary School Teachers' Federation, 60 Mobile Dr, Toronto, Ont. M4A 2P3
T: (416) 751-8300; Fax: (416) 751-3394
Founded: 1919; Members: 43000
Gen Secr: Malcolm Buchanan
Focus: Educ *02294*

Ontario Society for Cable Television Engineers, 4560 Fieldgate Dr, Mississauga, Ont. L4W 3W6
T: (416) 629-1111
Pres: Karl Poirier
Focus: Eng *02295*

Ontario Society for Industrial Archaeology, 88 Upper Canada Dr, North York, Ont. M2P 1S4
T: (416) 207-5872; Fax: (416) 207-5911
Founded: 1982; Members: 150
Pres: Ian Livsey
Focus: Archeol *02296*

Ontario Society of Clinical Hypnosis, 200 Saint Clair Av W, Ste 402, Toronto, Ont. M4V 1R1
T: (416) 251-2442
Founded: 1970; Members: 500
Focus: Anesthetics *02297*

Ontario Society of Occupational Therapists, 55 Eglinton Av E, Ste 210, Toronto, Ont. M4P 1G8
T: (416) 322-3011; Fax: (416) 322-6705
Founded: 1920; Members: 1263
Focus: Therapeutics *02298*

Ontario Teachers' Federation, 1260 Bay St, Ste 700, Toronto, Ont. M5R 2B5
T: (416) 966-3424; Fax: (416) 966-5450
Founded: 1944; Members: 134000
Pres: Bill Martin
Focus: Educ *02299*

Ontario Thoracic Society, 573 King St E, Ste 201, Toronto, Ont. M5A 4L3
T: (416) 864-9911; Fax: (416) 864-9916
Members: 250
Focus: Pulmon Dis
Periodical
The Ontario Thoracic Review (bi-annually) *02300*

Ontario Veterinary Medical Association, 245 Commercial St, Milton, Ont. L9T 2J3
T: (905) 875-0756; Fax: (905) 875-0958
Members: 1300
Focus: Vet Med
Periodical
Update (bi-monthly) *02301*

Operation Eyesight Universal, 4 Parkdale Cres NW, Calgary, Alta. T2N 3T8
T: (403) 283-6323; E-Mail: oeuca@cadvision.com; Fax: (403) 270-1899
Founded: 1963
Focus: Ophthal
Periodical
Newsletter (bi-monthly) *02302*

Organization of Military Museums of Canada / Organisation des Musées Militaires du Canada, 72 Robertson Rd, POB 26106, Nepean, Ont. K2H 9R6
T: (613) 829-0280; Fax: (613) 829-0280
Founded: 1967; Members: 300
Focus: Military Sci; Archives *02303*

Osteoporosis Society of Canada, 33 Laird Dr, Toronto, Ont. M4G 3S9
T: (416) 696-2663; Fax: 696-2673
Founded: 1982; Members: 14000
Gen Secr: Joyce Gordon
Focus: Pathology
Periodical
Osteoporosis: Bulletin for Physicians (semi-annually) *02304*

Ottawa-Carleton Safety Council, 200 Elgin St, Ste 501, Ottawa, Ont. K2P 0L5
T: (613) 238-1513; Fax: (613) 238-8744
Founded: 1957; Members: 100
Focus: Safety *02305*

Pacific Coast Family Therapy Training Association, 1545 62 Av W, Vancouver, B.C. V6P 2E8
T: (604) 736-3664
Focus: Therapeutics *02306*

Parkinson Foundation of Canada / Fondation Canadienne du Parkinson, 390 Bay St, Ste 710, Toronto, Ont. M5H 2Y2
T: (416) 366-0099; Fax: (416) 366-9190
Founded: 1965; Members: 15000
Focus: Neurology
Periodical
Network Newsletter (5 times annually) . *02307*

Pharmacological Society of Canada, c/o Dept of Pharmacology, Faculty of Medicine, Dalhousie University, Halifax, N.S. B3H 4H7
T: (902) 494-2596; E-Mail: sawydalu@ac.dal.ca; Fax: (902) 494-1388
Founded: 1956; Members: 300
Gen Secr: Dr. Jana Sawynak
Focus: Pharmacol
Periodical
Canadian Journal of Physiology and Pharmacology *02308*

Pharmacy Association of Nova Scotia, POB 3214, Station South, Halifax, N.S. B3J 3H5
T: (902) 422-9583; Fax: (902) 422-2619
Founded: 1979; Members: 700
Focus: Pharmacol *02309*

Photographic Historical Society of Canada, 1712 Avenue Rd, POB 54620, Toronto, Ont. M5M 4N5
T: (416) 691-1555; E-Mail: phsc@onramp.ca; Fax: (416) 693-0018
Founded: 1974; Members: 250
Pres: L. Jones
Focus: Photo
Periodical
Photographic Canadiana (bi-monthly) . . *02310*

Physiotherapy Association of British Columbia (PABC), 1755 Broadway W, Ste 402, Vancouver, B.C. V6J 4S5
T: (604) 736-5130; E-Mail: pabc@unixg.ubr.ca; Fax: (604) 736-5606
Founded: 1927; Members: 1650
Gen Secr: Joyce Statton
Focus: Physical Therapy
Periodical
PABC Report (monthly) *02311*

Planning Institute of British Columbia, 10551 Shellbridge Way, Ste 20, Richmond, B.C. V6X 2W9
T: (604) 270-2061; Fax: (604) 660-2271
Founded: 1958; Members: 460
Focus: Urban Plan *02312*

Pollution Probe Foundation, 12 Madison Av, Toronto, Ont. M5R 2S1
T: (416) 926-1907; E-Mail: pprobe@web.net; Fax: (416) 926-1601
Founded: 1969; Members: 35000
Gen Secr: Ken Ogilvie
Focus: Ecology *02313*

Postal History Society of Canada, 216 Mailey Dr, Carleton Place, Ont. K7C 3X9
T: (613) 257-5453
Founded: 1972; Members: 700
Focus: Cultur Hist *02314*

Potash and Phosphate Institute of Canada, CN Tower, Midtown Plaza, Sakatoon, Sask. S7K 1J5
T: (306) 652-3535; Fax: (306) 664-8941
Founded: 1971
Focus: Agri *02315*

Prince Edward Island Association of Medical Radiation Technologists, 15 Westview Dr, Charlottetown, P.E.I. C1A 3A4 k702=bmurley@peinet.pe.ca
Founded: 1982; Members: 68
Focus: Radiology; Nucl Med *02316*

Prince Edward Island Cerebral Palsy Association, POB 2702, Charlottetown, P.E.I. C1A 8C3
T: (902) 892-9494; Fax: (902) 566-2214
Founded: 1953; Members: 150
Pres: Richard Montigny
Focus: Neurology *02317*

Prince Edward Island Dietetic Association, POB 2575, Charlottetown, P.E.I. C1A 8C2
T: (902) 892-6004
Members: 50
Pres: Margie Kays
Focus: Nutrition *02318*

Prince Edward Island Institute of Agrologists, POB 2712, Charlottetown, P.E.I. C1A 8C3
T: (902) 629-1229; E-Mail: kimpinskij@em.agr.ca; Fax: (902) 629-1229
Members: 113
Pres: Les Haliday
Focus: Agri *02319*

Prince Edward Island Lung Association, 1 Rochford St, Charlottetown, P.E.I. C1A 9L2
T: (902) 892-5957; Fax: (902) 368-7281
Founded: 1936
Gen Secr: Vicki Bryanton
Focus: Pulmon Dis *02320*

Prince Edward Island Professional Librarians Association, c/o Robertson Library Reference Dept, 550 University Av, Charlottetown, P.E.I. C1A 4P3
T: (902) 368-4637
Founded: 1982; Members: 35
Gen Secr: B. Stanfield
Focus: Libraries & Bk Sci *02321*

Prince Edward Island Society of Medical Technologists, c/o Queen Elizabeth Hospital, POB 6600, Charlottetown, P.E.I. C1A 8T5
T: (902) 894-2329; Fax: (902) 894-2415
Members: 115
Pres: Eunice Tanton
Focus: Med; Eng *02322*

Prince Edward Island Speech and Hearing Association, 65 McGill Av, Charlottetown, P.E.I. C1A 2K1
T: (902) 368-5807; Fax: (902) 368-6468
Founded: 1979; Members: 20
Pres: Pat Ellis
Focus: Logopedy *02323*

Prince Edward Island Teachers' Federation, POB 6000, Charlottetown, P.E.I. C1A 8B4
T: (902) 569-4157; Fax: (902) 569-3682
Founded: 1880; Members: 1505
Gen Secr: Bob MacRae
Focus: Educ *02324*

Prince Edward Island Veterinary Medical Association, POB 100, Montague, P.E.I. C0A 1R0
T: (902) 838-2281; Fax: (902) 838-5077
Founded: 1920; Members: 80
Gen Secr: Dr. David Lister
Focus: Vet Med *02325*

Printing Trades Accident Prevention Association, c/o IAPA District 4 Office, 1090 Don Mills Rd, North York, Ont. MC3 3R6
T: (416) 449-5755
Focus: Safety *02326*

Professional Development Institute, 79 Fentiman Av, POB 1181, Station B, Ottawa, Ont. K1S 0T7
T: (613) 730-7777; Fax: (613) 235-1115
Founded: 1973; Members: 121
Focus: Econ *02327*

Professional Marketing Research Society / Société Professionnelle de Recherche en Marketing, 2175 Sheppard Av E, Ste 110, Toronto, Ont. M2J 1W8
T: (416) 493-4060; Fax: (416) 491-1670
Founded: 1960; Members: 1200
Focus: Marketing *02328*

Provincial Association of Catholic Teachers, 5800 Blvd Metropolitain Est, Ste 330, Montréal, Qué. H1S 1A7
T: (514) 252-7946; Fax: (514) 252-9003
Founded: 1969; Members: 3500
Pres: Michel Palumbo
Focus: Educ *02329*

Provincial Association of Protestant Teachers of Québec / Association Provinciale des Enseignants Protestants du Québec, 17035 Brunswick Blvd, Ste 1, Kirkland, Qué. H9H 5G6
T: (514) 694-9777; Fax: (514) 694-0189
Founded: 1864; Members: 6000
Focus: Educ *02330*

Psychological Society of Saskatchewan, POB 4528, Regina, Sask. S4P 3W7
T: (306) 694-3750
Founded: 1966; Members: 204
Pres: Francis Stewart
Focus: Psych *02331*

Pulp and Paper Research Institute of Canada, 570 Blvd Saint-Jean, Pointe Claire, Qué. H9R 3J9
T: (514) 630-4100; Fax: (514) 630-4105
Founded: 1925; Members: 50
Pres: Dr. Joseph D. Wright
Focus: Materials Sci; Chem; Bio; Eng; Physics
Periodicals
Annual Report (annually)
Trend (1-2 times annually) *02332*

Quebec Association of Independent Schools / Association des Ecoles Privées du Québec, 410 Rue Gratton, Ste 206, Saint-Laurent, Qué. H4M 2E2
T: (514) 744-6711; Fax: (514) 744-6523
Founded: 1965; Members: 24
Pres: Elizabeth Scanlan; Gen Secr: Soryl Naymark
Focus: Educ *02333*

Reinforcing Steel Institute of Canada, 70 Leek Cres, Richmond Hill, Ont. L4B 1H1
T: (416) 499-4000 ext 28; Fax: (416) 707-0610
Founded: 1976; Members: 40
Gen Secr: J. Warren Webster
Focus: Metallurgy *02334*

Reinsurance Research Council / Conseil de Recherche en Réassurance, 18 King St E, Ste 800, Toronto, Ont. M5C 1C4
T: (416) 601-4651; Fax: (416) 368-0333
Founded: 1973; Members: 37
Focus: Insurance *02335*

Richard Ivey Foundation, 630 Richmond St, London, Ont. N6A 3G6
T: (519) 673-1280; E-Mail: 102704.353@compuserve.com; Fax: (519) 672-4790
Founded: 1947
Focus: Sci *02336*

Royal Architectural Institute of Canada / Institut Royal d'Architecture du Canada, 55 Murray St, Ste 330, Ottawa, Ont. K1N 5M3
T: (613) 241-3600; Fax: (613) 241-5750
Founded: 1907; Members: 4000
Gen Secr: Timothy Kehoe
Focus: Archit
Periodicals
RAIC Bulletin (quarterly)
RAIC Practice Notes (quarterly) *02337*

Royal Astronomical Society of Canada / Société Royale d'Astronomie du Canada, 136 Dupont St, Toronto, Ont. M5R 1V2
T: (416) 924-7973; Fax: (416) 924-7973
Founded: 1903; Members: 2300
Gen Secr: R.C. Brooks
Focus: Astronomy
Periodicals
Journal (bi-monthly)
Observer's Handbook (annually) *02338*

Royal Canadian Academy of Arts / Académie Royale des Arts du Canada, 163 Queen St E, POB 2, Toronto, Ont. M5A 1S1
T: (416) 363-9612; Fax: (416) 363-9612
Founded: 1880; Members: 793
Pres: Ernest Annau; Gen Secr: V. Hubel
Focus: Arts *02339*

Royal Canadian Geographical Society / Société Géographique Royale du Canada, 39 McArthur Av, Vanier, Ont. K1L 8L7
T: (613) 745-4629; Fax: (613) 744-0947
Founded: 1929; Members: 238000
Pres: Dr. Denis Saint-Onge
Focus: Geography *02340*

Royal Canadian Institute, 196 Carleton St, Toronto, Ont. M5A 2K8
T: (416) 928-2096
Founded: 1849; Members: 800
Pres: Veronika Huta
Focus: Sci 02341

Royal Canadian Military Institute, 426 University Av, Toronto, Ont. M5G 1S9
T: (416) 597-0286; Fax: (416) 597-6919
Founded: 1890; Members: 2700
Gen Secr: Norbert Luth
Focus: Military Sci 02342

Royal College of Dental Surgeons of Ontario, 6 Crescent Rd, Toronto, Ont. M4W 1T1
T: (416) 961-6555; Fax: (416) 961-5814
Founded: 1868; Members: 6400
Focus: Dent 02343

Royal College of Physicians and Surgeons of Canada (RCPSC), 774 Echo Dr, Ottawa, Ont. K1S 5N8
T: (613) 730-8177; Fax: (613) 730-8833
Founded: 1929; Members: 28500
Pres: Dr. Luc Deschênes; Gen Secr: Hugh M. Scott
Focus: Surgery; Physiology
Periodical
Annals RCPSC (bi-monthly) 02344

Royal Nova Scotia Historical Society (RNSHS), POB 2097, Dartmouth, N.S. B2W 3B8
T: (902) 422-4610; Fax: (902) 422-4610
Founded: 1878; Members: 331
Pres: Donald F. Maclean; Gen Secr: Rosemary Barbour
Focus: Hist; Genealogy
Periodicals
Collections (irregularly)
The Nova Scotia Genealogist (3 times annually) 02345

Royal Society of Canada / Société Royale du Canada, 225 Metcalfe St, Ste 308, Ottawa, Ont. K2P 1P9
T: (613) 991-6990; E-Mail: adminrsc@rsc.ca; Fax: (613) 991-6996
Founded: 1882; Members: 1150
Pres: Robert H. Haynes
Focus: Sci
Periodicals
Calendar: Annuaire
Presentation (annually)
Proceedings and Transaction: Délibérations et Memoirs (annually) 02346

Rural Education and Development Association, 14815 119 Av NW, Edmonton, Alta. T5L 2N9
T: (403) 451-5959; Fax: (403) 452-5385
Founded: 1958
Gen Secr: John Melicher
Focus: Educ 02347

Sandford Fleming Foundation, c/o University of Waterloo, 4300 Carl Pollock Hall, Waterloo, Ont. N2L 3G1
T: (519) 888-4008; Fax: (519) 746-1457
Founded: 1976; Members: 46
Gen Secr: Jeff D. Weller
Focus: Sci 02348

Saskatchewan Association of Library Technicians, POB 9388, Saskatoon, Sask. S7K 7E9
T: (306) 477-2743; Fax: (306) 975-7521
Members: 100
Pres: Louise Hajlasz
Focus: Libraries & Bk Sci 02349

Saskatchewan Association of Medical Radiation Technologists, 514 Wilkinson Cres, Saskatoon, Sask. S7N 3M1
Founded: 1956; Members: 400
Focus: Radiology; Nucl Med 02350

Saskatchewan Dietetic Association (SDA), POB 3894, Regina, Sask. S4P 3R8
T: (306) 359-3040; Fax: (306) 757-8161
Founded: 1958; Members: 171
Pres: Michael Chan
Focus: Nutrition
Periodical
SDA Newsletter (bi-monthly) 02351

Saskatchewan Genealogical Society, 1870 Lorne St, Regina, Sask. S4P 2L7
T: (306) 780-9207; E-Mail: margethomas.sgs@cabler.cableregina.com; Fax: (306) 781-6021
Founded: 1969; Members: 1700
Focus: Genealogy
Periodical
Bulletin (quarterly) 02352

Saskatchewan Geological Society, POB 234, Regina, Sask. S4P 2Z6
Founded: 1952; Members: 130
Gen Secr: Brian Brunskill
Focus: Geology 02353

Saskatchewan Horticultural Association, POB 68, Parkside, Sask. S0J 2A0
T: (306) 747-3296
Founded: 1927
Gen Secr: Alan Daku
Focus: Hort 02354

Saskatchewan Institute of Agrologists, 3012 Louise St, Ste 7, Saskatoon, Sask. S7J 3L8
T: (306) 242-2606; Fax: (306) 955-5561
Founded: 1946; Members: 1100
Focus: Agri
Periodical
Newsletter (bi-monthly) 02355

Saskatchewan Library Association, POB 3388, Regina, Sask. S4P 3H1
T: (306) 780-9413; E-Mail: sla@pleis.lib.sk.ca; Fax: (306) 780-9447
Founded: 1942; Members: 270
Focus: Libraries & Bk Sci
Periodical
Forum (5 times annually) 02356

Saskatchewan Lung Association, 1231 Eighth St, Sakatoon, Sask. S7H 0S5
T: (306) 343-9511; E-Mail: info@sk.Jung.ca; Fax: (306) 343-7007
Founded: 1911
Focus: Pulmon Dis 02357

Saskatchewan Medical Association, 211 Fourth Av S, Ste 200, Saskatoon, Sask. S7K 1N1
T: (306) 244-2196; Fax: (306) 653-1631
Founded: 1906; Members: 1170
Gen Secr: Dr. Brian Scharfstein
Focus: Med 02358

Saskatchewan Pharmaceutical Association, 2631 28 Av, Ste 301, Regina, Sask. S4S 6X3
T: (306) 584-2292; Fax: (306) 584-9695
Founded: 1911; Members: 1300
Focus: Pharmacol 02359

Saskatchewan Psychiatric Association, 222 Av P South, Saskatoon, Sask. S7M 2W2
T: (306) 652-8777; Fax: (306) 665-3304
Members: 40
Focus: Psychiatry 02360

Saskatchewan Safety Council, 445 Hoffer Dr, Regina, Sask. S4N 6E2
T: (306) 757-3197; Fax: (306) 569-1907
Founded: 1956; Members: 300
Gen Secr: H.P. Toupin
Focus: Safety 02361

Saskatchewan Society of Medical Laboratory Technologists, POB 3837, Regina, Sask. S4P 3R8
T: (306) 352-6791; Fax: (306) 352-6791
Founded: 1983; Members: 1000
Focus: Med 02362

Saskatchewan Society of Occupational Therapists, POB 9089, Saskatoon, Sask. S7K 7E7
T: (306) 384-1276; Fax: (306) 655-3801
Founded: 1971; Members: 150
Focus: Therapeutics
Periodical
NBTA News (14 times annually) 02363

Saskatchewan Teachers' Federation, 2317 Arlington Av, POB 1108, Saskatoon, Sask. S7K 3N3
T: (306) 373-1660; Fax: (306) 374-1122
Founded: 1933; Members: 11778
Pres: George Georget
Focus: Educ
Periodical
Saskatchewan Bulletin (15 times annually) 02364

Saskatchewan Veterinary Medical Association, 112 Research Dr, Ste 104, Saskatoon, Sask. S7N 3R3
T: (306) 955-7862
Members: 458
Focus: Vet Med 02365

Science for Peace / Science et Paix, c/o University College, University of Toronto, Toronto, Ont. M5S 3H8
T: (416) 978-3606; E-Mail: sfp@physics.utoronto.ca
Founded: 1981; Members: 260
Pres: Prof. Peter Nicholls; Gen Secr: Helmut Burkhardt
Focus: Prom Peace
Periodicals
Canadian Papers in Peace Studies (irregularly)
Science for Peace Bulletin (quarterly) . . 02366

Sculptors' Society of Canada / Société des Sculpteurs du Canada, Exchange Tower, First Canadian Pl, 130 King St W, POB 40, Station First Canadian Pl, Toronto, Ont. M5X 1B5
T: (416) 214-0389; E-Mail: sculpcan@lglobal.com
Founded: 1928; Members: 160
Pres: Desmond Scott
Focus: Arts 02367

Serena Canada, 151 Holland Av, Ottawa, Ont. K1Y 0Y2
T: (613) 728-6536
Members: 1000
Gen Secr: Marie-Paule Doyle
Focus: Family Plan
Periodical
Serena Canada (quarterly) 02368

Sex Information and Education Council of Canada (SIECCAN) / Conseil du Canada d'Information et Education Sexuelles, 850 Coxwell Av, East York, Ont. M4C 5R1
T: (416) 466-5304; Fax: (416) 778-0785
Founded: 1964; Members: 895
Focus: Educ
Periodicals
SIECCAN Journal (quarterly)
SIECCAN Newsletter (2-3 times annually) 02369

Sir Joseph Flavelle Foundation, c/o National Trust Co., 1 Financial Pl, 1 Adelaide St E, Toronto, Ont. M5C 2W8
T: (416) 361-4096; Fax: (416) 361-3717
Founded: 1945; Members: 320
Gen Secr: D.R. Windeyer
Focus: Sci 02370

Société d'Archéologie et de Numismatique de Montréal / Antiquarian and Numismatic Society of Montréal, 280 Rue Notre Dame Est, Montréal, Qué. H2Y 1C5
T: (514) 861-3708; Fax: (514) 861-8317
Founded: 1862; Members: 310
Focus: Archeol; Numismatics 02371

Société de Criminologie du Québec, 425 Rue Viger Ouest, Ste 620, Montréal, Qué. H2Z 1X2
T: (514) 873-4239; Fax: (514) 873-6460
Founded: 1960; Members: 450
Gen Secr: Samir Rizkalla
Focus: Criminology
Periodical
Ressources et Vous (bi-monthly) 02372

Société de Généalogie de Québec, CP 9066, Sainte-Foy, Qué. G1K 4A8
T: (418) 651-9127; Fax: (418) 651-2643
Founded: 1961; Members: 1200
Focus: Genealogy 02373

Societe d'Entomologie du Quebec, 472 Rue Maisonneuve, Saint-Jean-sur-Richelieu, Qué. J3B 1G2
T: (514) 348-8515
Founded: 1873; Members: 194
Focus: Entomology 02374

Société des Auteurs, Recherchistes, Documentalistes et Compositeurs, 1229 Rue Panet, Montréal, Qué. H2L 2Y6
T: (514) 526-9196; Fax: (514) 526-4124
Founded: 1949; Members: 716
Gen Secr: Yves Légaré
Focus: Lit; Doc; Music 02375

Société des Ecrivains Canadiens, c/o Fondation Macdonald-Stewart, 1195 Rue Sherbrooke Ouest, Montréal, Qué. H3A 1H9
T: (514) 733-0754; Fax: (514) 342-3866
Founded: 1936; Members: 300
Focus: Lit 02376

Société Généalogique Canadienne-Française, CP 335, Succ Place d'Armes, Montréal, Qué. H2Y 3H1
T: (514) 729-8366; Fax: (514) 729-1180
Founded: 1943; Members: 3700
Pres: Normand Robert
Focus: Genealogy
Periodical
Mémoires (quarterly) 02377

Société Historique Acadienne (SHA), CP 632, Moncton, N.B. E1C 8M7
T: (506) 855-5918
Founded: 1960; Members: 450
Pres: Léone Boudreau-Nelson
Focus: Hist
Periodical
Cahiers de la Société Historique Acadienne (quarterly) 02378

Société Historique de Québec, 171 Rue Grande-Allée Ouest, Québec, Qué. G1R 2H1
T: (418) 694-0085; Fax: (418) 649-0085
Founded: 1937; Members: 654
Focus: Hist
Periodical
Québecensia (bi-monthly) 02379

Société Historique du Saguenay, CP 456, Chicoutimi, Qué. G7H 5C8
T: (418) 549-2805
Founded: 1934; Members: 726
Focus: Hist 02380

Société Québécoise d'Assainissement des Eaux, 1055 René Lévesque Est, Montréal, Qué. H2L 4S5
T: (514) 873-7411; Fax: (514) 873-7879
Founded: 1980
Pres: Guy Leclerc
Focus: Ophthal 02381

Society for Indian and Northern Education, c/o College of Education, University of Saskatchewan, Saskatoon, Sask. S7N 0W0
T: (303) 343-3139
Gen Secr: Del Koenig
Focus: Educ 02382

Society for the Study of Architecture in Canada / Société pour l'Etude de l'Architecture au Canada, POB 2302, Station D, Ottawa, Ont. K1P 5W5
Founded: 1974; Members: 430
Focus: Archit
Periodical
Nouvelle: News (bi-monthly) 02383

Society for the Study of Egyptian Antiquities, POB 578, Station P, Toronto, Ont. M5S 2T1
T: (416) 978-6838; E-Mail: ssea@bigfoot.com; Fax: (416) 978-5294
Founded: 1969; Members: 518
Pres: Gayle Gibson; Gen Secr: Patricia Paice
Focus: Cultur Hist; Archeol 02384

Society of Christian Schools in British Columbia, 7600 Glover Rd, Langley, B.C. V3A 6H4
T: (604) 888-6366; Fax: (604) 888-2791
Founded: 1976; Members: 45
Focus: Educ 02385

Society of Commercial Seed Technologists (SCST), POB 579, Rivers, Man. R7A 6S3
T: (204) 328-5313; Fax: (204) 328-7400
Founded: 1922; Members: 225
Focus: Agri
Periodical
Seed Technologist News (3 times annually) 02386

Society of Composers, Authors and Music Publishers of Canada, 41 Valleybrook Dr, North York, Ont. M3B 2S6
T: (416) 445-8700; Fax: (416) 445-7108
Founded: 1990; Members: 58000
Gen Secr: Michael R. Rock
Focus: Music; Lit
Periodicals
The Canadian Composer (quarterly)
Probe (monthly) 02387

Society of Management Accountants of Canada, 120 King St W, Ste 850, POB 176, Hamilton, Ont. L8N 3C3
T: (905) 525-4100; Fax: (905) 525-4533
Founded: 1920
Focus: Business Admin
Periodicals
Cost & Management (bi-monthly)
RIA Digest (bi-monthly) 02388

Society of Obstetricians and Gynaecologists of Canada / Société des Obstétriciens et Gynécologues du Canada, 774 Echo Dr, Ottawa, Ont. K1N 5N8
T: (613) 730-4192; Fax: (613) 730-4314
Founded: 1944; Members: 1350
Gen Secr: Dr. André Lalonde
Focus: Gynecology
Periodical
Bulletin (bi-monthly) 02389

Spectroscopy Society of Canada, POB 332, Station A, Ottawa, Ont. K1N 8V3
T: (613) 597-1067
Founded: 1957; Members: 500
Pres: Dr. Ralph M. Paroli
Focus: Physics
Periodical
Canadian Journal of Spectroscopy . . . 02390

Speech and Hearing Association of Nova Scotia, POB 775, Halifax Central CRO, Halifax, N.S. B3J 2V2
T: (902) 423-9331; Fax: (902) 423-0981
Founded: 1978; Members: 120
Pres: Rachael Tabor
Focus: Logopedy 02391

Speech Foundation of Ontario, 10 Buchan Ct, North York, Ont. M2J 1V2
T: (416) 491-7771; Fax: (416) 491-7215
Founded: 1977
Pres: Gerald Brown
Focus: Logopedy 02392

Spina Bifida and Hydrocephalus Association of Ontario, 35 Mc Caul St, Ste 310, Toronto, Ont. M5T 1V7
T: (416) 979-5514; Fax: (416) 979-0849
Founded: 1973; Members: 800
Pres: Bonnie Charbonneau
Focus: Pathology
Periodical
Current: Pamphlet (quarterly) 02393

Spina Bifida Association of British Columbia, 9460 140 St, Surrey, B.C. V3V 5Z4
T: (604) 584-1361; Fax: (604) 521-3454
Founded: 1976; Members: 50
Pres: Colleen Talbot
Focus: Pathology 02394

Spina Bifida Association of Canada, 388 Donald St, Ste 220, Winnipeg, Man. R3B 2J4
T: (204) 957-1784; E-Mail: spinab@mts.net; Fax: (204) 957-1794
Founded: 1981; Members: 11
Pres: Wally Sagansky
Focus: Pathology 02395

Sport Medicine and Science Council of Canada, 1600 James Naismith Dr, Gloucester, Ont. K1B 5N4
T: (613) 748-5671; Fax: (613) 748-5729
Founded: 1978
Gen Secr: Rick Nickelchok
Focus: Med; Sci 02396

Statistical Society of Canada (SSC) / Société Statistique du Canada, c/o Carleton University, 1125 Colonel By Dr, Rm 4356 HP, London, Ont. K1S 5B6
T: (613) 788-3988; Fax: (613) 788-3822
Founded: 720; Members: 650
Focus: Stats
Periodicals
Canadian Journal of Statistics (semi-annually)
SSC Newsletter (quarterly) 02397

Sugar Industry Technologists (SIT), RR 2, POB B2, Arundel, Qué. J0T 1A0
T: (819) 687-2881; Fax: (819) 687-8138
Founded: 1941; Members: 600
Gen Secr: Bruce A. Foster
Focus: Food
Periodical
Annual Technical Meeting Proceedings (annually) *02398*

Thyroid Foundation of Canada / Fondation du Canada pour les Maladies Thyroidiennes, 1040 Gardiners Rd, Kingston, Ont. K7P 1R7
T: (613) 634-3426; E-Mail: thyroid@io.org; Fax: (613) 634-3483
Founded: 1980; Members: 3500
Pres: Don McKelvie
Focus: Endocrinology *02399*

Tiger Hills Arts Association, POB 58, Holland, Man. R0G 0X0
T: (204) 526-2063
Founded: 1978; Members: 147
Gen Secr: L. Robertson
Focus: Arts *02400*

Toronto Health Libraries Association, c/o Science and Medicine Library, University of Toronto, 7 King's College Circle, Toronto, Ont. M5S 1A5
T: (416) 978-1331; E-Mail: wright@library.utoronto.ca; Fax: (416) 978-7666
Founded: 1965; Members: 130
Gen Secr: Elaine Wright
Focus: Libraries & Bk Sci *02401*

Toronto Society of Model Engineers, 166 Millard Av, Newmarket, Ont. L3Y 1Y9
T: (905) 895-2197
Founded: 1933; Members: 120
Pres: Don Cart
Focus: Eng *02402*

Traffic Injury Research Foundation of Canada / Fondation de Recherches sur les Blessures de la Route au Canada, 171 Nepean St, Ste 200, Ottawa, Ont. K2P 0B4
T: (613) 238-5235; E-Mail: tirf@sonetics.com; Fax: (613) 238-5292
Founded: 1963; Members: 225
Focus: Transport *02403*

Transport 2000 Canada, 111 Metcalfe St, Ste 102, POB 858, Station B, Ottawa, Ont. K1P 5P9
T: (613) 594-3290; Fax: (613) 594-3271
Founded: 1977; Members: 1100
Gen Secr: Anton Turittin
Focus: Transport *02404*

Turner's Syndrome Society / Association du Syndrome de Turner, 7777 Keele St, Concord, Ont. L4K 1Y7
T: (905) 660-7766; Fax: (905) 660-7450
Founded: 1982; Members: 500
Gen Secr: Sandi Hofbauer
Focus: Endocrinology *02405*

Urban Development Institute of Canada, 717 Pender St W, Vancouver, B.C. V6C 1G9
T: (604) 669-9585; Fax: (604) 689-8691
Members: 1200
Gen Secr: Maureen Enser
Focus: Urban Plan *02406*

Vancouver Museum Association, 1100 Chestnut St, Vancouver, B.C. V6J 3J9
T: (604) 736-4431; Fax: (604) 736-5417
Founded: 1968; Members: 2020
Gen Secr: Wilma Wood
Focus: Hist; Anthro *02407*

Vancouver Natural History Society, POB 3021, Vancouver, B.C. V6B 3X5
T: (604) 737-3074
Founded: 1918; Members: 1160
Pres: Linda Kingston
Focus: Nat Sci
Periodical
Discovery (quarterly) *02408*

Vancouver Neurological Association, 2805 Kingsway Av, Vancouver, B.C. V5R 5H9
T: (604) 451-5511; Fax: (604) 451-5651
Founded: 1978
Gen Secr: Laney Bryenton
Focus: Neurology *02409*

Vancouver Secondary Teachers Association, 2929 Commercial Dr, Ste 105, Vancouver, B.C. V5N 4C8
T: (604) 873-5570; Fax: (604) 873-3916
Focus: Educ *02410*

Victoria Foundation, 645 Fort St, Ste 118, Victoria, B.C. V8W 1G2
Founded: 1936
Gen Secr: Sheila Henley
Focus: Sci *02411*

Victoria Librarians Association, POB 8634, Victoria, B.C. V8W 3S2
T: (250) 477-3185
Founded: 1962; Members: 85
Gen Secr: Philip Chiddell
Focus: Libraries & Bk Sci *02412*

Victoria Natural History Society, POB 5220, Station B, Victoria, B.C. V8R 6N4
T: (250) 477-9952
Founded: 1944; Members: 720
Gen Secr: Tom Gillespie
Focus: Hist; Nat Sci *02413*

Visual Arts Manitoba, 100 Arthur St, Ste 221, Winnipeg, Man. R3B 1H3
T: (204) 943-1056
Founded: 1983
Pres: Jennifer Woodbury
Focus: Arts *02414*

Visual Arts Nova Scotia, 1809 Barrington St, Ste 901, Halifax, N.S. B3J 3K8
T: (902) 423-4694; Fax: (902) 422-0881
Founded: 1977; Members: 527
Gen Secr: Andrew Terris
Focus: Arts *02415*

Visual Arts Ontario, 439 Wellington St W, Toronto, Ont. M5V 1E7
T: (416) 591-8883; Fax: (416) 591-2432
Founded: 1974; Members: 3500
Gen Secr: Hennie L. Wolff
Focus: Arts
Periodicals
Agenda (quarterly)
Artviews (quarterly) *02416*

Wallaceburg and District Historical Society, 505 King St, Wallaceburg, Ont. N8A 1J1
T: (519) 627-8962; Fax: (519) 627-9859
Founded: 1973; Members: 60
Pres: George VanSnick
Focus: Hist *02417*

Waterloo Centre for Groundwater Research, 200 University Av W, Waterloo, Ont. N2L 3G1
T: (519) 888-4567 ext 2892; E-Mail: wcgr@sciborg.uwaterloo.ca; Fax: (519) 725-8720
Founded: 1988; Members: 24
Gen Secr: Art Headlam
Focus: Water Res *02418*

Waterloo Historical Society, c/o Kitchener Public Library, 85 Queen St N, Kitchener, Ont. N2H 2H1
T: (519) 743-0271 ext 252; Fax: (519) 570-1360
Founded: 1912; Members: 300
Pres: James Breithaupt
Focus: Hist *02419*

Waterloo Regional Arts Council, 25 Frederick St, Kitchener, Ont. N2H 6M8
T: (519) 744-4552; Fax: (519) 744-9342
Founded: 1980; Members: 391
Gen Secr: Deborah Budd
Focus: Arts *02420*

Welland Historical Society, POB 412, Welland, Ont. L3B 5P7
T: (905) 732-3285
Founded: 1965; Members: 40
Pres: George Foss; Gen Secr: W. Laing
Focus: Hist *02421*

West Coast Environmental Law Research Foundation, 207 Hastings St W, Ste 1001, Vancouver, B.C. V6B 1H7
T: (604) 684-7378; E-Mail: admin@wcel.org.; Fax: (604) 684-1312
Founded: 1974; Members: 300
Gen Secr: William J. Andrews
Focus: Law *02422*

Western Board of Music, 11044 90 Av, Edmonton, Alta. T6G 1A7
T: (403) 492-3264; Fax: (403) 492-0200
Founded: 1934; Members: 300
Gen Secr: Leslie Vermeer
Focus: Music *02423*

Western Canada Water and Wastewater Association, POB 6168, Station A, Calgary, Alta. T2H 2L4
T: (403) 259-4041; Fax: (403) 258-1631
Founded: 1948; Members: 2000
Pres: Steve Blonsky
Focus: Water Res
Periodical
Bulletin (bi-monthly) *02424*

Western Communities Arts Council, POB 7279, Station Victoria LCD 4, Victoria, B.C. V9B 4Z3
Founded: 1988
Pres: Lois Klages
Focus: Arts *02425*

Winnipeg Film Group, 100 Arthur St, Winnipeg, Man. R3B 1H3
T: (204) 942-6795; Fax: (204) 942-6799
Founded: 1974
Gen Secr: L. Pendergast
Focus: Cinema *02426*

Winnipeg Jewish School Teachers Association, 427 Matheson Av, Winnipeg, Man. R2W 0E1
T: (204) 586-8366
Members: 90
Pres: Judy Doctoroff
Focus: Educ *02427*

Woodworkers' Accident Prevention Association, c/o IAPA District 2 Office, 73 Water St N, Ste 407, Cambridge, Ont. N1R 7L6
T: (519) 624-4272; Fax: (519) 624-5200
Focus: Safety; Forestry *02428*

Workers' Educational Association of Canada, 736 Bathurst St, Ste 3, Toronto, Ont. M5S 2R4
T: (416) 538-4947; Fax: (416) 531-6214
Founded: 1917
Gen Secr: Karen Ferguson
Focus: Adult Educ *02429*

Writers Association for Romance and Mainstream, 436 Terrasse Talbot, Ste 7, Longueuil, Qué. J4L 1T5
T: (514) 468-5410
Founded: 1983; Members: 100
Pres: Jeanette Paul
Focus: Lit *02430*

York Technology Association, POB 71572, Aurora, Ont. L4G 6S9
T: (905) 471-9547; Fax: (905) 471-4651
Founded: 1982; Members: 120
Gen Secr: Joan Embury
Focus: Eng
Periodicals
Yorktech Directory (annually)
Yorktech Newsletter (bi-monthly) *02431*

Yorkton Natural History Society, 510 Circlebrook Dr, Yorkton, Sask. S3N 2Y3
T: (306) 783-0392
Pres: Warren Hjertaas
Focus: Nat Sci; Hist *02432*

Youth Science Foundation, 151 Slater St, Ste 904, Ottawa, Ont. K1P 5H3
T: (613) 238-1671; Fax: (613) 238-1677
Founded: 1966; Members: 230
Focus: Sociology *02433*

Yukon Historical and Museums Association, 3126 Third Av, POB 4357, Whitehorse, Y.T. Y1A 3T5
T: (403) 667-4704
Founded: 1977; Members: 167
Pres: Brent Slobodin
Focus: Hist; Arts *02434*

Yukon Medical Association, 406 Lambert St, Whitehorse, Y.T. Y1A 1Z7
T: (403) 667-4421; Fax: (403) 668-3736
Members: 46
Pres: Dr. Roger Mitchell
Focus: Med *02435*

Yukon Teacher-Librarians' Association, 2064 Second Av, Whitehorse, Yuk. Y1A 1A9
T: (403) 668-2426; Fax: (403) 667-4324
Members: 15
Focus: Educ; Libraries & Bk Sci . . . *02436*

Yukon Teachers' Association, 2064 Second Av, Whitehorse, Y.T. Y1A 1A9
T: (403) 668-6777; Fax: (403) 667-4324
Founded: 1955; Members: 381
Pres: Terry Price
Focus: Educ *02437*

Zoological Society of Metropolitan Toronto, POB 370, Scarborough, Ont. M1E 4Y9
T: (416) 392-9100; Fax: (416) 392-9115
Founded: 1969; Members: 20000
Pres: Calvin White
Focus: Zoology *02438*

Zoological Society of Montréal, 2055 Rue Peel, Montréal, Qué. H3A 1V4
T: (514) 845-8317
Founded: 1964; Members: 500
Focus: Zoology *02439*

Chile

Academia Chilena de Bellas Artes, Clasificador 1349, Correo Central, Santiago
T: (02) 6331902
Founded: 1964; Members: 10
Pres: Carlos Riesco Grez; Gen Secr: Gonzalo Cienfuegos
Focus: Arts
Periodical
Boletín *02440*

Academia Chilena de Ciencias, Clasificador 1349, Correo Central, Santiago
T: (02) 6382847; Fax: 6332129
Founded: 1964; Members: 57
Pres: Dr. Jorge E. Allende; Gen Secr: Dr. José Corvalán Díaz
Focus: Sci
Periodical
Boletín (irregularly) *02441*

Academia Chilena de Ciencias Naturales, Medinacelli 1233, Santiago
Founded: 1926
Pres: Dr. Hugo Gunckel L.; Gen Secr: Hans Niemeyer F.
Focus: Nat Sci
Periodical
Anales *02442*

Academia Chilena de Ciencias Sociales, Politicas y Morales, Clasificador 1349, Correo Central, Santiago
T: (02) 6331902; Fax: 6326649
Founded: 1964; Members: 36
Pres: Juan de Dios Vial Larrain; Gen Secr: H. Godoy Urzúa
Focus: Poli Sci; Sociology; Educ
Periodicals
Anales/Societas (annually)
Boletín (3 times annually)
Folletos *02443*

Academia Chilena de la Historia, Almirante Montt 453, Santiago
T: (02) 6399323; Fax: 6399323
Founded: 1933; Members: 36
Pres: Javier González Echenique; Gen Secr: Ricardo Couyoundjian Bergamali
Focus: Hist
Periodicals
Archivo de D. Bernardo O'Higgins
Boletín de la Academia *02444*

Academia Chilena de la Lengua, Clasificador 1349, Correo Central, Santiago
T: (02) 6382847
Founded: 1885; Members: 36
Pres: Alfredo Matus Olivier; Gen Secr: José Luis Samaniego Aldazábal
Focus: Ling
Periodical
Boletín de la Academia Chilena de la Lengua *02445*

Academia Chilena de Medicina, Clasificador 1349, Correo Central, Santiago
T: (02) 6331902
Founded: 1964; Members: 108
Pres: Dr. Armando Roa; Gen Secr: Dr. Jaime Perez-Olea
Focus: Med
Periodicals
Boletín (annually)
Proceedings of the Chilean History of Medicine *02446*

Asociación Chilena de Astronomía y Astronáutica, Casilla 3904, Santiago
T: (02) 6327556
Founded: 1957; Members: 350
Pres: Hernan Villarroel Leo; Gen Secr: Elías Riuz
Focus: Astronomy; Aero *02447*

Asociación Chilena de Informatica y Computación en Educación (ACHICE), Lo Barnechea 1772, Santiago
T: (02) 2167602; E-Mail: sinie@reuna.cl; Fax: 2161071
Founded: 1990; Members: 2250
Pres: Fidel Oteiza; Gen Secr: Maria A. Palavicino
Focus: Computer & Info Sci *02448*

Asociación Chilena de Microbiología (A.Ch.M.), Casilla 59, Santiago 22
T: (02) 2093503; E-Mail: 2258427
Founded: 1964; Members: 194
Pres: Dr. Eugenio Spencer; Gen Secr: Dr. Matilde Jashes
Focus: Microbio
Periodical
Acta Microbiologica (bi-annually) *02449*

Asociación Chilena de Sismología e Ingeniería Antisísmica / Chilean Association of Seismology and Earthquake Engineering, Casilla 2796, Santiago
Founded: 1963
Pres: Dr. Patricio Ruiz
Focus: Geophys *02450*

Asociación Científica y Técnica de Chile, Carlos Antúnez 1885, Dpto 205, Santiago
Founded: 1965
Pres: Héctor Cathalifaud Argandoña
Focus: Sci; Eng *02451*

Asociación de Psicólogos Infanto-Juveniles, Bustamante 30, Santiago
Pres: Sofia Lecaros; Gen Secr: Gabriele Sepulveda
Focus: Psych *02452*

Asociación Interamericana de Ingeniería Sanitaria y Ambiental, San Martín 352, Santiago
T: (02) 6984028
Founded: 1979
Pres: Guillermo Ruiz Troncoso; Gen Secr: Julio Hevia Medel
Focus: Eng *02453*

Asociación Judicial de Chile, Santo Domingo 1373, Santiago
Focus: Law *02454*

Asociación Plástica Latina Internacional de Chile, Av P. de Valdivia 1781, Casilla 177, Correo 29, Santiago
T: (02) 2233444; Fax: 2233444
Founded: 1990
Pres: Alicia Argandoña R.; Gen Secr: Angelina Soffia. S.
Focus: Arts *02455*

Colegio de Arquitectos de Chile, Av Libertador Bernardo O'Higgins 115, Casilla 13377, Santiago
T: (02) 6398744; Fax: 6398769
Founded: 1942; Members: 5500
Pres: Fernando Merino de la Cerda; Gen Secr: E. Luebert Cid
Focus: Archit; Eng; Energy; Civil Eng
Periodicals
Bienal de Arquitectura (bi-annually)
Boletín (monthly)
Revista CA (quarterly) *02456*

Colegio de Bibliotecarios de Chile / Chilean Librarianship Association, Diagonal Paraguay 383, Depto 122, Casilla 3741, Santiago
T: (02) 2225652
Founded: 1969; Members: 1439
Pres: Esmeralda Ramos Ramos
Focus: Libraries & Bk Sci

Periodical
Micronoticias (irregularly) 02457

Colegio de Ingenieros de Chile, Av Santa Maria 0508, Casilla 13745, Santiago
T: (02) 7779530; Fax: 7778681
Founded: 1958; Members: 18000
Pres: Maximo H. Alamos
Focus: Eng 02458

Colegio de Ingenieros Forestales, San Isidro 22, Of 503, Casilla 9686, Santiago
T: (02) 6393289
Founded: 1972; Members: 350
Pres: Jorge I. Correa Drubi
Focus: Forestry 02459

Colegio de Químico-Farmacéuticos de Chile, Casilla 1136, Santiago
T: (02) 6392505
Founded: 1942; Members: 2500
Pres: Antonio Morris
Focus: Pharmacol 02460

Comisión Chilena de Energía Nuclear, Amunategui 95, Casilla 188D, Santiago
T: (02) 6990070; Fax: 6991618
Founded: 1965
Pres: Eduardo Bobadilla López; Gen Secr: Germán Piderit Alvear
Focus: Nucl Res
Periodical
Nucleotecnica (semi-annually) 02461

Comité Oceanográfico Nacional, Casilla 324, Valparaíso
T: (032) 282697; E-Mail: cona@huelen.reuna.cl; Fax: 283537
Founded: 1971; Members: 26
Pres: Hugo Gorziglia A.; Gen Secr: Mario Caceres M.
Focus: Oceanography 02462

Commission on Livestock Development in Latin America and the Caribbean, c/o FAO Office for Latin America and the Caribbean, Av Dag Hamarskjold 3, Casilla 10095, Santiago
T: (02) 3372234; E-Mail: Carlos.Arellano-Sota@field.fao.org; Fax: 3372001
Founded: 1987
Gen Secr: Carlos Arellano Sota
Focus: Animal Husb 02463

Consejo de Rectores de Universidades Chilenas (CRUCH), Moneda 673, Casilla 14798, Santiago
T: (02) 6397415
Founded: 1954
Pres: Agustín Toro Davilla
Focus: Sci 02464

Corporación para el Desarrollo de la Ciencia (CODECI), Marcoleta 250, Casilla 10332, Santiago
T: (02) 2354137
Founded: 1978; Members: 120
Pres: Fernando Diaz; Gen Secr: Héctor Cathalifaud
Focus: Anthro; Archeol; Geology
Periodical
Revista CODECI (trimestrial) 02465

Instituto de Chile, Almirante Montt 453, Santiago
T: (02) 6382847; Fax: 6326649
Founded: 1964
Pres: Juan de Dios Vial Larraín; Gen Secr: Prof. Carlos Riesco
Focus: Sci
Periodical
Boletín 02466

Instituto de Estudios y Publicaciones Juan Molina, Casilla de Correo 2974, Santiago
T: (02) 7455066; Fax: 7455176
Founded: 1976; Members: 28
Pres: Alfredo Ugarte
Focus: Nat Sci 02467

Instituto de Ingenieros de Chile, San Martín 352, Casilla 487, Santiago
T: (02) 6984028; Fax: 6971136
Founded: 1888; Members: 800
Focus: Eng
Periodicals
Anales
Revista Chilena de Ingeniería 02468

Instituto de Ingenieros de Minas de Chile, Av Bulnes 197, Casilla 14668, Correo 21, Santiago
T: (02) 6953849; Fax: 6972351
Founded: 1930; Members: 1000
Pres: Esteban Domic; Gen Secr: Ricardo Simian
Focus: Eng; Mining
Periodical
Minerales (quarterly) 02469

Instituto Geográfico Militar, Nueva Santa Isabel 1640, Santiago
T: (02) 6968221; Fax: 6988278
Founded: 1922; Members: 400
Gen Secr: Enrique Gillmore Callejas
Focus: Geography 02470

Liga Marítima de Chile, Av Errázuriz 471, Casilla 117V, Valparaíso
Founded: 1914; Members: 1350
Pres: Eri Solis Oyarzún
Focus: Navig 02471

Oficina Regional de Educación de la UNESCO para América Latina y el Caribe, Enrique Depiano 2058, Casilla 3187, Santiago
T: (02) 2049032; Fax: 2091875
Founded: 1963; Members: 40
Gen Secr: Ernesto Schiefelbein
Focus: Educ
Periodicals
Boletin Bibliografico (monthly)
Boletin de Educación (3 times ammually)
Contacto (quarterly)
FBEDOC Informa (quarterly) 02472

Servicio Médico Legal, Av La Paz 1012, Casilla 10095, Santiago
T: (02) 7371268; Fax: 7371323
Founded: 1915; Members: 305
Gen Secr: Dr. Marco Antonio Medina Molina
Focus: Med 02473

Sistema Nacional de Información en Educación (SINIE) / National Educational Information System, c/o Ministerio de Educación, Centro de Perfeccionamiento, Experimentación e Investigaciones Pedagogicas, Nido de Aguilas s/n, Casilla 16162, Correo 9, Santiago
T: (02) 2167602; E-Mail: sinie@reuha.cl; Fax: 2167662
Founded: 1983; Members: 72
Pres: Maria A. Palavicino
Focus: Educ
Periodical
INRED: Indices y Resumenes en Educación (annually) 02474

Sociedad Agronómica de Chile, MacIver 120, Of 36, Santiago
T: (02) 6384881
Founded: 1910; Members: 1900
Pres: Dr. L. Antonio Lizana; Gen Secr: Hector E. Núñez
Focus: Agri 02475

Sociedad Arqueológica de la Serena, Casilla 125, La Serena
Founded: 1944
Focus: Archeol 02476

Sociedad Chilena de Alergia e Immunología, Pérez Valenzuela 163, Santiago
T: (02) 743559
Founded: 1978
Gen Secr: Dr. F. Galleguillos M.
Focus: Immunology; Med
Periodical
Acta Médica FAB (monthly) 02477

Sociedad Chilena de Cancerología, c/o Fundación Arturo López Pérez, Rancagua 878, Santiago
T: (02) 6250063
Founded: 1964; Members: 64
Pres: Dr. Luis Orlandi; Gen Secr: Dr. Nelson Romero
Focus: Cell Biol & Cancer Res 02478

Sociedad Chilena de Cardiología y Cirugía Cardiovascular / Chilean Society of Cardiology and Cardiovascular Surgery, Esmeralda 678, Santiago
Founded: 1949; Members: 353
Pres: Dr. Carlos Akel A.; Gen Secr: Dr. Jorge Carabantes C.
Focus: Cardiol 02479

Sociedad Chilena de Cirugía Plástica y Reparadora, Av Santa María 410, Santiago
Founded: 1944
Focus: Surgery 02480

Sociedad Chilena de Citología, Casilla 10-D, Correo 13, San Miguel, Santiago
Fax: (02) 492247
Founded: 1970; Members: 103
Pres: Dr. R. Gonzalez Munizaga
Focus: Cell Biol & Cancer Res
Periodical
Cito-Notícias (quarterly) 02481

Sociedad Chilena de Dermatología y Venereología, c/o Depto Dermatología, Hospital J.J. Aguirre, Santos Dumont 999, Santiago
T: (02) 779484
Founded: 1938
Pres: Dr. Julia Quiroz M.
Focus: Derm 02482

Sociedad Chilena de Endocrinología y Metabolismo, Casilla 166, Correo 55, Santiago
T: (02) 3412909; Fax: 3512909
Founded: 1961
Pres: Dr. Gloria López Stewart
Focus: Endocrinology 02483

Sociedad Chilena de Enfermedades Respiratorias, Bernarda Morín 488, Santiago
T: (02) 2238946; Fax: 2238946
Founded: 1930; Members: 530
Pres: Dr. Patricia Díaz A.; Gen Secr: Dr. Tamara Soler V.
Focus: Med 02484

Sociedad Chilena de Entomología, Casilla 21132, Santiago
Founded: 1922; Members: 150
Pres: Dr. Rene Covarrubias B.; Gen Secr: Dr. Freisia Rojas A.
Focus: Entomology
Periodical
Revista Chilena de Entomología (annually) 02485

Sociedad Chilena de Física, Casilla 73, Correo 5, Santiago
T: (02) 3412723; Fax: 2258427
Founded: 1965; Members: 278
Pres: Sergio Hojman
Focus: Physics 02486

Sociedad Chilena de Fotogrametría y Percepción Remota, Nueva Santa Isabel 1640, Santiago
T: (02) 6968221; Fax: 6988278
Pres: Enrique Gillmore Callejas
Focus: Surveying 02487

Sociedad Chilena de Gastroenterología, Casilla 166, Correo 55, Santiago
T: (02) 6343106; Fax: 3413836
Founded: 1938
Pres: Dr. E. Saenz F.
Focus: Gastroenter 02488

Sociedad Chilena de Gerontología, Av Bulnes 377, Santiago
T: (02) 6967176
Founded: 1961; Members: 60
Pres: Dr. José Froimovich S.; Gen Secr: Dr. Jaime Pereira G.
Focus: Geriatrics 02489

Sociedad Chilena de Hematología, CLasificador 1, Correo 27, Santiago
T: (02) 2243175
Founded: 1943; Members: 90
Pres: Dr. Diego Mezzano A.; Gen Secr: Dr. Jaime Pereira G.
Focus: Hematology 02490

Sociedad Chilena de Historia Natural, Casilla 787, Santiago
Founded: 1926
Focus: Nat Sci 02491

Sociedad Chilena de Historia y Geografía, Casilla 1386, Santiago
T: (02) 6382489
Founded: 1911; Members: 387
Pres: Martínez Baeza; Gen Secr: Rene Artigas Moreira
Focus: Geography; Hist
Periodical
Revista Chilena de Historia y Geografía 02492

Sociedad Chilena de Immunología, Casilla 70061, Santiago
T: (02) 370081
Founded: 1972; Members: 55
Pres: Dr. Alicia Ramos
Focus: Immunology 02493

Sociedad Chilena de la Ciencia del Suelo, Casilla 6177, Santiago
Founded: 1973
Pres: Renato Grez Z.; Gen Secr: Ricardo Honorato P.
Focus: Agri 02494

Sociedad Chilena de Lingüística (SOCHIL), La Verbena 3882, Santiago
Founded: 1971; Members: 100
Pres: Ambrosio Rabanales; Gen Secr: Mario Bernales
Focus: Ling 02495

Sociedad Chilena de Neurocirugía, Casilla 3717, Santiago
T: (02) 2237109
Pres: Dr. Jorge Méndez S.
Focus: Surgery 02496

Sociedad Chilena de Obstetricia y Ginecología / Chilean Society of Obstetrics and Gynecology, Román Díaz 205, Of 205, Providencia, Santiago
T: (02) 2359133; Fax: 2351294
Founded: 1935; Members: 248
Pres: Dr. Jorge Tisné T.; Gen Secr: Dr. C. Miranda V.
Focus: Gynecology
Periodical
Revista Chilena de Obstetricia y Ginecología (bi-monthly) 02497

Sociedad Chilena de Oftalmología, Casilla 16197, Correo 9, Santiago
T: (02) 776645
Founded: 1931; Members: 320
Pres: Dr. Edgardo Carreño S.
Focus: Ophthal 02498

Sociedad Chilena de Ortopedía y Traumatología, Jofre 039, Dpto 41, Casilla 117, Correo 22, Santiago
T: (02) 2227233; Fax: 2227233
Founded: 1949; Members: 400
Pres: Dr. Jaime Paulos A.; Gen Secr: Eduardo Zamudio A.
Focus: Orthopedics; Traumatology . . . 02499

Sociedad Chilena de Otorrinolaringología, Providencia 2019, Santiago
Pres: Dr. Angel Fernández P.; Gen Secr: Dr. Werner Konow F.
Focus: Otorhinolaryngology 02500

Sociedad Chilena de Parasitología, Condell 303, Casilla 50470, Santiago
T: (02) 6785532; Fax: 5416840
Founded: 1964; Members: 150
Pres: Dr. Texia Gorman G.; Gen Secr: Myriam Lorca H.
Focus: Microbio
Periodical
Parasitología al Día (semi-annually) . . . 02501

Sociedad Chilena de Patología de la Adaptación y del Mesenquima, c/o Hospital J.J. Aguirre, Santos Dumont 999, Santiago
Founded: 1954
Focus: Pathology 02502

Sociedad Chilena de Pediatría, Av Eliodoro Yañez 1984, Santiago
T: (02) 2254393; Fax: 2232351
Founded: 1922; Members: 1230
Pres: Dr. Nelson Vargas Catalan; Gen Secr: Dr. Carmen Larrañaga L.
Focus: Pediatrics
Periodical
Revista Chilena de Pediatria (bi-monthly) 02503

Sociedad Chilena de Producción Animal, Santa Rosa 11735, Santiago
T: (02) 5587042 ext 307
Founded: 1979; Members: 115
Pres: Dr. Alejandro López V.
Focus: Animal Husb 02504

Sociedad Chilena de Química, Casilla 2613, Concepción
T: (041) 227815; Fax: 235819
Founded: 1945; Members: 1000
Pres: Dr. Guillermo Contreras; Gen Secr: Dr. Eduardo Delgado
Focus: Chem
Periodical
Boletin de la Sociedad Chilena de Química (quarterly) 02505

Sociedad Chilena de Reumatología, Casilla 23-D, Santiago
Founded: 1950
Pres: Dr. Gonzalo Astorga P.; Gen Secr: Dr. Alberto Valdés S.
Focus: Rheuma 02506

Sociedad Chilena de Sanidad, c/o Ministerio de Salud Pública, Huérfanos 1273, Santiago
Founded: 1947
Focus: Public Health 02507

Sociedad Chilena de Tecnología de Alimentos, Casilla 3755, Santiago
Founded: 1962
Pres: Bernardo Poloni G.; Gen Secr: Julia Vinagre
Focus: Eng; Food
Periodicals
Anuario de la Minería (annually)
Boletín (irregularly)
Carta Geológica de Chile (irregularly)
Carta Hidrogeológica de Chile (irregularly)
Carta Magnética de Chile (irregularly)
Revista Geográfica de Chile
Revista Geológica de Chile (semi-annually) 02508

Sociedad Chilena de Tisiología y Enfermedades Broncopulmonares, c/o Hospital del Tórax, J.M. Infante 717, Santiago
Founded: 1931
Focus: Pulmon Dis 02509

Sociedad Chilena de Urología, Casilla 51, Correo 29, Santiago
Founded: 1935
Pres: Dr. Juan Prieto W.; Gen Secr: Dr. Javier Aviles J.
Focus: Urology 02510

Sociedad Científica Chilena Claudio Gay, Casilla 2974, Santiago
T: (02) 7455066; Fax: 7455176
Founded: 1946; Members: 143
Pres: Luis Peña G.; Gen Secr: Alfredo Ugarte
Focus: Sci 02511

Sociedad Científica de Chile, Rosa Eguiguren 813, Casilla 696, Santiago
Founded: 1891; Members: 250
Focus: Sci 02512

Sociedad de Anatomía Normal y Patológica de Chile, c/o Museo Histórico, Santiago
Founded: 1938
Focus: Anat; Pathology 02513

Sociedad de Anestesiología de Chile, Casilla 4259, Santiago
Founded: 1946
Focus: Anesthetics 02514

Sociedad de Bibliófilos Chilenos, Casilla 895, Santiago
Founded: 1945; Members: 100
Gen Secr: Ramón Eyzaguirre
Focus: Ling
Periodical
El Bibliófilo Chileno (annually) 02515

Sociedad de Biología de Chile, Casilla 16164, Santiago
Founded: 1928; Members: 565
Pres: Dr. Eugenio Spencer Ossa; Gen Secr: Dr. Manuel Santos
Focus: Bio
Periodicals
Archivos de Biología y Medicina Experimentales
Revista Chilena de Historia Natural . . 02516

Sociedad de Biología de Concepción, c/o Escuela de Química y Farmacía y Bioquímica, Casilla 29, Concepción
Founded: 1927
Focus: Bio 02517

Sociedad de Bioquímica de Concepción, c/o Escuela de Química y Farmacía y Bioquímica, Casilla 237, Concepción
Founded: 1957
Pres: Mario Pozo López
Focus: Biochem 02518

Sociedad de Bioquímica y Biología Molecular de Chile, Casilla 16164, Correo 9, Santiago
T: (02) 2093503; Fax: 2258427
Founded: 1971; Members: 110
Pres: Dr. Emilio Cardemil; Gen Secr: Dr. Ana María Jabalquinto
Focus: Biochem; Microbio 02519

Sociedad de Cirujanos de Chile, Román Díaz 205, Of 401, Casilla 2843, Santiago
T: (02) 2362831; Fax: 2351741
Founded: 1949; Members: 640
Pres: Dr. Sergio Guzman B.
Focus: Surgery
Periodicals
Informaciones de Secretaría (monthly)
Revista Chilena de Cirugía (quarterly) . 02520

Sociedad de Farmacología de Chile, Casilla 70000, Correo 7, Santiago
T: (02) 776560 ext 5262; Fax: 2225515
Founded: 1979; Members: 88
Pres: Dr. J. Pablo Huidobro Tobo; Gen Secr: M. Verónica Donoso G.
Focus: Pharmacol 02521

Sociedad de Genética de Chile, Casilla 70061, Correo 7, Santiago
T: (02) 776560
Founded: 1964; Members: 100
Pres: Dr. Raúl Godoy Herrera; Gen Secr: Prof. Laura Walker B.
Focus: Genetics
Periodicals
Biological Research (quarterly)
Revista Chilena de Historia Natural . . 02522

Sociedad de Matemática de Chile, Casilla 653, Santiago
T: (02) 2713882; Fax: 2713882
Founded: 1976; Members: 250
Pres: Patricio Felmer; Gen Secr: Oscar Barriga
Focus: Math 02523

Sociedad de Medicina Veterinaria de Chile, Av Italia 1045, Casilla 13384, Correo 21, Santiago
T: (02) 2093471; Fax: 3415408
Founded: 1926; Members: 152
Pres: Dr. Lautaro Gomez Ramos
Focus: Vet Med 02524

Sociedad de Neurología, Psiquiatría y Neurocirugía de Chile, Carlos Silva V 1292, Plaza Las Lilas, Providencia, Santiago
T: (02) 2329347; Fax: 2319287
Founded: Casilla 3757, Correo 21 1932
Pres: Dr. César Ojeda F.; Gen Secr: Fredy Holzer M.
Focus: Neurology; Psychiatry; Surgery . . 02525

Sociedad de Ortodoncía de Chile, Casilla 9895, Santiago
Founded: 1942; Members: 200
Pres: Dr. Jorge Pavic M.; Gen Secr: Dr. Alejandro Illanes V.
Focus: Dent 02526

Sociedad de Otorinolaringología de Valparaíso, Blas Cuenas 964, Valparaíso
Founded: 1945
Focus: Otorhinolaryngology 02527

Sociedad de Pediatría de Valparaíso, Av Brasil 1689, Valparaíso
Founded: 1932; Members: 45
Focus: Pediatrics 02528

Sociedad de Vida Silvestre de Chile, Casilla 1705, Temuco
T: (045) 210773 ext 310
Founded: 1975; Members: 300
Pres: Darcy Rios Leal; Gen Secr: Enrique Hauenstein Barra
Focus: Ecology 02529

Sociedad Geológica de Chile, Valentin Letelier 20, Dept 401, Casilla 13667, Correo 21, Santiago
T: (02) 6980481
Founded: 1962; Members: 434
Pres: E. Godoy; Gen Secr: Waldo Vivallo
Focus: Geology 02530

Sociedad Médica de Concepción, Casilla 60C, Concepción
Founded: 1886
Pres: Dr. Enrique Bellolioz
Focus: Med 02531

Sociedad Médica de Santiago, Casilla 168, Correo 55, Santiago
T: (02) 2748985; Fax: 3413068
Founded: 1869; Members: 1500
Pres: Dr. H. Iturriaga
Focus: Med
Periodical
Revista Médica de Chile (monthly) . . . 02532

Sociedad Médica de Valparaíso, Hontaneda 2653, Valparaíso
Founded: 1913; Members: 271
Pres: Dr. Arturo Villagran Valdes
Focus: Med 02533

Sociedad Nacional de Agricultura, Tenderini 187, Casilla 40D, Santiago
T: (02) 6396710; E-Mail: SOCNADEA;
Fax: 6337771
Founded: 1838
Pres: Ernesto Correa Gatica
Focus: Agri
Periodicals
Boletín de Mercado (monthly)
Boletín Económico (monthly)
Revista El Campesino 02534

Sociedad Nacional de Minería, Teatinos 20, Of 33, Casilla 1807, Santiago
Founded: 1883
Pres: Walter Riesco Salvo; Gen Secr: Julio Ascuí Latorre
Focus: Mining
Periodical
Boletín Minero 02535

Sociedad Odontológica de Concepción (SOC), Casilla 2107, Concepción
T: (041) 258997
Founded: 1924; Members: 300
Pres: Dr. Eduardo Navarete
Focus: Dent 02536

China, People's Republic

Academy of Overseas Services, H13 2/F Pretitcoin House, 297 Ma Tin Rd, Hong Kong
T: 24780061
Gen Secr: Stella Liu
Focus: Educ 02537

Acoustical Society of China, 17 Zhongguancun St, Beijing 100080
T: (010) 62553765
Founded: 1985; Members: 3035
Pres: Tong Chen; Gen Secr: Chaohuan Hou
Focus: Acoustics
Periodicals
Acta Acustica (bi-monthly)
Applied Acoustics (quarterly)
Chinese Journal of Acoustics (quarterly)
Noise and Vibration Control (bi-monthly) . 02538

Architectural Society of China, Baiwanzhuang, West District, Beijing 100835
T: (010) 68393559, 68394122; Fax: 68393428, 68311585
Founded: 1953; Members: 14000
Pres: Rutang Ye; Gen Secr: Yide Dou
Focus: Archit
Periodicals
Architectural Journal (monthly)
Architectural Knowledge
Journal of Building Structures (monthly) . 02539

Asian Pacific Federation of Human Resource Management (APFHRM), c/o Hong Kong Institute of Human Resource, Ste 1203, Salisbury Plaza, 68 Yee Wo St, Causeway Bay, GPOB 4404, Hong Kong
T: 28815113; E-Mail: info@hkihrm.org;
Fax: 28816062
Founded: 1968
Focus: Business Admin
Periodical
APFHRM Newsletter 02540

Biophysical Society of China, 15 Datun Rd, Chaoyang District, Beijing 100101
T: (010) 62027837
Founded: 1980; Members: 2000
Pres: Dongcai Liang; Gen Secr: Prof. Shen Xun Shen
Focus: Biophys 02541

Botanical Society of China, 141 Xizhimenwai Tajie, Beijing
Founded: 1933
Pres: Fuxiang Wang
Focus: Botany
Periodicals
Acta Botanica Sinica (quarterly)
Acta Mycologica Sinica (quarterly)
Acta Phytoecologica et Geobotanica Sinica (quarterly)
Acta Phytotaxonimica Sinica (quarterly)
Bulletin of Biology (bi-monthly)
Bulletin of Botany (bi-monthly)
Plants 02542

Chemical Industry and Engineering Society of China, POB 911, Beijing
T: (01) 466025
Founded: 1922; Members: 40000
Pres: Guangqi Yang; Gen Secr: Delin Yin
Focus: Eng 02543

China Academy of Traditional Chinese Medicine, 18 Beixincang, Dongzhimennai, Beijing 100900
T: (01) 446661
Founded: 1955
Pres: Shaowu Chen
Focus: Med
Periodicals
Chinese Acupuncture and Moxibustion (bi-monthly)
Journal of Traditional Chinese Medicine . 02544

China Association for Science and Technology, 54 Sanlihe Rd, Beijing 100863
T: (010) 68321924; Fax: 68321914
Founded: 1958
Pres: Guangya Zhu
Focus: Sci; Eng
Periodicals
Knowledge is Power (monthly)
Science and Technology Review (monthly) 02545

China Association of Traditional Chinese Medicine (CATCM), A4 Yinghualu, Hepingli Dongjie, Beijing 100029
T: (010) 64212828; Fax: 64220867
Founded: 1979; Members: 80000
Pres: Yuli Cui
Focus: Med
Periodical
China Journal of TCM (bi-monthly) . . . 02546

China Association of Zhenjiu, 18 Beixincang Dongcheng Qu, Beijing 100700
T: (010) 64014411
Founded: 1979; Members: 10050
Pres: Ximing Hu; Gen Secr: Weiheng Li
Focus: Med
Periodical
Chinese Acupuncture and Moxibustion . 02547

China Coal Society, Hepingli, Beijing 100013
T: (010) 64931628
Founded: 1962; Members: 43000
Pres: Weitang Fan; Gen Secr: Huizheng Pan
Focus: Mining
Periodical
Journal of the China Coal Society (bi-monthly) 02548

China Electrotechnical Society, 46 Sanlihe Rd, POB 2133, Beijing 100823
T: (010) 68595355; Fax: 68511242
Founded: 1981; Members: 50000
Pres: Mingsheng Zhao; Gen Secr: Heliang Zhou
Focus: Electric Eng 02549

China Energy Research Society, 54 San Li He St, Beijing
T: (010) 68011816
Founded: 1981; Members: 18000
Pres: Jike Yang
Focus: Energy 02550

China Engineering Graphics Society, POB 85, Beijing 100083
T: (010) 62015346
Pres: Fuxi Zhu
Focus: Graphic & Dec Arts, Design; Eng 02551

China Fire Protection Association, 14 Dong Chang An St, Beijing
T: (010) 66068788; Fax: 66089640
Founded: 1984; Members: 3062000
Pres: Lei Ju; Gen Secr: Qi-Hong Wu
Focus: Eng 02552

China Law Society, 6 Xizhi Men Nan Da Jie, Beijing 100035
T: (010) 668971; Fax: 68317502
Founded: 1982; Members: 5260
Pres: Yu Zou; Gen Secr: Shutao Song
Focus: Law 02553

China Society of Fisheries, 31 Minfeng Ln, Beijing 100032
T: (010) 66020794; Fax: 66002346
Members: 15000
Pres: Yanxi Zhang
Focus: Fisheries 02554

Chinese Abacus Association, Sidaokou, Xizhimenwai, Shidaokou, Beijing
T: (010) 896275
Founded: 1979; Members: 500000
Pres: Xi-An Zhu; Gen Secr: Jing Hu
Focus: Med 02555

Chinese Academy of Agricultural Sciences, 30 Bai Shi Qiao Rd, Beijing 100081
T: (010) 68314433; Fax: 68316545
Founded: 1957
Pres: Lian Zheng Wang
Focus: Agri 02556

Chinese Academy of Forestry, Wan Shou Shan, Beijing 100091
T: (010) 62582211; Fax: 62584229
Founded: 1958; Members: 4700
Pres: Zehui Jiang
Focus: Forestry 02557

Chinese Academy of Geological Sciences (CAGS), 26 Baiwanzhuang Rd, Beijing 100037
T: (010) 68310893; Fax: 68310894
Founded: 1959; Members: 5000
Pres: Yuchuan Chen
Focus: Geology
Periodical
Bulletin (irregularly) 02558

Chinese Academy of Medical Sciences, 9 Dongdan Santiao, Beijing 100730
T: (010) 553447; Fax: 5124876
Founded: 1956
Pres: Dr. Denian Ba
Focus: Med 02559

Chinese Academy of Meteorological Sciences, 7 Block 11, Hepingli, Beijing
T: (010) 64211631; Fax: 64218703
Focus: Geophys 02560

Chinese Academy of Sciences, 52 San Li He Rd, Beijing 100864
T: (010) 68597219; Fax: 68511095
Founded: 1949; Members: 597
Pres: Guangzhao Zhou; Gen Secr: Xuan Kzhu
Focus: Sci 02561

Chinese Academy of Social Sciences, 5 Jianguomen Nei Da Jie, Beijing 100732
T: (010) 65137744
Founded: 1977; Members: 4865
Pres: Qiaomu Hu; Gen Secr: Yi Mei
Focus: Soc Sci
Periodicals
Archaeology
Literary Review
Philosophical Research
Social Sciences in China (bi-monthly)
Studies in Law
Studies on Chinese History
Studies on Economics
World Economy 02562

Chinese Academy of Space Technology, 31 Baishiqiao, POB 2417, Beijing 100081
T: (010) 68379439; Fax: 68378237
Pres: Faren Qi
Focus: Aero 02563

Chinese Aerodynamics Research Society, POB 2425, Beijing
Pres: Genggan Zhuang
Focus: Physics 02564

Chinese Agricultural Economics Society, Agro-Exhibition, Beijing
Pres: Ziwei Cai
Focus: Agri 02565

Chinese Anti-Cancer Association, Huan-hu-xi Rd, Ti-yuan-bei, 300060 Tianjin
T: (022) 23359958; Fax: 23359958
Founded: 1985; Members: 18000
Pres: Tian-Ze Zhang; Gen Secr: Shu-Ling Li
Focus: Cell Biol & Cancer Res 02566

Chinese Anti-Tuberculosis Society, 42 Dung-si-xi-da St, Beijing
T: (010) 553685
Pres: Dingchen Huang
Focus: Pulmon Dis 02567

Chinese Archives Society, 21 Fengshen Hutong, Beijing
T: (010) 665797
Founded: 1981; Members: 3783
Pres: Zizhi Feng
Focus: Archives 02568

Chinese Association for European Studies, 5 Jiannei, Beijing 100732
T: (010) 65138428
Founded: 1981; Members: 1000
Pres: Prof. Leming Chen
Focus: Ethnology 02569

Chinese Association for Mental Health, 5 An Kang Hutong, De Wai, Beijing
T: (010) 62013448
Founded: 1985; Members: 5000
Pres: Xue Shi Chen; Gen Secr: Quan Run Wen
Focus: Psych 02570

Chinese Association for Physiological Sciences, 42 Dongsixidajie, Beijing 100710
Pres: Mengqin Chen
Focus: Physiology 02571

Chinese Association of Agricultural Science Societies, c/o Ministry of Agriculture and Fisheries, 11 Nongzhanguan Nanli, Beijing 100026
Founded: 1917
Pres: Fuzeng Hong; Gen Secr: Huaizhi Li
Focus: Agri 02572

Chinese Association of Animal Science and Veterinary Medicine, 33 Dongdaqiao Nongfengli, Chao Yang District, Beijing 10020
T: (010) 65066533; Fax: 65005670
Founded: 1936; Members: 40000
Pres: Yaochun Chen; Gen Secr: Hanping Yan
Focus: Vet Med; Zoology 02573

Chinese Association of Automation, POB 2728, Beijing 100080
T: (010) 62544415; E-Mail: wangh@sunserver.ia.ac.cn; Fax: 62620908
Founded: 1957; Members: 30000
Pres: Hanfu Chen; Gen Secr: Weihou Ling
Focus: Eng
Periodicals
Acta Automatica Sinica
Automation Panorama
Information and Control
Pattern Recognition and Artificial Intelligence
Robot and Automation 02574

Chinese Association of Integrated Traditional and Western Medicine, 18 Beixincang, Dongzhimennei, Beijing
T: (010) 64014411 ext 3026
Founded: 1981; Members: 20000
Pres: Yueli Cui; Gen Secr: Weibo Lu
Focus: Med 02575

Chinese Association of Natural Science Museums, 126 Tian Qiao South St, Beijing 100050
T: (010) 67024431; Fax: 67021254
Founded: 1979; Members: 1520
Gen Secr: Yenghuan Xie
Focus: Nat Sci 02576

Chinese Association of Political Science, c/o Chinese Academy of Social Sciences, 5 Jianguomennei Av, Beijing
T: (010) 65125048
Founded: 1980; Members: 1025
Pres: Liu Jiang; Gen Secr: Zhirong Zhang
Focus: Poli Sci 02577

Chinese Astronomical Society, c/o Purple Mountain Observatory, Nanjing 210008
Founded: 1922; Members: 1662
Pres: Qibin Li
Focus: Astronomy
Periodicals
Acta Astronomica Sinica (quarterly)
Acta Astrophysica Sinica (quarterly)
Astronomical Circular (irregularly)
Progress in Astronomy (quarterly) . . . 02578

Chinese Ceramic Society, Bai Wan Zhuang, Beijing 100831
T: (010) 68313364; Fax: 68311497
Pres: Dongsheng Yan
Focus: Materials Sci 02579

Chinese Chemical Society, POB 2709, Beijing 100080
T: (010) 62568157, 62564020; E-Mail: giuxb@infoc3.icas.ac.cn; Fax: 62568157
Founded: 1932; Members: 50000
Pres: Prof. Fu Xi; Gen Secr: Prof. Chunli Bai
Focus: Chem
Periodicals
Chinese Chemical Letters (monthly)
Chinese Journal of Chemistry (bi-monthly)
Chinese Journal of Polymer Science (quarterly)
Daxue Huaxue (bi-monthly)
Dian Huaxue (quarterly)
Fenxi Huaxue (monthly)
Gaofenzi Tongbao (quarterly)
Gaofenzi Xuebao (bi-monthly)
Huaxue Jiaoyu (monthly)
Huaxue Tongbao (monthly)
Huaxue Tongxun (bi-monthly)
Huaxue Xuebao (monthly)
Journal of Molecular Sciences (quarterly)
Sepu (bi-monthly)
Wuji Huaxue (quarterly)
Wuli Huaxue (monthly)
Yingyong Huaxue (bi-monthly)
Youji Huaxue (bi-monthly) 02580

Chinese Civil Engineering Society, Bai Wan Zhuang, POB 2500, Beijing 100835
T: (010) 68311313; Fax: 68313669
Founded: 1953
Pres: Yisheng Mao; Gen Secr: Xichun Zhao
Focus: Eng 02581

Chinese Computer Federation, POB 2704, Beijing
T: (010) 62567724
Founded: 1985; Members: 23590
Pres: Xiaoxiang Zhang; Gen Secr: Shukai Chen
Focus: Electronic Eng 02582

Chinese Education Society, 35 Damucang Ln, Beijing 100816
Pres: Chengxian Zhang
Focus: Educ 02583

Chinese Geophysical Socitey (CGS), POB 941, Beijing
Founded: 1948; Members: 4000
Pres: Gongxu Gu; Gen Secr: Chengyi Fu
Focus: Geophys
Periodicals
Acta Geophysica Sinica (bi-monthly)
Bulletin of the Chinese Geophysical Society (irregularly) 02584

Chinese High-Energy Physics Society, POB 918, Beijing
T: (010) 68213344; Fax: 68213374
Founded: 1981; Members: 820
Pres: Xueying Zheng
Focus: Physics 02585

Chinese Historical Society, 5 Jianguomennei St, Beijing 100732
Focus: Hist 02586

Chinese Hydraulic Engineering Society, 2-2 Bai Guang Rd, Beijing 100053
T: (010) 63202171; Fax: 63202824
Founded: 1931; Members: 80000
Pres: Keqiang Yan; Gen Secr: Liandi Zheng
Focus: Mach Eng 02587

Chinese Information Processing Society, POB 2704, Beijing
Pres: Weichang Qian
Focus: Computer & Info Sci 02588

Chinese Legal History Society, c/o Law Dept, Beijing University, Haidian District, Beijing 100871
T: (010) 62561166
Founded: 1979; Members: 300
Pres: Prof. Guohua Zhang; Gen Secr: Xinxian Rao
Focus: Law; Hist
Periodical
Review of Legal History 02589

Chinese Light Industry Society, B22 Fuchengmenwai Av, Beijing 100307
T: (010) 894147
Founded: 1979
Pres: Long Ji
Focus: Eng 02590

Chinese Mathematical Society, Zong Guan Cun, Beijing
T: (010) 281022
Founded: 1935
Pres: Yuan Wang; Gen Secr: Zhong Li
Focus: Math 02591

Chinese Mechanical Engineering Society (CMES), Sanlihe Rd, Beijing 100823
T: (010) 68695319; Fax: 68533613
Founded: 1936; Members: 180000
Pres: Guangyuan He; Gen Secr: Ruiquan Cheng
Focus: Eng
Periodical
Journal of Mechanical Engineering (quarterly) 02592

Chinese Medical Association, 42 Dongsi Xidajie, Beijing
T: (010) 551943
Founded: 1915
Pres: Xiqing Bai
Focus: Med
Periodicals
Chinese Medical Journal (monthly)
National Medical Journal of China (monthly) 02593

Chinese Meteorological Society, 46 Baishiqiao Rd, Beijing 100081
Founded: 1924; Members: 21000
Pres: Jingmeng Zhou; Gen Secr: Guangyi Peng
Focus: Geophys 02594

Chinese Nuclear Physics Society, POB 275, Beijing
T: (010) 69357487; Fax: 69357008
Founded: 1979; Members: 1300
Pres: Zuxun Sun; Gen Secr: Jincheng Xu
Focus: Nucl Res; Physics 02595

Chinese Nuclear Society, POB 2125, Beijing 100822
Founded: 1980
Pres: Shengjie Jiang
Focus: Nucl Res 02596

Chinese Nursing Association, 42 Dongsi Xidajie, Beijing 100710
Founded: 1909
Pres: Ju Ying Lin
Focus: Med 02597

Chinese Nutrition Society, 29 Nanwei Rd, Beijing 100050
T: (010) 63043472; Fax: 63011875
Founded: 1981
Pres: Xiaoshu Chen
Focus: Food 02598

Chinese Petroleum Society, Liu Pu Kang, POB 766, Beijing 100724
T: (010) 62095615; Fax: 62014787
Founded: 1979; Members: 60000
Pres: Zhongchao Jin; Gen Secr: Jimeng Lu
Focus: Petrochem 02599

Chinese Pharmaceutical Association, A38 Lishi Rd N, Beijing 100810
T: (010) 68316576
Founded: 1907
Pres: Maijia Qi
Focus: Pharmacol 02600

Chinese Pharmacological Society, 1 Xian Nong Tan St, Beijing 100050
T: (010) 63013366 ext 404; Fax: 63017757
Founded: 1979
Pres: Prof. Juntian Zhang; Gen Secr: Prof. Zhibin Lin
Focus: Pharmacol 02601

Chinese Physics Society, c/o Institute of Physics, Academia Sinica, Zhongguancun, Beijing 100080
T: (010) 62562425
Pres: Kun Huang; Gen Secr: Guozhen Yang
Focus: Physics 02602

Chinese Psychological Society, c/o Institute of Psychology, Chinese Academy of Sciences, Beijing 100012
T: (010) 449664
Founded: 1921; Members: 2600
Pres: Prof. Su Wang
Focus: Psych 02603

Chinese Railway Society, 10 Fuxing Rd, POB 2499, Beijing
Pres: Jianzhang Liu; Gen Secr: Xichun Zhao
Focus: Transport; Eng 02604

Chinese Research Society for the Modernization of Management, c/o China Association for Science and Technology, Sanlihe, Xijiao, Beijing
T: (010) 68318877 ext 524
Founded: 1978
Pres: Shaoming Xie
Focus: Business Admin 02605

Chinese Sericulture Society, Sibaidu, Zhenjiang, Jiangsu 212018
T: 626721 ext 317; Fax: 622507
Founded: 1963
Pres: Zhuwen Zhu
Focus: Animal Husb 02606

Chinese Society for Anatomical Sciences, 42 Dongsi Xidajie, Beijing 100710
T: (010) 65133311 ext 247; Fax: 65123754
Founded: 1947; Members: 5000
Pres: Shepu Xue; Gen Secr: Changen Bem
Focus: Anat 02607

Chinese Society for EU Studies, c/o Institute of World Economy, Fudan University, 220 Handan Rd, Shanghai
T: (021) 65492222 ext 2668; E-Mail: bkdei@mobors.fudan.edu.cn; Fax: 65483331
Founded: 1984; Members: 100

Pres: Yikang Wu; Gen Secr: Bingran Dai
Focus: Econ; Poli Sci; Law
Periodical
European Integration Studies (quarterly) . 02608

Chinese Society for Future Studies, 32 Baishiqiao Rd, Haidian District, Beijing 100081
Founded: 1979; Members: 1000
Gen Secr: Dagong Du
Focus: Futurology 02609

Chinese Society for Horticultural Science, 30 Baishiqiao Rd, Beijing 100081
T: (010) 62174433 ext 2629
Founded: 1930
Pres: Chingyang Xiang
Focus: Hort 02610

Chinese Society for Metals, 46 Dongsi Xidajie, Beijing 100711
T: (010) 65133322 ext 3390; Fax: 65124122
Founded: 1956; Members: 90000
Pres: Ming Li
Focus: Metallurgy 02611

Chinese Society for Microbiology, Zhong-Guan Cun, Beijing 100080
T: (010) 62554677
Founded: 1952
Pres: Ji-Lun Li
Focus: Microbio 02612

Chinese Society for Oceanology and Limnology (C.S.O.L.), 7 Nanhai Rd, Qingdao 266071
T: (0532) 2879062; Fax: 2870882
Founded: 1950; Members: 7000
Pres: Yunshan Qin; Gen Secr: Mingjiang Zhou
Focus: Hydrology; Oceanography
Periodicals
Chinese Journal of Oceanology and Limnology (quarterly)
Oceanologia et Limnologia Sinica (bi-monthly) 02613

Chinese Society for Rock Mechanics, Jia 11, Anwai Datun Lu, POB 9701, Bejing
T: (010) 6201118; Fax: 62031995
Founded: 1985; Members: 8043
Pres: Jia Zheng Pan; Gen Secr: Bingjun Fu
Focus: Eng 02614

Chinese Society for Scientific and Technical Information, 15 Fuxinglu, Beijing
T: (010) 68014024; Fax: 68014025
Founded: 1964; Members: 13000
Pres: Heng Wu
Focus: Computer & Info Sci; Sci; Eng . 02615

Chinese Society for the Science and Technology of Labour Protection, POB 4711, Beijing
T: (010) 64215300
Founded: 1983; Members: 15000
Pres: Guang He; Gen Secr: Yiyong Su
Focus: Eng 02616

Chinese Society for Theoretical and Applied Mechanics, 15 Zhong Guan-Cun, Beijing 100080
T: (010) 62559588; Fax: 62561284
Founded: 1957; Members: 21000
Gen Secr: Prof. Ren Wang
Focus: Eng 02617

Chinese Society for Urban Studies, Bai Wanzhuang, Beijing 100835
T: (010) 68992424
Founded: 1984; Members: 30000
Pres: Zhong Lian; Gen Secr: Mengbai Li
Focus: Urban Plan 02618

Chinese Society of Aeronautics and Astronautics (CSAA), 5 Liangguochang Rd, Dongcheng District, Beijing
T: (010) 64021416; Fax: 64021413
Founded: 1964; Members: 30000
Pres: Yu-Li Zhu; Gen Secr: Jiaqi Zhou
Focus: Aero 02619

Chinese Society of Agricultural Machinery, 1 Beishatan, Deshengmen Wai, Beijing 100083
T: (010) 62017131 ext 2233; Fax: 62017326
Founded: 1963; Members: 26245
Pres: Shouren Li; Gen Secr: Yuanen Gao
Focus: Agri 02620

Chinese Society of Astronautics, POB 838, Beijing
T: (010) 68584077; Fax: 68372081
Founded: 1979; Members: 5600
Pres: Jiyuan Liu; Gen Secr: Jingsheng Liu
Focus: Aero 02621

The Chinese Society of Biochemistry and Molecular Biology, c/o Institute of Biophysics, Academia Sinica, 15 Datun Rd, Beijing
T: (010) 64963554; E-Mail: csbmb@sun5.ibp.ac.cn; Fax: 62027837
Founded: 1979; Members: 1500
Pres: C.L. Tsou; Gen Secr: F.Y. Yang
Focus: Biochem; Bio
Periodicals
Chemistry of Life (bi-monthly)
Chinese Journal of Biochemistry and Molecular Biology (bi-monthly) 02622

Chinese Society of Electrical Engineering, 1 Lane 2, Baiguang Rd, Beijing 100076
Pres: Fengxiang Zhang
Focus: Electric Eng 02623

Chinese Society of Engineering Thermophysics, Zhong Guan Cun, POB 2706, Beijing
Founded: 1978; Members: 5000
Pres: Jianzhong Xu; Gen Secr: Prof. Tianzhong Xu
Focus: Eng
Periodicals
Journal of Engineering Thermophysics (quarterly)
Proceedings of Engineering Thermophysics Conference (annually) 02624

Chinese Society of Environmental Sciences, 115 Xizhimennei Nanxiaojie, Beijing
T: (010) 661006
Founded: 1979; Members: 22000
Pres: Jingzhao Li; Gen Secr: Geping Qu
Focus: Ecology 02625

Chinese Society of Forestry, Wanshoushan, 100091 Beijing
T: (010) 62583561; E-Mail: csf@csf.forstry.ac.cn; Fax: 62582317
Founded: 1917; Members: 70000
Pres: Yuhe Liu; Gen Secr: Changyi Song
Focus: Forestry 02626

Chinese Society of Geodesy, Photogrammetry and Cartography, Baiwanzhuang, Beijing
T: (010) 68311564, 68346614, 68339095; E-Mail: fanbsm@public.bta.net.cn; Fax: 68311564
Founded: 1959; Members: 3000
Pres: Xiangwen Jin; Gen Secr: Menghua Feng
Focus: Cart; Surveying
Periodical
Acta Geodetica et Cartographica Sinica . 02627

Chinese Society of Library Science, 39 Bai Shi Qiao Rd, Beijing 100081
T: (010) 68415566 ext 5563; Fax: 68419271
Founded: 1979; Members: 10150
Pres: Deyou Liu
Focus: Libraries & Bk Sci 02628

Chinese Society of Mineralogy, Petrology and Geochemistry, POB 91, Guiyang, Guizhou 550002
T: (0851) 522982
Founded: 1978; Members: 6000
Pres: Guangchi Tu
Focus: Mineralogy; Petrochem; Chem . 02629

Chinese Society of Naval Architects and Marine Engineers, POB 817, Beijing
T: (010) 68340527; Fax: 68133380
Founded: 1943
Pres: Rongsheng Wang; Gen Secr: Shoudao Wang
Focus: Mach Eng 02630

Chinese Society of Oceanography, 10 Fuxingmenwai, Beijing
Pres: Deqing Peng
Focus: Oceanography 02631

Chinese Society of Oceanology and Limnology, 4 Nanhai Rd, Qingdao 266071
T: (0532) 2879062 ext 3402; Fax: 2870882
Founded: 1950; Members: 6500
Pres: Yun-Shan Qin
Focus: Oceanography; Zoology 02632

Chinese Society of Plant Physiology, 300 Fongling Rd, Shanghai
T: (021) 4042090; Fax: 4332385
Founded: 1963; Members: 4000
Pres: Prof. Y.G. Shen
Focus: Botany 02633

Chinese Society of Space Sciences, 1 S Lane 2, Zhongguancun, Beijing 100080
T: (010) 289882
Founded: 1980
Pres: Baowei Lu
Focus: Aero
Periodical
Chinese Journal of Space Science (quarterly) 02634

Chinese Society of the History of International Relations, 12 Poshangcun, Haidian District, Beijing
Pres: Shengzu Wang
Focus: Hist; Poli Sci 02635

Chinese Society of the History of Science and Technology, 137 Chao Nei St, Beijing 100010
T: (010) 64043989; Fax: 64017637
Founded: 1980; Members: 1500
Focus: Hist; Sci; Eng 02636

Chinese Society of Theoretical and Applied Mechanics, c/o Institute of Mechanics, Zhong Guan Cun, Beijing
T: (010) 62554107; 62559588; E-Mail: cstam@sun.ihep.ac.cn; Fax: 62559588, 62554107
Founded: 1957; Members: 21000
Pres: Fenggan Zhuang; Gen Secr: Youshi Hong
Focus: Eng 02637

Chinese Society of Tropical Crops, Baodao Xincun, Danzhou, Hainan
Founded: 1978; Members: 4088
Pres: Yanqing Pan; Gen Secr: Wenrong Zheng
Focus: Agri 02638

Chinese Sociological Research Society, c/o Chinese Academy of Social Sciences, 5 Jiang Nei Da Jie, Beijing
Founded: 1979
Pres: Xiaotong Fei; Gen Secr: Kang Wang
Focus: Sociology 02639

Chinese Study of Religion Society, Xi'anmen Av, Beijing
Pres: Jiyu Ren
Focus: Rel & Theol 02640

Chinese Textile Engineering Society, 3 Middle St, Yanjin Li, East Suburb, Beijing 100025
T: (010) 65016537; Fax: 65016538
Founded: 1930; Members: 60000
Pres: Guobiao Ji
Focus: Textiles; Eng 02641

Chinese Writers' Association, 2 Shatanbeijie, Beijing 100720
Pres: Jin Ba
Focus: Lit
Periodical
Chinese Writers (bi-monthly) 02642

Chinese Zoological Society, 19 Zhong Guan Cun Lu, Beijing
T: (010) 62561873; Fax: 62565689
Founded: 1934
Pres: Daxiang Song
Focus: Zoology 02643

Crop Science Society of China, c/o Institute of Crop Breeding and Cultivation, 30 Bai Shi Qiao Rd, Beijing 100081
T: (010) 62176667 ext 2116; Fax: 62174865
Founded: 1961; Members: 22000
Pres: Linazheng Wang; Gen Secr: Chunhua Li
Focus: Agri 02644

Ecological Society of China, 19 Zhongguancun Lu, Beijing 100080
T: (010) 62565694; Fax: 62565689
Founded: 1979; Members: 5000
Pres: Prof. Zuwang Wang; Gen Secr: Prof. Rusong Wang
Focus: Ecology 02645

Entomological Society of China, 19 Zhongguancun Lu, Haidian, Beijing 100080
T: (010) 62630062; E-Mail: zss@panda.ioz.ac.cn; Fax: 62565689
Members: 1100
Pres: J.D. Quin; Gen Secr: M.Y. Liu
Focus: Entomology
Periodicals
Acta Entomologica (quarterly)
Acta Zootaxonomia Sinica (quarterly)
Entomologia Sinica (quarterly)
Kunchong zhishi: Entomological Knowledge (bi-monthly) 02646

Genetics Society of China, 917 Datun Rd, Andingmenwai, Beijing 100101
T: (010) 64919944; Fax: 64914896
Founded: 1978; Members: 6600
Pres: Zhengsheng Li; Gen Secr: Shouyi Chen
Focus: Genetics
Periodical
Acta Genetica Sinica 02647

Geographical Society of China, 917 Datun Rd, Beijing 100101
T: (010) 64911104; Fax: 64911844
Founded: 1909; Members: 15000
Pres: Chuanjun Wu; Gen Secr: Jiazhen Zhang
Focus: Geography
Periodical
Acta Gepographica Sinica (bi-monthly) . 02648

Geological Society of China (G.S.C.), Pai Wan Chuang, Fuchengmenwai, 100037 Beijing
T: (010) 68311539
Founded: 1922; Members: 77040
Pres: Ruixiang Song; Gen Secr: Milly Wang
Focus: Geology
Periodicals
Acta Geologia (quarterly)
Geological Review (bi-monthly) 02649

Hong Kong Chinese PEN Centre, POB 78521, Hong Kong
Founded: 1955; Members: 92
Pres: Chih-Tai Chu; Gen Secr: William Hsu
Focus: Lit 02650

Hong Kong Library Association (HKLA), GPOB 10095, Hong Kong
T: 468161
Founded: 1958; Members: 520
Pres: Mary Leong; Gen Secr: Edward Spodick
Focus: Libraries & Bk Sci
Periodicals
HKLA Journal (semi-annually)
Newsletter (8 times annually) 02651

Hong Kong Management Association, Fairmont House, 8 Cotton Tree Dr, Central, Hong Kong
T: 5266516; Fax: 5721660
Founded: 1960
Pres: David K.P. Li; Gen Secr: Elizabeth Shing
Focus: Business Admin 02652

Hong Kong Medical Association, 15 Hennessy Rd, Hong Kong
T: 28650943; Fax: 25278285
Founded: 1920; Members: 4600
Pres: Dr. Lee Kin Hung; Gen Secr: Dr. Ko Wing Man
Focus: Med 02653

Hunan Academy of Agricultural Sciences, Changsha 410125
T: (0731) 4691204; Fax: 4691124
Founded: 1938; Members: 2600
Pres: Jirong Tian
Focus: Agri
Periodicals
Hunan Agricultural Research Newsletter (quarterly)
Hunan Agricultural Sciences (bi-monthly)
Hybrid Rice (bi-monthly)
Tea Bulletin (bi-monthly) 02654

Law Society of Hong Kong, 1403-1413 Swire House, 11 Chater Rd, Hong Kong
T: 28460500; Fax: 28450387
Founded: 1907; Members: 3600
Pres: Christopher Chan
Focus: Law
Periodical
Hong Kong Lawyer 02655

Nonferrous Metals Society of China, B12 Fuxing Rd, Beijing 100814
T: (010) 68515387; Fax: 68515387
Founded: 1984
Pres: Jianching Wu; Gen Secr: Fukang Ma
Focus: Metallurgy 02656

Palaeontological Society of China (PSC), 39E Beijing Rd, Nanjing 210008
T: (025) 3358784; Fax: 3357026
Founded: 1929; Members: 1230
Pres: Miman Zhang; Gen Secr: Xinan Mu
Focus: Paleontology
Periodical
Acta Palaeontologica Sinica (bi-monthly) . 02657

Royal Asiatic Society, Hong Kong Branch, GPOB 3864, Hong Kong
Founded: 1847; Members: 560
Pres: Dr. Dan Waters; Gen Secr: Claire Hockadey
Focus: Ethnology; Hist; Cultur Hist
Periodical
Journal (annually) 02658

Seismological Society of China, 5 Minzu Xueyuan Banhu, Beijing 100081
T: (010) 68417858
Founded: 1979; Members: 4771
Pres: Prof. Yuntai Chen
Focus: Geophys 02659

Society of Autmotive Engineering of China, 46 Fucheng Rd, Beijing 100036
T: (010) 68121894; Fax: 68125556
Founded: 1963; Members: 1520
Pres: Xingye Zhang
Focus: Eng 02660

Soil Science Society of China, POB 821, Nanjing 210008
T: (025) 713360; Fax: 712663
Founded: 1945; Members: 15000
Pres: Qiguo Zhao
Focus: Agri 02661

Systems Engineering Society of China, c/o Institute of Systems Science, Zhongguancun, Beijing 100080
T: (010) 62541827; Fax: 62568364
Founded: 1980; Members: 3150
Pres: Jifa Gu; Gen Secr: Guangya Chen
Focus: Eng 02662

China, Republic

Academia Historica, 406 Pei Yi Rd, Section 406, Hsintien, Taipei
T: (02) 2171535; Fax: 2171640
Founded: 1947; Members: 158
Pres: Shao-Hwa Chu; Gen Secr: Chung-Sheng Chu
Focus: Hist 02663

Academia Sinica, Nankang, Taipei
T: (02) 7823142
Founded: 1928; Members: 181
Pres: Dr. Yuan-Tseh Lee; Gen Secr: Dr. Hsi-Chiang Liu
Focus: Sci 02664

Agricultural Association of China, 14 Wenchow St, Taipei
T: (02) 3636681
Founded: 1917; Members: 2550
Pres: Zsong-Shien Wu
Focus: Agri
Periodical
Journal (quarterly) 02665

Asia-Pacific Office Automation Council (APOAC), c/o CACCI, 122 Tunhua North Rd, Taipei 10590
T: (02) 7163016, 7164250; Fax: 7163683
Focus: Business Admin 02666

Asian-Australian Association of Animal Production Societies (AAAP), c/o Pig Research Institute, POB 23, Chunan, Miaoli 350
Focus: Animal Husb
Periodical
Asian-Australian Journal of Animal Science (quarterly) 02667

Asian Crystallographic Association (ASCA), c/o Dept of Chemistry, National Taiwan University, Taipei 10764
Focus: Chem 02668

Asian Ecological Society, c/o Tunghai University, POB 843, Taichung 40704
T: (04) 3590991; E-Mail: edgarlin@ms5.hinet.net; Fax: 3590379
Founded: 1977; Members: 100
Pres: Yun-Li Lin
Focus: Ecology
Periodical
Journal of Asian Ecology (irregularly) . . 02669

Asian Food Council, c/o CACCI, 122 Tunhua North Rd, Taipei 10590
T: (02) 7163016; Fax: 7183683
Focus: Food 02670

Asian Vegetable Research and Development Center (AVRDC), POB 42, Shanhua, Tainan 74199
T: (06) 5837801; Fax: 5830009
Founded: 1971; Members: 9
Focus: Hort
Periodicals
Centerpoint Newsmagazine (semi-annually)
Soybean Rust Newsletter (annually) . . 02671

Association of Child Education of the Republic of China, 94 Hoping East Rd, Section 3, Taipei
Founded: 1930
Focus: Educ 02672

The Association of Obstetrics and Gynecology of the Republic of China, c/o Dept of Obstetrics and Gynecology, Veterans General Hospital, 201 Shihpai Rd, Section 2, Taipei
Fax: (02) 8739512
Founded: 1961
Focus: Gynecology 02673

Astronautical Society of the Republic of China, c/o National Taiwan Science Hall, 41 Nanhai Rd, Taipei
Founded: 1958
Focus: Aero 02674

Astronomical Society of the Republic of China, c/o Taipei Observatory, Yuan Shan, Taipei 104
Founded: 1958; Members: 200
Pres: Dr. M.H. Wu; Gen Secr: Chang-Hsien Tsai
Focus: Astronomy 02675

Atomic Energy Council, 67 Lane 144, Keelung Rd, Section 4, Taipei 106
T: (02) 3634180; Fax: 3635377
Founded: 1955; Members: 15
Pres: Dr. Yih-Yun Hsu; Gen Secr: Kuang-Chi Liu
Focus: Nucl Res
Periodicals
Chinese AEC Bulletin (bi-monthly)
Nuclear Science Journal (quarterly) . . . 02676

Biological Society of China, c/o Dept of Biology, National Taiwan Normal University, 162 Hoping East Rd, Section 1, Taipei
Founded: 1959
Focus: Bio 02677

Chemical Society, POB 609, Taipei
T: (02) 3313176; E-Mail: CCSWWW@gate.sinica.edu.tw; Fax: 3118464
Founded: 1932; Members: 8200
Pres: Chun-Chen Liao; Gen Secr: Tashin J. Chow
Focus: Chem
Periodicals
Chemistry (bi-monthly)
Journal 02678

China Association of the Five Principles of Administrative Authority, 26 Ningpo West St, Taipei
Founded: 1962
Focus: Business Admin 02679

China Education Society, c/o National Taiwan Normal University, Hoping East Rd, Taipei
Founded: 1933
Focus: Educ 02680

China International Education Research Association, 173 Sinyi Rd, Section 2, Taipei
Founded: 1959
Focus: Educ 02681

China National Association of Literature and the Arts, 4 Lane 22, Nuigpo St West, Taipei
Focus: Lit; Arts 02682

China Social Education Society, 5 Chungshan South Rd, Taipei
Founded: 1931
Focus: Educ; Sociology 02683

China Society, 7 Lane 52, Wenchow St, Taipei
Founded: 1960; Members: 100
Pres: Dr. Chi-Lu Chen
Focus: Ethnology
Periodical
Journal (annually) 02684

China Spiritual Therapy Study Association, 5 Alley 11, Lane 131, Olung St, Taipei
Founded: 1926
Focus: Therapeutics 02685

Chinese Association for Folklore, 422 Fulin Rd, Shihlin, POB 681292, Taipei
Founded: 1932; Members: 47
Pres: Prof. Lou-Kuang Lou; Gen Secr: Amy Lou
Focus: Ethnology 02686

Chinese Association for the Advancement of Science, 5 Chungshan South Rd, Taipei
Founded: 1917
Pres: Tien-Fong Cheng
Focus: Sci
Periodical
Science Education 02687

Chinese Association of Psychological Testing, c/o Psychological Laboratory, National Taiwan Normal Univeristy, Hoping East Rd, Taipei
Founded: 1935
Focus: Psych 02688

Chinese Buddhist Association, 23 Chungsiao East Rd, Section 1, Taipei
Founded: 1912
Focus: Rel & Theol 02689

Chinese Center, International PEN, 33 Lane 180, Kwang-Fu South Rd, Taipei 105
Founded: 1935
Focus: Lit
Periodical
The Chinese PEN (quarterly) 02690

Chinese Classical Music Association, 1 Lane 3, Linyi St, Taipei 100
Founded: 1951; Members: 1100
Focus: Music 02691

Chinese Film Critic's Association of China, 18 Hsining South Rd, Taipei
Founded: 1964
Focus: Cinema 02692

Chinese Forestry Association (C.F.A.), 2 Hang Chow-South Rd , Section 1, Taipei
T: (02) 3515441
Founded: 1948; Members: 1545
Pres: Chi-You Hsu
Focus: Forestry
Periodicals
Journal of Chinese Forestry (quarterly)
Taiwan's Forestry Monthly (quarterly) . . 02693

Chinese Foundrymen's Association, 1001 Kao-Nan Hwy, Kaohsiung 811
T: (07) 3534791/92; E-Mail: 63605@mail.kscgeb.edu.tw; Fax: 3524989
Founded: 1966; Members: 2389
Pres: M.H. Hung; Gen Secr: S.C. Mao
Focus: Metallurgy
Periodicals
Casting (monthly)
Journal of the Chinese Foundrymen's Association (quarterly) 02694

Chinese Historical Association, c/o College of Liberal Arts, National Taiwan University, Roosevelt Rd, Taipei
Founded: 1954
Focus: Hist 02695

Chinese Home Education Promotion Association, 7-1 Alley 6, Lane 238, Tun Hua North Rd, Taipei 104
T: (02) 7520944
Founded: 1960; Members: 5767
Focus: Home Econ; Educ 02696

Chinese Institute of Civil and Hydraulic Engineering, POB 499, Taipei
Founded: 1973; Members: 7500
Pres: Cheng Yu
Focus: Civil Eng
Periodical
Civil and Hydraulic Engineering (quarterly) 02697

Chinese Institute of Engineers, 1 Jen. Ai Rd, Section 2, Taipei
T: (02) 3925128; Fax: 3973003
Founded: 1912; Members: 11500
Pres: M. Hsia Han
Focus: Eng
Periodicals
CIE Newsletter (bi-monthly)
Engineering Journal (monthly)
Journal of the Chinese Institute of Engineers (bi-monthly) 02698

Chinese Institute of Mining and Metallurgical Engineers (CIMME), 2F, 38-1 Chin Nan Rd, Section 2, Taipei 100
T: (02) 3517046, 3960202; Fax: 3975377
Founded: 1926
Focus: Mining; Metallurgy
Periodicals
The Metallurgy of Iron and Steel
Symposium on Steel Production Technology 02699

Chinese Language Society, c/o Taiwan Normal University, Hoping East Rd, Taipei
Founded: 1953
Gen Secr: Tzu-Shui Mao
Focus: Ling
Periodical
Chinese Language Monthly (monthly) . . 02700

Chinese Mathematical Society, c/o National Taiwan University, Taipei
Members: 550
Focus: Math 02701

Chinese Medical Association, 201 Shih-Pai Rd, Section 2, Taipei
T: (010) 551943
Founded: 1915; Members: 1672
Pres: Dr. Kwang-Jujei Lo; Gen Secr: Dr. Yang-Te Tsai
Focus: Med
Periodical
Chinese Medical Journal (quarterly) . . . 02702

Chinese Medical History Association, 6 Lane 120, Hsinsheng Rd, Section 1, Taipei
Founded: 1963
Focus: Hist 02703

Chinese National Association for Mental Hygiene, c/o National Taiwan University Hospital, 1 Changteh St, Taipei
Founded: 1936
Focus: Hygiene 02704

Chinese National Foreign Relations Association, 94 Nanchang St, Section 1, Taipei
Pres: Kuo-Shu Huang
Focus: Poli Sci 02705

Chinese Physiological Society, 1 Jenai Rd, Section 1, Taipei
Founded: 1928
Focus: Physiology 02706

Chinese Psychological Association (CPA), c/o Dept of Psychology, National Taiwan University, Taipei 106
T: (02) 3630231 ext 2374; Fax: 3629909
Founded: 1962; Members: 500
Focus: Psych
Periodical
Chinese Journal of Psychology (semi-annually)
. . . . 02707

Chinese Society for Electronic Data Processing, 66 Nanchang St, Section 1, Taipei
Founded: 1966
Focus: Computer & Info Sci 02708

Chinese Society for Materials Science, 195 Chung Hsing Rd, Section 4, Chutung, Hsinchu 31015
Founded: 1966; Members: 1281
Focus: Materials Sci
Periodical
Chinese Journal of Materials Science (quarterly)
. . . . 02709

Chinese Society of Budgetary Management, 69-2 Lane 189, Antung St, Taipei
Founded: 1965
Focus: Finance 02710

Chinese Society of International Law, 187 Kinhwa St, Taipei
Founded: 1958
Focus: Law 02711

Chinese Statistical Association, 1 Nan Chung Rd, Section 1, Taipei
Founded: 1941; Members: 1082
Pres: C.C. Lee
Focus: Stats
Periodical
Chinese Statistical Journal 02712

The Chinese Taipei Pediatric Association, 11 Ching-Tao West, 4F-4, Taipei 100
T: (02) 3314917; Fax: 3142184
Founded: 1960; Members: 2200
Focus: Pediatrics
Periodical
Acta Pediatrica Sinica (bi-monthly) . . . 02713

Chinese Women Writer's Association, 16-5 Lane 61, Linyi St, Taipei
Founded: 1969
Focus: Lit 02714

Chinese Youth Academic Research Association, 219 Sungchiang Rd, Taipei
Founded: 1958
Focus: Sci 02715

Committee on the Promotion of the Peaceful Uses of Atomic Energy, 110 Yenping South Rd, Taipei
Pres: Milton J.T. Shieh
Focus: Energy 02716

Confucius-Mencius Society of the Republic of China, 45 Nanhai Rd, Taipei
Founded: 1960; Members: 3900
Pres: Dr. Li-Fu Chen; Gen Secr: Chung-Lin Hua
Focus: Philos
Periodicals
Confucius-Mencius Monthly (monthly)
Journal of the Confucius-Mencius Society 02717

Cooperative League of the Republic of China, 11-2 Fu Chow St, Taipei
Founded: 1928
Focus: Business Admin; Econ 02718

Council of Agriculture, 37 Nanhai Rd, Taipei
T: (02) 3812991; E-Mail: coa@mail.coa.gov.tw; Fax: 3310341
Founded: 1984; Members: 351
Pres: Tso-Kwei Peng; Gen Secr: Te-Yeh Ku
Focus: Agri
Periodical
General Report (annually) 02719

Early Childhood Education Society of the Republic of China, 321 Lane 124, Hu-lin St, Taipei
Founded: 1959
Focus: Educ 02720

Ethnological Society of China, c/o Institute of Ethnology, Academia Sinica, Nankang, Taipei
Founded: 1934
Focus: Ethnology 02721

Finance Association of China, 63-9 Hangchow South Rd, Section 1, Taipei
Founded: 1941
Focus: Finance 02722

The Geographical Society of China (Taipei), 162 Ho-ping East Rd, Section 1, Taipei 106
T: (02) 3930874; Fax: 3691770
Founded: 1934; Members: 1600
Pres: Dr. Kuo-Yan Chen; Gen Secr: Dr. Sheng-I Hsu
Focus: Geography
Periodical
Bulletin (annually) 02723

Geological Society of China, POB 3317, Taipei
Focus: Geology
Periodicals
Memoir
Proceedings 02724

Graphic Arts Association of China, 71 Paochao Rd, Hsientien, Taipei
Founded: 1956
Focus: Arts 02725

Historical Research Commission of Taiwan, 111 Yenping South Rd, Taipei
Founded: 1949
Focus: Hist 02726

International Academy of Chest Physicians and Surgeons of the American College of Chest Physicians, Republic of China Chapter, c/o National Taiwan University Hospital, 1 Changteh St, Taipei
T: (02) 3123456 ext 2527
Founded: 1969; Members: 166
Focus: Cardiol 02727

International Education Association of China, 173 Hsinyi Rd, Section 2, Taipei
Founded: 1959
Focus: Educ 02728

International House Association, Taipei Chapter, 18 Hsin Yi Rd , Section 3, Taipei
Focus: Urban Plan 02729

Library Association of China (LAC), c/o National Central Library, 20 Chungshan South Rd, Taipei
T: (02) 3312475; Fax: 3820747
Founded: 1953; Members: 2312
Pres: James S.C. Hu; Gen Secr: Teresa Wang Chang
Focus: Libraries & Bk Sci
Periodical
Bulletin (annually) 02730

Malacological Society of China, 2 Siangyang Rd, Taipei
Founded: 1970; Members: 400
Focus: Zoology
Periodical
Bulletin of Malacology (annually) . . . 02731

Mathematical Society of the Republic of China, c/o Dept of Mathematics, National Cheng Kung University, Tainan 70101
Fax: (06) 2743191
Pres: Yuh-Jia Lee; Gen Secr: Young-Ye Huang
Focus: Math 02732

The Meteorological Society of the Republic of China, 64 Kung-Yuan Rd, Taipei
T: (02) 3491094
Founded: 1958; Members: 400
Pres: Shin-Liang Shieh; Gen Secr: Ming-Shing Lin
Focus: Geophys
Periodicals
Atmospheric Science (quarterly)
Bulletin of the Meteorological Society of the Republic of China (semi-annually) . . . 02733

Modern Fine Arts Association of Southern Taiwan, 17 Shulin St, Tainan
Founded: 1967
Focus: Arts 02734

Museum Association of China, 49 Nanhai Rd, Taipei
Founded: 1964
Focus: Arts 02735

National Audio-Visual Education Association of China, 162 Hoping East Rd, Section 1, POB 2225, Taipei 106
T: (02) 3511472
Founded: 1959; Members: 1500
Focus: Educ
Periodical
AV Newsletter (irregularly) 02736

National Bar Association, 124 Chungking South Rd , Section 1, Taipei
Focus: Law 02737

National Institute for Compilation and Translation, 247 Choushan Rd, Taipei
Fax: (02) 3629256
Founded: 1932
Focus: Ling
Periodicals
The Institute Periodical (semi-annually)
News Bulletin (quarterly) 02738

National Music Council of China, 162 Hoping East Rd, Section 1, Taipei
Founded: 1957
Focus: Music 02739

National Science Council, 2 Canton St, Taipei
Founded: 1959
Pres: Li-An Chen
Focus: Sci

Periodicals
Abstracts of Research Papers (annually)
National Science (monthly)
The NSC Review (annually)
NSC Special Publication (irregularly)
NSC Symposium Series (irregularly)
Proceedings (quarterly)
Science Bulletin (monthly) 02740

National Tax Research Association of China, 63-9 Hangchow South Rd, Section 1, Taipei
Founded: 1951
Focus: Law 02741

National Young Writers Association of China, 51 Hanchung St, Taipei
Founded: 1953
Focus: Lit 02742

Ophthalmological Society of the Republic of China, c/o Dept of Ophthalmology, National Taiwan University Hospital, 1 Chang-Teh St, Taipei 100
Fax: (02) 3832310
Founded: 1959
Focus: Ophthal
Periodical
Transactions of the Ophthalmological Society of the Republic of China (quarterly) . . 02743

Physical Society of China, POB 2330, Taipei
Focus: Physics
Periodical
Chinese Journal of Physics (quarterly) . 02744

Physics Education Society of the Republic of China, 88 Ting-Chou Rd, Section 4, Taipei
T: (02) 9346620; E-Mail: cnnchang@ms8.hinet.net; Fax: 9326408
Founded: 1975; Members: 500
Pres: Prof. Chu-Nan Chang; Gen Secr: Prof. Tzuen-Rong Yang
Focus: Educ; Physics 02745

Playwriters Association of the Republic of China, 218-1 Roosevelt Rd, Section 3, Taipei
Founded: 1970
Focus: Lit 02746

Population Association of China, 107 Roosevelt Rd, Section 4, Taipei
Founded: 1956
Focus: Sociology 02747

Public Administration Society of China, c/o Dept of Public Administration, College of Law and Commerce, National Chung-Hsing University, 53 Ho-Chiang St, Taipei
Founded: 1954
Focus: Business Admin 02748

The Radiological Society of the Republic of China, c/o Dept of Radiology, Veterans General Hospital, Shih-Pai, Taipei 11217
Fax: (02) 8733643
Founded: 1951
Focus: Radiology
Periodical
Chinese Journal of Radiology (quarterly) . 02749

Republic of China Society of Cardiology (ROCSOC), c/o Tri-Service General Hospital, No. 8, Sect. 3, Ting-Chow Rd, Taipei 100
T: (02) 3687720; Fax: 3687926
Founded: 1960; Members: 882
Focus: Cardiol
Periodical
Acta Cardiologica Sinica (quarterly) . . . 02750

School Health Association of the Republic of China, 162 Hoping East Rd, Section 1, Taipei
Founded: 1962
Focus: Public Health 02751

The Society of Anaesthesiologist of the Republic of China (SAROC), 271 Roosevelt Rd, Section 3, Taipei 10764
T: (02) 3633912; E-Mail: saroc@tpts5.seed.net.tw; Fax: 3633912
Founded: 1956; Members: 1800
Pres: Prof. Shung-Tai Ho; Gen Secr: Chen-Hwan Cheng
Focus: Anesthetics
Periodical
Acta Anaesthesiologica Sinica (5 times annually)
. . . . 02752

Society of Chinese Acupuncture and Cauterizing, Chung Ching Bldg. 66-1, Chung Ching South Rd, Section 1, Taipei
Founded: 1955; Members: 3500
Focus: Anesthetics 02753

Society of Chinese Constitutional Law, 170 Keelung Rd, Section 2, Taipei
Founded: 1951
Focus: Law 02754

Society of the Chinese Borders History and Languages, c/o National Taiwan University Library, Taipei
Founded: 1958
Focus: Hist; Ling 02755

Special Education Association of the Republic of China, 320 Chungching North Rd, Section 3, Taipei
Founded: 1967
Focus: Educ 02756

Surgical Association of the Republic of China, c/o Dept of Surgery, National Taiwan University Hospital, Taipei
T: (02) 7642409; Fax: 7656630
Founded: 1967; Members: 4100
Pres: Shu-Hsun Chu; Gen Secr: King-Jen Chang
Focus: Surgery
Periodical
Journal (bi-monthly) 02757

Taiwan Otolaryngological Society, No. 201, Sec. 2, Shih-Pai Rd, Taipei 10112
T: (02) 8733776; Fax: 8733692
Founded: 1965; Members: 1242
Pres: Shyue-Yih Chang; Gen Secr: An-Suey Shiao
Focus: Otorhinolaryngology
Periodical
The Journal of Taiwan Otolaryngological Society (bi-monthly) 02758

Television Academy of Arts and Sciences of the Republic of China, 10 Pateh Rd, Section 3, Taipei
Founded: 1969
Focus: Arts; Sci 02759

World Wide Ethical Society (WES), 264 Chien Kang Rd, Taipei
T: (02) 7670401
Founded: 1920; Members: 52000
Focus: Philos
Periodical
Morality Quarterly (quarterly) 02760

Colombia

Academia Antioqueña de Historia, Carrera 43, No 53-37, Apdo Aéreo 7175, Medellín
T: (04) 395576
Founded: 1903; Members: 60
Pres: Jaime Sierra Garcia; Gen Secr: Alicia Giraldo Gómez
Focus: Hist
Periodicals
Bolsilibros
Repertorio Histórico (3 times annually) . 02761

Academia Boyacense de Historia, Casa del Fundador, Tunja
T: (087) 3441
Founded: 1905; Members: 30
Pres: Javier Ocampo Lopez; Gen Secr: Ramón Correa
Focus: Hist
Periodical
Repertorio Boyacense (semi-annually) . . 02762

Academia Colombiana de Ciencias Exactas, Físicas y Naturales, Carrera 3A, No 17-34, Apdo Aéreo 44763, Bogotá
T: (01) 3414805; Fax: 2838552
Founded: 1933; Members: 46
Pres: Luis Eduardo Mora-Osejo; Gen Secr: José A. Lozano
Focus: Nat Sci; Physics
Periodical
Revista 02763

Academia Colombiana de Historia, Calle 10, No 8-95, Apdo Aéreo 14428, Bogotá
Founded: 1902; Members: 40
Pres: Dr. Germán Arciniegas; Gen Secr: Roberto Velandia
Focus: Hist
Periodical
Boletín de Historia y Antigüedades . . . 02764

Academia Colombiana de Jurisprudencia, Calle 17, No 4-95, Of 210, Bogotá
T: (01) 2414716
Founded: 1894; Members: 50
Pres: Hernando Morales M.
Focus: Law
Periodicals
Anuario
Revista (semi-annually) 02765

Academia Colombiana de la Lengua, Apdo Aéreo 13922, Bogotá
Founded: 1871; Members: 79
Gen Secr: José Manuel Rivas Sacconi
Focus: Ling
Periodicals
Anuario
Boletín 02766

Academia de la Historia de Cartagena de Indias, Casa de la Inquisición, Plaza Bolívar, Cartagena
T: (053) 645432
Founded: 1918; Members: 120
Pres: Donaldo Bossa Herazo; Gen Secr: Celedonio Piñeres de la Espriella
Focus: Hist
Periodical
Boletín Historial (quarterly) 02767

Academia Nacional de Medicina, Calle 60A, No 5-29, Apdo Aéreo 23224, Bogotá
T: (01) 2493122
Founded: 1890; Members: 228
Pres: Dr. Juan Jacobo Muñoz; Gen Secr: César Augusto Pantoja
Focus: Med
Periodicals
Medicina (3 times annually)
Temas Médicos (annually) 02768

Asociación Colombiana de Bibliotecarios (ASCOLBI), Calle 10, No 3-16, Apdo Aéreo 30883, Bogotá
T: (01) 2694219
Founded: 1942; Members: 1200
Pres: Saul Sanchez Toro; Gen Secr: B.N. Cardona de Gil
Focus: Libraries & Bk Sci
Periodical
Boletín (quarterly) 02769

Asociación Colombiana de Facultades de Medicina, Calle 39A, No 28-63, Bogotá
T: (01) 3686711
Founded: 1959; Members: 1512
Pres: Héctor Raul Echavarría; Gen Secr: Dr. Julio Enrique Ospina
Focus: Med
Periodical
Boletín de Medicamentos y Terapéutica: Boletín Informativo de Ascofame (quarterly) . . 02770

Asociación Colombiana de Fisioterapía, Carrera 23, No 47-51, Of 3N-06-A, Bogotá
T: (01) 2876106
Founded: 1953; Members: 950
Pres: Elisa Jaramillo de Lopez
Focus: Physical Therapy 02771

Asociación Colombiana de Sociedades Científicas, c/o Hospital Militar Central, Apdo Aéreo 6658, Bogotá
T: Transversal 5a, No 49-00 (01) 2454481
Founded: 1957; Members: 3692
Gen Secr: Dr. Rafael Sarmiento Montero
Focus: Sci 02772

Asociación Colombiana de Universidades (ASCUN), Calle 93, No 16-43, Apdo Aéreo 252367, Bogotá
T: (01) 2185145; Fax: 2185098
Founded: 1957; Members: 68
Pres: Dr. Alfonso Ocampo L.; Gen Secr: Dr. Jaime Tobón V.
Focus: Sci
Periodical
Mundo Universitario (quarterly) 02773

Asociación Colombiana de Usarios de Computadores, Calle 39A, No 14-58, Apdo 4542, Bogotá
T: (01) 2455932
Founded: 1970; Members: 400
Pres: José Guillermo Jaramillo G.
Focus: Agri 02774

Asociación de Universidades Confiadas a la Compañía de Jesús en América Latina (AUSJAL) / Organization of Latin American Jesuit Universities and Faculties, Carrera 7, No 40-76, Of 501, Apdo 56710, Bogotá
T: (01) 2875584, 2881511 ext 204; Fax: 2857524
Founded: 1985
Focus: Educ
Periodical
Carta de AUSJAL (quarterly) 02775

Capitolo Colombiano de las Federaciones Latinoamericanas de Asociaciones de Cancer, c/o Clínica del Country, Carrera 15, No 84-13, Bogotá
T: (01) 2361168
Founded: 1983
Pres: Calixto Noguera
Focus: Cell Biol & Cancer Res 02776

Centro Interamericano de Fotointerpretación (CIAF), Carrera 30, No 47A-57, Apdo Aéreo 53754, Bogotá
T: (01) 2680300
Focus: Surveying
Periodical
Revista CIAF (irregularly) 02777

Centro Interamericano de Vivienda y Planeamiento, Apdo Aéreo 6209, Bogotá
Founded: 1952
Focus: Sociology; Urban Plan 02778

Centro Internacional de Agricultura Tropical (CIAT), Apdo Aéreo 6713, Cali
T: (02) 680111; E-Mail: CINATROP
Focus: Agri; Develop Areas
Periodicals
Abstracts on Cassava (3 times annually)
Abstracts on Phaseolus Vulgaris (3 times annually)
Boletín Informativo de Pastos Tropicales (3 times annually)
Cassava Newsletter (semi-annually)
CIAT International (3 times annually)
CIAT Report (annually)
Hojas de Frijol (3 times annually)
Jojas de Arroz (3 times annually)
Resumenes Pastos Tropicales (3 times annually) 02779

Centro Regional para el Fomento del Libro en América Latina (CERLAL), Calle 70, No 9-52, Apdo Aéreo 57348, Bogotá
T: (01) 3217501; Fax: 3217503
Founded: 1972
Pres: Carmen Barvo Barcenas
Focus: Libraries & Bk Sci 02780

Comité Nacional del Consejo Internacional de Museos (ICOM), c/o División de Museos y Restauración, Calle 24, No 5-60, Of 211, Bogotá
Focus: Arts; Ethnology 02781

Confederación Interamericana de Educación Católica, Apdo Aéreo 7478, Bogotá
Founded: 1945
Focus: Educ 02782

Confederación Latinoamericana de Sociedades de Anestesiología (CLASA), Calle 118, No 20-08, Bogotá
T: (01) 2138174
Founded: 1962; Members: 7000
Focus: Anesthetics 02783

Corporación Latinoamericana de Investigación para el Desarrollo del Sector Rural y Zona Costeros, Apdo 102279, Bogotá
Focus: Develop Areas 02784

Federación Médica Colombiana, Calle 72, No 6-44, Bogotá
T: (01) 2110208
Founded: 1935
Pres: Ismael Roldan Valencia; Gen Secr: Sergio Robleda Riaga
Focus: Med 02785

Instituto Caro y Cuervo, Carrera 11, No 64-37, Apdo Aéreo 51502, Bogotá
T: (01) 2557753
Founded: 1942; Members: 20
Pres: Dr. Ignacio Chaves Cuevas; Gen Secr: Dr. Guillermo Ruiz Lara
Focus: Ling; Lit; Hist
Periodicals
Anuario Bibliográfico Colombiano
Noticias Culturales (bi-monthly)
Thesaurus: Boletín Cuadrimestral 02786

Instituto Colombiano Agropecuario, Calle 37, No 8-43, Apdo Aéreo 7984, Bogotá
Founded: 1962
Focus: Agri 02787

Instituto Colombiano Agropecuario (ICA), Apdo Aéreo 151123, Mosquera
T: 813080
Focus: Agri 02788

Instituto Colombiano de Antropología (ICAN), Carrera 7, No 28-66, Apdo Aéreo 407, Bogotá
T: (01) 2836647, 2454843
Founded: 1941; Members: 32
Focus: Anthro
Periodical
Revista Colombiana de Antropologia: Informes Antropologicos (irregularly) 02789

Instituto Colombiano de Bienestar Familiar (ICBF), Av 68, Calle 64, Apdo Aéreo 18116, Bogotá
T: (01) 314556
Focus: Sociology 02790

Instituto Colombiano de Crédito Educativo y Estudios Técnicos en el Exterior (ICETEX), Carrera 3, No 18-24, Apdo Aéreo 5735, Bogotá
Founded: 1950
Focus: Eng; Educ
Periodicals
Boletín desde Colombia (quarterly)
Carta Informativa (semi-annually) 02791

Instituto Colombiano de Cultura, Calle 8, No 6-97, Bogotá
T: (01) 2828596; Fax: 2820854
Founded: 1968
Pres: Liliana Bonilla Otoya
Focus: Lit; Arts 02792

Instituto Colombiano de Cultura Hispánica, Calle 12, No 2-41, Apdo 5454, Bogotá
T: (01) 3413857; Fax: 2811051
Founded: 1951
Pres: William Jaramillo Mejla
Focus: Lit; Hist 02793

Instituto Colombiano de la Reforma Agraria (INCORA), Av El Dorado, Apdo Aéreo 151046, Bogotá
Focus: Agri 02794

Instituto Colombiano de Normas Técnicas (ICONTEC), Carrera 37, No 52-95, Apdo Aéreo 14237, Bogotá
Fax: (01) 2221435
Founded: 1963; Members: 950
Focus: Standards; Eng
Periodicals
Boletín Bibliográfico (quarterly)
Boletín Informativo (monthly)
Normas y Calidades (semi-annually)
Standards (monthly) 02795

Instituto Colombiano de Oncologia Pediatrica / Colombian Institute of Pediatric Oncology, Calle 120, No 8-23, Bogotá
T: 2133067
Founded: 1982; Members: 6
Focus: Cell Biol & Cancer Res; Pediatrics 02796

Instituto Colombiano de Pedagogía (ICOLPE), Carrera 7, No 27-52, Apdo Aéreo 52976, Bogotá
T: (01) 822270
Focus: Educ 02797

Instituto Colombiano para el Fomento de la Educación Superior (ICFES) / Colombian Institute for the Development of Higher Education, Calle 17, No 3-40, Apdo Aéreo 6319, Bogotá
T: (01) 2819311; Fax: 2868045
Founded: 1968; Members: 520
Focus: Educ; Adult Educ
Periodicals
Directorio de la Educación Superior en Colombio (bi-annually)
Educación Superior y Desarrollo (quarterly) 02798

Instituto de Ciencias Naturales (ICN-MHN), Apdo Aéreo 7495, Bogotá
T: (01) 2442387
Founded: 1936; Members: 57
Focus: Nat Sci; Botany; Geology; Zoology
Periodicals
Biblioteca José Jerónimo Triana (irregularly)
Caldasía: Boletín (irregularly)
Catalogo Ilustrado de las Plantas de Cundinamarca (irregularly)
Flora de Colombia (irregularly)
Lozanía: Acta Zoológica Colombiana (irregularly)
Mutisía: Acta Botánica Colombiana (irregularly) 02799

Instituto Nacional de Investigaciones Geológico-Mineras (INGENOMINAS), Diagonal 53, No 34-53, Apdo Aéreo 4865, Bogotá
T: (01) 2125400, 2121811
Founded: 1968; Members: 480
Focus: Geology; Mining 02800

Instituto Nacional de Salud (INPES), Av el Dorado, Carrera 50, Apdo Aéreo 80334, Bogotá
Founded: 1968
Focus: Public Health 02801

Junta Nacional de Folclore, c/o Instituto Caro y Cuervo, Apdo Aéreo 51502, Bogotá
Focus: Ethnology 02802

Liga Colombiana de Lucha Contra el Cancer, Calle 80, No. 5-77, Bogotá
T: (01) 2116981, 2118894, 2118828
Founded: 1961
Focus: Cell Biol & Cancer Res 02803

PEN Club de Colombia, Apdo Aéreo 51748, Bogotá
Founded: 1983; Members: 50
Pres: David Mejía Velilla; Gen Secr: Maruja Vieira
Focus: Lit
Periodical
Noticias del PEN (monthly) 02804

Servicio Interamericana de Geodesía, c/o Instituto Geográfico Augustín Codazzi, Carrera 30, No 48-51, Bogotá
Focus: Surveying 02805

Servicio Nacional de Aprendizaje (SENA), Av Caracas, No 13-88, Apdo Aéreo 9801, Bogotá
T: (01) 832965
Focus: Educ 02806

Sociedad Americana de Oftalmologia y Optometria, Apdo 091019, Bogotá
Focus: Ophthal 02807

Sociedad Antioqueña de Ingenieros y Architectos, Calle 71, No 65-100, Apdo 4754, Medellín
T: (04) 573900
Founded: 1913; Members: 950
Pres: Joel Moreno Santos
Focus: Archit; Eng 02808

Sociedad Bolivariana de Colombia, Calle 19A, No 4-40E, Apdo 11812, Bogotá
T: (01) 2431166
Founded: 1924; Members: 20
Pres: Alberto Lozano
Focus: Hist 02809

Sociedad Colombiana de Biologí, Calle 73, No 10-10, Apdo 301, Bogotá
Founded: 1942; Members: 36
Pres: Dr. Gonzalo Montes; Gen Secr: Margaret Ordóñez-Smith
Focus: Bio 02810

Sociedad Colombiana de Cardiología, Carrera 19, No 80-36, Apdo Aéreo 1875, Bogotá
T: (01) 2191388; Fax: 2191399
Founded: 1950; Members: 245
Pres: Dr. Camilo Roa Amaya; Gen Secr: Dr. Germán Gómez Segura
Focus: Cardiol 02811

Sociedad Colombiana de Cirugía, Calle 97A, No 10-65, Apdo 503, Bogotá
T: (01) 2563007
Founded: 1973; Members: 300
Pres: Dr. Erix Bozon Martinez; Gen Secr: Dr. Jaime Escallón
Focus: Surgery
Periodical
Revista 02812

Sociedad Colombiana de Cirugía Ortopedica y Traumatología, Transv 14, No 126-10, Of 210, Bogotá
T: (01) 6260077; Fax: 615563
Founded: 1959; Members: 640
Pres: Germán Carillo A.
Focus: Surgery; Orthopedics; Traumatology 02813

Sociedad Colombiana de Economistas, Carrera 20, No 36-41, Apdo Aéreo 8429, Bogotá
T: (01) 2459637
Founded: 1957; Members: 5500
Pres: Jorge Valencia Jaramillo; Gen Secr: Luis Alberto Avila
Focus: Econ
Periodical
Revista (bi-monthly) 02814

Sociedad Colombiana de Ingenieros, Carrera 4, No 10-41, Apdo 340, Bogotá
T: (01) 2862200
Founded: 1887; Members: 5000
Pres: Luis E. Laverde Leguizamo
Focus: Eng 02815

Sociedad Colombiana de la Ciencia del Suelo (SCCS), Carrera II, No 66-34, Of 204, Apdo Aéreo 51791, Bogotá
Founded: 1955; Members: 400
Focus: Agri 02816

Sociedad Colombiana de Matemáticas (SCM), Apdo Aéreo 2521, Bogotá
T: (01) 2216829
Founded: 1955; Members: 800
Pres: Victor Samuel Albis Gonzalez
Focus: Math
Periodicals
Lecturas Matematicas (3 times annually)
Revista Colombiana de Matemáticas (quarterly) 02817

Sociedad Colombiana de Obstetricia y Ginecologia (SCOG) / Colombian Society of Obstetrics and Gynecology, Carrera 23, No 39-82, Apdo Aéreo 34188, Bogotá
T: (01) 2681485
Founded: 1943; Members: 300
Pres: Dr. Maria Teresa Ferro Camargo
Focus: Gynecology
Periodical
Revista Colombina de Obstetricia y Ginecologia (bi-monthly) 02818

Sociedad Colombiana de Patología, c/o Dpto de Patología, Universidad del Valle, Cali
Founded: 1955; Members: 155
Pres: Dr. Edgar Duque; Gen Secr: Dr. José A. Dorado
Focus: Pathology 02819

Sociedad Colombiana de Pediatría, Av 4 Norte, No 16-23, Apdo 3124, Cali
T: (02) 611407; Fax: 673614
Founded: 1917; Members: 150
Pres: Cesar A. Villamizar Luna; Gen Secr: Alberto Levy F.
Focus: Pediatrics
Periodical
Pediatría (quarterly) 02820

Sociedad Colombiana de Psiquiatría, Apdo 52053, Bogotá
T: (01) 561148; Fax: 6162706
Founded: 1961; Members: 350
Pres: Dr. Roberto Chaskel; Gen Secr: Dr. Alvaro Franco
Focus: Psychiatry
Periodical
Revista Colombiana de Psiquiatría (quarterly) 02821

Sociedad Colombiana de Químicos e Ingenieros Químicos / Columbian Society of Chemists and Chemical Engineers, Apdo Aéreo 10968, Bogotá
T: (01) 2411480
Founded: 1941; Members: 250
Pres: Francisco Varela A.
Focus: Chem; Eng
Periodical
Química e Industria (quarterly) 02822

Sociedad Colombiana de Radiología, Carrera 13A, No 90-18, Of 208, Bogotá
T: (01) 6183895; Fax: 6183775
Founded: 1945; Members: 400
Pres: Cayo Duarte
Focus: Dent 02823

Sociedad de Antropología de Antioquía, c/o Universidad de Antioquia, Medellín
Founded: 1946
Focus: Anthro 02824

Sociedad de Ciencias Naturales Caldas, Apdo Aéreo 1180, Medellín
Founded: 1938
Gen Secr: Marco A. Serna D.
Focus: Nat Sci 02825

Sociedad de Pediatría y Puericultura del Atlántico, c/o Hospital Infantil San Francisco de Paula, Barranquilla
Founded: 1955
Focus: Pediatrics 02826

Sociedad Geográfica de Colombia, c/o Observatorio Astronómico Nacional, Apdo Nacional 2584, Bogotá
T: (01) 2348893
Founded: 1903; Members: 40
Pres: Clemente Garavito; Gen Secr: Rafael Convers Pinzon
Focus: Geography 02827

Sociedad Jurídica de la Universidad Nacional, c/o Universidad Nacional, Apdo Aéreo 14490, Bogotá
Founded: 1908
Pres: Alvaro Menese S.; Gen Secr: Luis Alberto Patiño
Focus: Law 02828

Unión Nacional de Escritores, Carrera 6, No 10-42, Of 402, Apdo 28846, Bogotá
T: (01) 2439814
Founded: 1980
Pres: Jaime Mejia Dique
Focus: Lit 02829

Congo, Democratic Republic

African Bureau of Educational Sciences, BP 1764, Kinshasa 1
T: (012) 22006
Founded: 1973; Members: 39
Focus: Educ
Periodicals
Annuaire Africain des Sciences de l'Education (3 times annually)
Bulletin d'Information (quarterly)
Répertoire Africain des Institutions de Recherche (annually)
Revue Africaine des Sciences de l'Education (semi-annually) 02830

Association des Institutions d'Enseignement Théologique en Afrique Occidentale (ASTHEOL-WEST), c/o Faculté de Théologie, BP 4745, Kinshasa
Focus: Rel & Theol; Educ 02831

Association Zaïroise des Archivistes, Bibliothécaires et Documentalistes, BP 805, Kinshasa
Founded: 1973
Focus: Archives; Libraries & Bk Sci; Doc 02832

Central African Regional Branch of the International Council on Archives (CENARBICA), c/o Archives Nationales, BP 3428, Kinshasa
T: (012) 31083
Founded: 1982
Focus: Archives 02833

Centrale des Enseignants Zairois (CEZ), BP 8814, Kinshasa
Founded: 1957
Focus: Educ 02834

Centre for the Coordination of Research and Documentation in Social Science for Sub-Saharan Africa / Centre de Coordination des Recherches et de Documentation en Sciences Sociales desservant l'Afrique Sub-Saharienne, BP 836, Kinshasa
T: (012) 27003
Founded: 1974
Focus: Soc Sci
Periodical
CERDAS Liaison (quarterly) 02835

Conférence des Recteurs des Universités Francophones d'Afrique (CRUFA), c/o Présidence des Universités du Zaïre, BP 13399, Kinshasa
T: (012) 78681
Founded: 1978
Focus: Educ 02836

Société des Historiens Zairois, BP 7246, Lubumbashi
Founded: 1974
Pres: Prof. Ndaywel E. Nziem; Gen Secr: Prof. Dr. T.-B.M. Kabet
Focus: Hist
Periodical
Likundoli (semi-annually) 02837

Congo, Republic

Association for Health Information and Libraries in Africa (AHILA), c/o WHO/AFRO, POB 6, Brazzaville
T: 813860
Founded: 1980
Focus: Public Health 02838

PEN Centre de Congo, BP 2181, Brazzaville
T: 813601; Fax: 813601
Pres: E.B. Dongala
Focus: Lit 02839

Union Panafricaine de la Science et de la Technologie, BP 2339, Brazzaville
T: 836535; Fax: 832185
Founded: 1987; Members: 409
Pres: Prof. Edward S. Ayensu
Focus: Sci; Eng 02840

Costa Rica

Academia Costarricense de la Lengua, Paseo de los Estudiantes, Apdo 157-1002, San José
Founded: 1923; Members: 18
Pres: Arturo Aguero Chaves; Gen Secr: Virginia Sandoval de Fonseca
Focus: Ling
Periodical
Boletín 02841

Academia Costarricense de Periodoncia, Apdo 1435, San José
Founded: 1965
Focus: Dent 02842

Academia de Geografía e Historia de Costa Rica, Apdo 4499, San José
Members: 31
Pres: Carlos Meléndez; Gen Secr: Dr. Oscar Aguilar
Focus: Hist
Periodical
Anales 02843

Asociación Costarricense de Bibliotecarios, Apdo 3308, San José
Founded: 1949
Pres: Efraim Rojas R.
Focus: Libraries & Bk Sci 02844

Asociación Costarricense de Cirurgíca, Apdo 548, San José
Founded: 1954; Members: 150
Pres: Dr. Eduardo Flores Montero; Gen Secr: Dr. Luis Morales Alfaro
Focus: Surgery 02845

Asociación Costarricense de Pediatría, Apdo 1654, San José
T: 2216821; Fax: 2216821
Founded: 1951; Members: 250
Pres: Dr. Manuel Soto
Focus: Pediatrics
Periodical
Carta Pediátrica (3 times annually) . . . 02846

Asociación de Cardiología, Apdo 527, Pavas, San José
T: 2220122
Founded: 1978; Members: 36
Pres: Dr. A. Castro Bermúdez
Focus: Cardiol 02847

Asociación de Medicina Interna, c/o Hospital San Juan de Díos, San José
Focus: Intern Med 02848

Asociación de Obstetricia y Ginecología, c/o Hospital San Juan de Díos, San José
Focus: Gynecology 02849

Central American Institute for Business Administration, Apdo 960, Alajuela
T: 412255
Founded: 1961
Focus: Business Admin
Periodical
Revista INCAE (semi-annually) 02850

Central American Institute of Public Administration, Edificio Schyfter, Av Central y Calle 2, Apdo 10025, San José
T: 223133
Founded: 1954
Focus: Public Admin
Periodical
Revista Centroamericana de Administración Pública (semi-annually) 02851

Central American Institute of Social Studies, Coronado 2200, Apdo 75, San José
T: 290152; Fax: 293077
Founded: 1964
Focus: Soc Sci 02852

Central American, Mexican and Caribbean Network for Bean Research, c/o PROFRIJOL, Coronado 2200, Apdo 55, San José
T: 294741
Founded: 1978
Focus: Crop Husb 02853

Central American University Confederation, Ciudad Universitaria Rodrigo Facio, Apdo 37, San José
T: 252744; Fax: 220478
Founded: 1948; Members: 7
Focus: Educ
Periodicals
Carta Informativa de la Secretaría General (monthly)
Cuadernos de Investigación (monthly)
Estadísticas Universitarias (semi-annually) 02854

Comisión de Energía Atómica de Costa Rica, Calle 5, No 555, Apdo 6681, San José
T: 2241591; Fax: 2241293
Founded: 1969
Pres: Enrique Góngora Trejos
Focus: Energy 02855

Confederación Centroamericana de Medicina del Deporte / Central American Federation of Sports Medicine, Apdo 172, Heredía 3000
Founded: 1986; Members: 7
Focus: Med 02856

Consejo Superior Universitario Centroemericano (CSUCA), Ciudad Universitaria Rodrigo Facio, Apdo 37, San José
T: 252744
Founded: 1948
Focus: Adult Educ; Sci 02857

Instituto Centroamericano de Administración Pública (ICAP), Apdo 10025, San José
T: 223133
Founded: 1954
Focus: Poli Sci; Public Admin; Develop Areas
Periodical
Central American Journal of Public Administration (semi-annually) 02858

Instituto Centroamericano de Extensión de la Cultura (ICECU), Apdo 2948, 1000 San José
Founded: 1963
Focus: Educ
Periodical
Libro Almanaque Escuela para Todos (annually) 02859

Instituto Interamericano de Cooperación para la Agricultura (IICA) / Inter-American Institute for Cooperation on Agriculture, Coronado 2200, Apdo 55, San José
T: 290222; E-Mail: IICA San José
Founded: 1942
Focus: Agri
Periodicals
Desarrollo Rural en las Américas (quarterly)
Turrialba (quarterly) 02860

Instituto Latinoamericano de las Naciones Unidas para la Prevención del Delito y Tratamiento del Delincuente, Apdo 10338, San José
Founded: 1975
Focus: Law 02861

Inter-American Association of Agricultural Librarians and Documentalists, c/o Centro de Enseñanza e Investigación, Catie 7170, Turrialba
Founded: 1953
Focus: Libraries & Bk Sci; Doc
Periodicals
AIBDA Actualidades (irregularly)
Boletín Especial (irregularly)
Boletín Informativo de AIBDA (quarterly)
Páginas de Contenido: Ciencias de la Información (quarterly)
Revista AIBDA 02862

Junta Nacional de Planeamiento Económico, c/o Consejo Nacional de Producción, San José
Focus: Econ 02863

Organización de Estudios Tropicales, Apdo 676-2050, San Pedro
T: 2406696; Fax: 406783
Founded: 1963
Pres: Charles E. Schnell
Focus: Geography 02864

Croatia

Croatian Geographic Society, Marulićev trg 19, 41000 Zagreb
T: (01) 446728
Founded: 1897; Members: 600
Pres: Dr. Zlatko Pepeonik
Focus: Geography 02865

Croatian Medical Association, Šubićeva ul 9, 41000 Zagreb
T: (01) 416820; Fax: 416820
Founded: 1874; Members: 8500
Pres: Prof. Dr. Ante Dražančić; Gen Secr: Prof. Dr. Ivan Bakran
Focus: Med 02866

Croatian Pharmaceutical Society, Masarykova 2, 41000 Zagreb
T: (01) 427944; Fax: 431301
Founded: 1945; Members: 1040
Pres: K. Rukavina
Focus: Pharmacol 02867

Društvo Ekonomista Hrvatske / Economists' Society of Croatia, Berislavićeva 6, 41000 Zagreb
T: (01) 445206
Focus: Econ 02868

Drustvo za Proučavanje i Unapredenje Pomorstva / Society for Research and Promotion of Maritime Sciences, Rade Končara 44, POB 391, Rijeka
Founded: 1962; Members: 323
Pres: B. Pecotić; Gen Secr: Dr. D. Crnković
Focus: Navig; Oceanography
Periodical
Pomorski Zbornik: Maritime Annals (annually) 02869

Hrvatska Akademija Znanosti i Umjetnosti / Croatian Academy of Sciences and Arts, Zrinski trg 11, 41000 Zagreb
T: (01) 433661; Fax: 433383
Founded: 1866; Members: 164
Pres: Dr.Ivan Super; Gen Secr: Dr. M. Moguš
Focus: Sci; Arts
Periodicals
Bulletin International Starine
Ljetopis (annually)
Rad 02870

Hrvatsko Bibliotekarsko Društvo / Croatian Library Association, Marulićev trg 21, 41000 Zagreb
T: (01) 446322; Fax: 426676
Founded: 1948; Members: 820
Pres: D. Kunštek; Gen Secr: Dunja Gabrijel
Focus: Libraries & Bk Sci
Periodical
Vjesnik Bibliotekara Hrvatske (quarterly) . 02871

Hrvatsko Muzejsko Drustvo, Habdelićeva 2, 41000 Zagreb
T: (01) 431404
Founded: 1945; Members: 500
Pres: Nada Vrkljan-Križić
Focus: Arts 02872

Hrvatsko Numizmatičko Društvo (HND) / Croatian Numismatic Society, Habdeliceva 2, POB 181, 41000 Zagreb
T: (01) 431426
Founded: 1928; Members: 500
Pres: E. Fabry
Focus: Numismatics
Periodicals
Numizmatičke vijesti
Numizmatika
Obol 02873

Hrvatsko Prirodoslovno Društvo / Croatian Society of Natural Sciences, Ilica 16, 41000 Zagreb
T: (01) 425288
Founded: 1885; Members: 30000
Pres: Dr. Vlatko Silobrčić; Gen Secr: Dr. Damir Kralj
Focus: Nat Sci
Periodicals
Periodicum Biologorum (quarterly)
Priroda (monthly) 02874

Pedagoško-Književni zbor, Savez Pedagoških Društava Hrvatske, Trg Maršala Tita 4, 41000 Zagreb
T: (01) 420601
Founded: 1871; Members: 3000
Pres: H. Vrgoč; Gen Secr: A. Bikić
Focus: Educ 02875

Union of the Societies of Engineers and Technicians of Croatia, Berislavićeva 6, 41000 Zagreb
Founded: 1970; Members: 3017
Pres: Prof. Dr. E. Nonveiller
Focus: Psychiatry 02876

Cuba

Academia Cubana de la Lengua, Av 19, No. 502, Vedado, La Habana
Founded: 1926
Pres: Dr. Dulce M. Loynaz; Gen Secr: Dr. Delio Carreras
Focus: Ling 02877

Academia de Ciencias de Cuba, Capitolio Nacional, La Habana 10200
T: (07) 626606; Fax: 338054
Founded: 1962
Pres: Prof. Dr. Rosa Elena Simeón Negrin
Focus: Sci 02878

Asociación Latinoamericana de Micología, c/o Jardín Botánica Nacional, Carretesa del Roci0 km 3 1/2, Calabazar, La Habana
Founded: 1990
Focus: Botany 02879

Ateneo de La Habana, Av 5, No 608, Vedado, La Habana
Founded: 1902
Pres: Dr. José M. Chacón y Calvo; Gen Secr: Dr. José Enrique Heymann y de la Gándara
Focus: Educ 02880

Casa de las Américas, Calle 3 Esq a G., El Vedado, La Habana 10400
T: (07) 323587; Fax: 334554
Founded: 1959
Pres: Roberto Fernández Retamar
Focus: Cultur Hist 02881

Centro de Investigación Forestal / Forest Research Center, Calle 174, No. 1723, 17-B y 17-C, Siboney, La Habana
Founded: 1969; Members: 418
Focus: Forestry
Periodical
Revista Foresta Baracoa (semi-annually) . 02882

Centro de Investigaciones Pesqueras, Av 1 y 26, Miramar, Marianao, La Habana
Founded: 1959
Focus: Agri 02883

Centro Nacional de Información de Ciencias Médicas, Calle 23, No. 177, entre N y O, Vedado, La Habana
Focus: Med 02884

Centro Nacional de Investigaciones Científicas (CNIC), Av 25, Calle 158, Reparto Cubanacán, Apdo 6990, La Habana
Founded: 1964
Focus: Bio; Chem; Physics
Periodicals
Revista de Ciencias Biológicas (annually)
Revista de Ciencias Químicas (annually) 02885

Consejo Nacional de Tuberculosis Paulina Aldina, Calzada de Colombia y Octava, Marianao, La Habana
Founded: 1946
Focus: Pulmon Dis 02886

Consejo Nacional de Universidades, c/o Ministerio de Educación Superior, Ciudad Libertad, La Habana
Founded: 1960
Pres: José Ramón Fernández; Gen Secr: Miguel Marrero Vallet
Focus: Educ 02887

Grupo Nacional de Radiología, c/o Ministerio de Salud Pública, 23 y N, Vedado, La Habana
Founded: 1968
Focus: Radiology 02888

Sociedad Cubana de Hipnosis, CP 6773, La Habana 10600
T: (07) 791410; Fax: 8686150
Founded: 1986; Members: 300
Pres: Dr. B. Martínez Perigod; Gen Secr: Dr. M. Asís
Focus: Psych 02889

Sociedad Cubana de Historia de la Ciencia y de la Técnica, Cuba 460, La Habana
Founded: 1967
Focus: Nat Sci; Eng 02890

Sociedad Cubana de Historia de la Medicina, Calle 4, No 407, E/ 17 y 19, La Habana
Pres: Dr. Rafael O. Pedraza; Gen Secr: Dr. A.R. Guzmán
Focus: Med; Cultur Hist 02891

Sociedad Cubana de Ingenieros, Av de Bélgica 258, La Habana
Founded: 1908; Members: 500
Pres: Gustavo Sterling; Gen Secr: Honrato Colete
Focus: Eng 02892

Sociedad Cubana de Radiología, Calle L 406 esq 23 y N, Vedado, La Habana, 10400
Founded: 1968
Pres: Prof. Dr. Carlus Ugarte; Gen Secr: Prof. Dr. Jorge Banasco
Focus: Radiology 02893

Sociedad Económica de Amigos del País, Av Salvador Allende 710, La Habana
Founded: 1928
Focus: Econ 02894

Unión de Escritores y Artistas de Cuba, Calle 17, No. 351, Vedado, La Habana
Founded: 1961; Members: 66
Focus: Arts; Lit 02895

Cyprus

Association of Sports Medicine of the Balkan (ASMB), POB 5137, Nicosia
T: (02) 455762; Fax: 464355
Founded: 1967
Focus: Med 02896

Cyprus Astronautical Society, POB 3332, Limassol
Focus: Aero 02897

Cyprus Bibliophiles Association, POB 1722, Nicosia
Focus: Libraries & Bk Sci 02898

Cyprus Civil Engineers and Architects Association, Zena de Tyras Palace, POB 1825, Nicosia
T: (02) 41221
Founded: 1950; Members: 400
Focus: Archit 02899

Cyprus Economic Association, POB 1632, Nicosia
Focus: Econ 02900

Cyprus Geographical Association (CGA), POB 3656, Nicosia
T: (02) 463205
Founded: 1968; Members: 200
Pres: Andreas Sophocleous; Gen Secr: Andreas Christodoulou
Focus: Geography
Periodical
The Geographical Chronicles (annually) . 02901

Cyprus Joint Technical Council, POB 1825, Nicosia
Focus: Eng 02902

Cyprus Numismatic Society (CNS), POB 3703, Nicosia
T: (02) 336241; Fax: 337879
Founded: 1970; Members: 250
Pres: Andreas G. Pitsillides; Gen Secr: Antonios Apostolides
Focus: Numismatics
Periodical
Numismatic Report (annually) 02903

Cyprus Ophthalmological Society, POB 406, Larnaca
T: (04) 631011; Fax: 631370
Founded: 1970; Members: 45
Focus: Ophthal 02904

Cyprus Photogrammetric Society, G. Christoferou 9, Nicosia 112
Focus: Surveying 02905

Cyprus Research Centre / Kentron Epistemonikon Erevnon, POB 1952, Nicosia
Founded: 1967
Pres: Dr. Costas Yiangoullis
Focus: Hist; Sociology
Periodicals
Epeteris (annually)
Publications
Texts and Studies of the History of Cyprus
. . . . 02906

Etaireia Kypriakon Spoudon / Society of Cypriot Studies, POB 1436, Nicosia
T: (02) 463205
Founded: 1936; Members: 250
Pres: Dr. Kypros Chrysanthis; Gen Secr: A. Spyridakis
Focus: Archeol; Hist; Ethnology; Ling
Periodical
Deltion: Bulletin (annually) 02907

Library Association of Cyprus, POB 1039, Nicosia
Founded: 1962; Members: 45
Pres: Costas D. Stephanou; Gen Secr: P.G. Rossos
Focus: Libraries & Bk Sci 02908

Pancyprian Medical Association, Zena de Tyras Palace, Nicosia
Focus: Med 02909

Czech Republic

Asociace Hudebních Umělcu a Vedcu, Maltézské nám 1, 118 01 Praha 1
T: (02) 533661
Founded: 1990; Members: 1200
Pres: L. Sluka
Focus: Music 02910

Česká Akademie Věd (ČSAV) / Czech Academy of Sciences, Národní tř 3, 111 42 Praha 1
T: (02) 24220384; Fax: 24240531
Founded: 1952; Members: 412
Pres: Prof. R. Zahradnik; Gen Secr: L. Kopriva
Focus: Sci
Periodicals
Acta Entomologica Bohemoslovaca (bi-monthly)
Acta Technica (bi-monthly)
Acta Virologica (bi-monthly)
Aplikace matematiky (bi-monthly)
Archeologické rozhledy (bi-monthly)
Archiv orientální (quarterly)
Biologia Plantarum (bi-monthly)
Biologické listy (quarterly)
Bulletin of the Czech Astronomical Institute (bi-monthly)
Byzantinoslavica (semi-annually)
Časopis pro mineralogii a geologii (quarterly)
Časopis pro pěestování matematiky (quarterly)
Česká fysiologie (bi-monthly)
Česká literatura (bi-monthly)
Česká mykologie (quarterly)
Česká psychologie (bi-monthly)
Česká rusistika (5 times annually)
Český časopis historický (bi-monthly)
Český časopis pro fyziku (bi-monthly)
Český lid (quarterly)
Chemické listy (monthly)
Collection of Czech Chemical Publications (monthly)
Czech Journal of Physics (monthly)
Czech Mathematical Journal (quarterly)
Dějiny věd a techniky (quarterly)
Ekonomicko-matematicky obzor (quarterly)
Estetika (quarterly)
Filozofický časopis (bi-monthly)
Folia Biologica (bi-monthly)
Folia Geobotanica e Phytotaxonomica (quarterly)
Folia Microbiologica (bi-monthly)
Folia Morphologica (quarterly)
Folia Parasitologica (quarterly)
Folia Zoologica (quarterly)
Hudební věda (quarterly)
Kybernetika (bi-monthly)
Lidé a země (monthly)
Listy filologické (quarterly)
Naše řeč (5 times annually)
Nový orient (10 times annually)
Památky archeologické (semi-annually)
Pedagogika (bi-monthly)
Philologica Pragensia (quarterly)
Photosynthetica (quarterly)
Physiologia Bohemoslovaca (bi-monthly)
Pokroky matematiky, fyziky a astronomie (bi-monthly)
Politická ekonomie (monthly)
Právník (monthly)
Preslia (quarterly) 02911

Česká Akademie Zemědělských Věd, Těšnov 65, 117 05 Praha 1
T: (02) 2320582; Fax: 2328898
Founded: 1924; Members: 179
Focus: Agri
Periodicals
Agricultural Literature (quarterly)
Lesnictví (monthly)
Metodiky pro Zavádění Výzkumu do Praxe (monthly)
Přehled Lesnické a Myslivecké literatury (monthly)
Rostlinná Vároba (monthly)
Scientia Agriculturae Bohemoslovaca (quarterly)
Zemědělská Ekonomika (monthly)
Zemědělská Informatika (monthly)
Zemědělská Technika (monthly)
Živočišná Výroba (monthly) 02912

Česká Archeologická Společnost (ČAS) / Czech Archaeological Society, Letenská 4, 118 01 Praha 1
T: (02) 57320942
Founded: 1919; Members: 550
Pres: Karel Sklenář; Gen Secr: P. Vařeka
Focus: Archeol
Periodical
Zprávy ČAS: ČAS News (irregularly) . 02913

Česká Astronomická Společnost, Královská obora 233, 170 00 Praha 7
T: (02) 370840
Founded: 1917; Members: 700
Pres: Dr. J. Grygar
Focus: Astronomy 02914

Česká Biologicka Společnost, Joštova 10, 662 43 Brno
T: (05) 42126268; Fax: 42126200
Founded: 1922; Members: 1550
Pres: Prof. O. Nečas; Gen Secr: Prof. R. Janisch
Focus: Bio 02915

Česká Botanická Společnost, Benátská 2, 128 01 Praha 2
T: (02) 21953117; E-Mail: botspol@ prfdee.natur.cuni.cz
Founded: 1912; Members: 980

Pres: Dr. J. Holub; Gen Secr: Dr. L. Hrouda
Focus: Botany
Periodicals
Preslia (quarterly)
Zprávy ČSBS (semi-annually) 02916

Česká Demografická Společnost, W. Churchilla nám 4, 130 67 Praha 3
Founded: 1964; Members: 450
Pres: Z. Pavlik
Focus: Soc Sci 02917

Česká Geografická Společnost, Oldřichova 19, 128 00 Praha 2
Founded: 1894; Members: 805
Pres: Prof. I. Bičik; Gen Secr: Dr. D. Drbohlav
Focus: Geography
Periodical
Sborník: Journal (quarterly) 02918

Česká Geologická Společnost / Czech Geological Society, Holešovičkách 41, 182 09 Praha 8
T: (02) 66009323; Fax: 66410649
Founded: 1923; Members: 920
Pres: Dr. F. Veselovský
Focus: Mineralogy; Geology
Periodical
Journal of the Czech Geological Society (quarterly) 02919

Česká Hudební Společnost, Janáčkovo 59, 150 00 Praha 5
T: (02) 530868
Founded: 1973; Members: 5000
Pres: M. Smetáčkova
Focus: Sci 02920

Česká Imunologická Společnost, Vídeňská 1083, 142 20 Praha 4
T: (02) 4719740; Fax: 4713221
Founded: 1986; Members: 500
Pres: Prof. Dr. Jaroslav Šterzi
Focus: Immunology 02921

Česká Komise pro UNESCO, Hradčanské nám 5, 118 00 Praha 1
T: (02) 24310542; Fax: 24310543
Focus: Arts; Cultur Hist 02922

Česká Lékařská Společnost J.E. Purkyně / Czech Medical Association J.E. Purkyně, Sokolská 31, 120 26 Praha 2
T: (02) 24915195; Fax: 24216836
Founded: 1947; Members: 35000
Pres: Prof. Jaroslav Blahoš
Focus: Med
Periodicals
Anesteziologie a neodkladná péče: Anaesthesiology and Emergency Care (bi-monthly)
Časopis lékařu českých: Czech Medical Journal (bi-weekly)
Central European Journal of Public Health (quarterly)
Česká revmatologie: Czech Rheumatology (quarterly)
Česko-slovenská dermatologie: Czecho-Slovak Dermatology (quarterly)
Česko-slovenská epidemiologie, mikrobiologie, immunologie: Czecho-Slovak Epidemiology, Microbiology, Immunology (quarterly)
Česko-slovenská farmacie: Czecho-Slovak Pharmacy (bi-monthly)
Česko-slovenská gastroenterologie a výživa: Czecho-Slovak Gastroenterology and Nutrition (bi-monthly)
Česko-Slovenská gynekologie: Czecho-Slovak Gynaecology (bi-monthly)
Česko-Slovenská hygiena: Czecho-Slovak Hygiene (bi-monthly)
Česko-Slovenská neurologie a neurochirurgie: Czecho-Slovak Neurology and Neurosurgery (bi-monthly)
Česko-slovenská oftalmologie: Czecho-Slovak Ophthalmology (bi-monthly)
Česko-Slovenská otolaryngologie a foniatrie: Czecho-Slovak Otorhinolaryngology and Phoniatrics (quarterly)
Česko-slovenská patologie s přílohou Soudní lékařství: Czecho-Slovak Pathology with Supplement on Forensic Medicine (quarterly)
Česko-Slovenská pediatrie: Czecho-Slovak Paediatrics (monthly)
Česko-Slovenská psychiatrie: Czecho-Slovak Psychiatry (bi-monthly)
Česko-Slovenská radiologie: Czecho-Slovak Radiology (quarterly)
Česko-Slovenská stomatologie: Czecho-Slovak Stomatology (bi-monthly)
Československá fyziologie: Czecho-Slovak Physiology (quarterly)
Klinická biochemie a metabolismus: Clinical Biochemistry and Metabolism (quarterly)
Klinická onkologie: Clinical Oncology (bi-monthly)
Lékař a technika: Biomedical Engineering (bi-monthly)
Pracovní lékařství: Occupational Medicine (bi-monthly)
Praktické zubní lékařství: General Dentistry (bi-monthly)
Praktický lékař: General Practitioner (bi-weekly)
Rozhledy v chirurgii: Surgical Review (8 times annually)
Vnitřní lékařství: Internal Medicine (monthly) 02923

Česká Meteorologická Společnost, Šabatce 17, 143 06 Praha
T: (02) 85762548

Founded: 1958; Members: 230
Pres: Dr. Jan Bednar
Focus: Geophys 02924

Česká Oftalmologická Společnost (ČOS) / Czech Society of Ophthalmology, c/o Eye Dept, Vinohrady Hospital, Srobarova 50, 100 34 Praha 10
T: (02) 67162390; E-Mail: kuchynka@mbox.vol.cz; Fax: 67162491
Founded: 1926; Members: 850
Pres: Prof. Pavel Kuchynka; Gen Secr: Michal Janek
Focus: Ophthal
Periodical
Česká a Slovenská oftalmologie (bi-monthly)
. . . . 02925

Česká Parazitologická Společnost / Czech Society of Parasitology, Viničná 7, 128 44 Praha 2
T: (02) 21953206; E-Mail: horak@mail.natur.cuni.cz; Fax: 299713
Founded: 1993; Members: 170
Pres: Prof. Dr. Jaroslav Kulda; Gen Secr: Dr. Petr Horák
Focus: Biochem
Periodical
Zprávy České Parazitologické Společnosti (quarterly) 02926

Česká Pedagogická Společnost / Czech Society for Education, Poříčí 31, 603 00 Brno
T: (05) 320211; Fax: 33545416
Founded: 1964; Members: 500
Pres: Prof. Dr. B. Bližkovský
Focus: Educ
Periodical
Bulletin for Members (semi-annually) . . 02927

Česká Psychologická Společnost / Czech Psychological Association, U háje 12/268, 147 00 Praha 4
T: (02) 462568
Founded: 1927; Members: 2700
Pres: Prof. Dr. K. Pavlica; Gen Secr: Prof. Dr. E. Bedrnová
Focus: Psych 02928

Česká Radiologická Společnost / Czech Radiological Society, c/o Clinic for Diagnostic Radiology, Budínova 2, 180 81 Praha 8
T: (02) 822431
Founded: 1934; Members: 100
Pres: Prof. Dr. Luboš Vyhnánek; Gen Secr: Prof. Dr. Jaromír Kolář
Focus: Radiology
Periodical
Česká radiologie (bi-monthly) 02929

Česká Společnost Antropologická, Salmovská 5, 120 00 Praha 2
T: (02) 298323
Founded: 1964; Members: 180
Pres: Dr. J. Jelínek
Focus: Anthro 02930

Česká Společnost Bioklimatologická (ČSBKS) / Czech Society of Bioclimatology, Bočni II 1401, 141 31 Praha 4
T: (02) 67103321; Fax: 761549
Founded: 1965; Members: 140
Pres: Dr. V. Krečmer; Gen Secr: Dr. V. Pasák
Focus: Bio
Periodical
Zypravodaj (annually) 02931

Česká Společnost Chemická / Czech Chemical Society, Ul Pelléova 24, 160 00 Praha 6
T: (02) 329265; Fax: 329265
Founded: 1866; Members: 2350
Pres: Prof. Dr. J. Horák
Focus: Chem
Periodical
Chemické Listy (monthly) 02932

Česká Společnost Ekonomická / Czech Economic Association, Politických Vězňu 11, 110 00 Praha 1
T: (02) 24210571
Founded: 1962; Members: 600
Gen Secr: Pavel Kysilka
Focus: Econ 02933

Česká Společnost Entomologická / Czech Entomological Society, Viničná 7, 128 00 Praha 2
T: (02) 298726
Founded: 1904; Members: 1300
Pres: Dr. Ivan Hrdy; Gen Secr: Dr. Ivo Novak
Focus: Entomology
Periodical
European Journal of Entomology: Klapalekiana (quarterly) 02934

Česká Společnost Histo- a Cytochemnická / Czech Society for Histochemistry and Cytochemistry, Studničkova 2, 120 00 Praha 2
T: (02) 291751
Founded: 1962; Members: 210
Pres: Prof. Dr. Z. Lojda; Gen Secr: Dr. I. Juliš
Focus: Chem
Periodical
Proceedings (annually) 02935

Česká Společnost Mikrobiologická (CSM) / Czech Society for Microbiology, Vídeňská 1083, 142 20 Praha 4
T: (02) 4752494; Fax: 4713221
Founded: 1928; Members: 1000

Pres: Prof. Libor Ebringer; Gen Secr: Dr. F. Kunc
Focus: Microbio
Periodicals
Bulletin České Společnosti Mikrobiologicke (quarterly)
Folia Microbiologica (bi-monthly) 02936

Česká Společnost pro Biomechaniku, Prosecká 74, 190 00 Praha 9
T: (02) 884189 ext 273; Fax: 884634
Founded: 1990; Members: 150
Pres: V. Kafka
Focus: Bio 02937

Česká Společnost pro Mechaniku / Czech Society for Mechanics, Dolejškova 5, 182 00 Praha 8
T: (02) 8587784; E-Mail: csm@bivoj.it.cas.cz; Fax: 8587784
Founded: 1966; Members: 634
Pres: Prof. Dr. Ladislav Frýba; Gen Secr: Dr. Miloslav Okrouhlik
Focus: Mach Eng
Periodical
Bulletin (3 times annually) 02938

Česká Společnost pro Mezinárodní Právo, Národni tř 18, 116 91 Praha 1
T: (02) 24912258; Fax: 24910495
Founded: 1969; Members: 96
Pres: Dr. V. Mikulka
Focus: Law 02939

Česká Společnost pro Politické Vědy / Czech Society for Political Sciences, Nam W. Churchilla 4, 137 60 Praha 3
T: (02) 24095204; Fax: 24220657
Founded: 1964; Members: 173
Pres: Prof. Jan Škaloud; Gen Secr: V. Prorok
Focus: Poli Sci 02940

Česká Společnost pro Vědy Zemědělské, Lesnické, Veterinárni a Potravinářské / Czech Society for Agriculture, Veterinary Sciences and Food Technology, Suchdol VŠZ, 160 21 Praha 6
T: (02) 323640
Founded: 1968; Members: 750
Pres: Prof. F. Hron; Gen Secr: Dr. M. Valla
Focus: Agri
Periodical
Informační Zpravodaj (annually) 02941

Česká Společnost Zoologická / Czech Zoological Society, Viničná 7, 128 44 Praha 2
T: (02) 294606
Founded: 1927; Members: 500
Pres: Dr. I. Heraň; Gen Secr: Dr. K. Absolon
Focus: Zoology
Periodical
Věstník České Společnosti Zoologické (quarterly)
. . . . 02942

Česká Vědecká Společnost pro Mykologii / Czech Society for Mycology, POB 106, 111 21 Praha 1
T: (02) 24497259
Founded: 1946; Members: 220
Pres: Dr. Z. Pouzar; Gen Secr: Dr. Alena Kubátová
Focus: Botany, Specific
Periodical
Česká Mykologie: Czech Mycology (quarterly)
. . . . 02943

Český Esperantský Svaz, Jilská 10, 110 01 Praha 1
T: (02) 220262
Focus: Ling 02944

Český Filmový a Televizní Svaz, Pod Nuselskými schody 3, 120 00 Praha 2
T: (02) 6910310; Fax: 6911375
Founded: 1966; Members: 810
Pres: Martin Skyba
Focus: Cinema; Mass Media 02945

Český Spolek pro Komorní Hudbu, c/o Česka Filharmonie Rudolfinum, Palachovo nám 5, 110 00 Praha 5
Founded: 1894; Members: 3500
Focus: Music 02946

Český Svaz Vědeckotechnických Společností, Novotného lávka 5, 116 68 Praha 1
T: (02) 21082295; Fax: 24227836
Founded: 1990
Pres: Dr. Z. Trojan
Focus: Sci; Eng 02947

Czech Anatomical Society, U Nemocnice 3, 128 00 Praha 2
T: (02) 24915003; Fax: 297692
Founded: 1954; Members: 100
Pres: Prof. Dr. Pavel Petrovický; Gen Secr: Prof. Josef Stingl
Focus: Anat 02948

Czech Centre of International PEN, Valdšteinké nám 5, 118 00 Praha 1
Founded: 1925; Members: 165
Pres: J. Mucha
Focus: Lit 02949

Divadelní Obec, Valdšteinské nám 3, 118 00 Praha 1
T: (02) 539257
Founded: 1990; Members: 1000
Pres: B. Srba
Focus: Perf Arts 02950

Divadelní Ustav, Celetná 17, 110 01 Praha 1
T: (02) 24812754; Fax: 2326100
Founded: 1956
Pres: Helena Albertová
Focus: Perf Arts 02951

Jednota Českých Matematiků a Fysiků / Union of Czech Mathematicians and Physicists, Žitná 25, 117 10 Praha 1
T: (02) 24230877; Fax: 24227633
Founded: 1862; Members: 2700
Pres: S. Zajac
Focus: Math; Physics
Periodical
Pokroky matematiky, fyziky a astronomie (bi-monthly) 02952

Literárněvědná Společnost / Literary Society, Valentinská 1, 110 00 Praha 1
T: (02) 2320167
Founded: 1934; Members: 285
Pres: Dr. S. Wollman; Gen Secr: J. Vlášek
Focus: Lit 02953

Masarykova Česká Sociologická Společnost / Masaryk's Czech Sociological Association, Husova 4, 110 00 Praha 1
T: (02) 24220997
Founded: 1964; Members: 548
Pres: Dr. J. Šiklová
Focus: Sociology 02954

Matice Moravská, Gorkého 14, 602 00 Brno
T: (05) 750050; Fax: 753050
Founded: 1849; Members: 560
Pres: Prof. Dr. Jan Janák; Gen Secr: J. Malir
Focus: Hist; Lit
Periodical
Časopis Matice moravské (semi-annually) 02955

Národopisná Společnost, Národní třída 3, 111 42 Praha 1
T: (02) 65152331; Fax: 65155212
Founded: 1893; Members: 270
Pres: Jiřina Veselská; Gen Secr: Dr. Helena Mevaldová
Focus: Ethnology 02956

Obec Architektů / The Society of Czech Architects, Letenská 5, 118 45 Praha 1
T: (02) 57321068; Fax: 3114926
Founded: 1990; Members: 1200
Pres: Jiří Mojžíš; Gen Secr: Karel Dušek
Focus: Archit 02957

Obec Spisovatelu, Narodni 11, 111 47 Praha 1
T: (02) 2358388
Pres: Dr. Milan Jungmann
Focus: Lit 02958

Spektroskopická Společnost Jana Marca Marci / Jana Marca Marci Spectroscopic Society, Thákurova 7, 166 29 Praha 6
T: (02) 3112343; Fax: 3112343
Founded: 1967; Members: 928
Pres: Prof. Karel Volka; Gen Secr: Pavla Vampolová
Focus: Physics; Chem
Periodical
Bulletin Spektroskopické Společnosti Jana Marca Marci 02959

Společnost pro Dějiny Věd a Techniky, Podbabská 13, 166 12 Praha 6
T: (02) 341486
Founded: 1965; Members: 350
Pres: Dr. P. Drábek
Focus: Hist; Sci; Eng 02960

Společnost pro Estetiku, Husová 4, 110 00 Praha 1
T: (02) 24229436
Founded: 1969
Pres: Dr. V. Svatoň
Focus: Arts 02961

Unie Výtvarných Umělcu, Masarykovo nábr 250, 110 00 Praha 1
T: (02) 292215; Fax: 292442
Founded: 1990; Members: 3000
Pres: Jaroslav Zapletal
Focus: Arts 02962

Vědecká Společnost pro Nauku o Kovech / Society for Metal Science, Žižkova 22, 616 62 Brno
T: (05) 7268417; Fax: 41212301
Founded: 1966; Members: 190
Pres: V. Cihal
Focus: Metallurgy 02963

Denmark

Akademiet for de Tekniske Videnskaber (ATV) / Danish Academy of Technical Sciences, Lundtoftevej 266, 2800 Lyngby
T: 42881311; Fax: 45931377
Founded: 1937; Members: 615
Pres: Prof. Dr. Jens R. Rostrup-Nielsen; Gen Secr: Vibeke Q. Zeuthen
Focus: Eng
Periodicals
Report, DK-edition (annually)
Report, UK-edition (annually) 02964

Almindelige Danske Laegeforening, Trondhjemsgade 9, 2100 København Ø
T: 31385500; Fax: 31426678
Founded: 1857; Members: 18000
Pres: J. Reedtz Funder
Focus: Med 02965

Arktisk Institut / Arctic Institute, Strandgade 100h, 1401 København K
T: 32880150; Fax: 32880151
Founded: 1954
Pres: C.C. Resting-Jeppesen; Gen Secr: Jens S. Fabricius
Focus: Geography
Periodical
Acta Arctica 02966

Association of European Cancer Leagues (ECL), c/o Danish Cancer Society, Rosenvaengets Hovedvej 35, 2100 København
T: 31268866; Fax: 31264560
Founded: 1980
Focus: Intern Med 02967

Billedkunstnernes Forbund, Vingrådstraede 21, 1070 København K
T: 33128170
Members: 1000
Pres: Jane Ring
Focus: Arts 02968

Biologisk Selskab / Danish Biological Society, c/o Dept of Cell Biology and Anatomy, Institute of Zoology, Universitetsparken 15, 2100 København
T: 35321227; Fax: 35321200
Founded: 1896; Members: 670
Pres: Michael G. Palmgren; Gen Secr: Cornelis Grimmelikhuijzen
Focus: Bio 02969

Byggecentrum / Building Centre, Dr. Neergaards Vej 15, 2970 Hørsholm
T: 45767373; E-Mail: byggec@byggecentrum.dk; Fax: 45767669
Founded: 1956
Gen Secr: Jørn Vibe Andreasen
Focus: Urban Plan; Archit 02970

Chakoten Dansk Militaershistorisk Selskab, Violvej 36, 3500 Vaerløse
T: 44484342
Founded: 1944; Members: 250
Pres: Hans Chr. Wolter
Focus: Military Sci; Hist
Periodical
Chakoten (quarterly) 02971

Danish Cancer Society, Strandboulevarden 49, 2100 København Ø
T: 35257500; Fax: 35257701
Founded: 1928; Members: 366509
Focus: Cell Biol & Cancer Res 02972

Danks Biblioteks Center, Tempovej 7-11, 2750 Ballerup
T: 44867777; Fax: 44867891
Founded: 1991
Focus: Libraries & Bk Sci 02973

Danmarks Biblioteksforening (DB) / Danish Library Association, Telegrafvej 5, 2750 Ballerup
T: 44681466; Fax: 44681103
Founded: 1905; Members: 2117
Pres: Mogens Damm; Gen Secr: Jens Thorhauge
Focus: Libraries & Bk Sci
Periodicals
Biblioteksvejviser: Library Directory (annually)
Bogens Verden: Periodical on Culture and Librarianship (bi-monthly)
Danmarks Biblioteker: Newsletter from D.L.A. (10 times annually) 02974

Danmarks Farmaceutiske Selskab / The Pharmaceutical Society of Denmark, Universitetsparken 2, 2100 København Ø
T: 31370850
Founded: 1912; Members: 765
Pres: Prof. Ebba Holme Hansen; Gen Secr: Jens Overø
Focus: Pharmacol 02975

Danmarks Forskningsbiblioteksforening / Danish Research Library Association, c/o Odense Universitetsbibliotek, Campusvej 55, 5239 Odense
T: 66156768; Fax: 66158162
Founded: 1978; Members: 140
Pres: Mette Stockmarr
Focus: Libraries & Bk Sci
Periodical
DF-Revy 02976

Danmarks Jordbrugsvidenskabelige PhD-Forening (DJP), Strandvejen 863, 2930 Klampenborg
Founded: 1937; Members: 150
Focus: Agri 02977

Danmarks Jurist- og Økonomforbund, Gothersgade 133, 1123 København K
T: 33142920; Fax: 33325805
Founded: 1972; Members: 25000
Gen Secr: Rolf Tvedt
Focus: Law; Econ 02978

Danmarks Naturfredningsforening (DN) / Danish Society for the Conservation of Nature, Noerregade 2, 1165 København F
T: 33322021; Fax: 33322202
Founded: 1911; Members: 265000
Pres: Prof. Svend Bichel; Gen Secr: Lone Johnsen
Focus: Ecology
Periodical
Tidsskrift Natur og Miljø (quarterly) . . . 02979

Danmarks Skolebibliotekarforening / The Danish Association of School Librarians, Gøgevej 1, 4130 Viby
T: 42393440
Founded: 1953; Members: 2300
Focus: Libraries & Bk Sci
Periodical
Skolebiblioteket (9 times annually) . . . 02980

Danmarks Skolebiblioteksforening (DSF), Vesterbrogade 20, 1620 København V
T: 33253222; E-Mail: KomSkolBib@intenet.dk; Fax: 33253223
Founded: 1933; Members: 250
Pres: Poul Erik Sørensen; Gen Secr: Niels Jacobsen
Focus: Libraries & Bk Sci
Periodicals
Børn & Bøger (8 times annually)
Skolebiblioteksårbog (annually) 02981

Dansk Agronomforening (DA), Strandvejen 863, 2930 Klampenborg
T: 39970100; E-Mail: post@ jordbrugsakademikerne.dk; Fax: 39970119
Founded: 1896; Members: 3640
Pres: Svend D. Vesterlund; Gen Secr: Henrik Jessen Toft
Focus: Agri
Periodical
Jord og Viden (26 times annually) . . . 02982

Dansk Anaestesiologisk Selskab (DAS), c/o Arhus Amtssygehus, 8000 Arhus C
Founded: 1949; Members: 260
Focus: Anesthetics 02983

Dansk Automationsselskab (DAu), c/o Symbion Science Park, Fruebjergvej 3, 2100 Københanh
T: 39179999; Fax: 31205521
Founded: 1962; Members: 116
Focus: Eng
Periodical
Medlemsnyt (quarterly) 02984

Dansk Betonforening, c/o Ingeniørforeningen i Danmark, Vester Farimagsgade 31, 1606 København V
T: 33156565
Founded: 1947; Members: 1030
Focus: Materials Sci 02985

Dansk Biblioteks Center / Danish Library Centre, Tempovej 7-11, 2750 Ballerup
Founded: 1991
Focus: Libraries & Bk Sci 02986

Dansk Billedhuggersamfund, Høgstedgård, Hyrup, 7140 Stouby
T: 75897515
Founded: 1905; Members: 120
Pres: Markan Christensen
Focus: Arts 02987

Dansk Biologisk Selskab, c/o Tumorbiologisk Institut, Frederik den V's Vey 11, 2100 København Ø
Founded: 1896; Members: 660
Focus: Bio 02988

Dansk Botanisk Forening, Sølvgade 83, 1307 København K
T: 33141703
Founded: 1840; Members: 1350
Pres: Poul Møller Pederson
Focus: Botany
Periodical
URT (quarterly) 02989

Dansk Byplanlaboratorium / Danish Town Planning Institution, Peder Skrams Gade 2b, 1054 København
T: 33137281; Fax: 33143435
Founded: 1921
Focus: Urban Plan
Periodical
Byplan (bi-monthly) 02990

Dansk Cardiologisk Selskab (DCS) / Danish Society of Cardiology, c/o Cardiological Dept, University Hospital, Herlev Hospital, 2730 Herlev
T: 86126866; Fax: 86193075
Founded: 1960; Members: 550
Focus: Cardiol
Periodical
Newsletter (bi-monthly) 02991

Dansk Cerealforening (DCF), c/o Dept of Biotechnology, DTH, Block 223, 2800 Lyngby
Founded: 1932; Members: 84
Focus: Agri 02992

Dansk Dataforening, Kronprinsensgade 14, 1114 København K
Founded: 1958; Members: 3500
Focus: Computer & Info Sci
Periodical
DATA posten (bi-monthly) 02993

Dansk Dendrologisk Forening, Kirkegårdsvej 3a, 2970 Hørsholm
T: 35283628; Fax: 35283629
Founded: 1949
Focus: Forestry
Periodical
Dansk Dendrologisk Årsskrift 02994

Dansk Dermatologisk Selskab (DDS), c/o H. Fogh, Dermatological Dept, Bispebjerg Hospital, Bispebjerg Bakke, 2400 København NV
T: 35313105; Fax: 35313950
Founded: 1899; Members: 210
Focus: Derm 02995

Dansk Epilepsiforening / Danish Epilepsy Society, c/o University Clinic of Neurology, Hvidovre Hospital, Kettegård Alle 30, 2650 Hvidovre
T: 36323632; Fax: 31473941
Founded: 1970; Members: 39
Focus: Neurology 02996

Dansk Exlibris Selskab, Postboks 1519, 2700 Brønshøj
T: 46769166; E-Mail: 113071.3716@compuserve.com; Fax: 46769167
Founded: 1941; Members: 250
Focus: Libraries & Bk Sci; Arts 02997

Dansk Farmaceutforening / Association of Danish Pharmacists, Toldbodgade 36a, 1253 København K
Founded: 1873; Members: 3200
Pres: Gerd Askaa
Focus: Pharmacol
Periodical
Farmaceutisk Tidende (weekly) 02998

Dansk Farmacihistorisk Selskab, c/o Danmarks Farmaceutiske Højskole, Universitetsparken 2, 2100 København Ø
Founded: 1953; Members: 300
Focus: Hist; Pharmacol
Periodical
Theriaca (annually) 02999

Dansk Føderation for Informationsbehandling og Virksomhedsstyring (DANFIP), Kronprinsensgade 14, 1114 København K
Founded: 1968; Members: 4
Focus: Computer & Info Sci 03000

Dansk Forening for Europaret (DFE), c/o Plesner & Lunoe, Esplanaden 34, 1263 København K
Fax: 33120014
Founded: 1973; Members: 240
Focus: Law 03001

Dansk Forening for Jordbundsvidenskab / Danish Society of Soil Science, c/o Chemistry Dept, Royal Veterinary and Agricultural University, Thorvaldsensvej 40, 1871 Frederiksberg C
T: 35282419; Fax: 35282398
Founded: 1928; Members: 60
Pres: O.K. Borggaard; Gen Secr: B.T. Christensen
Focus: Agri 03002

Dansk Forening for Retssociologi, c/o Institute of Organisation, Howitzvej 60, 2000 København F
Founded: 1967; Members: 115
Focus: Law; Sociology 03003

Dansk Forfatterforening / Danish Writers' Association, Strandgade 6, 1401 København K
T: 32955100; Fax: 31540115
Founded: 1894; Members: 1380
Pres: Mette Koefoed Bjørnsen
Focus: Lit
Periodical
Forfatteren 03004

Dansk Fysisk Forening / Danish Physical Society, Blegdamsvej 17, 2100 København Ø
Founded: 1908; Members: 220
Focus: Physics 03005

Dansk Fysisk Selskab, c/o Prof. Preben Alstrøm, Niels Bohr Institute, Blegdamsvej 17, 2100 København Ø
Founded: 1972; Members: 500
Pres: Preben Alstrøm
Focus: Physics
Periodical
Kvant (quarterly) 03006

Dansk Gastroenterologisk Selskab (DGS) / Danish Society of Gastroenterology, c/o Peter Funck-Jensen, Hvidovre Hospital, Kettegård Allé 30, 2650 Hvidovre
T: 36322259; Fax: 31473311
Founded: 1970; Members: 600
Focus: Gastroenter 03007

Dansk Geofysisk Forening (DGF), Juliane Maries Vej 30, 2100 København Ø
T: 35320602; Fax: 35365357
Founded: 1936; Members: 102
Pres: Peter Skjellerup
Focus: Geophys 03008

Dansk Geologisk Forening (DGF), Øster Voldgade 5-7, 1350 København K
T: 33322354; Fax: 35322325
Founded: 1893; Members: 800
Pres: Lars Clemmensen
Focus: Geology
Periodical
Bulletin of the Geological Society of Denmark (2-3 times annually) 03009

Dansk Geoteknisk Forening (DGF), Maglebjergvej 1, 2800 Lyngby
T: 45884444; Fax: 45881240
Founded: 1950; Members: 240
Pres: Jens Kammer Mortensen; Gen Secr: John Frederiksen
Focus: Civil Eng 03010

Dansk Gerontologisk Selskab / Danish Gerontological Society, c/o Langtidsmedicinsk Afdeling, Centralsygehuset, 4700 Naestved
Founded: 1957; Members: 175
Focus: Geriatrics 03011

Dansk Grafologisk Selskab (DGS), Mothsvej 49, 2840 Holte
Founded: 1952; Members: 59
Focus: Graphology 03012

Dansk Haematologisk Selskab (DHS), c/o Dept of Medicine and Haematology, Gentofte Hospital, 2900 Hellerup
Founded: 1972; Members: 62
Focus: Hematology 03013

Dansk Historielaererforening, c/o Jørgen Riskaer-Jørgensen, Bakkebøllevej 12, 4760 Vordingborg
T: 53776616
Founded: 1960; Members: 3000
Focus: Hist; Educ
Periodical
Historie & Samtid (quarterly) 03014

Dansk Hortonomforening (DH), Strandvejen 863, 2930 Klampenborg
T: 39970100; E-Mail: post@jordbrugsakademikerne.dk; Fax: 39970119
Founded: 1915; Members: 575
Pres: Morten Brøgger Kristensen
Focus: Hort
Periodical
Jord og Viden (26 times annually) . . . 03015

Dansk Husflidsselskab / Danish Society of Domestic Crafts, Tyrebakken 11, 5300 Kerteminde
T: 65322096; Fax: 65325611
Founded: 1873; Members: 6000
Focus: Home Econ
Periodical
Husflid (bi-monthly) 03016

Dansk Idraetslaererforening, Egernvaenget 143, 5800 Nyborg
Members: 5000
Focus: Sports 03017

Dansk Industrimedicinsk Selskab, Bindesbøllsvej 23, 2920 Charlottenlund
T: 31642220
Founded: 1950; Members: 342
Focus: Med; Hygiene 03018

Dansk Ingeniørforening, Vester Farimagsgade 31, 1780 København V
T: 33156565; Fax: 33937171
Founded: 1892; Members: 20500
Pres: Hans-Ole Skougaard; Gen Secr: Helge S. Henriksen
Focus: Energy
Periodical
Ingeniøren (weekly) 03019

Dansk Kerneteknisk Selskab, c/o Dansk Ingeniørforening, Vester Farimagsgade 31, 1606 København V
Focus: Nucl Res 03020

Dansk Kirurgisk Selskab, c/o Kirurgisk Afdeling, Amtssygehuset, 2970 Hørsholm
Founded: 1908
Focus: Surgery 03021

Dansk Køleforening, c/o Refrigeration Laboratory, Danmarks Tekniske Højskole, Bygning 402, 2800 Lyngby
T: 42404590; Fax: 42404207
Founded: 1911; Members: 612
Focus: Electric Eng
Periodical
Scandinavian Refrigeration (bi-monthly) . 03022

Dansk Komponistforening / Danish Composers' Society, Graebroedtorv 16, 1154 København K
T: 33135405; Fax: 33143219
Founded: 1913; Members: 165
Pres: Holm Mogens Winkel; Gen Secr: Kirsten Wrem
Focus: Music
Periodical
Danske Komponister af i Dag: Danish Composers of Today – Dänische Komponisten von heute 03023

Dansk Kriminalistforening, Skt. Peders Str 19, 1453 København K
Founded: 1899; Members: 450
Pres: Vagh Greve
Focus: Criminology; Law 03024

Dansk Kulturhistorisk Museumsforening (DKM), Nr. Madsbadvej 6, 7884 Fur
Fax: 97593163
Founded: 1929; Members: 167
Pres: Inger Tolstrup; Gen Secr: Kirsten Rex Andersen
Focus: Hist 03025

Dansk Kunstmuseumsforening, c/o Statens Museum for Kunst, Sølvgade, 1307 København K
Founded: 1913
Focus: Arts 03026

Dansk Laererforeningen, Rosenørns Allé 18, 1970 København V
Founded: 1885; Members: 5213
Focus: Ling; Educ 03027

Dansk Lokalhistorisk Forening, c/o Ebbe Fels, Bondehavevej 146, 2880 Bagsvaerd
Founded: 1967; Members: 142
Focus: Hist 03028

Dansk Mathematisk Forening (DMF), Universitetsparken 5, 2100 København Ø
Founded: 1873; Members: 350
Focus: Math
Periodicals
MAT-NYT (weekly)
Mathematica Scandinavia (semi-annually)
normat (annually) 03029

Dansk Medicinsk-Historisk Selskab, c/o Medicinsk-Historisk Museum, Bredgade 62, 1260 København K
T: 35323800
Founded: 1917; Members: 350
Pres: Mogens Norn; Gen Secr: Henrik Permin
Focus: Med; Cultur Hist
Periodical
Danish Medical Historical Yearbook (annually) 03030

Dansk Medicinsk Selskab (DMS) / Danish Medical Society, Kristianiagade 14, 2100 København
Founded: 1919; Members: 18081
Pres: Jørn Nerup; Gen Secr: Karsten Bech
Focus: Med
Periodical
Danish Medical Bulletin (quarterly) . . . 03031

Dansk Medikoteknisk Selskab, Bakkefaldet 44, 2840 Holte
Founded: 1973; Members: 370
Focus: Eng; Med 03032

Dansk Mejeringeniør Forening / Dairy Engineerings Association, Cikorievej 8, 5220 Odense SØ
Founded: 1887; Members: 1700
Focus: Dairy Sci; Eng
Periodicals
Danish Dairy and Food Industry
Maelkeritidende (bi-weekly) 03033

Dansk Mejeristforening (AC), Cikorievej 8, 5220 Odense sØ
T: 66124025
Founded: 1887; Members: 900
Pres: K. Mark Christensen
Focus: Food 03034

Dansk Metallurgisk Selskab (DMS), c/o Danmarks Tekniske Højskole, Bygning 204, 2800 Lyngby
T: 42884022
Founded: 1933; Members: 300
Focus: Metallurgy
Periodical
Dansk Metallurgisk Selskabs Arbog (annually) 03035

Dansk Musikbiblioteksforening / Association of Danish Music Libraries, c/o Dansk Musik Informations Center, Graabrødretorv 16, 1154 København K
T: 33112016; Fax: 33322016
Founded: 1961; Members: 150
Focus: Libraries & Bk Sci; Music
Periodical
MUS'en (quarterly) 03036

Dansk Musikpaedagogisk Forening (DMpF), Nørrebrogade 45a, 2200 København N
T: 31356333; Fax: 31350698
Founded: 1898; Members: 1300
Pres: Ole Helby; Gen Secr: Lars Møller
Focus: Music; Educ
Periodical
Modus: Music Magazine (bi-monthly) . . 03037

Dansk Naturhistorisk Forening, Universitetsparken 15, 2100 København Ø
T: 35321120; Fax: 35321010
Founded: 1833; Members: 525
Pres: Ole E. Heie
Focus: Hist; Nat Sci
Periodical
Dansk Naturhistorisk Forening Arsskrift (annually) 03038

Dansk Nefrologisk Selskab, c/o Prof. Steen Olsen, University Institute of Pathology, Arhus Kommunehospital, 8000 Arhus C
Focus: Intern Med 03039

Dansk Neurologisk Selskab (DNS), c/o Per Hübbe, Nordkrog 16, 2900 Hellerup
Members: 259
Focus: Neurology 03040

Dansk Numismatisk Forening, c/o Preben Nielsen, Hallandsparken 134, 2630 Taastrup
T: 43521918
Founded: 1885
Pres: Preben Nielsen
Focus: Numismatics
Periodical
numismatisk rapport (quarterly) 03041

Dansk Odontologisk Selskab, c/o Fritz Bundgård-Jørgensen, Standvejen 296b, 2930 Klampenborg
Founded: 1923
Focus: Dent 03042

Dansk Oftalmologisk Selskab / Danish Ophthalmological Society, c/o Rigshospitalets Øjenafdeling, Blegdamsvej 9, 2100 København
Founded: 1901; Members: 250
Focus: Ophthal
Periodicals
Acta Ophthalmalogica Scandinavica
Transactions 03043

Dansk Økologisk Forening Oikos, c/o Institutet for Økologisk Botanik, Øster Farimagsgade 2d, 1353 København K
Focus: Ecology 03044

Dansk Ornithologisk Forening (DOF), Vesterbrogade 140, 1620 København V
T: 31314404; E-Mail: dof@post2.tele.dk; Fax: 31312435
Founded: 1906; Members: 12000
Pres: Christian Hjorth; Gen Secr: Claus Oppermann
Focus: Ornithology
Periodicals
Dansk Ornitologisk Forenings Tidsskrift (quarterly)
Fugle (quarterly) 03045

Dansk Ortopaedisk Selskab (DOS), c/o Rigshospitalet, Blegdamsvej, 2100 København Ø
Founded: 1946; Members: 172
Focus: Orthopedics 03046

Dansk Oto-laryngologisk Selskab (DOS), c/o University ENT-Clinic, Gentofte Hospital, 2900 Hellerup
Founded: 1899; Members: 292
Focus: Otorhinolaryngology 03047

Dansk Pediatrisk Selskab (DPS), c/o Dr. Flemming Hart Hansen, Abrinken 155, 2830 Virum
Founded: 1908; Members: 200
Focus: Pediatrics 03048

Dansk Pneumologisk Selskab, c/o Dr. Finn V. Rasmussen, Sandholmgårdsvej 16B, 3450 Allrød
Founded: 1921; Members: 120
Focus: Pulmon Dis 03049

Dansk Pressehistorisk Selskab, c/o Berlingske Tidende, Pilestraede 34, 1147 København K
T: 33157575; Fax: 33131012
Members: 390
Focus: Hist; Journalism 03050

Dansk Psykoanalytisk Selskab, c/o Bispebjerg Hospital, Psychiatric Dept E, 2400 København NV
Members: 25
Focus: Psych; Psychoan
Periodical
The Scandinavian Psychoanalytic Review (semi-annually) 03051

Dansk Psykolog Forening (DP), Stockholmsgade 27, 2100 København Ø
T: 35269955; Fax: 35269755
Founded: 1947; Members: 4500
Pres: Johanne Bratbo; Gen Secr: Ole Münster
Focus: Psych
Periodical
Psykolog Nyt (23 times annually) . . . 03052

Dansk Radiologisk Selskab (DRS), c/o Radiological Dept, Herlev Hospital, 2730 Herlev
T: 02942733
Founded: 1921; Members: 500
Focus: Radiology 03053

Dansk Reumatologisk Selskab (D.S.F.), c/o Dept of Physical Medicine and Rheumatology, Bispebjerg Hospital, 2400 København N
Founded: 1921; Members: 353
Focus: Rheuma; Rehabil 03054

Dansk Selskab for Akupunktur, c/o Dr. Ole Dahl, H.C. Andersens Blvd 49, 1553 København V
Founded: 1974; Members: 382
Focus: Pathology 03055

Dansk Selskab for Allergologi og Immunologi, c/o University Hospital, Blegdamsvej 9, 2100 København Ø
Founded: 1946; Members: 161
Focus: Immunology 03056

Dansk Selskab for Bygningsstatik (DSBy), c/o Danmarks Tekniske Højskole, Bygning 118, 2800 Lyngby
Founded: 1928; Members: 674
Focus: Civil Eng
Periodical
Bygningsstatische Meddelelser (quarterly) . 03057

Dansk Selskab for Cancerforskning, c/o Rigshospitalet, Blegdamsvej 9, 2100 København Ø
Fax: 31356906
Founded: 1964
Focus: Cell Biol & Cancer Res 03058

Dansk Selskab for Europaforskning, Studiestrade 6, 1455 København K
T: 35322626; Fax: 35323203
Founded: 1975; Members: 132
Pres: Prof. H. Rasmussen
Focus: Poli Sci
Periodical
Nyt om Euroforskning 03059

Dansk Selskab for Fotogrammetri og Landmåling (DSFL) / Danish Society for Photogrammetry and Surveying, Ålborg Universitet, Fibigerstråde 11, 9220 Ålborg
Fax: 98156541
Founded: 1934; Members: 475
Focus: Surveying
Periodical
DSFL Meddelelser (monthly) 03060

Dansk Selskab for Intern Medicin (DSIM), c/o Steno Memorial Hospital, 2820 Gentofte
T: 44439101; E-Mail: tmpo@novo.dk;
Fax: 44438232
Founded: 1916; Members: 1052
Pres: Thomas Mandrup-Poulsen; Gen Secr: Jørn Merrstedt
Focus: Intern Med 03061

Dansk Selskab for Materialprøvning og -forskning, c/o Dansk Ingeniørforening, Vester Farimagsgade 31, 1606 København V
Focus: Materials Sci 03062

Dansk Selskab for Musikforskning / Danish Musicological Society, c/o Musikvidenskabeligt Institut, Klerkegade 2, 1308 København K
Founded: 1954
Focus: Music
Periodical
Danish Yearbook of Musicology (annually) 03063

Dansk Selskab for Obstetrik og Gynaekologi / Danish Society for Obstetrics and Gynaecology, c/o Aarhus University Hospital, Skejby Sygehus, Brendstrupgaardsvej, 8200 Aarhus N
T: 89496458; Fax: 89496460
Founded: 1898; Members: 815
Pres: Dr. Aksel Lange
Focus: Gynecology 03064

Dansk Selskab for Oldtids- og Middelalderforskning (DSOM), c/o Nationalmuseet, Frederiksholms Kanal 12, 1220 København K
Founded: 1934; Members: 120
Pres: Rikke Agnete Olsen; Gen Secr: Keld Grunde Hansen
Focus: Hist 03065

Dansk Selskab for Oligofreniforskning, Svanevanget 32, 2100 København
Focus: Psychiatry 03066

Dansk Selskab for Optometri (DSO), c/o Jens Rahlff, Gongesletten 5, 2950 Vedbaek
Founded: 1954; Members: 300
Focus: Optics 03067

Dansk Selskab for Opvarmnings- og Ventilationsteknik (DSOV), c/o Dansk Ingeniørforening, Vester Farimagsgade 29, 1606 København V
Founded: 1945
Focus: Air Cond; Eng 03068

Dansk Selskab for Patologi / Danish Society of Pathology, c/o Bartholin Instituttet, Øster Farimagsgade 5, 1399 København K
Focus: Pathology; Microbio 03069

Dansk Selskab for Rumfartsforskning / Danish Astronautical Society, Postboks 31, 1002 København K
T: 35840855; E-Mail: dsr@inet.uni-c.dk;
Fax: 35840855
Founded: 1949; Members: 130
Pres: Thomas A.E. Andersen; Gen Secr: Bjarne M. Johansen
Focus: Eng 03070

Dansk Selskab for Social Medicin, c/o Afdeling for Scial Medicin, Odense Universitet, J.B. Winsløwsvej 17, 5000 Odense C
Founded: 1967; Members: 215
Focus: Hygiene 03071

Dansk Selskab for Teoretisk Statistik (DSTS), c/o Institut for Matematisk Statistik, Universitetsparken 5, 2100 København Ø
Founded: 1971; Members: 250
Focus: Stats 03072

Dansk Skattevidenskabelig Forening (DSF), Palaegade 4, 1261 København K
Founded: 1938; Members: 300
Focus: Law 03073

Dansk Skovforening / Danish Forestry Society, Amalievej 20, 1875 Frederiksberg C
T: 33244266; E-Mail: info@skovenes-hus.dk;
Fax: 33240242
Founded: 1888; Members: 800
Pres: Gustav Berner; Gen Secr: Henrik Studsgaard
Focus: Forestry
Periodical
Dansk Skovforenings Tidsskrift and Skoven 03074

Dansk Socialradgiverforening (DSF) / Danish Association of Social Workers, Toldbodgade 19a, 1253 København K
T: 33913033; Fax: 33913069
Founded: 1938; Members: 8000
Pres: Anna Marie Møller
Focus: Sociology
Periodical
Socialradgiveren (bi-weekly) 03075

Dansk Sociologisk Selskab, Howitzvej 60, 2000 København F
Focus: Sociology 03076

Dansk Sprogvaern, c/o B.T.Persson, Weirsoevej 10, 3500 Vaerløse
Founded: 1955
Focus: Ling 03077

Dansk Svejseteknisk Landsforening / Danish Welding Society, Gregersensvej 8, 2630 Taastrup
T: 43719041; Fax: 43504422
Founded: 1939
Focus: Eng
Periodical
Svejsning: Welding (bi-monthly) 03078

Dansk Tandlaegeforening (DTF), Amaliegade 17, Postboks 143, 1004 København K
T: 33157711; Fax: 33151637
Founded: 1873; Members: 5633
Focus: Dent
Periodical
Tandlägebladet (bi-weekly) 03079

Dansk Teknisk Laererforening (DTL), Rosenvångets Hovedvej 14, 2100 København Ø
Founded: 1907; Members: 2300
Focus: Educ
Periodical
DTL-Nyt (monthly) 03080

Dansk Vandteknisk Forening / Danish Water Supply Association, Vilhelm Becks Vej 60, 8260 Viby
T: 86112333
Founded: 1926; Members: 550
Focus: Water Res
Periodical
Vandteknik (10 times annually) 03081

Dansk Veterinaerhistorisk Samfund / Danish Veterinary History Society, Svalgaardsvej 20, Sjørring, 7700 Thisted
T: 97971001; Fax: 97971567
Founded: 1934; Members: 300
Pres: Anton Rosenbom
Focus: Vet Med; Hist 03082

Det Danske Afrika Selskab, c/o J. Konnild, Fragariavej 9, 2900 Hellerup
Focus: Ethnology 03083

Den Danske Aktuarforening, c/o DIP, Slotsholmsgade 1, 1216 København K
T: 33326565
Founded: 1901; Members: 245
Focus: Insurance 03084

Danske Arkitekters Landsforbund (DAL) / Akademisk Arkitektforening / Federation of Danish Architects, Bredgade 66, Postboks 1163, 1269 København K
T: 33131290; Fax: 33931203
Founded: 1879; Members: 6000
Pres: Viggo Grunnet; Gen Secr: B. Budholm
Focus: Archit
Periodicals
Arkitekten (18 times annually)
Arkitektur DK (bi-monthly)
Artur (18 times annually) 03085

Danske Bibelselskab, Frederiksborggade 50, 1360 København K
T: 33127835
Founded: 1814; Members: 7500
Pres: G. Frimodt Møller
Focus: Rel & Theol 03086

Danske Dermato-Venerologers Organisation, c/o Dr. Thais Hattel, Vesterbro 99, 9000 Alborg
Founded: 1970
Focus: Derm; Venereology 03087

Den Danske Dyrlaegeforening (DdD), Rosenlunds Allé 8, 2720 Vanlöse
T: 38710888; E-Mail: ddd@ddd.dk; Fax: 38710322
Founded: 1849; Members: 2336
Pres: N.O. Bjerregaard; Gen Secr: Lars Holsaae
Focus: Vet Med
Periodical
Dansk Veterinaertidsskrift (Danish Veterinary Journal) (bi-monthly) 03088

Danske Forstkandidaters Forening (DFF) / Association of Danish Graduates in Forestry, Strandvejen 863, 2930 Klampenborg
T: 39970100; E-Mail: post@jordbrugsakademikerne.dk; Fax: 39970119
Founded: 1897; Members: 670
Pres: J.C. Briand Petersen
Focus: Forestry
Periodical
Jord og Viden (26 times annually) . . . 03089

Danske Fysioterapeuter (D.F.) / Association of Danish Physiotherapists, Nørre Voldgade 90, 1358 København K
T: 33138211; Fax: 33938214
Founded: 1918; Members: 6015
Focus: Therapeutics
Periodical
Danske Fysioterapeuter (bi-weekly) . . . 03090

Det Danske Hedeselskab (DDH) / Danish Land Development Service, Klostermarken 12, 8800 Viborg
T: 86676111; Fax: 86675101
Founded: 1866; Members: 10000
Focus: Agri; Forestry; Ecology
Periodical
Vaekst: Hedeselskabets Tidsskrift (bi-monthly) 03091

Den Danske Historiske Forening, Njalsgade 102, 2300 København S
T: 35328245; Fax: 35328241
Founded: 1839
Pres: Prof. Dr. E. Ladewig Petersen; Gen Secr: Carsten Due-Nielsen; Anders Monrad Møller
Focus: Hist
Periodical
Historisk Tidsskrift (semi-annually) . . . 03092

Danske Interne Medicineres Organisation (DIMO), c/o Helsehuset, Hold-An Vej 5, 2750 Ballerup
T: 44681212; Fax: 44684464
Founded: 1947; Members: 430
Pres: J. Meibom; Gen Secr: H. Toft
Focus: Intern Med 03093

Danske Komité for Historikernes Internationale Samarbejde / Danish Committee for International Historical Cooperation, c/o Institute of History, University, Njalsgade 102, 2300 København
Founded: 1926; Members: 45
Focus: Hist; Int'l Relat 03094

Danske Lunglaegers Organisation, c/o Jacob Winslow, Ringstedvej 6b, 4300 Holbaek
Members: 50
Focus: Pulmon Dis 03095

Danske Nervelaegers Organisation (DNO), c/o Odense Sygehus, 5000 Odense
Founded: 1915
Focus: Neurology 03096

Det Danske Orgelselskab, c/o Erik Poppe, Dønnerupvej 2, 2720 Vanløse
Founded: 1970; Members: 600
Focus: Music
Periodical
Orglet (semi-annually) 03097

Danske Radiologers Organisation (DRO) / Danish Association of Medical Imaging, c/o Dept of Radiology, Sønderborg Sygehus, 6400 Sønderborg
T: 74430311
Founded: 1921; Members: 220
Focus: X-Ray Tech 03098

Det Danske Shakespeare Selskab, Østerbrogade 144, 2100 København Ø
Founded: 1961
Pres: Søs Haugaard
Focus: Lit 03099

Danske Sprog- og Litteraturselskab, Frederiksholms Kanal 18a, 1220 København
Founded: 1911; Members: 70
Pres: Dr. Iver Kjaer
Focus: Ling; Lit 03100

Danske Veterinårhygiejnikeres Organisation (DVO), c/o Veterinårkontrollen, Volden 11, 4200 Slagense
Founded: 1898; Members: 510
Focus: Vet Med; Food; Hygiene 03101

danvak VVS Teknisk Forening / Danish Society of Heating, Ventilating and Airconditioning Engineers, Orholmvej 40b, 2800 Lyngby
T: 45877611; Fax: 45877677
Founded: 1964
Focus: Eng
Periodical
VVS danvak 03102

DJKV, Strandvejen 863, 2930 Klampenborg
T: 39970100; Fax: 39970119
Founded: 1976; Members: 5100
Pres: Knud Aavang Jensen
Focus: Agri
Periodical
Jord og Viden (irregularly) 03103

DTL – Dansk Forening for Information og Dokumentation (DTL), c/o DTV, Anker Engelunds Vej 1, 2800 Lyngby
T: 45257302
Founded: 1959; Members: 317
Focus: Lit
Periodical
Skriftserie (semi-annually) 03104

Elektroteknisk Forening, Ehlersvej 11, 2900 Hellerup
T: 49201819; Fax: 49201839
Founded: 1903; Members: 3000
Gen Secr: Aage Hansen
Focus: Electric Eng 03105

Entomologisk Forening, c/o Zoological Museum, Universitetsparken 15, 2100 København Ø
Founded: 1868; Members: 360
Pres: Niels Peder Kristensen; Gen Secr: Ole Gudik-Sørensen
Focus: Entomology
Periodical
Entomologiske Meddelelser (quarterly) . . 03106

Euroenviron, Aaboulevard 13, 1635 København V
T: 31394344; Fax: 31354344
Founded: 1989; Members: 13
Focus: Ecology 03107

European Academy of Allergology and Clinical Immunology, c/o Munksgaard International Publishers Ltd., Norre Sogade 35, Postboks 2148, 1016 København K
T: 33127030; E-Mail: hfr@mail.munksgaard.dk;
Fax: 33129387
Focus: Immunology
Periodical
Allergy: European Journal of Allergy and Clinical Immunology (monthly) 03108

European Advisory Committee on Health Research (EACHR), c/o WHO, Scherfigsvej 8, 2100 København
T: (01) 290111; Fax: 181120
Founded: 1975; Members: 31
Focus: Public Health 03109

European Association for Haematopathology (EAHP), c/o Laboratory of Immunohistology, Finsengade 12, 8000 Aarhus C
T: 86125555 ext 3841; Fax: 86182386
Members: 300
Focus: Pathology 03110

European College of Neuropsychopharmacology (ECNP), c/o Dept of Psychiatry, Frederiksborg General Hospital, 3400 Hillerød
T: 42261500; Fax: 86600244
Founded: 1985
Focus: Pharmacol 03111

European Council of National Associations of Independent Schools (ECNAIS), Japanvej 36, 4200 Slagelse
T: 58531845; E-Mail: friegsk@inet.uni-c.dk;
Fax: 58532588
Founded: 1988
Pres: Per Kristensen; Gen Secr: Kjeld Peter A. Olesen
Focus: Educ 03112

Filologisk-Historiske Samfund, c/o Institute of Classical Studies, University of Copenhagen, Nialsgade 92, 2300 København S
Founded: 1854; Members: 300
Pres: Prof. Minna Skafte Jensen
Focus: Ling; Lit
Periodical
Studier fra Sprog- og Oldtidsforskning . 03113

Folkeuniversitetsudvalget, c/o University of Odense, 5230 Odense
Founded: 1898
Pres: Carl F. Wandel
Focus: Educ 03114

FORCE Institutterne / FORCE Institutes, Park Allé 345, 2600 Glostrup
T: 43969800; Fax: 43962636
Focus: Eng 03115

Foreningen af Danske Biologer. / The Association of Danish Biologists, c/o Kristian Lauridsen, Lindevangsvej 16B, 3460 Birkerød
Founded: 1976
Focus: Educ; Bio
Periodical
Biofag (bi-monthly) 03116

Foreningen af Danske Civiløkonomer (FDC), Börsen, Slotsholmsgade, 1216 København K
Founded: 1954; Members: 5300
Focus: Business Admin; Econ 03117

Foreningen af Danske Kunstmuseer, Nr. Madsbadvej 6, 7884 Fur
Fax: 97593163
Founded: 1978; Members: 50
Pres: Lars Kaerulf Møller; Gen Secr: Kirsten Rex Andersen
Focus: Arts 03118

Foreningen af Danske Museumsmaend, c/o Zoologisk Museum, Universitetsparken 15, 2100 København Ø
Founded: 1928; Members: 250
Pres: Tove Hatting; Gen Secr: Anne Kromann
Focus: Arts 03119

Foreningen af Geografilaerere ved de Gymnasiale Uddannelser, Blokvej 2e, 6760 Ribe
Focus: Geography; Educ
Periodical
Geo-Nyt (quarterly) 03120

Foreningen af Medarbejdere ved Danmarks Forskningsbiblioteker, c/o Danmarks Tekniske Bibliotek, Anker Engelundsvej 1, 2800 Lyngby
T: 45939979
Founded: 1934
Focus: Libraries & Bk Sci
Periodical
DF-Revy (10 times annually) 03121

Foreningen af Speciallåger (FAS) / The Danish Association of Medical Specialists, Trondhjemsgade 9, 2100 København Ø
T: 31385500; Fax: 31386807
Founded: 1935; Members: 5233
Focus: Med 03122

Foreningen for Danske Lanbrugsskoler, c/o Grevevej 20, 2670 Greve
Founded: 1903; Members: 300
Focus: Adult Educ; Agri 03123

Foreningen for National Kunst / Society for National Art, Landemarkt 3, 1000 København K
Founded: 1900
Focus: Arts 03124

Frankslaererforeningen, c/o Jørgen Lykke Petersen, Fuglebo 4, 2000 København F
Members: 500
Focus: Ling; Educ 03125

Det Grønlandske Selskab (DGS), L.E. Bruuns Vej 10, 2920 Charlottenlund
Founded: 1905; Members: 1300
Pres: Helge Schultz-Lorentzen; Gen Secr: Jørn Würtz
Focus: Geography

Periodicals
Grønland (8 times annually)
Saerskrifter (annually) *03126*

Gymnasieskolernes Laererforening, Lyngbyvej 32, 2100 København Ø
T: 31209591; Fax: 31207447
Founded: 1890; Members: 10000
Focus: Educ
Periodical
Gymnasieskolen (bi-weekly) *03127*

Historisk Samfund for Sønderjylland, Haderslevvej 45, 6200 Abenrå
T: 74624683
Focus: Hist
Periodicals
Sønderjysk Maanedsskrift (monthly)
Sønderjyske Aarbøger (annually) *03128*

Historisk-Topografisk Selskab, Solbjergvej 25, 2000 Frederiksberg
Founded: 1944; Members: 375
Focus: Hist *03129*

Ingeniør-Sammenslutningen, Domus Technica, Ved Stranden 18, 1061 København K
T: 31121311; Fax: 33934622
Founded: 1937; Members: 23000
Gen Secr: Jesper Ginnerup
Focus: Eng *03130*

International Association of Geodesy, c/o University of Copenhagen, Dept. og Geophysics, Juliane Maries Vej 30, 2100 København
T: 35320582; E-Mail: iag@gfy.ku.dk; Fax: 35365357
Founded: 1922; Members: 78
Pres: K.P. Schwarz; Gen Secr: C.C. Tscherning
Focus: Surveying *03131*

International Association of Physical Education and Sports for Girls and Women (IAPESGW), Vestermøllevej 11, 8800 Viborg
Founded: 1953; Members: 400
Focus: Sports
Periodical
Bulletin of IAPESGW *03132*

International Banking Research Institute, c/o Privatbanken A/S, Torvegade 2, 1249 København K
T: 31111111
Founded: 1951; Members: 55
Focus: Finance *03133*

International Council for the Exploration of the Sea (ICES), Palaegade 2-4, 1261 København K
T: 33154225; Fax: 33934215
Founded: 1902; Members: 18
Focus: Oceanography
Periodicals
Bulletin Statistique (annually)
Cooperative Research Report (6-8 times annually)
Fiches d'Identification du Plancton (irregularly)
ICES Oceanographic Data Lists and Inventories (3-4 times annually)
Identification Leaflets for Diseases and Parasites of Fish and Shellfish (irregularly)
Journal du Conseil (2-3 times annually)
Rapports et Procès-Verbaux des Réunions (irregularly)
Techniques in Marine Environmental Sciences (irregularly) *03134*

International Law Association – Danish Branch, c/o A. Kaufmann, Skoubogade 1, 1158 København K
Founded: 1925
Pres: Prof. Allan Philip
Focus: Law *03135*

International Society for Prosthetics and Orthotics (ISPO), Borgervaenget 5, 2100 København Ø
T: 31207501; Fax: 31207501
Founded: 1970; Members: 2800
Pres: Seishi Sawamura; Gen Secr: B. McHugh
Focus: Dent
Periodical
Prosthetics and Orthotics International (3 times annually) *03136*

International Society of Libraries and Museums of the Performing Arts, c/o Museum of Decorative Art, Bredgade 68, 1260 København
Founded: 1954; Members: 320
Focus: Libraries & Bk Sci; Perf Arts . . *03137*

International Work Group for Indigenous Affairs (IWGJA), Fiolstraede 10, 1171 København K
T: 33124724
Founded: 1968; Members: 1400
Focus: Anthro
Periodicals
Documents (semi-annually)
Newsletter (quarterly)
Yearbook (annually) *03138*

Izlenzka Fraedafélag, Helsevej 21, 3400 Hillerød
Founded: 1912
Gen Secr: P. Jonasson
Focus: Lit *03139*

Juridisk Forening, Esplanaden 34, 1263 København K
Founded: 1881; Members: 460
Focus: Law *03140*

Jysk Arkaeologisk Selskab (JAS), Moesgård, 8270 Højbjerg
T: 89424504; E-Mail: FARKLL@moes.hum.aau.dk; Fax: 86272378
Founded: 1951; Members: 1500
Pres: H. Steen; Gen Secr: Hans Jørgen Madsen
Focus: Archeol
Periodical
Kuml: Journal of the JAS *03141*

Jysk Forening for Naturvidenskab, c/o Poul Hansen, Naturhistorisk Museum, 8000 Arhus C
Founded: 1903
Focus: Nat Sci *03142*

Jysk Selskab for Fysik og Kemi (JSFK), c/o Dept of Chemistry, University, Langelandsgade 140, 8000 Arhus C
Founded: 1934; Members: 200
Focus: Chem; Physics *03143*

Jysk Selskab for Historie, c/o Historisk Institut, Aarhus Universitet, Nørrebrogade, 8000 Aarhus C
T: 89422023; Fax: 89422047
Founded: 1866; Members: 900
Pres: Prof. Dr. Henning Poulsen; Gen Secr: Prof. Dr. Henning Poulsen
Focus: Hist
Periodicals
Historie (semi-annually)
Nyt fra Historien (semi-annually) *03144*

Kemisk Forening, c/o H.C. Ørsted Institutet, Universitetsparken 5, 2100 København Ø
T: 35320287; Fax: 35320299
Founded: 1879; Members: 900
Pres: Poul Erik Hansen; Gen Secr: I. Trabjerg
Focus: Chem *03145*

Kirkeligt Centrum, Storegade 7, 6240 Løgumkloster
Founded: 1899
Pres: A. Kristoffersen
Focus: Rel & Theol *03146*

Det Kongelige Danske Geografiske Selskab, Øster Voldgade 10, 1350 København K
Founded: 1876; Members: 450
Gen Secr: Prof. S. Christiansen
Focus: Geography
Periodical
Geografisk Tidsskrift *03147*

Kongelige Danske Landhusholdnings-selskab / Royal Danish Agricultural Society, Mariendalsvej 27, 2000 Frederiksberg
T: 38886688; E-Mail: NJF-GS@inet.uni.c.dk; Fax: 38886111
Founded: 1769; Members: 1700
Pres: J. Krabbe; I. Tesdorpf; B. Shall Holberg; Gen Secr: Jens Wulff
Focus: Agri
Periodical
Tidsskrift for landøkonomi (quarterly) . . *03148*

Kongelige Danske Selskab for Faedrelandest Historie, c/o Kgl. Mønt- og Medaillesamling, National Museet, Frederiksholms Kanal 12, 1220 København k615=K
T: 33143414
Founded: 1745; Members: 80
Pres: Vagn Skovgaard-Petersen; Gen Secr: J. Steen Jensen
Focus: Archeol *03149*

Det Kongelige Danske Videnskabernes Selskab (KDVS) / The Royal Danish Academy of Sciences and Letters, H.C. Andersens Blvd 35, 1553 København V
T: 33113240; Fax: 33910736
Founded: 1742; Members: 471
Pres: Prof. Dr. Birger Munk von Olsen; Gen Secr: Prof. Dr. Thor A. Bak
Focus: Sci
Periodicals
Biologiske Skrifter (irregularly)
Historisk-filosofiske Meddelelser (irregularly)
Historisk-filosofiske Skrifter (irregularly)
Matematisk-fysiske Meddelelser (irregularly)
Oversigt over Selskabets Virksomhed (annually) *03150*

Det Kongelige Nordiske Oldskriftselskab, Prinsens Palais, Frederiksholms Kanal 12, 1220 København K
Founded: 1825; Members: 1200
Pres: Queen Margrethe II; Gen Secr: Peter V. Petersen
Focus: Hist; Archeol
Periodicals
Aarbøger for Nordisk Oldkyndighed og Historie (annually)
Nordiske Fortidsminder, Serie B – in quarto (irregularly) *03151*

Det Krigsvidenskabelige Selskab, c/o Haerens Officersskole, Frederiksberg Slot, Postboks 214, 2000 Frederiksberg
T: 31162244 ext 243; Fax: 36440160
Founded: 1871; Members: 1100
Focus: Military Sci
Periodical
Militaert tidsskrift (8 times annually) . . *03152*

Kunstforeningen, Gammel Strand 48, 1202 København K
T: 33360260; E-Mail: Admin@Kunstforeninge.dk; Fax: 33360266
Founded: 1825; Members: 3000
Pres: Steffen Gulmann; Gen Secr: Helle Behrndt
Focus: Arts *03153*

Kunstnerforeningen af 18. November / Artists' Association of the 18th of November, Frederiksgade 8, 1265 København K
T: 33159614
Founded: 1842; Members: 150
Pres: Niels Wamberg; Gen Secr: Søren Birk Pedersen
Focus: Arts *03154*

Det Laerde Selskab i Aarhus, c/o Aarhus Universitet, 8000 Aarhus C
Founded: 1945; Members: 150
Focus: Sci *03155*

Landsforeningen af Foldterapeuter, Bjelkes Allé 43, 2200 København N
Founded: 1932; Members: 700
Focus: Therapeutics
Periodical
Fodterapeuten (10 times annually) . . . *03156*

Landsforeningen for Sukkersyge, Skt. Anne Plads 4, 5000 Odense C
Focus: Diabetes
Periodical
Tidsskrift for Sukkersyge (quarterly) . . . *03157*

Landskabsarkitekternes Fagforening (LAF) / Association of Danish Graduates in Landscape Architecture, Strandvejen 863, 2930 Klampenborg
T: 31631166; Fax: 31631790
Founded: 1992
Pres: Kim Tang Jørgensen
Focus: Archit
Periodical
Jord og Viden (26 times annually) . . . *03158*

Lepidopterologisk Forening, Skovskellet 35a, 2840 Holte
Founded: 1941; Members: 500
Focus: Zoology
Periodical
Lepidoptera (semi-annually) *03159*

Levnedsmiddelselskabet (LEVS) / Danish Society of Food Science and Technology, c/o Dansk Ingeniørforening, Vester Farimagsgade 29, 1780 København V
T: 33156565; Fax: 33937171
Founded: 1959; Members: 1800
Focus: Food *03160*

Lysteknisk Selskab (LTS), Engholmvej 19, Postbox 28 Stenløse
T: 47171800; Fax: 47170832
Founded: 1948; Members: 725
Pres: Mogens Munk; Gen Secr: Joergen Klausen
Focus: Electric Eng
Periodical
Lys (quarterly) *03161*

Matematiklaererforeningen, Pilegårdsparken 93, 3460 Birkerød
Founded: 1931; Members: 1048
Focus: Math; Educ *03162*

Det Medicinske Selskab i København / The Medical Society of Copenhagen, Trondhjemsgade 9, 2100 København Ø
T: 31380984; Fax: 35448503
Founded: 1772; Members: 2596
Pres: Gerda Krag Jacobsen; Gen Secr: Marianne Pontoppidan
Focus: Med *03163*

Mellemfolkeligt Samvirke / Danish Association for International Cooperation, Borgergade 10-14, 1300 København K
T: 33326244; Fax: 33156243
Founded: 1944; Members: 6000
Gen Secr: Bjoern Foerde
Focus: Int'l Relat
Periodicals
Kontakt (8 times annually)
MS Biblioteksnyt (18 times annually)
MS Revy (8 times annually)
ZAPP (bi-monthly) *03164*

Militaerteknisk Forening (MtF) / Danish Military Technical Society, c/o Ingeniørforeningen i Danmark, Vester Farimagsgade 29, 1780 København V
T: 33156565; Fax: 33937171
Members: 625
Focus: Eng; Military Sci *03165*

Nationaløkonomisk Forening, c/o Danmarks Nationalbank, Havnegade 5, 1093 København K
T: 31141411; Fax: 33913041
Founded: 1873; Members: 1500
Pres: Niels Christian Nielsen; Gen Secr: Lisbeth Borup
Focus: Econ
Periodical
Nationaløkonomisk Tidsskrift (3 times annually) *03166*

Naturhistorisk Forening for Jylland, c/o Natural History Museum, 8000 Arhus C
T: 86129777
Founded: 1911
Focus: Hist; Nat Sci
Periodical
Flora og Fauna (quarterly) *03167*

Naturhistorisk Forening for Nordsjaelland, Hyttebakken 4, 3400 Hillerød
Founded: 1967
Focus: Hist; Nat Sci *03168*

Nordforsk, H. C. Andersens Blvd 18, 1553 København V
Focus: Sci *03169*

Nordic Federation for Medical Education, c/o Rigshospitalet, Tagensvej 18, København N
T: 35375252; Fax: 46307750
Founded: 1966
Gen Secr: Jørgen Nystrup
Focus: Adult Educ; Med; Educ *03170*

Nordic Society for Cell Biology, Bülowsvej 13, 1870 København
Founded: 1960; Members: 350
Focus: Cell Biol & Cancer Res *03171*

Nordisk Akustik Selskab (NAS) / Acoustical Society of Scandinavia, c/o Technical University of Denmark, Lundtoftevej 100, 2800 Lyngby
Founded: 1956; Members: 800
Focus: Acoustics
Periodical
NAS-Proceedings *03172*

Nordisk Byggedag (NBD) / Nordic Building Conference, Pakhus 12, Dampfaergevej 10, 2100 København Ø
T: 35430055; Fax: 35431055
Founded: 1927; Members: 222
Gen Secr: Kirsten Sørensen
Focus: Urban Plan
Periodical
Congress Literature *03173*

Nordisk Cerealist Foreningen, c/o Afdeling for Teknisk Biokemi, Danmarks Tekniske Højskole, 2800 Lyngby
Founded: 1931; Members: 300
Focus: Agri *03174*

Nordisk Forening for Celleforskning, c/o Biological Institute of the Carlsberg Foundation, Tagensvej 16, 2200 København N
Focus: Cell Biol & Cancer Res *03175*

Nordisk Forening for Rettssociologi, c/o Copenhagen School of Economics, Howitzvej 60, 2000 København F
Founded: 1966
Focus: Law; Sociology
Periodical
Newsletter (semi-annually) *03176*

Nordisk Institut for Asienstudier (NIAS) / Nordic Institute of Asian Studies, Leifsgade 33, 2300 København S
T: 31548844; E-Mail: sec@nias.ku.dk; Fax: 32962530
Founded: 1967
Gen Secr: Thommy Svensson
Focus: Humanities; Soc Sci
Periodical
NIASnytt: Nordic Newsletter of Asian Studies (quarterly) *03177*

Nordisk Institut for Teoretisk Fysik (NORDITA), Blegdamsvej 17, 2100 København
T: 35325500; E-Mail: nordita@nordita.dk; Fax: 31389157
Founded: 1957; Members: 5
Pres: P. Hoyer
Focus: Physics
Periodicals
NORDITA Årsberetning: NORDITA Annual Report (annually)
NORDITA Preprint *03178*

Nordisk Kollegium for Fysisk Oceanografi, c/o Institut for Fysisk Oceanografi, Haraldsgade 6, 2200 København N
Fax: 1822565
Founded: 1965
Focus: Oceanography *03179*

Nordisk Laederforskningsråd (NLFR), Gregersensvej, 2630 Taastrup
T: 43710663
Founded: 1960; Members: 13
Focus: Materials Sci *03180*

Nordisk Neurokirurgisk Forening (NNF), c/o Neurosurgical Dept, Arhus Kommunehospital, Nørrebrogade 44, 8000 Arhus C
T: 86125555; Fax: 86139597
Founded: 1945; Members: 95
Focus: Surgery *03181*

Nordisk Numismatisk Union, c/o Den Kgl. Mønt- og Medaillesamling, Nationalmuseet, 1220 København K
Fax: 33155521
Focus: Numismatics
Periodical
Nordisk Numismatisk Unions Medlemsblad (8 times annually) *03182*

Nordisk Statistisk Sekretariat, Sejrøgade 11, 2100 København Ø
Fax: 1184801
Founded: 1969
Focus: Stats
Periodicals
Nordisk Statistik Arsbok: Yearbook of Nordic Statistics (annually)
Nordisk Statistik Skriftserie (irregularly)
Tekniske Rapporter (semi-annually) . . . *03183*

Orientalsk Samfund, c/o University of Copenhagen, Njalsgade 80, 1200 København S
Founded: 1915; Members: 50
Pres: Dr. Leif Littrup; Gen Secr: Prof. J.P. Asmussen
Focus: Ethnology
Periodical
Acta Orientalia 03184

Orlogsmuseetsvenner – Marinehistorisk Selskab, c/o Orlogsmuseet, Overgade 58, 1415 København K
Founded: 1951; Members: 1000
Pres: Per Wessel-Tolvig
Focus: Military Sci; Hist; Transport
Periodical
Marinehistorisk Tidsskrift (quarterly) . . . 03185

Paedagogisk Forening, c/o Hanne Thorsen, Gernersgade 1, 1319 København K
Founded: 1940; Members: 700
Focus: Sociology; Educ
Periodical
Det Paedagogiske Selskab: Dansk Paedagogisk Tidsskrift (9 times annually) 03186

Polymerteknisk Selskab (PTS), c/o Dansk Ingeniørforening, Vester Farimagsgade 31, 1606 København V
Founded: 1957; Members: 330
Focus: Eng 03187

Polyteknisk Forening, c/o Danmarks Tekniske Universitet, Anker Engelunds Vej 1, 2800 Lyngby
T: 45881104; Fax: 45881353
Founded: 1845; Members: 4200
Focus: Eng
Periodicals
PF nyt (weekly)
Polygraphus (bi-monthly)
Rusbogen (annually) 03188

Rektorkollegiet, c/o Undervisningsministeriet, Frederiksholms Kanal 26, 1220 København K
T: 33925403; E-Mail: cb@rks.dk; Fax: 33925075
Founded: 1967
Pres: Hans Peter Jensen; Gen Secr: Ellen Hansen
Focus: Educ 03189

Samfundet for Dansk Genealogi og Personalhistorie, Groenneves 23, 2830 Virum
Founded: 1879; Members: 1100
Pres: Finn Andersen; Gen Secr: Poul Steen
Focus: Genealogy
Periodical
Personalhistorisk Tidsskrift (semi-annually) 03190

Samfundet til Udgivelse af Dansk Musik, Gråbrøreståde 18, 1156 København K
Founded: 1871; Members: 150
Focus: Music
Periodical
Bulletin (bi-annually) 03191

Sammenslutningen af Danmarks Forskningsbiblioteker (SDF), c/o Danmarks Tekniske Bibliotek, Anker Engelundsvej 1, 2800 Lyngby
T: 45939979
Founded: 1949; Members: 135
Focus: Libraries & Bk Sci
Periodical
DF-Revy (10 times annually) 03192

Sammenslutningen af Danske Kunstforeninger / National Committee of Danish Art Societies, Skt. Annae Pl 10c, 1250 København K
Founded: 1942; Members: 15000
Pres: Bodil Olesen; Gen Secr: Eidenert
Focus: Arts 03193

Sammenslutningen af Lokalarkiver, Postbox 235, 7100 Vejle
T: 75840898; Fax: 75831801
Founded: 1949; Members: 430
Focus: Archives
Periodical
OmSLAget (monthly) 03194

Sammenslutningen af Medieforskere i Danmark, c/o Institut for Uddannelse og Socialisering, Alborg Universitetscenter, 9100 Alborg
Members: 71
Focus: Journalism 03195

Sammenslutningen af Praktiserende Dyrlaeger (SAPD), Rosenlunds Allé 8, 2720 Vanløse
T: 31710888
Founded: 1966; Members: 875
Focus: Vet Med 03196

Scandinavian Society for Economic and Social History, c/o University of Odense, Campusvej 55, 5230 Odense M
Fax: 65932974
Focus: Hist; Econ; Sociology
Periodical
The Scandinavian Economic History Review (3 times annually) 03197

Scandinavian Sociological Association, c/o Munksgrad, Nørre Sogade 35, 1370 København K
Focus: Sociology 03198

Sektionen for Klinisk Neurofysiologi / Danish Society of EEG and Clinical Neurophysiology, c/o A. Fuglsang-Frederiksen, Brogaardsvej 26, 2680 Gentofte
Founded: 1946; Members: 39
Focus: Physiology 03199

Selskab for Arbejdsmiljø, c/o Ingeniørforeningen i Danmark, Vester Farimagsgade 31, 1606 København V
T: 33156565
Focus: Sociology
Periodical
Loke (bi-monthly) 03200

Selskab for Nordisk Filologi, c/o Institut for Navneforskning, Københavns Universitet Amager, Njalsgade 80, 2300 København S
T: 35328561; Fax: 35328568
Founded: 1912; Members: 150
Pres: H. Galberg Jacobsen; Gen Secr: M. Lerche Nielsen
Focus: Ling; Lit
Periodical
Selskab for Nordisk Filologi Årsberetning (bi-annually) 03201

Selskabet for Danmarks Kirkehistorie, c/o Institut for Kirkehistorie, Købmagergade 44-46, 1150 København K
T: 35323611; Fax: 35323639
Founded: 1849; Members: 650
Pres: Prof. Dr. Martin Schwarz-Leusten; Gen Secr: Maria Rasmussen
Focus: Hist; Rel & Theol
Periodical
Kirkehistoriske Samlinger (annually) . . . 03202

Selskabet for Dansk Kulturhistorie, c/o Botanisk Centralbibliotek, Sølvgade 83, 1307 København K
Founded: 1936; Members: 30
Pres: Steffen Heiberg; Gen Secr: Peter Wagner
Focus: Hist
Periodical
Kulturminder (irregularly) 03203

Selskabet for Dansk Skolehistorie, c/o Dr. Vagn Skovgaard-Petersen, Taffelbays Allé 15, 2900 Hellerup
Founded: 1966
Focus: Hist; Educ
Periodical
Årbog for Dansk Skolehistorie: Yearbook on History of Danish Schools (Education) (annually) 03204

Selskabet for Dansk Teaterhistorie, c/o B. Lemvigh-Müller, Gruntvigsvej 27b, 1864 København V
Founded: 1911
Focus: Hist; Perf Arts 03205

Selskabet for Filosofi og Psykologi, Kobmagergade 50, 1150 København K
Founded: 1926
Focus: Philos; Psych 03206

Selskabet for Københavns Historie, c/o Stadsarkivet, Radhuset, 1599 København V
T: 33662370; Fax: 33159212
Founded: 1935; Members: 1000
Focus: Hist 03207

Selskabet for Naturlaerens Udbredelse, c/o UNI-C, Vermundsgade 5, 2100 København Ø
Founded: 1824; Members: 200
Pres: Prof. Dorte Olesen; Gen Secr: Dr. J.J. Christiansen
Focus: Nat Sci
Periodical
Kwant (quarterly) 03208

Selskabet for Tekniske Uddanelsespørgsmal, c/o Dansk Ingeniørforening, Vester Farimagsgade 31, 1606 København V
Focus: Educ; Eng 03209

Selskabet til Udgivelse af Danske Mindesmaerker, c/o Nivaagaards Malerisamling, Gammel Strandvej 2, 2990 Nivaa
Founded: 1919; Members: 200
Focus: Hist; Arts 03210

Skandinavisk Museumsforbund, Danish Section, c/o Den Hirschsprungske Samling, Stockholmsgade 20, 2100 København Ø
T: 31420336; E-Mail: hirsch@post3.tele.dk; Fax: 35433510
Founded: 1915; Members: 150
Pres: Brigitte Kjaer; Gen Secr: Jens Peter Munk
Focus: Arts; Cultur Hist 03211

Socialpaedagogernes Landsforbund, Brolaeggerstraede 9, 1211 København K
T: 33140058; Fax: 33930604
Focus: Educ; Sociology
Periodical
Socialpaedagogen (bi-weekly) 03212

Societas Heraldica Scandinavica / Heraldisk Selskab, c/o Carsten Frölich, Maltevangen 15, 2820 Gentofte
Founded: 1959; Members: 700
Focus: Genealogy
Periodical
Heraldisk Tidsskrift (semi-annually) . . . 03213

Société Internationale pour l'Enseignement Commercial, Hunderupvej 122A, 5230 Odense M
T: 66121966; Fax: 66145794
Founded: 1901; Members: 2400
Focus: Adult Educ
Periodical
Revue Internationale pour l'Enseignment Commercial (semi-annually) 03214

Sønderjyllands Amatørarkaeologer, c/o Johan Jessen, Lindsnakkevej 7, 6200 Abenrå
Founded: 1966
Focus: Archeol 03215

Teknisk Skoleforening, c/o Ejnar Bo Pedersen, Munkehatten 28, 5220 Odense Ø
T: 66158725; Fax: 66154555
Founded: 1891; Members: 63
Focus: Educ; Eng 03216

Teologisk Forening ved Københavns Universitet, Valkendorfsgade 23, 1151 København K
Founded: 1905; Members: 227
Focus: Rel & Theol 03217

Tysklaererforeningen for Gymnasiet og Hf., c/o Nanna Bjargum, Egebjergvej 263, 4500 Nykøbing
T: 59328544
Founded: 1933; Members: 900
Focus: Ling; Educ
Periodical
Meddelelser FRA Tysklaererforeningen for Gymnasiet og Hf. (bi-monthly) 03218

Det Udenrigspolitiske Selskab, Amaliegade 40a, 1256 København K
T: 33148886; E-Mail: udenrigs@udenrigs.dk; Fax: 33148520
Founded: 1946; Members: 1400
Pres: Uffe Ellemann-Jensen; Gen Secr: Klaus Carsten Pedersen
Focus: Poli Sci
Periodicals
Udenrigs (quarterly)
Udenrigspolitiske Skrifter (irregularly) . . 03219

Dominican Republic

Academia Dominicana de la Historia, Calle Mercedes 50, Santo Domingo
T: 6894584; Fax: 5357891
Founded: 1931; Members: 67
Pres: Hugo E. Polanco Brito; Gen Secr: Manuel de J.S. Mañon Arredondo
Focus: Hist
Periodical
Clio (quarterly) 03220

Academia Dominicana de la Lengua, Av Tiradentes 66, Ensanche La Fe, Santo Domingo
Members: 13
Pres: Mariano Lebrón Saviñón; Gen Secr: Manuel Goico Castro
Focus: Ling 03221

Asociación Dominicana de Bibliotecarios (ASODOBI), c/o Biblioteca Nacional, Plaza de la Cultura, César Nicolás Penson 91, Santo Domingo
T: 6884086
Founded: 1974; Members: 90
Pres: P.J. Mella Chavier; Gen Secr: V. Regús
Focus: Libraries & Bk Sci
Periodical
El Papiro (quarterly) 03222

Asociación Dominicana de Rectores de Universidades, Calle Luperón esq Hostos, Edif Comisioń de Monumentos, Zona Colonial, Apdo 2465, Santo Domingo
T: 6894931; Fax: 6877401
Founded: 1981
Gen Secr: Dr. G. Mieses
Focus: Educ 03223

Asociación Dominicana pro Bienestar de la Familia, Apdo 1053, Santo Domingo
Focus: Family Plan
Periodicals
Población y Desarrollo
Resúmenes sobre Población Dominicana 03224

Asociación Médica de Santiago, Apdo 445, Santiago de los Caballeros
Founded: 1941; Members: 65
Pres: Dr. Rafael Fernández Lazala
Focus: Med 03225

Asociación Médica Dominicana, Apdo 1237, Santo Domingo
Founded: 1941; Members: 1551
Pres: Dr. Angel S. Chan Aquino
Focus: Med 03226

Grupo Bibliográfico Nacional de la República Dominicana, c/o Archivo General de la Nación, Calle Chiclana de la Frontera, Santo Domingo
Focus: Libraries & Bk Sci 03227

Servicio de Documentación y Biblioteca, Palacio de Educación, Santo Domingo
Founded: 1958
Focus: Libraries & Bk Sci; Doc 03228

Sociedad Amantes de la Luz, España Esquina Av Central, Santiago de los Caballeros
Founded: 1874
Focus: Arts 03229

Ecuador

Academia Ecuatoriana de la Lengua, Apdo 3460, Quito
Founded: 1875
Pres: Galo René Pérez; Gen Secr: Piedad Larrea Borja
Focus: Lit
Periodicals
Memorias (quarterly)
Obras de la Literatura Ecuatoriana (quarterly) 03230

Academia Ecuatoriana de Medicina, c/o Casa de la Cultura Ecuatoriana, Apdo 67, Quito
Founded: 1958
Focus: Med 03231

Agence Latinoaméricaine d'Information (ALAI), Pasaje San Luis 104, Of 304, Casilla 596-A, Suc 3, Quito
T: (02) 572689; Fax: 580835
Founded: 1976
Focus: Computer & Info Sci
Perindical
ALAI Servicio Mensual de Información y Documentación (monthly) 03232

Andean Institute of Popular Arts, Calle Diego de Atienza y Av América, Quito
T: (02) 563096
Founded: 1977; Members: 8
Focus: Arts
Periodicals
Bocina de los Andes (monthly)
Revista IADAP (semi-annually) 03233

Asociación Ecuatoriana de Bibliotecarios (AEB), c/o Casa de la Cultura, Apdo 67, Quito
T: 528840
Focus: Libraries & Bk Sci 03234

Asociación Ecuatoriana de Museos (ASEM) / Ecuadorian Association of Museums, Caldas 340, Apdo 175B, Quito
Founded: 1977; Members: 60
Focus: Archives; Anthro; Nat Sci; Educ
Periodical
Boletín (quarterly) 03235

Asociación Latinoamericana de Educación Radiofónica (ALER) / Latin American Association for Education by Radio, Valladolid 479, Casilla 4639-A, Quito
T: (02) 524358; Fax: 503996
Founded: 1972; Members: 54
Focus: Educ
Periodical
Boletín Informativo ALER (bi-monthly) . . 03236

Asociación Latinoamericana de Escuelas y Facultades de Enfermería (ALADEFE) / Latin American Association of Nursing Science Schools and Departments, Casilla 1395-A, Suc 3, Quito
T: (02) 521053, 230764; Fax: 521053
Founded: 1986
Focus: Educ
Periodicals
Boletín Informativo ALADEFE (semi-annually)
Revista ALADEFE 03237

Casa de la Cultura Ecuatoriana, Av 6 de Diciembre 794, Apdo 67, Quito
Founded: 1944; Members: 25
Pres: Camilo Restrepo
Focus: Lit 03238

Centro Andino de Tecnología Rural (CATER), Av Pío Jamarillo Avarado y Pedro Vaca de la Cadena, Casilla 399, Loja
T: 961329
Founded: 1980
Focus: Eng 03239

Centro de Investigaciones Históricas, Apdo 7110, Guayaquil
Founded: 1930; Members: 15
Focus: Hist 03240

Centro Médico Federal del Azuay, Apdo 233, Cuenca
Founded: 1944
Focus: Med 03241

Comisión Ecuatoriana de Energía Atómica, Av González Suárez 2351, Apdo 17-01-2517, Quito
T: (02) 458013; Fax: 253097
Founded: 1958; Members: 40
Gen Secr: Celiano Almeida
Focus: Nucl Res 03242

Federación Nacional de Médicos del Ecuador, Av de los Estadios e Iñaquito, Quito
Founded: 1942; Members: 1435
Pres: Dr. Leonardo Malo Borrero; Gen Secr: Dr. Alfredo Pérez Hueda
Focus: Med 03243

Instituto Latinoamericano de Investigaciones Sociales (ILDIS) / Latin American Social Science Research Institute, Av Colón 1346, Apdo 367A, Quito
T: 543000
Founded: 1974
Focus: Sociology; Econ; Poli Sci . . . 03244

Sociedad Ecuatoriana de Alergía y Ciencias Afinas (SEACA), Av 12 de Octubre 2206, Apdo 2339, Quito
T: 235632
Founded: 1960; Members: 25
Focus: Immunology 03245

Sociedad Ecuatoriana de Astronomía, Apdo 165, Quito
Founded: 1956
Focus: Astronomy 03246

Sociedad Ecuatoriana de Pediatría, Apdo 5865, Guayaquil
Founded: 1945
Pres: Dr. Isidoro Martinez McKliff
Focus: Pediatrics 03247

Sociedad Latinoamericana de Farmacología, Apdo 8884-S7, Quito
T: 235632
Founded: 1960; Members: 1450
Focus: Pharmacol 03248

Egypt

Academy of Scientific Research and Technology, 101 Sharia Kasr El-Aini, Cairo
T: (02) 3542714; Fax: 356280
Founded: 1971
Pres: Prof. Dr. Ali A. Hebeish
Focus: Sci; Eng 03249

Academy of the Arabic Language, 15 Aziz Abaza St, Zamalek, Cairo
T: (02) 3405931, 3405983; E-Mail: aal@idsc-gov.eg; Fax: 3412002
Founded: 1932; Members: 40
Pres: Prof. Dr. Ahmed k712 Abdel Megged, Ibrahim Shawky Dheif
Focus: Ling
Periodicals
Councils and Conferences Proceedings (annually)
Review (semi-annually) 03250

African Society, 5 Ahmed Hishmat St, Zamalek, Cairo
T: (02) 3407658
Founded: 1972
Gen Secr: M. Fouad El-Bidewy
Focus: Int'l Relat
Periodicals
Africa Newsletter
African Studies (irregularly) 03251

African Soil Science Association (ASSS), c/o Dept of Soil Science, Faculty of Agriculture, Ain Shams University, Shobra El-Khema, Cairo
T: (02) 2201296; Fax: 2913059
Founded: 1986; Members: 66
Focus: Agri 03252

Afro-Asian Philosophy Association (AAPA), c/o Faculty of Education, Heliopolis, Cairo
T: (02) 2460531
Founded: 1978
Focus: Philos 03253

Alexandria Medical Association, 4 Sharia G. Carducci, Alexandria
Founded: 1921; Members: 1200
Pres: Prof. H.S. El-Badawi; Gen Secr: Prof. Dr. T. Aboul-Azi
Focus: Med
Periodical
The Alexandria Medical Journal (quarterly) 03254

Arab Aerospace Educational Organization, 11 Emad Al-Din St, Cairo
T: (02) 918561
Founded: 1986; Members: 11
Pres: M.F. Rayan; Gen Secr: Shawky I. Sarg
Focus: Aero 03255

Arab Center for Energy Studies (ACES), c/o OAPEC, POB 108, Cairo
T: (02) 3542660; Fax: 3542601
Founded: 1983
Focus: Develop Areas 03256

Arab Commission for International Law, c/o LAS, POB 11642, Cairo
T: (02) 750511; Fax: 740331
Focus: Law 03257

Arab Council for Childhood and Development (ACCD), POB 15, Orman, Cairo
T: (02) 3408011/12; E-Mail: accd@link.com.eg; Fax: 3408013
Founded: 1987
Pres: Prince Talal Bin Abdul Aziz Al Saud
Focus: Educ
Periodicals
Khatwa (quarterly)
The State of the Child in the Arab World (annually) 03258

Arab Higher Committee for Pharmacological Affairs, c/o LAS, POB 11642, Cairo
T: (02) 750511; Fax: 740331
Focus: Pharmacol 03259

Arab Institute of Navigation (AIN), POB 1029, Alexandria
T: (03) 5467221; Fax: 4311882
Founded: 1978; Members: 276
Focus: Transport
Periodical
AIN News Bulletin (semi-annually) . . . 03260

Arab Management Society (AMS), 23 Wadi El-Nil, Mahandesseen, Cairo
T: (02) 3446729; Fax: 3445729
Founded: 1989
Focus: Business Admin 03261

Arab Organization for Standardization and Metrology, 27 Sharia Dokki, Cairo
T: 818580
Founded: 1965
Focus: Standards 03262

Arab Scientific Advisory Committee for Blood Transfer, c/o LAS, Social Affairs Dept, POB 11642, Cairo
T: (02) 750511; Fax: 740331
Focus: Med 03263

Arab States Regional Centre for Functional Literacy in Rural Areas (ASFEC), Sirs El-Layyan, Menoufia
Founded: 1952
Focus: Adult Educ 03264

Armenian Artistic Union (A.A.U.), 3 Sharia Soliman, El-Halaby, POB 1060, Cairo
T: (02) 742282
Founded: 1920; Members: 300
Pres: Vahag Depoyan
Focus: Arts 03265

Association for Medical Education in the Middle East, POB 1517, Alexandria
T: (03) 4930090; Fax: 4838916
Focus: Educ; Med 03266

Association of African Maritime Training Institutes (AAMTI) / Association des Instituts Africains de Formation Maritime, Gamal Abdel Nasser St, POB 1029, Alexandria
T: (03) 5600245; Fax: 5602144
Founded: 1985; Members: 18
Pres: Dr. Gamal Mokhtar; Gen Secr: Dr. Refaat Rashad
Focus: Navig; Educ
Periodical
AAMTI Newsletter (semi-annually) . . . 03267

Association of Agricultural Research Institutions in the Near East and North Africa, c/o FAO Regional Office for the Near East, 11 Eslah El Zeraie St, Cairo, POB 2223
T: (202) 3602324; E-Mail: Ibrahim.Hamdan@Field.Fao.org; Fax: 3495981
Founded: 1985; Members: 16
Pres: Dr. A. Arifi; Gen Secr: Dr. Ibrahim Hamdan
Focus: Agri 03268

Atelier / Groupement d'Artistes et d'Ecrivains, 6 Victor Bassili St, Alexandria
T: (03) 4820526; Fax: 4837662
Founded: 1934; Members: 350
Pres: Prof. Dr. Naima El-Shishiny; Gen Secr: Prof. Dr. Farouk Wahba
Focus: Arts; Lit; Photo; Music 03269

Cairo Odontological Society, 39 Kasr El-Nil, Cairo
Pres: Dr. A.M. Abdel-Azim; Gen Secr: Dr. J. Alcée
Focus: Dent 03270

Eastern Mediterranean Hand Society, 13 Messaha St, Dokki, Cairo
T: (02) 3484483
Founded: 1980
Focus: Surgery 03271

Egyptian Association for Library and Information Science, c/o Dept of Archives, Librarianship and Information Science, Faculty of Arts, University of Cairo, Cairo
T: (02) 728211
Founded: 1956; Members: 4000
Pres: Dr. M. El-Shenity; Gen Secr: Hamed Diab
Focus: Libraries & Bk Sci; Computer & Info Sci 03272

Egyptian Association for Mental Health, 1 Sharia Tlhami, Qasr Al-Doubara, Cairo
Founded: 1948; Members: 630
Focus: Psych 03273

Egyptian Association for Psychological Studies, Tager Bldg, 1 Osiris St, Garden City, Cairo
T: (02) 3541857
Founded: 1948; Members: 1200
Pres: Dr. Fouad A.-L.H. Abou-Hatab
Focus: Psych
Periodical
Yearbook of Psychology (annually) . . . 03274

Egyptian Association of Archives, Librarianship and Information Science (EALJS), c/o Dept of Library and Information Science, Faculty of Arts, University, Cairo
T: 22167
Founded: 1978
Focus: Archives; Libraries & Bk Sci; Computer & Info Sci 03275

Egyptian Botanical Society, 1 Ozoris St, Garden City, Cairo
Founded: 1956; Members: 230
Pres: Prof. Dr. A.M. Salama; Gen Secr: Dr. Mohamed Fawzy
Focus: Botany
Periodical
Egyptian Journal of Botany (3 times annually) 03276

Egyptian Dental Federation, 42 Sharia Kasr El-Aini, Cairo
Focus: Dent
Periodical
Egyptian Dental Journal (quarterly) . . . 03277

Egyptian Geographical Society, Sharia Kasr El-Aini, Jardin du Ministère d'Irrigation, Cairo
T: (02) 3545450
Founded: 1875
Pres: Soliman A. Huzzayn
Focus: Geography
Periodical
Bulletin 03278

Egyptian Horticultural Society, POB 46, Cairo
Founded: 1915
Focus: Hort 03279

Egyptian Medical Association, 42 Sharia Kasr El-Aini, Cairo
Founded: 1919; Members: 2142
Pres: Prof. Dr. A. El-Kater; Gen Secr: Prof. Dr. A.H. Shaaban
Focus: Med
Periodical
Journal (monthly) 03280

Egyptian Organization for Biological Products and Vaccines, 51 Sharia Wezarat El Zeraa, Agouza, Giza
Focus: Bio 03281

Egyptian Orthopaedic Association, Dar El-Hekmah, 42 Sharia Kasr El-Aini, Cairo
Founded: 1948; Members: 350
Pres: Dr. Mohammed Abdulla
Focus: Orthopedics 03282

Egyptian School Library Association (ESLA), 35 Sharia Alhalaa, Cairo
Focus: Libraries & Bk Sci 03283

The Egyptian Society for the Dissemination of Universal Culture and Knowledge (ESDUCK), 1081 Corniche El-Nil St, POB 24, Cairo
T: 20295, 25079
Focus: Ethnology; Cultur Hist 03284

Egyptian Society of Dairy Science, 1 Ouziris St, Garden City, Cairo
Founded: 1972
Pres: Dr. Ismael Yousry
Focus: Dairy Sci
Periodical
Egyptian Journal of Dairy Science . . . 03285

Egyptian Society of Engineers, 28 Sharia Ramses, Cairo
Founded: 1920
Pres: Prof. Dr. Ibrahim Adham El-Demirdash; Gen Secr: Dr. Mohamed M. El-Hashimy
Focus: Eng 03286

Egyptian Society of International Law, 16 Sharia Ramses, Cairo
T: (02) 743162
Founded: 1945; Members: 650
Pres: Dr. Fouad Abdel Moncim Riad; Gen Secr: Dr. Moufeed Chehab
Focus: Law
Periodical
Revue Egyptienne de Droit International (annually) 03287

Egyptian Society of Medicine and Tropical Hygiene, 2 Sharia Fouad I, Alexandria
Founded: 1927
Pres: Dr. Ahmed Helmi; Gen Secr: Dr. Ibrahim Abdel-Sayed
Focus: Hygiene; Trop Med 03288

Egyptian Society of Parasitology, Tager Bldg, 1 Ozoris St, Garden City, Cairo
Founded: 1967; Members: 350
Pres: Prof. Mahmoud Hafez
Focus: Stats 03289

Egyptian Society of Political Economy, Statistics and Legislation, 16 Sharia Ramses, POB 732, Cairo
T: (02) 750797
Founded: 1909; Members: 3020
Pres: Dr. Atif Sidky; Gen Secr: Mahmoud Hafez Ghanem
Focus: Law; Stats; Poli Sci; Econ
Periodical
L'Egypte Contemporaine (quarterly) . . . 03290

General Organization for Housing and Building Research, POB 1770, Cairo
T: (02) 3556853; E-Mail: hbrc@idscl.gov.eg; Fax: 3367179
Founded: 1956; Members: 651
Pres: Prof. Dr. Omaima Ahmed Salah; Gen Secr: Prof. Dr. A. El-Mallwany
Focus: Urban Plan; Civil Eng 03291

Hellenic Society of Ptolemaic Egypt, 20 Sharia Fouad I, Alexandria
Founded: 1908
Pres: Dr. G. Partheniadis; Gen Secr: Costa A. Sandi
Focus: Hist 03292

High Council of Arts and Literature, 9 Sharia Hassan Sabri, Zamalek, Cairo
Founded: 1956
Focus: Arts; Lit 03293

High Council of Culture, 9 Sharia Hassan Sabri, Zamalek, Cairo
T: 818910, 814899
Founded: 1980
Focus: Arts; Lit 03294

Institut d'Egypte, 13 Sharia Sheikh Rihane, Cairo
Founded: 1798; Members: 160
Pres: Dr. Sileman Hazien; Gen Secr: P. Ghalioungui
Focus: Int'l Relat; Ethnology
Periodical
Bulletin (annually) 03295

Institute of Arab Music, 2 Sharia Tewfik, Alexandria
Pres: Ahmed Bey Hassan; Gen Secr: Aly Saad
Focus: Music 03296

Institute of Arab Music, 22 Sharia Ramses, Cairo
T: (02) 750702
Founded: 1924
Pres: Hassan taker Mok; Gen Secr: Farzy Rashad
Focus: Music 03297

National Centre for Educational Research, Central Ministry of Education, 33 Sharia Falaky, Cairo
Founded: 1972
Focus: Educ
Periodicals
Contemporary Trends in Education (semi-annually)
Educational Information Bulletin (monthly) 03298

National Information and Documentation Centre (NIDOC), Sharia Al-Tahrir, Dokki, Cairo
T: (02) 701696
Founded: 1955
Pres: Esmat El-Sarha
Focus: Doc; Computer & Info Sci
Periodical
Arab Science Abstracts 03299

National Research Centre, Al-Tahrir St, Dokki, Cairo
T: 701010
Founded: 1956
Focus: Sci
Periodical
Bulletin 03300

Ophthalmological Society of Egypt, Dar El-Hekma, 42 Sharia Kasr El-Aini, Cairo
Founded: 1902; Members: 480
Pres: Prof. Dr. El-Said Khalil Abou Shousa; Gen Secr: Dr. Ahmad Ez El-Din Naim
Focus: Ophthal
Periodical
Annual Bulletin (annually) 03301

Société Archéologique d'Alexandrie, 6 Sharia Mahmoud Moukhtar, POB 815, Alexandria
T: (03) 4820650
Founded: 1893; Members: 248
Pres: Dr. A. Sadek; Gen Secr: M. El-Abadi
Focus: Archeol
Periodical
Bulletin 03302

Société Entomologique d'Egypte, 14 Sharia Ramses, POB 430, Cairo
Founded: 1907; Members: 502
Pres: Prof. Mahmoud Hafez; Gen Secr: Dr. A.H.M. Kamel
Focus: Entomology 03303

Society for Coptic Archaeology, 222 Sharia Ramses, Cairo
Founded: 1934; Members: 360
Pres: Wassif Boutros Ghali; Gen Secr: Dr. A. Khater
Focus: Archeol
Periodical
Bulletin (annually) 03304

Supreme Council of Universities, University Buildings, Giza, Cairo
T: (02) 5738583; Fax: 5728722
Founded: 1950
Gen Secr: Prof. Dr. Ali El-Din Hijal
Focus: Educ 03305

World Aerospace Education Organization, 20 Saray El-Guezirah St, Zamalek, Cairo
T: (02) 3409323 703=3924270
Founded: 1978; Members: 179
Pres: Kamal Naguib; Gen Secr: Jule Zumwalt
Focus: Educ; Aero 03306

Zoological Society of Egypt, c/o Giza Zoo, Giza, Cairo
Members: 260
Pres: Dr. Hassan A. Hafez; Gen Secr: Mohamed H. Amer
Focus: Soc Sci
Periodical
Bulletin 03307

El Salvador

Academia Salvadoreña, Calle Poniente 13, San Salvador
Members: 22
Pres: Alfredo Martínez Moreno; Gen Secr: Prof. Alfredo Betancourt
Focus: Sci 03308

Academia Salvadoreña de la Historia, Km 10 Planes de Renderoz, Col. Los Angeles, Villa Lilia 13, San Salvador
Founded: 1925; Members: 18
Pres: Jorge Lardé y Larín; Gen Secr: Pedro Escalante Mena
Focus: Hist
Periodical
Boletín (irregularly) 03309

Asociación de Bibliotecarios de El Salvador, c/o Biblioteca Nacional, Av Norte y Calle Delgado 8a, San Salvador
T: 216312
Focus: Libraries & Bk Sci 03310

Asociación de Radiólogos de América Central y Panamá, c/o Dr. Raúl Argüello, 5a Av Norte 48, San Salvador
Focus: Radiology 03311

Ateneo de El Salvador, Av España 225, Edificio Quán, Apdo 13a, San Salvador
Founded: 1912; Members: 132
Focus: Arts 03312

Central American Dermatological Society, 95 Av Norte 626, San Salvador 01117
Founded: 1957
Focus: Derm 03313

Central American Paediatric Society, c/o Sociedad de Pediatría de El Salvador, Arce 1403, San Salvador
Focus: Pediatrics 03314

Central American Public Health Council, c/o ODECA, San Salvador
Focus: Public Health 03315

Centro de Estudios e Investigaciones Geotécnicas, Apdo 109, San Salvador
Founded: 1964
Focus: Geology 03316

Colegio Médico de El Salvador, Final Pasaje 10, Col. Miramonte, San Salvador
T: 267403
Founded: 1943; Members: 1710
Pres: Dr. Miguel Oquelí Colindres
Focus: Med 03317

Comisión Salvadoreña de Energía Nuclear, c/o Ministerio de Economía, Calle Poniente 1A y Av Norte 73, San Salvador
Founded: 1961
Focus: Energy 03318

Dirección General de Estadística y Censos, Arce 953, San Salvador
Founded: 1881
Focus: Stats 03319

Dirección General de Investigaciones Agronómicas, c/o Centro Nacional de Agronomía, Santa Tecla
Focus: Agri 03320

Sociedad de Anestiología de El Salvador, Gustavo Guerrero 640, San Salvador
Founded: 1958
Focus: Anesthetics 03321

Sociedad de Ginecología y Obstetricia de El Salvador, c/o Colegio Médico, Final Pasaje 10, Col. Miramonte, San Salvador
Founded: 1947; Members: 96
Pres: Dr. Douglas Jarquín
Focus: Gynecology 03322

Sociedad Médica de Salud Pública, c/o Colegio Médico, Final Pasaje 10, Col. Miramonte, San Salvador
Founded: 1960; Members: 85
Focus: Public Health 03323

Estonia

Estonian Academy of Sciences, Kohtu 6, 0001 Tallinn
T: (02) 442129; Fax: 451805
Founded: 1938; Members: 68
Pres: J. Engelbrecht; Gen Secr: U. Margna
Focus: Sci
Periodicals
Eesti Loodus: Nature of Estonia
Gorjutsie Slantsö: Oil Shale
Keel ja Kirjandus: Language and Literature
Toimetised: Proceedings
Uralica Linguistica 03324

Ethiopia

African Association of Science Editors (AASE), POB 2302, Addis Ababa
T: (01) 159813
Founded: 1985
Focus: Lit
Periodical
AASE Newsletter 03325

African Forum for Mathematical Ecology (AFME), c/o Asmara University, POB 32896, Asmara
Founded: 1990
Focus: Math; Ecology 03326

African Mountain Association (AMA), c/o University of Asmara, POB 1220, Asmara
T: (04) 113600
Founded: 1986
Focus: Geology
Periodical
African Mountains and Highlands Newsletter (annually) 03327

African Small Ruminant Research Network, POB 5689, Addis Ababa
T: (01) 613215; Fax: 611892
Focus: Agri
Periodical
Newsletter (quarterly) 03328

African Training and Research Centre for Women (ATRCW), POB 3001, Addis Ababa
T: (01) 517200, 517000
Founded: 1975; Members: 51
Focus: Sociology
Periodical
ATRCW Update (semi-annually) 03329

All Africa Leprosy and Rehabilitation Training Center (ALERT), POB 165, Addis Ababa
T: (01) 711110; Fax: 711199
Founded: 1965; Members: 18
Focus: Rehabil
Periodical
ALERT (annually) 03330

Association for the Advancement of Agricultural Sciences in Africa (AAASA), POB 30087, Addis Ababa
T: (01) 443536
Founded: 1968; Members: 1200
Gen Secr: Prof. M. El-Fouly
Focus: Agri
Periodicals
AAASA Newsletter (quarterly)
African Journal of Agricultural Sciences (semi-annually) 03331

Desert Locust Control Organization for Eastern Africa (DLCO-EA), POB 4255, Addis Ababa
Founded: 1962
Pres: Dr. A.M.H. Karrar
Focus: Ecology
Periodical
Annual Report (annually) 03332

Ethiopian Library and Information Association, POB 30530, Addis Ababa
T: (01) 110844
Founded: 1961; Members: 150
Pres: Mulugeta Hunde; Gen Secr: Girma Makonnen
Focus: Libraries & Bk Sci; Computer & Info Sci
Periodicals
Bulletin (semi-annually)
Directory of Ethiopian Libraries 03333

Ethiopian Medical Association, POB 2179, Addis Ababa
Founded: 1961
Pres: Dr. Abebe Haregewoin
Focus: Med
Periodical
Ethiopian Medical Journal (quarterly) . . 03334

Fiji

Fiji Law Society, POB 144, Ba
Pres: K.N. Govind; Gen Secr: G.P. Shankar
Focus: Law 03335

Fiji Medical Association, 2 Brown St, POB 1116, Suva
T: 315388; Fax: 315869
Founded: 1960; Members: 250
Pres: Dr. Sachida Mudaliar
Focus: Med 03336

Fiji Society, POB 1205, Suva
Founded: 1936; Members: 50
Pres: Ivan Williams
Focus: Sci
Periodical
Transactions (irregularly) 03337

Finland

Äidinkielen Opettajain Liitto (ÄOL), Vilppulantie 2, 00700 Helsinki
T: (09) 3511763; E-Mail: ajopet@freene.hnt.fi; Fax: 3511764
Founded: 1948; Members: 2700
Pres: Leena Kirstina; Gen Secr: Anne Helttunen
Focus: Ling; Educ; Lit
Periodicals
Virke (bi-monthly)
Yearbook (annually) 03338

Agronomiliitto / Association of Academic Agronomists, P. Makasiinikatu 6 A 8, 00130 Helsinki
T: (09) 171201; Fax: 171251
Founded: 1897; Members: 5000
Gen Secr: P. Rinne
Focus: Agri; Nutrition; Home Econ . . . 03339

Arkistoyhdistys / Archival Association, PL 755, 00101 Helsinki
T: (09) 176911
Founded: 1947; Members: 260
Focus: Archives
Periodical
Arkisto (irregularly) 03340

Cancer Society of Finland, Liisankatu 21 B 9, 00170 Helsinki
Pres: Risto Johansson; Gen Secr: Liisa Elovainio
Focus: Cell Biol & Cancer Res 03341

Ekonomiska Samfundet i Finland / Economic Society of Finland, c/o Svenska Handelshögskolan, Arkadiagatan 22, PL 479, 00101 Helsinki
T: (09) 431331; Fax: 43133382
Founded: 1894; Members: 873
Pres: Harald Bo; Gen Secr: Jan-Erik Krusberg
Focus: Econ
Periodical
Ekonomiska Samfundets Tidskrift (3 times annually) 03342

European Association for Environmental History, c/o Dept of Economic History, University of Helsinki, PL 54, 00014 Helsinki
T: (09) 1918900; E-Mail: Timo.Myllyntans@Helsinki.Fi; Fax: 1918924
Founded: 1988
Gen Secr: Timo Myllyntaus
Focus: Nat Sci; Hist 03343

Finlands Svenska Författareförening (FSF), Runebergsgatan 32 C 27, 00100 Helsinki
T: (09) 446871
Founded: 1919; Members: 190
Pres: Agneta Ara; Gen Secr: Mette Jensen
Focus: Lit 03344

Finska Kemistsamfundet / Chemical Society of Finland, Hietaniemenkatu 2, 00100 Helsinki
Founded: 1891; Members: 574
Pres: Olle Teleman; Gen Secr: Urban Wiik
Focus: Chem 03345

Finska Läkaresällskapet / Medical Society of Finland, PL 316, 00171 Helsinki
T: (09) 665576; Fax: 1356463
Founded: 1835; Members: 1000
Pres: Prof. Leif Anderson; Gen Secr: Dr. Marianne Grippenberg
Focus: Med
Periodical
Finska Läkaresällskapets Handlingar (semi-annually) 03346

Finska Vetenskaps-Societeten, Mariankatu 5A, 00170 Helsinki
T: (09) 633005; Fax: 661065
Founded: 1838; Members: 323
Pres: Prof. Henrik Wallgren; Gen Secr: Prof. Carl G. Gahmberg
Focus: Sci 03347

Geofysiikan Seura / Geophysical Society of Finland, Betonimiehenkuja 4, 02150 Espoo
T: (09) 46932448; Fax: 462205
Founded: 1926; Members: 300
Pres: Esko Kuusisto; Gen Secr: Satu Mertanen
Focus: Physics; Geophys; Oceanography
Periodicals
Geofysiikan päivät
Geophysica (semi-annually) 03348

Geologian Tutkimuskeskus / Geological Survey of Finland, Betonimiehenkuja 4, 02150 Espoo
T: (0205) 5011; Fax: 5012
Founded: 1886; Members: 800
Pres: Raimo Matikainen
Focus: Geology
Periodicals
Geologian tutkimuskeskus, Opas (annually)
Geologian tutkimuskeskus, Toimintakertomus
Geologian tutkimuskeskus, Tutkimusraportti
Geological Survey of Finland, Bulletin
Geological Survey of Finland, Special Paper 03349

Hallinnon Tutkimuksen Seura, c/o Dept of Administrative Sciences, University of Tampere, PL 607, 33101 Tampere
Founded: 1981; Members: 606
Pres: Prof. Iris Aaltio-Marjorola; Gen Secr: Jyri Lehtinen
Focus: Public Admin 03350

Historian Ystäväin Liitto / Society of the Friends of History, Kaupinkatu 22 A 5, 33500 Tampere
Founded: 1926; Members: 1500
Gen Secr: M. Linna
Focus: Hist
Periodicals
Historiallinen Aikakauskirja: Suuomen Historiallinen (quarterly)
Historiallinen Kirjasto (semi-annually)
Historian Aitta (irregularly) 03351

International Association of Technological University Libraries, c/o Dr. Sinikka Koskiala, Helsinki University of Technology, 02150 Espoo
T: (9) 4514112; E-Mail: sinikka.koskiala@hut.fi; Fax: 4514132
Founded: 1955; Members: 202
Pres: Dr Nancy Fjällbrant; Gen Secr: Sinikka Koskiala
Focus: Libraries & Bk Sci 03352

International Law Association: Finnish Branch, c/o Klaus Lagus, Tehtaankatu 4 B 11, 00140 Helsinki
T: (09) 666726; Fax: 631054
Founded: 1946; Members: 105
Pres: Prof. Bengt Broms; Gen Secr: Matti Tupamäki
Focus: Law; Int'l Relat 03353

International Peat Society (IPS), Kuokkalantie 4, 40420 Jyskä
T: (014) 674042; E-Mail: peatsocinternat@peatso.pp.fi; Fax: 677405
Founded: 1968; Members: 1200
Pres: Dr. Jens Dieter Becker-Platen; Gen Secr: Raimo Sopo
Focus: Geology; Ecology
Periodicals
Bulletin of the IPS (annually)
International Peat Journal (irregularly)
Proceedings of International Peat Congresses (every fourth year) 03354

Ius Gentium Association, 00171 Helsinki, PL 208
T: (09) 1912468; Fax: 1913076
Founded: 1983
Pres: Juhani Kortteinen
Focus: Law 03355

Juridiska Föreningen i Finland / Law Society of Finland, c/o Konow Rehn, Mannerheimvägen 8, 00100 Helsinki
Founded: 1862; Members: 778
Pres: Per Lindholm
Focus: Law
Periodical
Tidskrift utgiven av Juridiska Föreningen i Finland 03356

Kalevalaseura, Hallituskatu 1, 00170 Helsinki
T: (09) 131231; E-Mail: sirkka-liisamettomaki@helsinki.fi; Fax: 13123220
Founded: 1919; Members: 372
Pres: Pekka Laaksonen; Gen Secr: Sirkka-Liisa Mettomäki
Focus: Folklore; Ethnology; Ling; Hist
Periodical
Kalevalaseuran vuosikirja (annually) . . . 03357

Kansantaloudellinen Yhdistys / Finnish Economic Association, c/o Sinimaaria Ranki, Bank of Finland, PL 160, 00101 Helsinki
Founded: 1884; Members: 1012
Pres: Sinikka Salo; Gen Secr: Sinimaaria Ranki
Focus: Econ
Periodical
Kansantaloudellinen Aikakauskirja: The Finnish Economic Journal (quarterly) 03358

Kasvinsuojeluseura, c/o Agricultural Research Centre, 31600 Jokioinen
T: (016) 1881
Founded: 1931; Members: 1500
Pres: Risto Tahvonen; Gen Secr: Minna-Maria Linna
Focus: Agri 03359

Kemiallisteknillinen Yhdistys, Hietaniemenkatu 2, 00100 Helsinki
Founded: 1970; Members: 816
Pres: Jaakko E. Laine
Focus: Eng 03360

Klassillis-Filologinen Yhdistys / Klassisk-filologiska Föreningen / Classical Association of Finland, Vuorikatu 3 A, PL 4, 00014 Helsingin Yliopisto
T: (09) 1912682; Fax: 1912161
Founded: 1882; Members: 140
Pres: Prof. Dr. Heikki Solin; Gen Secr: Nicola Nykopp
Focus: Lit; Hist; Archeol
Periodical
Arctos: Acta philologica Fennica (annually) 03361

Kotikielen Seura, Castrenianum, PL 3, 00014 Helsingin Yliopisto
T: (09) 8746761; E-Mail: Hanna.Lappalainen@Helsinki.fi; Fax: 1913329
Founded: 1876; Members: 600
Pres: Pirkko Nuolijairi; Gen Secr: Hanna Lappalainen
Focus: Ling; Lit
Periodical
Virittäjä (quarterly) 03362

Maanmittaustieteiden Seura, PL 84, 00521 Helsinki
Fax: (09) 465077
Founded: 1926; Members: 960
Pres: Henrik Haggren
Focus: Surveying 03363

Maataloustuottajain Keskusliitto (MTK), Simonkatu 6, 00100 Helsinki
T: (09) 131151; Fax: 13115425
Founded: 1917
Focus: Agri 03364

Meijeritieteellinen Seura, c/o Dept of Food Technology, 00014 Helsingin Yliopisto, PL 27
Founded: 1938; Members: 300
Pres: Prof. Dr. Esko Uusi-Rauva
Focus: Food 03365

Museovirasto / National Board of Antiquities, PL 913, 00101 Helsinki
T: (09) 40501; E-Mail: Forename.Surname@NBA.fi; Fax: 4050300
Founded: 1884

Pres: Henrik Lilius
Focus: Hist; Ethnology; Preserv Hist Monuments; Numismatics; Archeol
Periodicals
Arkeologia Suomessa: Archaeology in Finland (annually)
Museoviraston arkeologian julkaisuja
Museoviraston rakennushistorian osaston raportteja: Annual Report (annually)
Museoviraston työväenkulttuurijulkaisuja
Nautica Fennica (annually)
Rakennushistorian osaston julkaisuja
Suomen kirkot: Finland's Churches . . . 03366

Nordic Council for Scientific Information, PL 237, 00171 Helsinki
T: (09) 1800480; Fax: 1800482
Founded: 1976; Members: 9
Pres: Lennart Thörnqvist; Gen Secr: Ylva Lindholm-Romantschuk
Focus: Computer & Info Sci; Libraries & Bk Sci
Periodicals
NORDINFO-publikation (irregularly)
NORDINFO-rapport (quarterly) 03367

Nordisk Odontologisk Förening, c/o Institute of Dentistry, University of Helsinki, Mannerheimintie 172, 00014 Helsingin Yliopisto
T: (09) 19127272; E-Mail: Jukka.Meurman@Helsinki.Fi; Fax: 19127517
Founded: 1917
Gen Secr: Prof. Jukka H. Meurman
Focus: Dent
Periodical
European Journal of Oral Sciences (bi-monthly) 03368

Rakenteiden Mekaniikan Seura, c/o Faculty of Information Technology, Helsiniki University of Technology, Tietotie 1, 02150 Espoo
T: (09) 4513498; Fax: 4513493
Founded: 1979; Members: 253
Pres: Kaj Riska; Gen Secr: Mika Reivivem
Focus: Eng 03369

Säteilyturvakeskus (STUK), PL 14, 00881 Helsinki
T: (09) 759881; Fax: 75988500
Founded: 1958
Pres: Jukka Laaksonen; Gen Secr: Antti Niittylä
Focus: Radiology; Safety
Periodicals
ST-guides
STUK-A-series
YVL-guides 03370

Scandinavian Association for Dental Research, c/o Institute of Dentistry, Mannerheimintie 172, PL 41, 00014 Helsingin Yliopisto
T: (09) 19127284; E-Mail: Jukka.Meurman@Helsinki.Fi; Fax: 19127517
Founded: 1866; Members: 1500
Focus: Dent 03371

Societas Amicorum Naturae Ouluensis, c/o Dept of Biology, University of Oulu, 90570 Oulu
T: (081) 5531535; Fax: 5531500
Founded: 1925; Members: 436
Pres: Dr. J. Lumme; Gen Secr: S. Kontunen-Soppela
Focus: Botany 03372

Societas Biochemica, Biophysica et Microbiologica Fenniae, c/o Div of Genetics, Dept of Biosciences, Jarma Institute, Viikinkaari 5, PL 56, 00014 Helsingin Yliopisto
Founded: 1945; Members: 1100
Pres: Prof. Tuula Teeri; Gen Secr: Dr. Jarmo Juuti
Focus: Biophys; Biochem; Microbio . . . 03373

Societas Biologica Fennica Vanamo, Unioninkatu 44, PL 7, 00014 Helsingin Yliopisto
T: (09) 1918620; E-Mail: Pertti.Uotila@Helsinki.Fi; Fax: 1918656
Founded: 1896; Members: 1600
Pres: Prof. Pertti Uotila; Gen Secr: K. Vainio-Mattila
Focus: Bio
Periodicals
Acta Botanica Fennica (irregularly)
Acta Zoologica Fennica (irregularly)
Annales Botanici Fennici (quarterly)
Annales Zoologici Fennici (quarterly)
Luonnon Tutkija: The Naturalist (5 times annually) 03374

Societas Entomologica Fennica, P. Rautatiekatu 13, 00100 Helsinki
T: (09) 1917392; Fax: 19174443
Founded: 1935
Pres: Dr. Antti Pekkarinen
Focus: Bio
Periodical
Entomologica Fennica (quarterly) 03375

Societas Medicinae Physicalis et Rehabilitationis Fenniae, c/o KYS Dept of Physical Medicine and Rehabilitation, PL 1777, 70211 Kuopis
T: (017) 173455; E-Mail: kpuustja@messl.uku.fi; Fax: 173466
Founded: 1956; Members: 150
Pres: Dr. Olavi Airaksinen; Gen Secr: Dr. Kaija Puustjärvi
Focus: Rehabil; Physiology; Physical Therapy 03376

Societas pro Fauna et Flora Fennica (SFFF), c/o Botanical Museum, PL 47, 00014 Helsingin Yliopisto
T: (09) 7084787; E-Mail: roland.skyten@helsinki.fi; Fax: 7084830
Founded: 1821; Members: 940
Pres: Dr. K.-G. Widen; Gen Secr: R. Skyten
Focus: Botany; Zoology
Periodicals
Acta Botanica Fennica (irregularly)
Acta Zoologica Fennica (irregularly)
Annales Botanici Fennici (quarterly)
Annales Zoologici Fennici (quarterly)
Memoranda Societatis pro Fauna et Flora Fennica (quarterly) 03377

Societas Scientiarum Fennica (SSF) / The Finnish Society of Sciences and Letters, Mariankatu 5, 00170 Helsinki
T: (09) 633005
Founded: 1838; Members: 170
Pres: Prof. Henrik Wallgren; Gen Secr: Prof. Carl G. Gahmberg
Focus: Sci 03378

Suomalainen Lääkäriseura Duodecim / The Finnish Medical Society Duodecim, Kalevankatu 11 A, 00100 Helsinki
T: (09) 618851; Fax: 61885200
Founded: 1881; Members: 14300
Focus: Med
Periodicals
Annals of Medicine (bi-monthly)
Lääketieteellinen Aikakauskirja Duodecim (bi-weekly) 03379

Suomalainen Lakimiesyhdistys, Bulevardi 32B, 00120 Helsinki
T: (09) 603567; Fax: 604668
Founded: 1898; Members: 4100
Focus: Law 03380

Suomalainen Teologinen Kirjallisuusseura (STKS), Aleksanterinkatu 7, PL 33, 00014 Helsingin Yliopisto
T: (09) 19122076; Fax: 19123033
Members: 1890
Pres: Dr. Eeva Martikainen
Focus: Rel & Theol
Periodical
Suomalainen Teologisen Kirjallisuusseuran julkaisuja 03381

Suomalainen Tiedeakatemia / Finnish Academy of Science and Letters, Mariankatu 5, 00170 Helsinki
T: (09) 636800; Fax: 660117
Founded: 1908; Members: 425
Pres: Heikki Solin; Gen Secr: Pentti Kauranen
Focus: Lit
Periodicals
Annales Academiae Scientiarum Fennicae
Folklore Fellows' Communications
Year Book (annually) 03382

Suomalais-Ugrilainen Seura (SUS) / Société Finno-Ougrienne, Mariankatu 7, PL 320, 00171 Helsinki
T: (09) 662149; E-Mail: Riho.Grunthal@Helsinki.Fi; Fax: 632501
Founded: 1883; Members: 800
Pres: Seppo Suhonen; Gen Secr: Riho Grünthal
Focus: Ling
Periodicals
Finnisch-Ugrische Forschungen (annually)
Hilfsmittel für das Studium der finnisch-ugrischen Sprachen (irregularly)
Journal de la Société Finno-Ougrienne (annually)
Lexica Societatis Fenno-Ugricae (irregularly)
Mémoires de la Société Finno-Ougrienne (irregularly) 03383

Suomalaisen Kirjallisuuden Seura (SKS) / Finnish Literature Society, Hallituskatu 1, PL 259, 00171 Helsinki
T: (09) 131231
Founded: 1831; Members: 3400
Pres: Prof. Anna-Leena Siikala; Gen Secr: Urpo Vento
Focus: Lit; Folklore; Ling
Periodicals
Kirjallisuudentutkijain Seuran vuosikirja: Yearbook of the Literary Research Society (annually)
Studia Fennica (annually)
Yearbook of the Kalerala Society (annually) 03384

Suomalaisten Kemistien Seura (SKS), Hietaniemenkatu 2, 00100 Helsinki
T: (09) 4542040; E-Mail: sks@kemia.pp.fi; Fax: 499940
Founded: 1919; Members: 3700
Pres: Reija Jokela; Gen Secr: H. Karnus
Focus: Chem 03385

Suomen Akatemia (SA), PL 57, 00551 Helsinki
T: (09) 77581; Fax: 7748299
Founded: 1947
Pres: Reijo Vihko; Gen Secr: Heikki Kallio
Focus: Sci 03386

Suomen Allergologi- ja Immunologiyhdistys / Finnish Society of Allergology and Immunology, c/o Finnish Institute of Occupational Health, Topeliuksenkatu 41a, 00250 Helsinki
T: (09) 47471; E-Mail: helena.keskinen@occuphealth.fi; Fax: 4584761
Founded: 1946; Members: 335
Pres: Henrik Nordman; Gen Secr: Helena Keskinen
Focus: Immunology 03387

Suomen Antropologinen Seura, PL 322, 00171 Helsinki
T: (09) 19123094; Fax: 19123006
Founded: 1975; Members: 500
Pres: Jukka Siikala; Gen Secr: Kari Huit
Focus: Anthro 03388

Suomen Atomiteknillinen Seura (ATS), c/o Technical Research Centre, Nuclear Engineering Laboratory, PL 208, 02151 Espoo
Fax: (09) 4565000
Founded: 1966; Members: 600
Pres: Prof. Rainer Salomaa; Gen Secr: Jussi Palmu
Focus: Nucl Res; Energy
Periodical
DiA-kunta 03389

Suomen Autoteknillinen Liitto (SATL), Köydenpunojankatu 8, 00180 Helsinki
T: (09) 6944724; E-Mail: heikki.haapaniemi@satl.inet.fi; Fax: 6944027
Founded: 1934; Members: 5500
Pres: Matti Juhala; Gen Secr: Heikki Haapaniemi
Focus: Auto Eng
Periodical
Suomen Autolehti (10 times annually) . . 03390

Suomen Betoniyhdistys / Finska Betongföreningen, Mikonkatu 18B, 00100 Helsinki
T: (09) 651411; Fax: 651145
Founded: 1925; Members: 700
Pres: Bengt Jansson; Gen Secr: Klaus Söderlund
Focus: Materials Sci
Periodicals
Betoni (quarterly)
Nordic Concrete Research (semi-annually) 03391

Suomen Egyptologinen Seura (SES) / Finnish Egyptological Society, c/o Erja Salmenkiri, Runeberginkatu 6 BA 9, 00100 Helsinki
T: (09) 19123688
Founded: 1969; Members: 600
Focus: Archeol; Preserv Hist Monuments
Periodical
SES-ESF tiedotuslehti (irregularly) . . . 03392

Suomen Eläinlääkäriliitto, Makelankatu 2C, 00500 Helsinki
T: (09) 7011388; Fax: 7018397
Founded: 1892; Members: 1320
Focus: Vet Med
Periodical
Suomen Eläinlääkärilehti: Finsk Veterinärtidskrift (monthly) 03393

Suomen Englanninopettajat, Rautatieläisenkatu 6A, 00520 Helsinki
T: (09) 145414
Founded: 1948; Members: 2900
Pres: Tuula Penttila
Focus: Ling; Educ
Periodical
Tempus (8 times annually) 03394

Suomen Farmaseuttinen Yhdistys, c/o Dept of Pharmacy, University of Helsinki, PL 56, 00014 Helsingin Yliopisto
T: (09) 70859137; Fax: 70859138
Founded: 1887; Members: 300
Pres: Liisa Turabba; Gen Secr: Sirkku Saarela
Focus: Pharmacol 03395

Suomen Filosofinen Yhdistys (SFY) / Philosophical Society of Finland, PL 24, 00014 Helsingin Yliopisto
T: (09) 1911; Fax: 1917627
Founded: 1873; Members: 580
Focus: Philos
Periodicals
Acta Philosophica Fennica (quarterly)
Ajatus-yearbook (annually) 03396

Suomen Fysiologiyhdistys / Societas Physiologicae Finlandiae / Finnish Physiological Society, c/o Dept of Biology, 90570 Oulu
E-Mail: Esa.Hontola@oulu.fi; Fax: (08) 5531242
Founded: 1961; Members: 350
Pres: Osmo Hänninen; Gen Secr: Seppo Turunen
Focus: Physiology 03397

Suomen Fysioterapeuttiliitto / Finlands Fysioterapeutförbund / Finnish Association of Physiotherapists, Asemamiehenkatu 4, 00520 Helsinki
T: (09) 146817; Fax: 1483054
Founded: 1943; Members: 6500
Focus: Therapeutics
Periodical
Fysioterapia (8 times annually) 03398

Suomen Fyysikkoseura / Finnish Physical Society, Siltavuorenpenger 20 M, PL 9, 00014 Helsingin Yliopisto
T: (09) 1918375; Fax: 1918378
Founded: 1947; Members: 1100
Focus: Physics
Periodicals
Arkhimedes (quarterly)
Fysiikka Tänään (quarterly) 03399

Suomen Gastroenterologiayhdistys / Finnish Society of Gastroenterology, c/o Duodecim, PL 713, 00101 Helsinki
T: (09) 611523; Fax: 611004
Founded: 1956; Members: 482
Focus: Gastroenter 03400

Suomen Gemmologinen Seura / Gemmological Society of Finland, Vuorikatu 3 A 10, 00100 Helsinki
T: (09) 660562
Founded: 1960; Members: 160
Focus: Mineralogy
Periodical
Gemmologian Työsaralta (semi-annually) . 03401

Suomen Geologinen Seura, Betonimiehent. 4, 02150 Espoo
T: (0205) 5011; Fax: 5012
Founded: 1886; Members: 922
Pres: Veli-Pekka Salonen; Gen Secr: Pekka Salonsaari
Focus: Geology
Periodical
Bulletin (1-2 times annually) 03402

Suomen Geoteknillinen Yhdistys / Finnish Geotechnical Society, c/o VTT-YKI, PL 19031, 02044 Espoo
T: (09) 4561; Fax: 463251
Founded: 1951; Members: 550
Focus: Mining; Geomorph 03403

Suomen Hammaslääkäriliitto, Bulevardi 30 B 5, 00120 Helsinki
T: (09) 6803120; Fax: 646263
Founded: 1892; Members: 5800
Pres: Prof. Jorma Tenovuo; Gen Secr: Dr. Pirkko Hult
Focus: Dent 03404

Suomen Hammaslääkäriseura (SHS) / Finnish Dental Society, Rautatieläisenkatu 6, 00520 Helsinki
T: (09) 15021; Fax: 146317
Founded: 1891; Members: 5400
Focus: Dent
Periodical
Proceedings of the Finnish Dental Society (quarterly) 03405

Suomen Historiallinen Seura, Arkadiankatu 16 B 28, 00100 Helsinki
T: (09) 440369; Fax: 441468
Founded: 1875; Members: 850
Pres: Toivo J. Nygård; Gen Secr: Rauno Enden
Focus: Hist
Periodicals
Bibliotheca Historica (8-12 times annually)
Historiallinen Arkisto (2-3 times annually)
Historiallisia Tutkimuksia (2-5 times annually)
Käsikirjoja
Studia Historica (3-5 times annually)
Suomen Historian Lähteitä 03406

Suomen Hitsausteknillinen Yhdistys, Mäkelänkatu 36 A, 00510 Helsinki
T: (09) 7732199; Fax: 7732661
Members: 3500
Focus: Eng
Periodical
Hitsaustekniikka-Svetsteknik (bi-monthly) . 03407

Suomen Itämainen Seura / Finnish Oriental Society, c/o Dept of Asian and African Studies, University of Helsinki, PL 13, 00014 Helsingin Yliopisto
Fax: (09) 1912094
Founded: 1917; Members: 150
Focus: Ethnology
Periodical
Studia Orientalia (1-2 times annually) . . 03408

Suomen Kansanopistoyhdistys / Finnish Folk High School Association, P. Rautatiekatu 15 B 12, 00100 Helsinki
T: (09) 444413; Fax: 445619
Founded: 1907; Members: 789
Focus: Adult Educ 03409

Suomen Kasvatustieteellinen Seura / Finnish Society for Educational Research, c/o Oulun Yliopisto Kasvatustieteiden Tiedekunta, PL 222, 90571 Oulu
T: (081) 5531011; Fax: 5533600
Founded: 1967; Members: 275
Focus: Educ
Periodical
The Finnish Journal of Education . . . 03410

Suomen Kemian Seura / Association of Finnish Chemical Societies, Hietaniemenkatu 2, 00100 Helsinki
T: (09) 4542040; E-Mail: skka@kemia.pp.fi; Fax: 408780
Founded: 1970; Members: 4700
Pres: Dr. Sirpa Herve
Focus: Chem 03411

Suomen Kielen Seura / Finnish Language Society, c/o Humanistinen Tiedekunta, Turun Yliopisto, 20500 Turku
Fax: (021) 6336360
Focus: Ling
Periodical
Sananjalka (annually) 03412

Suomen Kirjailijaliitto / Association of Finnish Authors, Runeberginkatu 32 C, 00100 Helsinki
T: (09) 449752; E-Mail: suomen.kirjailijaliitto@cultnet.fi; Fax: 492278
Founded: 1897; Members: 520
Pres: Jarkko Laine; Gen Secr: Päivi Liedes
Focus: Lit
Periodicals
Suomalaiset kertojat
Suomen Runotar 03413

Suomen Kirjastoseura / Finnish Library Association, Kansakouluk 10 A 19, 00100 Helsinki
T: (09) 6941858; E-Mail: fla@fla.fi; Fax: 6941859
Founded: 1910; Members: 2100
Pres: Kaarina Dromberg; Gen Secr: Tuula Haavisto
Focus: Libraries & Bk Sci
Periodical
Kirjastolehti (monthly) *03414*

Suomen Kirkkohistoriallinen Seura (SKHS) / Finnish Society for Church History, Aleksanterinkatu, PL 33, 00014 Helsingin Yliopisto
T: (09) 19123040; E-Mail: Hannu.Mustakalli@helsinki.fi; Fax: 19123033
Founded: 1891; Members: 900
Pres: Prof. Simo Heininen; Gen Secr: Dr. Hannu Mustakallio
Focus: Hist; Rel & Theol
Periodicals
Suomen kirkkohistoriallisen seuran toimituksia (bimonthly)
Suomen kirkkohistoriallisen seuran vuosikirja (annually) *03415*

Suomen Kirurgiyhdistys, Mäkeländkatu 2 A, 00500 Helsinki
T: (09) 3930768; Fax: 3930801
Founded: 1925; Members: 1000
Focus: Surgery
Periodical
Annales Chirurgiae & Gynaecologiae (quarterly) *03416*

Suomen Kliinisen Neurofysiologian Yhdistys, c/o Dept of Clinical Neurophysiology, University Central Hospital of Helsinki, Haartmaninkatu 4, 00290 Helsinki
Fax: (09) 4714009
Founded: 1972; Members: 95
Focus: Physiology *03417*

Suomen Lainopillinen Yhdistys, Alexandersgatan 48 A, 00100 Helsinki
T: (09) 630302
Founded: 1862
Focus: Law *03418*

Suomen Lakimiesliitto / Union of Finnish Lawyers, Uudenmaankatu 4-6 B, 00120 Helsinki
T: (09) 649201
Founded: 1944; Members: 14200
Focus: Law
Periodicals
Finnish Law I: Common Law
Finnish Law II: Public law
The Finnish Legal System: The English Language Publication *03419*

Suomen Lintutieteellinen Yhdistys, P. Rautatiekatu 13, 00014 Helsingin Yliopisto
T: (09) 1917453; Fax: 1917443
Founded: 1924; Members: 645
Pres: Dr. Jari Kouki; Gen Secr: Jaakko Jarvinen
Focus: Ornithology
Periodical
Ornis Fennica (quarterly) *03420*

Suomen Maantieteellinen Seura / Geographical Society of Finland, c/o Dept of Geography, PL 4, 00014 Helsingin Yliopisto
T: (09) 19122627; Fax: 1912641
Founded: 1888; Members: 1300
Pres: H. Vesajoki; Gen Secr: L. Houtsonen
Focus: Geography
Periodicals
Fennia (semi-annually)
Terra (quarterly) *03421*

Suomen Maataloustieteellinen Seura / Scientific Agricultural Society of Finland, c/o Dept of Applied Chemistry and Microbiology, Section of Agricultural Chemistry and Microbiology, 00014 Helsingin Yliopisto
T: (09) 70851; Fax: 7085212
Founded: PL 27 1909; Members: 580
Pres: Prof. Asko Maki-Tanila
Focus: Agri; Hort
Periodical
Journal (5-6 times annually) *03422*

Suomen Matemaattinen Yhdistys / Finnish Mathematical Society, c/o Dept of Mathematics, PL 4, 00014 Helsingin Yliopisto
T: (09) 1913206; Fax: 1913213
Founded: 1868; Members: 360
Pres: Antti Kupiainen; Gen Secr: Jari Taskinen
Focus: Math
Periodical
Arkhimedes (quarterly) *03423*

Suomen Metsätieteellinen Seura / The Society of Forestry in Finland, Unioninkatu 40B, 00014 Helsingin Yliopisto
T: (09) 658707; Fax: 1917619
Founded: 1909; Members: 800
Pres: Seppo Vehkamaki; Gen Secr: Eero Nikinmaa
Focus: Forestry
Periodicals
Acta Forestalia Fennica (5-8 times annually)
Silva Fennica (quarterly) *03424*

Suomen Muinaismuistoyhdistys (SMY), PL 913, 00101 Helsinki
T: (09) 662672
Founded: 1870; Members: 600
Pres: Dr. Torsten Edgren; Gen Secr: Marianne Schauman-Lönnqvist
Focus: Archeol; Ethnology; Hist

Periodicals
Aikakauskirja
Finskt Museum (annually)
Iskos
Kansatieteellinen Arkisto
Suomen Museo (annually) *03425*

Suomen Museoliitto (SML) / Finnish Museums Association, Annankatu 16 B 50, 00120 Helsinki
T: (09) 649001; E-Mail: museoliitto@museoliitto.fi; Fax: 608330
Founded: 1923; Members: 246
Pres: Matti Rossi; Gen Secr: Anja-Tuulikki Huovinen
Focus: Arts
Periodicals
Museo (quarterly)
Suomen museoliiton julkaisuja (semi-annually) *03426*

Suomen Musiikkitieteellinen Seura, Vironkatu 1, PL 35, 00014 Helsingin Yliopisto
T: (09) 8252452; Fax: 1917955
Founded: 1925; Members: 250
Pres: Prof. Eero Tarasti; Gen Secr: Tarja Taurula
Focus: Music *03427*

Suomen Näytelmäkirjailijaliitto / Dramatists' League of Finland, Vironkatu 12 B, 00170 Helsinki
Founded: 1921
Pres: Esko Salervo; Gen Secr: Pirjo Westman
Focus: Perf Arts *03428*

Suomen Palontorjuntaliitto / Finlands Brandvärnsförbund / Finnish Fire Protection Association, Iso Roobertinkatu 7 A 4, 00120 Helsinki
T: (09) 649233
Founded: 1968; Members: 26
Focus: Safety *03429*

Suomen Psykologiliitto, Rautatieläisenkatu 6, 00520 Helsinki
T: (09) 150021; Fax: 141716
Founded: 1957; Members: 3300
Focus: Psych
Periodical
Psykologiumtiset (monthly) *03430*

Suomen Radiologiyhdistys, PL 963, 00101 Helsinki
Founded: 1924; Members: 703
Focus: Radiology *03431*

Suomen Säveltäjät / Society of Finnish Composers, Runeberginkatu 15 A 11, 00100 Helsinki
T: (09) 445589; E-Mail: ttuomela@siba.fi; Fax: 440181
Founded: 1945; Members: 113
Pres: Mikko Heiniö; Gen Secr: Annu Mikkonen
Focus: Music *03432*

Suomen Standardisoimisliitto / Finnish Standards Association, Maistraatinportti 2, PL 116, 00240 Helsinki
T: (09) 1499331; E-Mail: Finnstandard
Founded: 1924
Focus: Standards
Periodicals
SFS Catalogue (annually)
SFS-tiedotus (bi-monthly) *03433*

Suomen Sukututkimusseura (SSS) / Genealogiska Samfundet i Finland / Genealogical Society of Finland, Liisankatu 16 A, 00170 Helsinki
T: (09) 179189; Fax: 626929
Founded: 1917; Members: 2600
Pres: J. Paaskoski; Gen Secr: Pertti Vuorinen
Focus: Genealogy
Periodicals
Genos: Suomen Sukututkimusseuran aikakauskirja (quarterly)
Suomen Sukututkimusseuran julkaisuja: Skrifter (irregularly)
Suomen Sukututkimusseuran vuosikirja: Årsskrift (irregularly) *03434*

Suomen Syöpäyhdistys / Cancer Society of Finland, Liisankatu 21 B, 00170 Helsinki
T: (09) 135331; E-Mail: society@cancer.fi; Fax: 1351093
Founded: 1936; Members: 130000
Pres: Prof. Jussi Huttunen; Gen Secr: Liisa Elovainio
Focus: Cell Biol & Cancer Res
Periodical
Syöpä-Cancer (bi-monthly) *03435*

Suomen Taideyhdistys / Finska Konstföreningen, Nervanderinkatu 3, 00100 Helsinki
T: (09) 45420611; Fax: 45420610
Founded: 1846; Members: 3000
Pres: Jaakko Iloniemi; Gen Secr: Timo Valjakka
Focus: Arts *03436*

Suomen Taiteilijaseura, Yrjönkatu 11, 00120 Helsinki
T: (09) 607171; Fax: 607561
Founded: 1864
Pres: Kari Jylhä; Gen Secr: Esko Vesikansa
Focus: Arts *03437*

Suomen Tekstiiliteknillinen Liitto, PL 433, 33101 Tampere
T: (03) 3184113; Fax: 2617482
Founded: 1936; Members: 700
Focus: Eng *03438*

Suomen Tieteellinen Kirjastoseura / Finnish Research Library Association, PL 217, 00171 Helsinki
T: (09) 3653148; Fax: 3652907
Founded: 1929; Members: 700
Pres: Arja-Riitta Haarala
Focus: Libraries & Bk Sci
Periodicals
Guide to Research Libraries and Information Services in Finland (irregularly)
Signum (8 times annually) *03439*

Suomen Tilastoseura / Statistiska Samfundet i Finland / Finnish Statistical Society, c/o Statistics Finland, PL 4A, 00022 Statistics Finland
T: (09) 17341; Fax: 17343554
Founded: 1920; Members: 500
Pres: Risto Lehtonen; Gen Secr: Jorma Heimonen
Focus: Stats
Periodicals
Scandinavian Journal of Statistics
Vuosikirja: Yearbook *03440*

Suomen Vesttieteen Yhdistys / Demographic Society of Finland, c/o Statistics Finland, PL 4B, 00022 Statistics Finland
Founded: 1973; Members: 169
Gen Secr: Mauri Nieminen
Focus: Stats *03441*

Suomen Yliopistojen Rehtorien, PL 3, 00014 Helsingin Yliopisto
T: (09) 19122335; Fax: 19122194
Pres: Dr. Ossi V. Lindqvist; Gen Secr: Dr. T. Markkanen
Focus: Educ *03442*

Suomen Ympäristöoikeustieteen Seura, c/o Institute of Environmental Law, Helsinki University of Technology, Otakaari 1, 02150 Espoo
T: (09) 4513861; Fax: 465077
Founded: 1980; Members: 400
Pres: E.J. Hollo; Gen Secr: M. Kuoppala
Focus: Law *03443*

Svenska Litteratursällskapet i Finland (SLS) / Society of Swedish Literature in Finland, Mariegatan 8, 00170 Helsinki
T: (09) 2285000; Fax: 632820
Founded: 1885; Members: 1100
Pres: Prof. Johan Wrede; Gen Secr: Prof. Ann-Marie Ivars
Focus: Lit
Periodical
Skrifter utgivna av Svenska Litteratursällskapet i Finland (5-6 times annually) *03444*

Svenska Tekniska Vetenskapsakademien i Finland (STV) / Swedish Academy of Engineering Sciences in Finland, Teknikvägen 12, 02150 Espoo
T: (09) 4554565; Fax: 4554626
Founded: 1921; Members: 159
Pres: Prof. Johan Gullichsen; Gen Secr: Prof. Kenneth Holmberg
Focus: Eng
Periodicals
Förhandlingar Proceedings
Meddelanden-Reports (semi-annually) . *03445*

Tähtitieteellinen Yhdistys Ursa (URSA) / URSA Astronomical Association, Raatimiehenkatu 3 A 2, 00140 Helsinki
T: (09) 174048; Fax: 657728
Founded: 1921; Members: 7000
Pres: Esko Valtaoja; Gen Secr: Seppo Linnaluoto
Focus: Astronomy
Periodicals
Tähdet: Stars (annually)
Tähdet ja Avaruus: Stars and Space (bi-monthly)
Ursa minor: Ursan jaostojentiedotuslehti (bi-monthly) *03446*

Taidehistorian Seura, Unioninkatu 34, 00014 Helsingin Yliopisto
Founded: 1974; Members: 425
Pres: Ville Lukkarinen
Focus: Hist *03447*

Taloushistoriallinen Yhdistys, c/o Dept of Economic and Social History, 00014 University of Helsinki
Founded: 1952; Members: 55
Pres: Dr. Riitta Hjerppe
Focus: Econ; Hist *03448*

Taloustieteellinen Seura / Finnish Society for Economic Research, c/o Bank of Finland, Rauhankatu 19, 00170 Helsinki
T: (09) 1832541; E-Mail: mikko.spolander@bof.fi; Fax: 1832227
Founded: 1936; Members: 550
Pres: Olli-Pekka Ruuskanen; Gen Secr: Mikko Spolander
Focus: Econ
Periodical
Finnish Economic Papers (bi-annually) . *03449*

Tekniikan Akateemisten Liitto / Finnish Association of Graduate Engineers, Ratavartijankatu 2, 00520 Helsinki
T: (09) 229121; Fax: 22912911
Founded: 1896; Members: 43000
Pres: Markku Markkula; Gen Secr: Heikki Kauppi
Focus: Eng *03450*

Teknillisten Oppilaitosten Opettajainliitto (TOOL), Rautatieläisenkatu 6, 00520 Helsinki
T: (09) 1502687; E-Mail: tool@too.fi; Fax: 1481449
Founded: 1946; Members: 1500
Pres: Seppo Pahlman; Gen Secr: Tarja Halenius
Focus: Adult Educ *03451*

Teknillisten Tieteiden Akatemia (TTA) / Finnish Academy of Technology, Tekniikantie 12, 02150 Espoo
T: (09) 4554565; Fax: 4554626
Founded: 1957; Members: 381
Pres: Dr. Matti Kankaanpää; Gen Secr: Prof. Eino Tunkelo
Focus: Eng
Periodical
Acta Polytechnica Scandinavica (irregularly) *03452*

Tekniska Föreningen i Finland, Banvaktsg 2, 00520 Helsinki
T: (09) 4767718
Founded: 1880; Members: 2650
Pres: Henrik Janson; Gen Secr: Frej Gustafsson
Focus: Eng
Periodical
Forum för Ekonomi och Teknik *03453*

Tieteellisten Seurain Valtuuskunta, Mariankatu 5, 00170 Helsinki
T: (09) 22869222; Fax: 22869291
Founded: 1899; Members: 208
Pres: Prof. P. Tommila; Gen Secr: Hannu Heikkilä
Focus: Sci *03454*

Tietohuollon Neuvottelukunta / Finnish Council Council for Information Provision, c/o' Ministry of Education, Meritullinkatu 10, PL 293, 00171 Helsinki
T: (09) 134171; Fax: 656765
Founded: 1979; Members: 10
Pres: Veikko Litzen; Gen Secr: Annu Jylha-Pyykönen
Focus: Sci; Libraries & Bk Sci . . . *03455*

Tietopalveluseura / Finnish Society for Information Services, Harakantie 2, 02600 Espoo
T: (09) 518138; Fax: 518167
Founded: 1947; Members: 752
Focus: Computer & Info Sci
Periodical
Tietopalelu (bi-monthly) *03456*

Turun Historiallinen Yhdistys (THY) / Turku Historical Society, c/o Institute of History, University of Turku, Henrikinkatu 2, 20500 Turku
T: (021) 6335365; Fax: 6336585
Founded: 1923; Members: 604
Focus: Hist
Periodical
Turun Historiallinen Arkisto *03457*

Turun Soitannollinen Seura / Musical Society of Turku, c/o Sibelius Museum, Piispankatu 17, 20500 Turku
T: (02) 2313789; Fax: 2518528
Founded: 1790; Members: 625
Pres: Alarik Repo; Gen Secr: Ilpo Tolvas
Focus: Music *03458*

Työtehoseura / Work Efficiency Institute, Melkonkatu 16 A, 00210 Helsinki
T: (09) 29041200; Fax: 6922084
Founded: 1924; Members: 2900
Gen Secr: Dr. Tarmo Luoma
Focus: Business Admin; Agri; Forestry; Home Econ; Educ
Periodical
TEHO (bi-monthly) *03459*

Uusfilologinen Yhdistys (UFY) / Modern Language Society, Yliopistonkatu 3, PL 4, 00014 Helsingin Yliopisto
T: (09) 19122115; E-Mail: pekka.kuusisto@helsinki.fi; Fax: 19123072
Founded: 1887; Members: 300
Pres: Prof. Olli Välikangas; Gen Secr: Pekka Kuusisto
Focus: Ling; Lit
Periodicals
Mémoires de la Société Néophilologique: Monograph Series (irregularly)
Neuphilologische Mitteilungen (quarterly) . *03460*

Valtiotieteellinen Yhdistys / Finnish Political Science Association, c/o Faculty of Political Science, University of Helsinki, PL 54, 00014 Helsingin Yliopisto
T: (09) 1911; Fax: 1918832
Founded: 1935; Members: 500
Pres: Erkki Berndtson; Gen Secr: Pasi Saukkonen
Focus: Poli Sci
Periodical
Politiikka Géorges (quarterly) *03461*

France

Académie d'Agriculture de France, 18 Rue de Bellechasse, 75007 Paris
T: 0147051037; Fax: 0145550978
Founded: 1761; Members: 370
Pres: Suzanne Mériaux
Focus: Agri
Periodical
Comptes rendus de l'Académie d'Agriculture de France *03462*

Académie d'Architecture, 9 Pl des Vosges, 75004 Paris
T: 018878310, 018878574
Founded: 1840; Members: 100
Pres: Roger Saubot; Gen Secr: Janine Robert-Gardent
Focus: Archit 03463

Académie d'Arles, c/o Musée Arlaten, Rue de la République, 13200 Arles
Focus: Sci 03464

Académie de Chirurgie, 15 Rue de l'Ecole de Médecine, 75006 Paris
T: 0143540232; Fax: 0143293444
Founded: 1935; Members: 120
Gen Secr: Philippe Boutelier
Focus: Surgery
Periodical
Chirurgie (monthly) 03465

Académie de Marine, BP 11, 00300 Armées
T: 0144384033; Fax: 0144384065
Founded: 1752; Members: 90
Pres: Paul Boquin; Gen Secr: Claude Blanc
Focus: Navig
Periodical
Communications et Mémoires (3 times annually) 03466

Académie de Nîmes, 16 Rue Dorée, 30000 Nîmes
Founded: 1682; Members: 60
Focus: Sci
Periodicals
Bulletin Trimestriel (3 times annually)
Mémoires (annually) 03467

Académie de Pharmacie de Paris, 4 Av de l'Observatoire, 75270 Paris Cedex 06
T: 0143255449; Fax: 0143290592
Founded: 1803; Members: 345
Focus: Pharmacol 03468

Académie de Savoie, Château des Ducs, BP 1801, 73018 Chambéry Cedex
Founded: 1819; Members: 200
Pres: Prof. Louis Terreaux; Gen Secr: Paul Dupraz
Focus: Sci; Lit; Arts 03469

Académie des Beaux-Arts, 23 Quai de Conti, 75006 Paris
Founded: 1648; Members: 115
Pres: A. d' Hauterives; Gen Secr: Bernard Zehrfuss
Focus: Arts
Periodical
Annuaire (annually) 03470

Académie des Belles-Lettres, Sciences et Arts de La Rochelle, 30 Rue Gargoulleau, 17000 La Rochelle
Founded: 1732; Members: 50
Focus: Lit; Hist 03471

Académie des Inscriptions et Belles-Lettres, 23 Quai de Conti, 75006 Paris
T: 013269282
Founded: 1663; Members: 145
Gen Secr: Jean Leclant
Focus: Lit
Periodicals
Journal des Savants
Mémoires 03472

Académie des Jeux Floraux, Hôtel d'Assézat et Clémence Isaure, Pl d'Assézat, 31000 Toulouse
T: 0561212285
Founded: 1324; Members: 64
Focus: Sci; Lit
Periodical
Recueil de l'Académie des Jeux Floraux (annually) 03473

Académie des Sciences, 23 Quai de Conti, 75006 Paris
T: 0144414367
Founded: 1666; Members: 540
Pres: Marianne Grunberg-Manago; Gen Secr: Jean Dercourt
Focus: Sci
Periodical
Comptes-Rendus de l'Académie des Sciences 03474

Académie des Sciences, Agriculture, Arts et Belles-Lettres d'Aix, 2a Rue du 4 Septembre, 13100 Aix-en-Provence
T: 0442383895
Founded: 1829; Members: 150
Pres: Baron de Vitrolles; Gen Secr: Georges Souville
Focus: Arts; Agri; Sci; Lit; Hist
Periodical
Bulletin (annually) 03475

Académie des Sciences, Arts et Belles-Lettres de Dijon, 5 Rue de l'Ecole de Droit, 21000 Dijon
Founded: 1740; Members: 550
Pres: Pierre Feuilée; Gen Secr: Martine Chauney-Boiuillot
Focus: Arts; Sci; Lit; Hist
Periodical
Mémoires (bi-annually) 03476

Académie des Sciences, Belles-Lettres et Arts de Clermont, 19 Rue Bardoux, 63000 Clermont-Ferrand
Founded: 1747; Members: 542
Focus: Sci; Lit; Arts 03477

Académie des Sciences, Belles-Lettres et Arts de Lyon, Palais Saint-Jean, 4 Av Adolphe Max, 69005 Lyon
T: 0478382654
Founded: 1700; Members: 52
Pres: J. Boidin; Gen Secr: P. Malapert
Focus: Sci; Lit; Arts
Periodical
Mémoires de l'Académie (annually) . . . 03478

Académie des Sciences, Belles-Lettres et Arts de Rouen, 190 Rue Beauvoisine, 76000 Rouen
Founded: 1744; Members: 50
Focus: Sci; Lit; Arts 03479

Académie des Sciences d'Outre-Mer (ASOM), 15 Rue La Pérouse, 75116 Paris
T: 0147208793; Fax: 0147208972
Founded: 1922; Members: 275
Pres: M. Decraene; Gen Secr: Gilbert Mangin
Focus: Geography; Hist; Law
Periodicals
Hommes et Destins
Mondes et Cultures (semi-annually) . . . 03480

Académie des Sciences et Lettres de Montpellier, c/o Bibliothèque Interuniversitaire, 4 Rue Ecole Mage, 34000 Montpellier
Founded: 1847
Focus: Sci; Lit
Periodical
Bulletin de l'Académie des Sciences et Lettres de Montpellier (annually) 03481

Académie des Sciences, Lettres et Arts d'Amiens, 60 Blvd de Saint-Quentin, 80090 Amiens
T: 0322952910
Founded: 1750; Members: 50
Gen Secr: René Lenoir
Focus: Sci; Humanities; Arts 03482

Académie des Sciences, Lettres et Arts d'Arras, c/o Archives Départementales, 12 Pl de la Préfecture, 62000 Arras
Focus: Sci; Lit; Arts
Periodical
Mémoires (irregularly) 03483

Académie des Sciences, Lettres et Arts de Marseille, c/o Castel France, Saint-Loup, 13010 Marseille
Founded: 1715; Members: 40
Focus: Sci; Lit; Arts 03484

Académie des Sciences Morales et Politiques, 23 Quai de Conti, 75006 Paris
T: 0144414326; Fax: 0144414327
Founded: 1832; Members: 50
Pres: Roger Arnaldez; Gen Secr: Pierre Messmer
Focus: Philos; Poli Sci; Law; Econ
Periodical
Revue des Sciences Morales et Politiques: Nouvelle Série (quarterly) 03485

Académie Diplomatique Internationale (A.D.I.), 4bis Av Hoche, 75008 Paris
T: 0142276618
Founded: 1926; Members: 586
Focus: Poli Sci 03486

Académie d'Orléans – Agriculture, Sciences, Belles-Lettres et Arts, 5 Rue Antoine Petit, 45000 Orléans
Founded: 1809; Members: 73
Focus: Agri; Sci; Lit; Arts 03487

Académie Française, 23 Quai de Conti, 75006 Paris
T: 0144414300; Fax: 0143294745
Founded: 1635; Members: 40
Gen Secr: Maurice Druon
Focus: Ling; Lit
Periodicals
Annuaire de l'Académie Française (annually)
Discours de réception des académiciens 03488

Académie Goncourt, c/o Drouant, Pl Gaillon, 75002 Paris
Founded: 1896; Members: 10
Pres: F. Nourissier; Gen Secr: Didier Decoin
Focus: Lit 03489

Académie Internationale de Science Politique et d'Histoire Constitutionnelle, c/o Université de Paris I, 12 Pl du Panthéon, 75000 Paris
Founded: 1936
Focus: Poli Sci; Hist 03490

Académie Mallarmé, 38 Rue du Faubourg Saint-Jacques, 75014 Paris
Members: 30
Pres: Jean Orizet; Gen Secr: Charles Dobzynski
Focus: Lit 03491

Académie Montaigne, Le Doyenné, 72140 Sillé-le-Guillaume
Founded: 1924; Members: 20
Gen Secr: Constant Hubert
Focus: Lit 03492

Académie Nationale de Chirurgie Dentaire, 22 Rue Emile Ménier, 75116 Paris
T: 0147046540
Members: 190
Focus: Surgery
Periodical
Bulletin (annually) 03493

Académie Nationale de Médecine, 16 Rue Bonaparte, 75272 Paris Cedex 06
T: 0142345770; Fax: 0140468755
Founded: 1820; Members: 130
Pres: Paul Lechat; Gen Secr: Raymond Bastin
Focus: Med
Periodical
Bulletin (9 times annually) 03494

Académie Nationale de Metz, 20 en Nexirue, 57000 Metz
Focus: Sci; Hist
Periodicals
Bibliographie Lorraine (irregularly)
Mémoires de l'Académie Nationale de Metz (annually) 03495

Académie Nationale de Pharmacie de Paris, 4 Av de l'Observatoire, 75006 Paris
Founded: 1803
Focus: Pharmacol 03496

Académie Nationale des Sciences, Belles-Lettres et Arts de Bordeaux, 1 Pl Bardineau, 33000 Bordeaux
Founded: 1712; Members: 40
Focus: Sci; Lit; Arts 03497

Académie Polonaise des Sciences, 74 Rue Lauriston, 75116 Paris
T: 0145536691
Focus: Sci
Periodical
Conférences (semi-annually) 03498

Académie Vétérinaire de France, 60 Blvd Latour-Maubourg, 75007 Paris
Founded: 1844; Members: 44
Focus: Vet Med
Periodical
Bulletin (quarterly) 03499

Amici Thomae Mori (ATM), BP 808, 49008 Angers Cedex 01
Fax: 0241887442
Founded: 1962; Members: 900
Focus: Lit; Hist; Rel & Theol
Periodicals
Gazette (annually)
Moreana (quarterly) 03500

Amis de Guy de Maupassant, 60 Rue Vaneau, 75007 Paris
Focus: Lit 03501

Amis de Rimbaud, c/o Pierre Petitfils, 13 Rue P.-L. Courier, 75007 Paris
T: 0145483420
Founded: 1927; Members: 350
Focus: Lit 03502

Arab Music Rostrum, c/o IMC, 1 Rue Miollis, 75732 Paris Cedex 15
T: 0145682550; Fax: 0143068798
Founded: 1990
Focus: Music 03503

Arab World Institute, 23 Quai Saint-Bernard, 75005 Paris
T: 0140513838
Founded: 1980; Members: 21
Focus: Cultur Hist
Periodical
Al-Moukhtarat (3 times annually) 03504

Asian Music Rostrum (ASMR), c/o UNESCO, 1 Rue Miollis, 75732 Paris Cedex 15
T: 0145682550; Fax: 0143068798
Founded: 1969
Focus: Music 03505

Asocio de Studado Internacia pri Spiritaj kaj Teologiaj Instruoj (ASISTI), c/o Foyer de Culture Internationale, Le Presbytère, 09800 Balagué
T: 0561047066; E-Mail: shinto@alpha-web.or.jp; Fax: 0561047066
Founded: 1989; Members: 450
Pres: Yoshimi Umeda; Gen Secr: Christian Lavarenne
Focus: Rel & Theol
Periodical
Asistilo (quarterly) 03506

Association Aéronautique et Astronautique de France (AAAF), 6 Rue Galilée, 75016 Paris
T: 0147230749
Founded: 1972; Members: 1800
Pres: J.C. Poggi
Focus: Aero
Periodical
L'Aéronautique et l'Astronautique (bi-monthly) 03507

Association Centrale des Vétérinaires (A.C.V.), 10 Pl Léon Blum, 75011 Paris
T: 0143562102
Founded: 1889; Members: 3000
Pres: Dr. J.-P. Marty
Focus: Vet Med 03508

Association des Amis de la Revue de Géographie de Lyon, 74 Rue Pasteur, 69007 Lyon
Founded: 1923
Focus: Geography 03509

Association des Archivistes Français, 60 Rue des Francs-Bourgeois, 75141 Paris Cedex 03
T: 0140276000
Founded: 1904; Members: 700
Pres: Jean-Luc Eichenlaub; Gen Secr: Jean Le Pottier
Focus: Archives
Periodical
La Gazette des Archives (quarterly) . . 03510

Association des Bibliothécaires Français (ABF), 7 Rue des Lions Saint-Paul, 75004 Paris
T: 0148879787; Fax: 0148879713
Founded: 1906; Members: 2500
Pres: Claudine Belache; Gen Secr: Mairie-Martine Tomitch
Focus: Libraries & Bk Sci
Periodical
Bulletin d'Informations (quarterly) 03511

Association des Chimistes, Ingénieurs et Cadres des Industries Agricoles et Alimentaires, 51 Rue Jean-Jacques Rousseau, 75001 Paris
T: 0101401391; Fax: 0101401391
Founded: 1883; Members: 2000
Focus: Chem
Periodical
Revue IAA (10 times annually) 03512

Association des Conservateurs de Bibliothèques (ACB), 16 Rue Claude Bernard, 75005 Paris
T: 0144081786; Fax: 0144081784
Founded: 1992; Members: 600
Pres: Philippe Dupont; Gen Secr: Antonieta Moellon
Focus: Libraries & Bk Sci
Periodicals
ABC Infos (quarterly)
Annuaire des Associations de Bibliothécaires et Documentalistes (bi-annually) 03513

Association des Epidémiologists de Langue Française (ADELF), c/o INSERM U 88, Hôpital National, 94410 Saint-Maurice
T: 0145183850; E-Mail: P.lopes@st-maurice.insern.f; Fax: 0145183889
Founded: 1976
Gen Secr: S. Briançon
Focus: Med 03514

Association des Etudes Tsiganes / Association for Gypsy Studies, 2 Rue d'Hautpoul, 75019 Paris
T: 0140400905; Fax: 0142067511
Founded: 1949
Pres: Jacqueline Charlemagne
Focus: Ethnology
Periodical
Etudes Tsiganes (semi-annually) 03515

Association des Géographes Français (AGF), 191 Rue Saint-Jacques, 75005 Paris
T: 0144331400; Fax: 0145291340
Founded: 1920; Members: 450
Pres: A. Metton; Gen Secr: J.-P. Charvet
Focus: Geography
Periodical
Bulletin de l'Association de Géographes Français (quarterly) 03516

Association des Professeurs de Langues Vivantes (APLV), 19 Rue de la Glacière, 75013 Paris
Founded: 1902; Members: 3000
Pres: Christian Puren; Gen Secr: Sylvestre Vanuxem
Focus: Educ; Ling 03517

Association des Professionnels de l'Information et de la Documentation, 25 Rue Claude Tiller, 75012 Paris
T: 0143722525; Fax: 0143723041
Founded: 1963; Members: 5000
Pres: Jean Michel; Gen Secr: Olivier Thiebeauld
Focus: Libraries & Bk Sci; Doc
Periodical
Documentaliste – Sciences de l'Information (5 times annually) 03518

Association d'Etudes et d'Informations Politiques Internationales, 86 Blvd Haussmann, 75008 Paris
Founded: 1949
Focus: Poli Sci 03519

Association du Salon d'Automne, Grand Palais, Porte H, Av Winston Churchill, 75008 Paris
Founded: 1903
Focus: Arts 03520

Association Européenne des Enseignants, Section Française (AEDE), BP 24507, 75327 Paris Cedex
Founded: 1956; Members: 600
Pres: Prof. Y.-H. Nouailhat; Gen Secr: Monique Jeanmichel
Focus: Educ
Periodicals
Context (bi-monthly)
Education européenne (5 times annually) 03521

Association Française d'Astronomie (AFA), c/o Observatoire du Parc Montsouris, 17 Rue Emile Deutsch de la Meurthe, 75014 Paris
T: 0145898144; E-Mail: ceespace@francenet.fr; Fax: 0145650895
Founded: 1946; Members: 12000
Pres: Olivier Las Vergnas
Focus: Astronomy
Periodical
Ciel et Espace (monthly) *03522*

Association Française de Chirurgie (AFC), 26 Blvd Raspail, 75007 Paris
Founded: 1884; Members: 2000
Focus: Surgery *03523*

Association Française de Formation, 63 Blvd des Batignolles, 75017 Paris
T: 0142935281
Focus: Adult Educ *03524*

Association Française de Formation, Coopération, Promotion et Animation d'Entreprises, 12 Av Marceau, 75008 Paris
T: 0142253762
Focus: Adult Educ *03525*

Association Française de Gemmologie (AFG), 14 Rue Cadet, 75009 Paris
Fax: 0142465016
Founded: 1964; Members: 1100
Focus: Mineralogy
Periodical
Revue de Gemmologie (quarterly) . . . *03526*

Association Française de Génie Rural (AFGR), 30 Rue Las Cases, 75340 Paris Cedex 07
T: 0145559550
Founded: 1947; Members: 164
Focus: Agri
Periodical
Génie Rural: Column (monthly) *03527*

Association Française de l'Eclairage (AFE), 52 Blvd Malesherbes, 75008 Paris
T: 0143872121; Fax: 0143871698
Founded: 1930; Members: 2000
Focus: Electric Eng
Periodicals
Lux: La Revue de l'Eclairage
Recommandations Relatives à l' Eclairage (irregularly) *03528*

Association Française de l'Ecole Paysanne, 11 Rue de Clichy, 75009 Paris
T: 0148746848
Focus: Educ *03529*

Association Française de Management (CNOF), 119 Rue de Lille, 75007 Paris
T: 0145443880
Founded: 1926; Members: 1150
Focus: Business Admin; Econ
Periodical
Management France (bi-monthly) *03530*

Association Française de Normalisation (AFNOR) / French Association for Standardization, Tour Europe, 92080 Paris La Défence Cedex 07
T: 0142915555; Fax: 0142915656
Founded: 1926; Members: 5500
Pres: Philippe Boulin; Gen Secr: Bernard Vaucelle
Focus: Standards
Periodical
Enjeux (monthly) *03531*

Association Française de Prévention des Accidents de Travail et Incendie, 17 Rue Salneuve, 75017 Paris
T: 0147665151
Focus: Safety *03532*

Association Française de Psychiatrie, 23 Rue Pradier, 92410 Ville d'Avray
T: 0147091177; Fax: 0147506275
Founded: 1979; Members: 2200
Focus: Psychiatry
Periodicals
La Lettre de Psychiatrie Française (monthly)
Psychiatrie Française *03533*

Association Française de Recherches d'Essais sur les Matériaux et les Constructions (AFREM), 12 Rue Brancion, 75015 Paris
T: 0145392233
Founded: 1948; Members: 65
Focus: Materials Sci; Civil Eng *03534*

Association Française de Science Economique (A.F.S.E.), c/o Université des Scienas Sociales, Pl Anatole France, 31042 Toulouse Cedex
Founded: 1952; Members: 700
Focus: Econ *03535*

Association Française de Science Politique (AFSP), 224 Blvd Saint-Germain, 75007 Paris
T: 0145499221; Fax: 0145489945
Founded: 1949; Members: 1058
Pres: Jean-Louis Quermonne; Gen Secr: Jean-Luc Parodi
Focus: Poli Sci
Periodical
Revue Française de Science Politique (bi-monthly) *03536*

Association Française des Arabisants, c/o Collège de France, 52 Rue Cardinal Lemoine, 75005 Paris
T: 0142507025; Fax: 0142507025
Founded: 1973; Members: 300
Pres: Floréal Sanagustin
Focus: Ethnology; Ling; Lit; Educ . . . *03537*

Association Française des Enseignants de Français, 19 Rue des Martyrs, 75009 Paris
T: 0145264141; Fax: 0140169338
Founded: 1967; Members: 4000
Focus: Educ; Ling
Periodical
Le Francais Aujourd'hui: Le Supplément au Français Aujourd'hui (quarterly) *03538*

Association Française des Femmes Médecins, 123 Rue de Lille, 75007 Paris
T: 0145512929
Focus: Med *03539*

Association Française des Hémophiles, 6 Rue Alexandre Cabanel, 75015 Paris
T: 0145677767; Fax: 0145678544
Pres: Dr. Patrick Wallet
Focus: Hematology
Periodical
L'Hémophile (3 times annually) *03540*

Association Française des Historiens Economistes, 54 Blvd Raspail, 75006 Paris
T: 0149542501; E-Mail: AFHE@ehess.fr; Fax: 0149542496
Founded: 1965; Members: 200
Focus: Hist; Econ *03541*

Association Française des Ingénieurs, Chimistes et Techniciens des Industries du Cuir (AFICTIC), BP 7003, 69342 Lyon Cedex 07
Founded: 1939; Members: 300
Focus: Chem; Eng
Periodical
Revue Technique des Industries du Cuir . *03542*

Association Française des Instituts de Recherche sur le Développement (AFIRD), c/o Institut d'Etude du Développement Economique et Social, 58 Blvd Arago, 75013 Paris
T: 0143362355
Founded: 1975; Members: 45
Focus: Econ *03543*

Association Française des Professeurs de Langues Vivantes, 19 Rue de la Glacière, 75013 Paris
T: 0147079482
Founded: 1902; Members: 4000
Pres: François Monnanteuil; Gen Secr: Sylvestre Vanuxem
Focus: Ling
Periodical
Les Langues Modernes (quarterly) . . . *03544*

Association Française des Russisants (A.F.R.), 9 Rue Michelet, 75006 Paris
Pres: Hélène Mélat
Focus: Educ; Ling; Lit; Hist; Soc Sci; Econ
Periodicals
Bulletin de l'A.F.R. (quarterly)
La Revue Russe (semi-annually) *03545*

Association Française des Sociétés d'Etudes et de Conseils Exportatrices, 3 Rue Leon Bonnat, 75016 Paris
T: 0145244353
Focus: Econ *03546*

Association Française d'Etude des Relations Professionnelles (C.N.A.M.), 33 Rue du Regard, 94260 Fresnes
Founded: 1969
Focus: Sociology *03547*

Association Française d'Etudes Américaines (AFEA), 1 Pl de l'Odéon, 75006 Paris
T: 0146330248
Founded: 1967; Members: 300
Focus: Ethnology *03548*

Association Française d'Observateurs d'Etoiles Variables, c/o Observatoire Astronomique, 11 Rue de l'Université, 67000 Strasbourg
T: 0388843711
Founded: 1921; Members: 110
Pres: E. Schweitzer
Focus: Astronomy
Periodical
Bulletin (quarterly) *03549*

Association Française du Froid (AFF), 17 Rue Guillaume Apollinaire, 75263 Paris Cedex 06
T: 0145445252 k703=01 42220042; Fax: 0162220042
Founded: 1908
Pres: Michel Barth; Gen Secr: Louis Millot
Focus: Air Cond; Eng
Periodical
Revue Générale du Froid (monthly) . . *03550*

Association Française d'Urologie, c/o Convergences, 120 Av Gambetta, 75020 Paris
T: 0143647777; Fax: 0140310165
Founded: 1896
Focus: Urology *03551*

Association Française Inter Médicale, 2 Rue de Clichy, 75009 Paris
T: 0148747329
Focus: Med *03552*

Association Française pour la Cybernetique Economique et Technique, 156 Blvd Péreire, 75017 Paris
T: 0147662419; Fax: 0142679312
Founded: 1968
Focus: Cybernetics *03553*

Association Française pour la Protection des Eaux (AFPE), 195 Rue Saint-Jacques, 75005 Paris
T: 0143267053
Founded: 1960; Members: 1100
Focus: Ecology *03554*

Association Française pour la Recherche et la Création Musicales, 9 Rue Chaptal, 75009 Paris
Founded: 1971
Focus: Music *03555*

Association Française pour le Développement de la Stomatologie, c/o Institut de Stomatologie, Faculté de Médecine, 47 Blvd de l'Hôpital, 75013 Paris
T: 0143364927
Focus: Stomatology *03556*

Association Française pour l'Etude du Cancer (A.F.E.C.), 26 Rue d'Ulm, 75231 Paris Cedex 05
T: 0143291242
Founded: 1907; Members: 300
Focus: Cell Biol & Cancer Res
Periodical
Bulletin du Cancer (5 times annually) . *03557*

Association Française pour l'Etude du Quaternaire (A.F.E.Q.), c/o Centre Géomorphologie, CNRS, 24 Rue des Tilleuls, 14000 Caen
T: 0231565718; Fax: 0231565757
Founded: 1962; Members: 650
Pres: M. T. Morzadec; Gen Secr: D. Lefèvre
Focus: Geology
Periodical
Quaternaire: Bulletin de l'Association Française pour l'Etude du Quaternaire (quarterly) . *03558*

Association Française pour l'Etude du Sol (A.F.E.S.), Domaine de Limère, Av de la Pomme de Pin, 45160 Ardon
Founded: 1934; Members: 950
Pres: J.C. Remy
Focus: Agri; Geomorph
Periodicals
Etude et Gestion des Sols (semi-annually)
European Journal of Soil Science (quarterly) *03559*

Association Française pour l'Information en Economie Ménagère, 11 Rue Toussaint Feron, 75013 Paris
T: 0140334551
Focus: Home Econ *03560*

Association Francophone de Spectrométrie des Masses Solides, c/o Centre National d'Etudes des Télécommunications, 22301 Lannion
Founded: 1975
Focus: Physics *03561*

Association Francophone d'Education Comparée (AFEC), 1 Av Léon Journault, 92310 Sèvres
T: 0145076000
Founded: 1973; Members: 100
Pres: Jean-Michel Leclercq; Gen Secr: Antoine Bevort
Focus: Educ
Periodicals
Education Comparée (annually)
Etudes d'Education Comparée (irregularly) *03562*

Association Francophone Internationale des Groupes d'Animation de la Paraplégie (AFIGAP), c/o Centre de Rééducation Neurologique, Rte de Liverdy, 77170 Coubert
T: 0164422081; Fax: 0164422082
Founded: 1979; Members: 200
Gen Secr: Dr. Jean-François Désert
Focus: Rehabil *03563*

Association Générale des Conservateurs des Collections Publiques de France (AGCCPFI), 6 Rue des Pyramides, 75041 Paris Cedex 01
T: 0140153649; Fax: 0147034482
Founded: 1922; Members: 1000
Pres: Jean-Marcl Humbert
Focus: Arts
Periodical
Musées et Collections Publiques de France (quarterly) *03564*

Association Générale des Hygiénistes et Techniciens Municipaux (AGHTM), 9 Rue de Phalsbourg, 75017 Paris
T: 0144151550
Founded: 1905; Members: 1350
Focus: Hygiene; Eng
Periodical
Techniques, Sciences, Methodes (monthly) *03565*

Association Générale des Médecins de France (A.G.M.F.), 60 Blvd de Latour-Maubourg, 75327 Paris Cedex 07
T: 0147054528
Pres: P. Baudouin; Gen Secr: Dr. A. Tochard
Focus: Med
Periodical
Bulletin *03566*

Association Guillaume Budé (CSSF), 95 Blvd Raspail, 75006 Paris
T: 0142226915
Founded: 1917; Members: 3200
Focus: Lit *03567*

Association Internationale de Droit Pénal (AIDP), BP 1146, 64011 Pau Cedex
Fax: 0559807559
Founded: 1924
Gen Secr: H. Epp
Focus: Law
Periodicals
Nouvelles Etudes Pénales
Revue Internationale de Droit Pénal (semi-annually) *03568*

Association Internationale de l'Inspection du Travail (AIIT) / International Association of Labour Inspections, c/o Direction Régionale du Travail, 66 Rue de Mouzaia, 75935 Paris Cedex 19
T: 0142003300
Founded: 1972
Focus: Business Admin *03569*

Association Internationale de Littérature Comparée / International Comparative Literature Association, c/o Université de Paris-Sorbonne, 1 Rue Victor-Cousin, 75230 Paris Cedex 05
T: 0132911213
Founded: 1955; Members: 2800
Pres: Prof. E. Miner; Gen Secr: José Lambert; Prof. Lore Metzger
Focus: Lit *03570*

Association Internationale de Médecine et de Biologie de l'Environnement (AIMBE), 115 Rue de la Pompe, 75116 Paris
T: 0145534504; Fax: 0145534175
Founded: 1971
Focus: Med; Bio; Ecology *03571*

Association Internationale de Pédiatrie / Asociación Internacional de Pediatría / International Pediatric Association, Château de Longchamp, Bois de Boulogne, 75016 Paris
T: 0145271590; Fax: 0145257367
Founded: 1912; Members: 110
Pres: Prof. Perla D. Santos-Ocampo; Gen Secr: Prof. Ihsan Dogramaci
Focus: Pediatrics
Periodical
International Child Health (quarterly) . . *03572*

Association Internationale de Psychologie du Travail de Langue Française / International Association of French-Speaking Psychologists of the Working Environment, c/o Dépt de Psychologie, Université de Rouen, 76821 Motn Saint-Aignan Cedex
T: 0235146104
Founded: 1980
Pres: Prof. Claude Lemoine
Focus: Psych *03573*

Association Internationale de Recherche en Informatique Toxicologique (AIRIT), c/o CAP, Hôpital Fernand Widal, 200 Rue du Faubourg Saint-Denis, 75475 Paris
Founded: 1973
Focus: Computer & Info Sci; Toxicology *03574*

Association Internationale d'Epigraphie Grecque et Latine (A.I.E.G.L.), c/o Bibliothèque de la Sorbonne, 47 Rue des Ecoles, 75230 Paris Cedex 05
Founded: 1963
Focus: Ling
Periodical
Nouvelles de l'A.I.E.G.L. *03575*

Association Internationale des Amis de Vasile Stanciu, 49 Blvd de Port Royal, 75013 Paris
T: 0160841151
Founded: 1987
Focus: Criminology *03576*

Association Internationale des Arts Plastiques (AIAP), c/o UNESCO, 1 Rue Miollis, 75732 Paris Cedex 15
T: 0145682655
Founded: 1952; Members: 80
Gen Secr: C. Rubalcava
Focus: Arts
Periodical
Art-Journal of the Professional Artist (annually) *03577*

Association Internationale des Critiques de Théâtre (AICT), 6 Rue de Braque, 75003 Paris
Founded: 1956
Focus: Perf Arts
Periodical
Prospectus (3 times annually) *03578*

Association Internationale des Critiques Littéraires (AICL), 58 Rue Claude-Bernard, 75005 Paris
Fax: 0143549299
Founded: 1969; Members: 700
Pres: Robert André
Focus: Lit
Periodical
Revue de l'AICL (semi-annually) *03579*

Association Internationale des Démographes de Langue Française (AIDELF) / International Association of French-Language Demographers, 27 Rue du Commandeur, 75675 Paris Cedex 14

T: 0143201345; Fax: 0143277240
Founded: 1977
Gen Secr: Alain Parant
Focus: Soc Sci 03580

Association Internationale des Docteurs en Economie du Tourisme (A.I.D.E.T.), 6 Av de Grassi, 13100 Aix-en-Provence
T: 0442966497; Fax: 0442233720
Members: 740
Pres: Dr. Jean-Maurice Thurot; Gen Secr: Dr. Christine Richter
Focus: Business Admin 03581

Association Internationale des Ecoles des Sciences de l'Information (AIESI), c/o Institut d'Etudes Politiques, Cycle Gestion de l'Information dans l'Entreprise, 9 Rue de l'Abbaye, 75006 Paris
T: 0144072864; E-Mail: martine.prévot@sciences-po.fr
Founded: 1977; Members: 23
Pres: Martine Prévot-Hubert
Focus: Educ; Computer & Info Sci . . . 03582

Association Internationale des Educateurs de Jeunes Inadaptés (AIEJI), 3 Rue Pierre Brossolette, 64000 Pau
T: 0559025962; Fax: 0559026283
Founded: 1951; Members: 92
Focus: Educ 03583

Association Internationale des Etudes de l'Asie du Sud-Est (AIEAS), 22 Av du Président Wilson, 75116 Paris
T: 0145537301
Founded: 1973
Gen Secr: Prof. P.B. Lafont
Focus: Ethnology
Periodical
Lettre d'Information (semi-annually) . . . 03584

Association Internationale des Etudes Françaises (AIEF), 11 Pl Marcelin Berthelot, 75005 Paris
T: 0143291211
Founded: 1949
Gen Secr: Prof. Robert Garapon
Focus: Ling; Lit
Periodical
Cahiers (annually) 03585

Association Internationale des Professeurs et Maîtres de Conférences des Universités, 21 Rue Isabey, 54000 Nancy
T: 0383281221
Founded: 1945
Gen Secr: L.-P. Laprévote
Focus: Sci 03586

Association Internationale des Sciences Juridiques (AISJ) / International Association of Legal Science, c/o CISS-UNESCO, 1 Rue Miollis, 75732 Paris Cedex 15
T: 0145682558; Fax: 0143068798
Founded: 1950
Gen Secr: M. Leker
Focus: Law 03587

Association Internationale des Sociologues de Langue Française (AISLF), c/o Université de Toulouse-le-Mirail, 5 Allée Antonio Machado, 31058 Toulouse Cedex
T: 0561504374; Fax: 0561504374
Founded: 1956; Members: 1115
Gen Secr: Christiane Rondi
Focus: Sociology
Periodicals
Annuaire de l'AISLF
Bulletin de l'AISLF (annually) 03588

Association Internationale des Statisticiens d'Enquêtes (AISE) / International Association of Survey Statisticians, 18 Blvd Adolphe Pinard, Bureau 1059, 75675 Paris Cedex 14
T: 0141175300
Founded: 1973; Members: 1435
Gen Secr: A. Charraud
Focus: Stats
Periodicals
International Statistical Information
International Statistical Review
Survey Statistician (semi-annually) . . . 03589

Association Internationale des Techniciens Biologistes de Langue Française (ASSITEB), 109 Av Gabriel Peri, 94170 Le Perreux
T: 0248711451
Founded: 1982
Pres: Nelly Marchal
Focus: Eng
Periodicals
Le Courier de l'ASSITEB
L'Information du Technicien Biologiste . . 03590

Association Internationale des Travaux en Souterrain (AITES) / International Tunnelling Association, 25 Av François Mitterand, 69674 Bron Cedex
T: 4178260455; Fax: 4172372406
Founded: 1974; Members: 45
Gen Secr: C. Berenguier
Focus: Civil Eng
Periodicals
Tribune: Newsletter of the ITA
Tunnelling and Underground Space Technology (quarterly) 03591

Association Internationale d'Histoire Economique / International Economic History Association, c/o Centre de Recherches Historiques, Ecole des Hautes Etudes en Sciences Sociales, 54 Blvd Raspail, 75270 Paris Cedex 06
T: 0149542440; E-Mail: aihe@ehess.fr
Founded: 1965
Gen Secr: Prof. Joseph Goy
Focus: Hist; Econ 03592

Association Internationale d'Information Scolaire, Universitaire et Professionnelle (AIISUP), 20 Rue de l'Estrapade, 75005 Paris
T: 0143541027
Founded: 1956
Focus: Computer & Info Sci
Periodicals
Bibliographical Bulletin
Informations Universitaires et Professionnelles Internationales (bi-monthly) 03593

Association Internationale d'Irradiation Industrielle (AIII) / Association of International Industrial Irradiation, 59 Rte de Paris, 69260 Charbonnières-les-Bains
T: 0478871165; Fax: 0478878831
Founded: 1970
Pres: Pierre E. Vidal; Gen Secr: N. Studer
Focus: Eng
Periodical
Newsletter (semi-annually) 03594

Association Internationale d'Océanographie Médicale / International Association of Medical Oceanography, c/o CERBOM, Parc de la Côte, Av Jean Lorrain, 06000 Nice
Founded: 1975
Focus: Oceanography 03595

Association Internationale Données pour le Développement (DPD) / Data for Development International Association, 122 Av de Hambourg, 13008 Marseille
T: 0491739018; Fax: 0491730138
Founded: 1975; Members: 198
Focus: Computer & Info Sci
Periodical
Data for Development Newletters (quarterly) 03596

Association Internationale Francophone de Recherche Odontologique (AIFRO), c/o Faculté de Chirurgie Dentaire, 2 Pl Pasteur, 35000 Rennes
Founded: 1977
Focus: Dent 03597

Association Internationale pour le Développement de l'Odonto-Stomatologie Tropicale / International Association for the Development of Tropical Odonto-Stomatology, c/o UER d'Odontologie, 146 Rue Léo Saignat, 33076 Bordeaux Cedex
T: 0556909124
Founded: 1988
Gen Secr: Christine Canet
Focus: Stomatology; Dent
Periodical
Revue d'Odonto-Stomatologie Tropicale . 03598

Association Internationale pour le Développement des Gommes Naturelles / Association of International Development of Natural Gums, 4 Rue Frédéric Passy, 92200 Neuilly-sur-Seine
T: 0247471850; Fax: 0247471891
Founded: 1974
Focus: Materials Sci 03599

Association Internationale pour le Développement des Universités Internationales et Mondiales (AIDUM) / International Association for the Development of International and World Universities, 31 Av de Mun, 93600 Aulnay-sous-Bois
T: 0248666698
Founded: 1953
Gen Secr: Marc Bullio
Focus: Sci
Periodical
Memoranda 03600

Association Internationale pour le Management du Sport, BP 149, 91240 Saint-Michel
T: 0545391237
Founded: 1987
Pres: Robert Trottein
Focus: Business Admin 03601

Association Internationale pour l'Etude de la Paléontologie Humaine, c/o Institut de Paléontologie Humaine, 1 Rue René Panhard, 75013 Paris
T: 0143316291
Founded: 1982
Gen Secr: Prof. Henry de Lumley
Focus: Paleontology 03602

Association Interprofessionnelle de France (AINF), Rue Marcel Dassault, Zone Industrielle, BP 259, 59472 Seclin Cedex
T: 0320329900; Fax: 0320325166
Founded: 1894; Members: 3500
Pres: C. Bloch
Focus: Safety 03603

Association Interprofessionnelle des Centres Médicaux et Sociaux de la Région Parisienne (A.C.M.S.), 132 Rue du Faubourg Saint-Denis, 75010 Paris
T: 0142091800
Focus: Med; Sociology 03604

Association Interprofessionnelle pour la Formation Permanente dans le Commerce Textile, 69 Rue de Richelieu, 75001 Paris
T: 012975493
Focus: Adult Educ; Textiles 03605

Association Les Amis de Gustave Courbet, c/o Musée Maison Natale Gustave Courbet, Pl Robert Fernier, 25290 Ornans
T: 0381622330; Fax: 0145244700
Founded: 1938; Members: 500
Pres: Comte Balthazar Klossowski de Rok; Gen Secr: Roland Laheurte
Focus: Arts
Periodical
Bulletin des Amis de Gustave Courbet (semi-annually) 03606

Association Linguistique Franco-Européenne (A.L.F.E.), 117 Rue de Rennes, 75006 Paris
T: 0145484563
Focus: Ling 03607

Association Littéraire et Artistique Internationale (ALAI), 55 Rue des Mathurins, 75008 Paris
T: 0142650445
Founded: 1878
Gen Secr: André Françon
Focus: Arts; Lit
Periodical
Bulletin de l'ALAI 03608

Association Lyonnaise de Criminologie et Anthropologie Sociale, 12 Av Rockefeller, 69008 Lyon
T: 0472344858; Fax: 0472120075
Founded: 1967
Focus: Criminology; Anthro 03609

Association Marc Bloch, 54 Blvd Raspail, 75006 Paris
Founded: 1949
Focus: Hist 03610

Association Maria Montessori, 51 Av Bugeaud, 75016 Paris
T: 0147235230
Focus: Educ 03611

Association Médico-Sociale Protestante de Langue Française, 68 Rue Marcel Bourdarias, 94140 Alfortville
T: 0248992783, 0243760666; Fax: 0248980334
Founded: 1948
Gen Secr: Pierre-Yves Le Renard
Focus: Soc Sci; Med
Periodical
Ouvertures (quarterly) 03612

Association Mondiale des Vétérinaires Microbiologistes, Immunologistes et Spécialistes des Maladies Infectieuses (A.M.V.M.I.), c/o Service de Microbiologie, Ecole Nationale Vétérinaire d'Alfort, 7 Av du Général de Gaulle, 94704 Maisons Alfort Cedex
T: 0143759211
Founded: 1967; Members: 240
Pres: Prof. Pilet
Focus: Vet Med
Periodical
Comparative Immunology Microbiology and infection disease (quarterly) 03613

Association Nationale de la Recherche Technique (A.N.R.T), 101 Av Raymond Poincaré, 75116 Paris
T: 0145017227; Fax: 0145018529
Founded: 1953; Members: 264
Pres: Francis Mer
Focus: Eng
Periodical
La Lettre Européenne du Progrés Technique (10 times annually) 03614

Association Nationale des Bibliothécaires, c/o Mlle Pintaparis, Cité Administrative, 17 Blvd Morland, 75004 Paris
Focus: Libraries & Bk Sci 03615

Association Nationale des Cours Professionnels pour les Préparateurs en Pharmacie, 41 Blvd de Magenta, 75010 Paris
T: 0142065900
Focus: Adult Educ; Pharmacol 03616

Association Nationale des Docteurs en Droit, 38bis Rue Faber, 75007 Paris
T: 0147051165
Members: 4000
Focus: Law
Periodical
Droit et Economie (3 times annually) . . 03617

Association Nationale des Educateurs de Jeunes Inadaptés (ANEJ), 27 Rue de Maubeuge, 75009 Paris
T: 0148783917
Founded: 1947; Members: 2000
Focus: Educ 03618

Association Nationale des Professeurs en Economie Sociale et Familiale, 28 Pl Saint-Georges, 75009 Paris
T: 0142800782
Focus: Sociology; Educ 03619

Association Nationale pour la Formation et la Promotion Professionnelle dans l'Industrie et le Commerce de la Chaussure et des Cuirs et Peaux (A.F.P.I.C.), 5 Rue Joseph Sansboeuf, 75008 Paris
T: 0145222888
Focus: Adult Educ 03620

Association Nationale pour la Protection des Eaux, 195 Rue Saint-Jacques, 75005 Paris
T: 0143267053
Founded: 1960; Members: 800
Focus: Ecology 03621

Association Nationale pour la Protection des Villes d'Art, 39 Av de la Motte-Picquet, 75007 Paris
T: 0147053771
Founded: 1963
Focus: Preserv Hist Monuments 03622

Association Nationale pour la Réhabilitation Professionnelle par le Travail Protégé, 59 Blvd de Belleville, 75011 Paris
T: 0143571365
Focus: Rehabil 03623

Association Nationale pour l'Etude de la Neige et des Avalanches (ANENA), 15 Rue Ernest Calvat, 38000 Grenoble
T: 0476513939; Fax: 0476428166
Founded: 1971; Members: 800
Pres: Jean-Guy Cupillard; Gen Secr: François Sivardière
Focus: Geophys
Periodical
Neige et Avalanches (quarterly) 03624

Association of African Geological Surveys / Association des Services Géologiques Africains, c/o CIFEG, Av de Concyr, BP 6517, 45065 Orléans Cedex 2
T: 0238643347; Fax: 0238643472
Founded: 1929
Pres: G.O. Kesse; Gen Secr: M. Bensaid
Focus: Geology
Periodical
African Geology (semi-annually) 03625

Association of European Schools and Colleges of Optometry / Association Européenne des Ecoles et Collèges d'Optométrie, 134 Rte de Chartres, 91440 Bures-sur-Yvette
T: 0469076737; Fax: 0469287806
Founded: 1979; Members: 58
Gen Secr: Jean-Paul Roosen
Focus: Ophthal
Periodical
Communications (5 times annually) . . . 03626

Association of French-Speaking Planetariums, c/o Planetarium de Strasbourg, Université Louis Pasteur, Rue de l'Observatoire, 67000 Strasbourg
T: 0388361251
Gen Secr: Agnes Acker
Focus: Astronomy 03627

Association Philotechnique, 47 Rue Saint-André des Arts, 75006 Paris
T: 0143264828
Focus: Ling 03628

Association pour la Fondation Internationale du Cinéma et de la Communication Audiovisuelle (AFICCA), 33 Rue Washington, 75008 Paris
T: 0153752700; Fax: 0153752701
Founded: 1987; Members: 153
Pres: André Holleaux; Gen Secr: René Thevenet
Focus: Comm Sci; Cinema
Periodical
Script (quarterly) 03629

Association pour la Formation aux Professions Immobilières, 2 Impasse Mont Tonnerre, 75015 Paris
T: 0145672082
Focus: Adult Educ 03630

Association pour la Formation des Cadres de l'Industrie et du Commerce, 31 Av Pierre Ier de Serbie, 75784 Paris Cedex 16
T: 0147236158
Focus: Adult Educ 03631

Association pour la Formation Professionnelle dans les Industries Céréalières (A.F.P.I.C), 66 Rue La Boétie, 75008 Paris
Focus: Adult Educ 03632

Association pour la Formation Professionnelle dans les Industries de l'Ameublement (A.F.P.I.A.), 28 Av Daumesnil, 75012 Paris
T: 0143075907
Focus: Adult Educ 03633

Association pour la Médiathèque Public (AMP), c/o Bibliothèque Municipale, 37 Rue Saint-Georges, 59400 Cambrai
T: 0327813520
Focus: Libraries & Bk Sci; Doc
Periodical
Médiathèques Publiques (quarterly) . . . 03634

Association pour la Prévention de la Pollution Atmosphérique (APPA), 58 Rue du Rocher, 75008 Paris
T: 0142936207; Fax: 0142934199
Founded: 1958; Members: 1000
Pres: Prof. B. Festy; Gen Secr: Dr. W. Dab

Focus: Ecology 03635

Association pour la Promotion de la Pédagogie Nouvelle, 11 Rue Coetlogon, 75006 Paris
T: 0145445576
Focus: Educ 03636

Association pour la Recherche et le Développement en Informatique Chimique, 25 Rue Jussieu, 75005 Paris
T: 0143362525
Focus: Chem 03637

Association pour la Recherche Interculturelle (ARIC), c/o UFR de Psychologie, Université de Paris VIII, 2 Rue de la Liberté, 93526 Saint-Denis Cedex
Founded: 1984
Focus: Cultur Hist 03638

Association pour la Rééducation de la Parole et du Langage Oral et Ecrit et de la Voix (A.R.P.L.O.E.V.), 10 Rue de l'Arrivée, 75015 Paris
T: 0145444885
Founded: 1956; Members: 600
Focus: Logopedy
Periodical
Rééducation Orthophonique (quarterly) . . 03639

Association pour le Développement de la Formation Professionnelle Continue dans les Industries Lourdes du Bois, 30 Av Marceau, 75008 Paris
T: 0142561732, 0142561739
Focus: Adult Educ 03640

Association pour le Développement de la Formation Professionnelle dans les Transports, 46 Av de Villiers, 75017 Paris
T: 0147660360
Focus: Adult Educ 03641

Association pour le Développement de la Recherche en Toxicologie Expérimentale, 4 Av de l'Observatoire, 75006 Paris
T: 0143267122
Focus: Toxicology 03642

Association pour le Développement de la Stomatologie, 47 Blvd de l'Hôpital, 75013 Paris
T: 0143364927
Focus: Stomatology 03643

Association pour le Développement de la Traduction Automatique et de Linguistique Appliqué, 11 Rue de Lille, 75007 Paris
Focus: Ling 03644

Association pour le Développement de l'Enseignement et des Recherches Scientifiques auprès des Universités de la Région Parisienne (A.D.E.R.P.), 31 Av Pierre Ier de Serbie, 75116 Paris
T: 0147236158
Focus: Sci 03645

Association pour le Développement des Etudes Biologiques en Psychiatrie, 1 Rue Cabanis, 75014 Paris
T: 0145814557
Focus: Bio; Psychiatry 03646

Association pour le Développement des Relations Médicales entre la France et les Pays Etrangers, 16 Rue Bonaparte, 75272 Paris Cedex 06
Focus: Med 03647

Association pour le Développement des Techniques de Transport, d'Environnement et de Circulation (ATEC), 38 Av Emile Zola, 75015 Paris
T: 0145755611
Founded: 1973; Members: 1330
Focus: Transport
Periodical
T.E.C. (bi-monthly) 03648

Association pour le Développement du Droit Mondial, 28 Rue Saint-Guillaume, 75007 Paris
Focus: Law 03649

Association pour l'Enseignement de l'Assurance, 8 Rue Chaptal, 75009 Paris
T: 0148747539
Focus: Insurance; Educ
Periodical
La Lettre d'Information (semi-annually) . 03650

Association pour l'Innovation Scientifique, 41 Rue de Vaugirard, 75006 Paris
T: 0145480789
Focus: Sci 03651

Association Psychoanalytique de France, 24 Pl Dauphine, 75001 Paris
T: 0143298511; Fax: 0143261346
Members: 40
Focus: Psychoan 03652

Association Régionale d'Education Permanente, 22 Rue de Varenne, 75007 Paris
T: 0142220025
Focus: Educ 03653

Association Régionale des Oeuvres Educatives et des Vacances de l'Education Nationale (A.R.O.E.V.E.N.), 18 Passage Turquetil, 75011 Paris
T: 0143704501
Focus: Educ 03654

Association Régionale d'Informations Sociales, 30 Rue Gramont, 75002 Paris
T: 0142962336
Focus: Sociology 03655

Association Scientifique des Médecins Acupuncteurs de France (A.S.M.A.F.), 2 Rue du Général de Larminat, 75015 Paris
T: 0142733726
Founded: 1945; Members: 1500
Pres: Dr. Georges Cantoni; Gen Secr: Dr. H. Olivo
Focus: Anesthetics
Periodical
Méridiens (quarterly) 03656

Association Scientifique et Technique pour l'Exploitation des Océans, Immeuble Ile de France, 4 Pl de la Pyramide, La Défense 9, 92070 Paris-La Défense Cedex 33
T: 0147672532
Founded: 1967
Focus: Oceanography 03657

Association Stomatologique Internationale (ASI) / International Stomatological Association, 66 Rue La Boétie, 75008 Paris
Founded: 1907
Focus: Stomatology 03658

Association Technique de la Fonderie (ATF), 2 Rue de Bassano, 75116 Paris
T: 0147235550
Founded: 1911; Members: 2800
Focus: Metallurgy
Periodical
Hommes et Fondérie (monthly) 03659

Association Technique de la Réfrigération et de l'Equipement Ménager (A.T.R.E.M.), 28 Av Hoche, 75008 Paris
T: 0147662134, 015630200
Members: 4
Focus: Eng; Air Cond 03660

Association Technique de la Sidérurgie Française (ATS), 11 Cours Valmy, 92072 Paris la Défense Cedex
T: 0141255800; Fax: 0141255858
Founded: 1946; Members: 1100
Pres: Daniel Meyer; Gen Secr: Jean Louis Gatelais
Focus: Metallurgy 03661

Association Technique de l'Industrie du Gaz en France (ATG), 62 Rue de Courcelles, 75008 Paris
T: 0147660351
Founded: 1874; Members: 2150
Focus: Energy
Periodicals
Gaz d'Aujourd'hui (10 times annually)
Médiagaz (11 times annually) 03662

Association Technique de l'Industrie Papetière (ATIP), 154 Blvd Haussmann, 75008 Paris
T: 0145621191; Fax: 0145635309
Founded: 1947; Members: 1220
Pres: B. Mathieu; Gen Secr: Daniel Gomez
Focus: Eng
Periodical
Revue ATIP (bi-monthly) 03663

Association Technique Maritime et Aéronautique (ATMA), 47 Rue Monceau, 75008 Paris
T: 0145619911
Founded: 1889; Members: 1050
Focus: Eng; Aero
Periodical
Bulletin ATMA (annually) 03664

Association Technique pour l'Etude de la Gestion des Institutions Publiques et des Entreprises Privées (ATEGIPE), 2 Av de la Bourbonnais, 75007 Paris
Founded: 1950; Members: 220
Focus: Business Admin 03665

Association Universitaire pour le Développement de l'Enseignement et de la Culture en Afrique et à Madagascar (AUDECAM), 100 Rue de l'Université, 75007 Paris
T: 0145555638
Focus: Adult Educ 03666

Astronomical Data Centre, c/o Observatoire de Strasbourg, 11 Rue de l'Université, 67000 Strasbourg
T: 03388358218; Fax: 0388250160
Founded: 1972
Pres: Dr. Michel Crézé
Focus: Astronomy
Periodical
Bulletin d'Information du CDS (semi-annually) 03667

Atlantic Gas Research Exchange (AGRE), c/o Gaz de France, 361 Av du Président Wilson, BP 33, 93211 La Plaine-Saint-Denis
Founded: 1978
Focus: Energy 03668

Bureau International de Documentation (BILD), 13 Av de l'Opéra, 75001 Paris
T: 0142603200
Focus: Doc 03669

Bureau International de Liaison et de Documentation (BILD), 50 Rue de Laborde, 75008 Paris
Founded: 1945
Focus: Int'l Relat
Periodicals
Documents
Revue des Questions Allemandes . . . 03670

Bureau International des Poids et Mesures (BIPM), Pavillon de Breteuil, 92310 Sèvres
T: 0145077070; Fax: 0145342021
Founded: 1875; Members: 47
Pres: Dr. D. Kind; Gen Secr: Dr. T.J. Quinn
Focus: Standards
Periodicals
Procès-Verbaux des séances du CIPM (annually)
Sessions des Comités Consultatifs (8): Electricité, Photométrie et Radiométrie, Thermométrie, Définition du Mètre, Définition de la Seconde, Etalons des Mesure des Reyonnement Ionisants, Unités, Masse et grandeurs apparentées (irregularly) 03671

Center for Studies, Research and Training in International Understanding and Cooperation (CERFCI), c/o FMACU-WFUCA, 1 Rue Miollis, 75015 Paris
T: 0145682818
Focus: Soc Sci; Econ 03672

Centre d'Archives et de Documentation Politiques et Sociales, 86 Blvd Haussmann, 75008 Paris
Founded: 1949
Focus: Poli Sci; Soc Sci 03673

Centre de Coopération Internationale en Recherche Agronomique pour le Développement (CIRAD), 42 Rue Scheffer, 75116 Paris
T: 0147043215; Fax: 0147551530
Founded: 1984
Focus: Agri
Periodical
Agritrop Tropical and Subtropical (semi-annually) 03674

Centre de Coopération pour les Recherches Scientifiques Relatives au Tabac (CORESTA) / Cooperation Centre for Scientific Research Relative to Tobacco, 53 Quai d'Orsay, 75347 Paris Cedex 07
T: 0145566019
Founded: 1956; Members: 130
Pres: Günther Hayn; Gen Secr: F. Jacob
Focus: Agri; Chem; Standards; Tobacco
Periodical
Bulletin du CORESTA (quarterly) 03675

Centre de Perfectionnement des Industries Textiles Rhône-Alpes (CEPITRA), 55 Montée de Choulans, 69323 Lyon Cedex 04
T: 0472564926; Fax: 0472564929
Focus: Eng; Textiles 03676

Centre de Rencontres et d'Etudes des Dirigeants des Administrations Fiscales (CREDAF), 51 Rue de Rome, 75008 Paris
T: 0143874433; Fax: 0143874433
Founded: 1982
Gen Secr: Jacques Carion
Focus: Business Admin 03677

Centre d'Etudes, de Documentation, d'Information et d'Action Sociales (CEDIAS), 5 Rue Las Cases, 75007 Paris
T: 0145516610, 0147059246
Founded: 1894
Pres: Dr. M. Montalembert; Gen Secr: Brigitte Bouquet
Focus: Sociology; Doc; Poli Sci; Hist
Periodicals
Manuel de Placement (annually)
Vie Sociale (bi-monthly) 03678

Centre d'Etudes Supérieures de Civilisation Médiévale, 24 Rue de la Chaine, 86022 Poitiers
T: 0549454563; Fax: 0549454573
Founded: 1954; Members: 60
Pres: G. Bianciotto
Focus: Hist
Periodical
Cahiers de Civilisation Médiévale (5 times annually) 03679

Centre d'Histoire Militaire et d'Etudes de Défense Nationale (CHMM), c/o Université Paul Valery, BP 5043, 34032 Montpellier Cedex
Founded: 1938
Focus: Hist; Military Sci
Periodical
Les Cahiers de Montpellier: Forces Armées et Politiques de Défense (semi-annually) . . 03680

Centre Européen de Formation des Statisticiens Economistes des Pays en Voie de Développement (CESD), 3 Av Pierre Larousse, 92241 Malakoff Cedex
T: 0145401007; Fax: 0140921191
Founded: 1962
Gen Secr: L. Diop
Focus: Stats 03681

Centre Européen de Recherches sur les Congrégations et Ordres Religieux (CERCOR), c/o Maison Rhône-Alpes des Sciences de l'Homme, 35 Rue du 11 Novembre, 42023 Saint-Etienne
T: 0477389667
Founded: 1981; Members: 1400
Pres: Prof. Marcel Pacaut
Focus: Rel & Theol 03682

Centre for the Advancement and Study of the European Currency, 16 Av Berthelot, 69007 Lyon
T: 0472732820; Fax: 0472734604
Founded: 1982; Members: 39
Pres: Michel Coste
Focus: Finance 03683

Centre Français de Droit Comparé, 28 Rue Saint-Guillaume, 75007 Paris
T: 0144398623; Fax: 0144398628
Founded: 1951
Pres: Prof. Jacques Robert; Gen Secr: Didier Lamèthe
Focus: Law
Periodical
Lettre du Centre Français de Droit Comparé (3 times annually) 03684

Centre International de Cyto-Cybernétique (C.I.C. CYB.), 9 Av Niél, 75017 Paris
Founded: 1966; Members: 1280
Focus: Cybernetics 03685

Centre International de l'Enfance, Château de Longchamp, Bois de Boulogne, 75016 Paris
T: 0145207992; Fax: 0145257367
Founded: 1949
Pres: Prof. Claude Griscelli; Gen Secr: Michèle Puybasset
Focus: Educ
Periodicals
Bulletins bibliographiques
L'Enfant en Milieu Tropical: Children's in the Tropics (bi-monthly)
El Niño en el Tropico 03686

Centre International de Recherches et d'Etudes Touristiques (CIRET), 6 Av de Grassi, 13100 Aix en Provence
T: 0442969935; Fax: 0442233720
Founded: 1997
Pres: Dr. René Baretje; Gen Secr: Dr. Jean-Maurice Thurot
Focus: Econ 03687

Centre International de Synthèse, 12 Rue Colbert, 75002 Paris
T: 0142975068; E-Mail: synthese@filnet.fr;
Fax: 0142974646
Founded: 1924; Members: 36
Pres: Jean-Claude Perrot; Gen Secr: M. Laigneau
Focus: Sci; Philos
Periodicals
Revue de Synthèse (quarterly)
Revue d'Histoire des Sciences (quarterly) 03688

Centre International d'Etude des Textiles Anciens (CIETA), 34 Rue de la Charité, 69002 Lyon
Founded: 1954; Members: 235
Focus: Hist; Textiles
Periodical
Bulletin du CIETA (annually) 03689

Centre International d'Etudes Latines (C.I.E.L.), 25 Rue du Mont Thabor, 75001 Paris
T: 0142608484
Focus: Ling 03690

Centre International d'Etudes Romanes (CIER), 13 Cour du Cloitre, 71700 Tournus
T: 0385325454; Fax: 038531898
Founded: 1952; Members: 400
Pres: Gislain de Gislain de Bontin; Gen Secr: Marguerite Thibert
Focus: Archeol 03691

Centre International du Film pour l'Enfance et la Jeunesse (CIFEJ) / International Centre of Films for Children and Young People, 9 Rue Bargue, 75015 Paris
Founded: 1957
Focus: Cinema
Periodicals
News from ICFCYP
Young Cinema International (semi-annually) 03692

Centre International Scolaire de Correspondance Sonore (CISCS), Chanteloup, 10300 Sainte-Savine
Focus: Educ 03693

Centre National de la Recherche Scientifique (CNRS), 20-22 Rue Saint-Armand, 75015 Paris
T: 0155761716; Fax: 0155761717
Founded: 1939
Focus: Sociology; Humanities
Periodicals
Annuaire de l'Afrique du Nord (annually)
Annuaire des Pays de l'Océan Indien (annually)
Annuaire Français de Droit International (annually)
Antiquités Africaines (annually)
Archaeonautica (annually)
Bibliographie Annuelle de l'Histoire de France (annually)
Cahiers de Micropaléontologie (semi-annually)
Cahiers du Seminaire d'Econométrie (semi-annually)
Etudes Celtiques (annually)
Gallia (annually)
Hermes (semi-annually)
Paleorient (semi-annually)
Paroisses et Communes de France (semi-annually)
Patrimoine au Présent (semi-annually)
Revue Archéologie Médiévale (annually)

Revue Archéologique de l'Est et du Centre-Est (semi-annually)
Revue Archéologique de Narbonnaise (annually)
Les Voies de la Création Théatrale (irregularly) . . . 03694

Centre National d'Etudes Spatiales, 2 Pl Maurice Quentin, 75001 Paris
Founded: 1961
Focus: Aero . . . 03695

Centre National du Livre, 53 Rue de Verneuil, 75007 Paris
T: 0149546868; Fax: 0145491021
Founded: 1946
Focus: Libraries & Bk Sci . . . 03696

Centre Naturopa, c/o Conseil de l'Europe, 67075 Strasbourg Cedex
T: 0388412000; Fax: 0388412715
Focus: Ecology
Periodicals
Environment Features (bi-monthly)
Library Bulletin (bi-monthly)
Naturopa (3 times annually)
Naturopa-Newsletter (monthly) . . . 03697

Centre Technique et de Promotion des Laitiers Sidérurgiques (C.T.P.L.), Immeuble Pacific, 92070 Paris La Défense Cedex
T: 0141256154; Fax: 0141258048
Founded: 1948; Members: 3
Focus: Dairy Sci
Periodical
Revue Laitiers Sidérurgiques (2-3 times annually) . . . 03698

Cercle d'Etudes Architecturales, 38 Blvd Raspail, 75006 Paris
T: 0145483144
Focus: Archit . . . 03699

Cercle d'Etudes Pédiatriques (CEP), 153 Rue de Saussure, 75017 Paris
T: 0142671215
Founded: 1967; Members: 85
Pres: Dr. Jean Feigelson; Gen Secr: Dr. Marie F. Merklen
Focus: Pediatrics . . . 03700

Chambre Syndicale des Sociétés d'Etudes et de Conseils, 3 Rue Léon Bonnat, 75016 Paris
T: 0145244353
Focus: Sci
Periodicals
Lettre de l'Ingénieur (quarterly)
Lettre de Syntec-Informatique (quarterly) . 03701

Club Européen d'Histoire de la Neurologie, c/o Service de Neurologie, Hôpital de l'Antiquaille, 1 Rue de l'Antiquaille, 69321 Lyon Cedex 05
T: 0478258090
Gen Secr: M. Boucher
Focus: Neurology . . . 03702

Club of Rome (COR), 34 Av d'Eylau, 75116 Paris
T: 0147044525; E-Mail: cor.bs@Dialup.Francenet.fr; Fax: 0147044523
Founded: 1968; Members: 100
Pres: Ricardo Diez-Hochleitner; Gen Secr: Bertrand Schneider
Focus: Econ; Poli Sci; Soc Sci . . . 03703

Collège International pour l'Etude Scientifique des Techniques de Production Mécanique (CIRP), 10 Rue Mansart, 75009 Paris
T: 0145262180; E-Mail: cirp@lurpa.ens-cachan.fr; Fax: 0140164075
Founded: 1950; Members: 490
Gen Secr: M. Véron
Focus: Eng
Periodical
CIRP Annals (semi-annually) . . . 03704

Comité d'Education Sanitaire et Sociale de la Pharmacie Française, 4 Av Ruysdael, 75008 Paris
T: 0146225428
Focus: Adult Educ; Pharmacol . . . 03705

Comité d'Entente des Ecoles de Formation en Economie Sociale Familiale, 28 Pl Saint-Georges, 75009 Paris
T: 0142800883
Focus: Educ; Sociology . . . 03706

Comité des Travaux Historiques et Scientifiques, 1 Rue Descartes, 75005 Paris
T: 0146344757; Fax: 0146344760
Founded: 1834
Focus: Hist; Sci . . . 03707

Comité d'Etudes et de Liaison des Amendements Calcaires (C.E.L.A.C.), 30 Av de Messine, 75008 Paris
T: 0145630266; Fax: 0153750213
Focus: Agri . . . 03708

Comité d'Etudes et de Liaison Interprofessionnel de la Haute-Marne (C.E.L.I.H.M.), Résidence Gigny Val d'Ornel, BP 86, 52103 Saint-Dizier
Focus: Adult Educ . . . 03709

Comité d'Etudes et de Liaison Interprofessionnel du Département de l'Aisne (C.E.L.I.D.A.), 12 Blvd Roosevelt, 02100 Saint-Quentin
Focus: Adult Educ . . . 03710

Comité d'Etudes Fiscales et Contentieuses, 5 Rue La Boétie, 75008 Paris
T: 0142660850
Focus: Law . . . 03711

Comité d'Etudes pour un Nouveau Contrat Social, 17 Blvd Raspail, 75007 Paris
T: 0142221265
Focus: Sociology . . . 03712

Comité du Film Ethnographique (C.I.F.H.), c/o Musée de l'Homme, Pl du Trocadéro, 75016 Paris
T: 0147043820; Fax: 0145535282
Founded: 1952; Members: 20
Focus: Cinema . . . 03713

Comité Européen Permanent de Recherches pour la Protection des Populations contre les Risques d'Intoxication à Long Terme, c/o Faculté des Sciences Pharmaceutiques et Biologiques, Université René Descartes, 4 Av de l'Observatoire, 75006 Paris
T: 0143267122
Founded: 1957
Gen Secr: Prof. René Truhaut
Focus: Toxicology . . . 03714

Comité Européen pour l'Education des Enfants et Adolescents Précoces, Doués, Talentueux (EUROTALENT), c/o ALREP, 33 Av Franklin Roosevelt, 30000 Nîmes
T: 0466648251
Focus: Educ; Adult Educ . . . 03715

Comité Français de l'Electricité, Espace ELEC, 92053 Paris-La Défense
T: 0141265700; Fax: 0141265760
Pres: Lucien Emmanuel Blanc; Gen Secr: Michel Guenot
Focus: Electric Eng
Periodicals
Bâtiment Relations ELEC (bi-monthly)
Industries Relations ELEC (bi-monthly) . 03716

Comité Français d'Education et d'Assistance de l'Enfance Déficiente, 185 Rue de Charonne, 75011 Paris
T: 0143712570
Focus: Educ . . . 03717

Comité Historique du Centre-Est, 86 Rue Pasteut, 69007 Lyon
Focus: Hist . . . 03718

Comité International de l'AISS pour la Prévention des Risques Professionnels du Bâtiment et des Travaux Publics, c/o OPPBTP, Tour Amboise, 204 Rond Point du Pont de Sèvres, 92516 Boulogne-Billancourt Cedex
T: 0146092654; Fax: 0146092740
Founded: 1968; Members: 40
Gen Secr: Patrice Leroy
Focus: Safety . . . 03719

Comité International de Paléographie Latine (CIPL), c/o IRHT, 40 Av d'Iéna, 75116 Paris
T: 0147238939
Founded: 1953
Gen Secr: Denis Muzerelle
Focus: Ling . . . 03720

Comité International des Sciences Historiques (CISH), c/o Institut d'Histoire du Temps Présent, 44 Rue de l'Amiral Mouchez, 75014 Paris
T: 0145809046; Fax: 0145654350
Founded: 1926; Members: 95
Pres: Prof. Ivan T. Berend; Gen Secr: Prof. François Bédarida
Focus: Hist
Periodical
Bulletin d'Information di CISH (annually) . 03721

Comité International pour l'Information et la Documentation en Sciences Sociales (CIDSS), 27 Rue Saint-Guillaume, 75341 Paris Cedex 07
T: 0144495050
Founded: 1950
Gen Secr: Prof. Jean Meyriat
Focus: Doc; Sociology
Periodicals
Current Sociology (3 times annually)
International Bibliography of the Social Sciences: Sociology, Political Science, Economics, Social and Cultural Anthropology (annually)
International Political Science Abstracts (bi-monthly) . . . 03722

Comité National contre les Maladies Respiratoires et la Tuberculose (CNTMR), 66 Blvd Saint-Michel, 75006 Paris
T: 0146345880; Fax: 0143290658
Founded: 1916; Members: 200000
Pres: F. Bonnaud
Focus: Pulmon Dis . . . 03723

Comité National de l'Enseignement Libre, 277 Rue Saint-Jacques, 75005 Paris
T: 0140331459
Focus: Educ . . . 03724

Comité National des Conseillers de l'Enseignement Technique, 39 Rue de la Roquette, 75011 Paris
T: 0148050608
Focus: Adult Educ; Eng . . . 03725

Comité National des Ecoles Françaises de Service Social, 9 Rue de l'Isly, 75008 Paris
T: 0142936322
Gen Secr: M.F. Marques
Focus: Educ; Sociology . . . 03726

Comité National Français de Géodesie et Géophysique, 136bis Rue de Grenelle, 75007 Paris
T: 0145554345
Members: 470
Focus: Surveying; Geophys . . . 03727

Comité National Français de Géographie, 191 Rue Saint-Jacques, 75005 Paris
Pres: J.R. Pitte; Gen Secr: P.K. Thumerelle
Focus: Geography . . . 03728

Comité National Français de Mathématiciens, c/o P. Pansu, Département de Mathématiques, Université Paris Sud, 91405 Orsay
T: 0169417561; Fax: 0169416348
Founded: 1951
Pres: Pansu. P.; Gen Secr: P. Arnoux
Focus: Math . . . 03729

Comité National Français des Recherches Antarctiques (CNFRA), 34Rue Francis Baulier, 42023 saint Etienne Cedxex 2
T: 0477421752; Fax: 0477421799
Members: 150
Pres: J.Q. Hureau; Gen Secr: A. Giret
Focus: Geography
Periodical
Report (annually) . . . 03730

Comité pour les Données Scientifiques et Technologiques (CODATA) / Committee on Data for Science and Technology, 51 Blvd de Montmorency, 75016 Paris
T: 015250496
Founded: 1966
Focus: Computer & Info Sci
Periodicals
CODATA Bulletin (monthly)
CODATA Newsletter (monthly)
Conference Proceedings (semi-annually) . 03731

Comité Scientifique du Club Alpin Français, 24 Av de Laumière, 75019 Paris
T: 0153728713; Fax: 0153728716
Founded: 1874
Focus: Geography . . . 03732

Comité Universitaire d'Information Pédagogique, 29 Rue d'Ulm, 75005 Paris
Focus: Educ; Adult Educ . . . 03733

Commission de la Carte Géologique du Monde / Commission for the Geological Map of the World, 77 Rue Claude Bernard, 75005 Paris
T: 0147072284; E-Mail: CCGM@club-internet.fr; Fax: 0143369518
Founded: 1881; Members: 150
Pres: Jean Dercourt; Gen Secr: Philippe Bouysse
Focus: Cart
Periodical
CGMW Bulletin (annually) . . . 03734

Commission de l'Enseignement Supérieur en Biologie, 1 Rue Victor Cousin, 75005 Paris
Focus: Educ; Bio . . . 03735

Commission Internationale de Bibliographie / International Bibliographic Commission, c/o Institut de Recherche et d'Histoire des Textes, 40 Av d'Iéna, 75016 Paris
Focus: Libraries & Bk Sci . . . 03736

Commission Internationale des Grands Barrages (CIGB) / International Commission on Large Dams, 151 Blvd Haussmann, 75008 Paris
T: 0140426824
Founded: 1928
Gen Secr: J. Cotillon
Focus: Civil Eng
Periodical
ICOLD Technical Bulletin (3-4 times annually) . . . 03737

Commission Internationale d'Etudes Historiques Latinoaméricaines et des Caraïbes (CIOHL), 28 Rue Saint-Guillaume, 75007 Paris
T: 0142223593
Founded: 1982
Gen Secr: Prof. Frédéric Mauro
Focus: Cultur Hist
Periodical
Newsletter (annually) . . . 03738

Commission Internationale d'Histoire des Mouvements Sociaux et des Structures Sociales, 9 Rue de Valence, 75005 Paris
T: 0147072864
Founded: 1953; Members: 26
Gen Secr: Denise Fauvel Rouif
Focus: Hist; Sociology . . . 03739

Commission Océanographique Intergouvernementale (COI) / Intergovernmental Oceanographic Commission, c/o UNESCO, Pl de Fontenoy, 75700 Paris
T: 0145681000
Founded: 1960; Members: 117
Gen Secr: Dr. Gunnar Kullenberg
Focus: Oceanography . . . 03740

Committee for European Marine Biology Symposia (EMBS), c/o Laboratoire d'Océanographie Biologique, Université de Bretagne Occidentale, 6 Av Le Gorgeu, 29287 Brest Cedex
Founded: 1966
Focus: Oceanography . . . 03741

Committee for International Cooperation in National Research in Demography (CICRED), 27 Rue du Commandeur, 75675 Paris Cedex 14
T: 0143201345; Fax: 0143277240
Founded: 1972; Members: 300
Pres: Jean Bourgeois-Pichat
Focus: Soc Sci
Periodicals
CICRED Bulletin (semi-annually)
Directory of Demographic Research Centres (quarterly) . . . 03742

Committee on Data for Science and Technology (CODATA), 51 Blvd de Montmorency, 75016 Paris
T: 0145250496; Fax: 0142889431
Founded: 1966
Gen Secr: Phyllis Glaeser
Focus: Computer & Info Sci . . . 03743

Committee on Space Research (COSPAR), 51 Blvd de Montmorency, 75016 Paris
T: 0145250679; E-Mail: cospar@paris7.jussiev.fr; Fax: 0140509827
Founded: 1958; Members: 5052
Pres: Prof. G. Haerendel; Gen Secr: S. Grzedzielski
Focus: Astronomy
Periodicals
Advances in Space Research (monthly)
COSPAR Directory of Organization and Members (bi-annually)
COSPAR Information Bulletin (3 times annually) . . . 03744

Community of European Management Schools (CEMS), 1 Rue de la Libération, 78350 Jouy-en-Josas
T: 0239677457; Fax: 0239677440
Founded: 1988; Members: 65
Pres: Prof. Heinz Hauser; Gen Secr: Nicole de Fontaines
Focus: Educ; Business Admin . . . 03745

Compagnie des Experts-Architectes près la Cour d'Appel de Paris, 22 Rue de Vouille, 75015 Paris
T: 0148560530; Fax: 0147560883
Founded: 1928; Members: 125
Pres: P.C. Parlebas; Gen Secr: G. Colard
Focus: Archit . . . 03746

Confédération des Sociétés Scientifiques Françaises (CSSF), 11 Rue Pierre et Marie Curie, 75005 Paris
Founded: 1919
Focus: Sci . . . 03747

Confédération des Syndicats Médicaux Français (CSMF), 60 Blvd de Latour-Maubourg, 75340 Paris Cedex 07
T: 0140626800; Fax: 0145519758
Founded: 1930; Members: 16000
Pres: Dr. Maffioli; Gen Secr: Dr. Wannepain
Focus: Med
Periodical
Le Médecin de France (weekly) . . . 03748

Confédération Européenne pour la Thérapie Physique (CETP), 24 Rue des Petits-Hôtels, 75010 Paris
T: 0142468007
Founded: 1938
Gen Secr: F. Chambon
Focus: Therapeutics . . . 03749

Confédération Internationale des Associations de Médecines Alternatives Naturelles (CIAMAN), Av Becquerel, BP 37, 26700 Pierrelatte Cedex
T: 0175040336
Founded: 1974
Gen Secr: M. Monneret
Focus: Med
Periodical
Revue de Médecine Biotique . . . 03750

Confédération Internationale des Sociétés d'Auteurs et Compositeurs (CISAC), 11 Rue Keppler, 75116 Paris
T: 0145535937
Founded: 1926; Members: 99
Gen Secr: J.A. Ziegler
Focus: Music; Lit
Periodical
Interauteurs (annually) . . . 03751

Confédération Nationale des Syndicats Dentaires (CNSD), 22 Av de Villiers, 75017 Paris
T: 0147660232; Fax: 0147632671
Founded: 1935; Members: 18000
Pres: Dr. Jacques Reignault; Gen Secr: Dr. Philippe Eveilleau
Focus: Dent
Periodical
Le Chirurgien-Dentiste de France (weekly) 03752

Conférence des Présidents d'Université, 12 Rue de l'Ecole de Médecine, 75270 Paris Cedex 06
T: 0143545049; Fax: 0143251651
Founded: 1971; Members: 86

Focus: Adult Educ 03753

Conférence des Recteurs Français,
c/o Chancellerie des Universités de Paris, 47 Rue des Ecoles, 75005 Paris
T: 0140462211
Founded: 1967
Focus: Educ 03754

Conférence Internationale des Doyens des Facultés de Médecine d'Expression Française (CIDMEF), c/o Faculté de Médecine, Université François Rabelais, BP 3223, 37032 Tours Cedex
T: 0247376673; Fax: 0247366099
Founded: 1981
Focus: Educ; Med
Periodical
Revue d'Education Médicale 03755

Conférence Internationale des Facultés de Droit ayant en Commun l'Usage du Français (CIFDUF), c/o Université de Droit, d'Economie et des Sciences, 3 Av Robert Schuman, 13628 Aix-en-Provence
T: 0442201905
Founded: 1991
Pres: Louis Favoreu
Focus: Law; Educ 03756

Conférence Internationale des Facultés, Instituts et Ecoles de Pharmacie d'Expression Française (CIFPEF), 4 Av de l'Observatoire, 75270 Paris Cedex 06
T: 0146613325
Founded: 1987
Pres: Charles Souleau
Focus: Educ; Pharmacol 03757

Conférence Internationale des Formations d'Ingénieurs et Techniciens d'Expression Française (CITEF), c/o INSA, 20 Av Albert Einstein, 89821 Villeurbanne Cedex
T: 0478948112
Founded: 1986
Gen Secr: N. Mongereau
Focus: Educ; Eng 03758

Conférence Internationale des Grands Réseaux Electriques à Haute Tension (CIGRE) / International Conference on Large High Voltage Electric Systems, 21 Rue d'Artois, 75008 Paris
T: 0153891290; E-Mail: cigre@world.net.set.fr; Fax: 0153891299
Founded: 1921
Gen Secr: Yves G. Thomas
Focus: Electric Eng
Periodical
Electra (bi-monthly) 03759

Conférence Internationale des Responsables des Universités et Instituts à Dominante Scientifique et Technique d'Expression Française (CIRUISEF), c/o Université de Bordeaux I, 351 Cours de la Libération, 33405 Talence Cedex
T: 0556846040
Founded: 1988
Pres: Jean Lascombe
Focus: Sci; Educ; Eng 03760

Conference on the Development and the Planning of Urban Transport in Developing Countries, c/o CODATU Association, Grande Arche, 92055 La Défense Cedex 04
T: 0140812304; Fax: 0140812393
Founded: 1980; Members: 9
Gen Secr: Christian Curé
Focus: Transport 03761

Congrès de Psychiatrie et de Neurologie de Langue Française, c/o Hôpital Universitaire Dupuytren, 2 Av Martin-Luther-King, 87042 Limoges Cedex
T: 0555056182; Fax: 0555056667
Founded: 1890
Focus: Neurology; Psychiatry
Periodical
Annual Report (annually) 03762

Congrès des Psychoanalystes de Langues Romanes, 187 Rue Saint-Jacques, 75005 Paris
Focus: Psychoan 03763

Congrès International de Médecine Légale et de Médecine Sociale de Langue Française / International French-Language Congresses of Forensic and Social Medicine, 2 Pl Mazas, 75012 Paris
T: 0143434254
Founded: 1911
Gen Secr: Prof. A.J. Chaumont
Focus: Hygiene 03764

Conité Européen Lex Informatica Mercatoriaque (CELIM), 868 Rte de Ganges, 34090 Montpellier
T: 0467606586; Fax: 0467604231
Founded: 1985
Focus: Computer & Info Sci 03765

Conseil International de la Danse (CIDD) / International Dance Council, c/o UNESCO, 1 Rue Miollis, 75732 Paris Cedex 15
T: 0145669422
Founded: 1973
Gen Secr: Nicole Luc-Marèchal
Focus: Music; Perf Arts 03766

Conseil International de la Langue Française, 11 Rue de Navarin, 75009 Paris
T: 0148787395; Fax: 0148784928
Founded: 1967; Members: 525
Pres: M. Goosse; Gen Secr: M. Joly
Focus: Ling
Periodicals
La Banque des Mots
Le Français Moderne 03767

Conseil International de la Musique (CIM), 1 Rue Miollis, 75732 Paris Cedex 15
T: 0145682550; Fax: 0143068798
Founded: 1949
Focus: Music
Periodical
Resonance (3 times annually) 03768

Conseil International de la Philosophie et des Sciences Humaines (CIPSH), c/o UNESCO, 1 Rue Miollis, 75732 Paris Cedex 15
T: 0145682685; Fax: 0140659480
Founded: 1949; Members: 13
Pres: Jean d' Ormesson; Gen Secr: Annelise Gaborieau
Focus: Humanities; Philos
Periodical
Diogenes (quarterly) 03769

Conseil International des Monuments et des Sites / International Council on Monuments and Sites, 75 Rue de Temple, 75003 Paris
T: 0142773576; Fax: 0142775742
Founded: 1965; Members: 4500
Pres: Roland Silva; Gen Secr: H. Stovel
Focus: Preserv Hist Monuments
Periodical
Icomos News (quarterly) 03770

Conseil International des Moyens du Film d'Enseignement (CIME) / International Council for Educational Media, c/o Institut Pédagogique National, 29 Rue d'Ulm, 75005 Paris
T: 0143261490
Founded: 1950
Gen Secr: R. Lefranc
Focus: Cinema 03771

Conseil International des Sciences Sociales (CISS), 1 Rue Miollis, 75732 Paris Cedex 15
T: 0145682558; E-Mail: issclak@zcc.net; Fax: 0143068798
Founded: 1952; Members: 42
Pres: Else Øyers; Gen Secr: Leszek Kosiuski
Focus: Econ; Law; Poli Sci; Psych; Anthro; Geography
Periodical
ISSC Newsletter (quarterly) 03772

Conseil International des Unions Scientifiques (CIUS) / International Council of Scientific Unions, 51 Blvd de Montmorency, 75016 Paris
T: 0145250329; Fax: 0142889431
Founded: 1919; Members: 104
Gen Secr: J. Marton-Lefèvre
Focus: Sci
Periodical
ICSU Yearbook (annually) 03773

Conseil International pour l'Information Scientifique et Technique / International Council for Scientific and Technical Information, 51 Blvd de Montmorency, 75016 Paris
T: 0145256592; Fax: 0142151262
Founded: 1984; Members: 51
Gen Secr: Daniel Confland
Focus: Computer & Info Sci
Periodical
Forum (quarterly) 03774

Conseil Mondial d'Ethique des Droits de l'Animal (COMEDA), 10 Rue Gallieni, 92600 Asnières
T: 0134781416; Fax: 0134782192
Focus: Ecology 03775

Conseil National de l'Ordre des Architectes, 7 Rue de Chaillot, 75116 Paris
Founded: 1977
Focus: Archit 03776

Conseil National des Ingénieurs et des Scientifiques de France, 7 Rue Lamennais, 75008 Paris
T: 0144136688; Fax: 0142898250
Founded: 1848
Focus: Eng; Sci 03777

Demeure Historique, 57 Quai de la Tournelle, 75005 Paris
T: 0143290286; Fax: 0143293644
Founded: 1924; Members: 3000
Pres: Marquis de Breteuil
Focus: Hist
Periodical
La Demeure Historique (quarterly) . . . 03778

Dialogue et Coopération, 140 Av Daumesnil, 75012 Paris
T: 0143440506
Founded: 1965
Pres: Jacqueline Cretté
Focus: Educ 03779

Dickens Fellowship, 29 Blvd Mariette, 62200 Boulogne-sur-Mer
Focus: Lit 03780

Division de Chimie Physique de la Société Française de Chimie, 10 Rue Vauquelin, 75005 Paris
T: 0147075448; Fax: 0143314222
Founded: 1908; Members: 1400
Focus: Chem
Periodical
Journal de Chimie physique et de physico-chimie biologique (monthly) 03781

Ecole Internationale de Bordeaux (EIB), 43 Rue Pierre Noailles, 33405 Talence Cedex
T: 0556375059; Fax: 0556044201
Founded: 1972
Focus: Educ 03782

Ecole Internationale d'Informatique de l'AFCET, 156 Blvd Péreire, 75017 Paris
T: 0147662419
Focus: Educ; Computer & Info Sci . . . 03783

Equipe de Recherche Associée au C.N.R.S.- Laboratoire de Génétique, 351 Cours de la Libération, 33405 Talence
Focus: Genetics 03784

Esperanto Academy / Académie d'Espéranto, 5 Rue Léon Cogniet, 75017 Paris
T: 0142278916
Founded: 1905; Members: 45
Gen Secr: Jean Thierry
Focus: Ling 03785

Etudes Préhistoriques, 34 Av Limburg, 69110 Sainte-Foy-lès-Lyon
Founded: 1967; Members: 975
Focus: Hist
Periodical
Etudes Préhistoriques (annually) 03786

Euro-African Asscociation for the Anthropology of Social Change and Development, BP 5045, 34032 Montpellier Cedex
T: 0467617400; Fax: 0467547800
Founded: 1991
Gen Secr: Jean-Pierre Chauveau
Focus: Anthro 03787

Eurocoast, c/o BRGM, Domaine de Luminy, 13009 Marseille
T: 0491412446; Fax: 0491411510
Founded: 1988
Gen Secr: Dr. L. Galtier
Focus: Geology; Eng 03788

EUROLAT – European Network for Studies on Laterites and Tropical Environment, c/o Institut de Géologie, Université Louis Pasteur, 1 Rue Blessig, 67084 Strasbourg
T: 0388358564; Fax: 0388607550
Founded: 1984; Members: 20
Pres: Prof. Yves Tardy
Focus: Geology 03789

European Academic and Research Network (EARN), c/o CIRCE, BP 167, 91403 Orsay Cedex
T: 0469823973; Fax: 0469285273
Founded: 1985
Gen Secr: H. Decers
Focus: Sci 03790

European Academy of Anaesthesiology / Académie Européenne d'Anesthésiologie, c/o Service d'Anesthésie et de Réanimation, Hôpital de Hautepierre, Av Molière, 67098 Strasbourg
T: 0388289000; Fax: 0388285464
Founded: 1976
Gen Secr: Prof. J.C. Otteni
Focus: Anesthetics 03791

European Aggregate Association (UEPG), 3 Rue Alfred Roll, 75849 Paris Cedex 17
Focus: Mach Eng 03792

European and Mediterranean Plant Protection Organization (EPPO), 1 Rue Le Nôtre, 75016 Paris
T: 0145207794; E-Mail: hq@eppo.fr; Fax: 0142248943
Founded: 1951; Members: 38
Pres: Dr. R. Petzold; Gen Secr: Dr. I.M. Smith
Focus: Ecology
Periodicals
EPPO-Bulletin (quarterly)
Quarantine Pests for Europe
Reporting Service: Special Sheets for Quick Delivery of Urgent Information (monthly) . 03793

European Association for American Studies (EAAS), c/o Dépt d'Anglais, Faculté des Langues, Université Lyon II, 86 Rue Pasteur, 69007 Lyon
T: 0478695601
Founded: 1954
Focus: Hist; Arts; Lit; Soc Sci
Periodical
European Contributions to American Studies 03794

European Association for Chinese Studies (EACS) / Association Européenne d'Etudes Chinoises, c/o Ecole des Hautes Etudes en Sciences Sociales, 54 Blvd Raspail, 75006 Paris
T: 0149542368; Fax: 0145449311
Founded: 1975
Gen Secr: Dr. Viviane Alleton
Focus: Cultur Hist
Periodical
AEDEC Newsletter (annually) 03795

European Association for the International Space Year (EUREG), 16bis Av Bosuet, 75007 Paris
T: 0147051779; Fax: 0145519923
Gen Secr: J. Gomérieux
Focus: Aero 03796

European Association for the Study of Dreans (EASD) / Association Européenne pour l'Etude du Rêve, c/o Association Française pour l'Etude du Rêve, BP 30, 93451 Ile-Saint-Denis Cedex
Founded: 1987
Focus: Parapsych 03797

European Association of Contract Research Organizations (EACRO) / Association Européenne des Organisations de Recherche sous Contrat, c/o Bertin, BP 3, 78373 Plaisir Cedex
T: 0134818581
Founded: 1989; Members: 53
Pres: Georges Mordchelles-Regnier
Focus: Eng
Periodical
Eacronews (quarterly) 03798

European Association of Geochemistry, c/o Institut Physique du Globe, 4 Pl Jussieu, Tour 14-15, 3e Etage, 75252 Paris
Focus: Chem 03799

European Association of Marine Sciences and Techniques / Association Européenne des Sciences et Techniques de la Mer, c/o IGBA, 351 Cours de la Libération, 33405 Talence Cedex
T: 0556806050; Fax: 0556370774
Founded: 1985
Focus: Oceanography; Eng
Periodical
AESTM Newsletter (3 times annually) . . 03800

European Association of Museums of the History of Medical Sciences / Association Européenne des Musées de l'Histoire des Sciences Médicales, c/o Musée Claude Bernard, Saint-Julien en Beaujolais, 69440 Denicé
Founded: 1983
Focus: Med; Hist 03801

European Association of Plastic Surgeons (EURAPS) / Association Européenne des Chirurgiens Plastiques, 130 Rue de la Pompe, 75116 Paris
T: 0147274431; Fax: 0147276515
Founded: 1989; Members: 120
Gen Secr: Dr. Daniel Marchac
Focus: Surgery
Periodical
European Journal of Plastic Surgery . . 03802

European Association of Radiology, c/o Dept. of General Radiology, Hôpital de Bicêtre, 78 Rue du General Leclerc, 94275 Le Kremlin Bicêtre
T: 0145213209
Founded: 1962; Members: 34
Pres: Prof. Hans Ringertz
Focus: Radiology 03803

European Association of Urology / Association Européenne d'Urologie, c/o Hôpital Cochin, 27 Rue du Faubourg Saint-Jacques, 75014 Paris
Focus: Urology 03804

European Audio Phonological Centers Association (EAPCA) / Association Européenne des Centres d'Audiologie, 23 Av de la République, 42000 Saint-Etienne
T: 0477414720
Founded: 1967
Pres: Dr. Michel Courtoy; Gen Secr: Dr. P. Guichard-Duthel
Focus: Otorhinolaryngology 03805

European Brachytherapy Group, c/o Institut Gustave Roussy, 53 Rue Camille Desmoulins, 94805 Villejuif
T: 0545594566; Fax: 0545594727
Gen Secr: A. Gerbaulet
Focus: Therapeutics 03806

European Brain and Behaviour Society, c/o Institut des Neurosciences, UPML, 9 Quai St Bernard, 75005 Paris
E-Mail: ebbs@snv.jussieu.fr
Founded: 1969; Members: 500
Gen Secr: Dr. Susan J. Sara
Focus: Intern Med 03807

European Centre for Advanced Studies in Thermodynamics (ECAST), c/o LUAP Paris VII, Tour 33-2e, 52 Pl Jussieu, 75251 Paris Cedex 05
T: 0144277908
Founded: 1989
Pres: Prof. J. Chanu
Focus: Physics 03808

European Centre for Regional Development, 20 Pl des Halles, 67000 Strasbourg
T: 0388223883; Fax: 0388226482
Founded: 1985; Members: 71
Focus: Develop Areas 03809

European Chapter of Combinatorial Optimization, c/o PNN, Université de Versailles, 45 Av des Etats Unies, 78035 Versailles Cedex
Gen Secr: Prof. Catherine Roucairol
Focus: Philos 03810

European Committee for the Study of Salt (ECSS), 17 Rue Daru, 75008 Paris
T: 0147665290; Fax: 0147665266
Founded: 1958
Gen Secr: Bernard Moinier
Focus: Mineralogy 03811

European Committee of Construction Economists (CEEC), 234 Rue du Faubourg Saint-Honoré, 75008 Paris
T: 0142890805; Fax: 0142890806
Founded: 1979
Gen Secr: Gordon F. Wheatley
Focus: Civil Eng 03812

European Committee on Crime Problems, c/o Conseil de l'Europe, Div des Problèmes Criminels, 67075 Strasbourg Cedex
T: 0388412000; Fax: 0388412794
Founded: 1957
Gen Secr: H.-J. Bartsch
Focus: Criminology; Law
Periodical
Penological Information Bulletin (every 1-2 years) 03813

European Consortium for Ocean Drilling (ECOD), c/o European Science Foundation, 1 Quai Lezay Marnésia, 67080 Strasbourg Cedex
T: 0388767100; Fax: 0388370532
Gen Secr: M. Fratta
Focus: Eng 03814

European Council on African Studies (ECAS), c/o Centre de Géographie Appliquée, 3 Rue de l'Argonne, 67060 Strasbourg Cedex
T: 0388358247
Founded: 1983
Pres: A. Coupez; Gen Secr: J.-P. Blanck
Focus: Geography 03815

European Council on Chiropractic Education, 8 Chemin de Tison, 86000 Poitiers
T: 0549415825
Pres: Pierre Gruny
Focus: Educ 03816

European Council on Environmental Law, c/o CEDE, 6 Rue de la Haute-Vienne, 67800 Strasbourg
T: 0388834397
Founded: 1974; Members: 20
Pres: Prof. Alexandre Kiss; Gen Secr: Brigitte Brunner
Focus: Law 03817

European Documentation and Information System for Education (EUDISED), c/o Conseil de l'Europe, Direction de l'Enseignement, de la Culture et du Sport, BP 431R6, 67006 Strasbourg
T: 0388412000; Fax: 0388412788
Founded: 1968
Gen Secr: Dr. Michael Vorbeck
Focus: Educ 03818

European Dyslexia Association – International Organization for Specific Learning Disabilities (EDA), 46 Av de Port Royal des Champs, 78320 Le Mesnil-Saint-Denis
T: 0534619252
Founded: 1987
Pres: Marcel Seynave; Gen Secr: Anne-Marie Montarnal
Focus: Educ 03819

European Federation of AIDS Research (EFAR), 51 Rue Liancourt, 75014 Paris
T: 0143216975; Fax: 0143214231
Founded: 1988
Pres: Prof. Luc Montagnier
Focus: Derm 03820

European Marine and Polar Science (EMAPS) Boards, c/o ESF, 1 Quai Lezay Marnésia, 67080 Strasbourg
T: 0388767141; Fax: 0388251954
Founded: 1995; Members: 49
Pres: Dr. D. Cadet
Focus: Oceanography 03821

Euskaltzaindia/Bayonne Académie de la Langue Basque, 37 Rue Pannecau, 64100 Bayonne
T: 0559594559
Focus: Sci 03822

Expéditions Polaires Françaises, 47 Av Maréchal Fayolle, 75116 Paris
T: 0145041771; Fax: 0145031487
Focus: Geography 03823

Fédération Aéronautique Internationale (FAI), 10-12 Rue du Capitaine Ménard, 75015 Paris
T: 0145792477; Fax: 0145797315
Founded: 1905
Gen Secr: Max Bishop
Focus: Aero
Periodical
Air Sports International (3 times annually) 03824

Fédération Autonome de l'Education Nationale, 13 Av de Taillebourg, 75011 Paris
T: 0143732136; Fax: 0143700847
Focus: Educ
Periodical
Bulletin (quarterly) 03825

Fédération Caribe de Santé Mentale, c/o Charles Saint-Cyr, Ravine Vilaine, Fort de France
Focus: Public Health; Psychiatry 03826

Fédération d'Associations et Groupements pour les Etudes Corses (FAGEC), BP 85, 20291 Bastia
Founded: 1970; Members: 16
Focus: Hist 03827

Fédération de l'Education Nationale (FEN), 48 Rue La Bruyère, 75009 Paris Cedex 09
T: 0140167800; E-Mail: fen@fen.fr;
Fax: 0140167899
Founded: 1948; Members: 175000
Gen Secr: Jean Paul Roux
Focus: Educ; Sports
Periodicals
L'Enseignement Public (monthly)
F.E.N. HEBDO (weekly) 03828

Fédération des Amicales des Documentalistes et Bibliothcaires de l'Education Nationale, 29 Rue d'Ulm, 75007 Paris
Focus: Libraries & Bk Sci 03829

Fédération des Chambres Syndicales des Chirurgiens Dentistes de la Région de Paris, 32 Rue de la Victoire, 75009 Paris
T: 0148785573
Focus: Surgery; Dent 03830

Fédération des Gynécologues et Obstétriciens de Langue Française (FGOLF) / Federation of French-Language Gynecologists and Obstetricians, c/o Clinique Universitaire Baudelocque, 123 Blvd de Port-Royal, 75674 Paris Cedex 14
T: 0142341143; Fax: 0142341231
Founded: 1950; Members: 1000
Gen Secr: Prof. Jean René Zorn
Focus: Gynecology
Periodical
Journal de Gynécologie, Obstétrique et Biologie de la Réproduction (8 times annually) . 03831

Fédération des Médecins de France (FMF), 60 Rue Laugier, 75017 Paris
T: 0147634052
Founded: 1968
Focus: Med
Periodical
France Médecine (bi-monthly) 03832

Fédération des Sociétés Francaises de Généalogie, d'Héraldique et de Sigillographie, 11 Blvd Pershing, 78000 Versailles
T: 0239548516
Founded: 1969; Members: 9500
Focus: Genealogy
Periodical
Héraldique et Généalogie (bi-monthly) . . 03833

Fédération des Sociétes Historiques et Archéologiques de Paris et de l'Ile de France, 24 Rue Pavée, 75004 Paris
T: 0142744444
Founded: 1949; Members: 90
Pres: Prof. J. Jacquart; Gen Secr: Prof. M. Balard
Focus: Hist; Archeol
Periodical
Paris et Ile-de-France: Mémoires publiés par la Fédération des Sociétés Historiques et Archéologiques de Paris et de l'Ile de France (annually) 03834

Féderation des Sociétés Savantes de la Charente-Maritime, c/o Archives Départementales, 17000 La Rochelle
Founded: 1975
Focus: Hist; Archeol
Periodical
Revue de la Saintonge et de l'Aunis (annually) 03835

Fédération des Syndicats Dentaires Libéraux (F.S.D.L.), 32 Rue de la Victoire, 75009 Paris
T: 0148785573; Fax: 0148782204
Focus: Dent
Periodicals
Flash Info
Le Libéral de Chaine
Le Libéral Dentaire 03836

Fédération des Syndicats Pharmaceutiques de France, 13 Rue Ballu, 75009 Paris
T: 0145261250
Members: 98
Focus: Pharmacol 03837

Fédération Française de Spéléologie (FFS), 130 Rue Saint-Maur, 75011 Paris
T: 0143575654; Fax: 0149230096
Founded: 1963; Members: 16150
Pres: Claude Viala; Gen Secr: Jean Piotrowski
Focus: Speleology 03838

Fédération Française d'Education Physique et de Gymnastique Volontaire (FFEPGV), 2 Rue de Valois, 75001 Paris
T: 0142613844
Founded: 1888; Members: 76400
Focus: Sports
Periodical
Loisirs-Santé (5 times annually) 03839

Fédération Française des Sociétés d'Amis de Musées (FFSAM), Place Henry de Montherlant, Hôtel d'Orsay, 75116 Paris
T: 0147236520
Focus: Arts
Periodical
Bulletin (semi-annually) 03840

Fédération Française des Sociétés de Protection de la Nature (FFSPN), 57 Rue Cuvier, 75231 Paris Cedex 05
T: 0143367995
Founded: 1968; Members: 400000
Focus: Ecology 03841

Fédération Française des Sociétés de Sciences Naturelles, 57 Rue Cuvier, 75231 Paris Cedex 05
T: 0143382084
Founded: 1919; Members: 150
Pres: J. Lescure; Gen Secr: J.F. Voisin
Focus: Nat Sci; Ecology
Periodical
Revue de la FFSSN (annually) 03842

Fédération Française d'Etudes et de Sports Sous Marins, 24 Quai de Rive Neuve, 13007 Marseille
T: 0491339931
Focus: Oceanography
Periodical
Etudes et Sports Sous Marins (bi-monthly) 03843

Fédération Générale des Syndicats de Biologistes, 133 Blvd du Montparnasse, 75006 Paris
T: 0143203910
Focus: Bio 03844

Fédération Historique de Provence, c/o Archives Départementales, 66b Rue Saint-Sébastien, 13259 Marseille Cedex 6
T: 0491720400; Fax: 0491720498
Founded: 1950; Members: 750
Pres: R. Bertrand; Gen Secr: P. Santoni
Focus: Hist
Periodical
Provence Historique 1950-1996 03845

Fédération Hospitalière de France, 33 Av d'Italie, 75013 Paris
T: 0145843250
Focus: Med
Periodical
Revue Hospitalière de France (bi-monthly) 03846

Fédération Internationale Catholique d'Education Physique et Sportive (FICEP), 22 Rue Oberkampf, 75011 Paris
T: 0143385057; Fax: 0143140665
Founded: 1911; Members: 2500000
Pres: Akiel Diegenant; Gen Secr: Jacques Gautheron
Focus: Sports 03847

Fédération Internationale des Associations d'Instituteurs, 3 Rue La Rochefoucauld, 75009 Paris
T: 0148745844; Fax: 0142852736
Focus: Educ 03848

Fédération Internationale des Centres d'Entraînement aux Méthodes d'Education Active (FICEMEA) / International Federation of Training Centres for the Promotion of Progressive Education, 76 Blvd de la Villette, 75940 Paris Cedex 19
Founded: 1954
Focus: Educ
Periodical
FICEMEA Bulletin 03849

Fédération Internationale des Mouvements d'Ecole Moderne (FIMEN), 189 Av Francis Tonner, BP 109, 06322 Cannes-La Bocca Cedex
Founded: 1957
Focus: Educ
Periodicals
Art Enfantin (quarterly)
Bibliothèque de travail (bi-weekly)
L'Educateur (monthly) 03850

Fédération Internationale des Professeurs de Français (FIPF), 1 Av Léon Journault, 92310 Sèvres
T: 0146265316; Fax: 0146268169
Founded: 1969; Members: 125
Pres: Raymond Le Loch; Gen Secr: Jean Souillat
Focus: Ling; Educ
Periodicals
Dialogues et Cultures (annually)
Une Lettre de la FIPF (quarterly) . . . 03851

Fédération Internationale des Universités Catholiques (FIUC) / International Federation of Catholic Universities, 51 Rue Orfila, 75341 Paris
T: 0147972660; Fax: 0147972942
Founded: 1948; Members: 176
Pres: Prof. Julio Teran Dutari; Gen Secr: Marc Caudron
Focus: Sci
Periodical
News in Brief (quarterly) 03852

Fédération Internationale pour l'Economie Familiale (FIEF) / International Federation for Home Economics, 5 Av de la Porte Brancion, 75015 Paris
T: 0148423474
Founded: 1908
Gen Secr: Odette Goncet
Focus: Home Econ
Periodical
Economie Familiale-Home Economics-Hauswirtschaft (quarterly) 03853

Fédération Internationale pour l'Education des Parents (F.I.E.P.), 1 Av Léon Journault, 92311 Sèvres Cedex
T: 0145072164; Fax: 0146266927
Founded: 1964; Members: 120
Pres: Jean Auba; Gen Secr: Micheline Ducray
Focus: Adult Educ
Periodical
Lettre d'Information (semi-annually) . . . 03854

Fédération interuniversitaire de l'enseignement à distance français (FIED), c/o Bureau E217, Université de Paris X, 200 Av de la République, 92001 Nanterre Cedex
T: 0140977551; Fax: 0147291821
Founded: 1987
Focus: Educ 03855

Fédération Métallurgique Française, 6 Av de Massine, 75008 Paris
T: 0145221062
Focus: Metallurgy 03856

Fédération Nationale Aéronautique, 52 Rue Galilée, 75008 Paris
T: 0147203975; Fax: 0127203032
Focus: Aero
Periodical
Info Pilote (monthly) 03857

Fédération Nationale des Médecins Radiologues et Spécialistes en Imagerie Diagnostique et Thérapeutique, 60 Blvd la Tour-Maubourg, 75327 Paris Cedex 07
Founded: 1907
Focus: Radiology; Med 03858

Fédération Nationale des Syndicats Départementaux de Médecins Electro-Radiologistes Qualifiés, 60 Blvd Latour-Maubourg, 75327 Paris Cedex 07
T: 0145517784
Founded: 1907; Members: 3000
Pres: Dr. J. Moinard
Focus: Radiology
Periodical
Bulletin 03859

Fondation pour la Recherche Sociale, 14 Rue Saint-Benoît, 75006 Paris
Founded: 1965; Members: 15
Focus: Sociology; Econ
Periodical
Recherche Sociale (quarterly) 03860

Fondation Saint-John Perse, 8-10 Rue des Allumettes, 13098 Aix-en-Provence Cedex 2
T: 0442259885; Fax: 0442271186
Founded: 1975; Members: 400
Pres: Joëlle Gardes Tamine
Focus: Lit
Periodicals
Cahiers Saint-John Perse (13 times annually)
Souffle de Perse (annually) 03861

France Intec, 43 Rue Decamps, 75016 Paris
Founded: 1895; Members: 10000
Focus: Eng 03862

Futuribles International (AIF), 55 Rue de Varenne, 75434 Paris Cedex 07
T: 0142226310; E-Mail: futurib@pratique.fr;
Fax: 0142226554
Founded: 1960
Pres: Jacques Lesourne; Gen Secr: Hugues de Jouvenel
Focus: Futurology
Periodicals
Revue Futuribles (monthly)
Vigie info (quarterly) 03863

Groupe de Recherche et pour l'Education et la Prospective (G.R.E.P.), 13-15 Rue des Petites Ecuries, 75010 Paris
T: 0148245036; E-Mail: grep@wanadoo.fr;
Fax: 0148240054
Founded: 1963
Pres: Jean-Marie Marx
Focus: Educ
Periodical
Pour (3 times annually) 03864

Groupe de Recherche Génétique Epidémiologique, Château de Longchamp, Bois de Boulogne, 75016 Paris
T: 0147727791
Focus: Genetics; Immunology 03865

Groupe des Méthodes Pluridisciplinaires Contribuant à l'Archéologie (GMPCA), c/o L. Langouet, Laboratoire d'Archéométrie, Université de Rennes 1, 35042 Rennes Cedex
T: 0299286070; Fax: 0299286934
Founded: 1976; Members: 110
Pres: L. Langovët; Gen Secr: C. Oberlin
Focus: Archeol
Periodical
Revue d'Archéométrie (annually) 03866

Groupe d'Etude et de Synthèse des Microstructures, c/o Ecole Supérieure de Physique et Chimie Industrielle de la Ville de Paris, 10 Rue Vauquelin, 75231 Paris Cedex
Founded: 1970
Focus: Chem; Physics 03867

Groupe Leibniz, c/o Groupe d'Etude pour la Traduction Automatique, Université de Grenoble, 38000 Grenoble Cedex 53
Founded: 1974
Focus: Ling 03868

Groupe Phonétique de Paris, c/o Institut de Phonétique, Université de Paris III, 19 Rue des Bernardins, 75005 Paris
Focus: Ling
Periodical
Report (annually) 03869

Groupe pour l'Avancement des Sciences Analytiques, 88 Blvd Malesherbes, 75008 Paris
T: 0145639304; Fax: 0149530434
Gen Secr: J. Tranchant; D. Sandino
Focus: Physics; Chem
Periodical
Bulletin d'Information GAMS (bi-monthly) . 03870

Groupe Rhône-Alpes de Recherche et d'Etudes en Gestion, c/o Université Jean Moulin, BP 155, 69224 Lyon Cedex 1
Focus: Geography 03871

Groupement des Associations Dentaires Francophones (GADEF), 22 Av de Villiers, 75017 Paris
T: 0147660232
Founded: 1971
Pres: Dr. M. Pirard
Focus: Dent
Periodical
Bulletin du GADEF 03872

Groupement des Bureaux Médicaux, 8 Rue Botzaris, 75019 Paris
T: 0142056068
Focus: Med 03873

Groupement d'Etudes et de Réalisations Médicales, 154 Rue du Faubourg Saint-Denis, 75010 Paris
T: 0142088255
Focus: Med 03874

Groupement Industriel Européen d'Etudes Spatiales, 16 Av Bosquet, 75007 Paris
T: 0145558353
Founded: 1961; Members: 74
Focus: Aero
Periodical
Eurospace Bulletin (quarterly) 03875

Groupement Médical d'Etudes sur l'Alcoolisme (GMEA), 6 Allée Dugay-Trouin, 44000 Nantes
Founded: 1942; Members: 950
Focus: Hygiene 03876

Groupement Médical Saint-Augustin, 43 Blvd Malesherbes, 75008 Paris
T: 0142654810
Focus: Med 03877

Groupement National d'Etude des Médecins du Bâtiment et des Travaux Publics, 6 Rue Paul Valery, 75016 Paris
T: 0147201020
Focus: Orthopedics; Traumatology . . . 03878

Groupement Professionnel National de l'Informatique, 43 Rue de Trevise, 75009 Paris
T: 0148246650
Focus: Computer & Info Sci 03879

Institut de France, c/o Académie des Sciences, 23 Quai de Conti, 75006 Paris
T: 0144414441; Fax: 0144414341
Founded: 1795; Members: 160
Pres: Marcel Landowski; Gen Secr: Eric Peuchot
Focus: Sci
Periodicals
Les comptes rendus de l'Académie des Sciences
Les nouvelles de l'Académie des Sciences
La vie des sciences 03880

Institut des Actuaires Français, 59 Rue de la Boétie, 75008 Paris
T: 0145636135
Founded: 1890; Members: 600
Pres: Jean Berthon
Focus: Insurance; Finance
Periodical
Bulletin de l'Institut des Actuaires Français (3 times annually) 03881

Institut des Sciences Historiques / Société Archéologique de France, 45 Rue Rémy Dumoncel, 75014 Paris
T: 0143275045; Fax: 0140470409
Founded: 1816; Members: 150
Pres: Philippe Montillet; Gen Secr: Fabien Gandrille
Focus: Hist
Periodical
La Science Historique (quarterly) 03882

Institut Français d'Analyse de Groupe et de Psychodrame, 12 Rue Emile Deutsch de la Meurthe, 75014 Paris
T: 0145882322; Fax: 0145893242
Founded: 1958
Pres: Prof. Michel Laxenaire; Gen Secr: Claude Ouzilou
Focus: Sociology; Psych; Therapeutics . 03883

Institut Français de l'Energie (I.F.E.), 3 Rue Henri Heine, 75016 Paris
T: 0145244614; Fax: 0140500754
Founded: 1952; Members: 46
Pres: Albert Robin; Gen Secr: Yves Chainet
Focus: Energy
Periodical
Actualité Combustibles Energie (monthly) 03884

Institut Français des Relations Internationales, 6 Rue Ferrus, 75683 Paris Cedex 14
T: 0140789100
Founded: 1979
Focus: Poli Sci 03885

Institut Français d'Etudes Byzantines, 14 Rue Séguier, 75006 Paris
T: 0143261236
Founded: 1897
Focus: Cultur Hist 03886

Institut Français d'Histoire Sociale, c/o Centre de Documentation et de Recherche, Archives Nationales, 60 Rue des Francs-Bourgeois, 75141 Paris Cedex 03
T: 0140276449
Founded: 1948; Members: 200
Pres: Jean-Pierre Chaline; Gen Secr: Denise Fauvel-Rouif
Focus: Hist 03887

Institut Géographique National, 136bis Rue de Grenelle, 75700 Paris
T: 0143988000; Fax: 0143988400
Founded: 1940; Members: 2000
Focus: Geography
Periodical
Bulletin d'Information de l'Institut Géographique National (semi-annually) 03888

Institut International d'Administration Publique, 2 Av de l'Observatoire, 75006 Paris
Fax: 0146332638
Focus: Public Admin
Periodical
Revue Française d'Administration Publique (quarterly) 03889

Institut International de Droit d'Expression et d'Inspiration Françaises (I.D.E.F.), 27 Rue Oudinot, 75007 Paris
T: 0153692028; Fax: 0153692030
Founded: 1964
Pres: Raymond Barre; Gen Secr: Pierre Decheix
Focus: Law
Periodicals
Bulletin de l'I.D.E.F. (semi-annually)
Indépendance et Coopération (quarterly) . 03890

Institut International de Planification de l'Education (IIPE) / International Institute for Educational Planning, 7 Rue Eugène Delacroix, 75116 Paris
Fax: 0140728366
Founded: 1963
Pres: Victor Urquidi; Gen Secr: Jacques Hallak
Focus: Educ
Periodical
IIEP Newsletter (quarterly) 03891

Institut International des Droits de l'Homme / International Institute of Human Rights, 1 Quai Lezay-Marnésia, 67000 Strasbourg
Fax: 0388363855
Founded: 1969
Pres: Denise Bindschedler-Robert; Gen Secr: Jean-Bernard Marie
Focus: Law 03892

Institut International du Froid (IIF) / International Institute of Refrigeration, 177 Blvd Malesherbes, 75017 Paris
T: 0142273235; E-Mail: iifiir@ibm.net;
Fax: 0147631798
Founded: 1908; Members: 800
Gen Secr: L. Lucas
Focus: Air Cond; Mach Eng
Periodicals
Bulletin (bi-monthly)
International Journal of Refrigeration (8 times annually) 03893

Institut International du Théâtre (IIT), 1 Rue Miollis, 75732 Paris Cedex 15
T: 0145682650; Fax: 0143068798
Founded: 1948; Members: 88
Gen Secr: André-Louis Perinetti
Focus: Perf Arts 03894

Intergovernmental Council for the International Hydrological Programme (IHP), c/o UNESCO, Pl de Fontenoy, 75700 Paris
Founded: 1975; Members: 30
Focus: Water Res
Periodicals
Studies and Reports in Hydrology
Technical Documents in Hydrology
Technical Papers in Hydrology 03895

International Academy of the History of Science (IAHS), 12 Rue Colbert, 75002 Paris
Founded: 1929; Members: 300
Focus: Hist; Sci
Periodical
Archives Internationales d'Histoire des Sciences (semi-annually) 03896

International Association of Agricultural Information Specialists, BP 5035, 34032 Montpellier Cedex 1
Fax: 0467615820
Founded: 1955; Members: 660
Gen Secr: Dr. J. Van der Burg
Focus: Doc; Agri
Periodical
Bulletin (quarterly) 03897

International Association of Engineering Geology (I.A.E.G.), c/o Laboratoire Central des Ponts et Chaussées, 58 Blvd Lefèbvre, 75732 Paris Cedex 15
T: 0140435243
Founded: 1964; Members: 5000
Pres: Prof. Ricardo Oliveira; Gen Secr: Dr. L. Primel
Focus: Geology
Periodical
Newsletter of the IAEG (semi-annually) . 03898

International Association of Sanskrit Studies, 52 Rue du Cardinal Lemaire, 75231 Paris Cedex 05
Founded: 1973
Focus: Lit; Ling; Cultur Hist; Arts; Archeol
Periodicals
Indologica Taurinensia
Newsletter 03899

International Association of Universities (IAU), 1 Rue Miollis, 75732 Paris Cedex 15
T: 0145682545; E-Mail: iau@unesco.org;
Fax: 0147347605
Founded: 1950; Members: 650
Pres: Dr. Wataru Mori; Gen Secr: Dr. Franz Eberhard
Focus: Educ
Periodicals
Higher Education Policy (quarterly)
IAU Newsletter (bi-monthly) 03900

International Astronautical Association (IAA), 3-5 Rue Mario Nikis, 75015 Paris
T: 0145674260; Fax: 0142737537
Founded: 1950; Members: 125
Gen Secr: Michelle Claudin
Focus: Aero
Periodical
Journal of the IAA (monthly) 03901

International Commission for Plant-Bee Relationships (ICPBR), c/o Laboratoire de Zoologie, INRA, 86600 Lusignan
T: 0549556000; E-Mail: tasei@lusignan.inra.fr;
Fax: 0549556088
Founded: 1951; Members: 225
Pres: Prof. Ingrid Williams; Gen Secr: J.N. Tasei
Focus: Botany; Bio
Periodical
Reports of Meetings 03902

International Council of Museums (ICOM), 1 Rue Miollis, 75732 Paris Cedex 15
T: 0147340500; E-Mail: secretariat@icom.org;
Fax: 0143067862
Founded: 1946; Members: 13000
Pres: S. Ghose; Gen Secr: Elisabeth Des Portes
Focus: Arts
Periodical
ICOM News (quarterly) 03903

International Council on Archives (ICA), 60 Rue des Francs-Bourgeois, 75003 Paris
T: 0140276306; E-Mail: 100640.54@compuserve.com; Fax: 0142722065
Founded: 1948; Members: 1500
Pres: Gang Wang; Gen Secr: Dr. Charles Kecskemeti
Focus: Archives
Periodicals
Archivum: International Review on Archives (annually)
Bulletin CIA (semi-annually)
Janus (semi-annually) 03904

International Economic Association (I.E.A.), 23 Rue Campagne Première, 75014 Paris
T: 0143279144; Fax: 0142799216
Founded: 1950; Members: 60
Gen Secr: Jean-Paul Fitoussi
Focus: Econ
Periodical
Newsletter (1-2 times annually) 03905

International Research Council on Biokinetics of Impacts (IRCOBI), 109 Av Salvador Allende, 69500 Bron
T: 0472362420; Fax: 0472362437
Founded: 1973
Focus: Traumatology
Periodical
Proceedings (annually) 03906

International Union for Health Education, 15 Rue de l'Ecole de Médecine, 75270 Paris Cedex 06
Founded: 1951; Members: 1200
Focus: Educ
Periodical
HYGIE: International Journal of Health Education (quarterly) 03907

International Union of Microbiological Societies (IUMS), c/o Institut de Biologie Moléculaire et Cellulaire du CNRS, 15 Rue Descartes, 67084 Strasbourg
T: 0388417022; Fax: 0388610680
Founded: 1927; Members: 68
Pres: Rita Colwell; Gen Secr: Marc H.V. Van Regenmortel
Focus: Microbio
Periodicals
Archives of Virology (monthly)
International Journal of Food Microbiology (monthly)
International Journal of Systematic Bacteriology (monthly)
Journal of Medical and Veterinary Mycology (annually)
World Journal of Microbiology and Biotechnology (bi-monthly) 03908

Jeunesses Littéraires de France, 117 Blvd Saint-Germain, 75279 Paris Cedex 06
Focus: Lit 03909

Jeunesses Musicales de France, 20 Rue Geoffroy l'Asnier, 75004 Paris
T: 0144618686
Founded: 1944; Members: 3800
Pres: J.M. Tournier; Gen Secr: Robert Berthier
Focus: Music 03910

Joint Committee on Climatic Changes and the Ocean, c/o UNESCO, 7 Pl de Fontenoy, 75700 Paris
T: 0145681000; Fax: 0143061122
Focus: Oceanography; Physics 03911

Ligue Française contre la Sclérose en Plaques (L.F.S.E.P.), 17 Blvd Auguste Blanqui, 75013 Paris
T: 0140786900; E-Mail: lfsep@hantinews.com;
Fax: 0140786933
Founded: 1986; Members: 7
Pres: Prof. René Marteau; Gen Secr: Guy Pailliez
Focus: Pathology
Periodical
Courrier de la SEP (3 times annually) . 03912

Ligue Française de l'Enseignement et de l'Education Permanente, 3 Rue Récamier, 75341 Paris Cedex 07
T: 0145443871
Founded: 1866; Members: 3400000
Focus: Educ; Adult Educ 03913

Ligue Française de l'Enseignement Oroleis de Paris, 23 Rue Dagorno, 75012 Paris
T: 0143075930
Focus: Educ 03914

Ligue Française d'Hygiène Mentale (L.F.H.M.), 11 Rue Tronchet, 75008 Paris
T: 0142662070; Fax: 0142664489
Members: 100
Pres: Dr. Claude Leroy; Gen Secr: Natalie Alessandrini
Focus: Hygiene 03915

Ligue Internationale de l'Enseignement, de l'Education et de la Culture Populaire (LIEEP), 3 Rue Récamier, 75007 Paris Cedex 07
T: 0143589730
Founded: 1947; Members: 48
Gen Secr: F. Coursin
Focus: Educ
Periodical
Informations Internationales (quarterly) . . 03916

Ligue Nationale contre le Cancer, 1 Av Stéphen Pichon, 75013 Paris
T: 0144068080; Fax: 0145865678
Founded: 1920; Members: 700000
Focus: Cell Biol & Cancer Res
Periodical
Vivre (quarterly) 03917

Ligue pour la Protection des Oiseaux (LPO), La Corderie Royale, BP 263, 17305 Rochefort Cedex 05
T: 0546821250
Founded: 1912; Members: 17000
Pres: Allan B. Dubourg; Gen Secr: Michel Terrasse
Focus: Ornithology
Periodical
L'Oiseau (quarterly) 03918

Médecins sans Frontières, 8 Rue Saint-Sabin, 75011 Paris
T: 0140212929; Fax: 0148066868
Founded: 1971; Members: 2600
Pres: Dr. Rony Brauman; Gen Secr: Dr. Bernard Pécoul
Focus: Public Health; Med
Periodical
MSF: Bulletin (quarterly) 03919

Mouvement Français pour la Qualité (MFQ), 5 Esplanade Charles de Gaulle, 92733 Nanterre Cedex
T: 0147290929; Fax: 0147253221
Founded: 1991; Members: 3500
Focus: Econ
Periodicals
Newsletter (11 times annually)
Newsletter: Qualité en Mouvement (5 times annually)
Regard sur la Qualité (monthly) 03920

Mouvement Universel de la Responsabilité Scientifique (MURS) / Universal Movement for Scientific Responsibility, 127 Blvd Saint-Michel, 75005 Paris
T: 0143264398; Fax: 0143543550
Founded: 1974
Pres: Jean Dausset; Gen Secr: Michel Barrault
Focus: Sci
Periodicals
Cahiers du MURS (3-4 times annually)
Lettre aux Générations 2000 03921

Naturalistes Parisiens, 45 Rue de Buffon, 75005 Paris
Founded: 1904; Members: 450
Pres: Claude Dupuis; Gen Secr: Pierre Fesolowicz

Focus: Nat Sci
Periodical
Cahiers des Naturalistes: Bulletin des Naturalistes Parisiens (quarterly) 03922

Office Général du Bâtiment et des Travaux Publics (O.G.B.T.P.), 55 Av Kléber, 75784 Paris Cedex 16
T: 0140695100
Founded: 1918
Pres: Michel Marconnet
Focus: Civil Eng 03923

Office International de l'Eau, c/o Direction de la Documentation et des Bonnes, Rue Edouard Chamberland, 87065 Limoges Cedex
T: 0555114780; Fax: 0555777224
Founded: 1949; Members: 450
Focus: Water Res
Periodical
Bulletin (11 times annually) 03924

Office National d'Etudes et des Recherches Aérospatiales, 29 Av de la Division Leclerc, 92320 Chatillon
Focus: Aero 03925

Office National d'Information sur les Enseignements et les Professions (O.N.I.S.E.P.), BP 86, Lognes, 77423 Marne la Vallée
T: 0164803500; Fax: 0164803501
Founded: 1970; Members: 576
Pres: Michel Valdiguié
Focus: Adult Educ; Educ
Periodicals
Avenirs (monthly)
Les Cahiers 03926

Ordre des Architectes, 140 Av Victor Hugo, 75016 Paris
T: 0147205856, 01477205864
Founded: 1940
Focus: Archit
Periodical
Architectes (monthly) 03927

Ordre des Chirurgiens Dentistes, 174 Rue de Rivoli, 75001 Paris
T: 0142604973
Focus: Surgery; Dent 03928

Ordre des Géomètres-Experts (O.G.E.), 40 Av Hoche, 75008 Paris
T: 0145632426
Founded: 1946; Members: 2000
Pres: Jean Lamaison; Gen Secr: Marie Hélène Vellieux
Focus: Surveying
Periodical
Géomètre (monthly) 03929

Ordre National des Chirurgiens Dentistes, 7bis Rue Merimée, 75016 Paris
T: 0147235062
Focus: Surgery; Dent 03930

Ordre National des Médecins, 180 Blvd Haussmann, 75008 Paris Cedex 08
T: 0153893200; Fax: 0153893201
Focus: Med
Periodical
Bulletin de l'Ordre des Médecins (monthly)
. . . . 03931

Organisation de la Jeunesse Esperantiste Française / French Youth Esperanto Organization, 4bis Rue de la Cerisaie, 75004 Paris
T: 0142786886
Founded: 1969; Members: 300
Pres: Bruno Flochon
Focus: Ling
Periodicals
Jefo Informa (bi-monthly)
Koncize (bi-monthly) 03932

Organisation Européenne pour l'Equipement de l'Aviation Civile, 17 Rue Hamelin, 75783 Paris Cedex 16
T: 0145057188; Fax: 0145530393
Founded: 1963; Members: 70
Pres: Jean Paul Lepeytre; Gen Secr: F. Grimal
Focus: Electronic Eng 03933

Organisation Internationale contre le Trachome, c/o Hôpital de Créteil, Université Paris XII, 40 Av de Verdun, 94010 Créteil
Fax: 0148987787
Founded: 1929; Members: 600
Pres: Prof. Gabriel Coscas
Focus: Ophthal
Periodical
International Review of Trachoma (quarterly)
. . . . 03934

Organisation Internationale de Métrologie Légale (OIML), 11 Rue Turgot, 75009 Paris
T: 0148781282, 0142852711; Fax: 0142821727
Founded: 1955; Members: 50
Focus: Standards
Periodicals
Bulletin de l'Organisation Internationale de Métrologie Légale (quarterly)
OIML International Recommendations and International Documents 03935

Organisation Internationale de Recherche sur la Cellule, c/o UNESCO, Div of Scientific Research and Higher Education, 1 Rue Miollis, 75015 Paris
T: 0145688378; E-Mail: icro@unesco.org;
Fax: 0145685818
Founded: 1962; Members: 395
Pres: Prof. E. Carafoli; Gen Secr: Dr. G.N. Cohen
Focus: Cell Biol & Cancer Res 03936

Organisation Scientifique des Industries du Bâtiment, 53 Blvd Lannes, 75116 Paris
T: 0145047089
Focus: Civil Eng 03937

Paris et son Histoire, 82 Rue Taitbout, 75009 Paris
T: 0145262677
Founded: 1952; Members: 5000
Focus: Hist
Periodical
Bulletin Paris et son Histoire (monthly) . 03938

Le Pays Bas-Normand, 21 Rue de la Planchette, 61100 Flers
T: 0233643387
Founded: 1908; Members: 420
Pres: Louise Gérard; Gen Secr: Yves Letortu
Focus: Hist; Arts
Periodical
Revue (quarterly) 03939

PEN Club de Suisse Romande, c/o Brigitte Mantilleri, 217 Rte de Vovray, 74160 Collonges
Founded: 1949; Members: 70
Pres: Jean-Pierre Moulin; Gen Secr: Brigitte Mantilleri
Focus: Lit
Periodical
Lettre de Information (1-2 times annually) 03940

P.E.N. Maison Internationale, 6 Rue François Miron, 75004 Paris
T: 0142773787; Fax: 0142786487
Founded: 1921; Members: 600
Pres: Jean Orizet; Gen Secr: Bertrand Galimard Flavigny
Focus: Lit
Periodical
Informations (bi-monthly) 03941

Program on Man and the Biosphere (MAB), c/o UNESCO, 1 Rue Miollis, 75352 Paris Cedex 15
T: 0145684067; E-Mail: mab@unesco.org;
Fax: 0145685804
Founded: 1971; Members: 112
Pres: Peter Bridgewater; Gen Secr: Pierre Lasserre
Focus: Ecology
Periodical
InfoMAB (bi-annually) 03942

Réunion Internationale des Laboratoires d'Essais et de Recherche sur les Matériaux et les Constructions (RILEM) / International Union of Testing and Research Laboratories for Materials and Structures, 61 Av du Président Wilson, 94235 Cachan Cedex
T: 0147402397; E-Mail: sg@rilem.ens-cachan.fr;
Fax: 0147400113
Founded: 1947; Members: 800
Pres: Prof. Dr. Folker H. Wittmann; Gen Secr: Michel Brusin
Focus: Civil Eng; Materials Sci 03943

Scientific Committee on Problems of the Environment (SCOPE), 51 Blvd de Montmorency, 75016 Paris
Fax: 0142881466
Founded: 1969; Members: 55
Pres: Prof. J.W.B. Stewart; Gen Secr: Prof. P. Bourdeau
Focus: Ecology
Periodicals
Newsletter (3 times annually)
SCOPE Series 03944

Societas Oto-Rhino-Laryngologia Latina, c/o Clinique ORL, 34000 Montpellier
Focus: Otorhinolaryngology 03945

Société Académique des Arts Libéraux de Paris, 3 Av Chanzy, BP 49, 94210 La Varenne Saint-Hilaire
T: 0142833603
Focus: Arts 03946

Société Africaine de Culture (SAC), 18 Rue des Ecoles, 75005 Paris
T: 0143297572
Founded: 1956
Focus: Ethnology 03947

Société Anatole France, 15 Rue Gustave Courbet, 75116 Paris
T: 0145537093
Founded: 1933; Members: 350
Focus: Lit 03948

Société Anatomique de Paris, 45 Rue des Saints-Péres, 75270 Paris Cedex 06
Founded: 1802
Focus: Anat
Periodical
Bulletins (annually) 03949

Société Archéologique de Touraine (SAT), c/o Bibliothèque Municipale, 37042 Tours Cedex
Founded: 1840; Members: 1300
Focus: Archeol
Periodicals
Bulletin (annually)
Mémoires (irregularly) 03950

Société Archéologique et Historique du Limousin, 54 Rue Bourneville, 87032 Limoges Cedex
T: 0555509760
Founded: 1845; Members: 650
Focus: Archeol; Hist
Periodical
Bulletin de la Société Archéologique et Historique du Limousin (annually) 03951

Société Asiatique (S.A.), 3 Rue Mazarine, 75006 Paris
T: 0144414314; Fax: 0144414316
Founded: 1822; Members: 725
Pres: Danile Gimaret
Focus: Ethnology
Periodical
Journal Asiatique (bi-annually) 03952

Société Astronomique de Bordeaux, 71 Rue du Loup, 33000 Bordeaux
Founded: 1909; Members: 75
Focus: Astronomy 03953

Société Astronomique de France (S.A.F.), 3 Rue Beethoven, 75016 Paris
T: 0142241374; Fax: 0142307547
Founded: 1887; Members: 3000
Pres: Jean-Claude Ribes; Gen Secr: Joel Minois
Focus: Astronomy
Periodicals
L'Astronomie (monthly)
Observations et Travaux (quarterly) . . . 03954

Société Astronomique de Lyon, c/o Observatoire de Lyon, 69230 Saint-Genis-Laval
Founded: 1901; Members: 160
Focus: Astronomy 03955

Société Botanique de France (S.B.F.), c/o Pharmaceutical Faculty, 4 Av de l'Observatoire, 75270 Paris Cedex 06
Founded: 1854; Members: 500
Pres: B. Descoings; Gen Secr: M. Botineau
Focus: Botany
Periodical
Acta Botanica Gallica (quarterly) 03956

Société Cartographique de France, 48 Rue de Charenton, 75012 Paris
T: 0143072533
Focus: Cart 03957

Société Centrale d'Apiculture, 41 Rue Pernety, 75014 Paris
T: 0143062908
Focus: Bio 03958

Société d'Anthropologie de Paris (S.A.P.), c/o Musée de l'Homme, 17 Pl du Trocadéro, 75116 Paris
T: (01) 44057265; Fax: 0144057241
Founded: 1859; Members: 310
Pres: Olivier Dutour; Gen Secr: Alain Froment
Focus: Anthro
Periodical
Bulletins et Mémoires (quarterly) 03959

Société d'Archéologie et d'Histoire de la Manche, BP 600, 50010 Saint-Lo Cedex
Focus: Archeol; Hist 03960

Société d'Archéologie et d'Histoire de l'Aunis, Muséum Lafaille, 51 Rue du Canada, 17000 La Rochelle
Founded: 1970; Members: 250
Focus: Hist; Archeol 03961

Société de Biogéographie, 57 Rue Cuvier, 75231 Paris Cedex 05
Founded: 1924; Members: 350
Gen Secr: Mauries. J.P.
Focus: Geography
Periodicals
Compte Rendu des Séances
Mémoires 03962

Société de Biologie, c/o Collége de France, 11 Pl M. Berthelot, 75231 Paris Cedex 05
T: 0144271340; Fax: 0144271340
Founded: 1848; Members: 510
Pres: Prof. Jacques Picard; Gen Secr: Prof. Jacques Polonovski
Focus: Bio
Periodical
Compte rendus de la Société de Biologie (bi-monthly) 03963

Société de Biométrie Humaine, 41 Rue Gay Lussac, 75005 Paris
T: 0146330596
Founded: 1932; Members: 300
Gen Secr: J. Delmas
Focus: Bio; Anthro
Periodical
Cahiers d'Anthropologie et Biométrie Humaine (quarterly) 03964

Société de Chimie Biologique, 4 Av de l'Observatoire, 75270 Paris Cedex 06
T: 0143251260
Founded: 1914; Members: 1129
Pres: P. Louisot; Gen Secr: J. Agneray; J.P. Ebel
Focus: Biochem
Periodicals
Biochimie (monthly)
Regard sur la Biochimie (quarterly) . . . 03965

Société de Chimie Industrielle, 28 Rue Saint-Dominique, 75007 Paris
T: 0153590210; E-Mail: sci.fr@wanadoo.fr;
Fax: 0145554033
Founded: 1917; Members: 12000
Pres: Philippe Tripard; Gen Secr: Georges Mattioda
Focus: Chem 03966

Société de Chimie Thérapeutique (SCT), 3 Rue Jean-Baptiste Clement, 92290 Châtenay Malabry
Founded: 1966; Members: 750
Focus: Chem 03967

Société de Chirurgie de Marseille, Hôtel Dieu, 13000 Marseille
Focus: Surgery 03968

Société de Chirurgie de Toulouse, 18 Rue de Languedoc, 31000 Toulouse
Focus: Surgery 03969

Société de Chirurgie Thoracique et Cardio-Vasculaire de Langue Française, c/o Hôpital Marie Lannelongue, 133 Av de la Résistance, 92350 Le Plessis Robinson
T: (01409) 42800
Founded: 1948; Members: 643
Gen Secr: Dr. R. Nottin
Focus: Surgery
Periodical
Annales de chirurgie (semi-annually) . . 03970

Société de Démographie Historique, 54 Blvd Raspail, 75006 Paris
T: 0149542556
Founded: 1963
Pres: Jean-Pierre Bardet; Gen Secr: Fauve-Chamoux
Focus: Hist
Periodicals
Annales de démographie historique (annually)
Bulletin dh (3 times annually) 03971

Société de Géographie, 184 Blvd Saint-Germain, 75006 Paris
T: 0145485462
Founded: 1821; Members: 700
Gen Secr: M. Florin
Focus: Geography
Periodical
Acta Geographica (quarterly) 03972

Société de Géographie Commerciale de Bordeaux, 71 Rue du Loup, 33000 Bordeaux
Focus: Geography 03973

Société de Géographie Commerciale de Paris, 8 Rue Roquépine, 75008 Paris
T: 0142664626
Founded: 1873; Members: 490
Pres: Jacques Augarde
Focus: Geography
Periodical
Revue Economique Française (quarterly) . 03974

Société de Géographie de Lille, 77 Rue Nationale, 59800 Lille
T: 0320572745
Founded: 1880; Members: 1500
Focus: Geography
Periodical
Hommes et Terres du Nord (quarterly) . 03975

Société de Géographie de Lyon, 74 Rue Pasteur, 69007 Lyon
Founded: 1873
Focus: Geography
Periodical
Revue de Géographie de Lyon (quarterly) 03976

Société de Géographie de Toulouse, Hôtel d'Assézat, Pl d'Assézat, 31000 Toulouse
T: 0561522806; Fax: 0561504441
Founded: 1882; Members: 195
Focus: Geography 03977

Société de Géographie Humaine de Paris, 8 Rue Roquépine, 75008 Paris
Founded: 1873
Focus: Geography 03978

Société de Législation Comparée, 28 Rue Saint-Guillaume, 75007 Paris
T: 0144398623; Fax: 0144398628
Founded: 1869; Members: 1300
Pres: Xavien Blauc-Jouvan; Gen Secr: Marie-Anne Gallot Le Lorier
Focus: Law
Periodicals
Journées de la Société de Legislation Comparée (annually)
Revue Internationale de Droit Comparé (quarterly)
. . . . 03979

Société de l'Histoire de France, c/o Ecole des Chartes, 19 Rue de la Sorbonne, 75005 Paris
Founded: 1834; Members: 400
Pres: Henri Dubois; Gen Secr: Philippe Contamine
Focus: Hist
Periodicals
Annuaire-Bulletin (annually)
Mémoires 03980

Société de l'Histoire de l'Art Français, 1 Rue Berbier du Mets, 75013 Paris
Founded: 1873; Members: 1000
Pres: Jean Coural; Gen Secr: Bruno Foucart
Focus: Hist; Arts; Cultur Hist

Periodicals
Archives de l'Art Français (annually)
Bulletin de la Société de l'Histoire de l'Art Français (annually) 03981

Société de l'Histoire du Protestantisme Français, 54 Rue des Saints-Pères, 75007 Paris
T: 0145486207; Fax: 0145449487
Founded: 1852
Focus: Hist; Rel & Theol 03982

Société de Linguistique de Paris, c/o Ecole Pratique des Hautes Etudes, 47 Rue des Ecoles, 75005 Paris
Founded: 1864; Members: 800
Pres: Prof. J. Perrot; Gen Secr: Prof. B. Caron
Focus: Ling
Periodicals
Bulletin de la Société de Linguistique de Paris (annually)
Collection linguistique (irregularly) 03983

Société de Linguistique Romane, 8 Quai Rouget de Lisle, 67000 Strasbourg
T: 0388350084
Founded: 1925; Members: 1000
Pres: Prof. Dr. M. Pfister; Gen Secr: Prof. Dr. G. Straka
Focus: Ling 03984

Société de Médecine, Chirurgie et Pharmacie de Toulouse, Pl d'Assézat, 31000 Toulouse
Focus: Surgery; Med; Pharmacol 03985

Société de Médecine de Strasbourg, c/o Faculté de Médecine, 4 Rue Kirschleger, 67085 Strasbourg Cedex
Founded: 1919; Members: 450
Pres: Dr. P. Haegele; Gen Secr: Dr. Moise
Focus: Med
Periodical
Bulletin (monthly) 03986

Société de Médecine et de Chirurgie de Bordeaux, 15 Rue du Professeur Demons, 33000 Bordeaux
Focus: Surgery; Med 03987

Société de Médecine et d'Hygiène du Travail, 15 Rue de l'Ecole de Médecine, 75006 Paris
T: 016331188
Members: 250
Focus: Hygiene 03988

Société de Médecine Légale et de Criminologie de France, 2 Pl Mazas, 75012 Paris
T: 0143434254
Founded: 1868; Members: 400
Pres: Prof. L. Arbus; Gen Secr: M. Penneau
Focus: Criminology; Med; Forensic Med; Toxicology
Periodicals
Droit Médical
Médecine Légale (monthly) 03989

Société de Mythologie Française, 3 Rue Saint-Laurent, 75010 Paris
T: 0142053057
Founded: 1950; Members: 300
Pres: H. Fromage
Focus: Hist
Periodicals
Bulletin (3 times annually)
Bulletin de la Société de Mythologie Française 03990

Société de Neurochirurgie de Langue Française, 60 Blvd Latour-Maubourg, 75327 Paris Cedex 7
Founded: 1948; Members: 700
Pres: J.P. Brotchi; Gen Secr: J.P. Houtteville
Focus: Surgery
Periodical
Neurochirurgie (bi-monthly) 03991

Société de Neurophysiologie Clinique de Langue Française, c/o Hôpital Sainte-Anne, 1 Rue Cabanis, 75674 Paris Cedex 14
T: 0140488203
Founded: 1948; Members: 520
Pres: Prof. F. Maugière; Gen Secr: Dr. B. Gueguen
Focus: Med; Physiology; Neurology
Periodical
Neurophysiologie Clinique 03992

Société de Neuropsychologie de Langue Française, c/o Service de Neuropsychologie, Hôpital Purpan, 31059 Toulouse Cedex
T: 0561779500; E-Mail: agniel@purpan.inserm.fr
Founded: 1977; Members: 450
Gen Secr: Alain Agniel
Focus: Psych
Periodical
Revue de Neuropsychologie (quarterly) . 03993

Société de Nutrition et de Diététique de Langue Française, Hôtel Dieu, 1 Pl du Parvis Notre Dame, 75004 Paris
T: 0142348452; Fax: 0140510057
Founded: 1963
Focus: Nutrition
Periodical
Cahiers de Nutrition et de Diététique (bi-monthly) 03994

Société de Pathologie Comparée, 4 Rue Théodule Ribot, 75017 Paris
T: 0146225319
Founded: 1901
Focus: Pathology 03995

Société de Pathologie Exotique, 25 Rue du Docteur Roux, 75015 Paris
T: 0145668869; E-Mail: socpatex@club-internet.fr; Fax: 0145668869
Founded: 1908; Members: 850
Pres: Prof. Marc Gentilini; Gen Secr: Dr. Alain Chippaux
Focus: Pathology; Trop Med
Periodical
Bulletin de la Société de Pathologie Exotique (5 times annually) 03996

Société de Pharmacie de Bordeaux, c/o Faculté de Pharmacie, 3 Pl de la Victoire, 33076 Bordeaux Cedex
T: 0556913424
Founded: 1834; Members: 300
Focus: Pharmacol
Periodical
Bulletin (quarterly) 03997

Société de Pharmacie de Lyon, 8 Av Rockefeller, 69373 Lyon Cedex 08
Focus: Pharmacol
Periodical
Bulletin des Travaux de la Société de Pharmacie de Lyon (semi-annually) 03998

Société de Pharmacie de Marseille, 92 Rue Blanqui, 13001 Marseille
Focus: Pharmacol 03999

Société de Philosophie de Toulouse, 4 Rue Albert Lantmann, 31000 Toulouse
Focus: Philos 04000

Société de Pneumologie de Langue Française, 66 Blvd Saint-Michel, 75006 Paris
Focus: Intern Med 04001

Société de Psychologie Médicale de Langue Française, 95 Blvd Pinel, 69677 Bron
T: 0472358694; Fax: 0472358593
Founded: 1960; Members: 2
Pres: Dr. P. Moron; Gen Secr: Prof. M. Marie-Cardine
Focus: Psych
Periodical
Revue Française de Psychiatrie et de Psychologie Médicale (10 times annually) 04002

Société de Réanimation de Langue Française (S.R.L.F.) / French-Language Society for Reanimation, 27 Rue du Dessous des Berges, 75013 Paris
T: 0145867444
Founded: 1971; Members: 1100
Gen Secr: Prof. J.F. Dhainaut
Focus: Med
Periodical
Réanimation-Urgences 04003

Société de Recherches et d'Etudes Historiques Corses, c/o Musée Fesch, 20000 Ajaccio
Focus: Hist 04004

Société de Recherches Géophysiques, 81 Rue Laugier, 75017 Paris
T: 0147544391
Focus: Geophys 04005

Société de Recherches Pharmaceutiques et Cientifiques, 6 Rue Lincoln, 75008 Paris
T: 0142252265
Focus: Pharmacol 04006

Société de Recherches Psychothérapiques de Langue Française, c/o Dr. J.C. Benoit, 1bis Rue Deroisin, 78000 Versailles
T: 0239514868
Founded: 1961; Members: 250
Focus: Therapeutics
Periodical
Annales de Psychothérapie (annually) . 04007

Société de Statistique, d'Histoire et d'Archéologie de Marseille et de Provence, Palais de la Bourse, 13231 Marseille
Founded: 1827; Members: 600
Focus: Archeol; Hist; Stats 04008

Société de Stomatologie de France, 20 Passage Dauphine, 75006 Paris
Focus: Stomatology; Surgery 04009

Société de Transplantation, 2 Pl du Docteur Fournier, 75010 Paris
Founded: 1966
Focus: Surgery 04010

Société d'Economie et de Science Sociales, 80 Rue Vaneau, 75007 Paris
Founded: 1856; Members: 300
Focus: Sociology; Econ
Periodical
Les Etudes Sociales (semi-annually) . . 04011

Société d'Economie Politique, c/o Librairie Dalloz-Sirey, 14 Rue Soufflot, 75005 Paris
Pres: Charles Vallée; Gen Secr: M. de Nussac
Focus: Econ; Poli Sci
Periodical
Annales d'Economie Politique 04012

Société d'Emulation du Bourbonnais, 4 Pl de l'Ancien Palais, 03000 Moulins
T: 0470443903
Founded: 1846
Focus: Hist; Sci; Arts; Lit 04013

Société d'Emulation Historique et Littéraire d'Abbéville, 81 Pl du Général de Gaulle, 80000 Abbéville
Founded: 1797; Members: 300
Focus: Hist; Lit
Periodical
Bulletin (annually) 04014

Société d'Encouragement pour l'Industrie Nationale (S.E.I.N.), 4 Pl Saint-Germain-des-Prés, 75006 Paris
T: 0145485561
Founded: 1801
Focus: Econ
Periodical
L'Industrie Nationale 04015

Société des Africanistes, c/o Musée de l'Homme, 17 Pl du Trocadéro, 75116 Paris
T: 0147277255
Founded: 1931; Members: 400
Gen Secr: M.H. Piault
Focus: Ethnology
Periodical
Journal des Africanistes (semi-annually) . 04016

Société des Agriculteurs de France (SAF), 8 Rue d'Athènes, 75009 Paris
T: 0142857227
Focus: Agri 04017

Société des Américanistes, c/o Musée de l'Homme, 17 Pl du Trocadéro, 75116 Paris
T: 0147046311
Founded: 1895; Members: 500
Pres: Claude Baudez; Gen Secr: Dominique Michelet
Focus: Ethnology; Archeol
Periodical
Journal (annually) 04018

Société des Amis de la Revue de Géographie de Lyon, 18 Rue Chevreul, 69362 Lyon Cedex 07
Founded: 1923
Focus: Geography
Periodical
Revue de Géographie de Lyon (quarterly) 04019

Société des Amis de Marcel Proust et des Amis d'Illiers-Combray, 49 Rue Vineuse, 75016 Paris
Focus: Lit 04020

Société des Amis d'Eugène Delacroix, 6 Pl Furstenberg, 75006 Paris
T: 0145622934
Founded: 1928; Members: 245
Focus: Arts 04021

Société des Amis du Louvre, 34 Quai du Louvre, 75001 Paris
T: 0140205354; Fax: 0140205967
Founded: 1897; Members: 56000
Pres: Marc Fumaroli; Gen Secr: Serge-Antoine Tchekhoff
Focus: Fine Arts
Periodical
Bulletin des Amis du Louvre (quarterly) . 04022

Société des Amis du Musée de l'Homme, c/o Musée de l'Homme, Pl du Trocadéro, 75116 Paris
T: 0147046210
Focus: Ethnology; Anthro; Hist 04023

Société des Anciens Textes Français (S.A.T.F), c/o Ecole des Chartes, 19 Rue de la Sorbonne, 75005 Paris
T: 0146334182
Founded: 1875
Pres: Prof. A. Vernet; Gen Secr: Prof. J. Monfrin
Focus: Lit 04024

Société des Artistes Décorateurs (SAD), Grand Palais, Porte H, Av Winston Churchill, 75008 Paris
T: 0143596610; Fax: 0145637113
Founded: 1901
Focus: Arts 04025

Société des Artistes Français, Grand Palais, Porte H, Av Winston Churchill, 75008 Paris
T: 0143595249; Fax: 0145628597
Founded: 1882
Focus: Arts 04026

Société des Artistes Indépendants, Grand Palais des Champs-Elysées, Porte H, Av Winston Chrchill, 75008 Paris
Founded: 1884
Focus: Arts 04027

Société des Auteurs, Compositeurs et Editeurs de Musique, 225 Av Charles de Gaulle, 92521 Neuilly-sur-Seine Cedex
T: 0147154715
Founded: 1851; Members: 72000
Pres: Gerard Calvi
Focus: Music; Lit 04028

Société des Auteurs et Compositeurs Dramatiques, 11bis Rue Ballu, 75009 Paris
T: 0140234444; Fax: 0145267428
Founded: 1777
Pres: Marcel Bluwal
Focus: Lit 04029

Société des Bibliophiles de Guyenne, c/o Bibliothèque Municipale, 3 Rue Mably, 33075 Bordeaux
T: 0557870447; Fax: 0557873361
Founded: 1866; Members: 800
Focus: Libraries & Bk Sci
Periodical
Revue Française d'Histoire du Livre (quarterly) 04030

Société des Ecoles du Dimanche, 152 Rue Léon Maurice Nordmann, 75013 Paris
T: 0143318659
Focus: Educ 04031

Société des Electriciens et des Electroniciens (SEE), 48 Rue de la Procession, 75724 Paris Cedex 15
T: 0144496000; Fax: 0144496049
Founded: 1883
Focus: Electric Eng 04032

Société des Etudes Historiques, 44 Rue de Rennes, 75006 Paris
Founded: 1833
Focus: Hist 04033

Société des Etudes Latines (CSSF), 1 Rue Victor-Cousin, 75230 Paris Cedex 05
Founded: 1923
Pres: Prof. Alain Michel
Focus: Lit
Periodicals
Collection d'Etudes Latines
Revue des Etudes Latines 04034

Société des Etudes Renaniennes, 167 Blvd Malesherbes, 75017 Paris
Focus: Rel & Theol 04035

Société des Experts-Chimistes de France, 39bis Rue de Dantzig, 75015 Paris
T: =145311480
Founded: 1912; Members: 1200
Pres: Paul Laugel; Gen Secr: Colette Courcelles
Focus: Chem
Periodical
Annales des Falsifications de l'Expertise Chimique et Toxicologique 04036

Société des Explorateurs et des Voyageurs Français, 9bis Av de Montespan, 75116 Paris
T: 0147042272
Focus: Geography 04037

Société des Gens de Lettres, 38 Rue du Faubourg Saint-Jacques, 75014 Paris
T: 0140513300; Fax: 43549299
Founded: 1838
Pres: Paul Fournel; Gen Secr: Georges-Olivier Chateaureynaud
Focus: Lit 04038

Société des Lépidopteristes Français, c/o Muséum d'Histoire Naturelle, 45bis Rue Buffon, 75005 Paris
Focus: Entomology 04039

Société des Lettres, Sciences et Arts La Haute-Auvergne, c/o Archives Départementales, Rue du 139. R.I., 15012 Aurillac Cedex
Founded: 1898; Members: 650
Pres: René Monboisse; Gen Secr: Jean Vezole
Focus: Geology; Botany; Hist; Lit; Archeol 04040

Société des Médecins-Chefs des Compagnies Européennes d'Aviation, c/o Service Médical d'Air France, 1 Sq Max Hymans, 75015 Paris
Focus: Med 04041

Société des Océanistes, c/o Musée de l'Hommes, Pl du Trocadéro, 75116 Paris
T: 0147046340; Fax: 0147046340
Founded: 1938; Members: 560
Pres: Michel Panoff; Gen Secr: Philippe Missotte
Focus: Ethnology
Periodicals
Journal (quarterly)
Publications 04042

Société des Poètes Français, 38 Rue du Faubourg Saint-Jacques, 75014 Paris
T: 0164203805
Founded: 1902; Members: 1600
Pres: Brigitte Level; Gen Secr: Jean Baillon
Focus: Lit
Periodical
Bulletin (quarterly) 04043

Société des Professeurs de Dessin et d'Arts Plastiques de l'Enseignement Secondaire, c/o Lycée Buffon, 16 Blvd Pasteur, 75015 Paris
Founded: 1901; Members: 1050
Focus: Educ; Arts 04044

Société des Sciences, Arts et Belles-Lettres de Bayeux (S.A.B.L.), Hôtel de Ville, 14400 Bayeux
Founded: 1891; Members: 100
Focus: Arts; Lit; Sci 04045

Société des Sciences Historiques et Naturelles de la Corse, c/o Lycée Marbeuf, 20200 Bastia
Focus: Hist; Nat Sci 04046

Société des Sciences Naturelles de Bourgogne, c/o Mus. Hist. Nat., 1 Av Albert Ier, 21000 Dijon
T: 0380768276; Fax: 0380768277
Founded: 1913; Members: 40
Focus: Nat Sci

Periodical
Bulletin Scientifique de Bourgogne (semi-annually) 04047

Société des Sciences Physiques et Naturelles de Bordeaux, c/o Université de Bordeaux, 351 Cours de la Libération, 33405 Talence
Founded: 1850; Members: 300
Focus: Nat Sci; Physics 04048

Société d'Ethnographie de Paris, 6 Rue Champfleury, 75007 Paris
Founded: 1859; Members: 400
Focus: Ethnology; Soc Sci
Periodical
L'Ethnographie (semi-annually) 04049

Société d'Ethnologie Française (SEF), 6 Av du Mahatma Gandhi, 75116 Paris
T: 0144176042
Founded: 1947; Members: 500
Pres: A. Abeles; Gen Secr: D. Laborde
Focus: Ethnology
Periodical
Ethnologie Française (quarterly) 04050

Société d'Ethnozoologie et d'Ethnobotanique (SEZEB), c/o Laboratoire d'Ethnobotanique, Muséum National d'Histoire Naturelle, 57 Rue Cuvier, 75005 Paris
T: 0143316957
Members: 120
Focus: Zoology; Botany 04051

Société d'Etude de Psychodrame Pratique et Théorique (SEPT), 10 Rue des Lions, 75004 Paris
Founded: 1964; Members: 150
Focus: Psych
Periodical
Psychodrame (3 times annually) 04052

Société d'Etude du Dix-Septième Siècle, c/o Collège de France, 11 Pl Marcelin Bethelot, 75231 Paris Cedex 05
Founded: 1949; Members: 1250
Pres: J. Berenger
Focus: Hist; Lit; Philos; Arts
Periodical
XVIIe Siècle (quarterly) 04053

Société d'Etudes Ardennaises (SEA), c/o Archives Départementales des Ardennes, BP 831, 08011 Charleville-Mézières
Founded: 1955; Members: 550
Focus: Hist
Periodical
Revue Historique Ardennaise (annually) . 04054

Société d'Etudes Dantesques, c/o Centre Universitaire Méditerranéen, 65 Promenade des Anglais, 06000 Nice
Founded: 1935; Members: 21
Gen Secr: Simon Lorenzi
Focus: Lit
Periodical
Bulletin 04055

Société d'Etudes Economiques et Comptables, 62 Rue Jouffroy, 75017 Paris
T: 019241353
Focus: Econ; Law 04056

Société d'Etudes et de Contrôles Juridiques, 12 Rue de la Paix, 75002 Paris
T: 0142616558
Focus: Law 04057

Société d'Etudes et de Documentation Economiques, Industrielles et Sociales (SEDEIS), 1 Av Edouard Belin, 92856 Rueil-Malmaison
T: 0241299921
Founded: 1948
Pres: Albert Merlin
Focus: Doc; Sociology; Econ
Periodicals
Analyses de la SEDEIS (bi-monthly)
Chroniques d'Actualité (monthly) 04058

Société d'Etudes et de Recherches Biologiques (S.E.R.B.), 53 Rue Villiers de l'Isle Adam, 75020 Paris
T: 0146368853
Focus: Bio 04059

Société d'Etudes et de Recherches en Sciences Sociales (S.E.R.E.S.), 10 Rue Richer, 75009 Paris
T: 0147706471
Focus: Sociology 04060

Société d'Etudes et de Recherches pour la Connaissance de l'Homme (S.E.R.C.H.), 5 Rue du Commandant Marchand, 75016 Paris
T: 0145003727
Focus: Ethnology 04061

Société d'Etudes et de Soins pour les Enfants Paralysés (SESEP), Château de Longchamp, Bois de Boulogne, 75016 Paris
T: 0145275979
Founded: 1947; Members: 550
Focus: Educ Handic; Pediatrics 04062

Société d'Etudes Ferroviaires, 13 Rue Chardin, 75016 Paris
T: 0148706282
Focus: Transport 04063

Société d'Etudes Financières et Meunières (S.E.F.I.M.), 66 Rue La Boétie, 75008 Paris
T: 0143594580
Focus: Finance; Eng 04064

Société d'Etudes Folkloriques du Centre-Ouest (SEFCO), Maison de Jeannette, Les Granges, 17400 Saint-Jean d'Angely
Founded: 1962; Members: 2950
Focus: Ethnology; Ling
Periodicals
Aguiaine (bi-monthly)
Le Subiet (bi-monthly) 04065

Société d'Etudes Hispaniques et de Diffusion de la Culture Française à l'Etranger, 65 Rue Solférino, 24000 Périgueux
Focus: Ethnology 04066

Société d'Etudes Historiques, c/o Ecole des Hautes Etudes, La Sorbonne, 47 Rue des Ecoles, 75005 Paris
Founded: 1833
Focus: Hist 04067

Société d'Etudes Italiennes, Grand Palais, Perron Alexandre III, Cours La Reine, 75008 Paris
Focus: Ethnology 04068

Société d'Etudes Jaurésiennes, 21 Blvd Lefebvre, 75015 Paris
T: 0148282589
Founded: 1959; Members: 300
Pres: Madeleine Reberioux; Gen Secr: Vincent Duclert
Focus: Poli Sci
Periodical
Bulletin (quarterly) 04069

Société d'Etudes Juives, 39 Rue Broca, 75005 Paris
T: 0142171092
Founded: 1880; Members: 245
Focus: Rel & Theol; Hist; Lit; Sociology; Arts
Periodical
Revue des Etudes Juives 04070

Société d'Etudes Juridiques, Economiques et Fiscales (S.E.J.E.F.), 191 Rue Saint-Honoré, 75001 Paris
T: 0142606880
Focus: Law; Econ 04071

Société d'Etudes Linguistiques et Anthropologiques de France (SELAF), 52 Blvd Saint-Michel, 75005 Paris
T: 0140518920; Fax: 0140518105
Founded: 1964
Pres: J.M.C. Thomas; Gen Secr: L. Bouquiaux
Focus: Ling; Anthro; Ethnology
Periodicals
Acquisition du language et pathologie
Applications et Transferts
Arctique
Bibliothèque de la SELAF
Description de langues et monographies ethnolinguistiques
Ethnomusicologie
Ethnosciences
Etudes ethnolinguistiques Maghreb-Sahara
Europe de tradition orale
LACITO-Documents
Langues et cultures africaines
Langues et cultures du Pacifique
Langues et sociétés de l'Amérique traditionnelle
Linguistique générale
Numéros spéciaux
Oralité – Documents et Etudes
Sociolinguistique: systèmes de langues et interaction sociales et culturelles
Tradition Orale 04072

Société d'Etudes Minières, Industrielles et Financières, 7 Blvd de la Madeleine, 75001 Paris
T: 0142611337
Focus: Mining; Eng; Finance 04073

Société d'Etudes Ornithologiques des France (SOF), c/o Muséum National d'Histoire Naturelle, 55 Rue de Buffon, 75005 Paris
T: 0140793834; Fax: 0140793063
Founded: 1993; Members: 800
Pres: Bernard Frachot; Gen Secr: Jacques Perrn de Brichambaut
Focus: Ornithology 04074

Société d'Etudes pour le Développement Economique et Social (S.E.D.E.S), 105 Rue de Lille, 75007 Paris
T: 0145558759
Founded: 1958; Members: 285
Focus: Sociology; Econ 04075

Société d'Etudes Psychiques, 2 Rue des Fabriques, 54000 Nancy
Focus: Psychiatry 04076

Société d'Etudes Robespierristes, c/o Faculté de Lettres, Université de Paris I, 17 Rue de la Sorbonne, 75231 Paris Cedex 05
Focus: Hist
Periodical
Annales Historiques de la Révolution Française (quarterly) 04077

Société d'Etudes Romantiques, c/o Prof. Dr. Jacques Saint-Gérand, 29 Blvd Gergovia, 63037 Clermont-Ferrand Cedex
T: 0473346502
Focus: Hist; Lit; Philos
Periodical
Romantique (quarterly) 04078

Société d'Etudes Scientifiques et de Recherches (SEURI), 10ter Chemin du Parc, 95220 Herblay
T: 0134500007; Fax: 0139970799
Focus: Sci 04079

Société d'Etudes Techniques, 13 Blvd de Strasbourg, 75010 Paris
T: 0147705251
Focus: Eng 04080

Société d'Histoire de Bordeaux, 71 Rue du Loup, 33000 Bordeaux
Focus: Hist 04081

Société d'Histoire de la Médecine Hébraïque, c/o Dr. I. Simon, 177 Blvd Malesherbes, 75017 Paris
Focus: Hist
Periodicals
Revue d'Histoire de la Médecine Hébraique
Revue Trimestrielle (3 times annually) . 04082

Société d'Histoire de la Pharmacie (S.H.P.), 4 Av de l'Observatoire, 75270 Paris Cedex 06
T: 0143258315
Founded: 1913; Members: 1300
Pres: Jean Flahaut; Gen Secr: Christian Warolin
Focus: Hist
Periodical
Revue d'Histoire de la Pharmacie (quarterly) 04083

Société d'Histoire du Droit (S.H.D.), 158 Rue Saint-Jacques, 75005 Paris
Founded: 1913; Members: 550
Pres: Prof. Olivier Guillot; Gen Secr: A. Lefebvre
Focus: Hist; Law 04084

Société d'Histoire du Droit Normand, c/o Faculté de Droit, Université, 14000 Caen
Focus: Hist; Law 04085

Société d'Histoire du Théâtre, 98 Blvd Kellermann, 75013 Paris
T: 0145884655; Fax: 0145898763
Founded: 1948
Pres: François Périer; Gen Secr: Rose Marie Moudoues
Focus: Hist; Perf Arts
Periodical
Revue d'Histoire du Théâtre (quarterly) . 04086

Société d'Histoire et d'Archéologie de Bretagne, 20 Av Jules Ferry, 35700 Rennes
T: 0299380370; Fax: 0299871074
Founded: 1919; Members: 750
Focus: Hist; Archeol
Periodical
Archives Historiques (quarterly) 04087

Société d'Histoire et d'Archéologie de la Lorraine (SHAL), c/o Archives Départementales de la Lorraine, 1 Allée du Château, 57070 Saint Julien les Metz
Founded: 1888; Members: 1200
Focus: Hist; Archeol
Periodical
Les Cahiers Lorrains (quarterly) 04088

Société d'Histoire et d'Archéologie Le Vieux Montmartre, c/o Musée de Montmartre, 12 Rue Cortot, 75018 Paris
T: 0146066111, 0149258937; Fax: 0145063075
Founded: 1886; Members: 800
Pres: Jean-Marc Tarrit
Focus: Arts; Lit 04089

Société d'Histoire Générale et d'Histoire Diplomatique, 13 Rue Soufflot, 75005 Paris
T: 0143540597; Fax: 46340760
Founded: 1887; Members: 400
Focus: Hist; Poli Sci
Periodical
Revue d'Histoire Diplomatique 04090

Société d'Histoire Littéraire de la France, 112 Rue Monge, 75005 Paris
T: 0145872330
Founded: 1894
Focus: Hist; Lit 04091

Société d'Histoire Moderne et Contemporaine, 47 Blvd Bessières, 75017 Paris
T: 0146277074
Founded: 1901; Members: 1100
Pres: Jean Mycinski; Gen Secr: Guy Boquet
Focus: Hist 04092

Société d'Histoire Religieuse de la France, 26 Rue d'Assas, 75006 Paris
Founded: 1914; Members: 900
Focus: Hist
Periodical
Revue d'Histoire de l'Eglise de France (semi-annually) 04093

Société d'Hygiène International, 5 Sq Henri Delormel, 75014 Paris
T: 015429590
Focus: Hygiene 04094

Société d'Obstétrique et de Gynécologie de Marseille, c/o Hôpital de la Conception, 13001 Marseille
Focus: Gynecology 04095

Société d'Obstétrique et de Gynécologie de Toulouse (S.O.G.T.), c/o Hôpital de la Grave, 31052 Toulouse
Fax: 0561777934
Founded: 1908; Members: 58
Focus: Gynecology
Periodical
Journal de Gynécologie Obstétrique et Biologie de la Reproduction 04096

Société d'Océanographie de France, 195 Rue Saint-Jacques, 75005 Paris
Founded: 1897
Focus: Oceanography 04097

Société d'Ophtalmologie de l'Est de la France, 133 Rue Saint-Dizier, 54000 Nancy
Focus: Ophthal 04098

Société d'Ophtalmologie de Lyon, c/o Hôpital Edouard Herriot, Pavillon C, Pl d'Arsonval, 69437 Lyon Cedex 03
T: 0472116211; Fax: 0472116211
Founded: 1906; Members: 697
Pres: Carole Burillon; Gen Secr: Philippe Gain
Focus: Ophthal 04099

Société d'Ophtalmologie de Paris (SOP), 108 Rue du Bac, 75007 Paris
Founded: 1888; Members: 200
Gen Secr: Dr. Jean-Paul Boissin
Focus: Ophthal
Periodical
Bulletin (monthly) 04100

Société d'Oto-Neuro-Ophthalmologie du Sud-Est de la France, c/o Hôpital de la Timone, 13001 Marseille
Focus: Otorhinolaryngology; Neurology; Ophthal 04101

Société du Salon d'Automne, Grand Palais, Porte H, Av W. Churchill, 75008 Paris
T: 0143594607
Founded: 1903
Focus: Arts 04102

Société Entomologique de France, c/o Muséum d'Histoire Naturelle, 45 Rue Buffon, 75005 Paris
T: 0140793384
Founded: 1832; Members: 600
Pres: G. Perrault; Gen Secr: H. Piguet
Focus: Entomology
Periodicals
Annales (quarterly)
Bulletin (5 times annually) 04103

Société Européenne de Radiologie Cardio-Vasculaire et de Radiologie d'Intervention / European Society of Cardio-Vascular Radiology and Interventional Radiology, c/o Dépt de Radiologie, Hôpital Cardio-Vasculaire, 69393 Lyon Cedex 03
Founded: 1975; Members: 200
Focus: Radiology
Periodical
Annales de Radiologie 04104

Société Européenne de Radiologie Pédiatrique, c/o Hôpital des Enfants Malades, 149 Rue de Sèvres, 75730 Paris Cedex 15
Focus: Radiology 04105

Société Financière Européenne / European Financial Society, 20 Rue de la Paix, 75002 Paris
T: 0142615747
Focus: Finance 04106

Société Française d'Acoustique, 33 Rue Croulebarbe, 75013 Paris
T: 0145355400; Fax: 0143317426
Founded: 1948; Members: 1200
Focus: Physics; Acoustics
Periodical
Acta Acustica (bi-monthly) 04107

Société Française d'Allergologie et d'Immuno-Allergie Clinique, c/o Institut Pasteur, 25 Rue du Dr. Roux, 75015 Paris
T: 0145688241; Fax: 0140613160
Founded: 1947; Members: 860
Pres: Prof. B. David
Focus: Immunology
Periodical
Revue Française d'Allergologie et d'Immunologie Clinique (5 times annually) 04108

Société Française d'Anesthésie et de Réanimation, 74 Rue Raynouard, 75016 Paris
T: 0145258525; Fax: 0140503522
Founded: 1934; Members: 3500
Pres: Prof. C. Conseiller; Gen Secr: Prof. J.L. Pourriat
Focus: Anesthetics
Periodical
Annales Francaises d'Anesthésie et de Réanimation (8 times annually) 04109

Société Française d'Angéiologie, 153 Av Berthelot, 69007 Lyon
T: 0478723898
Founded: 1947; Members: 350
Pres: Dr. H. Bureau du Colombier
Focus: Hematology
Periodical
Angéiologie (8 times annually) 04110

Société Française d'Archéocivilisation et de Folklore, c/o Ecole des Hautes Etudes en Sciences Sociales, 54 Blvd Raspail, 75006 Paris
T: 0145443979
Founded: 1928
Focus: Archeol 04111

Société Française d'Archéologie (S.F.A.), c/o Musée des Monuments Français, Palais de Chaillot, 1 Pl du Trocadéro, 75116 Paris
T: 0147047896; Fax: 0144059425
Founded: 1834; Members: 2850
Pres: Jean Mesqui; Gen Secr: Philippe Dubost
Focus: Archeol
Periodicals
Bulletin Monumental (quarterly)
Congrès Archéologique de France (annually) 04112

Société Française d'Art Contemporain, 28bis Blvd de Sebastopol, 75004 Paris
T: 0142773846
Focus: Arts 04113

Société Française de Biochimie et Biologie Moléculaire, 4 Av de l'Observatoire, 75270 Paris Cedex 06
Founded: 1914
Focus: Biochem; Microbio 04114

Société Française de Biologie Clinique, c/o Laboratoire de Chimie Clinique et Biologie Moléculaire, 15 Rue de l'Ecole de Médecine, 75270 Paris Cedex 06
Gen Secr: Prof. L. Hartmann
Focus: Biochem; Biophys 04115

Société Française de Cardiologie, 15 Rue de Madrid, 75008 Paris
T: 0143879514; Fax: 0143871714
Founded: 1937; Members: 2200
Focus: Cardiol
Periodical
Archives des Maladies du Coeur et des Vaisseaux (monthly) 04116

Société Française de Céramique (SFC), 23 Rue de Cronstadt, 75015 Paris
T: 0140432300; Fax: 0145315804
Founded: 1945
Focus: Arts 04117

Société Française de Chimie, 250 Rue Saint-Jacques, 75005 Paris
T: 0140467160; E-Mail: sfc@sfc.fr; Fax: 0140467161
Founded: 1984; Members: 5000
Pres: Marc Julia; Gen Secr: Jean-Claude Brunie
Focus: Chem
Periodicals
L'Actualité Chimique
Bulletin de la Société Chimique de France
Journal de Chimie Physique 04118

Société Française de Chirurgie Orthopédique et Traumatologique (SOFCOT), c/o Hôpital Cochin, 27 Rue du Faubourg Saint-Jacques, 75014 Paris
T: 0146336479
Members: 1950
Pres: J.M. Thomine
Focus: Surgery; Orthopedics; Traumatology
Periodical
Revue de Chirurgie Orthopédique . . . 04119

Société Française de Chirurgie Pédiatrique (SPCP), c/o Hôpital Debrousse, 29 Rue Soeur Bouvier, 69322 Lyon Cedex 05
T: 0472385651; Fax: 0472385883
Founded: 1959
Focus: Surgery
Periodicals
Chirurgie Pédiatrique (monthly)
European Journal of Pediatric Surgery . 04120

Société Française de Chirurgie Plastique et Reconstructive (SFCPR), 40 Rue Bichat, 75010 Paris
T: 0142066244
Founded: 1953; Members: 360
Pres: Dr. A. de Coninck; Gen Secr: Prof. P. Banzet
Focus: Surgery 04121

Société Française de Chronométrie et de Microtechnique (SFCM), 39 Av de l'Observatoire, 25003 Besançon Cedex
Founded: 1931; Members: 350
Focus: Eng 04122

Société Française de Composition, 24 Rue de la Banque, 75002 Paris
T: 0142612332
Focus: Music 04123

Société Française de Dermatologie et de Syphiligraphie, 37 Rue Galilée, 75016 Paris
Focus: Derm; Venereology 04124

Société Française de Droit Aérien et Spatial (SFDAS), 17 Av de Lamballe, 75016 Paris
T: 0145244650
Founded: 1954; Members: 321
Focus: Law
Periodical
Revue Française de Droit Aérien et Spatial (3 times annually) 04125

Société Française de Génétique (SFG) / French Society of Genetics, c/o R. Motta, C.S.E.A.L.-C.N.R.S., 3b Rue de la Férollerie, 45071 Orléans Cedex 2
T: 0238515438
Founded: 1987; Members: 533
Pres: Ethel Moustacchi; Gen Secr: Roland Motta
Focus: Genetics
Periodical
Bulletin de la SFG (3 times annually) . 04126

Société Française de Géographie Economique, 148 Blvd Malesherbes, 75017 Paris
T: 0146223457
Founded: 1936
Focus: Geography 04127

Société Française de Graphologie, 5 Rue Las Cases, 75007 Paris
T: 0145554694
Focus: Graphology
Periodical
La Graphologie (3 times annually) . . . 04128

Société Française de Gynécologie (SFG), 20 Rue Clément Marot, 75008 Paris
T: 0147208781
Founded: 1931; Members: 582
Pres: J.P. Wolff; Gen Secr: André Gorins
Focus: Gynecology
Periodical
Gynécologie (bi-monthly) 04129

Société Française de Malacologie (SFM), c/o Laboratoire de Biologie des Invertébrés Marins et de Malacologie, Muséum National d'Histoire Naturelle, 55 Rue de Buffon, 75005 Paris
T: 0140793091
Founded: 1969; Members: 350
Focus: Zoology
Periodical
Haliotis (annually) 04130

Société Française de Médecine Aérospatiale, c/o Laboratoire de Médecine Aérospatiale, Centre d'Essais au Vol, 91228 Bretigny Cedex
T: 0169882380; Fax: 0169882725
Founded: 1960; Members: 1200
Focus: Med; Physiology
Periodical
Médecine Aéronautique et Spatiale (quarterly) 04131

Société Française de Médecine du Sport (SFMS), 1 Rue Lacretelle, 75015 Paris
T: 0148285562
Founded: 1921; Members: 3000
Focus: Med; Physical Therapy 04132

Société Française de Médecine du Trafic (SFMT), 21 Rue de l'Ecole de Médecine, 75006 Paris
T: 0146035373
Focus: Med 04133

Société Française de Médecine Esthétique (SFME), 154 Rue A. Silvestre, 92400 Courbevoie
T: 0145063259; Fax: 0145063911
Founded: 1973; Members: 200
Pres: J.J. Legrand
Focus: Surgery; Derm
Periodical
Journal de Médecine Esthétique et de Chirurgie Dermatologique (quarterly) 04134

Société Française de Médecine Générale (S.F.M.G.), 27 Blvd Gambetta, 92130 Issy les Moulineaux
T: 0141909820; E-Mail: sfmgqg@compuserve.com; Fax: 0141909821
Founded: 1973; Members: 500
Pres: Dr. Pascal Clerc
Focus: Med
Periodical
Documents de Recherches en Médecine Générale (bi-monthly) 04135

Société Française de Médecine Orthopédique et Thérapeutique Manuelle, 6 Rue Jean Richepin, 75116 Paris
T: 0145041048
Founded: 1965; Members: 240
Pres: Prof. Philippe Vautravers; Gen Secr: Dr. Marie-José Teyssandier
Focus: Orthopedics; Therapeutics
Periodical
Revue de Médecine Orthopédique (quarterly) 04136

Société Française de Médecine Préventive et Sociale, 60 Blvd de Latour-Maubourg, 75340 Paris Cedex 07
T: 0142605438
Founded: 1953; Members: 700
Focus: Hygiene
Periodical
Bulletin de Liaison (semi-annually) . . . 04137

Société Française de Médecine Psychosomatique, 22 Rue Legendre, 75017 Paris
Focus: Psychiatry
Periodical
Revue de Médecine Psychosomatique (quarterly) 04138

Société Française de Mesothérapie (S.F.M.), 87 Blvd Suchet, 75016 Paris
Founded: 1964
Focus: Therapeutics
Periodical
S.F.M. Bulletin (3 times annually) . . . 04139

Société Française de Métallurgie et de Matériaux (SFMM), 1 Rue de Craïova, 92024 Nanterre Cedex
T: 0141020390; Fax: 0141020388
Founded: 1945; Members: 1400
Pres: Yves Farge; Gen Secr: Yves Franchot
Focus: Metallurgy; Materials Sci 04140

Société Française de Microbiologie, c/o Institut Pasteur, 28 Rue du Docteur Roux, 75724 Paris Cedex 15
T: 0145688179; E-Mail: cmurphy@pasteur.fr; Fax: 0145674698
Founded: 1937; Members: 2600
Pres: Prof. Jean-Pierre Flandrois; Gen Secr: Dr. Patrick Boiron
Focus: Microbio 04141

Société Française de Microscopie Electronique (S.F.M.E.), 9 Quai Saint-Bernard, 75005 Paris
T: 0144272621; Fax: 0144272622
Founded: 1959; Members: 1600
Pres: Prof.Richard Portier
Focus: Electronic Eng
Periodicals
Biology of the Cell (9 times annually)
Journal de Microscopie et de Spectroscopie Electronique (bi-monthly) 04142

Société Française de Minéralogie et de Cristallographie, 4 Pl Jussieu, Tour 16m Casier 115, 75252 Paris Cedex 05
T: 0144276024; Fax: 0144276024
Founded: 1878; Members: 600
Gen Secr: H. Suquet
Focus: Mineralogy
Periodical
European Journal of Mineralogy (quarterly) 04143

Société Française de Musicologie, 2 Rue Louvois, 75002 Paris
T: 0147037549
Founded: 1917; Members: 550
Pres: Jean Gribenski; Gen Secr: Arik Devries-Lesure
Focus: Music
Periodical
Revue de Musicologie (semi-annually) . . 04144

Société Française de Mycologie Médicale, c/o Institut Pasteur, 25 Rue du Docteur Roux, 75724 Paris Cedex 15
T: 0140613254; Fax: 0140688480
Founded: 1956; Members: 500
Pres: J.Y. Rastide
Focus: Botany, Specific
Periodical
Journal de Mycologie Médicale (quarterly) 04145

Société Française de Néonatologie, c/o Hôpital Port Royal, 123 Blvd de Port Royal, 75679 Paris Cedex 14
T: 0142341260; E-Mail: jean-pierre.relier@cch.ap-hop-paris.fr; Fax: 0143290338
Founded: 1975; Members: 1200
Focus: Pediatrics; Physiology; Pathology
Periodical
Progrès en Néonatologie (annually) . . . 04146

Société Française de Neurologie, c/o Masson Editeur, 120 Blvd Saint-Germain, 75006 Paris
T: 0140466000; Fax: 0140466231
Founded: 1899
Focus: Neurology
Periodical
Revue Neurologique (10 times annually) . 04147

Société Française de Numismatique (SFN), c/o Bibliothèque Nationale, Cabinet des Médailles, 58 Rue de Richelieu, 75084 Paris Cedex 02
T: 0147038344
Founded: 1865; Members: 700
Pres: Olivier Picard; Gen Secr: Jacqueline Pilet-Lemière
Focus: Numismatics
Periodicals
Bulletin (10 times annually)
Revue Numismatique (annually) 04148

Société Française de Pathologie Respiratoire, 66 Blvd Saint-Michel, 75005 Paris
Founded: 1945
Focus: Pathology 04149

Société Française de Pédagogie (SFP), 6 Rue du Champ de l'Alouette, 75013 Paris
Founded: 1902; Members: 10000
Pres: M. Bonissel; Gen Secr: M. Gevrey
Focus: Educ
Periodical
Bulletin Trimestriel (3 times annually) . . 04150

Société Française de Pédiatrie, c/o Hôpital des Enfants Malades, 149 Rue de Sèvres, 75743 Paris Cedex 15
Founded: 1929; Members: 1050
Focus: Pediatrics
Periodical
Archives Françaises de Pédiatrie (monthly) 04151

Société Française de Philosophie, 12 Rue Colbert, 75002 Paris
Founded: 1901; Members: 180
Pres: Bernard Bourgeois; Gen Secr: Christiane Menasseyre
Focus: Philos
Periodicals
Bulletin de la Société Française de Philosophie (quarterly)
Revue de Metaphysique et de Morale (quarterly) 04152

Société Française de Phlébologie, 46 Rue Saint-Lambert, 75015 Paris
T: 0145330271; Fax: 0142507518
Founded: 1947; Members: 1700
Pres: Michel Perrin; Gen Secr: F. Vin
Focus: Med
Periodical
Phlébologie: Annales Vasculaires (quarterly) 04153

Société Française de Phoniatrie, c/o Clinique ORL, Hôpital Lariboisière, Rue Ambroise Paré, 75010 Paris
Founded: 1934; Members: 320
Focus: Otorhinolaryngology 04154

Société Française de Photogrammétrie et de Télédétection, 2 Av Pasteur, 94160 Saint-Mandé
T: 0143988073; Fax: 0143988541
Founded: 1959; Members: 615
Pres: Gérard Begni; Gen Secr: Isabelle Veillet
Focus: Surveying
Periodical
Bulletin (quarterly) 04155

Société Française de Photographie, 4 Rue Vivienne, 75002 Paris
T: 0147037539
Founded: 1854; Members: 1200
Pres: Michel Poivert
Focus: Photo 04156

Société Française de Physiologie Végétale, 4 Pl Jussieu, 75230 Paris Cedex 05
Founded: 1955; Members: 600
Pres: P. Mazliak; Gen Secr: B. Camara
Focus: Botany
Periodical
Physiologie Végétale 04157

Société Française de Physique (SFP), 33 Rue Croulebarbe, 75013 Paris
T: 0147073298; Fax: 0143317426
Founded: 1873; Members: 2500
Pres: Marianne Lambert; Gen Secr: Claude Sebenne
Focus: Physics
Periodicals
Bulletin (quarterly)
Journal de Physique (monthly)
Lettres et Journal de Physique (bi-weekly)
Revue de Physique Appliquée (monthly) . 04158

Société Française de Phytiatrie et de Phytopharmacie, c/o C.N.R.A., Rte de Saint-Cyr, 78000 Versailles
T: 0549507522
Founded: 1951; Members: 1000
Focus: Pharmacol; Botany 04159

Société Française de Psychologie (S.F.P.), 28 Rue Serpente, 75006 Paris
T: 0140519936; Fax: 0140469651
Founded: 1922; Members: 1000
Pres: Bernard Bisseret; Gen Secr: Bernard Lespes
Focus: Psych
Periodical
Psychologie Française (quarterly) 04160

Société Française de Radiologie et d'Imagerie Médicale, c/o Hôpital Laënnec, 42 Rue de Sèvres, 75007 Paris
Founded: 1909; Members: 1960
Gen Secr: G. Frija
Focus: Radiology
Periodicals
Diagnostic and Interventional Radiology
Revue d'Imagerie Médicale 04161

Société Française de Santé Publique (S.F.S.P.), c/o Centre de Médecine Préventive, BP 7, 54501 Vandoeuvre lès Nancy Cedex
T: 0383443917; E-Mail: afsp@camp.u-nancy.fr; Fax: 0383443776
Founded: 1877; Members: 730
Pres: Marc Brodin; Gen Secr: Yves Chaspak
Focus: Public Health
Periodicals
Santé et Société (quarterly)
Santé Publique (bi-monthly) 04162

Société Française de Sciences et Techniques Pharmaceutiques, 9 Rue de la Montagne Sainte-Geneviève, 75005 Paris
T: 0143268137; Fax: 0143298252
Members: 1200
Focus: Pharmacol
Periodical
Sciences et Techniques Pharmaceutiques (10 times annually) 04163

Société Française de Sexologie Clinique / French Society for Clinical Sexology, 32 Av Carnot, 75017 Paris
T: 0145726762
Founded: 1974; Members: 300
Pres: Dr. C. Marc; Gen Secr: Dr. Nicole Arnaud-Beauchamps
Focus: Public Health
Periodical
Cahiers de Sexologie Clinique (bi-monthly) 04164

Société Française de Sociologie (S.F.S.), 59-61 Rue Pouchet, 75849 Paris Cedex 17
T: 0140251099; Fax: 0142289544
Founded: 1962; Members: 545
Pres: Dominique Schnapper; Gen Secr: Gérard Mauger
Focus: Sociology 04165

Société Française de Thérapeutique et de Pharmacologe Clinique, c/o Doin Editeur, 8 Pl de l'Odéon, 75006 Paris
Founded: 1866; Members: 1000
Focus: Therapeutics
Periodical
Thérapie (bi-monthly) 04166

Société Française de Toxicologie, 4 Av de l'Observatoire, 75006 Paris
Founded: 1974; Members: 90
Focus: Toxicology 04167

Société Française d'Ecologie, c/o Muséum National d'Histoire Naturelle, 4 Av du Petit Château, 91800 Brunoy
Focus: Ecology 04168

Société Française d'Economie Rurale (SFER), 16 Rue Claude Bernard, 75341 Paris Cedex 05
T: 0147074786; Fax: 0144081842
Founded: 1949; Members: 400
Focus: Agri
Periodical
Economie Rurale (bi-monthly) 04169

Société Française d'Egyptologie (SFE), Collège de France, 11 Pl Marcelin-Berthelot, 75231 Paris Cedex 05
T: 0143256211
Founded: 1923; Members: 850
Pres: J. Vercoutter; Gen Secr: V. Laurent
Focus: Archeol; Hist
Periodicals
Bulletin
Revue d'Egyptologie 04170

Société Française d'Endocrinologie, c/o Masson Editeur, 120 Blvd Saint-Germain, 75280 Paris Cedex 06
T: 0140466000; Fax: 0140466231
Founded: 1939; Members: 550
Focus: Endocrinology
Periodical
Annales d'Endocrinologie (bi-monthly) . . 04171

Société Française d'Energie Nucléaire (S.F.E.N.), 48 Rue de la Procession, 75015 Paris
T: 0145670770
Focus: Energy; Nucl Res
Periodicals
Bulletin de Liaison (monthly)
Revue Générale Nucléaire (bi-monthly) . 04172

Société Française des Architectes, 55 Rue du Cherche-Midi, 75006 Paris
T: 0145485310; Fax: 0142840199
Founded: 1877
Focus: Archit 04173

Société Française des Physiciens d'Hôpital (S.F.P.H.), c/o Institut Curie, 26 Rue d'Ulm, 75231 Paris Cedex 05
Founded: 1972; Members: 340
Pres: Suzanne Naudy; Gen Secr: Bendedicte Perrin
Focus: Physics
Periodicals
Cancer-Radiothérapie (quarterly)
Physica Medica (quarterly) 04174

Société Française des Thermiciens (SFT), 3 Rue Henri Heine, 75016 Paris
T: 0142245935; Fax: 0140500754
Members: 4000
Focus: Eng
Periodical
Revue Générale de Thermique (monthly) 04175

Société Française des Urbanistes (S.F.U.), 38 Rue Eugène Oudiné, 75013 Paris
T: 0145850220
Focus: Urban Plan 04176

Société Française d'Etude du Dix-Huitième Siècle, c/o Gerhardt Stenger, UFR de Lettres, Chemin de la Censive du Tertre, 44312 Nantes Cedex 3
T: 0240141201; E-Mail: stenger.g@humana.univ.nantes.fr; Fax: 0240141201
Founded: 1864; Members: 1700
Pres: Jean Mondot; Gen Secr: Claude Lauriol
Focus: Hist; Lit; Philos
Periodical
Dix Huitième Siècle (annually) 04177

Société Française d'Etudes des Phénomènes Psychiques, 1 Rue des Gâtines, 75020 Paris
T: 0143493080
Founded: 1893; Members: 1000
Pres: A. Croonenberghs
Focus: Psych
Periodical
La Tribune Psychique (quarterly) . . . 04178

Société Française d'Etudes et de Réalisations Cartographiques, 5 Rue Papillon, 75009 Paris
T: 0145230491
Focus: Cart 04179

Société Française d'Etudes Juridiques, 101 Av Raymond Poincaré, 75016 Paris
T: 0147238768
Focus: Law 04180

Société Française d'Hématologie, 96 Rue Didot, 75014 Paris
Focus: Hematology 04181

Société Française d'Héraldique et de Sigillographie, 60 Rue des Francs-Bourgeois, 75141 Paris Cedex 03
Founded: 1937; Members: 200
Focus: Genealogy
Periodical
Revue française d'héraldique et de sigillographie (annually) 04182

Société Française d'Histoire de la Médecine (S.F.H.M), 38bis Rue de Courlancy, 51100 Reims
T: 0326483260; Fax: 0326483271
Founded: 1902; Members: 700
Pres: Prof. Guy Pallardy; Gen Secr: Prof. Alain Ségal
Focus: Med; Cultur Hist
Periodical
Histoire des Sciences Médicales (quarterly) 04183

Société Française d'Histoire d'Outre-Mer (SFHOM), 15 Rue Catulienne, 93200 Saint-Denis
T: 0148130989; Fax: 0148130991
Founded: 1913; Members: 500
Pres: Marc Michel; Gen Secr: Daniel Leveuvre
Focus: Hist
Periodical
Revue Française d'Histoire d'Outre Mer (quarterly) 04184

Société Française d'Hydrologie et de Climatologie Médicales, 1 Rue Monticelli, 75014 Paris
T: 0145406330
Founded: 1853; Members: 413
Pres: Dr. Claude Loisy; Gen Secr: Dr.André Authier
Focus: Water Res; Geophys
Periodical
La Presse Thermale et Climatique (quarterly) 04185

Société Française d'Ichtyologie (S.F.I.), c/o Muséum National d'Histoire Naturelle, 43 Rue Cuvier, 75231 Paris Cedex 05
T: 0140793756; E-Mail: meunier@mnhn.fr; Fax: 0140793771
Founded: 1976; Members: 300
Pres: J. Allardi; Gen Secr: G. Duhamel
Focus: Zoology; Ecology; Fisheries
Periodical
Cybium: Annuaire des Ichtyologistes Français (quarterly) 04186

Société Française d'Ophthalmologie (SFO), 9 Rue Mathurin Régnier, 75015 Paris
T: 0147342021
Founded: 1883; Members: 7200
Pres: Dr.J. Flament; Gen Secr: Dr. J.L. Dufier
Focus: Ophthal
Periodicals
Ophthalmologie
Rapport (annually) 04187

Société Française d'Optique Physiologique, c/o Laboratoire de Physique du Muséum, 43 Rue Cuvier, 75231 Paris Cedex 05
T: 0145873898
Founded: 1966
Focus: Optics; Physiology 04188

Société Française d'Orthopédie, 7 Rue de Duras, 75008 Paris
T: 0142652899
Focus: Orthopedics 04189

Société Française d'Oto-Rhino-Laryngologie et de Pathologie Cervico-Faciale, 9 Rue Villebois-Mareuil, 75017 Paris
Founded: 1880; Members: 1500
Pres: Dr. R. Batisse; Gen Secr: Prof. Charles Freche
Focus: Otorhinolaryngology
Periodicals
Comptes Rendus
Rapports Discutés au Congrès 04190

Société Française du Cancer, 34 Rue d'Ulm, 75231 Paris Cedex 05
Founded: 1920
Focus: Cell Biol & Cancer Res . . . 04191

Société Française du Vide (S.F.V.), 19 Rue du Renard, 75004 Paris
T: 0142781582; Fax: 0142786320
Founded: 1945; Members: 2000
Focus: Eng
Periodical
Le Vide, les Couches Minces (quarterly) 04192

Société Française d'Urologie, 6 Av Constant Coquelin, 75007 Paris
Founded: 1919; Members: 50
Pres: Dr. Boissonnat
Focus: Urology
Periodical
Journal d'Urologie 04193

Société Française pour le Droit International (SFDI), c/o CEDIN, Université de Paris X, 200 Av de la République, 92001 Nanterre Cedex
T: 0140977722; Fax: 0140974710
Founded: 1967; Members: 500
Pres: Prof. Hubert Thierry; Gen Secr: Prof. Emmanuel Decaux
Focus: Law 04194

Société Géologique de France (SGF), 77 Rue Claude Bernard, 75005 Paris
T: 0143317735; E-Mail: sgfr@worldnet.fr; Fax: 0145357910
Founded: 1830; Members: 2500
Focus: Geology
Periodicals
Bulletin de la Société Géologique de France (bi-monthly)
Géochronique (quarterly)
Géologie de la France (quarterly)
Mémoires de la Société Géologique de France (irregularly) 04195

Société Géologique et Minéralogique de Bretagne (SGMB), c/o Institut de Géologie, Faculté des Sciences, Av du Général Leclerc, 35042 Rennes Cedex
T: 0299364815
Founded: 1920; Members: 230
Focus: Geology; Mineralogy
Periodicals
Bulletin (semi-annually)
Mémoires (irregularly) 04196

Société Historique, Archéologique et Littéraire de Lyon, c/o Archives Municipales de Lyon, 4 Av Adolphe Max, 69005 Lyon
Founded: 1807; Members: 100
Focus: Archeol; Hist; Lit
Periodical
Bulletin de la Société Historique, Archéologique et Littéraire de Lyon (annually) . . 04197

Société Historique de la Province de Maine, 26 Rue des Chanoines, 72000 Le Mans
Focus: Hist
Periodical
La Province du Maine (quarterly) . . . 04198

Société Historique du Bas-Limousin, c/o Robert Joudoux, 13 Pl Municipale, 19000 Tulle
Focus: Hist 04199

Société Historique et Archéologique du Périgord, 18 Rue du Plantier, 24000 Périgueux
Founded: 1874
Focus: Hist; Archeol
Periodical
Bulletin de la Société Historique et Archéologique du Périgord (quarterly) 04200

Société Hydrotechnique de France, 199 Rue de Grenelle, 75007 Paris
T: 0147051337; Fax: 0145569746
Founded: 1912; Members: 600
Pres: Georges Maurin; Gen Secr: Max Perrin
Focus: Eng; Hydrology
Periodical
La Houille Blanche: Revue Internationale de l'Eau (8 times annually) 04201

Société Internationale de Bibliographie Classique (SIBC) / International Society of Classical Bibliography, 11 Av René Coty, 75014 Paris
T: 0143276790
Founded: 1923
Gen Secr: Pierre Paul Corsetti
Focus: Libraries & Bk Sci
Periodical
L'Année Philologique: Bibliographie Critique et Analytique de l'Antiquité Gréco-Latine (annually) 04202

Société Internationale de Biologie Mathématique, 11bis Av de la Providence, 92160 Antony
Founded: 1962
Focus: Bio; Math
Periodical
Revue de Bio-Mathématique (quarterly) . 04203

Société Internationale de Criminologie (SIC) / International Society of Criminology, 4 Rue de Mondovi, 75001 Paris
T: 0142618022 ext 5825
Founded: 1934; Members: 1200
Gen Secr: Georges Picca
Focus: Criminology
Periodical
Newsletter 04204

Société Internationale de Podologie Médico-Chirurgicale, 93 Av du Docteur Picaud, 06150 Cannes-la-Bocca
Focus: Surgery 04205

Société Internationale de Psycho-Prophylaxie Obstétricale, 31 Rue Saint-Guillaume, 75007 Paris
T: 0145481513
Founded: 1958
Gen Secr: Dr. Pierre Vellay
Focus: Gynecology
Periodical
Bulletin (quarterly) 04206

Société Internationale de Psychopathologie de l'Expression (SIPE) / International Society of Art and Psychopathology, c/o Clinique des Maladies Mentales et de l'Encephale, 100 Rue de la Santé, 75014 Paris
T: 0145895521
Founded: 1959; Members: 600
Pres: Prof. Robert Volmat
Focus: Psychiatry
Periodical
Newsletter 04207

Société Internationale de Recherches pour l'Environnement et la Santé, 4 Rue Pérignon, 75007 Paris
T: 0147342168
Founded: 1979
Focus: Ecology; Public Health 04208

Société Internationale de Transfusion Sanguine (SITS) / International Society of Blood Transfusion, c/o CNTS, BP 100, 91943 Les Ulis Cedex
T: 0169072040
Founded: 1937; Members: 1780
Pres: G. Archer; Gen Secr: G. Garretta
Focus: Hematology
Periodical
Transfusion Today (quarterly) 04209

Société Internationale des Amis de Montaigne, BP 913, 75073 Paris Cedex 02
Founded: 1912; Members: 780
Focus: Lit
Periodical
Bulletin (semi-annually) 04210

Société Internationale d'Urologie (SIU), 9 Blvd du Temple, 75003 Paris
T: 0142784009
Founded: 1910; Members: 1500
Gen Secr: Prof. Dr. A. Jardin
Focus: Urology 04211

Société Internationale pour la Lutte contre le Cancer du Sein / International Society Against Breast Cancer, 26 Rue de la Faisanderie, 75116 Paris
Founded: 1973
Focus: Cell Biol & Cancer Res 04212

Société J. S. Bach, 95 Rue Vaugirard, 75006 Paris
Focus: Music 04213

Société Juridique et Fiscale de France, 2bis Rue de Villiers, 92309 Levallois Perret Cedex
Focus: Law 04214

Société Linnéenne de Provence, c/o Lycée Thiers, Pl du Lycée, 13001 Marseille
Founded: 1909; Members: 350
Focus: Nat Sci 04215

Société Longuédocienne de Géographie, c/o Université P. Valéry, BP 5043, 34032 Montpellier Cedex
T: 0467142183
Focus: Geography 04216

Société Mathématique de France (S.M.F.), c/o Institut H. Poincaré, 11 Rue Pierre et Marie Curie, 75005 Paris Cedex 05
T: 0144276796; E-Mail: smf@dmi.ens.fr; Fax: 0140469096
Founded: 1872; Members: 1800
Pres: Jean-Jacques Risler; Gen Secr: Claire Ropartz
Focus: Math
Periodicals
Astérisque (monthly)
Bulletin et Mémoires de la S.M.F. (quarterly)
Gazette des Mathématiciens (quarterly)
Officiel des Mathématiques (monthly)
Revue d'Histoire des Mathématiques (semi-annually) 04217

Société Médicale des Hôpitaux de Paris, 45 Quai de la Tournelle, 75005 Paris
T: 0143257195; Fax: 0143254092
Founded: 1848; Members: 600
Focus: Med
Periodical
Annales de Médecine Interne 04218

Société Médicale d'Imagerie, Enseignement et Recherche (SMIER), c/o Hôpital Saint-Antoine, 75571 Paris Cedex 12
T: 0149282460; Fax: 0149282687
Founded: 1955
Pres: F. Vicari; Gen Secr: C. Florent
Focus: Radiology
Periodical
Acta Endoscopica (bi-monthly) 04219

Société Médico-Chirurgicale des Hôpitaux et Formations Sanitaires des Armées, 277bis Rue Saint-Jacques, 75005 Paris
Founded: 1969
Focus: Surgery 04220

Société Médico-Chirurgicale des Hôpitaux Libres, 1 Pl d'Iéna, 75016 Paris
Focus: Surgery 04221

Société Médico-Psychologique, 14-16 Av R. Schuman, 92100 Boulogne
Founded: 1852; Members: 675
Pres: Prof. Michel Laxenaire; Gen Secr: Dr. Pierre Marchais
Focus: Med; Psych; Psychiatry
Periodical
Annales Médico-Psychologiques (10 times annually) 04222

Société Météorologique de France (SMF), 73-77 Rue de Sèvres, 92100 Boulogne-Billancourt
Founded: 1852; Members: 950
Focus: Geophys

Periodical
La Météorologie 04223

Société Mycologique de France, 18 Rue de l'Ermitage, 75020 Paris
T: 0143663540; Fax: 0143663540
Founded: 1884; Members: 1800
Pres: René Hontic; Gen Secr: Patrick Vanhecke
Focus: Botany, Specific
Periodical
Bulletin Trimestriel (3 times annually) . . 04224

Société Nationale Académique de Cherbourg, 21 Rue Bonhomme, 50100 Cherbourg
T: 0233532806
Founded: 1755; Members: 40
Pres: André Poirier; Gen Secr: Claude Dréno
Focus: Sci
Periodical
Mémoires (every 4-5 years) 04225

Société Nationale de Protection de la Nature (SNPN), 9 Rue Cels, 75014 Paris
T: 0143201539; Fax: 0143201571
Founded: 1854; Members: 8500
Pres: François Ramade
Focus: Ecology
Periodicals
Le Courrier de la Nature (bi-monthly)
La Terre et la Vie (quarterly) 04226

Société Nationale de Transfusion Sanguine (SNTS), 6 Rue A. Cabanel, 75739 Paris Cedex 15
T: 0143067000
Founded: 1955; Members: 510
Focus: Hematology
Periodicals
Blood Transfusion and Immunhematology (bi-monthly)
Revue Française de Transfusion et Hémobiologie 04227

Société Nationale des Architectes de France, 8 Rue Albert Samain, 75017 Paris
Founded: 1872; Members: 500
Focus: Archit
Periodical
Le Monitor des Architectes 04228

Société Nationale des Beaux-Arts (S.N.B.A.), 11 Rue Berryer, 75008 Paris
Founded: 1890; Members: 800
Pres: F. Baboulet; Gen Secr: Roger Grellet
Focus: Arts 04229

Société Nationale des Sciences Naturelles et Mathématiques de Cherbourg, 21 Rue Bonhomme, 50100 Cherbourg
T: 0233532806
Focus: Math; Nat Sci; Chem; Physics
Periodical
Mémoires 04230

Société Nationale d'Horticulture de France (SNHF), 84 Rue de Grenelle, 75007 Paris
T: 0144397878; Fax: 0145449657
Founded: 1827; Members: 13000
Pres: Michel Cointat; Gen Secr: Philippe Giraut
Focus: Hort
Periodical
Jardins de France (10 times annually) . 04231

Société Nationale Française de Gastro-Entérologie (SNFGE), Hôpital de Brabois, 54511 Vandoeuvre Cedex
T: 0383153585; Fax: 0383442389
Founded: 1911; Members: 570
Gen Secr: Prof. Marc-André Bigard
Focus: Gastroenter 04232

Société Nationale Française de Rééducation et Réadaption Fonctionnelles, 13 Blvd Raspail, 75007 Paris
Focus: Rehabil 04233

Société Odontologique de Paris (S.O.P.), 239 Rue du Faubourg Saint-Martin, 75010 Paris
T: 0142092913
Members: 2500
Pres: Dr. E. Hazan; Gen Secr: Dr. Y. Bismuth
Focus: Dent
Periodical
Revue d'Odonto-Stomatologie (bi-monthly) 04234

Société Parisienne d'Etudes et de Recherches Foncières (SOPEREF), 88bis Rue Jouffroy, 75017 Paris
T: 0142670023
Focus: Geology 04235

Société Parisienne d'Etudes Spéciales, 10 Rue Castagnary, 75015 Paris
T: 0148420939
Focus: Sci 04236

Société Phycologique de France, c/o Laboratoire de Biologie Végétale Marine, Université Paris VI, 7 Quai Saint-Bernard, 75230 Paris Cedex 05
Founded: 1950; Members: 150
Focus: Botany 04237

Société pour la Protection des Paysages, Sites et Monuments, 39 Av de La Motte-Picquet, 75007 Paris
T: 0147053771
Founded: 1901; Members: 7000
Pres: Paule Albrecht
Focus: Ecology
Periodical
Sites et Monuments (quarterly) 04238

Société Provençale de Pédiatrie, c/o Hôpital de la Conception, 13001 Marseille
Focus: Pediatrics 04239

Société Psychoanalytique de Paris, 187 Rue Saint-Jacques, 75005 Paris
T: 0146333290
Founded: 1926; Members: 285
Focus: Psychoan 04240

Société Racinienne, 52 Rue J. Dulud, 92200 Neuilly-sur-Seine
Focus: Lit 04241

Société Saint-Simon, 11d Allée d'Honneur, 92330 Sceaux
T: 0145788270
Founded: 1972; Members: 360
Pres: Philippe Hourcade; Gen Secr: Hélène Himelfarb
Focus: Hist 04242

Société Savoisienne d'Histoire et d'Archéologie, 6 Av de Bassens, 73000 Chambéry
T: 0479334448
Focus: Hist; Archeol 04243

Société Scientifique de Bretagne, c/o Faculté des Sciences, 35000 Rennes
Founded: 1924; Members: 280
Focus: Sci 04244

Société Scientifique d'Hygiène Alimentaire (SSHA), 16 Rue de l'Estrapade, 75005 Paris
T: 0143251185
Founded: 1904; Members: 1182
Pres: Dr. Guy Ebrard
Focus: Hygiene 04245

Société Technique d'Etudes Mécaniques et d'Outillage (S.T.E.M.O.), 22 Passage Dumas, 75011 Paris
T: 0143713513
Focus: Eng 04246

Société Théosophique de France, 4 Sq Rapp, 75007 Paris
T: 0145513179
Focus: Rel & Theol 04247

Société Vétérinaire Pratique de France (S.V.P.F.), 10 Pl Léon Blum, 75011 Paris
Founded: 1879; Members: 1730
Focus: Vet Med
Periodical
Bulletin de la Société Vétérinaire Pratique de France (monthly) 04248

Société Zoologique de France, 195 Rue Saint-Jacques, 75005 Paris
T: 0140793110
Founded: 1876; Members: 750
Pres: Prof. T. Hourdry; Gen Secr: Prof. J.-L. d' Hondt
Focus: Zoology
Periodicals
Bulletin (quarterly)
Mémoires (irregularly) 04249

Sociétés de Statistique de Paris et de France, 18 Blvd Pinard, 75675 Paris Cedex 14
Founded: 1860; Members: 1040
Gen Secr: Annie Morin
Focus: Stats
Periodical
Journal de la Société de Statistique de Paris (3 times annually) 04250

Syndicat des Chirurgiens Dentistes de Paris, 4 Rue La Vrillière, 75001 Paris
T: 0142964339
Focus: Surgery; Dent
Periodical
Le Chirurgien-Dentiste de Paris (monthly) 04251

Syndicat des Ecrivains, 38 Rue du Faubourg Saint-Jacques, 75014 Paris
T: 0143220647
Focus: Lit 04252

Syndicat des Enseignants, 209 Blvd Saint-Germain, 75007 Paris
T: 0144392300; E-Mail: enseign-@fen.fr; Fax: 0144392313
Founded: 1920; Members: 110000
Gen Secr: Herré Baro
Focus: Educ 04253

Syndicat des Psychiatres Français (SPF), 23 Rue Pradier, 92410 Ville d'Avray
T: 0147091177; Fax: 0147506275
Founded: 1967; Members: 1500
Focus: Psychiatry
Periodicals
Annuaire des Psychiatres Français (bi-annually)
La Lettre de Psychiatrie Française (monthly)
Psychiatrie Française (quarterly) 04254

Syndicat des Spécialistes Français en Orthopédie Dento-Faciale (SSFODF), 92 Av de Wagram, 75017 Paris
T: 0142278900
Founded: 1961; Members: 600
Focus: Orthopedics 04255

Syndicat des Vétérinaires de la Région Parisienne, 8 Rue Pierre Guerin, 75016 Paris
T: 0142886799
Focus: Vet Med 04256

Syndicat Général de l'Education Nationale, 5 Rue des Feuillantines, 75005 Paris
T: 0143266243
Focus: Educ 04257

Syndicat Général des Personnels de l'Éducation Nationale, 55 Rue Pixerecourt, 75020 Paris
T: 0146367693
Focus: Educ 04258

Syndicat National de l'Enseignement Supérieur, 78 Rue du Faubourg Saint-Denis, 75010 Paris
T: 0147709035
Founded: 1937; Members: 10780
Focus: Educ 04259

Syndicat National de l'Enseignement Technique, 74 Rue de la Fédération, 75015 Paris
T: 0147836130; Fax: 0147832669
Members: 11000
Focus: Adult Educ 04260

Syndicat National de l'Intendance de l'Éducation Nationale, 22bis Rue de Paradis, 75010 Paris
T: 0145231991
Focus: Educ 04261

Syndicat National de l'Orthopédie Française, 18 Blvd des Filles du Calvaire, 75011 Paris
T: 0143556220
Focus: Orthopedics 04262

Syndicat National des Allergologistes Français, 19 Rue Eupatoria, 37000 Tours
T: 0247543276
Founded: 1959; Members: 400
Pres: Dr. Paul Fleury; Gen Secr: Dr. F. Duguet
Focus: Immunology 04263

Syndicat National des Anesthésistes-Réanimateurs Français, 185 Rue Saint-Maur, 75010 Paris
T: 0142380868
Pres: Dr. Frayssinhes; Gen Secr: Dr. Chapus
Focus: Anesthetics 04264

Syndicat National des Auteurs et Compositeurs de Musique (SNAC), 80 Rue Taitbout, 75442 Paris Cedex 09
T: 0148749630
Founded: 1946
Pres: Antoine Duhamel; Gen Secr: Emmanuel Rengervé
Focus: Music; Lit
Periodical
Le Bulletin des Auteurs (3 times annually) 04265

Syndicat National des Chefs d'Etablissements d'Enseignement Libre, 277 Rue Saint-Jacques, 75005 Paris
T: 0143296550; Fax: 0146340884
Focus: Educ
Periodical
Fiches Syndicales (monthly) 04266

Syndicat National des Chirurgiens Français (SNCF), c/o Confédération des Syndicats Médicaux Français, 60 Blvd de Latour-Maubourg, 75007 Paris
T: 0147053751
Members: 1200
Focus: Surgery 04267

Syndicat National des Chirurgiens Plasticiens, 32 Blvd de Courcelles, 75017 Paris
T: 0149246154
Founded: 1968; Members: 125
Focus: Surgery 04268

Syndicat National des Collèges de la Région Parisienne, 20 Rue Neuve des Boulets, 75011 Paris
T: 0143714043
Focus: Educ 04269

Syndicat National des Collèges et des Lycées, 13 Av Taillebourg, 75011 Paris
T: 0143732136; Fax: 0143700847
Focus: Educ
Periodical
Bulletin (monthly) 04270

Syndicat National des Enseignements de Second Degré (S.N.E.S.), 1 Rue de Courty, 75007 Paris
T: 0140632900; Fax: 0140632909
Founded: 1928
Focus: Educ
Periodical
L'Université Syndicaliste (bi-monthly) . . 04271

Syndicat National des Instituteurs et Professeurs de Collège, 5 Rue Paul Louis Courier, 75007 Paris
T: 0142221021
Founded: 1920; Members: 320000
Focus: Educ 04272

Syndicat National des Lycées et Collèges (SNALC), 4 Rue de Trévise, 75009 Paris
T: 0145230514; Fax: 0142462660
Founded: 1905; Members: 15000
Pres: Françoise Angoulvant
Focus: Educ
Periodicals
Quinzaine Universitaire (bi-monthly)
SNALC-Info S. 1 (monthly) 04273

Syndicat National des Médecins Acupuncteurs de France, 14 Blvd de Courcelles, 75017 Paris
T: 0146222975
Founded: 1946; Members: 1500
Focus: Anesthetics 04274

Syndicat National des Médecins Anatomo-Cyto-Pathologistes Français, c/o Faculte X Bichat, 16 Rue Henri Huchard, 75018 Paris
T: 0142633534
Pres: Dr. Marie Claire Imbert; Gen Secr: Dr. Jean Paul Donzel; Jacques Hassoun
Focus: Anat; Pathology 04275

Syndicat National des Médecins Biologistes, 133 Blvd de Montparnasse, 75006 Paris
T: 0143203838
Founded: 1927
Pres: Dr. Gérard Gallez; Gen Secr: Dr. Jean Gayraud
Focus: Med; Bio 04276

Syndicat National des Médecins de Groupe, 26 Rue de Clichy, 75009 Paris
T: 0142800607
Focus: Med
Periodicals
Lettre Hebdomadaire des Médecins de Groupe (weekly)
Médecins de Groupe (monthly) 04277

Syndicat National des Médecins des Hôpitaux Publics, 60 Blvd Latour-Maubourg, 75007 Paris
T: 014556018
Focus: Med
Periodical
Médecine Hospitaliére (bi-monthly) . . . 04278

Syndicat National des Médecins du Sport (S.N.M.S.), 60 Blvd de Latour-Maubourg, 75340 Paris Cedex 07
T: 0147053751; E-Mail: monroche@dial.oleane.com
Founded: 1948
Focus: Med
Periodicals
Cinésiologie: La Revue Internationale des Médecins du Sport (bi-monthly)
Lettre Syndicale (bi-monthly) 04279

Syndicat National des Médecins Electro-Radiologistes Qualifiés, 60 Blvd Latour-Moubourg, 75007 Paris
T: 0145517784
Focus: Radiology 04280

Syndicat National des Médecins Français Spécialistes des Maladies du Coeur et des Vaisseaux, 147 Blvd Brune, 75014 Paris
T: 0145430810
Founded: 1948; Members: 10
Pres: Dr. Jacques Vadot; Gen Secr: Dr. Gérard Rousselet
Focus: Cardiol 04281

Syndicat National des Médecins Homéopathes Français, c/o Domus Medica, 60 Blvd de la Tour Maubourg, 75007 Paris
T: 0240717777; Fax: 0240737833
Founded: 1932; Members: 870
Pres: Dr. François Gassin; Gen Secr: Dr. Michèle Daut
Focus: Homeopathy 04282

Syndicat National des Médecins Ostéothérapeutes Français (SNMOF), 67 Rue Raymond Poincaré, 54000 Nancy
T: 0383406061; Fax: 0383273460
Founded: 1953; Members: 600
Pres: Dr. Jean-Louis Garcia; Gen Secr: Dr. Daniel Le Corgne
Focus: Therapeutics 04283

Syndicat National des Médecins Phlébologues Français, c/o Dr. Sapin, 55 Rue de Varenne, 75007 Paris
Focus: Physiology 04284

Syndicat National des Médecins Rhumatologues, 19 Blvd Pierre Brossolette, 92160 Antony
T: 0442373888
Pres: Dr. Yves Lac de Fougères; Gen Secr: Dr. Raymond Cohen
Focus: Rheuma 04285

Syndicat National des Médecins Spécialisés en Phoniatrie, 16 Rue des Ursulines, 93200 Saint-Denis
Founded: 1966
Focus: Otorhinolaryngology 04286

Syndicat National des Médecins Spécialistes de l'Endocrinologie et de la Nutrition, 71 Av des Ternes, 75017 Paris
T: 0145741919
Founded: 1960; Members: 200
Pres: Dr. Nicolas Gueritée; Gen Secr: Dr. Jean Michel Daninos
Focus: Endocrinology; Nutrition 04287

Syndicat National des Médecins Spécialistes en Stomatologie et Chirurgie Maxillo-Faciale, c/o Dr. Etienne Alexandre, 3 Rue de Rivoli, 75004 Paris
T: 0142728960
Pres: Dr. Etienne Alexandre; Gen Secr: Dr. Francis Dujarric
Focus: Stomatology 04288

Syndicat National des Oto-Rhino-Laryngologistes Français, 12 Rue de Logelbach, 75017 Paris
Founded: 1907; Members: 1250
Focus: Otorhinolaryngology 04289

Syndicat National des Pédiatres Français (SNPF), c/o Dr. J.L. Boy, 28 Rue August Audollent, 63000 Clermont-Ferrand
Founded: 1952; Members: 800
Focus: Pediatrics 04290

Syndicat National des Personnels de Direction de l'Enseignement Secondaire (SNPDES), c/o Lycée Jacquard, 2 Rue Bouret, 75019 Paris
Members: 3400
Focus: Educ 04291

Syndicat National des Professeurs d'Arts Martiaux (S.N.P.A.M.), 68 Rue Castagnary, 75015 Paris
T: 0145314129
Founded: 1957; Members: 250
Pres: Luc Levannier
Focus: Sports 04292

Syndicat National des Professeurs des Ecoles Normales d'Instituteurs (SNPEN), 48 Rue La Bruyère, 75009 Paris
Founded: 1946; Members: 1600
Focus: Educ 04293

Syndicat National des Vétérinaires Français, 10 Pl Léon Blum, 75011 Paris
T: 0143791152
Focus: Vet Med
Periodicals
La Dépêche Technique (bi-monthly)
La Dépêche Vétérinaire (weekly) 04294

Syndicat National Français des Dermatologistes et Vénéréologistes, 60 Blvd de Latour-Maubourg, 75007 Paris
T: 0144186230; Fax: 0145515270
Founded: 1928; Members: 1200
Pres: Dr. J. Martel; Gen Secr: Dr. G. Reuter
Focus: Derm; Venereology
Periodical
La Lettre du Président (bi-monthly) . . . 04295

Syndicat National Professionnel des Médecins du Travail (SNPMT), 12 Impasse Mas, 31000 Toulouse
T: 0561992077; Fax: 0561627566
Founded: 1949
Focus: Hygiene
Periodical
Revue Médecine et Travail 04296

Union Astronomique Internationale (UAI) / International Astronomical Union, 98bis Blvd Arago, 75014 Paris
T: 0143258358; E-Mail: ian@iap.fr;
Fax: 0143252616
Founded: 1919; Members: 8500
Gen Secr: Johannes Andersen
Focus: Astronomy
Periodicals
Colloquium Proceedings (2-3 times annually)
IAU/UAI Information Bulletin (semi-annually)
Symphosium Proceedings (bi-monthly) . . 04297

Union Centrale des Arts Décoratifs (U.C.A.D.), 107 Rue de Rivoli, 75001 Paris
T: 0142603214
Founded: 1864; Members: 2200
Pres: Antoine Riboud; Gen Secr: Pierre Lambertin; Thierry Bondoux
Focus: Arts 04298

Union des Biologistes de France, 4 Rue Pasquier, 75008 Paris
T: 0142651597; Fax: 0142655805
Pres: Adrien Bedossa; Gen Secr: Michèle Hanne
Focus: Bio; Med
Periodical
Le Nouveau Biologiste (10 times annually) 04299

Union des Océanographes de France, 195 Rue Saint-Jacques, 75005 Paris
T: 0143256310; Fax: 0140517316
Founded: 1901
Focus: Oceanography
Periodical
Journal de Recherche Océanographique . 04300

Union des Physiciens, 44 Blvd Saint-Michel, 75270 Paris Cedex 06
T: 0143297308
Founded: 1906; Members: 9500
Pres: Prof. A. Duruphty
Focus: Physics; Chem; Educ
Periodical
Bulletin (monthly) 04301

Union des Professeurs de Spéciales (Mathématiques et Sciences Physiques) (U.P.S.), 3 Rue de l'Ecole Polytechnique, 75005 Paris
T: 0143269792; Fax: 0143269792
Founded: 1928; Members: 2500
Pres: M. Rooy; Gen Secr: M. di Valentin
Focus: Educ 04302

Union des Travailleurs Espérantistes des Pays de Langue Française / SAT-AMIKARO, 67 Av Gambetta, 75020 Paris
T: 0147978705; E-Mail: sat-esp@worldnet.net;
Fax: 0147977190
Founded: 1937; Members: 800
Pres: Jean Selle; Gen Secr: Henri Masson
Focus: Ling 04303

Union Fédérative des Sociétés d'Education Physique et de Préparation Militaire, 23 Rue La Sourdière, 75001 Paris
T: 0142612774
Focus: Sports; Military Sci 04304

Union Française des Organismes de Documentation (U.F.O.D.), 16 Rue Jules Claretie, 75016 Paris
T: 0145040771
Founded: 1932
Focus: Doc 04305

Union Française pour l'Espéranto, 4bis Rue de la Cerisaie, 75004 Paris
T: 0142786886
Focus: Ling
Periodical
Franca Esperantisto: Revue Française d'Espéranto (8 times annually) 04306

Union Générale des Auteurs et Musiciens Professionnels, 71 Rue du Faubourg Saint-Martin, 75010 Paris
T: 0142082290
Focus: Lit; Music 04307

Union Géodésique et Géophysique Internationale (UGGI), c/o Bureau Gravimétrique International, 18 Av Edouard Belin, 31055 Toulouse Cedex
T: 0561332989; Fax: 0561253098
Founded: 1919
Gen Secr: Dr. Georges Balmino
Focus: Geology; Geophys
Periodical
Chronique UGGI (quarterly) 04308

Union Internationale de Phlébologie, 106 Av de Suffren, 75015 Paris
T: 0143069909; Fax: 0143069057
Founded: 1960; Members: 16
Pres: André Davy; Gen Secr: Dr. Pierre Wallois
Focus: Med
Periodical
Phlébologie (quarterly) 04309

Union Internationale d'Electrothermie (UIE) / International Union for Electroheat, Tour Atlantique, 92080 Paris-La Défense Cedex 06
T: 0147789934; Fax: 0149060373
Founded: 1953
Pres: J. Finet; Gen Secr: G. Vanderschueren
Focus: Electric Eng 04310

Union Internationale des Architectes (UIA) / International Union of Architects, 51 Rue Raymonard, 75016 Paris
T: 0145243688; Fax: 0145240278
Founded: 1948; Members: 900000
Gen Secr: Vassilis Sgoutas
Focus: Archit
Periodical
Bulletin d'Information (monthly) 04311

Union Internationale des Etudes Orientales et Asiatiques (UIEOA) / International Union for Oriental and Asian Studies, 77 Quai du Port-au-Fouarre, 94100 Saint-Maur
Founded: 1951
Focus: Ethnology 04312

Union Internationale des Femmes Architectes (UIFA) / International Union of Women Architects, 14 Rue Dumont d'Urville, 75116 Paris
T: 0147208882
Members: 1000
Pres: S. d' Herbez de la Tour
Focus: Archit 04313

Union Internationale des Sciences Biologiques (UIBS) / International Union of Biological Sciences, 51 Blvd de Montmorency, 75016 Paris
T: 0145250009
Founded: 1922
Gen Secr: Dr. Talal Younès
Focus: Bio
Periodical
Biology International (semi-annually) . . . 04314

Union Internationale des Sociétés d'Aide à la Santé Mentale, 39 Rue Charles Monselet, 33000 Bordeaux
T: 0556816005
Founded: 1972
Focus: Psychiatry 04315

Union Internationale pour la Liberté d'Enseignement (UILE) / International Union for the Liberty of Education, 17 Rue Monceau, 75006 Paris
Founded: 1950
Focus: Educ
Periodical
Congress Report 04316

Union Internationale Thérapeutique, 8 Pl de l'Odéon, 75006 Paris
Founded: 1934
Focus: Therapeutics 04317

Union Nationale des Médecins Spécialistes Confédérés, 60 Blvd de Latour-Maubourg, 75340 Paris Cedex 07
T: 0147053751; Fax: 0145415270
Members: 9000
Focus: Med 04318

Union Nationale des Techniciens Biologistes (UNATEB), 109 Av Gabriel Péri, 94170 Le Perreux
T: 0148714344; Fax: 0148711431
Founded: 1963; Members: 3000
Focus: Bio
Periodicals
Le Biotechnologiste (quarterly)
UNATEB Actualités (quarterly) 04319

Union Nationale Patronale des Prothésistes Dentaire, 27 Av Stephen Pichon, 75013 Paris
T: 0145870104
Focus: Dent 04320

Union Professionnelle des Professeurs, Cadres et Techniciens du Secrétariat et de la Comptabilité, 21 Rue Croulebarbe, 75013 Paris
T: 0143312248
Focus: Adult Educ 04321

Union Syndicale Nationale des Angiologues, 102 Av du Général Leclerc, 75014 Paris
T: 0145436458
Pres: Dr. Daniel Paitel; Gen Secr: Dr. Roger Elkrieff
Focus: Hematology 04322

Union Technique de l'Automobile, du Motocycle et du Cycle (U.T.A.C.), 157 Rue Lecourbe, 75015 Paris
T: 0148425390
Focus: Auto Eng
Periodicals
Album des Normes de l'Automobile
Bulletin Mensuel de Documentation (monthly)
. . . . 04323

Union Technique de l'Electricité (UTE), Immeuble L'Avoisier, 92052 Paris-La Défense Cedex 64
T: 0147685020
Founded: 1907; Members: 7
Focus: Electric Eng
Periodicals
Bulletin (3 times annually)
Catalogue (annually) 04324

Universités Unies pour l'Environnement, c/o AIMBE, 115 Rue de la Pompe, 75116 Paris
T: 0145534504, 0145530970; Fax: 0145534175
Focus: Ecology 04325

Vieilles Maisons Françaises (VMF), 93 Rue de l'Université, 75007 Paris
T: 0140626171; Fax: 0145511226
Founded: 1962; Members: 16000
Pres: Baron de Grandmaison; Gen Secr: Evelyne de Ladoncette
Focus: Archit
Periodical
Vieilles Maisons Françaises 04326

World Federation of Scientific Workers, BP 404, 93514 Montreuil Cedex
T: 0148184584; E-Mail: 100764.1427@compuserve.com; Fax: 0148188003
Founded: 1946; Members: 400000
Pres: André Jaeglé; Gen Secr: M.A. Jaeglé
Focus: Sci
Periodical
Scientific World (quarterly) 04327

World Medical Association (WMA), 28 Av des Alpes, BP 6363, 01212 Ferney-Voltaire Cedex
Fax: 0450405937
Founded: 1947; Members: 59
Gen Secr: Dr. André Wynen
Focus: Med
Periodical
World Medical Journal (bi-monthly) . . . 04328

French Polynesia

Société des Etudes Océaniennes (S.E.O.), BP 110, Papeete, Tahiti
T: 419603
Founded: 1917; Members: 450
Pres: Robert Koenig
Focus: Ethnology; Archeol
Periodical
Bulletin (quarterly) 04329

Gambia

Gambia Ornithological Society, Banjul, POB 757
T: 27233
Founded: 1974; Members: 56
Pres: Chris White; Gen Secr: M. Dale
Focus: Ornithology
Periodical
Report 04330

Georgia

Amateur Society of Basque Language, Rustaveli 52, 380008 Tbilisi
Pres: S.V. Dzidziguri
Focus: Ling 04331

Commission for the Study of Production Forces and Natural Resources, Paliashvili 87, 380030 Tbilisi
T: 223216
Focus: Econ 04332

Commission on Biosphere and Ecology Research, Rustaveli 52, 380008 Tbilisi
Focus: Biophys; Ecology 04333

Council on Co-ordinating Scientific Studies of the Georgian Language, Dzerzhinski 8, 380007 Tbilisi
Focus: Ling 04334

Council on the History of Natural Sciences and Technology, Rustaveli 52, 380008 Tbilisi
Focus: Hist; Sci; Eng 04335

Georgian Academy of Sciences, Pr Rustaveli 52, 380008 Tbilisi
T: 998891; Fax: 998823
Members: 121
Pres: A.N. Tavkhelidze; Gen Secr: L.K. Gabunia
Focus: Sci
Periodicals
Bulletin (monthly)
Matsne: Herald (monthly)
Metsnierba da Technika (monthly)
Yearbook of Iberian-Caucasian Linguistics (annually) 04336

Georgian Bio-Mecico-Technical Society, Telavi 51, 380003 Tbilisi
Pres: K.S. Nadreishvili
Focus: Med 04337

Georgian Botanical Society, Kodzhorskoe Shosse, 380007 Tbilisi
Pres: G.S. Nakhutsrishvili
Focus: Botany, Specific 04338

Georgian Commission on Archaeology, Rustaveli 52, 380008 Tbilisi
Focus: Archeol 04339

Georgian Geographical Society, Ketskhoveli 11, 380007 Tbilisi
Pres: V.S. Dzhaoshvili
Focus: Geography 04340

Georgian Geological Society, Rustaveli 52, 380008 Tbilisi
Pres: S.A. Adamia
Focus: Geology 04341

Georgian History Society, Rustaveli 52, 380008 Tbilisi
Pres: A.M. Apakidze
Focus: Hist 04342

Georgian National Committee on UNESCO Long-Term Programme „Man and the Biosphere", Rustaveli 52, 380008 Tbilisi
Focus: Biophys 04343

Georgian National Speleological Society, Rukhadze 1, 380093 Tbilisi
Pres: Z.K. Tatashidze
Focus: Geology 04344

Georgian Philosophy Society, Rustaveli 29, 380008 Tbilisi
Pres: N.Z. Chavchavadze
Focus: Philos 04345

Georgian Society of Biochemists, University 2, 380043 Tbilisi
T: 312184
Pres: N.G. Aleksidze
Focus: Biochem 04346

Georgian Society of Genetics and Selectionists, Gotua 3, 380060 Tbilisi
T: 374227
Pres: T.G. Chanishvili
Focus: Genetics 04347

Georgian Society of Helminthologists, Chavchavadze 3, 380030 Tbilisi
Pres: Prof. B.E. Kurashvili
Focus: Zoology 04348

Georgian Society of Patho-Anatomists, V. Pshavela 27b, 380077 Tbilisi
Pres: T.I. Dekanosidze
Focus: Anat 04349

Georgian Society of Physiologists, Gudamakari 2, 380092 Tbilisi
Pres: V.M. Okudzjava
Focus: Physiology 04350

Georgian Society of Psychologists, Jashvili 22, 380007 Tbilisi
Pres: N.Z. Nadirashvili
Focus: Psych 04351

Scientific-Technical Council on Computer Technology, Mathematical Modelling, Automation of Scientific Research and Instrument Making, Rustaveli 52, 380008 Tbilisi
Focus: Computer & Info Sci; Math; Eng 04352

Germany

Aachener Geschichtsverein, Fischmarkt 3, 52062 Aachen
Focus: Hist
Periodicals
Aachener Beiträge für Baugeschichte und Heimatkunst (irregularly)
Zeitschrift des Aachener Geschichtsvereins (annually) 04353

Ärztegesellschaft für Erfahrungsheilkunde e.V., Im Weiher 10, 69121 Heidelberg
T: (06221) 489469; Fax: 489584
Founded: 1966; Members: 1400
Gen Secr: Dr. Ewald Fischer
Focus: Med
Periodical
Erfahrungsheilkunde (monthly) 04354

Ärztekammer Berlin, Flottenstr 28-42, 13407 Berlin
T: (030) 408060
Focus: Med
Periodical
Berliner Ärzte (monthly) 04355

Ärztekammer Bremen, Schwachhauser Heerstr 26-28, 28209 Bremen
T: (0421) 340051
Focus: Med 04356

Ärztekammer des Saarlandes, Faktoreistr 4, 66111 Saarbrücken
T: (0681) 40030
Focus: Med
Periodical
Saarländisches Ärzteblatt (monthly) . . . 04357

Ärztekammer des Saarlandes, Abteilung Zahnärzte, Puccinistr 2, 66119 Saarbrücken
T: (0681) 586080; Fax: 5860814
Members: 810
Pres: Dr. Wolfgang Weis; Gen Secr: Bernhard Kuntz
Focus: Dent 04358

Ärztekammer Frankfurt, Georg-Voigt-Str 15, 60325 Frankfurt
T: (069) 79201
Focus: Med 04359

Ärztekammer Hamburg, Humboldtstr 56, 22083 Hamburg
T: (040) 228020
Focus: Med
Periodical
Hamburger Ärzteblatt (monthly) 04360

Ärztekammer Mecklenburg-Vorpommern, Humboldtstr 6, 18055 Rostock
T: (0381) 22265
Focus: Med 04361

Ärztekammer Niedersachsen, Berliner Allee 20, 30175 Hannover
T: (0511) 38002; Fax: 3802240
Focus: Med
Periodical
Niedersächsisches Ärzteblatt (bi-weekly) . 04362

Ärztekammer Nordrhein (ÄKNo), Tersteegenstr 31, 40474 Düsseldorf
T: (0211) 43020; E-Mail: aeknowes@www.aekno.de; Fax: 4302200
Founded: 1945; Members: 42000
Pres: Prof. Dr. Jörg D. Hoppe; Gen Secr: Dr. Wolfgang Klitzsch; Dr. Robert D. Schäfer
Focus: Med
Periodical
Rheinisches Ärzteblatt (monthly) 04363

Ärztekammer Sachsen-Anhalt, Doctor-Eisenbart-Ring 2, 39120 Magdeburg
T: (0391) 60546; Fax: 6054700
Founded: 1990; Members: 8829
Pres: Prof. Dr. Walter Brandstätter; Gen Secr: Dr. Jutta Synowitz
Focus: Med 04364

Ärztekammer Schleswig-Holstein, Bismarckallee 8-12, 23795 Bad Segeberg
T: (04551) 8030
Focus: Med
Periodical
Schleswig-Holsteinisches Ärzteblatt (monthly) 04365

Ärztekammer Westfalen-Lippe, Kaiser-Wilhelm-Ring 4-6, 48145 Münster
T: (0251) 37500; Fax: 3750450
Focus: Med
Periodical
Westfälisches Ärzteblatt (monthly) . . . 04366

Ärztliche Gesellschaft für Physiotherapie, Kneippärztebund e.V., Seb.-Kneipp-Promenade 28-30, 53902 Bad Münstereifel
T: (02253) 911
Founded: 1894; Members: 700
Focus: Therapeutics 04367

AgaS Arbeitsgemeinschaft für angewandte Sozialforschung GmbH, Blutenburgstr 93, 80634 München
T: (089) 132005; E-Mail: AgaS.Muenchen@t-online.de; Fax: 1689285
Founded: 1978
Pres: Karl-Heinz Neumann
Focus: Sociology 04368

Agnes-Miegel-Gesellschaft e.V. (AMG), Landsberger Str 52, 45481 Mülheim a.d. Ruhr
T: (0208) 466010; Fax: 466011
Focus: Lit 04369

Agrarsoziale Gesellschaft e.V. (ASG), Kurze Geismarstr 33-35, 37073 Göttingen
T: (0551) 497090; Fax: 4970916
Founded: 1947; Members: 580
Pres: Manfred Merforth; Gen Secr: Dr. Dieter Czech
Focus: Agri
Periodicals
Geschäfts- und Arbeitsbericht (annually)
Kleine Reihe (irregularly)
Ländlicher Raum: Rundbrief der ASG (monthly)
Materialsammlung (irregularly)
Schriftenreihe für Ländliche Sozialfragen (irregularly) 04370

aid Auswertungs- und Informationsdienst für Ernährung, Landwirtschaft und Forsten e.V., Konstantinstr 124, 53179 Bonn
T: (0228) 84990; E-Mail: aid@dainet.de; Fax: 9526952
Pres: Dr. K. Padberg; Gen Secr: Dr. Michael Vogt
Focus: Agri; Forestry; Nutrition
Periodicals
aid Verbraucherdienst: Zeitschrift für Fach-, Lehr- und Beratungskräfte im Bereich Ernährung (monthly)
Ausbildung und Beratung in Land- und Hauswirtschaft: Monatsschrift für Lehr- und Beratungskräfte (monthly) 04371

Akademie der Arbeit in der Universität Frankfurt/Main, Alte Mainzer Gasse 17-19, 60311 Frankfurt
T: (069) 772021; Fax: 7073469
Focus: Sociology; Law; Econ
Periodical
Mitteilungen (annually) 04372

Akademie der Bayerischen Presse e.v. (ABP), Arnulfstr 44, 80335 München
T: (089) 5490020; Fax: 54900222
Focus: Journalism 04373

Akademie der Diözese Rottenburg-Stuttgart, Im Schellenkönig 61, 70184 Stuttgart
T: (0711) 16406; E-Mail: AkademieRS@t-online.de homepage: http://www.kirchen.de/akademie/rs; Fax: 1640777
Founded: 1951
Pres: Dr. Gebhard Fürst
Focus: Rel & Theol 04374

Akademie der Künste, Hanseatenweg 10, 10557 Berlin
T: (030) 390070; Fax: 3900771
Founded: 1696; Members: 256
Focus: Arts; Fine Arts 04375

Akademie der Politischen Bildung der Friedrich-Ebert-Stiftung e.v. (APB), Godesberger Allee 149, 53175 Bonn
T: (0228) 8830; Fax: 883695
Focus: Poli Sci 04376

Akademie der Wissenschaften in Göttingen, Theaterstr 7, 37073 Göttingen
T: (0551) 395362; Fax: 395365
Founded: 1751; Members: 311
Pres: Prof. Dr. Rudolf Smend; Gen Secr: Prof. Dr. Heinz Georg Wagner
Focus: Sci
Periodicals
Abhandlungen: I. Philologisch-Historische Klasse, II. Mathematisch-Physikalische Klasse (irregularly)
Göttingische Gelehrte Anzeigen (semi-annually)
Jahrbuch (annually)
Nachrichten: I. Philologisch-Historische Klasse, II. Mathematisch-Physikalische Klasse (irregularly) 04377

Akademie der Wissenschaften und der Literatur zu Mainz, Geschwister-Scholl-Str 2, 55131 Mainz
T: (06131) 5770
Founded: 1949; Members: 220
Pres: Prof. Dr. Clemens Zintzen; Gen Secr: Dr. Wulf Thommel
Focus: Sci
Periodicals
Abhandlungen: Geistes- und Sozialwissenschaftliche Klasse (irregularly)
Abhandlungen: Klasse der Literatur (irregularly)
Abhandlungen: Mathematisch-Naturwissenschaftliche Klasse (irregularly)
Altern und Entwicklung: Aging and Development (irregularly)
Basic Aspects of Glaucoma Research (irregularly)
Biona Report (irregularly)
Colloquia Academica: Akademievorträge junger Wissenschaftler (irregularly)
Erdwissenschaftliche Forschung: Kommission für Erdwissenschaftliche Forschung (irregularly)
Forschungen zur Antiken Sklaverei: Kommission für Geschichte des Altertums (irregularly)
Forschungen zur neueren Medizin- und Biologiegeschichte (irregularly)
Fortschritte der Zoologie (irregularly)
Funktionsanalyse Biologischer Systeme (irregularly)
Historische Forschungen (irregularly)
Hydronymia Europaea (irregularly)
Hydronymia Germaniae (irregularly)
Indices zur lateinischen Literatur der Renaissance (irregularly)
Information Processing in Animals (irregularly)
Jahrbuch (annually)
Karl-August-Forster-Lectures: Mathematisch-Naturwissenschaftliche Klasse (irregularly)
Kiniogenases (irregularly)
Mainzer Reihe (irregularly)
Medizinhistorisches Journal: Kommission für Geschichte der Medizin und der Naturwissenschaften (irregularly)
Medizinische Forschung (irregularly)
Microfauna Marina: Mathematisch-Naturwissenschaftliche Klasse (irregularly)
Musikalische Denkmäler (irregularly)
Neue Studien zur Musikwissenschaft (irregularly)
Ökosystemanalyse und Umweltforschung (irregularly)
Paläoklimaforschung (irregularly)
Research in Molecular Biology: Mathematisch-Naturwissenschaftliche Klasse (irregularly)
Soemmering-Forschungen (irregularly)
Studien zu den Bogazköy-Texten (irregularly)
Studien zu den Fundmünzen der Antike (irregularly)
Tropische und Subtropische Pflanzenwelt (irregularly)
Untersuchungen zur Sprach- und Literaturgeschichte der Romanischen Völker (irregularly)
Veröffentlichungen: Orientalische Kommission (irregularly)
Verschollene und Vergessene (irregularly)
Winckelmann-Edition (irregularly) 04378

Akademie der Wissenschaften zu Berlin / Academy of Sciences and Technology in Berlin, Griegstr. 5-7, 14193 Berlin
T: (030) 8209050
Founded: 1987; Members: 31
Focus: Sci 04379

Akademie des Deutschen Buchhandels, Literaturhaus München, Salvatorpl 1, 80333 München
T: (089) 4709293; Fax: 4709285
Focus: Libraries & Bk Sci 04380

Akademie Deutscher Genossenschaften e.V. (ADG), Schloß, 56410 Montabaur
T: (02602) 140; Fax: 14147
Focus: Econ 04381

Akademie Führung und Organisation (AfürO), Kaiserstr 3, 53113 Bonn
T: (0228) 210021; Fax: 218858
Focus: Business Admin 04382

Akademie für Arbeit und Sozialwesen, Fritz-Dobisch-Str 6-8, 66111 Saarbrücken
T: (0681) 4005229; Fax: 4005410
Focus: Sociology 04383

Akademie für Arbeitsmedizin und Umweltmedizin Berlin (AfAUM), Lorenzweg 5, 12099 Berlin
T: (030) 75795311/13; Fax: 75795399
Focus: Med 04384

Akademie für Beruf, Jugend und Kultur e.V. (ABJK), Torgauer Str 14, 03253 Doberlug-Kirchhain
T: (035322) 2217; Fax: 4242
Focus: Educ 04385

Akademie für Fernstudium und Weiterbildung Bad Harzburg, Golfstr 11, 38667 Bad Harzburg
T: (05322) 54091; Fax: 2014
Founded: 1990; Members: 3
Focus: Educ 04386

Akademie für Führungskräfte der Wirtschaft e.V. (AFW), Postfach 1116, 38667 Bad Harzburg
T: (05322) 730
Founded: 1956
Focus: Business Admin
Periodical
Management heute (monthly) 04387

Akademie für Kinderheilkunde und Jugendmedizin e.V., Mielenforster Str 2, 51069 Köln
T: (0221) 6805627; Fax: 63204
Focus: Med 04388

Akademie für Kommunikation Baden-Württemberg e.V. (AFK), Kölner Str 7, 70376 Stuttgart
T: (0711) 541789; Fax: 544207
Focus: Comm Sci 04389

Akademie für Kurzschrift, Maschinenschreiben und Bürowirtschaft e.V., Lindenstr 1, 24966 Sörup
T: (04635) 618
Focus: Educ 04390

Akademie für Natur- und Umweltschutz beim Ministerium für Umwelt und Verkehr Baden-Württemberg, Dillmannstr 3, 70193 Stuttgart
T: (0711) 1262807; Fax: 2237668
Focus: Ecology 04391

Akademie für öffentliches Gesundheitswesen (AföG), Auf'm Hennekamp 70, 40225 Düsseldorf
T: (0211) 310960; Fax: 3109669
Founded: 1971; Members: 7
Focus: Public Health
Periodical
Blickpunkt (quarterly) 04392

Akademie für Organisation, Kaiserstr 3, 53113 Bonn
T: (0228) 210021
Focus: Business Admin 04393

Akademie für Politische Bildung, Buchensee 1, 82323 Tutzing
T: (08158) 2560; Fax: 25614
Founded: 1957
Focus: Poli Sci 04394

Akademie für Publizistik in Hamburg e.V., Magdalenenstr 64a, 20148 Hamburg
T: (040) 4147960; Fax: 41479690
Focus: Journalism 04395

Akademie für Raumforschung und Landesplanung (ARL), Hohenzollernstr 11, 30161 Hannover
T: (0511) 348420; E-Mail: ARL@mbox.arl.uni-hannover.de; Fax: 3484241
Founded: 1946; Members: 450
Pres: Prof. Dr. Klaus Wolf; Gen Secr: Dr. Martin Junkernheinrich
Focus: Urban Plan
Periodical
Raumforschung und Raumordnung (bi-monthly) 04396

Akademie gemeinnütziger Wissenschaften, Anger 37-38, 99084 Erfurt
T: (03641) 635784
Focus: Sociology 04397

Akademie Gesellschaft und Wissenschaft e.V. (AGW), Bäckerstr 23-24, 38640 Goslar
T: (05321) 34000; Fax: 340099
Focus: Sociology; Sci 04398

Akademie Klausenhof, Klausenhofstr 100, 46499 Hamminkeln
T: (02852) 890; Fax: 89300
Focus: Educ 04399

Akademie Kontakte der Kontinente, Langenbachstr 1, 53113 Bonn
Focus: Poli Sci 04400

Akademie Remscheid für musische Bildung und Medienerziehung e.V. (ARS), Küppelstein 34, 42857 Remscheid
T: (02191) 7940; Fax: 794205
Founded: 1958
Focus: Arts; Educ
Periodicals
kulturarbeit aktuell (quarterly)
RAT – Remscheider Arbeitshilfen und Texte (irregularly) 04401

Akademie Sankelmark, 24988 Sankelmark
T: (04630) 550; Fax: 628
Focus: Poli Sci 04402

Akademie Schwerin e.V., Arsenalstr 2, 19053 Schwerin
T: (0385) 565078; Fax: 565078
Focus: Poli Sci 04403

Akademikergesellschaft für Erwachsenenfortbildung mbH (AKAD), Maybachstr 8, 70469 Stuttgart
T: (0711) 814950; Fax: 8179750
Focus: Adult Educ 04404

Akademischer Verein Hütte, Carmerstr 12, 10623 Berlin
Founded: 1846
Focus: Metallurgy 04405

Aktion Bildungsinformation e.V. (AB), Alte Poststr 5, 70173 Stuttgart
T: (0711) 299335
Focus: Educ 04406

Aktion Psychisch Kranke / Vereinigung zur Reform der Versorgung psychisch Kranker e.V., Gaurheindorfer Str 15, 53111 Bonn
T: (0228) 631545
Focus: Psychiatry 04407

Aktionsgemeinschaft Natur- und Umweltschutz Baden-Württemberg, Olgastr 19, 70182 Stuttgart
T: (0711) 241460; Fax: 2360556
Focus: Ecology 04408

Aktionsgemeinschaft Soziale Marktwirtschaft e.V. (ASM), Mohlstr 26, 72074 Tübingen
T: (07071) 550600; Fax: 550601
Founded: 1953
Focus: Econ
Periodical
ASM-Bulletin (quarterly) 04409

Aktuelles Forum NRW e.V. (AF), Hohenstaufenallee 1-5, 45888 Gelsenkirchen
T: (0209) 15371; Fax: 148146
Focus: Poli Sci 04410

Albertus-Magnus-Institut, Adenauerallee 19, 53111 Bonn
T: (0228) 201460; E-Mail: ami@ami.bn.shuttle.de; Fax: 2014630
Founded: 1931; Members: 7
Pres: Prof. Dr. Ludger Honnefelder; Gen Secr: Dr. Mechthild Dreyer
Focus: Rel & Theol; Philos 04411

Alfred Toepfer Akademie für Naturschutz (NNA), Hof Möhr, 29640 Schneverdingen
T: (05199) 9890; Fax: 432
Focus: Ecology 04412

Allgemeine Ärztliche Gesellschaft für Psychotherapie (AÄGP), Friedrich-Lau-Str 7, 40474 Düsseldorf
T: (0211) 450741; Fax: 450741
Founded: 1926; Members: 1583
Focus: Therapeutics 04413

Allgemeine Gesellschaft für Philosophie in Deutschland e.V., Augustuspl 9, 04109 Leipzig
T: (0341) 9735800; Fax: 9735849
Focus: Philos 04414

Allgemeiner Cäcilien-Verband für Deutschland (ACV), Andreasstr 9, 93059 Regensburg
T: (0941) 84339; Fax: 84339
Founded: 1868; Members: 318000
Pres: Prof. Dr. Wolfgang Bretschneider
Focus: Music
Periodicals
Kirchenmusikalisches Jahrbuch (annually)
Musica Sacra (bi-monthly) 04415

Anatomische Gesellschaft, c/o Institut für Anatomie, Medizinische Universität, Ratzeburger Allee 160, 23538 Lübeck
T: (0451) 5004030; Fax: 5004034
Founded: 1886; Members: 1025
Gen Secr: Prof. Dr. Wolfgang Kühnel
Focus: Anat
Periodical
Anatomischer Anzeiger: Annals of Anatomy (bi-monthly) 04416

Anna-Seghers-Gesellschaft Berlin und Mainz e.V., Anna Seghers-Str 81, 12489 Berlin
T: (030) 6774725
Focus: Lit 04417

Annette von Droste-Gesellschaft e.V. (AvDG), Am Rüschhaus 81, 48161 Münster
T: (02533) 31091317; Fax: 3109
Focus: Lit 04418

Anthropos Institut, Arnold-Janssen-Str 20, 53754 Sankt Augustin
T: (02241) 2371; E-Mail: anthropos@t-online.de; Fax: 205823
Founded: 1932; Members: 33
Pres: Prof. Dr. Joachim Piepke
Focus: Anthro
Periodical
Anthropos: International Review of Ethnology and Linguistics Internationale Zeitschrift für Völker- und Sprachenkunde (semi-annually) 04419

Anthroposophische Gesellschaft in Deutschland, Zur Uhlandshöhe 10, 70188 Stuttgart
T: (0711) 1643121; Fax: 1643130
Gen Secr: Friedhelm Dörmann; Charlotte Roder
Focus: Humanities; Educ; Philos
Periodical
die Drei: Zeitschrift für Anthroposophie in Wissenschaft, Kunst und sozialem Leben (monthly) 04420

Arbeit und Leben / Arbeitskreis für die Bundesrepublik Deutschland e.V., Tersteegenstr 61-63, 40474 Düsseldorf
T: (0211) 434686; Fax: 459593
Focus: Sociology; Poli Sci; Educ . . . 04421

Arbeitsausschuß Wälzlager im DIN Deutsches Institut für Normung e.V., Kamekestr 2-8, 50672 Köln
T: (0221) 57131
Focus: Standards; Eng 04422

Arbeitsgemeinschaft Allensbach e.V., Kappeler-Berg-Str 54, 78476 Allensbach
Focus: Stats
Periodical
Allensbacher Almanach 04423

Arbeitsgemeinschaft außeruniversitärer historischer Forschungseinrichtungen in der Bundesrepublik Deutschland e.V. (AHF), Aldringenstr 11, 80639 München
T: (089) 134729; Fax: 134739
Focus: Hist 04424

Arbeitsgemeinschaft Berufliche Bildung der deutschen Zeitungsverlage (ABZV), Riemenschneiderstr 10, 53175 Bonn
T: (0228) 8100433; Fax: 8100434
Focus: Educ; Mass Media 04425

Arbeitsgemeinschaft Demokratischer Bildungswerke e.V. (ADB), Ahornweg 27, 53177 Bonn
T: (0228) 321023; Fax: 326821
Focus: Poli Sci 04426

Arbeitsgemeinschaft der Archive und Bibliotheken in der evangelischen Kirche, Veilhofstr 28, 90489 Nürnberg
Fax: (0911) 5819683
Focus: Archives; Libraries & Bk Sci . . 04427

Arbeitsgemeinschaft der Deutschen Werkkunstschulen, Am Wandrahm 23, 28195 Bremen
Focus: Arts 04428

Arbeitsgemeinschaft der kirchlichen Büchereiverbände, Wittelsbacherring 9, 53115 Bonn
T: (0228) 72580; Fax: 7258189
Members: drei
Gen Secr: Rolf Pitsch
Focus: Libraries & Bk Sci 04429

Arbeitsgemeinschaft der Leiter musikpädagogischer Studiengänge in der Bundesrepublik Deutschland (ALMS), c/o HdK Berlin, FB 8/KWE 2, Fasanenstr 1, 10623 Berlin
T: (030) 31850, 31852399
Focus: Educ; Music 04430

Arbeitsgemeinschaft der Musikakademien, Konservatorien und Hochschulinstitute, Ludwigshöhstr 120, 64285 Darmstadt
T: (06151) 96640; Fax: 966413
Focus: Music 04431

Arbeitsgemeinschaft der Ordenshochschulen (AGO), Pallottistr 3, 56179 Vallendar
T: (0261) 64021
Focus: Rel & Theol; Educ 04432

Arbeitsgemeinschaft der Parlaments- und Behördenbibliotheken (APBB), c/o Bundesamt für die Anerkennung ausländischer Flüchtlinge, Bibliothek, 90469 Nürnberg
T: (0911) 9435504; Fax: 9435598
Founded: 1955; Members: 500
Pres: Gaby Wecker
Focus: Libraries & Bk Sci
Periodicals
Arbeitshefte der Arbeitsgemeinschaft der Parlaments- und Behördenbibliotheken (annually)
Mitteilungen der Arbeitsgemeinschaft der Parlaments- und Behördenbibliotheken (semi-annually) 04433

Arbeitsgemeinschaft der Regionalbibliotheken / Joint Association of Regional Libraries, c/o Saarländische Universitäts- und Landesbibliothek, Universität des Saarlandes, 66123 Saarbrücken
T: (0681) 3022070; E-Mail: sulb@rz.uni-sb.de; Fax: 3022796
Pres: Bernd Hagenau
Focus: Libraries & Bk Sci 04434

Arbeitsgemeinschaft der Sozialdemokraten im Gesundheitswesen (ASG), Ollenhauerstr 1, 53113 Bonn
T: (0228) 532456
Focus: Public Health 04435

Arbeitsgemeinschaft der Spezialbibliotheken e.V. (ASpB), c/o Kekulé-Bibliothek, Bayer AG, Bayerwerk, 51373 Leverkusen
T: (0214) 307819; Fax: 307407
Founded: 1946; Members: 671
Focus: Libraries & Bk Sci
Periodical
Report 04436

Arbeitsgemeinschaft der wissenschaftlichen Institute des Handwerks der EG-Länder / Working Committee of the Scientific Institutes for Crafts in the EEC Countries, c/o Institut für Handwerkswirtschaft, Max-Joseph-Str 4, 80333 München
T: (089) 593671; Fax: 553453
Founded: 1961
Focus: Econ 04437

Arbeitsgemeinschaft Deutsche Lateinamerika-Forschung (ADLAF), c/o Zentralinstitut für Lateinamerika-Studien, Katholische Universität Eichstätt, Ostenstr 26-28, 85071 Eichstätt
T: (08421) 931249; E-Mail: karl.kohuta@ku-eichstaett.de, ingrid.adam@ku-eichstaett.de; Fax: 1446
Founded: 1965; Members: 280
Pres: Prof. Dr. Karl Kohut
Focus: Sci
Periodical
ADLAF-Info (quarterly) 04438

Arbeitsgemeinschaft Deutscher Chorverbände e.V. (ADC), Adersheimer Str 60, 38304 Wolfenbüttel
T: (05331) 46016; Fax: 43723
Focus: Music 04439

Arbeitsgemeinschaft Deutscher Tumorzentren e.V. (ADT), c/o Klinikum Großhadern, Med. Klinik III, Marchioninistr 15, 81366 München
T: (089) 70954563; Fax: 70958834
Focus: Cell Biol & Cancer Res 04440

Arbeitsgemeinschaft deutscher wirtschaftswissenschaftlicher Forschungsinstitute e.V., Königin-Luise-Str 5, 14195 Berlin
Founded: 1949; Members: 10
Pres: Prof. Dr. K.H. Oppenländer
Focus: Econ
Periodical
Gemeinschaftsdiagnose: Die Lage der Weltwirtschaft und der westdeutschen Wirtschaft im Frühjahr und im Herbst eines jeden Jahres (semi-annually) 04441

Arbeitsgemeinschaft deutschsprachiger Autoren (ADA), von-Schildeck-Str 12, 36043 Fulda
T: (0661) 23274; Fax: 23274
Focus: Lit 04442

Arbeitsgemeinschaft Evangelischer Schulbünde e.V., Im Tiergarten 5-7, 57076 Siegen
T: (0271) 72171; Fax: 76597
Focus: Educ 04443

Arbeitsgemeinschaft Fernwärme e.V. (AGFW), Stresemannallee 30, 60596 Frankfurt
T: (069) 63041; Fax: 6304289
Founded: 1971; Members: 381
Focus: Air Cond
Periodical
Fernwärme International: District Heating/Chauffage Urbain (bi-monthly) 04444

Arbeitsgemeinschaft Freier Schulen, Vereinigungen und Verbände gemeinnütziger Schulen in freier Trägerschaft, Am Schlachtensee 2, 14163 Berlin
T: (030) 8012079; Fax: 8022392
Founded: 1951; Members: 10
Pres: Herbert Oehel; Gen Secr: Prof. Dr. Johann Peter Vogel
Focus: Educ 04445

Arbeitsgemeinschaft Friedensforschung und Europäische Sicherheitspolitik e.V. (AFES), Alte Bergsteige 47, 74821 Mosbach
T: (06261) 12912; Fax: 15695
Focus: Poli Sci; Prom Peace 04446

Arbeitsgemeinschaft Friedhof und Denkmal e.V. (AFD), Weinbergstr 25-27, 34117 Kassel
T: (0561) 918930; Fax: 9189310
Focus: Preserv Hist Monuments 04447

Arbeitsgemeinschaft für betriebliche Altersversorgung e.V. (ABA), Postfach 101208, 69002 Heidelberg
T: (06221) 21422, 20619; Fax: 24210
Founded: 1938; Members: 1200
Focus: Soc Sci; Poli Sci
Periodical
Betriebliche Altersversorgung (8 times annually) 04448

Arbeitsgemeinschaft für Jugendhilfe, Haager Weg 44, 53127 Bonn
T: (0228) 910240; Fax: 9102466
Focus: Poli Sci
Periodical
Forum Jugendhilfe (quarterly) 04449

Arbeitsgemeinschaft für juristisches Bibliotheks- und Dokumentationswesen (AJBD), c/o Juristisches Seminar der Universität, Domerschulstr 16, 97070 Würzburg
T: (0931) 312315; E-Mail: Ziegler@bibliothek.uni-wuerzburg.de; Fax: 312317
Founded: 1971; Members: 163
Pres: Dr. Hans-Peter Ziegler
Focus: Libraries & Bk Sci; Doc; Law
Periodical
Recht, Bibliothek, Dokumentation (3 times annually) 04450

Arbeitsgemeinschaft für Kieferchirurgie innerhalb der Deutschen Gesellschaft für Zahn-, Mund- und Kieferheilkunde, Arnold-Heller-Str 16, 24105 Kiel
T: (0431) 5972833
Founded: 1956; Members: 300
Focus: Surgery
Periodical
Deutsche zahnärztliche Zeitschrift (annually) 04451

Arbeitsgemeinschaft für Krebsbekämpfung des Landes Niedersachsen e.V. / Niedersächsische Krebsgesellschaft, Ellernstr 36, 30175 Hannover
T: (0511) 815091
Focus: Cell Biol & Cancer Res 04452

Arbeitsgemeinschaft für Landschaftsentwicklung (AGL), Godesberger Allee 142-148, 53175 Bonn
T: (0228) 8100239
Founded: 1970; Members: 9
Focus: Ecology 04453

Arbeitsgemeinschaft für medizinisches Bibliothekswesen / Joint Association for Medical Librarianship, c/o Boehringer Mannheim GmbH, Zentralbibliothek, Sandhofer Str 116, 68305 Mannheim
T: (0621) 7592376; Fax: 7594419
Focus: Libraries & Bk Sci 04454

Arbeitsgemeinschaft für Osteuropaforschung, Wilhelmstr 36, 72074 Tübingen
Focus: Geography 04455

Arbeitsgemeinschaft für Umweltfragen e.V. (AGU), Matthias-Grünewald-Str 1-3, 53175 Bonn
T: (0228) 375005; Fax: 375515
Focus: Ecology
Periodical
Das Umweltgespräch: Schriftenreihe . . . 04456

Arbeitsgemeinschaft für wirtschaftliche Verwaltung e.V. (AWV), Düsseldorfer Str 40, 65760 Eschborn
T: (06196) 495388; Fax: 496351
Focus: Business Admin
Periodical
AWV-Informationen (monthly) 04457

Arbeitsgemeinschaft für zeitgemässes Bauen e.V., Walkerdamm 17, 24103 Kiel
T: (0431) 63064
Focus: Civil Eng
Periodical
Mitteilungsblätter (3-4 times annually) . . 04458

Arbeitsgemeinschaft Getreideforschung e.V. (AGF) / Association of Cereal Research, Schützenberg 10, 32756 Detmold
T: (05231) 25530; Fax: 20505
Focus: Agri
Periodical
Getreide, Mehl und Brot (bi-monthly) . . 04459

Arbeitsgemeinschaft Grünland und Futterbau in der Gesellschaft für Pflanzenbauwissenschaften, Atzenberger Weg 99, 88326 Aulendorf
T: (07525) 942351; Fax: 942333
Founded: 1957; Members: 100
Pres: Dr. Martin Elsaesser
Focus: Agri 04460

Arbeitsgemeinschaft Hauswirtschaft e.V., Poppelsdorfer Allee 15, 53115 Bonn
T: (0228) 224063; Fax: 210827
Pres: Siglinde Porsch
Focus: Home Econ 04461

Arbeitsgemeinschaft Historischer Kommissionen und Landesgeschichtlicher Institute e.V. / Association of Historic Councils and Regional History Institutes, c/o Johann-Gottfried-Herder-Institut, Gisonenweg 5-7, 35037 Marburg
T: (06421) 1840; Fax: 184139
Founded: 1898; Members: 55
Pres: Prof. Dr. Roderich Schmidt; Gen Secr: Dr. Winfried Irgang
Focus: Hist
Periodical
Mitteilungsblatt (irregularly) 04462

Arbeitsgemeinschaft industrieller Forschungsvereinigungen „Otto von Guericke" e.V., Bayenthalgürtel 23, 50968 Köln
T: (0221) 376800; Fax: 3768027
Founded: 1954; Members: 104
Focus: Eng
Periodical
Akzente, Profile, Innovationen (irregularly) 04463

Arbeitsgemeinschaft Kartoffelforschung e.V., Am Schützenberg 10, 32756 Detmold
T: (05231) 25530; Fax: 20505
Focus: Agri 04464

Arbeitsgemeinschaft kath.-sozialer Bildungswerke in der Bundesrepublik Deutschland (AKSB), Heilsbachstr 6, 53123 Bonn
T: (0228) 645058; Fax: 6420910
Focus: Educ 04465

Arbeitsgemeinschaft katholisch-theologischer Bibliotheken (AKThB), Leostr 21, 33098 Paderborn
T: (05251) 290480; Fax: 282575
Founded: 1947; Members: 139
Focus: Libraries & Bk Sci
Periodical
Mitteilungsblatt (annually) 04466

Arbeitsgemeinschaft Katholischer Fachkrankenhäuser für Suchtkranke, Karlstr 40, 79104 Freiburg
T: (0761) 200368; Fax: 200350
Focus: Rehabil 04467

Arbeitsgemeinschaft Kirchlicher Museen und Schatzkammern, Hinter dem Dom 6, 54290 Trier
T: (0651) 7105233
Focus: Arts; Rel & Theol 04468

Arbeitsgemeinschaft Korrosion e.V., Theodor-Heuss-Allee 25, 60486 Frankfurt
T: (069) 7564209; Fax: 7564201
Members: 26
Focus: Metallurgy
Periodical
Werkstoffe und Korrosion 04469

Arbeitsgemeinschaft Literarischer Gesellschaften e.V. (ALG), Am Sandwerder 5, 14109 Berlin
T: (030) 81699618; Fax: 81699619
Focus: Lit 04470

Arbeitsgemeinschaft Literatur im Deutschen Kulturrat, c/o Archiv für Kulturpolitik, Am Hofgarten 17, 53113 Bonn
T: (0228) 211059; Fax: 217493
Focus: Lit 04471

Arbeitsgemeinschaft Media-Analyse e.V. (AG.MA), Wolfsgangstr 92, 60322 Frankfurt
T: (069) 550391
Focus: Mass Media
Periodical
Media-Analyse (MA) (annually) 04472

Arbeitsgemeinschaft Rosalia Chladek in Deutschland e.V. (ARC-D), Martin-Opitz-Str 9, 13357 Berlin
T: (030) 4656280
Focus: Perf Arts 04473

Arbeitsgemeinschaft Sozialwissenschaftlicher Institute e.V. (ASI), Lennéstr 30, 53113 Bonn
T: (0228) 22810; Fax: 2281120
Founded: 1949; Members: 102
Pres: Prof. Dr. Heinz Sahner; Gen Secr: Matthias Stahl
Focus: Soc Sci
Periodical
Soziale Welt: Zeitschrift für sozialwissenschaftliche Forschung und Praxis (quarterly) 04474

Arbeitsgemeinschaft Spina bifida und Hydrocephalus e.V. (ASbH), Münsterstr 13, 44145 Dortmund
T: (0231) 834777; Fax: 833911
Focus: Physiology
Periodical
ASbH-Brief (quarterly) 04475

Arbeitsgemeinschaft staatlich anerkannter evangelischer Ausbildungsstätten für Altenpflege im DEVA, Bleekstr 20, 30559 Hannover
T: (0511) 5109170
Focus: Educ 04476

Arbeitsgemeinschaft Verstärkte Kunststoffe e. V., Am Hauptbahnhof 10, 60329 Frankfurt
T: (069) 250920; Fax: 250919
Focus: Materials Sci 04477

Arbeitsgemeinschaft Versuchsreaktor (AVR), Auf der Lausward, 40221 Düsseldorf
Focus: Nucl Res 04478

Arbeitsgemeinschaft wildbiologischer und jagdkundlicher Forschungsstätten, c/o Forschungsstelle für Jagdkunde und Wildschadenverhütung des Landes Nordrhein-Westfalen, Forsthaus Hardt, Pützchens Chaussee 228, 53229 Bonn
T: (0228) 482115
Focus: Forestry; Bio 04479

Arbeitsgemeinschaft zur Preußischen Geschichte e.V. (APG), c/o Friedrich-Meinecke-Institut, Habelschwerdter Allee 45, 14195 Berlin
T: (030) 7792448; Fax: 7762213
Focus: Hist 04480

Arbeitsgruppe für strukturelle Molekularbiologie in der Max-Planck-Gesellschaft, Notkerstr 85, 22603 Hamburg
T: (040) 89982801; Fax: 891314
Focus: Bio 04481

Arbeitskreis Bildung und Politik Rheinland, Hauptstr 77, 53424 Remagen
T: (02642) 644
Focus: Educ; Poli Sci 04482

Arbeitskreis Chemische Industrie, Palmstr 17, 50672 Köln
Focus: Chem; Ecology 04483

Arbeitskreis der Musikbildungsstätten in der Bundesrepublik Deutschland, Schloßpl 13, 38304 Wolfenbüttel
T: (05331) 808411; Fax: 808413
Focus: Educ; Music 04484

Arbeitskreis deutscher Bildungsstätten e.V., Haager Weg 44, 53127 Bonn
T: (0228) 910280; Fax: 299030
Focus: Educ; Adult Educ
Periodical
Außerschulische Bildung (quarterly) . . . 04485

Arbeitskreis Entwicklungspolitik e.V. (AKE), Burgstr 1, 32602 Vlotho
T: (05733) 95739; Fax: 18154
Focus: Poli Sci 04486

Arbeitskreis Ethnomedizin, Curschmannstr 33, 20251 Hamburg
Focus: Med; Ethnology
Periodical
Ethnomedizin (semi-annually) 04487

Arbeitskreis für Betriebsführung München (ABM), Waldhaus, 86943 Thaining
T: (08172) 249
Focus: Business Admin 04488

Arbeitskreis für Hochschuldidaktik, Schlüterstr 28, 20146 Hamburg
Focus: Adult Educ 04489

Arbeitskreis für Jugendliteratur e.V. (AKJ), Schlörstr 10, 80634 München
T: (089) 1684052; Fax: 1684066
Focus: Lit 04490

Arbeitskreis für Schulmusik und allgemeine Musikpädagogik e.V., Winterleitenweg 65, 97082 Würzburg
T: (0931) 71315; Fax: 71315
Founded: 1953; Members: 2000
Pres: Prof. Dr. Volker Schütz; Gen Secr: Winfried Noack
Focus: Music; Educ
Periodical
AfS-Magazin (semi-annually) 04491

Arbeitskreis Gesundheitskunde e.V., Feldbergstr 11, 78112 Sankt Georgen
T: (07724) 6148
Focus: Public Health 04492

Arbeitskreis Hauptschule e.V. (AKH), Westfalendamm 247, 44141 Dortmund
T: (0231) 433861/-63; Fax: 433864
Focus: Educ 04493

Arbeitskreis katholischer Schulen in freier Trägerschaft in der Bundesrepublik Deutschland, Kaiserstr 163, 53113 Bonn
T: (0228) 103250, 103255; Fax: 103201
Pres: Dr. Eckhard Nordhofen; Gen Secr: Nikolaus Kircher
Focus: Educ; Rel & Theol
Periodical
Engagement: Zeitschrift für Erziehung und Schule (quarterly) 04494

Arbeitskreis Musikpädagogische Forschung e.V. (AMPF), An der Schule 12, 29342 Wienhausen
T: (05149) 503
Focus: Educ; Music 04495

Arbeitskreis Rhetorik in Wirtschaft, Politik und Verwaltung, Auf dem Steinchen 8, 53127 Bonn-Ippendorf
T: (0228) 281900, 281989; E-Mail: ProfGLANGE@AOL.com; Fax: 281989
Founded: 1987
Pres: Prof. Dr. Gerhard Lange
Focus: Ling 04496

Arbeitskreis Studium populärer Musik e.V. (ASPM), Ahornweg 154, 25469 Halstenbek
T: (04101) 44840
Focus: Music 04497

Arbeitskreis Verkehr und Umwelt e.V. (UMKEHR), Exerzierstr 20, 13357 Berlin
T: (030) 4927473; Fax: 4927972
Focus: Transport; Ecology 04498

Arbeitswissenschaft im Landbau e.V., Fruwirthstr 48, 70539 Stuttgart
T: (0711) 4592816
Founded: 1941; Members: 100
Focus: Agri; Eng; Standards 04499

Arbeo-Gesellschaft e.V., 85777 Bachenhausen
Focus: Hist; Lit 04500

Archäologische Gesellschaft zu Berlin, Podbielskiallee 69-71, 14195 Berlin
T: (030) 830080
Founded: 1842; Members: 240
Pres: Prof. Dr. Adolf H. Borbein; Gen Secr: Dr. Antje Krug
Focus: Archeol
Periodical
Berliner Winckelmannsprogramm (irregularly)
. . . . 04501

Arnold-Bergstraesser-Institut für kulturwissenschaftliche Forschung e.V. / Forschungsinstitut zu Politik und Gesellschaft überseeischer Länder, Windausstr 16, 79110 Freiburg
T: (0761) 85091; E-Mail: abifr@ruf.uni-freiburg.de; Fax: 892967
Founded: 1960; Members: 22
Pres: Prof. Dr. Theodor Hanf; Prof. Dr. Dieter Oberndörfer; Gen Secr: Dr. Heribert Weiland
Focus: Poli Sci; Ethnology; Sociology; Econ
. . . . 04502

Arzneimittelkommission der Deutschen Ärzteschaft, Aachener Str 233-237, 50931 Köln
T: (0221) 4004525/26; Fax: 4004539
Focus: Pharmacol 04503

ASB Management-Zentrum-Heidelberg e.V., Gaisbergstr 11-13, 69115 Heidelberg
T: (06221) 9888; Fax: 988682
Focus: Business Admin
Periodical
ASB-Aktuell (semi-annually) 04504

Association Européenne pour l'Enseignement de l'Architecture (AEEA) / European Association for the Teaching of Architecture, c/o Fachbereich Architektur, Gesamthochschule, Henschelstr 2, 34127 Kassel
Focus: Educ; Archit 04505

Association Internationale des Professeurs de Philosophie (AIPPHi) / International Association of Teachers of Philosophy, Am Schirrhof 11, 32427 Minden
T: (0571) 23474
Founded: 1964
Focus: Philos
Periodical
Bulletin d'Information AIPPHi 04506

Association of European Federations of Agro-Engineers (AEFA), Auf der Helte 23, 53604 Bad Honnef
T: (02224) 6124
Founded: 1974
Focus: Agri 04507

Association of European Geological Societies, c/o Fachbereich 9, Universität Essen, Universitätsstr, 45141 Essen
T: (0201) 1833103; E-Mail: jens.wiegand@uni-essen.de; Fax: 1833101
Gen Secr: Jens Wiegand
Focus: Geology 04508

Astronomische Gesellschaft e.V. (A.G.), c/o Universitäts-Sternwarte, Schillergäßchen 2, 07745 Jena
Founded: 1863; Members: 800
Pres: Prof. Dr. Werner Pfau; Gen Secr: Dr. Reinhard E. Schielicke
Focus: Astronomy
Periodicals
AG Abstract Series (annually)
Mitteilungen der Astronomischen Gesellschaft (annually)
Reviews in Modern Astronomy (annually) 04509

ASUE (Arbeitsgemeinschaft für sparsamen und umweltfreundlichen Energieverbrauch e.V.) (ASUE), Heidenkampsweg 101, 20097 Hamburg
T: (040) 234509; Fax: 23663361
Founded: 1977; Members: 41
Pres: Ulrich Hartmann; Gen Secr: Jörg Christiansen; Klaus Telges
Focus: Energy 04510

ATV (Abwassertechnische Vereinigung e.V.) (ATV), Theodor-Heuss-Allee 17, 53773 Hennef
T: (02242) 8720; E-Mail: 101623.1642@compuserve.com http://www.atv.de; Fax: 872135
Founded: 1948; Members: 13500
Pres: Prof. Hermann H. Hahn; Gen Secr: Dr. Sigurd van Riesen
Focus: Eng
Periodical
Korrespondenz Abwasser (monthly) . . . 04511

Augustin Wibbelt-Gesellschaft e.V. (AWG), Stiftsherrenstr 23, 48143 Münster
T: (0251) 45428
Focus: Lit 04512

Auslandsgesellschaft Nordrhein-Westfalen e.V., Postfach 103334, 44033 Dortmund
T: (0231) 838000; E-Mail: agnw@cww.de; Fax: 8380055
Founded: 1946; Members: 2300
Pres: Jürgen Alexander Fischer; Gen Secr: Günter Löb
Focus: Int'l Relat
Periodical
Brücken (quarterly) 04513

Ausschuss Normenpraxis im DIN Deutsches Institut für Normung e.V. (ANP), Burggrafenstr 6, 10787 Berlin
T: (030) 26012337
Members: 700
Focus: Standards 04514

Autonomes Bildungs-Centrum e.V. (ABC), Bauernreihe 1, 21706 Drochtersen
T: (04775) 529
Focus: Educ 04515

AW produktplanung / Arbeitsgemeinschaft der Wirtschaft für Produktdesign und Produktplanung e.V., Holteyer Str 6, 45289 Essen
T: (0201) 570294
Focus: Graphic & Dec Arts, Design . . 04516

AWV-Fachausschuss Mikrofilm/Optische Informationssysteme, Düsseldorfer Str 40, 65760 Eschborn
T: (06196) 495374
Focus: Doc
Periodical
AWV-Informationen (monthly) 04517

Bach-Verein Köln e.V., Minoritenstr 7, 50667 Köln
T: (0221) 2576663; Fax: 2578468
Founded: 1931; Members: 750
Pres: Ursula Thorn Prikken; Gen Secr: Andreas Braun
Focus: Music 04518

Baden-Württembergischer Sportärzteverband, Bezirksgruppe Süd-Baden, Hugstetter Str 55, 79106 Freiburg
T: (0761) 2011
Focus: Med 04519

Badischer Landesverein für Naturkunde und Naturschutz e.V. (BLNN), Gerberau 32, 79098 Freiburg
T: (0761) 2163325; Fax: 21636717
Founded: 1882; Members: 600
Focus: Ecology
Periodical
Mitteilungen des Badischen Landesvereins für Naturkunde und Naturschutz (annually) . 04520

Baltische Gesellschaft in Deutschland e. V., Titurelstr 9, 81925 München
T: (089) 980542
Founded: 1954; Members: ca. 900
Pres: Dr. Olgred Aule
Focus: Hist; Poli Sci; Cultur Hist
Periodical
Mitteilungen aus Baltischem Leben (quarterly)
. . . . 04521

Bankakademie e.V., Oeder Weg 16-18, 60318 Frankfurt/Main
T: (069) 1540080; Fax: 551461
Founded: 1957; Members: 13
Focus: Finance 04522

Battelle-Institut e.V., Am Römerhof 35, 60486 Frankfurt
T: (069) 79080; Fax: 790880
Founded: 1952
Focus: Nat Sci; Eng
Periodical
Battelle-Information 04523

Bayerische Akademie der Schönen Künste, Max-Joseph-Pl 3, 80539 München
T: (089) 2900770
Founded: 1948; Members: 200
Focus: Arts 04524

Bayerische Akademie der Werbung, Orléansstr 34, 81667 München
T: (089) 48090910; Fax: 48090919
Focus: Advert 04525

Bayerische Akademie der Wissenschaften, Marstallpl 8, 80539 München
T: (089) 230310; Fax: 23031100
Founded: 1759; Members: 286
Pres: Prof. Dr. Dr. Horst Fuhrmann; Gen Secr: Monika Stoermer
Focus: Sci
Periodicals
Abhandlungen und Sitzungsberichte: Mathematisch-Naturwissenschaftliche Klasse (annually)
Abhandlungen und Sitzungsberichte: Philosophisch-Historische Klasse (5-10 times annually)
Jahrbuch (annually) 04526

Bayerische Akademie für Arbeits-, Sozial- und Umweltmedizin, Pfarrstr 3, 80538 München
T: (089) 21840; Fax: 2184226
Founded: 1968
Focus: Med; Hygiene 04527

Bayerische Akademie für Fernsehen e.V. (BAF), Martin-Kollar-Str 13, 81829 München
T: (089) 4274320; Fax: 42743223
Focus: Mass Media 04528

Bayerische Akademie für Naturschutz und Landschaftspflege (ANL), Seethaler Str 6, 83410 Laufen
T: (08682) 89630; Fax: 896317, 1560
Focus: Ecology 04529

Bayerische Botanische Gesellschaft (BBG), Menzinger Str 67, 80638 München
T: (089) 17861264; Fax: 17861193
Founded: 1890; Members: 900
Pres: Dr. W. Lippert
Focus: Botany
Periodical
Berichte (annually) 04530

Bayerische Kommission für die Internationale Erdmessung, Marstallpl 8, 80539 München
T: (089) 23031112, 23031111; E-Mail: a2101aa@bek.badw-muenchen.de; Fax: 23031100
Founded: 1868
Pres: Prof. Dr. Rudolf Sigl
Focus: Surveying 04531

Bayerische Krebsgesellschaft e.V., Tumblinger Str 4, 80337 München
T: (089) 531175, 539524
Founded: 1925
Focus: Cell Biol & Cancer Res
Periodical
Rundschreiben 04532

Bayerische Landesärztekammer, Mühlbaurstr 16, 81677 München
T: (089) 41471
Focus: Med
Periodical
Bayerisches Ärzteblatt (monthly) 04533

Bayerische Landeszahnärztekammer (BLZK), Fallstr 34, 81369 München
T: (089) 724010
Members: 11000
Focus: Dent
Periodical
Bayerisches Zahnärzteblatt (BZB) (monthly) 04534

Bayerische Röntgengesellschaft, c/o Städt. Krankenanstalten, Jakob-Henle-Str 1, 90766 Fürth
Focus: X-Ray Tech 04535

Bayerische Theaterakademie im Prinzregententheater, Prinzregentenpl 12, 81675 München
T: (089) 218502; Fax: 21852813
Focus: Educ 04536

Bayerischer Holzwirtschaftsrat, Prannerstr 9, 80333 München
T: (089) 294561
Focus: Forestry 04537

Bayerischer Landesdenkmalrat, Salvatorstr 2, 80333 München
T: (089) 21862370; Fax: 21862813
Focus: Preserv Hist Monuments 04538

Bayerischer Landesverein für Familienkunde e.V., Ludwigstr 14, 80539 München
Focus: Genealogy
Periodical
Blätter (3 times annually) 04539

Bayerischer Lehrer- und Lehrerinnenverband (BLLV), Bavariaring 37, 80336 München
T: (089) 7210010; E-Mail: sekrlgf@bllv.spacenet.de; Fax: 7250324
Founded: 1861; Members: 55000
Pres: Albin Dannhäuser; Gen Secr: Dr. Dieter Reithmeier
Focus: Educ
Periodical
Bayerische Schule (monthly) 04540

Bayerischer Sportärzteverband e.V., Nymphenburger Str 81, 80636 München
Focus: Med
Periodical
Sportärztliche Mitteilungen (quarterly) . . 04541

Bayerischer Volkshochschulverband e.V., Fäustlestr 5a, 80339 München
T: (089) 510800
Pres: Josef Deimer; Gen Secr: Wilhelm F. Lang
Focus: Adult Educ
Periodical
Das Forum: Zeitschrift der Volkshochschulen in Bayern (quarterly) 04542

Beilstein-Institut für Literatur der Organischen Chemie, Varrentrappstr 40-42, 60486 Frankfurt
T: (069) 7917251; Fax: 7917669
Focus: Chem

Periodical
Beilstein: Handbuch der Organischen Chemie (17 times annually) 04543

Bergbau-Forschung, Franz-Fischer-Weg 61, 45307 Essen
T: (0201) 1051
Focus: Mining 04544

Bergischer Geschichtsverein e. V., Friedrich-Engels-Allee 89-91, 42285 Wuppertal
Focus: Hist
Periodicals
Romerike Berge (quarterly)
Zeitschrift des Bergischen Geschichtsvereins (annually) 04545

Berlin-Brandenburgische Akademie der Wissenschaften, Jägerstr 22-23, 10117 Berlin
T: (030) 20370620; E-Mail: bbaw@bbaw.de; Fax: 20370500
Founded: 1992; Members: 107 ord., 34 außerord., 3 Ehrenmitgl.
Pres: Prof. Dr. Dieter Simon; Gen Secr: Diepold Salvini-Plawen
Focus: Sci 04546

Berliner Arbeitskreis Information, c/o Universitätsbibliothek der TU Berlin, Str des 17. Juni 135, 10623 Berlin
T: (030) 31424429, 31422217; E-Mail: penke@ub.tu-berlin.de; http://es.tu-berlin.de/rbak/; Fax: 31424743
Founded: 1963; Members: 400
Pres: Prof. Dr. Wolfrudolf Laux; Gen Secr: Kurt Penke
Focus: Doc; Computer & Info Sci
Periodical
Weitblick (quarterly) 04547

Berliner Gesellschaft für Anthropologie, Ethnologie und Urgeschichte / Berlin Society for Anthropology, Ethnology and Prehistory, Schloß Charlottenburg, Langhansbau, 14059 Berlin
T: (030) 3209116
Founded: 1869; Members: 285
Pres: Dr. Herbert Ullrich; Gen Secr: Dr. Claudius Müller
Focus: Anthro; Hist; Ethnology
Periodical
Mitteilungen (annually) 04548

Berliner Institut für Lehrerfort- und -weiterbildung und Schulentwicklung, Uhlandstr. 97, 10715 Berlin
T: (030) 86871; Fax: 8687266
Members: 150
Pres: Egbert Jancke
Focus: Educ; Adult Educ 04549

Berliner Mathematische Gesellschaft e.V., Str des 17. Juni 136, 10623 Berlin
Founded: 1899
Focus: Math
Periodical
Sitzungsberichte 04550

Berliner Medizinische Gesellschaft, Fregestr 73, 12159 Berlin
Focus: Med 04551

Berliner Orthopädische Gesellschaft e.V., Clayallee 229-233, 14195 Berlin
T: (030) 3311660; Fax: 810041
Focus: Orthopedics 04552

Berliner Sportärztebund e.V., Forckenbeckstr 20, 14199 Berlin
T: (030) 8232056; Fax: 8238870
Founded: 1950; Members: 510
Focus: Med 04553

Bert Brecht Kreis Augsburg e.V., c/o Staats- u. Stadtbibliothek, Schaetzlerstr 25, 86152 Augsburg
T: (0821) 3242737; Fax: 3242127
Focus: Lit 04554

Berufliche Fortbildungszentren der Bayerischen Arbeitgeberverbände e.V. (bfz), Landshuter Allee 174, 80637 München
T: (089) 159260; Fax: 155128
Focus: Adult Educ 04555

Berufsbildungswerk der Deutschen Versicherungswirtschaft e.V. (BWV), Arabellastr 29, 81925 München
T: (089) 92200130; Fax: 92200144
Focus: Educ; Insurance 04556

Berufsverband der Ärzte für Kinderheilkunde und Jugendmedizin Deutschland e.V., Mielenforster Str 2, 51069 Köln
T: (0221) 689090; Fax: 683204
Members: 9900
Pres: Dr. Wolfgang Meinrenken; Gen Secr: St. Eßer
Focus: Pediatrics
Periodical
der kinderarzt: Zeitschrift für Kinderheilkunde und Jugendmedizin (monthly) 04557

Berufsverband der Ärzte für Orthopädie e.V., Stephanienstr 88, 76133 Karlsruhe
T: (0721) 25820
Members: 2300
Focus: Orthopedics
Periodical
Informationen (bi-monthly) 04558

Berufsverband der Allgemeinärzte Deutschlands - Hausärzteverband - e.V. (BDA), Theodor-Heuss-Ring 14, 50668 Köln
T: (0221) 160670; Fax: 1606735
Founded: 1960; Members: 22000
Pres: Dr. Klaus-Dieter Kossow; Gen Secr: Dieter Robert Adam
Focus: Med
Periodical
Zeitschrift für den Hausarzt (20 times annually) 04559

Berufsverband der Augenärzte Deutschlands e.V. (BVA), Wildenbruchstr 21, 40545 Düsseldorf
T: (0211) 570310; Fax: 579912
Founded: 1950
Focus: Ophthal
Periodical
Der Augenarzt (bi-monthly) 04560

Berufsverband der Berliner Hals-, Nasen-, Ohren-Ärzte, Hohenzollerndamm 91, 14199 Berlin
T: (030) 8262021
Focus: Otorhinolaryngology 04561

Berufsverband der Deutschen Chirurgen (BDC), Wendemuthstr 5, 22041 Hamburg
T: (040) 682059; Fax: 684821
Founded: 1960; Members: 10000
Focus: Surgery
Periodical
Der Chirurg BDC: Informationen des Berufsverbandes der Deutschen Chirurgen (monthly) 04562

Berufsverband der Deutschen Fachärzte für Urologie, Julius-Leber-Str 10, 22765 Hamburg
Founded: 1953
Focus: Urology 04563

Berufsverband der Deutschen Radiologen und Nuklearmediziner e.V., Sonnenstr 3, 80331 München
T: (089) 592690
Focus: Radiology; Nucl Med
Periodicals
Mitglieder-Info (10 times annually)
Röntgenpraxis (monthly) 04564

Berufsverband der Deutschen Urologen e.V., Erdingerstr 17, 84405 Dorfen
T: (08081) 41313
Focus: Urology
Periodical
Der Urologe (bi-monthly) 04565

Berufsverband Deutscher Hörgeschädigtenpädagogen / Berufsverband der Lehrer an Gehörlosen- und Schwerhörigenschulen, Borsteler Chaussee 163, 22453 Hamburg
T: (040) 5537174, 2369730; Fax: 5537174
Founded: 1894
Pres: Christiane Hartmann-Börner
Focus: Educ Handic
Periodicals
Das bunte Blatt (monthly)
Hörgeschädigtenpädagogik (quarterly) . . 04566

Berufsverband Deutscher Nervenärzte e.V. (BVDN), Goethestr 21, 60313 Frankfurt
T: (069) 285974
Members: 1600
Focus: Neurology 04567

Berufsverband Deutscher Psychologinnen und Psychologen e.V., Heilsbachstr 22-24, 53123 Bonn
T: (0228) 987310; Fax: 9873170
Founded: 1946; Members: 22000
Pres: Lothar J. Hellfritsch; Gen Secr: Gerd Pulverich
Focus: Psych
Periodical
Report Psychologie (monthly) 04568

Berufsverband Deutscher Soziologen e.V. (BDS), c/o Institut für Soziologie der FU Berlin, Babelsberger Str 14-16, 10715 Berlin
T: (030) 85002229; Fax: 85002138
Founded: 1976; Members: 600
Pres: Prof. Dr. H. Bücker-Gärtner
Focus: Sociology
Periodical
Sozialwissenschaften und Berufspraxis (quarterly) 04569

Berufsverband Deutscher Yogalehrer e.V. (BDY), Heinrich-Grob-Str 48, 97250 Erlabrunn
T: (09364) 4797; Fax: 7208
Focus: Educ 04570

Berufsverband Geprüfter Graphologen/Psychologen e.V. (BGG/P), Cimbernstr 70c, 81377 München
T: (089) 7145880
Founded: 1952; Members: 85
Focus: Graphology; Psych
Periodical
Angewandte Graphologie und Charakterkunde (3 times annually) 04571

Beta Beta Delta, c/o Fachhochschule für Bibliothekswesen, Wolframstr 32, 70191 Stuttgart
Founded: 1983
Focus: Libraries & Bk Sci 04572

Beton-Verein Berlin e.V., Bundesallee 23, 10717 Berlin
T: (030) 860301
Focus: Materials Sci 04573

Betriebswirtschafts-Akademie e.V. (BWA), Taunusstr 54, 65183 Wiesbaden
T: (06121) 5341
Founded: 1961
Focus: Business Admin 04574

Bettina-von-Arnim-Gesellschaft e.V., Veitstr 24, 13507 Berlin
T: (030) 4345486
Focus: Lit 04575

Bevensen Tagung e.V., Lindenstr 1, 29549 Bad Bevensen
T: (05821) 89151; Fax: 89490
Focus: Lit 04576

Bezirksärztekammer Koblenz, Emil-Schüller-Str 45-47, 56068 Koblenz
T: (0261) 390010
Focus: Med 04577

Bezirksärztekammer Nordwürttemberg (BÄK NW), Jahnstr 32, 70597 Stuttgart
T: (0711) 769810; Fax: 7698139
Founded: 1955; Members: 13600
Pres: Dr. Karl-Heinz Kamp; Gen Secr: Dr. Helmut Paris
Focus: Med
Periodical
Ärzteblatt Baden-Württemberg (monthly) . 04578

Bezirksärztekammer Pfalz, Maximilianstr 22, 67433 Neustadt
T: (06321) 8930
Focus: Med 04579

Bezirksärztekammer Trier, Balduinstr 10-14, 54290 Trier
T: (0651) 45011
Focus: Med 04580

Bezirkszahnärztekammer Koblenz, Bahnhofstr 32, 56068 Koblenz
T: (0261) 36681
Focus: Med 04581

Bezirkszahnärztekammer Pfalz, Brunhildenstr 1, 67059 Ludwigshafen
T: (0621) 519111; Fax: 622972
Focus: Med 04582

Bezirkszahnärztekammer Rheinhessen, Eppichmauergasse 1, 55116 Mainz
T: (06131) 287760; Fax: 225706
Focus: Med 04583

Bezirkszahnärztekammer Trier, Saarstr 52, 54290 Trier
T: (0651) 45150
Focus: Med 04584

Bildung, Begegnung, Zeitgeschehen Bernau e.V. (BBZ), Breitscheidstr 41, 16321 Bernau
T: (03338) 763270; Fax: 764458
Focus: Educ; Poli Sci 04585

Bildungsforum Potsdam e.V., Lindenstr 54, 14467 Potsdam
T: (0331) 77507; Fax: 77507
Focus: Educ 04586

Bildungswerk der Bayerischen Wirtschaft e.V. (bbw), Brienner Str 7, 80333 München
T: (089) 2900260; Fax: 29002655
Focus: Adult Educ 04587

Bildungswerk der Hessischen Wirtschaft e.V. (BWHW), Emil-von-Behring-Str 4, 60439 Frankfurt/Main
T: (069) 958080; Fax: 95808259
Focus: Adult Educ 04588

Bildungswerk der Humanistischen Union NRW e.V., Kronprinzenstr 15, 45128 Essen
T: (0201) 227982; Fax: 235505
Focus: Poli Sci 04589

Bildungswerk der Konrad-Adenauer-Stiftung, Politische Akademie der Konrad-Adenauer-Stiftung, Urfelder Str 221, 50389 Wesseling
T: (02236) 7071
Focus: Poli Sci
Periodical
Eichholzbrief (quarterly) 04590

Bildungswerk der Nordrhein-Westfälischen Wirtschaft e.V., Brunnenstr 24-28, 58332 Schwelm
T: (02336) 40080; Fax: 4008150
Focus: Adult Educ 04591

Bildungswerk der Rheinland-Pfälzischen Wirtschaft e.V. (BWRP), Hölderlinstr 1, 55131 Mainz
T: (06131) 557575; Fax: 557539
Focus: Business Admin 04592

Bildungswerk der Sächsischen Wirtschaft e.V. (bsw), Flügelweg 6, 01157 Dresden
T: (0351) 425020; Fax: 4250250
Focus: Business Admin 04593

Bildungswerk der Thüringer Wirtschaft e.V. (BWTW), Wilhelm-Wolff-Str 6, 99086 Erfurt
T: (0361) 4262717; Fax: 4262777
Focus: Business Admin 04594

Bildungswerk des Instituts für angewandte Kommunikationsforschung in der außerschulischen Bildung e.V. (IKAB), Poppelsdorfer Allee 92, 53115 Bonn
T: (0228) 636460; Fax: 694848
Focus: Comm Sci; Educ 04595

Bildungswerk Rhythmik e.V. (BWR), Loignystr 32, 28211 Bremen
T: (0421) 230452
Focus: Music 04596

Bildungszentrum Tannenfelde, Studien- und Fördergesellschaft der Schleswig-Holsteinischen Wirtschaft e.V. (StFG), Tannenfelde, 24613 Aukrug
T: (04873) 180; Fax: 1888
Focus: Business Admin 04597

Brandenburgischer Volkshochschulverband e.V., Neustädtische Wassertorstr 16-17, 14776 Brandenburg
T: (03381) 522304; Fax: 522304
Focus: Adult Educ 04598

Braunschweigische Wissenschaftliche Gesellschaft (BWG), Fallersleber-Tor-Wall 16, 38100 Braunschweig
T: (0531) 3914596
Founded: 1944; Members: 110
Focus: Sci 04599

Bremer Ausschuss für Wirtschaftsforschung (BAW), Schlachte 10-11, 28195 Bremen
T: (0421) 3978804; Fax: 3978810
Founded: 1947
Pres: Dr. Peter Frankenfeld
Focus: Econ
Periodicals
BAW-Monatsbericht (monthly)
Bremer Zeitschrift für Wirtschaftspolitik (quarterly)
Regionalwirtschaftliche Studien (irregularly) 04600

Bremer Gesellschaft für Wirtschaftsforschung e.V., Am Brill 21-23, 28195 Bremen
T: (0421) 500807
Pres: Prof. Dr. Rolf Stuchtey; Gen Secr: Prof. Dr. Alfons Lemper
Focus: Econ 04601

Bremer Sportärztebund, Horner Str 70, 28203 Bremen
T: (0421) 44925144
Focus: Med 04602

Brüder Grimm-Gesellschaft e.V. (BGG), Brüder-Grimm-Pl 4a, 34117 Kassel
T: (0561) 103235; Fax: 713299
Focus: Lit 04603

Bund demokratischer Wissenschaftlerinnen und Wissenschaftler e.V. (BdWi), Gisselberger Str 7, 35037 Marburg
T: (06421) 21395; Fax: 24654
Focus: Sci 04604

Bund der Freien Waldorfschulen e.V., Heidehofstr 32, 70184 Stuttgart
T: (0711) 210420; Fax: 2104219
Focus: Educ
Periodical
Erziehungskunst (monthly) 04605

Bund Deutscher Architekten (BDA), Ippendorfer Allee 14b, 53127 Bonn
T: (0228) 285011; Fax: 285465
Focus: Archit
Periodical
Der Architekt (monthly) 04606

Bund Deutscher Baumeister, Architekten und Ingenieure (BDB), Kennedyallee 11, 53175 Bonn
T: (0228) 376784; Fax: 376057
Focus: Archit
Periodical
Deutsche Bauzeitung (monthly) 04607

Bund Deutscher Kunsterzieher e.V. (BDK), Jakobistr 40, 30163 Hannover
T: (0511) 662229; Fax: 662229
Pres: Jutta Johannsen
Focus: Arts; Educ
Periodical
BDK-Mitteilungen (quarterly) 04608

Bund deutscher Volksbühnen e.V., Am Handelshof 9, 45127 Essen
T: (0201) 222253
Focus: Perf Arts 04609

Bund Freiheit der Wissenschaft e.V., Elisabethstr 3, 53177 Bonn
T: (0228) 352083; Fax: 358658
Focus: Sci
Periodical
Freiheit der Wissenschaft (quarterly) . . 04610

Bund für Deutsche Schrift und Sprache, Postfach 1110, 26189 Ahlhorn
T: (04435) 1313; Fax: 3623
Founded: 1918
Focus: Lit; Ling
Periodical
Die Deutsche Schrift: Vierteljahreshefte zur Förderung der deutschen Sprache und Schrift (quarterly) 04611

Bund für freie und angewandte Kunst e.V., Herdweg 29, 64285 Darmstadt
T: (06151) 64371
Focus: Arts 04612

Bund für Lebensmittelrecht und Lebensmittelkunde e.V. (BLL), Godesberger Allee 157, 53175 Bonn
T: (0228) 819930; Fax: 375069
Founded: 1955; Members: 500
Focus: Food; Law

Periodical
BLL-Schriftenreihe (irregularly) 04613

Bund für Umwelt und Naturschutz Deutschland e.V. (BUND), Im Rheingarten 7, 53225 Bonn
T: (0228) 400970; Fax: 4009740
Founded: 1975; Members: 220000
Focus: Ecology
Periodical
Natur & Umwelt (quarterly) 04614

Bund für Umwelt und Naturschutz Deutschland, Landesverband Hessen e.V., Kelsterbacher Str 28, 64546 Mörfelden-Walldorf
T: (06105) 44041; Fax: 44691
Focus: Ecology
Periodical
Natur und Umwelt (quarterly) 04615

Bund katholischer Erzieher Deutschlands (BKED), Hedwig-Dransfeld-Pl 4, 45143 Essen
T: (0201) 623029
Focus: Educ 04616

Bund Naturschutz in Bayern e.V., Dr.-Johann-Maier-Str 4, 93049 Regensburg
T: (0941) 297200; Fax: 2972030
Founded: 1913
Pres: Hubert Weinzierl; Gen Secr: Helmut Steininger
Focus: Ecology 04617

Bund Technischer Experten e.V., Busestr 42, 28213 Bremen
T: (0421) 211014/15
Founded: 1924
Focus: Eng 04618

Bundes-Arbeitsgemeinschaft Akademischer Räte in der Bundesrepublik, c/o Institut für Datenverarbeitung, Arcisstr 21, 80333 München
Members: 10000
Focus: Public Admin 04619

Bundesärztekammer (BÄK), Herbert-Lewin-Str 1, 50931 Köln
T: (0221) 40040
Founded: 1947
Focus: Med
Periodicals
Deutsches Ärzteblatt: Publikationsorgan der deutschen Ärzteschaft (weekly)
Medizin Heute: Zeitschrift für Patienten (monthly)
. . . . 04620

Bundesakademie für musikalische Jugendbildung Trossingen, Postfach 1158, 78635 Trossingen
T: (07425) 94930; Fax: 949321
Focus: Music; Educ 04621

Bundesakademie für öffentliche Verwaltung, Deutschherrnstr 93, 53177 Bonn
T: (0228) 331005
Focus: Adult Educ 04622

Bundesarbeitsgemeinschaft der Musikinitiativen e.V. (BA Rock), Emil-Meyer-Str 20, 30165 Hannover
T: (0511) 3504723; Fax: 3504726
Focus: Music 04623

Bundesarbeitsgemeinschaft der Träger psychiatrischer Krankenhäuser, c/o Landschaftsverband Rheinland, Hermann-Pünder-Str 1, 50663 Köln
T: (0221) 8096619; Fax: 8096657
Focus: Psychiatry 04624

Bundesarbeitsgemeinschaft Evangelischer Familien-Bildungsstätten e.V., Deutenbacher Str 1, 90547 Stein
T: (0911) 670460; Fax: 6806177
Focus: Adult Educ 04625

Bundesarbeitsgemeinschaft für Darstellendes Spiel in der Schule e.V., Walter-Kolb-Str 4, 60594 Frankfurt/Main
T: (069) 21232044; Fax: 21232070
Focus: Perf Arts 04626

Bundesarbeitsgemeinschaft für Rehabilitation, Walter-Kolb-Str 9-11, 60594 Frankfurt
T: (069) 6050180
Focus: Rehabil
Periodicals
BAR-REHA-INFO (irregularly)
Die Rehabilitation (quarterly) 04627

Bundesarbeitsgemeinschaft katholischer Familienbildungsstätten, Prinz-Georg-Str 44, 40477 Düsseldorf
T: (0211) 4499245; Fax: 4499259
Founded: 1956; Members: 120
Focus: Adult Educ
Periodical
BAG-Magazin (3 times annually) 04628

Bundesarbeitsgemeinschaft Schule-Wirtschaft, Gustav-Heinemann-Ufer 84-88, 50968 Köln
T: (0221) 4981722, 4981723
Pres: Dr. Roland Delbos; Ullrich Wiethaup; Gen Secr: Hans-Jürgen Brackmann; Marion Hüchtermann
Focus: Educ
Periodical
Schule-Wirtschaft (quarterly) 04629

Bundesarbeitsgemeinschaft Spiel und Theater e.V., Falkenstr 20, 30449 Hannover
T: (0511) 4581799; Fax: 4583105
Focus: Perf Arts 04630

Bundesarbeitsgemeinschaft von Familienbildung und Beratung e.V. (AGEF), Hamburger Str 137, 25337 Elmshorn
T: (04121) 71938; Fax: 787238
Focus: Adult Educ; Family Plan 04631

Bundesarbeitsgemeinschaft zur Förderung haltungsgefährdeter Kinder und Jugendlicher e.V., Fischtorpl 17, 55116 Mainz
T: (06131) 227440
Focus: Orthopedics; Rehabil
Periodical
Haltung und Bewegung (quarterly) . . . 04632

Bundesarbeitskreis der Seminar- und Fachleiter e.V. (BAK), Hebelstr 17, 76698 Ubstadt-Weiher
T: (07251) 63454; Fax: 63454
Focus: Educ 04633

Bundesarchitektenkammer, Königswinterer Str 709, 53227 Bonn
T: (0228) 441051; Fax: 442760
Focus: Archit 04634

Bundesausschuß Betriebswirtschaft (BBW), Düsseldorfer Str 40, 65760 Eschborn
T: (06196) 495255; Fax: 495392
Pres: Dr. Hannspeter Neubert; Gen Secr: Bernhard Feldhaar
Focus: Business Admin 04635

Bundesausschuß der Ärzte und Krankenkassen, Herbert-Lewin-Str 3, 50931 Köln
T: (0221) 40050; Fax: 408039
Focus: Med 04636

Bundeselternvereinigung für anthroposophische Heilpädagogik und Sozialtherapie e.V., Schloßstr 9, 61209 Echzell
T: (06035) 81190; Fax: 81217
Focus: Educ; Therapeutics 04637

Bundesfachgruppe Musikpädagogik e.V., Fürvelser Str 31, 51069 Köln
T: (0221) 683635; Fax: 688718
Focus: Educ; Music 04638

Bundestierärztekammer e.V., Oxfordstr 10, 53111 Bonn
T: (0228) 725460; Fax: 7254666
Members: 31
Pres: Prof. Dr. Günter Pschorn; Gen Secr: Eberhardt Rösener
Focus: Vet Med
Periodical
Deutsches Tierärzteblatt (monthly) . . . 04639

Bundesverband beruflicher Naturschutz (ABN), Konstantinstr 110, 53179 Bonn
T: (02228) 8491116; Fax: 8491200
Founded: 1947; Members: 700
Pres: Prof. Dr. Lothar Finke; Gen Secr: Prof. Dr. Wolfgang Erz
Focus: Ecology
Periodical
Jahrbuch für Naturschutz und Landschaftspflege (semi-annually) 04640

Bundesverband Bildender Künstlerinnen und Künstler (BBK) / Bundesgeschäftsstelle, Weberstr. 61, 53113 Bonn
T: (0228) 216107; Fax: 216105
Members: 15000
Pres: Hans Wilhelm Sotrop; Gen Secr: Dr. Ursula Cramer
Focus: Fine Arts
Periodical
Kulturpolitik (quarterly) 04641

Bundesverband der Apotheker im öffentlichen Dienst e.V. (BApöD), Im Kirschensand 4, 64665 Alsbach
T: (06151) 126242; Fax: 125789
Focus: Pharmacol 04642

Bundesverband der beamteten Tierärzte, Kronacher Str 30, 96215 Lichtenfels
T: (09571) 5676; Fax: 18123
Focus: Vet Med 04643

Bundesverband der Bibliotheken und Museen für Darstellende Künste e.V., Galeriestr 4a, 80539 München
T: (089) 2106910; Fax: 29160789
Focus: Libraries & Bk Sci; Perf Arts . . 04644

Bundesverband der Diplom-Ingenieure Gartenbau und Landespflege e.V. (BDGL), Godesberger Allee 142-148, 53175 Bonn
T: (0228) 376711/12; Fax: 373260
Focus: Hort; Ecology 04645

Bundesverband der freiberuflichen und unabhängigen Sachverständigen für das Kraftfahrzeugwesen e.V. (BVSK), Kantering 57, 53639 Königswinter
T: (02223) 22000
Focus: Auto Eng 04646

Bundesverband der Friedrich-Bödecker-Kreise e.V., Fischtorpl 23, 55116 Mainz
T: (06131) 288900; Fax: 230333
Founded: 1981
Focus: Lit
Periodical
Autoren lesen vor Schülern – Autoren sprechen mit Schülern (irregularly) 04647

Bundesverband der Jugendkunstschulen und Kulturpädagogischen Einrichtungen e.V. (BJkE), Luisenstr 22, 59425 Unna
T: (02303) 69324; Fax: 65057
Focus: Educ; Arts 04648

Bundesverband der Lebensmittelchemiker/innen im öffentlichen Dienst e.V., Rudolfstr 12, 47447 Moers
T: (02841) 61631
Focus: Chem; Nutrition 04649

Bundesverband der Lehrkräfte der russischen Sprache e.V., Birkhofstr 45, 41564 Kaarst
T: (02131) 514073; Fax: 514073
Focus: Educ; Ling 04650

Bundesverband der öffentlichen angestellten und vereidigten Chemiker e.V., Grosse Bleichen 34, 20354 Hamburg
T: (040) 343435, 345210
Focus: Chem 04651

Bundesverband der Pneumologen, Schloßstr 22, 45468 Mülheim
T: (0208) 474608
Focus: Pulmon Dis 04652

Bundesverband der Vertrauens- und Rentenversicherungsärzte, Ubbo-Emmius-Str 2, 26603 Aurich
T: (04941) 2933
Focus: Med 04653

Bundesverband der Zahnärzte des öffentlichen Gesundheitsdienstes e.V. (BZÖG), Krausniekstr 3, 10115 Berlin
T: (030) 2814878
Focus: Dent 04654

Bundesverband Deutscher Ärzte für Mund-Kiefer-Gesichtschirurgie e.V., Harburger Rathausstr 41, 21073 Hamburg
T: (040) 777070; Fax: 779606
Focus: Surgery 04655

Bundesverband Deutscher Autoren e.V. (B.A.), Lehrter Str 69/119, 10557 Berlin
T: (030) 3944697; Fax: 3944697
Focus: Lit 04656

Bundesverband Deutscher Gesangspädagogen, Gellertstr 55, 30175 Hannover
T: (0511) 852437; Fax: 281571
Focus: Educ; Music 04657

Bundesverband Deutscher Privatkrankenanstalten e.V. (BDPK), Bonn-Center, Bundeskanzlerpl 2-10, 53113 Bonn
T: (0228) 211001/02; Fax: 212211
Focus: Med 04658

Bundesverband Deutscher Privatschulen (VDP), Darmstädter Landstr 85a, 60598 Frankfurt am Main
T: (069) 614058; Fax: 626763
Founded: 1946; Members: 480
Pres: Dr. Rainer Köllner; Gen Secr: Christian Lucas
Focus: Educ
Periodical
Freie Bildung und Erziehung (semi-annually)
. . . . 04659

Bundesverband Deutscher Verwaltungs- und Wirtschafts-Akademien e.V. (VWA), Eschersheimer Landstr 230, 60320 Frankfurt/Main
T: (069) 9200670; Fax: 568549
Focus: Public Admin; Law 04660

Bundesverband Evangelischer Erzieherinnen und Sozialpädagoginnen e.V., Kurt-Schumacher-Str 2, 34117 Kassel
T: (0561) 107696; Fax: 107601
Focus: Educ 04661

Bundesverband Freier Theater e.V. (BFT), Museumstr 6, 76437 Rastatt
T: (07222) 37585; Fax: 33770
Focus: Perf Arts 04662

Bundesverband für den Selbstschutz, Deutschherrenstr 93-95, 53177 Bonn
T: (0228) 8401
Focus: Eng
Periodical
Zivilschutz Magazin: Fachzeitschrift für Zivilschutz, Katastrophenschutz und Selbstschutz (monthly)
. . . . 04663

Bundesverband für Tanztherapie Deutschland e.V. (BVT), Hofstr 16, 40789 Monheim
T: (02173) 56573; Fax: 30619
Focus: Therapeutics; Perf Arts 04664

Bundesverband Hilfe für das autistische Kind e.V., Bebelallee 141, 22297 Hamburg
T: (040) 5115604; Fax: 5110813
Focus: Educ Handic; Therapeutics
Periodical
Autismus (semi-annually) 04665

Bundesverband junger Autoren und Autorinnen e.V. (BVjA), Kannenbäckerstr 9, 53340 Meckenheim
T: (02225) 7889; Fax: 7889
Focus: Lit 04666

Bundesverband Katholischer Ingenieure und Wirtschaftler Deutschlands, Bendenweg 101, 53121 Bonn
T: (0228) 9875220; Fax: 9875222
Founded: 1961; Members: 170
Pres: Dr. Max Haneke
Focus: Eng; Econ 04667

Bundesverband Legasthenie e.V., Gneisenaustr 2, 30175 Hannover
T: (0511) 853465; Fax: 858065
Focus: Psych; Educ Handic
Periodical
LRS (quarterly) 04668

Bundesverband Museumspädagogik e.V., c/o Sprengel-Museum, Kurt-Schwitters-Pl, 30169 Hannover
T: (0511) 1683736; Fax: 1685093
Focus: Educ; Arts 04669

Bundesverband Neue Erziehung e.V. (BNE), Am Schützenhof 4, 53119 Bonn
T: (0228) 6640; Fax: 667793
Focus: Educ 04670

Bundesverband Rhythmische Erziehung e.V., Küppelstein 34, 42857 Remscheid
T: (02191) 794257; Fax: 794389
Focus: Educ; Music 04671

Bundesverband Solarenergie e.V. (BSE), Kruppstr 5, 45128 Essen
T: (0201) 1223006; Fax: 1215143
Focus: Energy 04672

Bundesverband Theaterpädagogik e.V. (BUT), Genter Str 23, 50672 Köln
T: (0221) 9521093/94; Fax: 9521095
Focus: Educ; Perf Arts 04673

Bundesverband unabhängiger deutscher Sicherheitsberater und -Ingenieure e.V., Dörpfeldstr 12, 12489 Berlin
T: (030) 6718840/41; Fax: 67198842
Focus: Eng 04674

Bundesverband wissenschaftlicher Vogelschutz e.V. (BWV), Olshausenstr 40, 24118 Kiel
T: (0431) 8804502; Fax: 8801389
Focus: Ornithology; Ecology 04675

Bundesverein der Bibliotheks-Assistenten/innen und anderer Mitarbeiter/innen an Bibliotheken e.V. (BBA e.V.), c/o Bibliothek des Deutschen Wetterdienstes, Frankfurter Str 135, 63067 Offenbach
T: (069) 80622273; Fax: 80622486
Members: 600
Pres: Sabine Rust
Focus: Libraries & Bk Sci 04676

Bundesvereinigung der Oberstudiendirektoren, Bundes-Direktoren-Konferenz (BDK), Pelzacker 4a, 79194 Gundelfingen
T: (0761) 580176; Fax: 589184
Focus: Educ 04677

Bundesvereinigung Deutscher Bibliotheksverbände e.V. (BDB), c/o Prof. Birgit Dankert, Fachbereich Bibliothek, Fachhochschule Hamburg, Grindelhof 30, 20146 Hamburg
Focus: Libraries & Bk Sci 04678

Bundesvereinigung Deutscher Blas- und Volksmusikverbände e.V. (BDBV), König-Karl-Str 13, 70372 Stuttgart
T: (0711) 552523; Fax: 568397
Focus: Music 04679

Bundesvereinigung für Gesundheit e.V., Heilsbachstr 30, 53123 Bonn
T: (0228) 987270; Fax: 6420024
Founded: 1954; Members: 260
Pres: Dr. Hans-Peter Voigt; Gen Secr: Dr. Uwe Primel-Philippsen
Focus: Public Health
Periodical
Gesundheits-Informations-Dienst (irregularly) 04680

Bundesvereinigung Kulturelle Jugendbildung e.V., Küppelstein 34, 42857 Remscheid
T: (02191) 794390; E-Mail: info@bkj.de;
Fax: 794389
Founded: 1963; Members: 48 Verbände & Institutionen
Pres: Dr. Max Fuchs; Gen Secr: Hildegard Bockhorst
Focus: Educ 04681

Bundesvereinigung Lebenshilfe für geistig Behinderte e.V., Raiffeisenstr 18, 35043 Marburg
T: (06421) 43007/09
Focus: Educ Handic
Periodical
Die Lebenshilfe-Zeitung (bi-monthly) . . . 04682

Bundesvereinigung Logistik e.V. (BVL), Schlachte 31, 28195 Bremen
T: (0421) 173840; Fax: 167800
Members: 2700
Pres: Dr. Hanspeter Stabenau; Gen Secr: Manfred Schaar
Focus: Econ; Marketing
Periodical
Logistik Heute (10 times annually) . . . 04683

Bundeszahnärztekammer (BDZ), Universitätsstr 71, 50931 Köln
T: (0221) 40010; Fax: 404035
Founded: 1953; Members: 17
Pres: Dr. Fritz-Josef Willmes; Gen Secr: Dr. Detlef Schulze-Wilk
Focus: Dent
Periodical
Zahnärztliche Mitteilungen (bi-weekly) . . 04684

Carl-Cranz-Gesellschaft e.V. / Gesellschaft für technisch-wissenschaftliche Weiterbildung, Postfach 1112, 82234 Weßling
T: (08153) 28413; Fax: 281345
Founded: 1961
Focus: Eng; Adult Educ 04685

Carl Duisberg Gesellschaft e.V., Weyerstr 79-83, 50676 Köln
T: (0221) 20980; Fax: 2098111
Founded: 1949; Members: 1000
Focus: Sci
Periodicals
Carl Duisberg Forum (quarterly)
Echo aus Deutschland (bi-monthly) . . . 04686

Carl Einstein Gesellschaft, Universitätsstr 30, 95447 Bayreuth
T: (09209) 16378; Fax: 553641
Focus: Lit 04687

Carl-Zuckmayer-Gesellschaft Mainz e.V., Schillerstr 11, 55299 Nackenheim
T: (06135) 2835
Focus: Lit 04688

Catholic Media Council / Publizistische Medienplanung für Entwicklungsländer e.V., Anton-Kurze-Allee 2, 52074 Aachen
T: (0241) 73081; E-Mail: cameco@compuserve.com; Fax: 73462
Founded: 1969
Focus: Journalism; Mass Media; Develop Areas
Periodical
Mediaforum (quarterly) 04689

CENELEC Electronic Components Committee (CECC), Gartenstr 179, 60596 Frankfurt
T: (069) 639171; Fax: 639427
Founded: 1970
Focus: Electronic Eng 04690

Center for International Research on Economic Tendency Surveys (CIRET), Poschingerstr 5, 81679 München
T: (089) 92241; Fax: 985369
Founded: 1969
Focus: Econ 04691

Chopin-Gesellschaft in der Bundesrepublik Deutschland e.V., Kasinostr 3, 64293 Darmstadt
T: (06151) 25957, 55897
Focus: Music 04692

Clara Viebig-Gesellschaft e.V., Clara-Viebig-Str 1, 56864 Bad Bertrich
T: (02674) 1506; Fax: 1507
Focus: Lit 04693

Claudius-Gesellschaft e.V., Pappelweg 24a, 22949 Ammersbek
T: (04102) 59595
Focus: Lit 04694

Collegium Carolinum e.V., Hochstr 8, 81669 München
T: (089) 4488393; Fax: 486196
Focus: Hist 04695

Confederation of European Laryngectomees, Luisenstr 20, 36179 Bebra
Focus: Otorhinolaryngology 04696

Conference of Baltic Oceanographers (CBO), c/o Institut für Meereskunde, Universität Kiel, Düsternbrooker Weg 20, 24105 Kiel
T: (0431) 5971
Founded: 1957
Focus: Oceanography 04697

Conseil International des Associations de Bibliothèques de Théologie, Postfach 250104, 50517 Köln
T: (0221) 3382110; Fax: 3382103
Founded: 1961; Members: 12
Pres: Dr. André Geuns; Gen Secr: Dr. Isolde Dumke
Focus: Libraries & Bk Sci 04698

Cusanus-Institut, Domfreihof 3, 54290 Trier
T: (0651) 99415401
Founded: 1960; Members: 230
Pres: Prof. Dr. Klaus Kremer; Prof. Dr. Klaus Reinhardt
Focus: Philos; Law; Rel & Theol
Periodicals
Kleine Schriften der Cusanus-Gesellschaft
Mitteilungen und Forschungsbeiträge der Cusanus-Gesellschaft 04699

Dachverband Psychosozialer Hilfsvereinigungen e.V., Graurheindorfer Str 15, 53111 Bonn
T: (0228) 631548
Focus: Rehabil; Psych; Therapeutics . . 04700

Dachverband wissenschaftlicher Gesellschaften der Agrar-, Forst-, Ernährungs-, Veterinär- und Umweltforschung e.V., Eschborner Landstr 122, 60489 Frankfurt
T: (069) 24788104; Fax: 24788110
Founded: 1973; Members: 28
Focus: Ecology; Vet Med; Agri; Nutrition; Forestry
Periodicals
Agrarspectrum (irregularly)
Agrarspectrum: Schriftenreihe 04701

Dauthendey-Gesellschaft, Otto-Hahn-Str 136, 97218 Gerbrunn
T: (0931) 708040
Focus: Lit 04702

Design Zentrum Nordrhein-Westfalen e.V., Hindenburgstr 25-27, 45127 Essen
T: (0201) 820210; Fax: 231903
Founded: 1954
Focus: Graphic & Dec Arts, Design . . 04703

Deutsch-Pazifische Gesellschaft e.V. (DPG)/German Pacific Society (GPS) (DPG), c/o Dr. Dr. F. Steinbach, Feichtmayrstr 25, 80992 München
T: (089) 151158; E-Mail: dr.friedrich.steinbauer@ibm.net; //or steinld@ibm.net; Fax: 151833
Founded: 1974; Members: 400
Pres: Dr. F. Steinbauer
Focus: Int'l Relat
Periodical
Bulletins: Informationshefte (quarterly) . . 04704

Deutsche Akademie der Darstellenden Künste e.V., Siesmayerstr 61, 60323 Frankfurt/Main
T: (069) 745428; Fax: 745428
Focus: Perf Arts 04705

Deutsche Akademie der Naturforscher Leopoldina, August-Bebel-Str 50a, 06108 Halle
T: (0345) 2025014; Fax: 2021727
Founded: 1652; Members: 1000
Focus: Nat Sci; Med
Periodicals
Acta Historica Leopoldina: Abhandlungen aus dem Archiv für Geschichte der Naturforschung und Medizin der Deutschen Akademie der Naturforscher Leopoldina (irregularly)
Informationen (semi-annually)
Leopoldina: Mitteilungen der Deutschen Akademie der Naturforscher Leopoldina, Reihe 3 (annually)
Nova Acta Leopoldina: Abhandlungen der Deutschen Akademie der Naturforscher Leopoldina (irregularly) 04706

Deutsche Akademie des Tanzes e.V., Gleißbühlstr 12, 90402 Nürnberg
T: (0911) 9923999; Fax: 468584
Focus: Perf Arts 04707

Deutsche Akademie für Kinder- und Jugendliteratur e.V., Hauptstr 42, 97332 Würzburg
T: (0931) 4355
Founded: 1976; Members: 30
Focus: Lit
Periodical
Volkacher Bote: Mitteilungsblatt 04708

Deutsche Akademie für Landeskunde e.V., Senckenberganlage 36, 60325 Frankfurt/Main
T: (069) 79822404/416; Fax: 79828173
Focus: Geography 04709

Deutsche Akademie für medizinische Fortbildung, Schöne Aussicht 2, 34117 Kassel
Focus: Med; Adult Educ 04710

Deutsche Akademie für Nuklearmedizin, Karl-Wiechert-Allee 9, 30625 Hannover
Founded: 1968; Members: 80
Focus: Nucl Med 04711

Deutsche Akademie für Sprache und Dichtung e.V., Alexandraweg 23, 64287 Darmstadt
T: (06151) 40920; Fax: 409299
Founded: 1949; Members: 134
Focus: Ling; Lit
Periodical
Jahrbuch der Deutschen Akademie (annually) 04712

Deutsche Akademie für Städtebau und Landesplanung, Kurfürstendamm 188, 10707 Berlin
T: (030) 8854936; Fax: 8854936
Founded: 1922; Members: 450
Focus: Urban Plan
Periodical
Mitteilungen (semi-annually) 04713

Deutsche Alzheimer Gesellschaft e.V., Büchsenstr 34-36, 70174 Stuttgart
T: (0711) 2268598; Fax: 2268519
Focus: Neurology 04714

Deutsche Anwalt-Akademie (DAA), Ellerstr 48, 53119 Bonn
T: (0228) 9836677; Fax: 9836666
Focus: Law 04715

Deutsche Arbeitsgemeinschaft für Paradontologie, Bäckerstr 102, 38640 Goslar
Focus: Dent 04716

Deutsche Arbeitsgemeinschaft Genealogischer Verbände e.V., c/o Nordrhein-Westfälisches Personenstandsarchiv Rheinland, Schloßstr 12, 50321 Brühl
T: (02232) 42948; Fax: 42948
Focus: Genealogy
Periodical
Genealogie (quarterly) 04717

Deutsche Botanische Gesellschaft e.V., Untere Karspüle 2, 37073 Göttingen
T: (0551) 33347
Founded: 1882
Focus: Botany
Periodical
Botanica Acta: Berichte der Deutschen Botanischen Gesellschaft (3 times annually) 04718

Deutsche Bunsen-Gesellschaft für Physikalische Chemie e.V. (DBG), Varrentrappstr 40-42, 60486 Frankfurt
T: (069) 7917201; E-Mail: H.Behret@gdch.de; Fax: 7917450
Founded: 1894; Members: 1800
Pres: Dr. K. Nothnagel; Gen Secr: Dr. Heinz Behret
Focus: Chem
Periodical
Berichte der Bunsen-Gesellschaft für Physikalische Chemie: An International Journal of Physical Chemistry (monthly) 04719

Deutsche Burgenvereinigung e.V. (DBV), Marksburg, 56338 Braubach
T: (02627) 536; Fax: 8866
Focus: Preserv Hist Monuments; Archit . 04720

Deutsche Chopin-Gesellschaft e.V., Wilhelm-Külz-Str 16, 03046 Cottbus
T: (0355) 702637; Fax: 702637
Focus: Music 04721

Deutsche Dante-Gesellschaft e.V. (DDG), Finkensteig 13, 39110 Magdeburg
T: (0391) 7218246
Focus: Lit 04722

Deutsche Dekane- und Abteilungsleiterkonferenz für Architektur, Raumplanung und Landschaftsarchitektur (DARL), Schloßwender Str 1, 30159 Hannover
T: (0511) 7622117, 413121; Fax: 233492
Focus: Archit; Urban Plan 04723

Deutsche Dendrologische Gesellschaft, Hünstollenstr 32, 37136 Waake
T: (05507) 91389; Fax: 91388
Founded: 1892
Focus: Forestry
Periodical
Mitteilungen (annually) 04724

Deutsche Dermatologische Gesellschaft, Schittenhelmstr 7, 24105 Kiel
Founded: 1888
Focus: Derm 04725

Deutsche Diabetes-Gesellschaft, c/o Diabetesklinik, Wielandstr 23, 32445 Bad Oeynhausen
T: (05731) 9702
Members: 685
Focus: Diabetes
Periodical
Diabetologie-Informationen (quarterly) . . 04726

Deutsche Dostojewskij-Gesellschaft e.V., Breite Str 159, 22767 Hamburg
T: (040) 388689; Fax: 388689
Focus: Lit 04727

Deutsche EEG-Gesellschaft, Wissmannstr 1a, 14193 Berlin
Founded: 1950; Members: 1200
Focus: Med; Neurology 04728

Deutsche Elektrotechnische Kommission im DIN und VDE (DKE), Stresemannallee 15, 60596 Frankfurt
T: (069) 63080; Fax: 6312925
Founded: 1970
Focus: Electric Eng; Standards
Periodicals
DIN-Mitteilungen + elektronorm (monthly)
Elektrotechnische Zeitschrift (bi-weekly) . 04729

Deutsche Epilepsievereinigung e.V. (DE), Zillestr 102, 10585 Berlin
T: (030) 3424414; Fax: 3424466
Focus: Neurology 04730

Deutsche Evangelische Arbeitsgemeinschaft für Erwachsenenbildung e.V. (DEAE), Schillerstr 58, 76135 Karlsruhe
T: (0721) 849016; Fax: 853527
Focus: Adult Educ 04731

Deutsche Exlibris Gesellschaft e.V., Am Löwentor 46, 56075 Koblenz
T: (0261) 57885; Fax: 57885
Founded: 1891
Pres: Dr. Gernot Blum; Gen Secr: Birgit Göbel
Focus: Libraries & Bk Sci
Periodicals
Jahrbuch für Exlibriskunst und Graphik (annually)
Mitteilungen (3 times annually) 04732

Deutsche farbwissenschaftliche Gesellschaft e.V. (DfwG), Unter den Eichen 87, 12203 Berlin
T: (030) 81045400, 81045409
Founded: 1974; Members: 200
Focus: Materials Sci 04733

Deutsche Film- und Fernsehakademie Berlin, Heerstr 18-20, 14052 Berlin
T: (030) 3009050; Fax: 30090461
Focus: Cinema 04734

Deutsche Forschungs- und Versuchsanstalt für Luft- und Raumfahrt e.V. / German Aerospace Research Establishment, Linder Höhe, 51147 Köln
T: (02203) 6010; Fax: 67310
Founded: 1969; Members: 130
Focus: Aero
Periodicals
DFVLR-Forschungsberichte (irregularly)
DFVLR-Mitteilungen (irregularly)
DFVLR-Nachrichten (irregularly)
Wissenschaftliche Berichte der Forschungsbereiche
Zeitschrift für Flugwissenschaften und Weltraumforschung (bi-monthly) 04735

Deutsche Forschungsgemeinschaft (DFG), Kennedyallee 40, 53175 Bonn
T: (0228) 8851; Fax: 8852777
Founded: 1951; Members: 87
Pres: Prof. Dr. Wolfgang Frühwald; Gen Secr: Dr. Reinhard Grunwald
Focus: Sci
Periodicals
Forschung (quarterly)
German Research (3 times annually) . . 04736

Deutsche Forschungsgesellschaft für Oberflächenbehandlung e.V., Adersstr 94, 40215 Düsseldorf
T: (0211) 370457; Fax: 370459
Founded: 1949; Members: 170
Pres: Dr. K.W. Thomer; Gen Secr: Helmut Vesper
Focus: Eng 04737

Deutsche Ganghofer-Gesellschaft e.V. (DGG), Königsberger Str 10, 87600 Kaufbeuren
T: (08341) 18033, 94765; Fax: 74042
Focus: Lit 04738

Deutsche Gartenbauwissenschaftliche Gesellschaft e.V., Herrenhäuser Str 2, 30419 Hannover
T: (0511) 7622638; E-Mail: dgg@gem.uni-hannover.d400.de; Fax: 7623606
Founded: 1961; Members: 390
Pres: Prof. Dr. M. Schenk; Gen Secr: Dr. A. Fricke
Focus: Hort 04739

Deutsche Gemmologische Gesellschaft e.V. / Deutsche Gesellschaft für Edelsteinkunde / Gemmological Association of Germany, Professor-Schlossmacher-Str 1, 55743 Idar-Oberstein
T: (06781) 43011; Fax: 41616
Founded: 1932; Members: ca. 1900
Pres: Prof.Dr. Hermann Bank; Gen Secr: Dr. Ulrich Henn
Focus: Mineralogy
Periodical
Gemmologie: Zeitschrift der Deutschen Gemmologischen Gesellschaft (quarterly) . 04740

Deutsche Geodätische Kommission (DGK), Marstallpl 8, 80539 München
T: (089) 23031113; Fax: 23031100
Founded: 1952; Members: 34
Focus: Surveying; Cart 04741

Deutsche Geologische Gesellschaft (D.G.G.), Postfach 510153, 30631 Hannover
T: (0511) 6432507; Fax: 6432304
Founded: 1848; Members: 2700
Pres: Prof. Dr. Peter Neumann-Mahlkau
Focus: Geology
Periodicals
Nachrichten Deutsche Geologische Gesellschaft (quarterly)
Zeitschrift der Deutschen Geologischen Gesellschaft (quarterly) 04742

Deutsche Geophysikalische Gesellschaft e.V. (DGG), Corrensstr 24, 48149 Münster
T: (0251) 834733; Fax: 838397
Founded: 1922; Members: 880
Focus: Geophys
Periodicals
Geophysical Journal International (monthly)
Mitteilungen (quarterly) 04743

Deutsche Gesellschaft für Aesthetische Medizin, Augustenburger Pl 1, 13353 Berlin
Focus: Med 04744

Deutsche Gesellschaft für Agrarrecht / Vereinigung für Agrar- und Umweltrecht e.V., Postfach 1969, 53009 Bonn
T: (0228) 703140; Fax: 703498
Founded: 1964; Members: 500
Pres: Prof. Dr. Hans-Joachim Hötzel; Gen Secr: Marianne May
Focus: Law; Agri
Periodical
Agrarrecht: Zeitschrift für das gesamte Recht der Landwirtschaft, der Agrarmärkte und des ländlichen Raumes (monthly) 04745

Deutsche Gesellschaft für Allergie- und Immunitätsforschung, c/o BG-Kliniken Bergmannsheil, Gilsingstr 14, 44789 Bochum
Founded: 1951
Focus: Immunology
Periodical
Allergo Journal (bi-monthly) 04746

Deutsche Gesellschaft für Allergieforschung, Liebermeisterstr 8, 72076 Tübingen
Focus: Immunology 04747

Deutsche Gesellschaft für allgemeine und angewandte Entomologie e.V. (DGaaE), c/o Biologische Bundesanstalt, Institut für Pflanzenschutz im Obstbau, Schwabenheimerstr 101, 69221 Dossenheim
Founded: 1976; Members: 900
Pres: Prof. Dr. E. Dickler; Gen Secr: Dr. Heidrun Vogt
Focus: Entomology
Periodical
Mitteilungen der Deutschen Gesellschaft für allgemeine und angewandte Entomologie (annually) 04748

Deutsche Gesellschaft für Alternative Medizin e.V. (DGAM), Landschaftsstr 2, 30926 Seelze
T: (05137) 5272; Fax: 5272
Focus: Med 04749

Deutsche Gesellschaft für Amerikastudien e.V. (DGfA), c/o Institut für Anglistik und Amerikanistik, Gimritzer Damm 2, 06099 Halle/Saale
T: (0345) 5523511; Fax: 5527044
Founded: 1953; Members: 504
Focus: Ethnology
Periodical
Amerikastudien/American Studies: Vierteljahresschrift (quarterly) 04750

Deutsche Gesellschaft für Anästhesiologie und Intensivmedizin (DGAI) / German Society of Anaesthesiology and Intensive Medicine, Roritzerstr 27, 90419 Nürnberg
T: (0911) 933780; Fax: 3938195
Founded: 1953; Members: 8500
Pres: Prof. Dr. Gunter Hempelmann; Gen Secr: Prof. Dr. Klaus van Ackern
Focus: Anesthetics; Med
Periodical
Anästhesiologie und Intensivmedizin (monthly) 04751

Deutsche Gesellschaft für Analytische Psychologie e.V. (DGAP), Wedellstr 16-18, 12247 Berlin
T: (030) 7745561
Founded: 1961; Members: 350
Focus: Psych; Psychoan
Periodical
Analytische Psychologie (quarterly) . . . 04752

Deutsche Gesellschaft für angewandte Optik e.V. (DGaO), c/o Carl Zeiss, Oberkochen, 73446 Oberkochen
T: (07364) 203428; E-Mail: merkle@zeiss.de; Fax: 204601
Founded: 1923; Members: 683
Pres: Dr. F. Merkle; Gen Secr: Prof. Dr. T. Tschudi
Focus: Optics
Periodical
Optik (monthly) 04753

Deutsche Gesellschaft für Angiologie, c/o Medizinische Klinik, Hirschlandstr 97, 73730 Esslingen
T: (07365) 31031
Founded: 1971; Members: 400
Focus: Hematology 04754

Deutsche Gesellschaft für Arbeitsmedizin e.V., Pfarrstr 3, 80538 München
T: (089) 2184259/60
Members: 720
Focus: Hygiene 04755

Deutsche Gesellschaft für Asienkunde e.V. / German Association for Asian Studies, Rothenbaumchaussee 32, 20148 Hamburg
T: (040) 445891
Founded: 1967; Members: 735
Pres: Dr. Christian Schwarz-Schilling
Focus: Ethnology; Poli Sci; Econ; Arts
Periodical
Asien: Deutsche Zeitschrift für Politik, Wirtschaft und Kultur (quarterly) 04756

Deutsche Gesellschaft für Auswärtige Politik e.V. (DGAP), Adenauerallee 131, 53113 Bonn
T: (0228) 26750; Fax: 2675173
Founded: 1955; Members: 1600
Pres: Dr. Werner Lamby
Focus: Poli Sci
Periodical
Internationale Politik: Europa-Archiv (monthly) 04757

Deutsche Gesellschaft für Baukybernetik e.V (DGBK), Riemenschneiderstr 9, 37603 Holzminden
T: (05531) 4040
Focus: Civil Eng; Cybernetics
Periodical
Bauen mit Kopf (bi-annually) 04758

Deutsche Gesellschaft für Baurecht e.V., Kettenhofweg 126, 60325 Frankfurt/Main
T: (069) 748893; Fax: 7411775
Members: 550
Focus: Law 04759

Deutsche Gesellschaft für Biomedizinische Technik e.V., Markgrafenstr 11, 10969 Berlin
T: (030) 25375237, 2537520; E-Mail: DGBMT.BLN@T-Online.de; Fax: 2517248
Founded: 1961; Members: ca. 600
Focus: Eng; Med; Bio
Periodical
Biomedizinische Technik: Biomedical Engineering (10 times annually) 04760

Deutsche Gesellschaft für Biophysik, c/o Fakultät für Physik, Technische Universität München, James-Franck-Str, 85748 Garching
T: (089) 32092552
Founded: 1961
Focus: Biophys 04761

Deutsche Gesellschaft für Bluttransfusion und Immunhämatologie e.V., Sandhofstr 1, 60528 Frankfurt
T: (069) 6782283, 6782204
Focus: Hematology
Periodical
Blut (monthly) 04762

Deutsche Gesellschaft für Chemisches Apparatewesen, Chemische Technik und Biotechnologie e.V. (DECHEMA), Theodor-Heuss-Allee 25, 60486 Frankfurt
T: (069) 75640; E-Mail: info@dechema.de; Fax: 7564201
Founded: 1926; Members: 4100
Pres: Prof. Dr. Dr. Utz-Hellmuth Felcht; Gen Secr: Prof. Dr. Gerhard Kreysa
Focus: Eng
Periodicals
Biotechnology: Apparatus, Plant and Equipment (monthly)
Chemie-Ingenieur-Technik (monthly)
Current Biotechnology (monthly)
Environmental and Safety Technology (monthly)
Materialwissenschaft und Werkstofftechnik: Journal of Materials Technology and Testing (monthly)
Process and Chemical Engineering (monthly)
Theoretical Chemical Engineering (monthly)
Werkstoffe und Korrosion: Materials and Corrosion (monthly) 04763

Deutsche Gesellschaft für Christliche Kunst e.V., Wittelsbacherpl 2, 80333 München
T: (089) 282548; Fax: 288645
Founded: 1893; Members: 900
Focus: Arts
Periodical
Hefte der Deutschen Gesellschaft für christliche Kunst (annually) 04764

Deutsche Gesellschaft für Chronometrie e.V. (DGC), Ziehrerweg 8, 71254 Ditzingen
T: (07156) 951640; Fax: 951640
Founded: 1949; Members: 750
Pres: Prof. Dr. Friedrich Assmus
Focus: Eng; Electronic Eng; Astronomy
Periodical
DGC-Mitteilungen (quarterly) 04765

Deutsche Gesellschaft für das Badewesen e.V. (DGfdB), Postfach 340201, 45074 Essen
T: (0201) 879690; Fax: 8796920
Founded: 1899
Pres: Felix Zimmermann; Gen Secr: Friedrich R. Kunze
Focus: Public Health
Periodical
Archiv des Badewesens (monthly) . . . 04766

Deutsche Gesellschaft für die Bekämpfung der Muskelkrankheiten e.V., Rennerstr 4, 79106 Freiburg
T: (0761) 277932, 278024; Fax: 281043
Focus: Pathology
Periodical
Muskelreport (quarterly) 04767

Deutsche Gesellschaft für die Erforschung des 18. Jahrhunderts (DGEJ), Schloßplatz 4, 38304 Wolfenbüttel
T: (05331) 808202; Fax: 808266
Focus: Hist 04768

Deutsche Gesellschaft für die Vereinten Nationen e.V., Poppelsdorfer Allee 55, 53115 Bonn
T: (0228) 213646; Fax: 217492
Focus: Poli Sci
Periodical
Vereinte Nationen (bi-monthly) 04769

Deutsche Gesellschaft für Dokumentation e.V. (DGD), Ostbahnhofstr 13, 60314 Frankfurt/Main
T: (069) 430313; Fax: 4909096
Founded: 1948; Members: 1800
Focus: Doc
Periodicals
DGD-Newsletter (bi-monthly)
Nachrichten für Dokumentation (bi-monthly)
OLBG-INFO (bi-monthly) 04770

Deutsche Gesellschaft für Dynamische Psychiatrie (DGDP), Geiselgasteigstr 203, 81545 München
T: (089) 644017
Founded: 1980
Focus: Psychiatry 04771

Deutsche Gesellschaft für Eisenbahngeschichte e.V. (DGEG), Kleinsorgenring 14, 59457 Werl
T: (02922) 84970; Fax: 84970
Focus: Hist 04772

Deutsche Gesellschaft für Elektroakustische Musik e.V., Treuchtlinger Str 8, 10779 Berlin
T: (030) 2185960; Fax: 2139816
Focus: Music 04773

Deutsche Gesellschaft für Elektronenmikroskopie e.V. (DGE), c/o Fritz-Haber-Institut der Max-Planck-Gesellschaft, Faradayweg 4-6, 14195 Berlin
Founded: 1949; Members: 750
Focus: Nat Sci
Periodical
Elektronenmikroskopie (semi-annually) . . 04774

Deutsche Gesellschaft für Endokrinologie, Postfach 650311, 14129 Berlin
T: (030) 4685802; Fax: 46916614
Founded: 1953; Members: 1200
Focus: Endocrinology
Periodical
Endokrinologie-Informationen (bi-monthly) . 04775

Deutsche Gesellschaft für Erd- und Grundbau e.V. (DGEG), Kronprinzenstr 35A, 45128 Essen
T: (0201) 227677
Founded: 1951; Members: 950
Focus: Civil Eng
Periodicals
Dokumentation für Bodenmechanik, Grundbau, Felsmechanik, Ingenieurgeologie
Geotechnical Abstracts (monthly)
Geotechnik (quarterly) 04776

Deutsche Gesellschaft für Ernährung e.V. (DGE), Feldbergstr 28, 60323 Frankfurt
T: (069) 9714060; Fax: 97140699
Founded: 1953; Members: 2000
Focus: Nutrition
Periodical
Ernährungs-Umschau: Organ der DGE (monthly) 04777

Deutsche Gesellschaft für Erziehungswissenschaft (DGfE), c/o Fachbereich Erziehungswissenschaft, Freie Universität, Arnimallee 10, 14195 Berlin
T: (030) 8385295; Fax: 8385889
Founded: 1963; Members: 1400
Focus: Educ
Periodicals
Arbeitsberichte (bi-annually)
Tagungsberichte 04778

Deutsche Gesellschaft für Fettwissenschaft e.V., Soester Str 13, 48155 Münster
T: (0251) 64745
Founded: 1935
Focus: Materials Sci
Periodical
Fett-Wissenschaft, Technologie (14 times annually) 04779

Deutsche Gesellschaft für Film- und Fernsehforschung, Willroiderstr 6, 81545 München
T: (089) 646948
Focus: Cinema 04780

Deutsche Gesellschaft für Filmdokumentation, Traubenstr 9, 65207 Wiesbaden
Focus: Cinema; Doc 04781

Deutsche Gesellschaft für Forschung im Graphischen Gewerbe, Brunnerstr 2, 80804 München
Founded: 1951
Focus: Eng 04782

Deutsche Gesellschaft für Galvano- und Oberflächentechnik e.V. (DGO), Horionpl 6, 40213 Düsseldorf
T: (0211) 132381; Fax: 327199
Founded: 1961; Members: 1800
Pres: Willi Metzger; Gen Secr: Dr. H.-P. Wilbert
Focus: Eng 04783

Deutsche Gesellschaft für Gartenkunst und Landschaftspflege e.V. (DGGL), Wartburgstr 42, 10823 Berlin
T: (030) 7881125; Fax: 7874337
Focus: Hort; Ecology
Periodical
Garten und Landschaft (monthly) 04784

Deutsche Gesellschaft für Geographie (DGfG) (DGfG), c/o Fach Geographie im FB 6, Universität Duisburg, Lotharstr 65, 47048 Duisburg
T: (0203) 3792250, 3792909; E-Mail: hh227wo@unidui.uni-duisburg.de; Fax: 3793516
Pres: Prof. Dr. Hans Heinrich Blotevogel; Gen Secr: Dr. Gerald Wood
Focus: Geography 04785

Deutsche Gesellschaft für Gerontologie und Geriatrie, c/o Medizinische Universität, Ratzeburger Allee 160, 23538 Lübeck
T: (0451) 5002400; Fax: 5006518
Founded: 1992; Members: 1100
Pres: Prof. Dr. Rudolf-M. Schütz
Focus: Geriatrics 04786

Deutsche Gesellschaft für Geschichte der Medizin, Naturwissenschaft und Technik e.V., c/o Institut für Philosophie, Universitätsstr 31, 93040 Regensburg
T: (0941) 9433659
Founded: 1901; Members: 701
Focus: Cultur Hist; Med; Nat Sci; Eng
Periodical
Nachrichtenblatt (3 times annually) . . . 04787

Deutsche Gesellschaft für Geschlechtserziehung e.V. (DGG), Olshausenstr 75, 24118 Kiel
T: (0431) 8801256
Focus: Educ 04788

Deutsche Gesellschaft für Gesetzgebung e.V. (DGG), Schlüterstr 28, 20146 Hamburg
T: (040) 41233023; Fax: 447854
Focus: Law 04789

Deutsche Gesellschaft für Gesundheitsvorsorge e.V. (DGGV), Driescher Hecke 19, 51375 Leverkusen
T: (0214) 56744
Founded: 1968; Members: 800
Focus: Public Health 04790

Deutsche Gesellschaft für Gynäkologie und Geburtshilfe, c/o Städtisches Marienkrankenhaus, Mariahilfbergweg 7, 92224 Amberg
Founded: 1885
Focus: Gynecology 04791

Deutsche Gesellschaft für Hämatologie und Onkologie e.V., c/o Medizinische Klinik III, Klinikum Großhadern, Marchioninistr 15, 81377 München
T: (089) 70956403
Members: 580
Focus: Hematology; Cell Biol & Cancer Res
Periodicals
Ann. Haemat. (monthly)
Onkologie (bi-monthly) 04792

Deutsche Gesellschaft für Hals-Nasen-Ohren-Heilkunde, Kopf- und Hals-Chirurgie, Hittorfstr 7, 53129 Bonn
T: (0228) 231770; Fax: 239325
Founded: 1922; Members: 3500
Pres: Prof. Dr. Wolfgang Steiner; Gen Secr: Prof. Dr. Henning Hildmann
Focus: Surgery; Otorhinolaryngology
Periodical
HNO-Informationen (quarterly) 04793

Deutsche Gesellschaft für Heereskunde e.V. (DGfHK), Goethestr 18, 76532 Baden-Baden
Founded: 1898; Members: 1100
Focus: Military Sci
Periodical
Zeitschrift für Heereskunde: Wissenschaftliches Organ für die Kulturgeschichte der Streitkräfte, ihrer Bekleidung, Bewaffnung und Ausrüstung, für heeresmuseale Nachrichten und Sammler-Mitteilungen (quarterly) 04794

Deutsche Gesellschaft für Herpetologie und Terrarienkunde e.V. (DGHT), Postfach 1421, 53351 Rheinbach
T: (02255) 950106; Fax: 1726
Founded: 1964; Members: 6700
Pres: Ingo Pauler
Focus: Zoology
Periodicals
elaphe (quarterly)
Salamandra: Zeitschrift für Herpetologie und Terrarienkunde (quarterly) 04795

Deutsche Gesellschaft für Holzforschung e.V. (DGfH), Schwanthalerstr 79, 80336 München
T: (089) 5389057; Fax: 531657
Founded: 1942; Members: 600
Focus: Forestry
Periodicals
DGfH-Nachrichten
Informationsdienste Holz der Entwicklungsgemeinschaft Holzbau in der DGfH
Merkhefte
Mitteilungshefte 04796

Deutsche Gesellschaft für Hopfenforschung e.V. (DGfH), Hüll 5 1/3, 85283 Wolnzach
T: (08442) 3597; Fax: 2871
Founded: 1926; Members: 150
Pres: Georg Balk; Gen Secr: Hermann Schlicker
Focus: Agri
Periodical
Forschungsberichte (annually) 04797

Deutsche Gesellschaft für Hydrokultur e.V., Kurt-Schumacher-Str 36, 45699 Herten
Focus: Hydrology 04798

Deutsche Gesellschaft für Hygiene und Mikrobiologie e.V. (DGHM), c/o Hygiene-Institut, Universität, Im Neuenheimer Feld 324, 69120 Heidelberg
T: (06221) 568310; E-Mail: Hans-Guenther Sonntag@krzmail.krz-heidelberg.de; Fax: 565857
Founded: 1906; Members: 1700
Pres: Prof. Dr. J. Hacker; Gen Secr: Prof. Dr. Hans-G. Sonntag
Focus: Microbio; Hygiene 04799

Deutsche Gesellschaft für Immunologie e.V., c/o Behringwerke AG, Emil-von-Behring-Str 76, 35041 Marburg
T: (06421) 392338; Fax: 394663
Founded: 1968; Members: 1460
Pres: Prof. Dr. Günter J. Hämmerling; Gen Secr: Dr. Friedrich R. Seiler
Focus: Immunology 04800

Deutsche Gesellschaft für Innere Medizin, Humboldtstr 14, 65189 Wiesbaden
T: (0611) 307946; Fax: 378260
Founded: 1882; Members: 4000
Focus: Intern Med
Periodical
Supplement der Medizinischen Klinik (annually) 04801

Deutsche Gesellschaft für Internistische Intensivmedizin, Rübenkamp 148, 22307 Hamburg
Members: 950
Focus: Intern Med 04802

Deutsche Gesellschaft für Kardiologie – Herz- und Kreislaufforschung, c/o Institut für Experimentelle Chirurgie, Heinrich-Heine-Universität Düsseldorf, Universitätsstr 1, 40225 Düsseldorf
T: (0211) 8115255; E-Mail: dgk@uni-duesseldorf.de http://www.uni-duesseldorf.de/WWW/DGK/; Fax: 8113550
Founded: 1927; Members: 3500
Pres: Prof. Dr. P. Hanrath; Gen Secr: Prof. Dr. G. Arnold

Focus: Cardiol
Periodical
Zeitschrift für Kardiologie (annually) . . . 04803

Deutsche Gesellschaft für Kartographie (D.G.f.K.), Karlstr 6, 80333 München
T: (089) 12652619; Fax: 12652698
Founded: 1950; Members: 2300
Focus: Cart
Periodical
Kartographische Nachrichten (bi-monthly) . 04804

Deutsche Gesellschaft für Kieferorthopädie e.V., c/o Poliklinik für Kieferorthopädie, Poliklinik für Kiefernorthopädie, Im Neuenheimer Feld 400, 69120 Heidelberg
T: (06221) 566560; Fax: 565753
Founded: 1907; Members: 2000
Pres: Prof. Dr. Gerda Komposch; Gen Secr: Dr. Oscar Paur
Focus: Dent
Periodical
Fortschritte der Kieferorthopädie: Journal of Orofacial Orthopedics (bi-monthly) . . . 04805

Deutsche Gesellschaft für Kinder- und Jugendpsychiatrie und Psychotherapie e.V., Hans-Sachs-Str 6, 35039 Marburg
T: (06421) 6258; Fax: 8975
Founded: 1950; Members: 680
Pres: Prof. Dr. Michael Scholz; Gen Secr: Prof. Dr. Andreas Warnke
Focus: Psychiatry
Periodical
Zeitschrift für Kinder- und Jugendpsychiatrie und Psychotherapie 04806

Deutsche Gesellschaft für Kinderheilkunde, c/o Kinderklinik, Medizinische Hochschule, Konstanty-Gutschow-Str 8, 30625 Hannover
T: (0511) 5323212
Founded: 1883; Members: 6000
Focus: Pediatrics
Periodical
Monatsschrift für Kinderheilkunde (monthly) 04807

Deutsche Gesellschaft für Kommunikationsforschung, Willroider Str 6, 81545 München
T: (089) 646948
Focus: Comm Sci 04808

Deutsche Gesellschaft für Laboratoriumsmedizin e.V., Witzelstr 63, 40225 Düsseldorf
T: (0211) 340556; Fax: 341930
Members: 600
Focus: Med 04809

Deutsche Gesellschaft für Lichtforschung, Hochstädter Landstr 23, 63454 Hanau
Founded: 1927
Focus: Physics 04810

Deutsche Gesellschaft für Logistik e.V. (DGFL), Joseph-von-Fraunhofer-Str 20, 44227 Dortmund
T: (0231) 9700121
Founded: 1973; Members: 1000
Pres: Dr. Wolfgang Zwillich; Gen Secr: Dr. Jörg Breker
Focus: Marketing; Econ
Periodical
Logistik Spektrum: Logistik in Industrie, Handel und Dienstleistung (quarterly) 04811

Deutsche Gesellschaft für Luft- und Raumfahrt e.V. (DGLR), Godesberger Allee 70, 53175 Bonn
T: (0228) 376726; Fax: 374755
Founded: 1968; Members: 3500
Focus: Aero
Periodical
Luft- und Raumfahrt (bi-monthly) 04812

Deutsche Gesellschaft für Luft- und Raumfahrtmedizin e.V. (DGLRM), c/o Abt. Neurologie, Bundeswehrkrankenhaus, Oberer Eselsberg, 89081 Ulm
T: (0731) 1712060
Founded: 1961
Focus: Med 04813

Deutsche Gesellschaft für Lungenkrankheiten und Tuberkulose, Hugstetter Str 55, 79106 Freiburg
Focus: Pulmon Dis 04814

Deutsche Gesellschaft für Manuelle Medizin e.V., Heerstr 162, 56154 Boppard
T: (06742) 5917
Founded: 1953; Members: 1300
Focus: Med 04815

Deutsche Gesellschaft für Materialkunde e.V. (DGM), Hamburger Allee 26, 60486 Frankfurt
T: (069) 7917750; E-Mail: ma@mail.dgm.mcs.de; Fax: 7917733
Founded: 1919; Members: 3200
Pres: Prof. Dr. F. Jeglitsch; Gen Secr: Dr. P.P. Schepp
Focus: Metallurgy
Periodicals
DGM-Aktuell (semi-annually)
Zeitschrift für Metallkunde (monthly) . . 04816

Deutsche Gesellschaft für Medizinische Informatik, Biometrie und Epidemiologie (GMDS), Herbert-Lewin-Str 1, 50931 Köln
T: (0221) 4004865
Founded: 1955; Members: 1370
Pres: Prof. Dr. Karl-Heinz Jöckel; Gen Secr: Thomas Banasiewicz
Focus: Doc; Med; Stats
Periodical
Mitteilungsblatt der GMDS (3 times annually) 04817

Deutsche Gesellschaft für Medizinische Soziologie, Am Hochsträß 8, 89081 Ulm
T: (0731) 1762927; Fax: 1762038
Focus: Sociology
Periodical
Medizinsoziologie (semi-annually) 04818

Deutsche Gesellschaft für Missionswissenschaft (DGMW), Kisselgasse 1, 69117 Heidelberg
T: (06221) 543308
Founded: 1918; Members: 128
Focus: Rel & Theol 04819

Deutsche Gesellschaft für Moor- und Torfkunde e.V. / German Society for Bog and Peat Research, Alfred-Bentz-Haus, Stilleweg 2, 30655 Hannover
T: (0511) 6432241; Fax: 6432304
Founded: 1970; Members: 320
Pres: Prof. Dr. J.-D. Becker-Platen
Focus: Geology
Periodical
TELMA 04820

Deutsche Gesellschaft für Mund-, Kiefer- und Gesichtschirurgie (DGMKG), c/o Klinik und Poliklinik für Mund-, Kiefer- und Gesichtschirurgie, Welschnonnenstr 17, 53111 Bonn
T: (0228) 2872452; Fax: 2872604
Founded: 1951; Members: 600
Pres: Prof. Dr. Dr. Jürgen Reuther; Gen Secr: Prof. Dr. Dr. Rudolf H. Reich
Focus: Surgery
Periodical
Mund-, Kiefer- und Gesichtschirurgie (bi-monthly) 04821

Deutsche Gesellschaft für Musik des Orients e.V., Arnimallee 23-27, 14195 Berlin
T: (030) 8301241
Focus: Music 04822

Deutsche Gesellschaft für Musiktherapie e.V. (DGMT), Weichselstr 48, 12045 Berlin
T: (030) 6247364; Fax: 6247489
Focus: Therapeutics; Music 04823

Deutsche Gesellschaft für Neurochirurgie, Hufelandstr 55, 45147 Essen
Founded: 1950; Members: 244
Focus: Surgery 04824

Deutsche Gesellschaft für Neurologie, Josef-Schneider-Str 11, 97080 Würzburg
Founded: 1906
Focus: Neurology 04825

Deutsche Gesellschaft für Neuropathologie und Neuroanatomie e.V., c/o Institut für Neuropathologie der Universität, Thalkirchner Str 36, 80337 München
Focus: Neurology 04826

Deutsche Gesellschaft für Neuroradiologie, Josef-Schneider-Str. 11, 97080 Würzburg
Focus: Radiology 04827

Deutsche Gesellschaft für Nuklearmedizin, Hugstetter Str 55, 79106 Freiburg
T: (0761) 2703913; Fax: 2703930
Founded: 1963; Members: 1150
Pres: Prof. Dr. Dr. E. Moser; Gen Secr: Dr. Th. Krause
Focus: Nucl Med
Periodical
Nuklearmedizin (8 times annually) . . . 04828

Deutsche Gesellschaft für Orthopädie und Traumatologie e.V. (DGOT), Marienburgstr 2, 60528 Frankfurt/Main
T: (069) 6705377; Fax: 6705376
Founded: 1901
Pres: Prof. Dr. R. Kotz; Gen Secr: Prof. Dr. H. Cotta
Focus: Orthopedics
Periodical
Mitteilungsblatt der Deutschen Gesellschaft für Orthopädie und Traumatologie (quarterly) 04829

Deutsche Gesellschaft für Ortung und Navigation e.V. (DGON), Pempelforter Str 47, 40211 Düsseldorf
T: (0211) 369909; Fax: 351645
Founded: 1951; Members: 165
Focus: Navig
Periodical
Ortung und Navigation (3 times annually) 04830

Deutsche Gesellschaft für Osteuropakunde e.V. (DGO), Schaperstr 30, 10719 Berlin
T: (030) 21478412; E-Mail: dgo@zedat.fu-berlin.de; Fax: 21478414
Founded: 1913; Members: 800
Pres: Dr. Otto Wolff von Amerongen; Gen Secr: Dr. Thomas Bremer
Periodicals
Osteuropa (monthly)
Osteuropa-Recht (quarterly)
Osteuropa-Wirtschaft (quarterly) 04831

Deutsche Gesellschaft für Parasitologie e.V. (DGP), c/o Behringwerke AG, Postfach 1140, 35001 Marburg
T: (06421) 392606; Fax: 394757
Founded: 1961; Members: 628
Focus: Med; Vet Med; Zoology 04832

Deutsche Gesellschaft für Parodontologie (DGP), Sierichstr 60, 22301 Hamburg
T: (040) 2793335
Founded: 1925; Members: 1980
Focus: Dent
Periodical
DGP-Nachrichten (quarterly) 04833

Deutsche Gesellschaft für Pathologie, c/o Senckenbergisches Zentrum der Pathologie der Universität, Theodor-Stern-Kai 7, 60596 Frankfurt
T: (069) 63015364
Founded: 1897; Members: 950
Focus: Pathology 04834

Deutsche Gesellschaft für Perinatale Medizin, c/o Frauenklinik, Pulsstr 4, 14059 Berlin
T: (030) 6253081
Focus: Gynecology
Periodical
Perinatal-Medizin (semi-annually) 04835

Deutsche Gesellschaft für Personalführung e.V., Niederkasseler Lohweg 16, 40547 Düsseldorf
T: (0211) 59780; Fax: 5978199
Focus: Business Admin 04836

Deutsche Gesellschaft für Pharmakologie und Toxikologie, Postfach 4119, 64271 Darmstadt
T: (06151) 722592; Fax: 713314
Members: 2200
Focus: Pharmacol; Toxicology
Periodical
Naunyn-Schmiedeberg's Archive of Pharmacology (monthly) 04837

Deutsche Gesellschaft für Phlebologie, c/o Allergie- und Hautklinik, Lippestr 9-11, 26548 Norderney
T: (04932) 805404; Fax: 805200
Founded: 1953; Members: 1200
Focus: Physiology; Pathology; Gastroenter
Periodical
Phlebologie und Proktologie (3 times annually) 04838

Deutsche Gesellschaft für Photogrammetrie und Fernerkundung e.V., c/o Fachgebiet Photogrammetrie und Kartographie, TU Berlin, Straße des 17. Juni 135, 10623 Berlin
T: (030) 31423331; E-Mail: zephir@fpk.tu-berlin.de; Fax: 31421104
Founded: 1909; Members: 880
Pres: Prof. Dr. Jörg Albertz
Focus: Surveying
Periodical
Photogrammetrie-Fernerkundung-Geoinformation (bi-monthly) 04839

Deutsche Gesellschaft für Photographie e.V. (DGPh), Rheingasse 8-12, 50676 Köln
T: (0221) 2402037; Fax: 2402035
Founded: 1951; Members: 700
Focus: Photo
Periodical
DGPh Intern (quarterly) 04840

Deutsche Gesellschaft für Physikalische Medizin und Rehabilitation, K.-Gutschow-Str 8, 30625 Hannover
Focus: Rehabil; Physiology; Physical Therapy
Periodical
Zeitschrift Physikalische Medizin, Rehabilitationsmedizin, Kurortmedizin (bi-monthly) 04841

Deutsche Gesellschaft für Pilzkunde, Kaiserstr 2, 76131 Karlsruhe
Founded: 1921
Focus: Botany, Specific 04842

Deutsche Gesellschaft für Plastische und Wiederherstellende Chirurgie e.V., c/o Diakoniekrankenhaus, Elise-Averdieck-Str 17, 27342 Rotenburg
T: (04261) 772127; Fax: 772128
Founded: 1961; Members: 427
Focus: Surgery 04843

Deutsche Gesellschaft für Pneumologie (DGP), c/o Pneumologische Klinik, Waldhof Elgershausen, 35753 Greifenstein
T: (06449) 927261; Fax: 927399
Pres: Prof. Dr. R. Dierkesmann; Gen Secr: Prof. Dr. H. Morr
Focus: Pulmon Dis
Periodical
Pneumologie (monthly) 04844

Deutsche Gesellschaft für Poesie- und Bibliotherapie e.V. (DGPB), Alteburger Str 7, 50678 Köln
Focus: Therapeutics 04845

Deutsche Gesellschaft für Polarforschung (DeGePo), Columbusstr, 27568 Bremerhaven
T: (0471) 4831210
Founded: 1936; Members: 370
Focus: Geography; Geology; Geophys; Bio
Periodical
Polarforschung (semi-annually) 04846

Deutsche Gesellschaft für Psychiatrie und Nervenheilkunde e.V. (DGPN), Joseph-Stelzmann-Str 9, 50931 Köln
T: (0221) 4786357; Fax: 4786398
Founded: 1842; Members: 1100
Focus: Neurology; Psychiatry
Periodicals
Nervenarzt
Spektrum 04847

Deutsche Gesellschaft für Psychologie e.V. (DGfPs), c/o Psychologisches Institut IV, Fliednerstr 21, 48149 Münster
T: (0251) 834153; Fax: 838319
Founded: 1904; Members: 1500
Focus: Psych
Periodical
Psychologische Rundschau (quarterly) . . 04848

Deutsche Gesellschaft für Psychosomatische Medizin e.V. (DGPM), Geiselgasteigstr 203, 81545 München
T: (089) 641016
Focus: Psychiatry; Neurology; Psych . . 04849

Deutsche Gesellschaft für Publizistik- und Kommunikationswissenschaft e.V., c/o Prof. Dr. Günter Bentele, Institut für Kommunikationswissenschaft und Medienwissenschaft, Augustuspl 9, 04109 Leipzig
T: (0341) 9735730; E-Mail: beutele@rz.uni-leipzig.de; Fax: 9735748
Founded: 1963; Members: 500
Pres: Prof. Dr. Günter Beutele
Focus: Journalism; Sociology; Comm Sci
Periodical
Aviso: Informationsdienst der Deutschen Gesellschaft für Publizistik- und Kommunikationswissenschaft (3 times annually) 04850

Deutsche Gesellschaft für Qualität e.V. (DGQ), Kurhessenstr 95, 60431 Frankfurt
T: (069) 520128
Focus: Materials Sci
Periodical
Qualität und Zuverlässigkeit: Zeitschrift für industrielle Qualitätssicherung (monthly) . 04851

Deutsche Gesellschaft für Qualitätsforschung (Pflanzliche Nahrungsmittel) e.V. (DGQ), c/o Lehrstuhl für Obstbau, TU Weihenstephan, 85354 Freising
T: (08161) 713753; Fax: 714499
Founded: 1955
Pres: Dr. D. Treutter; Gen Secr: Dr. J. Habben
Focus: Botany
Periodical
Proceedings der Jahreskongresse (annually) 04852

Deutsche Gesellschaft für Rechtsmedizin, Melatengürtel 60-62, 50823 Köln
T: (0221) 4784280; Fax: 4784261
Founded: 1904; Members: 400
Focus: Forensic Med
Periodical
Zeitschrift für Rechtsmedizin: Journal of Legal Medicine (quarterly) 04853

Deutsche Gesellschaft für Rheumatologie e.V., c/o Rheumaklinik, 24576 Bad Bramstedt
Founded: 1927; Members: 657
Focus: Rheuma
Periodical
Zeitschrift für Rheumatologie (bi-monthly) 04854

Deutsche Gesellschaft für Säugetierkunde e.V., c/o Universität Osnabrück, FB Biologie/Chemie, Barbarastr 11, 49069 Osnabrück
T: (0541) 9692847; E-Mail: schro@fuchs.biologie.uni-osnabrueck.de; Fax: 9692862
Founded: 1926; Members: 650
Pres: Prof. Dr. Hans Erkert; Gen Secr: Prof. Dr. Rüdiger Schröpfer
Focus: Zoology
Periodical
Zeitschrift für Säugetierkunde: International Journal of Mammalian Biology (bi-monthly) . . . 04855

Deutsche Gesellschaft für Sexualforschung e.V. (DGfS), c/o Sexualberatungsstelle der Abteilung für Sexualforschung, Universität, Poppenhusenstr 12, 22305 Hamburg
Founded: 1950; Members: 220
Focus: Psych
Periodical
Beiträge zur Sexualforschung 04856

Deutsche Gesellschaft für Sonnenenergie e.V. (DGS), Augustenstr 79, 80333 München
T: (089) 524071
Members: 6000
Focus: Energy
Periodical
Sonnenenergie (bi-monthly) 04857

Deutsche Gesellschaft für Soziale Psychiatrie e.V. (DGSP), Stuppstr 14, 50823 Köln
T: (0221) 511002; Fax: 529903
Founded: 1970; Members: 2700
Pres: Ruth Vogel; Gen Secr: Richard Suhre
Focus: Psychiatry
Periodical
Soziale Psychiatrie (quarterly) 04858

Deutsche Gesellschaft für Sozialmedizin und Prävention e.V., Overbergstr 17, 44801 Bochum
T: (0234) 7004868; Fax: 7007922
Founded: 1964; Members: 400
Focus: Hygiene
Periodical
Sozial- und Präventivmedizin (bi-monthly) 04859

Deutsche Gesellschaft für Sozialpädiatrie und Jugendmedizin e.V. (DGSP), Heiglhofstr 63, 81377 München
T: (089) 71009232, 71009233; Fax: 71009248
Founded: 1909; Members: 2203
Pres: Prof. Dr. Hubertus von Voss
Focus: Pediatrics 04860

Deutsche Gesellschaft für Soziologie, c/o Universität, Schloss, 68163 Mannheim
Focus: Sociology
Periodical
Soziologie (semi-annually) 04861

Deutsche Gesellschaft für Sprach- und Stimmheilkunde, Kardinal-von-Galen-Ring 10, 48149 Münster
Founded: 1925
Focus: Logopedy 04862

Deutsche Gesellschaft für Sprachheilpädagogik e.V. (DGS), Goldammerstr 34, 12351 Berlin
T: (030) 6616004; Fax: 6616024
Founded: 1927; Members: 6000
Pres: Kurt Bielfeld; Gen Secr: Volker Maihack
Focus: Logopedy
Periodical
Die Sprachheilarbeit (bi-monthly) 04863

Deutsche Gesellschaft für Sprachwissenschaft / German Society for Linguistics, c/o Philosophische Fakultät, Universität Passau, Innstr 40, 94030 Passau
Founded: 1978; Members: 800
Focus: Ling
Periodicals
Bulletin (semi-annually)
Zeitschrift für Sprachwissenschaft (semi-annually) 04864

Deutsche Gesellschaft für Sprechwissenschaft und Sprecherziehung e.V. (DGSS), Goethestr 8, 69115 Heidelberg
T: (06221) 29548; Fax: 29548
Founded: 1920; Members: 360
Focus: Ling; Educ 04865

Deutsche Gesellschaft für Suchtforschung und Suchttherapie e.V., Wilhelmstr 125, 59067 Hamm
T: (02381) 417998; Fax: 417999
Pres: Prof. Dr. Karl-Artur Kovar; Gen Secr: Edit Göcke
Focus: Public Health; Educ; Sociology; Psych; Med
Periodical
Sucht: Zeitschrift für Wissenschaft und Praxis 04866

Deutsche Gesellschaft für Tanztherapie (DGT), Königsberger Str 60, 50259 Puhlheim
T: (02234) 83008; Fax: 83008
Focus: Educ; Perf Arts 04867

Deutsche Gesellschaft für Technische Zusammenarbeit (GTZ), Dag-Hammarskjöld-Weg 1-5, 65726 Eschborn
T: (06196) 790; E-Mail: Internet: http://www.gtz.de; Fax: 791115
Founded: 1975; Members: Inlandsmitarbeiter: 1297 Auslandsmitarbeiter: 1586
Pres: Gerold Dieke; Dr. Bernd Eisenblätter; Dr. Hans-Dietrich Pallmann; Gen Secr: Wighard Härdtl
Focus: Eng; Develop Areas
Periodicals
Akzente (quarterly)
Gate (quarterly) 04868

Deutsche Gesellschaft für Thorax-, Herz- und Gefässchirurgie, c/o Kerckhoff-Institut, Parkstr 1, 61231 Bad Nauheim
Founded: 1971; Members: 700
Pres: Prof. Dr. M. Polonius; Gen Secr: Prof. Dr. K. H. Leitz
Focus: Surgery
Periodical
The Thoracic and Cardiovascular Surgeon (monthly) 04869

Deutsche Gesellschaft für Umwelterziehung e.V. (DGU), Frauenthal 25, 20149 Hamburg
T: (040) 4106921; Fax: 456129
Focus: Ecology; Educ 04870

Deutsche Gesellschaft für Unfallheilkunde e.V., Theodor-Stern-Kai 7, 60596 Frankfurt
Focus: Surgery
Periodical
Unfallheilkunde: Traumatology (monthly) . 04871

Deutsche Gesellschaft für Urologie, Humboldtstr 5, 30169 Hannover
Focus: Urology 04872

Deutsche Gesellschaft für Verdauungs- und Stoffwechselkrankheiten, c/o Medizinische Hochschule Hannover (6810), Carl-Neuberg-Str 1, 30625 Hannover
T: (0511) 5324237; E-Mail: manns.michael@mh-hannover.de; Fax: 5324896
Founded: 1913; Members: 2177
Pres: Prof. Dr. J.F. (1997) Riemann; Prof. Dr. U. (1998) Fölsch; Gen Secr: Prof. Dr. M.P. Manns
Focus: Intern Med
Periodical
Zeitschrift für Gastroenterologie, Endoscopy (monthly) 04873

Deutsche Gesellschaft für Verhaltenstherapie e.V. (DGVT), Postfach 1343, 72003 Tübingen
T: (07071) 41211
Founded: 1968
Focus: Therapeutics
Periodical
Verhaltenstherapie und Psychosoziale Praxis (quarterly) 04874

Deutsche Gesellschaft für Versicherungsmathematik e.V., Komödienstr 44, 50667 Köln
T: (0221) 9125540; Fax: 91255444
Founded: 1944; Members: 1300
Pres: Dr. Martin Balleer; Gen Secr: Klaus Allerdissen
Focus: Insurance
Periodical
Blätter (semi-annually) 04875

Deutsche Gesellschaft für Völkerkunde e.V. (DGV), Schaumainkai 35, 60594 Frankfurt/M., 60594 Frankfurt/Main
T: (069) 21235391
Founded: 1929; Members: 800
Focus: Ethnology
Periodical
Zeitschrift für Ethnologie 04876

Deutsche Gesellschaft für Völkerrecht, c/o Institut für Völkerrecht, Adenauerallee 24-42, 53113 Bonn
Founded: 1917
Focus: Law 04877

Deutsche Gesellschaft für Volkskunde e.V. (DGV), Friedländer Weg 2, 37085 Göttingen
Founded: 1904; Members: 1150
Pres: Prof. Dr. Rolf Wilhelm Brednich
Focus: Folklore
Periodicals
dgv informationen (quarterly)
Zeitschrift für Volkskunde (semi-annually) 04878

Deutsche Gesellschaft für Wehrtechnik e.V. (DWT), Bertha-von-Suttner-Pl 1-7, 53111 Bonn
T: (0228) 7668282; Fax: 656366
Founded: 1957; Members: 1350
Pres: Dr. Ernst Grosch; Gen Secr: Dr. Heinz Gläser
Focus: Military Sci
Periodical
Wehrtechnik (monthly) 04879

Deutsche Gesellschaft für Windenergie e.V. (DGW), Lutherstr 14, 30171 Hannover
T: (0511) 282363; Fax: 282377
Focus: Energy 04880

Deutsche Gesellschaft für Wirtschaftliche Fertigung und Sicherheitstechnik e.V. (DGW), Gilbachweg 18, 41564 Kaarst
T: (02101) 68212
Focus: Safety; Mach Eng 04881

Deutsche Gesellschaft für Wohnmedizin und Bauhygiene e.V., Nelkenweg 5, 76291 Spöck-Stutensee
T: (07249) 6932
Focus: Hygiene
Periodical
Wohnmedizin 04882

Deutsche Gesellschaft für Zahn-, Mund- und Kieferheilkunde, Lindemannstr 96, 40237 Düsseldorf
T: (0211) 682296
Founded: 1859; Members: 9500
Focus: Dent
Periodical
Deutsche Zahnärztliche Zeitschrift: DZZ (quarterly) 04883

Deutsche Gesellschaft für Zahnärztliche Prothetik und Werkstoffkunde e.V. (DGZPW), Strempelstr 13, 18057 Rostock
T: (0381) 4946500; Fax: 4946503
Pres: Prof. Dr. H. von Schwanewede; Gen Secr: Dr. M. Wichmann
Focus: Dent 04884

Deutsche Gesellschaft für Zahnerhaltung, Prinzregentenstr 1, 10717 Berlin
Focus: Dent 04885

Deutsche Gesellschaft für Zerstörungsfreie Prüfung e.V. (DGZfP), Unter den Eichen 87, 12205 Berlin
T: (030) 8114001; Fax: 8114003
Founded: 1933; Members: 1100
Focus: Eng
Periodical
Materialprüfung 04886

Deutsche Gesellschaft für Züchtungskunde e.V. (DGfZ), Adenauerallee 174, 53113 Bonn
T: (0228) 213411; Fax: 223497
Founded: 1905; Members: 1000
Focus: Zoology
Periodical
Züchtungskunde (bi-monthly) 04887

Deutsche Gesellschaft zum Studium des Western e.V., c/o Univ., Engl. Seminar, Johannisstr 12-20, 48143 Münster
T: (0251) 834595; Fax: 834827
Focus: Lit 04888

Deutsche Gesellschaft zur Bekämpfung von Fettstoffwechselstörungen und ihren Folgeerkrankungen e.V. (DGFF), Waldklausenweg 20, 81733 München
T: (089) 7191001; Fax: 7142687
Focus: Med 04889

Deutsche Gesellschaft zur Förderung der Gehörlosen und Schwerhörigen e.V., Veit-Stoß-Str 14, 80687 München
T: (089) 588848
Founded: 1962; Members: 12
Focus: Rehabil; Educ Handic
Periodical
hörgeschädigte kinder (quarterly) 04890

Deutsche Gesundheitshilfe e.V. (DGH), Hausener Weg 61, 60489 Frankfurt/Main
T: (069) 780042; Fax: 787700
Focus: Public Health 04891

Deutsche Glastechnische Gesellschaft e.V. (DGG), Mendelssohnstr 75-77, 60325 Frankfurt
T: (069) 9758610; Fax: 97586199
Founded: 1922; Members: 1460
Pres: Manfred Werner; Gen Secr: Prof. Dr. Helmut A. Schaeffer
Focus: Eng
Periodical
Glass Science and Technology: Glastechnische Berichte (monthly) 04892

Deutsche Graphologische Vereinigung e.V. (DGV) / Berufsverband Deutscher Graphologen, Postfach 4031, 58239 Schwerte
T: (02304) 73024
Focus: Graphology 04893

Deutsche Gruppenpsychotherapeutische Gesellschaft e.V. (DGG), Kantstr 120-121, 10625 Berlin
T: (030) 3132698; Fax: 3136959
Focus: Therapeutics
Periodical
Dynamische Psychiatrie: Internationale Zeitschrift für Psychiatrie und Psychoanalyse (bi-monthly) 04894

Deutsche Hämophilieberatung / Verein zur Beratung bei Blutungskrankheiten e.V., Lessingstr 61, 45772 Marl-Hüls
T: (02365) 21503
Focus: Hematology 04895

Deutsche Hämophiliegesellschaft zur Bekämpfung von Blutungskrankheiten e.V., Halenseering 3, 22149 Hamburg
T: (040) 6722970; Fax: 6724944
Founded: 1956
Focus: Hematology
Periodical
Hämophilie-Blätter (semi-annually) 04896

Deutsche Hauptstelle gegen die Suchtgefahren e.V. (DHS), Postfach 1369, 59003 Hamm
T: (02381) 90150; Fax: 15331
Pres: anna Fett; Gen Secr: Rolf Hüllinghorst
Focus: Public Health; Educ; Sociology; Psych; Med
Periodical
Sucht: Zeitschrift für Wissenschaft und Praxis (6 times annually) 04897

Deutsche Hörfunkakademie, Nollendorfpl 2, 44339 Dortmund
T: (0231) 988900; Fax: 9889025
Focus: Mass Media 04898

Deutsche Ileostomie-Colostomie-Urostomie-Vereinigung e.V., Postfach 1265, 85312 Freising
T: (08161) 84911; Fax: 85521
Focus: Rehabil
Periodical
ILCO-Praxis: Organ der Deutschen Ileostomie-Colostomie-Urostomie-Vereinigung (quarterly) 04899

Deutsche Informatik-Akademie (DIA), Ahrstr 45, 53175 Bonn
T: (0228) 302145; Fax: 378690
Focus: Computer & Info Sci 04900

Deutsche Jazz-Föderation e.V., Rabanstr 32, 74921 Helmstedt
T: (07263) 911094; Fax: 911095
Focus: Music 04901

Deutsche Johann Strauss Gesellschaft e.V. (DJStG), Untere Anlage 2, 96450 Coburg
T: (09561) 95016; Fax: 90467
Focus: Music 04902

Deutsche Journalistenschule e.V. (DJS), Altheimer Eck 3, 80331 München
T: (089) 266021; Fax: 268733
Focus: Educ; Journalism 04903

Deutsche Kakteen-Gesellschaft e.V., Betzenriedweg 44, 72800 Eningen
T: (07121) 82392; Fax: 82392
Founded: 1892; Members: 10000
Focus: Hort
Periodical
Kakteen und andere Sukkulenten (monthly) 04904

Deutsche Kautschuk-Gesellschaft e.V. (DKG), Zeppelinallee 69, 60487 Frankfurt
T: (069) 7936153; Fax: 7936155
Founded: 1926; Members: 1550
Focus: Materials Sci 04905

Deutsche Keramische Gesellschaft e.V. (DKG), Frankfurter Str 196, 51147 Köln
T: (02203) 69069; Fax: 69301
Founded: 1919; Members: 1400
Focus: Materials Sci
Periodicals
Ceramic Forum International: Berichte (10 times annually)
Fachausschussberichte (irregularly)
Fortschrittsberichte (quarterly) 04906

Deutsche Kommission für die Bearbeitung der Regesta Imperii e.V. bei d. Akad. d. Wiss. u. d. Lit. zu Mainz, Geschwister-Scholl-Str 2, 55131 Mainz
T: (06131) 57734; Fax: 57740
Focus: Hist 04907

Deutsche Kommission für Ingenieurausbildung, Graf-Recke-Str 84, 40239 Düsseldorf
T: (0211) 6214277; Fax: 6214575
Focus: Adult Educ; Eng 04908

Deutsche Krankenhausgesellschaft (DKG), Tersteegenstr 9, 40474 Düsseldorf
T: (0211) 454730; Fax: 4547361
Focus: Med 04909

Deutsche Krebsgesellschaft e.V., Paul-Ehrlich-Str 41, 60596 Frankfurt
T: (069) 6300960; Fax: 639130
Founded: 1970; Members: 3650
Pres: Prof. Dr. Ch. Herfarth; Gen Secr: Prof. Dr. P. Drings
Focus: Cell Biol & Cancer Res
Periodicals
FORUM-Mitgliederzeitschrift (6-8 times annually)
Journal of Cancer Research and Clinical Oncology (bi-monthly)
Der Onkologe (bi-monthly) 04910

Deutsche Landjugend-Akademie Fredeburg e.V. (DLA), In der Wehrhecke 1, 53125 Bonn
T: (0228) 919290; Fax: 9192930
Founded: 1948; Members: 6
Focus: Agri
Periodical
Fredeburger Hefte (irregularly) 04911

Deutsche Landwirtschafts-Gesellschaft e.V. (DLG), Eschborner Landstr 122, 60489 Frankfurt
T: (069) 247880; E-Mail: SB-TT@DLG-Frankfurt.de; Fax: 24788110
Founded: 1885; Members: 16000
Pres: Philip Freiherr von dem Bussche; Gen Secr: Dr. Dietrich Rieger
Focus: Agri
Periodical
DLG-Mitteilungen (monthly) 04912

Deutsche Leopardi-Gesellschaft (DLG), Habelschwerdter Allee 45, 14195 Berlin
T: (030) 8382191; Fax: 8382235
Focus: Lit 04913

Deutsche Lichttechnische Gesellschaft e.V., Burggrafenstr 6, 10787 Berlin
T: (030) 26012439; Fax: 26011255
Founded: 1912; Members: 2700
Gen Secr: Dr. Michael Seidl
Focus: Electric Eng 04914

Deutsche Liga zur Bekämpfung des hohen Blutdruckes e.V., Deutsche Hypertonie Gesellschaft, Berliner Str 46, 69120 Heidelberg
T: (06221) 474300; Fax: 402274
Focus: Hematology 04915

Deutsche Malakozoologische Gesellschaft (DMG), c/o Forschungsinstitut Senckenberg, Senckenberganlage 25, 60325 Frankfurt
T: (069) 75421237; Fax: 746238
Founded: 1868; Members: 270
Pres: Dr. Vollrath Wiese; Gen Secr: Dr. Ronald Janssen
Focus: Zoology
Periodicals
Archiv für Molluskenkunde (annually)
Mitteilungen der Deutschen Malakozoologischen Gesellschaft (semi-annually) 04916

Deutsche Management Akademie Niedersachsen (DMAN), Welfenallee 32, 29225 Celle
T: (05141) 9730; Fax: 973200
Focus: Business Admin 04917

Deutsche Mathematiker-Vereinigung e.V. (DMV), Albertstr 24, 79104 Freiburg
T: (0761) 278020; Fax: 272698
Founded: 1890; Members: 2600
Focus: Math
Periodical
Jahresbericht (quarterly) 04918

Deutsche Medizinische Arbeitsgemeinschaft für Herd- und Regulationsforschung e.V. (DAH), Scharnhorststr 21, 52351 Düren
T: (02421) 34842
Founded: 1950
Focus: Intern Med 04919

Deutsche MERU Gesellschaft, Am Berg 2, 49143 Bissendorf
T: (05402) 8833; Fax: 7149
Founded: 1973; Members: 500
Focus: Sci
Periodical
Mitteilungsblätter der Deutschen MERU-Gesellschaft (semi-annually) 04920

Deutsche Meteorologische Gesellschaft e.V. (DMG), Mont Royal, 56841 Traben-Trarbach
T: (06541) 18205
Founded: 1883; Members: 1733
Focus: Geophys; Oceanography
Periodicals
Beiträge zur Physik der Atmosphäre (quarterly)
Meteorologische Zeitschrift (bi-monthly) . 04921

Deutsche Meteorologische Gesellschaft e.V., Zweigverein Hamburg (DMG), Bernhard-Nocht-Str 76, 20359 Hamburg
T: (040) 31908824; Fax: 31908803
Founded: 1883; Members: 398
Pres: Prof. Dr. Burkhard Brömmer
Focus: Oceanography; Geophys 04922

Deutsche Mineralogische Gesellschaft e.V. (DMG), c/o Mineralogisch-Petrologisches Institut, Poppelsdorfer Schloß, 53115 Bonn
T: (0228) 732733; Fax: 732763
Founded: 1908; Members: 1700
Gen Secr: Prof. Dr. S. Hoernes
Focus: Mineralogy
Periodical
European Journal of Mineralogy (bi-monthly)
. . . . 04923

Deutsche Montessori Gesellschaft, Postfach 5461, 97004 Würzburg
Focus: Educ
Periodical
Das Kind: Halbjahresschrift für Montessori-Pädagogik (semi-annually) 04924

Deutsche Morgenländische Gesellschaft e.V., c/o Südasien-Institut, Im Neuenheimer Feld 330, 69120 Heidelberg
T: (6221) 548900; Fax: 544998
Founded: 1845; Members: 698
Pres: Prof. Dr. Herrmann Jungraithmayr; Gen Secr: Manfred Hake
Focus: Ling; Lit; Hist; Ethnology; Arts; Archeol
Periodicals
Journal of the Nepal Research Centre (annually)
ZDMG (semi-annually) 04925

Deutsche Mozart-Gesellschaft e.V. (DMG), Mozarthaus, Frauentorstr 30, 86152 Augsburg
T: (0821) 518588; Fax: 157228
Founded: 1951; Members: 3500
Pres: Dr. Friedhelm Brusniak; Gen Secr: Brigitte Löder
Focus: Music
Periodical
Acta Mozartiana (semi-annually) 04926

Deutsche Multiple Sklerose Gesellschaft Bundesverband e.V. (DMSG), Vahrenswalderstr 205-207, 30165 Hannover
T: (0511) 968340; Fax: 9683450
Founded: 1952; Members: 36000
Pres: Prof. Dr. Dr. Hermann Hoffmann; Gen Secr: Dorothea Pitschnau
Focus: Med
Periodical
Aktiv (quarterly) 04927

Deutsche Myastenie Gesellschaft e.V. (DMG), Langemarckstr 106, 28199 Bremen
T: (0421) 592060; Fax: 508226
Focus: Med 04928

Deutsche Narkolepsie-Gesellschaft (DNG), Auf den Schollen 7, 42781 Haan
T: (02129) 53723; Fax: 32945
Focus: Anesthetics 04929

Deutsche Neurovegetative Gesellschaft, Rosspfad 19, 40489 Düsseldorf
T: (0211) 402236
Founded: 1960
Focus: Neurology 04930

Deutsche Numismatische Gesellschaft / Verband der Deutschen Münzvereine e.V., Hans-Purrmann-Allee 26, 67346 Speyer
T: (06232) 92458
Focus: Numismatics
Periodical
Numismatisches Nachrichtenblatt (monthly) 04931

Deutsche Ophthalmologische Gesellschaft Heidelberg e.V. (DOG), Berliner Str 14, 69120 Heidelberg
T: (06221) 411787; Fax: 484616
Founded: 1857; Members: 3500
Pres: Dr. Jochen Kammann; Gen Secr: Prof. Dr. Hans Eberhard Völcker
Focus: Ophthal
Periodical
Der Ophthalmologe (monthly) 04932

Deutsche Orchideen-Gesellschaft, Flößweg 11, 33758 Schloß Holte-Stukenbrock
T: (05207) 920607; Fax: 920608
Focus: Botany
Periodical
Die Orchidee (bi-monthly) 04933

Deutsche Orient-Gesellschaft e.V. (DOG), c/o Altorientalisches Seminar der FU, Bitterstr 8-12, 14195 Berlin
T: (030) 8383347
Founded: 1898; Members: 800
Pres: Prof. Dr. Gernot Wilhelm
Focus: Archeol; Hist
Periodical
Mitteilungen der Deutschen Orient-Gesellschaft (annually) 04934

Deutsche Ornithologen-Gesellschaft e.V., Möggingen, 78315 Radolfzell
Founded: 1850; Members: 2200
Focus: Ornithology
Periodical
Journal für Ornithologie (quarterly) . . . 04935

Deutsche Parlamentarische Gesellschaft e.V., Dahlmannstr 7, 53113 Bonn
T: (0228) 212654
Focus: Poli Sci 04936

Deutsche Paul-Tillich-Gesellschaft e.V., c/o Institut für Evangelische Theologie, Universität, Im Stadtwald, 66123 Saarbrücken
T: (0681) 3022949
Founded: 1960; Members: 239
Focus: Rel & Theol 04937

Deutsche Pharmakologische Gesellschaft e.V., Postfach 101709, 42017 Wuppertal
T: (0202) 368327
Members: 1540
Focus: Pharmacol
Periodical
Naunyn-Schmiedeberg's Archives of Pharmacology
. . . . 04938

Deutsche Pharmazeutische Gesellschaft e.V. (DPhG), Hamburger Allee 26-28, 60486 Frankfurt am Main
T: (069) 7917555; Fax: 7917553
Founded: 1890; Members: 6000
Pres: Prof. Dr. H.P.T. Ammon; Gen Secr: Peter Ditzel
Focus: Pharmacol
Periodicals
Archiv der Pharmazie (monthly)
Pharmazie in unserer Zeit (bi-monthly) . 04939

Deutsche Phono-Akademie e.V., Grelckstr 36, 22529 Hamburg
T: (040) 581935; Fax: 580833
Founded: 1973; Members: 32
Pres: Gerd Gebhardt; Gen Secr: Prof. Werner Hay
Focus: Music 04940

Deutsche Physikalische Gesellschaft e.V. (DPG), Hauptstr 5, 53604 Bad Honnef
T: (02224) 92320; Fax: 923250
Founded: 1845; Members: 25000
Pres: Prof. Dr. M. Schwoerer; Gen Secr: Dr. V. Häselbarth
Focus: Physics
Periodicals
Physikalische Blätter (monthly)
Verhandlungen der DPG (irregularly) . . 04941

Deutsche Physiologische Gesellschaft e.V., Im Neuenheimer Feld 326, 69120 Heidelberg
T: (06221) 564033; Fax: 564561
Founded: 1904; Members: 820
Focus: Physiology 04942

Deutsche Phytomedizinische Gesellschaft e.V. (DPG), Nussallee 9, 53115 Bonn
T: (0228) 732442; Fax: 732442
Founded: 1949; Members: 1798
Pres: Prof. Dr. H.-W. Dehne; Gen Secr: Dr. E.-Ch. Oerke
Focus: Agri 04943

Deutsche Psychoanalytische Gesellschaft e.V. (DPG), Nussbaumstr 7, 80336 München
Founded: 1910; Members: 300
Focus: Psychoan
Periodicals
Praxis der Kinderpsychologie und Kinderpsychiatrie
Zeitschrift für Psychosomatische Medizin und Psychoanalyse 04944

Deutsche Psychoanalytische Vereinigung e.V. (DPV), Sulzaer Str 3, 14199 Berlin
T: (030) 8264547; Fax: 8266090
Founded: 1950; Members: 712
Focus: Psych 04945

Deutsche Puschkin-Gesellschaft e.V., Lennéstr 1, 53113 Bonn
T: (02225) 18350; Fax: 702253
Focus: Lit 04946

Deutsche Quartärvereinigung (Deuqua), Postfach 510153, 30631 Hannover
T: (0511) 6432487; Fax: 6432304
Founded: 1950; Members: 650
Focus: Geology
Periodical
Eiszeitalter und Gegenwart (annually) . . 04947

Deutsche Rechtspflegervereinigung e.V. (DRV), Prämienstr 71, 52076 Aachen
T: (0241) 517576; Fax: 81818
Focus: Law 04948

Deutsche Religionsgeschichtliche Studiengesellschaft, Droste-Hülshoff-Str 9b, 48341 Altenberge
Founded: 1970
Pres: Prof. Dr. M.L.G. Dietrich
Focus: Rel & Theol
Periodical
Mitteilungen für Anthropologie und Religionsgeschichte 04949

Deutsche Rheologische Gesellschaft e.V. (DRG), Unter den Eichen 87, 12205 Berlin
T: (030) 81041610
Founded: 1951; Members: 250
Pres: Prof. Dr. M.H. Wagner; Gen Secr: Prof. Dr. W. Mielke
Focus: Materials Sci 04950

Deutsche Rheuma-Liga Bundesverband e.V., Rheinallee 69, 53173 Bonn
T: (0228) 957500; Fax: 9575020
Focus: Rheuma
Periodical
Mobil: Das Rheuma-Magazin (bi-monthly) 04951

Deutsche Richterakademie, Tagungsstätte Trier, Berliner Allee 7, 54295 Trier
T: (0651) 93610; Fax: 300210
Founded: 1973
Pres: Renate Schmidt-Hanemann
Focus: Law 04952

Deutsche Röntgengesellschaft (DRG), Frankfurter Str 231, 63263 Neu-Isenburg
T: (06102) 4032
Founded: 1905; Members: 1950
Focus: Bio; Radiology; X-Ray Tech; Nucl Med
. . . . 04953

Deutsche Schillergesellschaft e.V. (DSG), Schillerhöhe 8-10, 71672 Marbach
T: (07144) 8480
Founded: 1895; Members: 4000
Pres: Prof. Dr. Eberhard Lämmert; Gen Secr: Dr. Ulrich Ott
Focus: Lit
Periodicals
Jahrbuch der Deutschen Schillergesellschaft (annually)
Marbacher Arbeitskreis für Geschichte der Germanistik, Mitteilungen (2-3 times annually)
Marbacher Magazin (quarterly) 04954

Deutsche Schmerzliga e.V., Roßmarkt 23, 60311 Frankfurt/Main
T: (069) 29988075; Fax: 29988033
Focus: Med 04955

Deutsche Sekretärinnen-Akademie e.V., Wielandstr 14, 23558 Lübeck
T: (0451) 8717119; Fax: 8717112
Focus: Adult Educ 04956

Deutsche Sektion der Internationalen Juristen-Kommission e.V. (IJK), Nowackanlage 15, 76137 Karlsruhe
T: (0721) 388699; Fax: 358263
Focus: Law 04957

Deutsche Sektion der Internationalen Liga gegen Epilepsie, Herforder Str 5-7, 33602 Bielefeld
T: (0521) 124192; Fax: 124172
Founded: 1957; Members: 1500
Pres: Prof. Dr. D. Rating; Gen Secr: Dr. C. Benninger
Focus: Pathology
Periodical
Rundbrief (3 times annually) 04958

Deutsche Sektion des Internationalen Instituts für Verwaltungswissenschaften, Gaurheindorferstr 198, 53117 Bonn
Focus: Public Admin
Periodicals
Schriften der Deutschen Sektion (annually)
Verwaltungswissenschaftliche Informationen (3 times annually) 04959

Deutsche Shakespeare-Gesellschaft e.V., Markt 13, 99423 Weimar
T: (03643) 64076; Fax: 64076
Founded: 1864; Members: 2700
Focus: Lit
Periodical
Shakespeare-Jahrbuch (annually) 04960

Deutsche Statistische Gesellschaft (DStG), c/o Universität, 78464 Konstanz
T: (07531) 883758
Founded: 1911; Members: 800
Focus: Stats
Periodical
Allgemeines Statistisches Archiv (quarterly) 04961

Deutsche Stendhal-Gesellschaft e.V., c/o TU, Institut für Romanische Literaturwissenschaft, Ernst-Reuter-Pl 7, 10587 Berlin
T: (030) 31422958; Fax: 31425479
Focus: Lit 04962

Deutsche Stiftung für internationale Entwicklung, Hans-Böckler-Str 5, 53225 Bonn
T: (0228) 40010
Focus: Int'l Relat; Econ
Periodical
Entwicklung und Zusammenarbeit (monthly) 04963

Deutsche Straßenliga e.V. / Vereinigung zur Förderung des Straßen- und Verkehrswesen, Herderstr 56, 53173 Bonn
T: (0228) 956830
Members: 99
Focus: Transport
Periodicals
Straße und Wirtschaft (semi-annually)
Straße-Verkehr-Wirtschaft: (SVW)-Infodienst (monthly) 04964

Deutsche Studiengesellschaft für Publizistik (Stupu), Königstr 1a, 70173 Stuttgart
T: (0711) 293165, 294353
Founded: 1956; Members: 47
Focus: Journalism 04965

Deutsche Thomas-Mann-Gesellschaft e.V., Königstr 67a, 23552 Lübeck
T: (0451) 1600632
Focus: Lit 04966

Deutsche Tropenmedizinische Gesellschaft e.V. (DTG), Bernhard-Nocht-Str 74, 20359 Hamburg
T: (040) 31182500; Fax: 31182512
Founded: 1962; Members: 705
Pres: Dr. R. Korte; Gen Secr: Prof. Dr. R. Horstmann
Focus: Trop Med 04967

Deutsche Vereinigung für die Rehabilitation Behinderter e.V., Friedrich-Ebert Anlage 9, 69117 Heidelberg
T: (06221) 25485; Fax: 166009
Pres: Dr. Wolfgang Blumenthal; Gen Secr: Martin Schmollinger
Focus: Rehabil
Periodical
Die Rehabilitation: Zeitschrift für alle Fragen der medizinischen, schulisch-beruflichen und sozialen Eingliederung (quarterly) 04968

Deutsche Vereinigung für Finanzanalyse und Anlageberatung e.V. (DVFA), Einsteinstr. 5, 63303 Dreieich
T: (06103) 58330; E-Mail: info@dvfa.de; Fax: 583333
Founded: 1960; Members: 900
Gen Secr: Ulrike Diehl
Focus: Finance
Periodical
Beiträge zur Wertpapieranalyse (irregularly) 04969

Deutsche Vereinigung für gewerblichen Rechtsschutz und Urheberrecht e.V., Theodor-Heuss-Ring 19-21, 50668 Köln
T: (0221) 77160; Fax: 7716110
Members: 3200
Pres: Dr. Wolfgang Gloy; Gen Secr: Dr. Michael Loschelder
Focus: Law
Periodical
Gewerblicher Rechtsschutz und Urheberrecht (GRUR) (monthly) 04970

Deutsche Vereinigung für Internationales Steuerrecht, Gustav-Heinemann-Ufer 84-88, 50968 Köln
T: (0221) 3708586
Founded: 1852; Members: 500
Focus: Finance 04971

Deutsche Vereinigung für internationales Steuerrecht im Verband der Fiscal Association, Bayerische Sektion e.V., Galeriestr 6a, 80539 München
T: (089) 292244
Focus: Finance 04972

Deutsche Vereinigung für Parlamentsfragen e.V., Bundeshaus, 53113 Bonn
T: (0228) 1622442, 1622250; Fax: 1626671
Pres: Joachim Hörster; Gen Secr: Gunter Gabrysch
Focus: Poli Sci
Periodical
Zeitschrift für Parlamentsfragen (quarterly) 04973

Deutsche Vereinigung für Politische Wissenschaft (DVPW), Residenzschloss, 64283 Darmstadt
T: (06151) 163197; E-Mail: dvpw@hrz1.hrz.th-darmstadt.de; Fax: 162397
Founded: 1951; Members: 1200
Pres: Prof. Dr. Michael Th. Greven; Gen Secr: Felix W. Wurm
Focus: Poli Sci
Periodicals
Politische Vierteljahresschrift (quarterly)
PVS-Literatur (semi-annually) 04974

Deutsche Vereinigung für Religionsgeschichte (DVRG), c/o Seminar für Religionswissenschaft, Wilhelm-Busch-Str 22, 30167 Hannover
Founded: 1950; Members: 154
Focus: Rel & Theol 04975

Deutsche Vereinigung für Sportwissenschaft, Bei der Neuen Münze 4a, 22145 Hamburg
T: (040) 67941212; E-Mail: dvs.Hamburg@t-online.de; Fax: 67941213
Founded: 1976; Members: ca. 750
Pres: Prof. Dr. Klaus Zieschang; Gen Secr: Frederik Borkenhagen
Focus: Sports
Periodical
dvs-Informationen (quarterly) 04976

Deutsche Vereinigung für Verbrennungsforschung e.V., c/o VGB, Postfach 103932, 45039 Essen
T: (0201) 8128216
Focus: Eng 04977

Deutsche Vereinigung zur Bekämpfung der Viruskrankheiten e.V. (DVV), Pettenkoferstr 9a, 80336 München
T: (089) 533401
Focus: Immunology; Microbio 04978

Deutsche Verkehrswissenschaftliche Gesellschaft e.V. (DVWG), Brüderstr 53, 51427 Bergisch Gladbach
T: (02204) 60027; E-Mail: dvwghgs@t-online.de; Fax: 67743
Founded: 1908; Members: 4000
Pres: Prof. Dr. Paul Baron; Gen Secr: Sigurd Rielke
Focus: Transport
Periodical
Internationales Verkehrswesen (monthly) . 04979

Deutsche Veterinärmedizinische Gesellschaft e.V. (DVG), Frankfurter Str 89, 35392 Giessen
T: (0641) 24466
Founded: 1952; Members: 4000
Focus: Vet Med 04980

Deutsche Werbewissenschaftliche Gesellschaft e.V. (DWG), Königswinterer Str 552, 53227 Bonn
T: (0228) 444560; Fax: 441148
Founded: 1919
Pres: Prof. Dr. Claudia Fantopie-Altobelli; Gen Secr: Lutz E. Weidner
Focus: Advert
Periodical
Werbeforschung und Praxis (bi-monthly) . 04981

Deutsche Wissenschaftliche Kommission für Meeresforschung, Palmaille 9, 22767 Hamburg
T: (040) 389050; Fax: 38905129
Focus: Oceanography
Periodical
Archive of Fishery and Marine Research: Archiv für Fischerei und Meeresforschung (2-3 times annually) 04982

Deutsche Zentrale für Volksgesundheitspflege e.V. (DZV), Münchener Str 48, 60329 Frankfurt
T: (069) 235761/62
Founded: 1955; Members: 70
Focus: Public Health 04983

Deutsche Zöliakie Gesellschaft e.V. (DZG), Filderhauptstr 61, 70599 Stuttgart
T: (0711) 454514; Fax: 4567817
Focus: Med 04984

Deutsche Zoologische Gesellschaft e.V. (DZG), Postfach 202136, 80021 München
Founded: 1890; Members: 1860
Pres: Prof. Dr. G. Heldmaier; Gen Secr: Prof. Dr. W. Schortau
Focus: Zoology
Periodical
Verhandlungen (annually) 04985

Deutscher Ärztinnenbund e.V., Herbert-Lewin-Str 1, 50931 Köln
T: (0221) 4004540; Fax: 4004541
Founded: 1924; Members: 2000
Pres: Dr. Ingeborg Retzlaff; Dr. Ute Otten
Focus: Med
Periodical
Ärztin: Mitteilungsblatt des Deutschen Ärztinnenbundes (bi-monthly) 04986

Deutscher Akademikerinnenbund e.V. (DAB), Guido-Hauck-Str 27, 74076 Heilbronn
T: (07131) 178540; E-Mail: DABeV@t-online.de; Fax: 166985
Founded: 1926; Members: 2000
Pres: Monika Schmitz
Focus: Sci
Periodical
Mitteilungsblatt des Deutschen Akademikerinnenbundes e.V. (annually) . 04987

Deutscher Akademischer Austauschdienst (DAAD), Kennedyallee 50, 53175 Bonn
T: (0228) 8820; E-Mail: postmaster@daad.de; Fax: 882444
Founded: 1925; Members: 220 Hochschulen
Pres: Prof. Dr. Theodor Berchem; Gen Secr: Dr. Christian Bode
Focus: Sci
Periodical
Hochschule und Ausland (quarterly) . . 04988

Deutscher Akkordeonlehrer-Verband e.V. (DALV), Löhrstr 32, 78647 Trossingen
T: (07425) 20448
Focus: Educ; Music 04989

Deutscher Allergie- und Asthmabund e.V. (DAAB), Hindenburgstr 110, 41061 Mönchengladbach
T: (02161) 814940; Fax: 208502
Focus: Med 04990

Deutscher Altphilologen-Verband, Wilhelmshavener Str 62, 10551 Berlin
T: (030) 3967261
Members: 6000
Focus: Ling; Lit
Periodical
Mitteilungsblatt des Deutschen Altphilologenverbandes (quarterly) 04991

Deutscher Arbeitsgerichtsverband e.V., Blumenthalstr 33, 50670 Köln
T: (0221) 7740347; Fax: 7740356
Focus: Law
Periodical
Mitteilungen (semi-annually) 04992

Deutscher Arbeitsring für Lärmbekämpfung e.V. (DAL), Frankenstr 25, 40476 Düsseldorf
T: (0211) 488499; Fax: 442634
Founded: 1952; Members: 620
Pres: Prof. Dr. Rainer Guski; Gen Secr: Ludger Visse
Focus: Public Health
Periodical
Zeitschrift für Lärmbekämpfung (bi-monthly) 04993

Deutscher Ausschuss für Stahlbau (DASt), Ebertpl 1, 50668 Köln
T: (0221) 77310
Focus: Civil Eng 04994

Deutscher Autoren-Verband e.V. (DAV), Sophienstr 2, 30159 Hannover
T: (0511) 322068
Founded: 1946; Members: 150
Focus: Lit 04995

Deutscher Bäderverband e.V., Schumannstr 111, 53113 Bonn
T: (0228) 262040
Founded: 1892; Members: 5
Pres: Dr. Christoph Kirschner; Gen Secr: Heike Wilms-Kegel
Focus: Public Health
Periodical
Heilbad und Kurort: Zeitschrift für das gesamte Bäderwesen (monthly) 04996

Deutscher Berufsverband der Hals-Nasen-Ohrenärzte e.V., Mühlenhof 2-4, 24534 Neumünster
T: (04321) 45035; Fax: 44348
Founded: 1951; Members: 3500
Focus: Otorhinolaryngology
Periodical
HNO-Mitteilungen (bi-monthly) 04997

Deutscher Berufsverband der Sozialarbeiter und Sozialpädagogen e.V. (DBS), Schützenbahn 17, 45127 Essen
T: (0201) 239666; Fax: 200259
Founded: 1916; Members: 3500
Focus: Educ; Sociology; Adult Educ
Periodicals
DBS Pressedienst (irregularly)
Der Sozialarbeiter (bi-monthly) 04998

Deutscher Berufsverband für Tanzpädagogik e.V. (DBfT), Hollestr 1, 45127 Essen
T: (0201) 228883; Fax: 226444
Focus: Educ; Perf Arts 04999

Deutscher Beton-Verein e.V. (DBV), Bahnhofstr 61, 65185 Wiesbaden
T: (0611) 14030
Founded: 1898; Members: 640
Focus: Materials Sci; Graphic & Dec Arts, Design; Standards
Periodical
Vorträge Betontag 05000

Deutscher Bibliotheksverband e.V. (DBV), Bundesallee 184-185, 10717 Berlin
T: (030) 8505274; Fax: 8542240
Founded: 1949; Members: 2300
Focus: Libraries & Bk Sci
Periodical
DBV-INFO (annually) 05001

Deutscher Bühnenverein e.V. (DBV), St.-Apern-Str 17-21, 50667 Köln
T: (0221) 208120; Fax: 2081228
Focus: Perf Arts 05002

Deutscher Bundesverband Tanz e.V. (DBT), Küppelstein 34, 42857 Remscheid
T: (02191) 794241; Fax: 794292
Focus: Perf Arts 05003

Deutscher Dampfkesselausschuss (DDA), Kurfürstenstr 56, 45138 Essen
T: (0201) 284881
Focus: Eng 05004

Deutscher Diabetiker-Verband e.V., Hahnbrunner Str 46, 67659 Kaiserslautern
T: (0631) 76488; Fax: 97222
Focus: Diabetes
Periodical
Diabetes aktuell / Hallo Du auch (quarterly) 05005

Deutscher Erfinderring e.V., Schlegelstr 17, 90491 Nürnberg
Focus: Eng
Periodical
Erfinder und Neuheitendienst (bi-monthly) 05006

Deutscher Evangelischer Krankenhausverband e.V., Gänsheidestr 83, 70186 Stuttgart
T: (0711) 233441; Fax: 2369569
Focus: Med 05007

Deutscher Fakultätentag für Elektrotechnik (DFTE), c/o Fakultät Elektronik, Mommsenstr 13, 01062 Dresden
T: (0351) 4633569; Fax: 4637740
Focus: Electric Eng 05008

Deutscher Fernschulverband e.V. (DFV), Ostendstr 3, 64319 Pfungstadt
T: (06157) 80654; Fax: 80658
Focus: Educ 05009

Deutscher Forstverein e.V. (DFV), Stresemannallee 61, 60596 Frankfurt
T: (069) 638674; Fax: 6312981
Focus: Forestry
Periodical
Tagungsbericht (every second year) . . 05010

Deutscher Forstwirtschaftsrat e.V. (DFWR), Münstereifeler Str 19 Postfach 1229, 53349 Rheinbach
T: (02226) 2350; Fax: 5792
Founded: 1950; Members: 64
Pres: Hermann Ilaender; Gen Secr: Martin Strittmatter
Focus: Forestry
Periodical
DFWR-Dreijahresbericht (every 3 years) . 05011

Deutscher Germanistenverband, c/o Germanistisches Seminar, Am Hof 1d, 53113 Bonn
T: (0228) 737478; Fax: 735579
Focus: Ling; Lit
Periodical
Mitteilungen des Deutschen Germanistenverbandes (quarterly) 05012

Deutscher Harmonika-Verband e.V. (DHV), Rudolf-Maschke-Pl 6, 78647 Trossingen
T: (07425) 20221
Focus: Music 05013

Deutscher Hispanistenverband (DHV), c/o Ibero-Amerik. Institut, Potsdamer Str 37, 10785 Berlin
T: (030) 2662502; Fax: 2662503
Focus: Ling; Lit 05014

Deutscher Hochschulverband, Rheinallee 18, 53173 Bonn
T: (0228) 364002; E-Mail: dhv@hochschulverband.de; Fax: 353403
Founded: 1950; Members: 16000
Pres: Prof.Dr. Hartmut Schiedermair; Gen Secr: Dr. Michael Hartmer
Focus: Educ
Periodical
Forschung & Lehre (monthly) 05015

Deutscher Ingenieurinnenbund e.V. (dib), Mainzer Str 1a, 80803 München
T: (089) 336029
Focus: Eng 05016

Deutscher Juristen-Fakultätentag, Carl-Zeiss-Str 3, 07743 Jena
T: (03641) 631670; Fax: 631668
Members: 40
Focus: Law 05017

Deutscher Juristentag e.V., Oxfordstr 21, 53111 Bonn
T: (0228) 9839135; Fax: 630283
Founded: 1860; Members: 8200
Focus: Law 05018

Deutscher Juristinnenbund, Vereinigung der Juristinnen, Volkswirtinnen und Betriebswirtinnen e.V. (DJB), Reuterstr 241, 53113 Bonn
T: (0228) 915100; Fax: 211009
Focus: Law; Business Admin; Econ . . 05019

Deutscher Kälte- und Klimatechnischer Verein e.V. (DKV), Pfaffenwaldring 10, 70569 Stuttgart
T: (0711) 6853200; Fax: 6853242
Founded: 1909; Members: 1200
Focus: Air Cond 05020

Deutscher Kassenarztverband e.V., Am Rain 4, 86845 Großaitingen
T: (08203) 90202; Fax: 5669
Founded: 1969; Members: 10300
Pres: Dr. Hans-Peter Krepp
Focus: Med 05021

Deutscher Kommunikationsverband BDW e.V., Königswinterer Str 552, 53227 Bonn
T: (0228) 444560; Fax: 441148
Members: 3012
Pres: Rudolf L. Dautzenberg; Gen Secr: Lutz E. Weidner
Focus: Advert
Periodical
Highway (bi-monthly) 05022

Deutscher Komponisten-Interessenverband e.V., Kadettenweg 80b, 12205 Berlin
T: (030) 8334121; Fax: 8330713
Founded: 1954; Members: 1450
Pres: Karl Heinz Wahren; Gen Secr: Manuel Neuendorf
Periodical
Informationen (annually) 05023

Deutscher Künstlerbund e.V., Zeughofstr 20, 10997 Berlin
T: (030) 6189191; Fax: 6117082
Focus: Arts 05024

Deutscher Kulturrat (DKR), Weberstr 59a, 53113 Bonn
T: (0228) 201350; Fax: 2013521
Focus: Cultur Hist 05025

Deutscher Lehrerverband (DL), Burbacher Str 8, 53129 Bonn
T: (0228) 211212/22; Fax: 211224
Focus: Educ 05026

Deutscher Lehrerverband Niedersachsen, Grosse Packhofstr 28, 30159 Hannover
Focus: Educ 05027

Deutscher Markscheider-Verein e.V. (DMV), Shamrockring 1, Shamrockring 1, 44623 Herne
T: (02323) 152977; Fax: 153980
Founded: 1879; Members: 500
Pres: Manfred Böhmer; Gen Secr: Jörg Glocker
Focus: Mining
Periodical
Das Markscheidewesen (3 times annually) 05028

Deutscher Medizinischer Informationsdienst e.V. (DMI), Siesmayerstr 15, 60323 Frankfurt
T: (069) 745882
Focus: Public Health; Educ 05029

Deutscher Museumsbund e.V. (DMB), Lingnerpl 1, 01069 Dresden
T: (0351) 4846324; Fax: 4955162
Founded: 1917; Members: 1200
Pres: Dr. Martin Roth; Gen Secr: Dr. Werner Hilgers
Focus: Archives; Arts
Periodical
Museumskunde (quarterly) 05030

Deutscher Musikrat e.V. (DMR), Weberstr 59, 53113 Bonn
T: (0228) 20910; Fax: 2091200
Founded: 1953; Members: 86
Focus: Music
Periodical
Musikforum: Referate und Informationen des Deutschen Musikrates (semi-annually) . . 05031

Deutscher Naturheilbund e.V., Kreuzbergstr 45, 74564 Crailsheim
T: (07951) 5504; Fax: 45568
Founded: 1889; Members: 1800
Pres: Dr. Rainer Matejka; Gen Secr: Alfred Adis
Focus: Med
Periodical
Der Naturarzt (monthly) 05032

Deutscher Naturkundeverein e.V., Zavelsteinstr 38b, 70469 Stuttgart
T: (0711) 855896
Focus: Nat Sci 05033

Deutscher Naturschutzring e.V., Dachverband der deutschen Natur- und Umweltschutzverbände (DNR), Am Michaelshof 8-10, 53177 Bonn
T: (0228) 359005; E-Mail: dnr@bonn.comlink.apc.org; Fax: 359096
Founded: 1950; Members: 108 Natur- und Umweltschutzverbände
Pres: Prof. Dr. Wolfgang Engelhardt; Gen Secr: Helmut Röscheisen
Focus: Ecology
Periodical
Deutschland-Rundbrief (monthly) 05034

Deutscher Nautischer Verein von 1868 e.V., Striepenweg 31, 21147 Hamburg
T: (040) 7960105; Fax: 7960806
Founded: 1868; Members: 4210
Pres: Frank Leonhardt; Gen Secr: Garrit Leemrijze
Focus: Navig 05035

Deutscher Philologenverband e.V. (DPhV), Bahnhofsweg 8, 82008 Unterhaching
T: (089) 6251619; Fax: 6251818
Founded: 1904
Pres: Heinz Durner; Gen Secr: Gabriele Lipp
Periodical
Prolit (10 times annually) 05036

Deutscher Politologen-Verband e.V. (dp), Peter-Schwingen-Str 11, 53177 Bonn
T: (0228) 321000; E-Mail: 0228810050-0001@T-Online.de; Fax: 326500
Founded: 1965; Members: 600
Pres: Heinz J.H. Fleischhauer
Focus: Poli Sci 05037

Deutscher Rat für Landespflege (DRL), Konstantinstr 110, 53179 Bonn
T: (0228) 331097; Fax: 334727
Founded: 1962; Members: 27
Pres: Prof. Dr. Dr. Wolfgang Haber; Gen Secr: Prof. Dr. Klaus Borchard
Focus: Ecology
Periodical
Schriftenreihe des DRL (semi-annually) . 05038

Deutscher Romanistenverband (DRV), c/o Roman. Seminar, Bispinghof 3a, 48143 Münster
T: (0251) 834522; Fax: 838351
Focus: Ling; Lit 05039

Deutscher Skilehrerverband e.V. (DSLV), Sohnckestr 17, 81479 München
T: (089) 799051/52; Fax: 790185
Focus: Educ; Sports 05040

Deutscher Spanischlehrerverband (DSV), Findelgasse 2, 90402 Nürnberg
T: (0911) 5302655; Fax: 5302658
Focus: Educ; Ling 05041

Deutscher Sportärztebund (DSÄB) / Deutsche Gesellschaft für Sportmedizin e.V., Bergheimer Str 118, 69115 Heidelberg
T: (06221) 601880; Fax: 601881
Founded: 1950; Members: 5500
Focus: Med; Physical Therapy
Periodicals
Abdruck von durchzuführenden Weiterbildungs- und Fortbildungskursen (semi-annually)
Deutsche Zeitschrift für Sportmedizin (monthly) 05042

Deutscher Sportbund, Otto-Fleck-Schneise 12, 60528 Frankfurt
T: (069) 67000; Fax: 674906
Founded: 1950; Members: 93 Sportverbände mit 85938 Sportvereinen
Pres: Manfred von Richthofen; Gen Secr: Dr. Wulf Preising
Focus: Sports 05043

Deutscher Sportlehrerverband e.V. (DSLV), Am Rasselberg 16, 35578 Wetzlar
T: (06441) 28444; Fax: 26697
Founded: 1949; Members: 12000
Focus: Sports 05044

Deutscher Stahlbau-Verband (DSTV), Ebertpl 1, 50668 Köln
T: (0221) 77310
Members: 163
Focus: Civil Eng
Periodical
Stahlbau-Nachrichten (bi-monthly) 05045

Deutscher Stenografielehrerverband e.V. / Verband der Lehrer für Bürowirtschaft, Kurzschrift und Maschinenschreiben, Carsten-Meyn-Weg 6, 22399 Hamburg
T: (040) 6028135
Focus: Adult Educ 05046

Deutscher Tanzrat/Deutscher Ballettrat e.V., Graurheindorfer Str 23, 53111 Bonn
T: (0228) 633578
Focus: Perf Arts 05047

Deutscher Textdichter-Verband e.V. (DTV), Teneverstr 3b, 28325 Bremen
T: (0421) 423245; Fax: 423245
Focus: Lit 05048

Deutscher Tonkünstlerverband e.V. (DTKV), Linprunstr 16, Rückgebäude, 80335 München
T: (089) 5420235; Fax: 529704
Founded: 1844
Focus: Music
Periodicals
Musik und Bildung (bi-monthly)
Neue Musikzeitung (bi-monthly) 05049

Deutscher Verband Evangelischer Büchereien e.V. / Zentralstelle der Büchereiarbeit in der Evangelischen Kirche in Deutschland, Bürgerstr 2, 37073 Göttingen
T: (0551) 74917
Focus: Libraries & Bk Sci
Periodicals
Buchauswahl (annually)
Der Evangelische Buchberater (quarterly) 05050

Deutscher Verband Farbe (DVF), Unter den Eichen 87, 12203 Berlin
T: (030) 81045400
Founded: 1976; Members: 500
Focus: Materials Sci 05051

Deutscher Verband Forstlicher Forschungsanstalten (DVFFA), Schloss, 67705 Trippstadt
T: (06306) 9110; Fax: 2821
Founded: 1872; Members: 72
Pres: Prof. Dr. Axel Roeder
Focus: Forestry 05052

Deutscher Verband für das Skilehrwesen e.V. (DVS), Postfach 1425, 87554 Oberstdorf
T: (08322) 80126; Fax: 80226
Founded: 1951
Pres: Dr. Harald Kiedaisch; Gen Secr: Kurt Kreismeyer
Focus: Sports 05053

Deutscher Verband für Materialforschung und -prüfung e.V. (DVM), Unter den Eichen 87, 12205 Berlin
T: (030) 8113066; Fax: 8119359
Founded: 1896; Members: 350
Focus: Materials Sci
Periodical
Materialprüfung – Materials Testing – Matériaux Essais et Recherches (monthly) 05054

Deutscher Verband für Physiotherapie / Zentralverband der Physiotherapeuten/Krankengymnasten e.V., Postfach 210280, 50528 Köln
T: (0221) 9810270; E-Mail: 106417.3057@compuserve.com; Fax: 98102725
Founded: 1949; Members: 31000
Pres: Eckhardt Böhle; Gen Secr: Heinz Christian Esser
Focus: Therapeutics 05055

Deutscher Verband für Schweisstechnik e.V. (DVS), Postfach 101965, 40010 Düsseldorf
T: (0211) 15910; Fax: 1575950
Founded: 1947; Members: 20000
Focus: Eng
Periodicals
Der Praktiker (monthly)
Schweissen und Schneiden (monthly)
Verbindungstechnik in der Elektronik (quarterly)
. . . . 05056

Deutscher Verband für Wasserwirtschaft und Kulturbau e.V. (DVWK) / German Association for Water Resources and Land Improvement, Gluckstr 2, 53115 Bonn
T: (0228) 983870; E-Mail: dvwk@aol.com; Fax: 9838733
Members: 2400
Pres: Dr. Joachim Renner; Gen Secr: Dr. Wolfram Dirksen
Focus: Hydrology; Water Res; Agri
Periodicals
Wasser und Boden (monthly)
Wasserwirtschaft (monthly) 05057

Deutscher Verband technisch-wissenschaftlicher Vereine (DVT), Graf-Recke-Str 84, 40239 Düsseldorf
T: (0211) 6214499; Fax: 6214172
Founded: 1916; Members: 91
Pres: Dr. H. Gassert; Gen Secr: Dr. Jörg Debelius
Focus: Eng 05058

Deutscher Verband Technischer Assistenten in der Medizin e.V., Spaldingstr 110b, 20097 Hamburg
T: (040) 231436; Fax: 233373
Pres: Heidi Schramm; Gen Secr: Almuth Never
Focus: Med
Periodical
mta (monthly) 05059

Deutscher Verein des Gas- und Wasserfaches e.V. (DVGW), Hauptstr 71-79, 65727 Eschborn
T: (06196) 70170; Fax: 481152
Founded: 1859; Members: 6010
Focus: Water Res; Energy
Periodical
gwf – Das Gas- und Wasserfach: Ausgaben Gas/Erdgas und Wasser/Abwasser (monthly)
. . . . 05060

Deutscher Verein für Internationales Seerecht e.V. (DVIS), Esplanade 6, 20354 Hamburg
T: (040) 350970
Founded: 1898; Members: 330
Pres: Dr. Hans-Christian Albrecht
Focus: Law 05061

Deutscher Verein für Kunstwissenschaft e.V., Jebensstr 1, 10623 Berlin
T: (030) 3139932
Founded: 1908; Members: 1150
Focus: Arts
Periodical
Zeitschrift des Deutschen Vereins für Kunstwissenschaft (3 times annually) . . 05062

Deutscher Verein für Vermessungswesen e.V. (DVW), Akademiestr 3, 69117 Heidelberg
Founded: 1871; Members: 3300
Focus: Surveying
Periodical
Zeitschrift für Vermessungswesen (monthly) 05063

Deutscher Verein für Versicherungswissenschaft e.V. (DVfVW), Johannisberger Str 31, 14197 Berlin
T: (030) 8212031; Fax: 8222875
Founded: 1899; Members: 1670
Pres: Prof. Dr. Dr. Robert Schwebler; Gen Secr: Dr. Ulrich Schlie
Focus: Insurance
Periodical
Zeitschrift für die gesamte Versicherungswissenschaft (quarterly) . . 05064

Deutscher Verkehrssicherheitsrat e.V. (DVR), Beueler Bahnhofspl 16, 53222 Bonn
T: (0228) 400010; Fax: 4000167
Members: 270
Pres: Dr. Gerhard Schork; Gen Secr: Siegfried Werber
Focus: Transport; Safety
Periodical
DVR-report (quarterly) 05065

Deutscher Volkshochschul-Verband e.V. (DVV), Obere Wilhelmstr 32, 53225 Bonn
T: (0228) 975690; Fax: 9756930
Founded: 1953; Members: 16
Focus: Adult Educ
Periodicals
Adult Education and Development (semi-annually)
Agenda (quarterly)
Volkshochschule (bi-monthly) 05066

Deutscher Werkbund e.V., Weißadlergasse 4, 60311 Frankfurt
T: (069) 290658; Fax: 2979991
Focus: Educ
Periodical
Werk und Zeit (quarterly) 05067

Deutscher Wissenschaftler Verband, Höhlenweg 31, 38642 Goslar
Focus: Humanities
Periodical
DWV-Mitteilungen (quarterly) 05068

Deutscher Zentralausschuss für Chemie (DZfCh), Varrentrappstr 40-42, 60486 Frankfurt
T: (069) 7917323; E-Mail: htd@gdch.de; Fax: 7917322
Pres: Prof. Dr. Dr. Lutz F. Tietze; Gen Secr: Prof. Dr. Heindirk tom Dieck
Focus: Chem 05069

Deutscher Zentralverein Homöopathischer Ärzte e.V., Münsterstr 10, 53111 Bonn
Founded: 1829; Members: 2500
Focus: Homeopathy
Periodicals
AHZ: Allgemeine homöopathische Zeitung (monthly)
KHZ: Klassische hom. Zeitung (monthly) . 05070

Deutsches Anwaltsinstitut e.V., Brüderstr 2, 44787 Bochum
T: (0234) 12566
Focus: Law 05071

Deutsches Archäologisches Institut, Podbielskiallee 69-71, 14195 Berlin
T: (030) 830080; Fax: 83008168
Founded: 1829
Pres: Prof. Dr. Helmut Kyrieleis
Focus: Archeol
Periodicals
Archäologische Berichte aus dem Yemen
Archäologische Bibliographie als CD oder auf Disketten (annually)
Archäologische Mitteilungen aus Iran (annually)
Archäologischer Anzeiger (quarterly)
Athenische Mitteilungen (annually)
Baghdader Mitteilungen (annually)
Beiträge zur Allgemeinen und Vergleichenden Archäologie (annually)
Berichte der Römisch-Germanischen-Kommission (annually)
Chiron (annually)
Damaszener Mitteilungen (annually)
Eurasia Antiqua (annually)
Germania (annually)
Istanbuler Mitteilungen (annually)
Jahrbuch des Deutschen Archäologischen Instituts (annually)
Madrider Mitteilungen (annually)
Mitteilungen des Deutschen Archäologischen Instituts, Abteilung Kairo (annually)
Römische Mitteilungen (annually) 05072

Deutsches Atomforum e.V. (DAtF), Heussallee 10, 53113 Bonn
T: (0228) 5070
Founded: 1959
Pres: Dr. Wilfried Steuer
Focus: Nucl Res 05073

Deutsches Bibliotheksinstitut (dbi) / German Library Institute, Alt-Moabit 101A, 10559 Berlin
T: (030) 390770; Fax: 39077100
Pres: Prof. Günter Beyersdorff
Focus: Libraries & Bk Sci
Periodicals
Bibliotheksdienst (monthly)
Bibliotheksinfo (monthly)
Forum Musikbibliothek (quarterly)
Schulbibliothek Aktuell (quarterly) 05074

Deutsches Elektronen-Synchrotron (DESY), Notkestr 85, 22607 Hamburg
T: (040) 89980; E-Mail: desyinfo@desy.de; Fax: 89983282
Founded: 1959; Members: 1390
Focus: Physics
Periodicals
DESY-Jahrbuch
Forschungsberichte
Jahresbericht HASYLAB (annually)
Pressespiegel DESY
Wissenschaftlicher DESY-Jahresbericht (annually)
. . . . 05075

Deutsches Forum für Erbrecht e.V., Rosental 10, 80331 München
T: (089) 2605207; Fax: 2605287
Focus: Law 05076

Deutsches Forum für Figurentheater und Puppenspielkunst e.V., Hattinger Str 467, 44795 Bochum
T: (0234) 47720; Fax: 47735
Focus: Perf Arts 05077

Deutsches Forum für zeitgenössischen Tanz e.V. (DFT), Melchiorstr 3, 50670 Köln
T: (0221) 722133; Fax: 7392020
Focus: Perf Arts 05078

Deutsches Handwerksinstitut e.V. (DHI), Max-Joseph-Str 4, 80333 München
T: (089) 593671, 594132; Fax: 553453
Focus: Eng; Educ; Law; Econ 05079

Deutsches High-Fidelity Institut e.V. (DHFI), Karlstr 19-21, 60329 Frankfurt
T: (069) 2556409; Fax: 236521
Focus: Acoustics 05080

Deutsches Institut für Ärztliche Mission, Paul-Lechler-Str 24, 72076 Tübingen
Fax: (07071) 27125
Focus: Med
Periodical
Nachrichten aus Ärztlicher Mission (quarterly)
. . . . 05081

Deutsches Institut für angewandte Kommunikation und Projektförderung e.V., Leibnizstr 69, 53177 Bonn
Focus: Comm Sci 05082

Deutsches Institut für Betriebswirtschaft e.V. (CIB) (DIB), Friedrichstr 10-12, 60323 Frankfurt
T: 971650
Founded: 1943
Gen Secr: Wolfgang Werner
Focus: Business Admin
Periodicals
Betriebliches Vorschlagswesen
Fachzeitschrift für die Praxis in Wirtschaft und Verwaltung (quarterly) 05083

Deutsches Institut für Erwachsenenbildung/Pädagogische Arbeitsstelle des Deutschen Volkshochschul-Verbandes e.V. / Pädagogische Arbeitsstelle des Deutschen Volkshochschul-Verbandes e.V., Hansaallee 150, 60320 Frankfurt
T: (069) 956260; E-Mail: die@die.f.shuttle.de; Fax: 95626174
Founded: 1957
Focus: Adult Educ 05084

Deutsches Institut für Filmkunde e.V. (DIF), Schaumainkai 41, 60596 Frankfurt
T: (069) 9612200; Fax: 620060
Pres: Claudia Dillmann-Kühn; Gen Secr: Helmut Poßmann
Focus: Cinema 05085

Deutsches Institut für Internationale Pädagogische Forschung (DIPF), Schloßstr 29, 60486 Frankfurt
T: (069) 247080; E-Mail: dipf@dipf.de; Fax: 24708444
Founded: 1951; Members: 120
Pres: Hans Krollmann
Focus: Educ
Periodical
Zeitschrift für internationale erziehungs- und sozialwissenschaftliche Forschung (semi-annually)
. . . . 05086

Deutsches Institut für medizinische Dokumentation und Information (DIMDI) / German Institute for Medical Documentation and Information, Weißhausstr 27, 50939 Köln
T: (0221) 47241; E-Mail: helpdesk@dimdi.de; Fax: 411429
Founded: 1969
Pres: Prof. Dr. Harald G. Schweim
Focus: Doc; Med; Computer & Info Sci . 05087

Deutsches Institut für Public Relations e.V. (DIPR), Habichtweg 1, 41548 Kaarst
T: (02131) 768970; Fax: 768971
Focus: Advert 05088

Deutsches Institut für Urbanistik (Difu) (Difu) / German Institute for Urban Affairs, Strasse des 17. Juni 112, 10623 Berlin
T: (030) 390010; E-Mail: difu@difu.de; Fax: 39001100
Founded: 1973; Members: rund 140 Mitgliedsstädte
Pres: Prof. Dr. Heinrich Mäding; Gen Secr: Dr. Rolf-Peter Löhr
Focus: Urban Plan
Periodicals
Arbeitshilfen (semi-annually)
Archiv für Kommunalwissenschaften (semi-annually)
Berichte (monthly)
Difu-Materialien (5-10 times annually)
Graue Literatur zur Orts-, Regional- und Landesplanung (semi-annually)
Informationen zur modernen Stadtgeschichte (semi-annually)
Kommunalwissenschaftliche Dissertationen (irregularly)
Occasional Papers (quarterly) 05089

Deutsches Institut für Vormundschaftswesen, Postfach 102020, 69010 Heidelberg
Fax: (06221) 981828
Focus: Family Plan
Periodical
Der Amtsvormund (monthly) 05090

Deutsches Institut für Wertanalyse e.V. (DIWA), Börsenpl 4, 60313 Frankfurt/Main
T: (069) 917650; Fax: 9716525
Focus: Business Admin 05091

Deutsches Institut für Wirtschaftsforschung (DIW), Königin-Luise-Str 5, 14195 Berlin
T: (030) 897890; Fax: 89789200
Founded: 1925
Pres: Prof. Dr. Lutz Hoffmann
Focus: Econ
Periodicals
Vierteljahrshefte zur Wirtschaftsforschung (quarterly)
Wochenbericht des DIW (weekly) . . . 05092

Deutsches Jugendinstitut e.V. (DJI), Freibadstr 30, 81543 München
T: (089) 623060; Fax: 62306162
Founded: 1961; Members: 140
Focus: Lit
Periodicals
Diskurs: Studien zu Kindheit, Jugend, Familie und Gesellschaft (semi-annually)
Dokumentation Bibliographie Jugendhilfe (annually)
. . . . 05093

Deutsches Jugendschriftenwerk e.V., Fischtorpl 23, 55116 Mainz
T: (06131) 288900; Fax: 230333
Focus: Lit 05094

Deutsches Komitee Instandhaltung e.V. (DKIN), Brehmstr 78, 40239 Düsseldorf
T: (0211) 623240; Fax: 625204
Founded: 1970; Members: 19
Pres: Rolf B. Neurath; Gen Secr: Katharina Schlosser
Focus: Eng
Periodical
DKIN-Empfehlungen (irregularly) 05095

Deutsches Krebsforschungszentrum (DKFZ), Postfach 101949, 69009 Heidelberg
T: (06221) 420; Fax: 422995
Founded: 1964
Pres: Prof. Dr. Dr. Harald zur Hausen; Gen Secr: Dr. Josef Puchta
Focus: Cell Biol & Cancer Res
Periodical
einblick: Zeitschrift des Deutschen Krebsforschungszentrums (3-4 times annually)
. . . . 05096

Deutsches Kunststoff-Institut, Schloßgartenstr 6, 64289 Darmstadt
T: (06151) 162104; Fax: 292855
Founded: 1957
Pres: Prof. Dr. Dietrich Braun
Focus: Materials Sci
Periodical
Mitteilungen aus dem Deutschen Kunststoff-Institut (semi-annually) 05097

Deutsches Kupfer-Institut e.V., Knesebeckstr 96, 10623 Berlin
T: (030) 310271; Fax: 3128826
Founded: 1927; Members: 65
Focus: Materials Sci 05098

Deutsches Nationales Komitee des Weltenergierats (DNK), Graf-Recke-Str 84, 40239 Düsseldorf
T: (0211) 6214499; Fax: 6214172
Pres: Dr. G. Ott; Gen Secr: Dr. J. Debelius
Focus: Energy 05099

Deutsches Nationalkomitee für Denkmalschutz, c/o Bundesministerium des Innern, Postfach 170290, 53108 Bonn
T: (0228) 6815563; Fax: 6814130
Founded: 1973
Pres: Dr. Christina Weiss; Gen Secr: Hans Günter Kowalski
Focus: Preserv Hist Monuments
Periodical
Denkmalschutz-Informationen (quarterly) . 05100

Deutsches Optisches Komitee, c/o Institut für medizinische Optik der Universität München, Theresienstr 37, 80333 München
T: (089) 23941
Focus: Optics 05101

Deutsches Orient-Institut, Mittelweg 150, 20148 Hamburg
T: (040) 441481; Fax: 441484
Founded: 1960
Focus: Ethnology; Hist; Poli Sci
Periodicals
Mitteilungen (irregularly)
Orient (quarterly) 05102

Deutsches P.E.N.-Zentrum (Ost), Kulturbrauerei, Schönhauser Allee 36-39, 10435 Berlin
T: (030) 4413904; Fax: 4413004
Focus: Lit 05103

Deutsches Textilforschungszentrum Nord-West e.V., Frankenring 2, 47798 Krefeld
Founded: 1990; Members: 100
Focus: Textiles 05104

Deutsches Übersee-Institut, Neuer Jungfernstieg 21, 20354 Hamburg
T: (040) 3562593; E-Mail: dnei@hwwa.uni-hamburg.de; Fax: 3562547
Founded: 1964
Pres: Dr. Werner Draguhn
Focus: Develop Areas; Int'l Relat
Periodicals
Jahrbuch Dritte Welt: Daten, Übersichten, Analysen (annually)
Nord-Süd aktuell (quarterly) 05105

Deutsches wissenschaftliches Steuerinstitut der Steuerberater e.V., Poppelsdorfer Allee 24, 53115 Bonn
T: (0228) 985710; Fax: 9857146
Pres: Dr. Wilfried Dann; Gen Secr: Katrin L. Schulz
Focus: Finance 05106

Deutsches Wollforschungsinstitut (DWI), Veltmanpl 8, 52062 Aachen
T: (0241) 44690; Fax: 4469100
Founded: 1952; Members: 106
Focus: Textiles
Periodical
DWI-Report (annually) 05107

Deutsches Zentralinstitut für soziale Fragen, Bernadottestr 94, 14195 Berlin
T: (030) 83900113; Fax: 8314750
Founded: 1893
Focus: Soc Sci
Periodical
Soziale Arbeit: Deutsche Zeitschrift für soziale und sozialverwandte Gebiete (monthly) . . . 05108

Deutsches Zentralkomitee zur Bekämpfung der Tuberkulose (DZK), c/o Abteilung für Pneumologie, Universitätsklinikum, Langenbeckstr 1, 55131 Mainz
T: (06136) 8424; Fax: 80022286
Founded: 1893; Members: 32
Focus: Pulmon Dis
Periodical
Pneumologie (monthly) 05109

Deutsches Zentrum für Altersfragen e.V., Manfred-von-Richthofen-Str 2, 12101 Berlin
T: (030) 7866071; Fax: 7854350
Founded: 1973
Focus: Geriatrics
Periodical
Altenhilfe: Beispiele, Informationen, Meinungen (monthly) 05110

Deutschsprachige Arbeitsgemeinschaft für Handchirurgie, c/o Abteilung für Handchirurgie und Plastische Chirurgie, Bergedorfer Str 10, 21033 Hamburg
T: (031) 643534; Fax: 262419
Founded: 1960; Members: 78
Focus: Surgery 05111

DIN Deutsches Institut für Normung e.V., Burggrafenstr 6, 10787 Berlin
T: (030) 26010; E-Mail: POSTMASTER@DIN.DE; http://www.din.de; Fax: 2601231
Founded: 1917; Members: 5763
Pres: Gottfried Kremer; Gen Secr: Prof. Dr. Helmut Reihlen
Focus: Standards
Periodical
DIN-Mitteilungen + elektronorm (monthly) . 05112

Dokumentationsring Elektrotechnik, c/o Siemens AG, Werner-von-Siemens-Str 50, 91052 Erlangen
Focus: Electric Eng 05113

Dramatiker-Union e.V., Babelsberger Str 43, 10715 Berlin
T: (030) 8539001; Fax: 8539004
Focus: Perf Arts 05114

Dramaturgische Gesellschaft e.V. (dg), Tempelherrenstr 4, 10961 Berlin
T: (030) 6932482; Fax: 6932654
Focus: Perf Arts 05115

E.-F.-Schumacher-Gesellschaft für politische Ökologie e.V. (EFSG), Görrestr 33, 80798 München
T: (089) 529770; Fax: 529770
Focus: Ecology 05116

Eichendorff-Gesellschaft e.V., Bahnhofstr 71, 40883 Ratingen
T: (02102) 9650
Founded: 1931; Members: 520
Pres: Prof. Dr. Peter H. Neumann; Gen Secr: Marie Luise Labrie
Focus: Lit
Periodicals
apropos Eichendorff: Kleine Beiträge zur klassisch-romantischen Zeit (irregularly)
Aurora: Jahrbuch der Eichendorff-Gesellschaft (annually)
Aurora-Buchreihe (irregularly) 05117

Elektrotechnischer Verein Berlin e.V., Bismarckstr 33, 10625 Berlin
T: (030) 3414566
Members: 1200
Focus: Electronic Eng
Periodical
ETV-Mitteilungen (bi-monthly) 05118

Elisabeth-Langgässer-Gesellschaft e.V., Friedenspl 4, 64283 Darmstadt
T: (06155) 64271
Focus: Lit 05119

Else-Lasker-Schüler-Gesellschaft e.V., c/o Stadtbibliothek, Kolpingstr 8, 42103 Wuppertal
T: (0202) 305198; Fax: 305198
Focus: Lit 05120

Energie- und Umweltzentrum am Deister e.V. (E.u.U.Z.), 31832 Springe-Eldagsen
T: (05044) 9750; Fax: 97566
Focus: Energy; Ecology
Periodical
Rundbrief des E.u.U.Z. (annually) . . . 05121

Energietechnische Gesellschaft im VDE, Stresemannallee 15, 60596 Frankfurt
T: (069) 6308346
Members: 6000
Focus: Energy
Periodicals
Elektrotechnische Zeitschrift (bi-weekly)
European Transactions on Electrical Power Engineering (monthly) 05122

Erich Maria Remarque-Gesellschaft e.V., Alte Münze 16, 49074 Osnabrück
T: (0541) 9694511, 9694674; Fax: 9694774
Focus: Lit 05123

Erich Mühsam-Gesellschaft e.V., Klaus-Groth-Str 3, 23564 Lübeck
T: (0451) 704491; Fax: 7020740
Focus: Lit 05124

Ernst Barlach Gesellschaft e.V., Mühlenstr 1, 22880 Wedel
T: (04103) 918291; Fax: 97135
Focus: Arts; Fine Arts; Lit 05125

Ernst-Bloch-Gesellschaft e.V., Jahnstr 16, 67434 Neustadt
T: (06321) 30715
Focus: Lit 05126

Ernst Meister Gesellschaft e.V., c/o Buchhandlung Backhaus, Trichtergasse 14, 52064 Aachen
T: (0241) 21957
Focus: Lit 05127

Erster Deutscher Fantasy Club e.V., Wolf-Huber-Str 8b, 94032 Passau
T: (0851) 58137
Focus: Lit 05128

ESTA-Bildungswerk e.V., Bismarckstr 8, 32545 Bad Oeynhausen
T: (05731) 1570; Fax: 157101
Focus: Adult Educ 05129

E.T.A. Hoffmann-Gesellschaft e.V., Nonnenbrücke 1, 96047 Bamberg
T: 28173
Focus: Lit
Periodical
Mitteilungen (annually) 05130

Euro-Handelsinstitut e.V., Spichernstr 55, 50672 Köln
T: (0221) 579930; Fax: 5799345
Founded: 1951
Pres: Karl-Josef Baum; Gen Secr: Dr. Bernd Hallier
Focus: Business Admin
Periodical
Dynamik im Handel 05131

Europa-Zentrum Baden-Württemberg e.V. (EZBW), Wöhrdstr 25, 72072 Tübingen
T: (07071) 133051; Fax: 31851
Focus: Poli Sci 05132

Europäische Akademie Bad Bevensen, Gustav-Stresemann-Institut in Niedersachsen e.V. (GSI), Klosterweg 4, 29549 Bad Bevensen
T: (05821) 9550; Fax: 955299
Focus: Poli Sci 05133

Europäische Akademie Bayern e.V., Hirtenstr 16, 80335 München
T: (089) 5491410; Fax: 5491419
Founded: 1976
Pres: Hans Zehetmair; Gen Secr: Michael Jörger
Focus: Educ 05134

Europäische Akademie Berlin e.V. (EAB), Bismarckallee 46/48, 14193 Berlin
T: (030) 8959510; Fax: 8266410
Founded: 1964; Members: 18
Pres: Dr. Giuseppe Vita; Gen Secr: Dr. Eckart D. Stratenschulte
Focus: Educ 05135

Europäische Akademie Hessen e.V. (EAH), Arthur-Zitscher-Str 4, 63065 Offenbach
T: (069) 884884; Fax: 880215
Focus: Poli Sci 05136

Europäische Akademie Mecklenburg-Vorpommern e.V. (EA-M-V), Am Eldenholz 23, 17192 Waren
T: (033991) 15370, 122428; Fax: 121369
Focus: Poli Sci 05137

Europäische Akademie Otzenhausen e.V. (EAO), Europahausstr, 66620 Nonnweiler
T: (06873) 6620; Fax: 662250
Founded: 1954; Members: 30
Focus: Poli Sci 05138

Europäische Akademie Schleswig-Holstein e.V. (EASH), Flensburger Str 18, 25917 Leck
T: (04662) 3043; Fax: 5427
Focus: Poli Sci 05139

Europäische Autorenvereinigung Die Kogge e.V., Kleiner Domhof 17, 32423 Minden
T: (0571) 89414; Fax: 89680
Focus: Lit 05140

Europäische Bildungs- und Aktionsgemeinschaft e.V. (EBAG), Kölnstr 1, 53111 Bonn
T: (0228) 657702, 654014; Fax: 657685
Focus: Educ 05141

Europäische Bildungs- und Begegnungszentren e.V. (EBZ), Taubenberg 84, 65510 Idstein
T: (06126) 3374; Fax: 54630
Founded: 1977; Members: 10
Focus: Educ 05142

Europäische Föderalismusakademie Bonn, Denglerstr 2, 53117 Bonn
T: (0228) 358440; Fax: 358449
Focus: Poli Sci 05143

Europäische Föderation Biotechnologie (EFB) / European Federation of Biotechnology, c/o Dechema, Postfach 150104, 60061 Frankfurt
T: (069) 7564279; Fax: 7564201
Founded: 1978
Pres: Prof. Dr. G. Kreysa
Focus: Biophys; Eng
Periodical
EFB-Newsletter (quarterly) 05144

Europäische Föderation für Chemie-Ingenieur-Wesen (EFCIW) / European Federation of Chemical Engineering, Theodor-Heuss-Allee 25, 60486 Frankfurt
T: (069) 7564235; Fax: 7564201
Founded: 1953; Members: 73
Focus: Eng; Chem
Periodical
EFCE Newsletter (semi-annually) 05145

Europäische Föderation Korrosion (EFK) / European Federation of Corrosion, c/o DECHEMA, Theodor-Heuss-Allee 25, 60486 Frankfurt
T: (069) 7564209; Fax: 7564201
Founded: 1955; Members: 75
Focus: Metallurgy
Periodical
EFC Newsletter (semi-annually) 05146

Europäische Märchengesellschaft e.V. (EMG), Schloß Bentlage, 48432 Rheine
T: (05971) 12117; Fax: 53046
Focus: Lit; Folklore 05147

Europäische Staatsbürger-Akademie e.V., Adenauerallee 59, 46399 Bocholt
T: (02871) 3430; Fax: 343101
Founded: 1961; Members: 26
Focus: Adult Educ 05148

Europäische Vereinigung für Eigentumsbildung, Hermann-Lindrath-Gesellschaft e.V., Am Südbahnhof 2, 30171 Hannover
T: (0511) 810906
Founded: 1960; Members: 250
Focus: Sociology; Finance
Periodical
Pressedienst (3-4 times annually) . . . 05149

Europäischer Erzieherbund e.V., Sektion Deutschland (EEB), Julius-Brecht-Str 16, 65824 Schwalbach
T: (06196) 85515; Fax: 85515
Founded: 1956
Focus: Educ 05150

Europäischer Verband für Produktivitätsförderung, c/o Dr. Helms, Elbchaussee 352, 22609 Hamburg
T: (040) 823011; Fax: 826594
Focus: Business Admin; Eng
Periodical
News Release (quarterly) 05151

European Association for Japanese Studies (EAJS), c/o Fachbereich 5, Universität Duisburg, Lotharstr 65, 47048 Duisburg
T: (0203) 3792002; E-Mail: eajs@uni-duisburg.de; Fax: 3792002
Founded: 1973; Members: 700
Pres: Dr. Peter Kornicki; Gen Secr: Dr. Gaye Rowley
Focus: Ethnology; Ling; Lit; Cultur Hist . 05152

European Association for Research and Development in Higher Education (EARDHE), c/o Freie Universität Berlin, Habelschwerdter Allee 34a, 14195 Berlin
T: (030) 8383389; E-Mail: berendt@math.fu-berlin.; Fax: 8329096
Founded: 1972; Members: 100
Pres: Dr. Brigitte Behrendt; Gen Secr: Ilona Yenal
Focus: Educ 05153

European Association for Special Education (EASE), Edgbaston, The University of Birgmingham, B 152 TT Birmingham
T: (0121) 4144865; E-Mail: H.R.J.Daniels@bham.ac.uk
Founded: 1970
Pres: Harry Daniels; Gen Secr: Věra Vojtová
Focus: Educ 05154

European Association for the Study of Diabetes (EASD), Auf'm Hennekamp 32, 40225 Düsseldorf
T: (0211) 316738; E-Mail: easd@rz.uni-duesseldorf.de; Fax: 3190987
Founded: 1964; Members: 5000
Pres: Prof. M. (retires 1998) Berger; Gen Secr: Dr. V. Jörgens
Focus: Diabetes
Periodical
Diabetologia (monthly) 05155

European Association of Experimental Social Psychology, c/o Psychologisches Institut, Universität Heidelberg, Hauptstr 47-51, 69117 Heidelberg
T: (06221) 547270; E-Mail: FIE@PSI-SV1.PSI.UNI-HEIDELBERG.DE; Fax: 547745
Founded: 1964; Members: 15
Pres: Prof. Dr. J.P. Leyens; Gen Secr: Prof. Dr. Klaus Fiedler
Focus: Metallurgy 05156

European Astronaut Centre (EAC) / Europäisches Astronautenzentrum, c/o ESA-EAC, Linder Höhe, 51147 Köln
T: (02203) 60010; Fax: 600166
Founded: 1990; Members: 21
Pres: Heinz Oser
Focus: Aero 05157

European Centre for the Development of Vocational Training / Europäisches Zentrum für die Förderung der Berufsbildung, Bundesallee 22, 10717 Berlin
T: (030) 884120; Fax: 88412222
Founded: 1975; Members: 12
Focus: Educ 05158

European Committee for Future Accelerators (ECFA), c/o III. Physikalisches Institut, Rheinisch-Westfälische Hochschule, Sommerfeldstr 26-28, 52074 Aachen
Founded: 1962
Focus: Eng 05159

European Council of Management (CECIOS), c/o RKW, Düsseldorfer Str 40, 65760 Eschborn
T: (06196) 495366; Fax: 495303
Focus: Business Admin 05160

European Fast Reactor Association, c/o Kernforschungszentrum Karlsruhe, Leopoldhafen 2, 76344 Eggenstein
Focus: Nucl Res 05161

European Federation of Corrosion (EFC), c/o DECHEMA, Theodor-Heuss-Allee 25, 60486 Frankfurt
T: (069) 7564209; Fax: 7564201
Founded: 1955
Focus: Metallurgy
Periodical
EFC Newsletter 05162

European Federation of Cytology Societies (EFCS), c/o Zentrum für Pathologie, Institut für Cytopathologie, Universität, Moorenstr 5, 40225 Düsseldorf
T: (0221) 3112524; Fax: 342229
Founded: 1969
Focus: Cell Biol & Cancer Res 05163

European Federation of the Associations of Dieticians, Neuhaus 22, 40833 Ratingen
T: (02102) 60358
Founded: 1978
Pres: Renate Frenz; Gen Secr: Judith Liddell
Focus: Nutrition 05164

European Guitar Teachers Association (EGTA), Marblicksweg 55, 59555 Lippstadt
T: (02941) 60445; Fax: 2471
Focus: Educ; Music 05165

European Piano Teachers Association, Sektion der Bundesrepublik Deutschland (EPTA), Schanzenstr 24, 34130 Kassel
T: (0561) 68082; Fax: 66778
Focus: Educ; Music 05166

European Society of Neuroradiology, c/o Institut für Neuroradiology, Universität des Saarlandes, 66421 Homburg
Fax: (06841) 164310
Focus: Radiology
Periodical
Neuroradiology 05167

European String Teachers Association (ESTA), Katzenberg 123, 55126 Mainz
T: (06131) 479568
Focus: Educ; Music 05168

European Water Pollution Control Association e.V. (EWPCA), Theodor-Heuss-Allee 17, 53773 Hennef
T: (02242) 8720; E-Mail: 101623.1473@comouserve.com; Fax: 872135
Founded: 1981; Members: 26
Pres: Dr. Peter Matthews; Gen Secr: Dr. Sigurd van Riesen
Focus: Ecology
Periodical
European Water Pollution Control (bi-monthly)
. . . . 05169

European Weed Research Society (EWRS), c/o Dr. Birgit Krauskopf, Bayer AG, Bayerwerk, Postfach E-Reg., 51368 Leverkusen
T: (02173) 384928; Fax: 383593
Founded: 1959; Members: 590
Focus: Botany
Periodical
Weed Research (bi-monthly) 05170

Evangelisch-theologischer Fakultätentag, Lahntor 3, 35037 Marburg
T: (06421) 284274/-75; Fax: 288968
Focus: Educ; Rel & Theol 05171

Evangelische Akademie Arnoldshain (EAA), Arnoldshain, 61389 Schmitten
T: (06084) 9440; Fax: 944138
Focus: Rel & Theol 05172

Evangelische Akademie Bad Boll, Akademieweg 11, 73087 Bad Boll
T: (07164) 790; Fax: 79440
Founded: 1945
Focus: Adult Educ
Periodicals
Aktuelle Gespräche (quarterly)
Arbeitshilfen (irregularly)
Dokumente, Texte und Tendenzen (irregularly)
. . . . 05173

Evangelische Akademie Baden (Bad Herrenalb), Postfach 76010, 76010 Karlsruhe
T: (0721) 9175380; Fax: 9175350
Founded: 1947
Pres: Hans Martin Leichle; Gen Secr: Ralf Stieber
Focus: Adult Educ
Periodical
Diskussionen: Zeitschrift für Freunde der Akademiearbeit 05174

Evangelische Akademie Berlin – Brandenburg, Goethestr 27-30, 10625 Berlin
T: (030) 3191297; Fax: 3191200
Focus: Rel & Theol 05175

Evangelische Akademie der Pfalz (EvAKPf), Dompl 5, 67346 Speyer
T: (06232) 60200; Fax: 25307
Focus: Rel & Theol 05176

Evangelische Akademie Görlitz, Schlaurother Str 11, 02827 Görlitz
T: (03581) 744261; Fax: 406818
Focus: Rel & Theol 05177

Evangelische Akademie Greifswald, Karl-Marx-Platz 15, 17489 Greifswald
T: (03834) 897490; Fax: 897490
Focus: Rel & Theol 05178

Evangelische Akademie Hofgeismar, Schlösschen Schönburg, Gesundbrunnen, 34369 Hofgeismar
T: (05671) 8810
Focus: Adult Educ
Periodical
Anstösse (quarterly) 05179

Evangelische Akademie im Saarland (eas), Großherzog-Friedrich-Str 44, 66111 Saarbrücken
T: (0681) 3870051/52; Fax: 3870056
Focus: Rel & Theol 05180

Evangelische Akademie Iserlohn, Berliner Platz 12, 58638 Iserlohn
T: (02371) 3520, 35243; Fax: 35289
Focus: Rel & Theol 05181

Evangelische Akademie Kurhessen-Waldeck, Gesundbrunnen 11, 34369 Hofgeismar
T: (05671) 8810; Fax: 881154
Focus: Rel & Theol 05182

Evangelische Akademie Loccum, Münchehäger Str 6, 31547 Rehburg-Loccum
T: (05766) 810; Fax: 81188
Founded: 1952
Focus: Adult Educ
Periodicals
Forum Loccum (quarterly)
Loccumer Protokolle 05183

Evangelische Akademie Meißen (EAM), Freiheit 16, 01662 Meißen
T: (03521) 47060; Fax: 470699
Focus: Rel & Theol 05184

Evangelische Akademie Mühlheim an der Ruhr, Uhlenhorstweg 29, 45479 Mühlheim a. d. Ruhr
T: (0208) 599060; Fax: 59906600
Focus: Rel & Theol 05185

Evangelische Akademie Nordelbien, Marienstr 31, 23795 Bad Segeberg
T: (04551) 80090; Fax: 800950
Focus: Rel & Theol 05186

Evangelische Akademie Oldenburg (EAO), Mühlenstr 126, 26180 Rastede
T: (04402) 92840, 928419; Fax: 82138
Focus: Rel & Theol 05187

Evangelische Akademie Sachsen-Anhalt, Otto-von-Guericke-Str 57, 39104 Magdeburg
T: (0391) 5619249/50; Fax: 5619249/50
Focus: Rel & Theol 05188

Evangelische Akademie Thüringen (EAT), Zinzendorfhaus, 99192 Neudietendorf
T: (036202) 98300; Fax: 82253
Focus: Rel & Theol 05189

Evangelische Akademie Tutzing, Schloßstr 2-4, 82327 Tutzing
T: (08158) 2510; Fax: 251133
Founded: 1947
Pres: Dr. Friedemann Greiner; Gen Secr: Martin Kurz
Focus: Adult Educ
Periodicals
Tutzinger Blätter (quarterly)
Tutzinger Materialien (irregularly) 05190

Evangelische Akademien in Deutschland e.V., Akademieweg 11, 73087 Bad Boll
T: (07164) 79230
Founded: 1947; Members: 19
Pres: Wolfgang Vogelmann; Gen Secr: Wolfgang Lenz
Focus: Adult Educ 05191

Evangelische Akademikerschaft in Deutschland e.V., Kniebisstr 29, 70188 Stuttgart
T: (0711) 282015; E-Mail: EvangAkadi@T-Online.de; Fax: 2628115
Members: 3000
Pres: Dr. Matthias Ahrens
Focus: Rel & Theol
Periodical
Evangelische Aspekte (quarterly) 05192

Evangelische Arbeitsgemeinschaft für Kirchliche Zeitgeschichte, Schellingstr 3, 80799 München
T: (089) 21802828
Focus: Hist; Rel & Theol 05193

Evangelische Landjugendakademie Altenkirchen, Dieperzbergweg 13, 57610 Altenkirchen
T: (02681) 95160; Fax: 70206
Focus: Rel & Theol 05194

Evangelische Medienakademie im GEP e.V. (cpa), Emil-von-Behring-Str 3, 60439 Frankfurt/Main
T: (069) 58098207; Fax: 58098254
Focus: Mass Media 05195

Evangelische Sozialakademie Friedewald, Schloßstr 2, 57520 Friedewald
T: (02743) 2091; Fax: 4645
Founded: 1949; Members: 10
Focus: Sociology; Rel & Theol; Econ . . 05196

Evangelische Studiengemeinschaft e.V. / Protestant Institute for Interdisciplinary Studies, Schmeilweg 5, 69118 Heidelberg
T: (06221) 14061
Founded: 1957; Members: 20
Focus: Rel & Theol; Philos; Nat Sci
Periodicals
Forschungen und Berichte
Texte und Materialien 05197

Evangelischer Erziehungs-Verband e.V. (EREV) / Bundesverband evangelischer Einrichtungen und Dienste, Lister Meile 87, 30161 Hannover
T: (0511) 660266; Fax: 660222
Founded: 1920; Members: 400
Focus: Educ
Periodicals
EREV-Schriftenreihe (quarterly)
Evangelische Jugendhilfe (5 times annually)
. . . . 05198

Fachgruppe Baudenkmalpflege des Deutschen Heimatbundes e.V. (DHB), Adenauerallee 68, 53113 Bonn
T: (0228) 224091; Fax: 215503
Focus: Preserv Hist Monuments 05199

Fachgruppe Frauenarbeit und Informatik in der Gesellschaft für Informatik e.V., Mendelssohnstr 42, 30173 Hannover
T: (0511) 801865, 9357230
Focus: Sociology; Computer & Info Sci . 05200

Fachgruppe Freie musikwissenschaftliche Forschungsinstitute, Hohle Gasse 5, 53177 Bonn
T: (0228) 658245, 326212; Fax: 692744
Focus: Music 05201

Fachinformationssystem Bildung / Koordinierungsstelle, c/o Deutsches Institut für Internationale Pädagogische Forschung, Schloßstr 29, 60486 Frankfurt
T: (069) 247080; Fax: 24708444
Founded: 1992; Members: 20 Einrichtungen
Pres: Alexander Botte
Focus: Educ
Periodicals
Bibliographie Pädagogik: Bibliographie Pédagogique (1-2 times annually)
CD Bildung (annually) 05202

Fachinformationszentrum Technik e.V., Ostbahnhofstr 13, 60314 Frankfurt
T: (069) 4308241; Fax: 4308200
Focus: Textiles
Periodical
Informationsdienst Textiltechnik Bekleidungstechnik Textilmaschinenbau (monthly) 05203

Fachkonferenz des Borromäusvereins, Wittelsbacherring 9, 53115 Bonn
T: (0228) 72580; Fax: 7258189
Founded: 1996
Pres: Joachim Pflug; Gen Secr: Norbert Brockmann
Focus: Libraries & Bk Sci 05204

Fachschaft Berliner Chirurgen e.V., Technowpromenade 65, 13437 Berlin
T: (030) 4112870
Focus: Surgery 05205

Fachverband Deutscher Berufschorleiter e.V. (FDB), Märker Str 29, 47169 Duisburg
T: (0203) 592708; Fax: 590115
Focus: Music 05206

Fachverband Deutscher Heilpraktiker e.V., Maarweg 10, 53123 Bonn
T: (0228) 611049; Fax: 627359
Members: ca. 53000
Pres: Peter A. Zizmann
Focus: Med
Periodical
Der Heilpraktiker & Volksheilkunde (monthly)
. . . . 05207

Fachverband Moderne Fremdsprachen (FMF), Marconistr 30b, 86179 Augsburg
T: (0821) 85237; Fax: 5985501
Founded: 1880; Members: 7500
Pres: Prof. Dr. Konrad Schröder
Focus: Ling
Periodical
Neusprachliche Mitteilungen aus Wissenschaft und Praxis (quarterly) 05208

Fachverband Pulvermetallurgie (Fpm), Postfach 921, 58009 Hagen
T: (02331) 958817; Fax: 51046
Founded: 1948; Members: 41
Pres: Dr. Lothar Albano-Müller; Gen Secr: Hans-Dieter Oelkers
Focus: Metallurgy
Periodicals
Metall (monthly)
powder metallurgy international (bi-monthly)
Pulvermetallurgie in Wissenschaft und Praxis (annually) 05209

Fachverband Textilunterricht e.V., Münzstr 6, 48143 Münster
T: (0251) 42595
Founded: 1975; Members: 500
Focus: Educ; Textiles
Periodical
Textil-Info für Unterricht & Bildung (quarterly)
. . . . 05210

Fachvereinigung Niederländisch e.V. (FN), Alter Steinweg 6-7, 48143 Münster
T: (0251) 4142227; Fax: 40061
Focus: Ling 05211

Fakultätentag für Bauingenieur- und Vermessungswesen, c/o Institut für Baumechanik, Mommsenstr 13, 01069 Dresden
T: (0351) 4635369; Fax: 4637200
Focus: Civil Eng 05212

Fakultätentag für Maschinenbau und Verfahrenstechnik, c/o Lehrstuhl für Hydr. Maschinen, Arcisstr 21, 80333 München
T: (089) 21052330; Fax: 21052333
Focus: Educ; Mach Eng; Eng 05213

Fakultätentag Informatik der Hochschulen in der Bundesrepublik Deutschland, c/o Universität, Geb. 20.20, Kaiserstr 12, 76128 Karlsruhe
T: (0721) 6083909; Fax: 370455
Focus: Educ; Computer & Info Sci . . . 05214

Faust-Gesellschaft, Nachtigallenstr 52, 75417 Mühlacker
Focus: Hist 05215

Fehrs-Gilde e.V., Wellingsbüttler Weg 97, 22391 Hamburg
T: (040) 5363172
Focus: Lit 05216

Ferdinand Tönnies-Gesellschaft e.V., Freiligrathstr 11, 24116 Kiel
T: (0431) 551107; Fax: 552993
Founded: 1956; Members: 130
Pres: Prof. Dr. Lars Clausen; Gen Secr: Dr. Uwe Carstens
Focus: Sociology; Philos
Periodical
Tönnies-Forum (semi-annually) 05217

Filmbewertungsstelle Wiesbaden (FBW), Postfach 120240, 65080 Wiesbaden
T: (0611) 9660040; Fax: 96600411
Founded: 1951; Members: Länder der BRD
Pres: Steffen Wolf
Focus: Cinema 05218

Filmkritiker Kooperative, Kreitmayerstr 3, 80335 München
Focus: Cinema
Periodical
Filmkritik (monthly) 05219

Fördergemeinschaft für Absatz- und Werbeforschung, Friedensstr 11, 60311 Frankfurt
Focus: Marketing; Advert 05220

Fördergemeinschaft für das Süddeutsche Kunststoff-Zentrum e.V. (FSKZ), Frankfurter Str 15-17, 97082 Würzburg
T: (0931) 41040; Fax: 4194177
Pres: Dr. Volker Hülck; Gen Secr: Dr. Franz Haaf
Focus: Materials Sci; Adult Educ; Eng . 05221

Fördergemeinschaft für Staatsbürgerliche Bildung e.V., Godesberger Allee 91, 53175 Bonn
T: (0228) 376567
Focus: Poli Sci 05222

Förderkreis Freie Literaturgesellschaft e.V. (FFL), Gerichtsweg 28, 04103 Leipzig
T: (0341) 9954163
Focus: Lit 05223

Förderkreis Phantastik in Wetzlar, c/o Phansastische Bibliothek, Friedrich-Ebert-Pl 3, 35578 Wetzlar
T: (06441) 99490; Fax: 99395
Focus: Lit 05224

Förderungsgemeinschaft der Kartoffelwirtschaft e.V., Dethlingen, 29633 Munster
T: (05192) 2282; Fax: 10979
Founded: 1949
Focus: Nutrition; Food; Agri
Periodical
Der Kartoffelbau: Fachzeitschrift über Züchtung, Vermehrung, Produktionstechnik, Verwertung und Ökonomik (monthly) 05225

FOGRA Forschungsgesellschaft Druck e.V., Postfach 800469, 81604 München
T: (089) 431820; E-Mail: fogra@fogra.org; Fax: 4316896
Founded: 1951; Members: 600
Pres: Jan te Neues; Gen Secr: Dr. Hans-Joachim Falge
Focus: Eng
Periodicals
FOGRA Aktuell (bi-monthly)
Fogra-Literatur-Profil (irregularly)
Fogra-Literaturdienst (monthly)
Fogra-Mitteilungen (semi-annually)
Fogra-Patentschau (monthly) 05226

Forschungs-Gesellschaft Verfahrenstechnik e.V., Graf-Recke-Str 84, 40239 Düsseldorf
T: (0211) 6214552; Fax: 6214159
Founded: 1951
Focus: Eng 05227

Forschungsgemeinschaft Angewandte Geophysik e.V., Postfach 3266, 30032 Hannover
T: (0511) 326331; Fax: 328501
Founded: 1954; Members: 16
Focus: Geophys 05228

Forschungsgemeinschaft Eisenhüttenschlacken e.V., Bliersheimer Str 62, 47229 Duisburg
T: (02065) 99450; Fax: 994510
Focus: Metallurgy; Ecology; Eng 05229

Forschungsgemeinschaft Feuerfest e.V., An der Elisabethkirche 27, 53113 Bonn
T: (0228) 915080; Fax: 9150866
Focus: Materials Sci
Periodical
Literaturbericht (quarterly) 05230

Forschungsgemeinschaft für Hochspannungs- und Hochstromtechnik e.V. (FGH), Hallenweg, 68219 Mannheim
T: (0621) 89970
Founded: 1921; Members: 77
Focus: Electric Eng 05231

Forschungsgemeinschaft für technisches Glas e.V. (FtG), Bronnbach 28, 97877 Wertheim
T: (09342) 92120; Fax: 921292
Founded: 1950; Members: 41
Focus: Materials Sci 05232

Forschungsgemeinschaft Hönn-Wolf, Markt 12, 98631 Römhild
Focus: Arts 05233

Forschungsgemeinschaft Industrieofenbau e.V., Lyoner Str 18, 60528 Frankfurt
T: (069) 66030; Fax: 6603692
Focus: Eng 05234

Forschungsgemeinschaft Kalk und Mörtel e.V., Annastr 67-71, 50969 Köln
T: (0221) 376920
Focus: Materials Sci
Periodical
Forschungsberichte der Forschungsgemeinschaft Kalk und Mörtel e.V. (irregularly) . . . 05235

Forschungsgemeinschaft Kraftpapiere und Papiersäcke, Nerotal 4, 65193 Wiesbaden
T: (0611) 524041/42
Focus: Materials Sci 05236

Forschungsgemeinschaft Naturstein-Industrie e.V., Annastr 67-71, 50968 Köln
T: (0221) 93467463; Fax: 93467464
Members: 12
Pres: Dr. Michael Pescher; Gen Secr: Dr. Ulrich Hahn
Focus: Materials Sci
Periodical
Die Naturstein-Industrie (monthly) 05237

Forschungsgemeinschaft Werkzeuge und Werkstoffe e.V. (FGW), Postfach 100320, 42803 Remscheid
T: (02191) 900300; E-Mail: FGW-Remscheid@t-online.de; Fax: 900320
Focus: Eng 05238

Forschungsgemeinschaft Zink e.V., Friedrich-Ebert-Str 37-39, 40210 Düsseldorf
T: (0211) 350867; Fax: 350869
Focus: Materials Sci 05239

Forschungsgesellschaft Druckmaschinen e.V. (FGD), Postfach 710864, 60498 Frankfurt
T: (069) 6603451; Fax: 6603675
Founded: 1955; Members: 24
Focus: Mach Eng 05240

Forschungsgesellschaft für Agrarpolitik und Agrarsoziologie e.V., Meckenheimer Allee 125, 53115 Bonn
T: (0228) 634781, 634788
Founded: 1953; Members: 61
Focus: Poli Sci; Econ; Sociology . . . 05241

Forschungsgesellschaft für Strassen- und Verkehrswesen e.V., Postfach 501362, 50973 Köln
T: (0221) 397035; Fax: 393747
Focus: Civil Eng; Transport
Periodicals
Arbeitsgruppe Asphaltstrassen: Schriftenreihe (irregularly)
Arbeitsgruppe Betonstrassen: Schriftenreihe (irregularly)
Arbeitsgruppe Erd- und Grundbau (irregularly)
Arbeitsgruppe Mineralstoffe im Strassenbau (irregularly)
Dokumentation Straße: Kurzauszüge aus dem Schrifttum über das Straßenwesen (monthly)
Forschung im Straßenwesen (irregularly)
Forschungsarbeiten aus dem Strassenwesen (irregularly)
Strasse und Autobahn (monthly)
Strassenverkehrstechnik (bi-monthly) . . . 05242

Forschungsgesellschaft Kunststoffe e.V., Schlossgartenstr 6, 64289 Darmstadt
T: (06151) 291150; Fax: 292855
Founded: 1953; Members: 168
Focus: Materials Sci
Periodical
Literaturschnelldienst: Kunststoffe, Kautschuk, Fasern (monthly) 05243

Forschungsgesellschaft Landschaftsentwicklung Landschaftsbau e.V., Colmantstr 32, 53115 Bonn
T: (0228) 691810; Fax: 650098
Focus: Ecology 05244

Forschungsgesellschaft Stahlverformung e.V., Postfach 4009, 58040 Hagen
T: (02331) 958841; Fax: 51046
Focus: Eng 05245

Forschungsgesellschaft Steinzeugindustrie e.V., Max-Planck-Str 6, 50858 Köln 40
Focus: Materials Sci 05246

Forschungsgruppe für Anthropologie und Religionsgeschichte e.V., Droste-Hülshoff-Str 9b, 48341 Altenberge
Founded: 1970
Focus: Anthro; Rel & Theol
Periodicals
Forschungen zur Anthropologie und Religionsgeschichte
Jahrbuch für Anthropologie und Religionsgeschichte (annually) 05247

Forschungsgruppe Köln, Barbarossapl 2, 50674 Köln
T: (0221) 235177/79
Focus: Sci 05248

Forschungsgruppe Modellprojekte e.V. (FGM), Römerstr 18, 69115 Heidelberg
T: (06221) 10085
Focus: Sci 05249

Forschungsinstitut für Arbeiterbildung e.V. (FIAB), Kirchpl 2, 45657 Recklinghausen
T: (02361) 57034; Fax: 183362
Founded: 1980
Focus: Adult Educ
Periodical
Jahrbuch Arbeit, Bildung, Kultur 05250

Forschungsinstitut für Pigmente und Lacke e.V., Allmandring 37, 70569 Stuttgart
T: (0711) 687800; E-Mail: fpl@fpl.uni-stuttgart.de; Fax: 6878079
Founded: 1951; Members: 37
Pres: Prof. Dr. Claus D. Eisenbach; Gen Secr: Dr. Johannes Reck
Focus: Materials Sci 05251

Forschungsinstitut für Rationalisierung e.V. / FIR, Pontdriesch 14-16, 52062 Aachen
T: (0241) 477050; Fax: 402401
Focus: Business Admin
Periodical
FIR+IAW-Mitteilungen (3 times annually) . 05252

Forschungsinstitut für Wärmeschutz e.V. München (FIW) (FIW), Postfach 1525, 82157 Gräfelfing
T: (089) 858000; Fax: 8580040
Founded: 1918; Members: 140
Pres: Peter Hefter; Gen Secr: Joachim Achtziger; Horst Zehendner
Focus: Civil Eng
Periodicals
FIW-Informationen
Mitteilungen aus dem Forschungsinstitut für Wärmeschutz 05253

Forschungskuratorium Gesamttextil / Ständiger Ausschuss des Gesamtverbandes der Textilindustrie in der Bundesrepublik Deutschland -Gesamttextil- e.V., Frankfurter Str 10-14, 65760 Eschborn
T: (06196) 9660; Fax: 42170
Founded: 1951
Pres: Dr. Ehrenfried Hennige; Gen Secr: Dr. Walter Begemann
Focus: Textiles
Periodical
Textilforschung: Bericht des Forschungskuratoriums Gesamttextil (annually) 05254

Forschungskuratorium Maschinenbau e.V., Lyoner Str 18, 60528 Frankfurt
T: (069) 66031
Focus: Mach Eng 05255

Forschungsrat Kältetechnik e.V., Lyoner Str 18, 60528 Frankfurt
T: (069) 6603277; Fax: 6603218
Focus: Air Cond 05256

Forschungsstelle der Deutschen Ziegelindustrie e.V., Schaumburg-Lippe-Str 4, 53113 Bonn
T: (0228) 9149315; Fax: 9149327
Founded: 1953; Members: 100
Pres: K.-H. Brakemeier
Focus: Materials Sci
Periodical
ZI – Ziegelindustrie International (monthly) 05257

Forschungsstelle für Acetylen, Marsbruchstr 186, 44287 Dortmund
T: (0231) 451194
Focus: Chem 05258

Forschungsstelle für den Handel Berlin (FfH) e.V. (FfH), Fehrbelliner Pl 3, 10707 Berlin
T: (030) 8630940; Fax: 86309444
Founded: 1929
Pres: Prof. Dr. Volker Trommsdorff; Gen Secr: Dr. Helmut Bunge
Focus: Commerce
Periodical
mitteilungen aus der FfH (quarterly) . . 05259

Forschungsstelle für internationale Agrar- und Wirtschaftsentwicklung e.V., Ringstr 19, 69115 Heidelberg
T: (06221) 183056; E-Mail: FIA@urz.uni-heidelberg.de; Fax: 167482
Founded: 1962; Members: 70
Pres: Prof. Dr. O. Gans; Gen Secr: Dr. O.C. Kirsch
Focus: Agri 05260

Forschungsverband für den Handelsvertreter- und Handelsmaklerberuf, Geleniusstr 1, 50931 Köln
T: (0221) 514043
Focus: Advert; Commerce 05261

Forschungsvereinigung Antriebstechnik e.V., Lyoner Str 18, 60528 Frankfurt
T: (069) 66030
Pres: Prof. Dr. Manfred Hirt; Gen Secr: Hartmut Rauen
Focus: Eng 05262

Forschungsvereinigung Automobiltechnik e.V. (FAT), Westendstr 61, 60325 Frankfurt
T: (069) 75701
Focus: Auto Eng 05263

Forschungsvereinigung der Deutschen Asphaltindustrie e.V., Geleitstr 105, 63067 Offenbach
T: (069) 883305
Focus: Materials Sci 05264

Forschungsvereinigung der Gipsindustrie e.V., Birkenweg 13, 64295 Darmstadt
T: (06151) 314310; Fax: 316549
Focus: Materials Sci 05265

Forschungsvereinigung der Rheinischen Bimsindustrie e.V., Sandkauler Weg 1, 56564 Neuwied
T: (02631) 22227/28
Focus: Materials Sci 05266

Forschungsvereinigung Elektrotechnik beim ZVEI e.V., Stresemannallee 19, 60596 Frankfurt
T: (069) 6302277
Focus: Electric Eng 05267

Forschungsvereinigung Feinmechanik und Optik e.V., Pipinstr 16, 50667 Köln
Founded: 1963
Focus: Eng; Optics 05268

Forschungsvereinigung für angewandte Schloß-, Beschlag- und präventive Sicherheitstechnik e.V., Offerstr 12, 42551 Velbert
T: (02051) 95060; Fax: 950620
Focus: Eng 05269

Forschungsvereinigung für Luft- und Trocknungstechnik e.V. (FLT), Lyoner Str 18, 60528 Frankfurt
T: (069) 660289; E-Mail: Maschinenverein Frankfurtmain
Founded: 1964; Members: 40
Focus: Air Cond
Periodical
Forschungsberichte aus dem Gebiet der Luft- und Trocknungstechnik (annually) 05270

Forschungsvereinigung Kalk-Sand e.V., Entenfangweg 15, 30419 Hannover
T: (0511) 793077; Fax: 750333
Focus: Materials Sci
Periodical
Forschungsberichte (quarterly) 05271

Forschungsvereinigung Porenbeton e.V., Postfach 1826, 65008 Wiesbaden
T: (0611) 85086; Fax: 809707
Focus: Materials Sci 05272

Forschungsvereinigung Programmiersprachen für Fertigungseinrichtungen e.V., Peterstr 17, 52062 Aachen
T: (0241) 25607
Focus: Computer & Info Sci 05273

Forschungsvereinigung Schweißen und Schneiden e.V., Aachener Str 172, 40223 Düsseldorf
T: (0211) 15910; Fax: 1591200
Focus: Metallurgy
Periodicals
Der Praktiker (monthly)
Schweißen und Schneiden: Welding and Cutting (monthly)
Verbindungstechnik in der Elektronik (quarterly)
. . . . 05274

Forschungsvereinigung Verbrennungskraftmaschinen e.V. (FVV), Postfach 710864, 60498 Frankfurt
T: (069) 66030
Founded: 1956; Members: 52
Focus: Auto Eng 05275

Forschungsvereinigung Ziegelindustrie, Schaumburg-Lippe-Str 4, 53113 Bonn
T: (0228) 914930; Fax: 9149327
Focus: Materials Sci 05276

Forschungszentrum des Deutschen Schiffbaues e.V., An der Alster 1, 20099 Hamburg
T: (040) 245505
Focus: Navig 05277

Forstlicher Fakultätentag, Büsgenweg 5, 37077 Göttingen
T: (0551) 393401; Fax: 399629
Focus: Educ; Forestry 05278

Fortbildungsakademie der Wirtschaft (FAW), Schönhauser Str 64, 50968 Köln
T: (0221) 376400; Fax: 3764040
Focus: Business Admin 05279

Fortbildungszentrum Gesundheits- und Umweltschutz Berlin e.V. (FGU), Eisenacher Str 11, 10777 Berlin
T: (030) 212953; Fax: 21295420
Focus: Public Health; Ecology 05280

Forum für Zukunftsenergien e.V., Godesberger Allee 90, 53175 Bonn
T: (0228) 959550; Fax: 9595550
Focus: Energy 05281

Fränkische Geographische Gesellschaft e.V., Kochstr 4, 91054 Erlangen
T: (09131) 852645; Fax: 852013
Founded: 1954; Members: 1050
Pres: Prof. Dr. Horst Kopp; Gen Secr: Prof. Dr. Hilmar Schröder
Focus: Geography
Periodical
Mitteilungen der Fränkischen Geographischen Gesellschaft 05282

Frank-Wedekind-Gesellschaft e.V. (FWG), Haardtring 100, 64295 Darmstadt
T: (06151) 168745; Fax: 168945
Focus: Lit 05283

Franken-Akademie Schloß Schney e.V., Friedrich-Puchta-Str 15, 95444 Bayreuth
T: (0921) 23066; Fax: 83930
Focus: Poli Sci 05284

Frankfurter Geographische Gesellschaft e.V. (FGG), Senckenberganlage 36, 60325 Frankfurt
T: (069) 7982913; Fax: 7988382
Founded: 1836; Members: 300
Focus: Geography
Periodical
Frankfurter Geographische Hefte (irregularly)
. . . . 05285

Frau und Musik, Internationaler Arbeitskreis e.V., Naumburger Str 40, 34127 Kassel
T: (0561) 8900061; Fax: 893642
Focus: Music 05286

Frauen in Naturwissenschaft und Technik e.V., Friedrichstr 165, 10117 Berlin
T: (030) 2291792
Focus: Nat Sci; Eng 05287

Fraunhofer-Gesellschaft zur Förderung der angewandten Forschung e.V., Leonrodstr 54, 80636 München
T: (089) 120501; Fax: 1205317
Founded: 1949
Focus: Nat Sci; Eng; Electronic Eng; Computer & Info Sci; Materials Sci; Civil Eng; Energy; Ecology; Public Health; Econ
Periodicals
Forschungsplan (annually)
Der Fraunhofer (quarterly)
Jahresbericht/Annual Report (annually)
Mediendienst/Research News (monthly)
Medienspiegel (annually) 05288

Freie Akademie der Künste in Hamburg e.V., Klosterwall 23, 20095 Hamburg
T: (040) 324632; Fax: 326929
Focus: Arts 05289

Freie Akademie der Künste Mannheim (AdK), R 7, 24, 68161 Mannheim
T: (0621) 154571; Fax: 154577
Focus: Arts 05290

Freie Vereinigung von Fachleuten öffentlicher Verkehrsbetriebe (FV), Bochumer Str 4, 45879 Gelsenkirchen
T: (0209) 1584230
Members: 270
Focus: Transport 05291

Freier Deutscher Autorenverband e.V. (FDA), Seifen 1, 57587 Birken-Honigsessen
T: (02742) 6651; Fax: 6651
Focus: Lit 05292

Freier Verband Deutscher Zahnärzte e.V., Mallwitzstr 16, 53177 Bonn
T: (0228) 85570; E-Mail: joe.fvdz@t-online.de; Fax: 347967
Founded: 1955; Members: 24000
Pres: Dr. Ralph Gutmann; Gen Secr: Manfred Gilles
Focus: Dent
Periodicals
Der Freie Zahnarzt (monthly)
Wissenschaftlicher Info-Dienst (bi-monthly) 05293

Freudenthal-Gesellschaft e.v., Rathaus, Poststr 12, 29614 Soltau
T: (05191) 82205
Focus: Lit 05294

Freundeskreis Deutscher Auslandsschulen e.V., Adenauerallee 148, 53113 Bonn
T: (0228) 104106; Fax: 104199
Pres: Hans Peter Stihl; Gen Secr: Philipp Graf von Walderdorff
Focus: Educ 05295

Freundeskreis Till Eulenspiegels e.V., Rathaus, Markt 3, 38170 Schöppenstedt
T: (05332) 6158; Fax: 938101
Focus: Lit 05296

Fridtjof-Nanse-Akademie für politische bildung (FNA), Wilhelm-Leuschner-Str 61, 55218 Ingelheim
T: (06132) 7900316; Fax: 7900322
Focus: Poli Sci 05297

Friedrich-Ebert-Stiftung e.V. / The Friedrich Ebert Foundation, Godesberger Allee 149, 53175 Bonn
T: (0228) 8830; Fax: 883396
Founded: 1925
Focus: Adult Educ; Hist
Periodicals
Archiv für Sozialgeschichte
Schriftenreihe des Forschungsinstituts der Friedrich-Ebert-Stiftung
Vierteljahresberichte des Forschungsinstituts der Friedrich-Ebert-Stiftung 05298

Friedrich Gerstäcker-Gesellschaft e.V., Am Uhlenbusch 17, 38108 Braunschweig
T: (0531) 350189; Fax: 352960
Focus: Lit 05299

Friedrich-Spee-Gesellschaft e.V., Bilker Str 12-14, 40213 Düsseldorf
T: (0211) 8995580; Fax: 8929044
Focus: Lit 05300

Friedrich-Spee-Gesellschaft e.V., Weberbach 25, 54290 Trier
T: (0651) 7182430; Fax: 7183432
Focus: Lit 05301

Fritz Reuter Gesellschaft e.V. (FRG), Neutorstr, Neues Tor, 17033 Neubrandenburg
T: (0395) 5442753; Fax: 5442753
Focus: Lit 05302

Frobenius-Gesellschaft e.V., Liebigstr 41, 60323 Frankfurt
T: (069) 7191990; Fax: 71919911
Founded: 1938; Members: 170
Pres: Werner Busch
Focus: Ethnology; Hist; Cultur Hist
Periodicals
Ergebnisse der Frobenius-Expeditionen
Paideuma-Mitteilungen zur Kulturkunde (annually)
Sonderschriften des Frobenius-Instituts
Studien zur Kulturkunde 05303

Frontinus-Gesellschaft e.V., Brüderstr 53, 51427 Bergisch Gladbach
T: (02204) 962159; Fax: 962160
Members: 400
Pres: Herbert Oster
Focus: Eng
Periodical
Frontinus-Schriftenreihe 05304

Fuldaer Geschichtsverein e.V., Schloßstr, 36037 Fulda
T: (0661) 102440; Fax: 102777
Founded: 1896; Members: 499
Focus: Hist
Periodical
Fuldaer Geschichtsblätter (annually) . . . 05305

Gaswärme-Institut e.V., Hafenstr 101, 45356 Essen
T: (0201) 341023/26
Focus: Air Cond 05306

GDMB Gesellschaft für Bergbau, Metallurgie, Rohstoff- und Umwelttechnik (GDMB), Postfach 1054, 38668 Clausthal-Zellerfeld
T: (05323) 93790; E-Mail: GDMB@tu-clausthal.de, http://www.tu-clausthal.de/gdmb; Fax: 937937
Founded: 1912; Members: 2000
Pres: Dr. Gernot Hänig; Gen Secr: Detlev Dornbusch
Focus: Mining; Metallurgy
Periodicals
Erzmetall (monthly)
Schriftenreihe der GDMB (irregularly) . . 05307

Gemeinnütziger Verein zur Förderung von Philosophie und Theologie e.V., Rheinsdorfer Burgweg 9, 53332 Bornheim
Focus: Philos; Rel & Theol 05308

Gemeinschaft katholischer Studierender und Akademiker, August-Bebel-Str 42, 68519 Viernheim
T: (06204) 4801
Focus: Sci 05309

Gemeinschaft zur Förderung der privaten deutschen Pflanzenzüchtung e.V. (GFP), Kaufmannstr 71, 53115 Bonn
T: (0228) 965410
Focus: Crop Husb 05310

Gemeinschaft zur Förderung von Kinder- und Jugendliteratur e.V. (GEM), Weinmeisterstr 5, 10178 Berlin
T: (030) 2829747; Fax: 2829769
Focus: Lit 05311

Gemeinschaftsausschuss Kaltformgebung e.V., Kaiserswerther Str 137, 40474 Düsseldorf
Focus: Metallurgy 05312

Gemeinschaftswerk der Evangelischen Publizistik e.V., Emil-von-Behring-Str 3, 60394 Frankfurt
T: (069) 580980; Fax: 58098100
Focus: Journalism; Rel & Theol
Periodicals
epd Film (monthly)
Evangelische Information (weekly)
medienpraktisch (quarterly)
medium (quarterly) 05313

Gemologisches Institut (GIE) / Gilde Internationaler Edelsteinexperten, Kaiserfeld 2, 55715 Idar-Oberstein
T: (06781) 36161; Fax: 36162
Founded: 1967
Pres: Peter O. Reiter
Focus: Mineralogy 05314

Genealogische Gesellschaft, Sitz Hamburg, e.V., Postfach 302042, 20307 Hamburg
Founded: 1918; Members: 567
Pres: Rolf Hillmer
Focus: Genealogy
Periodical
Zeitschrift für Niederdeutsche Familienkunde (quarterly) 05315

GEO-KART / Wirtschaftsverband für Geodäsie und Kartographie e.V., c/o Carl Zeiss, Postfach 1380, 73444 Oberkochen
T: (07364) 203722
Focus: Surveying; Cart 05316

Geographische Gesellschaft, Heinrich-Vogl-Str 7, 81479 München
Focus: Geography
Periodical
Mitteilungen (annually) 05317

Geographische Gesellschaft Bremen, c/o Übersee-Museum, Bahnhofspl 13, 28195 Bremen
T: (0421) 3619744
Founded: 1877
Focus: Geography; Ethnology 05318

Geographische Gesellschaft in Hamburg e.V., Bundesstr 55, 20146 Hamburg
T: (040) 41234910/4946; Fax: 41234981
Founded: 1873; Members: 430
Pres: Prof. Dr. Dieter Jaschke
Focus: Geography
Periodical
Mitteilungen der Geographischen Gesellschaft in Hamburg (1-2 times annually) 05319

Geographische Gesellschaft zu Hannover (GGH), Schneiderberg 50, 30167 Hannover
T: (0511) 7622233
Founded: 1878; Members: 600
Focus: Geography
Periodical
Hannoversche Geographische Arbeiten (1-2 times annually) 05320

Geologische Vereinigung e.V., Vulkanstr 23, 56743 Mendig
T: (02652) 989360; E-Mail: geol.ver@t-online.de; Fax: 989361
Founded: 1910; Members: 2300
Pres: Prof. Dr. Dietrich H. Welte; Gen Secr: Dr. Carl-Detlef Cornelius
Focus: Geology
Periodical
Geologische Rundschau (quarterly) . . . 05321

Georg-Agricola-Gesellschaft zur Förderung der Geschichte der Naturwissenschaften und der Technik e.V., Am Bergbaumuseum 28, 44791 Bochum
T: (0234) 5877140; Fax: 5877111
Founded: 1926; Members: 276
Pres: Dr. H. Gassert; Gen Secr: Dr. W. Kroker
Focus: Hist; Nat Sci; Eng 05322

Georg Büchner Gesellschaft e.v., Am Grün 1, 35037 Marburg
T: (06421) 284182
Focus: Lit 05323

Georg-Friedrich-Händel-Gesellschaft e.V., Große Nikolaistr 5, 06108 Halle/Saale
T: (0345) 50090223; Fax: 50090416
Founded: 1955
Focus: Music
Periodical
Händel-Jahrbuch (annually) 05324

Georg Groddeck-Gesellschaft e.V., Cronstettenstr 25, 60322 Frankfurt/Main
T: (069) 599585
Focus: Lit 05325

Georg-von-Vollmar-Akademie e.V., Landwehrstr 37, 80336 München
T: (089) 595223; Fax: 5503849
Focus: Poli Sci
Periodical
Kochel-Brief (semi-annually) 05326

Gerhart-Hauptmann-Gesellschaft e.V., Bismarckallee 14, 14193 Berlin
T: (030) 8928302
Focus: Lit 05327

Germana Esperanto Asocio r.a. / Deutscher Esperanto-Bund e.V., Rheinweg 15, 53113 Bonn
T: (0228) 235898
Founded: 1906; Members: 3000
Focus: Ling
Periodical
Esperanto aktuell (8 times annually) . . 05328

Germania Judaica / Kölner Bibliothek zur Geschichte des deutschen Judentums e.V., Josef-Haubrich-Hof 1, 50676 Köln
T: (0221) 232349
Founded: 1959
Focus: Hist 05329

Gertrud von le Fort-Gesellschaft e.V., Thüringer Str 50, 97078 Würzburg
T: (0931) 8884862
Focus: Lit 05330

GES-Gesellschaft für elektronische Systemforschung, 78476 Allensbach
Focus: Electronic Eng 05331

Gesamteuropäisches Studienwerk e.V. (GESW), Südfeldstr 2-4, 32602 Vlotho
T: (05733) 2258, 5110; Fax: 18804
Focus: Poli Sci 05332

Gesamtverein der deutschen Geschichts- und Altertumsvereine, Am Archiv 1, 30169 Hannover
T: (0511) 1062856; Fax: 1062910
Founded: 1852; Members: 248
Pres: Dr. Dieter Brosius; Gen Secr: Dr. Manfred Treml
Focus: Hist
Periodical
Blätter für Deutsche Landesgeschichte (annually) 05333

Geschäftsführendes Sekretariat des Kuratoriums für die Tagungen der Nobelpreisträger in Lindau, Postfach 1325, 88103 Lindau
Focus: Sci 05334

Gesellschaft anthroposophischer Ärzte, Trossinger Str 53, 70619 Stuttgart
Focus: Med
Periodical
Der Merkurstab: Beiträge zu einer Entwicklung der Heilkunst 05335

Gesellschaft der Arno-Schmidt-Leser e.V. (GASL), Grabenstr 33, 54516 Wittlich
T: (06571) 3255
Focus: Lit 05336

Gesellschaft der Bibliophilen e.V., Theresienstr 60, 80333 München
T: (089) 283682
Focus: Libraries & Bk Sci
Periodical
Wandelhalle der Bücherfreunde (quarterly) 05337

Gesellschaft der Europäischen Akademien e.V. (GEA), Kölnstr 1, 53111 Bonn
T: (0228) 657702; Fax: 657685
Focus: Poli Sci 05338

Gesellschaft der Freunde Romain Rollands in Deutschland e.V., Feuerbacher Weg 4, 70192 Stuttgart
T: (0711) 2566359
Focus: Lit 05339

Gesellschaft der Musik- und Kunstfreunde Heidelberg e.V., Wielandstr 1, 69251 Gaiberg
T: (06223) 970451; Fax: 970451
Founded: 1945; Members: 600
Pres: Hans Kühl
Focus: Music; Arts
Periodical
Die Gesellschaft (annually) 05340

Gesellschaft des Bauwesens e.V. (GdB), RKW-Haus, Düsseldorfer Str 40, 65760 Eschborn
T: (06196) 43143; Fax: 495393
Founded: 1962; Members: 1000
Pres: Wolfram Zeller; Gen Secr: Horst Wetzel
Focus: Civil Eng 05341

Gesellschaft Deutscher Chemiker e.V. (GDCh), Varrentrappstr 40-42, 60486 Frankfurt
T: 79171; E-Mail: gdch@gdch.de; Fax: 7917322
Founded: 1867; Members: 28000
Pres: Prof. Dr. Dr. E. Winterfeldt; Gen Secr: Prof. Dr. Dr. Tom Dieck
Focus: Chem
Periodicals
Angewandte Chemie (monthly)
Angewandte Chemie International Edition (monthly)
Chemie in unserer Zeit (bi-monthly)
Chemie-Ingenieur-Technik (monthly)
Chemische Berichte/Recueil (monthly)
Liebigs Annalen/Recueil (monthly)
Nachrichten aus Chemie, Technik und Laboratorium (monthly) 05342

Gesellschaft für Agrargeschichte, c/o Universität Hohenheim, Garbenstr 9-9a, 70593 Stuttgart
T: (711) 4592146; Fax: 4593404
Founded: 1953; Members: 250
Pres: Uwe Zimpelmann; Gen Secr: Dr. Klaus Herrmann
Focus: Hist; Agri
Periodical
Zeitschrift für Agrargeschichte und Agrarsoziologie (semi-annually) 05343

Gesellschaft für angewandte Informatik (GAI), Frankenstr 2, 61352 Bad Homburg
T: (06172) 47262
Focus: Computer & Info Sci 05344

Gesellschaft für Angewandte Mathematik und Mechanik (GAMM), c/o Technische Universität Dresden, Institut f. Festkörpermechanik, Mommsenstr 13, 01062 Dresden
T: (0351) 4634285; E-Mail: ulbricht@mfkrs1.mw.tu-dresden.de; Fax: 4637061
Founded: 1922; Members: 2600
Pres: Prof. Dr. R. Mennicken; Gen Secr: Prof. Dr. V. Ulbricht
Focus: Math; Eng
Periodical
GAMM-Mitteilungen (semi-annually) . . . 05345

Gesellschaft für Anlagen- und Reaktorsicherheit (GRS), Schwertnergasse 1, 50667 Köln
T: (0221) 20680; Fax: 2068442
Focus: Safety; Nucl Res
Periodicals
GRS-Bericht (irregularly)
GRS-Spektrum (quarterly) 05346

Gesellschaft für Anthropologie und Humangenetik, c/o Abt Humanbiologie/Anthropologie, Fachbereich Biologie, Universität, 28359 Bremen
Focus: Anthro; Genetics 05347

Gesellschaft für Arbeitswissenschaft e.V. (GfA), Ardeystr 67, 44139 Dortmund
T: (0231) 124243; Fax: 1084308
Founded: 1953; Members: 644
Focus: Business Admin
Periodical
Zeitschrift für Arbeitswissenschaft (quarterly) 05348

Gesellschaft für Arzneipflanzenforschung e.V. (GfA) / Society for Medicinal Plant Research, Am Grundbach 5, 97271 Kleinrinderfeld
T: (0931) 6102271; Fax: 6102275
Founded: 1953; Members: 900
Pres: Prof. Dr. G. Franz; Gen Secr: Dr. B. Frank
Focus: Pharmacol
Periodical
Planta Medica (bi-monthly) 05349

Gesellschaft für bedrohte Völker e.V., Postfach 2024, 37010 Göttingen
T: (0551) 499060; E-Mail: info@gfbv.de; Fax: 58028
Founded: 1970; Members: 8100
Pres: Zülch Tilman; Gen Secr: Günther Schierloh
Focus: Ethnology
Periodical
Pogrom: Zeitschrift für bedrohte Völker (bi-monthly) 05350

Gesellschaft für Bibliothekswesen und Dokumentation des Landbaues (GBDL), 85350 Freising
T: (08161) 713426; E-Mail: schlind@edv.agrar.tu-muenchen.de; Fax: 714409
Founded: 1958; Members: 150
Pres: Prof. Dr. W. Laux; Gen Secr: Dr. Birgid B. Schlindwein
Focus: Libraries & Bk Sci; Doc; Agri
Periodical
Mitteilungen der Gesellschaft für Bibliothekswesen und Dokumentation des Landbaues . . . 05351

Gesellschaft für Biochemie und Molekularbiologie e.V., Theodor-Stern-Kai 7, Haus 25b, 60590 Frankfurt am Main
T: (069) 63016925; Fax: 63016970
Founded: 1947; Members: 5000
Pres: Prof. Dr. H. Betz; Gen Secr: Prof. Dr. U. Brandt
Focus: Biochem; Microbio
Periodicals
BIOspektrum (bi-monthly)
Hoppe-Seyler's Zeitschrift für Physiologische Chemie (3 times annually) 05352

Gesellschaft für Biologische Krebsabwehr e.V. (GfBK), Hauptstr 27, 69117 Heidelberg
T: (06221) 161525; Fax: 183322
Focus: Cell Biol & Cancer Res 05353

Gesellschaft für Datenschutz und Datensicherung e.V. (GDD), Irmintrudisstr 1a, 53111 Bonn
T: (0228) 694313; Fax: 695638
Founded: 1976; Members: 1000
Focus: Law; Computer & Info Sci
Periodical
Recht der Datenverarbeitung (5 times annually) 05354

Gesellschaft für Deutsche Postgeschichte, Schaumainkai 53, 60552 Frankfurt 70
Focus: Hist; Public Admin
Periodical
Archiv für deutsche Postgeschichte (semi-annually) 05355

Gesellschaft für deutsche Sprache e.V. (GfdS), Spiegelgasse 11, 65183 Wiesbaden
T: (0611) 999550; Fax: 9995530
Founded: 1947; Members: 1950
Focus: Ling
Periodicals
Muttersprache: Zeitschrift zur Pflege und Erforschung der deutschen Sprache (quarterly)
Der Sprachdienst (bi-monthly) 05356

Gesellschaft für die Geschichte und Bibliographie des Brauwesens e.V., Seestr 13, 13353 Berlin
T: (030) 4509234, 4509264; E-Mail: Amylum Berlin; Fax: 4536069
Founded: 1913; Members: 250
Focus: Eng
Periodical
Jahrbuch (annually) 05357

Gesellschaft für Elektrische Hochleistungsprüfungen (PEHLA), Theodor-Stern-Kai 1, Hochhaus Süd, 60596 Frankfurt
T: (069) 66418148
Focus: Electric Eng 05358

Gesellschaft für empirische soziologische Forschung e.V., Marienstr 2, 90402 Nürnberg
T: (0911) 224333; E-Mail: ifes@rzmail.uni-erlangen.de; Fax: 225685
Founded: 1949; Members: 13
Pres: Walther Schüsser; Gen Secr: Dr. Rainer Wasilewski
Focus: Sociology 05359

Gesellschaft für Epilepsieforschung e.V., Karl-Siebold-Weg 11, 33617 Bielefeld
T: (0521) 4800; Fax: 1444048
Founded: 1955
Pres: P. Friedrich Schophaus; Gen Secr: Rolf Eichholt
Focus: Med 05360

Gesellschaft für Erd- und Völkerkunde, Meckenheimer Allee 166, 53115 Bonn
T: (0228) 737506
Founded: 1910; Members: 300
Focus: Geography; Ethnology 05361

Gesellschaft für Erd- und Völkerkunde zu Stuttgart e.V. (GEV), Hegelpl 1, 70174 Stuttgart
T: (0711) 20223; Fax: 2022590
Founded: 1882; Members: ca. 1600
Pres: Prof. Dr. Christoph Borcherdt
Focus: Geography; Ethnology 05362

Gesellschaft für Erdkunde zu Berlin (GFE), Arno-Holz-Str 14, 12165 Berlin
T: (030) 7919001; Fax: 7933249
Founded: 1828; Members: 500
Pres: Dr. Dieter Biewald; Gen Secr: Dr. Kirsten Gehrenkemper
Focus: Geography
Periodical
Die Erde (quarterly) 05363

Gesellschaft für Erdkunde zu Köln e.V., c/o Geographisches Institut, Universität, Albertus-Magnus-Pl, 50931 Köln
Focus: Geography 05364

Gesellschaft für Ernährungsbiologie e.V., Veterinärstr 13, 80539 München
Members: 200
Pres: Prof. Dr. G. Wolfram; Gen Secr: Dr. Bernhard Brunner
Focus: Nutrition; Bio 05365

Gesellschaft für Ernährungsphysiologie, Eschborner Landstr 122, 60489 Frankfurt
T: (069) 24788320; Fax: 24788114
Founded: 1953; Members: 155
Pres: Prof. Dr. J. Pallauf; Gen Secr: Dr. W. Staudacher
Focus: Nutrition
Periodical
Proceedings of the Society of Nutrition Physiology (1-2 times annually) 05366

Gesellschaft für Familienkunde in Franken e.V., Archivstr 17, 90408 Nürnberg
Focus: Genealogy
Periodical
Blätter für Fränkische Familienkunde (semi-annually) 05367

Gesellschaft für Geburtsvorbereitung Bundesverband e.V. (GfG), Dellestr 5, 40627 Düsseldorf
T: (0211) 252607; Fax: 202919
Focus: Gynecology 05368

Gesellschaft für Geistesgeschichte e.V., Am Neuen Palais 10, 14469 Potsdam
T: (0331) 9771036; Fax: 9771168
Founded: 1958; Members: 150
Focus: Hist; Humanities
Periodical
Zeitschrift für Religions- und Geistesgeschichte (quarterly) 05369

Gesellschaft für Goldschmiedekunst, Altstädter Markt 6, 63450 Hanau
T: (06181) 256556; Fax: 256554
Founded: 1932; Members: 500
Pres: Walter Behning; Gen Secr: Dr. C. Weber
Focus: Arts 05370

Gesellschaft für Historische Waffen- und Kostümkunde, c/o Historisches Museum, Pferdestr 6, 30159 Hannover
T: (0511) 1683965; Fax: 1685003
Founded: 1896; Members: 267
Pres: Dr. Alheidis von Rohr; Gen Secr: Gerhard Grosse-Löscher
Focus: Hist; Military Sci
Periodical
Zeitschrift für Historische Waffen- und Kostümkunde (annually) 05371

Gesellschaft für Informatik e.V. (GI) / Wissenschaftszentrum, Ahrstr 45, 53175 Bonn
T: (0228) 302145; E-Mail: gibonn@gmd.de; Fax: 302167
Founded: 1969; Members: 20000
Pres: Prof. Dr. Wolffried Stucky; Gen Secr: Dr. Hermann Rampacher
Focus: Computer & Info Sci
Periodical
Informatik-Spektrum (bi-monthly) 05372

Gesellschaft für Informationsverarbeitung in der Landwirtschaft (GIL), Birkheckenstr 100a, 70599 Stuttgart
Founded: 1980; Members: 180
Focus: Computer & Info Sci; Agri
Periodical
Infoagrar (semi-annually) 05373

Gesellschaft für Informationsvermittlung und Technologieberatung, Blumenstr 1, 80331 München
T: (089) 263060; Fax: 2608471
Focus: Business Admin; Econ; Electronic Eng; Electric Eng; Energy; Chem; Med; Bio . 05374

Gesellschaft für Interkulturelle Germanistik e.V. (GIG), c/o Institut für Internationale Kommunikation und Auswärtige Kulturarbeit, Jahnstr 8-10, 95444 Bayreuth
T: (0921) 515345; Fax: 511207
Focus: Ling; Lit 05375

Gesellschaft für internationale Geldgeschichte (GIG), Rotlintstr 66, 60318 Frankfurt
T: (069) 498921; Fax: 71356
Focus: Finance; Econ
Periodical
Geldgeschichtliche Nachrichten (bi-monthly) 05376

Gesellschaft für internationale Sprache e.V., Schaumanns Kamp 126, 21465 Reinbek
Focus: Ling
Periodical
Interlinguistika Informa Servo (quarterly) . 05377

Gesellschaft für Klassifikation e.V. (GfKl), c/o Institut für Entwicklungstheorie und Unternehmensforschung, Universität Karlsruhe, Postfach 6980, 76128 Karlsruhe, Postfach 6980, 76128 Karlsruhe
T: (0721) 608-3726; E-Mail: gaul@etu.wiwi.uni-Karlsruhe.de; Fax: 661227
Founded: 1977; Members: 340
Pres: Prof. Dr. Wolfgang Gaul
Focus: Standards 05378

Gesellschaft für Konsum-, Markt- und Absatzforschung (GfK), Nordwestring 101, 90319 Nürnberg
T: (0911) 3950; Fax: 3952209
Founded: 1934; Members: 840
Focus: Marketing 05379

Gesellschaft für Literatur in Nordrhein-Westfalen e.V., Wilmergasse 12, 48143 Münster
T: (0251) 46877
Founded: 1977
Focus: Lit 05380

Gesellschaft für Lungen- und Atmungsforschung e.V., Gilsingstr 14, 44789 Bochum
T: (0234) 3026444; Fax: 3026420
Founded: 1962; Members: 400
Focus: Pulmon Dis
Periodical
Atemwegs- und Lungenkrankheiten (monthly) 05381

Gesellschaft für Mathematik und Datenverarbeitung, Postfach 1316, 53731 Sankt Augustin
T: (02241) 141; Fax: 142619
Focus: Math; Computer & Info Sci . . . 05382

Gesellschaft für mathematische Forschung e.V., Lorenzenhof, 77709 Oberwolfach-Walke
T: (07834) 9790; E-Mail: admin@mfo.de; Fax: 97938
Founded: 1959; Members: 58
Pres: Prof. Dr. Gerd Fischer
Focus: Math
Periodical
Archiv der Mathematik (monthly) 05383

Gesellschaft für Medienpädagogik und Kommunikationskultur e.V. (GMK), Körnerstr 3, 33602 Bielefeld
T: (0521) 67788; Fax: 67727
Focus: Mass Media; Educ 05384

Gesellschaft für Mittelrheinische Kirchengeschichte, Karmeliterstr 1-3, 56068 Koblenz
T: (0261) 9129121
Founded: 1949
Focus: Hist; Rel & Theol
Periodical
Archiv für Mittelrheinische Kirchengeschichte (annually) 05385

Gesellschaft für Musikforschung e.V. (GfM), Heinrich-Schütz-Allee 35, 34131 Kassel
T: (0561) 3105255
Founded: 1947; Members: 1700
Focus: Music
Periodical
Die Musikforschung (quarterly) 05386

Gesellschaft für Musikpädagogik, Verband der Musikpädagogen e.V. (GMP/VMP), Heinrich-Schütz-Allee 35, 34131 Kassel
T: (0561) 3105131
Focus: Educ; Music 05387

Gesellschaft für Natur- und Völkerkunde Ostasiens e.V., c/o Japanisches Seminar, Von-Melle-Park 6, 20146 Hamburg
T: (040) 41234884; Fax: 41236200
Founded: 1873; Members: 202
Pres: Dr. Dieter Lorenz-Meyer; Gen Secr: Dr. Herbert Worm
Focus: Nat Sci; Ethnology
Periodicals
Kagami: Japanischer Zeitschriftenspiegel (3 times annually)
Nachrichten der Gesellschaft für Natur- und Völkerkunde Ostasiens e.V.: Zeitschrift für Kultur und Geschichte Ost- und Südostasiens (semi-annually) 05388

Gesellschaft für Naturkunde in Württemberg e.V., Rosenstein 1, 70191 Stuttgart
T: (0711) 89360
Founded: 1844; Members: 850
Focus: Ecology
Periodical
Jahreshefte 05389

Gesellschaft für öffentliche Wirtschaft e.V. (GöWG), Sarrazinstr 11-15, 12159 Berlin
T: (030) 8521045/46
Founded: 1951; Members: 100
Focus: Econ
Periodical
Zeitschrift für öffentliche und gemeinwirtschaftliche Unternehmen (quarterly) 05390

Gesellschaft für Pädagogik und Information e.V., Rathenaustr 16, 33102 Paderborn
T: (05251) 34024
Founded: 1964; Members: 400
Focus: Educ; Computer & Info Sci
Periodical
Pädagogik und Information 05391

Gesellschaft für Pädiatrische Radiologie, c/o Röntgenabteilung Universitäts Kinderklinik, Im Neuenheimer Feld 150, 69120 Heidelberg
Pres: Prof. Dr. J. Tröger
Focus: Radiology 05392

Gesellschaft für Politische Bildung e.V., Frankenwarte, 97082 Würzburg
T: (0931) 804640; Fax: 8046444
Focus: Poli Sci 05393

Gesellschaft für pommersche Geschichte, Altertumskunde und Kunst e.V., Gisonenweg 5-7, 35037 Marburg
T: (06421) 184101
Focus: Hist; Archeol; Arts 05394

Gesellschaft für prä- und postoperative Tumortherapie e.V., Sackgasse 8, 55278 Undenheim
T: (06737) 1298
Founded: 1969; Members: 150
Focus: Therapeutics 05395

Gesellschaft für praktische Energiekunde e.V. (GFPE), Am Blütenanger 71, 80995 München
T: (089) 1581210
Founded: 1949; Members: 177
Focus: Energy 05396

Gesellschaft für Programmierte Instruktion und Mediendidaktik e.V., c/o Seminar Anglistik/Didaktik, Justus-Liebig-Universität, Otto-Behaghel-Str 10, 35394 Giessen
Founded: 1964; Members: 600
Focus: Mass Media; Computer & Info Sci; Educ
Periodical
Neue Unterrichtspraxis 05397

Gesellschaft für Psychotherapie, Psychosomatik und Medizinische Psychologie e.V., Karl-Tauchnitz-Str 25, 04107 Leipzig
T: (0341) 9718850; Fax: 2131257
Founded: 1960; Members: 1800
Pres: Prof. Dr. M. Geyer
Focus: Psych; Therapeutics 05398

Gesellschaft für publizistische Bildungsarbeit e.V., Haus Busch, Helfe, 58099 Hagen
T: (02331) 365600; E-Mail: hans-busch@publ.ha.shuttle.de; Fax: 365690
Founded: 1960; Members: 19
Pres: Claus-Werner Koch; Gen Secr: Prof. Dr. Ulrich Pätzold
Focus: Journalism; Educ 05399

Gesellschaft für rationale Verkehrspolitik e.V. (GRV), Bromberger Str 5, 40599 Düsseldorf
T: (0211) 741507
Founded: 1970; Members: 242
Pres: Dr. Alfons Thoma; Gen Secr: Werner Kammer
Focus: Poli Sci
Periodical
GRV-Nachrichten (quarterly) 05400

Gesellschaft für Rationelle Energieverwendung e.V., Kaiserdamm 80, 14057 Berlin
T: (030) 3016090; Fax: 3019016
Focus: Energy
Periodical
Merkblätter (irregularly) 05401

Gesellschaft für Rechtsvergleichung e.V., Humboldtallee 15, 37073 Göttingen
T: (0551) 59035
Founded: 1950; Members: 1100
Focus: Law
Periodicals
Arbeiten zur Rechtsvergleichung
Ausländische Aktiengesetze
Mitteilungen (irregularly) 05402

Gesellschaft für Regionalforschung e.V. (GfR), c/o Gerlind Schütte, Großgörschenstr 18, 10829 Berlin
T: (030) 78704498; E-Mail: gerlind.schuette@f-online.de; Fax: 78704498
Founded: 1963; Members: 292
Pres: Prof. Dr. F.-J. Bade; Gen Secr: Gerlind Schütte
Focus: Sociology; Econ; Urban Plan; Poli Sci
Periodicals
Jahrbuch für Regionalwissenschaft (annually)
Seminarbericht (annually) 05403

Gesellschaft für Reichskammergerichtsforschung, Rosengasse 16, 35578 Wetzlar
T: (06441) 99610; Fax: 99614
Focus: Hist; Law 05404

Gesellschaft für Sicherheitswissenschaft e.V. (GfS), c/o Prof. Dr. Peter C. Compes, Bergische Universität, Gaußstr 20, 42097 Wuppertal
T: (0202) 4392060
Members: 250
Focus: Safety
Periodicals
Berichte über GfS-Sommer-Symposien
Sicherheitswissenschaftliche Monographien 05405

Gesellschaft für Sozial- und Wirtschaftsgeschichte, c/o Institut für Sozial- und Wirtschaftsgeschichte, Universität Heidelberg, Grabengasse 14, 69117 Heidelberg
T: (06221) 542933
Founded: 1961; Members: 220
Focus: Hist; Soc Sci; Econ 05406

Gesellschaft für Strahlen- und Umweltforschung (GSF), Ingolstädter Landstr 1, 91465 Ergersheim
T: (09847) 31870
Founded: 1964
Focus: Ecology; Nat Sci
Periodical
GSF-Bericht 05407

Gesellschaft für Tanzforschung e.V. (GTF), Bibliothekstr, 28359 Bremen
T: (0421) 2183152
Focus: Perf Arts 05408

Gesellschaft für Technologiefolgenforschung e.V. (GTF) (GTF), Hohenzollerndamm 91, 14199 Berlin
T: (030) 89502090; E-Mail: klaus.dette@gtf.b.shottle.de; Fax: 8258088
Founded: 1979
Pres: Dr. Klaus Dette
Focus: Eng; Ecology 05409

Gesellschaft für Theatergeschichte, Mecklenburgische Str 56, 14197 Berlin
T: (030) 82400123; Fax: 82400111
Focus: Cultur Hist 05410

Gesellschaft für Tribologie e.V. (GfT), Ernststr 12, 47443 Moers
T: (02841) 54213
Founded: 1959; Members: 410
Focus: Eng 05411

Gesellschaft für Übernationale Zusammenarbeit e.V., Bachstr 32, 53115 Bonn
T: (0228) 7290080
Founded: 1945
Focus: Poli Sci
Periodicals
Dokumente: Zeitschrift für den deutsch-französischen Dialog
Revue des questions allemandes – Documents 05412

Gesellschaft für Unternehmensgeschichte e.V., Zimmerweg 6, 60325 Frankfurt/Main
T: (069) 97203314; Fax: 97203308
Focus: Hist; Econ
Periodicals
Anno: Magazin für Unternehmensgeschichte (annually)
Zeitschrift für Unternehmensgeschichte (quarterly) 05413

Gesellschaft für Ursachenforschung bei Verkehrsunfällen e.V. (GUVU), Universitätsstr 5, 50937 Köln
T: (0221) 415894; E-Mail: 106406.2300@compuserve.com; Fax: 428255
Founded: 1959; Members: 130
Pres: Prof. Dr. Klaus Rompe; Gen Secr: Prof. Dr. Walter Schneider
Focus: Transport 05414

Gesellschaft für Versicherungswissenschaft und -gestaltung e.V. (GVG), Prälat-Otto-Müller-Pl 2, 50670 Köln
T: (0221) 726965; Fax: 730373
Founded: 1947
Focus: Insurance
Periodicals
Informationsdienst (10 times annually)
Schriftenreihe (2-3 times annually) . . . 05415

Gesellschaft für Wirbelsäulenforschung, c/o BG-Unfallklinik, Friedberger Landstr 430, 60389 Frankfurt
Focus: Anat 05416

Gesellschaft für Wirtschafts- und Sozialwissenschaften, Schackstr 4, 80539 München
T: (089) 21802740; Fax: 397303
Founded: 1872; Members: 1700
Pres: Prof. Dr. Hans-Werner Sinn; Gen Secr: Dr. Ronnie Schöb
Focus: Sociology; Econ
Periodical
Zeitschrift für Wirtschafts- und Sozialwissenschaften (quarterly) 05417

Gesellschaft für Wirtschaftskunde e.V., Albertus-Magnus-Str 2, 57072 Siegen
T: (0271) 52799
Focus: Econ 05418

Gesellschaft für wissenschaftliche Gesprächspsychotherapie e.V. (GwG), Richard-Wagner-Str 12, 50674 Köln
T: (0221) 237917
Members: 7300
Focus: Educ Handic
Periodicals
GwG-Zeitschrift (quarterly)
Informationsblätter der GwG (quarterly) . 05419

Gesellschaft für Wohnungsrecht und Wohnungswirtschaft Köln e.V., Klosterstr 79b, 50931 Köln
T: (0221) 4702311, 4705573; Fax: 407148
Pres: Prof. Dr. Johann Eekhoff; Gen Secr: Dr. Beate Thiemer
Focus: Urban Plan; Finance; Law . . . 05420

Gesellschaft für zeitgenössische Lyrik e.V. (GZL), Arndtstr 60, 04275 Leipzig
T: (0341) 4778519
Focus: Lit 05421

Gesellschaft Information Bildung e.V. (GIB), Arnimallee 10, 14195 Berlin
T: (030) 8385888; Fax: 8385889
Founded: 1992; Members: 72
Pres: Dr. Diann Rusch-Feja
Focus: Educ *05422*

Gesellschaft Rheinischer Ornithologen e.V., Schlesische Str 80, 40231 Düsseldorf
T: (0211) 214885
Focus: Ornithology
Periodical
Charadrius: Zeitschrift für Vogelkunde, Vogelschutz und Naturschutz in Nordrhein-Westfalen (quarterly) *05423*

Gesellschaft Sozialwissenschaftlicher Infrastruktureinrichtungen e.V. (GESIS), B2, 1, 68159 Mannheim
Founded: 1986; Members: 3
Focus: Soc Sci *05424*

Gesellschaft zum Studium strukturpolitischer Fragen e.V., Postfach 120333, 53045 Bonn
T: (0228) 691316; Fax: 697327
Founded: 1959; Members: 200
Pres: Dr. Ludolf von Wartenberg; Gen Secr: Hans-Hermann Lutzke
Focus: Poli Sci
Periodical
Die strukturpolitische Information (bi-weekly) *05425*

Gesellschaft zur Erforschung des Markenwesens e.V., Schöne Aussicht 59, 65193 Wiesbaden
T: (0611) 58670; Fax: 586727
Founded: 1954
Focus: Econ *05426*

Gesellschaft zur Förderung der Erforschung der Zuckerkrankheit e.V., Auf'm Hennekamp 65, 40225 Düsseldorf
T: (0211) 33821
Focus: Hematology *05427*

Gesellschaft zur Förderung der finanzwissenschaftlichen Forschung e.V., Zülpicher Str 182, 50937 Köln
T: (0221) 426979; Fax: 422352
Founded: 1949; Members: 150
Focus: Finance *05428*

Gesellschaft zur Förderung der Lufthygiene und Silikoseforschung e.V., Auf'm Hennekamp 50, 40225 Düsseldorf
T: (0211) 33890; Fax: 3190910
Founded: 1962; Members: 9
Focus: Pulmon Dis; Toxicology; Immunology; Hygiene
Periodicals
Jahresberichte
Umwelthygiene *05429*

Gesellschaft zur Förderung der Segelflugforschung e.V., Herrenstr 14-16, 79098 Freiburg
T: (0761) 52719
Focus: Aero *05430*

Gesellschaft zur Förderung der Spektrochemie und angewandten Spektroskopie e.V., Bunsen-Kirchhoff-Str 11, 44139 Dortmund
T: (0231) 13920; Fax: 1392120
Founded: 1952; Members: 45
Focus: Chem; Physics *05431*

Gesellschaft zur Förderung Pädagogischer Forschung e.V. (GFPF), Schloßstr 29, 60486 Frankfurt
T: (069) 7073890, 24708221; Fax: 24708444
Founded: 1950; Members: 350
Pres: Hans Krollmann; Gen Secr: P. Doebrich
Focus: Educ
Periodical
Zeitschrift für erziehungs- und sozialwissenschaftliche Forschung (semi-annually) *05432*

Gesellschaft zur Förderung von Bildung e.V. (GFB), Hauptstr 36, 53604 Bad Honnef
T: (02224) 73195
Focus: Educ *05433*

Gesellschaft zur Herausgabe des Corpus Catholicorum, Johannisstr 8-10, 48143 Münster
Founded: 1917
Focus: Rel & Theol *05434*

Gesundheitspolitische Gesellschaft e.V., Weimarer Str 8, 24106 Kiel
T: (0431) 338550
Focus: Poli Sci *05435*

Gesundheitstechnische Gesellschaft e.V. (GG), Alt-Marienfelde 12d, 12277 Berlin
T: (030) 7226046; Fax: 7226046
Founded: 1949; Members: 650
Pres: Dr. A. Jahn; Gen Secr: M. Samp
Focus: Eng; Public Health
Periodical
GG-Nachrichten (10 times annually) . . *05436*

GFM-GETAS Gesellschaft für Marketing-, Kommunikations- und Sozialforschung, Langelohstr 134, 22545 Hamburg
Founded: 1945
Focus: Marketing; Soc Sci *05437*

GKSS-Forschungszentrum Geesthacht (GKSS), Max-Planck-Str, 21502 Geesthacht
Founded: 1956; Members: 700
Focus: Eng
Periodical
GKSS-Information (quarterly) *05438*

Görres-Gesellschaft zur Pflege der Wissenschaft, Postfach 101618, 50456 Köln
T: (0221) 738317
Founded: 1876; Members: 3000
Pres: Prof. Dr. Dr. Paul Mikat; Gen Secr: Prof. Dr. Rudolf Schieffer
Focus: Sci
Periodicals
Historisches Jahrbuch
Jahrbuch für Volkskunde
Kirchenmusikalisches Jahrbuch
Literaturwissenschaftliches Jahrbuch
Oriens Christianus
Philosophisches Jahrbuch
Portugiesische Forschungen
Römische Quartalschrift (quarterly)
Spanische Forschungen
Vierteljahresschrift für wissenschaftliche Pädagogik
Zeitschrift für Psychologie, Psychiatrie und Psychotherapie *05439*

Goethe-Gesellschaft in Weimar e.V., Burgpl 4, 99423 Weimar
T: (03643) 202050; Fax: 202050
Founded: 1885; Members: 5000
Focus: Lit *05440*

Göttinger Arbeitskreis, Calsowstr 54, 37085 Göttingen
T: (0551) 55848; Fax: 486203
Pres: Prof. Dr. Dr. Boris Meissner; Gen Secr: Dr. Alfred Eisfeld
Focus: Hist
Periodical
Deutsche in der ehemaligen Sowjetunion (bi-monthly) *05441*

Göttinger Literarische Gesellschaft e.V., Zur Scharfmühle 10, 37083 Göttingen
T: (0551) 795733; Fax: 7989770
Focus: Lit *05442*

Gottfried-Wilhelm-Leibniz-Gesellschaft e.V., c/o Niedersächsische Landesbibliothek, Waterloostr 8, 30169 Hannover
T: (0511) 1267331; Fax: 1267202
Founded: 1966; Members: 385
Pres: Prof. Dr. E.G. Mahrenholz; Gen Secr: Prof. Dr. W. Totok
Focus: Philos
Periodicals
Studia Leibnitiana
Studia Leibnitiana Sonderhefte
Studia Leibnitiana Supplementa *05443*

Grabbe-Gesellschaft e.V., Buchstr 27, 32756 Detmold
T: (05231) 24400
Focus: Lit *05444*

Grimmelshausen-Gesellschaft e.V., Wilhelm-Röpke-Str 6a, 35039 Marburg
T: (06421) 21344
Focus: Lit *05445*

Gruppe Ökologie, c/o Institut für ökologische Forschung und Bildung e.V., Kleine Düwelstr 21, 30171 Hannover
T: (0511) 853055; Fax: 853062
Founded: 1981
Focus: Ecology *05446*

Gustav-Freytag-Gesellschaft e.V., Bahnhofstr 71, 40883 Ratingen
T: (02102) 9650; Fax: 60178
Focus: Lit
Periodical
Gustav-Freytag-Blätter (annually) *05447*

Gustav-Stresemann-Institut e.V. für übernationale Bildung und europäische Zusammenarbeit (GSI), Langer Grabenweg 68, 53175 Bonn
T: (0228) 81070; Fax: 8107198
Focus: Poli Sci *05448*

Gutenberg-Gesellschaft (GG) / Internationale Vereinigung für Geschichte und Gegenwart der Druckkunst, Liebfrauenpl 5, 55116 Mainz
T: (06131) 226420; Fax: 123488
Founded: 1901; Members: 1700
Pres: Jens Beutel; Gen Secr: Gertraude Benöhr
Focus: Hist; Libraries & Bk Sci *05449*

GVC/VDI-Gesellschaft Verfahrenstechnik und Chemieingenieurwesen / Prozess- und Umwelttechnik, Graf-Recke-Str 84, 40239 Düsseldorf
T: (0211) 6214256; Fax: 6214575
Founded: 1934; Members: 8000
Focus: Eng
Periodicals
Chemical Engineering and Technology (monthly)
Chemie-Ingenieur-Technik (monthly) . . . *05450*

Hafenbautechnische Gesellschaft e.V. (HTG), Dalmannstr 1, 20457 Hamburg
T: (040) 32852178; Fax: 32852179
Founded: 1914; Members: 1500
Pres: Prof. Dr. Jochen Müller; Gen Secr: Karlheinz Pöpping
Focus: Civil Eng
Periodicals
Binnenschiffahrt (bi-weekly)
Hansa (monthly) *05451*

Hahn-Schickard-Gesellschaft für angewandte Forschung e.V., Breitscheidstr 2b, 70174 Stuttgart
T: (0711) 293174; Fax: 2268304
Founded: 1954; Members: 80
Focus: Eng *05452*

Hamburger Autorenvereinigung e.V., Jürgensallee 13, 22609 Hamburg
T: (040) 876758
Founded: 1977
Focus: Lit *05453*

Hamburger Gesellschaft für Völkerrecht und Auswärtige Politik e.V., Rothenbaumchaussee 21-23, 20148 Hamburg
T: (040) 41234607; Fax: 41236262
Founded: 1968
Gen Secr: Dr. Karl-Andreas Hernekamp
Focus: Poli Sci; Law
Periodical
Verfassung und Recht in Übersee: Law and Politics in Africa, Asia and Latin America (quarterly) *05454*

Hannah-Arendt-Institut für Totalitarismusforschung e.V. (HAIT), Mommsenstr 13, 01062 Dresden
T: (0351) 4632802; Fax: 4636079
Focus: Hist *05455*

Hannoversches Forschungsinstitut für Fertigungsfragen e.V. (HFF), Welfengarten 1a, 30167 Hannover
T: (0511) 7622264
Focus: Standards; Eng *05456*

Hans-Fallada-Gesellschaft e.V. (HFG), Eichholz 3, 17258 Feldberg
T: (039831) 20560; Fax: 20560
Focus: Lit *05457*

Hans-Fallada-Verein Greifswald e.V., Bahnhofsstr 46-47, 17489 Greifswald
T: (03834) 863404; Fax: 863423
Focus: Lit *05458*

Hartmannbund / Verband der Ärzte Deutschlands e.V., Godesberger Allee 54, 53175 Bonn
T: (0228) 81040; Fax: 8104155
Founded: 1900; Members: 60000
Pres: Dr. Hans-Jürgen Thomas; Gen Secr: Dr. Bernd Hügle
Focus: Public Health
Periodical
Hartmannbund-Magazin (monthly) *05459*

Harzverein für Geschichte, Burgpl 1, 38100 Goslar
Pres: C. Römer
Focus: Hist
Periodical
Harz-Zeitschrift (annually) *05460*

Hauptschullehrerverband e.V. (HLV), Am Wellnerberg 3, 32760 Detmold
T: (05231) 47349
Focus: Educ *05461*

Haus der Technik e.V. (HDT), Hollestr 1, 45127 Essen
T: (0201) 18031; Fax: 1803269
Focus: Eng *05462*

Haus der Zukunft e.V. - Internationales Institut für deutschland- u. europa-politische Bildungsarbeit, Goethestr 37, 14163 Berlin
T: (030) 8013097; Fax: 8021698
Focus: Poli Sci *05463*

Hebbel-Gesellschaft e.V., Österstr 6, 25764 Wesselburen
T: (04833) 4190, 4188; Fax: 4191
Focus: Lit *05464*

Heidelberger Akademie der Wissenschaften, Karlstr 4, 69117 Heidelberg
T: (06221) 543265; E-Mail: marion.freerk@urz.uni-heidelberg.de; Fax: 543355
Founded: 1909; Members: 212
Pres: Prof. Dr. Gottfried Seebaß; Gen Secr: Gunther, M.A. Jost
Focus: Sci
Periodical
Zentralblatt für Mathematik und Grenzgebiete (bi-weekly) *05465*

Heinrich-Heine-Gesellschaft e.V. (HHG), Bolker Str 53, 40213 Düsseldorf
T: (0211) 8995575; Fax: 320679
Focus: Lit *05466*

Heinrich-Hoffmann-Gesellschaft e.V. (HHG), Bendergasse 1, 60311 Frankfurt/Main
T: (069) 555632
Focus: Lit *05467*

Heinrich Mann-Gesellschaft e.V. (HMG), Schillerhöhe 8-10, 71672 Marbach
T: (07144) 848111; Fax: 848191
Focus: Lit *05468*

Heinrich-von-Kleist-Gesellschaft e.V., Faberstr 7, 15230 Frankfurt/Oder
T: (0335) 531155; Fax: 5004945
Focus: Lit *05469*

Herder-Institut e.V., Gisonenweg 5-7, 35037 Marburg
T: (06421) 1840; E-Mail: herder@mailer.uni-marburg.de, WWW: http://www.uni-marburg.de/herder-institut; Fax: 184139
Founded: 1950; Members: 11
Pres: Dr. Eduard Mühle
Focus: Cultur Hist; Hist *05470*

Hermann von Helmholtzgemeinschaft Deutscher Forschungszentren (HGF), Ahrstr 45, 53175 Bonn
T: (0228) 308180; 376741; E-Mail: helmholtz@de; Fax: 3081830
Members: 16
Pres: Prof. Dr. Joachim Treusch; Gen Secr: Dr. Klaus Fleischmann
Focus: Sci *05471*

Herold, Verein für Heraldik, Genealogie und verwandte Wissenschaften, Archivstr 12-14, 14195 Berlin
T: (030) 83901100
Focus: Genealogy *05472*

Hessische Akademie für Bürowirtschaft e.V. (HAB), Kandelstr 7, 60528 Frankfurt
T: (069) 673857
Founded: 1965; Members: 420
Focus: Adult Educ
Periodical
HAB-Journal (semi-annually) *05473*

Hessische Historische Kommission Darmstadt, Karolinenpl 3, 64289 Darmstadt
T: (06151) 165900; Fax: 165901
Focus: Hist *05474*

Hessische Krebsgesellschaft e.V., Heinrich-Heine-Str 44, 35039 Marburg
T: (06421) 63324; Fax: 600711
Founded: 1952; Members: 130
Focus: Cell Biol & Cancer Res *05475*

Hessischer Philologen-Verband, Hellmundstr 5, 65183 Wiesbaden
Focus: Ling
Periodical
blickpunkt schule (8 times annually) . . *05476*

Hessischer Volkshochschulverband e.V. (HVV), Winterbachstr 38, 60320 Frankfurt/Main
T: (069) 5600080; Fax: 56000810
Focus: Adult Educ *05477*

Historische Kommision der Deutschen Gesellschaft für Erziehungswissenschaft, Lüerstr 3, 30175 Hannover
T: (0511) 7629412/13; Fax: 7623456
Founded: 1967; Members: 300
Focus: Hist; Educ
Periodical
Information zur erziehungs- und bildungshistorischen Forschung (IZEBF) (2-3 times annually) *05478*

Historische Kommission bei der Bay. Akademie der Wissenschaften, Marstallpl 8, 80539 München
T: (089) 23031151; Fax: 23031245
Focus: Hist *05479*

Historische Kommission des Börsenvereins des Deutschen Buchhandels, Grosser Hirschgraben 17-21, 60311 Frankfurt
T: (069) 1306287; Fax: 1306382
Founded: 1953; Members: 45
Pres: Prof. Dr. Klaus G. Saur; Gen Secr: Dr. Monika Estermann
Focus: Libraries & Bk Sci; Hist
Periodicals
Archiv für Geschichte des Buchwesens (semi-annually)
Buchhandelsgeschichte (quarterly) *05480*

Historische Kommission zu Berlin, Kirchweg 33, 14129 Berlin
T: (030) 8160010
Focus: Hist
Periodical
I.W.K.: Internationale wissenschaftliche Korrespondenz zur Geschichte der deutschen Arbeiterbewegung (quarterly) *05481*

Historische Kommission zur Erforschung des Pietismus, Jebensstr 3, 10623 Berlin
T: (030) 31001209; Fax: 31001200
Founded: 1964
Pres: Dr. Gerhard Schäfer
Focus: Hist; Rel & Theol
Periodical
Pietismus und Neuzeit: Ein Jahrbuch zur Geschichte des neueren Protestantismus (annually) *05482*

Historischer Verein Bamberg, Untere Sandstr 30a, 96049 Bamberg
T: (0951) 14412
Founded: 1830; Members: 953
Pres: Lothar Braun
Focus: Hist
Periodical
Bericht des Historischen Vereins Bamberg (annually) *05483*

Historischer Verein der Pfalz e.V., Postfach 1429, 67324 Speyer
Focus: Hist
Periodical
Mitteilungen (annually) *05484*

Historischer Verein Dillingen an der Donau, Örtelstr 10, 89407 Dillingen
Focus: Hist
Periodical
Jahrbuch (annually) *05485*

Historischer Verein für die Saargegend e.V., c/o Landesarchiv Saarbrücken, 102431, 66024 Saarbrücken
T: (0681) 399953; Fax: 3905204
Founded: 1839; Members: 850
Pres: Prof. Dr. Wolfgang Haubrichs; Gen Secr: Michael Sander
Focus: Hist
Periodical
Zeitschrift für die Geschichte der Saargegend (annually) 05486

Historischer Verein für Hessen, c/o Staatsarchiv, Karolinenpl 3, 64289 Darmstadt
T: (06151) 165900; Fax: 165901
Founded: 1833; Members: 460
Pres: Prof. Dr. Eckhart G. Franz
Focus: Hist
Periodicals
Archiv für Hessische Geschichte und Altertumskunde (annually)
Darmstädter Archivschriften (irregularly)
Hessische Beiträge zur Geschichte der Arbeiterbewegung (irregularly) 05487

Historischer Verein für Oberfranken e.V., Ludwigstr 25b, Postfach 110263, 95421 Bayreuth
T: (0921) 65307
Founded: 1827; Members: 1000
Pres: Wolfgang Winkler; Gen Secr: Norbert Hübsch
Focus: Hist
Periodical
Archiv für Geschichte von Oberfranken (annually) 05488

Historischer Verein für Schwaben, Schaezlerstr 25, 86152 Augsburg
Focus: Hist
Periodical
Zeitschrift des Historischen Vereins für Schwaben (annually) 05489

Historischer Verein für Württembergisch Franken, c/o Stadtarchiv, Postfach 100180, 74501 Schwäbisch Hall
Focus: Hist
Periodical
Württembergisch Franken (annually) . . . 05490

Historischer Verein Rupertiwinkel e.V., Postfach 1108, 83405 Laufen
Focus: Hist
Periodical
Das Salzfaß (semi-annually) 05491

Hochschullehrerbund e.V. (HLB), Rüngsdorfer Str 4c, 53173 Bonn
T: (0228) 352271; Fax: 354512
Founded: 1973
Focus: Educ
Periodical
Die Neue Hochschule (bi-monthly) . . . 05492

Hochschulrektorenkonferenz, Ahrstr 39, 53175 Bonn
T: (0228) 8870; E-Mail: uzr612@ibm.rhrz.uni-bonn.de; Fax: 887110
Founded: 1949; Members: 252
Pres: Prof. Dr. Klaus Landfried; Gen Secr: Dr. Josef Lange
Focus: Educ 05493

Hölderlin-Gesellschaft, Hölderlinhaus, Bursagasse 6, 72070 Tübingen
Founded: 1943; Members: 1500
Pres: Prof. Dr. Gerhard Kurz; Gen Secr: Valérie Lawitschka
Focus: Lit
Periodical
Hölderlin-Jahrbuch (bi-annually) 05494

Hoffman-von-Fallersleben-Gesellschaft e.V. (HvF), Schloß Fallersleben, 38442 Wolfsburg
T: (05362) 52623; Fax: 52623
Focus: Lit 05495

Hohenzollerischer Geschichtsverein, Postfach 526, 72482 Sigmaringen
T: (07571) 101558; Fax: 552
Focus: Hist
Periodicals
Hohenzollerische Heimat (quarterly)
Zeitschrift für Hohenzollerische Geschichte (annually) 05496

Hüttentechnische Vereinigung der Deutschen Glasindustrie e.V. (HVG), Mendelssohnstr 75-77, 60325 Frankfurt
T: (069) 9758610; Fax: 97586199
Founded: 1920; Members: 44
Pres: Prof. Dr. Jürgen Petzoldt; Gen Secr: Prof. Dr. Dr. Helmut A. Schaeffer
Focus: Eng; Materials Sci
Periodical
HVG-Mitteilungen (3 times annually) . . 05497

Hugo von Hofmannsthal-Gesellschaft e.V., Gartenstr 35, 72074 Tübingen
T: (0711) 247397; Fax: 248140
Focus: Lit 05498

Humanistische Union e.V., Bräuhausstr 2, 80331 München
T: (089) 226441/42
Focus: Poli Sci
Periodical
Vorgänge: Zeitschrift für Bürgerrechte und Gesellschaftspolitik 05499

Humboldt-Gesellschaft für Wissenschaft, Kunst und Bildung e.V., Riedlach 12, 68307 Mannheim
T: (0621) 771236
Founded: 1962; Members: 580
Focus: Sci; Arts
Periodical
Mitteilungen (1-2 times annually) 05500

HWWA – Institut für Wirtschaftsforschung – Hamburg, Neuer Jungfernstieg 21, 20354 Hamburg
T: (040) 35620
Focus: Econ; Commerce; Marketing; Int'l Relat; Develop Areas
Periodicals
Bibliographie der Wirtschaftspresse: Documentation of selected articles from periodicals
Intereconomics: Review of International Trade and Development
Konjunktur von Morgen: Brief fortnightly Survey of German and World Business Cycles and of the World's Commodity Marktets (bi-weekly)
Wirtschaftsdienst (quarterly)
Wirtschaftsdienst: A Monthly Magazine on Economic Policies (monthly) 05501

ICOM-Deutschland, Deutsches Nationalkomitee des Internationalen Museumsrates, c/o Museum für Mensch und Natur, Schloß Nymphenburg, 80638 München
T: (089) 1783336; Fax: 1783336
Focus: Arts 05502

Ifo Institut für Wirtschaftsforschung e.V. / Ifo Institute for Economic Research, Poschingerstr 5, 81679 München
T: (089) 92240; Fax: 985369
Founded: 1949
Focus: Econ
Periodicals
Ifo-Digest (quarterly)
Ifo-Schnelldienst (3 times monthly)
Ifo-Studien (quarterly)
Wirtschaftskonjunktur (monthly) 05503

IFRA (Inca-Fiej Research Association) (IFRA), Washingtonpl 1, 64287 Darmstadt
T: (06151) 7336; Fax: 733800
Founded: 1961; Members: 1200
Gen Secr: Günther W. Böttcher
Focus: Eng
Periodicals
Newspaper Techniques (monthly)
technique de presse (monthly)
Zeitungstechnik (monthly) 05504

Immermann-Gesellschaft e.V., Thiemstr 7, 39104 Magdeburg
T: (0391) 44995
Focus: Lit 05505

Immuno / Medizinisch-wissenschaftiche Information, Slevogtstr 3-5, 69126 Heidelberg
Focus: Doc; Med; Immunology 05506

Industrie-Gemeinschaft Aerosole e.V. (IGA), Karlstr 21, 60329 Frankfurt
T: (069) 25561508; Fax: 25561608
Founded: 1958; Members: 87
Pres: Josef Wilhelm; Gen Secr: Matthias Ibel
Focus: Chem 05507

INFODAS / Gesellschaft für Systementwicklung und Informationsverarbeitung, Rhonestr 2, 50765 Köln
T: (0221) 709120; Fax: 7091255
Founded: 1974
Focus: Computer & Info Sci 05508

Informatica / Gesellschaft für die EDV-Ausbildung, Ahastr 5, 64285 Darmstadt
T: (06151) 662646
Focus: Computer & Info Sci 05509

Informations- und Bildungszentrum Schloß Gimborn e.V. (IBZ), Schloßstr 10, 51709 Marienheide
T: (02264) 6091; Fax: 3713
Focus: Poli Sci 05510

Informationskreis Mundhygiene und Ernährungsverhalten (IME), Schwedlerstr 6, 60314 Frankfurt/Main
T: (069) 493530
Focus: Hygiene; Nutrition 05511

Informationstechnische Gesellschaft im VDE (ITG), Stresemannallee 15, 60596 Frankfurt
T: (069) 6308360; Fax: 6308273
Founded: 1954; Members: 10000
Pres: Dr. Hans Schüßler; Gen Secr: Dr. Volker Schanz
Focus: Electric Eng; Comm
Periodical
Nachrichtentechnische Zeitschrift: Communications Journal (monthly) 05512

Inklings-Gesellschaft für Literatur und Ästhetik e.V., Wilhelm-Tell-Str 3, 40219 Düsseldorf
T: (0211) 3981163; Fax: 3982638
Focus: Lit 05513

Institut der deutschen Wirtschaft e.V., Gustav-Heinemann-Ufer 84-88, 50968 Köln
T: (0221) 370801; E-Mail: Deutstitut; Fax: 3708192
Founded: 1951; Members: 116
Focus: Econ; Sociology
Periodical
iwd: Informationsdienst des Instituts der deutschen Wirtschaft (weekly) 05514

Institut der Hessischen Volkshochschulen, Winterbachstr 38, 60320 Frankfurt
T: (069) 5600080; Fax: 56000810
Pres: Dr. Lothar Arabin; Gen Secr: Dr. Enno Knobel
Focus: Adult Educ
Periodical
Hessische Blätter für Volksbildung (quarterly) 05515

Institut „Finanzen und Steuern" e.V. / Finance and Taxation Institute, Markt 10, 53111 Bonn
T: (0228) 982210; Fax: 9822150
Founded: 1949
Gen Secr: Dr. Adalbert Uelner
Focus: Finance
Periodical
IFST-Schriften (irregularly) 05516

Institut für angewandte Arbeitswissenschaft e.V. (IfaA), Marienburger Str 7, 50968 Köln
T: (0221) 376030
Focus: Sci
Periodical
Angewandte Arbeitswissenschaft (quarterly) 05517

Institut für Angewandte Geodäsie, Richard-Strauss-Allee 11, 60598 Frankfurt
T: (069) 63331; Fax: 6333235
Founded: 1952
Pres: Prof. Dr. Hermann Seeger
Focus: Surveying
Periodicals
Mitteilungen (irregularly)
Nachrichten aus dem Karten- und Vermessungswesen (irregularly) 05518

Institut für angewandte Verbraucherforschung e.V., Aachener Str 89, 50931 Köln
T: (02234) 71910; Fax: 71060
Focus: Sociology; Ecology 05519

Institut für Angewandte Wirtschaftsforschung (IAW), Ob dem Himmelreich 1, 72074 Tübingen
T: (07071) 98960; E-Mail: iaw@oe.uni-tuebingen.de; Fax: 989699
Founded: 1957; Members: 49
Pres: Prof. Dr. Gerd Ronning; Prof. Dr. Manfred Stadler
Focus: Econ
Periodical
Mitteilungen des Instituts für Angewandte Wirtschaftsforschung (quarterly) 05520

Institut für Auslandsbeziehungen, Charlottenpl 17, 70173 Stuttgart
T: (0711) 22250; E-Mail: Lyncker@ifa-ev.de; Fax: 2264346
Founded: 1917
Pres: Dr. Bernt Graf zu Dohna; Gen Secr: Udo Rossbach
Focus: Int'l Relat
Periodicals
Materialien zum Internationalen Kulturaustausch (irregularly)
Schriftenreihe Dokumentation (irregularly)
Zeitschrift für Kulturaustausch (quarterly) . 05521

Institut für Bauforschung e.V., An der Markuskirche 1, 30163 Hannover
T: (0511) 965160; Fax: 9651626
Founded: 1946; Members: 30
Pres: Prof. Dr. Joachim Arlt
Focus: Civil Eng 05522

Institut für Chemiefasern, Körschtalstr 26, 73770 Denkendorf
T: (0711) 3408101
Focus: Textiles 05523

Institut für den Wissenschaftlichen Film, Nonnenstieg 72, 37075 Göttingen
T: (0551) 50240; E-Mail: iwf-goe@iwf.gwdg.de; Fax: 5024400
Founded: 1956; Members: 110
Pres: Dr. Hanns Frhr. v. Spiegel; Gen Secr: Dr. Hartmut Rudolph
Focus: Cinema; Sci 05524

Institut für Energie- und Umweltforschung Heidelberg e.V. (IFEU), Wilkenstr 3, 69120 Heidelberg
T: (06221) 47670; E-Mail: ifeu@ifeu.com; Fax: 476719
Founded: 1978
Pres: Dr. Ulrich Höpfner
Focus: Energy; Ecology 05525

Institut für Europäische Umweltpolitik, Aloys-Schulte-Str 6, 53129 Bonn
T: (0228) 213810; Fax: 221982
Focus: Ecology; Eng 05526

Institut für Film und Bild in Wissenschaft und Unterricht, Postfach 260, 82026 Grünwald
T: (089) 64971; E-Mail: info-fwu@t-online.de; Fax: 6497300
Founded: 1950
Gen Secr: Manfred Gaibinger
Focus: Cinema; Educ; Photo
Periodical
FWU Magazin (bi-monthly) 05527

Institut für Gesellschaftswissenschaften Walberberg e.V., Simrockstr 19, 53113 Bonn
Focus: Sociology
Periodical
Die Neue Ordnung (bi-monthly) 05528

Institut für gewerbliche Wasserwirtschaft und Luftreinhaltung e.V. / Institute of Water Resources Management and Air Pollution Control, Wankelstr 33, 50996 Köln
Founded: 1956; Members: 2500
Focus: Water Res; Ecology
Periodicals
IWL-Forum (irregularly)
IWL-Umweltbrief (monthly) 05529

Institut für Handwerkswirtschaft München, Max-Joseph-Str 4, 80333 München
T: (089) 593671, 594132; Fax: 553453
Focus: Econ 05530

Institut für Länderkunde e.V., Schongauerstr 9, 04329 Leipzig
T: (0341) 2556500; Fax: 2556598
Founded: 1896 (Neugründung 1992)
Pres: Prof. Dr. Alois Mayr
Focus: Geography 05531

Institut für nationale und internationale Fleisch- und Ernährungswirtschaft, Rombachweg 11, 69118 Heidelberg
T: (06221) 80528, 80529; Fax: 809029
Founded: 1977
Focus: Nutrition; Food; Develop Areas; Doc 05532

Institut für Neue Musik und Musikerziehung e.V. (INMM), Olbrichweg 15, 64287 Darmstadt
T: (06151) 46667; Fax: 46647
Founded: 1948; Members: 300
Pres: Prof. Johannes Fritsch
Focus: Music; Educ
Periodical
Veröffentlichungen des INMM (annually) . 05533

Institut für Neue Technische Form e.V., Eugen-Bracht-Weg 6, 64287 Darmstadt
T: (06151) 48008; Fax: 46553
Focus: Standards 05534

Institut für ökologische Forschung und Bildung e.V., Kettelerstr 15, 48147 Münster
T: (0251) 26091
Focus: Ecology 05535

Institut für religiöse Volkskunde e.V., Breite Gasse 35, 48143 Münster
T: (0251) 57853
Focus: Rel & Theol 05536

Institut für Schadenverhütung und Schadenforschung der öffentlich-rechtlichen Versicherer e.V. (IfS), Preetzer Str 75, 24143 Kiel
T: (0431) 775780
Focus: Insurance
Periodical
IfS-Information (irregularly) 05537

Institut für Sozial- und Wirtschaftspolitische Ausbildung e.V. (ISWA), Gustav-Heinemann-Ufer 72, 50968 Köln
T: (0221) 3795174; Fax: 3795203
Focus: Sociology; Poli Sci 05538

Institut für Sozialarbeit und Sozialpädagogik e.V., Am Stockborn 5-7, 60439 Frankfurt/Main
T: (069) 957890; Fax: 95789190
Focus: Educ; Sociology; Adult Educ
Periodical
Migration und Soziale Arbeit (quarterly) . 05539

Institut für Sozialforschung und Sozialwirtschaft e.V., Trillerweg 68, 66117 Saarbrücken
T: (0681) 954240; Fax: 9542427
Founded: 1969
Focus: Sociology; Econ 05540

Institut für Technik der Betriebsführung im Handwerk, Karl-Friedrich-Str 17, 76133 Karlsruhe
T: (0721) 931030; Fax: 9310350
Focus: Business Admin 05541

Institut für technische Weiterbildung Berlin e.V. (ITW), Luxemburger Str 10, 13353 Berlin
T: (030) 456010; Fax: 4539039
Founded: 1967; Members: 26
Focus: Eng; Adult Educ 05542

Institut für Textil- und Faserforschung Stuttgart, Körschtalstr 26, 73770 Denkendorf
T: (0711) 34080
Focus: Textiles 05543

Institut für Wirtschaft und Gesellschaft Bonn e.V. (IWG Bonn) / Bonn Institute for Economic and Social Research, Ahrstr 45, 53175 Bonn
T: (0228) 372044; Fax: 375869
Founded: 1977
Focus: Econ; Poli Sci
Periodicals
IWG-Berichte
IWG-Impulse
IWG-Mitteilungen 05544

Institut für Wissenschaftliche Zusammenarbeit, Vogtshaldenstr 24, 72074 Tübingen
T: (07071) 5066; E-Mail: iwz@oe.uni-tuchingen.de; Fax: 26753
Founded: 1966; Members: 20

Pres: Prof. Dr. Dr. W. Voelter; Gen Secr: Prof. Dr. J.H. Hohnholz
Focus: Sci 05545

Institut für Zeitungsforschung, Münsterstr 9-11, 44122 Dortmund
T: (0231) 5023221; E-Mail: hbacker@stadtdo.de; Fax: 5026018
Founded: 1926
Pres: Prof. Dr. Hans Bohrmann
Focus: Journalism 05546

Institut für Ziegelforschung Essen e.V., Am Zehnthof 197-203, 45307 Essen
T: (0201) 5921301; Fax: 5921320
Focus: Materials Sci 05547

Institut Neue Wirtschaft e.V., Kurze Mühren 2, 20095 Hamburg
T: (040) 308010; Fax: 30801107
Focus: Econ 05548

Institut zur Förderung publizistischen Nachwuchses e.V. (IFP), Elisenstr 3a, 80335 München
T: (089) 553081; Fax: 5504486
Focus: Journalism 05549

Inter Nationes e.V., Kennedyallee 91-103, 53175 Bonn
T: (0228) 8801; Fax: 880457
Focus: Int'l Relat
Periodicals
Bildung und Wissenschaft (monthly)
Fikrun wa fan (Geist und Leben) (semi-annually)
hand in hand (3 times annually)
Humboldt (3 times annually)
Kulturchronik (bi-monthly) 05550

Interessengemeinschaft für Lederforschung und Häuteschädenbekämpfung im Verband der deutschen Lederindustrie e.V., Leverkuser Str 20, 65929 Frankfurt
Focus: Materials Sci 05551

International Academy of Cytology (IAC) / Universitäts-Frauenklinik, c/o Universitäts-Frauenklinik, Hugstettenstr 55, 79106 Freiburg
T: (0761) 2703012; Fax: 2703122
Founded: 1957; Members: 1950
Gen Secr: Manuel Hilgarth
Focus: Cell Biol & Cancer Res
Periodical
Acta Cytologica (bi-monthly) 05552

International Commission for Uniform Methods of Sugar Analysis (ICUMSA), c/o CSR Limited Central Laboratory, 37-41 Waterloo Road, NSW 2113 North Ryde, Australia
T: (9859) 1905; Fax: 1900
Members: 250
Pres: Dr. Murray R. Player; Gen Secr: R. McCowage
Focus: Nutrition 05553

International Commission of Sugar Technology, Donauwörther Str 50, 86641 Rain
T: (09002) 71210; Fax: 71346
Founded: 1949; Members: 200
Focus: Eng
Periodical
Proceedings of General Assemblies . . 05554

International Copyright Society, Rosenheimer Str 11, 81667 München
T: (089) 4800300; Fax: 48003408
Founded: 1954; Members: 402
Focus: Law
Periodical
Yearbook (irregularly) 05555

International Council of Environmental Law, Adenauerallee 214, 53113 Bonn
T: (0228) 2692240; Fax: 2692250
Founded: 1969; Members: 256
Focus: Law; Ecology
Periodical
Environmental Policy and Law (8 times annually)
. . . . 05556

International Council of Sport Science and Physical Education (ICSSPE), Am Kleinen Wannsee 6, 14109 Berlin
T: (030) 8050060; E-Mail: icsspe@zedat.fu-berlin.de; Fax: 8056386
Founded: 1958
Pres: Prof. Dr. Grdrun Doll-Tepper; Gen Secr: Christophe Mailliet
Focus: Sports
Periodical
ICSSPE Bulletin (semi-annually) 05557

International Council on Monuments and Sites ICOMOS, Deutsches Nationalkomitee, Hofgraben 4, 80539 München
T: (089) 2114260; Fax: 2114300
Focus: Preserv Hist Monuments 05558

International Geographical Union (IGU) (IGU), c/o Geographisches Institut, Universität, Meckenheimer Allee 166, 53115 Bonn
T: (0228) 739287; E-Mail: secretariat@igu.bn.eunet.de; Fax: 739272
Founded: 1923; Members: 83
Pres: Prof. Bruno Messerli; Gen Secr: Prof. Dr. Eckart Ehlers
Focus: Geography
Periodical
Bulletins (semi-annually) 05559

International Institute of Public Finance, c/o Universität, Postfach 1150, 66041 Saarbrücken
Focus: Finance
Periodical
Papers and Proceedings (annually) . . . 05560

International Mineralogical Association (IMA), c/o Institut für Mineralogie, Universität, Lahnberge, 35043 Marburg
T: (6421) 285617
Founded: 1958
Focus: Mineralogy
Periodical
IMA News 05561

International Society for Group Activity in Education (ISGE), Schlittweg 34, 69198 Schriesheim
T: (06203) 62717
Founded: 1972
Focus: Educ
Periodical
Forum Pädagogik: Zeitschrift für pädagogische Modelle und soziale Probleme (quarterly) 05562

International Society of Developmental Biologists (ISDS), c/o Max-Planck-Institut für Biophysikalische Chemie, Postfach 2841, 37070 Göttingen
T: (0551) 2011361; E-Mail: pgruss@gwdg.de; Fax: 2011504
Founded: 1950; Members: 800
Pres: Prof. P. Gruss
Focus: Bio
Periodical
ISDS Newsletter (semi-annually) 05563

Internationale Akademie für Pathologie, Deutsche Abteilung e.V., Röttgener Str 101, 53127 Bonn
T: (0228) 282404; Fax: 284796
Founded: 1964; Members: 1355
Focus: Pathology 05564

Internationale Alfred Döblin-Gesellschaft (IADG), Reinbeckstr 29c, 70565 Stuttgart
T: (0711) 744122; Fax: 744122
Focus: Lit 05565

Internationale Arbeitsgemeinschaft der Archiv-, Bibliotheks- und Graphikrestauratoren (IADA), c/o Staats- und Universitätsbibliothek, Frau Renate von Issem, Papendiek 14, 37073 Göttingen
T: (06421) 81758; Fax: 82506
Founded: 1957; Members: 530
Focus: Archives; Libraries & Bk Sci; Arts
Periodical
Restauro (bi-monthly) 05566

Internationale Arnold Zweig-Gesellschaft e.V., Gustav-Adolf-Str 150, 13086 Berlin
T: (030) 28538544
Focus: Lit 05567

Internationale Bachakademie Stuttgart, Johann-Sebastian-Bach-Pl, Hasenbergsteige 3, 70178 Stuttgart
T: (0711) 619210; Fax: 6192123
Focus: Music 05568

Internationale Biometrische Gesellschaft, Deutsche Region (IBS), Goethestr 23, 52064 Aachen
T: (0241) 8089796
Founded: 1953
Focus: Bio 05569

Internationale Gesellschaft der Bildenden Künste, Sektion der Bundesrepublik Deutschland (IGBK), Weberstr 61, 53115 Bonn
T: (0228) 216141; Fax: 216105
Focus: Arts 05570

Internationale Gesellschaft für Geschichte der Pharmazie, Graf-Moltke-Str 46, 28211 Bremen
T: (0421) 345525
Founded: 1926; Members: 1300
Focus: Hist; Pharmacol 05571

Internationale Gesellschaft für musikpädagogische Fortbildung e.V. (IGMF), c/o Deutsche Landjugendakademie, Johannes-Hummel-Weg 1, 57392 Schmallenberg
T: (02974) 9110; Fax: 911100
Focus: Educ; Music 05572

Internationale Gewässerschutzkommission für den Bodensee, c/o BUWAL – Bundesamt für Umwelt, Wald und Landschaft, 3003 Bern
T: (031) 3226968; Fax: 3230371
Founded: 1960; Members: 20 Delegierte, 22 Sachverständige
Pres: Dr. H.U. Schweizer; Gen Secr: Dr. B. Sollberger
Focus: Ecology 05573

Internationale Heinrich Schütz-Gesellschaft e.V. (ISG), Heinrich-Schütz-Allee 35, 34131 Kassel
T: (0561) 31050; Fax: 3105240
Founded: 1930; Members: 1500
Focus: Music
Periodicals
Acta Sagittariana (annually)
Schütz-Jahrbuch (annually) 05574

Internationale Kommission zum Schutze des Rheins gegen Verunreinigung / International Commission for the Protection of the Rhine against Pollution, Hohenzollernstr 18, 56068 Koblenz
T: (0261) 12495; Fax: 36572
Founded: 1963; Members: 6
Pres: Dominique Moyen; Gen Secr: Koos Wieriks
Focus: Ecology
Periodical
Zahlentafeln der Physikalisch-Chemischen Untersuchungen des Rheinwassers (annually)
. . . . 05575

Internationale Novalis Gesellschaft, Schäfergasse 6, 06333 Wiederstedt
T: (03476) 812359; Fax: 812359
Focus: Lit 05576

Internationale Peter Weiss-Gesellschaft e.V., Mommsenstr 47, 10629 Berlin
T: (030) 32701013; Fax: 32701014
Focus: Lit 05577

Internationale Robert-Musil-Gesellschaft e.V. (IRMG), c/o Universität des Saarlandes, Gde. 35/4, St. Johann, Stadtwald, 66123 Saarbrücken
T: (0681) 3023334
Focus: Lit 05578

Internationale Schubert-Gesellschaft e.V., Schulberg 2, 72070 Tübingen
T: (07071) 22810; Fax: 550617
Focus: Music 05579

Internationale Vereinigung der Musikbibliotheken, Musikarchive und Musikdokumentationszentren, Gruppe Bundesrepublik Deutschland (AIBM), c/o Deutsches Musikarchiv der Deutschen Bibliothek, Postfach 450229, 12172 Berlin
T: (030) 770020
Founded: 1951; Members: 240
Pres: Dr. Bettina von Seyfried; Gen Secr: Dr. Joachim Jaenecke
Focus: Libraries & Bk Sci
Periodical
Forum Musikbibliothek (quarterly) 05580

Internationale Vereinigung der Schallarchive – Ländergruppe Deutschland/Deutschschweiz (IASA), Bertramstr 8, 60320 Frankfurt/Main
T: (069) 15687150; Fax: 15687100
Focus: Archives; Music 05581

Internationale Vereinigung des Theaters für Kinder und Jugendliche Sektion BRD e.V. (ASSITEJ), Schützenstr 12, 60311 Frankfurt/Main
T: (069) 291538; Fax: 292354
Focus: Perf Arts 05582

Internationale Vereinigung für Rechts- und Sozialphilosophie e.V., c/o Juristisches Seminar, Georg-August-Universität, Pl der Göttinger Sieben 6, 37073 Göttingen
T: (0551) 397384; Fax: 394872
Founded: 1909
Focus: Law; Sociology; Philos 05583

Internationale Vereinigung für Vegetationskunde (IVV), Wilhelm-Weber-Str 2, 37073 Göttingen
T: (0551) 395700; Fax: 398449
Founded: 1937; Members: 1200
Focus: Botany
Periodical
Journal of Vegetation Science (5 times annually)
. . . . 05584

Internationale Vereinigung von Versicherungsjuristen (A.I.D.A.), Deutsche Landesgruppe, c/o Deutscher Verein für Versicherungswissenschaft e.V., Johannisberger Str 31, 14197 Berlin
T: (030) 8212031; Fax: 8222875
Founded: 1960
Pres: Prof. Dr. Ulrich Hübner
Focus: Law
Periodical
Zeitschrift für die gesamte Versicherungswissenschaft (quarterly) . . 05585

Internationale Wolfgang-Borchert-Gesellschaft e.v., Statthalterpl 3, 22605 Hamburg
T: (040) 41235918; Fax: 41233352
Focus: Lit 05586

Internationaler Arbeitskreis für Musik e.V. (IAM), Heinrich-Schütz-Allee 33 Post Office Box 410236, 34064 Kassel
T: (0561) 935170; Fax: 313772
Founded: 1923; Members: 5000
Pres: Prof. Diether de la Motte; Gen Secr: Adolf Lang
Focus: Music
Periodical
IAM-Journal (semi-annually) 05587

Internationaler Arbeitskreis Sonnenberg, Bankpl 8, 38100 Braunschweig
T: (0531) 49242; Fax: 42512
Focus: Sci
Periodicals
Internationale Briefe / International Journal / Revue Internationale (irregularly)
Sonnenberg-News (irregularly) 05588

Internationaler Kunstkritikerverband, Sektion der Bundesrepublik Deutschland e.V. (AICA), Maternusstr 29, 50678 Köln
T: (0221) 314641; Fax: 315337
Focus: Arts 05589

Internationales Dokumentations- und Studienzentrum für Jugendkonflikte, Gaußstr 20, 42119 Wuppertal
T: (0202) 4392308
Focus: Law
Periodical
Cahier (irregularly) 05590

Internationales Institut für Öffentliche Finanzen, c/o Universität des Saarlandes, 66123 Saarbrücken
T: (0681) 3023653; E-Mail: iipf@rz.uni-sb.de http://www.wiwi.uni-sb./iipf; Fax: 3024369
Founded: 1937; Members: 975
Pres: Prof Dr. Robert Haveman; Gen Secr: Birgit Schneider
Focus: Finance
Periodical
International Tax and Public Finance (quarterly)
. . . . 05591

Internationales Zentralinstitut für das Jugend- und Bildungsfernsehen, Rundfunkpl 1, 80335 München
T: (089) 59002140; Fax: 59002379
Founded: 1965
Focus: Mass Media; Educ
Periodical
Televizion (semi-annually) 05592

Interparlamentarische Arbeitsgemeinschaft, Postfach 120110, 53043 Bonn
T: (0228) 2692212, 2692228; Fax: 2692251
Pres: Dr. Elke Leonhard; Gen Secr: Dr. Wolfgang Burhenne
Focus: Poli Sci 05593

Intitut für Baustoffprüfung und Fußbodenforschung, Industriestr 19, 53842 Troisdorf
T: (02241) 42042; Fax: 404295
Focus: Civil Eng; Materials Sci 05594

Intitut für Bildungsmedien e.V., Zeppelinallee 33, 60325 Frankfurt
T: (069) 709046; Fax: 70790169
Founded: 1971
Pres: Andreas Baer
Focus: Mass Media; Educ 05595

Jean-Paul-Gesellschaft (JPGes.), Richard-Wagner-Str 48, 95444 Bayreuth
T: (0921) 757280; Fax: 7572822
Focus: Lit 05596

Joachim Jungius-Gesellschaft der Wissenschaften e.V. (JJG), Edmund-Siemers-Allee 1, 20146 Hamburg
T: (040) 417444
Founded: 1947; Members: 119
Focus: Humanities; Nat Sci 05597

Johann-Gottfried-Schnabel-Gesellschaft e.V. (JGSG), Neustadt 12, 06547 Stolberg
T: (030) 7971225
Focus: Lit 05598

Johann Heinrich Voß-Gesellschaft e.V., Schloßpl 4, 23701 Eutin
T: (04521) 701228; Fax: 701236
Focus: Lit 05599

Johannes-Althusius-Gesellschaft e.V. / Technische Universität, Mommsenstr. 13, 01062 Dresden
T: (0251) 4901
Pres: Prof. Dr. Dieter Wyduckel
Focus: Law; Hist 05600

Johannes Brahms-Gesellschaft Internationale Vereinigung e.V., Peterstr 39, 20355 Hamburg
T: (040) 452158
Focus: Music 05601

Jung-Stilling-Gesellschaft e.V., Postfach 100433, 57004 Siegen
T: (0271) 52799; E-Mail: Dr.Erich-Mertens@t-online.de; Fax: 80463
Pres: Prof. Dr. Gerhard Merk
Focus: Hist 05602

Kant-Gesellschaft, Am alten Forsthaus 16, 53125 Bonn
Founded: 1904
Focus: Philos 05603

Karl-Lamprecht-Gesellschaft Leipzig e.V. (KLG), Oststr 41, 04159 Leipzig
T: (0341) 9900440; Fax: 9900440
Focus: Hist 05604

Karl-May-Gesellschaft e.V. (KMG), Eitzenbachstr 22, 54343 Föhren
T: (06502) 20887
Focus: Lit 05605

Kassenärztliche Bundesvereinigung (KBV), Herbert-Lewin-Str 3, 50931 Köln
T: (0221) 40050; Fax: 408039
Founded: 1955
Focus: Med 05606

Kassenärztliche Vereinigung Bayerns, Mühlbaurstr 16, 81677 München
T: (089) 41471; Fax: 4147324
Focus: Med 05607

Kassenärztliche Vereinigung Berlin, Bismarckstr 95-96, 10625 Berlin
T: (030) 310031272; Fax: 31003210
Focus: Med
Periodical
Mitteilungsblatt (monthly) 05608

Kassenärztliche Vereinigung Bremen, Schwachhauser Heerstr 26-28, 28209 Bremen
T: (0421) 340051
Focus: Med 05609

Kassenärztliche Vereinigung Hamburg, Humboldtstr 56, 22083 Hamburg
T: (040) 228021
Focus: Med 05610

Kassenärztliche Vereinigung Hessen, Georg-Voigt-Str 15, 60325 Frankfurt
T: (069) 79201
Focus: Med 05611

Kassenärztliche Vereinigung Koblenz, Emil-Schüller-Str 14-16, 56073 Koblenz
T: (0261) 12552
Focus: Med 05612

Kassenärztliche Vereinigung Niedersachsen, Postfach 3167, 30175 Hannover
T: (0511) 38003
Focus: Med 05613

Kassenärztliche Vereinigung Nord-Württemberg, Albstadtweg 11, 70567 Stuttgart
T: (0711) 78750
Focus: Med
Periodical
Kassenarzt-aktuell (quarterly) 05614

Kassenärztliche Vereinigung Nordbaden, Postfach 3806, 76023 Karlsruhe
T: (0721) 5961151; Fax: 5961188
Focus: Med 05615

Kassenärztliche Vereinigung Nordrhein, Emanuel-Leutze-Str 8, 40547 Düsseldorf
T: (0211) 59701
Focus: Med 05616

Kassenärztliche Vereinigung Pfalz, Maximilianstr 22, 67433 Neustadt
T: (06321) 8930
Focus: Med 05617

Kassenärztliche Vereinigung Rheinhessen, Hindenburgstr 32, 55118 Mainz
T: (06131) 63020
Focus: Med 05618

Kassenärztliche Vereinigung Saarland, Faktoreistr 4, 66111 Saarbrücken
T: (0681) 40031
Focus: Med 05619

Kassenärztliche Vereinigung Schleswig-Holstein, Bismarckallee 1-3, 23795 Bad Segeberg
T: 890
Focus: Med
Periodical
Schleswig-Holsteinisches Ärzteblatt . . . 05620

Kassenärztliche Vereinigung Südbaden, Sundgauallee 27, 79114 Freiburg
T: (0761) 8840; Fax: 84107
Focus: Med 05621

Kassenärztliche Vereinigung Südwürttemberg, Wächterstr 76, 72074 Tübingen
T: (07071) 2080
Focus: Med 05622

Kassenärztliche Vereinigung Trier, Balduinstr 10-12, 54290 Trier
T: (0651) 45011
Focus: Med 05623

Kassenärztliche Vereinigung Westfalen-Lippe, Westfalendamm 45, 44141 Dortmund
T: (0231) 41071
Focus: Med 05624

Kassenzahnärztliche Bundesvereinigung (KZBV), Universitätsstr 71-73, 50931 Köln
T: (0221) 40010; Fax: 404035
Founded: 1955; Members: 17
Focus: Dent
Periodical
Zahnärztliche Mitteilungen: ZM (bi-weekly) 05625

Kassenzahnärztliche Vereinigung Berlin, Georg-Wilhelm-Str 16, 10711 Berlin
T: (030) 890040; Fax: 89004102
Focus: Dent
Periodical
Mitteilungsblatt der Berliner Zahnärzte (monthly) 05626

Kassenzahnärztliche Vereinigung für den Regierungsbezirk Freiburg, Schönauer Str 4, 79115 Freiburg
T: (0761) 490410
Focus: Dent 05627

Kassenzahnärztliche Vereinigung für den Regierungsbezirk Karlsruhe, Joseph-Meyer-Str 8-10, 68167 Mannheim
T: (0621) 23335
Focus: Dent 05628

Kassenzahnärztliche Vereinigung für den Regierungsbezirk Stuttgart, Heinrich-Baumann-Str 1-3, 70190 Stuttgart
T: (0711) 283243
Focus: Dent 05629

Kassenzahnärztliche Vereinigung für den Regierungsbezirk Tübingen, Bismarckstr 96, 72072 Tübingen
T: (07071) 9110; E-Mail: kzv-tuebingen@t-online.de; Fax: 911131
Focus: Dent 05630

Kassenzahnärztliche Vereinigung Hamburg, Katharinenbrücke 1, 20457 Hamburg
T: (040) 363011
Focus: Dent 05631

Kassenzahnärztliche Vereinigung Hessen, Lyoner Str 21, 60528 Frankfurt
T: (069) 66071
Focus: Dent
Periodical
Der hessische Zahnarzt: DHZ (monthly) . 05632

Kassenzahnärztliche Vereinigung im Lande Bremen, Emmastr 220, 28213 Bremen
T: (0421) 211035/39
Focus: Dent 05633

Kassenzahnärztliche Vereinigung Koblenz-Trier, Poststr 4-8, 56068 Koblenz
T: (0261) 38047
Focus: Dent 05634

Kassenzahnärztliche Vereinigung Niedersachsen, Berliner Allee 14, 30175 Hannover
T: (0511) 34931
Focus: Dent
Periodical
Niedersächsisches Zahnärzteblatt (monthly) 05635

Kassenzahnärztliche Vereinigung Nordrhein, Lindemannstr 36-42, 40237 Düsseldorf
T: (0211) 68850; Fax: 6885333
Focus: Dent
Periodical
Rheinisches Zahnärzteblatt (bi-monthly) . 05636

Kassenzahnärztliche Vereinigung Pfalz, Brunhildenstr 1, 67059 Ludwigshafen
T: (0621) 519111; Fax: 622972
Focus: Dent 05637

Kassenzahnärztliche Vereinigung Rheinhessen, Eppichmauergasse 1, 55116 Mainz
T: (06131) 287760; Fax: 225706
Focus: Dent 05638

Kassenzahnärztliche Vereinigung Saarland, Puccinistr 2, 66119 Saarbrücken
T: (0681) 586080
Focus: Dent 05639

Kassenzahnärztliche Vereinigung Schleswig-Holstein, Westring 498, 24106 Kiel
T: (0431) 38970; Fax: 389710
Focus: Dent 05640

Kassenzahnärztliche Vereinigung Westfalen-Lippe, Auf der Horst 25, 48147 Münster
T: (0251) 5070; Fax: 507117
Focus: Dent
Periodical
Zahnärzteblatt Westfalen-Lippe (bi-monthly) 05641

Katalyse-Umweltgruppe Köln e.V., Friesenstr 84, 50670 Köln
T: (0221) 122166
Focus: Ecology 05642

Katholische Ärztearbeit Deutschlands, Bendenweg 101, 53121 Bonn
T: (0228) 9875220; Fax: 9875222
Founded: 1958; Members: 670
Pres: Dr. Rudolf Giertler
Focus: Med
Periodical
Renovatio: Zeitschrift für das interdisziplinäre Gespräch (quarterly) 05643

Katholische Akademie Augsburg, Kappelberg 1, 86150 Augsburg
T: (0821) 3152295; Fax: 3152263
Focus: Rel & Theol 05644

Katholische Akademie Dresden e.V., Tiergartenstr 74, 01219 Dresden
T: (0351) 4710710; Fax: 4717669
Focus: Rel & Theol 05645

Katholische Akademie Hamburg (KAH), Herrengraben 4, 20459 Hamburg
T: (040) 369520; Fax: 36952101
Focus: Rel & Theol 05646

Katholische Akademie in Bayern, Mandlstr 23, 80802 München
T: (089) 381020; Fax: 38102103
Founded: 1957
Focus: Adult Educ
Periodicals
Schriften der Katholischen Akademie in Bayern
zur debatte: Themen der Katholischen Akademie in Bayern (bi-monthly) 05647

Katholische Akademie in Berlin (KAiB), Hannoversche Str 5, 10115 Berlin
T: (030) 2830950; Fax: 283095147
Focus: Rel & Theol 05648

Katholische Akademie Rabanus Maurus, OT Naurod, Wilhelm-Kempf-Haus 1, 65207 Wiesbaden
T: (06127) 77280; Fax: 77287
Focus: Rel & Theol 05649

Katholische Akademie Schwerte, Bergerhofweg 24, 58239 Schwerte
T: (02304) 4770; Fax: 47724
Focus: Rel & Theol 05650

Katholische Akademie Trier, auf der Jüngt 1, 54293 Trier
T: (0651) 81050; Fax: 8105434
Gen Secr: Dr. Herbert Hoffmann
Focus: Adult Educ 05651

Katholische Akademikerarbeit Deutschlands, Bendenweg 101, 53121 53121 Bonn
T: (0228) 9875220; Fax: 9875222
Founded: 1979; Members: 920000
Pres: Erich Hasselkuss
Focus: Sci
Periodical
Schriftenreihe der Katholischen Akademikerarbeit Deutschlands (irregularly) 05652

Katholische Bundesarbeitsgemeinschaft für berufliche Bildung, Kolpingpl 5-11, 50667 Köln
T: (0221) 20701142; Fax: 2070138
Focus: Educ 05653

Katholische Bundesarbeitsgemeinschaft für Erwachsenenbildung (KBE), René-Schickele-Str 10, 53123 Bonn
T: (0228) 643081; E-Mail: kbe-bonn@t-online.de; Fax: 643083
Founded: 1957; Members: 63
Pres: Erwin Müller-Ruckwitt; Gen Secr: Dr. Ralph Bergold
Focus: Adult Educ
Periodical
Erwachsenenbildung: Adult Education (quarterly) 05654

Katholische Erwachsenenbildung im Lande Niedersachsen e.V., Hohenzollernstr 22, 30161 Hannover
T: (0511) 348500; Fax: 3485033
Founded: 1956; Members: 101
Pres: Ferdinand Cloppenburg; Gen Secr: Hubert Stuntebeck
Focus: Adult Educ
Periodical
KEB-NordWest: Mitteilungsblatt für kath. Erwachsenenbildung (quarterly) 05655

Katholische Erziehergemeinschaft in Bayern (KEG), Herzogspitalstr 13, 80331 München
T: (089) 267041; Fax: 2606387
Pres: Prof. Dr. Konrad Macht; Gen Secr: Dr. Gottfried Dylong
Focus: Educ; Sociology
Periodicals
Christ und Bildung (monthly)
paed (bi-monthly)
Treffpunkt Kindergarten/Forum Sozialpädagogik (bi-monthly) 05656

Katholische Juristenarbeit Deutschlands, Bendenweg 101, 53121 Bonn
T: (0228) 9875220; Fax: 9875222
Founded: 1968; Members: 115
Pres: Dr. Horst-Harald Lewandowski
Focus: Law 05657

Katholische Pädagogenarbeit Deutschlands, Bendenweg 101, 53121 Bonn
T: (0228) 9875220; Fax: 9875222
Founded: 1978; Members: 100
Pres: Dr. Gabriele Peus
Focus: Educ 05658

Katholischer Akademikerverband Deutschlands (KAV), Bendenweg 101, 53121 Bonn
T: (0228) 9875220; Fax: 9875222
Founded: 1913
Pres: Norbert Darga
Focus: Sci
Periodical
Renovatio: Zeitschrift für das interdisziplinäre Gespräch (quarterly) 05659

Katholischer Akademischer Ausländer-Dienst, Hausdorffstr 151, 53129 Bonn
T: (0228) 917580; E-Mail: KAAD-de@t-online.de; Fax: 9175858
Founded: 1956
Pres: Prof. Dr. Peter Hünermann; Gen Secr: Dr. Hermann Weber
Focus: Sci
Periodical
Jahresbericht (annually) 05660

Katholischer Krankenhausverband Deutschlands e.V. (KKVD), Karlstr 40, 79104 Freiburg
T: (0761) 200351; Fax: 200609
Focus: Med 05661

Katholischer-Theologischer Fakultätentag (KThFT), c/o Kath.-Theol. Fakultät, Johannisstr 8, 48143 Münster
T: (0251) 832632; Fax: 838357
Focus: Educ; Rel & Theol 05662

Kestner-Gesellschaft, Warmbüchenstr 16, 30159 Hannover
T: (0511) 327081; Fax: 3681699
Founded: 1916; Members: 3000
Focus: Arts 05663

KfH-Kuratorium für Dialyse und Nierentransplantation e.V., Emil-von-Behring-Passage, 63263 Neu-Isenburg
T: (06102) 3590; Fax: 359344
Focus: Surgery; Hematology 05664

KIM Katholisches Institut für Medieninformation GmbH (KIM), Am Hof 28, 50667 Köln
T: (0221) 9254630; E-Mail: kimlux@NetCologne.de; Fax: 9254636
Focus: Mass Media
Periodicals
Fernseh-Dienst (weekly)
film-dienst (bi-weekly)
Funk-Korrespondenz (weekly) 05665

Kinder- und Jugendtheaterzentrum in der Bundesrepublik Deutschland, Schützenstr 12, 60311 Frankfurt/Main
T: (069) 296661; Fax: 292354
Focus: Perf Arts 05666

Klaus-Groth-Gesellschaft e.V., Uhlenhorst 14, 25746 Lohe-Rickelshof
T: (0481) 73513
Focus: Lit 05667

Klinische Forschungsgruppe für Multiple Sklerose, c/o Neurologische Klinik der Universität, Josef-Schneider-Str 11, 97080 Würzburg
T: (0931) 2012201; Fax: 2012697
Focus: Med 05668

Klinische Forschungsgruppe für Reproduktionsmedizin, c/o Frauenklinik der Universität, Steinfurter Str 107, 48149 Münster
T: (0251) 836096
Focus: Med 05669

Kneipp-Bund e.V. / Bundesverband für Gesundheitsförderung, Adolf-Scholz-Allee 6, 86825 Bad Wörishofen
T: (08247) 30020; Fax: 3002199
Focus: Public Health 05670

Kölner Schule – Institut für Publistik e.V. (KS), Gut Schillingsrott, 50996 Köln
T: (0221) 9355690; Fax: 93556918
Focus: Journalism 05671

Kollegium der Medizinjournalisten, Brünnsteinstr 13, 83080 Oberaudorf
T: (08033) 2327
Focus: Med; Journalism 05672

Kommission für Alte Geschichte und Epigraphik des Deutschen Archäologischen Instituts, Amalienstr 73, 80799 München
T: (089) 281045; Fax: 2805161
Focus: Archeol
Periodical
Chiron: Mitteilungen der Kommission für Alte Geschichte und Epigraphik des Deutschen Archäologischen Instituts (annually) . . . 05673

Kommission für Erforschung der Agrar- und Wirtschaftsverhältnisse des europäischen Ostens e.V., Otto-Behaghel-Str 10d, 35394 Gießen
T: (0641) 7022835; Fax: 7022837
Founded: 1957; Members: 8
Focus: Agri; Hist
Periodicals
Giessener Abhandlungen zur Agrar- und Wirtschaftsforschung des europäischen Ostens (8-10 times annually)
Osteuropastudien der Hochschulen des Landes Hessen: Reihe I (8-10 times annually) . 05674

Kommission für Geschichte des Parlamentarismus und der politischen Parteien e.V., Colmantstr 39, 53115 Bonn
T: (0228) 604830; Fax: 6048323
Founded: 1951; Members: 20
Pres: Prof. Dr. Rudolf Morsey; Gen Secr: Dr. Martin Schumacher
Focus: Hist; Poli Sci 05675

Kommission für geschichtliche Landeskunde in Baden-Württemberg, Eugenstr 7, 70182 Stuttgart
T: (0711) 2124266; Fax: 2124283
Founded: 1954; Members: 152
Pres: Dr. Gerhard Taddey
Focus: Hist
Periodicals
Zeitschrift für die Geschichte des Oberrheins (annually)
Zeitschrift für Württembergische Landesgeschichte (annually) 05676

Kommission für Sozial- und Wirtschaftsgeschichte der Bayerischen Akademie der Wissenschaften, Marstallpl 8, 80539 München
T: (089) 23031225; Fax: 23031100
Focus: Hist; Sociology; Econ 05677

Kommission für Zeitgeschichte e.V., Königstr 28, 53113 Bonn
T: (0228) 222030; Fax: 221205
Focus: Hist 05678

Kommission Reinhaltung der Luft (KRdL) im VDI und DIN, Postfach 101139, 40002 Düsseldorf
T: (0211) 6214532; E-Mail: Krdl@vdi.de; Fax: 6214157
Founded: 1957
Pres: Prof. Dr. Johann Hubert; Gen Secr: Prof. Dr. Klaus Grefen
Focus: Ecology
Periodical
Gefahrstoffe-Reinhaltung der Luft (monthly) 05679

Kommunalpolitische Vereinigung der CDU und CSU Deutschland, Friedrich-Ebert-Allee 73, 53113 Bonn
T: (0228) 544246
Focus: Poli Sci
Periodical
Kommunalpolitische Blätter (monthly) . . 05680

Konferenz der deutschen Akademien der Wissenschaften, Geschwister-Scholl-Str 2, 55131 Mainz
T: (06131) 57728; Fax: 57740
Founded: 1973; Members: 7
Gen Secr: N.N.

Focus: Sci 05681

Konferenz der Landesfilmdienste in der Bundesrepublik Deutschland e.V., Rheinallee 59, 53173 Bonn
T: (0228) 355002; Fax: 358269
Focus: Cinema 05682

Konferenz der Leiter der kirchlichen und der staatlichen Ausbildungsstätten für Kirchenmusik und der Landeskirchenmusikdirektoren, Untere Schmiedegasse 8, 90403 Nürnberg
T: (0911) 2418344; Fax: 223866
Focus: Music; Educ 05683

Konferenz der Leiter katholischer kirchenmusikalischer Ausbildungsstätten Deutschlands, c/o Amt für Kirchenmusik, Schoferstr 4, 79098 Freiburg
T: (0761) 2188244; Fax: 381083
Focus: Educ; Music 05684

Konferenz Sportwissenschaftlicher Hochschuleinrichtungen, Carl-Diem-Weg 6, 50933 Köln
T: (0221) 4982200; Fax: 4995505
Focus: Sports 05685

Kongreßgesellschaft für ärztliche Fortbildung e.V., Klingsorstr 21, 12167 Berlin
T: (030) 7913091; Fax: 7913994
Founded: 1952; Members: 13
Pres: Prof. Dr. Rudolf Häring; Gen Secr: Prof. Dr. R. Gotzen
Focus: Med; Adult Educ 05686

Konrad-Adenauer-Kreis für freiheitliche und europäische Politik e.V., In der Freiheit 34, 56179 Vallendar
T: (0261) 60075; Fax: 60076
Focus: Poli Sci 05687

Konstanzer Arbeitskreis für mittelalterliche Geschichte e.V. (AKfMA), Benediktinerpl 5, 78467 Konstanz
T: (07531) 61743; Fax: 61743
Focus: Hist 05688

Kritische Akademie Inzell, Salinenweg 45, 83334 Inzell
T: (08665) 820; Fax: 1854
Focus: Poli Sci 05689

Kulturinstitut Komponistinnen gestern-heute e.V., Theaterstr 11, 69117 Heidelberg
T: (06221) 166861; Fax: 182072
Focus: Music 05690

Kulturkreis der deutschen Wirtschaft im Bundesverband der Deutschen Industrie e.V., G.-Heinemann-Ufer 84-88, 50968 Köln
T: (0221) 3708406/506; Fax: 3708503
Focus: Cultur Hist 05691

Kulturpolitische Gesellschaft e.V., Weberstr 59a, 53113 Bonn
T: (0228) 201670; E-Mail: Kulturpol@aol.com; Fax: 2016733
Members: 1400
Pres: Dr. Oliver Scheytt; Gen Secr: Dr. Norbert Sievers
Focus: Poli Sci 05692

Kulturwerk für Südtirol e.V., Schwanthalerstr 73b, 80336 München
T: (089) 537474; Fax: 5439511
Focus: Cultur Hist 05693

Kunstrat im Deutschen Kulturrat, Weberstr 59a, 53113 Bonn
T: (0228) 201350; Fax: 216105
Focus: Arts 05694

Kunstwissenschaftler- und Kunstkritiker-Verband e.V, Postfach 540 PA 14, 10149 Berlin
T: (030) 2793566, 2794055; Fax: 2793076
Focus: Arts 05695

Kuratorium der Deutschen Wirtschaft für Berufsbildung, Adenauerallee 8a, 53113 Bonn
T: (0228) 915230; Fax: 212079
Focus: Adult Educ; Econ 05696

Kuratorium für Forschung und Technik der Zellstoff- und Papierindustrie, Adenauerallee 55, 53113 Bonn
Fax: (0228) 2670562
Focus: Eng 05697

Kuratorium für Technik und Bauwesen in der Landwirtschaft e.V. (KTBL), Bartningstr 49, 64289 Darmstadt
T: (06151) 70010; Fax: 700123
Focus: Civil Eng; Eng; Agri
Periodicals
Landtechnik: Fachzeitschrift für Agrartechnik und ländliches Bauen (monthly)
Schriften (irregularly) 05698

Kuratorium für Waldarbeit und Forsttechnik e.V. (KWF) / Federal Centre of Forest Operations and Techniques, Spremberger Str 1, 64823 Groß-Umstadt
T: (06078) 7850; E-Mail: kwf.info@t-online.de; Fax: 78550
Founded: 1962; Members: 1500
Focus: Forestry
Periodical
Forsttechnische Informationen: Mitteilungsblatt des KWF (monthly) 05699

Kurt Tucholsky-Gesellschaft e.V (KTG), Rebhuhngang 1, 27798 Hude
T: (04408) 1357; Fax: 1357
Focus: Lit 05700

Ländliche Erwachsenenbildung in Niedersachsen e.V. (LEB), Marienstr 9-11, 30171 Hannover
T: (0511) 304110; Fax: 3631615
Founded: 1951; Members: 80
Focus: Adult Educ 05701

Landesärztekammer Baden-Württemberg, Postfach 700361, 70573 Stuttgart
T: (0711) 769890
Pres: Prof. Dr. Friedrich-Wilhelm Kolkmann; Gen Secr: Dr. Kurt Seizinger
Focus: Public Health
Periodical
Ärzteblatt Baden-Württemberg, (ÄBW): Offizielles Organ der Landesärztekammer Baden-Württemberg (monthly) 05702

Landesärztekammer Brandenburg, Dreifort-Str 12, 03044 Cottbus
T: (0355) 780100; Fax: 7801036
Founded: 1990; Members: ca. 7300
Pres: Dr. Udo Walter; Gen Secr: Dr. Reinhard Heiber
Focus: Med 05703

Landesärztekammer Hessen, Im Vogelsgesang 3, 60488 Frankfurt
T: (069) 976720; Fax: 97672128
Founded: 1956; Members: 26000
Pres: Dr. Alfred Möhrle; Gen Secr: Dr. Michael Popovic
Focus: Med
Periodical
Hessisches Ärzteblatt (monthly) 05704

Landesärztekammer Rheinland-Pfalz, Deutschhauspl 3, 55116 Mainz
T: (06131) 288220; Fax: 2882288
Pres: Dr. Dieter Everz; Gen Secr: Dr. Jochen Wimmenauer
Focus: Med
Periodical
Ärzteblatt Rheinland-Pfalz (monthly) . . . 05705

Landesärztekammer Thüringen, Stoystr 2, 07743 Jena
T: (03641) 25541
Focus: Med 05706

Landesarbeitsgemeinschaft Jugend und Literatur NRW e.V., c/o Brigitte Müller-Beyreiss, Von-Werth-Str 159, 50259 Pulheim-Brauweiler
T: (02234) 84286; Fax: 89724
Founded: 1978; Members: 60
Focus: Lit; Educ 05707

Landesausschuß der Volkshochschulen des Landes Bremen, Schwachhauser Heerstr 67, 28211 Bremen
T: (0421) 3613666; Fax: 3613216
Focus: Adult Educ 05708

Landesverband der Volkshochschulen Niedersachsens e.V., Bödekerstr 16, 30161 Hannover
T: (0511) 348410; Fax: 3484125
Focus: Adult Educ 05709

Landesverband der Volkshochschulen Sachsen-Anhalt e.V., Liebknechtstr 91, 39110 Magdeburg
T: (0391) 7360154; Fax: 7360154
Focus: Adult Educ 05710

Landesverband der Volkshochschulen Schleswig-Holsteins e.V., Holstenbrücke 7, 24103 Kiel
T: (0431) 979840; Fax: 96685
Members: 170
Focus: Adult Educ 05711

Landesverband der Volkshochschulen von Nordrhein-Westfalen e.V., Heiliger Weg 7-9, 44135 Dortmund
T: (0231) 9520580; Fax: 9520583
Founded: 1947; Members: 142
Pres: Waldtraud Lehn; Gen Secr: Reiner Hammelrath
Focus: Adult Educ 05712

Landeszahnärztekammer Baden-Württemberg, Herdweg 50, 70174 Stuttgart
T: (0711) 227160; Fax: 295144
Focus: Dent
Periodical
Zahnärzteblatt Baden-Württemberg (monthly) 05713

Landeszahnärztekammer Hessen, Lyoner Str 21, 60528 Frankfurt
T: (069) 665815; Fax: 6666945
Pres: Dr. M. Frank; Gen Secr: K. Weis
Focus: Dent
Periodical
Der Hessische Zahnarzt (monthly) . . . 05714

Landeszahnärztekammer Rheinland-Pfalz, Frauenlobpl 2, 55118 Mainz
T: (06131) 618061; Fax: 672985
Focus: Dent
Periodical
Zahnärztliche Informationen (quarterly) . . 05715

Leiterkreis der Katholischen Akademien, c/o Akademie der Diözese Rottenburg-Stuttgart, Im Schellenkönig 61, 70184 Stuttgart
T: (0711) 16406; E-Mail: AkademieRS@t-online.de; Fax: 1640777
Founded: 1958; Members: 26
Pres: Dr. Gebhard Fürst
Focus: Adult Educ; Poli Sci; Cultur Hist; Rel & Theol; Econ 05716

Leonhard-Frank-Gesellschaft e.V. (LFG), Oberer Steinbachweg, 97082 Würzburg
T: (0931) 7841408
Focus: Lit 05717

Lernen Fördern – Bundesverband zur Förderung Lernbehinderter e.V., Rolandstr 61, 50677 Köln
T: (0221) 380666; Fax: 385954
Founded: 1968; Members: 15000
Pres: Jürgen Eppendorf; Gen Secr: Rudolf C. Zelfel
Focus: Rehabil; Educ Handic
Periodical
LERNEN FÖRDERN (quarterly) 05718

Lichtenberg-Gesellschaft e.V., Waldreiterring 25, 22359 Hamburg
T: (040) 6037165
Focus: Lit 05719

List Gesellschaft e.V., c/o Ruhr-Universität, GC 3/159, 44780 Bochum
T: (0234) 705151; Fax: 7094144
Founded: 1954; Members: 750
Pres: Dr. Friedrich Janssen
Focus: Econ
Periodical
List Forum für Wirtschafts- und Finanzpolitik (quarterly) 05720

Literarische Gesellschaft Lüneburg e.V., Am Ochsenmarkt 1, 21335 Lüneburg
T: (04131) 714404, 52248; Fax: 309688
Focus: Lit 05721

Literarische Gesellschaft Magdeburg e.V., Thiemstr 7, 39104 Magdeburg
T: (0391) 4044995
Focus: Lit 05722

Literarische Gesellschaft (Scheffelbund) e.V., Röntgenstr 6, 76133 Karlsruhe
T: (0721) 843818; Fax: 853544
Focus: Lit 05723

Literarische Gesellschaft Thüringen e.V., Goethepl 11, 99423 Weimar
T: (03643) 501848; Fax: 501848
Focus: Lit 05724

Literarische Vereinigung Braunschweig e.V., c/o Öffentliche Bücherei, Hintern Brüdern 23, 38100 Braunschweig
T: (0531) 4706800; Fax: 4706899
Focus: Lit 05725

Literarischer Gesprächskreis Ludwigsburg e.V., Häslenweg 17, 71642 Ludwigsburg
T: (07141) 55888
Focus: Lit 05726

Literarischer Verein in Stuttgart e.V. / Stuttgart Literary Society, Rosenbergstr 113, 70193 Stuttgart
T: (0711) 638264/65; Fax: 6369010
Founded: 1839
Focus: Lit
Periodical
Bibliothek: Editionsreihe (semi-annually) . 05727

Literarisches Colloquium Berlin e.V., Am Sandwerder 5, 14109 Berlin
T: (030) 8169960; Fax: 81699619
Focus: Lit
Periodical
Sprache im Technischen Zeitalter (quarterly) 05728

Literaturarchiv Sulzbach-Rosenberg e.V., Rosenberger Str 9, 92237 Sulzbach-Rosenberg
T: (09661) 2659, 3626; Fax: 3626
Focus: Lit 05729

Literaturbrücke Berlin e.V., Majakowskiring 46-48, 13156 Berlin
T: (030) 4824765; Fax: 4855712
Focus: Lit 05730

Literaturkreis Novalis e.V., Klosterstr 24, 06667 Weißenfels
T: (03443) 3703170
Focus: Lit 05731

Literaturverein Georg Kaiser e.V., Ernst-Thälmann-Str 66, 15537 Grünheide
T: (03362) 26622
Focus: Lit 05732

Literaturverein Münster e.V., Bispinghof 3a, 48143 Münster
T: (0251) 835418
Focus: Lit 05733

Mainzer Altertumsverein e.V., c/o Stadtarchoiv, Rheinallee 3b (Stadtarchiv), 55116 Mainz
T: (06131) 122656; Fax: 123569
Founded: 1844
Pres: 1844
Focus: Hist; Arts; Archeol
Periodical
Mainzer Zeitschrift (annually) 05734

Management Akademie München (MAM), Brienner Str 7, 80333 München
T: (089) 29002636; Fax: 29002655
Focus: Adult Educ
Periodicals
Handeln (semi-annually)
MA Spezial (semi-annually) 05735

Marburger Bund (MB) / Verband der angestellten und beamteten Ärzte Deutschlands e.V., Riehler Str 6, 50668 Köln
T: (0221) 733173, 724624; Fax: 733697
Founded: 1947; Members: 33000
Focus: Med
Periodical
Der Arzt im Krankenhaus und im Gesundheitswesen: Monatsschrift des Marburger Bundes (monthly) 05736

Marburger Literaturforum e.V. (MLF), Barfüßertor 10, 35037 Marburg
T: (06421) 26458; Fax: 26458
Focus: Lit 05737

Marcel Proust Gesellschaft, Brahmsstr 17, 50935 Köln
T: (0221) 4301091
Focus: Lit 05738

Margarine-Institut für gesunde Ernährung, Friesenweg 1, 22763 Hamburg
T: (040) 882091; Fax: 882093
Focus: Nutrition 05739

Mary Wigman-Gesellschaft e.V., Ubierring 58, 50678 Köln
T: (0221) 319198
Focus: Perf Arts 05740

Mathematisch-Naturwissenschaftlicher Fakultätentag, c/o Fachbereich Chemie, Friedemann-Bach-Pl 6, 06108 Halle/Saale
T: (0345) 8320; Fax: 2024652
Focus: Math; Nat Sci; Adult Educ . . . 05741

Mathematische Gesellschaft in Hamburg (MGH), Bundesstr 55, 20146 Hamburg
Founded: 1690; Members: 400
Focus: Math
Periodical
Mitteilungen der Mathematischen Gesellschaft in Hamburg (annually) 05742

Max-Eyth-Gesellschaft Agrartechnik im VDI, Graf-Recke-Str 84, 40239 Düsseldorf
T: (0211) 6214264; Fax: 6214163
Members: 1200
Pres: Prof. Dr. Dr. Th. Renius; Gen Secr: Dr. A. Simburger
Focus: Agri
Periodical
Jahrbuch (annually) 05743

Max-Planck-Gesellschaft zur Förderung der Wissenschaften e.V. (MPG), Hofgartenstr 2, 80539 München
T: (089) 21080; E-Mail: mpg@sap-Noe.mpg-gv.mpg.de; Fax: 21081111
Founded: 1948; Members: 1410
Pres: Prof. Dr. Hubert Markl; Gen Secr: Dr. Barbara Bludau
Focus: Sci
Periodical
MPG-Spiegel (bi-monthly) 05744

Mecklenburgische Evangelische Akademie, Herderstr 6, 18055 Rostock
T: (0381) 4907981; Fax: 4907988
Focus: Rel & Theol 05745

Mecklenburgische Literaturgesellschaft e.V., Wiekhaus 22 – 2. Ringstr, 17033 Neubrandenburg
T: (0395) 5441671; Fax: 5441671
Focus: Lit 05746

Mediävistenverband e.V., c/o Institut für Kunstgeschichte, Schinkelstr 1, 52062 Aachen
T: (0241) 805069
Focus: Hist 05747

MEDICA, Deutsche Gesellschaft zur Förderung der Medizinischen Diagnostik e.V., Postfach 700149, 70571 Stuttgart
T: (0711) 761454, 763443; Fax: 766992
Focus: Med
Periodical
Medica (monthly) 05748

Medical Women's International Association (MWIA), Herbert-Lewin-Str 1, 50931 Köln
T: (0221) 4004558; E-Mail: MWIA@aol.com; Fax: 4004557
Founded: 1919; Members: 20000
Pres: Dr. Florence (Kenya) Manguyu; Gen Secr: Dr. Carolyn Motzel
Focus: Med
Periodicals
Congress Report (every 2-3 years)
MWIA Update (quarterly) 05749

Medizinischer Fakultätentag der Bundesrepublik Deutschland (MFT) / Association of all Medical Faculties in the Federal Republic of Germany, Schillerstr 25/29, 91054 Erlangen
T: (09131) 856130; Fax: 852317
Founded: 1913
Pres: Prof. Dr. Dr. Gerhard Lehnert
Focus: Med 05750

Mommsen-Gesellschaft / Verband der deutschen Forscher auf dem Gebiete des griechisch-römischen Altertums, c/o Seminar für Klassische Philologie, Humboldtallee 19, 37073 Göttingen
T: (0551) 394743; Fax: 394682
Founded: 1949; Members: 570
Pres: Prof. Dr. Siegmar Döpp; Gen Secr: Dr. Marcus Deufert
Focus: Lit; Hist; Archeol 05751

Monumenta Germaniae Historica, Postfach 340223, 80099 München
T: (089) 28638384; E-Mail: schieffer@mgh.de Verlag@mgh.de; Fax: 281419
Founded: 1819
Pres: Prof. Dr. Rudolf Schieffer; Gen Secr: Dr. Wolfram Setz
Focus: Hist
Periodical
Deutsches Archiv für Erforschung des Mittelalters (semi-annually) . . . 05752

Moses Mendelssohn Zentrum für europäisch-jüdische Studien, Am Neuen Markt 8, 14467 Potsdam
T: (0331) 280940; E-Mail: moses@mmz.uni-potsdam.de; Fax: 2809450
Founded: 1992
Focus: Cultur Hist . . . 05753

Münchener Arbeitsgemeinschaft für Luftschadstoffe (MAGL), c/o GSF, Ingolstädter Landstr 1, 85758 Oberschleißheim
T: (089) 31872452; Fax: 31874431
Focus: Ecology . . . 05754

Münchener Tierärztliche Gesellschaft (MTG), Veterinärstr 13, 80539 München
T: (089) 21802900
Founded: 1873; Members: 180
Focus: Vet Med . . . 05755

Münchner Dermatologische Gesellschaft, c/o Dermatologische Universitäts-Klinik, Frauenlobstr 9-11, 80337 München
Focus: Derm
Periodical
Der Hautarzt (monthly) . . . 05756

Münchner Entomologische Gesellschaft e.V., Münchhausenstr 21, 81247 München
T: (089) 81070; Fax: 8107300
Founded: 1905; Members: 650
Pres: Dr. Roland Gerstmeier; Gen Secr: Dr. Klaus Schönitzer
Focus: Entomology
Periodicals
Mitteilungen der Münchner Entomologischen Gesellschaft (annually)
Nachrichtenblatt der Bayerischen Entomologen (quarterly) . . . 05757

Münchner Kreis / Übernationale Vereinigung für Kommunikationsforschung e.V., Tal 16, 80331 München
T: (089) 223238; Fax: 225407
Focus: Comm Sci
Periodical
Telecommunications (irregularly) . . . 05758

NABU (Naturschutzbund Deutschland e.V.), Herbert-Rabius-Str 26, 53225 Bonn
T: (0228) 975610; Fax: 9756190
Founded: 1899; Members: 200000
Pres: Jochen Flasbarth; Gen Secr: Uwe Huser; Gerd Billen
Focus: Ecology
Periodical
Naturschutz heute (quarterly) . . . 05759

Nah- und Mittelost-Verein e.V., Mittelweg 151, 20148 Hamburg
T: (040) 4503310; Fax: 45033131
Founded: 1950; Members: 500
Pres: Wolf-Elmar Warning; Gen Secr: Dr. Otto Plassmann
Focus: Ethnology . . . 05760

Nationalkomitee der Bundesrepublik Deutschland im International Council for Traditional Music (ICTM), Feldkirchenstr 21, 96052 Bamberg
T: (0951) 8631936; Fax: 59221
Focus: Music . . . 05761

Natur und Medizin e.V., Fördergemeinschaft für Erfahrungsheilkunde, Am Michaelshof 6, 53177 Bonn
T: (0228) 352503, 356888; Fax: 364344
Focus: Med . . . 05762

Naturforschende Gesellschaft Bamberg e.V., Bergstr 14, 96191 Viereth-Trunstadt
Founded: 1834; Members: 250
Focus: Nat Sci
Periodical
Berichte der Naturforschenden Gesellschaft Bamberg e.V. (annually) . . . 05763

Naturforschende Gesellschaft Freiburg, Albertstr 23b, 79104 Freiburg
Founded: 1821
Focus: Nat Sci
Periodical
Berichte der Naturforschenden Gesellschaft Freiburg (annually) . . . 05764

Naturhistorische Gesellschaft Hannover (NHG), Postfach 510153, 30631 Hannover
T: (0511) 2472463
Founded: 1797; Members: 580
Pres: Dr. J.D. Becker-Platen
Focus: Nat Sci
Periodicals
Beihefte zu den Berichten der Naturhistorischen Gesellschaft Hannover (irregularly)
Berichte der Naturhistorischen Gesellschaft Hannover (annually) . . . 05765

Naturhistorische Gesellschaft Nürnberg e.V. (NHG), Gewerbemuseumspl 4, 90403 Nürnberg
T: (0911) 227970; Fax: 2447441
Founded: 1801; Members: 2100
Pres: Rainer Ott; Gen Secr: Kathrin Göbel
Focus: Hist; Nat Sci; Ethnology; Anthro
Periodical
Natur und Mensch (annually) . . . 05766

Naturhistorischer Verein der Rheinlande und Westfalens, Nussallee 15a, 53115 Bonn
T: (0228) 692377
Focus: Nat Sci
Periodicals
Decheniana (annually)
Decheniana-Beihefte (irregularly) . . . 05767

Naturwissenschaftlicher und Historischer Verein für das Land Lippe e.V., Willi-Hofmann-Str 2, 32756 Detmold
T: (05231) 766110; Fax: 766114
Founded: 1835; Members: 870
Pres: Prof. Dr. Jürgen Döhl
Focus: Nat Sci; Hist
Periodical
Lippische Mitteilungen aus Geschichte und Landeskunde (annually) . . . 05768

Naturwissenschaftlicher Verein für das Fürstentum Lüneburg von 1851 e.V., Salzstr 26, 21335 Lüneburg
T: (04131) 403883; Fax: 403883
Founded: 1851; Members: 470
Pres: Dr. Johannes Prüter; Gen Secr: Prof. Dr. Kurt Horst
Focus: Nat Sci . . . 05769

Naturwissenschaftlicher Verein in Hamburg, Martin-Luther-King-Pl 3, 20146 Hamburg
Fax: (040) 41233937
Founded: 1837; Members: 600
Gen Secr: Prof. Dr. O. Kraus
Focus: Nat Sci
Periodicals
Abhandlungen (irregularly)
Verhandlungen (annually) . . . 05770

Naturwissenschaftlicher Verein zu Bremen, c/o Übersee-Museum, Bahnhofspl 13, 28195 Bremen
T: (0421) 171347; Fax: 3619291
Founded: 1864; Members: 492
Pres: Heinrich Kuhbier
Focus: Nat Sci
Periodical
Abhandlungen des Naturwissenschaftlichen Vereins zu Bremen (annually) . . . 05771

NAV-Virchowbund (NAV) / Verband der niedergelassenen Ärzte Deutschlands e.V., Belfortstr 9, 50668 Köln
Founded: 1949; Members: 17870
Focus: Med
Periodical
Der Niedergelassene Arzt (monthly) . . . 05772

Nephrologischer Arbeitskreis Saar-Pfalz-Mosel e.V., c/o Medizinische Klinik III, Städtisches Krankenhaus, 67653 Kaiserslautern
T: (0631) 2031256
Focus: Med . . . 05773

Neue Bachgesellschaft e.V., Thomaskirchhof 16, 04109 Leipzig
T: (0341) 9601463; Fax: 9601463
Founded: 1900
Focus: Music
Periodical
Bach-Jahrbuch (annually) . . . 05774

Neue Gesellschaft für Literatur Berlin e.V., Rosenthaler Str 38, 10178 Berlin
T: (030) 2829140; Fax: 2833984
Focus: Lit . . . 05775

Neue Gesellschaft für Literatur Erlangen e.V., Niendorfstr 25, 91054 Erlangen
T: (09131) 55106; Fax: 862717
Focus: Lit . . . 05776

Neue Kriminologische Gesellschaft / Wissenschaftliche Vereinigung deutscher, österreichischer und schweizerischer Kriminologen, c/o Institut für Kriminologie der Universität, Corrensstr 34, 72076 Tübingen
T: (07071) 2972931; Fax: 65104
Founded: 1988; Members: 250
Pres: Prof. Dr. Dieter Rössner
Focus: Criminology . . . 05777

Neue Leipziger Chopin-Gesellschaft e.V., Kirschbergstr 21, 04159 Leipzig
T: (0341) 9011453
Focus: Music . . . 05778

Niedersächsischer Bund für freie Erwachsenenbildung e.V., Marienstr 9-11, 30171 Hannover
T: (0511) 364910; Fax: 322925
Founded: 1954; Members: 6
Focus: Adult Educ
Periodical
Erwachsenenbildung: Berichte & Informationen der Erwachsenenbildung in Niedersachsen (semi-annually) . . . 05779

Niedersächsischer Landesverband der Heimvolkshochschulen e.V., Warmbüchenstr 17, 30159 Hannover
T: (0511) 326962; Fax: 329738
Founded: 1961; Members: 24
Focus: Adult Educ . . . 05780

Nordfriisk Instituut, Süderstr 30, 25821 Bräist
T: (04671) 2081; Fax: 1333
Founded: 1949; Members: 800
Pres: Hans-Meinert Redlin; Gen Secr: Dr. Thomas Steensen
Focus: Lit; Hist; Cultur Hist
Periodicals
Der Maueranker (quarterly)
Nordfriesisches Jahrbuch (annually)
Nordfriesland (quarterly) . . . 05781

Nordrhein-Westfälische Akademie der Wissenschaften, Palmenstr 16, 40217 Düsseldorf
T: (0211) 342051; Fax: 341475
Focus: Sci . . . 05782

Nordrhein-Westfälische Gesellschaft für Urologie, c/o Städtische Krankenanstalten, Caprivistr 1, 49076 Osnabrück
Focus: Urology . . . 05783

Nordwestdeutsche Gesellschaft für ärztliche Fortbildung e.V., Todendorfer Str 14, 22964 Steinburg
T: (04534) 8202
Focus: Med; Adult Educ . . . 05784

Nordwestdeutsche Gesellschaft für innere Medizin, Blankeneser Landstr 68, 22587 Hamburg
T: (040) 860720, 862024
Founded: 1924; Members: 10
Focus: Intern Med
Periodical
Kongressberichte der Tagungen der NWDGIM (semi-annually) . . . 05785

Nordwestdeutsche Vereinigung der Hals-Nasen-Ohrenärzte, c/o Universitäts-HNO-Klinik, Hospitalstr 20, 24105 Kiel
Focus: Otorhinolaryngology . . . 05786

Normenausschuss Akustik, Lärmminderung und Schwingungstechnik im DIN Deutsches Institut für Normung e.V., Burggrafenstr 6, 10787 Berlin
T: (030) 26012367; Fax: 26011231
Focus: Civil Eng; Standards . . . 05787

Normenausschuss Anstrichstoffe und ähnliche Beschichtungsstoffe im DIN Deutsches Institut für Normung e.V., Burggrafenstr 6, 10787 Berlin
T: (030) 26011
Focus: Materials Sci; Standards . . . 05788

Normenausschuss Armaturen im DIN Deutsches Institut für Normung e.V. (NAA), Kamekestr 8, 50672 Köln
T: (0221) 57130; E-Mail: richter@zwk.din.de; Fax: 5713414
Pres: Walter Siepmann; Gen Secr: Dr. Ingo Richter
Focus: Standards; Eng . . . 05789

Normenausschuss Bauwesen im DIN Deutsches Institut für Normung e.V., Burggrafenstr 6, 10787 Berlin
T: (030) 26012501; E-Mail: X400:C=DE;ADMD=D400;PRMD=DIN;S=VOGEL; Fax: 26011180
Founded: 1947; Members: 3500
Pres: Dr. Lothar Mayer; Gen Secr: Eckhard Vogel
Focus: Civil Eng; Standards
Periodical
Mitteilungen aus der Baunormung (bi-monthly) . . . 05790

Normenausschuss Bergbau im DIN Deutsches Institut für Normung e.V., Franz-Fischer-Weg 61, 45307 Essen
T: (0201) 1721558; E-Mail: Faberg@germany mail.com; Fax: 1721577
Founded: 1922
Pres: Friedrich-Wilhelm Lieneke; Gen Secr: Horst Michaely
Focus: Mining; Standards
Periodical
Bergbau-Verzeichnis (annually) . . . 05791

Normenausschuss Bibliotheks- und Dokumentationswesen im DIN Deutsches Institut für Normung e.V. (NABD), Burggrafenstr 6, 10787 Berlin
T: (030) 26012791; E-Mail: Lechner@nabd.din.de; Fax: 26011231
Founded: 1927
Pres: Dr. W. Neubauer; Gen Secr: Edith Lechner
Focus: Libraries & Bk Sci; Doc; Standards . . . 05792

Normenausschuss Bild und Film im DIN Deutsches Institut für Normung e.V. (photokinonorm), Burggrafenstr 6, 10787 Berlin
T: (030) 26012433; Fax: 26011255
Pres: Dr. Klaus Nieswandt; Gen Secr: Dr. Michael Seidl
Focus: Standards; Photo . . . 05793

Normenausschuss Bühnentechnik in Theatern und Mehrzweckhallen im DIN Deutsches Institut für Normung e.V. (FNTh), Burggrafenstr 6, 10787 Berlin
T: (030) 26012694
Focus: Standards; Arts . . . 05794

Normenausschuss Bürowesen im DIN Deutsches Institut für Normung e.V., Burggrafenstr. 4-6, 10787 Berlin
T: (030) 26011
Focus: Standards; Business Admin . . . 05795

Normenausschuss Chemischer Apparatebau im DIN Deutsches Institut für Normung e.V. (FNCA), Kamekestr 8, 50672 Köln
T: (0221) 5713522; Fax: 5713414
Founded: 1950
Focus: Standards; Eng
Periodical
DIN-Mitteilungen (monthly) . . . 05796

Normenausschuss Dental im DIN Deutsches Institut für Normung e.V., Westliche Karl-Friedrich-Str 56, 75172 Pforzheim
T: (07231) 918819
Founded: 1969
Pres: Dr. J. Eberlein; Gen Secr: Dr. H.-P. Keller
Focus: Standards; Dent . . . 05797

Normenausschuss Dichtungen im DIN Deutsches Institut für Normung e.V., Kamekestr 2-8, 50672 Köln
T: (0221) 57131
Focus: Standards; Eng . . . 05798

Normenausschuss Druck- und Reproduktionstechnik im DIN Deutsches Institut für Normung e.V. (NDR), Burggrafenstr 4-6, 10787 Berlin
T: (030) 26011
Focus: Eng; Standards . . . 05799

Normenausschuss Druckgasanlagen im DIN Deutsches Institut für Normung e.V., Burggrafenstr 4-10, 10787 Berlin
T: (030) 2602351
Focus: Standards; Eng . . . 05800

Normenausschuss Eisen-, Blech- und Metallwaren im DIN Deutsches Institut für Normung e.V. (NA EBM), Kaiserswerther Str 135, 40474 Düsseldorf
T: (0211) 454930; Fax: 4549369
Focus: Eng; Standards . . . 05801

Normenausschuß Eisen und Stahl im DIN Deutsches Institut für Normung e.V., Sohnstr 65, 40237 Düsseldorf
T: (0211) 88941
Founded: 1947
Focus: Metallurgy; Standards . . . 05802

Normenausschuss Erdöl- und Erdgasgewinnung im DIN Deutsches Institut für Normung e.V. (NÖG), Kamekestr 8, 50672 Köln
T: (0221) 5713522
Founded: 1975; Members: 25
Focus: Eng; Standards; Mining . . . 05803

Normenausschuss Ergonomie im DIN Deutsches Institut für Normung e.V., Burggrafenstr 6, 10787 Berlin
T: (030) 26011; Fax: 2601231
Focus: Standards . . . 05804

Normenausschuss Fahrräder im DIN Deutsches Institut für Normung e.V. (NAFA), Kamekestr 2-8, 50672 Köln
T: (0221) 57131
Focus: Eng; Standards . . . 05805

Normenausschuss Farbe im DIN Deutsches Institut für Normung e.V. (FNF), Burggrafenstr 6, 10787 Berlin
T: (030) 26012433
Members: 150
Focus: Materials Sci; Standards . . . 05806

Normenausschuss Feinmechanik und Optik im DIN Deutsches Institut für Normung e.V. (NAFuO), Westliche Karl-Friedrich-Str 56, 75172 Pforzheim
T: (07231) 91880; Fax: 356973
Founded: 1950
Pres: B.J.L. Kratzer; Gen Secr: Dr. K. Gindele
Focus: Standards; Optics; Eng . . . 05807

Normenausschuss Feuerwehrwesen im DIN Deutsches Institut für Normung e.V. (FNFW), Burggrafenstr 6, 10787 Berlin
T: (030) 2601340/41
Focus: Eng; Standards; Safety . . . 05808

Normenausschuss Gastechnik im DIN Deutsches Institut für Normung e.V., Hauptstr 71-76, 65760 Eschborn
T: (06196) 70170
Focus: Eng; Standards
Periodicals
gwf/Gas-Erdgas (monthly)
gwf/Wasser-Abwasser (monthly) . . . 05809

Normenausschuss Gebrauchstauglichkeit im DIN Deutsches Institut für Normung e.V. (NHW), Burggrafenstr 6, 10787 Berlin
T: (030) 260140
Focus: Standards; Home Econ . . . 05810

Normenausschuss Giessereiwesen im DIN Deutsches Institut für Normung e.V., Kamekestr 8, 50672 Köln
T: (0221) 57130; Fax: 5713414
Focus: Standards; Metallurgy . . . 05811

Normenausschuss Gleitlager im DIN Deutsches Institut für Normung e.V. (NGL), Kamekestr 2-8, 50672 Köln
T: (0221) 57131
Focus: Standards; Eng . . . 05812

Normenausschuss Graphische Symbole im DIN Deutsches Institut für Normung e.V. (NGS), Burggrafenstr 6, 10787 Berlin
T: (030) 26011463
Focus: Standards; Eng . . . 05813

Normenausschuss Grundlagen der Normung im DIN Deutsches Institut für Normung e.V. (NG), Burggrafenstr 6, 10787 Berlin
T: (030) 26011
Focus: Standards
Periodical
DIN-Mitteilungen + electronorm: Zentralorgan der deutschen Normung (monthly) 05814

Normenausschuss Heiz-, Koch- und Wärmegeräte im DIN Deutsches Institut für Normung e.V. (NH), Am Hauptbahnhof 10, 60329 Frankfurt
T: (069) 234157
Focus: Electric Eng; Standards 05815

Normenausschuss Heiz- und Raumlufttechnik im DIN Deutsches Institut für Normung e.V. (NHR), Burggrafenstr 6, 10787 Berlin
T: (030) 26012351; Fax: 26011231
Founded: 1929; Members: 800
Focus: Eng; Standards 05816

Normenausschuss Holzwirtschaft und Möbel im DIN Deutsches Institut für Normung e.V., Kamekestr 8, 50672 Köln
T: (0221) 57130; E-Mail: lorentzen@nasport.din.de; Fax: 5713414
Founded: 1949; Members: 480
Pres: Prof. Dr. D. Noack; Gen Secr: Holger Lorentzen
Focus: Econ; Standards
Periodical
NHM Info (annually) 05817

Normenausschuß Informationstechnik im DIN Deutsches Institut für Normung e.V. (NI), Burggrafenstr 6, 10772 Berlin
T: (030) 26012465
Pres: Ulrich Hartmann; Gen Secr: Dr. Ingo Wende
Focus: Computer & Info Sci; Standards
Periodical
DIN-Mitteilungen (monthly) 05818

Normenausschuss Instandhaltung im DIN Deutsches Institut für Normung e.V. (NIN), Kamekestr 8, 50672 Köln
T: (0221) 5713307
Pres: Prof. Dr. Tschuschke; Gen Secr: Dr. G. Hellwig
Focus: Eng; Standards 05819

Normenausschuss Kältetechnik im DIN Deutsches Institut für Normung e.V. (FNKä), Kamekestr. 2-8, 50672 Köln
T: (0221) 5713514
Focus: Eng; Standards
Periodical
DIN-Mitteilungen (monthly) 05820

Normenausschuss Kautschuktechnik im DIN Deutsches Institut für Normung e.V., Zeppelinallee 69, 60487 Frankfurt
T: (069) 79360; Fax: 7936150
Focus: Eng; Standards 05821

Normenausschuss Kerntechnik im DIN Deutsches Institut für Normung e.V. (NKe), Burggrafenstr 6, 10787 Berlin
T: (030) 26012701
Members: 450
Focus: Nucl Res; Standards
Periodical
IKN Informationen Kerntechnische Normung (semi-annually) 05822

Normenausschuss Kommunale Technik im DIN Deutsches Institut für Normung e.V. (NKT), Burggrafenstr 6, 10787 Berlin
T: (030) 2601340/41
Focus: Eng; Standards 05823

Normenausschuss Kraftfahrzeuge im DIN Deutsches Institut für Normung e.V., Westendstr 61, 60325 Frankfurt
T: (069) 75701
Focus: Eng; Standards; Auto Eng . . . 05824

Normenausschuss Kunststoffe im DIN Deutsches Institut für Normung e.V., Burggrafenstr 6, 10787 Berlin
T: (030) 26012352
Founded: 1946; Members: 600
Focus: Materials Sci; Standards 05825

Normenausschuss Laborgeräte und Laboreinrichtungen im DIN Deutsches Institut für Normung e.V., Theodor-Heuss-Allee 25, 60486 Frankfurt
T: (069) 7564255; E-Mail: din@dechema.de; Fax: 7564201
Founded: 1926; Members: 230
Pres: Dr. D. Reuschling; Gen Secr: Dr. B. Winter
Focus: Standards; Eng 05826

Normenausschuss Lebensmittel und Landwirtschaftliche Produkte im DIN Deutsches Institut für Normung e.V. (NAL), Burggrafenstr 6, 10787 Berlin
T: (030) 26012445; E-Mail: bohnsack@NAL.DIN.de; Fax: 26011186
Pres: Prof. Dr. K. Paulus; Gen Secr: Dr. Ulrike Bohnsack
Focus: Food; Standards 05827

Normenausschuss Lichttechnik im DIN Deutsches Institut für Normung e.V. (FNL), Burggrafenstr 6, 10787 Berlin
T: (030) 26012433
Members: 400
Focus: Electric Eng; Standards 05828

Normenausschuss Maschinenbau (NAM) im DIN Deutsches Institut für Normung e.V. (NAM), Lyoner Str 18, 60528 Frankfurt
T: (069) 66031341; E-Mail: nam@vdma.org; Fax: 66031557
Founded: 1949
Pres: Dr. Fritz Hochstein; Gen Secr: Harald Riekeles
Focus: Mach Eng; Standards 05829

Normenausschuss Materialprüfung im DIN Deutsches Institut für Normung e.V. (NMP), Burggrafenstr 6, 10787 Berlin
T: (030) 26012712
Focus: Materials Sci; Standards 05830

Normenausschuss Mechanische Verbindungselemente im DIN Deutsches Institut für Normung e.V., Kamekestr 8, 50672 Köln
T: (0221) 5713307
Pres: K. Kayser; Gen Secr: Dr. G. Hellwig
Focus: Eng; Standards 05831

Normenausschuss Medizin im DIN Deutsches Institut für Normung e.V. (NAMed), Burggrafenstr 6, 10772 Berlin
T: (030) 26012413; E-Mail: Deutschnormen Berlin; Fax: 26011231
Founded: 1967
Focus: Standards; Med
Periodical
DIN-Mitteilungen + elektronorm: Zentralorgan der deutschen Normung (monthly) 05832

Normenausschuss Nichteisenmetalle im DIN Deutsches Institut für Normung e.V., Kamekestr 8, 50672 Köln
T: (0221) 57130; Fax: 5713414
Focus: Standards; Metallurgy 05833

Normenausschuss Papier und Pappe im DIN Deutsches Institut für Normung e.V., Burggrafenstr 6, 10787 Berlin
T: (030) 26012685
Focus: Standards; Materials Sci 05834

Normenausschuss Persönliche Schutzausrüstung und Sicherheitskennzeichnung im DIN Deutsches Insitut für Normung e.V. (NPS), Burggrafenstr 4-10, 10787 Berlin
T: (030) 26011
Focus: Standards; Safety 05835

Normenausschuss Pigmente und Füllstoffe im DIN Deutsches Institut für Normung e.V. (NPF), Burggrafenstr 6, 10787 Berlin
T: (030) 26011
Focus: Materials Sci; Standards 05836

Normenausschuss Pulvermetallurgie im DIN Deutsches Institut für Normung e.V. (NPu), Kamekestr 2-8, 50672 Köln
T: (0221) 57131
Focus: Standards; Metallurgy 05837

Normenausschuss Rohre, Rohrverbindungen und Rohrleitungen im DIN Deutsches Institut für Normung e.V., Kamekestr 8, 50672 Köln
T: (0221) 57130; E-Mail: richter@zwk.din.de; Fax: 5713414
Pres: S. Szusdziara; Gen Secr: Dr. I. Richter
Focus: Standards; Eng
Periodical
DIN-Mitteilungen (monthly) 05838

Normenausschuss Rundstahlketten im DIN Deutsches Institut für Normung e.V. (NRK), Kamekestr 2-8, 50672 Köln
T: (0221) 57131
Focus: Standards; Eng 05839

Normenausschuss Schienenfahrzeuge im DIN Deutsches Institut für Normung e.V., Panoramaweg 1, 34131 Kassel
T: (0561) 935670; Fax: 9356755
Founded: 1958; Members: 75
Pres: H. Atzorn; Gen Secr: L. Gregel
Focus: Eng; Standards 05840

Normenausschuss Schmiedetechnik im DIN Deutsches Institut für Normung e.V., Goldene Pforte 1, 58093 Hagen
T: (02331) 958835
Focus: Standards; Eng 05841

Normenausschuss Schweisstechnik im DIN Deutsches Institut für Normung e.V. (NAS), Burggrafenstr 6, 10787 Berlin
T: (030) 26012342; Fax: 2601231
Founded: 1925
Focus: Standards; Eng 05842

Normenausschuss Sport- und Freizeitgerät im DIN Deutsches Institut für Normung e.V., Kamekestr 8, 50672 Köln
T: (0221) 5713512; E-Mail: lorentzen@nasport.din.de; Fax: 5713414
Pres: G. Boye; Gen Secr: H. Lorentzen
Focus: Standards; Eng; Sports
Periodical
NA Sport Info (semi-annually) 05843

Normenausschuss Stahldraht und Stahldrahterzeugnisse im DIN Deutsches Institut für Normung e.V., Kamekestr 8, 50672 Köln
T: (0221) 5713307
Pres: H. Stauch; Gen Secr: Dr. G. Hellwig
Focus: Standards; Eng 05844

Normenausschuss Technische Grundlagen im DIN Deutsches Institut für Normung e.V. (AEF), Burggrafenstr 6, 10787 Berlin
T: (030) 260124367; Fax: 26011231
Founded: 1996; Members: 630
Pres: Prof. Dr. Manfred Kochsiek; Gen Secr: Hans-Peter Grode
Focus: Standards 05845

Normenausschuss Terminologie im DIN Deutsches Institut für Normung e.V., Burggrafenstr 6, 10787 Berlin
T: (030) 26012318
Focus: Standards 05846

Normenausschuss Textil und Textilmaschinen im DIN Deutsches Institut für Normung e.V. (Textilnorm), Burggrafenstr 6, 10787 Berlin
T: (030) 26012431
Focus: Standards; Mach Eng; Textiles . 05847

Normenausschuss Transportkette im DIN Deutsches Institut für Normung e.V. (NTK), Burggrafenstr 6, 10787 Berlin
T: (030) 2601497; E-Mail: Deutschnormen Berlin; Fax: 2601231
Focus: Standards; Eng; Transport . . . 05848

Normenausschuss Überwachungsbedürftige Anlagen im DIN Deutsches Institut für Normung e.V., Kamekestr 8, 50672 Köln
T: (0221) 5713522; Fax: 5713414
Focus: Standards; Eng
Periodical
DIN-Mitteilungen (monthly) 05849

Normenausschuss Uhren und Schmuck im DIN Deutsches Institut für Normung e.V., Westliche Karl-Friedrich-Str 56, 75172 Pforzheim
T: (07231) 91880; Fax: 359200
Founded: 1941
Pres: W. Duckwitz; Gen Secr: Karl Wenzelewski
Focus: Eng; Standards 05850

Normenausschuss Vakuumtechnik im DIN Deutsches Institut für Normung e.V. (NAV), Kamekestr 2-8, 50672 Köln
T: (0221) 57131
Focus: Standards; Eng 05851

Normenausschuss Verpackungswesen im DIN Deutsches Institut für Normung e.V. (NAVp), Burggrafenstr 6, 10787 Berlin
T: (030) 26011; E-Mail: Deutschnormen Berlin; Fax: 2601231
Founded: 1948; Members: 5901
Focus: Standards; Materials Sci 05852

Normenausschuss Waagenbau im DIN Deutsches Institut für Normung e.V. (NWB), Burggrafenstr 6, 10787 Berlin
T: (030) 26012367; Fax: 26011231
Focus: Standards; Eng 05853

Normenausschuss Wärmebehandlungstechnik metallischer Werkstoffe im DIN Deutsches Institut für Normung e.V. (NWT), Kamekestr 2-8, 50672 Köln
T: (0221) 57131
Focus: Standards; Eng; Metallurgy . . . 05854

Normenausschuss Wasserwesen im DIN Deutsches Institut für Normung e.V. (NAW), Burggrafenstr 4-10, 10787 Berlin
T: (030) 2601421
Founded: 1952; Members: 750
Focus: Standards; Water Res 05855

Normenausschuss Werkzeuge und Spannzeuge im DIN Deutsches Institut für Normung e.V., Kamekestr 8, 50672 Köln
T: (0221) 57130; Fax: 5713414
Pres: Wilfried Nöll; Gen Secr: E. Barthel
Focus: Standards; Eng 05856

Normenausschuss Werkzeugmaschinen im DIN Deutsches Institut für Normung e.V. (NWM), Corneliusstr 4, 60325 Frankfurt
T: (069) 7560810; Fax: 7568111
Pres: Dr. I. Faulstich; Gen Secr: H.-P. Leonhardt
Focus: Eng; Standards; Mach Eng . . . 05857

Normenausschuss Zeichnungswesen im DIN Deutsches Institut für Normung e.V. (NZ), Burggrafenstr 6, 10787 Berlin
T: (030) 26012349; Fax: 26011163
Focus: Standards; Econ
Periodical
DIN-Mitteilungen + elektronorm: Zentralorgan der deutschen Normung (monthly) 05858

Numismatische Kommission der Länder in der Bundesrepublik Deutschland, c/o Staatliche Museen zu Berlin, Münzkabinett, Bodestr 1-3, 10178 Berlin
T: (030) 20905700; Fax: 20905702
Founded: 1950
Pres: Prof. Dr. Bernd Kluge; Gen Secr: Prof. Dr. Niklot Klüßendorf
Focus: Numismatics 05859

Oberrheinische Gesellschaft für Geburtshilfe und Gynäkologie, c/o Universitäts-Frauenklinik, Schleichstr 4, 72076 Tübingen
T: (07071) 222955
Founded: 1905; Members: 400
Focus: Gynecology 05860

Öko-Institut, Institut für angewandte Ökologie e.V., Postfach 6226, 79038 Freiburg
T: (0761) 452950; E-Mail: postmaster@Freiburg.oeko.de; Fax: 475437
Founded: 1977; Members: 5500
Gen Secr: Uwe Ilgemann
Focus: Ecology
Periodical
Öko-Mitteilungen (quarterly) 05861

Optikzentrum NRW e.V. (OZ), Universitätsstr 142, 44799 Bochum
T: (0234) 970700; Fax: 9707070
Focus: Optics 05862

Orchester-Akademie des Berliner Philharmonischen Orchesters e.V., Matthäikirchstr 1, 10785 Berlin
T: (030) 2628604
Focus: Music 05863

Orff-Schulwerk Gesellschaft e.V. (OSG), Hermann-Hummel-Str 25, 82166 Lochham
T: (089) 8542851; Fax: 8542953
Focus: Music 05864

Oskar Maria Graf-Gesellschaft e.V., Steebstr 17, 82229 Seefeld
T: (08152) 70218; Fax: 70203
Focus: Lit 05865

Ost-Akademie e.V., Herderstr 1-11, 21335 Lüneburg
T: (04131) 42094; Fax: 406084
Members: 50
Focus: Hist; Poli Sci; Cultur Hist
Periodical
Deutsche Studien (quarterly) 05866

Ost-West-Wirtschafts-Akademie (OWWA), Koenigsallee 20a, 14193 Berlin
T: (030) 8969980; Fax: 8921050
Focus: Econ 05867

Osteuropa-Institut München, Scheinerstr 11, 81679 München
T: (089) 9983960; Fax: 9810110
Founded: 1952
Focus: Hist; Econ; Ethnology
Periodicals
Economic Systems (semi-annually)
Jahrbücher für Geschichte Osteuropas (quarterly) 05868

Oswald von Wolkenstein-Gesellschaft e.V., Myliusstr 25, 60323 Frankfurt/Main
T: (069) 726661; Fax: 174416
Focus: Lit 05869

Outward Bound – Deutsche Gesellschaft für Europäische Erziehung e.V., Nymphenburger Str 42, 80335 München
T: (089) 1215110; Fax: 12151110
Founded: 1950
Focus: Educ 05870

Pädagogisches Zentrum Rheinland-Pfalz (PZ), Europapl 7-9, 55543 Bad Kreuznach
T: (0671) 840880; Fax: 8408810
Focus: Educ 05871

Paläontologische Gesellschaft, c/o Dr. Werner, Senckenberg-Institut, Senckenberg-Anlage 25, 60325 Frankfurt
T: (069) 7940046
Founded: 1912; Members: 938
Focus: Paleontology
Periodical
Paläontologische Zeitschrift (semi-annually) 05872

Paritätisches Bildungswerk Bundesverband e.V., Heinrich-Hoffmann-Str 3, 60528 Frankfurt
T: (069) 6706274; Fax: 6706203
Focus: Educ 05873

Paul-Ernst-Gesellschaft e.V., Oberthürstr 11, 97070 Würzburg
T: (0931) 13807
Focus: Lit 05874

Pegnesischer Blumenorden e.V., Verein zur Pflege der deutschen Sprache und Dichtkunst, An der Fleischbrücke 2, 90403 Nürnberg
T: (0911) 2419286; Fax: 2419773
Focus: Lit 05875

P.E.N.-Zentrum Bundesrepublik Deutschland, Sandstr 10, 64283 Darmstadt
T: (06151) 23120; Fax: 293414
Founded: 1951; Members: 488
Focus: Lit 05876

Percussion Creativ e.V. (PC), Hastverstr 31, 90408 Nürnberg
T: (0911) 3659768; Fax: 3659768
Focus: Music 05877

Peter-Hille-Gesellschaft e.V., Am Enskeberg 13, 33039 Nieheim
T: (05274) 404
Focus: Lit 05878

Peter-Schwingen-Gesellschaft e.V., Muffendorfer Hauptstr 62, 53177 Bonn
T: (0228) 9323134; Fax: 9323135
Pres: Dr. Pia Heckes
Focus: Arts; Cultur Hist 05879

Pfalzakademie e.V., Franz-Hartmann-Str 9, 67466 Lambrecht
T: (06325) 18000; Fax: 180026
Focus: Poli Sci 05880

Pharma-Dokumentationsring e.V. (PDR), Pharma Research Centre, 42096 Wuppertal
T: (0202) 368495; Fax: 364200
Founded: 1958; Members: 27
Focus: Pharmacol 05881

Philosophia e.V., Hans-Loch-Str 53, 99099 Erfurt
T: (0361) 345253; Fax: 345253
Focus: Philos 05882

Philosophischer Fakultätentag, c/o Fachbereich 5.2, Universität, Im Stadtwald 8, 66123 Saarbrücken
T: (0681) 3022949; Fax: 3022992
Focus: Educ; Philos 05883

Physikalisch-Medizinische Sozietät zu Erlangen, Universitätsstr 40, 91054 Erlangen
Focus: Med; Physics
Periodical
Sitzungsberichte der Physikalisch-Medizinischen Sozietät zu Erlangen (1-2 times annually) 05884

Pirckheimer-Gesellschaft e.V., Friedrichstr 120, 10117 Berlin
T: (030) 2826343, 2810525; Fax: 2826343
Focus: Lit 05885

Politische Akademie Biggesee, Ewiger Str 7-9, 57439 Attendorn
T: (02761) 7090; Fax: 709453
Founded: 1951; Members: 110
Focus: Poli Sci
Periodical
Meinungen, Informationen, Nachrichten (semi-annually) 05886

Politischer Arbeitskreis Schulen (PAS), Wachsbleiche 28, 53111 Bonn
T: (0228) 636102; Fax: 696489
Focus: Educ 05887

POLLICHIA e.V., Saarlandstr 13, 76855 Annweiler
T: (06346) 7353; Fax: 7245
Founded: 1840; Members: 3800
Pres: Prof. Dr. Günter Preuß; Gen Secr: Prof. Dr. Norbert Hailer
Focus: Nat Sci; Ecology
Periodicals
Mitteilungen der POLLICHIA (annually)
Pfälzer Heimat (quarterly)
POLLICHIA-Kurier (quarterly) 05888

Postakademie, Schloss, 63924 Kleinheubach
Focus: Adult Educ 05889

Pro Familia / Deutsche Gesellschaft für Familienplanung, Sexualpädagogik und Sexualberatung e.V., Stresemannallee 3, 60596 Frankfurt/Main
T: (069) 639002; Fax: 639852
Founded: 1952
Focus: Sociology; Family Plan
Periodical
pro familia magazin: Sexualpädagogik und Familienplanung (bi-monthly) 05890

Prüf- und Forschungsinstitut für die Schuhherstellung e.V., Hans-Sachs-Str 2, 66955 Pirmasens
T: (06331) 74017
Focus: Materials Sci 05891

Psychobiologische Gesellschaft, Freundhofweg 5, 45479 Mülheim
T: (0208) 485041
Founded: 1953; Members: 130
Focus: Bio; Psych 05892

Public Relations Akademie e.V., Dachsstr 33, 65207 Wiesbaden
T: (06122) 13163; Fax: 16658
Focus: Advert 05893

Quickborn – Vereinigung für niederdeutsche Sprache und Literatur e.V., Alexanderstr 16, 20099 Hamburg
T: (040) 240809
Focus: Lit 05894

Raabe-Gesellschaft e.V., c/o Braunschweig. Landesmuseum, Burgpl 1, 38100 Braunschweig
T: (0531) 4842629; Fax: 4842607
Focus: Lit 05895

Rabanus-Maurus-Akademie, Eschenheimer Anlage 21, 60318 Frankfurt
T: (069) 554538
Focus: Rel & Theol 05896

Ranke-Gesellschaft – Vereinigung für Geschichte im öffentlichen Leben e.V., Olshausenstr 40, 24118 Kiel
T: (0431) 8802301; Fax: 8801524
Focus: Hist 05897

Rat für Baukultur im Deutschen Kulturrat, Schliepersberg 115, 45241 Essen
T: (0201) 486061; Fax: 481357
Focus: Archit 05898

Rat für Darstellende Künste im Deutschen Kulturrat, c/o Deutscher Bühnenverein, St. Apern-Str 17-21, 50667 Köln
T: (0221) 208120; Fax: 2081228
Focus: Perf Arts 05899

Rat für Formgebung, Postfach 150311, 60063 Frankfurt
T: (069) 747919; E-Mail: german-design-wuniccil@ipf.de; Fax: 7410911
Founded: 1953
Pres: Prof. Dr. Dieter Rams; Gen Secr: Dr. Hans Höger
Focus: Graphic & Dec Arts, Design
Periodical
Design Report (monthly) 05900

Rat für Soziokultur im Deutschen Kulturrat, Weberstr 59a, 53113 Bonn
T: (0228) 2420210; Fax: 2420212
Focus: Cultur Hist 05901

Rat von Sachverständigen für Umweltfragen, Gustav-Stresemann-Ring 11, 65189 Wiesbaden
T: (0611) 754210; Fax: 731269
Focus: Ecology 05902

Rationalisierungs-Gemeinschaft Bauwesen im RKW, Düsseldorfer Str 40, 65760 Eschborn
T: (06196) 495313; Fax: 495393
Founded: 1952
Pres: Gabriele Jany; Gen Secr: Horst Wetzel
Focus: Business Admin; Civil Eng
Periodical
Informationen Bau-Rationalisierung ibp (6-8 times annually) 05903

Rationalisierungs-Gemeinschaft Verpackung im RKW, Düsseldorfer Str 40, 65760 Eschborn
T: (06196) 495200; Fax: 495303
Focus: Business Admin
Periodical
Informationsdienst Verpackung IV (monthly) 05904

Rationalisierungs-Kuratorium der Deutschen Wirtschaft e.V. (RKW), Düsseldorfer Str 40, 65760 Eschborn
T: (06196) 4951
Founded: 1921; Members: 8000
Focus: Business Admin
Periodical
Wirtschaft & Produktivität (monthly) . . . 05905

Rationalisierungs-Kuratorium der Deutschen Wirtschaft e.V., Landesgruppe Baden-Württemberg, Königstr 49, 70173 Stuttgart
T: (0711) 229980; Fax: 2299810
Pres: Richard Hirschmann; Gen Secr: Dr. Albrecht Fridrich
Focus: Business Admin
Periodical
Ratio (quarterly) 05906

Rationalisierungs-Kuratorium der Deutschen Wirtschaft e.V., Landesgruppe Berlin, Rankestr 5-6, 10789 Berlin
T: (030) 8844800; Fax: 88448025
Founded: 1921
Pres: Ernst-Henning Graf von Hardenberg; Gen Secr: Hans-Jürgen Buschmann
Focus: Business Admin 05907

Rationalisierungs-Kuratorium der Deutschen Wirtschaft e.V., Landesgruppe Bremen, Balgebrückstr 3-5, 28195 Bremen
T: (0421) 323316; Fax: 326218
Focus: Business Admin 05908

Rationalisierungs-Kuratorium der Deutschen Wirtschaft e.V., Landesgruppe Hamburg, Hammer Steindamm 40, 22089 Hamburg
T: (040) 2094160; Fax: 20941650
Pres: Ralf Bacia; Gen Secr: Alois Vilgis
Focus: Business Admin 05909

Rationalisierungs-Kuratorium der Deutschen Wirtschaft e.V., Landesgruppe Hessen, Düsseldorfer Str 40, 65760 Eschborn
T: (06196) 495358; Fax: 495368
Focus: Business Admin 05910

Rationalisierungs-Kuratorium der Deutschen Wirtschaft e.V., Landesgruppe Niedersachsen, Friesenstr 14, 30161 Hannover
T: (0511) 338030; Fax: 3380338
Founded: 1921; Members: 450
Pres: Günter Schwank; Gen Secr: Alois Vilgis
Focus: Business Admin
Periodical
wir produktiv (quarterly) 05911

Rationalisierungs-Kuratorium der Deutschen Wirtschaft e.V., Landesgruppe Nord-Ost, Holtenauer Str 94, 24105 Kiel
T: (0431) 563075
Focus: Business Admin
Periodical
Wirtschaft & Produktivität (monthly) . . . 05912

Rationalisierungs-Kuratorium der Deutschen Wirtschaft e.V., Landesgruppe Nordrhein-Westfalen, Sohnstr 70, 40237 Düsseldorf
T: (0211) 680010; E-Mail: info@rkw.d.eunet.de; Fax: 6800168
Founded: 1950; Members: 670
Focus: Business Admin 05913

Rationalisierungs-Kuratorium der Deutschen Wirtschaft e.V., Landesgruppe Rheinland-Pfalz, Schillerstr 26-28, 55116 Mainz
T: (06131) 286610; Fax: 286619
Focus: Business Admin
Periodical
RKW Kompass (annually) 05914

Rationalisierungs-Kuratorium für Landwirtschaft e.V., Am Kamp 13, 24783 Osterrönfeld
T: (04331) 847940; E-Mail: rkl.info@t-online.de; Fax: 847950
Founded: 1958; Members: 1700
Pres: Eberhard Herweg; Gen Secr: Dr. Hardwin Traulsen
Focus: Agri 05915

Rechts- und Staatswissenschaftliche Vereinigung Düsseldorf e.V., Cecilienallee 3, 40474 Düsseldorf
T: (0211) 4971515
Founded: 1949; Members: 360
Focus: Poli Sci; Law 05916

REFA-Verband für Arbeitsstudien und Betriebsorganisation e.V., Wittichstr 2, 64295 Darmstadt
T: (06151) 88010; Fax: 8801109
Founded: 1924; Members: 45600
Focus: Business Admin
Periodicals
Fortschrittliche Betriebsführung und Industrial Engineering (bi-monthly)
REFA-Nachrichten (bi-monthly) 05917

Regionale Organisation der FDI für Europa (ERO), Universitätsstr 71-73, 50931 Köln
T: (0221) 4001204; Fax: 4001214
Founded: 1965; Members: 30 Länder
Pres: A. Schneider; Gen Secr: Dr. E. Cimbura
Focus: Dent 05918

Reinhold-Schneider-Gesellschaft e.V. (RSG), Friedrich-Ebert-Str 52, 33102 Paderborn
T: (05251) 31230, 24905; Fax: 37646
Focus: Lit 05919

Rheinisch-Westfälische Akademie der Wissenschaften, Palmenstr 16, 40217 Düsseldorf
T: (0211) 342051; Fax: 341475
Founded: 1950
Focus: Humanities; Eng; Econ; Philos
Periodicals
Abhandlungen (irregularly)
Jahrbuch (irregularly)
Jahresprogramm (irregularly)
Sitzungsberichte (irregularly) 05920

Rheinisch-Westfälische Vereinigung für Lungen- und Bronchialheilkunde, Tüschener Weg 40, 45239 Essen
T: (0201) 4309201; Fax: 4309498
Focus: Pulmon Dis 05921

Rheinisch-Westfälisches Institut für Wirtschaftsforschung, Hohenzollernstr 1-3, 45128 Essen
T: (0201) 81490; Fax: 8149200
Pres: Prof. Dr. Paul Klemmer; Prof. Dr. Ullrich Heilemann
Focus: Econ; Marketing
Periodicals
RWI-Handwerksberichte (annually)
RWI-Konjunkturberichte (semi-annually)
RWI-Konjunkturbriefe (irregularly)
RWI-Mitteilungen (quarterly)
RWI-Papiere (irregularly)
Schriftenreihe des RWI (irregularly)
Untersuchungen des RWI (irregularly) . . 05922

Rheinische Adalbert-Stifter-Gemeinschaft, Altenberger Str 124, 51381 Leverkusen
T: (02171) 53189
Focus: Lit 05923

Rheinische Naturforschende Gesellschaft, Reichklarastr 1, 55116 Mainz
Focus: Nat Sci
Periodicals
Mainzer Naturwissenschaftliches Archiv (annually)
Mitteilungen der Rheinischen Naturforschenden Gesellschaft (annually)
Museumsführer (irregularly) 05924

Rheinische Vereinigung für Volkskunde, Am Hofgarten 22, 53113 Bonn
T: (0228) 737618; Fax: 737562
Founded: 1947; Members: 220
Pres: Prof. Dr. H.L. Cox
Focus: Folklore
Periodicals
Rheinisch-Westfälische Zeitschrift für Volkskunde (annually)
Rheinisches Jahrbuch für Volkskunde (bi-annually) 05925

Richard-Strauss-Gesellschaft e.V., Viktualienmarkt 3, 80331 München
T: (089) 2283985; Fax: 29162019
Focus: Music 05926

Richard-Wagner-Verband Bayreuth e.V., Weberhof 4, 95448 Bayreuth
T: (0921) 21512; Fax: 854366
Founded: 1910; Members: 850
Pres: Paul Götz
Focus: Music 05927

Robert Schumann-Gesellschaft e.V. (RSG), Bilker Str 4-6, 40213 Düsseldorf
T: (0211) 133240
Focus: Music 05928

Robert Schumann-Gesellschaft Zwickau e.V., Hauptmarkt 5, 08056 Zwickau
T: (0375) 215269; Fax: 281101
Focus: Music 05929

Rolf-Dieter-Brinkmann-Gesellschaft e.V., Immentun 2a, 49377 Vechta
T: (04441) 7821; Fax: 15447
Focus: Lit 05930

Rudolf Borchardt-Gesellschaft e.V., Rinding 2, 85560 Ebersberg
T: (08092) 22671; Fax: 20318
Focus: Lit 05931

Rückert-Gesellschaft e.V., Schrittturm/Petersgasse 3, 97421 Schweinfurt
T: (09721) 25377
Focus: Lit 05932

Saarländisch-Pfälzische Internistengesellschaft e.V., c/o Medizinische Klinik C, Bremserstr 79, 67063 Ludwigshafen
T: (0621) 5084100
Focus: Intern Med 05933

Saarländische Gesellschaft für zahnärztliche Fortbildung, Puccinistr 2, 66119 Saarbrücken
T: (0681) 586080; Fax: 5860814
Founded: 1973; Members: 300
Pres: Prof. Dr. Dr. J. Dumbach
Focus: Dent 05934

Saarländischer Gymnasiallehrerverband e.V., Losheimer Str 16, 66679 Losheim
T: 2216
Focus: Educ 05935

Sachverständigenrat für die Konzertierte Aktion im Gesundheitswesen (BMG), Am Propsthof 78a, 53121 Bonn
T: (0228) 9412294/95; Fax: 9414915
Focus: Public Health 05936

Sächsische Akademie der Wissenschaften zu Leipzig (SAW), Karl-Tauchnitz-Str 1, 04107 Leipzig
T: (0341) 711530
Founded: 1846; Members: 140
Pres: Prof. Dr. Gotthard Lerchner
Focus: Sci
Periodicals
Abhandlungen (irregularly)
Sitzungsberichte (irregularly) 05937

Sächsischer Volkshochschulverband e.V., Leipziger Str 162, 09114 Chemnitz
T: (0371) 373275; Fax: 373274
Focus: Adult Educ 05938

Salomon Ludwig Steinheim-Institut für deutsch-jüdische Geschichte e.V., Geibelstr 41, 47057 Duisburg
T: (0203) 370071/72; Fax: 373380
Focus: Hist 05939

Sankt Ingberter Literaturforum (ILF), Kaiserstr 71, 66386 Sankt Ingbert
T: (06894) 922515
Focus: Lit 05940

Sartre-Gesellschaft, Kurfürstendamm 211, 10719 Berlin
T: (030) 8859020
Focus: Lit 05941

Schiffbautechnische Gesellschaft e.V. (STG), Lämmersieth 72, 22305 Hamburg
T: (040) 6904910; Fax: 6900341
Founded: 1899; Members: 2000
Focus: Eng
Periodical
Jahrbuch der Schiffbautechnischen Gesellschaft (annually) 05942

Schmalenbach-Gesellschaft / Deutsche Gesellschaft für Betriebswirtschaft e.V., Nonnendammallee 101, 13629 Berlin
T: (030) 3827024
Founded: 1978; Members: 1500
Focus: Business Admin
Periodical
Schmalenbachs Zeitschrift für betriebswirtschaftliche Forschung (monthly) 05943

Schopenhauer-Gesellschaft e.V., c/o Philologisches Institut, Universität Bonn, Am Hof 1a, 53113 Bonn
Founded: 1911; Members: 915
Focus: Philos
Periodical
Schopenhauer-Jahrbuch (annually) . . . 05944

Schostakowitsch-Gesellschaft e.V. (SchoG), Klaustaler Str 2, 13187 Berlin
T: (030) 4827570; Fax: 4830251
Focus: Music 05945

Schutzgemeinschaft Alt Bamberg e.V., Schillerpl 9, 96047 Bamberg
T: (0951) 202521
Founded: 1968; Members: 300
Focus: Preserv Hist Monuments
Periodical
Informationsheft (semi-annually) 05946

Senckenbergische Naturforschende Gesellschaft (SNG), Senckenberganlage 25, 60325 Frankfurt
T: (069) 75420; Fax: 746238
Founded: 1817; Members: 5000
Pres: Alexander Rasor; Gen Secr: Prof. Dr. Fritz F. Steininger
Focus: Nat Sci 05947

SNV Studiengesellschaft Verkehr, Lokstedter Weg 24, 20251 Hamburg
T: (040) 460680; Fax: 4608155
Founded: 1971
Focus: Transport 05948

Sorbisches Institut e.V., Bahnhofstr 6, 02625 Bautzen
T: (03591) 49720; Fax: 497214
Focus: Ethnology 05949

Sozialakademie Dortmund, Hohe Str 141, 44139 Dortmund
T: (0231) 126059; Fax: 126165
Founded: 1947
Focus: Sociology 05950

Sportärztebund Hamburg, Eppendorfer Baum 8, 20249 Hamburg
T: (040) 483880
Focus: Med 05951

Sportärztebund Hessen, Otto-Fleck-Schneise 10, 60528 Frankfurt
T: (069) 67800923; Fax: 6708505
Focus: Med
Periodical
Sportärzteverband Hessen – aktuell (semi-annually) 05952

Sportärztebund Niedersachsen, Sprangerweg 2, 37075 Göttingen
T: (0551) 22414
Focus: Med 05953

Sportärztebund Nordrhein, Bernhard-Letterhaus-Str 17, 51377 Leverkusen
T: (0214) 51804
Focus: Med 05954

Sportärztebund Rheinland-Pfalz, Roonstr 10, 67655 Kaiserslautern
T: (0631) 16079; Fax: 25021
Focus: Med 05955

Sportärzteverband Schleswig-Holstein, Olshausenstr 40-60, 24098 Kiel
T: (0431) 8803775; Fax: 8803777
Founded: 1948; Members: 280
Pres: Prof. Dr. Hans Rieckert
Focus: Med 05956

Sprachverband Deutsch für ausländische Arbeitnehmer e.V., Raimundistr 2, 55118 Mainz
T: (06131) 964440; E-Mail: Sprachverband@T-Online.de; Fax: 9644444
Founded: 1974; Members: 34
Pres: Heinz Seidel; Gen Secr: Gerhard Fiedler
Focus: Ling
Periodicals
Bildungsarbeit in der Zweitsprache Deutsch: Konzepte und Materialien (3 times annually)
Deutsch lernen: Zeitschrift für den Sprachunterricht mit ausländischen Arbeitnehmern (quarterly) 05957

Staats- und Wirtschaftspolitische Gesellschaft e.V., Parkallee 84, 20144 Hamburg
T: (040) 446541/42
Focus: Econ; Poli Sci
Periodical
Deutschland-Journal (semi-annually) . . . 05958

Ständige Konferenz Schauspielausbildung (SKS), Wedeler Landstr 49, 22559 Hamburg
T: (040) 817272; Fax: 810156
Focus: Educ; Perf Arts 05959

Ständiger Ausschuss für geographische Namen (StAGN) (StAGN), Richard-Strauss-Allee 11, 60598 Frankfurt
T: (069) 6333317; E-Mail: beinstein@ifag.de; Fax: 6333441
Founded: 1959
Pres: Dr. Jörn Sievers; Gen Secr: Bernd E. Beinstein
Focus: Ling 05960

Stefan-Andres-Gesellschaft e.V., Hofgartenstr 26, 54338 Schweich
T: (06502) 6524
Focus: Lit 05961

Stifterverband für die Deutsche Wissenschaft, Postfach 164460, 45224 Essen
T: (0201) 84010; E-Mail: Stifterverband@compuserve.com; Fax: 8401301
Founded: 1920; Members: 4000
Pres: Prof. Dr. Karlheinz Kaske; Gen Secr: Prof. Dr. Manfred Erhardt
Focus: Sci
Periodicals
Arbeitsschriften Forschung und Entwicklung in der Wirtschaft (bi-annually)
Jahresberichte über die Tätigkeit des Stifterverbands
Materialien aus dem Stiftungszentrum (irregularly)
Materialien zur Bildungspolitik (irregularly)
Wirtschaft und Wissenschaft (quarterly) . 05962

Stifterverband Metalle / Gesellschaft zur Förderung der Metallforschung, Tersteegenstr 28, 40474 Düsseldorf
T: (0211) 454710; Fax: 4647111
Focus: Metallurgy 05963

Studiengemeinschaft für Fertigbau e.V., Panoramaweg 11, 65191 Wiesbaden
T: (06121) 562191; Fax: 564699
Focus: Civil Eng 05964

Studiengemeinschaft Holzleimbau e.V., Füllenbachstr 6, 40474 Düsseldorf
T: (0211) 434635; Fax: 452314
Focus: Civil Eng 05965

Studiengesellschaft für den kombinierten Verkehr e.V. (SGKV), Börsenpl 1, 60313 Frankfurt
T: (069) 283571; E-Mail: Cserve 100104,64; Fax: 285920
Founded: 1928; Members: 100
Pres: Ewald Stöwe; Gen Secr: Dr. Christoph Seidelmann
Focus: Transport 05966

Studiengesellschaft für Holzschwellenoberbau e.V., Mainzer Str 64, 65185 Wiesbaden
T: (06121) 300020; Fax: 309175
Focus: Materials Sci
Periodical
Die Holzschwelle (annually) 05967

Studiengesellschaft für Stahlleitplanken e.V., Spandauer Str 25, 57072 Siegen
T: (0271) 53039
Focus: Materials Sci 05968

Studiengesellschaft für unterirdische Verkehrsanlagen e.V. (STUVA), Mathias-Brüggen-Str 41, 50827 Köln
T: (0221) 597950; E-Mail: 101610.3545@compuserve.com; Fax: 5979550
Founded: 1960; Members: 230
Pres: Prof. Dr. Dr. Günter Girnau; Gen Secr: Prof. Dr. Alfred Haack
Focus: Transport
Periodical
Tunnel (8 times annually) 05969

Studiengesellschaft Stahlanwendung e.V., Breite Str 69, 40213 Düsseldorf
T: (0211) 829382
Focus: Eng
Periodical
Forschungsberichte (irregularly) 05970

Studiengruppe für Sozialforschung e.V., 83250 Marquartstein
T: (08641) 7130; Fax: 63242
Founded: 1972
Pres: Prof. Albrecht Goeschel; Gen Secr: Dr. Margarete Landenberger
Focus: Sociology 05971

Studiengruppe Unternehmer in der Gesellschaft, Ölmühlweg 37b, 61462 Königstein
T: (06174) 7348
Focus: Econ 05972

Studienkreis für Presserecht und Pressefreiheit, Königstr 1a, 70173 Stuttgart
T: (0711) 293165; Fax: 2991857
Founded: 1956
Focus: Law; Mass Media 05973

Studienkreis für staatsbürgerliche Arbeit e.V., Peter-Schwingen-Str 11, 53177 Bonn
T: (0228) 321000; Fax: 326500
Focus: Poli Sci 05974

Studienzentrum Weikersheim e.V. (SZW), Mörikestr 30, 70178 Stuttgart
T: (0711) 603530; Fax: 6493747
Focus: Poli Sci 05975

Süddeutsches Kunststoff-Zentrum (SKZ) / Institut für Kunststoffverarbeitung, -anwendung und -prüfung, Frankfurter Str 15-17, 97082 Würzburg
T: (0931) 41040; Fax: 4194177
Focus: Materials Sci; Adult Educ . . . 05976

Südostdeutsche Historische Kommission, Mohlstr 18, 72074 Tübingen
T: (07071) 2002513; Fax: 2002535
Focus: Hist 05977

Südosteuropa-Gesellschaft e.V. (SOG), Widenmayerstr 49, 80538 München
T: (089) 2121540; E-Mail: Suedosteuropa-Gesellschaft@t-online.de; Fax: 2289469
Founded: 1952
Pres: Dr. Walter Althammer; Gen Secr: Dr. Hansjörg Brey
Focus: Ethnology; Econ; Int'l Relat; Hist; Arts; Ling
Periodical
Südosteuropa-Mitteilungen (quarterly) . . 05978

Südwestdeutsche Akademie für Marketing und Kommunikation e.V., Königstr 1b, 70173 Stuttgart
T: (0711) 291714
Focus: Business Admin; Comm Sci . . 05979

Technikerschule für Druck und Papierverarbeitung, Pranckhstr 2, 80335 München
T: (089) 555761; Fax: 5504418
Founded: 1927
Pres: Dietmar Leischner; Gen Secr: Oberstudiendirektor/Schulleitung
Focus: Eng 05980

Technische Akademie Esslingen e.V. (TAE), In den Anlagen 5, 73760 Ostfildern
T: (0711) 340080; Fax: 3400843
Focus: Eng 05981

Technische Akademie Wuppertal e.V. (TAW), Hubertusallee 18, 42117 Wuppertal
T: (0202) 74950; Fax: 8063006
Founded: 1948
Focus: Eng 05982

Technische Fördergemeinschaft Holzsilo (TFS), Malterer Str 18f, 79102 Freiburg
T: (0761) 32321
Focus: Materials Sci 05983

Technische Vereinigung der Großkraftwerksbetreiber e.V. (VGB), Klinkestr 27-31, 45136 Essen
Focus: Energy
Periodical
VGB Kraftwerkstechnik (monthly) 05984

Theodor-Däubler-Gesellschaft e.V., Domitianstr 33, 60439 Frankfurt/Main
T: (069) 589176
Focus: Lit 05985

Theodor Fontane Gesellschaft e.V., Am Alten Gymnasium 1-3, 16816 Neuruppin
T: (03391) 652772; Fax: 652772
Focus: Lit 05986

Theodor-Storm-Gesellschaft e.V., Wasserreihe 31, 25813 Husum
T: (04841) 666270
Focus: Lit 05987

Thomas-Morus-Akademie Bensberg, Overather Str 51, 51429 Bergisch Gladbach
T: (02204) 408472; E-Mail: tma.bensberg@t-online.de; Fax: 408420
Founded: 1953
Pres: Dr. Wolfgang Isenberg
Focus: Rel & Theol; Adult Educ; Soc Sci
Periodicals
Bensberger Manuskripte (irregularly)
Bensberger Protokolle (irregularly)
TMA Journal (irregularly) 05988

Thüringer Volkshochschulverband e.V., Konrad-Zuse-Str 3, 07745 Jena
T: (03641) 620976/-77; Fax: 620978
Focus: Adult Educ 05989

Thüringische Literaturhistorische Gesellschaft Palmbaum e.V., Johannispl 26, 07743 Jena
T: (03641) 443731; Fax: 619005
Focus: Lit 05990

Tübinger Förderkreis zur Erforschung der Troas – Freunde von Troia, c/o Prof. Dr. Manfred Korfmann, Institut für Ur- und Frühgeschichte und Archäologie des Mittelalters, Schloß Hohentübingen, 72070 Tübingen
T: (07071) 2974394; E-Mail: troia.projekt@uni-tuebingen.de; Fax: 295269
Focus: Archeol 05991

TÜV-Akademie Rheinland, Am Grauen Stein, 51105 Köln
T: (0221) 8063000; Fax: 8063006
Focus: Auto Eng 05992

TÜV Akademie Westfalen, Herner Str 45, 44787 Bochum
T: (0234) 96802; Fax: 3232
Focus: Auto Eng 05993

Tusculum e.V., Kurneystr 10, 48161 Münster
T: (02533) 97078; Fax: 97079
Focus: Educ 05994

Unabhängiger Ärzteverband Deutschlands e.V., Hohenstaufenring 39, 50674 Köln
T: (0221) 217659
Members: 1250
Focus: Med
Periodical
Der freie Arzt (bi-monthly) 05995

Union Internationale de la Marionnette, UNIMA-Zentrum Bundesrepublik Deutschland e.V., c/o Die Schaubude, Greifswalder Str 81-84, 10405 Berlin
T: (030) 4286059; Fax: 4234310
Focus: Perf Arts 05996

Urania Berlin e.V., Kleiststr 13, 10787 Berlin
T: (030) 2189091; Fax: 2110398
Focus: Sci 05997

VDD-Berufsverband Dokumentation, Information, Kommunikation, Postfach 2509, 53111 Bonn
T: (040) 330261
Founded: 1961; Members: 400
Focus: Doc
Periodical
VDD-Schriftenreihe (irregularly) 05998

VDE/VDI-Gesellschaft Mikroelektronik, Stresemannallee 15, 60596 Frankfurt
T: (069) 6308330; E-Mail: Elektrobund; Fax: 6308273
Founded: 1987; Members: 3300
Focus: Electronic Eng
Periodical
mikroelektronik: Entwicklung und Produktion – Technik und Wirtschaft (bi-monthly) . . . 05999

VDE/VDI-Gesellschaft Mikroelektronik, Mikro- und Feinwerktechnik, Postfach 101139, 40002 Düsseldorf
T: (0211) 6214230; Fax: 6214575
Founded: 1996; Members: 11000
Gen Secr: Dr. Helmut Lauruschkat
Focus: Eng
Periodical
F & M: Feinwerktechnik, Mikroelektronik & Meßtechnik (8 times annually) 06000

VDE Verband Deutscher Elektrotechniker e.V. (VDE), Stresemannallee 15, 60596 Frankfurt
T: (069) 63080
Members: 36000
Pres: Hermann Wolters; Gen Secr: Dr. Friedrich Dankward Althoff
Focus: Electric Eng
Periodicals
dialog (bi-monthly)
etz-Archiv (monthly)
etz Elektrotechnische Zeitschrift (bi-weekly)
ntz-Archiv (monthly)
ntz Nachrichtentechnische Zeitschrift (monthly) 06001

VDEh-Gesellschaft zur Förderung der Eisenforschung, Breite Str 27, 40213 Düsseldorf
T: (0211) 88941
Founded: 1966; Members: 50
Focus: Metallurgy 06002

VDI-Gesellschaft Bautechnik / VDI-Society for Civil Engineering, Graf-Recke-Str 84, 40239 Düsseldorf
T: (0211) 6214531; Fax: 6214177
Founded: 1856; Members: 8000
Pres: Prof. Dr. Manfred Nussbaumer; Gen Secr: Reinhold Jesorsky
Focus: Civil Eng
Periodical
Bauingenieur (monthly) 06003

VDI-Gesellschaft Energietechnik, Graf-Recke-Str 84, 40239 Düsseldorf
T: (0211) 6214416; Fax: 6214161
Pres: K.O. Abt; Gen Secr: Dr. E.-G. Hencke
Focus: Energy 06004

VDI-Gesellschaft Entwicklung Konstruktion Vertrieb (VDI-EKW), Graf-Recke-Str 84, 40239 Düsseldorf
T: (0211) 6214239; E-Mail: internet http://www.vdi.de; Fax: 6214171
Founded: 1973; Members: 20000
Focus: Eng
Periodicals
Absatzwirtschaft: Zeitschrift für Marketing (monthly)
Konstruktion: Zeitschrift für Konstruktion und Entwicklung im Maschinen-, Apparate- und Gerätebau (monthly) 06005

VDI-Gesellschaft Fahrzeug- und Verkehrstechnik, Graf-Recke-Str 84, 40239 Düsseldorf
T: (0211) 6214264; Fax: 6214163
Members: 10600
Pres: D. Frank; Gen Secr: Dr. A. Simburger
Focus: Auto Eng; Transport
Periodical
Jahrbuch (annually) 06006

VDI-Gesellschaft Fördertechnik Materialfluss Logistik, Graf-Recke-Str 84, 40239 Düsseldorf
T: (0211) 6214258; Fax: 6214155
Focus: Eng 06007

VDI-Gesellschaft Kunststofftechnik, Graf-Recke-Str 84, 40239 Düsseldorf
T: (0211) 62141
Members: 6500
Focus: Eng 06008

VDI-Gesellschaft Produktionstechnik, Graf-Recke-Str 84, 40239 Düsseldorf
T: (0211) 6214231/32; Fax: 6214575
Focus: Eng
Periodical
WT-Werkstattechnik (monthly) 06009

VDI-Gesellschaft Technische Gebäudeausrüstung (VDI-TGA) / VDI-Society for Technical Building Services, Graf-Recke-Str 84, 40239 Düsseldorf
T: (0211) 6214251; Fax: 6214575
Founded: 1935; Members: 8200
Pres: Bernd Pasterkamp; Gen Secr: Undine Stricker-Berghoff
Focus: Eng
Periodical
HLH Heizung Lüftung/Klima Haustechnik (monthly) 06010

VDI-Gesellschaft Werkstofftechnik, Graf-Recke-Str 84, 40239 Düsseldorf
T: (0211) 62140
Focus: Materials Sci
Periodicals
Ingenieur-Werkstoffe (monthly)
Materialprüfung (monthly) 06011

VDI-Kommission Lärmminderung, Graf-Recke-Str 84, 40239 Düsseldorf
T: (0211) 62141
Focus: Eng; Ecology 06012

VDI/VDE-Gesellschaft Mess- und Automatisierungstechnik (GMA), Postfach 101139, 40002 Düsseldorf
T: (0211) 6214224; E-Mail: gma@vdi.de; Fax: 6214161
Founded: 1973; Members: 15500
Pres: Dr. Gerhard Lausterer; Gen Secr: Manfred Schatz
Focus: Eng 06013

Verband Bildung und Erziehung e.V. (VBE), Dreizehnmorgenweg 36, 53175 Bonn
T: (0228) 959930; E-Mail: VBE-Bund@T-Online.de; Fax: 378934
Founded: 1974; Members: 140000
Pres: Dr. Ludwig Eckinger; Gen Secr: Michael Zimmermann
Focus: Educ; Adult Educ
Periodical
Forum E (monthly) 06014

Verband der Betriebs- und Werksärzte e.V. (VDBW) / Berufsverband deutscher Arbeitsmediziner, Marie-Alexandra-Str 36, 76135 Karlsruhe
T: (0721) 33660; Fax: 30245
Focus: Med 06015

Verband der Bibliotheken des Landes Nordrhein-Westfalen e.V., Königsholz 2, 58453 Witten
T: (02302) 83704; Fax: 83704
Founded: 1949; Members: 320
Focus: Libraries & Bk Sci
Periodical
Mitteilungsblatt (quarterly) 06016

Verband der deutschen Höhlen- und Karstforscher e.V., Hehner Str 100, 41069 Mönchengladbach
T: (02161) 837653; Fax: 837918
Founded: 1955; Members: 603
Focus: Geology; Speleology
Periodicals
Die Höhle: Zeitschrift für Karst- und Höhlenkunde (quarterly)
Karst und Höhle (annually)
Mitteilungen des Verbandes der deutschen Höhlen- und Karstforscher e.V. (quarterly) . . . 06017

Verband der deutschen Kritiker e.V., Volbedingstr 31, 04357 Leipzig
T: (0341) 6017639
Focus: Lit 06018

Verband der Dozenten an Deutschen Ingenieurschulen, Lorscher Str 13, 55129 Mainz
Focus: Adult Educ; Eng 06019

Verband der Gemeinde-Tierärzte Baden-Württembergs, c/o Städtischer Schlachthof, Bahnackerstr 14, 76532 Baden-Baden
Focus: Vet Med 06020

Verband der Gemeinschaften der Künstlerinnen und Kunstfreunde e.V. (GEDOK), Einern 29, 42279 Wuppertal
T: (0202) 524642; E-Mail: GEDOK.Ma.Wpt@T-Online.de; Fax: 522539
Founded: 1926; Members: 4500
Pres: Dr. Renate Massmann
Focus: Arts 06021

Verband der Geographen an Deutschen Hochschulen (VGDH), Arcisstr 21, 80333 München
T: (089) 28922811/13; Fax: 28922804
Focus: Geography 06022

Verband der Geographen an Deutschen Hochschulen (VGDH) (VGDH), c/o Fach Geographie im FB 6, Universität Duisburg, Lotharstr 65, 47048 Duisburg
T: (0203) 3792250, 3792909; E-Mail: hh227wo@unidui.uni-duisburg.de; Fax: 3793516
Members: ca. 650
Pres: Prof. Dr. Hans Heinrich Blotevogel; Gen Secr: Dr. Gerald Wood
Focus: Geography 06023

Verband der Geschichtslehrer Deutschlands e.V., Sankt-Annen-Str 23, 38723 Seesen
T: (05381) 93740; Fax: 9374474
Founded: 1949; Members: 5000
Focus: Hist; Educ
Periodicals
Geschichte in Wissenschaft und Unterricht (monthly)
Geschichte, Politik und ihre Didaktik (semi-annually)
Geschichte und Politik in der Schule (semi-annually)
Informationen für den Geschichts- und Gemeinschaftskundelehrer (semi-annually) . 06024

Verband der Hermann-Löns-Kreise in Deutschland und Österreich e.V. (Löns-Verb.), Hermann-Löns-Str 2, 29664 Walsrode
T: (05161) 977219
Focus: Lit 06025

Verband der Historiker Deutschlands, c/o Institut für europäische Geschichte, Alte Univesitätsstr 19, 55116 Mainz
T: (06131) 399360; E-Mail: ieg2@inst-euro-history.uni-mainz.de; Fax: 237988
Founded: 1893; Members: 2000
Pres: Prof. Dr. Johannes Fried; Gen Secr: Prof. Dr. Heinz Duchhardt
Focus: Hist 06026

Verband der Landesarchäologen in der Bundesrepublik Deutschland, Schloß Wiligrad, 19069 Lübstorf
T: (03867) 240
Focus: Archeol 06027

Verband der leitenden Krankenhausärzte Deutschlands e.V., Tersteegenstr 9, 40474 Düsseldorf
T: (0211) 454990; Fax: 451834
Members: 5200
Pres: Prof. Dr. Dr. Hermann Hoffmann
Focus: Med
Periodical
Arzt und Krankenhaus (monthly) 06028

Verband der Materialprüfungsämter e.V. (VMPA), Rudower Chaussee 5, Geb 13.7, 12484 Berlin
T: (030) 67059190; Fax: 67059195
Founded: 1948; Members: 54
Pres: Prof. Dr. Horst Falkner
Focus: Materials Sci 06029

Verband der Technischen Überwachungs-Vereine e.V. (VdTÜV), Kurfürstenstr 56, 45138 Essen
T: (0201) 89870; Fax: 8987120
Founded: 1949; Members: 16
Pres: Prof. Dr. Ernst Schadow; Gen Secr: Dr. Lutz K. Wessely
Focus: Eng; Safety
Periodical
TÜ-Technische Überwachung (monthly) . 06030

Verband der Tierheilpraktiker e.V., Am Postbichl 29, 86405 Meitingen
T: (08271) 1322
Focus: Vet Med 06031

Verband der Volkshochschulen des Landes Bremen, Schwachhauser Heerstr 67, 28211 Bremen
T: (0421) 4963666
Focus: Adult Educ 06032

Verband der Volkshochschulen des Saarlandes e.V., Bahnhofstr 47-49, 66111 Saarbrücken
T: (0681) 36680, 36660; Fax: 36610
Founded: 1959; Members: 16
Pres: Dr. Brunhilde Peter; Gen Secr: Dr. Detlef Oppermann
Focus: Adult Educ 06033

Verband der Volkshochschulen von Rheinland-Pfalz e.V., Postfach 4069, 55030 Mainz
T: (06131) 288890; E-Mail: VHS-Verband-RP@T-Online.de; Fax: 2888930
Founded: 1947; Members: 78
Pres: Joachim Mertes; Gen Secr: Lothar Bentin
Focus: Adult Educ 06034

Verband Deutsche Puppentheater e.V. (VDP), Moorweg 1, 21337 Lüneburg
T: (04131) 84415; Fax: 84415
Focus: Perf Arts 06035

Verband Deutscher Agrarjournalisten e.V. (VDAJ), Kasernenstr 14, 53111 Bonn
T: (0228) 694813; Fax: 9630511
Members: 700
Pres: Hans-Heinrich Matthiesen; Gen Secr: Ilona Busch
Focus: Journalism; Agri 06036

Verband Deutscher Badeärzte e.V., Elisabethstr 7, 32545 Bad Oeynhausen
T: (05731) 21203; Fax: 260880
Members: 1100
Pres: Dr. Wolfram Enders; Gen Secr: Dr. Dirk Kühn
Focus: Med
Periodical
Physikalische Medizin, Rehabilitationsmedizin, Kurortmedizin (bi-monthly) 06037

Verband Deutscher Biologen e.V. (VDBiol) / German Association of Biologists, c/o Institut 9, Fachbereich 06, Universität Hamburg, Von-Melle-Park 8, 20146 Hamburg
Focus: Bio
Periodical
Biologen in unserer Zeit (bi-monthly) . . 06038

Verband Deutscher Diplom-Trainer (VDDT), Gensemerstr 5, 53225 Bonn
T: (0228)469329; Fax: 420722
Focus: Educ; Sports 06039

Verband Deutscher Freilichtbühnen e.V. (VDF), Gebrüder-Funke-Weg 3, 59073 Hamm
T: (02381) 6934; Fax: 675692
Focus: Perf Arts 06040

Verband Deutscher Konzert-Chöre e.V. (VDKC), Kempener Str 5, 41749 Viersen
T: (02162) 67058; Fax: 67058
Focus: Music 06041

Verband Deutscher Kunsthistoriker e.V., c/o Zentralinstitut für Kunstgeschichte, Meiserstr 10, 80333 München
T: (089) 553488; Fax: 5504352
Founded: 1948
Focus: Hist; Arts; Cultur Hist 06042

Verband Deutscher Landwirtschaftlicher Untersuchungs- und Forschungsanstalten (VDLUFA), Bismarckstr 41a, 64293 Darmstadt
T: (06151) 26485; Fax: 293370
Founded: 1888
Pres: Prof. Dr. Gerhard Breitschuh; Gen Secr: Dr. Christof Braun
Focus: Agri
Periodicals
Landwirtschaftliche Forschung (quarterly)
VDLUFA-Schriftenreihe (irregularly) . . . 06043

Verband Deutscher Lehrer im Ausland e.V., Pellwormer Str 13, 25813 Husum
T: (04841) 3126
Focus: Educ 06044

Verband Deutscher Meteorologen e.V. (VDM), Frankfurter Str 135, 63067 Offenbach
T: (069) 80622593; Fax: 80622012
Focus: Geophys 06045

Verband deutscher Musikschulen e.V., Plittersdorfer Str 93, 53173 Bonn
T: (0228) 957060; E-Mail: VdM-Musikschulen@t-online.de; Fax: 9570633
Founded: 1952; Members: 977 Musikschulen
Pres: Dr. Gerd Eicker; Gen Secr: Rainer Mehlig
Focus: Music; Educ 06046

Verband Deutscher Physikalischer Gesellschaften, Gänsheidestr 15a, 70184 Stuttgart
Focus: Physics 06047

Verband Deutscher Realschullehrer im Deutschen Beamtenbund (VDR), Viersener Str 57b, 41751 Viersen
T: (02162) 52246
Focus: Educ 06048

Verband Deutscher Schiffahrts-Sachverständiger e.V. (V.D.S.S.), Steinhöft 11, 20459 Hamburg
T: (040) 373062; Fax: 373474
Focus: Navig 06049

Verband deutscher Schriftsteller in der IG Medien (VS), Friedrichstr 15, 70174 Stuttgart
T: (0711) 20180, 2018237; Fax: 2018300
Focus: Lit 06050

Verband Deutscher Schulgeographen e.V., Breslauer Str 26, 30938 Großburgwedel
T: (05139) 1205; Fax: 2646
Founded: 1912; Members: 4900
Focus: Geography; Educ 06051

Verband Deutscher Schullandheime e.V., Mendelssohnstr 86, 22761 Hamburg
T: (040) 8901541; Fax: 898639
Focus: Educ 06052

Verband Deutscher Schulmusiker e.V. / Interessenverband der Musiklehrer an allgemeinbildenden Schulen und der diese Berufsgruppe ausbildenden Hochschullehrer, Weihergarten 5, 55116 Mainz
T: (06131) 234049; Fax: 234006
Pres: Prof. Dr. Hans Bäßler; Gen Secr: Monika Heinrich
Focus: Educ; Music
Periodical
Musik & Bildung: Praxis Musikunterricht (11 times annually) 06053

Verband Deutscher Sonderschulen e.V. (vds), Ohmstr 7, 97076 Würzburg
T: (0931) 24020; Fax: 24023
Focus: Educ 06054

Verband Deutscher Städtestatistiker (VDSt), Schwartzstr 73, 46045 Oberhausen
T: (0208) 8252387; Fax: 8255120
Focus: Stats 06055

Verband Deutscher Tennislehrer e.V. (VDT), Hafenstr 10, 45356 Essen
T: (0201)660058; Fax: 610991
Focus: Educ; Sports 06056

Verband Deutscher Tierarztfrauen und Tierärztinnen e.V., Bismarckstr 4, 26316 Varel
T: (04451) 82795
Focus: Vet Med 06057

Verband Deutscher Tonmeister e.V. (VDT), Masurenallee 8-14, 14057 Berlin
T: (030) 30313628; Fax: 3656088
Focus: Music 06058

Verband deutscher Waldvogelpfleger und Vogelschützer, Monestr 25, 76669 Bad Schönborn
T: (07259) 7433
Founded: 1953; Members: 2500
Pres: Dr. J. Steinbacher; Gen Secr: Herbert Geitner
Focus: Ornithology 06059

Verband deutscher Werkbibliotheken e.V., c/o Bayer AG, Nobelstr 33b, 51373 Leverkusen
T: (0214) 41097; Fax: 44386
Focus: Libraries & Bk Sci 06060

Verband Deutscher Zoodirektoren, Am Vogelgesang 12, 39124 Magdeburg
T: (0391) 280900; Fax: 2809012
Founded: 1887
Pres: Wolfgang Puschmann
Focus: Zoology
Periodical
Der Zoologische Garten (bi-monthly) . . 06061

Verband evangelischer Kirchenmusikerinnen und Kirchenmusiker in Deutschland, Dompl 5, 67346 Speyer
T: (06232) 664112; Fax: 664130
Focus: Music 06062

Verband Forschender Arzneimittelhersteller (VFA) e.V. (VFA), Johanna-Kinkel-Str 24, 53175 Bonn
T: (0228) 819990; Fax: 8199999
Founded: 1994; Members: 36
Pres: Dr. Horst Freisler; Gen Secr: Cornelia Yzer
Focus: Pharmacol 06063

Verband für anthroposophische Heilpädagogik, Sozialtherapie und soziale Arbeit e.V., Schloßstr 9, 61209 Echzell
T: (06035) 81190; Fax: 81217
Focus: Educ; Therapeutics; Sociology . 06064

Verband für Lied, Folk und Weltmusik in Deutschland e.V. (PROFOLK), Pappelallee 32a, 10437 Berlin
T: (030) 4446886; Fax: 4446886
Focus: Music 06065

Verband für Waffentechnik und -geschichte e.V. (VdW), Klever Str 80, 40477 Düsseldorf
T: (0211) 464844; Fax: 489035
Focus: Military Sci; Hist 06066

Verband Hochschule und Wissenschaft im Deutschen Beamtenbund (VHW), Dreizehnmorgenweg 36, 53175 Bonn
T: (0228) 378331
Founded: 1973; Members: 2500
Focus: Adult Educ; Sci
Periodical
VHW-Mitteilungen (quarterly) 06067

Verband Katholischer Landvolkshochschulen Deutschlands, Drachenfelsstr 4, 53604 Bad Honnef
T: (02224) 93800; Fax: 938080
Founded: 1948; Members: 21
Focus: Adult Educ 06068

Verband Physikalische Therapie / Vereinigung für die physiotherapeutischen Berufe e.V., Hofweg 15, 22085 Hamburg
T: (040) 2201236; Fax: 2205537
Focus: Therapeutics
Periodical
Physikalische Therapie in Theorie und Praxis (monthly) 06069

Verein Arbeitsgemeinschaft Deutsche Musikwettbewerbe, Rosenheimer Str 11, 81667 München
T: (089) 48003204; Fax: 48003240
Focus: Music 06070

Verein der Bibliothekare an Öffentlichen Bibliotheken e.V. (VBB), Gartenstr 18, 72764 Reutlingen
T: (07121) 34910; Fax: 300433
Founded: 1949; Members: 4500
Focus: Libraries & Bk Sci
Periodical
Buch und Bibliothek (BuB) (10 times annually) 06071

Verein der Diplom-Bibliothekare an wissenschaftlichen Bibliotheken e.V. (VdDB), c/o Bundesinstitut für Ostwissenschaftliche und internationale Studien, Lindenbornstr 22, 50823 Köln
T: (0221) 5747161; E-Mail: biost.koeln@mail.rrz.uni-koeln.de; Fax: 5747110
Founded: 1948; Members: 3200
Pres: Susanne Oehlschläger; Gen Secr: Martina Leibold
Focus: Libraries & Bk Sci
Periodical
Rundschreiben (quarterly) 06072

Verein der Textilchemiker und Coloristen e.V. (VTCC), Rohrbacher Str 76, 69115 Heidelberg
T: (06221) 21865
Founded: 1948; Members: 1450
Focus: Chem 06073

Verein der Zellstoff- und Papier-Chemiker und -Ingenieure e.V., Berliner Allee 56, 64295 Darmstadt
T: (06151) 33264; Fax: 311076
Founded: 1905; Members: 2000
Pres: W. Heinrich; Gen Secr: R. Weidenmüller
Focus: Materials Sci
Periodical
Das Papier (monthly) 06074

Verein Deutscher Archivare (VDA), c/o Westfälisches Archivamt, Warendorfer Str 24, 48145 Münster
T: (0251) 5913886; Fax: 591269
Founded: 1947; Members: 1800
Focus: Archives
Periodicals
Der Archivar (quarterly)
Archive und Archivare in der Bundesrepublik Deutschland, Österreich und der Schweiz (irregularly) 06075

Verein Deutscher Bibliothekare e.V. (VDB), c/o Universitäts- und Landesbibliothek Münster, Krummer Timpen 3-5, 48143 Münster
T: (0251) 8324032; E-Mail: hilgema@uni-muenster.de; Fax: 8328398
Founded: 1900; Members: 1550
Pres: Dr. Klaus Hilgemann; Gen Secr: Dr. Lydia Jungnickel
Focus: Libraries & Bk Sci
Periodicals
Jahrbuch der Deutschen Bibliotheken (annually)
Zeitschrift für Bibliothekswesen und Bibliographie (bi-monthly) 06076

Verein Deutscher Eisenhüttenleute (VDEh), Sohnstr 65, 40237 Düsseldorf
T: (0211) 67070; Fax: 6707310
Founded: 1860; Members: 10000
Focus: Metallurgy
Periodicals
Literaturschau Stahl und Eisen (bi-weekly)
MPT Metallurgical Plant and Technology International (bi-monthly)
Stahl und Eisen (monthly)
Steel Research (monthly) 06077

Verein Deutscher Emailfachleute e.V., Zehlendorfer Str 24, 58097 Hagen
T: (02331) 10880; Fax: 108833
Focus: Eng
Periodical
Mitteilungen (monthly) 06078

Verein Deutscher Giessereifachleute e.V. (VDG), Sohnstr 70, 40237 Düsseldorf
T: (0211) 68710; Fax: 6871333
Founded: 1909; Members: 3900
Focus: Metallurgy
Periodicals
Casting Plant and Technology: CP+T International (quarterly)
Giesserei (26 times annually)
Giesserei-Literaturschau (monthly)
Giessereiforschung (quarterly) 06079

Verein Deutscher Ingenieure (VDI) / Association of German Engineers, Graf-Recke-Str 84, 40239 Düsseldorf
T: (0211) 62140; Fax: 6214575
Founded: 1856
Focus: Eng
Periodicals
Forschung im Ingenieurwesen (bi-monthly)
Umwelt (bi-monthly)
VDI-Nachrichten (weekly)
VDI-Zeitschrift (bi-weekly) 06080

Verein Deutscher Zuckertechniker (VDZ), c/o Nordharzer Zucker AG, 38315 Schladen
Focus: Food 06081

Verein für bayerische Kirchengeschichte, Veilhofstr 28, 90489 Nürnberg
Fax: (0911) 5819683
Focus: Hist; Rel & Theol
Periodical
Zeitschrift für bayerische Kirchengeschichte (annually) 06082

Verein für das Forschungsinstitut für Edelmetalle und Metallchemie e.V., Katharinenstr 17, 73525 Schwäbisch Gmünd
T: (07171) 10060; E-Mail: FEMMAIL@compuserve.de; Fax: 100654
Founded: 1922
Gen Secr: Dr. H.A. Jehn
Focus: Metallurgy 06083

Verein für die Geschichte Berlins, gegr. 1865, Roedernstr 48, 13465 Berlin
T: (030) 4041449
Focus: Hist 06084

Verein für europäische Binnenschiffahrt und Wasserstraßen e.V., Dammstr 15-17, 47118 Duisburg
T: (0203) 8000627; Fax: 8000621
Pres: Prof. D. Schröder; Gen Secr: G. Dütemeyer
Focus: Transport
Periodical
Binnenschiffahrt: Zeitschrift für Binnenschiffahrt und Wasserstraßen (ZfB) (monthly) 06085

Verein für Familien- und Wappenkunde in Württemberg und Baden e.V., Postfach 105441, 70047 Stuttgart
T: (0711) 2124490
Founded: 1920; Members: 1343
Pres: Dr. Volker Trugenberger; Gen Secr: Dr. Volker Trugenberger
Focus: Genealogy
Periodical
Südwestdeutsche Blätter für Familien- und Wappenkunde (quarterly) 06086

Verein für Familienforschung in Ost- und Westpreussen e.V., In de Krümm 10, 21147 Hamburg
Focus: Genealogy
Periodical
Altpreussische Geschlechterkunde 06087

Verein für Forstliche Standortskunde und Forstpflanzenzüchtung e.V., Wonnhaldestr 4, 79100 Freiburg
T: (0761) 4018283
Founded: 1951; Members: 1050
Focus: Forestry
Periodical
Mitteilungen des Vereins für Forstliche Standortskunde und Forstpflanzenzüchtung (annually) 06088

Verein für Gerberei-Chemie und -Technik e.V. (VGCT), Camerloherstr 83, 80689 München
T: (089) 565711
Focus: Chem; Eng
Periodical
Das Leder (monthly) 06089

Verein für Geschichte des Hegaus e.V., August-Ruf-Str 7, 78224 Singen
T: 85244; Fax: 85243
Focus: Hist
Periodical
Hegau (annually) 06090

Verein für Geschichte und Landeskunde von Osnabrück, Schloßstr 29, 49074 Osnabrück
T: (0541) 28577
Founded: 1847; Members: 850
Pres: Dr. Gerd Steinwascher
Focus: Hist
Periodicals
Heimatkunde des Osnabrücker Landes in Einzelbeispielen (irregularly)
Osnabrücker Geschichtsquellen und Forschungen (irregularly)
Osnabrücker Mitteilungen (annually)
Osnabrücker Urkundenbuch (irregularly) . 06091

Verein für Grüne Solararchitektur zur Förderung der Wohn- und Umweltqualität e.V., Sindelfinger Str 85, 72070 Tübingen
T: (07071) 42918; Fax: 44436
Focus: Archit; Energy 06092

Verein für Kommunalwissenschaften e.V., Strasse des 17. Juni 112, 10623 Berlin
T: (030) 390010; Fax: 390010
Founded: 1951
Pres: Prof. Dr. Heinrich Mäding; Gen Secr: Dr. Rolf-Peter Löhr
Focus: Poli Sci
Periodicals
Archiv für Kommunalwissenschaften (semi-annually)
Informationen zur modernen Stadtgeschichte
. . . . 06093

Verein für Reformationsgeschichte e.V. (VRG), c/o Historisches Institut, Am Neuen Palais 10, 14469 Potsdam
T: (0331) 9771323, 9771850
Focus: Hist; Rel & Theol 06094

Verein für technische Holzfragen e.V., Bienroder Weg 54e, 38108 Braunschweig
T: (0531) 39090
Focus: Materials Sci 06095

Verein für Versicherungs-Wissenschaft und -Praxis Nordhessen e.V., Kölnische Str 108, 34119 Kassel
T: (0561) 7881131
Focus: Insurance 06096

Verein für Wasser-, Boden- und Lufthygiene e.V., Postfach 311420, 10644 Berlin
T: (030) 27065746; Fax: 4145800
Focus: Hygiene
Periodicals
Literaturberichte über Wasser, Abwasser und feste Abfallstoffe (bi-monthly)
Schriftenreihe (irregularly) 06097

Verein für Westfälische Kirchengeschichte, Altstädter Kirchpl 1-3, 33602 Bielefeld
Focus: Hist; Rel & Theol
Periodical
Jahrbuch für Westfälische Kirchengeschichte (annually) 06098

Verein für Zahnhygiene e.V. (VfZ), Feldbergstr 40, 64293 Darmstadt
T: (06151) 894814; Fax: 895198
Focus: Hygiene; Dent 06099

Verein katholischer deutscher Lehrerinnen e.V. (VkdL), Hedwig-Dransfeld-Pl 4, 45143 Essen
T: (0201) 623029; Fax: 621587
Founded: 1885; Members: 10000
Pres: Nelly Friedrich
Focus: Educ
Periodical
Katholische Bildung (monthly) 06100

Verein Naturschutzpark e.V., 29646 Niederhaverbeck
T: (05198) 408; E-Mail: Verein Naturschutzpark@t-online.de; Fax: 668
Founded: 1909; Members: 5000
Gen Secr: Dr. Eberhard Jüttner
Focus: Ecology 06101

Verein Nordfriesisches Institut e.V., Süderstr 30, 25821 Bredstedt
T: (04671) 2081; Fax: 1333
Focus: Hist; Lit; Ling
Periodicals
Der Maueranker (quarterly)
Das nordfriesische Jahrbuch (annually)
Nordfriesland (quarterly) 06102

Verein von Altertumsfreunden im Rheinlande, Colmantstr 14-16, 53115 Bonn
T: (0228) 72941; Fax: 7294299
Founded: 1848; Members: 1500
Pres: Prof. Dr. Hartmut Galsterer
Focus: Hist; Cultur Hist
Periodical
Bonner Jahrbücher (annually) 06103

Verein zur Förderung der deutschen Tanz- und Unterhaltungsmusik e.V., Friedrich-Wilhelm-Str 31, 53113 Bonn
Founded: 1966
Focus: Music 06104

Verein zur Förderung der Gießerei-Industrie e.V., Sohnstr 70, 40237 Düsseldorf
T: (0211) 68711
Focus: Metallurgy 06105

Verein zur Förderung der Versicherungswissenschaft in Hamburg e.V., Überseering 45, 22297 Hamburg
T: (040) 63761
Focus: Insurance 06106

Verein zur Förderung der Versicherungswissenschaft in München e.V., Schackstr 3, 80539 München
T: (089) 390460; Fax: 390836
Focus: Insurance
Periodical
Schriftenreihe des Vereins zur Förderung der Versicherungswissenschaft in München e.V. (3-6 times annually) 06107

Verein zur Förderung von Community Education in der Bundesrepublik Deutschland e.V. (COMED), Burgholzstr 150, 44145 Dortmund
T: (0231) 815026; Fax: 815026
Focus: Educ 06108

Vereinigung Bayerischer Augenärzte, c/o Augenklinik des Klinikums rechts der Isar, Ismaninger Str 22, 81675 München
Focus: Ophthal 06109

Vereinigung der Ärzte der Medizinaluntersuchungsämter, Alte Poststr 11, 49074 Osnabrück
Focus: Med 06110

Vereinigung der Bayerischen Chirurgen e.V., c/o Kreiskrankenhaus Alt/Neuötting, Vinzenz-von-Paul-Str 10, 84503 Altötting
T: (08671) 509211; Fax: 509290
Founded: 1911; Members: 780
Focus: Surgery 06111

Vereinigung der Freunde der Mineralogie und Geologie e.V. (VFMG), Blumenthalstr 40, 69120 Heidelberg
T: (06221) 413411; Fax: 413411
Founded: 1950
Pres: Horst Welzel
Focus: Mineralogy; Geology
Periodical
Der Aufschluss (bi-monthly) 06112

Vereinigung der Hochschullehrer für Zahn-, Mund- und Kieferheilkunde, c/o Zahnärztliches Institut, Universität, Ludwig-Rehn-Str 14, 60596 Frankfurt
Focus: Adult Educ; Dent 06113

Vereinigung der Landesdenkmalpfleger in der Bundesrepublik Deutschland, c/o Bayerisches Landesamt für Denkmalpflege, Hofgraben 4, 80539 München
T: (089) 2114286; Fax: 2114300
Founded: 1949; Members: 354
Focus: Preserv Hist Monuments 06114

Vereinigung der unabhängigen freiberuflichen Versicherungs- und Wirtschaftsmathematiker in der Bundesrepublik Deutschland e.V. (I.A.C.A.) / Deutsche Sektion der International Association of Consulting Actuaries, Nördliche Münchner Str 5, 82031 Grünwald
T: (089) 6416040; Fax: 64160420
Founded: 1968; Members: 20
Focus: Math; Insurance; Econ 06115

Vereinigung der Versicherungs-Betriebswirte e.V. (VVB), Landgrafenstr 1, 50931 Köln
T: (0221) 404398
Founded: 1951; Members: 1250
Focus: Insurance; Business Admin
Periodical
Versicherungs-Betriebswirt (6 times annually)
. . . . 06116

Vereinigung Deutscher Gewässerschutz e.V. (VDG), Matthias-Grünewald-Str 1-3, 53175 Bonn
T: (0228) 375007; Fax: 375515
Focus: Ecology 06117

Vereinigung deutscher Landerziehungsheime, Am Schlachtensee 2, 14163 Berlin
T: (030) 8012079; Fax: 8022392
Founded: 1924; Members: 18
Pres: Gerald Becker; Gen Secr: Prof. Dr. Johann Peter Vogel
Focus: Educ 06118

Vereinigung Deutscher Musik-Bearbeiter e.V., Kiesstr 44a, 12209 Berlin
T: (030) 7726241
Focus: Music 06119

Vereinigung Deutscher Neuropathologen und Neuroanatomen, c/o Prof. Dr. W. Schachenmayr, Institut für Neuropathologie, Arndtstr 16, 35392 Giessen
Focus: Anat; Pathology; Neurology . . . 06120

Vereinigung deutscher Wirtschaftsarchivare e.V. (VdW), Am Bergbaumuseum 28, 44791 Bochum
T: (0234) 5877154; Fax: 5877111
Focus: Archives 06121

Vereinigung für angewandte Botanik, Grisebachstr 6, 37077 Göttingen
T: (0551) 393748; E-Mail: hkoch@gwdg.de; Fax: 393759
Founded: 1902; Members: 300
Pres: Prof. Dr. Reinhard Lieberei; Gen Secr: Prof. Dr. Hans-Jürgen Jäger
Focus: Botany
Periodical
Angewandte Botanik (3 times annually) . 06122

Vereinigung für Bankbetriebsorganisation e.V., Schaumainkai 69, 60596 Frankfurt
T: (069) 625011; Fax: 628631
Focus: Finance
Periodical
vbo-informationen (quarterly) 06123

Vereinigung für Stadt-, Regional- und Landesplanung e.V., Köpenicker Str 48/49, 10179 Berlin
T: (030) 30862060; Fax: 30862062
Founded: 1969; Members: 1880
Pres: Ludwig Krause; Gen Secr: Rainer Bohne
Focus: Urban Plan
Periodical
PlanerIn (quarterly) 06124

Vereinigung Getreide-, Markt- und Ernährungsforschung e.V. (GMF), Kronprinzenstr 51, 53173 Bonn
T: (0228) 355019, 355010; Fax: 356972
Focus: Marketing; Nutrition 06125

Vereinigung katholischer Schulen in Ordenstradition, In den Strubben 11, 49809 Lingen
T: (0591) 4091; Fax: 58075
Focus: Educ 06126

Vereinigung Süddeutscher Orthopäden e.V., Maria-Viktoria-Str 9, 76530 Baden-Baden
Focus: Orthopedics
Periodical
Orthopädische Praxis (monthly) 06127

Vereinigung Südwestdeutscher Dermatologen, c/o Universitäts-Hautklinik, Hauptstr 7, 79104 Freiburg
Focus: Derm 06128

Vereinigung Südwestdeutscher HNO-Ärzte, c/o Prof. Dr. Matzker, Neufelder Str 32, 51067 Köln
Focus: Otorhinolaryngology 06129

Vereinigung Südwestdeutscher Radiologen und Nuklearmediziner (VSRN) (VSRN), c/o Dr. S. Bosnjakovic-Büscher, Radiologische Abteilung, Städt. Krankenhaus Sindelfingen, 71065 Sindelfingen
T: (07031) ??????
Focus: Med; X-Ray Tech; Nucl Med . . 06130

Vereinigung Westdeutscher Hals-, Nasen- und Ohrenärzte, c/o HNO-Klinik, Städtische Krankenanstalten, Neufelder Str 32, 51067 Köln
Founded: 1897; Members: 1370
Focus: Otorhinolaryngology 06131

Vereinigung zur Erforschung der Neueren Geschichte e.V., Argelanderstr 59, 53115 Bonn
T: (0228) 216205
Founded: 1957
Pres: Prof. Dr. Konrad Repgen; Gen Secr: Dr. A. Oschmann
Focus: Hist 06132

Vereinigung zur Förderung der technischen Optik e.V., Ernst-Leitz-Str 30, 35578 Wetzlar
Focus: Optics 06133

Vereinigung zur Förderung des Deutschen Brandschutzes e.V. (VFDB), Postfach 1231, 48338 Altenberge
T: (02505) 2617; Fax: 2468
Founded: 1950; Members: 1727
Pres: Hans Jochen Blätte; Gen Secr: Hanns-Helmuth Spohn
Focus: Eng
Periodicals
vfdb-Zeitschrift: Forschung und Technik im Brandschutz (quarterly)
vfdb-Zeitschrift: Forschung und Technik im Brandschutz (quarterly) 06134

Vereinigung zur Förderung des Instituts für Kunststoffverarbeitung in Industrie und Handwerk an der Rhein.-Westf. Technischen Hochschule Aachen e.V., Pontstr 49, 52062 Aachen
T: (0241) 803806; Fax: 8888262
Founded: 1951; Members: 309
Gen Secr: Prof. Dr. Walter Michaeli
Focus: Materials Sci 06135

Versicherungswissenschaftlicher Verein in Hamburg e.V., Schlüterstr 28, 20146 Hamburg
T: (040) 41232629; Fax: 41236252
Members: 723
Focus: Insurance 06136

Versuchsgrubengesellschaft, Tremoniastr 13, 44137 Dortmund
T: (0231) 9144840; Fax: 91448477
Founded: 1927
Focus: Mining
Periodical
Grubensicherheitliche Kurzberichte (quarterly)
. . . . 06137

Veterinärmedizinischer Fakultätentag, c/o Tierärztl. Hochschule, Bünteweg 2, 30559 Hannover
T: (0511) 9530; Fax: 9538050
Focus: Educ; Vet Med 06138

VGB-Forschungsstiftung / Forschungsstiftung der VGB Technische Vereinigung der Großkraftwerksbetreiber e.V., Klinkestr 27-31, 45136 Essen
T: (0201) 8128216; Fax: 8128345
Founded: 1970
Pres: Prof. Dr. H.-D. Schilling; Gen Secr: Prof. Dr. J. Jacobs
Focus: Eng; Energy
Periodical
VGB-Kraftwerkstechnik (monthly) 06139

Volks- und Betriebswirtschaftliche Vereinigung im Rheinisch-Westfälischen Industriegebiet e.V., Mercatorstr 22-24, 47051 Duisburg
T: (0203) 2821288; Fax: 26533
Founded: 1920; Members: 100
Pres: Hans-Jürgen Reitzig; Gen Secr: Theodor Friedhoff
Focus: Econ; Business Admin 06140

Volkshochschulverband Baden-Württemberg e.V., Raiffeisenstr 14, 70771 Leinfelden-Echterdingen
T: (0711) 759000; Fax: 7590041
Pres: Frieder Birzele; Gen Secr: Dr. Hermann Huba
Focus: Adult Educ 06141

Volkshochschulverband Mecklenburg-Vorpommern e.V., Bertha-von-Suttner-Str 5, 19061 Schwerin
T: (0385) 3031550; Fax: 3031555
Focus: Adult Educ 06142

Volkskundliche Kommission für Westfalen / Landschaftsverband Westfalen-Lippe, Dompl 23, 48143 Münster
T: (0251) 834404; Fax: 838393
Founded: 1928; Members: 40
Focus: Ethnology
Periodical
Rheinisch-Westfälische Zeitschrift für Volkskunde (annually) 06143

Von Recklinghausen-Gesellschaft e.V., Langenhorner Chaussee 560, 22419 Hamburg
T: (040) 52712822; Fax: 5277462
Focus: Med 06144

Weltbund für Erneuerung der Erziehung, Deutschsprachige Sektion (WEE), Keplerstr 87, 69120 Heidelberg
T: (06221) 477502
Founded: 1920
Focus: Educ
Periodical
Forum Pädagogik (quarterly) 06145

Werkgemeinschaft Musik e.V., Carl-Mosterts-Pl 1, 40477 Düsseldorf
T: (0211) 4693191; Fax: 4693159
Focus: Music 06146

West- und Süddeutscher Verband für Altertumsforschung, Schillerstr 11, 55116 Mainz
T: (06131) 392667; Fax: 393227
Founded: 1900; Members: 140
Focus: Archeol 06147

Westdeutsche Gesellschaft für Familienkunde e.V. (WGfF), Wallstr 96, 51063 Köln
T: (0221) 628512
Founded: 1913; Members: 800
Focus: Genealogy
Periodical
Mitteilungen (quarterly) 06148

Westdeutscher Medizinischer Fakultätentag (WMFT), Schillerstr 25, 91054 Erlangen
Founded: 1913; Members: 29
Focus: Med; Adult Educ 06149

Westfälische Gesellschaft für Zahn-, Mund- und Kieferheilkunde, Waldeyerstr 30, 48149 Münster
T: (0251) 8347084; Fax: 8347083
Founded: 1957; Members: 300
Pres: Dr. Dr. Ludger Figgener
Focus: Dent 06150

Wilhelm-Busch-Gesellschaft e.V., Georgengarten 1, 30167 Hannover
T: (0511) 714076/77; Fax: 7011222
Founded: 1930; Members: 3600
Pres: Prof. Dr. Dr. Hinrich Seidel; Gen Secr: Dr. Hans Joachim Neyer
Focus: Graphic & Dec Arts, Design
Periodical
Wilhelm-Busch-Jahrbuch (annually) . . . 06151

William-Stern-Gesellschaft für Begabungsförderung Begabtenförderung e.V. (WSG), Von-Melle-Park 8, 20146 Hamburg
T: (040) 41235465/66; Fax: 41235492
Focus: Educ 06152

Willibald Pirckheimer Gesellschaft zur Erforschung von Renaissance und Humanismus e.V., c/o Institut für Buchwesen, Saarstr 21, 55122 Mainz
T: (06131) 392580; Fax: 395487
Focus: Lit 06153

Wirtschafts- und Sozialwissenschaftlicher Fakultätentag (WISOFT), Schloß, 68131 Mannheim
T: (0621) 2925684; Fax: 2923331
Focus: Educ; Econ; Sociology 06154

Wirtschaftsakademie für Lehrer e.V., Hindenburgring 12a, 38667 Bad Harzburg
T: (05322) 730
Founded: 1959
Focus: Econ 06155

Wirtschaftspolitische Gesellschaft von 1947 e.V., Myliusstr 27, 60323 Frankfurt/Main
T: (069) 723254
Founded: 1947
Focus: Poli Sci
Periodical
Offene Welt (irregularly) 06156

Wissenschaftliche Gesellschaft an der Johann Wolfgang Goethe-Universität Frankfurt am Main, Postfach 111932, 60054 Frankfurt
T: (069) 79822139
Founded: 1906; Members: 80
Pres: Prof. Dr. Werner Thomas
Focus: Sci
Periodical
Sitzungsberichte, Frankfurter Wissenschaftliche Beiträge (irregularly) 06157

Wissenschaftliche Gesellschaft für Europarecht, c/o Universität Trier, Postfach 3825, 54296 Trier
T: (0651) 2012512
Founded: 1962; Members: 480
Focus: Law
Periodical
Europarecht (quarterly) 06158

Wissenschaftliche Gesellschaft für Theologie e.V., Liebermeisterstr 12, 72076 Tübingen
T: (07071) 2972591; E-Mail: eilert.herms@uni-tuebingen.de; Fax: 295415
Founded: 1973; Members: 620
Pres: Prof. Dr. Eilert Herms
Focus: Rel & Theol 06159

Wissenschaftliche Vereinigung für Augenoptik und Optometrie e.V. (WVAO), Adam-Karrillon-Str 32, 55118 Mainz
T: (06131) 613061; Fax: 614872
Founded: 1949; Members: 2500
Pres: Malte Volz; Gen Secr: Hartmut Glaser
Focus: Ophthal; Optics
Periodical
Optometrie (quarterly) 06160

Wissenschaftlicher Verein für Verkehrswesen e.V. (WVV), Postfach 500500, 44221 Dortmund
T: (0231) 7552270; Fax: 751532
Founded: 1971; Members: 165
Focus: Transport 06161

Wissenschaftliches Forum für internationale Sicherheit e.V. (WIFIS), Blomkamp 61, 22549 Hamburg
T: (040) 8005416; Fax: 8005688
Focus: Prom Peace 06162

Wissenschaftsförderung der Sparkassenorganisation e.V., Simrockstr 4, 53113 Bonn
T: (0228) 204241; Fax: 204705
Founded: 1955; Members: 572
Pres: Dr. H. Berndt; Gen Secr: Dr. E. Ketzel
Focus: Finance 06163

Wissenschaftsforum Berlin, Jägerstr 22-23, 10117 Berlin
T: (030) 20370366; Fax: 20370680
Focus: Sci 06164

Wissenschaftsgemeinschaft Blaue Liste e.V. (WBL), Ahrstr 45, 53175 Bonn
T: (0228) 308150; Fax: 3081555
Focus: Sci 06165

Wissenschaftskolleg zu Berlin e.V., Wallotstr 19, 14193 Berlin
T: (030) 890010; Fax: 89001300
Focus: Sci 06166

Wissenschaftsrat, Brohlerstr 11, 50968 Köln
T: (0221) 37760; E-Mail: post@wrat.de; Fax: 388440
Founded: 1957
Pres: Prof. Dr. Dagmar Schipanski; Gen Secr: Dr. Winfried Benz
Focus: Sci
Periodical
Empfehlungen und Stellungnahmen (annually) 06167

Wissenschaftszentrum – Gemeinsame Dienste e.V., Ahrstr 45, 53175 Bonn
T: (0228) 3020; Fax: 302270
Focus: Sci 06168

Wissenschaftszentrum Nordrhein-Westfalen, Reichsstr 45, 40217 Düsseldorf
T: (0211) 387900; Fax: 37058
Focus: Sci 06169

Wittheit zu Bremen e.V., Baumwollbörse, Zimmer 334, 28195 Bremen
T: (0421) 323347; Fax: 327019
Founded: 1924; Members: 150
Pres: Dr. Martina Rudloff
Focus: Sci 06170

Wolfram von Eschenbach-Gesellschaft e.V., Rebdorferstr 90c, 85072 Eichstätt
T: (08421) 8631
Focus: Lit 06171

World Veterinary Poultry Association (W.V.P.A.), c/o Prof. Dr. E.F. Kaleta, Institut für Geflügelkrankheiten, Justus-Liebig-Universität, Frankfurter Str 87, 35392 Giessen
T: (0641) 9938430; E-Mail: erhard.f.kaleta@vetmed.uni-giessen.de; Fax: 201548
Founded: 1960; Members: 1500
Pres: Dr. L.N. Payne; Gen Secr: Prof. Dr. E.F. Kaleta
Focus: Vet Med 06172

Württembergische Bibliotheksgesellschaft, Vereinigung der Freunde der Landesbibliothek, Postfach 105441, 70047 Stuttgart
T: (0711) 2124428; Fax: 2124422
Founded: 1946; Members: 500
Pres: Dr. Wulf von Lucius
Focus: Libraries & Bk Sci 06173

Wuppertaler Kreis e.V. / Deutsche Vereinigung zur Förderung der Weiterbildung von Führungskräften, Gustav-Heinemann-Ufer 84-88, 50968 Köln
T: (0221) 372018; E-Mail: Wuppertaler.Kreis@t-online.de; Fax: 385952
Founded: 1954; Members: 49
Pres: Helmut G. Düsterloh; Gen Secr: Carsten R. Löwe
Focus: Adult Educ; Business Admin . . 06174

Zahnärztekammer Berlin, Stallstr 1, 10585 Berlin
T: (030) 348080
Focus: Dent 06175

Zahnärztekammer Bremen, Emmastr 220, 28213 Bremen
T: (0421) 211035/39
Focus: Dent 06176

Zahnärztekammer Hamburg, Möllner Landstr 31, 22111 Hamburg
T: (040) 7334050; Fax: 7325828
Focus: Dent
Periodical
Hamburger Zahnärzteblatt (monthly) . . . 06177

Zahnärztekammer Niedersachsen, Hildesheimer Str 35, 30169 Hannover
T: (0511) 853085
Focus: Dent
Periodical
Niedersächsisches Zahnärzteblatt (monthly) 06178

Zahnärztekammer Nordrhein, Emanuel-Leutze-Str 8, 40547 Düsseldorf
T: (0211) 526050; Fax: 5260521
Pres: Dr. Joachim Schulz-Bongert
Focus: Dent
Periodical
Rheinisches Zahnärzteblatt (monthly) . . 06179

Zahnärztekammer Schleswig-Holstein, Westring 498, 24106 Kiel
T: (0431) 3897200; Fax: 3897210
Focus: Dent
Periodical
Mitteilungsblatt (8 times annually) . . . 06180

Zahnärztekammer Westfalen-Lippe, Auf der Horst 29, 48147 Münster
T: (0251) 490902; Fax: 4909117
Founded: 1954
Focus: Dent
Periodical
Zahnärzteblatt Westfalen-Lippe (bi-monthly) 06181

Zentralausschuss für Deutsche Landeskunde e.V., Postfach 111932, 60054 Frankfurt
T: (069) 7982404
Founded: 1882
Focus: Geography
Periodicals
Berichte zur deutschen Landeskunde (semi-annually)
Deutsche Landschaften: Landeskundliche Erläuterungen zur Topographischen Karte 1:50000 (irregularly)
Forschungen zur deutschen Landeskunde (1-2 times annually)
Schrifttumsberichte zur deutschen Landeskunde (irregularly) 06182

Zentralinstitut für Kunstgeschichte, Meiserstr 10, 80333 München
T: (089) 5591547; Fax: 5504352
Founded: 1946
Focus: Cultur Hist
Periodical
Kunstchronik (monthly) 06183

Zentralstelle für Agrardokumentation und -information (ZADI), Villichgasse 17, 53177 Bonn
T: (0228) 95480; E-Mail: zadi@zadi.de; Fax: 9548149
Founded: 1969
Gen Secr: Dr. Jan Mark Pohlmann
Focus: Agri; Doc; Ecology 06184

Zentralstelle für Berufsbildung im Einzelhandel e.V. (zbb), Gothaer Allee 2, 50969 Köln
T: (0221) 9365502; Fax: 93655819
Focus: Educ; Commerce 06185

Zentralstelle für Pilzforschung und Pilzverwertung, Breslauer Str 3, 68753 Waghäusel
T: (07254) 74271
Founded: 1951
Focus: Botany, Specific 06186

Zentrum Bundesrepublik Deutschland des Internationalen Theater-Instituts e.V. (ITI), Schloßstr 48, 12165 Berlin
T: (030) 7911777; Fax: 7911874
Focus: Perf Arts 06187

Zentrum für Türkeistudien e.V. (ZfT), Overbergstr 27, 45141 Essen
T: (0201) 311041/42; Fax: 311043
Focus: Ethnology 06188

Zoologische Gesellschaft Frankfurt von 1858 e.V. (ZGF), Alfred-Brehm-Pl 16, 60316 Frankfurt/Main
T: (069) 21234410; Fax: 439348
Focus: Zoology 06189

Ghana

All Africa Teachers' Organization (AATO), POB 7431, Accra
T: (021) 221515
Founded: 1974
Focus: Educ
Periodical
All Africa Teachers' Organization Newsletter (quarterly) 06190

Arts Council of Ghana, POB 2738, Accra
T: (021) 64099
Founded: 1958
Focus: Arts 06191

Association of African Universities (AAU) / Association des Universités Africaines, POB 5744, Accra
T: (021) 663281; Fax: 664293
Founded: 1987; Members: 95
Focus: Educ
Periodical
AAU Newsletter (3 times annually) . . . 06192

Council for Scientific and Industrial Research (CSIR), POB M32, Accra
T: (021) 777651; Fax: 777655
Founded: 1958
Focus: Sci; Eng
Periodicals
Annual Report (annually)
CSIR Handbook
Ghana Journal of Agricultural Science
Ghana Journal of Science 06193

Economic Society of Ghana, POB 57, Legon, Accra
Founded: 1957; Members: 500
Focus: Econ
Periodicals
Economic Bulletin of Ghana
Social and Economic Affairs (quarterly) . 06194

Geological Survey of Ghana, POB M80, Accra
T: (021) 228093
Founded: 1913
Gen Secr: G.O. Kesse
Focus: Geology
Periodical
Annual Report (annually) 06195

Ghana Academy of Arts and Sciences, POB M32, Accra
T: (021) 777651; Fax: 777655
Founded: 1959; Members: 73
Pres: Prof. D.A. Bekoe; Gen Secr: Prof. E.V. Doku
Focus: Arts; Sci
Periodicals
J.B. Danquah Memorial Lectures (annually)
Proceedings (annually) 06196

Ghana Association of Writers, POB 4414, Accra
Founded: 1957
Pres: A. Okai; Gen Secr: J.E. Allotey-Pappoe
Focus: Lit
Periodicals
Angla (annually)
Takra (monthly) 06197

Ghana Bar Association, POB 4150, Accra
T: (021) 226748
Pres: N. Kyenyehia; Gen Secr: Paul Adu-Gymafi
Focus: Law 06198

Ghana Geographical Association (G.G.A.), c/o Dept of Geography, University, Accra
Founded: 1955
Pres: Prof. E.V.T. Engmann; Gen Secr: Dr. J.L. Gyamfi-Fenteng
Focus: Geography
Periodical
Bulletin (annually) 06199

Ghana Institute of Architects, POB M272, Accra
T: (021) 75676
Founded: 1962; Members: 203
Pres: E.L. Akita; Gen Secr: H.D.L. Yartey
Focus: Archit 06200

Ghana Institution of Engineers, POB 7042, North, Accra
T: (021) 772005
Founded: 1968; Members: 1000
Pres: K. Ofori-Kurago
Focus: Eng 06201

Ghana Library Association, POB 4105, Accra
T: (021) 668731
Founded: 1962
Pres: E.S. Asiedu; Gen Secr: A.W.K. Insaidoo
Focus: Libraries & Bk Sci
Periodical
Ghana Library Journal (irregularly) . . . 06202

Ghana Science Association, POB 7, Legon, Accra
Founded: 1959
Pres: Prof. Aba B. Andam; Gen Secr: Dr. A.B.C. Dadson
Focus: Sci
Periodical
The Ghana Journal of Science 06203

Ghana Sociological Association, c/o Dept of Sociology, University of Ghana, Legon, Accra
Founded: 1961; Members: 215
Pres: Prof. J.M. Assimeng; Gen Secr: E.H. Mends
Focus: Sociology
Periodical
Ghana Journal of Sociology 06204

Historical Society of Ghana, POB 12, Legon, Accra
Founded: 1952; Members: 600
Pres: T.A. Osae; Gen Secr: R. Addo-Fening
Focus: Hist
Periodicals
Transactions (semi-annually)
West African Journal for History Teachers (annually) 06205

Pharmaceutical Society of Ghana, POB 2133, Accra
Founded: 1939; Members: 900
Pres: David Anim Addo; Gen Secr: Czarina Ribeiro
Focus: Pharmacol 06206

West African Examinations Council (WAEC), POB 125, Accra
T: (021) 221511; Fax: 222905
Founded: 1952
Pres: Prof. J.A. kamara
Focus: Educ
Periodicals
Annual Report (annually)
WAEC News (quarterly) 06207

West African Science Association, c/o Botany Dept, University of Ghana, POB 7, Legon, Accra
Founded: 1953; Members: 7
Pres: Prof. André Dovi Kuevi; Gen Secr: Dr. J.K.B.A. Ata
Focus: Sci
Periodical
Journal (annually) 06208

Gibraltar

Gibraltar Ornithological and Natural History Society, c/o Gibraltar Natural History Field Centre, Jew's Gate, Upper Rock Nature Reserve, POB 843, Gibraltar
T: 72639, 74022; E-Mail: gonhs@gibnet.gi; Fax: 74022
Founded: 1978; Members: 231
Gen Secr: J.E. Cortes
Focus: Ornithology; Botany
Periodicals
Alectoris (annually)
Gibraltar Nature News (bi-annually)
Strait of Gibraltar Bird Observation Report (bi-annually) 06209

Gibraltar Teachers' Association (GTA), 40 Town Range, Gibraltar
T: 76308; Fax: 76308
Founded: 1962; Members: 300
Pres: B. Gonzalez; Gen Secr: F. Ferro
Focus: Educ 06210

Greece

Akadimia Athinon, Panepistimiou 28, Athinai
T: (01) 3614552
Founded: 1926; Members: 211
Pres: M. Manoussakas; Gen Secr: P. Sakellaridis
Focus: Sci
Periodicals
Mnimeia Ellinikis Historias: Documents of Greek History
Pragmateiai: Papers
Praktika tes Akademias Athinon: Proceedings (annually) 06211

Archaeologiki Hetairia / Archaeological Society of Athens, Panepistimiou 22, 10672 Athinai
T: (01) 3609689; Fax: 3644996
Founded: 1837; Members: 498
Pres: George Dontas; Gen Secr: Basil Petrakos
Focus: Archeol
Periodicals
Archaeologiki Ephimeris (annually)
Ergon (annually)
O Mentor (quarterly)
Praktika (annually) 06212

Constantine Porphyrogenetus / Planning and Regional Development Studies Association, 1 Smirnis St, 15772 Zografou
T: (01) 6123631; Fax: 6123631
Pres: Prof. John Karkazis
Focus: Urban Plan 06213

Elliniki Anaisthisiologiki Etaireia, Ionos Dragoumi 34, Athinai
T: (01) 7242566
Members: 205
Focus: Anesthetics
Periodical
Acta Anaesthisiologica Hellenica (quarterly) 06214

Elliniki Astronautiki Etaireia, Voulis 14, Athinai
T: (01) 3227666
Founded: 1957; Members: 75
Focus: Aero 06215

Elliniki Cheirourgiki Etaireia, Papadiamantopoulou 150, Athinai
T: (01) 7701813
Members: 300
Focus: Surgery 06216

Elliniki Etaireia Orologias / Hellenic Society for Terminology, S. Tsakona 5, 15236 Penteli
T: (01) 8042313; Fax: 8068299
Founded: 1992; Members: 180
Pres: V.A. Filopoulos; Gen Secr: K. Valeontis
Focus: Standards 06217

Elliniki Geografiki Etaireia / Hellenic Geographical Society, Voucourestiou 11, 10671 Athinai
T: (01) 3631112
Founded: 1919; Members: 148
Pres: Dimitrios Dimitriades; Gen Secr: George S. Ivantchos
Focus: Geography
Periodical
Bulletin 06218

Elliniki Kardiologiki Etairia, Sisini 17, 11528 Athinai
T: (01) 7221633; Fax: 7226139
Focus: Cardiol
Periodical
Hellenic Cardiological Review (quarterly) . 06219

Elliniki Ktiniatriki Eteria / Hellenic Veterinary Medical Society, Kentrikon Tachydromeion, POB 3546, 10210 Athinai
T: (01) 5241189; Fax: 5241189
Founded: 1924; Members: 830
Pres: Dr. T. Ananiadis; Gen Secr: Dr. Vasilios Kontos
Focus: Vet Med
Periodical
Bulletin of the Hellenic Veterinary Medical Society (quarterly) 06220

Elliniki Laographiki Etaireia, Didotou 12, Athinai
T: (01) 633110
Focus: Ethnology 06221

Elliniki Mathimatiki Eteria (H.M.E.), Odos Panepistimiou 34, 10679 Athinai
T: (01) 3616532; Fax: 3641025
Founded: 1918; Members: 13000
Pres: Prof. N. Alexandris; Gen Secr: C.G. Salaris
Focus: Math
Periodicals
Bulletin
Enimerossi (quarterly)
Euclides (5 times annually)
Mathematical Review 06222

Elliniki Microbiologiki Etaireia, c/o Dept of Microbiology, Univeristy, POB 1540, Athinai
T: (01) 7785638
Founded: 1947; Members: 1330
Focus: Microbio 06223

Elliniki Nomismatiki Etaireia / Hellenic Numismatic Society, Didotou 45, 10680 Athinai
T: (01) 3615585; Fax: 3634296
Founded: 1970; Members: 350
Pres: Anastasios P. Tzamalis; Gen Secr: Panos Tazedakis
Focus: Numismatics
Periodical
Numismatika Khronika (annually) 06224

Elliniki Paidiatriki Etairia, Hippokratous 65, POB 1519, Athinai
T: (01) 3638602
Focus: Pediatrics 06225

Elliniki Pharmakeutiki Etaireia, Emm. Benakis 30, 10678 Athinai
T: (01) 3609108
Founded: 1932; Members: 550
Focus: Pharmacol
Periodical
Archeia tis Pharmakeftikis (bi-monthly) . . 06226

Elliniki Spilaiologiki Etaireia, Spilaiologiki Etaireia, Athinai
T: (01) 617824
Focus: Speleology 06227

Ellinikon Kentron Paragogikotitos, Kapodistriou 28, Athinai
T: (01) 3600411
Founded: 1953
Focus: Business Admin 06228

Ellinikos Organismos Tipopoiisis (ELOT) / Hellenic Organization for Standardization, Acharnon 313, 11145 Athinai
T: (01) 2280001; E-Mail: prds@elot.gr; Fax: 2283034
Founded: 1976; Members: 110
Pres: G. Varoufakis; Gen Secr: P. Theofalopoulos
Focus: Standards
Periodical
Catalogue of Hellenic Standards (annually) 06229

Enosis Ellinon Bibliothekarion / Greek Library Association, Skouleniou 4, 10561 Athinai
T: (01) 3226625; Fax: 3226625
Founded: 1968; Members: 1000
Pres: K. Xatzopoulos; Gen Secr: A. Salomou
Focus: Libraries & Bk Sci
Periodical
Bibliothikes kai Plicophocis: Bibliothèques et information (irregularly) 06230

Enosis Ellinon Chimikon / Association of Greek Chemists, Odos Kaningos 27, 10682 Athinai
T: (01) 3621524
Founded: 1924; Members: 5000
Pres: P. Hamakiotis; Gen Secr: D. Psomas
Focus: Chem
Periodical
Chimika Chronika 06231

Enosis Ellinon Physikon, Grivaion 6, Athinai
T: (01) 3635701
Founded: 1930; Members: 1500
Focus: Physics 06232

Enosis Hellinon Mousourgon / League of Greek Composers, Odos Mitropoleos 38, Athinai
T: (01) 3223302; Fax: 3223302
Founded: 1931; Members: 135
Pres: Theodoros Antoniou; Gen Secr: Georgios Koucoupos
Focus: Music 06233

Epimelitirion Ikastikon Technon Ellados, Odos Nikis 11, 10557 Athinai
T: (01) 3231230; Fax: 3240296
Founded: 1945; Members: 2120
Pres: Yannis Gourzis
Focus: Eng 06234

Etaireia Byzantinon Spoudon / Society for Byzantine Studies, Odos Aristeidou 8, 10559 Athinai
Founded: 1919; Members: 250
Pres: A. Orlandos; Gen Secr: N.B. Tomadakis
Focus: Cultur Hist
Periodical
Epetiris Etairias Byzantinin Spoudon: EEBS (annually) 06235

Etaireia Makedonikon Spoudon (EMS) / Society for Macedonian Studies, Ethnikis Amynis 4, 54621 Thessaloniki
T: (031) 271195, 270343; Fax: 271501
Founded: 1939; Members: 508
Focus: Hist
Periodicals
Ellinika: Classical studies (semi-annually)
Makedonika: History, Folklore, Archaeology of North Greece (annually) 06236

Etaireia Odontostomatologikis Ereunis, M. Asias 70, 11527 Athinai
T: (01) 7780671
Founded: 1948; Members: 70
Focus: Dent; Stomatology
Periodical
Odontostomatological Progress (bi-monthly) 06237

European Institute of Environmental Cybernetics, Agias Sophias 81, 16232 Athinai
T: (01) 7628676; Fax: 7628675
Founded: 1970
Pres: C.K. Cyrilov
Focus: Cybernetics; Med; Ecology . . . 06238

Greek National Committee for Astronomy, c/o Akademia Athinon, Odos Anagnostopoulou 14, 10673 Athinai
Fax: (01) 3631606
Focus: Astronomy 06239

Greek National Committee for Space Research, c/o Akademia Athinon, Odos Anagnostopoulon 14, 10673 Athinai
Fax: (01) 3631606
Focus: Astronomy 06240

Hellenic Association of University Women, Voulis 44a, 10557 Athinai
Pres: Irene Dilari; Gen Secr: Flora Kamari
Focus: Adult Educ 06241

Hellenic Institute of International and Foreign Law, Solonos 73, 10679 Athinai
Fax: (01) 3619777
Founded: 1939
Focus: Int'l Relat; Law
Periodical
Revue Hellénique de Droit International (annually) 06242

Helliniki Epitropi Atomikis Energhias / Greek Atomic Energy Commission, Aghia Paraskevi, POB 60092, 15310 Athinai
T: (01) 6515194; Fax: 6533939
Founded: 1954
Pres: Anastasios Katsanos
Focus: Nucl Res 06243

Hetaireia Hellenon Philologon / Society of Greek Philologists, POB 3373, 10210 Athinai
Fax: (01) 3213363
Founded: 1948; Members: 1900
Pres: Prof. N. Livadaras; Gen Secr: Prof. Georgia Xanthaki-Karamanou
Focus: Ling; Lit; Hist
Periodical
Platon (annually) 06244

Hetairia Hellinon Logotechnon / Society of Greek Men of Letters, Gennadiou 8, 10678 Athinai
T: (01) 3634559
Founded: 1934; Members: 700
Pres: Ilias Simopoulos; Gen Secr: Panos Panagiotounis
Focus: Lit 06245

Hetairia Hellinon Thetricon Syngrapheon / Greek Playwrights' Association, Asklipiou 33, 10680 Athinai
Fax: (01) 3614219
Founded: 1908; Members: 120
Pres: Dimitri Ioannopoulos; Gen Secr: Dimitri Yanoukakis
Focus: Lit 06246

Istoriki kai Ethnologiki Etaireia tis Ellados / Historical and Ethnological Society of Greece, Old Parliament, Stadiou, Athinai
T: (01) 3226370
Founded: 1882
Pres: Dimitrios A. Gerondas; Gen Secr: V.C. Mazarakis-Aenian
Focus: Ethnology; Hist
Periodical
Bulletin (annually) 06247

Kallitechnikon Epimelitirion Ellados (K.E.E.), Mitropoleos 38, Athinai
T: (01) 3231230
Founded: 1944; Members: 1100
Focus: Arts 06248

Omospondia Didaskaliki Ellados, Xenofontos 15a, Athinai
T: (01) 3236547
Members: 15000
Focus: Educ 06249

Omospondia Panellinios Syndesmon Dasoponon, Veranzerou 42, Athinai
T: (01) 5237512
Focus: Forestry 06250

Panellinios Enosis Technikon (PET), Vranzerou 34, Athinai
T: (01) 5233756
Founded: 1957; Members: 6500
Focus: Eng 06251

Panellinios Omospondia Syndesmon Geoponon, L. Katsoni 12, Athinai
T: (01) 6467516
Focus: Agri 06252

PEN Centre, Skoufa 60a, Athinai
Focus: Lit 06253

Syllogos Architktonon Diplomatouchon Anotaton Scholon (SADAS), Ipitou 3, Athinai
T: (01) 3236431
Founded: 1922; Members: 2100
Focus: Archit 06254

Syllogos pros Diadosin ton Hellenikon Grammaton / Society for the Promotion of Greek Education, Odos Pindarou 15, Athinai
T: (01) 3612370
Founded: 1869; Members: 9
Pres: Philip Dragoumis; Gen Secr: A. Panayotis
Focus: Educ 06255

World Society for Ekistics (W.S.E.), Strat. Syndesmou 24, 10673 Athinai
T: (01) 3623216, 3623373; Fax: 3629337
Founded: 1965; Members: 250
Pres: Charles Correa; Gen Secr: P. Psomopoulos
Focus: Anthro; Sociology; Urban Plan; Archit 06256

Grenada

Grenada National Trust and Historical Society, c/o Grenada National Museum, Young St, Saint George's
T: 4403725
Founded: 1967; Members: 240
Pres: Paul Finlay; Gen Secr: Jean Pitt
Focus: Hist 06257

Guatemala

Academia de Ciencias Médicas, Físicas y Naturales de Guatemala, 13 Calle 1-25, Zona 1, Apdo 569, Guatemala City
Founded: 1945; Members: 125
Pres: Dr. Roberto Lembke; Gen Secr: Carlos Rolz Asturias
Focus: Med; Nat Sci; Physics
Periodical
Annals (irregularly) 06258

Academia de Geografía e Historia de Guatemala (AGHG), 3a Av 8-35, Zona 1, Guatemala City
T: (02) 535141
Founded: 1923; Members: 45
Pres: Ana María Urruela de Quezada; Gen Secr: Ramiro Ordoñez Jonama
Focus: Geography; Hist
Periodical
Anales de la Academia de Geografía e Historia (annually) 06259

Academia de la Lengua Maya Quiché, 7a Calle 11-27, Zona 1, Quezaltenango
Founded: 1959; Members: 20
Pres: Prof. Adrián Ines Chávez; Gen Secr: Prof. Víctor Salvador de León Toledo
Focus: Ling
Periodical
El Idioma Quiché y su Grafía 06260

Academia Guatemalteca de la Lengua, 12 Calle 6-60, Zona 9, Guatemala City
T: (02) 322824
Founded: 1887
Pres: David Vela; Gen Secr: Mario Alberto Carrera
Focus: Sci
Periodical
Boletín 06261

Asociación Bibliotecológica Guatemalteca, c/o Biblioteca Nacional, 5a Av 7-26, Zona 1, Guatemala City
Founded: 1969
Focus: Libraries & Bk Sci 06262

Asociación de Ortodoncistas de Guatemala, 13 Calle 3-43, Zona 10, Guatemala City
Founded: 1946
Focus: Dent 06263

Asociación Guatemalteca de Historia Natural (AGHN), c/o Jardín Botánico, Universidad de San Carlos, Mariscal Cruz 1-56, Zona 10, Guatemala City
Founded: 1960; Members: 86
Pres: Dr. Mario Sary Rivera
Focus: Nat Sci; Hist 06264

Asociacion Latinoamericana de Escuelas de Cirurgía Dental, Av las Américas 21-69, Zona 10, Guatemala City
Founded: 1946
Focus: Dent 06265

Asociación Pediátrica de Guatemala, 12 Av 12-72, Zona 1, Guatemala City
Founded: 1945
Focus: Pediatrics 06266

Center for Meso American Studies on Appropriate Technology, 1a Av 32-21, Zona 12, Apdo 1160, Guatemala City
T: (02) 762018; E-Mail: (02) 762355
Founded: 1976
Focus: Eng
Periodical
Boletín RED (quarterly) 06267

Central American Research Institute for Industry, Av La Reforma 4-47, Zona 10, Apdo 1552, Guatemala City
T: (02) 310631; Fax: 317466
Founded: 1956; Members: 6
Focus: Econ
Periodical
Revista ICAITI 06268

Colegio de Ingenieros de Guatemala, 7 Av 39-60, Zona 8, Guatemala City
Founded: 1947; Members: 1342
Pres: Carlos Gerardo Bran Guzmán
Focus: Eng 06269

Federación de Universidades Privadas de América Central (FUPAC), c/o Universidad Rafael Landivar, Apdo 1273, Guatemala City
Founded: 1966
Focus: Sci 06270

Instituto Centroamericano de Investigación y Tecnología (ICAITI), Av La Reforma 4-47, Zona 10, Apdo 1552, Guatemala City
E-Mail: ICAITI
Founded: 1956
Focus: Eng 06271

Sociedad Centroamericana de Dermatologia, 4a Av 1-56, Zona 1, Guatemala City
Founded: 1957
Focus: Derm 06272

Sociedad Pro-Arte Musical, 12 Calle 2-09, Zona 3, Apdo 980, Guatemala City
Founded: 1945; Members: 200
Focus: Music 06273

Guinea

PEN Centre de Guinée, BP 440, Conakry
T: 441475
Founded: 1989; Members: 32
Pres: A. Fanye; Gen Secr: Roger Gotto Zomou
Focus: Lit
Periodical
Pour Mémoire 06274

Guyana

Adult Education Association of Guyana, POB 101111, Georgetown
T: (02) 50757
Founded: 1957
Pres: Adola Grandsoult; Gen Secr: Newton L. Profitt
Focus: Adult Educ 06275

Guyana Institute of International Affairs, POB 101176, Georgetown
T: (02) 77768; Fax: 77768
Founded: 1965; Members: 100
Pres: Donald A.B. Trotman
Focus: Poli Sci
Periodical
Annual Journal of International Affairs (irregularly) 06276

Guyana Library Association (GLA), c/o National Library, 76-77 Main St, POB 10240, Georgetown
T: (02) 62690
Founded: 1968; Members: 48
Pres: Hetty London; Gen Secr: Jean Harripersaud
Focus: Libraries & Bk Sci
Periodical
Guyana Library Association Bulletin (semi-annually) 06277

Pan-American Health Organization – Guyana Office, Lot 8, Brickdam, Stabroek, POB 10960, Georgetown
T: (02) 53000; Fax: 66654
Founded: 1949
Gen Secr: Peter R. Carr
Focus: Public Health 06278

Haiti

Conseil National des Recherches Scientifiques, c/o Département de la Santé Publique et de la Population, Port-au-Prince
Founded: 1963
Pres: Prof. Victor Noel; Gen Secr: M. Douyon
Focus: Sci 06279

Honduras

Academia Hondureña, Apdo 38, Tegucigalpa
Founded: 1949; Members: 28
Pres: Miguel R. Ortega; Gen Secr: Jorge Fidel Durón
Focus: Sci
Periodical
Boletín 06280

Academia Hondureña de Geografía e Historia, Apdo 619, Tegucigalpa
Founded: 1968; Members: 21
Pres: Dr. Ramón E. Cruz; Gen Secr: Fernando Ferrari Bustillo
Focus: Geography; Hist
Periodical
Revista 06281

Asociación de Bibliotecarios y Archiveros de Honduras (ABAH), 11a Calle, 1a y 2a Av 105, Comayagüela, Tegucigalpa
Founded: 1951; Members: 53
Pres: Francisca de Escoto Espinoza
Focus: Libraries & Bk Sci; Archives . . 06282

Colegio de Arquitectos de Honduras, Apdo 1974, Tegucigalpa
T: 334768
Founded: 1979; Members: 140
Focus: Med 06283

Hungary

Bör-, Cipö-, és Börfeldolgozóipari Tudományos Egyesület / Scientific Society of the Leather, Shoe and Allied Industries, Fö utca 68, 1027 Budapest
T: (01) 2020182; Fax: 2020182
Founded: 1930
Pres: Dr. T. Karnitscher
Focus: Materials Sci
Periodical
Bör és Cipötechnika: Leather and Shoemaking 06284

Bólyai János Matematikai Társulat / János Bolyai Mathematical Society, Fö utca 68, 1027 Budapest
T: (01) 2017656; Fax: 2016974
Founded: 1891; Members: 1850
Pres: András Hajnal
Focus: Math
Periodicals
A Matematika Tanitása
Combinatorica
Középiskolai Matematikai Lapok
Matematikai Lapok
Periodica Mathematica Hungarica 06285

Energiagazdálkodási Tudományos Egyesület (ETE), Kossuth Lajos tér 6-8, 1055 Budapest
T: (01) 1532751; Fax: 1533894
Founded: 1949; Members: 4300
Pres: Dr. T. Zettner; Gen Secr: G. Wiegand
Focus: Energy
Periodicals
Energia és Atomtechnika (bi-monthly)
Energiagazdálkodás (monthly) 06286

Eötvös Loránd Fizikai Társulat / Roland Eötvös Physical Society, Fö utca 68, 1027 Budapest
T: (01) 2068182; Fax: 2068182
Founded: 1891; Members: 1180
Pres: Prof. György Marx; Gen Secr: Prof. D.J. Nagy
Focus: Physics
Periodical
Fizikai Szemle (monthly) 06287

Epitéstudományi Egyesület / Scientific Society for Building, Fö utca 68, 1027 Budapest
T: (01) 2018416; Fax: 1561215
Founded: 1949; Members: 3400
Pres: Dr. Celesztia Meszléry; Gen Secr: Pál Seeuger
Focus: Civil Eng; Archit
Periodicals
Magyar Epitöipar: Hungarian Building Industry (monthly)
Magyar Epületgépészet: Sanitary Engeneering (monthly) 06288

Faipari Tudományos Egyesület / Scientific Society of the Timber Industry, Fö utca 68, 1027 Budapest
T: (01) 2019929
Founded: 1950; Members: 1800
Pres: Dr. Sándor Molnár
Focus: Eng
Periodical
Faipar 06289

Gépipari Tudományos Egyesület (GTE) / Scientific Society of Mechanical Engineers, Fö utca 68, 1027 Budapest
T: (01) 2020582; Fax: 2020252
Founded: 1949; Members: 11000
Pres: Dr. J. Rittinger
Focus: Eng
Periodicals
Gép: Machine
Gépgyártástechnológia: Manufacturing Processes
Gépipar: Machine Industry
Jármüvek, Epitöipari és Mezögazdasági Gépek: Vehicles, Building and Agricultural Machines
Müanyag és Gumi: Plastics and Rubber 06290

Hiradástechnikai Tudományos Egyesület / Scientific Society for Telecommunication, Kossuth Lajos tér 6-8, 1055 Budapest
T: (01) 1531027; E-Mail: hiradastechnika@mtesz.hu; Fax: 1530451
Founded: 1949; Members: 3000
Pres: Dr. László Pap; Gen Secr: Gábor Huszty
Focus: Electric Eng
Periodicals
Híradástechnika: Telecommunication (monthly)
Hírlevél: Newsletter (monthly) 06291

John von Neumann Computer Society, Báthory utca 16, 1054 Budapest
T: (01) 3329390; E-Mail: h10339tit@ella.hu; Fax: 1318140
Founded: 1968; Members: 3600
Pres: Prof. D. Sima; Gen Secr: I. Alföldi
Focus: Computer & Info Sci 06292

Károlyi Mihály Társaság, Mihály utca 16, 1053 Budapest
T: (01) 1173611
Founded: 1988; Members: 128
Pres: János Péter
Focus: Hist 06293

Közlekedéstudományi Egyesület (KTE) / Scientific Society for Transport, Kossuth Lajos tér 6-8, 1055 Budapest
T: (01) 1532005; Fax: 1532005
Founded: 1949; Members: 4500
Pres: Dr. Sándor Gyurkovics
Focus: Transport 06294

Liszt Ferenc Társaság / F. Liszt Society, Vörösmarty utca 35, 1064 Budapest
T: (01) 3421573
Founded: 1893; Members: 750
Pres: Prof. István Lantos; Gen Secr: Dr. Klára Hamburger
Focus: Music 06295

Magyar Agrártudományi Egyesület (MAE) / Hungarian Society of Agricultural Sciences, Kossuth Lajos tér 6-8, 1055 Budapest
T: (01) 1530651; Fax: 1531950
Founded: 1951; Members: 8500
Pres: Dr. P. Horn; Gen Secr: Dr. V. Marillai
Focus: Agri
Periodical
Agrárvilág 06296

Magyar Anatómus Társaság, c/o Dept of Anatomy, Semmelweis University Medical School, Tüzoltó utca 58, POB 95, 1450 Budapest
T: (01) 2156598; E-Mail: rethelyi@ana.sote.hu; Fax: 2155158
Founded: 1966; Members: 121
Pres: Dr. Miklós Réthelyi; Gen Secr: Dr. Gyula Lázár
Focus: Anat; Bio; Neurology 06297

Magyar Asztronautikai Egyesület / Hungarian Astronautical Society, Fö utca 68, 1027 Budapest
T: (01) 2018443
Founded: 1956; Members: 450
Pres: Dr. I. Almár
Focus: Eng 06298

Magyar Biofizikai Társaság (MBFT) / Hungarian Biophysical Society, Fö utca 68, POB 433, 1027 Budapest
T: (01) 2021216; Fax: 2021216
Founded: 1961; Members: 450
Pres: Prof. Lajos Keszthelyi; Gen Secr: Dr. Sándor Györgyi
Focus: Physics
Periodicals
Bulletin of the Hungarian Biophysical Society
Magyar Biofizikai Társaság Ertesitöje (every 3 years)
Newsletter (quarterly)
Newsletter (quarterly) 06299

Magyar Biokemiai Társaság / Hungarian Biochemical Society, Karolina utca 29, 1113 Budapest
T: (01) 1665856
Founded: 1949
Pres: Dr. Peter Friedrich
Focus: Biochem
Periodical
Biokémia 06300

Magyar Biológiai Társaság (MBT) / Hungarian Biological Society, Fö utca 68, 1061 Budapest
T: (01) 2016484
Founded: 1952; Members: 1500
Pres: Dr. T. Pócs
Focus: Bio 06301

Magyar Biomassza Társaság, Páter Károly utca 1, 2103 Gödöllö
T: (028) 310200
Founded: 1991
Pres: István Barótfi
Focus: Biophys 06302

Magyar Diabetes Társaság / Hungarian Diabetes Association, Pihenö utca 1, POB 1, 1529 Budapest
T: (01) 2607619; Fax: 2607619
Founded: 1970; Members: 700
Pres: Tamás Halmos; Gen Secr: György Jermendy
Focus: Diabetes
Periodical
Diabetologia Hungarica (quarterly) . . . 06303

Magyar Elektrotechnikai Egyesület (MEE) / Hungarian Electrotechnical Association, Kossuth Lajos tér 6-8, 1055 Budapest
T: (01) 1530117; Fax: 1534069
Founded: 1900; Members: 6500
Pres: Dr. I. Krómer
Focus: Electric Eng
Periodical
Elektrotechnika (monthly) 06304

Magyar Elelmezésipari Tudományos Egyesület (METE) / Hungarian Scientific Society for the Food Industry, Akadémia utca 1-3, 1361 Budapest
T: (01) 1122859; Fax: 1310288
Founded: 1949; Members: 9800
Pres: Prof. P. Biacs; Gen Secr: Dr. Zoltán Hernádi
Focus: Food
Periodical
Élelmezési Ipar (monthly) 06305

Magyar Elettani Társaság / Hungarian Physiological Society, Nagyvárad tér 4, POB 370, 1445 Budapest
T: (01) 2104409; Fax: 2104409
Founded: 1931; Members: 600
Pres: Prof. E. Monos; Gen Secr: Prof. L.G. Szollár
Focus: Pathology; Physiology 06306

Magyar Filozófiai Társaság, POB 107, 1364 Budapest
T: (01) 2664195; Fax: 2664195
Founded: 1987; Members: 400
Pres: Kristóf Nyiri
Focus: Philos 06307

Magyar Fögorvosok Egyesülete (MFE), Szentdirályi utca 40, 1088 Budapest
T: (01) 330970
Founded: 1878; Members: 100
Focus: Dent 06308

Magyar Földmérési, Térképészeti és Távérzélési Társaság, Fö utca 68, 1027 Budapest
T: (01) 2018642; Fax: 1561215
Founded: 1956; Members: 2000
Pres: Akos Detrekói
Focus: Surveying; Cart 06309

Magyar Földrajzi Társaság (MFT), Andrássy utca 62, 1062 Budapest
T: (01) 1117688; Fax: 1117688
Founded: 1872; Members: 1300
Pres: Sandor Marosi
Focus: Geography
Periodical
Földrajzi Közlemenyek: Geographical Review (quarterly) 06310

Magyar Geofizikusok Egyesülete (MGE), Fö utca 68, POB 433, 1371 Budapest
T: (01) 2019815; E-Mail: geophysic@mtesz.hu; Fax: 2019815
Founded: 1954; Members: 700
Pres: András Pályi; Gen Secr: Lászlo Verö
Focus: Geophys
Periodical
Magyar Geofizika (quarterly) 06311

Magyar Gerontológiai Társaság / Hungarian Association of Gerontology, c/o Gerontology Center, Semmelweis Medical University, Rökk Szilárd utca 13, POB 45, 1428 Budapest
Founded: 1967; Members: 240
Focus: Geriatrics; Bio; Soc Sci 06312

Magyar Gyógyszerészeti Társaság / Hungarian Pharmaceutical Society, Zrinyi utca 3, 1051 Budapest
T: (01) 181573
Founded: 1924; Members: 3000
Pres: Dr. Z. Vincze; Gen Secr: Dr. J. Lipták
Focus: Pharmacol
Periodicals
Acta Pharmaceutica Hungarica (bi-monthly)
Gyógyszerészet (monthly) 06313

Magyar Hidrológiai Társaság / Hungarian Hydrological Society, POB 433, 1371 Budapest
T: (01) 2017655; Fax: 2027244
Founded: 1917; Members: 5000
Pres: Prof. Dr. J. Juhász
Focus: Water Res; Hydrology
Periodicals
Hidrológiai Közlöny (bi-monthly)
Hidrológiai Tájékoztató (semi-annually) . . 06314

Magyar Immunológiai Társaság, c/o Országos Reuma- és Fizioterápiás Intézet, POB 114, 1502 Budapest
Founded: 1972
Focus: Immunology
Periodical
Acta Microbiologica et Immunologica Hungarica 06315

Magyar Iparjogvédelmi és Szerzöi Jogi Egyesület (MIE) / Hungarian Association for the Protection of Industrial Property, Kossuth Lajos tér 6-8, 1055 Budapest
T: (01) 1531661, 1531780; E-Mail: 1.mie@mtesz.hu; Fax: 1531780
Founded: 1962; Members: 1650
Pres: Prof. Endre Lontai; Gen Secr: Györgi Marosi
Focus: Eng
Periodical
MIE Közlemények 06316

Magyar Irodalomtörténeti Társaság / Society of Hungarian Literary History, Piarista köz 1, 1052 Budapest
T: (01) 1377819
Founded: 1912
Pres: Dezsö Keresztury
Focus: Lit
Periodical
Irodalomtörténet: Literary History (quarterly) 06317

Magyar Irók Irószövetség, Bajza utca 18, 1062 Budapest
Founded: 1945
Pres: Béla Pomogáts
Focus: Lit
Periodicals
Kortárs (monthly)
Magyar Napló (monthly) 06318

Magyar Jogász Egylet (MJSZ) / Hungarian Lawyers Association, Szemere utca 10, 1054 Budapest
Founded: 1949; Members: 9000
Focus: Law
Periodicals
Jogásnapló (annually)
Jogász Szövetségi Értekezések (semi-annually)
Magyar Jog (monthly) 06319

Magyar Kardiologusok Társasága / Hungarian Society of Cardiology, POB 88, 1450 Budapest
T: (01) 2151220, 2155217; Fax: 2157067, 2155217
Founded: 1957; Members: 1150
Pres: Prof. Dr. Károly Lozsádi; Gen Secr: Prof. Dr. István Préda
Focus: Cardiol
Periodical
Cardiologia Hungarica (quarterly) 06320

Magyar Karszt- és Barlangkutató Társulat, Fö utca 68, 1027 Budapest
T: (01) 2019493; Fax: 1561215
Founded: 1910; Members: 1000
Pres: Dr. Attila Hevesi
Focus: Speleology
Periodicals
Beszámoló (annually)
Karszt és Barlang (semi-annually) . . . 06321

Magyar Kémikusok Egyesülete (MKE) / Hungarian Chemical Society, Fö utca 68, 1027 Budapest
T: (01) 2016883; E-Mail: maill.mke@mtesz.hu; Fax: 2018056
Founded: 1907; Members: 5500
Pres: Dr. A. Kálmán; Gen Secr: Dr. L. Harsányi
Focus: Chem
Periodicals
Magyar Kémiai Folyóirat: Hungarian Journal of Chemistry (monthly)
Magyar Kémikusok Lapja: Hungarian Chemical Journal (monthly) 06322

Magyar Kisérletes és Klinikai Farmakológiai Társaság, POB 370, 1445 Budapest
T: (01) 2104400, 2104416; E-Mail: kecsval@net.sore.hu; Fax: 2104400, 2104412
Founded: 1962; Members: 530
Pres: Prof. Sylvester E. Vizi; Gen Secr: Prof. Valeria Kecskemeti
Focus: Pharmacol 06323

Magyar Könyvtárosok Egyesülete (MKE) / Association of Hungarian Librarians, Szabó Ervin tér 1, 1088 Budapest
T: (01) 1182050; Fax: 1182050
Founded: 1935; Members: 2400
Pres: Dr. Tibor Horváth; Gen Secr: István Papp
Focus: Libraries & Bk Sci
Periodical
Hírlevél Magyar Könyvtárosok Egyesülete tagjaihoz (monthly) 06324

Magyar Levéltárosok Egyesülete, Hess tér 5, 1014 Budapest
T: (01) 1557122
Founded: 1986; Members: 500
Gen Secr: Dr. Vilma Alföldi
Focus: Archives 06325

Magyar Meteorológiai Társaság / Hungarian Meteorological Society, Fö utca 68, 1027 Budapest
T: (01) 2017525; Fax: 1561215
Founded: 1925; Members: 450
Pres: Dr. Pál Ambrózy
Focus: Geophys 06326

Magyar Mikrobiológiai Társaság (MMT) / Hungarian Society of Microbiology, POB 64, 1966 Budapest
T: (01) 1760044; E-Mail: mini@microbi.hu; Fax: 1760409
Founded: 1951; Members: 200
Pres: Prof. Dr. Lajos Gergely; Gen Secr: Janos Minarovits
Focus: Microbio 06327

Magyar Müvelödési Intézet, POB 33, 1251 Budapest
T: (01) 2013766; Fax: 2015764
Founded: 1951
Gen Secr: Peter Halász
Focus: Cultur Hist 06328

Magyar Néprajzi Társasag / Hungarian Ethnographical Society, Kossuth Lajos tér 12, 1055 Budapest
T: (01) 2691272; E-Mail: mnt@post.hem.hu; Fax: 2691272
Founded: 1889; Members: 1318S011-856-5
Pres: László Kósa; Gen Secr: Imre Gráfik
Focus: Ethnology
Periodicals
Ethnographia (quarterly)
Néprajzi Hirek 06329

Magyar Numizmatikai Társulat, Csepreghu utca 4, 1088 Budapest
Founded: 1901; Members: 507
Focus: Numismatics
Periodicals
Evkönyv (annually)
Numizmatikai Közlöny (semi-annually) . . 06330

Magyar Nyelvtudományi Társaság (MNyT) / Hungarian Linguistic Society, Piarista köz 1, 1052 Budapest
T: (01) 1376819
Founded: 1904; Members: 660
Pres: L. Benkó
Focus: Ling
Periodicals
Magyar Nyelv (quarterly)
Magyar Nyelvtudományi Társaság Kiadványai (irregularly) 06331

Magyar Orvostudományi Társaságok és Egyesületek Szövetsége / Federation of Hungarian Medical Societies, Nádor utca 36, 1051 Budapest
T: (01) 3123807; Fax: 1837918
Members: 80
Focus: Med
Periodical
MOTESZ Magazin 06332

Magyar Pathológusok Társasága, c/o Dept of Pathology, Haynal Imre University of Health Sciences, Szabolcs utca 35, 1389 Budapest
T: (01) 2704730
Members: 400
Pres: Prof. Mikó Tivadar; Gen Secr: László Vass
Focus: Pathology
Periodicals
Morphologia és Igazságügyi Orvosi Szemle (quarterly)
Pathologia (semi-annually) 06333

Magyar PEN Club / Hungarian PEN Club, Károlyi Mihály utca 16, 1056 Budapest
T: (01) 1184143
Founded: 1926; Members: 300
Pres: Miklós Hubay; Gen Secr: Tamás Ungvari
Focus: Lit
Periodicals
The Hungarian PEN
Le PEN Hongrois (irregularly) 06334

Magyar Pszichológiai Társaság / Hungarian Psychological Association, Teréz krt 13, POB 220, 1536 Budapest
T: (01) 1426178
Founded: 1928; Members: 1225
Pres: István Czigler
Focus: Psych
Periodical
Pszichológiai Szemle: Psychological Review 06335

Magyar Radiológusok Társasága / Societas Radiologorum Hungarorum / Society of the Hungarian Radiologists, Mohai utca 2, 1115 Budapest
T: (01) 2033639; Fax: 2033639
Founded: 1922; Members: 500
Pres: Dr. Béla Fornet; Gen Secr: Dr. János Gyarmati
Focus: Radiology
Periodical
Magyar Radiologia (bi-monthly) 06336

Magyar Régészeti és Müvészettörténeti Társulat / Hungarian Society of Archaeology and History of Fine Arts, Múzeum krt 14, 1088 Budapest
Founded: 1878
Pres: Dr. J. Fitz
Focus: Fine Arts; Archeol
Periodicals
Archaeológiai Ertesítö
Müvészettörténeti Értesítö 06337

Magyar Rovartani Társaság, Barross utca 13, 1088 Budapest
T: (01) 1850666
Founded: 1910; Members: 300
Pres: Dr. Z. Mészáros; Gen Secr: A. Podlusány
Focus: Entomology
Periodical
Folia Entomologica Hungarica 06338

Magyar Sebész Társaság / Societas Chirurgica Hungarica, Ra1th Gy utca 7-9, 1122 Budapest
Founded: 1906; Members: 1345
Focus: Surgery
Periodical
Magyar Sebészet (bi-monthly) 06339

Magyar Szociológiai Társaság, Benczur utca 33, 1068 Budapest
T: (01) 3225265; Fax: 3221843
Founded: 1978; Members: 760
Pres: Dénes Némedi; Gen Secr: Imre Kovách
Focus: Sociology 06340

Magyar Történelmi Társulat / Hungarian Historical Society, I. Uri utca 51-53, 1014 Budapest
T: (01) 1759011
Founded: 1867
Pres: István Diószegi; Gen Secr: Klára Hegyi
Focus: Hist
Periodicals
Magyarország Ujabbkori Forrásai
Századok 06341

Magyar Traumatológus Társaság / Hungarian Society for Trauma Surgery, Fiumei utca 17, POB 21, 1430 Budapest
T: (01) 3337599; Fax: 3330966
Founded: 1966; Members: 488
Pres: Prof. Dr. Tamás Salacz; Gen Secr: Dr. Károly Fekete
Focus: Traumatology
Periodical
Magyar Traumatologia, Orthopaedia, Kézsebézet Plasztikai Sebészet (quarterly) 06342

Magyar Tudományos Akadémia / Hungarian Academy of Sciences, Roosevelt tér 9, 1051 Budapest
T: (01) 1382344; Fax: 1328943
Founded: 1825; Members: 545
Pres: Domokos Kosáry; Gen Secr: László Keviczky
Focus: Sci
Periodicals
Acta Agronomica
Acta Alimentaria
Acta Antiqua
Acta Archaeologica
Acta Biochimica et Biphysica
Acta Biologica
Acta Botanica
Acta Chimica
Acta Chirurgica
Acta Ethnographica
Acta Geodaetica, Geophysica et Montanistica
Acta Geologica
Acta Historiae Artium
Acta Historica
Acta Juridica
Acta Linguistica
Acta Litteraria
Acta Mathematica
Acta Medica
Acta Microbiologica
Acta Morphologica
Acta Oeconomica
Acta Orientalia
Acta Paediatrica
Acta Physica
Acta Physiologica
Acta Phytopathologica
Acta Technica
Acta Veterinaria
Acta Zoologica
Studia Musicologica
Studia Scientiarium Mathematicarum
Studia Slavica 06343

Magyar Ujságirók Országos Szövetsége, Andrássy utca 101, 162 Budapest
T: (01) 3221699; Fax: 3221881
Members: 6800
Pres: András Kereszty
Focus: Lit 06344

Magyar Zenei Tanács / Hungarian Music Council, V. Vörösmarty tér 1, POB 47, 1364 Budapest
T: (01) 1184267; E-Mail: hmic@mail.c3.hu; Fax: 1178267
Founded: 1990; Members: 56
Pres: Adrienne Csenfery; Gen Secr: Eva Csébfalvi
Focus: Music
Periodicals
Magyar Zene (quarterly)
Polifónia (quarterly) 06345

Magyar Zenemüvészeti Társaság, Attila utca 103, 1012 Budapest
T: (01) 1753946
Founded: 1987; Members: 60
Pres: Zsolt Durkó
Focus: Music 06346

Magyarhoni Földtani Társulat / Hungarian Geological Society, Fö utca 68, 1027 Budapest
T: (01) 2019129; Fax: 1561215
Founded: 1848; Members: 1400
Pres: Dr. Tibor Kecskeméti; Gen Secr: DSr. János Halmai
Focus: Geology
Periodicals
Általános Földtani Szemle: General Geological Review (semi-annually)
Annals of the History of Hungarian Geology: Földtani Tudománytörténeti Évkönyv (annually)
Discussiones Palaeontologicae: Öslénytani Viták (semi-annually)
Engineering Geological Review: Mérnökgeológiai-Környezetföldtani Szemle (semi-annually)
Földtani Közlöny (quarterly) 06347

Méréstechnikai és Automatizálási Tudományos Egyesület (MATE) / Scientific Society of Measurement and Automation, Kossuth Lajos tér 6-8, 1055 Budapest
T: (01) 1531406
Founded: 1952; Members: 3000
Pres: Prof. Dr. I. Martos
Focus: Eng
Periodical
Mérés és Automatika: Measurement and Automation (monthly) 06348

Müszaki és Természettudományi Egyesületek Szövetsége / Federal Chamber of Technical and Scientific Societies, Kossuth L. tér 6-8, 1055 Budapest
T: (01) 1534795; Fax: 1530317
Founded: 1948; Members: 34
Pres: M. Havass
Focus: Eng; Nat Sci
Periodical
Müszaki Magazin 06349

Optikai, Akusztikai, Filmtechnikai és Színháztechnikai Tudományos Egyesület, Fö utca 68, 1027 Budapest
T: (01) 2020452; Fax: 2020452
Founded: 1933; Members: 1700
Pres: Olivér Petrik; Gen Secr: László Fuszfás
Focus: Cinema; Optics; Eng 06350

Országos Erdészeti Egyesület / Hungarian Forestry Association, Fö utca 68, 1027 Budapest
T: (01) 2016293; Fax: 2017737
Founded: 1866; Members: 4200
Pres: András Schmotzer; Gen Secr: Dr. Dezsö Szikra
Focus: Forestry
Periodical
Erdészeti Lapok: Forestry Bulletin (monthly) 06351

Országos Magyar Bányászati és Kohászati Egyesület (OMBKE) / Hungarian Mining and Metallurgical Society, Fö utca 68, 1027 Budapest
T: (01) 2017337; Fax: 2017337
Founded: 1892; Members: 6000
Pres: Dr. István Tóth; Gen Secr: Dr. Pál Tardy
Focus: Mining; Metallurgy
Periodicals
Bányászat: Mining (monthly)
Bohászat: Metallurgy (monthly)
Köolaj és Földgáz: Oil and Gas
Öntöde: Foundry 06352

Országos Magyar Cecília Társulat (OMCE) / National Hungarian Cecilia Society, Fehérvári utca 82, 1119 Budapest
Founded: 1897; Members: 2800
Pres: G. Szakos
Focus: Music 06353

Országos Színháztörténeti Múzeum és Intézet, Kristina krt 57, 1013 Budapest
T: (01) 1751184; Fax: 1751184
Founded: 1957; Members: 50
Gen Secr: Dr. Nina Király
Focus: Perf Arts 06354

Papir- és Nyomdaipari Müszaki Egyesület / Technical Association of the Paper and Printing Industry, Fö utca 68, POB 433, 1027 Budapest
T: (01) 2018495; Fax: 2020256
Founded: 1948; Members: 3800
Pres: Miklós Balog
Focus: Eng
Periodicals
Magyar Grafika (bi-monthly)
Papiripar (bi-monthly) 06355

Széchenyi Irodalmi és Müvészeti Akadémia, Roosevelt tér 9, 1051 Budapest
T: (01) 1314117; Fax: 1314117
Founded: 1825; Members: 69
Pres: Miklós Jancsó; Gen Secr: Aniko Kovács
Focus: Humanities; Arts 06356

Szervezési és Vezetési Tudományos Társaság / Society for Organization and Management Science, Fö utca 68, 1027 Budapest
T: (01) 2021456; Fax: 2020856
Founded: 1970; Members: 5000
Pres: Dr. Ferenc Trethon
Focus: Business Admin; Public Admin
Periodical
Ipar-Gazdaság: Industry-Economy (monthly) 06357

Szilikátipari Tudományos Egyesület, Fö utca 68, 1027 Budapest
T: (01) 2019360; Fax: 2019360
Founded: 1949; Members: 2300
Pres: J. Vig
Focus: Eng
Periodical
Epitöanyog: Building Materials (bi-monthly) 06358

Textilipari Müszaki és Tudományos Egyesület (TMTE) / Hungarian Society of Textile Technology and Science, Fö utca 68, 1027 Budapest
T: (01) 2018782; Fax: 1561215
Founded: 1948; Members: 7200
Pres: Dr. Frigyes Geleji
Focus: Eng; Textiles
Periodicals
Hungarian Textile Technology
Textile Cleaning 06359

Tudományos Ismeretterjesztö Társulat / Society for Dissemination of Sciences, Bródy Sándor utca 16, 1088 Budapest
T: (01) 1382496; Fax: 1383320
Founded: 1841; Members: 17000
Gen Secr: Eszter Piróth
Focus: Nat Sci
Periodicals
Békési Élet: Békés Life (quarterly)
Borsodi Szemle: Borsodi Review (quarterly)
Egészég: Health
Élet és Tudomány: Life and Science (weekly)
Föld és Ég: Earth and Sky (bi-monthly)

Műemlékvédelem: Care of Ancient Monuments (quarterly)
Természet Világa: World of Nature (monthly)
Valóság: Reality (monthly) 06360

Iceland

Arkitektafélag Islands / Icelandic Architects' Association, Freyjugata 41, 101 Reykjavik
Members: 2226
Pres: Ormar P. Gudmundsson
Focus: Arts
Periodical
Arkitídindi (3 times annually) 06361

Bandalag Islenzkra Listamanna / Union of Icelandic Artists, POB 637, 121 Reykjavik
Founded: 1928; Members: 1712
Pres: Hjalmar H. Ragnarsson
Focus: Arts 06362

Bókavardafélag Islands (BVFI), POB 1497, 121 Reykjavik
T: 5642050; E-Mail: wrafnah@kopavogur.is; Fax: 5643877
Founded: 1960; Members: 370
Pres: Hrafn A. Hardarson; Gen Secr: Hrafnhiidur Hreinsdottir
Focus: Libraries & Bk Sci 06363

Félag Bókavarda í Rannsókarbókasöfnum / Islandic Research Librarians Association, POB 5382, 125 Reykjavik
Focus: Libraries & Bk Sci 06364

Félag Islenzkra Myndlistarmanna / Association of Icelandic Visual Artists, POB 637, 121 Reykjavik
Members: 263
Pres: K. Steingrimur Jónsson
Focus: Arts 06365

Félag Kvikmyndagerdarmanna / Icelandic Film Makers' Association, POB 5162, Reykjavik
Members: 156
Pres: E. Thorsteinsson
Focus: Cinema 06366

Gedverndarfélag Islands, Hafnarstraeti 5, POB 467, Reykjavik
Founded: 1949; Members: 893
Focus: Psychiatry 06367

Hid Islenska Nattúrufraedifélag, POB 5355, 125 Reykjavik
T: 5624757; Fax: 5620815
Founded: 1889; Members: 1500
Pres: Freysteinn Sigurdsson
Focus: Nat Sci
Periodical
Náttúrufrädingurinn (quarterly) 06368

Hid Islenzka bókmennatafélag / Islandic Literary Society, Sidumuli 21, POB 8935, 128 Reykjavik
Founded: 1816; Members: 1450
Pres: Sigurdur Líndal
Focus: Lit
Periodicals
Annual Journal (semi-annually)
Skirnir 06369

Hid Islenzka Fornleifafélag, c/o National Museum of Iceland, Sudurgötu 41, POB 1489, 101 Reykjavik
T: (1) 5528888
Founded: 1879; Members: 550
Pres: Thor Magnusson; Gen Secr: Thorhallur Vilmundarson
Focus: Archeol
Periodical
Arbók (annually) 06370

International PEN Centre, Kartavogur 40, Reykjavik
Gen Secr: Thor Vilhjalmsson
Focus: Lit 06371

Izlenzka Fornleifafélag / Icelandic Archaeological Society, Sudurgötu 41, 101 Reykjavik
Members: 700
Pres: T. Vilmundarson
Focus: Archeol 06372

Kennarasamband Islands (K.I.) / Icelandic Teachers Association, Laufásvegur 81, 101 Reykjavik
Founded: 1980; Members: 3800
Focus: Educ
Periodicals
Félagsblad K.I. (monthly)
Nýmenntamál (semi-annually) 06373

Loeknafélag Islands (L.I.) / Icelandic Medical Association, Domus Medica, Egilsgötu 3, 101 Reykjavik
Founded: 1918; Members: 850
Focus: Med
Periodicals
Fréttabréf Laekna: Physicians News (10 times annually)
Laeknabladid: Icelandic Medical Journal (19 times annually) 06374

Menntamálarád / Arts Council, POB 1398, Reykjavik
Founded: 1928
Focus: Arts
Periodicals
Almanak
Andvari
Studia Islandica 06375

Rannsóknarád Ríkisins / National Research Council, Laugavegur 13, 101 Reykjavik
Founded: 1987; Members: 7
Focus: Sci
Periodicals
Newsletter in Icelandic (quarterly)
Report on Research in Iceland (semi-annually) 06376

Rannsóknastofnun Fiskidnadarins / Icelandic Fisheries Laboratories, Skúlagata 4, 101 Reykjavik
T: 5620240; E-Mail: info@rfisk.is; Fax: 5620740
Founded: 1934
Focus: Food 06377

Rithöfundasamband Islands / Icelandic Writers' Association, POB 949, Reykjavik
Members: 350
Pres: I. Haraldsdöttir
Focus: Lit 06378

Skógraektarfélag Islands / Forest Association of Iceland, Ránargötu 18, Reykjavik
Founded: 1930; Members: 7000
Focus: Forestry
Periodical
Yearbook (annually) 06379

Sögufélag / Historical Society, POB 1078, 121 Reykjavik
Founded: 1902; Members: 1600
Pres: Heimir Porleifsson; Gen Secr: Sveinbjörn Rafnsson
Focus: Hist
Periodical
Saga: Ný saga (annually) 06380

Surtseyjarfélagid / Surtsey Research Society, POB 352, Reykjavik
Founded: 1965; Members: 65
Focus: Nat Sci
Periodical
Surtsey Research Progress Reports . . 06381

Svaefingalaeknafélag Islands / Icelandic Society of Anesthesiologists, POB 5095, 105 Reykjavik
T: 5601375
Founded: 1960; Members: 39
Pres: Adalbjörn Thorsteinsson
Focus: Anesthetics 06382

Tannlaeknafélag Islands (T.F.I.) / Icelandic Dental Associatio, Sídumúli 35, POB 8596, 105 Reykjavik
Founded: 1927; Members: 240
Focus: Dent
Periodical
Tannlaeknabladid (semi-annually) 06383

Tónlistarfélagid / Music Society, Gardastrati 17, 101 Reykjavik
Founded: 1930
Pres: Baldvin Tryggvason; Gen Secr: Rut Magnússon
Focus: Music 06384

Tónskáldafélag Islands / Icelandic Composers' Society, Laufásvegi 40, 101 Reykjavik
Members: 50
Pres: John Speight
Focus: Music 06385

Verkfraedingafélag Islands / Association of Chartered Engineers in Iceland, POB 1745, Reykjavik
Founded: 1912; Members: 1100
Pres: Petur Stefansson; Gen Secr: Edda Gudbjörnsdóttir
Focus: Eng
Periodicals
Arbók (annually)
Fréttabréf (weekly) 06386

Vísindafélag Islendinga / Icelandic Academy of Sciences, Bárugötu 3, 101 Reykjavik
Founded: 1918; Members: 159
Pres: Sigurdur Steinthorsson
Focus: Sci
Periodical
RIT (irregularly) 06387

India

Academy of Architecture, Plot 267, Shankar Ghanekar Marg, next to Tyresoles Co., Prabhadevi, Mumbai 400025
Founded: 1955
Pres: P.P. Amberkar
Focus: Archit 06388

Academy of Sanskrit Research, Melkote 571431
T: (08232) 38741
Founded: 1978
Pres: M.A.S. Rajan
Focus: Ling 06389

Academy of Zoology, Church Rd 2/95, Civil Lines, Agra 282002
Founded: 1954; Members: 1500
Pres: Dr. D.P.S. Bhati
Focus: Zoology 06390

Aeronautical Society of India, 13-B, Indraprastha Estate, New Delhi 110002
T: (011) 3317516
Founded: 1948; Members: 2500
Pres: Dr. A.P.J. Abdul Kalam; Gen Secr: J.R. Bhaskar
Focus: Aero 06391

Agri-Horticultural Society of India, Alipur Rd, Calcutta 700027
T: (033) 4791713
Founded: 1820; Members: 1300
Pres: S.G. Khaitan; Gen Secr: Dr. S.K. Basu
Focus: Agri; Hort
Periodicals
Horticultural Bulletin (quarterly)
Monthly Garden News Sheet (monthly) . 06392

Agri-Horticultural Society of Madras, Cathedral PO, Madras 600086
Founded: 1835; Members: 3410
Pres: R. Sadasivam; Gen Secr: Prof. J. Ramchandran
Focus: Hort; Agri
Periodicals
Horticultural Bulletin (quarterly)
Monthly Garden News Sheet (monthly) . 06393

Ahmedabad Textile Industry's Research Association (ATIRA), PO Ambavadi Vistar, Ahmadabad 380015
T: (079) 442671; Fax: 6569874
Founded: 1949; Members: 350
Gen Secr: A.R. Garde
Focus: Textiles
Periodical
ATIRA Communications on Textiles (quarterly) 06394

All-India Fine Arts and Crafts Society, Old Mill Rd, New Delhi 110001
T: (011) 3711315
Founded: 1928; Members: 600
Pres: Prof. J. Chopra; Gen Secr: S.S. Bhagat
Focus: Arts
Periodicals
Arts News (monthly)
Roopa Lekha (semi-annually) 06395

All-India Ophthalmological Society, c/o Dr. A.K. Gupta, V1/10 Maulana Azad Medical College Campus, Kotla Rd, New Delhi 110002
T: (011) 3318813
Founded: 1937; Members: 4690
Pres: Dr. C.P. Gupta; Gen Secr: Dr. A.K. Gupta
Focus: Ophthal 06396

All-India Oriental Conference, c/o Bhandarkar Oriental Research Institute, Pune 411004
Founded: 1919; Members: 1350
Pres: Prof. R.N. Danekar; Gen Secr: Prof. S.D. Joshi
Focus: Ethnology; Cultur Hist 06397

Allahabad Mathematical Society, 10 C.S.P. Singh Marg, Allahabad 211001
T: (0532) 623553
Founded: 1958; Members: 270
Gen Secr: Dr. P. Srivastava
Focus: Math
Periodicals
Bulletin
Indian Journal of Mathematics (3 times annually) 06398

Anjuman-i-Islam Islamic Research Association, 92 Dadabhoy Nowroji Rd, Mumbai 400001
Pres: Dr. M.I. Jamkhanawala
Focus: Rel & Theol 06399

Anthropological Society of Mumbai, 209 Dr. Dadabhaj Naoroji Rd, Fort, Mumbai 400001
Founded: 1886
Pres: Dr. J.F. Bulsara; Gen Secr: Sapur F. Desai
Focus: Anthro 06400

Anthropological Survey of India, 27 Jawaharlal Nehru Rd, Calcutta 700016
T: (033) 2498731; Fax: 2497696
Founded: 1945
Gen Secr: Dr. R.K. Bhattacharya
Focus: Anthro
Periodicals
Annual Report (annually)
Folklore Series (irregularly)
Human Science
Linguistic Series (irregularly)
Memoir (quarterly)
Newsletter (bi-monthly)
Occasional Publication (irregularly) . . . 06401

Art Society of India, Sandhurst House, 524 S.V.P. Rd, Bombay 400004
T: (022) 3888550
Founded: 1918; Members: 650
Pres: D. Dahanukar Prafulla; Gen Secr: B.R. Kulkarni
Focus: Arts 06402

Asian and Pacific Centre for Transfer of Technology (APCTT), POB 4575, New Delhi 110016
T: (011) 6856276, 6856255; E-Mail: gen@apett.ernet.in; Fax: 6856274
Founded: 1977
Gen Secr: Dr. Jürgen H. Bischoff
Focus: Eng
Periodicals
Asia-Pacific Tech Monitor (bi-monthly)
VATIS Update (bi-monthly) 06403

Asian Center for Organization, Research and Development (ACORD), C-126 Greater Kailash I, New Delhi 110048
T: (011) 6410616, 6435993; E-Mail: acord@delz.vsnl.net.in; Fax: 6479397
Founded: 1981
Pres: Prof. M.D.G. Koreith; Gen Secr: Kiron Wadnera
Focus: Business Admin 06404

Asiatic Society, 1 Park St, Calcutta 700016
T: (033) 290779; Fax: 290355
Founded: 1784; Members: 1292
Pres: Dr. M. Chakrabarty; Gen Secr: Dr. Chandan Roychoudhury
Focus: Ethnology
Periodicals
Bibliotheka Indica
Journal
Monthly Bulletin (monthly)
Year Book (annually) 06405

Asiatic Society of Mumbai, Town Hall, Mumbai 400023
T: (022) 2660956; E-Mail: asbl@iasbom2.vsne.net.in
Founded: 1804; Members: 1970
Pres: Dr. D.R. Sardesai; Gen Secr: Vimal Shah
Focus: Ethnology
Periodical
Journal (annually) 06406

Association of Indian Universities, AIU House, 16 Kotla Marg, New Delhi 110002
T: (011) 3315105
Founded: 1925; Members: 212
Pres: Prof. A. Gnaman; Gen Secr: Prof. K.B. Powar
Focus: Sci 06407

Association of Medical Physicists of India, c/o Radiological Physics Div, Bhabba Atomic Research Centre, Mumbai 400085
T: (022) 556060 ext 2201; Fax: 5560750
Founded: 1976; Members: 680
Pres: Dr. P.S. Iyer; Gen Secr: Dr. M.S.S. Murthy
Focus: Med; Physics 06408

Association of Microbiologists of India, c/o Div of Microbiology, Indian Agricultural Research Institute, New Delhi 110012
T: (011) 587649
Founded: 1938; Members: 1200
Pres: Dr. S. Ramchandran
Focus: Microbio 06409

Association of Surgeons of India, 18 Swamy Sivananda Salai, Adams Rd, Chepauk, Madras 600005
T: (044) 567095
Founded: 1938; Members: 6500
Pres: Dr. S.S. Deshmukh; Gen Secr: Dr. B. Krishna Rau
Focus: Surgery
Periodical
Indian Journal of Surgery (monthly) . . 06410

Astronomical Society of India, c/o Dept of Astronomy, Osmania University, Hyderabad 500007
T: (040) 7017306, 7018951 ext 247; E-Mail: kilambi@ouastr.ernet.in
Founded: 1973; Members: 500
Pres: Dr. K. Kasturirangan; Gen Secr: Dr. G.S.D. Babu
Focus: Astronomy
Periodical
Bulletin of the Astronomical Society of India (quarterly) 06411

Automotive Research Association of India, POB 832, Vetal Hill, Pune 411004
T: (0212) 337185
Founded: 1966
Focus: Auto Eng
Periodical
Newsletter (quarterly) 06412

Bal Bhavan Society, Kotla Rd, New Delhi 110002
Founded: 1958
Pres: B.B. Latif; Gen Secr: Madhu Pant
Focus: Educ 06413

Bar Association of India, Chamber 93, Supreme Court Bldg, New Dehli 110001
Focus: Law
Periodical
The Indian Advocate (quarterly) 06414

Bharata Ganita Parisad, c/o Dept of Mathematics and Astronomy, University, Lucknow
T: (0522) 75944
Founded: 1950; Members: 450
Pres: Prof. K.D. Singh; Gen Secr: Dr. D. Singh
Focus: Math
Periodical
Ganita 06415

Bharata Itihasa Samshodhaka Mandala, 1321 Sadashiva Peth, Poona 411030
T: (0212) 472581
Founded: 1910; Members: 750
Gen Secr: Dr. S.M. Bhave
Focus: Hist
Periodical
Journal (quarterly) 06416

Bihar Research Society, Museum Bldgs, Patna 800001
Founded: 1915; Members: 180
Pres: Dr. J.C. Jha; Gen Secr: M.S. Pandey
Focus: Hist
Periodical
Journal 06417

Botanical Survey of India, P/8 Brabourne Rd, Calcutta 700001
T: (033) 2424922; Fax: 2429330
Founded: 1890
Gen Secr: Dr. B.D. Sharma
Focus: Botany
Periodicals
Bulletin (quarterly)
Indian Floras
Records and Reports (annually) 06418

Calcutta Mathematical Society (C.M.S.), Ssutosh Bhavan, AE374, Sector I, Saltlake City, Calcutta 700064
T: (033) 3378882; Fax: 376290
Founded: 1908; Members: 845
Pres: Prof. M. Dutta; Gen Secr: Prof. R. Nath Sten
Focus: Math
Periodicals
The Bulletin of the Calcutta Mathematical Society (bi-monthly)
News Bulletin (10 times annually) . . . 06419

Cereals and Legumes Asia Network, c/o ICRISAT, Patancheru 502324
T: (040) 596161; E-Mail: clan@cgnet.com; Fax: 241239
Founded: 1992
Gen Secr: C.L.L. Gonda
Focus: Agri 06420

Commonwealth Veterinary Association (CVA), 123, 7th B Main Rd, IV Block West, Jayanagar, Bangalore 560011
T: (080) 6635210; E-Mail: rahman.cva@sm4.sprintrpg.ems.vsnl.net.in; Fax: 6635210
Founded: 1968; Members: 52
Pres: Dr. W.J. Pryor; Gen Secr: Dr. S. Abdul Rahman
Focus: Vet Med
Periodical
CVA News (semi-annually) 06421

Council of Scientific and Industrial Research, Rafi Marg, New Delhi
T: (011) 3710472; E-Mail: csirkq@sirnet.d.ernet.in; Fax: 3710018
Founded: 1942
Gen Secr: Dr. R.A. Mashelkar
Focus: Sci; Eng
Periodicals
CSIR News (bi-weekly)
Current Literature on Science of Science (monthly)
Indian Journal of Biochemistry & Biophysics (bi-monthly)
Indian Journal of Chemical Technology (bi-monthly)
Indian Journal of Chemistry, Section A (monthly)
Indian Journal of Chemistry, Section B (monthly)
Indian Journal of Engineering and Materials Sciences (bi-monthly)
Indian Journal of Experimental Biology (monthly)
Indian Journal of Fibre and Textile Research (quarterly)
Indian Journal of Marine Sciences (quarterly)
Indian Journal of Pure and Applied Physics (monthly)
Indian Journal of Radio and Space Physics (bi-monthly)
Journal of Intellectual Property Rights (bi-monthly)
Journal of Scientific and Industrial Research (monthly)
Medicinal & Aromatic Plants Abstracts (bi-monthly)
Science-Ki-Duniya (quarterly)
Science Reporter (monthly)
Vigyan Pragati (monthly) 06422

Crafts Council of Western India, 59 L. Jagmohandas Marg, Mumbai 40006
T: (022) 814125
Founded: 1972; Members: 155
Pres: Roshan Kalapesi
Focus: Arts 06423

Crop Improvement Society of India, c/o Dept of Plant Breeding, Punjab Agricultural University, Ludhiana 141004
T: 401960 ext 224
Founded: 1974; Members: 200
Pres: Dr. P.S. Phul
Focus: Agri 06424

Education for All Network, c/o IFHD, 12-13-705/ Ioagb, Gokulnagar, Yacharam, 500017 Hyderabad
T: (040) 674189; E-Mail: UNRLVNR@Pennahit.uvnet.in; Fax: 7154118
Founded: 1991
Pres: Rao Chelikani; Gen Secr: Moreau Odile
Focus: Educ 06425

Electrochemical Society of India, c/o Indian Institute of Science, Bangalore 560012
T: (080) 340977; Fax: 341683
Founded: 1964; Members: 640
Pres: Prof. D.J. Padma; Gen Secr: G.V. Mahesh
Focus: Electrochem

Periodical
The Journal of the Electrochemical Society of India (quarterly) 06426

Ethnographic and Folk Culture Society, L-II/31, Sector B, Aliganj, POB 209, Lucknow 226024
Founded: 1945; Members: 575
Focus: Ethnology; Anthro
Periodicals
The Eastern Anthropologist (quarterly)
Indian Journal of Physical Anthropology and Human Genetics (bi-annually)
Manav (quarterly) 06427

Federation of Obstetric and Gynaecological Societies of India, Purandare Griha, 31/C Dr. N.A. Purandare Marg, Mumbai 400007
T: (022) 3614011
Founded: 1950; Members: 10100
Pres: Dr. V.B. Patwardhan; Gen Secr: Dr. D.K. Tank
Focus: Gynecology 06428

Geographical Society of India, c/o Dept of Geography, University of Calcutta, 35 Ballygunge Circular Rd, Calcutta 700019
T: (033) 4753681
Founded: 1933; Members: 715
Pres: Prof. P.K. Sircar; Gen Secr: Dr. P.K. Saha
Focus: Geography
Periodical
Geographical Review of India (quarterly) . 06429

Geological, Mining and Metallurgical Society of India, c/o Geology Dept, University of Calcutta, 35 B.C. Rd, Calcutta 700019
T: (033) 4753681
Founded: 1924; Members: 315
Pres: Prof. A.K. Banerji
Focus: Mining; Geology; Metallurgy
Periodicals
Bulletin (irregularly)
Journal (quarterly) 06430

Geological Survey of India, 27 Jawaharlal Nehru Rd, Calcutta 700016
T: (033) 2497645
Founded: 1851
Gen Secr: D.B. Dimri
Focus: Geology
Periodicals
Bulletin
Catalogue Series
Geological Survey of India News
Indian Minerals
Manual Series
Memoirs
Palaeontologica Indica
Records
Special Publications 06431

Gujarat Research Society, Dr. Madhuri Shah Campus, Ramkrishna Mission Marg, Khar West, Mumbai 400052
T: (022) 6462691; Fax: 6047398
Founded: 1936
Pres: K.P. Hazarat
Focus: Hist
Periodical
Journal (quarterly) 06432

Helminthological Society of India, c/o Dept of Parasitology, U.P. College of Veterinary Science and Animal Husbandry, Mathura
Pres: Prof. S.N. Singh; Gen Secr: Prof. B.P. Pande
Focus: Vet Med
Periodical
Indian Journal of Helminthology (semi-annually) 06433

Hyderabad Educational Conference, 19 Bachelors' Quarters, Jawaharlal Nehru Rd, Hyderabad
Founded: 1913
Pres: Syed Masood Ali
Focus: Educ 06434

India International Photographic Council, c/o Modern School, Barakhamba Rd, New Delhi 110001
T: (011) 3327762
Founded: 1983; Members: 4000
Pres: B.W. Jatkar; Gen Secr: C. Sharma
Focus: Photo 06435

India Society of Engineers, 12-B Netaji Subhas Rd, Calcutta 700001
Founded: 1934; Members: 8000
Pres: A.C. Sinha
Focus: Eng
Periodical
Science and Engineering (monthly) . . . 06436

Indian Academy of Sciences, C.V. Raman Av, Sadashivanagar, POB 8005, Bangalore 560080
T: (080) 3344592, 3342546; E-Mail: madhavan@ias.ernet.in; Fax: 3346094
Founded: 1934; Members: 770
Pres: Prof. P. Rama Rao; Gen Secr: N. Viswanadham; R. Gadaqkar; G. Madhavan
Focus: Sci
Periodicals
Bulletin of Materials Science (bi-monthly)
Current Science (bi-weekly)
Journal of Astrophysics & Astronomy (quarterly)
Journal of Biosciences (quarterly)
Journal of Genetics (quarterly)
Pramana: Journal of Physics (monthly)

Proceedings (Chemical Sciences) (bi-monthly)
Proceedings (Earth and Planetary Sciences) (quarterly)
Proceedings (Mathematical Sciences) (quarterly)
Resonance: Journal of Science Education (monthly)
Sadhana: Engineering Sciences (quarterly) 06437

Indian Adult Education Association (I.A.E.A.), 17-B Indraprastha Marg, New Delhi 110002
T: (011) 3319282, 3722206; Fax: 3355306
Founded: 1939; Members: 1200
Pres: B.S. Garg; Gen Secr: K.C. Choudhary
Focus: Adult Educ
Periodicals
I.A.E.A. Newsletter (monthly)
Indian Journal of Adult Education (quarterly)
Jagoo aur Jagao (monthly)
Proudh Shiksha (monthly) 06438

Indian Anthropological Association, c/o Dept of Anthropology, University of Delhi, Delhi 110007
Founded: 1964; Members: 400
Pres: Prof. Dr. R.S. Mann
Focus: Anthro
Periodicals
Anthropologists in India (every 2-3 years)
Indian Anthropologist (semi-annually)
News Bulletin (annually) 06439

Indian Association of Biological Sciences, c/o Life Science Centre, University of Calcutta, Calcutta 700019
T: (033) 473681
Founded: 1968; Members: 400
Pres: Prof. T.M. Das
Focus: Bio 06440

Indian Association of Geohydrologists, c/o Geological Survey of India, 4 Chowringhee Lane, Calcutta 700016
Founded: 1964; Members: 440
Pres: V. Subramanyam; Gen Secr: A.K. Roy
Focus: Water Res
Periodical
Indian Geohydrology 06441

Indian Association of Parasitologists, 110 Chittaranjan Av, Calcutta 700012
Pres: Dr. H.N. Ray; Gen Secr: Dr. A.B. Chaudhury
Focus: Microbio 06442

Indian Association of Special Libraries and Information Centres (IASLIC), P-291 CIT Scheme 6-M Kankurgachi, Calcutta 700054
T: (033) 359651
Founded: 1955; Members: 1700
Pres: Prof. M.G. Som; Gen Secr: J.N. Satpathi
Focus: Libraries & Bk Sci; Computer & Info Sci
Periodicals
IASLIC Bulletin (quarterly)
Indian Library Science Abstracts (annually)
Information Superhighway: Its Impaction Library and Information Services in India (annually)
. . . . 06443

Indian Association of Systematic Zoologists, c/o Zoological Survey of India, 34 Chitteranjan Av, Calcutta 700012
Founded: 1947
Pres: Dr. A.P. Kapur
Focus: Zoology 06444

Indian Biophysical Society, c/o Saha Institute of Nuclear Physics, 92 Acharya Prafulla Chandra Rd, Calcutta 700009
T: (033) 354281
Founded: 1965; Members: 200
Pres: Prof. N.N. Saha; Gen Secr: Prof. D.P. Burma
Focus: Biophys
Periodical
Prodeedings (annually) 06445

Indian Botanical Society, c/o Dept of Botany, University of Madras, Chepauk, Madras 600005
Pres: K.S. Thind; Gen Secr: Prof. K.S. Bhargava
Focus: Botany
Periodical
Journal 06446

Indian Brain Research Association, c/o Dept of Biochemstry, Calcutta University, 35 Ballygunge Circular Rd, Calcutta 700019
Founded: 1964; Members: 300
Pres: Prof. J.J. Ghosh
Focus: Neurology
Periodical
Brain News (semi-annually) 06447

Indian Cancer Society, c/o Lady Ratan Tata Medical & Research Centre, Cooperage, M. Karve Rd., Mumbai 400021
T: (022) 2029941, 2048742
Founded: 1951
Gen Secr: Dr. D.J. Jussawalla
Focus: Cell Biol & Cancer Res
Periodical
Indian Journal of Cancer (quarterly) . . 06448

The Indian Ceramic Society, c/o Central Glass and Ceramic Research Institute, Calcutta 700032
T: (033) 4733469; Fax: 4730957
Founded: 1928; Members: 2000
Pres: Dr. N.R. Sircar; Gen Secr: D. Amit Kumar
Focus: Materials Sci
Periodical
Transactions (bi-monthly) 06449

Indian Chemical Society, 92 Acharya Prafulla Chandra Rd, Calcutta 700009
T: (033) 353478
Founded: 1924; Members: 2000
Pres: Dr. D.S. Bhakuni; Gen Secr: Dr. D.C. Mukherjee
Focus: Chem
Periodical
Journal (monthly) 06450

Indian College Library Association, 19/2/01/B/66 Ranjan Colony, Hyderabad 500053
T: (040) 525282
Founded: 1965; Members: 1000
Pres: A.P. Jain; Gen Secr: K.R. Soundar Rajan
Focus: Libraries & Bk Sci 06451

Indian Council of Agricultural Research, Krishi Anusandhan Bhavan, Dr. Rajendra Prasad Rd, New Delhi 110001
T: (011) 388991; Fax: 387293
Founded: 1929; Members: 79
Pres: B.R. Jakhar; Gen Secr: Dr. V.L. Chopra
Focus: Agri 06452

Indian Council of Historical Research, 35 Ferozeshah Rd, New Delhi 110001
T: (011) 3384347; Fax: 3383421
Pres: Prof. S. Settar; Gen Secr: Dr. T.R. Sareen
Focus: Hist
Periodical
The Indian Historical Review (semi-annually)
. . . . 06453

Indian Council of Medical Research (I.C.M.R.), Medical Enclave, Ansari Nagar, POB 4911, New Dehli 110029
T: (011) 6963980, 667136; E-Mail: icmrhqd@ren.nic.in; Fax: 6868662
Founded: 1911
Gen Secr: Dr. G.V. Satyavati
Focus: Med
Periodicals
Annual Report (annually)
Indian Journal of Medical Research (monthly)
. . . . 06454

Indian Council of Social Science Research (ICSSR), JNU Institutional Area, Asuna Asaf Ali Marg, New Dehli 110067
T: (011) 6176771; Fax: 3388037
Founded: 1969
Pres: Prof. A. Debai
Focus: Sociology
Periodicals
ICSSR Journal of Abstracts and Reviews: Economics
ICSSR Journal of Abstracts and Reviews: Geography
ICSSR Journal of Abstracts and Reviews: Political Science
ICSSR Journal of Abstracts and Reviews: Sociology and Social Anthropology
ICSSR Newsletter (quarterly)
ICSSR Research Abstracts (quarterly)
Indian Dissertation Abstracts
Indian Journal of Social Science (quarterly)
Indian Psychological Abstracts 06455

Indian Council of World Affairs (I.C.W.A.), Sapru House, Barakhamba Rd, New Delhi 110001
T: (011) 3317248, 3319055
Founded: 1943; Members: 2625
Pres: Harcharan Singh Josh; Gen Secr: S.C. Parasher
Focus: Poli Sci
Periodicals
Foreign Affairs Report (monthly)
India Quarterly (quarterly) 06456

Indian Dairy Association (IDA), IDA House, Sector IV, R.K. Puram, New Dehli 110022
Members: 3000
Focus: Agri
Periodicals
Dairying-in-India (annually)
Indian Dairyman (monthly)
Indian Journal of Dairy Science (quarterly) 06457

Indian Economic Association, c/o Delhi School of Economics, Dehli 110009
Founded: 1918
Pres: Prof. V.M. Dandekar; Gen Secr: Prof. K.A. Naqvi
Focus: Econ
Periodical
Indian Economic Journal 06458

Indian Geologists' Association, c/o Dept of Geology, Panjab University, Chandigarh 160014
T: (0172) 22740; Fax: 54549
Founded: 1968; Members: 250
Focus: Geology
Periodical
Bulletin of the Indian Geologists' Association (semi-annually) 06459

Indian Institute of Architects, Prospect Chambers Annexe, Dr. D.N. Rd, Mumbai 40001
T: (022) 204972; Fax: 2832516
Founded: 1929; Members: 8800
Pres: A.C. Desai
Focus: Archit 06460

Indian Institute of Metals (IIM), 33 Chowringhee Rd, Calcutta 700071
T: (033) 294648
Founded: 1946; Members: 10000
Pres: Dr. R. Krishnan; Gen Secr: Dr. S.S. Das Gupta

Focus: Metallurgy
Periodicals
Journal of Alloy Phase Diagrams (3 times annually)
Metal News (quarterly) 06461

Indian Law Institute, Opp. Supreme Court, Bhagwandas Rd, New Delhi 110001
T: (011) 389429
Founded: 1956
Gen Secr: Prof. P.M. Bakshi
Focus: Law
Periodicals
Index to Indian Legal Periodicals (semi-annually)
Journal of the Indian Law Institute (quarterly) 06462

Indian Library Association (ILA), A/40-41, Flat 201, Ansal Bldgs, Dr. Mukherjee Nagar, Delhi 110009
T: (011) 7117743
Founded: 1933; Members: 2500
Pres: Dr. P.S.G. Kumar; Gen Secr: A.P. Gakhar
Focus: Libraries & Bk Sci
Periodical
Bulletin (quarterly) 06463

Indian Mathematical Society, c/o Dr. S.P. Arya, Maitreyi College, Bapu Dham Complex, Chanakyapuri, New Delhi 110021
Founded: 1907; Members: 1000
Pres: Prof. A.R. Singal; Gen Secr: Dr. S.P. Arya
Focus: Math
Periodical
Journal of the Indian Mathematical Society: Mathematics Student (quarterly) 06464

Indian Medical Association (IMA), IMA House, Indraprastha Marg, New Dehli 110002
T: (011) 3319009; Fax: 3316270
Founded: 1928; Members: 90367
Pres: Dr. B.C. Chaparwal; Gen Secr: Dr. J.C. Sobti
Focus: Med
Periodicals
Annals of IMA Academy of Medical Specialities (semi-annually)
Bulletin on Continuing Medical Education (bi-monthly)
Journal of the Indian Medical Association (monthly) 06465

Indian Musicological Society, Jambu Bet, Dandia Bazar, Baroda 390001
T: (0265) 425388
Founded: 1970
Pres: Krishna A. Khatau; Gen Secr: Prof. R.C. Mehta
Focus: Music
Periodical
Journal of the Indian Musicological Society (annually) 06466

Indian National Academy of Engineering, 117, Visiting Faculty, Nalanda House, IIT Campus, Hauz Khas, New Delhi 110016
T: (011) 6968475, 6968635; Fax: 6856635
Founded: 1987; Members: 266
Pres: Prof. P.V. Indiresan; Gen Secr: J.C. Ahluwalia
Focus: Eng 06467

Indian National Science Academy, Bahadur Shah Zafar Marg, New Delhi 110002
T: (011) 3313153; Fax: 3716648
Founded: 1935; Members: 774
Pres: Prof. S.K. Joshi
Focus: Sci
Periodicals
Indian Journal of History of Science
Indian Journal of Pure and Applied Mathematics
Proceedings: Pt.A: Physical Sciences
Proceedings: Pt.B: Biological Sciences
Yearbook 06468

Indian Optometric Association, POB 2812, New Delhi 110060
T: (011) 5599839
Founded: 1961
Focus: Ophthal
Periodical
Optometry Today (quarterly) 06469

Indian Pharmaceutical Association (I.P.A.), Kalina, Santacruz East, Mumbai 400098
T: (022) 6122401; Fax: 6140480
Founded: 1935; Members: 6500
Pres: S.N. Desai; Gen Secr: Dr. J.K. Lalla
Focus: Pharmacol
Periodicals
Indian Journal of Pharmaceutical Sciences (bi-monthly)
Pharmatimes (monthly) 06470

Indian Physical Society, 2-3 Raja Subodh Mallick Rd, Jadavpur, Calcutta 700032
T: (033) 473971; Fax: 4732805
Founded: 1934; Members: 168
Pres: Prof. D. Chakravorty; Gen Secr: Prof. S.P. Sen Gupta
Focus: Hist; Nat Sci
Periodical
Physics Teacher (quarterly) 06471

Indian Phytopathological Society (I.P.S.), c/o Division of Plant Pathology, Indian Agricultural Research Institute, New Dehli 110012
T: (011) 5782438, 5788418; E-Mail: anuc@naasdel.ren.nic.in; Fax: 5753678, 5766420
Founded: 1947; Members: 1500
Pres: C.D. 1947 Mayee; Gen Secr: D.V. Singh
Focus: Botany
Periodical
Indian Phytopathology (quarterly) 06472

Indian Political Science Association, c/o Centre for Anna Studies, University of Madras, Madras 600005
T: (044) 568778
Founded: 1937; Members: 3000
Focus: Poli Sci 06473

Indian Psychometric and Educational Research Association, c/o Dept of Education, Patna Training College, Patna 800004
Founded: 1969; Members: 330
Pres: Dr. A.K.P. Sinha; Gen Secr: Dr. R.P. Singh
Focus: Educ
Periodical
Indian Journal of Psychometry and Education 06474

Indian Public Health Association, 110 Chittaranjan Av, Calcutta 700073
Focus: Public Health
Periodical
Indian Journal of Public Health (quarterly) 06475

Indian Rubber Manufacturers Research Association (I.R.M.R.A.), Plot B-88, Rd U-2, Wagle Industrial Estate, Thane 400604
T: 593910
Founded: 1959
Gen Secr: Dr. W. Millns
Focus: Materials Sci 06476

Indian Science Congress Association (ISCA), 14 Dr. Biresh Guha St, Calcutta 700017
T: (033) 2474530; Fax: 402551
Founded: 1914; Members: 11876
Pres: Dr. S.K. Joshi
Focus: Sci; Eng; Med
Periodicals
Everyman's Science (bi-monthly)
Proceedings (annually) 06477

Indian Society for Medical Statistics, c/o Dept of Biostatistics, All-India Institute of Medical Sciences, Ansari Nagar, New Delhi 110029
T: (011) 661123; Fax: 6862663
Founded: 1983; Members: 483
Pres: Prof. S.S.P. Sundar Rao; Gen Secr: Dr. K.R. Sundaram
Focus: Med; Stats 06478

Indian Society for Nuclear Techniques in Agriculture and Biology, c/o Nuclear Research Laboratory, Indian Agricultural Research Institute, New Delhi 110012
T: (011) 5711902; Fax: 5766420
Members: 350
Pres: Dr. P. Sachdev; Gen Secr: Dr. M.S. Sachdev
Focus: Nucl Res; Agri; Bio 06479

Indian Society of Afro-Asian Studies, 297 Sarswati Kunj, Patpargani, New Delhi 110092
T: (011) 2248246; Fax: 3329273
Founded: 1980; Members: 820
Pres: L. Bhasin
Focus: Ethnology 06480

Indian Society of Agricultural Economics (ISAE), 46-48 Esplanade Mansions, Mahatma Gandhi Rd, Mumbai 400001
T: (022) 2842542
Founded: 1939; Members: 1000
Pres: Prof. A. Vaidyanathan; Gen Secr: Dr. Tara Shukla
Focus: Agri
Periodical
Indian Journal of Agricultural Economics (quarterly) 06481

Indian Society of Anaesthetists, c/o Dept of Anaesthesiology, K.E.M. Hospital, Parel, Mumbai 400012
Founded: 1947; Members: 4000
Pres: Dr. D. Das Gupta
Focus: Anesthetics
Periodical
Indian Journal of Anaesthesia (bi-monthly) 06482

Indian Society of Criminology, c/o University of Madras, Madras 600005
Founded: 1970; Members: 600
Focus: Criminology
Periodical
Indian Journal of Criminology (semi-annually) 06483

Indian Society of Earthquake Technology, Roorkee 247667
T: (01332) 71490; E-Mail: iset@rurkiu.ernet.in; Fax: 73560
Founded: 1962; Members: 960
Pres: Dr. N.C. Nigam; Gen Secr: Prof. Dr. H.R. Wason
Focus: Geophys 06484

Indian Society of Genetics and Plant Breeding, c/o Genetics Div, Indian Agricultural Research Institute, New Dehli 110012
Founded: 1941; Members: 1400
Pres: Prof. V.L. Chopra; Gen Secr: Dr. R.B. Mehra
Focus: Botany; Genetics
Periodical
Journal 06485

Indian Society of Mechanical Engineers (ISME), c/o Dept of Mechanical Engineering, Indian Institute of Technology, New Delhi 110016
T: (011) 654187; Fax: 6862037
Founded: 1975
Pres: Prof. G.S. Sekhon; Gen Secr: Dr. S.G. Deshmukh
Focus: Eng
Periodical
Journal of Engineering Production (quarterly) 06486

Indian Society of Oriental Art (I.S.O.A.), 15 Park St, Calcutta 700016
Founded: 1907; Members: 300
Gen Secr: Indira Nag Chaudhuri
Focus: Arts
Periodical
The Journal of the Indian Society of Oriental Art (annually) 06487

Indian Society of Soil Science, c/o Div of Soil Science and Agricultural Chemistry, Indian Agricultural Research Institute, New Delhi 110012
T: (011) 5720991
Founded: 1934; Members: 2200
Pres: Dr. G. Dev; Gen Secr: Dr. G. Narayanasamy
Focus: Agri
Periodicals
Bulletin of the Indian Society of Soil Science (irregularly)
Journal of the Indian Society of Soil Science (quarterly) 06488

Indian Space Research Organization (ISRO), c/o Dept of Space, Antariksh Bhavan, New Bel Rd, Bangalore 560094
T: (080) 334474; Fax: 334229
Founded: 1969
Focus: Astronomy 06489

Indian Standards Institution (ISI), 9 Bahadur Shah Zafar Marg, Manak Bhavan, New Dehli 110002
T: (011) 270131, 272166
Founded: 1947
Focus: Standards
Periodicals
Current Published information on Standardization (monthly)
ISI Annual Report (annually)
ISI Bulletin (monthly)
ISI Handbook (annually)
Manakdoot (quarterly)
Standards Worldover (monthly) 06490

Indo-British Historical Society, 21 Rajaram Mehta Av, Madras 600029
T: (044) 4802404
Founded: 1968; Members: 675
Pres: Dharma Vira; Gen Secr: G.T. Verghese
Focus: Hist
Periodical
Indo-British Review (quarterly) 06491

Inland Fisheries Society of India, c/o Central Inland Capture Fisheries Research Institute, Barrackpore 743101
T: (033) 5601190/91; E-Mail: CICFRI@niegw.nic.in; Fax: 5600388
Founded: 1969; Members: 800
Pres: Dr. M. Sinha; Gen Secr: K.K. Vass
Focus: Fisheries 06492

Institute of Chartered Accountants of India, Indraprastha Marg, New Delhi 110002
T: (011) 3312055; Fax: 372334
Founded: 1949; Members: 62000
Pres: N.P. Sarda; Gen Secr: A.K. Majumdar
Focus: Business Admin 06493

Institution of Electronics and Telecommunication Engineers, 2 Institutional Area, Lodi Rd, New Dehli 110003
T: (011) 4631810
Founded: 1953; Members: 40000
Pres: S.V.S. Chowdhry
Focus: Eng; Electric Eng; Electronic Eng 06494

Institution of Engineers (India), 8 Gokhale Rd, Calcutta 700020
T: (033) 288311; Fax: 288345
Founded: 1920; Members: 300000
Gen Secr: K.N. Majumdar
Focus: Eng
Periodical
Bulletin (monthly) 06495

International Academy of Indian Culture, J-22 Hauz Khas Enclave, New Delhi 110016
T: (011) 6515800, 6515494
Founded: 1935
Pres: Dr. L. Chandra
Focus: Ethnology
Periodical
Satapitaka Series (irregularly) 06496

International Society of Plant Morphologists, c/o Dept of Botany, University of Delhi, Dehli 110007
T: (011) 2918983
Founded: 1951; Members: 500
Gen Secr: N.N. Bhandari
Focus: Botany
Periodical
Phytomorphology: An International Journal of Plant Morphology (quarterly) 06497

International Tamil People Promotive Organization, c/o Thamizh Nilam, 5 Arunachala St, Chepauk, Chennai 600005
T: 847829
Founded: 1968; Members: 20000
Gen Secr: P. Arivan
Focus: Ling; Lit; Hist; Cultur Hist
Periodicals
Tamil Chittu (monthly)
Tamil Nilam (weekly)
Thenmozhi (monthly) 06498

Jammu and Kashmir Academy of Art, Culture and Languages, Srinagar 32379
T: 542640; Fax: 542640
Founded: 1958
Pres: K.V. Krishna Rao; Gen Secr: B. Thakur
Focus: Arts; Ethnology; Ling; Lit
Periodical
Sheeraza (monthly) 06499

Karnatak Historical Research Society, Diwan Bahadur Rodda Rd, Dharwar
Founded: 1914; Members: 100
Pres: S.G. Acharya
Focus: Hist
Periodical
Karnatak Historical Review (semi-annually) 06500

Linguistic Society of India, c/o Deccan College, Pune 411006
T: (0212) 27231
Founded: 1928; Members: 700
Pres: Dr. D.S. Dwivedi; Gen Secr: Dr. S.R. Sharma
Focus: Ling
Periodical
Indian Linguistics (annually) 06501

Madras Literary Society, College Rd, Madras 600006
T: (044) 827966
Pres: M. Gopalakrishnan; Gen Secr: Ramesh Rao. U.
Focus: Lit 06502

Medical Council of India, Aiwan-e-Galib Marg, Kotla Rd, New Dehli 110002
T: (011) 3235178; Fax: 3236604
Founded: 1933
Pres: Dr. P. Narasimha Rao; Gen Secr: Dr. M. Sachdeva
Focus: Med
Periodical
Indian Medical Register 06503

Mineralogical Society of India, Manasa Gangotri, Mysore
Founded: 1959; Members: 400
Pres: Dr. A. Viswanathiah; Gen Secr: Dr. P.N. Satish
Focus: Mineralogy
Periodical
The Indian Mineralogist (annually) . . . 06504

Mumbai Art Society (BAS), c/o Jehangir Art Gallery, Mumbai 400023
T: (022) 2044058
Founded: 1888; Members: 800
Pres: K.K. Hebbar; Gen Secr: G.S. Adivrekar
Focus: Arts
Periodical
Art Journal 06505

Mumbai Medical Union, Blavatsky Lodge Bldg, Chowpatty, Mumbai 400007
Founded: 1883; Members: 250
Pres: Dr. U.N. Bastodkar; Gen Secr: Dr. S.M.K. Thacker
Focus: Med 06506

Mumbai Natural History Society, Hornbill House, Shaheed Bhagat Singh Rd, Mumbai 400023
T: (022) 2821811; Fax: 2837615
Founded: 1883; Members: 2500
Pres: B.G. Deshmukh; Gen Secr: Dr. Asad Rahmani
Focus: Nat Sci; Ecology
Periodicals
Hornbill (quarterly)
Journal of the Bombay Natural History Society (3 times annually) 06507

Mumbai Textile Research Association (BTRA), L.B. Shastri Marg, Ghatkopar, Mumbai 400086
T: (022) 5003651; Fax: 5000459
Founded: 1954
Focus: Textiles
Periodicals
BTRA Bulletin (monthly)
BTRA Cleanings (quarterly)
BTRA Current Textile Literature (monthly)
BTRA Scan (quarterly) 06508

Museums Association of India (MAI), c/o State Museum, Lucknow 226001
Founded: 1944; Members: 700
Pres: Dr. R.C. Sharma; Gen Secr: Dr. S.D. Trivedi
Focus: Arts
Periodicals
Journal of Indian Museums
Museums Newsletter 06509

Mythic Society, 2 Nrupathunga Rd, Bangalore 560002
T: (080) 2215034
Founded: 1909; Members: 404

Pres: Dr. Suryyanath U. Kamath; Gen Secr: Dr. M.K.L.N. Sastry
Focus: Philos
Periodical
Journal of the Mythic Society (quarterly) 06510

National Academy of Art, Rabindra Bhavan, New Dehli 110001
T: (011) 387241
Founded: 1934
Gen Secr: Prof. C.L. Porinchukutty
Focus: Arts
Periodical
Lalit Kala (annually) 06511

National Academy of Sciences, 5 Lajpat Rai Rd, Allahabad 211002
T: (0532) 640224; E-Mail: ExSec@NASI.Wiprobt.ems.vsnl.net.in; Fax: 641183
Founded: 1930; Members: 2957
Pres: Prof. P.N. Tandon; Gen Secr: Prof. Alok K. Gupta; Dr. V.P. Kamboj
Focus: Sci
Periodicals
Annual Number (annually)
National Academy of Sciences Letters (monthly)
Proceedings Sec. A: Physical Sciences (quarterly)
Proceedings Sec. B: Biological Sciences (quarterly)
. . . . 06512

National Atlas and Thematic Mapping Organisation, 50A Gariahat Rd, Calcutta 700019
T: (033) 479924
Founded: 1956
Gen Secr: A.K. Kundu
Focus: Cart 06513

National Book Trust India, A-5, Green Park, New Dehli 110016
T: (011) 664667
Founded: 1957
Pres: Anand Sarup; Gen Secr: Dr. Arvind Kumar
Focus: Libraries & Bk Sci 06514

National Council for Cement and Building Materials, P-21, South Extension II, New Delhi Ghosh, Dr. S.P. 110049
T: (011) 6440133; Fax: 6468868
Founded: 1966
Focus: Materials Sci 06515

National Council of Applied Economic Research (NCAER), Parisila Bhavan, 11 Indraprastha Estate, New Delhi 110002
T: (011) 3317860; Fax: 3327164
Founded: 1956
Gen Secr: S.L. Rao
Focus: Econ 06516

National Council of Educational Research and Training, Sri Aurobindi Marg, New Dehli 110016
T: (011) 666047; Fax: 6868419
Founded: 1961
Gen Secr: Dr. K. Gopalan
Focus: Educ
Periodicals
Indian Educational Review (quarterly)
Journal of Indian Education (bi-monthly)
School Science (quarterly) 06517

National Geographical Society of India, c/o Dept of Geography, Banaras Hindu University, Varanasi 221005
Fax: (0542) 312059
Founded: 1948; Members: 502
Focus: Geography
Periodical
National Geographical Journal of India (quarterly)
. . . . 06518

National Productivity Council, 5-6 Institutional Area, Lodi Rd, New Delhi 110003
Fax: (011) 4615002
Founded: 1958
Gen Secr: Siladitya Ghosh
Focus: Business Admin
Periodicals
Energy Management (quarterly)
Maintenance (bi-monthly)
Productivity (quarterly)
Productivity News (monthly) 06519

Optical Society of India (OSI), c/o Applied Physics Dept, University of Calcutta, 92 Acharya Prafulla Chandra Rd, Calcutta 700009
T: (033) 3508386
Founded: 1965; Members: 410
Pres: Prof. R.S. Sirohi; Gen Secr: A.K. Datta
Focus: Optics
Periodical
Journal of Optics (quarterly) 06520

Palynological Society of India, c/o Environmental Resources Research Centre, POB 1230, Peroorkada P.O., Thiruvananthapuram 695005
T: (047) 435115
Founded: 1965; Members: 60
Pres: Dr. P.K.K. Nair; Gen Secr: Prof. P.M. Mathew
Focus: Botany
Periodical
Journal of Palynology (semi-annually) . . 06521

PEN All-India Centre, 40 New Marine Lines, Mumbai 400020
Founded: 1933; Members: 375
Pres: Annada Sankar Ray; Gen Secr: N. Ezekiel
Focus: Lit
Periodical
The Indian PEN (quarterly) 06522

Pharmacy Council of India, Combined Councils' Bldg, Temple Lane, Kotla Rd, POB 7020, New Dehli 110002
Founded: 1949
Pres: Dr. J.L. Kaul
Focus: Pharmacol 06523

Rajasthan Academy of Science, c/o Birla College, Pilani 333031
Founded: 1951
Focus: Sci
Periodical
Proceedings 06524

Research Designs and Standards Organization, c/o Ministry of Railways, Manak Nagar, Lucknow 226011
T: (0522) 50667; Fax: 56421
Founded: 1957
Gen Secr: O.P. Jala
Focus: Eng; Standards
Periodicals
Documentation Notes (bi-monthly)
Indian Railway: Technical Bulletin (quarterly)
. . . . 06525

Sahitya Akademi / National Academy of Letters, Rabindra Bhavan, 35 Ferozshah Rd, New Dehli 110001
Founded: 1954
Pres: Prof. U.R. Anantha Murthy; Gen Secr: Prof. K. Satchidanandan
Focus: Lit
Periodicals
Indian Literature (bi-monthly)
Samakaleena Bharateeya Sahitya (bi-monthly)
Samskrita Pratibha (semi-annually) . . . 06526

Sangeet Natak Akademi, Rabindra Bhavan, 35 Feroze Shah Rd, New Delhi 110001
T: (011) 385715; Fax: 385715
Founded: 1953
Pres: J.J. Bhabha; Gen Secr: U. Malik
Focus: Music
Periodical
Sangeet Natak (quarterly) 06527

Sanskrita Academy, Sanskrit College Bldgs, 84 Thiru Vi. Ka. Rd, Mylapore, Madras 600004
T: (044) 847320
Founded: 1927; Members: 200
Pres: B. Madhavan
Focus: Ling 06528

Silk and Art Silk Mills' Research Association (SASMIRA), Sasmira Marg, Worli, Mumbai 400025
T: (022) 4935351; Fax: 4930225
Founded: 1950; Members: 151
Pres: H. Doshi Maganlal; Gen Secr: M.K. Bardhan
Focus: Textiles
Periodicals
Man-made Textiles India (monthly)
Sasmira Bulletin (monthly)
Sasmira Technical Digest (quarterly) . . 06529

Society of Biological Chemists, India, c/o Indian Institute of Science, Bangalore 560012
Founded: 1930; Members: 1600
Pres: Dr. P.M. Bhargava
Focus: Biochem; Bio
Periodicals
Biochemical Review (quarterly)
Proceedings: Abstract of Papers Presented at the Annual Meeting 06530

Society of Young Scientists (S.Y.S.), c/o All India Institute of Medical Sciences, 111 Ashwini Block, Ansaringar, New Dehli 110029
Founded: 1974; Members: 351
Focus: Sci 06531

South India Society of Painters, No 13, 11 Trust Cross, Madras 600028
Focus: Arts 06532

South India Textile Research Association, POB 3205 Coimbatore 641014
T: (0422) 574367; Fax: 571896
Focus: Textiles 06533

Tamil Association, Karanthai Tamil Sangam, Thanjavur, Tamil Nadu
T: 21149
Founded: 1911; Members: 216
Pres: S. Ramanathan; Gen Secr: T.K.P. Govindasami
Focus: Ling
Periodical
Tamil Pozhil (monthly) 06534

Tamil Nadu Tamil Development and Research Council, Fort Saint George, Madras 600009
Founded: 1959
Focus: Ling
Periodical
Tamil Nadu Tamil Bibliography (quarterly) 06535

Theosophical Society, c/o Theosophy Science Centre, Adyar, Chennai 600020
T: (044) 417198
Founded: 1990; Members: 500
Gen Secr: Dr. A. Kannan
Focus: Philos; Parapsych; Sociology; Rel & Theol
Periodical
Holistic Science and Human Vlues (irregularly)
. . . . 06536

United Lodge of Theosophists, 40 New Marine Lines, Mumbai 400020
T: (091) 2039024; E-Mail: ambika.sirkar@gems.vsnl.net.in
Founded: 1929
Focus: Rel & Theol; Philos
Periodical
The Theosophical Movement: A Magazine devoted to the Living of the Higher Life (monthly) 06537

United Schools International (USI), USO House, 6 Special Institutional Area, New Dehli 110057
T: (011) 661103, 663998
Founded: 1961
Focus: Educ
Periodical
World Informo (monthly) 06538

Uttar Pradesh Zoological Society, c/o Dept of Zoology, Sanatan Dharm College, Muzaffarnagar 251001
T: 4936
Founded: 1981; Members: 125
Pres: Prof. S.C. Rastogi; Gen Secr: Dr. S.C. Goel
Focus: Zoology 06539

Zoological Society of India, c/o Zoological Survey of India, 34 Chittaran Av, Calcutta 700012
Founded: 1916
Focus: Zoology 06540

Zoological Survey of India, M Block, New Aipur, Calcutta 700053
Founded: 1916
Gen Secr: Dr. A.K. Ghosh
Focus: Zoology
Periodical
Records (quarterly) 06541

Indonesia

Akademi Teknologi Kulit, Djalan Diponegoro 101, Jogjakarta
Focus: Eng 06542

ASEAN Council of Teachers (ACT), c/o Persatuan Guru Republik Indonesia, Djalan Tanah Abang Tiga 24, Jakarta
Founded: 1978
Focus: Educ 06543

ASEAN Energy Management and Research Training Centre (AEEMTRC), c/o ASEAN, Djalan Sisingamangaraja 70A, POB 2072, Jakarta
T: (021) 716451, 712991, 711988
Focus: Business Admin 06544

ASEAN Federation of Endocrine Societies (AFES), c/o Div of Endocrinology and Metabolism, Dept of Medicine, University of Indonesia, Salemba 6, Jakarta 10430
Focus: Endocrinology
Periodical
Journal of AFES 06545

ASEAN Law Association (ALA), c/o MKK, Wisma Metropolitan II Lantai 14, Djalan Jenderal Sudirman, Jakarta
Founded: 1979
Focus: Law
Periodicals
ALA Newsletter
ASEAN Law Journal 06546

ASEAN Population Coordination Unit (APCU), POB 186, Jakarta 10002
T: (02) 8195251, 8191308
Founded: 1979; Members: 6
Focus: Soc Sci 06547

ASEAN Population Information Network (ASEANPOPIN), c/o APCU, Djalan Lt. Jen. M.T. Harijono 9-11, POB 186, Jakarta 10002
T: (02) 8195251, 8191308
Focus: Soc Sci 06548

Asia Pacific League against Rheumatism (APLAR), c/o Seroja Arthritis Centre, Djalan Seroja Dalam 7, Semarang 50241
Founded: 1963; Members: 17
Focus: Rheuma 06549

Asia Soil Conservation Network for the Humid Tropics (ASOCON), POB 133, Jakarta 10270
Fax: (02) 5700263
Focus: Geology 06550

Asian Physics Education Network (ASPEN), c/o UNESCO/ROTSEA, Djalan M.H. Thamrin 14, Tromolpos, Jakarta 10012
T: (021) 321308; Fax: 334498
Founded: 1981
Focus: Educ; Physics
Periodicals
Asia-Pacific Journal of Physics Education
Asia-Pacific Physics News
ASPEN Newsletter (annually) 06551

Asian Society of Oto-Rhino-Laryngology, Djalan Proklamasi 42c, Jakarta 10320
Focus: Otorhinolaryngology 06552

Asosiasi Perpustakaan, Arsip dan Dokumentasi Indonesia (APADI), Medan Merdeka Selatan 11, Jakarta
Focus: Libraries & Bk Sci; Doc; Archives 06553

Astronomical Association of Indonesia, c/o Jakarta Planetarium, Cikini Raya 73, Jakarta
Founded: 1920
Pres: Prof. Dr. B. Hidayat; Gen Secr: Dr. W. Sutantyo
Focus: Astronomy 06554

Balai Pengetahuan Umum Bandung, c/o Universitas Bandung, Djalan Merdeka 27, Bandung
Founded: 1946
Pres: Prof. Dr. L. Van der Pijl; Gen Secr: F.J. Suyderhoud
Focus: Sci 06555

Himpunam Pustakawan Chusus Indonesia (HPCI), Djalan Raden Saleh 43, Jakarta
Focus: Libraries & Bk Sci 06556

Ikatan Dokter Indonesia, Djalan Dr. Sam Ratulangi 29, Jakarta 10350
Fax: (021) 3900473
Founded: 1950; Members: 12650 12650
Gen Secr: Dr. I. Oetama
Focus: Med 06557

Ikatan Pustakawan Indonesia (IPI) / Indonesian Library Association, Djalan Imam Bonjol 1, POB 3624, Jakarta 10002
T: (021) 342529
Founded: 1954
Pres: M.H. Prakoso
Focus: Libraries & Bk Sci
Periodical
Majalah Ikatan Pustakawan Indonesia . . 06558

Jajasan Dana Normalisasi Indonesia, Djalan Braga 38, Bandung
Founded: 1920
Focus: Standards 06559

Perkumpulan Penggemar Alam di Indonesia, c/o Herbarium Bogoriense, Bogor
Founded: 1911
Focus: Hist; Nat Sci 06560

Persatuan Insinyur Indonesia / Indonesian Institute of Engineers, Kompleks Pertamina, Simprug Staff Houses R-08, Djalan Sinabung II, Terusan, Kebayoran Baru, Jakarta 12120
T: (021) 7398858; Fax: 7392255
Members: 27000
Pres: A. Bakrie; Gen Secr: I.S. Umar
Focus: Eng
Periodical
Majalah Insinyur Indonesia (bi-monthly) . 06561

Iran

Ancient Iran Cultural Society, Jomhorie Eslamie Av, Shahrokh St, Teheran
Founded: 1961
Pres: A. Quoreshi
Focus: Hist 06562

Iran Management Association, POB 15855-359, Teheran
Members: 550
Gen Secr: P. Bayat
Focus: Business Admin 06563

Iranian Mathematical Society, POB 13145-418, Teheran
Founded: 1971; Members: 2300
Gen Secr: R. Zaare-Nahandi
Focus: Math 06564

Islamic Republic of Iran Society of Microbiology, POB 13445-583, Teheran
T: (021) 8791160; Fax: 8791160, 8773488
Founded: 1940; Members: 250
Pres: Dr. Reza Amiri Gharagozloo; Gen Secr: Dr. Bahram Fatollah-Zadeh
Focus: Microbio 06565

PEN Club of Iran, 55 Kechvardoust St, Djomhoury Av, Teheran
T: (021) 641828
Gen Secr: Dr. S. Vahidnia
Focus: Lit 06566

Sazemane Pachuhesh va Barnamerizi Amuzeshi / Organization of Research and Educational Planning, c/o Ministry of Education, Iranshahr Av, Martyr Musavi Bldg, POB 14367, Teheran
T: (021) 839262/64
Founded: 1972; Members: 250
Focus: Educ; Public Admin
Periodical
Roshd: Educational Journal for Students and Teachers (monthly) 06567

Iraq

Arab Academy of Music, POB 6150, Baghdad
T: (01) 5373891
Founded: 1971; Members: 20
Focus: Music
Periodical
Arab Music Magazine (quarterly) 06568

Arab Dental Federation, 38 Al-Sabragh St, Baghdad
Founded: 1969
Focus: Dent 06569

Arab Federation for Technical Education (AFTE), POB 718, Baghdad
T: (01) 7189801
Founded: 1981
Focus: Educ
Periodicals
Arab Journal for Technical Education (3 times annually)
Arab Technical Education Newsletter (bi-monthly)
. . . . 06570

Arab Historians Association (AHA), POB 4085, Baghdad
T: (01) 4438868; Fax: 740331
Founded: 1974
Focus: Hist
Periodicals
Arab Historian (quarterly)
The Union News (quarterly) 06571

Arab Industrial Development and Mining Organization (AIDMO), POB 3156, Sadoon, Baghdad
T: (01) 7748546; Fax: 7184658
Focus: Econ; Mining 06572

Arab Literacy and Adult Education Organization (ARLO), POB 3217, Al-Saadoon, Baghdad
T: (01) 7186246
Founded: 1966
Gen Secr: Hashim Abu Zeid El-Safi
Focus: Educ; Lit
Periodical
Education of the Masses (semi-annually)   06573

Arab Petroleum Training Institute (APTI), POB 6037, Al-Tajeyat, Baghdad
T: (01) 5234100
Founded: 1978; Members: 11
Focus: Petrochem
Periodical
Arabic Training (bi-monthly) 06574

Arab Union of Veterinary Surgeons, POB 27098, Baghdad
Focus: Vet Med 06575

Association of Arab Geologists / Association des Géologues Arabes, c/o Iraq National Oil Company, Al-Khulani Sq, Baghdad
Focus: Geology 06576

Federation of Arab Scientific Councils, POB 13027, Baghdad
T: (01) 5381090
Founded: 1976
Gen Secr: Dr. Taha T. Al-Naimi
Focus: Sci 06577

Iraq Academy, Waziriyah, Baghdad
Founded: 1947
Pres: Dr. Saleh A. Al-Ali; Gen Secr: Dr. N.H. Al-Qissi
Focus: Sci
Periodicals
Arabs before Islam
Bulletin (semi-annually)
Majallat al Majimma'al Ilmi al Iraqi (quarterly)
. . . . 06578

Iraqi Medical Society, Maari St, Al Mansoor, Baghdad
Founded: 1920; Members: 871
Pres: F.H. Ghali; Gen Secr: A.K. Al-Khateer
Focus: Med 06579

Scientific Research Council, POB 2441, Baghdad
Founded: 1963
Pres: Dr. N.M. Khalil
Focus: Sci 06580

Society of Iraqi Artists, Damascus St, Baghdad
Founded: 1956
Pres: Noori Al-Rawi; Gen Secr: Amer Alubidi
Focus: Arts 06581

Ireland

Aosdana, 70 Merrion Sq, Dublin 2
T: (01) 6611840; Fax: 6761302
Founded: 1981; Members: 200
Focus: Arts 06582

Apothecaries' Hall, 95 Merrion Sq, Dublin 2
T: (01) 6762147
Founded: 1791
Focus: Lit 06583

Architectural Association of Ireland (AAI), 8 Merrion Sq, Dublin 2
T: (01) 6761703
Founded: 1896; Members: 450
Pres: Sean Mahon
Focus: Archit
Periodicals
AAI Green Book (annually)
AAI Newsletter (monthly) 06584

The Arts Council, 70 Merrion Sq, Dublin 2
T: (01) 6611840; E-Mail: info@artscouncil.ie;
Fax: 6761302
Founded: 1951
Gen Secr: Patricia Quinn
Focus: Arts
Periodicals
Annual Report (annually)
Art Matters (quarterly) 06585

Association of Irish Jurists, c/o Law Library, Four Courts, Dublin 7
T: (01) 8720622; Fax: 8720455
Founded: 1981; Members: 20
Pres: Peter Charleton
Focus: Law 06586

Association of Secondary Teachers, Ireland, ASTI House, Winetavern St, Dublin 8
T: (01) 719144; E-Mail: asti@iol.ie; Fax: 719280
Founded: 1909; Members: 15250
Gen Secr: C.M. Lennon
Focus: Educ
Periodicals
ASTIR (9 times annually)
Issues in Education (annually) 06587

Bird Watch Ireland, Ruttledge House, 8 Longford Pl, Monkstown, Co. Dublin
T: (01) 2804322; E-Mail: bird@indigo.ie;
Fax: 2844407
Founded: 1969; Members: 5000
Pres: A.P. Kelly; Gen Secr: O. O'Sullivan
Focus: Ornithology
Periodicals
Irish Birds (annually)
Wings' Magazine (quarterly) 06588

Brainwave – Irish Epilepsy Association, 249 Crumlin Rd, Dublin 12
T: (01) 4557500; E-Mail: brainwve@iol.ie;
Fax: 4557013
Founded: 1967
Pres: Dr. J.G. Kirker
Focus: Pathology
Periodical
Epilepsy News (3 times annually) . . . 06589

The Bram Stoker Society (BSS), Regent House, Trinity College, Dublin 2
Fax: (01) 6772694
Founded: 1980; Members: 200
Pres: Leslie Shepard; Gen Secr: David Lass
Focus: Lit 06590

Church Education Society, 28 Bachelor's Walk, Dublin 1
Founded: 1839
Gen Secr: A. Wilson
Focus: Rel & Theol; Educ
Periodical
Annual Report (annually) 06591

Conradh na Gaeilge / Gaelic League, 6 Sráid Fhearchair, Dublin 2
T: (01) 4757401; Fax: 4757844
Founded: 1893; Members: 5500
Gen Secr: Séan Mac Mathúna
Focus: Ling
Periodicals
An tUltach (monthly)
Feasto (monthly) 06592

Cork Historical and Archaeological Society (CHAS), Ballysheehy Lodge, Clogheen, Cork Co. Cork
Founded: 1891; Members: 500
Pres: John J. Sheehan; Gen Secr: Patrick Holohan
Focus: Archeol; Hist 06593

County Louth Archaeological and Historical Society (C.L.A.H.S.), 5 Oliver Plunkett Park, Dundalk, Co. Louth
Founded: 1903; Members: 650
Focus: Archeol; Hist
Periodical
County Louth Archaeological and Historical Journal (annually) 06594

Cystic Fibrosis Association of Ireland, 24 Lower Rathmines Rd, Dublin 6
T: (01) 962433
Focus: Physiology
Periodical
Newsletter (quarterly) 06595

Dental Council, 57 Merrion Sq, Dublin 2
T: (01) 6762069
Founded: 1928; Members: 19
Pres: Dr. Daniel I. Keane; Gen Secr: Thomas Farren
Focus: Dent
Periodical
Register of Dentists (annually) 06596

Dublin University Biological Association, c/o Trinity College, Dublin
Founded: 1874; Members: 400
Pres: Prof. Ian Temperley; Gen Secr: Emer Loughrey
Focus: Bio 06597

Engineering and Scientific Association of Ireland, Green Hills, 13 Mather Rd South, Mount Merrion, Co. Dublin
Founded: 1903; Members: 100
Pres: T.A. McInerney; Gen Secr: M.J. Higgins
Focus: Eng; Sci
Periodical
Annual Report (annually) 06598

European Healthcare Management Association (EHMA), Vergemount Hall, Clonskeagh, Dublin 6
T: (01) 2839299; E-Mail: ehma@iol.ie;
Fax: 2838653
Founded: 1966; Members: 210
Pres: Prof. T.E.D. van der Grinten; Gen Secr: Philip C. Berman
Focus: Public Health

Periodical
Newsletter (bi-monthly) 06599

Federation of Irish Film Societies, 65 Harcourt St, Dublin 2
T: (01) 712982
Founded: 1977; Members: 4000
Focus: Cinema 06600

Folklore of Ireland Society, c/o Dept of Irish Folklore, University College, Belfield, Dublin 4
T: (01) 2693244
Founded: 1927
Gen Secr: Hennigan. D.
Focus: Ethnology; Hist
Periodical
Béaloideas: Journal (annually) 06601

Friends of Medieval Dublin (FMD), c/o Dept of Medieval History, University College, Belfield, Dublin 4
T: (01) 7068100; Fax: 7068602
Founded: 1976; Members: 25
Pres: Dr. H.B. Clarke; Gen Secr: Emer Purcell
Focus: Hist; Archeol 06602

Genealogical Office, c/o State Heraldic Museum, Kildare St, Dublin
T: (01) 6030302/03; Fax: 6766690
Founded: 1552
Pres: F. Gillespie
Focus: Genealogy 06603

Geographical Society of Ireland (G.S.I.), c/o Dept of Geography, Trinity College, Dublin
T: (01) 7021143; Fax: 6713397
Founded: 1934; Members: 200
Pres: Dr. P. Duffy; Gen Secr: Michael Quigley
Focus: Geography
Periodicals
Geonews (bi-annually)
Irish Geography (bi-annually) 06604

Health Research Board, 73 Lower Baggot St, Dublin 2
T: (01) 6761176; Fax: 6611856
Founded: 1987
Focus: Public Health
Periodical
Annual Report (annually) 06605

Honorable Society of King's Inns, Henrietta St, Dublin 1
T: (01) 8744840; Fax: 8726048
Founded: 1542; Members: 900
Focus: Law 06606

Incorporated Law Society of Ireland, Solicitors' Buildings, Blackhall Pl, Dublin 7
T: (01) 6710711; Fax: 6710704
Founded: 1841; Members: 5000
Gen Secr: N.C. Ryan
Focus: Law
Periodicals
Gazette (monthly)
Law Directory (annually) 06607

Institiúid Teangeolaíochta Eireann / Linguistics Institute of Ireland, 31 Fitzwilliam Pl, Dublin 2
T: (01) 6765489; Fax: 6610004
Founded: 1972; Members: 23
Pres: Cliona de Bhaldraithe-Marsh; Gen Secr: Eoghan MacAogain
Focus: Ling
Periodicals
Annual Report (annually)
Language, Culture and Curriculum (tri-annually)
Teangeolas (semi-annually) 06608

Institute of Chartered Accountants in Ireland, 87-89 Pembroke Rd, Ballsbridge, Dublin 4
T: (01) 6680400; Fax: 668042
Founded: 1888; Members: 8500
Pres: R.F. Hussey; Gen Secr: B. Walsh
Focus: Stats 06609

Institute of Chemistry of Ireland / Institiúid Ceimice Na hEireann, c/o Royal Dublin Society, Science Section, Ballsbridge, Dublin 4
Founded: 1950; Members: 850
Pres: D.M.X. Donnelly; Gen Secr: Dr. James P. Ryan
Focus: Chem
Periodicals
Irish Chemical News (3 times annually)
Irish Chemical Newsletter (bi-annually) . 06610

Institute of Industrial Engineers (IIE), 35-39 Shelbourne Rd, Dublin 4
T: (01) 686244
Focus: Eng 06611

Institute of Management Consultants in Ireland, Harcourt House, Harcourt St, Dublin 2
T: (01) 757971
Focus: Business Admin 06612

Institute of Public Administration (IPA), 57-61 Lansdowne Rd, Dublin 4
T: (01) 2697011; E-Mail: sales@ipa.ie;
Fax: 2698644
Founded: 1957
Focus: Advert
Periodical
Administration: Journal (quarterly) . . . 06613

Institution of Civil Engineers (Republic of Ireland), 2 Putland Rd, Bray, Co. Wicklow
T: 2860517
Founded: 1818; Members: 550

Pres: Don N. McEntee; Gen Secr: Gabriel Dennison
Focus: Eng
Periodicals
Municipal Engineer (quarterly)
New Civil Engineer (weekly) 06614

Institution of Electrical Engineers (Irish Centre), Telecom Eireann, Saint Stephen's Green West, Dublin 2
Pres: P. Roche; Gen Secr: J.A. Lysaght
Focus: Electric Eng 06615

Institution of Engineers of Ireland (IEI), 22 Clyde Rd, Ballsbridge, Dublin 4
T: (01) 6684341; Fax: 6685509
Founded: 1835; Members: 12000
Pres: John Killeeen; Gen Secr: P.F. Callanan
Focus: Eng
Periodicals
Monthly Journal (monthly)
Transactions 06616

Insurance Institute of Ireland, 32 Nassau St, Dublin 2
T: (01) 6772753; Fax: 6772621
Focus: Insurance 06617

International Political Science Association (IPSA), c/o Dept. of Politics, University College Dublin, Belfield, Dublin 4
T: (01) 7068182; E-Mail: IPSA@ollamh.ucd.ie;
Fax: 7061171
Pres: Jean Leca; Gen Secr: John Coakley
Focus: Poli Sci 06618

International Union of Food Science and Technology, c/o National Food Centre, Dunsinea, Castleknock, Dublin 15
T: (01) 383222
Founded: 1970; Members: 43
Focus: Food
Periodical
IUFost Newsletter (semi-annually) . . . 06619

Irish Academy of Letters, c/o School of Irish Studies, Thomas Prior House, Merrion Rd, Dublin 4
Founded: 1932
Gen Secr: Sean J. White
Focus: Lit 06620

Irish Association for Economic Geology, c/o Geological Survey of Ireland, Haddington Rd, Dublin 4
T: (01) 6715233; Fax: 6691782
Founded: 1973
Focus: Geology
Periodical
IAEG Annual Review (annually) 06621

Irish Astronomical Society, POB 2547, Dublin 14
T: (01) 2980181
Founded: 1937; Members: 105
Pres: Patricia Carroll; Gen Secr: James O'Connor
Focus: Astronomy
Periodicals
Orbit (bi-monthly)
Sky-High (annually) 06622

Irish Cancer Society, 22 Earlsfoot Terrace, Dublin 2
T: (01) 757048
Founded: 1963
Focus: Cell Biol & Cancer Res 06623

Irish Computer Society, 17 Earlsfort Terrace, Dublin 2
Fax: (01) 6620788
Founded: 1972
Focus: Computer & Info Sci 06624

Irish Dental Association (IDA), 10 Richview Office Park, Clonskeagh Rd, Dublin 14
T: (01) 2830499
Founded: 1922
Focus: Dent
Periodical
Journal of the Irish Dental Association (quarterly)
. . . . 06625

Irish Family Planning Association (IFPA), 16-17 Lower O'Connell St, Dublin 1
T: (01) 8780366; E-Mail: ifpa@iol.ie;
Fax: 8780375
Founded: 1969; Members: 250
Pres: Catherine Forde; Gen Secr: Tony O'Brien
Focus: Family Plan
Periodicals
Annual Report (annually)
Newsletter (quarterly) 06626

Irish Federation of University Teachers (IFUT), 11 Merrion Sq, Dublin 2
T: (01) 6610910; Fax: 6610909
Focus: Educ
Periodical
IFUT News 06627

Irish Georgian Society (IGS), 42 Merrion Sq, Dublin 2
T: (01) 6767053
Founded: 1958
Focus: Hist; Archit
Periodical
Bulletin (annually) 06628

Irish Grassland and Animal Production Association, Belclare, Tuam, Co. Galway
T: (091) 798140, 55455; Fax: 55430
Founded: 1946; Members: 900
Pres: Maurice Keane; Gen Secr: Dr. Sean Flanagan
Focus: Animal Husb; Agri 06629

Irish Institute of Purchasing and Materials Management, 90 Saint Stephen's Green, Dublin 2
T: (01) 752552
Focus: Materials Sci; Commerce 06630

Irish Management Institute (IMI), Sandyford Rd, Dublin 14
T: (01) 2956911
Founded: 1952
Focus: Business Admin 06631

Irish Manuscripts Commission (I.M.C.), 73 Merrion Sq, Dublin 2
T: (01) 6761610
Founded: 1928; Members: 18
Pres: Brian Trainor
Focus: Hist
Periodical
Analecta Hibernica 06632

Irish Maritime Law Association, Merrion Hall, Strand Rd, Dublin 4
T: (01) 695522
Focus: Law 06633

Irish Medical Association (IMA), 10 Fitzwilliam Pl, Dublin 2
T: (01) 6767273; E-Mail: im@101.ie;
Fax: 6612758
Founded: 1936; Members: 3700
Pres: Dr. Neil Brennan; Gen Secr: George McNeice
Focus: Med
Periodical
Irish Medical Journal (bi-monthly) . . . 06634

Irish Mining and Quarrying Society, 87-89 Waterloo Rd, Dublin 4
T: (01) 685193
Focus: Mining 06635

Irish National Teachers' Organisation (I.N.T.O.), 35 Parnell Sq, Dublin 1
T: (01) 8722533; Fax: 8422462
Founded: 1868; Members: 24000
Focus: Educ
Periodicals
Education Today (3 times annually)
Tuarascail (10 times annually) 06636

Irish PEN, 26 Rosslyn, Killarney Rd, Bray, Co. Wicklow
Founded: 1921; Members: 62
Pres: F.J.A. Gaughan; Gen Secr: Arthur Flynn
Focus: Lit 06637

Irish Productivity Centre (IPC), 35-39 Shelbourne Rd, Dublin 4
T: (01) 6686244; Fax: 6686525
Founded: 1963
Focus: Business Admin; Econ 06638

Irish Psychoanalytical Association, 2 Belgrave Terrace, Monkstown, Dublin
Founded: 1942; Members: 8
Focus: Psychoan 06639

Irish Quality Control Association, 3 Saint Stephen's Green, Dublin 2
T: (01) 781755
Focus: Materials Sci 06640

Irish Society for Design and Craftwork, 112 Ranelagh, Dublin 6
Founded: 1894
Pres: Prof. Domnall O'Murcada; Gen Secr: Angela O'Brien
Focus: Arts 06641

Irish Society of Arts and Commerce, 55 Fairview Strand, Dublin
Founded: 1911
Pres: Edward Kissane; Gen Secr: A. von Muntz
Focus: Arts 06642

Irish Welding Association, Fitzwilton House, Wilton Pl, Dublin 2
T: (01) 760306, 682222; E-Mail: Colybrand Dublin
Focus: Eng 06643

Library Association of Ireland, 53 Upper Mount St, Dublin 2
T: (01) 6619000; E-Mail: laisec@id.ie;
Fax: 6761628
Founded: 1928; Members: 650
Pres: Liam Ronayre; Gen Secr: B. Teeling
Focus: Libraries & Bk Sci
Periodical
An Leabharlann: The Irish Library (quarterly)
. . . . 06644

Maritime Institute of Ireland, Haigh Terrace, Dun Laoghaire, Co. Dublin
T: (01) 800969
Focus: Navig 06645

The Marketing Society, 19-22-Upper Pembroke St, Dublin 2
T: (01) 761196
Founded: 1971; Members: 360
Focus: Advert 06646

Medical Council, Lynn House, Lower Rathmines Rd, Dublin 6
T: (01) 4965588; Fax: 4965972
Founded: 1978
Focus: Med
Periodical
General Register of Medical Practitioners (every 5 years) 06647

Medical Research Council of Ireland (M.R.C.I.), 9 Clyde Rd, Ballsbridge, Dublin 4
Founded: 1937; Members: 9
Focus: Med
Periodical
Annual Report (annually) 06648

Mental Health Association of Ireland, 2 Herbert Av, Dublin 4
T: (01) 695096
Focus: Psychiatry 06649

Military History Society of Ireland, c/o University College Dublin, Newman House, 86 Saint Stephen's Green, Dublin 2
Fax: (01) 962094
Founded: 1949; Members: 1000
Focus: Hist; Military Sci
Periodical
The Irish Sword (semi-annually) 06650

Music Association of Ireland, 5 North Frederick St, Dublin 1
Founded: 1948; Members: 850
Pres: Marion Doherty; Gen Secr: Margot Doherty
Focus: Music
Periodicals
Annual Report (annually)
Soundpost (bi-monthly) 06651

National Council for Educational Awards, 26 Mountjoy Sq, Dublin 1
T: (01) 8556526; Fax: 8554250
Founded: 1972
Pres: P. MacDiarmada
Focus: Educ 06652

National Safety Council, 4 Northbrook Rd, Ranelagh, Dublin 6
T: (01) 4963422; E-Mail: info@national-safety.council.ie; Fax: 4963306
Founded: 1988
Pres: C. Finegan; Gen Secr: P.C. Costello
Focus: Safety 06653

Old Dublin Society, City Assembly House, 58 South William St, Dublin 2
Founded: 1934; Members: 15000
Pres: Anthony P. Behan; Gen Secr: Sheila Smith
Focus: Hist
Periodical
Dublin Historical Record (quarterly) . . . 06654

Pharmaceutical Society of Ireland, 37 Northumberland Rd, Dublin 4
T: (01) 6600699, 6600551; E-Mail: pharm.soc@indigo.ie; Fax: 6681461
Founded: 1875; Members: 2053
Pres: Tom Holly; Gen Secr: Eugenie Canavan
Focus: Pharmacol
Periodicals
Calendar (annually)
The Irish Pharmacy Journal (monthly) . . 06655

Psychological Society of Ireland, 13 Adelaide Rd, Dublin 2
T: (01) 4783916
Founded: 1970; Members: 806
Pres: Paul Gilligan; Gen Secr: Isolde Blau
Focus: Psych 06656

Royal Academy of Medicine, 6 Kildare St, Dublin 2
T: (01) 6767650; E-Mail: secretary@rami.iol.ie;
Fax: 6611684
Founded: 1882; Members: 2000
Pres: Kevin O'Malley; Gen Secr: Brain L. Sheppard
Focus: Med
Periodical
Irish Journal of Medical Science (quarterly)
. . . . 06657

Royal College of Physicians of Ireland, 6 Kildare St, Dublin 2
T: (01) 6616677
Founded: 1654
Focus: Med 06658

Royal College of Surgeons in Ireland (RCSI), 123 Saint Stephen's Green, Dublin 2
T: (01) 4780200; Fax: 4782100
Founded: 1784
Focus: Surgery
Periodicals
Journal of the Irish College of Physicians and Surgeons (quarterly)
Nursing Review (quarterly) 06659

Royal Dublin Society (R.D.S.), Ballsbridge, Dublin 4
T: (01) 6680866; E-Mail: Carol.Power@Rds.ie;
Fax: 6604014
Founded: 1731; Members: 12000
Pres: Liam Connellan; Gen Secr: Carol Power
Focus: Sci
Periodical
Royal Dublin Society Seminar Proceedings (irregularly) 06660

Royal Hibernian Academy of Arts, 15 Ely Pl, Dublin 2
T: (01) 6766212
Founded: 1823; Members: 68
Pres: Carey Clarke; Gen Secr: Arthur Gibney
Focus: Archit; Arts 06661

Royal Horticultural Society of Ireland, Swanbrook House, Bloomfield Av, Morehampton Rd, Donnybrook, Dublin 4
Founded: 1830
Pres: Rita Rutherfoord; Gen Secr: Monica Nolan
Focus: Hort 06662

Royal Institute of Architects of Ireland (RIAI), 8 Merrion Sq, Dublin 2
T: (01) 6761703; E-Mail: info@riai.ie;
Fax: 6610948
Founded: 1839; Members: 1600
Gen Secr: John Graby
Focus: Archit
Periodicals
Irish Architect (bi-monthly)
RIAI Yearbook (annually) 06663

Royal Irish Academy (R.I.A.), 19 Dawson St, Dublin 2
T: (01) 6762570, 6764222; E-Mail: Admin@ria.ie;
Fax: 6762346
Founded: 1785; Members: 275
Pres: Prof. M. Herity; Gen Secr: Patrick Buckley
Focus: Sci; Humanities; Soc Sci
Periodicals
Erill (annually)
Irish Journal of Earth Sciences (annually)
Irish Studies in International Affairs (annually)
Proceedings of the Royal Irish Academy (annually) 06664

Royal Irish Academy of Music (RIAM), 36 Westland Row, Dublin 2
T: (01) 6764412; Fax: 6622798
Founded: 1856; Members: 135
Pres: John O'Conor; Gen Secr: Dorothy Shiel
Focus: Music 06665

The Royal Society of Antiquaries of Ireland (R.S.A.I.), 63 Merrion Sq, Dublin 2
T: (01) 6761749; Fax: 6761749
Founded: 1849; Members: 1050
Pres: Prof. P. Nt. Chathain; Gen Secr: Dr. Dorothy Kelly
Focus: Archeol
Periodical
Journal of The Royal Society of Antiquaries of Ireland (annually) 06666

Society of Chartered Surveyors in the Republic of Ireland, 5 Wilton Pl, Dublin 2
T: (01) 6765500
Pres: A.P. Smith
Focus: Surveying 06667

Society of Irish Foresters, c/o Royal Dublin Society, Ballsbridge, Dublin 4
Founded: 1942; Members: 630
Pres: Eugene Hendrick; Gen Secr: Pat O'Sullivan
Focus: Forestry
Periodical
Irish Forestry 06668

Society of the Irish Motor Industry, 5 Upper Pembroke St, Dublin 2
T: (01) 6761690; Fax: 6619213
Founded: 1968
Focus: Auto Eng
Periodical
Irish Motor Industry (monthly) 06669

Statistical and Social Inquiry Society of Ireland (SSISI), c/o AIB Group, Bankcentre, Ballsbridge, Dublin 4
T: (01) 6600311
Founded: 1847; Members: 500
Pres: Prof. D. McAlees
Focus: Sociology; Stats
Periodical
Journal of the Statistical and Social Inquiry Society of Ireland (annually) 06670

Theosophical Society in Ireland, 31 Pembroke Rd, Dublin 4
Founded: 1919; Members: 10
Pres: W. Woods; Gen Secr: M. Newham
Focus: Rel & Theol; Philos 06671

University Philosophical Society (U.P.S.), c/o Trinity College, Dublin 2
T: (01) 7022089; Fax: 6778996
Founded: 1684; Members: 1150
Pres: Joseph Guerin; Gen Secr: Nick Royle
Focus: Philos
Periodical
Laws 06672

Veterinary Council, 53 Lansdowne Rd, Dublin 4
T: (01) 6684402; Fax: 6604373
Founded: 1931; Members: 1905
Gen Secr: P.J. O'Connor
Focus: Vet Med 06673

Zoological Society of Ireland (R.Z.S.I.), Phoenix Park, Dublin 8
T: (01) 6771425; Fax: 6771660
Founded: 1830; Members: 9000
Pres: Joseph McCullough; Gen Secr: Dorothy Kilroy
Focus: Zoology
Periodical
Annual Report (annually) 06674

Israel

Academy of the Hebrew Language, POB 3449, Jerusalem 91034
T: (02) 5632242; Fax: 5617065
Founded: 1953; Members: 50
Pres: Prof. M. Bar-Asher; Gen Secr: G. Birenbaum
Focus: Ling
Periodicals
Lamed Lĕšonĕkha (bi-monthly)
Lĕšonénu: A Quarterly for the Study of the Hebrew Language and Cognate Subjects (quarterly)
Lĕšonénu Laam (quarterly) 06675

Agricultural Research Organization, c/o Volcani Center, POB 6, Bet Dagan
T: (03) 968311; Fax: 993998
Founded: 1921
Pres: Prof. E. Sadan
Focus: Agri 06676

Arthur Rubinstein International Music Society, 12 Huberman, Tel Aviv 61060
T: (03) 6856684, 6856628; E-Mail: arims@netvision.net.il; Fax: 6854924
Founded: 1980
Pres: Jan Jacob Bistritzky
Focus: Music
Periodical
Bulletin (annually) 06677

Association for the Advancement of Science in Israel, c/o Dept of Physics, Bar-Ilan University, Ramat-Gan 52100
T: (03) 5318433; Fax: 5353298
Founded: 1953; Members: 5200
Pres: Prof. M. Jammer
Focus: Sci
Periodical
Proceedings of Congress of Scientific Societies
. . . . 06678

Association for the Archaeological Survey of Israel, c/o Israel Museum, POB 1299, Jerusalem 91012
T: (02) 638421
Founded: 1964; Members: 130
Pres: R. Cohen
Focus: Archeol 06679

Association Internationale des Etudes Arméniennes (AIEA), POB 16174, Jerusalem 91161
T: (02) 6412906; E-Mail: weitenberg@rullet.leidenuniv.nl
Founded: 1982; Members: 200
Pres: Prof. Dr. Michael Edward Stone; Gen Secr: Prof. Dr. J.J.S. Weitenberg
Focus: Lit; Hist; Ling 06680

Association of Engineers and Architects in Israel, 200 Dizengoff Rd, POB 3082, Tel Aviv 63462
T: (03) 5240274; Fax: 5235993
Founded: 1922; Members: 20000
Pres: S. Sorek
Focus: Archit
Periodicals
Bulletin (monthly)
Handassa 06681

Association of Religious Writers, POB 7440, Jerusalem
Founded: 1963; Members: 100
Pres: J.E. Chen
Focus: Lit
Periodical
Mabua (annually) 06682

Biochemical Society of Israel, c/o Dept of Chemical Immunology, Weizmann Institute of Science, Rehovot
Fax: (08) 466966
Members: 350
Pres: Prof. M. Wilchet
Focus: Biochem 06683

Botanical Society of Israel, c/o Dept of Biology, Technion-Israel Institute of Technology, Haifa 32000
T: (04) 294211; Fax: 225153
Founded: 1936; Members: 300
Pres: Prof. Shimon Gepstein; Gen Secr: Prof. Peter Newmann
Focus: Botany 06684

Council for Higher Education, Jerusalem 91040, POB 4037
T: (02) 663131; Fax: 660625
Founded: 1958; Members: 25
Gen Secr: Gury Zilkha
Focus: Educ 06685

Development Study Center (DSC), POB 2355, Rehovot 76122
T: (08) 9474111; Fax: 9475884
Founded: 1963; Members: 30
Pres: Prof. Raanan Weitz; Gen Secr: Dr. Dafna Schwartz
Focus: Develop Areas 06686

Entomological Society of Israel, POB 6, Bet-Dagan
T: (03) 9683520; Fax: 9604180
Founded: 1965; Members: 120
Pres: Dr. Manes Wysoki
Focus: Bio 06687

Hebrew Writers Association in Israel, POB 7111, Tel Aviv
T: (03) 6953256; Fax: 6919681
Founded: 1921; Members: 400
Focus: Lit
Periodical
Moznayim (monthly) 06688

Hechal Shlomo, King George St, Jerusalem
Focus: Rel & Theol 06689

Historical Society of Israel, POB 4179, Jerusalem 91041
T: (02) 5637171; Fax: 5662135
Founded: 1936; Members: 1000
Pres: Prof. Yosef Kaplan; Gen Secr: Zvi Yekutiel
Focus: Hist
Periodical
Zion (quarterly) 06690

International Association of Jewish Lawyers and Jurists, 10 Daniel Frish St, Tel Aviv 64731
T: (03) 6910673; Fax: 6953855
Founded: 1969
Pres: H. Ben-Itto; Gen Secr: O. Kidron
Focus: Law 06691

International Society of Computerized and Quantitative EMG, POB 9117, Jerusalem 91090
T: (02) 6731050; Fax: 6713086
Founded: 1981
Pres: Dr. Arieh N. Gilai; Gen Secr: Prof. Joe F. Jabre
Focus: Physiology; Med; Neurology . . . 06692

The Israel Academy of Sciences and Humanities, 43 Jabotinsky Rd, Einstein Sq, POB 4040, Jerusalem 91040
T: (02) 5676222, 5676233; Fax: 5666059
Founded: 1959; Members: 50
Pres: Prof. Joshua Jortner; Gen Secr: Dr. Meir Zadok
Focus: Humanities; Sci 06693

Israel Association of Archaeologists, POB 39299, Tel Aviv 61392
Founded: 1955
Pres: David Ilan
Focus: Archeol 06694

Israel Atomic Energy Commission, 26 Rh. Hauniversita, Ramat Aviv, POB 17120, Tel Aviv 61070
T: (03) 422922; Fax: 422974
Founded: 1952
Gen Secr: Dr. S.Y. Ettinger
Focus: Nucl Res 06695

Israel Bar Association, 10 Daniel Frish St, POB 34022, Tel Aviv 64731
Members: 14000
Pres: D. Hoter-Ishai
Focus: Law
Periodical
Od-Maida (quarterly) 06696

Israel Chemical Society, 66 Nordau Blvd, Tel Aviv 62381
Pres: Dr. Herbert Bernstein; Gen Secr: Dr. I. Blank
Focus: Chem 06697

Israel Crystallographic Society (ICS), c/o Dept of Chemistry, Israel Institute of Technology, Haifa 32000
T: (04) 8293716; Fax: 8233735
Founded: 1952; Members: 50
Pres: Frank H. Herbstein; Gen Secr: M. Harel
Focus: Mineralogy 06698

Israel Dermatological Society, c/o Dermatology Outpatient Clinic, Meir General Hospital, Kfar Saba
Fax: (09) 7472769 7410596
Founded: 1927; Members: 238
Pres: Prof. R. Friedman-Birnbaum; Gen Secr: D. Abraham
Focus: Derm 06699

Israel Exploration Society (I.E.S.), 5 Avida St, POB 7041, Jerusalem 91070
T: (02) 6257991; E-Mail: ies@vms.huji.ac.il; Fax: 6247772
Founded: 1913; Members: 5500
Pres: Prof. Avraham Biran; Gen Secr: Joseph Aviram
Focus: Archeol
Periodicals
Eretz-Israel (annually)
Israel Exploration Journal (quarterly)
Qadmoniot (quarterly) 06700

Israel Geographical Society (IGS), c/o Dept of Geography, The Hebrew University, Jerusalem
T: (02) 883017
Founded: 1962; Members: 300
Gen Secr: Prof. Gabriel Lipshitz
Focus: Geography 06701

Israel Geological Society, POB 1239, Jerusalem
Members: 400
Pres: Y. Mimran; Gen Secr: I. Gavrieli
Focus: Geology
Periodical
Abstracts of Annual Meeting (annually) . 06702

Israel Gerontological Society (IGS), POB 1105, Ramat Gan 52111
T: (03) 232725
Founded: 1956; Members: 600
Focus: Bio; Soc Sci; Med

Periodicals
Gerontology (quarterly)
Yedyion Haaguda (quarterly) 06703

Israel Institute of Productivity (I.I.P.), 4 Henrietta Szold St, POB 33010, Tel Aviv 61330
T: (03) 6920296; Fax: 6916890
Founded: 1951; Members: 2500
Pres: Ram Gabison
Focus: Business Admin
Periodical
Ha Mif'al: The Enterprise (monthly) . . . 06704

Israel Librarians' Association (ILA), POB 303, Tel Aviv 61002
Founded: 1952; Members: 850
Pres: Benjamin Schachter; Gen Secr: Naama Ravid
Focus: Libraries & Bk Sci
Periodicals
Meida La Sefran
Yad-La-Kore 06705

Israel Mathematical Union, c/o Dept of Mathematics and Computer Science, Bar-Ilan University, Ramat Gan 52900
T: (03) 5314807/08; E-Mail: imu@wisdom.weizmann.ac.il; Fax: 5353325
Founded: 1953; Members: 210
Pres: Prof. L. Zalcman; Gen Secr: Dr. J. Schiff
Focus: Math
Periodical
Proceedings of the Annual Meeting of the Israel Mathematical Union (annually) 06706

Israel Medical Association (I.M.A.), 35 Jabotinsky St, POB 3604, Ramat Gan 52900
T: (03) 6100444; Fax: 5753303
Founded: 1912; Members: 20000
Pres: Dr. Yoram Blachar; Gen Secr: Leah Wapner
Focus: Med
Periodicals
Harefuha (bi-weekly)
Mikhtav Lekhaver (monthly) 06707

Israel Music Institute, POB 3004, Tel Aviv 61030
T: (03) 5246475; Fax: 5245276
Founded: 1961
Pres: Ruth Talgam
Focus: Music 06708

Israel Oriental Society (I.O.S.), c/o Hebrew University, Jerusalem 91905
T: (02) 5883633
Founded: 1949; Members: 2500
Pres: T. Kollek; Gen Secr: O. Barak
Focus: Ethnology
Periodical
Hamizrah Hehadash: The New East . . 06709

Israel Painters and Sculptors Association, 9 Alharizi St, Tel Aviv 64244
T: (03) 246685
Founded: 1922; Members: 2000
Pres: Rachel Shavit
Focus: Arts 06710

Israel Pediatric Association, c/o Soroka Medical Center, Beer Sheva 84101
T: (07) 6400828; Fax: 6403500
Founded: 1935
Pres: Manuel Katz; Gen Secr: Shmuel Rigler
Focus: Pediatrics 06711

Israel Physical Society (IPS), c/o Dept of Physics, Bar-Ilan University, Ramat-Gan 52900
T: (03) 5318431; Fax: 5353298
Founded: 1954; Members: 350
Pres: Prof. S. Havlin; Gen Secr: Prof. V. Halpern
Focus: Physics
Periodical
IPS Bulletin (annually) 06712

Israel Plastics and Rubber Center, Technion City, Nveh Sha'anan, Haifa 32000
T: (04) 8225174; Fax: 8320157
Founded: 1986; Members: 45
Gen Secr: S. Kenig
Focus: Materials Sci 06713

Israel Political Science Association, c/o Dept of Political Science, Hebrew University, Jerusalem
Founded: 1921
Pres: Emanuel Gutmann; Gen Secr: Moshe Abalo
Focus: Poli Sci 06714

Israel Prehistoric Society, POB 1502, Jerusalem 91014
Founded: 1958
Pres: A. Gopher; Gen Secr: N. Goren
Focus: Anthro
Periodical
Mitekufat Haeven: Journal of the Israel Prehistoric Society (annually) 06715

Israel Psychological Association, 74 Frishman St, POB 65244, Tel Aviv 61652
T: (03) 5239393; Fax: 5230763
Founded: 1958; Members: 2620
Pres: Masha Sheinman
Focus: Psych 06716

Israel Radiological Society, POB 8833, Haifa 31087
T: (04) 530880
Founded: 1927; Members: 200
Focus: Radiology 06717

Israel Society for Biblical Research, c/o World Jewish Bible Center, 2 Ha Askan, Jerusalem
T: (02) 759152
Focus: Rel & Theol
Periodical
Beth Mikra (quarterly) 06718

Israel Society for Experimental Biology and Medicine, c/o Weizmann Institute of Science, Rehovoth
Founded: 1962
Focus: Bio; Med 06719

Israel Society for Gastroenterology, c/o Israel Medical Association, 1 Heftman St, Tel Aviv
Founded: 1953
Focus: Gastroenter 06720

Israel Society for Hematology and Blood Transfusion, c/o Dr. A. Eldor, Dept of Hematology, POB 12000, Jerusalem 91120
Founded: 1957; Members: 162
Focus: Hematology 06721

Israel Society for Microbiology (ISM), POB 9095, Jerusalem 52190
T: (03) 6355038; E-Mail: eliora@post.tau.ac.il; Fax: 5351103
Founded: 1932; Members: 600
Pres: Prof. Eliora Ron; Gen Secr: Prof. Benzion Cavari
Focus: Microbio
Periodical
Newsletter (5 times annually) 06722

Israel Society of Aeronautics and Astronautics (I.S.A.A.), POB 2956, Tel Aviv 61028
Founded: 1951; Members: 400
Pres: Dov Sa'ar; Gen Secr: Yehuda Borovik
Focus: Aero
Periodical
Bi'af (quarterly) 06723

Israel Society of Allergology, 23 Balfour St, Tel Aviv
Founded: 1949; Members: 30
Pres: Dr. N. Lass
Focus: Immunology 06724

Israel Society of Anesthesiologists (I.S.A.), c/o Dr. G. Gurman, Haifa City Medical Center (Rothschild), Haifa
T: 671671
Founded: 1952
Focus: Anesthetics
Periodical
I.S.A. Newsletter (quarterly) 06725

Israel Society of Clinical Neurophysiology (ISCN), POB 9117, Jerusalem 91090
T: (02) 2412251; Fax: 2713086
Founded: 1960
Focus: Med; Physiology; Neurology . . . 06726

Israel Society of Clinical Pediatrics, c/o J. Sack, Dept of Pediatrics A, Sheba Medical Centre, Ramat Gan 52621
T: (03) 710111
Founded: 1953; Members: 200
Pres: J. Sack
Focus: Pediatrics 06727

Israel Society of Criminology, Jerusalem 91905
T: Mount Scopus (02) 882502; Fax: 881725
Founded: 1972; Members: 250
Pres: J.M. Talgam
Focus: Criminology 06728

Israel Society of Geriatric Medicine, c/o Sheba Medical Centre, Ramat Gan
T: (03) 753171
Founded: 1963
Pres: M. Fisher
Focus: Geriatrics 06729

Israel Society of Internal Medicine, c/o Div of Medicine, Hadassah University Hospital, POB 12000, Jerusalem 91120
T: (02) 776449
Founded: 1958
Pres: Prof. M. Levy
Focus: Intern Med 06730

Israel Society of Logic and Philosophy of Science, c/o Hebrew University, Jerusalem
Founded: 1959
Focus: Philos 06731

Israel Society of Pathologists, c/o Prof. Jed Goldstein, Institute of Pathology, Soroka Medical Center, Beer-Sheva 84101
T: (07) 6403446; Fax: 6232770
Founded: 1950; Members: 100
Pres: Prof. Jed Goldstein
Focus: Pathology 06732

Israel Society of Soil Mechanics and Foundation Engineering, c/o Association of Engineers and Architects in Israel, 200 Dizengoff Rd, Tel Aviv
Founded: 1948
Focus: Agri 06733

Israel Society of Soil Science, c/o National and University Institute of Agriculture, Rehovoth
Founded: 1951
Focus: Agri 06734

Israel Society of Special Libraries and Information Centers (ISLIC), 31 Ha-Barzel St, Ramat Ha-Hayal, Tel Aviv 69710
T: (03) 6480592
Founded: 1966; Members: 900
Pres: Karen Sitton
Focus: Libraries & Bk Sci; Computer & Info Sci
Periodical
Bulletin (semi-annually) 06735

Israel Veterinary Medical Association, POB 1871, Tel Aviv
Founded: 1922
Focus: Vet Med 06736

Israeli Center for Libraries, POB 242, Jerusalem 91002
T: (02) 252949; Fax: 250620
Founded: 1965
Pres: Dr. Dan Ronen; Gen Secr: Iris Chai
Focus: Libraries & Bk Sci 06737

Jerusalem Philosophical Society, c/o Hebrew University, Jerusalem
T: (02) 883747; Fax: 322545
Founded: 1943; Members: 130
Focus: Philos
Periodical
IYYUN: The Jerusalem Philosophical Quarterly (quarterly) 06738

Mekize Nirdamim Society, POB 4344, Jerusalem
T: (02) 636072
Founded: 1861; Members: 600
Pres: Prof. S. Abramson; Gen Secr: Prof. I. Ta-Shma
Focus: Lit 06739

Museums Association of Israel, POB 71117, Jerusalem 631833
Founded: 1964; Members: 55
Pres: Dr. Martin Weyl
Focus: Arts 06740

National Council for Research and Development (NCRD), POB 18195, Jerusalem 91181
T: (02) 277060
Founded: 1950; Members: 40
Focus: Sci
Periodical
Scientific Research in Israel (every 2-3 years) 06741

The Natural Resources Research Organization, 38 Keren Hayesod St, Jerusalem
Focus: Geology 06742

Oto-Laryngological Society of Israel, c/o Israel Medical Association, 1 Heftman St, Tel Aviv
Founded: 1925
Focus: Otorhinolaryngology 06743

PEN Centre for Palestinian Writers, Wadi Al-Juz, 4 Al-Khaldi St, Jerusalem
T: (02) 815185; Fax: 894620
Pres: Hanan Awwad
Focus: Lit 06744

Society for Medicine and Law in Israel, POB 6451, Haifa 31063
T: (04) 8381587; Fax: 8381587
Founded: 1972; Members: 2300
Pres: A. Carmi
Focus: Med; Law 06745

Society for the Protection of Nature in Israel (SPNI), 4 Hashfela St, Tel Aviv 66183
T: (03) 335063; Fax: 377695
Founded: 1953; Members: 45000
Pres: Y. Sagi; Gen Secr: Eitan Gedalizon
Focus: Ecology
Periodicals
Eretz Magazine (quarterly)
Pashosh (monthly)
Teva Ve'Aretz (monthly) 06746

Society of Authors, Composers and Music Publishers in Israel (ACUM), 118 Rothschild Blvd, POB 14220, Tel Aviv 65271
T: (03) 6841414; Fax: 5620119
Founded: 1936; Members: 2360
Pres: Shlomo Tanny; Gen Secr: Ran Kedar
Focus: Lit; Music
Periodical
Zman ACUM (quarterly) 06747

Society of Municipal Engineers of Israel, 200 Dizengoff St, Tel Aviv
Founded: 1937
Gen Secr: J. Kornblum
Focus: Eng 06748

Society of Orthopedic Surgeons of the Israel Medical Association, 1 Heftman St, Tel Aviv
Founded: 1934
Focus: Surgery; Orthopedics 06749

Technion Research and Development Foundation Ltd, Senate House, Technion City, Haifa 32000
Founded: 1952
Focus: Eng; Materials Sci
Periodicals
Hamatechet
In the Field of Building
Research Report 06750

Tel Aviv Astronomical Association, 13 de Haas St, Tel Aviv
Founded: 1961
Focus: Astronomy 06751

Verband deutschsprachiger Schriftsteller in Israel, POB 1356, Tel Aviv 61013
Focus: Lit
Periodical
Rundschreiben (5-6 times annually) . . . 06752

Yad Izhak Ben-Zvi, POB 7660, Jerusalem 91076
T: (02) 5635432; Fax: 5638310
Founded: 1964
Pres: Dr. Zvi Zameret
Focus: Hist; Cultur Hist
Periodicals
Cathedra: History of Palestine Studies (quarterly)
Pe'amim: Studies in the Cultural Heritage of Oriental Jewry (quarterly) 06753

Yeshivat Dvar Yerushalayim / Jerusalem Academy of Jewish Studies, 53 Katzenellenbogen, Har Nof, POB 5454, Jerusalem 91053
T: (02) 6522817; E-Mail: dvar@netmedia.net.il; Fax: 6522827
Founded: 1970; Members: 100
Pres: R. Horovitz; Gen Secr: D. Horovitz
Focus: Rel & Theol; Hist
Periodical
Jewish Studies Magazine (annually) . . 06754

Zoological Society of Israel, c/o Dept of Zoology, Tel-Aviv University, Ramat Aviv
Founded: 1940; Members: 300
Pres: B.S. Galil
Focus: Zoology 06755

Italy

Academia Belgica, Via Omero 8, 00197 Roma
T: (06) 3201889; Fax: 3208361
Founded: 1939
Gen Secr: Prof. Jacqueline Hamesse
Focus: Sociology; Law; Econ 06756

Academia Cardinalis Bessarionis / Cultus et Lectura Patrum, c/o Convento di S. Giacomo, Lungotevere Farnesina 12, 00165 Roma
T: (06) 655758
Founded: 1975; Members: 14
Focus: Rel & Theol
Periodical
Bessarione: Atti Convegni sul Paleocristiano 06757

Academia Española de Bellas Artes en Roma, Piazza San Pietro in Montorio 3, 00153 Roma
Founded: 1873
Pres: Prof. Venencio Blanco Martin
Focus: Arts 06758

Academia Gentium Pro Pace (A.GEN.P.P.), CP 6326, 00195 Roma
T: (06) 3335449
Founded: 1967; Members: 2750
Focus: Rel & Theol; Philos; Physics; Med; Lit; Fine Arts
Periodicals
AGENPP Press: Agenzia di Stampa Quotidiana
Annali dell'Athenaeum
Annuario 06759

Academia Petrarca di Lettere, Arti e Scienze, Via dell'Orto, 52100 Arezzo
T: (0575) 24700; Fax: 24700
Founded: 1810; Members: 413
Focus: Lit; Arts; Sci
Periodicals
Atti e Memorie
Studi Petrarcheschi 06760

Accademia Agraria, Via Mazza 9, 61100 Pesaro
Founded: 1828
Focus: Agri
Periodical
Esercitazioni della Accademia Agraria di Pesaro 06761

Accademia Albertina di Belle Arti, Via Accademia Albertina 6, 10123 Torino
T: (011) 889020; Fax: 8125688
Founded: 1652
Pres: Prof. P. Delle Roncole; Gen Secr: Prof. Carlo Giuliamo
Focus: Arts 06762

Accademia Ambrosiana Medici Umanisti e Scrittori (A.A.M.U.S.), Viale Lunigiana 5, 20125 Milano
T: (02) 603715
Focus: Humanities 06763

Accademia Americana, Via Angelo Masina 5, 00153 Roma
T: (06) 588653
Founded: 1894
Focus: Sci 06764

Accademia Anatomico-Chirurgica, c/o Biblioteca della Facoltà di Medicina e Chirurgia, Università degli Studi, Policlinico, XIV Settembre 1860, Via Enrico dal Pozzo, CP 72 Succ 3, 06100 Perugia
T: (075) 5733923
Founded: 1802
Focus: Surgery; Anat
Periodical
Annali della Facoltà di Medicina e Chirurgia dell'Università degli Studi di Perugia e Atti dell'Accademia Anatomico-Chirurgica (quarterly) 06765

Accademia Artistica Internazionale Pinocchio d'Oro (A.A.I.P.D.), Via Foria 26, 80137 Napoli
T: (081) 445780
Founded: 1964
Focus: Perf Arts
Periodical
Il Malcontento (monthly) 06766

Accademia Biella Cultura, c/o Circolo Sociale Biellese, CP 383, 13051 Biella
Focus: Arts
Periodical
Premio Biella Poesia Junior: Biella Poetry Junior Price (annually) 06767

Accademia Corale Stefano Tempia, Via del Carmine 28, 10122 Torino
T: (011) 547372
Founded: 1875
Focus: Music 06768

Accademia Cosentina, Piazza XV Marzo 7, 87100 Cosenza
T: (0984) 25007
Founded: 1507
Focus: Humanities
Periodical
Atti (annually) 06769

Accademia Culturale d'Europa, Viale IV Novembre, Villa Silvera, 01030 Bassano Romano
T: 634115
Focus: Humanities
Periodical
Il Torchio Artistico e Letterario (monthly) 06770

Accademia Culturale di Rapallo, c/o Ufficio Stampa del Comune, 16035 Rapallo
T: (0185) 50201
Founded: 1978
Focus: Humanities; Adult Educ 06771

Accademia degli Abruzzi per le Scienze e le Arti (A.A.S.A.), Via Saline 18, 66010 Chieti
T: (0871) 684708
Founded: 1965
Focus: Sci; Adult Educ
Periodical
Quaderni del Sapere Scientifico (monthly) 06772

Accademia degli Euteleti, Piazza XX Settembre, CP 30, 56027 San Miniato
Founded: 1644
Focus: Lit; Hist; Sci; Arts
Periodical
Bollettino dell'Accademia degli Euteleti (annually) 06773

Accademia degli Incamminati, Via del Cappuccini, 47015 Modigliana
T: 91131
Founded: 1650
Focus: Sci; Lit; Arts; Agri; Business Admin 06774

Accademia degli Incolti, c/o Collegio Nazareno, Largo del Nazareno 25, 00187 Roma
T: (06) 6990990; Fax: 8417725
Founded: 1658; Members: 70
Pres: Alberto Gaffi; Gen Secr: Dr. Maria Grazia Cicchetti
Focus: Educ 06775

Accademia degli Ottimi, Via Bezzecca 1b, 00185 Roma
T: (06) 480251
Focus: Educ 06776

Accademia degli Sbalzati, Via XX Settembre 46, 52037 Sansepolcro
T: 76909
Founded: 1964
Focus: Arts; Perf Arts 06777

Accademia dei Filedoni, Piazza Italia 2, 06100 Perugia
Founded: 1816
Focus: Sci 06778

Accademia dei Filodrammatici, Piazza Paolo Ferrari 6, 20121 Milano
T: (02) 872564
Founded: 1796
Focus: Arts; Perf Arts 06779

Accademia dei Filopatridi (Rubiconia), Piazza Borghesi 11, 47039 Savignano sul Rubicone
T: (0541) 945107
Founded: 1651; Members: 239
Focus: Hist; Lit; Arts; Sci
Periodical
Quaderni della Rubiconia Accademia dei Filopatridi (annually) 06780

Accademia dei Gelati, Piazza San Rocco, 67038 Scanno
Focus: Hist; Arts 06781

Accademia dei Georgofili, Logge degli Uffizi, 50122 Firenze
T: (055) 213360; Fax: 2302754
Founded: 1753; Members: 314
Pres: Prof. Franco Scaramuzzi
Focus: Agri 06782

Accademia dei Sepolti, Via Buomparenti 7, 56048 Volterra
T: (0588) 86558
Founded: 1597
Focus: Sci
Periodical
Rassegna Volterrana (annually) 06783

Accademia della Crusca, Via di Castello 46, 50141 Firenze
T: (055) 454277/78; Fax: 454279
Founded: 1583; Members: 15
Pres: Prof. Giovanni Nencioni; Gen Secr: Silvia Franchini
Focus: Sci; Ling
Periodicals
Studi di Filologia Italiana: Bollettino dell'Accademia della Crusca (annually)
Studi di Grammatica Italiana (irregularly)
Studi di Lessicografia Italiana (irregularly) 06784

Accademia delle Scienze dell'Istituto di Bologna, Via Zamboni 31, 40126 Bologna
T: (051) 222596
Founded: 1711; Members: 260
Pres: Prof. Dario Graffi; Gen Secr: Prof. Silvano Leghissa
Focus: Sci 06785

Accademia delle Scienze di Ferrara, Via Romei 3, 44100 Ferrara
T: (0532) 205209
Founded: 1823; Members: 270
Pres: Prof. Gabriele Battaglia; Gen Secr: Vincenzo Caputo
Focus: Sci
Periodical
Atti dell'Accademia e Supplementi (semi-annually) 06786

Accademia delle Scienze di Torino, Via Maria Vittoria 3, 10123 Torino
T: (011) 5620047
Founded: 1783; Members: 250
Pres: Prof. Roberto Malaroda
Focus: Sci
Periodicals
Atti dell'Accademia delle Scienze di Torino: Classe di Scienze fisiche (annually)
Atti dell'Accademia delle Scienze di Torino: Classe di Scienze morali (annually)
Memorie dell'Accademia delle Scienze di Torino (irregularly)
Memorie dell'Accademia delle Scienze di Torino: Classe di Scienze morali (irregularly) . . 06787

Accademia delle Scienze e delle Arti degli Ardenti di Viterbo, Largo Cesare Battisti 2, 01100 Viterbo
T: (0761) 30220
Founded: 1480
Focus: Cultur Hist 06788

Accademia delle Scienze Mediche di Palermo, c/o Clinica Chirurgica B, Via Liborio Giuffrè 5, 90127 Palermo
T: (091) 230808
Founded: 1621
Pres: Prof. P. di Voti; Gen Secr: Prof. Pietro Bazan
Focus: Med
Periodical
Atti (annually) 06789

Accademia di Agricoltura di Torino, Via Andrea Doria 10, 10123 Torino
T: (011) 511689
Founded: 1785; Members: 150
Pres: Prof. Pier Luigi Ghisleni
Focus: Agri
Periodical
Annali dell'Accademia di Agricoltura di Torino (annually) 06790

Accademia di Agricoltura Scienze e Lettere, Palazzo Erbisti, Via Leoncino 6, 37121 Verona
T: (045) 8003668
Focus: Sci; Agri; Ling
Periodical
Atti e Memorie (annually) 06791

Accademia di Belle Arti, Via Belle Arti 54, 40126 Bologna
T: (051) 243064
Founded: 1710
Pres: Prof. A. Baccilieri; Gen Secr: Prof. M.V. Riccardi Scassellati
Focus: Arts 06792

Accademia di Belle Arti, Via Ricasoli 66, 50122 Firenze
T: (055) 215449
Founded: 1801
Pres: L. Bausi; Gen Secr: Prof. D. Viggiano
Focus: Arts 06793

Accademia di Belle Arti, Via Libertini 3, 73100 Lecce
Pres: Prof. S. Spedicato
Focus: Arts 06794

Accademia di Belle Arti, Via Brera 28, 20121 Milano
T: (02) 86461929; Fax: 86403643
Founded: 1776
Pres: Walter Fontana; Gen Secr: Dr. Daniela Palazzoli
Focus: Arts 06795

Accademia di Belle Arti, Via S.M. Constantinopoli 107a, 80138 Napoli
Founded: 1838
Pres: Prof. C. Lorenzetti
Focus: Arts 06796

Accademia di Belle Arti, Via Papireto 20, 90134 Palermo
T: (091) 585620
Focus: Arts 06797

Accademia di Belle Arti, Piazza S. Francesco al Prato 5, 06123 Perugia
T: (075) 5730631; Fax: 5730632
Founded: 1573; Members: 143
Pres: Claudio Spinelli; Gen Secr: Prof. Edgardo Abbozzo
Focus: Arts 06798

Accademia di Belle Arti, Via di Roma 13, 48100 Ravenna
T: (0544) 482874; E-Mail: ravac@sbn.provincia.ra.it; Fax: 213641
Founded: 1827
Pres: Vittorio D'Augusta; Gen Secr: Patrizia Poggi
Focus: Arts 06799

Accademia di Belle Arti, Via Ripetta 222, 00186 Roma
T: (06) 3227025; Fax: 3218007
Founded: 1873
Pres: Prof. Antonio Passa
Focus: Arts 06800

Accademia di Belle Arti, Campo della Carità 1050, 30123 Venezia
T: (041) 5225396; Fax: 5230129
Founded: 1750
Pres: Prof. Nedo Fiorentin
Focus: Arts 06801

Accademia di Belle Arti e Liceo Artistico, Piazza dell' Accademia 1, 54033 Carrara
Focus: Arts 06802

Accademia di Costume e di Moda, Libero Istituto di Studi Superiori di Belle Arti, Piazza Farnese 144, 00186 Roma
T: (06) 6568169, 6564132
Founded: 1964
Focus: Graphic & Dec Arts, Design . . 06803

Accademia di Danimarca, Via Omero 18, 00197 Roma
T: (06) 3265931; E-Mail: accademia@dkinst-rom.dk; Fax: 3222717
Founded: 1956
Focus: Sci
Periodical
Analecta Romana Instituti Danici (annually) 06804

Accademia di Francia, Viale Trinità dei Monti 1, 00187 Roma
T: (06) 67611; Fax: 6761305
Founded: 1666
Focus: Sci 06805

Accademia di Medicina di Torino, Via Po 18, 10123 Torino
Founded: 1846
Focus: Med
Periodical
Giornale dell'Accademia di Medicina di Torino (annually) 06806

Accademia di Paestum Eremo Italico, Via Trieste 9, 84085 Mercato San Severino
T: 879191
Founded: 1949
Focus: Lit; Sci; Arts; Archeol; Journalism
Periodical
Fiorisce un Cenacolo (monthly) 06807

Accademia di Relazioni Pubbliche (A.R.P.), Via XX Settembre 26, 00187 Roma
T: (06) 4950350
Founded: 1970
Focus: Comm Sci 06808

Accademia di Romania, Piazza Josè de San Martin 1, Valle Giulia, 00197 Roma
T: (06) 3601898, 3601594
Founded: 1920
Focus: Ethnology; Sci
Periodicals
Bollettino Bibliografico
Notiziario dell'Accademia di Romania . . 06809

Accademia di Scienze, Lettere e Arti, Palazzo del Liceo Classico, 55100 Lucca
Founded: 1819
Focus: Cultur Hist; Hist 06810

Accademia di Scienze, Lettere e Arti, Via Beato Odorico da Pordenone 9, 33100 Udine
Founded: 1606
Focus: Lit; Sci; Sociology; Arts
Periodical
Atti dell'Accademia di Scienze, Lettere e Arti (annually) 06811

Accademia di Scienze, Lettere e Belle Arti degli Zelanti e dei Dafnici, Piazza Duomo 1, 95024 Acireale
T: (095) 604557
Founded: 1934
Focus: Sci; Lit; Arts
Periodical
Memorie e Rendiconti (annually) 06812

Accademia di Scienze, Lettere ed Arti, Piazza Indipendenza 17, 90129 Palermo
T: (091) 420862
Focus: Arts; Lit; Sci
Periodical
Atti dell'Accademia di Scienze, Lettere ed Arti di Palermo (annually) 06813

Accademia Etrusca, Palazzo Casali, Piazza Signorelli, 52044 Cortona-Arezzo
T: (0575) 630415
Founded: 1727; Members: 210
Pres: Dr. Guglielmo Maetzke; Gen Secr: Prof. Dr. E. Mirri
Focus: Sci
Periodicals
L'Annuario (annually)
Fonti e Testi (monthly)
Note e Documenti (quarterly) 06814

Accademia Euro-Afro-Asiatica del Turismo, c/o Espomanifestotur, CP 170, 95100 Catania
T: (095) 7273122; Fax: 7273122
Founded: 1966
Focus: Travel
Periodical
Euroturismo Progetto 2000 06815

Accademia Europea Dentisti Implantologi (A.E.D.I.), Piazza Bertarelli 4, 20122 Milano
T: (02) 879298
Founded: 1978
Focus: Dent
Periodical
Rivista Europea di Implantologia (quarterly) 06816

Accademia Filarmonica di Bologna (Reale), Via F. Guerrazzi 13, 40125 Bologna
T: (051) 222997
Founded: 1666
Focus: Music 06817

Accademia Filarmonica di Verona, Via dei Mutilati 4l, 37100 Verona
Founded: 1543
Focus: Music 06818

Accademia Filarmonica Romana, Via Flaminia 118, 00196 Roma
T: (06) 3201752; E-Mail: filarmonica@mail.nexus.it; Fax: 3210410
Founded: 1821; Members: 1000
Pres: Roman Vlad
Focus: Music
Periodical
Il Giornale della Filarmonica (monthly) . 06819

Accademia Fulginia di Arti, Lettere, Scienze, Via Tasso 6, 06034 Foligno
T: (0742) 21469
Founded: 1961
Focus: Arts; Lit; Sci
Periodical
Bollettino Storico della Città di Foligno . 06820

Accademia Georgica, Piazza della Repubblica 9, 62010 Treia
T: 515138
Founded: 1430
Focus: Agri 06821

Accademia Gioenia di Scienze Naturali, Corso Italia 55, 95129 Catania
T: (095) 371668
Founded: 1824; Members: 84
Pres: Prof. A. Agodi; Gen Secr: Prof. G. Montaudo
Focus: Nat Sci
Periodicals
Atti
Bolletino delle Sedute 06822

Accademia Gli Amici Dei Sacri Lari, Terrazza Nunzienza, Viale Enrico Fermi 4, 24100 Bergamo
T: (035) 237458
Founded: 1961
Focus: Rel & Theol; Lit 06823

Accademia Il Tetradramma, Via IV Novembre 152, 00187 Roma
T: (06) 6784964, 6784991
Focus: Arts; Lit; Sci 06824

Accademia Internazionale d'Arte Moderna (A.I.A.M.), Via Giulio Sacchetti 10, 00167 Roma
T: (06) 6373303
Founded: 1975
Focus: Arts; Educ
Periodical
Il Notiziario dell'Accademia Internazionale d'Arte Moderna (quarterly) 06825

Accademia Internazionale della Tavola Rotonda, Via Zante 21, 20138 Milano
T: (02) 7490506; Fax: 7490506
Founded: 1957
Focus: Arts; Sci; Hist; Educ
Periodical
La Tavola Rotonda (monthly) 06826

Accademia Internazionale di Medicina Legale e di Medicina Sociale, Viale Regina Elena 336, 00161 Roma
Founded: 1938
Focus: Med; Hygiene
Periodical
Acta Medicinae Legalis et Medicinae Socialis 06827

Accademia Internazionale per le Scienze Economiche, Sociali e Sanitarie (A.I.S.E.S.S.), Via Francesco d'Ovidio 135, 00137 Roma
T: (06) 8280261
Focus: Econ; Soc Sci; Hygiene 06828

Accademia Italiana di Economia Aziendale, Via Cairoli 11, 40121 Bologna
T: (051) 558798; Fax: 6492446
Founded: 1813; Members: 360
Pres: Umberto Bertini
Focus: Econ 06829

Accademia Italiana di Medicina Omeopatica Hahnemanniana (AIMOH), Piazza Navona 49, 00186 Roma
T: (06) 659030
Focus: Homeopathy
Periodical
Rassegna Italiana di Medicina Omeopatica (quarterly) 06830

Accademia Italiana di Scienze Forestali, Piazza Edison 11, 50133 Firenze
T: (055) 570348; Fax: 575724
Founded: 1952; Members: 240
Pres: Prof. A. Mancini
Focus: Forestry
Periodicals
Annali dell'Accademia Italiana di Scienze Forestali (annually)
Bollettino della Bibliografia Forestale Italiana (annually)
L'Italia Forestale e Montana (bi-monthly) . 06831

Accademia Italiana di Stenografia e di Dattilografia Giuseppe Aliprandi, Via Ricasoli 9, 50122 Firenze
T: (055) 2398641; Fax: 289719
Focus: Educ
Periodical
Specializzazione (quarterly) 06832

Accademia Italiana di Storia della Farmacia (A.I.S.F.), Via G. Pardo Roquez 1, 56100 Pisa
T: (050) 27397
Focus: Pharmacol 06833

Accademia Italiana di Studi Filatelici e Numismatici, Piazza Battisti 1, CP 102, 42100 Reggio Emilia
Founded: 1975
Focus: Numismatics 06834

Accademia Lancisiana di Roma, Borgo S. Spirito 3, 00193 Roma
T: (06) 68308539
Founded: 1715
Focus: Humanities
Periodical
Atti dell'Accademia Lancisiana di Roma . 06835

Accademia Letteraria Italiana, Arcadia, c/o Biblioteca Angelica, Piazza S. Agostino 8, 00186 Roma
T: (06) 655874
Founded: 1690
Focus: Lit
Periodicals
Atti e Memorie: Serie Terza
Quaderni dell'Accademia Arcadia 06836

Accademia Ligure di Scienze e Lettere, Piazza G. Matteotti 5, 16123 Genova
T: (010) 565570; Fax: 566080
Founded: 1890; Members: 180
Pres: Prof. L. Brian; Gen Secr: Dr. G.P. Peloso
Focus: Sci; Lit
Periodical
Atti della Accademia Ligure di Scienze e Lettere (annually) 06837

Accademia Ligustica de Belle Arti, Piazza Raffaele de Ferrari 5, 16121 Genova
T: (010) 581957
Focus: Arts; Ling 06838

Accademia Lunigianese di Scienze Giovanni Capellini, Via XX Settembre 148, 19100 La Spezia
Focus: Sci; Geography 06839

Accademia Medica, Via Benedetto XV 6, 16132 Genova
Founded: 1885
Focus: Med 06840

Accademia Medica di Roma, c/o Policlinico Umberto I, Viale del Policlinico, 00161 Roma
T: (06) 4957818
Founded: 1876; Members: 400
Focus: Med
Periodical
Bollettino ed Atti dell'Accademia Medica di Roma 06841

Accademia Medica Lombarda, c/o Ospedale Policlinico, Padiglione Monteggia, Via Francesco Sforza 35, 20122 Milano
T: (02) 598941
Founded: 1912
Focus: Med; Bio
Periodical
Atti dell'Accademia Medica Lombarda (quarterly) 06842

Accademia Medica Pistoiese Filippo Pacini, c/o Ospedale Civile, Piazza Giovanni XXIII, 51100 Pistoia
T: (0573) 372209
Founded: 1928
Focus: Med; Surgery
Periodical
Bollettino (annually) 06843

Accademia Medico-Chirurgica del Piceno, c/o Ospedale Civile Umberto 1, 60100 Ancona
Founded: 1932
Focus: Med; Surgery
Periodical
Rassegna Medico-Chirurgica del Piceno . 06844

Accademia Medico-Fisica Fiorentina, c/o Istituto di Radiologia, Policlinico Universitario di Careggi, Viale Morgagni, 50134 Firenze
T: (055) 410084
Focus: Med; Physiology 06845

Accademia Musicale Chigiana, Via di Città 89, 53100 Siena
T: (0577) 46152
Founded: 1932
Pres: Prof. Giovanni Grotanelli de' Santi
Focus: Music
Periodical
Chigiana: Rivista annuale di studi musicologici (annually) 06846

Accademia Musicale Ottorino Respighi (A.M.O.R.), Via di Villa Maggiorani 20, 00168 Roma
T: (06) 336261
Founded: 1978
Focus: Music
Periodicals
Atti dei Convegni Musicologici Annuali
Libro dei Programmi Annuali 06847

Accademia Nazionale dei Lincei, Via della Lungara 10, 00165 Roma
T: (06) 6838831; Fax: 6893616
Founded: 1603; Members: 511
Pres: Prof. Sabatino Moscati
Focus: Sci
Periodicals
Adunanze straordinarie per il conferimento dei premi A. Feltrinelli (annually)
Annuario (annually)
Atti dei Convegni Lincei (irregularly)
Bollettino dei Classici (annually)
Celebrazioni lincee (irregularly)
Contributi del Centro Linceo Interdisciplinare B. Segre (irregularly)
Indici e sussidi bibliografici della Biblioteca (irregularly)
Memorie della classe di scienze morali, storiche e filologiche (irregularly)
Memorie lincee, matematica e applicazioni (irregularly)
Monumenti Antichi (irregularly)
Notizie degli scavi di antichità (annually)
Problemi attuali di scienza e di cultura (irregularly)
Rendiconti della classe di scienze morali, storiche e filologiche (annually)
Rendiconti delle Adunanze Solenni (annually)
Rendiconti lincei, scienze fisiche e naturali (annually) 06848

Accademia Nazionale dei Sartori, Largo dei Lombardi 21, 00186 Roma
T: (06) 6794041
Founded: 1947
Focus: Sci
Periodical
Il Maestro Sarto (quarterly) 06849

Accademia Nazionale delle Scienze, detta dei XL, Via Cassia Antica 35, 00191 Roma
T: (06) 3297667; Fax: 36300057
Founded: 1782; Members: 62
Pres: Prof. G.T. Scarascia Mugnozza; Gen Secr: Prof. E. Manelli
Focus: Nat Sci
Periodicals
Annali
Annuario dell'Accademia Nazionale dei XL
Rendiconti dell'Accademia Nazionale dei XL (annually)
Studi e Documenti 06850

Accademia Nazionale di Agricoltura (ANA), Via Castiglione 11, 40124 Bologna
T: (051) 268809
Founded: 1807; Members: 220
Pres: Prof. Giuseppe Medici; Gen Secr: Dr. Tullio Romualdi
Focus: Agri
Periodical
Annali (quarterly) 06851

Accademia Nazionale di Arte Drammatica Silvio d'Amico, Via Vincenzo Bellini 16, 00198 Roma
T: (06) 8543680; Fax: 8542505
Founded: 1935
Pres: Prof. Luigi Maria Musati
Focus: Perf Arts 06852

Accademia Nazionale di Belle Arti di Parma, Viale Paolo Toschi 1, 43100 Parma
T: (0521) 22270
Founded: 1752
Focus: Arts 06853

Accademia Nazionale di Danza, Largo Arrigo VII 5, Castello dei Cesari, 00153 Roma
T: (06) 5743284; Fax: 5780994
Founded: 1948
Pres: Carlo Scarascia; Gen Secr: Lia Calizza
Focus: Perf Arts 06854

Accademia Nazionale di Entomologia, Via Romana, 50125 Firenze
T: (055) 220531
Focus: Entomology 06855

Accademia Nazionale di Marina Mercantile, Via Garibaldi 4, 16124 Genova
Founded: 1945; Members: 50
Focus: Navig
Periodical
Atti della Accademia Nazionale di Marina Mercantile 06856

Accademia Nazionale di San Luca, Piazza dell'Accademia di San Luca 77, 00187 Roma
T: (06) 6798850; Fax: 6789243
Members: 211
Focus: Arts
Periodical
Annuario dell'Accademia Nazionale di San Luca 06857

Accademia Nazionale di Santa Cecilia, Via Vittoria 6, 00187 Roma
T: (06) 6790389; E-Mail: Concerti Roma; Fax: 6782796
Founded: 1566; Members: 100
Pres: Francesco Siciliani
Focus: Music
Periodicals
Annuario dell'Accademia Nazionale di Santa Cecilia
Studi Musicali 06858

Accademia Nazionale di Scienze, Lettere e Arti, Corso Vittorio Emanuele II 59, 41100 Modena
T: (059) 225566; Fax: 225566
Founded: 1683; Members: 130
Focus: Arts; Lit; Sci
Periodical
Atti e Memorie 06859

Accademia Nazionale di Scienze, Lettere ed Arti, Piazza Indipendenza 17, 90129 Palermo
T: (091) 420862
Pres: Prof. Giuseppe Le Grutte; Gen Secr: Prof. Romualdo Giuffrida
Focus: Sci; Arts; Humanities 06860

Accademia Nazionale Italiana di Entomologia, c/o Istituto Sperimentale per la Zoologia Agraria, Via Romana 15-17, 50125 Firenze
T: (055) 220531
Focus: Entomology 06861

Accademia Nazionale Virgiliana di Scienze, Lettere e Arti di Mantova, Via Accademia 47, 46100 Mantova
T: (0376) 320314; Fax: 222774
Founded: 1562; Members: 150
Focus: Arts; Lit; Sci
Periodical
Atti e Memorie (annually) 06862

Accademia Olimpica, Largo Goethe 3, 36100 Vicenza
T: (0444) 324376, 320396; Fax: 321875
Founded: 1555; Members: 159
Pres: Lorenzo Pellizzari; Gen Secr: Osvaldo Petrella
Focus: Nat Sci; Econ; Philos; Arts; Lit; Hist; Eng; Ling; Law
Periodical
Odeo Olimpico 06863

Accademia Petrarca di Lettere, Arti e Scienze, Via dell'Orto, 52100 Arezzo
T: (0575) 24700
Founded: 1810; Members: 413
Pres: Prof. Alberto Fatucchi; Gen Secr: Dr. Tullio Bensi
Focus: Humanities; Arts; Sci 06864

Accademia Polacca delle Scienze / Polska Akademia Nauk, Palazzo Doria, Vicolo Doria 2, 00187 Roma
T: (06) 6792170; Fax: 6794087
Founded: 1927
Pres: Prof. Krzysztof Zaboklicki
Focus: Humanities; Soc Sci
Periodical
Conferenze (semi-annually) 06865

Accademia Pomposiana, Via Roma 31, 44021 Codigoro
T: 93484
Founded: 1972
Focus: Arts; Lit
Periodical
Seriarte (bi-weekly) 06866

Accademia Pontaniana, Via Mezzocannone 8, 80134 Napoli
T: (081) 207075
Founded: 1443
Focus: Sci; Lit; Arts
Periodicals
Atti dell'Accademia Pontaniana
Fonti Aragenesi
Quaderni
Registri della Cancelleria Angioina . . . 06867

Accademia Pratese di Medicina e Scienze, c/o Ospedale Civile, Piazza Ospedale 5, 50047 Prato
T: (0574) 49001
Founded: 1958
Focus: Med; Sci 06868

Accademia Prenestina del Cimento di Musica, Lettere, Scienze, Arti Visive e Figurative, Via Orazio Marucchi 5, 00036 Palestrina
T: (06) 9558935
Founded: 1977
Focus: Music; Lit; Comm Sci; Arts . . . 06869

Accademia Pugliese delle Scienze, Piazza Umberto I, 70121 Bari
T: (080) 314578
Founded: 1925; Members: 160
Pres: Prof. Luigi Ambrosi
Focus: Sci 06870

Accademia Raffaello, Via Raffaello 57, 61029 Urbino
T: (0722) 4735
Founded: 1869
Focus: Cultur Hist; Fine Arts 06871

Accademia Romana di Cultura, Via Vittorio Fiorini 15, 00179 Roma
T: (06) 723543
Founded: 1949
Focus: Arts; Lit; Sci 06872

Accademia Romana di Scienze Mediche e Biologiche, Via IV Novembre 152, 00187 Roma
T: (06) 6784964
Focus: Med; Bio
Periodicals
Messaggio Medico: Il Corriere di Roma (bi-weekly)
Quaderni Scientifico-Tecnici 06873

Accademia Roveretana degli Agiati, Via Canestrini 1, 38068 Rovereto
T: (0464) 436663; Fax: 436663
Founded: 1750
Focus: Sci; Lit
Periodical
Atti (annually) 06874

Accademia Salentina di Lettere ed Arti, Via Idomeneo 77a, 73100 Lecce
T: (0832) 41127
Founded: 1949
Focus: Lit; Arts 06875

Accademia Scientifica, Letteraria, Artistica del Frignano Lo Scoltenna, c/o Liceo Scientifico Barbieri, Via Tamburu 53, 41027 Pievepelago
T: (0536) 71470
Founded: 1902; Members: 295
Pres: Antonio Galli; Gen Secr: Marisella Casolari
Focus: Lit; Arts; Hist
Periodical
Rassegna Frignanese: Rivista di Cultura e di Studi Regionali (annually) 06876

Accademia Senese degli Intronati, Palazzo Patrizi Piccolomini, Via di Città 75, 53100 Siena
T: (0577) 284073
Founded: 1528
Focus: Lit; Arts; Hist
Periodical
Bullettino Senese di Storia Patria (annually) 06877

Accademia Simba, Via XX Settembre 49, 00187 Roma
T: (06) 483572, 4755592
Focus: Econ; Soc Sci; Poli Sci
Periodical
Corriere Africano: Mensile di Relazioni Africa-Europa-Medio Oriente (monthly) 06878

Accademia Spagnola di Belle Arti, Piazza S. Pietro in Montorio 3, 00153 Roma
T: (06) 5816013, 5818607, 582806
Founded: 1873
Focus: Arts 06879

Accademia Spoletina, Palazzo Mauri, Via Brignone, 06049 Spoleto
T: (0743) 221203
Founded: 1477; Members: 200
Pres: Filippo De Marchis
Focus: Hist; Cultur Hist; Arts
Periodical
Spoletium (annually) 06880

Accademia Tedesca Villa Massimo / Deutsche Akademie Villa Massimo, Via Angelo Masina 5, 00153 Roma
T: (06) 58461; Fax: 5810788
Founded: 1894
Pres: Adele Chatfield-Taylor; Gen Secr: Caroline Bruzelius
Focus: Arts; Lit; Music 06881

Accademia Tiberina, Via del Vantaggio 22, 00186 Roma
T: (06) 3619305
Founded: 1813; Members: 2200
Pres: Prof. Dr. Igor Istomin-Duranti; Gen Secr: Silvia Ramini
Focus: Sci 06882

Accademia Toscana di Scienze e Lettere La Colombaria, Via S. Egidio 23, 50122 Firenze
T: (055) 2396628; E-Mail: colombaria@dada.it; Fax: 2396628
Founded: 1735
Focus: Sci; Lit
Periodical
Atti e Memorie (annually) 06883

Accademia Universale Citta' Eterna, Via Vincenzo Brunacci 15, 00146 Roma
T: (06) 5576604, 5577188
Founded: 1970
Focus: Lit; Arts; Sociology
Periodicals
Città Eterna (weekly)
VIP Gran Premio 06884

Accademia Universale Guglielmo Marconi, Via Ugo Fleres 27, 00137 Roma
T: (06) 825848
Founded: 1978
Focus: Arts; Lit; Sci
Periodical
Teleuropa: Mensile di Cultura, Arte e Attualità (monthly) 06885

Accademia Valdarnese del Poggio, Via Poggio Bracciolini 40, 52025 Montevarchi
T: 981227
Founded: 1450
Focus: Geology; Paleontology
Periodical
Memorie Valdarnesi 06886

Accademia XXXX dei Georgofili, Loggiato degli Uffizi, 50122 Firenze
T: (055) 213360
Founded: 1753
Focus: Econ; Agri
Periodicals
Agraria dei Georgofili
I Georgofili: Atti della Accademia XXXX deo Georgofili
Rivista di Storia dell'Agricoltura 06887

Agricultural Libraries Network (AGLINET), c/o FAO, Via delle Terme di Caracalla, 00100 Roma
T: (06) 57971
Founded: 1971; Members: 27
Focus: Libraries & Bk Sci 06888

Apimondia, Corso Vittorio Emanuele 101, 00186 Roma
T: (06) 6512286; Fax: 6548578
Founded: 1949; Members: 77
Focus: Entomology
Periodicals
Agrindex (monthly)
Apiacta (quarterly) 06889

Aquatic Sciences and Fisheries Information System (ASFIS), c/o FAO, Fisheries Dept, Fishery Information, Data and Statistics Service, Via delle Terme di Caracalla, 00100 Roma
T: (06) 57971; Fax: 5146172
Founded: 1972; Members: 12
Focus: Fisheries 06890

Arbeitsgemeischaft der Kunst- und Museumsbibliotheken, c/o Deutsches Archäologisches Institut Rom, Via Sardegna 79, 00187 Roma
T: (06) 4817812; Fax: 4884973
Focus: Libraries & Bk Sci 06891

Association of Advisers on Education in International Religious Congregations (EDUC International), c/o International School Sisters of Notre-Dame, Via della Stazione Aurelia 95, 00165 Roma
T: (06) 6808065
Founded: 1967
Focus: Educ 06892

Association of European Operational Research Societies (EURO), c/o Dip di Elettronica, Informatica e Sistemistica, Università di Bologna, Viale Risorgimento 2, 40136 Bologna
T: (051) 6443028
Founded: 1975
Focus: Computer & Info Sci
Periodicals
EURO Bulletin
European Journal of Operational Research (monthly) 06893

Associazione Alessandro Scarlatti, Piazza dei Martiri 58, 80121 Napoli
T: (081) 406011
Founded: 1919
Focus: Music 06894

Associazione Anestesisti Rianimatori Ospedalieri Italiani (AAROI), Via Massimo Stanzione 15, 80129 Napoli
T: (081) 378724
Founded: 1959; Members: 1400
Focus: Anesthetics 06895

Associazione Archaeologica Romana, Vicolo del Governo Vecchio 8, 00186 Roma
Founded: 1902; Members: 500
Focus: Archeol 06896

Associazione Archeologica Allumiere Adolfo Klitsche de la Grange, c/o Museo Civico, 00051 Allumiere
Founded: 1954
Focus: Archeol
Periodical
Notiziario del Museo Civico (annually) . 06897

Associazione Archeologica Centumcellae, Piazza Leandro 5, 00053 Civitavecchia
T: (0766) 500783
Founded: 1911
Focus: Archeol
Periodical
Bollettino d'Informazioni 06898

Associazione Archeologica Romana, Piazza B. Cairoli 117, 00186 Roma
T: (06) 64565647
Founded: 1902; Members: 400
Pres: Dr. V. Santa Maria Scrinari; Gen Secr: Dr. Leandro Sperduti
Focus: Archeol
Periodical
Romana Gens (monthly) 06899

Associazione Archivistica Ecclesiastica, Piazza S. Calisto 16, 00153 Roma
T: (06) 67015228
Founded: 1956
Focus: Archives
Periodicals
Archiva Ecclesiae
Notiziario: Organo di Collegamento (semi-annually) 06900

Associazione Astrofili Bolognesi (A.A.B.), CP 313, 40100 Bologna
T: (051) 517800
Founded: 1967; Members: 250
Focus: Astronomy
Periodical
Giornale dell' A.A.B. (quarterly) 06901

Associazione Bresciana di Ricerche Economiche (A.B.R.E.), c/o Camera di Commercio, Via Luigi Einaudi 23, 25100 Brescia
T: (030) 45061
Founded: 1960
Focus: Econ 06902

Associazione Campana degli Insegnanti di Scienze Naturali (ACISN), c/o Università degli Studi, Via Mezzocannone 8, 80134 Napoli
T: (081) 612849
Founded: 1969
Focus: Nat Sci
Periodical
ACISN: Bollettino Periodico delle Attività . 06903

Associazione Centri di Orientamento Scolastico Professionale e Sociale (COSPES), Piazza Ateneo Salesiano 1, 00139 Roma
T: (06) 8184641
Focus: Educ 06904

Associazione Criogenica Italiana (A.Cr.I.), c/o Istituto di Scienze Fisiche, Facoltà di Scienze, Università degli Studi, Via Dodecaneso 33, 16146 Genova
T: (010) 59931
Founded: 1980
Focus: Eng; Air Cond 06905

Associazione degli Africanisti Italiani, c/o Dipartimento di Studi Politici e Sociali, Sezione di Studi Afro-Asiatici, Via Strada Nuova 65, 27100 Pavia
T: (0382) 37358
Founded: 1967; Members: 70
Focus: Ethnology
Periodical
Bollettino (quarterly) 06906

Associazione degli Statistici, Via Roma 12, 33100 Udine
T: (0432) 204198
Founded: 1976
Focus: Stats
Periodical
Statistica (semi-annually) 06907

Associazione dei Critici Letterari Italiani, Via Bu Meliana 12, 00195 Roma
T: (06) 3565003
Founded: 1969
Focus: Lit 06908

Associazione dei Geografi Italiani (A.GE.I.), c/o Istituto dell'Enciclopedia Italiana, Piazza Paganica 4, 00186 Roma
T: (06) 650881
Founded: 1977
Focus: Geography 06909

Associazione di Cultura Lao Silesu, Piazza Quintino Sella 34, 09016 Iglesias
T: (0781) 41902
Founded: 1963
Focus: Lit; Arts; Folklore
Periodical
La Questione Sarda-Autonomia (bi-monthly) 06910

Associazione di Cultura Romana Te Roma Sequor, Via Gregoriana 25, 00187 Roma
Founded: 1925
Focus: Hist
Periodical
Te Roma Sequor (quarterly) 06911

Associazione di Ricerca e Interventi Psicosociali e Psicoterapeutici (ARIPS), Via Brescia 6, 25080 Molinetto di Mazzano
T: (030) 2620589, 2120130; E-Mail: arips@iol.it; Fax: 2120130
Founded: 1978
Pres: Margherita Sberna
Focus: Sociology; Psych
Periodicals
Gruppi, Organizzazioni, Comunità (semi-annually)
Notizie ARIPS (quarterly) 06912

Associazione Educatrice Italiana (AEI), Via Trinita dei Pelligrini 16, 00186 Roma
T: (06) 6861555; Fax: 6893261
Founded: 1927
Focus: Educ 06913

Associazione Elettrotecnica ed Elettronica Italiana, Viale Monza 259, 20129 Milano
T: (02) 257791
Founded: 1896
Pres: P. Chizzolini
Focus: Electric Eng; Electronic Eng . . 06914

Associazione Forense Italiana, Palazzo Giustizia, Piazza Cavour, 00193 Roma
Focus: Law 06915

Associazione Forestale Italiana, Via Guido d'Arezzo 16, 00198 Roma
Pres: Dr. Alfonso Froncillo
Focus: Forestry 06916

Associazione Genetica Italiana (AGI), c/o Prof. G.A. Danieli, Dipartimento di Biologia, Via Trieste 75, 35100 Padova
T: (049) 8071978
Founded: 1953; Members: 450
Focus: Genetics
Periodical
Atti dell'Associazione Genetica Italiana (annually) 06917

Associazione Geo-Archeologica Italiana, c/o Instituto di Archeologia Università di Roma, Piazzale Aldo Moro 5, 00185 Roma
T: (06) 857540
Founded: 1968
Focus: Geology; Archeol
Periodical
Geo-Archeologia (semi-annually) 06918

Associazione Geofisica Italiana (AGI), c/o C.N.R.-I.F.A., Piazzale Luigi Sturzo 31, 00144 Roma
T: (06) 59293011; Fax: 5915790
Founded: 1951; Members: 300
Pres: Marcello Pagliari; Gen Secr: Dr. M. Aversa
Focus: Geophys
Periodical
Bollettino Geofisico (monthly) 06919

Associazione Geotecnica Italiana, Via Giorgio Baglivi 5, 00161 Roma
T: (06) 44249272; Fax: 44249274
Founded: 1947; Members: 1500
Pres: Sandro Martinetti; Gen Secr: Sergio Di Maio
Focus: Mining
Periodicals
Atti dei Convegni Nazionale di Geotecnica
Rivista Italiana di Geotecnica (quarterly) . 06920

Associazione Giacomo Boni per la Difesa dei Monumenti di Roma Antica, c/o Direzione del Palatino e del Foro Romano, Piazza S. Maria Nova 53, 00186 Roma
T: (06) 6790333
Founded: 1973
Focus: Preserv Hist Monuments 06921

Associazione Grafologica Italiana (A.G.I.), Scale San Francesco 8, 60100 Ancona
T: (071) 206100; Fax: 206100
Founded: 1976; Members: 1200
Focus: Graphology
Periodical
Attualità Grafologica (quarterly) 06922

Associazione Idrotecnica Italiana (AII), Viale Regina Margherita 239, 00198 Roma
T: (06) 4404493
Founded: 1923; Members: 1500
Pres: Dr. Umberto Ucelli; Gen Secr: Dr. Pasquale Penta
Focus: Water Res
Periodical
Idrotecnica (bi-monthly) 06923

Associazione Internazionale Centro Studi di Storia e Documentazione delle Regioni, Stradone Vescovado 3, 42100 Reggio Emilia
T: (0522) 35621
Focus: Doc; Hist 06924

Associazione Internazionale di Archeologia Classica (AIAC), Piazza S. Marco 49, 00186 Roma
T: (06) 6798798
Founded: 1945; Members: 450
Focus: Archeol
Periodicals
Annuario
Fasti Archaeologici (annually) 06925

Associazione Internazionale di Diritto Nucleare, Via S. Ilaria 2, 00199 Roma
Founded: 1970; Members: 150
Focus: Law 06926

Associazione Internazionale di Poesia, Via Angelo Poliziano 69, 00184 Roma
Focus: Lit
Periodical
Il Giornale dei Poeti 06927

Associazione Internazionale Giuristi Italia-USA, Via Castelfranco Veneto 90, 00191 Roma
T: (06) 3277781
Founded: 1979
Focus: Law 06928

Associazione Internazionale per lo Studio del Diritto Canonico, c/o Istituto di Diritto Canonico, Facoltà di Giurisprudenza, Università degli Studi, Città Universitaria, Piazzale delle Scienze, 00185 Roma
T: (06) 491319
Focus: Rel & Theol 06929

Associazione Italiana Biblioteche (AIB), CP 2461, 00100 Roma
T: (06) 4463532; Fax: 4441139
Founded: 1930; Members: 3000
Pres: Dr. Rossella Caffo; Gen Secr: Dr. Luca Bellingeri
Focus: Libraries & Bk Sci
Periodicals
AIB Notizie (monthly)
Bolletino AIB (quarterly) *06930*

Associazione Italiana Condizionamento dell'Aria, Riscaldamento e Refrigerazione, Via Sardegna 32, 20146 Milano
Founded: 1960
Focus: Air Cond
Periodical
Condizionamento dell'Aria (monthly) . . . *06931*

Associazione Italiana degli Insegnanti di Geografia (AIIG), c/o G. Valussi, Via P. Valussi 2, 34141 Trieste
Members: 2080
Focus: Educ; Geography
Periodical
La Geografia nelle Scuole (bi-monthly) . *06932*

Associazione Italiana degli Slavisti (A.I.S.), c/o Istituto di Filologia Slava, Facoltà di Lettere e Filosofia, Università di Pisa, Via del Collegio Ricci 10, 56100 Pisa
T: (050) 28466
Founded: 1971
Focus: Ling; Lit
Periodicals
Europa Orientalis: Studi e Ricerche sulle Culture dell'Est Europeo
Ricerche Slavistiche *06933*

Associazione Italiana dei Chimici del Cuoio, c/o Prof. Giuseppe De Simone, Via Salerno 37, 10152 Torino
Focus: Chem
Periodical
Cuoio, Pelli e Materie Concianti *06934*

Associazione Italiana dei Giuristi Europei, Via Nomentana 76, 00161 Roma
Focus: Law *06935*

Associazione Italiana di Aeronautica e Astronautica (AIDAA), Via Po 50, 00198 Roma
T: (06) 8445894
Founded: 1920; Members: 1000
Pres: Prof. Ernesto Vallerani; Gen Secr: Dr. Antonio Castellani
Focus: Aero
Periodical
L'Aerotecnica-Missili e Spazio (quarterly) . *06936*

Associazione Italiana di Anestesia Odontostomatologica, CP 1630, 40100 Bologna
T: (051) 247784
Founded: 1971
Focus: Anesthetics; Dent
Periodical
Giornale di Anestesia Stomatologica (quarterly) *06937*

Associazione Italiana di Anglistica (A.I.A.), Via della Faggiola 7, 56126 Pisa
Focus: Ling
Periodical
Textus (semi-annually) *06938*

Associazione Italiana di Cardiostimolazione (A.I.C.), Viale Gramsci 14, 56125 Pisa
T: (050) 21051; Fax: 21051
Founded: 1978; Members: 508
Focus: Cardiol
Periodical
Cardiostimolazione *06939*

Associazione Italiana di Cartografia (AIC), c/o Istituto di Geografia dell'Università, Largo S. Marcellino 10, 80138 Napoli
Founded: 1963
Focus: Cart
Periodical
Bollettino dell'Associazione Italiana di Cartografia *06940*

Associazione Italiana di Chimica Tessile e Coloristica (AICTC), Viale Sarca 223, 20126 Milano
Focus: Chem; Textiles
Periodical
Bollettino dell'Associazione Italiana di Chimica Tessile e Coloristica (quarterly) *06941*

Associazione Italiana di Cinematografia Scientifica, Via Alfonso Borelli 50, 00161 Roma
T: (06) 490820
Focus: Cinema *06942*

Associazione Italiana di Cultura Classica, c/o Istituto di Filologia Classica, Università, Piazza Brunelleschi 4, 50121 Firenze
Focus: Ethnology *06943*

Associazione Italiana di Dietetica e Nutrizione Clinica, Via dei Penitenzieri 13, 00193 Roma
Members: 200
Pres: Prof. P. Montenero
Focus: Hematology *06944*

Associazione Italiana di Diritto Marittimo, Via Po 1, 00198 Roma
Gen Secr: Camilla Dagna
Focus: Law *06945*

Associazione Italiana di Documentazione e di Informazione (AIDI), Via Vittoria Colonna 39, 00193 Roma
T: (06) 3604841
Founded: 1966
Focus: Doc; Computer & Info Sci . . . *06946*

Associazione Italiana di Fisica Sanitaria e di Protezione contro le Radiazioni (AIFSPR), c/o Centro Studi Fisico-Biologici, Corso Polonia 14, 10126 Torino
T: (011) 693358
Focus: Public Health; Ecology *06947*

Associazione Italiana di Genio Rurale (AIGR), Via Gradenigo 6, 35131 Padova
T: (049) 8071065; Fax: 8070615
Founded: 1959; Members: 373
Focus: Civil Eng; Agri
Periodical
Rivista di Ingegneria Agraria (quarterly) . *06948*

Associazione Italiana di Immuno-Oncologia Clinico-Pratica, c/o Istituti Ospedalieri, Viale Albertoni, 46100 Mantova
T: (0376) 329261
Founded: 1978
Focus: Immunology *06949*

Associazione Italiana di Ingegneria Chimica, Corso Venezia 16, 20121 Milano
T: (02) 791175
Founded: 1958
Focus: Eng; Chem
Periodical
Rivista I.C.P. *06950*

Associazione Italiana di Ingegneria Medica e Biologica (A.I.I.M.B.), c/o Facolta di Ingegneria, Via Claudio 21, 80125 Napoli
T: (081) 620522
Founded: 1966; Members: 160
Focus: Med; Bio; Eng *06951*

Associazione Italiana di Medicina Aeronautica e Spaziale (AIMAS), Via Piero Gobetti 2a, 00185 Roma
T: (06) 463538
Founded: 1952
Pres: Prof. Aristide Scano
Focus: Med *06952*

Associazione Italiana di Medicina dell'Assicurazione Vita, Viale Regina Elena 336, 00161 Roma
Focus: Med
Periodical
Atti del Convegno Nazionale di Medicina dell'Assicurazione Vita *06953*

Associazione Italiana di Metallurgia (A.I.M.), Piazzale Rodolfo Morandi 2, 20121 Milano
T: (02) 76021132; E-Mail: ASSOMETAL Milano; Fax: 784236
Founded: 1946; Members: 2000
Pres: Dr. Giuseppe Orlando; Gen Secr: Aurelio Ciccocioppo
Focus: Metallurgy
Periodical
La Metallurgia Italiana (monthly) *06954*

Associazione Italiana di Microbiologia Applicata (SIMA), Via Novara 89, 20153 Milano
T: (02) 48779245; Fax: 40090010
Founded: 1975; Members: 250
Focus: Microbio *06955*

Associazione Italiana di Oncologia Medica (A.I.O.M.), Via G. Venezian 1, 20133 Milano
T: (02) 2664352, 2390676; Fax: 2367404
Founded: 1973; Members: 1400
Pres: Prof. Maurizio Tonato; Gen Secr: Dr. Roberto Labianca
Focus: Cell Biol & Cancer Res
Periodicals
Abstracts Tumori
Association News
Update in Medical Oncology *06956*

Associazione Italiana di Protezione contro le Radiazione (A.I.R.P.), c/o Enea, Viale G.B. Ercolani 8, 40138 Bologna
T: (051) 498259; Fax: 498131
Founded: 1958
Focus: Radiology
Periodical
Bollettino A.I.R.P. (bi-monthly) *06957*

Associazione Italiana di Psicologia dello Sport (A.I.P.S.), Via Aldighieri 7, 40100 Ferrara
T: (0532) 34401
Founded: 1974
Focus: Psych; Sports *06958*

Associazione Italiana di Radiobiologia Medica e Medicina Nucleare, c/o III Cattedra di Radiologia, Istituto di Radiologia, Policlinico Umberto I, 00161 Roma
Pres: Prof. Carissimo Biagini; Gen Secr: Prof. Vincenzo Cavallo
Focus: Bio; Radiology *06959*

Associazione Italiana di Radiologia e Medicina Nucleare (A.I.R.M.N.), c/o Istituto di Radiologia, Università degli Studi La Sapienza, Policlinico Umberto Primo, 00161 Roma
Founded: 1959
Focus: Radiology; Nucl Med
Periodicals
La Radiologia Medica (monthly)
Il Radiologo (quarterly) *06960*

Associazione Italiana di Ricerca Operativa (AIRO), c/o ILVA, Via Ilva 3, 16128 Genova
T: (010) 314415
Founded: 1961; Members: 500
Focus: Business Admin
Periodical
Ricerca Operativa (3 times annually) . . *06961*

Associazione Italiana di Robotica (S.I.R.I.), c/o UCIMU, Viale Fulvio Testi 128, 20092 Cinisello Balsamo
T: (02) 783051
Focus: Electronic Eng *06962*

Associazione Italiana di Scienze Politiche e Sociali (AISPS), Viale Bruno Buozzi 105, 00197 Roma
Focus: Poli Sci; Sociology *06963*

Associazione Italiana di Sociologia (AIS), Via del Quadraro 14, 00174 Roma
T: (06) 7672209
Founded: 1972
Focus: Sociology *06964*

Associazione Italiana di Strumentisti, Via Giulio Carcano 24, 20141 Milano
T: (02) 8435844
Focus: Eng *06965*

Associazione Italiana di Studi Semiotici (A.I.S.S.), Strade Comunale di Pecetto 244, 10131 Torino
T: (011) 658052
Focus: Ling *06966*

Associazione Italiana di Studio delle Relazioni Industriali, Via Brescia 29, 00198 Roma
Focus: Business Admin *06967*

Associazione Italiana di Tecnica Navale (ATENA), Salita S. Caterina 10, 16123 Genova
T: (010) 542254
Founded: 1946
Focus: Navig *06968*

Associazione Italiana di Tecnologia Alimentare (A.I.T.A.), c/o Istituto di Tecnologie Alimentari, Via Celoria 2, 20133 Milano
T: (02) 70631971; Fax: 70638625
Founded: 1979
Focus: Nutrition
Periodical
Tecnologie Alimentari: Sistemi per Produrre *06969*

Associazione Italiana di Terapia Occupazionale (A.I.T.O.), Via Peralba 9, 00141 Roma
Founded: 1977
Focus: Psychiatry
Periodical
Il Bagatto (semi-annually) *06970*

Associazione Italiana Giuristi Democratici (A.I.G.D.), Viale Carso 51, 00195 Roma
T: (06) 315664
Founded: 1946
Focus: Law
Periodical
Democrazia e Diritto: Trimestrale di Diritto e Giurisprudenza (quarterly) *06971*

Associazione Italiana per gli Studi di Marketing (AISM), Via Olmetto 3, 20123 Milano
T: (02) 863293 72002889; E-Mail: aism@vnet.ecs.net
Founded: 1954; Members: 350
Pres: Sergio Meacci
Focus: Marketing *06972*

Associazione Italiana per la Difesa degli Interessi di Diabetici, Via del Scofa 14, 00186 Roma
T: (06) 6543784
Focus: Diabetes *06973*

Associazione Italiana per la Promozione degli Studi e delle Ricerche per l'Edifizia (AIRE) / Italian Association for the Promotion of Building Research and Studies, Via B. Angelico 3, 20133 Milano
T: (02) 716281; Fax: 716295
Founded: 1964; Members: 5
Focus: Civil Eng *06974*

Associazione Italiana per la Psicologia Umanistica e Transpersonale (I.A.H.P.), Via Adolfo Ravà 61, 00142 Roma
T: (06) 5402291
Focus: Psych *06975*

Associazione Italiana per la Qualità (AICQ), Piazza Armando Diaz 2, 20123 Milano
T: (02) 8052285
Founded: 1955; Members: 2000
Focus: Materials Sci
Periodicals
Lettera Circolare Qualità
Qualità (quarterly) *06976*

Associazione Italiana per la Ricerca Industriale (A.I.R.I.), Viale Gorizia 25, 00198 Roma
T: (06) 8848871; Fax: 8552949
Founded: 1974
Focus: Eng; Econ
Periodical
Notizie A.I.R.I. (bi-monthly) *06977*

Associazione Italiana per la Ricerca nell'Impiego degli Elastomeri (AIRIEL), Via San Vittore 36, 20123 Milano
T: (02) 466020; Fax: 435432
Founded: 1968; Members: 44
Pres: Arrigo Pini
Focus: Materials Sci
Periodical
L'Industria della Gomma/Elastica (monthly) *06978*

Associazione Italiana per l'Analisi delle Sollecitazioni (A.I.A.S.), c/o Dipartimento di Energetica, Università, Via Valerio 10, 34127 Trieste
T: (040) 6763430; Fax: 568469
Founded: 1971; Members: 400
Focus: Eng
Periodical
Notiziario A.I.A.S. (quarterly) *06979*

Associazione Italiana per le Ricerche di Storia del Cinema, Via Tuscolana 1522, 00173 Roma
Founded: 1964
Focus: Cinema
Periodical
Bollettino dell'Associazione (annually) . . *06980*

Associazione Italiana per L'Educazione Sanitaria (A.I.E.S.), c/o Centro Sperimentale per l'Educazione Sanitaria, Via del Giochetto, 06100 Perugia
T: (075) 28377
Founded: 1967
Focus: Hygiene
Periodical
Notiziario in La Salute Umana (semi-annually) *06981*

Associazione Italiana per l'Informatica et il Calcolo Automatico, Piazzale Rodolfo Morandi 2, 20121 Milano
T: (02) 784970, 76014082; E-Mail: aica@iol.it; Fax: 76015717
Founded: 1961; Members: 1500
Focus: Computer & Info Sci
Periodical
Informatica (quarterly) *06982*

Associazione Italiana per lo Studio del Dolore (A.I.S.D.), c/o Clinica Medica, Università degli Studi, Viale G.B. Morgagni 85, 50134 Firenze
T: (055) 412063
Founded: 1976
Focus: Pathology
Periodical
Bollettino dell'Associazione Italiana per lo Studio del Dolore (quarterly) *06983*

Associazione Italiana per lo Studio della Psicologia Analitica (A.I.P.A.), Via Cola di Rienzo 28, 00192 Roma
T: (06) 388210
Founded: 1961
Focus: Psych; Psychoan
Periodical
Rivista di Psicologia Analitica *06984*

Associazione Italiana per lo Sviluppo Internazionale (AISI), Via Luigi Lilio 19, 00143 Roma
T: (06) 5146089
Founded: 1977
Focus: Int'l Relat
Periodicals
Note Informative AISI (irregularly)
Quaderni AISI (irregularly) *06985*

Associazione Italiana Santa Cecilia per la Musica Sacra (AISC), Piazza S. Calisto 16, 00153 Roma
Founded: 1877; Members: 3000
Focus: Music
Periodical
Bollettino Ceciliano (monthly) *06986*

Associazione Italiana Scientifica di Metapsichica (A.I.S.M.), Via S. Vittore 19, 20123 Milano
Focus: Parapsych
Periodical
Metapsichica (quarterly) *06987*

Associazione Italiana Sclerosi Multipla (AISM), Via della Magliana 279, 00146 Roma
T: (06) 5267923
Focus: Pathology
Periodical
Notiziario AISM (quarterly) *06988*

Associazione Italiana Socioanalisi Individuale (A.I.S.I.), Via del Don 6, 20123 Milano
T: (02) 8358328
Founded: 1976
Focus: Psych; Sociology *06989*

Associazione Italiana Studi Americanisti (A.I.S.A.), Corso Solferino 29, 16122 Genova
T: (010) 814737
Founded: 1964
Focus: Ethnology; Hist; Archeol; Anthro
Periodical
Terra America (annually) *06990*

Associazione Italiana Tecnico-Economica del Cemento (AITEC), Via di S. Teresa 23, 00193 Roma
T: (06) 8548505; Fax: 8416176
Founded: 1960; Members: 45
Focus: Civil Eng

Periodicals
Cemento (quarterly)
L'Industria Italiana del Cemento (monthly) 06991

Associazione Italiana tra Foniatri e Logopedisti, c/o Centro Medico di Foniatria, Via Bergamo 10, 35100 Padova
Focus: Logopedy 06992

Associazione La Nostra Famiglia, 22037 Ponte Lambro
T: (031) 625111; E-Mail: Zanella@pl1.lnf.it; Fax: 625275
Founded: 1948; Members: 110
Focus: Educ Handic
Periodicals
Notiziario d'Informazione del Gruppo Amici de La Nostra Famiglia
Saggi: Rivista di Neuropsicologia Infantile, Psicopedagogia, Riabilitazione 06993

Associazione Medica Italiana di Idroclimatologia, Talassologia e Terapia Fisica, Via Roverto 11, 00198 Roma
T: (06) 863505
Founded: 1896
Focus: Physical Therapy; Therapeutics
Periodical
La Clinica Termale (bi-monthly) 06994

Associazione Medica Italiana per lo Studio della Ipnosi (A.M.I.S.I.), Via Paisiello 28, 20131 Milano
T: (02) 2365493; Fax: 2365493
Founded: 1959
Focus: Psychoan
Periodical
Rivista Italiana di Ipnosi Clinica e Sperimentale 06995

Associazione Medici Dentisti Italiani (AMDI), Via Savoia 78, 00198 Roma
T: (06) 8540535; Fax: 8414133
Members: 4000
Focus: Dent; Stomatology
Periodicals
Bollettino AMDI: Annuario degli Atti Ufficiali dell'Associazione (quarterly)
Fronte Stomatologico (monthly)
Rivista Italiana di Stomatologia (monthly) 06996

Associazione Micologica ed Ecologica Romana (A.M.E.R.), c/o Cattedra di Micologia Orto Botanico, Università degli Studi, Largo Cristina di Svezia 24, 00165 Roma
Founded: 1973
Focus: Ecology; Botany, Specific 06997

Associazione Nazionale Archivistica Italiana (ANAI), Via di Ponziano 15, 00152 Roma
T: (06) 585067
Founded: 1948
Focus: Archives
Periodical
Archivi e Cultura (annually) 06998

Associazione Nazionale Assistenti Sociali (AssNAS), c/o CISS, Via Duilio, 00192 Roma
T: (06) 318696
Focus: Sociology 06999

Associazione Nazionale degli Urbanisti (ASSURBANISTI), CP 348, 31100 Treviso
Founded: 1977; Members: 250
Focus: Urban Plan
Periodical
Il Giornale degli Urbanisti: Organo Ufficiale (quarterly) 07000

Associazione Nazionale dei Musei Italiani, Piazza S. Marco 49, 00186 Roma
T: (06) 6791343; Fax: 6791343
Founded: 1955; Members: 615
Pres: Prof. D. Bernini; Gen Secr: Dr. L. Barbacani
Focus: Arts
Periodical
Musei e Gallerie d'Italia 07001

Associazione Nazionale dei Periti Grafici a Base Psicologica (ANPGP), Corso XXII Marzo 57, 20129 Milano
T: (02) 7388427; Fax: 7491051
Founded: 1969; Members: 98
Focus: Psych; Graphology 07002

Associazione Nazionale del Libero Pensiero Giordano Bruno, Casella Postale 6089, Roma-Prati
T: (06) 3274807
Founded: 1903
Focus: Philos
Periodical
La Ragione (bi-monthly) 07003

Associazione Nazionale di Ingegneria Nucleare, Piazza Sallustio 24, 00187 Roma
T: (06) 486415
Pres: Maurizio Cumo; Gen Secr: Guido Botta
Focus: Nucl Res 07004

Associazione Nazionale di Ingegneria Sanitaria (ANDIS), Piazza Sallustio 24, 00187 Roma
T: (06) 487397
Founded: 1953
Focus: Eng
Periodical
Ingegneria Sanitaria (bi-monthly) 07005

Associazione Nazionale di Meccanica (ASMECCANICA), c/o F.A.S.T., Piazzale Rodolfo Morandi 2, 20121 Milano
T: (02) 784991
Founded: 1970
Focus: Eng
Periodical
La Meccanica Italiana (monthly) 07006

Associazione Nazionale Disegno di Macchine (A.D.M.), Viale delle Scienze, 90128 Palermo
T: (091) 427238
Founded: 1974
Focus: Mach Eng
Periodical
Disegno di Macchine 07007

Associazione Nazionale Esercenti Teatri (ANET), Via Villa Patrizi 10, 00161 Roma
Focus: Perf Arts 07008

Associazione Nazionale Famiglie di Fanciulli e Adulti Subnormali (ANFFAS), Borgo Sant'Angelo 19, 00193 Roma
T: (06) 6547454
Focus: Educ Handic 07009

Associazione Nazionale Filosofia Arti Scienze (FAS), Via Oberdan 15, 40126 Bologna
T: (051) 232506
Founded: 1958
Focus: Philos; Sci
Periodical
Quaderni FAS 07010

Associazione Nazionale Industria Meccanica Varia ed Affine (A.N.I.M.A.), Piazza Armando Diaz 2, 20123 Milano
T: (02) 809006
Founded: 1945
Focus: Eng
Periodical
L'Industria Meccanica (monthly) 07011

Associazione Nazionale Ingegneri ed Architetti Italiani (ANIAI), Piazza Sallustio 24, 00187 Roma
T: (06) 486415, 4744397
Focus: Archit; Eng
Periodicals
Bollettino di Informazione ANIAI (bi-weekly)
Il Giornale dell'Ingegnere (bi-weekly)
L'Ingegnere: Rivista Tecnica di Ingegneria e di Architettura (monthly)
Ingegneria Nucleare (bi-monthly)
Ingegneria Sanitaria (bi-monthly)
Quaderni ANIAI
Tecnica Ospedaliera (monthly) 07012

Associazione Nazionale Ingegneri Minerari (A.N.I.M.), Piazza Sallustio 24, 00187 Roma
T: (06) 4744397
Founded: 1962
Focus: Mineralogy 07013

Associazione Nazionale Insegnanti di Disegno (ANID), c/o Prof. Luigi Varone, Salita Arenella 13a, 80129 Napoli
T: (081) 378927
Focus: Adult Educ 07014

Associazione Nazionale Italiana Esperti Scientifici del Turismo (ANIEST), Via C. Federici 2, 00147 Roma
T: (06) 5134973
Founded: 1964; Members: 125
Focus: Econ
Periodical
Rassegna di Studi Turistici (quarterly) . . 07015

Associazione Nazionale Italiana per l'Automazione (ANIPLA), Piazzale Rodolfo Morandi 2, 20121 Milano
T: (02) 702311
Members: 800
Focus: Eng 07016

Associazione Nazionale per i Centri Storico-Artistici, Palazzo dei Consoli, 06024 Gubbio
Founded: 1961
Focus: Cultur Hist
Periodical
Bollettino dell'Associazione (bi-monthly) . 07017

Associazione Nazionale per il Progresso della Scuola Italiana, Palazzo Odescalchi, Piazza SS. Apostoli 80, 00186 Roma
T: (06) 6780004
Founded: 1970
Focus: Educ
Periodical
Politica della Scuola (quarterly) 07018

Associazione Nazionale per la Scuola Italiana (ANSI), Via Paolo Emilio 57, 00192 Roma
T: (06) 383632
Founded: 1945
Focus: Educ
Periodical
Rinnovare la Scuola (bi-monthly) 07019

Associazione Nazionale per lo Studio dei Problemi del Credito, Via Lisbona 9, 00198 Roma
T: (06) 863036
Focus: Finance 07020

Associazione Nazionale Professori Universitari di Ruolo (ANPUR), c/o Prof. Dr. V. Castellano, Via Ippolerate 79, 00161 Roma
Focus: Adult Educ 07021

Associazione Otologica Ospedaliera Italiano (AOOI), c/o Prof. Lucio Coppo, Via Boezio 14, 00192 Roma
T: (06) 353264
Founded: 1947; Members: 1126
Focus: Otorhinolaryngology
Periodical
Acta Otorhinolaryngologica Italica (bi-monthly) 07022

Associazione Ottica Italiana (AOI), Largo Enrico Fermi 1, 50125 Firenze
T: (055) 221163
Founded: 1926
Focus: Optics
Periodical
Luce e Immagini (bi-monthly) 07023

Associazione Pedagogica Italiana, Via Zamboni 34, 40126 Bologna
T: (051) 258442; Fax: 228847
Founded: 1950; Members: 5000
Pres: Sira Serenella Macchietti; Gen Secr: Aldo D'Alfonso
Focus: Educ
Periodicals
Bollettino della As.Pe.I.
Prospettiva E.P. (semi-annually) 07024

Associazione per il Diabete Infantile e Giovanile (A.D.I.G.), c/o Servizio di Diabetologia, Istituto di Clinica Pediatrica, Università degli Studi, Policlinico Umberto 1, Viale Regina Elena 324, 00161 Roma
T: (06) 490962
Founded: 1976
Focus: Diabetes; Pediatrics
Periodical
Scritti in Favore dei Bambini Diabetici (annually) 07025

Associazione per Imola Storico-Artistica (I.S.A.), Via Emilia 125, 40026 Imola
T: (0542) 20908; Fax: 55082
Founded: 1938
Focus: Preserv Hist Monuments; Arts; Hist 07026

Associazione per la Conservazione delle Tradizioni Popolari, Palazzo Fatta, Piazza Marina 19, 90133 Palermo
T: (091) 328060
Founded: 1965
Focus: Ethnology; Folklore; Perf Arts
Periodical
Studi e Materiali per la Storia della Cultura Popolare (irregularly) 07027

Associazione per l'Agricoltura Biodinamica, Via Privata Vasto 4, 20121 Milano
T: (02) 29002544; Fax: 29002544
Founded: 1947
Focus: Agri
Periodical
Terra Biodinamica (quarterly) 07028

Associazione per le Previsioni Econometriche (PROMETEIA), Via Santa 12, 40125 Bologna
T: (051) 226789
Focus: Econ 07029

Associazione per lo Studio del Problema Mondiale dei Rifugiati, Sezione Italiana / Association for the Study of the World Refugee Problem, A.W.R., Piazzale di Porta Pia 121, 00198 Roma
T: (06) 8445514
Founded: 1960
Focus: Poli Sci; Sociology 07030

Associazione per lo Sviluppo degli Studi di Banca e Borsa (ASSBB), c/o Banca Popolare Commercio e Industria, Via Moscova 33, 20121 Milano
Founded: 1973
Focus: Finance 07031

Associazione per lo Sviluppo delle Scienze Religiose in Italia, Via San Vitale 114, 40125 Bologna
T: (051) 239532; Fax: 230658
Founded: 1961; Members: 182
Focus: Rel & Theol; Hist 07032

Associazione per lo Sviluppo dell'Istruzione e della Formazione Professionale (A.S.I.P.), Via Federico Cesi 30, 00193 Roma
T: (06) 310429
Founded: 1971
Focus: Develop Areas
Periodical
Sviluppo, Formazione, Economia, Cooperazione Internazionale (quarterly) 07033

Associazione per lo Sviluppo di Studi e Ricerche nell'Industria Tessile Laniera Oreste Rivetti, Piazza Lamarmora 5, 13051 Biella
T: (015) 20490, 21655
Focus: Textiles 07034

Associazione Piemontese di Studi Filosofici, Via Torino 55, 13051 Biella
T: (015) 22756
Focus: Philos 07035

Associazione Professionale Italiana Medici Oculisti (APIMO), Via degli Scialoia 18, 00196 Roma
T: (06) 3610333
Focus: Ophthal 07036

Associazione Psicanalitica Italiana, Via Crivelli 15, 20122 Milano
T: (02) 588804
Founded: 1976
Focus: Psychoan
Periodicals
Clinica: Rivista Internazionale di Psichiatria
Vel: Collana Periodica di Psicanalisi (semi-annually) 07037

Associazione Romana di Entomologia (ARDE), c/o Museo Civico di Zoologia, Via Ulisse Aldrovandi 18, 00197 Roma
T: (06) 3216586; E-Mail: aletardi@casaccia.enea.it
Founded: 1945; Members: 340
Focus: Entomology
Periodical
Bollettino dell'Associazione Romana di Entomologia (quarterly) 07038

Associazione Scientifica di Produzione Animale (ASPA), c/o Istituto Zootecnico Università, Via F. Delpino 1, 80137 Napoli
T: (081) 441273
Founded: 1973; Members: 130
Focus: Zoology
Periodical
Zootecnica e Nutrizione Animale (bi-monthly) 07039

Associazione Siciliana per le Lettere e le Arti (A.S.L.A.), Via XX Settembre 68, 90141 Palermo
T: (091) 211410
Focus: Lit; Arts 07040

Associazione Sociologi Lucani, Via Ammiraglio Ruggiero 71, 85044 Lauria Inferiore
Focus: Sociology 07041

Associazione Sole Italico, Corso Ovidio 191, 67039 Sulmona
T: 51606
Founded: 1971
Focus: Ethnology; Arts
Periodical
Bollettino Informativo (bi-weekly) 07042

Associazione Studi sull'Informazione (A.S.I.), Viale Ferdinando di Savoia 5, 20124 Milano
Founded: 1975
Focus: Comm
Periodical
Problemi dell'Informazione (quarterly) . . 07043

Associazione Tecnica Italiana per la Cellulosa e la Carta (ATICLCA), Via Sandro Botticelli 19, 20133 Milano
T: (02) 2664141; Fax: 2664141
Founded: 1967; Members: 1160
Focus: Eng
Periodical
Industria della Carta (monthly) 07044

Associazione Tecnica Italiana per la Cinematografia (A.T.I.C.), Viale Regina Margherita 286, 00198 Roma
T: (06) 44259622; Fax: 4404128
Founded: 1947; Members: 150
Focus: Cinema
Periodicals
Note di Tecnica Cinematografica (quarterly)
Notiziario (irregularly) 07045

Associazione Teologica Italiana per lo Studio della Morale (A.T.I.S.M.), c/o Seminario Vescovile, Via Monte S. Gabriele 60, 28100 Novara
T: (0321) 21783
Founded: 1965
Focus: Philos
Periodical
Rivista di Teologia Morale 07046

Associazione Termotecnica Italiana (ATI), c/o FAST, Piazzale R. Morandi 2, 20121 Milano
T: (02) 795208; Fax: 76009442
Founded: 1946; Members: 2000
Pres: Daniele L. Milvio; Gen Secr: Prof. Giancarlo Chiesa
Focus: Air Cond
Periodicals
Annuario ATI
Atti dei Congressi Nazionali
La Termotecnica (monthly) 07047

Associazione Urania / Associazione Ligure per lo Studio e la Divulgazione dell'Astronomia e dell'Astronautica, c/o Museo Civico di Storia Naturale Giacomo Doria, Via Brigata Liguria 9, 16121 Genova
T: (010) 8352882; E-Mail: urania@aleph.it
Founded: 1951; Members: 98
Focus: Astronomy 07048

Automazione Energia Informazione (AEI), Viale Monza 259, 20126 Milano
T: (02) 257791; Fax: 2570512
Founded: 1896; Members: 11600
Focus: Electronic Eng
Periodicals
Alta Frequenza: Rivista di Elettronica (bi-monthly)
L'Elettrotecnica (monthly)
L'Energia Elettrica (monthly)

ETT-European Transactions on Telecommunications and Related Technologies (bi-monthly) . 07049

Bioelectrochemical Society (BES), c/o Dipartimento di Biologia, Via Irnerio 42, 40126 Bologna
T: (051) 351293; Fax: 242576
Focus: Biochem 07050

Cenacolo Triestino, Piazza della Borsa 14, 34121 Trieste
T: (040) 64210
Founded: 1946
Pres: Beniamino Antonini
Focus: Doc; Humanities 07051

Centre for Coordination of Research of the International Federation of Catholic Universities, Piazza della Pilotta 4, 00187 Roma
T: (06) 6786253; Fax: 6786253
Founded: 1975
Focus: Educ 07052

Centre for Human Evolution Studies, Via Antonio Bertoloni 29, 00197 Roma
T: (06) 8073420, 8085944; Fax: 8077306
Founded: 1978
Pres: Prof. Michele Trimarchi; Gen Secr: Luisa Papeschi
Focus: Educ; Public Health; Law; Ecology; Soc Sci
Periodicals
The Brain and the Integration of Sciences (semi-annually)
Cultura e Natura (quarterly) 07053

Centro Camuno di Studi Preistorici (CCSP), 25044 Capo di Ponte
T: (0364) 42091; E-Mail: ccsp@globalnet.it; Fax: 42572
Founded: 1964; Members: 500
Pres: Caterina Agostini; Gen Secr: Emmanuel Anati
Focus: Ethnology; Arts; Archeol; Anthro; Hist
Periodicals
B.C. Notizie (annually)
Bollettino del Centro Camuno di Studi Preistorici (annually) 07054

Centro Di, Piazza de Mozzi 1, 50125 Firenze
Founded: 1968
Pres: F. Marchi
Focus: Ling 07055

Centro di Documentazione, Via degli Orafi 29, CP 347, 51100 Pistoia
T: (0573) 977353; E-Mail: centrodocumpt@comune.pistoia.pr.; Fax: 977353
Founded: 1977
Pres: Giorgio kl715= 100 Lima
Focus: Doc
Periodicals
Fogli di Informazione (monthly)
Notiziario del Centro (monthly)
Per il Sessantotto (semi-annually) . . . 07056

Centro di Ricerca per il Teatro (C.R.T.), Viale Alemagna, 6, 20121 Milano
T: (02) 861901; Fax: 863813
Founded: 1974
Focus: Perf Arts 07057

Centro di Ricerca Pergamene Medievali e Protocolli Notarili, Via di Ponziano 15, 00162 Roma
T: (06) 585067
Founded: 1965
Gen Secr: Prof. Maria Luisa Lombardo
Focus: Archives; Hist 07058

Centro di Ricerche Biopsichiche di Padova (C.R.B.), Via Dante 60, 35100 Padova
T: (049) 657996
Founded: 1957
Pres: Prof. Conte Giorgio Foresti; Gen Secr: Dr. Carla Berlanda
Focus: Psych; Therapeutics
Periodical
Centro Ricerche Biopsichiche (annually) . 07059

Centro di Studi Atesini, c/o p. Menapace, Corso Libertà 119, 00197 Roma
T: (0338) 2103595
Founded: 1968; Members: 4
Pres: Dr. Ferruccio Bravi; Gen Secr: Carla Menapace
Focus: Hist; Ling 07060

Centro di Studi e Ricerche di Museologia Agraria, c/o Museo Lombardo di Storia dell'Agricoltura, CP 908, 20101 Milano
T: (02) 211304; Fax: 6678722
Founded: 1975
Pres: Dr.Giuseppe Barbiano di Belgiojoso
Focus: Cultur Hist; Agri
Periodical
Acta Museorum Italicorum Agriculturae: Rivista di Storia dell'Agricoltura (annually) 07061

Centro di Studi Storici Maceratesi, CP 49, 62100 Macerata
T: (0733) 235654
Founded: 1965
Pres: Prof. Pio Cartechini; Gen Secr: Prof. Luciana Fermani Paoloni
Focus: Hist
Periodical
Studi Maceratesi: Collana 07062

Centro Emilia-Romagna per la Storia del Giornalismo (C.E.R.S.G.), c/o Dipartimento di Discipline Storiche, Piazza S. Giovanni in Monte 2, 40124 Bologna
T: (051) 6457623; Fax: 6457620
Founded: 1975; Members: 80
Focus: Journalism 07063

Centro Internazionale della Pace (C.I.P.), Corso Re Umberto 38, 10128 Torino
Founded: 1967
Focus: Prom Peace
Periodical
Civitas Pacis (bi-monthly) 07064

Centro Internazionale di Documentazione e Comunicazione (IDOC) / International Documentation and Communication Center, Via S. Maria dell'Anima 30, 00186 Roma
T: (06) 6868332; Fax: 6832766
Founded: 1965
Focus: Doc; Comm Sci
Periodical
IDOC Internazionale (quarterly) 07065

Centro Internazionale di Ipnosi Medica e Psicologica / International Center of Medical and Psychological Hypnosis, c/o Istituto di Indagini Psicologiche, Corso XXII Marzo 57, 20129 Milano
T: (02) 70126489; Fax: 7491051
Founded: 1969; Members: 155
Pres: Prof. Rolando Marchesan; Gen Secr: Dr. Aurora Zavertanik
Focus: Med; Psych; Depth Psych; Therapeutics 07066

Centro Internazionale di Ricerche sulle Strutture Ambiente Pio Manzù, 47040 Verucchio
Focus: Ecology 07067

Centro Internazionale di Scienze Meccaniche (CISM) / International Centre for Mechanical Sciences, Piazza Garibaldi 18, 33100 Udine
T: (0432) 294989, 22523
Founded: 1968
Focus: Eng
Periodical
Mechanics Research Communications . . 07068

Centro Internazionale di Studi Archeologici Maiuri, Via Quattro Orologi, 80056 Ercolano
T: 32417
Focus: Archeol 07069

Centro Internazionale di Studi di Architettura Andrea Palladio, Domus Comestabilis, Basilica Palladiana, CP 835, 36100 Vicenza
T: (0444) 323014; Fax: 322869
Founded: 1959
Pres: Giuseppina Dal Santo
Focus: Archit
Periodical
Annali di Architettura (annually) 07070

Centro Internazionale di Studi e Documentazione sulle Comunità Europee (C.I.S.D.C.E.), Corso Magenta 61, 20123 Milano
T: (02) 48009072; Fax: 48009067
Founded: 1958
Focus: Econ
Periodical
Euroinformazioni (weekly) 07071

Centro Internazionale di Studi Rosminiani, Corso Umberto I 15, 28049 Stresa
T: (0323) 30091; Fax: 31623
Founded: 1966
Focus: Rel & Theol; Poli Sci; Philos
Periodicals
Bollettino Charitas: Di Spiritualità
Rivista Rosminiana: Di Cultura e Filosofia 07072

Centro Internazionale di Studi Sardi (C.I.S.S.), c/o Dipartimento di Biologia Sperimentale, Facoltà di Scienze Matematiche, Fisiche e Naturali, Università degli Studi, Via G.T. Porcell 2, 09100 Cagliari
T: (070) 659294
Founded: 1955
Focus: Ethnology; Folklore
Periodical
Atti Congresso Internazionale di Studi Sardi 07073

Centro Internazionale di Studi Umanistici, c/o Facoltà di Filosofia, Università, Via Nomentana 118, 00161 Roma
Founded: 1978
Focus: Humanities; Philos
Periodical
Archivio di Filosofia 07074

Centro Internazionale Magistrati Luigi Severini, c/o Palazzo di Giustizia, 06100 Perugia
T: (075) 28214, 24254
Founded: 1954
Focus: Law 07075

Centro Internazionale per gli Studi sulla Irrigazione, Piazza Pradaval 16, 37100 Verona
T: (045) 24682
Founded: 1953
Focus: Water Res
Periodical
L'Irrigazione (bi-monthly) 07076

Centro Internazionale per l'Avanzamento della Ricerca e dell'Educazione, Via Rivetti 61, 13069 Vigliano Biellese
Founded: 1974
Focus: Educ
Periodical
Yoga & Ayurveda (bi-monthly) 07077

Centro Internazionale per le Communicazione Sociali (CISCOM), Via della Pisana 1111, CP 9092, 00163 Roma
T: (06) 656121; E-Mail: ans@sdb.org; Fax: 65612709
Focus: Soc Sci 07078

Centro Internazionale per l'Educazione Artistica della Fondazione Giorgio Cini (C.I.ED.ART.), Isola di San Giorgio Maggiore, 30124 Venezia
T: (041) 8990
Focus: Educ; Arts 07079

Centro Internazionale per l'Iniziativa Giuridica (C.I.I.G.), Via Foggia 6, 00161 Roma
T: (06) 5242540/06
Founded: 1973
Focus: Law
Periodical
Iniziativa Giuridica 07080

Centro Internazionale per lo Studio dei Papiri Ercolanesi (C.I.S.P.E.), c/o Dipartimento di Filologia Classica, Università degli Studi di Napoli Federico II, Via Porta di Massa 1, 80133 Napoli
Founded: 1969
Pres: Prof. Giovanni Pugliese Carratelli; Gen Secr: Prof. Marcello Gigante
Focus: Materials Sci
Periodical
Cronache Ercolanesi (annually) 07081

Centro Internazionale Ricerche sulle Strutture Ambientali Pio Manzu (C.I.R.S.A.) / International Research Centre on the Habitat Pio Manzu, 47040 Verucchio
T: (0541) 678139; Fax: 670172
Founded: 1969
Focus: Develop Areas
Periodical
Strutture Ambientali (semi-annually) . . . 07082

Centro Internazionale Sonnenberg per l'Italia, c/o Luciano Mosso, Corso Turati 11/C, 10128 Torino
T: (011) 5683598; Fax: 5683598
Founded: 1964
Focus: Econ; Educ
Periodical
Sonnenberg Internationale Briefe, International Journal, Revue Internationale: Rivista Trilingue (Tedesco, Inglese, Francese) (quarterly) . 07083

Centro Internazionale Studi Famiglia (C.I.S.F.), Via Duccio di Boninsegna 10, 20145 Milano
T: (02) 48012040; E-Mail: cisfdoc@stpauls.it; Fax: 48009938
Founded: 1973; Members: 12
Focus: Family Plan 07084

Centro Internazionale Studi Musicali (C.I.S.M.), Largo del Nazareno 8, 00187 Roma
T: (06) 6790360
Founded: 1962
Focus: Music 07085

Centro Internazionale Studi Umanistici Scientifici Psicologici, Via Rosa Raimondi Garibaldi 42, 00145 Roma
T: (06) 5134891
Focus: Psych 07086

Centro Isec, Iniziative per Studi e Convegni, Piazza Cinque Giornate 2, 00192 Roma
T: (06) 3216657; Fax: 3215143
Founded: 1969
Focus: Educ 07087

Centro Italiano Ricerca e Informazione Economica (CIRIEC), Via Flavia 47, 00187 Roma
T: (06) 482890
Focus: Econ 07088

Centro Italiano Ricerche e Studi Assicurativi (C.I.R.S.A.), Via del Corso 184, 00168 Roma
T: (06) 6789127, 6798847
Focus: Insurance 07089

Centro Italiano Ricerche e Studi Trasporto Aereo (CIRSTA), Via Toscani 78, 00152 Roma
T: (06) 5313952
Founded: 1978
Focus: Aero; Transport 07090

Centro Italiano Studi Containers (CISCo), Via Garibaldi 4, 16124 Genova
Founded: 1967; Members: 140
Focus: Transport
Periodicals
CISCo-News: Notiziario (monthly)
Quaderni CISCo 07091

Centro Italiano Studi Politici Economici Sociali (C.I.S.P.E.S.), Via del Tritone 62, 00187 Roma
T: (06) 6797672, 6796539
Founded: 1963
Focus: Econ 07092

Centro Italiano Studi sull'Arte dello Spettacolo (C.I.S.A.S.), Via Angelo Poliziano 51, 00184 Roma
T: (06) 733092
Founded: 1965
Focus: Cinema; Perf Arts
Periodicals
Agenzia Giornalistica SAFJ-Press
Corriere di Roma 07093

Centro Italiano Sviluppo Impieghi Acciaio (C.I.S.I.A.), Piazza Velasca 8, 20122 Milano
T: (02) 865840, 8059692, 8057046
Founded: 1954
Focus: Materials Sci
Periodical
Acciaio (monthly) 07094

Centro Italo-Nipponico di Studi Economici (C.I.N.S.E.), Piazza Armando Diaz 7, 20123 Milano
T: (02) 802896
Founded: 1973
Focus: Econ
Periodical
Nuovo Giappone (monthly) 07095

Centro Lattiero Caseario di Assistenza e Sperimentazione Antonio Bizzozero, Via Pomponio Torelli 17, 43100 Parma
T: (0521) 44916
Founded: 1956
Focus: Dairy Sci
Periodical
Bollettino Tecnico (quarterly) 07096

Centro Ligure di Storia Sociale, Piazza Campetto 8a, 16123 Genova
T: (010) 297408
Founded: 1955
Focus: Hist; Sociology; Socialism
Periodical
Movimento Operaio e Socialista (quarterly) 07097

Centro Luigi Lavazza per gli Studi e Ricerche sul Caffe', Corso Novara 59, 10154 Torino
T: (011) 2398
Focus: Coffee, Tea, Cocoa 07098

Centro Nazionale di Dietobiologia ed Igiene della Alimentazione, Via Mario Pagano 31a, 20145 Milano
T: (02) 496303
Focus: Nutrition 07099

Centro Nazionale di Studi Urbanistici, Via Antonio Bertoloni 31, 00197 Roma
T: (06) 805101, 805103
Founded: 1964
Focus: Urban Plan 07100

Centro per gli Studi di Tecnica Navale (CE.TE.NA.), Via Al Molo Giano, 16126 Genova
T: (010) 590521, 589349, 542481
Founded: 1962
Focus: Navig 07101

Centro per gli Studi e le Applicazioni delle Risorse Energetiche (C.S.A.R.E.), Corso del Popolo 261, 45100 Rovigo
T: (0425) 26478
Founded: 1977
Focus: Energy
Periodical
Bollettino del C.S.A.R.E. (monthly) . . . 07102

Centro per gli Studi sui Mercati Esteri (CEME), Via Giulio Alberoni 8a, 00198 Roma
T: (06) 854144
Founded: 1956
Focus: Econ; Marketing; Int'l Relat
Periodical
Mondo Aperto 07103

Centro per gli Studi sui Sistemi Distributivi e il Turismo (CESDIT), Corso Venezia 49, 20121 Milano
T: (02) 7750
Founded: 1977
Focus: Commerce; Travel 07104

Centro per la Diffusione del Libro Lucano, Via Pretoria 210, 85100 Potenza
T: (0971) 24570
Focus: Hist 07105

Centro per la Documentazione Automatica (C.D.A.), Via Cusani 10, 20121 Milano
T: (02) 870444
Founded: 1962
Focus: Doc; Law 07106

Centro per la Riforma del Diritto di Famiglia, c/o Avv. Giuliana Fuà, Via Enrico Dandolo 4, 20122 Milano
T: (02) 705136
Founded: 1967
Focus: Family Plan 07107

Centro per la Statistica Aziendale, Via A. Baldesi 20, 50131 Firenze
T: (055) 50713
Founded: 1935
Focus: Econ
Periodicals
Circolare (monthly)
La Congiuntura in Toscana (monthly)
Index (monthly)
Lettere d'Affari (monthly)
Previsioni a Breve Termine (monthly)

Prontuario Economico del Turista: Spesa Giornaliera del Viaggiatore in 42 Paesi (annually) *07108*

Centro per la Storia della Tradizione Aristotelica Nel Veneto, Via Accademia 5, 35100 Padova
T: (049) 24034
Focus: Cultur Hist; Philos *07109*

Centro per lo Studio dei Dialetti Veneti dell'Istria, c/o Istituto di Glottologia, Università degli Studi, Via dell'Università 1, 34100 Trieste
T: (040) 722274
Founded: 1970
Focus: Ling
Periodical
Bollettino del Centro per lo Studio dei Dialetti Veneti dell'Istria (annually) *07110*

Centro Piombinese di Studi Storici, c/o Biblioteca Comunale, Via Cavour 152, 57025 Piombino
T: 33110
Focus: Hist *07111*

Centro Polesano di Studi Storici, Archeologici ed Etnografici (C.P.S.S.A.E.), c/o Museo delle Civiltà in Polesine, Piazzale S. Bortolo 18, CP 106, 45100 Rovigo
T: (0425) 21021
Founded: 1964
Focus: Ethnology; Hist; Archeol
Periodicals
Padusa
Padusa Notiziario (quarterly) *07112*

Centro Provinciale Impiego Combinato Tecniche Agricole (Centro I.C.T.A.), c/o Camera di Commercio, Piazza della Costituzione 8, 40128 Bologna
T: (051) 519061
Founded: 1960
Focus: Agri; Eng *07113*

Centro Psico-Pedagogico Didattico (Ce.Psi.Pe.Di.), Via Galeotti 5, 40127 Bologna
T: (051) 502842
Founded: 1978
Focus: Educ; Psych
Periodical
Problemi d'Oggi: Bimestrale di Scienze Umane e Formazione Sociale (bi-monthly) *07114*

Centro Regionale di Studi Sociali V.G. Galati, Piazza Stocco 21, Lamezia Terme
T: 23889
Focus: Sociology *07115*

Centro Ricerche Applicazione Bioritmo (C.R.A.B.), Viale dell'Università 25, 00185 Roma
T: (06) 4951759
Focus: Med; Genetics *07116*

Centro Ricerche Archeologiche e Scavi di Torino per il Medio Oriente e l'Asia, Via Gaudenzio Ferrari 1, 10124 Torino
Founded: 1963
Focus: Archeol
Periodical
Mesopotamia *07117*

Centro Ricerche Cosmetologiche, Via Montoggio 49, 00168 Roma
T: (06) 6378788
Founded: 1972
Focus: Pharmacol
Periodical
Journal of Applied Cosmetology (quarterly) *07118*

Centro Ricerche di Storia e Arte Bitontina (C.R.S.A.B.), Viale Giovanni XXIII 129, 70032 Bitonto
Founded: 1968
Focus: Cultur Hist; Ethnology; Archeol; Music
Periodicals
Studi Bitontini
La tua Città *07119*

Centro Ricerche Didattiche Ugo Morin (C.R.D.M.), Via S. Giacomo 4, 31010 Paderno del Grappa
T: (0423) 330441; Fax: 539098
Founded: 1976
Focus: Educ
Periodical
L'Insegnamento della Matematica e delle Scienze Integrate (monthly) *07120*

Centro Ricerche Economiche ed Operative della Cooperazione (C.R.E.O.C.), Piazza S. Maria degli Angeli a Pizzofalcone 1, 80132 Napoli
T: (081) 400711
Founded: 1972
Focus: Econ *07121*

Centro Ricerche Economiche Sociologiche e di Mercato nell'Edilizia (C.R.E.S.M.E.), Via Sebenico 2, 00198 Roma
T: (06) 850158, 865952, 867227
Founded: 1962
Focus: Econ; Sociology; Marketing
Periodicals
Bulletins (irregularly)
Cahiers (irregularly)
Volumes (irregularly) *07122*

Centro Ricerche Metapsichiche e Psicofoniche (Ce.Ri.Me.Ps.), Via Mancini 3, 63023 Fermo
T: (0734) 24231
Founded: 1977
Focus: Parapsych *07123*

Centro Ricerche Socio-Religiose, Largo Donnaregina 22, 80138 Napoli
T: (081) 449589
Founded: 1966
Focus: Rel & Theol; Sociology
Periodical
Annuario dell'Archidiocesi di Napoli (annually) *07124*

Centro Ricerche Urbanistiche e di Progettazione, Via Beato Angelico 23, 20133 Milano
T: (02) 7387917
Founded: 1975
Focus: Urban Plan *07125*

Centro Romano per lo Studio dei Problemi di Attualita' Sociale, Via dei Savorelli 38, 00165 Roma
T: (06) 6221865
Focus: Sociology; Poli Sci *07126*

Centro Rossiniano di Studi, c/o Fondazione Gioacchino Rossini, Piazza Olivieri 5, 61100 Pesaro
T: (0721) 30053
Founded: 1869
Focus: Music
Periodical
Bollettino del Centro Rossiniano di Studi *07127*

Centro Sperimentale di Cinematografia (C.S.C.), Via Tuscolana 1524, 00173 Roma
T: (06) 740046; Fax: 7111619
Founded: 1935
Focus: Cinema
Periodical
Bianco e Nero *07128*

Centro Sperimentale Italiano di Giornalismo, Viale Caldara 13, 20122 Milano
T: (02) 584223
Focus: Journalism *07129*

Centro Sperimentale Metallurgico, Via di Castel Romano, 00129 Roma
T: (06) 64951
Founded: 1963
Focus: Metallurgy *07130*

Centro Studi Archaeologici di Boscoreale, Boscotrecase e Trecase, c/o Biblioteca Comunale Francesco Cangemi, Piazza Pace 36, 80041 Boscoreale
Founded: 1974
Focus: Archeol
Periodicals
Bollettino del Centro Studi Archaeologici (annually)
Rivista sull'Arte, la Storia e il Folklore di Somma Vesuviana (quarterly) *07131*

Centro Studi Assicurativi Piero Sacerdoti, Corso Venezia 8, 20121 Milano
T: (02) 794235
Founded: 1951
Focus: Insurance
Periodical
Diritto e Pratica nell'Assicurazione (quarterly) *07132*

Centro Studi Cinematografici (C.S.C.), Via Gregorio VII 6, 00165 Roma
T: (06) 6382605; Fax: 6382605
Founded: 1963
Pres: Carlo Tagliabve; Gen Secr: Cesare Frioni
Focus: Cinema
Periodical
Notiziario del C.S.C. (bi-monthly) *07133*

Centro Studi della Cooperazione nel Veneto, Piazzale del Mutilato 6, 36100 Vicenza
T: (0444) 24226
Founded: 1961
Focus: Econ; Agri *07134*

Centro Studi di Diritto del Lavoro, c/o Palazzo di Giustizia, Corso Porta Vittoria, 20122 Milano
Focus: Law *07135*

Centro Studi di Diritto Fluviale e della Navigazione Interna, S. Marco, Calle Avvocati 392, 30124 Venezia
T: (041) 5220762; Fax: 5236357
Focus: Navig; Law *07136*

Centro Studi di Diritto Sportivo (CE.S.DI.S.), c/o Studio Legale Dal Lago, Contrà Canove Nuove 3, 36100 Vicenza
T: (0444) 44044
Founded: 1972
Focus: Law; Sports *07137*

Centro Studi di Economia Applicata all'Ingegneria (C.S.E.I.), c/o Facoltà di Ingegneria, Università degli Studi, Viale Japigia 182, 70126 Bari
T: (080) 580639
Founded: 1975
Focus: Econ; Eng *07138*

Centro Studi di Economia Applicata all'Ingegneria (C.S.E.I.), c/o Facoltà d'Ingegneria, Università degli Studi, Via Claudio 21, 80125 Napoli
T: (081) 614641
Founded: 1968
Focus: Econ; Eng
Periodical
Notizie C.S.E.I. (irregularly) *07139*

Centro Studi di Estimo e di Economia Territoriale (Ce.S.E.T.), c/o Istituto di Economia e Politica Agraria, Facoltà di Agraria, Università degli Studi, Piazzale delle Cascine 18, 50144 Firenze
T: (055) 352051
Focus: Econ *07140*

Centro Studi di Poesia e di Storia delle Poetiche, Via Bu Meliana 12, 00195 Roma
Focus: Lit *07141*

Centro Studi di Politica Economica (CEEP), Via San Francesco da Paola 17, 10123 Torino
T: (011) 8170449
Founded: 1973
Focus: Econ; Poli Sci
Periodical
Ambiente (weekly) *07142*

Centro Studi di Psicologia e Sociologia Applicate ad Indirizzo Adleriano (C.E.P.S.A.), Via Michele Amari 47, 00179 Roma
T: (06) 7807897, 7857216
Founded: 1969
Focus: Psych; Econ
Periodical
Cepsa-Informa (3 times annually) . . . *07143*

Centro Studi di Psicoterapia e Psicologia Clinica, Via Antonio Cecchi 3, 16129 Genova
T: (010) 541092
Founded: 1971
Focus: Psychiatry
Periodical
Aggiornamenti di Psicoterapia e Psicologia Clinica (semi-annually) *07144*

Centro Studi di Storia Locale, Via Dante 37, 54100 Massa
T: (0585) 41720
Founded: 1974
Focus: Hist *07145*

Centro Studi Diritto Comunitario, Via in Lucina 10, 00186 Roma
T: (06) 6789560, 6783144
Focus: Law *07146*

Centro Studi e Applicazioni in Tecnologie Avanzate (C.S.A.T.A.), c/o Istituto di Fisica, Università degli Studi, Via G. Amendola 173, 70126 Bari
T: (080) 583388
Founded: 1969
Focus: Eng *07147*

Centro Studi e Archivio della Comunicazione, Università di Parma, Piazzale della Pace 7a, 43100 Parma
T: (0521) 270847; Fax: 207125
Focus: Photo *07148*

Centro Studi e di Educazione Civica Enrico Mattei, Via Giovanni Cravero 45, 10154 Torino
T: (011) 267880
Founded: 1963
Focus: Educ
Periodical
Opinioni Libere (monthly) *07149*

Centro Studi e Documentazione della Cultura Armena (CSDCA), Via Cherubini 6, 20145 Milano
T: (02) 4814921; Fax: 4694548
Founded: 1967; Members: 3
Pres: Prof. A. Novello
Focus: Hist; Arts; Music; Preserv Hist Monuments
Periodical
Documents of Armenian Architecture (semi-annually) *07150*

Centro Studi e Iniziative Pier Santi Mattarella (C.S.I.P.M.), Piazza Malta 27-29, 9110 Trapani
T: (0923) 22241, 22881
Founded: 1981
Focus: Educ
Periodical
Faro (bi-weekly) *07151*

Centro Studi e Ricerche per la Conoscenza della Liguria Attraverso le Testimonianze dei Viaggiatori Stranieri / Research Institute for Foreign travellers in Italy, Via F. Mignone 46, 16133 Genova
T: (010) 3450119
Focus: Hist; Geography; Travel
Periodicals
Architettura Navale agli Inizi del'600 (quarterly)
Il Porto di Genova agli Inizi del'600 (quarterly)
Viaggiare in Liguria (quarterly)
Viaggiatori Stranieri in Liguria (quarterly)
Viaggiatori Tedeschi del'700 (quarterly) . *07152*

Centro Studi e Ricerche sui Rapporti Umani, Via dei Lucchesi 21a, 00187 Roma
T: (06) 67015283
Focus: Soc Sci *07153*

Centro Studi Economici (CE.S.E.), Piazza Colonna 355, 00187 Roma
T: (06) 6794065
Focus: Econ *07154*

Centro Studi Economici e Sociali Giuseppe Toniolo, Piazza Giuseppe Toniolo 2, 56100 Pisa
T: (050) 571181
Founded: 1966
Focus: Econ
Periodical
Studi Economici e Sociali (3 times annually) *07155*

Centro Studi Economici per l'Alta Italia, Via Alessandro Manzoni 31, 20121 Milano
T: (02) 639634
Focus: Econ *07156*

Centro Studi ed Esperienze Scout Baden Powell, Via Achille Papa 17, 00195 Roma
T: (06) 3603618
Founded: 1974
Focus: Educ
Periodical
Esperienze e Progetti (bi-monthly) . . . *07157*

Centro Studi Filippo e Marta Larizza per la Formazione Permanente degli Educatori e per la Prevenzione del Disadattamento Giovanile, c/o Istituto Vescovile Graziani, Via Ca' Rezzonico 6, 36061 Bassano del Grappa
T: (0424) 524369
Founded: 1979
Pres: Prof. Luigi Secco
Focus: Educ
Periodical
Larizza Informazioni (quarterly) *07158*

Centro Studi Mario Mazza, Via Fassolo 29, 16126 Genova
T: (010) 267155; Fax: 267155
Founded: 1962
Focus: Educ
Periodical
Strade Aperte (monthly) *07159*

Centro Studi Mutualistici Emancipazione e Partecipazione (S.M.S.), Via Francesco d'Ovidio 135, 00137 Roma
T: (06) 8280261
Founded: 1974
Focus: Educ; Hist; Sociology *07160*

Centro Studi Nord e Sud, Via Chiatamone 7, 80121 Napoli
T: (081) 418347
Focus: Geography; Sociology
Periodical
Nord e Sud (quarterly) *07161*

Centro Studi Parlamentari, Via della Rosetta 5, 00186 Roma
T: (06) 6547838
Focus: Poli Sci *07162*

Centro Studi per il Mezzogiorno A. Ajon, Palazzo Grasso, Viale de Gasperi, 95024 Acireale
T: (095) 605705
Focus: Poli Sci; Hist; Econ *07163*

Centro Studi per il Progresso della Educazione Sanitaria e del Diritto Sanitario (STUDES), Via Azuni 9, 00196 Roma
T: (06) 3600093
Founded: 1962
Focus: Public Health; Educ
Periodical
Rassegna Amministrativa della Sanità (monthly) *07164*

Centro Studi per la Programmazione Economica e Sociale (C.S.P.E.S.), Via della Vite 27, 00187 Roma
Focus: Econ; Sociology *07165*

Centro Studi per la Valorizzazione delle Risorse del Mezzogiorno, Corso Umberto I 22, 80138 Napoli
T: (081) 5527744
Founded: 1990
Focus: Econ; Poli Sci
Periodicals
Incontri di Studio: Collana di Quaderni Meridionalistici (irregularly)
Politica Meridionalista: Rivista Mensile di Cultura Economia Attualità (monthly) *07166*

Centro Studi Piero Gobetti, Via Antonio Fabro 6, 10122 Torino
T: (011) 531429; E-Mail: bibto95@itocsivm.csi.it; Fax: 531429
Founded: 1961; Members: 134
Focus: Hist
Periodical
Mezzosecolo (annually) *07167*

Centro Studi Pietro Mancini, Corso Telesio 53, 87100 Cosenza
T: (0984) 29983
Focus: Perf Arts; Cinema; Journalism . . *07168*

Centro Studi Politici e Sociali Alcide de Gasperi, Via Nicola Serra 123, 87100 Cosenza
T: (0984) 32865
Founded: 1964
Focus: Poli Sci; Educ; Sociology
Periodical
Prospettive *07169*

Centro Studi Politico-Sociali Achille Grandi, Piazza Sant'Ambrogio 15, 20123 Milano
T: (02) 893838, 867148, 871110
Founded: 1961
Focus: Poli Sci; Sociology *07170*

Centro Studi Problemi Medici (C.S.P.M.), Corso Sempione 77, 20149 Milano
T: (02) 3189587
Focus: Med 07171

Centro Studi Ricerche e Documentazioni per l'Agricoltura Siciliana, Via Milano 58, 00184 Roma
T: (06) 461893
Focus: Agri 07172

Centro Studi Ricerche Ligabue, S. Croce 499, 30135 Venezia
T: (041) 5225127; Fax: 791661
Founded: 1978
Focus: Archeol; Paleontology; Anthro; Nat Sci 07173

Centro Studi Santa Veronica Giuliani, Via del Marchese Paolo 13, 06012 Città di Castello
Founded: 1978; Members: 350
Focus: Rel & Theol 07174

Centro Studi Storici di Mestre (C.S.S.), c/o Centro Culturale Villa Pozzi, Via Gazzera Alta 46, 30174 Mestre
T: (041) 5298600
Founded: 1961
Gen Secr: Prof. Roberto Stevanato
Focus: Cultur Hist 07175

Centro Studi Storici Sociali, Via Castiglione 6, 40124 Bologna
T: (051) 223979
Focus: Hist 07176

Centro Studi sulla Resistenza, Piazza della Repubblica 3, 61029 Urbino
Focus: Poli Sci 07177

Centro Studi Wilhelm Reich, Salita Cupa Caiafa 36, 80122 Napoli
T: (081) 664389
Focus: Psych 07178

Centro Studi Zingari, Via dei Barbieri 22, 00186 Roma
T: (06) 6833181; Fax: 6868760
Founded: 1970
Focus: Ethnology
Periodical
Lacio Drom: Bimestrale di Studi Zingari (bi-monthly) 07179

Centro Superiore di Logica e Scienze Comparate (C.S.L.S.C.), Via Belmeloro 3, 40126 Bologna
T: (051) 235471
Focus: Logic 07180

Centro Sviluppo Impiego Diesel (CE.S.I.D.), Via Italo Svevo 1, 34144 Trieste
Founded: 1980
Focus: Auto Eng 07181

Centro Thomas Mann, Via Zanardelli 36, 00186 Roma
T: (06) 659766
Focus: Lit 07182

Cineteca Italiana Archivio Storico del Film, Villa Comunale, Via Palestro 16, 20121 Milano
T: (02) 799224
Founded: 1947
Focus: Cinema 07183

Circolo Filosofico di Studi Tomistici, Largo Angelicum 1a, 00184 Roma
T: (06) 681261
Founded: 1912
Focus: Rel & Theol; Philos
Periodical
Idea: Rivista di Cultura e di Vita Sociale (monthly) 07184

Circolo Giuridico Italiano, Via della Conciliazione 15, 00193 Roma
T: (06) 6569941
Focus: Law 07185

Circolo Speleologico Romano (CSR), Via Ulisse Aldrovandi 18, 00197 Roma
T: (06) 3216223
Founded: 1904; Members: 150
Focus: Speleology
Periodicals
Notiziario del Circolo Speleologico Romano (semi-annually)
Quaderni di Speleologia 07186

CIRGIS, Via Manzoni 45, 20121 Milano
T: (02) 6552167
Founded: 1979; Members: 400
Pres: Prof. Francesco Ogliari; Gen Secr: Giuseppe Aglialoro
Focus: Law 07187

Club Turati, Via Brera 18, 20121 Milano
T: (02) 877903, 877873
Focus: Poli Sci 07188

Codex Coordinating Committee for Africa, Via Terme di Caracalla, 00100 Roma
T: (06) 57971; Fax: 57973152
Founded: 1974
Focus: Food 07189

Collegio degli Ingegneri Ferroviari Italiani (C.I.F.I.), Via Giovanni Giolitti 34, 00185 Roma
T: (06) 4882129; Fax: 4742987
Founded: 1899
Focus: Transport
Periodicals
L'Ingegneria Ferroviaria
La Tecnica Professionale 07190

Collegio dei Tecnici dell' Acciaio (CTA), Piazzale Rodolfo Morandi 2, 20121 Milano
T: (02) 784711
Founded: 1966; Members: 600
Focus: Eng; Metallurgy
Periodical
Costruzioni Metalliche: Organo Ufficiale del CTA 07191

Collegium Biologicum Europa, Via Agrigento 6, 00161 Roma
Focus: Bio 07192

Collegium Internationale Neuro-Psychopharmacologicum (CINP), c/o Centre of Neuropharmacology, University of Milano, Via Balzaretti 9, 20133 Milano
T: (02) 20488331
Founded: 1957
Focus: Pharmacol 07193

Collegium Musicum di Latina (C.M.L.), Via Antonio Rosmini 10, 04100 Latina
Founded: 1968
Focus: Music 07194

Comitato dei Geografi Italiani, Via Giorgio Baglivi 3, 00161 Roma
T: (06) 866070
Founded: 1965; Members: 105
Focus: Geography 07195

Comitato Elettrotecnico Italiano (C.E.I.), Viale Monza 259, 20126 Milano
Pres: Dr. Germano Bonanni
Focus: Electric Eng 07196

Comitato Glaciologico Italiano (CGI), Via Accademia delle Scienze 5, 10123 Torino
T: (011) 553525; Fax: 6707155
Founded: 1914; Members: 40
Focus: Geology
Periodical
Geografia Fisica e Dinamica Quaternaria: Bollettino del Comitato Claciologico Italiano (annually) 07197

Comitato Italiano per l'Educazione Sanitaria (C.I.E.S.), c/o Centro Sperimentale per l'Educazione Sanitaria, Via del Giochetto, 06100 Perugia
T: (075) 28377
Focus: Public Health; Educ
Periodicals
Educazione Sanitaria e Medicina Preventiva (quarterly)
La Salute Umana (bi-monthly) 07198

Comitato Italiano per lo Studio dei Problemi della Popolazione (CISP), Via Nomentana 41, 00161 Roma
T: (06) 859555
Founded: 1928
Focus: Sociology
Periodical
Genus: Rivista fondata da Corrado Gini edita sotto il Patrocinio del Consiglio Nazionale delle Ricerche semestrale 07199

Comitato Italiano per lo Studio del Dolore in Oncologia (C.I.S.D.O.), c/o Istituto Regina Elena, Viale Regina Elena 291, 00161 Roma
T: (06) 497931
Focus: Cell Biol & Cancer Res 07200

Comitato Nazionale Italiana per l'Organizzazione Scientifica (ENIOS), Palazzo della Civiltá del Lavoro, 00144 Roma
T: (06) 595147
Focus: Business Admin 07201

Comitato Nazionale per la Ricerca e la Sviluppo dell'Energia Nucleare e delle Energie Alternative, Viale Regina Margherita 125, 00198 Roma
Founded: 1960
Pres: Umberto Colombo; Gen Secr: Luigi Noe
Focus: Energy 07202

Comitato per Bologna Storica-Artistica, Strada Maggiore 71, 40125 Bologna
T: (051) 347764
Focus: Hist; Arts 07203

Comitato Termotecnico Italiano (C.T.I.), c/o Dip de Energetica, Politecnico di Milano, Piazzale Leonardo da Vinci 32, 20133 Milano
T: (02) 257731; Fax: 25773210
Founded: 1933
Pres: Prof. Pierangelo Andreini; Gen Secr: Prof. Giovanni Riva
Focus: Air Cond 07204

Commission for Controlling the Desert Locust in the Eastern Region of its Distribution Area in South West Asia (DL/SWA), c/o Migrant Pest Group, FAO, Via delle Terme di Caracalla, 00100 Roma
T: (06) 5794021; Fax: 5146172
Founded: 1964; Members: 4
Focus: Agri 07205

Commissione di Studio dei Fenomeni di Corrosione Elettrolitica, Viale Risorgimento 2, Bologna
Focus: Metallurgy 07206

Committee for the European Development of Science and Technology, c/o ENEA, Viale Regina Margherita 125, 00198 Roma
T: (06) 85281
Founded: 1982
Focus: Sci; Eng 07207

Committee on Forest Development in the Tropics, c/o FAO, Via delle Terme di Caracalla, 00100 Roma
Founded: 1967; Members: 41
Focus: Forestry 07208

Community of Mediterranean Universities (CMU), c/o Università degli Studi, Piazza Umberto I 1, 70121 Bari
T: (080) 360786; Fax: 369108
Founded: 1983; Members: 100
Focus: Educ
Periodical
CMU Bulletin (semi-annually) 07209

Consiglio Nazionale degli Architetti, Corso Rinascimento 11, 00186 Roma
T: (06) 6561374
Focus: Archit 07210

Consiglio Nazionale dei Chimici, c/o Comprofessionist, Via Sicilia 57, 00187 Roma
T: (06) 42824076; E-Mail: ene@chimiei.it;
Fax: 42823622
Founded: 1928; Members: 9000
Focus: Chem 07211

Consiglio Nazionale delle Ricerche (CNR), Piazzale Aldo Moro 7, 00185 Roma
T: (06) 49931; E-Mail: CORICERCHE;
Fax: 4957241
Founded: 1923
Pres: Prof. Enrico Garaci; Gen Secr: Dr. Nunzio De Rensis
Focus: Sci
Periodicals
Bollettino Ufficiale del CNR
Monografie Scientifiche del CNR 07212

Consiglio Nazionale Forense, Via Arenula 71, 00186 Roma
T: (06) 6542689
Focus: Forensic Med 07213

Consiglio Nazionale per i Beni Culturali e Ambientali, c/o Ministry of Culture and the Environment, Via del Collegio Romano 27, 00186 Roma
T: (06) 6789529
Focus: Cultur Hist; Ecology
Periodical
Piceno (semi-annually) 07214

Consociatio Internationalis Musicae Sacrae (CIMS), Via di Rossa 21, 00165 Roma
T: (06) 6638792
Founded: 1963; Members: 663
Focus: Music 07215

Deputazione di Storia Patria per gli Abruzzi, Corso Umberto 19, 67100 L'Aquila
T: (0862) 22581
Founded: 1888
Focus: Hist
Periodical
Bollettino della Deputazione Abruzzese di Storia Patria (annually) 07216

Deputazione di Storia Patria per il Friuli, Palazzo Mantica, Via Manin 18, CP 319, 33100 Udine
T: (0432) 21924
Founded: 1918
Focus: Hist
Periodical
Memorie Storiche Forogiuliesi 07217

Deputazione di Storia Patria per la Calabria (D.S.P.C.), c/o Museo Nazionale, Piazza G. de Nava 26, 89100 Reggio Calabria
T: (0985) 21949
Founded: 1957
Focus: Hist
Periodical
Rivista Storica Calabrese (Nuova Serie) (quarterly) 07218

Deputazione di Storia Patria per la Lucania, Piazza Vittorio Emanuele 14, 85100 Potenza
Founded: 1957
Focus: Hist
Periodical
Bollettino Storico della Basilicata 07219

Deputazione di Storia Patria per la Sardegna, Via Cadello 9bis, 09100 Cagliari
T: (070) 4092764; Fax: 502521
Founded: 1955
Focus: Hist 07220

Deputazione di Storia Patria per la Toscana, Piazza dei Giudici 1, 50122 Firenze
T: (055) 23251
Founded: 1862
Focus: Hist
Periodical
Archivio Storico Italiano (quarterly) . . . 07221

Deputazione di Storia Patria per le Antiche Province Modenesi, c/o Aedes Muratoriana, Via Pomposa 1, 41100 Modena
T: (059) 241104; Fax: 241104
Founded: 1860; Members: 800
Focus: Hist
Periodical
Atti e Memorie (annually) 07222

Deputazione di Storia Patria per le Marche, Piazza B. Stracca 3, 60100 Ancona
T: (071) 29411
Founded: 1863
Focus: Hist
Periodical
Atti e Memorie della Deputazione di Storia Patria per le Marche (annually) 07223

Deputazione di Storia Patria per le Province di Romagna, c/o Istituto di Discipline Storiche e Giuridiche, Facoltà di Magistero, Largo Trombetti 1, 40126 Bologna
T: (051) 236210
Focus: Hist
Periodical
Atti e Memorie della Deputazione di Storia Patria per le Province di Romagna (annually) . 07224

Deputazione di Storia Patria per le Province Parmensi, Borgo Schizzati 3, 43100 Parma
T: (0521) 238661
Founded: 1860
Focus: Hist
Periodical
Archivio Storico per le Province Parmensi 07225

Deputazione di Storia Patria per le Venezie, S. Croce, Calle del Tintor 1583, 30135 Venezia
T: (041) 524487
Founded: 1871
Focus: Hist
Periodical
Archivio Veneto 07226

Deputazione di Storia Patria per l'Umbria, Palazzo della Penna, Via Podiani 11, 06100 Perugia
T: (075) 5727057
Founded: 1896
Focus: Hist
Periodical
Bollettino della Deputazione di Storia Patria per l'Umbria (annually) 07227

Deputazione Provinciale Ferrarese di Storia Patria, Via Cairoli 13, 44100 Ferrara
Founded: 1884
Focus: Hist
Periodical
Atti e Memorie della Deputazione Provinciale Ferrarese di Storia Patria 07228

Deputazione Reggiana di Storia Patria, Via I. Pindemonte 12, 42100 Reggio Emilia
Focus: Hist
Periodical
Bollettino Storico Reggiano (quarterly) . . 07229

Deputazione Subalpina di Storia Patria, Via Principe Amedeo 5, 10123 Torino
T: (011) 537226
Founded: 1833
Focus: Hist
Periodical
Bollettino Storico Bibliografico Subalpino (semi-annually) 07230

Documentation and Research Centre, Via dei Verbiti 1, CP 5080, 00100 Roma
T: (06) 5741350
Founded: 1964; Members: 69
Focus: Doc; Rel & Theol
Periodical
SEDOS Bulletin (monthly) 07231

Earthnet Programme Office (EPO), c/o ESRIN, Via Galileo Galilei, CP 65, 00044 Frascati
T: (06) 941801; Fax: 94180361
Founded: 1978; Members: 13
Focus: Geology
Periodical
Earth Observation Quarterly (quarterly) . 07232

Ente Autonomo La Biennale de Venezia, S. Marco 1364a, 30100 Venezia
T: (041) 700311
Focus: Arts; Archit; Perf Arts; Music; Cinema 07233

Ente di Unificazione Navale (UNAV) / Marine Standardization Office, Via al Nolo Giano, Calata Grazie, 16126 Genova
T: (010) 5995795; Fax: 5995790
Founded: 1938
Focus: Navig
Periodicals
Note di Informazioni Trimestrali e Note su Attività Tecnica
Tabelle Italiane Navali 07234

Ente Eugenio e Claudio Faina per l'Istruzione Professionale Agraria, Via Torino 45, 00184 Roma
T: (06) 4751735
Founded: 1912
Focus: Agri; Educ 07235

Ente Fauna Siciliana, CP 76, 96017 Noto
Fax: (0931) 813273
Founded: 1973
Focus: Ecology; Botany
Periodical
Atti del Convegno Siciliano di Ecologia . 07236

Ente Friulano di Economia Montana, c/o Palazzo della Provincia, Piazza Patriarcato 3, 33100 Udine
T: (0432) 22804, 61233
Focus: Econ 07237

Ente Istruzione Professionale Artigiana (E.I.P.A.), Piazzetta Pattari 4, 20122 Milano
T: (02) 802851/54
Focus: Adult Educ 07238

Ente Nazionale Francesco Petrarca, c/o Università degli Studi, Palazzo del Bo, Via VIII Febbraio 2, 35122 Padova
T: (049) 8803763; Fax: 8273007
Founded: 1971
Focus: Lit
Periodicals
Censimento dei Codici Petrarcheschi
Lectura Petrarce
Studi sul Petrarca 07239

Ente Nazionale Italiano di Unificazione (UNI), Via Battistotti Sassi 11, 20123 Milano
T: (02) 70105955; E-Mail: Unificazione Milano
Founded: 1921
Pres: Dr. Giacomo Elias; Gen Secr: Dr. Enrico Martinotti
Focus: Standards
Periodical
L'Unificazione (monthly) 07240

Ente per la Valorizzazione dei Vini Astigiani (E.V.V.A.), c/o Camera di Commercio, Piazza Medici 8, 14100 Asti
T: (0141) 53011
Founded: 1967
Focus: Wines 07241

Ente per le Nuove Tecnologie, l'Energia e l'Ambiente, Lungotevere Thaon di Revel 76, 00196 Roma
T: (06) 36271; Fax: 36272591
Founded: 1960
Pres: Nicola Cabibbo
Focus: Eng; Energy; Sci 07242

Ente Studi Economici per la Calabria (E.S.E.C.), Via A. Arabia 7, 87100 Cosenza
Founded: 1950
Focus: Econ 07243

ESRIN, Via Galileo Galilei, CP 64, 00044 Frascati
T: (06) 941801; Fax: 94180280
Founded: 1966; Members: 13
Focus: Aero 07244

Europa Club, Sezione Italiana (EKIS) / Associazione per il Superamento delle Barriere Linguistiche in Europa, Via Rovereto 14, 37126 Verona
T: (045) 915837
Focus: Ling 07245

European Academy of Allergology and Clinical Immunology (EAACI), Via Ugo di Carolis 59, 00134 Roma
T: (06) 35346840; Fax: 35403017
Founded: 1956; Members: 32
Gen Secr: Prof. Sergio Bonini
Focus: Immunology 07246

European Association for Bioeconomic Studies (EABS), Via Larga, 20122 Milano
Founded: 1991
Focus: Econ 07247

European Association for the Visual Studies of Man (EAVSoM), c/o Instituto di Antropologia, Via di Proconsolo 12, 50122 Firenze
T: (055) 214049
Focus: Anthro 07248

European Association of Perinatal Medicine, c/o Prof. Gian Carlo di Renzo, Centre of Perinatal Medicine, University of Perugia, University Hospital Monteluce, 06122 Perugia
T: (075) 5720574; E-Mail: direnzo@unipg.it; Fax: 5729271
Founded: 1968; Members: 3000
Pres: Prof. Asim Kurjak; Gen Secr: Prof. Gian Carlo di Renzo
Focus: Med 07249

European Association of Remote Sensing Laboratories (EARSeL), c/o DISIS, Piazzale Tecchio 80, 80125 Napoli
T: (081) 7682159; Fax: 7682160
Founded: 1977; Members: 230
Pres: Prof. S. Vetrella
Focus: Geology
Periodical
EARSeL News (quarterly) 07250

European Association of Senior Hospital Physicians, c/o Primario Divisione Medicina d'Urgenza, 33100 Udine
Founded: 1965
Focus: Med 07251

European Association of Social Medicine, Via Sacchi 24, 10128 Torino
T: (011) 517017
Founded: 1955
Focus: Med 07252

European Cell Biology Organization (ECBO), c/o Dept of Pharmacology, University of Milan, Via Vanvitelli 32, 20129 Milano
T: (02) 70146254; Fax: 7490937
Founded: 1969
Focus: Cell Biol & Cancer Res 07253

European Centre for Research and Development in Primary Health Care (EuroCentre-PHC), Via Marzia 16, 06100 Perugia
T: (075) 6962487; Fax: 6963904
Founded: 1991
Focus: Public Health 07254

European Centre for the Validation of Alternative Methods (ECVAM), c/o Joint Research Centre, Environment Institute, 21020 Ispra
T: (0332) 785996; Fax: 785336
Founded: 1991; Members: 35
Focus: Materials Sci 07255

European Centre for Training Craftsmen in the Conservation of the Architectural Heritage, Isola di San Servolo, CP 676, 30100 Venezia
T: (041) 5268546; Fax: 2760211
Founded: 1977
Focus: Preserv Hist Monuments 07256

European Centre of Environmental Studies (ECES), Via Po 14, 10123 Torino
T: (011) 8127167; Fax: 832870
Founded: 1990
Focus: Ecology 07257

European Commission for the Control of Foot-and-Mouth Disease (EUFMD), c/o FAO, Viale delle Terme di Caracalla, 00100 Roma
T: (06) 52255528, 52252635; E-Mail: yves.leforban@fao.org; Fax: 52255749
Founded: 1954; Members: 33
Pres: Dr. R. Marabelli; Gen Secr: Dr. Yves Leforban
Focus: Vet Med 07258

European Communities Biologists Association (ECBA), c/o Ordine Nazionale dei Biologi, Via icilio 7, 00153 Roma
T: (06) 571061; E-Mail: Dumontet@unibas.it; Fax: 57106235
Founded: 1975
Focus: Bio 07259

European Consortium for Church and State Research, c/o Sezione Relazioni tra Stato e Confessioni Religiose, Università degli Studi di Firenze, Via Laura 48, 50121 Firenze
Focus: Poli Sci 07260

European Coordinating Committee for Artificial Intelligence (ECCAI), c/o Istituto per la Ricerca Scientifica e Tecnologica, Loc Panté di Povo, 38050 Povo
T: (0461) 814444; Fax: 810851
Founded: 1982; Members: 25
Focus: Computer & Info Sci 07261

European Council for Social Research on Latin America, Via Arcangelo Corelli 10, 00198 Roma
T: (06) 79237364; Fax: 79200083
Founded: 1971
Focus: Soc Sci 07262

European Federation for the Advancement of Anaesthesia in Dentistry, CP 1630, 40100 Bologna
T: (051) 247784
Founded: 1973
Focus: Anesthetics 07263

European Network of Scientific Information Referral Centres (EUSIREF), CP 64, 00044 Frascati
Focus: Sci 07264

European Renal Association – European Dialysis and Transplant Association (ERA-EDTA), CP 474, Parma Sud, 43100 Parma
T: (0521) 989078; E-Mail: eraedta@ ipruniv.cce.unipr.it; Fax: 291777
Founded: 1964; Members: 4500
Pres: Prof. François Berthoux; Gen Secr: Dr. Fernando Carrera
Focus: Surgery; Hematology 07265

European Safeguards Research and Development Association (ESARDA), c/o Commission of the European Communities Joint Research Centre, 21020 Ispra
T: (0332) 789372; Fax: 789509
Founded: 1969; Members: 10
Focus: Eng
Periodical
ESARDA Bulletin (semi-annually) 07266

European Society for Clinical Respiratory Physiology, c/o Fondazione Menarini, Piazza del Carmine 4, 20121 Milano
T: (02) 874932
Founded: 1966
Focus: Physiology
Periodical
SEPCR Newsletter (quarterly) 07267

European Society for the Study of Ultrasonics, c/o Centro Minerva Medica, Via L. Spallanzani, 00161 Roma
Focus: Physics 07268

European Society of Hypnosis in Psychotherapy and Psychosomatic Medicine-Italian Constituent Society, c/o Centro Studi di Ipnosi Clinica H. Bernheim, Via Valverde 65, 37100 Verona
T: (045) 30795
Founded: 1964
Focus: Therapeutics
Periodical
International Journal of Clinical and Experimental Hypnosis 07269

Famiglia e Libertà / Comitato Tecnico Permanente per lo Studio della Legislazione e dei Rimedi, Via della Conciliazione 15, 00193 Roma
T: (06) 6544841
Founded: 1965
Focus: Family Plan; Sociology 07270

Federazione delle Associazioni Scientifiche e Tecniche (FAST), Piazzale Rodolfo Morandi 2, 20121 Milano
T: (02) 76015672; Fax: 782485
Founded: 1961; Members: 35
Pres: Prof. Walter Nicodemi; Gen Secr: Dr. Alberto Pieri
Focus: Sci; Eng
Periodicals
Alta Frequenza
Automazione e Strumentazione
L'Elettrotecnica
La Fonderia Italiana
La Meccanica Italiana
La Metallurgia Italiana
Notiziario della FAST
La Termotecnica 07271

Federazione delle Istituzioni Antropologiche Italiane (F.I.A.I.), c/o Istituto di Antropologia Fisica, Università degli Studi, Via Balbi 4, 16126 Genova
T: (010) 204654
Founded: 1977
Focus: Anthro 07272

Federazione Europea di Zootecnia (F.E.Z.) / Fédération Européenne de Zootechnie / European Association for Animal Production, Via A. Tortonia 15a, 00161 Roma
T: (06) 8840785; Fax: 8441733
Founded: 1949
Focus: Zoology
Periodical
Livestock Production Science (monthly) . 07273

Federazione Italiana contro la Tubercolosi e le Malattie Polmonari Sociali, Via G. da Procida 7, 00162 Roma
T: (06) 44240682; Fax: 44240682
Focus: Pulmon Dis
Periodical
Lotta contro la Tubercolosi e le Malattie Polmonari Sociali (quarterly) 07274

Federazione Italiana dei Cineclub (FEDIC), Via de Villa Patrizi 10, 00161 Roma
T: (06) 421901
Founded: 1949
Focus: Cinema
Periodical
Giornale dello Spettacolo: Notiziario FEDIC 07275

Federazione Italiana delle Scienze e delle Attività Motorie (F.I.S.A.M.), Via Federico Cesi 30, 00193 Roma
T: (06) 315577
Founded: 1965
Focus: Auto Eng
Periodical
Società Domani, Dibattiti 07276

Federazione Italiana Dottori in Agraria e Forestali (FEDERAGRONOMI), Via Livenza 6, 00198 Roma
T: (06) 8416036; Fax: 8555961
Founded: 1944; Members: 74
Focus: Agri; Forestry
Periodical
Il Dottore in Scienze Agrarie e Forestali (monthly) 07277

Federazione Medico-Sportiva Italiana (FMSI), Viale Tiziano 70, 00196 Roma
T: (06) 394670, 393221; Fax: 36858206
Focus: Med; Sports
Periodical
Medicina dello Sport (bi-monthly) 07278

Federazione Nazionale Collegi Tecnici di Radiologia Medica, c/o G.C. Luisetti, Viale S. Marco 56, 30173 Mestre
Focus: Radiology 07279

Federazione Nazionale degli Ordini dei Medici Chirurghi e Odontoiatri, Piazza Cola di Rienzo 80a, 00192 Roma
T: (06) 362031
Founded: 1946; Members: 34
Focus: Med
Periodicals
Federazione Medica (monthly)
Il Medico d'Italia 07280

Federazione Nazionale degli Ordini dei Veterinari Italiani (FNOVI), Via del Tritone 125, 00186 Roma
T: (06) 485923
Focus: Vet Med 07281

Federazione Nazionale Insegnanti Educazione Fisica (FNIEF), Via Pasquale Revoltella 41, 00152 Roma
T: (06) 533417
Focus: Sports 07282

Federazione Nazionale pro Natura, c/o Istituto per lo Sviluppo Economico dell'Appennino, Via Marchesana 12, 40124 Bologna
T: (051) 231999
Founded: 1959
Focus: Ecology
Periodical
Natura Società (bi-monthly) 07283

Fondazione Centro di Documentazione Ebraica Contemporanea (F.C.D.E.C.), Via Eupili 8, 20145 Milano
T: (02) 316338, 316092
Founded: 1955
Focus: Hist 07284

Forum Italiano dell'Energia Nucleare (FIEN), Via Paisello 26-28, 00198 Roma
T: (06) 868291
Founded: 1958; Members: 233
Focus: Nucl Res 07285

Gruppi Archeologici d'Italia (G.A.I.), Via Tacito 41, 00193 Roma
T: (06) 6874028
Founded: 1960; Members: 3000
Focus: Archeol
Periodical
Archeologia (monthly) 07286

Gruppo Automazione Navale e Problemi delle Navi di Grande Tonnellaggio, Via Al Molo Giano, Calata Grazie, 16126 Genova
T: (010) 5995460; Fax: 5995790
Gen Secr: Prof. Bruno Della Loggia
Focus: Eng 07287

Gruppo di Ricerca per i Virus e Virosi delle Piante, c/o Istituto di Patologia Vegetale, Università, Via E. de Nicola, 07100 Sassari
T: (079) 210731
Gen Secr: Prof. Ulisse Prota
Focus: Botany 07288

Gruppo di Ricerca per la Patologia delle Piante Ortensi, c/o Istituto di Patologia Vegetale, Università, Via Pietro Giuria 15, 10126 Torino
T: (011) 6509617
Gen Secr: Prof. Alberto Matta
Focus: Botany 07289

Gruppo di Ricerca sulle Alte Tensioni, c/o Dip di Energia Elettrica, Università, Via Eudossiana 18, 00184 Roma
T: (06) 4825051; Fax: 4883236
Gen Secr: Prof. Carlo Mazzetti di Pietralata
Focus: Electric Eng 07290

Gruppo di Ricerca sulle Macchine Elettriche, c/o Dip di Ingegneria Elettrica, Università La Sapienza, Via Eudossiana 18, 00184 Roma
T: (06) 4817981; Fax: 4883235
Gen Secr: Prof. Augusto Di Napoli
Focus: Electric Eng 07291

Gruppo Interdisciplinare per la Ricerca Sociale, c/o Facoltà di Scienze Statistiche Demografiche, Piazza Aldo Moro 5, 00185 Roma
T: (06) 4453828
Founded: 1937
Focus: Soc Sci 07292

Gruppo Italiano di Fisica Cosmica, Via Tiburtina 770, 00159 Roma
T: (06) 4392974; Fax: 4392974
Gen Secr: Prof. F. Mariani
Focus: Astrophys 07293

Gruppo Italiano di Linguistica Applicata (GILA), c/o Istituto del Consiglio Nazionale delle Richerche, Via S. Maria 36, 56100 Pisa
Focus: Ling 07294

Gruppo Nazionale di Cibernetica e Biofisica, c/o Instituto di Biofisica del CNR, Via San Lorenzo 26, 56127 Pisa
T: (050) 501501
Gen Secr: Prof. Carlo Frediani
Focus: Biophys; Physics 07295

Gruppo Nazionale di Elettronica Quantistica e Plasmi, Via Panciatichi 64, 50127 Firenze
T: (055) 4222793; Fax: 410893
Gen Secr: Giancarlo Righini
Focus: Electronic Eng 07296

Gruppo Nazionale di Geofisica della Terra Solida, c/o Dip di Idraulica, Trasporti e Strade, Università La Sapienza, Via Eudossiana 18, 00184 Roma
T: (06) 44585076; Fax: 44585080
Gen Secr: Prof. Marcello Bernabini
Focus: Geophys 07297

Gruppo Nazionale di Sistemistica e di Informatica dell'Ingegneria, c/o Dip di Informatica e Sistemistica, Università, Via Claudio 21, 80125 Napoli
T: (081) 7683188
Gen Secr: Prof. C. Savy
Focus: Eng 07298

Gruppo Nazionale di Struttura della Materia, Viale dell'Università 11, 00185 Roma
T: (06) 4462489; Fax: 4941159
Gen Secr: Prof. Francesco Paolo Ricci
Focus: Materials Sci 07299

Gruppo Nazionale per la Difesa dai Terremoti, Via Nizza 128, 00198 Roma
T: (06) 866129
Focus: Geology 07300

Gruppo Nazionale per la Fisica Matematica, Via di Santa Marta 13a, 50139 Firenze
T: (055) 474389; Fax: 475915
Gen Secr: Prof. V. Boffi
Focus: Math 07301

Gruppo Nazionale per l'Analisi Funzionale e le sue Applicazioni, Via di Santa Marta 13a, 53139 Firenze
T: (055) 496912; Fax: 475915
Gen Secr: Prof. D- Pagani
Focus: Math 07302

Gruppo Nazionale per l'Astronomia, c/o Reparto di Planetologia, Istituto di Astrofisica Spaziale, Viale dell'Università 11, 00185 Roma
T: (06) 4958230; Fax: 4454969
Gen Secr: Dr. Angioletta Coradini
Focus: Astronomy 07303

Gruppo Nazionale per le Strutture Algebriche e Geometriche e loro Applicazioni, Via di Santa Marta 13a, 50139 Firenze
T: (055) 474389; Fax: 475915
Gen Secr: Prof. A. Conte
Focus: Math 07304

Gruppo Nazionale per l'Informatica Matematica, Via di Santa Marta 13a, 50139 Firenze
T: (055) 474389; Fax: 475915
Gen Secr: Prof. I. Galligani
Focus: Math 07305

Gruppo per i Problemi Geologici della Regione Alpino-Padana, c/o Istituto di Mineralogia e Petrologia, Università, Corso Garibaldi 37, 35122 Padova
T: (049) 663122
Gen Secr: Prof. Giuseppe O. Gatto
Focus: Geology 07306

Institutio Santoriana, Via Maggiolini 1, 20122 Milano
T: (02) 76006417; Fax: 799404
Founded: 1992
Pres: Luca M. Pedrotti dell'Acqua
Focus: Med; Ecology 07307

International Association for the Study of Canon Law, c/o Universitá degli Studi, Cittá Universitaria, 00100 Roma
Founded: 1973
Focus: Rel & Theol; Law 07308

International Association for Veterinary Homeopathy, Via Soresina 16, 20144 Milano
Focus: Vet Med
Periodical
International Journal for Veterinary Homeopathy (semi-annually) 07309

International Association for Water Law (IAWL), Via Montevideo 5, 00198 Roma
T: (06) 8548932; Fax: 8548932
Founded: 1967; Members: 200
Focus: Law
Periodicals
Annales Juris Aquarum (irregularly)
Aquaforum (irregularly) 07310

International Association of Biblicists and Orientalists, Piazza Duomo 4, 48100 Ravenna
T: (0544) 23432
Founded: 1967
Focus: Rel & Theol; Ethnology
Periodical
Biblia Revuo (quarterly) 07311

International Association of Engineering Geology, Sezione Italiana, c/o Istituto di Geologia Applicata e Geotecnica, Facoltà di Ingegneria, Università degli Studi, Via Re David 200, 70125 Bari
T: (080) 228369
Founded: 1972
Focus: Eng; Geology
Periodical
Bulletin of the International Association of Engineering Geology 07312

International Board for Plant Genetic Resources (IBPGR), Via delle Sette Chiese 142, 00145 Roma
T: (06) 518921; Fax: 5750309
Founded: 1974
Focus: Genetics
Periodical
Plant Genetic Resources Newsletter (quarterly) 07313

International Centre for Advanced Technical and Vocational Training / Centre International de Perfectionnement Professionnel et Technique, Corso Unità d'Italia 125, 10127 Torino
T: (011) 633733; E-Mail: INTERLAB Torino;
Fax: 638842
Founded: 1963
Focus: Adult Educ; Eng; Sociology; Econ; Marketing; Finance; Travel; Energy; Educ; Develop Areas; Animal Husb; Agri; Fisheries; Doc
Periodical
Bulletin (3 times annually) 07314

International Centre for Mechanical Sciences, Piazza Garibaldi 18, 33100 Udine
T: (0432) 294989
Founded: 1968
Focus: Eng
Periodical
Mechanics Research Communications (bi-monthly) 07315

International Centre for Theoretical Physics (ICTP), CP 586, 34100 Trieste
T: (040) 2240111; E-Mail: sci_info@ictp.trieste.it;
Fax: 224163
Founded: 1964
Pres: Prof. Miguel Virasoro
Focus: Physics; Math
Periodicals
Annual Report of Scientific Activities (annually)
News from ICTP (quarterly) 07316

International Committee for Recording the Productivity of Milk Animals (ICRPMA), Via A. Torlonia 15a, 00161 Roma
T: (06) 8840785; Fax: 8441733
Founded: 1951
Focus: Agri 07317

International Council of Museums (I.C.O.M.) / Comitato Nazionale Italiano, c/o Museo Nazionale della Scienza e della Tecnica, Via S. Vittore 19, 20123 Milano
Founded: 1976
Focus: Archives
Periodical
Notiziario (bi-monthly) 07318

International Institute for the Unification of Private Law (Unidroit), Via Panisperna 28, 00184 Roma
T: (06) 69941372; Fax: 69941394
Founded: 1926; Members: 58
Pres: Prof. Luigi Ferrari Bravo; Gen Secr: Walter Rodino
Focus: Law
Periodicals
NEWS Bulletin (semi-annually)
Uniform Law Review (quarterly) 07319

International Juridical Organization for Environment and Development (IJO), Via Barberini 3, 00187 Roma
T: (06) 4742117; E-Mail: Juricountries Rome;
Fax: 4745779
Founded: 1964
Focus: Law; Energy; Ecology
Periodical
IJO Newsletter (quarterly) 07320

International Law Association, Sezione Italiana (I.L.A.), Via delle Quattro Fontane 15, 00184 Roma
T: (06) 4883979, 4880981; Fax: 4820686
Focus: Law 07321

International League of Esperantist Teachers, Via Palestro 36, 54100 Massa
T: (0585) 41756
Founded: 1949; Members: 2700
Focus: Ling; Educ
Periodical
IPORO Internacia Pedagogia Revuo (3 times annually) 07322

International Linguistic Club, Via San Tommaso 29, 10121 Torino
T: (011) 533121; Fax: 533121
Gen Secr: Prof. Andrea Rastelli
Focus: Ling 07323

International Poplar Commission (IPC), c/o FAO, Viale delle Terme di Caracalla, 00153 Roma
T: (06) 57971; Fax: 5795137
Founded: 1947; Members: 35
Focus: Forestry
Periodical
Session Report 07324

International Society for Medical and Psychological Hypnosis (ISMPH), c/o Istituto di Indagini Psicologiche, Corso XXII Marzo 57, 20129 Milano
T: (02) 70126489; Fax: 7491051
Founded: 1985; Members: 175
Pres: Prof. Rolando Marchesan; Dr. Milton V. Kline; Gen Secr: Dr. Aurora Zavertanik
Focus: Med; Psych; Therapeutics . . . 07325

International Society for the Study of Infectious and Parasitic Diseases, c/o Ospedale Amadeo di Savoia, Corso Svizzera 164, 10149 Torino
Focus: Microbio; Immunology 07326

International Society for Twin Studies (ISTS), c/o Mendel Institute, Piazza Galeno 5, 00162 Roma
Founded: 1974; Members: 227
Focus: Behav Sci; Genetics; Med
Periodicals
Acta Geneticae Medicae et Gemellologiae/Twin Research (quarterly)
Twins (semi-annually) 07327

International Society of Theoretical and Experimental Hypnosis (ISTEH), c/o Istituto di Indagini Psicologiche, Corso XXII Marzo 57, 20129 Milano
T: (02) 7388427; Fax: 7401051
Founded: 1988; Members: 65
Focus: Psychoan 07328

International Solar Energy Society, Sezione Italiana (I.S.E.S.), Via Francesco Crispi 72, 80121 Napoli
T: (081) 666684
Founded: 1964
Focus: Energy
Periodicals
Energie Alternative: Bimestrale della Sezione Italiana (bi-monthly)
ISES News (quarterly)
Solar Energy
Sun World 07329

International Study Group for Steroid Hormones (ISGSH), c/o Clinica Medica, Policlinico Umberto I, 00161 Roma
T: (06) 4940568; Fax: 490530
Founded: 1961
Focus: Pathology
Periodical
Proceedings of the Meetings 07330

Istituto Agronomico per l'Oltremare (I.A.O.), Via Antonio Cocchi 4, 50131 Firenze
T: (055) 573201; Fax: 580314
Founded: 1904; Members: 50
Gen Secr: Dr. Gian Curotti
Focus: Agri
Periodical
Rivista di Agricoltura Subtropicale e Tropicale (quarterly) 07331

Istituto Centrale per la Patologia del Libro, Via Milano 76, 00184 Roma
T: (06) 482911; Fax: 4814968
Founded: 1938; Members: 77
Pres: Prof. Carlo Federici
Focus: Libraries & Bk Sci 07332

Istituto Cooperativo per l'Innovazione (ICIE) / Istituto Nazionale per la Ricerca Applicata ed il Trasferimento Tecnologico della Lega Nazionale delle Cooperative e Mutue / Cooperative Institute for Innovation, Via Nomentana 133, 00161 Roma
T: (06) 8845848; Fax: 8550250
Founded: 1972; Members: 30
Focus: Archit
Periodical
Innovazione: Trimestrale di Informazione Tecnico-Scientifica (quarterly) 07333

Istituto Cooperazione Economica Internazionale (I.C.E.I.), Via Tommaso Salvini 3, 20122 Milano
T: (02) 799144, 784723
Founded: 1978
Focus: Econ; Int'l Relat 07334

Istituto di Diritto Romano e dei Diritti dell'Oriente Mediterraneo, c/o Facoltà di Giurisprudenza, Piazzale Aldo Moro 5, 00185 Roma
Founded: 1937
Pres: Feliciano Serrano
Focus: Archit; Cultur Hist 07335

Istituto di Sociologia Internazionale di Gorizia (I.S.I.G.) / Institute of International Sociology, Gorizia, Via Mazzini 13, 34170 Gorizia
T: (0481) 32580; Fax: 532094
Founded: 1968
Focus: Sociology; Int'l Relat; Poli Sci
Periodicals
Futuribili (quarterly)
ISIG (quarterly) 07336

Istituto di Studi Nucleari per l'Agricoltura (ISNA), Via IV Novembre 152, 00187 Roma
T: (06) 6784964
Founded: 1959
Pres: Prof. Giuseppe Gesualdi; Gen Secr: Pof. M.L. Scarselli
Focus: Eng; Agri 07337

Istituto Elettrotecnico Nazionale Galileo Ferraris (IEN), Corso Massimo d'Azeglio 42, 10125 Torino
T: (011) 39191; Fax: 6507611
Founded: 1934; Members: 123
Pres: Sigfrido Leschiutta
Focus: Electric Eng
Periodical
Pubblicazioni IEN (annually) 07338

Istituto Geografico Militare (IGMI), Via Cesare Battisti 10, 50100 Firenze
T: (055) 27751; Fax: 282172
Founded: 1872; Members: 404
Gen Secr: D. Costantino Maglio
Focus: Geography
Periodicals
Bollettino di Geodesia e Scienze Affini (quarterly)
L'Universo (bi-monthly) 07339

Istituto Internazionale delle Comunicazioni (I.I.C.), Villa Piaggio, Via Pertinace, 16125 Genova
T: (010) 294683/84; Fax: 200883
Founded: 1962
Focus: Comm
Periodical
Notiziario I.I.C.: Mensile d'Informazione (monthly) 07340

Istituto Internazionale di Diritto Umanitario (IIDU), Corso Cavallotti 115, 18038 San Remo
T: (0184) 541848; Fax: 541600
Founded: 1970; Members: 119
Focus: Law 07341

Istituto Internazionale di Studi Liguri (IISL), Via Romana 39, 18012 Bordighera
T: (0184) 263601; Fax: 266421
Founded: 1947; Members: 1500
Pres: Cosimo Costa; Gen Secr: Dr. Orazio Sappa
Focus: Hist
Periodicals
Cahiers Ligures de Préhistoire et de Protohistoire (annually)
Giornale Storico della Lunigiana e del Territorio Lucense (annually)
Rivista di Studi Liguri (annually)
Rivista Ingauna e Intemelia (annually)
Studi Genuensi (annually) 07342

Istituto Internazionale di Vulcanologia, Viale Regina Margherita 6, 95123 Catania
Focus: Geology 07343

Istituto Italiano degli Attuari, Via del Corea 3, 00186 Roma
T: (06) 3226051
Founded: 1930; Members: 355
Focus: Insurance
Periodical
Giornale (annually) 07344

Istituto Italiano del Marchio di Qualità, Via Quintiliano 43, 20138 Milano
T: (02) 50731; Fax: 5073271
Founded: 1951
Pres: Lorenzo Frangali Casanuova
Focus: Materials Sci 07345

Istituto Italiano della Saldatura, Lungobisagno Istria 15, 16141 Genova
T: (010) 83411; E-Mail: iis@assicomitalia.it;
Fax: 8367780
Founded: 1948; Members: 800
Focus: Eng
Periodical
Rivista Italiana della Saldatura (bi-monthly) 07346

Istituto Italiano di Arti Grafiche, Via Zanica 92, 24100 Bergamo
Focus: Graphic & Dec Arts, Design . . 07347

Istituto Italiano di Numismatica (IIN), Palazzo Barberini, Via Quattro Fontane 13, 00184 Roma
T: (06) 4743603; Fax: 4743603
Founded: 1912
Focus: Numismatics
Periodical
Annali dell'Istituto Italiano di Numismatica (annually) 07348

Istituto Italiano di Paleontologia Umana (I.I.P.U.), Piazza Mincio 2, 00198 Roma
T: (06) 8557598
Founded: 1913; Members: 250
Pres: Prof. Dr. A. Ascenzi; Gen Secr: Prof. A. Bietti
Focus: Paleontology
Periodicals
Memorie
Quaternaria Nova: Atti – pubblicati nella rivista 07349

Istituto Italiano di Pubblicismo (I.I.P.), c/o Facoltà di Scienze Statistiche, Università degli Studi, Piazzale delle Scienze 2, 00185 Roma
Founded: 1947
Focus: Journalism; Comm Sci
Periodicals
Bibliografia Italiana sull'Informazione (annually)
Saggi e Studi di Pubblicistica (annually) . 07350

Istituto Italiano di Storia della Chimica, Via G. B. Morgagni 32, 00161 Roma
Focus: Chem; Cultur Hist 07351

Istituto Italiano di Studi Germanici, Via Calandrelli 25, 00153 Roma
T: (06) 582465, 5897577; Fax: 5835929
Founded: 1932
Focus: Ling; Lit
Periodical
Studi Germanici (3 times annually) . . . 07352

Istituto Italiano per il Medio ed Estremo Oriente (ISMEO), Via Merulana 248, 00185 Roma
T: (06) 732741
Founded: 1933
Focus: Ethnology
Periodicals
Cina (annually)
East and West (quarterly)
Il Giappone (annually) 07353

Istituto Italiano per la Storia Antica, Via Milano 76, 00184 Roma
T: (06) 4880597
Founded: 1935; Members: 5
Pres: Prof. S. Accame
Focus: Hist 07354

Istituto Italiano per la Storia della Musica (IISM), c/o Accademia Nazionale di Santa Cecilia, Via Vittoria 6, 00187 Roma
T: (06) 36000146
Founded: 1938
Pres: Prof. Raffaello Monterosso
Focus: Hist; Music 07355

Istituto Italiano per l'Africa e l'Oriente, Via Merulana 248, 00185 Roma
T: (06) 4874273; Fax: 4873138
Founded: 1995
Pres: Prof. Gherardo Gnoli; Gen Secr: Giancarlo Gargaruti
Focus: Ethnology; Hist; Econ; Poli Sci . 07356

Istituto Italiano Studi di Ipnosi Clinica e Psicoterapia, Via Valverde 54, 37122 Verona
T: (045) 8030795; Fax: 8030795
Founded: 1965; Members: 130

Pres: Dr. Giulio Guerra; Gen Secr: Dr. Michele Modenese
Focus: Therapeutics
Periodical
Acta Hypnologica (3 times annually) . . 07357

Istituto Lombardo Accademia di Scienze e Lettere, Via Brera 28, 20121 Milano
T: (02) 86461388; Fax: 86461388
Founded: 1802
Pres: Prof. Luigi Amerio
Focus: Sci; Humanities 07358

Istituto Nazionale delle Assicurazioni (I.N.A.), Via Sallustiana 51, 00187 Roma
T: (06) 4882497; Fax: 47224595
Founded: 1912
Focus: Insurance
Periodical
Assicurazioni: Bimestrale di Diritto, Economia e Finanza delle Assicurazioni Private (bi-monthly) 07359

Istituto Nazionale di Archeologia e Storia dell'Arte, Piazza San Marco 49, 00186 Roma
T: (06) 6780817; Fax: 6798804
Founded: 1922
Gen Secr: Paolo Pellegrino
Focus: Archeol; Arts; Hist 07360

Istituto Nazionale di Architettura, Via Catalana 5, 00186 Roma
T: (06) 68802254
Founded: 1959
Pres: Paolo Baratta
Focus: Archit 07361

Istituto Nazionale di Ottica (INO), Largo Enrico Fermi 6, 50125 Firenze
T: (055) 23081; Fax: 2337755
Founded: 1927; Members: 32
Focus: Optics 07362

Istituto Nazionale di Studi Etruschi ed Italici, Via della Pergola 65, 50121 Firenze
T: (055) 2396846
Founded: 1932; Members: 215
Pres: Dr. Guglielmo Maetzke; Gen Secr: Prof. G. Camporeale
Focus: Ethnology; Cultur Hist 07363

Istituto Nazionale di Studi Verdiani, Strada della Repubblica 56, 43100 Parma
T: (0521) 286044; Fax: 287949
Founded: 1960
Pres: Alberto Carrara Verdi; Gen Secr: Pierluigi Petrobelli
Focus: Music 07364

Istituto Nazionale di Urbanistica (INU), Via S. Caterina da Siena 46, 00186 Roma
T: (06) 6793559; E-Mail: inunaz@mbox.vol.it; Fax: 6780929
Founded: 1929; Members: 3095
Focus: Urban Plan
Periodicals
Urbanistica (quarterly)
Urbanistica Informazioni (bi-monthly) . . 07365

Istituto per gli Studi di Politica Internazionale (ISPI), Via Clerici 5, 20121 Milano
T: (02) 878266/68
Founded: 1933; Members: 80
Focus: Poli Sci
Periodicals
Quaderni-Papers (10-12 times annually)
Relazioni Internazionali (quarterly) . . . 07366

Istituto per il Rinnovamento Economico (IRE), Via Petronio Arbitro 4, 00136 Roma
Founded: 1924
Pres: G. Di Domenico
Focus: Econ 07367

Istituto per la Cooperazione Economica Internazionale e i Problemi di Sviluppo (I.C.E.P.S.) / Institute for International Economic Cooperation and Development, Via Cola di Rienzo 11, 00192 Roma
T: (06) 3215095; Fax: 3214690
Founded: 1966; Members: 55
Focus: Econ; Int'l Relat; Develop Areas
Periodical
Booklets and Documents (monthly) . . . 07368

Istituto per la Cooperazione Universitaria (I.C.U.), Viale G. Rossini 26, 00198 Roma
T: (06) 85300722; Fax: 8554646
Founded: 1967
Pres: Prof. Raffaello Cortesini; Gen Secr: Prof. Umberto Farri
Focus: Adult Educ
Periodical
SIPE – Servizio Stampa Educazione e Sviluppo: Notiziario d'informazione (monthly) . . . 07369

Istituto per la Storia del Risorgimento Italiano (ISTOR), Piazza Venezia, Vittoriano, 00186 Roma
T: (06) 6793589; Fax: 6782572
Founded: 1935; Members: 3400
Pres: Prof. Giuseppe Talamo; Gen Secr: Alberto M. Arpino
Focus: Hist
Periodical
Rassegna Storica del Risorgimento (quarterly) 07370

Istituto per l'Economia Europea, Via C. Colombo 70, 00147 Roma
Founded: 1960; Members: 62
Pres: Prof. Gaetano Stammati; Gen Secr: Dr. Silvano Palumbo
Focus: Econ 07371

Istituto per l'Oriente (I.P.O.), Via Alberto Caroncini 19, 00197 Roma
T: (06) 804106
Founded: 1921; Members: 200
Focus: Ethnology
Periodicals
Oriens Antiquus
Oriente Moderno
Rassegna di Studi Etiopici 07372

Istituto Storico Italiano per il Medio Evo, Piazza dell'Orologio 4, 00186 Roma
T: (06) 68802075; Fax: 6877059
Founded: 1883
Pres: Prof. Girolamo Arnaldi
Focus: Hist 07373

Istituto Storico Italiano per l'Età Moderna e Contemporanea, Via Michelangelo Caetani 32, 00186 Roma
T: (06) 68806922; Fax: 6875127
Founded: 1934
Pres: Prof. Luigi Lotti
Focus: Hist
Periodical
Annuario dell'Istituto Storico Italiano per l'Età moderna e contemporanea (bi-annually) . 07374

Istituto Veneto di Scienze, Lettere ed Arti, San Marco 2945, 30124 Venezia
T: (041) 5210177; Fax: 5210598
Founded: 1838; Members: 180
Pres: Prof. Feliciano Benvenuti
Focus: Humanities; Sci; Arts 07375

ITALCONSULT / Società Generale per Progettazioni, Consulenze e Partecipazioni, Via Giorgione 163, 00147 Roma
T: (06) 54671
Founded: 1957
Focus: Eng 07376

Italia Nostra – Associazione Nazionale per la Tutela del Patrimonio Storico Artistico e Naturale della Nazione, Via Nicolò Porpora 22, 00198 Roma
T: (06) 8542333
Founded: 1955; Members: 20000
Pres: Floriano Villa; Gen Secr: Gala Pallottino
Focus: Preserv Hist Monuments
Periodical
Italia Nostra 07377

ITALSIEL / Società Italiana Sistemi Informativi Elettronici, Via Isonzo 21b, 00198 Roma
T: (06) 841351
Founded: 1969
Focus: Electronic Eng; Computer & Info Sci 07378

Keats-Shelley Memorial Association (KSMA), Piazza di Spagna 26, 00187 Roma
T: (06) 6784235; Fax: 6784167
Founded: 1907
Focus: Lit
Periodicals
Keats-Shelley Bulletin (annually)
Keats-Shelley Journal (annually) 07379

Latin-Mediterranean Society of Pharmacy, Via Belmeloro 6, 40126 Bologna
Founded: 1953
Focus: Pharmacol 07380

Lega Italiana per la Lotta contro i Tumori, Via Alessandro Torlonia 15, 00161 Roma
T: (06) 867382, 8845024; Fax: 8450362
Focus: Cell Biol & Cancer Res 07381

Ordine Nazionale degli Attuari, Via del Corea 3, 00186 Roma
T: (06) 6794014
Focus: Insurance 07382

PEN International Centre, Via Daverio 7, 20122 Milano
Pres: Maria Bellonci; Gen Secr: Rosario Assunto
Focus: Lit 07383

Sezione di Training Autogeno del Centro Internazionale de Ipnosi, c/o Istituto di Indagini Psicologiche, Corso XXII Marzo 57, 20129 Milano
T: (02) 7388427; Fax: 7491051
Members: 72
Focus: Psych 07384

Sindacato Autonomo Scuola Media Italiana (SASMI), Viale Trastevere 60, 00153 Roma
T: (06) 5803367
Focus: Educ 07385

Sindacato Nazionale Autori Drammatici (SNAD), Via dei Baullari 4, 00186 Roma
Founded: 1948
Focus: Lit 07386

Sindacato Nazionale Istruzione Artistica (S.N.I.A.), Via Antonino Pio 40, 00145 Roma
Focus: Arts; Educ
Periodical
Mensile di Informazione Sindacale sull'Istruzione Artistica (monthly) 07387

Sindacato Nazionale Scrittori (SNS), Via Basento 52d, 00198 Roma
T: (06) 8440837
Founded: 1945; Members: 1400
Focus: Lit 07388

Società Adriatica di Scienze (SAS) / Adriatic Society of Sciences, Via Orsera 3, CP 1029, 34145 Trieste
Founded: 1874; Members: 200
Pres: Prof. Dulio Lausi; Gen Secr: Dr. Tiziana C. Velari
Focus: Sci
Periodical
Bollettino della Società Adriatica di Scienze (irregularly) 07389

Società Archeologica Comense, c/o Civico Museo, Giovio, Piazzale delle Medaglie d'Oro Comasche 1, 22100 Como
T: (031) 211343, 269022
Founded: 1902
Focus: Archeol
Periodical
Rivista Archeologica della Antica Provincia e Diocesi di Como (annually) 07390

Società Archeologica Viterbese Pro Ferento, Via S. Pietro 80, 01100 Viterbo
T: 1927
Focus: Archeol 07391

Società Astronomica Italiana, Largo E. Fermi 5, 50125 Firenze
T: (055) 2752270; Fax: 220039
Founded: 1920; Members: 700
Pres: Prof. Massimo Capaccioli
Focus: Astronomy
Periodicals
Giornale di Astronomica (quarterly)
Memorie della Società Astronomica Italiana (quarterly) 07392

Società Botanica Italiana (S.B.I.), c/o Dipartimento di Biologia Vegetale, Facoltà di Scienze Matematiche, Fisiche e Naturali, Università degli Studi, Via Giorgio La Pira 4, 50121 Firenze
T: (055) 2757379; Fax: 2757379
Founded: 1888; Members: 1300
Focus: Botany
Periodicals
Giornale Botanico Italiano: Plant Biosystems (quarterly)
Informatore Botanico Italiano (quarterly) . 07393

Società Chimica Italiana (SCI), Viale Liegi 48, 00198 Roma
T: (06) 8549691; Fax: 8548734
Founded: 1909; Members: 4800
Pres: Prof. Bruno Scrosati
Focus: Chem
Periodicals
Annali di Chimica (bi-monthly)
La Chimica e l'Industria: Quaderni dell'Ingegnere Chimico Italiano (monthly)
Chimica nella Scuola (bi-monthly)
Il Farmaco (monthly)
Gazzetta Chimica Italiana (monthly) . . . 07394

Società Dalmata di Storia Patria, c/o Società Dante Alighieri, Palazzo Firenze, Piazza Firenze 27, 00186 Roma
T: (06) 686992
Focus: Hist
Periodical
Atti e Memorie 07395

Società Dante Alighieri, Piazza Firenze 27, 00186 Roma
T: (06) 6873694
Founded: 1889
Gen Secr: Dr. Giuseppe Cota
Focus: Lit
Periodical
Pagine della Dante (3 times annually) . 07396

Società Dantesca Italiana (S.D.I.), Via dell'Arte della Lana 1, 50123 Firenze
T: (055) 287134; E-Mail: sdi@leonet.it; Fax: 211316
Founded: 1888; Members: 290
Pres: Prof. Francesco Mazzoni
Focus: Lit
Periodicals
Quaderni degli Studi Danteschi
Quaderni del Centro di Documentazione Dantesca e Medievale
Studi Danteschi (annually) 07397

Società Dauna di Cultura, c/o Palazzetto della Cultura e dell'Arte, Via Ferdinando Galiani 1, 71100 Foggia
T: (0881) 23042
Founded: 1947
Focus: Lit; Arts; Eng
Periodical
Rassegna di Studi Dauni (quarterly) . . 07398

Società degli Amici del Museo Civico di Storia Naturale Giacomo Doria, Via Brigata Liguria 9, 16121 Genova
T: (010) 585753
Founded: 1927; Members: 238
Focus: Mineralogy; Paleontology; Botany; Zoology 07399

Società degli Ingegneri e degli Architetti in Torino, Corso Massimo d'Azeglio 42, 10125 Torino
T: (011) 6508511; Fax: 6508168
Founded: 1866
Focus: Archit; Eng
Periodicals
Atti e Rassegna Tecnica della Società degli Ingegneri e degli Architetti in Torino (monthly) 07400

Società dei Naturalisti in Napoli, Via Mezzocannone 8, 08134 Napoli
T: (081) 207922
Founded: 1881; Members: 350
Focus: Nat Sci
Periodicals
Bollettino della Società dei Naturalisti in Napoli
Memorie: Supplemento al Bollettino (annually) 07401

Società di Etnografia Italiana, Via Tacito 50, 00193 Roma
T: (06) 359512
Founded: 1911; Members: 170
Pres: Prof. Pablo Toschi
Focus: Ethnology 07402

Società di Fotogrammetria e Topografia (SIFET), Piazzale Rodolfo Morandi 2, 20121 Milano
Founded: 1951
Focus: Surveying 07403

Società di Letture e Conversazioni Scientifiche, Piazza Fontane Marose 6, 16100 Genova
Founded: 1866
Gen Secr: P. Bozzo-Costa
Focus: Lit; Sci 07404

Società di Linguistica Italiana (S.L.I.), Via M. Caetani 32, 00186 Roma
T: (06) 651613; Fax: 66987044
Founded: 1966; Members: 1000
Focus: Ling
Periodical
Bollettino della S.L.I. (quarterly) 07405

Società di Medicina Legale e delle Assicurazioni, c/o Istituto di Medicina Legale e delle Assicurazione, Università degli Studi, Viale Regina Elena 336, 00161 Roma
T: (06) 4952941
Founded: 1907
Focus: Public Health
Periodical
Zacchia (quarterly) 07406

Società di Minerva, Piazza A. Hortis 4, 34123 Trieste
Founded: 1810; Members: 150
Pres: Luigi Pavan
Focus: Hist
Periodical
Archeografo Triestino 07407

Società di Ortopedia e Traumatologia dell'Istituto Meridionale ed Insulare (S.O.T.I.M.I.), c/o Clinica Ortopedica I, Facoltà di Medicina, Università degli Studi, Via S. Andrea delle Dame 4, 80138 Napoli
T: (081) 459824
Founded: 1956
Focus: Traumatology
Periodical
Atti e Memorie della S.O.T.I.M.I. (annually) 07408

Società di Scienze Farmacologiche Applicate (S.S.F.A.), Via G. Jan 18, 20129 Milano
T: (02) 29513303; Fax: 29520179
Founded: 1963; Members: 700
Focus: Pharmacol
Periodical
Bolletino di Informazione (bi-monthly) . . 07409

Società di Scienze Naturali del Trentino, c/o Museo Tridentino di Scienze Naturali, Via Calepina 14, 38100 Trento
T: (0461) 234760
Founded: 1948
Focus: Nat Sci
Periodical
Natura Alpina (quarterly) 07410

Società di Storia Patria di Terra di Lavoro, Palazzo Reale, 81100 Caserta
T: (0823) 326037
Founded: 1952
Focus: Hist; Sociology
Periodical
Archivio Storico di Terra di Lavoro (annually) 07411

Società di Storia Patria per la Puglia, Piazza Umberto 2, 70121 Bari
T: (080) 237538
Focus: Hist
Periodical
Archivio Storico Pugliese (quarterly) . . 07412

Società di Storia Patria per la Sicilia Orientale, Piazza Stesicoro 29, 95124 Catania
T: (095) 316920; Fax: 316920
Founded: 1903; Members: 260
Pres: Prof. Paolo Mario Sipala; Gen Secr: Prof. Rosalba Galvagno
Focus: Hist

Periodicals
Archivio Storico per la Sicilia Orientale (quarterly)
Quaderni di Filologia e Letteratura Siciliana . . . 07413

Società di Studi Celestiniani (S.S.C.), c/o Biblioteca Comunale, 86170 Isernia
T: 2372
Founded: 1919
Focus: Hist; Rel & Theol . . . 07414

Società di Studi Geografici (S.S.G.), Via S. Gallo 10, 50129 Firenze
T: (055) 2757956
Founded: 1895; Members: 600
Pres: Paolo Roberto Federici; Gen Secr: Laura Cassi
Focus: Geography
Periodical
Rivista Geografica Italiana (quarterly) . . . 07415

Società di Studi Romagnoli (S.S.R.), c/o Biblioteca Malatestiana, Piazza Bufalini 1, 47023 Cesena
T: (0547) 21297
Founded: 1949
Focus: Hist; Geography
Periodical
Studi Romagnoli (annually) . . . 07416

Società di Studi Trentini di Scienze Storiche, Via Petrarca 36, 38100 Trento
T: (0461) 983383
Focus: Hist . . . 07417

Società di Studi Valdesi, Via Beckwith 3, 10066 Torre Pellice
Founded: 1881; Members: 650
Focus: Hist
Periodical
Bollettino (semi-annually) . . . 07418

Società d'Incoraggiamento d'Arti e Mestieri, Via Santa Maria 18, 20123 Milano
T: (02) 86450125
Founded: 1838
Pres: Massimo Scortecci; Gen Secr: Danilo Cancellieri
Focus: Arts; Commerce . . . 07419

Società Ecologica Friulana (S.E.F.), Viale delle Rose 60, 33030 Campoformido
T: (0432) 69716
Founded: 1973
Focus: Hist; Lit; Poli Sci; Ecology
Periodical
Corriere del Friuli . . . 07420

Società Economica di Chiavari, Via Ravaschieri 15, 16043 Chiavari
T: 309941
Founded: 1791
Focus: Econ
Periodicals
Atti della Società Economica di Chiavari
Enciclopedia Araldica . . . 07421

Società Emiliana Pro Montibus et Silvis, c/o Accademia Nazionale di Agricoltura, Via Castiglione 11, 40124 Bologna
T: (051) 268809
Focus: Ecology
Periodical
Natura & Montagna (quarterly) . . . 07422

Società Entomologica Italiana, Via Brigata Liguria 9, 16121 Genova
Founded: 1869; Members: 900
Focus: Entomology
Periodicals
Bollettino
Memorie: Supplemento al Bollettino . . . 07423

Società Europea di Cultura / Société Européenne de Culture, Giudecca 54, 30133 Venezia
T: (041) 5230210; Fax: 5231033
Founded: 1950
Focus: Arts; Int'l Relat
Periodical
Comprendre (irregularly) . . . 07424

Società Europea di Patologia / European Society of Pathology, c/o Istituto di Anatomia e Istologia Patologica, Via Francesco Sforza 38, 20122 Milano
T: (02) 874214
Focus: Pathology . . . 07425

Società Farmaceutica del Mediterraneo Latino, c/o Istituto di Farmacognosia, Facoltà di Farmacio dell'Universita, Villaggio Annunziata, 98100 Messina
T: (090) 1632
Founded: 1953
Focus: Pharmacol
Periodical
Pharmacia Mediterranea . . . 07426

Società Filarmonica di Trento, Via Verdi 30, 38100 Trento
T: (0461) 21830
Founded: 1795
Focus: Music . . . 07427

Società Filologica Friulana G.I. Ascoli (S.F.F.), Via Manin 18, 33100 Udine
T: (0432) 501598; Fax: 511766
Founded: 1919
Focus: Ling; Lit
Periodicals
Ce Fastu? (semi-annually)
Sot la Nape (quarterly)
Strolic (annually) . . . 07428

Società Filologica Romana, Piazzale Aldo Moro, Città Universitaria, 00185 Roma
T: (06) 491919
Founded: 1901
Pres: Prof. Aurelio Roncaglia
Focus: Ling; Lit
Periodical
Studi Romanzi . . . 07429

Società Filosofica Calabrese (S.F.C.), Via C. Battisti 12, 89015 Palmi
T: 22523
Founded: 1948
Focus: Philos . . . 07430

Società Filosofica Italiana (S.F.I.), c/o Prof. E. Spinelli, Via C. Bertinoro 13, 00162 Roma
T: (06) 44291035
Founded: 1906; Members: 1405
Pres: Prof. Enrico Berti; Gen Secr: Prof. Emilio Spinelli
Focus: Philos
Periodical
Bollettino della Società Filosofica Italiana (quarterly) . . . 07431

Società Filosofica Romana, c/o Istituto di Filosofia, Università, Città Universitaria, 00185 Roma
T: 4991
Focus: Philos . . . 07432

Società Gallaratese per gli Studi Patri, Chiostro di S. Francesco, Via Borgo Antico 2, 2013 Gallarate
T: 795092
Founded: 1896
Focus: Hist
Periodical
Rassegna Gallaratese di Storia e d'Arte (quarterly) . . . 07433

Società Geografica Italiana (S.G.I), Via della Navicella 12, 00184 Roma
T: (06) 7008279; E-Mail: mc2944@melink.it; Fax: 7004677
Founded: 1867; Members: 1300
Focus: Geography
Periodicals
Bibliografia Geografica della Regione Italiana (annually)
Bollettino della Società Geografica Italiana (quarterly)
Memorie della S.G.I.: Monografie scientifiche . . . 07434

Società Geologica Italiana (S.G.I.), c/o Dip di Scienze della Terra, Università La Sapienza, Piazzale Aldo Moro 5, 00185 Roma
T: (06) 4959390
Founded: 1881; Members: 2400
Gen Secr: Dr. Achille Zuccari
Focus: Geology
Periodicals
Bollettino (quarterly)
Memorie (quarterly) . . . 07435

Società Incoraggiamento Arti e Mestieri, Via S. Maria 18, 20123 Milano
Founded: 1838
Focus: Arts . . . 07436

Società Internazionale di Diritto Penale Militare e di Diritto della Guerra, Gruppo Italiano / Société Internationale de Droit Penal Militaire et de Droit de la Guerre; Groupe Italiennne, Viale delle Milizie 5c, 00192 Roma
T: (06) 386052
Founded: 1956
Focus: Law; Int'l Relat
Periodical
Rivista di Diritto Penale e di Diritto della Guerra . . . 07437

Società Internazionale di Psicologia della Scrittura (S.I.P.S.) / International Society for the Psychology of Writing, Corso XXII Marzo 57, 20129 Milano
T: (02) 70126489
Founded: 1961; Members: 208
Pres: Prof. Rolando Marchesan; Gen Secr: Prof. Luigina Lazzaroni
Focus: Lit; Psych; Graphology . . . 07438

Società Internazionale di Studi Francescani, Piazza del Comune 27, 06081 Assisi
T: (075) 813210; Fax: 813210
Founded: 1972
Focus: Rel & Theol; Hist . . . 07439

Società Internazionale di Studi Gemellari / International Society for Twin Studies, c/o Istituto Gregorio Mendel, Piazza Galeno 5, 00162 Roma
T: (06) 862055
Focus: Gynecology; Bio; Genetics
Periodicals
Acta Genetica Medicae et Gemellologiae: Twin Research (quarterly)
Twins (semi-annually) . . . 07440

Società Internazionale di Tecnica Idrotermale (S.I.T.H.), Via de Gasperi 144, 80053 Castellamare di Stabia
T: 8715322
Focus: Hydrology; Water Res . . . 07441

Società Istriana di Archeologia e Storia Patria (S.I.A.S.P.), c/o Archivio di Stato, Via La Marmora 17, 34139 Trieste
Founded: 1884
Focus: Hist; Archeol; Folklore; Geography; Ling; Numismatics
Periodical
Atti e Memorie (annually) . . . 07442

Società Italiana Amici dei Fiori, Via dei Tavolini 8, 50123 Firenze
Founded: 1931
Focus: Hort; Botany
Periodical
Il Giardino Fiorito (monthly) . . . 07443

Società Italiana Attività Nervosa Superiore (SIANS), c/o Clinica Psychiatrica Romeo Vuoli, Via G.F. Besta 1, 20161 Milano
T: (02) 584100
Focus: Neurology . . . 07444

Società Italiana Calcolo Ricerca Economica Operativa (S.I.C.R.E.O.), Via Polistena 10, 00173 Roma
T: (06) 7485435, 7485476, 7485480
Founded: 1960
Focus: Econ . . . 07445

Società Italiana degli Autori e Editori, Viale della Letteratura 30, 00144 Roma
T: (06) 59901; Fax: 59647050
Founded: 1882; Members: 50000
Gen Secr: Lucio Capograssi
Focus: Lit; Journalism . . . 07446

Società Italiana degli Economisti, Via Pizzecolli 68, 60121 Ancona
Founded: 1950; Members: 594
Pres: Prof. S. Lombardini; Gen Secr: Prof. M. Crivellini
Focus: Econ
Periodical
Bollettino (annually) . . . 07447

Società Italiana della Continenza, c/o Cattedra l'Patologia Ostetrica e Ginecologica, Università di Roma, Policlinico Umberto I, 00161 Roma
T: (06) 4959341
Focus: Pathology; Gynecology . . . 07448

Società Italiana della Scienza del Suolo (S.I.S.S.), c/o Istituto Sperimentale per lo Studio e la Difesa del Suolo, Piazza M. D'Azeglio 30, 50121 Firenze
T: (055) 2477242; Fax: 241485
Members: 250
Focus: Geology
Periodical
Bollettino della Società Italiana della Scienza del Suolo: Nuova Serie (semi-annually) . . . 07449

Società Italiana della Trasfusione del Sangue, Corso Principe Oddone 18, 10153 Torino
T: (011) 471515
Founded: 1936; Members: 150
Focus: Hematology
Periodical
Rivista di Emoterapia ed Immunoematologia . . . 07450

Società Italiana delle Scienze Veterinarie, Via Antonio Bianchi 1, 25124 Brescia
T: (030) 223244; Fax: 2420569
Founded: 1947; Members: 1700
Pres: Prof. Orazio Catarsini
Focus: Vet Med
Periodical
Atti (annually) . . . 07451

Società Italiana di Agopuntura, Corso Principe Oddone 18, 10153 Torino
T: (011) 471515
Founded: 1968
Focus: Anesthetics
Periodical
Rivista Italiana di Agopuntura . . . 07452

Società Italiana di Agronomia (SIA) / Italian Society of Agronomy, c/o Istituto di Agronomia, Facoltà di Agraria, Università degli Studi, Via Filippo Re 6-8, 40126 Bologna
T: (051) 351510; Fax: 351511
Founded: 1966
Focus: Agri
Periodical
Rivista di Agronomia (quarterly) . . . 07453

Società Italiana di Allergologia e Immunologia Clinica, c/o Policlinico Umberto I, Viale del Policlinico, 00100 Roma
T: (06) 4950068
Founded: 1953
Focus: Immunology
Periodical
Folia Allergologica et Immunologica Clinica (bi-monthly) . . . 07454

Società Italiana di Anatomia, c/o Istituto di Anatomia Umana Normale, Policlinico di Careggi, 50134 Firenze
T: (055) 410084
Founded: 1929; Members: 300
Focus: Anat . . . 07455

Società Italiana di Anatomia Patologica, Via P. Castelli, 98100 Messina
T: (090) 44895
Focus: Anat; Pathology . . . 07456

Società Italiana di Andrologia (S.I.A.) / Society of Andrology, c/o Centro di Andrologia, 1. Clinica Medica, Università degli Studi, Policlinico S. Chiara, 56100 Pisa
T: (050) 26135
Founded: 1976; Members: 400
Focus: Pathology
Periodicals
Andrologia
Archives of Andrology
Fertility and Sterility
Infertility
International Journal of Andrology
Journal of Andrology
Journal of Endocrinological Investigation . 07457

Società Italiana di Anestesia, Analgesia, Rianimazione e Terapia Intensiva, c/o Istituto di Anestesiologia e Rianimazione, Università degli Studi di Firenze, Viale Morgagni 85, 50134 Firenze
Fax: (055) 430393
Members: 4000
Focus: Anesthetics
Periodicals
Acta Anesthesiologica Italia (bi-monthly)
Minerva Anesthesiologica (monthly) . . . 07458

Società Italiana di Anestesiologia e Rianimazione (S.I.A.R.), c/o Istituto di Anestesiologia e Rianimazione, Nuovo Policlinico, Viale Bracci 53, 53100 Siena
T: (0577) 50103
Founded: 1934; Members: 2000
Pres: Prof. Gualtiero Bellucci; Gen Secr: Dr. Andrea di Massa
Focus: Anesthetics . . . 07459

Società Italiana di Antropologia e Etnologia, Via del Proconsolo 12, 50122 Firenze
T: (055) 2396449; Fax: 219438
Founded: 1871; Members: 200
Pres: Prof. Cleto Corrain
Focus: Anthro; Ethnology
Periodical
Archivio per l'Antropologia e l'Etnologia (annually) . . . 07460

Società Italiana di Audiologia e Foniatria (SIA), c/o Clinica ORL, Università, Policlinico Umberto I, Viale del Policlinico, 00161 Roma
T: (06) 490054
Founded: 1967; Members: 300
Focus: Otorhinolaryngology
Periodical
Bollettino di Audiologia e Foniatria (bi-monthly) . . . 07461

Società Italiana di Aziendologia, Viale dei Mille 38, 20129 Milano
T: (02) 7490247
Focus: Business Admin
Periodical
Tecniche Direzionali (monthly) . . . 07462

Società Italiana di Biochimica, c/o Istituto di Chimica Biologica, Università, Via del Giochetto, CP 3, 06100 Perugia
Founded: 1951
Focus: Chem; Biochem . . . 07463

Società Italiana di Biochimica Clinica e Biologia Molecolare Clinica, Via Farini 70, 20159 Milano
T: (02) 6887556; Fax: 6887026
Founded: 1969; Members: 2500
Pres: G. Tettamanti
Focus: Biochem; Bio . . . 07464

Società Italiana di Biogeografia (S.I.B.), c/o Istituto di Biologia Generale, Università degli Studi, Via T. Pendola 62, 53100 Siena
T: (0577) 284173; Fax: 263509
Founded: 1954; Members: 400
Focus: Botany; Paleontology; Zoology
Periodical
Biogeographia . . . 07465

Società Italiana di Biologia Marina (S.I.B.M.), c/o Acquario Comunale, Piazzale Mascagni 1, 57100 Livorno
T: (0586) 805504
Founded: 1969
Focus: Bio; Oceanography . . . 07466

Società Italiana di Biologia Sperimentale (S.I.B.S.), c/o Catedra di Biofisica, Facoltà di Medicina e Chirurgia, Università degli Studi di Napoli Federico II, Via Sergio Pansini 5, 80131 Napoli
T: (081) 7463220; Fax: 5453045
Founded: 1925; Members: 524
Pres: Prof. Alfredo Ruffo; Gen Secr: Prof. Giovanni Pizzuti
Focus: Bio
Periodical
Bollettino Società Italiana di Biologia Sperimentale: Journal of Biological Research (monthly) 07467

Società Italiana di Biometria (SIB), c/o Dipartimento di Statistica e Matematica, Via Curtatone 1, 50123 Firenze
T: (055) 284845
Founded: 1963
Focus: Bio . . . 07468

Società Italiana di Buiatria, c/o Istituto di Patologia Speciale e Clinica Medica Veterinaria, Facoltà di Medicina Veterinaria, Università degli Studi, Via Nizza 52, 10126 Torino
T: (011) 651828, 688769

Focus: Vet Med
Periodicals
Atti della Società Italiana di Buiatria (annually)
Notiziario Buiatrico (irregularly) 07469

Società Italiana di Cancerologia, c/o Istituto di Anatomia, Università di Napoli, Via L. Armanni 5, 80100 Napoli
Pres: Prof. P. Verga; Gen Secr: Prof. P. Bucalossi
Focus: Cell Biol & Cancer Res 07470

Società Italiana di Cardiologia, Corso di Francia 197, 00191 Roma
T: (06) 36309819; Fax: 36308197
Founded: 1934; Members: 2000
Pres: Prof. Salvatore Caponnetto; Gen Secr: Prof. Salvatore Novo
Focus: Cardiol
Periodical
Cardiologia (monthly) 07471

Società Italiana di Chemioterapia (SIC), c/o Istituto C. Forlanini, Viale Taramelli 5, 27100 Pavia
T: (0382) 23707; Fax: 422267
Founded: 1953; Members: 210
Focus: Therapeutics
Periodical
Giornale Italiano di Chemioterapia (semi-annually) 07472

Società Italiana di Chirurgia, Viale di Villa Massimo 21, 00161 Roma
T: (06) 4881818
Founded: 1882
Pres: Prof. G. di Matteo; Gen Secr: Prof. L. Angelini
Focus: Surgery
Periodicals
Archivio ed Atti (annually)
Bollettino (bi-monthly) 07473

Società Italiana di Chirurgia Cardiaca e Vascolare, c/o Istituto di Chirurgia del Cuore e Grossi Vasi, Policlinico Umberto I, Lungotevere Flaminio 30, 00196 Roma
T: (06) 3230227; Fax: 3220744
Founded: 1963; Members: 720
Focus: Surgery
Periodical
Archivio di Chirurgia Toracica e Cardiovascolare (bi-monthly) 07474

Società Italiana di Chirurgia Clinica, c/o Policlinico, Clinica Chirurgia B, 00161 Roma
T: (06) 4956239
Founded: 1882; Members: 220
Focus: Surgery 07475

Società Italiana di Chirurgia della Mano, Largo Piero Palagi 1, 50139 Firenze
T: (055) 427811
Focus: Surgery
Periodical
Rivista Italiana di Chirurgia della Mano . 07476

Società Italiana di Chirurgia d'Urgenza, di Pronto Soccorso e di Terapia Intensiva Chirurgica, c/o Istituto di Chirurgia d'Urgenza, Facoltà di Medicina e Chirurgia, Università degli Studi, Via Sforza 35, 20122 Milano
T: (02) 581635
Focus: Surgery 07477

Società Italiana di Chirurgia Estetica, Via della Camilluccia 643, 00135 Roma
T: (06) 36304165; Fax: 36303204
Founded: 1970
Focus: Surgery 07478

Società Italiana di Chirurgia Pediatrica, c/o Ospedale Bambino Gesu, Piazza S. Onofrio 4, 00165 Roma
T: (06) 68591; Fax: 8592443
Founded: 1963; Members: 379
Focus: Surgery; Pediatrics
Periodical
Rassegna Italiana di Chirurgia Pediatrica (quarterly) 07479

Società Italiana di Chirurgia Plastica, c/o Div Chirurgia Plastica, Azienda Ospedaliera, 37126 Verona
T: (045) 8072412; E-Mail: plastic.surgery@ntt.it; Fax: 8072069
Founded: 1951; Members: 800
Focus: Surgery 07480

Società Italiana di Chirurgia Toracica, Via Augusto Murri 4, 00161 Roma
T: (06) 4958300
Founded: 194
Focus: Surgery 07481

Società Italiana di Citologia Clinica e Sociale, c/o Istituto Regina Elena, Viale Regina Elena 291, 00161 Roma
T: (06) 497931
Founded: 1961
Focus: Cell Biol & Cancer Res
Periodical
Citologia Informazioni 07482

Società Italiana di Criminologia, c/o Istituto di Antropologia Criminale, Via Bartolo Longo 72, 00156 Roma
T: (06) 416671
Founded: 1957
Focus: Criminology
Periodical
Rassegna di Criminologia (semi-annually) 07483

Società Italiana di Dermatologia e Sifilografia (SIDES), c/o Istituto S. Gallicano, Via S. Gallicano 25a, 00153 Roma
T: (06) 5813741, 5892390
Founded: 1883; Members: 330
Focus: Derm; Venereology 07484

Società Italiana di Diabetologia, c/o Ospedale S. Giovanni Battista e della Città di Torino, Istituto di Endocrinologia, Corso Polonia 14, 10126 Torino
Focus: Diabetes 07485

Società Italiana di Diabetologia e Endocrinologia Pediatrica, c/o Istituto di Clinica Pediatrica III dell'Università, Via G.B. Grassi 74, 20157 Milano
T: (02) 3556241
Focus: Diabetes 07486

Società Italiana di Economia Agraria (S.I.D.E.A.), c/o Istituto di Zooeconomia, Coviolo, 42100 Reggio Emilia
T: (0522) 21745
Founded: 1962; Members: 300
Pres: Prof. Giulio Zucchi
Focus: Agri
Periodical
Rivista di Economia Agraria: Atti del Convegno di Studi (annually) 07487

Società Italiana di Economia, Demografia e Statistica (SIEDS), c/o Dip di Teoria Economica e Metodi Quantitativi per le Scelte Politiche, Università La Sapienza, Piazzale Aldo Moro 5, CP 12003, Belsito, 00185 Roma
T: (06) 4462991
Founded: 1938; Members: 600
Pres: Prof. Franco Giusti; Gen Secr: Prof. Marcello Natale
Focus: Econ; Stats
Periodicals
Atti Sociali
Collano di Studi e Monografie
Rivista Italiana di Economia, Demografia e Statistica (quarterly) 07488

Società Italiana di Elettroencefalografia e Neurofisiologia, c/o Clinica Neurologica, Facoltatà di Medicina, Università degli Studi, Via Ugo Foscolo 7, 40123 Bologna
T: (051) 585158
Founded: 1949; Members: 270
Focus: Neurology; Physiology 07489

Società Italiana di Ematologia, c/o Istituto di Clinica Medica Generale e Terapia Medica I, Padiglione Granelli, Policlinico, Via S. Sforza 35, 20122 Milano
T: (02) 573166
Focus: Hematology
Periodical
Haematologica (bi-monthly) 07490

Società Italiana di Endocrinologia (SIE), Via Cosenza 8, 00161 Roma
T: (06) 44231346; Fax: 4404294
Founded: 1951; Members: 851
Focus: Endocrinology
Periodical
Journal Endocrinological Investigation (monthly) 07491

Società Italiana di Ergonomia (S.I.E.), Via S. Barnaba 8, 20122 Milano
T: (02) 57992613, 55902197; Fax: 55187172
Founded: 1961; Members: 250
Pres: Prof. Sebastiano Bagnara; Gen Secr: Prof. Gabriella Caterina
Focus: Sociology
Periodical
Notiziario S.I.E. (quarterly) 07492

Società Italiana di Ergonomia Stomatologica (S.I.E.S.), Via Commenda 10, 20122 Milano
T: (02) 593593
Founded: 1968
Focus: Stomatology; Physiology 07493

Società Italiana di Farmacologia, Via Giorgio Jam 18, 20129 Milano
T: (02) 29520311; E-Mail: sifcese@imivcca.csi.unimi.it; Fax: 29520179
Founded: 1939; Members: 1105
Pres: Prof. Giancarlo Pepeu; Gen Secr: Prof. Vincenzo Cuomo
Focus: Pharmacol
Periodicals
Pharmacological Research (monthly)
SIF-Notizie (3 times annually) 07494

Società Italiana di Farmacologia Clinica, c/o Istituto di Farmacologia, Facoltà di Medicina e Chirurgia, Università degli Studi, Via Roma 55, 56100 Pisa
T: (050) 22312, 46009
Focus: Pharmacol
Periodical
Drugs under Experimental and Clinical Research (bi-monthly) 07495

Società Italiana di Filosofia Giuridica e Politica, c/o Facoltà di Giurisprudenza, Università La Sapienza, 00185 Roma
T: (06) 490489; Fax: 49910951
Founded: 1936; Members: 200
Focus: Philos; Law; Poli Sci
Periodicals
Proceedings of the Società Italiana di Filosofia Giuridica e Politica (bi-annually)
Rivista Internazionale di Filosofia del Diritto (quarterly) 07496

Società Italiana di Fisica, Via Castiglione 101, 40136 Bologna
T: (051) 331554; E-Mail: sif@sif.it; Fax: 581340
Founded: 1897; Members: 1023
Pres: Prof. R.A. Ricci
Focus: Physics
Periodicals
Europhysics Letters (3 times per month)
Giornale di Fisica (quarterly)
Il Nuovo Cimento A (monthly)
Il Nuovo Cimento B (monthly)
Il Nuovo Cimento C (bi-monthly)
Il Nuovo Cimento D (monthly)
Il Nuovo Saggiatore (bi-monthly)
Rivista del Nuovo Cimento (monthly) . . 07497

Società Italiana di Fisiologia, c/o Istituto di Fisiologia Umana, Viale Margagni 65, 50134 Firenze
Focus: Physiology 07498

Società Italiana di Foniatria, c/o Clinica ORL, Ospedale Garibaldi, Università, 95100 Catania
Focus: Otorhinolaryngology 07499

Società Italiana di Fotobiologia, c/o Laboratorio di Radiobiologia Animale del C.N.E.N., Località Casaccia, 00060 S. Maria di Galeria
Focus: Radiology; Bio 07500

Società Italiana di Fotogrammetria e Topografia (S.I.F.E.T.), Piazzale Morandi 2, 20121 Milano
T: (02) 296621; Fax: 23996550
Founded: 1951; Members: 1500
Focus: Surveying
Periodical
Bollettino della Società Italiana di Fotogrammetria e Topografia (quarterly) 07501

Società Italiana di Gastroenterologia (SIGE), Clinica Medica, Università S. Orsola, 40100 Bologna
Founded: 1937
Focus: Gastroenter 07502

Società Italiana di Genetica Agraria (SIGA) / Italian Society of Agricultural Genetics, c/o Istituto Sperimentale per la Cerealicoltura, S.S. 16 km. 675, 71100 Foggia
T: (0881) 42972; Fax: 693150
Founded: 1954; Members: 400
Focus: Genetics 07503

Società Italiana di Geofisica e Meteorologia, c/o Università degli Studi, Via Balbi 30, 16126 Genova
Focus: Geophys
Periodical
Rivista Italiana di Geofisica e Scienze Affini 07504

Società Italiana di Gerontologia e Geriatria, Via G.C. Vanini 5, 50129 Firenze
T: (055) 474330; Fax: 461217
Members: 2500
Focus: Geriatrics
Periodicals
Giornale della Arteriosclerosi
Giornale di Gerontologia (monthly) . . . 07505

Società Italiana di Ginecologia ed Ostetricia, Via dei Soldati 25, 00186 Roma
T: (06) 6875119; Fax: 6868142
Founded: 1892; Members: 1500
Pres: Prof. U. Montemagno; Gen Secr: Prof. D. Arduini
Focus: Pediatrics; Gynecology 07506

Società Italiana di Ginnastica Medica, Medicina Fisica e Riabilitazione (SIGM), Via Crivelli 20, 20122 Milano
T: (02) 5453328
Founded: 1952
Focus: Rehabil; Physical Therapy
Periodical
La Ginnastica Medica (quarterly) 07507

Società Italiana di Glottologia (S.I.G.), c/o Istituto di Glottologia, Via S. Maria 36, 56100 Pisa
Founded: 1970
Focus: Ling 07508

Società Italiana di Immunologia e di Immunopatologia (S.I.I.I.), c/o Istituto di Clinica Medica a, Università degli Studi, Policlinico, 70124 Bari
T: (080) 360713, 369728
Founded: 1968
Focus: Immunology; Pathology
Periodical
Proceedings 07509

Societá Italiana di Ingegneria, Aerofotogrammetria e Topografia (S.I.A.T.), Via Giuseppe Armellini 35, 00143 Roma
T: (06) 5920946
Founded: 1961
Focus: Surgery 07510

Società Italiana di Ippologia, c/o Istituto di Clinica Chirurgica Veterinaria, Facoltà di Veterinaria, Università degli Studi, Strada Comunale del Cornocchio, 43100 Roma
T: (06) 96287
Focus: Vet Med 07511

Società Italiana di Laringologia, Otologia, Rinologia e Patologia Cervico-Facciale, c/o Istituto di Clinica Otorinolaringolatrica I, Facoltà di Medicina e Chirurgia, Università degli Studi, Viale del Policlinico, 00161 Roma
T: (06) 490051
Focus: Otorhinolaryngology
Periodical
Acta O.R.L. Italica (bi-monthly) 07512

Società Italiana di Liposcultura, Via della Camilluccia 643, 00135 Roma
T: (06) 36304792; Fax: 36303204
Founded: 1986
Focus: Med 07513

Società Italiana di Malacologia (S.I.M.), c/o Acquario Civico, Viale Gadio 2, 20121 Milano
T: (02) 872867; Fax: 325721
Founded: 1965
Focus: Zoology
Periodicals
Bollettino Malacologico (quarterly)
Lavori S.I.M. (irregularly)
Notiziario S.I.M. (bi-monthly) 07514

Società Italiana di Medicina del Lavoro e di Igiene Industriale, Via Severino Boezio 24, 27100 Pavia
T: (0382) 301221
Founded: 1906; Members: 1000
Focus: Med; Hygiene
Periodical
Bollettino Lavoro 07515

Società Italiana di Medicina del Traffico (SIMT), c/o Clinica Ortopedica e Traumatologica dell'Università, Piazzale delle Scienze, 00185 Roma
T: (06) 491672
Founded: 1958; Members: 700
Focus: Traumatology; Orthopedics; Surgery
Periodical
Rassegna di Medicina del Traffico (quarterly) 07516

Società Italiana di Medicina e Igiene della Scuola, Via Vincenzo Monti 57, 20145 Milano
T: (02) 4817404, 48007052
Founded: 1951
Focus: Med; Hygiene
Periodical
Rivista Italiana di Medicina e Igiene della Scuola (quarterly) 07517

Società Italiana di Medicina Estetica, Viale Mazzini 13, 00195 Roma
T: (06) 351514, 385377
Founded: 1975
Focus: Physiology
Periodical
La Medicina Estetica (quarterly) 07518

Società Italiana di Medicina Fisica e Riabilitazione (S.I.M.F.E.R.), c/o Centro F. Cornaglia, Corso Savona 25, 10024 Moncalieri
T: (011) 645596
Focus: Physiology; Rehabil 07519

Società Italiana di Medicina Interna (SIMI), Via Savoia 37, 00198 Roma
T: (06) 8554388; Fax: 8559067
Founded: 1888
Pres: Prof. Alberico Borghetti; Gen Secr: Prof. Giuseppe Licata
Focus: Intern Med
Periodical
Annali Italiani di Medicina Interna (quarterly) 07520

Società Italiana di Medicina Legale e delle Assicurazioni (S.I.M.L.A.), Via Falloppio 50, 35100 Padova
T: (049) 8272200; Fax: 663155
Pres: Prof. Francesco Introna; Gen Secr: G. Umani Romchi
Focus: Med
Periodical
Minerva Medico-Legale (quarterly) . . . 07521

Società Italiana di Medicina Preventiva e Sociale (S.I.M.P.S.), Via Caffaro 19, 16124 Genova
Founded: 1966
Focus: Hygiene; Public Health 07522

Società Italiana di Medicina Psicosomatica (SIMP), Via della Camilluccia 195, 00135 Roma
T: (06) 3420230
Founded: 1966; Members: 1000
Focus: Psychiatry
Periodical
Medicina Psicosomatica (quarterly) . . . 07523

Società Italiana di Medicina Sociale (SIMS), Corso Bramante 83, 10126 Torino
T: (011) 687272
Founded: 1947; Members: 500
Focus: Hygiene
Periodical
Rivista Italiana di Medicina Sociale e Preventiva (semi-annually) 07524

Società Italiana di Medicina Subacquea ed Iperbarica (S.I.M.S.I.), Via Schipa 68, 80122 Napoli
T: (081) 664462
Focus: Therapeutics 07525

Società Italiana di Medicina Trasfusionale e di Immunoematologia (SIMTI), Via Principe Amedeo 149/D, 00185 Roma
T: (06) 4452669, 4452751; Fax: 4441439
Founded: 1954; Members: 1600
Pres: Franco Biffoni; Gen Secr: Augusto D'Angiolino
Focus: Hematology; Immunology
Periodical
La Trasfusione del Sangue (bi-monthly) . 07526

Società Italiana di Mesoterapia, Viale Mazzini 13, 00195 Roma
T: (06) 351514
Focus: Therapeutics 07527

Società Italiana di Meteorologia Applicata (S.I.M.A.), Via Flavia 104, 00187 Roma
T: (06) 486415, 4744397
Founded: 1979
Focus: Geophys 07528

Società Italiana di Microangiologia e Microcorcolazione, c/o Athenaeum Angiologicum Santorianum, Domus Camilliana, Via S. Ranierino 9, 56100 Pisa
T: (050) 26358
Focus: Microbio 07529

Società Italiana di Microbiologia, c/o Istituto di Microbiologia, Via Androne 81, 95124 Catania
T: (095) 312633; Fax: 312633
Founded: 1962
Pres: Prof. Giovanni A. Meloni; Gen Secr: Prof. Giovanni Russo
Focus: Bio; Microbio 07530

Società Italiana di Mineralogia e Petrologia (SIMP), c/o Museo di Storia Naturale, Corso Venezia 55, 20121 Milano
T: (02) 702018
Founded: 1941; Members: 530
Focus: Mineralogy; Petrochem
Periodical
Rendiconti (semi-annually) 07531

Società Italiana di Musicologia (SIDM), Piazza S. Croce in Gerusalemme 9/A, 00185 Roma
Founded: 1964; Members: 630
Pres: Prof. Alberto Basso
Focus: Music
Periodicals
Le Fonti Musicali Italiane (annually)
Monumenti Musicali Italiani
Quaderni della Rivista Italiana di Musicologia (annually)
Rivista Italiana di Musicologia (bi-annually) 07532

Società Italiana di Neurochirurgia (SIN), c/o Ospedale Generale Regionale, 60100 Ancona
T: (071) 56636
Founded: 1948; Members: 220
Focus: Surgery
Periodical
Journal of Neurosurgical Sciences . . . 07533

Società Italiana di Neurologia, c/o Istituto di Clinica Neurologica, Università Cattolica del S. Cuore, Via Pineta Sacchetti 526, 00168 Roma
Founded: 1905; Members: 785
Focus: Neurology 07534

Società Italiana di Neuropediatria, c/o Istituto di Clinica Pediatrica, Facoltà di Medicina e Chirurgia, Università degli Studi, Via Mattioli 10, 53100 Siena
T: (0577) 283284
Focus: Pediatrics; Neurology 07535

Società Italiana di Neuropsichiatria Infantile (SINPI), c/o Cattedra di Neuropsichiatria Infantile, Via Pansini 5, 80131 Napoli
Focus: Psychiatry 07536

Società Italiana di Neuroradiologia, Via Generale Orsini 40, 80100 Napoli
T: (081) 393483
Pres: Prof. Enzo Valentino
Focus: Radiology 07537

Società Italiana di Neurosonologia (S.I.N.S.), Via Casaglia 65, 40135 Bologna
T: (051) 589092
Founded: 1970
Focus: Neurology 07538

Società Italiana di Nipiologia, c/o Istituto di Clinica Pediatrica II, Viale Regina Elena 324, 00161 Roma
T: (06) 4951738, 490962
Founded: 1915
Focus: Pediatrics
Periodical
Minerva Nipiologica (quarterly) 07539

Società Italiana di Nutrizione Umana, c/o Cattedra di Scienza dell'Alimentazione, Viale Forlanini 1, 00161 Roma
T: (06) 858276, 860584
Focus: Food; Nutrition 07540

Società Italiana di Odontoiatria Infantile (SIOI), Viale Shakespeare 47, 00144 Roma
T: (06) 596443
Founded: 1956; Members: 250
Focus: Dent
Periodical
Bollettino della SIOI (quarterly) 07541

Società Italiana di Odontostomatologia e Chirurgia Maxillo-Facciale (S.I.O.C.M.F.), c/o Clinica Odontostomatologica, Via Verdi 28, 67100 L'Aquila
T: (0862) 411176; Fax: 411176
Founded: 1957; Members: 2000
Pres: Prof. Sergio Tartaro; Gen Secr: Prof. Franco Marci
Focus: Dent; Stomatology; Surgery
Periodical
Minerva Stomatologica (monthly) 07542

Società Italiana di Oncologia Ginecologica, Via O. Tommasini 1, 00162 Roma
Founded: 1977
Focus: Cell Biol & Cancer Res; Gynecology
. . . . 07543

Società Italiana di Ortopedia e Traumatologia (S.I.O.T.), c/o Clinica Ortopedica, Università, Piazzale Aldo Moro 5, 00185 Roma
Founded: 1906; Members: 3100
Pres: Prof. Mario Gandolfi; Gen Secr: Prof. Marcello Pizzetti
Focus: Orthopedics; Traumatology . . . 07544

Società Italiana di Ostetricia e Ginecologia (S.I.O.G.), c/o Policlinico Umberto I, 00161 Roma
T: (06) 4954292
Founded: 1892; Members: 1050
Focus: Gynecology
Periodical
Notiziario e Bollettino 07545

Società Italiana di Oto-Neuro-Oftalmologia, c/o Clinica Oculista, Università degli Studi, 40138 Bologna
T: (051) 392948
Founded: 1923
Focus: Otorhinolaryngology; Neurology; Ophthal
. . . . 07546

Società Italiana di Otorinolaringologia e Chirurgia Cervico Facciale (S.I.O.e Ch.C.-F.), c/o II. Clinica Otorinolaringolatrica, Policlinico Umberto I, Viale del Policlinico, 00161 Roma
T: (06) 490051
Founded: 1893; Members: 850
Focus: Otorhinolaryngology
Periodical
Acta O.R.L. Italica (annually) 07547

Società Italiana di Otorinolaringologia Pediatrica (S.I.O.P.), c/o Ospedale Bambino Gesù, Piazza S. Onofrio 4, 00165 Roma
T: (06) 68592498; Fax: 68592522
Founded: 1978; Members: 391
Focus: Otorhinolaryngology; Pediatrics
Periodical
L'Otorinolaringologia Pediatrica (3 times annually)
. . . . 07548

Società Italiana di Parassitologia, c/o Istituto di Parassitologia, Università degli Studi di Roma La Sapienza, Piazzale Aldo Moro 5, 00185 Roma
T: (06) 49914932; E-Mail: coluzzi@axrma.uniroma1.it; Fax: 49914644
Founded: 1959; Members: 337
Pres: Prof. Mario Coluzzi; Gen Secr: Dr. Michele Maroli
Focus: Med
Periodical
Parassitologia (3 times annually) 07549

Società Italiana di Patologia, c/o Istituto di Anatomia e Istologia Patologica, Via Francesco Sforza 38, 20122 Milano
T: (02) 874200, 874214
Founded: 1948; Members: 400
Focus: Pathology
Periodicals
Atti
Bollettino 07550

Società Italiana di Patologia Aviare (S.I.P.A.), c/o Istituto di Patologia Generale e Anatomia Patologica, Via S. Costanzo 4, 06100 Perugia
T: (075) 5854534; Fax: 5854532
Founded: 1960; Members: 152
Focus: Vet Med
Periodical
Zootecnica International: Atti del Convegno Annuale (annually) 07551

Società Italiana di Patologia e di Allevamento degli Ovini e dei Caprini (S.I.P.A.O.C.), c/o Sezione Diagnostica dell'Istituto Zooprofilattico, Via Passo Gravina 193, 95125 Catania
T: (095) 338585
Founded: 1974
Focus: Vet Med 07552

Società Italiana di Patologia ed Allevamento dei Suini / Italian Society of Swine Pathology and Breeding, c/o Clinica Medica Veterinaria, Università, Via del Taglio 8, 43100 Parma
T: (0521) 293853; Fax: 293302
Founded: 1974; Members: 500
Pres: Prof. Paolo Martelli; Gen Secr: Dr. Pierfilippo Guadagnini
Focus: Vet Med
Periodical
Atti Proceedings (annually) 07553

Società Italiana di Patologia Vascolare (S.I.P.V.), Via Nazionale 230, 00184 Roma
T: (06) 4757192
Focus: Pathology; Physiology; Biochem . 07554

Società Italiana di Pediatria (S.I.P.), c/o Clinica Pediatrica, Università, Viale Regina Elena 324, 00100 Roma
T: (06) 4951738, 5870442
Founded: 1936; Members: 5500
Focus: Pediatrics
Periodical
Rivista Italiana di Pediatria 07555

Società Italiana di Pneumologia, c/o Edizioni Minerva Medica, Corso Bramante 83, 10126 Torino
T: (011) 678282; Fax: 3121736
Focus: Pulmon Dis
Periodical
Minerva Pneumologica (quarterly) 07556

Società Italiana di Psichiatria (SIP), c/o Istituto di Clinica Psichiatrica, Via Francesco Sforza 35, 20100 Milano
T: (02) 5483075
Focus: Psychiatry
Periodical
Bollettino 07557

Società Italiana di Psichiatria Biologica, c/o Clinica Psichiatrica, Largo Madonna delle Grazie, 80138 Napoli
T: (081) 5666502
Focus: Psychiatry; Bio
Periodical
Bollettino di Psichiatria Biologica (quarterly)
. . . . 07558

Società Italiana di Psicologia (S.I.Ps.), Via Due Macelli 66, 00187 Roma
Focus: Psych
Periodical
Psicologia Italiana (bi-monthly) 07559

Società Italiana di Psicologia Individuale (S.I.P.I.), Via Giasone del Maino 19, 20146 Milano
T: (02) 4985505; Fax: 4985505
Founded: 1969; Members: 255
Focus: Psych
Periodical
Rivista di Psicologia Individuale (semi-annually)
. . . . 07560

Società Italiana di Psicologia Scientifica (SIPS), c/o Istituto di Psicologia, Università Policlinico Filciuzza, 90121 Palermo
Founded: 1971
Focus: Psych 07561

Società Italiana di Psicosintesi Terapeutica (S.I.P.T.), Via San Domenico 16, 50133 Firenze
T: (055) 570140; Fax: 570140
Founded: 1973; Members: 52
Pres: Massimo Rosselli; Gen Secr: Elia Iapalucci
Focus: Therapeutics
Periodical
Rivista di Terapeutica (semi-annually) . . 07562

Società Italiana di Psicoterapia Analitica Immaginativa (S.I.P.A.I.), Via Mantova 5, 26100 Cremona
T: (0372) 430334
Founded: 1975
Focus: Therapeutics 07563

Società Italiana di Radiologia Medica e di Medicina Nucleare, c/o Prof. Aldo Perussia, Via Comelico 2, 20135 Milano
T: (02) 540766
Founded: 1913
Focus: Radiology; Nucl Med 07564

Società Italiana di Reologia (S.R.I.), c/o Istituto Principi Ingegneria Chimica, Università, Piazza V. Tecchio, 80125 Napoli
T: (081) 611800, 610966
Founded: 1970; Members: 87
Focus: Physics 07565

Società Italiana di Reumatologia, c/o Ospedale Maggiore, Via Gramsci 14, 43100 Parma
Pres: Prof. U. Carfassi; Gen Secr: Prof. U. Ambanelli
Focus: Rheuma
Periodical
Reumatismo 07566

Società Italiana di Scienze Farmaceutiche (SISF), Via Giorgio Jan 18, 20129 Milano
T: (02) 29513303; Fax: 29520179
Founded: 1953; Members: 350
Pres: Prof. Rodolfo Paoletti; Gen Secr: Prof. Franco Bonati
Focus: Pharmacol
Periodical
Cronache Farmaceutiche (bi-monthly) . . 07567

Società Italiana di Scienze Fisiche e Matematiche Mathesis, c/o Istituto Matematico, Facoltà di Scienze Matematiche, Fisiche e Naturali, Università degli Studi, Via Vicenza 23, 00185 Roma
T: (06) 4954641
Focus: Math; Physics 07568

Società Italiana di Scienze Naturali, c/o Museo Civico di Storia Naturale, Corso Venezia 55, 20121 Milano
T: (02) 62085405
Founded: 1857; Members: 900
Pres: Prof. Bruno Parisi; Gen Secr: Dr. Bona Bianchi Potenza
Focus: Nat Sci
Periodicals
Atti della Società Italiana di Scienze Naturali e del Museo Civico di Storia Naturale di Milano
Memorie della Società Italiana di Scienze Naturali e del Museo Civico di Storia Naturale di Milano
Natura: Rivista di Scienze Naturali (quarterly)
Paleontologia Lombarda: Nuova Serie
Rivista Italiana di Ornitologia 07569

Società Italiana di Senologia, Via Lazzaro Spallanzani 11, 00161 Roma
T: (06) 862289
Focus: Med
Periodical
Giornale Italiano di Senologia (quarterly) . 07570

Società Italiana di Sessuologia Clinica, Via Luigi Rizzo 50, 00136 Roma
T: (06) 311384
Focus: Venereology 07571

Società Italiana di Sessuologia Medica, Via di Tor Fiorenza 13, 00199 Roma
T: (06) 8391557
Focus: Venereology 07572

Società Italiana di Sociologà, Piazza delle Scienze 5, 00185 Roma
Founded: 1937
Focus: Sociology 07573

Società Italiana di Statistica (SIS), Salita de Crescenzi 26, 00186 Roma
T: (06) 6869845; Fax: 68806742
Founded: 1939; Members: 1000
Pres: Prof. Luigi Biggeri; Gen Secr: Prof. Giuseppe Gesano
Focus: Stats
Periodicals
Journal of the Italian Statistical Society (quarterly)
SIS-Bollettino (quarterly)
SIS-Informazioni (monthly) 07574

Società Italiana di Storia della Medicina (S.I.S.MED.), Viale Oriani 42, 40137 Bologna
T: (051) 344750
Founded: 1956
Focus: Med; Cultur Hist
Periodical
Rivista di Storia della Medicina 07575

Società Italiana di Studi sul Secolo XVIII, c/o Accademia Letteraria dell'Arcadia, Piazza S. Agostino 8, 00186 Roma
T: (06) 655874
Founded: 1978
Focus: Hist
Periodical
Bollettino 07576

Società Italiana di Terapia Familiare, Via Reno 60, 00198 Roma
T: (06) 864261
Founded: 1976
Focus: Therapeutics
Periodical
Terapia Familiare (semi-annually) 07577

Società Italiana di Tossicologia, Via Giorgio Jan 18, 20129 Milano
T: (02) 29520311; E-Mail: sifcese@imiucca.csi.unimi.it; Fax: 29520179
Founded: 1967
Pres: Rodolfo Paoletti; Gen Secr: Marina Marinovich
Focus: Toxicology
Periodical
Sitox Informa (3 times annually) 07578

Società Italiana di Traumatologia della Strada, c/o Istituto di Clinica Ortopedica e Traumatologica dell'Università La Sapienza, Piazzale Aldo Moro 5, 00185 Roma
T: (06) 49914846
Founded: 1984; Members: 150
Pres: Andrea Costanzo; Gen Secr: Dr. Roberto Sapia
Focus: Traumatology 07579

Società Italiana di Urodinamica, c/o Clinica Urologica, Policlinico S. Orsola, Via Massarenti 9, 40138 Bologna
T: (051) 397931
Founded: 1977
Focus: Urology 07580

Società Italiana di Urologia (S.I.U.) / Italian Urological Association, Viale Cortina d'Ampezzo 49, 00135 Roma
T: (06) 3273328
Founded: 1922; Members: 1500
Focus: Urology
Periodicals
Acta Urologica Italica (bi-monthly)
Aula Medica (3 times annually)
Journal of Nephrology (3 times annually)
La Settimana degli Ospedali (semi-annually)
. . . . 07581

Società Italiana Medica del Training Autogeno (S.I.M.T.A.), c/o Istituto di Psicologia, Facoltà di Medicina e Chirurgia, Università degli Studi, Viale Berti Pichat 5, 40127 Bologna
T: (051) 276610
Focus: Therapeutics *07582*

Società Italiana Medici e Operatori Geriatrici, Via Ippolito Nievo 16, 50129 Firenze
T: (055) 474510
Founded: 1965; Members: 800
Focus: Geriatrics
Periodical
Medicina Geriatrica (bi-monthly) *07583*

Società Italiana Medico-Chirurgica di Pronto Soccorso, c/o Pronto Soccorso del Policlinico S. Orsola, Via Massarenti 9, 40136 Bologna
T: (051) 342416
Founded: 1973
Focus: Surgery *07584*

Società Italiana Musica Contemporanea, Piazza Buenos Aires 20, 00198 Roma
T: (06) 868012
Pres: M. Peragallo; Gen Secr: M.R. Mann
Focus: Music *07585*

Società Italiana Organi Artificiali, c/o Patologia Chirugica, Policlinico Umberto I, Università degli Studi, 00161 Roma
T: (06) 4950741/43
Focus: Surgery *07586*

Società Italiana per gli Archivi Sanitari Ospedalieri (S.I.A.S.O.), c/o Ospedale Versilia, Direzione Sanitaria, Via A. Fratti, 55049 Viareggio
T: (0584) 31438, 47283
Founded: 1975
Focus: Doc; Med *07587*

Società Italiana per gli Studi Filosofici e Religiosi, c/o Università Cattolica del Sacro Cuore, Piazza S. Ambrogio 9, 20123 Milano
Pres: Prof. Gustavo Bontadini; Gen Secr: Prof. Luciana Vigone
Focus: Philos; Rel & Theol *07588*

Società Italiana per il Progresso della Zootecnia, Via Monte Ortigara 35, 20137 Milano
T: (02) 576527
Focus: Zoology *07589*

Società Italiana per il Progresso delle Scienze, Viale Regina Margherita 202, 00198 Roma
T: (06) 8554156
Founded: 1839
Pres: Prof. Arnaldo M. Angelini; Gen Secr: Prof. Rocco Capasso
Focus: Sci *07590*

Società Italiana per la Organizzazione Internazionale (S.I.O.I.), Via S. Marco 3, 00186 Roma
T: (06) 6793566; E-Mail: sioi@ats.it; Fax: 6789102
Founded: 1944; Members: 1000
Pres: Umberto La Rocca; Gen Secr: Luigi Vittorio Ferraris
Focus: Business Admin; Law; Poli Sci
Periodical
La Comunità Internazionale (quarterly) . . *07591*

Società Italiana per l'Antropologia e la Etnologia (SIAE), Via del Proconsolo 12, 50122 Firenze
T: (055) 2396449
Members: 160
Focus: Anthro; Ethnology
Periodical
Archivio per l'Antropologia e la Etnologia (annually) *07592*

Società Italiana per l'Archeologia e la Storia delle Arti (S.I.A.S.A.), c/o Facoltà di Architettura, Università degli Studi, Via Monteoliveto 3, 80134 Napoli
T: (081) 320878
Focus: Archeol; Arts; Cultur Hist *07593*

Società Italiana per le Scienze Ambientali: Biometeorologia, Bioclimatologia ed Ecologia (S.I.S.A.), c/o Cattedra di Idrologia e Climatologia Medica, Università degli Studi, Via Luigi Vanvitelli 32, 20129 Milano
T: (02) 7386914
Founded: 1970
Focus: Ecology; Geophys *07594*

Società Italiana per l'Educazione Musicale (S.I.E.M.), Via Clerici 10, 20121 Milano
Founded: 1969
Focus: Music; Educ
Periodical
Musica Domani: Trimestrale di Pedagogia Musicale (quarterly) *07595*

Società Italiana per lo Studio della Cancerogenesi Ambientale ed Epidemiologia dei Tumori (S.I.S.C.A.), c/o Istituto di Oncologia, Università degli Studi, Viale Benedetto XV 10, 16132 Genova
T: (010) 302754, 300767
Founded: 1977
Focus: Public Health; Cell Biol & Cancer Res *07596*

Società Italiana per lo Studio della Fertilità e della Sterilità, c/o Clinica Ostetrico-Ginecologico, 00168 Roma
T: (06) 33054979
Focus: Venereology; Gynecology *07597*

Società Italiana per lo Studio dell'Arteriosclerosi (S.I.S.A.), c/o Istituto di Clinica Medica la Università degli Studi, Policlinico, 70124 Bari
T: (080) 369728
Founded: 1964
Focus: Pathology *07598*

Società Italiana per lo Studio delle Sostanze Grasse, Via del Lauro 3, 20121 Milano
T: (02) 897280
Focus: Materials Sci *07599*

Società Italiana per lo Studio e l'Applicazione del Pirodiserbo, c/o Istituto di Patologia Vegetale, Facoltà di Agraria, Università Cattolica del S. Cuore, 29100 Piacenza
T: (0523) 62600
Founded: 1968
Focus: Ecology *07600*

Società Italiana per l'Organizzazione Internazionale, c/o Piazza di S. Marco 51, 00186 Roma
T: (06) 6793566; Fax: 6789102
Founded: 1944
Pres: Umberto La Rocca; Gen Secr: Luigi Vittorio Ferraris
Focus: Business Admin *07601*

Società Italiana pro Deontologia Sanitaria (S.I.De.S.), Piazza S. Agostino 24, 20123 Milano
T: (02) 490887
Founded: 1958
Focus: Hygiene
Periodical
Medicina Sociale: Organo della S.I.De.S. e della Società Italiana di Medicina Sociale . . *07602*

Società Jonico-Salentina de Medicina e Chirurgia, c/o Ospedale Regionale, Via Bruno, 74100 Taranto
Focus: Med; Surgery
Periodical
Bollettino della Società Jonico Salentina di Medicina e Chirurgia *07603*

Società Laziale Abruzzese di Medicina del Lavoro, Viale Regina Elena 336, 00162 Roma
T: (06) 492515
Focus: Hygiene; Pathology *07604*

Società Laziale – Abruzzese Marchigiana Molisana di Ostetricia e Ginecologia (L.A.M.), c/o Istituto di Clinica Ostetrica e Ginecologica, Policlinico Umberto I, Viale Regina Elena 326, 00181 Roma
T: (06) 4955260
Founded: 1900
Focus: Gynecology
Periodical
Aggiornamenti in Ostetricia e Ginecologia (bi-monthly) *07605*

Società Letteraria, Piazzetta Scalette Rubiani 1, 37100 Verona
T: (045) 8030641; Fax: 595949
Founded: 1808
Pres: Dr. Giovanni Battista Ruffo
Focus: Lit
Periodical
Bollettino della Società Letteraria di Verona (annually) *07606*

Società Ligure di Storia Patria, Piazza Matteotti 5, 16123 Genova
T: (010) 591358; Fax: 591358
Founded: 1857; Members: 440
Focus: Hist
Periodical
Atti (semi-annually) *07607*

Società Lombarda di Criminologia, Via Carlo Crivelli 20, 20122 Milano
T: (02) 76820
Founded: 1956
Focus: Criminology *07608*

Società Mazziniana Pensiero e Azione, Via Angelo Brunetti 60, 00186 Roma
T: (06) 687410
Founded: 1921
Focus: Hist; Poli Sci *07609*

Società Medica Chirurgica di Bologna, Piazza Galvani 1, 40124 Bologna
T: (051) 231488
Founded: 1823; Members: 330
Pres: Prof. Emilio Pisi; Gen Secr: Prof. Michele Fiorentino
Focus: Surgery
Periodical
Bollettino delle Scienze Mediche (quarterly) *07610*

Società Medico-Chirugica, Facoltà di Medicina e Chirugia, Università degli Studi, Via Crisanzio 3, 70122 Bari
T: (080) 218849
Focus: Surgery *07611*

Società Medico-Chirurgica di Ferrara, c/o Sez. di Chirurgia Pediatrica, Arcispedale S. Anna, Corso Giovecca 203, 44100 Ferrara
T: (0532) 395580
Founded: 1956
Focus: Surgery *07612*

Società Medico-Chirurgica di Modena, c/o Clinica Chirurgica Generale dell'Università degli Studi, Policlinico, Via del Pozzo, 41100 Modena
Founded: 1873
Focus: Surgery
Periodical
Bollettino (bi-monthly) *07613*

Società Medico-Psicologica (AITP), Corso XXII Marzo 57, 20129 Milano
T: (02) 7388427, 70126489
Founded: 1978
Focus: Psych *07614*

Società Messinese di Storia Patria, c/o Palazzo dell'Università, 98100 Messina
T: 1900
Focus: Hist
Periodical
Archivio Storico Messinese *07615*

Società Napoletana di Chirurgia, c/o Istituto di Chirurgia d'Urgenza. I Facoltà di Medicina e Chirugia, Università degli Studi, Piazza Miraglia, 80138 Napoli
T: (081) 446765
Founded: 1945
Focus: Surgery *07616*

Società Napoletana di Storia Patria, Piazza Municipio Maschio Angioino, 80133 Napoli
T: (081) 5510353; Fax: 5529238
Founded: 1876; Members: 650
Focus: Hist
Periodical
Archivio Storico per le Province Napoletane (annually) *07617*

Società Naturalisti Veronesi F. Zorzi, c/o Museo Civico di Storia Naturale, Lungadige Porta Vittoria 9, 37129 Verona
T: (045) 8001987
Focus: Nat Sci *07618*

Società Nazionale di Informatica delle Camere di Commercio per la Gestione dei Centri Elettronici Reteconnessi Valutazione Elaborazione Dati (CERVED), Piazza Sallustio 21, 00187 Roma
T: (06) 4741268, 486403
Founded: 1974
Focus: Electronic Eng; Computer & Info Sci *07619*

Società Nazionale di Scienze, Lettere ed Arti, Via Mezzacannone 8, 80134 Napoli
T: (081) 324634
Pres: Prof. A. Vallone; Gen Secr: Prof. F. Tessitore
Focus: Arts; Lit; Sci *07620*

Società Nucleare Italiana (S.N.I.), CP 414, 50100 Firenze
T: (055) 4392854
Founded: 1975
Focus: Nucl Res *07621*

Società Oftalmologica Italiana, c/o Istituto di Clinica Oculistica, Facoltà di Medicina, Università degli Studi, Via Massarenti 5, 40138 Bologna
T: (051) 392848
Founded: 1942
Focus: Ophthal *07622*

Società Ornitologica Italiana (S.O.I.), c/o Museo Ornitologico e di Scienze Naturali Loggetta Lombardesca, 48100 Ravenna
T: (0544) 35625
Focus: Ornithology
Periodical
Gli Uccelli d'Italia (quarterly) *07623*

Società Ornitologica Reggiana (S.O.R.), c/o Ferdinando Messori, Via del Cristo 6, 42100 Reggio Emilia
T: (0522) 37865
Founded: 1938
Focus: Ornithology
Periodicals
Il Giornale degli Uccelli (monthly)
Italia Ornitologica: Organo Ufficiale della Federazione Ornicoltori Italiani (bi-monthly)
Uccelli (monthly) *07624*

Società Orticola Italiana (S.O.I.), Piazza G. Puccini 4, 50144 Firenze
T: (055) 361688
Founded: 1953
Focus: Forestry; Ecology; Hort
Periodical
Notiziario di Ortoflorofrutticoltura (bi-monthly) *07625*

Società Pavese di Storia Patria, Via Belli 9, 27100 Pavia
T: (0382) 22154
Focus: Hist *07626*

Società per gli Studi Storici, Archeologici ed Artistici della Provincia di Cuneo (SSSAA), c/o Biblioteca Civica, Via Cacciatori delle Alpi 9, 12100 Cuneo
T: (0171) 634367
Founded: 1929
Focus: Hist; Archeol; Arts
Periodical
Bollettino della SSSAA (semi-annually) . *07627*

Società per la Formazione la Ricerca e l'Addestramento per le Aziende e le Organizzazioni (FORRAD), Via Fabio Filzi 25a, 20124 Milano
T: (02) 6570941
Founded: 1968
Focus: Econ; Business Admin
Periodical
Forrad Informazioni *07628*

Società per la Matematica e l'Economia Applicate (SOMEA), Piazza del Collegio Romano 2, 00186 Roma
T: (06) 6798443, 6798487
Founded: 1967
Focus: Math; Econ *07629*

Società per le Belle Arti ed Esposizione Permanente, c/o Palazzo Sociale, Via Filippo Turati 34, 20121 Milano
T: (02) 639803, 661445
Founded: 1884
Focus: Fine Arts
Periodical
Società per le Belle Arti ed Esposizione Permanente (quarterly) *07630*

Società Piemontese, Ligure, Lombarda di Ortopedia e Traumatologia, c/o Istituto di Clinica Ortopedica, Facoltà di Medicina e Chirurgia, Università degli Studi, Ospedale S. Martino, 16132 Genova
T: (010) 502739
Focus: Orthopedics; Traumatology . . . *07631*

Società Pistoiese di Storia Patria, Via Abbi Pazienza 1, CP 339, 51100 Pistoia
T: (0573) 977317
Founded: 1898
Focus: Hist
Periodical
Bullettino Storico Pistoiese (annually) . . *07632*

Società Promotrice di Belle Arti, Casina Pompeiana nella Villa Comunale, 80121 Napoli
T: (081) 425188
Founded: 1861
Focus: Fine Arts *07633*

Società Reggiana d'Archeologia, Via Lero 6, 42100 Reggio Emilia
T: (0522) 433029
Founded: 1968
Focus: Archeol *07634*

Società Reggiana di Studi Storici, Corso Cairoli 6, 42100 Reggio Emilia
T: (0522) 451328; Fax: 454610
Founded: 1978
Pres: Prof. Davide Dazzi; Gen Secr: Prof. Aurelia Fresta
Focus: Hist
Periodical
Reggio Storia (quarterly) *07635*

Società Ricerche Impianti Nucleari (SORIN), 13100 Vercelli
Focus: Nucl Res *07636*

Società Romana di Chirurgia, c/o Patologia Speciale Chirurgica, Università degli Studi, Policlinico Umberto I, 00161 Roma
T: (06) 4954876
Founded: 1939
Focus: Surgery *07637*

Società Romana di Storia Patria, Piazza della Chiesa Nuova 18, 00186 Roma
T: (06) 68307513
Founded: 1876; Members: 100
Pres: Prof. Letizia Ermini Pani; Gen Secr: Pasquale Smiraglia
Focus: Hist
Periodical
Archivio della Società Romana di Storia Patria (annually) *07638*

Società Sassarese per le Scienze Giuridiche, c/o Isituto Giuridico dell'Università, Piazza Università, 07100 Sassari
Focus: Law *07639*

Società Savonese di Storia Patria (S.S.S.P.), Piazza della Maddalena 14, CP 358, 17100 Savona
T: (019) 811960; Fax: 811960
Founded: 1885; Members: 274
Focus: Hist; Archeol
Periodicals
Atti e Memorie (annually)
Sabazia (semi-annually) *07640*

Società Siciliana per la Storia Patria, Piazza S. Domenico 1, 90133 Palermo
T: (091) 582774
Founded: 1872
Focus: Hist
Periodical
Archivio Storico Siciliano (annually) . . . *07641*

Società Siracusana di Storia Patria, c/o Villa Reimann, Via Necropoli Grotticelle 14, 96100 Siracusa
Focus: Hist
Periodical
Archivio Storico Siracusano (annually) . . *07642*

Società Storica Catanese, Via Etnea 248, 95131 Catania
T: (095) 434782
Founded: 1955
Focus: Hist *07643*

Società Storica di Terra d'Otranto, Palazzo Adorni, Via Umberto I 32, 73100 Lecce
T: (0832) 41938
Founded: 1966
Focus: Hist
Periodical
Rivista Storica del Mezzogiorno (semi-annually) 07644

Società Storica Lombarda, Via Morone 1, 20121 Milano
T: (02) 860118; Fax: 72002108
Founded: 1874; Members: 316
Pres: Gaetano Barbiano Di Belgiojoso; Gen Secr: Luigi Orombelli
Focus: Hist
Periodical
Archivio Storico Lombardo (annually) . . 07645

Società Storica Novarese, Via S. Gaudenzio 15, 28100 Novara
Fax: (0321) 34339
Founded: 1907
Focus: Hist
Periodical
Bollettino Storico per la Provincia di Novara (semi-annually) 07646

Società Storica Pisana, c/o Dipartimento di Medievistica, Facoltà di Lettere, Università degli Studi, Via Derna 1, 56126 Pisa
T: (050) 29475; Fax: 40949
Focus: Hist
Periodical
Bollettino Storico Pisano 07647

Società Tarquiniense d'Arte e Storia, Via delle Torri 29-33, 01016 Tarquinia
T: (0766) 858194
Founded: 1917
Focus: Arts; Hist; Cultur Hist
Periodical
Bolletino (annually) 07648

Società Teosofica in Italia (S.T.I.), Via Enrico Toti 3, 34131 Trieste
Founded: 1901
Focus: Rel & Theol
Periodical
Rivista Italiana di Teosofia (monthly) . . 07649

Società Tiburtina di Storia e d'Arte, Villa d'Este, 00019 Tivoli
T: (0774) 22187
Founded: 1919
Focus: Hist; Arts; Cultur Hist
Periodical
Atti e Memorie della Società Tiburtina di Storia e d'Arte (annually) 07650

Società Torricelliana di Scienze e Lettere, Corso Garibaldi 2, CP 179, 48018 Faenza
Founded: 1947
Focus: Lit; Sci
Periodical
Torricelliana (annually) 07651

Società Toscana di Orticoltura, Via delle Terme 4, 50123 Firenze
T: 1852
Focus: Hort
Periodical
Rivista della Ortoflorofrutticoltura Italiana . 07652

Società Toscana di Scienze Naturali (STSN), Via S. Maria 53, 56100 Pisa
T: (050) 22413
Founded: 1847; Members: 412
Gen Secr: Prof. Marco Tongiorgi
Focus: Nat Sci
Periodical
Atti della Società Toscana di Scienze Naturali 07653

Société de la Flore Valdôtaine (S.F.V.), Piazza Emile Chanoux 8, 11100 Aosta
Founded: 1858; Members: 300
Focus: Nat Sci
Periodicals
Bulletin (quarterly)
Revue Valdôtaine d'Histoire Naturelle (annually) 07654

Society for International Development (SID), Palazzo Civiltà del Lavoro, 00144 Roma
T: (06) 5917897; Fax: 5919836
Founded: 1957; Members: 9000
Focus: Int'l Relat
Periodicals
Compass (quarterly)
Development (quarterly)
Development Hotline (bi-weekly)
Meridian (bi-monthly) 07655

Studio Teologico Accademico Bolognese (S.T.A.B.), Piazza S. Domenico 13, 40124 Bologna
T: (051) 265756, 232238
Founded: 1978
Focus: Rel & Theol
Periodical
Sacra Doctrina 07656

SVP Italia, Via Piccinni 3, 20131 Milano
T: (02) 2043451; Fax: 29531000
Founded: 1962
Focus: Doc; Stats
Periodical
Notiziario SVP (bi-weekly) 07657

Tecnagro, Via Tommaso Grossi 6, 00184 Roma
T: (06) 7008896; Fax: 7009380
Founded: 1976
Focus: Agri 07658

Tecneco, Via Papiria, 61032 Fano
T: (0721) 86741
Founded: 1971
Focus: Energy; Water Res 07659

Tecnocasa, Viale Lombardia 43, 67100 L'Aquila
T: (0862) 61223
Founded: 1972
Focus: Civil Eng 07660

Tecnocentro Italiano (T.I.), c/o Dr. Fasola, Via Donizetti 45, 20122 Milano
T: (02) 780848
Founded: 1965
Focus: Law; Poli Sci 07661

Tecnofarmaci / Società Consortile per Azioni per lo Sviluppo della Ricerca Farmaceutica, Piazza Indipendenza 24, 00040 Pomezia
T: (06) 9111961; Fax: 9111956
Founded: 1974
Focus: Pharmacol 07662

Tecnotessile / Centro di Ricerche, Via Valentini 14, 50047 Prato
T: (0574) 35741/42
Founded: 1972
Focus: Textiles 07663

Union Generela di Ladins dla Dolomites, Val Gardena-Cësa di Ladins-Str Rezia 83, 39046 Ortisei-Urtijëi
Founded: 1949
Focus: Ethnology
Periodical
La Usc di Ladins (weekly) 07664

Union Ladins Val Badia (ULVB), S. Leonardo Scola Vedla, Pedraces
Founded: 1967
Focus: Ling; Ethnology; Lit
Periodical
La Usc di Ladins (monthly) 07665

Union Mondiale des Enseignants Catholiques (UMEC) / World Union of Catholic Teachers, Piazza S. Calisto 16, 00153 Roma
T: (06) 69887286
Founded: 1950; Members: 45
Focus: Educ
Periodicals
Nouvelles UMEC (quarterly)
Proceedings of the World Congress (every 3 years)
WUCT Newsletter (quarterly) 07666

Unione Accademica Nazionale (U.A.N.), Via della Lungara 230, 00165 Roma
T: (06) 6875024; Fax: 6869066
Founded: 1923
Focus: Hist; Archeol 07667

Unione Antropologica Italiana (U.A.I.), c/o Istituto di Antropologia, Via Selmi 1, 40126 Bologna
T: (051) 243272
Founded: 1972
Focus: Anthro
Periodical
Antropologia Contemporanea (quarterly) . 07668

Unione Associazioni Regionali (UN.A.R.), Corso Vittorio Emanuele 24, 00186 Roma
T: (06) 6797491, 6797717, 6782779, 8393783
Founded: 1977
Focus: Sociology
Periodical
Presenze Regionali (weekly) 07669

Unione Bolognese Naturalisti (U.B.N.), c/o Dipartimento di Biologia, Università degli Studi, Via S. Giacomo 9, 40126 Bologna
Founded: 1950
Focus: Nat Sci
Periodicals
Natura e Montagna (quarterly)
Notiziario (bi-monthly) 07670

Unione Cattolica Italiana Insegnanti Medi (UCIIM), Via Crescenzio 25, 00193 Roma
T: (06) 6875584, 6542701
Founded: 1944; Members: 20000
Focus: Educ
Periodical
La Scuola l'Uomo (monthly) 07671

Unione Consultori Italiani Prematrimoniali e Matrimoniali (U.C.I.P.E.M.), Via Giuseppe Garibaldi 3, 40124 Bologna
T: (051) 224531
Founded: 1968
Focus: Family Plan 07672

Unione della Legion d'Oro (U.L.D.O.), Via del Vantaggio 22, 00186 Roma
T: (06) 6788658
Founded: 1954
Focus: Sci
Periodical
La Voce dell'Unione: Atti Annuali (annually) 07673

Unione Erpetologica Italiana, Via Ulisse Aldrovandi 18, 00197 Roma
T: (06) 873586
Focus: Zoology 07674

Unione Giuristi Cattolici Italiani (U.G.C.I.), Via della Conciliazione 1, 00193 Roma
T: (06) 6564865
Founded: 1948
Focus: Rel & Theol; Law
Periodicals
Iustitia (quarterly)
Quaderni di Justitia (annually)
Vita dell'Unione: Bollettino Mensile (monthly) 07675

Unione Italiana Lotta alla Distrofia Muscolare (U.I.L.D.M.), Via P.P. Vergerio 17, 35126 Padova
T: (049) 757361, 8021001; E-Mail: dmredaz@tin-it; Fax: 757033
Founded: 1961; Members: 18000
Pres: Roberto Bressanello; Gen Secr: Renzo Renato Franco
Focus: Physical Therapy; Psych; Soc Sci
Periodical
DM – Distrofia Muscolare (quarterly) . . 07676

Unione Matematica Italiana (UMI), Piazza Porta San Donato 5, 40127 Bologna
T: (051) 229909
Founded: 1922; Members: 2850
Focus: Math
Periodicals
Bollettino (bi-monthly)
Bollettino di Storia delle Science Matematiche (semi-annually)
Notiziario (monthly) 07677

Unione Micologica Italiana (U.M.I.), c/o Centro di Micologia, Via Filippo Re 8, 40126 Bologna
T: (051) 351401
Founded: 1969
Focus: Botany, Specific
Periodical
Micologia Italiana (quarterly) 07678

Unione Tecnica Italiana Farmacisti (UTIFar), Via Casaregis 52, 16129 Genova
T: (010) 587345; Fax: 587013
Founded: 1959
Focus: Pharmacol
Periodical
Collegamento (monthly) 07679

World Association for Animal Production, Via A. Torlonia 15a, 00161 Roma
T: (06) 44238013; E-Mail: zoorec@rmnet.it; Fax: 44241466
Focus: Animal Husb 07680

World Future Studies Federation (WFSF), CP 6203, 00100 Roma
T: (06) 872529
Founded: 1973; Members: 500
Focus: Futurology
Periodical
WFSF Newsletter (quarterly) 07681

Ivory Coast

Académie Régionale des Sciences et Techniques de la Mer d'Abidjan / Regional Maritime Academy, Abidjan, BP V 158, Abidjan
T: 452830
Members: 15
Focus: Oceanography 07682

African Institute for Economic and Social Development, BP 08 BP8, Abidjan
T: 441594; Fax: 440641
Founded: 1962
Focus: Develop Areas; Soc Sci; Econ . 07683

African Oil Palm Development Association (AFOPDA), BP 15 341, Abidjan
T: 251518
Founded: 1985
Focus: Botany
Periodical
Africa Palm (quarterly) 07684

Société pour le Développement Minier de la Côte d'Ivoire (SODEMI), 01 BP 2816, Abidjan
T: 442995; Fax: 440821
Founded: 1962; Members: 200
Gen Secr: J. N'zi
Focus: Mining 07685

Jamaica

Association for Commonwealth Language and Literature Studies (ACLALS), c/o Dept of English, University of the West Indies, Mona, Kingston 7
Founded: 1965
Focus: Ling; Lit
Periodical
ACLALS Newsletter 07686

Association of Caribbean Economists (ACE), POB 735, Kingston 8
T: (0809) 9278283; Fax: 92724096
Focus: Econ 07687

Caribbean Council of Engineering Organizations (CCEO), 2-4 Ruthven Rd, 122, Kingston 10
Focus: Eng 07688

Caribbean Council of Legal Education (CLE), Mona Campus, Kingston 7
Founded: 1971
Focus: Law; Educ 07689

Caribbean Energy Information System (CEIS), c/o Scientific Research Council, POB 350, Kingston 6
Focus: Energy 07690

Caribbean Institute of Mass Communications (CARIMAC), c/o University of the West Indies, Mona
Founded: 1974
Focus: Comm Sci
Periodicals
CARIMAC Newsletter
Crossover (3 times annually) 07691

Caribbean Regional Drug Testing Laboratory (CRDTL), c/o Government Chemist Dept, Hope Gardens, Kingston 6
Founded: 1975; Members: 14
Focus: Pharmacol 07692

Commonwealth Association of Planners (CAP), The Professional Centre, 2-4 Ruthven Rd, Kingston 10
T: 92988805; Fax: 9299242
Founded: 1971; Members: 11500
Focus: Urban Plan
Periodical
CAP News (quarterly) 07693

Commonwealth Caribbean Medical Research Council (CCMRC), c/o Tropical Metabolism Research Unit, University of the West Indies, Mona, Kingston
Founded: 1972; Members: 20
Focus: Med 07694

Commonwealth Library Association (COMLA), POB 40, Mandeville
T: 9620703; E-Mail: COMLA; Fax: 9622770
Founded: 1972; Members: 52
Focus: Libraries & Bk Sci
Periodical
COMLA Newsletter (quarterly) 07695

Geological Society of Jamaica, c/o Dept of Geology, University of the West Indies, Mona, Kinston 7
T: 9272728; Fax: 9271640
Founded: 1958; Members: 80
Focus: Geology
Periodical
The Journal of the Geological Society of Jamaica (annually) 07696

Institute of Jamaica, 12-16 East St, Kingston
T: 9220620; Fax: 9221147
Founded: 1879
Gen Secr: Dr. Elaine Fisher
Focus: Anthro; Ethnology; Hist 07697

International P.E.N. Club, c/o Institute of Jamaica, 12-16 East St, Kingston
Founded: 1947; Members: 50
Focus: Lit 07698

Jamaica Historical Society, 14-16 East St, Kingston
Focus: Hist 07699

Jamaica Institution of Engineers, 2 3/4 Ruthven Rd, Kingston 10
Founded: 1977; Members: 16
Gen Secr: Dr. Rae Davis
Focus: Eng
Periodical
JIE News (monthly) 07700

Jamaica Library Association (JLA), POB 58, Kingston 5
Founded: 1949; Members: 211
Pres: P. Kerr; Gen Secr: F. Salmon
Focus: Libraries & Bk Sci
Periodicals
Jamaica Library Association Annual Report (annually)
Jamaica Library Association Bulletin (annually)
JLA News (quarterly) 07701

Jamaica National Trust Commission, 79 Duke St, POB 8934, Kingston
Founded: 1959
Pres: Herbert D. Repole
Focus: Urban Plan 07702

Jamaican Association of Sugar Technologists, c/o Sugar Industry Research Institute, Mandeville
T: 9622241; Fax: 9621288
Founded: 1937; Members: 266
Pres: Michael G. Hylton; Gen Secr: H.M. Thompson
Focus: Food 07703

Jamaican Geographical Society, c/o Geography Dept, University of the West Indies, Mona, Kingston 7
Focus: Geography
Periodical
Newsletter (semi-annually) 07704

Jamaican Institute of Architects, POB 251, Kingston 10
T: 9268060; Fax: 9268060
Founded: 1957; Members: 80
Pres: Lincoln Deane
Focus: Archit 07705

Medical Association of Jamaica (MAJ), 3a Paisley Av, Kingston 5
T: 95829
Founded: 1966; Members: 707
Pres: Dr. K.O. Barrow
Focus: Med
Periodical
Newsletter (bi-monthly) 07706

Medical Research Council Laboratories (MRC LABS), c/o University of the West Indies, Mona, Kingston 7
T: 9272471
Founded: 1962; Members: 22
Focus: Hematology 07707

Scientific Research Council, POB 350, Kingston 6
T: 9271771; Fax: 9275347
Gen Secr: Dr. G.A. Taylor
Focus: Sci 07708

Japan

Ajia Seikei Gakkai / Society for Asian Political and Economic Studies, c/o Prof. S. Amako, School of International Politics, Economics and Business, Aoyama Gakuin University, 4-4-25 Shibuya, Shibuya-ku, Tokyo 150
Founded: 1953; Members: 900
Pres: T. Watanabe
Focus: Poli Sci; Econ
Periodical
Ajia Kenkyu (quarterly) 07709

Asia Crime Prevention Foundation (ACPF), 60 Sunshine Bldg, 1-1 Higashi-Ikebukuro 3-chome, Toshima-ku, Tokyo 170
T: (03) 39871444; Fax: 59512505
Founded: 1982; Members: 3440
Pres: Sugiichiro Watari; Gen Secr: Tetsurou Takizawa
Focus: Criminology
Periodicals
Asian Journal of Crime Prevention and Criminal Justice
Newsletter of the Asia Crime Prevention Foundation 07710

Asian and Oceanian Thyroid Association (AOTA), c/o Radiation Effects Research Foundation, 5-2 Hijiyama Park, Minami-ku, Hiroshima 732
T: (082) 2613131; E-Mail: nagataki@rerf.or.jp; Fax: 2637279
Founded: 1975
Pres: Prof. Shigenobu Nagataki
Focus: Intern Med 07711

Asian Parasite Control Organization (APCO), c/o Hokenkaikan Bekkan, 1-2 Sadohara-cho, Ichigaya, Shinjuku-ku, Tokyo 162
T: (03) 32681800; Fax: 32668767
Founded: 1974
Gen Secr: Ohtsuru Masamitsu
Focus: Med 07712

Asian Productivity Organization (APO), 4-14 Akasaka 8-chome, Minato-ku, Tokyo 107
T: (03) 34087221; E-Mail: apo@gol.com; Fax: 34087220
Founded: 1961; Members: 18
Gen Secr: Kenichi Yanagi
Focus: Business Admin 07713

Association of Medical Doctors of Asia (AMDA), c/o Suganami Hospital, 1/310 Narazu, Okayama 701-12
T: (086) 2847730; E-Mail: webmaster@mail.amda.or.jp; Fax: 2848959
Founded: 1984; Members: 1700
Pres: Dr. Shigeru Suganami; Gen Secr: Yuji Kondo
Focus: Med 07714

Bigaku-Kai / The Japanese Society for Aesthetics, c/o Faculty of Letters, Seijo University, 6-1-20 Seijo, Setagaya-ku, Tokyo 157
Founded: 1950; Members: 1500
Pres: Keiji Asanuma
Focus: Philos
Periodicals
Aesthetics (bi-annually)
Bigaku (quarterly) 07715

Bijutsu-shi Gakkai / Japanese Art History Society, c/o Tokyo National Research Institute of Cultural Properties, 13-27 Ueno Park, Taito-ku, Tokyo 110
Founded: 1949; Members: 665
Focus: Hist; Arts
Periodical
Journal (quarterly) 07716

Butsuri Tansa Gakkai / Society of Exploration Geophysicists of Japan, San-es Bldg, 2-2-18 Nakamagome, Ota-ku, Tokyo
Founded: 1948; Members: 1420
Pres: T. Kawamura
Focus: Geophys
Periodical
Butsuri Tansa (bi-monthly) 07717

Chigaku Dantai Kenkyu-Kai / The Association for the Geological Collaboration in Japan, Kawai Bldg, 2-24-1, Minami-Ikebukuro, Toshima-ku, Tokyo 171
T: (03) 39833378; E-Mail: chidanken@tokyo.e-mail.ne.jp; Fax: 39837527
Founded: 1947; Members: 2800
Pres: Kawabe Takayuki; Gen Secr: Kobayashi Tadao
Focus: Geology
Periodical
Chikyu-kagaku: Earth Science (bi-monthly) 07718

Chikyudenjiki Chikyuwakuseiken Gakkai, c/o Japan Academic Societies Business Centre, 5-16-9 Honkomagome, Bunkyo-ku, Tokyo 113
T: (03) 58145810; Fax: 58145820
Founded: 1947; Members: 730
Pres: M. Kono; Gen Secr: N. Iwagami
Focus: Physics
Periodical
Earth, Planets and Space (monthly) . . 07719

Danchi-Nogaku Kenkyu-Kai / Southern Agricultural Society, c/o Faculty of Agriculture, Miyazaki University, 3-210 Funatsuka-cho, Miyazaki 880
Founded: 1947; Members: 200
Pres: Shigeo Asano
Focus: Agri 07720

Denki Gakkai / Institute of Electrical Engineers of Japan, 1-12-1, Yuraku-cho, Chiyoda-ku, Tokyo 100
T: (03) 32010983
Founded: 1888; Members: 26000
Pres: Hisao Oka
Focus: Chem
Periodical
Denki Kagaku 07721

Denshi Joho Tsushin Gakkai / Institute of Electronics, Information and Communication Engineers of Japan, Kikai-Shinko-Kaikan Bldg, 3-5-8 Shibakoen, Minato-ku, Tokyo 105
T: (03) 34336691; Fax: 34336659
Founded: 1917; Members: 40000
Pres: Shigeo Tsuji
Focus: Electronic Eng; Comm Sci
Periodicals
Journal, Transactions (monthly)
Original Contributions in English and Abstracts in English from the Transactions (monthly) . 07722

Doboku-Gakkai / Japan Society of Civil Engineers, 1 Yotsuya, Shinjuku-ku, Tokyo 160
T: (03) 3553441; Fax: 53790125
Founded: 1914; Members: 37155
Pres: Dr. Minoru Matsuo; Gen Secr: Hiroshi Kono
Focus: Civil Eng
Periodicals
Civil Engineering in Japan
Coastal Engineering in Japan (annually)
Journal (monthly)
Proceedings (monthly) 07723

Doshitsu Kogakkai / Japanese Society of Soil Mechanics and Foundation Engineering, 4F Sugayama Bldg, Kanda Awaji-cho 2-23, Chiyoda-ku, Tokyo 101
T: (03) 32517661; Fax: 32516688
Founded: 1949; Members: 13000
Pres: Y. Yoshima
Focus: Civil Eng
Periodicals
Soils and Foundations (quarterly)
Tsuchi to Kiso (monthly) 07724

Engei Gakkai / Japanese Society for Horticultural Science, c/o Business Center for Academic Societies Japan, 16-9, Honkomagome 5-chome, Bunkyo-ku, Tokyo 113
T: (03) 58145801; Fax: 58145820
Founded: 1923; Members: 2855
Pres: S. Iwahori; Gen Secr: N. Sugiyama
Focus: Hort
Periodical
Journal (quarterly) 07725

Gakujutsu Bunken Fukyu-Kai / Association for Science Documents Information, c/o Tokyo Institute of Technology, 2-15-1, O-okayama, Meguro-ku, Tokyo 152
Founded: 1933
Pres: S. Kanbara
Focus: Doc
Periodical
Reports on Progress in Polymer Physics in Japan 07726

Gyogyo Keizai Gakkai / Fisheries Economic Society, c/o Tokyo-Suisan University, 4-5-7 Kohnan, Minato-ku, Tokyo 108
Founded: 1953; Members: 220
Pres: Ryuzo Takayama
Focus: Fisheries 07727

Hassei Seibutsu Gakkai / Japanese Society of Developmental Biologists, c/o Dept of Life Science, University of Tokyo, 3-8-1 Komaba, Meguro-ku, Tokyo 153
T: (03) 54542904
Founded: 1968; Members: 1320
Pres: M. Okada
Focus: Bio 07728

Hikaku-ho Gakkai / Japan Society of Comparative Law, c/o Faculty of Law, Tokyo University, Hongo, Bunkyo-ku, Tokyo 113
Founded: 1950; Members: 780
Pres: H. Tanaka
Focus: Law
Periodical
Hikakuhô Konkyû: Comparative Law Journal (annually) 07729

Hiroshima Shikagu Kenkyukai, c/o Hiroshima Daigaku Bungakubu, Kagamiyama 1-2-3, Higashihiroshima 739
T: (0824) 246643; E-Mail: h660270@ipc.hiroshima-u.ac.jp; Fax: 240315
Founded: 1929; Members: 879
Pres: Jun Teraji
Focus: Hist
Periodical
Shigaku-Kenkyu: Review of Historical Studies (quarterly) 07730

Hogaku Kyokai / Jurisprudence Association, c/o Faculty of Law, University of Tokyo, 7-3-1 Hongo, Bunkyo-ku, Tokyo 113
T: (03) 38122111; Fax: 38167375
Founded: 1884; Members: 600
Pres: Y. Aoyama
Focus: Law
Periodical
Hogaku Kyokai Zassi (monthly) 07731

Hosei-shi Gakkai / Legal History Association, c/o Tohoku University, Kawauchi, Aoba-ku, Sendai 980-77
T: (022) 2176237; Fax: 2176249
Founded: 1949; Members: 470
Pres: S. Koyama
Focus: Hist; Law
Periodical
Legal History Review (annually) 07732

Hosokai / Lawyers' Association, 1-1 Kasumigaseki, Chiyoda-ku, Tokyo
Founded: 1891; Members: 20000
Pres: R. Kusaba; Gen Secr: Isao Imai
Focus: Law
Periodical
Hoso Jiho 07733

Ikomasan Tenmon Kyokai / Ikomasan Astronomical Society, Ikoma-Sanzyo, Ikoma-gun, Nara Ken
Founded: 1942; Members: 705
Pres: Joe Ueta; Gen Secr: H. Hamane
Focus: Astronomy
Periodical
Tenmon Kyositu: Astronomical Class (monthly) 07734

Information Processing Society of Japan (IPSJ), Shibaura-Maekawa Bldg, 3-16-20, Shibaura, Minato-ku, Tokyo 108
T: (03) 54843535; E-Mail: tsuchi@ipsj.or.jp; Fax: 54843534
Founded: 1960; Members: 30000
Pres: Dr. I. Toda; Gen Secr: H. Iizuka
Focus: Computer & Info Sci
Periodicals
Joho Shori: Journal of the Information Processing Society of Japan (monthly)
Joho Shori Gakkai Ronbunshi: Transactions of the Information Processing Society of Japan (monthly) 07735

The Japan Gas Association, 15-12, Toranomon 1-chome, Minato-ku, Tokyo 105
T: (03) 35020652; Fax: 35020013
Founded: 1947; Members: 244
Pres: Hiroshi Watanabe; Gen Secr: Koshiro Goda
Focus: Energy
Periodical
Journal (monthly) 07736

Japan Oil Chemists' Society, Yushi Kogyo Kaikan, 3-13-11 Nihonbashi, Chuo-ku, Tokyo 103
T: (03) 32717463; Fax: 32717464
Founded: 1951; Members: 2500
Pres: Toru Takagi; Gen Secr: Osamu Tsuji
Focus: Petrochem
Periodical
Journal (monthly) 07737

Japan PEN Club, Rm 265, Syiwa Residential Hotel, 9-1-7 Akasaka, Minato-ku, Tokyo
T: (03) 34021171; Fax: 34025951
Founded: 1935; Members: 1485
Pres: Markoto Ooka
Focus: Lit
Periodical
Japanese Literature Today (annually) . . 07738

Japan Society of Blood Transfusion, Central Blood Center, The Japanese Red Cross, 4-1-31, Shibuya-ku, Tokyo
T: (03) 54856020; Fax: 34067892
Founded: 1954; Members: 2800
Pres: M. Shimizu
Focus: Hematology
Periodical
Journal (bi-monthly) 07739

Japan Techno-Economics Society (JATES), Masuda Bldg, 2-4-5 Iidabashi, Chiyoda-ku, Tokyo 102
T: (03) 32635501; Fax: 32635504
Founded: 1966; Members: 2210
Pres: Shoichi Saba; Gen Secr: Yoshio Ishikawa
Focus: Business Admin
Periodical
Technology and Economy (monthly) . . 07740

Japan Weather Association, Kaiji Center Bldg, 4-5 Kojimachi, Chiyoda-ku, Tokyo
Founded: 1950
Pres: Naoshi Machida
Focus: Geophys
Periodicals
Geophysical Magazine
Journal of Meteorological Research (monthly)
Oceanographical Magazine (quarterly) . . 07741

Japanese Circulation Society, c/o Kinki Invention Center, 14 Yoshida Kawahara-cho, Sakyo-ku, Kyoto 606
T: (075) 7518643; E-Mail: admin@kardia.netjcs.or.jp; Fax: 7713060
Founded: 1935; Members: 19515
Pres: Yoshio Yazaki; Gen Secr: Masatoshi Fujita
Focus: Cardiol
Periodical
Japanese Circulation Journal (monthly) . 07742

Japanese College of Angiology, c/o Gakkai Jimu Center, 5-16-9 Honkomagome, Bunkyo-ku, Tokyo 113
T: (03) 58145801; Fax: 58145820
Founded: 1960; Members: 4000
Pres: Prof. Yoshio Mishima; Gen Secr: Prof. Hiroshi Shigematsu
Focus: Sci 07743

Japanese Society for Stereotactic and Functional Neurosurgery, c/o Dept of Neurosurgery, Nihon University, 30-1 Ohyaguchi Kamimachi, Itabashi-ku, Tokyo
T: (03) 39728111 Youichik@bekkoame.or.jp; Fax: 35540425
Founded: 1963; Members: 550
Pres: Prof. C. Ohye; Gen Secr: Prof. Y. Katayama
Focus: Neurology; Surgery
Periodical
Functional Neurosurgery (annually) . . . 07744

Japanese Society for the Study of Pain, c/o Dept of Anaesthesia, Kyoto University, 54 Kawahara-cho Syogoin, Sakyo-ku, Kyoto 606-01
T: (075) 7513433; Fax: 7523259
Founded: 1973; Members: 700
Gen Secr: K. Mori
Focus: Anesthetics 07745

Joho Kagaku Gijutsu Kyokai / Information Science and Technology Association, Sasaki Bldg, 2-5-7 Koisikawa, Bunkyo-ku, Tokyo
Founded: 1950; Members: 1550
Pres: T. Gondoh
Focus: Computer & Info Sci
Periodical
Journal (monthly) 07746

Kagaku Gijutsu Shinko Jigyodan / Japan Science and Technology Corporation, Kawaguchi Center Bldg, 4-1-8, Hon-cho, Kawaguchi-shi, Saitama 332
T: (048) 2265628; Fax: 2265652
Founded: 1996; Members: 410
Pres: M. Nakamura
Focus: Doc
Periodicals
Current Bibliography on Science and Technology: Kagaku Gijutsu Bunken Sokuho (bi-weekly)
Journal of Information Processing and Management: Joho Kanri
Proceedings of the Annual Meeting on Information Science and Technology 07747

Kagaku Kisoron Gakkai / Japan Association for Philosophy of Science, c/o Dept of Philosophy, Rissyo University, 4-2-16, Oosaki, Shinagawa-ku, Tokyo 141
T: (03) 54873362; Fax: 54873321
Founded: 1954; Members: 550
Pres: Natuhiko Yoshida; Gen Secr: Murakami Yoichiro
Focus: Philos
Periodicals
Annals of the Japan Association for Philosophy of Science (annually)
Kagaku Kisoron Kenkyu (semi-annually) . 07748

Kaiyoo Kisho Gakkai / Oceanographical and Meteoroligical Society, 7-chome, Ikutaku, Kboe
Founded: 1921; Members: 310
Pres: Hayato Oida
Focus: Oceanography 07749

Kansai Zosen Kyokai / Kansai Society of Naval Architects, c/o Dept of Naval Architecture, Osaka University, 2-1 Yamada-oka, Suita, Osaka 565
T: (06) 8797593; Fax: 8785364
Founded: 1912; Members: 2400
Pres: S. Furuta
Focus: Eng
Periodicals
Bulletin of the Kansai Society of Naval Architects (quarterly)
Journal of The Kansai Society of Naval Architects (semi-annually) 07750

Keikinzoku Gakkai / Japanese Institute of Light Metals, Nihonbashi Asahiseimei Bldg, 1-3, Nihonbashi 2-chome, Chuo-ku, Tokyo 103
T: (03) 32753688; Fax: 32132918
Founded: 1951; Members: 2234
Pres: S. Sato
Focus: Metallurgy
Periodical
Journal (monthly) 07751

Keisoku Jidouseigyo Gakkai SICE / Society of Instrument and Control Engineers, 35-28-303 Hongo 1-chome, Bunkyo-ku, Tokyo 113
T: (03) 38144121; Fax: 38144699
Founded: 1962; Members: 10124

Pres: Ichiro Ido
Focus: Eng 07752

Keizai Chiri Gakkai / Japan Association of Economic Geographers, c/o Institute of Economic Geography, Hitotsubashi University, 2-1 Naka, Kunitachi-shi, Tokyo 186
T: (0425) 721101 ext 5374; Fax: 711893
Founded: 1954; Members: 700
Pres: K. Takeuchi
Focus: Geography
Periodical
Annals of the Japan Association of Economic Geographers (quarterly) 07753

Keizai-ho Gakkai / Association of Economic Jurisprudence, c/o Hitotsubashi University, Kunitachi, Tokyo 186
Founded: 1951; Members: 280
Focus: Law
Periodical
Journal (annually) 07754

Keizai Riron Gakkai / Japan Society of Political Economy, c/o Faculty of Economics, Rikkyo University, 3 Ikebukuro, Toshima-ku, Tokyo
Founded: 1959; Members: 865
Pres: H. Oouchi
Focus: Poli Sci; Econ 07755

Keizaigaku-shi Gakkai / Japan Society for the History of Economic Thought, c/o School of Economics, Kwansei Gakuin University, Uegahara, Nishinomiya, Hyogo
T: (0789) 536111; Fax: 510944
Founded: 1949; Members: 810
Pres: M. Tanaka
Focus: Hist; Econ; Sociology
Periodical
Annual Bulletin (annually) 07756

Kinyu Gakkai / Financial Science Association, c/o Toyo Keizai, Motoishi, 1-4 Nihonbashi, Chuo-ku, Tokyo
Founded: 1943; Members: 460
Pres: T. Takagaku
Focus: Finance 07757

Kobunshi Gakkai / Society of Polymer Science, 3 Nagaoka Bldg, 2-4-7 Tsukiji, Chuo-ku, Tokyo 104
T: (03) 35433765; Fax: 35458560
Founded: 1951; Members: 12800
Pres: M. Kamachi
Focus: Physics; Chem
Periodicals
Kobunshi (monthly)
Polymer Journal (monthly)
Polymer Preprints, Japan (semi-annually) 07758

Kogyo Kayaku Kyokai / Industrial Explosives Society of Japan, Gumma Bldg, 2-3-21 Nihonbashi, Chuo-ku, Tokyo 103
T: (03) 80716715; Fax: 32717592
Founded: 1939; Members: 971
Pres: I. Fukuyama
Focus: Eng
Periodical
Journal (bi-monthly) 07759

Kokka Gakkai, c/o Tokyo Daigaku Hogakubu, 7-3-1 Hongo, Bunkyo-ku, Tokyo 113
T: (03) 38122111; Fax: 381673575
Founded: 1877
Pres: M. Nishio
Focus: Poli Sci; Sociology 07760

Kokugo Gakkai / Society for the Study of Japanese Language, c/o Faculty of Letters, University of Tokyo, Hongo, Bunkyo-ku, Tokyo 113
Founded: 1944; Members: 1500
Pres: E. Iwabuchi
Focus: Ling
Periodical
Studies in the Japanese Language (quarterly) 07761

Kokusaiho Gakkai / Association of International Law, c/o Faculty of Law, University of Tokyo, Hongo, Bunkyo-ku, Tokyo 113
T: (03) 38122111
Founded: 1897; Members: 804
Pres: S. Kozai
Focus: Law
Periodical
Journal of International Law and Diplomacy (bi-monthly) 07762

Kokushi Gakkai / Society of Japanese Historical Research, c/o Kokugakuin University, 4-10-28 Higashi, Shibuya-ku, Tokyo
Founded: 1910
Gen Secr: H.R. Tsubaki
Focus: Hist 07763

Kuki-Chowa Eisei Kogakkai / Society of Heating, Airconditioning and Sanitary Engineers of Japan, 1-8-1 Kitashinjuku, Shinjuku-ku, Tokyo
Founded: 1917; Members: 18000
Pres: S. Yoshizawa
Focus: Eng; Air Cond
Periodicals
Journal (monthly)
Transactions (3 times annually) 07764

Kyoiku Tetsugakkai / Society of Educational Philosophy, c/o Sophia University, Kioi-cho, Chiyoda-ku, Tokyo 102
Founded: 1957; Members: 510
Pres: T. Oura
Focus: Educ; Philos
Periodical
Studies in the Philosophy of Education . 07765

Manyo Gakkai / Society for Manyo Studies, c/o Kansai University, Senriyama Suita-shi, Osaka 564
Founded: 1951; Members: 810
Focus: Sci
Periodical
Manyo (quarterly) 07766

Minji Soshoho Gakkai / Japan Association of Civil Procedure Law, c/o Chuuo Daigaku Hogakubu, Higashinakano 742-1, Hachioji-shi, Tokyo 192-03
Founded: 1949
Focus: Law
Periodical
Journal of Civil Procedure (annually) . . 07767

Minzokugaku Shinkokai / Japanese Society of Ethnology, 3-1-17 Higashi-cho, Hoya-shi, Tokyo 188
T: (0424) 215003
Focus: Folklore 07768

Moralogy Kenkyusho / Institute of Moralogy, 2-1-1 Hikarigaoka, Kashiwa-shi, Chiba 277
Fax: (0471) 761177
Founded: 1926
Pres: M. Hiroike
Focus: Philos
Periodical
Studies in Moralogy 07769

National Cancer Center, 5-1-1 Tsukiji, Chuo-ku, Tokyo 104
T: (03) 5422511; Fax: 5453567
Founded: 1962; Members: 800
Focus: Cell Biol & Cancer Res
Periodicals
Annual Report (annually)
Bone Tumor Registration in Japan (annually)
Clinical Staging of Lung Cancer
Collected Papers (annually)
Japanese Journal of Clinical Oncology (semi-annually)
Registration and Clinical Statistics of Stomach Cancer in Japan
Report of Hematologic Neoplasmas Registration in Japan (annually) 07770

Nichibei Hogakkai / Japanese American Society for Legal Studies, c/o Faculty of Law, University of Tokyo, Hongo, Bunkyo-ku, Tokyo 113
Founded: 1964; Members: 980
Gen Secr: T. Kinoshita
Focus: Law
Periodical
Amerika Ho: Law in the United States (semi-annually) 07771

Nihon Aisotopu Kyokai / Japan Radioisotope Association, 28-45 Hon-Komagome 2-chome, Bunkyo-ku, Tokyo 113
T: (03) 39467111; E-Mail: Japanisotope Tokyo; Fax: 39462640
Founded: 1951; Members: 7500
Focus: Eng; Chem; Radiology
Periodicals
Isotope News (monthly)
Radioisotopes (monthly) 07772

Nihon Arerugi Gakkai / Japanese Society of Allergology, 33-19-802, Hakusan-1, Bunkyo-ku, Tokyo 113
T: (03) 8160280
Founded: 1952; Members: 4300
Focus: Med
Periodical
Japanese Journal of Allergology (monthly) 07773

Nihon Bearingu Kogyokai / Japan Bearing Industrial Assocation, Kikaishinkokaikan, 3-5-8 Shibakoen, Minato-ku, Tokyo 105
T: (03) 4330927
Focus: Mach Eng 07774

Nihon Bunseki Kagaku-Kai / Japan Society for Analytical Chemistry, Gotanda Sanhaitsu, 26-2, Nishigotanda 1-chome, Shinagawa-ku, Tokyo 141
T: (03) 4903351; Fax: 34903572
Founded: 1952; Members: 9108
Pres: M. Tanaka; Gen Secr: Dr. T. Fujinuki
Focus: Chem
Periodicals
Analytical Sciences (bi-monthly)
Bunseki
Bunseki Kagaku (monthly) 07775

Nihon Chugoku Gakkai, c/o Yushima Seido, 1-4-25 Yushima, Bunkyo-ku, Tokyo 113
Founded: 1949
Focus: Ling; Lit 07776

Nihon Denpun Gakkai / Japanese Society of Starch Science, c/o National Food Research Institute, Ministry of Agriculture, Forestry and Fisheries, 2-1-2 Kannondai, Tsukuba, Ibaraki 305
Founded: 1952; Members: 1200
Focus: Food
Periodical
Denpun Kagaku: Journal for Starch and Its Related Carbohydrates and Enzymes . . 07777

Nihon Denshi Kogyo Shinko Kyokai / Japan Electronic Industry Developent Assocation, Kikai Shinko Kaikan, 3-5-8 Shibakoen, Minato-ku, Tokyo 105
T: (03) 4348211
Focus: Electronic Eng 07778

Nihon Do Senta / Japan Copper Development Association, Konwa Bldg, 1-12-22 Tsukiji, Chuo-ku, Tokyo 104
T: (03) 5426631
Focus: Metallurgy 07779

Nihon Dobutsu Shinri Gakkai / The Japanese Society for Animal Psychology, c/o Institute of Psychology, University of Tsukuba, 1-1-1 Ten'noudai, Tsukuba 305
T: (0298) 534720
Founded: 1933; Members: 410
Pres: Shigehisa Sekiguchi; Gen Secr: Toshiyuki Mori
Focus: Vet Med
Periodical
Dobutsu-shinrigaku-kenkyu: The Japanese Journal of Animal Psychology (semi-annually) . . 07780

Nihon Dokubun Gakkai / Japanische Gesellschaft für Germanistik, c/o Ikubundo, Hongo 5-30-21, Bunkyo-ku, Tokyo 113
Founded: 1947; Members: 2600
Pres: S. Inoue
Focus: Lit
Periodical
Doitsu Bungaku: German Literature (semi-annually) 07781

Nihon Eibungakkai / The English Literary Society of Japan, 501 Kenkyusha Bldg, 9 Surugadai 2-chome, Kanda, Chiyoda-ku, Tokyo 101
T: (03) 32937528; Fax: 32333398
Founded: 1917; Members: 4400
Pres: Y. Fujikawa
Focus: Lit; Ling
Periodical
Studies in English Literature (3 times annually) 07782

Nihon Eisei Gakkai / Japanese Society for Hygiene, c/o Dept of Hygiene and Preventive Medicine, Hokkaido University School of Medicine, Nishi 7-chome, Kita 15-jo, Kita-ku, Sapporo 060
T: (011) 7065553; Fax: 7171140
Founded: 1902; Members: 2750
Gen Secr: Prof. Kazuo Saito
Focus: Hygiene
Periodical
Japanese Journal of Hygiene (bi-monthly) 07783

Nihon Engeki Gakkai / Japanese Society for Theatre Research, c/o Waseda University, 1-6-1 Nishi-Waseda, Shinjuku-ku, Tokyo
Founded: 1949
Pres: T. Mori
Focus: Perf Arts 07784

Nihon Esperanto Gakkai / Japana Esperanto-Instituto / Japan Esperanto Institute, Waseda-mati 12-3, Sinzyuku-ku, Tokyo 162
T: (03) 32034581; Fax: 32034582
Founded: 1919; Members: 1435
Pres: Y. Seiko; Gen Secr: Yosio Isino
Focus: Ling
Periodical
La Revuo Orienta: Esperanto (monthly) . 07785

Nihon Gakko-hoken Gakkai / Japanese Association of School Health, c/o Dept of Health Education, Faculty of Education, University of Tokyo, 7-3-1 Hongo, Bunkyo-ku, Tokyo 113
T: (03) 38122111
Founded: 1954; Members: 1500
Pres: A. Eguchi
Focus: Public Health
Periodical
Gakko-hoken Kenkyu (monthly) 07786

Nihon Gakujutsu Kaigi / Science Council of Japan, 7-22-34 Roppongi, Minato-ku, Tokyo 106
T: (03) 34036291; Fax: 34036224
Founded: 1949; Members: 210
Pres: Masao Ito
Focus: Sci 07787

Nihon Gakujutsu Shinko-kai / Japan Society for the Promotion of Science, 5-3-1 Kojimachi, Chiyoda-ku, Tokyo 102
T: (03) 32631721; Fax: 32378238, 32221986
Founded: 1967
Pres: Kenichi Fukui; Gen Secr: Nitoshi Osaki
Focus: Nat Sci; Humanities; Sociology
Periodicals
Annual Report (annually)
Japanese Scientific Monthly (monthly)
JSPS Newsletter (bi-monthly) 07788

Nihon Gengogakkai / The Linguistic Society of Japan, Shimotachiuri Ogawa Higashi, Kamikyoku, Kyoto 602
Fax: (075) 4153662
Founded: 1938; Members: 1900
Pres: Shibatani Masayoshi; Gen Secr: Kubozono Haruo
Focus: Ling
Periodical
Gengo Kenkyu: Journal of the Linguistic Society of Japan (semi-annually) 07789

Nihon Genshiryoku Gakkai / Atomic Energy Society of Japan, 1-1-13, Shimbashi, Minato-ku, Tokyo 105
T: (03) 35081261; Fax: 35816128
Founded: 1959; Members: 6630
Focus: Nucl Res
Periodicals
Journal of Nuclear Science and Technology (monthly)
Journal of the Atomic Energy Society of Japan (monthly) 07790

Nihon Gomu Kyokai, 5-26 Motoakasaka, 1-chome, Minato-ku, Tokyo 107
T: (03) 4012957
Founded: 1928; Members: 3500
Focus: Materials Sci 07791

Nihon Hikaku Kyoiku Gakkai / Japan Comparative Education Society, c/o NIER, 6-5-22 Shimomeguro, Meguro-ku, Tokyo 153
T: (03) 57215040; Fax: 37143653
Founded: 1965; Members: 663
Pres: S. Kawanobe
Focus: Educ 07792

Nihon Hinyokika Gakkai / Japanese Urological Association, Taisei Bldg, 3-14-10 Hongo, Bunkyo-ku, Tokyo
Founded: 1912; Members: 6200
Pres: Osamu Yoshida
Focus: Urology 07793

Nihon Hoken Gakkai, Shinkokusai Bldg, 4-1, Marunouchi 3-chome, Chiyoda-ku, Tokyo 100
T: (03) 2130661
Founded: 1940; Members: 850
Focus: Insurance 07794

Nihon Hoken Igakkai / Association of Life Insurance Medicine of Japan, c/o Life Insurance Association of Japan, Shi-Kokusai Bldg, 3-4-1 Marunouchi, Chiyoda-ku, Tokyo 100
T: (03) 2862735
Founded: 1901; Members: 982
Focus: Med 07795

Nihon Hozon Shika Gakkai, c/o Nihon Shika Daigaku, 1-9-20 Fujimi-cho, Chiyoda-ku, Tokyo 102
Founded: 1955
Focus: Dent 07796

Nihon Iden Gakkai / Genetics Society of Japan, c/o National Institute of Genetics, 1, 111 Yata, Mishima, Shizuoka 411
Fax: (0559) 756240
Founded: 1920
Focus: Genetics
Periodical
Japanese Journal of Genetics (bi-monthly) 07797

Nihon Ikushu Gakkai / Japanese Society of Breeding, c/o Faculty of Agriculture, University of Tokyo, 1-1-1 Yayoi, Bunkyo-ku, Tokyo 113
Founded: 1951; Members: 2000
Pres: Genkichi Takeda; Gen Secr: Hisashi Hirano
Focus: Bio
Periodical
Breeding Science (quarterly) 07798

Nihon Indogaku Bukkyogaku Kai / Japanese Association of Indian and Buddhist Studies, c/o Dept of Indian Philosophy and Buddhist Studies, University of Tokyo, 7-3-1 Hongo, Bunkyo-ku, Tokyo 113
T: (03) 38122111; Fax: 38160949
Founded: 1951; Members: 2400
Pres: Y. Ejima; Gen Secr: K. Kimura
Focus: Philos; Rel & Theol
Periodical
Journal of Indian and Buddhist Studies (semi-annually) 07799

Nihon Ishi-Kai / Japan Medical Association, 2-28-16, Honkomagome, Bunkyo-ku, Tokyo 113
Founded: 1916; Members: 121510
Pres: E. Tsuboi
Focus: Med
Periodicals
Asian Medical Journal (monthly)
Journal of The Japan Medical Association (bi-weekly) 07800

Nihon Ishinkin Gakkai, c/o Juntendo Daigaku, 2-1-1 Hongo, Bunkyo-ku, Tokyo 113
Founded: 1956
Focus: Botany, Specific
Periodical
Japanese Journal of Medical Mycology (quarterly) 07801

Nihon Jinrui Iden Gakkai / Japan Society of Human Genetics, c/o Dept of Human Genetics, Tokyo Medical and Dental University, 1-5-45 Yushima, Bunkyo-ku, Tokyo
T: (03) 38136111
Founded: 1956; Members: 1050
Pres: E. Matsunaga
Focus: Genetics 07802

Nihon Jui Gakkai / Japanese Society of Veterinary Science, Rakunokaikan Bldg, 1-37-20 Yoyogi, Shibuya-ku, Tokyo 151
T: (03) 33790636; Fax: 33790636
Founded: 1885; Members: 4530
Pres: Prof. Dr. Tomotari Mitsuoka
Focus: Vet Med
Periodical
The Journal of Veterinary Medical Science (bi-monthly) 07803

Nihon Kagakushi Gakkai / History of Science Society of Japan, 201 West Pine Bldg, 2-15-19 Hirakawa-cho, Chiyoda-ku, Tokyo 102
Founded: 1941; Members: 1000
Pres: T. Kikuchi
Focus: Hist; Sci 07804

Nihon Kairui Gakkai / The Malacological Society of Japan, c/o National Science Museum, 3-23-1 Hyakunin-cho, Shinjuku-ku, Tokyo 169
T: (03) 33642311
Founded: 1928; Members: 928
Pres: T. Okutani; Gen Secr: H. Saito
Focus: Zoology
Periodicals
Chiribotan (quarterly)
Venus (quarterly) *07805*

Nihon Kakuigakukai / Japanese Society of Nuclear Medicine, c/o Japan Radioisotope Association, 2-28-45 Hon-Komagome, Bunkyo-ku, Tokyo
Fax: (03) 39472535
Founded: 1963; Members: 3500
Pres: J. Konishi
Focus: Med
Periodical
Japanese Journal of Nuclear Medicine (monthly) *07806*

Nihon Kandenchi Kogyokai / Japan Dry Battery Assocation, Dai 9 Mori Bldg, 1-2-2 Atago, Minato-ku, Tokyo 105
T: (03) 4362471
Focus: Electrochem *07807*

Nihon Kasai Gakkai / Japanese Association for Fire Science and Engineering, c/o Business Center for Academic Societies, 2-4-16 Yayoi, Bunkyo-ku, Tokyo 113
Founded: 1951; Members: 2000
Pres: H. Saito
Focus: Econ
Periodicals
Bulletin (semi-annually)
Kasai (bi-monthly) *07808*

Nihon Kensetsu Kikaika Kyokai, Kikai Shinko Bldg, 5-8, 3-chome, Shiba Park, Minato-ku, Tokyo 105
T: (03) 4331501
Founded: 1949; Members: 1527
Focus: Civil Eng *07809*

Nihon Kikai Gakkai / Japan Society of Mechanical Engineers, 5F Shinanomachi-Rengakan, 35 Shinanomachi, Shinjuku-ku, Tokyo
T: (03) 53603500
Founded: 1897; Members: 47000
Pres: H. Abe
Focus: Eng
Periodical
Journal (monthly) *07810*

Nihon Kikaku Kyokai Gaikoku Kikaku Raiburari / Nihon Kikaku Kyokai Gaikoku Kikaku Raiburari / Japanese Standards Assocation, 4-1-24 Akasaka, Minato-ku, Tokyo 107
T: (03) 5838001
Focus: Standards *07811*

Nihon Kin Gakkai / Mycological Society of Japan, c/o Business Center for Academic Societies, 4-1 Yayoi 2-chome, Bunkyo-ku, Tokyo 113
T: (03) 8151903
Founded: 1956; Members: 1100
Focus: Botany, Specific
Periodicals
News (semi-annually)
Transactions (quarterly) *07812*

Nihon Kirisutokyo Gakkai / The Japan Society of Christian Culture, c/o Tokyo Union Theological Seminary, 3-10-30, Osawa, Mitaka, Tokyo 181
T: (0422) 324185; Fax: 330667
Founded: 1952; Members: 648
Pres: Toshio Sato; Gen Secr: Katsuhiko Kondo
Focus: Rel & Theol
Periodical
Nihon no Shingaku: Theological Studies in Japan (annually) *07813*

Nihon Kobutsu Gakkai, c/o Tokyo Daigaku Kyoyobu, 3-8-1 Komaba, Meguro-ku, Tokyo 153
Founded: 1952
Focus: Mineralogy *07814*

Nihon Koho Gakkai / Japan Public Law Association, c/o Faculty of Law, University of Tokyo, Hongo, Bunkyo-ku, Tokyo 113
Founded: 1948; Members: 1100
Pres: H. Shiono
Focus: Law
Periodical
Koho-Kenkyu (annually) *07815*

Nihon Koko Geka Gakkai / Japanese Society of Oral Surgeons, Tokyo Joshi Ika Daigaku, 10 Kawada-cho, Shinjuku-ku, Tokyo
Founded: 1952; Members: 2000
Gen Secr: M. Murase
Focus: Surgery; Med
Periodical
Japanese Journal of Oral Surgery (quarterly) *07816*

Nihon Kokogaku Kyokai / The Japanese Archaeological Association, 5-15-5, Hirai, Edogawa-ku, Tokyo 132
T: (03) 36186608; Fax: 36186625
Founded: 1948; Members: 3313
Pres: Takuya Iwasaki
Focus: Archeol
Periodical
Archaeologia Japonica: Nihon Kokogaku (annually) *07817*

Nihon Koku Eisei Gakkai / Japanese Society for Dental Health, c/o Koku Hoken Kyokai, 44-2 Komagome, 1-chome, Toshima-ku, Tokyo 170
Founded: 1952; Members: 2000
Focus: Dent
Periodical
Journal (quarterly) *07818*

Nihon Kokukai Gakkai / Japanese Stomatological Society, Dept of Oral Surgery, School of Medicine, University of Tokyo, 7-3-1, Hongo, Bunkyo-ku, Tokyo
T: (03) 8155411
Founded: 1947; Members: 3600
Gen Secr: I. Yamashita
Focus: Stomatology
Periodical
Journal of the Japanese Stomatological Society (quarterly) *07819*

Nihon Kokusai Kyoiku Kyokai / Association of International Education, 4-5-29 Komaba, Meguro-ku, Tokyo 153
T: (03) 4673521
Focus: Int'l Relat; Educ
Periodical
ABC's of Study in Japan (annually) . . *07820*

Nihon Kontyu Gakkai / Entomological Society of Japan, c/o Dept of Zoology, National Science Museum (Natural History), 3-23-1 Hyakunun-cho, Shinjuku-ku, Tokyo 169
Founded: 1917; Members: 1300
Pres: M. Saskawa
Focus: Zoology
Periodical
Japanese Journal of Entomology (quarterly) *07821*

Nihon Kotsu Igakkai / Japanese Association of Transportation Medicine, c/o Chuo Tetsudo Byouin, 2-1-3 Yoyogi, Shibuya-ku, Tokyo 151
T: (03) 3791111
Founded: 1947; Members: 5000
Focus: Med
Periodical
Journal of Transportation Medicine (bi-monthly) *07822*

Nihon Kotsu Kyokai Toshokan / Japan Transportation Association, Shin-Kokusai Bldg, 3-4 Marunouchi, Chiyoda-ku, Tokyo 100
T: (03) 216-4082
Focus: Transport *07823*

Nihon Kyobu Geka Gakkai, c/o Tokyo Daigaku Igakubu, 7-3-1 Hongo, Bunkyo-ku, Tokyo 113
Founded: 1948
Focus: Surgery *07824*

Nihon Kyoiku Gakkai / Japanese Society for the Study of Education, 5-26-5-901 Hongo, Bunkyo-ku, Tokyo 113
T: (03) 8182505; Fax: 8166898
Founded: 1941; Members: 3200
Pres: T. Horio
Focus: Educ
Periodical
Japanese Journal of Educational Research (quarterly) *07825*

Nihon Kyoiku-shakai Gakkai / Japan Society for the Study of Educational Sociology, c/o Faculty of Education, University of Tokyo, 7-3-1 Hongo, Bunkyo-ku, Tokyo 113
T: (03) 58006813; Fax: 58006814
Founded: 1949; Members: 1110
Pres: Ikuo Amano
Focus: Educ; Sociology
Periodical
Journal of Educational Sociology (semi-annually) *07826*

Nihon Kyoiku-shinri Gakkai / Japanese Association of Educational Psychology, c/o Faculty of Education, University of Tokyo, 7-3-1 Hongo, Bunkyo-ku, Tokyo 113
Founded: 1955; Members: 4400
Pres: S. Takano
Focus: Educ; Psych
Periodicals
The Annual Report of Educational Psychology in Japan (annually)
The Japanese Journal of Educational Psychology (quarterly) *07827*

Nihon Kyosei Shikagakkai / Japan Orthodontic Society, c/o Koku Hoken Kyokai, 1-44-2 Komagome, Toshima-ku, Tokyo 170
T: (03) 39478891; Fax: 39478341
Founded: 1932; Members: 4200
Pres: Kazuo Yamauchi; Gen Secr: M. Sebato
Focus: Dent
Periodical
The Journal of the Japan Orthodontic Society (quarterly) *07828*

Nihon Masui Gakkai / Japan Society of Anesthesiology, TY Bldg, 3-18-11 Hongo, Bunkyo-ku, Tokyo 113
Founded: 1954; Members: 3711
Pres: M. Hirakawa
Focus: Anesthetics
Periodical
Journal of Anesthesia (semi-annually) . . *07829*

Nihon Mendel Kyokai / Japan Mendel Society, Toshin Bldg, 2-27-2 Hongo, Bunkyo-ku, Tokyo 113
Members: 1100
Pres: N. Tanaka
Focus: Bio *07830*

Nihon Naika Gakkai / Japanese Society of Internal Medicine, Hongo Daiichi Bldg, 3-34-3 Hongo, Bunkyo-ku, Tokyo 113
T: (03) 38135991
Founded: 1903; Members: 70000
Pres: Ichiro Kanazawa
Focus: Med
Periodicals
Internal Medicine (monthly)
Journal (monthly) *07831*

Nihon Nettai Igakkai / Japanese Society of Tropical Medicine, c/o Institute of Tropical Medicine, Nagasaki University, 1-12-4 Sakamoto, Nagasaki 852
T: (0958) 472111; Fax: 476607
Founded: 1959
Focus: Med
Periodical
Japanese Journal of Tropical Medicine and Hygiene (quarterly) *07832*

Nihon Oyo Shinri-gakkai / Japan Association of Applied Psychology, c/o Dept of Psychology, College of Humanities and Sciences, Nihon University, 3-25-40 Sakurajosui, Setagaya-ku, Tokyo
T: (03) 3291151
Founded: 1931
Pres: H. Yamamoto; Gen Secr: K. Mural
Focus: Psych *07833*

Nihon Oyo Toshitsu Kagaku Kai / Japanese Society of Applied Glycoscience, c/o National Food Research Institute, 2-1-2 Kannondai, Tsubuka, Ibaraki 305
T: (0298) 388053; Fax: 3881222
Founded: 1952; Members: 4430
Pres: S. Hizukuri
Focus: Chem *07834*

Nihon PEN Kurabu / Japan PEN Club, Room 265, Syuwa Residential Hotel, 9-1-7, Akasaka, Minato-ku, Tokyo 107
T: (03) 4021171; Fax: 44025951
Founded: 1935; Members: 1000
Focus: Lit
Periodical
Japanese Literature Today (annually) . . *07835*

Nihon Reito Kyokai / Japanese Association of Refrigeration, Sanei Bldg, 8 San-ei-cho, Shinguku-ku, Tokyo 160
T: (03) 33595231; Fax: 33595233
Founded: 1925; Members: 6000
Focus: Electric Eng
Periodicals
Nihon Reito Kyokai Ronbunshu: JAR Transactions (3 times annually)
Reito: Refrigeration (monthly) *07836*

Nihon Rinrigakukai / Japanese Society for Ethics, c/o Dept of Ethics, Faculty of Letters, University of Tokyo, Bunkyo-ku, Tokyo 113
Founded: 1950; Members: 800
Pres: Y. Yazima
Focus: Philos
Periodical
Rinrigakukaironshu (annually) *07837*

Nihon Rinsho Byori Gakkai / Japan Society of Clinical Pathology, Well-Stone Heights 203, 2-11-10, Hongo, Bunkyo-ku, Tokyo 113
Fax: (03) 8138150
Founded: 1951; Members: 3500
Focus: Pathology
Periodical
The Japanese Journal of Clinical Pathology (monthly) *07838*

Nihon Ronen Igakukai / Japan Geriatrics Society, Kyorin Bldg 702, 4-2-1 Yushima, Bunkyo-ku, Tokyo 113
Founded: 1959; Members: 4500
Pres: Prof. H. Orimo
Focus: Geriatrics
Periodical
Japanese Journal of Geriatrics (bi-monthly) *07839*

Nihon Sakumotsu Gakkai / Crop Science Society of Japan, c/o Faculty of Agriculture, University of Tokyo, Bunkyo-ku, Tokyo 113
T: (03) 38122111; Fax: 38155851
Founded: 1927; Members: 1800
Pres: R. Ishii; Gen Secr: M. Kokubun
Focus: Crop Husb; Agri
Periodical
Japanese Journal of Crop Science and Plant Production Science (quarterly) *07840*

Nihon Sangyo Eisei Gakkai, c/o Koei Biru, 1-29-8 Shinjuku, Tokyo 160
Fax: (03) 33561536
Founded: 1929
Focus: Sci
Periodical
Japanese Journal of Industrial Health (bi-monthly) *07841*

Nihon Sanshi Gakkai / Japanese Society of Sericultural Science, c/o National Institute of Sericultural and Entomological Science, Owashi 1-2, Tsubuka, Ibaraki 305
T: 66070
Founded: 1929; Members: 1313
Focus: Agri
Periodical
The Journal of Sericultural Science of Japan (bi-monthly) *07842*

Nihon Seibutsu Butsuri Gakkai / Biophysical Society of Japan, c/o Dept of Biophysical Engineering, Faculty of Engineering Science, Osaka University, Machikaneyama, Toyonaka, Osaka 560
T: (06) 8440943; Fax: 8439354
Founded: 1960; Members: 3000
Focus: Biophys
Periodical
Seibutsu Butsuri: Biophysics (bi-monthly) . *07843*

Nihon Seibutsu Kankyo Chosetsu Kenkyukai / Japanese Society of Environment Control in Biology, c/o Dept of Agricultural Engineering, University of Tokyo, Tokyo 113
T: (03) 8122111 ext 5356
Founded: 1969; Members: 752
Focus: Bio
Periodical
Environment Control in Biology (quarterly) *07844*

Nihon Seibutsu-kogaku Kai / Society for Fermentation and Bioengineering Japan, c/o Faculty of Engineering, Osaka University, 2-1 Yamadaoka, Suita, Osaka 565
T: (06) 8762731; Fax: 8792034
Founded: 1923; Members: 4000
Pres: Prof. T. Kodama
Focus: Eng; Agri *07845*

Nihon Seishin Shinkei Gakkai / Japanese Society of Psychiatry and Neurology, Hongo Sky Bldg 38-11, 3-chome, Hongo, Bunkyo-ku, Tokyo 113
Founded: 1902; Members: 8200
Pres: Masahiro Asai
Focus: Neurology; Psychiatry
Periodical
Seishin Shinkeigaku Zasshi (monthly) . . *07846*

Nihon Sen'i Kikai Gakkai / Textile Machinery Society of Japan, c/o Osaka Kagaku Gijutsu Senta, 1-8-4, Utsubo-Honmachi, Nishi-ku, Osaka 550
T: (06) 4434691; E-Mail: JDH04707@niftyserve.or.jp; Fax: 4434694
Founded: 1948; Members: 7000
Pres: Dr. K. Kazama
Focus: Mach Eng
Periodicals
Journal: English Edition (quarterly)
Journal: Japanese Edition (monthly) . . *07847*

Nihon Setchakuzai Kogyokai Toshoshitsu / Japan Adhesive Industry Association, Fukushima Bldg, 1-15-10 Uchikanda, Chiyoda-ku, Tokyo 101
T: (03) 2913303
Focus: Materials Sci *07848*

Nihon Shakai Shinri Gakkai / The Japanese Society of Social Psychology, c/o Dept of Psychology, Tokyo Woman's Christian University, 2-6-1, Zempukuji, Suginami-ku, Tokyo 167
Founded: 1960; Members: 1400
Pres: Tomio Kinoshita
Focus: Psych
Periodical
Japanese Journal of Social Psychology: Bulletin of the Japanese Society of Social Psychology (3 times a year) *07849*

Nihon Shika Hoshasen Gakkai / Japanese Society for Oral and Maxillofacial Radiology, c/o Dept of Oral and Maxillofacial Radiology, Faculty of Dentistry, Osaka University, 1-8 Yamadaoka, Suita, Osaka 565
T: (06) 8792967; Fax: 8755834
Founded: 1951; Members: 1200
Gen Secr: H. Fuchihata
Focus: Radiology
Periodical
Dental Radiology (quarterly) *07850*

Nihon Shinku Kyokai, Kikai Shinko Kaikan, 21-1-5 Shiba-koen, Minato-ku, Tokyo 105
Founded: 1958
Focus: Physics *07851*

Nihon Shinrigakkai / Japanese Psychological Association, 2-40-14-902, Hongo, Bunkyo-ku, Tokyo 113
Founded: 1927; Members: 4800
Focus: Psych
Periodicals
Japanese Journal of Psychology (bi-monthly)
Japanese Psychological Research (quarterly) *07852*

Nihon Shiritsu Daigak Kyokai / Association of Private Universities of Japan, c/o Shigaku Kaikan, 4-2-25 Kudan-Kita, Chiyoda-ku, Tokyo 102
T: (03) 32617048; Fax: 32610769
Founded: 1946; Members: 250
Pres: Dr. S. Kittaka
Focus: Educ *07853*

Nihon Shokaki Naishikyo Gakkai / Japan Gastroenterological Endoscopy Society, 3-22, Taimei Bldg 2F, Ogawa-machi, Kanda, Chiyoda-ku, Tokyo 101
T: (03) 32914111; Fax: 32915568
Founded: 1961; Members: 25341
Pres: Hirohumi Niwa
Focus: Gastroenter
Periodical
Gastroenterological Endoscopy (monthly) . *07854*

Nihon Shoni Geka Gakkai / Japanese Society of Pediatric Surgeons, c/o Business Center for Academic Societies, 2-4-16 Yayoi, Bunkyo-ku, Tokyo 113
Founded: 1964
Focus: Pediatrics
Periodical
Journal (7 times annually) 07855

Nihon Shonika Gakkai / Societas Paediatrica Japonica / Japan Pediatric Society, 4 Daiichi Magami Bldg, 1-1-5, Koraku, Bunkyo-ku, Tokyo 112
T: (03) 38180091
Founded: 1896; Members: 15600
Pres: N. Matsuo
Focus: Pediatrics
Periodical
Acta Paediatrica Japonica (bi-monthly) . 07856

Nihon Shukyo Gakkai / Japanese Association for Religious Studies, 1-29-7-295 Hongo, Bunkyo-ku, Tokyo 113
T: (03) 56845473; Fax: 56845474
Founded: 1930; Members: 2000
Pres: N. Tamaru
Focus: Rel & Theol
Periodical
Journal of Religious Studies (quarterly) . 07857

Nihon Syoyakuga Gakkai / Japanese Society of Pharmacognosy, c/o Business Center for Academic Societies, 2-4-16 Yayoi, Bunkyo-ku, Tokyo 113
Founded: 1946; Members: 1030
Pres: M. Konoshima
Focus: Pharmacol 07858

Nihon Tairyoku Igakkai, c/o Tokyo Jieikai Ika Dagaku, Minato-ku, Tokyo 105
Founded: 1949
Focus: Med 07859

Nihon Tenmon Gakkai / Astronomical Society of Japan, c/o National Astronomical Observatory, Osawa Mitaka, Tokyo
Fax: (0422) 311359
Founded: 1908; Members: 2028
Focus: Astronomy
Periodicals
The Astronomical Herold (monthly)
Publications (bi-monthly) 07860

Nihon Tetsugakkai, c/o Toyo Daigaku Bungakubu, 5-28-20 Hakusan, Bunkyo-ku, Tokyo 112
Founded: 1949
Focus: Philos 07861

Nihon Tokei Gakkai / Japan Statistical Society, c/o Institute of Statistical Mathematics, 4-6-7 Minami-azabu, Minato-ku, Tokyo 106
T: (03) 4425801
Founded: 1931; Members: 1310
Pres: Kiyoshi Takeushi
Focus: Stats
Periodical
Journal (semi-annually) 07862

Nihon Toshokan Kyokai / Japan Library Association, 1-10, 1-chome, Taishido, Setagaya-ku, Tokyo 154
T: (03) 34106411; E-Mail: jla@ar.aix.or.jp; Fax: 34217588
Founded: 1892; Members: 8300
Pres: Michio Nagai; Gen Secr: Reiko Sakagawa
Focus: Libraries & Bk Sci
Periodicals
Gendai no Toshokan (quarterly)
Nihon no Sankotosho Shikiban (quarterly)
Toshokan Zasshi (monthly) 07863

Nihon Uirusu Gakkai / Society of Japanese Virologists, c/o Business Centre for Academic Societies, 4-16 Yayoi 2-chome, Bunkyo-ku, Tokyo 113
Founded: 1958; Members: 2141
Focus: Med
Periodicals
Microbiology and Immunology
Virus (semi-annually) 07864

Nihon Yakuri Gakkai / Japanese Pharmacological Society, 2-4-16 Yayoi, Bunkyo-ku, Tokyo 113
T: (03) 38144828
Founded: 1927; Members: 6500
Pres: Tomoh Masaki
Focus: Pharmacol
Periodicals
Folia Pharmacologica Japonica (monthly)
The Japanese Journal of Pharmacology (monthly) 07865

Nihon Yosetsu Kyokai, Sampo Sakuma Bldg 1-11, Kanda Sakuma-cho, Chiyoda-ku, Tokyo 101
T: (03) 2530581
Founded: 1949; Members: 750
Focus: Eng 07866

Nihon Zairyo Gakkai, 1-101 Yoshida-Izumidono-machi, Sakyo-ku, Kyoto 606
Founded: 1952
Focus: Materials Sci 07867

Nihon Zairyo Kyodo Gakkai, c/o Research Institute for Stenght and Facture of Materials, Tohoku University, Armaki-Aoba, Sendai 980
Founded: 1966; Members: 1068
Focus: Materials Sci 07868

Nihon Zaisei Gakkai / Japanese Association of Fiscal Studies, c/o Hitotsubashi University, Kunitachi, Tokyo 186
Founded: 1940; Members: 195
Focus: Finance 07869

Nihon Zoen Gakkai / Japanese Institute of Landscape Architects, c/o Faculty of Architecture, University of Tokyo, Hongo, Bunkyo-ku, Tokyo 113
Founded: 1924; Members: 1800
Pres: Akira Homma
Focus: Archit 07870

Nihon Zosen Gakkai / Society of Naval Architects of Japan, Sempaku-Shinko Bldg, 15-16 Toranomon, 1-chome, Minato-ku, Tokyo 105
Founded: 1897; Members: 4400
Pres: H. Ohba
Focus: Eng
Periodicals
Bulletin (monthly)
Journal (semi-annually)
Naval Architecture and Ocean Engineering (annually) 07871

Nippon Afurika Gakkai, c/o Tokyo Daigaku Rigakubu, 7-31 Hongo, Bunkyo-ku, Tokyo 113
Founded: 1964
Focus: Ethnology 07872

Nippon Bitamin Gakkai / Vitamin Society of Japan, c/o Nippon Italy Kyoto-Kaikan, 4-Ushinomiya-cho, Yoshida, Sakyo-ku, Kyoto 606
T: (075) 7510314
Founded: 1947; Members: 2000
Pres: Dr. K. Okuda
Focus: Nutrition; Food; Pharmacol; Med; Agri; Chem
Periodicals
Journal of Nutritional Science and Vitaminology (bi-monthly)
Vitamins (monthly) 07873

Nippon Bungaku Kyokai / Japanese Literature Association, 2-17-10 Minami-otsuka, Toyoshima-ku, Tokyo 170
T: (03) 39412740; Fax: 39412740
Founded: 1946; Members: 1500
Pres: Mamoru Takada
Focus: Lit
Periodical
Japanese Literature (monthly) 07874

Nippon Bunko Gakkai / Spectroscopial Society of Japan, Clean Bldg, 1-13 Kanda-Awaji-cho, Chiyoda-ku, Tokyo 101
Founded: 1951; Members: 1200
Pres: K. Shibata; Gen Secr: Y. Nihei
Focus: Physics; Chem
Periodical
Journal (bi-monthly) 07875

Nippon Butsuri Gakkai / The Physical Society of Japan, Room 211, Kikai-Shinko Bldg, 3-5-8 Shiba-Koen, Minato-ku, Tokyo 105
T: (03) 34342671; Fax: 34320997
Founded: 1977; Members: 17062
Pres: Katsuhiko Sato; Gen Secr: Yuki Kiyota
Focus: Physics
Periodicals
Butsuri (monthly)
Japanese Journal of Applied Physics (bi-weekly)
Journal of the Physical Society of Japan (monthly)
Progress of Theoretical Physics (monthly) 07876

Nippon Butsuri-Kagaku Kenkyukai / Physico-Chemical Society of Japan, c/o Research Institute for Production Development, 15 Simogamo Morimoto-cho, Sakyo-ku, Kyoto 606
T: (075) 7811107
Founded: 1926; Members: 360
Focus: Physics; Chem 07877

Nippon Byori Gakkai / Japanese Society of Pathology, 4F New Akamon Bldg, 2-40-9 Hongo Bunkyo-ku, Tokyo 113
Founded: 1911; Members: 4200
Gen Secr: R. Machinami
Focus: Pathology
Periodicals
Annual of Pathological Autopsy Cases in Japan
Pathologica Japonica (bi-monthly)
Transactions 07878

Nippon Chikusan Gakkai / Japanese Society of Zootechnical Science, 201, Nagatani Corporas, Ikenohata 2-9-4, Taito-ku, Tokyo 110
T: (03) 38288409; Fax: 38287649
Founded: 1924; Members: 2500
Pres: S. Sugano; Gen Secr: Y. Kanai
Focus: Zoology
Periodical
Animal Science and Technology (monthly) 07879

Nippon Chiri Gakkai / Assocation of Japanese Geographers, c/o Bldg of Academic Societies Centre, 2-4-16, Yayoi, Bunkyo-ku, Tokyo 113
T: (03) 38151912; Fax: 38151672
Founded: 1925; Members: 3000
Pres: K. Nakamura
Focus: Geography
Periodical
Geographical Review of Japan: Chirigaku Hyoron (monthly) 07880

Nippon Chishitsu Gakkai / Geological Society of Japan, Maruishi Bldg, 1-10-4 Kajicho, Chiyoda-ku, Tokyo 101
T: (03) 2527242; Fax: 52565676
Founded: 1893; Members: 5280
Pres: Hakuyu Okada
Focus: Geology
Periodical
Journal (monthly) 07881

Nippon Chô Gakkai / Ornithological Society of Japan, c/o Dept of Zoology, Faculty of Science, Osaka City University, 3-3-138 Sugimoto, Sumiyoshi-ku, Osaka 558
Founded: 1912; Members: 900
Pres: S. Yamagishi
Focus: Ornithology
Periodical
Japanese Journal of Ornithology (quarterly) 07882

Nippon Dai-Yonki Gakkai / Japan Association for Quaternary Research, c/o Business Center for Academic Societies, Honkomagome 5-16-9, Bunkyo-ku, Tokyo 113
T: (03) 58145801; Fax: 58145820
Founded: 1956; Members: 2000
Pres: K. Chinzei
Focus: Geology
Periodical
The Quaternary Research (quarterly) . . 07883

Nippon Denki Kyokai Chosabu Chosaka / The Japan Electric Association, Danki Bldg, 1-7-1 Yuraku-cho, Chiyoda-ku, Tokyo 100
T: (03) 2160551
Focus: Energy 07884

Nippon Denshi Kenbikyo Gakkai / Japanese Society of Electron Microscopy, c/o Business Centre for Academic Societies, 2-4-16 Yayoi, Bunkyo-ku, Tokyo 113
Founded: 1949; Members: 2690
Pres: K. Ogawa
Focus: Physics
Periodical
Journal (quarterly) 07885

Nippon Dobutsu Gakkai / The Zoological Society of Japan, Toshin Bldg, 2-27-2 Hongo, Bunkyo-ku, Tokyo 113
T: (03) 38145461; E-Mail: ny02-zsj@t3.rim.or.jp; Fax: 38145352
Founded: 1878; Members: 2680
Pres: Koscak Mayuyama
Focus: Zoology
Periodical
Zoological Science (bi-monthly) 07886

Nippon Dojo-Hiryo Gakkai / Japanese Society of Soil Science and Plant Nutrition, 26-10-202 Hongo, 2-chome, Bunkyo-ku, Tokyo
Founded: 1914; Members: 2300
Pres: T. Tadano
Focus: Agri
Periodical
Journal (bi-monthly) 07887

Nippon Dokumenesyon Kyokai / Japan Documentation Society, 5-7, Koisikaw 2, Bunkyo-ku, Tokyo 112
T: (03) 8133791
Founded: 1950; Members: 1200
Focus: Doc
Periodicals
Informant: Microfiche-Editon (semi-annually)
Journal (monthly) 07888

Nippon Dokyo Gakkai / Japan Society of Taoistic Research, c/o Dept of International Studies, Obirin University, 3758, Tokiwa-machi, Machioda, Tokyo 194-02
T: (0427) 972661
Founded: 1950; Members: 650
Pres: T. Noguchi
Focus: Ethnology; Rel & Theol
Periodical
The Journal of Eastern Religions (semi-annually) 07889

Nippon Eisei-Dobutsu Gakkai / Japanese Society of Medical Entomology and Zoology, c/o Business Center for Academic Societies, 5-16-9 Honkomagome, Bunkyo-ku, Tokyo 113
T: (03) 58145801; Fax: 58145820
Founded: 1943; Members: 750
Pres: Dr. Y. Wada
Focus: Vet Med; Zoology 07890

Nippon Engeki Gakkai / Japanese Society for Theatre Research, c/o Waseda University, 1-6-1 Nishi-Waseda, Shinjuku-ku, Tokyo
T: (0427) 398092; E-Mail: mori@lit.tamagawa.ac.jp; Fax: 398092
Founded: 1949; Members: 600
Pres: M. Mori; Gen Secr: T. Norizuki
Focus: Perf Arts
Periodical
Kiyo (annually) 07891

Nippon Gakushiin / Japan Academy, 7-32 Ueno Park, Taito-ku, Tokyo 110
T: (03) 38222101; Fax: 38222105
Founded: 1879; Members: 150
Pres: Prof. Yoshio Fujita; Gen Secr: Prof. Teiji Ichiko
Focus: Nat Sci
Periodicals
Nippon Gakusshiin Kiyo (3 times annually)
Proceedings (10 times annually) 07892

Nippon Gan Gakkai / Japanese Cancer Association, c/o Cancer Institute, Kami-Ikebukuro 1-37-1, Toshima-ku, Tokyo 170
T: (03) 39180111 ext 4231; Fax: 39185776
Founded: 1907; Members: 16980
Pres: Dr. Fumimato Takaku
Focus: Cell Biol & Cancer Res
Periodicals
Gann-Monograph on Cancer Research (irregularly)
Japanese Journal of Cancer Research (monthly) 07893

Nippon Ganka Gakkai / Japanese Ophthalmological Society, 2-4-11-402 Sarugaku-cho, Chiyoda-ku, Tokyo 101
Founded: 1897; Members: 8800
Pres: Yasuo Uemura
Focus: Ophthal
Periodical
Acta Societatis Ophthalmologicae Japonicae (monthly) 07894

Nippon Ganseki Kobutsu Kosho Gakkai / Japanese Association of Mineralogists, Petrologists and Economic Geologists, c/o Faculty of Science, Tohoku University, Aoba, Sendai 980
T: (022) 2243852; Fax: 2243852
Founded: 1928; Members: 1000
Focus: Geology; Mineralogy; Petrochem
Periodical
Journal of Mineralogy, Petrology and Economic Geology (monthly) 07895

Nippon Geka Gakkai / Japan Surgical Society, Hakuoh Bldg, 2-3-10, Koraku, Bunkyo-ku, Tokyo 101
Founded: 1899; Members: 37405
Pres: K. Isono
Focus: Surgery
Periodical
Journal (monthly) 07896

Nippon Gyosei Gakkai / Japanese Society for Public Administration, c/o Meiji University, Kanda-Surugadai 1-1, Chiyoda-ku, Tokyo
Founded: 1945; Members: 400
Pres: A. Sato
Focus: Business Admin
Periodical
Nenpo (annually) 07897

Nippon Hifuka Gakkai / Japanese Dermatological Association, 3-14-10 Hongo, Bunkyo-ku, Tokyo 113
T: (03) 38115099; Fax: 38126790
Founded: 1901; Members: 8140
Pres: S. Harada
Focus: Derm
Periodicals
The Journal of Dermatology (monthly)
Nihon Hifuka Gakkai Zasshi (14 times annually) 07898

Nippon Hikaku Bungakukai / Comparative Literature Society of Japan, c/o Aoyamagakiun University, Shibuya-ku, Tokyo 150
Founded: 1948; Members: 400
Pres: K. Nakajima
Focus: Lit
Periodicals
Bulletin (quarterly)
Journal (annually) 07899

Nippon Hinyoki-ka Gakkai / The Japanese Urological Association, Taisei Bldg, Hongo 3-14-10, Bunkyo-ku, Tokyo
T: (03) 38147921; Fax: 38144117
Founded: 1912; Members: 5780
Focus: Urology
Periodical
The Japanese Journal of Urology (13 times annually) 07900

Nippon Hoi Gakkai / Medico-Legal Society of Japan, c/o Dept of Forensic Medicine, Faculty of Medicine, University of Tokyo, 7-3-1 Hongo, Bunkyo-ku, Tokyo 113
T: (03) 58005416
Founded: 1914; Members: 1400
Pres: Shogo Misawa
Focus: Med; Law
Periodical
Journal (bi-monthly) 07901

Nippon Hoshakai Gakkai / Japan Association of Sociology of Law, c/o University of Tokyo, Hongo, Bunkyo-ku, Tokyo 113
Founded: 1947; Members: 800
Pres: N. Toshitani
Focus: Law; Sociology
Periodical
Sociology of Law (annually) 07902

Nippon Hoshasen Eikyo Gakkai / Japan Radiation Research Society, c/o National Institute of Radiological Sciences, 4-9-1 Anagawa, Inage-ku, Chiba 263
T: (0472) 2512111; Fax: 2569616
Founded: 1969; Members: 964
Pres: Akihiro Shima
Focus: Radiology
Periodical
Journal of Radiation Research (quarterly) 07903

Nippon Hotetsu Gakkai / Japanese Association for Legal Philosophy, c/o Faculty of Law, Kyoto University, Yoshida Honmachi, Sakyo-ku, Kyoto 606-01
T: (075) 7533204; Fax: 7533290

Founded: 1948; Members: 486
Pres: Prof. Shigeaki Tanaka
Focus: Philos; Law
Periodical
The Annals of Legal Philosophy (annually) 07904

Nippon Hotetsu Shika Gakkai / Japan Prosthodontic Society, c/o Koku Hoken Kyokai, 1-44-2 Komagome, Toshima-ku, Tokyo
Founded: 1931; Members: 4500
Pres: Tsuneo Tabata
Focus: Dent
Periodical
Journal of the Japan Prosthodontic Society (bi-monthly) 07905

Nippon Iden Gakkai / Genetics Society of Japan, c/o National Institute of Genetics, 1-111 Yata, Mishima 411
Founded: 1920; Members: 1510
Pres: M. Sekiguchi
Focus: Genetics 07906

Nippon Igaku Hoshasen Gakkai / Japan Radiological Society, Room 301, Akamon Habitation, 5-29-13, Hongo, Bunkyo-ku, Tokyo
T: (03) 8143077; Fax: 56844075
Founded: 1923; Members: 6000
Pres: Y. Onoyama
Focus: Radiology
Periodical
Nippon Acta Radiologca (monthly) . . . 07907

Nippon Imono Kyokai, 8-12-13 Ginza, Chuo-ku, Tokyo 104
T: (03) 5412758
Founded: 1932; Members: 7
Focus: Metallurgy 07908

Nippon Jibi-Inkoka Gakkai / The Oto-Rhino-Laryngological Society of Japan, c/o Chateau-Takanawa, 3-23-14 Takanawa, Minato-ku, Tokyo
T: (03) 34433085; Fax: 34433037
Founded: 1893; Members: 10000
Pres: Atsushi Komatsuzuki
Focus: Otorhinolaryngology
Periodical
Journal of Otolaryngology of Japan (monthly) 07909

Nippon Jidoseigyo Kyokai / Japan Association of Automatic Control Engineers, 14, Kawahara-cho, Yoshida, Sakyo-ku, Kyoto
Founded: 1957; Members: 1964
Focus: Eng
Periodical
Systems and Control (monthly) 07910

Nippon Jinrui Iden Gakkai / The Japan Society of Human Genetics, c/o Dept of Human Genetics, Tokyo Medical and Dental University, 1-5-45 Yushima, Bunkyo-ku, Tokyo 113
Founded: 1957; Members: 900
Pres: Dr. Ei Matsunaga; Gen Secr: Dr. Takashi Imamura
Focus: Genetics 07911

Nippon Jinruigaku Kai / Anthropological Society of Nippon, c/o Business Center for Academic Societies, 5-16-9 Honkomagome, Bunkyo-ku, Tokyo 113
T: (03) 58145801; Fax: 58145820
Founded: 1884; Members: 1050
Pres: Hidemi Ishida
Focus: Anthro
Periodical
Journal of the Anthropological Society of Nippon (quarterly) 07912

Nippon Junkan-ki Gakkai / Japanese Circulation Society, 14 Yoshida Kawahara-cho, Sakyo-ku, Kyoto 606
T: (075) 7518643; Fax: 7713060
Founded: 1935; Members: 19105
Gen Secr: T. Sugimoto
Focus: Med
Periodical
Japanese Circulation Journal (monthly) . 07913

Nippon Junkatsu Gakkai / Japan Society of Lubrication Engineers, Kikai Shinko Kaikan 407-2, 3-5-8 Shiba Koen, Minato-ku, Tokyo 105
T: (03) 4341926
Founded: 1956; Members: 2700
Focus: Med
Periodical
Journal (monthly) 07914

Nippon Kagaku-Gijutsu Joho Sentah / Japan Information Center of Science and Technology, Tokyo, POB 1478
Founded: 1957; Members: 330
Pres: M. Nakamura
Focus: Sci; Eng
Periodical
Journal of Information Processing and Management 07915

Nippon Kagaku Kyoiku Gakukai / Japan Society for Science Education, c/o National Institute for Educational Research, 6-5-22, Shimomeguro, Meguro-ku, Tokyo 153
Founded: 1977; Members: 1050
Pres: Dr. M. Oki
Focus: Educ
Periodicals
Journal (quarterly)
Letter (bi-monthly) 07916

Nippon Kagakukai / Chemical Society of Japan, 1-5 Kanda-Surugadai, Chiyoda-ku, Tokyo
Founded: 1878; Members: 38000
Pres: Hideki Sakurai
Focus: Chem
Periodicals
Bulletin (monthly)
Chemistry Letters
Kagaku to Kogyo
Nippon Kagaku Kaishi 07917

Nippon Kaibo Gakkai / Japanese Association of Anatomists, c/o Business Center for Academic Societies Japan, 5-16-9 Honkomagome, Bunkyo-ku, Tokyo 113
Founded: 1893; Members: 2700
Pres: Dr. Shigeo Uchino
Focus: Anat
Periodical
Acta Anatomica Nipponica (bi-monthly) . 07918

Nippon Kaiho Gakkai / Maritime Law Association of Japan, c/o Chuo University, Higashinakano, Hachioji-shi, Tokyo
Founded: 1950; Members: 165
Pres: T. Ishii
Focus: Law
Periodical
Report 07919

Nippon Kaisui Gakkai / Society of Sea Water Science, Japan, c/o Japan Salt Industry Association, 7-15-14, Roppongi, Minato-ku, Tokyo 106
T: (03) 4026414
Founded: 1950; Members: 485
Pres: Shoji Imura
Focus: Water Res 07920

Nippon Kaiyo Gakkai / The Oceanographic Society of Japan, MK Bldg 202, 1-6-14 Minamidai, Nakano-ku, Tokyo 164
T: (03) 33773951; Fax: 33789419
Founded: 1941; Members: 2044
Pres: K. Taira
Focus: Oceanography
Periodical
Journal of Oceanography (bi-monthly) . . 07921

Nippon Kango Kyokai / Japanese Nursing Assocation, 1-2-3 Umezono, Kiyoseshi, Tokyo 204
T: (0424) 927466
Founded: 1946
Focus: Med 07922

Nippon Kansenshoh Gakkai / Japanese Association for Infectious Diseases, 6F Sankei 8 Bldg, 1-8-7 Ebisu, Shibuya-ku, Tokyo 150
T: (03) 34735095; Fax: 34421196
Founded: 1926; Members: 5300
Pres: Kaoru Shimada
Focus: Med
Periodical
Journal (monthly) 07923

Nippon Kazan Gakkai / Volcanological Society of Japan, Earthquake Research Institute, University of Tokyo, 1-1-1, Yayoi-cho, Bunkyo-ku, Tokyo 113
T: (03) 8137421
Founded: 1932; Members: 1090
Pres: K. Aoki
Focus: Geophys
Periodicals
Bulletin (quarterly)
Bulletin of Volcanic Eruptions (annually) . 07924

Nippon Keiei Gakkai / Japan Society of Business Administration, Institute of Business Research, Hitotsubashi University, 2-1 Naka, Kunitachi, Tokyo 186
T: (0425) 721101 ext 3782
Founded: 1926; Members: 2030
Pres: A. Mori
Focus: Business Admin
Periodical
Keieigaku Ronshu (annually) 07925

Nippon Keiho Gakkai / Criminal Law Society of Japan, c/o University of Tokyo, Hongo, Bunkyo-ku, Tokyo
Founded: 1949; Members: 1000
Pres: S. Suzuki
Focus: Criminology
Periodical
Journal (quarterly) 07926

Nippon Keizai Seisaku Gakkai / Japan Economic Policy Association, c/o Keio University, Mita, Minato-ku, Tokyo 108
Founded: 1940; Members: 862
Pres: T. Yamanaka
Focus: Poli Sci
Periodical
Annals 07927

Nippon Kekkaku-byo Gakkai / Japanese Society for Tuberculosis, 3-1-24 Matsuyama, Kiyose-shi, Tokyo 204
Founded: 1925; Members: 3000
Pres: Dr. T. Aoyagi
Focus: Pulmon Dis
Periodical
Kekkaku (monthly) 07928

Nippon Kessho Gakkai / Crystallographic Society of Japan, 8F Cosmos Hongo Bldg, 4-1-4 Hongo, Bunkyo-ku, Tokyo 113
T: (03) 38158514; Fax: 38158529
Founded: 1950; Members: 1000
Pres: H. Iwasaki
Focus: Mineralogy
Periodical
Journal (bi-monthly) 07929

Nippon Ketsueki Gakkai / Japan Haematological Society, c/o Dept of Hematology and Oncology, Graduate School of Medicine, Kyoto University, Kawahara, Shogoin, Sakyo-ku, Kyoto 606
T: (075) 7518982; E-Mail: ijh-ind@umin.u-tokyo.ac.jp; Fax: 7520761
Founded: 1937; Members: 5518
Pres: F. Takaku
Focus: Hematology
Periodical
International Journal of Hematology (8 times annually) 07930

Nippon Kikan-Shokudo-ka Gakkai / Japan Bronco-Esophagological Society, 5F Hakuo Bldg, 2-3-10, Koraku, Bunkyo-ku, Tokyo 112
T: (03) 38183030; Fax: 38152810
Founded: 1949; Members: 3600
Pres: Dr. Y. Murakami
Focus: Pulmon Dis
Periodical
Journal (bi-monthly) 07931

Nippon Kin Gakkai / Mycological Society of Japan, c/o Business Center for Academic Societies, 5-16-9 Honkomagome, Bunkyo-ku, Tokyo 113
T: (03) 58145801; Fax: 58145820
Founded: 1956; Members: 1600
Pres: Makoto Miyaji
Focus: Bio 07932

Nippon Kinzoku Gakkai / Japan Institute of Metals, Aoba Aramaki, Aoba-ku, Sendai 980
T: (022) 2233685; Fax: 2236312
Founded: 1937; Members: 11000
Pres: Hiroshi Oikawa
Focus: Metallurgy
Periodicals
Bulletin (monthly)
Journal (monthly)
Transactions (monthly) 07933

Nippon Kisei-chu Gakkai / Japanese Society of Parasitology, c/o Institute of Medical Science, University of Tokyo, Minato-ku, Tokyo 108
Founded: 1926; Members: 1000
Gen Secr: Prof. S. Kojima
Focus: Microbio
Periodical
Japanese Journal of Parasitology (bi-monthly) 07934

Nippon Kisho Gakkai / Meteorological Society of Japan, c/o Japan Meteorological Agency, 1-3-4 Ote-machi, Chiyoda-ku, Tokyo 100
Founded: 1882; Members: 4300
Pres: T. Asai
Focus: Geophys
Periodicals
Journal of the Meteorological Society of Japan (bi-monthly)
Papers in Meteorology and Geophysics (quarterly)
Tenki (monthly) 07935

Nippon Kogakukai / Japan Federation of Engineering Societies, Nogizaka Bldg, 9-6-41 Akasaka, Minato-ku, Tokyo 107
Founded: 1879; Members: 64
Focus: Eng
Periodical
Journal (quarterly) 07936

Nippon Kokai Gakkai / Japan Institute of Navigation, c/o Tokyo University of Mercantile Marine, 2-1-6 Etchujima, Koto-ku, Tokyo 135
T: (03) 36303093; Fax: 36303093
Founded: 1948; Members: 1047
Pres: Prof. T. Yamada; Gen Secr: Prof. S. Kuwashima
Focus: Navig
Periodicals
Journal (semi-annually)
Navigation (quarterly) 07937

Nippon Kokogaku Kyokai / Japanese Archaeological Association, 5-15-5 Hirai, Edogawa-ku, Tokyo 132
T: (03) 36186608
Founded: 1948; Members: 3200
Pres: T. Iwasaki
Focus: Archeol 07938

Nippon Koku Uchu Gakkai / Japan Society for Aeronautical and Space Sciences, 18-2 Shinbashi 1-chome, Minato-ku, Tokyo 105
T: (03) 35010463
Founded: 1934; Members: 4400
Pres: Prof. K. Kato
Focus: Eng
Periodicals
Journal (monthly)
Transactions (quarterly) 07939

Nippon Kokusai Seiji Gakkai / Japan Association of International Relations, c/o Hosei University, Fujimi-cho, Chiyoda-ku, Tokyo
Founded: 1956; Members: 510
Pres: H. Kamikawa
Focus: Poli Sci
Periodical
International Relations (3 times annually) 07940

Nippon Kontyu Gakkai / Entomological Society of Japan, c/o Dept of Zoology, National Science Museum (Natural History), 3-23-1 Hyakunin-cho, Shinjuku, Tokyo 160
T: (03) 3642311
Founded: 1917; Members: 1200
Focus: Entomology
Periodical
Kontyu (quarterly) 07941

Nippon Koseibutsu Gakkai / Palaeontological Society of Japan, c/o Business Center for Academic Societies, Honkomagome 5-16-9, Bunky-ku, Tokyo 113
Founded: 1935; Members: 1000
Pres: N. Ikeya; Gen Secr: H. Kitazato
Focus: Paleontology
Periodicals
Fossils (semi-annually)
Paleontological Research (quarterly)
Special Papers (annually) 07942

Nippon Koshu-Eisei Kyokai / Japan Public Health Association, Koei Bldg, 29-8, Shinjuku 1-chome, Shinjuku-ku, Tokyo
Founded: 1883; Members: 5000
Pres: M. Seijo
Focus: Public Health
Periodicals
Japanese Journal of Public Health (monthly)
Public Health Information (monthly) . . . 07943

Nippon Kumo Gakkai / Arachnological Society of Japan, c/o Biological Laboratory, Otemon Gakuin University, 2-1-15 Nishi-Ai, Ibaraki, Osaka 567
T: (0726) 435421; Fax: 435427
Founded: 1936; Members: 340
Pres: Dr. Y. Nishikawa
Focus: Bio
Periodical
Acta Arachnologica (semi-annually) . . . 07944

Nippon Mokuzai Gakkai / Japan Wood Research Society, 21-4-407, Hongo 6-chome, Bunkyo-ku, Tokyo 113
T: (03) 38160396; Fax: 38186568
Founded: 1955; Members: 2240
Pres: Dr. Ken Okano
Focus: Forestry
Periodical
Mokuzai Gakkaishi: Journal of the Japan Wood Reseach Society (monthly) 07945

Nippon Naibumpigaku-Kai Tobu-bukai / Eastern Branch of the Japan Endocrinological Society, c/o Dept of Urology, School of Medicine, Gumma University, Maebashi
Founded: 1954; Members: 1300
Pres: K. Shida
Focus: Endocrinology 07946

Nippon Nensho Gakkai / Combustion Society of Japan, c/o Dept of Reaction Chemistry, Faculty of Engineering, University of Tokyo, 7 Hongo, Bunkyo-ku, Tokyo 113
Fax: (03) 356842509
Founded: 1953; Members: 580
Focus: Chem; Eng
Periodical
Nensho Kenkyu (quarterly) 07947

Nippon Nensho Kenkyukai / The Japanese Section of the Combustion Institute / Combustion Society of Japan, c/o Kyoto Daigaku Kogakubu, Yoshida, Sakyo-ku, Kyoto 606
Founded: 1954; Members: 400
Focus: Eng
Periodical
Nensho-Kenkyu (3 times annually) . . . 07948

Nippon Netsushori Gijutsu Kyokai / The Japan Society for Heat Treatment, Shinsen Bldg 4F, 8-2 Shinsen, Shibuya-ku, Tokyo 150
T: (03) 4617116
Focus: Energy
Periodical
Netsu Shori: Journal of the Japan Society for Heat Treatment (bi-monthly) 07949

Nippon No-Shinkei Gek Gakkai / The Japan Neurosurgical Society, Akamon-mae Iwata Bldg, 5-27-8 Hongo, Bunkyo-ku, Tokyo 113
T: (03) 38126226; E-Mail: jns@ssij4u.ot.jp;
Fax: 38122090
Founded: 1948; Members: 6686 5905
Pres: T. Hayakawa; Gen Secr: Jakaaki Kirino
Focus: Neurology; Surgery
Periodical
Neurologia medico-chirurgica II (monthly) . 07950

Nippon Nogei Kagaku Kai / Japan Society for Bioscience, Biotechnology and Agrochemistry, 2-4-16 Yayoi, Bunkyo-ku, Tokyo 113
Fax: (03) 38151920
Founded: 1924; Members: 15170
Pres: Teruhiko Beppu
Focus: Agri; Chem; Bio
Periodicals
Bioscience, Biotechnology and Biochemistry (monthly)
Journal of the Japan Society for Bioscience, Biotechnology and Agrochemistry (monthly) 07951

Nippon Nogyo-Kisho Gakkai / Society of Agricultural Meteorology of Japan, c/o Dept of Agricultural Engineering, Faculty of Agriculture, University of Tokyo, Yayoi 1-1-1, Bunkyo-ku, Tokyo 113
T: (03) 38122111 ext 5355

Founded: 1942; Members: 1169
Focus: Agri; Geophys
Periodical
Nogyo-Kisho: Journal of Agricultural Meteorology (quarterly) 07952

Nippon Noritsu Kyokai Shiryoshitsu / Japan Management Association, Kyoritsu Bldg, 3-1-22 Shiba-koen, Minato-ku, Tokyo 105
T: (03) 4346211
Focus: Business Admin 07953

Nippon Ongaku Gakkai / Musicological Society of Japan, c/o Tokyo National University of Fine Arts and Music, Ueno-Park, Taito-ku, Tokyo 110
T: (03) 56857500
Founded: 1952; Members: 1350
Pres: I. Sumikura
Focus: Music
Periodical
Ongaku Gaku: Journal of the Musicological Society of Japan (quarterly) 07954

Nippon Onkyo Gakkai / Acoustical Society of Japan, Ikeda Bldg, 2-7-7 Yoyogi, Shibuya-ku, Tokyo 151
T: (03) 33791200; Fax: 33791456
Founded: 1936; Members: 3600
Pres: T. Sone
Focus: Acoustics
Periodicals
Journal (monthly)
The Journal (E): English Edition (bi-monthly)
Reports of Spring and Autumn Meetings (semi-annually) 07955

Nippon Onsei Gakkai / Phonetic Society of Japan, 1-3-1 Sarugaku, Chiyoda-ku, Tokyo 101
T: (03) 32921718
Founded: 1926; Members: 780
Pres: M. Sugito
Focus: Ling
Periodical
Bulletin (3 times annually) 07956

Nippon Orient Gakkai / Society for Near Eastern Studies in Japan, c/o Tokyo Tenrikyokan, 1-9 Nishiki-cho, Kanda, Chiyoda-ku, Tokyo 101
Founded: 1954; Members: 910
Pres: Dr. Namio Egami
Focus: Ethnology
Periodical
Bulletin of the Society for Near Eastern Studies in Japan 07957

Nippon Oyo-Dobutsu-Konchu Gakkai / Japanese Society of Applied Entomology and Zoology, c/o Japan Plant Protection Association, 1-11-43 Komagome, Toshima-ku, Tokyo 170
Founded: 1957; Members: 2000
Pres: Yoshio Tamaki
Focus: Entomology; Zoology
Periodicals
Applied Entomology and Zoology (quarterly)
Japanese Journal of Applied Entomology and Zoology (quarterly) 07958

Nippon Rai Gakkai / Japanese Leprosy Association, 4-2-1, Aoba-cho, Higashimurayama-shi, Tokyo 189
T: (0423) 918211; Fax: 949092
Founded: 1927; Members: 355
Pres: Toshiharu Ozawa
Focus: Derm
Periodical
La Lepro (bi-monthly) 07959

Nippon Rikusui Gakkai / Japanese Society of Limnology, c/o Faculty of Education, Shiga University, 2-5-1 Hiratsu, Otsu 520
T: (0775) 377735; Fax: 377840
Founded: 1931; Members: 1300
Pres: Prof. T. Okino; Gen Secr: Prof. S. Endoh
Focus: Hydrology; Bio; Chem; Physics
Periodical
Rikusui-gaku Zasshi: Japanese Journal of Limnology (quarterly) 07960

Nippon Ringakukai / The Japanese Forestry Society, c/o Japan Forest Technical Association, 7 Rokubancho, Chiyoda-ku, Tokyo 102
T: (03) 32612766; Fax: 32612766
Founded: 1914; Members: 2800
Pres: Y. Kohohira; Gen Secr: T. Inamura
Focus: Forestry
Periodicals
Journal of Forestry Research (bi-monthly)
Transactions of the Japanese Forestry Society (annually) 07961

Nippon Rodo-ho Gakkai / Japanese Labour Law Association, c/o University of Tokyo, 7-3-1 Hongo, Bunkyo-ku, Tokyo
T: (03) 38122111 ext 3243; Fax: 38167375
Founded: 1950; Members: 595
Pres: Y. Yamamoto
Focus: Sci
Periodical
Journal (semi-annually) 07962

Nippon Rosiya Bungakkai / Russian Literary Society in Japan, c/o Baba-ken, Tokyo Institute of Technology, 2-12-1, O-okayama, Meguro-ku, Tokyo 152
Members: 380
Pres: Masanobu Togo; Gen Secr: T. Egawa
Focus: Ling; Lit
Periodical
Bulletin 07963

Nippon Saikingakkai / Japanese Society for Bacteriology, c/o Oral Health Association of Japan, 1-44-2 Komagome, Toshima-ku, Tokyo 170
Founded: 1927; Members: 3400
Pres: Dr. Y. Takeda
Focus: Sci
Periodical
Japanese Journal of Bacteriology, Microbiology and Immunology 07964

Nippon Sakumotsu Gakkai / Crop Science Society of Japan, c/o Faculty of Agriculture, University of Tokyo, Hongo, Bunkyo-ku, Tokyo 113
Founded: 1927; Members: 1900
Pres: R. Ishii
Focus: Agri 07965

Nippon Sanka-Fujinka Gakkai / Japan Society of Obstetrics and Gynaecology, Hoken Kaikan Bldg, 1-1 Sadohara-cho, Ichigaya, Shinjuku-ku, Tokyo 162
Founded: 1949; Members: 16000
Pres: Prof. Y. Takeda
Focus: Gynecology
Periodical
Acta Obstetrica et Gynaecologica Japonica (monthly) 07966

Nippon Sanshi Gakkai / Japanese Society of Sericultural Science, c/o National Institute of Sericultural and Entomological Science, Tsukuba, Ibaraki 305
T: (0298) 386056
Founded: 1930; Members: 1127
Pres: A. Shimazaki
Focus: Agri 07967

Nippon Seibutsu Kankyo Chosetsu Kenkyukai / Japanese Society of Environmental Control in Biology, c/o Faculty of Agriculture, University of Tokyo, 1-1-1 Yayoi, Bunkyo-ku, Tokyo 113
T: (03) 38132437
Founded: 1963; Members: 1090
Pres: T. Takakura
Focus: Bio; Ecology 07968

Nippon Seibutsuchiri Gakkai / Biogeographical Society of Japan, 2-26-12 Sendagi, Bunkyo-ku, Tokyo 113
T: (03) 38280445
Founded: 1928; Members: 300
Pres: Seiroku Sakai
Focus: Geography
Periodical
Bulletin 07969

Nippon Seikei Geka Gakkai / Japanese Orthopaedic Association, 40-17, Hongo 2-chome, Bunkyo-ku, Tokyo 113
Fax: (03) 38182337
Founded: 1926; Members: 16545
Pres: Takahide Turokawa
Focus: Orthopedics
Periodical
Journal of Orthopaedic Science (bi-monthly) 07970

Nippon Seiri Gakkai / Physiological Society of Japan, Fuse Bldg, Hongo 3-30-10, Bunkyo-ku, Tokyo 113
Founded: 1922; Members: 3700
Pres: Masao Ito
Focus: Physiology
Periodical
Journal 07971

Nippon Seitai Gakkai / The Ecological Society of Japan, c/o Dept of Biology, University of Tokyo, Komaba, Meguro-ku, Tokyo 153
T: (03) 54544322; E-Mail: cmatsu@komaba.ecc.u-tokyo.ac.jp; Fax: 54544322
Founded: 1954; Members: 2600
Gen Secr: Keiichi Masuko
Focus: Ecology
Periodicals
Ecological Research (3 times annually)
Japanese Journal of Ecology (3 times annually) 07972

Nippon Seiyoshi Gakkai / Japanese Society of Western History, c/o Osaka University, 1-1 Toyonaka-shi, Machikaneyama-cho, Osaka 560
Founded: 1948; Members: 800
Pres: Prof. S. Aisaka
Focus: Hist
Periodical
Studies in Western History (quarterly) . . 07973

Nippon Seizi Gakkai / Japanese Political Science Association, c/o Faculty of Law, Rikkyo University, 3-34-1, Nishi-Ikebukuro, Toshima-ku, Tokyo 171
Members: 820
Pres: Jiro Kamishima
Focus: Poli Sci 07974

Nippon Seramikkusu Kyokai / The Ceramic Society of Japan, 22-17, 2-chome, Hyakunin-cho, Shinjuku-ku, Tokyo 169
Fax: (03) 33625714
Founded: 1891; Members: 7500
Pres: Soga. N.; Gen Secr: Y. Suzuki
Focus: Materials Sci
Periodicals
Bulletin of the Ceramic Society of Japan (monthly)
Journal of the Ceramic Society of Japan (monthly) 07975

Nippon Shakai Gakkai / Japanese Sociological Society, c/o Dept of Sociology, Faculty of Letters, University of Tokyo, 7-3-1 Hongo, Bunkyo-ku, Tokyo
Founded: 1923; Members: 2500
Pres: Tamito Yoshida
Focus: Sociology
Periodicals
International Journal of Japanese Sociology (annually)
Shakaigaku Hyóron: Japanese Sociological Review (quarterly) 07976

Nippon Shakai Shinri Gakkai / Japanese Society of Social Psychology, c/o Dept of Social Psychology, Tokyo University, Hongo, Bunkyo-ku, Tokyo 113
Founded: 1960; Members: 1400
Pres: K. Hirota
Focus: Psych
Periodical
Bulletin (quarterly) 07977

Nippon Shashin Gakkai / Society of Photographic Science and Technology of Japan, c/o Tokyo Polytechnic Institute, 2-9-5 Hon-cho, Nakano-ku, Tokyo 164
Founded: 1925; Members: 1550
Pres: T. Wakabayashi
Focus: Eng
Periodical
Journal (bi-monthly) 07978

Nippon Shashin Sokuryo Gakkai / Japan Society of Photogrammetry and Remote Sensing, Daichi Honan Bldg 502, 2-8-17 Minami Ikebukuro, Toshima-ku, Tokyo 171
Fax: (03) 39847402
Founded: 1962; Members: 1038
Focus: Surveying
Periodical
Journal (quarterly) 07979

Nippon Shiho Gakkai / Japan Association of Private Law, c/o University of Tokyo, Hongo, Bunkyo-ku, Tokyo 113
Founded: 1948; Members: 688
Pres: T. Suzuki
Focus: Law
Periodical
Journal (annually) 07980

Nippon Shika Hoshasen Gakkai / Japanese Society of Dental Radiology, c/o Tokyo Dental College, 2-9-18, Misakicho, Chiyoda-ku, Tokyo
Founded: 1951; Members: 319
Focus: Radiology
Periodical
Dental Radiology (annually) 07981

Nippon Shika Hozon Gakkai / Japanese Society of Conservative Dentistry, c/o Tokyo Dental University, 1 Misaki-cho Kanda, Chiyoda-ku, Tokyo
Founded: 1955; Members: 826
Pres: E. Sekine
Focus: Dent
Periodical
Journal (semi-annually) 07982

Nippon Shika Igakkai / Japanese Association for Dental Science, 4-1-20 Kudan-kita, Chiyoda-ku, Tokyo
T: (03) 32629214; Fax: 32629885
Founded: 1949; Members: 80000
Pres: Prof. H. Sekine
Focus: Dent
Periodicals
Dentistry in Japan (annually)
Journal (annually) 07983

Nippon Shimbun Gakkai / Japan Society for Studies in Journalism and Mass Communication, c/o Institute of Journalism and Communication Studies, University of Tokyo, 7-3-1 Hongo, Bunkyo-ku, Tokyo 113
T: (03) 8122111 ext 5921
Founded: 1951; Members: 830
Pres: A. Haruhara
Focus: Journalism
Periodical
Japanese Journalism Review (annually) . 07984

Nippon Shinkei Gakkai / Japanese Society of Neurology, Ichimaru Bldg, 2-31-21 Yushima, Bunkyo-ku, Tokyo 113
T: (03) 8151080; Fax: 8151931
Founded: 1960; Members: 6900
Pres: Nobuo Yanagisawa
Focus: Neurology
Periodical
Rinsho Shinkei: Clinical Neurology (monthly) 07985

Nippon Shinkeikagaku Gakkai / Japan Neuroscience Society, c/o Business Center for Academic Societies, 5-16-9 Honkomagome, Bunkyo-ku, Tokyo 113
Founded: 1974; Members: 2750
Pres: Masao Ito
Focus: Neurology
Periodicals
Neuroscience News (quarterly)
Neuroscience Research (monthly) . . . 07986

Nippon Shogyo Gakkai / Japan Society of Commercial Sciences, c/o Meiji University, 1-1 Surugadai, Kanda, Chiyoda-ku, Tokyo 101
Founded: 1951; Members: 429
Pres: K. Fukuda
Focus: Business Admin 07987

Nippon Shokaki-byo Gakkai / Japanese Society of Gastroenterology, Ginza Orient Bldg, Ginza 8-9-13, Chuo-ku, Tokyo 104
T: (03) 35734297; Fax: 32892359
Founded: 1899; Members: 24000
Pres: T. Takemoto
Focus: Gastroenter
Periodicals
Gastroenterologia Japonica (bi-monthly)
Nihon Shokaki-byo Gakkai Zasshi (monthly) 07988

Nippon Shokubutsu-Byori Gakkai / Phytopathological Society of Japan, Shokubo Bldg, 1-43-11, Toshima-ku, Tokyo 170
T: (03) 39436021; Fax: 39436021
Founded: 1916; Members: 1880
Pres: T. Tsuchizaki
Focus: Crop Husb
Periodical
Annals of the Phytopathological Society of Japan (bi-monthly) 07989

Nippon Shokubutsu Gakkai / Botanical Society of Japan, Toshin Bldg, 2-27-2 Hongo, Bunkyo-ku, Tokyo
T: (03) 38145675; Fax: 38145461
Founded: 1882; Members: 2300
Pres: K. Iwatsuki
Focus: Botany
Periodical
Journal of Plant Research (quarterly) . . 07990

Nippon Shokubutsu Seiri Gakkai / Japanese Society of Plant Physiologists, Shimotachiuri Ogawa Higashi, Kamikyo-ku, Kyoto 602
T: (075) 4153661; E-Mail: jspp@nacos.com; Fax: 4153662
Founded: 1959; Members: 2990
Pres: Hiroh Shibaoka; Gen Secr: Moritoshi Iino
Focus: Botany
Periodical
Plant and Cell Physiology (monthly) . . 07991

Nippon Sokuchi Gakkai / Geodetic Society of Japan, c/o Geogaphical Survey Institute, 1 Kitazato, Tsukuba-shi, Ibaraki 305
T: (0298) 641111; E-Mail: geod-soc@vldb.gsi-mc.go.jp; Fax: 641802
Founded: 1954; Members: 600
Pres: T. Tanaka
Focus: Surveying
Periodical
Journal of the Geodetic Society of Japan (quarterly) 07992

Nippon Sugaku Kai / Mathematical Society of Japan, 25-9-203 Hongo 4-chome, Bunkyo-ku, Tokyo 113
Founded: 1877; Members: 5000
Pres: Kazuo Okamoto
Focus: Math
Periodicals
Japanese Journal of Mathematics (semi-annually)
Journal of the Mathematical Society of Japan (quarterly)
Publications of the Mathematical Society of Japan (irregularly)
Sugaku (quarterly) 07993

Nippon Sugaku Kyoiku Gakkai / Japan Society of Mathematical Education, Koishikawa, POB 18, Tokyo 112
T: (03) 9462267
Founded: 1919; Members: 3394
Pres: Prof. Y. Sugiyama
Focus: Math; Educ
Periodicals
Journal (monthly)
Report on Mathematical Education (semi-annually)
Supplementary Issue 07994

Nippon Suisan Gakkai / Japanese Society of Fisheries Science, c/o Tokyo University of Fisheries, 4-5-7 Konan, Minato-ku, Tokyo 108
T: (03) 34712165; Fax: 34712054
Founded: 1932; Members: 4790
Pres: Prof. K. Hashimoto
Focus: Fisheries
Periodical
Bulletin: Nippon Suisan Gakkaishi (bi-monthly) 07995

Nippon Syoyakugakkai / Japanese Society of Pharmacognosy, c/o Business Centre for Academic Societies, 4-16 Yayoi 2-chome, Bunkyo-ku, Tokyo 113
T: (03) 8151903
Founded: 1946; Members: 1027
Focus: Pharmacol
Periodical
Japanese Journal of Pharmacognosy (quarterly) 07996

Nippon Taiiku Gakkai / Japanese Society of Physical Education, c/o School of Physical Education, University of Tokyo, Hongo 7-3-1, Bunkyo-ku, Tokyo 113
Founded: 1950; Members: 2315
Pres: M. Matsui
Focus: Sports
Periodicals
Journal of Health and Physical Education (monthly)
Research Journal (quarterly) 07997

Nippon Tekko Kyokai / The Iron and Steel Institute of Japan, Keidanren Kaikan, 9-4, Ohtemachi 1-chome, Chiyoda-ku, Tokyo 100
T: (03) 32796021; Fax: 32451355
Founded: 1915; Members: 10160
Pres: Tadayoshi Noda; Gen Secr: Jin Shimada
Focus: Metallurgy
Periodicals
Ferrum (monthly)
ISIJ International (monthly)
Tetsu-to-Hagane (monthly) 07998

Nippon Tonyo-byo Gakkai / Japan Diabetes Society, 403 Hongo Sky Bldg, 3-38-11 Hongo, Bunkyo-ku, Tokyo 113
Founded: 1958; Members: 8500
Pres: Yasuo Akanuma
Focus: Diabetes
Periodical
The Journal of the Japan Diabetes Society 07999

Nippon Toshi Keikaku Gakkai / City Planning Institute of Japan, 6F Ichibancho-West Bldg, 10 Ichibancho, Chiyoda-ku, Tokyo 102
Founded: 1951; Members: 5322
Pres: Kazuo Yoda
Focus: Urban Plan
Periodical
City Planning Review (bi-monthly) . . . 08000

Nippon Toshokan Gakkai / Japan Society of Library Science, c/o Faculty of Sociology, Toyo University, 28-20 Hakusan 5-chome, Bunkyo-ku, Tokyo 112
T: (03) 39457444
Founded: 1953; Members: 570
Pres: Masao Nagasawa; Gen Secr: Shinichi Toda
Focus: Libraries & Bk Sci
Periodicals
Annals of the Japan Society of Library Science (quarterly)
Bibliography of Library and Information Science (annually) 08001

Nippon Tribologi Gakkai / Japanese Society of Tribologists, c/o Kikai Shinko Kaikan, No 407-2, 3-5-8 Shibakoen, Minato-ku, Tokyo 105
T: (03) 34341926; Fax: 34343556
Founded: 1956; Members: 3044
Pres: K. Nakajima
Focus: Eng
Periodical
Tribologists (monthly) 08002

Nippon Uirusu Gakkai / Society of Japanese Virologists, c/o Business Center for Academic Societies, 5-16-9 Honkomagome, Bunkyo-ku, Tokyo 113
Founded: 1953; Members: 3000
Pres: Dr. H. Yoshikura
Focus: Med 08003

Nippon Yakugaku-Kai / The Pharmaceutical Society of Japan, 12-15, Shibuya 2-chome, Shibuya-ku, Tokyo 150
T: (03) 34063321; E-Mail: koho_win@pharm.or.jp; Fax: 34981835
Founded: 1881; Members: 21541
Gen Secr: Kishino Masaaki
Focus: Pharmacol; Chem
Periodicals
Biological Pharmaceutical Bulletin (monthly)
Chemical Pharmaceutical Bulletin (monthly)
Eiseikagaku (bi-monthly)
Farumashia (monthly)
Yakugaku Zasshi (monthly) 08004

Nogyo-Doboku Gakkai / Japanese Society of Irrigatin, Drainage and Reclamation Engineering, Nogyo Doboku-Kaikan, 34-4 Shinbashi 5-chome, Tokyo 105
T: (03) 34363418; Fax: 34358494
Founded: 1929; Members: 13000
Pres: Prof. Masashi Nakano
Focus: Sci
Periodicals
Journal (monthly)
Transactions (bi-monthly) 08005

Nogyo-Ho Gakkai / Japan Agricultural Law Association, c/o Faculty of Law, University of Nihon, Chiyoda-ku, Tokyo 101
Founded: 1956; Members: 200
Pres: T. Ogura
Focus: Agri
Periodical
Nogyo-ho Kenkyu (annually) 08006

Nogyokikai Gakkai / Society of Agricultural Machinery, c/o BRAIN, 1-40-2 Nisshin-cho, Omiya, Saitama 331
Founded: 1937; Members: 1677
Pres: O. Kitani
Focus: Eng
Periodical
Journal (irregularly) 08007

Okinawa Kyokai Chosa Engoka, Gloria Bldg, 3-6-15 Kasumigaseki, Chiyoda-ku, Tokyo 100
T: (03) 5800641
Focus: Poli Sci 08008

Oyo-buturi Gakkai (JJAP) / Japan Society of Applied Physics, Kikai-Shinko Bldg, 3-5-8 Shiba-Koen, Minato-ku, Tokyo 105
Founded: 1932; Members: 9000
Focus: Physics
Periodicals
JJAP (monthly)
Oyo-buturi 08009

Raten Amerika Kyokai Kenkyubu / Latin-American Association, Dai-2 Jingumae Bldg, 2-6-14 Jingumae, Shibuya-ku, Tokyo 150
T: (03) 4032661
Focus: Econ; Law 08010

Riron Keiryo Keizai Gakkai / Japan Association of Economics and Econometrics, c/o Institute of Statistical Research, 1-18-16 Shinbashi, Minato-ku, Tokyo 105
Fax: (03) 35952220
Founded: 1934; Members: 2250
Pres: M. Aoki
Focus: Econ 08011

Rissho Koseikai / Rissho Koseikai Fuzoku Kosei Toshokan, Gyogakuen Bldg, 1-2-8 Wada, Suginami-ku, Tokyo 166
T: (03) 3840111
Focus: Rel & Theol 08012

San-yo Gijutsu Shinkokai / Sanyo Association for Advancement of Science and Technology, 16-1-1 Hon-machi, Kurashiki-shi, Okayama-ken 710
T: (0846) 226655
Focus: Sci; Eng 08013

Sapporo Norin Gakkai / Sapporo Society of Agriculture and Fisheries, c/o Faculty of Agriculture, Hokkaido University, Kita-ku, kita 9, Nishi 9, Sapporo 060
T: (011) 7162111; Fax: 7160879
Founded: 1908; Members: 700
Pres: Dr. Chosei Shichinohe
Focus: Forestry; Agri
Periodical
Journal (irregularly) 08014

Seisan Gijutsu Kenkyusho / Institute of Industrial Science, c/o University of Tokyo, 7-22-1 Roppongi, Minato-ku, Tokyo 106
T: (03) 34026231; Fax: 34025078
Founded: 1949
Pres: Prof. Dr. M. Suzuki
Focus: Business Admin
Periodical
Report (6-8 times annually) 08015

Seito Kogyokai Jimubu Chosaka / Japan Sugar Refiners' Assocation, 5-7, Samban-cho, Chiyoda-ku, Tokyo 102
T: (03) 2620176
Focus: Agri; Econ 08016

Sekiyu Gijutsu Kyokai, Keidanren Kaikan, 1-9-4 Otemachi, Chiyoda-ku, Tokyo 100
Founded: 1933
Focus: Eng 08017

Sekiyu Remmei Kohobu Shiryoka / Petroleum Association of Japan, Keidanren Bldg, 1-9-4 Otemachi, Chiyoda-ku, Tokyo 100
T: (03) 32793816; E-Mail: pajpr@mars.dtinet.or.jp; Fax: 32464740
Founded: 1955; Members: 24
Pres: Yuji Idemitsu; Gen Secr: Isamu Noto
Focus: Petrochem 08018

Sen-i Gakkai / Society of Fibre Science and Technology, 3-3-9-208 Kamiosaki, Shinagawa-ku, Tokyo 141
Founded: 1943; Members: 3000
Pres: H. Inagaki
Focus: Eng
Periodical
Journal (monthly) 08019

Senshokutai Gakkai, c/o International Christian University, 1500 Ozawa, Mitaka-shi, Tokyo 181
Founded: 1949
Focus: Bio 08020

Shakai Keizaishi Gakkai, c/o Dept of Economics, Sophia University, Kioi-cho, Chiyoda-ku, Tokyo 102
T: (03) 32383090; Fax: 32383090
Founded: 1930; Members: 1179
Focus: Hist; Econ
Periodical
Shakai-Keizai-Shigaku (bi-monthly) . . . 08021

Shakai Seisaku Gakkai, c/o Hosei Daigaku Ohara Shakai Mondai Kenkyusho, 2-17-1 Fujimi-cho, Chiyoda-ku, Tokyo 102
Founded: 1950
Focus: Poli Sci 08022

Shigaku-kai / Historical Society of Japan, c/o Faculty of Letters, University of Tokyo, Hongo, Bunkyo-ku, Tokyo 113
Founded: 1889; Members: 2470
Pres: O. Naruse
Focus: Hist
Periodical
Shigaku-Zasshi 08023

Shigaku Kenkyukai, c/o Kyoto Daigaku Bungakubu, Yoshida Honmachi, Sakyo-ku, Kyoto 606
T: (075) 7532787
Founded: 1908; Members: 1460
Focus: Hist; Archeol; Geography
Periodical
The Shirin or the Journal of History (bi-monthly) 08024

Shika Kiso Igakkai, c/o Tokyo Shika Daigaku, 2-9-18 Misaki-cho, Chiyoda-ku, Tokyo 101
Founded: 1967
Focus: Otorhinolaryngology 08025

Shinto Gakkai, c/o Izumo Taisha Bunshi, 7-18-5 Rappongi, Minato-ku, Tokyo 105
Founded: 1938
Focus: Rel & Theol 08026

Shinto Shukyo Gakkai, c/o Kokugakuin Daigaku, 4-10-28 Higashi, Shibuya-ku, Tokyo 150
Founded: 1947
Focus: Rel & Theol 08027

Shokubai Gakkai / Catalysis Society of Japan, 302 Shin-Ikedayama Mansions, 5-21-13 Higashi-Gotanda, Shinagawa-ku, Tokyo 141
T: (03) 34442126; Fax: 34448794
Founded: 1958; Members: 2261
Pres: T. Inui
Focus: Chem
Periodical
Shokubai: Catalyst (bi-monthly) 08028

Shokubutsu Bunrui Chiri Gakkai / Phytogeographical Society, c/o Faculty of Integrated Human Studies, Kyoto University, Kyoto 606-01
T: (075) 7536847; E-Mail: nagamasu@gaia.h.kyoto-u.ac.jp; Fax: 7536608
Founded: 1932; Members: 490
Pres: N. Kitagawa
Focus: Botany
Periodical
Acta Phytotaxonomica et Geobotanica (bi-annually) 08029

The Society of Fermentation and Bioengineering, Japan, c/o Faculty of Engineering, Osaka University, 2-1 Yamadaoka, Suita, Osaka 565
T: (06) 8762731; Fax: 8762773
Founded: 1923; Members: 3100
Focus: Food
Periodicals
Journal of Fermentation and Bioengineering (monthly)
Seibutsu-kogaku Kaishi (bi-monthly) . . . 08030

Society of Japanese Historical Research, c/o Kokugakuin University, 4-10-28 Higashi, Shibuya-ku, Tokyo 150
Founded: 1910
Focus: Hist
Periodical
Kokushigaku 08031

Suifumeitokukai Shokokan, 1215-1, Migawa-machi, Mito-shi, Ibaraki-ken 310
T: (0292) 412721
Focus: Cultur Hist 08032

Tensor Society, c/o Kawaguchi Institute of Mathematical Sciences, 2-7-15 Matsu-ga-oka, Chigasaki 253
Founded: 1937; Members: 550
Focus: Math
Periodical
Tensor 08033

Tetsugaku-kai / Philosophical Society, c/o Faculty of Letters, University of Tokyo, 7-3-1 Hongo, Bunkyo-ku, Tokyo 113
Founded: 1884; Members: 500
Pres: J. Katsura
Focus: Philos
Periodical
Tetsugaku-zasshi (annually) 08034

Toa Igaku Kyokai, 2-20 Shin-Ogawa, Shinjuku-ku, Tokyo 162
Founded: 1954
Focus: Med 08035

Toa Kumo Gakkai, c/o Oitemon Gakuin Daigaku, Ibaraki-shi, Osaka 567
Founded: 1936
Focus: Sci 08036

Tochi Seidoshi Gakkai, c/o Institute of Social Science, University of Tokyo, 3-1, Hongo 7-chome, Bunkyo-ku, Tokyo 113
Founded: 1948; Members: 950
Focus: Hist; Econ; Agri
Periodical
Tochi Seido Shigaku: The Journal of Agrarian History (quarterly) 08037

Todai Chugoku Gakkai / The Sinological Society, c/o Faculty of Letters, The University of Tokyo, Bunkyo-ku, Tokyo
T: (03) 8122111, 8123746
Founded: 1985; Members: 800
Focus: Ethnology
Periodical
Hugoku-Shakai to Bunka: China-Society and Culture 08038

Toho Gakkai / Institute of Eastern Culture, 2-4-1 Nishi Kanda, Chiyoda-ku, Tokyo 101
T: (03) 32627221; Fax: 32627227
Founded: 1947; Members: 1560
Pres: Dr. Jikido Takasaki; Gen Secr: Hiroshi Yanase
Focus: Hist; Lit; Ling; Philos
Periodicals
Acta Asiatica (semi-annually)
Books and Articles on Oriental Subjects published in Japan (annually)
Tohogaku (semi-annually)
Transactions of the International Conference of Orientalists in Japan (annually) 08039

Tokei Kagaku Kenkyukai / Research Association of Statistical Sciences, c/o Kyushu University 33, Fukuoka 812
Founded: 1941
Focus: Stats; Cybernetics
Periodical
Bulletin of Informatics and Cybernetics (annually) 08040

Tokyo Bengoshikai Toshokan / Tokyo Bar Association, 1-1-4 Kasumigaseki, Chiyoda-ku, Tokyo 100
T: (03) 35812201; Fax: 35810865
Founded: 1911; Members: 3340
Focus: Law
Periodicals
Libra (semi-annually)
Toben Shinbun (monthly) 08041

Tokyo Chigaku Kyokai / Tokyo Geographical Society, Chigaku-Kaikan, 12-2, Nibancho, Chiyoda-ku, Tokyo 102
Fax: (03) 32630257
Founded: 1879; Members: 812
Pres: Prof. Hisashi Sato; Gen Secr: Dr. Takahiko Mikami
Focus: Geology; Geography; Geophys
Periodical
Journal of Geography (7 times annually) 08042

Tokyo Daigaku Keizai Gakkai / Society of Economics, c/o Faculty of Economics, University of Tokyo, Bunkyo-ku, Tokyo 113
Founded: 1922; Members: 500
Pres: M. Nakamura
Focus: Econ
Periodical
Journal of Economics (quarterly) 08043

Toshi Kaihatsu Kyokai Joho Sabisu Senta Shiryoshitsu / Urban Developers' Association of Japan, Akasaka Tokyu Bldg, 2-14-3 Nagat-cho, Chiyoda-ku, Tokyo 100
T: (03) 5803871
Focus: Urban Plan 08044

Toyo Ongaku Gakkai / The Society for Research in Asiatic Music, c/o Dept of Musicology, Faculty of Music, Tokyo University of Fine Art and Music, 12-8 Ueno Park, Taito-ku, Tokyo 110
Founded: 1936; Members: 750
Focus: Music
Periodical
Journal of the Society for Research in Asiatic Music (annually) 08045

Toyoshi Kenkyu-Kai / Society of Oriental Research, c/o Kyoto University, Sakyo-ku, Kyoto 606
T: (075) 7532790
Founded: 1935; Members: 1400
Pres: I. Miyazaki
Focus: Hist
Periodical
The Toyoshi-Kenkyu: The Journal of Oriental History (quarterly) 08046

Un-yu Chosakyoku Johobu Toshoshitsu / Institute of Transportation Economics, 7-1-1, Ueno, Taito-ku, Tokyo 110
T: (03) 8414101; Fax: 8414030
Focus: Transport
Periodical
Unyu-To-Keizai: Transportation & Economy (monthly) 08047

Waka Bungakkai, c/o Showa Joshi Daigaku Kenkyukan, 1-7-57 Taishido, Setagaya-ku, Tokyo 154
Focus: Lit 08048

World Association of Societies of Pathology (Anatomic and Clinical) (WASP), c/o Japan Clinical Pathology Foundation for International Exchange, Sakura-Sugamo Bldg 7F, Sugamo 2-11-1, Toshima-ku, Tokyo 170
T: (03) 39188161; Fax: 39496168
Founded: 1947; Members: 50
Focus: Pathology
Periodical
News Bulletin (2-3 times annually) . . . 08049

Yosetsu Gakkai / Japan Welding Society, 1-11 Sakuma-cho, Kanda, Chiyoda-ku, Tokyo 101
T: (03) 32530488; Fax: 32533059
Founded: 1925; Members: 5000
Pres: Prof. Dr. Y. Mukai
Focus: Eng
Periodicals
Journal (monthly)
Transactions (semi-annually) 08050

Zisin Gakkai / Seismological Society of Japan, c/o Earthquake Research Institute, University of Tokyo, 1-1-1 Yayoi, Bunkyo-ku, Tokyo
T: (03) 38137421; Fax: 56842549
Founded: 1929; Members: 1700
Pres: Masataka Amdo
Focus: Geophys
Periodicals
Journal of Physics of the Earth (bi-monthly)
Zisin: Journal (quarterly) 08051

Jordan

Arab Biosciences Network (ARABN), c/o Higher Council for Science and Technology, POB 560, Jubaiha
T: (06) 840401
Founded: 1983
Focus: Bio
Periodical
Arab Biosciences Newsletter 08052

Association of Arab Universities (AARU) / Association des Universités Arabes, POB 401, Jubeyha, Amman
T: (06) 845131; Fax: 832994
Founded: 1964; Members: 70
Focus: Educ
Periodical
AARU Bulletin (annually) 08053

Islamic Academy of Sciences, POB 830036, Amman
T: (06) 8222104; Fax: 821803
Founded: 1986
Pres: Prof. M.A. Kazi; Gen Secr: M.R. Zoubi
Focus: Sci 08054

Jordan Library Association, POB 6289, Amman
T: (06) 629412
Founded: 1963; Members: 600
Pres: Anwar Akroush; Gen Secr: Y.A. Ajamieh
Focus: Libraries & Bk Sci
Periodicals
The Jordanian National Bibliography (annually)
Rissalat al-Maktaba: Message of the Library (quarterly) 08055

Royal Academy for Islamic Civilization Research, POB 950361, Amman
T: (06) 815471; Fax: 826471
Founded: 1980
Pres: Dr. Nassir El-Din El-Assad
Focus: Rel & Theol; Cultur Hist
Periodical
Arab Journal of Administration (quarterly) 08056

Royal Scientific Society (R.S.S.), POB 925819, Amman
T: (06) 844701; Fax: 844806
Founded: 1970; Members: 350
Pres: Dr. Hani Mulki
Focus: Sci
Periodicals
Current List of Periodical Holdings
Monthly Accession List (monthly) 08057

Kazakhstan

Kazakhstan Academy of Sciences, Ul Shevchenko 28, 480021 Almaty
T: (03272) 695150; Fax: 696116
Members: 144
Pres: V.S. Shkolnik; Gen Secr: M.K. Suleimenov
Focus: Sci
Periodicals
Izvestiya: Bulletin
Vestnik: Herald 08058

Kenya

African Academy of Sciences (AAS), POB 14798, Nairobi
T: (02) 884401/05; Fax: 884406
Founded: 1985; Members: 80
Focus: Nat Sci
Periodicals
Discovery and Innovations (quarterly)
Whydah (quarterly) 08059

African Association for Literacy and Adult Education (AALAE), Finance House, Loita St, Nairobi
T: (02) 22391, 331512; Fax: 340849
Founded: 1984
Focus: Adult Educ 08060

African Association of Insect Scientists (AAIS), POB 59862, Nairobi
T: (02) 802501, 602509; Fax: 803360
Founded: 1978; Members: 2000
Focus: Entomology
Periodicals
Bulletin of African Insect Science
Insect Science and its Application . . . 08061

African Centre for Technology Studies (ACTS), POB 45917, Nairobi
T: (02) 744047; Fax: 743995
Founded: 1982
Focus: Eng 08062

African Commission on Mathematics Education, c/o Bureau of Educational Research, POB 43844, Nairobi
T: (02) 817356
Focus: Educ; Math 08063

African Council for Communication Education (ACCE), POB 47495, Nairobi
T: (02) 27043
Founded: 1976; Members: 333
Focus: Educ; Comm Sci
Periodicals
Africa Media Review (3 times annually)
AFRICOM Newsletter (3 times annually) . 08064

African Economic Research Consortium (AERC), POB 47543, Nairobi
T: (02) 225234, 228057; Fax: 218840
Founded: 1988
Focus: Econ
Periodical
AERC Newsletter (semi-annually) 08065

African Elephant and Rhino Specialist Group (AERSG), c/o Wildlife Conservation International, POB 62844, Nairobi
T: (02) 221699; Fax: 215969
Founded: 1982
Focus: Zoology
Periodical
Pachyderm 08066

African Institute for Higher Technical Training and Research (AIHTTR), c/o Kenya Regional Training Institution, POB 53763, Nairobi
T: (02) 335661, 220060
Founded: 1979; Members: 15
Focus: Eng 08067

African Medical and Research Foundation (AMREF), POB 30125, Nairobi
T: (02) 501301, 500508; Fax: 506112
Founded: 1957; Members: 12
Focus: Med 08068

African Network of Scientific and Technological Institutions (ANSTI), POB 30592, Nairobi
T: (02) 622620; Fax: 215991
Founded: 1980; Members: 85
Focus: Nat Sci; Eng
Periodicals
African Journal of Science and Technology
ANSTI Newsletter 08069

African Regional Organization for Standardization (ARSO), City Hall Annexe, Muindi Mbingu St., POB 57363, Nairobi
T: (02) 24561, 330882; Fax: 729228
Founded: 1977; Members: 23
Focus: Standards
Periodical
ARSO Newsletter (semi-annually) 08070

African Society for Environmental Studies Programme (ASESP), POB 44777, Nairobi
T: (02) 747960, 740817
Founded: 1968; Members: 17
Focus: Ecology
Periodical
African Social Studies Forum (semi-annually) 08071

African Training Centre for Literacy and Adult Education, c/o AALAE, Finance House, Loita St, POB 50768, Nairobi
T: (02) 22391, 331512; Fax: 340849
Founded: 1991
Focus: Adult Educ; Lit 08072

African Trypanotolerant Livestock Network, c/o ILCA, POB 46847, Nairobi
T: (02) 292013, 592093
Focus: Vet Med 08073

African Water Network, c/o KWAHO, POB 61470, Nairobi
Founded: 1988
Focus: Water Res 08074

Agricultural Society of Kenya, POB 30176, Nairobi
T: (02) 566655
Founded: 1901; Members: 12000
Pres: R.W. Walukano; Gen Secr: W.E. Adero
Focus: Agri
Periodical
The Kenya Farmer (monthly) 08075

Association for Teacher Education in Africa, POB 45869, Nairobi
Focus: Educ 08076

Association of Faculties of Science in African Universities (AFSAU), c/o University of Nairobi, POB 30197, Nairobi
T: (02) 43181
Founded: 1977
Focus: Nat Sci 08077

Association of International Schools in Africa (AISA), c/o International School of Kenya, POB 14103, Nairobi
T: (02) 582578; Fax: 582451
Members: 61
Focus: Educ
Periodical
AISA Newsletter (bi-monthly) 08078

Association of Surgeons of East Africa, POB 30726, Nairobi
T: (02) 340930
Founded: 1950; Members: 500
Pres: M.Y.D. Kodwavwala; Gen Secr: K.C. Rankin
Focus: Surgery
Periodical
Proceedings 08079

Association of Theological Institutions of Eastern Africa (ATIEA), POB 50784, Nairobi
Focus: Rel & Theol 08080

Basic Education Resource Centre (BERC), c/o Kenyatta University, POB 43844, Nairobi
T: (02) 810901
Founded: 1975
Focus: Educ 08081

Centre for African Family Studies (CAFS), POB 60054, Nairobi
T: (02) 747144; Fax: 747160
Founded: 1975
Focus: Family Plan
Periodical
CAFS Newsletter (semi-annually) 08082

Church Organization Research and Advisory Trust of Africa (CARAT AFRICA), POB 42493, Nairobi
T: (02) 331698
Founded: 1975
Focus: Business Admin 08083

Climate Network Africa, c/o KC, POB 21136, Nairobi
T: (02) 226028; Fax: 336742
Founded: 1991
Focus: Geophys 08084

Committee of International Development Institutions on the Environment (CIDIE), c/o UNEP, POB 30552, Nairobi
T: (02) 230800; Fax: 226886
Founded: 1980
Focus: Develop Areas; Ecology 08085

Commonwealth Association of Polytechnics in Africa (CAPA), POB 52428, Nairobi
T: (02) 338156
Founded: 1978; Members: 110
Focus: Educ
Periodicals
CAPA Journal of Technical Education and Training (semi-annually)
CAPA Newsletter (quarterly) 08086

Desert Locust Control Organization for Eastern Africa (DLCOEA), POB 30023, Nairobi
T: (02) 501704; Fax: 611648
Founded: 1962
Focus: Geology
Periodical
Desert Locus Situation Report (monthly) . 08087

Earthwatch, c/o UNEP, POB 30552, Nairobi
T: (02) 333930; Fax: 520711
Founded: 1972
Focus: Ecology 08088

East Africa Natural History Society (EANHS), POB 44486, Nairobi
T: (02) 749957; Fax: 741049
Founded: 1909; Members: 1400
Pres: Dr. L. Bennun
Focus: Nat Sci; Hist 08089

East African Academy, POB 47288, Nairobi
T: 22976
Focus: Sci 08090

East African Engineering Consultants (EAEC), Madison Insurance House, Upper Hill Rd, POB 30707, Nairobi
T: (02) 711415; Fax: 569389
Founded: 1967
Focus: Eng 08091

East African Industrial Research Organization, POB 30650, Nairobi
Founded: 1948
Focus: Eng 08092

East African Library Association (EALA), POB 46031, Nairobi
Founded: 1956; Members: 200
Pres: P.S. Weche
Focus: Libraries & Bk Sci 08093

East African Wildlife Society (E.A.W.L.S.), Nairobi Hilton Bldg, Mama Ngina St, POB 20110, Nairobi
T: (02) 748170; Fax: 746868
Founded: 1961; Members: 16000
Gen Secr: N.K. Arap Rotich
Focus: Ecology
Periodicals
The African Journal of Ecology (quarterly)
Swara Magazine: Wildlife News (bi-monthly) 08094

East Asian Seas Action Plan, c/o UNEP, POB 30552, Nairobi
T: (02) 333930; Fax: 520711
Founded: 1981
Focus: Oceanography 08095

Eastern Africa Environment Network (EAEN), Museum Hill Centre, Museum Hill Rd, POB 20110, Nairobi
T: (02) 748170; Fax: 746868
Founded: 1001
Focus: Ecology 08096

Eastern and Southern African Regional Branch of the International Council on Archives (ESARBICA), c/o Kenya National Archives, POB 49210, Nairobi
T: (02) 28979
Founded: 1969; Members: 13
Focus: Archives
Periodical
ESARBICA Journal (irregularly) 08097

Historical Association of Kenya, POB 43844, Nairobi
Founded: 1966
Pres: Prof. B.A. Ogot
Focus: Hist
Periodicals
Hadith Series (annually)
Kenya Historical Review (semi-annually) . 08098

Institution of Engineers of Kenya, POB 41346, Nairobi
T: (02) 721022
Founded: 1945; Members: 1500
Gen Secr: A.V. Otieno
Focus: Eng 08099

Kenya Dental Association (KDA), POB 20059, Nairobi
Founded: 1943; Members: 110
Focus: Dent 08100

Kenya Library Association, POB 46031, Nairobi
Founded: 1956; Members: 200
Focus: Libraries & Bk Sci
Periodicals
Kelias News (bi-monthly)
Maktaba: Official Journal (semi-annually) . 08101

Kenya Medical Association, POB 48502, Nairobi
T: (02) 724617
Founded: 1962; Members: 1500
Pres: Prof. W. Kore
Focus: Med 08102

Kenya National Academy of Sciences, POB 47288, Nairobi
Founded: 1977; Members: 200
Pres: Prof. R.M. Munavu
Focus: Arts; Sci
Periodicals
The Kenya Journal of Sciences: Series A (semi-annually)
The Kenya Journal of Sciences: Series B (semi-annually)
The Kenya Journal of Sciences: Series C (semi-annually) 08103

Law Society of Kenya, POB 72219, Nairobi
T: (02) 225558; Fax: 223997
Founded: 1949; Members: 1385
Gen Secr: P.M. Mwangi
Focus: Law 08104

National Council for Science and Technology, POB 30623, Nairobi
T: (02) 336173
Founded: 1977; Members: 35
Gen Secr: Prof. P. Gach
Focus: Sci; Eng 08105

Ophthalmological Society of East Africa (OSEA), c/o Kenyatta National Hospital, POB 20723, Nairobi
Focus: Ophthal 08106

Standing Conference of African University Libraries (SCAUL), c/o University, POB 30197, Nairobi
T: (02) 334244
Founded: 1964
Focus: Libraries & Bk Sci 08107

Korea, Democratic People's Republic

Academy of Agricultural Science, Ryongsong Dictrict, Pyongyang
Founded: 1948
Pres: Yong Gyun Li
Focus: Agri 08108

Academy of Fisheries, Namgang-dong, Sung Ho District, Pyongyang
Founded: 1969
Pres: Gyong Ho Ho
Focus: Zoology 08109

Academy of Forestry Science, Samsin-dong, Taesong District, Pyongyang
Founded: 1948
Pres: Rok Jae Im
Focus: Forestry 08110

Academy of Light Industry Science, Kangan 1-dong, Songyo District, Pyongyang
Founded: 1954
Pres: Ju Ung Li
Focus: Eng; Econ 08111

Academy of Medical Sciences, Saemaul-dong, Pyongchon District, POB 305, Pyongyang
T: (02) 46924
Pres: Guy Dong Lyu
Focus: Med 08112

Academy of Railway Sciences, Namgyo-dong, Hyongjaesan District, Pyongyang
Pres: Byong Hak An
Focus: Eng 08113

Academy of Sciences, Ryonmot-dong, Jangsan St, Sosong District, Pyongyang
T: (02) 51956
Founded: 1952
Pres: Song Gun Kim
Focus: Sci
Periodical
Journal (bi-monthly) 08114

Academy of Social Sciences, Central District, Pyongyang
Founded: 1952
Pres: Sok Hyong Kim
Focus: Sociology 08115

Library Association of the Democratic People's Republic of Korea, c/o State Central Library, Pyongyang
Founded: 1953
Focus: Libraries & Bk Sci 08116

Korea, Republic

Academy of Korean Studies, 50 Unjung-dong, Songman-si, Pundang-gu, Kyonggi-do
T: (0342) 7098111; Fax: 7091531
Founded: 1978
Pres: Young-Dug Lee
Focus: Hist; Cultur Hist 08117

Asia Foundation, Gwang Wha Moon, POB 738, Seoul 110-607
T: (02) 7322044; E-Mail: tafkoz@mcimail.com; Fax: 7396022
Founded: 1954
Gen Secr: David I. Steinberg
Focus: Int'l Relat 08118

Asia-Pacific Lawyers Association, Korea Re-Insurance Bldg, 80 Soosong-Dong, Chongro-ku, Seoul
T: (02) 7355661; Fax: 7355206
Founded: 1984
Focus: Law 08119

Asian Association of Open Universities (AAOU), c/o Korea National Open University, 169 Xongsung-dong, Chongro-gu, Seoul
T: (02) 7404323; E-Mail: ide@av9500.knou.ac.kr; Fax: 7477100
Founded: 1987
Pres: Dr. Wan-Sang Han
Focus: Educ 08120

Asian Pacific Association for the Study of the Liver, c/o Dept of Internal Medicine, Catholic University Medical College, 62 Youido-gu, Seoul 150010
Focus: Intern Med 08121

Asian-Pacific Society of Cardiology (APSC), c/o Seoul National University Hospital, Room 9326, Seoul 110744
Fax: (02) 7442819
Founded: 1956
Focus: Cardiol
Periodical
APSC Newsletter (annually) 08122

Asian Regional Association for Home Economics (ARAHE), c/o College of Home Economics, Yonsei University, 134 Shinchon-dong, Sudaemun-ku, Seoul 120749
Focus: Home Econ 08123

Asian Society of Agricultural Economists, c/o Korea Rural Economic Institute, 4-102 Hoegi-dong, Dongdaemun-ku, Seoul 130-050
T: (02) 9627311; E-Mail: jsupchoi@kreisun.krei.re.kr; Fax: 9656959
Founded: 1991; Members: 200
Pres: Dr. Beddu Amang; Gen Secr: Dr. Yang Boo Choe
Focus: Agri 08124

International Cultural Society of Korea (ICSK), Daewoo Foundation Bldg 526, 5-ga, Namdaemunno, Chung-gu, CPO 2147, Seoul 100-095
Fax: (02) 7572049
Founded: 1972
Focus: Int'l Relat
Periodicals
Le Courrier de la Corée (weekly)
Korea Newsreview (weekly)
Koreana: English Edition (quarterly)
Koreana: Japanese Edition (quarterly) . . 08125

Korean Association for the Biological Sciences, c/o Sung Kyun Kwan University, Seoul
Focus: Bio 08126

Korean Association of Sinology, c/o Asiatic Research Center, Korea University, Anam-dong, Seoul
Founded: 1955; Members: 100
Pres: Jun-Yop Kim
Focus: Ethnology
Periodical
Journal of Chinese Studies 08127

Korean Chemical Society, 35, 5-ga, Anam-Dong, Seongbuk-gu, Seoul 136-075
T: (02) 9265457; Fax: 9235589
Founded: 1946; Members: 2595
Pres: Bong Young Chung; Gen Secr: Si-Joong Kim
Focus: Chem
Periodicals
Bulletin (bi-monthly)
Chemical Education (quarterly)
ChemWorld (monthly)
Journal of the Korean Chemical Society (monthly)
The Korean Journal of Medicinal Chemistry (semi-annually) 08128

Korean Economic Association, 45, 4-ga Namdae-mun-ro, Chung-gu, Seoul
Founded: 1952; Members: 3000
Pres: Chinkeun Park; Gen Secr: Sungkeun Ha
Focus: Econ
Periodical
Korean Economic Review (bi-annually) . 08129

Korean Forestry Society, c/o Dept of Forest Resources, Seoul National University, Suwon, Kyonggido 441-744
T: (0331) 2902330
Founded: 1960; Members: 800
Pres: Jing Hwa Youn; Gen Secr: Prof. Joo Sang Chung
Focus: Forestry
Periodical
Journal of the Korean Forestry Society (quarterly) 08130

Korean Geographical Society, c/o Dept of Geography, College of Social Sciences, Seoul National University, Seoul 151-742
T: (02) 8806449; Fax: 8855272
Founded: 1945; Members: 585
Pres: Bo-Woong Chang; Gen Secr: Sam Ock Park
Focus: Geography
Periodical
Chirihak (semi-annually) 08131

Korean Historical Association, 2-5, Myong-nuyun-dong 3-ga, Chongno-ku, Seoul
Founded: 1952; Members: 400
Focus: Hist
Periodical
Yoksa Hakbo (quarterly) 08132

Korean Library Association, San 60-1, Panpo-Dong, Seocho-Gu, Seoul
T: (02) 5354868; Fax: 5355616
Founded: 1955; Members: 2500
Pres: Chul Sakong; Gen Secr: Won-Ho Jo
Focus: Libraries & Bk Sci
Periodical
KLA Bulletin (bi-monthly) 08133

Korean Medical Association (KMA), CPOB 2062, Seoul
T: (02) 7942414; Fax: 7921296
Founded: 1908
Pres: Sung Hee Ryu; Gen Secr: In Soo Tschoi
Focus: Med
Periodicals
Journal of the Korean Medical Association (monthly)
Newspaper (bi-weekly) 08134

Korean Micro-Library Association, c/o Library Association, Central National Library Bldg, 6 Sogong-dong, 6 Chung-ku, Seoul
Focus: Libraries & Bk Sci 08135

Korean Psychological Association, c/o Dept of Psychology, Seoul National University, Shinrim 2-dong, Kwanak-gu, Seoul
T: (02) 8770101 ext 2528
Founded: 1946; Members: 420
Pres: Bongyun Suh; Gen Secr: Jungoh Kim
Focus: Psych
Periodicals
Korean Journal of Clinical Psychology (semi-annually)
Korean Journal of Industrial Psychology (annually)
Korean Journal of Psychology (semi-annually)
Korean Journal of Social Psychology (annually) 08136

Korean Research and Development Library Association, POB 131, Cheongryang, Seoul
T: (02) 9673692; Fax: 29634013
Founded: 1979
Pres: Ke Hong Park; Gen Secr: Keon Tak Oh
Focus: Libraries & Bk Sci 08137

The Korean Society of Pharmacology, c/o Dept of Pharmacology, Yonsei University College of Medicine, 134 Shin-Chon-Dong, Seo-Dae-Moon-ku, Seoul 120-752
Founded: 1947; Members: 335
Focus: Pharmacol
Periodical
The Korean Journal of Pharmacology . . 08138

Music Association of Korea, Room 303, FACO Bldg, 81-6, Sejongro, Chongno-gu, Seoul
Founded: 1961; Members: 700
Pres: Dr. Tai Joon Park; Gen Secr: Dae Yup Sohn
Focus: Music 08139

National Academy of Arts, 1 Sejongro, Chongno-gu, Seoul 50
T: (02) 7203902
Founded: 1954
Focus: Arts
Periodicals
Bibliography
Bulletin
Journal
Survey of Korean Arts 08140

National Academy of Sciences, San 94, Panpo-dong, Seocho-gu, Seoul 137-044
T: (02) 5340737; Fax: 5373183
Founded: 1954; Members: 150
Pres: Byong Ik Koh; Gen Secr: Chang Whan Kim
Focus: Sci
Periodicals
Bibliography
Bulletin
Journal
Report on International Symposium . . . 08141

Royal Asiatic Society, Korea Branch, Seoul, POB 255
Fax: (02) 7639483 7663796
Founded: 1900; Members: 1600
Gen Secr: Sue J. Bae
Focus: Arts; Hist; Lit; Cultur Hist . . . 08142

Kuwait

Arab Center for Medical Literature (ACML), POB 5225, 13053 Safat
T: 5338610; Fax: 5338618
Founded: 1988; Members: 21
Gen Secr: Dr. Abdel Rahman Al-Awadi
Focus: Lit 08143

Arab Planning Institute Kuwait, POB 5834, 13059 Safat
T: 4843130; Fax: 4842935
Founded: 1966
Gen Secr: Dr. E. Al-Shareedah
Focus: Econ 08144

National Council for Culture, Arts and Literature, POB 23996, 13100 Safat
T: 4877085; Fax: 4873694
Founded: 1973
Gen Secr: Al-Omar. Dr. F.
Focus: Cultur Hist; Arts; Lit 08145

Kyrgyzstan

Kyrgyz Academy of Sciences, Chuy pr 265a, 720071 Bishkek
T: (03312) 264541
Founded: 1954; Members: 84
Pres: T. Kolchuev; Gen Secr: A.V. Frlov
Focus: Sci
Periodical
Izvestiya: Bulletin 08146

Kyrgyz Genetics and Selection Society, Chuy pr 265A, 720071 Bishkek
T: (03312) 243994
Pres: M.M. Tokobaev
Focus: Genetics 08147

Kyrgyz Geographical Society, Bul Erkindik 30, 720081 Bishkek
T: (03312) 264721
Pres: S.U. Umurzakov
Focus: Geography 08148

Kyrgyz Philosophical Society, c/o Kyrgyz Academy of Sciences, Chuy pr 265A, 720071 Bishkek
Pres: A.A. Saliev
Focus: Philos 08149

Laos

Lao Buddhist Fellowship, Maha Kudy, That Luang, Vientiane
Founded: 1964
Pres: Thong Khoune Anantasunthone; Gen Secr: Siho Sihavong
Focus: Rel & Theol 08150

Latvia

Latvian Academy of Sciences, Turgeneva iela 19, 1524 Riga
T: (02) 225361; Fax: 228784
Members: 248
Pres: T. Millers; Gen Secr: A. Silins
Focus: Sci
Periodicals
Khimiya Geterotsiklicheskikh Soedinenii: Chemistry of Heterocyclic Compounds
Latvijas Fizikas un Tehnisko Zinatnu Zurnals: Latvian Journal of Physics and Technical Sciences
Latvijas Kimijas Zurnals: Latvian Chemical Journal
Magnitnaya Gidrodinamika: Magnetic Hydrodynamics
Mekhanika Kompozitnykh Materialov: Mechanics of Composite Materials
Vestis: Proceedings 08151

Lebanon

Association Libanaise des Sciences Juridiques, c/o Faculté de Droit et des Sciences Economiques, Université Saint Joseph, BP 293, Beirut
T: (01) 200629
Founded: 1963; Members: 40
Pres: Pierre Gannagé; Gen Secr: Meline Topakian
Focus: Law
Periodicals
Etudes Juridiques
Proche-Orient 08152

Association of Theological Institutes in the Middle East (ATIME), c/o Dept of Theological Concerns, Immeuble DEEB, Rue Makhoul, BP 5376, Beirut
T: (01) 3448994
Founded: 1967; Members: 11
Focus: Rel & Theol 08153

Lebanese Library Association, c/o University Library, American University of Beirut, BP 113/5367, Beirut
T: (01) 340740 ext 2603
Founded: 1960
Pres: M. Rafi; Gen Secr: Linda Sadaka
Focus: Libraries & Bk Sci 08154

Lesotho

Lesotho Library Association, Private Bag A26, Maseru
Founded: 1978; Members: 22
Pres: E.M. Nthunya
Focus: Libraries & Bk Sci 08155

Liberia

Geological, Mining and Metallurgical Society of Liberia, POB 902, Monrovia
Founded: 1964; Members: 78
Pres: C.S. Wotorson; Gen Secr: Dr. M.-H. Neufville
Focus: Geology; Mining; Metallurgy
Periodical
Bulletin (semi-annually) 08156

Liberia Arts and Crafts Association, POB 885, Monrovia
Founded: 1964; Members: 14
Pres: R.V. Richards
Focus: Arts 08157

Society of Liberian Authors, POB 2468, Monrovia
Founded: 1959
Focus: Lit
Periodical
Kaafa (semi-annually) 08158

Libya

National Academy for Scientific Research, POB 8004, Tripoli
Fax: (021) 39841
Founded: 1981; Members: 330
Gen Secr: Dr. T.H. Jehemi
Focus: Sci 08159

Union of Libyan Authors, Writers and Artists, POB 1017, Tripoli
Founded: 1980; Members: 800
Pres: Amin Mazen
Focus: Arts; Lit 08160

Liechtenstein

CIPRA Internationale Alpenschutzkommission, Im Bretscha 22, 9494 Schaan
T: (075) 2374030; E-Mail: 101662.3043@compuserve.com; Fax: 2374031
Founded: 1952
Pres: Andreas Weissen; Gen Secr: Andreas Götz
Focus: Ecology
Periodical
Info-Bulletin (quarterly) 08161

Historischer Verein für das Fürstentum Liechtenstein, 9495 Triesen
T: (075) 3921747; Fax: 3921961
Founded: 1901; Members: 800
Pres: Dr. Rupert Quaderer; Gen Secr: Klaus Biedermann
Focus: Hist
Periodical
Jahrbuch des Historischen Vereins für das Fürstentum Liechtenstein 08162

Liechtensteinische Gesellschaft für Umweltschutz (LGU), Im Bretscha 22, 9494 Schaan
T: (075) 2325262; E-Mail: lgu@lgu.LOL.li; Fax: 2374031
Founded: 1973; Members: 726
Pres: Barbara Rheinberger; Gen Secr: Regula Imhof
Focus: Ecology
Periodicals
LGU-Mitteilungen (quarterly)
Liechtensteiner Umweltbericht (2-3 times annually) 08163

Liechtensteinischer Ärzteverein, Postfach 464, 9490 Vaduz
Focus: Med 08164

Lithuania

Lithuanian Academy of Sciences, Gedimino pr 3, 2600 Vilnius
T: (02) 613651; Fax: 618464
Founded: 1941; Members: 105
Pres: Prof. B. Juodka; Gen Secr: Prof. A. Sileika
Focus: Sci
Periodicals
Astronomical Bulletin
Lithuanian Mathematical Journal
Lithuanistika: Lithuanian Studies
Mokelas ir Tekhnika: Science and Technology
Trudy Akademii Nauk Litvy: Bulletin of the Lithuanian Academy 08165

PEN Centre of Lithuania, Sirvydo 6, 2600 Vilnius
T: (02) 628643
Founded: 1989; Members: 36
Pres: Kornelijus Platelis; Gen Secr: Galina Bauzyte-Cepinskiene
Focus: Lit 08166

Luxembourg

Association des Médecins et Médecins-Dentistes du Grand-Duché de Luxembourg, 29 Rue de Vianden, 2680 Luxembourg
T: 444033; Fax: 458349
Founded: 1904; Members: 820
Focus: Med; Dent
Periodical
Le Corps Médical (bi-monthly) 08167

Association des Professeurs de l'Enseignement Secondaire et Supérieur du Grand-Duché de Luxembourg (APESS), 389 Rte d'Arlon, 8011 Strassen
T: 808358; Fax: 802813
Founded: 1905; Members: 1000
Pres: Carlo Felten; Gen Secr: André Bauler
Focus: Educ 08168

Association of European Psychiatrists / Association Européenne de Psychiatrie, c/o Centre Hospitalier de Luxembourg, 4 Rue Barble, 1210 Luxembourg
T: 44112706; E-Mail: aep@chl.lu; Fax: 4412247
Founded: 1983; Members: 1000
Gen Secr: Prof. C. Pull
Focus: Psychiatry 08169

Collège Mé1dical, 57 Blvd de la Pétrusse, 2320 Luxembourg
Founded: 1818
Pres: Dr. Georges Arnold; Gen Secr: Pierre Schroeder
Focus: Med 08170

Commission Grand-Ducale d'Instruction, 29 Rue Aldringen, 2926 Luxembourg
T: 4785211; E-Mail: gerard.gretsch@ci.educ.lu; Fax: 466815
Founded: 1843; Members: 10
Pres: Jean-Pierre Kraemer; Gen Secr: Gérard Gretsch
Focus: Educ 08171

European Association for the Transfer of Technologies, Innovations and Industrial Information (TII) / Association Européenne pour le Transfert des Technologies, de l'Innovation et de l'Information Industrielle, 3 Rue des Capucins, 1313 Luxembourg
T: 463035; Fax: 462185
Founded: 1984; Members: 470
Focus: Eng 08172

European Association of Information Services / Association Européenne des Centres de Dissémination des Informations Scientifiques, BP 1416, 1014 Luxembourg
T: 422474; Fax: 422474
Founded: 1970; Members: 200
Focus: Computer & Info Sci 08173

European Centre for Parliamentary Research and Documentation (ECPRD), c/o Parlement Européen, 2929 Luxembourg
T: 43002447; E-Mail: jwittenberg@europarl.eu.int; Fax: 43009021
Founded: 1977; Members: 40
Gen Secr: Dick Toornstra; Wojciech Sawicki
Focus: Poli Sci 08174

Société des Naturalistes Luxembourgeois (SNL), CP 327, Luxembourg
Founded: 1890; Members: 480
Pres: Claude Meisch; Gen Secr: M. Molitor
Focus: Nat Sci
Periodical
Bulletin de la Société des Naturalistes Luxembourgeois (annually) 08175

Société Luxembourgeoise de Radiologie, 29 Rue de Vianden, 2680 Luxembourg
T: 444033; Fax: 458349
Founded: 1968; Members: 40
Pres: Dr.Guy Scheifer; Gen Secr: Dr. Armand Wildanger
Focus: Radiology 08176

Syndicat National des Enseignants (S.N.E.), BP 2437, Luxembourg
T: 481118
Founded: 1948; Members: 2300
Focus: Educ
Periodical
Ecole et Vie: Bulletin dınformation syndical, pédagogique et culturel (8 times annually) 08177

Macao

Associação de Ciências Socias de Macau, Edifício Tak On, Estrada Adolfo Loureiro 3A, CP 957, Macau
T: 319880; Fax: 319880
Founded: 1985; Members: 40
Pres: Wei-Wen Huang
Focus: Soc Sci
Periodical
Huo Keng (semi-annually) 08178

Circulo de Cultura Musical / Circle of Musical Culture, Largo de Santo Agostinho 3, Macao 68
Founded: 1952; Members: 68
Gen Secr: Francisco Xavier Freire Garcia
Focus: Music 08179

Macedonia

Društvo na Istoričarite na Umetnosta od Makedonija / Society of Art Historians of Macedonia, c/o Arheološki Muzej na Makedonija, Curčiska bb, 91000 Skopje
Founded: 1970; Members: 130
Focus: Arts; Cultur Hist
Periodical
Likovna Umetnost: Plastic Arts 08180

Društvo na Kompozitorite na Makedonija / Society of Macedonian Composers, Maksim Gorki 18, 91000 Skopje
Founded: 1950; Members: 40
Focus: Music
Periodical
Bilten: Bulletin 08181

Društvo na Likovnite Umetnici na Makedonija / Society of Plastic Arts of Macedonia, c/o Umetnička Galerija, Kruševska 1a, 91000 Skopje, (041) 10110
Founded: 1944; Members: 150
Focus: Fine Arts 08182

Društvo na Literaturnite Preveduvači na Makedonija / Society of Literary Translators of Macedonia, POB 3, 91000 Skopje
Founded: 1955; Members: 102
Focus: Lit 08183

Društvo na Muzejskite Rabotnici na Makedonija / Museum Society of Macedonia, c/o Muzei na Grad Skopje, Mito Hadži-Vasilev-Jasmin bb, 91000 Skopje
Founded: 1951; Members: 100
Focus: Archives 08184

Društvo na Pisatelite na Makedonija / Society of Writers of Macedonia, Maksim Gorki 18, 91000 Skopje
T: (091) 236205
Founded: 1951; Members: 194
Focus: Lit 08185

Društvo za Filozofija, Sociologija i Politikologija na Makedonija / Society for Philosophy, Sociology and Politics of Macedonia, c/o Institut za Sociološki i Političko-Pravni Istražuvanja, Bul Partizanski Odredi bb, 91000 Skopje
Founded: 1960; Members: 170
Focus: Philos; Sociology; Poli Sci
Periodical
Zbornik: Collected Papers 08186

Društvo za Nauka i Umetnost / Association of Sciences and Art, POB 145, 97000 Bitola
T: (097) 22683
Founded: 1960
Pres: Sotir Panovski; Gen Secr: Trajko Ognenovski
Focus: Psych 08187

Farmaceutsko Društvo na Makedonija / Pharmacological Society of Macedonia, Ivo Ribar Lola 6, 91000 Skopje
Focus: Pharmacol
Periodical
Bilten: Bulletin 08188

Geografsko Društvo na Makedonija / Geographical Society of Macedonia, c/o Geografski Institut pri Prirodomatematički Fakultet, POB 146, 91000 Skopje
Founded: 1949; Members: 600
Focus: Geography
Periodicals
Geografski Razgledi: Geographical Surveys
Geografski Vidik: Geographical Look . . 08189

Makedonska Akademija na Naukite i Umetnostite (MANU) / Macedonian Academy of Sciences and Art, Bul Krste Misirkov 2, POB 428, 91000 Skopje
T: (091) 114200; Fax: 115903
Founded: 1967; Members: 75
Pres: Ksente Bogoev; Gen Secr: T. Georgievski
Focus: Sci; Arts
Periodicals
Letopis (annually)
Prilozi na Oddelenieto za Bioloski i Medicinski Nauki (semi-annually)
Prilozi na Oddelenieto za Matematicko-Tehnicki Nauki
Prilozi na Oddelenieto za Opstestveni Nauki (semi-annually) 08190

Makedonsko Geološko Društvo / Macedonian Geological Society, c/o Geološki Zavod, POB 28, 91001 Skopje
T: (091) 230873
Founded: 1954; Members: 300
Focus: Geology 08191

Makedonsko Lekarsko Društvo / Medical Society of Macedonia, Gradski zid blok 11/6, 91000 Skopje
Founded: 1946; Members: 2000
Focus: Med
Periodical
Makedonski Medicinski Pregled: Macedonian Medical Review 08192

Republički Zavod za Zaštita na Spomenicite na Kulturata / Institute for the Protection of Cultural Monuments of Macedonia, Maršal Tito bb, Gorče Petrov, 91000 Skopje
Founded: 1949
Focus: Preserv Hist Monuments
Periodical
Kulturno-Istorisko Nasledstvo na Makedonija: The Cultural and Historical Heritage of Macedonia
. . . . 08193

Sojuz na Društvata na Arhivskite Rabotnici na Makedonija / Union of Societies of Archivists of Macedonia, Ul Gligor Prličev br 3, 91000 Skopje
T: (091) 237211; Fax: 234461
Founded: 1954; Members: 340
Focus: Archives
Periodical
Makedonski Arhivist (annually) 08194

Sojuz na Društvata na Bibliotekarite na Makedonija / Union of Librarians' Associations of Macedonia, Bul Goce Delčev br 6, 91000 Skopje
Founded: 1949; Members: 550
Focus: Libraries & Bk Sci
Periodical
Bibliotekarska iskra (quarterly) 08195

Sojuz na Društvata na Istoričarite na Makedonija / Union of Societies of Historians of Macedonia, c/o Institut za Nacionalna Istorija, Ul Gligor Prličev br 3, POB 591, 91000 Skopje
T: (091) 239036
Founded: 1952
Focus: Hist
Periodical
Istorija: History 08196

Sojuz na Društvata na Matematičarite i Informatičarite na Makedonija / Society of Mathematicians and Computerists of Macedonia, POB 162, 91000 Skopje
T: (091) 261330; Fax: 228141
Founded: 1950
Focus: Math; Computer & Info Sci
Periodical
Matematički Bilten: Mathematical Bulletin . 08197

Sojuz na Društvata na Veterinarnite Lekari i Tehničari na Makedonija / Union of Associations of Veterinary Surgeons and Technicians of Macedonia, c/o Veterinaren Institut, Lazar Pop-Trajkov 5, POB 95, 91000 Skopje
Founded: 1950; Members: 450
Focus: Vet Med
Periodical
Makednonski Veterinaren Pregled: Macedonian Veterinary Review 08198

Sojuz na Društvata za Makedonski Jazik i Literatura / Union of Associations for Macedonian Language and Literature, c/o Filološki Fakultet, Bul Krste Misirkov bb, 91000 Skopje
Founded: 1954; Members: 700
Focus: Lit
Periodical
Literaturen Zbor: Literary Word 08199

Sojuz na Ekonomistite na Makedonija / Union of Economists of Macedonia, c/o Ekonomiski Fakultet, K. Misirkov bb, 91000 Skopje
T: (091) 224311; Fax: 224973
Founded: 1950; Members: 3000
Focus: Econ
Periodical
Stopanski pregled: Economic Review . . 08200

Sojuz na Inženeri i Tehničari na Makedonija / Society of Engineers and Technicians of Macedonia, Nikola Vapcarov bb, 91000 Skopje
Founded: 1945; Members: 27000
Focus: Eng 08201

Sojuz na Inženeri i Tehničari po Sumarstvo i Industrija za Prerabotka na Drvo na Makedonija / Union of Forestry Engineers and Technicians of Macedonia, c/o Šumarski Institut, Engelsova 2, 91000 Skopje
Founded: 1952; Members: 500
Focus: Forestry
Periodical
Sumarski Pregled: Forester's Review . . 08202

Sojuz na Združenijata na Pravnicite na Makedonija / Union of Associations of Jurists of Macedonia, XII Udarna Brigada 2, 91000 Skopje
Founded: 1946; Members: 4000
Focus: Law
Periodical
Pravna misla 08203

Sojuz na Zemjodelskite Inženeri i Tehničari na SR Makedonija / Union of Agricultural Engineers and Technicians of Macedonia, c/o Zemjodelskošumarski Fakultet, 91000 Skopje
Founded: 1945; Members: 5000
Focus: Agri
Periodical
Socijalističko Zemjodelstvo: Socialist Agriculture
. . . . 08204

Združenie na Arheolozite na Makedonija / Archaeological Society of Macedonia, c/o Muzej na Makedonija, 91000 Skopje
T: (091) 220222
Founded: 1970; Members: 150
Focus: Archeol
Periodical
Macedoniae Acta Archaeologica 08205

Združenie na Folkloristite na Makedonija / Association of Folklorists of Macedonia, c/o Institut za Folklor, Ruzveltova 3, 91000 Skopje
T: (091) 233876; Fax: 233319
Founded: 1952; Members: 60
Focus: Folklore 08206

Madagascar

Académie Malgache, Tsimbazaza, BP 6217, Antananarivo
T: (02) 21084; Fax: 21084
Founded: 1902; Members: 200
Pres: Dr. C. Rabenoro
Focus: Sci
Periodicals
Bulletin
Mémoires 08207

Association des Bibliothécaires, Documentalistes, Archivistes et Muséographes de Madagascar, c/o Bibliothèque Nationale, BP 257, Antananarivo
T: (02) 25872
Founded: 1976
Pres: Christiane Andriamirado; Gen Secr: Samoela Andriankotonirina
Focus: Libraries & Bk Sci; Doc; Archives; Arts
. . . . 08208

Malawi

Geological Survey of Malawi, Liwonde Rd, POB 27, Zomba
T: 522166
Founded: 1921
Pres: F.R. Phiri
Focus: Surveying
Periodicals
Bulletin
Memoirs
Records 08209

Malawi Library Association, POB 429, Zomba
T: 522222; Fax: 523225
Founded: 1976; Members: 340
Pres: J.J. Uta; Gen Secr: Vote D. Somba
Focus: Libraries & Bk Sci
Periodical
Bulletin 08210

Medical Association of Malawi, POB 30605, Chichiri, Blantyre
T: 630333; Fax: 631353
Founded: 1967; Members: 100
Pres: Dr. B. Mwale; Gen Secr: Dr.E. Mtitimila
Focus: Med
Periodical
Malawi Medical Journal 08211

Society of Malawi, POB 125, Blantyre
Founded: 1948; Members: 400
Pres: A. Schwarz; Gen Secr: P. Royle
Focus: Hist; Sci
Periodical
Journal (semi-annually) 08212

Malaysia

Academy of Family Physicians of Malaysia, MMA House, 124 jalan Pahang, 53000 Kuala Lumpur
T: (03) 4417735; Fax: 4425206
Founded: 1973; Members: 800
Pres: Dr. Ruby Abdul Majeed
Focus: Med
Periodical
The Family Physician (3 times annually) 08213

ASEAN Plant Quarantine Centre and Training Institute (PLANTI), PMB 209, 43400 Serdang
T: (03) 9486010, 9486016; Fax: 9486023
Founded: 1980
Focus: Botany, Specific
Periodical
Plantinews (3 times annually) 08214

Asia Pacific Forum on Women, Law and Development (APWLD), APWLD Bldg, Persiaran Duta, POB 12224, 50770 Kuala Lumpur
T: (03) 2550648; Fax: 2541371
Founded: 1986
Focus: Soc Sci; Law 08215

Asia-Pacific People's Environment Network (APPEN), c/o Sahabat Alam Malaysia, 43 Salween Rd, 10050 Penang
T: (04) 376930; Fax: 375705
Founded: 1983
Focus: Ecology 08216

Asian Association of National Languages (ASANAL), c/o Language Center, University of Malaya, 59100 Kuala Lumpur
T: (03) 7560181
Focus: Ling 08217

Asian Institute for Development Communication (AIDCOM), APDC Bldg, Persiaran Duta, 50480 Kuala Lumpur
T: (03) 2542558; Fax: 2543785
Founded: 1986
Focus: Comm Sci
Periodicals
AIDCOM Information
Journal of Development Communication . 08218

Asian Wetland Bureau (AWB), c/o Institute of Advanced Studies, University of Malaya, Lembah Pantai, 59100 Kuala Lumpur
T: (03) 7572176; Fax: 7571225
Founded: 1983
Focus: Geology 08219

Association for Medical Education in the Western Pacific Region (AMEWPR), c/o Dept of Medical Education, Faculty of Medicine, University, Jalan Raja Muda Abdul Aziz, 50300 Kuala Lumpur
T: (03) 2923066; Fax: 2912659
Founded: 1988
Focus: Educ; Med 08220

Association of Development Research and Training Institutes of Asia and the Pacific (ADIPA), c/o APDC, Pesiaran Duta, POB 12224, 50770 Kuala Lumpur
T: (03) 2548088; Fax: 2550316
Founded: 1973; Members: 100
Focus: Develop Areas
Periodical
ADIPA Newsletter 08221

Commonwealth Association of Scientific Agricultural Societies (CASAS), c/o FPM, Menara Boustead, Jalan Raja Chulan, 50200 Kuala Lumpur
Founded: 1978
Focus: Agri
Periodical
CASAS Newsletter (semi-annually) . . . 08222

Dewan Bahasa dan Pustaka, POB 10803, 50926 Kuala Lumpur
T: (03) 2481011
Founded: 1956
Gen Secr: Haji Jumaat Mohd Noor
Focus: Ling; Lit 08223

Geological Survey of Malaysia, Scrivenor Rd, Ipoh, Perak
Founded: 1903; Members: 792
Gen Secr: E.H. Yin
Focus: Surveying; Geology
Periodicals
Annual Report (annually)
District Memoirs
Economic Bulletins
Map Bulletins
Professional Papers (West)
Regional Memoirs
Reports and Bulletins (East) 08224

Geological Survey of Malaysia, POB 560, 93712 Kuching, Sarawak
T: (082) 240152; Fax: 415390
Founded: 1949; Members: 117
Gen Secr: Dr. Chen Shick-Pei
Focus: Geology
Periodicals
Annual Report (annually)
Bulletin
Geological Papers
Memoirs
Report 08225

Library Association of Malaysia, POB 12545, 50782 Kuala Lumpur
T: (03) 273114; Fax: 2731167
Founded: 1955; Members: 600
Pres: Chew Wing Foong; Gen Secr: Raslim Bakar
Focus: Libraries & Bk Sci
Periodicals
Berita PPM (quarterly)
Majalah PPM (annually) 08226

Malayian Nature Society, POB 10750, 50724 Kuala Lumpur
Founded: 1940; Members: 2650
Focus: Hist; Nat Sci
Periodical
The Malayan Nature Journal (quarterly) . 08227

Malaysian Biochemical Society, c/o Biochemistry Dept, University of Malaya, 59100 Kuala Lumpur
T: (03) 7502884; Fax: 7573661
Founded: 1973; Members: 120
Pres: Prof. P. Ramsamy
Focus: Biochem
Periodical
Proceedings of Annual Conference (annually) 08228

Malaysian Economic Association, Jalan Pantai Bahru, POB 1178, 59700 Kuala Lumpur
T: (03) 7560075; Fax: 7573661
Founded: 1962; Members: 600
Gen Secr: Dr. M. Zainal-Abidin
Focus: Econ
Periodicals
Ekonomika (quarterly)
Malaysian Journal of Economic Studies (semi-annually) 08229

Malaysian Historical Society, 958 Jalan Hose, Kuala Lumpur
T: (03) 481469
Founded: 1953; Members: 160
Pres: Dato Musa Hitam
Focus: Hist
Periodicals
Malaysia Dari Segi Sejarah (annually)
Malaysia in History 08230

Malaysian Institute of Architects, 4-6 Jalan Tangsi, POB 10855, 50726 Kuala Lumpur
T: (03) 2928733; Fax: 2982878
Founded: 1967; Members: 1983
Pres: Henry Lee Inn Seong
Focus: Archit
Periodicals
Berita Akitek (monthly)
Majallah Akitek (quarterly)
Panduan Akitek (annually) 08231

Malaysian Medical Association (MMA), MMA House, 124 Jalan Pahang, 53000 Kuala Lumpur
T: (03) 4420617; Fax: 4418187
Founded: 1959; Members: 5500
Pres: Dr. R.S. McCoy; Gen Secr: Morgan S. Rajah
Focus: Med
Periodicals
Medical Journal of Malaysia (quarterly)
MMA Newsletter (monthly) 08232

Malaysian Nature Society, POB 10750, 60724 Kuala Lumpur
T: (03) 6165259; Fax: 6165258
Founded: 1940; Members: 5000
Focus: Ecology 08233

Malaysian Rubber Research and Development Board, 148 Jalan Ampang, POB 10508, 50716 Kuala Lumpur
Founded: 1959
Focus: Materials Sci
Periodicals
Annual Report (annually)
Getah Asli (quarterly)
Malaysian Rubber Review (quarterly)
Natural Rubber Technology (quarterly)
Rubber Developments (quarterly) 08234

Malaysian Scientific Association, POB 10911, 50728 Kuala Lumpur
Founded: 1955; Members: 356
Pres: Dr. Soon Ting Kueh; Gen Secr: Dr. N.S. Chin
Focus: Sci 08235

Malaysian Society of Anaesthesiologists, MMA House, 124 Jalan Pahang, Kuala Lumpur
T: (03) 980617
Members: 100
Focus: Anesthetics 08236

Malaysian Zoological Society, 301 Lee Yan Lian Bldg, Jalan Tun Perak, 50050 Kuala Lumpur
Pres: Y.B. Tan Dato
Focus: Zoology 08237

Royal Asiatic Society, Malaysian Branch, 130M Jalan Thamby Abdullah, Brickfields, 50470 Kuala Lumpur
T: (03) 2743458
Founded: 1877; Members: 1079
Pres: A. Bin Ali; Gen Secr: H.B. Bin Tajudin
Focus: Hist; Lit; Sociology; Anthro . . . 08238

Tamil Language Society, c/o Dept of Indian Studies, University of Malaysia, Kuala Lumpur
Founded: 1957; Members: 350
Pres: M. Jaykumar; Gen Secr: L. Krishnan
Focus: Ling
Periodical
Tamil Olu (annually) 08239

Malta

Agrarian Society, Palazzo de la Salle, 219 Republic St, Valletta
T: 26345
Founded: 1844; Members: 200
Pres: Prof. Joseph A. Micallef; Gen Secr: Joseph Borg
Focus: Agri 08240

Birdlife Malta, POB 498, Valletta
T: 230684; Fax: 225665
Founded: 1962; Members: 4000
Pres: John Grech; Gen Secr: Denis Cachia
Focus: Ornithology
Periodicals
Bird Talk (bi-monthly)
Il-Huttafa (bi-monthly)
Il-Merill (annually) 08241

Chamber of Architects and Civil Engineers, Medisle Village, Saint Andrews
T: 338851; Fax: 376540
Founded: 1910
Focus: Archit; Civil Eng 08242

Euro-Mediterranean Centre on Insular Coastal Dynamics, c/o Foundation for International Studies, University of Malta, Saint Paul St, Valletta
T: 240746; E-Mail: icod@maltanet.net; Fax: 230551
Founded: 1987; Members: 5
Gen Secr: Anton Micallef
Focus: Oceanography; Ecology 08243

Ghaqda Bibljotekarji, c/o University Library, Msida
Founded: 1969; Members: 125
Pres: Laurence V. Zerafa; Gen Secr: Marian Borg
Focus: Libraries & Bk Sci
Periodicals
Ghaqda Bibljotekarji: Library Association Newsletter (irregularly)
Occasional Papers Series (irregularly) . . 08244

Ghaqda Tal Folklor / Folklore Society, c/o Guido Lanfranco, 78 Saint Trophimus St, Sliema
T: 335382
Founded: 1964; Members: 150
Focus: Ethnology
Periodical
L-Imnara (annually) 08245

Malta Geographical Society, c/o E. Sambrook, 3 Saint Pancras Flats, Nazju Ellul St, Gzira
T: 511886
Founded: 1943; Members: 220
Focus: Geography 08246

Malta Historical Society (MHS), c/o Kosi Kot, Triq Guze Ellul Mercer, Qormi
T: 445799
Founded: 1950; Members: 450
Pres: Prof. Godfrey Wettinger; Gen Secr: Joseph F. Grima
Focus: Hist
Periodicals
Melita Historica (annually)
Proceedings of History Week (irregularly) 08247

Malta Society of Arts, Manufactures and Commerce, 219 Kingsway, Valletta
Focus: Arts; Commerce 08248

Malta Union of Teachers (MUT), 213 Republic St, Valletta
T: 27815, 22663
Founded: 1919; Members: 3400
Focus: Educ 08249

Medical Association of Malta (MAM), c/o Malta Federation of Professional Bodies, 1 Wilga St, Paceville
T: 38851
Members: 320
Focus: Med 08250

Professional Librarians of Malta Association (PLMA), c/o Malta Federation of Professional Bodies, 1 Wilga St, Paceville
T: 38851
Founded: 1971
Focus: Libraries & Bk Sci 08251

Society for the Study and Conservation of Nature, POB 459, Valletta
T: 248558
Founded: 1962; Members: 1500
Focus: Ecology; Botany; Paleontology
Periodicals
Central Mediterranean Naturalist (irregularly)
Il-Ballotra (irregularly)
In-Natura (semi-annually)
Potamon (irregularly) 08252

Mauritania

Association Mauritanienne des Bibliothécaires, Archivistes et Documentalistes, c/o Bibliothèque Nationale, BP 20, Nouakchott
Founded: 1979
Pres: O. Diouwara; Gen Secr: Sid'Ahmed Fall
Focus: Libraries & Bk Sci; Archives; Doc 08253

Mauritius

Royal Society of Arts and Sciences of Mauritius, c/o Sugar Industry Research Institute, Réduit
T: 4541061; Fax: 4541971
Founded: 1829; Members: 191
Pres: W. Owadally; Gen Secr: J. Guého
Focus: Arts; Sci
Periodical
Proceedings 08254

Société de l'Histoire de l'Ile Maurice, Rue de Froberville et Rue Curepipe, Port Louis
Founded: 1938; Members: 810
Gen Secr: G. Ramet
Focus: Hist
Periodical
Bulletin 08255

Société de Technologie Agricole et Sucrière de l'Ile Maurice, c/o Mauritius Sugar Industry Research Institute, Réduit
T: 4541061; Fax: 541971
Founded: 1910; Members: 395
Pres: Dr. J.C. Autrey; Gen Secr: C. Barbe
Focus: Agri; Eng
Periodical
La Revue Agricole et Sucrière de l'Ile Maurice (3 times annually) 08256

Mexico

Academia de Ciencias Históricas de Monterrey, Apdo 389, Monterrey, Nuevo León
Founded: 1947
Pres: Carlos Pérez-Maldonado
Focus: Hist 08257

Academia Mexicana de la Historia, Plaza Carlos Pacheco 21, Cuauhtémoc, 06070 México, D.F.
T: (5) 5219653; Fax: 5219653
Founded: 1919
Pres: Prof. Dr. Miguel León Portilla; Gen Secr: Dr. Gisela von Wobeser
Focus: Hist
Periodical
Memorias (quarterly) 08258

Academia Mexicana de la Lengua, Donceles 66, 06010 México, D.F.
Founded: 1957; Members: 28
Pres: José G. Moreno de Alba
Focus: Ling 08259

Academia Nacional de Ciencias, Av San Jerónimo 260, Col. Jardines de Pedregal, 04500 México, D.F.
T: (5) 5504000; E-Mail: academia@iserve.net.mx, aic@servidor.unam.mx; Fax: 5501143
Founded: 1959; Members: 1000
Pres: Juan Ramón de la Fuente; Gen Secr: Francisco Bolivar
Focus: Sci
Periodicals
Carta Informativa (semi-annually)
Ciencia (quarterly) 08260

Academia Nacional de Historia y Geografía, Londres 60, México D.F.
Founded: 1925; Members: 179
Pres: Antonio Fernández del Castillo
Focus: Geography; Hist
Periodical
Revista 08261

Academia Nacional de Medicina, c/o Centro Médico Nacional, Bloque B, V. Congresos, Av Cuauhtémoc 330, Apdo M 8075, 06725 México, D.F.
T: (5) 5782044; Fax: 5784271
Founded: 1864; Members: 460
Pres: Dr. Juan Rodríguez-Argüelles; Gen Secr: Dr. Maurio García-Sainz
Focus: Med
Periodical
Gaceta Médica de México (bi-monthly) . 08262

Asociación de Ingenieros y Arquitectos de México, Calle del Puente de Alvarado 58, México, D.F.
Founded: 1868; Members: 560
Pres: F. Dovali Ramos; Gen Secr: José Acosta Sánchez
Focus: Archit; Eng 08263

Asociación de Médicas Mexicanas, Oklahoma 151, México D.F.
Founded: 1923; Members: 3000
Pres: Dr. Irene Talamas V.
Focus: Med 08264

Asociación Interamericana de Gastroentereología (AIGA), Pizarras 171, México 20, D.F.
Founded: 1948
Focus: Gastroenter 08265

Asociación Latinoamericana de Ecodesarrollo / Latin American Association for Ecological Development, Apdo 1-110, 21000 Mexicali
Founded: 1978
Focus: Ecology 08266

Asociación Latinoamericana de Sociología (ALAS), c/o Instituto de Investigaciones Sociales, Torre de Humanidades, Universidad, México 20, D.F.
Focus: Sociology 08267

Asociación Médica del Hospital Beistegui, Regina 7, México, D.F.
Founded: 1963
Focus: Med 08268

Asociación Médica Franco-Mexicana, Dr. Balmis 148, México D.F.
Founded: 1928; Members: 600
Pres: Dr. Jorge Espino Vela
Focus: Med 08269

Asociación Mexicana de Administración Científica, Durango 167, México, D.F.
Focus: Law 08270

Asociación Mexicana de Bibliotecarios, AC (AMBAC) / Mexican Librarians Association, Angel Urraza 817A, Col. del Valle, 03100 México, D.F.
T: (5) 5751135, 5753396; E-Mail: ambac@solar.sar.net; Fax: 5751135
Founded: 1954; Members: 1002
Pres: Elsa M. Ramírez Leyva; Gen Secr: José Luis Almanza Morales
Focus: Libraries & Bk Sci
Periodicals
Memorias (annually)
Noticiero de la AMBAC (bi-monthly) . . 08271

Asociación Mexicana de Facultades y Escuelas de Medicina, Av V. Carranza 870, Apdo 836, San Luis de Potosí
Founded: 1957; Members: 30
Pres: Dr. Ramón Arrizabalaga
Focus: Med 08272

Asociación Mexicana de Géologos Petroleros, Torres Bodet 176, 06400 México D.F.
Founded: 1949; Members: 600
Pres: Javier Meneses Gyves
Focus: Geology 08273

Asociación Mexicana de Ginecologia y Obstetricia, Amsterdam 214, Col. Condesa, 06100 México D.F.
T: (5) 5645463; Fax: 2641745
Founded: 1946; Members: 1600
Pres: Dr. Manuel Villalobos Román
Focus: Gynecology
Periodical
Ginecologia y Obstetricia de México (monthly)
. . . . 08274

Asociación Mexicana de Profesores de Microbiología y Parasitología en Escuelas de Medicina, Tolsa 238, Guadalajara, Jalisco
Founded: 1962
Focus: Microbio 08275

Asociación Musical Manuel M. Ponce, Bucareli 12,, México D.F.
T: (5) 5217260
Founded: 1949
Pres: Luis Herrera de la Fuente
Focus: Music 08276

Asociación Nacional de Universidades e Institutos de Educación Superior, Insurgentes Sur 2133, 01000 México D.F.
T: (5) 5502755
Founded: 1950; Members: 99
Gen Secr: María Isabel Pallán Figueroa
Focus: Educ; Sci
Periodical
Revista de la Educación Superior (quarterly)
. . . . 08277

Asociación Panamericana de Cirurgía Pediátrica (APCP), Calzada de Tlalpan 4515, México 22, D.F.
T: 5730094
Founded: 1966; Members: 600
Focus: Surgery 08278

Ateneo de Ciencias y Artes de Chiapas, 3a Oriente 28, Tuxtla Gutiérrez
Founded: 1942; Members: 76
Focus: Arts 08279

Ateneo Nacional de Ciencias y Artes de México, Bucareli12, México D.F.
Founded: 1920; Members: 1000
Pres: Emilio Portes Gil; Gen Secr: José L. Cossio
Focus: Sci; Arts 08280

Ateneo Veracruzano, Independencia 924, Veracruz
Founded: 1933; Members: 68
Pres: C.P.T. Francisco Broissin A.
Focus: Educ 08281

Barra Mexicana-Colegio de Abogados, Varsovia 1, 06600 México D.F.
Fax: (5) 5336775
Founded: 1922; Members: 1685
Pres: Octavio Igartua Araiza; Gen Secr: Fabian Aguinaco Bravo
Focus: Law
Periodical
El Foro (3 times annually) 08282

Center for Economic and Social Studies in the Third World (CESSTEM), Porfirio Diaz 50, San Jerónimo Lidice, 10200 México, D.F.
T: (05) 5952088
Founded: 1976
Focus: Soc Sci; Econ 08283

Center of Coordination and Diffusion of Latin American Studies / Centro Coordinador y Difusor de los Estudios Latinoamericanos, Torre I de Humanidades, Ciudad Univ, 04510 México, D.F.
T: 5505745
Founded: 1978
Focus: Soc Sci; Geography; Hist
Periodical
Carta del CCYDEL (3 times annually) . 08284

Center of Regional Cooperation in Adult Education for Latin America, Quinta Eréndira s/n, 61600 Patzcuaro
T: (0454) 21475; Fax: 20092
Founded: 1951
Focus: Adult Educ
Periodicals
Cuadernos del CREFAL (quarterly)
Revista Interamericana de Educación de Adultos
. . . . 08285

Centre for Latin American Monetary Studies, Durango 54, Cuauhtemoc, Colonia Roma, 06700 México D.F.
T: (05) 5330300; E-Mail: cemlainF@mail.internet.com.mx; Fax: 5254432
Founded: 1952; Members: 65
Pres: Sergio Ghigliazza
Focus: Finance
Periodicals
CEMLA Bulletin (bi-monthly)
Money Affairs (semi-annually)
Montaria (quarterly) 08286

Centro Científico y Técnico Francés en México, Liverpool 67, Col. Juarez, 06600 México, D.F.
T: (5) 250180; Fax: 250183
Founded: 1960
Pres: Jean-Pierre Tihay
Focus: Eng; Nat Sci
Periodical
Interface (3 times annually) 08287

Centro de Estudios Económicos y Sociales del Tercer Mundo, Coronel Porfirio Díaz 50, Col. San Jeronimo Lidice, 10200 México, D.F.
T: 5955950
Focus: Econ; Sociology 08288

Centro de Estudios Educativos, Av Revolución 1291, México 20, D.F.
Founded: 1963
Focus: Educ 08289

Centro de Estudios Monetarios Latinoamericanos (CEMLA), Durango 54, México 7, D.F.
Founded: 1949
Focus: Finance 08290

Centro de Información Científica y Humanística, c/o Universidad Nacional Autónoma de México, Ciudad Universitaria, Apdo 70-392, 04510 México D.F.
T: (5) 6223960; Fax: 6162557
Founded: 1971
Focus: Humanities
Periodicals
Bibliografía Latinoamericana (semi-annually)
Clase: Citas Latinoamericanas en Sociología en Ciencias y Humanidades (quarterly)
Inforum (irregularly)
Periodica: Indice de Revistas Latinoamericanas en Ciencias (quarterly) 08291

Centro de Investigación de Computación, c/o Unidad Profesional Zacatenco IPN-Lindavista, 07738 México
T: (5) 5862990, 7296155; E-Mail: aguzman@pollux.cenac.ipn.mx; Fax: 5862936, 7296167
Founded: 1963; Members: 250
Pres: Dr. Adolfo Guzman; Gen Secr: Dr. Angel Kuri
Focus: Computer & Info Sci 08292

Centro de Investigación y de Estudios Avanzados del Instituto Politécnico Nacional, Av Instituto Politécnico Nacional 2508, Apdo 14-740, 07000 México, D.F.
T: (5) 7477091/92; E-Mail: Adolfo.Martínez@dirección.inf.cinvestav.mx; Fax: 7477093
Founded: 1961; Members: 470
Pres: Dr. Adolfo Martínez Palomo; Gen Secr: Dr. Manuel Méndez Nonell
Focus: Biochem; Physics; Electronic Eng; Math; Chem; Energy; Cell Biol & Cancer Res
Periodical
Avance y Perspectiva (quarterly) 08293

Centro Internacional de Mejoramiento de Maíz y Trigo (CIMMYT), Lisboa 27, Apdo 6-641, 06600 México, D.F.
Founded: 1966
Focus: Agri
Periodicals
Barley Yellow Dwarf Newsletter
CIMMYT Economics Working Paper
CIMMYT hechos y tendencias mundiales relacionadas con maíz
CIMMYT hechos y tendencias mundiales relacionadas con trigo
CIMMYT Hoy
CIMMYT IN
CIMMYT Réalité et tendances-le mais dans le monde: le potentiel maisicole de l'Afrique subsaharienne
CIMMYT Research Report
CIMMYT Today
CIMMYT Wheat Special Report
CIMMYT World Maize Facts and Trends
CIMMYT World Wheat Facts and Trends
Documento de trabajo de Programa de Economía del CIMMYT
Literature on Maize
Literature Update on Wheat, Barley and Triticale
Scientific Information Bulletin 08294

Centro Nacional de Ciencias y Tecnologías Marinas, Apdo 512, Veracruz
Founded: 1957; Members: 23
Focus: Eng 08295

Centro Regional de Educación de Adultos y Alfabetización Funcional para América Latina (CREFAL), Quinta Eréndira, 61600 Pátzcuaro
Fax: 20092
Founded: 1951
Focus: Educ; Adult Educ
Periodicals
Cuadernos del CREFAL (3 times annually)
Retablo de Papel (3 times annually)
Revista Interamericana de Educación de Adultos (semi-annually) 08296

Centro Vasco, Madero 6, México, D.F.
Founded: 1800
Focus: Lit; Hist 08297

Colegio Nacional, Luis González Obregón 23, 06020 México, D.F.
Fax: (5) 7021779
Founded: 1943; Members: 36
Gen Secr: Fausto Vega y Gómez
Focus: Educ
Periodical
Memoria de El Colegio Nacional (annually)
. . . . 08298

Comisión Latinoamericana de Investigadores en Sorgo (CLAIS), Apdo 6641, 06000 México D.F.
T: (05) 7613311; Fax: 41069
Focus: Crop Husb 08299

Commission of Studies for Latin American Church History, Celaya 21-402, Colonia Hipódromo, 06100 México, D.F.
T: (05) 5745661
Founded: 1971
Focus: Rel & Theol
Periodical
Boletín CEHILA (quarterly) 08300

Confederación de Educadores Americanos, Venezuela 38, México 1, D.F.
Focus: Educ 08301

Consejo Interamericano de Archiveros (CITA), c/o Archivo Nacional de México, México, D.F.
Focus: Libraries & Bk Sci 08302

Consejo Mexicano de Dermatología, Durango 324, Col. Roma, 06700 México D.F.
T: (5) 5534518
Founded: 1974; Members: 349
Gen Secr: Prof. Ernesto Macotela Ruíz
Focus: Derm 08303

Consejo Nacional de Ciencia y Tecnologia (CONACYT), Insurgentes Sur 1677, México 20, D.F.
Founded: 1970
Focus: Nat Sci; Eng 08304

Departamento de Antropología e Historia de Nayarit, Av México 91, Tepic, Nayarit
Founded: 1946
Pres: Everardo Peña Navarro
Focus: Anthro; Hist 08305

Departamento de Educación Audiovisual, c/o Instituto Politécnico Nacional, Prolongación de Carpio 475, México, D.F.
Focus: Educ 08306

Environmental Training Network for Latin America and the Caribbean, c/o Naciones Unidas, Oficina Regional para América Latina, Av Presidente Masaryk 29, Colonia Polanco, 11570 México, D.F.
T: (02) 2034975; Fax: 2034465
Founded: 1980
Focus: Ecology 08307

Equipe 7 des Arts Visuels, 2 Lerdo 35, Azcapotzalco, México 16, D.F.
T: 5611271
Focus: Arts 08308

Federación Latinoamericana de Parasitología (FLAP), c/o Departamento de Parasitología, Universidad, Apdo 20372, México 20, D.F.
Founded: 1963
Focus: Microbio 08309

Instituto de Ecología / Ecological Institute, Km 2,5 Carretera Antigua a Coatepec, Apdo 63, 91000 Xalapa
T: 86000, 86110, 86209, 86310, 86409; Fax: 86510
Founded: 1974; Members: 150
Focus: Ecology
Periodicals
Acta Botanica (3 times annually)
Acta Zoologica (3 times annually) . . . 08310

Instituto Indigenista Interamericano / Inter-American Indian Institute, Nubes 232, Col. Pedregal de San Angel, 01900 México, D.F.
T: (5) 5680819; Fax: 6521274
Founded: 1940
Focus: Ethnology
Periodicals
América Indígena (quarterly)
Anuario Indigenista (annually) 08311

Instituto Nacional de Bellas Artes, Paseo de la Reforma y Campo Marte,Atras del Auditorio Nacional, Bosque dee Chapultepec, Miguel Hidalgo, 11560 México D.F.
T: (5) 2805474
Founded: 1947 711=Estrada, Gerardo
Focus: Arts 08312

Instituto Nacional de Higiene, Calzada, Mariano Escobedo 20, México, D.F.
Fax: (5) 276693
Founded: 1904; Members: 153
Focus: Hygiene 08313

Instituto Nacional de Investigaciones Agrícolas, Apdo 6882, México 6, D.F.
Founded: 1960
Focus: Agri 08314

Instituto Panamericano de Geografía e Historia (IPGH) / Pan American Institute of Geography and History, Ex-Arzobispado 29, 11860 México, D.F.
Founded: 1928; Members: 21
Focus: Geography; Hist
Periodicals
Boletín de Antropología Americana (semi-annually)
Folklore Americano (semi-annually)
Revista Cartográfica (semi-annually)
Revista de Historia de Amercia (semi-annually)
Revista Geofísica (semi-annually)
Revista Geográfica (semi-annually) . . . 08315

International Association of Gerontology (IAG), c/o Dr. Samuel Bravo, Jojutla 91, Tlalpan, México, D.F.
T: (5) 5735056; Fax: 6795842
Founded: 1950; Members: 53
Focus: Geriatrics
Periodicals
Gerontology: International Journal of Experimental and Clinical Gerontology (bi-monthly)
IAG Newsletter (quarterly) 08316

International Communication Agency (ICA), Libertad 1492, Guadalajara, Jalisco
Founded: 1949
Focus: Lit 08317

International Communication Agency (ICA), Londres 16, México 6, D.F.
Founded: 1942
Focus: Lit 08318

International Communication Agency (ICA), Av Constitución 411, Apdo 152, Monterrey
Founded: 1949
Focus: Lit 08319

PEN Club de México, Medellín 162, 06700 México D.F.
T: (5) 5645078
Founded: 1924; Members: 62
Pres: Eduardo Lizalde
Focus: Lit 08320

Sociedad Agronómica Mexicana, Mariano Azuela 121, México, D.F.
Focus: Agri 08321

Sociedad Astronómica de México, Jardín Felipe Xicotencath, Col. Alamos, México D.F.
T: (5)5194730
Founded: 1902; Members: 500
Pres: Marte Trejo Sandoval
Focus: Astronomy 08322

Sociedad de Educación, c/o Sección Educacional, Edificio del Banco de Londres y México, México, D.F.
Focus: Educ 08323

Sociedad de Estudios Biológicos, Balderas 94, México, D.F.
Focus: Bio 08324

Sociedad de Oftalmología del Hospital de Oftalmológico de Nuestra Señora de la Luz, c/o Escuela de Medicina, Ezequiel Montes 135, México, D.F.
Founded: 1893
Focus: Ophthal 08325

Sociedad Forestal Mexicana, JesúsTerán 11, México D.F.
Founded: 921; Members: 225
Gen Secr: Rigoberto Vásquez de la Parra
Focus: Forestry 08326

Sociedad Geológica Mexicana, Jaime Torres Bodet 176, Col. Santa Maria La Ribera, 06400 México
T: (5) 5472666
Founded: 1904; Members: 1000
Pres: Bernardo Martell Andrade
Focus: Geology
Periodical
Boletín de la Sociedad Geológica Mexicana (semi-annually) 08327

Sociedad Interamericana de Cardiología (IASC), Juan Badiano 1, México 22, D.F.
T: 5732911
Founded: 1946; Members: 4000
Focus: Cardiol 08328

Sociedad Latinoamericana de Alergología, Dr. Márquez 162, México, D.F.
Founded: 1964; Members: 485
Pres: Dr. Luis Gómez Orazco
Focus: Immunology 08329

Sociedad Matemática Mexicana (SMM), Apdo 70-450, 04510 México, D.F.
T: (5) 6224520; Fax: 5489499
Founded: 1943; Members: 1120
Pres: Dr. José Carlos Gómez L.
Focus: Math
Periodical
Miscelanea Matematica: Boletín de la Sociedad Matematica Mexicana and Aportaciones Matematicas 08330

Sociedad Médica del Hospital General, Dr. Balmis y Dr. Pasteur, México, D.F.
Founded: 1939
Focus: Med 08331

Sociedad Médica del Hospital Oftalmológico de Nuestra Señora de la Luz, Ezequiel Montes 135, México, D.F.
Founded: 1966
Focus: Ophthal 08332

Sociedad Mexicana de Antropología (S.M.A.), Apdo 105-100, 11581 México, D.F.
Founded: 1937; Members: 350
Pres: Dr. Linda Manzanilla Naim
Focus: Anthro

Periodical
Revista Mexicana de Estudios Antropológicos (bianual) 08333

Sociedad Mexicana de Bibliografía, c/o Hemeroteca Nacional, Carmen y San Ildefonso, México, D.F.
Founded: 1945; Members: 91
Focus: Libraries & Bk Sci 08334

Sociedad Mexicana de Cardiología (SMC) / Mexican Society of Cardiology, Juan Badiano 1, Tlalpan, 14080 México, D.F.
T: (5) 5732911 ext 295; E-Mail: smcardio@starnet.net.mx; Fax: 5732111
Founded: 1935; Members: 975
Pres: José F. Guadalajara-Boo; Gen Secr: David Huerta-Hernández
Focus: Cardiol
Periodical
Quehacer cardiológico 08335

Sociedad Mexicana de Entomología, Apdo 63, 91300, Xalapa Veracruz
Founded: 1952; Members: 650
Pres: C. Deloya López
Focus: Entomology
Periodical
Folia Entomológica Mexicana (quarterly) . 08336

Sociedad Mexicana de Estudios Psico-Pedagógicos, Nayarit 86, México, D.F.
Focus: Educ; Psych 08337

Sociedad Mexicana de Eugenesia, Acapulco 44, México, D.F.
Founded: 1931; Members: 150
Pres: Dr. Eugenio Echeverría Arnaux
Focus: Genetics 08338

Sociedad Mexicana de Fitogenética (SOMEFI), Apdo 21, Capingo, Edo de México, 56230 México D.F.
T: (5) 42200 ext 5795; Fax: 46652
Founded: 1965; Members: 1000
Pres: Dr. Hilda Susana Azpiroz Rivero; Gen Secr: Dr. Fernando Castillo Gonzalez
Focus: Botany
Periodical
Fitotecnia (annually) 08339

Sociedad Mexicana de Fitopatología (SMF), c/o Colegio de Postgraduados, Instituto de Fitosanidad, 56230 Montecillo
T: (595) 10220, 11580; E-Mail: fitsanid@colpos.colpos.mx; Fax: 10220, 11580
Founded: 1960; Members: 400
Pres: Dr. Guillermo Fuentes; Gen Secr: Dr. Daniel Teliz
Focus: Botany
Periodical
Revista Mexicana de Fitopatologia: El Vector (semi-annually) 08340

Sociedad Mexicana de Geografía y Estadística, Justo Sierra 19, Apdo 10739, 06020 México, D.F.
T: (5)5427340
Founded: 1833; Members: 1844
Pres: Irene Alicia Suárez Sarabia
Focus: Geography; Stats
Periodical
Boletín (3 times annually) 08341

Sociedad Mexicana de Historia de la Ciencia y la Tecnología, Apdo 21873, 04000 México D.F.
Fax: (5) 6596406
Founded: 1964
Pres: Dr. Juan José Saldaña
Focus: Hist; Sci; Eng
Periodical
Anales (irregularly) 08342

Sociedad Mexicana de Historia Natural, Av Dr. Vertiz 724, México D.F.
Founded: 1868; Members: 400
Pres: Dr. Raul Gio Argaez
Focus: Nat Sci 08343

Sociedad Mexicana de Historia y Filosofía de la Medicina, Apdo 107-035, 06741 México, D.F.
Founded: 1957; Members: 275
Pres: Juan Somolinos Palencia
Focus: Hist
Periodical
Boletín (quarterly) 08344

Sociedad Mexicana de Neurologia y Psiquiatria, Tlalpan, 14410 México, D.F.
T: 5732822 ext 29
Founded: 1947; Members: 400
Focus: Neurology; Psychiatry
Periodical
Revista de Neurologia, Neurocirugia y Psiquiatria (quarterly) 08345

Sociedad Mexicana de Nutrición y Endocrinología, Vasco de Quiroga 15, Col. Sección XVI, Tlalpan, 14000 México D.F.
T: (5)6551768; Fax: 6551768
Founded: 1960; Members: 456
Pres: Dr. Juan Manuel Malacara
Focus: Endocrinology; Food 08346

Sociedad Mexicana de Parasitología, Nicolás de San Juan 1015, Apdo 12813, México, D.F.
Founded: 1960; Members: 51
Pres: Luis Flores Barroeta
Focus: Med 08347

Sociedad Mexicana de Pediatría, Tehuantepec 86-503, Col. Roma Sur, 06760 México, D.F.
T: (5) 5648371; Fax: 5647739
Founded: 1930; Members: 1200
Pres: Dr. Carlos J. Arnaiz Toledo
Focus: Pediatrics
Periodical
Revista Mexicana de Pediatría (semi-annually) 08348

Sociedad Mexicana de Salud Pública, Leibnitz 32, 11560 México D.F.
Founded: 1944; Members: 1000
Pres: Dr. Juan Alberto Herrera Moro Gómez
Focus: Public Health 08349

Sociedad Mexicana de Seguridad Radiologica (SMSR) / Radiological Protection Mexican Association, Insurgentes Sur 1806, 01030 México, D.F.
T: 5349402, 5219045; Fax: 5341405, 5213792
Founded: 1975; Members: 120
Focus: Radiology
Periodical
Boletín SMSR (quarterly) 08350

Sociedad Mexicana de Tisiología, Av Coyoacán 1707, México 12, D.F.
Founded: 1932
Focus: Pulmon Dis 08351

Sociedad Nuclear Mexicana / Mexican Nuclear Society, Sierra Mojada 447, Col. Lomas de Barrilaco, 11010 México, D.F.
T: 5219402, 5406567; Fax: 5213798
Founded: 1988; Members: 250
Focus: Nucl Res 08352

Sociedad Nuevoleonesa de Historia, Geografía y Estadística, c/o Biblioteca Universitaria Alfonso Reyes, Apdo 1575, Monterrey
Founded: 1942; Members: 80
Focus: Geography; Hist; Stats 08353

Sociedad Química de México, Mar del Norte 5, Col. San Alvaro, Deleg. Azcapotzalco, 02090 México D.F.
Founded: 1956; Members: 2300
Pres: I.O.G. Espinosa Chavarría
Focus: Chem 08354

Unión de Universidades de América Latina, Ciudad Universitaria, Delegación Alvaro Obregon, Apdo 70232, 04510 México, D.F.
T: 5489786, 5480269; E-Mail: UDUAL-México
Founded: 1949; Members: 121
Focus: Sci
Periodicals
Gaceta UDUAL (monthly)
Universidades (quarterly) 08355

Moldova, Republic of

Entomological Society of Moldova, Str Academiei 1, 277028 Chişinău
T: (02) 739896
Focus: Zoology 08356

Geographic Society of Moldova, Bul Stefan cel Mare 1, 277012 Chişinău
T: (02) 228428
Focus: Geography 08357

Hydrobiological Society of Moldova, Str Academiei 1, 277028 Chişinău
T: (02) 739809
Focus: Bio 08358

Mendeleev Chemical Society, Str Academiei 3, 277028 Chişinău
T: (02) 739755
Focus: Chem 08359

Microbiological Society of Moldova, Str Academiei 1, 277028 Chişinău
T: (02) 739916
Focus: Microbio 08360

Moldovan Academy of Sciences, Bul Stefan cel Mare 1, 2001 Chişinău
T: (02) 261478; Fax: 223348
Founded: 1961; Members: 114
Pres: Andries Andries; Gen Secr: Gheorghe Siscanu
Focus: Sci
Periodicals
Elektronnaya Obrabotka Materialov: Electronic Processing of Materials (bi-monthly)
Izvestiya: Bulletin
Revista de Filozofie si Drept: Journal of Philosophy and Law (bi-monthly)
Revista de Istorie a Moldovei: Moldovan Historical Journal (quarterly)
Revista de Lingvistica si Stiinta Literara: Journal of Linguistics and Study of Literature (bi-monthly) 08361

Moldovan Society of Animal Protection, Str Academiei 1, 277028 Chişinău
T: (02) 739821
Focus: Ecology 08362

Moldovan Sociological Association, Str Puşkin 38, 279000 Beltsi
T: (02) 23222
Focus: Sociology 08363

Ornithological Society of Moldova, Str Academiei 1, 277028 Chişinău
T: (02) 737509
Pres: I.M. Ganea
Focus: Ornithology 08364

PEN Centre of Moldova, Bul Miron Costin 21, 277068 Chişinău
T: (02) 443540
Focus: Lit 08365

Physical Society of Moldova, Str Academiei 5, 277028 Chişinău
T: (02) 725887
Focus: Physics 08366

Protozoological Society of Moldova, Str Academiei 1, 277028 Chişinău
T: (02) 737511
Focus: Zoology 08367

Society of Botanists of Moldova, Str Padurilor 18, 277018 Chişinău
T: (02) 523896
Focus: Botany 08368

Society of Genetics of Moldova, Str Gribova 44, 277049 Chişinău
T: (02) 432308
Focus: Genetics 08369

Society of Plant Physiologists of Moldova, Str Padurilor 22, 277028 Chişinău
T: (02) 555514
Focus: Botany 08370

Teriological Society of Moldova, Str Academiei 1, 277028 Chişinău
T: (02) 725566
Focus: Nat Sci 08371

Monaco

Association Monégasque de Préhistoire (A.P.S.M.), c/o Musée d'Anthropologie Préhistorique de Monaco, Blvd du Jardin Exotique, 98000 Monaco
T: 93158006; Fax: 93300246
Founded: 1952; Members: 56
Pres: Suzanne Simone
Focus: Hist
Periodical
Bulletin du Musée d'Anthropologie Préhistorique de Monaco (annually) 08372

Commission Internationale pour l'Exploration Scientifique de la Mer Méditerranée (CIESM), 16 Blvd de Suisse, 98000 Monaco
T: 93303879; E-Mail: ciesm@ciesm.org; Fax: 92161195
Founded: 1910; Members: 2521
Pres: Prince Rainier III de Monaco; Gen Secr: Prof. F. Doumenge
Focus: Oceanography
Periodical
Proceedings of CIESM Congress . . . 08373

Organisation Hydrographique Internationale (OHI) / International Hydrographic Organization, 1 Quay Antoine 1er, Monte Carlo
T: 93108100; E-Mail: ihb@unice.fr; Fax: 93108140
Founded: 1921; Members: 63
Pres: Christian-R. Andreasen
Focus: Water Res
Periodicals
IHO Yearbook (annually)
International Hydrographic Bulletin (monthly)
International Hydrographic Review (semi-annually) 08374

Mongolia

Academy of Sciences, Sühbaatar Sq 3, Ulan Bator 11
T: (01) 322216; Fax: 321638
Founded: 1921
Pres: Dr.D. Baatar; Gen Secr: Dr. T. Boldsüh
Focus: Sci
Periodicals
Journal of the MPR Academy of Sciences (quarterly)
Studia Archaeologica
Studia Ethnographica
Studia Folklorica
Studia Historica
Studia Mongolica
Studia Museologica 08375

Morocco

Académie du Royaume du Maroc, Charia Imam Malik, BP 5062, Rabat
T: (07) 755113; Fax: 755101
Founded: 1977
Gen Secr: Dr. A. Berbich
Focus: Sci
Periodical
Academia 08376

African Network of Administrative Information (ANAI), BP 310, Tangiers
T: (09) 942652/91; E-Mail: cafradt@mail.sis.net.ma
Founded: 1981; Members: 26
Gen Secr: M. Lelo
Focus: Computer & Info Sci
Periodical
ANAI Index (annually) 08377

African Training and Research Centre in Administration for Development, Av Mohamed V, BP 310, Tangiers
T: (09) 942652; E-Mail: cafradt@mail.sis.net.ma; Fax: 941415
Founded: 1964; Members: 27
Pres: Messaoud Mansouri; Gen Secr: Dr. M.A. Wali
Focus: Public Admin 08378

Association des Amateurs de la Musique Andalouse, 133 Av Ziraoui, Casablanca
Founded: 1956
Gen Secr: H.D. Benjelloun
Focus: Music 08379

Association Nationale des Géographes Marocains, c/o Faculté des Lettres et des Sciences Humaines, Université Mohamed V, BP 1040, Rabat
T: (07) 771873; 771893, 775493; Fax: 772063
Founded: 1916; Members: 500
Gen Secr: T. Agoumy
Focus: Geography
Periodical
Revue de Géographie du Maroc (semi-annually) 08380

Association Nationale des Informatistes, BP 616, Chellah, Rabat
T: (07) 74907
Founded: 1982; Members: 400
Pres: L. Bachr; Gen Secr: N. El Fassi
Focus: Computer & Info Sci
Periodical
L'Informatiste (semi-annually) 08381

Centre National de Documentation, BP 826, Rabat
T: (07) 7774944; E-Mail: maghridoc@wizarat-sukkan.sukkan.gov.ma; Fax: 773134
Founded: 1968
Pres: Ahmed Fassi Fihri
Focus: Econ; Sociology; Doc
Periodicals
Index de la Documentation Économique, Scientifique et Technique (quarterly)
Index Rétrospectifs Specialisés (bi-monthly) 08382

Comité National de Géographie du Maroc, c/o Institut Universitaire de la Recherche Scientifique, Chari Ma Al Ainine, BP 6287, Rabat
Founded: 1959
Gen Secr: A. Laouina
Focus: Geography 08383

Société des Sciences Naturelles et Physiques du Maroc, c/o Institut Scientifique Chérifien, Av Moulay Chérif, Rabat
Founded: 1920; Members: 420
Pres: H. Faraj; Gen Secr: A. Sasson
Focus: Nat Sci; Physics
Periodicals
Bulletin
Bulletin de la Section des Naturalistes Enseignants 08384

Société d'Etudes Economiques, Sociales et Statistiques du Maroc, BP 535, Chellah, Rabat
Founded: 1933; Members: 20
Pres: Nacer El-Fassi
Focus: Econ; Sociology; Stats 08385

Mozambique

Associação dos Escritores Moçambicanos, Av 24 de Julho 1420, CP 4187, Maputo
Focus: Lit 08386

PEN Centre of Mozambique, c/o Associação dos Escritores Moçambicanos, Av 24 de Julho 1420, CP 4187, Maputo
Gen Secr: Pedro Chissano
Focus: Lit 08387

Myanmar

Central Research Organization, Kanbe, Yankin Post Office, Yangon
Gen Secr: Aung Koe
Focus: Sci 08388

Namibia

Namibia Institute of Architects, POB 1478, Windhoek
T: (061) 35119
Founded: 1952; Members: 86
Pres: D. Pretorius
Focus: Archit 08389

Namibia Scientific Society, POB 67, Windhoek
T: (061) 225372
Founded: 1925; Members: 1100
Pres: Dr. K.F.R. Budack
Focus: Sci
Periodicals
Dinteria
Journal SWA Scientific Society
Namibiana 08390

Nepal

National Council for Science and Technology, Kirtipur, Kathmandu
T: (01) 216348
Founded: 1976
Pres: P.R. Ligal; Gen Secr: D.D. Shakya
Focus: Sci; Eng 08391

Royal Nepal Academy, Kamaladi, Kathmandu
T: (01) 211283
Founded: 1957; Members: 178
Gen Secr: Dr.D.C. Gautam
Focus: Sci
Periodicals
Kabita
Prajna 08392

Royal Nepal Academy of Science and Technology, POB 3323, New Baneswor, Kathmandu
T: (01) 215316; Fax: 228690
Founded: 1982; Members: 157
Gen Secr: Rishi Shah
Focus: Sci; Eng 08393

Netherlands

Actuarieel Genootschap (AG), Postbus 540, 3440 AM Woerden
T: (0348) 439641; Fax: 430555
Founded: 1888; Members: 950
Pres: S. van Vuure; Gen Secr: R. van Dam
Focus: Insurance
Periodical
De Actuaris (bi-monthly) 08394

Algemene Nederlandse Vereniging voor Wijsbegeerte (A.N.V.W.), c/o Faculteit Wijsbegeerte, K.U.B., Postbus 90153, 5000 LE Tilburg
Founded: 1933; Members: 150
Pres: Dr. Marga Jager
Focus: Philos 08395

Association Européenne des Enseignants (AEDE) / European Association of Teachers, Koningsholster 64, 6573 VV Beek-Ubbergen
T: (02468) 42854; E-Mail: context@euronet.nl; Fax: 42902
Founded: 1956; Members: 25000
Pres: Yves-Henri Nouailhat; Gen Secr: Dr. Guus N.M. Wijngaards
Focus: Educ 08396

Association Internationale d'Etudes Occitanes (AIEO), Universitätscampus AAKH, Spitalgasse 2, Hof 8, 1090 Wien
Founded: 1981; Members: 350
Pres: Prof. Dr. Georg Kremnitz; Gen Secr: François Pic
Focus: Ethnology
Periodical
Bulletin de l'AIEO 08397

Association Internationale pour l'Histoire du Verre (AIHV) / International Association for the History of Glass, Postbus 177, 7240 AD Lochem
T: (0573) 256272; Fax: 256272
Founded: 1958; Members: 400
Pres: G. Meconcelli-Notarianni; Gen Secr: K. King
Focus: Hist 08398

Association Montessori Internationale / International Montessori Association, Koninginneweg 161, 1075 CN Amsterdam
T: (020) 6798932; E-Mail: 106203.452@compuserve.com; Fax: 6767341
Founded: 1929; Members: 3000
Pres: G.J. Portielje; Gen Secr: Renilde Montessori
Focus: Educ
Periodical
Communications (quarterly) 08399

Association of European Paediatric Cardiologists, c/o University Hospital Nijmegen, Kinderhartc., Geert Grooteplein 20, 6500 HB Nijmegen
T: (024) 3619060; E-Mail: O.Daniels@ckskhc.azn.nl; Fax: 3619052
Founded: 1964; Members: ca. 530
Pres: Prof. Dr. Fernando A. Maymone-Martins; Gen Secr: Dr. Otto Daniëls
Focus: Cardiol; Pediatrics 08400

Bataafsch Genootschap der Proefondervindelijke Wijsbegeerte, Postbus 597, 3000 AN Rotterdam
Founded: 1769; Members: 375
Pres: Prof. Dr. A.J. Man in't Veld; Gen Secr: Dr. J.R. ter Molen
Focus: Philos; Sci
Periodical
Nieuwe Verhandelingen (irregularly) . . . 08401

Benelux Society for Microcirculation, c/o Dept of Physiology, Free University, Van der Boechorstr 7, 1081 BT Amsterdam
Founded: 1986; Members: 40
Gen Secr: P. Sipkema
Focus: Biophys 08402

Bond Heemschut, Korenmetershuis, N.Z. Kolk 28, 1012 PV Amsterdam
T: (020) 6225292; Fax: 6240571
Founded: 1911; Members: 10000
Focus: Archit; Ecology
Periodical
Heemschut (monthly) 08403

Bond van Nederlandse Stedebouwkundigen (BNS), Waterlooplein 219, Postbus 19126, 1000 GC Amsterdam
T: (020) 6276820
Founded: 1935; Members: 425
Focus: Urban Plan
Periodical
Blauwekamer/Profiel (bi-monthly) 08404

Caribbean Institute of Perinatology (CIP), c/o Dept of Obstetrics and Gynaecology, University Hospital Groningen, Hanzeplein 1, 9713 EZ Groningen
T: (050) 3613173; E-Mail: e.r.boersma@med.rug.nl; Fax: 3611062
Founded: 1988; Members: 80
Pres: Prof. C. Berchel; Gen Secr: Prof. Dr. E. Rudy Boersma
Focus: Gynecology 08405

Center for Research and Documentation on the World Language Problem, c/o CED, Nieuwe Binnenweg 176, 3015 BJ Rotterdam
T: (010) 4361044; E-Mail: uea@inter.nl.net; Fax: 4361751
Founded: 1952
Gen Secr: Prof. H. Tonkin
Focus: Ling 08406

Centraal Bureau voor Genealogie / Central Bureau for Genealogy, Prins Willem Alexanderhof 22, Postbus 11755, 2502 AT Den Haag
T: (070) 3150500; Fax: 3478394
Founded: 1945
Focus: Genealogy
Periodicals
Genealogie (quarterly)
Jaarboek (annually)
Nederland's Adelsboek (annually)
Nederland's Patriciaat (annually) 08407

Centrum voor de Studie van het Onderwijs in Ontwikkelingslanden / Centre for the Study of Education in Developing Countries, Kortenaerkade 11, Postbus 29777, 2502 LT Den Haag
T: (070) 4260291; Fax: 4260299
Founded: 1963; Members: 19
Pres: Prof. Dr. L.F.B. Dubbeldam
Focus: Educ
Periodical
Verhandelingen 08408

Centrum voor Plantenveredelings- en Reproduktieonderzoek (CPRO) / Centre for Plant Breeding and Reproduction Research, Postbus 16, 6700 AA Wageningen
Focus: Agri; Crop Husb
Periodical
Annual Report (annually) 08409

Centrum voor Wiskunde en Informatica / Centre for Mathematics and Computer Science, Kruislaan 413, 1098 SJ Amsterdam
T: (020) 5929333; Fax: 5924199
Founded: 1946; Members: 150
Focus: Math; Computer & Info Sci
Periodicals
CWI Monographs
CWI Syllabus
CWI Tracts
Jaarverslagen: Annual Report (annually)
Report Series (irregularly) 08410

College van Toezicht, Keizersgracht 321, Postbus 19611, 1000 GP Amsterdam
Founded: 1988
Pres: H.B.A. Verhagen
Focus: Archit 08411

Comité International d'Histoire de l'Art, Kromme Nieuwegracht 29, 3512 HD Utrecht
T: (030) 314886; Fax: 314886
Focus: Hist; Arts; Cultur Hist 08412

Commission of Socialist Teachers of the European Community (CSTEC), Kanonsdijk 128, 7205 AE Zutphen
T: (05750) 12439
Focus: Educ 08413

Conference of European Computer User Associations (CECUA), c/o BSG, Postbus 432, 1400 AK Bussum
Founded: 1978
Focus: Computer & Info Sci 08414

Consortium of Institutions of Higher Education in Health and Rehabilitation in Europe (COHEHRE), Postbus, 6503 GL Nijmegen
T: (024) 3596666; Fax: 3596550
Founded: 1990
Pres: Cor Segeren; Gen Secr: Maj Aldskogius
Focus: Educ; Public Health; Rehabil
Periodical
COHEHRE Newsletter (quarterly) 08415

Esperanto Writers' Association, Volkerakstr 38, 1078 XT Amsterdam
T: (020) 6712664
Founded: 1957; Members: 83
Focus: Lit 08416

Europa Nostra/IBI, Lange Voorhout 35, 2514 EC Den Haag
T: (070) 3560333; Fax: 3617865
Founded: 1991; Members: 1200
Pres: Prince Consort of Denmark; Gen Secr: Antonio Marchini Camia
Focus: Preserv Hist Monuments 08417

European Asphalt Pavement Association (EAPA), Straatweg 68, Postbus 175, 3620 AD Breukelen
T: (03462) 66868; Fax: 63505
Founded: 1973
Focus: Civil Eng
Periodical
European Asphalt Magazine (quarterly) . 08418

European Association for Cancer Education (EACE), c/o BOOG, Blasingel 1, 9713 BZ Groningen
T: (050) 632888; Fax: 632883
Founded: 1987
Focus: Educ; Cell Biol & Cancer Res
Periodical
Journal of Cancer Education 08419

European Association for Cognitive Ergonomics (EACE), c/o Dept of Mathematics and Computer Science, Vrije Universiteit, De Boelelaan 1081A, 1081 HV Amsterdam
T: (020) 5485591; Fax: 6426275
Founded: 1987
Focus: Computer & Info Sci
Periodical
EACE Newsletter (semi-annually) 08420

European Association for Gastroenterology and Endoscopy (EAGE), c/o Academic Medical Center, Melbergdreef 9, 1105 AZ Amsterdam
Founded: 1970; Members: 352
Pres: Prof. J.P. Galmiche; Gen Secr: Prof. P. Malfertheimer
Focus: Gastroenter
Periodical
European Journal for Gastroenterology and Hepatology 08421

European Association for Grey Literature Exploitation (EAGLE), Postbus 40407, 2209 LK Den Haag
T: (070) 314028; Fax: 3140493
Founded: 1981
Focus: Lit 08422

European Association for Gynaecologists and Obstetricians, c/o Dept of Obstetrics and Gynecology, University Hospital, Postbus 9101, 6500 HB Nijmegen
T: (080) 514725; Fax: 540576
Founded: 1985; Members: 100
Focus: Gynecology
Periodical
European Journal of Obstetrics, Gynecology and Reproductive Biology 08423

European Association for International Education (EAIE), Van Diemenstr 344, 1013 CR Amsterdam
T: (020) 6252727; E-Mail: eaie@eaie.nl; Fax: 6209406
Founded: 1989
Pres: Giancarlo Spinelli; Gen Secr: Hilary Callan
Focus: Educ
Periodical
EAIE Newsletter (3 times annually) . . . 08424

European Association for Microprocessing and Microprogramming (EUROMICRO), Postbus 2346, 7301 EA Apeldoorn
T: (055) 557372; Fax: 557393
Founded: 1973
Focus: Computer & Info Sci 08425

European Association for Population Studies (EAPS), Postbus 11676, 2502 AR Den Haag
T: (070) 3565200; E-Mail: eaps@nidi.nl; Fax: 3647187
Founded: 1983; Members: 550
Pres: Graziella Caselli; Gen Secr: Nico van Nimwegen
Focus: Soc Sci
Periodicals
EAPS Newsletter (2-3 times annually)
European Journal of Population (quarterly) 08426

European Association for Potato Research (EAPR), Postbus 20, 6700 AA Wageningen
T: (0317) 483041; Fax: 484575
Founded: 1956; Members: 650
Pres: L.M. Monti; Gen Secr: P.C. Struik
Focus: Food 08427

European Association for Research on Plant Breeding (EUCARPIA), Postbus 315, 6700 AH Wageningen
T: (0317) 482838; E-Mail: marjo.dejeu@users.pv.wan.nl; Fax: 483457
Founded: 1956; Members: 1000
Pres: Dr. G.T. Scarascia Mugnozza; Gen Secr: Dr. M.J. de Jeu
Focus: Botany; Crop Husb; Genetics
Periodicals
EUCARPIA Bulletin (annually)
Proceedings of Section Meetings (irregularly) 08428

European Association for the Education of Adults (EAEA), Postbus 367, 3800 AJ Amersfoort
T: (033) 4654116; Fax: 4654116
Founded: 1953; Members: 160
Pres: P. Federighi; Gen Secr: W. Bax
Focus: Adult Educ
Periodicals
Conference Reports (irregularly)
Newsletter (quarterly) 08429

European Association for the Science of Air Pollution (EURASAP), c/o Prof. Peter Builtjes, TNO-MEP, POB 342, 7300 AH Apeldoorn
T: (055) 5493038; Fax: 5493252
Founded: 1986
Pres: Prof. Peter Builtjes
Focus: Ecology 08430

European Association of Diabetes Educators (EADE), Postbus 3023, 2301 DA Leiden
T: (071) 210905
Founded: 1986
Focus: Educ; Diabetes 08431

European Association of Distance Teaching Universities (EADTU), Valkenburgerweg 167, Postbus 2960, 6401 DL Heerlen
T: (045) 5762214; E-Mail: eadtu@ouh.nl; Fax: 5741473
Founded: 1987; Members: 18
Pres: Prof. J.M. Baissus; Gen Secr: P.H. Henderikx
Focus: Educ
Periodical
EADTU-News (quarterly) 08432

European Association of Geoscientists and Engineers (E.A.E.G.), Laan van Vollenhove 3039, Postbus 298, 3700 AG Zeist
T: (030) 6962655; E-Mail: cage@pobox.ruu.nl; Fax: 6962640
Founded: 1951; Members: 6000
Pres: J. Smethuest; Gen Secr: J.-C. Grosset
Focus: Geophys
Periodicals
First Break (monthly)
Geophysical Prospecting (8 times annually)
Petroleum Geoscience (8 times annually) 08433

European Association of Law and Economics, c/o University of Maastricht, Postbus 616, 6200 MD Maastricht
T: (043) 887060; Fax: 256538
Founded: 1984; Members: 280
Focus: Econ; Law 08434

European Association of State Veterinary Officers (EASVO), c/o Veterinaire Inspectie van de Volksgezondheid, Wijnhaven 78, 3011 WT Rotterdam
T: (010) 4132210; Fax: 4046064
Founded: 1980; Members: 15
Pres: Dr. J. Minderhoud; Gen Secr: J. Brodeziek
Focus: Vet Med 08435

European Association of Veterinary Pharmacology and Toxicology (EAVPT), c/o Dept of Veterinary Pharmacology and Toxicology, Faculty of Veterinary Medicine, University of Utrecht, Postbus 80176, 3508 TD Utrecht
Focus: Vet Med 08436

European Association of Zoos and Aquaria, c/o Amsterdam Zoo, Postbus 20164, 1000 HD Amsterdam
T: (020) 6207476, 6224934; E-Mail: nvdzoos@nvdzoos.nl; Fax: 6253931, 6253571
Founded: 1985; Members: 230
Pres: Prof. R. Wheater; Gen Secr: Dr. Koen Brouwer
Focus: Zoology 08437

European Calcified Tissue Society, c/o Dept of Oral Cell Biology, Van der Boechorststr 7, 1080 BT Amsterdam
Founded: 1981
Focus: Cell Biol & Cancer Res 08438

European Cartographic Institute, Laan Copes Van Cattenburch 79, 2585 EW Den Haag
T: (02) 2161545; Fax: 2163026
Focus: Cart 08439

European Centre for Development Policy Management (ECDPM), Onze Lieve Vrouweplein 21, 6211 HE Maastricht
T: (043) 3502900; E-Mail: info@ecdpm.org; Fax: 3502902
Founded: 1986
Gen Secr: Dr. L. de la Rive Box
Focus: Develop Areas; Poli Sci 08440

European Centre for Work and Society (ECWS), Hoogbrugstr 43, Postbus 3073, 6202 NB Maastricht
T: (043) 3216724; E-Mail: general@ecus.nl; Fax: 3255712
Founded: 1979; Members: 23
Pres: D. Wijgnerts
Focus: Soc Sci 08441

European College of Gerodontology (ECG), c/o Dept of Oral Function, Dental School Nijmegen, Postbus 9101, 6500 HB Nijmegen
Founded: 1990
Focus: Dent 08442

European College of Obstetrics and Gynaecology (ECOG), c/o Office of Post Graduate Medical Education, Erasmus University Medical School, Postbus 1738, 3000 DR Rotterdam
T: (010) 4087880
Founded: 1992
Focus: Gynecology 08443

European Committee for the Advancement of Thermal Sciences and Heat Transfer (EUROTHERM), c/o Delft University of Technology, Postbus 5046, 2600 GA Delft
T: (015) 784104; Fax: 622814

Founded: 1986
Focus: Eng *08444*

European Company Lawyers Association (ECLA), Prinses Beatrixlaan 5, Postbus 93093, 2509 AB Den Haag
T: (070) 3497397; Fax: 3819508
Founded: 1990
Focus: Law *08445*

European Development Education Curriculum Network (EDECN), Nassauplein 8, 1815 GM Alkmaar
T: (072) 118502; Fax: 151221
Founded: 1982; Members: 48
Focus: Educ *08446*

European Environmental Research Organization (EERO), General Foulkesweg 70, Postbus 191, 6700 AD Wageningen
T: (08370) 84817; Fax: 84818
Founded: 1987; Members: 50
Focus: Ecology *08447*

European Federation of Associations of Market Research Organizations (EFAMRO), c/o ESOMAR, J.J. Viottastr 29, 1071 JP Amsterdam
T: (020) 6642141; E-Mail: email@esomar.nl; Fax: 6642922
Founded: 1992; Members: 8
Pres: Claude Bénazeth; Gen Secr: Bryan A. Bates
Focus: Marketing *08448*

European Federation of Branches of the World's Poultry Science Association, c/o Spelderholt Institute for Poultry Research, Beekbergen
T: 1808
Founded: 1960; Members: 3900
Focus: Zoology
Periodical
World's Poultry Science Journal (3 times annually) *08449*

European Full-Scale Modelling Association (EFA), c/o Ruud van Wezel, Wageningen Agricultural University, POB 8060, 6700 DA Wageningen
T: (08370) 82088
Founded: 1986
Focus: Eng *08450*

European Grassland Federation, c/o Netherlands Fertilizer Institute, Badhuisweg 139, 2597 JN Den Haag
T: (070) 525071
Founded: 1963; Members: 20
Focus: Agri
Periodical
Proceedings (bi-annually) *08451*

European Society for Opinion and Marketing Research (ESOMAR) / Association Européenne pour les Etudes d'Opinion et de Marketing, J.J. Viottastr 29, 1071 JP Amsterdam
T: (020) 6642141; E-Mail: email@esomar.nl; Fax: 6642922
Founded: 1948; Members: 3500
Pres: Mario van Hamersveld; Gen Secr: Juergen Schwoerer
Focus: Marketing
Periodicals
Annual Congress Book of Papers (annually)
The ESOMAR Directory (annually)
Marketing and Research Today (quarterly)
Monograph Series (irregularly)
Newsbrief (monthly)
Seminar Books of Papers (8-10 times annually) *08452*

European Society of Cardiology (E.S.C.) / Société Européenne de Cardiologie, Postbus 23410, 3001 KK Rotterdam
T: (010) 186014145; Fax: 186014258
Founded: 1950
Focus: Cardiol
Periodical
European Heart Journal (monthly) . . . *08453*

Federatie van Organisaties van Bibliotheek-, Informatie-, Dokumentatiewezen (FOBID) / Federation of Library Information and Documentation Organisations, Postbus 398, 2600 AJ Delft
T: (03) 353092
Founded: 1975
Pres: Dr. R. van der Velde
Focus: Doc; Libraries & Bk Sci; Computer & Info Sci *08454*

Fédération Internationale d'Information et de Documentation (FID) / International Federation for Information and Documentation, Prins Willem-Alexanderhof 5, 2595 BE Den Haag
T: (070) 3140671; E-Mail: fid@python.konbib.nl; Fax: 3140667
Founded: 1895; Members: 425
Pres: Martha B. Stone
Focus: Doc
Periodicals
Education and Training Programmes for Information Personnel: ET Newsletter (quarterly)
FID Directory (bi-annually)
FID News Bulletin (monthly)
International Forum of Information and Documentation (quarterly) *08455*

FOM-Instituut voor Atoom- en Molecuulfysica / FOM Institute of Atomic and Molecular Physics, Kruislaan 407, Postbus 41883, 1009 DB Amsterdam
T: (020) 946711; Fax: 6684106
Founded: 1953; Members: 200
Focus: Nucl Res; Physics
Periodical
Annual Report (annually) *08456*

FOM-Instituut voor Plasmafysica Rijnhuizen / Institute of Plasmaphysics Rijnhuizen, Edisonbaan 14, Postbus 1207, 3430 BE Nieuwegein
Fax: (03402) 31204
Founded: 1959; Members: 120
Focus: Nucl Res
Periodical
Annual Status Report (annually) *08457*

Fries Genootschap van Geschied-, Oudheid- en Taalkunde, c/o Fries Museum, Turfmarkt 11, 8911 KS Leeuwarden
Founded: 1827; Members: 1800
Gen Secr: Dr. O.D.J. Roemeling
Focus: Archeol; Hist
Periodicals
Fryslân (quarterly)
De Vrije Fries (annually) *08458*

Fryske Akademy (FA) / Frisian Academy, Postbus 54, 8900 AB Leeuwarden
T: (058) 2131414; E-Mail: fa@fa.know.nl; Fax: 2131414
Founded: 1938; Members: 3000
Focus: Ling; Hist; Soc Sci
Periodicals
It Beaken (quarterly)
Ut de Smidte (quarterly)
De Vrije Fries (annually) *08459*

Gelre / Vereniging tot Beoefening van Gelderse Geschiedenis, Oudheidkunde en Recht, Markt 1, 6811 CG Arnhem
T: (085) 599335
Founded: 1897; Members: 800
Focus: Hist
Periodical
Bijdragen en Mededelingen (annually) . . *08460*

Genootschap Amstelodamum, Singel 436h, 1017 AV Amsterdam
T: (020) 246740
Focus: Hist *08461*

Genootschap Architectura et Amicitia, Waterlooplein 211, 1011 PG Amsterdam
T: (020) 6220188
Founded: 1855; Members: 225
Pres: Prof. M.E. Zwarts; Gen Secr: M. Pothoff
Focus: Archit *08462*

Genootschap ter Bevordering von Natuur-, Genees- en Heelkunde, Plantage Muidergracht 12, 1018 TV Amsterdam
T: (020) 5255125
Founded: 1790; Members: 900
Pres: Dr. P.J. Klopper
Focus: Med; Public Health *08463*

Genootschap voor Wetenschappelijke Filosofie, c/o Dr. G. Corver, Fazantweg 12, 9765 JM Paterswolde
Founded: 1933; Members: 100
Focus: Philos *08464*

Geschiedkundige Vereniging Die Haghe, Galvanistr 95, 2517 RB Den Haag
T: (070) 624562
Founded: 1890; Members: 1100
Focus: Hist
Periodical
Yearbook (annually) *08465*

Hague Academy of International Law (HAIL), Carnegieplein 2, 2517 KJ Den Haag
T: (070) 3024242
Founded: 1923; Members: 16
Pres: H.E.N. Valticos; Gen Secr: Prof. D. Bardonnet
Focus: Law *08466*

Historisch Genootschap De Maze, c/o Gemeentearchief, Robert Fruinstr 52, 3021 XE Rotterdam
T: (010) 775166
Founded: 1931; Members: 90
Focus: Hist *08467*

Historisch Genootschap Roterodamum, 's-Landswerf 177, 3063 GE (010) Rotterdam
T: 127869
Focus: Hist *08468*

Hollandsche Maatschappij der Wetenschappen (H.M.W.) / Dutch Society of Sciences, Postbus 9698, 2003 LR Haarlem
T: (023) 321773
Founded: 1752; Members: 450
Pres: M. Enschedé
Focus: Sci
Periodical
Haarlemse Voordrachten (annually) . . . *08469*

Institute for Esperanto in Commerce and Industry (IECI), Postbus 72, Valkenswaard
Founded: 1963
Focus: Ling *08470*

Instituut voor Mechanisatie, Arbeid en Gebouwen (IMAG) / Institute of Agricultural Engineering, Mansholtlaan 10-12, 6708 PA Wageningen
T: (08370) 76300; Fax: 25670
Founded: 1974; Members: 155
Focus: Agri
Periodicals
Annual Report (annually)
IMAG-publikaties (8 times annually)
IMAG-Research Reports *08471*

Instituut voor Onderwijskundige Dienstverlening, Postbus 9104, 6500 HE Nijmegen
T: (080) 612470; Fax: 615551
Focus: Educ *08472*

Instituut voor Toegepaste Sociale Wetenschappen (ITS) / Institute for Applied Social Sciences, Toernooiveld 5, Postbus 9048, 6500 KJ Nijmegen
T: (080) 653500; Fax: 653599
Founded: 1965; Members: 140
Focus: Soc Sci
Periodical
ITS-publikaties *08473*

Internationaal Instituut voor Sociale Geschiedenis (Stichting) (IISG) / International Institute of Social History, Cruquiusweg 31, 1019 AT Amsterdam
T: (020) 6685866; E-Mail: inf.gen@iisg.nl; Fax: 6654181
Founded: 1935
Pres: H.M. van de Kar
Focus: Hist
Periodicals
Annual Report (annually)
International Review of Social History (3 times annually) *08474*

International Academy of Management (IAM), c/o CIOS, Van Alkemadelaan 700, Postbus 90730, 2509 LS Den Haag
Founded: 1958; Members: 180
Focus: Business Admin *08475*

International Association for Hydraulic Research (IAHR), Rotterdamseweg 185, Postbus 177, 2600 MH Delft
T: (015) 2858585; E-Mail: iahr@wloelft.nl; Fax: 2858582
Founded: 1935; Members: 2360
Pres: Prof. Dr. H. Kobus; Gen Secr: H.J. Overbeek
Focus: Eng
Periodicals
IAHR Bulletin (bi-monthly)
Journal of Hydraulic Research (bi-monthly)
Proceedings of Biennial Congresses (bi-annually) *08476*

International Association for Media in Science (IAMS), Postbus 80125, 3508 TC Utrecht
T: (030) 534500; Fax: 515463
Focus: Mass Media
Periodical
Newsletter *08477*

International Association for Official Statistics, Prinses Beatrixlaan 428, Postbus 950, 2270 AZ Voorburg
T: (070) 3375737; Fax: 3860025
Founded: 1985; Members: 540
Focus: Stats *08478*

International Association for Statistical Computing (IASC), Prinses Beatrixlaan 428, Postbus 950, 2270 AZ Voorburg
T: (070) 3357737; E-Mail: Statist Voorburg; Fax: 3860025
Founded: 1977; Members: 775
Focus: Stats; Computer & Info Sci
Periodical
CSOA: Computational Statistics and Data Analysis (3 times annually) *08479*

International Association of Applied Psychology, Montessorilaan 3, 6525 HR Nijmegen
Founded: 1920; Members: 2122
Focus: Psych
Periodicals
International Review of Applied Psychology (quarterly)
Newsletter (bi-annually) *08480*

International Association of Wood Anatomists (IAWA), c/o Institute of Systematic Botany, Heidelberglaan 2, 3584 CS Utrecht
T: (030) 532643; Fax: 518061
Founded: 1931; Members: 500
Focus: Forestry
Periodical
IAWA Journal (quarterly) *08481*

International Bureau of Fiscal Documentation (IBFD), Sarphatistr 600, Postbus 20237, 1000 HE Amsterdam
T: (020) 6267726; E-Mail: Forintax; Fax: 6228658
Founded: 1938
Focus: Law; Doc
Periodicals
Bulletin for International Fiscal Documentation (monthly)
European Taxation (monthly)
International VAT Monitor (monthly) . . . *08482*

International Colour Association, c/o Philips Lighting, Postbus 80020, 5600 JM Eindhoven
Founded: 1967; Members: 28
Focus: Chem *08483*

International Commission for the Nomenclature of Cultivated Plants (ICNCP), c/o Government Institute for Research on Varieties of Cultivated Plants, Dept for Horticultural Botany, Postbus 32, 6700 AA Wageningen
Founded: 1955; Members: 24
Focus: Botany *08484*

International Commitee for Histochemistry and Cytochemistry (ICHC), Wassenaarseweg 62, 2333 AL Leiden
Founded: 1960
Focus: Chem *08485*

International Federation for Housing and Planning (IFHP), Wassenaarseweg 43, 2596 CG Den Haag
T: (070) 3244557; Fax: 3282085
Founded: 1913; Members: 1200
Focus: Civil Eng; Urban Plan
Periodicals
Congress Papers Proceedings (annually)
IFHP News Sheet (7 times annually) . . *08486*

International Federation of Library Associations and Institutions (IFLA), Prins Willem Alexanderhof 5, Postbus 95312, 2509 CH Den Haag
T: (070) 3140884; E-Mail: IFLA.HQ@IFLA.NL; Fax: 3834827
Founded: 1927; Members: 1530
Pres: Robert Wedgeworth; Gen Secr: Leo Voogt
Focus: Libraries & Bk Sci
Periodicals
IFLA Council Report (bi-annually)
IFLA Directory (bi-annually)
IFLA Journal (bi-monthly)
IFLA Medium Term Programme 1998-2002 (every 4 years) *08487*

International Huntington Association (IHA), c/o Gerrit Dommerholt, Callunahof 8, 7217 ST Harfsen
T: (0573) 431595; Fax: 3586174
Founded: 1979; Members: 32
Pres: Gerrit Dommerholt; Gen Secr: Robyn Kapp
Focus: Med
Periodical
Newsletter (semi-annually) *08488*

International Organisation for the Study of the Endurance of Wire Ropes, c/o Dept of Transport Technology, University of Technology Delft, Postbus 5034, 2600 GA Delft
T: (015) 782011; Fax: 781397
Founded: 1963
Focus: Materials Sci
Periodical
Bulletin (semi-annually) *08489*

International Organisation for the Study of the Old Testament, POB 9515, 2300 RA Leiden
T: (071) 5272577; Fax: 5272571
Founded: 1950
Pres: Prof. M. Saebø; Gen Secr: Prof. Arie van der Kooij
Focus: Rel & Theol *08490*

International Radiation Protection Association (IPRA), Postbus 662, 5600 MB Eindhoven
T: (040) 2473355; Fax: 2435020
Founded: 1966; Members: 13000
Pres: Dr. Klaus E. Duftschmid; Gen Secr: Chris J. Huyskens
Focus: Radiology
Periodical
IRPA-Bulletin (quarterly) *08491*

International Society for Horticultural Science (I.S.H.S.), De Dreijen 6, 6703 BC Wageningen
T: (08370) 21747
Founded: 1959; Members: 3000
Focus: Hort
Periodicals
Acta Horticulturae
Chronica Horticulturae (quarterly) *08492*

International Society for Soilless Culture (ISOSC), Postbus 52, 6700 AB Wageningen
T: (0317) 413809; Fax: 423457
Founded: 1955; Members: 405
Pres: Rick S. Donnan; Gen Secr: Abram A. Steiner
Focus: Agri *08493*

International Society of City and Regional Planners (ISoCaRP), Mauritskade 23, 2514 HD Den Haag
T: (070) 3462654; Fax: 3617909
Founded: 1965; Members: 432
Focus: Urban Plan
Periodical
The News Bulletin (semi-annually) . . . *08494*

International Society of Paediatric Oncology, Postbus 3283, 5203 DG 's-Hertogenbosch
T: (073) 6429285; E-Mail: imedex@pi.net; Fax: 6414766
Founded: 1969; Members: 891
Pres: Prof. S.O. Lie; Gen Secr: Prof. A.W. Craft
Focus: Pediatrics; Cell Biol & Cancer Res

Periodical
Medical and Paediatric Oncology (monthly) 08495

International Statistical Institute (ISI), Prinses Beatrixlaan 428, Postbus 950, 2270 AZ Voorburg
T: (070) 3375737; E-Mail: Statist Voorburg; Fax: 3860025
Founded: 1885; Members: 1800
Focus: Stats
Periodicals
International Statistical Review (3 times annually)
Short Book Reviews (3 times annually)
Statistical Theory and Method Abstracts (quarterly) 08496

International Technical and Scientific Organization for Soaring Flight (OSTIV), c/o DFVLR, Van Halewijnplein 37, 8031 Wessling
Founded: 1948
Focus: Eng; Sci 08497

IPO-Centrum voor Onderzoek naar Mens-Systeem Interactie (IPO) / Institute for Perception Research, Postbus 513, 5600 MB Eindhoven
T: (040) 2477100; Fax: 2431930
Founded: 1957; Members: 900
Focus: Biophys
Periodical
IPO Annual Progress Report (annually) . 08498

Katholiek Documentatie Centrum (KDC), Erasmuslaan 36, 6521 MG Nijmegen
Fax: (080) 615944
Focus: Hist; Sociology; Rel & Theol
Periodicals
Bronnen en Studies (irregularly)
Jaarboeken (annually)
Scripta (irregularly)
Sleutels (irregularly) 08499

Koninklijk Instituut van Ingenieurs (KIvI), Prinsessegracht 23, Postbus 30424, 2514 AP Den Haag
T: (070) 3919900; E-Mail: Kiribur@Technet.IAF.NL; Fax: 3919840
Founded: 1847; Members: 21000
Pres: J.M.H. van Engelshoven; Gen Secr: J.N.P. Haarsma
Focus: Eng
Periodicals
De Ingenieur (bi-weekly)
Ingenieursnieuws (bi-weekly)
Journal A: Automatic Control
Yearbook (bi-annually) 08500

Koninklijk Instituut voor Taal-, Land- en Volkenkunde (KITLV) / Royal Institute of Linguistics and Anthropology, Reuvensplaats 2, Postbus 9515, 2300 RA Leiden
T: (071) 5272295; Fax: 5272638
Founded: 1851; Members: 2000
Gen Secr: Prof. Dr. P. Boomgaard
Focus: Anthro; Ling; Ethnology
Periodicals
Bijdragen tot de Taal-, Land- en Volkenkunde (quarterly)
European Newsletter on Southeast Asian Studies (semi-annually)
Excerpta Indonesica (quarterly)
New West Indian Guide (quarterly) . . . 08501

Koninklijk Nederlands Aardrijkskundig Genootschap (K.N.A.G.) / Royal Dutch Geographical Society, Postbus 80123, 3508 TC Utrecht
T: (030) 2534056; Fax: 2535523
Founded: 1834; Members: 4000
Gen Secr: A. Harink
Focus: Geography
Periodicals
Geografisch Tijdschrift (5 times annually)
De Nieuwe Geografenkrant (10 times annually)
De Nieuwe Geografenkrant (10 times annually)
Tijdschrift voor Economische en Sociale Geografie: Journal of Economic and Social Geography (5 times annually) 08502

Koninklijk Nederlands Geologisch Mijnbouwkundig Genootschap (KNGMG) / Royal Geological and Mining Society of the Netherlands, Postbus 157, 2000 AD Haarlem
Fax: (023) 312328
Founded: 1912; Members: 1500
Pres: Prof. Dr. S.B. Kroonenberg; Gen Secr: Dr. L.J. Witte
Focus: Mining; Geology
Periodicals
Geologie en Mijnbouw: International Journal of the Royal Geological and Mining Society of the Netherlands (quarterly)
Nieuwsbrief (10 times annually)
Verhandelingen van het KNGMG (irregularly) 08503

Koninklijk Nederlands Historisch Genootschap, Postbus 90406, 2509 LK Den Haag
Founded: 1845; Members: 1800
Pres: Prof. C. Fasseur
Focus: Hist 08504

Koninklijk Nederlandsch Genootschap voor Geslacht- en Wapenkunde, Postbus 85630, 2508 CH Den Haag
T: (070) 3855965
Founded: 1983; Members: 1200
Pres: T.J. Versélewel Witt Hamer; Gen Secr: A.E.M. Landheer
Focus: Genealogy

Periodicals
De Nederlandsche Leeuw (monthly)
Nederlandse Genealogieen (every 3 years)
Series Publicaties (irregularly)
Series Werken (irregularly) 08505

Koninklijk Oudheidkundig Genootschap Amsterdam (K.O.G.), c/o Rijksmuseum, Stadhouderskade 42, Postbus 74888, 1071 ZD Amsterdam
Founded: 1858; Members: 500
Pres: Prof. Dr. D.P. Blok
Focus: Arts; Cultur Hist
Periodical
Annual Reports (every 4-5 years) . . . 08506

Koninklijke Landbouwkundige Vereniging, Postbus 79, 6700 AB Wageningen
T: (0317) 483539; E-Mail: office@users.klv.wau.nl; Fax: 483976
Founded: 1886; Members: 8000
Pres: W.M. Geluk; Gen Secr: S.J. van Prooijen
Focus: Agri
Periodicals
Adressenlijst: Address-List of all Alumni Wageningen Agricultural University (annually)
LT-Journal (monthly)
Netherlands Journal of Agricultural Science (quarterly) 08507

Koninklijke Maatschappij tot Bevordering der Bouwkunst, Bond van Nederlandse Architekten (B.N.A.), Postbus 19606, 1000 GP Amsterdam
T: (020) 5553666; Fax: 5953699
Founded: 1842; Members: 2750
Focus: Archit
Periodical
Architectuur/Bouwen (monthly) 08508

Koninklijke Maatschappij Tuinbouw en Plantkunde (K.M.T.P.), Postbus 87910, 2508 JK Den Haag
T: (070) 3514551; Fax: 3522579
Founded: 1872; Members: 60000
Focus: Hort; Botany
Periodical
Groei & Bloei (monthly) 08509

Koninklijke Maatschappij voor Natuurkunde onder de Zinspreuk Diligentia, Lange Voorhout 5, 2514 EA Den Haag
Founded: 1793; Members: 530
Focus: Nat Sci
Periodical
Natuurkundige Voordrachten, Nieuwe Reeks (annually) 08510

Koninklijke Nederlandsche Heidemaatschappij, Utrechtseweg 68, 6812 AG Arnhem
T: (085) 4455146; E-Mail: publ@knhm.nl; Fax: 4437827
Founded: 1888; Members: 1900
Pres: Dr. C.J. Rijnvos; Gen Secr: M.A.E. Chorus-Menken
Focus: Ecology
Periodical
Heidemijtijdschrift (bi-monthly) 08511

Koninklijke Nederlandsche Maatschappij tot Bevordering der Geneeskunst (KNMG), Lomanlaan 103, 3526 XD Utrecht
T: (030) 2823911; E-Mail: info@bureau.unmg.nl; Fax: 2823326
Founded: 1849; Members: 19000
Pres: Prof. Dr. J.M. Minderhoud; Gen Secr: Th. M.G. van Berkesrijn
Focus: Med 08512

Koninklijke Nederlandse Akademie van Wetenschappen, Kloveniersburgwal 29, Postbus 19121, 1000 GC Amsterdam
T: (020) 5510700; E-Mail: bureau@know.nl; Fax: 6204941
Founded: 1808; Members: 200
Pres: Prof. Dr. P.J. Zandbergen; Gen Secr: Prof. A.S. Hartkamp
Focus: Sci
Periodicals
Akademie Nieuws (5 times annually)
Medelingen: Nieuwe Reeks, Letterkunde
Proceedings: Series A: Mathematical Sciences; Series B: Palaeontology, Geology, Chemistry, Physics and Anthropology; Series C: Biological and Medical Sciences (quarterly)
Verhandelingen: Nieuwe Reeks, Letterkunde
Verhandelingen, Series I, II: Transactions 08513

Koninklijke Nederlandse Bosbouw Vereniging, Postbus 139, 6800 AC Arnhem
T: (026) 3778221; Fax: 4455994
Founded: 1910; Members: 320
Focus: Forestry
Periodical
Nederlands Bosbouw Tijdschrift (monthly) 08514

Koninklijke Nederlandse Botanische Vereniging (K.N.B.V.), c/o Biologisch Laboratorium, Vrije Universiteit, De Boelelaan 1087, 1081 HV Amsterdam
T: (020) 5485538
Founded: 1845; Members: 800
Focus: Botany
Periodicals
Acta Botanica Neerlandica (quarterly)
Bionieuws (bi-weekly) 08515

Koninklijke Nederlandse Chemische Vereniging (KNCV), Burnierstr 1, 2596 HV Den Haag
T: (070) 3469406
Founded: 1903; Members: 15000
Gen Secr: E.J. de Ryck van der Gracht
Focus: Chem 08516

Koninklijke Nederlandse Maatschappij ter Bevordering der Pharmacie / Royal Netherlands Association for Advancement of Pharmacy, Alexanderstr 11, 2514 JL Den Haag
T: (070) 3624111; Fax: 3106530
Founded: 1842; Members: 3500
Pres: Dr. B.H. Graatsma; Gen Secr: Dr. L.H.A.J. Arts
Focus: Pharmacol
Periodical
Pharmaceutisch Weekblad 08517

Koninklijke Nederlandse Maatschappij voor Diergeneeskunde (K.N.M.v.D.), Julianalaan 10, 3581 NT Utrecht
T: (030) 510111; Fax: 511707
Founded: 1862; Members: 3420
Focus: Vet Med
Periodicals
Tijdschrift voor Diergeneeskunde (23 times annually)
Veehouder en Dieren Arts (quarterly)
Veterinary Quarterly (quarterly) 08518

Koninklijke Nederlandse Natuurhistorische Vereniging (KNNV), Oudegracht 237, 3511 NK Utrecht
T: (030) 2314797; Fax: 2368907
Founded: 1901; Members: 10000
Pres: V.P.A. Lukkien
Focus: Bio; Nat Sci
Periodicals
Natura (11 times annually)
Wetenschappelijke Mededelingen (10 times annually) 08519

Koninklijke Nederlandse Toonkunstenaars-vereniging / Royal Netherlands Association of Musicians, Keizersgracht 480, 1017 EG Amsterdam
T: (020) 6200229
Founded: 1875; Members: 3400
Pres: Rein Verhagen; Gen Secr: Dick Visser
Focus: Music
Periodical
Muziek en Dans 08520

Koninklijke Nederlandse Vereniging voor Luchtvaart (KNVL), Jozef Israelsplein 8, 2596 AS Den Haag
T: (070) 245457
Founded: 1907; Members: 14000
Focus: Eng 08521

Koninklijke Vereniging van Leraren in de Lichamelijke Opvoeding, Zinzendorflaan 9, Postbus 398, 3700 AJ Zeist
T: (030) 6920847; Fax: 6912810
Founded: 1862; Members: 8000
Pres: Dr. O. Loopstra; Gen Secr: G.W. van den Gugten
Focus: Sports
Periodical
Lichamelijke Opvoeding (18 times annually) 08522

Kristana Esperantista Ligo Internacia (KELI) / International Christian Esperanto Association, Koningsmantel 4, 2403 HZ Alphen a/d Rijn
Founded: 1911; Members: 800
Pres: A. Burkhardt; Gen Secr: E.A. van Dijk
Focus: Ling 08523

Landelijke Huisartsen Vereniging, Lomanlaan 103, 3526 XD Utrecht
T: (030) 2823733; Fax: 2890400
Focus: Med 08524

Limburgs Geschied- en Oudheidkundig Genootschap (LGOG), Postbus 83, 6200 AB Maastricht
T: (043) 3212586; Fax: 3218572
Founded: 1863; Members: 3200
Focus: Hist
Periodicals
Archeologie in Limburg (quarterly)
Limb. Tijdschrift voor Genealogie (quarterly)
De Maasgouw (quarterly)
Werken LGOG (irregularly) 08525

Maatschappij Arti et Amicitiae, Rokin 112, 1012 LB Amsterdam
T: (020) 6233508
Founded: 1839; Members: 1000
Pres: Henk Rijzinga
Focus: Arts 08526

Maatschappij der Nederlandse Letterkunde, c/o Universiteitsbibliotheek, Witte Singel 27, POB 9501, 2300 RA Leiden
Fax: (071) 5272836
Founded: 1766; Members: 1300
Pres: Dr. E.K. Grootes; Gen Secr: Dr. L.L. van Maris
Focus: Lit; Ling; Hist
Periodical
Jaarboek van de Maatschappij der Nederlandse Letterkunde te Leiden (annually) 08527

Maatschappij tot Bevordering der Toonkunst, Jacob van Campenstr 59, 1072 BD Amsterdam
T: (020) 6713091
Founded: 1829; Members: 6500
Pres: F.M. Bot-Tiddens
Focus: Music 08528

Mijnbouwkundige Vereeniging, Mijnbouwstr 120, 2628 RX Delft
T: (015) 2786039; E-Mail: MV@mp.tudelft.nl; Fax: 2781611
Founded: 1892; Members: 1700
Pres: M.C. de Roos; Gen Secr: R.A. Jansen
Focus: Mining
Periodical
Jaarboek 08529

Monumentenraad / Monuments and Historic Buildings Council, Broederplein 41, 3703 CD Zeist
Founded: 1961; Members: 40
Focus: Preserv Hist Monuments
Periodical
Kunstreisboek voor Nederland: Annual Report 08530

Nationale Vereniging voor Economisch Onderwijs, Kapelweidtje 9, 1861 JH Bergen
Focus: Educ; Econ 08531

Natuurhistorisch Genootschap in Limburg (NHG) / Society of Natural History in Limburg, Postbus 882, 6200 AW Maastricht
T: (043) 213671
Founded: 1910; Members: 1132
Pres: Dr. A.J.W. Lenders; Gen Secr: H. Schmitz
Focus: Hist; Nat Sci
Periodicals
Limburgse Vogels (2-3 times annually)
Natuurhistorisch Maandblad (monthly)
SOK-medelingen (irregularly) 08532

Nederlands Bibliotheek en Lektuur Centrum / Dutch Centre for Public Libraries and Literature, Taco Scheltemastraat 5, Postbus 93054, 2509 AB Den Haag
T: (070) 3141500; Fax: 3141600
Founded: 1972
Focus: Lit; Libraries & Bk Sci
Periodical
Bibliotheek en Samenleving 08533

Nederlands Bureau voor Bibliotheekwezen en Informatieverzorging (NBBI) / Netherlands Organization for Libraries and Information Services, Burg. Van Karnebeeklaan 19, 2585 BA Den Haag
T: (070) 3607833; Fax: 3615011
Founded: 1987
Focus: Libraries & Bk Sci; Computer & Info Sci 08534

Nederlands Economisch Instituut / Netherlands Economic Institute, K.P. van der Mandelelaan 11, Postbus 4175, 3006 AD Rotterdam
T: (010) 4538800; E-Mail: market@nei.nl; Fax: 4530768
Founded: 1929
Pres: Prof. Dr. W.T.M. Molle; Gen Secr: P. Taselaar
Focus: Econ
Periodical
Economisch Statistische Berichten (weekly) 08535

Nederlands Filosofisch Genootschap, P.J. Oudlaan 2, 3705 VP Zeist
T: (03404) 15987
Focus: Philos 08536

Nederlands Genootschap van Leraren (NGL), Postbus 407, 3300 AK Dordrecht
T: (078) 131611; Fax: 130178
Founded: 1972; Members: 20000
Focus: Educ
Periodical
NGL blad (weekly) 08537

Nederlands Genootschap voor Fysiotherapie (N.G.v.F.), Postbus 240, 3800 AE Amersfoort
T: (033) 622400; Fax: 616462
Founded: 1889; Members: 14000
Focus: Therapeutics
Periodicals
Fysiovisie (11 times annually)
Nederlands Tijdschrift voor Fysiotherapie (11 times annually)
Nederlands Tijdschrift voor Manuele Therapie (quarterly) 08538

Nederlands Historisch Genootschap (N.H.G.), Postbus 90406, 2509 LK Den Haag
Founded: 1845; Members: 1700
Focus: Hist
Periodicals
Bijdragen en Mededelingen betreffende de Geschiedenis der Nederlanden
Nederlandse Historische Bronnen
Werken NHG 08539

Nederlands Huisartsen Genootschap (N.H.G.), Lomanlaan 103, 3526 XD Utrecht
T: (030) 2881700; E-Mail: nhgmail@nhg.knmg.nl; Fax: 2870668
Founded: 1956; Members: 6600
Pres: W.A.B. Stalman; Gen Secr: J.P.M. van der Voort
Focus: Med

Periodicals
Huisarts en Wetenschap (13 times annually)
NHG-Standards for GP's (8 times annually)
. . . . 08540

Nederlands Instituut voor Internationale Betrekkingen Clingendael / Netherlands Institute of International Relations Clingendael, Clingendael 7, Postbus 93080, 2597 VH Den Haag
T: (070) 3245384; Fax: 3282002
Founded: 1983; Members: 900
Focus: Int'l Relat
Periodical
Internationale Spectator (monthly) . . . 08541

Nederlands Instituut voor Marketing (NIMA) / Netherlands Institute of Marketing, Hogehilweg 8, Postbus 7352, 1007 JJ Amsterdam
T: (020) 6974821; Fax: 6913971
Founded: 1966; Members: 3200
Focus: Marketing
Periodical
Tijdschrift voor Marketing (monthly) . . . 08542

Het Nederlands Kanker Instituut / Netherlands Cancer Institute, c/o Antoni van Leeuwenhoek Hospital, Plesmanlaan 121, 1066 CX Amsterdam
T: (020) 5129111; Fax: 6172625
Founded: 1913
Pres: Prof. Dr. P. Borst; Gen Secr: Dr. P. van Asselt
Focus: Cell Biol & Cancer Res; Biochem; Genetics; Immunology
Periodical
Scientific Annual Report (annually) . . . 08543

Nederlands Oogheelkundig Gezelschap (NOG), c/o J. Hennink, Postbus 6711, 6503 GE Nijmegen
E-Mail: j.hennink@ohk.azn.nl; Fax: (024) 3562461
Founded: 1892; Members: 826
Pres: Prof. Dr. G. van Rij; Gen Secr: Prof. Dr. J.E.E. Keunen
Focus: Ophthal 08544

Nederlands Psychoanalytisch Genootschap (N.P.G.), Maliestr 1a, 3581 SH Utrecht
T: (030) 333300; Fax: 343883
Founded: 1947; Members: 170
Gen Secr: Dr. J.H. Scheffer
Focus: Psychoan
Periodical
Psychoanalytisch Forum (quarterly) . . . 08545

Nederlands Verpakkingscentrum, Postbus 164, 2800 AD Gouda
T: (0182) 512411; Fax: 512769
Founded: 1953; Members: 500
Gen Secr: M.W.C.M. Nieuwesteg
Focus: Materials Sci 08546

Nederlands-Zuidafrikaanse Vereniging / Netherlands South African Society, Keizersgracht 141, 1015 CK Amsterdam
Fax: (020) 6382596
Founded: 1881; Members: 1000
Focus: Int'l Relat
Periodicals
Annual Report (annually)
Zuid-Afrika (monthly) 08547

Nederlandsche Internisten Vereeniging (NIV), c/o Domus Medica, Postbus 20066, 3502 LB Utrecht
T: (030) 2823229; E-Mail: secr@niv.knmg.nl; Fax: 2882298
Founded: 1931; Members: 1900
Pres: Dr. H.P. Muller; Gen Secr: T. Huis in't Veld-Schimmel
Focus: Intern Med
Periodicals
The Netherlands Journal of Medicine (monthly)
The Newsletter (quarterly) 08548

Nederlandsche Maatschappij tot Bevordering der Tandheelkunde / Dutch Dental Organization, Postbus 2000, 3430 CA Nieuwegein
T: (03402) 76276; Fax: 48994
Founded: 1914; Members: 7200
Focus: Dent
Periodical
Nederlands Tandartsenblad: Dutch Dental Journal (bi-weekly) 08549

Nederlandsche Vereniging voor Druk- en Boekkunst / Netherlands Society for the Art of Printing and Book Production, J. van Banningstr 2c, 2381 AV Zoeterwoude
Founded: 1938; Members: 300
Pres: Dr. C.J. Keyser; Gen Secr: Dr. K. Thomassen
Focus: Graphic & Dec Arts, Design; Libraries & Bk Sci
Periodical
Mededelingen (irregularly) 08550

Nederlandse Anatomen Vereniging, c/o Laboratorium voor Anatomie en Embryologie, Vrije Universiteit, Postbus 7161, 1007 MC Amsterdam
Focus: Anat 08551

Nederlandse Astronomenclub, c/o Dr. J.B.G.M. Bloemen, Leiden Observatory, Postbus, 2300 RA Leiden
T: (071) 275818
Focus: Astronomy 08552

Nederlandse Bond voor Natuurgeneeswijze, Frans van Mierisstr 57, 1071 RL Amsterdam
T: (020) 723552
Focus: Med 08553

Nederlandse Dendrologische Vereniging, Vogellaan 6, 2771 JX Boskoop
T: 4266
Focus: Forestry 08554

Nederlandse Dierkundige Vereniging (NDV), c/o Dept of Aquatic Ecology, University of Amsterdam, Kruislaan 320, 1098 SM Amsterdam
Founded: 1872; Members: 610
Pres: Prof. Dr. J.W.M. Osse
Focus: Zoology
Periodical
Netherlands Journal of Zoology (quarterly) 08555

Nederlandse Entomologische Vereniging (NEV), Plantage Middenlaan 64, 1018 DH Amsterdam
T: (020) 5256246; E-Mail: biblionev@bio.uva.nl; Fax: 5256528
Founded: 1845; Members: 600
Focus: Entomology
Periodicals
Catalogue of Palaeartic Heteroptera (annually)
Entomologia Experimentalis et Applicata (bi-monthly)
Entomologische Berichte (monthly)
Monografieën van de Nederlandse Entomologische Vereniging (irregularly)
Proceedings Section Experimental and Applied Entomology (annually)
Tijdschrift voor Entomologie (bi-monthly) . 08556

Nederlandse Genealogische Vereniging, Postbus 976, 1000 AZ Amsterdam
T: (020) 766780
Focus: Genealogy
Periodical
Gens Nostra (monthly) 08557

Nederlandse Genetische Vereniging, c/o Dr. W. Ferro, Dept of Radiation Genetics and Chemical Mutagenesis, Postbus 9503, 2300 RA Leiden
T: (071) 5276153; E-Mail: ferro@RULLF2.LeidenUniv.nl; Fax: 5221615
Founded: 1915; Members: 250
Pres: Prof. C. Heyting; Gen Secr: Dr. W. Ferro
Focus: Genetics 08558

Nederlandse Museumvereniging (NMV), Postbus 74683, 1070 BR Amsterdam
T: (020) 6701100; Fax: 6701101
Founded: 1926; Members: 380
Gen Secr: Dr. P.M. van Vlijmen
Focus: Arts 08559

Nederlandse Mycologische Vereniging (N.M.V.), c/o Biologisch Station, Kampsweg 27, 9418 PD Wyster
T: (0593) 562441
Founded: 1908; Members: 600
Pres: Dr. E.J.M. Arnolds; Gen Secr: M.T. Veerkamp
Focus: Botany, Specific
Periodical
Coolia: Journal (quarterly) 08560

Nederlandse Natuurkundige Vereniging, Postbus 302, 1170 AL Badhoevedorp
T: (020) 6580228; Fax: 6592477
Founded: 1921; Members: 3800
Pres: Prof. Dr. P.J. Brussaard; Gen Secr: Dr. A.M. Hoohenboom
Focus: Nat Sci 08561

Nederlandse Organisatie voor Internationale Samenwerking in het Hoger Onderwijs (NUFFIC) / Netherlands Organisation for International Cooperation in Higher Education, Kortenaerkade 11, Postbus 29777, 2502 LT Den Haag
T: (070) 4260260; Fax: 4260399
Founded: 1952
Pres: Dr. P.J.C. van Dijk
Focus: Educ 08562

Nederlandse Organisatie voor Wetenschappelijk Onderzoek / Netherlands Organization for Scientific Research, Laan van Nieuw Oost Indië 131, Postbus 93138, 2509 AC Den Haag
T: (070) 3440640; Fax: 3850971
Focus: Humanities; Soc Sci; Bio; Eng; Med; Nat Sci
Periodical
Jaarboek: Annual Report (annually) . . . 08563

Nederlandse Ornithologische Unie (N.O.U.), Akelei 42, 4102 JM Culemborg
Founded: 1901; Members: 950
Pres: Prof. Dr. R.H. Drent; Gen Secr: Dr. T.J. Boudewijn
Focus: Ornithology
Periodicals
Ardea (semi-annually)
Limosa (quarterly) 08564

Nederlandse Orthopaedische Vereniging (N.O.V.), Postbus 9011, 6500 GM Nijmegen
T: (024) 3659134; Fax: 3659261
Founded: 1898; Members: 550
Pres: Dr. R.J. Sanders; Gen Secr: Dr. L.P.A. Bom
Focus: Orthopedics 08565

Nederlandse Patholoog Anatomen Vereniging (NPAV), c/o Prof. Dr. J.W. Arends, Afd Pathologie, Academisch Ziekenhuis, Postbus 1910, 6201 BX Maastricht
Founded: 1920; Members: 200
Focus: Anat; Pathology 08566

Nederlandse Sint-Gregoriusvereniging, Plompekovengracht 1, 3512 CA Utrecht
T: (030) 2331010
Focus: Music
Periodical
Gregoriusblad (quarterly) 08567

Nederlandse Toonkunstenaarsraad / Council of Organisations of Musicians in the Netherlands, Valeriusplein 20, Amsterdam
Founded: 1948 Kappeyne van de Coppelio, Dr. N.J.C.M.; Members: 3000
Focus: Music
Periodical
A Musical Guide for Holland 08568

Nederlandse Tuinbouwraad, Schiefbaanstr 29, 2596 RC Den Haag
T: (070) 3450600; Fax: 3453902
Founded: 1908; Members: 10
Gen Secr: J.M. Gerritsen
Focus: Hort 08569

Nederlandse Vereniging van Artsen voor Revalidatie en Physische Geneeskunde (VRA), Van Swietenlaan 4, 9700 RM Groningen
T: (050) 266810
Founded: 1955; Members: 230
Focus: Rehabil; Physical Therapy; Physiology
. . . . 08570

Nederlandse Vereniging van Bibliothecarissen, Documentalisten en Literatuuronderzoekers, Plompetorengracht 11, 3512 CA Utrecht
T: (030) 231163; Fax: 2311830
Founded: 1912; Members: 3000
Pres: Dr. H.C. Kooyman-Tibbles; Gen Secr: Dr. A.C.G.M. Eyffinger
Focus: Libraries & Bk Sci; Doc; Lit . . 08571

Nederlandse Vereniging van biomedisch Laboratoriumsmedewerkers, Wilhelminapark 52, 3581 NM Utrecht
T: (030) 2523792
Founded: 1946; Members: 4500
Focus: Med
Periodical
Analyse (10 times annually) 08572

Nederlandse Vereniging van Gieterijtechnici (NVvGT), c/o AVNEG, Boerhaavelaan 40, Postbus 190, 2700 AD Zoetermeer
T: (079) 3514516; E-Mail: hor@fme.nl; Fax: 3531365
Founded: 1927; Members: 350
Pres: R. Britstra; Gen Secr: P.H.J. Ket
Focus: Metallurgy
Periodical
Gietwerk Perspektief (bi-monthly) 08573

Nederlandse Vereniging van Neurochirurgen (NVvN), c/o Neurochirurgische Afdeling, Academisch Ziekenhuis Rotterdam, Dr. Molewaterplein 40, 3015 GD Rotterdam
Fax: (010) 4633735
Founded: 1952; Members: 87
Focus: Surgery
Periodical
Clinical Neurology and Neurosurgery: CNN (quarterly) 08574

Nederlandse Vereniging van Pedagogen en Onderwijskundigen, Korte Elisabethstr 11, 3511 JG Utrecht
T: (030) 2322407; Fax: 2369749
Founded: 1962; Members: 3000
Focus: Educ
Periodical
Nederlands Tijdschrift voor Opvoeding, Vorming en Onderwijs 08575

Nederlandse Vereniging van Radiologische Laboranten (NVRL), Catharijnesingel 73, 3511 GM Utrecht
T: (030) 2318842; E-Mail: 2321362
Founded: 1950; Members: 3100
Pres: D. Pronk-Larive; Gen Secr: G.J.R. Bos
Focus: Radiology; Nucl Med
Periodical
Gamma (monthly) 08576

Nederlandse Vereniging van Specialisten in den Dento-Maxillaire Orthopaedie, Weezenhof 14-16, Nijmegen
Founded: 1963
Pres: Dr. H.S. Duterloo
Focus: Orthopedics; Dent 08577

Nederlandse Vereniging van Wiskundeleraren (NVvW), Burg. Bijleveldstr 38, 8052 AP Hattem
T: (038) 4447017
Founded: 1925; Members: 3400
Pres: Dr. J. van Lint; Gen Secr: W. Kuipers
Focus: Educ; Math
Periodical
Euclides (10 times annually) 08578

Nederlandse Vereniging voor Afvalwaterbehandeling en Waterkwaliteitsbeheer, Postbus 70, 2280 AB Rijswijk
T: (070) 902720
Founded: 1958; Members: 1900
Focus: Water Res
Periodical
H20-Journal (bi-weekly) 08579

Nederlandse Vereniging voor Algemene Gezondheidszorg (NVAG), Postbus 70032, 3000 LP Rotterdam
T: (010) 4339615
Founded: 1980; Members: 300
Focus: Public Health; Hygiene
Periodical
NVAG-Bulletin (semi-annually) 08580

Nederlandse Vereniging voor Anesthesiologie (NVA), Lomanlaan 103, Postbus 20063, 3502 HB Utrecht
T: (030) 2823385; Fax: 2881853
Founded: 1948; Members: 1250
Pres: J.S. Pöll; Gen Secr: A.P.K. Verkaaik
Focus: Anesthetics
Periodical
Nederlands Tijdschrift voor Anesthesiologie NTVA (quarterly) 08581

Nederlandse Vereniging voor Cardiologie, c/o Dept of Cardiology, Sint Antonius Hospital, Koekoekslaan 1, 3435 CM Nieuwegein
T: (03402) 47669; Fax: 34420
Focus: Cardiol
Periodical
Netherlands Journal of Cardiology (bi-monthly)
. . . . 08582

Nederlandse Vereniging voor Dermatologie en Venereologie, Nieuwe Ginnekenstr 14, 4811 NR Breda
T: (076) 137596
Founded: 1896; Members: 450
Focus: Derm; Venereology 08583

Nederlandse Vereniging voor Gastro-Enterologie (NVGE), Postbus 657, 2003 RR Haarlem
T: (023) 5513016; Fax: 5513087
Founded: 1913; Members: 900
Pres: Prof. Dr. C.B.H.W. Lamers; Gen Secr: Dr. W. Hameeteman
Focus: Gastroenter 08584

Nederlandse Vereniging voor Geodesie (NVG), Waltersingel 1, 7314 NK Apeldoorn
T: (055) 5285111
Founded: 1970; Members: 500
Focus: Surveying
Periodical
NGT Geodesia (monthly) 08585

Nederlandse Vereniging voor Heelkunde, Lomanlaan 103, Postbus 20061, 3502 LB Utrecht
T: (030) 2823327; Fax: 2823329
Founded: 1902; Members: 1400
Gen Secr: Dr. B.C. de Vries
Focus: Surgery
Periodical
The European Journal of Surgery . . . 08586

Nederlandse Vereniging voor Internationaal Recht (NVIR) / Netherlands Branch of the International Law Association, Alexanderstr 20-22, Postbus 30461, 2500 GL Den Haag
T: (070) 3420300; Fax: 3420359
Founded: 1910; Members: 560
Pres: A.H.A. Soons; Gen Secr: E.N. Frohn
Focus: Law
Periodical
Mededelingen (semi-annually) 08587

Nederlandse Vereniging voor Kindergeneeskunde, c/o Pediatric Dept, Free University Hospital, De Boelelan 1117, 1081 HV Amsterdam
T: (020) 5482395
Focus: Pediatrics 08588

Nederlandse Vereniging voor Logica en Wijsbegeerte der Exacte Wetenschappen, Postbus 80103, 3508 TC Utrecht
Founded: 1947; Members: 150
Pres: J.-J. C. Meyer
Focus: Philos 08589

Nederlandse Vereniging voor Luchtvaarttechniek (NVvL), Anthony Fokkerweg 2, 1059 CM Amsterdam
T: (020) 5113113; Fax: 178024
Founded: 1941; Members: 330
Focus: Aero
Periodical
NVvL Jaarboek (annually) 08590

Nederlandse Vereniging voor Management (NIVE), Neuhuyskade 40, Postbus 90730, 2509 LS Den Haag
T: (070) 180180
Founded: 1925; Members: 2515
Focus: Business Admin 08591

Nederlandse Vereniging voor Medisch Onderwijs / Dutch Association for Medical Education, Universiteitsweg 100, Postbus 80030, 3508 TA Utrecht
T: (030) 2538344; E-Mail: M.Sterman@med.ruu; Fax: 2539039
Founded: 1972; Members: 500
Pres: Prof. Dr. H.J.M. van Rossum
Focus: Med; Educ
Periodical
Bulletin Medisch Onderwijs: Officieel Blad (quarterly) 08592

Nederlandse Vereniging voor Medische Microbiologie, c/o Laboratorium voor de Volksgezondheid in Friesland, Postbus 21020, 8900 JA Leeuwarden
T: (058) 2939495; Fax: 2939200
Founded: 1992; Members: 380
Pres: Prof. Dr. H.A. Verbrugh; Gen Secr: Dr. D. Veenendaal
Focus: Microbio 08593

Nederlandse Vereniging voor Microbiologie (NVvM) / Netherlands Society for Microbiology, c/o R.I.V.M., Postbus 1, 3720 BA Bilthoven
T: (030) 2742040; Fax: 2744413
Founded: 1911; Members: 1200
Pres: Prof. Dr. J.G. Kuenen; Gen Secr: Dr. M. Rutgers
Focus: Microbio
Periodical
Bionieuws (20 times annually) 08594

Nederlandse Vereniging voor Mondziekten en Kaakchirurgie, Sportlaan 600, 2566 TP Den Haag
Founded: 1956; Members: 300
Focus: Otorhinolaryngology; Surgery . . 08595

Nederlandse Vereniging voor Neurologie, Postbus 20050, 3502 LB Utrecht
T: (030) 823343
Founded: 1871; Members: 800
Pres: Dr. J.J. van der Sande; Gen Secr: Dr. A.R. Wintzen
Focus: Neurology
Periodical
Clinical Neurology and Neurosurgery (quarterly) 08596

Nederlandse Vereniging voor Obstetrie en Gynaecologie, Lomanlaan 103, 3526 XD Utrecht
T: (030) 823328; Fax: 823329
Focus: Gynecology
Periodical
Nederlands Tijdschrift voor Obstetrie en Gynaecologie 08597

Nederlandse Vereniging voor Orthodontische Studie (NVOS), Schelluinsevliet 5, 4203 NB Gorinchem
T: (0183) 635476; E-Mail: Booij@Zeeland.net.nl; Fax: 633177
Founded: 1946; Members: 750
Pres: Prof. Dr. A.M. Kuijpers-Jagtman; Gen Secr: J.W. Booij
Focus: Dent 08598

Nederlandse Vereniging voor Parasitologie, c/o Dept of Clinical Microbiology, Erasmus University, Dr. Molewaterplein 40, 3015 GD Rotterdam
T: (010) 4633874; E-Mail: sluiters@bacl.azr.nl; Fax: 4633875
Founded: 1961; Members: 150
Pres: Prof. Dr. A.W.C.A. Cornelissen; Gen Secr: Dr. J.F. Sluiters
Focus: Microbio 08599

Nederlandse Vereniging voor Pathologie, c/o Dr. R.W.M. Giard, Afd Pathologie, St. Clara Ziekenhuis, Olympiaweg 350, 3078 HT Rotterdam
Focus: Pathology 08600

Nederlandse Vereniging voor Personeelbeleid (NVP), Catharijnesingel 53, Postbus 19124, 3501 DC Utrecht
T: (030) 367101; Fax: 343991
Focus: Business Admin
Periodical
Personeelbeleid (monthly) 08601

Nederlandse Vereniging voor Produktieleiding (NPL), Van Alkemadelaan 700, 90730, 2509 LS Den Haag
T: (070) 264341
Founded: 1970
Focus: Business Admin
Periodical
Bedrijfsvoering (monthly) 08602

Nederlandse Vereniging voor Psychiatrie, Postbus 20062, 3502 LB Utrecht
T: (030) 2823303; Fax: 2888400
Founded: 1871; Members: 1950
Pres: Prof. Dr. W. van Tilburg; Gen Secr: F. Polak
Focus: Psychiatry 08603

Nederlandse Vereniging voor Thoraxchirurgie, c/o Dept of Cardiothoracic Surgery, University Hospital Groningen, Postbus 30001, 9700 RB Groningen
Focus: Surgery 08604

Nederlandse Vereniging voor Toegepaste Taalwetenschap, c/o Instituut voor Toegepaste Taalkunde, Rijksuniversiteit, Wilhelminapark 11, 3581 NC Utrecht
Founded: 1972; Members: 400
Focus: Ling
Periodical
Toegepaste Taalwetenschap: Publications in Applied Linguistics (quarterly) 08605

Nederlandse Vereniging voor Tropische Geneeskunde (N.V.T.G.), Postbus 244, 3970 AE Driebergen-Rijsenburg
T: (0343) 517126; E-Mail: nadamo@worldacces.nl; Fax: 517126
Founded: 1907; Members: 950
Focus: Trop Med
Periodical
Medicus Tropicus, Tropical & International Health: A European Journal 08606

Nederlandse Vereniging voor Urologie / Dutch Urological Association, Postbus 20061, 3502 LB Utrecht
T: (030) 2823218; E-Mail: NVU@xs4all.nl; Fax: 2803956
Founded: 1908
Focus: Urology 08607

Nederlandse Vereniging voor Veiligheidskunde (NVVK) / Netherlands Society on Safety Engineering, c/o GAK, Afd AB, Postbus 8300, 1005 CA Amsterdam
T: (020) 455351
Founded: 1947; Members: 950
Focus: Safety
Periodical
NVVK-Nieuws (5 times annually) 08608

Nederlandse Vereniging voor Zeegeschiedenis, c/o Dr. J.P. Sigmond, Leeuerikstr 14, 2333 VZ Leiden
Founded: 1961; Members: 487
Focus: Hist; Transport 08609

Nederlandse Werkgroep van Praktizijns in de Natuurlijke Geneeskunst (NWP), Ruige Velddreef 133, 3831 PG Leusden
T: (033) 4953133; Fax: 4953133
Focus: Med 08610

Nederlandse Zootechnische Vereniging, Deylerweg 99, 2241 AC Wassenaar
T: (01751) 12617
Founded: 1930; Members: 850
Pres: D. Oostendorp; Gen Secr: J.J. Bakker
Focus: Zoology 08611

Netherlands Centre of the PEN International, Graafseweg 3, 6512 BM Nijmegen
T: (024) 3241045; Fax: 3603857
Founded: 1923; Members: 350
Pres: Hans van de Waarsenburg; Gen Secr: Daan Cartens
Focus: Lit
Periodical
PEN-Nieuws Brief (semi-annually) . . . 08612

Orde van Medisch Specialisten (LSV), Lomanlaan 103, Postbus 20057, 3502 LB Utrecht
T: (030) 2823301
Founded: 1946; Members: 7500
Focus: Med 08613

Permanent International Committee of Linguists, c/o Instituut voor Nederlandse Lexicologie, Witte Singel, Matthias de Vrieshof 2-3, 2311 BZ Leiden
Founded: 1928; Members: 50
Focus: Ling
Periodical
Linguistique Bibliographie 08614

Pharma-Dokumentationsring e.V., c/o Organon International B.V., POB 20, 5340 BH Oss
T: (04120) 62409
Focus: Pharmacol 08615

Protestants-Christelijke Onderwijsvakorganisatie (PCO), Postbus 87868, 2508 DG Den Haag
T: (070) 3522541; Fax: 3522841
Focus: Educ
Periodical
Magazine (weekly) 08616

Raad Cultuur, R.J. Schimmelpenninckiaan 3, 2517 JN Den Haag
T: (070) 3106686; E-Mail: cultuur@cultuur. nl; Fax: 3614727
Founded: 1995; Members: 60
Pres: J. Jessurun; Gen Secr: A. Nicolai
Focus: Cultur Hist
Periodicals
Knipselkrant (weekly)
Recommendations (irregularly) 08617

Rectoren College, Postbus 19270, 3501 DG Utrecht
T: (030) 334441; Fax: 333540
Pres: Dr. T.J.M. van Els
Focus: Educ 08618

Research Group for European Migration Problems (REMP), Pauwenlaan 17, 2566 TA Den Haag
T: (070) 647784
Founded: 1952; Members: 178
Focus: Sociology 08619

Rijksbureau voor Kunsthistorische Documentatie (R.K.D.) / Netherlands Institute for Art History, Prins Willem-Alexanderhof 5, Postbus 90418, 2509 LK Den Haag
T: (070) 3471514; Fax: 3475005
Founded: 1932
Focus: Arts; Hist; Doc
Periodical
Periodical Oud Holland (quarterly) . . . 08620

Samenwerkingsverband van de Universiteitsbibliotheken, de Koninklijke Bibliotheek en de Bibliotheek van de Koninklijke Nederlandse Akademie van Wetenschappen (UKB), c/o Bibliotheek der Vrije Universiteit, De Boelelaan 1103, 1081 HV Amsterdam
T: (020) 4445140; Fax: 4445259
Founded: 1977; Members: 15
Pres: Dr. A.C. Klugkist; Gen Secr: J.H. de Swart
Focus: Libraries & Bk Sci 08621

Société Universitaire Européenne de Recherches Financières (SUERF), Herengracht 205, 1016 BE Amsterdam
T: (020) 5208565; E-Mail: suerf@worldaccess.nl; Fax: 5208606
Founded: 1963
Pres: Franco Bruni; Gen Secr: Joop van Kessel
Focus: Finance
Periodicals
SUERF Papers on Monetary Policy and Financial Systems
SUERF Reprints
SUERF Series
SUERF Studies
SUERF Translations 08622

Stichting Centrale Raad voor de Academies van Bouwkunst / Central Council of the Academies for Architecture, Keizersgracht 321, 1016 EE Amsterdam
Focus: Archit; Urban Plan 08623

Stichting Economisch Instituut voor de Bouwnijverheid / Economic Institute for the Building Industry, De Cuserstr 89, 1081 CN Amsterdam
Founded: 1956
Focus: Civil Eng
Periodical
Bouw Werk: De Bouw in Feiten, Cijfers en Analyses (quarterly) 08624

Stichting Koninklijk Zoölogisch Genootschap Natura Artis Magistra / Royal Zoological Society, Plantage Kerklaan 40, 1018 CZ Amsterdam
T: (02) 5233400; Fax: 5233419
Founded: 1838
Pres: Dr. M.T. Frankenhuis
Focus: Zoology
Periodical
Dieren 08625

Stichting Natuur en Milieu, Donkerstr 17, 3511 KB Utrecht
T: (030) 2331328; Fax: 2331311
Founded: 1972; Members: 7000
Pres: A.J.M. van den Biggelaar
Focus: Ecology
Periodical
Natuur en Milieu (monthly) 08626

Stichting Nederlands Agronomisch-Historisch Instituut / Netherlands Agronomic-Historical Foundation, Oude Kijk in 't Jatstr 26, 9712 EK Groningen
Founded: 1949
Focus: Agri; Hist
Periodical
Historia Agriculturae 08627

Stichting Verenigd Nederlands Filminstituut / Netherlands Film and TV Academy, Steynlaan 8, Postbus 515, Hilversum
Founded: 1948
Focus: Cinema
Periodicals
Groepsmedia (quarterly)
Skoop (monthly) 08628

Stichting voor Fundamenteel Onderzoek der Materie (FOM) / Foundation for Fundamental Research on Matter, Van Vollenhovenlaan 659, Postbus 3021, 3502 GA Utrecht
T: (030) 923211; Fax: 946099
Founded: 1946
Focus: Physics 08629

Stichting voor Wetenschappelijk Onderzoek van de Tropen (WOTRO) / Foundation for the Advancement of Tropical Research, Laan van Nieuw Oost Indië 131, Postbus 93138, 2509 AC Den Haag
Founded: 1964
Focus: Develop Areas
Periodical
Annual Report (annually) 08630

Studievereniging voor Psychical Research (SPR), Eemwijkplein 16, 2271 RA Voorburg
T: (070) 863732
Founded: 1919; Members: 600
Focus: Psych 08631

Theater Instituut Nederland, Herengracht 168, 1016 BP Amsterdam
T: (020) 6235104
Founded: 1993
Pres: D. Klaic
Focus: Perf Arts
Periodicals
Dansjaarboek (annually)
Theaterjaarboek (annually)
Toneel Theatraal 08632

Trans European Research and Education Networking Association (TERENA), Singel 466-468, 1017 AW Amsterdam
T: (020) 6391131; E-Mail: secretariat@terena.nl; Fax: 6393289
Founded: 1987; Members: 51
Pres: St. Trumpy; Gen Secr: K. Veitsch
Focus: Sci; Educ 08633

Unitas Malacologica, c/o Nationaal Natuurhistorisch Museum, Postbus 9517, 2300 RA Leiden
T: (071) 133344
Founded: 1962; Members: 400
Focus: Zoology 08634

Universal Esperanto Association (UEA), Nieuwe Binnenweg 176, 3015 BJ Rotterdam
T: (010) 4361044; E-Mail: uea@inter.nl.net; Fax: 4361751
Founded: 1908; Members: 22271
Pres: Prof. Chong-Yeong Lee; Gen Secr: M. Lipari
Focus: Ling
Periodicals
Esperanto (monthly)
Kontakto (bi-monthly) 08635

Vereniging Glere, Markt 1, 6811 CG Arnhem
Founded: 1897
Focus: Hist 08636

Vereniging Het Nederlandsch Economisch-Historisch Archief, Cruquiusweg 31, 1019 AT Amsterdam
T: (020) 6685866; E-Mail: neha@iisg.nl; Fax: 6654181
Founded: 1914
Focus: Hist; Econ
Periodicals
Economisch- en sociaal-historisch Jaarboek (annually)
NEHA-Bulletin (semi-annually) 08637

Vereniging Natuurmonumenten, Noordereinde 60, 1243 JJ 's-Graveland
T: (035) 6559933; Fax: 6563174
Founded: 1905; Members: 870000
Pres: Dr. P. Winsemius; Gen Secr: F.W.R. Evers
Focus: Ecology
Periodical
Natuurbehoud (quarterly) 08638

Vereniging NBLC, 2504 AH Den Haag, Postbus 43300
T: (070) 3090100; Fax: 3090200
Founded: 1972
Pres: R. van der Velde
Focus: Libraries & Bk Sci 08639

Vereniging Sint Lucas, Zomerdijkstr 20, 1079 XB Amsterdam
Founded: 1880
Pres: Bart Peitel
Focus: Arts 08640

Vereniging tot Bevordering der Homoeopathie in Nederland, Postbus 82027, 2500 NA Den Haag
Focus: Homeopathy 08641

Vereniging van Archivarissen in Nederland (VAN), Postbus 897, 8901 Leeuwarden
Founded: 1891; Members: 750
Focus: Archives
Periodicals
Nederlands Archievenblad (quarterly)
Nieuws van Archieven (monthly) 08642

Vereniging van Docenten in Geschiedenis en Staatsrichting in Nederland (VGN), Driehoek 72, 3328 KJ Dordrecht
T: (078) 6540195; E-Mail: cweltevr@worldaccess.nl; Fax: 6540235
Founded: 1958; Members: 2500
Pres: Dr. C. Weltevrede
Focus: Hist; Adult Educ
Periodical
Kleio (10 times annually) 08643

Vereniging van Homoeopathische Artsen in Nederland, Eykmanlaan 8, 3571 JS Utrecht
T: (030) 711606
Focus: Homeopathy 08644

Vereniging van Katholieke Leraren Sint-Bonaventura (V.K.L.), Reviusstr 68, 7552 GL Hengelo
Founded: 1918; Members: 5000
Focus: Educ 08645

Vereniging van Nederlandse Kunsthistorici (VNK), Oude Boteringestr 81, 9712 GG Groningen
Members: 481
Focus: Arts; Hist 08646

Vereniging van Samenwerkende Nederlandse Universiteiten, 3501 DG Utrecht, Postbus 19270
T: (030) 2363888; Fax: 2333540
Gen Secr: Dr. F.E.H. van Eijkern
Focus: Educ 08647

Vereniging voor Agrarisch Recht (VAR) / Agricultural Law Association, Hollandseweg 1, 6706 KN Wageningen
Fax: (0317) 483483
Founded: 1959; Members: 400
Gen Secr: Dr. I.P. de Visser
Focus: Law 08648

Vereniging voor Arbeidsrecht, Postbus 132, 3440 AC Woerden
T: (0348) 421752; Fax: 418460
Founded: 1946; Members: 825
Pres: S. de Laat; Gen Secr: M.J. Broeckx
Focus: Law
Periodical
Reeks van de Vereniging voor Arbeidsrecht (annually) 08649

Vereniging voor Bouwrecht, Wassenaarseweg 23, 2596 CE Den Haag
T: (070) 3245544; Fax: 3282074
Founded: 1972; Members: 900

Pres: Prof. Dr. J. de Jong; Gen Secr: M.A. van Voorst van Beest
Focus: Law 08650

Vereniging voor Calvinistische Wijsbegeerte (V.v.C.W.), Postbus 2156, 3800 CD Amersfoort
T: (033) 4657078; Fax: 4657304
Founded: 1935; Members: 600
Pres: Prof. Dr. S. Griffioen; Gen Secr: Dr. W. Vollbehr
Focus: Philos
Periodicals
Beweging (bi-monthly)
Philosophia Reformata (semi-annually) . . 08651

Vereniging voor de Staathuishoudkunde, c/o De Nederlandsche Bank NV, Postbus 98, 1000 AB Amsterdam
T: (020) 5242280; Fax: 5242525
Founded: 1862; Members: 3200
Pres: Prof. Dr. A. Knoester; Gen Secr: Dr. T. de Swaan
Focus: Poli Sci 08652

Vereniging voor Filosofie-Onderwijs, D. van Polderveldweg 283, 6523 CW Nijmegen
T: (080) 237711
Founded: 1995; Members: 300
Gen Secr: Jo Martens
Focus: Philos; Educ 08653

Vereniging voor het Theologisch Bibliothecariaat (VTB), Postbus 289, 6500 AG Nijmegen
T: (024) 3615528
Founded: 1947; Members: 80
Focus: Libraries & Bk Sci
Periodicals
Bibliografie Doctorale Scripties Theologie (annually)
Mededelingen van de VTB (quarterly) . . 08654

Vereniging voor Hoger Beroepsonderwijs, Europaboulevard 23, 1079 PC Amsterdam
T: (020) 429333
Focus: Adult Educ 08655

Vereniging voor Nederlandse Muziekgeschiedenis (VNM), Postbus 1514, 3500 BM Utrecht
T: (030) 735004
Founded: 1868; Members: 570
Focus: Hist; Music
Periodical
Tijdschrift van de Vereniging voor Nederlandse Muziekgeschiedenis (semi-annually) . . . 08656

Vereniging voor Penningkunst, Van der Meystr 1, 1815 GP Alkmaar
T: (072) 120041
Founded: 1925; Members: 700
Focus: Numismatics
Periodical
De Beeldenaar (bi-monthly) 08657

Vereniging voor Statistiek (V.V.S.), Postbus 331, 2990 AH Barendrecht
T: (0180) 623796; E-Mail: hwander@oi.net; Fax: 623670
Founded: 1945; Members: 1260
Pres: Prof. Dr. R. Delcker; Gen Secr: Dr. A. Koning
Focus: Stats
Periodicals
Kwantitatieve Methoden (3 times annually)
Statistica Neerlandica (quarterly)
V.V.S.-Bulletin (10 times annually) . . . 08658

Vereniging voor Wijsbegeerte des Rechts, Valeriusstr 253, 175 GB Amsterdam
T: (020) 6791470
Founded: 1918; Members: 300
Gen Secr: F.C.L.M. Jacobs
Focus: Law; Philos
Periodicals
Journal for Legal Philosophy and Jurisprudence (3 times annually)
Rechtsfilosofie en rechtstheorie (3 times annually)
. . . . 08659

Vereniging voor Wijsbegeerte te s'-Gravenhage, c/o S. Simons, Van der Capellenstr 20, 2593 XD Den Haag
T: (070) 3835081
Founded: 1907; Members: 100
Focus: Philos 08660

Vereniging voor Zuivelindustrie en Melkhygiëne (VVZM), Laan van Meerdervoort 18-20, 2517 AK Den Haag
T: (070) 634936
Focus: Food 08661

Volkenrechtelijk Instituut, c/o Utrecht University, Janskerkhof 3, 3512 BK Utrecht
T: (030) 2537060; Fax: 2537073
Founded: 1955
Focus: Law
Periodical
Nova et Vetera Iuris Gentium 08662

Wagnervereeniging / Wagner Society, Gabriël Metsustr 32, Amsterdam
Founded: 1883
Pres: W.T. Doyer
Focus: Music 08663

Wiskundig Genootschap (W.G.), c/o Technical University Delft, Postbus 5031, 2600 GA Delft
T: (015) 787286; Fax: 787255
Founded: 1778; Members: 1270
Pres: Prof. Dr. J.C. Willems; Gen Secr: Dr. J.A.M. van der Weide
Focus: Math
Periodicals
Mededelingen van het Wiskundig Genootschap (quarterly)
Nieuw Archief voor Wiskunde (quarterly) . 08664

World Federation of Neurosurgical Societies (WFNS), Bergweg 12, 6523 MD Nijmegen
T: (080) 231146
Founded: 1955; Members: 52
Focus: Surgery 08665

New Caledonia

Société des Etudes Mélanésiennes, Nouméa
T: 272342
Founded: 1938
Focus: Ethnology
Periodical
Etudes Mélanésiennes (annually) 08666

New Zealand

Agronomy Society of New Zealand, c/o Plant Science Dept, Lincoln University, POB 84, Canterbury
T: (03) 3252811; E-Mail: McKenzie@Lincoln.ac.nz; Fax: 3253880
Founded: 1970; Members: 295
Pres: B. McCloy; Gen Secr: Dr. B.A. McKenzie
Focus: Agri 08667

Australasian Universities Language and Literature Association (AULLA), c/o Dept of French, University of Canterbury, Private Bag 4800, Christchurch
T: (03) 3667001; E-Mail: m.downer@fren.canterbury.ac.nz; Fax: 3642522
Founded: 1950; Members: 654
Gen Secr: Michele Downer
Focus: Ling; Lit
Periodical
AUMLA (semi-annually) 08668

Australian Association of Clinical Biochemists – New Zealand Branch, c/o Hamilton Medical Laboratory, POB 52, Hamilton
Founded: 1967; Members: 60
Gen Secr: G. Scheurich
Focus: Biochem
Periodical
Newsletter (quarterly) 08669

Commonwealth Heraldry Board, POB 23-056, Papatoetoe, Auckland
T: (09) 2787415
Founded: 1969
Pres: Dr. A.E. Tonson
Focus: Cultur Hist
Periodical
Commonwealth Heraldry Bulletin (annually) 08670

Creative New Zealand, POB 3806, Wellington
T: (04) 4730880; Fax: 4712865
Founded: 1963; Members: 7
Pres: Brian Stevenson; Gen Secr: Peter Scott
Focus: Arts
Periodical
Arts Fines (quarterly) 08671

Entomological Society of New Zealand, c/o S. Millar, 8 Maymorn Rd, Te Marua, Upper Hutt
T: (04) 5267440; E-Mail: millark@ihuq.co.nz
Founded: 1951; Members: 250
Gen Secr: S. Millar
Focus: Entomology
Periodicals
New Zealand Entomologist (annually)
Weta (semi-annually) 08672

Geological Society of New Zealand (GSNZ), c/o kInstitute of Geological and Nuclear Sciences, POB 30368, Lower Hutt
T: (04) 5701444; Fax: 5666168
Founded: 1955; Members: 820
Pres: R. Norris; Gen Secr: D. Lee
Focus: Geology
Periodical
Newsletter (quarterly) 08673

Hawke's Bay Medical Research Foundation, POB 596, Napier
Focus: Med 08674

Institute of Energy (New Zealand Section), c/o Dr. E.R. Palmer, 7 Ngahere St, Stokes Valley, Wellington
Members: 96
Focus: Energy 08675

Institute of Geological and Nuclear Sciences, POB 30368, Lower Hutt
T: (04) 5701444; Fax: 5690600
Founded: 1992; Members: 250
Pres: Dr. David Ross; Gen Secr: Graham Clarke
Focus: Geophys; Geology
Periodical
Newsletter (3 times annually) 08676

Institution of Professional Engineers New Zealand, 101 Molesworth St, POB 12241, Wellington
Founded: 1914; Members: 6000
Focus: Eng
Periodical
New Zealand Engineering (monthly) . . 08677

Medical Research Council of New Zealand (MRCNZ), Wellesley St, POB 5541, Auckland
T: (09) 798227
Founded: 1950; Members: 14
Focus: Med
Periodical
Research Review (annually) 08678

Meteorological Society of New Zealand, POB 6523, Wellington
T: (04) 4729379
Founded: 1979; Members: 410
Focus: Geophys
Periodical
Newsletter (quarterly) 08679

Microscopy New Zealand, c/o School of Medical Science, POB 913, Dunedin
T: (03) 4797301; E-Mail: richard.easingwood@; Fax: 4797254
Founded: 1980; Members: 160
Pres: Adya Singh; Gen Secr: Mark Gould
Focus: Optics; Electronic Eng
Periodical
Microscopy in Focus (semi-annually) . . 08680

Museums Association of Aotearoa New Zealand Te Ropu Hanga Kaupapa, c/o Museum of New Zealand, POB 467, Wellington
T: (04) 3859609; Fax: 3857157
Founded: 1947; Members: 200
Pres: Steve Lowndes; Gen Secr: Wallace Lynda
Focus: Arts; Archives
Periodicals
AGMANZ News (quarterly)
New Zealand Museum Journal (semi-annually)
Newsletter (bi-monthly) 08681

New Zealand Academy of Fine Arts, Buckle St, Private Bag, Wellington
T: (04) 859267, 844911
Founded: 1882; Members: 2000
Focus: Arts 08682

New Zealand Archaeological Association (N.Z.A.A.), POB 6337, Dunedin North
Founded: 1957; Members: 500
Pres: C. Tacomb; Gen Secr: M. White
Focus: Archeol
Periodicals
Archaeology in New Zealand (quarterly)
New Zealand Journal of Archaeology (annually)
. . . . 08683

New Zealand Association of Clinical Biochemists, c/o Wellington Hospital, POB 47, Wellington
Members: 150
Focus: Biochem
Periodical
Newsletter (bi-monthly) 08684

New Zealand Association of Scientists, POB 1874, Wellington
E-Mail: mimrmb@wnmeds.ac.nz; Fax: (04) 3895095
Founded: 1940; Members: 300
Pres: Brian Jarvis; Gen Secr: Mike Berridge
Focus: Sci
Periodical
New Zealand Science Review (bi-monthly) 08685

New Zealand Association of Soil Conservators, POB 204, Blenheim
Members: 262
Focus: Ecology 08686

New Zealand Book Council, Book House, Boulcott St, POB 11377, Wellington
T: (04) 4991569
Founded: 1972; Members: 1180
Focus: Libraries & Bk Sci 08687

New Zealand Cartographic Society, POB 12454, Thorndon
Founded: 1971; Members: 220
Focus: Cart
Periodicals
Cartogram Newsletter (quarterly)
New Zealand Cartographic Journal (semi-annually)
. . . . 08688

New Zealand Computer Society, POB 10044, Wellington
T: (04) 4731043; Fax: 4731025
Founded: 1960; Members: 2000
Focus: Electronic Eng
Periodical
Journal of Computing (semi-annually) . . 08689

New Zealand Council for Educational Research, POB 3237, Wellington
T: (04) 3847939; E-Mail: info@nzcer.org.nz; Fax: 3847933
Founded: 1934; Members: 40
Gen Secr: Dr. E.A. Meade
Focus: Educ
Periodicals
Annual Report (annually)
Newsletter (semi-annually)
Set: Research Information for Teachers (semi-annually) 08690

New Zealand Dairy Technology Society, c/o Dairy Science Section, Anchor Products Ltd, Waitoa
T: (07) 8893989
Members: 250
Focus: Eng 08691

New Zealand Dietetic Association, POB 5065, Wellington
Members: 372
Focus: Nutrition
Periodical
Journal (semi-annually) 08692

New Zealand Ecological Society, POB 25178, Christchurch
Members: 474
Focus: Ecology 08693

New Zealand Electronics Institute (NZEI), POB 755, Auckland
Founded: 1946; Members: 419
Focus: Electronic Eng
Periodicals
Newelectronics Journal (monthly)
NZEI Ralph Slade Memorial Lecture (annually)
. . . . 08694

New Zealand Fertiliser Manufacturers Research Association (NZFMRA), 61 Otara Rd, POB 23637, Auckland
T: (09) 2747184
Founded: 1947; Members: 27
Focus: Chem
Periodicals
NZFMRA Annual Report (annually)
Proceedings, NZFMRA Symposia (semi-annually)
Proceedings, NZFMRA Technical Conferences (semi-annually) 08695

New Zealand Genetical Society, c/o Crop Research Div, DSIR, Private Bag, Christchurch
T: (03) 252511; Fax: 252074
Founded: 1949; Members: 131
Focus: Genetics 08696

New Zealand Geographical Society, c/o Dept of Geography, University of Waikato, Private Bag 3105, Hamilton
T: (07) 8384913; E-Mail: jey@waikato.ac.nz; Fax: 8562158
Founded: 1944; Members: 900
Pres: Dr. Graeme Campbell; Gen Secr: Dr. Peter Ulrich
Focus: Geography
Periodicals
New Zealand Geographer (semi-annually)
New Zealand Journal of Geography (semi-annually)
Proceedings (bi-annually) 08697

New Zealand Historic Places Trust, POB 2629, Wellington
T: (04) 4724341; E-Mail: nzhistoricplaces@xtra.co.nz; Fax: 4990669
Founded: 1954; Members: 23500
Pres: Dame Catherine Tizard; Gen Secr: Peter Atkinson
Focus: Hist 08698

New Zealand Historical Association, c/o History Dept, Canterbury University, Christchurch
T: (03) 677001; Fax: 642999
Founded: 1979; Members: 300
Focus: Hist
Periodical
Newsletter (quarterly) 08699

New Zealand Hydrological Society (NZHS), POB 12300, Wellington
T: (03) 3256701; Fax: 3252418
Founded: 1961; Members: 500
Pres: A. Fenemor; Gen Secr: B.D. Fahey
Focus: Water Res
Periodical
Journal of Hydrology (New Zealand) (semi-annually) 08700

New Zealand Institute of Agricultural Science (NZIAS), POB 19560, Christchurch
T: (03) 3842432; Fax: 3842432
Founded: 1954; Members: 1007
Focus: Agri
Periodicals
Bulletin of Agricultural and Horticultural Sciences (bi-monthly)
New Zealand Agricultural Science (annually)
. . . . 08701

New Zealand Institute of Architects, Greenock House, 102-112 Lambton Quay, POB 438, Wellington
T: (04) 4735346; Fax: 4720182
Founded: 1905; Members: 2380
Gen Secr: A.K. Purdie
Focus: Archit 08702

New Zealand Institute of Chemistry, POB 12347, Wellington 6038
T: (04) 4739444; E-Mail: nzic@ipenz.org.nz; Fax: 4732324
Founded: 1931; Members: 1500
Pres: R.S. Whitney; Gen Secr: A.A. Turner
Focus: Chem
Periodical
Chemistry in New Zealand (bi-monthly) . 08703

New Zealand Institute of Food Science and Technology (N.Z.I.F.S.T.), POB 35187, Browns Bay, Auckland
T: (09) 4793188; E-Mail: coralie@nzifast.org.nz; Fax: 4793188
Founded: 1965; Members: 770
Pres: Prof. Andrew Cleland; Gen Secr: Coralie Spencer
Focus: Eng; Food

Periodical
Food Technologist (quarterly) *08704*

New Zealand Institute of Forestry, POB 19840, Christchurch
T: (03) 3942432; Fax: 3942432
Founded: 1926; Members: 800
Focus: Forestry
Periodical
New Zealand Forestry (quarterly) . . . *08705*

New Zealand Institute of International Affairs (N.Z.I.I.A.), c/o Victoria University of Wellington, POB 600, Wellington
T: (04) 4715356; Fax: 4731261
Founded: 1934; Members: 600
Pres: G.M. Davidson; Gen Secr: Bryce Harland
Focus: Poli Sci
Periodical
New Zealand International Review (bi-monthly) *08706*

The New Zealand Institute of Management (NZIM), 101 Molesworth St, Wellington
Founded: 1945; Members: 5980
Focus: Business Admin *08707*

New Zealand Institute of Physics (NZIP), c/o Dept of Physics, University of Auckland, Private Bag, Auckland
Founded: 1982; Members: 360
Focus: Physics *08708*

New Zealand Institute of Surveyors, POB 831, Wellington
T: (04) 4711774; Fax: 4711907
Founded: 1888; Members: 1300
Focus: Eng
Periodical
Journal (semi-annually) *08709*

New Zealand Law Society, 26 Waring Taylor St, POB 5041, Wellington
T: (04) 4727837; E-Mail: inquiries@nz-lawson.org.nz; Fax: 4737909
Founded: 1869; Members: 7413
Pres: I.L. Haynes; Gen Secr: A.D. Ritchie
Focus: Law
Periodical
Law Talk (bi-weekly) *08710*

New Zealand Leather and Shoe Research Association (LASRA), Dairy Farm Rd, Private Bag 11333, Palmerston North
T: (06) 3559028; E-Mail: lasra@xtra.co.nz; Fax: 3541185
Founded: 1928; Members: 162
Pres: J. Clark; Gen Secr: A. Passman
Focus: Materials Sci; Microbio
Periodicals
Annual Conference of Fellmongers and Hide Processors
Annual Conference of Leather Technicians
Annual Report (annually) *08711*

New Zealand Library Association (NZLA), 20 Brandon St, POB 12212, Wellington
T: (04) 735834; Fax: 4991480
Founded: 1910; Members: 1700
Focus: Libraries & Bk Sci
Periodicals
Library Life (monthly)
New Zealand Libraries (quarterly) . . . *08712*

New Zealand Limnological Society, POB 6016, Rotorua
Founded: 1968; Members: 200
Focus: Hydrology
Periodical
Newsletter (annually) *08713*

New Zealand Maori Arts and Crafts Institute, POB 334, Rotorua
T: (073) 489047; Fax: 489045
Founded: 1963
Focus: Arts
Periodical
Whaka *08714*

New Zealand Marine Sciences Society, POB 297, Wellington
T: (04) 3861029; Fax: 3861299
Founded: 1960; Members: 317
Focus: Oceanography
Periodical
Newsletter (annually) *08715*

New Zealand Mathematical Society, c/o Royal Society of New Zealand, POB 598, Wellington
T: (03) 4797758; Fax: 4798427
Founded: 1972; Members: 250
Pres: Prof. R. Goldblatt; Gen Secr: Dr. Stephen Joe
Focus: Math
Periodicals
New Zealand Journal of Mathematics (3 times annually)
Newsletter (3 times annually) *08716*

New Zealand Medical Association, POB 156, Wellington
T: (04) 4724741; Fax: 4710838
Founded: 1887; Members: 4500
Focus: Med
Periodical
The New Zealand Medical Journal (bi-weekly) *08717*

New Zealand Microbiological Society, c/o Dept of Oral Sciences and Orthodontics, University of Otago, POB 647, Dunedin
T: (03) 4797081; E-Mail: richard.cannon@stonebow.otago.ac.nz; Fax: 4790673
Founded: 1956; Members: 460
Pres: Prof. G.W. Tannock; Gen Secr: Dr. R.D. Cannon
Focus: Microbio
Periodical
Newsletter: New Zealand Microbiology (quarterly) *08718*

The New Zealand National Society for Earthquake Engineering, POB 17268, Wellington
T: (04) 4766866; Fax: 4766866
Founded: 1968; Members: 700
Focus: Civil Eng
Periodical
Bulletin (quarterly) *08719*

New Zealand Pottery and Ceramics Research Association (PACRA), 2 Bell Rd, Gracefield, Lower Hutt
T: 666919
Founded: 1947; Members: 7
Focus: Materials Sci *08720*

New Zealand Psychological Society, POB 4092, Wellington
T: (04) 8015414; E-Mail: psychsoc@actrix.gen.nz; Fax: 8015366
Founded: 1962; Members: 800
Gen Secr: Dr. W. Whittaker
Focus: Psych
Periodicals
Bulletin (quarterly)
NZ Journal of Psychology (semi-annually) *08721*

New Zealand Society for Biochemistry and Molecular Biology, c/o AgResearch Dairy Science Group, Ruakura Research Centre, Private Bag 3123, Hamilton
E-Mail: wheelert@agresearch.cri.nz; Fax: (07) 8385099 8385628
Members: 350
Pres: Dr. M.R. Grigor; Gen Secr: Dr. T.T. Wheeler
Focus: Biochem; Microbio *08722*

New Zealand Society for Horticultural Science, POB 19560, Christchurch
T: (03) 3842432 3842432; E-Mail: MPLMIB@dslak.co.nz
Founded: 1981; Members: 350
Pres: Dr. Chris Hale; Gen Secr: Marleene Boyd
Focus: Hort *08723*

New Zealand Society for Parasitology, c/o Ruakura Agricultural Centre, Private Bag, Hamilton
T: (07) 8385558
Founded: 1972; Members: 100
Focus: Microbio; Zoology; Immunology; Entomology
Periodical
Proceedings (annually) *08724*

New Zealand Society of Animal Production, c/o Ruakura Agricultural Centre, Private Bag, Hamilton
T: (07) 8562839; E-Mail: NZSAP.animal@xtra.co.nz; Fax: 8569150
Founded: 1940; Members: 746
Pres: Prof. D.J. Garrick; Gen Secr: Dr. R.M.W. Sumner
Focus: Agri
Periodical
Proceedings of the New Zealand Society of Animal Production (annually) *08725*

New Zealand Society of Dairy Science and Technology (NZSDST), c/o Technical Services, Bay Milk Products Ltd, Private Bag, Edgecumbe
T: (076) 49011
Founded: 1963; Members: 285
Focus: Food; Eng *08726*

New Zealand Society of Plant Physiologists, c/o Crop and Food Research Institute of New Zealand, Private Bag 4005, Levinj
T: (06) 3687059; E-Mail: heyes@crop.cri.nz; Fax: 3675656
Founded: 1978; Members: 144
Pres: K.R. Sharrock; Gen Secr: J. Heyes
Focus: Botany *08727*

New Zealand Society of Soil Science (NZSSS), c/o Dept of Soil Science, Lincoln University, POB 84, Canterbury
T: (03) 252811; Fax: 252994
Founded: 1952; Members: 300
Focus: Agri
Periodical
Soil News (bi-monthly) *08728*

New Zealand Statistical Association, POB 1731, Wellington
T: (06) 3582905
Founded: 1950; Members: 600
Pres: J.J. Hunter; Gen Secr: S. Ganesh; G.C. Arnold
Focus: Stats
Periodicals
Newsletter (quarterly)
Statistician (2-3 times annually) *08729*

New Zealand Veterinary Association (N.Z.V.A.), POB 27499, Wellington
T: (04) 843632
Founded: 1923; Members: 1150
Focus: Vet Med
Periodical
New Zealand Veterinary Journal (quarterly) *08730*

Nutrition Society of New Zealand, c/o Dept of Human Nutrition, University of Otago, POB 56, Dunedin
Members: 200
Focus: Food
Periodical
Proceedings of thr Nutrition Society of New Zealand (irregularly) *08731*

Operational Research Society of New Zealand, POB 904, Wellington
T: (04) 121855
Founded: 1964; Members: 170
Focus: Computer & Info Sci
Periodical
New Zealand Operational Research (semi-annually) *08732*

Ornithological Society of New Zealand (OSNZ), POB 12397, Wellington
T: (09) 2948334; E-Mail: osnz@ibm.net; Fax: 2948334
Founded: 1939; Members: 1050
Pres: Christopher J.R. Robertson; Gen Secr: R.A. Empson
Focus: Ornithology
Periodical
Notornis: OSNZ News (quarterly) . . . *08733*

Palmerston North Medical Research Foundation, POB 648, Palmerston North
Founded: 1959
Focus: Med
Periodical
Annual Report (annually) *08734*

P.E.N. New Zealand, 631 Birkenhead, POB 34, Auckland
Founded: 1934; Members: 650
Focus: Lit
Periodical
The New Zealand Author (bi-monthly) . . *08735*

Physiological Society of New Zealand, c/o Dept of Physiology, University of Otago, POB 913, Dunedin
T: (03) 4797334; E-Mail: pat.crogg@stonebow.otago.ac.nz; Fax: 4797323
Founded: 1972; Members: 174
Gen Secr: Dr. P.A. Cragg
Focus: Physiology
Periodical
Proceedings of the Physiological Society of New Zealand (annually) *08736*

Polynesian Society, c/o Anthropology Dept, University of Auckland, Private Bag, Auckland
T: (09) 737999; Fax: 3033429
Founded: 1892; Members: 1100
Focus: Ethnology; Anthro; Hist; Antique
Periodicals
Journal of Polynesian Society
Memoirs (irregularly) *08737*

Population Association of New Zealand, POB 225, Wellington
T: (04) 4716146; Fax: 4714412
Founded: 1974; Members: 132
Focus: Soc Sci
Periodical
New Zealand Population Review (semi-annually) *08738*

Royal Aeronautical Society, New Zealand Division, c/o BP Oil Nz Ltd, POB 892, Wellington
Founded: 1945; Members: 230
Focus: Aero *08739*

Royal Agricultural Society of New Zealand, POB 3095, Wellington
T: (04) 4724190; E-Mail: 100254.2140@compuserve.com; Fax: 4712278
Founded: 1924
Pres: Ken McKenzie; Gen Secr: Chris Mason
Focus: Agri
Periodical
Onshow (3 times annually) *08740*

Royal Astronomical Society of New Zealand (R.A.S.N.Z.), POB 3181, Wellington
Founded: 1920; Members: 347
Pres: A. Gilmore; Gen Secr: G. Whiteford
Focus: Astronomy
Periodicals
Newsletter (monthly)
Southern Stars (quarterly) *08741*

Royal Society of New Zealand (RSNZ), POB 598, Wellington
T: (04) 4727421; E-Mail: ceo@rsnz.gout.nz; Fax: 4731841
Founded: 1867; Members: 17000
Pres: Prof. P.M. Black; Gen Secr: V.R. Moore
Focus: Sci
Periodicals
Bulletin (irregularly)
Journal (quarterly)
Proceedings (annually) *08742*

Systematics Association of New Zealand, c/o Dept of Botany, University of Otago, Dunedin
Members: 180
Focus: Botany *08743*

Veterinary Services Council, POB 417, Wellington
Founded: 1946
Focus: Vet Med *08744*

Waikato Geological and Lapidary Society, POB 62, Hamilton
Founded: 1966
Focus: Geology *08745*

Wellington Medical Research Foundation, c/o The Secretary, POB 14240, Wellington
T: (04) 888179
Focus: Med *08746*

Nicaragua

Academia Nicaragüense de la Lengua, Apdo 2711, Managua
Founded: 1928; Members: 13
Pres: Pablo Antonio Cuadra; Gen Secr: Julio Ycaza Tigerino
Focus: Ling *08747*

Asociación Nicaragüense de Bibliotecarios y Profesionales afines, Apdo 3257, Managua
Founded: 1983
Focus: Libraries & Bk Sci *08748*

Sociedad de Oftalmología Nicaragüense, c/o Clínica Especializada, Managua
Founded: 1949
Focus: Ophthal *08749*

Sociedad Nicaragüense de Psiquiatría y Psicología, c/o Centro México, Managua
Founded: 1962
Focus: Psychiatry; Psych *08750*

Nigeria

Accrediting Council for Theological Education in Africa (ACTEA), PMB 2049, Kaduna
Founded: 1976
Focus: Educ
Periodicals
ACTEA Bulletin
ACTEA Tools and Studies
ASTIN Bulletin (semi-annually)
TEE Newsletter *08751*

Africa Genetics Association, POB 10123, Ugbowo, Benin City
Founded: 1982
Focus: Genetics *08752*

Africa Leadership Forum, POB 2286, Abeokuta, Ogun State
Founded: 1988
Focus: Poli Sci *08753*

Africa Regional Centre for Information Science (ARCIS), c/o University of Ibadan, 6 Benue Rd, Ibadan
T: (022) 400550 ext 2654
Founded: 1990
Focus: Computer & Info Sci *08754*

African Association of Political Science (AAPS), c/o Dept of Social Sciences, Lagos State University, Badagry Express-Way Ojo, Lagos
T: (01) 884209
Founded: 1973
Focus: Poli Sci
Periodicals
AAPS Newsletter
African Journal of Political Economy
African Review *08755*

African Centre for Fertilizer Development (ACFD), c/o OAU, 26-28 Marina, Lagos
Focus: Agri *08756*

African Council of Food and Nutrition Sciences (AFRONUS), POB 5160, Harare
T: 728991
Founded: 1988
Focus: Nutrition; Food *08757*

African Curriculum Organization (ACO), c/o Institute of Education, University of Ibadan, Ibadan
T: (022) 62550
Members: 20
Focus: Soc Sci *08758*

African Feed Resources Research Network, c/o ILCA Liaison Office, POB 3211, Harare
Founded: 1991
Focus: Agri *08759*

African Mathematical Union (AMU), c/o Dept of Mathematics, University of Ibadan, Ibadan
Focus: Math
Periodical
Afrika Mathematika *08760*

African Peace Research Institute (APRI), POB 51757, Falomo Ikoyi, Lagos
T: (01) 633437
Founded: 1985
Focus: Prom Peace
Periodical
APRI Journal (bi-monthly) *08761*

African Regional Centre for Engineering Design and Manufacturing (ARCEDEM), PMB 19, Ull Post Office, Ibadan
T: (022) 710180
Founded: 1979; Members: 25
Focus: Eng
Periodical
ARCEDEM Bulletin (quarterly) 08762

African Regional Network for Microbiology (ARNM), c/o School of Biological Sciences, Imo State University, PMN 2000, Okigwi
T: (083) 232214
Founded: 1977
Focus: Microbio
Periodical
Newsletter 08763

African Statistical Association (AFSA), c/o Federal Office of Statistics, 36-38 Broad St, PMB 12528, Lagos
Focus: Stats 08764

Alley Farming Network for Tropical Africa (AFNETA), c/o ITA, Oyo Rd, PMB 5320, Ibadan
T: (022) 400300, 400314
Founded: 1988
Focus: Agri
Periodical
Afnetan (quarterly) 08765

Ecological Society of Nigeria, c/o Dept of Biological Sciences, University of Lagos, Lagos
Founded: 1973; Members: 100
Focus: Ecology 08766

Entomological Society of Nigeria, c/o Dept of Crop Protection, Ahmadu Bello University, Zaria
T: (069) 50681; Fax: 50563, 51355
Founded: 1965; Members: 170
Pres: Dr. B.A. Okwakpam; Gen Secr: Dr. O.C. Umeozor
Focus: Entomology
Periodicals
The Nigerian Entomologists' Magazine (annually)
Nigerian Journal of Entomology (annually)
Occasional Publications of the Entomological Society of Nigeria (irregularly) 08767

Fisheries Society of Nigeria, PMB 12529, Lagos
Founded: 1976; Members: 500
Focus: Zoology
Periodicals
Advisory Notes
Fishery Bulletin
Nigerian Journal of Fisheries and Hydrobiology
Proceedings 08768

Forestry Association of Nigeria, POB 4185, Ibadan
Founded: 1970; Members: 400
Pres: Alh. A.M. Danyaro; Gen Secr: Patrick C. Obiaga
Focus: Forestry
Periodicals
Nigerian Journal of Forestry (annually)
Proceedings of Annual Conferences (annually)
. . . . 08769

Genetics Society of Nigeria, c/o International Institut of Tropical Agriculture, Oyo Rd, PMB 5320, Ibadan
Founded: 1972; Members: 75
Focus: Genetics
Periodical
Proceedings 08770

Geological Survey of Nigeria, PMB 2007, Kaduna South
T: 212003
Founded: 1919
Focus: Geology
Periodicals
Annual Report (annually)
Bulletin
Occasional Papers
Records 08771

Historical Society of Nigeria, c/o Dept of History, University of Lagos, Lagos
Founded: 1955
Focus: Hist
Periodicals
Bulletin of News (quarterly)
Journal
Tarikh (semi-annually) 08772

The Medical and Dental Council of Nigeria, 25 Ahmed Onibudo St, Victoria Island, PMB 12611, Lagos
T: (01) 613323, 611299; Fax: 617667
Founded: 1963; Members: 50
Gen Secr: Dr. C.O. Ezeani
Focus: Med; Stomatology
Periodical
Medical and Dental Register (annually) . 08773

Nigeria Educational Research Council, POB 8058, Lagos
Founded: 1965; Members: 30
Focus: Educ 08774

Nigerian Academy of Science, c/o Dept of Computer Science, University of Lagos, PMB 1004, University of Lagos Post Office, Akoka
Founded: 1977; Members: 45
Focus: Sci
Periodicals
The Discourses of the Academy (semi-annually)
The Proceedings of the Academy (semi-annually)
. . . . 08775

Nigerian Bar Association, 25 Odion Rd, POB 403, Warri
Founded: 1962
Focus: Law 08776

Nigerian Economic Society, c/o Dept of Economics, University of Ibadan, Ibadan
Founded: 1957; Members: 1000
Focus: Econ
Periodicals
Nigerian Journal of Economic and Social Studies (3 times annually)
Proceedings of Annual Conferences . . 08777

Nigerian Geographical Association, c/o Dept of Geography, University of Ibadan, Ibadan
Founded: 1955; Members: 500
Focus: Geography
Periodical
Nigerian Geographical Journal 08778

Nigerian Institute of International Affairs, Kofo Abayomi Rd, GPOB 1727, Lagos
T: (01) 615606; E-Mail: Internations, Lagos
Founded: 1961
Focus: Poli Sci
Periodicals
Bulletin (semi-annually)
Dialogue Series (irregularly)
Lecture Series (quarterly)
Monograph Series (irregularly)
Nigerian Forum (monthly)
Nigerian Journal of International Affairs (semi-annually) 08779

Nigerian Institute of Management (NIM), Plot 22, Idowu Taylor St, Victoria Island, POB 2557, Lagos
T: (01) 615105, 616203; Fax: 614116
Founded: 1961; Members: 28000
Gen Secr: Prof. G.O. Olusanya
Focus: Business Admin
Periodical
Management in Nigeria (quarterly) . . . 08780

Nigerian Library Association (NLA), c/o National Library of Nigeria, PMB 12626, Lagos
Founded: 1962; Members: 1000
Focus: Libraries & Bk Sci
Periodicals
Nigerian Libraries (semi-annually)
NLA Newsletter (semi-annually) 08781

Nigerian Society for Microbiology, c/o Dept of Medical Microbiology, University College Hospital, Ibadan
Founded: 1973; Members: 130
Focus: Microbio
Periodical
Nigerian Journal for Microbiology (semi-annually)
. . . . 08782

Nigerian Veterinary Medical Association, c/o Nigerian Veterinary Research Institute, POB 38, Vom, Plateau State
Founded: 1963; Members: 2155
Focus: Vet Med
Periodical
Nigerian Veterinary Journal (semi-annually) 08783

Nutrition Society of Nigeria, c/o Dept of Food Science and Technology, Obafemi Amolowo University, Ile-Ife
Founded: 1966; Members: 350
Focus: Food
Periodical
Nigerian Nutrition Newsletter 08784

Organization of African Unity – Scientific, Technical and Research Commission, PMB 2359, Lagos
T: (01) 2633430, 2633289; E-Mail: Oaustrc-Lagos@rcl.dircom.co.uk; Fax: 2636093
Founded: 1965; Members: 54
Pres: Johnson Ekpere
Focus: Sci; Eng; Poli Sci
Periodicals
African Soils (3 times annually)
Bulletin des Epizooties en Afrique (quarterly)
Bulletin Interafricain d'Informations Phytosanitaires (quarterly)
Bulletin of Epizootic Diseases of Africa (quarterly)
Inter-African Phytosanitary Bulletin (quarterly)
Journal of African Meldicinal Plants (semi-annually)
. . . . 08785

Pan African Association of Neurological Sciences, c/o Prof. T.O. Dada, 346 Herbert Macaulay St, POB 457, Yaba, Lagos
Focus: Neurology 08786

West African Association of Agricultural Economists, c/o Dept of Agricultural Economics, University of Ibadan, Ibadan
Fax: (087) 222872
Founded: 1972; Members: 275
Focus: Agri
Periodical
West African Journal of Agricultural Economics
. . . . 08787

Norway

Committee on Conceptual and Terminological Analysis (COCTA), c/o Institute of Political Science, Postboks 1097, Blindern, Oslo 3
Founded: 1970; Members: 150
Focus: Poli Sci
Periodicals
COCTA News (annually)
Journal of Theoretical Politics (annually) . 08788

Foreningen til Norske Fortidsminnesmerkers Bevaring / Society for the Preservation of Ancient Monuments in Norway, Dronningensgst 11, 0152 Oslo
T: 22422732; Fax: 22421894
Founded: 1844; Members: 8000
Pres: Johan S. Helberg; Gen Secr: Terje Forseth
Focus: Preserv Hist Monuments
Periodicals
Årbok for Foreningen til norske Fortidsminnesmerkers Bevaring (annually)
Fortidsvern (quarterly) 08789

Den Geofysiske Kommisjon / Geophysical Commission, c/o Det Norske Meteorologiske Institutt, Niels Henrik Abels vei 40, Postboks 320, Blindern, 0313 Oslo
Founded: 1917; Members: 5
Focus: Geophys
Periodical
Geofysiske Publikasjoner 08790

Høyokoleutdannedes Forbund, Postboks 9200, Grønland, 0134 Oslo
Founded: 1956; Members: 900
Focus: Business Admin
Periodical
Etcetera (quarterly) 08791

Institute of Transport Economics / Norwegian Centre for Transport Research, Grensesvingen 7, Postboks 6110, Etterstad, 0602 Oslo
T: 22573800; Fax: 22570290
Founded: 1964
Focus: Transport
Periodical
Samferdsel: Communication 08792

Joint Committee of the Nordic Natural Science Research Councils / The Research Council of Norway, Postboks 2700, St. Hanshaugen, 0131 Oslo
T: 22037000; Fax: 22037001
Founded: 1967; Members: 5
Focus: Nat Sci 08793

Kirkehistorisk Samfunn / Church History Society, Markalléen 7, 1320 Stabekk
Founded: 1956; Members: 52
Pres: Prof. Jan Schumacher; Gen Secr: Peder A. Eidberg
Focus: Rel & Theol; Hist
Periodical
Norvegia Sacra 08794

Kommunale Bibliotekarbeiderers Forening / Municipal Librarians' Association, c/o Kari Hjelde, Oppegårdbibliotekene, 1410 Kolbotn
Focus: Libraries & Bk Sci
Periodical
Kontakten (bi-monthly) 08795

Kongelige Norske Videnskabers Selskab, Erling Skakkesgt 47c, 7004 Trondheim
T: 73592157; Fax: 73595895
Founded: 1760; Members: 402
Pres: Prof. Peder Borgen
Focus: Sci
Periodical
Fordhandliger 08796

Landslaget for Lokalhistorie, c/o Historisk Institutt, 7055 Dragvoll
T: 73596433; E-Mail: Jostein.Molde@hf.utnu.no; Fax: 73596441
Founded: 1920; Members: 347
Pres: Egil Nysaeter; Gen Secr: Jostein Molde
Focus: Hist
Periodicals
Heimen (quarterly)
Lokalhistorisk magasin (quarterly) 08797

Landslaget for Språklig Samling (LSS), Postboks 636, Sentrum, 0106 Oslo
Founded: 1959
Focus: Ling
Periodical
Språklig Samling (quarterly) 08798

Landslaget Musikk i Skolen, Toftesgt 69, 0552 Oslo
T: 22714646; Fax: 22375511
Founded: 1956
Focus: Educ; Music 08799

Medicinske Selskap i Bergen / Medical Society of Bergen, c/o Med. Dept B, Haukeland Hospital, 5016 Bergen
Founded: 1831; Members: 220
Focus: Med
Periodical
Medicinsk Revue (weekly) 08800

Nordic Road Safety Council, c/o Samferdselsdepartementet, Möllergatan 1-3, Oslo 3
Fax: 2349570
Members: 5
Focus: Transport
Periodical
Rapporte (irregularly) 08801

Nordisk Anaesthesiologisk Forening (NAF) / The Scandinavian Society of Anaesthesiologists, c/o Dept of Anaesthesia, Ullevaal Hospital, Oslo
Founded: 1950; Members: 900
Focus: Anesthetics
Periodical
Acta Anaesthesiologica Scandinavica (bi-monthly)
. . . . 08802

Norges Fiskeriforskningsråd (NFFR) / The Norwegian Fisheries Research Council, Postboks 1853, 7001 Trondheim
Founded: 1971; Members: 33
Focus: Fisheries 08803

Norges Geologiske Undersökelse (NGU) / Geological Survey of Norway, Postboks 3006, Lade, 7002 Trondheim
Founded: 1858
Focus: Geology
Periodicals
Bulletin
Skrifter 08804

Norges Geotekniske Institutt / Norwegian Geotechnical Institute, Postboks 3930, Ullevaal Hageby, 0806 Oslo
T: 22230388; Fax: 22230448
Founded: 1953; Members: 130
Focus: Geophys 08805

Norges Kunstnerråd / Norwegian Artists' Council, Postboks 643, Sentrum, 0106 Oslo
T: 22478040; E-Mail: kunstner@raadet.filmenshus.no; Fax: 22424040
Founded: 1940
Pres: Eva Sevaldson; Gen Secr: Carl Morten Iversen
Focus: Arts 08806

Norges Landbruksvitenskapelige Forskningsråd / The Agricultural Research Council of Norway, Ökernvn 145, Postboks 8154, Dep, 0033 Oslo
Founded: 1949; Members: 30
Focus: Agri 08807

Norges Standardiseringsforbund (NSF) / Norwegian Standards Association, Postboks 7020, Homansbyen, 0306 Oslo
E-Mail: Standardisering; Fax: 2464457
Founded: 1923; Members: 180
Focus: Standards
Periodicals
Catalogue of Norwegian Standards (annually)
Standardisering (bi-monthly) 08808

Norges Teknisk-Naturvitenskapelige Forskningsråd (NTNF) / Royal Norwegian Council for Scientific and Industrial Research, Sognsvn 72, Tåsen, Oslo
Founded: 1946; Members: 40
Focus: Nat Sci; Eng 08809

Norges Tekniske Vitenskapsakademi / Norwegian Academy of Technological Sciences, 7034 Trondheim
T: 73595463; E-Mail: ntvae@chembio.ntnv.no; Fax: 73590830
Founded: 1955; Members: 390
Pres: Johannes Moe; Gen Secr: Hein Johnson
Focus: Eng 08810

Norks Bibliotekforening, Malerhaugveien 20, 0661 Oslo
T: 22688550; Fax: 22672368
Founded: 1913; Members: 3900
Pres: Froda Baken; Gen Secr: B. Aaker
Focus: Libraries & Bk Sci
Periodical
Nordiatrans Newspaper (semi-annually) . 08811

Norsk Anestesiologisk Forening, c/o Gjövik Fylkessykehus, 2800 Gjövik
Founded: 1949; Members: 160
Focus: Anesthetics 08812

Norsk Arkeologisk Selskap, Frederiksgt 2, Oslo
Founded: 1936; Members: 1000
Focus: Archeol 08813

Norsk Astronautisk Forening / Norwegian Astronautical Society, Postboks 52, Blindern, 0313 Oslo
T: 22293961
Founded: 1951; Members: 400
Pres: Per Arne Marthinsen; Gen Secr: Johannes Fossen
Focus: Eng; Aero
Periodical
Nytt om Romfart (quarterly) 08814

Norsk Bibliotekforening (NBF) / Norwegian Library Association, Malerhaugvn 20, 0661 Oslo
T: 22688550; Fax: 22672368
Founded: 1913; Members: 3600
Focus: Libraries & Bk Sci
Periodical
Internkontakt (11 times annually) 08815

Norsk Botanisk Forening (NBF) / Norwegian Botanical Association, c/o Botanisk Museum, Trondheimsvn 23b, 0562 Oslo
E-Mail: jan.wesenberg@lu.nioslo.no; Fax: 22851835
Founded: 1935; Members: 1250
Pres: Jan Wesenberg; Gen Secr: Anders Often
Focus: Botany
Periodical
Blyttia (quarterly) 08816

Norsk Faglaererlag (NF), Waldemar Thranesgt 1a, 0171 Oslo
Founded: 1914; Members: 7400
Focus: Adult Educ
Periodical
Yrke (10 times annually) 08817

Norsk Forening for Internasjonal Rett (NFIR) / Norsk Avdeling av International Law Association, Fridtjof Nansens plass 4, Postboks 1600, Vika, Oslo
Founded: 1925; Members: 102
Focus: Law 08818

Norsk Forening for Mikrobiologi, c/o Dept of Microbiology, Agricultural University, Postboks 40, 1432 Aas
Founded: 1959; Members: 220
Focus: Microbio 08819

Norsk Forening mot Støy, Kingosgt 22, Oslo
Founded: 1963
Focus: Ecology 08820

Norsk Forsikringsjuridisk Forening, c/o Sparebanken Oslo Akershus, Grensen 3, Oslo
Founded: 1934; Members: 900
Focus: Law
Periodical
Average (annually) 08821

Norsk Fysiologisk Forening, c/o Institutt for ernäringsforskning, Universitetet i Oslo, Postboks 1046, Blindern, Oslo
Focus: Physiology 08822

Norsk Fysisk Selskap (NFS), c/o Dept of Physics, University of Oslo, Postboks 1048, Blindern, 0316 Oslo
T: 22855641; E-Mail: tove.svendby@fys.uio.no; Fax: 22855671
Founded: 1951; Members: 1180
Pres: Thormod Henriksen; Gen Secr: Tove Svendby
Focus: Physics
Periodical
Fra Fysikkens Verden (quarterly) 08823

Norsk Gastroenterologisk Selskap, c/o Dept of Surgery, Aker Hospital, Oslo
Members: 30
Focus: Gastroenter 08824

Norsk Geofysisk Forening (NGF), c/o River and Harbour Laboratory, Klaebuvn 153, 7000 Trondheim
Founded: 1918; Members: 167
Focus: Geophys 08825

Norsk Geologisk Forening, Postboks 3006, Lade, 7002 Trondheim
Founded: 1905; Members: 900
Focus: Geology
Periodical
Norsk Geologisk Tidsskrift (annually) . . 08826

Norsk Geoteknisk Forening (NGF) / Norwegian Geotechnical Society, Sognsvn 72, Postboks 3930, Ullevål Hageby, 0806 Oslo
T: 22023000; Fax: 22230448
Founded: 1950; Members: 343
Focus: Eng; Mining 08827

Norsk Heraldisk Forening, Postboks 313, Sentrum, 0103 Oslo
Founded: 1969
Focus: Genealogy 08828

Norsk Homøopatisk Pasientforening, Postboks 412, 7001 Trondheim
T: 73532307; E-Mail: aslak-s@online.no
Founded: 1951; Members: 1500
Pres: Thore Aalberg; Gen Secr: Aslak Steinsbekk
Focus: Homeopathy
Periodical
Homøopatisk Tidsskrift (quarterly) 08829

Norsk Institutt for By- og Regionforskning (NIBR) / Norwegian Institute for Urban and Regional Research, Gaustadalléen 21, Postboks 44, Blindern, 0313 Oslo
T: 22958800; Fax: 22607774
Founded: 1965; Members: 80
Focus: Urban Plan
Periodicals
NIBR Notater
NIBR Rapport 08830

Norsk Kirurgisk Forening / Norwegian Surgical Society, Fjellvn 5, 1324 Lysaker
Founded: 1911; Members: 730
Focus: Surgery
Periodical
Vitenskapelige Forhandlinger: Scientific Proceedings (annually) 08831

Norsk Kjemisk Selskap (NKS) / Norwegian Chemical Society, Postboks 1107, Blindern, 0317 Oslo
T: 22855531; Fax: 22855441
Founded: 1893; Members: 2200
Focus: Chem
Periodical
KJEMI (10 times annually) 08832

Norsk Korrosjonsteknisk Forening, Rosenkrantzgt 7, Oslo
T: 22426870; E-Mail: polytekn@online.no
Members: 150
Focus: Metallurgy 08833

Norsk Laererlag / Norwegian Union of Teachers, Rosenkrantzgt 15, Oslo
T: 2415875
Founded: 1892; Members: 59000
Focus: Educ
Periodical
Norsk Skoleblad (weekly) 08834

Norsk Logopedlag (NLL) / Norwegian Association of Logopedists, 7041 Trondheim
Founded: 1948; Members: 1000
Focus: Logopedy
Periodical
Norsk Tidsskrift for Logopedi (quarterly) . 08835

Norsk Lokalhistorisk Institutt (NLI) / Norwegian Institute of Local History, Folke Bernadottes vei 21, Kringsja, 0862 Oslo
T: 22022606; E-Mail: nli@riksarkivet.dep.telemax.no; Fax: 22237489
Founded: 1955
Focus: Hist 08836

Norsk Matematisk Forening, c/o Matematisk Institutt, Universitetet i Oslo, Postboks 1053, Blindern, 0316 Oslo
Fax: 22854349
Founded: 1918
Focus: Math
Periodical
Nordisk Matematisk Tidskrift (quarterly) . 08837

Norsk Metallurgisk Selskap, Rosenkrantzgt 7, Oslo
T: 22426870; E-Mail: polytekn@online.no; Fax: 22425887
Founded: 1936; Members: 440
Focus: Metallurgy 08838

Norsk Meteorologforening (NMF) / The Norwegian Association of Meteorologists, c/o Det Norske Meteorologiske Institutt, Postboks 43, Blindern, 0313 Oslo
T: 22963000; Fax: 22963050
Founded: 1961; Members: 110
Focus: Geophys 08839

Norsk Musikkinformasjon / Norwegian Music Information Centre, Toftesgt 69, 0552 Oslo
T: 22370909; Fax: 22356938
Founded: 1978
Focus: Music
Periodical
Listen to Norway (3 times annually) . . 08840

Norsk Naturforvalterforbund / Norwegian Association of Agriculture Graduates, Parkvn 37, Oslo
Founded: 1970; Members: 4098
Focus: Agri
Periodical
NaFo-nytt (23 times annually) 08841

Norsk Operasjonsanalyseforening, c/o Norwegian State Railways Executive Offices, Storgt 33, Oslo
Founded: 1959; Members: 190
Focus: Computer & Info Sci 08842

Norsk P.E.N., Urtegt 50, 0187 Oslo
T: 22571220
Focus: Lit 08843

Norsk Radiologisk Forening (NRF), c/o Røntgenavd, Ullevål Sykehus, 0407 Oslo
Founded: 1920; Members: 280
Focus: Radiology
Periodical
Noraforum (quarterly) 08844

Norsk Regnesentral / Norwegian Computing Centre, Gaustadalléen 23, Postboks 114, Blindern, 0314 Oslo
Founded: 1952
Focus: Computer & Info Sci 08845

Norsk Samfunnsgeografisk Forening (NSGF), c/o Geografisk Institutt, Universitetet i Trondheim, 7055 Dragvoll
Founded: 1974; Members: 200
Focus: Geography
Periodicals
NSGF-Meldingsblad: Newsletter (5-6 times annually)
Skrifter fra NSGF: Conference Proceedings (annually) 08846

Norsk Slektshistorisk Forening, Postboks 9562, Egertorvet, 0128 Oslo
Founded: 1926; Members: 1300
Focus: Genealogy 08847

Norske Akademi for Sprog og Litteratur, Inkognitogt 24, 0256 Oslo
T: 22562950; Fax: 22553743
Founded: 1953; Members: 42
Pres: Lars Roar Langslet
Focus: Ling; Lit 08848

Den Norske Aktuarforening, Hansteens gt 2, Postboks 2429, Solli, 0202 Oslo
Founded: 1904; Members: 215
Focus: Insurance; Stats
Periodical
Scandinavian Actuarial Journal: Published in cooperation with the societies of actuaries in Denmark, Finland and Sweden (quarterly) 08849

Norske Arkitekters Landsforbund (NAL), Josefinesgt 34, 0351 Oslo
T: 22602290; Fax: 22695948
Founded: 1911; Members: 3020
Focus: Archit
Periodicals
Arkitektnytt (20 times annually)
Byggekunst (8 times annually) 08850

Norske Billedkunstnere / The Association of Norwegian Visual Artists, Kongensgt 3, 0153 Oslo
T: 22421357
Founded: 1888; Members: 1900
Focus: Fine Arts
Periodical
Billedkunstneren (10 times annually) . . 08851

Norske Fagbibliotek Forening (NFF), c/o Vigdis Nass, Høgskolen i Sør-Trøndelag, Bibl. v/ økon.-adm. utd., 7005 Trondheim
T: 73559916; E-Mail: vigdis.nass@aoa.hist.no; Fax: 73559910
Founded: 1947; Members: 730
Pres: V. Naess
Focus: Libraries & Bk Sci 08852

Norske Forfatterforening / Norwegian Authors' Society, Rådhusgata 7, Oslo
Founded: 1893; Members: 400
Focus: Lit 08853

Norske Fysioterapeuters Forbund (NFF) / Norwegian Physiotherapist Association, Pilestredet 56, Postboks 7009, Majorstua, 0306 Oslo
T: 22933050; E-Mail: Fysioterapi@online.no; Fax: 22565825
Founded: 1936; Members: 6620
Pres: Anne L. Lexow; Gen Secr: Kari Haug
Focus: Therapeutics
Periodical
Fysioterapeuten (15 times annually) . . 08854

Det Norske Geografiske Selskap, c/o Avd for Samfunnsgeografi, Iks, Universitetet i Oslo, Postboks 1056, Blindern, 0316 Oslo
T: 22856943; Fax: 22854828
Founded: 1889; Members: 500
Focus: Geography
Periodical
Norsk Geografisk Tidsskrift (quarterly) . . 08855

Det Norske Hageselskap, Motzfeldtsgt 1, Postboks 9008, Grønland, 0133 Oslo
T: 22173360; Fax: 22172319
Founded: 1884
Focus: Hort 08856

Norske Havforskeres Forening (NHF), c/o Svein Sundby Havforskningsinst., Postboks 1870, 5011 Nordnes
Founded: 1949; Members: 260
Focus: Oceanography 08857

Den Norske Historiske Forening, c/o Historisk Institutt, Postboks 1008, Blindern, 0315 Oslo
T: 22856759; Fax: 22854828
Founded: 1869; Members: 1500
Pres: Ellen Schrumpf; Gen Secr: Nils Ivar Agøy
Focus: Hist 08858

Norske Kunst- og Kulturhistoriske Museer, Ullevålsvn 11, 0165 Oslo
T: 22201402; Fax: 22112337
Founded: 1918; Members: 331
Focus: Arts; Hist
Periodical
Museumsnytt (quarterly) 08859

Den Norske Laegeforening (DNLF), Fjellvn 5, 1324 Lysaker
T: 67124600; Fax: 67124620
Founded: 1886; Members: 11700
Focus: Med 08860

Det Norske Medicinske Selskab, Drammensvn 44, 0271 Oslo
T: 22440644
Founded: 1833; Members: 600
Focus: Med 08861

Norske Meierifolks Landsforening, Nedre Slottsgt 23, Postboks 398, Sentrum, 0103 Oslo
T: 22422520; Fax: 22413801
Founded: 1914; Members: 1344
Gen Secr: Steinar Husby
Focus: Dairy Sci
Periodical
Meieriposten (monthly) 08862

Den Norske Mikrobionomforening (DNM), c/o Statens Institutt for Folkehelse, Postuttak, Oslo
Founded: 1973; Members: 294
Focus: Microbio 08863

Norske Musikklaereres Landsforbund (N.M.L.L.), Östre Strandgt 17a, 4600 Kristiansand
Founded: 1914; Members: 750
Focus: Music; Educ 08864

Norske Naturhistoriske Museers Landsforbund (NNML), c/o Tromsø Museum, 9000 Tromsø
Founded: 1938; Members: 165
Focus: Hist; Nat Sci
Periodical
Museumsnytt (quarterly) 08865

Det Norske Samlaget, Trondheimsvegen 15, Postboks 4672, Sofienberg, 0506 Oslo
T: 22687600; Fax: 22687502
Founded: 1868; Members: 3500
Focus: Lit
Periodicals
Maal og Minne (semi-annually)
Norsk Litterår Årbok (annually)
Syn og Segn (quarterly) 08866

Norske Sivilingeniørers Forening / Norwegian Society of Chartered Engineers, Postboks 2312, Solli, 0201 Oslo
T: 22947500; Fax: 22947501
Founded: 1874; Members: 30000
Focus: Civil Eng
Periodicals
Bygg
Elektro (bi-weekly)
Sivilingeniören (bi-monthly)
Teknisk Ukeblad (weekly) 08867

Det Norske Skogselskap, Wergelandsvn 23b, 0167 Oslo
T: 22469857; E-Mail: skegsel@online.no; Fax: 22604189
Founded: 1898; Members: 12500
Pres: Tertit Hørstad; Gen Secr: Olav Kaveldiget
Focus: Forestry
Periodical
Norsk Skogbruk (monthly) 08868

Den Norske Tannlegeforening (NTF) / The Norwegian Dental Association, Frederik Stangsgt 20, Postboks 3063, Elisenberg, 0207 Oslo
T: 22547400; Fax: 22551109
Founded: 1884; Members: 4500
Focus: Dent
Periodical
Den Norske Tannlegeforenings Tidende (17 times annually) 08869

Den Norske Veterinaerforening (DNV), General Birchsgt 16, 0454 Oslo
T: 22591650; Fax: 22690450
Founded: 1888; Members: 1800
Focus: Vet Med
Periodical
Norsk Veterinaertidsskrift (monthly) . . . 08870

Det Norske Videnskaps-Akademi / The Norwegian Academy of Science and Letters, Drammensvn 78, Postboks 2814, Solli, 0204 Oslo
T: 22444296; E-Mail: dnva@online.no; Fax: 22562656
Founded: 1857; Members: 747
Pres: Prof. Aagfinn Føllesdal; Gen Secr: Prof. Leif Mohle
Focus: Sci 08871

Norwegian Council of Cultural Affairs, Grev Wedels plass 1, 0151 Oslo
T: 22334042; Fax: 22428919
Founded: 1965
Focus: Arts
Periodical
The Norwegian Cultural Fund 08872

Organization of Nordic Teachers Associations, c/o Norsk Laererlag, Rosenkrantzgt 15, 0160 Oslo
Founded: 1968
Focus: Educ 08873

Papirindustriens Forskningsinstitutt / The Norwegian Pulp and Paper Research Institute, Postboks 24, Blindern, 0319 Oslo
Fax: 22468014
Founded: 1923; Members: 60
Focus: Materials Sci 08874

Den Polytekniske Forening, Rosenkrantzgt 7, 0155 Oslo
T: 22426870; E-Mail: polytekn@online.no; Fax: 22425887
Founded: 1852; Members: 8000
Pres: Nils Holme; Gen Secr: Nils C. Tommeraas
Focus: Eng; Business Admin
Periodical
Teknisk Ukeblad (weekly) 08875

Research Council of Norway, POB 2700, St. Hanshaugen, 0131 Oslo
T: 22037000; Fax: 22037001
Founded: 1971; Members: 27
Pres: Viggo Mohr; Gen Secr: Roald Vaage
Focus: Sci 08876

Riksbibliotektjenesten / National Office for Research and Special Libraries, Bygdøy Allé 21, Postboks 2439, Solli, 0201 Oslo
T: 22430880; Fax: 22560981
Focus: Libraries & Bk Sci
Periodicals
Annual Report (annually)
Skrifter (irregularly)
Synopsis (bi-monthly) 08877

Scandinavian Society for Electron Microscopy, c/o National Institute of Public Health, Oslo
Founded: 1948; Members: 600
Focus: Nat Sci 08878

Selskapet for Lyskultur, Blommenholmvn 1, Postboks 18, 1301 Sandvika
T: 67547930, 67547948
Founded: 1936; Members: 405
Focus: Eng
Periodical
News from Lightening Culture (semi-annually) 08879

Selskapet til Vitenskapenes Fremme / Society for the Advancement of Science, c/o Fysisk Institutt, Universitetet i Bergen, Allégt 55, 5007 Bergen
T: 55582717; E-Mail: arvid.erdal@fi.uib.no; Fax: 55589440
Founded: 1927; Members: 277
Pres: Solveig Aasheim; Gen Secr: Arvid Erdal
Focus: Sci 08880

Skogbrukets og Skogindustrienes Forskningsforening (SSFF) / The Norwegian Forestry and Forest Industry Association, Hoegskolevn 12, 1432 Aas
T: 64949000; Fax: 64942980
Founded: 1947
Focus: Forestry *08881*

Sosialøkonomenes Forening (SF), Youngstorget, Postboks 8872, 0028 Oslo
T: 22170035; Fax: 22173155
Founded: 1908; Members: 946
Focus: Econ
Periodicals
Norsk Økonomisk Tidsskrift
Sosialøkonomen *08882*

Standardiseringsforeningen, c/o Norges Standardiseringsforbund, Haakon Vii's gt 2, Oslo
T: 2416820
Founded: 1974; Members: 110
Focus: Standards *08883*

Statistik Sentralbyrå / Statistics Norway, Kongensgt 6, Postboks 8131 Dep, 0033 Oslo
T: 22864500; E-Mail: ssb@ssb.no; Fax: 22864973
Founded: 1876; Members: 800
Focus: Stats
Periodicals
Official Statistics of Norway
Social and Economic Studies (SES)
Statistical Analyses (SA)   . . .   *08884*

Statsøkonomisk Forening, Dronningensgt 16, Oslo
T: 2413820
Founded: 1883; Members: 400
Focus: Econ
Periodical
Statsøkonomisk Tidsskrift (semi-annually)   .   *08885*

Stiftelsen for Industriell og Teknisk Forskning ved Norges Tekniske Høgskole (SINTEF) / The Foundation for Scientific and Industrial Research at the Norwegian Institute of Technology, 7034 Trondheim NTH
Founded: 1950
Focus: Eng
Periodical
Reports *08886*

The Teachers' Union, Wergelandsvn 15, 0167 Oslo
T: 22030000; Fax: 22110542
Founded: 1993; Members: 33500
Focus: Educ
Periodical
Skoleforum (bi-weekly) *08887*

Teko Teknisk Forening (TTF), Postboks 51, 5036 Fantoft
T: 55574088; Fax: 55574081
Founded: 1941; Members: 405
Focus: Textiles *08888*

Oman

Historical Association of Oman, POB 3941, Ruwi
Founded: 1971; Members: 145
Focus: Hist
Periodical
Bulletin (monthly) *08889*

Pakistan

Academy of Letters, 36 48 St, Islamabad
Founded: 1979
Focus: Lit *08890*

All-Pakistan Educational Conference, Conference Hall, 1-J45/10, Syed Altaf Ali Brelvi Rd, Karachi
T: (021) 611196
Founded: 1951; Members: 118
Focus: Educ
Periodical
Al-Ilm (quarterly) *08891*

Architects Regional Council Asia (ARCASIA), 404 Noor Estate, Shara El-Faisal, Karachi 75350
Founded: 1979; Members: 12
Focus: Archit *08892*

Arts Council of Pakistan, M.R. Kayani Rd, Karachi
T: (021) 2635108
Founded: 1956; Members: 1850
Pres: Zia-Ul-Islam; Gen Secr: Q. Akbar
Focus: Arts *08893*

Asia Foundation, POB 1165, Islamabad
T: (051) 820507
Focus: Int'l Relat; Lit *08894*

Baluchi Academy, Mekran House, Sariab Rd, Quetta
T: 440274
Founded: 1961; Members: 63
Pres: Jan Muhammad Dashti; Gen Secr: Abdul Qaadir Shahwani
Focus: Ling; Lit *08895*

College of Physicians and Surgeons Pakistan, 7 Central St, Karachi 75500
T: (021) 5892801; Fax: 5887513
Founded: 1962; Members: 5877
Pres: Prof. Haq Nawaz; Gen Secr: Prof. Saghir Ahmed
Focus: Surgery; Med *08896*

Federal Library Association, 169 Sawar Rd, Rawalpindi
Focus: Libraries & Bk Sci *08897*

Idarah-i-Yadgar-i-Ghalib, Nazimabad 2, POB 2268, Karachi 18
T: (021) 6686998
Founded: 1968; Members: 10
Pres: A.M. Malik; Gen Secr: M. Zaman
Focus: Lit
Periodical
Ghalib (semi-annually) *08898*

Institute of Cost and Management Accountants of Pakistan, Soldier Bazaar, POB 7284, Karachi 3
T: (021) 719907
Founded: 1951; Members: 825
Focus: Econ; Business Admin
Periodicals
Industrial Accountant (quarterly)
Professional Information Bulletin (bi-monthly)
Students' Handbook (annually)   . . .   *08899*

Institute of Islamic Culture, Club Rd, Lahore 3
T: (042) 53908; E-Mail: ICULT
Founded: 1950
Focus: Lit; Ethnology
Periodical
Al-Ma'arif (monthly) *08900*

Institution of Electrical Engineers, 4 Lawrence Rd, Lahore
Founded: 1969
Focus: Electric Eng
Periodicals
Journal (quarterly)
Newsletter (monthly) *08901*

Institution of Engineers – Pakistan (IEP), IEP Round About, Engineering Centre, Gulberg III, Lahore 54660
T: (042) 5754043, 5756974; E-Mail: hq@iep.edunet.sdnpk.undp.org; Fax: 5759449
Founded: 1948; Members: 48615
Pres: I.A. Omsani; Gen Secr: Ch. Muhammad Rshind Kahn
Focus: Eng
Periodical
The Pakistan Engineer (monthly)   . . .   *08902*

Iqbal Academy Pakistan, GPOB 1308, Lahore
T: (042) 6314510; E-Mail: dhikr@lhr.infolink.net.pk; Fax: 6314496
Founded: 1951
Pres: Minister for Culture; Gen Secr: M.Suheyl Umar
Focus: Ling; Lit
Periodicals
Iqbal Review (English) (semi-annually)
Iqbaliat Farsi (Arabic-Turkish-Persian) (annually)
Iqbaliat (Urdu) (semi-annually) *08903*

Jamiyat-ul-Falah, Akbar Rd, Saddar, POB 7141, Karachi 74400
T: (021) 7721394
Founded: 1950; Members: 300
Gen Secr: Prof. A.Q. Saleem
Focus: Rel & Theol
Periodical
Voice of Islam (monthly) *08904*

Karachi Theosophical Society, Jamshed Memorial Hall, M.A. Jinnah Rd, Karachi 1
T: (021) 721275
Founded: 1896; Members: 124
Focus: Rel & Theol
Periodical
Theosophy in Karachi (monthly) *08905*

Lok Virsa / National Institute of Folk and Traditional Heritage, Garden Av, Shakatparian Hills, Box 1184, Islamabad
T: (051) 813756; Fax: 813756
Founded: 1974
Focus: Cultur Hist; Ethnology; Folklore   .   *08906*

Mehran Library Association, POB 126, Hyderabad
Focus: Libraries & Bk Sci
Periodical
Newsletter *08907*

National Book Council of Pakistan, Block 14-D, Al-Markaz F/8, Islamabad
T: (051) 850892
Founded: 1981
Focus: Libraries & Bk Sci; Lit
Periodical
Kitab (monthly) *08908*

National Science Council of Pakistan, 63 School Rd, Islamabad
Founded: 1961
Focus: Sci *08909*

Pakistan Academy of Letters, H-8/1, Islamabad
T: (051) 855447
Founded: 1976
Focus: Lit

Periodicals
Academy (monthly)
Adbiyat (quarterly) *08910*

Pakistan Academy of Sciences, 3 Constitution Av, G-3, Islamabad
Founded: 1953; Members: 53
Focus: Sci
Periodicals
Monographs (irregularly)
Proceedings (quarterly)
Proceedings of Symposia (irregularly)   .   *08911*

Pakistan Anti Tuberculosis Association, Rm 8, Block 55, Karachi 72400
T: (021) 5688011
Focus: Intern Med
Periodical
The Challenge (quarterly) *08912*

Pakistan Atomic Energy Commission, POB 1114, Islamabad
Fax: (051) 819031 ext 2550
Founded: 1956
Focus: Nucl Res
Periodical
The Nucleus (quarterly) *08913*

Pakistan Board for Advancement of Literature, Narsing Das Garden, Club Rd, Lahore
Focus: Lit *08914*

Pakistan Concrete Institute, 11 Bambino Chambers, Garden Rd, Karachi 0310
Focus: Eng; Civil Eng *08915*

Pakistan Council of Architects and Town Planners, c/o Defence Housing Authority, E-6 Fourth Gizri St, Karachi 46
T: (021) 537416
Founded: 1983
Focus: Archit; Urban Plan *08916*

Pakistan Council of Scientific and Industrial Research (PCSIR), c/o Press Centre, Shahrah-e-Kemal Ataturk, Karachi 1
T: (021) 212256; Fax: 2636704
Founded: 1953
Focus: Sci; Business Admin
Periodicals
Karawan-e-Science (quarterly)
Pakistan Journal of Scientific and Industrial Research (bi-monthly)
Science Chronicle (quarterly)
Technology Digest (monthly) *08917*

Pakistan Historical Society, c/o New Karachi Co-operative Housing Society, 30 Dr. Moinul Haq Rd, Karachi 74700
T: (021) 4557847; E-Mail: huve@cyber.net.pk; Fax: 6641766
Founded: 1951
Pres: H.M. Said; Gen Secr: Dr. A.Z. Khan
Focus: Hist
Periodical
Journal (quarterly) *08918*

Pakistan Institute of International Affairs, Aiwan-e-Sadar Rd, Karachi 1
T: (021) 512891
Founded: 1947; Members: 650
Focus: Poli Sci
Periodical
Pakistan Horizon (quarterly) *08919*

Pakistan Library Association, c/o University of Karachi, POB 8455, Karachi
Founded: 1957; Members: 800
Focus: Libraries & Bk Sci
Periodicals
Conference Proceedings (annually)
Journal (semi-annually)
Newsletter (bi-monthly) *08920*

Pakistan Medical Association (PMA), PMA House, Garden Rd, POB 7267, Karachi 3
T: (021) 714632
Focus: Med *08921*

Pakistan Medical Research Council (PMRC), 162/0/III, Minhas House, PECHS, Karachi 29
T: (021) 416522
Founded: 1953; Members: 19
Focus: Med
Periodical
Pakistan Journal of Medical Research (quarterly) *08922*

Pakistan Museum Association, c/o National Museum, Burns Garden, Karachi
T: (021) 211341
Founded: 1949
Focus: Arts
Periodicals
Museum Studies
Museums Journal of Pakistan (semi-annually) *08923*

Pakistan Philosophical Congress, c/o Dept of Philosophy, University of the Punjab, New Campus, Lahore 20
T: (042) 85134
Founded: 1954
Focus: Philos
Periodicals
Annual Proceedings (annually)
Pakistan Philosophical Journal (semi-annually) *08924*

Pashto Academy, c/o University of Peshawar, Peshawar
T: (0521) 41009
Founded: 1955; Members: 22
Pres: Prof. Dr. Wali Shah Khattak
Focus: Ling; Lit
Periodical
Pakhto (monthly) *08925*

Punjab Bureau of Education, 15A Mahmud Ghaznavi Rd, Lahore 54000
Founded: 1958
Focus: Educ
Periodicals
Educational Statistics Higher Education (annually)
Educational Statistics (Schools) (annually)
Sanvi Taleem (irregularly)
Taleem-e-Tadrees (irregularly)   . . .   *08926*

Punjab Text Board, 21 E-11, Gulberg III, Lahore
Focus: Lit *08927*

Punjab University Historical Society, University Hall, Lahore
Founded: 1911
Focus: Hist *08928*

Punjabi Adabi Academy, 12-G, Model Town, Lahore 14
Founded: 1957
Focus: Ling; Lit *08929*

Quaid-i-Azam Academy, 297 M.A. Jinnah Rd, POB 894, Karachi 74800
T: (021) 7218184, 7214027; Fax: 7219175
Founded: 1976
Gen Secr: Muhammad Ali Siddiqui
Focus: Sci
Periodical
Journal of Pakistan Studies *08930*

Research Society of Pakistan, c/o University of the Punjab, 2 Narsingdas Garden, Club Rd, Lahore 3
T: (042) 65907
Founded: 1963
Focus: Hist; Cultur Hist
Periodical
Journal (quarterly) *08931*

Scientific Society of Pakistan, c/o University, University Campus, Karachi 32
T: (021) 463144
Founded: 1954; Members: 3500
Focus: Sci
Periodicals
Jadeed Science (bi-monthly)
Proceedings of Annual Science Conferences
Science Bachchon Key Liye (monthly)
Science Name (bi-weekly) *08932*

Shah Waliullah Academy, Hyderabad
T: (0221) 24154
Founded: 1963
Focus: Philos
Periodical
Alwali (monthly) *08933*

Sind Library Association, POB 126, Hyderabad
Founded: 1966
Focus: Libraries & Bk Sci *08934*

Sindhi Adabi Board, Sindh University Campus, Tamshoro, Sindh
Founded: 1951
Focus: Lit
Periodicals
Gul Phul (monthly)
Mehran (quarterly) *08935*

Society for the Promotion and Improvement of Libraries, c/o Hamdard Library, Al-Majeed Centre, Nazimabad, Karachi 18
Focus: Libraries & Bk Sci *08936*

Urdu Academy, 33C Model Town A, Bahawalpur
T: 2381
Founded: 1959
Focus: Ling; Lit
Periodical
Az-Zubair (quarterly) *08937*

Panama

Academia Panameña de la Historia, Apdo 973, Zona 1, Panamá City
Founded: 1921
Pres: Miguel A. Martín; Gen Secr: Rogelio Alfaro
Focus: Hist
Periodical
Boletín *08938*

Academia Panameña de la Lengua, Apdo 1748, Zona 1, Panamá City
Members: 12
Pres: Ismael García S.; Gen Secr: T. Díaz Blaitry
Focus: Ling
Periodical
Boletín (annually) *08939*

Asociación Centroamericana de Sociología (ACAS) / Central American Association of Sociology, Apdo 63093, El Dorado, Panamá City
T: 2320028
Founded: 1974; Members: 150
Focus: Sociology *08940*

Asociación de Bibliotecarios Graduados del Istmo de Panamá, c/o Biblioteca de la Universidad de Panamá, Panamá City 3
T: 238786
Focus: Libraries & Bk Sci 08941

Asociación Panameña de Bibliotecarios, Apdo 3435, Panamá City
Focus: Libraries & Bk Sci 08942

Asociación Panamericana de Oftalmología, Apdo 1189, Panamá City 1
Founded: 1940; Members: 4000
Focus: Ophthal 08943

Association for Cooperation in Banana Research in the Caribbean and Tropical America, c/o UPEB, Apdo 4273, Panamá City 5
T: 636310
Founded: 1965
Focus: Agri 08944

Central American Society of Pharmacology, c/o Faculdad de Medicina, Universidad de Panamá, Panamá City
T: 643701; Fax: 635622
Founded: 1975
Focus: Pharmacol 08945

Centro para el Desarrollo de la Capacidad Nacional de Investigación, c/o Estafeta Universitaria, Universidad de Panamá, Panamá City
Founded: 1976
Focus: Sci
Periodicals
Carta Informativa
Revista Scientia 08946

Comisión Nacional de Arqueología y Monumentos Históricos (CONAMOH), Apdo 662, Panamá City
T: 628130
Founded: 1953
Focus: Archeol; Preserv Hist Monuments 08947

Consejo de Economía Nacional, Av 3a, Panamá City
Focus: Econ 08948

Consejo Nacional de Ciencia, Apdo 3277, Panamá City
Founded: 1963
Focus: Sci 08949

Educational and Development Foundation of the Latin American Confederation of Credit Unions, c/o FECOLAC, Apdo 3280, Panamá City 3
T: (0507) 273322; Fax: 273768
Founded: 1979; Members: 2518
Focus: Educ 08950

Federación Odontológica de Centro América y Panamá, Apdo 4115, Panamá City 5
Founded: 1953
Focus: Dent 08951

Inter-American Statistical Institute (IASI), Apdo 5139, Panamá City 5
T: (507) 641349, 64367; Fax: 644601
Founded: 1940
Focus: Stats
Periodicals
Estadística (semi-annually)
Newsletter (2-3 times annually) 08952

Papua New Guinea

Papua New Guinea Library Association (PNGLA), POB 5368, Boroko
Founded: 1973; Members: 200
Focus: Libraries & Bk Sci
Periodicals
Directory of Libraries in Papua New Guinea
PNGLA Librarian's Calendar (monthly)
PNGLA Nius (semi-annually)
Toktok bilong haus buk (quarterly) . . . 08953

Papua New Guinea Scientific Society, c/o National Museum, POB 5560, Boroko
Founded: 1949; Members: 203
Focus: Sci
Periodical
Proceedings (irregularly) 08954

Papua New Guinea Teachers' Association, POB 6546, Boroko
Founded: 1971; Members: 10500
Focus: Educ 08955

Paraguay

Academia de la Lengua y Cultura Guaraní, Calle España y Mompox, Asunción
Founded: 1975
Pres: Dr. Rufino Arevalo Paris; Gen Secr: Antonio E. Gonzáles
Focus: Ling; Lit; Hist
Periodical
Revista 08956

Academia Paraguaya, Av España y Mompox, Asunción
Founded: 1927
Pres: Julio C. Chaves; Gen Secr: Lezcano Luis A.
Focus: Sci 08957

Asociación de Bibliotecarios del Paraguay, Casilla 1505, Asunción
Focus: Libraries & Bk Sci 08958

Asociación de Bibliotecarios Universitarios del Paraguay, c/o Escuela de Bibliotecología, Universidad Nacional, Av España 1098, Asunción
Focus: Libraries & Bk Sci 08959

Centro Paraguayo de Estudios de Desarrollo Económico y Social, Casilla 1189, Asunción
Focus: Sociology; Econ 08960

Comisión Paraguaya de Documentación e Información, c/o Instituto de Ciencias, Universidad Nacional, Av España 1098, Asunción
Focus: Doc 08961

Federación Universitaria del Paraguay, c/o Universidad, Colón 63, Asunción
Focus: Adult Educ 08962

Instituto Nacional de Parasitología, c/o Instituto de Microbiología, Facultad de Medicina, Casilla 1102, Asunción
Founded: 1963; Members: 5
Focus: Microbio 08963

Servicio Cooperativo Interamericano de Salud Pública (SCISP), Av Pettirossi y Brasil, Asunción
Focus: Public Health 08964

Servicio Técnico Interamericano de Cooperación Agrícola, Casilla 819, Asunción
Founded: 1943
Focus: Agri; Eng 08965

Sociedad Científica del Paraguay, Av España 505, Asunción
Founded: 1921; Members: 80
Focus: Sci
Periodical
Revista 08966

Sociedad de Pediatría y Puericultura del Paraguay, 25 de Mayo y Tacuaí, Asunción
Founded: 1928; Members: 28
Focus: Pediatrics 08967

Unión Sudamericana de Asociaciones de Ingenieros (USAI), Casilla 336, Asunción
Founded: 1935
Focus: Eng 08968

Peru

Academia de Estomatología del Perú, Apdo 2467, Lima
Founded: 1929
Focus: Stomatology
Periodicals
Actualidades Académicas
Boletín 08969

Academia Nacional de Ciencias Exactas, Físicas y Naturales de Lima, Casilla 1979, Lima
Founded: 1939
Focus: Nat Sci; Physics
Periodical
Actas 08970

Academia Nacional de Medicina, Camaná 773, Apdo 987, Lima
Founded: 1884; Members: 106
Focus: Med 08971

Academia Peruana de Cirurgía, Camaná 773, Lima
Founded: 1940; Members: 100
Focus: Surgery
Periodical
Revista 08972

Academia Peruana de la Lengua, Jr. Conde de Superunda 298, Lima 1
Fax: (01) 457424
Founded: 1887; Members: 30
Pres: Dr. Luis Jaime Cisneros; Gen Secr: Dr. Martha Hildebrandt
Focus: Hist
Periodical
Boletín (annually) 08973

Agrupación de Bibliotecas para la Información Socio-Económica (ABIISE), Apdo 2874, Lima 100
T: 351760
Focus: Libraries & Bk Sci 08974

Andean Commission of Jurists, Los Sauces 285, San Isidro, Lima 27
T: (014) 407907, 428094; Fax: 426468
Founded: 1980
Focus: Law
Periodicals
Andean Newsletter (monthly)
Boletin de la Comisión Andina de Juristas (quarterly) 08975

Andean Institute for Population Studies and Development, Lola Pardo Vargas 325, Urbanización Aurora Miraflores, Lima 18
Focus: Soc Sci 08976

Andean Institute of Social Studies, Av Arequipa 2064, Lima 1
T: (014) 289929
Focus: Soc Sci 08977

Andean Technological Information System, c/o JUNAC, Paseo de la República 3895, Casilla 181177, Lima 27
T: (014) 414212; Fax: 420911
Founded: 1980
Focus: Computer & Info Sci
Periodical
Boletin Informativo SAIT (quarterly) . . . 08978

Asociación de Artistas Aficionados, Ica 323, Lima
Founded: 1938; Members: 254
Focus: Arts; Perf Arts 08979

Asociación de Bibliotecarios y Documentalistas Agrícolas del Perú (ABYDAP) / Peruvian Association of Agricultural Librarians and Documentalists, c/o Biblioteca Agrícola Nacional, Universidad Nacional Agraria, Apdo 456, Lima
Founded: 1976
Focus: Agri
Periodicals
ABYDAP Informa (irregularly)
Boletín Técnico (irregularly) 08980

Asociación de Ingenieros Civiles del Perú, Nicolás de Piérola 788, Lima
Focus: Civil Eng 08981

Asociación Electrotécnica Peruana, Av República de Chile 284, Lima
Founded: 1943
Focus: Electric Eng 08982

Asociación Latinoamericana Científico de Plantas, c/o Universidad Agraria, Apdo 456, Lima
Focus: Botany 08983

Asociación Médica Peruana Daniel A. Carrión, Jirón Ucayali 218, Lima
Founded: 1920; Members: 1500
Focus: Med 08984

Asociación Nacional de Escritores y Artistas (ANEA), Puno 421, Lima 1
Founded: 1938; Members: 954
Focus: Lit 08985

Asociación Peruana de Archiveros, c/o Archivo Nacional, Palacio de la Nación Justicia, Apdo 3124, Lima
Focus: Archives 08986

Asociación Peruana de Astronomía (A.P.A.), Enrique Palacios 374, Chorrillos, Lima 9
Founded: 1946; Members: 400
Focus: Astronomy 08987

Asociación Peruana de Bibliotecarios, Apdo 3760, Lima
Focus: Libraries & Bk Sci 08988

Center for Andean Regional Studies Bartolomé de las Casas, Pampa de la Alianza 465, Apdo 477, Cusco
T: (084) 232544
Founded: 1974
Focus: Hist 08989

Centro de Estudios Histórico-Militares del Perú, Paeso Colón 190, Lima 1
Focus: Hist; Military Sci 08990

Centro de Investigación y Restauración de Bienes Monumentales del Instituto Nacional de Cultura, Casilla 5247, Lima
Focus: Preserv Hist Monuments 08991

Centro del PEN Internacional, Apdo 1161, Lima
Founded: 1940; Members: 25
Focus: Lit 08992

Centro Latinoamericana de Estudios y Difusión de la Construcción en Tierra (CLEDTIERRA), Apdo 5603, Correo Central, Lima
T: (014) 406027
Focus: Eng 08993

Centro Nacional de Patologia Animal, Apdo 1128, Lima
Focus: Vet Med 08994

CIAT Andean Zone Network for Bean Research, Apdo 14-0185, Lima 14
T: 411711; Fax: 411711
Founded: 1988
Focus: Crop Husb 08995

Colegio de Arquitectos del Perú, Av San Felipe 999, Lima 11
Founded: 1962; Members: 1611
Focus: Archit
Periodical
Habitar 08996

Consejo Andino de Cienccia y Tecnología (CACYT), c/o Depto de Tecnología, JUNAC, Casilla 548, Lima 18
T: 414212; Fax: 420911
Founded: 1983
Focus: Sci; Eng 08997

Consejo Nacional de la Universidad Peruana, Calle Aldabas 3, Surco, Apdo 4664, Lima 33
Founded: 1969; Members: 33
Focus: Sci 08998

Federación de Sociedades Latinoamericanas del Cáncer, Apdo 4135, Lima
Focus: Cell Biol & Cancer Res 08999

Federación Médica Peruana, Apdo 4439, Lima
Founded: 1942; Members: 1230
Focus: Med
Periodical
Boletín de la Federación Médica Peruana 09000

Instituto de Zoonosis e Investigación Pecuaria (IZIP), Camilo Carrillo 402, Apdo 1128, Lima
T: 248530
Founded: 1940; Members: 150
Focus: Zoology 09001

Instituto Geográfico Nacional, Apdo 2038, Lima
Founded: 1921; Members: 260
Focus: Geography
Periodical
Boletín Informativo 09002

Instituto Peruano de Ingenieros Mecánicos, Av República de Chile 284, Lima
Focus: Eng 09003

Junta de Control de Energía Atómica, Espinar 250, San Miguel, Apdo 914, Lima
Focus: Nucl Res 09004

Liga Nacional de Higiene y Profilaxia Social, Apdo 2563, Lima
Founded: 1923
Focus: Hygiene 09005

Servicio de Investigación y Promoción Agraria, c/o Estación Experimental de la Molina, Apdo 2791, Lima
Founded: 1927
Focus: Agri 09006

Sociedad de Ingenieros del Perú, Av N. de Piérola 788, Apdo 1314, Lima
Focus: Eng 09007

Sociedad Entomológica del Perú, Apdo 4796, Lima
Founded: 1956; Members: 600
Focus: Entomology
Periodical
Revista Peruana de Entomología . . . 09008

Sociedad Geográfica de Lima, Jirón Puno 456, Apdo 100-1176, Lima 100
Founded: 1888
Focus: Geography
Periodicals
Anuario Geográfico del Perú (annually)
Boletín de la Sociedad Geográfica de Lima (quarterly)
Diccionario Geográfico del Perú (irregularly)
. . . . 09009

Sociedad Geológica del Perú (SGP), Arnaldo Marquez 2277, Lima
T: 623948
Founded: 1924; Members: 700
Focus: Geology 09010

Sociedad Latinoamericana de Investigación Pediátrica, Jirón Hancayo 190, Lima
Focus: Pediatrics 09011

Sociedad Nacional Agraria, A. Miró Quesada 327-341, Apdo 350, Lima
Founded: 1824
Focus: Agri 09012

Sociedad Nacional de Minería, Pl San Martín 917, Lima
Focus: Mining 09013

Sociedad Peruana de Espeleología, Porta 540, Miraflores, Lima
Founded: 1965
Focus: Speleology 09014

Sociedad Peruana de Eugenesia, Apdo 2563, Lima
Founded: 1943
Focus: Genetics 09015

Sociedad Peruana de Historia de la Medicina, Apdo 987, Lima
Founded: 1939; Members: 110
Focus: Med; Cultur Hist
Periodical
Anales 09016

Sociedad Peruana de Ortopedía y Traumatología, Villalta 218, Lima
Focus: Orthopedics; Traumatology . . . 09017

Sociedad Peruana de Tisiología y Enfermedades Respiratorias, Domingo Casanova 116, Lince, Lima
Founded: 1935
Focus: Pulmon Dis 09018

Sociedad Química del Perú, Apdo 891, Lima, 100
Founded: 1933
Focus: Chem
Periodical
Boletín (quarterly) 09019

Philippines

Academia Filipina, 47 Juan LUna St, San Lorenzo Village, 1223 Manila
Members: 15
Pres: Josef Rodriguez
Focus: Sci 09020

Agricultural Economics Society of South East Asia (AESSEA), c/o Land Bank of the Philippines, Manila
Founded: 1975
Focus: Agri 09021

ASEAN Association for Planning and Housing (AAPH), Strata Bldg, Emerald Av, Pasig, Manila
T: (02) 6313462
Founded: 1979
Focus: Urban Plan
Periodicals
AAPH Bulletin (irregularly)
AAPH Data Resouces (bi-monthly)
Interlink (quarterly) 09022

ASEAN Neurological Society, Room 205, PCS Bldg, 992 EDSA, Quezon City, Manila
T: (02) 984973
Focus: Neurology 09023

ASEAN Training Centre for Preventive Drug Education, c/o Dept of Health Education, College of Education, University of the Philippines, Diliman, Quezon City, Manila 3004
T: (02) 999756; Fax: 992863
Founded: 1980; Members: 6
Focus: Educ 09024

Asia Pacific Physics Teachers and Educators Association (APPTEA), c/o ISMED, University of the Philippines, Diliman, Quezon City, Manila
Founded: 1986
Focus: Educ; Physics 09025

Asia Pacific Quality Organization (APQO), 11 Barrion St, BF Homes, Quezon City
T: (02) 9319696; E-Mail: qcine@ginet.net; Fax: 9324148
Founded: 1981; Members: 93
Pres: José Gonzalez y Prado; Gen Secr: Miflora M. Gatchalian
Focus: Materials Sci 09026

Asian Alliance of Appropriate Technology Practitioners (APPROTECH ASIA), c/o Philippine Social Development Center, Magallanes corner Real Sts, Intramuros, Manila
T: (02) 479918, 497041; Fax: 8189720
Founded: 1980; Members: 17
Focus: Eng 09027

Asian Association for Biology Education (AABE), c/o ISMED, University of the Philippines, Diliman, Quezon City, Manila
T: (02) 9283545; E-Mail: director@ismed.upd.edu.ph; Fax: 9282624
Founded: 1965; Members: 70
Pres: Carmen Kanapi; Gen Secr: Lourdes R. Carale
Focus: Educ; Bio 09028

Asian Association of Agricultural Colleges and Universities (AAACU), c/o SEARCA College, Laguna 4031
T: (0942) 2576, 2290
Focus: Educ; Agri 09029

Asian Confederation of Teachers (ACT), POB 163, Manila
Focus: Educ 09030

Asian Fisheries Society (AFS), c/o MOC, POB 1501, Makati, Manila
T: (02) 8180466
Founded: 1984; Members: 1000
Focus: Fisheries
Periodical
Asian Fisheries Science (semi-annually) . 09031

Asian Institute of Management (AIM), 123 Paseo de Roxas, Makati, Manila 3117
T: (02) 863260, 874011; Fax: 8179240
Founded: 1968
Focus: Business Admin
Periodical
The Asian Manager (quarterly) 09032

Asian Institute of Tourism (AIT), c/o University of the Philippines, Dilman, Quezon City, Manila 3004
T: (02) 969071
Founded: 1976
Focus: Econ
Periodical
AIT Newsbrief 09033

Asian NGO Coalition for Agrarian Reform and Rural Development (ANGOC), POB 870, Makati, Manila 1200
T: (02) 8163033, 8151198; Fax: 8151198
Founded: 1979
Focus: Agri
Periodicals
Information Notes (bi-monthly)
Lok Niti (quarterly) 09034

Asian-Pacific Weed Science Society (APWSS), C-214 Bioscience Bldg, U.P. Los Banos College, Laguna 4031
Founded: 1967; Members: 300
Focus: Agri; Botany; Hort
Periodicals
APWSS Newsletter (2-3 times annually)
Proceedings of Conferences 09035

Asian Recycling Association (ARA), Prosamapi, Isarog Farms, Palestina, Camarines Sur
Founded: 1978
Gen Secr: Portia A. Nayve
Focus: Ecology
Periodical
ARA Newsletter (quarterly) 09036

Asian Regional Training and Development Organization (ARTDO), V.V. Soliven Bldg, Ste 2039, EDA Greenhills, San Juan, Manila 1500
T: (02) 707742
Founded: 1974
Focus: Educ
Periodicals
ARTDO Journal (semi-annually)
ARTDO Report (quarterly) 09037

Asian Rice Farming Network, c/o IRRI, POB 933, Manila
Founded: 1974
Focus: Agri 09038

Asian Women's Research and Action Network (AWRAN), c/o Philippina, 12 Pasajede La Paz, Project 4, Quezon City, Manila
Founded: 1982
Focus: Soc Sci 09039

Association for Engineering Education in Southeast Asia and the Pacific, c/o College of Engineering, University of the Philippines, Diliman, Quezon City
T: (02) 4343641, 9224714; E-Mail: rvea@engg.upd.edu.ph; Fax: 4343641
Founded: 1973; Members: 210
Pres: B. Vea Reynaldo; Gen Secr: C. Matias Aura
Focus: Educ; Eng 09040

Association of Deans of Southeast Asian Graduate Schools of Management (ADSGM), Paseo de Roxas 123, Legaspi Village, Makati City
T: (02) 8160683; Fax: 8179240
Founded: 1985; Members: 25
Pres: Felipe B. Alfonso; Gen Secr: Anna Marie L. Yalung
Focus: Educ; Business Admin 09041

Association of Pediatric Societies of the Southeast Asian Region (APSSEAR), c/o Medical Center of Manila, 1122 General Luna St, Ste 326, POB EA 100, Manila
T: (02) 5247874; Fax: 5261238
Founded: 1974; Members: 20
Pres: Dr. Chok-Wan Chan; Gen Secr: Dr. Perla D. Santos Ocampo
Focus: Pediatrics
Periodical
Bulletin of the Association of Pediatric Societies of the Southeast Asian Region (quarterly) 09042

Association of Special Libraries of the Philippines (ASLP), c/o College of Public Administration Library, University of the Philippines, POB 474, Manila
Founded: 1954; Members: 300
Focus: Libraries & Bk Sci
Periodicals
ASLP Bulletin (quarterly)
ASLP Newsletter (irregularly) 09043

Los Baños Biological Club / Baños Biological Club, c/o College, Laguna
Founded: 1923
Focus: Bio 09044

Colombo Plan Staff College for Technician Education (CPSC), Bldg Block C, DECS Complex, Meralco Av, Pasic City
T: (02) 6310991/95; E-Mail: cpscdir@dostmis.dost.gov.ph; Fax: 6310996 (02) 6730891
Founded: 1974; Members: 19
Gen Secr: Dr. Bernardo Adiviso
Focus: Educ
Periodical
CPSC Quarterly (quarterly) 09045

Confederation of Medical Associations in Asia and Oceania (CMAAO), 862 Guillermo Masangkay St, Binondo, Manila 1006
T: (02) 216405
Founded: 1956
Focus: Med 09046

Conference of Asian-Pacific Pastoral Institutes (CAPPI), c/o EAPI, POB 221, UP Campus, Manila
T: (02) 983182
Founded: 1986
Focus: Rel & Theol
Periodical
CAPPI Newsletter (semi-annually) . . . 09047

Crop Science Society of the Philippines, c/o Institute of Plant Breeding, UPLB, Laguna
Founded: 1970; Members: 2500
Focus: Agri
Periodical
Philippine Journal of Crop Science (3 times annually) 09048

East Asian Pastoral Institute (EAPI), c/o Ateneo de Manila University, Quezon City, Manila
T: (02) 9240561; E-Mail: eapisec@pusit.admi.edu.ph; Fax: 9244359
Founded: 1966
Pres: José Mario C. Francisco; Gen Secr: Geoffrey King
Focus: Rel & Theol
Periodicals
The Bridge Newsletter (semi-annually)
East Asian Pastoral Review (quarterly) . 09049

Eastern Regional Organization for Public Administration (EROPA), POB 464, Manila
T: (02) 993861
Founded: 1958; Members: 91
Focus: Public Admin
Periodicals
Asian Review of Public Administration
EROPA Bulletin (quarterly) 09050

Ecumenical Association of Third World Theologians, c/o Dr. Mary John Mananzan, OSB, POB 3153, Manila
Founded: 1976
Gen Secr: Dr. Mary John Mananzan
Focus: Rel & Theol 09051

ESCAP/WMO Typhoon Committee (TC), ATB Bldg, 1424 Quezon Av, Quezon City
T: (02) 9228055; E-Mail: tes@cyber.cyb-live.com; Fax: 9228413
Founded: 1968; Members: 3
Gen Secr: Roman L. Kintanar
Focus: Geophys
Periodicals
ESCAP/WMO Newsletter
Typhoon Committee Annual Review . . 09052

International Association of Historians of Asia (IAHA), National Archives, T.M. Kalaw St, Manila
Founded: 1961
Focus: Hist 09053

National Research Council of the Philippines (NRCP), Bicutan Taguig, Manila
Founded: 1933
Focus: Sci
Periodicals
NRCP Research Bulletin (quarterly)
NRCP Technical Bulletin (annually) . . . 09054

Philippine Association of Nutrition, c/o Food and Nutrition Research Institute, Corner Taft Av and Pedro Gil St, Ermita, Manila
Founded: 1947; Members: 1100
Focus: Food
Periodical
Philippine Journal of Nutrition (quarterly) . 09055

Philippine Council of Chemists, 2227 Severino Reyes St, Santa Cruz, POB 1202, Manila 2805
Founded: 1958; Members: 200
Focus: Chem 09056

Philippine Historical Association (PHA), c/o University of the East, Sampaloc, Manila
Founded: 1955; Members: 500
Focus: Hist
Periodical
PHA Bulletin (quarterly) 09057

Philippine Institute of Architects, POB 350, Manila
Founded: 1933; Members: 405
Focus: Archit 09058

Philippine Library Association, c/o National Library, T.M. Kalaw St, Room 301, Manila
T: (02) 590177
Founded: 1923; Members: 1025
Focus: Libraries & Bk Sci
Periodicals
Bulletin (semi-annually)
Newsletter 09059

Philippine Medical Association (P.M.A.), P.M.A. House, North Av, Quezon City
T: (02) 973514, 974974; Fax: 974974
Founded: 1903; Members: 140
Focus: Med
Periodical
P.M.A. Newsletter 09060

Philippine Paediatric Society, POB 3527, Manila
Founded: 1947; Members: 620
Focus: Pediatrics
Periodical
Philippine Journal of Paediatrics (semi-annually) 09061

Philippine Pharmaceutical Association, Cardinal Bldg, Corner Herran and F. Agoncillo Sts, Ermita, Manila
Founded: 1920; Members: 4300
Focus: Pharmacol
Periodical
Journal 09062

Philippine Society of Parasitology, c/o College of Public Health, University of the Philippines, 625 Pedro Gil St, POB EA-460, Ermita, Manila 1000
T: (02) 596808; Fax: 5211394
Founded: 1930; Members: 450
Focus: Med 09063

Philippine Veterinary Medical Association (PVMA), c/o College of Veterinary Medicine, University of the Philippines, Diliman, Quezon City 1101
T: (02) 995436, 8161107
Founded: 1907; Members: 2800
Focus: Vet Med 09064

Philosophical Association of the Philippines, POB 3797, Manila
Founded: 1973; Members: 200
Focus: Philos
Periodical
Philippine Journal of Philosophy (annually) 09065

Radioisotope Society of the Philippines (RSP), c/o Philippine Nuclear Research Institute, Don Marino Marcos Av, Diliman, Quezon City
Founded: 1961; Members: 2500
Focus: Nucl Res
Periodical
The Nucleus (annually) 09066

Society for the Advancement of Research, c/o Los Baños College, University of the Philippines, Laguna
Founded: 1930; Members: 530
Focus: Agri 09067

Society for the Advancement of the Vegetable Industry (SAVI), c/o Los Baños College, University of the Philippines, Laguna
Founded: 1967
Focus: Food
Periodical
Proceedings of Annual Seminar-Workshop 09068

United Technological Organizations of the Philippines, 512-516 Samanillo Bldg, Escolta, Manila
Founded: 1946
Focus: Eng 09069

Poland

Bialostockie Towarzystwo Naukowe / Bailystok Scientific Society, Rynek Kosciuszki 22, 15-426 Bialystok
T: (085) 326126
Pres: Prof. Dr. S. Alexandrowicz; Gen Secr: Dr. W. Jarmolik
Focus: Sci
Periodical
Bialostoczyzna (quarterly) 09070

Bydgoskie Towarzystwo Naukowe (BTN), Ul Jezuicka 4, 85-102 Bydgoszcz
T: (052) 222009
Founded: 1959; Members: 531
Pres: Prof. Dr.R. Mazur; Gen Secr: Prof. Dr. K. Kwasniewska
Focus: Sci 09071

Czestochowskie Towarzystwo Naukowe / Czestochowa Scientific Society, II Aleja 22, 42-200 Czestochowa
T: (034) 42449
Pres: Prof. Dr. M. Glowacki; Gen Secr: Prof. Dr. A. Zakrzewski
Focus: Sci 09072

Gdánskie Towarzystwo Naukowe (GTN) / Gdánsk Scientific Society, Ul Grodzka 12, 80-841 Gdánsk
T: (058) 312124
Founded: 1922; Members: 532
Pres: Prof. Dr. Marek Latoszek; Gen Secr: Prof. Dr. Jan Majewski
Focus: Sci
Periodicals
Acta Biologica (irregularly)
Acta Technica Gedanensia (irregularly)
Gdańsk Wczesnośredniowieczny (irregularly)
Gdańskie Studia Jezykoznawcze (irregularly)
Peribalticum (irregularly)
Pomorskie Monografie Toponomastyczne (irregularly)
Pomorze Gdańskie (annually)
Rocznik Gdański (semi-annually)
Seria Zródel (irregularly) 09073

Karkonoskie Towarzystwo Naukowe / Karkonosze Mountains Scientific Society, Ul Bartka Zwyciezcy 1, 58-500 Jelenia Góra
T: (075) 24410
Pres: Dr. T. Bugaj; Gen Secr: Dr. Marian Iwanek
Focus: Sci 09074

Katowickie Towarzystwo Spoleczno-Kulturalne / Katowice Social and Cultural Society, Ul Slowackiego 26, 40-093 Katowice
T: (032) 588467
Pres: Karol Szarowski; Gen Secr: A. Topol
Focus: Sci; Cultur Hist 09075

Kieleckie Towarzystwo Naukowe / Kielce Scientific Society, Ul Zamkowa 5, 25-009 Kielce
T: (041) 45453
Founded: 1958
Pres: Prof. Dr. Adam Massalski; Gen Secr: Prof. Dr. Marta Meducka
Focus: Sci 09076

Lódzkie Towarzystwo Naukowe (LTN) / Lodz Scientific Society, Piotrkowska 179, 90-447 Lódż
T: (042) 361026
Founded: 1936; Members: 365
Pres: Prof. Dr. Stanislaw Liszewski; Gen Secr: Prof. Dr. Ewa Marynowicz-Hetka
Focus: Sci

Periodicals
Acta Archaeologica Lodziensia (annually)
Acta Geographica Lodziensia
Biuletyn Peryglacjalny (annually)
Bulletin de la Société des Sciences et des Lettres de Łódź
Prace Polonistyczne (annually)
Przeglad Socjologiczny (annually)
Rozprawy Komisji Jezykowej (annually)
Sprawozdania z Czynności i Posiedzeń Naukowych /various/
Studia Prawno-Ekonomiczne (semi-annually)
Sylwetki Lódzkich Uczonych (bi-monthly)
Szlakami nauki (semi-annually)
Zagadnienia Rodzajów Literackich (annually) . . . 09077

Lomzynskie Towarzystwo Naukowe im. Wagow / Brothers Waga Lomza Scientific Society, Ul Plac Kosciuszki 2, 18-400 Lomza
T: 163256
Founded: 1975; Members: 250
Pres: Prof. Dr. Michal Gnatowski; Gen Secr: E. Zegalska
Focus: Sci . . . 09078

Lubelskie Towarzystwo Naukowe / Lublin Scientific Society, Plac Litewski 5, 20-080 Lublin
T: (081) 21300
Founded: 1957; Members: 722
Pres: Prof. Dr. Edmund K. Prost; Gen Secr: Prof. Dr. Jan Malarczyk
Focus: Sci . . . 09079

Lubuskie Towarzystwo Naukowe / Ziemia Lubuska Region Scientific Society, Ul Gwardii Ludowej 14, 65-536 Zielona Gora
T: (068) 63375
Pres: Prof. Dr. J. Korbicz; Gen Secr: Bogdan Biegalski
Focus: Sci
Periodicals
Przeglad Lubuski
Rocznik Lubuski . . . 09080

Opolskie Towarzystwo Przyjaciol Nauk (OTPN) / Opole Society of Friends of Science, Ul Zamkowa 2, 45-016 Opole
T: (077) 32112
Founded: 1955; Members: 378
Pres: Prof. Dr. Feliks Pluta
Focus: Sci
Periodicals
Wydział Języka i Literatury
Wydział Nauk Historyczno-Społecznych
Wydział Nauk Medycznych
Wydział Nauk Przyrodniczych . . . 09081

Polska Akademia Nauk (PAN), Palac Kultury i Nauki, POB 24, 00-901 Warszawa
T: (022) 6204349, 6566264; E-Mail: panpk@warman.com.pl; Fax: 6203374
Founded: 1952; Members: 507
Pres: Leszek Kuznicki
Focus: Sci
Periodical
Bulletin (quarterly) . . . 09082

Polski Klub Literacki P.E.N. / Polish P.E.N. Centre, Palac Kultury i Nauki, 00-901 Warszawa
T: (022) 263948
Founded: 1925; Members: 270
Focus: Lit . . . 09083

Polski Komitet Pomiarów Automatyki, c/o Naczelna Organizacja Techniczna w Polsce, UL Czackiego 3-5, 00-043 Warszawa
Focus: Eng . . . 09084

Polskie Lekarskie Towarzystwo Radiologiczne (PLTR), Bamacha 1a, 02-097 Warszawa
T: (022) 223005; Fax: 223005
Founded: 1925; Members: 1280
Focus: Radiology
Periodical
Polski Przeglag Radiologii (quarterly) . . . 09085

Polskie Towarzystwo Anatomiczne, Chalubinskiego 5, 02-004 Warszawa
T: (022) 281041
Founded: 1923; Members: 400
Focus: Anat . . . 09086

Polskie Towarzystwo Antropologiczne, Al Paderewskiego 35, 51-612 Wroclaw
T: (071) 3487077; Fax: 482281
Founded: 1925; Members: 500
Pres: Prof. Pawel Bergman; Gen Secr: Dr. A. Nowacka-Chiari
Focus: Anthro . . . 09087

Polskie Towarzystwo Astronautyczne (PTA), c/o Military Institute of Aviation Medicine, Ul Krasińskiego 54, 01-755 Warszawa
Founded: 1954 I711; Members: 420
Focus: Aero
Periodicals
Astronautyka: Astronautics (bi-monthly)
Postepy Astronautyki: Progress in Astronautics (quarterly) . . . 09088

Polskie Towarzystwo Astronomiczne (PTA), Bartycka 18, 00-716 Warszawa
T: (022) 410041 ext 146; E-Mail: mig@camk.edu.pl
Founded: 1923; Members: 232
Pres: Prof. Jerzy Kreiner; Gen Secr: Dr. M. Giersz
Focus: Astronomy . . . 09089

Polskie Towarzystwo Balneologii, Bioklimatologii i Medycyny Fizykalnej, Ul Slowackiego 8-10, 60-823 Poznan
T: (061) 46338, 46547
Founded: 1954; Members: 500
Focus: Physiology; Physical Therapy . . . 09090

Polskie Towarzystwo Biochemiczne / Polish Biochemical Society, Ul Pasteura 3, 02-093 Warszawa
T: (022) 6582099; E-Mail: ptbioch@nencki.gov.pl; Fax: 225342
Founded: 1958; Members: 1320
Pres: Prof. Liliana Konarska; Gen Secr: Dr. Malgorzata Balinska
Focus: Microbio; Biochem
Periodicals
Monografie Biochemiczne: Biochemical Monographs (irregularly)
Postepy Biochemii: Acta Biochimica Polonica (quarterly) . . . 09091

Polskie Towarzystwo Botaniczne, Ul Rekowiecka 26-30, 02-528 Warszawa
T: (022) 499340
Founded: 1922; Members: 1200
Focus: Botany
Periodicals
Acta Agrobotanica (semi-annually)
Acta Myologica (semi-annually)
Acta Societatis Botanicorum Poloniae (quarterly)
Monographiae Botanicae (annually)
Rocznik Dendrologiczny (annually)
Wiadomości Botaniczne (quarterly) . . . 09092

Polskie Towarzystwo Chemiczne (PTCh), Ul Freta 16, 00-227 Warszawa
T: (022) 311304
Founded: 1918; Members: 2900
Focus: Chem
Periodical
Wiadomości Chemiczne (monthly) . . . 09093

Polskie Towarzystwo Dermatologiczne (PTD), c/o Dept of Dermatology, Warsaw School of Medicine, Ul Koszykowa 82a, 02-008 Warszawa
T: (022) 215180; Fax: 6226781
Founded: 1922; Members: 1300
Pres: Prof. Dr. Wieslaw Glinski; Gen Secr: Dr. Anna Górkiewicz-Petkow
Focus: Derm
Periodical
Przeglad Dermatologiczny: Polish Journal of Dermatology (quarterly) . . . 09094

Polskie Towarzystwo Ekonomiczne (PTE) / Polish Economic Society, Nowy Swiat 49, 00-042 Warszawa
T: (022) 274857
Founded: 1918; Members: 11500
Focus: Econ
Periodical
Ekonomista (bi-monthly) . . . 09095

Polskie Towarzystwo Endokrynologiczne, Plac Starynkiewicza 3, 02-015 Warszawa
T: (022) 281159
Founded: 1951; Members: 400
Focus: Endocrinology
Periodical
Endokrynologia Polska (bi-monthly) . . . 09096

Polskie Towarzystwo Entomologiczne (PTE), Sienkiewicza 21, 50-335 Wroclaw
T: (071) 225041; Fax: 222817
Founded: 1920; Members: 800
Pres: Prof. Dr. Jaroslaw Buszko; Gen Secr: Dr. Marek Bunalski
Focus: Entomology . . . 09097

Polskie Towarzystwo Farmaceutyczne, Dluga 16, 00-238 Warszawa
T: (022) 8311542; Fax: 8310243
Founded: 1947
Pres: Prof. Dr. Witold Wieniawski
Focus: Pharmacol
Periodicals
Acta Poloniae Pharmaceutica (bi-monthly)
Bromatologia i Chemia Toksykologiczna (quarterly)
Farmacja Polska (bi-weekly) . . . 09098

Polskie Towarzystwo Filologiczne (PTF), Nowy Swiat 72, 00-350 Warszawa
T: (02) 8265231 ext 256; E-Mail: ptf@obta.uw.edu.pl; Fax: 8269128
Founded: 1893; Members: 547
Pres: Jerzy Axer; Gen Secr: Robert A. Sucharski
Focus: Ling; Lit . . . 09099

Polskie Towarzystwo Filozoficzne (PTF), Palac Staszica, 00-330 Warszawa
Founded: 1904; Members: 738
Focus: Philos
Periodical
Ruch Filozoficzny: Philosophical Movement (quarterly) . . . 09100

Polskie Towarzystwo Fizjologiczne, Jaczewskiego 8, 20-090 Lublin
T: (081) 26510
Founded: 1936; Members: 669
Focus: Physiology . . . 09101

Polskie Towarzystwo Fizyczne (PTF) / Polish Physical Society, Hoza 69, 00-681 Warszawa
T: (02) 6212668; Fax: 6212668
Founded: 1919; Members: 1840
Focus: Physics
Periodicals
Acta Physica Polonica ser. A: Europhysics Journal (monthly)
Acta Physica Polonica ser. B: Europhysics Journal (monthly)
Delta (monthly)
Postepy Fizyki: Advances in Physics (bi-monthly)
Reports on Mathematical Physics (bi-monthly) . . . 09102

Polskie Towarzystwo Fizyki Medycznej, Wawelska 15, 02-034 Warszawa
T: (022) 224431
Founded: 1965; Members: 380
Focus: Physiology
Periodical
Postępy Fizyki Medycznej: Progress in Medical Physics (quarterly) . . . 09103

Polskie Towarzystwo Geograficzne (PTG) / Polish Geographical Society, Krakowskie Przedmieście 30, 00-325 Warszawa
T: (022) 261794
Founded: 1918; Members: 2300
Focus: Geography
Periodicals
Czasopismo Geograficzne (quarterly)
Fotointerpretacja w Geografii (annually)
Polski Przeglad Kartograficzny (quarterly)
Poznaj Świat (monthly) . . . 09104

Polskie Towarzystwo Geologiczne (PTG) / Geological Society of Poland, Oleandry 2a, 30-063 Kraków
T: (012) 332041
Founded: 1921; Members: 1450
Focus: Geology
Periodical
Annales Societatis Geologorum Poloniae: Rocznik Polskiego Towarzystwa Geologicznego . . . 09105

Polskie Towarzystwo Ginekologiczne, Ul Karowa 2, 00-315 Warszawa
T: (022) 261754
Founded: 1922; Members: 2025
Focus: Gynecology . . . 09106

Polskie Towarzystwo Gleboznawcze (P.T.G.), Ul Wisniowa 61, 02-520 Warszawa
T: (022) 494816
Founded: 1937; Members: 1070
Focus: Agri . . . 09107

Polskie Towarzystwo Hematologiczne, Ul Marcinkowskiego 1, 50-368 Wroclaw
T: (071) 224959
Founded: 1950; Members: 280
Focus: Hematology . . . 09108

Polskie Towarzystwo Higieny Psychicznej, Ul Targowa 59, 03-729 Warszawa
T: (022) 186599
Founded: 1958; Members: 450
Focus: Hygiene
Periodicals
Zagadnienia Wychowawcze a Zdrowie Psychiczne: Upbringing Problems and Mental (quarterly)
Zdrowie Psychiczne: Mental Health (quarterly) . . . 09109

Polskie Towarzystwo Historii Medycyny i Farmacji / Polish Society of History of Medicine and Pharmacy, Ul Długa 16, 00-238 Warszawa
T: (022) 310241
Founded: 1957; Members: 400
Focus: Med; Pharmacol; Cultur Hist
Periodical
Archiwum Historii Medycyny (quarterly) . . . 09110

Polskie Towarzystwo Historyczne (PTH), Rynek Starego Miasta 29-31, Warszawa
T: (022) 316341
Founded: 1886; Members: 3000
Focus: Hist . . . 09111

Polskie Towarzystwo Immunologii Doswiadczalnej i Klinicznej, Pawinskiego 5, 02-106 Warszawa
T: (022) 6086405, 6685316; Fax: 6685334
Founded: 1969; Members: 439
Pres: Prof. Waldemar L. Olszewski; Gen Secr: Dr. Irena Grzelak
Focus: Immunology . . . 09112

Polskie Towarzystwo Jezykoznawcze (PTJ), Al A. Mickiewicza 9-11, 31-120 Kraków
Founded: 1925; Members: 763
Focus: Ling
Periodical
Biuletyn Polskiego Towarzystwa Jezykoznawczego: Bulletin de la Société Polonaise de Linguistique (annually) . . . 09113

Polskie Towarzystwo Kardiologiczne (P.T.K.), Nowogrodzka 59, 02-006 Warszawa
T: (022) 283507
Founded: 1962; Members: 1236
Focus: Cardiol . . . 09114

Polskie Towarzystwo Lekarski (PTL), Al Ujazdowskie 24, 00-478 Warszawa
T: (022) 288699
Founded: 1951; Members: 20000
Focus: Med . . . 09115

Polskie Towarzystwo Lesne (PTL), Ul Bitwy Warszawskiej 1920 R.3, 02-362 Warszawa
T: (022) 221470; Fax: 224935
Founded: 1882; Members: 3229
Focus: Forestry
Periodical
Sylwan (monthly) . . . 09116

Polskie Towarzystwo Ludoznawcze (PTL) / Polish Ethnological Society, Szewska 36, 50-139 Wroclaw
T: (071) 443832, 444613
Founded: 1895; Members: 1154
Focus: Ethnology
Periodicals
Archiwum Ethnograficzne: Ethnographic Archives (irregularly)
Atlas Polskich Strojów Ludowych: Atlas of Polish Folk Costumes (irregularly)
Biblioteka Popularnonaukowa: Library of Popular Science (irregularly)
Literatura Ludowa: Folk Literature (bi-monthly)
Łódzkie Studia Etnograficzne: Ethnographic Works and Materials (annually)
Lud: The People (annually)
Prace Ethnologiczne: Ethnological Works (irregularly)
Prace i Materiały Etnograficzne: Ethnographic Works and Materials (irregularly) . . . 09117

Polskie Towarzystwo Matematyczne (PTM) / Polish Mathematical Society, Ul Sniadeckich 8, 00-950 Warszawa
T: (022) 299592
Founded: 1919; Members: 2115
Focus: Math
Periodicals
Commentationes Mathematicae (annually)
Dydaktyka Matematyki (irregularly)
Fundamenta Informaticae (semi-annually)
Matematyka Stosowana (irregularly)
Wiadomości Matematyczne (irregularly) . . . 09118

Polskie Towarzystwo Mechaniki Teoretycznej i Stosowanej / Polish Society of Theoretical and Applied Mechanics, c/o Wydzial Inzynierii Ladowej Politechniki Warszawskiej, Al Armii Ludowej 16, Pok 650, 00-637 Warszawa
T: (022) 257180; E-Mail: ptmts@omk.il.pw.edu.pl
Founded: 1958; Members: 1192
Pres: Prof. Jerzy Maryniak; Gen Secr: Prof. Józef Kubik
Focus: Eng; Physics
Periodical
Mechanika Teoretyczna i Stosowana: Journal of Theoretical and Applied Mechanics (quarterly) . . . 09119

Polskie Towarzystwo Medycyny Pracy, Ul B. Bieruta 20, 41-200 Sosnowiec
T: 660640
Founded: 1969; Members: 2590
Focus: Med . . . 09120

Polskie Towarzystwo Mikrobiologów / Polish Society of Microbiology, Ul Chocimska 24, 00-791 Warszawa
Founded: 1927; Members: 600
Focus: Microbio
Periodicals
Acta Microbiologica Polonica (quarterly)
Medycyna Doswiadczalna i Mikrobiologia (quarterly)
Postepy Mikrobiologii (quarterly) . . . 09121

Polskie Towarzystwo Milosników Astronomii, Ul Solskiego 30, 31-027 Kraków
T: (012) 23892
Founded: 1921; Members: 2500
Focus: Astronomy . . . 09122

Polskie Towarzystwo Mineralogiczne, Al Mickiewicza 30, 30-059 Kraków
T: (012) 34330
Founded: 1969; Members: 150
Focus: Mineralogy . . . 09123

Polskie Towarzystwo Nauk Weterynaryjnych (PTNW) / Polish Society of Veterinary Sciences, Ul Grochowska 272, 03-849 Warszawa
T: (022) 103397
Founded: 1953; Members: 2620
Focus: Vet Med
Periodical
Medycyna Weterynaryjna (monthly) . . . 09124

Polskie Towarzystwo Nautologiczne (PTN) / Polish Nautological Society, Sienkiewicza 3, 81-374 Gdynia
T: (058) 204975
Founded: 1958
Focus: Navig
Periodical
Nautologia (quarterly) . . . 09125

Polskie Towarzystwo Neofilologiczne (PTN), Ul Mielczynskiego 27-29, 61-725 Poznan
T: (061) 532682
Founded: 1929; Members: 2120
Focus: Ling; Lit
Periodical
Neofilolog (semi-annually) . . . 09126

Polskie Towarzystwo Neurologiczne (P.T.N.) / Polish Neurological Society, c/o Neurological Rehabilitation Hospital, Ul Ujejskiego 37, 05-510 Konstancin-Jeziorna
T: 7564041; Fax: 7564972
Founded: 1934; Members: 1400
Focus: Neurology
Periodical
Neurologia i Neurochirurgia Polska (quarterly) . . . 09127

Polskie Towarzystwo Numizmatyczne (PTAiN), Jezuicka 6, 00-958 Warszawa
T: (022) 8313928
Founded: 1991; Members: 6200
Pres: Lech Kokociński; Gen Secr: Adam Zajac

Focus: Archeol; Numismatics
Periodical
Biuletyn Numizmatyczny (quarterly) . . . 09128

Polskie Towarzystwo Orientalistyczne (PTO) / Polish Oriental Society, Ul Sniadeckich 8, 00-656 Warszawa
T: (022) 217332
Founded: 1922; Members: 300
Focus: Ethnology
Periodical
Przegląd Orientalistyczny: Oriental Review (quarterly) 09129

Polskie Towarzystwo Ortopedyczne i Traumatologiczne / Polish Orthopedic and Traumatologic Society, Ul Lindleys, 02-005 Warszawa
T: (058) 418652
Founded: 1928; Members: 1625
Focus: Orthopedics; Traumatology
Periodical
Chirurgia Narządów Ruchu i Ortopedia Polska (bi-monthly) 09130

Polskie Towarzystwo Otolaryngologiczne (PTOL) / Polish Otolaryngological Society, Ul Banacha 1A, 02-097 Warszawa
T: (022) 235975
Founded: 1889; Members: 1340
Focus: Otorhinolaryngology
Periodical
Otolaryngologia Polska: Polish Journal of Otolaryngology (bi-monthly) 09131

Polskie Towarzystwo Parazytologiczne / Polish Parasitological Society, Ul C. Norwida 29, 50-375 Wroclaw
T: (071) 226661
Founded: 1948; Members: 410
Focus: Microbio
Periodicals
Katalog Fauny Pasozytniczej Polski (irregularly)
Monografie parazytologiczne (irregularly)
Wiadomości Parazytologiczne (bi-monthly) 09132

Polskie Towarzystwo Patologów / Polish Society of Pathologists, Ul S. Żeromskiego 113, 90-549 Łódź
T: (042) 25145
Founded: 1958; Members: 700
Focus: Pathology
Periodical
Patologia Polska (quarterly) 09133

Polskie Towarzystwo Pediatryczne (PTP), Ul Karowa 31, 00-324 Warszawa
T: (022) 267147
Founded: 1908; Members: 5600
Focus: Pediatrics
Periodicals
Pediatria Polska (monthly)
Przeglad Pediatryczny (bi-monthly) . . . 09134

Polskie Towarzystwo Przyrodników im. Kopernika, Ul Rakowiecka 36, 02-532 Warszawa
T: (022) 490171
Founded: 1875; Members: 2300
Focus: Nat Sci
Periodicals
Kosmos (quarterly)
Wszechświat (monthly) 09135

Polskie Towarzystwo Psychiatryczne (P.T.P.) / Polish Psychiatric Association, Al Sobieskiego 1-9, 02-957 Warszawa
T: (022) 427588; Fax: 427588
Founded: 1920; Members: 1000
Pres: Prof. Adam Bilikiewicz; Gen Secr: Joanna Meder
Focus: Psychiatry
Periodicals
Psychiatria Polska (bi-monthly)
Psychoterapia (quarterly) 09136

Polskie Towarzystwo Psychologiczne (PTP) / Polish Psychological Association, Ul Stawki 5-7, 00-183 Warszawa
T: (022) 8311368
Founded: 1950; Members: 2000
Pres: Dr. M. Toeplitz-Winiewska; Gen Secr: Barbara Weigl
Focus: Psych
Periodicals
Nowiny Psychologiczne (quarterly)
Przeglad Psychologiczny (quarterly) . . . 09137

Polskie Towarzystwo Semiotyczne (PTS), Palac Kultury i Nauki, 00-901 Warszawa
Founded: 1968; Members: 115
Focus: Ling
Periodical
Studia Semiotyczne: Semiotic Studies (annually) 09138

Polskie Towarzystwo Socjologiczne (PTS) / Polish Sociological Association, Nowy Swiat 72, 00-330 Warszawa
T: (022) 8267737; Fax: 8267737
Founded: 1957; Members: 1003
Pres: Prof. Antoni Sulek; Gen Secr: Dr. Malgorzata Melchior
Focus: Sociology
Periodical
Polish Sociological Review (quarterly) . . 09139

Polskie Towarzystwo Stomatologiczne (PTS) / Polish Dental Association, Ul Nowotki 21, 90-202 Łódź
T: (042) 321735
Founded: 1951; Members: 9017
Focus: Stomatology
Periodicals
Czasopismo Stomatologiczne (monthly)
Protetyka Stomatologiczna (bi-monthly) . . 09140

Polskie Towarzystwo Urologiczne (PTU), Ul Warszawska 52, Katowice
T: (032) 30978
Founded: 1949; Members: 280
Focus: Urology 09141

Polskie Towarzystwo Zoologiczne, Sienkiewicza 21, 50-335 Wroclaw
T: (071) 225041, 222817; Fax: 282817
Founded: 1937; Members: 1100
Focus: Zoology
Periodicals
Notatki Ornitologiczne (semi-annually)
Przeglad Zoologiczny (semi-annually)
The Ring (annually)
Zoologica Poloniae (annually) 09142

Polskie Towarzystwo Zootechniczne (PTZ) / Polish Society of Animal Production, Ul Kaliska 9, 02-316 Warszawa
T: (022) 221723, 6689671; Fax: 221723
Founded: 1922; Members: 1290
Pres: Dr. J. Luchowiec; Gen Secr: Anna Zablocka-Idczak
Focus: Animal Husb
Periodicals
Animal Production Review (monthly)
Animal Production Review Applied Sciences Report (annually) 09143

Poznánskie Towarzystwo Przyjaciól Nauk (PTPN) / Poznán Society of Friends of Arts and Sciences, Ul Sew. Mielzyńskiego 27-29, 61-725 Poznan
T: (061) 527441
Founded: 1857; Members: 1023
Pres: Prof. Dr A. Karlowska-Kamzowa; Gen Secr: Dr. S. Jakobczyk
Focus: Sci; Arts
Periodicals
Badania Fizjograficzne: Seria A, B, C (irregularly)
Badania z Dziejów Spolecznych i Gospodarczych (irregularly)
Bulletin: Série D: Sciences Biologiques (annually)
Fizyka Dielektryków i Radiospektroskopia (annually)
Lingua Posnaniensis (annually)
Prace Komisji Archeologicznej (irregularly)
Prace Komisji Automatyki (irregularly)
Prace Komisji Biologicznej (irregularly)
Prace Komisji Etnograficznej (irregularly)
Prace Komisji Filologicznej (irregularly)
Prace Komisji Filozoficznej (irregularly)
Prace Komisji Geologiczno-Geograficznej (irregularly)
Prace Komisji Historii Sztuki (irregularly)
Prace Komisji Historycznej (irregularly)
Prace Komisji Jezykoznawczej (irregularly)
Prace Komisji Nauk Ekonomicznych (irregularly)
Prace Komisji Nauk Rolniczych i Komisji Nauk Leśnych (annually)
Prace Komisji Nauk Spolecznych (irregularly)
Prace Monograficzne nad Przyroda Wielkopolskiego Parku Narodowego pod Poznaniem (irregularly)
Roczniki Dziejów Spolecznych i Gospodarczych
Roczniki Historyczne (annually)
Slavia Occidentalis (annually)
Sprawozdania (annually)
Studia nad Historia Prawa Polskeigo (irregularly)
Wydawnictwa Źródlowe Komisji Historycznej (irregularly) 09144

Radomskie Towarzystwo Naukowe / Radom Scientific Society, Slowackiego 1, 26-600 Radom
T: (048) 27259
Pres: Dr. K. Orzechowski; Gen Secr: Dr. Helena Kisiel
Focus: Sci 09145

Stowarzyszenie Autorów ZAIKS / Society of Authors ZAIKS, Hipoteczna 2, 00-092 Warszawa
T: (022) 276061; Fax: 6351347, 6351563
Founded: 1918; Members: 7000
Pres: Antoni Marianowicz; Gen Secr: Witold Kolodziejski
Focus: Lit 09146

Stowarzyszenie Bibliotekarzy Polskich / Polish Librarians Association, Konopczyńskiego 5-7, 00-953 Warszawa
Founded: 1917; Members: 13500
Focus: Libraries & Bk Sci
Periodicals
Bibliotekarz (monthly)
Poradnik Bibliotekarza (monthly)
Przeglad Biblioteczny (quarterly) 09147

Stowarzyszenie Historyków Sztuki (SHS) / Association of Art Historians in Poland, Rynek Starego Miasta 27, 00-272 Warszawa
T: (022) 313773
Founded: 1934; Members: 1602
Focus: Arts; Cultur Hist; Preserv Hist Monuments
Periodical
Kronika Stowarzyszenia Historyków Sztuki (quarterly) 09148

Stowarzyszenie Zydowski Instytut Historyczny w Polsce / Jewish Historical Institute Association of Poland, ul Tlomackie 3-5, 00-090 Warszawa
T: (022) 8279225; E-Mail: zih@it.com.pl;
Fax: 8279225
Founded: 1947; Members: 200
Pres: Michael Friedman; Gen Secr: Dr. Grazyna Pawlak
Focus: Hist
Periodicals
Biuletyn ZIH (quarterly)
Bleter far Geszichte (annually) 09149

Szczecinskie Towarzystwo Naukowe / Szczecin Scientific Society, Ul Wojska Polskiego 96, 70-481 Szczecin
T: (091) 231862
Founded: 1956
Pres: Prof. Dr. Jozef Rutkowski; Gen Secr: Prof. Dr. Jerzy Straszko
Focus: Sci 09150

Towarzystwo Anestezjologów Polskich (TAP), Ul Dluga 1-2, 61-848 Poznan
T: (061) 51021
Founded: 1958; Members: 1350
Focus: Anesthetics 09151

Towarzystwo Chirurgów Polskich (TChP), Ul Banacha 1a, 00-957 Warszawa
T: (022) 236411 ext 467
Founded: 1889; Members: 2100
Focus: Surgery 09152

Towarzystwo imienia Fryderyka Chopina (TiFC) / Frederick Chopin Society, Okólnik 1, 00-368 Warszawa
T: (022) 275471; Fax: 279599
Founded: 1934; Members: 750
Focus: Music
Periodical
Rocznik Chopinowski: Chopin Studies . . 09153

Towarzystwo Internistów Polskich (TIP), Pasteura 4, 50-367 Wroclaw
T: (071) 210765
Founded: 1906; Members: 3000
Focus: Intern Med 09154

Towarzystwo Literackie im. Adama Mickiewicza, Nowy Swiat 72, 00-330 Warszawa
T: (022) 265231 ext 79
Founded: 1886; Members: 1500
Focus: Lit
Periodical
Rocznik Towarzystwa Literackiego im. Adama Mickiewicza (annually) 09155

Towarzystwo Milosników Historii i Zabytków Krakowa (TMHiZK), Swietego Jana 12, 31-018 Kraków
T: (012) 25398
Founded: 1820; Members: 405
Focus: Preserv Hist Monuments; Hist . . 09156

Towarzystwo Milosnikow Jezyka Polskiego (TMJP) / Society of Friends of Polish Language, Straszewskiego 27, 31-113 Kraków
T: (012) 222699
Founded: 1920; Members: 800
Focus: Ling
Periodical
Jezyk Polski (5 times annually) 09157

Towarzystwo Naukowe Organizacji i Kierownictwa / Scientific Society of Organization and Management, Koszykowa 6, 00-564 Warszawa
T: (022) 292127; Fax: 292127
Founded: 1925; Members: 32000
Focus: Business Admin
Periodicals
Organization Review (monthly)
Organizational Problems (quarterly) . . . 09158

Towarzystwo Naukowe Plockie / Societas Scientiarum Plocensis / Scientific Society of Płock, Plac Narutowicza 8, 09-402 Płock
T: (024) 622604, 629477
Founded: 1820; Members: 471
Pres: Dr. Jakub Chojnacki; Gen Secr: Dr. Wieslaw Konski
Focus: Sci
Periodical
Sprawozdanie roczne, Notatki Płockie: Yearbook (annually) 09159

Towarzystwo Naukowe w Toruniu (TNT), Ul Wysoka 16, 87-100 Torun
T: (056) 23941
Founded: 1875; Members: 528
Pres: Prof. Dr. Marian Biskup; Gen Secr: Prof. Marian Kallas
Focus: Sci; Hist
Periodicals
Fontes (irregularly)
Prace Archeologiczne (irregularly)
Prace Popularnonaukowe (irregularly)
Prace Wydziału Filologiczno-Filozoficznego (irregularly)
Roczniki TNT (3 times annually)
Sprawozdania TNT (annually)
Studia Iuridica (irregularly)
Studia Societatis Scientiarum Torunensis: Sectio C - geographia et geologia (irregularly)
Studia Societatis Scientiarum Torunensis: Sectio D - botanica (irregularly)
Studia Societatis Scientiarum Torunensis: Sectio E - zoologia (irregularly)
Studia Societatis Scientiarum Torunensis: Sectio F - astronomia (irregularly)
Studia Societatis Scientiarum Torunensis: Sectio G - physiologia (irregularly)
Studia Societatis Scientiarum Torunensis: Sectio H - medicina
Zapiski Historyczne TNT (quarterly) . . . 09160

Towarzystwo Naukowe Warszawskie / Warsaw Scientific Society, Nowy Swiat 72, 00-330 Warszawa
T: (022) 265231 exz 226
Founded: 1907; Members: 360
Pres: Prof. Dr. Witold Rudowski; Gen Secr: , Prof. Dr. Ewa Rzetelska-Feleszko
Focus: Sci 09161

Towarzystwo Przjaciol Nauk w Miedzyrzecu Podlaskim / Society of Friends Science in Miedzyrzec Podlaski, Ul Warszawska 37, 21350 Warszawa
T: (022) 714126
Pres: Dr. Marian Kowalski; Gen Secr: L. Bernat
Focus: Sci 09162

Towarzystwo Przyjaciól Nauk w Przymyslu (TPN), Rynek 4, 37-700 Przemysl
T: (010) 785601
Founded: 1909; Members: 285
Pres: Prof. Dr. Zdzislaw Budzynski; Gen Secr: Maciej Dalecki
Focus: Sci
Periodicals
Biblioteka Przemyska
Rocznik Przemyski (annually) 09163

Towarzystwo Przyjaciól w Legnicy / Society of Friends of Science in Legnica, Ul Zmakowa 2, 59-220 Legnica
T: (076) 22634
Members: 110
Pres: Dr. W. Morawiec; Gen Secr: Dr. K. Kostrzanowski
Focus: Sci 09164

Towarzystwo Urbanistów Polskich (T.U.P.), Plac Zamkowy 10, 00-277 Warszawa
T: (022) 310773, 312830
Founded: 1923; Members: 2900
Focus: Urban Plan
Periodical
Miasto: The Town (monthly) 09165

Towarzystwo Wiedzy Powszechnej / Society for the Propagation of Knowledge, Palac Kultury y Nauki, 00-901 Warszawa
T: (022) 266504
Founded: 1957; Members: 42410
Gen Secr: Dr. Marek Zukowski
Focus: Sci 09166

Towarzystwo Wolnej Wszechnicy Polskiej / Society of the Polish Free University, Ul Górnóslaska 20, 00-484 Warszawa
T: (022) 6217355; Fax: 6253934
Members: 1000
Pres: Dr. M. Lipowski
Focus: Educ 09167

Wloclawskie Towarzystwo Naukowe (WTN) / Wloclawek Scientific Society, Pl Wolnosci 20, 51-616 Wloclawek
T: (054) 322808
Founded: 1979; Members: 450
Pres: Prof. S.L. Bagdzinski; Gen Secr: S. Kunikowski
Focus: Sci
Periodicals
Annales Silesiae (annually)
Litteraria (annually)
Rozprawy Komisji Jezykowej (annually)
Sprawozdania: Reports A and B (annually) 09168

Wroclawskie Towarzystwo Naukowe / Wroclaw Scientific Society, Ul Parkowa 13, 51-616 Wroclaw
T: (071) 484961
Founded: 1946; Members: 482
Pres: Prof. Dr. Marian Piekarski; Gen Secr: Prof. Jan Zarzycki
Focus: Sci 09169

Zamojskie Towarzystwo Przyjaciól Bauk / Zamosc Society of Friends of Science, Ul Akademicka 8, 22-400 Zamosc
T: (084) 2206
Pres: Dr. Bogdan Szyszka
Focus: Sci 09170

Zrzeszenie Polskich Towarzystw Medycznych (ZPTM) / Federation of Polish Medical Societies, Ul Karowa 31, 00-324 Warszawa
T: (022) 8266320; E-Mail: isobotka@plearn.edu.pl;
Fax: 8268236
Founded: 1965; Members: 70
Pres: Prof. B. Górnicki; Prof. P. Januszewicz; Gen Secr: Prof. C. Korczak
Focus: Med
Periodicals
Activities of the Federation of Polish Medical Societies
Problemy Medycyny i Farmacji (1-2 times annually)
Register of the Federation of Polish Medical Societies (2-3 times annually) 09171

Portugal

Academia das Ciências de Lisboa, Rua da Academia das Ciências 19, 1200 Lisboa
T: (01) 3219730; Fax: 3420395
Founded: 1779; Members: 163
Pres: Prof. Manuel José de Abreu Faro;
Gen Secr: Prof. Justino Mendes de Almeida
Focus: Sci

Periodicals
Anuário Académico
Boletim 09172

Academia Internacional da Cultura Portuguesa, Rua do Salitre62, 1200 Lisboa
Members: 50
Pres: Prof. J. Pereira Neto
Focus: Cultur Hist; Ling; Lit 09173

Academia Nacional de Belas-Artes, Largo da Academia Nacional de Belas-Artes, Lisboa
Founded: 1932; Members: 20
Pres: Prof. P. Ayres de Carvalho; Gen Secr: Prof. Augusto Brandão
Focus: Arts
Periodicals
Belas Artes: Revista-Boletim
Boletim 09174

Academia Portuguesa da História, Largo da Rosa 5, Lisboa
T: (01) 868997
Founded: 1720; Members: 40
Pres: Prof. J.V. Serrão; Gen Secr: Henrique Rema
Focus: Hist
Periodicals
Anais
Boletim
Documentos Medievais Portugueses . . 09175

Associação dos Arqueólogos Portugueses, c/o Museu Arqueológico, Largo do Carmo, Lisboa
T: (01) 3460473
Founded: 1863; Members: 640
Pres: Dr. José Morais Arnaud; Gen Secr: Jacinta Bugalho
Focus: Archeol
Periodical
Arqueólogia e História (annually) 09176

Associação Portuguesa de Bibliotecários, Arquivistas e Documentalistas, Rua Morais Soares 43, 1900 Lisboa
T: (01) 8154479; E-Mail: badbn@mail.telepac.pt; Fax: 8154479
Founded: 1973; Members: 1200
Pres: António José Pina Falcão; Gen Secr: Eloy Rodrigues
Focus: Libraries & Bk Sci; Archives; Doc
Periodicals
Cadernos de Biblioteconomia, Arquivistica e Documentagão (3 times annually)
Noticia (quarterly) 09177

Associação Portuguesa de Economistas, Rua da Estrela 8, 1200 Lisboa
T: (01) 661584
Founded: 1976; Members: 3500
Pres: José de Almeida Serra; Gen Secr: Guilherme Vaz
Focus: Econ 09178

Associação Portuguesa de Escritores (APE), Rua de S. Domingos à Lapa 17, 1200 Lisboa
Founded: 1973; Members: 600
Pres: José Manuel Mendes
Focus: Lit
Periodical
Loreto 13 (quarterly) 09179

Associação Portuguesa de Fisioterapeutas, Av Pedro Alvares Cabral 1a, Lisboa
T: (01) 658656
Focus: Therapeutics 09180

Associação Portuguesa de Fotogrametria, c/o Instituto Geográfico e Cadastral, Praça de Estrela, 1200 Lisboa
T: (01) 666023
Focus: Surveying 09181

Associação Portuguesa de Fundição (APF), Rua do Campo Alegre 672, Porto
T: (02) 690675, 6000764
Founded: 1964 I712; Members: 200
Focus: Metallurgy
Periodicals
Anuario (annually)
Fundigao (quarterly) 09182

Associação Portuguesa de Management (APM), Rua Rodrigo da Fonseca 182, 1000 Lisboa
Fax: (01) 3883266
Focus: Business Admin 09183

Associação Portuguesa de Odontologia, Br. Sabrosa 91, Lisboa
T: (01) 841633
Focus: Dent 09184

Associação Portuguesa de Otorinolaringologia e Cirurgia Cérvico-Facial, Av Almirante Gago Coutinho 151, 1700 Lisboa
T: (01) 8470654; Fax: 847121
Members: 450
Pres: Manuel Filipe Rodrigues; Gen Secr: António Migueis
Focus: Otorhinolaryngology
Periodical
Revista Portuguesa de Otorrinolaringologia (quarterly) 09185

Associação Portuguesa para a Qualidade Industrial, Praça das Indústrias, 1300 Lisboa
T: (01) 636443; E-Mail: INDUSTRIPORT
Focus: Materials Sci
Periodical
Qualidade (3 times annually) 09186

Associação Protectora dos Diabéticos de Portugal (A.P.D.P.), Rua do Salitre 118-120, 1200 Lisboa
T: (01) 3880041; Fax: 659371
Founded: 1926; Members: 767
Focus: Diabetes
Periodical
Bulletin A.P.D.P. (every 3 years) . . . 09187

Associação Técnica da Indústria do Cimento (ATIC), Av 5 Outubro 54, 1050 Lisboa
T: (01) 3547538; Fax: 3525099
Founded: 1965; Members: 5
Focus: Eng
Periodical
ATIC Magazine (semi-annually) 09188

Association of Paediatric Education in Europe (APEE), c/o Serv Pediatri-HSM, Av Prof. Egas Moniz, 1699 Lisboa Codex
Fax: (01) 764059
Founded: 1970; Members: 70
Focus: Educ
Periodical
APEE Bulletin 09189

Associção dos Arquitectos Portugueses (AAP) / Portuguese Architects' Association, Av 24 de Julho 52, 1200 Lisboa
T: (01) 3951401
Founded: 1978; Members: 5020
Focus: Archit
Periodical
Journal Arquitectos (10 times annually) . 09190

Centro de Estudos de História e Cartografia Antiga, Rua da Junqueira 30, 1300 Lisboa
T: (01) 3622621/25; Fax: 3622626
Founded: 1958; Members: 9
Pres: E. Madeira Santos
Focus: Hist; Cart 09191

Colégio Ibero-Latino-Americano de Dermatologia (C.I.L.A.D.), Av da Liberdade 90, 1298 Lisboa Codex
T: (01) 322540
Founded: 1948; Members: 1500
Focus: Derm 09192

Conselho de Reitores das Universidades Portuguesas, Campo dos Mártires da Pátria 2, 1100 Lisboa
T: (01) 549170
Pres: Prof. Esperanza Pina; Gen Secr: Dr. Mario Marchante
Focus: Educ 09193

Instituto Açoriano de Cultura, Apdo 67, 9701 Angra do Heroismo Codex
Founded: 1956
Pres: Dr. Jorge A. Paulus Banno; Gen Secr: Dr. A. Fraga Barcelos
Focus: Educ 09194

Instituto de Coímbra, Rua da Ilha, Coímbra
Founded: 1851; Members: 599
Pres: Prof. Luis . Mendonça de Albuquerque; Gen Secr: Armando Carneida Silva
Focus: Educ 09195

Instituto dos Actuarios Portugueses (IAP), Rua Rodrigo da Fonseca 76, Lisboa
T: (01) 557830
Founded: 1945; Members: 150
Focus: Insurance 09196

Instituto Nacional de Estatistica, c/o Ministério do Planeamento e da Administração do Território, Av Dr. A.J .Aldeia, 1078 Lisboa Codex
T: (01) 8470050; Fax: 8478578
Focus: Stats 09197

Instituto Portugués de Arqueologia, História e Etnografia / Portuguese Archaeological, Historical and Ethnographical Institute, Praça do Imperio, Edificio dos Jerónimos, Belém, Lisboa
Gen Secr: Dr. João L. Saavedra Machado
Focus: Hist
Periodical
Ethnos 09198

International Society for Rock Mechanics (ISRM), c/o Laboratório Nacional de Engenharia Civil, Av do Brasil 101, 1799 Lisboa Codex
T: (01) 8482131; E-Mail: delgado@fnec.pt; Fax: 8478187
Founded: 1962; Members: 5000
Pres: Charles Fairhurst; Gen Secr: José Delgado Rodrigues
Focus: Geology
Periodical
Journal (quarterly) 09199

Junta Nacional de Investigação Científica e Tecnológica (JNICT/CDCT) / Centro de Documentação Cinetífica e Técnica, Av Prof. Gama Pinto 2, 1699 Lisboa
T: (01) 772886, 731300, 731350; Fax: 7965622
Founded: 1936
Focus: Doc 09200

Ordem dos Engenheiros / Association of Engineers, Av de António Augusto de Aguiar 3-D, 1096 Lisboa Codex
T: (01) 3562438; Fax: 3524632
Founded: 1936
Pres: E.J. Leandro Maranha das Neves; Gen Secr: H.P. Pereira
Focus: Eng
Periodical
Review Ingenium (monthly) 09201

Ordem dos Farmacêuticos / Portuguese Pharmaceutical Society, Rua da Sociedade Farmacêutica 18, 1150 Lisboa
T: (01) 3141424; Fax: 3524480
Founded: 1835; Members: 6800
Pres: João Silveira; Gen Secr: Maria José Serra
Focus: Pharmacol
Periodical
Revista Portuguesa de Farmácia (quarterly) 09202

Ordem dos Médicos / Medical Association, Av Almirante Reis 242, 1000 Lisboa
T: (01) 805492
Founded: 1938; Members: 24851
Pres: Manuel Machado Macedo
Focus: Med
Periodical
Revista (monthly) 09203

Real Instituto Arqueológico de Portugal, Praça Rainha D. Filipa 4, 1600 Lisboa
T: (01) 7591109
Founded: 1868
Pres: Dr. J.P. Caxaria; Gen Secr: Dr. J.A. Falcao
Focus: Archeol 09204

Real Sociedade Arqueológica Lusitana, 7540 Santiago do Cacém
T: 826380
Founded: 1849; Members: 167
Pres: Dr. José António Falcão; Gen Secr: Dr. Lilia Ribeiro da Silva
Focus: Archeol; Hist; Arts
Periodicals
Anais da Real Sociedade Arqueológica Lusitana (annually)
Memórias da Real Sociedade Arqueológica Lusitana (annually)
Repertorium Fontium Artis Historiae Portugaliae Instaurandum
Trabalhos da Real Sociedade Arqueológica Lusitana (annually) 09205

Sindicato Nacional dos Odontologistas Portuguesas, Arroios 179, Lisboa 1
T: (01) 546389
Focus: Dent 09206

Sindicato Nacional dos Professionais de Serviço Social, Rua Luciano Cordeiro 18, Lisboa
T: (01) 537963
Focus: Sociology 09207

Sindicato Nacional dos Professores, Conde Redondo 22, Lisboa 1
T: (01) 573014
Founded: 1940; Members: 6000
Focus: Educ 09208

Sindicato Nacional dos Protésicos Dentários, Palmira 66, Lisboa 1
T: (01) 840075
Focus: Dent 09209

Sociedade Anatómica Luso-Hispano-Americana / Portuguese-Spanish-Latin American Anatomical Society, Av Egas Moniz, Lisboa 4
T: 1935
Pres: Prof. Dr. Armando dos Santos Ferreira
Focus: Anat
Periodicals
Actas dos Congressos
Anuário Estatistico: Continente e Ilhas Adjacentes
Arquivo de Anatomia e Antropologia
Boletim Mensal de Estatistica
Comércio Externo (annually)
Estatisticas Agricolas
Estatisticas da Educação
Estatisticas Demográficas
Estatisticas Industriais
Estatisticas Monetárias e Financeiras
Folha Mensal do Estado das Culturas e Previsão de Colheitas 09210

Sociedade Anatómica Portuguesa (SAP), c/o Lab de Anatomia Normal, Faculdade de Medicina de Coímbra, 3049 Coímbra Codex
T: (039) 28121 ext 532; Fax: 23236
Founded: 1930; Members: 184
Pres: António Miguéis; Gen Secr: Jorge Miguéis
Focus: Anat 09211

Sociedade Astronómica de Portugal, Edificio Faculdade de Ciencias, Rua da Escola Politecnica, Lisboa
T: (01) 661521
Focus: Astronomy 09212

Sociedade Broteriana, c/o Dept de Botânica, Universidade, 3049 Coimbra
T: (039) 22897; Fax: 20780
Founded: 1880; Members: 300
Pres: Prof. Dr. José Firmino Moreira Mesquita; Gen Secr: Jorge Paiva
Focus: Botany
Periodicals
Anuário da Sociedade Broteriana (annually)
Boletim da Sociedade Broteriana (annually)
Memórias da Sociedade Broteriana (irregularly) 09213

Sociedade Científica da Universidade Católica Portuguesa, c/o Universidade Católica Portuguesa, Palma de Cima, 1600 Lisboa
T: (01) 7265817; Fax: 7260546
Founded: 1980; Members: 240
Pres: José da Cruz Policarpo
Focus: Sci; Rel & Theol; Philos; Law; Lit; Arts 09214

Sociedade das Ciências Médicas de Lisboa, Av da República 34, 1000 Lisboa
T: (01) 772730
Founded: 1822; Members: 2000
Focus: Med 09215

Sociedade de Ciências Agrárias de Portugal, Rua da Junqueira 299, 1300 Lisboa
T: (01) 3633719
Focus: Agri
Periodical
Revista de Ciencias Agrarias (quarterly) . 09216

Sociedade de Estudos Açoreanos Afonso Chaves / Society for Research on the Azores, Ponta Delgada
Founded: 1932; Members: 100
Focus: Nat Sci; Geophys
Periodical
Açoreana (annually) 09217

Sociedade de Estudos Técnicos SARL-SETEC, Rua Joaquin António de Aguiar 73, Lisboa
Members: 10000
Pres: Armando Lencastre; Gen Secr: Jorge Ramiro
Focus: Eng
Periodical
Boletim Informativo Nacional (monthly) . 09218

Sociedade de Geografia de Lisboa, Rua das Portas de Santo Antão 100, 1150 Lisboa
T: (01) 3425401; Fax: 3464553
Founded: 1875; Members: 1500
Pres: António E. Sousa Leitão; Gen Secr: Nuno Pedro da Silva
Focus: Geography
Periodical
Boletim (semi-annually) 09219

Sociedade de Lingua Portuguesa, Rua São José 41, Lisboa 2
T: (01) 363949
Founded: 1949; Members: 8000
Focus: Ling 09220

Sociedade Geológica de Portugal, c/o Escola Politécnica, Faculty of Science, University, Rue Escola Politecnica, 1294 Lisboa Codex
T: (01) 605850; Fax: 2957668
Founded: 1940; Members: 600
Pres: Prof. R. Rocha; Gen Secr: Dr. Filomena Diniz
Focus: Geology
Periodicals
Boletim (annually)
Maleo 09221

Sociedade Histórica da Independência de Portugal, Palacio da Independencia, Largo de São Domingo 11, 1200 Lisboa
T: (01) 3428987; Fax: 3460754
Focus: Hist
Periodicals
Independência: Society's Review
Report (semi-annually) 09222

Sociedade Martins Sarmento / Martins Sarmento Society, Rua de Paio Galvão, Guimarães
Fax: (053) 415969
Founded: 1881; Members: 540
Pres: J. Simões
Focus: Lit
Periodical
Revista de Guimarães: Boletim da Sociedade Martins Sarmento 09223

Sociedade Nacional de Belas Artes / National Society of Fine Arts, c/o Palacio das Belas Artes, Rua Barata Salgueiro 36, Lisboa
T: (01) 3138510; Fax: 3138519
Founded: 1901
Pres: Fernando de Azevedo
Focus: Arts 09224

Sociedade Portuguesa de Alergologia e Imunologia Clínica (SPAIC) / Portuguese Society of Allergology and Clinical Immunology, c/o Faculdade de Medicina, Av Egas Moniz, 1699 Lisboa
T: (01) 764673
Members: 140
Focus: Immunology
Periodical
Allergologia e Imunologia Clinica: Boletim (semi-annually) 09225

Sociedade Portuguesa de Anestesiologia, Av da República 34, Lisboa 1
Founded: 1955; Members: 145
Focus: Anesthetics 09226

Sociedade Portuguesa de Antropologia e Etnologia, Praça Gomes Teixeira, 4050 Porto
T: (02) 2084656; Fax: 2084656
Founded: 1918; Members: 500
Pres: Prof. Dr. V. Oliveira Jorge; Gen Secr: Henrique G. Araújo
Focus: Anthro; Ethnology; Archeol
Periodical
Trabalhos de Antropologia e Etnologia (annually) 09227

Sociedade Portuguesa de Autores, Av Duque de Loulé 31, 1098 Lisboa Codex
T: (01) 3530257; Fax: 3530257
Founded: 1925; Members: 15000
Pres: Dr. Luiz Francisco Rebello
Focus: Lit

Periodical
Autores (quarterly) 09228

Sociedade Portuguesa de Bioquímica, c/o Instituto de Química Fisiológica, Faculdade de Medicina, Lisboa
Members: 230
Focus: Biochem 09229

Sociedade Portuguesa de Cardiologia, Campo Grande 28, 1700 Lisboa
T: (01) 7970685; Fax: 7931095
Focus: Cardiol
Periodicals
Boletim da Sociedade Portuguesa de Cardiologia
Revista Portuguesa de Cardiologia: Portuguese Journal of Cardiology 09230

Sociedade Portuguesa de Ciências Naturais, c/o Faculdade de Ciências, Rua da Escola Politécnica, 1294 Lisboa Codex
T: (01) 661521
Founded: 1907
Focus: Nat Sci
Periodicals
Boletim
Natura
Naturalia 09231

Sociedade Portuguesa de Ciências Veterinárias, Rua D. Dinis 2a, 1250 Lisboa
T: (01) 3880188
Founded: 1902; Members: 590
Pres: Prof. A. Martins Mendes; Gen Secr: Prof. Manuel d' Almeida Bernardo
Focus: Vet Med
Periodical
Revista Portuguesa de Ciências Veterinárias (quarterly) 09232

Sociedade Portuguesa de Dermatologia e Venereologia, c/o Hospital do Desterro, Lisboa
Founded: 1942; Members: 105
Focus: Derm; Venereology 09233

Sociedade Portuguesa de Educação Médica, Av da República 34, 1000 Lisboa
Fax: (01) 7977578
Members: 130
Focus: Educ
Periodical
Boletim da Sociedade Portuguesa de Educação Médica (3 times annually) 09234

Sociedade Portuguesa de Especialistas de Pequenos Animales / Portuguese Society of Specialists in Small Animals, Rua de D. Dinis 2-A, 1200 Lisboa
Focus: Zoology 09235

Sociedade Portuguesa de Espeleologia, Rua Saraiva Carvalho 233, 1300 Lisboa
T: (01) 666291
Founded: 1948; Members: 150
Focus: Speleology
Periodical
Algar (annually) 09236

Sociedade Portuguesa de Gastroenterologia, c/o Dr. J.M.C. Ribeiro, Av Infante Santo 55, Lisboa 3
Members: 145
Focus: Gastroenter 09237

Sociedade Portuguesa de Hemorreologia e Microcirculação, Apdo 4098, 1502 Lisboa Codex
Fax: (01) 7977578
Members: 242
Focus: Med
Periodical
Boletim da Sociedade Portuguesa de Hemorreologia e Microcirculação (quarterly) 09238

Sociedade Portuguesa de Higiene Alimentar, Rua de D. Dinis 2a, 1200 Lisboa
Focus: Nutrition 09239

Sociedade Portuguesa de Medicina Fisica e Reabilitação (S.P.M.F.R.) / Portuguese Society of Physical Medicine and Rehabilitation, Av Almirante Gago Coutinho 151, 1700 Lisboa
T: (01) 8470654; Fax: 8471215
Members: 300
Pres: Dr. Maria Lidia Ramalho; Gen Secr: Prof. João Pinheiro
Focus: Rehabil
Periodical
Medicina Fisica e de Reabilitação (semi-annually) 09240

Sociedade Portuguesa de Neurologia e Psiquiatria, c/o Hospital Miguel Bombarda, Rua da Cruz Carreira, Lisboa
T: (01) 49849
Focus: Neurology; Psychiatry 09241

Sociedade Portuguesa de Numismática (SPN), Rua Costa Cabral 664, Porto
T: (02) 496029
Founded: 1952; Members: 1600
Focus: Numismatics 09242

Sociedade Portuguesa de Nutrição e Alimentação Animal, Rua de D. Dinis 2a, 1200 Lisboa
Focus: Agri 09243

Sociedade Portuguesa de Oftalmologia, Av Almirante Gago Countinho 151, 1700 Lisboa
T: (01) 8470654; E-Mail: spo@mailtelepac.pt; Fax: 8471215
Founded: 1939; Members: 660
Pres: Prof. Dr. Joaquim Neto Murta; Gen Secr: Dr. Pita Negrad
Focus: Ophthal
Periodical
Revista da Sociedade Portuguesa de Oftalmologia (3 times annually) 09244

Sociedade Portuguesa de Ortopedia e Traumatologia, Av Cons. Barjona Freitas 5, Lisboa 4
T: (01) 784541
Focus: Orthopedics; Traumatology . . . 09245

Sociedade Portuguesa de Patologia, Rua Botelho 24, 1500 Lisboa
Pres: Prof. Dr. Maria-Ana Marques
Focus: Pathology 09246

Sociedade Portuguesa de Pediatria, c/o Hospital Santa Maria, Av 28 de Maio, Lisboa 4
Focus: Pediatrics 09247

Sociedade Portuguesa de Química (SPQ), Av da República 37, 1000 Lisboa
T: (01) 734637
Founded: 1974; Members: 2000
Pres: S. Formosinho
Focus: Chem
Periodicals
Boletim da Sociedade Portuguesa de Química (quarterly)
Revista Portuguesa de Qúimica (quarterly) 09248

Sociedade Portuguesa de Reprodução Animal, Rua de D. Dinis 2a, 1200 Lisboa
Focus: Agri 09249

Sociedade Portuguesa de Reumatologia (SPR) / Portugese Society of Rheumatology, Rua de Dona Estefânia 177, 1000 Lisboa
T: (01) 3534395
Founded: 1972; Members: 248
Pres: Dr. José António Melo Gomes; Gen Secr: Dr. António Carlos Alves de Matos
Focus: Rheuma
Periodical
Acta Reumatológica Portuguesa (bi-monthly) 09250

Sociedade Portuguesa Veterinária de Anatomia Comparativa / Portuguese Veterinary Society of Comparative Anatomy, Av E.U.A. 96-R.D, 1700 Lisboa
Founded: 1974
Pres: Dr. Paulo 715=47 Marques
Focus: Vet Med; Anat 09251

Sociedade Portuguesa Veterinária de Estudos Sociológicos / Portuguese Society of Sociological Veterinary Studies, Rua Abel Botelho 24, 1500 Lisboa
Founded: 1965; Members: 39
Pres: Prof. Dr. Maria-Ana Marques
Focus: Vet Med; Sociology 09252

Sociedade Portuguese de Estomatologia (S.P.E.), Av Rainha D. Amélia 36, 1600 Lisboa
T: (01) 793948
Members: 533
Focus: Stomatology 09253

Puerto Rico

Academia Puertorriqueña de la Historia, Apdo 1446, San Juan
Founded: 1932; Members: 40
Pres: Luis E. González Vales
Focus: Hist 09254

Academia Puertorriqueña de la Lengua Española, Apdo 4008, San Juan, PR 00936
Founded: 1955; Members: 22
Pres: Manuel Alvarez Nazario; Gen Secr: María Vaquero de Ramírez
Focus: Ling
Periodical
Boletín (quarterly) 09255

Ateneo de Ponce, Apdo 1923, Ponce, PR 00731
Founded: 1956
Pres: Hilda Chavier; Gen Secr: Vicente Ruiz
Focus: Arts; Lit 09256

Ateneo Puertorriqueño, Apdo 1180, San Juan, PR 00902
T: (787) 721-3877; Fax: 725-3873
Founded: 1876; Members: 600
Pres: Eduardo Morales Coll; Gen Secr: Prof. Roberto Ramos Perea
Focus: Arts; Lit 09257

Caribbean Studies Association (CSA), POB X, UPR Station, Rio Piedras, PR 00931
T: (809) 763-0812
Founded: 1974; Members: 650
Focus: Ethnology 09258

PEN Club de Puerto Rico, Calle San Sebastián 270, San Juan, PR 00901
Members: 40
Gen Secr: Ernesto Juan Fonfrías
Focus: Lit 09259

Sociedad de Bibliotecarios de Puerto Rico, Apdo 22898, San Juan, PR 00931-2898
T: (787) 764-0000 ext 5034
Founded: 1961; Members: 275
Pres: Annie F. Thompson; Gen Secr: Laura Hernánadez
Focus: Libraries & Bk Sci 09260

Sociedad Mayagüezana por Bellas Artes, Apdo %004, Mayaguez, PR 00709
Founded: 1977; Members: 300
Pres: Dr. Luis E. Bacó Rodriguez
Focus: Arts 09261

Réunion

Académie de l'Ile de la Réunion, 142 Rue Jean-Catel, 97400 Saint-Denis
T: 201009
Founded: 1913; Members: 25
Pres: Serge Ycard; Gen Secr: Yves Drouhet
Focus: Sci
Periodical
Bulletin 09262

Association Historique Internationale de l'Océan Indien, c/o Archives Départementales de la Réunion, Le Chaudron, 97490 Sainte-Clotilde
Founded: 1960; Members: 86
Pres: C. Wanquet; Gen Secr: B. Jullien
Focus: Hist 09263

Romania

Academia de Stiinte Agricole si Silvice Gheorghe Ionescu-Sisesti, Bdul Màràsti 61, Bucuresti
T: (01) 6180699
Founded: 1969; Members: 164
Pres: Corneliu Rauta
Focus: Forestry; Agri
Periodicals
Buletinul informativ al Academiei de Stiinte Agricole si Silvice (annually)
Bulletin de l'Académie des Sciences Agricoles et Forestières (annually) 09264

Academia de Stiinte Medicale (A.S.M.) / Academy of Medical Sciences, Bdul 1 Mai 11, 79173 Bucuresti
T: (01) 502393
Founded: 1969; Members: 96
Pres: Prof. Stefan M. Milcu; Gen Secr: Dr. M. Zamfirescu
Focus: Med
Periodical
Buletinul (quarterly) 09265

Academia de Stiinte Sociale e Politice ((A.S.S.P.)) / Academy of Social and Political Sciences, Str Onesti 11, 70119 Bucuresti
T: (01) 157620
Founded: 1970; Members: 27
Focus: Lit
Periodicals
Dacia: Revue d'Archéologie et d'Histoire Ancienne (semi-annually)
Revista de filozofie: Journal of Philosophy (bi-monthly)
Revista de istorie: Journal of History (monthly)
Revista de istorie şi teorie literarâ: Journal of Literary History and Theory (quarterly)
Revista de psihologie: Journal of Psychology (quarterly)
Revue des Etudes Sud-Est Européennes (quarterly)
Revue Roumaine des Science Sociales: Série des Sociologie/Série des Sciences Economiques (semi-annually)
Revue Roumaine des Sciences Sociales: Série de Psychologie (semi-annually)
Revue Roumaine des Scienes Sociales: Série de Sciences Juridiques (semi-annually)
Revue Roumaine des Scienes Sociales: Série des Philosophie et Logique (quarterly)
Revue Roumaine d'Etudes Internationales (bi-monthly)
Revue Roumaine d'Histoire (quarterly)
Revue Roumaine d'Histoire de l'Art: Série Théâtre, Musique, Cinéma (annually)
Revue Roumaine d'Histoire de l'Art/Serie Beaux-Arts (annually)
Studii şi cercetări de istoria artei, seria Artâ plasticâ: Studies and Researches in Art History/Fine Arts Series (annually)
Studii şi cercetări de istoria artei, seria Teatru, muzicâ, cinematografie: Studies and Researches in Art History/Theatre, Music, Cinematography Series (annually)
Studii şi cercetări de istorie veche şi arheologie: Studies and Researches in Ancient History and Archeology (quarterly)
Studii şi cercetări juridice: Juridical Studies and Researches (quarterly)
Synthesis: Bulletin du Comité National de Littérature Comparée (annually)
Thraco-dacica (semi-annually)
Viitorul social: The Social Future, Journal of Sociology and Political Science (bi-monthly) 09266

Academia Romana, Calea Victoriei 125, 71102 Bucuresti
T: (01) 3122760, 3124699; E-Mail: vnc@aix.acad.ro; Fax: 3120209
Founded: 1866; Members: 181
Pres: Virgilio Nicolae Constantinescu; Gen Secr: Marius Peculea
Focus: Sci
Periodicals
L'Analyse Numérique et la Théorie de l'Approximation
Annuaire Roumain d'Anthropologie
Cahiers de Linguistique Théoretique et Appliquée
Cellulose Chemistry and Technology
Mathematica-Revue d'Analyse Numérique et de Théorie del 'Approximation
Revue Romaine de Physique
Revue Roumaine de Biochimie
Revue Roumaine de Biologie: Série de Biologie Animale
Revue Roumaine de Biologie: Série de Biologie Végétale
Revue Roumaine de Chimie
Revue Roumaine de Géologie, Géophysique et Géographie
Revue Roumaine de Linguistique
Revue Roumaine de Mathématiques Pures et Appliquées
Revue Roumaine des Sciences Techniques Série de Mécanique Appliquée
Studii si cercetari matematice: Studies and Research in Mathematics 09267

Asociatia Bibliotecarilor din Romania, c/o Biblioteca Centrala de Stat, Str Jop Ghica 4, 70018 Bucuresti
T: (01) 503765
Founded: 1956
Focus: Libraries & Bk Sci 09268

Asociaţia Generala a Economiştilor din Romania (A.G.E.R.) / Romanian General Association of Economists, Calea Griviţei 21, 78101 Bucuresti
T: (01) 6507820; Fax: 3129717
Founded: 1990; Members: 20000
Pres: Prof. Nicolae N. Constantinescu; Gen Secr: Dinu Marin
Focus: Econ
Periodical
Economistul (quarterly) 09269

Asociatia Medicala Romana, Str Progresul 10, 70754 Bucuresti
T: (01) 6141071; Fax: 3121357
Founded: 1873
Pres: Prof. Dr. Zorel Filipescu
Focus: Med 09270

Asociatia Oamenilor de Stiinta din Romania (AOS), Str Gabriel Péri 1, 70148 Bucuresti
T: (01) 136234
Founded: 1956
Focus: Sci 09271

Asociaţia Psihiatricâ Românâ (A.P.R.) / Romanian Psychiatric Association, M. Kogâlniceanu av 95a, 70603 Bucuresti
T: (01) 3113471
Founded: 1918
Focus: Psychiatry
Periodical
The Romanian Review of Psychiatry, Child Psychiatry and Clinical Psychiatry (quarterly) 09272

Asociatia Psihologilor din Romania, Str Onesti 11, 70119 Bucuresti
Founded: 1964
Focus: Psych
Periodicals
Revista de Psihologie
Revue des Sciences Sociales, Série de Psychologie 09273

Asociatia Romana de Ştiinte Politice / Romanian Association of Political Sciences, Sos. Kiseleff 47, 71268 Bucuresti
Founded: 1968; Members: 357
Focus: Poli Sci
Periodical
Viitorul social 09274

Balkan Medical Union / Union Médicale Balkanique, G. Clemenceau 1, CP 149, 70148 Bucuresti
T: (01) 6137857; Fax: 3121570
Founded: 1932; Members: 2000
Pres: Prof. Dr. Niki Agnantis; Gen Secr: Prof. Dr. V. Cândea
Focus: Med
Periodicals
Annuaire (annually)
Archives (bi-monthly)
Bulletin (semi-annually) 09275

Comitetul National al Geologilor din Romania (C.N.G.R.S.R.), Str Mendeleev 36, 70169 Bucuresti
Founded: 1962
Focus: Geology 09276

Entente Médicale Méditerranéenne (EMM), c/o Union Médicale Balkanique, Strada Gabriel Péri 1, CP 149, 70148 Bucuresti
T: (0) 137857
Founded: 1980
Focus: Med 09277

European Centre for Higher Education, c/o CEPES-UNESCO, Palatul Kretulescu, Strada Stirbei Voda 39, Bucuresti
T: (01) 6130839; Fax: 6415025
Founded: 1972; Members: 44
Focus: Educ
Periodical
Higher Education in Europe (quarterly) . 09278

European Committee for Scientific and Cultural Relations with Romania, Strada Politechicii, 77213 Bucuresti
Focus: Sci 09279

International Association of South-East European Studies, Str Ion Frimu 9, Bucuresti
T: (01) 507410, 507470
Founded: 1963
Focus: Ethnology
Periodicals
Bulletin d'Archéologie Sud-Est Européenne
Bulletin de l'AIESEE (semi-annually) . . 09280

Latin Language Mathematicians' Group, c/o Institut de Mathématiques, Académie des Sciences de la RSR, Calea Grivitei 21, Bucuresti
Founded: 1955
Focus: Math 09281

PEN Club, Calea Victoriei 113, Bucuresti
Members: 27
Pres: Ana Blandiana; Gen Secr: Mircea Martin
Focus: Lit 09282

Romanian Medical Association, Sos. Berceni 10, 75622 Bucuresti
T: (01) 6827570 ext 160; Fax: 3129867
Members: 90000
Focus: Med
Periodical
Viața Medicală (monthly) 09283

Societatea de Anestezie si Terapie Intensiva, Str Progresului 10, 70754 Bucuresti
Founded: 1973; Members: 46
Focus: Anesthetics; Therapeutics 09284

Societatea de Balneologie, c/o USSM, Str Progresului 10, 70754 Bucuresti
Focus: Physical Therapy 09285

Societatea de Cardiologie, c/o USSM, Str Progresului 10, 70754 Bucuresti
Founded: 1947
Focus: Cardiol 09286

Societatea de Chirurgie, c/o A.M.R., Str Progresului 10, 70754 Bucuresti
T: (01) 6140845; Fax: 3121357
Founded: 1898; Members: 457
Pres: Prof. Dr. Angelescu Nicolae; Gen Secr: Prof. Dr. Popa Florin
Focus: Surgery
Periodical
Chirurgie (bi-monthly) 09287

Societatea de Dermato-Venerologie, c/o USSM, Str Progresului 10, 70754 Bucuresti
Founded: 1928
Focus: Derm; Venereology
Periodical
Dermato-Venerologia (quarterly) 09288

Societatea de Endocrinologie, c/o USSM, Str Progresului 10, 70754 Bucuresti
Founded: 1918
Focus: Endocrinology 09289

Societatea de Farmacie, c/o USSM, Str Progresului 10, 70754 Bucuresti
Founded: 1880; Members: 1200
Focus: Pharmacol
Periodical
Farmacia (quarterly) 09290

Societatea de Fiziologie, c/o USSM, Str Progresului 10, 70754 Bucuresti
Founded: 1949
Focus: Physiology 09291

Societatea de Ftiziologie, c/o USSM, Str Progresului 10, 70754 Bucuresti
Founded: 1930
Focus: Pathology 09292

Societatea de Gastroenterologie, c/o USSM, Str Progresului 10, 70754 Bucuresti
Founded: 1959; Members: 60
Focus: Gastroenter 09293

Societatea de Gerontologie, c/o USSM, Str Progresului 10, 70754 Bucuresti
Founded: 1956
Focus: Geriatrics 09294

Societatea de Histochimie si Citochimie, c/o USSM, Str Progresului 10, 70754 Bucuresti
Founded: 1964
Focus: Chem 09295

Societatea de Igiena si Sànàtate Publica, c/o USSM, Str Progresului 10, 70754 Bucuresti
Founded: 1949
Focus: Public Health; Hygiene
Periodical
Igiena 09296

Societatea de Istorie Medicinei, c/o USSM, Str Progresului 10, 70754 Bucuresti
Founded: 1929
Focus: Hist 09297

Societatea de Medici si Naturalisti / The Society of Physicians and Natural Scientists, Independentei Blvd 16, POB 25, 66000 Iasi
T: (098) 142980; Fax: 142980
Founded: 1830
Focus: Med
Periodical
Revista Medico-Chirurgicala: Medical Surgical Journal (quarterly) 09298

Societatea de Medicinà Generalà, c/o USSM, Str Progresului 10, 70754 Bucuresti
Founded: 1961
Focus: Med 09299

Societatea de Medicinà Internà, c/o USSM, Str Progresului 10, 70754 Bucuresti
Founded: 1919; Members: 50
Focus: Intern Med
Periodical
Medicina Interna (bi-monthly) 09300

Societatea de Medicinà Sportiva, c/o AMR, Str Progresului 10, 70754 Bucuresti
Founded: 1932
Focus: Physical Therapy; Sports 09301

Societatea de Microbiologie, c/o Institutul Cantacuzino, Bucuresti
Focus: Microbio
Periodical
Bacteriologia, Virusologia, Parazitologia si Epidemiologia (quarterly) 09302

Societatea de Obstetricà si Ginecologie, c/o USSM, Str Progresului 10, 70754 Bucuresti
Founded: 1900
Focus: Gynecology
Periodical
Obstetrica si Ginecologia (quarterly) . . 09303

Societatea de Oftalmologie, c/o USSM, Str Progresului 10, 70754 Bucuresti
Founded: 1922
Focus: Ophthal
Periodical
Oftalmologia (quarterly) 09304

Societatea de Oto-Rino-Laringologie, c/o USSM, Str Progresului 10, 70754 Bucuresti
Founded: 1908; Members: 100
Focus: Otorhinolaryngology
Periodical
Oto-Rino-Laringologie (quarterly) 09305

Societatea de Patologie Infectioasà, c/o USSM, Str Progresului 10, 70754 Bucuresti
Founded: 1958
Focus: Pathology 09306

Societatea de Pediatrie, c/o USSM, Str Progresului 10, 70754 Bucuresti
Founded: 1925; Members: 100
Focus: Pediatrics
Periodical
Pediatrie (quarterly) 09307

Societatea de Radiologie, c/o USSM, Str Progresului 10, 70754 Bucuresti
Founded: 1924
Focus: Radiology
Periodical
Radiologie (quarterly) 09308

Societatea de Stiinte Biologice din Romania, Alleea Portocalilor 1-3, 76258 Bucuresti
T: (01) 496602
Founded: 1949; Members: 9000
Focus: Bio 09309

Societatea de Stiinte Farmaceutice / Society of Pharmaceutical Sciences, c/o Asociatia Medicala Romana, Str Progresului 10, 79754 Bucuresti
T: (01) 6141071
Founded: 1880; Members: 320
Focus: Pharmacol
Periodical
Farmacia (quarterly) 09310

Societatea de Stiinte Filologice din Romania (S.S.F.), Bd Schitul Magureanu 1, 79664 Bucuresti
T: (01) 6151792
Founded: 1949; Members: 12000
Pres: Ion Coteanu; Gen Secr: Mircea Franculescu
Focus: Ling; Lit
Periodicals
Buletinul SSF (annually)
Limba si literatura (quarterly)
Limba si literatura romana (quarterly) . . 09311

Societatea de Stiinte Fizice si Chimice din Romania, Bd Schitu Magureanu 1, 70626 Bucuresti
T: (01) 147508
Founded: 1964; Members: 8000
Focus: Chem; Physics
Periodicals
Buletin de fizica si chimie (annually)
Revista de Fizica si Chimie (monthly) . 09312

Societatea de Stiinte Geografice din Romania, Bd Nicolae Bàlcescu 1, 70111 Bucuresti
T: (01) 149350
Founded: 1875; Members: 5000
Focus: Geography
Periodicals
Buletinul S.S.G.: Bulletin de la Société Roumaine de Géographie
In ajutorul profesorului de geografie: A l'Aide du Professeur de Géographie
Lecturi geografice: Des Lectures Géographiques
Terra (quarterly) 09313

Societatea de Stiinte Geologice din Romania, Str Berzei 46, Bucuresti
Founded: 1930; Members: 850
Focus: Geology 09314

Societatea de Stiinte Matematice din Romania (SSM), Str Academiei 14, 70109 Bucuresti
T: (01) 144653; E-Mail: socmat@math.math.unibuc.ro; Fax: 3124072
Founded: 1895; Members: 14000
Pres: Prof. Petru Mocanu; Gen Secr: Prof. Florin Diac
Focus: Math
Periodicals
Bulletin Mathématique (quarterly)
Gazeta Mathematica (monthly) 09315

Societatea de Stomatologie, c/o USSM, Str Progresului 10, 70754 Bucuresti
Founded: 1938
Focus: Stomatology
Periodical
Stomatologie (quarterly) 09316

Societatea de Studii Clasice din Romania, Str Spiru Haret 12, 70738 Bucuresti
Focus: Archeol
Periodical
Studii clasice (annually) 09317

Societatea Nationala de Medicina Generala din Romania (SNMG) / National Society of General Practice of Romania, Str Progresului 10, 70754 Bucuresti
T: (01) 6141062; Fax: 3121357
Founded: 1961; Members: 6000
Focus: Med
Periodical
Revista Medicala Romana: Romanian Medical Journal (bi-monthly) 09318

Societatea Nationala Romana pentru Stiinta Solului (S.N.R.S.S.) / National Romanian Society for Soil Science, Bd Màràsti 61, 71331 Bucuresti
T: (01) 2227620, 2225979; Fax: 2225979
Founded: 1961; Members: 600
Pres: Dr. Lacatusu Radu; Gen Secr: Dr. Nitu Ion
Focus: Agri
Periodical
Stiința Solului (semi-annually) 09319

Societatea Numismatica Romana (SNR), Str I.C. Frimu 11, Sect 1, 71119 Bucuresti
T: (01) 503410
Founded: 1903; Members: 1810
Focus: Numismatics
Periodical
Buletinul (annually) 09320

Societatea Romana de Linguistica, Bd Republicii 13, 70031 Bucuresti
T: (01) 141717
Founded: 1970
Focus: Ling 09321

Societatea Romana de Neurochirurgie / Romanian Society of Neurosurgery, c/o AMR, Sos. Berceni 10, 75622 Bucuresti
T: (01) 6827570 ext 160; Fax: 3129867
Founded: 1982; Members: 115
Focus: Surgery; Neurology
Periodical
Romanian Neurosurgery (annually) . . . 09322

Societatea Românǎ de Ortopedie și Traumatologie (SOROT) / Romanian Society for Orthopaedics and Traumatology, Str Progresului 10, 70754 Bucuresti
T: (01) 6141062
Founded: 1935; Members: 312
Focus: Orthopedics; Traumatology
Periodical
Revista de Ortopedie si Traumatologie (quarterly)
. . . . 09323

Societatea Romana de Sprijia a Virstnicilor Suferinzi de Afectiuni de tip Alzheimer (R.S.S.P.S.A.D.) / Romanian Support Society for People Suffering of Alzheimer Type Diseases, Str Gh. Marinescu 3, Bucuresti
T: (01) 3113471; Fax: 3212268
Founded: 1992; Members: 171
Focus: Neurology
Periodical
Romanian Alzheimer Newsletter 09324

Uniunea Arhitectilor din Romania, Str Academiei 18-20, 70109 Bucuresti
T: (01) 6140743; Fax: 3120956
Founded: 1952; Members: 3000
Pres: Alexandru Beldiman; Gen Secr: Stefan Lungu
Focus: Archit
Periodical
Arhitectura (bi-monthly) 09325

Uniunea Artistilor Plastici din Romania, Str Nicolae Iorga 21, Bucuresti
T: (01) 507380
Founded: 1950; Members: 1650
Focus: Arts
Periodical
Arta (monthly) 09326

Uniunea Cineaştilor din Romania / Cinema Workers' Association of Romania, Str Mendeleev 28-30, Sector 1, 70169 Bucuresti
T: (01) 6505741; Fax: 3111246
Founded: 1963; Members: 900
Pres: Mihnea Gheorghiu
Focus: Cinema 09327

Uniunea Scriitorilor din Romania / Writers' Union of the SRR, Calea Victoriei 115, Bucuresti
T: (01) 507245
Founded: 1877
Focus: Lit
Periodicals
Convorbiri literare
Igaz Szó
Knijevni Jivot
Luceafaírul
Orizont
România Literaraí
Secolul 20
Steaua
Utunk
Vatra
Viata Româneascaí 09328

Russia

Agro-Industrial Society, Ul Kirova 13, 101000 Moskva
T: (095) 9243809
Pres: V.I. Fisinin
Focus: Agri; Econ 09329

Aircraft Building Society, Leningradskii Pr 24a, 125040 Moskva
T: (095) 2142288
Pres: A.M. Batkov
Focus: Aero 09330

Association of Economic Scientific Institutions, Krasikova 27, 117218 Moskva
T: (095) 1290427
Focus: Econ 09331

Association of International Law, Ul Frunze 10, 119841 Moskva
Pres: Prof. G.I. Tunkin
Focus: Law 09332

Association of Orientalists, Ul Rozhdestvenka 12, 103753 Moskva
T: (095) 9285764
Pres: M.S. Kapitsa
Focus: Ethnology 09333

Association of Political Sciences, Ul Frunze 10, 118941 Moskva
Pres: Dr. G.K. Shakhnazarov
Focus: Poli Sci 09334

Association of Sinologists, Ul Krasikova 27, 117848 Moskva
Pres: M.L. Titarenko
Focus: Ethnology 09335

Astronomical and Geodesical Society, Sadovo-Kudrinskaya ul 24, 103001 Moskva
Pres: Y.D. Bulanzhe
Focus: Astronomy 09336

Automobile and Road Building Society, B. Ovchinnikovsky per 12, 113184 Moskva
T: (095) 2314813
Pres: A.K. Vasilev
Focus: Auto Eng; Civil Eng 09337

Biochemical Society, Ul Vavilova 34, 117991 Moskva
T: (095) 1359779
Pres: S.E. Severin
Focus: Biochem 09338

Biological Engineering Society, Ul Lesteva 18, 113809 Moskva
T: (095) 2366075
Pres: V.E. Matveyev
Focus: Eng 09339

Civil Engineering Society, Podsosensky per 25, 103062 Moskva
T: (095) 2978799
Pres: I.I. Ishenko
Focus: Eng 09340

Co-ordination Council for Information on Achievements, Leninskii Pr 61, 117333 Moskva
T: (095) 2344485
Pres: I.M. Makarov
Focus: Sci 09341

Co-ordination Council for Scientific Problems Linked with Ecological Consequences of the Use of New Technological Systems, Leninskii Pr 14, 117901 Moskva
Pres: A.P. Aleksandrov
Focus: Ecology 09342

Commission for Scientific and Technical Co-operation of the Academy of Sciences and Organizations of Moscow Oblast, Ul Vavilova 34, 117995 Moskva
T: 2229393
Pres: V.N. Melkishev
Focus: Eng; Sci 09343

Commission for the European (Vienna) Centre for Co-ordination of Research and Documentation in Social Sciences, Ul Krasikova 28, 117418 Moskva
T: 1286851
Pres: V.A. Vinogradov
Focus: Soc Sci 09344

Commission on Terminology, Leninskii pr 265a, 720071 Bishkek
Pres: S.T. Tabysahaliev
Focus: Humanities 09345

Council for International Co-operation in Social Sciences, Ul Dimitrova 35, 113095 Moskva
T: (096) 2387600
Pres: P.N. Fedoseev
Focus: Soc Sci 09346

Council for Links between the Academy of Sciences and Higher Education, Leninskii Pr 14, 117901 Moskva
T: (095) 2325801
Pres: A.A. Logunov
Focus: Educ 09347

Council for Metrological Provision and Standardization, Bolshoi Pr 612, 199178 St. Petersburg
T: (095) 2178602
Pres: N.S. Solomenko
Focus: Standards 09348

Council for the Study of Productive Forces, Ul Vavilova 7, 117822 Moskva
T: 1356358
Focus: Business Admin 09349

Council of Scientific Medical Societies, Rakhmanovskii per 3, 101431 Moskva
Focus: Med 09350

Council on International Cooperation in Research and Uses of Outer Space (INTERCOSMOS), Leninskii Pr 14, 117901 Moskva
T: (095) 2343828
Founded: 1970
Focus: Aero 09351

D.I. Mendeleev Chemical Society, Krivokolenniy per 12, 101907 Moskva
T: 9257285
Focus: Chem 09352

Economics Society, B. Cheremushkinskaya ul 34, 117259 Moskva
T: 1201321
Focus: Econ 09353

Entomological Society, Universitetskaya Nab. 1, 199034 St. Petersburg
T: 2181212
Focus: Zoology 09354

Federation of Anaesthesiologists and Reanimatologists, Botkin Hospital kv 3, 125101 Moskva
T: 9459725; Fax: 9459725
Founded: 1991
Focus: Anesthetics 09355

Ferrous Metallurgy Society, Baumanskaya ul 9, 107865 Moskva
T: 2670988
Focus: Metallurgy 09356

Flour, Fodder and Grain Storage Society, Chistoprudnyi bul 12a, 101859 Moskva
T: 9286733
Focus: Agri 09357

Geological Society, 2-Roshinskaya ul 10, 113191 Moskva
T: 2373333
Focus: Geology 09358

Geomorphological Commission, Staromonetnii 29, 109017 Moskva
T: 2380360
Focus: Geology 09359

Group of the Far Eastern Division, Ul Vavilova 44, 117333 Moskva
T: 1359019
Focus: Sci 09360

Hydrobiological Society, Ul Gorkogo 27, 103050 Moskva
Focus: Bio 09361

I.I. Polzunov Science Production Association for Research and Design of Power Equipment, Politekhnicheskaya ul 24, 194021 St. Petersburg
T: 2779213
Focus: Mach Eng 09362

Institute for Standardization, Pr Kalinina 56, 121205 Moskva
T: 2908789
Founded: 1962
Focus: Standards
Periodical
Aspects of Standardization (quarterly) . . 09363

International Confederation of Theatre, Tverskaya ul 12, 103009 Moskva
T: 2092436 app 228; Fax: 2095249
Founded: 1992
Focus: Perf Arts 09364

International Society for Pathophysiology, Ul Baltiiskaya 8, 124315 Moskva
T: 1528655; Fax: 1518540
Members: 1200
Focus: Physiology 09365

I.P. Pavlov Physiological Society, Pogodinskaya ul 6, 119121 Moskva
Focus: Physiology 09366

Mapping and Prospecting Engineering Society, Ul Krzhizhanovskogo 14, 117801 Moskva
T: 1243560
Focus: Eng 09367

Mational Scientific Medical Society of Forensic Medical Officers, Ul Sadovaya-Kudrinskaya 32, 123242 Moskva
Focus: Forensic Med 09368

Mechanical Engineering Society, Ul Chkalova 64, 109004 Moskva
T: 9258332
Focus: Eng 09369

Medical Engineering Society, Ul Kasatkina 3, 129301 Moskva
T: 2839784
Focus: Eng 09370

Microbiological Society, Pr 60-letiya Oktyabrya 7, 117811 Moskva
Focus: Microbio 09371

Mining Engineering Society, Karetnyi ryad 10, 103006 Moskva
T: 2998815
Focus: Mining 09372

Moscow Science-Production Association, Ul Ulsacheva 35, 119048 Moskva
T: 2455656
Focus: Sci 09373

Moscow Society of Naturalists, Ul Gertsena 6, 103009 Moskva
T: 2036704
Founded: 1805; Members: 2700
Focus: Nat Sci
Periodical
Byulleten Moskovskogo Obshchestva Ispytatelei Prirody (bi-monthly) 09374

Municipal Economy Soiety, Trekhprudny per 11-13, 103001 Moskva
T: 2998300
Focus: Econ 09375

Museum Council, Ul Dm. Ulyanova 19, 117036 Moskva
T: 1251121
Focus: Arts 09376

National Committee for the Collection and Assessment of Numerical Data in Science and Technology, Leninskii Pr 14, 117901 Moskva
T: 2324205
Focus: Computer & Info Sci 09377

National Committee for Thermal Analysis, Leninskii Pr 312, 117907 Moskva
T: 2323420
Focus: Physics 09378

National Committee of Biochemists, Leninskii Pr 33, 117071 Moskva
Focus: Biochem 09379

National Committee of Biologists, Leninskii Pr 33, 117071 Moskva
Focus: Bio 09380

National Committee of Chemists, Ul A.N. Kosygina 2b, Moskva
Focus: Chem 09381

National Committee of Finno-Ugric Philologists, Ul Semashko 1, 103009 Moskva
Focus: Ling; Lit 09382

National Committee of Geologists, Pyzhevsky per 7, 109017 Moskva
T: 2308151
Focus: Geology 09383

National Committee of History and Philosophy of Natural Science and Technology, Volkhonka 14, 119842 Moskva
T: 2039320
Focus: Hist; Philos; Nat Sci; Eng . . . 09384

National Committee of Mathematicians, Ul Vavilova 42, 117966 Moskva
Focus: Math 09385

National Committee of Russian Historians, Ul Dm. Ulyanova 19, 117036 Moskva
T: 1260529
Focus: Hist 09386

National Committee of Slavonic Philologists, Volkhonka 18, 121019 Moskva
Focus: Ling; Lit 09387

National Committee of the International Council of Scientific Unions, Leninskii Pr 14, 117901 Moskva
Focus: Sci 09388

National Committee of the International Scientific Radio Union, Pr Marksa 18, 103907 Moskva
Focus: Mass Media 09389

National Committee of the Pacific Ocean Research Association, Ulyanovskaya ul 51, 109004 Moskva
T: 2724786
Focus: Oceanography 09390

National Committee of the Scientific Committee for Problems of the Environment, Ul Vavilova 40, 117697 Moskva
T: 1352489
Focus: Ecology 09391

National Committee of Turkish Philologists, Ul Semashko 1, 103009 Moskva
Focus: Ling; Lit 09392

National Committee on Automatic Control, Profsoyuznaya 65, Moskva
Focus: Mach Eng 09393

National Committee on the International Biological Programme, Leninskii Pr 14, 117901 Moskva
Focus: Bio 09394

National Committee on Theoretical and Applied Mechanics, Pr Vernadskogo 101, 177526 Moskva
Focus: Mach Eng 09395

National Immunological Society, Kashirskoe shosse 24, 115478 Moskva
T: 1118333; Fax: 1171027
Founded: 1983; Members: 600
Focus: Immunology 09396

National Medical and Technical Scientific Society, Ul Kasatkina 3, 129301 Moskva
T: 1879723; Fax: 1873734
Founded: 1968
Focus: Med; Eng
Periodical
Biomedical Engineering (bi-monthly) . . . 09397

National Ophthalmological Society, Ul Sadovo-Chernogryazskaya 14, 103064 Moskva
Focus: Ophthal 09398

National Pharmaceutical Society, Ul Krasikova 34, 117418 Moskva
Focus: Pharmacol 09399

National Scientific Medical Society of Anatomists, Histologists and Embryologists, Ul Ostrovityanova 1, 117869 Moskva
Focus: Anat; Physiology 09400

National Scientific Medical Society of Endocrinologists, Ul Dm. Ulyanova 11, 117036 Moskva
Focus: Endocrinology 09401

National Scientific Medical Society of Gastroenterologists, Ul Pogodinskaya 5, 119435 Moskva
Focus: Gastroenter 09402

National Scientific Medical Society of Haematologists and Transfusiologists, Novozykovskii Pr 4a, 125167 Moskva
Focus: Hematology 09403

National Scientific Medical Society of History of Medicine, Petroverigskii per 6-8, 101838 Moskva
Focus: Hist; Med 09404

National Scientific Medical Society of Hygienists, Mechnikova per 5, 103064 Moskva
Focus: Hygiene 09405

National Scientific Medical Society of Infectionists, Botkinskii per 3, 125284 Moskva
Focus: Med 09406

National Scientific Medical Society of Medical Geneticists, Ul Moskvoreche 1, 115478 Moskva
T: 1118594; Fax: 3240702
Founded: 1978; Members: 1500
Focus: Genetics 09407

National Scientific Medical Society of Nephrologists, Ul Rossolimo 11a, 119021 Moskva
T: 2485333
Founded: 1969
Focus: Med 09408

National Scientific Medical Society of Neuropathologists and Psychiatrists, Ul Kropotkinskii per 23, 119034 Moskva
Focus: Pathology; Psychiatry 09409

National Scientific Medical Society of Neurosurgeons, Ul Fadeeva 5, 125047 Moskva
Focus: Surgery 09410

National Scientific Medical Society of Obstetricians and Gynaecologists, Ul Shabolovka 57, 113163 Moskva
Focus: Gynecology 09411

National Scientific Medical Society of Oncologists, Ul St. Petersburgskaya 68, 188646 St. Petersburg
Focus: Cell Biol & Cancer Res 09412

National Scientific Medical Society of Oto-Rhino-Laryngologists, Bolshaya Pirogovskaya 6, 119435 Moskva
Focus: Otorhinolaryngology 09413

National Scientific Medical Society of Paediatriciams, Lomonosovskii Pr 2, 117963 Moskva
Focus: Pediatrics 09414

National Scientific Medical Society of Phtisiologists, Ul 6 kilometr Severnoi Zheleznoi Dorogi, 107564 Moskva
Focus: Med 09415

National Scientific Medical Society of Physical Therapists and Health-Resort Physicians, Kalinina Pr 50, 121099 Moskva
Focus: Physical Therapy; Med 09416

National Scientific Medical Society of Physicians-Analysts, Ul Sadovaya-Kudrinskaya 3, 123242 Moskva
Focus: Med 09417

National Scientific Medical Society of Physicians in Curative Physical Culture and Sports Medicine, Lomonovskii Pr 2, 117963 Moskva
Focus: Med 09418

National Scientific Medical Society of Rheumatologists, Kashirskoye shosse 34a, 115522 Moskva
T: 1144490
Founded: 1928; Members: 1418
Focus: Rheuma
Periodical
Revmatologhia (quarterly) 09419

National Scientific Medical Society of Roentgenologists and Radiologists, Ul Profsoyuznaya 86, 117837 Moskva
Focus: X-Ray Tech; Radiology 09420

National Scientific Medical Society of Stomatologists, Ul Pogodinskaya 5, 119435 Moskva
Focus: Stomatology 09421

National Scientific Medical Society of Surgeons, Abrikosovskii per 2, 119874 Moskva
Focus: Surgery 09422

National Scientific Medical Society of Therapists, Cherepkovskaya 15, 121500 Moskva
Focus: Therapeutics 09423

National Scientific Medical Society of Toxicologists, Ul Bekhtereva 1, 193019 St. Petersburg
Focus: Toxicology 09424

National Scientific Medical Society of Traumatic Surgeons and Orthopaedists, Ul Priorova 10, 125299 Moskva
Focus: Surgery; Orthopedics 09425

National Scientific Medical Society of Venereologists and Dermatologists, Ul Korolenko 3, 107076 Moskva
Focus: Venereology; Derm 09426

National Scientific Society of Urological Surgeons, 3-ya Parkovaya 51, 105483 Moskva
T: 1649652
Founded: 1925; Members: 5500
Focus: Urology; Surgery
Periodical
Urology and Nephrology (bi-monthly) . . 09427

Paper and Wood-Working Society, Ul 25 Oktyabrya 8, 103012 Moskva
T: 9244728
Focus: Forestry 09428

Permanent Commission of Gosplan, Ul Vavilova 44, 117333 Moskva
T: 1969331
Focus: Energy 09429

Petroleum and Gas Society, Leninskii Pr 63, 117876 Moskva
T: 1358866
Focus: Energy 09430

Philosophy Society, Smolensky bul 20, 121002 Moskva
T: 2012402
Focus: Philos 09431

Power and Electrical Power Engineering Society, Stremyannaya ul 10, 191025 St. Petersburg
T: 3113277
Focus: Electric Eng; Energy 09432

Press and Publishing Engineering Society, Volkov per 7-9, 123376 Moskva
T: 2521431
Focus: Eng 09433

Programme Committee Surface Physics, Chemistry and Mechanics, Chenogolovka, 142342 Moskva
T: 2374532
Focus: Chem; Physics; Eng 09434

Pushkin Commission, Nab. Makarova 4, 199034 St. Petersburg
T: 2181601
Focus: Lit 09435

Radio Engineering, Electronics and Telecommunications Society, Kuznetskii Most 20, 103897 Moskva
T: 9217108
Focus: Electric Eng; Electronic Eng . . 09436

Rersearch Council for Applied Mathematics, Ul Vavilova 44, 117333 Moskva
Focus: Math 09437

Russian Academy of Agricultural Sciences, Bolshoi Kkaritonevsky per 21, 107814 Moskva
T: (095) 2073942
Founded: 1992
Pres: V.P. Shishkov
Focus: Agri
Periodicals
Doklady: Proceedings
Mekhanizatsiya i Elektrificatsiya Selskogo Khozyaistva: Mechanization and Electrification of Agriculture
Selektsiya i Semenovodstvo: Selection and Seed Science
Selskokhozyaisstvennaya Biologiya: Agricultural Biology
Vestnik Selskokhozyaistvennoi Nauki: Agricultural Science Journal 09438

Russian Academy of Arts, UlPrechistenka 21, 119034 Moskva
T: (095) 2902088
Founded: 1757; Members: 131
Pres: N.A. Ponomarev; Gen Secr: M.M. Kurilko-Ryumin
Focus: Arts 09439

Russian Academy of Medical Sciences, Ul Solyanka 14, 109801 Moskva
T: (095) 9170504; Fax: 9237052
Founded: 1944; Members: 480
Pres: V.I. Pokrovskii; Gen Secr: D.S. Sarkisov
Focus: Med
Periodicals
Arkhiv Anatomii, Gistologii i Embriologii: Anatomy, Histology and Embryology Archive
Arkhiv Patologii i Meditsiny: Pathology and Medicine Archive
Byulleten Eksperimentalnoi Biologii i Meditsiny: Bulletin of Experimental Biology and Medicine
Byulleten Sibirskogo Otdeleniya Rossiiskoi AMN: Bulletin of the Siberian Division of the Russian Academy of Medical Sciences
Immunologiya: Immunology
Meditsinskaya Radiologiya: Medical Radiology
Patologicheskaya Fiziologiya i Eksperimentalnaya Terapiya: Pathological Physiology and Experimental Therapy
Pharmakologiya i Toksikologiya: Pharmacology and Toxicology
Vestnik Rossiiskoi Akademii Meditsinskikh Nauk: Journal of the Russian Academy of Medical Sciences
Voprosy Meditsinskoi Khimii: Problems of Medical Chemistry
Voprosy Virusologii Khimii: Problems of Virology 09440

Russian Academy of Pedagogical Sciences, Pogodinskaya ul 8, 119905 Moskva
T: 2451641
Founded: 1943
Focus: Educ
Periodicals
Defektologiya: Defectology (bi-monthly)
Kavnt: Quantum (monthly)
Pedagogika: Pedagogics (monthly)
Russkii Yazyk i Natsionalnoi Shkole: Russian in the National School
Semya i Shkola: Family and School (monthly)
Voprosy Psikhologii: Problems of Psychology (monthly) 09441

Russian Academy of Sciences, Leninsky pr 14, 117901 Moskva
T: (095) 9542153; Fax: 9382144
Founded: 1725
Pres: Y.S. Osipov; Gen Secr: I.M. Makarov
Focus: Sci
Periodicals
Agrokhimiya: Agrochemistry (monthly)
Akusticheskii Zhurnal: Acoustics Journal (bi-monthly)
Algebra i Analiz: Algebra and Analysis (bi-monthly)
Astronomicheskii Vestnik: Astronomical Herald (quarterly)
Astronomicheskii Zhurnal: Astronomy Journal (bi-monthly)
Atomnaya Energiya: Atomic Energy (bi-monthly)
Avtomekhanika i Telemekhanika: Automation and Telemechanics (monthly)
Avtometriya: Autometry (bi-monthly)
Aziya i Afrika Segodnya: Asia and Africa Today (monthly)
Biofizika: Biophysics (bi-monthly)
Biokhimiya: Biochemistry (monthly)
Biologicheski Membrany: Biological Membranes (monthly)
Biologiya Morya: Biology of the Sea (bi-monthly)
Bioorganicheskaya Khimiya: Bioorganic Chemistry (monthly)
Botanicheskii Zhurnal: Journal of Botany (monthly)
Chelovek: Man
Defektokopiya: Defectoscopy (monthly)
Diskretnaya Matematika: Discrete Mathematics
Doklady Akademii Nauk Rossiiskoi: Proceedings of the Russian Academy of Sciences (3 times monthly)
Ekologiya: Ecology (bi-monthly)
Ekonomika i Matematicheskie Metody: Economics and Mathematical Methods (bi-monthly)
Ekonomika i Organizatsiya Promyshlennogo Proizvodstva: Economics amd the Organisation of Industrial Production (monthly)
Elektrichestvo: Electricity (monthly)
Elektrokhimiya: Electrochemistry (monthly)
Elektronnoe Modelirovanie: Electronic Modelling (bi-monthly)
Energiya: Energy (monthly)
Entomologicheskoe Obozrenie: Entomological Survey (quarterly)
Fizika Goreniya i Vzryva: Physics of Combustion and Explosion (bi-monthly)
Fizika i Khimiya Obrabotki Materialov: Physics and Chemistry of Materials Processing (bi-monthly)
Fizika i Khimiya Stekla: Physics and Chemistry of Glass (bi-monthly)
Fizika i Tekhnika Poluprovodnikov: Semiconductor Physics and Technology
Fizika Metallov i Metallovedenie: Physics of Metals and Metal Science (monthly)
Fizika Plazmy: Plasma Physics (monthly)
Fizika Tverdogo Tela: Solid State Physics (monthly)
Fiziko-Tekhnicheskie Problemy Razrabotki Poleznykh Iskopaemykh: Physical and Technical Problems of Mineral Exploitation (bi-monthly)
Fiziologicheskii Zhurnal: Physiological Journal (monthly)
Fiziologiya Cheloveka: Human Physiology (bi-monthly)
Fiziologiya Rastenii: Plant Physiology (bi-monthly)
Funktsionalnyi Analiz i Ego Prilozhenie: Functional Analysis and its Application (quarterly)
Genetika: Genetics (monthly)
Geografiya i Prirodnya Resursy: Geography and Natural Resources (quarterly)
Geokhimiya: Geochemistry (monthly)
Geologiya i Geofizika: Geology and Geophysics (monthly)
Geologiya Rudnykh Mestorozhdenii: Geology of Ore Deposits (bi-monthly)
Geomagnetizm i Aeronomiya: Geomagnetism and Aeronomy (bi-monthly)
Geomorfologiya: Geomorphology (quarterly)
Geotekhtonika: Geotectonics (bi-monthly)
Inzhnernaya Geologiya: Engineering Geology (bi-monthly)
Issledovanie Zemli iz Kosmosa: Investigation of the Earth from Space (bi-monthly)
Izvestiya Rossiiskoi Akademii Nauk: Bulletin of the Russian Academy of Sciences
Izvestiya Sibirskogo Otdeleniya Rossiiskoi Akademii Nauk: Bulletin of the Siberian Branch of the Russian Academy of Sciences
Khimicheskaya Fizika: Chemical Physics (monthly)
Khimiya i Tekhnologiya Topliv i Masel: Chemistry and Technology of Fuels and Oils (monthly)
Khimiya i Tekhnologiya Vody: Water Chemistry and Technology (bi-monthly)
Khimiya i Zhizn: Chemistry and Life (monthly)
Khimiya Prirodnykh Soedinenii: Chemistry of Natural Compounds (bi-monthly)
Khimiya Tverdogo Topliva: Solid Fuel Chemistry (bi-monthly)
Khimiya Vysokikh Energii: High Energy Chemistry (bi-monthly)
Kinetika i Kataliz: Kinetics and Catalysis (bi-monthly)
Kolloidny Zhurnal: Colloids Journal (bi-monthly)
Kompleksnoe Ispolzovanie Mineralnogo Syrya: Comprehensive Utilisation of Mineral Raw Materials (monthly)
Koordinatsionnaya Khimiya: Coordination Chemistry (monthly)
Kosmicheskie Issledovaniya: Space Research (bi-monthly)
Kristallografiya: Crystallography (bi-monthly)
Kvant: Quantum (monthly)
Kvantovaya Elektronika: Quantum Electronics (monthly)
Latinskaya Amerika: Latin America (monthly)
Lesovedenie: Forestry Studies (bi-monthly)
Litologiya i Poleznye Iskopaemye: Lithology and Minerals
Magnitnyi Rezonans i ego Primenenie: Magnetic Resonance and its Application
Matematicheskii Sbornik: Mathematical Collection (monthly)
Matematicheskii Zametki: Mathematical Notes (monthly)
Mikrobiologiya: Microbiology (bi-monthly)
Mikroelektronika: Microelectronics (bi-monthly)
Mineralogicheskii Zhurnal: Mineralogical Journal (bi-monthly)
Mirovaya Ekonomika i Mezhdunarodnye Otnosheniya: World Economics and International Relations (monthly)
Molekulyarnaya Biologiya: Molecular Biology (bi-monthly)
Nauchnoe Proborostroenie: Scientific Instrumentation (quarterly)
Nauka v Rossii: Science in Russia (bi-monthly)
Neftekhimiya: Petrochemistry
Neirofiziologiya: Neurophysiology (bi-monthly)
Neirokhimiya: Neurochemistry (quarterly)
Novaya i Noveishaya Istoriya: Modern and Contemporary History (bi-monthly)
Obshchestvennye Nauki: Social Sciences (bi-monthly)
Okeanologiya: Oceanology (bi-monthly)
Ontogenez: Ontogenesis (bi-monthly)
Optika Atmosfery: Optics of Atmosphere (monthly)
Optika i Spektroskopiya: Optics and Spectroscopy (monthly)
Otechestvennaya Istoriya: The Nation's History (bi-monthly)
Otechestvennye Arkhivy: National Archives (bi-monthly)
Paleontologicheskii Zhurnal: Palaeontological Journal (quarterly)
Parazitologiya: Parasitology (bi-monthly)
Pochvovedenie: Soil Science (monthly)
Poverkhnost: Fizika, Khimiya, Mekhanika: Surface: Physics, Chemistry, Mechanics (monthly)
Pribory i Tekhnika Eksperimenta: Instruments and Equipment for Experiments (bi-monthly)
Prikladnaya Biokhimiya i Mikrobiologiya: Applied Biochemistry and Microbiology (bi-monthly)
Prikladnaya Matematika i Mekhanika: Applied Mathematics and Mechanics (bi-monthly)
Priroda: Nature (monthly)
Problemy Dalnego Vostoka: Problems of the Far East (bi-monthly)
Problemy Mashinostroeniya i Nadezhnosti Mashin: Problems of Engineering and Machine Reliability (bi-monthly)
Problemy Peredachi Informatsii: Problems of Information Transmission (quarterly)
Programmirovanie: Programming (bi-monthly)
Psikhologicheskii Zhurnal: Psychological Journal (bi-monthly)
Radiobiologiya: Radiobiology (bi-monthly)
Radiokhimiya: Radiochemistry (bi-monthly)
Rastitelnye Resursy: Plant Resources (quarterly)
Rossiiskaya Arkheologiya: Russian Archaeology (quarterly)
Rossiiskii Musei: Russian Museums (bi-monthly)
Russkaya Literatura: Russian Literature (quarterly)
Russkaya Rech: Russian Speech (bi-monthly)
Sibirskii Matematicheskii Zhurnal: Siberian Mathematical Journal (bi-monthly)
Slavyanovedenie: Slavonic Studies (bi-monthly)
Sotsiologicheskie Issledovaniya: Sociological Research (bi-monthly)
Sverkhverdye Materialy: Superhard Materials (bi-monthly)
Teoreticheskaya i Matematicheskaya Fizika: Theoretical and Mathematical Physics (monthly)
Teoreticheskie Osnovy Khimicheskoi Tekhnologii: Theoretical Foundations of Chemical Technology (bi-monthly)
Teoriya Veroyatnostei i ee Primenenie: Probability Theory and its Application (quarterly)
Teploenergetika: Heat and Power Engineering (monthly)
Teplofizika Vysokikhk Temperatur: High Temperature Thermal Physics (bi-monthly)
Tikhookeanskaya Geologiya: Pacific Ocean Geology (bi-monthly)
Trenie i Iznos: Friction and Wear (bi-monthly)
Tsitologiya: Cytology (monthly)
Uspekhi Fizicheskikh Nauk: Progress of Physics (monthly)
Uspekhi Fiziologicheskikh Nauk: Progress of Physiology (quarterly)
Uspekhi Khimii: Progress in Chemistry (monthly)
Uspekhi Matematicheskikh Nauk: Progress in Mathematics (quarterly)
Uspekhi Sovremennoi Biologii: Progress in Modern Biology (bi-monthly)
Vestnik Dalnevostochnogo Otdeleniya Rossiiskoi Akademii Nauk: Journal of the Far Eastern Division of the Russian Academy of Sciences
Vestnik Drevnei Istorii: Journal of Ancient History (quarterly)
Vestnik Rossiiskoi Akademii Nauk: Journal of the Russian Academy of Sciences (monthly)
Vodnye Resursy: Water Resources (bi-monthly)
Voprosy Ekonomiki: Economic Questions (monthly)
Voprosy Filosofii: Questions of Philosophy (monthly)
Voprosy Ikhtiologii: Questions of Ichthyology (bi-monthly)
Voprosy Istorii: Questions of History (monthly)
Voprosy Istorii Estestvoznaniya i Tekhniki: History of Natural Sciences and Technology (quarterly)
Voprosy Literatury: Questions of Literature (monthly)
Voprosy Yazykoznaniya: Questions of Linguistics (bi-monthly)
Vostok: East (bi-monthly)
Vulkanologiya i Seismologiya: Vulcanology and Seismology (bi-monthly)
Vysokomolekulyarnye Soedineniya: High Molecular Compounds (monthly)
Yadernaya Fizika: Nuclear Physics (monthly)
Zapiski Mineralogo Obshchestva: Notes of the Mineralogical Society (bi-monthly)
Zaschita Metallov: Protection of Metals (bi-monthly)
Zemlya i Vselennaya: Earth and Universe (bi-monthly)
Zhurnal Analiticheskoi Khimii: Journal of Analytical Chemistry (bi-monthly)
Zhurnal Eksperimentalnoi i Teoreticheskoi Fiziki: Journal of Experimental and Theoretical Physics (monthly)
Zhurnal Evolyutsionnoi Biokhimii i Fiziologii: Journal of Evolutionary Biochemistry and Physiology (bi-monthly)
Zhurnal Fizicheskoi Khimii: Journal of Physical Chemistry (monthly)
Zhurnal Nauchnoi i Prikladnoi Fotografii i Kinematografii: Journal of Scientific and Applied Photography and Cinematography (bi-monthly)
Zhurnal Neorganicheskoi Khimii: Journal of Inorganic Chemistry (monthly)
Zhurnal Obshchei Biologii: Journal of General Biology (bi-monthly)
Zhurnal Obshschei Khimii: Journal of General Chemistry (monthly)
Zhurnal Organicheskoi Khimii: Journal of Organic Chemistry (monthly)
Zhurnal Prikladnoi Khimii: Journal of Applied Chemistry (monthly)
Zhurnal Prikladnoi Mekhaniki i Tekhnicheskoi Fiziki: Journal of Applied Mechanics and Technical Physics (bi-monthly)
Zhurnal Strukturnoi Khimii: Journal of Structural Chemistry (bi-monthly)
Zhurnal Tekhnicheskoi Fiziki: Journal of Technical Physics (monthly)
Zhurnal Vychislityelnoi Matematiki i Matematicheskoy Fiziki: Journal of Computational Mathematics and Mathematical Physics (monthly)
Zhurnal Vysshei Nervnoi Deyatelnosti: Journal of Higher Nervous Activity (bi-monthly)
Zoologicheskii Zhurnal: Zoological Journal (monthly) 09442

Russian Association for Comparative Literature, Ul Vorovskogo 25a, 121069 Moskva
T: 2901709
Focus: Lit 09443

Russian Botanical Society, Ul Prof. Popova 2, 197022 St. Petersburg
T: 2340092
Focus: Botany 09444

Russian Geographical Society, Per Grivtsova 10, 190000 St. Petersburg
T: 3156312
Focus: Geography 09445

Russian Linguistics Society, Ul Semashko 1, 103009 Moskva
Focus: Ling 09446

Russian Mineralogical Society, V.O. Liniya 2, 199026 St. Petersburg
T: 2188640
Focus: Mineralogy 09447

Russian Palaeontological Society, Srednii Pr 74, 199026 St. Petersburg
T: 2189121
Focus: Paleontology 09448

Russian Palestine Society, Volkhonka 14, 119842 Moskva
T: 2039398
Focus: Hist 09449

Russian PEN Centre, Ul Neglinnaya 18, 103031 Moskva
T: 2094589; Fax: 2000293
Founded: 1989; Members: 121
Focus: Lit 09450

Russian Pharmacological Society, Ul Baltiiskaya 8, 125315 Moskva
T: (095) 1511881; Fax: 1511261
Founded: 1958; Members: 615
Pres: D.A. Kharkevich; Gen Secr: S.A. Borisenko
Focus: Pharmacol
Periodical
Farmakologia i Toksikologia: Pharmacology and Toxicology (bi-monthly) 09451

Russian Pugwash Committee, Leninskii Pr 14, 117901 Moskva
T: 1373545
Focus: Eng 09452

Russian Society of Genetics and Breeders, Ul Fersmana 11, 117312 Moskva
Focus: Genetics; Animal Husb 09453

Russian Union of Composers, Ul Nezhdanovoi 8-10, Moskva
T: (095) 2295218; Fax: 2004273
Founded: 1960; Members: 1500
Pres: V. Kazenin
Focus: Music
Periodicals
Musical Life
Musical Review
Muzikalnaya Akademia 09454

Scientific Medical Society of Anatomists-Pathologists, Bolshaya Serpuhovskaya 27, 109801 Moskva
Focus: Anat; Pathology 09455

Scientific-Technical Association, Pr Ogorodnikova 26, 198103 St. Petersburg
T: 2512850
Focus: Eng 09456

Shipbuilding Engineering Society, Nevskii Pr 44, 191011 St. Petersburg
T: 3155027
Focus: Eng 09457

Society for Railway Transport, Ul K. Marksa 11, 107262 Moskva
T: 2626180
Focus: Transport 09458

Society for Trade and Commerce, Gogolevskii bul 9, 121019 Moskva
T: 2032246
Focus: Commerce 09459

Society of Cardiology, Petroverigskii ul 10, 101953 Moskva
T: 9238636
Founded: 1958
Focus: Cardiol
Periodical
Kardiologiya: Cardiology (monthly) . . . 09460

Society of Herminthologists, B. Cheremushkinskaya 28, 117259 Moskva
Focus: Bio 09461

Society of Light Industry, Ul Vavilova 69, 117846 Moskva
T: 1347009
Focus: Mach Eng 09462

Society of Mammalogists, Ul Vavilova 44, 117033 Moskva
T: 2322088
Focus: Zoology 09463

Society of Non-Ferrous Metallurgy, Per Pechatnikova 7, 103045 Moskva
T: 2084838
Focus: Metallurgy 09464

Society of Ornithologists, I.Y. Kotelnichesky per 10, 109240 Moskva
T: 2974496
Focus: Ornithology 09465

Society of Protozoologists, Tikhoretskii per 4, 194064 St. Petersburg
T: 2474496
Focus: Zoology 09466

Society of Psychologists, Yarovslavskaya ul 13, 129366 Moskva
T: 2827212
Focus: Psych 09467

Society of the Food Industry, Kuznetskii most 19, 103031 Moskva
T: 9252611
Focus: Food 09468

Society of the Instrument Building Industry, Pr K. Marksa 17, 121019 Moskva
T: 2033503
Focus: Mach Eng 09469

Society of the Timber and Forestry Industry, Ul Chernyshevskogo 29, 103062 Moskva
T: (095) 9239570
Pres: Y.A. Yagodnikov
Focus: Forestry 09470

Sociological Association, Ul Krzhizhanovskogo 24, 117418 Moskva
T: 1208257
Focus: Sociology 09471

Soil Science Society, Pyzhevskii per 7, 109017 Moskva
T: (095) 2314359
Pres: G.V. Dobrovolsky
Focus: Geology 09472

Theatre Union of the Russian Federation, Ul Gorkogo 16, 103009 Moskva
T: 2299152
Members: 30124
Focus: Perf Arts
Periodicals
Information from the Secretariat (quarterly)
Problems of Contemporary Theatre . . . 09473

Tropical Committee, Leninskii Pr 33, 117071 Moskva
T: 2341209
Focus: Geography 09474

Union of Arts of the Russian Federation, Ul Pokrovka 37, 103062 Moskva
Focus: Arts 09475

Union of Russian Architects, Ul Shchuseva 3, 103889 Moskva
T: (095) 2902579
Founded: 1932; Members: 20000
Gen Secr: Y.P. Platonov
Focus: Archit 09476

Union of Russian Filmmakers, Vasilevskaya 13, 123825 Moskva
T: 2515370
Focus: Cinema 09477

Union of Russian Writers, Ul Vorovskogo 52, Moskva
T: (095) 2916350
Founded: 1935; Members: 9500
Pres: G.M. Markov
Focus: Lit
Periodicals
Inostrannaya Literatura (monthly)
Literaturnaya Gazeta (weekly)
Novyi Mir (monthly) 09478

Union of Scientific and Learned Societies, Kursovoi per 17, 119034 Moskva
T: (095) 2915943
Pres: A.Y. Ishlinskii
Focus: Sci 09479

Water Management Society, Staropansky per 3, 103012 Moskva
T: (095) 9252446
Focus: Water Res 09480

Znanie, Proezd Servova 4, 101813 Moskva
T: (095) 9213381
Founded: 1947; Members: 3300000
Pres: N.G. Basov
Focus: Sci
Periodical
Science and Life (monthly) 09481

Rwanda

African and Mauritian Institute of Statistics and Applied Economics, BP 1109, Kigali
T: (07) 84989
Founded: 1975; Members: 9
Focus: Stats; Econ 09482

Saint Lucia

Caribbean Association for Rehabilitation Therapists (CARDA), c/o CART, POB 1068, Castries
Founded: 1979
Focus: Rehabil; Therapeutics 09483

Caribbean Environmental Health Institute (CEHI), POB 1111, Castries
T: (045) 4521412; Fax: 4532721
Members: 16
Focus: Ecology 09484

San Marino

European Centre for Disaster Medicine, c/o Ospedale di Stato, Via Toscana, 47031 San Marino
T: (0541) 994535, 903706
Founded: 1986
Focus: Med 09485

Saudi Arabia

Arab Bureau of Education for the Gulf States (ABEGS), POB 3908, Riyadh 11481
T: (01) 4774644; Fax: 4783165
Founded: 1975; Members: 6
Gen Secr: Dr. Ali Al-Towagry
Focus: Educ
Periodicals
Arab Gulf Journal of Scientific Research (semi-annually)
Risalat Ul-Khalee Al-Arabi (quarterly) . . 09486

Arab Regional Branch of the International Council on Archives (ARBICA), POB 205, Riyadh 11141
T: (01) 4761600 ext 462
Members: 20
Pres: A. Tamini; Gen Secr: Fahd Al-Askar
Focus: Archives 09487

Arab Security Studies and Training Center (ASSTC), POB 6830, Riyadh 11452
T: (01) 246344; Fax: 2464713
Focus: Criminology 09488

Arab Urban Development Institute (AUDI), POB 6892, Riyadh 11452
T: (01) 4419158, 4419876, 4418100; Fax: 4418235
Founded: 1980; Members: 35
Pres: Abdullah Al-Ali Al-Nuaim; Gen Secr: Ahmed Al-Salloum
Focus: Urban Plan 09489

Center for Research in Islamic Education, POB 1034, Mecca
T: (02) 5586707
Founded: 1980; Members: 15
Pres: A.A. Zafar
Focus: Educ 09490

Commission for Controlling the Desert Locust in the Near East (CCDLNE), POB 327, Jeddah
T: (02) 6445941; Fax: 6799563
Founded: 1965; Members: 13
Focus: Agri 09491

King Abdul Aziz Research Centre, POB 2945, Riyadh 11461
Fax: (01) 4417020
Founded: 1972
Gen Secr: Dr. Fahd Al-Semmari
Focus: Hist; Geography; Lit; Arts
Periodical
Addarah (quarterly) 09492

King Faisal Centre for Research and Islamic Studies, 51049, Riyadh 11543
T: (01) 4652255; Fax: 4659993
Founded: 1983
Pres: Prince Turki Al-Faisal; Gen Secr: Dr. Zaid A. Ak-Husain
Focus: Rel & Theol 09493

Saudi Biological Society, c/o Botany and Microbiology Department, Faculty of Science, King Saud University, POB 2455, Riyadh 11451
T: (01) 4675835; Fax: 4675833
Founded: 1975; Members: 341
Pres: Dr. Ibrahim A. Arif; Gen Secr: Dr. F. Al-Mana
Focus: Bio
Periodicals
Abstract and Programme of Annual Conference
Saudi Journal of Biological Sciences (bi-annually)
. . . . 09494

Society of Esaff Alkhairia, Mecca
Founded: 1946
Focus: Hist 09495

Senegal

African Biosciences Network (ABN), c/o UNESCO-BREDA, BP 3311, Dakar
T: 235083, 234614
Founded: 1981
Focus: Bio
Periodical
ABN Newsletter (quarterly) 09496

African Centre for Monetary Studies (ACMS), 15 Blvd Franklin Roosevelt, Dakar
T: 233821; Fax: 217760
Founded: 1978; Members: 34
Focus: Finance
Periodicals
ACMS Research Report
Financial Journal
Financial News Analysis 09497

African Council for Social and Human Sciences, c/o BREDA, BP 3311, Dakar
Founded: 1990
Focus: Soc Sci 09498

African Institute for Economic Development and Planning, BP 3186, Dakar
T: 231020, 214831; Fax: 212158
Founded: 1962; Members: 51
Focus: Develop Areas; Econ 09499

African Network for Integrated Development (ANID), BP 12085, Dakar
T: 224495; Fax: 221544
Founded: 1985
Focus: Develop Areas
Periodicals
Impact (semi-annually)
Jef-Jel (monthly) 09500

African Regional Centre for Technology (ARCT), BP 2435, Dakar
T: 227712; Fax: 257712
Founded: 1977
Focus: Eng 09501

African Standing Conference on Bibliographic Control (ASCOBIC), Immeuble Administratif, Av Roume, Dakar
T: 21507223
Members: 13
Focus: Libraries & Bk Sci 09502

Agency for the Safety of Aerial Navigation in Africa, BP 8132, Dakar
T: 201080, 231041; Fax: 200600
Founded: 1959
Focus: Aero 09503

Association de Radiologie d'Afrique Francophone, 41bis Rue Carnot, BP 3566, Dakar
Focus: Radiology 09504

Association des Bibliothèques de l'Enseignement Supérieure de l'Afrique de l'Ouest Francophone (ABESAO) / Association of Higher Education Libraries in French-Speaking West Africa, c/o Bibliothèque Universitaire, BP 2006, Dakar
T: 246981; Fax: 242379
Founded: 1986
Focus: Libraries & Bk Sci 09505

Association des Etablissements d'Enseignement Vétérinaire Totalement ou Partiellement de Langue Française (AEEVTPLF), c/o EISVM, BP 5077, Dakar
T: 230545, 256692; Fax: 254283
Founded: 1982
Focus: Vet Med 09506

Association des Facultés ou Etablissements de Lettres et Sciences Humaines des Universités d'Expression Française (AFELSH), c/o Faculté des Lettres et Sciences Humaines, Université Cheikh Anta Diop, Fann, Dakar
T: (0221) 213158
Founded: 1988
Focus: Humanities 09507

Association des Professionnelles Africaines de la Communication (APAC), BP 4234, Dakar
Founded: 1984; Members: 300
Focus: Comm Sci
Periodical
La Satellite (quarterly) 09508

Association of African Women for Research and Development (AAWORD) / Association des Femmes Africaines pour la Recherche sur le Développement, BP 3304, Dakar
T: 252572, 230211; Fax: 241289
Founded: 1977; Members: 400
Focus: Develop Areas
Periodical
Flash: African Trade (bi-monthly) 09509

Association of Maize Researchers in Africa (AMRA), BP 6236, Dakar
Founded: 1985
Focus: Agri 09510

Association Sénégalaise de Bibliothécaires, Archivistes et Documentalistes (ASBAD), BP 3252, Dakar
T: 246981; Fax: 242379
Founded: 1988
Pres: Marietou Diongue Diop; Gen Secr: Emmanuel Kabou
Focus: Libraries & Bk Sci; Archives; Doc 09511

Centre Africain d'Etudes Supérieures en Gestion (CESAG), BP 3802, Dakar
T: 219254; Fax: 213215
Founded: 1983; Members: 7
Focus: Business Admin 09512

Comité Scientifique Inter-Africain Post-Récolte / Inter-African Scientific Committee Post-Harvest, c/o Bureau Africain de l'AUPELF, BP 10017, Liberté, Dakar
T: 212927
Founded: 1980
Focus: Food 09513

Conférence des Facultés et Ecoles de Médecine d'Afrique d'Expression Française, c/o Faculté de Médecine et de Pharmacie, Fann, Dakar
Focus: Educ; Med 09514

Council for the Development of Economic and Social Research in Africa (CODESRIA), BP 3304, Dakar
T: 230211; Fax: 241289
Founded: 1973
Focus: Sociology; Econ
Periodicals
Africa Development (quarterly)
CODESRIA Bulletin (quarterly) 09515

Ecole de Bibliothécaires, Archivistes et Documentalistes (EBAD), c/o University Cheikh Anta Diop de Dakar, BP 3252, Dakar
T: 257660; Fax: 252883
Founded: 1963
Focus: Doc; Libraries & Bk Sci; Archives 09516

Environmental Development in the Third World, 4-5 Rue Kléber, BP 3370, Dakar
T: 224229; Fax: 222695
Founded: 1972
Focus: Ecology 09517

Sierra Leone

Historical Society of Sierra Leone (HSSL), c/o Dept of History, Fourah Bay College, University of Sierra Leone, Freetown
T: 281
Founded: 1975; Members: 30
Pres: G. S. Anthony; Gen Secr: Dr. A.J.G. Wyse
Focus: Hist
Periodical
Journal (semi-annually) 09518

Sierra Leone Association of Archivists, Librarians and Information Scientists, 7 Percival St, POB 326, Freetown
Founded: 1970; Members: 50
Pres: O. Campbell; Gen Secr: Agnes Morovia
Focus: Libraries & Bk Sci
Periodical
Bulletin (semi-annually) 09519

Sierra Leone Medical and Dental Assication, POB 850, Freetown
Founded: 1961
Pres: Dr. S.U.M. Jah; Gen Secr: Dr. Desmond Wright
Focus: Med; Dent 09520

Sierra Leone Science Association, c/o Dept of Physics, Fourah Bay College, University of Sierra Leone, Freetown
T: (022) 231617; Fax: 224439
Founded: 1960
Pres: Dr. Ernest H. Wright
Focus: Sci 09521

Singapore

Academy of Medicine, Singapore, College of Medicine Bldg, 16 College Rd, Singapore 0316
T: 2238968; Tx: 40173; Fax: 2255155
Founded: 1957; Members: 708
Pres: Dr. Ngoh Chuan Tan; Gen Secr: Y.L. Lam
Focus: Med
Periodical
Annals of the Academy (bi-monthly) . . 09522

Asia and Oceania Federation of Obstetrics and Gynecology (AOFOG), c/o Dept of Obstetrics and Gynecology, National University Hospital, Lower Kent Ridge Rd, Singapore 0511
Founded: 1957; Members: 21
Focus: Gynecology
Periodical
Asia-Oceania Journal of Obstetrics and Gynecology (bi-monthly) 09523

Asian-Pacific Association for Laser Medicine and Surgery (APALMS), 3 Mount Elizabeth, 06-03 Mount Elizabeth Medical Centre, Singapore 0922
Focus: Surgery 09524

Asian Pacific Dental Federation (APDF), 841 Mountbatten Rd, Singapore 1543
T: 3453125; Fax: 3442116
Founded: 1955
Focus: Dent
Periodical
APDF Newsletter (semi-annually) 09525

Asian-Pacific Political Science Association (APPSA), c/o Dept of Political Science, University of Singapore, 10 Kent Ridge Crescent, Singapore 0511
T: 7723970; Fax: 7770751
Founded: 1984
Focus: Poli Sci
Periodical
APPSA Newsletter (3 times annually) . . 09526

Asian Pacific Section of the International Confederation for Plastic and Reconstructive Surgery, c/o Dept of Plastic and Reconstructive Surgery, Singapore General Hospital, Outram Rd, Singapore 0316
Founded: 1970
Focus: Surgery
Periodical
Asian Pacific Section of IPRS Newsletter 09527

Asian-Pacific Tax and Investment Research Centre (APTIRC), 2 Nassim Rd, Singapore 1025
T: 2351954; Fax: 7331540
Founded: 1982
Focus: Finance
Periodical
Asian-Pacific Tax and Investment Bulletin (monthly) 09528

Association for Theological Education in South East Asia (ATESEA), 324 Onan Rd, Singapore 1542
T: 3447316; Fax: 3447316
Founded: 1957
Focus: Educ
Periodical
Asia Journal of Theology (semi-annually) 09529

Centre for the Study of Transitional Economies, c/o Dept of Economics and Statistics, National University of Singapore, 10 Kent Ridge Crescent, Singapore 119260
T: 7726108; E-Mail: ecslud@nus.sg; Fax: 7752646
Founded: 1993
Pres: Dr. Lu Ding
Focus: Econ 09530

The China Society, Maxwell Rd, POB 3738, Singapore 9057
Founded: 1948; Members: 148
Focus: Ethnology
Periodical
Journal 09531

Chinese Language and Research Centre, Jurong Campus, Upper Jurong Rd, Singapore 2264
Focus: Ling 09532

Indian Fine Arts Society, St. Michael's Mansion, St. Michael's Rd, POB 2812, Singapore 12
Founded: 1949
Focus: Arts 09533

Institute of Physics - Singapore, c/o Dept of Physics, National University of Singapore, Kent Ridge, Singapore 0511
Fax: 7722605 7776126
Founded: 1973; Members: 153
Pres: Prof. Tang Seung Mun; Gen Secr: Dr. Kuok Meng Hau
Focus: Physics
Periodicals
Bulletin (quarterly)
Physics Update (bi-annually)
Singapore Journal of Physics 09534

Institute of Southeast Asian Studies, Heng Mui Keng Terrace, Pasir Panjang, Singapore 0511
Fax: 7781735
Founded: 1968
Focus: Sociology; Poli Sci; Econ
Periodicals
ASEAN Economic Bulletin (3 times annually)
Contemporary Southeast Asia (quarterly)
SOJOURN: Social Issues in Southeast Asia (semi-annually)
Southeast Asian Affairs (annually) . . . 09535

Library Association of Singapore (LAS), POB 0693, Singapore 911599
Founded: 1955; Members: 338
Pres: Choy Fatt Cheong; Gen Secr: Siti Harifeh
Focus: Libraries & Bk Sci
Periodicals
LAS Newsletter (quarterly)
Singapore Libraries (bi-annually) 09536

Singapore Art Society, 6001 Neach Rd, 18-08 Mile Tower, Singapore 0719
T: 2924244
Founded: 1949
Pres: Ho Kok Hoe; Gen Secr: Quek Kian Guan
Focus: Arts 09537

Singapore Association for the Advancement of Science, c/o Singapore Science Centre, Science Centre Rd off Town Hall Rd, Singapore 2260
T: 5603316; Fax: 5659533
Founded: 1976
Pres: Prof. Ang Kok Peng; Gen Secr: Dr. Leo Tan Wee Hin
Focus: Sci 09538

Singapore Institute of Architects (SIA), 20 Orchard Rd, Singapore
T: 3388977; Fax: 3368708
Founded: 1923; Members: 1000
Pres: Edward da Silva; Gen Secr: Johnny Tan
Focus: Archit
Periodicals
SIA Journal (bi-monthly)
Yearbook (annually) 09539

Singapore Institute of International Affairs (SIIA), 6 Nassim Rd, Singapore 1025
T: 7349600; Fax: 7336217
Founded: 1961; Members: 80
Pres: Dr. Lau Teik Soon; Gen Secr: M. Rajaretnam
Focus: Int'l Relat 09540

Singapore Mathematical Society, c/o Mathematics Dept, National University of Singapore, Kent Ridge, Singapore 119260
Founded: 1952; Members: 576
Pres: Prof. Koh Khee Meng; Gen Secr: Dr. Ling San
Focus: Math
Periodical
Mathematical Medley (semi-annually) . . 09541

Singapore Medical Association (SMA), Alumni Medical Centre, 2 College Rd, Singapore 169850
T: 2231264; E-Mail: sma@sma.org.sg; Fax: 2247827
Founded: 1959; Members: 2900
Pres: Dr. Pak Yean Cheong; Gen Secr: Dr. Chiang Yin Wong
Focus: Med
Periodical
Singapore Medical Journal (monthly) . . 09542

Singapore National Academy of Science (SNAS), c/o Singapore Science Centre Bldg, Science Centre Rd off Town Hall Rd, Singapore 2260
T: 5603316; Fax: 5659533
Founded: 1971; Members: 1000
Pres: Prof. Leo Tau Wee Hin; Gen Secr: Dr. Chia Woon Kim
Focus: Sci
Periodical
Journal of the Singapore National Academy of Science (annually) 09543

Singapore Society of Asian Studies, Kent Ridge, Singapore 9111, POB 1976
Founded: 1982
Pres: Lim Guan Hock; Gen Secr: Dr. YeoMang Thong
Focus: Ling; Lit; Cultur Hist
Periodical
Asian Culture (annually) 09544

Slovakia

Asociácia pre Výskum Slovenskej a Svetovej Ekonomiky, Šancová 56, 811 05 Bratislava
T: (07) 395480; Fax: 395106
Founded: 1997; Members: 400
Pres: Dr. Eduard Mikelka; Gen Secr: Tatiana Žáryová
Focus: Econ 09545

Jednota Slovenských Matematikov a Fyzikov / Association of Slovak Mathematicians and Physicists, Gorkého 5, 811 01 Bratislava
T: (07) 59094
Founded: 1862
Focus: Math; Physics 09546

Kružok Moderných Filológov / Union for Modern Philology, Gondova 2, 818 01 Bratislava
T: (07) 56471
Founded: 1956; Members: 205
Focus: Ling; Lit 09547

Organizačné Stredisko Vedeckých Spoločností pri SAV / Organization Centre of the Scientific Societies of the SAS, Gorkého 13, 811 01 Bratislava
T: (07) 330084
Founded: 1973
Focus: Sci 09548

Slovenská Akadémia Vied (SAV) / Slovak Academy of Sciences, Štefánikova 49, 814 38 Bratislava
T: (07) 492751; Fax: 494391
Founded: 1953; Members: 60
Pres: Štefan Luby; Gen Secr: Štefan Markus
Focus: Sci
Periodicals
Acta Physica Slovaca
Acta Virologica
Slavica Slovaca
Sociológia 09549

Slovenská Antropologická Spoločnost / Slovak Anthropological Society, Mlynská dolina B2, 842 15 Bratislava
T: (07) 796742; E-Mail: antropologia@fns.uniba.sk
Founded: 1965; Members: 109
Pres: Dr. M. Pospíšil; Gen Secr: Dr. E. Neščáková
Focus: Anthro 09550

Slovenská Archeologická Spoločnost / Slovak Archaeological Society, Akademiická 2, 949 21 Nitra
T: (087) 35739; Fax: 35618
Founded: 1956; Members: 330
Pres: Dr. D. Čaplovič; Gen Secr: Dr. K. Kuzmová
Focus: Archeol 09551

Slovenská Astronomická Spoločnost / Slovak Astronomical Society, 055 60 Tatranská Lomnica
T: (0969) 467866; Fax: 467656
Founded: 1959; Members: 353
Pres: Dr. V. Rušin; Gen Secr: Dr. R. Komžík
Focus: Astronomy 09552

Slovenská Biochemiká Spoločnost / Slovak Biochemical Society, Kalinčiakova 8, 832 32 Bratislava
T: (07) 65356
Founded: 1959; Members: 450
Focus: Biochem 09553

Slovenská Bioklimatologická Spoločnost / Slovak Bioclimatology Society, Mickiewiczova 13, 812 54 Bratislava
T: (07) 54430
Founded: 1966; Members: 180
Focus: Biophys 09554

Slovenská Biologická Spoločnost / Slovak Biological Soiety, Sasinkova 4, 811 08 Bratislava
T: (07) 685415
Founded: 1967; Members: 180
Focus: Bio 09555

Slovenská Botanická Spoločnost / Slovak Botanical Society, Dúbravská 14, 842 23 Bratislava
T: (07) 3782680; E-Mail: botuhsip@savba.savba.sk
Founded: 1955; Members: 410
Pres: Dr. O. Erdelská; Gen Secr: H. Šipossová
Focus: Botany 09556

Slovenská Chemická Spoločnost / Slovak Chemical Society, Radlinského 9, 812 37 Bratislava
T: (07) 395205
Founded: 1940; Members: 1100
Pres: D. Berek; Gen Secr: Dr. Dalma Gyepesová
Focus: Chem
Periodical
Chemical Papers: Chemické zvesti (bi-monthly) 09557

Slovenská Demografická a Štatistická Spoločnost / Slovak Demographic and Statistical Society, Obrancov mieru 4, 812 86 Bratislava
T: (07) 671692
Founded: 1968; Members: 152
Focus: Stats 09558

Slovenská Entonologická Spoločnost / Slovak Entomology Society, c/o Katedra Zoológie pri FUK, Mylanská dolina B-1, 842 15 Bratislava
T: (07) 796249
Founded: 1957; Members: 230
Pres: Dr. L. Jedlička; Gen Secr: Dr. Z. Bianchi
Focus: Zoology 09559

Slovenská Geografická Spoločnost / Slovak Geographical Society, Stefánikova 49, 814 73 Bratislava
T: (07) 492751
Founded: 1945; Members: 480
Focus: Geography 09560

Slovenská Geologická Spoločnost / Slovak Geological Society, Mlynská dolina 1, 817 04 Bratislava
T: (07) 3705111; Fax: 371940
Founded: 1965; Members: 640
Pres: Dr. P. Reichwalder; Gen Secr: Dr. M. Elečko
Focus: Geology 09561

Slovenská Historická Spoločnost / Slovak Historical Society, Klemensova 19, 813 64 Bratislava
T: (07) 56321
Founded: 1946; Members: 785
Pres: Dr. L. Lipták; Gen Secr: Dr. J. Lukačka
Focus: Hist 09562

Slovenská Jazykovedná Spoločnost / Slovak Linguistics Society, Panská 26, 813 64 Bratislava
T: (07) 331763; E-Mail: slavoo@savba.sk; Fax: 5331756
Founded: 1957; Members: 260
Pres: Prof. Dr. S. Ondrejovič; Gen Secr: Dr. M. Nábělková
Focus: Ling 09563

Slovenská Jednota Klassických Filológov / Slovak Association of Classical Philologists, Gondova 2, 818 01 Bratislava
T: (07) 58041
Founded: 1969
Focus: Ling; Lit 09564

Slovenská Lekárska Společnost (SLS) / Slovak Medical Society, Legionárska 4, 813 22 Bratislava
T: (07) 5424015, 5422424; Fax: 5422363
Founded: 1969; Members: 33061
Pres: Prof. Rastislav Dzurik; Gen Secr: Prof. Peter Kristufek
Focus: Med 09565

Slovenská Literárnovedná Spoločnost / Slovak Literary Society, Konventná 13, 813 64 Bratislava
T: (07) 5313391, 5312701; E-Mail: postmaster@usvl.savba.sk; Fax: 5316025
Founded: 1958; Members: 320
Pres: Dr. J. Koška; Gen Secr: Dr. Gazdík M. Kusá
Focus: Lit 09566

Slovenská Meteorologická Spoločnost / Slovak Meteorological Society, Jeséniova 17, 833 15 Bratislava
T: (07) 42030
Founded: 1960; Members: 170
Focus: Astrophys 09567

Slovenská Národopisná Spoločnost / Slovak Ethnography Society, Jakubovo nám 12, 813 64 Bratislava
T: (07) 334956
Founded: 1958; Members: 400
Focus: Ethnology 09568

Slovenská Orientalistická Spoločnost / Slovak Society for Oriental Studies, Klemensova 19, 813 64 Bratislava
T: (07) 56321
Founded: 1960; Members: 42
Focus: Ethnology 09569

Slovenská Parazitologická Spoločnost / Slovak Society for Parasitology, Hlinkova 3, 040 01 Košice
T: (095) 6334455; E-Mail: pausav@linux1.saske.sk; Fax: 6331414
Founded: 1992; Members: 85
Pres: Prof. P. Dubinský; Gen Secr: Prof. V. 011-814-6 Letková
Focus: Med
Periodical
Správy Slovenskej Parazitologickej Spoločnosti (irregularly) 09570

Slovenská Pedagogická Spoločnost / Slovak Education Society, c/o Filozofická Fakulta UPJS, 080 01 Prešov
T: (0791) 32869
Founded: 1965; Members: 365
Focus: Educ 09571

Slovenská Pneumologická a Ftizeologická Společnost / Slovak Society of Pneumology and Phtisiology, Krajinska 93-103, 825 56 Bratislava
T: (07) 2401398; Fax: 243622
Founded: 1968; Members: 504
Focus: Pulmon Dis 09572

Slovenská Psychologická Spoločnost / Slovak Psychological Society, Gondova 2, 818 01 Bratislava
T: (07) 56471
Founded: 1959; Members: 1400
Focus: Psych 09573

Slovenská Spoločnost Medzinárodné Právo / Slovak Society for International Law, Klemensova 19, 813 64 Bratislava
T: (07) 56321
Founded: 1969; Members: 63
Focus: Law 09574

Slovenská Spoločnost pre Dejiny Vied a Techniky pri SAV / Slovak Society for History of Science and Technology, Klemensova 19, 813 64 Bratislava
T: (07) 57645
Founded: 1965; Members: 300
Focus: Cultur Hist 09575

Slovenská Spoločnost pre Kybernetiku a Informatiku / Slovak Society for Cybernetics and Informatics, Dúbravská cesta 9, 842 37 Bratislava
T: (07) 373271; Fax: 376045
Founded: 1966; Members: 270
Focus: Cybernetics; Computer & Info Sci 09576

Slovenská Spoločnost pre Mechaniku / Slovak Society for Mechanics, Dúbravská cesta 9, 842 20 Bratislava
T: (07) 3782530; Fax: 372494
Founded: 1967; Members: 225
Pres: Prof. Dr. J. Brilla; Gen Secr: Dr. V. Sládek
Focus: Physics; Eng 09577

Slovenská Spoločnost pre Vedy Polnohospodarske, Lesnické a Potravinárské / Slovak Society for Agriculture, Forestry and Food, 900 28 Ivanka pri Dunaji
T: 943456
Founded: 2968; Members: 300
Focus: Agri; Forestry; Food 09578

Slovenská Zoologická Spoločnost / Slovak Zoological Society, Obrancov mieru 3, 814 34 Bratislava
T: (07) 335435
Founded: 1956; Members: 300
Focus: Zoology 09579

Slovenské Filozofické Združenie (SFZ) / The Slovak Philosophical Association, Klemensova 19, 813 64 Bratislava
T: (07) 321215; Fax: 321215
Founded: 1990; Members: 280
Focus: Philos 09580

Spolok Architektov Slovenska / Slovak Architects Society, Panská 15, 811 01 Bratislava
T: (07) 5335711, 5331431; Fax: 5335744
Founded: 1956; Members: 1400
Pres: Martin Kusy; Gen Secr: Frantisek Kyselica
Focus: Archit 09581

Zväz Slovenských Knihovníkov a Informatikov / Association of the Slovak Librarians and Information Workers, Michalská 1, 814 17 Bratislava
T: (07) 330557
Founded: 1969; Members: 2907
Focus: Libraries & Bk Sci
Periodicals
Ročenka knihovníckej sekcie ZKI (annually)
Zborník INFOS (annually)
Zväzový bulletin (quarterly) 09582

Slovenia

Arhivsko Društvo Slovenije (ADS), Zvezdarska 1, 1000 Ljubljana
T: (061) 20002
Founded: 1954; Members: 131
Focus: Archives 09583

Association of Engineers and Technicians of Slovenia, Erjavčeva 15, 1000 Ljubljana
Founded: 1953
Pres: Tone Tribušon
Focus: Eng
Periodical
Nova Proizvodnja (bi-weekly) 09584

Društvo Matematikov, Fizikov i Astronomov Slovenije / Association of Mathematicians, Physicists and Astronomers of Slovenia, POB 2964, 1111 Ljubljana
T: (061) 1766500
Founded: 1949; Members: 1100
Pres: Dr. Egon Zakrajšek
Focus: Math; Physics; Astronomy
Periodicals
Kujizuica Sipma (annually)
Obzornik za matematiko in fiziko (bi-monthly)
Presek: list za mlade matematike, fizike in astronome (bi-monthly) 09585

Društvo Slovenskih Skladateljev (DSS) /
Society of Slovene Composers, Trg Francoske
Revolucije 6, 1000 Ljubljana
T: (061) 213487; Fax: 213487
Founded: 1945; Members: 106
Pres: Janez Gregorc; Gen Secr: M. Strmčnik
Focus: Music
Periodical
Edicije DSS 09586

Društvo za Medicinsku i Biološku Tehniku,
c/o Faculty of Electrical Engineering, 1000
Ljubljana
T: (061) 61342
Members: 57
Focus: Eng 09587

Jamarska zveza Slovenije (JZS) /
Speleological Association of Slovenia, POB 44,
1109 Ljubljana
T: (061) 315666
Founded: 1889; Members: 1000
Pres: B. Urbar; Gen Secr: Miran Erič
Focus: Speleology
Periodical
Naše jame (semi-annually) 09588

Prirodoslovno Društvo Slovenije v Ljubljani,
Novi trg 4, 1000 Ljubljana
T: (061) 22786
Founded: 1934; Members: 3000
Focus: Sci 09589

Raziskovalna Skupnost Slovenije / Research
Community of Slovenia, Tržaška 42, 1115
Ljubljana
Fax: (061) 261125
Founded: 1953
Focus: Eng; Nat Sci
Periodical
Raziskovalec: Researcher (monthly) . . . 09590

Slavistično Društvo Slovenije / Society for
Slavonic Studies in Slovenia, Aškerčeva 12, 1000
Ljubljana
T: (061) 332611 ext 274
Founded: 1935; Members: 1500
Focus: Ling; Lit
Periodicals
Jezik in Slovstvo (8 times annually)
Slavistična Revija (quarterly) 09591

**Slovenska Akademija Znanosti in Umetnosti
(SAZU)** / Slovenian Academy of Sciencesand Art,
Novi Trg 3, 1000 Ljubljana
T: (061) 1256068; Fax: 1253423
Founded: 1938; Members: 91
Pres: F. Bernik; Gen Secr: M. Drovenik
Focus: Sci
Periodicals
Arheološki vestnik: Acta Archaeologica (annually)
Biblioteka (irregularly)
Dela: Opera (irregularly)
Geografski zbornik: Acta Geographica (annually)
Krasoslovni zbornik: Acta Carsologica (annually)
Letopis-Yearbook (annually)
Razprave: Dissertations (irregularly)
Slovenski biografski leksikon (irregularly)
Traditiones (annually) 09592

Slovenska Matica / Slovenian Society,
Kongresni trg 8, 1000 Ljubljana
T: (061) 214200
Founded: 1864; Members: 2800
Pres: Prof. Dr. Joža Mahnič; Gen Secr: Drago
Jančar
Focus: Ling; Lit 09593

**Slovensko Umetnostno Zgodovinsko
Društvo** / Slovenian Society of Historians of Art,
Aškerčeva 12, 1000 Ljubljana
T: (061) 150001 ext 247; Fax: 159337
Founded: 1921; Members: 299
Focus: Cultur Hist
Periodical
Archives d'Histoire de l'Art: Zbornik za
Umetnostno Zgodovino 09594

Society for Natural Sciences of Slovenia,
Novi trg 4, 1000 Ljubljana
Founded: 1934; Members: 3000
Focus: Nat Sci
Periodical
Proteus (10 times annually) 09595

Society of Jurists of Slovenia, Dalmati-nova
4, 1000 Ljubljana
Founded: 1947; Members: 1073
Pres: Jože Pavličič
Focus: Law
Periodical
Jurist 09596

**Zveza Bibliotekarskih Društev Slovenije
(DBS)** / Library Association of Slovenia, Turjaška
1, 1000 Ljubljana
T: (061) 1255014; Fax: 1259257
Founded: 1947; Members: 970
Pres: Nada Češnovar; Gen Secr: Liljana Hubej
Focus: Libraries & Bk Sci
Periodical
Knjižnica (quarterly) 09597

Zveza Društev Arhitektov Slovenije (ZDAS),
Erjagavčeva 15, 1000 Ljubljana
T: (061) 21608
Founded: 1951; Members: 622
Focus: Archit 09598

Zveza Društev za Varilno Tehniko Slovenije,
Erjavčeva 15, 1000 Ljubljana
T: (061) 221631
Focus: Eng
Periodical
Varilna Tehnika (quarterly) 09599

Zveza Ekonomistov Slovenije, Trubarjeva 3,
1000 Ljubljana
T: (061) 224433
Focus: Econ 09600

Zveza Geografskih Društev Slovenije /
Association of the Geographical Societies of
Slovenia, Aškerčeva 2, 1000 Ljubljana
T: (061) 1769315; Fax: 1259337
Founded: 1922; Members: 700
Pres: Prof. Dr. Andrej Černe
Focus: Geography
Periodicals
Geografski obzornik (quarterly)
Geografski vestnik (annually)
Zborniki geografskih zborovanj: Congress
Proceedings 09601

Zveza Pedagoskih Društev Slovenije /
Pedagocical Society of Slovenia, Gosposka ulica
3, 1000 Ljubljana
Founded: 1920
Focus: Educ
Periodical
Sodobna pedagogika (monthly) . . . 09602

Zveza Zgodovinskih Društev Slovenije /
Slovenian Historical Association, Aškerčeva 2,
1000 Ljubljana
T: (061) 150001 ext 210; Fax: 159337
Founded: 1839; Members: 1649
Pres: Prof. Dr. Franc Rozman
Focus: Hist 09603

South Africa

**Aerial Survey, Photogrammetric and Remote
Sensing Research Group**, c/o Dept of Land
Surveying, University of Natal, King George V Av,
Durban 4001
T: (031) 352461
Focus: Surveying 09604

Aeronautical Society of South Africa /
Lugvaartkundige Vereniging van Suid-Afrika, POB
130774, Bryanston 2021
T: (011) 7063763
Founded: 1911; Members: 621
Focus: Aero
Periodical
Journal (annually) 09605

Africa Institute of South Africa, Corner
Hamilton and Belvedere Sts, Arcadia, POB 630,
Pretoria 0001
T: (012) 286970; E-Mail: africain@iafrica.com;
Fax: 3238163
Founded: 1960; Members: 450
Pres: Dr. T.D. Venter; Gen Secr: B.C. Fisher
Focus: Ethnology; Econ; Geography; Poli Sci; Int'l
Relat
Periodical
Africa Insight (quarterly) 09606

**African Association for the Study of Liver
Diseases**, c/o Dept of Medicine, Liver Research
Centre, University of Cape Town, Cape Town
T: (021) 471250; Fax: 4486815
Focus: Intern Med 09607

**African Library Association of South Africa
(ALASA)**, c/o University of the North Library,
Private Bag X5090, Pietersburg 0700
T: Sovenga 33
Founded: 1964
Focus: Libraries & Bk Sci 09608

**Associated Scientific and Technical
Societies of South Africa (ASTS)**,
c/o Observatory, 18a Gill St, Johannesburg 2198
T: (011) 4871512; Fax: 6481876
Founded: 1920; Members: 78000
Pres: Dr. R.P. Viljoen; Gen Secr: J.A. Nel
Focus: Sci; Eng
Periodical
Annual Proceedings (quarterly) 09609

Association of Surgeons of South Africa /
Chirurgiese Vereniging van Suid-Afrika, POB
52027, Saxonwold, Johannesburg 2132
T: (011) 8371011
Founded: 1945; Members: 250
Pres: P. Perdikis; Gen Secr: V.E. Sorour
Focus: Surgery
Periodical
South African Journal of Surgery . . . 09610

Astronomical Society of Southern Africa,
POB 9, Observatory 7935
T: (021) 470025; E-Mail: assa@saao.ac.za;
Fax: 473639
Founded: 1922; Members: 450
Pres: Dr. R.S. Stobie; Gen Secr: B. Skinner
Focus: Astronomy
Periodicals
Handbook (annually)
Mnassa (monthly) 09611

Birdlife South Africa, POB 84394, Greenside,
Johannesburg 2034
T: (011) 8884147; E-Mail: info@birdlife.org.za;
Fax: 7827013
Founded: 1930; Members: 6000
Pres: Dr. U. Tarboton; Gen Secr: Dr. Aldo
Berruti
Focus: Ornithology
Periodical
Ostrich (quarterly) 09612

The Botanical Society of South Africa,
Kirstenbosch, Claremont 7735
T: (021) 7972090; Fax: 7972376
Founded: 1913; Members: 20000
Focus: Botany; Ecology; Hort
Periodicals
S.A. Wild Flower Guide Series (irregularly)
Veld & Flora (quarterly) 09613

Cancer Association of South Africa, 139
Smit St, Braamfontein 2017
T: (011) 4032825; Fax: 4031946
Founded: 1931
Focus: Cell Biol & Cancer Res
Periodical
S.A.-Cancer Bulletin (quarterly) 09614

**Carbohydrate and Lipid Metabolism
Research Group**, c/o Dept of Medicine, Medical
School, University of the Witwatersrand, 7 York
Rd, Parktown, Johannesburg 2193
T: (011) 4883818; E-Mail: 015bar@
chiron.wits.ac.za; Fax: 6432935
Founded: 1970; Members: 10
Pres: Prof. B.I. Joffe; Gen Secr: J. Pieters
Focus: Med 09615

Chemical Engineering Research Group,
c/o Dept of Chemical Engineering, University of
Natal, King George V Av, Durban 4001
T: (031) 253411
Focus: Chem; Eng 09616

Classical Association of South Africa,
c/o Dept of Classics, University of Cape Town,
Cape Town 7700
T: (021) 6502607; E-Mail: classec@
beattie.uct.ac.za; Fax: 6503726
Founded: 1956; Members: 350
Pres: Prof. J.D. Scourfield; Gen Secr: Dr. S.
Thom
Focus: Ling; Lit; Hist
Periodicals
Acta Classica (annually)
Akroterion (quarterly) 09617

Climatology Research Group, c/o Dept of
Geography and Environmental Studies, University
of the Witwatersrand, Johannesburg 2001
T: (011) 7162986; E-Mail: steve@
crg.bpb.wits.ac.za; Fax: 7163161
Founded: 1975
Pres: Prof. P.D. Tyson
Focus: Geophys; Ecology 09618

The College of Medicine of South Africa, 17
Milner Rd, Rondebosch 7700
T: (021) 6899533; E-Mail: cmsa-adm@iafrica.com;
Fax: 6853766
Members: 4500
Gen Secr: Bernise Bothma
Focus: Med
Periodical
Transactions of the College of Medicine of South
Africa (semi-annually) 09619

CSIR, POB 395, Pretoria 0001
T: (012) 8412911; Fax: 8413789
Founded: 1945; Members: 3100
Focus: Sci; Eng
Periodicals
Chemdata (semi-annually)
CSIR Annual Report (annually)
Technobrief (monthly)
Watertek Newsletter (quarterly) 09620

Dental Association of South Africa (DASA) /
Tandheelkundige Vereniging van Suid-Afrika,
Private Bag 1, Houghton 2041
T: (011) 4845288; E-Mail: dasa.jhb.lia.net;
Fax: 6425718
Founded: 1922; Members: 2900
Gen Secr: Dr. J.T. Barnard
Focus: Dent
Periodical
Journal of the Dental Association of South Africa
(monthly) 09621

**Diffuse Obstructive Pulmonary Syndrome
Research Group**, c/o Dept of Internal Medicine,
Medical School, University of Stellenbosch, POB
63, Tygerberg 7505
Focus: Intern Med 09622

Division of Energy Technology (Enertek),
c/o Scientia, POB 395, Pretoria 0001
T: (012) 8414946; Fax: 8412135
Focus: Chem; Eng 09623

Economic Society of South Africa, POB 929,
Pretoria 0001
T: (011) 3133300
Founded: 1925; Members: 700
Pres: P.D.F. Strydom; Gen Secr: Else Krüger-
Cloete
Focus: Econ
Periodical
The South African Journal of Economics
(quarterly) 09624

**The Electron Microscopy Society of
Southern Africa**, c/o Electron Microscope Unit,
Medical School, POB 17039, Congella, Durban
4013
Founded: 1962; Members: 335
Focus: Optics
Periodical
Proceedings (annually) 09625

English Academy of Southern Africa, POB
124, Wits 2050
T: (011) 7163683; Fax: 7163683
Founded: 1961
Pres: Prof. M.I. Leveson; Gen Secr: B.E.J.
Garmeson
Focus: Ling
Periodical
English Academy Review (annually) . . 09626

Entomological Society of Southern Africa,
POB 103, Pretoria 0001
Founded: 1937; Members: 450
Focus: Entomology
Periodicals
African Entomology (semi-annually)
Memoirs (irregularly) 09627

**Federasie van Afrikaanse Kultuurvereniginge
(F.A.K.)**, POB 91050, Auckland Park 2006
T: (011) 7267134; Fax: 7262073
Founded: 1929; Members: 4000
Pres: Prof. C. Swanepoel; Gen Secr: H.C. de
Wet
Focus: Hist
Periodical
Handhaaf Newsletter (quarterly) 09628

Federasie van Rapportryerskorpse, POB
91001, Aucklandpark 2006
Founded: 1961; Members: 11500
Pres: Dr. C. Stander; Gen Secr: J.G. du Plessis
Focus: Ling; Lit
Periodical
Die Rapportryer (bi-monthly) 09629

Genealogical Society of South Africa,
Postnet X2600, Houghton, Johannesburg 2041
Founded: 1963; Members: 850
Pres: Martin Zollner; Gen Secr: E. van Rooyen
Focus: Genealogy
Periodical
Familia (quarterly) 09630

**The Geological Society of South Africa
(GSSA)** / Die Geologiese Vereniging van Suid-
Afrika, POB 44283, Linden 2104
T: (011) 8882288; Fax: 8882181
Founded: 1895; Members: 1900
Focus: Geology
Periodical
South African Journal of Geology . . . 09631

Heraldry Society of Southern Africa, POB
4839, Cape Town 8000
Founded: 1953; Members: 150
Pres: Dr. C. Pama; Gen Secr: Michael Purcell
Focus: Genealogy
Periodical
Arma (quarterly) 09632

Herpetological Association of Africa (H.A.A.),
c/o Port Elizabeth Museum, POB 13147, Port
Elizabeth 6013
T: (041) 561051; Fax: 562175
Members: 300
Focus: Zoology
Periodicals
African Herp News
Journal of the Herpetological Association of Africa
. . . . 09633

Human Sciences Research Council / Raad
vir Geesteswetenskaplike Navorsing, 134 Pretorius
St, Private Bag X41, Pretoria 0001
T: (012) 2029111; E-Mail: RAGEN, Pretoria;
Fax: 3265362
Focus: Humanities; Sociology; Arts
Periodicals
Afford Ability (semi-annually)
Africa 2001 Dialogue with the Future (semi-
annually)
CSD/SWO Bulletin
HSRC Centre for Constitution Analysis
HSRC/RGN In Focus (bi-monthly)
Information Update (annually)
Prodder Newsletter (quarterly)
Tharnbodala 09634

Institute of Bankers in South Africa, POB
61420, Marshalltown 2107
T: (011) 8321371; Fax: 8346592
Founded: 1904; Members: 15500
Gen Secr: J. Hodges
Focus: Finance
Periodical
The South African Banker (quarterly) . . 09635

Institute of South African Architects, The
Pines, 9 Gordon Hill, Parktown, POB 2093,
Houghton 2041
T: (011) 4861683
Founded: 1927; Members: 3500
Pres: M. Knoetze
Focus: Archit
Periodical
Architecture (SA) (bi-monthly) 09636

Joint Council of Scientific Societies, POB 13480, Yeoville 2143
Founded: 1968
Focus: Sci 09637

The Medical Association of South Africa (M.A.S.A.), 428 King's Hwy, Lynnwood 0081
T: (012) 4812000; E-Mail: masamvw@iafrica.com; Fax: 4812100
Founded: 1927; Members: 13240
Pres: Ephraim Mokgokong; Gen Secr: Dr. Hendrik Hanekom
Focus: Med
Periodicals
Continuing Medical Education Journal (monthly)
Medigram (bi-weekly)
South African Medical Journal (monthly) . 09638

Medical Graduates' Association of the University of the Witwatersrand, c/o Medical School, Hospital St, Johannesburg 2000
Founded: 1934; Members: 1100
Focus: Med 09639

Medical Research Council, c/o Dental Research Institute, School of Dentistry, University of the Witwatersrand, Private Bag 3, PO Wits, Johannesburg 2050
T: (011) 7164163; E-Mail: 078pec@cosmos.wits.ac.za; Fax: 7163879
Founded: 1954; Members: 15
Pres: Prof. P. Cleaton-Jones
Focus: Dent 09640

Mintek, 200 Hans Strijdom Dr, Private Bag X3015, Randburg 2125
T: (011) 7094111; Tx: 424867; E-Mail: Minteksa, Johannesburg
Pres: Dr. A. Edwards
Focus: Mineralogy
Periodicals
Annual Report (annually)
Mintek Bulletin: Mintek Research Digest (bi-monthly) 09641

National Association for Clean Air (NACA), POB 5777, Johannesburg 2000
T: (011) 6462210
Founded: 1969; Members: 450
Focus: Ecology
Periodical
Clean Air Journal (semi-annually) . . . 09642

The National Association of Scientists, Lynnwood, POB 11346, Pretoria 0001
Founded: 1968; Members: 1180
Focus: Sci 09643

Natural Products Chemistry Research Group, c/o Dept of Chemistry, University of the Witwatersrand, Johannesburg 2001
T: (011) 7163185; E-Mail: jmichael@aurum.chem.wits.ac.za; Fax: 3397967
Members: 15
Pres: Prof. J.P. Michael
Focus: Chem 09644

The Nutrition Society of Southern Africa, c/o J. Lochner, POB 1697, Brits 0250
T: (012) 5214259; Fax: 5213510
Founded: 1957; Members: 305
Pres: Prof. H.H. Vorster; Gen Secr: P.M.N. Kuzwayo
Focus: Food
Periodical
SA Journal of Food Science and Nutrition (quarterly) 09645

Oral and Dental Research Institute, POB X1, Tygerberg 7505
T: (021) 9312246; Fax: 9312287
Focus: Dent
Periodicals
Archives of Environmental Health
Clinical Preventive Dentistry
Community Dentistry and Oral Epidemiology
International Journal of Pediatric Otorhinolaryngology
Journal of Clinical Orthodontics
Journal of Oral Pathology and Medicine
Journal of the Dental Association of South Africa
South African Medical Journal 09646

Organic Soil Association of South Africa, POB 47100, Parklands 2121
Founded: 1948; Members: 999
Focus: Agri; Hort; Nutrition; Public Health
Periodical
Soil News (bi-monthly) 09647

Physiological and Biochemical Society of Southern Africa, c/o Dept of Physiology, University, Pretoria 0002
Founded: 1971; Members: 76
Focus: Physiology; Biochem 09648

Pollution Research Group, c/o Dept of Chemical Engineering, King George V Av, Durban 4001
T: (031) 8163375; Fax: 8163131
Founded: 1970
Focus: Chem; Eng; Ecology 09649

Preclinical Diagnostic Chemistry Research Group of the South African Medical Research Council, c/o Dept of Chemical Pathology, University of Natal, 719 Umbilo Rd, Congella 4013
T: 254211
Focus: Chem; Pathology 09650

Pretoria Horticultural Society, POB 1186, Pretoria 0001
Founded: 1916; Members: 700
Focus: Hort 09651

Primate Behaviour Research Group, c/o University of Witwatersrand, PO Wits, Johannesburg 2050
Focus: Behav Sci 09652

Prosthodontics Society of South Africa, Private Bag X1, Houghton 2041
Founded: 1970; Members: 250
Focus: Dent 09653

Psychological Society of South Africa, POB 74119, Lynnwood Ridge 0040
T: (012) 8071740; Fax: 8071776
Founded: 1982; Members: 1600
Focus: Psych
Periodical
South African Journal of Psychology (quarterly) 09654

Research Group for Lung Metabolism, c/o Dept of Medical Physiology and Biochemistry, Faculty of Medicine, POB 63, Tygerberg 7505
T: (021) 933131
Focus: Pulmon Dis 09655

Research Group for Neurochemistry, c/o Dept of Chemical Pathology, Medical School, University of Stellenbosch, POB 63, Tygerberg 7505
T: (021) 9310111
Founded: 1977
Focus: Neurology; Chem 09656

Royal Aeronautical Society, Southern Africa Division, POB 130774, Bryanston 2021
Founded: 1945; Members: 130
Focus: Aero 09657

Royal Society of South Africa, P.D. Hahn Bldg, POB 594, Cape Town 8000
T: (021) 6502543; Fax: 6502710
Founded: 1877; Members: 400
Pres: Dr. O.W. Prozesky; Gen Secr: Prof. D.E. Rawlings
Focus: Sci
Periodical
Transactions (irregularly) 09658

The Science Writers' Association of South Africa, POB 686, Johannesburg 2000
Founded: 1959; Members: 30
Focus: Lit 09659

Society for Endocrinology, Metabolism and Diabetes of Southern Africa, POB 783155, Sandton 2146
T: (011) 7837275
Founded: 1960; Members: 87
Focus: Diabetes; Endocrinology 09660

Society for Experimental Biology, c/o South African Institute for Medical Research, Hospital St, Johannesburg 2001
Founded: 1951; Members: 44
Focus: Bio 09661

Society of Physiologists, Biochemists and Pharmacologists, c/o Dept of Biochemistry, University, Pretoria 0002
Members: 50
Focus: Pharmacol; Physiology; Biochem . 09662

Society of South African Geographers (S.A.G.S.), POB 128, Wits 2050
T: (011) 3391951; Fax: 4037281
Founded: 1917; Members: 490
Pres: Prof. U.J. Fairhurst; Gen Secr: Prof. H.L. Zietsmans
Focus: Geography
Periodicals
South African Geographical Journal (semi-annually)
South African Landscape Series (irregularly) 09663

Soil Science Society of Southern Africa (S.S.S.S.A.), POB 1821, Pretoria 0001
Founded: 1953; Members: 200
Focus: Agri 09664

South African Academy of Science and Arts / Suid-Afrikaanse Akademie vir Wetenskap en Kuns, POB 538, Pretoria 0001
T: (012) 3285082; Fax: 3285091
Founded: 1909; Members: 1700
Pres: Prof. F.P. Retief; Gen Secr: Dr. D.J.C. Geldenhuys
Focus: Sci; Arts
Periodicals
Jaarverslag (annually)
Nuusbrief
SA Tydskrif vir Natuurwetenskappe en Tegnologie
Tydskrif vir Geesteswetenskappe 09665

South African Archaeological Society (S.A.A.S.), POB 15700, Vlaeberg 8012
T: 243330
Founded: 1945; Members: 1250
Pres: Prof. T.N. Huffman; Gen Secr: M. Leslie-Brooker
Focus: Archeol
Periodicals
The Digging Stick (3 times annually)
Goodwin Series (irregularly)
Monograph Series (irregularly)
S.A. Archaeological Bulletin (semi-annually) 09666

The South African Association for Food Science and Technology (SAAFoST), POB 2140, Edenvale 1610
T: (011) 6096322; Fax: 4524928
Founded: 1961; Members: 1200
Focus: Food; Med
Periodicals
Food Review (bi-monthly)
The SA Journal of Food Science & Nutrition (quarterly) 09667

South African Association for Technical and Vocational Education (S.A.A.T.V.E), POB 40684, Arcadia 0007
T: (012) 3236851; Fax: 3230185
Founded: 1895; Members: 4800
Focus: Adult Educ; Educ
Periodical
Journal of Technical and Vocational Education in South Africa (quarterly) 09668

South African Association of Arts, POB 6188, Pretoria 0001
T: (012) 3287109; E-Mail: 3231275
Founded: 1945; Members: 5000
Pres: Conrad Theys
Focus: Arts
Periodical
South Africa Arts Calendar (semi-annually) 09669

The South African Association of Botanists, c/o Botany Dept, University of Fort Hare, Alice 5700
Founded: 1968; Members: 230
Focus: Botany 09670

The South African Association of Physicists in Medicine and Biology, c/o Div of Production Technology, POB 395, Pretoria 0001
Founded: 1960; Members: 61
Focus: Bio; Med; Physiology
Periodical
Congress Brochure (annually) 09671

South African Biological Society / Suid-Afrikaanse Biologiese Vereniging, POB 820, Pretoria 0001
Founded: 1907; Members: 144
Focus: Bio
Periodical
Journal (annually) 09672

South African Ceramic Society, POB 13702, Northmead 1511
T: (011) 8490856; Fax: 4251698
Founded: 1967
Gen Secr: G. Sneddon
Focus: Materials Sci
Periodicals
Conference Proceedings (annually)
Keramicos (quarterly) 09673

The South African Chemical Institute (S.A.C.I.), POB 93480, Yeoville 2143
T: (011) 4871543; Fax: 4871543
Founded: 1912; Members: 1700
Pres: Prof. E.L.J. Breet; Gen Secr: Dr. D. Groot
Focus: Chem
Periodicals
Chemical Processing SA (monthly)
SA Journal of Chemistry (quarterly) . . 09674

South African Council for Automation and Computation (S.A.C.A.C.), POB 395, Pretoria 0001
Founded: 1961; Members: 60
Focus: Electric Eng; Computer & Info Sci 09675

South African Crystallographic Society, c/o Prof. G.J. Kruger, Chemistry Dept, POB 524, Johannesburg 2000
Fax: (011) 4892363
Founded: 1958
Focus: Mineralogy 09676

South African Dietetics and Home Economics Association, POB 3046, Stellenbosch 7600
Founded: 1953; Members: 300
Focus: Hematology; Home Econ 09677

South African Filtration Society (SAFJL), 159 Duxbury Rd, Hillcrest 0181
T: 747346
Founded: 1978; Members: 453
Focus: Eng 09678

South African Genetics Society, c/o Dept of Genetics, University, Stellenbosch 7600
T: (021) 8084443; E-Mail: lw@maties.sun.ac.za; Fax: 8084336
Founded: 1956; Members: 148
Pres: Prof. E.H. Meyer; Gen Secr: Dr. L. Warnich
Focus: Genetics 09679

South African Institute for Librarianship and Information Science (SAJBJ), POB 36575, Menlo Park, Pretoria 0102
Founded: 1930; Members: 2851
Pres: Prof. S.P. Manaka; Gen Secr: Prof. A. Louw
Focus: Libraries & Bk Sci; Computer & Info Sci
Periodicals
Newsletter (monthly)
South African Journal for Librarianship and Information Science (quarterly) 09680

The South African Institute for Medical Research, Hospital St, POB 1038, Johannesburg 2000
T: (011) 7250511; E-Mail: BACTERIA, Johannesburg
Focus: Med 09681

South African Institute of Aeronautical Engineers (SAIAeE), POB 27335, Sunnyside 0132
T: (011) 9273162
Founded: 1977; Members: 140
Focus: Aero; Eng
Periodical
Aeronautica Meridiana (annually) 09682

South African Institute of Assayers and Analysts, Kelvin House, 2 Hollard St, POB 61019, Mashalltown 2107
Founded: 1919; Members: 181
Focus: Eng
Periodical
Bulletin (quarterly) 09683

The South African Institute of International Affairs, Jan Smuts House, University of the Witwatersrand, POB 31596, Braamfontein 2017
T: (011) 3392021; Fax: 3392154
Founded: 1934; Members: 3500
Focus: Poli Sci
Periodicals
Bibliographical Series (annually)
Bradlow Series (annually)
South African Journal of International Affairs (semi-annually)
Special Studies (irregularly) 09684

The South African Institute of Mining and Metallurgy, Cape Towers, 11-13 MacLaren St, POB 61127, Marshalltown 2107
T: (011) 8341273; Fax: 8385923
Founded: 1884; Members: 2186
Focus: Mining; Metallurgy; Physics
Periodical
Journal of the South African Institute of Mining and Metallurgy (monthly) 09685

The South African Institute of Organization and Methods, POB 693, Pretoria 0001
Founded: 1960
Focus: Business Admin
Periodical
Organization & Methods Newsletter (quarterly) 09686

The South African Institute of Physics (S.A.I.P.), POB 72, Faure 7131
Founded: 1955; Members: 600
Focus: Physics 09687

South African Institute of Printing (S.A.I.P.), Pearl Assurance House, Heerengracht, Cape Town 8001
T: (021) 254210; Fax: 215485
Founded: 1969; Members: 137
Focus: Eng; Graphic & Dec Arts, Design 09688

South African Institute of Race Relations, POB 31044, Braamfontein 2017
Founded: 1929; Members: 2200
Focus: Sociology; Poli Sci; Educ
Periodicals
Race Relations News (quarterly)
Race Relations Survey (annually) . . . 09689

The South African Institution of Civil Engineering, POB 93495, Yeoville 2143
T: (011) 6481184; E-Mail: siace@cis.co.za; Fax: 6487427
Founded: 1903; Members: 7706
Pres: A.T. Visser; Gen Secr: D.B. Botha
Focus: Civil Eng
Periodicals
Civil Engineering (monthly)
Journal of the South African Institution of Civil Engineering (quarterly) 09690

South African Market Research Association (SAMRA), POB 9858, Johannesburg 2000
Founded: 1963; Members: 494
Focus: Marketing
Periodical
Report (annually) 09691

The South African Mathematical Society (SAMS), POB 395, Pretoria 0001
T: (012) 869211
Founded: 1957; Members: 300
Focus: Math
Periodical
Quaestiones Mathematicae (quarterly) . . 09692

The South African Medical Research Council, Francie van Zijl Av, Parowvallei, POB 19070, Tygerberg 7505
T: (021) 9380911; E-Mail: lgething@eagle.mrc.ac.za; Fax: 9380200
Founded: 1969; Members: 350
Pres: Dr. O.W. Prozesky
Focus: Med; Public Health
Periodicals
AIDS Bulletin (quarterly)
CAPFSA Reporter (quarterly)
Documentum (quarterly)
Health Promotion Newsletter
MRC Annual Report and Health Impact Report (annually)
MRC News (bi-monthly)
Trauma Review (quarterly)
Urbanisation and Health Newsletter (quarterly) 09693

The South African National Committee on Illumination (SANCI), POB 395, Pretoria 0001
T: (012) 869211
Founded: 1954; Members: 200
Focus: Electric Eng 09694

South African National Group of the International Society for Rock Mechanics (S.A.N.G.O.R.M.), POB 61809, Marshalltown 2107
T: (011) 7263020; E-Mail: Bullion, Johannesburg; Fax: 7265405
Founded: 1969; Members: 417
Focus: Mining; Civil Eng 09695

South African National Multiple Sclerosis Society, 295 Villiers Rd, Walmer 6070
T: (041) 512900; Fax: 515705
Founded: 1963
Pres: Seámus Fitzpatrick; Gen Secr: Isobel Henderson
Focus: Pathology; Med 09696

South African National Tuberculosis Association (SANTA), 621 Leisk House, Corner Bree and Rissik Sts, Johannesburg 2001
T: (011) 3369636/38; E-Mail: santatb@iafrica.com; Fax: 3339057
Founded: 1947; Members: 252
Pres: J. Pender-Smith; Gen Secr: J. Hylton Smith
Focus: Pulmon Dis
Periodical
SANTA TB and Health News (bi-monthly) 09697

The South African Numismatic Society, POB 1689, Cape Town 8000
T: (021) 244412
Founded: 1941; Members: 340
Focus: Numismatics
Periodical
Bulletin (monthly) 09698

South African Optometric Association, POB 3966, Pretoria 0001
Founded: 1924; Members: 714
Focus: Optics
Periodical
South African Optometrist (quarterly) . . 09699

South African Orthopaedic Association, 129 Northwold, Saxonwold, Johannesburg 2129
T: (011) 4474627; E-Mail: saoa@megaweb.co.za; Fax: 4474564
Founded: 1942; Members: 650
Pres: James B. Craig; Gen Secr: S.M. Young
Focus: Orthopedics
Periodical
Journal of Bone and Joint Surgery . . 09700

South African PEN Centre, 2 Scott Rd, Claremont 7735
Founded: 1960; Members: 100
Gen Secr: A. Naudé
Focus: Lit
Periodical
Newsletter 09701

The South African Rheumatism and Arthritis Association, c/o Brenthurst Clinic, 4 Park Lane, Parktown, Johannesburg 2001
Focus: Rheuma 09702

South African Society for Photogrammetry, Remote Sensing and Cartography, POB 69, Newlands 7725
Founded: 1958; Members: 300
Focus: Cart
Periodical
South African Journal of Photogrammetry, Remote Sensing and Cartography (semi-annually) 09703

The South African Society of Anaesthesists (SASA), Suite 101, Cargo corner Sevemth Av, Rosebank 2196
Focus: Anesthetics 09704

South African Society of Otorhinolaryngology, 532 Louis Leipoldt Medical Centre, Bellville 7530
Members: 100
Focus: Otorhinolaryngology 09705

The South African Society of Physiotherapy, POB 11151, Johannesburg 2000
Founded: 1925; Members: 1400
Focus: Therapeutics
Periodical
The South African Journal of Physiotherpy: Die Soid-Afrikaanse Tydskrif Fisioterapie (monthly) 09706

South African Speech and Hearing Association / Suid-Afrikaanse Vereniging vir Spraak- en Gehoorheelkunde, POB 31782, Braamfontein 2017
T: (011) 394011 ext 660
Founded: 1946; Members: 600
Focus: Logopedy
Periodical
The South African Journal of Communication Disorders (annually) 09707

The South African Statistical Association, POB 27321, Sunnyside 0132
T: (011)4981623
Founded: 1953; Members: 400
Focus: Stats
Periodical
South African Statistical Journal (semi-annually) 09708

South African Veterinary Association, POB 25033, Monument Park 0105
T: (012) 3461150; Fax: 3462929
Founded: 1903; Members: 1364
Focus: Vet Med
Periodical
Journal of the South African Veterinary Association (quarterly) 09709

Southern Africa Cardiac Society, c/o Chelmsford Medical Centre, Saint Augustine's Hospital, 107 Chelmsford, Durban 4001
Members: 300
Focus: Cardiol 09710

Southern African Association for the Advancement of Science, Jakaranda 301, Beckettstr 304, Arcadia 0083
T: (012) 4202169; Fax: 433254
Founded: 1902; Members: 124
Focus: Sci 09711

Southern African Institute of Forestry (SAIF), POB 1022, Pretoria 0001
T: (012) 473479; Fax: 473479
Founded: 1967; Members: 502
Pres: P.J. Keyworth; Gen Secr: C. Viljoen
Focus: Forestry
Periodical
Southern African Forestry Journal (quarterly) 09712

Southern African Museums Association (SAMA), POB 29294, Sunnyside 0132
T: (012) 3416531; Fax: 3416146
Founded: 1936; Members: 660
Pres: B. Wilmot; Gen Secr: G. Balkwill
Focus: Arts
Periodicals
SAMAB: Southern African Museums Association Bulletin (quarterly)
Samantix (quarterly) 09713

Southern African Society of Aquatic Scientists, c/o Dr. Chris Dickens, Umgeni Water, POB 9, Pietermaritzburg 3200
E-Mail: chrisd@umgeni.co.za; Fax: (0331) 3411349
Founded: 1963; Members: 350
Pres: Dr. Chris Dickens; Gen Secr: Mark Graham
Focus: Hydrology
Periodical
Journal (semi-annually) 09714

Spectroscopic Society of South Africa, c/o Dept of Chemistry, University of Pretoria, Pretoria 0002
T: (012) 4202511; E-Mail: crademey@scientia.up.ac.za; Fax: 432963
Founded: 1969; Members: 400
Pres: Prof. C.J. Rademeyer; Gen Secr: Prof. J. Willis
Focus: Chem
Periodical
SASV/SASS Newsletter (quarterly) . . . 09715

Succulent Society of South Africa, POB 1193, Pretoria 0001
Founded: 1962; Members: 2500
Focus: Botany
Periodical
Aloe: Journal of the Succulent Society of South Africa 09716

The Tree Society of Southern Africa, POB 4116, Johannesburg 2000
Founded: 1948; Members: 500
Focus: Forestry
Periodicals
Newsletter (semi-annually)
Trees in South Africa (semi-annually) . . 09717

Van Riebeeck Society (VRS), c/o South African Library, POB 496, Cape Town 8000
T: (021) 238424
Founded: 1918; Members: 1400
Pres: Dr. F.R. Bradlow; Gen Secr: A. Adema
Focus: Hist 09718

Water Research Commission, 491 18 Av, Rietfontein, Pretoria 0001
T: (012) 3300340; E-Mail: WATERKOM, Pretoria; Fax: 3312565
Focus: Hydrology
Periodicals
SA Water Bulletin
Water SA 09719

Water Systems Research Group, c/o Dept of Civil Engineering, University of the Witwatersrand, 1 Jan Smuts Av, PO Wits, Johannesburg 2050
Focus: Hydrology; Water Res 09720

Wildlife Society of Southern Africa, POB 44189, Linden 2104
Founded: 1902; Members: 26000
Focus: Ecology
Periodicals
African Wildlife (bi-monthly)
Toktokki (bi-monthly) 09721

Zoological Society of Southern Africa (ZSSA), c/o Dept of Zoology, University of the Witwatersrand, Private Bag 3, Wits, Johannesburg 2000
E-Mail: nevillep@gecko.biol.wits.ac.za
Members: 500
Pres: Prof. A. van Jaarsveld; Gen Secr: Dr. N. Pillay
Focus: Zoology
Periodical
South African Journal of Zoology (quarterly) 09722

Spain

Academia de Ciencias Exactas, Físicas, Químicas y Naturales de Zaragoza, c/o Facultad de Ciencias, Ciudad Universitaria, Zaragoza
Founded: 1916; Members: 40
Pres: Horacio Marco Moll; Gen Secr: Mariano Gasca
Focus: Chem; Nat Sci; Physics; Math
Periodical
Revista (quarterly) 09723

Academia de Ciencias Médicas de Bilbao, Lersundi 9, Apdo 5073, 48080 Bilbao
T: (04) 4233768
Founded: 1895; Members: 1300
Pres: Dr. C. Aguirre Errasti; Gen Secr: Dr. Javier Garrós Garay
Focus: Med
Periodical
Gaceta Médica de Bilbao (bi-monthly) . 09724

Academia Española de Dermatología y Sifilografía, Sandoval 7, 28010 Madrid
Founded: 1909; Members: 489
Pres: José Gómez Piera; Gen Secr: R. Morán López
Focus: Derm; Venereology
Periodical
Actas Dermosifiliográficas 09725

Academia Médico-Quirúrgica Española, Villanueva 11, 28001 Madrid
Founded: 1891; Members: 492
Pres: Prof. Eduardo Arias Vallejo; Gen Secr: Dr. Julio Múniz González
Focus: Surgery; Med
Periodical
Anales 09726

Arxiu Històric de la Ciutat de Barcelona, Casa de l'Ardiaca, Carrer Santa Lúcia 1, 08002 Barcelona
T: (03) 3181195; Fax: 3178327
Founded: 1917
Focus: Hist 09727

Asociación Amics del Museus de Catalunya / Friends of the Catalan Museums Association, Palau de la Virreina, La Rambla 99, 08002 Barcelona
T: (03) 3014379; Fax: 3189421
Founded: 1933; Members: 935
Pres: Josep Ma Garrut; Gen Secr: Fauusto Serra de Dalmases
Focus: Archives
Periodical
Historiales 09728

Asociación de Escritores y Artistas Españoles, Leganitos 10, 28013 Madrid
T: (01) 5599067; Fax: 5599067
Founded: 1872; Members: 645
Pres: Luis Cervera Vera; Gen Secr: José Gerardo Manrique de Lara
Focus: Lit 09729

Asociación Española de Archiveros, Bibliotecarios, Museólogos y Documentalistas (ANABAD), Recoletos 5, 28001 Madrid
T: (01) 5751727
Founded: 1949; Members: 1620
Pres: Julia M. Rodríguez Barrero; Gen Secr: Carmen Cayetano Martín
Focus: Libraries & Bk Sci; Archives; Archeol
Periodical
Boletín de la ANABAD (quarterly) . . . 09730

Asociación Española de Entomología / Spanish Entomological Association, c/o Facultad de Ciencias Biológicas, Universidad de Valencia, 46100 Burjasot
Founded: 1977
Pres: Dr. Eduardo Galante Patiño
Focus: Zoology 09731

Asociación Española de Logopedia, Foniatría y Audiología (AELFA), Provenza 319, 08037 Barcelona
T: (03) 2577818; Fax: 3173766
Founded: 1960; Members: 1231
Pres: J. Perelló; Gen Secr: E. Bardina
Focus: Logopedy; Otorhinolaryngology
Periodical
Revista de Logopedia (quarterly) 09732

Asociación Española de Pediatría, Villanueva 11, 28001 Madrid
T: (91) 4354916; E-Mail: aep@telprof.es; Fax: 4355043
Founded: 1949; Members: 7000
Pres: Prof. Manuel Moya; Gen Secr: Prof. Luis Madero
Focus: Pediatrics 09733

Asociación Española de Pintores y Escultores / Association of Spanish Artists and Sculptors, Infantas 30, 28004 Madrid
T: (01) 5224961; Fax: 5225508
Founded: 1910
Focus: Arts 09734

Asociación Iberoamericana de Educación Superior a Distancia, c/o UNED, Apdo 50487, 28080 Madrid
Founded: 1981; Members: 53
Pres: Dr. Jenardo Costas; Gen Secr: Dr. D. Luis Tejero Escribano
Focus: Educ
Periodical
Revista Iberoamericana de Educación Superior a Distancia (quarterly) 09735

Asociación Nacional de Químicos de España / National Association of Chemists, Lagasca 83, 28006 Madrid
Founded: 1945; Members: 9000
Pres: José Luis Negro López; Gen Secr: Joaquín Copado López
Focus: Chem
Periodical
Química e Industria (monthly) 09736

Association for Dental Education in Europe (ADEE), c/o Faculdad de Odontologia, Universidad, Madrid
T: (91) 3941906; E-Mail: marsan@eucmax.sim.ucm.es; Fax: 3941910
Founded: 1975; Members: 90
Pres: D. Shanley; Gen Secr: Dr. Mariano Sanz
Focus: Educ; Dent 09737

Ateneo Científico, Literario y Artístico, Calle del Prado 21, 28014 Madrid
T: (01) 4296251
Founded: 1820; Members: 6500
Pres: José Prat García; Gen Secr: David M. Rivas Infante
Focus: Arts; Lit 09738

Ateneo Científico, Literario y Artístico / Scientific, Literary and Artistic Athenaeum, Cifuentes 25, Mahón, Minorca
Founded: 1905; Members: 630
Pres: F. Tutzó Bennasar; Gen Secr: Miguel Angel Limón Pons
Focus: Lit; Arts
Periodical
Revista de Menorca (quarterly) 09739

Ateneu Barcelonés / Barcelona Athenaeum, Canuda 6, 08002 Barcelona
Founded: 1860; Members: 3200
Pres: Heribert Barrera Costa; Gen Secr: Isidor Cònsul Giribet
Focus: Arts; Lit 09740

Centro de Documentación y Estudios SiiS, Reina Regente 5, 20003 San Sebastián
T: (943) 423656; Fax: 293007
Founded: 1972
Focus: Poli Sci; Educ Handic; Sociology 09741

Centro de Estudios Constitucionales / Centre for Constitutional Studies, Pl de la Marina Española 9, 28013 Madrid
Fax: (01) 5478549
Founded: 1977
Pres: Carmen Iglesias Cano; Gen Secr: Daniel Villagra Blanco
Focus: Poli Sci; Law
Periodicals
Boletín del Centro de Estudios Constitucionales (3 times annually)
Derecho Privado y Constitución (annually)
Revista de Administración Pública (quarterly)
Revista de Derecho Comunitario Europeo (semi-annually)
Revista de Economía Política
Revista de Estudios Internacionales (quarterly)
Revista de Estudios Políticos (3 times annually)
Revista Española de Derecho Constitucional (quarterly) 09742

Col-legi Notaris / College of Notaries, Notariat 4, 08001 Barcelona
T: (03) 3174800
Members: 346
Pres: R. Folla Camps
Focus: Law 09743

Col-legi Oficial d'Enginyers Industrials de Catalunya, Via Layetana 39, 08003 Barcelona
T: (03) 08003; Fax: 3100681
Founded: 1950; Members: 20000
Pres: Ramón Garriga i Saperas; Gen Secr: Kosep M. Rovira i Ragué
Focus: Eng 09744

Colegio de Abogados de Barcelona / Barcelona College of Lawyers, Mallorca 283, 08037 Barcelona
T: (03) 4872814; Fax: 4871128
Founded: 1832; Members: 6200
Pres: E. Gay Montalvo; Gen Secr: José Gasch Riudor
Focus: Law
Periodicals
Anuario de Sociologia y Psicologia Juridicas
Revista Juridica de Cataluña 09745

Collegi d'Arquitectes de Catalunya / College of Architects of Catalonia, Pl Nova 5, 08002 Barcelona
T: (93) 3015000; E-Mail: coacnet@coac.es; Fax: 4123964
Founded: 1931; Members: 6080
Pres: Joan B. Mur i Soteras; Gen Secr: Pere Serra i Amengual
Focus: Archit
Periodical
Quaderns d'Arquitectura i Urbanisme (quarterly) 09746

Comité International Permanent des Etudes Mycéniennes, c/o Universidad del País Vasco, 01006 Vitoria
T: (045) 139811; E-Mail: ecpmejij@vc.ehu.es; Fax: 138227
Founded: 1956

Gen Secr: Prof. José L. Melena
Focus: Cultur Hist 09747

Comité Nacional Español del Consejo Internacional de la Música / National Committee of the International Music Council, Martín de los Héroes 56, 28001 Madrid
Gen Secr: M. Iglesias
Focus: Music 09748

Conferencia de Rectores de las Universidades del Estado, c/o Universidad de Sevilla, San Fernando 4, 41071 Sevilla
T: (05) 4551012; Fax: 4211294
Founded: 1978; Members: 37
Pres: Prof. Javier Pérez Royo
Focus: Educ 09749

Consejo de Universidades, Cuidad Universitaria s/n, 28040 Madrid
T: (01) 4497437
Founded: 1983; Members: 52
Gen Secr: F. Michavila
Focus: Educ 09750

Consejo General de Colegios Oficiales de Doctores y Licenciados en Filosofía y Letras y en Ciencias / General Council of Official Colleges of Doctors and Licenciates in Philosophy, Letters and Science, Bolsa 11, 28012 Madrid
T: (01) 5224597
Founded: 1944; Members: 55800
Pres: Dr. Luis Negro Fernández; Gen Secr: Dr. Roberto Salmerón Sanz
Focus: Lit; Philos 09751

Consejo General de Colegios Oficiales de Farmacéuticos, Villanueva 11, 28001 Madrid
Founded: 1942; Members: 13500
Pres: Ernesto Marco Cañizares
Focus: Pharmacol
Periodical
Boletín de Información 09752

Departamento de Historia del Arte Diego Velázquez, c/o Centro de Estudios Históricos, Duque de Medinaceli 6, 28014 Madrid
T: (01) 5856000; Fax: 5854878
Founded: 1939; Members: 9
Gen Secr: Enrique Arias Angles
Focus: Arts
Periodical
Archivo Español de Arte (3 times annually) 09753

Dirección General de Relaciones Culturales y Científicas / Cultural and Scientific Relations Department, c/o Ministerio de Ascuntos Exteriores, Calle José Abascal 41, 28003 Madrid
T: (01) 4411600; Fax: 4414417
Founded: 1926
Gen Secr: Santiago Cabanas
Focus: Poli Sci; Sci 09754

Federación de Urbanismo y de la Vivienda, Pl del Cordon 1, Madrid
Focus: Urban Plan 09755

Federación Española de Religiosos de Enseñanza (FERE) / Spanish Federation of Religious Teaching, Conde de Peñalver 45, Apdo 53052, 28006 Madrid
T: (01) 4021300; Fax: 3091740
Founded: 1957
Pres: María J. Fernández; Gen Secr: Angel Astorgano Ruiz
Focus: Rel & Theol; Educ
Periodicals
Boletín de la FERE (monthly)
Educadores (bi-monthly) 09756

Ilustre Consejo General de Colegios Oficiales de Odontólogos y Estomatólogos de España, Villanueva 11, 28001 Madrid
T: (91) 5770638; E-Mail: consejo@lander.es; Fax: 5770639
Members: 14560
Pres: Dr. Manuel Alfonso Villa Virgil; Gen Secr: Dr. José Font Buxó
Focus: Dent; Stomatology
Periodical
RCOE-Revista (monthly) 09757

Institución Fernando el Católico, Palacio Provincial, Plaza de España 2, 50004 Zaragoza
T: (976) 288879; E-Mail: ifc@mail.sendanet.es; Fax: 288869
Founded: 1943; Members: 150
Pres: Guillermo Fatàs; Gen Secr: José Barranco López
Focus: Arts; Ling; Lit; Hist; Music; Law . 09758

Institut Agrícola Català de Sant Isidre / Catalan Agricultural Institute, Pl Sant Josep Oriol 4, 08002 Barcelona
T: (03) 3011740; Fax: 3173005
Founded: 1851; Members: 2000
Pres: Joaqim d' Abadal; Gen Secr: F. de Muller
Focus: Agri
Periodicals
Boletín (monthly)
Calendari del Pagés (annually)
Revista (quarterly) 09759

Institut Amatller d'Art Hispànic / Institute os Hispanic Art, Passeig de Gràcia 41, 08007 Barcelona
T: (03) 2160175; Fax: 4875827
Founded: 1942
Focus: Arts 09760

Institut del Teatre / Theatrical Institute, Sant Sant Pere més baix 7, 08003 Barcelona
T: (03) 2682078; Fax: 2681070
Founded: 1913
Pres: P. Monterde
Focus: Perf Arts
Periodical
Estudis escènics (3 times annually) . . 09761

Institut d'Estudis Catalans / Institute of Catalan Studies, Carrer del Carme 47, 08001 Barcelona
T: (03) 3185516; Fax: 4122994
Founded: 1907; Members: 165
Pres: Manuel Castellet i Solanas; Gen Secr: J.R. Rafel i Fontanals
Focus: Hist 09762

Instituto Aula de Mediterráneo, c/o Universidad de Valencia, Valencia
Founded: 1942; Members: 545
Pres: Dr. F. Sánchez Castañer
Focus: Lit 09763

Instituto de España, San Bernardo 49, 28015 Madrid
T: (01) 5224885; Fax: 5210654
Founded: 1938
Pres: Margarita Salas Falgueras; Gen Secr: Pedro García Barreno
Focus: Sci
Periodical
Anuario (annually) 09764

Instituto de Filologia, Duque de Medinaceli 6, 28014 Madrid
T: (91) 4290626
Founded: 1985; Members: 15
Pres: María Teresa Ortega
Focus: Ling; Lit
Periodicals
Al-Qantara (semi-annually)
Anales Cervantinos (annually)
Emerita (semi-annually)
Revista de Dialectologia y Tradiciones Populares (annually)
Revista de Filología Española
Revista de Literatura (semi-annually)
Sefarad (semi-annually) 09765

Instituto de Historia y Cultura Naval, Juan de Mena 1, 28071 Madrid
T: (01) 3795050
Founded: 1942; Members: 10
Pres: José I. González Aller
Focus: Hist; Transport 09766

Instituto Geográfico Nacional, General Ibáñez de Ibero 3, 28003 Madrid
T: (01) 5333800; Fax: 5333444
Founded: 1870; Members: 1200
Gen Secr: Angel Arévalo Barroso
Focus: Geography 09767

Instituto Nacional de Administración Pública / National Institut of Public Administration, Atocha 106, 28012 Madrid
T: (01) 3493147; Fax: 3493160
Founded: 1940
Focus: Public Admin 09768

Instituto Nacional de Estadística (INE), Paseo de la Castellana 183, 28046 Madrid
T: (01) 5839100; Fax: 5792713
Founded: 1945
Focus: Stats
Periodicals
Anuario Estadística de España (annually)
Boletín Mensual de Estadística (monthly)
Revista Estadística Española 09769

Instituto Nacional de Meteorología, Ciudad Universitaria, 28040 Madrid
T: (01) 5819882; Fax: 5819845
Founded: 1887; Members: 5011
Pres: M.J. Prieto Laffargue
Focus: Geophys
Periodical
Boletin Meteorológico 09770

International Association for Shell and Spatial Structures (IASS), Alfonso XII 3, 28014 Madrid
T: (91) 3357409; E-Mail: palaejos@cedex.es; Fax: 3357422
Founded: 1959; Members: 700
Pres: Prof. S. Medwadowski; Gen Secr: Dr. P. Alaejos Gutiérrez
Focus: Civil Eng
Periodical
IASS Journal (3 times annually) 09771

Organización Médica Colegial – Consejo General de Colegios Médicos de Espanña, Villanueva 11, 28001 Madrid
T: (01) 2258410
Founded: 1930; Members: 21
Pres: José Fornes Ruiz
Focus: Med
Periodicals
Boletín Formativo e Informativo (monthly)
Medicina de España 09772

Real Academia de Bellas Artes de la Purísima Concepción, Rastro, Casa de Cervantes, 47001 Valladolid
T: (983) 308810; Fax: 390703
Founded: 1783; Members: 30
Pres: Dr. Javier López de Uribe y Laya; Gen Secr: D. Jesús Urrea Fernández
Focus: Arts 09773

Real Academia de Bellas Artes de San Fernando, Alcalá 13, 28014 Madrid
T: (01) 5321546; Fax: 5231599
Founded: 1752
Pres: Ramón Gonzáles de Amezúa; Gen Secr: Enrique Pardo Canlis
Focus: Arts
Periodical
Boletín 09774

Real Academia de Bellas Artes de San Telmo, Málaga
Founded: 1849; Members: 28
Pres: José Luis Estrada Segalerva
Focus: Arts 09775

Real Academia de Bellas Artes de Santa Isabel de Hungria, Abades 12-14, 41004 Sevilla
T: (05)4221198
Founded: 1660; Members: 36
Pres: Antonio de la Banda y Vargas; Gen Secr: Ramón Corzo Sánchez
Focus: Arts
Periodical
Boletin de Bellas Artes y Temas de Estetica y Arte (annually) 09776

Real Academia de Bellas Artes y Ciencias Históricas de Toledo, Esteban Illán 9, 45002 Toledo
T: (025) 214322
Founded: 1916; Members: 25
Pres: Dr. D. Felix del Valle y Diaz; Gen Secr: Luis Alba Gonzalez
Focus: Hist; Arts
Periodical
Toletum (semi-annually) 09777

Real Acadèmia de Bones Letres / Royal Academy of Belles Lettres, Bisbe Caçador 3, 08002 Barcelona
T: (03)3150010
Founded: 1700; Members: 36
Focus: Lit 09778

Real Academia de Ciencias Exactas, Físicas y Naturales, Valverde 22-24, 28004 Madrid
T: (01) 5212529; Fax: 5325716
Founded: 1847; Members: 160
Pres: Angel Martín Municio; Gen Secr: José Javier Etayo Miqueo
Focus: Nat Sci; Physics; Sci
Periodicals
Anuario (annually)
Memoria
Revista 09779

Real Academia de Ciencias Morales y Políticas (R.A.C.M.Y.P.), Pl de la Villa 2, 28005 Madrid
T: (01) 5481330, 5595739, 5595805; E-Mail: secre@racmyp.es; Fax: 5481975
Founded: 1857; Members: 36
Pres: Enrique Fuentes Quintana; Gen Secr: S. del Campo Urbano
Focus: Philos; Poli Sci
Periodicals
Anales (annually)
Catalogo (irregularly) 09780

Real Academia de Ciencias Veterinarias de España / Royal Academy of Veterinary Sciences of Spain, c/o Prof. Dr. Mariano Illera Martín, Dept. de Fisiología, Facultad de Veterinaria, Ciudad Universitaria, 28040 Madrid
T: (01) 3943867; Fax: 3943864
Founded: 1975
Focus: Vet Med 09781

Real Academia de Ciencias y Artes de Barcelona (RACAB), Rambla de los Estudios 115, 08002 Barcelona
T: (03) 3170536
Founded: 1764; Members: 95
Pres: Dr. Ramón Parés Farrás; Gen Secr: Prof. Dr. Manuel Puigcerver Zanón
Focus: Sci; Arts
Periodical
Memorias de la Real Academia de Ciencias y Artes de Barcelona (4-6 times annually) 09782

Real Academia de Córdoba de Ciencias, Bellas Letras y Nobles Artes, Ambrosio de Morales 9, 14003 Córdoba
T: (057) 413168
Founded: 1810; Members: 70
Pres: Dr. Manuel Pelaéz del Rosal; Gen Secr: Joaquin Criado Costa
Focus: Arts; Lit
Periodical
Boletín (semi-annually) 09783

Real Academia de Doctores, Calle de San Bernardo 49, 28015 Madrid
T: (01) 5319522; Fax: 5319522
Founded: 1920
Pres: Prof. Gustavo Villapalos; Gen Secr: Dr. Guillermo Suárez Fernández
Focus: Med 09784

Real Academia de Farmacia, Farmacia 11, 28004 Madrid
T: (01) 5310307
Founded: 1589; Members: 42
Pres: Rafael Cadórniga Carro; Gen Secr: Antonio Portolés Alonso
Focus: Pharmacol
Periodical
Anales (quarterly) 09785

Real Academia de Jurisprudencia y Legislación, Marqués de Cubas 13, 28014 Madrid
T: (91) 52222069; Fax: 5234021
Founded: 1730; Members: 40
Pres: Juan Vallet de Goytisolo; Gen Secr: José M. Castán Vázquez
Focus: Law 09786

Real Academia de la Historia, León 21, 28014 Madrid
T: (91) 4290611
Founded: 1738; Members: 36
Pres: Antonio Rumeu de Armas; Gen Secr: Eloy Benito Ruano
Focus: Hist
Periodical
Boletín 09787

Real Academia de la Lengua Vasca – Euskaltzaindia, Plaza Barria 15, 48005 Bilbao
T: (04) 4158155; Fax: 4158144
Founded: 1919; Members: 24
Pres: Jean Haritschelhar; Gen Secr: Patxi Goenaga
Focus: Ling
Periodicals
Euskararen Lekukoak
Euskera (quarterly)
Iker
Jagon
Onomasticon Vasconiae 09788

Real Academia de Medicina y Cirugía de Palma de Mallorca, Morei 20, 07001 Palma de Mallorca
Members: 19
Pres: José Sampol Vidal; Gen Secr: Santiago Forteza Forteza
Focus: Surgery; Med 09789

Real Academia de Nobles y Bellas Artes de San Luis, Pl de Los Sitios 6, 50001 Zaragoza
Founded: 1792; Members: 12
Pres: Angel Canellas López; Gen Secr: Jorge Albareda Agüeras
Focus: Arts
Periodical
Boletín (irregularly) 09790

Real Academia Española, Felipe IV 4, 28014 Madrid
T: (01) 4201478
Founded: 1713; Members: 100
Pres: Fernando Lazaro Carreter; Gen Secr: Victor García de la Concha
Focus: Ling; Lit 09791

Real Academia Gallega, Tabernas 11, 15001 La Coruña
Founded: 1905; Members: 40
Pres: Domingo García-Sabell; Gen Secr: Marino Donéga Rozas
Focus: Sci
Periodical
Boletín 09792

Real Academia Hispano-Americana, Almirante Vierna 14, Apdo 16, 11009 Cádiz
Founded: 1910; Members: 29
Pres: Antonio Orozco Acuaviva; Gen Secr: Juan I. Varela Gilabert
Focus: Sci
Periodical
Boletín 09793

Real Academia Nacional de Medicina, Arrieta 12, 28013 Madrid
T: (01) 5470318 703=5470320
Founded: 1732; Members: 198
Pres: H. Durán Sacristán; Gen Secr: Dr. V. Matilla Gómez
Focus: Med
Periodicals
Anales
Biblioteca Clásica de la Medicina Española 09794

Real Academia Sevillana de Buenas Letras, Abades 14, 41004 Sevilla
T: (05) 4225200
Founded: 1751; Members: 135
Pres: Eduardo Ybarra Hidalgo; Gen Secr: Dr. Rogelio Reyes Canó
Focus: Lit
Periodical
Boletín (annually) 09795

Real Institutode Estudios Asturianos / Institute of Asturian Studies, Pl Porlier 9, Oviedo
T: (05) 211760
Founded: 1946; Members: 50
Focus: Cultur Hist 09796

Real Sociedad Arqueológica Tarraconense (R.S.A.T.), Calle Mayor 35, Apdo 573, Tarragona
T: (977) 233789; E-Mail: rsat@tinet.fut.es; Fax: 233789
Founded: 1844; Members: 750
Pres: Gabriel R. Costa; Gen Secr: M. Güell Junkert
Focus: Archeol
Periodical
Butlleti Arqueologic (quarterly) 09797

Real Sociedad Bascongada de los Amigos del País, Donostia, Apdo 992, 20003 San Sebastián
T: (022) 424478

Founded: 1764; Members: 24
Pres: I.M. Barrila Irigoyen
Focus: Hist
Periodicals
Anuario de Eusko-Folklore Aranzadiana Orria
Boletín (quarterly)
Boletín de Estudios Históricos sobre San Sebastián (annually)
Boletín de la Cofradía Vasca de Gastronomía Egan
Munibe 09798

Real Sociedad Económica de Amigos del País de Tenerife / Royal Economic Society of Friends of Tenerife, San Agustín 23, Tenerife
Founded: 1777; Members: 490
Pres: Marqués de Villanueva del Pardo; Gen Secr: Manuel D. Quintana
Focus: Ethnology; Econ 09799

Real Sociedad Española de Historia Natural, c/o Facultades de Biología y Geología, Ciudad Universitaria, 28040 Madrid
T: (01) 3945000
Founded: 1871; Members: 800
Focus: Hist; Nat Sci
Periodicals
Actas (annually)
Boletín: Sección Biológica (quarterly)
Boletín: Sección Geológica (quarterly) . . 09800

Real Sociedad Española de Química, c/o Facultad de Ciencias Químicas, Ciudad Universitaria, 28040 Madrid
T: (01) 3944361; Fax: 5433879
Founded: 1903; Members: 2900
Pres: J. Antonio Rodríguez Renuncio; Gen Secr: Ballester Pérez. Antonio
Focus: Chem
Periodical
Anales de Quimica 09801

Real Sociedad Fotográfica Española (RSF), Príncipe 16, 28012 Madrid
T: (01) 5224300
Founded: 1899; Members: 1320
Pres: María Teresa Gutierrez Barranco; Gen Secr: Juan Carlos Martín Martín
Focus: Arts
Periodical
Boletín (monthly) 09802

Real Sociedad Geográfica, Pinar 25, 28006 Madrid
T: (01) 5617825; Fax: 5625567
Founded: 1876; Members: 433
Pres: Dr. Rodolfo Nuñez de las Cuevas; Gen Secr: Dr. J. Bosque Maurel
Focus: Geography
Periodicals
Boletín (annually)
Hoja Informativa (monthly) 09803

Real Sociedad Matemática Española (R.S.M.E.), Serrano 123, 28006 Madrid
T: (01) 2619800
Founded: 1911; Members: 600
Pres: Pedro Luis García Pérez; Gen Secr: Juan Llovet Verdugo
Focus: Math
Periodical
Revista Matemática Iberoamericana . . . 09804

Reial Acadèmia Catalana de Belles Arts de Sant Jordi, Casa Llozja, Passeig d'Isabel II 1, 08003 Barcelona
T: (03) 319432; Fax: 3192432
Founded: 1849
Pres: Joan Bassegoda Nonell; Gen Secr: L: Gil Nebot
Focus: Lit
Periodicals
Boletín
Memorias 09805

Seminario de Filología Vasca Julio de Urquijo / Julio de Urquijo Seminary of Basque Philology, Palacio de la Diputación de Guipúzcoa, San Sebastián
Founded: 1953
Pres: I. Sarasola
Focus: Ling; Lit
Periodical
Anuario 09806

Servicio de Investigación Prehistórica de la Excelentísima Diputación Provincial (S.I.P.), Corona 36, 46003 Valencia
T: (06) 3883587
Founded: 1927; Members: 30
Pres: Bernardo Marti Oliver
Focus: Hist
Periodicals
Archivo de Prehistoria Levantina (bi-annually)
Serie de Trabajos Varios: Monografias (quarterly) 09807

Sociedad Astronómica de España y América / Astronomical Society of Spain and America, Av Diagonal 377, 08008 Barcelona
Founded: 1911; Members: 250
Focus: Astronomy 09808

Sociedad de Ciencias Aranzadi Zientzi Elkartea, c/o Museo de San Telmo, Pl de I. Zuloaga, 20003 San Sebastián
T: (043) 422945; Fax: 421316
Founded: 1947; Members: 1944
Pres: Jesús Altuna; Gen Secr: Francisco Etxeberria
Focus: Nat Sci; Anthro; Archeol
Periodicals
Aranzadiana (annually)
Boletín de Astronomia (quarterly)
Munibe (Antropologia-Arkeologia) (annually)
Munibe (Ciencias Naturales) (annually) . 09809

Sociedad de Ciencias, Letras y Artes / Scientific, Literary and Art Society, c/o El Museo Canario, Dr. Chil 25, Las Palmas
T: (028) 315600; E-Mail: emuseo@ext.step.es; Fax: 314998
Founded: 1879; Members: 410
Pres: Lothar Siemens Hernández; Gen Secr: Julio Cuench Sanabria
Focus: Lit; Arts; Ethnology; Archeol
Periodical
El Museo Canario (quarterly) 09810

Sociedad de Estadística e Investigación Operativa (S.E.I.O.), Serrano 123, 28004 Madrid
T: (01) 3082474
Founded: 1962; Members: 650
Pres: Jesus T. Pastor Civrana; Gen Secr: Domingo Morales Gonzalez
Focus: Computer & Info Sci; Stats
Periodicals
TEST (semi-annually)
TOP (semi-annually) 09811

Sociedad de Pediatría de Madrid y Castilla La Mancha, Villanueva 11, 28001 Madrid
Founded: 1913; Members: 750
Pres: M. Moro Serrano; Gen Secr: A. Rodrígalvarez
Focus: Pediatrics 09812

Sociedad Española de Bioquímica y Biología Molecular (SEB), Vitruvio 8, 28006 Madrid
T: (91) 5613381; E-Mail: bmsgro@; Fax: 5613299
Founded: 1960; Members: 1800
Pres: Dr. Joan Guinovart Cirera; Gen Secr: García Ruiz
Focus: Biochem; Bio 09813

Sociedad Española de Cerámica y Vidrio / Spanish Society of Ceramic and Glass, Carretera de Valencia km 24.300, Arganda del Rey, 28005 Madrid
T: (01) 8711800; Fax: 8700550
Founded: 1960; Members: 730
Gen Secr: Emilio Criado
Focus: Materials Sci
Periodical
Boletín (bi-monthly) 09814

Sociedad Española de Cirugía Plástica, Reparadora y Estética, Santa Isabel 51, Apdo 2454, 28080 Madrid
T: (9) 4155995; Fax: 4155995
Founded: 1956; Members: 550
Pres: José María Serra Renom; Gen Secr: Julio Millán Mateo
Focus: Surgery
Periodical
Cirugía Plástica Iberolatinoamericana (quarterly) 09815

Sociedad Española de Diabetes, Santa Isabel 51, 28012 Madrid
T: (91) 4682940; Fax: 5396306
Founded: 1954; Members: 700
Pres: Dr. José Luis Herrera Pombo; Gen Secr: Dr. Adela Rovira Loscos
Focus: Diabetes 09816

Sociedad Española de Etología / Spanish Ethological Society, c/o Museu de Zoologia, Apdo 593, Parc Ciutadella, 08080 Barcelona
T: (03) 3196912; Fax: 3104999
Focus: Zoology 09817

Sociedad Española de Mecánica del Suelo y Cimentaciones, Alfonso XII 3, 28014 Madrid
T: (91) 3357337; Fax: 3357322
Founded: 1964; Members: 230
Pres: S. Uriel
Focus: Civil Eng
Periodical
Boletin de la Sociedad Española de Mecanica del Suelo y Cimentaciones (quarterly) . . . 09818

Sociedad Española de Patología Digestiva y de la Nutrición, Almagro 38, 28904 Madrid
Founded: 1933; Members: 800
Pres: Dr. H.G. Mogena
Focus: Pathology; Nutrition
Periodical
Revista Española de las Enfermedades del Aparato Digestivo y de la Nutrición . . 09819

Sociedad Española de Radiología Medica (S.E.R.M.), Goya 38, 28001 Madrid
Founded: 1946; Members: 3250
Pres: Dr. R. Casanova Gómez
Focus: Radiology; Nucl Med
Periodical
Radiología (bi-monthly) 09820

Sociedad General de Autores de España (SGAE) / General Society of Spanish Authors, Fernando VI 4, 28004 Apdo 484, 28004 Madrid
Founded: 1932
Pres: Enrique Loras García; Gen Secr: Javier Moscoso del Prado
Focus: Lit
Periodical
Boletín (quarterly) 09821

Sociedad Geológica de España / Geological Society of Spain, c/o Fundatión Gómez Pardo, Alenza 1, 28003 Madrid
T: (01) 4417138
Founded: 1985; Members: 980
Focus: Geology 09822

Sociedad Ibero-Americana de Estudios Numismáticos, c/o Museo Casa de la Moneda, Jorge Juan 106, 28009 Madrid
T: (91) 5666536
Founded: 1951
Pres: Antonio Beltrán; Gen Secr: Julio Torres
Focus: Numismatics 09823

Sociedad Veterinaria de Zootecnica de España / Spanish Veterinary Society of Zootechnics, Isabel la Católica 12, 28937 Madrid
T: (01) 2471838; Fax: 5416902
Founded: 1945; Members: 3750
Pres: Prof. Dr. C.L. de Cuenca; Gen Secr: Prof. Dr. J.M. Cid Diaz
Focus: Zoology; Animal Husb
Periodical
Zootecnia (quarterly) 09824

Societat Arqueològica Lul-liana (S.A.L.), Monti-Sion 9, 07010 Palma de Mallorca
T: (071) 213912
Founded: 1880; Members: 600
Pres: María Barceló Crespí; Gen Secr: Gabriel Ensenyat Pujol
Focus: Archeol
Periodical
Butlleti de la Societat Arqueològica Lul-liana (annually) 09825

Societat Catalana de Medicina Aerospacial, Subaquàtica i Ambiental, Passeig de la Bonanova 47, 08017 Barcelona
T: (93) 2124382; E-Mail: aerosub@acmcb.es; Fax: 4188729
Founded: 1960; Members: 147
Pres: Pere A. Martinez-Carpio
Focus: Med 09826

Sri Lanka

Archaeological Society of Sri Lanka, c/o Dept of Archaeology, Sir Marcus Fernando Mawata, Colombo 7
Founded: 1966
Pres: Prof. C. Wikkramahamage
Focus: Archeol 09827

Arts Council of Sri Lanka, Sethsiripausa, Battaramulla
T: 872031
Founded: 1952
Pres: R.A.A. Ranaweera; Gen Secr: H.K. Premadasa
Focus: Arts 09828

Buddhist Academy of Ceylon, 109 Rosmead Pl, Colombo
Focus: Rel & Theol 09829

Ceylon Geographical Society, 61 Abdul Caffoor Mawatha, Colombo 3
Founded: 1938; Members: 100
Pres: Prof. K. Kularatnam
Focus: Geography
Periodical
The Ceylon Geographer (annually) . . . 09830

Ceylon Humanist Society, Rutnam Institute Bldg, University Lane, Jaffna 7
Pres: J.T. Rutnam; Gen Secr: O.M. de Alwis
Focus: Philos
Periodical
Journal (irregularly) 09831

Ceylon Institute of World Affairs, c/o M. de Silva, 82B Ward Pl, Colombo 7
Founded: 1957
Pres: Anton Muttukumaru
Focus: Poli Sci 09832

Ceylon Society of Arts, c/o Art Gallery, Ananda Coomarassamy Mawatha, Colombo 7
T: (01) 693067
Founded: 1887
Pres: K.A. Weerakkody; Gen Secr: D. Jayasuriya
Focus: Arts 09833

English Speaking Union of Sri Lanka, 14A, 16K Lane Galle Rd, Colombo 3
T: (01) 575843
Founded: 1981
Pres: Dr. T. Amerasinghe
Focus: Ling; Lit 09834

Institution of Engineers – Sri Lanka, 120/15 Wijerama Mawatha, Colombo 7
Founded: 1906; Members: 4000
Pres: K.R.L. Perera; Gen Secr: D.D.S. Jayawardena
Focus: Eng 09835

National Academy of Sciences of Sri Lanka, 120/10 Wijerama Mawatha, Colombo 7
Founded: 1976; Members: 104
Pres: Eric M.U.S. Sultanbawa
Focus: Sci 09836

National Education Society of Ceylon, c/o Dept of Humanities Education, University of Colombo, POB 1490, Colombo 3
Focus: Educ 09837

Royal Asiatic Society of Sri Lanka, c/o Mahaveli Centre, 96 Ananda Coomaraswanuy Mawatha, Colombo 7
T: (01) 699249
Founded: 1845; Members: 500
Pres: R.C. de Manukulaseeriya
Focus: Ethnology; Hist; Ling; Lit; Arts; Soc Sci
Periodical
Journal (annually) 09838

Sri Lanka Association for the Advancement of Science, 120/10 Wijerama Mawatha, Colombo 7
T: (01) 691681
Founded: 1944; Members: 2600
Pres: Prof. Valentine Basnayake; Gen Secr: Dr. W.L. Sumathipala
Focus: Sci
Periodicals
Proceedings
Vidya Viyapathi 09839

Sri Lanka Library Association, c/o The Professional Centre, 175/75 Bauddhaloka Mawatha, Colombo 7
T: (01) 589103
Founded: 1960; Members: 113
Pres: P. Vidanapathirana; Gen Secr: W. Ranasinghe
Focus: Libraries & Bk Sci
Periodical
Ceylon Library Review (annually) . . . 09840

Sri Lanka Medical Association, 6 Wijerama Mawatha, Colombo 7
T: (01) 93324; Fax: 698802
Founded: 1887; Members: 985
Pres: Dr. J.B. Peiris
Focus: Med
Periodical
The Ceylon Medical Journal (quarterly) . 09841

Theosophical Society of Ceylon, 49 Peterson Lane, Colombo 6
Focus: Rel & Theol 09842

Sudan

Association des Professeurs de Français en Afrique (APFA) / Association of French Teachers in Africa, c/o Dept of French, Faculty of Arts, University of Khartoum, POB 321, Khartoum
T: (011) 78201
Founded: 1981; Members: 20
Focus: Educ; Ling
Periodical
JAFTA Journal (annually) 09843

Commission for Archaeology, POB 178, Khartoum
Focus: Archeol 09844

National Centre for Research, POB 2404, Khartoum
T: (011) 779040; Fax: 770701
Founded: 1991
Focus: Sci 09845

Philosophical Society, POB 526, Khartoum
Founded: 1946
Focus: Philos
Periodicals
Proceedings of Annual Conferences
Sudan Notes and Records 09846

Sudan Academy for Administrative Sciences, POB 2003, Khartoum
Founded: 1980
Gen Secr: Dr. Osman Elzuberi Ahmed
Focus: Public Admin 09847

Sudan Library Association, POB 32, Khartoum North
Focus: Libraries & Bk Sci 09848

Suriname

Centre for Agricultural Research in Suriname, POB 1914, Paramaribo
T: 60244
Founded: 1965
Focus: Agri 09849

Geologisch Mijnbouwkundige Dienst, Kleine Waterstr 2-6, Paramaribo
Focus: Mining; Geology 09850

Stichting Cultureel Centrum Suriname, POB 1241, Paramaribo
Fax: 10555
Founded: 1947
Focus: Arts; Hist; Lit 09851

Swaziland

Royal Swaziland Society of Science and Technology, c/o University, Private Bag, Kwaluseni
T: 84011; Fax: 85276
Founded: 1977; Members: 100
Pres: Prof. L.P. Makhubu; Gen Secr: R. Martin
Focus: Sci; Eng 09852

Swaziland Art Society, POB 812, Mbabane
Founded: 1970; Members: 60
Focus: Arts 09853

Swaziland Library Association, POB 2309, Mbabane
T: 43101; Fax: 42641
Founded: 1984; Members: 120
Pres: L. Dlamini; Gen Secr: P. Muswazi
Focus: Libraries & Bk Sci *09854*

Sweden

Akademikerförbundet SSR, Mariedalsv 4, Box 12800, 112 51 Stockholm
T: (08) 6174400; E-Mail: kansli@akademssr.se; Fax: 6174401
Founded: 1958; Members: 35500
Pres: Agneta Bygdell; Gen Secr: Jan-Åke Porsgren
Focus: Sociology; Soc Sci; Econ; Business Admin; Public Admin
Periodicals
Socionomen (8 times annually)
SSR-tidningen (22 times annually) . . . *09855*

Association of Nordic Paper Historians, St Eriksgt 130, 113 43 Stockholm
T: (08) 338369
Founded: 1968
Focus: Hist *09856*

Baltic Marine Biologists (BMB), c/o Institute of Marine Research, Box 4, 453 21 Lysekil
T: (0523) 18700; E-Mail: b.j.dybern@imr.se; Fax: 13977
Founded: 1968; Members: 400
Pres: Prof. Evald Ojaveer; Gen Secr: Dr. Bernt I. Dybern
Focus: Bio; Oceanography
Periodicals
The Baltic Marine Biologists Publications (irregularly)
Proceedings of the Baltic Marine Biological Symposia (bi-annually) *09857*

Bergianska Stiftelsen / Bergius Foundation, Box 50017, 104 05 Stockholm
Founded: 1976
Focus: Hort; Botany *09858*

Bibliotekarieförbundet (BF), c/o DIK-förbundet, Box 760, 131 24 Nacka
T: (08) 4662400; E-Mail: dik@akademikerhuset.se; Fax: 4662424
Founded: 1997; Members: 5100
Pres: Bo Ekengren
Focus: Libraries & Bk Sci
Periodical
DIK-forum (18 times annually) *09859*

Cancerfonden – Riksföreningen mot Cancer / Swedish Cancer Society, Box 17096, 104 62 Stockholm
T: (08) 7722800; Fax: 7202208
Founded: 1951
Focus: Cell Biol & Cancer Res
Periodicals
Forskning Nu (bi-monthly)
Rädda Livet (bi-monthly) *09860*

Carl Johans Förbundet, c/o Bexell, Geijersgt 18a, 752 28 Uppsala
T: (018) 536244; E-Mail: oloph.bexell@ted.uu.se; Fax: 536244
Founded: 1848; Members: 800
Pres: Jan-Erik Wikström; Gen Secr: Prof. Dr. Oloph Bexell
Focus: Hist *09861*

Centre for the Study of International Relations, Döbelnsgt 81, Box 19112, 104 32 Stockholm
Fax: (08) 6120592
Founded: 1971
Focus: Int'l Relat
Periodical
Review *09862*

Chemical Societies of the Nordic Countries, c/o Svenska Kemistsamfundet, Wallingt 24, 111 24 Stockholm
T: (08) 4115260; E-Mail: agneta@chemsoc.se; Fax: 106678
Focus: Chem *09863*

Coalition Clean Baltic (CCB), c/o SNF, Box 4510, 102 65 Stockholm
Founded: 1990; Members: 14
Focus: Ecology *09864*

Committee on Family Research (CFR), c/o Sociologiska Institutionen, Uppsala Universitet, Thunbergsv 3, Box 821, 751 08 Uppsala
Founded: 1950; Members: 210
Focus: Sociology
Periodical
CFR-Gazette (3 times annually) *09865*

Conference of the Baltic Oceanographers, c/o Hans Dahlin, Swedish Meteorological and Hydrological Institute, 601 76 Norrköping
Focus: Oceanography *09866*

Council of Nordic Teachers' Associations, c/o Sveriges Lärarförbund, Box 12229, 102 26 Stockholm
T: (08) 7376500; Fax: 569415
Founded: 1968
Focus: Educ *09867*

Dag Hammarskjöld Foundation, Dag Hammarskjöld Centre, Övre Slottsgt 2, 753 10 Uppsala
T: (018) 127272; Fax: 122072
Founded: 1962
Gen Secr: Olle Nordberg
Focus: Develop Areas
Periodical
Development Dialogue (semi-annually) . . *09868*

Esperantist Ornithologists' Association, Telegrafgt 5, 149 00 Nynäshamn
Founded: 1961
Focus: Ornithology *09869*

European Association of Labour Economists (EALE), c/o Swedish Institute for Social Research, University of Stockholm, 106 91 Stockholm
T: (08) 8163448; Fax: 8154670
Founded: 1989
Focus: Soc Sci
Periodical
EALE Newsletter *09870*

European Association of Perinatal Medicine, c/o Unit of Pediatric Physiology, University Hospital, 751 85 Uppsala
T: (018) 167515
Founded: 1968
Focus: Pediatrics *09871*

European Drosophila Centre, c/o Dept of Genetics, Umea University, 901 87 Umea
T: (090) 165000
Members: 10
Focus: Genetics *09872*

European Ecological Federation, c/o University of Lund, Ecology Bldg, 223 62 Lund
T: (046) 148188
Focus: Ecology *09873*

European Federation of Productivity Services (EFPS), c/o Sveriges Rationaliseringsförbund, Box 4324, 102 67 Stockholm
T: (08) 249225; Fax: 6433061
Founded: 1961
Focus: Business Admin *09874*

European Incoherent Scatter Scientific Association (EISCAT), Box 812, 981 28 Kiruna
T: (0980) 79153; Fax: 791533
Founded: 1975
Pres: Dr. Jürgen Röttger; Gen Secr: Anette Snällfot
Focus: Sci
Periodical
Annual Report (annually) *09875*

Flygtekniska Föreningen (FTF), c/o Swedish Space Corporation, Box 4107, 171 04 Stockholm
T: (08) 6276298; Fax: 987069
Founded: 1933; Members: 1867
Pres: Lasse Karlsen; Gen Secr: Kay Lundahl
Focus: Aero *09876*

Förbundet Sveriges Arbetsterapeuter (FSA) / Swedish Association of Occupational Therapists, Box 760, 131 24 Nacka
T: (08) 7162850; Fax: 7185392
Founded: 1979; Members: 6600
Focus: Therapeutics
Periodical
Arbetsterapeuten (16 times annually) . . *09877*

Föreningen för Vattenhygien (FVH), Box 519, 162 15 Vällingby 5
T: 228580, 316097
Founded: 1944; Members: 1200
Focus: Hygiene
Periodical
Vatten (quarterly) *09878*

Föreningen Svenska Tonsättare (F.S.T.) / Society of Swedish Composers, Sandhamsgt 79, Box 27327, 102 54 Stockholm
T: (08) 7838842
Founded: 1918; Members: 133
Focus: Music *09879*

Företagsekonomiska Föreningen, c/o Gunnar Bergström, Dalagt 36, 113 24 Stockholm
T: (08) 313192
Founded: 1936
Focus: Business Admin *09880*

Forskningsrådsnämnden (FRN), Regeringsg 56, Box 7101, 103 87 Stockholm
T: (08) 4544100; Fax: 45444144
Founded: 1977
Focus: Sci
Periodical
Källa *09881*

Fylkingen / Society of Contemporary Music and Intermedia Art, Münchenbryggeriet, Söder Mälarstrand 27, 102 66 Stockholm
T: (08) 845443; Fax: 6693868
Founded: 1933; Members: 130
Focus: Music
Periodical
Hz: The Fylkingen Bulletin (quarterly) . . *09882*

Geografilärarnas Riksförening, c/o Gegrafiska Institutionen, Sölvegt 13, 223 62 Lund
T: (046) 108414; Fax: 108401
Founded: 1933; Members: 1150
Focus: Geography; Educ
Periodical
Geografiska Notiser (quarterly) *09883*

Geografiska Förbundet (GF), c/o Dept of Physical Geography, 106 91 Stockholm
T: (08) 340860
Members: 360
Focus: Geography *09884*

Geologiska Föreningen / Geological Society, c/o SGU, Box 670, 751 28 Uppsala
T: (018) 179276; E-Mail: gff@sgu.se; Fax: 516767
Founded: 1871; Members: 650
Pres: Jan Bergström; Gen Secr: Per Sandgren
Focus: Geology
Periodical
GFF (quarterly) *09885*

Göteborgs Läkarförening, Storgt 35, 411 38 Göteborg
T: (031) 119654
Focus: Med *09886*

Humanistisk-Samhällsvetenskapliga Forskningsrådet (HSFR) / Swedish Council for Research in the Humanities and Social Sciences, Box 7120, 103 87 Stockholm
T: (08) 4544310; Fax: 4544320
Founded: 1977; Members: 11
Pres: Prof. Olof Ruin; Gen Secr: Prof. Anders Jeffner
Focus: Humanities; Soc Sci
Periodicals
Brytpunkt
Tvärsnitt (quarterly) *09887*

Ingenjörsvetenskapsakademien (IVA), Grev Turegt 14, Box 5073, 102 42 Stockholm
T: (08) 7912900; Fax: 6115623
Founded: 1919; Members: 1030
Pres: Prof. Kurt Östlund
Focus: Eng
Periodicals
IVA-Newsletter (semi-annually)
IVA-Nytt (4-5 times annually) *09888*

International Association for the Evaluation of Educational Achievement (IEA), c/o Institutionen för Internationell Pedagogik, Universitet, 106 91 Stockholm
T: 154000
Founded: 1959; Members: 36
Focus: Educ
Periodical
IEA Newsletter (semi-annually) *09889*

International Association of Medical Laboratory Technologists (IAMLT), Adolf Fredriks Kyrkog 11, 111 37 Stockholm
T: (08)103031; Fax: 109061
Founded: 1954; Members: 200050
Pres: Marja-Kaarina Koskinen; Gen Secr: Margareta Haag
Focus: Med
Periodical
Med Tec International (semi-annually) . . *09890*

International Association of Sound and Audiovisual Archives (IASA), c/o Arkivet för Ljud och Bild, Box 24124, 104 51 Stockholm
T: (08) 7833710; E-Mail: sven.allerstrand@alb.se; Fax: 6631811
Founded: 1969; Members: 375
Pres: Sven Allerstrand; Gen Secr: Albrecht Häfner
Focus: Archives
Periodical
IASA Journal (semi-annually) *09891*

International Association on Mechanization of Field Experiments (IAMFE), Box 7033, 750 07 Uppsala
T: (018) 671000; Fax: 673529
Founded: 1964
Focus: Agri
Periodical
Proceeding of IAMFE Conferences . . . *09892*

International Law Association, Swedish Branch, Box 16050, 103 22 Stockholm
T: (08) 231200
Founded: 1922
Focus: Law; Int'l Relat *09893*

International Research Group on Wood Preservation (IRG), c/o IRG Secretariat, KTM, Brinellvägen 34, 114 86 Stockholm
T: (08) 101453; E-Mail: irg@sp.se; Fax: 108081
Founded: 1969; Members: 300
Pres: Prof. John N.R. Ruddick; Gen Secr: Jörán Jermer
Focus: Forestry
Periodicals
Annual Report (annually)
IRG Documents (more than 100 times annually) *09894*

International Society for Applied Ethnology, c/o Dept. of Animal Hygiene, Swedish University of Agricultural Sciences, POB 345, 53224 Skara
T: (0511) 67220; E-Mail: linda.keeling@hhyg.slu.se; Fax: 67204
Founded: 1966; Members: 500
Focus: Folklore *09895*

International Society for Fat Research (ISF), c/o AB Karlshamns Oljefabriker, 292 00 Karlshamn
T: (0454) 82000
Founded: 1954; Members: 1500
Focus: Food *09896*

Karolinska Förbundet, c/o Ulla Johanson, Kungsgt 77, 112 27 Stockholm
Founded: 1910; Members: 1000
Focus: Hist
Periodical
Karolinska Förbundets årsbok (annually) . *09897*

Kartografiska Sällskapet, c/o Lantmäteriverket, 801 82 Gävle
T: (026) 153000
Founded: 1908; Members: 1300
Focus: Cart
Periodical
Kartbladet (quarterly) *09898*

Kommittén för Petrokemisk Forskning och Utveckling, Box 5073, 161 05 Stockholm
Focus: Petrochem *09899*

Konsthistoriska Sällskapet, c/o Institutet för Konstvetenskap, Universitet, Box, 106 91 Stockholm 50
T: (08) 150160
Founded: 1914; Members: 550
Focus: Hist; Arts *09900*

Kungliga Akademien för de fria Konsterna, Fredsgt 12, Box 16317, 103 26 Stockholm
T: (08) 232945; Fax: 7905924
Founded: 1735; Members: 120
Pres: Henry Montgomery; Gen Secr: Bo Sylvan
Focus: Arts
Periodical
Exhibition Catalogues (annually) *09901*

Kungliga Fysiografiska Sällskapet i Lund, Stortorget 6, 222 23 Lund
T: (046) 132528; Fax: 104439
Founded: 1772; Members: 470
Pres: Prof. Birger Bergh; Gen Secr: Prof. Rolf Elofsson
Focus: Sci; Med; Eng
Periodical
Arsbok (bi-annually) *09902*

Kungliga Gustav Adolfs Akademien för Svensk Folkkultur (KGAA), Klostergt 2, 753 21 Uppsala
T: (018) 548783; E-Mail: gustav.adolfs.akademien@mbox200.swipnet.se; Fax: 548783
Founded: 1932; Members: 220
Pres: Prof. Carl Göran Andrae; Gen Secr: Prof. Lennart Elmevik
Focus: Ethnology
Periodicals
Ethnologia Scandinavica (annually)
Namn och Bygd (annually) *09903*

Kungliga Humanistiska Vetenskaps-Samfundet i Uppsala / Royal Society of the Humanities at Uppsala, Box 513, 751 20 Uppsala
Founded: 1889
Pres: Prof. Harry Lenhammar; Gen Secr: Prof. Bo Utas
Focus: Humanities
Periodicals
Arsbok
Skrifter: Acta
Yearbook *09904*

Kungliga Krigsvetenskapsakademien / Royal Swedish Academy of Military Sciences, 107 87 Stockholm
Founded: 1796; Members: 360
Focus: Military Sci
Periodical
Handlingar och Tidskrift (bi-monthly) . . *09905*

Kungliga Musikaliska Akademien (KMA), Blasieholmstorg 8, 111 48 Stockholm
T: (08) 6115720; Fax: 6118718
Founded: 1771; Members: 150
Pres: Anders R. Öhman; Gen Secr: Bengt Holmstrand
Focus: Music
Periodicals
Årsskrift (annually)
Musica Sveciae *09906*

Kungliga Samfundet för Utgivande av Handskrifter rörande Skandinaviens Historia, c/o National Archives, Box 12541, 102 29 Stockholm
Founded: 1821; Members: 100
Focus: Hist
Periodical
Kunglig Samfundets Handlinger (annually) *09907*

Kungliga Skogs- och Lantbruksakademien (KSLA), Drottninggt 95b, Box 6806, 113 86 Stockholm
T: (08) 7360900; Fax: 322130
Founded: 1811; Members: 270
Pres: Valfrid Paulsson; Gen Secr: Prof. Sven-Uno Skarp
Focus: Forestry; Agri
Periodicals
Acta Agriculturae Scandinavica (quarterly)
Kungl. Skogs- och Lantbruksakademiens Tidskrift (quarterly)
Scandinavian Journal of Forest Research (quarterly) *09908*

Kungliga Vetenskaps- och Vitterhets-Samhället i Göteborg / Royal Society of Arts and Science of Göteborg, Box 5096, 402 22 Göteborg
Founded: 1778; Members: 207
Gen Secr: Prof. Jan Hult
Focus: Arts; Sci

Periodicals
Årsbok (annually)
Botanica (irregularly)
Geophysica (irregularly)
Humaniora (irregularly)
Interdisciplinaria (irregularly)
Minnestal: Obituaries (annually)
Zoologica (irregularly) 09909

Kungliga Vetenskaps-Societeten i Uppsala, Larsgt 1, 753 10 Uppsala
T: (018) 131270
Founded: 1710; Members: 230
Pres: Prof. Marten Carlsson; Gen Secr: Prof. Lars-Olof Sundelöf
Focus: Sci
Periodicals
Arsbok (annually)
Nova Acta 09910

Kungliga Vetenskapsakademien (KVA) / Royal Swedish Academy of Sciences, Lilla Frescativ 4, Box 50005, 104 05 Stockholm
T: (08) 6739500; Fax: 155670
Founded: 1739; Members: 501
Pres: Prof. Kerstin Fredga; Gen Secr: Prof. Carl-Olof Jacobson
Focus: Sci
Periodicals
Acta Mathematica (semi-annually)
Acta Zoologica (quarterly)
Ambio (8 times annually)
Arkiv för Matematik (annually)
Chemica Scripta (quarterly)
Physica Scripta (semi-annually)
Zoologica Scripta (annually) 09911

Kungliga Vitterhets Historie och Antikvitets Akademien (KVHAA) / The Royal Academy of Letters, History and Antiquities, Villagt 3, Box 5622, 114 86 Stockholm
T: (08) 200936; Fax: 200981
Founded: 1753; Members: 130
Pres: Prof. I. Jonsson; Gen Secr: Prof. S. Helmfrid
Focus: Archeol; Hist; Lit
Periodical
Fornvännen (quarterly) 09912

Lärarförbundet, Segelbåtsvägen 15, Box 12229, 102 26 Stockholm
T: (08) 7376500; Fax: 6569415
Founded: 1991; Members: 195000
Focus: Educ 09913

Lärarnas Riksförbund (LR), Sveavägen 50, Box 3529, 103 69 Stockholm
T: (08) 6132700; Fax: 219136
Founded: 1884; Members: 55000
Focus: Educ
Periodical
Skolvärlden (32 times annually) 09914

Legitimerade Sjukgymnasters Riksförbund, Vasagt 48, Box 3196, 103 63 Stockholm
T: (08) 6969730
Founded: 1943; Members: 8200
Focus: Therapeutics
Periodical
Sjukgymnasten (monthly) 09915

Litteraturfrämjandet, Bellmansgt 30, 116 47 Stockholm
T: (08) 449175; Fax: 701646
Focus: Lit
Periodical
En bok för alla 09916

Lunds Botaniska Förening (LBF) / Botanical Society of Lund, c/o The Botanical Museum, Ö. Vallgt 18, 223 61 Lund
E-Mail: britt.snogerup@sysbot.lu.se; Fax: (046) 2224234
Founded: 1858; Members: 500
Pres: Prof. Sven Snogerup; Gen Secr: Alf Porenius
Focus: Botany
Periodical
Lungs Botaniska Förening Medlemsblad (2-3 times annually) 09917

Lunds Matematiska Sällskap, c/o Matematiska Institutionen, Box 118, 221 00 Lund
T: (046) 2224010
Founded: 1923; Members: 150
Focus: Math 09918

Matematiska Föreningen, c/o Dept of Mathematics, Uppsala University, Lägerhyddsvägen 2, Box 480, 751 06 Uppsala
T: (018) 183200; Fax: 183201
Founded: 1853; Members: 50
Focus: Math 09919

Medicinska Forskningsrådet / Medical Research Council, Box 6713, 113 85 Stockholm
Fax: (08) 6100777
Founded: 1945
Focus: Med 09920

Musikaliska Konstföreningen / Musical Art Association, Blasieholmstorg 8, 111 48 Stockholm
T: (08) 116920
Founded: 1859; Members: 150
Focus: Music 09921

Nationalekonomiska Föreningen / Swedish Economic Association, c/o Stockholm School of Economics, Box 6501, 113 83 Stockholm
T: (08) 7369207; Fax: 313207
Founded: 1877; Members: 1200
Pres: Prof. Lars Bergman; Gen Secr: Dr. Anders Paalzow
Focus: Econ
Periodical
Ekonomisk Debatt (8 times annually) . . 09922

Naturvetenskapliga Forskningsrådet / Swedish Natural Science Research Council, Box 7142, 103 87 Stockholm
T: (08) 4544200; E-Mail: nfr@nfr.se; Fax: 4544250
Founded: 1977
Pres: Arne Wittlöv; Gen Secr: Prof. Gunnar Öquist
Focus: Nat Sci
Periodicals
Annual Report (monthly)
Yearbook 09923

Nobelstiftelsen / Nobel Foundation, Nobel House, Sturegt 14, Box 5232, 102 45 Stockholm
T: (08) 6630920; Fax: 6603847
Founded: 1900
Focus: Sci 09924

Nordic Association of Applied Geophysics, University of Luleå, 951 87 Luleå
T: (0920) 91000
Founded: 1964; Members: 400
Focus: Geophys 09925

Nordisk Förening för Tillämpad Geofysik, c/o Geological Survey of Sweden, 104 05 Stockholm 50
Founded: 1964; Members: 174
Focus: Geophys 09926

Nordisk Genetikerforening, c/o Wallenberg Laboratory, Universitet, 104 05 Stockholm 50
Founded: 1960; Members: 282
Focus: Genetics 09927

Nordiska Afrikainstitutet / Scandinavian Institute of African Studies, Box 1703, 751 47 Uppsala
T: (018) 562200; E-Mail: nai@nai.uu.se; Fax: 695629
Founded: 1962
Pres: Lennart Wohlgemuth
Focus: Develop Areas
Periodicals
Africana
Annual Newsletter (annually)
Research Report
Seminar Proceedings 09928

Nordiska Institutet för Samhällsplanering / Nordic Institute for Studies in Urban and Regional Planning, Box 1658, 111 86 Stockholm
Fax: (08) 6115105
Founded: 1968
Focus: Urban Plan
Periodicals
Arsrapport (annually)
Grupparbeten
Rapporter 09929

Nordiska Samarbetskommittén för Internationell Politik, inklusive Konflikt- och Fredsforskning, Box 1253, 111 82 Stockholm
T: (08) 234060
Founded: 1966; Members: 5
Focus: Poli Sci; Military Sci
Periodicals
Cooperation and Conflict: Nordic Journal of International Politics
Newsletter: International Studies in the Nordic Countries 09930

Nordiska Samfundet för Latinamerika-forskning (NOSALF) / Scandinavian Association for Research on Latin America, c/o Latinamerika-Institutet, 106 91 Stockholm
T: (08) 162884
Focus: Int'l Relat
Periodicals
Nordic Journal of Latin American Studies
Studies on Latin America 09931

Oikos, Ecology Bldg, University of Lund, 223 62 Lund
T: (046) 2223791; E-Mail: oikos@ekol.lu.se; Fax: 2223790
Founded: 1949
Focus: Ecology
Periodicals
Ecography (bi-monthly)
Oikos (9 times annually) 09932

PEN Klubben, c/o Wahlström & Widstrand, Box 5587, 114 85 Stockholm
Founded: 1922; Members: 500
Pres: Monica Nagler; Gen Secr: Jonas Modig
Focus: Lit 09933

Riksföreningen för Lärarna i Moderna Språk (LMS), Box 41, 425 02 Hisings Kärra
T: (031) 571640; Fax: 572643
Founded: 1938; Members: 5200
Focus: Ling; Educ
Periodicals
LMS-Lingua (quarterly)
Moderna Språk (semi-annually) 09934

SACO Sveriges Akademikers Centralorganisation, Lilla Nygt 14, Box 2206, 103 15 Stockholm
T: (08) 6134800; Fax: 247701
Founded: 1975; Members: 407000
Pres: Anders Milton
Focus: Sci
Periodical
SACO Tidningen Akademiker (quarterly) . 09935

Samfundet De Nio, c/o Anders R. Öhman, Villagt 14, 114 32 Stockholm
T: (08) 4111542; Fax: 211915
Founded: 1913; Members: 9
Pres: I. Jonsson; Gen Secr: Anders R. Öhman
Focus: Lit 09936

Scandinavian Forum for Lipid Research and Technology, c/o SIK, Box 27022, 400 23 Göteborg
T: (031) 400120
Founded: 1969; Members: 400
Focus: Cell Biol & Cancer Res 09937

Scandinavian Orthopaedic Association, c/o Ortopedkliniken, Karolinska Sjukhuset, 104 01 Stockholm
Focus: Orthopedics 09938

Skogs- och Jordbrukets Forskningsråd (SJFR) / Council for Forestry and Agricultural Research, Box 6488, 113 82 Stockholm
T: (08) 7360910; Fax: 332915
Focus: Forestry; Agri
Periodical
SJFR Eltgottråd (5 times annually) . . . 09939

Skolledarna (SLF), Vasagt 48, Box 3266, 103 65 Stockholm
T: (08) 6969780; E-Mail: post@skolledarna.se; Fax: 249844
Founded: 1966; Members: 6300
Pres: Lars Stenbäck; Gen Secr: Björn Wickström
Focus: Educ
Periodical
Skolledaren (10 times annually) 09940

Standardiseringskommissionen i Sverige (SIS) / Swedish Standards Institution, Tegnergt 11, Box 3295, 103 66 Stockholm
T: (08) 6135200; E-Mail: standardis stockholm; Fax: 4117035
Founded: 1922; Members: 24
Focus: Standards
Periodicals
Månadens Standard (monthly)
Nyhetsbrev Europa Standardisering (bi-monthly)
Nytt om Niotusen (monthly)
Teknik & Standard (bi-monthly) 09941

Statens Kulturråd / Swedish Council for Cultural Affairs, Box 7843, 103 98 Stockholm
T: (08) 6797260; E-Mail: statens.kulturrad@se; Fax: 6111349
Founded: 1974
Pres: Maj-Britt Theoriu; Gen Secr: Göran Lannegren
Focus: Cultur Hist; Poli Sci
Periodical
Kulturrådet 09942

Statens Råd för Byggnadsforskning (BFR) / Swedish Council for Building Research, Sankt Göransgt 66, 112 98 Stockholm
T: (08) 6177300; Fax: 6537462
Founded: 1960
Focus: Archit; Energy
Periodicals
Documents: Research Reports in English (bi-monthly)
Newsletter (3 times annually)
Rapporter: Research Reports in Swedish (150 times annually)
Synopses (9 times annually) 09943

Statistika Föreningen / Statistical Society, c/o Statistika Centralbyran (Statistics Sweden), Statsistika Centralbyrån, 115 81 Stockholm
Founded: 1901; Members: 600
Focus: Stats 09944

Statsvetenskapliga Förbundet / Swedish Political Science Association, c/o Statsvetenskapliga Institutionen, Lundsuniversitet, Box 52, 221 00 Lund
T: (046) 2220000
Founded: 1971; Members: 300
Focus: Poli Sci
Periodical
Politologen (semi-annually) 09945

Strindbergssällskapet / The Strindberg Society, c/o C.O. Johansson, Danneliden 2, 439 34 Onsala
T: (0300) 61333
Founded: 1945; Members: 850
Focus: Lit
Periodical
Strindbergiana (annually) 09946

Studieförbundet Närnigsliv och Samhälle (SNS), Sköldungagt 2, 114 27 Stockholm
T: (08) 232520
Founded: 1948
Focus: Econ 09947

Styrelsen för Teknisk Utveckling / Swedish National Board for Technical Development, Liljeholmsvägen 32, Box 43200, 100 72 Stockholm
T: (08) 7754000
Focus: Eng
Periodicals
Energiteknik (bi-monthly)
Energy Technology (5 times annually)
New Swedish Technology (semi-annually)
Technik i Tiden (quarterly) 09948

Svensk Flyghistorisk Förening / Swedish Aviation Historical Society, Box 308, 101 26 Stockholm
Focus: Hist; Aero
Periodical
Svensk Flyghistorisk Tidskrift (bi-monthly) 09949

Svensk Förening för Anatomi, c/o Dept of Anatomy, University of Umeå, 901 87 Umeå
Fax: (090) 165480
Founded: 1969; Members: 50
Focus: Anat 09950

Svensk Förening för Anestesi och Intensivvård (SAFI) / Swedish Society for Anaesthesia and Intensive Care, c/o Dept of Anaesthesiology, Linköping University Hospital, 581 85 Linköping
Fax: (013) 222836
Founded: 1946; Members: 1220
Focus: Anesthetics 09951

Svensk Förening för Gastroenterologi och Gastrointestinal Endoskopi (SFGGE), c/o Dept of Surgery, Helsingborg Hospital, 251 87 Helsingborg
Fax: (042) 242731
Founded: 1954; Members: 500
Focus: Gastroenter 09952

Svensk Förening for Radiofysik, c/o Dept of Medical Physics, Danderyd Hospital, 182 03 Danderyd
Focus: Physics 09953

Svensk Kirurgisk Förening (SKF) / Swedish Surgical Society, c/o Kirurgiska Kliniken, Akademiska Sjukhuset, 751 85 Uppsala
T: (08) 7292000
Founded: 1905; Members: 1400
Focus: Surgery
Periodical
Svensk Kirurgi (quarterly) 09954

Svensk Otolaryngologisk Förening, c/o Sabbatsbergs Sjukhus, Box 6401, 113 82 Stockholm
Members: 350
Focus: Otorhinolaryngology 09955

Svenska Akademien, Box 2118, 103 13 Stockholm
T: (08) 106524; E-Mail: sekretariat@SvenskaAkademien.se; Fax: 244225
Founded: 1786; Members: 18
Focus: Ling; Lit
Periodical
Svenska Akademiens Handlingar (annually) 09956

Svenska Akademiska Rektorskonferensen, c/o Uppsala University, Box 256, 751 05 Uppsala
T: (018) 182500; Fax: 111853
Founded: 1966; Members: 24
Focus: Educ 09957

Svenska Aktuarieföreningen / Swedish Insurance Federation, Box 1436, 111 84 Stockholm
T: (08) 7837150
Founded: 1904; Members: 228
Pres: Harry Wide; Gen Secr: Roland Svensk
Focus: Insurance
Periodical
Scandinavian Actuarial Journal (semi-annually) 09958

Svenska Akustiska Sällskapet (SAS) / Acoustical Society of Sweden, Box 276, 401 24 Göteborg
Founded: 1945; Members: 275
Focus: Acoustics 09959

Svenska Arkeologiska Samfundet / Swedish Archaeological Society, Box 5405, 114 84 Stockholm
T: (08) 7839000
Founded: 1947
Pres: Dr. Henrik Klackenberg; Gen Secr: Inga Ullén
Focus: Archeol
Periodical
Current Swedish Archaeology (annually) . 09960

Svenska Arkitekters Riksförbund (SAR) / National Association of Swedish Architects, Norrlandsgt 18, 111 43 Stockholm
T: (08) 240230
Founded: 1936; Members: 3600
Focus: Archit
Periodical
Arkitekttidningen (16 times annually) . . 09961

Svenska Arkivsamfundet / The Swedish Archival Association, c/o Riksarkivet, Fyrverkarbacken 13-17, Box 12541, 10229 Stockholm
T: (08) 7376350; Fax: 7376474
Founded: 1952; Members: 650
Pres: Anna-Christina Ulfsparre; Gen Secr: Petra Dornbusch
Focus: Archives
Periodical
Arkiv, samhälle och forskning: Svenska arkiv samfundets skriftserie (3 times annually) . 09962

Svenska Astronomiska Sällskapet, c/o Stockholms Observatorium, 133 36 Saltsjöbaden
T: (08) 164477164463; Fax: 7174719
Founded: 1919; Members: 1250
Pres: Hans Rickman; Gen Secr: Dan Kiselman
Focus: Astronomy

Periodical
Astronomisk Tidsskrift (quarterly) 09963

Svenska Bergmannaföreningen (SBF), Box 5283, 102 46 Stockholm
T: (08) 6639905
Founded: 1941; Members: 1800
Focus: Mining
Periodical
Bergsmannen med JKA (bi-monthly) . . 09964

Svenska Bibliotekariesamfundet (SBS), c/o Kerstin Assarsson-Rizzi, Vitterhetsakademiens Bibliotek, Box 5405, 114 84 Stockholm
T: (08) 7839325; E-Mail: kaz@rashm.se; Fax: 6633528
Founded: 1921; Members: 1100
Pres: Kerstin Assarsson-Rizzi
Focus: Libraries & Bk Sci
Periodical
Bibliotekariesamfundet meddelar (quarterly) 09965

Svenska Botaniska Föreningen, c/o Naturhistoriska Riksmuseet, Box 50007, 104 05 Stockholm
Founded: 1907; Members: 2800
Focus: Botany
Periodical
Svensk Botanisk Tidskrift (bi-monthly) . . 09966

Svenska Brandförsvarsföreningen (SBF), 115 87 Stockholm
T: (08) 7837200; E-Mail: bibliotek.sbt@stockholm.mail.telia.com; Fax: 6612284
Founded: 1919; Members: 2200
Pres: Lars Erik Jernberg
Focus: Safety
Periodical
Brand & Räddning (10 times annually) . 09967

Svenska Färgeritekniska Riksförbundet (SFR), c/o Arne Wärnegard, Valasgt 16, 412 74 Göteborg
Founded: 1924; Members: 363
Focus: Eng 09968

Svenska Föreningen för Ljuskultur, Box 5512, 114 85 Stockholm
T: (08) 675834
Founded: 1926; Members: 39
Focus: Electric Eng 09969

Svenska Föreningen för Medicinsk Teknik och Fysik / Swedish Society for Medical Engineering and Medical Physics, c/o Dept of Biomedical Engineering, University Hospital, 901 85 Umea
Fax: (090) 136717
Founded: 1956; Members: 932
Focus: Med; Physiology; Eng 09970

Svenska Föreningen för Mikrobiologi / Swedish Society for Microbiology, c/o Dept of Microbiological Ecology, Lund University, Helgonavägen 5, 223 62 Lund
T: (046) 109614; Fax: 104158
Founded: 1964; Members: 400
Focus: Microbio 09971

Svenska Försäkringsföreningen / Swedish Insurance Society, Slöjdgt 9, 111 57 Stockholm
T: (08) 242860; Fax: 241320
Founded: 1875; Members: 3000
Pres: Björn Wolrath; Gen Secr: Anders Kleverman
Focus: Insurance
Periodicals
Scandinavian Insurance Quarterly (quarterly)
Swedish Insurance Yearbook (annually) . 09972

Svenska Fornminnesföreningen, c/o Statens Historika Museum, Box 5405, 114 84 Stockholm
T: (08) 7839311; Fax: 7839195
Founded: 1871; Members: 350
Pres: Prof. Jan Svanberg
Focus: Archeol; Archit 09973

Svenska Fornskriftsällskapet (SFS), c/o Kungliga Biblioteket, Box 5039, 102 41 Stockholm
T: (08) 241040
Founded: 1843; Members: 230
Focus: Lit 09974

Svenska Fysikersamfundet / Swedish Physical Society, c/o Svedberg Laboratory, Uppsala University, Box 533, 751 21 Uppsala
T: (018) 183112; Fax: 183833
Founded: 1920; Members: 1000
Focus: Physics
Periodicals
Fysik-Aktuellt (quarterly)
Kosmos (annually) 09975

Svenska Geofysiska Föreningen (SGF), c/o Swedish Meteorological and Hydrological Institute, 601 76 Norrköping
T: (011) 108000
Founded: 1920; Members: 210
Focus: Geophys
Periodical
Tellus 09976

Svenska Geotekniska Föreningen (SGF) / Swedish Geotechnical Society, 581 93 Linköping
T: (013) 115100; Fax: 131696
Founded: 1950; Members: 700
Focus: Geology; Eng
Periodical
SGF Rapport (5 times annually) 09977

Svenska Gymnastikläraresällskapet (SGS), Björnstigen 13, 165 71 Hässelby
T: (08) 899701; Fax: 7393084
Founded: 1884; Members: 4000
Pres: Ingrid Eliasson
Focus: Sports
Periodical
Tidskrift i Gymnastik & Idrott (10 times annually) 09978

Svenska Historiska Föreningen, Box 5405, 114 84 Stockholm
T: (08) 7832502; Fax: 7832515
Founded: 1881; Members: 2200
Pres: Jarl Torbacke; Gen Secr: Pär Frohnert
Focus: Hist
Periodical
Historisk Tidskrift (quarterly) 09979

Svenska Kemistsamfundet, Wallingt 24, 111 24 Stockholm
T: (08) 4115260; E-Mail: agneta@chemsoc.se; Fax: 106678
Founded: 1883; Members: 4300
Gen Secr: Agneta Sjögren
Focus: Chem
Periodicals
Acta Chemica Scandinavica (10 times annually)
Kemisk Tidskrift/Kemivärlden (monthly) . . 09980

Svenska Klassikerförbundet, c/o Institutionen för Klassiska Språk, Stockholms Universitet, Universitetsvägen 10e, 106 91 Stockholm
T: (08) 163465; Fax: 164307
Founded: 1935; Members: 490
Pres: Gunhild Vidén; Gen Secr: Peter Ståhl
Focus: Hist; Ling 09981

Svenska Kriminalistföreningen, c/o Ministry of Justice, Box, 103 30 Stockholm
T: (08) 7634625
Founded: 1911; Members: 450
Focus: Criminology
Periodical
Nordisk Tidskrift for Kriminalvidenskab (quarterly) 09982

Svenska Kyltekniska Föreningen / The Swedish Society of Refrigeration, Box 4113, 175 04 Järfälla
T: (08) 58026135; Fax: 58081793
Founded: 1942; Members: 1800
Pres: Tage Magnusson; Gen Secr: Urban Flyckt
Focus: Eng 09983

Svenska Kyrkohistoriska Föreningen, c/o Teologiska Institutionen, Box 1604, 751 46 Uppsala
Founded: 1900; Members: 337
Focus: Hist; Rel & Theol 09984

Svenska Läkaresällskapet (SLS), Klara Östra Kyrkogt 10, Box 738, 101 35 Stockholm
T: (08) 243350
Founded: 1807; Members: 13000
Focus: Med
Periodical
Svenska Läkaresällskapets Handlingar: Hygiea (irregularly) 09985

Svenska Linné-Sällskapet / Swedish Linnaeus Society, Box 1530, 751 45 Uppsala
T: (018) 136540
Founded: 1917; Members: 600
Focus: Nat Sci; Sci
Periodical
Yearbook of the Swedish Linnaeus Society (bi-annually) 09986

Svenska Litteratursällskapet, c/o Litteraturvetenskapliga Institutionen, Slottet, 752 37 Uppsala
T: (018) 182946
Founded: 1880; Members: 400
Pres: Prof. Bengt Landgren
Focus: Lit
Periodical
Samlaren: Tidskrift för svensk litteraturvetenskaplig forskning (annually) 09987

Svenska Livsmedelstekniska Föreningen, Katarinavägen 20, 116 45 Stockholm
T: (08) 7145045; Fax: 408045
Focus: Eng; Food
Periodical
Livsmedelsteknik (9 times annually) . . . 09988

Svenska Matematikersamfundet, c/o Dept of Mathematics, University of Lulea, 971 87 Lulea
T: (0920) 91000; E-Mail: sms@sm.luth.se; Fax: 91073
Founded: 1950; Members: 540
Pres: Prof. Lars-Erik Persson; Gen Secr: Yuanji Cheng
Focus: Math
Periodicals
Mathematica Scandinavia
Nordisk Matematisk Tidskrift 09989

Svenska Museiföreningen / The Swedish Museums Association, Linnégt 89, Box 27151, 102 52 Stockholm
T: (08) 7832960; Fax: 6606034
Founded: 1906; Members: 1350
Focus: Arts
Periodical
Svenska Museer: Debate and Information on Museum Policies and Museology (quarterly) 09990

Svenska Nationalkomittén för Geologi, c/o Prof. Dr. Tryggve Troedsson, Dept of Forest Soils, Box 7001, 750 07 Uppsala
Founded: 1959; Members: 12
Focus: Geology 09991

Svenska Nationalkommittén för Kristallografi, Box 50005, 104 05 Stockholm
T: (08) 6739500; Fax: 155670
Focus: Mineralogy 09992

Svenska Naturskyddsföreningen (SNF) / The Swedish Society for Nature Conservation, Box 4625, 116 91 Stockholm
T: (08) 7026500; Fax: 7020855
Founded: 1909; Members: 200000
Focus: Ecology
Periodical
Sveriges Natur (7 times annually) . . . 09993

Svenska Österbottens Litteraturförening / Swedish Österbottens Literary Assocoiation, c/o Olof Haegerstrand, Fasanvaegen 4, 775 00 Krylbo
Focus: Lit
Periodical
Horisont 09994

Svenska Ogonläkareföreningen, c/o Dept of Ophthalmology, Karolinska Hospital, 104 01 Stockholm
Focus: Ophthal 09995

Svenska Operationsanalysföreningen (SORA), Box 20, 104 50 Stockholm
Founded: 1959; Members: 600
Focus: Computer & Info Sci 09996

Svenska Psykoanalytiska Föreningen, Västerlånggt 60, 111 29 Stockholm
T: (08) 108095; E-Mail: svpsyko@algonet.se; Fax: 108095
Founded: 1934; Members: 76
Focus: Psychoan 09997

Svenska Sällskapet för Antropologi och Geografi (SSAG), c/o Naturgeografiska Institutionen, Stockholms Universitet, 106 91 Stockholm
Fax: (08) 164818
Founded: 1880; Members: 1100
Focus: Anthro; Geography
Periodicals
Atlas of Sweden
Geografiska Annaler
Ymer 09998

Svenska Samfundet för Musikforskning / Swedish Society for Musicology, Box 7448, 103 91 Stockholm
T: (08) 6112058
Founded: 1919; Members: 330
Pres: Gunnar Ternhag
Focus: Music
Periodicals
Monumenta Musicae Svecicae
Svensk Tidskrift för Musikforskning (annually) 09999

Svenska Växtgeografiska Sällskapet, c/o Växtbiologiska Institutionen, Box 559, 751 22 Uppsala
T: (018) 139955
Founded: 1923; Members: 430
Focus: Botany; Bio
Periodicals
Acta Phytogeographica Suecica (annually)
Växtekologiska Studier (irregularly) . . . 10000

Svenska Yrketsutbildningsföreningen, Box 172, 771 01 Ludvika
Focus: Educ 10001

Sveriges Allmänna Biblioteksförening (SAB), Box 3127, 103 62 Stockholm
T: (08) 7230082
Founded: 1915; Members: 2500
Focus: Libraries & Bk Sci
Periodical
Biblioteksbladet 10002

Sveriges Allmänna Konstförening (S.A.K.), Stora Nygt 5, Box 2151, 103 14 Stockholm
T: (08) 104676/77
Founded: 1832; Members: 22000
Focus: Arts
Periodical
Art publications (annually) 10003

Sveriges Arkivtjänstemäns Förening, c/o DIK-Förbundet, Box 760, 131 24 Nacka
T: (08) 4662400; E-Mail: dik@akademikerhuset.se; Fax: 4662424
Founded: 1936; Members: 700
Pres: Per Matsson
Focus: Archives
Periodical
DIK-forum (18 times annually) 10004

Sveriges Civilingenjörsförbund (CF) / The Swedish Association of Graduate Engineers, Malmskillnadsgt 48, Box 1419, 111 84 Stockholm
T: (08) 142000
Founded: 1861; Members: 45000
Focus: Civil Eng
Periodicals
Civilingenjören (monthly)
Ny Teknik (weekly) 10005

Sveriges Författarförbund / Swedish Writers' Union, Drottninggt 88b, 111 36 Stockholm
T: (08) 7912280; Fax: 7912285
Founded: 1893; Members: 2000
Focus: Lit
Periodical
Författaren 10006

Sveriges Gemmologiska Riksförening, c/o Jonas Gevers, Box 19121, 104 32 Stockholm
Fax: (08) 8207317
Founded: 1947
Focus: Mineralogy 10007

Sveriges Geologiska Undersökning (SGU), Villavägen 18, 751 28 Uppsala
T: (018) 179000
Founded: 1858; Members: 267
Focus: Geology 10008

Sveriges Museimannaförbund / Swedish Association of Museum Curators, DIK-förbundet, Box 760, 131 24 Nacka
T: (08) 4662400; E-Mail: dik@akademikerhuset.se; Fax: 4662424
Members: 5200
Pres: Olof Stroh
Focus: Arts
Periodical
DIK-forum (18 times annually) 10009

Sveriges Praktiserande Läkares Förening, Villagt 5, Box 5610, 114 86 Stockholm
T: (08) 224740
Focus: Med 10010

Sveriges Rationaliseringsförbund (SRF), Box 4324, 102 67 Stockholm
T: (08) 249225; Fax: 6433061
Founded: 1956; Members: 257
Focus: Business Admin
Periodical
SRF-Information (quarterly) 10011

Sveriges Tandläkarförbund (STF) / The Swedish Dental Association, Nybrogt 53, Box 5843, 102 48 Stockholm
T: (08) 6661500; E-Mail: info@tandlakarforbundet.se; Fax: 6625842
Founded: 1908; Members: 11600
Pres: Dr.Leif Leisnert; Gen Secr: Gunnar Luthman
Focus: Dent
Periodicals
Swedish Dental Journal (bi-monthly)
Tandläkartidningen: The Journal of the S.D.A. (every third week) 10012

Sveriges Vetenskapliga Specialbiblioteks Förening (SVSF), c/o Utrikesdepartementels Bibliotek, Box 16121, 103 23 Stockholm
Founded: 1945; Members: 200
Focus: Libraries & Bk Sci 10013

Sveriges Veterinärförbund (SVF), Kungsholms Hamnplan 7, Box 12709, 112 94 Stockholm
T: (08) 6542480; Fax: 6517082
Founded: 1860; Members: 2200
Pres: Erik Kjellgren; Gen Secr: Aase Tronstad
Focus: Vet Med
Periodical
Svensk Veterinärtidning (15 times annually) 10014

Svetstekniska Föreningen (SVF), Box 5073, 102 42 Stockholm
T: (08) 220760; Fax: 808) 6799404
Founded: 1941; Members: 3200
Focus: Eng
Periodical
Svetsen (bi-monthly) 10015

Swedish Society for Dermatology and Venerology, c/o Svenska Läkaresällskapet, Klara Östra Kyrkogt 10, 101 27 Stockholm
T: (08) 243350; E-Mail: thomas.andersson@hud.us.lio.se; Fax: 222562
Founded: 1901; Members: 480
Pres: Prof. Inger Rosdahl; Gen Secr: Dr. Thomas Andersson
Focus: Derm; Venereology 10016

Teknikkonsulterna (SKIF) / Swedish Association of Consulting Engineers, Kungsholmstorg 1, Box 22076, 104 22 Stockholm
Fax: (08) 6502972
Founded: 1910; Members: 200
Focus: Eng
Periodical
Konsulttidningen (quarterly) 10017

Tekniska Litteratursällskapet / Swedish Society for Technical Documentation, Box 55580, 102 04 Stockholm
T: (08) 6782320; E-Mail: kansliet@tls.se; Fax: 6782301
Members: 1350
Pres: Lise-Lotte Lindskog; Gen Secr: Katarina Wahl
Focus: Lit; Doc
Periodical
Tidskrift för Documentation (quarterly) . . 10018

Tekniska Samfundet i Göteborg, Viktor Rydbergsgt 14, 411 32 Göteborg
Focus: Eng 10019

Utrikespolitiska Institutet (U.I.), Box 1253, 111 82 Stockholm
T: (08) 234060; E-Mail: siia@ui.se; Fax: 201049
Founded: 1938
Pres: Leif Leifland; Gen Secr: Anders Mellbourn
Focus: Poli Sci

Periodicals
Internationella studier (5 times annually)
Världspolitikens dagsfrågor (monthly) . . 10020

Switzerland

Ala - Schweizerische Gesellschaft für Vogelkunde und Vogelschutz, Rüttenenweg 63, 4313 Möhlin
T: (061) 8511650; Fax: 8511650
Founded: 1909
Pres: Dr. Luc Schifferli; Gen Secr: Renate Horváth
Focus: Ornithology
Periodical
Der Ornithologische Beobachter (quarterly) 10021

Alkohol- und Suchtfachleute, Schweiz. Fachverband, Burgmatte 23, 6208 Oberkirch
T: (041) 9219844; Fax: 9219844
Focus: Soc Sci
Periodical
Sozialarbeit & Suchtprobleme (10 times annually) 10022

Allgemeine Anthroposophische Gesellschaft, c/o Goetheanum, 4143 Dornach
T: (061) 7014242
Founded: 1923
Focus: Philos 10023

Allgemeine Geschichtforschende Gesellschaft der Schweiz (AGGS), Länggassstr 49, 3000 Bern 9
T: (031) 6318093
Founded: 1841; Members: 1500
Focus: Hist
Periodical
Schweizerische Zeitschrift für Geschichte (quarterly) 10024

Antiquarische Gesellschaft in Zürich (AGZ), c/o Staatsarchiv, Postfach, 8057 Zürich
T: (01) 3633606; Fax: 3633606, 3641815
Founded: 1832; Members: 520
Pres: Dr. Jürg E. Schneider
Focus: Hist 10025

Arbeitsgemeinschaft der Hauswirtschaftslehrerinnen-Seminarien der Schweiz, Teuchelweg 42, 7000 Chur
T: (081) 2524631
Focus: Educ; Home Econ 10026

Arbeitsgemeinschaft für elementare Bildung, Postfach, 8048 Zürich
T: (01) 7304145; Fax: 7434080
Focus: Educ 10027

Arbeitsgemeinschaft Solar 91, 8033 Zürich, Postfach 2272
T: (01)2619873; Fax: 2518168
Founded: 1990
Gen Secr: Gallus Codonau
Focus: Energy 10028

Arbeitsgemeinschaft Solar 91, Sonneggstr 29, 8006 Zürich
T: (01) 2619873; Fax: 2518168
Focus: Energy 10029

Arbeitsgemeinschaft Wirtschaft und Gesellschaft (AWG), Neugasse 55, 9000 Sankt Gallen
T: (071) 2222353
Focus: Econ; Soc Sci 10030

Arbeitskreis Deutsch als Fremdsprache in der Schweiz, Postfach 365, 8046 Zürich
T: (01) 2412233
Focus: Educ 10031

Arzneimittelkommission der Schweizer Apotheker, Postfach 5247, 3001 Bern
T: (031) 9785825; Fax: 9785859
Focus: Pharmacol 10032

Association des Bibliothèques Internationales / Association of International Libraries, c/o International Federation of Red Cross and Red Crescent Societies, 1211 Genève 19
T: (022) 7304432; E-Mail: stoddart@ifrc.org; Fax: 7330395
Founded: 1963
Pres: Linda Stoddard
Focus: Libraries & Bk Sci 10033

Association des Ecoles Internationales / International Schools Association, CIC Case 20, 1211 Genève 20
T: (022) 7336717; Fax: 7347082
Founded: 1951; Members: 85
Focus: Educ
Periodical
ISA Bulletin (3 times annually) 10034

Association des Instituts d'Etudes Européennes (AIEE) / Association of Institutes of European Studies, c/o European Cultural Centre, 122 Rue de Lausanne, 1200 Genève
Founded: 1951
Focus: Cultur Hist 10035

Association des Sociétés Suisses des Professeurs de Langues Vivantes, Imfangring 10, 6005 Luzern
T: (041) 448771
Focus: Educ; Ling 10036

Association d'Etudes Baha'ies - Europe Francophone, c/o Centre Baha'i, 24 Rte de Malagnou, 1208 Genève
E-Mail: dalai@geneva.bic.org
Focus: Rel & Theol 10037

Association d'Histoire et de Science Politique (HISPO), Eichholzstr 96, 3084 Wabern
T: (031) 9610257
Founded: 1977; Members: 165
Focus: Hist; Poli Sci 10038

Association for Computational Linguistics-Europe, c/o IDSIA, Corso Elvezia 36, 6900 Lugano
T: (091) 228881
Focus: Computer & Info Sci 10039

Association for the International Collective Management of Audiovisual Works (AGICOA), 25 Rte de Ferney, 1202 Genève
T: (022) 7344580; Fax: 7344762
Founded: 1981; Members: 16
Focus: Law 10040

Association Internationale de la Securité Sociale, 4 Rue des Morillons, CP 1, 1211 Genève 22
T: (022) 7996617; E-Mail: AISS@ilo.org; Fax: 7998509
Founded: 1927; Members: 340
Focus: Sociology
Periodicals
International Social Security Review (quarterly)
Internationale Revue für soziale Sicherheit (quarterly)
Revista Internacional de Seguridad Social (quarterly)
Revue Internationale de Sécurité Sociale (quarterly)
Weltbibliographie der sozialen Sicherheit (semi-annually) 10041

Association Internationale des Directeurs d'Ecoles Hôtelières, c/o Ecole Hôtelière de Lausanne, 1000 Lausanne 25
T: (021) 7851111
Founded: 1955
Focus: Adult Educ
Periodical
EUHOFA International Journal (semi-annually) 10042

Association Internationale pour l'Histoire Contemporaine de l'Europe / International Association for Contemporary History of Europe, 132 Rue de Lausanne, 1211 Genève
Founded: 1968
Focus: Hist
Periodical
Bulletin de Liaison et d'Information . . . 10043

Association of European Universities / Association des Universités Européennes, 10 Rue du Conseil Général, 1211 Genève 4
T: (022) 3292644, 3292251; E-Mail: cre@uni2a.unige.ch; Fax: 3292821
Founded: 1959; Members: 520
Focus: Educ
Periodical
CRE-action (irregularly) 10044

Association of International Consultants on Human Rights, CP 529, 1211 Genève
T: (022) 7364452; Fax: 7364863
Founded: 1983
Focus: Law 10045

Association Olympique Internationale pour la Recherche Médico-Sportive (AIORMS), c/o COI, Château de Vidy, 1007 Lausanne
T: (021) 253271; Fax: 241552
Focus: Med 10046

Association Suisse de Droit Aérien et Spatial (ASDA), 18 Rue du Marché, 1204 Genève
T: (022) 286522
Founded: 1954; Members: 220
Focus: Law
Periodical
ASDA SVLR (3 times annually) 10047

Association Suisse des Ecoles Hôtelières, c/o Centre International de Glion, 1823 Glion-sur-Montreux
T: (021) 9634841; Fax: 9631384
Focus: Adult Educ 10048

Association Suisse des Professeurs de Français / Verein schweizerischer Französischlehrerinnen und Französischlehrer, Hagwiesenstr 11, 3122 Kehrsatz
T: (031) 9616055; Fax: 9616055
Members: 520
Pres: Urs Tschopp; Gen Secr: Elisabeth Kleiner
Focus: Ling; Lit; Educ
Periodical
Lettre Circulaire (quarterly) 10049

BBS - Verband der Bibliotheken und Bibliothekare/innen Schweiz (VSB), Effingerstr 35, 3008 Bern
T: (031) 3824240; E-Mail: bbs@bbs.ch; Fax: 3824648
Founded: 1897; Members: 2066
Focus: Libraries & Bk Sci
Periodical
ARBIDO-B; ARBIDO-R (8 times annually) 10050

Bernische Botanische Gesellschaft, Altenbergrain 21, 3013 Bern
T: (031) 654911; Fax: 422059
Founded: 1918; Members: 380
Pres: Dr. Klaus Ammann; Gen Secr: Christine Keller
Focus: Botany
Periodical
Sitzungsberichte (annually) 10051

Berufsbildungsverband der Versicherungswirtschaft (VBV), Bubenbergpl 10, Postfach 8625, 3001 Bern
T: (031) 3111722; Fax: 3117756
Focus: Insurance
Periodical
VBV/AFA Info-Bulletin (semi-annually) . . 10052

Budapest Union for the International Recognition of the Deposit of Microorganisms for the Purposes of Patent Procedure, c/o WIPO, 34 Chemin des Colombettes, CP 18, 1211 Genève 20
T: (022) 3389111; E-Mail: wipo-mail@wipo.int; Fax: 7335428
Founded: 1977
Focus: Law 10053

Bund für vereinfachte rechtschreibung, Postfach, 8022 Zürich
T: (01) 3724540; Fax: 3724540
Founded: 1924; Members: 1500
Focus: Ling
Periodical
Rechtschreibung: Mitteilungen des Bundes für vereinfachte rechtschreibung (3 times annually) 10054

Bund Schweizer Architekten (BSA), Keltenstr 45, 8044 Zürich
T: (01) 2522852
Founded: 1908; Members: 545
Focus: Archit
Periodical
Werk, Bauen und Wohnen (10 times annually) 10055

Bureau International de la Paix / International Peace Bureau, 41 Rue de Zürich, 1201 Genève
T: (022) 316429
Founded: 1891; Members: 79
Focus: Poli Sci; Prom Peace
Periodicals
Geneva Monitor-Disarmement
IPB Geneva News 10056

Bureau International d'Education - International Bureau of Education (BIE) / International Bureau of Education, CP 199, 1211 Genève 20
T: (022) 7981455; E-Mail: unesco.ibe.library@unesco.org; http://www.unicc.org/ibe; Fax: 7981486
Founded: 1925; Members: 185
Focus: Educ
Periodicals
Bulletin du Bureau International d'Education: Bulletin of the International Bureau of Education (quarterly)
Educational Innovation and Education (quarterly) 10057

Campagne d'Education Civique Européenne, c/o European Cultural Centre, 122 Rue de Lausanne, 1211 Genève 21
T: (022) 7322803
Founded: 1960
Focus: Educ 10058

Centre Européen de Réflexion et d'Etude en Thermodynamique (CERET), c/o Polytechnique de Lausanne, 1015 Lausanne
T: (021) 6933506
Focus: Physics 10059

Centre for the Independence of Judges and Lawyers (CIJL), 109 Rte de Chêne, BP 45, 1224 Genève
T: (022) 493545; Fax: 493145
Founded: 1978
Focus: Law
Periodical
CIJL Bulletin (semi-annually) 10060

Centre Suisse de Documentation en Matière d'Enseignement et d'Education (CESDOC) / Schweizerische Dokumentationsstelle für Schul- und Bildungsfragen, 15 Rte des Morillons, 1218 Grand-Saconnex
T: (022) 7984531; Fax: 7883173
Founded: 1962
Focus: Doc; Educ
Periodicals
Bibliographie Pédagogique Suisse (annually)
Bulletin: Mitteilungen (quarterly) 10061

Centre Suisse Romand des PEN-Clubs, 22 Blvd des Promenades, 1227 Carouge
Focus: Lit 10062

Christlicher Lehrer- und Erzieherverein der Schweiz, Zimmertalstr 2, 6060 Sarnen
T: (041) 6606420
Focus: Educ
Periodical
Schweizer Schule (bi-weekly) 10063

CIP International Study and Research Center in Psychosynteresis, CP 937, 1001 Lausanne
T: (032) 936674; Fax: 936740
Founded: 1984
Focus: Psychoan 10064

Collaborative International Pesticides Analytical Council (CIPAC), c/o Eidgenössische Forschungsanstalt für Obst, Wein und Gartenbau, 8820 Wädenswil
T: (01) 7836111
Founded: 1957
Focus: Agri 10065

Collegium Romanicum (CR), c/o Section d'Italien, Faculté des Lettres, Université de Lausanne, 1015 Lausanne
Founded: 1947; Members: 200
Pres: Prof. Dr. Jean-Jacques Marchand; Gen Secr: Dr. Denis Fachard
Focus: Ling; Lit
Periodicals
Versants (semi-annually)
Vox Romanica (annually) 10066

Commission Electrotechnique Internationale (CEI) / International Electrotechnical Commission, 3 Rue de Varembé, 1211 Genève 20
T: (022) 7340150; Fax: 7333843
Founded: 1906
Focus: Electric Eng
Periodicals
IEC Bulletin (bi-monthly)
IEC Yearbook (annually) 10067

Commission Médicale Chrétienne (CMC) / Christliche Gesundheitskommission / Christian Medical Commission, 150 Rte de Ferney, CP 2100, 1211 Genève 2
T: (022) 916111; Fax: 7910361
Founded: 1967
Focus: Public Health
Periodical
CMC Contact Newsletter (bi-monthly) . . 10068

Conférence intercantonale des chefs des départements de l'instruction publique de la Suisse romande et du Tessin, CP 610, 1000 Lausanne 17 Riponne
T: (021) 3128459; Fax: 3123719
Focus: Educ 10069

Conference of European Statisticians, c/o Statistical Div, ECE, Palais des Nations, 1211 Genève 10
T: (022) 9174144; E-Mail: John.kelly@unece.org; Fax: 9170040
Founded: 1953; Members: 55
Gen Secr: John Kelly
Focus: Stats
Periodical
Statistical Journal (quarterly) 10070

Conférence romande et tessinoise des chefs d'établissements secondaires (CROTCES), c/o Collège des Terreaux, CP 357, 2001 Neuchâtel
T: (032) 7244132; Fax: 7213864
Focus: Educ 10071

Conseil des Organisations Internationales des Sciences Médicales / Council for International Organizations of Medical Sciences, c/o World Health Organization, Via Appia, 1211 Genève 27
T: (022) 913406; Fax: 910746
Founded: 1949; Members: 60
Focus: Med
Periodicals
Calendar of Congresses of Medical Sciences (annually)
CIOMS Organization and Activities/Directory of Members (bi-annually) 10072

Conseil International sur les Problèmes de l'Alcoolisme et des Toxicomanies (CIPAT) / International Council on Alcohol and Addictions, CP 189, 1001 Lausanne
T: (021) 209865; Fax: 209817
Founded: 1907
Focus: Toxicology
Periodical
ICAA News (quarterly) 10073

Consultative Council for Postal Studies (CCPS), c/o UPU, Weltpoststr 4, 3000 Bern 15
T: (031) 432211; Fax: 432210
Founded: 1957
Focus: Eng 10074

Cooperative Programme für Monitoring and Evaluation of the Long-range Transmission of Air Pollutants in Europe/Convention on Long-range Transboundary Air Pollution (EMEP), c/o CEE, Palais des Nations, 1211 Genève 10
T: (022) 9172354; E-Mail: lars.nordberg@unece.org; Fax: 9070107
Founded: 1979; Members: 37 Parties in the ECE region (42 Partres to the Convention)
Focus: Ecology 10075

Deutschschweizerischer Sprachverein (DSSV), Kutscherweg 3, 3047 Bremgarten
T: (031) 234019
Focus: Ling
Periodical
Sprachspiegel (bi-monthly) 10076

Deutschschweizerisches PEN-Zentrum, Postfach 403, 3000 Bern 14
T: (031) 3724085
Founded: 1932; Members: 200
Pres: Beat Brechbühl; Gen Secr: B. Traber
Focus: Lit
Periodical
PEN-Brief (irregularly) 10077

Development Innovations and Networks, 3 Rue de Varembé, 1211 Genève 20
T: (022) 7341716; Fax: 7400011
Founded: 1980; Members: 159
Focus: Develop Areas
Periodical
IRED Forum (quarterly) 10078

Digital Equipment Computer Users Society (Decus Europe), CP 510, Petit Lancy, 1213 Genève 1
Focus: Computer & Info Sci 10079

Direktorenkonferenz der Ingenieurschulen (Abend-HTL) der Schweiz, 20 Av de Sévelin, Ecole d'ingenieurs, 1004 Lausanne
T: (021) 6261501; Fax: 6261505
Focus: Educ; Eng 10080

Direktorenkonferenz der Ingenieurschulen der Schweiz (DIS), Postfach 805, 8401 Winterthur
T: (052) 2677171; E-Mail: mr@TWI.CH; Fax: 2677395
Founded: 1986
Pres: Prof. Christian Kunze; Gen Secr: Prof. Adolf Müller
Focus: Eng 10081

Direktorenkonferenz der Ingenieurschulen der Schweiz (DIS), Postfach 805, 8401 Winterthur
T: (052) 2677204; Fax: 2677395
Focus: Educ; Eng 10082

Direktorenkonferenz der Ingenieurschulen (Tages-HTL) der Schweiz, c/o Ecole d'Ing., 47 Rte du Rawyl, 1950 Sion
Focus: Educ; Eng 10083

Direktorenkonferenz der landwirtschaftlichen Ingenieurschulen (HTL), c/o Bundesamt für Landwirtschaft EVD, Mattenhofstr 5, 3003 Bern
T: (031) 3222517
Focus: Educ; Eng; Agri 10084

Ecological and Toxicological Association of the Dyestuffs Manufacturing Industry (ETAD), Clarastr 4, 4005 Basel
T: (061) 68122; Fax: 6914278
Founded: 1974; Members: 32
Focus: Ecology; Toxicology 10085

Ecumenical Institute Bossey, Château de Bossey, 1298 Céligny
T: (022) 9609333; Fax: 7760169
Founded: 1946
Focus: Rel & Theol
Periodicals
Bossey Newsletter
Ministerial Formation 10086

Eidgenössischer Musikverband, c/o Josef Meier, 6252 Dagmersellen
T: (062) 861450; Fax: 861445
Members: 87000
Pres: Josef Meier
Focus: Music
Periodical
Schweizerische Blasmusikzeitung (bi-monthly)
. . . . 10087

ErgotherapeutInnen-Verband Schweiz, Stauffacherstr 96, Postfach, 8026 Zürich
T: (01) 2425464; Fax: 2915440
Founded: 1956; Members: 1400
Pres: Franziska van Oosterhout; Gen Secr: Erica Kuster
Focus: Therapeutics
Periodical
ERGOTHERAPIE (monthly) 10088

Euro-International Committee for Concrete / Comité Euro-International du Béton, c/o Dept de Génie Civil, Ecole Polytechnique de Lausanne, CP 88, 1015 Lausanne
T: (021) 6932747
Founded: 1953
Focus: Materials Sci 10089

Europäische Gesellschaft für Schriftpsychologie und Schriftexpertise e.V., Postfach 88, 8041 Zürich
T: (01) 4816218; Fax: 4816288
Founded: 1972; Members: 678
Pres: Rudolf Känzig; Gen Secr: Ingrid Salzwedel
Focus: Graphology; Psych
Periodical
EGS-Bulletin (semi-annually) 10090

Europäische Organisation für Qualität / European Organization for Quality, Postfach 5032, 3001 Bern
T: (031) 216166; Fax: 216951
Founded: 1957; Members: 25
Focus: Business Admin
Periodical
EOQ Quality (quarterly) 10091

Europäisches Zentrum für die Bildung im Versicherungswesen, Kirchlistr 2, 9010 Sankt Gallen
T: (071) 251515; Fax: 251392
Focus: Adult Educ; Insurance 10092

EUROPAN SUISSE – Verein zur Förderung des exemplarischen Wohnungsbaus, c/o IREC/DA/EPFL, CP 555, 1001 Lausanne
T: (021) 6934206/08; Fax: 6933840
Focus: Civil Eng 10093

European Association for Cardio-Thoracic Surgery (AECTS), c/o Clinic for Cardiovascular Surgery, University Hospital, 8091 Zürich
T: (01) 2553298
Founded: 1986
Focus: Surgery
Periodical
European Journal of Cardio-Thoracic Surgery (monthly) 10094

European Association for Computer Graphics / Association Européenne pour les Graphiques sur l'Ordinateur, CP 16, 1288 Aire-la-Ville
E-Mail: secretary@eg.org; Fax: (022) 7570318
Founded: 1980
Pres: W. Terry Hewitt; Gen Secr: Carlo Vandoni
Focus: Computer & Info Sci 10095

European Association for Signal Processing (EURASIP), CP 134, 1000 Lausanne 13
T: (021) 6932626; Fax: 6932603
Founded: 1978
Focus: Computer & Info Sci
Periodicals
EURASIP Newsletter (3 times annually)
Image Communication (quarterly)
Speech Communication (quarterly) . . . 10096

European Association for the Advancement of Radiation Curing by UV, EB and Laser Beams, Pérolles 24, 1700 Fribourg
T: (037) 226465; Fax: 226545
Founded: 1988; Members: 266
Focus: Radiology 10097

European Association of Development Research and Training / Association Européenne des Instituts de Recherche et de Formation en Matière de Développement, 10 Rue Richemont, CP 272, 1211 Genève 21
T: (022) 7314648; Fax: 7385797
Founded: 1975; Members: 200
Focus: Sci
Periodicals
EADI Newsletter (2-3 times annually)
European Journal of Development Research (semi-annually) 10098

European Association of Music Conservatories, Academies and High Schools, c/o Konservatorium für Musik und Theater, Kramgasse 36, 3011 Bern
T: (031) 226221; Fax: 212053
Founded: 1953; Members: 99
Focus: Music 10099

European Association of Music Festivals (EAMF) / Association Européenne des Festivals de Musique, 122 Rue de Lausanne, 1202 Genève
T: (022) 7322803; Fax: 7384012
Founded: 1951; Members: 53
Focus: Music 10100

European Association of Nuclear Medicine, c/o Service de Médecine Nucléaire – CHUV, Bugnon 46, 1011 Lausanne
T: (021) 3144346/7; E-Mail: Angelika.BischofDeleloye@chuv.hospvd.ch; Fax: 3144349
Founded: 1988
Pres: Dr. A. Bischof Delaloye; Gen Secr: Dr. M. Bourguignon
Focus: Nucl Med 10101

European Centre for Insurance Education and Training, Kirchlistr 2, 9010 Sankt Gallen
T: (071) 251515; Fax: 251392
Founded: 1957
Focus: Insurance; Educ 10102

European Chemoreception Research Organization (ECRO), c/o Universität Zürich-Irchel, Winterthurerstr 190, 8057 Zürich
T: (01) 2575413; Fax: 2574004
Founded: 1970
Focus: Chem 10103

European Council of Coloproctology, c/o Policlinique de Chirurgie, Hôpital Cantonal de Genève, 24 Rue Micheli-du-Crest, 1211 Genève 4
T: (022) 7327902
Focus: Surgery 10104

European Cytoskeletal Club, c/o Dépt de Pathologie, Faculté de Médecine CMU, Université de Genève, 1 Rue Michel Servet, 1211 Genève 4
Founded: 1980
Focus: Pathology 10105

European Nuclear Society (E.N.S.), Belpstr 23, Postfach 5032, 3001 Bern
T: (031) 3206111; E-Mail: ens@to.aey.ch; Fax: 3824466
Founded: 1975; Members: 20000
Pres: Ger Kupers; Gen Secr: Dr. Konrad Hädener
Focus: Nucl Res
Periodical
Nuclear Europe Worldscan (bi-monthly) . 10106

European Photochemistry Association, c/o Institut Phys. Chemie, Klingelbergstr 80, 4056 Basel
T: (061) 2673842; Fax: 2673855
Founded: 1968; Members: 980
Pres: Prof. Dr. Jakob Wirz
Focus: Chem 10107

European Society for Pediatric Nephrology (ESPN), c/o Universitäts-Kinderklinik, Steinwiesstr 75, 8032 Zürich
Founded: 1967; Members: 230
Focus: Pediatrics
Periodical
Abstracts of Communications 10108

Fachgruppe Carosserie- und Fahrzeugtechnik des STV, Kienbergweg 6, 4450 Sissach
T: (061) 983507
Focus: Eng; Auto Eng 10109

Fachgruppe für Arbeiten im Ausland des SIA (FAA), Selnaustr 16, Postfach, 8039 Zürich
T: (01) 2831515; Fax: 2016335
Focus: Eng; Archit 10110

Fachgruppe für Architektur des SIA, Selnaustr 16, 8039 Zürich
T: (01) 2831515; Fax: 2016335
Members: 710
Focus: Archit 10111

Fachgruppe für Betriebstechnik des STV, Im Geissacker 24, 8404 Winterthur
T: (052) 814832
Focus: Eng 10112

Fachgruppe für Brückenbau und Hochbau des SIA (FBH), Selnaustr 16, 8039 Zürich
T: (01) 2831515; E-Mail: sia@sia-ch; Fax: 2016335
Members: 1000
Focus: Civil Eng 10113

Fachgruppe für das Management im Bauwesen des SIA (FMB), Selnaustr 16, 8039 Zürich
T: (01) 2011570; Fax: 2016335
Focus: Business Admin 10114

Fachgruppe für Elektronik des STV, CP 958, 1001 Lausanne
T: (021) 391151
Focus: Electronic Eng 10115

Fachgruppe für industrielles Bauen des SIA, Selnaustr 16, 8039 Zürich
T: (01) 2831515; Fax: 2016335
Founded: 1970; Members: 203
Focus: Civil Eng 10116

Fachgruppe für Raumplanung und Umwelt des SIA, Selnaustr 16, 8039 Zürich
T: (01) 2831515; Fax: 2016395
Members: 300
Focus: Urban Plan; Ecology 10117

Fachgruppe für Untertagbau des SIA (FGU), Selnaustr 16, Postfach, 8039 Zürich
T: (01) 2831515; E-Mail: sia@sia.ch; Fax: 2016335
Members: 380 Einzel-, 170 Kollektiv-
Focus: Civil Eng
Periodical
FGU-Dokumentationsbulletin (quarterly) . . 10118

Fachgruppe für Verfahrenstechnik des SIA, c/o Hoffmann-La Roche, 4002 Basel
Focus: Eng 10119

Fachgruppe für Vermessung und Kulturtechnik (Deutsch-Schweiz) des STV, Weingartenstr, 8501 Weiningen
T: (054) 75765
Focus: Surveying 10120

Fédération des Ecoles Privées de la Suisse Romande, La Combe, 1180 Rolle
T: 752727
Focus: Educ 10121

Fédération des Sociétés d'Agriculture de la Suisse Romande (F.S.A.S.R.), 3 Av des Jordils, CP 186, 1000 Lausanne 6
T: (021) 6177477
Founded: 1881; Members: 28000
Focus: Agri
Periodical
Revue Suisse de Viticulture, d'Arboriculture et d'Horticulture (bi-monthly) 10122

Fédération Internationale des Associations d'Etudes Classiques (FIEC) / International Federation of the Societies of Classical Studies, 6 Chemin Aux-Folies, 1293 Bellevue
T: (022) 7742656
Founded: 1948; Members: 78
Focus: Hist; Ling; Lit; Archeol
Periodical
Année philologique (annually) 10123

Fédération Internationale des Femmes Diplômées des Universités (FIFDU) / International Federation of University Women, 37 Quai Wilson, 1201 Genève
T: (022) 7312380; Fax: 780440
Founded: 1919; Members: 230000
Focus: Sci
Periodical
IFUW Newsletter (bi-monthly) 10124

Fédération Internationale des Sociétés de Philosophie (FISP), c/o Séminaire de Philosophie, Université, Miséricorde, 1700 Fribourg
T: (026) 4242669; E-Mail: philosophie@unifr.ch; Fax: 3009786
Founded: 1948; Members: 118
Focus: Philos 10125

Fédération Suisse des Ecoles Privées, 40 Rue des Vollandes, 1211 Genève 6
T: (022) 355706
Focus: Educ 10126

Förderverein Schweizerisches Institut für Kunstwissenschaft, Zollikerstr 32, 8032 Zürich
T: (01) 3885151; Fax: 3815250
Focus: Arts 10127

Forschungsgemeinschaft für Nationalökonomie, Dufourstr 48, 9000 Sankt Gallen
T: (071) 2242300; Fax: 2242646
Focus: Econ 10128

Forum für verantwortbare Anwendung der Wissenschaft (Basel), Postfach, 4112 Flüth
T: (061) 7312272
Focus: Sci 10129

Geographisch-Ethnographische Gesellschaft Zürich (GEGZ), c/o Geographisches Institut, Universität Zürich-Irchel, Winterthurerstr 190, 8057 Zürich
T: (01) 2575111
Founded: 1889; Members: 520
Focus: Geography
Periodical
Geographica Helvetica (quarterly) 10130

Geographisch-Ethnologische Gesellschaft Basel (GEG), Klingelbergstr 16, 4056 Basel
T: (061) 2673660
Founded: 1923; Members: 530
Pres: Dr. Rudolf Marr
Focus: Ethnology; Geography
Periodicals
Basler Beiträge zur Geographie (irregularly)
Physiogeographica: Basler Beiträge zur Physiogeographie (irregularly)
Regio Basiliensis: Basler Zeitschrift für Geographie/Revue de Géographie de Bâle (3 times annually) 10131

Geographische Gesellschaft Bern, Hallerstr 12, 3012 Bern
T: (031) 6318869; E-Mail: Wiesmann@giub.unibe.ch; Fax: 6318544
Founded: 1873; Members: 600
Pres: Dr. U. Wiesmann
Focus: Geography
Periodicals
Berner Geographische Mitteilungen (annually)
Jahrbuch (bi-annually) 10132

Gesellschaft der Freunde alter Musikinstrumente, Bündtenweg 62, 4102 Binningen
T: (061) 4218363
Founded: 1953; Members: 170
Pres: Georg F. Senn
Focus: Music
Periodical
Glareana (semi-annually) 10133

Gesellschaft für Arzneipflanzenforschung e.V., c/o Pharmazeutisches Institut, ETH Zürich, ETH-Zentrum, 8092 Zürich
T: (01) 2563166
Focus: Pharmacol; Therapeutics 10134

Gesellschaft für das Schweizerische Landesmuseum, Museumstr 2, 8023 Zürich
T: (01) 2211010
Focus: Arts 10135

Gesellschaft für deutsche Sprache und Literatur in Zürich, c/o Deutsches Seminar der Universität, Schönberggasse 9, 8001 Zürich
T: (01) 6342571; E-Mail: uguenthe@ds.unizh.ch; Fax: 6344905
Founded: 1894; Members: 200
Pres: Dr. U. Günther
Focus: Ling; Lit 10136

Gesellschaft für die Volksmusik in der Schweiz (GVS), Bellariastr 82, 8038 Zürich
T: (01) 4856666
Focus: Music 10137

Gesellschaft für Forschung auf biophysikalischen Grenzgebieten (GFBG), Postfach 1347, 4133 Pratteln 1
T: (061) 8210280; Fax: 8210280
Focus: Biophys 10138

Gesellschaft für Führungspraxis und Personalentwicklung (GfP), Feldgüetliweg 69, 8706 Feldmeilen
T: (01) 9234466; Fax: 9236480
Focus: Business Admin 10139

Gesellschaft für Schweizerische Kunstgeschichte (GSK), Pavillonweg 2, 3001 Bern
T: (031) 3014281; Fax: 3016991
Founded: 1880; Members: 9500
Pres: Stefan Biffiger
Focus: Hist; Arts
Periodical
Unsere Kunstdenkmäler/Nos Monuments d'Art et d'Histoire/I nostri Monumenti Storici (quarterly)
. . . . 10140

Gesellschaft für Versuchstierkunde (GV), c/o Dr. U. Märki, BRL Ltd, Wölferstr 4, 4414 Füllinsdorf
Focus: Zoology 10141

Gesellschaft Pro Vindonissa, c/o Vindonissa-Museum, 5200 Brugg
T: (056) 4412184; Fax: 4624815
Pres: Hansjörg Brem
Focus: Archeol
Periodical
Jahresbericht der Gesellschaft Pro Vindonissa (annually) 10142

Gesellschaft schweizerischer Amtsärzte, c/o Bundesamt für Gesundheitswesen, Postfach, 3001 Bern
T: (031) 3229508
Focus: Med 10143

Gesellschaft Schweizerischer bildender Künstlerinnen (GSBK), Benkenstr 4, 4054 Basel
T: (061) 2818134
Focus: Arts 10144

Gesellschaft Schweizerischer Maler, Bildhauer und Architekten (GSMBA) / Société des Peintres, Sculpteurs et Architectes Suisses, Kirchpl 9, 4132 Muttenz
T: (061) 617480
Founded: 1865; Members: 1600
Focus: Archit
Periodical
Schweizer Kunst (quarterly) 10145

Gesellschaft Schweizerischer Tierärzte (GST), Länggassstr 8, Postfach 6324, 3001 Bern
T: (031) 3025500; Fax: 3028841
Founded: 1813; Members: 2000
Focus: Vet Med
Periodicals
GST-Bulletin (10 times annually)
Schweizer Archiv für Tierheilkunde (monthly)
. . . . 10146

Gesellschaft Schweizerischer Zeichenlehrerinnen und Zeichenlehrer, Vordermatten, 9410 Heidem
T: (071) (913138
Members: 600
Pres: Kurt Kleinert; Gen Secr: Edi Furrer
Focus: Educ; Arts 10147

Gesellschaft zur Förderung der industrieorientierten Forschung, Technoparkstr 1, 8005 Zürich
T: (01) 4451501/04; Fax: 4451499
Focus: Econ 10148

Gottfried keller-Gesellschaft Zürich, c/o Zentralbibliothek, Zähringerpl 6, 8025 Zürich
T: (01) 2683100; Fax: 2683290
Focus: Lit 10149

Groupement Romand du Marketing, 2 Av Agassiz, 1001 Lausanne
T: (021) 3197111
Founded: 1945; Members: 135
Focus: Marketing 10150

Gruppe Olten, Schweizer Autorengruppe, Industriestr 23, 8500 Frauenfeld
T: (052) 7288933; Fax: 7288932
Focus: Lit
Periodical
Mitteilungsblatt (3-5 times annually) . . . 10151

Heimverband Schweiz, Seegartenstr 2, Postfach, 8034 Zürich
T: (01) 3834948; Fax: 3835077
Founded: 1844
Focus: Sociology
Periodical
Fachzeitschrift Heim 10152

Hindemith-Institut, c/o Hr. G. Schubert, Direktor, Eschersheimer Landstr 29-39, 60322 Frankfurt/M.
T: (069) 5970362; E-Mail: @hindermith.de;
Fax: 5963104
Founded: 1974
Focus: Music
Periodical
Hindemith-Jahrbuch (annually) 10153

Historisch-Antiquarischer Verein Heiden, 9410 Heiden
Founded: 1874; Members: 140
Focus: Hist 10154

Historische und Antiquarische Gesellschaft zu Basel (HAG), c/o Universitätsbibliothek, Schönbeinstr 18-20, 4056 Basel
T: (061) 2673141; Fax: 2673103
Founded: 1836; Members: 600
Focus: Hist
Periodical
Basler Zeitschrift für Geschichte und Altertumskunde (annually) 10155

Historischer Verein des Kantons Bern, c/o Stadt- und Universitätsbibliothek, Münstergasse 61, 3000 Bern 7
Founded: 1847
Focus: Hist
Periodicals
Archiv des Historischen Vereins des Kantons Bern (annually)
Berner Zeitschrift für Geschichte und Heimatkunde (quarterly) 10156

ICOM – Conseil International des Musées, Comité National Suisse, Baselstr 7, 4500 Solothurn
T: (032) 6236710; Fax: 6238583
Focus: Arts 10157

Information Systems Co-ordination Committee (ISCC), Palais des Nations, 1211 Genève 10
T: (022) 7988591; Fax: 339879
Founded: 1983; Members: 35
Focus: Computer & Info Sci
Periodical
ACCIS Newsletter (bi-monthly) 10158

Ingenieurinnen und Ingenieure für Umweltschutz, 3000 Bern
T: (031) 3026500; Fax: 3026618
Focus: Ecology; Eng 10159

Institut de Recherche et de Documentation Pédagogique (IRDP), 43-45 Faubourg de l'Hôpital, CP 54, 2007 Neuchâtel 7
T: (032) 8896970; E-Mail: jacques.weiss@irdp.unine.ch; Fax: 8896971
Founded: 1969
Focus: Doc; Educ
Periodicals
Coordination
Report 10160

Institut International de Psychologie et de Psychothérapie Charles Baudouin, 25 Chemin des Rannaux, 1296 Coppet
T: (022) 7761839; E-Mail: 101560.504@compuserve.com
Founded: 1924; Members: 94
Focus: Psych; Therapeutics 10161

Institut National Genevois, 1 Promenade du Pin, 1204 Genève
Founded: 1853; Members: 850
Focus: Nat Sci; Humanities; Sci
Periodicals
Bulletin
Mémoires 10162

Institut Suisse de Recherches Expérimentales sur le Cancer / Schweizerisches Institut für Experimentelle Krebsforschung / Swiss Institute for Experimental Cancer Research, 155 Chemin des Boveresses, 1066 Epalinges
T: (021) 6925858; E-Mail: isrec@unil.ch;
Fax: 6526933
Founded: 1964; Members: 170
Focus: Cell Biol & Cancer Res
Periodical
International Journal of Cancer (monthly) 10163

Interessengemeinschaft der botanischen Gärten der Schweiz, c/o Jardin botanique de l'Université, 58 Pertuis du Sault, 2000 Neuchâtel
T: (032) 7182350
Focus: Botany 10164

Interessengemeinschaft für die Volkskultur in der Schweiz und dem Fürstentum Liechtenstein, Hummelwaldstr 38, 8645 Jona
T: (055) 2124331; Fax: 2124339
Focus: Cultur Hist 10165

International Association for the Study of Insurance Economics, 18 Chemin Rieu, 1208 Genève
T: (022) 3470938; Fax: 3472078
Founded: 1973
Focus: Insurance
Periodical
The Geneva Papers on Risk and Insurance (quarterly) 10166

International Board on Books for Young People (IBBY), Nonnenweg 12, Postfach, 4003 Basel
T: (061) 2722917; E-Mail: ibby@eye.ch;
Fax: 2722757
Founded: 1953
Pres: Carmen Diana Dearden; Gen Secr: Leena Maissen
Focus: Lit
Periodical
Bookbird: World of Children's Books (quarterly)
. . . . 10167

International Computing Centre (ICC), Palais des Nations, 1211 Genève 10
T: (022) 7913201; Fax: 7919746
Founded: 1971
Focus: Computer & Info Sci 10168

International Federation for Psychotherapy, c/o Prof. Dr. Edgar Heim, Murtenstr 21, 3010 Bern
Founded: 1934; Members: 4000
Focus: Psych; Therapeutics 10169

International Federation of Surgical Colleges, c/o Prof. S. William A. Gunn, La Panetière, 1279 Bogis-Bossey
T: (022) 7762161; Fax: 7766417
Founded: 1958 k711 Terblanche, Prof. John; Members: 42
Gen Secr: Prof. S. William Gunn
Focus: Educ; Surgery 10170

International Industrial Relations Association (IIRA), c/o International Labour Office, 1211 Genève 22
Fax: (022) 7884709
Founded: 1966; Members: 1500
Focus: Econ; Business Admin
Periodicals
IIRA Bulletin (quarterly)
IIRA Membership Directory (bi-annually)
Proceedings of IIRA World Congresses . 10171

International Institute for Management Development (IMD), CP 915, 1001 Lausanne
Founded: 1946
Focus: Business Admin 10172

International Organization for Biological Control of Noxious Animals and Plants, c/o Swiss Federal Research Station for Agronomy, Reckenholzstr 191-211, 8046 Zürich
Fax: (01) 3777201
Founded: 1956
Focus: Bio
Periodical
Entomophaga (quarterly) 10173

International Organization for Standardization, 1 Rue de Varembé, CP 56, 1211 Genève 20
T: (022) 7490111; Fax: 7333430
Founded: 1947; Members: 123
Pres: Liew Mun Leong; Gen Secr: Dr. Lawrence D. Eicher
Focus: Standards
Periodicals
ISO 9000 News (bi-monthly)
ISO Bulletin (monthly) 10174

International Public Relations Association (IPRA), CP 2100, 1211 Genève 2
T: (022) 7910550; Fax: 7880336
Founded: 1955; Members: 1000
Focus: Advert
Periodicals
Gold Papers
IPRA Newsletter (irregularly)
IPRA Review (quarterly)
Members Manual 10175

International Society for General Relativity and Gravitation, c/o Institute of Theoretical Physics, Sidlerstr 5, 3012 Bern
Founded: 1974; Members: 350
Focus: Physics
Periodical
General Relativity and Gravitation (monthly)
. . . . 10176

International Society of Internal Medicine (ISIM), c/o Regionalspital, 4900 Langenthal
T: (062) 9163102; E-Mail: r.streuli@rsl.ch;
Fax: 9164155
Founded: 1948; Members: 3000
Pres: Prof. A. Igata; Gen Secr: Prof. A. Rolf
Focus: Intern Med
Periodical
ISIM-Bulletin (quarterly) 10177

International Solarcar Federation, Postfach 2272, 8033 Zürich
T: (01) 2619873; Fax: 2518168
Founded: 1987
Pres: Howard G. Wilson; Gen Secr: Gallus Codonau
Focus: Auto Eng 10178

International Telecommunication Union (ITU), Pl des Nations, 1211 Genève 20
T: (022) 7305111; Fax: 7337256
Founded: 1865; Members: 172
Focus: Comm 10179

International Union for Conservation of Nature and Natural Resources (IUCN) / World Conservation Union, 28 Rue Mauverney, 1196 Gland
T: (022) 9990001; E-Mail: mail@hq.iucn.org; http://www.iucn.org; Fax: 9990002
Founded: 1948; Members: 895
Focus: Ecology
Periodicals
Interact (semi-annually)
IUCN Bulletin (quarterly) 10180

Internationale Architekten-Union, Sektion Schweiz, c/o SIA, Selnaustr 16, Postfach, 8039 Zürich
T: (01) 2831515; Fax: 2016335
Focus: Archit 10181

Internationale Föderation der Vereine der Textilchemiker und Coloristen (IFVTCC) / International Federation of Associations of Textile Chemists and Colourists, Hollenweg 8a, 4153 Reinach
Founded: 1930; Members: 11
Focus: Chem; Textiles 10182

Internationale Gesellschaft für Musikwissenschaft (IGMW) / Société Internationale de Musicologie / International Musicological Society, Postfach 1561, 4001 Basel
Founded: 1927; Members: 1400
Focus: Music
Periodical
Acta Musicologica (semi-annually) . . . 10183

Internationale Gewässerschutzkommission für den Bodensee (IGKB), c/o BUWAL – Bundesam für Umwelt, Wald und Landschaft, 3003 Bern
T: (031) 3226968; Fax: 3230371
Founded: 1960; Members: 42
Pres: Dr. H.U. Schweizer; Gen Secr: Dr. B. Sollberger
Focus: Ecology 10184

Internationale Union Demokratisch-Sozialistischer Erzieher (IUDSE), Amslergut, 5103 Wildegg
T: (064) 531562
Founded: 1951; Members: 18
Focus: Educ 10185

Internationale Vereinigung für Brückenbau und Hochbau (IVBH) (IABSE) / Association Internationale des Ponts et Charpentes (AIPC) / International Association for Bridge and Structural Engineering, c/o ETH-Hönggerberg, 8093 Zürich
T: (01) 6332647; E-Mail: IABSE Zürich;
Fax: 3712131
Founded: 1929; Members: 3900
Pres: Klaus Ostenfeld; Gen Secr: Alain Golay
Focus: Civil Eng
Periodicals
IABSE Congress Report
IABSE Report
Structural Engineering Documents
Structural Engineering International (quarterly)
. . . . 10186

Internationale Vereinigung für gewerblichen Rechtsschutz (IVfgR) / Association Internationale pour la Protection de la Propriété Industrielle / International Association for the Protection of Industrial Property, Bleicherweg 58, 8027 Zürich
T: (01) 2041212; Fax: 2027502
Founded: 1897; Members: 6980
Focus: Law
Periodical
AIPPI Newsletter (3-7 times annually) . . 10187

Internationale Vereinigung für Natürliche Wirtschaftsordnung (INWO) / Ligue Internationale pour l'Ordre Economique Naturel / International Association for a Natural Economic Order, Postfach, 5001 Aarau
Focus: Econ
Periodical
Evolution (11 times annually) 10188

Internationale Vereinigung für Saatgutprüfung / Association Internationale d'Essais de Semences / International Seed Testing Association, Postfach 412, 8046 Zürich
Founded: 1924; Members: 180
Pres: Dr. Kevin Boyce; Gen Secr: Prof. A. Lovato
Focus: Agri
Periodicals
ISTA News Bulletin (quarterly)
Seed Science and Technology (3 times annually)
. . . . 10189

Internationale Vereinigung für Walsertum (IVfW), Mattinistr 26, 3900 Brig
T: (027) 9233976
Focus: Hist 10190

Internationale Vereinigung gegen den Lärm, Hirschenpl 7, 6004 Luzern
T: (041) 4103013; Fax: 4109093
Founded: 1959
Pres: Karel Novotny; Gen Secr: Dr. Willy Aecherli
Focus: Ecology
Periodical
Informationsbulletin (semi-annually) . . . 10191

Internationale Vereinigung wissenschaftlicher Fremdenverkehrsexperten, Varnbüelstr 19, 9000 Sankt Gallen
T: (071) 2242530; Fax: 2242536
Founded: 1949; Members: 380
Focus: Econ; Ecology; Soc Sci
Periodical
Zeitschrift für Fremdenverkehr (quarterly) . 10192

Internationale Veterinäranatomische Nomenklatur-Kommission (IVANK) / International Committee on Veterinary Anatomical Nomenclature, Winterthurerstr 260, 8057 Zürich
Founded: 1957; Members: 23
Gen Secr: Dr. Josef Frewein
Focus: Vet Med 10193

Internationales Kali-Institut / International Potash Institute, Schneidergasse 27, Postfach 1609, 4001 Basel
T: (061) 2612922; Fax: 2612925
Founded: 1952
Focus: Agri
Periodicals
International Fertilizer Correspondent/Corresponsal Internacional Agrícola (bi-monthly)
Kali-Briefe/Potash Review/Revue de la Potassa/Revista de la Potasa (monthly) . 10194

Internationales Komitee Giessereitechnischer Vereinigungen, Konradstr 9, Postfach 7190, 8023 Zürich
T: (01) 2719090; Fax: 2719292
Founded: 1927
Focus: Metallurgy 10195

Junge Esperantisten der Schweiz (JES), CP 32, 2416 Les Brenets
T: (032) 9143078
Focus: Ling 10196

Kantonalverband der Zürcher Psychologinnen und Psycologen (ZüPP), Beckhammer 9, 8057 Zürich, Postfach 114
T: (01) 3641210
Focus: Psych 10197

Katholische Arbeitsgemeinschaft für Erwachsenenbildung der Schweiz und Liechtensteins (KAGEB), Hirschgraben 13, 6002 Luzern, Postfach 2069
T: (041) 2105055; Fax: 2105056
Focus: Adult Educ 10198

Kommission zur Förderung der wissenschaftlichen Forschung, Monbijoustr 28, Postfach 7023, 3001 Bern
T: (031) 3222143; Fax: 3222115
Founded: 1944; Members: 23
Pres: Prof. Dr. H. Sieber; Gen Secr: Dr. Peter Kuentz
Focus: Sci 10199

Konferenz der Direktoren der Schweizerischen Konservatorien und Musikhochschulen, Tössertobelstr 1, 8400 Winterthur
T: (052) 2133623
Focus: Educ; Music 10200

Konferenz Katholischer Schulen und Erziehungsinstitutionen der Schweiz (KKSE), Hirschgraben 13, 6002 Luzern, Postfach 2069
T: (041) 2105055; Fax: 2105056
Focus: Educ 10201

Konferenz Schweizerischer Gymnasialrektoren, c/o App. A. Rh. Kantonsschule, 9043 Trogen
T: (971) 3436111; E-Mail: kstrogenverw@access.ch; Fax: 3436161
Founded: 1912
Focus: Educ
Periodical
Colloquium (bi-monthly) 10202

Konferenz Schweizerischer Handelsschulkektoren, c/o Bündener Kantonschule, Arosastr 2, 7000 Chur
T: (081) 2522939; Fax: 2533463
Focus: Educ 10203

Konferenz Schweizerischer Handelsschulrektoren, Arosastr 2, 7000 Chur
T: (081) 2522939; Fax: 2533463
Founded: 1929; Members: 80
Focus: Adult Educ 10204

Konferenz Schweizerischer Oberstufenlehrkräfte (KSO), Marktgasse 5, 4460 Gelterkinden
T: (061) 9511143, 9514054
Focus: Educ 10205

Kunstverein Sankt Gallen, Museumstr 32, 9000 Sankt Gallen
T: (071) 253355
Founded: 1827; Members: 2700
Focus: Arts 10206

Laboratoire Européen pour la Physique des Particules, Meyrin, 1211 Genève 23
T: (022) 7676111; Fax: 7676555
Founded: 1954
Focus: Nucl Res
Periodicals
CERN Courier/Courrier (7 times annually)
Courrier CERN / CERN Courier (10 times annually) 10207

LCH – Dachverband Schweizerischer Lehrerinnen und Lehrer, Ringstr 54, Postfach 189, 8057 Zürich
T: (01) 3118303; Fax: 3118315
Founded: 1849; Members: 40000
Focus: Educ
Periodical
Schweizerische Lehrerinnen- und Lehrer-Zeitung SLZ (bi-weekly) 10208

Mouvement International des Intellectuels Catholiques/MIIC-Pax Romana / International Catholic Movement for Intellectual and Cultural Affairs/ICMICA-Pax Romana, 37-39 Rue de Vermont, CP 85, 1211 Genève 20
T: (022) 7336740; Fax: 7336749
Focus: Sci
Periodical
Convergence 10209

Naturforschende Gesellschaft des Kantons Glarus (NGG), Berglirain 12, 8750 Glarus
Founded: 1881; Members: 190
Focus: Nat Sci
Periodical
Mitteilungen der Naturforschenden Gesellschaft des Kantons Glarus (irregularly) 10210

Naturforschende Gesellschaft in Basel, c/o Universitätsbibliothek, 4056 Basel
Founded: 1817; Members: 680
Pres: Dr. L. Landmann
Focus: Nat Sci
Periodical
Verhandlungen der Naturforschenden Gesellschaft in Basel (annually) 10211

Naturforschende Gesellschaft in Bern (NGB), c/o Stadt- und Universitätsbibliothek, Münstergasse 61, 3000 Bern 7
T: (031) 3203231
Founded: 1786; Members: 480
Pres: Prof. R. Weingart
Focus: Nat Sci
Periodical
Mitteilungen (annually) 10212

Naturforschende Gesellschaft in Zürich (NGZ), c/o P. Bamert, Grütacherstr 8, 8624 Grüt
Founded: 1746; Members: 1200
Focus: Nat Sci
Periodicals
Neujahrsblatt
Vierteljahrsschrift (quarterly) 10213

Naturforschende Gesellschaft Luzern (NGL), Denkmalstr 4, 6006 Luzern
T: (041) 514340
Founded: 1855; Members: 680
Focus: Nat Sci
Periodical
Mitteilungen der Naturforschenden Gesellschaft Luzern (every 1-2 years) 10214

Naturforschende Gesellschaft Schaffhausen, Postfach 432, 8201 Schaffhausen
Founded: 1822; Members: 520
Focus: Nat Sci
Periodicals
Mitteilungen
Neujahrsblätter 10215

Naturforschende Gesellschaft Solothurn, c/o Dr. Peter Berger, Hofmatt, 4582 Bruggien
Founded: 1823; Members: 373
Focus: Nat Sci
Periodical
Mitteilungen der Naturforschenden Gesellschaft des Kantons Solothurn 10216

Naturwissenschaftliche Gesellschaft Winterthur, Frohbergstr 21, 8542 Wiesendangen
T: (052) 3372563; E-Mail: kaisers@bluewin.ch; Fax: 3374278
Founded: 1884; Members: 334
Pres: Dr. K.F. Kaiser; Gen Secr: Dr. W. Caprez
Focus: Nat Sci
Periodical
Monographie zu naturwissenschaftlichen Themen (every 6 years) 10217

Neue Schweizerische Chemische Gesellschaft, c/o Ciba, K-25.5.02, 4002 Basel
T: (061) 6966626; Fax: 6966985
Founded: 1901; Members: 2300
Pres: Prof. Dr. Alexander von Zelewsky;
Gen Secr: Dr. Roland Darms
Focus: Chem
Periodicals
CHIMIA (10 times annually)
Helvetica Chimica Acta (9 times annually) 10218

Opera Svizzera dei Monumenti d'Arte/Inventario Beni Culturali (OSMA), c/o Archivio Cantonale, 6501 Bellinzona
T: (091) 8041380; Fax: 8041389
Founded: 1963
Focus: Hist; Arts
Periodical
I Monumenti d'Arte e di Storia del Canton Ticino 10219

Organisation Internationale de Protection Civile (OIPC) / International Civil Defence Organization, 10-12 Chemin de Surville, 1213 Petit-Lancy
T: (022) 7934433; Fax: 7934428
Founded: 1931; Members: 48
Gen Secr: Sadok Znaidi
Focus: Eng
Periodical
Revue Internationale de Protection Civile (3 times annually) 10220

Organisation Météorologique Mondiale (OMM) / World Meteorological Organization, 41 Av Giuseppe Motta, CP 2300, 1211 Genève 2
T: (022) 7308111; Fax: 7342326
Founded: 1951; Members: 160
Focus: Geophys
Periodical
WMO Bulletin (quarterly) 10221

Permanent Working Group of European Junior Hospital Doctors, c/o VSAO, Postfach 229, 3000 Bern 6
Focus: Med 10222

Philosophische Gesellschaft Bern, c/o Institut für Philosophie, Länggassstr 49a, 3009 Bern
E-Mail: Linneweber@philo.unibe.ch
Members: ca.50
Pres: Dr. Helmut Linneweber-Lammerskitten;
Gen Secr: Dr. Martin Bondeli
Focus: Philos 10223

Physikalische Gesellschaft Zürich (PGZ), Schönberggasse 9, 8001 Zürich
T: (01) 2572903; Fax: 2616323
Founded: 1887; Members: 640
Pres: Prof. Dr. N. Straumann; Gen Secr: Dr. H. Keller
Focus: Physics 10224

Präsidentenkonferenz Schweizerischer Fremdsprachenlehrerverbände, c/o Charles Gallo, Obergrundstr 61, 6003 Luzern
T: (041) 2103744
Focus: Educ; Ling 10225

Pro Helvetia, Hirschengraben 22, 8024 Zürich
T: (01) 2677171; Fax: 2677106
Founded: 1939; Members: 345
Pres: Rosemarie Simmen; Gen Secr: Urs Frauchiger
Focus: Int'l Relat; Arts
Periodical
Passagen (semi-annually) 10226

Pro Lyrica, Schweizerische Lyrische Gesellschaft, Postfach 61, 8205 Schaffhausen
T: (052) 7413960
Focus: Lit 10227

Pro Natura, 21 Devin du Village, 1203 Genève ASPI
T: (061) 3179191; Fax: 3179166
Pres: Martin Boesch; Gen Secr: Valeria Sulomoni Vaissade
Focus: Educ; Ling 10228

Renaissance, Schweizerischer Verband katholischer Akademiker-Gesellschaften, c/o Rudolf Tuor, Oberseeburgrain 1, 6006 Luzern
Focus: Sci 10229

Rheinaubund, Schweizerische Arbeitsgemeinschaft für Natur und Heimat, Neustadt 29, Postfach 584, 8201 Schaffhausen
T: (053) 6252658; Fax: 6252658
Founded: 1960; Members: 4000
Focus: Ecology
Periodical
Natur und Mensch: Schweizerische Blätter für Natur und Heimatschutz (bi-monthly) . . 10230

Schweizer Forum für Kommunikationsrecht (SVUM), Frohburgstr 116, 8057 Zürich
T: (079) 3019581; Fax: 2148140
Founded: 1946
Pres: Prof. Dr. Manfred Rehbinder; Gen Secr: Dr. Reto M. Hilty
Focus: Law 10231

Schweizer Gesellschaft für Neue Musik (SGNM), 11bis Av du Grammont, 1000 Lausanne 13, CP 177
T: (021) 6143290; Fax: 6143299
Focus: Music 10232

Schweizer Musikrat, Bahnhofstr 78, 5000 Aarau
T: (062) 8229423; E-Mail: musikrat@mail.spiderweb.ch; Fax: 8244767
Founded: 1964
Focus: Music
Periodical
Musikalische Berufsstudien in der Schweiz: Etudes Musicales Professionnelles en Suisse . . 10233

Schweizer Olympischer Verband (SOV) /Sportmed, Laubeggstr 70, 3006 Bern
T: (031) 3597111; Fax: 3523380
Pres: Fredy Schindler; Gen Secr: F. Schindler
Focus: Med 10234

Schweizerische Ärztegesellschaft für Akupunktur, Hus am Sportpl, 8134 Adliswil
Focus: Anesthetics 10235

Schweizerische Ärztegesellschaft für Holistische Medizin (SAGHOM), Hus an Sportpl, 8134 Adliswil
Focus: Med; Hist 10236

Schweizerische Ärztegesellschaft für Manuelle Medizin, c/o Klinik Wilhelm Schulthess, Neumünsterallee 10, 8032 Zürich
T: (01) 3857431
Founded: 1959; Members: 1000
Focus: Med 10237

Schweizerische Afrika-Gesellschaft (SAG) / Société Suisse d'Etudes Africaines, Postfach 8212, 3000 Bern
T: (031) 3227043; E-Mail: beat.sottas@bk.admin.ch; Fax: 3227001
Founded: 1974; Members: 190
Focus: Ethnology
Periodical
Newsletter (quarterly) 10238

Schweizerische Akademie der medizinischen Wissenschaften (SAMW), Peterspl 13, 4051 Basel
T: (061) 2614977; Fax: 2614934
Founded: 1943; Members: 57
Focus: Med
Periodical
Bulletin (annually) 10239

Schweizerische Akademie der Naturwissenschaften (SNG), Bärenpl 2, 3011 Bern
T: (031) 3123375; E-Mail: sanw@sanw.unibe.ch; Fax: 3123291
Founded: 1815; Members: 28000
Focus: Nat Sci
Periodical
Jahrbuch der Schweizerischen Akademie der Naturwissenschaften (annually) 10240

Schweizerische Akademie der Sozial- und Geisteswissenschaften, Hirschengraben 11, 3001 Bern
T: (031) 3113376
Founded: 1946
Focus: Humanities; Soc Sci
Periodical
Bulletin (3-4 times annually) 10241

Schweizerische Akademie der Technischen Wissenschaften (SATW), Postfach, 8039 Zürich
T: (01) 2831616; E-Mail: gen-sec@satw.ch; Fax: 2831620
Founded: 1981; Members: 150
Focus: Eng 10242

Schweizerische Akademische Gesellschaft der Anglisten (SAGA) / Société Suisse d'Etudes Anglaises, c/o Département d'Anglais, Faculté des Lettres, Université de Genève, 22 Blvd des Philosophes, 1205 Genève
T: (022) 7057034, 7057027; Fax: 7810171
Founded: 1949; Members: 61
Focus: Ling; Lit
Periodicals
English Studies at Swiss Universities (annually)
Swiss Papers in English Language and Literature (bi-annually) 10243

Schweizerische Akademische Gesellschaft für Umweltforschung und Ökologie (SAGUF), c/o Geographisches Institut, ETH, Winterthurer Str 190, 8057 Zürich
T: (01) 2575215/11; Fax: 3625197
Focus: Ecology 10244

Schweizerische Aktuarvereinigung (SAV) (VSVM), c/o Schweizerische Rückversichungs-Gesellschaft, Mythenquai 50-60, Postfach, 8022 Zürich
T: (01) 2852681; Fax: 2853287
Founded: 1905; Members: 850
Focus: Insurance
Periodical
Mitteilungen (3 times annually) 10245

Schweizerische Arbeitsgemeinschaft der Höheren Fachschulen für Soziale Arbeit (SASSA), Waldstätterstr 9, 6002 Luzern, Postfach 4212
T: (041) 2102432; Fax: 2102712
Focus: Educ; Soc Sci 10246

Schweizerische Arbeitsgemeinschaft der Höheren Fachschulen für Sozialpädagogik (SAH), c/o HFS Ostschweiz, Müller-Friedberg-Str 34, 9401 Rorschach
T: (071) 8552842; Fax: 8552835
Focus: Educ; Soc Sci 10247

Schweizerische Arbeitsgemeinschaft für akademische Berufs- und Studienberatung (AGAB), Zentralstr 28, 6002 Luzern
T: (041) 2285252; Fax: 2109776
Founded: 1959
Focus: Educ 10248

Schweizerische Arbeitsgemeinschaft für hauswirtschaftliche Bildungs- und Berufsfragen, Kürbergstr 33, 8049 Zürich
T: (01) 3421484
Focus: Home Econ 10249

Schweizerische Arbeitsgemeinschaft für Jugendmusik und Musikerziehung (SAJM), 269, 7302 Landquart
T: (081) 3229033; Fax: 3226835
Founded: 1956; Members: 1700
Focus: Music; Educ
Periodical
SAJM (quarterly) 10250

Schweizerische Arbeitsgemeinschaft für orale Implantologie (ASIO), Bleicherweg 39, 8002 Zürich
T: (01) 2013613; Fax: 2025459
Focus: Otorhinolaryngology 10251

Schweizerische Arbeitsgemeinschaft für Raumfahrt (SAFR), Postfach 4215, 6002 Luzern
T: (041) 558567
Founded: 1959
Focus: Aero
Periodical
SAFR-Mitteilungen (bi-monthly) 10252

Schweizerische Arbeitsgemeinschaft für Rehabilitation SAR, c/o Dr. med. Mark Mäder, Im Burgfelderhof 40, 4055 Basel
T: (061) 3267502; E-Mail: sar@rehab.ch; Fax: 3210104
Founded: 1960; Members: 231
Focus: Rehabil 10253

Schweizerische Arbeitsgemeinschaft für Schul- und Jugendzahnpflege, 8135 Langnau
T: 7133287
Focus: Dent 10254

Schweizerische Arbeitsgruppe Gentechnologie (SAG), Postfach 1168, 8032 Zürich
T: (01) 2622563; Fax: 2622570
Focus: Genetics 10255

Schweizerische Asiengesellschaft (SA), c/o Ostasiatisches Seminar der Universität, Zürichbergstr 4, 8032 Zürich
T: (01) 2573181; E-Mail: office@oas.unizh.ch; Fax: 2615687
Founded: 1947; Members: 224
Focus: Ethnology; Philos; Rel & Theol; Lit; Soc Sci
Periodicals
Asiatische Studien/Etudes Asiatiques (quarterly)
Schweizer Asiatische Studien 10256

Schweizerische Astronomische Gesellschaft, Gristenbühl 13, 9315 Neukirch-Egnach
Focus: Astronomy 10257

Schweizerische Bibliophilen-Gesellschaft, Voltastr 43, 8044 Zürich
Founded: 1921; Members: 600
Pres: Dr. Conrad Ulrich
Focus: Libraries & Bk Sci
Periodicals
Librarium (3 times annually)
Stultifera Navis 10258

Schweizerische Bodenkundliche Gesellschaft, c/o GIUZ, Winterthurer Str 190, 8057 Zürich
T: (01) 2575122/21; Fax: 3625227
Focus: Agri 10259

Schweizerische Botanische Gesellschaft (SBG), c/o Geobotanisches Institut, Zollikerstr 107, 8008 Zürich
T: (01) 6325700; E-Mail: koenig@geobot.umnw.ethz.ch
Founded: 1890
Focus: Botany
Periodical
Botanica Helvetica (2-4 times annually) . . 10260

Schweizerische Dendrologische Gesellschaft, c/o O. Hugentobler, Tranter flurs, 7440 Andeer
T: (081) 6611362; Fax: 6611542
Focus: Botany 10261

Schweizerische Diabetes-Gesellschaft (SDG), Forchstr 95, 8032 Zürich
T: (01) 3831315; Fax: 4228912
Founded: 1957; Members: 22867
Focus: Diabetes
Periodical
Journal des Diabétiques (5 times annually) . . . 10262

Schweizerische Direktoren-Konferenz gewerblicher Berufs- und Fachschulen, Lorrainestr 1, Postfach 67, 3000 Bern 11
T: (031) 3359111; Fax: 3359160
Focus: Adult Educ . . . 10263

Schweizerische Energie-Stiftung, Sihlquai 67, 8005 Zürich
T: (01) 2715464; Fax: 2730369
Founded: 1977
Focus: Energy
Periodical
Energie + Umwelt (quarterly) . . . 10264

Schweizerische Entomologische Gesellschaft (SEG/SES) / Société Entomologique Suisse, c/o CSCF, Terreaux 14, 2000 Neuchâtel
T: (032) 7207960
Founded: 1858; Members: 385
Focus: Entomology
Periodicals
Insecta Helvetica (irregularly)
Mitteilungen der Schweizerischen Entomologischen Gesellschaft/ Bulletin de la Société Entomologique Suisse (semi-annually) . . . 10265

Schweizerische Esperanto-Gesellschaft, c/o CDELI, 33 Progrès, 2300 La Chaux-de-Fonds
Focus: Ling
Periodical
Svisa Esperanto-Societi Informas (9 times annually) . . . 10266

Schweizerische Ethnologische Gesellschaft (SEG) / Société Suisse d'Ethnologie, c/o Institut für Ethnologie, Länggasstr 49a, 3000 Bern 9
T: (031) 6318995; Fax: 6314212
Focus: Ethnology
Periodicals
Ethnologica Helvetica (annually)
SEG/SSE – Information (semi-annually) . 10267

Schweizerische Fachvereinigung für Energiewirtschaft (SAEE), Kornhauspl 14, 3000 Bern 7
T: (031) 3115777; Fax: 3116432
Focus: Energy . . . 10268

Schweizerische Franchising-Vereinigung (SFV), Schlossbergstr 22, Postfach 125, 8702 Zollikon
T: 3914477
Focus: Econ . . . 10269

Schweizerische Gemmologische Gesellschaft (SGG), 5 Rue du Canal, 2502 Bienne
T: (032) 3223266; Fax: 3223205
Focus: Mineralogy . . . 10270

Schweizerische Gesellschaft der Kernfachleute (SGK), c/o Schweizerische Vereinigung für Atomenergie, Belpstr 23, Postfach 5032, 3001 Bern
Founded: 1958; Members: 300
Focus: Nucl Res . . . 10271

Schweizerische Gesellschaft für Agrarwirtschaft, Sonneggstr 33, 8092 Zürich
T: (01) 6325331; Fax: 6321086
Members: 450
Pres: Hans Müller; Gen Secr: Michel Roux
Focus: Agri
Periodical
Schweizerische Zeitschrift für Agrarwirtschaft und Agrarsoziologie (semi-annually) . . . 10272

Schweizerische Gesellschaft für allgemeine und vergleichende Literaturwissenschaft, Länggassstr 41, Franz. Seminar, 3000 Bern 9
Focus: Lit . . . 10273

Schweizerische Gesellschaft für Allgemeinmedizin (SGAM), Oberplattenstr 73, 9620 Lichtensteig
T: (071) 9886640; Fax: 9886641
Focus: Med . . . 10274

Schweizerische Gesellschaft für Altertumswissenschaft, c/o Dr. Christoph Uehlinger, Biblisches Institut, Universität, Miséricorde, 1700 Fribourg
T: (026) 3007384; E-Mail: Christoph.kehlinger@unifr.ch; Fax: 3009754
Founded: 1977; Members: 200
Pres: Dr. Christoph Kehlinger
Focus: Hist; Cultur Hist; Archeol
Periodical
Orbis Biblicus et Orientalis (irregularly) . 10275

Schweizerische Gesellschaft für angewandte Berufsbildungsforschung (SGAB), Ausstellungsstr 80, 8005 Zürich
T: (01) 2731939; Fax: 2731915
Focus: Educ . . . 10276

Schweizerische Gesellschaft für angewandte Geographie (SGAG), Breitestr 92, 8400 Winterthur
T: (052) 2125841
Focus: Geography . . . 10277

Schweizerische Gesellschaft für Astrophysik und Astronomie, c/o Astronomisches Institut der Universität Basel, 4102 Binningen
T: (061) 2055454; Fax: 2055455
Founded: 1968; Members: 165
Focus: Astrophys; Astronomy . . . 10278

Schweizerische Gesellschaft für Aussenpolitik (SGA), Stapferhaus, Schloss, 5600 Lenzburg
T: (064) 515751
Founded: 1968; Members: 500
Pres: Dr. Raymond Probst; Gen Secr: M. Kirchhofer
Focus: Poli Sci . . . 10279

Schweizerische Gesellschaft für Automatik (SGA), c/o Institut für Autmatik, ETH, Zentrum-ETH, 8092 Zürich
T: (01) 6322271; Fax: 6321211
Founded: 1956; Members: 250
Pres: Prof. Dr. A.H. Glattfelder
Focus: Eng
Periodical
SGA-ASSPA-Bulletin (quarterly) . . . 10280

Schweizerische Gesellschaft für Balneologie und Bioklimatologie, c/o Dr. R. Eberhard, Heilbadzentrum, 7500 Sankt Moritz
T: (082) 37171
Founded: 1902; Members: 126
Pres: Dr. O. Knüsel; Gen Secr: Dr. R. Eberhard
Focus: Physical Therapy
Periodical
Congress report . . . 10281

Schweizerische Gesellschaft für Bildungs- und Erziehungsfragen, Höflistr 12, Postfach 313, 8135 Langnau
T: (01) 7090979
Focus: Educ
Periodical
Die Presserundschau (bi-monthly) . . . 10282

Schweizerische Gesellschaft für Bildungsforschung (SGBF), c/o Schweizerische Koordinierungsstelle für Bildungsforschung, Entfelderstr 61, 5000 Aarau
T: (062) 8352390; Fax: 8352399
Focus: Educ . . . 10283

Schweizerische Gesellschaft für Boden- und Felsmechanik, ETH-Hönggerberg, 8093 Zürich
T: (01) 3716656; Fax: 6331062
Focus: Eng . . . 10284

Schweizerische Gesellschaft für cystische Fibrose, Bellevuestr 166, 3095 Spiegel
T: (031) 9722828; Fax: 9722828
Focus: Cell Biol & Cancer Res; Pathology
Periodical
cf-Bulletin (quarterly) . . . 10285

Schweizerische Gesellschaft für Dermatologie und Venerologie, c/o Dermatolog. Ambulatorium Triemli, Herman Greulich-Str 70, 8004 Zürich
T: (01) 2988921
Focus: Derm; Venereology . . . 10286

Schweizerische Gesellschaft für die Erforschung des 18. Jarhunderts (SGEAJ), c/o Philosophisches Seminar, Universität, Culmannstr 1, 8006 Zürich
T: (01) 2572852
Focus: Hist . . . 10287

Schweizerische Gesellschaft für die Rechte der Urheber musikalischer Werke (SUISA) / Swiss Society for Rights of Authors of Musical Works, Bellariastr 82, 8038 Zürich
T: (01) 4856666; Fax: 4824333
Founded: 1942; Members: 10400
Pres: Hans Ulrich Lehmann; Gen Secr: Patrick Liechtl
Focus: Music; Law . . . 10288

Schweizerische Gesellschaft für ein Soziales Gesundheitswesen (SGSG), Postfach, 4007 Basel
T: (061) 6911332
Focus: Public Health . . . 10289

Schweizerische Gesellschaft für Endokrinologie, c/o Div. d'Endocrinologie et de Diabétologie, Hôpital cant. univ., 1211 Genève 4
T: (022) 3729302; Fax: 3729326
Focus: Endocrinology . . . 10290

Schweizerische Gesellschaft für Ernährungsforschung (SGE), c/o Geriatrische Universitätsklinik, Kantonsspital, 4031 Basel
T: (061) 2652954; Fax: 2652670
Focus: Food . . . 10291

Schweizerische Gesellschaft für Familienforschung (SGFF), Postfach 54, 3608 Thun
T: (033) 3452511
Members: 1000
Focus: Genealogy
Periodicals
Mitteilungen der SGFF (3 times annually)
SGFF-Jahrbuch (annually) . . . 10292

Schweizerische Gesellschaft für Feintechnik (SGFT), Kirchenweg 4, 8032 Zürich
T: (01) 478400
Focus: Eng . . . 10293

Schweizerische Gesellschaft für Fertilität, Sterilität und Familienplanung, c/o CHUV, Unité de Stérilité, 1011 Lausanne
T: (021) 3141111
Focus: Med; Family Plan . . . 10294

Schweizerische Gesellschaft für Gastroenterologie und Hepatologie, Service de médecine, Hôpital du Locle, 2400 Le Locle
T: (032) 9323144
Focus: Gastroenter . . . 10295

Schweizerische Gesellschaft für Gerontologie (SGG), c/o Zieglerspital, Postfach, 3001 Bern
T: (031) 9710124
Founded: 1953; Members: 950
Focus: Geriatrics . . . 10296

Schweizerische Gesellschaft für Geschichte der Medizin und der Naturwissenschaften / Société Suisse d'Histoire de la Médicine et des Sciences Naturelles, Bühlstr 26, 3000 Bern 9
T: (031) 6318486; E-Mail: boschung@mhi.unibe.ch; Fax: 6318491
Founded: 1921; Members: 320
Focus: Med; Cultur Hist
Periodical
Gesnerus (quarterly) . . . 10297

Schweizerische Gesellschaft für Gesetzgebung, Staatkanzlei, Postgasse 72, 3000 Bern 8
T: (031) 6337511
Focus: Law . . . 10298

Schweizerische Gesellschaft für Gesundheitspolitik (SGGP), Haldenweg 10a, 3074 Muri BE
T: (031) 9526655; Fax: 9526800
Focus: Public Health; Poli Sci . . . 10299

Schweizerische Gesellschaft für Gynäkologie, c/o CHUV Dept d'Obstétrique et de Gynécologie, 1011 Lausanne
T: (021) 3142523
Founded: 1964; Members: 690
Focus: Gynecology . . . 10300

Schweizerische Gesellschaft für Höhlenforschung (SGH), CP 37, 1020 Renens
Focus: Geology . . . 10301

Schweizerische Gesellschaft für Innere Medizin, c/o Medizinische Klinik Regionalspital, 4900 Langenthal
T: (062) 9163102; E-Mail: r.streuli@rsl.ch; Fax: 9164155
Founded: 1932; Members: 2300
Pres: Prof. Ph. Jaeger; Gen Secr: Prof. R. A. Streuli
Focus: Intern Med . . . 10302

Schweizerische Gesellschaft für Kardiologie / Société Suisse de Cardiologie, c/o Kantonsspital, Petersgraben 4, 4031 Bern
T: (031) 632111
Focus: Cardiol . . . 10303

Schweizerische Gesellschaft für Kartographie, c/o Institut für Kartographie, ETH, Hönggerberg, 8093 Zürich
T: (01) 6333033; Fax: 6331153
Founded: 1969; Members: 250
Pres: Prof. Ernst Spiess
Focus: Cart
Periodicals
Kartographische Nachrichten (bi-monthly)
Kartographische Schriftenreihe (irregularly) 10304

Schweizerische Gesellschaft für kaufmännisches Bildungswesen, c/o AKAD, Jungholzstr 43, Postfach, 8050 Zürich
T: (01) 3073245; Fax: 3025737
Focus: Adult Educ
Periodical
Schweizerische Zeitschrift für kaufmännisches Bildungswesen . . . 10305

Schweizerische Gesellschaft für Kinder- und Jugendpsychatrie, 16-18 Blvd St-Georges, 1211 Genève 8, CP 50
T: (022) 3274309
Focus: Psychiatry . . . 10306

Schweizerische Gesellschaft für klinische Chemie, c/o Abt. Klinische Chemie, Universitäts-Kinderklinik, Steinwiesstr 75, 8032 Zürich
T: (01) 2667542; Fax: 2667169
Focus: Chem . . . 10307

Schweizerische Gesellschaft für Kommunikations- und Medienwissenschaft (SGKM), c/o SRG Forschungsdienst, Giacomettistr 1, Postfach, 3000 Bern 15
T: (031) 3509432; Fax: 3509436
Founded: 1974; Members: 280
Pres: Prof. Dr. Matthias Steinmann; Gen Secr: Markus Jedele
Focus: Comm Sci
Periodical
SGKM-Bulletin (semi-annually) . . . 10308

Schweizerische Gesellschaft für Kulturgüterschutz (SGKGS), 6 Rue St-Pierre, 1701 Fribourg, CP 990
T: (026) 4662600, 3227321; Fax: 3226062
Focus: Preserv Hist Monuments . . . 10309

Schweizerische Gesellschaft für Lebensmittel-Wissenschaft und -Technologie (SGLWT), Postfach 561, 8820 Wädenswil
Members: 530
Focus: Food; Eng
Periodicals
Lebensmittel-Technologie (monthly)
Lebensmittel-Wissenschaft und -Technologie: Food Science & Technology (bi-monthly) . . . 10310

Schweizerische Gesellschaft für Lehrerinnen- und Lehrerbildung (SGL), Muesmattstr 27, 3012 Bern
T: (031) 6318316
Members: 500
Pres: Prof. Dr. Hans Badertscher
Focus: Educ; Psych
Periodical
Beiträge zur Lehrerbildung (3 times annually) . . . 10311

Schweizerische Gesellschaft für Logik und Philosophie der Wissenschaften, c/o Institut de Mathématiques Appliquées, Université de Lausanne, 1015 Lausanne
Fax: (021) 6923125
Founded: 1948; Members: 60
Focus: Philos . . . 10312

Schweizerische Gesellschaft für Marketing, Bleicherweg 21, 8022 Zürich
T: (01) 2023425
Founded: 1941; Members: 320
Focus: Marketing . . . 10313

Schweizerische Gesellschaft für Medizinische Radiologie, Bürgerspital, 4500 Solothurn
T: (032) 6273121
Focus: Radiology . . . 10314

Schweizerische Gesellschaft für Mikrobiologie, c/o Institut Microbion, CP, 1001 Lausanne
Focus: Microbio . . . 10315

Schweizerische Gesellschaft für Mikrotechnik, c/o VSM, 1 Rue Jaquet-Droz, CP 20, 2007 Neuchâtel
T: (038) 200900; Fax: 200990
Founded: 1962; Members: 95
Pres: P. Stauber; Gen Secr: C. Montandon
Focus: Electronic Eng . . . 10316

Schweizerische Gesellschaft für Muskelkranke (SGMK), Forchstr 136, 8032 Zürich
T: (01) 4221634; Fax: 4225931
Focus: Physiology; Pathology
Periodical
Mitteilungsblatt (1-2 times annually) . . . 10317

Schweizerische Gesellschaft für Neuroradiologie, Inselspital, 3010 Bern
T: (031) 6322655
Focus: Neurology; Radiology . . . 10318

Schweizerische Gesellschaft für Oberflächentechnik, Hänselsmatt 2, 2544 Bettlach
T: (065) 553574; Fax: 553038
Founded: 1955; Members: 550
Focus: Eng
Periodical
Oberfläche/Surface (monthly) . . . 10319

Schweizerische Gesellschaft für Onkologie, c/o Abt für klinisch-experimentelle Forschung, Universität, Tiefenaustr 120, 3004 Bern
Focus: Cell Biol & Cancer Res . . . 10320

Schweizerische Gesellschaft für Orthopädie (SGO), Postfach, 3000 Bern 25
T: (031) 3329619; Fax: 3329879
Pres: Dr. André Kaelin; Gen Secr: Dr. Beat Simmen
Focus: Orthopedics
Periodical
Nachrichten-Bulletin SGO (2-3 times annually) . . . 10321

Schweizerische Gesellschaft für Otorhinolaryngologie, Hals- und Gesichtschirurgie / Société Suisse d'Oto-Rhino-Laryngologie et de Chirurgie Cervico-Faciale, c/o Admicron, Schuppistr 13, 9016 Sankt Gallen
T: (071) 2885020; Fax: 2885054
Founded: 1913; Members: 250
Focus: Surgery; Otorhinolaryngology
Periodical
ORL-Verhandlungsberichte der wissenschaftlichen Frühjahrsversammlung (annually) . . . 10322

Schweizerische Gesellschaft für Pädiatrie, 97-99 Rue de Genève, 1226 Thônex
Focus: Pediatrics . . . 10323

Schweizerische Gesellschaft für Personalfragen (SGP), Löwenstr 20, 8001 Zürich
T: (01) 2119544
Founded: 1972; Members: 2200
Focus: Business Admin
Periodical
SGP Mitteilungen (quarterly) . . . 10324

Schweizerische Gesellschaft für Physikalische Medizin und Rehabilitation, c/o Rheumaliga, Renggerstr 71, 8038 Zürich
T: (01) 4825600; Fax: 4826439
Founded: 1946
Focus: Physiology . . . 10325

Schweizerische Gesellschaft für Pneumologie (SGP), Falkenpl 9, Postfach, 3001 Bern
T: (031) 3020822; Fax: 3028833
Members: 242
Focus: Pulmon Dis

Periodical
Tuberkulose und Lungenkrankheiten: Beilage zum Bulletin des Bundesamtes für Gesundheitswesen (8 times annually) 10326

Schweizerische Gesellschaft für Prävention und Gesundheitswesen, c/o ISPM, Universität, Steingraben 49, 4059 Basel
Focus: Public Health 10327

Schweizerische Gesellschaft für Prävention und Gesundheitswesen, Effingerstr 40, 3008 Bern
T: (031) 3899286; E-Mail: sgpg@swisscancer.ch; Fax: 3899288
Founded: 1972; Members: 660
Focus: Public Health
Periodical
Sozial- und Präventivmedizin: Médecine Sociale et Préventive (bi-monthly) 10328

Schweizerische Gesellschaft für praktische Sozialforschung, Bärenpl 2, 3011 Bern
T: (031) 3110806; Fax: 3110819
Focus: Soc Sci 10329

Schweizerische Gesellschaft für Psychatrie, Postfach 895, 3000 Bern 7
T: (031) 3110687; Fax: 3110688
Focus: Psychiatry 10330

Schweizerische Gesellschaft für Psychologie, c/o Psychologisches Institut Universität-Zürich, Schmelzbergstr 40, 8044 Zürich
Founded: 1943; Members: 400
Pres: Dr. R. Volkart
Focus: Psych
Periodicals
Psychologie
Swiss Journal of Psychology (quarterly) . 10331

Schweizerische Gesellschaft für Rheumatologie, c/o Rheumaliga, Renggerstr 71, 8038 Zürich
T: (01) 4825600; Fax: 4826439
Focus: Rheuma
Periodical
Zeitschrift für Rheumatologie 10332

Schweizerische Gesellschaft für Schicksalsanalytische Therapie, Allmeindlistr 10, 8864 Reichenburg
Focus: Therapeutics 10333

Schweizerische Gesellschaft für Skandinavische Studien (SGSS), c/o Deutsches Seminar, Abt für Nordische Philologie, Universität Zürich, Schönberggasse 9, 8001 Zürich
T: (01) 6342514; Fax: 6344905
Founded: 1961; Members: 230
Pres: Prof. Dr. Hans-Peter Naumann; Gen Secr: Susanna Flühmann
Focus: Ling; Lit
Periodical
Beiträge zur nordischen Philologie (annually) 10334

Schweizerische Gesellschaft für Soziologie / Société Suisse de Sociologie, Rämistr 69, 8001 Zürich
T: (01) 2611034; Fax: 2521054
Founded: 1955; Members: 580
Pres: Claudia Honegger; Jean Widmer; Gen Secr: Peter Rusterholz
Focus: Sociology
Periodicals
Bulletin (quarterly)
Schweizerische Zeitschrift für Soziologie: Revue Suisse de Sociologie (3 times annually) . 10335

Schweizerische Gesellschaft für Sportmedizin, Postfach 408, 3000 Bern 25
T: (031) 3330254; Fax: 3329879
Focus: Med 10336

Schweizerische Gesellschaft für Statistik und Volkswirtschaft / Société Suisse de Statistique et d'Economie Politique, c/o Bundesamt für Statistik, 3003 Bern
T: (031) 3236069; Fax: 3236081
Founded: 1864; Members: 1000
Focus: Stats; Econ
Periodical
Schweizerische Zeitschrift für Volkswirtschaft und Statistik (quarterly) 10337

Schweizerische Gesellschaft für Theaterkultur (SGTK), Postfach 1940, 4001 Basel
T: (061) 3211060; Fax: 3211075
Founded: 1927; Members: 550
Focus: Perf Arts
Periodicals
Mimos: Mitteilungen der SGIK (semi-annually)
Schriften der Schweizerischen Gesellschaft für Theaterkultur
Schweizer Theater-Jahrbuch (annually)
Szene Schweiz/Scène suisse/Scena svizzera 10338

Schweizerische Gesellschaft für Traumatologie und Versicherungsmedizin, c/o SUVA, Postfach, 6002 Luzern
T: (041) 4195111
Focus: Traumatology 10339

Schweizerische Gesellschaft für Tropenmedizin und Parasitologie, c/o Schweiz. Tropeninstitut, Socinstr 57, 4002 Basel
T: (061) 2848111
Focus: Trop Med 10340

Schweizerische Gesellschaft für Umweltschutz (SGU), Merkurstr 45, 8032 Zürich
T: (01) 2512826
Focus: Ecology
Periodical
SGU Bulletin (quarterly) 10341

Schweizerische Gesellschaft für Ur- und Frühgeschichte, Petersgraben 9-11, 4001 Basel
T: (061) 2613078; Fax: 2613078
Founded: 1907; Members: 2500
Pres: Dr. Stefan Hochuli; Gen Secr: Dr. Urs Niffeler
Focus: Archeol
Periodicals
Archäologie der Schweiz, Archéologie Suisse, Archeologia Svizzera (quarterly)
Jahrbuch SGUF, Annuaire SSPA, Annuario SSPA (annually) 10342

Schweizerische Gesellschaft für Urologie, c/o Serv. d'Urologie, CHUV, 1011 Lausanne
T: (021) 3144710
Focus: Urology 10343

Schweizerische Gesellschaft für Vakuum-Physik und -Technik, c/o Institut für Technische Physik, ETH, Hönggerberg, 8093 Zürich
Focus: Physics; Eng 10344

Schweizerische Gesellschaft für Verhaltenstherapie, Ch. De la Chapelle, 1964 Conthey
T: (027) 346 3451
Focus: Therapeutics 10345

Schweizerische Gesellschaft für Versicherungsrecht, Postfach 4338, 8022 Zürich
T: (01) 2843260
Focus: Law 10346

Schweizerische Gesellschaft für Verwaltungswissenschaften (SGVW), 3000 Bern
T: (031) 6335280; Fax: 6335380
Focus: Public Admin 10347

Schweizerische Gesellschaft für Volkskunde, Augustinergasse 19, 4051 Basel
T: (061) 2619900; Fax: 2619900
Founded: 1896; Members: 1900
Focus: Folklore
Periodicals
Folklore suisse / Folclore svizzero (3 times annually)
Schweizer Volkskunde: Korrespondenzblatt (quarterly)
Schweizerisches Archiv für Volkskunde / Archives Suisses des Traditions Populaires (semi-annually) 10348

Schweizerische Gesellschaft für wildtierbiologie, Chasa dal Parc, 7530 Zernez
T: (081) 8561378
Focus: Zoology 10349

Schweizerische Gesellschaft für Zerstörungsfreie Prüfung, c/o SVS, St Alban-Rheinweg 222, 4052 Basel
Focus: Materials Sci 10350

Schweizerische Gesellschaft Pro Technorama, Postfach 3, 8404 Winterthur
T: (052) 2430505; Fax: 2422967
Members: 5500
Focus: Eng; Cultur Hist
Periodical
Pro Technorama (quarterly) 10351

Schweizerische Graphische Gesellschaft, c/o C. Brunner, Kunsthaus, Heimpl 1, 8024 Zürich
T: (01) 2516765
Focus: Graphic & Dec Arts, Design . . 10352

Schweizerische Graphologische Berufsvereinigung, Maihölzlistr 17, 5621 Zufikon
T: (056) 6336420
Focus: Graphology 10353

Schweizerische Graphologische Gesellschaft, Bächlerweg 29, 8802 Kilchberg
T: (01) 7151563
Focus: Graphology 10354

Schweizerische Hämophilie-Gesellschaft (SHG), Postfach 531, 8027 Zürich
T: (01) 2810855; Fax: 9301194
Founded: 1965; Members: 700
Focus: Hematology
Periodical
Bulletin (quarterly) 10355

Schweizerische Heilpädagogische Gesellschaft, Brunnmattstr 38, Postfach, 3000 Bern 14
T: (031) 262629; Fax: 264521
Focus: Educ; Rehabil
Periodicals
Pages Romandes (quarterly)
Schweizerische Heilpädagogische Rundschau (SHR) (monthly) 10356

Schweizerische Heraldische Gesellschaft, Burgstr 32, 8706 Meilen
T: (01) 9231077; Fax: 2446184
Focus: Hist 10357

Schweizerische Hochschulkonferenz (SHK), Sennweg 2, 3012 Bern
T: (031) 3025533; Fax: 3021792
Founded: 1969; Members: 29
Pres: Augustin Wacheret; Gen Secr: N. Ischi
Focus: Adult Educ
Periodicals
Jahresbericht (annually)
Politique de le Science (4-6 times annually) 10358

Schweizerische Hochschulrektoren-Konferenz, Sennweg 2, 3012 Bern
T: (031) 3066034; E-Mail: wettstei@szfh.unibe.ch; Fax: 3026811
Focus: Educ 10359

Schweizerische Homöopatie-Gesellschaft (SHG/SGKH), Hus am Sportpl, 8134 Adliswil
Focus: Homeopathy 10360

Schweizerische Humanisten-Vereinigung, Postfach 10, 8612 Uster 2
T: (01) 9403850
Focus: Philos 10361

Schweizerische katholische Arbeitsgemeinschaft für Ausländerfragen (SKAF), Neustadtstr 7, 6003 Luzern
T: (041) 2100347; Fax: 2105846
Pres: Dr. Walter Gut; Gen Secr: Dr. Urs Köppel
Focus: Rel & Theol 10362

Schweizerische Konferenz der Direktoren der Lehrerbildungsinstitutionen (SKDL), c/o Bündener Lehrerseminar, Plessurquai 63, 7000 Chur
T: (081) 2521804; Fax: 2572186
Focus: Educ 10363

Schweizerische Konferenz der kantonalen Erziehungsdirektoren (EDK), Zähringerstr 25, 3001 Bern
T: (031) 3095111; Fax: 3095150
Focus: Educ 10364

Schweizerische Konferenz der Rektoren kaufmännischer Berufsschulen, Postfach 687, 8027 Zürich
T: (01) 2834549; Fax: 2834550
Focus: Adult Educ 10365

Schweizerische Konferenz der Schulleiter hauswirtschaftlicher Berufs- und Fachschulen (SKHF), c/o Schule für Haushalt und Lebensgestaltung, Wipkingerpl 4, 8037 Zürich
T: (01) 2724320
Focus: Educ; Home Econ 10366

Schweizerische Krebsliga, Monbijoustr 61, Postfach 8219, 3001 Bern
T: (031) 3722767; Fax: 3718301
Focus: Cell Biol & Cancer Res 10367

Schweizerische Kriminalistische Gesellschaft / Société Suisse de Droit Pénal, c/o Bezirksanwaltschaft, Postfach, 8026 Zürich
Focus: Law 10368

Schweizerische Lichttechnische Gesellschaft (SLG), Postgasse 17, 3011 Bern
T: (031) 3122251; Fax: 3121250
Focus: Electric Eng
Periodical
Mitteilung an die Mitglieder (quarterly) . 10369

Schweizerische Liga gegen den Lärm, Hirschenpl 7, 6004 Luzern
T: (041) 4103013; Fax: 4109093
Pres: Prof. Dr. Meinrad Schär; Gen Secr: Dr. Willy Aecherli
Focus: Ecology 10370

Schweizerische Liga gegen Epilepsie (SLgE), Feldeggstr 71, Postfach 129, 8032 Zürich
T: (01) 3835455; E-Mail: SLgE@bluewin.ch; Fax: 3835433
Pres: Prof. Dr. P.A. Despland
Focus: Pathology
Periodicals
Epilepsie: Informationsblatt (semi-annually)
Epilepsie-Selbsthilfe-Zeitung: Kontakte (semi-annually) 10371

Schweizerische Management-Gesellschaft (SMG) / Swiss Management Association, Bleicherweg 64a, Postfach, 8039 Zürich
T: (01) 2022325; Fax: 2022320
Founded: 1961; Members: 1000
Focus: Business Admin 10372

Schweizerische Mathematische Gesellschaft (SMG) / Société Mathématique Suisse, c/o Institute de Mathématiques, Université de Genève, CP 240, 1211 Genève 24
Founded: 1910; Members: 460
Focus: Math
Periodicals
Commentarii Mathematici Helvetici (quarterly)
Elemente der Mathematik (bi-monthly) . . 10373

Schweizerische Multiple Sklerose Gesellschaft (SMSG), Brinerstr 1, 8036 Zürich
T: (01) 4614600; Fax: 4510939
Members: 12500
Focus: Pathology
Periodical
MS Aktuell/SP Actuel/Attualità SM (quarterly) 10374

Schweizerische Musikforschende Gesellschaft, Petersgraben 27, 4051 Basel
T: (061) 2672800; E-Mail: Willimann@ubaclu.unibas.ch
Founded: 1916; Members: 700
Pres: Dr. Joseph Willimann; Gen Secr: Dr. Dorothea Baumann
Focus: Music
Periodicals
Jahrbuch (annually)
Schweizer Musikdenkmäler 10375

Schweizerische Neurologische Gesellschaft (SNG), c/o Neurologische Klinik Universitätsspital, 8051 Zürich
Founded: 1908; Members: 228
Focus: Neurology
Periodical
Schweizer Archiv für Neurologie 10376

Schweizerische Normen-Vereinigung (SNV), Mühlebachstr 54, 8008 Zürich
T: (01) 2545454; Fax: 2545474
Founded: 1919; Members: 500
Focus: Standards
Periodicals
SNV Bulletin (11 times annually)
switec Information 10377

Schweizerische Numismatische Gesellschaft / Société Suisse de Numismatique, c/o Stadt- und Universitätsbibliothek, Münstergasse 61, 3000 Bern 7
Members: 743
Focus: Numismatics
Periodicals
Schweizer Münzblätter: Gazette Numismatique Suisse (quarterly)
Schweizerische Numismatische Rundschau: Revue Suisse de Numismatique (annually)
Schweizerischer Münzkatalog (irregularly) . 10378

Schweizerische Ophthalmologische Gesellschaft (S.O.G.), Berneckerstr 26, 9435 Heerbrugg
T: (071) 7222233; Fax: 7222205
Founded: 1927; Members: 300
Focus: Ophthal 10379

Schweizerische Paläontologische Gesellschaft, c/o Musée d'Histoire Naturelle, 1 Rte de Malagnou, CP 6434, 1211 Genève 6
T: (022) 7353445; Fax: 7359130
Founded: 1921; Members: 255
Focus: Paleontology
Periodical
Bericht 10380

Schweizerische Philosophische Gesellschaft / Société Suisse de Philosophie, Sankt Gallerring 25, 4055 Basel
Founded: 1940; Members: 800
Pres: Prof. Dr. A. Hügli; Gen Secr: Dr. Eduard Marbach
Focus: Philos
Periodicals
Studia Philosophica (annually)
Supplementa (irregularly) 10381

Schweizerische Physikalische Gesellschaft / Société Suisse de Physique / Swiss Physical Society, 1 Rue A.-L. Breguet, 2000 Neuchâtel
T: (038) 256991; Fax: 24913
Founded: 1908; Members: 1400
Pres: Prof. Yves Baer
Focus: Physics
Periodical
Helvetica Physica Acta (8 times annually) 10382

Schweizerische Raumfahrt-Vereinigung (SRV), c/o Ingenieurschule HTL, Bittertenstr 15, 4702 Oensingen
T: (062) 3882525; Fax: 3882520
Focus: Aero 10383

Schweizerische Rheumaliga, Renggerstr 71, 8038 Zürich
T: (01) 4825600; Fax: 4826439
Focus: Rheuma
Periodical
Forum R (quarterly) 10384

Schweizerische Schillerstiftung / Fondation Schiller Suisse, Im Ring 2, 8126 Zumikon
Founded: 1905; Members: 300
Pres: Prof. Dr. Egon Wilhelm
Focus: Lit
Periodical
Jahresbericht (annually) 10385

Schweizerische Sprachwissenschaftliche Gesellschaft, c/o Institut de Linguistique et des Sciences du Langage, BFSH 2, 1015 Lausanne
Founded: 1947; Members: 207
Pres: Prof. Dr. Anne-Claude Berthoud; Gen Secr: Dr. Pascal Singh
Focus: Ling
Periodical
Cahiers Ferdinand de Saussure (annually) 10386

Schweizerische Stiftung für Alpine Forschungen / Swiss Foundation for Alpine Research, Binzstr 23, 8045 Zürich
T: (01) 4610147; Fax: 2871368
Founded: 1939; Members: 11
Pres: Dr. Jürg Marmet; Gen Secr: Dr. F.H. Schwarzenbach
Focus: Geography
Periodical
The Mountain World 10387

Schweizerische Stiftung für Angewandte Psychologie / Fondation Suisse pour la Psychologie Appliquée, c/o Dr. M. Notter, Schweiz. Bankverein, Bahnhofstr 45, 8021 Zürich
Founded: 1927; Members: 150
Pres: Dr. H. Schmid; Gen Secr: Dr. M. Notter
Focus: Psych
Periodical
Psychologie für die Praxis (3 times annually) . . . 10388

Schweizerische Studiengesellschaft für Kommunikation und Administration (SSKA), Postfach 8311, 3001 Bern
T: (031) 3819545, 3525687
Focus: Comm Sci; Public Admin . . . 10389

Schweizerische Studiengesellschaft für Raumordnungs- und Regionalpolitik (ROREP), c/o VCP-ASPAN, Schänzlihalde 21, 3013 Bern
T: (056) 4423634; Fax: 4422164
Focus: Poli Sci; Urban Plan . . . 10390

Schweizerische Studiengruppe für Konsumentenfragen, Hallerstr 58, 3012 Bern
Focus: Econ . . . 10391

Schweizerische Theologische Gesellschaft (SThG), Postfach 8204, 3001 Bern
Founded: 1965; Members: 250
Pres: Prof. Dr. M. Rose; Gen Secr: K. Hanke-Wehrle
Focus: Rel & Theol . . . 10392

Schweizerische Trachtenvereinigung / Fédération Nationale des Costumes Suisses, Mühlegasse 13, Postfach, 3400 Burgdorf
T: (034) 222239
Founded: 1926; Members: 28000
Pres: Hansruedi Spichiger
Focus: Folklore
Periodicals
Costumes et Coutures
Heimatleben . . . 10393

Schweizerische Vereinigung der Baufachlehrer (SVB), Bramberghöhe 3, 6004 Luzern
T: (041) 4108391
Focus: Educ; Civil Eng . . . 10394

Schweizerische Vereinigung der Beraterinnen und Inspektorinnen für den Handarbeits- und Hauswirtschaftsunterricht (SVBIH), Hofwiesenstr 71, 8057 Zürich
T: (01) 2592278
Focus: Educ; Home Econ . . . 10395

Schweizerische Vereinigung der Lack- und Farben-Chemiker (SVLFC), c/o Streit AG, Postfach 2006, 8502 Frauenfeld
T: (052) 7201144; Fax: 7201148
Founded: 1948; Members: 300
Pres: Dr. Hans Ruvenacht; Gen Secr: Jürg Sarbach
Focus: Chem
Periodical
Farbe und Lack (monthly) . . . 10396

Schweizerische Vereinigung der Lehrkräfte grafischer Berufe (LGB), Reichsgasse 17, 7001 Chur
T: (081) 2535813; Fax: 2535813
Focus: Educ; Graphic & Dec Arts, Design 10397

Schweizerische Vereinigung diplomierter Chemiker HTL (SVCT) / Swiss Association of Certified Chemists HTL, Postfach 46, 4007 Basel
T: (061) 3246561; Fax: 3246301
Founded: 1946; Members: 1100
Focus: Chem
Periodical
Mitglieder-Bulletin: à jour (quarterly) . . . 10398

Schweizerische Vereinigung für Altertumswissenschaft / Association Suisse pour l'Etude de l'Antiquité, c/o Seminar für klassische Philologie, Nadelberg 6, 4051 Basel
T: (061) 2618065
Founded: 1943; Members: 138
Focus: Archeol; Hist
Periodical
Museum Helveticum: Schweizerische Zeitschrift für klassische Altertumswissenschaft (quarterly) 10399

Schweizerische Vereinigung für Atomenergie (SVA), Belpstr 23, Postfach 5032, 3001 Bern
T: (031) 3115882; Fax: 3206831
Founded: 1958; Members: 600
Focus: Nucl Res
Periodicals
Bulletin (bi-weekly)
Kernpunkte (monthly) . . . 10400

Schweizerische Vereinigung für Datenverarbeitung, Postfach 373, 8037 Zürich
T: (057) 333705; Fax: 334100
Focus: Computer & Info Sci
Periodical
Output (monthly) . . . 10401

Schweizerische Vereinigung für die Vereinfachung der Verfahren im internationalen Handel (SWISSPRO), Laupenstr 10, 3001 Bern
T: (031) 3847606; Fax: 3817002
Focus: Commerce; Law . . . 10402

Schweizerische Vereinigung für Dokumentation (SVD), Weinbergstr 31, 8006 Zürich
T: (01) 2666474
Founded: 1939; Members: 600
Pres: S. Hollander; Gen Secr: W. Bruderer
Focus: Doc
Periodical
ARBIDO (monthly) . . . 10403

Schweizerische Vereinigung für Ernährung (SVE) / Swiss Association for Nutrition / Swiss Association for Nutrition, Postfach 8333, 3001 Bern
T: (031) 3818581; Fax: 3828515
Founded: 1965; Members: 6000
Pres: Dr. Stephanie Baumgartner; Gen Secr: Hansjörg Ryser
Focus: Food
Periodical
Tabula . . . 10404

Schweizerische Vereinigung für Erwachsenenbildung (SVEB) / Swiss Federation for Adult Education, Oerlikonerstr 38, 8057 Zürich
T: (01) 3116455; E-Mail: svebch@access.ch; Fax: 3116459
Founded: 1951; Members: 500
Focus: Adult Educ
Periodicals
Education permanente (quarterly)
SVEB-Bulletin (5 times annually) . . . 10405

Schweizerische Vereinigung für Filmkultur, Gerechtigkeitsgasse 22, 3011 Bern
T: (031) 224333
Focus: Cinema . . . 10406

Schweizerische Vereinigung für Gesundheitstechnik (SVG), Walchestr 33, Postfach 305, 8035 Zürich
Focus: Eng . . . 10407

Schweizerische Vereinigung für Internationales Recht, Postfach 690, 8027 Zürich
Founded: 1914; Members: 990
Pres: Prof. Dr. F. Knoepfler; Gen Secr: Dr. P.M. Gutzwiller
Focus: Law
Periodicals
Schweizerisches Jahrbuch für Internationales Recht (annually)
Swiss Studies in International Law . . . 10408

Schweizerische Vereinigung für Kleintiermedizin (SVK), c/o Gesellschaft Schweizerischer Tierärzte, Postfach 6324, 3001 Bern
Fax: (031) 3028841
Founded: 1969; Members: 530
Focus: Vet Med . . . 10409

Schweizerische Vereinigung für Landesplanung (VLP), Schänzlihalde 21, 3013 Bern
T: (031) 3326444; Fax: 3321428
Pres: Eduard Belser; Gen Secr: Rudolf Muggli
Focus: Urban Plan . . . 10410

Schweizerische Vereinigung für Militärgeschichte und Militärwissenschaft, c/o Eidgenössische Militärbibliothek und historischer Dienst, Bundeshaus-Ost, 3003 Bern
T: (031)3245098/99
Focus: Hist; Military Sci . . . 10411

Schweizerische Vereinigung für Parapsychologie, Werkgasse 22, 3018 Bern
T: (031) 9929291; Fax: 9927569
Focus: Parapsych . . . 10412

Schweizerische Vereinigung für Puppenspiel, Postfach 501, 8401 Winterthur
T: (052) 2136991; Fax: 2136991
Focus: Perf Arts . . . 10413

Schweizerische Vereinigung für Schiedsgerichtsbarkeit / Association Suisse de l'Arbitrage, c/o Rechtsanwälte Bär & Karrer, Seefeldstr 19, 8024 ZZürich
T: (01) 2615150; Fax: 2513025
Focus: Law
Periodical
Bulletin (quarterly) . . . 10414

Schweizerische Vereinigung für Sozialpolitik / Association Suisse de Politique Sociale, Affolternstr 123, 8050 Zürich
T: (01) 3113727
Focus: Poli Sci
Periodical
Das sozialpolitische Forum (semi-annually) 10415

Schweizerische Vereinigung für Steuerrecht, c/o Schweizerische Bankgesellschaft, Abt Steuerdienst, Bahnhofstr 45, 8021 Zürich
T: (01) 2342361
Focus: Law . . . 10416

Schweizerische Vereinigung für Studentengeschichte (SVSt), Bärenhubelstr 19, 4800 Zofingen
Focus: Educ; Hist . . . 10417

Schweizerische Vereinigung für Weltraumtechnik, Postfach 2613, 3001 Bern
T: (031) 220382
Focus: Aero . . . 10418

Schweizerische Vereinigung für Zukunftsforschung (SZF) / Swiss Society for Futures Research, c/o Gottlieb Duttweiler-Institut, Postfach 531, 8803 Rüschlikon
T: (01) 7246317; Fax: 7246262
Founded: 1970; Members: 440
Focus: Futurology
Periodical
Zukunftsforschung: Informationen über Zukunftsforschung, Planung und Zukunftsgestaltung (5 times annually) . . . 10419

Schweizerische Vereinigung gegen Tuberkulose und Lungenkrankheiten (SVTL), Falkenpl 9, Postfach, 3001 Bern
T: (031) 3020822; Fax: 3028833
Focus: Pulmon Dis
Periodical
Tuberkulose und Lungenkrankheiten: Beilage zum Bulletin des Bundesamtes für Gesundheitswesen (8 times annually) . . . 10420

Schweizerische Vereinigung zum Schutz und zur Förderung des Berggebietes (VSB), Neue Simplonstr 40, 3900 Brig
T: (028) 234212
Focus: Ecology
Periodical
VSB Bulletin (quarterly) . . . 10421

Schweizerische Verkehrswirtschaftliche Gesellschaft, c/o Institut für Verkehrswirtschaft, Universität Sankt Gallen, Varnbüelstr 19, 9000 Sankt Gallen
T: (071) 2242525; Fax: 2242536
Founded: 1950; Members: 300
Focus: Transport
Periodical
Jahrbuch der Schweizerischen Verkehrswirtschaft (annually) . . . 10422

Schweizerische Zahnärzte-Gesellschaft, Münzgraben 2, 3000 Bern 7
T: (031) 3117628; Fax: 3117470
Founded: 1886; Members: 4500
Focus: Dent
Periodical
Schweizerische Monatsschrift für Zahnmedizin (13 times annually) . . . 10423

Schweizerische Zentralstelle für Baurationalisierung (CRB), Zentralstr 153, 8040 Zürich
T: (01) 4564545; Fax: 4564566
Focus: Civil Eng; Business Admin . . . 10424

Schweizerische Zentralstelle für Heilpädagogik (SZH), Obergrundstr 61, 6003 Luzern
T: (041) 2263040; Fax: 2263041
Focus: Educ; Med . . . 10425

Schweizerische Zentralstelle für Hochschulwesen, Sennweg 2, 3012 Bern
T: (031) 3066045; Fax: 3026811
Founded: 1920
Focus: Educ . . . 10426

Schweizerische Zoologische Gesellschaft (SZG), c/o Zoologisches Museum, Universität Zürich-Irchel, Winterthurerstr 190, 8057 Zürich
Founded: 1893; Members: 630
Focus: Zoology
Periodical
Revue Suisse de Zoologie: Annales d'Histoire Naturelle de Genève (quarterly) . . . 10427

Schweizerischer Akkordeon-Lehrer-Verband (SALV), Kaspar-Kopp-Str 121, 6030 Ebikon
T: (041) 4207437; Fax: 4207437
Focus: Educ; Music . . . 10428

Schweizerischer Altphilologen-Verband, Kloster, 8840 Einsiedeln
T: (055) 4186336
Focus: Ling; Lit
Periodical
Bulletin (semi-annually) . . . 10429

Schweizerischer Anglistenverband, Bürglenweg 3, 8854 Galgenen
T: (055) 4408442
Focus: Ling; Lit . . . 10430

Schweizerischer Anwaltsverband, Bollwerk 21, 3001 Bern
T: (031) 3122505; Fax: 3123103
Founded: 1898; Members: 5400
Pres: Dr. Ulrich Hirt; Gen Secr: F. Meyer
Focus: Law
Periodical
Der Schweizer Anwalt (bi-monthly) . . . 10431

Schweizerischer Apotheker-Verein / Société Suisse de Pharmacie, Stationsstr 12, 3097 Bern-Liebefeld
T: (031) 7985858; Fax: 9785859
Founded: 1843; Members: 5200
Focus: Pharmacol
Periodicals
Index Nominum
Pharmaceutica Acta Helvetiae
Schweizerische Apothekerzeitung . . . 10432

Schweizerischer Arbeitermusikverband, Freiburgstr 41, 3178 Bösingen
T: (031) 7470646, 7406260; Fax: 7406226
Focus: Music . . . 10433

Schweizerischer Ausschuss für Prüfung und Zertifizierung (SAPUZ), c/o Geschäftsstelle SNV, Mühlebachstr 54, 8008 Zürich
T: (01) 2545454; Fax: 2545474
Focus: Transport . . . 10434

Schweizerischer Ballettlehrer-Verband, Holgass-Str 47, 8634 Hombrechtikon
T: (055) 424494
Focus: Educ; Perf Arts . . . 10435

Schweizerischer Berufsverband für Angewandte Psychologie (SBAP), Winkelweg 3, 8127 Forch
T: (01) 9803620; Fax: 9803620
Founded: 1952; Members: 380
Focus: Psych
Periodical
SBAP-Bulletin (quarterly) . . . 10436

Schweizerischer Berufsverband Soziale Arbeit SBS, Holligenstr 70, 3000 Bern 21
T: (031) 3822822; Fax: 3821125
Focus: Sociology; Educ
Periodicals
Sozialarbeit (monthly)
Travail Social (monthly) . . . 10437

Schweizerischer Bühnenverband, Farlifangstr 12, 8126 Zumikon, Postfach 9
T: (01) 9181880; Fax: 9181880
Focus: Perf Arts . . . 10438

Schweizerischer Bund für Elternbildung (SBE), Schaffhauserstr 78, 8001 Zürich
T: (01) 2592394
Focus: Adult Educ
Periodical
Bulletin SBE (quarterly) . . . 10439

Schweizerischer Bund für Jugendliteratur, Gewerbestr 8, 6330 Cham
T: (041) 7414130; Fax: 7400159
Focus: Lit . . . 10440

Schweizerischer Burgebverein, c/o IKL Treuhand, Schneidergasse 1, 4001 Basel, 1539
T: (061) 2619977
Focus: Preserv Hist Monuments . . . 10441

Schweizerischer Chemiker-Verband, Im Rehwechsel 19, 4102 Binningen
T: 329069
Focus: Chem
Periodical
Chimia (monthly) . . . 10442

Schweizerischer Elektrotechnischer Verein (SEV), Postfach, 8034 Zürich
T: (01) 3849222; Fax: 4221426
Founded: 1889; Members: 6700
Focus: Electric Eng . . . 10443

Schweizerischer Fachverband der diplomierten medizinischen Laborantinnen und Laboranten, Postgasse 17, 3011 Bern
Fax: (031) 3112656
Focus: Med; Eng
Periodical
Labor und Medizin (monthly) . . . 10444

Schweizerischer Fachverband für Schweiss- und Schneidmaterial (SFAS), Birchstr 230, 8050 Zürich
T: (01) 3012121
Focus: Materials Sci . . . 10445

Schweizerischer Fachverband Sozialdienst in Spitälern, c/o Käthi Lüthi, Zieglerspital, 3007 Bern
Focus: Sociology . . . 10446

Schweizerischer Feldenkrais-Verband, Butzenstr 26, 8910 Affoltern a.A.
T: (01) 7618495; Fax: 7618495
Focus: Psych . . . 10447

Schweizerischer Forstverein (SFV), c/o ETH-Zentrum, HG FO 21.1, 8092 Zürich
T: (01) 2565205
Founded: 1843; Members: 1100
Focus: Forestry
Periodical
Schweizerische Zeitschrift für Forstwesen (monthly) . . . 10448

Schweizerischer Handelslehrerverein / Société Suisse des Professeurs de Sciences Commerciales, Tutilostr 30, 9011 Sankt Gallen
T: (071) 2232741; Fax: 2232741
Focus: Adult Educ
Periodical
Schweizerische Zeitschrift für kaufmännisches Bildungswesen: Revue Suisse pour l'enseignement commercial (bi-monthly) . . . 10449

Schweizerischer Ingenieur- und Architekten-Verein (SIA), Selnaustr 16, 8039 Zürich
T: (01) 2831515; E-Mail: sia@sia.ch; Fax: 2016335
Founded: 1837; Members: 12000
Focus: Archit; Civil Eng
Periodicals
Ingénieurs et Architectes Suisses
Rivista Tecnica della Svizzera Italiana
Schweizer Ingenieur und Architekt . . . 10450

Schweizerischer Internationaler Lyceum-Club, 24 Rue G.-Reimann, 2504 Bienne
T: (032) 3413680
Focus: Ling; Lit . . . 10451

Schweizerischer Juristenverein, CP 3802, 1002 Lausanne
T: (021) 3189111, 7915911; Fax: 7915913
Focus: Law 10452

Schweizerischer Kunstverein, Zeughausstr 55, 8026 Zürich
T: (01) 2416301; Fax: 2416373
Focus: Arts 10453

Schweizerischer Musikpädagogischer Verband / Société Suisse de Pédagogie Musicale, Birchwilerstr 6, 8303 Bassersdorf
T: (01) 8364535
Founded: 1893; Members: 4500
Focus: Music; Educ
Periodicals
Agenda du Musicien: Musikerkalender
Bulletin Mensuel SSPM: Mitteilungsblatt
Feuillets Suisses de Pédagogie Musicale: Schweizer musikpädagogische Blätter . . 10454

Schweizerischer Notarenverband, Gerechtigkeitsgasse 50-52, 867, 3000 Bern 8
T: (031) 3105840; Fax: 3105850
Founded: 1920; Members: 1300
Pres: Bernhard Burkard; Gen Secr: Andreas B. Notter
Focus: Law 10455

Schweizerischer Physiotherapeuten-Verband (SPV), Stadtstr 30, Postfach, 6204 Sempach-Stadt
T: (041) 993388; Fax: 993381
Founded: 1920; Members: 3300
Focus: Therapeutics
Periodical
Der Physiotherapeut (monthly) 10456

Schweizerischer Schriftstellerinnen- und Schriftsteller-Verband (SSV), Kirchgasse 25, Postfach, 8022 Zürich
T: (01) 2613020; Fax: 2613153
Founded: 1912; Members: 650
Pres: Edith Gloor; Gen Secr: Lou Pflüger
Focus: Lit
Periodical
Forum der Schriftstellerinnen und Schriftsteller: Forum des Ecrivaines et Ecrivains (annually) 10457

Schweizerischer Technischer Verband STV (STV), Weinbergstr 41, 8023 Zürich
T: (01) 2683711; E-Mail: info@SwissEngineering.ch; Fax: 2683700
Founded: 1905; Members: 17000
Focus: Eng
Periodical
Schweizerische Technische Zeitschrift (monthly) 10458

Schweizerischer Übersetzer-, Terminologen- und Dolmetscher-Verband (SÜTDV), Postgasse 17, 3011 Bern
T: (031) 3123303; Fax: 3121250
Focus: Ling 10459

Schweizerischer Verband der Akademikerinnen, Masanserstr 93, 7000 Chur
T: (081) 273391
Focus: Sci 10460

Schweizerischer Verband der Betriebsausbilder (SVBA), Via Piro 6, 6948 Porza
T: (091) 9411759, 8075147
Focus: Educ 10461

Schweizerischer Verband der Dozenten an Höheren Technischen Lehranstalten, c/o Ingenieurschule, Quellgasse 21, 2501 Biel
T: (032) 3216111
Focus: Educ; Eng 10462

Schweizerischer Verband der Filmjournalistinnen und Filmjournalisten (SVFJ), Länggasstr 36, 3012 Bern
T: (031) 3014970; Fax: 3014970
Focus: Cinema 10463

Schweizerischer Verband der Gewerbe- und Hauswirtschaftslehrerinnen und -lehrer (SVGH), Niederbürerstr 36b, 9220 Bischofszell
Focus: Educ; Home Econ 10464

Schweizerischer Verband der Ingenieur-Agronomen und der Lebensmittel-Ingenieure / Association Suisse des Ingénieurs Agronomes et des Ingénieurs en Technologie Alimentaire, Länggasse 79, 3052 Zollikofen
T: (031) 570668; Fax: 574925
Founded: 1901; Members: 2200
Focus: Agri; Nutrition
Periodical
Bulletin 10465

Schweizerischer Verband der Lehrerinnen und Lehrer an kaufmännischen Berufsschulen, Stokarbergstr 1, 8200 Schaffhausen
T: (052) 6243541; Fax: 6243530
Focus: Adult Educ 10466

Schweizerischer Verband der Philosophielehrer an Mittelschulen, CP 43, 1912 Leytron
T: (027) 3222930; Fax: 3237920
Focus: Educ; Philos 10467

Schweizerischer Verband des Theaters für Kinder und Jugendliche (ASTEJ), Hardturmstr 130, 8005 Zürich
T: (01) 2730330; Fax: 2731094
Focus: Perf Arts 10468

Schweizerischer Verband für Betriebsorganisation und Fertigungstechnik (SVBF), Postfach 350, 8401 Winterthur
Founded: 1946; Members: 2900
Focus: Business Admin
Periodical
P+P, Planung + Produktion: Fachzeitschrift für Organisation, Rationalisierung, Informationsverarbeitung, Produktionstechnik (monthly) 10469

Schweizerischer Verband für die Materialtechnik (SVMT), c/o Mat Search, 15 Chemin Jean Pavillard, 1009 Pully
T: (021) 7290154; Fax: 7290156
Focus: Materials Sci
Periodical
Oberflächen-Werkstoffe (11 times annually) 10470

Schweizerischer Verband für die Wärmebehandlung der Werkstoffe (SVW), c/o Technikum Winterthur, Ingenieurschule, Postfach, 8401 Winterthur
T: (052) 826349
Focus: Eng 10471

Schweizerischer Verband für Fernunterricht / Swiss Association for Education by Correspondence, Postfach 866, 8280 Kreuzlingen 1
T: (071) 6724444; Fax: 6725562
Founded: 1971
Focus: Educ 10472

Schweizerischer Verband für Frauenrechte, Postfach, 9035 Grub (AR)
T: (071) 8914584; Fax: 8914584
Focus: Law
Periodical
Contact (semi-annually) 10473

Schweizerischer Verband für Landtechnik (SVLT), Postfach 55, 5223 Riniken
T: (056) 4412022; E-Mail: zs@agrartechnik.ch; Fax: 4416731
Founded: 1924; Members: 32000
Focus: Eng; Agri
Periodical
Schweizer Landtechnik: Technique Agricole (15 times annually) 10474

Schweizerischer Verband für Sport in der Schule (SVSS), Neubrückstr 155, Postfach, 3000 Bern 26
T: (031) 3028802; Fax: 3028812
Members: 8000
Focus: Sports; Educ
Periodical
Sporterziehung in der Schule (bi-monthly) 10475

Schweizerischer Verband kantonal approbierter Zahnärzte, Bäckerstr 15, 8004 Zürich
T: (01) 2424722
Focus: Dent 10476

Schweizerischer Verein der Chemiker-Coloristen (SVCC), Postfach 41, 4665 Oftringen
T: 431111
Founded: 1922
Focus: Chem 10477

Schweizerischer Verein des Gas- und Wasserfaches (SVGW) / Swiss Gas and Water Industry Association, SGWA, Grütlistr 44, Postfach 658, 8027 Zürich
T: (01) 2021633
Members: 1029
Focus: Water Res; Energy
Periodical
gwa: Gas Wasser Abwasser (monthly) . 10478

Schweizerischer Verein für die deutsche Sprache (SVDS), Alpenstr 7, 6004 Luzern
T: (041) 4101910; Fax: 4101710
Focus: Ling 10479

Schweizerischer Verein für Schule und Fortbildung (SVSF), Bennwiler Str 6, 4434 Hölstein
T: (061) 9512331/33; Fax: 9512355
Focus: Educ 10480

Schweizerischer Verein für Schweisstechnik, St. Alban-Rheinweg 222, 4006 Basel
T: (061) 3178484; Fax: 3178480
Pres: J. Imler; Gen Secr: Dr. P. Kunzmann
Focus: Eng
Periodical
Schweißtechnik als Bestandteil der Technica (9 times annually) 10481

Schweizerischer Verein für Umweltsimulation (SVU), 3000 Bern
Focus: Ecology 10482

Schweizerischer Verein für Vermessung und Kulturtechnik (SVVK), Postfach 732, 4501 Solothurn
T: (032) 6246503; Fax: 6246508
Founded: 1902; Members: 850
Pres: René Sonney; Gen Secr: Silvia Steiner
Focus: Surveying; Eng
Periodical
Vermessung, Photogrammetrie, Kulturtechnik (monthly) 10483

Schweizerischer Verkehrssicherheitsrat, Schwanengasse 3, 3001 Bern
T: (031) 3123638; Fax: 3121839
Founded: 1952; Members: 230
Focus: Transport 10484

Schweizerischer Werkbund (SWB), Limmatstr 118, 8031 Zürich
T: (01) 2727176; Fax: 2727506
Founded: 1913; Members: 1000
Pres: Ellen Meyrat-Schlee; Gen Secr: Leonhard Fünfschilling
Focus: Ecology; Archit; Mass Media
Periodical
SWB-Information (quarterly) 10485

Schweizerischer Wissenschaftsrat (SWR), Inselgasse 1, 3003 Bern
T: (031) 3229666; Fax: 3228070
Founded: 1965; Members: 22
Pres: Prof. Verena Meyer; Gen Secr: Dr. Edo Poglia
Focus: Sci
Periodicals
Futura/Fer: Ergebnisse des Projektes Forschungspolitische Früherkennung des Schweizerischen Wissenschaftsrates (quarterly)
Jahresbericht (annually)
Wissenschaftspolitik: Mitteilungsblatt der schweizerischen wissenschaftlichen Instanzen 10486

Schweizerisches Bildungswerkstatt, Arbeitsgemeinschaft für persönliche und politische Bildung, Pl 7, 8200 Schaffhausen
T: (052) 6245330, (031) 3013664
Focus: Educ 10487

Schweizerisches Institut für das Gesundheitswesen, Pfrundweg 14, 5001 Aarau
T: (064) 247161; Fax: 245138
Focus: Public Health 10488

Schweizerisches Institut für Kunstwissenschaft (SIK) / Institut Suisse pour l'Etude de l'Art, Zollikerstr 32, Postfach, 8032 Zürich
T: (01) 3885151; E-Mail: sik@sik.unizh.ch; Fax: 3815250
Founded: 1951; Members: 2000
Pres: Dr. Johannes Fulda; Gen Secr: Dr. Hans-Jörg Heusser
Focus: Arts
Periodicals
Jahresbericht (annually)
SIK-Bulletin (semi-annually) 10489

Schweizerisches Institut für Volkskunde, Augustinergasse 19, 4051 Basel
T: (061) 2619900; Fax: 2619900
Founded: 1937; Members: 1900
Focus: Folklore 10490

Schweizerisches Komitee für Kultugüterschutz, Bundesamt für Zivilschutz, Postfach, 3003 Bern
T: (031) 3225256
Focus: Preserv Hist Monuments 10491

Società Retorumantscha (SRR), Ringstr 34, 7000 Chur
T: (081) 223435; 2846642; Fax: 2846642
Founded: 1885; Members: 660
Focus: Ling
Periodicals
Annalas da la Società Retorumantscha (annually)
DRG, Dicziunari Rumantsch Grischun (3 times annually) 10492

Società Storica Locarnese (SSL), Via Cappuccini 8, 6600 Locarno
Founded: 1955; Members: 100
Pres: Dr. Ugo Romerio
Focus: Hist
Periodical
Bollettino SSL (annually) 10493

Societá Ticinese di Scienze Naturali, c/o Museo Cantonale di Storia Naturale, Viale Cattaneo 4, 6900 Lugano
T: (091) 9237827
Founded: 1903; Members: 300
Pres: Dr. R. Peduzzi
Focus: Nat Sci
Periodical
Bollettino (annually) 10494

Société Académique, c/o Université, 26 Av du 1er Mars, 2000 Neuchâtel
Founded: 1889; Members: 440
Focus: Sci 10495

Société Astronomique Suisse (SAG), Gristenbühl 13, 9315 Neukirch
T: (071) 4771743
Founded: 1938; Members: 3200
Focus: Astronomy
Periodical
Orion (bi-monthly) 10496

Société de Géographie de Genève, 2 Rue de l'Athénée, 1205 Genève
Founded: 1858; Members: 250
Pres: René Zwahlen
Focus: Geography
Periodical
Le Globe: Bulletin et Mémoires (annually) 10497

Société de Physique et d'Histoire Naturelle de Genève, c/o Muséum d'Histoire Naturelle, Rte de Malagnou, CP 6434, 1211 Genève 6
T: (022) 4186300; E-Mail: jean.wuest@mhn.ville-ge.ch; Fax: 4186301
Founded: 1790; Members: 237
Pres: P. Tissot; Gen Secr: J. Wüest
Focus: Hist; Nat Sci; Physics
Periodical
Archives des Sciences (3 times annually) 10498

Société des Professeurs d'Allemand en Suisse Romande et Italienne, 22 Chemin de la Gradelle, 1224 Genève
T: (022) 483944
Focus: Educ; Ling 10499

Société d'Histoire de la Suisse Romande, c/o Bibliothèque Cantonale et Universitaire, Dorigny, 1015 Lausanne
T: (021) 6923225
Founded: 1837; Members: 500
Focus: Hist
Periodical
Mémoires et Documents 10500

Société d'Histoire et d'Archéologie de Genève, c/o Bibliothèque Publique et Universitaire, Les Bastions, 1211 Genève 4
Founded: 1838; Members: 530
Focus: Archeol; Hist
Periodicals
Bibliographie genevoise (annually)
Bulletin (annually)
Mémoires et Documents (irregularly) . . 10501

Société et Fédération Internationale de Cardiologie (SIC) / International Society and Federation of Cardiology, ISFC, 34 Rue de l'Athénée, CP 117, 1211 Genève 12
T: (022) 3476755; E-Mail: 101764.2635@compuserve.com; Fax: 3471028
Founded: 1978; Members: 126 national organisations
Focus: Cardiol
Periodical
Heartbeat (quarterly) 10502

Société Fribourgeoise des Sciences Naturelles, c/o Faculté des Sciences, Université, Pérolles, 1700 Fribourg
T: (037) 826111
Founded: 1886; Members: 340
Focus: Nat Sci
Periodical
Bulletin de la Société Fribourgeoise des Sciences Naturelles (annually) 10503

Société Géologique Suisse / Schweizerische Geologische Gesellschaft, c/o Prof. G. Gorin, Dpmt. de Géologie, 13 Rue des Maraichers, 1211 Genève 4
T: (022) 7026607
Founded: 1882; Members: 986
Pres: Prof. G. Gorin; Gen Secr: Dr. M. Sartori
Focus: Geology
Periodical
Eclogae Geologicae Helvetiae (3 times annually) 10504

Société Internationale de Chirurgie (SIC) / International Society of Surgery, Hauptstr 63, Postfach 411, 4153 Reinach
T: (061) 7117036; Fax: 7117303
Founded: 1902; Members: 3500
Focus: Surgery
Periodical
The World Journal of Surgery (bi-monthly) 10505

Société Jean-Jacques Rousseau, c/o Charles Wirz, 26 Rue Voltaire, 1201 Genève
T: (022) 3448050
Founded: 1904
Pres: Alain Grosrichard; Gen Secr: Charles Wirz
Focus: Lit; Philos
Periodical
Annales de la Société Jean-Jacques Rousseau (irregularly) 10506

Société Médicale de la Suisse Romande, 8 Rue de la Dent-Blanche, 1950 Sion
T: (027) 220156
Focus: Med 10507

Société Neuchâteloise des Sciences Naturelles, c/o Bibliothèque Publique et Universitaire, 3 Pl Numa-Droz, 2000 Neuchâtel
T: (038) 207300
Founded: 1832; Members: 400
Focus: Nat Sci
Periodical
Bulletin (annually) 10508

Société Pédagogique de la Suisse Romande, CP 1442, 1227 Carouge
T: (022) 3486437; Fax: 3486437
Focus: Educ
Periodical
L'Educateur (29 times annually) 10509

Société Romande d'Audiophonologie et de Pathologie du Langage (SRAPL), 13 Pl de la Liberté, 2800 Delémont
Founded: 1968; Members: 500
Focus: Otorhinolaryngology 10510

Société Suisse de Chirurgie / Schweizerische Gesellschaft für Chirurgie, c/o Service de Chirurgie, CHUV, 1011 Lausanne
Founded: 1913; Members: 1000
Pres: Dr. J. Ammann; Gen Secr: Dr. J.-C. Givel
Focus: Surgery
Periodical
Helvetica Chirurgica Acta 10511

Société Suisse de Juristes, 1 Av Tribunal Fédéral, 1002 Lausanne
T: (021) 202265
Founded: 1861; Members: 3615
Focus: Law 10512

Société Suisse des Américanistes, 65-67 Blvd Carl-Vogt, 1205 Genève
Founded: 1949; Members: 220
Focus: Ethnology
Periodical
Bulletin (annually) 10513

Sociéte Suisse des Auteurs (SSA), 12 Rue Centrale, 1003 Lausanne, CP 3893, 1002 Lausanne
T: (021) 3126571; Fax: 3126582
Focus: Lit 10514

Société Suisse des Professeurs de Français, 15 Rue Chapeau-Râble, 2300 La Chaux-de-Fonds
T: (032) 9269418
Focus: Educ; Ling 10515

Société Suisse des Professeurs de Musique de l'Enseignement Secondaire, Alpstr 34, 6020 Emmenbrücke
T: (041) 554252
Founded: 1958
Focus: Music; Educ 10516

Société Suisse pour la Recherche en Education, 11 Rte de Drize, 1227 Carouge
T: (022) 209333
Focus: Educ
Periodical
Bildungsforschung und Bildungspraxis: Education et Recherche (3 times annually) 10517

Société Vaudoise des Sciences Naturelles, Palais de Rumine, 1005 Lausanne
T: (021) 3124334; Fax: 3124334
Founded: 1815; Members: 560
Focus: Nat Sci
Periodicals
Bulletin de la Société Vaudoise des Sciences Naturelles (semi-annually)
Mémoires de la Société Vaudoise des Sciences Naturelles (irregularly) 10518

Société Vaudoise d'Histoire et d'Archéologie (SVHA), c/o Archives Cantonales vandoises, 32 Rue de la Mouline, 1022 Chavannes-près-Renens
T: (021) 3163711
Founded: 1902; Members: 900
Focus: Archeol; Hist
Periodical
Revue historique vaudoise (annually) . . 10519

Stiftung für Humanwissenschaftliche Grundlagenforschung, Postfach 112, 8030 Zürich
T: (01) 3830922
Founded: 1970
Focus: Humanities 10520

Swiss Political Science Association, c/o Prof. Peter Knoepfel, 21 Rte de la Maladièse, 1022 Chavannes-près-Renens
T: (021) 6940643; E-Mail: serge.terribilini@idheap.unil.ch; Fax: 6940609
Founded: 1959; Members: 900
Focus: Poli Sci
Periodicals
Année Politique Suisse (annually)
Annuaire Suisse de Science Politique (annually)
Bulletin de l'Association Suisse de Science Politique (quarterly) 10521

Union Internationale contre le Cancer; International Union Against Cancer, 3 Rue du Conseil-Général, 1205 Genève
T: (022) 8091811; E-Mail: info@uicc.ch; http://www.uicc.ch; Fax: 8091810
Founded: 1933; Members: 286
Pres: Dr. N. Gray; Gen Secr: A.J. Turnbull
Focus: Cell Biol & Cancer Res
Periodicals
International Journal of Cancer (5 times annually)
UICC Calendar of International Meetings on Cancer (semi-annually)
UICC News (quarterly) 10522

Union Internationale pour la Protection des Obtentions Végétales (UPOV) / International Union for the Protection of New Varieties of Plants, 34 Chemin des Colombettes, 1211 Genève 20
T: (022) 3389111; E-Mail: wpow.mail@wipo.int; Fax: 7335428
Founded: 1961; Members: 32
Gen Secr: Arpad Bogsch
Focus: Law; Agri
Periodical
Plant Variety Protection (irregularly) . . . 10523

Verband der Bibliotheken und der Bibliothekare/innen derSchweiz (BBS), Effingerstr 35, 3008 Bern
T: (031) 3824240
Founded: 1894; Members: 1850
Pres: Edmund Wiss; Gen Secr: Myriam Boussina
Focus: Libraries & Bk Sci 10524

Verband der Heilpädagogischen Ausbildungsinstitute der Schweiz (VHpA) / Union Suisse des Instituts de Formation en Pédagogie Curative (UIPC), Obergrundstr 61, 6003 Luzern
T: (041) 2263040; E-Mail: szh@mail.tic.ch; Fax: 2263041
Founded: 1976; Members: 9 Ausbildungsinstitute
Pres: Thomas Hagmann
Focus: Educ; Rehabil 10525

Verband der Kantonschemiker der Schweiz, Muesmattstr. 19, Postfach, 3000 Bern 9
T: (031) 6331111
Focus: Chem 10526

Verband der Lehrerinnen und Lehrer für Bürofächer (VLMB), Neufeldstr 18a, 3604 Thun
T: (033) 3350700; Fax: 3350705
Members: 700
Focus: Adult Educ 10527

Verband der Lehrerinnen und Lehrer für Bürofächer, Neufeldstr 18, 3604 Thun
T: (033) 3365632
Focus: Educ 10528

Verband der Museen der Schweiz, Baselstr 7, 4500 Solothurn
T: (032) 6236710; E-Mail: vms.icom@bluewih.ch; Fax: 6238583
Founded: 1966; Members: 520
Pres: Dr. Josef Brülisauer; Gen Secr: Verena von Sury Zumsteg
Focus: Arts
Periodical
Information VMS/AMS (semi-annually) . . 10529

Verband der Schweizer Geographen / Association Suisse de Géographie, c/o Geographisches Institut, Universität Basel, Spalenring 145, 4055 Basel
T: (061) 2726480; Fax: 2726923
Founded: 1990; Members: 190
Pres: Dr. Daniel Schaub; Gen Secr: Hella Marti
Focus: Geography
Periodical
Geographica Helvetica (quarterly) 10530

Verband der Schweizerischen Volkshochschulen (AUPS) / Association des Universités Populaires Suisses, Hallerstr 58, 3000 Bern 26
T: (031) 3028209; Fax: 3025646
Founded: 1943; Members: 85
Focus: Adult Educ 10531

Verband deutschschweizerischer Ärzte-Gesellschaften (Vedag), Gässlistr 17, 8856 Tuggen
T: 512212
Focus: Med
Periodical
Sprechstunde: Das Magazin der Ärzte für Ihre Gesundheit (bi-monthly) 10532

Verband freierwerbender Schweizer Architekten (FSAI), Zeughausstr 12, 8853 Lachen
T: (055) 633263
Focus: Archit 10533

Verband Jüdischer Lehrer und Kantoren der Schweiz, Brandschenkesteig 12, 8002 Zürich
T: (01) 2020025
Founded: 1926; Members: 62
Pres: Erich A. Hausmann; Gen Secr: Michel Bollag
Focus: Educ
Periodical
Bulletin 10534

Verband Musikschulen Schweiz, Postfach 49, 4410 Liestal
T: (061) 9275530; Fax: 9275531
Members: 375
Pres: Hans Brupbacher
Focus: Educ; Music
Periodical
Animato (bi-monthly) 10535

Verband Schweizer Abwasser- und Gewässerschutzfachleute (VSA), Strassburgstr 10, Postfach 2443, 8026 Zürich
T: (01) 2412585; Fax: 2416129
Founded: 1944; Members: 1420
Focus: Eng; Ecology 10536

Verband Schweizerischer Assistenz- und Oberärzte (VSAO) / Association Suisse des Médecins Assistants et Chefs de Clinique, Dahlhölzliweg 3, Postfach 229, 3000 Bern 6
T: (031) 3511573; Fax: 3529008
Founded: 1945
Focus: Med
Periodical
Bulletin VSAO (bi-monthly) 10537

Verband Schweizerischer Handelsschulen (VSH), Seftigenstr 240, 3084 Wabern
T: (031) 3073030; Fax: 3025737
Focus: Educ; Commerce 10538

Verband Schweizerischer Marketing- und Sozialforscher (SMS), c/o IHA Institut für Marktanalysen AG, 6052 Hergiswil
T: (041) 952222
Focus: Marketing; Soc Sci
Periodical
Media-Trend-Journal (3 times annually) . 10539

Verband Schweizerischer Privatschulen (VSP), Christoffelgasse 3, 3011 Bern
T: (031) 3118900; Fax: 3110459
Focus: Educ 10540

Verband Schweizerischer Vermessungsfachleute (VSVT), c/o Marja Balmer, Weissersteinstr 15, 3400 Burgdorf
T: (034) 4229804; Fax: 4229804
Founded: 1929; Members: 1450
Focus: Surveying
Periodical
Vermessung-Photogrammetrie-Kulturtechnik (monthly) 10541

Verband technischer Schulen (VTS), 11a Ch. de la Rose, 2025 Chez-le-Bart
T: (032) 8353236; Fax: 8353157
Focus: Educ; Eng 10542

Verein der Freien Pädagogischen Akademie, Postfach, 8908 Hedingen
T: (01) 7615235
Focus: Educ 10543

Verein für wirtschaftshistorische Studien, Weidächerstr 66, 8706 Meilen
T: (01) 9232823; Fax: 9232813
Focus: Econ; Hist 10544

Verein Geschichte und Informatik, c/o Historisches Institut der Universität, Unitobler, Länggasstr 49, 3000 Bern 9
T: (031) 6318091; Fax: 6314410
Focus: Hist; Computer & Info Sci . . . 10545

Verein katholischer Lehrerinnen der Schweiz, Dammstr 11, 6280 Hochdorf
T: (041) 9101236
Founded: 1891
Pres: Marlina Blum; Gen Secr: Iwana Höltschi
Focus: Educ
Periodicals
Lehreragenda (annually)
Notenheft (annually)
Unterrichtsheft (annually)
Unterrichtsjournal (annually) 10546

Verein Scheizerischer Gymnasiallehrerinnen und Gymnasiallehrer (VSG), Waisenhauspl 14, 3001 Bern
T: (031) 3110779; Fax: 3110982
Focus: Educ 10547

Verein Schweizerdeutsch, Herrenbergstr 5, 8006 Zürich
T: (01) 3616230
Founded: 1938; Members: 1000
Focus: Ling
Periodical
Mundart: Forum des Vereins Schweizerdeutsch (quarterly) 10548

Verein Schweizerische Juristische Datenbank (VSJDB), 38-40 Rue de Lausanne, 1702 Fribourg, CP 90
T: (026) 3231303; Fax: 2321310
Focus: Law; Computer & Info Sci . . . 10549

Verein schweizerischer Deutschlehrer und Deutschlehrerinnen, Kantonschule Büelrain, 8401 Winterthur
T: (052) 2677411; Fax: 2677424
Focus: Educ; Ling 10550

Verein Schweizerischer Geographielehrerinnen und Geographielehrer (VSGg), Kantonsschule, 5610 Wohlen
T: (056) 6224994; Fax: 6227836
Focus: Educ; Geography 10551

Verein Schweizerischer Geschichtslehrer, Chesa de Perini, 7525 S-Chanf
T: (081) 8542613; E-Mail: 101356.220@compuserve.com; Fax: 8542613
Founded: 1913
Focus: Hist; Educ
Periodical
Bulletin (annually) 10552

Verein Schweizerischer Mathematik- und Physiklehrer, 69 Ch. du Levant, 1005 Lausanne
T: (021) 3126761
Focus: Educ; Math; Physics 10553

Verein Zürcher Graphologen, c/o Zürischer Graphologie Schule, Stationsstr 64c, 8907 Wettswil
T: (01) 7001657
Focus: Graphology 10554

Verein zur Förderung der Augenoptik, Holbeinstr 20, 8008 Zürich
T: (01) 344241
Focus: Optics 10555

Verein zur Förderung der Wasser- und Lufthygiene (VFWL), Spanweidstr 3, 8006 Zürich
T: (01) 3634922
Focus: Hygiene
Periodical
Boden-Wasser-Luft 10556

Vereinigung der Freunde antiker Kunst, c/o Archäologisches Seminar, Universität, Schönbeinstr 20, 4056 Basel
T: (061) 2673063; Fax: 2673068
Founded: 1956; Members: 725
Pres: Dr. Jean-Robert Gisler
Focus: Arts; Archeol
Periodical
Antike Kunst (semi-annually) 10557

Vereinigung der Gymnastiklehrer, Hirschgartnerweg 31, 8057 Zürich
T: (01) 469267
Focus: Adult Educ; Sports 10558

Vereinigung der Kunsthistorikerinnen und Kunsthistoriker in der Schweiz, c/o Schweizerisches Institut für Kunstwissenschaft (SIK), Zollikoferstr 32, 8032 Zürich
T: (01) 3885151
Focus: Hist; Arts 10559

Vereinigung der Schweizer Denkmalpfleger, c/o Denkmalpflege der Stadt Bern, Postfach 636, 3000 Bern 8
T: (031) 3216090
Focus: Preserv Hist Monuments 10560

Vereinigung der Schweizerischen Mittelschulturnlehrerinnen (VSMT), Fuchsweg 10, 4512 Bellach
T: (032) 6183784
Focus: Educ 10561

Vereinigung für Rechsstaat und Individualrechte, Benedikt-Hugi-Str 14, 4500 Solothurn
T: (065) 226795
Focus: Law 10562

Vereinigung für Schweizerische Kirchengeschichte, Wolfacher, 6026 Rain
T: (041) 4581851
Focus: Rel & Theol; Hist 10563

Vereinigung für Walsertum (VfW), Bachhalteweg 19, 3900 Brig
T: (028) 233389
Focus: Hist
Periodical
Wir Walser (semi-annually) 10564

Vereinigung für Wirtschaftsforschung Schweiz-Europa/Asien (ERASA), CP 36, 1211 Genève 21
T: (022) 7328310; Fax: 7383996
Focus: Econ 10565

Vereinigung Schweizerischer Archivare (VSA), c/o Schweizerisches Bundesarchiv, Archivstr 24, 3003 Bern
T: (031) 3228989
Founded: 1922; Members: 200
Pres: Dr. R. Aebersold
Focus: Archives
Periodicals
ARBIDO-Bulletin (8 times annually)
ARBIDO-Revue (quarterly) 10566

Vereinigung Schweizerischer Hochschuldozenten, Hohstalenweg 30, 3047 Bremgarten
T: (031) 3020395
Founded: 1919; Members: 1500
Focus: Educ
Periodical
Bulletin (quarterly) 10567

Vereinigung Schweizerischer Kinder- und Jugendpsychologen (SKJP), Bielstr 9, 4500 Solothurn
T: (032) 6272961; Fax: 6272274
Founded: 1969; Members: 472
Pres: Carla Lanini; Gen Secr: Paul Schmid
Focus: Psych
Periodical
Der Jugendpsychologe (semi-annually) . . 10568

Vereinigung Schweizerischer Naturwissenschaftslehrer (VSN), c/o Dr. Willy Bachmann, Heithigstr 37, 8173 Neerach
T: (01) 8581639
Members: 730
Focus: Nat Sci; Educ
Periodical
c+b: Chemie und Biologie (quarterly) . . 10569

Vereinigung Schweizerischer Petroleumgeologen und -Ingenieure, Schützenmattweg 13, 4460 Gelterkinden
T: (061) 992605
Focus: Geology 10570

Vereinigung Umwelt und Bevölkerung (ECOPOP) / Association Ecologie et Population, Postfach 313, 3052 Zollikofen
T: (031) 9113466; Fax: 9116994
Founded: 1971
Focus: Ecology; Sociology
Periodical
EWPOP-Bulletin (3 times annually) . . . 10571

Volksgesundheit Schweiz (VGS), Splügenstr 3, 8027 Zürich
T: (01) 2023433
Focus: Public Health
Periodical
VGS-Gesundheitsmagazin (monthly) . . . 10572

Waldwirtschaft Verband Schweiz, Rosenweg 14, 4501 Solothurn
T: (032) 6258800; E-Mail: admin@wvs.ch; Fax: 6258899
Founded: 1921; Members: 270
Focus: Forestry
Periodical
Wald + Holz, La Foret: Organe des Waldwirtschaftsverbandes Schweiz (monthly) 10573

Wissenschaftliche Vereinigung zur Pflege des Wirtschafts- und Konsumentenschutzrechts / Scientific Association for Commercial and Consumer Law, Löwenstr 55-57, 8023 Zürich
T: (01) 2118737; Fax: 2120122
Founded: 1978; Members: 210
Focus: Law
Periodical
Schriftenreihe zum Konsumentenschutzrecht 10574

Wissenschaftliche Vereinigung zur Pflege von Rhtorik, Informationsverarbeitung und Kommunikation (RIK), Löwenstr 55-57, 8001 Zürich
T: (01) 2110078
Focus: Ling; Computer & Info Sci; Comm Sci
. . . . 10575

World Association for the School as an Instrument of Peace, 5-7 Rue du Simplon, 1207 Genève
T: (022) 7352422; E-Mail: cifedhopatmail-box.ch; Fax: 7350653
Founded: 1967
Gen Secr: Monique Prindezis
Focus: Educ; Law
Periodical
Ecole et Paix (annually) 10576

World Confederation of Organizations of the Teaching Profession, 5 Av du Moulin, 1110 Morges
T: (021) 8017467; Fax: 8017469
Founded: 1952; Members: 191
Focus: Educ
Periodical
Echo (quarterly) 10577

World Health Organization (WHO), 1211 Genève 27
T: (022) 7912111; E-Mail: UNISANTE-Genève; Fax: 7910746
Founded: 1946; Members: 180
Focus: Public Health
Periodicals
Bulletin of the World Health Organization (bi-monthly)
International Digest of Health Legislation (quarterly)
Weekly Epidemiological Record (weekly)
WHO Drug Information (quarterly)
World Health (monthly)
World Health Forum (quarterly)
World Health Statistics Quarterly (quarterly)
. . . . 10578

World Intellectual Property Organization (WIPO), 34 Chemin des Colombettes, CP 18, 1211 Genève 20
T: (022) 3389111; E-Mail: wipo-mail@wipo.int; Fax: 7335428
Founded: 1967; Members: 164
Gen Secr: Dr. Arpad Bogsch
Focus: Law
Periodicals
Gazette OMPI des Marques Internationales (monthly)
Industrial Property and Copyright (monthly)
International Designs Bulletin (monthly)
PCT Gazette: Gazette of International Patent Applications (weekly)
La Propriété Industrielle et le Droit d'Auteur (monthly) 10579

World Psychiatric Association, c/o Hôpital Psychogériatrique, 1008 Prilly
T: (021) 6436111; Fax: 6436238
Founded: 1961; Members: 64000
Focus: Psychiatry 10580

Zentralverband Schweizer Volkstheater, Hirschgraben 8, 3011 Bern
T: (031) 3820403; Fax: 3817410
Focus: Perf Arts 10581

Syria

Académie Arabe de Damas / Arab Academy of Damascus, BP 327, Damascus
Founded: 1919; Members: 14
Gen Secr: Dr. Adnan Al-Khatib
Focus: Ling; Lit
Periodical
Revue de l'Académie Arabe de Damas (quarterly)
. . . . 10582

Arab Agronomists Union, POB 3800, Damascus
T: (011) 335852, 333017
Focus: Agri 10583

Arab Center for the Studies of Arid Zones and Dry Lands (ACSAD), POB 2440, Damascus
T: (011) 755713
Founded: 1971; Members: 17
Focus: Geology 10584

Arab Centre for Information Studies on Population, Development and Construction, 20 Av Yabroudi, POB 11542, Damascus
T: (011) 425303
Founded: 1974
Focus: Soc Sci; Computer & Info Sci . 10585

Arab Council for Medical Specialization, Elharsh St, El-Mazza, Damascus
T: (011) 248942
Focus: Med 10586

Arab Federation for the Organs of the Deaf (AFOD), POB 4230, Damascus
T: (011) 420652
Founded: 1972
Focus: Med
Periodical
AFOD Newsletter (00) 10587

Arab Institute for Forestry and Ranges, POB 142, Bouga, Lattakia
T: 22000, 28459
Focus: Forestry 10588

Arab States Regional Broadcasting Training Centre, POB 5333, Damascus
T: (011) 661206, 214449
Focus: Educ 10589

Arab Union for Cement and Building Materials (AUCBM), POB 9015, Damascus
T: (011) 665070
Founded: 1977; Members: 70
Focus: Materials Sci
Periodicals
Al-Omran Al-Arabi (quarterly)
AUCBM Journal (quarterly) 10590

Tajikistan

Tajik Academy of Sciences, Pr Rudaki 33, 734025 Dushanbe
T: (03772) 225083; Fax: 234917
Founded: 1951; Members: 69
Pres: S.K. Negmatullaev; Gen Secr: G.H Salibaev
Focus: Sci
Periodicals
Doklady: Report
Izvestiya: Bulletin
Problemy Gastroenterologii: Problems of Gastroenterology 10591

Tanzania

Association of Management Training Institutions of Eastern and Southern Africa (AMTIESA), POB 3030, Arusha
T: (057) 2881; Fax: 7776
Founded: 1985; Members: 27
Focus: Business Admin
Periodical
AMTIESA Bulletin (quarterly) 10592

Confederation of African Medical Associations and Societies (CAMAS), c/o Medical Association of Tanzania, POB 701, Dar es Salaam
Fax: (051) 46229
Founded: 1982
Focus: Med 10593

East Africa Association for Theological Education by Extension (EAATEE), POB 32, Njombe
Founded: 1982
Focus: Rel & Theol; Educ 10594

East Africa Medical Research Council (EAMRC), Town Centre, Arusha
T: (057) 2810
Founded: 1962
Focus: Med 10595

East African Agriculture and Forestry Research Organization (EAAFRO), c/o East African Co-operation, POB 1096, Arusha
T: (057) 42538; Fax: 4255
Founded: 1996; Members: 3
Focus: Forestry; Agri 10596

East African Literature Bureau, POB 1408, Dar es Salaam
Founded: 1948
Focus: Lit 10597

East, Central and Southern African College of Nursing (ECSACON), POB 1009, Arusha
T: (057) 2961; Fax: 2714
Founded: 1988
Focus: Educ; Med 10598

Eastern Africa Statistical Training Centre (EASTC), c/o University of Dar es Salaam, POB 35193, Dar es Salaam
Founded: 1965; Members: 12
Focus: Stats 10599

Eastern African Centre for Research on Oral Traditions and African National Languages (EACROTANAL), POB 600, Zanzibar
T: 30786
Founded: 1979
Focus: Ling
Periodical
EACROTANAL Newsletter 10600

Eastern and Southern African Management Institute (ESAMI), POB 3030, Arusha
T: (057) 2881; Fax: 7776
Founded: 1980; Members: 11
Focus: Business Admin
Periodicals
Africa Management Development Forum
ESAMI Newsletter (quarterly) 10601

Eastern and Southern African Mineral Resources Development Centre (ESAMRDC), POB 1250, Dodoma
T: (0611) 20364
Founded: 1975; Members: 18
Focus: Mineralogy
Periodical
ESAMRDC Newsletter (semi-annually) . . 10602

Eastern and Southern African Universities Research Programme (ESAURP), POB 35121, Dar es Salaam
T: (051) 73687; Fax: 26921
Founded: 1977
Focus: Educ 10603

Historical Association of Tanzania, POB 35050, Dar es Salaam
Founded: 1966; Members: 2000
Pres: Prof. I.N. Kimambo; Gen Secr: M.L. Sago
Focus: Law 10604

Society for Clinical and Experimental Pharmacology in SADC/COMESSA/PTA Countries (SOCEPTA), POB 65010, Dar-es-Salaam
T: (051) 150816, 151351; E-Mail: amassele@tan.healthnet.org; Fax: 151596
Founded: 1989; Members: 76
Pres: Prof. Gabriel M.P. Mwaluko; Gen Secr: Prof. Francis D. Juma
Focus: Pharmacol 10605

Tanzania Commission for Science and Technology, POB 4302, Dar es Salaam
T: (051) 75311; Fax: 75313
Founded: 1968
Focus: Sci; Eng
Periodicals
Annual Report (annually)
S & T News (quarterly) 10606

Tanzania Library Association (TLA), POB 2645, Dar es Salaam
Founded: 1965; Members: 200
Pres: Theophilus E. Mlaki; Gen Secr: M. Ngaiza
Focus: Libraries & Bk Sci
Periodicals
Matukio (irregularly)
Someni: Tanzania Library Association Journal (semi-annually) 10607

Tanzania Medical Association, POB 9083, Dar es Salaam
Focus: Med 10608

Tanzania Society, POB 511, Dar es Salaam
T: (051) 44311
Founded: 1936; Members: 1200
Focus: Ethnology; Hist
Periodical
Tanzania Notes and Records (annually) . 10609

Tanzania Veterinary Association (TVA), POB 3174, Morogoro
T: (056) 4647, 4980; Fax: 3177
Founded: 1968; Members: 380
Pres: Prof. U.M. Minga; Gen Secr: Dr. A.E. Pereka
Focus: Vet Med
Periodicals
Proceedings of the Tanzania Veterinary Association Scientific Conferences (annually)
Tanzania Veterinary Journal (semi-annually)
. . . . 10610

Thailand

Agricultural Information Development Scheme, c/o ESCAP, Agriculture and Rural Development Div, UN Bldg, Rajadammen Av, Bangkok 10200
T: (02) 2829161, 2829181
Founded: 1979
Focus: Computer & Info Sci
Periodical
Agricultural Information Development Bulletin (quarterly) 10611

Agricultural Science Society of Thailand, c/o Kasetsart University, POB 1070, Bangkok 10903
Founded: 1967
Focus: Agri 10612

Applied Scientific Research Corporation of Thailand, 196 Phahonyothin Rd, Bangkok
Focus: Sci 10613

ASEAN Federation of Engineering Organizations (AFEO), c/o Engineering Institute of Thailand, Henri Dunant Rd, Bangkok 10500
Founded: 1980; Members: 6
Focus: Eng 10614

ASEAN Federation of Plastic Surgeons, c/o Dept of Surgery, Chulalongkorn Hospital, Sirindhorn Bldg, Bangkok 10500
Focus: Surgery 10615

ASEAN Institute for Health Development (AIHD), c/o Mahidol University, 25/5 Putthamonthon 4, Salaya, Nakhon Chaisri, Nakhon Pathom 73170
T: (02) 4419040; Fax: 4419044
Founded: 1982
Focus: Public Health 10616

ASEAN Otorhinolaryngological Head and Neck Federation, c/o Dept of Otolaryngology, Siriraj Hospital, Mahidol University, Bangkok 10700
T: (02) 4113254, 4114816
Founded: 1980
Focus: Otorhinolaryngology 10617

ASEAN Sub Committee on Non-Conventional Energy Research (SCNCER), c/o King Mongkut's Institute of Technology, Thonburi, Bangkok 10140
T: (02) 4279242, 4275208; Fax: 4278077
Founded: 1979; Members: 6
Focus: Energy
Periodical
SCNCER Newsletter 10618

Asia and Pacific Commission on Agricultural Statistics (APCAS), c/o FAO Regional Office, Maliwan Mansion, 39 Phra Atit Rd, Bangkok 10200
T: (02) 2817844; Fax: 2800445
Founded: 1963
Focus: Stats; Agri 10619

Asia and Pacific Plant Protection Commission (APPPC), c/o FAO Regional Office, Maliwan Mansion, Phra Atit Rd, Bangkok 10200
T: (02) 2817844; E-Mail: Chongyao.Shen@field.fao.org.; Fax: 2800445
Founded: 1955; Members: 26
Gen Secr: Dr. Chongyao Shen
Focus: Agri 10620

Asia and Pacific Programme of Educational Innovation for Development (APED), c/o UNESCO PROAP, 920 Sukhumvit Rd, POB 967, Prakanong Post Office, Bangkok 10110
T: (02) 3910879; Fax: 3910866
Founded: 1973
Focus: Educ 10621

Asia Foundation, POB 1910, Bangkok 5
Focus: Educ; Econ; Sociology 10622

Asia-Pacific Forestry Commission (APFC), c/o FAO Regional Office, Maliwan Mansion, Phra Atit Rd, Bangkok 10200
T: (02) 2817844; Fax: 2800445
Founded: 1949
Focus: Forestry 10623

Asia-Pacific Information Network in Social Sciences (APINESS), c/o RUSHSAP, UNESCO Annex Office, 24/1 Sukhumvit Soi 59, POB 967, Bangkok 10110
T: (02) 3811347; Fax: 3910866
Founded: 1986
Focus: Soc Sci
Periodicals
APINESS Newsletter
APPEN Features Service
Asia-Pacific Environment Newsletter (quarterly)
Environmental News Digest (3 times annually)
. . . . 10624

Asia-Pacific Programme of Education for All (APPEAL), c/o UNESCO PROAP, 920 Sukhumvit Rd, POB 967, Prakanong Post Office, Bangkok 10110
T: (02) 3910879; Fax: 3910866
Founded: 1986; Members: 29
Focus: Educ 10625

Asian and Pacific Information Network on Medicinal and Aromatic Plants (APINMAP), c/o Ministry of University Affairs, 328 Sri Ayutthya Rd, Bangkok 10400
T: (02) 2589853, 2451157; Fax: 2871443
Founded: 1987
Focus: Botany 10626

Asian and Pacific Project for Labour Administration (ARPLA), Labour Dept Bldg, Fuangnakorn Rd, Bangkok
Focus: Business Admin 10627

Asian Association of Occupational Health (AAOH), c/o Occupational Health Dept, Faculty of Public Health, Mahidol University, 420/1 Rajvidhi Rd, Bangkok 10400
T: (02) 2457793; Fax: 2467765
Founded: 1964
Focus: Public Health 10628

Asian Centre of Educational Innovation for Development (ACEID), c/o UNESCO PROAP, 920 Sukhumvit Rd, POB 967, Prakanong Post Office, Bangkok 10110
T: (02) 3910879
Founded: 1973
Focus: Educ 10629

Asian Disaster Preparedness Center (ADPC), GPOB 2754, Bangkok 10501
T: (02) 5245353; Fax: 5245360
Founded: 1986
Focus: Eng 10630

Asian Institute of Technology Library and Regional Documentation Centre, POB 2754, Bangkok
Focus: Eng; Doc
Periodicals
Abstracts of AIT Reports and Publications on Energy (annually)
AGE Current Awareness Service (bi-monthly)
AGE News (quarterly)
AGE Refdex (annually)
ENFO Newsletter (quarterly)
Environmental Sanitation Abstracts (3 times annually)
Environmental Sanitation Reviews (semi-annually)
Ferrocement Abstracts (annually)
IFIC Do it yourself Series (irregularly)
IFIC Slide Presentation Series (irregularly)
IFIC Specialized Bibliographies (irregularly)
Journal of Ferrocement (quarterly)

RERIC Holdings List (annually)
RERIC International Energy Journal (semi-annually)
RERIC Membership Directory (annually)
RERIC News (quarterly) 10631

Asian-Pacific Federation of Therapeutic Communities (APFTC), 31/1 Eramai, 10 Ekamai Rd, Bangkok 10110
Founded: 1984
Focus: Therapeutics 10632

Asian Society for Environmental Protection (ASEP), c/o Asian Institute of Technology, AIT Center, Room B219, POB 4, Bangkok 12120
T: (02) 5245245; E-Mail: asep@ait.ac.th; Fax: 5245236
Founded: 1984; Members: 300
Pres: Augustine Koh; Gen Secr: Dr. Günter Tharun
Focus: Ecology
Periodical
ASEP Newsletter (quarterly) 10633

Association of Geoscientists for International Development (AGID), c/o Asian Institute of Technology, POB 2754, Bangkok 10501
T: (02) 5245514; Fax: 5162126
Founded: 1974
Focus: Geology
Periodicals
AGID News (quarterly)
Bulletin des Géosciences en Afrique de l'Ouest (quarterly)
Geociencias (quarterly)
Middle East Geoscience News (quarterly)
South and West Asian Geoscience Newsletter (3 times annually)
West African Geoscience Newsletter . . 10634

Association of Southeast Asian Institutions of Higher Learning (ASAIHL), c/o Chulalongkorn University, Ratasastra Bldg 2, Henri Dunant Rd., Bangkok 10330
T: (02) 256966; Fax: 2554441
Founded: 1956; Members: 120
Focus: Educ 10635

Association of Southeast Asian Marine Scientists, c/o Dept. of Marine Science, Chulalongkorn University, 10330 Bangkok
T: (02) 2185390/95; E-Mail: ssurapho@netserv.chala.ac.th; Fax: 2511951
Founded: 1986
Pres: Suraphol Sudara
Focus: Oceanography 10636

Committee for Co-ordination of Investigations of the Lower Mekong Basin, Pibultham Villa, Kasatsuk Bridge, Bangkok 10330
T: (02) 2250029; Fax: 2252796
Founded: 1957
Focus: Water Res 10637

Environmental Sanitation Information Center (ENSIC), c/o AIT, POB 2754, Bangkok 10501
T: (02) 5160110; Fax: 5162126
Founded: 1978
Focus: Ecology 10638

ESCAP/FAO/UNIDO Fertilizer, Development and Information Network for Asia and the Pacific, c/o FADINAP/ESCAP Agriculture and Rural Development Div, United Nations Bldg, Rajadamnern Av, Bangkok 10200
T: (02) 2829161; Fax: 2812402
Founded: 1978; Members: 25
Focus: Agri 10639

Geotechnical Engineering International Resources Center (GE-IRC), POB 4, Khlong Luang, Pathumthani 12120
T: (02) 5245862; E-Mail: geoferro@ait.ac.th; Fax: 5162126
Founded: 1973
Pres: Prof. R.D. Stuart; Gen Secr: Lilia Robles-Austriaco
Focus: Eng
Periodicals
Current Awareness Service (quarterly)
Geotechnical Engineering Bulletin (quarterly) 10640

Medical Association of Thailand, 3 Silom St, Bangkok
Founded: 1921; Members: 3057
Pres: Prof. Dr. S. Niyomsen; Gen Secr: Prof. Dr. S. Unakol
Focus: Med
Periodical
Journal 10641

National Culture Commission, Ratchadapisek Rd, Huay Khwang, Bangkok 10310
T: (02) 2470013
Founded: 1979
Focus: Sci 10642

Rectors' Conference, c/o Planning Div, Ministry of University Affairs, Si-Ayuthya Rd, Bangkok 10400
Founded: 1971; Members: 14
Pres: Prof. Dr. N. Bhamarapravati; Gen Secr: Prof. Dr. U. Boonprasert
Focus: Educ 10643

Royal Institute, The Royal Grand PalaceGounds, Na Phra Larn Rd, Bangkok 10200
T: (02) 2214822; Fax: 2249910
Founded: 1933; Members: 161
Pres: Prof. Dr. B. Chatamra
Focus: Arts; Sci
Periodicals
Journal (quarterly)
Saranukrom Thai (monthly) 10644

Science Society of Thailand, c/o Faculty of Science, Chulalongkorn University, Phya Thai Rd, Bangkok 10330
T: (02) 2527987; Fax: 2527987
Founded: 1948; Members: 2500
Pres: Dr. M. Chulavatnatol; Gen Secr: Dr. P. Ongsawasdi
Focus: Sci
Periodicals
Journal (quarterly)
Science (monthly) 10645

Siam Society, 131 Soi Asoke, Sukhumvit 21, POB 65, Bangkok
T: (02) 2602830; Fax: 2583491
Founded: 1904; Members: 1500
Pres: Dr. P. Krairiksh; Gen Secr: B. Sampatisiri
Focus: Ethnology
Periodicals
Journal (annually)
Natural History Bulletin (annually) . . . 10646

Southeast Asian Society of Soil Engineering, POB 2754, Bangkok
Focus: Eng 10647

Thai-Bhara Cultural Lodge and Swami Satyananda Puri Foundation, 136/I Siriphongs Rd, Bangkok
Founded: 1940; Members: 450
Focus: Ling; Lit; Philos 10648

Thai Library Association (TLA), 273 Vibhavadee Rangsit Rd, Phyathai, Bangkok 10400
T: (02) 2712084
Founded: 1954; Members: 1524
Pres: M. Chavalit; Gen Secr: K. Suckcharoen
Focus: Libraries & Bk Sci
Periodicals
TLA Bulletin (monthly)
The World of Books 10649

Togo

Association Togolaise pour le Développement de la Documentation, des Bibliothèques, Archives et Musées, c/o Bibliothèque de l'Université, BP 1515, Lomé
Founded: 1959; Members: 60
Pres: K. Attignon; Gen Secr: E. Amah
Focus: Doc; Archives; Arts 10650

Tonga

Tonga Library Association, c/o USP Tonga Cnetre, POB 278, Nuku'alofa
T: 29055; Fax: 29249
Founded: 1981; Members: 40
Pres: Judy Mailei; Gen Secr: Lomalani Kavapalu
Focus: Libraries & Bk Sci 10651

Trinidad and Tobago

Agricultural Society of Trinidad and Tobago, 44 Pembroke St, Port of Spain
Founded: 1894; Members: 528
Focus: Agri
Periodical
Journal (quarterly) 10652

Caribbean Agricultural Research and Development Institute (CARDI), UWI Campus, Saint Augustine
Founded: 1975; Members: 12
Focus: Agri 10653

Caribbean Agro-Economic Society, c/o Dept of Agricultural Economics and Farm Management, University of the West Indies, UWI Campus, Saint Augustine
Founded: 1974
Focus: Agri
Periodicals
Caribbean Agro-Economic Society Journal
Caribbean Agro-Economic Society Newsletter (semi-annually) 10654

Caribbean Association for Feminist Research and Action (CAFRA), PO Bag 442, Tunapuna Post Office, Tunapuna
Founded: 1985
Focus: Soc Sci
Periodicals
CAFRA News (quarterly)
Novedades CAFRA (quarterly) 10655

Caribbean Association of Nutritionists and Dieticians (CANDI), c/o University of the West Indies, 16 Rowland Rd, West Moorings
Founded: 1972
Focus: Nutrition 10656

Caribbean Council for Science and Technology (CCST), 22-24 Saint Vincent St, POB 1113, Port of Spain
Founded: 1980; Members: 13
Focus: Nat Sci; Eng
Periodical
CCST Newsletter (bi-monthly) 10657

Caribbean Documentation Centre (CDC), 22-24 Saint Vincent St, POB 1113, Port of Spain
Members: 21
Focus: Doc
Periodical
Current Awareness Bulletin (monthly) . . 10658

Caribbean Federation for Mental Health, c/o Saint Ann's Hospital, POB 65, Port of Spain
Focus: Psychiatry 10659

Caribbean Industrial Research Institute (CARIRI), Tunapuna PO, Tunapuna
Founded: 1970
Focus: Business Admin
Periodicals
Caribbean Biotechnology Newsletter (quarterly)
CARIRI Technochat (quarterly) 10660

Caribbean Information System for Economic and Social Planning (CARISPLAN), 22 Saint Vincent St, POB 1113, Port of Spain
Founded: 1979; Members: 21
Focus: Soc Sci; Econ
Periodical
CARISPLAN Abstracts (quarterly) 10661

Caribbean Information System for the Agricultural Sciences (CAGRIS), c/o Main Library, University of the West Indies, Saint Augustine
Focus: Agri
Periodicals
Cagrindex (quarterly)
CAGRIS Newsletter 10662

Caribbean Meteorological Organization (CMO), POB 461, Port of Spain
Founded: 1973; Members: 16
Focus: Geophys 10663

Caribbean Plant Protection Commission (CPPC), c/o Ministry of Food Production, Marine Exploitation, Forestry and the Environment, Research Div, Central Experiment Station, Centeno, Arima
Founded: 1967; Members: 22
Focus: Ecology 10664

Caribbean Regional Branch of the International Council on Archives (CARBICA), 105 Saint Vincent St, POB 763, Port of Spain
Founded: 1965
Focus: Archives 10665

Caribbean Sports Medicine Association (CASMA), 77 Picton St, Newton-Hooslook, Port of Spain
Founded: 1986
Focus: Med 10666

Eastern Caribbean Institute of Agriculture and Forestry (ECIAF), Centeno, Arima
Founded: 1954
Focus: Agri; Forestry 10667

Historical Society of Trinidad and Tobago, c/o Ministry of Culture, Eastern Main Rd, Laventille, Port of Spain
Focus: Hist 10668

Library Association of Trinidad and Tobago, POB 1275, Port of Spain
Founded: 1960
Pres: Jennifer Joseph; Gen Secr: Jewel Mathieson-Stewart
Focus: Libraries & Bk Sci
Periodical
Bulletin 10669

Sugar Technologist's Association of Trinidad and Tobago, 80 Abercromby St, POB 230, Port of Spain
Founded: 1967
Focus: Eng 10670

Theosophical Society of Trinidad, Eastern Main Rd, Guaico
Focus: Rel & Theol 10671

Tobago District Agricultural Society, Main St, Scarborough
Focus: Agri 10672

Trinidad Music Association, c/o Bishop Anstey High School, Abercromby St, Port of Spain
Founded: 1941; Members: 102
Focus: Music 10673

Tunisia

Arab Atomic Energy Agency (AAEA), El-Manzah 5, POB 402, 1004 Tunis
T: (01) 766010
Founded: 1988
Focus: Nucl Res 10674

Arab Committee for Ottoman Studies (ACOS), BP 50, 1118 Zaghouan
T: (02) 76446; E-Mail: 676710
Founded: 1983
Pres: Abdeljehil Temimi
Focus: Hist 10675

Arab Federation of Sports Medicine, 6 Rue d'Annaba, Tunis
Founded: 1982
Focus: Med 10676

Arab Information Network for Terminology (ARABTERM), c/o INNOPRI, BP 23, Belvedère, 1012 Tunis
Founded: 1989
Focus: Computer & Info Sci 10677

Arab League Educational, Cultural and Scientific Organization, BP 1120, Tunis
T: (01) 784466; Fax: 784965
Founded: 1964; Members: 20
Focus: Sci; Educ
Periodicals
Al-Lissan Al-Arabi Magazine
ALECSO Newsletter
Arab Culture Magazine
Arab Manuscripts Magazine
Bulletin of Arab Publications
Bulletin of Educational Statistics for the Arab States 10678

Arab Medical Union / Union des Médecins Arabes, BP 290, 1082 Tunis
T: (01) 886800; Fax: 889293
Founded: 1961; Members: 200000
Pres: Dr. Hassan Khreis; Gen Secr: Prof. Aziz El-Matri
Focus: Med
Periodical
Revue Médicale de l'Union des Médecins Arabes (quarterly) 10679

Arab Regional Branch of the International Council on Archives (ARBICA), BP 50, Zaghouan, Tunis
T: (02) 76446
Founded: 1972; Members: 19
Focus: Archives
Periodical
Arab Archives Journal (annually) 10680

Association Africaine de Microbiologie et d'Hygiène Alimentaire (AAMHA) / African Association of Microbiology and Food Hygiene, c/o Dept de Biochimie, Faculté de Médecine, Ibn El-Jazzar, 4000 Sousse
T: (03) 22600 ext 431
Founded: 1984
Focus: Microbio; Food
Periodical
Microbiologie et Hygiène Alimentaire (bi-monthly) 10681

Association Internationale des Archives Francophones (AIAF), c/o Archives Nationales de Tunisie, Premier Ministère, 1020 Tunis
T: (01) 560556; Fax: 560556
Pres: Moncef Fakhfakh; Gen Secr: Claude Minotto
Focus: Archives 10682

Association Maghrébine des Etudes de la Population, 9bis Rue Khaled Ibn El-Qualid, Mutuelleville, Tunis
T: (01) 204760
Focus: Sociology 10683

Association of Arab Institutes and Centres for Economic and Social Research (AICARDES) / Association des Instituts et des Centres Arabes pour les Recherches Economiques et Sociales, c/o Institut d'Economie Quantitative, 27 Rue du Liban, Belvédère, 1002 Tunis
T: (01) 283214, 283216
Founded: 1977
Focus: Soc Sci; Econ 10684

Association Tunisienne des Bibliothécaires, Documentalistes et Archivistes, BP 380, 1015 Tunis
Founded: 1965; Members: 150
Pres: K. Ahmed
Focus: Libraries & Bk Sci; Doc; Archives
Periodical
Rassid (3 times annually) 10685

Comité International d'Etudes Morisques, BP 50, 1118 Zaghouan
T: (02) 76446; E-Mail: 676710
Founded: 1983
Pres: Prof. Abdeljelil Temini
Focus: Ethnology; Hist 10686

Comité National des Musées, c/o Musée National du Bardo, Tunis
Founded: 1961
Pres: Nayla Attya
Focus: Arts
Periodical
Les Musées de Tunisie 10687

Conseil International sur les Mathématiques dans les Pays en Voie de Développement (ICOMIDC), c/o Dépt de Mathématiques, Faculté des Sciences de Tunis, 1060 Campus Universitaire, Tunis
Focus: Math 10688

Institut National d'Archéologie et d'Art, 4 Pl du Château, 1008 Tunis
T: (01) 261622, 261259
Founded: 1957; Members: 80
Focus: Archeol; Ethnology
Periodicals
Africa
Bibliothèque Archéologique
Cahiers des Arts et Traditions Populaires
Etudes Hispano-Andalouses
Notes et Documents 10689

Union Nationale des Arts Plastiques, Musée du Belvédère, Tunis
Focus: Fine Arts 10690

Turkey

Fizik Tedavi ve Rehabilitasyon Derneği / The Society of Physical Medicine and Rehabilitation, c/o Fiziksel Tip ve Rehabilitasyon Derneği, Capa, 34390 Istanbul
T: (0212) 6330505; E-Mail: ftrdern@netacc.net; Fax: 6328464
Founded: 1963; Members: 700
Pres: Prof. Dr. Fikret Tüzün; Gen Secr: Prof. Dr. Ülkü Akarirmak
Focus: Therapeutics; Rehabil
Periodical
Fizik Tedavi Rehabilitasyon Dergisi (quarterly) 10691

Istanbul Dişhekimleri Odasi, Cumhuriyet Cad, Safir Apt 361/3 Harbiye, Istanbul
T: (01) 2444442; Fax: 2445909
Focus: Dent
Periodicals
Dişhekimliğinde Klinik (quarterly)
Ido Dergi (bi-monthly) 10692

Jeoloji Mühendisleri Odasi / Chamber of Geological Engineers of Turkay, PK 464, Kizilay, 06424 Ankara
T: (04) 343601
Founded: 1946; Members: 3200
Focus: Geology
Periodical
Türkiye Kurum Bülteni (semi-annually) . . 10693

Otomatik Kontrol Türk Milli Komitesi / Turkish National Committee of Automatic Control, c/o Makina Fakültesi, Istanbul Teknik Üniversitesi, 80191 Gümüssuyu
T: (0212) 2931300 ext 2474; E-Mail: mkdinib@burgaz.mkn.itu.edu.tr; Fax: 2450795
Founded: 1959; Members: 100
Pres: Prof. Dr. A. Talha Dinibütün; Gen Secr: Prof. Dr. Ibrahim Eksin
Focus: Eng 10694

P.E.N. Yazarlar Derneği / P.E.N., Turkish Centre, Cağaloğlu Yokusu 40, Istanbul
Founded: 1951; Members: 70
Focus: Lit 10695

Türk Anesteziyoloji ve Reanimasyon Derneği (TARD), c/o Cerrahpasa Tip Fakültesi, Istanbul
T: (01) 5861526; Fax: 5295600
Founded: 1956; Members: 600
Focus: Anesthetics
Periodical
Türk Anesteziyoloji ve Reanimas yon Dernégi Mecmuasi (quarterly) 10696

Türk Biyoloji Derneği, PK 144, Sirkeci, Istanbul
Founded: 1949; Members: 200
Focus: Bio 10697

Türk Cerrahi Cemiyeti / Turkish Surgical Society, Valikonagi Cad 10, Harbiye, Istanbul
Founded: 1931; Members: 870
Focus: Surgery 10698

Türk Diabetler Cemiyeti, Meyva Sok 10, Hrabiye, Istanbul
Focus: Diabetes 10699

Türk Dil Kurumu (TDK) / Turkish Linguistic Society, Atatürk Bulvari 217, Ankara
Founded: 1932; Members: 40
Focus: Ling
Periodical
Türk Dili (monthly) 10700

Türk Eczacilari Birliği / Turkish Pharmaceutical Association, Farabi Sok 35, Cankaya, Ankara
T: (0312) 4672512; E-Mail: teb@neuron.ato.org.tr; Fax: 4677585
Founded: 1956; Members: 21500
Pres: Mehmet Domag; Gen Secr: Betül Bilgetekin
Focus: Pharmacol
Periodical
Türk Eczacilari Haberler (bi-monthly) . . 10701

Türk Fizik Derneği, c/o CNAEM, PK 1, Havaalani, Istanbul
T: (01) 737515
Founded: 1950; Members: 282
Focus: Physics 10702

Türk Gastroenterologii Derneği, c/o Dept of Gastroenterology, Gulhane Military Medical Academy, Ankara
Focus: Gastroenter 10703

Türk Hukuk Kurumu / Turkish Law Association, 2 Cad 55/6 Bahcelievler, Ankara
Founded: 1934
Focus: Law
Periodical
Türk Hukuk Lugati 10704

Türk Kanser Arastirma ve Savaş Kurumu, PK 1078, Yenisehir, Ankara
T: (0312) 4312950; Fax: 4313958
Founded: 1947; Members: 2014
Pres: Prof. Munevver Buyukpamukcu; Gen Secr: Prof. Tezer Kutluk
Focus: Cell Biol & Cancer Res
Periodical
Turkish Journal of Cancer 10705

Türk Kardiyoloji Derneği / Turkish Society of Cardiology, Ortaklar cad 4/7, Mecidiyeköy, 80290 Istanbul
T: (0212) 2884455; Fax: 2884433
Founded: 1963; Members: 450
Pres: Altan Onat; Gen Secr: Muzaffer Öztürk
Focus: Cardiol
Periodical
Archives of the TSC (9 times annually) . 10706

Türk Kütüphaneciler Derneği (TKD) / Turkish Librarians' Association, Elgün Sok 8/8, Kizilay, Yenisehir, 06440 Ankara
T: (0312) 2301325; Fax: 2320453
Founded: 1949; Members: 1500
Pres: A. Berberoglu; Gen Secr: Ayhan Kaygusuz
Focus: Libraries & Bk Sci
Periodical
Türk Kütüphaneciliği (quarterly) 10707

Türk Mikrobiyoloji Cemiyeti / Turkish Microbiological Society, PK 57, Beyazit, 34492 Istanbul
T: (0212) 6351186; Fax: 6351186
Founded: 1931; Members: 258
Pres: Prof. Dr. Özdem Ang; Gen Secr: Prof. Dr. Candan Bozok
Focus: Microbio
Periodicals
Infeksion Dergisi (quarterly)
Türk Mikrobiyoloji Cemiyeti Dergisi (quarterly) 10708

Türk Mühendis ve Mimar Odalari Birligi (TMMB) / Union of Chambers of Turkish Engineers and Architects, Konur Sok 4, Yenisehir, 06650 Ankara
T: (0312) 4181275, 4175238; E-Mail: tmmobm-o@tr-net.net.tr; Fax: 4174824
Founded: 1954; Members: 220000
Pres: Yavuz Önen; Gen Secr: Ismet Öztunali
Focus: Archit; Eng; Urban Plan
Periodicals
Elektrik Mühendisliği: Electrical Engineering (bi-monthly)
Endüstri Mühendisliği: Industrial Engineering (bi-monthly)
ETA Dergisi (bi-monthly)
Harita ve Kadastro Mühendisliği: Surveying Engineering (quarterly)
Jeofizik: Geophysics (semi-annually)
Jeoloji Mühendisliği: Geological Engineering (semi-annually)
Kimya Mühendisliği: Chemical Engineering (quarterly)
Madencilik: Mining (bi-monthly)
Metalurji: Metallurgy (bi-monthly)
Mimarlik: Architecture (bi-monthly)
Mühendis ve Makina: Engineers and Machines (monthly)
Orman Mühendisliği: Forest Engineering (bi-monthly)
Tarim ve Mühendislik: Agriculture and Engineering (quarterly)
Tekstil ve Mühendis: Textile and Engineering (every 5 months)
Tesisat Mühendisliği: Installation Engineering
Türkiye Mühendislik Haberleri: News of Engineering in Turkey (bi-monthly) . . . 10709

Türk Nöro-Psikiyatri Dernĕi, c/o I.Ü. Istanbul Tip Fakültesi, Psikiyatri Kliniği, 34390 Capa, Istanbul
Founded: 1914; Members: 1100
Pres: Prof. Dr. Özcan Köknel; Gen Secr: Dr. Rasit Tükel
Focus: Neurology; Psychiatry
Periodical
Nöroppsikiyatri Arsivi: Archives of Neuro-Psychiatry (quarterly) 10710

Türk Oftalmoloji Derneği, c/o Capa Göz Klinigi, Istanbul
Members: 300
Focus: Ophthal 10711

Türk Ortopedi ve Travmatoloji Dernegi / Turkish Association of Orthopaedics and Traumatology, c/o Istanbul Tip Fakültesi Ortopedi ve Travmatoloji Klinigi, Topkapi, 34390 Istanbul
T: (01) 5213687
Founded: 1939; Members: 510
Focus: Orthopedics; Traumatology
Periodical
Acta Orthopaedica et Traumatologica Turcica (5 times annually) 10712

Türk Oto-Rino-Laringoloji Cemiyeti, c/o Capa Kulak Bogaz, Burun Klinigi, Istanbul
Founded: 1930; Members: 150
Focus: Otorhinolaryngology 10713

Türk Sirfi ve Tatbiki Matematik Derneği / Turkish Society of Pure and Applied Mathematics, Dedeefendi Cad 8, Sehzadebasi, Istanbul
Founded: 1948; Members: 100
Focus: Math 10714

Türk Standartlari Enstitüsü (TSE), Necatibey Cad 112, Bakanliklar, Ankara
T: 187240
Founded: 1960
Focus: Standards
Periodical
Standard (monthly) 10715

Türk Tarih Kurumu (TTK) / Turkish Historial Society, Kizilay Sok 1, Ankara
T: (0312) 3102368; E-Mail: yusuf@ttk.gov.tr; Fax: 3101698
Founded: 1931; Members: 40
Pres: Prof. Dr. Yusuf Halacoglu; Gen Secr: Prof. Dr. Özer Ergenc
Focus: Hist
Periodicals
Belgeler (annually)
Belleten (3 times annually) 10716

Türk Tüberküloz Cemiyeti / Turkish Tuberculosis Society, Selime Hatun, Sağlik Sok, Taksim, Istanbul
Founded: 1937
Focus: Immunology 10717

Türk Üniversite Rektörleri Komitesi, YüksekÖgretim Kuruhu, Bilkent, Ankara
T: (0312) 225316
Founded: 1967
Pres: Prof. Dr. Ihsan Dogramaci; Gen Secr: Prof. Dr. Himmet Umunc
Focus: Educ 10718

Türk Uroloji Dernegi / Turkish Urological Society, c/o Dr. Cafer Yildiran, Talimhane Lamartin Cad 46/4, Eren ap Taksim, Istanbul
Founded: 1933; Members: 180
Focus: Urology
Periodical
Türk Uroloji Dergisi: Turkish Journal of Urology (quarterly) 10719

Türk Veteriner Hekimleri Dernegi / Turkish Veterinary Medicine Association, Saglik Sok 21-3, Yenisehir, Ankara
T: (0312) 4316274; Fax: 4357914
Founded: 1930; Members: 3000
Pres: Getin Escan; Gen Secr: Dr. Muzaffer Celebi
Focus: Vet Med 10720

Türkiyat Arastirmalari Entitüsü, Horhor C. Kavalali Sk 5/4 Fatih-IST, Istanbul
T: (0212) 5323507; Fax: 5349495
Founded: 1924
Pres: Prof. Dr. Osman Fikri Sertkayaq
Focus: Ling; Lit; Hist 10721

Türkiye Aktüerler Cemiyeti, Siraselviler Cad 87, Taksim, Istanbul
Focus: Insurance 10722

Türkiye Fitopatolji Derneği / Turkish Phytopathological Society, c/o Zirai Mücadele Araştirma Enstitüsü, Bornova, 35040 Izmir
T: (0232) 3880030; E-Mail: phyto@ziraat.ege.edu.tr; Fax: 3741653
Members: 250
Pres: Dr. Ülkü Yorganci; Gen Secr: Nursen Üstün
Focus: Bio
Periodical
The Journal of Turkish Phytopathology (2-3 times annually) 10723

Türkiye Ziraat Odalari Birligi / Union of Turkish Chambers of Agriculture, Izmir Cad 24, Yenisehir, 06440 Ankara
T: (04) 4171274; E-Mail: Ziraat Odalari; Fax: 4173068
Founded: 1963; Members: 425
Focus: Agri
Periodicals
Agricultural and Economic Report (semi-annually)
Farmer and Rural World (monthly) . . . 10724

Yeni Felsefe Cemiyeti / The New Philosophical Society, Isik Lisesi, Nisantasi, Istanbul
Founded: 1943
Focus: Philos 10725

Turkmenistan

Turkmen Academy of Sciences, Ul Gogolya 15, 744000 Ashkhabad
Members: 55
Pres: A.G. Babaev; Gen Secr: V.N. Nikolaev
Focus: Sci
Periodicals
Izvestiya: Bulletin
Problemy Osvoyeniya Pustyn: Problems of Desert Development 10726

Uganda

Association for Teacher Education in Africa, c/o Prof. J.C.B. Bigala, Makerere University, POB 7062, Kampala
Founded: 1970; Members: 50
Pres: Prof. M. Mohapeloa; Gen Secr: Prof. J.C.B. Bigala
Focus: Educ
Periodicals
Education in Eastern Africa
Journal of West African Education . . . 10727

East African Agricultural Economics Society, c/o Dept of Rural Economy and Extension, Makerere University, POB 7062, Kampala
Founded: 1967
Focus: Agri 10728

East African School of Librarianship (EASL), c/o Makerere University, POB 7062, Kampala
T: (041) 554342
Founded: 1963
Focus: Libraries & Bk Sci; Educ
Periodicals
EASL Bulletin
EASL Newsletter 10729

Inter-University Council for East Africa, POB 7110, Kampala
T: (041) 256251 703=242007
Founded: 1980; Members: 20
Gen Secr: E.K. Kigozi
Focus: Educ 10730

Uganda Library Association (ULA), POB 5894, Kampala
Founded: 1972; Members: 140
Pres: P. Birungi; Gen Secr: L.M. Ssengero
Focus: Libraries & Bk Sci
Periodical
Ugandan Libraries 10731

Uganda Medical Association, POB 243, Kampala
T: (041) 236539; Fax: 532591
Founded: 1961; Members: 850
Pres: Dr. Frank Mwesigye; Gen Secr: Dr. Francis O. Oriokot
Focus: Med 10732

Uganda Society, POB 4980, Kampala
Founded: 1933; Members: 600
Focus: Hist; Lit
Periodical
The Uganda Journal 10733

Ukraine

Academy of Pedagogical Sciences of Ukraine, Tryokhsvyatelska vul 8, 252601 Kiev
T: (04) 2263180; Fax: 2283834
Founded: 1992; Members: 88
Pres: Prof. Mykola D. Yarmachenko
Focus: Educ 10734

National Academy of Sciences of Ukraine, Volodymirska54, 252601 Kiev
T: (044) 2256366; Fax: 2243243
Founded: 1918; Members: 554
Pres: B.E. Paton; Gen Secr: A.P. Shpak
Focus: Sci
Periodicals
Arkheologiya: Archaeology
Avtomaticheskaya Svarka: Automatic Welding
Avtomatika: Automation
Biopolimery i Kletki: Biopolymers and Cells
Dopovidi Akademii Nauk Ukrainy: Report of the Ukrainian Academy of Sciences
Ekonomika Ukrainy: Economy of the Ukraine
Eksperimentalnaya Onkologyia: Experimental Oncology
Electronnoe Modelirovanie: Electronic Modelling
Filosofska i Sotsiologichna Dumka: Philosophy and Sociological Thought
Fizika Nizkikh Temperatur: Low-Temperature Physics
Fiziko-khimicheskaya Mekhanika Materialov: Physical and Chemical Mechanics of Materials
Fiziologicheskii Zhurnal: Physiological Journal
Fiziologiya i Biokhimiya Kulturnykh Rastenii: Physiology and Biochemistry of Cultivated Plants
Geofizicheskii Zhurnal: Geophysical Journal
Geologicheskii Zhurnal: Geological Journal
Gidrobiologicheskii Zhurnal: Hydrobiological Journal
Khimicheskaya Tekhnologiya: Chemical Technology
Khimiya i Tekhnologiya Vody: Water Chemistry and Engineering
Kibernetika, Kinematika i Fizika Nebesnykh Tel: Cybernetics, Kinematics and Physics of Heavenly Bodies
Kriobiologiya: Cryobiology
Literaturoznavstvo: Literary Studies
Metallofizika: Physics of Metals
Morskoi Gidrofizicheskii Zhurnal: Marine Hydrophysical Journal
Movoznavstvo: Linguistics
Narodna Tvorchist ta Etnografiya: Folk Art and Ethnography
Nikrobiologicheskii Zhurnal: Microbiological Journal
Poroshkovaya Metallurgiya: Powder Metallurgy
Prikladnaya Mekhanika: Applied Mechanics
Problemy Prochnosti: Problems of Strength
Problemy Spetsialnoi Elektrometallurgii: Problems of Special Electrometallurgy
Promyshlennaya Teplofizika: Industrial Thermal Physics
Radyanske Pravo: Soviet Law
Sverkhtverdye Materialy: Superhard Materials
Tekhnicheskaya Diagnostika i Nerazrushayushchii Kontrol: Technical Diagnostics and Non-destructive Testing
Tekhnicheskaya Elektrodinamika: Technical Electrodynamics
Teoreticheskaya i Eksperimentalnaya Khimiya: Theoretical and Experimental Chemistry
Tsitologiya i Genetika: Cytology and Genetics
Ukrainskii Biokhimicheskii Zhurnal: Ukrainian Biochemical Journal
Ukrainskii Botanichnyi Zhurnal: Ukrainian Botanical Journal
Ukrainskii Fizicheskii Zhurnal: Ukrainiam Physics Journal
Ukrainskii Istorichnyi Zhurnal: Ukrainian Historical Journal
Ukrainskii Khimicheskii Zhurnal: Ukrainian Chemical Journal
Ukrainskii Matematicheskii Zhurnal: Ukrainian Mathematical Journal
Upravlyayusshchie Sistemy i Mashiny: Control Systems and Computers
Vestnik Zoologiya: Zoological Journal
Visnyk Akademii Nauk Ukrainy: Journal of the Ukrainian Academy of Sciences 10735

Scientific and Technical Societies National Headquarters, Vul Artema 21, 252053 Kiev
T: (044) 2124234
Focus: Sci; Eng *10736*

Ukrainian Academy of Agrarian Sciences, Vul Suvorova 9, 252010 Kiev
T: (044) 2901085; Tx: 131487
Focus: Agri *10737*

Ukrainian Academy of Medical Sciences, Vul Gertsena 12, 254050 Kiev
T: (044) 2133411; Fax: 2193981
Members: 77
Pres: Prof. Yury I. Gubsky
Focus: Med *10738*

United Kingdom

Aberdeen-Angus Cattle Society, 6 King's Pl, Perth PH2 8AD
T: (01738) 22477; Fax: 36436
Founded: 1879; Members: 1100
Focus: Animal Husb
Periodicals
Aberdeen-Angus Herdbook (annually)
Aberdeen-Angus Review (annually) . . . *10739*

Abergavenny and Border Counties Agricultural Society, 5 Lion St, Abergavenny NP7 5PE
T: (01873) 3152
Focus: Agri *10740*

Abortion Law Reform Association (ALRA) / A Woman's Right to Choose Campaign, 11-13 Charlotte St, London W1P 1HD
T: (0171) 6377264; Fax: 4369011
Founded: 1936
Gen Secr: Jane Roe
Focus: Law
Periodical
ALRA Newsletter (quarterly) *10741*

Academi Gymreig / Welsh Academy, Mount Stuart House, Mount Stuart Sq, Cardiff CF1 6DQ
T: (01222) 492025
Founded: 1959; Members: 60
Pres: Nesta Wyn Jones; Gen Secr: Dafydd Rogers
Focus: Ling; Lit
Periodicals
Cyfres Cyfieith-iadau'r Academi
Taliesin *10742*

Academia Europaea, 31 Old Burlington St, London W1X 1LB
T: (0171) 7345402; E-Mail: acadeuro@compuserve.com; Fax: 2875115
Founded: 1988; Members: 1660
Pres: Prof. Stig Strömholm; Gen Secr: Peter Colyer
Focus: Educ; Poli Sci; Sci *10743*

Action Against Allergy (AAA), 43 The Downs, London SW20 8HG
Focus: Immunology *10744*

Action for Dysphasic Adults (ADA), 1 Royal St, London SE1 7LL
T: (0171) 2619572; Fax: 9289542
Founded: 1980
Focus: Logopedy
Periodical
Newsletter (quarterly) *10745*

Action in International Medicine (AIM), 46 Cleveland St, London W1P 6DB
T: (0171) 6363610; Fax: 6363612
Gen Secr: Prof. A.P. Haines
Focus: Med *10746*

Acton Society Trust, 15 Wilton Rd, London SW1V 1LT
Founded: 1948
Pres: Alan Farrant
Focus: Econ; Poli Sci *10747*

Acupuncture Scientific and Clinical Advisory Group, 19 Richmond Hill, Clifton, Bristol BS8 1BA
T: (01272) 739477
Focus: Anesthetics *10748*

Advertising Association (AA), Abford House, 15 Wilton Rd, London SW1V 1NJ
T: (0171) 8282771; Fax: 9310376
Founded: 1926; Members: 27
Pres: A. Brown; Gen Secr: D. Harper
Focus: Advert
Periodical
International Journal of Advertising (quarterly) *10749*

Advisory Centre for Education (ACE), 1b Aberdeen Studio, 22-24 Highbury Grove, London N5 2DY
T: (0171) 3548321; Fax: 3549060
Founded: 1960; Members: 130
Pres: Lord Young of Dartington; Gen Secr: Liz Williams
Focus: Educ
Periodical
ACE-Bulletin (bi-monthly) *10750*

Advisory Committee on Protection of the Sea (ACOPS), 57 Duke St, London W1M 5DH
T: (0171) 4990704; Fax: 4933092
Founded: 1952
Gen Secr: Dr. Viktor Sebek
Focus: Oceanography; Ecology

Periodicals
ACOPS News (quarterly)
ACOPS Yearbook (semi-annually) . . . *10751*

The Aeroplane Collection (TAC), 38 Saint Mark's Av, Oldfield Brow, Altrinchem WA14 4JB
Members: 36
Focus: Aero
Periodical
Control Column *10752*

The Aetherius Society, 757 Fulham Rd, London SW6 5UU
T: (0171) 7364187
Founded: 1955
Gen Secr: Dr. Richard Lawrence
Focus: Rel & Theol
Periodical
Cosmic Voice (quarterly) *10753*

AFASIC overcoming speech impairments, 347 Central Markets, London EC1A 9NH
T: (0171) 2363632
Founded: 1968; Members: 750
Pres: Duchess of Gloucester
Focus: Logopedy
Periodicals
Annual Report (annually)
Newsletter (quarterly) *10754*

African Society of International and Comparative Law, 22 Highbury Grove, London N6 2EA
T: (0171) 7040610
Gen Secr: Emile K.M. Yakpo
Focus: Law *10755*

African Studies Association of the United Kingdom (ASAUK), c/o Royal African Society, SOAS, Thornhaugh St, Russell Sq, London WC1H 0XG
T: (0171) 3236253
Founded: 1963; Members: 600
Pres: Prof. J.D.Y. Peel; Gen Secr: Dr. N. Nelson
Focus: Ethnology
Periodical
African Affairs (quarterly) *10756*

Agency for Cooperation and Research in Development, Francis House, Francis St, London SW1P 1DQ
T: (0171) 8287611; Fax: 9766113
Founded: 1974
Gen Secr: Mark Sinclair
Focus: Develop Areas *10757*

Agricultural and Food Research Council (AFCR), Polaris House, North Star Av, Swindon SN2 1UH
T: (01793) 413200; Fax: 413201
Founded: 1931
Pres: Sir Alistair Grant; Gen Secr: Prof. T.L. Blundell
Focus: Agri; Food
Periodicals
AFCR News
Annual Report (annually)
Corporate Plan
Handbook of Agricultural and Food Research *10758*

Agricultural Economics Society (AES), c/o Dept of Agricultural and Food Economics, Queens University of Belfast, Newforge Lane, Belfast BT9 5PX
T: (01232) 255204 ext 2204; Fax: 668384
Founded: 1926; Members: 700
Gen Secr: Dr. J. Davis
Focus: Agri
Periodical
Journal of Agricultural Economics (3 times annually) *10759*

Agricultural Education Association (AEA), c/o Askham Bryan College, York YO2 3PR
T: (01904) 772277; Fax: 772288
Founded: 1894; Members: 300
Focus: Adult Educ; Agri *10760*

Agricultural Research Institute of Northern Ireland, Large Park, Hillsborough BT26 6DR
T: (01846) 682484; Fax: 689594
Focus: Agri
Periodical
Report on Agricultural Research (annually) *10761*

Aircraft Research Association (ARA), Manton Ln, Bedford MK41 7PF
T: (01234) 350681; Fax: 328584
Founded: 1952; Members: 4
Pres: B.R. Timmins; Gen Secr: M.P. Carr
Focus: Aero *10762*

Airship Association, 20 Myddelton Gardens, Winchmore Hill, London N21
T: (0181) 3601357
Founded: 1971
Focus: Aero *10763*

Alcuin Club, 11 Abbey St, Chester CH1 2JF
T: (01244) 347811; E-Mail: tr.barker@mcmail.com; Fax: 347823
Founded: 1897; Members: 650
Gen Secr: T.R. Barker
Focus: Rel & Theol
Periodicals
Collections (annually)
Joint Liturgical Studies (3 times annually) *10764*

Alkan Society, 21 Heronswood, Salisbury SP2 8DH
T: (01722) 325771; Fax: 325771
Founded: 1977; Members: 140
Pres: Ronald Smith; Gen Secr: Peter Grove
Focus: Music
Periodical
Bulletin (3 times annually) *10765*

Alternative Society (AS), 9 Morton Av, Kidlington, Oxon
T: 3413
Founded: 1972
Focus: Sociology *10766*

Amateur Entomologists' Society (A.E.S.), 22 Salisbury Rd, Feltham TW13 5DP
Founded: 1935; Members: 2000
Focus: Entomology
Periodical
Bulletin: Wants & Exchange List (bi-monthly) *10767*

American Civil War Round Table, United Kingdom (ACWRTUK), 41 Templemere Oatlands Dr, Weybridge KT13 9PA
T: (01932) 846150
Founded: 1953; Members: 105
Focus: Hist
Periodicals
Crossfire (quarterly)
Newsletter (quarterly) *10768*

American Dental Society of Europe, 40 Harley St, London W1N 1AB
Fax: (0171) 4362015
Founded: 1873; Members: 145
Focus: Dent *10769*

An Comunn Gaidhealach (ACG) / The Highland Association, 109 Church St, Inverness IV1 1EU
T: (01463) 231226
Founded: 1891; Members: 2600
Gen Secr: Donald M. MacLean
Focus: Ethnology; Ling *10770*

Anaesthetic Research Society, c/o Academic Unit of Anaesthesia, Beckett St, Saint James's University Hospital, Leeds LS9 7TF
T: (0113) 2065274; E-Mail: p.m.hopkins@leeds.ac.uk; Fax: 2064140
Founded: 1958; Members: 700
Gen Secr: Dr. P.M. Hopkins
Focus: Anesthetics
Periodical
Proceedings *10771*

Anatomical Society of Great Britain and Ireland, c/o Dept of Anatomy and Cell Biology, Imperial College School of Medicine, Saint Mary's, Norfolk Pl, London W2 1PG
T: (0171) 5943743
Founded: 1887; Members: 700
Pres: Prof. B.A. Wood; Gen Secr: Prof. J.A. Firth
Focus: Anat
Periodical
Journal of Anatomy (bi-monthly) . . . *10772*

Ancient Monuments Society (AMS), Saint Ann's Vestry Hall, 2 Church, London EC4V 5HB
T: (0171) 2363934
Founded: 1924; Members: 2000
Focus: Preserv Hist Monuments
Periodical
Transactions (annually) *10773*

Anglo-Continental Dental Society (ACDS), 75 Wimpole St, London W1
T: (0171) 9353242
Founded: 1942
Focus: Dent *10774*

Anglo-European College of Chiropractic, 13 Parkwood Rd, Bournemouth BH5 2DF
T: (01202) 431021; Fax: 417352
Founded: 1965
Pres: Prof. Brian N. Kliger
Focus: Med *10775*

Anglo-Norman Text Society (ANTS), c/o Birkbeck College, Malet St, London WCIE 7HX
T: (0171) 6316170
Founded: 1938; Members: 370
Pres: Prof. William Rottwell; Gen Secr: Prof. Ian Short
Focus: Lit *10776*

Animal Breeding Research Organization (ABRO), King's Bldgs, West Main Rd, Edinburgh EH9 3JQ
T: (0131) 6676901
Founded: 1947
Focus: Animal Husb *10777*

Animal Diseases Research Association, c/o Moredun Research Institute, 408 Gilmerton Rd, Edinburgh EH17 7JH
T: (0131) 6643262; Fax: 6648001
Founded: 1920; Members: 2000
Pres: J. Stobo; Gen Secr: M.J. Mackenzie
Focus: Vet Med
Periodicals
Association Report and Accounts (annually)
Moredun Research Institute: Scientific Report (bi-annually) *10778*

Animal Health Trust, POB 5, Newmarket CB8 7DW
T: (01638) 661111; Fax: 665789
Pres: A.J. Higgins; Gen Secr: Eve Fremantle
Focus: Vet Med
Periodical
Annual Report (annually) *10779*

Anthroposophical Society in Great Britain, 35 Park Rd, London NW1 6XT
T: (0171) 7234400
Founded: 1923; Members: 2000
Focus: Philos *10780*

Antiquarian Horological Society (A.H.S.), New House, High St, Ticehurst, Wadhurst TN5 7AL
T: (01580) 200155; E-Mail: 106365.2114@compuserve.com; Fax: 201323
Founded: 1953; Members: 2000
Pres: Prof. Arnold Wolfendale; Gen Secr: Pauline Hossbach
Focus: Hist; Eng
Periodical
Antiquarian Horology (quarterly) *10781*

Appropriate Health Resources and Technologies Action Group (AHRTAG), 1 London Bridge St, London SE1 8SG
T: (0171) 3781403; Fax: 4036003
Founded: 1977
Gen Secr: K. Atawell
Focus: Public Health
Periodicals
AIDS Action (quarterly)
ARI News (quarterly)
CBR News (3 times annually)
Dialogue on Diarrhoea (quarterly) . . . *10782*

Arab Research Centre, 76-78 Notting Hill Gate, London W11 3HS
T: (0171) 2212425; Fax: 2215899
Founded: 1979; Members: 50
Pres: Abdel Majid Farid
Focus: Ethnology
Periodicals
Arab Paper (10 times annually)
The Arab Researcher *10783*

Arboricultural Association, Ampfield House, Romsey SO51 9PA
T: (01794) 68717; Fax: 68978
Founded: 1964; Members: 2000
Focus: Forestry
Periodical
Arboricultural Journal: The International Journal of Urban Forestry (quarterly) *10784*

Architects and Surveyors Institute (ASI), 15 Saint Mary St, Chippenham SN15 3WD
T: (01249) 444505; Fax: 443602
Founded: 1926; Members: 6000
Pres: C.W. Campbell; Gen Secr: C.G.A. Nash
Focus: Archit; Surveying
Periodical
ASI Journal (5 times annually) *10785*

Architectural and Archaeological Society of Durham and Northumberland, c/o Dept of Archaeology, Saddler St, Durham City DH1 3NU
T: (0191) 3743633
Founded: 1861; Members: 300
Focus: Archeol; Archit
Periodical
Durham Archaeological Journal (annually) *10786*

Architectural Association (AA), 34-36 Bedford Sq, London WC1B 3ES
T: (0171) 6360974; Fax: 4140782
Founded: 1847; Members: 3000
Pres: P. Gough; Gen Secr: E. Maistre
Focus: Archit
Periodical
AA Files (semi-annually) *10787*

The Aristotelian Society, c/o University of London, Senate House, Malet St, London WC1E 7HV
T: (0171) 2551724
Founded: 1880; Members: 1206
Gen Secr: A.C. Grayling
Focus: Philos
Periodicals
Monographs
Proceedings and Supplementary Proceedings (annually) *10788*

ARLIS UK and Ireland- Art Libraries Society of the United Kingdom and Ireland, 18 College Rd, Bromsgrove B60 2NE
T: (01527) 579298
Founded: 1969; Members: 670
Pres: Gillian Varley; Gen Secr: Sonia French
Focus: Libraries & Bk Sci
Periodicals
Art Libraries Journal (quarterly)
News-sheet (bi-monthly) *10789*

Arms and Armour Society of Great Britain, POB 10232, London SW19 2ZD
Founded: 1951
Focus: Military Sci
Periodical
Journal (semi-annually) *10790*

Arnold Bennett Literary Society, Burslem Leisure Centre, Market Pl, Stoke-on-Trent ST6 3DS
T: (01782) 813363
Founded: 1954
Focus: Lit *10791*

The Arthritis and Rheumatism Council (ARC), Copeman House, Saint Mary's Court, Chesterfield S41 7TD
T: (01246) 558033
Founded: 1937
Pres: Lord Dainton; Gen Secr: J. Norton
Focus: Rheuma
Periodical
Reports on Rheumatic Diseases (semi-annually) 10792

Arts Association, 227 Goldhawk Rd, London W12 8ER
T: (0181) 7434378
Founded: 1953; Members: 8500
Focus: Arts 10793

Arts Council of England, 14 Great Peter St, London SW1P 3NQ
T: (0171) 3330100; Fax: 9736590
Founded: 1940; Members: 20
Pres: Lord Gowrie; Gen Secr: Graham Devlin
Focus: Arts
Periodical
Report (annually) 10794

Arts Council of Northern Ireland, 181a Stranmillis Rd, Belfast BT9 5DU
Founded: 1943
Focus: Arts
Periodical
Annual Report (annually) 10795

Arts Council of Wales, 9 Museums Pl, Cardiff CF1 3NX
T: (01222) 394711; Fax: 221447
Focus: Arts 10796

Ashmolean Natural History Society of Oxfordshire (ANHSO), Pickets Heath, The Ridgeway, Boars Hill, Oxford OX1 5EZ
Founded: 1828; Members: 300
Focus: Hist; Nat Sci
Periodical
Fritillary (irregularly) 10797

Aslib – Association for Information Management, 20-24 Old St, London EC1N 9AP
T: (0171) 2534488; Fax: 4300514
Founded: 1924; Members: 2100
Gen Secr: Roger N. Bowes
Focus: Libraries & Bk Sci
Periodicals
Aslib Booklist (monthly)
Aslib Informations (monthly)
Aslib Proceedings (monthly)
Current Awareness Bulletin (monthly)
Forthcoming International Scientific and Technical Conferences (semi-annually)
Journal of Documentation (quarterly)
Program (quarterly) 10798

Association for Adult and Continuing Education (AACE), Hamilton House, Mabledon Pl, London WC1H 9BH
T: (0171) 3801314
Founded: 1978; Members: 3000
Focus: Adult Educ 10799

Association for Applied Hypnosis (AAH), 33 Abbey Park Rd, Grimsby DN32 0HS
T: (01472) 47702
Founded: 1980; Members: 25
Focus: Depth Psych 10800

Association for Brain Damaged Children, Clifton House, Saint Pauls Rd, Coventry CV6 5DE
T: (01203) 665450
Founded: 1969; Members: 100
Focus: Pediatrics; Logopedy 10801

Association for British Music (ABM), 2 Union Pl, Boston PE21 6PS
T: (01205) 60541
Founded: 1977; Members: 600
Focus: Music 10802

Association for Child Psychology and Psychiatry (ACPP), 70 Borough High St, London SE1 1XF
T: (0171) 4037458; Fax: 4037081
Founded: 1957; Members: 2500
Gen Secr: R. Whithear
Focus: Psych; Psychiatry; Soc Sci; Educ 10803

Association for Educational and Training Technology (A.E.T.T.), Higher Millbrook, Beavor Lane, Axminster EX13 5EQ
Founded: 1965
Focus: Educ
Periodicals
Aspects of Educational Technology (annually)
Educational and Training Technology International (quarterly)
International Yearbook of Educational and Training Technology (bi-annually) 10804

Association for Group and Individual Psychotherapy, 29 Saint Marles Crescent, London NW1
T: (0171) 4859141
Focus: Psych; Therapeutics 10805

Association for Independent Disabled Self-Sufficiency (AIDS), 7 Alfred St, Bath BA1 2QU
T: (01225) 25197
Founded: 1977; Members: 200
Focus: Educ Handic
Periodical
Phoenix (quarterly) 10806

Association for Industrial Archaeology (AIA), c/o The Wharfage, Ironbridge, Telford TF8 7AW
T: (01952) 432751
Founded: 1973; Members: 630
Gen Secr: A. Patrick
Focus: Archeol
Periodicals
AIA Bulletin (quarterly)
Industrial Archaeology Review (semi-annually) 10807

Association for Information Management (ASLIB), 20-24 Old St, London EC1V 9AP
T: (0171) 2534488; Fax: 4300514
Founded: 1924
Gen Secr: Roger Bowes
Focus: Business Admin
Periodicals
ASLIB Book List (monthly)
ASLIB Information (10 times annually)
ASLIB Proceedings (10 times annually)
Computing, Communications, Media and Socio-Technology-Trend Monitor (8 times annually)
Critique (10 times annually)
Current Awareness Bulletin (10 times annually)
Forthcoming International Scientific and Technical Conferences (quarterly)
Index to Theses with Abstracts (quarterly)
The Intelligent Enterprise (monthly)
IT Link incorporating Automation Notes (monthly)
Journal of Documentation (quarterly)
Online Notes (monthly)
Program-Automated Library and Information Systems (quarterly)
Records Management Journal (quarterly) . 10808

Association for International Cancer Research, Moor House, Cameron-Markby
Founded: 1979; Members: 9
Focus: Cell Biol & Cancer Res 10809

Association for Language Learning, 150 Railway Terrace, Rugby CV21 3HN
T: (01788) 546443; Fax: 544149
Founded: 1990; Members: 6500
Pres: Margaret Tumber; Gen Secr: Christine Wilding
Focus: Ling; Educ
Periodicals
Francophonie (semi-annually)
German Teaching (semi-annually)
Language Learning Journal (semi-annually)
Language World Newsheet (quarterly)
Rusistika (semi-annually)
Tuttitalia (semi-annually)
Vida Hispanica (semi-annually) 10810

Association for Latin Liturgy (ALL), 47 Western Park Rd, Leicester LE3 6HQ
T: (0116) 2856158; E-Mail: mjcr.latinlit@btinternet.com
Founded: 1969; Members: 400
Focus: Rel & Theol 10811

Association for Literary and Linguistic Computing (ALLC), c/o Dept of English, University College of North Wales, Bangor LL57 2DG
T: (01248) 351151
Founded: 1973; Members: 420
Gen Secr: Thomas M. Corns
Focus: Computer & Info Sci
Periodical
Literary & Linguistic Computing (quarterly) 10812

Association for Medical Deans in Europe (AMDE), c/o Dept of Medicine, Institute of Clinical Science, Grosvenor Rd, Belfast BT12 6HJ
T: (01232) 240503; Fax: 240899
Founded: 1979
Pres: Prof. A.H. Gary Love
Focus: Med 10813

Association for Medical Education in Europe (AMEE), c/o Centre for Medical Education, Ninewells Hospital and Medical School, Dundee DD1 9SY
T: (01382) 60111; Fax: 645748
Founded: 1972
Gen Secr: Prof. R.M. Harden
Focus: Educ; Med
Periodical
Medical Education (bi-monthly) 10814

Association for Medical Physics Technology (AMPT), 30 Burnham Av, Ickenham, Middx
Founded: 1952; Members: 242
Focus: Physics; Eng 10815

Association for Petroleum and Explosives Administration (APEA), c/o Trading Standards Dept, Hinchingbrooke Cottage, Brampton Rd, Huntington PE18 8NA
Founded: 1974; Members: 350
Focus: Safety
Periodical
The Bulletin (quarterly) 10816

Association for Professionals in Services for Adolescents (APSA), 13 Bonaly Dr, Edinburgh EH13 0EJ
T: (0131) 4411049
Founded: 1969; Members: 500
Focus: Psychiatry
Periodical
Journal of Adolescence (quarterly) 10817

Association for Radiation Research (ARR), c/o Dr. K.M. Prise, Gray Laboratory, Mount Vernon Hospital, POB 100, Northwood HA6 2JR
Founded: 1958; Members: 330
Focus: Radiology 10818

Association for Recurrent Education (ARE), c/o Dept of Education Management, 36 Collegiate Crescent, Sheffield
T: 56101
Founded: 1975; Members: 65
Focus: Educ 10819

Association for Religious Education (ARE), 17 Clover Close, Cumnor Hill OX2 9JH
T: (018676) 3030
Founded: 1968
Focus: Rel & Theol; Educ 10820

Association for Research in the Voluntary and Community Sector (ARVAC), Unit 29, Wivenhoe Business Centre, Brook St, Wivenhoe CO7 9DP
T: (01206) 824281
Founded: 1978; Members: 250
Gen Secr: Pat Marsden
Focus: Public Admin
Periodical
ARVAC Bulletin (quarterly) 10821

Association for Research into Restricted Growth (ARRG), 5 Teak Walk, Witham CM8 2SX
Founded: 1970; Members: 350
Focus: Pathology 10822

Association for Science Education (A.S.E.), College Ln, Hatfield AL10 9AA
T: (01707) 267411; Fax: 266532
Founded: 1963; Members: 23000
Gen Secr: Dr. David S. Moore
Focus: Educ; Sci
Periodicals
ASE Primary Science (3 times annually)
Education in Science (5 times annually)
Primary Science Review (3 times annually)
The School Science Review (quarterly) . 10823

Association for Scottish Literary Studies (ASLS), c/o Dept of English, University of Aberdeen, Aberdeen AB9 2UB
T: (01224) 40241
Founded: 1970; Members: 750
Focus: Lit
Periodicals
New Writing Scotland (annually)
Scottish Language (annually)
Scottish Literary Journal (semi-annually)
Scottish Literary Journal Supplements (semi-annually) 10824

Association for Spina Bifida and Hydrocephalus (ASBAH), 42 Park Rd, Peterborough PE1 2UQ
T: (01733) 555988; E-Mail: postmaster@sbah.demon.co.uk; Fax: 555985
Founded: 1966; Members: 10000
Focus: Med
Periodical
Link (bi-monthly) 10825

Association for Studies in the Conservation of Historic Buildings (ASCHB), c/o Institute of Archaeology, 31-34 Gordon Sq, London WC1H 0PY
T: (0171) 5809148
Founded: 1968; Members: 450
Focus: Preserv Hist Monuments
Periodicals
Newsletter (quarterly)
Transactions (annually) 10826

Association for the Education and Welfare of the Visually Handicapped (A.E.W.V.R.), Saint John's School House, Hadzor, Droitwich Spa WR9 7DR
Founded: 1979; Members: 328
Focus: Educ Handic
Periodical
British Journal of Visual Impairment (3 times annually) 10827

The Association for the Protection of Rural Scotland (A.P.R.S.), Gladstone's Land, 483 Lawnmarket, Edinburgh EH1 2NT
T: (0131) 2256592
Founded: 1926; Members: 1110
Gen Secr: Elizabeth Garland
Focus: Ecology
Periodicals
Annual Report (annually)
Newsletter (semi-annually) 10828

Association for the Reduction of Aircraft Noise (ARAN), 11 First St, London SW3
T: (0171) 5841848
Founded: 1964
Focus: Ecology 10829

Association for the Reform of the Latin Teaching (A.R.L.T.), 33 Lane End Drive, Knaphell, Woking GU21 2QQ
T: (0121) 4540895
Founded: 1911; Members: 1000
Focus: Ling; Educ
Periodical
Latin Teaching (annually) 10830

Association for the Study of Animal Behaviour (ASAB), c/o School of Biology and Medical Sciences, University of Saint Andrews, Saint Andrews KY169TS
Founded: 1936; Members: 1500
Pres: Prof. L. Partridge; Gen Secr: Dr. A.E. Magurran
Focus: Behav Sci
Periodical
Animal Behaviour (monthly) 10831

Association for the Study of German Politics (ASGP), c/o Dept of Business Studies and Languages, Sheffield City Polytechnic, Sheffield S17 4AB
Founded: 1974
Focus: Poli Sci 10832

Association for the Study of Medical Education (ASME), 2a-4 Perth Rd, Dundee DD1 4LN
Founded: 1957; Members: 800
Pres: Prof. David Shaw; Gen Secr: Prof. S.J. Leinster
Focus: Adult Educ; Med
Periodicals
Annual Report (annually)
Medical Education (bi-monthly) 10833

Association for the Teaching of Psychology (ATPsych), c/o The British Psychological Society, 48 Princess Rd East, Leicester LE1 7DR
T: (01533) 549568
Founded: 1971; Members: 1000
Focus: Psych; Educ
Periodical
Psychology Teaching (semi-annually) . . 10834

Association for the Teaching of the Social Sciences (ATSS), 19 Mandeville Gardens, Saint Albans Al1 40A
Founded: 1963; Members: 1081
Focus: Educ; Sociology
Periodicals
Briefings (3 times annually)
The Social Science Teacher (3 times annually) 10835

Association for Veterinary Clinical Pharmacology and Therapeutics, Cedar Cottage, Sutton Pl, Abinger Hammer, Dorking, Surrey
Focus: Vet Med; Pharmacol 10836

Association in Scotland to Research into Astronautics (ASTRA), 720 Glasgow Rd, Craigneuk, Wishaw, Lanarks
Focus: Astronomy
Periodicals
Asgard (irregularly)
Space Explorer (irregularly)
Spacereport (irregularly) 10837

Association of Advisers in Design and Technical Studies (AADTS), 33 Foxhill Crescent, Camberley GU15 1PR
T: (01276) 23846
Members: 120
Focus: Eng; Graphic & Dec Arts, Design 10838

Association of Agricultural Education Staffs (AAES), 43 Saint John's Rd, Mogerhanger MK44 3RJ
T: (01767) 40464
Founded: 1946; Members: 792
Focus: Adult Educ; Agri 10839

Association of Anaesthetists of Great Britain and Ireland, 9 Bedford Sq, London WC1B 3RA
T: (0171) 6311650; Fax: 6314352
Founded: 1932; Members: 6300
Pres: Dr. W.L.M. Baird; Gen Secr: Dr. D.J. Wilkinson
Focus: Anesthetics
Periodical
Anaesthesia (monthly) 10840

The Association of Applied Biologists (AAB), c/o Horticultural Research International, Wellesbourne, Warwick CV35 9EF
T: (01789) 470382; E-Mail: carol.aab@hri.ac.uk; Fax: 470234
Founded: 1904; Members: 1200
Pres: Prof. J. Moorby; Gen Secr: Dr. F.A. Langton
Focus: Bio
Periodical
Annals of Applied Biology (bi-monthly) . 10841

Association of Art Institutions (AAI), 24 Widemarsh St, Hereford HR4 9EP
T: (01432) 66653
Founded: 1942; Members: 500
Focus: Arts 10842

Association of Arts Centres in Scotland (AACS), 50 Forest Rd, Aberdeen AB2 4BP
T: (01224) 37115
Founded: 1970; Members: 40
Focus: Arts 10843

Association of Basic Science Teachers in Dentistry, c/o Oral Sciences Dept, Dental School, University of Glasgow, 378 Sauchiehall St, Glasgow G23JZ
T: (0141) 2119755; E-Mail: j.a.beeley@dental.gla.ac.uk; Fax: 3531593
Founded: 1978; Members: 120
Pres: Prof. Colin Robinson; Gen Secr: Dr. Josie Beeley
Focus: Dent 10844

Association of Beauty Teachers (ABT), 38a Portsmouth Rd, Southampton SO19 9AD
T: (01703) 422695; E-Mail: gr34@dial.pipex.com; Fax: 447968
Founded: 1967; Members: 300
Pres: W.S. Sharps; Gen Secr: J.M. Palmer
Focus: Educ
Periodical
International Therapist (bi-monthly) . . . 10845

Association of Blind and Partially-Sights Teachers and Students (ABAPSTAS), POB 6727, London WC1N 3XX
Founded: 1970; Members: 200
Focus: Educ; Educ Handic; Adult Educ . 10846

Association of British Climatologists (ABC), c/o Dept of Environmental and Geographical Studies, Roehampton Institute, Wimbledon Parkside, London SW19 5NN
T: (0181) 3923473
Founded: 1974; Members: 120
Focus: Geophys
Periodical
Directory of Climatologists 10847

Association of British Correspondence Colleges (A.B.C.C.), 6 Francis Grove, London SW19 4DT
T: (0181) 5449559
Founded: 1955; Members: 20
Focus: Educ 10848

Association of British Dispensing Opticians, 6 Hurlingham Business Park, Sulivan Rd, London SW6 3DU
T: (0171) 7365531; Fax: 7315531
Founded: 1985
Pres: Colin Lee; Gen Secr: M.P.J. Hunt
Focus: Optics 10849

Association of British Forensic Specialists, POB 389, Moseley, Birmingham
T: (0121) 4497735
Focus: Forensic Med 10850

Association of British Geodesists (ABG), c/o Dept of Land Surveying, Polytechnic of East London, Longbridge Rd, Dagenham RM8 2AS
T: (0181) 5907722
Founded: 1950; Members: 60
Focus: Surveying 10851

Association of British Neurologists, 9 Fitzroy Sq, London W1P 5AH
Founded: 1933; Members: 800
Pres: Dr. R.B. Godwin-Austen; Gen Secr: Dr. M.J. Donaghy
Focus: Neurology 10852

Association of British Paediatric Nurses (ABPN), c/o Central Nursing Office, Hospital for Sick Children, Great Ormond St, London WC1N 3JH
T: (0171) 4059200
Founded: 1938; Members: 1600
Focus: Pediatrics
Periodicals
Newssheet (semi-annually)
Spotlight on Children (quarterly) 10853

Association of British Science Writers (ABSW), c/o The British Association, 23 Saville Row, London W1X 2NB
T: (0171) 4391205; Fax: 9733051
Founded: 1947; Members: 600
Gen Secr: Barbara Drillsma
Focus: Lit; Sci
Periodical
The Science Reporter (monthly) 10854

Association of British Spectroscopists, c/o Dr. D.V. Bowen, Physical Sciences, Pfizer Central Research, Sandwich, Kent CT13 9NJ
T: (01304) 616438; Fax: 616726
Founded: 1969; Members: 50
Pres: Dr. D.V. Bowen
Focus: Physics; Chem; Bio 10855

Association of British Theological and Philosophical Libraries (ABTAPL), c/o Bible Society's Library, Cambridge University Library, West Rd, Cambridge CB3 9DR
T: (01223) 333000 ext 3075; Fax: 333160
Founded: 1956; Members: 290
Pres: Judith Powles; Gen Secr: Alan F. Jesson
Focus: Libraries & Bk Sci
Periodical
Bulletin (3 times annually) 10856

The Association of Building Engineers, Jubilee House, Billing Brook Rd, Weston Favell, Northampton NN3 8NW
T: (01604) 404121; Fax: 784220
Founded: 1925; Members: 5200
Pres: N.J. Hammans; Gen Secr: W.A. Black
Focus: Civil Eng
Periodicals
Building Engineer (10 times annually)
Fire Safety Engineering (bi-monthly) . . 10857

Association of Chief Architects of Scottish Local Authorities, c/o Lanark District Council, 57 High St, Lanark
T: (01786) 3111
Founded: 1952
Focus: Archit 10858

Association of Child Psychotherapists, Burgh House, New End Sq, London NW3
T: (0171) 7948881; Fax: 3616794
Members: 150
Focus: Therapeutics
Periodical
Journal of Child Psychology 10859

The Association of Clinical Biochemists (ACB), 2 Carlton House Terrace, London SW1Y 5AF
T: (0171) 9303333; E-Mail: 100673.3340@compuserve.com; Fax: 9303553
Founded: 1953; Members: 2300
Pres: Prof. G. Elder; Gen Secr: Dr. M. Thomas
Focus: Biochem
Periodicals
ACB News (monthly)
Annals of Clinical Biochemistry (bi-monthly)
. . . . 10860

Association of Clinical Pathologists (A.C.P.), 189 Dyke Rd, Hove BN3 1TL
T: (01273) 775700; E-Mail: info@pathologists.org.uk; Fax: 773303
Founded: 1927; Members: 2350
Pres: Prof. A.F. Winder; Gen Secr: J.S. Turner
Focus: Pathology
Periodical
Journal of Clinical Pathology and Molecular Pathology (bi-monthly) 10861

Association of Colleges for Further and Higher Education, Swindon College, Regent Circus, Swindon SN1 1PT
T: (01793) 513193
Founded: 1893; Members: 362
Gen Secr: C. Brain
Focus: Educ; Adult Educ 10862

Association of Commonwealth Archivists and Records Managers, c/o Institute of Commonwealth Studies, 28 Russell Sq, London WC1B 5DS
Founded: 1984
Focus: Archives
Periodical
Association of Commonwealth Archivists and Records Managers Newsletter 10863

Association of Commonwealth Teachers, 42 Camborne Av, London W13
T: (0181) 5673221
Focus: Educ 10864

Association of Commonwealth Universities (A.C.U.), 36 Gordon Sq, London WC1H 0PF
T: (0171) 3878572; E-Mail: pubinf@acu.ac.uk; Fax: 3872655
Founded: 1913; Members: 463
Pres: Prof. Brenda Gourley; Gen Secr: Prof. Michael Gibbons
Focus: Educ
Periodicals
A.C.U. Bulletin of Current Documentation (5 times annually)
Appointments in Commonwealth Universities (bi-weekly)
Commonwealth Universities Yearbook (annually)
. . . . 10865

Association of Community Health Councils for England and Wales, 362 Euston Rd, London NW1 3BL
T: (0171) 3884814
Focus: Public Health
Periodical
CHC News (10 times annually) 10866

Association of Consulting Actuaries (ACA), 39-45 Tottenham Court Rd, London W1P 0JP
T: (0171) 636777
Founded: 1951; Members: 140
Focus: Insurance 10867

Association of County Public Health Officers (AssCPHO's), 1 Cloatley Rd, Hankerton, Malmesbury, Wilts
T: (016667) 441
Founded: 1946; Members: 70
Gen Secr: N.J. Durnford
Focus: Public Health 10868

Association of Crematorium Medical Referees, 59 Kings Rd, Westcliff-on-Sea, Essex
T: (01702) 77878
Founded: 1953
Focus: Med 10869

Association of Dental Hospitals of Great Britain and Northern Ireland, Saint Chad's, Queensway, Birmingham B4 6NN
T: (0121) 2368611
Focus: Dent 10870

Association of Directors of Education in Scotland (A.D.E.S.), c/o Dept of Education, Dundee City Council, Tayside House, Dundee DD1 3RJ
T: (01382) 433088; E-Mail: anne-wilson@dundee-education-office.dundeecity.sch.uk; Fax: 433080
Founded: 1920; Members: 194
Pres: John Travers; Gen Secr: Anne Wilson
Focus: Educ 10871

Association of Directors of Social Services (ADSS), County Hall, Stockport SK1 3XE
T: (0161) 4744600; Fax: 4747895
Founded: 1971; Members: 161
Pres: R.J. Lewis
Focus: Sociology 10872

Association of Directors of Social Work (ADSW), c/o Social Work Dept, Newtown St, Boswells, Melrose TD6 0SA
T: (01835) 23366
Founded: 1969; Members: 68
Focus: Sociology 10873

Association of Disabled Professionals (ADP), 170 Benton Hill, Wakefield Rd, Horbury WF4 5HW
T: (01924) 283253; E-Mail: 76721.2160@compuserve.com; Fax: 283253
Founded: 1971; Members: 507
Pres: Maynard Campbell
Focus: Educ Handic 10874

Association of District Medical Officers, c/o Royal United Hospital, Combe Park, Bath BA1 3NG
Founded: 1974
Focus: Med 10875

Association of Educational Psychologists (AEP), 3 Sunderland Rd, Durham DH1 2LH
T: (0191) 3849512
Founded: 1962; Members: 450
Gen Secr: J.B. Harrison-Jennings
Focus: Educ; Psych
Periodical
Journal (quarterly) 10876

Association of European Latin Americanist Historians, c/o Institute of Latin American Studies, University of Liverpool, POB 147, Liverpool L69 3BX
T: (0151) 7943079
Founded: 1972
Gen Secr: Prof. John Fisher
Focus: Hist
Periodical
Historia Latinoamericana en Europa (semi-annually)
. . . . 10877

Association of European Open Air Museums (AEOM), c/o Weald and Downland Open Air Museum, Singleton, Chichester PO18 0EU
T: (0124363) 348
Founded: 1966
Pres: Christopher Zeuner
Focus: Cultur Hist 10878

Association of Genealogists and Record Agents (AGRA), 29 Badgers Close, Horsham RH12 5RU
Founded: 1968; Members: 100
Focus. Genealogy; Hist 10879

Association of General Practitioner Hospitals, c/o Saint Chad Health Centre, The Dimbles, Lichfield, Staffs
Founded: 1969
Focus: Public Health 10880

Association of Governing Bodies of Girls Public Schools (GBGSA), 27 Church Rd, Steep, Petersfield GU32 2DW
T: (01730) 4823
Founded: 1942; Members: 233
Focus: Educ 10881

Association of Governing Bodies of Public Schools (Boys) (GBA), 27 Church Rd, Steep, Petersfield GU32 2DW
T: (01730) 4823
Founded: 1941; Members: 247
Focus: Educ 10882

Association of Hairdressing Teachers in Colleges of Further Education, 4 Samuel St, Balby, Doncaster
T: 851815
Founded: 1964; Members: 360
Focus: Adult Educ 10883

Association of Head and Neck Oncologists of Great Britain, 330 Gray's Inn Rd, London WC1X 8DA
T: (0171) 8378855
Founded: 1968; Members: 150
Focus: Cell Biol & Cancer Res; Physiology
. . . . 10884

Association of Heads of Independent Schools (AHIS), c/o Eton College, 5 Gullivers, Windor SP8 4ER
T: (017535) 60902
Founded: 1924; Members: 120
Focus: Educ 10885

Association of Health Care Information and Medical Records Officers (AMRO), Whitecroft, Wilmore Hill Lane, Hopton ST18 0AW
Founded: 1948; Members: 1000
Focus: Med; Public Health 10886

Association of Health Service Treasurers (AHST), c/o South Warwickshire Health Authority, Westgate House, Market St, Warwick CV34 4DE
T: (01926) 493491
Members: 488
Focus: Public Health; Finance 10887

Association of Hispanists of Great Britain and Ireland (ABH), c/o Dept of Spanish, Queen Mary College, University of London, Mile End Rd, London E1 4NS
T: (0181) 9804811
Founded: 1955; Members: 400
Focus: Lit 10888

Association of Independent Libraries, c/o P.A. Fisher, Birmingham and Midland Institute, 9 Margaret St, Birmingham B3 8BS
Founded: 1989; Members: 20
Pres: Lord Quinton
Focus: Libraries & Bk Sci
Periodicals
Directory (annually)
Newsletter (annually) 10889

Association of Independent Research and Technology Organisations, POB 330, Cambridge CB5 8DU
T: (01223) 467831; E-Mail: airto@dial.pipex.com; Fax: 462051
Founded: 1975; Members: 42
Gen Secr: J.A. Bennett
Focus: Eng 10890

Association of Institute and School of Education In-Service Tutors (AJSEJT), c/o School of Education, Leazes Rd, Durham
Founded: 1970; Members: 36
Focus: Educ 10891

Association of International Accountants / Association des Experts-Comptables Internationaux, South Bank Bldg, Kingsway, Team Valley, Gateshead NE11 0JS
T: (0191) 4824409; Fax: 4825578
Founded: 1928
Gen Secr: J.R.A. Turnbull
Focus: Law 10892

The Association of Law Teachers (ALT), c/o Coalville Technical College, Bridge Rd, Coalville, Leicester LE6 2QR
T: (01533) 836136
Founded: 1965; Members: 700
Focus: Educ; Law 10893

Association of Lecturers in Accountancy (ALJA), 62 North Gyle Lane, Edinburgh EH12 8LD
T: (0131) 3396144
Founded: 1964; Members: 450
Focus: Adult Educ 10894

Association of Lecturers in Colleges of Education in Scotland (ALCES), Beech Grove KA8 0SR
T: (01292) 60321
Members: 1190
Focus: Educ 10895

Association of London Chief Librarians (ALCL), c/o Central Library, Barking IG11 7NB
T: (0181) 5178666; Fax: 5941156
Founded: 1965; Members: 34
Pres: G. Allen; Gen Secr: A.J. Hill
Focus: Libraries & Bk Sci
Periodical
Directory of London Public Libraries (irregularly)
. . . . 10896

Association of Manufacturing Chemists, 1 Wardrobe Pl, Carter Ln, London EC4V 5AJ
T: (0171) 2485971
Members: 250
Focus: Chem 10897

Association of Marine Engineering Schools (AMES), c/o Liverpool Polytechnic, Byrom St, Liverpool L3 3AF
T: (0151) 2073581
Founded: 1951; Members: 22
Focus: Adult Educ; Eng 10898

Association of Meat Inspectors (AMJ), 10 Shaftesbury Av, Barnet EN5 5JA
T: (0181) 4408712
Founded: 1965; Members: 620
Focus: Vet Med 10899

Association of Medical Advisers to the Pharmaceutical Industry, 41 Queen's Gate, London SW7 5HU
T: (0171) 5899076
Focus: Pharmacol 10900

Association of Municipal Engineers, 1 Great George St, London SW1P 3AA
T: (0171) 2227722; E-Mail: huxford-r@ice.org.uk; Fax: 2227500
Founded: 1873; Members: 9972
Pres: David Hodgkinson; Gen Secr: Robert Huxford
Focus: Eng
Periodical
Municipal Engineer (quarterly) 10901

Association of National European and Mediterranean Societies of Gastroenterology (ASNEMGE), c/o Gastroenterology Unit, Guy's Hospital, London SE1 9RT
T: (0171) 9554564; Fax: 4076689
Founded: 1947
Gen Secr: Prof. Dr. R.H. Dowling
Focus: Gastroenter 10902

Association of National Park Officers (ANPO), c/o Lake District National Park Authority, Kendal LA9 4CH
T: (01539) 24555
Members: 34
Gen Secr: R. Foster
Focus: Forestry; Ecology 10903

Association of Noise Consultants (ANC), 6 Trap Rd, Guilden Morden SG8 0JE
T: (01763) 852958
Founded: 1973; Members: 50
Pres: Sue Bird; Gen Secr: Philip Dunbavin
Focus: Eng 10904

Association of Northumberland Local History Societies, c/o Centre for Continuing Education, University of Newcastle-upon-Tyne, Newcastle-upon-Tyne NE1 7RV
T: (0191) 2225680
Founded: 1966; Members: 1000
Gen Secr: C.M. Fraser
Focus: Hist
Periodical
Tyne & Tweed (annually) 10905

Association of Official Architects (AOA), 66 Portland Pl, London W1N 4AD
T: (0171) 5805533
Founded: 1958; Members: 500
Focus: Archit 10906

Association of Painting Craft Teachers (A.P.C.T.), 5 Raven Court, Churchwood Dr, Saint Leonards-on-Sea TN38 9RL
Founded: 1921; Members: 380
Focus: Adult Educ 10907

Association of Police Surgeons (APSGB), 18a Mount Parade, Harrogate HG1 1BX
T: (01423) 566391
Members: 1000
Pres: Dr. R. Bunting; Gen Secr: Dr. M. Knight
Focus: Forensic Med
Periodical
Clinical Forensic Medicine (quarterly) . . 10908

Association of Principals of Colleges (APC), Turnford, Broxborn, Herts
Founded: 1921; Members: 600
Focus: Educ 10909

Association of Principals of Colleges (Northern Ireland Branch) (APC), c/o Technical College, Lisburn BT27 4SU
Members: 30
Focus: Educ; Eng; Arts; Sci; Econ; Business Admin 10910

Association of Professional Scientists and Technologists, 14 Harley St, London W1N 1AA
T: (0171) 6367021
Focus: Sci; Eng 10911

Association of Psychiatrists in Training (APJT), c/o Royal Edinburgh Hospital, Edinburgh EH10 5HG
T: (0131) 4472011
Founded: 1972; Members: 450
Focus: Psychiatry 10912

Association of Public Analysts (A.P.A.), Burlington House, Piccadilly, London W1V 0BN
Founded: 1953; Members: 100
Pres: A. Harrison; Gen Secr: Dr. P.N. Clare
Focus: Food; Ecology
Periodical
Journal (quarterly) 10913

Association of Recognised English Language Services (ARELS), 2 Pontypool Pl, London SE1 8QF
T: (0171) 2423136; Fax: 9289378
Founded: 1960; Members: 215
Gen Secr: Richard Walker-Arnott
Focus: Ling; Educ
Periodical
Learn English in Britain with ARELS (annually) 10914

Association of Religious in Education, 41 Cromwell Rd, London SW7 2DH
T: (0181) 9463788
Founded: 1969; Members: 1100
Pres: Josephine Egan; Gen Secr: Hilda Mitchell
Focus: Educ; Rel & Theol
Periodical
A.R.E. Bulletin (semi-annually) 10915

Association of Researchers in Medicine and Science (ARMS), c/o Clinical Science Laboratories, Guy's Hospital, London SE1 9RT
Founded: 1978; Members: 300
Focus: Med
Periodical
Newsletter (quarterly) 10916

Association of School Natural History Societies (ASNHS), c/o Lancing College, Lancing BN15 0RN
T: (017917) 2213
Founded: 1946; Members: 300
Focus: Hist; Nat Sci 10917

Association of Schools of Public Health in the European Region (ASPHER), c/o Dept of Community Health, University of Bristol, Canynge Hall, Whiteladies Rd, Bristol BS8 2PR
T: (01272) 24161 ext 1100
Founded: 1966
Focus: Educ; Public Health 10918

Association of Scientific, Technical and Managerial Staffs, 79 Camder Rd, London NW1 9ES
T: (0171) 2674422
Focus: Sci; Eng; Business Admin
Periodicals
Industry News (quarterly)
Medical World (quarterly) 10919

Association of Show and Agricultural Organisations (ASAO), The Showground, Winthorpe, Newark NG24 2NY
T: (01636) 702627
Founded: 1924; Members: 190
Gen Secr: J.N. Armitage
Focus: Agri
Periodical
Official List of Shows and Sales (annually) 10920

Association of Social Anthropologists of the Commonwealth (ASA), 50 Fitzroy St, London W1P 5HS
T: (0171) 3870455
Founded: 1946; Members: 550
Pres: Prof. P. Caplan; Gen Secr: Prof. N.J. Rapport
Focus: Anthro; Sociology; Psych
Periodicals
Annals (annually)
ASA Newsletter (annually)
ASA Studies (irregularly)
Monograph Series (annually)
Research Methods Series (irregularly) . . 10921

Association of Surgeons of Great Britain and Ireland, c/o Royal College of Surgeons, 35-43 Lincoln's Inn Fields, London WC2A 3PN
T: (0171) 9730300; Fax: 4309235
Founded: 1920; Members: 2000
Pres: A.E.B. Giddings; Gen Secr: R.H.S. Lane
Focus: Surgery 10922

Association of Swimming Therapy (AST), 4 Oak St, Shrewsbury SY3 7RH
T: (01743) 344393
Founded: 1952; Members: 30000
Gen Secr: Ted Cowen
Focus: Therapeutics
Periodical
Report (quarterly) 10923

Association of Teachers of Management (ATM), c/o Polytechnic of Central London, 35 Marylebone Rd, London NW1 5LS
T: (0171) 4865811
Founded: 1960
Focus: Business Admin; Educ 10924

Association of Teachers of Mathematics (A.T.M.), 7 Shaftesbury St, Derby DE23 8YB
Founded: 1952; Members: 4000
Pres: Ann Kitchen; Gen Secr: Annie Gammon
Focus: Math; Educ
Periodicals
Mathematics Teaching (quarterly)
Micromath
Termley 10925

Association of Track and Field Statisticians (ATFS), Poste Restante, Larkhill PO, Salisbury SP4 8PY
T: (01980) 33371 ext 5446
Founded: 1950
Gen Secr: David Martin
Focus: Stats
Periodical
ATFS Bulletin (3 times annually) . . . 10926

Association of Tutors (A.O.T.), 4 Hawthorn Way, Cambridge CB4 1AX
T: (01223) 313464; Fax: 355352
Founded: 1958; Members: 70
Focus: Adult Educ 10927

Association of Tutors in Adult Education (ATAE), 9 Northfolk Walk, Springfield Park, Sandiacre, Nottingham
Founded: 1912; Members: 450
Focus: Adult Educ 10928

Association of University Radiation Protection Officers (AURPO), c/o University Hospital of Wales, Heath Park, Cardiff CF6 4XW
T: (01222) 742003; Fax: 742012
Founded: 1962; Members: 122
Gen Secr: A.R. Richards
Focus: Radiology
Periodical
AURPO Newsletter (3 times annually) . 10929

Association of University Teachers (AUT), 9 Pembridge Rd, London W11 3HJ
T: (0171) 2214370; E-Mail: hq@aut.org.uk; Fax: 7276547
Founded: 1919; Members: 38000
Gen Secr: David Triesman
Focus: Adult Educ 10930

Association of University Teachers in Accounting (AUTA), c/o Div of Economic Studies, University, Sheffield S10 2TN
T: (01742) 78555
Founded: 1947; Members: 110
Focus: Business Admin 10931

Association of University Teachers (Scotland) (A.U.T.(S.)), c/o Dept of Statistics, University, Glasgow G12 8QW
T: (0141) 3304047
Founded: 1922; Members: 4800
Pres: J. Duffy; Gen Secr: P. Breeze
Focus: Educ 10932

Association of Veterinary Anaesthetists of Great Britain and Ireland (AVA), Worlington House, Worlington, Bury Saint Edmunds, Suffolk
T: (01934) 852581
Founded: 1964
Focus: Vet Med 10933

Association of Veterinary Teachers and Research Workers (A.V.T.R.W.), c/o Moredun Research Institute, 408 Gilmerton Rd, Edinburgh EH17 7JH
T: (0131) 6643262; E-Mail: spence@mri.sari.ac.uk; Fax: 6648001
Founded: 1948; Members: 800
Pres: Prof. M.S. McNulty; Gen Secr: Dr. M.T. Fox
Focus: Educ; Vet Med 10934

Association of Voluntary Aided Secondary Schools (AVASS), 10 C Reddons Rd, Beckenham BR3 1LZ
T: (0181) 7787270
Founded: 1968; Members: 125
Focus: Educ 10935

Association of Young Irish Archaeologists (AYJA), c/o Emily Murray, Palaeoecology Centre, School of Geosciences, The Queen's University of Belfast, Belfast BT7 1NN
T: (01232) 273128; E-Mail: e.v.murray@qub.ac.uk; Fax: 315779
Founded: 1968; Members: 125
Focus: Archeol 10936

Association to Combat Huntington's Chorea / Combat, 34a Station Rd, Hinckley LE10 1AP
T: (01455) 615558
Founded: 1971; Members: 6600
Pres: Winifred Walmsley; Gen Secr: R.V. Bates
Focus: Med
Periodical
Newsletter (semi-annually) 10937

Assurance Medical Society (AMS), 11 Chandos St, London W1M 0EB
T: (0171) 6366308; Fax: 5805793
Founded: 1893; Members: 260
Pres: Colin Trew; Gen Secr: Dr. Richard Croxson
Focus: Med
Periodical
Transactions (annually) 10938

Astronomical Society of Edinburgh (A.S.E.), City Observatory, Calton Hill, Edinburgh EH7 5AA
T: (0131) 6644857
Founded: 1924; Members: 100
Focus: Astronomy 10939

Atlantis Research Centre (ARC), 14 Montpelier Villas, Brighton BN1 3DG
T: (01273) 25544
Founded: 1947; Members: 300
Focus: Archeol 10940

Audio Engineering Society, British Section (AES, UK), 8 Granville Rd, Sevenoaks
Founded: 1970; Members: 365
Focus: Eng
Periodical
Journal (10 times annually) 10941

Aviation Environment Federation (AEF), 5 High Timber St, London EC4V 3NS
T: (0171) 3298159; E-Mail: 101455.1475@compuserve.com; Fax: 3298160
Founded: 1975
Gen Secr: Peter Fairhurst
Focus: Aero; Ecology
Periodical
Newsletter (semi-annually) 10942

The Avicultural Society (A.S.), Windsor Forest Stud, Mill Ride, Ascot SL5 8LT
T: (013447) 5444
Founded: 1894; Members: 1000
Focus: Ornithology 10943

Ayrshire Agricultural Association, 24 Beresford Terrace, Ayr KA7 2EL
T: (01292) 66168
Members: 1196
Focus: Agri 10944

Ayrshire Archaeological and Natural History Society (A.A.N.H.S.), 1 Portmark Av, Ayr KA7 4DD
T: (01292) 42077
Founded: 1947; Members: 250
Focus: Archeol; Hist; Nat Sci 10945

Balint Society, Tollgate Health Centre, 220 Tollgate Rd, London E6 4JS
T: (0171) 4457709; Fax: 4457715
Founded: 1970; Members: 150
Pres: Dr. Paul Sackin; Gen Secr: Dr. David Watt
Focus: Psych
Periodical
Journal of the Balint Society (annually) . 10946

The Bantock Society, 101 Crouch Hill, London N8
T: (0171) 7068055
Founded: 1946; Members: 100
Focus: Lit 10947

Baptist Historical Society (B.H.S.), Baptist House, 129 Broadway, POB 44, Oxford OX11 8RT
Founded: 1908; Members: 600
Pres: Dr. W.M.S. West; Gen Secr: S.L. Copson
Focus: Hist
Periodical
Baptist Quarterly (quarterly) 10948

Bar Association for Commerce, Finance and Industry, 63 Great Cumberland Pl, London W1H 7LJ
T: (0171) 7239556
Founded: 1965; Members: 550
Focus: Law 10949

Barbirolli Society, 8 Tunnel Rd, Retford DN22 7TA
Founded: 1972; Members: 240
Focus: Music
Periodical
Newsletter (semi-annually) 10950

Barge and Canal Development Association (BCDA), 33 Walnut Crescent, Peacock Estate, Wakefield WF2 0EU
T: (01924) 366677
Founded: 1972
Focus: Transport
Periodical
Report (quarterly) 10951

Bath and Camerton Archaeological Society, 61 Pulteney St, Bath BA2 4DN
T: (01225) 66272
Founded: 1947
Focus: Archeol 10952

Battery Vehicle Society (BVS), 3 Steyning Court, Steyning Av, Peacehaven BN9 8LU
T: 4193
Founded: 1973; Members: 109
Focus: Electric Eng 10953

BC Society, 2 Ham Farm Cottages, Hurst Rd, Hassocks BN6 9NN
T: (017918) 5013
Founded: 1977; Members: 210
Focus: Archeol
Periodical
BC News (quarterly) 10954

Bedfordshire Archaeological Council, 36 Saint Andrews Rd, Bedford
Founded: 1963
Focus: Archeol 10955

Bedfordshire Historical Record Society (BHRS), c/o County Record Office, County Hall, Bedford MK42 9AP
T: (01234) 228833
Founded: 1913; Members: 250
Pres: E. Whitbread; Gen Secr: Betty Chambers
Focus: Hist
Periodical
BHRS Publications (annually) 10956

Belfast Natural History and Philosophical Society (BNHPS), c/o Linen Hall Library, 17 Donegall Sq, Belfast
Founded: 1821; Members: 100
Focus: Hist; Nat Sci; Philos
Periodical
Proceedings and Reports 10957

Benesh Institute, 36 Battersea Sq, London SW11 3RA
T: (0171) 3268031; Fax: 3268033
Founded: 1962; Members: 100
Pres: Sir Peter Wright; Gen Secr: Andrew Ward
Focus: Music
Periodicals
The Choreologist (annually)
Newsletter (annually) 10958

Benslow Music Trust, Little Benslow Hills, Benslow Ln, Hitchin SG4 9RB
T: (01462) 459446; Fax: 440171
Founded: 1929; Members: 1500
Pres: Lady Evelyn Barbirolli; Gen Secr: Keith Stent
Focus: Music; Educ
Periodical
Course Brochure (semi-annually) 10959

Bertrand Russell Society, 9 Naseby Av, Higher Blackley, Manchester M9 2JJ
T: (0161) 7950307
Founded: 1974
Focus: Philos 10960

Berwickshire Naturalists' Club (BNC), The Hill, Coldingham, Eyemouth TD14 5QB
T: (013903) 209
Founded: 1831; Members: 350
Focus: Nat Sci; Antique
Periodical
HBNC (annually) 10961

The Bibliographical Society, c/o The Wellcome Institute, 183 Euston Rd, London NW1 2BE
T: (0171) 6117244; Fax: 6118703
Founded: 1892; Members: 1200
Pres: R. Myers; Gen Secr: D.R.S. Pearson
Focus: Libraries & Bk Sci
Periodical
The Library (quarterly) 10962

BIBRA International, Woodmansterne Rd, Carshalton SM5 4DS
T: (0181) 6521000; E-Mail: help@bibra.co.uk; Fax: 6617029
Founded: 1960; Members: 120
Pres: Eric A. Flack; Gen Secr: Dr. S.E. Jaggers
Focus: Bio
Periodicals
BIBRA Bulletin (monthly)
BIBRA Toxicity Profiles
Food and Chemical Toxicology (monthly)
Toxicology in Vitro (quarterly) 10963

Bio-dynamic Agricultural Association (BDAA), Woodman Lane, Clent, Stourbridge DY9 9PX
T: (01562) 884933; Fax: 882619
Founded: 1929; Members: 650
Focus: Agri
Periodical
Star and Furrow (semi-annually) 10964

Biochemical Society, 59 Portland Pl, London W1N 3AJ
T: (0171) 5805530; Fax: 6377626
Founded: 1911; Members: 9000
Pres: Prof. A.D.B. Malcolm; Gen Secr: G.D. Jones
Focus: Biochem
Periodicals
The Biochemical Journal (bi-weekly)
Biochemical Society Symposia (annually)
Biochemical Society Transactions (bi-monthly)
The Biochemist (bi-monthly)
Clinical Science (14 times annually)
Essays in Biochemistry (annually) . . . 10965

Biodeterioration Society, c/o International Mycological Institute, Ferry Ln, Kew TW9 3AF
T: (0181) 9404086; Fax: 3321171
Founded: 1969
Gen Secr: Dr. J. Kelley
Focus: Botany
Periodical
International Biodeterioration 10966

Biological Engineering Society (B.E.S.), c/o Royal College of Surgeons, Lincoln's Inn Fields, London WC2A 3PN
T: (0171) 2427750
Founded: 1960; Members: 600
Gen Secr: Dr. R.E. Trotman
Focus: Eng
Periodicals
Journal of Biomedical Engineering (bi-monthly)
Proceedings of Conferences and Symposia 10967

Biorhythmic Research Association, 22 Far Ln, Normanton-on-Soar, Loughborough, Leics
Focus: Bio 10968

Biotechnology and Biological Sciences Research Council (BBSRC), Polaris House, North Star Av, Swindon SN2 1UH
T: (01793) 413200; Fax: 413201
Founded: 1931
Focus: Eng; Bio 10969

Bird Life International, Wellsbrook Court, Girton Rd, Cambridge CB3 0NA
T: (01223) 277318; Fax: 277200
Founded: 1922
Focus: Ornithology
Periodicals
Annual Report (annually)
World Birdwatch (quarterly) 10970

Birmingham and Midland Institute (BMI), Margaret St, Birmingham B3 3BS
T: (0121) 2363591
Founded: 1854
Focus: Arts; Lit
Periodical
B.M.I. Magazine (monthly) 10971

Birmingham and Warwickshire Archaeological Society (B.W.A.S.), c/o Birmingham and Midland Institute, Margaret St, Birmingham B3 3BS
T: (0121) 2363591
Founded: 1870; Members: 250
Pres: Dr. L.H. Barfield; Gen Secr: S. Middleton
Focus: Archeol
Periodical
Birmingham and Warwickshire Archaeological Society Transactions (annually) 10972

Birmingham Bibliographical Society, c/o Main Library, University of Birmingham, Edgbaston, Birmingham B15 2TT
T: (0121) 4145814; Fax: 4714691
Founded: 1972; Members: 50
Focus: Libraries & Bk Sci 10973

The Birmingham Metallurgical Association, c/o Dept of Mechanical and Production Engineering, City of Birmingham Polytechnic, Franchise St, Birmingham B42 2SU
T: (0121) 3566911
Founded: 1903; Members: 1500
Focus: Metallurgy 10974

Birmingham Natural History Society (BNHS), 55 Selby Close, Yardley, Birmingham B26 6AP
Founded: 1858; Members: 173
Focus: Hist; Nat Sci 10975

Birmingham Transport Historical Group (BTHG), 43 Shorncliffe Rd, Folkestone CT20 2UD
T: (01303) 59243
Founded: 1963; Members: 26
Focus: Transport; Hist 10976

Blackcountry Society (BCS), 15 Claydon Rd, Wallheath, Kingswinford DY6 0HR
T: (01384) 293656
Founded: 1967; Members: 2000
Focus: Archeol; Hist
Periodical
The Blackcountry Man Quarterly Magazine (quarterly) 10977

Blair Bell Research Society (BBRS), c/o Dept of Obstetrics and Gynaecology, Clinical Science Bldg, Leicester Royal Infirmary, POB 65, Leicester LE2 2EG
T: (01533) 523164; Fax: 523107
Founded: 1962; Members: 532
Pres: Prof. William Dunlop; Gen Secr: Dr. James Drife
Focus: Gynecology 10978

Bliss Classification Association (BCA), c/o The Library, Fitzwilliam College, Cambridge CB3 0DG
Fax: (01223) 464162
Founded: 1967; Members: 130
Pres: Jack Mills; Gen Secr: Christina Panagiotidou
Focus: Libraries & Bk Sci
Periodical
Bliss Classification Bulletin (annually) . . 10979

BMRB International, 79-81 Uxbridge Rd, London W5 5SU
Focus: Marketing
Periodicals
Premier TGI (annually)
TGI (annually)
Youth TGI (annually) 10980

BMT Cortec, c/o Wallsend Research Station, Wallsend NE28 6UY
T: (0191) 2625242; Fax: 2638754
Founded: 1944
Focus: Eng
Periodical
BMT Abstracts (monthly) 10981

Boarding Schools Association (BSA), Ysgol Nant, Valley Rd, Llanfairfeuhan LL33 0ES
T: (01248) 680542; Fax: 680542
Founded: 1966; Members: 485
Focus: Educ
Periodicals
Boarding School (semi-annually)
Occasional Papers (irregularly)
Research Topics (irregularly) 10982

Bone and Tooth Society, c/o Bone Research Laboratory, Churchill Hospital, Headington, Oxford
T: (01865) 64811
Founded: 1950; Members: 248
Focus: Dent 10983

Book Trust, Book House, 45 East Hill, London SW18 2QZ
T: (0181) 8709055
Founded: 1925; Members: 1000
Pres: Sir Simon Horney; Gen Secr: Brian Perman
Focus: Lit
Periodical
Reading Matters (semi-annually) 10984

Bookplate Society, 9 Lyndale Av, London NW2 2QD
T: (0171) 4351059
Members: 300
Focus: Graphic & Dec Arts, Design; Libraries & Bk Sci
Periodicals
Journal (semi-annually)
Newsletter (quarterly) 10985

Border Union Agricultural Society (BUAS), Showground Office, Springwood Park, Kelso TD5 8LS
T: (015732) 2188
Founded: 1813; Members: 1065
Focus: Agri 10986

Borthwick Institute of Historical Research, Saint Anthony's Hall, Peaseholme Green, York YO1 2PW
T: (01904) 59861
Focus: Hist 10987

The Botanical Society of Scotland (B.S.S.), c/o Royal Botanic Garden, Inverleith Row, Edinburgh EH3 5LR
T: (0131) 5527171
Founded: 1836; Members: 570
Pres: John Proctor; Gen Secr: R. Galt
Focus: Botany
Periodical
Botanical Journal of Scotland (annually) . 10988

Botanical Society of the British Isles (B.S.B.I), c/o Dept of Botany, Natural History Museum, Cromwell Rd, London SW7 5BD
T: (0171) 9389123 ext 8701
Founded: 1836; Members: 2700
Pres: D. Pearman; Gen Secr: R.G. Ellis
Focus: Botany
Periodicals
BSBI Abstracts (annually)
Watsonia (semi-annually) 10989

Branch Line Society (BLS), 15 Springwood Hall Gardens, Gledholt, Huddersfield HD1 4HA
T: (01484) 25782
Founded: 1955; Members: 1000
Focus: Transport
Periodical
Branch Line News (bi-weekly) 10990

Brewery History Society, 10 Ringstead Court, Ringstead Rd, Sutton SM1 4SH
T: (0181) 6427189
Founded: 1972; Members: 700
Focus: Hist 10991

BRF International (BRF), Lyttel Hall, Nutfield RH1 4HY
Founded: 1948
Focus: Eng
Periodical
Industry Review (annually) 10992

Bristol and Gloucestershire Archaeological Society, 22 Beaumont Rd, Gloucester GL2 0EJ
T: (01452) 302610
Founded: 1876; Members: 1000
Pres: E. Price; Gen Secr: D.J.H. Smith
Focus: Archeol; Hist
Periodicals
Gloucestershire Record Series (annually)
Transactions (annually) 10993

Bristol Industrial Archaeological Society (BIAS), c/o City Museum, Queens Rd, Bristol BS8 1RL
T: (01272) 299771
Founded: 1967; Members: 300
Pres: Owen H. Ward
Focus: Archeol
Periodicals
BIAS Bulletin (3 times annually)
BIAS Journal (annually) 10994

British Academy (B.A.F.T.A.), 20-21 Cornwall Terrace, London NW1 4QP
T: (0171) 4875966; Fax: 2243807
Founded: 1901; Members: 621
Pres: Sir Keith Thomas; Gen Secr: P.W.H. Brown
Focus: Cinema
Periodicals
Annual Report (annually)
Proceedings (annually) 10995

British Academy of Film and Television Arts (BAFTA), 195 Piccadilly, London W1V 9LG
T: (0171) 734 0022; Fax: 7341792
Founded: 1976; Members: 2200
Focus: Cinema 10996

British Academy of Forensic Sciences (B.A.F.S.), c/o Anaesthetics Unit, The London Royal Hospital, Whitechapel, London E1 1BB
T: (0171) 3779201
Founded: 1959; Members: 500
Gen Secr: Dr. Patricia J. Flynn
Focus: Forensic Med
Periodical
Medicine, Science and the Law (quarterly) 10997

British Acupuncture Association and Register (BAAR), 34 Alderney St, London SW1V 4EU
T: (0171) 8341012
Founded: 1960; Members: 230
Pres: Dr. E.W. Johnson
Focus: Med; Physical Therapy
Periodical
The British Journal of Acupuncture (semi-annually) 10998

British Agricultural History Society (BAHS), c/o Dept of Economic and Social History, University of Exeter, Amory Bldg, Rennes Dr, Exeter EX4 4RJ
E-Mail: bahs@exeter.ac.uk; Fax: (01392) 263305
Founded: 1953; Members: 820
Pres: Dr. J. Thirsk; Gen Secr: Dr. R. Hoyle
Focus: Hist; Agri
Periodical
Agricultural History Review (semi-annually) 10999

British Agricultural Marketing Research Group (BAMRG), Cedar Cott, Upper Bolney, Henley-on-Thames
Founded: 1971
Focus: Marketing 11000

British and European Geranium Society (BEGS), 56 Shrigley Rd., Higher Poynton SK12 1TF
T: (01625) 873056
Founded: 1970; Members: 2000
Gen Secr: Doris P. Codling
Focus: Botany 11001

British and Foreign Bible Society (BFBS), Stonchill Green, Westlea, Swindon SN5 7DG
T: (01793) 513713; Fax: 512539
Founded: 1804
Gen Secr: Neil Crosbie
Focus: Rel & Theol
Periodical
Word in Action (quarterly) 11002

British and Irish Association of Law Librarians (BIALL), c/o Susan Frost, 26 Myton Crescent, Warwick CV34 6QA
T: (01926) 491717; E-Mail: 106033.52@compuserve.com; Fax: 491717
Founded: 1969; Members: 600
Focus: Libraries & Bk Sci
Periodicals
Law Librarian (quarterly)
Newsletter (quarterly) 11003

British Arachnological Society, 2 Egypt Wood Cottages, Egypt Ln, Farnham Common SL2 3LE
T: (01753) 645791
Founded: 1963; Members: 600
Gen Secr: Dr. Helen Read
Focus: Zoology
Periodicals
Bulletin (3 times annually)
Newsletter (3 times annually) 11004

British Archaeological Association (BAA), c/o Victorian Society, 1 Priory Gardens, Bedford Park, London W4 1TT
Founded: 1843; Members: 700
Pres: L. Keen
Focus: Arts; Cultur Hist
Periodicals
Conference Transactions (annually)
Journal (annually) 11005

British Arts, 227 Goldhawk Rd, London W12 8ER
Founded: 1953; Members: 10800
Focus: Arts 11006

British Association for Accident and Emergency Medicine (BAEM), c/o The Royal College of Surgeons of England, 35-43 Lincoln's Inn Fields, London WC2A 3PN
T: (0171) 8319405; Fax: 4050318
Founded: 1967; Members: 930
Pres: Christopher Cutting; Gen Secr: John Heyworth
Focus: Surgery; Med
Periodical
Journal of Accident and Emergency Medicine (bi-monthly) 11007

British Association for American Studies (BAAS), c/o School of Humanities, De Montfort University, Leicester LE1 9BH
T: (0116) 2577398; E-Mail: pjd@dmn.ae.uk; Fax: 2577199
Founded: 1955; Members: 500
Pres: Prof. J. Newman; Gen Secr: Philip Davies
Focus: Ethnology; Hist; Lit; Poli Sci; Cultur Hist
Periodicals
BAAS Newsletter (semi-annually)
Journal of American Studies (3 times annually) 11008

British Association for Applied Linguistics (BAAL), Frankfurt Lodge, Clevedon Hall, Victoria Rd, Clevedon BA21 7SJ
T: (01275) 87619
Founded: 1968; Members: 500
Pres: Rosamond Mitchell; Gen Secr: Ulrike Meinhof
Focus: Ling
Periodicals
Applied Linguistics (3 times annually)
Newsletter 11009

British Association for Brazing and Soldering (BABS), c/o The Welding Institute, Abington House, Cambridge CB1 6AL
T: (01223) 891162; Fax: 892588
Founded: 1970
Gen Secr: J.B. Dunkerton
Focus: Eng; Metallurgy
Periodical
Welding and Metal Fabrication (10 times annually) 11010

British Association for Canadian Studies (BACS), 21 George Sq, Edinburgh EH8 9LD
T: (0131) 6621117; E-Mail: jrobson@afb1.ssc.ed.ac.uk; Fax: 6621118
Founded: 1975; Members: 500
Pres: C.D. Rolfe; Gen Secr: J. Robson
Focus: Hist; Poli Sci; Lit
Periodical
British Journal of Canadian Studies (semi-annually) 11011

British Association for Cancer Research (BACR), c/o Institute of Biology, 20 Queensberry Pl, London SW7 2DZ
T: (0171) 5818333; Fax: 8239409
Founded: 1960; Members: 1100
Focus: Cell Biol & Cancer Res 11012

British Association for Counselling (BAC), 1 Regent Pl, Rugby CV21 2PJ
T: (01788) 550899; E-Mail: bac@bac.co.uk; Fax: 562189
Founded: 1977; Members: 14500
Pres: Dr. Mark Aveline; Gen Secr: Judith Baron
Focus: Therapeutics
Periodicals
Counselling (quarterly)
Counselling & Psychotherapy Resources Directory (annually)
Jobfile (bi-weekly)
Training in Counselling & Psychotherapy (annually)
The Voice of Counselling (quarterly) . . 11013

British Association for Immediate Care (BASICS), 7 Black Horse Ln, Ipswich ID1 2EF
T: (01473) 218407
Founded: 1977; Members: 2200
Gen Secr: R. Bailey
Focus: Med
Periodical
BASICS (3 times annually) 11014

British Association for Information and Libraries Education and Research, c/o Dept of Information Studies, University of Sheffield, Sheffield S1 4DP
Founded: 1952; Members: 18
Focus: Libraries & Bk Sci; Computer & Info Sci 11015

British Association for Paediatric Nephrology, c/o Birmingham Childrens Hospital, Ladwood, Middleway, Birmingham B16 8ET
T: (0121) 4544851; Fax: 4545715
Members: 70
Focus: Pediatrics 11016

British Association for Psychopharmacology (BAP), c/o Dept of Psychiatry, Guy's Hospital Medical School, London SE1 9RT
T: (0171) 4077600
Founded: 1974; Members: 315
Focus: Pharmacol 11017

British Association for the Advancement of Science (B.A.A.S.), Fortress House, 23 Savile Row, London W1X 2NR
T: (0171) 9733500; Fax: 9733051
Founded: 1831; Members: 2000
Pres: Sir Derek Roberts; Gen Secr: Dr. P. Briggs
Focus: Sci

Periodicals
Science & the Public (bi-monthly)
Scope (quarterly) 11018

British Association for the History of Religions, c/o Open University in Wales, 24 Cathedral Rd, Cardiff CF1 9SA
Founded: 1954; Members: 170
Pres: Prof. C.G. Williams; Gen Secr: Dr. T. Thomas
Focus: Hist; Rel & Theol
Periodical
Bulletin (3 times annually) 11019

British Association for the Study of Religions, c/o Dept of Theology and Religious Studies, University of Leeds, Leeds LS2 9JT
Founded: 1954; Members: 200
Pres: Prof. Brian Bocking; Gen Secr: Dr. K. Knott
Focus: Rel & Theol
Periodical
Bulletin (3 times annually) 11020

British Association of Academic Phoneticians, c/o Phonetics Laboratory, Dept of English Language, University of Glasgow, Glasgow G12 9QQ
T: (0141) 3304596; E-Mail: macmahon@arts.gla.ac.uk; Fax: 3303531
Founded: 1984; Members: 75
Pres: J.C. Wells; Gen Secr: M.K.C. MacMahon
Focus: Ling 11021

British Association of Advisers and Lecturers in Pysical Education (B.A.A.L.P.E.), Nelson House, 6 The Beacon, Exmouth EX8 2AG
T: (01395) 263247; E-Mail: 106365.720@compuserve.com; Fax: 276348
Founded: 1920; Members: 410
Pres: M. Hunt; Gen Secr: G.M. Edmondson
Focus: Sports
Periodical
Safe Practice in Physical Education (3 times annually) 11022

British Association of Art Therapists (BAAT), 11a Richmond Rd, Brighton BN2 3RL
Founded: 1964; Members: 600
Focus: Therapeutics
Periodical
Inscape (semi-annually) 11023

British Association of Blind Esperantists, 32 Benson St, Middlesborough T55 6JQ
Founded: 1935
Focus: Ling 11024

British Association of Clinical Anatomists (BACA), c/o Dept of Anatomy, University, Oxford Rd, Manchester M13 9PT
T: (0161) 2738241 ext 155
Founded: 1977; Members: 200
Focus: Anat; Surgery
Periodicals
LM & Rules
Proceedings of Meetings (semi-annually) . 11025

British Association of Cosmetic Surgeons (BACS), 17 Harley St, London W1N
T: (0171) 3235728
Founded: 1980; Members: 15
Focus: Surgery 11026

British Association of Crystal Growth (BACG), c/o Allen Clark Research Centre, The Plessey Company Ltd, Caswell, Towcester, Northants
T: 50581
Founded: 1969; Members: 240
Focus: Mineralogy 11027

British Association of Dental Nurses, 110 London St, Fleetwood FY7 6EU
T: (01253) 778631; Fax: 778800
Founded: 1940
Pres: Gloria Kemp; Gen Secr: P.A. Swain
Focus: Dent
Periodical
The British Dental Nurses Journal (quarterly) 11028

British Association of Friends of Museums (BAFM), 548 Wilbraham Rd, Manchester M21 1LB
T: (0161) 8818640
Founded: 1973; Members: 230
Pres: Sir John Hale; Gen Secr: Rosemary Marsh
Focus: Arts; Sci
Periodicals
Newsletter (quarterly)
Yearbook (annually) 11029

British Association of Hair Transplant Surgeons, 125 Worlds End Ln, Quinton, Birmingham B32 1JX
T: (0121) 4225282
Focus: Surgery 11030

British Association of Homoeopathic Pharmacists (BAHP), 19a Cavendish Sq, London W1M 9AD
T: (0171) 6293204/05
Founded: 1980; Members: 100
Focus: Homeopathy 11031

British Association of Homoeopathic Veterinary Surgeons (BHAVS), Chinham House, Stanford-in-the-Vale SN7 8NQ
T: (01367) 710324; Fax: 718243
Founded: 1981; Members: 150
Gen Secr: Christopher Day
Focus: Homeopathy; Vet Med
Periodical
Newsletter (semi-annually) 11032

British Association of Landscape Industries (BALI), 9 Henry St, Keighley BD21 3DR
T: (01535) 606139; Fax: 610269
Founded: 1972; Members: 750
Gen Secr: John Topping
Focus: Hort
Periodical
Newsletter (monthly) 11033

British Association of Numismatic Societies (BANS), c/o Philip Mernick, Bush Boake Allen, Blackhorse Ln, London E17 5QP
Founded: 1953
Pres: K. Sugden
Focus: Numismatics 11034

British Association of Oral and Maxillofacial Surgeons (BAOS), c/o Royal College of Surgeons, 35-43 Lincoln's Inn Fields, London WC2A 3PN
T: (0171) 4058074
Founded: 1962; Members: 1250
Gen Secr: Brian Avery
Focus: Surgery
Periodical
The British Journal of Oral & Maxillofacial Surgery (bi-monthly) 11035

British Association of Orthodontists (BAO), 16 Castle Hill, Maidenhead SL6 4JJ
T: (01628) 23279
Founded: 1965; Members: 200
Focus: Dent 11036

British Association of Otorhinolaryngologists, Head and Neck Surgeons (BAO), c/o Royal College of Surgeons of England, 35-43 Lincoln's Inn Fields, London WC2A 3PN
T: (0171) 4048373; Fax: 4044200
Founded: 1943; Members: 930
Pres: David Wright; Gen Secr: Patrick Beasley
Focus: Otorhinolaryngology; Surgery . . 11037

British Association of Paediatric Surgeons (B.A.P.S.), c/o Royal College of Surgeons, Nicolson St, Edinburgh EH8 9DW
T: (0131) 6683975; Fax: 6671905
Founded: 1954; Members: 744
Focus: Surgery; Pediatrics 11038

British Association of Picture Libraries, c/o Winton, 10 Cheyne Row, London SW3
T: (0171) 3525824
Focus: Libraries & Bk Sci 11039

British Association of Plastic Surgeons (BAPS), c/o Royal College of Surgeons, 35-43 Lincoln's Inn Fields, London WC2A 3PN
T: (0171) 8315161; Fax: 8314041
Founded: 1946; Members: 561
Pres: B.D.G. Morgan; Gen Secr: J.G. Boorman
Focus: Surgery
Periodical
British Journal of Plastic Surgery (8 times annually) 11040

British Association of Psychotherapists, 37 Mapesbury Rd, London NW2 4HJ
T: (0181) 4529823; Fax: 4525182
Founded: 1951; Members: 450
Focus: Psych; Therapeutics 11041

British Association of Seed Analysts (BASA), 3 Whitehall Court, London SW1A 2EQ
T: (0171) 9303611; Fax: 9303952
Founded: 1961
Focus: Agri 11042

British Association of Social Psychiatry (BASP), 16 Lichfield Rd, Kew TW9 3JR
Founded: 1964; Members: 125
Focus: Psychiatry
Periodical
The International Journal of Social Psychiatry 11043

British Association of Sport Medicine (BASM), 49 Blakes Ln, New Malden KT3 6N3, Surrey
T: 9490607
Members: 730
Focus: Med 11044

British Association of Surgical Oncology (BASO), c/o Royal College of Surgeons, 35-43 Lincoln's Inn Fields, London WC2A 3PN
T: (0171) 4055612
Founded: 1973; Members: 411
Gen Secr: T.G. Allen-Mersh
Focus: Surgery; Cell Biol & Cancer Res
Periodical
European Journal of Surgical Oncology (bi-monthly) 11045

British Association of Teachers of the Deaf (BATOD), The Rycroft Centre, Stanley Rd, Cheadle Hulme SK8 6RF
T: (0161) 4375951
Founded: 1976
Focus: Educ Handic
Periodical
Journal: Teacher of the Deaf (bi-monthly) 11046

British Association of the Experiment in International Living (EIL), Otesaga, Upper Wyche, Malvern WR14 4EN
T: (016845) 62577/78
Founded: 1932; Members: 2000
Focus: Int'l Relat; Travel 11047

British Association of Urological Surgeons (BAUS), c/o Royal College of Surgeons, 35-43 Lincoln's Inn Fields, London WC2A 3PN
T: (0171) 4051390
Founded: 1945; Members: 1100
Pres: R.T. Turner-Warwick; Gen Secr: M.G. Royle
Focus: Urology; Surgery 11048

British Association Representing Breeders (B.A.R.B.), 9 Portland St, King's Lynn, Norfolk PE30 1PB
T: (01553) 773094; Fax: 772804
Founded: 1973; Members: 58
Pres: Alec Cocker; Gen Secr: D. Dealtrey
Focus: Botany, Specific
Periodical
BARB News and Views (semi-annually) . 11049

British Astronomical Association (BAA), Burlington House, Piccadilly, London W1V 9AG
T: (0171) 7344145
Founded: 1890; Members: 4500
Pres: M.V. Gavin; Gen Secr: Rosa Atwell
Focus: Astronomy
Periodicals
British Astronomical Association Handbook (annually)
Journal of the British Astronomical Association (bi-monthly) 11050

British Aviation Preservation Council (BAPC), c/o Museum of Science and Industry, Liverpool Rd, Manchester M3 4JP
T: (0161) 8322244; E-Mail: all@mussci.u.net.com; Fax: 8345135
Founded: 1967; Members: 180
Pres: Sir Peter G. Masefield; Gen Secr: Nick Forder
Focus: Aero
Periodical
Update (quarterly) 11051

British Ballet Organization (B.B.O.), 39 Lonsdale Rd, London SW13 9JP
T: (0181) 7481241; Fax: 7481301
Founded: 1930; Members: 1000
Pres: John Travis
Focus: Perf Arts
Periodical
The Dancer Magazine (semi-annually) . . 11052

British Balloon and Airship Club (BBAC), 47 Vaughan Way, Leicester LE1 4SG
T: (0121) 6434050
Founded: 1966; Members: 2000
Focus: Aero
Periodical
The Aerostat (bi-monthly) 11053

British Biophysical Society, c/o Dr. W.A.Thomas, 28 Milton Av, Eaton Ford, Saint Neots PE19 3LE
Founded: 1960
Focus: Biophys 11054

British Bryological Society (BBS), c/o National Museum and Galleries of Wales, Cardiff CF1 3NP
T: (01222) 573217; Fax: 239829
Founded: 1896; Members: 580
Pres: A.R. Perry; Gen Secr: Dr. M.E. Newton
Focus: Botany
Periodicals
Bulletin of the British Bryological Society (semi-annually)
Journal of Bryology (semi-annually) . . . 11055

British Butterfly Conservation Society (BBCS), POB 222, Dedham, Colchester CO7 6EY
T: (01206) 322342
Founded: 1968; Members: 10100
Focus: Ecology
Periodical
News Bulletin (3 times annually) 11056

British Cardiac Society, 7 Fitzroy Sq, London W1P 5AH
T: (0171) 3833887; Fax: 3880903
Founded: 1937
Gen Secr: Dr. D. Dymond
Focus: Cardiol
Periodicals
British Heart Journal (monthly)
Cardiovascolar Research (monthly) . . . 11057

British Cartographic Society (BCS), c/o Royal Geographical Society, 1 Kensington Grove, London SW7 2AR
T: (01703) 781519; Fax: 781519
Founded: 1963; Members: 1006
Pres: R.W. Hill; Gen Secr: J.K. Atherton
Focus: Cart
Periodicals
The Cartographic Journal (semi-annually)
Newsletter (quarterly) 11058

British Caspian Trust (BCT), Colonsay, Hampton Lovett, Droitwich, Worcs
T: (0129923) 495
Founded: 1975; Members: 138
Focus: Folklore
Periodical
British Caspian Trust News-Letter (semi-annually) 11059

British Cave Research Association (B.C.R.A.), 6 Worcester Terrace, Bristol BS8 3JW
T: (01272) 741848
Founded: 1973; Members: 800
Focus: Speleology
Periodicals
Cave Science: The Transactions of the B.C.R.A. (quarterly)
Caves and Caving (quarterly) 11060

British Cement Association (BCA), Century House, Telford Av, Crowthorne RG11 6YS
T: (01344) 762676; Fax: 761214
Founded: 1935
Focus: Materials Sci 11061

British Ceramic Society (B.C.S.), Shelton House, Stoke Rd, Stoke-on-Trent ST4 2DR
T: (01782) 23116
Founded: 1900; Members: 960
Focus: Materials Sci 11062

British Ceramic Tile Council, Federation House, Stoke-on-Trent ST4 2RU
T: (01782) 747147
Founded: 1960; Members: 5
Focus: Materials Sci 11063

British Committee for Standards in Haematology (B.C.S.H.), c/o Dept of Haematology, Middlesex Hospital, Riding House St, London W1P 7LD
T: (0171) 6368333
Members: 6
Focus: Hematology 11064

British Compressed Air Society (BCAS), 8 Leicester St, London WC2H 7BN
T: (0171) 4370678
Focus: Eng 11065

British Computer Society (BCS), 1 Sanford St, Swindon 1
T: (01793) 417417; Fax: 480270
Founded: 1957; Members: 34000
Gen Secr: Judith M. Scott
Focus: Computer & Info Sci
Periodicals
Computer Bulletin (monthly)
Computer Journal (bi-monthly)
Formal Aspects of Computing (quarterly)
Interacting with Computers (quarterly)
IT in Nursing (quarterly)
Software Engineering Journal (quarterly)
What's on in Computing (quarterly) . . . 11066

British Council, 10 Spring Gardens, London SW1A 2NB
T: (0171) 9308466; Fax: 8396347
Founded: 1934
Focus: Ling; Lit 11067

British Cryogenics Council, c/o Institution of Mechanical Engineers, 1 Birdcage Walk, London SW1 7BU
T: (0115)9312896; Fax: 9312896
Founded: 1967; Members: 10
Pres: N.P. Hegarty; Gen Secr: J.S. Harris
Focus: Physics; Eng
Periodical
British Cryogenics Council Newsletter (quarterly) 11068

British Dental Association (BDA), 64 Wimpole St, London W1M 8AL
T: (0171) 9350875; E-Mail: bdainfo@mailbox.ulcc.ac.uk; Fax: 4875232
Founded: 1880; Members: 15000
Gen Secr: J.M.G. Hunt
Focus: Dent
Periodical
British Dental Journal (bi-weekly) 11069

British Dental Hygienists Association (B.D.H.A.), 64 Wimpole St, London W1M 8AL
T: (0171) 9350875
Founded: 1949; Members: 900
Focus: Dent 11070

British Diabetic Association (B.D.A.), 10 Queen Anne St, London W1M 0BD
T: (0171) 3231531; Fax: 6373644
Founded: 1934; Members: 160000
Pres: Prof. Harry Keen; Gen Secr: Michael Cooper
Focus: Diabetes
Periodicals
Balance (bi-monthly)
Diabetes Contents (quarterly)
Diabetic Medicine (10 times annually) . . 11071

The British Dietetic Association (BDA), Elizabeth House, 22 Suffolk St, Queensway, Birmingham B1 1LS
T: (0121) 6435483; E-Mail: bda@dial.pipex.com; Fax: 6334399
Founded: 1936; Members: 4300
Pres: A.M. Dobson; Gen Secr: J.C.J. Grigg
Focus: Nutrition
Periodical
Journal of Human Nutrition and Dietetics (bi-monthly) 11072

British Dyslexia Association (BDA), 98 London Rd, Reading RG1 5AU
T: (0118) 9662677; E-Mail: admin@bda-dyslexia.demon.co.uk; Fax: 9351927
Founded: 1972; Members: 12000
Pres: Baroness Warnock of Weeke; Gen Secr: George S. Yelland
Focus: Logopedy
Periodicals
Dyslexia Contact (semi-annually)
Dyslexia Journal (3 times annually) . . 11073

The British Ecological Society (B.E.S.), 26 Blades Court, Deodar Rd, Putney, London SW15 2NU
T: (0181) 8719797; E-Mail: general@ecology.demon.co.uk; Fax: 8719779
Founded: 1913; Members: 4900
Pres: Prof. J.A. Lee; Gen Secr: Dr. H.J. Norman
Focus: Ecology
Periodicals
Functional Ecology (bi-monthly)
Journal of Animal Ecology (bi-monthly)
Journal of Applied Ecology (bi-monthly)
Journal of Ecology (bi-monthly)
Symposium (annually) 11074

British Educational Management and Administration Society, c/o Sheffield Hallam University, Collegiate Crescent Campus, Sheffield S10 2BP
T: (0114) 2532328; E-Mail: bemas@shv.ac.uk; Fax: 2532324
Founded: 1971; Members: 850
Pres: Margaret Maden; Gen Secr: Viv Garrett
Focus: Educ
Periodicals
Educational Management and Administration (quarterly)
Management in Education (5 times annually)
. . . . 11075

British Electrophoresis Society, c/o Dept of Medical Microbiology, University of Aberdeen, Medical School Bldgs, Foresterhill, Aberdeen AB9 2ZD
T: (01224) 681818 ext 52505; Fax: 685604
Founded: 1982; Members: 225
Pres: Dr. Michael Dunn; Gen Secr: Dr. Phillip Cash
Focus: Chem 11076

British Endodontic Society (B.E.S.), 40 Wimpole St, London W1M 7AF
T: (0171) 4863648
Founded: 1963
Focus: Dent 11077

British Epilepsy Association (BEA), Anstey House, 40 Hanover Sq, Leeds LS3 1BE
T: (0113) 2439393; Fax: 2428804
Founded: 1950; Members: 20000
Focus: Pathology
Periodical
Epilepsy Today (quarterly) 11078

British Federation of Film Societies (BFFS), 81 Dean St, London W1V 6AA
T: (0171) 4374355
Founded: 1945; Members: 650
Focus: Cinema
Periodicals
BFFS Handbook (3 times annually)
BFFS Register (annually)
Film Magazine (monthly) 11079

British Federation of Women Graduates (BFWG), 4 Mandeville Courtyard, 142 Battersea Park Rd, London SW11 4NB
T: (0171) 4988037; Fax: 4988037
Founded: 1907; Members: 2000
Pres: F.M. Kirkby; Gen Secr: Annabel Stein
Focus: Sci
Periodicals
Awards to Women for Graduate Research (monthly)
BFWG News (bi-monthly) 11080

British Film Institute (BFI), 21 Stephen St, London W1P 1PL
T: (0171) 2551444; Fax: 4367950
Founded: 1933; Members: 26000
Gen Secr: W. Stevenson
Focus: Cinema
Periodicals
BFI Film and Television Handbook (annually)
Directions (annually)
Sight and Sound (monthly) 11081

The British Fluoridation Society, Sandlebrook, Mill Ln, Alderley Edge SK9 7TY
T: (01565) 872445; Fax: 873936
Founded: 1968
Pres: Prof. M.A. Lennon; Gen Secr: Ross Thomson
Focus: Public Health 11082

British Geological Survey, Keyworth NG12 5GG
T: (01602) 363100; Fax: 9363200
Founded: 1835
Focus: Geology 11083

British Geomorphological Research Group (BGRG), 1 Kensington Gore, London SW7 2AR
Founded: 1960; Members: 800
Focus: Geomorph; Geography; Geology . 11084

British Geotechnical Society (BGS), c/o Institution of Civil Engineers, 1-7 Great George St, London SW1P 3AA
T: (0171) 2227722
Founded: 1959; Members: 350
Focus: Eng 11085

British Geriatrics Society (B.G.S.), 1 Saint Andrews Pl, London NW1 4LB
T: (0171) 9354004; E-Mail: britishgeriatrics@dial.pipex.com; Fax: 2240454
Founded: 1947; Members: 1800
Pres: Dr. Arup K. Banerjee; Gen Secr: Dr. D. Black
Focus: Geriatrics
Periodical
Age and Ageing (bi-monthly) 11086

British Goat Society (BGS), 34-36 Fore St, Bovey Tracey TQ13 9AD
T: (01626) 833168
Founded: 1879; Members: 1500
Focus: Dairy Sci
Periodicals
The Herd Book (annually)
The Monthly Journal (monthly)
The Year Book (annually) 11087

British Herpetological Society (B.H.S.), c/o Zoological Society of London, Regent's Park, London NW1 4RY
Founded: 1948; Members: 860
Focus: Zoology
Periodicals
Bulletin (quarterly)
Herpetological Journal (quarterly) 11088

The British Homoeopathic Association (B.H.A.), 27a Devonshire St, London W1N 1RJ
T: (0171) 9352163
Founded: 1902; Members: 3750
Gen Secr: Enid Segall
Focus: Homeopathy
Periodical
Homoeopathy (bi-monthly) 11089

British Horological Institute (BHI), Upton Hall, Upton, Newark NG23 5TE
T: (01636) 813795; Fax: 812258
Founded: 1858; Members: 3400
Gen Secr: H. Bartlett
Focus: Eng
Periodical
Horological Journal (monthly) 11090

British Humanist Association (BHA), 14 Lamb's Conduit Passage, London WC1R 4RH
T: (0171) 4300908; Fax: 4301271
Founded: 1963
Focus: Philos
Periodical
Humanist News (8 times annually) . . . 11091

British Hypnosis Research Association (BHRA), 15 The Bank, Somersham PE17 3DJ
T: (0148) 840915
Founded: 1979
Focus: Depth Psych 11092

British Hypnotherapy Association (BHA), 67 Upper Berkeley St, London W1H 7DH
T: (0171) 7234443
Founded: 1958; Members: 364
Focus: Therapeutics 11093

British Ichthyological Society (BIS), 60 Newfields, Welwyn Garden City AL8 6YT
T: 29038
Founded: 1961; Members: 126
Focus: Zoology 11094

The British Institute for Brain Injured Children (BIBIC), Knowle Hall, Knowle, Bridgwater TA7 8PJ
T: (01278) 684060; Fax: 685573
Founded: 1972
Focus: Educ Handic
Periodical
Newsletter (quarterly) 11095

The British Institute of Cleaning Science (BICS), Whitworth Chambers, George Row, Northampton NN1 1DF
T: (01604) 230075
Founded: 1961; Members: 1975
Gen Secr: Peter Andrews
Focus: Eng 11096

British Institute of Human Rights (BIHR), Kings College London, Strand, London WC2R 2LS
T: (0171) 8732352; E-Mail: bihr@kcl.ac.uk; Fax: 8732048
Founded: 1970
Pres: Lord Scarman; Gen Secr: Dr. James J. Busuttil
Focus: Poli Sci
Periodical
Human Rights Case Digest (monthly) . . 11097

British Institute of Industrial Therapy (BIIT), Exmoor House, Methuen St, Southampton SO2 0FQ
T: (01703) 635345
Founded: 1980; Members: 500
Pres: Dr. Mounir Ekdawi; Gen Secr: Dr. Alan Whitehead
Focus: Therapeutics
Periodical
Industrial Therapy (quarterly) 11098

British Institute of International and Comparative Law (B.I.I.C.L.), 17 Russell Sq, London WC1B 5DR
T: (0171) 6365802; Fax: 3232016
Founded: 1958; Members: 2500
Pres: Lord Goff; Gen Secr: J.P. Gardner
Focus: Law
Periodicals
Bulletin of Legal Developments (bi-weekly)
International and Comparative Law (quarterly)
. . . . 11099

British Institute of Learning Disabilities, Wolverhampton Rd, Kidderminster DY10 3PP
T: (01562) 850251; Fax: 851970
Founded: 1972; Members: 2000
Focus: Educ Handic
Periodicals
Current Awareness Service (monthly)
Mental Handicap (quarterly)
Mental Handicap Bulletin (quarterly)
Mental Handicap Research (quarterly) . . 11100

British Institute of Musculoskeletal Medicine, 27 Green Ln, Northwood HA6 2PX
T: (01923) 820110; E-Mail: bimm.100733.2534@compuserve.com; Fax: 820110
Founded: 1992; Members: 357
Pres: Dr. M. Hutson; Gen Secr: Dr. P.G. Skew
Focus: Med
Periodical
Journal of Orthopaedic Medicine (quarterly)
. . . . 11101

The British Institute of Persian Studies, c/o The Institute of Archaeology, University College London, 31-34 Gordon Sq, London WC1H 0PY
Founded: 1961; Members: 500
Focus: Archeol; Arts; Anthro; Archit; Ling; Lit
Periodical
Iran (annually) 11102

British Institute of Practical Psychology (B.I.P.P.), 67 Highbury New Park, London N5 2EZ
T: (0171) 2263569
Founded: 1933; Members: 2652
Focus: Psych 11103

British Institute of Professional Photography, Fox Talbot House, Amwell End, Ware SG12 9HN
T: (01920) 464011; Fax: 487056
Founded: 1901; Members: 4000
Focus: Photo
Periodicals
The Photographer (monthly)
The Register of Members and Guide for Buyers of Photography (annually) 11104

British Institute of Radiology (B.I.R.), 36 Portland Pl, London W1N 4AT
T: (0171) 5804085; Fax: 2553209
Founded: 1897; Members: 2000
Pres: Dr. S. Golding; Gen Secr: Mary-Anne Piggett
Focus: Radiology
Periodical
The British Journal of Radiology 11105

British Institute of Surgical Technologists (B.I.S.T.), 1 Webbs Court, Buckhurst Av, Sevenoaks TN13 1LZ
Founded: 1935; Members: 1350
Focus: Surgery
Periodical
Journal (annually) 11106

British Insurance Law Association (B.I.L.A.), 229-230 Shoreditch High St, London E1 6PJ
T: (0171) 3750471
Founded: 1964; Members: 320
Pres: Prof. A.L. Diamond; Gen Secr: R. Hanson-James
Focus: Law
Periodical
BILA Bulletin (quarterly) 11107

British Interlingua Society, 14 Ventnor Court, Wostenholm Rd, Sheffield S7 1LB
T: (01742) 582931
Founded: 1955; Members: 26
Focus: Ling
Periodical
Lingua e Vita (3 times annually) . . . 11108

British Internal Combustion Engine Research Institute (BICERI), Malton Av, Slough SL1 4QA
T: (01753) 811899; E-Mail: john.bradley@biceri.co.uk; Fax: 811898
Founded: 1943; Members: 55
Pres: John R. Bradley; Gen Secr: Tony Reid
Focus: Mach Eng 11109

British International Studies Association, c/o Dept of Politics, University of Lancaster, Bailrigg LA1 4YF
Founded: 1975
Focus: Poli Sci 11110

British Interplanetary Society, 27-29 South Lambeth Rd, London SW8 1SZ
T: (0171) 7353160; E-Mail: bis.bis@virgin.net; Fax: 8201504
Founded: 1933; Members: 3500
Pres: Dr. P.T. Thompson; Gen Secr: S.A. Jones
Focus: Astronomy
Periodicals
Journal of the British Interplanetary Society (monthly)
Spaceflight (monthly) 11111

British Iris Society (BIS), 1 Sole Farm Close, Great Bookham KT23 3ED
T: (01372) 45481
Founded: 1922; Members: 900
Gen Secr: S.A. Ecklin
Focus: Botany, Specific
Periodical
The Iris Yearbook (annually) 11112

British Jazz Society, 10 Southfield Gardens, Twickenham, Middx
T: 8920133
Founded: 1964
Focus: Music 11113

British Kidney Patient Association (BKPA), Bordon, Hants
T: 2022
Founded: 1975
Focus: Otorhinolaryngology
Periodical
Silver Lining Appeal Brochure (annually) . 11114

British Kinematograph Sound and Television Society (BKSTS), Victoria House, Vernon Pl, London WC1B 4DF
T: (0171) 2428400; Fax: 4053560
Founded: 1931; Members: 2500
Focus: Cinema
Periodicals
BKSTS News (10 times annually)
Cinema Technology (quarterly)
Image Technology (10 times annually) . 11115

British Laboratory Animals Veterinary Association, c/o Chemical Defense Establishment, Porton, Salisbury, Wilts
Focus: Vet Med 11116

British Leather Confederation, Leather Trade House, Kings Park Rd, Moulton Park, Northampton NN3 1JD
T: (01604) 494131; Fax: 648220
Founded: 1920
Gen Secr: R.P. Pearson
Focus: Materials Sci 11117

British Leprosy Relief Association (LEPRA), Fairfax House, Causton Rd, Colchester CO1 1PU
T: (01206) 562286; Fax: 762151
Founded: 1924
Focus: Derm
Periodical
Leprosy Review (quarterly) 11118

British Library National Sound Archive, 96 Euston Rd, London NW1 2DB
T: (0171) 4127440; Fax: 4127441
Founded: 1955
Pres: Crispin Jewitt
Focus: Music
Periodical
Playback: Bulletin of the National Sound Archive (3 times annually) 11119

British Lichen Society, c/o Dept of Botany, Natural History Museum, London SW7 5BD
T: (0171) 9388852; Fax: 9389260
Founded: 1958; Members: 520
Gen Secr: O.W. Purvis
Focus: Botany
Periodicals
British Lichen Society Bulletin (semi-annually)
The Lichenologist (3 times annually) . . 11120

British Marine Aquarist Association (BMAA), 139 Bradford Av, Hull HU9 4LZ
Founded: 1970; Members: 300
Focus: Oceanography
Periodical
Marinews (bi-monthly) 11121

British Mass Spectrometry Society (BMSS), c/o Dr. Christine Eckers, Smith Kline Beecham Pharmaceuticals, Coldharbour Rd, Harlow CM19 5AQ
Founded: 1965
Gen Secr: Dr. Christine Eckers
Focus: Physics 11122

British Measures Group (BMG), 6 Park Rd, Teddington, Middx
Founded: 1973
Focus: Standards 11123

British Medical Association (BMA), BMA House, Tavistock Sq, London WC1H 9JP
T: (0171) 3874499; Fax: 3836400
Founded: 1832; Members: 114000
Gen Secr: E.M. Armstrong
Focus: Med
Periodical
British Medical Journal (weekly) 11124

British Microcirculation Society, c/o Centre for Medical and Biological Systems, Imperial College of Science, Technology and Medicine, London SW7 2BY
T: (0171) 5945172; E-Mail: m.j.kver@ic.ac.uk; Fax: 5945177
Founded: 1963; Members: 210
Pres: Prof. O. Hudučka; Gen Secr: Dr. M.J. Lever
Focus: Physiology; Intern Med 11125

British Migraine Association, 178a High Rd, West Byfleet KT14 7ED
T: (01932) 352468; Fax: 351257
Founded: 1958; Members: 15000
Pres: Ann Turner; Gen Secr: Brenda Jones
Focus: Med
Periodical
Newsletter (3 times annually) 11126

British Model Soldier Society (BMSS), 22 Lynwood Rd, Ealing, London, W5 1JJ
T: (0181) 9985230
Founded: 1935; Members: 850
Gen Secr: David Pearce
Focus: Military Sci
Periodical
The Bulletin (quarterly) 11127

British Morgan Horse Society (BMHS), George and Dragon Hall, Mary Pl, London W11
T: (0171) 2298155
Founded: 1975
Pres: Tony Phillips; Gen Secr: Emma Scheck
Focus: Zoology
Periodical
Morgan Horse Magazine (quarterly) . . . 11128

British Museum Society, c/o British Museum, Bloomsbury, London WC1B 3DG
T: (0171) 3238605; Fax: 3238614
Founded: 1968; Members: 12500
Pres: Sarah Cartrew
Focus: Arts
Periodical
British Museum Magazine (3 times annually) 11129

British Music Society (BMS), 7 Tudor Gardens, Upminster RM14 3DE
T: (01708) 224795
Founded: 1978; Members: 500
Pres: John Talbot; Gen Secr: Stephen Trowell
Focus: Music
Periodicals
Journal (annually)
Newsletter (quarterly) 11130

British Mycological Society (B.M.S.), c/o School of Biological Sciences, University of Portsmouth, King Henry I St, Portsmouth PO1 2DY
T: (01705) 842024; E-Mail: steve.moss@port.ac.uk; Fax: 525902
Founded: 1896; Members: 2000
Pres: Dr. Alan D.M. Rayner; Gen Secr: Dr. S.T. Moss
Focus: Bio
Periodicals
Mycological Research (monthly)
Mycologist (quarterly) 11131

British National Committee on Space Research, c/o The Royal Society, 6 Carlton House Terrace, London SW1Y 5AG
Founded: 1959
Focus: Astronomy 11132

British Natural Hygiene Society (BNHS), Shalimar, Harold Grove, Frinton-on-Sea CO13 9BD
T: (01255) 672823
Founded: 1959; Members: 300
Focus: Hygiene; Public Health
Periodical
The Hygienist (quarterly) 11133

British Naturalists' Association (B.E.N.A.), 48 Russell Way, Higham Ferrers NN10 8EJ
T: (01933) 314672; Fax: 314672
Founded: 1905; Members: 2500
Pres: Prof. David J. Bellamy; Gen Secr: Alan Massam
Focus: Ecology
Periodicals
British Naturalist (semi-annually)
Country-Side (bi-monthly) 11134

British Naturopathic and Osteopathic Association (BNOA), 6 Netherhall Gardens, London NW3 5RR
T: (0171) 4358728
Founded: 1925; Members: 250
Focus: Med; Public Health
Periodical
British Naturopathic Journal (quarterly) . 11135

British Nuclear Energy Society (BNES), 1-7 Great George St, London SW1P 3AA
T: (0171) 6652241; E-Mail: tillbrook_a@ice.org.uk; Fax: 7991325
Founded: 1962; Members: 1189
Pres: Dr. R. Garnsey; Gen Secr: A. Tillbrook
Focus: Nucl Res
Periodical
Nuclear Energy (bi-monthly) 11136

British Numismatic Society (B.N.S.), c/o Hunterian Museum, Glasgow University, Glasgow G12 8QQ
T: (0141) 3304221
Founded: 1903; Members: 530
Focus: Numismatics
Periodical
British Numismatic Journal (annually) . . 11137

British Nutrition Foundation (BNF), High Holborn House, 52-54 High Holborn, London WC1V 6RQ
T: (0171) 4046504; Fax: 4046747
Founded: 1967
Pres: Sir Douglas Black; Gen Secr: Dr. B.A. Wharton
Focus: Nutrition
Periodical
BNF Bulletin 11138

British Occupational Hygiene Society (B.O.H.S.), 1 Saint Andrews Pl, Regents Park, London NW1 4LB
T: (0171) 4864860
Founded: 1953; Members: 1287
Focus: Hygiene
Periodicals
Annals of Occupational Hygiene (bi-monthly)
Technical Guide Series (irregularly)
Technical Handbook Series (irregularly) . 11139

British Origami Society (BOS), 11 Yarningale Rd, Kings Heath, Birmingham B14 6LT
T: (0121) 4431330
Founded: 1967; Members: 250
Focus: Fine Arts
Periodical
British Origami (bi-monthly) 11140

British Ornithologists' Club (BOC), Dene Cottage, West Harting, Petersfield GU31 5PA
T: (01730) 825280; Fax: 825280
Founded: 1892; Members: 600
Gen Secr: M.B. Casement
Focus: Ornithology
Periodical
Bulletin of the British Ornithologists' Club (quarterly) 11141

British Ornithologists' Union (B.O.U.), c/o The Natural History Museum, Tring HP23 6AP
T: (01442) 890080; Fax: 890693
Founded: 1858; Members: 2000
Pres: Dr. John P. Croxall; Gen Secr: Neil Bucknell
Focus: Ornithology
Periodical
Ibis (quarterly) 11142

British Orthodontic Society, c/o BOS Office, Eastman Dental Hospital, Grays Inn Rd, London WC1X 8LD
T: (0171) 8372193
Founded: 1994
Focus: Dent 11143

British Orthopaedic Association (BOA), c/o Royal College of Surgeons, 35-43 Lincoln's Inn Fields, London WC2A 3PN
T: (0171) 4056507; Fax: 8312676
Founded: 1918; Members: 2850
Pres: P.J. Mulligan; Gen Secr: D.H.A. Jonas
Focus: Orthopedics 11144

British Orthoptic Society (B.O.S.), Tavistock House North, Tavistock Sq, London WC1H 9HX
T: (0171) 3877992; Fax: 3832584
Founded: 1937; Members: 1000
Pres: Lord Yourger of Prestwick; Gen Secr: Joanna Brown
Focus: Ophthal
Periodical
British Orthoptic Journal (annually) . . . 11145

British Pharmacological Society (B.P.S.), 16 Angel Gate, City Rd, London EC1V 2PT
T: (0171) 4170113; Fax: 4170114
Founded: 1931; Members: 2500
Gen Secr: Prof. N.G. Bowery
Focus: Pharmacol
Periodicals
British Journal of Clinical Pharmacology (monthly)
British Journal of Pharmacology (bi-monthly) 11146

British Photobiology Society (B.P.S.), c/o Dept of Optometry, City University, London EC1V 7DD
T: (0171) 2534399 ext 4309; Fax: 8378068
Founded: 1955; Members: 350
Pres: Dr. A.R. Young; Gen Secr: Dr. R.A. Douglas
Focus: Bio
Periodical
Photobiology Bulletin (quarterly) 11147

British Phycological Society (BPS), c/o Botany Dept, The Natural History Museum, London
T: (0171) 9389352
Founded: 1952; Members: 700
Pres: Dr. M.J. Dring; Gen Secr: Dr. E.J. Cox
Focus: Botany
Periodical
European Journal of Phycology (quarterly) 11148

British Postgraduate Medical Federation (BPMF), 33 Millman St, London WC1N 3EJ
T: (0171) 8316222
Founded: 1945
Focus: Med 11149

British Postmark Society (BPS), 21 Empress Way, Euxton, Chorley PR7 6QB
T: (01257) 269652
Founded: 1958; Members: 300
Focus: Cultur Hist
Periodical
Bulletin (quarterly) 11150

British Psycho-Analytical Society, 63 New Cavendish St, London W1M 7RD
T: (0171) 5804952
Founded: 1913; Members: 433
Gen Secr: M. Garfield
Focus: Psychoan
Periodical
International Journal of Psycho-Analysis (bi-monthly) 11151

The British Psychological Society (BPS), 48 Princess Rd East, Leicester LE1 7DR
T: (01162) 549568; Fax: 470787
Founded: 1901; Members: 28000
Pres: Prof. C. Cullen; Gen Secr: Dr. G. Mulhem
Focus: Psych
Periodicals
British Journal of Clinical Psychology (quarterly)
British Journal of Developmental Psychology (quarterly)
British Journal of Educational Psychology (quarterly)
British Journal of Mathematical and Statistical Psychology (quarterly)
British Journal of Medical Psychology (quarterly)
British Journal of Psychology (quarterly)
British Journal of Social Psychology (quarterly)
Journal of Legal and Criminological Psychology (quarterly)
Journal of Occupational and Organizational Psychology (quarterly)
The Psychologist (monthly)
Selection & Development Review (bi-monthly) 11152

The British Puppet and Model Theatre Guild (BPMTG), 18 Maple Rd, Yeading UB4 9LP
Founded: 1925; Members: 400
Focus: Perf Arts
Periodicals
Magazine (annually)
Newsletter (10 times annually) 11153

British Records Association (BRA), c/o London Metropolitan Archives, 40 Northampton Rd, London EC1R 0HB
T: (0171) 8330428; Fax: 8330415
Founded: 1932; Members: 1000
Pres: The Master of the Rolls; Gen Secr: Elizabeth Hughes
Focus: Hist
Periodicals
Archives (semi-annually)
Archives and the User (irregularly) . . . 11154

British Retinitis Pigmentosa Society (BRPS), POB 350, Buckingham MK18 5EL
T: (012806) 363; Fax: 515
Founded: 1975; Members: 2500
Gen Secr: L. Cantor
Focus: Ophthal
Periodical
BRPS Newsletter (quarterly) 11155

British Robot Association (BRA), Aston Science Park, Love Ln, Birmingham B7 4BJ
T: (0121) 6281745
Founded: 1977; Members: 85
Gen Secr: Don Pitt
Focus: Computer & Info Sci 11156

British Safety Council (BSC), 70 Chancellor's Rd, London W6 9RS
T: (0181) 7411231; E-Mail: dsc@mail.britishsafetycouncil.co.uk; Fax: 7414555
Founded: 1957; Members: 12500
Gen Secr: Sir Neville Purvis
Focus: Safety 11157

British Schools Exploring Society (BSES), c/o Royal Geographical Society, 1 Kensington Gore, London SW7 2AR
T: (0171) 5840710; Fax: 5817995
Founded: 1932
Focus: Educ
Periodical
Expedition Report (annually) 11158

British Science Fiction Association (BSFA), 1 Long Reed Close, Everdon, Daventry NN11 3BE
T: (01303) 252939; E-Mail: bsfa@enterpnse.net
Founded: 1958; Members: 800
Gen Secr: P. Billinger
Focus: Lit
Periodicals
Focus: New Writers Forum (semi-annually)
Matrix (bi-monthly)
Vector (bi-monthly) 11159

British Shell Collectors Club (BSCC), 368 Kingston Rd, New Maldon KT3 3RX
T: (0181) 5410110
Founded: 1973
Focus: Zoology
Periodical
BSCC Newsletter (quarterly) 11160

British Small Animal Veterinary Association (BSAVA), Kingsley House, Church Ln, Shurdington, Cheltenham GL51 5TQ
T: (01242) 862994; E-Mail: bsava@chelt-hq.demon.co.uk; Fax: 863009
Founded: 1957; Members: 4500
Pres: D.F. Wadsworth
Focus: Vet Med
Periodical
Journal of Small Animal Practice (monthly) 11161

British Social Biology Council (B.S.B.C.), 69 Eccleston Sq, London SW1V 1PJ
T: (0171) 8342091
Founded: 1935; Members: 15
Gen Secr: V. Box
Focus: Bio
Periodical
Social Biology and Human Affairs (semi-annually) 11162

British Society for Agricultural Labour Science (BSALS), c/o Work Science Laboratory, Dept of Agriculture and Horticulture, Reading University, Earley Gate, Reading RG6 2AT
T: (01734) 85123
Founded: 1969; Members: 140
Focus: Agri
Periodical
Agricultural Manpower (semi-annually) . . 11163

British Society for Allergy and Clinical Immunology (BSACI), c/o Wythenshawe Hospital, Manchester M13 9PT
Members: 500
Focus: Immunology
Periodical
Clinical Allergy (bi-monthly) 11164

British Society for Antimicrobial Chemotherapy (BSAC), c/o Birmingham Heartlands Hospital, Birmingham B9 5JT
T: (0121) 7731740; Fax: 7668752
Founded: 1971; Members: 850
Pres: Prof. D.C.E. Speller; Gen Secr: Dr. M.J. Wood
Focus: Therapeutics
Periodical
Journal of Antimicrobial Chemotherapy (monthly) 11165

British Society for Cell Biology (B.S.C.B.), c/o Dept of Zoology, Downing St, Cambridge CB2 3EJ
T: (01223) 336631, 336600
Founded: 1959; Members: 1400
Focus: Cell Biol & Cancer Res
Periodical
Newsletter (semi-annually) 11166

British Society for Clinical Cytology (BSCC), c/o Cytology Laboratory, Saint Mary's Hospital, Whitworth Park, Manchester M13 0JH
T: (0161) 2249633
Founded: 1962
Focus: Cell Biol & Cancer Res 11167

British Society for Developmental Biology (BSDB), c/o Dept of Developmental Biology, Marishal College, University of Aberdeen, Aberdeen AB9 1AS
T: (01224) 40241
Founded: 1964; Members: 330
Focus: Bio 11168

British Society for Eighteenth Century Studies (BSECS), c/o Dept of French, King's College, University of Aberdeen, Aberdeen AB9 2UB
T: (01224) 272148
Founded: 1971; Members: 450
Gen Secr: Dr. John Dunkley
Focus: Lit; Hist
Periodicals
Bulletin (quarterly)
Journal (semi-annually) 11169

British Society for Electronic Music (BSEM), 49 Deodar Rd, London SW15
T: (0181) 8742363
Founded: 1969; Members: 112
Focus: Music 11170

British Society for Haematology (B.S.H.), 2 Carlton House Terrace, London SW1Y 5AF
T: (0171) 6437305; E-Mail: janice@bshhya.demon.co.uk; Fax: 7700933
Founded: 1960; Members: 950
Pres: Prof. A.K. Burnett; Gen Secr: Dr. Isobel D. Walker
Focus: Hematology
Periodical
The British Journal of Haematology (16 times annually) 11171

British Society for Middle Eastern Studies, c/o CMEIS, University of Durham, South Rd, Durham DH1 3TG
T: (0191) 3747989; E-Mail: A.L.Haysey@durham.ac.uk; Fax: 3742830
Founded: 1973; Members: 750
Pres: Sir Roger Tomkys; Gen Secr: Dr. C. Hillenbrand
Focus: Sci
Periodicals
British Journal of Middle Eastern Studies (semi-annually)
Newsletter (3 times annually) 11172

British Society for Music Therapy (BSMT), 25 Rosslyn Av, East Bamet EN4 8DH
T: (0181) 3688879
Founded: 1958; Members: 400
Focus: Therapeutics
Periodicals
BSMT Bulletin (3 times annually)
Journal of British Music Therapy (semi-annually) 11173

British Society for Oral Medicine, c/o Eastman Dental Hospital, 256 Gray's Inn Rd, London WC1X 8LD
T: (0171) 9151172
Gen Secr: Dr. Joanna Zakrzewska
Focus: Dent *11174*

British Society for Plant Pathology (BSPP), c/o Plant Breeding International Cambridge, Maris Ln, Trumpington, Cambridge CB2 2LQ
T: (01223) 840411; E-Mail: graham.j.jellis@unilever.com; Fax: 844425
Founded: 1981; Members: 680
Gen Secr: Prof. G.J. Jellis
Focus: Botany; Agri; Microbio
Periodical
Plant Pathology (bi-monthly) *11175*

British Society for Research on Ageing (BSRA), c/o School of Biological Sciences, University of Manchester, Stopford Bldg, Oxford Rd, Manchester M13 9PT
T: (0161) 2755252; E-Mail: ioan.davies@man.ac.uk; Fax: 2755252, 2755363
Founded: 1945; Members: 150
Gen Secr: Dr. I. Davies
Focus: Geriatrics
Periodical
Lifespan (semi-annually) *11176*

British Society for Restorative Dentistry (B.S.R.D.), c/o Guy's Hospital Dental School, London Bridge, London SE1 9RT
T: (0171) 4077600 ext 3013/4
Founded: 1968; Members: 350
Focus: Dent *11177*

British Society for Rheumatology, 41 EagleSt, London WC1R 4AR
T: (0171) 2423313; Fax: 2423277
Founded: 1984; Members: 1400
Pres: Dr. A.G. Mowat; Gen Secr: Kate Baillie
Focus: Rheuma
Periodical
British Journal of Rheumatology (monthly) *11178*

British Society for Social Responsibility in Science (BSSRS), 25 Horsell Rd, London N5 1XL
T: (0171) 6079615
Founded: 1969; Members: 600
Focus: Sociology
Periodical
Science for People (quarterly) *11179*

British Society for Surgery of the Hand, c/o Royal College of Surgeons, 35-43 Lincoln's Inn Fields, London WC2A 3PN
T: (0171) 8315161; Fax: 8314041
Founded: 1969; Members: 636
Pres: F.D. Burke; Gen Secr: P.D. Burge
Focus: Surgery
Periodical
Journal of Hand Surgery (bi-monthly) . . *11180*

British Society for the History of Mathematics, c/o Faculty of Mathematics and Computing, Open University, Walton Hall, Milton Keynes MK7 6AA
T: (01908) 652351; Fax: 652140
Founded: 1971
Focus: Hist; Math
Periodical
The British Society for the History of Mathematics Newsletter (quarterly) *11181*

British Society for the History of Medicine, 149 Harley St, London W1N 1HG
T: (0171) 9354444
Founded: 1965
Focus: Hist *11182*

British Society for the History of Pharmacy (BSHP), c/o Royal Pharmaceutical Society of Great Britain, 36 York Pl, Edinburgh EH1 3HU
T: (0131) 5564386; E-Mail: 101561.@compuserve.com; Fax: 5588850
Founded: 1967; Members: 230
Gen Secr: Dr. L.C. Howden
Focus: Hist; Pharmacol
Periodical
Pharmaceutical Historian (quarterly) . . . *11183*

The British Society for the History of Science (BSHS), 31 High St, Stanford in the Vale, Faringdon SN7 8LH
T: (01367) 718963; E-Mail: bshs@hidex.demon.co.uk; Fax: 718963
Founded: 1947; Members: 850
Pres: Prof. John H. Brooke
Focus: Hist; Nat Sci
Periodicals
The British Journal for the History of Science
Monograph Series
Newsletter *11184*

British Society for the Philosophy of Science (BSPS), c/o Brasenose College, Oxford
Founded: 1948; Members: 520
Pres: R. Harre; Gen Secr: Dr. C. Daly
Focus: Philos
Periodical
The British Journal for the Philosophy of Science (quarterly) *11185*

British Society for the Promotion of Vegetable Research, c/o Institute of Horticultural Research, Wellesbourne CV35 9EF
T: (01789) 470382; Fax: 472552
Founded: 1949; Members: 220
Pres: Dr. H.G. Jones; Gen Secr: A.A. Dalby
Focus: Food
Periodical
Annual Report (annually) *11186*

British Society for the Study of Infection, c/o Eastern Hospital, Homerton Grove, London
Founded: 1974; Members: 452
Focus: Immunology *11187*

British Society for the Study of Orthodontics (BSSO), c/o Eastman Dental Hospital, 256 Grays Inn Rd, London WC1X 8LD
Founded: 1908; Members: 1140
Focus: Dent
Periodical
British Journal of Orthodontics (quarterly) *11188*

British Society of Aesthetics (BSA), c/o Faculty of Art and Design, Nottingham Trent University, Burton St, Nottingham NG1 4BU
T: (01602) 0418418; Fax: 9486403
Founded: 1960; Members: 360
Pres: Prof. Richard Wollheim; Gen Secr: Richard Woodfield
Focus: Philos
Periodical
British Journal of Aesthetics (quarterly) . *11189*

British Society of Animal Science, POB 3, Penicuik EH26 0RZ
Fax: (0131) 4454508 5353120
Founded: 1944; Members: 1300
Pres: Prof.J.D. Leaver; Gen Secr: M.A. Steele
Focus: Agri
Periodical
Animal Production (bi-monthly) *11190*

British Society of Audiology (B.S.A.), 80 Brighton Rd, Reading RG6 1PS
T: (0118) 9660622; E-Mail: bsa@cityscape.co.uk; Fax: 9351915
Founded: 1967; Members: 1500
Pres: Dr. Valerie C.G. Cleaver; Gen Secr: Andrew Reid
Focus: Otorhinolaryngology
Periodical
British Journal of Audiology (bi-monthly) . *11191*

The British Society of Dowsers (B.S.D.), Sycamore Barn, Hastingleigh, Ashford, TN25 5HW
T: (01233) 750253; Fax: 750253
Founded: 1933; Members: 1099
Pres: W.F. Cooper; Gen Secr: M.D. Rust
Focus: Geology; Hydrology; Public Health
Periodical
Journal (quarterly) *11192*

British Society of Flavourists (BSF), c/o International Flavours & Fragrances IFF (GB) Ltd, Flavour Division, Duddery Hill, Haverhill CB9 8LG
T: (01440) 704488
Founded: 1971; Members: 393
Focus: Botany; Food
Periodical
Newsletter (quarterly) *11193*

British Society of Gastroenterology (B.S.G.), 3 Saint Andrew's Pl, London NW1 4LB
T: (0171) 3873534; E-Mail: bsg@mailbox.ulcc.ac.uk; Fax: 4873735
Founded: 1937; Members: 1300
Pres: Prof. M.J.S. Langman; Gen Secr: Dr. T.K. Daneshmend
Focus: Gastroenter *11194*

British Society of Hypnotherapists (BSH), 51 Queen Anne St, London W1
T: (0171) 9357075
Founded: 1950
Focus: Therapeutics *11195*

British Society of Medical and Dental Hypnosis, 10 Chillerton Rd, London SW17
T: (0181) 6723025
Focus: Med; Dent *11196*

British Society of Painters in Oil, Pastels and Acrylic, c/o Leslie Simpson, 41 Lister St, Riverside Gardens, Ilkley LS29 9ET
T: (01943) 609075; Fax: 603753
Founded: 1986; Members: 50
Pres: David Shepherd; Gen Secr: Leslie Simpson
Focus: Fine Arts *11197*

British Society of Rheology, c/o Institute of Food Research, Norwich Research Park, Colney NR4 7UA
T: (01603) 255201; Fax: 507723
Founded: 1940; Members: 600
Pres: Prof. H.A. Barnes; Gen Secr: Dr. G.J. Brownsey
Focus: Materials Sci
Periodical
Rheology Abstracts (quarterly) *11198*

British Society of Scientific Glassblowers (BSSG), 24 Saint Michaels Av, Dunstable LU5 5DN
T: (01582) 867528; Fax: 867528
Founded: 1960; Members: 200
Gen Secr: William Fludgate
Focus: Materials Sci
Periodical
Journal (quarterly) *11199*

British Society of Soil Science (BSSS), c/o Macaulay Land Use Research Institute, Craigiebuckler, Aberdeen AB15 8QH
T: (01224) 318611
Founded: 1947; Members: 1000
Pres: Prof. K. Smith; Gen Secr: J.H. Gauld
Focus: Agri
Periodicals
European Journal of Soil Science (quarterly)
Soil Use and Management (quarterly) . . *11200*

The British Sociological Association (BSA), Unit 3G, Mountjoy Research Centre, Stockton Rd, Durham DH1 3UR
T: (0191) 3830839; E-Mail: britsol@dial.pipex.com; Fax: 3830782
Founded: 1951; Members: 2500
Pres: Prof. D. Morgan; Gen Secr: Nicola Boyne
Focus: Sociology
Periodical
Sociology, Work, Employment and Society (quarterly) *11201*

British Standards Institution (BSI), 389 Chiswick High Rd, London W4 4AL
T: (0181) 9969000 703=9967400
Founded: 1901
Gen Secr: Sir Neville Purvis
Focus: Standards
Periodicals
Annual Report (annually)
BSI News (monthly) *11202*

British Theatre Association (B.T.A.), c/o Darwin Bldg, Regent's College, Regent's Park, London NW1
T: (0171) 9352571
Founded: 1919; Members: 2500
Pres: Earl of Bessborough; Gen Secr: Sally Meades
Focus: Perf Arts
Periodical
Drama (quarterly) *11203*

British Theatre Institute (BTI), 30 Clareville St, London SW7
Focus: Perf Arts *11204*

British Tinnitus Association (BTA), c/o Tinnitus Support Service, 105 Gower St, London WC1E 6AH
T: (0171) 3878033, 3878079
Founded: 1979; Members: 6000
Focus: Otorhinolaryngology
Periodical
BTA Newsletter (quarterly) *11205*

British Trolleybus Society (BTS), 14 Ilkley Rd, Caversham, Reading RG4 7BD
Founded: 1961; Members: 365
Focus: Transport
Periodical
Trolleybus (monthly) *11206*

British Trust for Ornithology (BTO), The Nunnery, Thetford IP24 2PU
T: (01842) 750050; E-Mail: bto.staff@bto.org; Fax: 750030
Founded: 1933; Members: 11000
Pres: Sir F. Holiday; Gen Secr: Dr. J.J.D. Greenwood
Focus: Ornithology
Periodicals
Bird Study (3 times annually)
BTO News (bi-monthly)
Ringing and Migration (3 times annually) *11207*

British Tunnelling Society, c/o Institution of Civil Engineers, Great George St, London SW1
T: (0171) 2227722
Founded: 1971; Members: 700
Focus: Civil Eng *11208*

British Universities Association of Slavists (BUAS), c/o Dept of Russian, University of Reading, Reading RG6 2AA
T: (01734) 875123
Founded: 1956; Members: 300
Focus: Ling; Lit; Hist
Periodical
Research Work in Progress (annually) . *11209*

British Universities Film and Video Council (BUFVC), 55 Greek St, London WIV 5LR
T: (0171) 7343687; E-Mail: bufvc@open.ac.uk; Fax: 2873914
Founded: 1948; Members: 260
Pres: Prof. Michael Clark; Gen Secr: Murray Weston
Focus: Cinema
Periodical
Viewfinder Magazine (3 times annually) . *11210*

British Universities Industrial Relations Association (BUIRA), c/o Dept of Management Sciences, University of Manchester Institute of Science and Technology, POB 88, Manchester M60 1QD
T: (0161) 2363311
Founded: 1950; Members: 375
Focus: Stats *11211*

British Urban and Regional Information System Association (BURISA), c/o County Council, Social Services Dept, The Castle, Winchester SO23 8UQ
T: (01962) 847257
Founded: 1972
Pres: D. Ward
Focus: Computer & Info Sci
Periodical
Newsletter (6 times annually) *11212*

British Veterinary Association (BVA), 7 Mansfield St, London W1M0AT
T: (0171) 6366541; E-Mail: bva@netcomuk.co.uk; Fax: 4362970
Founded: 1882
Pres: Edward Chandler; Gen Secr: James Baird
Focus: Vet Med
Periodicals
In Practice (monthly)
Veterinary Record (weekly) *11213*

British Veterinary Radiology Association (BVRA), c/o Royal Veterinary College, Hawkshead Ln, North Mymms, Hatfield, Herts
Focus: Vet Med; Radiology
Periodical
BVRA Abstracts (annually) *11214*

British Veterinary Zoological Society, c/o B.V.A., 7 Mansfield St, London WC1
Founded: 1961
Pres: D.G. Lyon; Gen Secr: M.J. Fielding
Focus: Vet Med; Zoology
Periodical
Journal of the B.V.Z.S. *11215*

British Vexillological Society (BVS), 80 Copers Cope Rd, Beckenham, Herts
Founded: 1981; Members: 217
Focus: Cultur Hist
Periodical
Raising the Standard (quarterly) *11216*

British Watercolour Society, c/o Leslie Simpson, Ralston House, 41 Lister St, Riverside Gardens, Ilkley LS29 9ET
T: (01943) 609075; Fax: 603753
Founded: 1803; Members: 75
Pres: Kenneth Elmsley; Gen Secr: Leslie Simpson
Focus: Arts *11217*

British Wind Energy Association, c/o Dept of Technology (EM), Open University, Milton Keynes, Bucks
Focus: Energy *11218*

British Wood Preserving and Damp-proofing Association (BWPA), 4 Romford Rd, Stratford, London E15 4EA
T: (0181) 5192588; Fax: 5193444
Founded: 1930; Members: 400
Gen Secr: J. David
Focus: Ecology
Periodicals
Information Leaflets
News Sheet (quarterly) *11219*

British Zeolite Association (BZA), c/o Dept of Chemistry, The City University, Northampton, London ECIV OHB
T: (0171) 2534399
Founded: 1977; Members: 100
Focus: Mineralogy *11220*

Brittle Bone Society (BBS), 30 Guthrie St, Dundee DD1 5BS
T: (01382) 204446/47; Fax: 206771
Founded: 1972; Members: 1500
Focus: Physiology
Periodical
Newsletter (quarterly) *11221*

The Brontë Society, Brontë Parsonage, Haworth, Keighley BD22 8DR
T: (01535) 642323; Fax: 647131
Founded: 1893; Members: 3500
Pres: Lord Morris of Castle Morris; Gen Secr: Stephen Loftus
Focus: Lit
Periodicals
Gazette (bi-annually)
Transactions (annually) *11222*

Browning Society of London, 2 Sedlescombe Rd, London SW6
T: (0171) 3855361
Founded: 1970; Members: 70
Focus: Lit *11223*

Brunel Society, c/o Brunel Technical College, Ashley Down, Bristol BS7 9BU
T: (01272) 41241
Founded: 1968; Members: 303
Focus: Eng *11224*

Buckinghamshire Archaeological Society, c/o County Museum, Church St, Aylesbury HP20 2QP
T: (01296) 20984
Founded: 1847; Members: 557
Pres: Elliott Viney; Gen Secr: Graham Aylett
Focus: Archit; Archeol; Hist
Periodical
Records of Buckinghamshire (annually) . *11225*

The Buddhist Society, 58 Eccleston Sq, London SW1V 1PH
T: (0171) 8345858
Founded: 1924; Members: 3000
Focus: Rel & Theol
Periodical
The Middle Way (quarterly) *11226*

Building Services Research and Information Association (BSRIA), Old Bracknell Ln West, Bracknell RG12 7AH
T: (01344) 426511; Fax: 487575
Founded: 1959; Members: 760
Pres: G. Baker; Gen Secr: J. Turner
Focus: Civil Eng

Periodicals
International Building Services Abstracts (quarterly)
Statistics Bulletin (quarterly) 11227

The Burns Federation, c/o Dick Institute, Elmbank Av, Kilmarnock KA1 3BU
T: (01563) 26401; Fax: 29661
Founded: 1885; Members: 250
Focus: Lit 11228

Buteshire Natural History Society, Mecknoch Farm, Rothesay, Bute PA20 0QA
T: (01700) 502409
Founded: 1905; Members: 200
Pres: L. Cumming; Gen Secr: E.M. Johnston
Focus: Hist; Nat Sci
Periodical
Transactions of the Buteshire Natural History Society 11229

Byron Society, 6 Gertrude St, London SW10 0JN
T: (0171) 3525112
Founded: 1971; Members: 958
Focus: Lit
Periodical
The Byron Society Journal (annually) . . 11230

CAB International, Wallingford OX10 8DE
T: (01491) 832111; E-Mail: cabi@cabi.org; Fax: 833508
Founded: 1929; Members: 41
Pres: J. Gilmore
Focus: Agri; Forestry; Public Health; Nutrition; Ecology; Hort; Botany
Periodicals
Abstracts on Hygiene and Communicable Diseases (monthly)
Agbiotech News and Information (monthly)
Agricultural Engineering Abstracts (monthly)
Agroforestry Abstracts (quarterly)
Aids Newsletter (monthly)
AIDS Targeted Information (monthly)
Animal Breeding Abstracts (monthly)
Bibliography of Systematic Mycology (semi-annually)
Biocontrol News and Information (quarterly)
The British Journal of Nutrition (monthly)
Bulletin of Entomological Research (quarterly)
Crop Physiology Abstracts (monthly)
Dairy Science Abstracts (monthly)
Descriptions of Pathogenic Fungi & Bacteria (semi-annually)
Distribution Maps of Pests (semi-annually)
Distribution Maps of Plant Diseases (semi-annually)
Field Crop Abstracts (monthly)
Forest Products Abstracts (bi-monthly)
Forestry Abstracts (monthly)
Grasslands & Forage Abstracts (monthly)
Helminthological Abstracts (monthly)
Horticultural Abstracts (monthly)
Index of Current Research on Pigs (annually)
Index of Fungi (semi-annually)
Index Veterinarius (monthly)
Irrigation and Drainage Abstracts (quarterly)
Leisure, Recreation and Tourism Abstracts (quarterly)
Maize Abstracts (quarterly)
Nematological Abstracts (quarterly)
Nutrition Abstracts and Reviews: Human and Experimental (monthly)
Nutrition Abstracts and Reviews: Livestock Feeds and Feeding (monthly)
Nutrition Research Reviews (annually)
Ornamental Horticulture (bi-monthly)
Pig News and Information (quarterly)
Plant Breeding Abstracts (monthly)
Plant Genetic Resources Abstracts (quarterly)
Plant Growth Regulator Abstracts (bi-monthly)
Post Harvest News and Information (bi-monthly)
Potato Abstracts (bi-monthly)
Poultry Abstracts (monthly)
Proceedings of the Nutrition Society (3 times annually)
Protozoological Abstracts (monthly)
Review of Agricultural Entomology (monthly)
Review of Aromatic & Medicinal Plants (bi-monthly)
Review of Medical and Veterinary Entomology (monthly)
Review of Medical and Veterinary Mycology (monthly)
Review of Plant Pathology (monthly)
Rice Abstracts (monthly)
Rural Development Abstracts (quarterly)
Seed Abstracts (monthly)
Soils and Fertilizers (monthly)
Soyabean Abstracts (irregularly)
Sugar Industry Abstracts (bi-monthly)
Tropical Diseases Bulletin (monthly)
Veterinary Bulletin (monthly)
Weed Abstracts (monthly)
Wheat, Barley and Triticale Abstracts (quarterly)
World Agric. Econ. & Rural Sociology Abstract (monthly) 11231

CAB International Bureau of Crop Protection, c/o CAB International, Wallingford OX10 8DE
T: (01491) 32111; Fax: 33508
Founded: 1987
Gen Secr: Dr. P.R. Scott
Focus: Agri 11232

CAB International Bureau of Horticulture and Plantation Crops, c/o CAB International, Wallingford OX10 8DE
T: (01491) 32111; Fax: 33508
Founded: 1929
Gen Secr: S. Bhat
Focus: Hort; Agri 11233

CAB International Bureau of Plant Breeding and Genetics, c/o CAB International, Wallingford OX10 8DE
T: (01491) 32111; Fax: 33508
Founded: 1929; Members: 29
Gen Secr: Ray Watkins
Focus: Botany; Agri 11234

CAB International Department of Dairy Science and Technology, Wallingford OX10 8DE
T: (01491) 832111; Fax: 833508
Founded: 1938
Focus: Agri
Periodical
Dairy Science Abstracts (monthly) . . . 11235

CAB International Department of Soils, Wallingford OX10 8DE
T: (01491) 32111; Fax: 33508
Founded: 1929
Focus: Agri
Periodicals
Irrigation and Drainage Abstracts (quarterly)
Soils and Fertilizers (monthly) 11236

CAB International Division of Animal Health and Medical Parasitology, c/o CAB International, Wallingford OX10 8DE
T: (01491) 32111; Fax: 33508
Founded: 1929; Members: 29
Gen Secr: G. Phillips
Focus: Vet Med 11237

CAB International Division of Animal Production, Wallingford OX10 8DE
T: (01491) 83211; Fax: 833508
Founded: 1929
Focus: Genetics; Animal Husb
Periodicals
AgBiotech News and Information (bi-monthly)
Animal Breeding Abstracts (monthly)
Poultry Abstracts (monthly) 11238

CAB International Forestry Department, c/o CAB International, Wallingford OX10 8DE
T: (01491) 832111; E-Mail: cabi@cabi.org; Fax: 833508
Founded: 1938; Members: 29
Pres: Gillian Petrokofoky; Gen Secr: Dr. K. Becker
Focus: Forestry 11239

CAB International Institute of Entomology, 56 Queen's Gate, London SW7 5JR
T: (0171) 5840067; E-Mail: cabi-iie@cabi.org; Fax: 5811676
Founded: 1913
Pres: Prof. Valerie K. Brown
Focus: Entomology
Periodicals
Bulletin of Entomological Research (quarterly)
Distribution Maps of Pests (18 times annually)
Review of Applied Entomology, Series A (Agricultural), Series B (Medical and Veterinary) (monthly) 11240

Caernarvonshire Historical Society (CHS), Shire Hall St, Caernarfon LL55 1SH
T: (01286) 679088
Founded: 1938; Members: 600
Pres: Lady G. Roberts; Gen Secr: Ann Rhydderch
Focus: Hist
Periodical
Transactions (annually) 11241

Cambrian Archaeological Association, The Laurels, Westfield Rd, Newport NP9 4ND
T: (01633) 262449
Founded: 1846; Members: 850
Pres: Glyn Lewis Jones; Gen Secr: Dr. J.M. Hughes
Focus: Archeol
Periodical
Archaeologia Cambrensis 11242

Cambridge Bibliographical Society, c/o Cambridge University Library, West Rd, Cambridge CB3 9DR
T: (01223) 333000; Fax: 333160
Founded: 1949; Members: 500
Gen Secr: N. Thwaite
Focus: Libraries & Bk Sci
Periodicals
Monographs (irregularly)
Transactions (annually) 11243

Cambridge Philosophical Society, c/o Scientific Periodicals Library, Arts School, Benet St, Cambridge CB2 3PY
T: (01223) 334743; Fax: 334748
Founded: 1819; Members: 1900
Pres: S. Sam Edwards; Gen Secr: Judith M. Winton Thomas
Focus: Philos; Nat Sci
Periodicals
Biological Reviews (annually)
Mathematical Proceedings (semi-annually) 11244

Cambridge Refrigeration Technology (CRT) / Shipowners Refrigerated Cargo Research Association, 140 Newmarket Rd, Cambridge CB5 8HE
T: (01223) 65101; Fax: 461522
Founded: 1945; Members: 27
Focus: Transport
Periodical
Newsletter (quarterly) 11245

Cambridge Society for Industrial Archaeology (CSIA), Engineers House, Riverside, Cambridge
Founded: 1968; Members: 150
Focus: Archeol 11246

Campaign for the Advancement of State Education (C.A.S.E.), 43 Littleheath Charlton, London SE7
T: (0181) 3177213
Founded: 1960; Members: 2500
Focus: Educ 11247

Campaign for the Protection of Rural Wales (CPRW), 31 High St, Welshpool SY21 7JP
T: (01938) 552525, 556212; Fax: 552741
Founded: 1928; Members: 4000
Pres: Lord Williams of Elvel; Gen Secr: Dr. Neil Caldwell
Focus: Ecology
Periodical
Rural Wales Magazine (3 times annually) 11248

Campden Food and Drink Research Association (CFDRA), Chipping Campden, Glos
T: (01386) 840319; Fax: 841306
Founded: 1919; Members: 620
Pres: Lord King's Norton; Gen Secr: Prof. C. Dennis
Focus: Food 11249

Cancer Research Campaign (CRC), 10 Cambridge Terrace, London NW1 4JL
T: (0171) 2241333
Founded: 1923; Members: 104
Pres: Duke of Gloucester; Gen Secr: David de Peyer
Focus: Cell Biol & Cancer Res
Periodicals
Annual Report (annually)
British Journal of Cancer (monthly) . . . 11250

Canterbury and York Society, 15 Cusack Close, Twickenham TW1 4TB
T: (0181) 8920500
Founded: 1904; Members: 200
Focus: Hist 11251

Careers Research and Advisory Centre (CRAC), Sheraton House, Castle Park, Cambridge CB3 0AX
T: (01223) 260277
Founded: 1964
Focus: Adult Educ 11252

Carlyle Society of Edinburgh, 38 Grange Rd, Edinburgh EH9 1UL
Founded: 1929; Members: 65
Focus: Lit 11253

The Castings Development Centre, 7 East Bank Rd, Sheffield S2 3PT
T: (0114) 2728647; E-Mail: info@castinesden.com; Fax: 2730852
Founded: 1968; Members: 210
Pres: Dr. M.C. Ashton
Focus: Metallurgy 11254

Catholic Record Society (C.R.S.), 114 Mount St, London W1Y 6AH
Founded: 1904; Members: 800
Gen Secr: Dr. L. Gooch
Focus: Hist
Periodical
Recusant History (semi-annually) 11255

Central Bureau for Educational Visits and Exchanges, Seymour Mews House, Seymour Mews, London WIH 9PE
Fax: (0171) 9355741
Founded: 1948
Pres: J.A. Carter; Gen Secr: A.H. Male
Focus: Educ
Periodicals
Home from Home
Study Holidays
Teach Abroad
Volunteer Work
Working Holidays (annually)
A Year Between 11256

Central Council of Physical Recreation, Francis House, Francis St, London SW1P 1DE
T: (0171) 8283163; Fax: 6308820
Founded: 1935
Pres: Philip Duke of Edinburgh; Gen Secr: Peter Lawson
Focus: Sports 11257

Central Scotland Aviation Group (CSAG), Craigmount Av, Edinburgh EH12 8ED
Founded: 1965; Members: 662
Focus: Aero
Periodicals
Scottish Air News (monthly)
Scottish Fly-Over Supplement (monthly) . 11258

Central Sterilising Club, c/o Dept of Pathology, Kingston Hospital, Kingston-upon-Thames KT2 7BD
Founded: 1960; Members: 500
Focus: Physiology 11259

Centre for Alternative Technology, Machynlleth SY20 9AZ
T: (01654) 702400; E-Mail: info@catinfo.demon.co.uk; Fax: 702782
Founded: 1974; Members: 3000
Focus: Eng; Ecology
Periodical
Clean Slate (quarterly) 11260

Centre for Iberian Studies (ISSA), c/o University of Keele, Keele ST5 5BG
T: (01782) 621111; Fax: 613847
Founded: 1968; Members: 300
Pres: Dr. John Naylon
Focus: Soc Sci; Cultur Hist
Periodical
Iberian Studies (semi-annually) 11261

Centre for Research into Economics and Finance in Southern Africa (CREFSA), c/o London School of Economics, Houghton St, London WC2A 2AE
T: (0171) 9557280; E-Mail: crefsa@lse.ac.uk; Fax: 4301769
Founded: 1990
Pres: Dr. Jonathan Leape
Focus: Econ; Finance; Develop Areas . 11262

CERAM Research, Queens Rd, Penkhull, Stoke-on-Trent ST4 7LQ
T: (01782) 45431; Fax: 412331
Founded: 1948
Pres: Prof. Sir Ronald Mason; Gen Secr: Dr. N.E. Sanderson
Focus: Materials Sci
Periodicals
CERAM Research News (semi-annually)
CERAM Research Progress (semi-annually)
World Ceramics Abstracts (monthly) . . 11263

Challenger Society for Marine Science, c/o Southampton Oceanography Centre, Southampton SO14 3ZH
T: (01703) 596097; E-Mail: jxj@soc.soton.ac.uk; Fax: 596149
Founded: 1903; Members: 550
Pres: Prof. M. Whitfield; Gen Secr: Jennifer Jones
Focus: Oceanography
Periodical
Ocean Challenge (3 times annually) . . 11264

The Charles Lamb Society, 1a Royston Rd, Richmond TW10 6LT
T: (0181) 9403837
Founded: 1935; Members: 361
Pres: Prof. John Beer; Gen Secr: M.R. Huxstep
Focus: Lit
Periodical
The Charles Lamb Society Bulletin (quarterly) 11265

Charles Rennie Mackintosh Society (CRM Society), Queens Cross, 870 Garscube Rd, Glasgow G20 7EL
T: (0141) 9466600; Fax: 9452321
Founded: 1973; Members: 1600
Gen Secr: Patricia Douglas
Focus: Archit; Fine Arts
Periodical
Newsletter (3 times annually) 11266

Chartered Association of Certified Accountants, 29 Lincoln's Inn Fields, London WC2A 3EE
T: (0171) 2426855; Fax: 8318054
Founded: 1904; Members: 50000
Pres: P. Langard; Gen Secr: A.L. Rose
Focus: Law
Periodicals
Accountants' Guide
Certified Accountants (monthly)
List of Members
Students' Newsletter (monthly) 11267

Chartered Institut of Bankers in Scotland, 19 Rutland Sq, Edinburgh EH1 2DE
T: (0131) 2299869; Fax: 2291852
Founded: 1875
Focus: Finance 11268

Chartered Institute of Bankers, 4-9 Burgate Ln, Canterbury CT1 2XJ
T: (01227) 762600; Fax: 763788
Founded: 1879; Members: 75000
Pres: Andrew Buxton; Gen Secr: Gavin Shreeve
Focus: Finance
Periodical
Banking World (monthly) 11269

The Chartered Institute of Building, Englemere, Kings Ride, Ascot SL5 7TB
T: (01344) 630700; E-Mail: kbanbury@ciob.org.uk; Fax: 630777
Founded: 1834; Members: 35000
Pres: David Deas; Gen Secr: Keith Banbury
Focus: Civil Eng
Periodicals
Campus Construction (3 times annually)
Construction Computing (bi-monthly)
Construction Manager (10 times annually)
List of Building Courses
Yearbook & Directory of Members . . . 11270

Chartered Institute of Management Accountants, 63 Portland Pl, London W1N 4AB
T: (0171) 6372311
Founded: 1919; Members: 34000
Gen Secr: John Shane Chester
Focus: Finance
Periodicals
Management Accounting
Management Accounting Research . . . 11271

Chartered Institute of Marketing, Moor Hall, Cookham, Maidenhead SL6 9QH
T: (01628) 427500; E-Mail: marketing@cim.co.uk; Fax: 427499
Founded: 1911; Members: 24000
Pres: Dominic Cadbury
Focus: Marketing
Periodicals
Journal of Marketing Management (quarterly)
Marketing Business (10 times annually)
Marketing Success (quarterly)
State of Marketing (quarterly) 11272

Chartered Institute of Patent Agents (CIPA), Staple Inn Bldgs, High Holborn, London WC1V 7PZ
T: (0171) 4059450; Fax: 4300471
Founded: 1882; Members: 2500
Gen Secr: M.C. Ralph
Focus: Law
Periodicals
CIPA (monthly)
Register of Patent Agents (annually) . . 11273

Chartered Institute of Public Finance and Accountancy (CIPFA), 3 Robert St, London WC2N 6BH
T: (0171) 8958823; Fax: 8958825
Founded: 1885; Members: 15000
Gen Secr: N.P. Hepworth
Focus: Business Admin; Finance
Periodicals
Public Finance and Accountancy (weekly)
Public Money and Management (quarterly) 11274

Chartered Institute of Transport (CIT), 80 Portland Pl, London W1N 4DP
T: (0171) 6369952; Fax: 6370511
Founded: 1919; Members: 20000
Pres: Stuart Milne; Gen Secr: R.P. Botwood
Focus: Transport
Periodicals
Proceedings (quarterly)
Transport (bi-monthly) 11275

Chartered Institution of Building Services Engineers, 222 Balham High Rd, London SW12 9BS
T: (0181) 6755211; E-Mail: info@cibse.org; Fax: 6755449
Founded: 1897; Members: 1500
Pres: Dr. G. Brundrott; Gen Secr: A.V. Ramsay
Focus: Civil Eng
Periodicals
Building Services (monthly)
Building Services Engineering Research and Technology (quarterly)
Lighting Research and Technology (quarterly)
. . . . 11276

Chartered Institution of Water and Environment Management, 15 John St, London WC1N 2EB
T: (0171) 8313110; E-Mail: admin@ciwen.org.uk; Fax: 4054967
Founded: 1895; Members: 12000
Pres: David Woods; Gen Secr: Tony Bispham
Focus: Ecology; Hydrology
Periodicals
Journal of the Chartered Institution of Water and Environment Management (bi-monthly)
Water & Environment Manager (bi-monthly)
Year Book (annually) 11277

The Chartered Insurance Institute (C.I.I.), 20 Aldermanbury, London EC2V 7HY
T: (0181) 9898464; E-Mail: info@cii.co.uk; Fax: 7260131
Founded: 1897; Members: 73000
Pres: B. Kellett; Gen Secr: D.E. Bland
Focus: Insurance
Periodicals
C.I.I. Journal (bi-monthly)
Society of Fellows Journal (semi-annually) 11278

Chartered Society of Designers, 32-38 Saffron Hill, London EC1N 8FH
T: (0171) 8319777; E-Mail: csd@csd.org.uk; Fax: 8316277
Founded: 1930; Members: 8500
Pres: Nicholas Jenkins; Gen Secr: Brian Lymbery
Focus: Graphic & Dec Arts, Design
Periodical
Newsletter (monthly) 11279

The Chartered Society of Physiotherapy (CSP), 14 Bedford Row, London WC1R 4ED
T: (0171) 3066666; Fax: 3066611
Founded: 1894; Members: 33000
Pres: Pennie Roberts; Gen Secr: Paul Lambden
Focus: Therapeutics
Periodicals
Frontline
Physiotherapy (monthly) 11280

Chemicals Notation Association (CNA), c/o Wellcome Foudation Ltd, Temple Hill, Dartford DA1 5AH
Founded: 1969; Members: 77
Focus: Chem 11281

Chemometrics Society, c/o Pfizer Central Research, Sandwich CT13 9NJ
T: (013046) 3511
Founded: 1976; Members: 20
Focus: Chem 11282

Chester Society of Natural Science, Literatur and Art, c/o The Grosvenor Museum, Grosvenor St, Chester CH1 2DD
T: (01244) 21616
Focus: Arts; Lit; Nat Sci 11283

Chiltern Society, Silver How, Little Hollis, Great Missenden HP16 9HZ
T: 3524
Founded: 1965; Members: 3800
Focus: Preserv Hist Monuments; Ecology
Periodical
Chiltern News (quarterly) 11284

China Policy Study Group (CPSG), 62 Parliament Hill, London NW3 2TJ
T: (0171) 4353416
Founded: 1964
Focus: Poli Sci 11285

China Society, 31b Torrington Sq, London WC1
T: (0171) 6367985
Founded: 1906; Members: 150
Focus: Ethnology 11286

Chippendale Society, Temple Newsam House, Leeds LS15 0AE
T: (01532) 647321
Founded: 1963; Members: 405
Focus: Arts 11287

Chiropractic Advancement Association (CAA), 38 The Island, Thames Ditton KT7 0SQ
T: (0181) 3982098
Founded: 1965; Members: 2000
Focus: Orthopedics
Periodicals
The British Chiropractic Handbook
News Bulletin (bi-annually) 11288

Choir Schools Association, c/o Wells Cathedral School, Wells, Somerset
T: (01749) 672117
Founded: 1921; Members: 40
Focus: Educ; Music 11289

The Chopin Society, 42 Beechcroft Gardens, Wembley Park HA9 8EP
T: 9045962
Founded: 1971; Members: 60
Focus: Music
Periodical
Newsletter (quarterly) 11290

Christian Education Movement (CEM), Royal Buildings, Victoria St, Derby DE1 1GW
T: (01332) 296655; E-Mail: cem@org.uk; Fax: 343253
Founded: 1965; Members: 11000
Gen Secr: Dr. Stephen Orchard
Focus: Educ
Periodicals
The British Journal of Religious Education (3 times annually)
RE Today (3 times annually) 11291

Chromatographic Society, Ste 4, Clarendon Chambers, 32 Clarendon St, Nottingham NG1 5JD
T: (01115) 9500595; E-Mail: info@chromsoc.demon.co.uk; Fax: 9500614
Founded: 1956
Focus: Chem 11292

Cinema Organ Society (COS), 33 Idris Villas, Tywyn LL36 9AW
Founded: 1953; Members: 2500
Focus: Music
Periodical
Cinema Organ (quarterly) 11293

Cinema Theatre Association (CTA), 66 Harrowcleve Gardens, Teddington TW11 1DJ
Founded: 1967; Members: 400
Focus: Archit; Hist
Periodicals
Bulletin (bi-monthly)
Picture House (3 times annually) . . . 11294

Circle of State Librarians (CSL), c/o Prison Service HQ Library, John Islip St, London SW1P 4LH
T: (0171) 2175253; Fax: 2175209
Founded: 1946; Members: 550
Focus: Libraries & Bk Sci
Periodical
State Librarian (3 times annually) . . . 11295

Citizens Protection Society (CPS), 611 Collingwood House, Dolphin Sq, London SW1V 3NF
T: (0171) 8340887
Founded: 1970; Members: 50000
Focus: Criminology 11296

City and Guilds, 1 Giltspur St, London EC1A 9DD
T: (0171) 2942468; Fax: 2942400
Founded: 1878
Gen Secr: Dr. Nicholas Carey
Focus: Educ
Periodicals
Broadsheet (3 times annually)
Handbook (annually)
Report and Accounts (annually) 11297

City of Stoke on Trent Museum Archaeological Society (S.O.T.M.A.S.), c/o City Museum and Art Gallery, Bethesda St, Hanley, Stoke-on-Trent ST1 3DW
T: (01782) 232323
Founded: 1959; Members: 50
Pres: E.E. Royle; Gen Secr: R.H. Outram
Focus: Archeol
Periodicals
Newsletter (3 times annually)
Staffordshire Archaeological Studies – by Museum (annually) 11298

The Classical Association, c/o Dr. M. Schofield, Saint John's College, Cambridge CB2 1TP
Founded: 1903; Members: 4000
Pres: Lindsey Davis; Gen Secr: Dr. Malcolm Schofield
Focus: Lit
Periodicals
CA News (semi-annually)
Classical Quarterly (semi-annually)
Classical Review (semi-annually)
Greece and Rome (semi-annually)
Proceedings of the Classical Association (annually)
. . . . 11299

Cleveland Industrial Archaeology Society (CIAS), 8 Loweswater Crescent, Stockton-on-Tees, Cleveland TS18 4PY
Founded: 1965; Members: 73
Focus: Archeol 11300

Clinical Theology Association (CTA), Saint Mary's House, Church Westcote, Oxford OX7 6SF
T: (01993) 830209
Founded: 1962; Members: 1000
Pres: Richard Darby; Gen Secr: P.J. Van de Kasteele
Focus: Rel & Theol; Psych
Periodical
Contact (quarterly) 11301

Collaborative International Pesticides Analytic Council (CIPAC), 61 Finchley Court, Ballards Lane, London N3
Founded: 1957
Focus: Agri
Periodical
CIPAC Proceedings 11302

College of Ophthalmologists, 17 Cornwall Terrace, London NW1 4QW
T: (0171) 9350702; Fax: 9359838
Founded: 1880; Members: 1734
Pres: P. Wright; Gen Secr: P.A. Hunter
Focus: Ophthal
Periodical
Eye (bi-monthly) 11303

The College of Optometrists, 10 Knaresborough Pl, London SW5 0TG
T: (0171) 3737765; E-Mail: pleigh@bcoptom.demon.co.uk; Fax: 3731143
Founded: 1980; Members: 8059
Pres: I.M. Anderson; Gen Secr: P.D. Leigh
Focus: Optics
Periodical
Ophthalmic and Physiological Optics (bi-monthly)
. . . . 11304

The College of Preceptors, Coppice Row, Theydon Bois, Epping CM16 7DN
T: (01992) 812727; E-Mail: preceptor@mailbox.ulcc.ac.uk; Fax: 814690
Founded: 1846; Members: 3500
Pres: Prof. John D. Turner; Gen Secr: T.F. Wheatley
Focus: Educ
Periodical
Education Today (3 times annually) . . 11305

The College of Radiographers, 14 Upper Wimpole St, London W1M 8BN
T: (0171) 9355726/27
Founded: 1920; Members: 9500
Focus: Radiology
Periodicals
Radiography (monthly)
Radiography News (monthly) 11306

Colour Group (Great Britain), c/o Kodak Ltd, Research Division, Wealdstone, Harrow HA4 1TY
T: 4274380
Founded: 1960; Members: 300
Focus: Materials Sci 11307

Comité de Liaison des Géomètres-Experts Européens, 12 Great George St, London SW1P 3AD
T: (0171) 2227000; Fax: 2229430
Founded: 1972
Gen Secr: Alain Bourcy
Focus: Math 11308

Commemorative Collectors Society, Lumless House, Gainsborough Rd, Winthorpe, Newark NG24 2NR
T: (01636) 71377
Founded: 1972; Members: 5341
Gen Secr: S.N. Jackson
Focus: Graphic & Dec Arts, Design
Periodicals
Collecting Commemorabilia (quarterly)
Newsletter (annually) 11309

Commission Internationale de Marketing, c/o EMA Central Secretariat, 18 Saint Peters Steps, Brixham TQ5 9TE
T: (01803) 859575
Founded: 1971
Pres: Dr. P. Allen; Gen Secr: Prof. H.-J. Schlinder
Focus: Marketing
Periodicals
Journal of International Marketing and Marketing Research (3 times annually)
Journal of International Selling & Sales Management (semi-annually) 11310

Committee of Directors of Polytechnics, Kirkman House, 12-14 Whitfield St, London W1P 6AX
T: (0171) 6379939; Fax: 4364966
Founded: 1970; Members: 34
Pres: J.M. Stoddart; Gen Secr: Dr. R.J. Brown
Focus: Educ
Periodicals
First Destinations of Polytechnic Students (annually)
Polytechnic Courses: A Guide to Full-Time and Sandwich Courses (annually)
Polytechnic Courses Handbook (annually) 11311

Committee of Vice-Chancellors and Principals of the Universities of the United Kingdom (CVCP), 20 Tavistock Sq, London WC1H 9HQ
T: (0171) 4194111; E-Mail: info@cvcp.ac.uk; Fax: 3888649
Founded: 1918
Pres: Prof. Martin Harris; Gen Secr: Diana Warwick
Focus: Sci; Educ
Periodical
CVCP News (bi-monthly) 11312

Commons, Open Spaces and Footpaths Preservation Society, 25a Bell St, Henley-on-Thames RG9 2BA
T: (01491) 573535
Founded: 1865; Members: 2500
Gen Secr: Kate Ashbrook
Focus: Ecology
Periodical
Open Space (3 times annually) 11313

Commonwealth Association for Development (CAD), 168 Towerbridge Rd, London SE1 3LS
T: (0171) 3577017; Fax: 3577113
Founded: 1988
Gen Secr: Dr. Charles I. Kejeh
Focus: Develop Areas
Periodicals
CAD Newsletter (3 times annually)
Journal of the Commonwealth Association for Development (semi-annually)
Research in the Commonwealth (quarterly) 11314

Commonwealth Association for Mental Handicap and Developmental Disabilities (CAMHDD), 36a Osberton Pl, Sheffield S11 8XL
T: (01742) 682695
Founded: 1983
Gen Secr: Dr. V.R. Pandurangi
Focus: Rehabil
Periodical
CAMHDD Newsletter 11315

Commonwealth Association for Public Administration and Management (CAPAM), c/o COMSEC, Marlborough House, Pall Mall, London SW1Y 5HX
T: (0171) 8393411; Fax: 9300827
Focus: Public Admin; Business Admin . 11316

Commonwealth Association of Architects – Education Committee, 66 Portland Pl, London W1N 4AD
T: (0171) 6368276; Fax: 2551541
Founded: 1966
Gen Secr: George Wilson
Focus: Educ; Archit 11317

Commonwealth Association of Science and Mathematics Educators (CASME), c/o Commonwealth Secretariat, Marlborough House, Pall Mall, London SW1Y 5HX
T: (0171) 7476282; Fax: 7476287
Founded: 1974; Members: 200
Pres: Dr. Andrew Salisbury; Gen Secr: Dr. V. Goel
Focus: Educ; Sci; Math 11318

Commonwealth Association on Surveying and Land Economy, 15 Greycoat Pl, London SW1P 1SB
T: (0171) 2228961; Fax: 9768304
Founded: 1969; Members: 50
Focus: Surveying; Agri
Periodical
Survey Review (quarterly) 11319

Commonwealth Commercial Crime Unit (CCU), c/o Legal Div, Commonwealth Secretariat, Marlborough House, Pall Mall, London SW1Y 5HX
T: (0171) 8393411; Fax: 9300827
Founded: 1981
Focus: Law 11320

Commonwealth Council for Educational Administration and Management, c/o University of Lincolnshire and Humberside, IELC School of Management, Lincoln LN6 7TS
T: (01522) 886071; E-Mail: al-hody@lincoln.ac.nz 703=886023
Founded: 1970; Members: 5000
Pres: Prof. Angela Thody; Gen Secr: Prof. Hugh (Treasurer) Jenkins
Focus: Educ; Public Admin 11321

Commonwealth Defence Science Organisation (CDSO), c/o Ministry of Defence, Main Bldg, Whitehall, London SW1A 2HB
T: (0171) 2183294

Founded: 1946; Members: 14
Focus: Military Sci 11322

Commonwealth Dental Association, 64 Wimpole St, London W1M 8AL
Founded: 1991
Pres: Dr. A. Ratna Nesan; Gen Secr: Dr. S. Prince Akpabio Obe
Focus: Dent 11323

Commonwealth Education Liaison Committee (CELC), c/o Education Programme, Human Resource Development Group, Commonwealth Secretariat, Marlborough House, Pall Mall, London SW1Y 5HX
T: (0171) 8393411; Fax: 9300827
Founded: 1960
Focus: Educ 11324

Commonwealth Education Programme (CELC), Marlborough House, Pall Mall, London SW1Y 5HX
T: (0171) 8393411; Fax: 9300827
Founded: 1960
Focus: Educ
Periodical
Commonwealth Education News (3 times annually) 11325

Commonwealth Forestry Association (C.F.A.), c/o Oxford Forestry Institute, South Parks Rd, Oxford OX1 3RB
T: (01865) 275072; E-Mail: cfa@plants.ox.ac.uk; Fax: 275074
Founded: 1921; Members: 1400
Pres: Duke of Buccleuch and Queensberry; Gen Secr: J.S. Maini
Focus: Forestry
Periodical
Review (quarterly) 11326

Commonwealth Industrial Training and Experience Programme (CITEP), c/o Fellowships and Training Programme, Commonwealth Secretariat, Marlborough House, Pall Mall, London SW1Y 5HX
T: (0171) 8393411; Fax: 9300827
Founded: 1986
Focus: Educ 11327

Commonwealth Lawyers' Association (CLA), c/o Law Society, 114 Chancery Ln, London WC2A 1SX
T: (0171) 2421222; Fax: 8310057
Founded: 1969
Gen Secr: J. Goldsmith
Focus: Law
Periodicals
CLANews
The Commonwealth Lawyer 11328

Commonwealth Legal Education Association (CLEA), c/o Commonwealth Secretariat, Marlborough House, Pall Mall, London SW1Y 5HX
T: (0171) 8393411
Founded: 1971; Members: 189
Focus: Educ; Law
Periodical
Commonwealth Education (irregularly) . . 11329

Commonwealth Medical Association, BMA House, Tavistock Sq, London WC1H 9JP
T: (0171) 3836095; Fax: 3836195
Founded: 1962; Members: 39
Pres: Dr. John Havard; Gen Secr: Marianne Haslegrave
Focus: Med 11330

Commonwealth Music Association, 1b Berry Pl, London EC1V 0JD
T: (0171) 2530437; Fax: 6082394
Founded: 1990
Gen Secr: Anne McClellan
Focus: Music 11331

Commonwealth Partnership for Technology Management (CCGTM), 14 Queen Anne's Gate, London SW1H 9AA
T: (0171) 2223773; Fax: 9301543
Founded: 1995
Gen Secr: M.Y. Smith
Focus: Business Admin 11332

Commonwealth Pharmaceutical Association (CPA), 1 Lambeth High St, London SE1 7JN
T: (0171) 7359141; E-Mail: eharden@compuserve.com; Fax: 5823401
Founded: 1970
Gen Secr: Philip Green
Focus: Pharmacol
Periodical
CPA Newsletter (quarterly) 11333

Commonwealth Secretariat, Education Programme, Human Resource, Development Group, Marlborough House, Pall Mall, London SW1Y 5HX
T: (0171) 8393411
Gen Secr: Stephen A. Matlin
Focus: Educ
Periodical
Commonwealth Education News (3 times annually) 11334

Commonwealth Trust, 18 Northumberland Av, London WC2N 5BJ
T: (0171) 9306733; Fax: 9309705
Pres: Sir Oliver Forster; Gen Secr: Sir David Thorne
Focus: Sci
Periodical
Newsletter (3 times annually) 11335

The Company Chemists' Association (CCA), 1 Thane Rd West, Nottingham NG2 3AA
T: (01159) 506111
Founded: 1898; Members: 2000
Focus: Pharmacol 11336

Composers' Guild of Great Britain, 34 Hanway St, London W1P 9DE
T: (0171) 4360007 703=4361913
Founded: 1944; Members: 500
Pres: Sir Peter Maxwell Davies
Focus: Music
Periodical
Compass News (quarterly) 11337

Computer Arts Society (CAS), 50-51 Russell Sq, London WC1B 4JX
T: (0171) 6363783
Founded: 1969; Members: 480
Focus: Computer & Info Sci
Periodical
Page (quarterly) 11338

Conchological Society of Great Britain and Ireland, 26 Courtland Av, Ilford IG1 3DW
Founded: 1876; Members: 700
Focus: Zoology
Periodical
Journal of Conchology (semi-annually) . . 11339

Confederate Historical Society (CHS), 19 Montague Av, Leigh-on-Sea SS9 3SL
T: 78075
Founded: 1962
Focus: Hist 11340

Confederation of British Industry, Centre Point, 103 New Oxford St, London WC1A 1DU
T: (0171) 3797400; Fax: 2401578
Pres: Sir Bryan Nicholson; Gen Secr: Howard Davies
Focus: Eng
Periodicals
Economic Situation Report (monthly)
Financial Times Distributive Trades Survey (monthly)
Industrial Trends Survey (quarterly) . . . 11341

Construction Industry Computing Association (CICA), Guildhall Pl, Cambridge CB2 3QQ
T: (01223) 311246
Founded: 1973
Focus: Computer & Info Sci
Periodicals
Computer Newssheet
Construction Industry Software Selector
Evaluation Reports 11342

Construction Industry Research and Information Association (CIRIA), 6 Storey's Gate, London SW1P 3AU
T: (0171) 2228891; Fax: 2221708
Founded: 1967; Members: 600
Pres: Terrel Wyatt; Gen Secr: Dr. P. Bransby
Focus: Civil Eng 11343

Contemporary Art Society (C.A.S.), c/o Tate Gallery, 20 John Islip St, London SW1P 4LL
T: (0171) 8215323
Founded: 1910; Members: 1500
Pres: Gill Hedley; Gen Secr: Elizabeth Tulip
Focus: Arts 11344

The Contemporary Glass Society, 7 The Leather Market, Weston St, London SE1 3ER
T: (0171) 4032800; Fax: 4037778
Founded: 1997; Members: 16
Pres: Peter Layton
Focus: Fine Arts 11345

Cornish Methodist Historical Association (CMHA), 17 Knight's Meadow, Carnon Downs TR15 3AD
Founded: 1960; Members: 350
Focus: Hist; Rel & Theol 11346

Cornish Mining Development Association (CMDA), 33 Wellington Rd, Camborne TR14 7LH
T: (012092) 714245
Founded: 1948; Members: 120
Pres: L.J. Bullen; Gen Secr: C.J. Dungey
Focus: Mining 11347

Cornwall Archaeological Society (CAS), 7 Porthmeor Rd, Saint Austell PL25 3LT
T: (01726) 74763; Fax: 74763
Founded: 1961; Members: 600
Pres: P. Gathercole; Gen Secr: B.D. and S.I. Hammond
Focus: Archeol
Periodical
Cornish Archaeology (annually) 11348

COSPAS-SARSAT, c/o INMARSAT, 40 Melton St, London NW1 2EQ
T: (0171) 7281391; Fax: 3877480
Founded: 1979
Gen Secr: Daniel Levesque
Focus: Aero 11349

The Costume Society, c/o L.E. Robertson, 32 Nore Rd, Portishead, Bristol BS20 9HN
T: (01275) 843264
Founded: 1965; Members: 1000
Focus: Cultur Hist
Periodical
Costume (annually) 11350

Council for British Archaeology (CBA), Bowes Morrell House, 111 Walmgate, York YO1 2UA
T: (01904) 671417; E-Mail: archaeology@compuserve.com; Fax: 671384
Founded: 1944; Members: 4450
Pres: P. Dixen; Gen Secr: R. Morris
Focus: Archeol
Periodicals
British and Irish Archaeological Bibliography (semi-annually)
British Archaeological Yearbook (annually)
British Archaeology (10 times annually)
CBA Briefing (5 times annually) 11351

Council for British Geography, c/o Royal Geographical Society, 1 Kensington Gore, London SW7 2AR
T: (0171) 5913000; Fax: 5913001
Founded: 1988
Pres: Prof. R.J. Bennett
Focus: Geography 11352

Council for Dance Education and Training (CDET), 5 Tavistock Pl, Room 301, London WC1H 9SS
Founded: 1978
Focus: Perf Arts 11353

Council for Education in World Citizenship, 13 West Smithfield, London EC1A 9HY
T: (0171) 3291711; Fax: 3291712
Founded: 1939; Members: 1000
Gen Secr: Patricia Rogers
Focus: Educ
Periodicals
Broadsheet Digest
Current Affairs Broadsheet (bi-monthly)
Newsletter 11354

Council for Environmental Conservation, 80 York Way, London N1 9AG
T: (0171) 2784736
Founded: 1969
Pres: Duke of Wellington; Gen Secr: David Hughes
Focus: Ecology
Periodical
Habitat (10 times annually) 11355

Council for Environmental Education (CEE), c/o University of Reading, London Rd, Reading RG1 5AQ
T: (0118) 9756061; E-Mail: info@cee.i-way.co.uk; Fax: 9756264
Founded: 1968
Gen Secr: Tim Osborn Jones
Focus: Educ
Periodicals
Annual Review of Environmental Education (annually)
Earthlines (bi-monthly)
Newsheet (10 times annually) 11356

Council for the Accreditation of Correspondence Colleges (CACC), 27 Marylebone Rd, London NW1 5JS
T: (0171) 9355391; Fax: 9352540
Founded: 1969; Members: 44
Pres: T.B. Degenhardt
Focus: Educ
Periodical
Information Leaflet (annually) 11357

Council for the Care of Churches (CCC), Fielden House, Little College St, London SW1P 3SH
T: (0171) 223793; Fax: 2223794
Founded: 1921
Pres: Bishop of Hulme; Gen Secr: Thomas Cocke
Focus: Preserv Hist Monuments
Periodical
Churchscape (annually) 11358

Council for the Protection of Rural England, 25 Buckingham Palace Rd, London SW1W 0PP
T: (0171) 9766433; E-Mail: cpre@gn.apc.org; Fax: 9766373
Founded: 1926; Members: 45000
Pres: Jonathan Dimbleby; Gen Secr: Fiona Reynolds
Focus: Ecology
Periodicals
Membership Magazine (3 times annually)
Report (annually) 11359

Council of British Geography (COBRIG), c/o Royal Geographical Society, 1 Kensington Gore, London SW7 2AR
T: (0171) 5913000; Fax: 5913001
Founded: 1988
Pres: Prof. R.J. Bennett
Focus: Geography 11360

Council of Legal Education (C.L.E.), 39 Eagle St, London WC1R 4AJ
T: (0171) 4045787; Fax: 8314188
Founded: 1852
Pres: Justice Phillips; Gen Secr: M.A. Phillips
Focus: Educ; Law
Periodical
A Range of Information Publications (annually) 11361

Council of Professors of Building, c/o Dept of Engineering and Construction, University of Aston, Birmingham, B4 7ET
Founded: 1978; Members: 10
Focus: Archit 11362

County, City and Borough Architects' Association, Civic Centre, POB 26, Harrow HA1 2ZX
T: 8635611
Founded: 1950; Members: 300
Focus: Archit 11363

County Emergency Planning Officers Society (CEPO), County Hall, Worlester WR5 2NP
T: (01905) 353366 ext 3020
Founded: 1966; Members: 62
Focus: Educ 11364

County Museum Society, c/o Hereford and Worcester County Museum, Hartlebury Castle, Hartlebury, Kidderminster DY11 7XZ
T: (01299) 250416
Founded: 1965; Members: 90
Focus: Arts; Hist 11365

County Surveyors Society (CSS), c/o County Surveyors Dept, Northampton House, Northampton NN1 2HZ
T: (01604) 34833
Founded: 1885; Members: 120
Focus: Transport 11366

Coventry and District Archaeological Society (CADAS), 20 Harvey Close, Allesley, Coventry CV5 9FV
T: (01203) 402462
Focus: Archeol 11367

Critics' Circle, 7 Lloyd Sq, London WC1X 9BA
T: (0171) 8374379
Founded: 1913
Focus: Lit 11368

Critics' Guild, 9 Compayne Gardens, London NW6
T: (0171) 3280809
Founded: 1950
Focus: Journalism 11369

Cross and Cockade, Great Britain Society of World Ware One Aero Historians, 23A Winchester St, Farnborough GU14 6AJ
T: (01252) 547435
Founded: 1968; Members: 1200
Focus: Hist
Periodical
Journal (quarterly) 11370

Crown Imperial Society, 37 Wolsey Close, Southall UB2 4NQ
T: (0181) 5744425
Founded: 1973; Members: 370
Pres: Sir Walter Walker; Gen Secr: G. Fawcett
Focus: Hist
Periodical
Crown Imperial (quarterly) 11371

Cumberland and Westmorland Antiquarian and Archaeological Society (C.W.A.A.S.), 2 High Tenterfell, Kendal LA9 4PG
T: (01539) 728288
Founded: 1866; Members: 775
Pres: J.M. Todd; Gen Secr: R. Hall
Focus: Archeol; Hist
Periodical
Transactions (annually) 11372

Cutlery and Allied Trades Research Association (CATRA), Henry St, Sheffield S3 7EQ
T: (01742) 769736; Fax: 722151
Founded: 1960; Members: 100
Focus: Materials Sci 11373

Cymdeithas Hanes Sir Ddinbych, Cefn Ceirch Betws Gwerfil Goch, Corwen LL21 9PG
T: (01490) 460388
Founded: 1951; Members: 350
Gen Secr: A. Fletcher
Focus: Hist
Periodical
Transactions (annually) 11374

Cymdeithas yr Iaith Gymraeg, Pen Roc, Rhodfa'r Mor, Aberystwyth SY23 2AZ
T: (01970) 624501; Fax: 627122
Founded: 1962; Members: 5000
Focus: Ling 11375

Cystic Fibrosis Research Trust, Alexandra House, 5 Blyth Rd, Bromley BR1 3RS
T: (0181) 4647211; Fax: 3130472
Founded: 1964; Members: 20000
Pres: Sir John Batten; Gen Secr: G.J. Edkins
Focus: Physiology
Periodicals
CF News
Directory (quarterly)
Information Leaflets 11376

Dartmoor Pony Society, Puddaven Farm, North Bovey, Newton Abbot TQ13 8RJ
T: (01647) 433203
Founded: 1946; Members: 550
Focus: Animal Husb
Periodical
Dartmoor Diary 11377

Dartmoor Preservation Association (DPA), 4 Oxford Gardens, Mannamead, Plymouth PL3 4SF
T: (01752) 21875
Founded: 1883; Members: 1500
Focus: Ecology 11378

David Davis Memorial Institut of International Studies, 2 Chadwick St, Westminster, London SW1P 2EP
T: (0171) 2224063; Fax: 2332863
Founded: 1951
Focus: Poli Sci 11379

Delphinium Society, Birklands, Douglas Grove, Farnham GU10 3HP
Founded: 1928; Members: 1500
Focus: Zoology 11380

Derbyshire Archaeological Society (D.A.S.), 7 Ashleigh Dr, Uttoxeter ST14 7RC
T: 66568
Founded: 1878; Members: 675
Focus: Archeol
Periodical
Derbyshire Archaeological Journal (annually) 11381

Design and Industries Association (DIA), 12 Carlton House Terrace, London SW1
T: (0171) 9300540
Founded: 1915; Members: 1150
Focus: Eng 11382

Design Council, 1 Oxendon St, London SW1Y 4EE
T: (0171) 2082121; Fax: 8396033
Founded: 1944
Pres: John Sorrell; Gen Secr: Andrew Summers
Focus: Graphic & Dec Arts, Design
Periodicals
Design (monthly)
Designing (3 times annually)
Engineering (monthly) 11383

Designers and Art Directors Association of London (DADA), 12 Carlton House Terrace, London SW1Y 5AH
T: (0171) 8392964
Founded: 1962; Members: 157
Focus: Arts
Periodicals
Annual of the Best Advertising, Graphics, Television & Editorial Design (annually)
Design & Art Direction (monthly) . . . 11384

Devon and Cornwall Record Society, c/o Devon and Exeter Institution, 7 The Close, Exeter EX1 1EZ
T: (01392) 274727
Founded: 1904; Members: 775
Pres: Sir Richard Carew Pole
Focus: Hist
Periodicals
Extra Series (irregularly)
New Series (annually) 11385

Devon Archaeological Society (DAS), c/o City Museum, Queen St, Exeter, Devon
T: (01392) 72340
Founded: 1929; Members: 900
Pres: H. Quinnell; Gen Secr: D. Butler
Focus: Archeol 11386

The Devonshire Association for the Advancement of Science, Literature and Art (D.A.), 7 Cathedral Close, Exeter EX1 1EZ
T: (01392) 52461; Fax: 52461
Founded: 1862; Members: 1830
Pres: Sir Jack Boles; Gen Secr: E.A.K. Patrick
Focus: Arts; Lit; Sci
Periodical
Report & Transactions (annually) 11387

The Dickens Fellowship, 48 Doughty St, London WC1N 2LF
T: (0171) 4052127; Fax: 8315175
Founded: 1902; Members: 6000
Pres: Gabriel Woolf; Gen Secr: Edward G. Preston
Focus: Lit
Periodical
The Dickensian (3 times annually) . . . 11388

Diplomatic and Commonwealth Writers Association of Britain (DCWAB), 8 Plender Court, College Pl, London NW1 0DH
Founded: 1960
Focus: Lit 11389

Direct Investigation Group on Aerial Phenomena (DIGAP), 24 Bent Fold Dr, Unsworth, Bury BL9 8NG
T: (0161) 2803976
Founded: 1953; Members: 20
Pres: Arthur Tomlinson
Focus: Parapsych 11390

Disabled Living Foundation (DLF), 380-384 Harrow Rd, London W9 2HU
T: (0171) 2896111; Fax: 2662922
Founded: 1970
Pres: Lady Hamilton; Gen Secr: Susan Bennett
Focus: Educ Handic
Periodical
DLF Hamilton Index 11391

Disinfected Mail Study Circle (DMSC), 25 Sinclair Grove, London NW11 9JH
T: (0181) 4559190
Founded: 1974; Members: 130
Pres: V. Denis Vandervelde; Gen Secr: Maxwell Seshold
Focus: Med; Cultur Hist; Public Health
Periodical
Pratique (3 times annually) 11392

Distributive Trades Education and Training Council, 56 Russell Sq, London WC1M 4HP
T: (0171) 6369811
Focus: Adult Educ 11393

Dolmetsch Foundation, Lavant Park Farm, West Lavant, Chichester PO18 9AH
T: (01243) 528612
Founded: 1928; Members: 600
Pres: Lord Bridges; Gen Secr: Peter D. Ritchie
Focus: Music
Periodicals
Bulletin Newsletter (3 times annually)
The Consort (semi-annually) 11394

Dolmetsch Historical Dance Society (DHDS), 28 Mead Crescent, Swaythling, Southampton, Hants
T: (01703) 553252
Founded: 1970; Members: 120
Focus: Perf Arts
Periodical
Historical Dance (annually) 11395

The Donizetti Society, 56 Harbut Rd, London SW11 2RB
T: (0171) 2284928
Founded: 1973; Members: 820
Focus: Music
Periodical
Journal (bi-annually) 11396

Dorothy L. Sayers Society, Rose Cottage, Malthouse Ln, Hurstpierpoint BN6 9JY
T: (01273) 823444; E-Mail: info@sayers.org.uk; Fax: 835988
Founded: 1976; Members: 500
Gen Secr: Christopher J. Dean
Focus: Hist; Lit; Rel & Theol
Periodicals
Annual Seminar Proceedings
Bulletin (bi-monthly) 11397

The Dorset Natural History and Archaeological Society, 66 High West St, Dorchester DT1 1XA
T: (01305) 262735; Fax: 257180
Founded: 1875; Members: 2000
Focus: Archeol; Hist; Nat Sci
Periodicals
Dorset Monographs (irregularly)
Proceedings of the Dorset Natural History and Archaeological Society (annually) 11398

Dorset Record Society (DRS), c/o Dorset County Museum, High West St, Dorchester DT1 1XA
Founded: 1962; Members: 1900
Focus: Hist 11399

The Dozenal Society of Great Britain (DSGB), Walnut Bank, Underhill, Moulsford OX10 9JH
Founded: 1958; Members: 70
Gen Secr: Arthur F. Whillock
Focus: Standards
Periodical
The Dozenal Journal (annually) 11400

Drama Association of Wales (DAW) / Cymdeithas Ddrama Cymru, c/o Library, Singleton Rd, Cardiff CF2 2ET
T: (01222) 452200; Fax: 452277
Founded: 1924; Members: 700
Gen Secr: N. Jeffries
Focus: Perf Arts
Periodical
DAWN: DAWN Plus 11401

Drama Board Association, Witches Broom, Yester Park, Chilehurst BR7 5DQ
Focus: Perf Arts 11402

Dry Stone Walling Association, 1 The Old School, Pant Glas, Oswestry SY10 7HS
T: (01691) 654019
Founded: 1968; Members: 300
Focus: Civil Eng 11403

Dryland Professional Network, c/o IIED, 3 Endsleigh St, London WC1
Founded: 1987; Members: 56
Gen Secr: Dr. Camilla Toulmin
Focus: Geology 11404

The Dugdale Society, c/o The Shakespeare Centre, Stratford-upon-Avon CV37 6QW
T: (01789) 204016
Founded: 1920; Members: 330
Pres: Sir William Dugdale
Focus: Hist 11405

Durham County Local History Society, c/o Durham County Record Office, County Hall, Durham DH1 5UL
T: (0191) 3833575
Founded: 1964; Members: 230
Pres: W. Stokes; Gen Secr: D.J. Buxler
Focus: Hist 11406

Dyslexia Institute, 133 Gresham Rd, Staines TW18 2AJ
T: (01784) 463851; Fax: 460747
Founded: 1972; Members: 1000
Pres: Susan Hampshire; Gen Secr: Liz Brooks
Focus: Educ Handic
Periodicals
Dyslexia Review (3 times annually)
Parents Guide-Special Needs-Special Provision (annually) 11407

Early English Text Society (EETS), Christ Church, Oxford OX1 1DP
Founded: 1864; Members: 1663
Pres: Prof. John Burrow; Gen Secr: R.F.S. Hamer
Focus: Lit 11408

East Hertfordshire Archaeological Society (EHAS), 1 Marsh Ln, Stanstead Abbots, Ware SG12 8HH
T: (01920) 870664
Founded: 1898; Members: 150
Pres: R.J. Kiln; Gen Secr: M.C. Readman
Focus: Archeol; Hist
Periodical
Hertfordshire Archaeology (bi-annually) . . 11409

East London History Society, 18 Hawkdene Rd, London E4 7PF
T: (0181) 5244506
Founded: 1952; Members: 165
Focus: Hist 11410

East Lothian Antiquarian and Field Naturalists' Society, Inchgarth, East Links, Dunbar EH42 1LT
T: (01368) 63335
Founded: 1924; Members: 250
Pres: Prof. R. Mitchison; Gen Secr: Stephen A. Bunyan
Focus: Archeol; Hist; Nat Sci
Periodical
Transactions (tri-annually) 11411

East Midlands Arts Board, Mountfields House, Forest Rd, Loughborough LE11 3HU
T: (01509) 218292; Fax: 262214
Founded: 1969
Focus: Arts 11412

East of England Agricultural Society, East of England Showground, Peterborough PE2 6XE
T: (01733) 234451; E-Mail: info@eastofengland.org.uk; Fax: 370033
Founded: 1797; Members: 7267
Focus: Agri
Periodical
East of England Journal (bi-monthly) . . 11413

East Riding Archaeological Society (ERAS), 7 Mill Rd, Swanland, Hull HU14 3PJ
T: (01482) 632244
Founded: 1960; Members: 230
Focus: Archeol 11414

Ecclesiastical History Society (E.H.S.), c/o Dept of Medieval History, University of Glasgow, Glasgow G12 8QQ
T: (0141) 4230901; E-Mail: mjk@arts.gla.ac.uk; Fax: 3305056
Founded: 1961; Members: 950
Pres: Prof. S.G. Hall; Gen Secr: M.J. Kennedy
Focus: Hist; Rel & Theol
Periodical
Studies in Church History (annually) . . 11415

Ecclesiological Society, Saint Andrew-by-the-Wardrobe, Queen Victoria St, London EC4V 5DE
Founded: 1839; Members: 600
Pres: D.R. Buttress; Gen Secr: Prof. K.H. Murta
Focus: Rel & Theol
Periodicals
Ecclesiology Today (3 times annually)
Papers (annually) 11416

Ecological Physics Research Group, c/o Cranfield Institute of Technology, Cranfield, Bedford MK43 0AL
T: (01234) 750993
Focus: Ecology; Physics 11417

Economic and Social Science Research Association (ESSRA), 177 Vauxhall Bridge Rd, London SW1V 1ER
T: (0171) 8344979
Founded: 1969
Focus: Econ; Sociology 11418

Economic History Society, c/o Dept of Economics and Related Studies, University of York, Heslington YO1 5DD
T: (01904) 433757; E-Mail: dtj1@york.ac.uk; Fax: 433759
Founded: 1927; Members: 2000
Pres: Prof. Sir A.E. Wrigley; Gen Secr: Dr. D.T. Jenkins
Focus: Hist; Econ
Periodical
The Economic History Review (quarterly) 11419

Economic Study Association, 8 Rathbone Pl, London W1
T: (0171) 6360467
Founded: 1966
Focus: Econ 11420

The Economics and Business Education Association, 1a Keymer Rd, Hassocks BN6 6AD
T: (01273) 846033; Fax: 844646
Founded: 1948; Members: 3200
Pres: Chris Marsden
Focus: Econ; Educ 11421

Economists Advisory Group, 54b Tottenham Court Rd, London W1
T: (0171) 3234923
Focus: Econ 11422

Edinburgh Architectural Association (EAA), 15 Rutland Sq, Edinburgh EH1 2BE
T: (0131) 2297205
Founded: 1858
Focus: Archit 11423

Edinburgh Bibliographical Society (E.B.S.), c/o Dept of Special Collections, Edinburgh University Library, George Sq, Edinburgh EH8 9LJ
T: (0131) 6503412; E-Mail: m.simpson@ed.ac.uk; Fax: 6506863
Founded: 1890; Members: 200
Pres: B.P. Hillyard; Gen Secr: M.C.T. Simpson
Focus: Libraries & Bk Sci
Periodical
Transactions (every 2 years) 11424

The Edinburgh Highland Reel and Strathspey Society, 78 Milton Rd West, Edinburgh EH15 1QY
T: (0131) 6695927
Founded: 1881; Members: 120
Focus: Music 11425

Edinburgh Mathematical Society (E.M.S.), c/o Dept of Mathematics and Statistics, King's Bldgs, Mayfield Rd, Edinburgh EH9 3JZ
T: (0131) 6505060; Fax: 6506553
Founded: 1883; Members: 504
Pres: Prof. P.F. Smith; Gen Secr: Dr. C. J. Smyth
Focus: Math
Periodical
Proceedings (3 times annually) 11426

Edinburgh Medical Missionary Society (EMMS), 7 Washington Ln, Edinburgh EH11 2HA
T: (0131) 3133828; Fax: 3133828
Founded: 1841
Pres: Dr. James Wallace; Gen Secr: Fred M. Aitken
Focus: Med
Periodical
Healing Hand (3 times annually) 11427

Edinburgh Obstetrical Society, c/o Simpson Memorial Maternity Pavilion, Royal Infirmary, Edinburgh EH3 9YW
T: (0131) 2292477
Founded: 1840; Members: 100
Focus: Gynecology 11428

Edinburgh Royal Choral Union (ERCU), 43 Inverleith Gardens, Edinburgh EH3 5PR
T: (0131) 5523874; Fax: 4473398
Founded: 1858; Members: 100
Focus: Music 11429

Edinburgh Sir Walter Scott Club, 37 Queen St, Edinburgh
T: (0131) 2252914
Founded: 1894; Members: 475
Focus: Lit 11430

Edmonton Hundred Historical Society, c/o Town Hall, Green Lanes, London N13
T: (0181) 8866555 ext 15
Founded: 1936; Members: 356
Focus: Hist 11431

Education in CAAD in Europe (ECAADE), c/o Jelena Petric, Dept of Architecture, University of Strathclyde, Glasgow G4 0NG
T: (0141) 5524400
Gen Secr: Jelena Petric
Focus: Educ; Archit 11432

Educational Development Association (EDA), The Castle, Wisbech, Cambs
T: 61515
Founded: 1888; Members: 4000
Focus: Educ 11433

Educational Drama Association (E.D.A.), c/o Vauxhall Gardens School, Barrack St, Birmingham B7 4HA
Founded: 1948; Members: 380
Focus: Educ; Perf Arts 11434

The Educational Institute of Design, Craft and Technology (EIDCT), c/o Fred R. Willmore, 34 Burton St, Melton Mowbray LE13 1AF
T: (01664) 69754
Founded: 1891; Members: 1200
Gen Secr: Fred R. Willmore
Focus: Educ; Graphic & Dec Arts, Design; Eng
Periodicals
CDT Yearbook and Directory (bi-annually)
Designing and Making (3 times annually) 11435

Educational Institute of Scotland (EIS), 46 Moray Pl, Edinburgh EH3 6BH
T: (0131) 2256244; Fax: 2203151
Founded: 1847; Members: 47000
Pres: May Ferries; Gen Secr: Ronald A. Smith
Focus: Educ
Periodical
Scottish Educational Journal (monthly) . . 11436

Educational Television Association (E.T.A.), The King's Manor, Exhibition Sq, York YO1 2EP
T: (01904) 433929; Fax: 433929
Founded: 1965; Members: 200
Pres: Robert McPherson; Gen Secr: Josie Key
Focus: Educ
Periodical
Journal of Educational Television (2-3 times annually) 11437

Edwardian Studies Association, 125 Markyate Rd, Dagenham, Essex
Founded: 1975
Focus: Hist *11438*

Egypt Exploration Society (E.E.S.), 3 Doughty Mews, London WC1N 2PG
T: (0171) 2421880
Founded: 1882; Members: 2900
Gen Secr: Dr. Patricia Spencer
Focus: Ethnology
Periodicals
Graeco-Roman Memoirs (annually)
Journal of Egyptian Archaeology (annually) *11439*

Eighteen Nineties Society, 3 Kemplay Rd, London NW3 1TA
T: (0171) 7945030
Founded: 1963; Members: 80
Focus: Hist *11440*

Electoral Reform Society of Great Britain and Ireland, 6 Chancel St, London SE1 0UU
T: (0171) 9281622; E-Mail: ers@refor.demon.co.uk; Fax: 4017789
Founded: 1884; Members: 2000
Gen Secr: E.M. Syddique
Focus: Law
Periodical
Representation (quarterly) *11441*

Electric Railway Society (ERS), 17 Catherine Dr, Sutton Coldfield B73 6AX
T: (0121) 3548332
Founded: 1946; Members: 350
Gen Secr: Dr. I.D.O. Frew
Focus: Transport
Periodical
Journal (bi-monthly) *11442*

Electro Physiological Technologists' Association (E.P.T.A.), c/o EEG Dept, Staffordshire General Hospital, Staford ST16 3SA
T: (01785) 230245; Fax: 230237
Founded: 1949; Members: 620
Pres: Dr. N.J. Smith; Gen Secr: K.J. Woolcock
Focus: Physiology
Periodical
Journal of Electrophysiological Technology (quarterly) *11443*

Electroencephalographic Society (EEG Society), c/o Dept of Anatomy, Medical School, Birmingham University, Birmingham B15 2TJ
T: (0121) 4721301 ext 3346
Founded: 1943; Members: 170
Focus: Neurology
Periodical
The EEG Journal (monthly) *11444*

Elgar Society, The Ridge, Pilgrim Pl, Woldingham CR3 7AG
T: 3252
Founded: 1951; Members: 730
Focus: Music *11445*

Elgar Society (London), 7 Batchworth Ln, Northwood HA6 3AU
T: 22010
Founded: 1971; Members: 690
Focus: Music *11446*

Engineering Council, 10 Maltravers St, London WC2R 3ER
T: (0171) 2407891; Fax: 2407517
Founded: 1981
Pres: Alan Rudge; Gen Secr: Mike Heath
Focus: Eng
Periodical
Newsletter (semi-annually) *11447*

Engineering Equipment and Materials Users' Association (E.E.M.U.A.), 14-15 Belgrave Sq, London SW1X 8PS
T: (0171) 2355316; Fax: 2456937
Founded: 1950; Members: 18
Gen Secr: R.W. Snudden
Focus: Energy
Periodical
E.E.M.U.A. Publications (irregularly) . . . *11448*

The English Association, c/o University of Leicester, University Rd, Leicester LE1 7RH
T: (0116) 2523982; Fax: 2522301
Founded: 1906; Members: 2000
Pres: Prof. Gordon Campbell; Gen Secr: H. Lucas
Focus: Ling; Lit
Periodicals
English (3 times annually)
English 4-II (3 times annually)
Essays and Studies (annually)
Newsletter (3 times annually)
The Use of English (3 times annually)
The Year's Work in English Studies (annually)
. . . . *11449*

English Centre of International PEN, 7 Dilke St, London SW3 4JE
T: (0171) 3526303; Fax: 3510220
Founded: 1921
Focus: Lit *11450*

The English Folk Dance and Song Society (EFDSS), 2 Regent's Park Rd, London NW1 7AY
T: (0171) 4852206
Founded: 1932; Members: 6000
Pres: Princess Margaret; Gen Secr: Terry Stodell
Focus: Music

Periodicals
English Dance and Song (quarterly)
Folk Directory (annually)
Folk Music Journal (annually) *11451*

English Goethe Society (EGS), c/o Dept of German, University College, Gower St, London WC1E 6BT
T: (0171) 3877050
Founded: 1886
Focus: Lit
Periodical
Publications of the English Goethe Society (annually) *11452*

English Guernsey Cattle Society (EGCS), Bury Farm, Pednor Rd, Chesham HP5 2LA
Founded: 1884; Members: 800
Focus: Agri
Periodicals
EGCS Herdbook & Type & Production Register (annually)
Guernsey Breeders' Journal (semi-annually) *11453*

English Place-Name Society (EPNS), c/o School of English Studies, University of Nottingham, Nottingham NG7 2RD
T: (0115) 9515919; E-Mail: paul.cavill@nottingham.ac.uk; Fax: 9515924
Founded: 1923; Members: 650
Pres: Dr. Margaret Gelling
Focus: Ling
Periodical
Journal and Volume (annually) *11454*

English Speaking Board (International), 26a Princes St, Southport PR8 1EQ
T: (01704) 501730
Founded: 1953
Pres: Christabel Burniston
Focus: Ling
Periodical
Spoken English (semi-annually) *11455*

English Spelling Association (ISA), 11 First St, London SW3
Founded: 1974; Members: 77
Focus: Ling *11456*

English Sports Council, 16 Upper Woburn Pl, London WC1H 0QP
T: (0171) 2731500; Fax: 3835740
Founded: 1997
Focus: Sports *11457*

English Westerners Society (EWS), 39a Kildare Terrace, London W2
Founded: 1954; Members: 300
Focus: Hist
Periodicals
Brand Book (1-2 times annually)
Tally Sheet (3 times annually) *11458*

Environment Council, 21 Elizabeth Council, London SW1W 9RP
T: (0171) 8248411; Fax: 7309941
Founded: 1969
Gen Secr: Steve Robinson
Focus: Ecology
Periodical
Habitat (10 times annually) *11459*

The Ephemera Society (Ephsoc), 84 Marylebone High St, London W1M 3DE
T: (0171) 4874669; Fax: 9357305
Founded: 1975; Members: 950
Focus: Cultur Hist
Periodical
The Ephemerist (quarterly) *11460*

ERA Technology (ERA), Cleeve Rd, Leatherhead KT22 7SA
T: (01372) 367000; E-Mail: info@era.co.uk; Fax: 367099
Founded: 1920; Members: 390
Gen Secr: M.J. Withers
Focus: Electric Eng
Periodical
ERA Technology News (quarterly) . . . *11461*

Ergonomics Society (ES), Devonshire House, Devonshire Sq, Loughborough LE11 3DW
T: (01509) 234904; Fax: 234904
Founded: 1949; Members: 1200
Pres: D.A. Stubbs; Gen Secr: J.G. Scriven
Focus: Psych; Physiology; Anat; Eng
Periodicals
Applied Ergonomics (quarterly)
Ergonomic Abstracts
Ergonomics (monthly)
The Ergonomist (monthly) *11462*

Esperanto-Asocio de Britio (EAB), 140 Holland Park Av, London W11 4UF
T: (0171) 7277821; E-Mail: eab@esperanto.demon.co.uk; Fax: 2295784
Founded: 1976; Members: 800
Pres: Dr. Geoffrey Greatrex; Gen Secr: Martyn McClelland
Focus: Ling
Periodical
La Brita Esperantisto (bi-monthly) . . . *11463*

Esperanto Teachers Association (E.T.A.), 7 Fairacre Rd, Barwell, Leicester LE9 8HH
T: Earl Shilton 44403
Founded: 1939; Members: 160
Focus: Ling; Educ *11464*

Essex Agricultural Society, The Showground, Great Leighs, Chelmsford, Essex
T: (0124534) 259
Founded: 1858; Members: 1500
Focus: Agri
Periodical
Show Catalogue (annually) *11465*

Essex Archaeological and Historical Congress (EAHC), Low Hill House, Stratford Saint Mary CO7 6JX
T: (01206) 37239
Founded: 1964; Members: 70
Focus: Archeol; Hist
Periodicals
Essex Journal (3 times annually)
Newsletter (3 times annually) *11466*

Essex Society for Archaeology and History (EAS), Hollytrees, Colchester CO1 1UG
Founded: 1852; Members: 466
Focus: Archeol; Hist
Periodicals
Essex Archaeological News (3 times annually)
Essex Archaeology and History (annually) *11467*

Essex Wildlife Trust (ENT), c/o Fingringhoe Wick Conservation Centre, South Green Rd, Fingringhoe, Colchester CO5 7DN
T: (01206) 729678; Fax: 729298
Founded: 1959
Focus: Ecology
Periodical
Essex Wildlife Magazine (3 times annually)
. . . . *11468*

EUROMINERALS – Confederation of Learned/Engineering Societies in the Mineral Industry, c/o Institution of Mining and Metallurgy, 44 Portland Pl, London W1N 4BR
T: (0171) 5803802; Fax: 4365388
Founded: 1990; Members: 17
Pres: Dr. Pedro Fontanilla; Gen Secr: Michael J. Jones
Focus: Mining; Metallurgy *11469*

European Academy of Facial Plastic Surgery, 35-43 Lincoln's Inn Fields, London WC2A 3PN
T: (0171) 8313916; Fax: 4044200
Founded: 1977; Members: 470
Pres: Prof. G.J. Nolst Trenite; Gen Secr: M.P. Stearns
Focus: Surgery
Periodical
Monographs in Facial Plastic Surgery (quarterly)
. . . . *11470*

European Air Law Assciation (EALA), 66 Chartfield Av, London SW15 6HQ
T: (0181) 7883513; Fax: 7892467
Founded: 1988; Members: 230
Pres: Prof. P.D. Dagtoglou; Gen Secr: John Balfour
Focus: Law *11471*

European Association for Behaviour and Cognitive Therapies (EABT), c/o Dept of Psychology, Northwick Park Hospital, Watford Rd, Harrow HA1 3UJ
T: (0181) 8692326; E-Mail: Rod_Holland@compuserve.com; Fax: 9771017
Founded: 1970; Members: 10000
Pres: Prof. Paolo Moderato; Gen Secr: Dr. R. Holland
Focus: Therapeutics
Periodical
The European Behavioural and Cognitive Therapist (3 times annually) *11472*

European Association for Cancer Research (EACR), c/o Cancer Research Campaign Laboratories, University of Nottingham, Nottingham NG7 2RD
T: (0115) 951514; E-Mail: paul.saunders@nottingham.ac.uk; Fax: 9515115
Founded: 1968; Members: 2000
Pres: Prof. Ian Ponten; Gen Secr: Dr. Mike Price
Focus: Cell Biol & Cancer Res *11473*

European Association for Special Education, Edgbaston, The University of Birmingham, Birmingham B15 2TT
T: (0121) 4144865; E-Mail: H.R.J.Daniels@bham.ac.uk
Founded: 1970
Pres: Harry Daniels; Gen Secr: Vojtová Věra
Focus: Educ *11474*

European Association for the Conservation of Energy (EuroACE), Westgate House, Prebend St, London N1 8PT
T: (0171) 3598000; Fax: 3590863
Founded: 1991
Gen Secr: Andrew Warren
Focus: Energy *11475*

European Association for the Study of the Liver, c/o University Dept. of Medicine, Royal Free Hospital, Pond St, London NW3 2QG
T: (0171) 7940500ext.5996; Fax: 8302867
Founded: 1966; Members: 1109
Gen Secr: Dr. Andrew K. Burroughs
Focus: Intern Med *11476*

European Association of Establishments for Veterinary Education, Veterinary Field Station, Easter Bush, Roslin EH25 9RG
T: (0131) 6506294; Fax: 6506588
Founded: 1988; Members: 80 Inst.
Pres: Richard Halliwell; Gen Secr: Goram Dalin

Focus: Educ; Vet Med *11477*

European Centre for Medium-Range Weather Forecasts, Shinfield Park, Reading RG2 9AX
T: (0118) 9499000; Fax: 9869450
Founded: 1973; Members: 18
Gen Secr: Dr. David Burridge
Focus: Geophys *11478*

European Cetacean Society (ECS), c/o Dept of Zoology, University of Oxford, South Parks Rd, Oxford OX1 3PS
T: (01865) 727984; Fax: 727984
Founded: 1987
Gen Secr: Dr. P.G.H. Evans
Focus: Zoology *11479*

European College of Marketing and Marketing Research (ECMMR), 18 Saint Peters Steps, Brixham TQ5 9TE
T: (01803) 859575
Founded: 1969
Pres: Dr. T.A. Voss; Gen Secr: Dr. D.W. Newill
Focus: Marketing *11480*

European Committee for Civil Engineers (ECCE), c/o ICE, Great George St, London SW1P 3AA
T: (0171) 2227722; Fax: 2227500
Founded: 1985
Gen Secr: G. Hornby
Focus: Eng *11481*

European Committee on Radiopharmaceuticals, c/o Radiopharmacy Dept., City Hospital NHS Trust, Birmingham B18 7QH
Fax: (0121) 5075223
Pres: Dr. S.R. Hesslewood
Focus: Pharmacol; Radiology *11482*

European Communities Clinical Chemistry Committee, Burlington House, Piccadilly, London W1 0BN
T: (0171) 4378656; Fax: 4378883
Founded: 1973; Members: 12
Focus: Chem *11483*

European Confederation of Huntington Associations, c/o Stanley Coth, 108 Battersea High St, London SW11 3HP
T: (0171) 2237000; Fax: 2239489
Pres: Sue Watkin
Focus: Med *11484*

European Consortium for Political Research (ECPR), c/o University of Essex, Wivenhoe Park, Colchester CO4 3SQ
Fax: 872500
Founded: 1970; Members: 163
Gen Secr: Prof. Kenneth Newton
Focus: Poli Sci *11485*

European Consortium for Political Research (ECPR), c/o University of Essex, Wivenhoe Park, Colchester CO4 3SQ
T: (01206) 872501; Fax: 872500
Founded: 1970; Members: 175
Pres: Prof. Giorgio Freddi; Gen Secr: Prof. Ken Newton
Focus: Poli Sci
Periodicals
ECPR News (3 times annually)
European Journal of Political Research (8 times annually) *11486*

European Contact Dermatitis Society (ECDS), c/o Dept of Dermatology, Royal Victoria Hospital, Grosvenor Rd, Belfast BT12 6BA
T: (01232) 240503
Gen Secr: Dr. Desmond Burrows
Focus: Derm *11487*

European Contact Lens Society of Ophthalmologists (ECLSO), 143 Harley St, London W1N 1DJ
T: (0171) 9350886
Founded: 1969
Focus: Ophthal *11488*

European Council for Industrial Marketing, 18 Saint Peters Steps, Brixham TU5 9TE
T: (01803) 859575
Founded: 1968; Members: 25
Pres: J.A. Curtis; Gen Secr: Dr. A.J. Williamson
Focus: Business Admin *11489*

European Council of International Schools (ECIS), 21b Lavant St, Petersfield GU32 3EL
T: (01730) 268244; Fax: 267914
Founded: 1965
Gen Secr: Michael Maybury
Focus: Educ *11490*

European Council of Optics and Optometry (ECOO), 90 London Rd, London SE1 6LN
Founded: 1960
Pres: Prof. Dr. Theo Gumpelmayer
Focus: Optics *11491*

European Council of Town Planners (ECTP), c/o Royal Town Planning Institute, 26 Portland Pl, London W1N 4BE
T: (0171) 6369107; Fax: 3231582
Founded: 1985; Members: 17
Pres: Alvaro Gómez-Ferrer Bayo; Gen Secr: Robert Upton
Focus: Urban Plan *11492*

European Dental Society, 10 Pike's End, Eastcote, Pinner HA5 2EX
T: (0181) 8680837
Founded: 1943
Gen Secr: Dr. Caroline Shanbury
Focus: Dent *11493*

European Design Education Network (EDEN), 120 Bothwell St, Glasgow G2 7JP
Focus: Educ 11494

European Electrostatic Discharge Association (EESDA), c/o Marketplace PR, Technology House, Old Wokingham Rd, POB 90, Crowthorne RG11 6PX
T: (01344) 780022; Fax: 773231
Gen Secr: L. Ashburner
Focus: Materials Sci 11495

European Environmental Mutagen Society (EEMS), c/o Dept of Genetics, West Mains Rd, Edinburgh EH9 3JN
Focus: Genetics 11496

European Group for Organization Studies (EGOS), c/o Sociology Dept, Plymouth Polytechnic, Drake Circus, Plymouth PL4 8AA
T: (01752) 21312
Focus: Business Admin
Periodical
International Yearbook of Organization Studies (annually) 11497

European Industrial Marketing Research Society, c/o EMA, 9 Aston Rd, Nuneaton, Warwicks
Focus: Marketing 11498

European Mechanics Council (Euromech), c/o Dept of Applied Mathematics and Theoretical Physics, University of Cambridge, Cambridge CB3 9EW
Fax: (01223) 312984
Founded: 1964
Pres: Prof. D.G. Crighton; Gen Secr: Prof. B. Lundberg
Focus: Physics 11499

European Movement, 52 Horseferry Rd, London SW1P 2AF
Fax: (0171) 2331422 7992817
Founded: 1948
Gen Secr: S. Woodard
Focus: Econ
Periodicals
Enterprise Europe Bulletin (quarterly)
Facts (quarterly)
New Europe Papers (irregularly) 11500

European Organization for Caries Research (ORCA), c/o Div of Oral Biology, Leeds Dental Institute, Clarendon Way, Leeds LS2 9LU
Fax: (01532) 336158
Founded: 1953; Members: 320
Focus: Dent
Periodical
Caries Research (bi-monthly) 11501

European Orthodontic Society (E.O.S.), Flat 31, 49 Hallam St, London W1N 5LL
T: (0171) 9352795; Fax: 9352795
Founded: 1907; Members: 2354
Gen Secr: Prof. J.P. Moss
Focus: Dent
Periodical
European Journal of Orthodontics (semi-annually) 11502

European Psycho-Analytical Federation, 15 Elsworthy Rd, London NW3
T: (0171) 7220338
Founded: 1967
Focus: Psych 11503

European Society for Clinical Investigation, c/o Guy's Hospital Medical School, Guy's Tower, London SE1 9RT
Founded: 1967; Members: 880
Focus: Med 11504

European Society for Comparative Endocrinology, c/o Dept of Physiology and Biochemistry, University of Reading, Reading
T: (01734) 85123
Founded: 1965
Focus: Endocrinology 11505

European Space Association (ESA), 32 Carment Dr, Ardeer, Stevenston, Ayrs
T: 61740
Founded: 1977
Focus: Astronomy 11506

European Underseas Bio-Medical Society (EUBS), 6 Parkhill Av, Aberdeen AB2 0FP
Founded: 1971; Members: 300
Focus: Med 11507

Exeter Industrial Archaeology Group, c/o Dept of Economic History, Exeter University, Exeter EX4 4RJ
T: (01392) 77911
Founded: 1969; Members: 50
Focus: Archeol
Periodical
Bulletin (semi-annually) 11508

Experimental Psychology Society (EPS), c/o Dept of Psychology, University of Glasgow, 56 Hillhead St, Glasgow G12 8QB
Founded: 1946; Members: 480
Pres: Prof. J.A. Gray; Gen Secr: Prof. A. Burton
Focus: Psych
Periodical
Quarterly Journal of Experimental Psychology (quarterly) 11509

Fabian Society, 11 Dartmouth St, London SW1H 9BN
T: (0171) 2228877; E-Mail: fabian-society@geo2.poptel.org.uk; Fax: 9767153
Founded: 1884; Members: 5400
Pres: Peter Archer; Gen Secr: Stephen Twigg
Focus: Poli Sci
Periodicals
Fabian Discussion Papers (irregularly)
Fabian Pamphlet (irregularly)
Fabian Research Series (irregularly)
Fabian Review (quarterly)
Young Fabian Pamphlets (irregularly) . . 11510

Fabric Care Research Association (FCRA), c/o Forest House Laboratories, Knaresborough Rd, Harrogate HG2 7LZ
T: (01423) 885977; Fax: 880045
Founded: 1976; Members: 750
Pres: A.W. Jones; Gen Secr: C.J. Tebbs
Focus: Eng 11511

Faculty of Actuaries in Scotland, 40-44, Edinburgh EH2 1EN
T: (0131) 2204555; Fax: 2202280
Founded: 1856; Members: 1322
Gen Secr: W.W. Mair
Focus: Insurance
Periodicals
Transactions (irregularly)
Year Book 11512

Faculty of Advocates, c/o Advocates Library, Parliament House, Edinburgh EH1 1RF
T: (0131) 2265071; Fax: 2255341
Founded: 1532; Members: 618
Pres: G.N.H. Emslie; Gen Secr: Iain G. Armstrong
Focus: Law 11513

Faculty of Astrological Studies, BM 7470, London WC1N 3XX
Fax: (0171) 7006479
Founded: 1948
Focus: Parapsych 11514

Faculty of Dental Surgery, c/o The Royal College of Surgeons of England, 35-43 Lincoln's Inn Fields, London WC2A 3PN
T: (0171) 4053474; E-Mail: fds@rcseng.ac.uk; Fax: 8319438
Founded: 1947; Members: 6500
Pres: John Llewellyn Williams; Gen Secr: Albert de Looze
Focus: Surgery; Dent 11515

The Faculty of Homoeopathy, 2 Powis Pl, London WC1N 3HT
T: (0171) 8379469; E-Mail: pa@homtrustandfac.demon.co.uk; Fax: 2787900
Founded: 1950
Pres: Dr. D. Owen; Gen Secr: E. Wincott
Focus: Homeopathy
Periodical
The British Homeopathic Journal (quarterly) 11516

Faculty of Royal Designers for Industry, c/o Royal Society for the Encouragement of Arts Manufacturers and Commerce, John Adam St, London WC2N 6EZ
T: (0171) 9305115; E-Mail: rsa@rsa.ftec.co.uk; Fax: 8395805
Founded: 1936; Members: 120
Pres: Richard Onians; Gen Secr: Joanna Thackray
Focus: Graphic & Dec Arts, Design . . 11517

Fair Organ Preservation Society (FOPS), 47 Hawthorne Av, Hellesdon, Norwich, Norfolk
T: (01603) 412258
Founded: 1958; Members: 1600
Focus: Music 11518

The Family Planning Association (FPA), 27-35 Mortimer St, London W1N 7RJ
T: (0171) 6367866; Fax: 4363288
Founded: 1930
Focus: Family Plan
Periodicals
Family Planning Today (quarterly)
Latest Literature in Family Planning (quarterly) 11519

Farm and Food Society (FAFS), 4 Willifield Way, London NW11 7XT
T: (0181) 4550634
Founded: 1966
Focus: Agri; Food
Periodical
Farm and Food News (3 times annually) 11520

Farm Buildings Association (FBA), Roseleigh, Deddington, Oxford OX5 4SP
T: (01869) 38234
Founded: 1956; Members: 620
Focus: Agri; Archit 11521

Fauna and Flora International, Great Eastern House, Tenison Rd, Cambridge CB1 2DT
T: (01223) 46171; Fax: 47181
Founded: 1903; Members: 5000
Pres: Lindsay Bury
Focus: Ecology
Periodical
ORYX (quarterly) 11522

Federal Trust for Education and Research, 11 Tufton St, London SW1P 3QB
T: (0171) 7992818; Fax: 7992820
Founded: 1945
Gen Secr: Andrew Duff
Focus: Educ 11523

Federation for Ulster Local Studies, c/o John Dooher, 8 Fitzwilliam St, Belfast BT9 6AW
T: (01232) 235254; Fax: 434086
Founded: 1975; Members: 191
Pres: John Dooher; Gen Secr: Helen Rankin
Focus: Hist
Periodical
Ulster Local Studies (semi-annually) . . 11524

Fédération Internationale d'Education Physique (FIEP), 4 Cleevecroft Av, Bishops Cleeve, Cheltenham GL52 4JZ
T: (01242) 673674; Fax: 673674
Founded: 1923; Members: 116
Pres: John C. Andrews; Gen Secr: Robert Decker
Focus: Sports
Periodical
FIEP Bulletin (3 times annually) 11525

Federation of British Artists, 17 Carlton House Terrace, London SW1Y 5BD
T: (0171) 9306844; Fax: 8397830
Founded: 1961; Members: 9
Focus: Fine Arts; Arts 11526

Federation of European Veterinaries in Industry and Research (FEVIR), Squibb House, Animal Health Div, 141-149 Staines Rd, Hounslow TW3 3JB
Founded: 1975
Focus: Vet Med 11527

The Federation of Family History Societies (FFHS), c/o The Benson Room, Birmingham and Midland Institute, Margaret St, Birmingham B3 3BS
Founded: 1974; Members: 207
Focus: Genealogy
Periodical
Family History News & Digest (semi-annually) 11528

Federation of London Area Dental Committees, Tavistock House North, Tavistock Sq, London
T: (0171) 3871493
Focus: Dent 11529

Federation of Old Cornwall Societies (FOCS), Tremarsh, Launceston, Cornwall
T: (01566) 3509
Founded: 1924
Focus: Hist
Periodical
Old Cornwall (semi-annually) 11530

The Federation of Zoological Gardens of Great Britain and Ireland, c/o Zoological Gardens, Regent's Park, London NW1 4RY
T: (0171) 5860230; Fax: 7224427
Founded: 1965; Members: 52
Pres: Prof. R.J. Wheater; Gen Secr: P.J. Olney
Focus: Zoology
Periodical
Zoo Federation News (3 times annually) 11531

The Fellowship for Freedom in Medicine (FFM), Stockbury House, Church St, Storrington RH20 4LD
T: (019066) 2679
Founded: 1948; Members: 400
Focus: Med 11532

Fellowship of British Christian Esperantists (FBCE), 5 Osborne Close, Hornchurch RM11 1HJ
Founded: 1953
Focus: Ling 11533

Fellowship of Christian Writers, 104 Evelyn St, London SE8 5DD
T: (0181) 6925787
Founded: 1969; Members: 400
Focus: Lit
Periodical
Newsheet (quarterly) 11534

Fellowship of Postgraduate Medicine, 6 Saint Andrews Pl, London NW1 4LB
T: (0171) 9355556
Founded: 1919
Focus: Med
Periodical
Postgraduate Medical Journal (monthly) . 11535

Field Studies Council (FSC), Preston Montford, Montford Bridge, Shrewsburry SY4 1HW
T: (01743) 850674
Founded: 1943; Members: 6000
Pres: I. Mercer; Gen Secr: D.J. Stanbury
Focus: Nat Sci
Periodicals
Annual Report (annually)
Field Studies (annually)
Programmes of Courses 11536

Filtration Society (FS), 7 Manor Close, Oadby, Leicester LE2 4FE
T: (01533) 720536
Founded: 1964; Members: 1300
Gen Secr: Peter Swift
Focus: Ecology
Periodical
Filtration & Separation Magazine (bi-monthly) 11537

Fire Protection Association (FPA), Melrose Av, Borehamwood WD6 4QU
T: (0181) 2072345; E-Mail: info@lpc.co.uk; Fax: 2369701
Founded: 1946; Members: 6300
Pres: Dr. E.J. Denney
Focus: Eng 11538

Flag Institute, 10 Vicarage Rd, Chester CH2 3HZ
T: (01244) 351335; Fax: 341894
Founded: 1971; Members: 350
Pres: B.E. Nicolls; Gen Secr: W.G. Crampton
Focus: Hist
Periodical
Flagmaster (quarterly) 11539

Flintshire Historical Society (FHS), 69 Pen-y-Maes Av, Rhyl, Denbs LL18 4ED
T: (01745) 332220
Founded: 1911; Members: 350
Gen Secr: N.P. Parker
Focus: Hist; Archeol
Periodical
Journal 11540

Flora Europaea Organization (FEO), c/o Dept of Botany, Liverpool Museum, William Brown St, Liverpool L3 8EN
T: (0151) 2070001; E-Mail: flora_europaea@compuserve.com; Fax: 4784390
Founded: 1956
Gen Secr: Dr. J.R. Edmondson
Focus: Botany
Periodical
Notulae Systematicae ad Floram Europaeam Spectantes (irregularly) 11541

Flour Milling and Baking Research Association (FMBRA), Chorleywood, Rickmansworth WD3 5SH
T: (01923) 4111
Founded: 1967; Members: 600
Focus: Home Econ 11542

Folklore Society, c/o University College, Gower St, London WC1E 6BT
T: (0171) 3875894
Founded: 1878; Members: 1000
Pres: Dr. Juliette Wood; Gen Secr: Dr. Jacqueline Simpson
Focus: Ethnology
Periodical
Folklore (annually) 11543

Food Education Society (FES), 160 Piccadilly, London W1 0NQ
T: (0171) 5841001
Founded: 1908
Focus: Food 11544

The Forensic Science Society, 18a Mount Parade, Harrogate HG1 1BX
T: (01423) 506068; Fax: 530948
Founded: 1959
Focus: Law
Periodical
Journal (quarterly) 11545

Fort Cumberland and Portsmouth Militaria Society (FC & PMS), 49 Lichfield Rd, Portsmouth PO3 6DD
T: (01705) 668981, 754003
Founded: 1966
Focus: Military Sci; Hist
Periodicals
Point News: Historical Newssheets (semi-annually)
Point Papers Series (quarterly) 11546

Fortress Study Group (FSG), The Severals, Bentleys Rd, Market Drayton TF9 1LL
T: (01630) 653433
Founded: 1975; Members: 600
Gen Secr: B.C. Lowry
Focus: Military Sci
Periodicals
Casemate (3 times annually)
Fort (annually) 11547

Foundation for Business Responsibilities (FBR), 40 Doughty St, London WC1N 2LF
T: (0171) 4055195
Founded: 1966
Focus: Econ
Periodicals
Sir Frederick Hooper Essay Award (annually)
Sir George Earle Memorial Lecture (annually) 11548

Foundation for the Study of Infant Deaths / Cot Death Research and Support, 35 Belgrave Sq, London SW1X 8QB
T: (0171) 2350965; Fax: 8231986
Founded: 1971; Members: 150
Gen Secr: Joyce Epstein
Focus: Pediatrics
Periodical
Newsletter (3 times annually) 11549

Francis Bacon Society, Canonbury Tower, Islington, London N1 2NQ
T: (0171) 3701233
Founded: 1886
Pres: George Trevelyan
Focus: Lit
Periodicals
Baconiana (annually)
Jottings (annually) 11550

Freshwater Biological Association, Ferry House, Far Sawrey, Ambleside LA22 0LP
T: (015394) 42468; Fax: 46914
Founded: 1929; Members: 2000
Pres: Sir Frederick Holliday; Gen Secr: Prof. J.G. Jones
Focus: Bio; Hydrology
Periodicals
Freshwater Forum (annually)
Occasional Publications (irregularly)
Scientific Publications (irregularly) 11551

Friends Historical Society, Friends House, Euston Rd, London NW1 2BJ
Founded: 1903; Members: 400
Gen Secr: Howard F. Gregg
Focus: Hist
Periodical
Journal (annually) 11552

Friends of The National Libraries (FNL), c/o The British Library, Great Russell St, London WC1B 3DG
T: (0171) 3237559
Founded: 1931; Members: 850
Pres: Lord Egremont; Gen Secr: A. Payne
Focus: Libraries & Bk Sci
Periodical
Friends of the National Libraries (annually)
. . . . 11553

Furniture History Society (FHS), c/o Dept of Furniture and Woodwork, Victoria and Albert Museum, London SW7 2RL
T: (01444) 413845
Founded: 1964; Members: 1850
Pres: Sir Nicholas Goodeson; Gen Secr: L. Meinertas
Focus: Cultur Hist
Periodicals
Furniture History (annually)
Newsletter (quarterly) 11554

Furniture Industry Research Association (FIRA), Maxwell Rd, Stevenage SG1 2EW
T: (01438) 313433; Fax: 727607
Founded: 1961; Members: 700
Pres: K. Fullalove; Gen Secr: H.T. Davies
Focus: Eng
Periodical
FIRA Newsletter (quarterly) 11555

Galton Institute, 19 Northfields Prospect, Northfields, London SW18 1PE
T: (0181) 8747257
Founded: 1907; Members: 400
Pres: Robert Peel; Gen Secr: L. Brooks
Focus: Genetics
Periodical
Symposium Proceedings (annually) . . . 11556

The Game Conservancy Trust, Burgate Manor, Fordingbridge SP6 1EF
T: (01425) 652381; E-Mail: game-conservancy@ ukonline.co.uk; Fax: 655848
Founded: 1970; Members: 23000
Pres: Duke of Westminster; Gen Secr: Dr. G.R. Potts
Focus: Ecology
Periodicals
The Game Conservancy Review (annually)
Gamewise (semi-annually) 11557

Gemmological Association and Gem Testing Laboratory of Great Britain, 27 Greville St, London EC1N 8SU
T: (0171) 4043334; E-Mail: gagtl@btinternet.com; Fax: 4048843
Founded: 1931; Members: 4000
Pres: Prof. R.A. Howie
Focus: Mineralogy
Periodical
Journal of Gemmology (quarterly) . . . 11558

General Council and Register of Osteopaths (G.C.R.O.), 56 London St, Reading RG1 4SQ
T: (01734) 576585; Fax: 566246
Founded: 1936; Members: 1693
Focus: Med; Pathology 11559

General Council of the Bar, 3 Bedford Row, London WC1R 4DB
T: (0171) 2420082; Fax: 8319217
Founded: 1883; Members: 16000
Pres: Robert Owen; Gen Secr: H. Morison
Focus: Law
Periodicals
Code of Conduct
Counsel (bi-monthly) 11560

General Dental Council (G.D.C.), 37 Wimpole St, London W1M 8DQ
T: (0171) 4862171; Fax: 2243294
Founded: 1956; Members: 50
Pres: Dr. Margaret Seward
Focus: Dent
Periodicals
The Dentists Register (annually)
The Rolls of Dental Auxiliaries (annually) 11561

General Dental Practitioner's Association (GDPA), 49 Cromwell Grove, Levenshulme, Manchester M19 3QD
T: (0161) 2247442
Founded: 1954; Members: 2000
Focus: Dent
Periodical
The Probe (monthly) 11562

General Medical Council, 44 Hallam St, London W1N 6AE
T: (0171) 5807642
Founded: 1858; Members: 91
Pres: Prof. Sir Robert Kilpatrick
Focus: Med
Periodical
The Medical Register (annually) 11563

General Studies Association (G.S.A.), Swallowhurst, Sinnington, York Y06 6SH
T: Kirkbymoorside 31962
Founded: 1962; Members: 900
Focus: Educ 11564

General Teaching Council for Scotland, 5 Royal Terrace, Edinburgh EH7 5AF
T: (0131) 5560072; Fax: 5576773
Founded: 1965; Members: 49
Focus: Educ
Periodical
Link (3 times annually) 11565

The Genetical Society of Great Britain, c/o MRC Human Genetics Unit, Western General Hospital, Crewe Rd, Edinburgh EH4 2XU
T: (0131) 3432362; Fax: 3432620
Founded: 1919; Members: 1600
Pres: Prof. M. Ashburner; Gen Secr: Dr. J.F. Burke
Focus: Genetics
Periodicals
Genes and Development (monthly)
Heredity (monthly) 11566

The Geographical Association (G.A.), 343 Fulwood Rd, Sheffield S10 3BP
T: (0114) 2670666; Fax: 2670688
Founded: 1893; Members: 11500
Pres: W.J.M. Morgan; Gen Secr: F.M. Soar
Focus: Geography
Periodicals
Geography (quarterly)
Primary Geographer (quarterly)
Teaching Geography (quarterly) 11567

The Geological Society, Burlington House, Piccadilly, London W1V 0JU
T: (0171) 4349944; Fax: 4398975
Founded: 1807; Members: 8600
Pres: R. Hardman; Gen Secr: E. Nickless
Focus: Geology
Periodicals
Journal of the Geological Society (bi-monthly)
Petroleum and Geoscience (quarterly)
Quarterly Journal of Engineering Geology (quarterly) 11568

Geologists' Association (G.A.), Burlington House, Piccadilly, London W1V 9AG
T: (0171) 4349268; Fax: 2890280
Founded: 1858; Members: 2500
Pres: Dr. Bob Symes; Gen Secr: S.E. Stafford
Focus: Geology
Periodicals
Geologists' Association Circular (bi-monthly)
Proceedings (quarterly) 11569

George Eliot Fellowship, 71 Stepping Stones Rd, Coventry CV5 8JT
T: (01203) 592231
Founded: 1930; Members: 500
Gen Secr: Kathleen Adams
Focus: Lit
Periodical
Review (annually) 11570

Gilbert and Sullivan Society of Edinburgh, 35 Paisley Av, Edinburgh EH8 7LG
T: (0131) 6612528
Founded: 1924
Focus: Music 11571

Girl's Schools Association (GSA), c/o Headington School, Oxford OX3 7TD
T: (01865) 62711
Founded: 1973; Members: 207
Focus: Educ 11572

Glamorgan History Society (G.H.S.), c/o Glamorgan Record Office, Mid Glamorgan County Hall, Cathays Park, Cardiff CF1 3NE
Members: 350
Focus: Hist
Periodical
Morgannwg (annually) 11573

Glasgow Agricultural Society, 4 Halloway Park, Ayr
T: (01292) 64295
Focus: Agri 11574

Glasgow Archaeological Society (G.A.S.), 8 Tavistock Dr, Glasgow G43 2SJ
T: (0141) 3398855
Founded: 1856; Members: 250
Focus: Archeol
Periodicals
Bulletin (semi-annually)
Glasgow Archaeological Journal (annually) 11575

Glasgow Mathematical Association (GMA), c/o Dept of Mathematics, University of Glasgow, University Gardens, Glasgow G12 8QW
T: (0141) 3398855
Founded: 1927; Members: 60
Pres: R. Bailey; Gen Secr: S. Rowan
Focus: Math 11576

Glasgow Obstetrical and Gynaecological Society, c/o Deparment of Obstetrics and Gynaecology, Royal Maternity Hospital, Glasgow G4 0NA
T: (0141) 5522435
Founded: 1886; Members: 150
Focus: Gynecology 11577

Glenn Miller Society, 244 Edgware Rd, London W2 1DS
T: (0171) 2624604
Focus: Music 11578

Gloucestershire Society for Industrial Archaeology, Oak House, Hamshill, Coaley, Dursley GL11 5EH
T: (01453) 860595
Founded: 1964; Members: 250
Pres: A. Chatwin; Gen Secr: Dr. R. Wilson
Focus: Archeol
Periodicals
Journal (annually)
Newsletter (quarterly) 11579

Good Gardeners' Association (GGA), The Pinetum, Churcham GL2 8AD
T: (01452) 750402
Founded: 1960; Members: 300
Pres: Marchioness of Worcester; Gen Secr: David Wilkin
Focus: Hort
Periodical
Newsletter (quarterly) 11580

Gooseberry Society, 14 Hillary Rise, Barnet EN5 5AZ
T: (0181) 4413120
Founded: 1980
Focus: Nutrition 11581

Gower Society, c/o Royal Institution of South Wales, Victoria Rd, Swansea SA1 1SN
Founded: 1947; Members: 1600
Focus: Ecology
Periodical
Gower (annually) 11582

Great Western Society (GWS), Didcot OX11 7NJ
T: (01235) 817200; Fax: 510621
Founded: 1961; Members: 4200
Pres: G.A. Perry; Gen Secr: J. O'Hagan
Focus: Transport
Periodical
Great Western Echo (quarterly) 11583

Greater London Federation of Parent-Teacher Associations, 113 Kingston Rd, London SW19
T: (0181) 5409299
Focus: Educ 11584

The Greek Institute, 34 Bush Hill Rd, London N21 2DS
T: (0181) 3607968; Fax: 3607968
Founded: 1969; Members: 350
Pres: Dr. Kypros Tofallis
Focus: Ling; Lit; Hist
Periodical
Greek Review (quarterly) 11585

Group-Analytic Society (London), 90 Belsize Ln, London NW3
T: (0171) 7943116; Fax: 7944990
Founded: 1952; Members: 310
Pres: Dr. Stuart Whiteley; Gen Secr: Dr. Radha Bhat
Focus: Behav Sci
Periodical
Group Analysis (3 times annually) . . . 11586

Group and Association of County Medical Officers of Health of England and Wales, c/o Dr. G. Ramage, County Health Dept, Martin St, Stafford
Founded: 1902
Focus: Public Health 11587

Group for the Study of Irish Historic Settlement (GSIHS), c/o School of Earth Sciences, Northern Ireland Polytechnic, Jordanstown, Newtonabbey BT37 0QB
T: Whiteabbey 65131
Founded: 1969; Members: 250
Focus: Hist 11588

Guild of Catholic Doctors, White Lodge, Radnor Rd, Westbury-on-Trym, Bristol BS9 4DX
T: (01272) 624617
Founded: 1923; Members: 1700
Focus: Med 11589

Guild of Church Musicians, Hillbrow, Goldstone Rd, Blechingley, Surrey
T: (0188374) 3168
Founded: 1888
Gen Secr: John Ewington
Focus: Music
Periodicals
Laudate (2-3 times annually)
Year Book (annually) 11590

Guild of Health, 26 Queen Anne St, London W1M 9LB
T: (0171) 5802492
Founded: 1904
Focus: Med
Periodical
Way of Life (quarterly) 11591

Guild of Pastoral Psychology, POB 1107, London W3 6ZP
T: (0181) 9938366
Founded: 1936; Members: 550
Focus: Psych
Periodicals
Bulletin (quarterly)
Lectures (quarterly) 11592

Guild of Travel Writers (GTW), 31 Riverside Court, Reading RG4 8A2
T: (01734) 481384
Members: 100
Focus: Lit 11593

Gwent Wildlife Trust (OWL), 16 White Swan Court, Monmouth NP5 3NY
T: (01600) 715501; Fax: 715832
Founded: 1964; Members: 1500
Focus: Ecology
Periodical
Wild about Gwent (3 times annually) . . 11594

Haemophilia Society, 123 Westminster Bridge Rd, London SE1 7HR
T: (0171) 9282020; Fax: 6201416
Founded: 1950; Members: 4000
Gen Secr: David G. Watters
Focus: Hematology
Periodicals
Bulletin (quarterly)
Update (quarterly) 11595

The Hakluyt Society, c/o Map Library, British Library, Great Russell St, London WC1B 3DG
T: (01986) 86359; E-Mail: haksoc@pastou.co.uk; Fax: 868181
Founded: 1846; Members: 2400
Pres: Sarah Tyacke; Gen Secr: Anthony Payne
Focus: Geography; Hist
Periodicals
Hakluyt Society – Extra Series (irregularly)
Hakluyt Society – Second Series (semi-annually)
. . . . 11596

Haldane Society, 35 Wellington St, London WC2
Founded: 1930; Members: 500
Focus: Sociology 11597

Hampshire Field Club and Archaeological Society, c/o King Alfred's College, Winchester SO22 4NR
Founded: 1885; Members: 600
Focus: Archeol; Hist; Nat Sci
Periodicals
Newsletter (semi-annually)
Proceedings (annually) 11598

Hansard Society for Parliamentary Government, Saint Philip's Bldg, Sheffield St, London WC2A 2EX
T: (0171) 9557478; Fax: 9557492
Founded: 1944; Members: 400
Pres: Dr. David Butler; Gen Secr: David Harris
Focus: Poli Sci
Periodical
Parliamentary Affairs: A Journal of Comparative Politics (quarterly) 11599

Hardy Plant Society (HPS), Garden Cottage, 214 Ruxley Ln, West Ewell KT19 9EZ
Founded: 1957; Members: 1900
Focus: Hort
Periodicals
Bulletin (annually)
News Letter (3 times annually) 11600

The Harleian Society, c/o College of Arms, Queen Victoria St, London EC4V 4BT
T: (0171) 2367728; Fax: 2486448
Founded: 1869; Members: 320
Pres: J.P. Brooke-Little; Gen Secr: T.H.S. Duke
Focus: Genealogy 11601

The Harveian Society of London, 11 Chandos St, London W1M 0EB
T: (0171) 5801043; Fax: 5805793
Founded: 1831; Members: 448
Pres: Robin Price; Gen Secr: M.C. Griffiths
Focus: Med 11602

HATRA, 7 Gregory Blvd, Nottingham NG7 6LD
T: (01602) 623311; Fax: 625450
Founded: 1949; Members: 200
Pres: P.D. Smith; Gen Secr: C.J. Moye
Focus: Eng
Periodical
Knitstats (annually) 11603

Havergal Brian Society (HBS), 5 Eastbury Rd, Watford WD1 4PT
T: (01923) 224607; Fax: 224607
Founded: 1974; Members: 240
Gen Secr: Dr. A. Marshall
Focus: Music
Periodical
Newsletter (bi-monthly) 11604

Hawick Archaeological Society (H.A.S.), Orrock-House, Stirches Rd, Hawick TD9 7HF
T: (01450) 75546
Founded: 1856; Members: 550
Pres: A.V. Tokely; Gen Secr: Ian W. Landles
Focus: Archeol; Hist
Periodical
Transactions (annually) 11605

Hawk and Owl Trust, c/o Bird of Prey Section, Zoological Society of London, Regents Park, London NW1 4RY
T: (0171) 6037756; Fax: 6037756
Members: 475
Focus: Ornithology
Periodicals
Annual Report (annually)
Newsletter (3 times annually) 11606

Head Teachers' Association of Scotland (HAS), c/o University of Strathclyde, Jordanhill Campus, Southbrae Dr, Glasgow G13 1PP
T: (0141) 9503298; Fax: 9503268
Founded: 1936
Gen Secr: James MacNair
Focus: Educ 11607

Health Service Social Worker Group, 112 Wood St, Barnet, Herts
Focus: Public Health; Sociology 11608

Hearing Concern (BAHOH), 7-11 Armstrong Rd, London W3 7JL
T: (0181) 7431110; Fax: 7429043
Founded: 1947; Members: 6000
Pres: Prof. I.G. Taylor; Gen Secr: Marwood Braund
Focus: Rehabil
Periodical
Hark (quarterly) 11609

Heather Society, Denbeigh, All Saints Rd, Creeting Saint Mary, Ipswich IP6 8PJ
T: (01449) 711220; E-Mail: heathers@zetnet.co.uk; Fax: 711220
Founded: 1963; Members: 900
Pres: David J. Small; Gen Secr: Pamela B. Lee
Focus: Botany, Specific
Periodicals
Bulletin (3 times annually)
Yearbook (annually) 11610

Henry Bradshaw Society (H.B.S.), c/o School of Music, University of East Anglia, Norwich NR4 7TJ
T: (01603) 592454; Fax: 250454
Founded: 1890; Members: 300
Pres: H.E.J, Cowdrey; Gen Secr: David F.L. Chadd
Focus: Rel & Theol 11611

Henry Doubleday Research Association (HDRA), c/o National Centre for Organic Gardening, Ryton-on-Dunsmore, Coventry CV8 3LG
T: (01203) 303517; E-Mail: enquiry@hdra.org.uk; Fax: 639229
Founded: 1958; Members: 22000
Pres: Earl Kitchener; Gen Secr: Alan Gear
Focus: Hort; Agri
Periodical
Henry Doubleday Research Association Newsletter (quarterly) 11612

Henry Williamson Society, Ryburn House, Ryburn House, Freshwater PO40 9HJ
T: (01983) 752207
Members: 310
Focus: Lit
Periodical
Journal (semi-annually) 11613

Henty Society, 60 Painswick Rd, Cheltenham GL50 2ER
T: (01242) 516578
Founded: 1976; Members: 139
Focus: Lit
Periodicals
Bulletin (quarterly)
The Double Ressure (semi-annually) . . 11614

The Heraldry Society, POB 32, Maidenhead SL6 3FD
T: (0118) 9320210
Founded: 1947; Members: 1000
Pres: Duke of Norfolk; Gen Secr: M. Miles
Focus: Genealogy
Periodicals
The Coat of Arms (quarterly)
The Heraldry Gazette (quarterly) 11615

Hertfordshire Local History Council (HLHC), Lamb Cottage, Whitwell, Hitchin, Herts
Founded: 1951
Focus: Cultur Hist
Periodical
Hertfordshire's Past (semi-annually) . . . 11616

Hertfordshire Natural History Society and Field Club, 9 Hill Rise, Potters Bar EN6 2RX
T: (01707) 57586
Founded: 1875; Members: 400
Focus: Geology; Ornithology
Periodicals
Bird NL (monthly)
Transactions (annually) 11617

Hesketh Hubbard Art Society, 17 Carlton House Terrace, London SW1Y 5BD
T: (0171) 9306844; Fax: 8397830
Founded: 1930; Members: 100
Pres: Simon Whittle
Focus: Arts; Fine Arts 11618

H.G. Wells Society, 49 Beckingthorpe Dr, Bottesford, Nottingham NG13 0DN
Founded: 1960; Members: 200
Gen Secr: J.R. Hammond
Focus: Lit
Periodicals
Newsletter
Wellsian 11619

High Pressure Technology Association (H.P.T.A.), c/o Dept of Mechanical Engineering, Leeds University, Leeds LS2 9JT
T: (01532) 31751
Founded: 1967; Members: 200
Focus: Eng 11620

Higher Education Funding Council for England, Northavon House, Coldharbour Ln, Bristol BS16 1QD
T: (01272) 9317317; Fax: 9317173
Founded: 1992
Pres: Brandon Gough; Gen Secr: Prof. Brian Fender
Focus: Educ 11621

Hispanic and Luso-Brazilian Council, 2 Belgrave Sq, London SW1X 8PJ
T: (0171) 2352303
Founded: 1943; Members: 600
Pres: Viscount Montgomery of Alamein; Gen Secr: Sir Kenneth James
Focus: Ethnology; Hist; Geography; Lit
Periodical
Bulletin (semi-annually) 11622

Historic Society of Lancashire and Cheshire (H.S.L.C.), Stand Park Rd, Liverpool LI6 9JD
Founded: 1848; Members: 500
Focus: Hist
Periodical
Transactions (annually) 11623

Historical Association (HA), 59a Kennington Park Rd, London SE11 4JH
T: (0171) 7353901; Fax: 5824989
Founded: 1906; Members: 7000
Gen Secr: M. Stiles
Focus: Hist
Periodicals
The Historian (quarterly)
History (quarterly)
Primary History (3 times annually)
Teaching History (quarterly) 11624

Historical Breechloading Smallarms Association, POB 12778, London SE1 6XG
T: (0171) 4165270; Fax: 4165374
Founded: 1973; Members: 420
Pres: Christopher Roads; Gen Secr: David J. Penn
Focus: Hist; Military Sci 11625

The Historical Metallurgy Society (HMS), 22 Easterfield Dr, Southgate, Swansea SA3 2DB
T: (01792) 233223; E-Mail: petehutch@compuserve.com
Founded: 1962; Members: 500
Pres: Ian Standing; Gen Secr: Peter Hutchison
Focus: Hist; Metallurgy
Periodical
The Journal of the Historical Metallurgy Society (semi-annually) 11626

Historical Newspaper Service, 8 Monks Av, New Barnet EN5 1DB
T: (0181) 4403159
Focus: Lit; Journalism 11627

Historical Society of the Church in Wales, c/o Trinity College, Carmarthen SA31 3EP
T: 7971
Founded: 1946; Members: 430
Focus: Hist; Rel & Theol 11628

Historical Society of the Methodist Church in Wales, Llys Myfyr, Pwllheli, Caerns
T: 2608
Founded: 1944
Focus: Hist; Rel & Theol 11629

History of Education Society, c/o B.J. Starkey, 4 Marydene Dr, Leicester LE5 6HD
T: (0116) 2416899
Founded: 1967; Members: 450
Focus: Hist; Educ
Periodical
History of Education Society Bulletin (semi-annually) 11630

Honourable Society of Cymmrodorion, 30 Eastcastle St, London W1N 7PD
T: (0171) 6310502
Founded: 1751; Members: 1000
Pres: Prof. E. Jones; Gen Secr: Samuel Jonn
Focus: Arts; Lit
Periodical
Transactions (annually) 11631

Honours Graduate Teachers' Association (HGTA), 25 Montgomerie Terrace, Ayr KA7 1SL
T: 84964
Founded: 1964; Members: 200
Focus: Educ 11632

Horatian Society, 4 Breams Bldgs, London EC4A 1AQ
T: (0171) 3535835
Founded: 1934
Pres: Lord Templeman; Gen Secr: C.P. Sydenham
Focus: Lit 11633

Hospitals Consultants and Specialists Association (H.C.S.A.), 1 Kingslere Rd, Overton RG25 3JP
T: (01256) 771777; Fax: 770999
Founded: 1947; Members: 3120
Pres: Dr. F. Foster-Thompson; Gen Secr: S.J. Charkham
Focus: Med
Periodical
The Consultant (quarterly) 11634

Hotel and Catering International Management Associaton, 191 Trinity Rd, London SW17 7HN
T: (0181) 6724251; E-Mail: library@hcima.org.uk
Founded: 1972; Members: 23000
Pres: Dr. Nigel Hemmington; Gen Secr: David Wood
Focus: Econ 11635

The Housman Society (HS), 80 New Rd, Bromsgrove B60 2LA
T: (01527) 874136
Founded: 1973; Members: 300
Focus: Lit
Periodical
Journal (annually) 11636

Huguenot Society of Great Britain and Ireland, c/o The Huguenot Library, University College, Gower St, London WC1E 6BT
Founded: 1885; Members: 1432
Gen Secr: Mary Bayliss
Focus: Hist
Periodicals
Proceedings (annually)
Quarto Series (irregularly) 11637

Hunter Archaeological Society, 37 Chesterwood Dr, Sheffield S10 5DD
Founded: 1912; Members: 340
Focus: Archeol
Periodical
Transactions (semi-annually) 11638

Hunterian Society, Brampton House, 60 Grove End Rd, London NW8 9NH
T: (0181) 4450695; Fax: 4450695
Founded: 1819; Members: 450
Pres: Sir Montague Levine; Gen Secr: David Hunter
Focus: Med
Periodical
Transactions (annually) 11639

Huntingdonshire Local History Society, Old Red Lion House, Thurleigh, Beds
Founded: 1957; Members: 300
Focus: Hist
Periodical
Records (annually) 11640

Hyper Active Children's Support Group (HACSG), 71 Whyke Ln, Chichester PO19 2LD
T: (01903) 725182; E-Mail: hacsg@dial.pipex.com; Fax: 725182
Founded: 1978; Members: 2520
Pres: Sally Bunday; Gen Secr: Sally Bunday
Focus: Public Health; Educ Handic
Periodical
Newsletter (3 times annually) 11641

Ileostomy Association of Great Britain and Ireland, Amblehurst House, Black Scotch Lane, Mansfield NG18 4PF
T: (01623) 28099; Fax: 28099
Founded: 1956; Members: 9200
Pres: Prof. N.S. Williams; Gen Secr: David S. Eades
Focus: Gastroenter
Periodical
ia Journal (quarterly) 11642

Incorporated Association of Architects, Jubilee House, Billing Brook Rd, Weston Favell NN3 4NW
T: (01604) 404121
Founded: 1925; Members: 4800
Pres: E. Heading; Gen Secr: W.A. Black
Focus: Archit
Periodicals
Architect and Surveyor (monthly)
Fire Surveyor (bi-monthly) 11643

Incorporated Association of Organists, 11 Stonehill Dr, Bromyard HR7 4XB
T: (01885) 483155; Fax: 488609
Founded: 1913; Members: 7500
Pres: Dr. Peter Hurford; Gen Secr: Richard Popple
Focus: Music
Periodical
The Organists' Review (quarterly) . . . 11644

Incorporated Society of Musicians, 10 Stratford Pl, London W1N 9AE
T: (0171) 6294413; Fax: 4081538
Founded: 1882; Members: 5000
Pres: Prof. George Pratt; Gen Secr: Neil Hoyle
Focus: Music
Periodicals
Music Journal (monthly)
Register of Specialist Teachers (annually)
Yearbook (annually) 11645

Incorporated Society of Registered Naturopaths (ISRN), 293 Gilmerton Rd, Edinburgh EH16 5UL
T: (0131) 6643435
Founded: 1934; Members: 50
Pres: Peter Fenton; Gen Secr: Jean Lapsley
Focus: Med; Pathology 11646

Independent Schools Joint Committee (ISJC), 27 Church Rd, Steep, Petersfield GU32 2DW
Founded: 1974; Members: 10
Focus: Educ 11647

Indian Military Historical Society, 37 Wolsey Close, Southall UB2 4NQ
T: (0181) 5744425
Founded: 1983; Members: 150
Pres: Sir John Chapple; Gen Secr: A.N. McClenaghan
Focus: Hist; Military Sci 11648

Industrial Fire Protection Association of Great Britain (IFPA), Aldermary House, Queen St, London EC4
T: (0171) 2485222
Founded: 1941; Members: 800
Focus: Safety 11649

Industrial Society, 3 Carlton House Terrace, London SW1Y 5DG
T: (0171) 8394300
Founded: 1918; Members: 15000
Focus: Comm Sci
Periodicals
Directory of Sources
Industrial Society (quarterly) 11650

Institut of Actuaries, Staple Inn Hall, High Holborn, London WC1V 7QJ
T: (0171) 2420106; Fax: 4052482
Founded: 1848
Focus: Insurance 11651

Institut of Biomedical Science, 12 Coldbath Sq, London EC1R 5HL
T: (0171) 6368192
Focus: Med 11652

Institute for Animal Health, Compton, Newbury RG20 7NN
T: (01635) 578411; Fax: 577237
Focus: Agri; Vet Med
Periodical
Annual Report (annually) 11653

Institute for Animal Health Pirbright, c/o Pirbright Laboratory, Ash Rd, Pirbright Woking GU24 0NF
T: (01483) 232441; Fax: 232448
Pres: Dr. A.I. Donaldson
Focus: Immunology; Biochem; Genetics . 11654

Institute for Consumer Ergonomics (ICE), 75 Swingbridge Rd, Loughborough LE11 0JB
T: (01509) 236161; Fax: 610725
Founded: 1970
Gen Secr: I.A.R. Galer
Focus: Public Health 11655

Institute for Cultural Research (ICR), POB 13, Tunbridge Wells TN3 0HQ
T: (0189286) 2045
Founded: 1968; Members: 450
Pres: David Wade; Gen Secr: Henri Bortoft
Focus: Cultur Hist 11656

The Institute for Fiscal Studies (IFS), 7 Ridgmount St, London WC1E 7AE
T: (0171) 6363784; E-Mail: mailbox@ifs.org.uk; Fax: 3234780
Founded: 1969; Members: 1000
Pres: Lord Alexander of Weedon; Gen Secr: Andrew Dilnot
Focus: Econ
Periodical
Fiscal Studies (quarterly) 11657

Institute for Jewish Policy Research (IJA), 79 Wimpole St, London W1M 7DD
T: (0171) 9358266; E-Mail: jpr@ort.org.uk; Fax: 9353252
Founded: 1941
Pres: Lord Rothschild; Gen Secr: A. Lerman
Focus: Poli Sci
Periodicals
East European Jewish Affairs (semi-annually)
JPR Reports and Policy Papers (6-8 times annually)
Patterns of Prejudice (quarterly) 11658

Institute for Sex Education and Research (ISER), 40 School Rd, Birmingham B13 9SN
T: (0121) 4490892
Founded: 1969
Focus: Behav Sci 11659

Institute for Supervision and Management (ISM), Stowe Horse, Netherstone, Lichfield WS13 6TJ
T: (01543) 251346; E-Mail: ism@ismstone.demon.co.uk; Fax: 415804
Founded: 1947; Members: 20000
Pres: Bryan Santelle-Smith; Gen Secr: John Morris
Focus: Commerce
Periodical
Modern Management (bi-monthly) . . . 11660

Institute of Actuaries, Staple Inn Hall, High Holborn, London WC1V 7QJ
T: (0171) 2420106
Founded: 1848; Members: 8483
Pres: L.J. Martin; Gen Secr: A.G. Tait
Focus: Insurance
Periodical
Journal (3 times annually) 11661

Institute of Administrative Management (IAM), 40 Chatsworth Parade, Petts Wood, Orpington BR5 1RW
T: (01689) 75555; Fax: 8952569
Founded: 1915; Members: 10000
Gen Secr: M.J. Ainsworth
Focus: Business Admin
Periodicals
Office & Information Management International (10 times annually)
Office Job Evaluation Manual (annually)
Office Salaries Analysis (annually) . . . 11662

Institute of Bankers in Scotland, 19-20 Rutland Sq, Edinburgh EH1 2DE
T: (0131) 2299869
Founded: 1875; Members: 14500
Gen Secr: Dr. C.W. Munn
Focus: Adult Educ; Finance
Periodical
The Scottish Banker (quarterly) 11663

Institute of Biology, 20-22 Queensberry Pl, London SW7 2DZ
T: (0171) 5818333; E-Mail: info@iob.primex.co.uk; Fax: 8239409
Founded: 1950; Members: 15000
Pres: Prof. R.B. Heap; Gen Secr: Dr. R. Priestley
Focus: Bio
Periodicals
Biologist (5 times annually)
Journal of Biological Education (quarterly) 11664

Institute of Biomedical Science (IBS), 12 Coldbath Sq, London EC1R 5HL
T: (0171) 6368192; E-Mail: 101771.3572@compuserve.com; Fax: 4364946
Founded: 1912; Members: 14000
Focus: Med
Periodicals
Biomedical Scientist (monthly)
British Journal of Biomedical Science (quarterly) 11665

Institute of Business Administration, 25 Bridgeman Terrace, Wigan WN1 1TD
T: (01442) 43572; Fax: 829350
Founded: 1946
Focus: Business Admin
Periodical
Business Administrator (bi-monthly) . . . 11666

Institute of Ceramics, Shelton House, Stoke Rd, Shelton, Stoke-on-Trent ST4 2DR
T: (01782) 23116
Founded: 1900; Members: 2000
Gen Secr: S.B. Buchanan
Focus: Materials Sci
Periodicals
Proceedings
Transactions and Journal (annually) . . 11667

The Institute of Chartered Accountants in England and Wales, Chartered Accountants' Hall, Moorgate Pl, London EC2P 2BJ
T: (0171) 9208100; Fax: 9200547
Founded: 1880; Members: 110000
Pres: C.N. Lainé; Gen Secr: A.J. Colquhoun
Focus: Econ
Periodicals
Accountancy (monthly)
Accountants Digest (monthly)
Accounting and Business Research (quarterly) 11668

Institute of Chartered Accountants of Scotland, 27 Queen St, Edinburgh EH2 1LA
T: (0131) 2255673; E-Mail: icas@icas.org.uk; Fax: 2253813
Founded: 1854; Members: 14200
Pres: A.S. Hunter; Gen Secr: P.W. Johnston
Focus: Econ
Periodicals
Annual Report (annually)
CA Magazine (monthly)
Official Directory of Members (annually) . 11669

Institute of Chartered Foresters (IFGB), 7a Saint Colme St, Edinburgh EH3 6AA
T: (0131) 2252705; Fax: 2206128
Founded: 1925; Members: 1440
Pres: R.T. Bradley; Gen Secr: Margaret W. Dick
Focus: Forestry
Periodical
Forestry (quarterly) 11670

Institute of Chartered Secretaries and Administrators, 16 Park Crescent, London W1N 4AH
T: (0171) 5804741; Fax: 3231132
Founded: 1891; Members: 44000
Gen Secr: M.P. Nolan
Focus: Public Admin
Periodicals
Administrator (monthly)
Company Secretarial Practice 11671

Institute of Clay Technology (ICT), c/o Butterley Building Materials Ltd, Wellington St, Ripley DE5 3DZ
T: (01773) 3661
Founded: 1927; Members: 771
Focus: Materials Sci
Periodical
Euroclay (bi-monthly) 11672

Institute of Community Studies, 18 Victoria Park Sq, London E2 9PF
T: (0181) 9806263
Founded: 1954
Pres: M. Young
Focus: Sociology 11673

The Institute of Concrete Technology (ICT), POB 255, Beaconsfield HP9 1JE
T: (01494) 674572; Fax: 673533
Founded: 1972; Members: 600
Gen Secr: Roy Jolly
Focus: Civil Eng
Periodical
Convention Symposium Papers (annually) 11674

Institute of Construction Management (ICM), 397 City Rd, London EC1V 1NE
T: (0171) 2780471; Fax: 8373194
Founded: 1974; Members: 1300
Gen Secr: J.W. Lawrence
Focus: Civil Eng
Periodicals
Construction Management-Focus (quarterly)
ICM Reference Book and List of Members (annually) 11675

Institute of Contemporary Arts, Nash House, The Mall, London SW1Y 5AH
T: (0171) 8730051
Founded: 1947; Members: 6000
Pres: Mik Flood
Focus: Arts 11676

Institute of Contemporary History and Wiener Library, 4 Devonshire St, London W1N 2BH
T: (0171) 6367247; E-Mail: lib@wl.u-net.com; Fax: 4366428
Founded: 1933
Gen Secr: Prof. David Cesarani
Focus: Hist 11677

Institute of Corrosion, 4 Leck House, Lake St, Leighton Buzzard LU7 8TQ
T: (01525) 851771; Fax: 376690
Founded: 1975; Members: 1600
Pres: Don Harrop; Gen Secr: David Beacon
Focus: Metallurgy
Periodicals
Annual Report (annually)
Corrosion Science (monthly)
Industrial Corrosion (bi-monthly) 11678

Institute of Credit Management (ICM), Easton House, Easton on the Hill, Stamford PE90 3NH
T: (01780) 56777
Founded: 1939; Members: 3400
Focus: Finance
Periodical
Credit Management (bi-monthly) 11679

Institute of Data Processing Management (IDPM), 18 Henrietta St, London WC2E 8NU
T: (0171) 2403304
Founded: 1978; Members: 7000
Focus: Computer & Info Sci
Periodicals
DP International (annually)
DP International Quarterly Journal (quarterly) 11680

Institute of Directors (IOD), 116 Pall Mall, London SW1Y 5ED
T: (0171) 8391233; Fax: 9301949
Founded: 1903; Members: 38000
Focus: Business Admin
Periodical
The Director (monthly) 11681

Institute of Economic Affairs (IEA), 2 Lord North St, London SW1P 3LB
T: (0171) 7993745; Fax: 7992137
Founded: 1955
Gen Secr: John Blundell
Focus: Econ
Periodicals
Economic Affairs (bi-monthly)
Hobart Papers
IEA Readings
Occasional Papers
Research Monographs 11682

Institute of Electrolysis, 251 Seymour Grove, Manchester M16 0DS
T: (0161) 8815306
Founded: 1944; Members: 298
Focus: Physics 11683

Institute of Energy, 18 Devonshire St, London W1N 2AU
T: (0171) 5807124; Fax: 5804420
Founded: 1927; Members: 5000
Gen Secr: J. Leach
Focus: Energy
Periodicals
Energy World (10 times annually)
Energy World Yearbook (annually)
Fuel and Energy Abstracts (bi-monthly)
Journal of the Institute of Energy (quarterly) 11684

Institute of Engineers and Technicians (IE), 100 Grove Vale, London SE22 8DR
T: (0181) 6931255; Fax: 535468
Founded: 1948; Members: 5500
Pres: Frank Shaw; Gen Secr: Dr. Tony Deeson
Focus: Eng
Periodical
Journal (quarterly) 11685

Institute of Fisheries Management (IFM), Balmaha, Coldwells Rd, Holmer HR1 1LH
T: (01432) 276225
Founded: 1969; Members: 1200
Gen Secr: E. Staite
Focus: Fisheries
Periodical
Fish (quarterly) 11686

Institute of Food Research / Biotechnology and Biological Sciences Research Council, Earley Gate, Whiteknights Rd, Reading RG6 2EF
T: (01734) 357000; Fax: 267917
Gen Secr: Prof. Douglas Georgala
Focus: Nutrition; Agri
Periodicals
Newsletter (quarterly)
Report (annually) 11687

Institute of Food Science and Technology of The United Kingdom (IFST), 5 Cambridge Court, 210 Shepherd's Bush Rd, London W6 7NJ
T: (0171) 6036316
Founded: 1964; Members: 3500
Pres: D. Hicks; Gen Secr: H.G. Wild
Focus: Food; Eng
Periodicals
Food Science and Technology Today (quarterly)
International Journal of Food Science and Technology (bi-monthly) 11688

The Institute of Group-Analysis, 1 Daleham Gardens, London NW3 5BY
T: (0171) 4312693; Fax: 4317276
Founded: 1971; Members: 220
Pres: Dick Blackwell; Gen Secr: Anja Estermann
Focus: Behav Sci 11689

Institute of Health Education (IHE), c/o University Dental Hospital, Higher Cambridge St, Manchester M15 6FH
T: (0161) 2756610; E-Mail: anthony.blinkhorn@man.ac.uk; Fax: 2756610
Founded: 1962; Members: 800
Gen Secr: Prof. Anthony S. Blinkhorn
Focus: Public Health
Periodical
International Journal of Health Education (quarterly) 11690

Institute of Heraldic and Genealogical Studies (IHGS), Northgate, Canterbury CT1 1BA
T: (01227) 768664; E-Mail: ihgs@dial.pipex.com; Fax: 765617
Founded: 1961; Members: 300
Pres: Viscount Monckton of Brenchley
Focus: Genealogy
Periodical
Family History (quarterly) 11691

Institute of Housing, Octavia House, Westwood Business Park, Westwood Way, Coventry CV4 8JP
T: (01203) 694433
Founded: 1965; Members: 5400
Focus: Home Econ
Periodicals
Housing (monthly)
Inside Housing (weekly) 11692

Institute of Information Scientists, 44 Museum St, London WC1A 1LY
T: (0171) 8318003; Fax: 4301270
Founded: 1958; Members: 2750
Pres: Michael F. Lynch; Gen Secr: E.B. Hyams
Focus: Computer & Info Sci
Periodicals
Inform (10 times annually)
IT Link (bi-monthly)
Journal of Information Science 11693

Institute of Inventors, 19-21 Fosse Way, London W13 0BZ
Founded: 1964; Members: 700
Focus: Eng
Periodical
New Invention Lists (monthly) 11694

Institute of Investment Management and Research, 21 Ironmonger Ln, London EC2V 8EY
T: (0171) 7963000; Fax: 7963333
Founded: 1956; Members: 3500
Gen Secr: Sir David Dobson
Focus: Finance
Periodical
The Professional Investor (10 times annually) 11695

Institute of Leisure and Amenity Management (ILAM), Lower Basildon, Reading RG8 9NE
T: (01491) 874222; Fax: 874059
Founded: 1983; Members: 6000
Gen Secr: Alan Smith
Focus: Travel
Periodical
The Leisure Manager (monthly) 11696

Institute of Linguists, Saxon House, 48 Southwark St, London SE1 1UN
T: (0171) 9403100; Fax: 9403101
Founded: 1910; Members: 6700
Pres: John Drew; Gen Secr: Edda Ostarhild
Focus: Ling
Periodical
The Linguist (bi-monthly) 11697

Institute of Logistics (ILDM), Douglas House, Queens Sq, Corby NN 17 1PL
T: (01536) 205500; Fax: 400979
Founded: 1993; Members: 13500
Focus: Physics; Logic
Periodicals
Logistics Focus (monthly)
Members' Directory (annually)
Members' Reference Book & Buyers' Guide (annually) 11698

Institute of Management, 2 Savoy Court, Strand, London WC2R 0EZ
T: (0171) 4970580
Founded: 1992; Members: 70000
Pres: Roger D. Young; Gen Secr: Christine Hayhurst
Focus: Business Admin
Periodicals
Management Today (monthly)
Professional Manager (bi-monthly) . . . 11699

Institute of Management Services (IMS), 1 Cecil Court, London Rd, Enfield EN2 6DD
T: (0181) 3637452; Fax: 3678149
Founded: 1941; Members: 6000
Pres: Lord Chilver; Gen Secr: Paul Symes
Focus: Business Admin
Periodical
Management Services (monthly) 11700

Institute of Marine Engineers, 76 Mark Ln, London EC3R 7JN
T: (0171) 4818493; E-Mail: imare@imare.org.uk; Fax: 4881854
Founded: 1889; Members: 16500
Pres: D.R. Cusdin; Gen Secr: J.E. Sloggett
Focus: Eng
Periodicals
Bulletin (monthly)
Marine Engineers Review (monthly)
Offshore Technology (quarterly)
Technical Conference Reports
Technical Transactions 11701

Institute of Materials, 1 Carlton House Terrace, London SW1Y 5DB
T: (0171) 8394071; Fax: 8392078
Founded: 1993; Members: 18000
Pres: Prof. Anthony Kelly; Gen Secr: Dr. J.A. Catterall
Focus: Materials Sci
Periodicals
Historical Metallurgy (semi-annually)
Ironmaking and Steelmaking (bi-monthly)
Materials Science and Technology (monthly)
Metals and Materials (monthly)
Surface Engineering (quarterly) 11702

The Institute of Mathematics and its Applications (IMA), 16 Nelson St, Southend-on-Sea SS1 1EF
T: (01702) 354020; E-Mail: post@ima.org.uk; Fax: 354111
Founded: 1964; Members: 6000
Pres: Prof. D.G. Crighton; Gen Secr: Dr. A.M. Lepper
Focus: Math
Periodicals
IMA Journal of Applied Mathematics (bi-monthly)
IMA Journal of Mathematical Control and Information (quarterly)
IMA Journal of Mathematics Applied in Business and Industry (quarterly)
IMA Journal of Mathematics Applied in Medicine and Biology (quarterly)
IMA Journal of Numerical Analysis (quarterly)
Mathematics Today (bi-monthly)
Teaching Mathematics and its Applications (quarterly) 11703

Institute of Measurement and Control, 87 Gower St, London WC1E 6AA
T: (0171) 3874949; Fax: 3888431
Founded: 1944; Members: 6000
Pres: C.R. Howard; Gen Secr: M.J. Yates
Focus: Eng
Periodicals
Instrument Engineer's Yearbook (annually)
Measurement and Control (monthly)
Transactions (quarterly) 11704

The Institute of Metals, 1 Carlton House Terrace, London SW1Y 5DB
T: (0171) 8394071; Fax: 8392289
Founded: 1985; Members: 12500
Pres: C.E.H. Morris; Gen Secr: Dr. J.A. Catterall
Focus: Metallurgy
Periodicals
British Corrosion Journal (quarterly)
Historical Metallurgy (semi-annually)
International Materials Review (bi-monthly)
Ironmaking and Steelmaking (bi-monthly)
Materials Science and Technology (quarterly)
Metals and Materials (monthly)
Powder Metallurgy (quarterly)
Steel in The USSR (monthly)
Surface Engineering (quarterly) 11705

Institute of Municipal Building Management (IMBM), 30 Rhiw Rd, Colwyn Bay LL29 7TP
T: (01492) 31348
Founded: 1951; Members: 1660
Focus: Urban Plan 11706

Institute of Occupational Medicine, 8 Roxburgh Pl, Edinburgh EH8 9SU
T: (0131) 6675131; E-Mail: iom@iomhq.org.uk; Fax: 6670136

Founded: 1969
Pres: Dr. C.A. Soutar
Focus: Hygiene 11707

Institute of Packaging (IOP), Sysonby Lodge, Nottingham Rd, Melton Mowbray LE13 0NU
T: (01664) 500055; Fax: 64164
Founded: 1947; Members: 4000
Pres: Victor Watson; Gen Secr: Jerry Berragan
Focus: Eng
Periodical
Panorama (bi-monthly) 11708

Institute of Personnel and Development (IPD), IPD House, Camp Rd, London SW19 4UX
T: (0181) 9719700; Fax: 2633333
Founded: 1913; Members: 82000
Pres: Sir Michael Bett; Gen Secr: G. Armstrong
Focus: Business Admin
Periodicals
People Management (bi-weekly)
Personnel Management Plus 11709

Institute of Petroleum (IP), 61 New Cavendish St, London W1M 8AR
T: (0171) 4677100; Fax: 2551472
Founded: 1913; Members: 8000
Pres: D.L. Setchell; Gen Secr: Ian Ward
Focus: Petrochem
Periodicals
IP Statistics Service (quarterly)
Petroleum Review (monthly) 11710

Institute of Physics, 76 Portland Pl, London W1N 4AA
T: (0171) 4704800; Fax: 4704848
Founded: 1918; Members: 22000
Pres: Dr.Brian Manley; Gen Secr: Dr. A. Jones
Focus: Physics
Periodicals
Bioimaging (quarterly)
Classical and Quantum Gravity (monthly)
Distributed Systems Engineering (quarterly)
European Journal of Physics (bi-monthly)
High Performance Polymers (quarterly)
Inverse Problems (bi-monthly)
Journal of Hard Materials (quarterly)
Journal of Micromechanics and Microengineering (quarterly)
Journal of Physics A: Mathematical and General (18 times annually)
Journal of Physics B: Atomic, Molecular and Optical Physics (bi-weekly)
Journal of Physics C: Condensed Matter (weekly)
Journal of Physics D: Applied Physics (monthly)
Journal of Physics G: Nuclear Physics (monthly)
Journal of Radiological Protection (quarterly)
Measurement Science and Technology (monthly)
Modelling and Simulation in Materials Science and Engineering (bi-monthly)
Nano Technology (quarterly)
Network (quarterly)
Nonlinearity (bi-monthly)
Opto and Laser Europe (bi-monthly)
Physics Education (bi-monthly)
Physics in Medicine and Biology (monthly)
Physics World (monthly)
Physiological Measurement (quarterly)
Plasma Physics and Controlled Fusion (monthly)
Plasma Sources Science and Technology (quarterly)
Public Understanding of Science (quarterly)
Pure and Applied Optics (bi-monthly)
Quantum Optics (bi-monthly)
Reports on Progress in Physics (monthly)
Semiconductor Science and Technology (monthly)
Smart Materials and Structures (quarterly)
Superconductor Science and Technology (bi-monthly)
Waves in Random Media (quarterly) . . 11711

Institute of Printing (IOP), 8a Lonsdale Gardens, Tunbridge Wells TN1 1NU
T: (01892) 538118; E-Mail: zop@globalprint.com; Fax: 518028
Founded: 1961; Members: 2000
Pres: H. Roche; Gen Secr: D. Freeland
Focus: Graphic & Dec Arts, Design . . 11712

Institute of Professional Investigators (IPI), 31a Wellington St, Blackburn BB1 8AF
T: (01254) 680072; Fax: 59276
Founded: 1976; Members: 400
Pres: Stephen J. Grant; Gen Secr: James D. Cole
Focus: Adult Educ
Periodical
The Professional Investigator (bi-monthly) 11713

Institute of Psycho-Analysis, 63 New Cavendish St, London W1M 7RD
T: (0171) 5804952
Founded: 1924; Members: 433
Focus: Psychoan
Periodical
International Journal of Psycho-Analysis (bi-monthly) 11714

Institute of Psycho-Sexual Medicine, 11 Chandos St, London W1M 9DE
Focus: Med
Periodical
Institute of Psychosexual Medicine Journal (semi-annually) 11715

Institute of Quarrying, 7 Regent St, Nottingham NG1 5BY
T: (01602) 411315
Founded: 1917; Members: 5000
Gen Secr: J. Berridge
Focus: Mining
Periodical
Quarry Management (monthly) 11716

Institute of Race Relations, 2-6 Leeke St, London WC1X 9HS
T: (0171) 8370041; Fax: 2780623
Founded: 1958; Members: 200
Gen Secr: A. Sivanandan
Focus: Sociology
Periodical
Race and Class (quarterly) 11717

Institute of Refrigeration, Kelvin House, 76 Mill Ln, Carshalton SM5 2JR
T: (0181) 6477033; Fax: 7730165
Founded: 1899; Members: 2600
Pres: P.J. Cooper; Gen Secr: M.J. Horlick
Focus: Food; Eng
Periodical
Proceedings (annually) 11718

Institute of Sales and Marketing Management (Inst SMM), 24 Warwick Rd, Royal Leamington Spa CV32 5JH
T: (01926) 37621/4
Founded: 1967; Members: 16000
Focus: Marketing
Periodical
Sales & Marketing Management 11719

Institute of Science Technology (IST), Mansell House, 22 Bole St, Lichfield WS13 6LP
T: (01543) 251346; Fax: 415804
Founded: 1954; Members: 2000
Pres: Lord Perry of Walton; Gen Secr: D.C.J. Sayers
Focus: Eng
Periodical
Science Technology (quarterly) 11720

Institute of Scientific and Technical Communicators (ISTC), 2-16 Goodge St, London W1P 1FF
T: (0171) 4364425; E-Mail: istc@istc.org.uk; Fax: 483480
Founded: 1972; Members: 1266
Pres: G. Gentle; Gen Secr: A. Brobyn
Focus: Sci; Eng
Periodical
The Communicator (quarterly) 11721

Institute of Sheet Metal Engineering (ISME), Exeter House, 48 Holloway Mead, Birmingham B1 1NU
T: (0121) 6222560; Fax: 6666316
Founded: 1946; Members: 400
Pres: R. Jaf; Gen Secr: C. Bates
Focus: Eng
Periodicals
Oracle (quarterly)
Sheet Metal Industries: Trade Journal (monthly) 11722

Institute of Small Business (ISB), 57-61 Mortimer St, London W1
T: (0171) 6374383
Focus: Commerce
Periodical
Business Ideas Letter (monthly) 11723

Institute of Sports Medicine (ISM), 10 Nottingham Pl, London W1M 4AX
T: (0171) 4861303
Founded: 1963
Focus: Med 11724

Institute of Statisticians, 43 Saint Peter's Sq, Preston PR1 7BX
T: (01772) 204237; Fax: 204476
Founded: 1948; Members: 2500
Pres: Sir John Boreham; Gen Secr: D.A. Holland
Focus: Stats
Periodicals
The Professional Statistician (monthly)
The Statistician (quarterly) 11725

Institute of Technicians in Venereology, c/o Orsett Hospital, Orsett, Essex
Founded: 1951
Focus: Venereology 11726

Institute of Translation and Interpreting, 377 City Rd, London EC1V 1NA
T: (0171) 7137600; E-Mail: iti@compuserve.com; Fax: 7137650
Founded: 1986; Members: 2300
Pres: G. Cross; Gen Secr: J.A. Hibbert
Focus: Ling
Periodical
ITI Bulletin (bi-monthly) 11727

Institute of Trichologists (IT), 20-22 Queensberry Pl, London SW7 2DZ
T: (0171) 4917253
Founded: 1902; Members: 230
Pres: John Mason; Gen Secr: Alan Samuel
Focus: Med; Immunology
Periodical
Trichologist 11728

Institute of Value Management (IVM), c/o Delta Executive Devt Centre Ltd, 22 Cavendish Av, Buxton SK17 9AE
T: (01298) 2284
Founded: 1966; Members: 80
Focus: Econ
Periodical
Value (quarterly) 11729

Institute of Wood Science (IWSc), Hughenden Valley, High Wycombe HP14 4NU
T: (01494) 565374; Fax: 565395
Founded: 1955; Members: 1500
Gen Secr: M.W. Holloway
Focus: Forestry
Periodical
Journal (semi-annually) 11730

Institution of Agricultural Engineers (IAgrE), West End Rd, Silsoe, Bedford MK45 4DU
T: (01525) 861096; Fax: 861660
Founded: 1938; Members: 2o00
Gen Secr: Michael H. Hurst
Focus: Agri; Eng
Periodical
The Agricultural Engineer incorporating Soil & Water (quarterly) 11731

Institution of British Telecom Engineers (IPOEE), 8-10 Gresham St, London EC2V 7AG
T: (0171) 3568050
Founded: 1906; Members: 20000
Focus: Electric Eng
Periodical
BT Engineering Journal (quarterly) . . . 11732

The Institution of Chemical Engineers, 165-189 Railway Terrace, Rugby CV21 3HQ
T: (01788) 578214; E-Mail: library@icheme.org.uk; Fax: 560833
Founded: 1922; Members: 722
Gen Secr: Dr. T.J. Evans
Focus: Eng
Periodicals
Chemical Engineer (22 times annually)
Chemical Engineering Research & Design: Transactions of The Institution of Chemical Engineers (8 times annually)
Environmental Protection Bulletin (bi-monthly)
Loss Prevention Bulletin (bi-monthly) . . 11733

The Institution of Civil Engineers (ICE), 1-7 Great George St, London SW1P 3AA
T: (0171) 2227722; Fax: 2227500
Founded: 1818; Members: 76397
Gen Secr: Roger Dobson
Focus: Civil Eng
Periodicals
Advances in Cement Research (quarterly)
The Concrete Yearbook (annually)
Construction Today (monthly)
Geotechnique (quarterly)
Ground Engineering (monthly)
Ground Engineering Yearbook (annually)
Ground Improvement (quarterly)
Magazine of Concrete Research (quarterly)
Nuclear Energy (bi-monthly)
Offshore Engineer Yearbook (annually)
Proceedings: Civil Engineering (quarterly)
Proceedings: Municipal Engineer (quarterly)
Proceedings: Structures and Buildings (quarterly)
Proceedings: Transport (quarterly)
Proceedings: Water, Maritime and Energy (quarterly)
Steel Construction Yearbook (annually)
Underground Services Directory (annually)
Waste, Recycling and Environmental Yearbook (annually) 11734

Institution of Corrosion Science and Technology, POB 253, Leighton Buzzard LU7 7WB
T: (01525) 851771; Fax: 376690
Founded: 1975; Members: 1500
Pres: Dr. J.L. Bown; Gen Secr: K.M. Vincent
Focus: Metallurgy
Periodicals
Corrosion Science (monthly)
Industrial Corrosion (8 times annually) . 11735

Institution of Electrical Engineers (IEE), Savoy Pl, London WC2R 0BL
T: (0171) 2401871; E-Mail: postmaster@iee.org.uk; Fax: 2407735
Founded: 1871; Members: 138000
Pres: D.G. Jefferies; Gen Secr: Dr. J.C. Williams
Focus: Electric Eng; Electronic Eng
Periodicals
Computing & Control Engineering Journal (bi-monthly)
Electronics & Communication Engineering Journal (bi-monthly)
Electronics Letters (bi-weekly)
IEE Review (bi-monthly)
Power Engineering Journal (bi-monthly) . 11736

Institution of Electronics, 659 Oldham Rd, Rochdale OL16 4PE
Founded: 1930; Members: 2500
Gen Secr: W. Birtwistle
Focus: Electronic Eng
Periodical
Proceedings (quarterly) 11737

Institution of Electronics and Electrical Incorporated Engineers (IEEIE), Savoy Hill House, Savoy Hill, London WC2R 0BS
T: (0171) 8363357; E-Mail: iecie@dial.pipex.com; Fax: 4979006
Founded: 1965; Members: 30000
Pres: W.A. Bill Dennay; Gen Secr: A.C. Gingell
Focus: Electric Eng; Electronic Eng
Periodical
Electrotechnology (bi-monthly) 11738

Institution of Engineering Designers, Courtleigh, Westbury Leigh, Westbury BA13 3TA
T: (01373) 822801; E-Mail: ied@inst-engg-design.demon.co.uk; Fax: 858085
Founded: 1945; Members: 5300
Pres: Prof. P.C. Hills; Gen Secr: M.J. Osborne
Focus: Graphic & Dec Arts, Design; Eng
Periodical
The Engineering Designer (bi-monthly) . 11739

Institution of Engineers amd Shipbuilders in Scotland, 1 Atlantic Quay, Broomielaw, Glasgow G2 8JE
T: (0141) 2483721
Founded: 1857; Members: 800
Pres: I.C. Broadley; Gen Secr: E.W. Bell
Focus: Eng
Periodicals
Transactions (annually)
Year Book and List of Members (bi-annually) 11740

Institution of Environmental Health Officers (IEH), Chadwick House, 48 Rushworth St, London SE1 0QT
T: (0171) 9286006
Founded: 1883; Members: 6000
Pres: E. Foskett; Gen Secr: A.M. Tanner
Focus: Ecology
Periodicals
Environmental Health Journal (monthly)
Environmental Health News (weekly) . . 11741

Institution of Environmental Sciences, 14 Princes Gate, Hyde Park, London SW7 1PU
T: (01778) 394846; Fax: 394846
Founded: 1971; Members: 800
Pres: Duke of Westminster; Gen Secr: Dr. R.A. Fuller
Focus: Ecology
Periodical
The Environmental Scientist (bi-monthly) . 11742

Institution of Fire Engineers (IFE), 148 New Walk, Leicester LE1 7QB
T: (01533) 553654; Fax: 2471231
Founded: 1918; Members: 10000
Pres: K.J. Lloyd; Gen Secr: D.W. Evans
Focus: Eng
Periodicals
Dictionary of Fire Technology
Fire Technology – Calculations
Fire Technology – Chemistry & Combustion
How Did It Start?
Quarterly (quarterly) 11743

Institution of Gas Engineers (IGE), 21 Portland Pl, London W1N 3AF
T: (0171) 6366603; Fax: 6366602
Founded: 1863; Members: 6000
Gen Secr: Sandra Raine
Focus: Eng; Energy
Periodical
Gas Engineering & Management (10 times annually) 11744

Institution of Highways and Transportation, 6 Endsleigh St, London WC1H 0DZ
T: (0171) 3872525; Fax: 3872808
Founded: 1930; Members: 10500
Pres: Mike Kendrick; Gen Secr: Dr. M.R. Cragg
Focus: Civil Eng
Periodical
Highways and Transportation 11745

Institution of Lighting Engineers, 9 Lawford Rd, Rugby CV21 2DZ
T: (01788) 576492; Fax: 540145
Founded: 1924; Members: 1750
Pres: C.R. Lane; Gen Secr: R. Frost
Focus: Electric Eng
Periodical
Lighting Journal (bi-monthly) 11746

Institution of Mechanical Engineers (IMechE), 1 Birdcage Walk, London SW1H 9JJ
T: (0171) 2227899; E-Mail: enquiries@imeche.org.uk; Fax: 2224557
Founded: 1847; Members: 77000
Pres: Pam Liversidge; Gen Secr: Dr. R.A. Pike
Focus: Eng
Periodicals
Automotive Engineering (bi-monthly)
Environmental Engineering (monthly)
Journal of Strain Analysis for Engineering Design (monthly)
Professional Engineering (monthly) . . . 11747

Institution of Mechanical Incorporated Engineers (IMIE), 3 Birdcage Walk, London SW1H 9JN
T: (0171) 7991808; Fax: 7992243
Founded: 1988; Members: 8000
Pres: J.H. Hooper; Gen Secr: D.P. Davy
Focus: Eng
Periodical
Mechanical Incorporated Engineer (bi-monthly) 11748

Institution of Mining and Metallurgy (IMM), 44 Portland Pl, London W1N 4BR
T: (0171) 5803802; Fax: 4365388
Founded: 1892; Members: 4250
Pres: Dr. C.V. Phillips; Gen Secr: M.J. Jones
Focus: Mining; Metallurgy
Periodicals
IMM Abstracts (bi-monthly)
Minerals Industry International (bi-monthly)

Transactions (Three Sections) (3 times annually) 11749

The Institution of Mining Engineers (IMinE), Danum House, South Parade, Doncaster DN1 2DY
T: (01302) 320486; Fax: 340554
Founded: 1889; Members: 3968
Gen Secr: Dr. G.J.M. Woodrow
Focus: Eng; Mining
Periodical
Mining Technology (monthly) 11750

Institution of Nuclear Engineers (INucE), 1 Penerley Rd, London SE6 2LQ
T: (0181) 6981500; Fax: 6956409
Founded: 1959; Members: 1500
Gen Secr: Bill Hurst
Focus: Nucl Res
Periodical
The Nuclear Engineer (bi-monthly) . . . 11751

Institution of Physics and Engineering in Medicine an Biology, 4 Champleshon Rd, York YO2 1PE
T: (01904) 610821
Focus: Physics; Eng; Med; Bio 11752

Institution of Plant Engineers (IPE), 77 Great Peter St, London SW1P 2EZ
T: (0171) 2332855; Fax: 2332604
Founded: 1946; Members: 6000
Pres: R. Wilkinson; Gen Secr: P.F. Tye
Focus: Eng; Botany
Periodical
The Plant Engineer (bi-monthly) 11753

Institution of Polish Engineers in Great Britain (STP), 238-246 King St, London W6 0RF
T: (0181) 7411940
Founded: 1940; Members: 425
Focus: Eng; Ethnology
Periodicals
Bulletin (quarterly)
Technika i Nauka (quarterly) 11754

Institution of Railway Signal Engineers (IRSE), 1 Badlake Close, Badlake Hill, Dawlish EX7 9AY
T: (01626) 888096; Fax: 888571
Founded: 1912; Members: 2900
Gen Secr: R.L. Weedon
Focus: Eng
Periodical
Proceedings (annually) 11755

Institution of Structural Engineers, 11 Upper Belgrave St, London SW1X 8BH
T: (0171) 2354535; Fax: 2354294
Founded: 1908; Members: 23000
Pres: B.P. Clancy; Gen Secr: Dr. J.W. Dougall
Focus: Eng
Periodical
The Structural Engineer (monthly) . . . 11756

Intercontinental Church Society, 175 Tower Bridge Rd, London SE1 2AQ
T: (0171) 4074588; Fax: 3780541
Founded: 1823
Pres: Viscount Brentford; Gen Secr: John Moore
Focus: Rel & Theol
Periodical
Going Places (5 times annually) 11757

Intermediate Technology Development Group (ITDG), Myson House, Railway Terrace, Rugby CV21 3HT
T: (01788) 560631; Fax: 540270
Founded: 1965
Pres: Prince of Wales; Gen Secr: Christopher Underhill
Focus: Eng
Periodicals
Appropriate Technology (quarterly)
Food Chain (quarterly)
Small Enterprise Development (quarterly)
Waterlines (quarterly) 11758

International African Institute (IAI), Thornhaugh St, Russell Sq, London WC1H 0XG
T: (0171) 8313068
Founded: 1926
Pres: Prof. William A. Shack; Gen Secr: Prof. David Parkin
Focus: Ethnology; Rel & Theol
Periodical
Africa and Africa Bibliography (quarterly) 11759

International Anatomical Nomenclature Committee, c/o Dept of Anatomy, Guy's Hospital Medical School, London SE1 9RT
Focus: Anat; Standards 11760

International Association for Esperanto in Libraries, 14 Elmdale Rd, London N13 4UL
T: (0181) 8889411
Founded: 1971; Members: 100
Focus: Ling; Libraries & Bk Sci 11761

International Association for Mass Communication Research (IAMCR), c/o Centre for Mass Communication Research, University of Leicester, Leicester LE1 7LT
Founded: 1957; Members: 1000
Focus: Journalism 11762

International Association for Scandinavian Studies (IASS), c/o EUR, University of East Anglia, Norwich NR4 7TJ
T: (01603) 456161; Fax: 250599
Founded: 1962; Members: 145
Focus: Lit 11763

International Association of Agricultural Museums, c/o Rural History Centre, University of Reading, Reading RG6 2AG
T: (01734) 318660; Fax: 751264
Founded: 1968
Pres: Dr. Nitra Vontorcic
Focus: Agri
Periodical
Acta Museorum Agriculturae Pragae (irregularly) 11764

International Association of Applied Linguistics (IAAL), c/o Dept of Linguistics, University of Edinburgh, Edinburgh EH8 9LN
Founded: 1964; Members: 22
Focus: Ling 11765

International Association of Biological Standardization (IABS), South Wind, Streat, Hassocks BN6 8RT
T: 890366
Founded: 1955; Members: 600
Focus: Standards; Bio
Periodical
Journal of Biological Standardization (quarterly) 11766

International Association of Environmental Coordinators (IAEC), Corylus Burton Way, Chalfont Saint Gills
Founded: 1976; Members: 150
Focus: Ecology 11767

International Association of Institutes of Navigation, c/o Royal Insitute of Navigation, 1 Kensington Gore, London SW7 2AT
T: (0171) 5895021; Fax: 8238671
Founded: 1975
Focus: Navig 11768

International Association of Music Libraries, Archives and Documentation Centres (United Kingdom Branch), c/o County Libraries Headquarters, Walton St, Aylesbury HP20 1UU
T: (01296) 382266; Fax: 382274
Founded: 1953
Gen Secr: M. Roll
Focus: Libraries & Bk Sci
Periodical
BRIO (semi-annually) 11769

International Association of Paediatric Dentistry, c/o Dept of Child Dental Health, The London Hospital Medical College, Turner St, London E1 2AD
T: (0171) 3777058 ext 2199; Fax: 3777058
Founded: 1969
Focus: Dent
Periodical
Journal of The IAPD (quarterly) 11770

International Association of Teachers of English as a Foreign Language (IATEFL), 3 Kingsdown Chambers, Kingsdown Park, Whitstable CT5 2DJ
T: (01227) 276528; E-Mail: 100070.1327@compuserve.com; Fax: 274415
Founded: 1967; Members: 10500
Pres: Prof. David Crystal; Gen Secr: Pauline Robinson
Focus: Ling; Educ
Periodical
Newsletter (bi-monthly) 11771

International Association of University Professors of English (IAUPE), c/o Penwithian Higher Fore St, Marazion TR17 0BQ
Founded: 1951; Members: 660
Focus: Adult Educ; Ling
Periodical
Bulletin (bi-annually) 11772

International Association of Volcanology and Chemistry of the Earth's Interior, c/o Dept of Earth Siences, University, Leeds LS2 9JT
Founded: 1919
Focus: Geology; Chem 11773

International Association on Water Quality (IAWQ), Duchess House, 20 Masons Yard, Duke St, London SW1Y 6BU
T: (0171) 8398390; E-Mail: iawq@compuserve.com; Fax: 8398299
Founded: 1965; Members: 7000
Pres: Prof. T. Keinath; Gen Secr: A. Milburn
Focus: Water Res; Hygiene; Ecology
Periodicals
Scientific and Technical Reports (every 6-9 months)
Water Quality International (bi-monthly)
Water Research (monthly)
Water Science and Technology (bi-weekly) 11774

International Bar Association (IBA), 2 Harewood Pl, London W1R 9HB
Fax: (0171) 4090456
Founded: 1947; Members: 12500
Gen Secr: Madeleine May
Focus: Law
Periodicals
International Bar News (semi-annually)
International Business Lawyer (monthly)
International Legal Practioner (quarterly) . 11775

International Bee Research Association (IBRA), 18 North Rd, Cardiff CF1 3DY
T: (01222) 372409; E-Mail: ibra@cardiff.ac.uk; Fax: 665522
Founded: 1949; Members: 1500
Pres: Prof. R. Morse; Gen Secr: Richard Jones
Focus: Zoology
Periodicals
Apicultural Abstracts (quarterly)
Bee World (quarterly)
Journal of Apicultural Research (quarterly) 11776

International Cerebral Palsy Society (ICPS), 19 Saint Mary's Grove, Chiswick, London W4 3LL
T: (0171) 7949761
Founded: 1969; Members: 300
Focus: Rehabil 11777

International Commission for The History of Representative and Parliamentary Institutions, Arts Bldg, University of Sussex, Brighton BN1 9QN
T: (01273) 606755
Founded: 1936
Focus: Hist
Periodical
Parliaments, Estates and Representation (semi-annually) 11778

International Commission on Polar Meteorology (ICPM), c/o British Antarctic Survey, Atmospheric Sciences Division, Madingley Rd, Cambridge CB3 0ET
Focus: Geophys 11779

International Commission on Zoological Nomenclature (ICZN), c/o Natural History Museum, Cromwell Rd, London SW7 5BD
T: (0171) 9389387; E-Mail: iczn@nhm.ac.uk
Founded: 1895; Members: 29
Pres: Prof. A. Minelli; Gen Secr: Dr. P.K. Tubbs
Focus: Zoology; Standards
Periodical
Bulletin of Zoological Nomenclature (quarterly) 11780

International Conference on Social Science and Medicine, c/o Centre for Social Research, University of Sussex, Falmer, Brighton BN1 9RF
T: (01273) 66755
Founded: 1968; Members: 150
Focus: Med; Hygiene 11781

International Council of Kinetography (ICKL), 250 Burges Rd, London E6 2E5
Founded: 1959; Members: 79
Focus: Perf Arts
Periodical
Conference Proceedings (bi-annually) . . 11782

International Dental Federation (IDF), 7 Carlisle St, London W1V 5RG
Founded: 1900; Members: 350000
Focus: Dent
Periodicals
FDI Dental World (bi-monthly)
International Dental Journal (bi-monthly) . 11783

International Esperanto-Association of Jurists (IEAJ), 77 Grasmere Av, Wembley HA9 8TF
T: 9049081
Founded: 1957; Members: 305
Focus: Law
Periodical
Internacia Jura Revuo (semi-annually) . . 11784

International Federation for Modern Languages and Literatures, c/o The Queen's University of Belfast, Belfast BT7 1NN
Founded: 1928
Focus: Ling; Lit 11785

International Federation for Theatre Research (IFTR), c/o Dept of Theatre Studies, University of Lancaster, Bailrigg, Lancaster
Founded: 1955; Members: 164
Focus: Perf Arts 11786

International Federation of Airworthiness (IFA), 58 Whiteheath Av, Ruislip HA4 7PW
T: (01895) 672504; E-Mail: dksmith@rmplc.co.uk; Fax: 676656
Founded: 1975; Members: 122
Pres: Beard Craig; Gen Secr: Donald Smith
Focus: Eng
Periodical
International Airworthiness News (quarterly) 11787

International Federation of Cell Biology (IFCB), c/o Imperial Cancer Research Fund, Lincoln's Inn Fields, London WC2A 3PX
Founded: 1947
Focus: Cell Biol & Cancer Res
Periodical
Cell Biology International Reports (monthly) 11788

International Federation of Gynecology and Obstetrics (FIGO), 27 Sussex Pl, Regent's Park, London NW1 4RG
T: (0171) 7232951; E-Mail: secret@figo.win-uk.net; Fax: 2580737
Founded: 1954; Members: 100
Pres: M. Fathalla
Focus: Gynecology
Periodicals
International Journal of Gynecology an Obstetrics (monthly)
Newsletter (3 times annually) 11789

International Federation of Multiple Sclerosis Societies (I.F.M.S.S.), 10 Heddon St, London W1R 7LJ
T: (0171) 7349120; E-Mail: info@ifmss.org.uk; Fax: 2872587
Founded: 1967; Members: 34
Pres: James Cantalupo; Gen Secr: Richard Hamilton
Focus: Med
Periodicals
MS Research in Progress (biennially)
Therapeutic Claims in MS (biennially)
Update (bi-annually) 11790

International Federation of Practitioners of Natural Therapeutics (IFPNT), 21 Bingham Pl, London W1M 3FH
T: (0171) 9356933
Founded: 1963
Focus: Therapeutics 11791

International Federation of Sportive Medicine (IFSM), Farnham Fark Rehabilitation Centre, Farnham Royal, Slough SL2 3LR
Founded: 1928; Members: 20000
Focus: Med 11792

International Federation on Aging – European Office (IFA), Astral House, 1268 London Rd, London SW16 4EJ
T: (0181) 6798000; Fax: 6796069
Founded: 1973
Gen Secr: Sally Greengross
Focus: Geriatrics; Adult Educ
Periodical
Aging International (bi-annually) 11793

International Filariasis Association (IFA), c/o Dept of Helminthology, London School of Hygiene and Tropical Medicine, Kepped St, London WC1E 7HT
T: (0171) 8255154
Founded: 1963; Members: 200
Focus: Med; Immunology 11794

International Food Information Service (IFIS), Ln End House, Shinfield, Reading RG2 9BB
T: (01118) 9883895; E-Mail: ifis@ifis.org.uk; Fax: 9885065
Founded: 1968
Gen Secr: J.R. Metcalfe
Focus: Food
Periodicals
Food Science and Technology Abstracts (monthly)
Food Science Profiles (monthly) 11795

International Glaciological Society (IGS), c/o SPRI, Lensfield Rd, Cambridge CB2 1ER
T: (01223) 355974; E-Mail: 100751.1667@compuserve.com; Fax: 336543
Founded: 1936; Members: 800
Pres: Dr. N. Maen; Gen Secr: C.S.L. Ommanney
Focus: Geology; Oceanography
Periodicals
Annals of Glaciology: Conference Proceedings (1-2 times annually)
ICE-News Bulletin (3 times annually)
Journal of Glaciology (3 times annually) . 11796

International Humanist and Ethical Union, 47 Theobald's Rd, London WC1X 8SP
T: (0171) 8314817; E-Mail: babu@iheu.org; Fax: 4301271
Founded: 1952; Members: 600
Pres: Prof. Dr. R.A.P. Tielman
Focus: Philos 11797

International Hydrofoil Society (IHS), 17 Melcombe Court, Dorset Sq, London NW1 6EP
Founded: 1970
Focus: Eng; Oceanography 11798

The International Institute for Conservation of Historic and Artistic Works (IIC), 6 Buckingham St, London WC2N 6BA
T: (0171) 8395975; E-Mail: iicon@compuserve.com; Fax: 9761564
Founded: 1950; Members: 3800
Pres: Agnes Ballestrem; Gen Secr: David Bomford
Focus: Preserv Hist Monuments
Periodical
Studies in Conservation (quarterly) . . . 11799

International Institute of Social Economics (IISE), Enholmes Hall, Patrington, Hull HU12 0PR
T: (01964) 630033; Fax: 547143
Founded: 1972; Members: 168
Gen Secr: Prof. Barrie O. Pettman
Focus: Econ
Periodical
International Journal of Social Economics (monthly) 11800

International Language Union, 14 Stray Towers, Victoria Rd, Harrogate HG2 O1J
Founded: 1908
Focus: Ling 11801

International Law Association (ILA), 17 Russell Sq, London WC1B 5DR
T: (0171) 3232978; Fax: 3233580
Founded: 1873; Members: 4000
Pres: Prof. Bengt Broms; Gen Secr: D.J.C. Wyld
Focus: Law
Periodical
Conference Reports (bi-annually) 11802

International Lead and Zinc Study Group (ILZSG), Metro House, 58 Saint James St, London SW1A 1LD
T: (0171) 499-9373; Fax: 4933725
Founded: 1959; Members: 30
Focus: Metallurgy; Mining
Periodical
Lead and Zinc Statistics (monthly)   . . . 11803

International Management Centre from Buckingham (IMCB), 13 Castle St, Buckingham MK18 1BP
T: (01280) 817222; Fax: 813297
Founded: 1964; Members: 2800
Pres: Baroness Dr. Caroline Cox; Gen Secr: Dr. Barnie Pettman
Focus: Business Admin
Periodical
Management Decision (monthly)   11804

International Map Collector's Society (IMCS), Woodstock, Flyford Flavell WR7 4BS
Founded: 1980; Members: 200
Focus: Cart   11805

International Medical Society of Paraplegia, c/o National Spinal Injuries Centre, Stoke Mandeville Hospital, Aylesbury HP21 8AL
T: (01296) 315866; Fax: 315268
Founded: 1961; Members: 1000
Focus: Pathology   11806

International Mycological Institute (IMI), Bakeham Ln, Egham TW20 9TV
T: (01784) 470111; E-Mail: imi@cabi.org; Fax: 3321171
Focus: Botany, Specific
Periodicals
Bibliography of Systematic Mycology (semi-annually)
IMI Descriptions of Pathogenic Fungi and Bacteria (semi-annually)
IMI Distribution Maps of Plant Diseases (semi-annually)
Index of Fungi (semi-annually)
Mycopathologia
Systema Ascomycetum (semi-annually)   . 11807

International Numismatic Commission, c/o Dept of Coins and Medals, British Museum, London WC1B 3DG
T: (0171) 3238227; Fax: 3238171
Founded: 1936; Members: 132
Pres: Dr. Cécile Morrisson; Gen Secr: Dr. Andrew Burnett
Focus: Numismatics
Periodicals
Compte rendu (annually)
International Numismatic Newsletter (semi-annually)
. . . . 11808

International Organization of Palaeobotany (I.O.P.), c/o N.E. London Polytechnic, Romford Rd, London E15
T: (0181) 5907722
Founded: 1950; Members: 1300
Focus: Botany   11809

International P.E.N. Writers Association, 9-10 Charterhouse Bldgs, Goswell Rd., London EC1M 7AT
T: (0171) 2534308; Fax: 2535711
Founded: 1921; Members: 13000
Pres: Ronald Harwood; Gen Secr: Alexandre Blokh
Focus: Lit
Periodical
P.E.N. International (semi-annually)   . . . 11810

International Petroleum Industry Environmental Conservation Association (IPIECA), 110 Euston Rd, London NW1
Founded: 1974; Members: 19
Focus: Ecology   11811

International Phonetic Association (IPA), c/o Dept of Linguistics and Phonetics, University of Leeds, Leeds LS2 9JT
T: (01532) 333563
Founded: 1886; Members: 750
Focus: Ling
Periodical
Journal of The International Phonetic Association (bi-annually)   11812

International Psychoanalytical Association (IPA), Broomhills, Woodside Ln, London N12 8UD
T: (0181) 4468324; Fax: 4454729
Founded: 1910; Members: 7200
Focus: Psychoan
Periodicals
Bulletin (annually)
IPA Newsletter (quarterly)
IPA Roster (annually)   11813

International Rubber Study Group (IRSG), York House, Empire Way, Wembley HA9 0PA
T: (0181) 9037727; Fax: 9032848
Founded: 1944; Members: 21
Gen Secr: M.E. Cain
Focus: Materials Sci
Periodicals
International Rubber Digest (monthly)
Outlook for Elastomers (annually)
Proceedings of International Discussion Forum (annually)
Rubber Statistical Bulletin (monthly)
Rubber Statistics Yearbook (annually)   . . 11814

International Seismological Centre (ISC), Pipers Ln, Thatcham, Newbury RG13 4NS
T: (01635) 861022; Fax: 872351
Founded: 1964
Focus: Geology
Periodicals
Bibliography of Seismology (semi-annually)
Bulletin of The International Seismological Centre (monthly)
Felt and Damaging Earthquakes (annually)
Regional Catalogue of Earthquakes (semi-annually)
. . . . 11815

International Society for Microelectronics, Tapestries Coach House, Harbertonford, Devon
Focus: Electronic Eng   11816

International Society for Soil Mechanics and Foundation Engineering (ISSMFE), c/o Engineering Dept, University, Trumpington St, Cambridge CB2 1PZ
T: (01223) 355020; Fax: 359675
Founded: 1936
Focus: Eng
Periodical
ISSMFE News (quarterly)   11817

International Society of Audiology, 330 Gray's Inn Rd, London WC1
Founded: 1952
Focus: Otorhinolaryngology   11818

International Society of Development Biologists (ISDB), Bassett Crescent East, Southampton SO9 3TU
Founded: 1911; Members: 800
Focus: Bio
Periodical
All Differentiation (monthly)   11819

International Society of Neuropathology, c/o National Hospital for Nervous Diseases, Queen Sq, London WC1N 3BG
Focus: Pathology   11820

International Society of Radiographers and Radiological Technicians (ISRRT), 18 Merthyr Rd, Whitchurch, Cardiff CF4 1DG
Founded: 1959; Members: 52
Focus: Radiology   11821

International Special Committee on Radio Interference (CISPR), c/o British Standards Institution, 2 Park St, London W1A 2BS
T: (0171) 6299000; Fax: 6290506
Founded: 1933
Focus: Electric Eng   11822

International Study Group for Mathematics Learning (ISGML), c/o LVCE Research Institute, Ealing Technical College, Woodlands Av, Acton, London W3 9DN
T: (0181) 9926944
Founded: 1961
Focus: Educ; Math   11823

International Tar Conference (ITC), c/o BTJA, 132-135, Sloane St, London SW1X 9BB
T: (0171) 7305212
Founded: 1952
Focus: Materials Sci   11824

International Union Against The Venereal Diseases and The Treponematoses (IUVDT), c/o The Pread Street Clinic, Saint Mary's Hospital, London W2 1NY
T: (0171) 2621123
Founded: 1923
Focus: Venereology   11825

International Union for Quaternary Research, c/o London University, Egham TW20 0EX
T: (01273) 748919; Fax: 748919
Founded: 1928; Members: 37
Focus: Geology
Periodical
Quaternary International (quarterly)   . . . 11826

The International Union of Air Pollution Prevention and Environmental Protection Associations, 136 North St, Brighton BN1 1RG
T: (01273) 326313; E-Mail: admin@nsca.org.uk; Fax: 735802
Founded: 1964; Members: 34
Pres: Dr. A.D. Surridge; Gen Secr: Dr. T. Crossett
Focus: Ecology
Periodicals
Handbook (bi-annually)
Newsletter (quarterly)
World Congress Proceedings   11827

International Union of Crystallography (IUCr), 2 Abbey Sq, Chester CH1 2HU
T: (01244) 345431; E-Mail: execsec@ives.ac.uk; Fax: 344843
Founded: 1947; Members: 40
Pres: Prof. E.N. Baker; Gen Secr: M.H. Dacombe
Focus: Mineralogy
Periodicals
Acta Crystallographica, Section B (bi-monthly)
Acta Crystallographica, Section C (monthly)
Acta Crystallographica, Section D (bi-monthly)
Acta Cystallographica, Section A (monthly)
Journal of Applied Crystallography (bi-monthly)
Journal of Synchrotion Radiation (bi-monthly)
. . . . 11828

International Union of Independent Laboratories / Union Internationale des Laboratoires Independants, c/o Harry Stanger Ltd, The Laboratories, Fortune Ln, Elstree WD6 3HQ
T: (0181) 2073191; Fax: 2074706
Founded: 1960; Members: 780
Focus: Sci   11829

International Union of Nutritional Sciences (IUNS), c/o Institute of Biology, 20 Queensberry Pl, London SW7 2DZ
Founded: 1946; Members: 50
Focus: Nutrition
Periodicals
IUNS Directory (quarterly)
IUNS Newsletter (bi-annually)   11830

International Union of Pure and Applied Chemistry (IUPAC), Bank Court Chambers, 2-3 Pound Way, Templars Sq, Cowley, Oxford, OX4 3YF
T: (01865) 747744; Fax: 747510
Founded: 1919; Members: 45
Focus: Chem
Periodicals
Chemistry International (bi-monthly)
Pure and Applied Chemistry (monthly)   . 11831

International Waterfowl and Wetlands Research Bureau (IWRB), Slimbridge GL2 7BX
T: (01453) 890624, 890634
Founded: 1954
Focus: Ornithology
Periodical
IWRB News (semi-annually)   11832

International Wool Secretariat (IWS), Wool House, 6-7 Carlton Gardens, London SW1Y 5AE
T: (0171) 9307300
Founded: 1937; Members: 980
Focus: Marketing; Textiles   11833

International Wool Study Group (I.W.S.G.), 123 Victoria St, London SW1E 6RB
T: (0171) 2156214
Founded: 1946; Members: 17
Focus: Materials Sci
Periodicals
Wool (quarterly)
Wool Questionnaire (annually)   11834

Interplanetary Space Travel Research Association (ISTRA), 21 Hargwyne St, London SW9
T: (0171) 7334814
Founded: 1957; Members: 6000
Focus: Astronomy   11835

Intractable Pain Society of Great Britain and Ireland (IPS), c/o Dept of Anaesthetics, Derbyshire Royal Infirmary, London Rd, Derby DE1 2QJ
T: (01332) 47141
Founded: 1968; Members: 196
Focus: Anesthetics
Periodical
Forum (2-3 times annually)   11836

Irish Association for Cultural, Economic and Social Relations, 31 Castlehill Rd, Belfast
Focus: Econ; Sociology   11837

Irish Heritage, 32 The Grove, London N3 1QJ
T: (0181) 3462726
Founded: 1973; Members: 509
Pres: Ethna Kennedy
Focus: Lit; Music; Perf Arts   11838

Isle of Man Natural History and Antiquarian Society, c/o Manx Museum, Douglas
Founded: 1879; Members: 850
Focus: Hist; Nat Sci; Archeol
Periodical
Proceedings   11839

Isle of Wight Natural History and Archaeological Society, Island Countryside Centre, Rylstone Gardens, Shanklin PO37 6RG
T: (01983) 867016
Founded: 1919
Pres: Dr. Allan Insole; Gen Secr: Toni Goodley
Focus: Hist; Nat Sci; Archeol
Periodicals
Isle of Wight Birds (annually)
Proceedings (annually)   11840

The Jane Austen Society, Carton House, Medstead, Alton GU34 5PE
T: (01420) 562469; E-Mail: rosemary@sndc.demon.co.uk; Fax: 788842
Founded: 1940; Members: 2100
Pres: Richard Knight; Gen Secr: Susan McCartan
Focus: Lit
Periodicals
Annual Report (annually)
Newsletter (bi-annually)   11841

Jazz Centre Society (JCS), 35 Great Russell St, London WC1
T: (0171) 5808532
Founded: 1968
Focus: Music   11842

Jersey Association of The National Association of Schoolmasters, 3 Palace Close, Bagatelle, Saint Saviour's, Jersey
Focus: Educ   11843

The Jewish Historical Society of England (JHSE), 33 Seymour Pl, London W1H 5AP
T: (0171) 7235852; E-Mail: jhse@dircon.co.uk; Fax: 7235852
Founded: 1893; Members: 900
Pres: Malcolm Brown; Gen Secr: Cyril Drukker
Focus: Hist
Periodical
Transactions (bi-annually)   11844

Johann Strauss Society of Great Britain, 12 Bishams Court, Church Hill, Caterham, CR3 6SE
T: (1883) 349681; Fax: 349681
Founded: 1964; Members: 500
Gen Secr: V.E. Coates
Focus: Music
Periodical
Tritsch-Tratsch (semi-annually)   11845

Johnson Society, c/o Johnson Birthplace Museum, Breadmarket St, Lichfield WS13 6LG
T: (015432) 24972
Founded: 1910; Members: 590
Focus: Lit
Periodical
Transactions (annually)   11846

Johnson Society of London, The Manse, Tower Rd, Hindhead GU26 6SU
T: 4167
Founded: 1928
Focus: Lit   11847

The Joint Association of Classical Teachers (JACT), 31-34 Gordon Sq, London WC1H 0PY
Founded: 1962; Members: 2200
Focus: Hist; Educ
Periodicals
JACT Bulletin
JACT Review (semi-annually)
Omnibus   11848

The Josephine Butler Society, 60 Rotherwick Rd, London NW11 7DB
T: (0181) 4551664
Founded: 1870; Members: 160
Gen Secr: R.M. Cass
Focus: Law
Periodical
News and Views (annually)   11849

Jury System Reform Society (JSRS), 18 Faversham Rd, Beckenham BR3 3PN
Founded: 1979; Members: 1435
Focus: Law
Periodical
Justice for Whom?   11850

Keats-Shelley Memorial Association (K-SMA), 1 Lewis Rd, Radford Semele, Leamington Spa CV31 1UB
T: (0171) 4352062
Founded: 1906; Members: 252
Focus: Lit
Periodical
The Keats-Shelley Review   11851

Kent and Sussex Poetry Society, c/o D.M. Hulse, Costens, Carpenters Ln, Hadlow TN11 0EY
T: (01732) 851404
Founded: 1946; Members: 50
Focus: Lit
Periodical
Poetry Folio (annually)   11852

Kent Archaeological Society (K.A.S.), Three Elms, Woodlands Ln, Shorne, Gravesend DA12 3HH
T: (01474) 822280; E-Mail: 70374.1002@compuserve.com
Founded: 1857; Members: 1620
Pres: K.W.E. Gravett; Gen Secr: A.I. Moffat
Focus: Archeol
Periodical
Archaeologia Cantiana (annually)   . . . 11853

Kent County Agricultural Society, County Showground, Detling, Maidstone ME14 3JF
T: (01622) 630975; Fax: 630978
Founded: 1923; Members: 3000
Focus: Agri
Periodical
Kent View (semi-annually)   11854

Kilvert Society, 91 Hallow Rd, Worcester
Focus: Sci   11855

The Kipling Society, 2 Brownleaf Rd, Brighton BN2 6LB
T: (01273) 303719; Fax: 303719
Founded: 1927; Members: 1000
Pres: Dr. Michael Brock; Gen Secr: Michael Smith
Focus: Lit
Periodical
The Kipling Journal (quarterly)   11856

Laboratory Animal Science Association (LASA), c/o Charing Cross Hospital Medical School, Saint Dunstans Rd, London LS2 9JT
T: (0181) 7482040
Founded: 1963; Members: 360
Focus: Zoology   11857

Lace Research Association (LRA), 7 Gregory Blvd, Nottingham NG7 6LD
T: (01602) 623311
Founded: 1952; Members: 23
Focus: Materials Sci   11858

Lakeland Dialect Society (LDS), 8 Barras Close, Morton Park, Carlisle CA2 6PR
T: (01228) 20539
Founded: 1938; Members: 280
Focus: Ling *11859*

Lancashire and Cheshire Fauna Society, c/o Entomology Dept, Manchester Museum, The University, Manchester M13 9PL
T: (0161) 2733333
Founded: 1914; Members: 200
Focus: Zoology *11860*

Lancashire Dialect Society (L.D.S.), 30 Broadoak Rd., Bramhall, Stockport
T: (0161) 4408272
Founded: 1951; Members: 300
Focus: Ling
Periodical
Journal (annually) *11861*

Lancashire Parish Register Society (LPRS), 65 Hillfield Rd, Hemel Hempstead HP2 4AB
Founded: 1897
Focus: Hist *11862*

Landlife (RPA), The Old Police Station, Lark Ln, Liverpool L17
T: (0151) 7287011; E-Mail: info@landlife.u-net.com; Fax: 7288413
Founded: 1975
Pres: J. Delf; Gen Secr: Sandra Christie
Focus: Ecology
Periodical
Natterjack (semi-annually) *11863*

The Landscape Institute (LI), 6-8 Barnard Mews, London SW11 1QU
T: (0171) 7389166; E-Mail: landscape.institute@dial.pipex.com; Fax: 7389134
Founded: 1929; Members: 4300
Pres: Richard Burden; Gen Secr: Stuart Rayston
Focus: Hort
Periodicals
Landscape Design (10 times annually)
Register of Practices (annually) *11864*

Law Society, 113 Chancery Ln, London WC2A 1PL
T: (0171) 2421222; Fax: 8310344
Founded: 1825; Members: 62439
Gen Secr: Jane Betts
Focus: Law
Periodical
Gazette (weekly) *11865*

Law Society of Scotland, 26 Drumsheugh Gardens, Edinburgh EH3 7YR
T: (0131) 2267411; Fax: 2252934
Founded: 1949; Members: 8268
Focus: Law
Periodicals
Journal (monthly)
Scottish Civil Law Reports (quarterly)
Scottish Criminal Case Reports (quarterly) *11866*

League for the Exchange of Commonwealth Teachers (LECT), 7 Lion Yard, Tremadoc Rd, Clapham, London SW4 7NF
T: (0171) 4981101; Fax: 7205403
Founded: 1901; Members: 3000
Pres: Patricia Swain
Focus: Educ
Periodical
Exchange Teacher: Annual Report (annually)
. . . . *11867*

Leatherhead Food Research Association, Randalls Rd, Leatherhead KT22 7RY
T: (01372) 376761
Founded: 1919; Members: 800
Pres: P.J. Kierstan
Focus: Food
Periodical
Abstracts (monthly) *11868*

Leeds Philosophical and Literary Society, c/o City Museum, Calverley St, Leeds
T: (01532) 2452894
Founded: 1820; Members: 140
Gen Secr: J. Lydon
Focus: Lit; Philos
Periodical
Proceedings (irregularly) *11869*

Leicestershire Archaeological and Historical Society (LAHS), Guildhall, Leicester LE1 5FQ
Founded: 1855; Members: 700
Pres: T.G.M. Brocks; Gen Secr: A.D. McWhirr
Focus: Archeol; Hist *11870*

Leisure Studies Association (LSA), c/o Scottish Tourist Board, 23 Ravelston Terrace, Edinburgh EH4 3EU
T: (0131) 3322433; E-Mail: b.hay@stb.gov.uk; Fax: 3432023
Founded: 1975; Members: 200
Pres: Les Haywood; Gen Secr: Brian Hay
Focus: Travel
Periodicals
Conference Reports (annually)
Leisure Studies (3 times annually) . . . *11871*

Lewis Carroll Society, 55 Heath Cottages, Chislehurst Common BR7 5ND
T: 4675734
Founded: 1969; Members: 235
Focus: Lit *11872*

Library Association (L.A.), 7 Ridgmount St, London WC1E 7AE
T: (0171) 6367543; Fax: 4367218
Founded: 1877; Members: 25000
Gen Secr: Ross Shimmon
Focus: Libraries & Bk Sci
Periodicals
Library Association Record (monthly)
Year Book (annually) *11873*

The Library Association – Personnel, Training and Education Group, c/o Perry Library, South Bank University, 10b Borough Rd, London SE1 0AA
T: (0171) 8156644; Fax: 8156699
Founded: 1968; Members: 1200
Focus: Libraries & Bk Sci
Periodical
Personnel, Training and Education Journal (3 times annually) *11874*

Lincoln Record Society (L.R.S.), c/o Lincoln Cathedral Library, Lincoln LN2 1PZ
T: (01522) 544544; Fax: 511307
Founded: 1910; Members: 340
Pres: Prof. J.C. Holt; Gen Secr: N.H. Bennett
Focus: Hist *11875*

Linguistics Association of Great Britain (L.A.G.B.), c/o Dept of Language and Linguistics, University of York, York YO1 5DD
T: (01904) 432669
Founded: 1959; Members: 700
Pres: Prof. R. Hudson; Gen Secr: Dr. D. Adger
Focus: Ling
Periodical
Journal of Linguistics (semi-annually) . . *11876*

Linnean Society of London, Burlington House, Piccadilly, London W1V 0LQ
T: (0171) 4344479; Fax: 2879364
Founded: 1788; Members: 2000
Pres: Prof. B.G. Gardiner
Focus: Hist; Nat Sci
Periodicals
Biological Journal (monthly)
Botanical Journal (monthly)
The Linnean (3 times annually)
Zoological Journal (monthly) *11877*

The Liszt Society, 9 Burnside Close, Twickenham TW1 1ET
T: (0181) 2875518; E-Mail: 100707.47@compuserve.com; Fax: 2875518
Founded: 1950; Members: 300
Pres: Leslie Howard; Gen Secr: Jan Hoare
Focus: Music
Periodicals
The Liszt Society Journal (annually)
Newsletter (quarterly) *11878*

Literary and Philosophical Society of Liverpool, 13 Hilbre Av, Wallasey L44 5RR
T: (0151) 6384309
Founded: 1812; Members: 50
Focus: Lit; Philos *11879*

Literary and Philosophical Society of Newcastle upon Tyne, 23 Westgate Rd, Newcastle-upon-Tyne NE1 1ST
T: (0191) 2320192
Founded: 1793; Members: 1300
Focus: Lit; Philos; Hist *11880*

Local Population Studies Society (LPSS), 10 Holmbush Rd, London SW15
T: (0181) 7892571
Founded: 1973; Members: 370
Focus: Cultur Hist
Periodicals
Local Population Studies (semi-annually)
LPS Supplements (annually) *11881*

Loch Ness Phenomena Investigation Bureau (LNPIB), c/o Loch Ness Investigation, Drumnadrochit, Invernessshire
Founded: 1961
Focus: Zoology *11882*

London and Middlesex Archaeological Society (LAMAS), c/o Museum of London, 150 London Wall, London EC2Y 5HN
T: (0171) 6003699
Founded: 1855; Members: 608
Pres: Harvey Sheldon; Gen Secr: Malcolm Harden
Focus: Archeol; Hist
Periodicals
Newsletter (3 times annually)
Transactions (annually) *11883*

London Association of Science Teachers (LAST), 61 Crescent Ln, London SW4
Focus: Educ *11884*

London Mathematical Society (L.M.S.), Burlington House, Piccadilly, London W1V 0NL
T: (0171) 4375377; E-Mail: lms@lms.ac.uk; Fax: 4394629
Founded: 1865; Members: 2216
Pres: Prof. J.M. Ball; Gen Secr: Prof. J.S. Pym
Focus: Math
Periodicals
LMS Bulletin (bi-monthly)
LMS Journal (bi-monthly)
LMS Proceedings (bi-monthly)
Nonlinearity (bi-monthly) *11885*

London Medieval Society (LMS), 70 Culverden Rd, London SW12 9LS
T: (0181) 6750335
Founded: 1945; Members: 150
Gen Secr: Robert Webb
Focus: Hist; Ling; Lit; Arts; Hist *11886*

London Metallurgical Society, 43 Melbourne Rd, Wallington, Surrey
Founded: 1966
Focus: Metallurgy *11887*

London Natural History Society (LNHS), Flat 9, Pinewood Ct, London SW4 8LB
Founded: 1858; Members: 1250
Gen Secr: P.C. Holland
Focus: Hist; Nat Sci
Periodicals
London Bird Report (annually)
London Naturalist (annually) *11888*

London Record Society (L.R.S.), c/o Institute of Historical Research, Senate House, Malet St, London WC1E 7HU
T: (0171) 6360272; E-Mail: creaton@sas.ac.uk
Founded: 1964; Members: 360
Pres: H.S. Cobb; Gen Secr: H.J. Creaton
Focus: Hist *11889*

London Society, Senate House, Malet St, London WC1E 7HU
T: (0171) 5805537
Founded: 1912; Members: 520
Pres: Duke of Gloucester; Gen Secr: G.A. Wells
Focus: Urban Plan
Periodical
Journal (semi-annually) *11890*

London Subterranean Survey Association (LSSA), c/o Faculty of Design and The Built Environment, University of East London, Duncan House, High St, London E15 2JB
T: (0181) 5907722 ext 3256
Founded: 1968; Members: 25
Focus: Surveying
Periodical
London's Infrastructure (3 times annually) *11891*

London Topographical Society (LTS), 36 Old Deer Park Gardens, Richmond TW9 2TL
T: (0181) 9405419
Founded: 1880; Members: 900
Pres: Duke of Edinburgh; Gen Secr: Patrick Frazer
Focus: Hist
Periodical
London Topographical News (semi-annually)
. . . . *11892*

London Underground Railway Society (TLURS), 113 Wandle Rd, Morden SM4 6AD
Founded: 1961
Focus: Transport *11893*

London Wargames Section (LWS), 48 East View, Barnet EN5 5TN
Founded: 1967
Focus: Military Sci *11894*

London Welsh Association (LWA), 157 Gray's Inn Rd, London WC1
T: (0171) 8373722
Focus: Ling *11895*

The Lute Society, Southside Cottage, Brook Hill, Albury, Guildford GU5 9DJ
T: (01483) 202159; Fax: 203088
Founded: 1956; Members: 300
Pres: Robert Spencer; Gen Secr: Christopher Goodwin
Focus: Music *11896*

Macmillan Cancer Fund, 15-19 Britten St, London SW3 3TZ
T: (0171) 3517811; Fax: 3768098
Founded: 1911; Members: 5600
Focus: Cell Biol & Cancer Res *11897*

Maghreb Studies Association, c/o The Maghreb Bookshop, 45 Burton St, London WC1H 9AL
T: (0171) 3881840
Founded: 1981
Pres: Prof. H. Bouraoui; Gen Secr: M. Ben-Madani
Focus: Ethnology
Periodical
The Maghreb Review *11898*

Maha Bodhi Society of Sri Lanka (U.K.), The Avenue, London W4 1UD
T: (0181) 9959493; Fax: 9948130
Founded: 1926; Members: 175
Pres: Dr. M. Vajiragnana
Focus: Rel & Theol
Periodical
Samadhi (quarterly) *11899*

The Malacological Society of London, c/o Canterbury Christ Church College, North Holmes Rd, Canterbury CT1 1QU
Founded: 1893; Members: 386
Pres: Dr. J.D. Taylor; Gen Secr: Dr. G.B.J. Dussart
Focus: Zoology
Periodical
The Journal of Molluscan Studies (3 times annually) *11900*

Malone Society, c/o Anne Ashby, Arts and Reference Div, Oxford University Press, Walton St, Oxford OX2 6DP
T: (01865) 58229
Founded: 1906; Members: 750
Pres: Prof. Richard Proudfoot; Gen Secr: Prof. John Creaser
Focus: Lit
Periodicals
Annual Report (annually)
Bulletin (1-2 times annually) *11901*

Management Research Groups (MRG), c/o Institute of Management, Management House, Cottingham Rd, Corby NN17 1TT
T: (01536) 204222; Fax: 201651
Founded: 1926; Members: 280
Focus: Business Admin *11902*

Manchester Geographical Society, 6 Mount St, Manchester M2 5NS
T: (0161) 8342965
Founded: 1884; Members: 120
Gen Secr: Dr. B.P. Hindle
Focus: Geography
Periodical
The Manchester Geographer (annually) . *11903*

Manchester Literary and Philosophical Society, 56 Oxford St, Manchester M60 7HJ
T: (0161) 2283638; Fax: 2369482
Founded: 1781; Members: 500
Pres: Prof. A. Donnachie; Gen Secr: S.C. Diggines
Focus: Lit; Philos
Periodical
Memoirs and Proceedings (annually) . . *11904*

Manchester Medical Society, c/o John Rylands University Library, Oxford Rd, Manchester M13 9PP
T: (0161) 2736048; Fax: 2728046
Founded: 1834; Members: 2250
Focus: Med
Periodical
Annual Report *11905*

Manchester Region Industrial Archaeology Society (M.R.I.A.S.), 5 Hilton Rd, Disley SK12 2JV
T: (01663) 763346
Founded: 1964
Focus: Archeol
Periodical
Newsletter (3 times annually) *11906*

Manchester Statistical Society (MSS), CIS Bldg, Miller St, Manchester M60 0AL
T: (0161) 8374011; Fax: 8375477
Founded: 1833; Members: 220
Pres: David Buckley; Gen Secr: P.K. Berry
Focus: Poli Sci; Econ
Periodical
Transactions of the Manchester Statistical Society (annually) *11907*

Manorial Society of Great Britain (MSGB), 65 Belmont Hill, London SE13 5AX
T: (0181) 8520200
Founded: 1906; Members: 2300
Focus: Genealogy; Hist
Periodical
Bulletin (quarterly) *11908*

Manpower Society, c/o Shell Refining and Marketing Ltd, Shell Centre, London SE1
T: (0171) 9344518
Founded: 1970; Members: 570
Focus: Business Admin *11909*

Mansfield Law Club (MLC), c/o London Guildhall University, 84 Moorgate, London EC2M 6SQ
T: (0171) 3201000; Fax: 3201525
Founded: 1947; Members: 800
Focus: Law *11910*

The Manx Gaelic Society, 3 Glencrutchery Rd, Douglas, Isle of Man
Founded: 1899; Members: 200
Focus: Ling *11911*

Marine Biological Association of the United Kingdom (MBA), The Laboratory, Citadel Hill, Plymouth PL1 2PB
T: (01752) 222772; Fax: 670637
Founded: 1884; Members: 1540
Pres: Sir Crispin Tickell; Gen Secr: Dr. M. Whitfield
Focus: Bio; Oceanography
Periodicals
Journal of The Marine Biological Association of The United Kingdom (quarterly)
MBA News (semi-annually) *11912*

Marine Conservation Society (MCS), Candle Cottage, Kempley, Glos
Founded: 1979; Members: 580
Focus: Ecology
Periodical
Newsletter (quarterly) *11913*

Maritime Information Association (MLA), c/o Marine Society, 202 Lambeth Rd, London SE1 7JW
T: (0171) 2619535; Fax: 4012537
Founded: 1972; Members: 145
Pres: Stephen Rabson; Gen Secr: Mary Shepherd
Focus: Oceanography *11914*

Maritime Trust, 2 Greenwich Church St, London SE10 9BG
T: (0181) 8582698; Fax: 8586976
Founded: 1969; Members: 600
Pres: Philip Duke of Edinburgh; Gen Secr: Alan Stimson
Focus: Preserv Hist Monuments
Periodical
Newsletter of The Friends of The Maritime Trust (semi-annually) 11915

Marlowe Society, 8 Norhyrst Av, London SE26
T: (0181) 6532809
Founded: 1956; Members: 260
Focus: Perf Arts 11916

Marquetry Society, 2a The Ridgeway, Saint Albans AL4 9AU
T: 68241
Founded: 1952; Members: 700
Focus: Fine Arts
Periodical
Marquetarian (quarterly) 11917

Mathematical Association, 259 London Rd, Leicester LE2 3BE
T: (0116) 2703877; Fax: 2448508
Founded: 1871; Members: 6300
Pres: Dr. A.D. Gardiner; Gen Secr: E.R. Ashley
Focus: Math
Periodicals
The Mathematical Gazette (3 times annually)
Mathematics in School (5 times annually) 11918

Mathematical Instruction Subcommittee (MIS), c/o The Royal Society, 6 Carlton House Terrace, London SW1Y 5AG
Founded: 1984
Focus: Educ; Math
Periodical
MIS Newsletter (quarterly) 11919

Measurement and Instrumentation Centre (EVDG), c/o City University, Northampton Sq, London ECIV 0HB
T: (0171) 4778120
Founded: 1894; Members: 70
Focus: Electric Eng
Periodical
Electric Vehicle Developments (quarterly) 11920

Medau Society of Great Britain and Northern Ireland, 220 Balham High Rd, London SW12
T: (0181) 6737333
Founded: 1952; Members: 2140
Focus: Educ 11921

Media Studies Association (MSA), c/o The School of Communication, Trinity and All Saints' College, Browenberrie Ln, Horsforth, Leeds LS18 5HD
T: (01532) 584341
Founded: 1977; Members: 130
Focus: Mass Media
Periodical
Media Reporter (quarterly) 11922

Medical Contact Lens Association (MCLA), Elm Park Rd, London N21
Founded: 1965; Members: 80
Focus: Ophthal 11923

The Medical Defence Union (MDU), 3 Devonshire Pl, London W1N 2EA
T: (0171) 4866181; Fax: 9355503
Founded: 1885; Members: 150000
Focus: Med
Periodicals
Annual Report of The Medical Defence Union (annually)
Healthcare Risk Management Bulletin (quarterly)
International Journal of The Medical Defence Union (quarterly)
Journal of The Medical Defence Union (quarterly)
MDU Nurse (bi-annually) 11924

Medical Officers of Schools Association (M.O.S.A.), 11 Chandos St, London, W1M 0EB
T: (01732) 750586
Founded: 1884; Members: 400
Pres: Dr. Giles Smith; Gen Secr: Dr. Neil D. Arnott
Focus: Public Health
Periodical
Proceedings and Report (annually) . . . 11925

Medical Practices Committee, 80-94 Newington Causeway, London SE1 6EF
T: (0171) 9722930; Fax: 4722985
Focus: Med 11926

Medical Practitioners' Union (MPU), 50 Southwark St, London SE1 1VN
T: (0171) 3787255
Founded: 1914; Members: 5024
Focus: Med
Periodical
Medical World (quarterly) 11927

Medical Protection Society (MPS), 50 Hallam St, London W1N 6DE
T: (0171) 6370541; Fax: 6360690
Founded: 1892
Focus: Med 11928

Medical Research Council (MRC), 20 Park Crescent, London W1N 4AL
T: (0171) 6365422; E-Mail: Medresco London; Fax: 4366179
Founded: 1920
Focus: Med
Periodicals
Annual Report (annually)
Corporate Plan (annually)
Handbook (annually)
MRC News (quarterly)
Scientific Strategy (annually) 11929

Medical Research Society (MRS), c/o Dept of Medicine, Royal Free Hospital, Pond St, London NW3 2QG
T: (0171) 7940500
Focus: Med 11930

Medical Sciences Historical Society, c/o Dental Hospital and School of Dentistry, Liverpool University, Pembroke Pl, Liverpool L3 5PS
T: (0151) 7065201; Fax: 7065845
Focus: Med; Hist 11931

Medical Society for The Study of Radiesthesia (MSSR), 24 Browning Av, Bournemouth BH5 1NN
T: (202) 35149
Members: 19
Focus: Radiology 11932

Medical Society for the Study of Venereal Diseases, 1 Wimpole St, London W1M 8AE
T: (0171) 2902968; E-Mail: sarah.carney@roysocmed.ac.uk; Fax: 2903904
Founded: 1955; Members: 700
Pres: Prof. M.W. Adler; Gen Secr: Dr. Angela J. Robinson
Focus: Venereology 11933

The Medical Society of London, 11 Chandos St, London W1M 0EB
T: (0171) 5801043; Fax: 5805793
Founded: 1773; Members: 558
Focus: Med 11934

Medical Women's Federation (MWF), Tavistock House North, Tavistock Sq, London WC1H 9HX
T: (0171) 3877765; Fax: 3877765
Founded: 1917; Members: 2000
Pres: Dr. Ann Rennie; Gen Secr: Dr. Sheila Glendinning
Focus: Med
Periodical
Medical Woman (3 times annually) . . . 11935

Medico-Legal Society, 15 Saint Botolph St, London EC3A 7NJ
T: (0171) 2472277; Fax: 7828507
Founded: 1901; Members: 650
Pres: Dr. K. Allsopp; Gen Secr: E. Pygott
Focus: Med; Law
Periodical
Medico-Legal Journal (quarterly) 11936

Medieval Combat Society, 20 Winterfold Close, London SW19
T: (0181) 7899307
Focus: Hist 11937

Medieval Settlement Research Group, c/o Planning Dept, County Hall, Bedford MK42 9AP
T: (01234) 228072; Fax: 228232
Founded: 1986; Members: 500
Pres: Prof. Christopher Dyer; Gen Secr: Stephen Coleman
Focus: Hist; Archeol
Periodical
Annual Report (annually) 11938

Men of The Stones (MS), 25 Cromarty Rd, Stamford PE9 2TQ
T: (01780) 53527
Founded: 1947; Members: 600
Focus: Archit
Periodical
Yearbook & Directory (annually) 11939

Mercia Cinema Society, 64 Somerton Dr, Erdington, Birmingham B23 5ST
Founded: 1980; Members: 129
Focus: Cinema
Periodical
Mercia Bioscope (quarterly) 11940

Merioneth Agricultural Society, Tir Y Dail, Cader Rd, Dolgellau, Gwynedd
T: (01341) 422837
Founded: 1868; Members: 500
Focus: Agri
Periodical
Show Catalogue (annually) 11941

Merseyside Archaeological Society (MAS), 14 Southwood Rd, Saint Michaels, Liverpool L17 7BQ
T: (0151) 7288505
Founded: 1977; Members: 120
Focus: Archeol 11942

Mervyn Peake Society (MPS), c/o John Watney, Five Elm Park Gardens, Flat 36, London SW10 9QQ
Founded: 1975; Members: 123
Focus: Lit 11943

Metals Society (MS), 1 Carlton House Terrace, London SW1Y 5DB
T: (0171) 8394071
Founded: 1974; Members: 5000
Focus: Metallurgy
Periodicals
British Corrosion Journal
Metals Abstracts (monthly)
Metals Abstracts Index (monthly)
Metals & Materials (monthly)
Metals Science (monthly)
Metals Technology (monthly)
Powder Metallurgy (quarterly) 11944

Midlands Asthma and Allergy Research Association (MAARA), The Allergy and Asthma Treatment and Research Centre, 12 Vernon St, Derby DE1 1FT
T: (01332) 362461
Founded: 1968
Focus: Immunology 11945

Military Heraldry Society, 37 Wolsey Close, Southall UB2 4NQ
T: (0181) 5744425
Founded: 1951; Members: 325
Pres: W.Y. carman; Gen Secr: J. Barker
Focus: Military Sci
Periodical
Formation Sign (quarterly) 11946

Military Historical Society (MHS), 30 Edgeborough Way, Bromley BR1 2UA
T: (0181) 4607341
Founded: 1948
Focus: Hist; Military Sci
Periodical
Bulletin (quarterly) 11947

Mind Association, c/o Dept of Philosophy, University of Manchester, Manchester M13 9PL
Founded: 1900; Members: 2839
Gen Secr: Cynthia Macdonald
Focus: Philos
Periodical
Mind (quarterly) 11948

MIND – National Association for Mental Health, 15-19 Broadway, London E15 4BQ
T: (0181) 5192122; Fax: 5221725
Founded: 1946
Pres: David Peyer; Gen Secr: J. Clements
Focus: Psychiatry
Periodical
Open Mind (bi-monthly) 11949

Mineralogical Society of Great Britain and Ireland, 41 Queen's Gate, London SW7 5HR
T: (0171) 5847516; Fax: 8288021
Founded: 1876; Members: 1150
Pres: Prof. A.H. Rankin; Gen Secr: Dr. B.A. Cressey
Focus: Mineralogy
Periodicals
Clay Minerals (quarterly)
Mineralogical Abstracts (quarterly)
Mineralogical Magazine (bi-monthly)
Monographs (irregularly) 11950

Minerals Engineering Society (MES), 2 Alder Grove, Stapenhill, Burton-on-Trent DE15 9QR
T: 45510
Founded: 1958; Members: 730
Focus: Mining 11951

Minority Rights Group (MRG), 379 Brixton Rd, London SW9 7DE
T: (0171) 9789498; Fax: 7386265
Founded: 1967
Focus: Law
Periodical
MRG Reports (bi-monthly) 11952

Modern Churchpeople's Union (MCU), 25 Birch Grove, London W3 9SP
T: (0181) 9922333; E-Mail: 101607.2025@compuserve.com; Fax: 9935812
Founded: 1898; Members: 600
Pres: John Saxbee; Gen Secr: Nicholas Henderson
Focus: Rel & Theol
Periodical
Modern Believing (quarterly) 11953

Modern Humanities Research Association (MHRA), c/o Birkbeck College, Malet St, London WC1E 7HX
T: (0171) 6316103
Founded: 1918; Members: 1000
Focus: Lit
Periodicals
Annual Bibliography of English Language and Literature (annually)
Modern Language Review (quarterly)
Portuguese Studies (annually)
Slavonic and East European Review (quarterly)
Yearbook of English Studies (annually)
The Year's Work in Modern Language Studies (annually) 11954

The Montessori Society A.M.I. (UK), 26 Lyndhurst Gardens, London NW3 5NW
T: (0171) 4357874
Founded: 1935
Focus: Educ
Periodical
Quarterly (quarterly) 11955

Monumental Brass Society, c/o Society of Antiquaries of London, Burlington House, Piccadilly, London W1V 0HS
Founded: 1887; Members: 600
Pres: Dr. N.E. Saul; Gen Secr: H.M. Stuchfield
Focus: Preserv Hist Monuments
Periodicals
Bulletin (3 times annually)
Portfolio (irregularly)
Transaction (annually) 11956

Moray Society, 1 High St, Elgin, Moray IV30 1EQ
T: (01343) 543675; Fax: 543675
Founded: 1836; Members: 360
Pres: David Byatt; Gen Secr: Iain Sinclair
Focus: Hist; Archeol; Paleontology . . . 11957

The Morris Ring, 21 Eccles Rd, Ipswich IP2 9RG
T: (01473) 682540
Founded: 1934
Focus: Music 11958

Motor Industry Research Association (MIRA), Watling St, Nuneaton CV10 OTU
T: (01203) 355000; Fax: 355355
Founded: 1946; Members: 180
Pres: Sir John Collyear; Gen Secr: R. Barter
Focus: Auto Eng
Periodicals
Agest for Japan SAE Revlon (3 times annually)
Agest for SAE Publications (annually)
Automobile Abstracts (monthly)
Business News Index (bi-weekly) . . . 11959

The Multiple Sclerosis Society of Great Britain and Northern Ireland, 25 Effie Rd, London SW6 1EE
T: (0171) 6107171; E-Mail: info@mssociety.org.uk; Fax: 7369861
Founded: 1953; Members: 60000
Gen Secr: M. Willis
Focus: Med; Pathology
Periodical
MS Matters (bi-monthly) 11960

Muscular Dystrophy Group of Great Britain & Northern Ireland, 7-11 Prescott Pl, London SW4 6BS
T: (0171) 7208055; Fax: 4980670
Founded: 1959; Members: 425
Pres: Sir Richard Attenborough; Gen Secr: F. Logan
Focus: Med; Pathology
Periodicals
In Focus Newsletter (annually)
The Search (3 times annually) 11961

Museum Attendants Association, c/o City Museum and Art Gallery, Museum Rd, Old Portsmouth PO1 2LJ
T: (705) 811527
Focus: Arts 11962

Museum Training Institute, Glyde House, Glydegate, Bradford BD5 0UP
T: (01274) 391056; Fax: 394890
Founded: 1989
Gen Secr: Chris Newbery
Focus: Arts; Educ
Periodical
News (bi-monthly) 11963

Museums and Galleries Commission, 16 Queen Anne's Gate, London SW1H 9AA
T: (0171) 2334200; Fax: 2333686
Founded: 1931; Members: 15
Pres: James Joll; Gen Secr: Timothy Mason
Focus: Arts
Periodical
Annual Report (annually) 11964

The Museums Association, 42 Clerkenwell Close, London EC1R 0PA
T: (0171) 6082933; Fax: 6082933
Founded: 1889; Members: 3500
Pres: Barbara Woroncow; Gen Secr: Mark Taylor
Focus: Arts
Periodicals
Museum Practice (3 times annually)
Museums Journal (monthly)
Museums Yearbook (annually) 11965

Music Advisers' National Association (MANA), c/o Education Office, 22 Northgate St, Warwick CV34 4SR
T: (01926) 493431 ext 2149
Founded: 1947
Focus: Music; Educ 11966

Musical Box Society of Great Britain (MBSOGB), POB 299, Waterbeach, Cambridge CB4 4PJ
Founded: 1962; Members: 1000
Focus: Music 11967

Names Society, 32 Speer Rd, Thames Ditton KT7 OPW
T: 3980761
Founded: 1967; Members: 390
Focus: Ling 11968

Napoleonic Association (NA), 59 Grimbald Rd, Knaresborough HG5 8HD
T: (0142386) 4857
Founded: 1975; Members: 500
Focus: Military Sci
Periodical
Directory of Wargame Section (annually) 11969

Napoleonic Society, 4 Boscombe Av, London E10 6HY
T: (0181) 5393876
Founded: 1970; Members: 120
Focus: Hist 11970

Narrow Gauge Railway Society (NGRS), 47
Birchington Av, Birchencliffe, Huddersfield HD3
3RD
T: (01422) 74526
Founded: 1951; Members: 800
Focus: Transport *11971*

**National Adult School Organisation
(N.A.S.O.)**, Norfolk House, Smallbrook
Queensway, Birmingham B5 4LJ
T: (0121) 6439297
Founded: 1798; Members: 1500
Focus: Adult Educ
Periodicals
One and All Magazine (monthly)
Study Handbook (annually) *11972*

National Anti-Vivisection Society (NAVS), 261
Goldhawk Rd, London W12 9PE
T: (0171) 8469777; E-Mail: navs@cygnet.co.uk;
Fax: 8469712
Founded: 1875; Members: 30000
Pres: J. Creamer
Focus: Vet Med
Periodical
The Campaigner (bi-annually) *11973*

National Art-Collections Fund (NACF), 7
Cromwell Pl, South Kensington, London SW7 2JN
T: (0171) 8210404
Founded: 1903; Members: 36000
Focus: Arts
Periodical
NACF Magazine (annually) *11974*

**National Association for Environmental
Education (UK) (NAEE)**, c/o Wolverhampton
University, Walsall Campus, Gorway Rd, Walsall
WS1 3BD
T: (01922) 31200; Fax: 31200
Founded: 1960; Members: 1200
Pres: Prof. David Bellamy; Gen Secr: Brian
Milton
Focus: Educ; Ecology
Periodical
Environmental Education (3 times annually)
. . . . *11975*

**National Association for Multiracial
Education (NAME)**, The Northbrook Centre,
Penn Rd, Slough SL2 1PH
T: 23416
Founded: 1966; Members: 515
Focus: Educ *11976*

**National Association for Outdoor Education
(NAOE)**, c/o Scout Dike Outdoor Centre,
Penistone, Sheffield S30 6GF
T: Penistone 2285
Founded: 1969; Members: 450
Focus: Educ *11977*

**National Association for Road Safety
Instruction in Schools**, 16 Woodward Av,
Hendon, London NW4 4NY
T: (0181) 2025787
Founded: 1970
Focus: Educ; Transport *11978*

**National Association for Soviet and East
European Studies (NASEES)**, c/o Faculty of
Social Sciences, Open University, Milton Keynes
MK7 6AA
T: (01908) 653257
Members: 300
Focus: Ethnology *11979*

**National Association for The Relief of
Pagets Disease**, 413 Middleton Rd, Rhodes,
Manchester M24 4QZ
T: (0161) 6431998
Founded: 1973; Members: 500
Focus: Cell Biol & Cancer Res *11980*

**National Association for The Teaching of
English (N.A.T.E.)**, Broadfield Business Centre,
50 Broadfield Rd, Sheffield S8 0XJ
T: (01742) 555419; Fax: 555296
Founded: 1963; Members: 4500
Focus: Ling; Educ
Periodicals
English in Education (3 times annually)
NATE News (3 times annually) *11981*

**National Association of Careers and
Guidance Teachers (NACGT)**, 18 Broad Mead,
Townbridge BA14 9BX
T: 63482
Founded: 1969; Members: 1600
Focus: Adult Educ *11982*

**National Association of Drama Advisers
(NADA)**, c/o Havering Education Authority,
Mercury House, Mercury Gardens, Romford, Essex
T: 66999
Founded: 1960; Members: 75
Focus: Perf Arts *11983*

**National Association of Head Teachers
(NAHT)**, 1 Heath Sq, Boltro Rd, Haywards Heath
RH16 1BJ
T: (01444) 458133
Founded: 1897; Members: 19700
Focus: Educ
Periodical
Head Teachers Review *11984*

**National Association of Language Advisers
(NALA)**, c/o Association for Language Learning,
16 Regent Pl, Rugby CV21 2PN
T: (01788) 526443
Founded: 1983; Members: 140
Focus: Ling *11985*

**National Association of Principal
Agricultural Education Officers (NAPAEO)**,
c/o Bishop Burton College, Bishop Burton,
Beverley HU17 8QG
T: (01964) 550481; Fax: 551190
Members: 50
Focus: Adult Educ; Agri; Hort; Forestry; Fisheries;
Ecology *11986*

**National Association of Schoolmasters
(NASUWT)** / Union of Women Teachers,
Hillscourt Education Centre, Rednal, Birmingham
B45 8R5
T: (0121) 4536150; Fax: 4576209
Founded: 1919; Members: 165501
Gen Secr: Nigel de Gruchy
Focus: Educ
Periodicals
Career Teacher (10 times annually)
Teaching Today (3 times annually) . . . *11987*

**National Association of Teachers in Further
and Higher Education (NATFHE)**, Hamilton
House, Mabledon Pl, London WC1H 9BH
T: (0171) 3876806, 3882745
Founded: 1975; Members: 73000
Focus: Educ; Adult Educ
Periodical
NATFHE Journal (9 times annually) . . *11988*

**National Association of Teachers of The
Mentally Handicapped (NATMH)**, 25 Grecian
St, Aylesbury, Bucks
Founded: 1935
Focus: Educ Handic
Periodical
Teaching and Training (quarterly) . . . *11989*

**National Associations of Teachers of Home
Economics and Technology (NATHE)**,
Hamilton House, Mabledon Pl, London WC1H 9BJ
T: (0171) 3871441; Fax: 3837230
Founded: 1896; Members: 5000
Focus: Educ; Home Econ
Periodical
Modus (10 times annually) *11990*

National Asthma Campaign, Providence House,
Providence Pl, London N1 0NT
T: (0171) 2262260
Founded: 1927
Pres: Duchess of Gloucester
Focus: Pulmon Dis
Periodical
Asthma News (quarterly) *11991*

National Autistic Society (NAS), 276 Willesden
Ln, London NW2 5RB
Founded: 1963; Members: 3500
Focus: Rehabil
Periodicals
Communication (3 times annually)
Connection (3 times annually) *11992*

National Back Pain Association (BPA), 16
Elmtree Rd, Teddington TW11 8ST
T: (0181) 9775474; E-Mail: 101540.1065@
compuserve.com; Fax: 9435318
Founded: 1968; Members: 7500
Pres: Stanley W. Grundy; Gen Secr: John
Nicholas
Focus: Med
Periodical
Talkback (quarterly) *11993*

National Bible Society of Scotland (NBSS),
7 Hampton Terrace, Edinburgh EH12 5XU
T: (0131) 3379701
Founded: 1861
Focus: Rel & Theol *11994*

**National Campaign for Nursery Education
(NCNE)**, 23 Albert St, London NW1 7LU
Founded: 1966; Members: 180
Focus: Educ; Public Health *11995*

**National Christian Education Council
(NCEC)**, 1020 Bristol Rd, Selly Oak, Birmingham
B29 6LB
T: (0121) 4724242; E-Mail: ncec@netlink.co.uk;
Fax: 4727575
Founded: 1803
Focus: Educ *11996*

**National Conference of University
Professors**, c/o Biological and Nutritional
Sciences, University of Newcastle upon Tyne,
Newcastle upon Tyne NE1 7RU
T: (0191) 2227886; Fax: 2226720
Founded: 1989; Members: 640
Pres: Prof. J.E. Walsh; Gen Secr: Prof. W.J.
Cram
Focus: Educ *11997*

**National Council for Educational
Technology**, Milburn Hill Rd, Science Park,
Coventry CV4 7JJ
T: (01203) 416994; Fax: 411418
Founded: 1988; Members: 80
Gen Secr: Margaret Bell
Focus: Educ
Periodical
British Journal of Educational Technology (3 times
annually) *11998*

National Council of Corrosion Societies, 1
Carlton House Terrace, London SW1Y 5DB
Focus: Metallurgy *11999*

**National Council of Jewish Religious Day
Schools**, 5 The Bishop's Av, London N2
T: (0181) 4445117
Focus: Rel & Theol; Educ *12000*

National Council of Psycho-Therapists, 1
Clovelly Rd, London W5
T: (0181) 5670262
Focus: Psych; Therapeutics *12001*

National Eczema Society, 4 Tavistock Pl,
London WC1H 9RA
T: (0171) 3884097; Fax: 7130733
Founded: 1976; Members: 10000
Focus: Derm
Periodical
Exchange (quarterly) *12002*

National Education Association (NEA),
Highcroft, Tewin Close, Tewin Wood, Herts
T: 262
Founded: 1970; Members: 33000
Focus: Educ *12003*

**National Federation of Continuative
Teachers' Associations (NFCTA)**, 110 North
Cray Rd, Bexley DA5 3NA
T: 7038029
Founded: 1920
Focus: Adult Educ *12004*

**National Federation of Sailing Schools
(NFSS)**, c/o Lymington Seamanship and Sailing
Centre, 21 New St, Lymington SO4 9BH
T: (01590) 77601
Founded: 1964; Members: 48
Focus: Sports *12005*

**National Federation of Voluntary Literacy
Schemes (NFVLS)**, 131 Camberwell Rd, London
SE5 0HF
T: (0171) 7038083
Founded: 1977
Focus: Adult Educ
Periodical
Wall Paper (quarterly) *12006*

**National Foundation for Educational
Research in England and Wales (NFER)**,
The Mere, Upton Park, Slough SL1 2DQ
T: (0175) 74123
Founded: 1947
Focus: Educ; Adult Educ
Periodicals
Educational Research (3 times annually)
Educational Research News
Research Reports *12007*

**National Foundry and Engineering Training
Association (NFETA)**, Fleming House, Renfrew
St, Glasgow G3 6TG
T: (0141) 3320826
Founded: 1966; Members: 300
Focus: Adult Educ; Eng; Metallurgy . . *12008*

**National Housing and Town Planning
Council (NHTPC)**, 14-18 Old St, London EC1V
9AB
T: (0171) 2512363; Fax: 6082830
Founded: 1900; Members: 400
Pres: Kelvin MacDonald
Focus: Urban Plan
Periodical
Housing and Planning Review (bi-monthly) *12009*

National Institute for Medical Research, The
Ridgeway, Mill Hill, London NW7 1AA
T: (0181) 9593666
Founded: 1920
Focus: Med *12010*

National Institute for Social Work (NISW), 5
Tavistock Pl, London WC1H 9SN
T: (0171) 3879681; Fax: 3877968
Founded: 1961
Pres: Sir Peter Barclay; Gen Secr: Daphne
Statham
Focus: Sociology
Periodical
Social Care Update (monthly) *12011*

**National Institute of Adult Continuing
Education (England and Wales) (NIACE)**, 21
De Montfort St, Leicester LE1 7GE
T: (0116) 2551451; E-Mail: niace@niace.org.uk;
Fax: 2854514
Founded: 1949
Gen Secr: Alan Tuckett
Focus: Adult Educ
Periodicals
Adults Learning (monthly)
Studies in The Education of Adults (semi-
annually)
Time to Learn (semi-annually)
Year Book of Adult Continuing Education
(annually) *12012*

**National Institute of Agricultural Botany
(NIAB)**, Huntingdon Rd, Cambridge CB3 0LE
T: (01223) 76381
Founded: 1919; Members: 5340
Focus: Botany *12013*

**National Institute of Economic and Social
Research (NIESR)**, 2 Dean Trench St, London
SW1P 3HE
T: (0171) 2227665; E-Mail: jkirkland@niesr.oc.uk;
Fax: 2221435
Founded: 1938
Focus: Soc Sci; Econ

Periodicals
National Institute Discussion Papers (irregularly)
National Institute Economic Review (quarterly)
National Institute Occasional Papers (irregularly)
. . . . *12014*

**National Institute of Industrial Psychology
(NIIP)**, The Mere, Upton Park, Slough SL1 2DQ
Founded: 1921
Focus: Psych *12015*

**National Institute of Medical Herbalists
(NIMH)**, 56 Longbrook St, Exeter EX4 6AH
T: (01392) 426022; Fax: 498963
Founded: 1864; Members: 385
Pres: Christine Steward; Gen Secr: Janet Hicks
Focus: Med *12016*

National Materials Handling Centre (NMHC),
c/o Cranfield Institute of Technology, Cranfield,
Bedford MK43 0AL
T: (01234) 750323; Fax: 750875
Members: 300
Focus: Materials Sci
Periodical
International Distribution & Handling Review (bi-
monthly) *12017*

**National Operatic and Dramatic Association
(NODA)**, 1 Crestfield St, London WC1H 8AU
T: (0171) 8375655; Fax: 8330609
Founded: 1899; Members: 3000
Focus: Perf Arts
Periodical
NODA National News (semi-annually) . . *12018*

National Secular Society, 702 Holloway Rd,
London N19 3NL
T: (0171) 2721266
Founded: 1866
Focus: Philos *12019*

**National Society (Church of England) for
Promoting Religious Education**, Church
House, Great Smith St, London SW1P 3NZ
T: (0171) 2221672; Fax: 2332572
Founded: 1811
Gen Secr: Geoffrey Duncan
Focus: Rel & Theol; Educ
Periodicals
News (3-4 times annually)
Together with Children (9 times annually) *12020*

**National Society for Clean Air and
Environmental Protection (NSCA)**, 136 North
St, Brighton BN1 1RG
T: (01273) 326313; E-Mail: admin@nsca.org.uk;
Fax: 735802
Founded: 1899; Members: 1500
Pres: Dame Barbara Clayton; Gen Secr: Richard
Mills
Focus: Ecology
Periodicals
Clean Air and Environmental Protection (bi-
monthly)
NSCA Members' Handbook (annually)
Proceedings of Annual Conferences and Seminars
(annually)
Workshop Proceedings (annually) . . . *12021*

**National Society for Education in Art and
Design (NSEAD)**, The Gatehouse, Corsham
Court, Corsham SN13 0BZ
T: (01249) 714825; E-Mail: 100436.3040@
compuserve.com; Fax: 716138
Founded: 1888; Members: 2500
Pres: Prof. Arthur Hughes; Gen Secr: John
Steers
Focus: Arts; Educ
Periodical
Journal of Art & Design Education: NSEAD
Newsletter (3 times annually) *12022*

National Society for Epilepsy (N.S.E.),
Chalfont Centre for Epilepsy, Chalfont Saint Peter,
Gerrards Cross SL9 0RJ
T: (01494) 601300; Fax: 871927
Founded: 1892
Focus: Neurology *12023*

**National Society for Research into Allergy
(NSRA)**, POB 45, Hinckley LE10 1JY
T: (01455) 851546; E-Mail: allergy@dial.pipex.com;
Fax: 851546
Founded: 1980
Gen Secr: Eunice L. Rose
Focus: Immunology
Periodical
Reaction (quarterly) *12024*

National Society for Transplant Surgery, 11
Alma Rd, Cardiff CF2 5BD
T: (01222) 40039
Founded: 1968
Focus: Surgery *12025*

**National Strict Baptist Sunday School
Association (NSBSSA)**, 87 Pynchbek, Bishops
Stortford, Essex
Founded: 1938; Members: 200
Focus: Rel & Theol; Educ
Periodical
Go Teach (quarterly) *12026*

National Trolleybus Association (NTA), 10
Compton Close, Flitwick, Bedford MK45 1TA
T: (01525) 752077
Founded: 1963; Members: 650
Focus: Transport
Periodical
Trolleybus Magazine (bi-monthly) *12027*

National Trust for Places of Historic Interest or Natural Beauty, 36 Queen Anne's Gate, London SW1H 9AS
T: (0171) 2229251; Fax: 2225097
Founded: 1895; Members: 2400000
Pres: Charles Nunneley; Gen Secr: Martin Drury
Focus: Preserv Hist Monuments; Ecology
Periodicals
Annual Report (annually)
Members' and Visitors' Handbook
Newsletter
Properties of The National Trust 12028

National Trust for Scotland, 5 Charlotte Sq, Edinburgh EH2 4DU
T: (0131) 2265922; Fax: 2439501
Founded: 1931; Members: 237000
Focus: Preserv Hist Monuments; Ecology
Periodicals
The Educational Guide to NTS
Guide to Properties
Heritage Scotland (quarterly)
Welcome 12029

National Union of Teachers (N.U.T.), Hamilton House, Mabledon Pl, London WC1H 9BD
T: (0171) 3886191; Fax: 3878458
Founded: 1870; Members: 185500
Focus: Educ
Periodicals
Annual Report (annually)
Education Review (semi-annually)
The Teacher (8 times annually) 12030

Natural Environment Research Council (NERC), Polaris House, North Star Av, Swindon SN2 1EU
T: (01793) 411500; Fax: 411501
Founded: 1965
Focus: Nat Sci
Periodicals
Annual Report (annually)
NERC News (quarterly) 12031

The Natural History Society of Northumbria, c/o Hancock Museum, Newcastle-upon-Tyne NE2 4PT
T: (0191) 2326386
Founded: 1829; Members: 850
Pres: Duke of Northumberland; Gen Secr: David Noble-Rollin
Focus: Hist; Nat Sci
Periodical
Transactions (annually) 12032

The Nautical Institute, 202 Lambeth Rd, London SE1 7LQ
T: (0171) 9281351
Founded: 1972; Members: 6000
Focus: Navig
Periodical
Seaways (monthly) 12033

Navy Records Society, Chatsworth House, 66-70 Saint Mary Axe, London EC3A 8BD
Fax: (071) 3825400
Founded: 1893; Members: 800
Focus: Hist
Periodical
Annual Report (annually) 12034

Neonatal Society, c/o Dept of Child Health, Hospital, Nottingham NG7 2UH
T: (0115) 9709257; E-Mail: michael.symonds@nottingham.ac.uk; Fax: 9709382
Founded: 1959; Members: 400
Gen Secr: Dr. Michael Symonds
Focus: Physiology
Periodical
Early Human Development (3 times annually)
. . . . 12035

New English Art Club, 17 Carlton House Terrace, London SW1Y 5BD
T: (0171) 9306844; Fax: 8397830
Founded: 1886; Members: 55
Gen Secr: William Bowyer
Focus: Arts
Periodical
Catalogue of Annual Exhibition (annually) 12036

Newark and Nottinghamshire Agricultural Society, The Showground, Winthorpe, Newark NG24 2NY
T: (01636) 702627
Founded: 1799; Members: 2500
Focus: Agri
Periodical
Catalogue (annually) 12037

The Newcomen Society, c/o Science Museum, South Kensington, London SW7 2DD
T: (0171) 5891793; Fax: 5891793
Founded: 1920; Members: 1000
Focus: Hist; Eng
Periodicals
Bulletin (3 times annually)
Transactions (annually) 12038

Newcomen Society for the Study of the History of Engineering and Technology, c/o Science Museum, Exhibition Rd, South Kensington, London SW7 2DD
T: (0171) 5891793; Fax: 5891793
Founded: 1920
Focus: Hist; Eng 12039

Nicholas Roerich Society, 91 Fitzjohn's Av, London NW3 6NX
T: (0171) 4355490
Focus: Lit 12040

NICOD, 31 Ulsterville Av, Belfast BT9 7AS
T: (01232) 666188; Fax: 682400
Founded: 1941; Members: 150
Focus: Orthopedics
Periodical
Annual Report (annually) 12041

Norfolk and Norwich Archaeological Society, Garsett House, Saint Andrew's Hall Plain, Norwich NR3 1AT
T: (01603) 455913
Founded: 1846; Members: 609
Pres: Mary Manning; Gen Secr: Roger Bellinger
Focus: Archeol
Periodical
Norfolk Archaelogy (annually) 12042

Norfolk Record Society, 17 Christchurch Rd, Norwich NR2 2AE
T: (01603) 453004
Founded: 1931; Members: 250
Pres: Sir Timothy Colman; Gen Secr: B. Miller
Focus: Hist
Periodical
Anytitles (annually) 12043

The North of England Zoological Society (N.E.Z.S.), c/o Zoological Garden, Upton, Chester CH2 1LH
T: (01244) 380280; Fax: 371273
Founded: 1934; Members: 3300
Focus: Zoology
Periodical
Chester Zoo Life (3 times annually) . . 12044

North Somerset Agricultural Society, 5 Thiery Rd, Brislington, Bristol BS4 2NX
T: (01272) 778463
Focus: Agri 12045

North Staffordshire Field Club, c/o School of Sciences, Staffordshire University, College Rd, Stoke-on-Trent ST4 2DE
T: (01782) 744531
Founded: 1865; Members: 260
Focus: Archeol; Hist; Nat Sci
Periodical
Transactions (annually) 12046

North Tyne and Redesdale Agricultural Society, Stobswood House, Stobswood, Morpeth NE61 5QA
Focus: Agri 12047

North Wales Agricultural Society, Rhos-y-Wylfa, Nant-y-Garth, Portdinorwic LL56 4QB
T: (01248) 670531
Focus: Agri 12048

North Wales Arts Association, 10 Wellfield House, Bangor LL57 1ER
T: (01248) 353248; Fax: 351077
Founded: 1967
Focus: Arts
Periodicals
Ben Bowen Thomas Lecture (annually)
Report (annually) 12049

North West Regional Association of Industrial Safety Groups, 1 Moor Av, Penwortham, Preston PR1 0ND
T: (01305) 42603
Founded: 1959
Focus: Safety 12050

North Western Naturalists' Union (NWNU), 59 Moss Ln, Bramhall, Stockport SK7 1EQ
T: (0161) 4392899
Founded: 1929
Focus: Nat Sci
Periodicals
Newsletter (quarterly)
North Western Naturalist (annually) . . . 12051

North Western Society for Industrial Archaeology and History (NWSIAH), c/o Merseyside County Museum, William Brown St, Liverpool L3 8EN
T: (0151) 2070001
Founded: 1964; Members: 120
Focus: Archeol; Hist 12052

Northamptonshire Archaeological Society (NAS), 54 The Knoll, Earls Barton, Northants
Founded: 1974; Members: 180
Focus: Archeol 12053

Northamptonshire Natural History Society and Field Club (N.N.H.S.), Humfrey Rooms, 10 Castilian Terrace, Northampton NN1 1LD
T: (01604) 604529
Founded: 1876; Members: 440
Pres: A. Kingsland
Focus: Hist; Nat Sci; Archeol; Astronomy; Botany; Photo; Zoology; Ornithology; Geology
Periodical
Journal (annually) 12054

Northamptonshire Record Society, Wootton Hall Park, Northampton NN4 8BQ
T: (01604) 762297
Founded: 1920; Members: 1000
Pres: Sir Hereward Wake; Gen Secr: L.C. Skelton
Focus: Hist
Periodical
Northamptonshire Past & Present (annually)
. . . . 12055

Northern Horticultural Society, c/o Harlow Carr Botanical Gardens, Crag Ln, Harrogate HG3 1QB
T: (01423) 565418
Founded: 1946; Members: 10500
Focus: Hort
Periodicals
Index Seminum (annually)
The Northern Gardener (quarterly) . . . 12056

Northern Ireland Association for Mental Health, 80 University St, Belfast BT7 1HE
T: (01232) 328474; E-Mail: niamhbel@aol.com.; Fax: 200335
Founded: 1959; Members: 160
Pres: Dr. Ken Dannan; Gen Secr: Alan Ferguson
Focus: Psychiatry
Periodical
Mental Health Matters (3 times annually) 12057

Northern Ireland Chest, Heart and Stroke Association, 21 Dublin Rd, Belfast BT2 7FJ
T: (01232) 320184
Focus: Cardiol; Pulmon Dis; Rehabil
Periodical
Masterstroke (quarterly) 12058

Northern Ireland Polio Fellowship (NIPF), 198 Belvoir Dr, Belvoir Park, Belfast BT8 4PJ
T: (01232) 643367
Founded: 1948
Focus: Med 12059

Nutrition Society, 10 Cambridge Court, 210 Shepherds Bush Rd, London W6 7NJ
Founded: 1941; Members: 1350
Pres: Prof. A.J.F. Webster
Focus: Food
Periodicals
The British Journal of The Nutrition Society (bi-monthly)
The Proceedings of The Nutrition Society (3 times annually) 12060

Odinic Rite (O.R.), BCM Runic, London WC1N 3XX
Founded: 1973
Focus: Rel & Theol
Periodicals
OR Briefing (monthly)
Rimstock (annually) 12061

Oil and Colour Chemists' Association, 967 Harrow Rd, Wembley HA0 2SF
T: (0181) 9081086; E-Mail: enquiries@occa.org.uk; Fax: 9081219
Founded: 1918; Members: 2500
Pres: R. Staples; Gen Secr: C. Pacey-Day
Focus: Chem
Periodical
Surface Coating's International (monthly) . 12062

Omnibus Society (OS), 103a Streatham Hill, London SW2 4UD
T: (0181) 6745280
Founded: 1929; Members: 1000
Focus: Transport 12063

Open and Distance Learning Quality Council, 27 Marylebone Rd, London NW1 5JS
T: (0171) 9355391; Fax: 9352540
Founded: 1968
Focus: Educ 12064

Open Spaces Society, 25a Bell St, Henley-on-Thames RG9 2BA
T: (01491) 573535
Founded: 1865
Focus: Urban Plan 12065

Operational Research Society (ORS), Neville House, Waterloo St, Birmingham B2 5TX
T: (0121) 6430236; Fax: 6313485
Founded: 1954; Members: 3000
Focus: Computer & Info Sci
Periodicals
European Journal of Information Systems (monthly)
Insight (quarterly)
Journal of The Operational Research Society (monthly)
Newsletter (monthly) 12066

Orders and Medals Research Society (OMRS), 123 Turnpike Link, Croydon CR0 5NU
T: (0181) 6802701
Founded: 1942; Members: 2700
Gen Secr: N.G. Gooding
Focus: Military Sci; Hist
Periodical
Orders & Medals (quarterly) 12067

Organisation Internationale pour l'Etude de l'Endurance des Cables (OIPEEC), c/o Dept of Enigineering, University of Reading, POB 225, Reading RG6 6AY
T: (0118) 9318580; E-Mail: C.R.Chaplin@reading.ac.uk; Fax: 2358017
Founded: 1963
Pres: Prof. C.R. Chaplin
Focus: Materials Sci 12068

Organisation of Professional Users of Statistics (OPUS), Lancaster House, More Ln, Esher, Surrey
T: 63121
Members: 5
Focus: Stats 12069

Organisation of Teachers of Transport Studies (OTTS), c/o Southall College of Technology, Beaconsfield Rd, Southall UB1 1DP
T: (0181) 5743448
Founded: 1971; Members: 102
Focus: Educ; Transport
Periodical
Seminar & Annual Report (annually) . . 12070

The Oriental Ceramic Society (OCS), 30b Torrington Sq, London WC1E 7JL
T: (0171) 6367985; Fax: 5806749
Founded: 1921; Members: 1100
Pres: Dr. Jessica Rawson; Gen Secr: Jean Martin
Focus: Arts
Periodical
Transactions of The Oriental Ceramic Society (annually) 12071

Oriental Numismatic Society (ONS), 30 Warren Rd, Woodley, Reading RG5 3AR
T: (01189) 693528
Founded: 1970; Members: 535
Gen Secr: Michael Broome
Focus: Numismatics
Periodical
ONS Newsletter (5-6 times annually) . . 12072

Ornithological Society of The Middle East (OSME), The Lodge, Sandy SG19 2DL
T: (01767) 80551
Founded: 1967; Members: 850
Focus: Ornithology
Periodicals
Bulletin (semi-annually)
Sandgrouse (annually) 12073

Osteopathic Association of Great Britain (OAGB), 1-4 Suffolk St, London SW1Y 4HG
T: (011) 292056
Founded: 1925; Members: 347
Focus: Pathology
Periodicals
British Osteopathic Journal
Osteopathic Newsletter (monthly) 12074

Overseas Doctors Association in The UK (ODA), 28-32 Princess St, Manchester M1 4LB
T: (0161) 236 5594
Founded: 1975; Members: 61283
Focus: Med
Periodical
News Review (bi-monthly) 12075

Oxford Centre for Islamic Studies, c/o Saint Cross College, Oxford OX1 3TU
T: (01865) 725077; Fax: 248942
Founded: 1985
Focus: Rel & Theol
Periodical
Journal of Islamic Studies (semi-annually) 12076

Oxford Preservation Trust, 10 Turn Again Ln, Saint Ebbes, Oxford OX1 1QL
T: (01865) 242918
Founded: 1927; Members: 1000
Pres: Sir David Yardley; Gen Secr: Moyra Haynes
Focus: Preserv Hist Monuments; Ecology
Periodical
Annual Report (annually) 12077

Oxford University Archaeological Society (OUAS), c/o Ashmolean Museum, Oxford
Founded: 1911; Members: 300
Focus: Archeol 12078

Oxfordshire Architectural and Historical Society (OAHS), 3 Wytham St, Oxford OXI 4SO
T: (01865) 245262
Founded: 1839; Members: 370
Focus: Archit; Hist; Archeol
Periodical
Oxoniensia (monthly) 12079

Oxfordshire Record Society (O.R.S.), c/o Bodleian Library, Oxford OX1 3BG
Founded: 1919; Members: 350
Focus: Hist 12080

Paediatric Welfare and Research Association, 22 Tytherington Dr, Tytherington, Macclesfield, Cheshire
T: (01625) 25228
Founded: 1968; Members: 102
Focus: Pediatrics 12081

Paint Research Association (PRA), 8 Waldegrave Rd, Teddington TW11 8LD
T: (0181) 9774427; Fax: 9434705
Founded: 1926; Members: 180
Focus: Materials Sci
Periodicals
Coating Regulations and Environmental Issues (monthly)
Comet (monthly)
Paint Titles (weekly)
PRA Newsletter (6 times monthly)
World Surface Coating Abstracts (monthly) 12082

Palaeontographical Society, c/o British Geological Survey, Keyworth, Nottingham NG12 5GG
Founded: 1847
Pres: M. House; Gen Secr: S.P. Tunnicliff
Focus: Paleontology 12083

Palestine Exploration Fund, 2 Hinde Mews, Marylebone Ln, London W1M 5RR
T: (0171) 9355379
Founded: 1865
Pres: Archbishop of Canterbury; Gen Secr: Yolande Hodson
Focus: Geography; Archeol; Hist
Periodical
Palestine Exploration Quarterly (semi-annually) . . . 12084

Pali Text Society (PTS), 62 South Lodge, Circus Rd, London NW8 9ET
T: (0171) 2864280
Founded: 1881
Focus: Lit . . . 12085

Parkinson's Disease Society of The United Kingdom (PDS), 22 Upper Woburn Pl, London WC1H 0RA
T: (0171) 3833513; Fax: 3835754
Founded: 1969; Members: 40000
Gen Secr: Barry Brooking
Focus: Med; Neurology
Periodical
The Parkinson Newsletter (3-4 times annually) . . . 12086

Parliamentary and Scientific Committee, 16 Great College St, London SW1P 3RX
T: (0171) 2227085
Focus: Sci; Eng
Periodical
Science in Parliament (5 times annually) 12087

Parrot Society, 19A De Parys, Bedford
T: (01234) 58922
Founded: 1966; Members: 4000
Focus: Ornithology
Periodical
Magazine (monthly) . . . 12088

Pastel Society, 17 Carlton House Terrace, London SW1Y 5BD
T: (0171) 9306844; Fax: 8397830
Members: 60
Pres: Tom Coates
Focus: Arts; Fine Arts
Periodical
Annual Catalogue (annually) . . . 12089

Pathological Society of Great Britain and Ireland, 2 Carlton House Terrace, London SW1Y 5AF
T: (0171) 9761260; E-Mail: administrator@pathsoc.org.uk; Fax: 9761267
Founded: 1906; Members: 1600
Gen Secr: Prof. F. Walker
Focus: Pathology
Periodicals
Journal of Medical Microbiology (monthly)
Journal of Pathology (monthly)
Reviews in Medical Microbiology (quarterly) . . . 12090

Peak District Mines Historical Society (PDMHS), 85 Peveril Rd, Beeston, Nottingham
T: (01602) 257945
Founded: 1959
Focus: Mining; Hist . . . 12091

Peakland Archaeological Society, 12 The Crescent, Hayfield Rd, Chapel in le Frith, Stockport
Focus: Archeol . . . 12092

Pembrokeshire Agricultural Society, Withybush Airfield, Haverfordwest, Dyfed
Focus: Agri . . . 12093

Pembrokeshire Historical Society, Dolan Dwrbach, Scloddau Fishguard SA65 9RN
T: 3707
Founded: 1950; Members: 150
Focus: Hist
Periodical
Journal of The Pembrokeshire Historical Society (annually) . . . 12094

P.E.N. English Centre, 7 Dilke St, London SW3 4JE
T: (0171) 3526303
Founded: 1921
Focus: Lit . . . 12095

Perthshire Society of Natural Science (PSNS), c/o Museum, George St, Perth
T: (01738) 32488
Founded: 1867
Focus: Nat Sci
Periodical
The Journal of The Perthshire Society of Natural Science (bi-annually) . . . 12096

Peter Warlock Society, 32a Chipperfield House, Cale St, London SW3 3SA
T: (0171) 5899595; Fax: 5899595
Founded: 1963; Members: 250
Pres: Richard Rodney Bennett; Gen Secr: Malcolm Rudland
Focus: Music
Periodical
Newsletter (bi-annually) . . . 12097

Petroleum Exploration Society of Great Britain (PESGB), 6 Saint James's Sq, London SW1
Founded: 1965; Members: 960
Focus: Geology . . . 12098

Pharmaceutical Society of Northern Ireland (PSNI), 73 University St, Belfast BT7 1HL
T: (01232) 326927; Fax: 439919
Founded: 1925; Members: 1400
Focus: Pharmacol . . . 12099

The Philological Society, c/o School of Oriental and African Studies, Thornhaugh St, Russell Sq, London WC1H 0XG
T: (0171) 3236318; Fax: 4363844
Founded: 1842; Members: 704
Pres: Prof. R. Posner; Gen Secr: Prof. R.J. Hayward
Focus: Ling
Periodical
Transactions (semi-annually) . . . 12100

Philosophical Society of England, King George VI Bldg, University of Newcastle upon Tyne, Newcastle upon Tyne NE1 7RU
T: (0191) 2226796; Fax: 227090
Founded: 1913
Gen Secr: Michael Bavidge
Focus: Philos
Periodical
The Philosopher . . . 12101

Philosophy of Education Society of Great Britain, c/o Education Centre, New University of Ulster, Coleraine, Ulster
T: 4141
Founded: 1964; Members: 560
Focus: Philos; Educ . . . 12102

The Photogrammetric Society, c/o Dept of Photogrammetry and Surveying, University College London, Gower St, London WC1E 6BT
T: (0171) 3877050; Fax: 3800453
Founded: 1952; Members: 500
Pres: Dr. R.P. Kirby; Gen Secr: Dr. S. Robson
Focus: Surveying
Periodical
The Photogrammetric Record (semi-annually) . . . 12103

Physiological Society, POB 506, Oxford OX1 3XE
T: (01865) 798498; Fax: 798092
Founded: 1876; Members: 1800
Gen Secr: Dr. C.A.R. Boyd
Focus: Physiology
Periodicals
Experimental Physiology (bi-monthly)
The Journal of Physiology (14 times annually) . . . 12104

Phytochemical Society of Europe (PSE), c/o Department of Plant Sciences, University of Oxford, South Parks Rd, Oxford OX1 3RB
T: (01865) 275000; E-Mail: george.ratcliffe@plant.sciences.oxford.ac.uk; Fax: 275074
Founded: 1957; Members: 500
Focus: Botany; Chem; Biochem; Physiology; Pharmacol
Periodical
PSE Symposia (annually) . . . 12105

Pipe Roll Society, c/o Public Record Office, Chancery Ln, London WC2A 1LR
T: (0171) 4050741
Founded: 1883; Members: 300
Focus: Hist
Periodical
Annual Report (annually) . . . 12106

Pira International, Randalls Rd, Leatherhead KT22 7RU
T: (01372) 376161; Fax: 360104
Founded: 1965; Members: 1000
Focus: Eng
Periodicals
DTP Publishing Commentary (10 times annually)
International Packaging Abstracts (monthly)
Now-World Publishing Monitor
Paper and Board Abstracts (monthly)
Paper Technology (monthly)
Printing Abstracts (monthly)
UK Printing Industry Statistics (annually) . 12107

Plainsong and Mediaeval Music Society, c/o Dr. Stephen Farmer, Magdalene College, Cambridge CB3 0AG
Founded: 1888; Members: 320
Pres: Prof. Sir Henry Chadwick; Gen Secr: Dr. C. Page
Focus: Music
Periodical
Plainsong and Mediaeval Music (semi-annually) . . . 12108

Planning Officers Society (POS), c/o Thameside Metropolitan Borough Council, Wellington Rd, Ashton-under-Lyne OL6 6DL
T: (0161) 3423107; Fax: 3423111
Founded: 1997
Gen Secr: Keith Hamilton
Focus: Urban Plan
Periodical
Newsletter (quarterly) . . . 12109

The Plastics and Rubber Institute (PRI), 11 Hobart Pl, London SW1W 0HL
T: (0171) 2459555; Fax: 8231379
Founded: 1975; Members: 10000
Focus: Materials Sci
Periodicals
Plastics and Rubber International (bi-monthly)
Plastics and Rubber Processing and Applications (quarterly)
Progress in Rubber and Plastic Technology (quarterly) . . . 12110

Play Matters – National Association of Toy and Leisure Libraries, 68 Churchway, London NW1 1LT
T: (0171) 3879592; Fax: 3832714
Founded: 1976; Members: 950
Focus: Libraries & Bk Sci
Periodicals
ARK Newsletter (quarterly)
Good Toy Guide (annually) . . . 12111

The Plymouth Athenaeum, Derry's Cross, Plymouth PL1 2SW
T: (01752) 266079
Founded: 1812; Members: 430
Focus: Sci; Arts . . . 12112

Poetry Society (PS), 22 Betterton St, London WC2H 9BU
T: (0171) 2404810; Fax: 2404818
Founded: 1909
Gen Secr: Chris Meade
Focus: Lit
Periodical
Poetry Review (quarterly) . . . 12113

Poets' Theatre Guild, 44 Croham Park Av, South Croydon CR2 7HL
T: 6888803
Focus: Lit . . . 12114

Polish Educational Society, 238 King St, London W6
T: (0181) 7411993
Focus: Educ
Periodical
Hychowanie Ojczyste (quarterly) . . . 12115

Polish Medical Association, 14 Collingham Gardens, London SW5
T: (0171) 3731087
Focus: Med . . . 12116

Polish Underground Movement (1939-1945) Study Trust (PUMST), 11 Leopold Rd, London W5 3PB
Founded: 1947
Focus: Hist . . . 12117

Political and Economic Planning (PEP), 12 Upper Belgrave St, London SW1X 8BB
T: (0171) 2355271
Founded: 1931; Members: 800
Focus: Poli Sci; Econ . . . 12118

Political Studies Association of the United Kingdom (PSAUK), c/o Lynn Corken, Dept of Politics, Queen's University, Belfast BT7 1NN
T: (01232) 245133 ext 3288; Fax: 235373
Founded: 1950; Members: 1000
Pres: Prof. E. Meehan; Gen Secr: Dr. Charlie Jeffery
Focus: Poli Sci
Periodicals
Newsletter (quarterly)
Political Studies (5 times annually)
Politics (3 times annually) . . . 12119

Politics Association, 16 Gower St, London WC1E 6DP
T: (0171) 3231131
Founded: 1969; Members: 760
Focus: Poli Sci
Periodicals
Politics Association Resources Bank (irregularly)
Talking Politics incorporating Teaching Politics (3 times annually) . . . 12120

The Powys Society, Hamilton's, Kilmersdon BA3 5TE
T: (01761) 435134
Founded: 1967; Members: 300
Pres: Dr. Glen Cavaliero
Focus: Lit
Periodical
The Powys Journal (annually) . . . 12121

Prehistoric Society, c/o Institute of Archaeology, 31-34 Gordon Sq, London WC1M 0A7
T: (0171) 3787050
Founded: 1935; Members: 2000
Pres: Prof. T. Champion; Gen Secr: Dr. R. Bewley
Focus: Archeol
Periodical
Proceedings (annually) . . . 12122

Presbyterian Church of Wales Historical Society, The Manse, Caradog Rd, Aberystwyth SY23 3BU
T: 3391
Founded: 1914; Members: 650
Focus: Hist; Rel & Theol . . . 12123

Primate Society of Great Britain, c/o Dr. Hilary Box, Psychology Dept, University of Reading, Reading
Focus: Bio
Periodical
Primate Eye (3 times annually) . . . 12124

Printing Historical Society (PHS), c/o Saint Bride Institute, Bride Ln, Fleet St, London EC4Y 8EE
Founded: 1964; Members: 500
Pres: John Dreyfus; Gen Secr: Philip Wickens
Focus: Cultur Hist; Eng
Periodicals
Bulletin of The Printing Historial Society (semi-annually)
Journal of The Printing Historical Society (annually) . . . 12125

The Private Libraries Association (P.L.A.), Ravelston, South View Rd, Pinner HA5 3YD
Founded: 1956; Members: 900
Pres: Robin de Beaumont; Gen Secr: Frank Broomhead
Focus: Libraries & Bk Sci
Periodicals
The Private Library (quarterly)
Private Press Books: Annual Bibliography 12126

Processors and Growers Research Organisation (PGRO), c/o Research Station, Great North Rd, Thornhaugh, Peterborough PE8 6HT
T: (01780) 782585
Founded: 1944
Focus: Hort
Periodical
Vegetable Grower (quarterly) . . . 12127

Procurators Fiscal Society, Sheriff Court, Dumbarton
T: 63266
Founded: 1930; Members: 80
Focus: Law . . . 12128

Production Engineering Research Association (PERA), Melton Mowbray LE13 0PD
T: (01664) 501501
Founded: 1946; Members: 2000
Focus: Eng . . . 12129

Production Mangagement Action Group (PROMAG), c/o Administrative Staff College, Greenlands, Henley-on-Thames, Oxon
T: Hambleden 454
Founded: 1975; Members: 60
Focus: Business Admin . . . 12130

Professional Association of Teachers (PAT), 2 Saint James' Court, Friar Gate, Derby DE1 1BT
T: (01332) 372337; Fax: 290310
Founded: 1970; Members: 40000
Pres: Jane Reid; Gen Secr: John R. Andrews
Focus: Educ
Periodicals
Professional Lecturer (5 times annually)
Professional Teacher (5 times annually) . 12131

Psoriasis Association, 7 Milton St, Northampton NN2 7JG
T: (01604) 711129
Founded: 1968; Members: 10500
Focus: Derm
Periodical
Psoriasis (3 times annually) . . . 12132

Psywar Society, 8 Ridgway Rd, Barton Seagrave, Kettering, Northants
T: (01536) 2921
Founded: 1958; Members: 123
Focus: Hist . . . 12133

Pugwash Conferences on Science and World Affairs, 63a Great Russell St, London WC1B 3BJ
T: (0171) 4056661; E-Mail: pugwash@qmw.ac.uk; Fax: 8315651
Founded: 1957; Members: 2500
Pres: Prof. Joseph Rotblat; Gen Secr: Prof. Francesco Calogero
Focus: Sci; Poli Sci . . . 12134

Pure Water Preservation Society (PWPS), Ln End, Highlands Ln, Westfield, Woking GU22 9PU
T: (014862) 60385
Founded: 1967
Focus: Hydrology . . . 12135

Pushkin Club, 46 Ladbroke Grove, London W11 2PA
T: (0171) 7275311
Founded: 1954
Focus: Lit . . . 12136

Quaker Esperanto Society, 69 Twemlow Parade, Morecambe LA3 2AL
Founded: 1921
Focus: Ling . . . 12137

Queen's English Society (QES), 20 Jessica Rd, London SW18 2QN
T: (0181) 8742200; Fax: 8702356
Founded: 1972; Members: 740
Pres: Baroness Cox; Gen Secr: P.M.F. Raper
Focus: Ling; Lit
Periodical
Quest (quarterly) . . . 12138

Quekett Microscopical Club, c/o Dept. Natural History, British Museum, Cromwell Rd, London SW7 5BD
Founded: 1865
Focus: Microbio . . . 12139

Radio Society of Great Britain (R.S.G.B.), Lambda House, Cranborne Rd, Potters Bar EN6 3JE
T: (01707) 659015; Fax: 645105
Founded: 1913; Members: 32000
Gen Secr: Peter A. Kirby
Focus: Electric Eng
Periodical
Radio Communication (monthly) . . . 12140

Radius / The Religious Drama Society of Great Britain, Christ Church and Upton Chapel, Kennington Rd, London SE1 7QP
T: (0171) 4012422
Founded: 1929
Focus: Perf Arts
Periodical
Radius-Magazine (quarterly) 12141

Radnorshire Society, c/o The Radnor College of Further Education, Spa Rd East, Llandrindod Wells LD1 5ES
T: (01597) 2618
Founded: 1930; Members: 550
Focus: Hist
Periodical
Transactions (annually) 12142

Railway Correspondence and Travel Society (R.C.T.S.), 158a North View Rd, Hornsey, London
T: (0181) 3489081
Founded: 1928; Members: 5800
Focus: Transport 12143

Railway Development Association (RDA), 3 Hall Way, Purley, Surrey
T: 6606139
Founded: 1951; Members: 260
Focus: Transport 12144

RAPRA Technology, Shawbury, Shrewsbury SY4 4NR
T: (01939) 250383; Fax: 251118
Founded: 1919; Members: 600
Focus: Materials Sci
Periodical
RAPRA News (quarterly) 12145

Rare Poultry Society (R.P.S.), 8 Saint Thomas's Rd, Great Glenn LE8 0EG
Founded: 1969; Members: 445
Focus: Animal Husb
Periodicals
Breeders Lists (annually)
Newsletter (quarterly) 12146

The Ray Society, c/o The Natural History Museum, Cromwell Rd, London SW7 5BD
T: (0171) 9389263; E-Mail: nje@nhm.ac.uk; Fax: 9389158
Founded: 1844; Members: 350
Pres: D. MacFarlane; Gen Secr: Dr. N.J. Evans
Focus: Nat Sci; Zoology; Botany . . . 12147

Regency Society of Brighton and Hove, 33 Roedean Crescent, Brighton BN2 5RG
T: (01273) 66881
Founded: 1945; Members: 660
Focus: Archit 12148

Regional Studies Association (RSA), 15 Micawber St, London N1 7TB
T: (0171) 4901128; E-Mail: rsa@mailbox.ulcc.ac.uk; Fax: 2530095
Founded: 1965; Members: 800
Pres: Mark Hart; Gen Secr: Sally Hardy
Focus: Urban Plan
Periodicals
Debates & Reviews (annually)
Newsletter (bi-monthly)
Regional Studies
Special Issue (annually) 12149

Religious Society of Friends, 173-177 Euston Rd, London NW1 2BJ
T: (0171) 3873601; Fax: 3881977
Focus: Rel & Theol 12150

Remote Sensing Society (RSS), c/o Dept of Geography, University of Nottingham, Nottingham NG7 2RD
T: (01159) 515435; Fax: 515249
Founded: 1974; Members: 900
Pres: Lord Hesketh; Gen Secr: Keith Hilton
Focus: Geography; Cart; Computer & Info Sci
Periodicals
International Journal of Remote Sensing (quarterly)
Proceedings of Annual Technical Meetings (annually)
RSS Newsletter (quarterly) 12151

The Renal Association, Triangle House, Broomhill Rd, London SW18 4HX
T: (0181) 8752413; E-Mail: renal@immunology.org; Fax: 8779308
Founded: 1950; Members: 600
Pres: Prof. J. Walls; Gen Secr: Dr. T.H.J. Goodship
Focus: Med 12152

Research and Development Society, 47 Belgrave Sq, London SW1X 8QX
T: (0171) 2356111; Fax: 2596002
Founded: 1971; Members: 500
Focus: Sci; Eng 12153

Research Defence Society (RDS), 58 Great Marlborough St, London W1V 1DD
T: (0171) 2872818
Founded: 1908; Members: 2565
Focus: Sci
Periodicals
Conquest (annually)
Newsletter (quarterly) 12154

Research into Lost Knowledge Organisation (RILKO), 10 Kedleston Dr, Orpington BR5 2DR
T: (01689) 32265
Founded: 1969; Members: 420
Focus: Rel & Theol; Philos; Archit
Periodical
Newsletter (semi-annually) 12155

Research Society for Natural Therapeutics, 8 Stokewood Rd, Bournemouth BH3 7NA
T: (01202) 25997
Focus: Therapeutics 12156

Richard III Society, 4 Oakley St, Chelsea, London SW3 5NN
T: (0171) 3513391
Founded: 1924; Members: 4000
Pres: R. Hamblin; Gen Secr: E.M. Nokes
Focus: Hist
Periodical
The Ricardian (quarterly) 12157

Richard Jefferies Society, 6 Chickerell Rd, Swindon SN3 2RQ
T: (01793) 21512
Founded: 1950; Members: 350
Focus: Lit
Periodicals
Annual Report and Bulletin (annually)
Spring Newsletter (annually) 12158

Right to a Comprehensive Education (RtCE), 4 Hammersmith Terrace, London W6 9TS
T: (0181) 7489790
Founded: 1965; Members: 1500
Focus: Educ
Periodical
Comprehensive Education (3 times annually) 12159

River Thames Society (RTS), 2 Ruskin Av, Kew, Richmond TW9 4DJ
T: (0181) 8761520
Founded: 1962; Members: 2143
Focus: Hydrology; Ecology
Periodical
Lower Tideway Topics (quarterly) . . . 12160

Royal Academy of Arts in London (RA), Burlington House, Piccadilly, London W1V 0DS
T: (0171) 4397438; Fax: 4340837
Founded: 1768
Pres: Sir Philip Dowson; Gen Secr: David Gordon
Focus: Arts
Periodicals
R A Illustrated (annually)
R A Magazine (quarterly) 12161

Royal Academy of Dancing (RAD), 36 Battersea Sq, London SW11 3RA
T: (0171) 2230091; Fax: 9243129
Founded: 1920; Members: 20000
Focus: Perf Arts
Periodical
Dancing Gazette (3 times annually) . . 12162

Royal Academy of Dramatic Art (RADA), 62-64 Gower St, London WC1E 6ED
T: (0171) 6367076
Founded: 1904; Members: 200
Focus: Perf Arts 12163

Royal Academy of Engineering, 29 Great Peter St, London SW1P 3LW
T: (0171) 2222688; Fax: 2330054
Founded: 1976; Members: 1035
Pres: Sir David Davies; Gen Secr: J.R. Appleton
Focus: Eng
Periodicals
Annual Report (annually)
Newsletter (quarterly) 12164

Royal Academy of Music (RAM), Marylebone Rd, London NW1 5HT
T: (0171) 8737373; Fax: 8737374
Founded: 1822
Pres: Curtis Price
Focus: Music
Periodicals
Prospectus (annually)
RAM Magazine (3 times annually) . . . 12165

Royal Aeronautical Society, 4 Hamilton Pl, London W1V 0BQ
T: (0171) 4993515; E-Mail: raes@raes.org.uk; Fax: 4996230
Founded: 1866; Members: 11000
Pres: S.M. John; Gen Secr: R.J. Kennett
Focus: Aero
Periodicals
Aeronautical Journal (10 times annually)
Aerospace (monthly) 12166

The Royal African Society (RAS), SOAS, Thornhaugh St, Russell Sq, London WC1H 0XG
T: (0171) 3236253
Founded: 1901; Members: 800
Pres: Sir Michael Caine; Gen Secr: Lindsay Allan
Focus: Ethnology
Periodicals
African Affairs
Journal (quarterly) 12167

Royal Agricultural Society of England (RASE), c/o National Agricultural Centre, Stoneleigh Park CV8 2LZ
T: (01203) 696969; E-Mail: info@rase.org.uk; Fax: 696900
Founded: 1838; Members: 14000
Pres: Duke of Westminster; Gen Secr: C.D. Runge
Focus: Agri
Periodicals
Diary of Agricultural Show Dates (annually)
RASE Journal (annually)
RASE News (quarterly) 12168

Royal Anthropological Institute of Great Britain and Ireland (R.A.I.), 50 Fitzroy St, London W1P 5HS
T: (0171) 3870455; E-Mail: rei@cix.compulink.co.uk; Fax: 3834235
Founded: 1843; Members: 2250
Pres: Dr. John Davis; Gen Secr: Jonathan Benthall
Focus: Anthro
Periodicals
Anthropology Today (bi-monthly)
The Journal of the Royal Anthropological Institute (quarterly) 12169

Royal Archaeological Institute (R.A.I.), c/o Society of Antiquaries, Burlington House, Piccadilly, London W1V 0HS
Founded: 1843; Members: 1500
Pres: Prof. A.P. Quiney; Gen Secr: J.G. Coad
Focus: Archeol
Periodical
The Archaeological Journal (annually) . . 12170

Royal Asiatic Society of Great Britain and Ireland, 60 Queen's Gardens, London W2 3AF
T: (0171) 7244742
Founded: 1823; Members: 800
Gen Secr: L. Collins
Focus: Ethnology
Periodical
Journal of The Royal Asiatic Society (3 times annually) 12171

Royal Association for Disability and Rehabilitation (RADAR), 12 City Forum, 250 City Rd, London EC1V 8AF
T: (0171) 2503222; Fax: 2500212
Founded: 1977
Pres: Duke of Buccleuch; Gen Secr: Bert Massie
Focus: Rehabil
Periodical
Bulletin (monthly) 12172

Royal Astronomical Society (RAS), Burlington House, Piccadilly, London W1V 0NL
T: (0171) 7344582; Fax: 4940166
Founded: 1820; Members: 2800
Pres: Prof. M.S. Longair
Focus: Astronomy
Periodicals
Geophysical Journal (monthly)
Monthly Notices (monthly)
Quarterly Journal (quarterly) 12173

Royal Bath and West of England Society, The Showground, Shepton Mallet BA4 6QN
T: (01749) 823211; Fax: 823169
Founded: 1777; Members: 3500
Focus: Agri 12174

Royal Caledonian Horticultural Society (RCHS), 7 Melville Crescent, Edinburgh EH3 7NA
T: (0131) 2252041
Founded: 1809; Members: 1330
Focus: Hort 12175

Royal Cambrian Academy of Art (R.C.A.), Crown Ln, Conwy LL32 8BH
T: (01492) 593413; Fax: 593413
Founded: 1882; Members: 100
Pres: K. Williams; Gen Secr: Vicky Macdonald
Focus: Arts 12176

Royal Celtic Society, 23 Rutland St, Edinburgh EH1 2RN
T: (0131) 2286449; Fax: 2296987
Founded: 1820; Members: 142
Pres: Sir Donald Cameron of Lochiel; Gen Secr: J. Gordon Cameron
Focus: Ethnology 12177

Royal Choral Society (RCS), Royal Albert Hall, Kensington, London SW7 2AP
T: (0171) 5845216
Founded: 1871; Members: 250
Focus: Music
Periodicals
Prospectus (annually)
Voice 12178

The Royal College of Anaesthetists, 48-49 Russell Sq, London WC1B 4JY
T: (0171) 8131900; Fax: 8131876
Founded: 1988; Members: 5500
Pres: Prof. L. Strunin; Gen Secr: Sir Geoffrey de Deney
Focus: Anesthetics
Periodical
Newsletter (semi-annually) 12179

Royal College of General Practitioners (R.C.G.P.), 14 Princes Gate, London SW7 1PU
T: (0171) 5813232; Fax: 2253047
Founded: 1952; Members: 18500
Pres: Prof. Denis Pereira Gray; Gen Secr: Dr. W. Reith
Focus: Med
Periodical
British Journal of General Practice (monthly) 12180

Royal College of Midwives (RCM), 15 Mansfield St, London W1M 0BE
T: (0171) 5806523
Founded: 1881; Members: 33000
Focus: Gynecology
Periodicals
Current Awareness Service (quarterly)
Midwives Chronicle (monthly) 12181

Royal College of Music (R.C.M.), Prince Consort Rd, London SW7 2BS
T: (0171) 5893643; E-Mail: ssturrock@rcm.ac.uk; Fax: 5897740
Founded: 1882; Members: 650
Pres: Dr. Janet Ritterman
Focus: Music
Periodical
Royal College of Music Annual Review (annually) 12182

Royal College of Nursing of The United Kingdom (RCN), 20 Cavendish Sq, London W1M 0AB
T: (0171) 4093333; Fax: 3551379
Founded: 1916
Gen Secr: Christine Hancock
Focus: Med
Periodicals
Nursing Bibliography (monthly)
Nursing Standard (weekly)
Nursing The Elderly (10 times annually)
Paediatric Nursing (10 times annually)
Primary Health Care (10 times annually)
Senior Nurse (10 times annually) . . . 12183

Royal College of Obstetricians and Gynaecologists (R.C.O.G.), 27 Sussex Pl, London NW1 4RG
T: (0171) 2625425; Fax: 7230575
Founded: 1929; Members: 4300
Pres: Dr. Naren Patel; Gen Secr: P.A. Barnett
Focus: Gynecology
Periodical
Journal (monthly) 12184

Royal College of Ophthalmologists, 17 Cornwall Terrace, London NW1 4QW
T: (0171) 9350702; Fax: 9359838
Founded: 1988
Focus: Ophthal 12185

The Royal College of Organists (RCO), 7 Saint Andrew St, London EC4A 3LQ
T: (0171) 9363606; Fax: 3538244
Founded: 1864; Members: 3200
Pres: Martin Neary
Focus: Music
Periodicals
RCO Journal (annually)
RCO News (quarterly) 12186

Royal College of Paediatrics and Child Health (BPA), 5 Saint Andrew's Pl, London NW1 4LB
T: (0171) 4866151; Fax: 4866009
Founded: 1928; Members: 4107
Pres: Prof. David Baum; Gen Secr: Dr. Keith Dodd
Focus: Pediatrics
Periodical
Disease in Childhood (monthly) 12187

Royal College of Pathologists, 2 Carlton House Terrace, London SW1Y 5AF
T: (0171) 9305861; Fax: 3210523
Founded: 1962; Members: 2500
Pres: Prof. R.N.M. MacSween; Gen Secr: K. Lockyer
Focus: Pathology 12188

Royal College of Physicians (RCP), 11 Saint Andrew's Pl, London NW1 4LE
T: (0171) 9351174; Fax: 4875218
Founded: 1518; Members: 15000
Pres: Prof. Sir Leslie A. Turnberg; Gen Secr: D.B. Lloyd
Focus: Educ; Med
Periodical
Journal of The Royal College of Physicians 12189

Royal College of Physicians and Surgeons of Glasgow, 234-242 Saint Vincent St, Glasgow G2 5RJ
T: (0141) 2216072; Fax: 2211804
Founded: 1599; Members: 6000
Pres: Colin McKay; Gen Secr: Dr. Stefan D. Slater
Focus: Surgery; Med; Dent 12190

Royal College of Physicians of Edinburgh (R.C.P.E.), 9 Queen St, Edinburgh EH2 1JQ
T: (0131) 2257324; E-Mail: rcpe@ac.uk; Fax: 2203939
Founded: 1681; Members: 6000
Focus: Physiology
Periodical
Proceedings of The Royal College of Physicians of Edinburgh (quarterly) 12191

The Royal College of Psychiatrists, 17 Belgrave Sq, London SW1X 8PG
T: (0171) 2352351; E-Mail: rcpsycn@rcpsycn.ac.uk; Fax: 2451231
Founded: 1971; Members: 8300
Gen Secr: V. Cameron
Focus: Psychiatry
Periodical
British Journal of Psychiatry (monthly) . 12192

Royal College of Radiologists (RCR), 38 Portland Pl, London W1N 4JQ
T: (0171) 6364432; E-Mail: enquiries@rcr.ac.uk; Fax: 3233100
Founded: 1975; Members: 4900
Pres: M.J. Brindle; Gen Secr: A.J. Cowles
Focus: Radiology

Periodicals
Clinical Oncology (bi-monthly)
Clinical Radiology (monthly) *12193*

The Royal College of Surgeons of Edinburgh, Nicolson St, Edinburgh EH8 9DW
T: (0131) 5271600; Fax: 5576406
Founded: 1505
Pres: Prof. Sir Robert Shields; Gen Secr: A.S. Campbell
Focus: Surgery
Periodical
Journal (bi-monthly) *12194*

Royal College of Surgeons of England (R.C.S.E.), 35-43 Lincoln's Inn Fields, London WC2A 3PN
T: (0171) 4053474; Fax: 8319438
Founded: 1800; Members: 12900
Pres: Sir Rodney Sweetnam; Gen Secr: R.H.E. Duffett
Focus: Surgery
Periodicals
Almanack (annually)
Annals and Bulletin (bi-monthly)
Handbook (irregularly) *12195*

Royal College of Veterinary Surgeons (R.C.V.S.), 62-64 Horseferry Rd, London SW1P 2AF
T: (0171) 2222001; Fax: 2222004
Founded: 1844; Members: 16000
Pres: Prof. R.S. Jones; Gen Secr: Peter Woolley
Focus: Vet Med
Periodicals
Directory of Practices (annually)
RCVS Newsletter (quarterly)
Register of Members (annually) *12196*

Royal Commission for The Exhibition of 1851, c/o Imperial College of Science and Technology, Sherfield Bldg, London SW7
Focus: Hist *12197*

Royal Commission on Historical Manuscripts, Quality House, Quality Court, Chancery Ln, London WC2A 1HP
T: (0171) 2421198; Fax: 8313550
Founded: 1869; Members: 17
Gen Secr: C.J. Kitching
Focus: Hist
Periodicals
Annual Review (annually)
Reports to The Crown (irregularly) . . . *12198*

Royal Commonwealth Society, 18 Northumberland Av, London WC2N 5BJ
T: (0171) 9306733; Fax: 9309705
Founded: 1868; Members: 20000
Focus: Ethnology
Periodicals
Conference Reports
Library Notes
Newsletter (3 times annually) *12199*

The Royal Cornwall Agricultural Association (RCAA), The Showground, Wadebridge PL27 7JE, Cornwall
T: (01208) 812183; Fax: 812713
Founded: 1793; Members: 6000
Gen Secr: C.P. Riddle
Focus: Agri *12200*

Royal Drawing Society (RDS), 17 Carlton House Terrace, London SW1
Founded: 1888; Members: 175
Focus: Arts *12201*

Royal Economic Society (R.E.S.), c/o Dept of Economics, London Business School, Sussex Pl, Regents Park, London NW1 4SA
Fax: (071) 2625050
Founded: 1890; Members: 3300
Pres: Prof. R. Atkinson
Focus: Econ
Periodicals
Economic Journal (bi-monthly)
Newsletter (quarterly) *12202*

Royal Entomological Society of London (RES), 41 Queen's Gate, London SW7 5HU
T: (0171) 5848361; E-Mail: reg@ royensoc.demon.co.uk; Fax: 5818505
Founded: 1883
Pres: Prof. W.M. Blaney; Gen Secr: G.G. Bentley
Focus: Entomology
Periodicals
Antenna (quarterly)
Ecological Entomology (quarterly)
The Entomologist (quarterly)
Handbooks for The Identification of British Insects (irregularly)
Insect Molecular Biology (quarterly)
Medical & Veterinary Entomology (quarterly)
Physiological Entomology (quarterly)
Symposium Volumes (semi-annually)
Systematic Entomology (quarterly) . . . *12203*

The Royal Faculty of Procurators in Glasgow, 12 Nelson Mandela Pl, Glasgow G2 1BT
T: (0141) 3339104
Founded: 1668; Members: 592
Pres: C. White; Gen Secr: Alistair J. Campbell
Focus: Law *12204*

Royal Fine Art Commission, 7 Saint James's Sq, London SW1Y 4JU
T: (0171) 8396537; Fax: 8398475
Founded: 1924

Pres: Lord Saint John of Fawsley; Gen Secr: Francis Golding
Focus: Arts *12205*

Royal Fine Art Commission for Scotland, 9 Atholl Crescent, Edinburgh EH3 8HA
T: (0131) 2296031
Founded: 1927
Gen Secr: Charles Prosser
Focus: Fine Arts
Periodical
Report to Parliament (annually) *12206*

Royal Forestry Society of England, Wales and Northern Ireland (R.F.S.), 102 High St, Tring HP23 4AF
T: (01442) 822028; E-Mail: rfs_tring@ compuserve.com; Fax: 890395
Founded: 1882; Members: 4400
Pres: J. Bede Howell; Gen Secr: Dr. J.E. Jackson
Focus: Forestry
Periodical
Journal (quarterly) *12207*

Royal Geographical Society (R.G.S.), 1 Kensington Gore, London SW7 2AR
T: (0171) 5913000; Fax: 5913001
Founded: 1830; Members: 121500
Pres: Earl Selbourne; Gen Secr: Dr. Rita Gardner
Focus: Geography
Periodicals
Area (quarterly)
Geographical Journal (3 times annually)
Geographical Magazine (monthly)
Transactions (quarterly) *12208*

Royal Highland and Agricultural Society of Scotland (R.H.A.S.S.), Ingliston, Edinburgh EH28 8NF
T: (0131) 3332444; Fax: 3335236
Founded: 1784; Members: 14000
Gen Secr: H. Davies
Focus: Agri
Periodical
The Royal Highland News *12209*

Royal Historical Society, c/o University College, Gower St, London WC1E 6BT
T: (0171) 3877532
Founded: 1868
Pres: Prof. P.J. Marshall; Gen Secr: J.N. McCarthy
Focus: Hist
Periodicals
Camden (semi-annually)
Transactions of The Royal Historical Society (annually) *12210*

Royal Horticultural Society (RHS), 80 Vincent Sq, London SW1P 2PE
T: (0171) 8344333
Founded: 1804; Members: 170000
Pres: Sir Simon Hornby; Gen Secr: D.P. Hearn
Focus: Hort
Periodicals
Daffodils (annually)
The Garden (monthly)
The Orchid Review (monthly)
The Plantsman (quarterly)
Rhododendrons (annually) *12211*

Royal Incorporation of Architects in Scotland, 15 Rutland Sq, Edinburgh EH1 2BE
T: (0131) 2297545; E-Mail: rias@compuserve.com; Fax: 2282188
Founded: 1916; Members: 4200
Pres: George Wren; Gen Secr: Sebastian Tombs
Focus: Archit
Periodicals
Chartered Architect (monthly)
Practice Information (quarterly)
Prospect (quarterly) *12212*

Royal Institute of British Architects (RIBA), 66 Portland Pl, London W1N 4AD
T: (0171) 5805533; Fax: 2551541
Founded: 1834; Members: 28000
Pres: David A. Rock; Gen Secr: Dr. Alexander Reid
Focus: Archit
Periodical
RIBA Journal (monthly) *12213*

Royal Institute of International Affairs (RIIA), Chatham House, 10 Saint James's Sq, London SW1Y 4LE
T: (0171) 9575700; Fax: 9575710
Founded: 1920; Members: 3000
Pres: Lord Carrington; Lord Callaghan; Lord Jenkins of Hillhead; Gen Secr: Sir Timothy Garden
Focus: Poli Sci
Periodicals
Chatham House Papers (irregularly)
International Affairs (quarterly)
RIIA Discussion Papers (irregularly)
The World Today (monthly) *12214*

Royal Institute of Navigation (RIN), c/o Royal Geographical Society, 1 Kensington Gore, London SW7 2AT
T: (0171) 5895021; Fax: 8238671
Founded: 1947; Members: 3400
Focus: Navig
Periodicals
Journal of Navigation (3 times annually)
Navigation News (bi-monthly) *12215*

Royal Institute of Oil Painters, 17 Carlton House Terrace, London SW1Y 5BD
T: (0171) 9306844; Fax: 8397830
Founded: 1882
Pres: Frederick Beckett
Focus: Fine Arts *12216*

Royal Institute of Painters in Water Colours, 17 Carlton House Terrace, London SW1Y 5BD
T: (0171) 9306844; Fax: 8397830
Founded: 1831; Members: 64
Pres: Ronald Maddox
Focus: Arts; Fine Arts
Periodical
Catalogue of Exhibitions (annually) . . . *12217*

Royal Institute of Philosophy, 14 Gordon Sq, London WC1H 0AG
T: (0171) 3874130
Founded: 1925; Members: 850
Pres: Lord Quinton; Gen Secr: Ingrid Purkiss
Focus: Philos
Periodicals
Lecture Series (annually)
Philosophy (quarterly) *12218*

Royal Institute of Public Administration (RIPA), 3 Birdcage Walk, London SW1H 9JJ
T: (0171) 2222248
Founded: 1922
Focus: Poli Sci
Periodicals
Public Administration (quarterly)
Public Administration and Development (quarterly)
RIPA Report (quarterly) *12219*

The Royal Institute of Public Health and Hygiene, 28 Portland Pl, London W1N 4DE
T: (0171) 5802731; E-Mail: riphh@corpex.com; Fax: 5806157
Founded: 1886; Members: 2500
Gen Secr: R.A. Smith
Focus: Public Health; Hygiene; Nutrition
Periodicals
Health & Hygiene (quarterly)
Public Health (bi-monthly) *12220*

Royal Institution of Chartered Surveyors, 12 Great George St, London SW1P 3AD
T: (0171) 2227000; Fax: 2229430
Founded: 1868; Members: 92000
Pres: Jeremy Bayliss; Gen Secr: Claire Makin
Focus: Surveying
Periodicals
Chartered Quantity Surveyor (monthly)
Chartered Surveyor (weekly)
Surveying World (bi-monthly) *12221*

Royal Institution of Cornwall (RIC), c/o Royal Cornwall Museum, River St, Truro, Cornwall
T: (01872) 72205
Founded: 1818; Members: 1200
Focus: Sci; Archeol; Hist; Genealogy
Periodical
Journal of The Royal Institution of Cornwall (annually) *12222*

Royal Institution of Great Britain (R.I.G.B.), 21 Albemarle St, London W1X 4BS
T: (0171) 4092992; Fax: 6293569
Founded: 1799; Members: 2300
Pres: Duke of Kent; Gen Secr: Prof. K.J. Packer
Focus: Sci
Periodicals
Proceedings (annually)
Record (annually) *12223*

The Royal Institution of Naval Architects, 10 Upper Belgrave St, London SW1X 8BQ
T: (0171) 2354622; Fax: 2456959
Founded: 1860; Members: 5100
Pres: Dr. T.J. Parker; Gen Secr: T. Blakeley
Focus: Eng
Periodicals
The Naval Architect incorporating Warship Technology (monthly)
Ship and Boat International (monthly)
Ship Repair and Conversion Technology (quarterly)
Transactions (annually) *12224*

Royal Institution of South Wales (RISW), c/o Swansea Museum, Victoria Rd, Swansea SA1 1SN
T: (01792) 653763
Founded: 1830; Members: 362
Focus: Sci
Periodical
Minerva (annually) *12225*

Royal Isle of Wight Agricultural Society, 66 Carisbrooke Rd, Newport PO30 1BW
T: 2925
Founded: 1882
Focus: Agri *12226*

Royal Jersey Agricultural and Horticultural Society, c/o WJCB Centre, La Route de la Trinité, Trinity JE3 53P
T: (01534) 866555; Fax: 865619
Founded: 1833; Members: 1000
Focus: Agri; Hort
Periodical
Jersey at Home (annually) *12227*

Royal Lancashire Agricultural Society (RLAS), Ribby Hall, Wrea Green, Kirkham, Preston PR4 2RD
T: (01772) 3911
Founded: 1767; Members: 3423
Focus: Agri *12228*

Royal Liverpool Philharmonic Society, Hope St, Liverpool L1 9BP
T: (0151) 7092895
Founded: 1840; Members: 2000
Focus: Music *12229*

Royal London Aid Society (RLAS), 56-58 East India Dock Rd, London E14
T: (0171) 9873864
Founded: 1939; Members: 1000
Focus: Sociology *12230*

Royal Medical Society, Students' Centre, Bristo Sq, Edinburgh EH8 9AL
T: (0131) 6502672
Founded: 1737; Members: 900
Pres: Christopher Parsons; Gen Secr: Gillian Ostrowski
Focus: Med *12231*

Royal Meteorological Society, 104 Oxford Rd, Reading RG1 7LJ
T: (0118) 9568500; E-Mail: execsec@royal-met-soc.org.uk; Fax: 9568571
Founded: 1850; Members: 3500
Pres: Dr. D.J. Carson; Gen Secr: S.G. Cornford
Focus: Geophys
Periodicals
International Journal of Climatology (15 times annually)
Meteorological Applications (quarterly)
Quarterly Journal (8 times annually)
Weather (monthly) *12232*

Royal Microscopical Society (RMS), 37-38 Saint Clements, Oxford OX4 1AJ
T: (01865) 248768; E-Mail: info@rms.org.uk; Fax: 791237
Founded: 1839; Members: 1900
Pres: Dr. C.V. Howard; Gen Secr: P.B. Hirst
Focus: Nat Sci; Sci
Periodicals
Journal of Microscopy (monthly)
Proceedings (quarterly) *12233*

Royal Musical Association (R.M.A.), 100 Harvist Rd, London NW8 6HL
Founded: 1874; Members: 800
Pres: Julian Rushton; Gen Secr: Robin Anderton
Focus: Music
Periodicals
Journal (semi-annually)
Research Chronicle (annually) *12234*

Royal Naval Bird Watching Society (RNBWS), 23 Saint Davids Rd, Southsea PO5 1QH
T: (01705) 822981
Founded: 1946; Members: 440
Focus: Ornithology; Navig
Periodicals
News Bulletins (semi-annually)
Sea Swallow (annually) *12235*

Royal Norfolk Agricultural Association (RNAA), Showground, Dereham Rd, New Costessey, Norwich NR5 0TT
T: (01603) 748931; Fax: 748229
Founded: 1847; Members: 4000
Pres: Sir Timothy Colman; Gen Secr: Diana Akers
Focus: Agri
Periodical
Norfolk Mardler Show Catalogue (annually) *12236*

Royal Numismatic Society, c/o Dept of Coins and Medals, British Museum, London WC1B 3DG
T: (0171) 3238404
Founded: 1836; Members: 1000
Pres: D.M. Metcalf
Focus: Numismatics
Periodicals
Coin Hoards
Numismatic Chronicle (annually) *12237*

Royal Pharmaceutical Society of Great Britain, 1 Lambeth High St, London SE1 7JN
T: (0171) 7359141; Fax: 7357629
Founded: 1841; Members: 37830
Pres: A.M. Lewis; Gen Secr: J. Ferguson
Focus: Pharmacol
Periodicals
Annual Register of Pharmaceutical Chemists (annually)
Journal of Pharmacy and Pharmacology (monthly)
The Pharmaceutical Journal (weekly) . . *12238*

The Royal Philharmonic Society, 10 Stratford Pl, London W1N 9AE
T: (0171) 4918110; Fax: 4937463
Founded: 1813; Members: 550
Focus: Music
Periodical
Fanfare from The Royal Philharmonic Society (semi-annually) *12239*

Royal Philosophical Society of Glasgow, c/o Dept of Philosophy, University of Glasgow, West Quadrangle, Glasgow G12 8QQ
T: (0141) 3344144; Fax: 3304112
Founded: 1802; Members: 200
Pres: Dr.A.M. Shenkin
Focus: Philos *12240*

Royal Photographic Society of Great Britain, The Octagon, Milsom St, Bath BA1 1DN
T: (01225) 462841; Fax: 448688
Founded: 1853; Members: 10500
Pres: Bob Moore; Gen Secr: Barry Lane
Focus: Photo

Periodicals
The Journal of Photographic Science
Photographic Abstracts (bi-monthly)
The Photographic Journal (monthly) . . 12241

Royal Physical Society of Edinburgh, c/o Dept of Genetics, University of Edinburgh, Edinburgh
Founded: 1771; Members: 160
Focus: Physics
Periodical
Proceedings (irregularly) 12242

Royal Scottish Academy (R.S.A.), The Mound, Edinburgh EH2 2EL
T: (0131) 2256671; Fax: 2252349
Founded: 1826; Members: 70
Pres: W.J.L. Baillie; Gen Secr: Ian McKenzie Smith
Focus: Sci
Periodical
Annual Report (annually) 12243

Royal Scottish Forestry Society, Stables, Dalkeith Country Park, Dalkeith EH22 2NA
T: (0131) 6609480; Fax: 6609490
Founded: 1854; Members: 1200
Pres: Graham Jeffrey; Gen Secr: Michael Osborne
Focus: Forestry
Periodical
Scottish Forestry (quarterly) 12244

Royal Scottish Geographical Society (R.S.G.S.), 40 George St, Glasgow G1 1QE
T: (0141) 5523330; E-Mail: r.s.g.s.@strath.ac.uk; Fax: 5523331
Founded: 1884; Members: 2500
Pres: Lord Younger of Prestwick; Gen Secr: Dr. David M. Munro
Focus: Geography
Periodical
The Scottish Geographical Magazine (3 times annually) 12245

The Royal Society, 6 Carlton House Terrace, London SW1Y 5AG
T: (0171) 8395561; Fax: 9302170
Founded: 1660; Members: 1134
Pres: Sir Aaron Klug; Gen Secr: Stephen Cox
Focus: Nat Sci
Periodicals
Annual Report (annually)
Year Book (annually) 12246

Royal Society for Asian Affairs, 2 Belgrave Sq, London SW1X 8PJ
T: (0171) 2355122
Founded: 1901; Members: 1100
Pres: Lord Denman; Gen Secr: H.C. McKeag
Focus: Ethnology
Periodical
Journal (3 times annually) 12247

Royal Society for Nature Conservation (RSNC), The Green, Witham Park, Lincoln LN5 4JR
T: (01522) 544400; Fax: 595325
Founded: 1912; Members: 204000
Focus: Ecology
Periodical
Natural World: Annual Review (annually) 12248

Royal Society for the Encouragement of Arts, Manufactures and Commerce, 8 John Adam St, London WC2N 6EZ
T: (0171) 9305115
Founded: 1754; Members: 11000
Pres: Philip Duke of Edinburgh; Gen Secr: James Sandison
Focus: Arts; Educ; Commerce
Periodical
Journal (monthly) 12249

Royal Society for The Prevention of Accidents (ROSPA), Cannon House, Priory Queensway, Birmingham B4 6BS
T: (0121) 2002461; Fax: 2001254
Founded: 1916
Focus: Safety
Periodicals
Care in The Home (quarterly)
Care on The Road (bi-monthly)
Occupational Safety & Health (monthly)
Safety Education (3 times annually) . . 12250

Royal Society for the Protection of Birds (R.S.P.B.), The Lodge, Sandy SG19 2DL
T: (01767) 80551; Fax: 692365
Founded: 1889; Members: 925000
Pres: John Lawton; Gen Secr: Barbara Young
Focus: Ecology; Ornithology
Periodical
Birds (quarterly) 12251

Royal Society of Arts (RSA), 6-8 John Adam St, London WC2N 6EZ
T: (0171) 8392366
Founded: 1754; Members: 12000
Focus: Arts 12252

Royal Society of British Artists, 17 Carlton House Terrace, London SW1Y 5BD
T: (0171) 9306844; Fax: 8397830
Members: 119
Pres: Colin Hayes
Focus: Arts; Fine Arts
Periodical
Annual Catalogue (annually) 12253

Royal Society of British Sculptors, 108 Old Brompton Rd, London SW7 3RA
T: (0171) 3735554; Fax: 3733721
Founded: 1904; Members: 262
Pres: Philomena Davidson Davis; Gen Secr: Donna Loveday
Focus: Fine Arts 12254

The Royal Society of Chemistry (RSC), Burlington House, Piccadilly, London W1V 0BN
T: (0171) 4378656; Fax: 4378883
Founded: 1980; Members: 45000
Pres: Prof. E.W. Abel; Gen Secr: Dr. T.D. Inch
Focus: Chem
Periodicals
The Analyst
Analytical Abstracts
Chemical Business Newsbase
Chemical Communications
Chemical Engineering and Biotechnology Abstracts
Chemical Hazards in Industry
Chemistry in Britain (monthly)
Education in Chemistry
Journal of The Chemical Society
Laboratory Hazards Bulletin
Mass Spectrometry Bulletin
Natural Product Updates 12255

The Royal Society of Edinburgh (R.S.E.), 22-24 George St, Edinburgh EH2 2PQ
T: (0131) 2256057; E-Mail: rse@rse.org.uk; Fax: 2206889
Founded: 1783; Members: 1100
Pres: Prof. Malcolm Jeeves; Gen Secr: Prof. Peter Wilson
Focus: Sci; Lit
Periodicals
Annual Report (annually)
Proceedings A (Mathematics) (bi-monthly)
RSE News (quarterly)
Transactions: Earth Sciences (quarterly)
Year Book (annually) 12256

The Royal Society of Health (R.S.H.), R.S.H. House, 38 Saint George's Dr, London SW1V 4BH
T: (0171) 6300121; E-Mail: rsh@cygnet.co.uk; Fax: 9766847
Founded: 1876; Members: 11500
Pres: Dr. Bashir Qureshi
Focus: Public Health
Periodical
Journal of the Royal Society of Health (bi-monthly) 12257

Royal Society of Literature of the United Kingdom, 1 Hyde Park Gardens, London W2 2LT
T: (0171) 7235104
Founded: 1823; Members: 800
Pres: Lord Jenkins; Gen Secr: Maggie Fergusson
Focus: Lit
Periodicals
Report
Transactions 12258

Royal Society of Marine Artists, 17 Carlton House Terrace, London SW1Y 5BD
T: (0171) 9306844; Fax: 8397830
Members: 49
Pres: Mark Myers
Focus: Fine Arts 12259

Royal Society of Medicine (RSM), 1 Wimpole St, London W1M 8AE
T: (0171) 2902900
Founded: 1805; Members: 17000
Pres: Sir Christopher Paine
Focus: Med
Periodicals
Annual Report (annually)
Calendar (annually) 12260

Royal Society of Portrait Painters, 17 Carlton House Terrace, London SW1Y 5BD
T: (0171) 9306844; Fax: 8397830
Founded: 1891; Members: 41
Pres: Daphne Todd
Focus: Arts; Fine Arts
Periodical
Catalogue of Annual Exhibition (annually) 12261

The Royal Society of Tropical Medicine and Hygiene, 26 Portland Pl, London W1N 4EY
T: (0171) 5802127; E-Mail: mail@rstmh.org; Fax: 4361389
Founded: 1907; Members: 2617
Pres: Prof. David A. Warrell; Gen Secr: Dr. Douglas C. Barker
Focus: Hygiene; Trop Med; Public Health
Periodical
Transactions of The Royal Society of Tropical Medicine and Hygiene (bi-monthly) . . . 12262

Royal Society of Ulster Architects (RSUA), 51 Malone Rd, Belfast BT9 6RY
T: (01232) 668846
Founded: 1901
Focus: Archit 12263

Royal Statistical Society, 12 Errol St, London EC1Y 8LX
T: (0171) 6388998; Fax: 2567598
Founded: 1834; Members: 6000
Pres: Prof. A.F.M. Smith
Focus: Stats
Periodicals
Journal of The Royal Statistical Society, Series A: Statistics in Society (3 times annually)
Journal of The Royal Statistical Society, Series B: Methodological (3 times annually)
Journal of The Royal Statistical Society, Series C: Applied Statistics (3 times annually)
Journal of The Royal Statistical Society, Series D: The Statistician 12264

Royal Stuart Society, 26 Ovse Walk, Huntingdon PE18 6OL
T: (01480) 459427
Founded: 1926
Focus: Hist
Periodicals
Royal Stuart Papers (semi-annually)
Royal Stuart Review (semi-annually)
Royalist Focus (irregularly) 12265

Royal Television Society (RTS), Holborn Hall, 100 Gray's Inn Rd, London WC1X 8AL
T: (0171) 4301000; Fax: 4300924
Founded: 1927; Members: 3000
Pres: Andrea Wonfor; Gen Secr: Michael Bunce
Focus: Electric Eng
Periodical
Television (8 times annually) 12266

Royal Town Planning Institute (RTPI), 26 Portland Pl, London W1N 4BE
T: (0171) 6369107; Fax: 3231582
Founded: 1914; Members: 17000
Pres: Clif Hague; Gen Secr: Robert Upton
Focus: Urban Plan 12267

Royal Ulster Academy (RUA), 28 Woodeane, Lurgan, Armagh
Founded: 1879
Focus: Sci 12268

Royal Ulster Academy Association (R.U.A.A.), 3 Derryvolgie Park, Lambeg BT27 4DA
Founded: 1962; Members: 150
Focus: Sci 12269

Royal Ulster Agricultural Society (RUAS), The King's Hall, Balmoral, Belfast BT9 6GW
T: (01232) 665225
Founded: 1826; Members: 3500
Focus: Agri 12270

Royal Watercolour Society, c/o Bankside Gallery, 48 Hopton St, Blackfriars, London SE1 9JH
T: (0171) 9287521; Fax: 9282820
Founded: 1804; Members: 89
Pres: John Doyle; Gen Secr: Judy Dixey
Focus: Fine Arts 12271

Royal Welsh Agricultural Society, LLnlwedd, Builth-Wells, Powys LD2 3SY
T: (01982) 553683; Fax: 553563
Founded: 1904; Members: 14000
Gen Secr: D. Walters
Focus: Agri
Periodical
Annual Journal (annually) 12272

Royal West of England Academy, Queen's Rd, Clifton, Bristol BS8 1PX
T: (0117) 9735129; Fax: 9237874
Founded: 1844; Members: 160
Pres: Peter Thursby; Gen Secr: Rachel Fear
Focus: Arts 12273

The Royal Zoological Society of Scotland, c/o Scottish National Zoological Park, Murrayfield, Edinburgh EH12 6TS
T: (0131) 3349171; Fax: 3164050
Founded: 1909; Members: 13000
Pres: John Grant of Rothiemorchas; Gen Secr: Prof. Roger J. Wheater
Focus: Zoology
Periodical
Ark File (quarterly) 12274

RSNC Wildlife Trusts Partnership, The Green, Witham Park, Waterside South, Lincoln LN5 7JR
T: (01522) 544400; Fax: 511616
Founded: 1912; Members: 250000
Focus: Ecology 12275

Rugby Football Schools Union (RFSU), c/o Rugby Football Union, Twickenham TW1 1DZ
T: (0181) 8928161; Fax: 8929816
Founded: 1970; Members: 1500
Focus: Sports 12276

Rutland Agricultural Society, 8 High St, Oakham, Rutland LE15 6AL
T: (01572) 2018
Founded: 1830; Members: 500
Focus: Agri
Periodical
Schedule & Show Catalogue (annually) . 12277

Saint Albans and Hertfordshire Architectural and Archaeological Society (SAHAAS), 24 Rose Walk, Saint Albans AL4 9AF
T: (01727) 853204
Founded: 1845; Members: 550
Pres: D.J. Dean; Gen Secr: B.E. Moody
Focus: Archeol; Archit; Hist
Periodical
Hertfordshire Archaeology 12278

Saint John's Hospital Dermatological Society, c/o Saint John's Dermatology Centre, Saint Thomas' Hospital, London SE1 7EH
T: (0171) 9289292
Founded: 1911; Members: 500
Pres: Dr. C. Darley; Gen Secr: Dr. S. Neill
Focus: Derm
Periodical
Clinical and Experimental Dermatology (bi-monthly) 12279

Saintpaulia and Houseplant Society, 33 Church Rd, Newbury Park, Ilford IG2 7ET
Founded: 1956; Members: 720
Focus: Hort
Periodical
Bulletin (quarterly) 12280

Saltire Society, 9 Fountain Close, 22 High St, Edinburgh EH1 1TF
Founded: 1936; Members: 1640
Pres: Paul Scott; Gen Secr: Kathleen Munro
Focus: Arts 12281

SATRA Technology Centre, SATRA House, Rockingham Rd, Kettering NN16 9JH
T: (01536) 410000; E-Mail: admin@satra.co.uk; Fax: 410626
Founded: 1919; Members: 1200
Pres: Dr. R.E. Whittaker; Gen Secr: John Butcher
Focus: Eng
Periodical
Footwear Business International (monthly) 12282

Schizophrenia Association of Great Britain (SAGB), Bryn Hyfryd, The Crescent, Bangor LL57 2AG
T: (01248) 354048; Fax: 354048
Founded: 1970; Members: 2100
Pres: Dr. David Horrobin; Gen Secr: Gwynneth Hemmings
Focus: Psychiatry
Periodical
Newsletter (2-3 times annually) 12283

School Natural Science Society (SNSS), 22 Chada Av, Gillingham KT5 8QU
T: (01634) 51973
Founded: 1903; Members: 1400
Focus: Educ; Nat Sci
Periodical
Science Teaching (3 times annually) . . 12284

Science and Engineering Research Council (SERC), Polaris House, North Star Av, Swindon SN2 1ET
T: (01793) 411000; Fax: 411400
Founded: 1965
Focus: Astronomy; Bio; Chem; Eng; Math; Nucl Res; Physics
Periodicals
Annual Report (annually)
SERC Bulletin (3 times annually) . . . 12285

Scientific Committee on Antarctic Research (SCAR), c/o Scott Polar Research Institute, Lensfield Rd, Cambridge CB2 1ER
T: (01223) 62061
Founded: 1958
Focus: Geophys; Geography 12286

Scientific Exploration Society (SES), Home Farm, Mildenhall, Marlborough SN8 2LF
T: (01672) 2994
Founded: 1969; Members: 154
Focus: Geography 12287

Scope, 6-10 Market Rd, London N7 0PW
Founded: 1952
Pres: Duke of Westminster; Gen Secr: Richard Brewster
Focus: Rehabil
Periodicals
Clinics in Developmental Medicine (irregularly)
Developmental Medicine + Child Neurology (monthly)
Disability Now (monthly) 12288

Scots Ancestry Research Society, 29b Albany St, Edinburgh EH1 3QN
T: (0131) 5564220
Founded: 1945
Focus: Genealogy 12289

Scottish Arts Council (SAC), 12 Manor Pl, Edinburgh EH3 7DD
T: (0131) 2266051; Fax: 2259833
Founded: 1946; Members: 22
Pres: Magnus Linklater; Gen Secr: Seona Reid
Focus: Arts 12290

Scottish Association for Building Education and Training (SABET), c/o Reid Kerr College, Renfrew Rd, Paisley PA3 4DR
Founded: 1950
Focus: Adult Educ; Civil Eng 12291

The Scottish Association for Marine Science (SAMS), c/o Dunstaffnage Marine Laboratory, Oban PA34 4AD
T: (01631) 562244; Fax: 565518
Founded: 1897; Members: 500
Pres: Dr. David Smith; Gen Secr: Dr. Graham B. Shimmield
Focus: Bio; Oceanography
Periodicals
Annual Report (annually)
Newsletter (semi-annually) 12292

Scottish Association of Advisers in Physical Education, c/o Educational Dept, Strathclyde Regional Council, Regional Offices, Dumbarton G82 3PU
T: 65151
Founded: 1939
Focus: Sports 12293

Scottish Association of Geography Teachers (SAGT), 19 Auchingramont Rd, Hamilton ML3 6JD
T: (01698) 29531
Founded: 1970; Members: 580
Focus: Geography; Educ 12294

Scottish Association of Writers (SAW), 221 East Clyde St, Helensburgh Dunbartonshire
T: (0141) 3343164
Founded: 1970
Focus: Lit 12295

Scottish Business Education Council, 22 Great King St, Edinburgh EH3 6QH
T: (0131) 5774555
Focus: Adult Educ
Periodicals
Annual Report (annually)
Business Education Guide (annually)
Careers Leaflets (annually)
Handbook (annually) 12296

Scottish Catholic Historical Association (SCHA), c/o John S. Burns & Sons, 25 Finlas St, Glasgow G22 5DS
T: (0141) 3368678
Founded: 1950
Focus: Hist; Rel & Theol 12297

Scottish Church History Society, 1 Denham Green Terrace, Edinburgh EH5 3PG
T: (0131) 5524059; Fax: 5524059
Founded: 1922; Members: 290
Pres: Gavin White; Gen Secr: Peter H. Donald
Focus: Hist; Rel & Theol
Periodical
Records (annually) 12298

Scottish Design, 7 Nelson Mandela Pl, Glasgow G2 7JN
T: (0141) 2216121; Fax: 2218799
Founded: 1994
Gen Secr: Andrew Travers
Focus: Graphic & Dec Arts, Design . . 12299

Scottish Economic Society (SES), c/o Dept of Economy, Adam Smith Bldg, Glasgow University, Glasgow G12 8RT
T: (0141) 3398855; Fax: 3304940
Founded: 1954; Members: 200
Focus: Econ
Periodical
Scottish Journal of Political Economy (quarterly) 12300

Scottish Electrophysiological Society, c/o Physiology Dept, Bute Medical Buildings, University, Saint Andrews KY16 9TS
T: (01334) 76161
Focus: Electrochem 12301

Scottish Epilepsy Association (SEA), 48 Govan Rd, Glasgow G51 1JL
T: (0141) 4274911
Founded: 1954
Focus: Pathology 12302

Scottish Field Studies Association (SFSA), Kindrogan House Field Centre, Enochdhu, Blairgowrie PH10 7PG
T: (01250) 881286; Fax: 881433
Founded: 1945; Members: 400
Pres: Dr. A. Pike
Focus: Nat Sci
Periodical
Annual Report (annually) 12303

Scottish Gaelic Texts Society (SGTS), c/o Dept of Celtic, King's College, Aberdeen AB24 3UB
T: (01224) 272544; E-Mail: r.a.v.cox@abdn.ac.uk; Fax: 272562
Founded: 1934; Members: 150
Pres: Dr. Roderick MacLeod; Gen Secr: Dr. Richard Cox
Focus: Lit
Periodical
SGTS Publications (irregularly) 12304

The Scottish Genealogy Society, 15 Victoria Terrace, Edinburgh EH1 2JL
T: (0131) 2203677; E-Mail: scotgensoc@sol.co.uk; Fax: 2203677
Founded: 1953
Pres: Sir Malcolm Innes of Edingight; Gen Secr: J.P.S. Ferguson
Focus: Genealogy
Periodicals
Pre-1855 Monumental Inscription Lists (irregularly)
Register of Members' Interests (irregularly)
The Scottish Genealogist (quarterly) . . 12305

Scottish History Society, c/o Dept of Scottish History, University of Aberdeen, Aberdeen AB9 1FX
Founded: 1886; Members: 800
Pres: Dr. G.G. Simpson; Gen Secr: Dr. S.I. Boardman
Focus: Hist 12306

Scottish Industrial Heritage Society (SSIA), 129 Fotheringay Rd, Glasgow G41 4LG
T: (0141) 4231782
Founded: 1984; Members: 140
Gen Secr: Eric T. Watt
Focus: Archeol
Periodical
Newsletter (quarterly) 12307

Scottish Inland Waterways Association (SIWA), 139 Old Dalkeith Rd, Edinburgh EH16 4SZ
T: (0131) 6641070
Founded: 1971; Members: 240
Gen Secr: G.A. Hunter
Focus: Transport
Periodical
SIWA News (3 times annually) 12308

Scottish Language Society, 31 Braeside Park, Balloch, Inverness
T: Culloden Moor 689
Founded: 1969; Members: 485
Focus: Ling 12309

Scottish Library Association, Motherwell Business Centre, 124 Coursington Rd, Motherwell ML1 1PW
T: (01698) 252526; Fax: 252057
Founded: 1908; Members: 2200
Pres: John Hunter; Gen Secr: Robert Craig
Focus: Libraries & Bk Sci
Periodical
Scottish Libraries (bi-monthly) 12310

Scottish National Dictionary Association, 27 George Sq, Edinburgh EH8 9LD
T: (0131) 6504149; E-Mail: mail@snda.org.uk; Fax: 6504149
Founded: 1929; Members: 150
Pres: Sir Kenneth Alexander; Gen Secr: H.A. Pirie
Focus: Ling 12311

Scottish National Housing and Town Planning Council, 19 Bentinck Dr, Troon KA10 6HX
T: 314552
Founded: 1912; Members: 110
Focus: Urban Plan 12312

Scottish Ornithologists' Club (SOC), 21 Regent Terrace, Edinburgh EH7 5BT
T: (0131) 5566042
Founded: 1936; Members: 2600
Pres: Ian Darling; Gen Secr: Sylvia Laing
Focus: Ornithology
Periodicals
Scottish Bird News (quarterly)
Scottish Bird Report (annually)
Scottish Birds (semi-annually) 12313

Scottish Pharmaceutical Federation (SPF), 135 Buchanan St, Glasgow G1 2JQ
T: (0141) 2211235
Founded: 1924
Focus: Pharmacol 12314

Scottish Physical Education Association (SPEA), c/o Jordanhill College of Education, Glasgow G13 1PP
T: (0141) 9591232
Founded: 1973; Members: 1000
Focus: Sports 12315

Scottish Record Society, c/o Scottish History Dept, University of Glasgow, Glasgow G12 8QQ
T: (0141) 3398855 ext 5682
Founded: 1897; Members: 383
Pres: Prof. G.W.S. Barrow; Gen Secr: Dr. James Kirk
Focus: Hist; Genealogy 12316

Scottish Secondary Teachers' Association (SSTA), 15 Dundas St, Edinburgh EH3 6QG
T: (0131) 5565919, 5560605; Fax: 5561419
Founded: 1946; Members: 7500
Pres: William A.L. Guthrie; Gen Secr: David H. Eaglesham
Focus: Educ
Periodicals
Bulletin (bi-monthly)
Journal (quarterly) 12317

Scottish Society for Crop Research, c/o Scottish Crop Research Institute, Invergowrie, Dundee DD2 5DA
T: (01382) 562731; E-Mail: lhood@scri.sart.ac.uk; Fax: 562426
Founded: 1981; Members: 300
Gen Secr: D.L. Hood
Focus: Agri; Crop Husb
Periodical
Bulletin (irregularly) 12318

Scottish Society for Northern Studies (SSNS), c/o School of Scottish Studies, University of Edinburgh, 27 George Sq, Edinburgh EH8 9LD
T: (0131) 6504162; Fax: 6506534
Founded: 1967; Members: 275
Pres: Dr. Ian Morrsison; Gen Secr: Morag Redford
Focus: Ethnology; Archeol; Hist; Lit
Periodical
Northern Studies (annually) 12319

Scottish Society for The Preservation of Historical Machinery, c/o Glasgow University Mechanical Engineering Research Annexe, 49 Spencer St, Glasgow G13
Focus: Eng; Preserv Hist Monuments; Cultur Hist 12320

Scottish Society of The History of Medicine (SSHM), c/o Grampian Health Board Offices, Woolmanhill, Aberdeen AB9 1EF
T: (01224) 663456; Fax: 840791
Founded: 1948; Members: 180
Focus: Med; Cultur Hist
Periodicals
Newsletter (annually)
Report of Proceedings (annually) 12321

Scottish Tartans Society, FONAB House, Pitlochry PH16 5ND
Founded: 1963; Members: 1086
Focus: Hist
Periodicals
Proceedings (irregularly)
Tartans (semi-annually) 12322

Scottish Text Society (STS), 27 George Sq, Edinburgh EH8 9LD
T: (031) 6504147; E-Mail: lorna.pike@ed.ac.uk
Founded: 1882; Members: 220
Pres: Prof. R.J. Lyall; Gen Secr: Lorna Pike
Focus: Lit
Periodical
Publications (annually) 12323

Scottish Tramway Museum Society (STMS), POB 78, Glasgow G3 6ER
Founded: 1951; Members: 142
Focus: Transport
Periodical
Scottish Transport (semi-annually) . . . 12324

Scottish Wildlife Trust (SWT), Cramond House, Kirk Cramond, Cramond Glebe Rd, Edinburgh EH4 6NS
T: (0131) 3127765; Fax: 3128705
Founded: 1964; Members: 15000
Pres: Sir John Lister-Raye; Gen Secr: David Hughes Hallett
Focus: Ecology; Forestry
Periodical
Scottish Wildlife 12325

Seabird Group, c/o RSPB, The Lodge, Sandy SG19 2DL
Founded: 1966; Members: 300
Focus: Ornithology
Periodicals
Seabird: Annual Journal (annually)
Seabird Group Newsletter (3 times annually) 12326

Selborne Society, 89 Daryngton Dr, Greenford UB6 8BH
Founded: 1885; Members: 900
Gen Secr: R.J. Hall
Focus: Hist; Nat Sci
Periodical
The Selborne Magazine (quarterly) . . . 12327

Selden Society, c/o Faculty of Law, Queen Mary College, Mile End Rd, London E1 4NS
T: (0171) 9755136; E-Mail: selden-society@qmw.ac.uk; Fax: 9818733
Founded: 1887; Members: 1700
Pres: Lord Mustill; Gen Secr: Victor Tunkel
Focus: Hist; Law
Periodicals
Early Law Reports
Legal Records (annually) 12328

The Sempervivum Society, 11 Wingle Tye Rd, Burgess Hill RH15 9HR
T: (01444) 236848; E-Mail: sempervivum@platformll.org.uk; Fax: 236848
Founded: 1970; Members: 300
Gen Secr: Peter J. Mitchell
Focus: Ecology
Periodical
Newsletter 12329

Sexual Law Reform Society (SLRS), 31 Clapham Rd, London SW9 0JD
T: (0171) 5820972
Founded: 1968; Members: 100
Focus: Law 12330

Shakespeare Birthplace Trust, c/o The Shakespeare Centre, Stratford-upon-Avon CV37 6QW
T: (01789) 204016; Fax: 296083
Founded: 1847
Gen Secr: Roger Pringle
Focus: Lit; Preserv Hist Monuments . . 12331

Shakespeare Institue, c/o University of Birmingham, Mason Croft, Church St, Stratford-upon-Avon CV37 6HP
T: (01789) 293138; Fax: 414992
Founded: 1952
Pres: Prof. Peter Holland
Focus: Lit
Periodicals
Conference Report
Report of The International Shakespeare Conference 12332

Shakespeare Reading Society, 17 Lake Close, Lake Rd, London SW19 7EE
T: (0181) 9473036
Founded: 1875; Members: 50
Focus: Lit 12333

Sheffield Metallurgical and Engineering Association (SMEA), c/o British Steel Technical, Moorgate, Rotherham S60 3AR
T: (01709) 820166; Fax: 825337
Founded: 1963; Members: 600
Focus: Metallurgy; Eng 12334

Sherlock Holmes Society of London, 13 Crofton Av, Orpington BR6 8DU
T: (01689) 811314; Fax: 811314
Founded: 1951; Members: 1000
Pres: A.D. Howlett; Gen Secr: R.J. Ellis
Focus: Lit
Periodical
Sherlock Holmes Journal (semi-annually) . 12335

Shetland Council of Social Service, 4b Market St, Lerwick ZE1 0JN
T: (01595) 3816
Founded: 1959; Members: 130
Focus: Sociology 12336

Shropshire Archaeological and Parish Register Society (SAS), c/o Much Wenlock Museum, High St, Much Wenlock TF13 6HR
T: (01952) 727773; Fax: 461522
Founded: 1877; Members: 313
Focus: Archeol; Hist
Periodical
Transactions (annually) 12337

Simplified Speeling Society (SSS), 5 Gwyder Rd, Beckenham, Kent
T: 5841848
Founded: 1908
Focus: Ling 12338

Sira, South Hill, Chislehurst BR7 5EH
T: (0181) 4672636; Fax: 4676515
Founded: 1918; Members: 85
Pres: R.A. Brook; Gen Secr: M.A. Bowles
Focus: Eng; Optics
Periodical
Spotlight (quarterly) 12339

Social History Society of the United Kingdom (SHS), c/o Centre for Social History, Lancaster University, Lancaster LA1 4YG
T: (01524) 592605; E-Mail: L.Persson@lancaster.ac.uk; Fax: 846102
Founded: 1976; Members: 712
Pres: Lord Briggs; Gen Secr: Dr. Cynthia Hay
Focus: Hist
Periodical
Bulletin (semi-annually) 12340

Social Policy Association (SAA), c/o School of Social and Professional Studies, University of Humberside, Inglemire Av, Hull HU6 7LU
Founded: 1968; Members: 320
Focus: Public Admin
Periodical
Social Policy Review (annually) 12341

Social Research Association (SRA), c/o Dept of Applied Social Studies, Polytechnic of North London, Ladbroke House, Highbury Grove, London N5 2AD
T: (0171) 6072789 ext 5082/5000
Founded: 1978; Members: 491
Focus: Sociology 12342

Socialist Educational Association (SEA), 62 Thornhill Rd, Heaton Mersey, Stockport SK4 3HL
T: 4321409
Founded: 1960; Members: 650
Focus: Educ 12343

Socialist Health Association (SHA), 16 Charles Sq, London N1 6HP
T: (0171) 4900057; Fax: 4900057
Founded: 1930; Members: 1330
Focus: Public Health
Periodical
Socialism & Health (bi-monthly) 12344

La Société Guernesiaise, Candie Gardens, Saint Peter Port GY1 1UG
T: (01481) 725093; Fax: 726248
Founded: 1882; Members: 2050
Pres: N.M. Ozanne; Gen Secr: L.S. Sherwill
Focus: Nat Sci; Hist; Archeol; Preserv Hist Monuments
Periodical
Transactions (annually) 12345

Société Jersiaise, 7 Pier Rd, Saint Helier, Jersey
T: (01534) 58314; Fax: 888262
Founded: 1873; Members: 4300
Pres: Marie-Louise Backhurst; Gen Secr: Pauline Syvret
Focus: Nat Sci
Periodical
Bulletin (annually) 12346

Society for African Church History, c/o Dept of Religious Studies, King's College, University of Aberdeen, Aberdeen AB9 2UB
T: (01224) 40241
Founded: 1963
Focus: Hist; Rel & Theol 12347

Society for Applied Bacteriology (SAB), c/o Faculty of Agriculture, Food and Land Use, University of Ayrmouth, Newton Abbot TQ12 6NQ
Founded: 1931; Members: 1650
Focus: Microbio
Periodicals
Journal of Applied Bacteriology (semi-annually)
Symposium Series (annually)
Technical Series (annually) 12348

The Society for Army Historical Research, c/o The National Army Museum, Royal Hospital Rd, London SW3 4HT
Founded: 1921; Members: 1000
Pres: Sir John Chapple; Gen Secr: G. Evelyn
Focus: Hist; Military Sci
Periodical
Journal (quarterly) 12349

Society for Back Pain Research (SBPR), c/o Bone and Joint Research Unit, The London Hospital, London E1 1BB
T: (0171) 2475454
Founded: 1971; Members: 130
Focus: Med 12350

Society for Computers and Law (SCL), 10 Hurle Crescent, Clifton, Bristol BS8 2TA
T: (0117) 9237393; Fax: 9239305
Founded: 1973; Members: 2500
Pres: Justice Brooke; Gen Secr: Ruth Baker
Focus: Law; Computer & Info Sci
Periodical
Computers & Law (bi-monthly) 12351

Society for Cooperation in Russian and Soviet Studies, 320 Brixton Rd, London SW9 6AB
T: (0171) 2742282; Fax: 2743230
Founded: 1924; Members: 1500
Pres: Stanley Forman; Gen Secr: Jean Turner
Focus: Ethnology
Periodical
Newsletter (quarterly) 12352

Society for Earthquake and Civil Engineering Dynamics (SECED), c/o Institution of Civil Engineers, 1-7 Great George St, London SW1
T: (0171) 8399827; Fax: 2227500
Members: 150
Focus: Geophys; Civil Eng 12353

Society for Education in Film and Television (SEFT), 63 Old Compton St, London W1V 5PM
T: (0171) 7345455
Founded: 1950
Focus: Educ 12354

Society for Endocrinology, 17-18 The Courtyard, Woodlands, Almondsbury, Bristol BS12 4NQ
T: (01454) 616046; Fax: 616071
Founded: 1946; Members: 1434
Pres: S.G. Hillier; Gen Secr: S. Franks
Focus: Endocrinology
Periodicals
Endocrine-Related Cancer (quarterly)
Journal of Endocrinology (monthly)
Journal of Molecular Endocrinology (bi-monthly)
. . . . 12355

Society for Environmental Therapy (SET), c/o Dept of Bacteriology and Virology, University of Manchester, Manchester M13 9PT
T: (0161) 2738241 ext 68
Founded: 1980; Members: 300
Focus: Toxicology; Immunology; Pharmacol
Periodical
Newsletter (quarterly) 12356

The Society for Experimental Biology (SEB), Burlington House, Piccadilly, London WIV OLQ
T: (0171) 4398732; E-Mail: v.wragg@pop3.demon.co.uk; Fax: 2874786
Founded: 1923; Members: 2300
Pres: Prof. J.A. Raven
Focus: Bio
Periodicals
Journal of Experimental Botany (monthly)
The Plant Journal (monthly)
Seminar Series (2-3 times annually)
Symposia (annually) 12357

Society for Folk Life Studies, c/o Ulster Folk and Transport Museum, Cultra Manor, Hollywood BT18 0EU
T: 5411
Founded: 1961; Members: 600
Focus: Ethnology 12358

Society for General Microbiology, Marlborough House, Basingstoke Rd, Spencers Wood, Reading RG7 1AE
T: (01189) 885577; Fax: 885656
Founded: 1945; Members: 5000
Pres: Prof. H. Dalton; Gen Secr: Dr. R.S.S. Fraser
Focus: Microbio
Periodicals
Journal of General Virology (monthly)
Microbiology (monthly)
Society for General Microbiology Quarterly (quarterly) 12359

Society for Interactive Learning (SAGSET), 11 Lloyd St, Crawcrook, Ryton NE40 4DJ
T: (0191) 4132262; Fax: 4132262
Founded: 1970; Members: 166
Pres: Morry van Ments; Gen Secr: Peter Walsh
Focus: Adult Educ; Educ
Periodical
The International Gaming & Simulation Yearbook (annually) 12360

Society for Italic Handwriting, 59a Arlington Rd, London NW1
T: (0171) 3887117
Founded: 1952; Members: 1100
Focus: Ling 12361

Society for Libyan Studies, c/o Institute of Archaeology, 31-34 Gordon Sq, London WC1H 0PY
T: (071) 3877050 ext 7495
Founded: 1969; Members: 325
Pres: Sir Stephen Egerton
Focus: Ethnology; Geology; Archeol; Geography; Hist
Periodical
Libyan Studies (annually) 12362

Society for Lincolnshire History and Archaeology (S.L.H.A.), Jews' Court, Steep Hill, Lincoln LN2 1LS
T: (01522) 521337
Founded: 1974; Members: 850
Focus: Archeol; Hist
Periodicals
Lincolnshire History and Archaeology (annually)
Lincolnshire Past and Present (quarterly) 12363

Society for Low Temperature Biology (SLTB), c/o Institute of Biology, 20-22 Queensberry Pl, London SW7 2DZ
T: (0171) 5818333
Founded: 1964; Members: 220
Gen Secr: Dr. S.J. Paynter
Focus: Bio 12364

Society for Medicine Research, c/o Institute of Biology, 20 Queensberry Pl, London SW7 2DZ
T: (0171) 5818333
Founded: 1966
Focus: Pharmacol 12365

Society for Medieval Archaeology (SMA), c/o Archaeology Service, Information and Community Services, Winston Churchill Bldg, Radbrook Centre, Shrewsbury SY3 9BJ
Fax: (01743) 254009
Founded: 1957; Members: 1500
Pres: Prof. M. Biddle; Gen Secr: Dr. P. Stamper
Focus: Archeol
Periodical
Medieval Archaeology (annually) 12366

Society for Multivariate Experimental Psychology, c/o National Foundation for Educational Research, The Mere, Upton Park, Slough
Focus: Psych 12367

Society for Nautical Research (SNR), c/o National Maritime Museum, Greenwich, London SE10 9NF
T: (0171)2185449
Founded: 1910; Members: 2o00
Pres: Lord Lewin; Gen Secr: W.J.R. Gardner
Focus: Navig; Archeol; Hist
Periodical
The Mariners' Mirror (quarterly) 12368

Society for New Testament Study, c/o Dept 07 Religious Studies, University of Lancaster, Lancaster LA1 4YG
T: (01524) 65201 ext 4420
Founded: 1938; Members: 800
Focus: Rel & Theol
Periodical
New Testament Studies (quarterly) . . . 12369

Society for Popular Astronomy (SPA), 36 Fairway, Keyworth, Nottingham NG12 5DU
Founded: 1953; Members: 2500
Gen Secr: Guy N.H. Fennimore
Focus: Astronomy
Periodicals
Circular Newsletter (bi-monthly)
Popular Astronomy (quarterly) 12370

Society for Post-Medieval Archaeology (SPMA), c/o Dept of Medieval and Later Antiquities, British Museum, Great Russell St, London WC1B 3DG
T: (0171) 3238734; Fax: 3238496
Founded: 1967; Members: 800
Pres: D. Barker; Gen Secr: Dr. David Gaimster
Focus: Archeol
Periodicals
Journal (annually)
Newsheet (06) 12371

Society for Promoting Christian Knowledge (SPCK), Holy Trinity Church, Marylebone Rd, London NW1 4DU
T: (0171) 3875282; Fax: 3882352
Founded: 1698
Focus: Rel & Theol
Periodical
Theology (bi-monthly) 12372

Society for Promotion of Educational Reform through Teacher Training (SPERTTT), c/o Sidney Webb College, 9-12 Barrett St, London W1M 6DE
T: (0171) 4864771
Founded: 1969
Focus: Educ 12373

Society for Psychical Research, 49 Marloes Rd, London W8 6LA
T: (0171) 9378984; Fax: 9378984
Founded: 1882; Members: 1180
Pres: Prof. Dr. G. Fontana; Gen Secr: E.J. O'Keeffe
Focus: Parapsych
Periodicals
Journal of the Society for Psychical Research (quarterly)
The Paranormal Review (quarterly)
Proceedings (irregularly) 12374

Society for Psychosomatic Research, c/o Dept of Psychiatry, Westminster Hospital, Horseferry Rd, London SW1P 2AP
Founded: 1955; Members: 100
Focus: Neurology 12375

Society for Radiological Protection (SRP), c/o National Radiological Protection Board, Chilton, Didcot OX11 0RQ
T: (01235) 831600; Fax: 833891
Founded: 1963
Focus: Radiology
Periodical
Journal of Radiological Protection (quarterly)
. . . . 12376

Society for Renaissance Studies, c/o Dept of Italian, University of Bristol, Bristol BS8 1TE
T: (0117) 9287588; Fax: 9288143
Founded: 1967; Members: 550
Pres: Dr. F. Ames-Lewis; Gen Secr: Dr. Stephen Milner
Focus: Hist
Periodical
Bulletin of The Society for Renaissance Studies (semi-annually) 12377

Society for Research in The Psychology of Music and Music Education, c/o Faculty of Arts, North East London Polytechnic, Longsbridge Rd, Dagenham RM8 2AS
T: 5901640
Founded: 1972; Members: 330
Focus: Psych; Music; Educ 12378

Society for Research into Higher Education (SRHE), 344-354 Gray's Inn Rd, London WC1X 8BP
T: (0171) 8377880; Fax: 7130690
Founded: 1964; Members: 644
Focus: Educ
Periodicals
Abstracts (3 times annually)
Higher Education (quarterly)
International Newsletter (quarterly)
Proceedings (annually)
SRHE News (quarterly)
Studies in Higher Education (3 times annually)
. . . . 12379

Society for Research into Hydrocephalus and Spina Bifida, c/o Darlington Memorial Hospital, Hollyhurst Rd, Darlington DL3 6HX
T: (01325) 380100; Fax: 1325743622
Founded: 1957; Members: 306
Gen Secr: Carole A. Sobkowiak
Focus: Pathology
Periodical
European Journal of Paediatric Surgery . 12380

Society for South Asian Studies, c/o Dept. of Oriental Antiquities, British Museum, London WC1B 3DG
Founded: 1972
Focus: Cultur Hist; Ethnology 12381

Society for the Advancement of Anaesthesia in Dentistry (SAAD), 53 Wimpole St, London W1M 7DF
T: (0171) 9351656
Focus: Anesthetics
Periodical
SAAD Digest (quarterly) 12382

Society for The Development of Techniques in Industrial Marketing (SDTIM), 9 Aston Rd, Nuneaton CV11 5EL
T: 67161
Founded: 1967
Focus: Advert 12383

Society for The Health Education (SHE), 69 Cornwall Gardens, London SW7 4BA
T: (0171) 9372520
Founded: 1962; Members: 1077
Focus: Public Health; Educ 12384

Society for The History of Alchemy and Chemistry, c/o The Science Museum, South Kensington, London SW7 2DD
T: (0171) 9388045; Fax: 9388118
Founded: 1937; Members: 250
Focus: Chem; Hist
Periodical
Ambix (3 times annually) 12385

Society for The History of Natural History, c/o The Natural History Museum, London SW7 5BD
T: (0171) 9389306; E-Mail: c.mills@nhm.ac.uk
Founded: 1936; Members: 600
Pres: Iain Rolfe; Gen Secr: Christopher Mills
Focus: Hist; Nat Sci
Periodicals
Archives of Natural History (3 times annually)
Special Publications (irregularly) 12386

Society for the Promotion of Hellenic Studies, Senate House, Malet St, London WC1E 7HU
T: (0171) 3239590; E-Mail: hellenic@sas.ac.uk; Fax: 3239591
Founded: 1879; Members: 2800
Pres: Prof. P.E. Easterling; Gen Secr: F.J. Fisher-Hunt
Focus: Lit; Hist; Archeol
Periodical
The Journal of Hellenic Studies and Supplement Archaeological Reports (annually) 12387

Society for the Promotion of New Music, Francis House, Francis St, London SW1P 1DE
T: (0171) 8289696; Fax: 9319928
Founded: 1943; Members: 1400
Pres: Sir Peter Maxwell Davies; Gen Secr: Graham Cathy
Focus: Music
Periodical
New: Notes (monthly) 12388

Society for The Promotion of Principles, 47 Long Mynd Rd, Northfield, Birmingham B31 1HJ
Members: 8
Focus: Philos 12389

Society for the Promotion of Roman Studies, Senate House, Malet St, London WC1E 7HU
T: (0171) 3239583; E-Mail: romansoc@sas.ac.uk; Fax: 3239584
Founded: 1910; Members: 3500
Pres: Dr. Averil M. Cameron; Gen Secr: Dr. Helen M. Cockle
Focus: Hist; Archeol; Lit
Periodicals
Britannia (annually)
Britannia Monographs (irregularly)
Journal of Roman Studies (annually)
Journal of Roman Studies Monographs (irregularly)
. . . . 12390

Society for The Promotion of Vocational Training and Education, c/o South Bristol Technical College, Marksbury Rd, Bedminster, Bristol BS3 5JL
T: (01272) 661105
Founded: 1973
Focus: Adult Educ 12391

The Society for the Protection of Ancient Buildings (S.P.A.B), 37 Spital Sq, London E1 6DY
T: (0171) 3771644; Fax: 2475296
Founded: 1877; Members: 6000
Pres: Duke of Grafton; Gen Secr: Philip Venning
Focus: Preserv Hist Monuments
Periodical
S.P.A.B. News (quarterly) 12392

Society for The Protection of Science and Learning (SPSL), 3 Buckland Crescent, London NW3 5DH
T: (0171) 7222095
Founded: 1933
Focus: Sci; Educ 12393

Society for The Social History of Medicine (SSHM), c/o Wellcome Unit for The History of Medicine, Maths Tower, The University, Manchester M13 9PL
T: (0161) 2755910
Founded: 1969; Members: 600
Focus: Hist; Med
Periodical
Social History of Medicine (3 times annually)
. . . . 12394

Society for The Study of Addiction (SSA), c/o Saint Christopher's Day Hospital, 52 Hurst Rd, Horsham RH12 2EP
T: (01403) 4367
Founded: 1884; Members: 400
Focus: Med 12395

Society for the Study of Human Biology (SSHB), c/o School of Biological and Molecular Sciences, Oxford Broomes University, Oxford OX3 0BP
T: (01865) 483818; E-Mail: jhenry@broomes.ac.uk; Fax: 484017
Founded: 1958
Pres: Dr. C.G.N. Mascie-Taylor; Gen Secr: Prof. C.J.K. Henry
Focus: Bio
Periodicals
Annals of Human Biology (bi-monthly)
Symposia volumes (annually) 12396

Society for The Study of Inborn Errors of Metabolism (SSIEM), c/o Willink Laboratory, Royal Manchester Childrens Hospital, Manchester M27 1HA
T: (0161) 7944696 ext 2138
Founded: 1963; Members: 700
Focus: Med
Periodical
Journal of Inherited Metabolic Disease (bi-monthly)
. . . . 12397

Society for The Study of Information Transfer, 76c The Avenue, Beckenham BR3 2ES
Founded: 1973
Focus: Computer & Info Sci 12398

Society for The Study of Labour History, c/o Polytechnic of Central London, Regent St, London W1A 8AL
T: (0171) 5802021
Founded: 1960; Members: 1050
Focus: Hist; Sociology 12399

Society for the Study of Medieval Languages and Literature (SSMLL), 32 Great Clarendon St, Oxford OX2 6AT
Fax: (01865) 557775
Founded: 1932
Pres: Prof. C.N. Mann; Gen Secr: Dr. C. Larrington
Focus: Ling; Lit
Periodical
Medium Aevum (semi-annually) 12400

Society for The Study of Normal Psychology, 151 Talgarth Rd, London W14
Focus: Psych
Periodicals
The Bridge (bi-monthly)
Fresh Morning of Life 12401

The Society for Theatre Research (STR), c/o Theatre Museum, 1E Tavistock St, London WC2E 7PA
Founded: 1948; Members: 800
Pres: Prof. Glynne Wickham; Gen Secr: Eileen Cottis
Focus: Perf Arts
Periodical
Theatre Notebook (3 times annually) . . 12402

Society for Underwater Technology (SUT), 76 Mark Ln, London EC3R 7JN
T: (0171) 4810750; E-Mail: inlg@sutadmin.demon.co.uk; Fax: 4814001
Founded: 1965; Members: 1500
Pres: Sir Anthony Laughton; Gen Secr: I.N.L. Gallett
Focus: Eng; Sci
Periodical
Underwater Technology (quarterly) . . . 12403

Society of Antiquaries of London (S.A.L.), Burlington House, Piccadilly, London W1V 0HS
T: (0171) 7340193; E-Mail: soc.antiq.lond@dial.pipex.com; Fax: 2876967
Founded: 1707; Members: 2100
Pres: S.S. Jervis; Gen Secr: David M. Evans
Focus: Archeol
Periodicals
Antiquaries Journal (annually)
Archaeologia (every 3-4 years) 12404

Society of Antiquaries of Newcastle-upon-Tyne, Black Gate, Castle Garth, Newcastle-upon-Tyne NE1 1RQ
T: (0191) 2615390
Founded: 1813; Members: 730
Focus: Archeol
Periodical
Archaeologia Aeliana (annually) 12405

Society of Antiquaries of Scotland, c/o Royal Museum of Scotland, Chambers St, Edinburgh EH1 1JF
Founded: 1780; Members: 3300
Pres: Prof. Michael Lynch; Gen Secr: Fionna Ashmore
Focus: Archeol; Hist
Periodicals
Monographs (irregularly)
Proceedings (annually) 12406

Society of Archer Antiquaries, 62 Lambert Rd, Bridlington YO16 5RD
Founded: 1956; Members: 400
Focus: Archeol 12407

Society of Architectural Historians of Great Britain (SAHGB), Brandon Mead, Old Park Ln, Farnham GU9 0AJ
Founded: 1956; Members: 1100
Pres: Margaret Richardson; Gen Secr: Dr. Deborah Mays
Focus: Archit; Hist
Periodicals
Architectural History (annually)
Newsletter 12408

Society of Architectural Illustrators, POB 22, Stroud GL5 3DH
T: (01453) 882563; Fax: 882563
Founded: 1975; Members: 359
Pres: Philip Crowe; Gen Secr: Eric Monk
Focus: Graphic & Dec Arts, Design
Periodicals
Newsletter
Yearbook 12409

Society of Archivists (SA), c/o Information House, 20-24 Old St, London EC1V 9AP
T: (0171) 2535087; Fax: 2533942
Founded: 1947; Members: 1500
Pres: P. Cadell; Gen Secr: E. Shepherd
Focus: Archives
Periodicals
Journal (semi-annually)
Newsletter (monthly) 12410

Society of Assistants Teaching in Preparatory Schools (SATIPS), 222 Hale Rd, Hale, Altrincham WA15 8EB
T: (0161) 9802609
Founded: 1953; Members: 1200
Focus: Educ 12411

Society of Authors, 84 Drayton Gardens, London SW10 9SB
T: (0171) 3736642; E-Mail: authorsoc@writers.org.uk; Fax: 3735768
Founded: 1884; Members: 6000
Focus: Lit
Periodical
The Author (quarterly) 12412

Society of British Neurological Surgeons (SBNS), c/o Dept of Neurosurgery, Manchester Royal Infirmary, Oxford Rd, Manchester M13 9WL
Fax: (0161) 2764567 2764565
Founded: 1926; Members: 580
Pres: T. Hide; Gen Secr: R.H. Lye
Focus: Surgery; Neurology
Periodical
Journal of Neurology, Neurosurgery and Psychiatry (semi-annually) 12413

Society of Business Economists (SBE), 11 Bay Tree Walk, Watford WD1 3RX
T: (01923) 237287
Founded: 1953; Members: 650
Pres: Sir D. Lees; Gen Secr: Marian Marshall
Focus: Business Admin
Periodical
The Business Economist (3 times annually) 12414

Society of Cartographers (SUC), c/o Dept of Geography and Topographic Science, University of Glasgow, Glasgow G12 8QQ
T: (0141) 3398855; Fax: 3304894
Founded: 1964; Members: 250
Focus: Cart
Periodical
Bulletin of The Soiety of Cartographers (semi-annually) 12415

Society of Chemical Industry (SCI), 14-15 Belgrave Sq, London SW1X 8PS
T: (0171) 2353681; Fax: 8231698
Founded: 1881; Members: 5500
Pres: Ken Milton
Focus: Chem
Periodicals
Chemistry and Industry (bi-weekly)
Journal of Chemical Technology and Biotechnology (monthly)
Journal of The Science of Food and Agriculture (monthly)
Pesticide Science (monthly)
Polymer International (monthly) 12416

Society of Chief Architects of Local Authorities (SCALA), POB 73, Wirral L63 0QG
T: (01517) 3344068
Founded: 1974; Members: 260
Focus: Archit
Periodicals
SCALA Conference Papers (annually)
SCALA Maintenance Expenature Revue (annually)
SCALA Newsletter (quarterly)
SCALA Study Day Papers (annually) . . 12417

Society of Cirplanologists, 26 Roe Cross Green, Mottram, Hyde SK14 6LP
T: (01457) 763485
Founded: 1955; Members: 105
Pres: O.A. Beckerlegge; Gen Secr: E.A. Rose
Focus: Hist; Rel & Theol 12418

Society of Consulting Marine Engineers and Ship Surveyors, The Italian Bldg, Little London. 41 Dockhead, London SE1 2BS
T: (0171) 2373034; Fax: 2373888
Founded: 1920
Pres: Ian Green; Gen Secr: Peter Hicks
Focus: Eng 12419

Society of County Librarians (SCL), c/o County Library Headquarters, County Hall, Worcester WR5 2NP
T: (01905) 766230; Fax: 763000
Founded: 1966; Members: 47
Focus: Libraries & Bk Sci
Periodical
Information (quarterly) 12420

Society of County Museum Directors, c/o Kent County Museum Service, West Malling Air Station, West Malling ME19 6QE
T: (01732) 845845 ext 2114
Focus: Arts
Periodical
Guide to County Museum Services in England and Wales (irregularly) 12421

Society of Dairy Technology (S.D.T.), 72 Ermine St, Huntingdon PE18 6EZ
T: (01480) 450741; Fax: 431800
Founded: 1943; Members: 2000
Pres: G.C.J. Lee; Gen Secr: R.A. Gale
Focus: Dairy Sci
Periodical
Journal of Dairy Technology (quarterly) . 12422

Society of Designer Craftsmen, 24 Rivington St, London EC2A 3DU
T: (0171) 7393663; E-Mail: richard@societydesignercraft.org.uk; Fax: 7393663
Founded: 1888; Members: 750
Pres: Prof. Christopher Frayling; Gen Secr: Richard O'Donoghue
Focus: Graphic & Dec Arts, Design
Periodicals
The Designer-Craftsman (annually)
News-Sheet (bi-monthly) 12423

The Society of Dyers and Colourists, Perkin House, 82 Grattan Rd, POB 244, Bradford BD1 2JB
T: (01274) 725138; Fax: 392888
Founded: 1884; Members: 3600
Pres: P. Flesher; Gen Secr: Kenneth M. McGhee
Focus: Chem
Periodicals
Journal (10 times annually)
Resource File (annually)
Review of Progress in Coloration and Related Topics (annually) 12424

Society of Engineers, Guinea Wiggs, Nayland, Colchester CO6 4NF
T: (01206) 263332; Fax: 262624
Founded: 1854; Members: 3000
Pres: J.H. Wilkinson; Gen Secr: L.C.A. Wright
Focus: Eng
Periodical
Journal and Transactions (quarterly) . . 12425

Society of Feed Technologists, 156 Oxford Rd, Reading, Berks
T: (01734) 595458
Members: 260
Focus: Agri 12426

Society of Genealogists (SG), 14 Charterhouse Buildings, Goswell Rd, London, EC1M 7BA
T: (0171) 2518799; Fax: 2501800
Founded: 1911; Members: 13750
Pres: Prince Michael of Kent; Gen Secr: Anthony J. Camp
Focus: Genealogy
Periodicals
Computers in Genealogy (quarterly)
Genealogists Magazine (quarterly) . . . 12427

Society of Glass Technology (S.G.T.), 20 Hallam Gate Rd, Sheffield S10 5BT
T: (01142) 663168; E-Mail: gt@glass.demon.co.uk; Fax: 665252
Founded: 1916; Members: 1100
Pres: P. Sewell; Gen Secr: W. Simpson
Focus: Materials Sci
Periodicals
Glass Technology (bi-monthly)
Physics and Chemistry of Glasses (bi-monthly) 12428

Society of Health and Beauty Therapists, 77 New Bond St, London W1Y 9DB
T: (0171) 4933321
Founded: 1962; Members: 5000
Focus: Public Health; Therapeutics . . . 12429

Society of Hearing Aid Audiologists (S.H.A.A.), 54 Croham Manor Rd, South Croydon CR2 7BE
T: 6882503
Founded: 1954; Members: 600
Focus: Rehabil
Periodical
S.H.A.A. Journal (irregularly) 12430

Society of Homoeopaths, 59 Norfolk House Rd, London SW16
T: (0181) 6773260
Founded: 1978; Members: 110
Focus: Homeopathy
Periodical
The Homoeopath (quarterly) 12431

Society of Indexers, Mermaid House, 1 Mermaid Court, London SE1 1HR
T: (0171) 4034947
Founded: 1957; Members: 900
Pres: M. Piggott; Gen Secr: C. Shuttleworth
Focus: Standards; Educ
Periodical
The Indexer (semi-annually) 12432

Society of Industrial Tutors (SIT), c/o Teesside Polytechnic, Middlesbrough, Cleveland
T: (01642) 44176
Founded: 1968; Members: 330
Focus: Adult Educ 12433

Society of King Charles The Martyr, c/o Saint Mary le Strand Parish Office, 171 Strand, London WC2R 2LS
Founded: 1894
Focus: Rel & Theol
Periodical
Church and King (semi-annually) 12434

Society of Licensed Aircraft Engineers and Technologists, Grey Tiles, Kingston Hill, Kingston-upon-Thames KT2 7LW
Founded: 1944; Members: 6500
Focus: Eng
Periodical
Tech Air (monthly) 12435

The Society of Metaphysicians, Archers' Court, Stonestile Ln, The Ridge, Hastings TN35 4PG
T: (01424) 751577; Fax: 722387
Founded: 1944; Members: 62000
Focus: Philos
Periodicals
Borderline Science Series: Esoteric Series (quarterly)
Neo Metaphysical Digest (quarterly)
Neometaphysical Series (quarterly)
Neometaphysics & Current Affairs Series (quarterly) 12436

Society of Miniaturists, c/o Leslie Simpson, Ralston House, 41 Lister St, Ilkley LS29 9ET
T: (01943) 609075; Fax: 603753
Founded: 1895; Members: 75
Pres: Kenneth Elmsley; Gen Secr: Leslie Simpson
Focus: Fine Arts 12437

Society of Occupational Medicine (SOM), 6 Saint Andrew's Pl, London NW1 4LB
T: (0171) 4862641; Fax: 4860028
Founded: 1935; Members: 2000
Pres: Dr. A.J.M. Slovak; Gen Secr: Dr. G. Smith
Focus: Med; Hygiene
Periodical
Occupational Medicine (quarterly) 12438

Society of Protozoologists, British Section, c/o Dept of Anatomy, Guy's Hospital Medical School, London SE1 9RT
T: (0171) 4077600
Founded: 1962; Members: 150
Focus: Zoology 12439

The Society of Public Health, 31 Battye Av, Huddersfield HD4 5PW
Founded: 1856; Members: 1000
Pres: Dr. H.E.A. Carson; Gen Secr: Dr. P.A. Gardner
Focus: Public Health
Periodical
Public Health (bi-monthly) 12440

Society of Public Teachers of Law (SPTL), c/o School of Law, University of Buckingham, Buckingham MK18 1EG
T: (01280) 814080
Founded: 1908; Members: 1450
Focus: Educ; Law
Periodical
Legal Studies (3 times annually) 12441

Society of Remedial Gymnasts and Recreational Therapies (SRG), c/o Combingo Training Institute, Cardiff University Hospital of Wales, Cardiff, Wales
Founded: 1946; Members: 700
Focus: Therapeutics
Periodical
Journal (quarterly) 12442

Society of Scribes and Illuminators (SSI), 6 Queen Sq, London WC1N 3AR
T: (01483) 894155
Founded: 1921; Members: 1868
Gen Secr: Clare Turvey
Focus: Libraries & Bk Sci
Periodical
Journal (3 times annually) 12443

Society of Teachers in Business Education, 88 Springfield Rd, Sheffield S7 2GF
T: (01742) 363659
Founded: 1907; Members: 1600
Focus: Educ
Periodical
Focus on Business Education (3 times annually) 12444

Society of Technical Analysts, 28 Panton St, Cambridge CB2 1DH
T: (01223) 356251; Fax: 329806
Founded: 1969; Members: 700
Focus: Eng 12445

Society of Thoracic and Cardiovascular Surgeons of Great Britain and Ireland, c/o Cardiothoracic Unit, Walsgrave Hospital, Conventry CV2 2DX
T: (01203) 538936; Fax: 538829
Founded: 1933; Members: 500
Focus: Cardiol; Surgery 12446

Society of Town Planning Technicians (STPT), c/o Royal Town Planning Institute, 26 Portland Pl, London W1N 4BE
T: (0171) 6369107
Founded: 1972; Members: 350
Focus: Urban Plan
Periodical
Technical Planner (quarterly) 12447

Society of Wildlife Artists, 17 Carlton House Terrace, London SW1Y 5BD
T: (0171) 9306844; Fax: 8397830
Founded: 1963; Members: 66
Pres: Bruce Pearson
Focus: Arts; Fine Arts
Periodical
Annual Catalogue (annually) 12448

Society of Women Artists, Willow House, Ealing Green, London W5 5EN
Founded: 1855; Members: 135
Pres: Barbara Tate; Gen Secr: Joyce Rogerson
Focus: Arts; Fine Arts
Periodical
Annual Catalogue (annually) 12449

Society of Writers to Her Majesty's Signet, c/o Signet Library, Parliament Sq, Edinburgh EH1 1RF
T: (0131) 2254923; Fax: 2204016
Founded: 1594; Members: 1000
Pres: T.H. Drysdale; Gen Secr: J.R.C. Foster
Focus: Law; Hist 12450

Soil Association, 86 Colston St, Bristol BS1 5BB
T: (0117) 9290661; E-Mail: soilassoc@gn.apc.org; Fax: 9252504
Founded: 1946; Members: 6000
Pres: George McRobie; Gen Secr: Francis Blake
Focus: Agri
Periodicals
The Living Earth (quarterly)
New Farmer and Grower (quarterly) . . 12451

Somerset Archaeological and Natural History Society (S.A.N.H.S.), Taunton Castle, Taunton TA1 4AD
T: (01823) 72429
Founded: 1849; Members: 970
Focus: Archeol; Hist; Nat Sci 12452

Somerset Record Society, c/o Somerset Studies Library, Paul St, Taunton TA1 3XZ
T: (01823) 340300; Fax: 340301
Founded: 1889; Members: 250
Pres: H.G.M. Leighton; Gen Secr: D. Bromwich
Focus: Hist 12453

Sound Learning Society (SLS), 4 Plaitford Close, Rickmansworth WD3 1NJ
T: 75776
Founded: 1971; Members: 60
Focus: Educ 12454

South Bedfordshire Archaeological Society (SBAS), 27 Lords Ln, Bradwell, Great Yarmouth NR31 8NY
T: (01493) 68605
Founded: 1950; Members: 15
Focus: Archeol *12455*

South-Eastern Union of Scientific Societies (SEUSS), 53 The Drive, Shoreham-by-Sea BN4 5GD
T: 2478
Founded: 1896; Members: 70
Focus: Sci *12456*

South of England Agricultural Society, The Showground, Ardingly, Haywards Heath RH17 6TL
T: (01444) 892700; Fax: 892888
Founded: 1967; Members: 5000
Focus: Agri
Periodical
Show Times (quarterly) *12457*

South Place Ethical Society (SPES) / International Humanist Centre, Conway Hall, 25 Red Lion Sq, London WC1R 4RL
T: (0171) 2428032, 8317723
Founded: 1793; Members: 400
Focus: Philos; Educ
Periodical
The Ethical Record (10 times annually) . *12458*

South Staffordshire Archaeological and Historical Society, 307 Erdington Rd, Aldridge, Walsall WS9 0SB
T: (01922) 52097
Founded: 1959; Members: 260
Focus: Archeol; Hist
Periodical
Transactions of South Staffordshire Archaeological and Historical Society (annually) *12459*

South Wales Institute of Engineers (SWIE), Empire House, Mount Stuart Sq, Cardiff CF1 6DN
T: (01222) 481726; E-Mail: swie@celtic.co.uk; Fax: 451953
Founded: 1857; Members: 604
Pres: Dr. Jarmila Davies; Gen Secr: R.E. Lindsay
Focus: Eng
Periodical
Proceedings (bi-annually) *12460*

Southern Arts Board (SAB), 13 Saint Clement St, Winchester SO23 9DQ
T: (01962) 855099; E-Mail: sarts-info@geo2.poptel.org.uk; Fax: 861186
Members: 206
Focus: Arts
Periodicals
Artlook – Visual Arts and Crafts (quarterly)
Newsletter (bi-monthly) *12461*

Southern Skirmish Association (SoSkAN), 24 Adioham House, Pembury Rd, London E5
T: (0181) 9864709
Founded: 1967; Members: 542
Focus: Hist *12462*

Spohr Society of Great Britain, 123 Mount View Rd, Sheffield S8 8PJ
T: (0114) 2585420; E-Mail: ctuttsheffield123@compuserve.com
Founded: 1969; Members: 83
Pres: K. Warsop; Gen Secr: C.H. Tutt
Focus: Music
Periodical
Spohr Journal (annually) *12463*

Spring Research and Manufacturers Association (S.R.A.M.A.), Henry St, Sheffield S3 7EQ
T: (01742) 760771; Fax: 726344
Founded: 1945
Focus: Eng; Metallurgy *12464*

Staffordshire Agricultural Society, County Showground, Weston Rd, Stafford ST18 0BD
T: (01785) 58060; Fax: 46443
Founded: 1803; Members: 4200
Focus: Agri *12465*

Staffordshire Parish Registers Society, 91 Brenton Rd, Penn WV4 5NS
T: (01902) 341885
Founded: 1901; Members: 180
Focus: Hist *12466*

Staffordshire Record Society, c/o William Salt Library, Eastgate St, Stafford ST16 2LZ
Founded: 1879
Focus: Hist
Periodical
Collections for a History of Staffordshire (bi-annually) *12467*

Stair Society, 20 Castle Terrace, Edinburgh EH1 2ET
T: (0131) 2289900; Fax: 2281222
Founded: 1934; Members: 535
Pres: Lord Hope; Gen Secr: Lorna M. Smith
Focus: Hist; Law *12468*

Standing Committee on Commonwealth Forestry, c/o Forestry Commission, 231 Corstorphine Rd, Edinburgh EH12 7AT
T: (0131) 3146137; E-Mail: libby.jones@forestry.gov.uk; Fax: 3340442
Founded: 1920; Members: 53
Pres: David Bills; Gen Secr: Libby Jones
Focus: Forestry
Periodical
Newsletter (irregularly) *12469*

Standing Conference of Arts and Social Sciences, c/o Dr. S. Delamont, SOCAS, University of Wales College of Cardiff, 50 Park Pl, Cardiff CF1 3AT
T: (01222) 874035; Fax: 874175
Founded: 1984
Pres: Prof. J. Birkett
Focus: Arts; Soc Sci *12470*

The Standing Conference of National and University Libraries (SCONUL), 102 Euston St, London NW1 2HA
T: (0171) 3870317
Founded: 1950
Gen Secr: A.J.C. Bainton
Focus: Libraries & Bk Sci
Periodicals
Annual Review (annually)
Newsletter (3 times annually) *12471*

Standing Conference on Library Materials on Africa (SCOLMA), c/o Records Branch, Foreign and Commonwealth Space, Hanslope Park, Milton Keynes MK19 7BH
T: (01908) 511389; Fax: 511419
Founded: 1962; Members: 100
Focus: Libraries & Bk Sci
Periodical
African Research and Documentation (3 times annually) *12472*

Standing International Committee for Mycenaean Studies, c/o Downing College, Cambridge
Focus: Hist *12473*

Statute Law Society, 186 City Rd, London EC1V 2NU
T: (0171) 2511644; Fax: 2500801
Founded: 1968; Members: 150
Focus: Law
Periodical
Statute Law Review (quarterly) *12474*

Steel Construction Institute, Silwood Park, Ascot SL5 7QN
T: (01344) 23345; Fax: 22944
Founded: 1986
Pres: Dr. G.W. Owens
Focus: Materials Sci; Metallurgy
Periodical
New Steel Construction (bi-monthly) . . *12475*

Stephenson Locomotive Society (SLS), 2 Gainsborough Rd, London W4
Founded: 1909; Members: 1800
Focus: Transport *12476*

The Stroke Association, Stroke House, Whitecross St, London EC1Y 8JJ
T: (0171) 4907999
Founded: 1899
Pres: Duke of Kent
Focus: Med *12477*

Structural Fire Protection Association (SFPA), 37 Soho Sq, London W1
T: (0171) 4377107
Founded: 1975; Members: 25
Focus: Civil Eng *12478*

Suffolk Agricultural Association (SAA), Suffolk Showground, Bucklesham Rd, Ipswich IP3 8UH
T: (01473) 726847; Fax: 721973
Founded: 1831; Members: 3200
Focus: Agri *12479*

Suffolk Institute of Archaeology and History, Oak Tree Farm, Hitcham, Ipswich IP7 7LS
T: (01284) 722022
Founded: 1848; Members: 850
Focus: Hist; Archeol
Periodicals
Proceedings (annually)
Suffolk Archaeology & History Newsletter (bi-annually) *12480*

Suffolk Records Society (SRS), County Hall, Ipswich IP4 2JS
T: (01473) 230000
Founded: 1958; Members: 390
Focus: Hist *12481*

Sunday Shakespeare Society (SSS), Heathfield, Chestnut Walk, Felcourt, East Grinstead RH19 2LB
T: (01342) 870436
Founded: 1874; Members: 47
Pres: Dorothy Tutin; Gen Secr: Peter J. Cox
Focus: Lit *12482*

Surgical Research Society (SRS), c/o Dept of Surgery, The General Hospital, Gwendolen Rd, Glasgow G4 0SF
T: (0141) 5523535
Founded: 1953; Members: 400
Focus: Surgery *12483*

Surrey Archaeological Society (S.A.S.), Castle Arch, Guildford GU1 3SX
T: (01483) 32454
Founded: 1854; Members: 1065
Focus: Archeol
Periodical
S.A.S. Collections (irregularly) *12484*

Surrey Record Society (SRS), Castle Arch, Guildford GU1 3SX
Founded: 1913; Members: 210
Focus: Hist *12485*

Sussex Archaeological Society (S.A.S.), Barbican House, 169 High St, Lewes BN7 1YE
T: (01273) 486290; E-Mail: sussexpart@pairlion.co.uk; Fax: 486990
Founded: 1846; Members: 2000
Pres: Prof. Barry Cunliffe; Gen Secr: John Manley
Focus: Archeol; Hist
Periodicals
Newsletter (3 times annually)
Sussex Archaeological Collections (annually) *12486*

Sussex Industrial Archaeology Society (SIAS), 42 Falmer Av, Saltdean, Brighton BN2 8FG
T: (01273) 271330
Founded: 1967; Members: 300
Gen Secr: R.G. Martin
Focus: Archeol
Periodical
Sussex Industrial History (annually) . . . *12487*

The Swedenborg Society, 20 Bloomsbury Way, London WC1A 2TH
T: (0171) 4057986; E-Mail: swed.soc@netmatters.co.uk; Fax: 8315848
Founded: 1810; Members: 1000
Pres: G.P. Dawson; Gen Secr: M.G. Waters
Focus: Philos; Rel & Theol
Periodical
The Swedenborg Society Magazine (irregularly) *12488*

Systematics Association, c/o Dept of Geological Sciences, Durham University, South Rd, Durham DH1 3LE
T: (0191) 64971
Founded: 1937
Pres: Prof. A.J. Cain
Focus: Bio *12489*

Tavistock Institute of Medical Psychology (T.I.M.P.), 12 Keswick Close, Camberley GU15 1RN
T: (01276) 675266; Fax: 675266
Founded: 1929; Members: 32
Gen Secr: G.C. Hume
Focus: Psych *12490*

The Tennyson Society, c/o Tennyson Research Centre, Central Library, Free School Ln, Lincoln LN2 1EZ
T: (01522) 552851; Fax: 552858
Founded: 1960; Members: 550
Pres: Lord Tennyson; Gen Secr: J.K. Jefferson
Focus: Lit
Periodicals
Annual Report
Bulletin (annually) *12491*

Tensor Society of Great Britain (TSGB), 66 South Terrace, Surbiton KT6 6HU
T: (0181) 3992724
Founded: 1950
Focus: Sci; Eng
Periodical
The Matrix and Tensor (quarterly) . . . *12492*

The Textile Institute (TI), 10 Blackfriars St, Manchester M3 5DR
T: (0161) 8348457; Fax: 8353087
Founded: 1910; Members: 10258
Focus: Textiles
Periodicals
International Textile Calendar (bi-monthly)
Journal of The Textile Institute (quarterly)
Manual of Textile Technology (irregularly)
Textile Horizons (bi-monthly)
Textile Progress (quarterly)
Textiles (quarterly) *12493*

Theatre Arts Society (TAS), Wyndhams Theatre, Charing Cross Rd, London WC2 0DA
T: (0171) 8362671
Founded: 1969; Members: 3000
Focus: Perf Arts *12494*

Theatre Organ Preservation Society (TOPS), 8 Dale Court, Seymour Rd, Slough SL1 2NU
T: 36786
Founded: 1960; Members: 2000
Focus: Music *12495*

Theosophical Society in England (TS), 50 Gloucester Pl, London W1H 4EA
T: (0171) 9359261
Founded: 1875; Members: 1750
Gen Secr: L. Storey
Focus: Philos; Rel & Theol; Sci; Psych; Soc Sci
Periodical
The Theosophical Journal (bi-monthly) . *12496*

Theosophical Society in Europe, 2 Tekels Park, Camberley, Surrey
Founded: 1903
Focus: Rel & Theol *12497*

Theosophical Society in Scotland, 28 Great King St, Edinburgh EH3 6QH
T: (0131) 5565385
Founded: 1895; Members: 100
Focus: Rel & Theol *12498*

Thomas Paine Society U.K., 43 Wellington Gardens, Selsey PO20 0RF
T: (01243) 605730; E-Mail: tom paine society@mrm.co.uk
Founded: 1963; Members: 175
Pres: Michael Foot; Gen Secr: Eric Paine
Focus: Hist

Periodicals
Newsletter (irregularly)
T.P.S. Echo (2-3 times annually) . . . *12499*

Thomas Tallis Society (TTS), 13 Albury St, London SE8 3PT
T: (0181) 6918337; Fax: 6918337
Founded: 1965; Members: 60
Pres: Philip Simms; Gen Secr: Deborah Sandringham
Focus: Music *12500*

Thoracic Society, c/o Dept of Medicine, D Level, Center Block, Southampton
T: (01703) 777222
Founded: 1945; Members: 540
Focus: Pulmon Dis *12501*

Thoresby Society, 23 Clarendon Rd, Leeds LS2 9NZ
Founded: 1889; Members: 420
Focus: Hist
Periodical
Publications (annually) *12502*

The Thoroton Society of Nottinghamshire, Bromley House, Angel Row, Nottingham
T: (0115) 9473134
Founded: 1897; Members: 650
Pres: Miles Thoroton Hildyard; Gen Secr: P. Rowley
Focus: Archeol; Hist *12503*

Three Counties Agricultural Society (TCAS), The Showyard, Malvern WR13 6NW
T: (01684) 892751; Fax: 568236
Founded: 1797; Members: 8000
Focus: Agri *12504*

Timber Research and Development Association (TRADA), Chiltern House, Stocking Ln, Hughenden Valley, High Wycombe HP14 4ND
T: (01494) 563091; Fax: 565487
Founded: 1934
Pres: Andrew Abbott
Focus: Forestry; Civil Eng *12505*

Tobacco Research Council, Glen House, Stag Pl, London SW1E 5AG
T: (0171) 8282041; Fax: 6309638
Focus: Agri *12506*

Tolkien Society, c/o Annie Haward, Flat 6, 8 Staverton Rd, Oxford OX2 6XJ
Founded: 1969; Members: 1000
Focus: Lit
Periodicals
Amon Hen (bi-monthly)
Mallorn (annually) *12507*

Town and Country Planning Association (TCPA), 17 Carlton House Terrace, London SW1Y 5AS
T: (0171) 9308903; Fax: 9303280
Founded: 1899; Members: 1300
Pres: Baroness Sally Hamwec; Gen Secr: Tim Cordy
Focus: Urban Plan; Ecology
Periodical
Town and Country Planning (monthly) . *12508*

Tramway Museum Society (TMS), c/o The National Tramway Museum, Crich, Matlock DE4 5DP
T: (01773) 852565; Fax: 852326
Founded: 1955; Members: 2500
Pres: D. Senior; Gen Secr: R.J. Clarke
Focus: Transport
Periodical
TMS Journal (quarterly) *12509*

Trans-Antarctic Association (TAA), c/o British Antarctic Survey, High Cross, Madingley Rd, Cambridge CB3 0ET
T: (01223) 61188
Founded: 1960; Members: 3
Focus: Geography *12510*

Transplantation Society, c/o Dept of Immunology, Saint Mary's Hospital Medical School, London W2 1PC
Founded: 1966
Focus: Surgery *12511*

Transport Ticket Society, 24 Frankfield Rise, Tunbridge Wells TN2 5UF
T: (01892) 511544; E-Mail: transport.ticket@btinternet.com
Founded: 1946; Members: 500
Gen Secr: G.R. Croughton
Focus: Transport *12512*

Trinitarian Bible Society (TBS), Tyndale House, Dorset Rd, London SW19 3NN
T: (0181) 5437857; Fax: 5436370
Founded: 1831
Gen Secr: D.P. Rowland
Focus: Rel & Theol
Periodical
Record (quarterly) *12513*

Tuberous Sclerosis Association (TSA), Little Barnsley Farm, Catshill, Bromsgrove B61 0NQ
T: (01527) 871898; E-Mail: tsassn@compuserve.com; Fax: 579419
Founded: 1977; Members: 1200
Pres: Tom Carter; Gen Secr: Janet Medcalf
Focus: Pulmon Dis
Periodicals
TSA Fact Sheets (3 times annually)
TSA Scan (3 times annually) *12514*

Turner Society, BCM Box Turner, London WC1N 3XX
Founded: 1975; Members: 580
Focus: Fine Arts
Periodical
Turner Society News (3 times annually) . 12515

Twentieth Century Society, 70 Cowcross St, London EC1M 6BP
T: (0171) 2503851; Fax: 2518985
Founded: 1979; Members: 1566
Pres: Margaret Richardson; Gen Secr: Elain Harwood
Focus: Preserv Hist Monuments
Periodical
Journal (irregularly) 12516

TWI, Abington Hall, Cambridge CB1 6AL
T: (01223) 891162
Founded: 1968; Members: 7000
Gen Secr: A.B.M. Braithwaite
Focus: Eng
Periodicals
Connect (monthly)
Research Bulletin (bi-monthly)
Welding Abstracts (monthly)
The Welding Institute News Video (semi-annually) 12517

UK Council for Graduate Education, c/o CEDAR, University of Warwick, Coventry CV4 7AL
T: (01203) 524847; Fax: 524472
Founded: 1994
Focus: Educ 12518

Ulster Archaeological Society (UAS), c/o Dept of Archaeology, Queen's University, Belfast BT7 1NN
T: (01232) 273447
Founded: 1938
Focus: Archeol
Periodical
Ulster Journal of Archaeology (annually) . 12519

Ulster Archery Association (UAA), 35 Norglen Dr, Belfast BT11 8DG
Founded: 1956
Focus: Archeol 12520

Ulster Architectural Heritage Society (UAHS), 66 Donegall Pass, Belfast BT7 1BU
T: (01232) 550213
Founded: 1967; Members: 1251
Pres: C.E.B. Brett; Gen Secr: Joan Kinch
Focus: Archit; Preserv Hist Monuments
Periodical
Newsletter (annually) 12521

Ulster Chemists' Association (UCA), 73 University St, Belfast BT7 1HL
T: (01232) 320787
Founded: 1901; Members: 654
Focus: Chem 12522

Ulster Folklife Society, c/o Ulster Folk and Transport Museum, Cultra Manor, Holywood BT18 0EU
T: (012317) 428428; Fax: 428728
Founded: 1962; Members: 175
Pres: Dr. G.R. Thompson
Focus: Ethnology
Periodical
Ulster Folklife 12523

The Ulster Genealogical and Historical Guild / The Ulster Historical Foundation, 12 College Sq East, Belfast BT1 6DO
T: (01232) 332288; E-Mail: enquiry@uhf.dnet.co.uk; Fax: 239885
Founded: 1956; Members: 5000
Pres: Duke of Abercorn; Gen Secr: Shane McAteer
Focus: Genealogy; Hist
Periodicals
Directory of Irish Family History Research (annually)
Familia: The Ulster Genealogical Review (annually) 12524

Ulster Historical Foundation, 12 College Sq East, Belfast BT1 6DD
T: (01232) 332288; E-Mail: enquiry@uhf.dnet.co.uk; Fax: 239885
Founded: 1956; Members: 900
Pres: Duke of Abercorn; Gen Secr: Shane McAteer
Focus: Hist
Periodicals
Biographical Series
Educational Series
Gravestone Inscription Series (annually)
Historical Series 12525

Ulster Society for Irish Historical Studies (USIHS), 36 North Parade, Belfast BT7 2GG
T: (01232) 643229
Founded: 1936; Members: 85
Focus: Hist 12526

Ulster Society for The Preservation of The Countryside (USPC), West Winds, Carney Hill, Holywood BT18 0JR
T: 2300
Founded: 1937; Members: 500
Focus: Ecology
Periodical
The Countryside Recorder (semi-annually) 12527

Ulster Society in London, 11 Berkeley St, London W1 6BU
T: (0171) 4930601
Founded: 1896; Members: 100
Gen Secr: V.H. Cuttle
Focus: Hist
Periodical
Newsletter (5 times annually) 12528

Ulster Teachers' Union (UTU), 94 Malone Rd, Belfast BT9 5HP
T: (01232) 662216; Fax: 663055
Founded: 1919; Members: 5500
Focus: Educ
Periodical
UTU News (3 times annually) 12529

UMIST Association, POB 88, Manchester M60 1QD
T: (0161) 2003066; E-Mail: alumni@umist.ac.uk; Fax: 9558066
Members: 23500
Pres: Oates J. Keith; Gen Secr: Annette Babczuk
Focus: Sci; Eng; Econ
Periodical
Mainstream (semi-annually) 12530

Union of Educational Institutions (UEI), Norfolk House, Smallbrook Queensway, Birmingham B5 4NB
T: (0121) 6438924
Founded: 1895
Focus: Educ 12531

Union of Lancashire and Cheshire Institutes (ULCI), Town Hall, Walkden Rd Worsley, Manchester M28 4QE
Founded: 1839
Focus: Educ
Periodicals
General Regulations & Examinations Timetable (annually)
Regional Guide to Further Education Courses in The North West (annually)
Regional List of Colleges in The North West (annually) 12532

Unitarian Historical Society, 6 Ventnor Terrace, Edinburgh EH9 2BL
T: (0131) 6674360; E-Mail: andrew@unitarian.ednet.co.uk
Founded: 1915; Members: 250
Focus: Hist
Periodical
Transactions (annually) 12533

United Earth Sciences Exploration Group (UESEG), 8 Utton's Av, Leigh-on-Sea SS9 2EL
T: (01702) 710521
Founded: 1972; Members: 83
Focus: Geology
Periodical
Expedition Reports 12534

United Kingdom Association for European Law (U.K.A.E.L.), c/o King's College, Strand, London WC2R 2LS
T: (0171) 2400206
Founded: 1975; Members: 300
Focus: Law 12535

United Kingdom Home Economics Federation (UKHEF), 171 Whitechapel Rd, Cleckheaton BD19 6HW
T: (01274) 872488
Founded: 1954
Focus: Home Econ
Periodical
Bulletin: Conference Report (3 times annually) 12536

United Kingdom Institute for Conservation of Historic and Artistic Works, c/o Conservation Dept, Tate Gallery, 6 Whitehorse News, Westminster Bridge Rd, London SE1 7QD
Focus: Preserv Hist Monuments; Arts
Periodicals
Conservation News (3 times annually)
The Conservator (annually) 12537

United Kingdom Reading Association (UKRA), c/o Warrington Road C.P. School, Naylor Rd, Widnes WA8 0BP
T: (0151) 4202552
Founded: 1964; Members: 1500
Focus: Educ
Periodicals
Journal of Research in Reading (semi-annually)
Newsletter (3 times annually)
Reading (3 times annually) 12538

United Kingdom Science Park Association, Aston Science Park, Love Ln, Aston Triangle, Birmingham B7 4BJ
T: (0121) 3590981; Fax: 3335852
Founded: 1984; Members: 45
Pres: Dr.G. Hunter; Gen Secr: W. Herriot
Focus: Sci
Periodicals
UKSPA News (semi-annually)
UKSPA Science Park Directory 12539

United Reformed Church History Society, 86 Tavistock Pl, London WC1H 9RT
T: (0171) 9162020
Founded: 1972; Members: 600
Gen Secr: S.C. Orchard
Focus: Hist; Rel & Theol
Periodical
Journal (semi-annually) 12540

United Society for The Propagation of The Gospel (USPG), 157 Waterloo Rd, London SE1 8XA
T: (0171) 9288681; Fax: 9282371
Founded: 1701; Members: 7000
Pres: Archbishop of Canterbury; Gen Secr: Peter Price
Focus: Rel & Theol
Periodicals
Encounter (quarterly)
Thinking Mission (quarterly)
Transmission (quarterly)
USPG Yearbook (annually) 12541

United Society of Artists, York Hill Cottage, Alderney, Channel Islands
T: (0148182) 2226
Focus: Fine Arts
Periodical
Annual Catalogue (annually) 12542

United World Colleges, London House, Mecklenburgh Sq, London WC1N 2AB
T: (0171) 8332626; Fax: 8373102
Founded: 1962; Members: 41
Focus: Educ
Periodical
UWC Journal (quarterly) 12543

University Association for Contemporary European Studies (UACES), c/o King's College, London WC2R 2LS
T: (071) 2400206
Founded: 1968; Members: 90
Pres: Prof. M. Smith; Gen Secr: J. Gower
Focus: Educ; Hist
Periodicals
Register of Courses in European Studies in British Universities and Polytechnics
Register of Current Research into European Integration (bi-annually) 12544

University of Bristol Spelaeological Society (U.B.S.S.), c/o Students Union, Queens Rd, Clifton, Bristol BS8 1LN
Founded: 1919; Members: 350
Pres: A.M. Simon
Focus: Speleology; Archeol
Periodical
Proceedings U.B.S.S. (annually) 12545

UV Spectrometry Group (UVG), c/o Pye Unicam Ltd, York St, Cambridge CB1 2PX
Founded: 1948; Members: 170
Focus: Physics 12546

Vasectomy Advancement Society of Great Britain (VASofGB), 1 Ravenscroft Court, 56 Ravenscroft Av, London NW11 8BA
T: (0181) 4556541
Founded: 1972; Members: 150
Focus: Med 12547

Vernacular Architecture Group (V.A.G.), c/o Bob Meeson, 16 Falna Crescent, Coton Green, Tamworth B79 8JS
T: (01827) 69434; Fax: 69434
Founded: 1954; Members: 581
Pres: Sarah Pearson; Gen Secr: Bob Meeson
Focus: Archit
Periodical
Vernacular Architecture (annually) . . . 12548

Verulam Institute, Shopwyke Park, Chichester PO20 6BQ
T: (01243) 786863
Founded: 1971
Focus: Philos 12549

Veterinary History Society, 32 Belgrave Sq, London SW1X 8QP
T: (0171) 2356568
Founded: 1962; Members: 130
Focus: Vet Med
Periodical
Veterinary History 12550

The Victoria Institute or Philosophical Society of Great Britain, 41 Marne Av, Welling DA16 2EY
T: (0181) 3030465
Founded: 1865
Pres: Dr. David J.E. Ingram
Focus: Philos
Periodicals
Faith and Thought Bulletin (semi-annually)
Science & Christian Belief (semi-annually) 12551

Victorian Military Society (VMS), Arm Farm Cottage, Blisworth Arm, Northampton NN7 3EF
T: (01604) 858647
Founded: 1975; Members: 850
Focus: Hist; Military Sci
Periodicals
Soldiers of The Queen (quarterly)
Soldiers Small Book (irregularly) 12552

Victorian Society, 1 Priory Gardens, Bedford Park, London W4 1TT
T: (0181) 9941019; Fax: 9954895
Founded: 1958; Members: 3250
Gen Secr: William Filmer-Sawkey
Focus: Archit
Periodicals
Annual (annually)
Magazine (semi-annually) 12553

Viking Society for Northern Research, c/o Dept of Scandinavian Studies, University College London, Gower St, London WC1E 6BT
T: (0171) 3807176/77
Founded: 1892; Members: 700
Focus: Hist; Lit
Periodical
Saga-Book (annually) 12554

Vintage Light Music Society (VLMS), 4 Harvest Bank Rd, West Wickham BR4 9DJ
T: (0181) 4625641
Founded: 1968; Members: 450
Gen Secr: Stuart Upton
Focus: Music
Periodical
Vintage Light Music (quarterly) 12555

Viola da Gamba Society, 93a Sutton Rd, London N10 1HH
T: (0181) 8834677
Founded: 1948; Members: 250
Focus: Music
Periodicals
Chelys (annually)
Newsletter (quarterly)
Thematic Index of Music for Viols (irregularly) 12556

Virgil Society, c/o Dept of Classics, King's College, Strand, London WC2R 2LS
T: (0171) 8365454
Founded: 1944; Members: 700
Focus: Lit
Periodical
Proceedings of The Virgil Society . . . 12557

Visible Record and Minicomputer Society, 37 West St, Croydon CR0 1DJ
T: 6810417
Founded: 1971
Focus: Electric Eng; Electronic Eng . . 12558

Vivaldi Society, 67 Twyford Av, London N2
T: (0181) 8835266
Focus: Music 12559

Wagner Society, c/o Dr. J.J. Pritchard, 15 David Av, Wickford SS11 7BG
T: (0171) 6314048
Founded: 1952; Members: 651
Pres: Dame Gwyneth Jones; Gen Secr: Dr. J.J. Pritchard
Focus: Music 12560

The Walpole Society, c/o c/o Dept of Prints and Drawings, British Museum, London WC1B 3DG
T: (0171) 8238408
Founded: 1911; Members: 550
Pres: Dr. Brian Allen; Gen Secr: M. Trusted
Focus: Hist; Arts 12561

Water Research Centre (WRC), Henley Rd, Medmenham, POB 16, Marlow, Bucks SL7 2HD
T: (0149166) 531
Founded: 1974; Members: 500
Focus: Water Res; Ecology
Periodicals
Technical Reports (irregularly)
WRC Information (weekly) 12562

Webb Society, 7 Elvendon Rd, London N13 4SJ
T: (0181) 8887238
Founded: 1967; Members: 90
Focus: Astronomy 12563

Wedgwood Society, Roman Villa, Rockbourne, Fordingbridge SP6 3PG
T: Rockbourne 445
Founded: 1954; Members: 190
Focus: Arts 12564

Wellesbourne Vegetable Research Association, c/o Horticulture Research International, Warwick, Warwicks.
T: (01789) 470382
Founded: 1958; Members: 505
Focus: Hort 12565

Welsh Arts Council, Holst House, Museum Pl, Cardiff CF1 3NX
Focus: Arts
Periodical
CREFFT (quarterly) 12566

Welsh Baptist Historical Society, 13 Ty'r-fran Av, LLnlli, Dyfed
T: 3244
Founded: 1901; Members: 400
Focus: Hist; Rel & Theol 12567

Welsh Federation of Head Teachers' Associations, 970 Llangyfelach Rd, Tirdeunaw, Swansea
T: (01792) 71104
Focus: Educ 12568

Welsh Folk Dance Society, Bryn Mair, Llanfair Caereinion PE7 B70
Focus: Music 12569

Welsh Folk Song Society (WFSS), Ynys Ceti, Penrhyn-Coch, Aberystwyth SY23 3EH
T: 36088
Focus: Music
Periodical
Canu Gwerin: Folk Song (annually) . . 12570

Welsh Library Association, c/o University College of Wales, Llanbadarn Fawr, Aberystwyth SY23 3AS
T: (01970) 622174; Fax: 622190
Founded: 1933; Members: 980
Pres: Andrew Green
Focus: Lit
Periodical
Y Ddolen (quarterly) 12571

Welwyn Hall Research Association (W.H.R.A.), 11 White Lion House, Town Centre, Hatfield AL10 0JL
T: (017072) 71580
Founded: 1964; Members: 24
Focus: Archit 12572

Wesley Historical Society (WHS), 34 Spiceland Rd, Birmingham B31 1NJ
T: (0121) 4754914
Founded: 1893; Members: 820
Pres: Dr. John A. Newton; Gen Secr: Dr. E.D. Graham
Focus: Hist; Lit
Periodical
Proceedings (3 times annually) 12573

Wildlife Sound Recording Society (WSRS), Chadswell, Sandy Ln, Rushmoor, Tilford, Farnham GU10 2ET
T: Frensham 2673
Founded: 1968; Members: 252
Focus: Zoology 12574

Wilhelm Furtwängler Society, 37 Chester Way, London SE11 4UR
Founded: 1967; Members: 210
Focus: Music
Periodical
Newsletter (bi-monthly) 12575

William Morris Society, 26 Upper Mall, London W6 9TA
T: (0181) 7413735
Founded: 1955; Members: 1900
Gen Secr: Peter Faulkner
Focus: Arts; Hist; Lit; Poli Sci
Periodical
Journal (semi-annually) 12576

Wiltshire Archaeological and Natural History Society (W.A.N.H.S.), c/o The Museum, 41 Long St, Devizes SN10 1NS
T: (01380) 727369
Founded: 1853; Members: 1300
Focus: Archeol; Hist; Nat Sci
Periodical
Magazine (annually) 12577

Wiltshire Record Society (W.R.S.), c/o County Record Office, County Hall, Trowbridge BA14 8JG
T: (01225) 713136
Founded: 1938; Members: 308
Pres: C. Elrington; Gen Secr: J.N. D'Arcy
Focus: Hist
Periodical
Wiltshire Record Society: A Series of Historical Records of Local and National Interest (annually) 12578

Wireless Preservation Society (WPS), 32 Luccombe Rd, Shanklin
T: 2586
Founded: 1972
Focus: Electric Eng 12579

Wolverton and District Archaeological Society, 82 Clarence Rd, Stony Stratford, Milton Keynes MK11 1JD
T: (01908) 565481
Founded: 1955; Members: 120
Pres: Elizabeth Thomson; Gen Secr: A. Lambert
Focus: Archeol
Periodical
Newsletter (bi-monthly) 12580

Woolhope Naturalists' Field Club, c/o Hereford Library, Broad St, Hereford HR4 9AU
T: (01432) 272456; Fax: 359668
Founded: 1851; Members: 800
Focus: Archeol; Hist; Nat Sci
Periodical
Woolhope Club Transactions (annually) . 12581

Worcestershire Archaeological Society, 4 Orchard Rd, Malvern, Worcs
T: 4215
Founded: 1854; Members: 370
Focus: Archeol 12582

Workers' Educational Association (WEA), 17 Victoria Park Sq, London E2 9PB
T: (0181) 9831515; Fax: 9834840
Founded: 1903
Pres: Jake Bharrier; Gen Secr: R. Lochrie
Focus: Educ
Periodical
Reportback (semi-annually) 12583

Workers' Music Association (WMA), 236 Westbourne Park Rd, London W11 1EL
T: (0171) 7277005
Founded: 1936; Members: 321
Focus: Music 12584

World Bureau of Metal Statistics, 27a High St, London SG12 9BA
Founded: 1946
Focus: Stats; Metallurgy
Periodicals
World Flow of Unwrought Aluminium (annually)
World Flow of Unwrought Copper (annually)
World Flow of Unwrought Lead (annually)
World Flow of Unwrought Nickel (annually)
World Flow of Unwrought Tin (annually)
World Flow of Unwrought Zinc (annually)
World Metal Statistics (monthly)
World Metal Statistics Yearbook (annually)
World Stainless Steel Statistics (annually)
World Tin Statistics (monthly)
World Wrought Copper Statistics (annually) 12585

World Education Fellowship (WEF), 58 Dickens Rise, Chigwell IG7 6NY
T: (0181) 2817122; E-Mail: 106465.1075@compuserve.com; Fax: 2817122
Founded: 1921
Pres: Prof. Shinjo Okuda
Focus: Educ
Periodical
New Era in Education (3 times annually) 12586

World Federation for Medical Education, c/o Dept of Psychiatry, University of Edinburgh, Morningside Park, Edinburgh EH10 5HF
T: (0131) 4472011
Focus: Educ; Med
Periodical
Proceedings (annually) 12587

World Federation of Societies of Anaesthesiologists (WFSA), c/o Dept of Anaesthetics, University of Wales College of Medicine, Heath Park, Cardiff, CF4 4XN
T: (01222) 743110; Fax: 747203
Founded: 1955; Members: 45000
Focus: Anesthetics
Periodical
Newsletter (semi-annually) 12588

World Medical Tennis Association, c/o Poole General Hospital, Poole, Dorset
Focus: Therapeutics 12589

World Rabbit Science Association (W.R.S.A.), Tyning House, Shurdington, Cheltenham GL51 5XF
Founded: 1976
Focus: Zoology 12590

World Union of Pythagorean Organizations (WUPO), 17 Longfield, Lutton, Devon
Founded: 1964
Focus: Philos 12591

World-wide Education Service of The Bell Educational Trust, 10 Barley Mow Passage, London W4 4PH
T: (0181) 7478376
Founded: 1887
Focus: Educ 12592

Worshipful Society of Apothecaries of London, Apothecaries' Hall, Black Friars Lane, London EC4V 6EJ
Founded: 1617
Focus: Pharmacol 12593

Writers' Guild of Great Britain (WGGB), 430 Edgware Rd, London W2 1EH
T: (0171) 7238074
Founded: 1959
Focus: Lit 12594

Yorkshire Agricultural Society, Great Yorkshire Showground, Hookstone Oval, Harrogate HG2 8PW
T: (01423) 561536
Founded: (0423) 531112
Focus: Agri 12595

Yorkshire Archaeological Society (Y.A.S.), Claremont, 23 Clarendon Rd, Leeds LS2 9NZ
T: (0113) 2457910; E-Mail: j.heron@shef.ac.uk; Fax: 2441979
Founded: 1863; Members: 1500
Gen Secr: M.J. Heron
Focus: Archeol
Periodicals
Y.A.S. Parish Register Series (annually)
Y.A.S. Record Series (annually)
Y.A.S. Wakefield Court Rolls Series (annually)
Yorkshire Archaeological Journal (annually) 12596

Yorkshire Arts Association, Glyde House, Glydegate, Bradford BD5 0BQ
T: (01274) 723051/52
Founded: 1969; Members: 2650
Focus: Arts
Periodicals
Regional Arts and What's on Magazine
Yorkshire Artscene (10 times annually) . 12597

Yorkshire Dialect Society (Y.D.S.), c/o School of English, University, Leeds LS2 9JT
Founded: 1897; Members: 1230
Focus: Ling 12598

Yorkshire Geological Society (Y.G.S.), c/o S. Rogers, 4 Middledyke Ln, Cottingham HU16 4NH
Founded: 1837; Members: 1000
Pres: D. Holliday; Gen Secr: W.J. Varker
Focus: Geology
Periodical
Proceedings (semi-annually) 12599

Yorkshire Philosophical Society (Y.P.S.), The Lodge, Museum Gardens, York YO1 2DR
T: (01904) 656713
Founded: 1822; Members: 620
Focus: Philos
Periodical
Annual Report (annually) 12600

Zinc Development Association, 42 Weymouth St, London W1N 3LQ
T: (0171) 4996636; Fax: 4931555
Focus: Metallurgy 12601

Zoological Society of Glasgow and West of Scotland, c/o Glasgow Zoological Gardens, Calderpark Uddingston, Glasgow G71 7RZ
T: (0141) 7711185; Fax: 7712615
Founded: 1936; Members: 609
Pres: W. Mackenzie; Gen Secr: R. O'Grady
Focus: Zoology
Periodical
Annual Report (annually) 12602

Zoological Society of London (Z.S.L.), Regent's Park, London NW1 4RY
T: (0171) 7223333; Fax: 5865743
Founded: 1826; Members: 20000
Pres: Sir Martin Holdgate; Gen Secr: Prof. R. McNeil Alexander
Focus: Zoology
Periodicals
International Zoo Yearbook (annually)
Journal of Zoology (monthly)
Nomenclator Zoologicus (irregularly)
Symposia (irregularly)
Zoological Record (annually) 12603

Zoological Society of Northern Ireland, 33 Saratoga Av, Newtownards BT23 4BO
Founded: 1963; Members: 73
Focus: Zoology 12604

Uruguay

Academia Nacional de Ingeniería, Cuareim 1492, Montevideo
Founded: 1965; Members: 32
Pres: A. Tierno Abreu; Gen Secr: Aurelio Tilve
Focus: Eng 12605

Academia Nacional de Letras (ANL), 25 de Mayo 376, Montevideo
T: (02) 952374
Founded: 1946; Members: 10
Pres: Julio C. da Rosa; Gen Secr: Carlos Jones
Focus: Ling
Periodical
Boletín de la Academia Nacional de Letras (semi-annually) 12606

Academia Nacional de Medicina del Uruguay, 18 de Julio 2175, Montevideo
T: (02) 401444
Founded: 1976; Members: 27
Focus: Med
Periodical
Boletín (annually) 12607

Agrupacíon Bibliotecológica del Uruguay (ABU), Cerro Largo 1666 601=11200, Montevideo
Focus: Libraries & Bk Sci 12608

Asociación de Bibliotecólogos del Uruguay, Eduardo V. Haedo 2255, Casilla 1315, 11200 Montevideo
Founded: 1978; Members: 430
Pres: Raquel Schneider
Focus: Libraries & Bk Sci
Periodicals
Actualidades Bibliotecológicas (quarterly)
Panel de Noticias (monthly) 12609

Asociación de Ingenieros del Uruguay, Av Libertador Brigadier General Lavalleja 1464, Montevideo
Founded: 1950; Members: 800
Focus: Eng
Periodical
Ingeniería 12610

Asociación de Química y Farmacia del Uruguay, Av Libertador Brigadier General Lavalleja 1464, Montevideo
Founded: 1888; Members: 600
Focus: Chem; Pharmacol 12611

Asociación Ondontológica Uruguaya, Durazno 937-939, Montevideo
T: 901572; E-Mail: Odontur
Founded: 1946; Members: 3000
Focus: Dent
Periodical
Odontología Uruguaya: Revista Científica Gremial e Informativa (semi-annually) 12612

Asociación Rural del Uruguay, Uruguay 864, Montevideo
Founded: 1871
Focus: Agri 12613

Asociación Uruguaya de Escritores, Bartolomé Mitre 1260, Montevideo
Focus: Lit 12614

Association for the Study of Man Environment Relations (ASMER), Casilla 13125, Montevideo
Founded: 1985
Focus: Ecology 12615

Ateneo de Clínica Quirúrgica, Montevideo
Founded: 1934
Focus: Surgery
Periodical
Anales 12616

Centro de Investigaciones Agrícolas Alberto Boerger, La Estanzuela, Colonia
Founded: 1914
Focus: Agri 12617

Centro de Investigaciones y Estudios Familiares (CIEF), José Enrique Rodo 2115, Montevideo
T: (02) 400681
Founded: 1965; Members: 50
Focus: Family Plan
Periodical
Digesto Familiar (bi-monthly) 12618

Centro de Nacionales y Comercio Internacional del Uruguay (CENCI), Misiones 1361, Casilla 1510, Montevideo
Founded: 1956; Members: 1200
Focus: Stats; Econ
Periodicals
Manual Práctico Aduanero (monthly)
Manual Práctico del Contribuyente (monthly)
Manual Práctico del Exportador (monthly)
Manual Práctico del Importador (monthly)
Manual Práctico Sudamericano del Transporte Internacional por Carretera de Carga y Pasajeros (monthly) 12619

Centro Interamericano de Investigación y Documentación sobre Formación Profesional (CINTERFOR), Colonia 993, Montevideo
Focus: Adult Educ 12620

Comisión Nacional de Energía Atómica (CNEA), Soriano 1014, Montevideo
T: 986783, 901944, 915916
Founded: 1955
Focus: Nucl Res 12621

Consejo Nacional de Educación, Centro Nacional de Información y Documentación (CONAE-CENID), Av del Libertador Brigadier General Lavalleja 2025, Montevideo
T: 905293, 983557
Founded: 1974
Focus: Educ 12622

Consejo Nacional de Higiene, c/o Ministerio de Salud Pública, Av 18 de Julio 1892, Montevideo
Focus: Hygiene 12623

Consejo Nacional de Investigaciones Científicas y Técnicas, Sarandí 450, Montevideo
Founded: 1961; Members: 7
Focus: Eng; Sci 12624

Gremial Uruguaya de Médicos Radiólogos, Av Libertador Brigadier General Lavalleja 1464, Montevideo
Founded: 1972; Members: 70
Focus: Radiology 12625

Instituto de Investigaciones Biológicas Clemente Estable, Av Italia 3318, Montevideo
T: 811012, 811662
Founded: 1927; Members: 81
Focus: Bio 12626

Instituto Histórico y Geográfico del Uruguay, Convención 1366, Casilla 10999, Montevideo
T: 914441
Founded: 1843; Members: 40
Focus: Geography; Hist
Periodical
Revista del Instituto Histórico y Geográfico del Uruguay (annually) 12627

Instituto Uruguayo de Normas Técnicas, Av Libertador Brigadier General Lavalleja, Montevideo
Founded: 1939; Members: 400
Focus: Standards; Eng 12628

Library Association of Uruguay, Ibicuy 1276, Montevideo
Focus: Libraries & Bk Sci 12629

Liga Uruguaya contra la Tuberculosis (LUCT), Magallanes 1320, Montevideo
T: 43570, 497869
Founded: 1902; Members: 7
Focus: Pulmon Dis 12630

Sociedad de Amigos de Arqueología, Buenos Aires 652, Casilla 399, Montevideo
Founded: 1926; Members: 86
Focus: Archeol
Periodical
Revista 12631

Sociedad de Biología de Montevideo, Casilla 567, Montevideo
Founded: 1927
Focus: Bio 12632

Sociedad de Cirugía del Uruguay, Av Libertador Brigadier General Lavalleja 1464, Montevideo
Founded: 1920; Members: 426
Focus: Surgery
Periodical
Cirúgia del Uruguay (bi-monthly) 12633

Sociedad de Radiología del Uruguay, Av Libertador Brigadier General Lavalleja 1464, Montevideo
Founded: 1923; Members: 60
Focus: Radiology 12634

Sociedad Malacológica del Uruguay, Casilla 1401, Montevideo
Founded: 1957; Members: 210
Focus: Zoology 12635

Sociedad Uruguaya de Patología Clínica, Casilla 6147, Montevideo
T: 801515
Founded: 1954; Members: 140
Focus: Pathology
Periodical
Revista *12636*

Sociedad Uruguaya de Pediatría, Casilla 10906, Montevideo
Founded: 1927
Focus: Pediatrics
Periodical
Archivos de Pediatría del Uruguay (quarterly) *12637*

Sociedad Zoológica del Uruguay, Casilla 399, Montevideo
Founded: 1961
Focus: Zoology
Periodical
Boletín *12638*

U.S.A.

AACE International, c/o Melissa Moore, 209 Prairie Av, Morgantown, WV 26505
T: (304) 296-8444; E-Mail: 76543.1216@compuserve.com; Fax: (304) 291-5728
Founded: 1956; Members: 6000
Focus: Eng
Periodicals
Cost Engineering (monthly)
Cost Engineers Notebook
Directory of Members (annually)
Transactions (annually) *12639*

Aaron Burr Association (ABA), 4520 King Edward Ct, Annandale, VA 22003
T: (703) 256-7226; E-Mail: aba@enols.com; Fax: (703) 503-4571
Founded: 1946; Members: 250
Pres: Dr. F. Burr Anderson
Focus: Hist
Periodicals
The Chronicle (quarterly)
Newsletter *12640*

Aboriginal Research Club (ARC), c/o Dearborn Historical Museum, 915 S Brady Rd, Dearborn, MI 48124
T: (313) 565-4848; Fax: (313) 565-4848
Founded: 1940; Members: 30
Pres: Ronald Covietz
Focus: Ethnology *12641*

Abrasive Engineering Society (AES), 108 Elliott Dr, Butler, PA 16001-1118
T: (412) 282-6210; Fax: (412) 282-6210
Founded: 1957; Members: 400
Gen Secr: Ted Giese
Focus: Eng
Periodical
AES-Magazine (quarterly) *12642*

Academic Council on the United Nations System (ACUNS), c/o Watson Institute, Brown University, POB 1983, Providence, RI 02912-1983
T: (401) 863-1274; E-Mail: acuns@brown.edu; Fax: (401) 863-3808
Gen Secr: Thomas G. Weiss
Focus: Sci *12643*

Academy for Educational Development (AED), 1875 Connecticut Av NW, Washington, DC 20009
T: (202) 884-8000; Fax: (202) 862-1947
Founded: 1961
Focus: Educ
Periodicals
Academy News (3 times annually)
Newsletter *12644*

Academy for Implants and Transplants (AIT), POB 223, Springfield, VA 22150
T: (703) 451-0001; Fax: (703) 451-0004
Founded: 1972; Members: 268
Gen Secr: Anthony J. Viscido
Focus: Dent
Periodical
Implant Update (quarterly) *12645*

Academy for Interscience Methodology (AIM), 907 N Elm St, Ste 203, Hinsdale, IL 60521
T: (846) 675-6144
Founded: 1961; Members: 15
Gen Secr: Martin E. Persky
Focus: Sci *12646*

Academy for Peace Research, 4264 Topsail Ct, Soquel, CA 95073
T: (408) 462-1588
Gen Secr: Dr. Buryl Payne
Focus: Prom Peace *12647*

Academy of Ambulatory Foot Surgery (AAFS), POB 2730, Tuscaloosa, AL 35403
T: (205) 758-3678; Fax: (205) 758-3688
Founded: 1972; Members: 1500
Gen Secr: Dr. Stanford Rosen
Focus: Surgery
Periodicals
Directory
Journal of the Academy of Ambulatory Foot Surgery
Newsletter (bi-monthly) *12648*

Academy of American Franciscan History (AAFH), 1712 Euclid Av, Berkeley, CA 94709
T: (510) 548-1755; E-Mail: ANFRE@WELL.SF.CA.US; Fax: (510) 548-1231
Founded: 1944; Members: 301
Gen Secr: John Frederick Schwaller
Focus: Hist; Rel & Theol
Periodical
The Americas (quarterly) *12649*

Academy of American Poets (AAP), 584 Broadway, Ste 1208, New York, NY 10012
T: (212) 274-0343; Fax: (212) 274-9427
Founded: 1934; Members: 2400
Gen Secr: William Wadsworth
Focus: Lit
Periodical
Booklist (annually) *12650*

Academy of Aphasia (AA), c/o Dept of Linguistics, UCLA, Los Angeles, CA 90024
T: (310) 206-3206
Founded: 1962; Members: 189
Pres: Dr. Victoria A. Fromkin
Focus: Logopedy *12651*

Academy of Applied Science (AAS), 1 Maple St, Concord, NH 03301
T: (603) 225-2072; Fax: (603) 228-4730
Founded: 1962; Members: 300
Gen Secr: Howard S. Curtis
Focus: Sci *12652*

Academy of Arts and Sciences of the Americas (AASA), 9450 Old Cutler Rd, Miami, FL 33156
T: (305) 663-9897; Fax: (305) 667-8426
Founded: 1965; Members: 25
Pres: Julia Allen Field
Focus: Arts; Sci *12653*

Academy of Criminal Justice Sciences (ACJS), c/o Northern Kentucky University, 402 Nunn Hall, Nunn Dr, Highland Heights, KY 41099-5998
T: (606) 572-5634; Fax: (606) 572-6665
Founded: 1963; Members: 2400
Gen Secr: Patricia DeLancey
Focus: Educ; Law
Periodicals
ACJS Employment Bulletin (8 times annually)
ACJS Membership Directory (annually)
ACJS Today (quarterly)
Journal of Criminal Justice Education (semi-annually)
Justice Quarterly (quarterly) *12654*

Academy of Dental Materials (ADM), 3302 Gaston Av, Dallas, TX 75246
T: (214) 828-8378; Fax: (214) 828-8458
Founded: 1940; Members: 300
Focus: Dent
Periodicals
ADM Newsletter (annually)
Dental Materials (semi-annually) *12655*

Academy of Dentistry International (ADI), 5125 MacArthur Blvd NW, Washington, DC 20016-3315
T: (202) 364-8349; Fax: (202) 364-8349
Founded: 1974; Members: 1500
Gen Secr: Dr. Henry J. Sazima
Focus: Dent
Periodicals
International Communicator (quarterly)
Roster of ADI (semi-annually) *12656*

Academy of Dispensing Audiologists (ADA), 3008 Millwood Av, Columbia, SC 29205
T: (803) 252-5646; Fax: (803) 765-0860
Founded: 1977; Members: 525
Gen Secr: Carol H. Davis
Focus: Otorhinolaryngology
Periodical
ADA Feedback (quarterly) *12657*

Academy of General Dentistry (AGD), 211 E Chicago Av, Ste 1200, Chicago, IL 60611
T: (312) 440-4300; Fax: (312) 440-0559
Founded: 1952; Members: 33000
Gen Secr: Harold E. Donnell Jr.
Focus: Dent
Periodical
AGD Impact (10 times annually) *12658*

Academy of Improbable Research, c/o Annals of Improbable Research, POB 380853, Cambridge, MA 02238
T: (617) 491-4437; E-Mail: air@improb.com
Gen Secr: Marc Abrahams
Focus: Sci *12659*

Academy of International Business (AIB), c/o University of Hawaii at Manoa, 2404 Maile Way, Honolulu, HI 96822-2223
T: (808) 956-3665; Fax: (808) 956-3261
Founded: 1959; Members: 2400
Gen Secr: James R. Wills
Focus: Econ
Periodicals
Journal of International Business Studies (quarterly)
Membership Directory (annually)
Newsletter (quarterly) *12660*

Academy of Legal Studies in Business (ALSB), c/o Dept of Finance, Miami University, 120 Upham Hall, Oxford, OH 45056
T: (513) 529-2945; Fax: (513) 529-6992
Founded: 1923; Members: 1300
Gen Secr: Dr. Daniel J. Herron
Focus: Law
Periodicals
American Business Law Journal (quarterly)
Journal of Legal Studies Education (semi-annually)
Newsletter (semi-annually) *12661*

Academy of Management (AM), c/o PACE University, POB 3020, Briarcliff Manor, NY 10510-8020
T: (914) 923-2607; Fax: (914) 923-2615
Founded: 1936; Members: 8700
Gen Secr: Nancy Urbanowicz
Focus: Business Admin
Periodicals
Academy of Management Executive (quarterly)
Academy of Management Journal (quarterly)
Academy of Management Newsletter
Academy of Management Proceedings (annually)
Academy of Management Review (quarterly) *12662*

Academy of Marketing Science (AMS), c/o School of Business Administration, University of Miami, POB 248012, Coral Gables, FL 33124
T: (305) 284-6673; E-Mail: ssultan@sba01.msmail.miami.edu; Fax: (305) 284-3762
Founded: 1971; Members: 1200
Gen Secr: Harold W. Berkman
Focus: Business Admin
Periodicals
Academy of Marketing Science (quarterly)
Academy of Marketing Science News (quarterly)
Index of JAMS (annually)
Journal of the Academy of Marketing Science *12663*

Academy of Motion Picture Arts and Sciences (AMPAS), 8949 Wilshire Blvd, Beverly Hills, CA 90211
T: (310) 247-3000; Fax: (310) 247-9619
Founded: 1927; Members: 5210
Gen Secr: Bruce Davis
Focus: Cinema
Periodicals
Academy Players Directory (3 times annually)
Annual Index of Motion Picture Credits (annually) *12664*

The Academy of Natural Sciences of Philadelphia (ANSP), 1900 Benjamin Franklin Pkwy, Philadelphia, PA 19103-1195
T: (215) 299-1000; Fax: (215) 299-1028
Founded: 1812; Members: 9000
Pres: Phelan Fretz
Focus: Nat Sci
Periodicals
Academy News
Proceedings of the Academy of Natural Sciences of Philadelphia (annually) *12665*

Academy of Operative Dentistry (AOD), POB 177, Menomonie, WI 54751
T: (715) 235-4999; Fax: (715) 235-7628
Founded: 1972; Members: 900
Gen Secr: Dr. Greg Smith
Focus: Dent
Periodicals
Membership Roster
Operative Dentistry (quarterly) *12666*

Academy of Oral Dynamics (AOD), 8919 Sudley Rd, Manassas, VA 22110
T: (703) 368-8527
Founded: 1950; Members: 75
Gen Secr: Dr. E. Paul Byrne
Focus: Dent *12667*

Academy of Political Science (APS), 475 Riverside Dr, Ste 1274, New York, NY 10115-1274
T: (212) 870-2500; Fax: (212) 870-2202
Founded: 1880; Members: 8000
Pres: Demetrios Caraley; Gen Secr: Demetrios Caraley
Focus: Poli Sci
Periodicals
Political Science Quarterly (quarterly)
Proceedings *12668*

Academy of Psychosomatic Medicine (APM), 5824 N Magnolia, Chicago, IL 60660
T: (312) 784-2025; Fax: (312) 784-1304
Founded: 1954; Members: 1000
Gen Secr: Evelyne A. Hallberg
Focus: Psych
Periodical
Psychosomatics (quarterly) *12669*

Academy of Rehabilitative Audiology (ARA), POB 26532, Minneapolis, MN 55426
T: (612) 920-6098; E-Mail: ara@incnet.com; Fax: (612= 920-6098
Founded: 1966; Members: 300
Gen Secr: Frances J. Laven
Focus: Otorhinolaryngology
Periodicals
Journal of the Academy of Rehabilitative Audiology (annually)
Membership Directory (annually) *12670*

Academy of Religion and Psychical Research (ARPR), POB 614, Bloomfield, CT 06002-0614
T: (203) 242-4593
Founded: 1972; Members: 300
Gen Secr: Boyce Batey
Focus: Psych; Rel & Theol
Periodicals
ARPR Bulletin (quarterly)
The Journal of Religion and Psychical Research (quarterly) *12671*

Academy of Science Fiction, Fantasy and Horror Films (ASFFHF), 334 W 54 St, Los Angeles, CA 90037
T: (213) 752-5811
Founded: 1972; Members: 3000
Pres: Dr. Donald A. Reed
Focus: Cinema *12672*

Academy of Scientific Hypnotherapy (ASH), POB 12041, San Diego, CA 92112
T: (619) 427-6225; Fax: (619) 427-5650
Founded: 1977
Pres: William E. Kemery
Focus: Psych; Therapeutics
Periodicals
Bulletin
Hypnotherapy in Review *12673*

Academy of Security Educators and Trainees (ASET), Rte 2, Box 3644, Berryville, VA 22611
T: (703) 955-1129
Founded: 1980; Members: 510
Gen Secr: Dr. Richard W. Kobetz
Focus: Educ; Eng
Periodicals
ASET Membership (annually)
The Educator (quarterly) *12674*

Academy of Television Arts and Sciences (ATAS), 5220 Lankershim Blvd, North Hollywood, CA 91601
T: (818) 754-2800; Fax: (818) 761-2827
Founded: 1948; Members: 6500
Gen Secr: James L. Loper
Focus: Journalism
Periodical
Debut (semi-annually) *12675*

Academy of Veterinary Cardiology (AVC), 51 Atlantic Av, POB 208, Floral Park, NY 11002
T: (516) 358-4500
Founded: 1967; Members: 600
Gen Secr: Larry P. Tilley
Focus: Cardiol; Vet Med
Periodicals
Membership Directory (bi-annually)
Newsletter *12676*

Accordion Teacher's Guild (ATG), c/o Joan Sommers, POB 22342, Kansas City, MO 64113
T: (913) 722-5625
Founded: 1941; Members: 100
Pres: Joan Sommers
Focus: Music; Educ
Periodical
Accordion Teacher's Guild Newsletter (10 times annually) *12677*

Accreditation Association for Ambulatory Health Care (AAAHC), 9933 Lawler Av, Skokie, IL 60077-3708
T: (312) 676-9610; Fax: (708) 676-9628
Founded: 1979; Members: 12
Gen Secr: Christopher Damon
Focus: Med *12678*

Accreditation Board for Engineering and Technology (ABET), 111 Market Pl, Ste 1050, Baltimore, MD 21202
T: (410) 347-7700; Fax: (410) 625-2238
Founded: 1932; Members: 26
Gen Secr: George D. Peterson
Focus: Eng
Periodical
Accreditation Yearbook (annually) *12679*

Accrediting Association of Bible Colleges (AABC), POB 1523, Fayetteville, AR 72702
T: (501) 521-8164; E-Mail: rebell@aabc.org; Fax: (501) 521-9202
Founded: 1947; Members: 106
Gen Secr: Randall Bell
Focus: Rel & Theol
Periodical
AABC Newsletter (3 times annually) . . *12680*

Accrediting Bureau of Health Education Schools (ABHES), Oak Manor Office, 29089 U.S. 20 W, Elkhart, IN 46514
T: (219) 293-0124; Fax: (219) 295-8564
Founded: 1964; Members: 154
Gen Secr: Mary Lou Reed
Focus: Adult Educ; Med
Periodical
ABHES News *12681*

Accrediting Commission on Education for Health Services Administration (ACEHSA), 1911 N Fort Myer Dr, Ste 503, Arlington, VA 22209
T: (703) 524-0511; Fax: (703) 525-4791
Founded: 1968; Members: 62
Gen Secr: Dr. Sherril B. Gelmon
Focus: Public Health
Periodical
Official List of Accredited Programs (semi-annually) *12682*

Accrediting Council for Continuing Education and Training (ACCET), 1560 Wilson Blvd, Ste 900, Arlington, VA 22209
T: (703) 525-3000; Fax: (703) 525-3339
Founded: 1974; Members: 400
Pres: Roger J. Williams
Focus: Adult Educ

Periodical
Growing Edge (quarterly) 12683

Accrediting Council on Education in Journalism and Mass Communications (ACEJMC), c/o School of Journalism, University of Kansas, Stauffer-Flint Hall, Lawrence, KS 66045
T: (913) 864-3973
Founded: 1929; Members: 23
Gen Secr: Susanne Shaw
Focus: Adult Educ; Journalism
Periodical
Accredited Journalism and Mass Communications Education (annually) 12684

ACEC Research and Management Foundation (ACEC/RMF), 1015 15 St NW, Ste 802, Washington, DC 20005
T: (202) 347-7474; Fax: (202) 898-0068
Founded: 1974
Gen Secr: Thomas E. Kern
Focus: Eng
Periodical
RMF Newsletter (quarterly) 12685

Ackerman Institute for Family Therapy (AIFT), 149 E 78 St, New York, NY 10021
T: (212) 879-4900; Fax: (212) 744-0206
Founded: 1960
Gen Secr: Dr. Peter Steinglass
Focus: Therapeutics 12686

Acoustical Society of America (ASA), 500 Sunnyside Blvd, Woodbury, NY 11797
T: (516) 576-2360; Fax: (516) 576-2377
Founded: 1929; Members: 6700
Pres: Stanley L. Ehrlich; Gen Secr: Charles E. Schmid
Focus: Acoustics
Periodical
Journal of the Acoustical Society of America (monthly) 12687

Action in International Medicine (AIM), 1725 E 19 St, Ste 605, Tulsa, OK 74104-5425
T: (918) 747-2797; Fax: (918) 747-2797
Gen Secr: Dr. W. Reynolds
Focus: Med 12688

Actuarial Studies in Non-Life Insurance (ASTIN), c/o Wharton School, Dept of Insurance, University of Pennsylvania, 3641 Locust Walk, Philadelphia, PA 19104
T: (215) 898-7765
Founded: 1957
Gen Secr: Prof. Jean Lemaire
Focus: Insurance 12689

Acupuncture Research Institute (ARI), 313 W Andrix St, Monterey Park, CA 91754
T: (213) 722-7353
Founded: 1972; Members: 750
Gen Secr: Louis Gasper
Focus: Med; Physical Therapy
Periodical
The Meridian (quarterly) 12690

Addiction Research and Treatment Corporation (ARTC), 22 Chapel St, Brooklyn, NY 11201
T: (718) 260-2900
Founded: 1969
Gen Secr: Dr. Beny J. Primm
Focus: Med 12691

Adhesion Society (AS), c/o 2 Davidson Hall, Virginia Tech, Blacksburg, VA 24061-0201
T: (540) 231-7257; E-Mail: adhesoc@ut.edu;
Fax: (540) 231-3971
Founded: 1978; Members: 400
Pres: Guy Davis
Focus: Chem
Periodical
Newsletter (quarterly) 12692

Adirondack Historical Association (AHA), c/o Adirondack Museum, Blue Mountain Lake, NY 12812-0099
T: (518) 352-7311; Fax: (518) 352-7603
Founded: 1948; Members: 121
Gen Secr: Jacqueline Bay
Focus: Hist
Periodical
Guide Line (semi-annually) 12693

Adult Christian Education Foundation (ACEF), POB 8398, Madison, WI 53708
T: (608) 849-5933
Founded: 1959
Pres: Harley A. Swiggum
Focus: Adult Educ
Periodical
Annual Report (annually) 12694

Advanced Transit Association (ATRA), 2432 N Summit Circle Glen, Escondido, CA 92026
T: (619) 744-8853; E-Mail: landeagl@cts.com;
Fax: (619) 744-3846
Founded: 1976; Members: 100
Gen Secr: Thomas Richert
Focus: Transport
Periodicals
ATRA Updates
Journal of Advanced Transportation (quarterly)
. 12695

Advertising Research Foundation (ARF), 641 Lexington Av, New York, NY 10022
T: (212) 751-5656; Fax: (212) 319-5265
Founded: 1936; Members: 355

Pres: Michael J. Naples
Focus: Advert
Periodicals
ARF Transcript Proceedings
Journal of Advertising Research (bi-monthly)
. 12696

Aerospace Department Chairmen's Association (ADCA), c/o Dept of Aerospace Engineering, Texas A & M University, 701 H.R. Bright Bldg, College Station, TX 77843-3141
T: (409) 845-1600; Fax: (409) 845-9267
Founded: 1968; Members: 79
Pres: Walter Haisler
Focus: Aero 12697

Aerospace Education Foundation (AEF), 1501 Lee Hwy, Arlington, VA 22209-1198
T: (703) 247-5839; Fax: (703) 247-5853
Founded: 1956; Members: 2000
Gen Secr: Steven S. Lee
Focus: Educ; Aero
Periodicals
Foundation Forums (semi-annually)
Newsletter (quarterly) 12698

Aerospace Electrical Society (AES), POB 531548, Grand Prairie, TX 75053-1548
Founded: 1941; Members: 250
Pres: Lloyd P. Appelman
Focus: Electric Eng
Periodical
News & Views (monthly) 12699

Aerospace Medical Association (AsMA), 320 S Henry St, Alexandria, VA 22314
T: (703) 739-2240; Fax: (703) 739-9692
Founded: 1929; Members: 4000
Gen Secr: Russell B. Rayman
Focus: Med
Periodicals
Aviation, Space and Envivonmental Medicine (monthly)
Membership Directory (annually)
Scientific Papers (annually) 12700

Afghanistan Studies Association (ASA), c/o Center for Afghanistan Studies, University of Nebraska at Omaha, ASH 238, Omaha, NE 68182-0006
T: (402) 554-2901; Fax: (402) 554-3242
Founded: 1971; Members: 125
Gen Secr: Thomas E. Gouttierre
Focus: Ethnology
Periodicals
Afghanistan Studies Journal (semi-annually)
ASA Newsletter (quarterly) 12701

Africa Fund (AF), 17 John St, New York, NY 10038-4010
T: (212) 962-1210; E-Mail: africa-fund@igc.apc.org;
Fax: (212) 964-5870
Founded: 1966; Members: 5000
Gen Secr: Jennifer Davis
Focus: Poli Sci
Periodical
Southern Africa Literature List (semi-annually)
. 12702

African-American Institute (AAI), 380 Lexington Av, New York, NY 10168-4298
T: (212) 949-5666; Fax: (212) 682-6174
Founded: 1953
Gen Secr: Frank Ferrari
Focus: Poli Sci 12703

African American Museum (AAM), 1765 Crawford Rd, Cleveland, OH 44106
T: (216) 791-1700
Founded: 1953; Members: 37
Gen Secr: Dr. Eleanor Engram
Focus: Hist
Periodical
African American Museum Newsletter (bi-monthly)
. 12704

African Association for the Study of Religions (AASR), c/o Univ. of California, African-American and African Studies Program, Davis, CA 95616
Gen Secr: Prof. Jacob Olupona
Focus: Rel & Theol 12705

African Heritage Center for African Dance and Music (AHCADM), 4018 Minnesota Av NE, Washington, DC 20019
T: (202) 399-5252
Founded: 1973; Members: 20
Gen Secr: Melvin Deal
Focus: Ethnology 12706

African Literature Association (ALA), c/o Africana Studies and Research Center, Cornell University, 310 Triphammer Rd, Ithaca, NY 14850-2599
T: (607) 255-0534; Fax: (607) 255-7116
Focus: Lit 12707

African Medical and Research Foundation (AMREF), 420 Lexington Av, New York, NY 10170
T: (212) 986-1835; Fax: (212) 599-5064
Gen Secr: Bruce Bodner
Focus: Med; Sci 12708

African Studies Association (ASA), c/o Emory University, Credit Union Bldg, Atlanta, GA 30322
T: (404) 329-6410; Fax: (404) 329-6433
Founded: 1957; Members: 2300
Pres: Prof. Iris Berger; Gen Secr: Christopher Koch
Focus: Ethnology

Periodicals
African Studies Review (3 times annually)
ASA News (quarterly)
History in Africa (annually)
Issue (semi-annually) 12709

Afro-American Historical and Genealogical Society (AAHGS), POB 73086, Washington, DC 20056
T: (202) 234-5350
Founded: 1977; Members: 1000
Pres: Sylvia Cooke Martin
Focus: Genealogy; Hist
Periodicals
Journal (quarterly)
Newsletter (quarterly) 12710

Afro-Asian Center (AAC), POB 337, Saugerties, NY 12477
T: (914) 246-7828
Founded: 1972
Gen Secr: Robert Carroll
Focus: Ethnology 12711

Agency for Instructional Technology (AIT), Box A, Bloomington, IN 47402-0120
T: (812) 339-2203; Fax: (812) 333-4218
Founded: 1970
Gen Secr: Michael F. Sullivan
Focus: Educ
Periodical
TECHNOS (quarterly) 12712

Agri-Energy Roundtable (AER), 1312 18 St NW, Ste 300, Washington, DC 20006
T: (202) 887-0528, 887-0238; Fax: (202) 887-9178
Gen Secr: Nicholas E. Hollis
Focus: Energy 12713

Agricultural Communicators in Education (ACE), c/o University of Florida, Bldg 116, 601 IFAS, Gainesville, FL 32611
T: (904) 392-9588; Fax: (904) 392-8583
Founded: 1913; Members: 700
Gen Secr: Ashley Wood
Focus: Agri
Periodical
Journal of Applied Communications (quarterly)
. 12714

Agricultural History Society (AHS), 1301 New York Av NW, Rm 928, Washington, DC 20005-4788
T: (202) 219-0787
Founded: 1919; Members: 1400
Pres: Robert McMath; Gen Secr: Lowell K. Dyson
Focus: Hist; Agri
Periodicals
Agricultural History (quarterly)
Symposium Proceedings (annually) . . . 12715

Agriservices Foundation, 648 W Sierra Av, POB 429, Clovis, CA 93612
T: (209) 299-2263; Fax: (209) 299-2098
Founded: 1964
Pres: Dr. Marion E. Ensminger
Focus: Agri 12716

Aid for International Medicine (AIM), POB 119, Rockland, DE 19732
T: (302) 655-8290
Founded: 1965
Focus: Med 12717

AIDIS-USA Section, 601 Wythe St, Alexandria, VA 22314-1994
T: (703) 684-2400; Fax: (703) 684-2492
Founded: 1946; Members: 20000
Pres: Dr. Richard F. Cole
Focus: Eng; Hygiene
Periodicals
Ingeniera Sanitaria (quarterly)
Newsletter (quarterly) 12718

AIESEC – United States, 135 W 50 St, New York, NY 10020
T: (212) 757-3774; Fax: (212) 757-4062
Founded: 1948; Members: 5000
Pres: Chelle Izzi
Focus: Econ
Periodicals
AIESEC-U.S. Annual Report (annually)
Linkletter (quarterly) 12719

Air and Waste Management Association (AWMA), 1 Gateway Ctr, Pittsburgh, PA 15222
T: (412) 232-3444; Fax: (412) 232-3450
Founded: 1907; Members: 17000
Gen Secr: John Thorner
Focus: Ecology
Periodical
Journal of the Air and Waste Management Association (monthly) 12720

Air National Guard Optometric Society (ANGOS), c/o Lyman Nordan, 5517 Afton Dr, Birmingham, AL 35242
T: (205) 991-8663
Founded: 1975; Members: 50
Pres: Lyman Nordan
Focus: Optics
Periodical
Newsletter (3 times annually) 12721

Aircraft Electronics Association (AEA), POB 1963, Independence, MO 64055-0963
T: (816) 373-6565; Fax: (816) 478-3100
Founded: 1958; Members: 862
Gen Secr: Monte Mitchell
Focus: Electronic Eng

Periodical
Avionics News (monthly) 12722

Airship Association – U.S. (AA), 8512 Cedar St, Silver Spring, MD 20910
T: (301) 588-7916; Fax: (301) 588-2085
Founded: 1953
Gen Secr: Frank G. McGuire
Focus: Aero
Periodical
Advanced Lighter-Than-Air Review (monthly)
. 12723

Alcor Life Extension Foundation (ALEF), 7895 E Acoma Dr, Ste 110, Scottsdale, AZ 85260-6916
T: (602) 922-9013; E-Mail: info@alcor.org;
Fax: (602) 922-9027
Founded: 1972; Members: 920
Pres: Stephen W. Bridge
Focus: Med
Periodical
Cryonics (monthly) 12724

Alexander Graham Bell Association for the Deaf (AGBAD), 3417 Volta Pl NW, Washington, DC 20007-2778
T: (202) 337-5220
Founded: 1890; Members: 5000
Gen Secr: Dr. Donna McCord Dickman
Focus: Educ Handic
Periodicals
Newsounds (10 times annually)
Our Kids Magazine (2-3 times annually) 12725

Alfred Adler Institute (AAI), 24 E 21 St, New York, NY 10010-7200
T: (212) 254-1048
Founded: 1950
Gen Secr: Robert Ellenbogen
Focus: Psych
Periodicals
Bulletin (annually)
Journal of Individual Psychology (quarterly)
Newsletter (quarterly) 12726

ALI-ABA Committee on Continuing Professional Education, 4025 Chestnut St, Philadelphia, PA 19104-3099
T: (215) 243-1600; Fax: (215) 243-1664
Founded: 1947
Gen Secr: Paul A. Wolkin
Focus: Educ
Periodicals
ALI-ABA CLR Review (weekly)
ALI-ABA Course Materials Journal (bi-monthly)
ALI-ABA Reporter (quarterly) 12727

Alliance for Alternatives in Healthcare (AAH), POB 6279, Thousand Oaks, CA 91359-6279
T: (805) 494-7818; Fax: (805) 494-8528
Founded: 1983; Members: 1500
Pres: Steve Gorman
Focus: Marketing 12728

Alliance for Environmental Education (AEE), POB 658, Marshall, VA 22115-0658
T: (703) 330-5667; Fax: (703) 253-5811
Founded: 1972; Members: 300
Pres: Steven C. Kussmann
Focus: Ecology
Periodical
Network Exchange (bi-monthly) 12729

Alliance to Save Energy (ASE), 1725 K St NW, Ste 509, Washington, DC 20006-1401
T: (202) 857-0666; Fax: (202) 331-9588
Founded: 1977; Members: 1500
Pres: William A. Nitze
Focus: Energy
Periodicals
Alliance Update (quarterly)
Annual Report (annually) 12730

ALSAC – Saint Jude Children's Research Hospital, 501 Saint Jude Pl, POB 3704, Memphis, TN 38105
T: (901) 522-9733
Founded: 1957; Members: 2000
Gen Secr: Richard C. Shadyac
Focus: Pediatrics
Periodicals
ALSAC News (quarterly)
Partners in Hope (quarterly) 12731

Alternative Energy Resources Organization (AERO), 25 S Ewing, Rm 214, Helena, MT 59601
T: (406) 443-7272; E-Mail: aero@desktop.org;
Fax: (406) 442-9120
Founded: 1974; Members: 600
Gen Secr: Pam Mavrolas
Focus: Energy; Econ; Agri
Periodicals
AERO Sun-Times (quarterly)
Sustainable Farming (quarterly) 12732

Alzheimer's Association, 919 N Michigan Av, Ste 1000, Chicago, IL 60611
T: (312) 335-8700; Fax: (312) 335-1110
Founded: 1980; Members: 30000
Pres: Edward Truschke
Focus: Med
Periodical
Alzheimer's Association Newsletter (quarterly)
. 12733

Alzheimer's Disease International (ADI), POB 2672, Chicago, IL 60690-2672
T: (312) 335-5777
Founded: 1984; Members: 56
Gen Secr: Rachel BNillington
Focus: Med
Periodical
ADI Global Perspective (quarterly) . . . 12734

AMA International, 135 W 50 St, New York, NY 10020
T: (212) 586-8100; Fax: (212) 713-1652
Founded: 1956; Members: 10000
Pres: Domenico A. Fanelli
Focus: Business Admin 12735

Ambulatory Pediatric Association (APA), 6728 Old McLean Village Dr, McLean, VA 22101
T: (703) 556-9222
Founded: 1960; Members: 1200
Gen Secr: M. Degnon
Focus: Pediatrics
Periodicals
Membership Directory (bi-annually)
Newsletter (3 times annually) 12736

Amdahl Users Group (AUG), c/o Jim Caitlan, 10900 NE Fourth St, Ste 1600, Bellevue, WA 98004
T: (206) 453-0271
Founded: 1976; Members: 350
Gen Secr: Jim Caitlan
Focus: Computer & Info Sci
Periodical
Directory (annually) 12737

American Academy for Cerebral Palsy and Developmental Medicine (AACPDM), 6300 N River Rd, Ste 727, Rosemont, IL 60018
T: (847) 698-1635; Fax: (847) 823-0536
Founded: 1947; Members: 1600
Gen Secr: Sheril King
Focus: Med; Neurology
Periodicals
Journal of Developmental Medicine and Child Neurology (monthly)
Newsletter (semi-annually) 12738

American Academy for Jewish Research (AAJR), 3080 Broadway, New York, NY 10027
T: (212) 678-8864; Fax: (212) 678-8947
Founded: 1919; Members: 460
Gen Secr: C. Frost
Focus: Hist; Ethnology; Rel & Theol
Periodicals
Monograph Series
Monograph Studies
Proceedings of the American Academy for Jewish Research (annually) 12739

American Academy of Actuaries (AAA), 1100 17 St NW, Washington, DC 20036
T: (202) 223-8196; Fax: (202) 872-1948
Founded: 1965; Members: 13000
Gen Secr: Wilson W. Wyatt
Focus: Insurance
Periodicals
Actuarial Update (monthly)
Contingencies (bi-monthly)
Enrolled Actuaries Report (5 times annually) 12740

American Academy of Advertising (AAA), c/o Dr. Robert L. King, School of Business, University of Richmond, Richmond, VA 23173
T: (804) 289-8902; Fax: (804) 289-8878
Founded: 1958; Members: 675
Gen Secr: Dr. Robert L. King
Focus: Advert
Periodicals
AAA Newsletter (quarterly)
Journal of Advertising (quarterly)
Proceedings of the Conference (annually) 12741

American Academy of Allergy, Asthma and Immunology (AAAI), 611 E Wells St, Milwaukee, WI 53202
T: (414) 272-6071; Fax: (414) 276-3349
Founded: 1943; Members: 5200
Pres: Dr. Philip Fireman
Focus: Immunology
Periodical
The Journal of Allergy and Clinical Immunology 12742

American Academy of Arts and Letters (AAAL), 633 W 155 St, New York, NY 10032-7599
T: (212) 368-5900; Fax: (212) 491-4615
Founded: 1898; Members: 250
Pres: Kevin Roche; Gen Secr: Virginia Dajani
Focus: Arts; Lit
Periodicals
Proceedings (annually)
Yearbook (annually) 12743

American Academy of Arts and Sciences (AAAS), Northon's Woods, 136 Irving St, Cambridge, MA 02138
T: (617) 576-5000; Fax: (617) 576-5050
Founded: 1780; Members: 3900
Pres: Jaroslav Pelikan; Gen Secr: Howard H. Hiatt
Focus: Arts; Sci
Periodicals
Bulletin (8 times annually)
Daedalus (quarterly) 12744

American Academy of Child and Adolescent Psychiatry (AACAP), 3615 Wisconsin Av NW, Washington, DC 20016
T: (202) 966-7300; Fax: (202) 966-2891
Founded: 1953; Members: 5000
Gen Secr: Virginia Q. Anthony
Focus: Psychiatry
Periodicals
Journal of the AACAP (bi-monthly)
Membership Directory
Newsletter (quarterly) 12745

American Academy of Clinical Psychiatrists (AACP), POB 3212, San Diego, CA 92163
T: (619) 298-0538
Founded: 1975; Members: 600
Gen Secr: Alicia A. Munoz
Focus: Psychiatry
Periodicals
Annals of Clinical Psychiatry (quarterly)
Clinical Psychiatry Quarterly (quarterly) . 12746

American Academy of Cosmetic Surgery (AACS), 401 N Michigan Av, Chicago, IL 60611-4212
T: (312) 527-6713; Fax: (312) 644-1815
Founded: 1985; Members: 1250
Gen Secr: Jeffrey P. Knezovich
Focus: Surgery
Periodicals
American Journal of Cosmetic Surgery (quarterly)
Membership Roster (annually)
Newsletter (quarterly) 12747

American Academy of Crisis Interveners (AACI), c/o Edward S. Rosenbluth, 215 Breckinridge Ln, Ste 102, Louisville, KY 40207
T: (502) 896-0200
Founded: 1977; Members: 200
Pres: Edward S. Rosenbluth
Focus: Psych 12748

American Academy of Dental Electrosurgery (AADE), POB 374, Planetarium Station, New York, NY 10024
T: (212) 595-1925
Founded: 1963; Members: 200
Gen Secr: Maurice J. Oringer
Focus: Surgery; Dent
Periodical
Current Events (quarterly) 12749

American Academy of Dental Group Practice (AADGP), 5110 N 40 St, Ste 250, Phoenix, AZ 85018
T: (602) 381-1185; Fax: (602) 381-1093
Founded: 1973; Members: 1575
Focus: Dent
Periodicals
Directory (bi-annually)
Newsletter (quarterly) 12750

American Academy of Dental Practice Administration (AADPA), c/o Kathleen Uebel, 1063 Whippoorwill Ln, Palatine, IL 60067
T: (708) 934-4404
Founded: 1958; Members: 250
Gen Secr: Kathleen Uebel
Focus: Dent
Periodicals
Communicator (quarterly)
Essay Tapes (annually)
Journal of Dental Practice Administration (quarterly)
Proceedings (annually) 12751

American Academy of Dermatology (AAD), 930 N Meacham Rd, Schaumburg, IL 60173-6016
T: (708) 330-0230; Fax: (708) 330-0050
Founded: 1938; Members: 11200
Gen Secr: Bradford W. Claxton
Focus: Derm
Periodicals
Bulletin (bi-monthly)
Journal of the American Academy of Dermatology (monthly) 12752

American Academy of Environmental Engineers (AAEE), 130 Holiday Ct, Annapolis, MD 21401
T: (301) 266-3311; Fax: (301) 266-7653
Founded: 1955; Members: 2600
Gen Secr: William C. Anderson
Focus: Eng
Periodicals
Environmental Engineer (quarterly)
Environmental Engineering Selection Guide (annually) 12753

American Academy of Esthetic Dentistry (AAED), 500 N Michigan Av, Ste 1920, Chicago, IL 60611
T: (708) 355-0424
Founded: 1975; Members: 100
Gen Secr: Sharon Bennett
Focus: Dent
Periodical
Esthetics (3 times annually) 12754

American Academy of Facial Plastic and Reconstructive Surgery (AAFPRS), 1110 Vermont Av NW, Ste 220, Washington, DC 22005
T: (202) 842-4500; Fax: (202) 371-1514
Founded: 1964; Members: 3200
Gen Secr: Stephen C. Duffy
Focus: Surgery
Periodicals
Face Facts (quarterly)
Facial Plastic Surgery Today (quarterly)
Facial Plastic Times (monthly) 12755

American Academy of Family Physicians (AAFP), 8880 Ward Pkwy, Kansas City, MO 64114
T: (816) 333-9700; Fax: (816) 822-0580
Founded: 1947; Members: 80000
Pres: Patrick B. Harr; Gen Secr: Robert Graham
Focus: Med; Physiology
Periodicals
American Family Physician (monthly)
FP Report (monthly) 12756

American Academy of Fixed Prosthodontics, POB 1409, Bodega Bay, CA 94923-1409
T: (707) 875-3040; Fax: (707) 875-2927
Founded: 1952; Members: 535
Gen Secr: Dr. Robert S. Staffanou
Focus: Dent
Periodicals
Journal of Prosthetic Dentisty (monthly)
Newsletter (semi-annually) 12757

American Academy of Forensic Sciences (AAFS), 410 N 21 St, Ste 203, Colorado Springs, CO 80901-0669
T: (719) 636-1100; Fax: (719) 636-1993
Founded: 1948; Members: 3500
Gen Secr: Anne H. Warren
Focus: Law
Periodical
Journal of Forensic Sciences (bi-monthly) 12758

American Academy of Gnathologic Orthopedics (AAGO), POB 548, Richmond, TX 77406-0548
T: (713) 341-5250
Founded: 1970; Members: 700
Gen Secr: L.M. Alderson
Focus: Orthopedics
Periodicals
Journal (quarterly)
Membership Roster (annually) 12759

American Academy of Gold Foil Operators (AAGFO), 17922 Tall Grass Ct, Noblesville, IN 46060
T: (317) 867-3011
Founded: 1952; Members: 400
Gen Secr: Dr. Ronald K. Harris
Focus: Dent
Periodicals
Journal of Operative Dentistry (quarterly)
Roster (annually) 12760

American Academy of Implant Dentistry (AAID), 211 E Chicago Av, Ste 750, Chicago, IL 60611
T: (312) 335-1550
Founded: 1952; Members: 2300
Gen Secr: Joyce Sigmon
Focus: Dent
Periodicals
Journal of Oral Implantology (quarterly)
Newsletter (quarterly) 12761

American Academy of Implant Prosthodontics (AAIP), 5555 Peachtree-Dunwoody Rd NE, Ste 140, Atlanta, GA 30342
T: (404) 847-9200; Fax: (404) 257-1201
Founded: 1980; Members: 300
Gen Secr: Donna P. Vaughn
Focus: Dent
Periodicals
Membership Directory
Newsletter (3 times annually) 12762

American Academy of Insurance Medicine (AAIM), c/o Paul R. Bell, 2211 Congress St, Portland, ME 04122
T: (207) 770-2946
Founded: 1889; Members: 800
Gen Secr: Paul R. Bell
Focus: Insurance; Med
Periodicals
Journal of Life Insurance Medicine (quarterly)
Transactions (annually) 12763

American Academy of Kinesiology and Physical Education, c/o Dept of Kinesiology, Louisiana State University, Baton Rouge, LA 70803-7101
T: (504) 388-3548; Fax: (504) 388-3680
Founded: 1926; Members: 125
Gen Secr: Richard Magill
Focus: Sports
Periodical
The Academy Papers (annually) 12764

American Academy of Matrimonial Lawyers / AAML, 150 N Michigan Av, Ste 2040, Chicago, IL 60601
T: (312) 263-6477
Founded: 1962; Members: 1300
Gen Secr: Lorraine J. West
Focus: Law
Periodicals
Journal of the American Academy of Matrimonial Lawyers (annually)
Newsletter 12765

American Academy of Maxillofacial Prosthetics (AAMP), 865 Fonake Cir, Indianapolis, IN 46278
T: (317) 274-5628; Fax: (317) 274-9544
Founded: 1953; Members: 148
Gen Secr: Dr. Carl Andres
Focus: Dent
Periodical
Journal of Prosthetic Dentistry (monthly) . 12766

American Academy of Mechanics (AAM), c/o ESM Dept, Virginia Tech, Blacksburg, VA 24061-0219
T: (703) 231-6841; Fax: (703) 231-4574
Founded: 1969; Members: 1300
Gen Secr: Dean T. Mook
Focus: Eng 12767

American Academy of Medical Administrators (AAMA), 30555 Southfield Rd, Ste 150, Southfield, MI 48076-7747
T: (313) 540-4310
Founded: 1957; Members: 2000
Pres: Thomas R. O'Donovan
Focus: Med
Periodical
Executive (bi-monthly) 12768

American Academy of Microbiology (AAM), 1325 Massachusetts Av NW, Washington, DC 20005-4171
T: (202) 942-9226
Founded: 1955; Members: 1000
Gen Secr: Carol A. Colgan
Focus: Microbio
Periodical
Directory of Fellows of the American Academy of Microbiology (triennial) 12769

American Academy of Neurological Surgery (AANS), c/o University Hospital, 2128 Taubman, Ann Arbor, MI 48109
T: (313) 936-5015; Fax: (313) 936-9294
Founded: 1938; Members: 168
Gen Secr: Dr. Julian Hoff
Focus: Surgery; Neurology 12770

American Academy of Ophthalmology (AAO), 655 Beach St, San Francisco, CA 94109
T: (415) 561-8500; Fax: (415) 561-8533
Founded: 1896; Members: 20777
Gen Secr: H. Dunbar Hoskins
Focus: Ophthal
Periodicals
Argus (monthly)
Directory (bi-annually)
Ophthalmology (monthly) 12771

American Academy of Optometry (AAO), 4330 East West Hwy, Ste 1117, Bethesda, MD 20814-4408
T: (301) 718-6500; Fax: (301) 656-0989
Founded: 1921; Members: 3850
Gen Secr: David Lewis
Focus: Ophthal
Periodical
Optometry and Vision Science (monthly) . 12772

American Academy of Oral and Maxillofacial Radiology (AAOMR), POB 55722, Jackson, MS 39296
T: (601) 984-6060; E-Mail: ocarroll@umsmed.edu; Fax: (601) 984-6086
Founded: 1949; Members: 500
Gen Secr: Dr. M. Kevin O. Carroll
Focus: Dent; Radiology
Periodical
Roster of Membership (annually) 12773

American Academy of Oral Medicine (AAOM), 631 29 St S, Arlington, VA 22202-2312
T: (703) 684-6649; E-Mail: brownr@medlib.georgetown.edu; Fax: (703) 684-2008
Founded: 1946; Members: 800
Gen Secr: Ronald S. Brown
Focus: Otorhinolaryngology
Periodicals
Journal of Oral Medicine (quarterly)
Newsletter (quarterly) 12774

American Academy of Orofacial Pain (AAOP), 10 Joplin Ct, Lafayette, CA 94549
T: (510) 945-9298; Fax: (510) 945-9299
Founded: 1975; Members: 220
Gen Secr: Martha Boam
Focus: Dent
Periodical
Journal of Craniomandibular Disorders Head and Neck Pain 12775

American Academy of Orthodontics for the General Practitioner (AAOGP), 920 Bascom Hill Dr, Baraboo, WI 53913-1281
Founded: 1959; Members: 250
Gen Secr: Jackie Hemmrich
Focus: Dent
Periodicals
Academic Calendar (annually)
International Journal of Orthodontics (semi-annually) 12776

American Academy of Orthopaedic Surgeons (AAOS), 6300 N River Rd, Rosemont, IL 60018-4226
T: (708) 823-7186; Fax: (708) 823-8125
Founded: 1933; Members: 15100
Gen Secr: Thomas C. Nelson
Focus: Surgery; Orthopedics
Periodical
Bulletin (quarterly) 12777

American Academy of Orthotists and Prosthetists (AAOP), 1650 King St, Ste 500, Alexandria, VA 22314
T: (703) 836-7118; Fax: (703) 836-0838
Founded: 1970; Members: 1700

Gen Secr: Dr. Ian R. Horen
Focus: Rehabil
Periodical
Journal of Prosthetics and Orthotics: C.P.O. (quarterly) 12778

American Academy of Osteopathy (AAO), 3500 DePauw Blvd, Ste 1080, Indianapolis, IN 46268-1136
T: (317) 879-1881; Fax: (317) 879-0563
Founded: 1937; Members: 3500
Gen Secr: Stephen J. Noone
Focus: Med; Pathology
Periodical
AAO Journal (quarterly) 12779

American Academy of Otolaryngic Allergy (AAOA), 8455 Colesville Rd, Ste 745, Silver Spring, MD 20910-9998
T: (301) 588-1800; Fax: (301) 588-2454
Founded: 1941; Members: 1900
Gen Secr: Donald J. Clark
Focus: Immunology; Otorhinolaryngology; Ophthal
Periodicals
Directory (annually)
Newsletter (quarterly)
Transactions (annually) 12780

American Academy of Pediatric Dentistry (AAPD), 211 E Chicago Av, Ste 1036, Chicago, IL 60611
T: (312) 337-2169
Founded: 1947; Members: 3300
Gen Secr: Dr. John A. Bogert
Focus: Dent
Periodicals
Newsletter (bi-monthly)
Pediatric Dentistry (bi-monthly) 12781

American Academy of Pediatrics (AAP), 141 NW Point Blvd, POB 927, Elk Grove Village, IL 60009-0927
T: (312) 228-5005; Fax: (312) 228-5097
Founded: 1930; Members: 46000
Gen Secr: Dr. Joe M. Sanders
Focus: Pediatrics
Periodicals
Pediatrics (monthly)
Pediatrics in Review 12782

American Academy of Periodontology (AAP), 737 N Michigan Av, Ste 800, Chicago, IL 60611
T: (312) 787-5518; Fax: (312) 787-3670
Founded: 1914; Members: 5300
Pres: Dr. Robert Ferris
Focus: Dent
Periodicals
Journal of Periodontology (monthly)
Newsletter (monthly)
Roster of Members (annually) 12783

American Academy of Physical Medicine and Rehabilitation (AAPMR), 1 IBM Plaza, Chicago, IL 60611-3604
T: (312) 464-9700; Fax: (312) 464-0227
Founded: 1938; Members: 3200
Gen Secr: Ronald A. Heinrichs
Focus: Med; Rehabil
Periodicals
Academy PM&R News (monthly)
Archives of Physical Medicine and Rehabilitation (monthly) 12784

American Academy of Physician Assistants (AAPA), 950 N Washington St, Alexandria, VA 22314-1552
T: (703) 836-2272; Fax: (703) 684-1924
Founded: 1968; Members: 15000
Gen Secr: Harry A. Bradley
Focus: Physiology
Periodicals
AAPA Bulletin (monthly)
Newsletter (monthly)
PA Job Find (bi-weekly) 12785

American Academy of Physiologic Dentistry (AAPD), c/o William Kopperud, 567 S Washington St, Naperville, IL 60540
T: (708) 355-2625
Founded: 1958; Members: 75
Gen Secr: William Kopperud
Focus: Dent 12786

American Academy of Podiatric Administration (AAPO), 836 Farmington Av, Ste 105, West Hartford, CT 06119
T: (203) 236-2564; Fax: (203) 233-0251
Founded: 1961; Members: 200
Pres: Harvey Lederman
Focus: Public Admin
Periodical
AAPO Newsletter (quarterly) 12787

American Academy of Podiatric Sports Medicine (AAPSM), 1729 Glastonberry Rd, Potomac, MD 20854
T: (301) 424-7440
Founded: 1970; Members: 800
Gen Secr: Larry I. Shane
Focus: Orthopedics
Periodicals
Membership Directory (annually)
Newsletter (quarterly) 12788

American Academy of Political and Social Science (AAPSS), 3937 Chestnut St, Philadelphia, PA 19104
T: (215) 386-4594; Fax: (215) 386-4630
Founded: 1889; Members: 5000
Pres: Marvin E. Wolfgang; Gen Secr: Mary Parker
Focus: Poli Sci; Sociology
Periodical
The Annals (bi-monthly) 12789

American Academy of Psychiatrists in Alcoholism and Addictions (AAPAA), POB 376, Greenbelt, MD 20770
T: (301) 220-0951; Fax: (301) 220-0941
Founded: 1985; Members: 1000
Gen Secr: Alice Conde
Focus: Psychiatry
Periodicals
American Journal of Addictions (quarterly)
Newsletter 12790

American Academy of Psychiatry and the Law (AAPL), 1 Regency Dr, POB 30, Bloomfield, CT 06002-0030
T: (860) 242-5450; Fax: (860) 286-0787
Founded: 1969; Members: 1550
Gen Secr: Jacquelyn T. Coleman
Focus: Psychiatry; Law
Periodicals
Bulletin of the American Academy of Psychiatry and the Law (quarterly)
Newsletter (3 times annually) 12791

American Academy of Psychoanalysis (AAP), 47 E 19 St, New York, NY 10003-1323
T: (212) 475-7980; Fax: (212) 475-8101
Founded: 1956; Members: 775
Gen Secr: Vivian Mendelsohn
Focus: Psychoan
Periodicals
The Academy Forum (quarterly)
Journal of the American Academy of Psychoanalysis (quarterly) 12792

American Academy of Psychotherapists (AAP), POB 607, Decatur, GA 30031
T: (404) 299-6336
Founded: 1955; Members: 725
Gen Secr: Nancy Hunt
Focus: Therapeutics
Periodicals
AAP Newsletter (monthly)
Directory (bi-annually)
Voices (quarterly) 12793

American Academy of Religion (AAR), 1703 Clifton Rd NE, Ste G5, Atlanta, GA 30329-4075
Founded: 1909; Members: 7500
Pres: Lawrence E. Sullivan; Gen Secr: Ronald M. Green
Focus: Rel & Theol
Periodicals
Academy Series (4-6 times annually)
Monograph Series (4-6 times annually) . 12794

American Academy of Restorative Dentistry (AARD), c/o Donald H. Downs, 1235 Lake Plaza Dr, Colorado Springs, CO 80906
T: (719) 576-8840
Founded: 1928; Members: 285
Gen Secr: Donald H. Downs
Focus: Dent
Periodicals
Journal of Prosthetic Dentistry
Roster (annually) 12795

American Academy of Safety Education (AASE), c/o Robert L. Baldwin, Central Missouri State University, Safety Center, Humphreys Bldg, Warrensburg, MO 64093
T: (816) 543-4281
Founded: 1962; Members: 107
Gen Secr: Robert L. Baldwin
Focus: Safety
Periodical
Ideas: Issues and Readings in Safety (annually) 12796

American Academy of Sanitarians (AAS), c/o James W. Pees, 829 Brookside Dr, Miami, OK 74354
T: (918) 540-2025
Founded: 1966; Members: 400
Gen Secr: James W. Pees
Focus: Adult Educ; Med
Periodicals
Newsletter (semi-annually)
Register of Professional Sanitarians
Roster of Diplomates (annually) 12797

American Academy of Sports Physicians (AASP), 17445 Oak Creek Court, Encino, CA 91316
T: (818) 501-4433; Fax: (818) 501-8855
Founded: 1979; Members: 150
Gen Secr: Janie Zimmer
Focus: Med; Sports
Periodical
Newsletter (quarterly) 12798

American Academy of Teachers of Singing (AATS), c/o William Gephart, 75 Bank St, New York, NY 10014
T: (212) 242-1836
Founded: 1922; Members: 35
Gen Secr: William Gephart
Focus: Music; Educ 12799

American Academy of the History of Dentistry (AAHD), c/o Aletha A. Kowitz, 100 S Vail Av, Arlington Heights, IL 60005-1866
T: (847) 670-7561
Founded: 1951; Members: 600
Gen Secr: Aletha A. Kowitz
Focus: Hist; Dent
Periodicals
Bulletin of the History of Dentistry (semi-annually)
Newsletter of the American Academy of History of Dentistry (semi-annually) 12800

American Academy of Veterinary Dermatology (AAVD), c/o Dr. Nita Gulbas, Desert Sage Veterinary Clinic, 2249 W Bethany Home Rd, Phoenix, AZ 85015
T: (602) 433-0198
Founded: 1964; Members: 348
Pres: Dr. Nita Gulbas
Focus: Vet Med; Derm
Periodicals
Derm-Dialogue (quarterly)
Membership Directory (annually)
Newsletter (semi-annually) 12801

American Accounting Association (AAA), 5717 Bessie Dr, Sarasota, FL 34233-2399
T: (813) 921-7747; Fax: (813) 923-4093
Founded: 1916; Members: 13000
Pres: katherine Schipper; Gen Secr: Paul L. Gerhardt
Focus: Business Admin
Periodicals
Accounting Review (quarterly)
Newsletter 12802

American Aging Association (AGE), 2129 Providence Av, Chester, PA 19013-5506
T: (610) 874-7550; E-Mail: ameraging@aol.com; Fax: (610) 876-7715
Founded: 1970; Members: 500
Gen Secr: Arthur K. Balin
Focus: Geriatrics
Periodical
AGE (quarterly) 12803

American Agricultural Economics Association (AAEA), 1110 Buckeye Av, Ames, IA 50010-8063
T: (515) 233-3202; E-Mail: lchristo@iastate.edu; Fax: (515) 233-3101
Founded: 1910; Members: 4500
Gen Secr: Rueben C. Buse
Focus: Agri; Econ
Periodicals
American Journal of Agricultural Economics (5 times annually)
Choices (quarterly)
Newsletter (bi-monthly) 12804

American Agricultural Law Association (AALA), c/o University of Arkansas, Leflar Law Center, Fayetteville, AR 72701
T: (501) 575-7389; Fax: (501) 575-5830
Founded: 1980; Members: 900
Gen Secr: William Babione
Focus: Agri; Law
Periodicals
Agricultural Law Update (monthly)
American Agricultural Law Association Membership Directory (bi-annually) 12805

American Allergy Association (AAA), POB 640, Menlo Park, CA 94026
T: (415) 855-8036
Founded: 1978
Focus: Immunology
Periodical
Living with Allergies (annually) 12806

American Alliance for Health, Physical Education, Recreation and Dance (AAHPERD), 1900 Association Dr, Reston, VA 22091
T: (703) 476-3400; Fax: (703) 476-9527
Founded: 1885; Members: 42000
Gen Secr: Millie Puccio
Focus: Sports
Periodicals
Health Education (bi-monthly)
Journal of Physical Education, Recreation & Dance (9 times annually)
Research Quarterly for Exercise & Sport (quarterly)
Strategies (bi-monthly)
Update (9 times annually) 12807

American Alliance for Theatre and Education (AATE), c/o Theatre Dept, Arizona State University, POB 873411, Tempe, AZ 85287-3411
T: (602) 965-6064; Fax: (602) 965-5351
Founded: 1987; Members: 1500
Gen Secr: Barbara Salisbury Wills
Focus: Perf Arts
Periodical
The O'Neill (semi-annually) 12808

American Animal Hospital Association (AAHA), POB 150899, Denver, CO 80215-0899
T: (303) 986-2800; Fax: (303) 986-1700
Founded: 1933; Members: 14000
Gen Secr: John W. Albers
Focus: Vet Med
Periodicals
AAHA Trends (bi-monthly)
Journal of the AAHA (bi-monthly)
Proceedings (annually) 12809

American Anorexia/Bulimia Association (AA/BA), 293 Central Park W, Ste 1R, New York, NY 10024
T: (212) 501-8351
Founded: 1978; Members: 2000
Focus: Med
Periodical
Newsletter (quarterly) 12810

American Anthropological Association (AAA), 4350 N Fairfax Dr, Ste 640, Arlington, VA 22203-1620
T: (703) 5281902
Founded: 1902; Members: 10000
Pres: Yolanda Moses
Focus: Anthro
Periodicals
American Anthropologist (quarterly)
American Ethnologist (quarterly)
Anthropology Newsletter (9 times annually) 12811

American Antiquarian Society (AAS), 185 Salisbury St, Worcester, MA 01609
T: (508) 755-5221
Founded: 1812; Members: 555
Pres: Ellen S. Dunlap
Focus: Hist
Periodical
Proceedings of the American Antiquarian Society (semi-annually) 12812

American Apitherapy Society (AAS), c/o Dr. Christopher Kim, 252 Broad St, Red Bank, NJ 07701
T: (908) 842-5700; Fax: (908) 530-7220
Founded: 1978; Members: 300
Pres: Dr. Christopher Kim
Focus: Therapeutics 12813

American Arbitration Association (AAA), 140 W 51 St, New York, NY 10020
T: (212) 484-4000; Fax: (212) 765-4874
Founded: 1926; Members: 5400
Pres: Robert Coulson
Focus: Law
Periodicals
Arbitration Journal (quarterly)
Arbitration Times (quarterly)
Newsletter (monthly) 12814

American Architectural Foundation (AAF), 1735 New York Av NW, Washington, DC 20006
T: (202) 626-7500; Fax: (202) 626-7420
Founded: 1942
Pres: Norman L. Koonce
Focus: Archit
Periodical
Forum (quarterly) 12815

American Art Therapy Association (AATA), 1202 Allanson Rd, Mundelein, IL 60060
T: (708) 949-6064; Fax: (708) 566-4580
Founded: 1969; Members: 3600
Gen Secr: Edward J. Stygar
Focus: Therapeutics
Periodicals
Journal (3 times annually)
Newsletter (quarterly)
Proceedings of Annual Conference . . . 12816

American Assembly (AA), c/o Columbia University, 475 Riverside Dr, Rm 456, New York, NY 10115
T: (212) 870-3500
Founded: 1950
Focus: Poli Sci 12817

American Assembly of Collegiate Schools of Business (AACSB), 600 Emerson Rd, Ste 300, Saint Louis, MO 63141-6762
T: (314) 872-8481; Fax: (314) 872-8495
Founded: 1916; Members: 900
Focus: Adult Educ; Econ
Periodicals
Business and Management Education Funding Alert (5 times annually)
Newsline (quarterly) 12818

American Association for Accreditation of Laboratory Animal Care (AAALAC), 11300 Rockville Pike, Ste 1211, Rockville, MD 20852-3035
T: (301) 231-5353; Fax: (301) 231-8282
Founded: 1965; Members: 36
Gen Secr: Albert E. New
Focus: Vet Med
Periodical
Communique 12819

American Association for Adult and Continuing Education (AAACE), 1200 19 St NW, Ste 300, Washington, DC 20036
T: (202) 429-5131; Fax: (202) 223-4579
Founded: 1982; Members: 6000
Gen Secr: Dr. Drew Allbritten
Focus: Adult Educ
Periodicals
AAACE Newsletter (10 times annually)
Adult Education (quarterly)
Lifelong Learning (8 times annually)
Membership Directory (annually) 12820

American Association for Aerosol Research (AAAR), 1330 Kemper Meadow Dr, Cincinnati, OH 45240-1634
T: (513) 742-2227
Founded: 1981; Members: 800
Focus: Chem
Periodicals
Aerosol Science and Technology (8 times annually)
Newsletter (quarterly) 12821

American Association for Agricultural Education (AAAE), c/o Agricultural Education, Pennsylvania State University, 337 Agricultural Administration Bldg, University Park, PA 16802-2601
T: (814) 863-7852; Fax: (814) 863-4753
Founded: 1959; Members: 300
Gen Secr: Dennis Scanlon
Focus: Agri; Educ
Periodicals
Directory
Journal (quarterly)
Summaries of Studies (semi-annually)   . . *12822*

American Association for Artificial Intelligence (AAAI), 445 Burgess Dr, Menlo Park, CA 94025
T: (415) 328-3123; Fax: (415) 321-4457
Founded: 1979; Members: 13000
Gen Secr: Carol M. Hamilton
Focus: Computer & Info Sci
Periodicals
AI Magazine (quarterly)
Conference Proceedings (annually)
Tutorial Syllabus (annually) *12823*

American Association for Budget and Program Analysis (AABPA), POB 1157, Falls Church, VA 22041
T: (703) 941-4300; Fax: (703) 941-1535
Founded: 1976; Members: 550
Gen Secr: Christine LaChance
Focus: Finance
Periodicals
Journal of Public Budgeting and Finance (quarterly)
Newsletter (monthly) *12824*

American Association for Cancer Education (AACE), c/o Dr. Robert M. Chamberlain, Dept of Epidemiology, 1515 Holcombe Blvd, Houston, TX 77030
T: (713) 792-3020; Fax: (713) 792-0807
Founded: 1966; Members: 550
Gen Secr: Dr. Robert M. Chamberlain
Focus: Cell Biol & Cancer Res
Periodical
Directory of Members (annually) *12825*

American Association for Cancer Research (AACR), c/o Margaret Foti, Public Ledger Bldg, 150 S Independence Mall West, Ste 816, Philadelphia, PA 19106-3483
T: (215) 440-9300; Fax: (215) 440-9313
Founded: 1907; Members: 10000
Pres: Donald Coffey; Gen Secr: Margaret Foti
Focus: Cell Biol & Cancer Res
Periodicals
Cancer Research (monthly)
Directory (annually)
Proceedings (annually) *12826*

American Association for Career Education (AACE), 2900 Amby Pl, Hermosa Beach, CA 90254-2216
T: (310) 376-7378; Fax: (310) 374-1360
Founded: 1980; Members: 900
Pres: Dr. Pat Nellor Wickwire
Focus: Educ
Periodical
Newsletter *12827*

American Association for Chinese Studies (AACS), 300 Bricker Hall, Ohio State University, Columbus, OH 43210
T: (614) 292-6681
Founded: 1958; Members: 357
Gen Secr: Prof. Wen-Lang Li
Focus: Ling; Adult Educ *12828*

American Association for Clinical Chemistry (AACC), 2101 L St NW, Ste 202, Washington, DC 20037-1526
T: (202) 857-0717; Fax: (202) 887-5083
Founded: 1948; Members: 10000
Gen Secr: Richard Flaherty
Focus: Chem; Med
Periodicals
Annual Report (annually)
Clinical Chemistry Journal (monthly)
Clinical Chemistry News (monthly)
Clinical Chemistry Reference Edition (monthly)
. . . . *12829*

American Association for Correctional Psychology (AACP), c/o Robert Smith, West Virginia Graduate College, 100 Angus E. Peyton Dr, South Charleston, WV 25303-1600
T: (304) 746-1929
Founded: 1953; Members: 400
Gen Secr: Robert Smith
Focus: Psych
Periodicals
Clinical Justice and Behavior (quarterly)
Newsletter (quarterly) *12830*

American Association for Crystal Growth (AACG), c/o Dr. Anthony L. Gentile, POB 3233, Thousand Oaks, CA 91359-0233
T: (805) 492-7047; Fax: (805) 492-4062
Founded: 1969; Members: 700
Gen Secr: Dr. Anthony L. Gentile
Focus: Chem; Geology; Physics
Periodicals
Membership Directory (annually)
Newsletter (quarterly) *12831*

American Association for Dental Research (AADR), 1111 14 St NW, Ste 1000, Washington, DC 20005
T: (202) 898-1050; Fax: (202) 789-1033
Founded: 1972; Members: 5000
Gen Secr: John J. Clarkson
Focus: Dent
Periodicals
Around (bi-monthly)
Journal of Dental Research (monthly)
Membership Directory *12832*

American Association for Functional Orthodontics (AAFO), 106 S Kent St, Winchester, VA 22601
T: (703) 662-2200
Founded: 1981; Members: 1800
Pres: Dr. Craig C. Stoner
Focus: Dent
Periodical
Functional Orthodontist (bi-monthly)   . . . *12833*

American Association for Geodetic Surveying (AAGS), 5410 Grosvenor Ln, Bethesda, MD 20814
T: (301) 493-0200; Fax: (301) 493-8245
Members: 1500
Gen Secr: John Lisack
Focus: Surveying *12834*

American Association for Geriatric Psychiatry (AAGP), 7910 Woodmont Av, Bethesda, MD 20814
T: (301) 654-7850; E-Mail: AAGPAOL@AOL.COM; Fax: (301) 654-4137
Founded: 1978; Members: 1468
Gen Secr: Janet L. Pailet
Focus: Geriatrics; Psychiatry
Periodicals
Membership Directory
Newsletter (bi-monthly) *12835*

American Association for Hand Surgery (AAHS), 444 E Algonquin Rd, Arlington Heights, IL 60005
T: (847) 228-9758; Fax: (847) 228-6509
Founded: 1970; Members: 1100
Gen Secr: Laura M. Downes
Focus: Surgery
Periodical
Hand Surgery Newsletter (3 times annually)
. . . . *12836*

American Association for Higher Education (AAHE), 1 Dupont Circle, Ste 360, Washington, DC 20036
T: (202) 293-6440; Fax: (202) 293-0073
Founded: 1969; Members: 8500
Pres: Russell Edgerton
Focus: Educ
Periodicals
AAHE Bulletin (monthly)
Change (bi-monthly) *12837*

American Association for International Aging (AAIA), 1900 L St NW, Ste 510, Washington, DC 20036-5002
T: (202) 833-8893; Fax: (202) 833-8762
Gen Secr: Helen K. Kerschner
Focus: Geriatrics *12838*

American Association for Laboratory Accreditation (AALA), 656 Quince Orchard Rd, Gaithersburg, MD 20878-1409
T: (301) 670-1377; Fax: (301) 869-1495
Founded: 1978; Members: 260
Pres: John W. Locke
Focus: Chem
Periodicals
Directory of Accredited Laboratories (annually)
Newsletter (bi-monthly) *12839*

American Association for Laboratory Animal Science (AALAS), 70 Timber Creek, Ste 5, Cordova, TN 38018
T: (901) 754-8620; Fax: (901) 753-0046
Founded: 1949; Members: 6000
Gen Secr: Donald W. Keene
Focus: Vet Med
Periodicals
Bulletin (bi-monthly)
Laboratory Animal Science (bi-monthly)   . *12840*

American Association for Marriage and Family Therapy (AAMFT), 1133 15 St NW, Ste 300, Washington, DC 20005
T: (202) 452-0109; Fax: (202) 223-2329
Founded: 1942; Members: 19000
Focus: Therapeutics
Periodicals
Journal (quarterly)
Membership Directory (bi-annually)
Newspaper (bi-monthly) *12841*

American Association for Medical Transcription (AAMT), POB 576187, Modesto, CA 95357-6187
T: (209) 551-0883; Fax: (209) 551-9317
Founded: 1978; Members: 9000
Gen Secr: Claudia Tessier
Focus: Med
Periodical
Journal (bi-monthly) *12842*

American Association for Music Therapy (AAMT), POB 80012, Valley Forge, PA 19484
T: (215) 265-4006; Fax: (215) 265-4006
Founded: 1971; Members: 650
Gen Secr: Katie H. Opher
Focus: Therapeutics

Periodicals
International Newsletter (annually)
Music Therapy (annually)
Tuning In (quarterly) *12843*

American Association for Paralegal Education (AAFPE), POB 40244, Overland, KS 66204
T: (913) 381-4458; Fax: (913) 381-9308
Founded: 1981; Members: 330
Gen Secr: Sandra L. Sabanske
Focus: Educ
Periodicals
Journal of Paralegal Education and Practice (annually)
The Paralegal Educator (quarterly)   . . . *12844*

American Association for Pediatric Ophthalmology and Strabismus (AAPO&S), POB 193832, San Francisco, CA 94119
T: (415) 561-8505; Fax: (415) 561-8575
Founded: 1974; Members: 570
Gen Secr: Sue A. Brown
Focus: Ophthal
Periodicals
Journal (bi-monthly)
Membership Directory (annually) *12845*

American Association for Social Psychiatry (AASP), 2021 K St NW, Ste 206, Washington, DC 20006
T: (202) 785-9328
Founded: 1971; Members: 500
Focus: Psychiatry
Periodicals
The American Journal of Social Psychiatry (quarterly)
Newsletter (quarterly) *12846*

American Association for State and Local History (AASLH), 530 Church St, Ste 600, Nashville, TN 37219
T: (615) 255-2971; Fax: (615) 255-2979
Founded: 1940; Members: 6000
Gen Secr: Terry L. Davis
Focus: Hist
Periodicals
History News (quarterly)
History News Dispatch (monthly) *12847*

American Association for Study of Neoplastic Diseases (AASND), 1768 S Belvoir Rd, South Euclid, OH 44121
T: (216) 382-0031
Founded: 1929; Members: 361
Focus: Cell Biol & Cancer Res *12848*

American Association for Textile Technology (AATT), POB 99, Gastonia, NC 28053
T: (704) 824-3522; Fax: (704) 824-5358
Founded: 1933; Members: 500
Gen Secr: Jim H. Conner
Focus: Textiles
Periodicals
Annual Conference Proceedings
Membership Directory
Newsletter (bi-monthly) *12849*

American Association for the Advancement of Science (AAAS), 1200 New York Av NW, Washington, DC 20005
T: (202) 326-6427; Fax: (202) 289-4958
Founded: 1848; Members: 144000
Pres: Rita R. Colwell; Gen Secr: Richard S. Nicholson
Focus: Sci
Periodicals
Handbook (annually)
Research and Development in Federal Budget (annually)
Science (weekly)
Science Books and Films (5 times annually)
Science Education News (quarterly)   . . *12850*

American Association for the Advancement of Slavic Studies (AAASS), c/o Stanford University, 125 Panama St, Stanford, CA 94305-4130
T: (415) 723-9668; E-Mail: ab.cde@stanford.edu; Fax: (415) 725-7737
Founded: 1948; Members: 4000
Gen Secr: Dorothy Atkinson
Focus: Sci
Periodicals
American Bibliography of Slavic & East European Studies (annually)
Directory of Members (triennially)
Directory of Programs in Societ & East European Studies (every 3 years)
Newsletter (quarterly)
Slavic Review (quarterly) *12851*

American Association for the History of Medicine (AAHM), c/o School of Medicine, Boston University, 80 E Concord St, Boston, MA 02118-2394
T: (617) 638-4328; Fax: (617) 638-4329
Founded: 1925; Members: 1300
Gen Secr: J. Worth Estes
Focus: Med; Cultur Hist
Periodicals
Bulletin of the History of Medicine (quarterly)
Membership Directory (bi-annually)
Newsletter (3 times annually) *12852*

American Association for the Study of Headache (AASH), 875 Kings Hwy, Ste 200, Woodbury, NJ 08096
T: (609) 845-0322; Fax: (609) 384-5811

Founded: 1959; Members: 950
Gen Secr: Robert K. Talley
Focus: Med; Neurology
Periodical
Headache (10 times annually) *12853*

American Association for the Study of Liver Diseases (AASLD), 6900 Grove Rd, Thorofare, NJ 08086
T: (609) 848-1000; Fax: (609) 848-5274
Founded: 1950; Members: 1450
Gen Secr: Susan Nelson
Focus: Intern Med
Periodicals
Hepatology (monthly)
Journal (bi-monthly)
Newsletter (2-3 times annually) *12854*

American Association for Thoracic Surgery (AATS), 13 Elm St, POB 1565, Manchester, MA 01944
T: (508) 526-8330; Fax: (508) 526-4018
Founded: 1917; Members: 900
Gen Secr: William T. Maloney
Focus: Surgery
Periodical
Journal of Thoracic and Cardiovascular Surgery (monthly) *12855*

American Association for Vocational Instructional Materials (AAVIM), 220 Smithonia Rd, Winterville, GA 30683-9527
T: (706) 742-5355; Fax: (706) 742-7005
Founded: 1949; Members: 6
Gen Secr: George W. Smith
Focus: Adult Educ *12856*

American Association for Women in Community Colleges (AAWCC), c/o Amarillo College, POB 447, Amarillo, TX 79178-0001
T: (806) 371-5175; E-Mail: drcox@actx.edu; Fax: (806) 371-5370
Founded: 1973; Members: 2700
Pres: Diana H. Cox
Focus: Educ
Periodicals
AAWCJC Journal (annually)
AAWCJC Quarterly (quarterly) *12857*

American Association for World Health (AAWH), 1825 K St NW, Ste 1207, Washington, DC 20006
T: (202) 466-5883
Founded: 1953; Members: 1200
Focus: Public Health
Periodicals
Newsletter (quarterly)
World Health Magazine (monthly)   . . . *12858*

American Association of Anatomists (AAA), c/o Dept of Anatomy, Tulane Medical Center, 1430 Tulane Av, New Orleans, LA 70112
T: (504) 584-2727; Fax: (504) 584-1687
Founded: 1888; Members: 2753
Pres: Dr. Charles E. Slonecker; Gen Secr: Dr. Robert D. Yates
Focus: Anat
Periodicals
Anatomical Record (monthly)
Developmental Dynamics *12859*

American Association of Avian Pathologists (AAAP), c/o New Bolton Center, University of Pennsylvania, Kennett Square, PA 19348
T: (215) 444-4282; Fax: (215) 444-5387
Founded: 1957; Members: 1016
Gen Secr: Dr. Robert J. Eckroade
Focus: Vet Med; Pathology
Periodical
Avian Diseases (quarterly) *12860*

American Association of Behavioral Therapists, POB 1737, Ormond Beach, FL 32175
T: (904) 248-0508
Founded: 1987; Members: 1156
Gen Secr: Dan J. Allen
Focus: Therapeutics *12861*

American Association of Blacks in Energy (AABE), 927 15 St NW, Ste 200, Washington, DC 20005
T: (202) 371-9530
Founded: 1977; Members: 800
Focus: Energy
Periodicals
Bulletin (quarterly)
Energy News (bi-monthly) *12862*

American Association of Blood Banks (AABB), 8101 Glenbrook Rd, Bethesda, MD 20814-2749
T: (301) 907-6977; Fax: (301) 907-6895
Founded: 1947; Members: 11500
Gen Secr: Joel M. Solomom
Focus: Public Health
Periodicals
News Briefs (monthly)
Transfusion (bi-monthly) *12863*

American Association of Botanical Gardens and Arboreta (AABGA), 786 Church Rd, Wayne, PA 19087
T: (215) 688-1120; Fax: (215) 293-0149
Founded: 1940; Members: 1800
Gen Secr: Susan H. Lathrop
Focus: Botany

Periodicals
Arboretum and Botanical Garden Bulletin (quarterly)
Newsletter (monthly)
Proceedings (annually) 12864

American Association of Bovine Practitioners (AABP), c/o Dr. James A. Jarrett, Box 1755, Rome, GA 30162
T: (706) 232-2220
Founded: 1965; Members: 5000
Gen Secr: Dr. James A. Jarrett
Focus: Vet Med
Periodicals
Bovine Practitioner (annually)
Directory (annually)
Newsletter (monthly)
Proceeding of Annual Meeting (annually) 12865

American Association of Cardiovascular and Pulmonary Rehabilitation (AACVPR), 7611 Elmwood Av, Ste 201, Middleton, WI 53562
T: (608) 831-6989; Fax: (608) 831-5122
Founded: 1985; Members: 2500
Gen Secr: Jane C. Shepard
Focus: Cardiol; Rehabil
Periodical
Journal of Cardiopulmonary Rehabilitation (bi-monthly) 12866

American Association of Cereal Chemists (AACC), 3340 Pilot Knob Rd, Saint Paul, MN 55121-2097
T: (612) 454-7250; E-Mail: AACC@scisoc.org; Fax: (612) 454-0766
Founded: 1915; Members: 4000
Gen Secr: Steven C. Nelson
Focus: Chem
Periodicals
Cereal Chemistry (bi-monthly)
Cereal Foods World (monthly) 12867

American Association of Certified Allergists (AACA), 85 W Algonquin Rd, Ste 550, Arlington Heights, IL 60005
T: (708) 427-8111; E-Mail: acaal@aol.com; Fax: (708) 427-1294
Founded: 1968; Members: 510
Gen Secr: Richard Stawny
Focus: Med 12868

American Association of Certified Orthoptists (AACO), c/o Texas Children's Hospital, 6411 Fannin, Houston, TX 77030-2399
T: (713) 770-3225
Founded: 1940; Members: 400
Focus: Orthopedics
Periodicals
American Orthoptic Journal (annually)
Directory (annually)
The Prism (quarterly) 12869

American Association of Chairmen of Departments of Psychiatry (AACDP), c/o Frederick G. Guggenheim, University of Arkansas Medical Sciences Center, 4301 W Markham, Little Rock, AR 72205
T: (501) 686-5480; Fax: (501) 686-8154
Founded: 1967; Members: 136
Gen Secr: Frederick G. Guggenheim
Focus: Psychiatry
Periodical
Membership List 12870

American Association of Christian Schools (AACS), POB 2189, Independence, MO 64055
T: (816) 795-7709; Fax: (816) 795-7462
Founded: 1972; Members: 1250
Pres: Dr. Carl Herbster
Focus: Educ 12871

American Association of Colleges for Teacher Education (AACTE), 1 Dupont Circle NW, Ste 610, Washington, DC 20036
T: (202) 293-2450; Fax: (202) 457-8095
Founded: 1948; Members: 721
Gen Secr: David G. Imig
Focus: Adult Educ; Educ
Periodicals
AACTE Policy Papers
The Journal of Teacher Education . . . 12872

American Association of Colleges of Nursing (AACN), 1 Dupont Circle NW, Ste 530, Washington, DC 20036
T: (202) 463-6930; Fax: (202) 785-8320
Founded: 1969; Members: 414
Gen Secr: Dr. Geraldine Bednash
Focus: Adult Educ; Med
Periodicals
Annual Report (annually)
Journal of Professional Nursing (bi-monthly)
Newsletter (monthly) 12873

American Association of Colleges of Osteopathic Medicine (AACOM), 6110 Executive Blvd, Rockville, MD 20852
T: (301) 468-0990
Founded: 1898; Members: 15
Gen Secr: Sherry R. Arnstein
Focus: Pathology
Periodicals
Annual Organizational Guide (annually)
Annual Statistical Report (annually) . . . 12874

American Association of Colleges of Pharmacy (AACP), 1426 Prince St, Alexandria, VA 22314
T: (703) 739-2330
Founded: 1900; Members: 2100
Gen Secr: Carl E. Trinca
Focus: Adult Educ; Pharmacol
Periodicals
AACP News (monthly)
American Journal of Pharmaceutical Education (quarterly)
Pharmacy School Admission Requirements (semi-annually) 12875

American Association of Colleges of Podiatric Medicine (AACPM), 1350 Piccard Dr, Ste 322, Rockville, MD 20850
T: (301) 990-7400; Fax: (301) 990-2807
Founded: 1932
Pres: Anthony J. McNevin
Focus: Adult Educ; Orthopedics
Periodical
Newsletter (3 times annually) 12876

American Association of Community Colleges (AACC), c/o National Center for Higher Education, 1 Dupont Circle NW, Ste 410, Washington, DC 20036-1176
T: (202) 728-0200; E-Mail: mlatif@aacc.nche.edu; Fax: (202) 833-2467
Founded: 1920; Members: 1113
Pres: David Pierce
Focus: Educ
Periodicals
Community, Technical and Junior College Journal (quarterly)
Community, Technical and Junior College Times (bi-weekly)
International Update (bi-monthly) 12877

American Association of Community Theatre (AACT), 4712 Enchanted Oaks, College Station, TX 77845
T: (409) 774-0611; E-Mail: angeloaact@aol.com; Fax: (409) 776-8718
Founded: 1986; Members: 800
Gen Secr: Julie Angelo
Focus: Perf Arts 12878

American Association of Cosmetology Schools (AACS), 901 N Washington St, Ste 206, Alexandria, VA 22314-1535
T: (703) 845-1333; Fax: (703) 845-1336
Founded: 1956; Members: 1000
Pres: Ronald E. Smith
Focus: Adult Educ
Periodicals
NAACS News (monthly)
Washington Report (monthly) 12879

American Association of Critical-Care Nurses (AACN), 101 Columbia, Aliso Viejo, CA 92656
T: (714) 362-2000; Fax: (714) 362-2020
Founded: 1969; Members: 77000
Gen Secr: Sarah Sanford
Focus: Med
Periodicals
AACN Clinical Issues in Critical Care Nursing (quarterly)
American Journal of Critical Care (bi-monthly)
Critical Care Nurse (bi-monthly) 12880

American Association of Dental Examiners (AADE), 211 E Chigago Av, Ste 844, Chigago, IL 60611
T: (312) 440-7464
Founded: 1883; Members: 850
Gen Secr: Molly S. Nadler
Focus: Dent
Periodicals
Bulletin (3-4 times annually)
Proceedings (annually) 12881

American Association of Dental Schools (AADS), 1625 Massachusetts Av NW, Washington, DC 20036
T: (202) 667-9433; Fax: (202) 667-0642
Founded: 1923; Members: 3600
Gen Secr: Preston Littleton
Focus: Adult Educ; Dent
Periodicals
Admissions Requirements at U.S. and Canadian Dental Schools (annually)
Directory of Institutional Members (annually)
Journal of Dental Education (monthly)
Journal of Public Health Dentistry (quarterly)
. . . . 12882

American Association of Diabetes Educators (AADE), 444 N Michigan Av, Ste 1240, Chicago, IL 60611-3901
T: (312) 644-2233; Fax: (312) 644-4411
Founded: 1974; Members: 7000
Gen Secr: Kate Doyle
Focus: Educ; Diabetes
Periodicals
The Diabetes Educator (bi-monthly)
Newsletter (monthly) 12883

American Association of Electrodiagnostic Medicine (AAEM), 21 Second St SW, Ste 103, Rochester, MN 55902
T: (507) 288-0100
Founded: 1953; Members: 2700
Gen Secr: Ella M. Van Laningham
Focus: Neurology; Rehabil
Periodicals
AAEE Annual Courses
AAEE Annual Meetings
AAEE Case Reports
AAEE Minimonographs 12884

American Association of Endodontists (AAE), 211 E Chicago Av, Ste 1100, Chicago, IL 60611
T: (312) 266-7255; Fax: (312) 266-9867
Founded: 1943; Members: 3950
Gen Secr: Irma S. Kudo
Focus: Dent
Periodicals
Communique (3 times annually)
Journal (monthly)
Membership Roster (annually) 12885

American Association of Engineering Societies (AAES), 1111 19 St NW, Ste 608, Washington, DC 20036
T: (202) 296-2237; Fax: (202) 296-1151
Founded: 1979; Members: 22
Gen Secr: Mitchell Bradley
Focus: Eng 12886

American Association of Entrepreneurial Dentists (AAED), 420 Magazine St, Tupelo, MS 38801
T: (601) 842-1036
Founded: 1983
Gen Secr: Dr. Charles E. Moore
Focus: Dent
Periodical
Entrepreneurial News 12887

American Association of Equine Practitioners (AAEP), 4075 Iron Works Pike, Lexington, KY 40511
T: (606) 233-0147; Fax: (606) 233-1968
Founded: 1955; Members: 5000
Gen Secr: Gary L. Carpenter
Focus: Vet Med
Periodicals
Directory (annually)
Newsletter (bi-monthly)
Proceedings (annually) 12888

American Association of Family and Consumer Sciences, 1555 King St, Alexandria, VA 22314
T: (703) 706-4600; Fax: (703) 706-4663
Founded: 1909; Members: 24000
Gen Secr: Dr. Mary Jane Kolar
Focus: Home Econ
Periodicals
AHEA Action (bi-monthly)
Home Economics Research Journal (quarterly)
Journal of Home Economics (quarterly) . 12889

American Association of Feed Microscopists (AAFM), c/o Marjorie McCutcheon, POB 5246, Charleston, WV 25361
T: (304) 558-2208
Founded: 1953; Members: 210
Gen Secr: Marjorie McCutcheon
Focus: Food
Periodical
Newsletter (bi-monthly) 12890

American Association of Genito-Urinary Surgeons (AAGUS), c/o Baylor College of Medicine, School of Medicine, University of Virginia, POB 422, Charlottesville, VA 22908
T: (804) 982-4004
Founded: 1886; Members: 180
Gen Secr: Stuart S. Howards
Focus: Surgery; Urology 12891

American Association of Gynecological Laparoscopists (AAGL), 13021 E Florence Av, Santa Fe Springs, CA 90670
T: (310) 946-8774
Founded: 1972; Members: 5200
Pres: Jordan M. Phillips
Focus: Gynecology
Periodical
News-Scope (3 times annually) 12892

American Association of Handwriting Analysts (AAHA), 820 W Maple, Hinsdale, IL 60521
T: (708) 325-2266
Founded: 1962; Members: 400
Pres: Liz Mills
Focus: Graphology
Periodicals
Annals
Directory
Newsletter (bi-monthly) 12893

American Association of Hospital Dentists (AAHD), 211 E Chicago Av, Chicago, IL 60611
T: (312) 440-2661; Fax: (312) 440-7494
Founded: 1960; Members: 900
Gen Secr: John S. Rutkauskas
Focus: Dent
Periodicals
Bulletin of Hospital Dental Practice (quarterly)
Special Care in Dentistry (bi-monthly) . . 12894

American Association of Hospital Podiatrists (AAHP), 420 74 St, Brooklyn, NY 11209
T: (718) 836-1017
Founded: 1950; Members: 800
Gen Secr: Dr. Louis J. Arancia
Focus: Orthopedics
Periodicals
Hospital Podiatrist (annually)
Newsletter (annually) 12895

American Association of Housing Educators (AAHE), c/o College of Architecture, Texas A & M University, College Station, TX 77843-3137
T: (409) 845-0986; Fax: (409) 845-4491
Founded: 1965; Members: 350
Gen Secr: Paul Woods
Focus: Educ
Periodicals
Housing and Society (3 times annually)
Newsletter (2-3 times annually)
Proceedings (annually) 12896

American Association of Immunologists (AAI), 9650 Rockville Pike, Bethesda, MD 20814
T: (301) 530-7178; Fax: (301) 571-1816
Founded: 1913; Members: 6000
Pres: Katherine L. Knight; Gen Secr: M. Michele Hogan
Focus: Immunology
Periodical
Journal of Immunology (bi-monthly) . . . 12897

American Association of Industrial Veterinarians (AAIV), c/o Caroline & Co, 1015 E Broadway, Columbia, MO 65201
T: (314) 449-3109
Founded: 1954; Members: 450
Gen Secr: Curt Schafer
Focus: Vet Med
Periodicals
AAIV Highlights (3 times annually)
Directory (annually) 12898

American Association of Jurists (AAJ), POB 673, Berkeley, CA 94701
T: (510) 848-0599; Fax: (510) 848-6008
Gen Secr: Camilo Perez Bustillo
Focus: Law 12899

American Association of Language Specialists (TAALS), 1000 Connecticut Av NW, Ste 9, Washington, DC 20036
T: (202) 986-1542
Founded: 1957; Members: 200
Gen Secr: D. Horowitz
Focus: Ling
Periodical
Yearbook (annually) 12900

American Association of Law Libraries (AALL), 53 W Jackson Blvd, Chicago, IL 60604
T: (312) 939-4764; Fax: (312) 431-1097
Founded: 1906; Members: 5000
Pres: Frank G. Houdek; Gen Secr: Suzsan P. Siebers
Focus: Libraries & Bk Sci
Periodicals
Directory of Law Libraries (annually)
Index to Foreign Legal Periodicals (quarterly)
Law Library Journal (quarterly) 12901

American Association of Medical Assistants (AAMA), 20 N Wacker Dr, Ste 1575, Chicago, IL 60606-2903
T: (312) 899-1500; Fax: (312) 899-1259
Founded: 1956; Members: 12000
Gen Secr: Donald A. Balasa
Focus: Med
Periodicals
Byline: AAMA (bi-monthly)
The Professional Medical Assistant (bi-monthly)
. . . . 12902

American Association of Medical Milk Commissions (AAMMC), c/o Paul Fleiss, 1824 N Hillhurst Av, Los Angeles, CA 90027
T: (213) 664-1977
Founded: 1907; Members: 35
Pres: Paul Fleiss
Focus: Med
Periodical
Methods and Standards for the Production of Certified Milk (annually) 12903

American Association of Medical Society Executives (AAMSE), 515 N State St, Chicago, IL 60610
T: (312) 464-2555; Fax: (312) 464-2467
Founded: 1947; Members: 1000
Gen Secr: Robin Kriegel
Focus: Med
Periodicals
Hotline (monthly)
The Medical Executive (quarterly) . . . 12904

American Association of Medico-Legal Consultants (AAMC), The Barclay, Rittenhouse Sq, Ste 11D, Philadelphia, PA 19103
T: (215) 545-6363
Founded: 1972; Members: 1200
Pres: Evelyn M. Goldstein
Focus: Law 12905

American Association of Mental Health Professionals in Corrections (AAMHPC), c/o John S. Zil, POB 163359, Sacramento, CA 95816-9359
T: (707) 864-0910; Fax: (707) 864-0910
Founded: 1940; Members: 2000
Pres: John S. Zil
Focus: Psych; Psychiatry
Periodical
Corrective and Social Psychiatry and Journal of Behavior Technology Methods and Therapy (quarterly) 12906

American Association of Meta-Science, POB 1182, Huntsville, AL 35807
T: (205) 882-2717
Founded: 1977; Members: 200
Focus: Sci 12907

American Association of Museums (AAM), 1225 Eye St NW, Ste 200, Washington, DC 20005
T: (202) 289-1818; Fax: (202) 289-6578
Founded: 1906; Members: 1200
Pres: Able Edward
Focus: Arts
Periodicals
Aviso (monthly)
Museum News (bi-monthly) *12908*

American Association of Neurological Surgeons (AANS), 22 S Washington St, Ste 100, Park Ridge, IL 60068-4287
T: (708) 692-9500; Fax: (708) 692-2589
Founded: 1931; Members: 3470
Gen Secr: Carl H. Hauber
Focus: Neurology; Surgery
Periodicals
Bulletin (quarterly)
Journal of Neurosurgery (monthly)
Neurosurgical Topics (quarterly) *12909*

American Association of Neuropathologists (AANP), c/o Jeannette J. Townsend, Dept of Pathology, University of Utah School of Medicine, 50 N Medical Dr, Salt Lake City, UT 84132
T: (901) 581-2507; Fax: (901) 585-3831
Founded: 1924; Members: 660
Gen Secr: Jeannette J. Townsend
Focus: Pathology; Neurology
Periodicals
Journal of Neuropathology and Experimental Neurology (bi-monthly)
Roster of Members (annually) *12910*

American Association of Oral and Maxillofacial Surgeons (AAOMS), 9700 W Bryn Mawr Av, Rosemont, IL 60018-5701
T: (708) 678-6200; Fax: (708) 678-6286
Founded: 1918; Members: 5891
Gen Secr: Bernard J. Degen
Focus: Dent
Periodicals
Forum (bi-monthly)
Journal of Oral and Maxillofacial Surgery (monthly) *12911*

American Association of Orthodontists (AAO), 401 N Lindbergh Blvd, Saint Louis, MO 63141-7816
T: (314) 993-1700; Fax: (314) 997-1745
Founded: 1901; Members: 11000
Gen Secr: Ronald S. Moen
Focus: Dent
Periodicals
American Journal of Orthodontics and Dentofacial Orthopedics (monthly)
Membership Directory (bi-annually)
Orthodontic Bulletin (quarterly) *12912*

American Association of Orthopedic Medicine (AAOM), 315 Boulevard NE, Ste 336, Atlanta, GA 30312
T: (404) 577-5455; Fax: (404) 681-4401
Founded: 1982; Members: 300
Gen Secr: Alan Lippitt
Focus: Orthopedics
Periodicals
AAOM Membership Directory (annually)
AAOM News (quarterly) *12913*

American Association of Petroleum Geologists (AAPG), Box 979, Tulsa, OK 74101-0979
T: (918) 584-2555; Fax: (918) 584-0469
Founded: 1917; Members: 32000
Gen Secr: Fred A. Dix
Focus: Geology
Periodicals
Bulletin (monthly)
Explorer (monthly)
Geobyte (quarterly) *12914*

American Association of Philosophy Teachers (AAPT), c/o Dept of Philosophy, University of Tennessee, Knoxville, TN 37996-0480
T: (615) 974-3255
Founded: 1979; Members: 300
Focus: Educ; Philos
Periodical
AAPT News (3 times annually) *12915*

American Association of Phonetic Sciences (AAPS), POB 14095, University Station, Gainesville, FL 32604
T: (904) 392-2046; Fax: (904) 382-6170
Founded: 1973; Members: 200
Gen Secr: Dr. W.S. Brown
Focus: Ling
Periodical
Newsletter (semi-annually) *12916*

American Association of Physical Anthropologists (AAPA), c/o Eugenie C. Scott, 925 Kearney St, El Cerrito, CA 94530-2810
T: (510) 526-1674
Founded: 1930; Members: 1500
Gen Secr: Eugenie C. Scott
Focus: Anthro *12917*

American Association of Physicists in Medicine (AAPM), 1 Physics Ellipse, College Park, MD 20740-3846
T: (301) 209-3350; E-Mail: strofi@aapm.acp.org; Fax: (301) 209-0862
Founded: 1958; Members: 4300
Gen Secr: Sal Trofi Jr.
Focus: Physiology

Periodicals
Medical Physics (bi-monthly)
Physics in Medicine & Biology (bi-monthly) *12918*

American Association of Physics Teachers (AAPT), 1 Physics Ellipse, College Park, MD 20740-3842
T: (301) 345-1857
Founded: 1930; Members: 11000
Gen Secr: Dr. Bernard V. Khoury
Focus: Educ; Physics
Periodicals
American Journal of Physics (monthly)
The Physics Teacher (9 times annually)   *12919*

American Association of Plastic Surgeons (AAPS), c/o R. Barrett Noone, 888 Glenbrook Av, Bryn Mawr, PA 19010
T: (610) 527-4833; Fax: (610) 527-3568
Founded: 1921; Members: 425
Gen Secr: R. Barrett Noone
Focus: Surgery *12920*

American Association of Poison Control Centers (AAPCC), 3201 New Mexico Av, Ste 310, Washington, DC 20016
T: (202) 362-7217
Founded: 1958; Members: 1000
Gen Secr: Rose Ann Soloway
Focus: Toxicology
Periodicals
Annual Report (annually)
Membership Directory (annually) *12921*

American Association of Presidents of Independent Colleges and Universities (AAPICU), 8346 ASB, Provo, UT 84602
T: (801) 378-5605; Fax: (801) 378-7521
Founded: 1968; Members: 180
Gen Secr: John B. Stohlton
Focus: Sci
Periodical
Private Higher Education (annually)   . . . *12922*

American Association of Pro Life Obstetricians and Gynecologists (AAPLOG), 850 Elm Grove Rd, Elm Grove, WI 53122
T: (414) 789-7984; Fax: (414) 782-8788
Founded: 1973; Members: 800
Pres: David V. Foley
Focus: Gynecology
Periodical
Newsletter (quarterly) *12923*

American Association of Professional Hypnotherapists (AAPH), POB 29, Boones Mill, VA 24065
T: (703) 334-3035
Founded: 1980; Members: 1550
Gen Secr: William S. Brink
Focus: Therapeutics
Periodical
Hypnotherapy Today (quarterly) *12924*

American Association of Professors of Yiddish (AAPY), NSF 350, Queens College, Flushing, NY 11367
T: (718) 997-3622
Founded: 1974; Members: 300
Gen Secr: Joseph C. Landis
Focus: Ling; Educ
Periodicals
Yiddish (quarterly)
Yiddish Studies Newsletter (quarterly)   . . *12925*

American Association of Psychiatric Administrators (AAPA), c/o Dr. Dave Davis, 1938 Peachtree Rd NW, Ste 505, Atlanta, GA 30304-1253
T: (404) 355-2914; Fax: (404) 355-2917
Founded: 1960; Members: 300
Pres: Dr. Dave Davis
Focus: Psychiatry
Periodicals
Journal
List of Members (semi-annually)
Newsletter (quarterly) *12926*

American Association of Psychiatric Services for Children (AAPSC), 1200C Scottsville Rd, Ste 225, Rochester, NY 14624
T: (716) 235-6910; Fax: (716) 235-0654
Founded: 1948; Members: 165
Gen Secr: Dr. Sydney Koret
Focus: Psychiatry
Periodicals
Journal of Child Psychiatry and Human Development (quarterly)
Membership Directory (bi-annually)
Newsletter (bi-monthly) *12927*

American Association of Public Health Dentistry (AAPHD), 10619 Jousting Ln, Richmond, VA 23235
T: (804) 272-8344
Founded: 1937; Members: 650
Pres: Jack Dillenberg
Focus: Dent
Periodicals
Communique (quarterly)
Journal of Public Health Dentistry (quarterly) *12928*

American Association of Public Health Physicians (AAPHP), c/o Armand Start, Dept of Family Practice, 777 South Mills St, Madison, WI 53715
T: (608) 263-1326; Fax: (608) 263-5813
Founded: 1954; Members: 200

Gen Secr: Armand Start
Focus: Public Health; Physiology
Periodical
Bulletin *12929*

American Association of School Librarians (AASL), 50 E Huron St, Chicago, IL 60611
T: (312) 944-6780; Fax: (312) 664-7459
Founded: 1951; Members: 7611
Focus: Libraries & Bk Sci
Periodicals
AASL Presidential Hotline (semi-annually)
School Library Media (quarterly)   . . . *12930*

American Association of School Personnel Administrators (AASPA), 2330 Alhambra Blvd, Sacramento, CA 95817
T: (916) 362-0300; Fax: (916) 362-0303
Founded: 1940; Members: 1700
Gen Secr: Herb Salinger
Focus: Educ *12931*

American Association of Sex Educators, Counselors and Therapists (AASECT), 435 N Michigan Av, Ste 1717, Chicago, IL 60611
T: (312) 644-0828; Fax: (312) 644-8557
Founded: 1967; Members: 2600
Focus: Educ
Periodicals
Contemporary Sexuality Newsletter (monthly)
Journal of Sex Education & Therapy (semi-annually) *12932*

American Association of Small Ruminant Practitioners (AASRP), 1675 Ellis Hollow Rd, Ithaca, NY 14850
T: (607) 539-6181; Fax: (607) 539-6181
Founded: 1969; Members: 1200
Focus: Vet Med
Periodical
Wool and Wattles (quarterly) *12933*

American Association of State Colleges and Universities (AASCU), 1 Dupont Circle NW, Ste 700, Washington, DC 20036-1192
T: (202) 293-7070; Fax: (202) 296-5819
Founded: 1961; Members: 405
Pres: James B. Appleberry
Focus: Sci
Periodical
Memo (bi-weekly) *12934*

American Association of Suicidology (AAS), 4201 Connecticut Av NW, Ste 310, Washington, DC 20008
T: (202) 237-2280; Fax: (202) 237-2282
Founded: 1968; Members: 1100
Gen Secr: Dr. Alan Berman
Focus: Psychiatry
Periodicals
Newslink (quarterly)
Suicide and Life (quarterly) *12935*

American Association of Teachers of Arabic (AATA), c/o Brigham Young University, 280 HRCB, Provo, UT 84602
T: (801) 378-6531; E-Mail: 22ta@yvax.byn.edu; Fax: (801) 378-5866
Founded: 1963; Members: 180
Gen Secr: R. Kirk Belnap
Focus: Ling; Educ
Periodicals
Al-Arabiyya (annually)
Bulletin of the Pan American Health Organization *12936*

American Association of Teachers of Esperanto (AATE), c/o Dorothy Holland, 5140 San Lorenzo Dr, Santa Barbara, CA 93111-2521
T: (805) 967-5241
Founded: 1961; Members: 80
Gen Secr: Dorothy Holland
Focus: Ling; Educ
Periodical
Bulteno (quarterly) *12937*

American Association of Teachers of French (AATF), 57 E Armory Av, Champaign, IL 61820
T: (217) 333-2842; Fax: (217) 333-2842
Founded: 1927; Members: 11000
Focus: Ling; Educ
Periodicals
French Review (bi-monthly)
National Bulletin (quarterly) *12938*

American Association of Teachers of German (AATG), 112 Haddontowne Ct, Cherry Hill, NJ 08034
T: (609) 795-5553; Fax: (609) 795-9398
Founded: 1926; Members: 7300
Focus: Ling; Educ
Periodicals
The German Quarterly (quarterly)
Newsletter (5 times annually)
Rundbrief (monthly)
Die Unterrichtspraxis (semi-annually)   . . *12939*

American Association of Teachers of Spanish and Portuguese (AATSP), c/o University of Colorado, 106 Gunter Hall, Greeley, CO 80639
T: (303) 351-1090; Fax: (303) 351-1095
Founded: 1917; Members: 13000
Gen Secr: Lynn A. Sandstedt
Focus: Ling; Educ
Periodicals
Directory (annually)
Hispania (quarterly) *12940*

American Association of Teachers of Turkic Languages (AATTL), c/o Dept of Near Eastern Studies, Princeton University, 110 Jones Hall, Princeton, NJ 08544-1008
T: (609) 424-2686; Fax: (609) 258-1242
Founded: 1985; Members: 100
Gen Secr: Prof. Erika Gilson
Focus: Educ; Ling
Periodical
AATT Newsletter (semi-annually) *12941*

American Association of Textile Chemists and Colorists (AATCC), POB 12215, Research Triangle Park, NC 27709-2215
T: (919) 549-8141; Fax: (919) 549-8933
Founded: 1921; Members: 7188
Focus: Chem; Textiles
Periodicals
AATCC Technical Manual (annually)
Textile Chemist and Colorist (monthly)   . *12942*

American Association of Tissue Banks (AATB), 1350 Beverly Rd, Ste 220-A, McLean, VA 22101
T: (703) 827-9582
Founded: 1976; Members: 800
Focus: Surgery
Periodicals
Membership Directory
Newsletter (quarterly) *12943*

American Association of University Professors (AAUP), 1012 14 St, Ste 500, Washington, DC 20005
T: (202) 737-5900
Founded: 1915; Members: 44000
Pres: James E. Perley; Gen Secr: Mary Burgan
Focus: Adult Educ
Periodicals
Academe: Bulletin of the AAUP (bi-monthly)
Collective Bargaining Newsletter (bi-monthly) *12944*

American Association of University Women (AAUW), 1111 16 St NW, Washington, DC 20036
T: (202) 785-7700; Fax: (202) 872-1425
Founded: 1881; Members: 135000
Gen Secr: Anne L. Bryant
Focus: Adult Educ
Periodicals
Action Alert (monthly)
Graduate Woman (9 times annually)
Leader in Action (quarterly)
On Campus with Women (quarterly)   . . *12945*

American Association of University Women Educational Foundation (AAUWEF), 1111 16 St NW, Washington, DC 20036
T: (202) 728-7602; Fax: (202) 872-1425
Founded: 1958; Members: 135000
Gen Secr: Anne L. Bryant
Focus: Educ *12946*

American Association of Variable Star Observers (AAVSO), 25 Birch St, Cambridge, MA 02138
T: (617) 354-0484; Fax: (617) 354-0665
Founded: 1911; Members: 1300
Focus: Astronomy
Periodicals
AAVSO Circular (monthly)
AAVSO Report (irregularly)
Bulletin (annually)
Journal of the AAVSO (semi-annually)
Solar Bulletin (monthly) *12947*

American Association of Veterinary Anatomists (AAVA), c/o Dr. Paul F. Rumph, Dept of Anatomy and Histology, College of Veterinary Medicine, Auburn University, Auburn, AL 36849
T: (205) 844-6743
Founded: 1949; Members: 250
Focus: Vet Med; Anat
Periodicals
Directory (bi-annually)
Newsletter (semi-annually) *12948*

American Association of Veterinary Laboratory Diagnosticians (AAVLD), c/o Dr. Harvey Gosser, Veterinary Medical Diagnostic Laboratory, POB 6023, Columbia, MO 65205
T: (314) 882-6811; Fax: (314) 882-1411
Founded: 1957; Members: 700
Focus: Vet Med
Periodicals
Journal of Veterinary Diagnostic Investigation (quarterly)
Newsletter (semi-annually) *12949*

American Association of Veterinary Parasitologists (AAVP), c/o Mallinckrodt Veterinary, 421 E Howley, Mundelein, IL 60060
T: (708) 970-4514; Fax: (708) 970-4513
Founded: 1956; Members: 450
Gen Secr: Dr. Tom Kennedy
Focus: Vet Med
Periodicals
Directory (Biennial)
Newsletter (quarterly)
Proceedings (annually) *12950*

American Association of Veterinary State Boards (AAVSB), POB 1702, Jefferson City, MO 65102
T: (314) 761-9937; E-Mail: aausbl@socketis.net; Fax: (314) 761-9938
Founded: 1957; Members: 54

Gen Secr: Charlotte P. Roman
Focus: Vet Med 12951

American Association of Wildlife Veterinarians (AAWV), c/o Southeastern Cooperative Wildlife Disease Study, University of Georgia, Athens, GA 30602-7387
T: (706) 542-1741; Fax: (706) 542-5865
Founded: 1979; Members: 350
Gen Secr: Dr. Victor F. Nettles
Focus: Vet Med
Periodicals
Membership Directory
Newsletter (quarterly) 12952

American Association of Women Dentists (AAWD), 401 N Michigan Av, Chicago, IL 60611-4267
T: (312) 644-6610; Fax: (312) 245-1084
Founded: 1921; Members: 2000
Focus: Dent
Periodicals
Chronicle (bi-monthly)
Newsletter (bi-monthly) 12953

American Association of Zoo Keepers (AAZK), c/o Topeka Zoological Park, 635 SW Gage Blvd, Topeka, KS 66606-2066
T: (913) 273-1980; Fax: (913) 273-1980
Founded: 1967; Members: 2700
Pres: Ric Urban
Focus: Zoology
Periodical
Animal Keeper's Forum (monthly) . . . 12954

American Association of Zoo Veterinarians (AAZV), 3400 W Girard Av, Philadelphia, PA 19104-1196
T: (215) 387-9094; Fax: (215) 387-2165
Founded: 1947; Members: 1100
Gen Secr: Dr. Wilbur Amand
Focus: Vet Med
Periodicals
AAZV Newsletter (quarterly)
Conference Proceedings (annually)
Journal of Zoo and Wildlife Medicine (quarterly)
Membership Directory (annually) . . . 12955

American Association of Zoological Parks and Aquariums (AAZPA), c/o Oglebay Park, Rte 88, Wheeling, WV 26003
T: (304) 242-2160; Fax: (304) 242-2283
Founded: 1924; Members: 6200
Focus: Zoology 12956

American Association on Mental Retardation (AAMR), 444 n Capitol St NW, Ste 846, Washington, DC 20001-1512
T: (202) 387-1968; Fax: (202) 387-2193
Founded: 1876; Members: 9500
Gen Secr: M. Doreen Croser
Focus: Psych; Educ Handic; Soc Sci; Med
Periodical
American Journal of Mental Deficiency (bi-monthly) 12957

American Astronautical Society (AAS), 6352 Rolling Mill Pl, Ste 102, Springfield, VA 22152
T: (703) 866-0020; Fax: (703) 866-3526
Founded: 1952; Members: 1600
Focus: Aero
Periodicals
Journal of the Astronautical Sciences (quarterly)
Newsletter (bi-monthly) 12958

American Astronomical Society (AAS), c/o Dept of Physics and Astronomy, Louisiana State University, Baton Rouge, LA 70803-4001
T: (504) 388-1160; Fax: (504) 334-1098
Founded: 1899; Members: 6570
Gen Secr: Dr. Arlo U. Landolt
Focus: Astronomy
Periodicals
The Astronomical Journal (monthly)
Astrophysical Journal (3 times annually)
Bulletin (quarterly) 12959

American Auditory Society (AAS), 512 E Canterbury Ln, Phoenix, AZ 85022
T: (602) 789-0755; Fax: (602) 942-1486
Founded: 1973; Members: 3000
Gen Secr: Wayne J. Staab
Focus: Otorhinolaryngology
Periodicals
The Bulletin of the AAS (3 times annually)
Ear and Hearing (bi-monthly) 12960

American Automatic Control Council (AACC), c/o EECS, Northwestern University, 2145 Sheridan Rd, Evanston, IL 60208-3118
T: (708) 491-3641; Fax: (708) 491-4455
Founded: 1957; Members: 7
Focus: Eng
Periodicals
Newsletter (semi-annually)
Proceedings of the American Control Conference (annually) 12961

American Aviation Historical Society (AAHS), 2333 Otis St, Santa Ana, CA 92704
T: (714) 549-4818
Founded: 1956; Members: 4332
Focus: Aero
Periodicals
Catalog (irregularly)
Index
Journal (quarterly)
Newsletter (quarterly) 12962

American Bamboo Society (ABS), 2655 Ellentown Rd, La Jolla, CA 92037-1147
T: (619) 453-0334; E-Mail: gshor@vesd.edu; Fax: (619) 453-0334
Founded: 1979; Members: 980
Pres: George Shor
Focus: Botany
Periodicals
Journal of the American Bamboo Society (semi-annually)
Newsletter (bi-monthly) 12963

American Baptist Historical Society (ABHS), POB 851, Valley Forge, PA 19428-0851
T: (610) 768-2378
Founded: 1853; Members: 270
Gen Secr: Beverly Carlson
Focus: Hist; Rel & Theol
Periodicals
American Baptist Quarterly (quarterly)
The Associate 12964

American Bar Association (ABA), 750 N Lake Shore Dr, Chicago, IL 60611
T: (312) 988-5000; Fax: (312) 988-6281
Founded: 1878; Members: 310700
Gen Secr: Thomas H. Gonser
Focus: Law
Periodicals
ABA Journal (monthly)
Administrative Law Review (quarterly)
Antitrust (3 times annually)
Antitrust Law Journal (quarterly)
Barrister (quarterly)
The Brief (quarterly)
Business Lawyer (quarterly)
China Law Reporter (quarterly)
Communications Law (quarterly)
The Compleat Lawyer (quarterly)
Criminal Justice (quarterly)
The Entertainment and Sports Lawyer (quarterly)
Environmental Law (quarterly)
Family Advocate (quarterly)
Family Law Quarterly (quarterly)
Fidelity and Security News (quarterly)
Franchise Law Journal (quarterly)
Human Rights (3 times annually)
Intelligence Report (monthly)
International Lawyer (quarterly)
The Judge's Journal (quarterly)
Jurimetrics: Journal of Law, Science and Technology (quarterly)
Juvenile and Child Welfare Law Reporter (monthly)
Labor Lawyer (quarterly)
Law Practice Management (8 times annually)
Letter (monthly)
Litigation (quarterly)
Probate and Property (bi-monthly)
Public Contract Law Journal (quarterly)
Student Lawyer (monthly)
The Tax Lawyer (quarterly)
Tort and Insurance Law Journal (quarterly)
The Urban Lawyer (quarterly) 12965

American Beethoven Society (ABS), c/o Center for Beethoven Studies, San Jose State University, 1 Washington Sq, San Jose, CA 95192-0171
T: (408) 924-4590; Fax: (408) 924-4365
Founded: 1985; Members: 300
Focus: Music
Periodical
The Beethoven Newsletter (3 times annually) 12966

American Biblical Encyclopedia Society (ABES), 24 W Maple Av, Monsey, NY 10952
T: (914) 352-4609
Founded: 1930
Focus: Rel & Theol 12967

American Birding Association (ABA), POB 6599, Colorado Springs, CO 80934-6599
T: (719) 578-1614; E-Mail: gregb@aba.org; Fax: (719) 578-1480
Founded: 1969; Members: 18000
Gen Secr: Gregory S. Butcher
Focus: Ornithology
Periodicals
Birding (bi-monthly)
Directory 12968

American Board for Certification in Orthotics and Prosthetics (ABC), 1650 King St, Ste 500, Alexandria, VA 22314
T: (703) 836-7114; Fax: (703) 836-0838
Founded: 1948; Members: 3200
Focus: Rehabil
Periodical
Registry of Accredited Facilities and Certified Practitioners (annually) 12969

American Board of Abdominal Surgery (ABAS), 675 Main St, Melrose, MA 02176
T: (617) 665-6101
Founded: 1957; Members: 1865
Focus: Surgery 12970

American Board of Allergy and Immunology (ABAI), c/o University City Science Center, 3624 Market St, Philadelphia, PA 19104
T: (215) 349-9466
Founded: 1972
Focus: Immunology 12971

American Board of Anesthesiology (ABA), 4101 Lake Boone Trail, Ste 510, Raleight, NC 27607-7506

T: (919) 881-2570; Fax: (919) 881-2575
Founded: 1938; Members: 12
Gen Secr: Francis P. Hughes
Focus: Anesthetics 12972

American Board of Bioanalysis (ABB), 818 Olive, Ste 918, Saint Louis, MO 63101-1598
T: (314) 241-1445; Fax: (314) 241-1449
Founded: 1968
Focus: Bio; Med
Periodical
Test of the Month (monthly) 12973

American Board of Colon and Rectal Surgery (ABCRS), 20600 Eureka Rd, Ste 713, Taylor, MI 48180
T: (313) 282-9400; Fax: (313) 282-9402
Founded: 1934
Focus: Surgery
Periodical
Newsletter to Diplomates (annually) . . . 12974

American Board of Dental Public Health (ABDPH), c/o Stanley Lotzkar, 1321 NW 47 Terrace, Gainesville, FL 32605
T: (904) 378-6301
Founded: 1950; Members: 5
Focus: Dent
Periodical
Newsletter (annually) 12975

American Board of Dermatology (ABD), c/o Henry Ford Hospital, 1 Ford Pl, Detroit, MI 48202-3450
T: (313) 874-3450; Fax: (313) 872-3221
Founded: 1932; Members: 15
Gen Secr: Harry J. Hurley
Focus: Derm
Periodical
Booklet of Information (annually) 12976

American Board of Endodontics (ABE), 211 E Chicago Av, Ste 1501, Chicago, IL 60611
T: (312) 266-7310
Focus: Dent
Periodical
Membership Roster (annually) 12977

American Board of Funeral Service Education (ABFSE), POB 1305, Brunswick, ME 04011
T: (207) 798-5801; Fax: (207) 798-5988
Founded: 1946; Members: 48
Gen Secr: Dr. Gordon S. Bigelow
Focus: Educ 12978

American Board of Health Physics (ABHP), 1313 Dolley Madison Blvd, Ste 402, McLean, VA 22101-3926
T: (703) 790-1745; Fax: (703) 790-9063
Founded: 1960; Members: 8
Gen Secr: Richard J. Burk Jr.
Focus: Public Health 12979

American Board of Internal Medicine (ABIM), 3624 Market St, Philadelphia, PA 19104
T: (215) 243-1500
Founded: 1936; Members: 40
Focus: Intern Med
Periodical
Policies and Procedures (annually) . . . 12980

American Board of Master Educators (ABME), 345 24 Av N, Ste 200, Nashville, TN 37203
T: (615) 327-2984; Fax: (615) 327-2935
Founded: 1983; Members: 450
Gen Secr: Dr. Jack Miller
Focus: Educ
Periodical
Master Educator (semi-annually) 12981

American Board of Neurological Surgery (ABNS), 6550 Fannin St, Houston, TX 77030-2722
T: (713) 790-6015
Founded: 1940; Members: 14
Focus: Neurology; Surgery
Periodical
Newsletter to Diplomates (annually) . . . 12982

American Board of Nuclear Medicine (ABNM), 900 Veteran Av, Los Angeles, CA 90024-1786
T: (310) 825-6787; Fax: (310) 825-9433
Founded: 1971; Members: 12
Focus: Nucl Med 12983

American Board of Nutrition (ABN), c/o University of Alabama at Birmingham, 1675 University Blvd, Birmingham, AL 35294
T: (205) 975-8788; Fax: (205) 934-7049
Founded: 1948; Members: 524
Gen Secr: Treva McAboy
Focus: Food 12984

American Board of Obstetrics and Gynecology (ABOG), 2915 Vine St, Dallas, TX 75204-1069
T: (214) 871-1619; Fax: (214) 871-1943
Founded: 1927; Members: 15
Gen Secr: Norman F. Gant
Focus: Gynecology
Periodical
Bulletin (annually) 12985

American Board of Ophthalmology (ABO), 111 Presidential Blvd, Ste 241, Bala Cynwyd, PA 19004
T: (215) 664-1175
Founded: 1916; Members: 17
Focus: Ophthal 12986

American Board of Opticianry (ABO), 10341 Democracy Ln, Fairfax, VA 22030
T: (703) 691-8356; Fax: (703) 691-3929
Founded: 1947
Focus: Optics
Periodical
Bulletin of Information for Candidates . . 12987

American Board of Oral and Maxillofacial Pathology (AMBOP), 4830 W Kennedy Blvd, Ste 690, POB 25915, Tampa, FL 33622-5915
T: (813) 286-2444; Fax: (813) 289-5279
Founded: 1948; Members: 260
Gen Secr: Clarita Wendrich
Focus: Pathology
Periodical
Oral Surgery, Oral Medicine, Oral Pathology (monthly) 12988

American Board of Orthodontics (ABO), 401 N Lindbergh Blvd, Ste 308, Saint Louis, MO 63141
T: (314) 432-6130
Founded: 1929; Members: 1695
Focus: Dent
Periodical
American Board of Orthodontics Directory (annually) 12989

American Board of Orthopedic Surgery (ABOS), 400 Silver Cedar Ct, Chapel Hill, NC 27514
T: (919) 929-7103
Founded: 1934; Members: 12
Focus: Surgery; Orthopedics 12990

American Board of Otolaryngology (ABO), 2211 Norfolk, Ste 800, Houston, TX 77098-4044
T: (713) 528-6200
Founded: 1924
Gen Secr: Dr. Robert W. Cantrell
Focus: Otorhinolaryngology
Periodical
Newsletter (semi-annually) 12991

American Board of Pathology (ABP), Lincoln Center, 5401 W Kennedy Blvd, POB 25915, Tampa, FL 33622
T: (813) 286-2444
Founded: 1936; Members: 12
Focus: Pathology
Periodicals
The American Board of Pathology (2-3 times annually)
Information Booklet (annually) 12992

American Board of Pediatric Dentistry (ABPD), 1193 Woodgate Dr, Carmel, IN 46033
T: (317) 573-0877; Fax: (317) 846-7235
Founded: 1940; Members: 831
Focus: Dent 12993

American Board of Pediatrics (ABP), 111 Silver Cedar Ct, Chapel Hill, NC 27514
T: (919) 929-0461; Fax: (919) 929-9255
Founded: 1933; Members: 18
Focus: Pediatrics 12994

American Board of Periodontology (ABP), c/o Baltimore College of Dental Surgery, University of Maryland, 666 W Baltimore St, Baltimore, MD 21201
T: (410) 328-2432; Fax: (410) 328-0074
Founded: 1939
Focus: Dent 12995

American Board of Physical Medicine and Rehabilitation (ABPMR), 21 First St SW, Ste 674, Rochester, MN 55902
T: (507) 282-1776
Founded: 1947; Members: 4024
Focus: Physiology; Rehabil 12996

American Board of Plastic Surgery (ABPS), 1635 Market St, Ste 400, Philadelphia, PA 19103
T: (215) 587-9322
Founded: 1937; Members: 19
Focus: Surgery 12997

American Board of Podiatric Orthopedics and Primary Medicine (ABPOPPM), 401 N Michigan Av, Chicago, IL 60611-4267
T: (312) 321-5139; Fax: (312) 321-5144
Founded: 1975; Members: 2041
Pres: Joseph R. Agostinelli
Focus: Orthopedics
Periodicals
Directory of Diplomates (annually)
Newsletter (semi-annually) 12998

American Board of Podiatric Surgery (ABPS), 1601 Dolores St, San Francisco, CA 94110-4906
T: (415) 826-3200; Fax: (415) 826-4640
Founded: 1975; Members: 3000
Focus: Surgery; Orthopedics 12999

American Board of Preventive Medicine (ABPM), 9950 W Lawrence Av, Ste 106, Schiller Park, IL 60176
T: (708) 671-1750; Fax: (708) 671-1751
Founded: 1948; Members: 17
Gen Secr: Alice R. Ring
Focus: Med; Hygiene
Periodical
Bulletin 13000

American Board of Professional Psychology (ABPP), 2100 E Broadway, Ste 313, Columbia, MO 65201
T: (314) 875-1267; Fax: (314) 443-1199
Founded: 1947; Members: 3750

Focus: Psych
Periodical
Newsletter (semi-annually) 13001

American Board of Prosthodontics (ABP), c/o Dr. William D. Culpepper, POB 8437, Atlanta, GA 30306
T: (706) 876-2625; Fax: (404) 872-8804
Focus: Dent 13002

American Board of Psychiatry and Neurology (ABPN), 500 Lake Cook Rd, Ste 335, Deerfield, IL 60015
T: (708) 945-7900; Fax: (708) 945-1146
Founded: 1934; Members: 36960
Focus: Neurology; Psychiatry 13003

American Board of Psychological Hypnosis (ABPH), c/o North Shore Counseling Center, 23 Broadway, Beverly, MA 01915
T: (508) 922-2280; Fax: (508) 927-1758
Founded: 1959; Members: 350
Gen Secr: Samuel M. Migdole
Focus: Psych 13004

American Board of Radiology (ABR), 5255 E. Williams Cir, Ste 6800, Tucson, AZ 85711-7401
T: (520) 790-2900; Fax: (520) 790-3200
Founded: 1934; Members: 23
Gen Secr: M. Paul Capp
Focus: Radiology 13005

American Board of Surgery (ABS), 1617 John F. Kennedy Blvd, Philadelphia, PA 19103
T: (215) 568-4000
Founded: 1937; Members: 28
Focus: Surgery
Periodical
Booklet of Information (annually) 13006

American Board of Thoracic Surgery (ABTS), 1 Rotary Center, Ste 803, Evanston, IL 60201
T: (708) 475-1520; Fax: (708) 475-6240
Founded: 1948
Focus: Surgery 13007

American Board of Urology (ABU), 31700 Telegraph Rd, Ste 150, Bingham Farms, MI 48025
T: (313) 646-9720
Founded: 1935
Focus: Urology 13008

American Board of Vocational Experts (ABVE), 4700 W Lake, Glenview, IL 60025-1485
T: (847) 375-4714; Fax: (847) 375-4777
Founded: 1980; Members: 380
Gen Secr: Jeffrey W. Engle
Focus: Educ
Periodicals
National Directory of Vocational Experts (annually)
The Vocational Expert (quarterly) . . . 13009

American Boccaccio Association (ABA), c/o Dept of Romance Languages and Literatures, Washington University, 1 Brookings Dr, Campus Box 1077, Saint Louis, MO 63130-4899
T: (314) 935-5175; Fax: (314) 726-3494
Members: 100
Gen Secr: Michael Sherberg
Focus: Lit
Periodical
Boccaccio Newsletter (semi-annually) . . 13010

American Boxwood Society (ABS), Box 85, Boyce, VA 22620
T: (703) 939-4646
Founded: 1961; Members: 800
Focus: Forestry
Periodical
Boxwood Bulletin (quarterly) 13011

American Brain Tumor Association (ABTA), 2720 River Rd, Ste 146, Des Plaines, IL 60018
T: (847) 827-9910; E-Mail: ABTA@aol.com; Fax: (847) 827-9918
Founded: 1973; Members: 20000
Gen Secr: Naomi Berkowitz
Focus: Neurology
Periodical
Message Line (semi-annually) 13012

American Broncho-Esophagological Association (ABEA), 1 Children's Pl, Rm 3535, Saint Louis, MO 63110
T: (314) 454-2138; Fax: (314) 454-2174
Founded: 1917; Members: 300
Gen Secr: Rodney P. Lusk
Focus: Otorhinolaryngology
Periodical
Transactions (annually) 13013

American Bryological and Lichenological Society (ABLS), c/o Robert J. Thomas, Biology Dept, Bates College, Lewiston, ME 04240
T: (207) 786-6105; Fax: (207) 786-6123
Founded: 1898; Members: 501
Gen Secr: Robert J. Thomas
Focus: Botany
Periodical
The Bryologist (quarterly) 13014

American Bureau for Medical Advancement in China (ABMAC), 1216 Fifth Av, New York, NY 10029
T: (212) 860-1990; Fax: (212) 860-1994
Founded: 1937; Members: 52
Gen Secr: Hope N.F. Phillips
Focus: Med

Periodical
Annual Report (annually) 13015

American Burn Association (ABA), c/o Cornell Medical Center, New York Hospital, 525 E 68 St, Rm L-706, New York, NY 10021
T: (212) 746-5078; Fax: (212) 746-8991
Founded: 1967; Members: 3500
Gen Secr: Cleon W. Goodwin
Focus: Traumatology
Periodicals
Burn Care Services in North America (annually)
Journal of Burn Care and Rehabilitation (bi-monthly) 13016

American-Canadian Genealogical Society (ACGS), POB 6478, Manchester, NH 03108
T: (603) 622-1554
Founded: 1973; Members: 2500
Pres: Roger Lawrence
Focus: Genealogy
Periodical
The Genealogist (semi-annually) 13017

American Canal Society (ACS), c/o William H. Shank, 809 Rathton Rd, York, PA 17403
T: (717) 843-4035
Founded: 1972; Members: 850
Focus: Eng; Hist
Periodical
American Canal Guides (quarterly) . . . 13018

American Cancer Society (ACS), 19 W 56 St, New York, NY 10019
Founded: 1913
Gen Secr: G. Robert Gadberry
Focus: Cell Biol & Cancer Res
Periodicals
Annual Report (annually)
CA-A Cancer Journal for Clinicians (bi-monthly)
Cancer Facts and Figures (annually)
Cancer News (3 times annually)
Cancer Nursing News (quarterly)
World Smoking and Health (3 times annually)
. . . . 13019

American Carbon Society (ACS), c/o Carbone of America, 215 Stackpole St, Saint Marys, PA 15857
T: (814) 781-8410
Founded: 1957; Members: 500
Focus: Physics
Periodical
Extended Abstracts and Proceedings from Biennial Carbon Conferences (bi-annually) 13020

American Cartographic Association (ACA), c/o American Congress on Surveying and Mapping, 5410 Grosvenor Ln, Bethesda, MD 20814
T: (301) 493-0200
Members: 1600
Focus: Cart 13021

American Catholic Historical Association (ACHA), c/o The Catholic University of America, Mullen Library, Rm 305, Washington, DC 20064
T: (202) 319-5079; Fax: (202) 319-4967
Founded: 1919; Members: 1146
Gen Secr: Robert Trisco
Focus: Hist
Periodical
Catholic Historical Review (quarterly) . . 13022

American Catholic Philosophical Association (ACPA), c/o Catholic University of America, Administration Bldg, Rm 403, 620 Michigan Av NE, Washington, DC 20064
T: (202) 319-5518; Fax: (202) 319-5047
Founded: 1926; Members: 1100
Focus: Philos
Periodical
The New Scholasticism (quarterly) . . . 13023

American Celiac Society (ACS), 58 Mussano Ct, West Orange, NJ 07052
T: (201) 325-8837
Founded: 1970; Members: 4000
Focus: Hematology; Gastroenter; Nutrition
Periodical
Newsletter (3 times annually) 13024

American Center for Design (ACD), 233 E Ontario, Ste 500, Chicago, IL 60611
T: (312) 787-2018; Fax: (312) 649-9518
Founded: 1927; Members: 3000
Focus: Graphic & Dec Arts, Design
Periodical
Creative Communicator Magazine (monthly) 13025

American Center for the Alexander Technique (ACAT), 129 W 67 St, New York, NY 10023
T: (212) 799-0468
Founded: 1964; Members: 80
Focus: Sports
Periodical
ACAT News 13026

American Ceramic Society (ACerS), POB 6136, Westerville, OH 43086-6136
T: (614) 890-4700; Fax: (614) 899-6109
Founded: 1899; Members: 11610
Gen Secr: W. Paul Holbrook
Focus: Materials Sci
Periodicals
Advanced Ceramic Materials (bi-monthly)
Cements Research Progress (annually)
Ceramic Abstracts (bi-monthly)
Ceramic Bulletin (monthly)

Ceramic Engineering and Science Proceedings (bi-monthly)
Journal of the American Ceramic Society (monthly) 13027

American Cetacean Society (ACS), POB 1391, San Pedro, CA 90733
T: (310) 548-6279; E-Mail: acs@pobox.com; Fax: (310) 548-6950
Founded: 1967; Members: 2000
Pres: Pete Major
Focus: Bio; Water Res
Periodicals
Whale News (quarterly)
The Whalewatcher (quarterly) 13028

American Chemical Society (ACS), 1155 16 St NW, Washington, DC 20036
T: (202) 872-4600; Fax: (202) 872-4615
Founded: 1876; Members: 151000
Gen Secr: John K. Crum
Focus: Chem
Periodicals
Accounts of Chemical Research
Analytical Chemistry
Biochemistry (weekly)
Bioconjugate Chemistry
Biotechnology Progress
Chemical & Engineering News
Chemical Research in Toxicology
Chemical Reviews
Chemistry of Materials
CHEMTECH
Energy & Fuels
Environmental Science & Technology
Industrial & Engineering Chemistry Research
Inorganic Chemistry
Journal of Agricultural and Food Chemistry (monthly)
Journal of Chemical and Engineering Data
Journal of Chemical Information and Computer Sciences
Journal of Medicinal Chemistry
The Journal of Organic Chemistry
Journal of Physical and Chemical Reference Data
The Journal of Physical Chemistry
Journal of the American Chemical Society
Langmuir (monthly)
Macromolecules (bi-weekly)
Organometallics 13029

American Chestnut Foundation (ACF), POB 4044, Bennington, VT 05201
T: (802) 447-0110; Fax: (802) 447-3712
Founded: 1983; Members: 2000
Gen Secr: John Herrington
Focus: Botany
Periodical
Journal of the American Chestnut Foundation (annually) 13030

American Chiropractic Association (ACA), 1701 Clarendon Blvd, Arlington, VA 22209
T: (703) 276-8800; Fax: (703) 243-2593
Founded: 1930; Members: 20000
Focus: Orthopedics
Periodicals
Journal of Chiropractic (monthly)
Membership Directory (annually) 13031

American Classical League (ACL), c/o Miami University, Oxford, OH 45056
T: (513) 529-7741; Fax: (513) 529-7742
Founded: 1918; Members: 3400
Gen Secr: Geri Dutra
Focus: Ling; Educ
Periodical
The Classical Outlook (quarterly) 13032

American Cleft Palate-Craniofacial Association (ACPA), 1218 Grandview Av, Pittsburgh, PA 15211
T: (412) 481-1376; Fax: (412) 481-0847
Founded: 1943; Members: 2500
Focus: Otorhinolaryngology
Periodicals
Cleft Palate Journal (quarterly)
Craniofacial: Cleft Palate Bibliography (quarterly)
. . . . 13033

American Clinical and Climatological Association (ACCA), c/o Mayo Clinic, 200 First St SW, Ste 1601, Rochester, MN 55905
T: (507) 284-3320; Fax: (507) 284-2053
Founded: 1884; Members: 375
Gen Secr: Dr. Lynwood H. Smith
Focus: Physical Therapy; Surgery
Periodical
Transactions (annually) 13034

American Cocoa Research Institute (ACRI), 7900 Westpark Dr, Ste A-320, McLean, VA 22102
T: (703) 790-5011
Founded: 1945
Focus: Coffee, Tea, Cocoa 13035

American College Health Association (ACHA), POB 28937, Baltimore, MD 21240-8937
T: (410) 859-1500; Fax: (410) 859-1510
Founded: 1920; Members: 3900
Focus: Public Health
Periodicals
Action Newsletter (bi-monthly)
Journal of American College Health (bi-monthly)
. . . . 13036

American College of Allergy and Immunology (ACAI), 55 W Algonquin Rd, Ste 550, Arlington Heights, IL 60005
T: (708) 427-1200; Fax: (708) 427-1294
Founded: 1942; Members: 3800
Gen Secr: James R. Slawny
Focus: Immunology 13037

American College of Apothecaries (ACA), POB 341266, Memphis, TN 38184-1266
T: (901) 383-8119; Fax: (901) 383-8882
Founded: 1940; Members: 1000
Gen Secr: Dr. D.C. Huffman
Focus: Pharmacol
Periodicals
Newsletter (monthly)
The Voice of the Pharmacist (quarterly) . 13038

American College of Cardiology (ACC), 9111 Old Georgetown Rd, Bethesda, MD 20814
T: (301) 897-5400; Fax: (301) 897-9745
Founded: 1949; Members: 19617
Focus: Cardiol
Periodical
Journal of the American College of Cardiology (monthly) 13039

American College of Chest Physicians (ACCP), 3300 Dundee Rd, Northbrook, IL 60062-2348
T: (847) 498-1400; E-Mail: chestp@ad.com; Fax: (847) 498-5460
Founded: 1935; Members: 15000
Gen Secr: Alvin Lever
Focus: Cardiol; Pulmon Dis
Periodicals
Bulletin (quarterly)
Chest (monthly)
Membership Directory 13040

American College of Chiropractic Orthopedists (ACCO), c/o William P. Valusek, 1030 Broadway, Ste 101, El Centro, CA 92243
T: (619) 352-1452; Fax: (619) 352-3966
Founded: 1964; Members: 716
Pres: William P. Valusek
Focus: Orthopedics
Periodical
Ortho-Briefs (quarterly) 13041

American College of Clinical Pharmacology (ACCP), 3 Ellinwood Court, New Hartford, NY 13413-1105
T: (315) 768-6117; Fax: (315) 768-6119
Founded: 1969; Members: 1000
Gen Secr: Susan Ulrich
Focus: Pharmacol
Periodical
Journal of Clinical Pharmacology (monthly) 13042

American College of Cryosurgery (ACC), POB 4014, Schaumburg, IL 60168-4014
T: (708) 330-0230; Fax: (708) 869-4382
Founded: 1977; Members: 336
Focus: Surgery 13043

American College of Dentists (ACD), 839-J Quince Orchard Blvd, Gaithersburg, MD 20878
T: (301) 977-3223; Fax: (301) 977-3330
Founded: 1920; Members: 7000
Gen Secr: Dr. Sherry Keramidas
Focus: Dent
Periodicals
Journal (quarterly)
News and Views (quarterly) 13044

American College of Emergency Physicians (ACEP), POB 619911, Dallas, TX 75261-9911
T: (214) 550-0911; Fax: (214) 580-2816
Founded: 1968; Members: 15700
Focus: Med
Periodicals
ACEP News (monthly)
Annals of Emergency Medicine (bi-monthly)
. . . . 13045

American College of Foot and Ankle Orthopedics and Medicine (ACFAOM), 4603 Hwy 95 S, POB 39, Cocolla, ID 83813-0039
T: (208) 265-3900; Fax: (208) 683-3700
Founded: 1949; Members: 1300
Gen Secr: Judith A. Baerg
Focus: Orthopedics
Periodical
Newsletter (quarterly) 13046

American College of Foot and Ankle Pediatrics (ACFAP), Eighth and Race St, Philadelphia, PA 19107
T: (215) 625-5361; Fax: (215) 629-0199
Founded: 1977; Members: 200
Pres: P.J. Bresnahan
Focus: Orthopedics; Pediatrics
Periodical
Newsletter (quarterly) 13047

American College of Foot and Ankle Surgeons (ACFAS), 515 Busez Hwy, Park Ridge, IL 60068
T: (708) 292-2237; Fax: (708) 292-2022
Founded: 1942; Members: 4500
Gen Secr: Ronald J. Bordui
Focus: Surgery; Orthopedics
Periodical
Journal of Foot Surgery (bi-monthly) . . 13048

American College of Gastroenterology (ACG), 4900B S 31 St, Arlington, VA 22206-1656
T: (703) 820-7400; Fax: (703) 931-4520

Founded: 1932; Members: 4000
Focus: Gastroenter
Periodical
American Journal of Gastroenterology (monthly) . . . 13049

American College of Healthcare Executives (ACHE), 1 N Franklin, Ste 1700, Chicago, IL 60606-3491
T: (312) 424-2800; Fax: (312) 424-0023
Founded: 1933; Members: 28000
Pres: Thomas C. Dolan
Focus: Adult Educ; Med
Periodicals
Healthcare Executive Magazine (bi-monthly)
Hospital & Health Services Administration (quarterly) . . . 13050

American College of Heraldry (ACH), Drawer CG, Tuscaloosa, AL 35486-2870
Founded: 1972; Members: 1054
Focus: Genealogy
Periodicals
The Armiger's News (quarterly)
The Heraldic Register of America (irregularly) . . . 13051

American College of International Physicians (ACIP), 711 Second St NE, Ste 200, Washington, DC 20002
T: (202) 544-7498; Fax: (202) 546-7105
Founded: 1975; Members: 1300
Focus: Physics
Periodical
Bulletin (quarterly) . . . 13052

American College of Medical Practice Executives, 104 Inverness Terrace E, Englewood, CO 80112-5306
T: (303) 397-7869; Fax: (303) 643-4427
Founded: 1956; Members: 2800
Gen Secr: Andrea M. Rossiter
Focus: Med; Dent . . . 13053

American College of Medical Toxicology (ACMT), 777 E Park Dr, POB 8820, Harrisburg, PA 17105-8820
T: (717) 558-7846; Fax: (717) 558-7841
Founded: 1993; Members: 210
Focus: Toxicology
Periodicals
American Board of Medical Toxicology Journal (annually)
Veterinary and Human Toxicology (bi-monthly) . . . 13054

American College of MOHS Micrographic Surgery and Cutaneous Oncology (ACMMSCO), POB 4014, Schaumburg, IL 60168-4014
T: (708) 330-0230; Fax: (708) 330-0050
Founded: 1967; Members: 260
Gen Secr: Michael G. Thompson
Focus: Cell Biol & Cancer Res; Surgery
Periodical
Bulletin (3 times annually) . . . 13055

American College of Musicians (ACM), 808 Rio Grande, POB 1807, Austin, TX 78767
T: (512) 478-5775
Founded: 1929; Members: 14867
Focus: Music . . . 13056

American College of Neuropsychiatrists (ACN), 28595 Orchard Lake Rd, Ste 200, Farmington Hills, MI 48334
T: (313) 553-9877; Fax: (313) 553-5957
Founded: 1937; Members: 420
Focus: Psychiatry; Neurology
Periodicals
Directory (annually)
Journal (quarterly) . . . 13057

American College of Neuropsychopharmacology (ACNP), 320 Centre Bldg, 2014 Broadway, Nashville, TN 37203
T: (615) 322-2075; E-Mail: acnp@ctrvax.vanderbilt.edu; Fax: (615) 343-0662
Founded: 1961; Members: 713
Gen Secr: Oakley Ray
Focus: Pharmacol
Periodicals
Mailings (monthly)
Roster (annually) . . . 13058

American College of Nuclear Physicians (ACNP), 1200 19 St NW, Ste 300, Washington, DC 20036
T: (202) 857-1135; Fax: (202) 223-4579
Founded: 1974; Members: 1600
Gen Secr: Carol A. Lively
Focus: Nucl Med; Physiology
Periodicals
Directory (annually)
Scanner (10 times annually) . . . 13059

American College of Nurse-Midwives (ACNM), 1522 K St NW, Ste 1000, Washington, DC 20005
T: (202) 728-9860; Fax: (202) 289-4395
Founded: 1955; Members: 3000
Gen Secr: Ronald E. Nitzsche
Focus: Adult Educ; Med
Periodicals
ACNM Membership Directory (annually)
Journal of Nurse-Midwifery (bi-monthly)
Quickening (bi-monthly) . . . 13060

American College of Nutrition (ACN), 301 E 17 St, New York, NY 10003
T: (212) 777-1037; Fax: (212) 777-1103
Founded: 1959; Members: 1170
Gen Secr: Stanley Wallach
Focus: Hematology
Periodicals
Journal (bi-monthly)
Newsletter (quarterly) . . . 13061

American College of Obstetricians and Gynecologists (ACOG), 409 12 St SW, POB 96920, Washington, DC 20090-6920
T: (202) 638-5577
Founded: 1951; Members: 37000
Gen Secr: Dr. Ralph Hale
Focus: Gynecology
Periodical
Obstetrics and Gynecology (monthly) . . . 13062

American College of Oral and Maxillofacial Surgeons (ACOMS), c/o James E. Bauerle, 1100 NW Loop 410, Ste 500, San Antonio, TX 78213-2266
T: (210) 344-5674; Fax: (210) 344-9754
Founded: 1975; Members: 1500
Focus: Doc
Periodical
Newsletter (quarterly) . . . 13063

American College of Orgonomy (ACO), POB 490, Princeton, NJ 08542
T: (908) 821-1144; Fax: (908) 821-0174
Founded: 1968; Members: 12
Focus: Physiology
Periodical
Journal of Orgonomy (semi-annually) . . . 13064

American College of Osteopathic Family Physicians (ACFP), 330 E Algonquin, Arlington Heights, IL 60005
T: (847) 228-6090; Fax: (847) 228-9755
Founded: 1950; Members: 14000
Gen Secr: George Nyhart
Focus: Med; Surgery; Pathology
Periodicals
Membership Directory (annually)
Newsletter (monthly)
Official Journal (bi-monthly) . . . 13065

American College of Osteopathic Internists (ACOI), 300 Fifth St NE, Washington, DC 20002
T: (202) 546-0095; Fax: (202) 543-5584
Founded: 1943; Members: 1300
Focus: Pathology
Periodicals
Directory (annually)
Newsletter (quarterly) . . . 13066

American College of Osteopathic Obstetricians and Gynecologists (ACOOG), 900 Auburn Rd, Pontiac, MI 48342-3365
T: (313) 332-6360; Fax: (313) 332-4607
Founded: 1934; Members: 565
Focus: Gynecology
Periodicals
ACOOG Newsletter (quarterly)
Directory of Members (annually) . . . 13067

American College of Osteopathic Pediatricians (ACOP), 5301 Wisconsin Av, Ste 630, Washington, DC 20015
T: (202) 362-3229; Fax: (202) 537-1362
Founded: 1940; Members: 365
Gen Secr: David Kushner
Focus: Pathology; Pediatrics
Periodicals
Membership Directory (annually)
Newsletter (quarterly) . . . 13068

American College of Osteopathic Surgeons (ACOS), 123 N Henry St, Alexandria, VA 22314-2903
T: (703) 684-0416
Founded: 1927; Members: 1350
Focus: Surgery; Pathology
Periodicals
Membership Directory and By-laws (annually)
News (monthly) . . . 13069

American College of Physicians (ACP), Independence Mall W, Sixth St at Race, Philadelphia, PA 19106
T: (215) 351-2400; Fax: (215) 351-2448
Founded: 1915; Members: 39712
Gen Secr: John R. Ball
Focus: Physiology
Periodicals
Annals of Internal Medicine (bi-weekly)
Directory
Medical Knowledge Self-Assessment
Observer (monthly) . . . 13070

American College of Preventive Medicine (ACPM), 1660 L St, Ste 206, Washington, DC 20036-5603
T: (202) 466-2044; E-Mail: info@acpm.org; Fax: (202) 466-2662
Founded: 1954; Members: 2000
Gen Secr: Hazel K. Keimowitz
Focus: Med; Hygiene
Periodicals
American Journal of Preventive Medicine
Membership Roster
Newsletter (bi-monthly) . . . 13071

American College of Prosthodontists (ACP), 211 E Chicago Av, Ste 1000, Chicago, IL 60611-2616
T: (312) 573-1260; Fax: (312) 573-1257
Founded: 1970; Members: 2350
Gen Secr: Dr. David Schwab
Focus: Dent
Periodical
Newsletter (quarterly) . . . 13072

American College of Psychiatrists (ACP), POB 365, Greenbelt, MD 20768
T: (301) 345-3534; Fax: (301) 474-0219
Founded: 1963; Members: 800
Focus: Psychiatry
Periodical
ACP Newsletter (quarterly) . . . 13073

American College of Psychoanalysts (ACPA), 520 Breck Ct, Benicia, CA 94510-1372
T: (707) 746-7674; Fax: (707) 746-7677
Founded: 1969; Members: 225
Gen Secr: Angela Clark
Focus: Psychoan
Periodical
Bulletin (3 times annually) . . . 13074

American College of Rheumatology (ACR), 60 Executive Park Dr S, Ste 150, Atlanta, GA 30329
T: (404) 633-3777; Fax: (404) 633-1870
Founded: 1934; Members: 4700
Focus: Rheuma
Periodicals
ARA Membership Directory (annually)
ARA Scientific Program (annually)
Arthritis and Rheumatism (monthly)
Rheumatism Review (bi-annually) . . . 13075

American College of Sports Medicine (ACSM), POB 1440, Indianapolis, IN 46206-1440
T: (317) 637-9200; Fax: (317) 634-7817
Founded: 1954; Members: 12800
Focus: Med; Physical Therapy
Periodicals
ACSM Membership Directory (annually)
Medicine and Science in Sports and Exercise (bi-monthly)
Sports Medicine Bulletin (quarterly) . . . 13076

American College of Surgeons (ACS), 55 E Erie St, Chicago, IL 60611
T: (312) 664-4050; Fax: (312) 440-7014
Founded: 1913; Members: 53510
Pres: Paul A. Ebert; Gen Secr: Dr. Kathryn D. Anderson
Focus: Surgery
Periodicals
Bulletin (monthly)
Journal of the American College of Surgeons (monthly)
Surgery, Gynecology and Obstetrics (monthly)
Surgical Forum (annually) . . . 13077

American College of Veterinary Internal Medicine (ACVIM), 7175 W Jefferson Av, Ste 2125, Lakewood, CO 80235
T: (303) 980-7136; Fax: (303) 980-7137
Founded: 1972; Members: 678
Gen Secr: June Johnson
Focus: Vet Med
Periodical
Proceedings of the Annual Veterinary Medical Forums (annually) . . . 13078

American College of Veterinary Pathologists (ACVP), 875 King Hwy, West Deptford, NJ 08096
T: (609) 848-7784; Fax: (609) 853-0411
Founded: 1948; Members: 921
Focus: Vet Med
Periodicals
Membership List (annually)
Proceedings (annually)
Veterinary Pathology (bi-monthly) . . . 13079

American College of Veterinary Radiology (ACVR), c/o Dr. M. Bernstein, POB 87, Glencoe, IL 60022
T: (708) 251-5517; Fax: (708) 446-8618
Founded: 1964; Members: 135
Focus: Radiology; Vet Med
Periodical
Veterinary Radiology (bi-monthly) . . . 13080

American College Testing (ACT), Box 168, Iowa City, IA 52243
T: (319) 337-1000; Fax: (319) 337-1551
Founded: 1959
Focus: Educ
Periodical
ACTivity (quarterly) . . . 13081

American Collegiate Retailing Association (ACRA), c/o Dr. Michael M. Pearson, College of Business, Loyola University, 6363 Saint Charles, New Orleans, LA 70118
T: (504) 865-2448; Fax: (504) 865-3496
Founded: 1948; Members: 300
Gen Secr: Dr. Michael M. Pearson
Focus: Business Admin
Periodicals
Directory of Members (annually)
Newsletter (quarterly) . . . 13082

American Committee for International Conservation (ACIC), c/o Roger E. McManus, Center for Marine Conservation, 1725 DeSales St NW, Ste 500, Washington, DC 20036
T: (202) 429-5609; Fax: (202) 872-0619
Founded: 1930; Members: 25
Focus: Bio; Ecology . . . 13083

American Committee for the Weizmann Institute of Science (ACWIS), 51 Madison Av, Ste 117, New York, NY 10010
T: (212) 779-2500; Fax: (212) 779-3209
Founded: 1944
Focus: Sci
Periodical
Weizmann Now (annually) . . . 13084

American Committee to Advance the Study of Petroglyphs and Pictographs (ACASPP), c/o Joseph J. Snyder, POB 158, Shepherdstown, WV 25443
T: (304) 876-3208; Fax: (304) 876-3208
Founded: 1979; Members: 237
Gen Secr: Joseph J. Snyder
Focus: Archeol
Periodicals
Membership Directory
Newsletter (quarterly)
Rock Art (semi-annually) . . . 13085

American Comparative Literature Association (ACLA), 5242 University of Oregon, Eugene, OR 97403-5242
T: (503) 346-0737; Fax: (503) 346-3240
Founded: 1960; Members: 1000
Pres: Eugene Eoyang; Gen Secr: Roland Greene
Focus: Lit
Periodical
Bulletin (semi-annually) . . . 13086

American Concrete Institute (ACI), POB 19150, Detroit, MI 48219
T: (313) 532-2600; Fax: (313) 538-0655
Founded: 1905; Members: 19500
Focus: Civil Eng
Periodicals
ACI Materials Journal (bi-monthly)
ACI Structural Journal (bi-monthly)
Concrete Abstracts (bi-monthly)
Concrete International: Design & Construction (monthly) . . . 13087

American Conference for Irish Studies (ACIS), 108 Limestone Ln, Syracuse, NY 13219
T: (315) 469-2612; E-Mail: mackillj@oliath.sunyocc.edu; Fax: (315) 469-2597
Founded: 1962; Members: 1650
Gen Secr: James MacKillop
Focus: Ethnology
Periodical
Newsletter (3 times annually) . . . 13088

American Conference of Academic Deans (ACAD), 1818 R St NW, Washington, DC 20009
T: (202) 387-3760
Founded: 1944; Members: 600
Focus: Adult Educ
Periodical
Proceedings (annually) . . . 13089

American Conference of Governmental Industrial Hygienists (ACGIH), 1330 Kemper Meadow Dr, Cincinnati, OH 45240
Fax: (513) 742-2020 (513) 742-3355
Founded: 1938; Members: 5500
Gen Secr: Richard A. Strano
Focus: Hygiene
Periodical
Applied Industrial Hygiene (monthly) . . . 13090

American Congress of Rehabilitation Medicine (ACRM), 4700 W Lake Av, Glenview, IL 60025-1485
T: (847) 375-4725; E-Mail: acrm@amctec.com
Founded: 1923; Members: 2000
Gen Secr: Diane Burgher
Focus: Rehabil
Periodicals
Archives of Physical Medicine and Rehabilitation (monthly)
Membership Directory (annually) . . . 13091

American Congress on Surveying and Mapping (ACSM), 5410 Grosvenor Ln, Bethesda, MD 20814-2122
T: (301) 493-0200; Fax: (301) 493-8245
Founded: 1941; Members: 10500
Focus: Surveying; Cart
Periodicals
American Cartographer (semi-annually)
Bulletin (bi-monthly)
News (bi-monthly)
Surveying and Mapping (quarterly)
Technical Papers (semi-annually) . . . 13092

American Conservation Association (ACA), 30 Rockefeller Plaza, Rm 5402, New York, NY 10112
T: (212) 649-5600; Fax: (212) 649-5921
Founded: 1958
Focus: Ecology . . . 13093

American Consulting Engineers Council (ACEC), 1015 15 St NW, Washington, DC 20005
T: (202) 347-7474; Fax: (202) 898-0068
Founded: 1956; Members: 5000
Gen Secr: Howard M. Messner
Focus: Eng
Periodical
Membership Directory (annually) . . . 13094

American Correctional Association (ACA), 4380 Forbes Blvd, Lanham, MD 20706-4322
T: (301) 918-1800; Fax: (301) 918-1900
Founded: 1870; Members: 20980
Gen Secr: James A. Gondles
Focus: Criminology; Educ
Periodicals
Corrections Today (bi-monthly)
On the Line (bi-monthly) 13095

American Correctional Health Services Association (ACHSA), POB 2307, Dayton, OH 45401-2307
T: (513) 223-9630; Fax: (513) 223-6307
Founded: 1975; Members: 1600
Focus: Public Health
Periodical
Corhealth (bi-monthly) 13096

American Coucil for an Energy Efficient Economy (ACEEE), 1001 Connecticut Av NW, Ste 801, Washington, DC 20036
T: (202) 429-8873; Fax: (202) 429-2248
Founded: 1980
Focus: Energy
Periodical
Conference Proceedings (bi-annually) . . 13097

American Council for Construction Education (ACCE), 1300 Hudson Ln, Ste 3, Monroe, LA 71201-6054
T: (318) 323-2413; Fax: (318) 323-2413
Founded: 1974; Members: 150
Gen Secr: Daniel E. Dupree
Focus: Educ 13098

American Council for International Studies (ACIS), 19 Bay state Rd, Dept CS, Boston, MA 02215-9802
T: (617) 236-2051; E-Mail: edu_travel@acis.com; Fax: (617) 236-4703
Gen Secr: Michael I. Eizenberg
Focus: Poli Sci 13099

American Council for the Arts (ACA), 1 E 53 St, New York, NY 10022-4201
T: (212) 223-2787; Fax: (212) 223-4415
Founded: 1960; Members: 1500
Pres: Luis R. Cancel
Focus: Arts
Periodical
UpDate (monthly) 13100

American Council of Applied Clinical Nutrition (ACACN), POB 509, Florissant, MO 63032
T: (314) 921-3997
Founded: 1974; Members: 500
Focus: Hematology 13101

American Council of Independent Laboratories (ACIL), 1629 K St NW, Washington, DC 20006
T: (202) 887-5872; E-Mail: acil@ix.netcom.com; Fax: (202) 887-0021
Founded: 1937; Members: 400
Gen Secr: Joseph F. O'Neil
Focus: Finance; Insurance
Periodicals
Directory (bi-annually)
Newsletter (monthly) 13102

American Council of Learned Societies (ACLS), 228 E 45 St, New York, NY 10017
T: (212) 697-1505; Fax: (212) 949-8058
Founded: 1919; Members: 56
Pres: Stanley N. Katz
Focus: Soc Sci
Periodicals
Annual Report (annually)
Newsletter (quarterly) 13103

American Council of the International Institute of Welding (ACIIW), 550 NW LeJeune Rd, POB 351040, Miami, FL 33135
T: (305) 443-9353; Fax: (305) 443-7559
Founded: 1948
Focus: Metallurgy; Eng 13104

American Council on Consumer Interests (ACCI), 240 Stanley Hall, University of Missouri, Columbia, MO 65211
T: (314) 882-3817; Fax: (314) 884-4807
Founded: 1953; Members: 1600
Focus: Econ 13105

American Council on Education (ACE), 1 Dupont Circle NW, Ste 800, Washington, DC 20036
T: (202) 939-9300; Fax: (202) 833-4760
Founded: 1918; Members: 1800
Pres: Robert H. Atwell
Focus: Educ
Periodicals
Educational Record (quarterly)
Higher Education – National Affairs (bi-weekly)
. . . . 13106

American Council on Pharmaceutical Education (ACPE), 311 W Superior St, Ste 512, Chicago, IL 60610
T: (312) 664-3575; Fax: (312) 664-4652
Founded: 1932; Members: 10
Focus: Adult Educ; Pharmacol
Periodicals
Colleges and Schools of Pharmacy, Accredited Professional Degree Programs (annually)
Continuing Pharmaceutical Education, Approved Providers (annually) 13107

American Council on Schools and Colleges (ACSC), c/o Dr. Fredrick R. O'Keefe, 13014 N Dale Mabry, Ste 363, Tampa, FL 33618-2814
T: (813) 933-1575; E-Mail: fredrick_okeefe@msn.com
Founded: 1927; Members: 18
Gen Secr: Dr. Fredrick R. O'Keefe
Focus: Educ 13108

American Council on the Teaching of Foreign Languages (ACTFL), 6 Executive Plaza, Yonkers, NY 10701-6801
T: (914) 963-8830; Fax: (914) 963-1275
Founded: 1967; Members: 7000
Focus: Ling; Educ
Periodicals
ACTFL Foreign Language Education Series (annually)
Foreign Language Annals (bi-monthly) . . 13109

American Counseling Association (ACA), 5999 Stevenson Av, Alexandria, VA 22304
T: (703) 823-9800; Fax: (703) 823-0252
Founded: 1952; Members: 57000
Gen Secr: John Jaco
Focus: Educ
Periodicals
The Career Development (quarterly)
Counseling and Values (3 times annually)
Counselor Education and Supervision (quarterly)
Elementary School Guidance and Counseling (quarterly)
Guidepost (18 times annually)
Journal for Specialists in Group Work (quarterly)
The Journal of College Student Personnel (bi-monthly)
The Journal of Counseling & Development (bi-monthly)
Journal of Employment Counseling (quarterly)
The Journal of Humanistic Education and Development (quarterly)
Journal of Multicultural Counseling & Development
Guidance (quarterly)
Journal of Offender Counseling (semi-annually)
Measurement and Evaluation in Counseling & Development (quarterly)
Rehabilitation Counseling Bulletin (quarterly)
The School Counselor (5 times annually) 13110

American Criminal Justice Association – Lambda Alpha Epsilon (ACJA-LAE), POB 61047, Sacramento, CA 95860
T: (916) 484-6553; Fax: (916) 488-4757
Founded: 1937; Members: 4000
Focus: Criminology; Law
Periodical
Journal of the American Criminal Justice Association (semi-annually) 13111

American Cryonics Society (ACS), POB 1509, Cupertino, CA 95015
T: (408) 734-4200; Fax: (408) 734-4441
Founded: 1969; Members: 204
Focus: Med
Periodicals
American Cryonics (semi-annually)
American Cryonics News (bi-monthly) . . 13112

American Crystallographic Association (ACA), POB 96, Ellicott Station, Buffalo, NY 14205-0096
T: (716) 856-9600; Fax: (716) 852-4846
Founded: 1949; Members: 2000
Pres: Elinor Adman; Gen Secr: Vivian Cody
Focus: Geology; Chem; Physics; Biochem
Periodicals
ACA Monographs (irregularly)
ACA Newsletter (bi-monthly)
ACA Program and Abstracts (annually)
ACA Transactions (annually) 13113

American Dairy Science Association (ADSA), 1111 N Dunlap Av, Savoy, IL 61874
T: (217) 356-3182; Fax: (217) 398-4119
Founded: 1906; Members: 4654
Pres: L.D. Satter; Gen Secr: Carl D. Johnson
Focus: Food
Periodical
Journal of Dairy Science (monthly) . . . 13114

American Dance Therapy Association (ADTA), 2000 Century Plaza, Ste 108, Columbia, MD 21044
T: (301) 997-4040
Founded: 1966; Members: 1200
Focus: Therapeutics
Periodicals
American Journal of Dance Therapy (annually)
Newsletter (quarterly) 13115

American Deafness and Rehabilitation Association (ADARA), POB 251554, Little Rock, AR 72225
T: (501) 868-8850; E-Mail: adarahuie@kaol.com; Fax: (501) 868-8812
Founded: 1966; Members: 1000
Pres: Steve Larew
Focus: Rehabil
Periodicals
Journal of Rehabilitation of the Deaf (quarterly)
Newsletter (bi-monthly) 13116

American Dental Assistants Association (ADAA), 203 N LaSalle St, Ste 1320, Chicago, IL 60601-1225
T: (312) 541-1550; Fax: (312) 541-1496
Founded: 1923; Members: 16000
Gen Secr: Lawrence H. Sepin
Focus: Dent
Periodical
The Dental Assistant (bi-monthly) . . . 13117

American Dental Association (ADA), 211 E Chicago Av, Chicago, IL 60611
Fax: (312) 440-2707
Founded: 1859; Members: 146000
Gen Secr: John S. Zapp
Focus: Dent
Periodicals
American Dental Directory (annually)
Dental Abstracts (monthly)
Dental Literature (quarterly)
Journal (monthly)
News (bi-weekly)
Special Care in Dentistry (bi-monthly) . . 13118

American Dental Hygienists' Association (ADHA), 444 N Michigan Av, Ste 3400, Chicago, IL 60611
T: (312) 440-8929; Fax: (312) 440-8929
Founded: 1923; Members: 30000
Focus: Hygiene; Dent
Periodicals
Access (quarterly)
Dental Hygiene (monthly) 13119

American Dental Society of Anesthesiology (ADSA), 211 E Chicago Av, Ste 948, Chicago, IL 60611
T: (312) 664-8270; Fax: (312) 642-9713
Founded: 1953; Members: 3200
Focus: Anesthetics; Dent
Periodicals
ADSA Directory (annually)
Anesthesia Progress (bi-monthly)
Pulse (bi-monthly) 13120

American Dermatologic Society of Allergy and Immunology (ADSAI), c/o Dr. R.S. Rogers, Dept of Dermatology, Mayo Clinic, Rochester, MN 55905
T: (507) 284-2555; Fax: (507) 284-2072
Founded: 1974; Members: 150
Focus: Immunology 13121

American Dermatological Association (ADA), c/o Dept of Dermatology, Medical College of Georgia, Augusta, GA 30912-2900
T: (706) 721-6496; Fax: (706) 721-3318
Founded: 1876; Members: 350
Gen Secr: Donald C. Abele
Focus: Derm 13122

American Design Drafting Association (ADDA), POB 799, Rockville, MD 20848-0799
T: (301) 460-6875; Fax: (301) 460-8591
Founded: 1959; Members: 2000
Focus: Graphic & Dec Arts, Design
Periodical
Design and Drafting News (bi-monthly) . 13123

American Diabetes Association (ADA), 1660 Duke St, POB 25757, Alexandria, VA 22314
T: (703) 549-1500; Fax: (703) 836-7439
Founded: 1940; Members: 280000
Focus: Diabetes
Periodicals
Clinical Diabetes (bi-monthly)
Diabetes (monthly)
Diabetes Care (bi-monthly)
Forecast (monthly) 13124

American Dialect Society (ADS), c/o Dept of English, MacMurray College, 1611 N Kent St, Jacksonville, IL 62650
T: (217) 479-7049; Fax: (217) 245-0405
Founded: 1889; Members: 750
Pres: Walt Wolfram; Gen Secr: Allan A. Metcalf
Focus: Ling
Periodicals
American Speech (quarterly)
Newsletter (3 times annually)
Publication of the ADS 13125

American Dietetic Association (ADA), 216 W Jackson Blvd, Ste 800, Chicago, IL 60606-6995
T: (312) 899-0040; Fax: (312) 899-0008
Founded: 1917; Members: 68000
Focus: Nutrition
Periodical
Journal (monthly) 13126

American Diopter and Decibel Society (ADDS), 3518 Fifth Av, Pittsburgh, PA 15213
T: (412) 682-6300; Fax: (412) 682-8137
Founded: 1960; Members: 200
Gen Secr: Albert W. Biglan
Focus: Ophthal
Periodicals
Directory (annually)
Seminar Transactions of Meetings (bi-annually)
. . . . 13127

American Economic Association (AEA), 2014 Broadway, Ste 305, Nashville, TN 37203-2418
T: (615) 322-2595; Fax: (615) 343-7590
Founded: 1885; Members: 25000
Gen Secr: John Siegfried
Focus: Econ
Periodicals
American Economic Review (quarterly)
Journal of Economic Literature (quarterly)
Papers and Proceeding (annually) . . . 13128

American Economic Development Council (AEDC), 9801 W Higgins Rd, Ste 540, Rosemont, IL 60018-4726
T: (708) 692-9944; Fax: (708) 696-2990
Founded: 1926; Members: 2740
Pres: James Ahr
Focus: Develop Areas 13129

American Education Association (AEA), POB 463, Center Moriches, NY 11934
Founded: 1938
Focus: Educ
Periodical
Newsletter 13130

American Educational Research Association (AERA), 1230 17 St NW, Washington, DC 20036-3078
T: (202) 223-9485; Fax: (202) 775-1824
Founded: 1915; Members: 23000
Gen Secr: William J. Russell
Focus: Educ
Periodicals
American Educational Research Journal (quarterly)
Educational Evaluation and Policy Analysis (quarterly)
Educational Researcher (9 times annually)
Journal of Educational Statistics (quarterly)
Review of Educational Research (quarterly)
Review of Educational Research (annually) 13131

American Educational Studies Association (AESA), c/o Dr. Denise R. Knapik, Graduate Studies and Research, Hiram College, Hiram, OH 44234
T: (330) 569-5273
Founded: 1968; Members: 650
Pres: Bernardo P. Gallegos; Gen Secr: Dr. Denise R. Knapik
Focus: Depth Psych
Periodical
Educational Studies (quarterly) 13132

American Electroencephalographic Society (AEEGS), 1 Regency Dr, POB 30, Bloomfield, CT 06002
T: (203) 243-3977
Founded: 1946; Members: 1320
Focus: Neurology
Periodical
Journal of Clinical Neurophysiology (quarterly)
. . . . 13133

American Electrology Association (AEA), 106 Oak Ridge Rd, Trumbull, CT 06611
T: (203) 374-6667
Founded: 1958; Members: 2000
Focus: Med
Periodicals
Electrolysis World (quarterly)
Journal of the American Electroly Association (semi-annually)
Roster (annually) 13134

American Electronics Association (AEA), 5201 Great America Pkwy, Ste 520, Santa Clara, CA 95054
T: (408) 987-4200; Fax: (408) 970-8565
Founded: 1943; Members: 3500
Focus: Electronic Eng 13135

American Electroplaters and Surface Finishers Society (AESFS), 12644 Research Pkwy, Orlando, FL 32826
T: (407) 281-6441; Fax: (407) 281-6446
Founded: 1909; Members: 10000
Focus: Metallurgy
Periodical
Plating and Surface Finishing (monthly) . 13136

American Endodontic Society (AES), 1440 N Harbor Blvd, Ste 719, Fullerton, CA 92635
T: (714) 870-5590
Founded: 1969; Members: 10000
Focus: Dent
Periodicals
Hotline
Newsletter (quarterly) 13137

American Entomological Society (AES), c/o Academy of Natural Sciences of Philadelphia, 1900 Race St, Philadelphia, PA 19103
T: (215) 561-3978; Fax: (215) 299-1028
Founded: 1859; Members: 350
Focus: Entomology
Periodicals
Entomological News (5 times annually)
Memoirs
Transactions (quarterly) 13138

American Epilepsy Society (AES), 638 Prospect Av, Hartford, CT 06105-4298
T: (203) 586-7565; Fax: (203) 586-7550
Founded: 1946; Members: 1850
Gen Secr: Suzanne C. Berry
Focus: Pathology
Periodical
Epilepsia (bi-monthly) 13139

American Equilibration Society (AES), 8726 N Ferris Av, Morton Grove, IL 60053
T: (708) 965-2888; Fax: (708) 965-4888
Founded: 1955; Members: 1100
Focus: Dent
Periodical
Newsletter (quarterly) 13140

American Ethnological Society (AES), c/o Dept of Cultural Anthropology, Duke University, POB 90091, Durham, NC 27708-3852
T: (503) 737-3852; E-Mail: cpiot@acpub.duke.edu; Fax: (919) 681-3264
Founded: 1842; Members: 2628
Gen Secr: Charles Piots
Focus: Ethnology

Periodicals
American Ethnologist (quarterly)
Monograph Series
Unit News in Anthropology Newsletter (monthly) . . . 13141

American Family Therapy Association (AFTA), 2020 Pennsylvania Av NW, Ste 273, Washington, DC 20006
T: (202) 994-2776; Fax: (202) 994-4812
Founded: 1977; Members: 900
Focus: Therapeutics
Periodicals
Membership Directory (annually)
Newsletter (quarterly) . . . 13142

American Farm Bureau Research Foundation (AFBRF), 225 Touhy Av, Park Ridge, IL 60068
T: (312) 399-5700
Founded: 1967
Focus: Agri . . . 13143

American Federation for Clinical Research (AFCR), 6900 Grove Rd, Thorofare, NJ 08086
T: (609) 848-7072; Fax: (609) 384-6504
Founded: 1940; Members: 12500
Pres: W.A. Hsueh
Focus: Med
Periodical
Clinical Research (quarterly) . . . 13144

American Federation of Arts (AFA), 41 E 65 St, New York, NY 10021
T: (212) 988-7700; Fax: (212) 861-2487
Founded: 1909; Members: 500
Pres: Robert M. Meltzer; Gen Secr: Serena Rattazzi
Focus: Arts
Periodicals
AFA Newsletter (semi-annually)
Journal (3 times annually) . . . 13145

American Federation of Astrologers (AFA), POB 22040, Tempe, AZ 85285-2040
T: (602) 838-1751
Founded: 1938
Focus: Parapsych
Periodical
Today's Astrologer (monthly) . . . 13146

American Federation of Mineralogical Societies (AFMS), POB 26523, Oklahoma City, OK 73126-0523
T: (405) 525-2692
Founded: 1947; Members: 52000
Gen Secr: Dan McLennan
Focus: Mineralogy
Periodical
Newsletter (9 times annually) . . . 13147

American Fern Society (AFS), c/o Botany Dept, Smithsonian Institution, Washington, DC 20560
T: (202) 357-2568
Founded: 1893; Members: 900
Gen Secr: Dr. David B. Lellinger
Focus: Botany
Periodicals
American Fern Journal (quarterly)
Fiddlehead Forum (bi-monthly) . . . 13148

American Film Institute (AFI), c/o John F. Kennedy Center for the Performing Arts, Washington, DC 20566
T: (202) 828-4000
Founded: 1967; Members: 135000
Focus: Cinema
Periodicals
American Film (monthly)
Guide to College Film Courses (bi-annually) . . . 13149

American Finance Association (AFA), c/o Stern School of Business, New York University, 44 W Fourth St, Ste 9-19, New York, NY 10012
Founded: 1940; Members: 4000
Gen Secr: Dr. Michael Keenan
Focus: Finance
Periodical
Journal of Finance (5 times annually) . 13150

American Fine Arts Society (AFAS), 215 W 57 St, New York, NY 10019
T: (212) 247-4510
Founded: 1889
Focus: Arts . . . 13151

American Fisheries Society (AFS), 5410 Grosvenor Ln, Ste 110, Bethesda, MD 20814-2199
T: (301) 897-8616; E-Mail: 73312.1155@compuserve.com; Fax: (301) 897-8096
Founded: 1870; Members: 8400
Gen Secr: Paul Brouha
Focus: Fisheries
Periodicals
Journal of Aquatic Animal Health (quarterly)
North American Journal of Fisheries Management (quarterly)
The Progressive Fish-Culturist (quarterly)
Transactions of the American Fisheries Society (bi-monthly) . . . 13152

American Folklore Society (AFS), 4350 N Fairfax Dr, Ste 640, Arlington, VA 22203
Founded: 1888; Members: 1540
Gen Secr: Shalom Staub
Focus: Ethnology
Periodicals
American Folklore Society Newsletter (bi-monthly)
Journal of American Folklore (quarterly) . 13153

American Foreign Law Association (AFLA), c/o Irving & Lynch, 60 E 42 St, New York, NY 10165-0089
Founded: 1925; Members: 650
Gen Secr: J. Gregory Lynch
Focus: Law . . . 13154

American Forensic Association (AFA), Box 256, River Falls, WI 54022
T: (715) 425-3198; Fax: (715) 425-9533
Founded: 1949; Members: 900
Focus: Law
Periodicals
Journal (quarterly)
Newsletter . . . 13155

American Forests, POB 2000, Washington, DC 20013
Founded: 1875; Members: 35000
Gen Secr: Deborah Gangloff
Focus: Forestry
Periodicals
American Forests Magazine (monthly)
Resource Hotline (bi-monthly) . . . 13156

American Forum for Global Education (AFGE), 120 Wall St, Ste 2600, New York, NY 10005
T: (212) 742-8232; E-Mail: ncode@igc.org; Fax: (212) 742-8752
Founded: 1987
Pres: Andrew F. Smith
Focus: Educ
Periodical
Access (monthly) . . . 13157

American Foundation for Aids Research (AmFAR), 733 Third Av, New York, NY 10017
T: (212) 682-7440; Fax: (212) 682-9812
Founded: 1985
Pres: Mervyn F. Silverman
Focus: Immunology
Periodical
Aids/HIV Treatment Directory (quarterly) . 13158

American Foundation for Vision Awareness (AFVA), 243 N Lindbergh Blvd, Saint Louis, MO 63141
T: (800) 927-2382; Fax: (314) 991-4101
Founded: 1927; Members: 5000
Gen Secr: Huck Roberts
Focus: Ophthal
Periodical
In Focus (bi-monthly) . . . 13159

American Foundrymen's Society (AFS), 505 State St, Des Plaines, IL 60016-8399
T: (708) 824-0181; Fax: (708) 824-7848
Founded: 1896; Members: 13500
Focus: Metallurgy
Periodical
Modern Casting (monthly) . . . 13160

American Fracture Association (AFA), 2416 E Washington, Ste D-3, Bloomington, IL 61704
T: (309) 663-6272
Founded: 1938; Members: 500
Gen Secr: Barbara J. Dehority
Focus: Surgery; Orthopedics
Periodicals
Directory
Orthopedic Transactions (annually) . . . 13161

American-French Genealogical Society (AFGS), POB 2113, Pawtucket, RI 02861
T: (401) 765-6141; Fax: (401) 765-6141
Founded: 1978; Members: 1000
Pres: Roger Beaudry
Focus: Genealogy
Periodical
Je Me Souviens (quarterly) . . . 13162

American Friends of Cambridge University (AFCU), c/o Stephen C. Price, 708 Third Av, New York, NY 10017
T: (212) 880-2840
Founded: 1967; Members: 9000
Pres: Stephen C. Price
Focus: Educ
Periodical
Annual Report (annually) . . . 13163

American Friends of Lafayette (AFL), c/o Daniel A. Evans, Skillman Library, Lafayette College, Easton, PA 18042
T: (610) 250-5161; E-Mail: EvansD@Lafayette.edu; Fax: (610) 252-0370
Founded: 1932; Members: 125
Gen Secr: Daniel A. Evans
Focus: Hist
Periodical
Gazette (irregularly) . . . 13164

American Gastroenterological Association (AGA), 7910 Woodmont Av, Ste 914, Bethesda, MD 20814
T: (301) 654-2055; Fax: (301) 654-5920
Founded: 1897; Members: 6400
Focus: Gastroenter
Periodicals
AGA News (quarterly)
Gastroenterology (monthly)
Viewpoints on Digestive Diseases (5 times annually) . . . 13165

American Genetic Association (AGA), POB 257, Buckeystown, MD 21717
T: (301) 695-9292; Fax: (301) 695-9292
Founded: 1903; Members: 1500
Focus: Genetics
Periodical
Journal of Heredity (bi-monthly) . . . 13166

American Geographical Society (AGS), 156 Fifth Av, Ste 600, New York, NY 10010-7002
T: (212) 242-0214; Fax: (212) 989-1583
Founded: 1851; Members: 1800
Focus: Geography
Periodicals
Focus (quarterly)
Geographical Review (quarterly) . . . 13167

American Geological Institute (AGI), 4220 King St, Alexandria, VA 22302-1502
T: (703) 379-2480; Fax: (703) 379-7563
Founded: 1948; Members: 29
Gen Secr: Dr. Marcus E. Milling
Focus: Geology
Periodicals
Bibliography and Index of Geology (monthly)
Earth Science (quarterly)
Geotimes (monthly) . . . 13168

American Geophysical Union (AGU), 2000 Florida Av NW, Washington, DC 20009
T: (202) 462-6900; Fax: (202) 328-0566
Founded: 1919; Members: 30000
Pres: Sean C. Solomon; Gen Secr: A.F. Spilhaus
Focus: Geophys
Periodicals
Earth in Space (7 times annually)
Geophysical Research Letters (monthly)
Global Biogeochemical Cycyles (quarterly)
Journal of Geophysical Research (monthly)
Paleoceanography (bi-monthly)
Planetology Papers (monthly)
Radio Science (bi-monthly)
Reviews of Geophysics and Space Physics (quarterly)
Tectonics (monthly)
Tectonics (bi-monthly)
Water Resources Research (monthly) . . 13169

American Geriatrics Society (AGS), 770 Lexington Av, Ste 300, New York, NY 10021
T: (212) 308-1414; Fax: (212) 832-8646
Founded: 1942; Members: 6022
Pres: Dr. Gregg A. Warshaw; Gen Secr: Linda Hiddemen Barondess
Focus: Geriatrics
Periodicals
Journal (monthly)
Newsletter (bi-monthly) . . . 13170

American Group Practice Association (AGPA), 1422 Duke St, Alexandria, VA 22314
T: (703) 838-0033; Fax: (703) 548-1890
Founded: 1949; Members: 300
Focus: Med
Periodicals
Directory (annually)
Executive News Service (bi-weekly)
Group Practice Journal (bi-monthly) . . . 13171

American Group Psychotherapy Association (AGPA), 25 E 21 St, New York, NY 10010
T: (212) 477-2677; Fax: (212) 979-6627
Founded: 1942; Members: 3500
Focus: Therapeutics
Periodicals
International Journal of Group Psychotherapy (quarterly)
Membership Directory (bi-annually)
Newsletter (quarterly) . . . 13172

American Guild of Hypnotherapists (AGH), 2200 Veterans Blvd, Ste 108, Kenner, LA 70062-4005
T: (504) 468-3223; Fax: (504) 468-3213
Founded: 1975; Members: 984
Pres: Reg Sheldrick
Focus: Psych
Periodical
American Journal of Hypnotherapy (quarterly) . . . 13173

American Gynecological and Obstetrical Society (AGOS), c/o University of Virginia, Charlottesville, VA 22908
Founded: 1993; Members: 335
Gen Secr: Dr. Paul B. Underwood
Focus: Gynecology
Periodical
Transactions (annually) . . . 13174

American Harp Society (AHS), c/o Jane Weldensaul, 1874 Academy Ln, Teaneck, NJ 07666-2112
T: (201) 836-8909
Founded: 1962; Members: 3300
Gen Secr: Jane Weldensaul
Focus: Music
Periodical
American Harp Journal (semi-annually) . 13175

American Health Information Management Association, 919 N Michigan Av, Ste 1400, Chicago, IL 60690
T: (312) 787-2672
Founded: 1928; Members: 31000
Focus: Med
Periodicals
The Gavel (quarterly)
Journal (monthly) . . . 13176

American Health Planning Association (AHPA), 7245 Arlington Blvd, Ste 300, Falls Church, VA 22042
T: (202) 371-1515; Fax: (202) 887-0812
Founded: 1970
Gen Secr: Dean Montgomery
Focus: Public Health
Periodicals
Directory of State and Local Health Planning Agencies
Today in Health Planning (bi-weekly) . . 13177

American Hearing Research Foundation (AHRF), 55 E Washington St, Ste 2022, Chicago, IL 60602
T: (312) 726-9670
Founded: 1956; Members: 1585
Focus: Pathology
Periodicals
Newsletter (quarterly)
Progress Report (semi-annually) . . . 13178

American Heart Association (AHA), 7272 Greenville Av, Dallas, TX 75231
T: (214) 373-6300; Fax: (214) 706-1341
Founded: 1924; Members: 3629000
Gen Secr: Dudley H. Hafner
Focus: Cardiol
Periodicals
Arteriosclerosis and Trombosis
Cardiovascular Nursing
Circulation
Circulation Research
Current Concepts
Heart Disease and Stroke (bi-monthly)
Hypertension
Stroke . . . 13179

American Herb Association (AHA), POB 1673, Nevada City, CA 95959
T: (916) 265-9552
Founded: 1981; Members: 1000
Gen Secr: Kathi Keville
Focus: Botany
Periodicals
Herb Gardens of the U.S. (semi-annually)
Newsletter (quarterly) . . . 13180

American Historical Association (AHA), 400 A St SE, Washington, DC 20003
T: (202) 544-2422; Fax: (202) 544-8307
Founded: 1884; Members: 16000
Gen Secr: Sandria B. Freitag
Focus: Hist
Periodicals
AHA Perspectives: Newsletter (9 times annually)
American Historical Review (8 times annually)
Recently Published Articles (3 times annually) . . . 13181

American Historical Society of Germans from Russia (AHSGR), 631 D St, Lincoln, NE 68502-1199
T: (402) 474-3363
Founded: 1968; Members: 6000
Focus: Folklore; Genealogy
Periodicals
Journal (quarterly)
Newsletter (quarterly) . . . 13182

American Hobbit Association (AHA), POB 51, Mason, OH 45040
T: (513) 398-4742
Founded: 1977; Members: 175
Gen Secr: Renee A. Alper
Focus: Lit
Periodical
The Rivendell Review (quarterly) . . . 13183

American Holistic Medical Association (AHMA), 4101 Lake Boone Tr, Ste 201, Raleigh, NC 27607
T: (919) 787-5181; Fax: (919) 787-4916
Founded: 1978; Members: 500
Gen Secr: Susan Kruse
Focus: Lit
Periodical
Holistic Medicine (bi-monthly) . . . 13184

American Holistic Medical Foundation (AHMF), 4101 Lake Boone Tr, Ste 201, Raleigh, NC 27607
T: (919) 787-5181; Fax: (919) 787-4916
Founded: 1974; Members: 450
Gen Secr: Susan Kruse
Focus: Med
Periodical
Holistic Medicine (bi-monthly) . . . 13185

American Horticultural Society (AHS), 600 Cameron St, Alexandria, VA 22314-2562
T: (703) 836-4606; Fax: (703) 836-2024
Founded: 1903; Members: 5000
Focus: Hort
Periodical
American Horticulturist (monthly) . . . 13186

American Horticultural Therapy Association (AHTA), 362A Christopher Av, Gaithersburg, MD 20879
T: (301) 948-3010
Founded: 1973; Members: 691
Focus: Therapeutics; Rehabil; Hort
Periodicals
Journal of Therapeutic Horticulture (annually)
People Plant Connection (11 times annually) . . . 13187

American Hospital Association (AHA), 1 N Franklin, Chicago, IL 60606
T: (312) 422-3000
Founded: 1898; Members: 44500
Pres: Richard J. Davidson
Focus: Public Health
Periodicals
AHA News (weekly)
Cross Reference (The Hospital Manager)
Discharge Planning Update
Hospital Literature Index
Hospital Technology Alerts
Hospitals and Health Networks (bi-weekly)
Infection Control Digest
Medical Staff Forum
Outreach
Trustee (monthly) 13188

American Hungarian Educators' Association (AHEA), c/o Eniko Molnar Basa, 707 Snider Ln, Silver Spring, MD 20905
T: (301) 384-4657
Founded: 1975; Members: 250
Focus: Educ
Periodical
The Educator (3 times annually) 13189

American Hungarian Library and Historical Society (AHLHS), 213 E 82 St, New York, NY 10021
T: (212) 744-5298
Founded: 1955; Members: 450
Focus: Hist 13190

American Indian Culture Research Center (AICRC), Box 98, Blue Cloud Abbey, Marvin, SD 57251
T: (605) 432-5528; Fax: (605) 432-4754
Founded: 1967
Focus: Hist 13191

American Indian Lore Association (AILA), 960 Walhonding Av, Logan, OH 43138
T: (614) 385-7136
Founded: 1957
Focus: Ethnology 13192

American Indian Science and Engineering Society (AISES), 1630 30 St, Ste 301, Boulder, CO 80301
T: (303) 492-8658; Fax: (303) 492-3400
Founded: 1977; Members: 2000
Focus: Eng; Sci
Periodicals
Annual Report (annually)
Science Education Newsletter (quarterly)
Winds of Change (quarterly) 13193

American Industrial Health Council (AIHC), 2001 Pennsylvania Av NW, Ste 760, Washington, DC 20006
T: (202) 833-2131; E-Mail: membershipservice@ainc.com; Fax: (202) 833-2201
Founded: 1977; Members: 47
Gen Secr: Gaylen M. Camera
Focus: Cell Biol & Cancer Res; Public Health
Periodical
Newsletter (quarterly) 13194

American Industrial Hygiene Association (AIHA), 2700 Prosperity Av, Ste 250, Fairfax, VA 22031
T: (703) 849-8888; E-Mail: infonet@aiha.org; Fax: (703) 207-3561
Founded: 1939; Members: 11500
Gen Secr: O. Gordon Banks
Focus: Hygiene
Periodicals
Directory (annually)
Journal (monthly) 13195

American Institute for Conservation of Historic and Artistic Works (AIC), 1717 K St NW, Ste 301, Washington, DC 20006
T: (202) 452-9545; E-Mail: vnyaic@aol.com; Fax: (202) 452-9328
Founded: 1972; Members: 3500
Gen Secr: Sarah Rosenberg
Focus: Hist; Arts
Periodicals
Journal (semi-annually)
Newsletter (bi-monthly) 13196

American Institute for Contemporary German Studies (AICGS), 1400 16 St NW, Ste 420, Washington, DC 20036
T: (202) 332-9312; Fax: (202) 265-9531
Founded: 1983; Members: 100
Gen Secr: J. Janes
Focus: Ling 13197

American Institute for CPCU, 720 Providence Rd, POB 3016, Malvern, PA 19355-0716
T: (610) 644-2100; Fax: (610) 640-9576
Founded: 1942; Members: 900
Pres: Dr. N.A. Baglini
Focus: Insurance
Periodical
Institute Insights (semi-annually) 13198

American Institute for Economic Research (AIER), Great Barrington, MA 01230
T: (413) 528-1216
Founded: 1933; Members: 8000
Focus: Econ
Periodicals
Economic Education Bulletin (monthly)
Research Report (bi-weekly) 13199

American Institute for Foreign Study (AIFS), 102 Greeenwich Av, Greenwich, CT 06830
T: (203) 869-9090; Fax: (203) 869-1173
Founded: 1964; Members: 300000
Focus: Educ 13200

American Institute for Maghreb Studies, c/o School of Advanced International Studies, The Johns Hopkins Univ., 1740 Massachusetts Av NW, Washington, DC 20036
T: (202) 663-5680; Fax: (202) 663-5683
Gen Secr: Dr. William Zartman
Focus: Geography 13201

American Institute for Patristic and Byzantine Studies (AIPBS), R.R. 1, Box 353A, Minuet Ln, Kingston, NY 12401
T: (915) 336-8797
Founded: 1967; Members: 390
Focus: Cultur Hist 13202

American Institute for Verdi Studies (AIVS), c/o Dept of Music, Faculty of Arts and Science, New York University, 24 Waverly Pl, Rm 268, New York, NY 10003
T: (212) 998-2587; Fax: (212) 995-4147
Founded: 1976; Members: 300
Focus: Music
Periodical
Verdi Newsletter (annually) 13203

American Institute of Aeronautics and Astronautics (AIAA), 370 L'Enfant Promenade SW, Washington, DC 20024-2518
T: (202) 646-7400; Fax: (202) 646-7508
Founded: 1930; Members: 45000
Pres: Robert A. Fuhrman; Gen Secr: C. Durocher
Focus: Aero
Periodicals
Aerospace America (monthly)
AIAA Journal (monthly)
International Aerospace Abstracts (bi-weekly)
Journal of Aircraft (bi-monthly)
Journal of Guidance, Control and Dynamics (bi-monthly)
Journal of Propulsion and Power (bi-monthly)
Journal of Spacecraft and Rockets (bi-monthly)
Journal of Thermophysics and Heat Transfer (quarterly) 13204

American Institute of Architects (AIA), 1735 New York Av NW, Washington, DC 20006
T: (202) 626-7300; Fax: (202) 626-7426
Founded: 1857; Members: 54000
Gen Secr: Terrence M. McDermott
Focus: Archit
Periodical
Memo 13205

American Institute of Biological Sciences (AIBS), 730 11 St NW, Washington, DC 20001-4521
T: (202) 628-1500; Fax: (202) 628-1509
Founded: 1947; Members: 6940
Pres: W. Hardy Eshbaugh; Gen Secr: Clifford J. Gabriel
Focus: Bio
Periodicals
BioScience (monthly)
Forum (bi-monthly)
Membership Directory (semi-annually) . . 13206

American Institute of Biomedical Climatology (AIBC), 313 S 17 St, Philadelphia, PA 19103
T: (215) 968-9296; E-Mail: zgwkking@mail.comcat.com
Founded: 1958; Members: 48
Gen Secr: Richmond G. Kent
Focus: Bio
Periodical
ABC Bulletin (quarterly) 13207

American Institute of Building Design (AIBD), 991 Post Rd E, Westport, CT 06880
T: (203) 227-3640; Fax: (203) 227-8624
Founded: 1950; Members: 1200
Gen Secr: Tammy Crosby
Focus: Civil Eng; Archit
Periodicals
Bulletin
Professional Designers Newsletter (quarterly)
Roster of Members (annually) 13208

American Institute of Chemical Engineers (AIChE), 345 E 47 St, New York, NY 10017
T: (800) 242-4363; Fax: (212) 752-3294
Founded: 1908; Members: 57000
Pres: Basil Doumas; Gen Secr: Dr. Glenn Taylor
Focus: Chem
Periodicals
Chemical Engineering Progress (monthly)
Environmental Progress (quarterly)
International Chemical Engineering (quarterly)
Plant/Operations Progress (quarterly) . . 13209

American Institute of Chemists (AIC), 501 White St, Alexandria, VA 22314-1917
T: (703) 836-2090; Fax: (703) 836-2091
Founded: 1923; Members: 6000
Pres: Roger R. Festa; Gen Secr: Sharon Dobson
Focus: Chem
Periodicals
The Chemist (9 times annually)
Professional Directory (annually) 13210

American Institute of Constructors (AIC), 466 94 Av, Saint Petersburg, FL 33702
T: (813) 578-0317; Fax: (813) 578-9982
Founded: 1971; Members: 1600

Gen Secr: Cheryl P. Harris
Focus: Civil Eng
Periodicals
American Professional Constructor (semi-annually)
Register (bi-annually) 13211

American Institute of Graphic Arts (AIGA), 164 Fifth Av, New York, NY 10010
T: (212) 807-1990; Fax: (212) 807-1799
Founded: 1914; Members: 6700
Gen Secr: Richard Grefe
Focus: Graphic & Dec Arts, Design
Periodical
AIGA Journal of Graphic Design (monthly) 13212

American Institute of Homeopathy (AIH), 925 E 17 Av, Denver, CO 80218-1407
Founded: 1844; Members: 160
Gen Secr: Karen Kaiser Nossaman
Focus: Homeopathy
Periodicals
Journal of the American Institute of Homeopathy (quarterly)
Newsletter (monthly) 13213

American Institute of Indian Studies (AILS), 1130 E 59 St, Rm 412, Chicago, IL 60637
T: (312) 702-8638
Founded: 1961; Members: 47
Focus: Ethnology
Periodicals
Annual Report (annually)
Ethnomusicology Newsletter 13214

American Institute of Iranian Studies (AIIS), c/o Dr. Marilyn R. Waldman, 106 Dulles Hall, Ohio State University, 230 W 17 Av, Columbus, OH 43210-1311
T: (614) 292-1265; Fax: (614) 292-2282
Founded: 1967; Members: 20
Focus: Ethnology
Periodical
Newsletter 13215

American Institute of Islamic Studies (AIIS), POB 100398, Denver, CO 80250
T: (303) 936-0108
Founded: 1965
Focus: Ethnology; Hist; Rel & Theol . . 13216

American Institute of Life Threatening Illness and Loss (FT), 630 W 168 St, New York, NY 10032
T: (212) 928-2066
Founded: 1967; Members: 400
Focus: Psychiatry 13217

American Institute of Management (AIM), POB 7039, Quincy, MA 02269
T: (617) 472-0277
Founded: 1948; Members: 1500
Focus: Business Admin
Periodicals
The Associates Digest (monthly)
The Executive Counselor (monthly)
The Institute Bulletin (irregularly)
National Biographies
The Presidents Journal (monthly) . . . 13218

American Institute of Mining, Metallurgical and Petroleum Engineers (AIME), 345 E 47 St, New York, NY 10017
T: (212) 705-7695; Fax: (212) 371-9622
Founded: 1871; Members: 73000
Gen Secr: Robert H. Marchum
Focus: Mining 13219

American Institute of Musical Studies (AIMS), 6621 Snider Plaza, Dallas, TX 75205-1351
T: (214) 363-2683; Fax: (214) 363-6474
Founded: 1969
Gen Secr: Nora Sands
Focus: Music
Periodical
AIMS Bulletin (bi-annually) 13220

American Institute of Nutrition (AIN), 9650 Rockville Pike, Bethesda, MD 20814
T: (301) 530-7050; Fax: (301) 571-1892
Founded: 1928; Members: 3100
Pres: J. Dwyer; Gen Secr: Martin. R.J.
Focus: Nutrition
Periodical
The Journal of Nutrition (monthly) . . . 13221

American Institute of Oral Biology (AIOB), POB 7184, Loma Linda, CA 92354-7184
T: (909) 824-4671; Fax: (909) 824-4211
Founded: 1943; Members: 150
Gen Secr: June J. Barrientos
Focus: Dent 13222

American Institute of Parliamentarians (AIP), 10535 Metropolitan Av, Kensington, MD 20895-2627
T: (301) 946-9220; Fax: (301) 949-5255
Founded: 1958; Members: 1350
Gen Secr: Veda J. Price
Focus: Poli Sci
Periodical
Parliamentary Journal (quarterly) 13223

American Institute of Physics (AIP), 335 E 45 St, New York, NY 10017
T: (212) 661-9404; Fax: (212) 949-0473
Founded: 1931; Members: 95600
Gen Secr: Kenneth W. Ford
Focus: Physics

Periodicals
The Astronomical Journal (monthly)
Current Physics Index (quarterly)
Journal of Applied Physics: Microfiche Edition (bi-weekly)
Journal of Chemical Physics: Microfiche Edition (bi-weekly)
Journal of Lightware Technology: Microfiche Edition (quarterly)
Journal of Physical and Reference Data (quarterly)
Journal of Vacuum Science and Technology A&B (8 times annually)
Mathematical Physics: Microfiche Edition (monthly)
Medical Physics (quarterly)
Optics Letters: Microfiche Edition (annually)
Optics News (bi-monthly)
Physical Review A, B, C, D: Microfiche Edition(s) (72 times annually)
Physical Review Abstracts (bi-weekly)
Physical Review Letters: Microfiche Edition (52 times annually)
Physics Briefs (bi-weekly)
Physics Briefs of Fluids: Microfiche Edition (monthly)
Physics Today: Microfiche Edition (monthly)
Reviews of Modern Physics: Microfiche Edition (quarterly)
Reviews of Scientific Instruments: Microfiche Edition (monthly) 13224

American Institute of Plant Engineers (AIPE), 8180 Corporate Paril Dr, Ste 306, Cincinnati, OH 45242
T: (513) 489-2473; Fax: (513) 247-7422
Founded: 1954; Members: 10000
Focus: Eng
Periodical
AIPE Facilities Management, Operations and Engineering (bi-monthly) 13225

American Institute of Steel Construction (AISC), 1 E Wacker Dr, Ste 3100, Chicago, IL 60601-2001
T: (312) 670-2400; Fax: (312) 670-5403
Founded: 1921; Members: 2512
Focus: Civil Eng
Periodical
Engineering Journal (quarterly) 13226

American Institute of the History of Pharmacy (AIHP), Pharmacy Bldg, 425 N Charter St, Madison, WI 53706
T: (608) 262-5378
Founded: 1941; Members: 1000
Gen Secr: Gregory J. Higby
Focus: Pharmacol; Cultur Hist
Periodical
Pharmacy in History (quarterly) 13227

American Institute of Timber Construction (AITC), 7012 S Revere Pky, Ste 140, Englewood, CO 80112
T: (303) 792-9559; Fax: (303) 792-0669
Founded: 1952; Members: 400
Gen Secr: Matthew Mathias
Focus: Eng
Periodical
Lam Lines (quarterly) 13228

American Institute of Ultrasound in Medicine (AIUM), 14750 Sweetzer Ln, Ste 100, Laurel, MD 20707-5906
T: (301) 498-4100; Fax: (301) 498-4450
Founded: 1951; Members: 11000
Gen Secr: James S. Packer
Focus: Med
Periodicals
AIUM Newsletter (monthly)
Journal of Ultrasound in Medicine (monthly)
Membership Directory (bi-annually)
Scientific Proceedings (irregularly) . . . 13229

American Institutes for Research in the Behavioral Sciences (AIR), 3333 K St NW, Ste 300, Washington, DC 20007
T: (202) 342-5000; Fax: (202) 342-5033
Founded: 1946
Pres: Dr. David A. Goslin
Focus: Behav Sci 13230

American Intellectual Property Law Association (AIPLA), 2001 Jefferson Davis Hwy, Ste 203, Arlington, VA 22202
T: (703) 415-0780; Fax: (703) 415-0786
Founded: 1897; Members: 7200
Focus: Law 13231

American Irish Historical Society (AIHS), 991 Fifth Av, New York, NY 10028
T: (212) 288-2263; Fax: (212) 628-7927
Founded: 1897; Members: 800
Gen Secr: Paul Ruppert
Focus: Hist
Periodical
The Recorder (semi-annually) 13232

American Iron and Steel Institute (AISI), 1101 17 St NW, Washington, DC 20036
T: (202) 452-7100; Fax: (202) 463-6573
Founded: 1908; Members: 2000
Pres: Andrew G. Sharkey
Focus: Metallurgy 13233

American Italian Historical Association (AIHA00), 209 Flagg Pl, Staten Island, NY 10304
T: (718) 667-6628
Founded: 1966; Members: 500
Focus: Hist

Periodical
Newsletter (quarterly) 13234

American Jewish Historical Society (AJHS), 2 Thornton Rd, Waltham, MA 02154
T: (617) 891-8110; Fax: (617) 899-9208
Founded: 1892; Members: 3200
Pres: Justin L. Wyner; Gen Secr: Michael J. Feldberg
Focus: Hist
Periodicals
American Jewish History (quarterly)
Heritage (bi-annually) 13235

American Joint Committee on Cancer (AJCC), 55 E Erie St, Chicago, IL 60611
T: (312) 664-4050; Fax: (312) 440-7144
Founded: 1959; Members: 40
Focus: Cell Biol & Cancer Res 13236

American Judges Association (AJA), 300 Newport Av, Williamsburg, VA 23187-8798
T: (804) 259-1841; Fax: (804) 229-7899
Founded: 1959; Members: 3000
Gen Secr: Shelley R. Rockwell
Focus: Law
Periodical
Court Review (quarterly) 13237

American Judicature Society (AJS), 180 N Michigan Av, Ste 600, Chicago, IL 60601
T: (312) 558-6900; Fax: (312) 558-9175
Founded: 1913; Members: 10000
Gen Secr: Frances K. Zemans
Focus: Law
Periodical
Judicature (bi-monthly) 13238

American Kinesiotherapy Association, POB 614, Wheeling, IL 60090-0614
Founded: 1946; Members: 450
Gen Secr: Carol A. Holsman
Focus: Rehabil
Periodical
Journal (bi-monthly) 13239

American Laryngological Association (ALA), c/o Children's Hospital, 300 Longwood Av, Boston, MA 02115
T: (617) 355-6417; Fax: (617) 735-8041
Founded: 1879; Members: 190
Gen Secr: Gerald B. Healy
Focus: Otorhinolaryngology; Surgery
Periodical
Transactions (annually) 13240

American Laryngological, Rhinological and Otological Society (ALROS), 10 S Broadway, Ste 1401, Saint Louis, MO 63102
T: (314) 621-6550; Fax: (314) 621-6688
Founded: 1895; Members: 750
Gen Secr: Dr. Robert H. Miller
Focus: Otorhinolaryngology 13241

American Law Institute (ALI), 4025 Chestnut St, Philadelphia, PA 19104
T: (215) 243-1600; Fax: (215) 243-1664
Founded: 1923; Members: 3685
Pres: Charles Alan Wright; Gen Secr: Geoffrey C. Hazard
Focus: Law
Periodical
Proceedings of Annual Meetings (annually) 13242

American Leather Chemists Association (ALCA), c/o University of Cincinnati, POB 210014, Cincinnati, OH 45221-0014
T: (513) 556-1197
Founded: 1903; Members: 700
Gen Secr: Velma Becker
Focus: Chem
Periodical
Journal of the American Leather Chemists Association (monthly) 13243

American Legal Studies Association (ALSA), c/o Program in Law, Policy and Society, Northeastern University, 341 Cushing Hall, Boston, MA 02115
T: (617) 437-5211; Fax: (617) 437-4691
Founded: 1975; Members: 427
Focus: Law
Periodical
Legal Studies Forum: A Journal of Interdisciplinary Legal Studies (quarterly) 13244

American Leprosy Missions (ALM), 1 ALM Way, Greenville, SC 29601
T: (803) 271-7040; Fax: (803) 271-7062
Founded: 1906
Focus: Derm
Periodical
Word and Deed (quarterly) 13245

American Library Association (ALA), 50 E Huron St, Chicago, IL 60611
T: (312) 944-6780; Fax: (312) 440-a9374
Founded: 1876; Members: 55000
Gen Secr: Elizabeth Martinez
Focus: Libraries & Bk Sci
Periodicals
ALA Handbook of Organization and Membership Directory (annually)
American Libraries (monthly)
Booklist (bi-weekly)
Choice (11 times annually)
Library Video Magazine (quarterly)
Washington Newsletter (monthly) 13246

American Library Trustee Association (ALTA), 50 E Huron St, Chicago, IL 60611
T: (312) 280-2161; Fax: (312) 280-3257
Founded: 1890; Members: 1880
Focus: Libraries & Bk Sci
Periodicals
Newsletter (bi-monthly)
Trustee Digest (quarterly) 13247

American Liszt Society (ALS), c/o Fernando Laires, 210 Devonshire Dr, Rochester, NY 14625-1905
T: (716) 586-9922; Fax: (716) 381-1144
Founded: 1964; Members: 550
Focus: Music
Periodicals
Journal of the American Liszt Society (semi-annually)
Newsletter of the American Liszt Society (semi-annually) 13248

American Literary Translators Association (ALTA), c/o University of Texas at Dallas, POB 830688, Richardson, TX 75083-0688
T: (214) 690-2093; Fax: (214) 690-2989
Founded: 1978; Members: 1000
Focus: Lit
Periodicals
Newsletter (quarterly)
Translation Review (3 times annually) . . 13249

American Littoral Society (ALS), c/o Sandy Hook, Highlands, NJ 07732
T: (908) 291-0055
Founded: 1961; Members: 9000
Focus: Zoology
Periodicals
Coastal Reporter (quarterly)
Underwater Naturalist (quarterly) 13250

American Longevity Association (ALA), 1000 W Carson St, Torrance, CA 90509
T: (310) 544-7057
Founded: 1980
Focus: Geriatrics
Periodical
Longevity Letter (monthly) 13251

American Lunar Society (ALS), POB 209, East Pittsburgh, PA 15112
T: (412) 829-0399
Founded: 1982; Members: 120
Pres: David O. Darling
Focus: Astronomy
Periodical
Selenology (quarterly) 13252

American Lung Association (ALA), 1740 Broadway, New York, NY 10019-4374
T: (212) 315-8700; Fax: (212) 265-5642
Founded: 1904; Members: 11000
Gen Secr: Marilyn Hansen
Focus: Pulmon Dis
Periodicals
American Journal of Respiratory and Critical Care Medicine (monthly)
American Journal of Respiratory Cell and Molecular Biology (monthly) 13253

The American Malacological Union (AMU), c/o Dept of Zoology, University of Rhode Island, Kingston, Ri 02881
Founded: 1931; Members: 750
Pres: Robert C. Bullock; Gen Secr: Richard E. Petit
Focus: Zoology
Periodicals
American Malacological Bulletin (semi-annually)
Membership List (annually)
Newsletter (semi-annually) 13254

American Management Association International, 135 W 50 St, New York, NY 10020
T: (212) 586-8100; Fax: (212) 581 6538
Founded: 1923; Members: 70000
Focus: Business Admin
Periodicals
Comp Flash (monthly)
Compensation and Benefits Review (bi-monthly)
Management Review (monthly)
The President (monthly) 13255

American Marketing Association (AMA), 250 S Wacker Dr, Ste 200, Chicago, IL 60606
T: (312) 648-0536; Fax: (312) 993-7542
Founded: 1915; Members: 53000
Focus: Marketing
Periodicals
AMA Annual Membership Roster & International Buyers' Guide (annually)
Journal of Marketing (quarterly)
Journal of Marketing Research (quarterly)
Marketing News (bi-weekly) 13256

American Massage Therapy Association (AMTA), 820 Davis St, Ste 100, Evanston, IL 60201-4444
T: (708) 864-0123; Fax: (708) 864-1178
Founded: 1943; Members: 22000
Focus: Therapeutics
Periodicals
Massage Journal (quarterly)
Yearbook and Registry 13257

American Mathematical Association of Two Year Colleges (AMATYC), c/o State Technical Institute at Memphis, 5983 Macon Cove, Memphis, TN 38134
T: (901) 383-4643; E-Mail: amatyc@stim.tec.tn.us; Fax: (901) 383-4503
Founded: 1974; Members: 2800
Pres: Wanda Garmer
Focus: Math; Educ
Periodicals
AMATYC News (3 times annually)
AMATYC Review (semi-annually)
Annual Developmental Mathematics Committee Report (annually)
Newsletter (semi-annually) 13258

American Mathematical Society (AMS), POB 6248, Providence, RI 02940
T: (401) 455-4000; Fax: (401) 331-3842
Founded: 1888; Members: 27000
Gen Secr: John Ewing
Focus: Math
Periodicals
Abstracts of Papers Presented to the American Mathematical Society (7 times annually)
Bulletin of the American Mathematical Society (quarterly)
Current Mathematical Publications (bi-weekly)
Journal of the American Mathematical Society (quarterly)
Mathematical Reviews (monthly)
Mathematics of Computation (quarterly)
Memoirs (bi-monthly)
Notices (8 times annually)
Proceedings of the American Mathematical Society (monthly)
Transactions (monthly) 13259

American Matthay Association (AMA), c/o David Watkins, 168 Lake Forest Dr, Acworth, GA 30102
Founded: 1925; Members: 170
Pres: David Watkins
Focus: Music
Periodical
Matthay News (semi-annually) 13260

American Meat Science Association (AMSA), c/o National Live Stock and Meat Board, 444 N Michigan Av, Chicago, IL 60611
T: (312) 467-5520
Founded: 1964; Members: 900
Focus: Food
Periodical
Proceedings of Reciprocal Meat Conference (annually) 13261

American Medical Associaction Auxiliary (AMAA), 515 N State St, Chicago, IL 60610-0174
T: (312) 464-4470; Fax: (312) 464-5838
Founded: 1922; Members: 70000
Gen Secr: Hazel J. Lewis
Focus: Public Health
Periodical
Facets (monthly) 13262

American Medical Association (AMA), 515 N State St, Chicago, IL 60610-4377
T: (312) 464-5000
Founded: 1847; Members: 296000
Gen Secr: Dr. P. John Seward
Focus: Med
Periodicals
American Medical News (weekly)
Archives of Dermatology (monthly)
Archives of General Psychiatry (monthly)
Archives of Internal Medicine (monthly)
Archives of Neurology (monthly)
Archives of Ophthalmology (monthly)
Archives of Otolaryngology, Head & Neck Surgery (monthly)
Archives of Pathology & Laboratory Medicine (monthly)
Archives of Surgery (monthly)
JAMA: The Journal of the American Medical Association (weekly) 13263

American Medical Association Education and Research Foundation (AMA-ERF), 515 N State St, Chicago, IL 60610
T: (312) 464-5000; Fax: (312) 464-4184
Founded: 1962
Focus: Educ; Med 13264

American Medical Electroencephalographic Association (AMEEGA), 850 Elm Grove Rd, Elm Grove, WI 53122
T: (414) 797-7800; Fax: (414) 782-8788
Founded: 1964; Members: 850
Focus: Neurology
Periodical
Clinical EEG (quarterly) 13265

American Medical Fly Fishing Association (AMFFA), c/o Veryl Frye, POB 768, Lock Haven, PA 17745
T: (717) 769-7375
Founded: 1969; Members: 220
Focus: Ecology; Med 13266

American Medical Informatics Association (AMIA), 4915 Saint Elmo Av, Ste 302, Bethesda, MD 20814
T: (301) 657-1291
Founded: 1981; Members: 850
Focus: Med; Computer & Info Sci
Periodical
Proceedings (semi-annually) 13267

American Medical Technologists (AMT), 710 Higgins Rd, Park Ridge, IL 60068
T: (708) 823-5169; Fax: (708) 823-0458
Founded: 1939; Members: 29000
Pres: Linda Cromeans
Focus: Med
Periodicals
AMT Events (quarterly)
Journal (bi-monthly) 13268

American Medical Women's Association (AMWA), 801 N Fairfax St, Ste 400, Alexandria, VA 22314
T: (703) 838-0500; Fax: (703) 549-3864
Founded: 1915; Members: 11000
Focus: Med
Periodicals
Journal (bi-monthly)
Quarterly Newsletter (quarterly) 13269

American Medical Writers' Association (AMWA), 9650 Rockville Pike, Bethesda, MD 20814-3998
T: (301) 493-0003; Fax: (301) 493-0005
Founded: 1940; Members: 3700
Focus: Lit; Med
Periodicals
AMWA Freelance Directory of Medical Communication Services (annually)
AMWA Journal (quarterly)
AMWA Membership Directory (annually) . 13270

American Mensa, 201 Main St, Ste 1101, Fort Worth, TX 76102
T: (817) 332-2600; Fax: (817) 332-7299
Founded: 1960; Members: 45000
Gen Secr: Dorothy Bloom
Focus: Philos
Periodical
Mensa Research Journal (3 times annually) 13271

American Merchant Marine Library Association (AMMLA), 1 World Trade Center, Ste 2161, New York, NY 10048
T: (212) 775-1038; Fax: (212) 432-5492
Founded: 1921
Focus: Libraries & Bk Sci
Periodical
AMMLA Annual Report (annually) . . . 13272

American Meteor Society (AMS), c/o Dept of Physics and Astronomy, SUNY-Geneseo, 1 College Cir, Geneseo, NY 14454
T: (716) 245-5282; E-Mail: meisel@uno.cc.geneseo.edu; Fax: (716) 245-5288
Founded: 1911; Members: 100
Gen Secr: David D. Meisel
Focus: Geophys
Periodicals
Annual Report (annually)
Meteor News (quarterly) 13273

American Meteorological Society (AMS), 45 Beacon St, Boston, MA 02108
T: (617) 227-2425; Fax: (617) 742-8718
Founded: 1919; Members: 11000
Pres: Paul D. Try; Gen Secr: Dr. Richard E. Hallgren
Focus: Geophys
Periodicals
AMS Newsletter
Bulletin (monthly)
Journal of Applied Meteorology (monthly)
Journal of Atmospheric and Oceanic Technology (bi-monthly)
Journal of Climate (monthly)
Journal of Physical Oceanography (monthly)
Journal of the Atmospheric Sciences (bi-weekly)
Meteorological and Geoastrophysical Abstracts (monthly)
Monthly Weather Review (monthly)
Weather and Forecasting (quarterly) . . 13274

American Microchemical Society (AMS), c/o Leonard Klein, FMC Corp, POB 8, Princeton, NJ 08543
T: (609) 951-3422; Fax: (609) 951-3809
Founded: 1935; Members: 150
Focus: Chem
Periodical
Microchemical Journal (bi-monthly) . . . 13275

American Microscopical Society (AMS), c/o Dept of Biology, Washington College, Chestertown, MD 21620
T: (410) 778-2800; Fax: (410) 778-0151
Founded: 1878; Members: 695
Focus: Electronic Eng
Periodical
Invertebrate Biology (quarterly) 13276

American Montessori Society (AMS), 150 Fifth Av, Ste 203, New York, NY 10011
T: (212) 924-3209
Founded: 1960; Members: 12000
Focus: Educ
Periodicals
Annual Report (annually)
Constructive Triangle (quarterly)
School Directory (annually) 13277

American Mosquito Control Association (AMCA), POB 5416, Lake Charles, LA 70606
T: (318) 474-2723; Fax: (318) 478-9434
Founded: 2000; Members: 2000
Focus: Entomology
Periodicals
Mosquito News Journal of the American Mosquito Control Association (quarterly)
Mosquito Systematics (3 times annually) . 13278

American Music Conference (AMC), 5140 Av Encinas, Carlsbad, CA 92008-4391
T: (619) 431-9124; Fax: (619) 438-7327
Founded: 1947; Members: 175
Focus: Music
Periodical
Music USA-Industry Statistics (annually) . 13279

American Musical Instrument Society (AMIS), c/o Albert R. Rice, 1664 Corbin Av, Tarzana, CA 91356-1011
T: (818) 776-9446; E-Mail: al-rice@cvcmail.claremont.edu; Fax: (818) 471-1278
Founded: 1971; Members: 850
Gen Secr: Albert R. Rice
Focus: Music
Periodicals
Journal (annually)
Membership Directory (annually)
Newsletter (3 times annually) 13280

The American Musicological Society (AMS), c/o University of Pennsylvania, 201 S 34 St, Philadelphia, PA 19104-6313
T: (215) 898-8698
Founded: 1934; Members: 3500
Focus: Music
Periodicals
Directory (annually)
Newsletter (semi-annually) 13281

American Name Society (ANS), c/o Dept of Modern Languages and Comparative Literature, Baruch College, 17 Lexington Av, Box G-1224, New York, NY 10010-5526
T: (212) 387-1570; Fax: (212) 387-1591
Founded: 1951; Members: 900
Gen Secr: Prof. Wayne H. Finke
Focus: Ling
Periodical
Names (quarterly) 13282

American Naprapathic Association (ANA), c/o Roy P. Krueger, 5913 W Montrose Av, Chicago, IL 60634
T: (312) 685-6020
Founded: 1909; Members: 300
Focus: Med
Periodicals
Directory
The Voice of Naprapathy (quarterly) . . 13283

American National Standards Institute (ANSI), 11 W 42 St, New York, NY 10036
T: (212) 642-4900; Fax: (212) 398-0023
Founded: 1918; Members: 1775
Pres: Sergio Mazza
Focus: Standards
Periodicals
Reporter (monthly)
Standards Action (bi-weekly) 13284

American Natural Hygiene Society (ANHS), POB 30630, Tampa, FL 33630
T: (813) 855-6607
Founded: 1948; Members: 6500
Focus: Hygiene
Periodical
Health Science Magazine (bi-monthly) . . 13285

American Nature Study Society (ANSS), c/o John A. Gustafson, 5881 Cold Brook Rd, Homer, NY 13077
T: (607) 749-3655
Founded: 1908; Members: 850
Focus: Nat Sci
Periodicals
Nature Study (quarterly)
News (irregularly) 13286

American Neurological Association (ANA), 108 Cedar Lake Rd, Office 5841, Minneapolis, MN 55416
T: (612) 545-6284
Founded: 1875; Members: 1000
Pres: Dr. John N. Whitaker; Gen Secr: S. Richard Baringer
Focus: Neurology
Periodicals
Abstract Program (annually)
Annals of Neurology 13287

American Nuclear Society (ANS), 555 N Kensington Av, La Grange Park, IL 60526
T: (312) 352-6611; Fax: (312) 352-0499
Founded: 1954; Members: 14050
Pres: Dr. Alan E. Waltar; Gen Secr: James G. Toscas
Focus: Nucl Res
Periodicals
Fusion Technology (semi-annually)
Nuclear News (monthly)
Nuclear Science & Engineering (monthly)
Nuclear Technology (monthly) 13288

American Numismatic Association (ANA), 818 N Cascade Av, Colorado Springs, CO 80903-3279
T: (719) 632-2646; Fax: (719) 634-4085
Founded: 1891; Members: 30000
Focus: Numismatics
Periodical
The Numismatist (monthly) 13289

American Numismatic Society (ANS), Broadway at 155 St, New York, NY 10032
T: (212) 234-3130; Fax: (212) 234-3381
Founded: 1858; Members: 2077
Pres: Arthur A. Houghton; Gen Secr: Leslie A. Elam
Focus: Numismatics
Periodicals
American Journal of Numismatics (annually)
ANS Museum Notes (annually)
ANS Numismatic Studies (irregularly)
Numismatic Literature (semi-annually)
Numismatic Notes and Monographs (irregularly)
Sylloge Nummorum Graecorum/The Collection of the American Numismatic Society (irregularly)
. . . . 13290

American Occupational Therapy Association (AOTA), 4720 Montgomery Ln, Bethesda, MD 20814
Founded: 1917; Members: 56000
Pres: Mary Foto; Gen Secr: Jeannette Bair
Focus: Adult Educ; Therapeutics
Periodical
American Journal of Occupational Therapy (10 times annually) 13291

American Oil Chemists' Society (AOCS), POB 3489, Champaign, IL 61826-3489
T: (217) 359-2344; Fax: (217) 351-8091
Founded: 1909; Members: 4200
Focus: Chem
Periodicals
Journal: JAOCS (monthly)
Lipids (monthly) 13292

American Ophthalmological Society (AOS), c/o W. Banks Anderson, Eye Center, Duke University, Durham, NC 27710
T: (919) 684-5365
Founded: 1864; Members: 225
Focus: Ophthal
Periodical
Transactions of the American Ophthalmological Society (annually) 13293

American Optometric Association (AOA), 243 N Lindbergh Blvd, Saint Louis, MO 63141
T: (314) 991-4100; Fax: (314) 991-4101
Founded: 1898; Members: 31000
Pres: Dr. T. Joel Byars; Gen Secr: Jeffrey G. Mays
Focus: Ophthal
Periodicals
Journal (quarterly)
News (bi-weekly) 13294

American Orchid Society (AOS), 6000 S Olive Av, West Palm Beach, FL 33405
T: (305) 585-8666; Fax: (305) 585-0654
Founded: 1921; Members: 27000
Focus: Botany 13295

American Oriental Society (AOS), c/o Hatcher Library, Room 111E, University of Michigan, Ann Arbor, MI 48109-1205
T: (313) 747-4760
Founded: 1842; Members: 1350
Pres: Jack M. Sasson; Gen Secr: Jonathan Rodgers
Focus: Ethnology; Hist; Lit; Ling; Arts; Archeol
Periodicals
American Oriental Series
American Oriental Series Essays
Journal (quarterly) 13296

American Ornithologists' Union (AOU), c/o Div of Birds, National Museum of Natural History, Washington, DC 20560
T: (202) 357-2051; Fax: (202) 3571932
Founded: 1883; Members: 5000
Pres: Richard C. Banks; Gen Secr: Mary V. McDonald
Focus: Ornithology
Periodicals
The Autz (quarterly)
Ornithological Monographs (irregularly)
Ornithological Newsletter (bi-monthly) . . 13297

American Orthodontic Society (AOS), 11884 Greenville Av, Dallas, TX 75243-3537
T: (214) 234-4000; Fax: (214) 234-4290
Founded: 1974; Members: 1900
Gen Secr: D. Glenn Whitten
Focus: Dent
Periodicals
Newsletter (quarterly)
Technique Directory 13298

American Orthopaedic Association (AOA), 6300 N River Rd, Ste 300, Rosemont, IL 60018-4263
T: (703) 318-7330
Founded: 1887; Members: 300
Focus: Orthopedics
Periodical
The Manual of Orthopaedic Surgery . . 13299

American Orthopaedic Foot and Ankle Society (AOFAS), 701 16 Av, Seattle, WA 98122
T: (206) 720-1070; Fax: (708) 823-0536
Founded: 1969; Members: 850
Gen Secr: Richard Cantrall
Focus: Orthopedics
Periodicals
In-Stride (quarterly)
Journal of the Foot and Ankle (annually) 13300

American Orthopaedic Society for Sports Medicine (AOSSM), 6300 N River Rd, Ste 200, Rosemont, IL 60018
T: (847) 292-4900; Fax: (847) 292-4905
Founded: 1972; Members: 1100
Pres: Arthur Boland
Focus: Orthopedics
Periodical
American Journal of Sports Medicine (bi-monthly)
. . . . 13301

American Orthopsychiatric Association (AOA), 330 Seventh Av, New York, NY 10001-3010
T: (212) 564-5930; E-Mail: amerortho@aol.com; Fax: (212) 564-6180
Founded: 1924; Members: 5200
Gen Secr: Gale Siegel
Focus: Psychiatry; Psych; Pediatrics; Educ; Soc Sci; Law
Periodical
American Journal of Orthopsychiatry (quarterly)
. . . . 13302

American Orthoptic Council (AOC), c/o Leslie France, 3914 Nakoma Rd, Madison, WI 53711
T: (608) 233-5383; Fax: (608) 263-7694
Members: 19
Focus: Ophthal
Periodical
American Orthoptic Journal (annually) . . 13303

American Orthotic and Prosthetic Association (AOPA), 1650 King St, Ste 500, Alexandria, VA 22314
T: (703) 836-7116; Fax: (703) 836-0838
Founded: 1917; Members: 1250
Focus: Rehabil
Periodicals
Almanac (monthly)
Journal of Orthotics and Prosthetics (quarterly)
. . . . 13304

American Osteopathic Academy of Addictionology, 270 Tavistock, Cherry Hill, NJ 08034-4017
T: (609) 795-0026; Fax: (609) 354-8029
Founded: 1986; Members: 225
Focus: Orthopedics 13305

American Osteopathic Academy of Sclerotherapy (AOAS), 107 Maple Av, Wilmington, DE 19809
T: (302) 792-9280
Founded: 1954; Members: 145
Gen Secr: Judy Wilbank
Focus: Therapeutics; Pathology
Periodical
Get the Point! (semi-annually) 13306

American Osteopathic Academy of Sports Medicine (AOASM), 7611 Elmwood Av, Ste 201, Middleton, WI 53562
T: (608) 831-4400; Fax: (608) 831-5122
Founded: 1975; Members: 750
Focus: Sports; Med
Periodical
Journal of Osteopathic Sports Medicine (quarterly)
. . . . 13307

American Osteopathic Association (AOA), 142 E Ontario St, Chicago, IL 60611
T: (312) 280-5800; Fax: (312) 280-5893
Founded: 1897; Members: 21735
Focus: Pathology
Periodicals
The D.O. (monthly)
Journal of AOA (monthly)
Yearbook & Directory (annually) 13308

American Osteopathic College of Allergy and Immunology (AOCAI), 10140 E Celtic Dr, Scottsdale, AZ 85260-7251
T: (602) 949-8898
Founded: 1975; Members: 70
Gen Secr: William Higgins
Focus: Immunology
Periodical
Newsletter (annually) 13309

American Osteopathic College of Anesthesiologists (AOCA), 17201 E US Hwy 40, Independence, MO 64055
T: (816) 373-4700; Fax: (816) 373-1529
Founded: 1952; Members: 500
Focus: Anesthetics; Pathology
Periodicals
Membership Directory (annually)
Newsletter (3 times annually) 13310

American Osteopathic College of Dermatology (AOCD), POB 7525, Kirksville, MO 63501-7525
T: (816) 665-2184; Fax: (816) 626-2714
Founded: 1955; Members: 220
Gen Secr: Rebecca A. Mansfield
Focus: Derm
Periodicals
Directory (annually)
Newsletter (quarterly) 13311

American Osteopathic College of Pathologists (AOCP), c/o Joan Gross, 12368 NW 13 Ct, Pembroke Pines, FL 33026
T: (305) 432-9640; Fax: (305) 432-9640
Founded: 1954; Members: 180
Focus: Pathology
Periodicals
American Osteopathic College of Pathologists Directory (annually)
Nova (quarterly) 13312

American Osteopathic College of Proctology (AOCPr), 1020 Galloping Hill Rd, Union, NJ 07083
T: (908) 687-2062
Members: 155
Focus: Pathology; Gastroenter 13313

American Osteopathic College of Radiology (AOCR), 119 E Second St, Milan, MO 63556
T: (816) 265-4011; Fax: (816) 265-3494
Founded: 1940; Members: 600
Focus: Educ
Periodical
Viewbox (quarterly) 13314

American Osteopathic College of Rehabilitation Medicine (AOCRM), 9058 W Church, Des Plaines, IL 60016
T: (708) 699-0048; Fax: (708) 296-1366
Founded: 1954; Members: 125
Focus: Rehabil; Pathology
Periodicals
Annual Directory (annually)
Newsletter 13315

American Otological Society (AOS), c/o Loyola University Medical School, 2160 S First Av, Maywood, IL 60153
T: (708) 216-8526; Fax: (919) 748-4204
Founded: 1868; Members: 220
Focus: Otorhinolaryngology
Periodical
Transactions (annually) 13316

American Pancreatic Association (APA), c/o Surgical Service, VA Hospital, 16111 Plummer St, Sepulveda, CA 91343
T: (818) 895-9461; Fax: (818) 895-9535
Founded: 1970; Members: 325
Focus: Gastroenter 13317

American Parkinson Disease Association (APDA), 1250 Hylan Blvd, Ste 4B, Staten Island, NY 10305
T: (718) 981-8001; Fax: (718) 981-4399
Founded: 1961; Members: 2000
Pres: Salvatore J. Esposito Jr.
Focus: Neurology; Psychiatry
Periodicals
Annual Report (annually)
Newsletter (semi-annually) 13318

American Peace Society (APS), 1319 18 St NW, Washington, DC 20036-1802
T: (202) 296-6267
Founded: 1828; Members: 110
Pres: Dr. Evron M. Kirkpatrick; Gen Secr: L. Eugene Hedberg
Focus: Poli Sci
Periodical
World Affairs (quarterly) 13319

American Peanut Research and Education Society (APRES), c/o Oklahoma State University, 376 AG Hall, Stillwater, OK 74078
T: (405) 744-9634; Fax: (405) 744-5269
Founded: 1969; Members: 550
Gen Secr: J.R. Sholar
Focus: Food 13320

American Pediatric Society (APS), POB 14871, Saint Louis, MO 63178
Founded: 1888; Members: 855
Gen Secr: David Goldring
Focus: Pediatrics
Periodicals
Pediatric Research-Program Issue (annually)
Program and Abstracts of Annual Meeting 13321

American Petroleum Institute (API), 1220 L St NW, Washington, DC 20005
T: (202) 682-8000; Fax: (202) 682-8030
Founded: 1919; Members: 250
Focus: Energy
Periodicals
API Report (quarterly)
Directory (annually)
Imported Crude Oil and Petroleum Products (monthly)
Inventories of Natural Gas Liquids and Liquefied Refinery Gases (monthly) 13322

American Pharmaceutical Association (APhA), 2215 Constitution Av NW, Washington, DC 20037
T: (202) 628-4410; Fax: (202) 783-2351
Founded: 1852; Members: 50000
Gen Secr: Dr. John A. Gans
Focus: Pharmacol
Periodicals
Academy Reporter (quarterly)
American Pharmacy (monthly)
Journal of Pharmaceutical Sciences (monthly)
The Pharmacy Student (quarterly)
Pharmacy Today (bi-weekly) 13323

American Philological Association (APA), c/o Dept of Classics, Holy Cross College, Worcester, MA 01610-2395
T: (508) 793-2203; Fax: (508) 793-3428
Founded: 1869; Members: 3000
Gen Secr: William J. Ziobro
Focus: Lit
Periodicals
American Classical Studies (irregularly)
Newsletter (bi-monthly)
Philological Monographs (irregularly)
Textbook Series (irregularly)
Transactions (annually) 13324

American Philosophical Association (APA), c/o University of Delaware, Newark, DE 19716
T: (302) 831-1112; Fax: (302) 831-8690
Founded: 1900; Members: 9000
Pres: Philip L. Quinn; Gen Secr: Erik Hoffman
Focus: Philos

Periodicals
APA Newsletter (semi-annually)
Jobs for Philosophers (5 times annually) 13325

American Philosophical Society (APS), 104 S Fifth St, Philadelphia, PA 19106-3387
T: (215) 440-3400; Fax: (215) 440-3436
Founded: 1743; Members: 720
Pres: Arlin M. Adams; Gen Secr: Herman H. Goldstine
Focus: Hist; Sci; Archeol
Periodicals
Proceedings (quarterly)
Transactions (8 times annually) 13326

American Physical Society (APS), 1 Physics Ellipse, College Park, MD 20740
T: (301) 209-3629; Fax: (301) 209-0865
Founded: 1899; Members: 43000
Pres: Dr. Robert Schrieffer; Gen Secr: Dr. Judy R. Franz
Focus: Physics
Periodicals
Bulletin (monthly)
Membership Directory (bi-annually)
Physical Review (monthly)
Physical Review Letters (weekly)
Reviews of Modern Physics (monthly) 13327

American Physical Therapy Association (APTA), 1111 N Fairfax St, Alexandria, VA 22314
T: (703) 684-2782
Founded: 1921; Members: 68070
Gen Secr: Francis J. Mallon
Focus: Therapeutics
Periodicals
Physical Therapy (monthly)
Physical Therapy Resource and Buyer's Guide (annually)
Progress Report (monthly)
PT – The Magazine of Physical Therapy 13328

American Physicians Association of Computer Medicine (APACM), 10 N Main St, Pittsford, NY 14534
T: (716) 586-8159
Founded: 1984; Members: 350
Focus: Med; Computer & Info Sci 13329

American Physicians Fellowship for Medicine in Israel (APF), 2001 Beacon ST, Brookline, MA 02146
T: (617) 232-5382
Founded: 1950; Members: 8500
Focus: Physiology
Periodicals
Koroth (semi-annually)
News (semi-annually) 13330

American Physiological Society (APS), 9650 Rockville Pike, Bethesda, MD 20814-3991
T: (301) 530-7164; Fax: (301) 571-1814
Founded: 1887; Members: 8250
Gen Secr: Martin Frank
Focus: Physiology
Periodicals
American Journal of Physiology (monthly)
Journal of Applied Physiology (monthly)
Journal of Neurophysiology (monthly)
News in Physiological Sciences (bi-monthly)
Physiological Reviews (quarterly)
The Physiologist (bi-monthly) 13331

American Phytopathological Society (APS), 3340 Pilot Knob Rd, Saint Paul, MN 55121
T: (612) 454-7250; Fax: (612) 454-0766
Founded: 1908; Members: 5000
Pres: Laurence V. Madden; Gen Secr: Steven C. Nelson
Focus: Botany
Periodicals
Biological and Cultural Tests for Control of Plant Diseases (annually)
Molecular Plant-Microbe Interactions (bi-monthly)
Phytopathology (monthly)
Plant Disease (monthly) 13332

American Planning Association (API), 1776 Massachusetts Av NW, Washington, DC 20036
T: (202) 872-0611; Fax: (202) 872-0643
Founded: 1909; Members: 28000
Gen Secr: Michael Barker
Focus: Econ
Periodicals
APA Journal (quarterly)
JobMart (22 times annually)
Land Use Law and Zoning Digest (monthly)
Planning Advisory Service Report (8 times annually)
Planning Magazine (monthly)
Zoning News (monthly) 13333

American Podiatric Medical Association (APMA), 9312 Old Georgetown Rd, Bethesda, MD 20814
T: (301) 571-9200; Fax: (301) 530-2752
Founded: 1912; Members: 9200
Focus: Orthopedics
Periodicals
Journal (monthly)
News (monthly) 13334

American Polar Society (APS), c/o Brian Shoemaker, POB 692, Reedsport, OR 97467
T: (503) 759-3589; E-Mail: iceman@presys.com; Fax: (503) 759-3403
Founded: 1934; Members: 2060
Gen Secr: Brian Shoemaker
Focus: Geography
Periodical
The Polar Times (semi-annually) 13335

American Political Science Association (APSA), 1527 New Hampshire Av NW, Washington, DC 20036
T: (202) 483-2512; Fax: (202) 483-2657
Founded: 1903; Members: 14500
Gen Secr: Catherine E. Rudder
Focus: Poli Sci
Periodicals
The American Political Science Review (quarterly)
PS: Political Science and Politics (quarterly) 13336

American Pomological Society (APS), 102 Tyson Bldg, University Park, PA 16802
T: (814) 863-6163; Fax: (814) 863-6139
Founded: 1848; Members: 1000
Gen Secr: Dr. Robert M. Grassweller
Focus: Hort; Food
Periodical
Fruit Varieties Journal (quarterly) 13337

American Poultry Historical Society (APHS), c/o G. Carpenter, Div of Animal and Veterinary Science, University of West Virginia, Agricultural Science Bldg, Morgantown, WV 26506-6108
T: (304) 293-5229; Fax: (304) 293-6954
Founded: 1952; Members: 240
Focus: Agri; Hist
Periodical
Newsletter (quarterly) 13338

American Press Institute (API), 11690 Sunrise Valley Dr, Reston, VA 22091
T: (703) 620-3611; Fax: (703) 620-5814
Focus: Journalism
Periodical
Bulletin (annually) 13339

American Printing History Association (APHA), POB 4922, Grand Central Station, New York, NY 10163
T: (212) 930-9220; Fax: (212) 302-4815
Founded: 1974; Members: 900
Gen Secr: Stephen Crook
Focus: Libraries & Bk Sci; Hist
Periodicals
APHA Newsletter (bi-monthly)
Printing History Journal (semi-annually) 13340

American Prosthodontic Society (APS), 919 N Michigan Av, Ste 460, Chicago, IL 60611
T: (312) 944-7618
Founded: 1928; Members: 1300
Focus: Dent
Periodical
Journal of Prosthetic Dentistry (monthly) 13341

American Psychiatric Association (APA), 1400 K St NW, Washington, DC 20005
T: (202) 682-6000; Fax: (202) 682-6114
Founded: 1844; Members: 40050
Gen Secr: Melvin Sabshin
Focus: Psychiatry
Periodicals
American Journal of Psychiatry (monthly)
American Psychiatric Press Review of Psychiatry (annually)
Hospital & Community Psychiatry (monthly) 13342

American Psychoanalytic Association (APsaA), 309 E 49 St, New York, NY 10017
T: (212) 752-0450; Fax: (212) 593-1571
Founded: 1911; Members: 3025
Focus: Psychiatry
Periodicals
Journal (quarterly)
Newsletter (quarterly) 13343

American Psychological Association (APA), 750 First St NE, Washington, DC 20002-4242
T: (202) 336-5500
Founded: 1892; Members: 142000
Gen Secr: Raymond D. Fowler
Focus: Psych
Periodicals
American Psychologist (monthly)
APA Monitor (monthly)
Behavioral Neuroscience (bi-monthly)
Comparative Psychology and Behavior (quarterly)
Contemporary Psychology (monthly)
Developmental Psychology (bi-monthly)
Journal of Abnormal Psychology (quarterly)
Journal of Applied Psychology (quarterly)
Journal of Consulting and Clinical Psychology (bi-monthly)
Journal of Counseling Psychology (quarterly)
Journal of Educational Psychology (bi-monthly)
Journal of Experiment Psychology: General (quarterly)
Journal of Experimental Psychology: Animal Behavior Processes (quarterly)
Journal of Experimental Psychology: Human Perception and Performance (bi-monthly)
Journal of Experimental Psychology: Learning, Memory and Cognition (quarterly)
Journal of Personality and Social Psychology (monthly)
Professional Psychology (bi-monthly)
Psychological Abstracts (monthly)
Psychological Bulletin (bi-monthly)
Psychological Documents (quarterly)
Psychological Review (quarterly)
PsycSCAN: Applied Psychology (quarterly)
PsycSCAN: Clinical Psychology (quarterly)
PsycSCAN: Development Psychology (quarterly)
PsycSCAN: LD/MR (quarterly)
PsycSCAN Series from PsycINFO (quarterly) 13344

American Psychology-Law Society (AP-LS), c/o Dept of Psychology, Medical College of Pennsylvania/Hehnenman, Broad and Vine Sts, Philadelphia, PA 19102-1192
T: (215) 762-8084
Founded: 1968; Members: 1700
Pres: Kirk Heilbrun
Focus: Psych; Law
Periodicals
Journal of Law and Human Behavior (quarterly)
Newsletter (quarterly) 13345

American Psychopathological Association (APPA), c/o Dept of Psychiatry, Washington University Medical School, 4940 Children's Pl, Saint Louis, MO 63110
T: (314) 362-7005; Fax: (314) 362-5594
Founded: 1912; Members: 500
Gen Secr: Dr. Robert Cloninger
Focus: Psychiatry
Periodicals
Comprehensive Psychiatry (quarterly)
Proceedings of Annual Meeting 13346

American Public Health Association (APHA), 1015 15 St NW, Washington, DC 20005
T: (202) 789-5600; Fax: (202) 789-5661
Founded: 1872; Members: 32000
Gen Secr: Dr. Fernando M. Treviño
Focus: Public Health
Periodicals
American Journal of Public Health (monthly)
The National Health (monthly) 13347

American Quaternary Association (AMQUA), c/o Julie Brigham-Grette, Dept of Geology and Geography, University of Massachusetts, Amherst, MA 01003
T: (413) 545-4840; Fax: (413) 545-1200
Founded: 1969; Members: 1200
Focus: Nat Sci
Periodical
Newsletter (quarterly) 13348

American Quilt Study Group (AQSG), 660 Mission St, Ste 400, San Francisco, CA 94105-4007
T: (415) 495-0163; Fax: (415) 495-3516
Founded: 1980; Members: 900
Gen Secr: Sarah K. Howard
Focus: Hist
Periodical
Blanket Statements (quarterly) 13349

American Radium Society (ARS), 1101 Market St, Philadelphia, PA 19107
T: (215) 574-3179; Fax: (215) 928-0153
Founded: 1916; Members: 850
Focus: Radiology
Periodical
Membership Directory (annually) 13350

American Real Estate and Urban Economics Association (AREUEA), c/o School of Business, Indiana University, Bloomington, IN 47405
T: (812) 855-7794; Fax: (812) 855-8679
Founded: 1965; Members: 1260
Focus: Econ
Periodicals
Journal (quarterly)
Newsletter (semi-annually) 13351

American Registry of Radiologic Technologists (ARRT), 1255 Northland Dr, Mendota Heights, MN 55120
T: (612) 687-0048
Founded: 1922; Members: 186000
Focus: Radiology
Periodical
Annual Directory of Registered Technologists (annually) 13352

American Rehabilitation Association, 1910 Association Dr, Ste 200, Reston, VA 22091
T: (703) 648-9300; Fax: (703) 648-0346
Founded: 1969; Members: 812
Pres: S. Schlossman
Focus: Rehabil
Periodical
Rehabilitation Review (monthly) 13353

American Rehabilitation Counseling Association (ARCA), c/o American Counseling Association, 5999 Stevenson Av, Alexandria, VA 22304
T: (703) 823-9800; Fax: (703) 823-0252
Founded: 1958; Members: 3000
Focus: Rehabil
Periodicals
Newsletter (quarterly)
Rehabilitation Counseling Bulletin (quarterly) 13354

American Research Institute in Turkey (ARIT), c/o University Museum, 33 and Spruce Sts, Philadelphia, PA 19104
T: (215) 898-3474; E-Mail: leinwand@sas.upenn.edu; Fax: (215) 898-0657
Founded: 1964; Members: 32
Pres: G. Kenneth Sams
Focus: Ethnology 13355

American Revolution Round Table (ARRT), c/o James W. Davis, 147-37 Beech Av, Flushing, NY 11355
T: (516) 944-8623
Founded: 1958; Members: 120
Pres: Thomas Fleming
Focus: Hist
Periodical
Newsletter (5 times annually) 13356

American Rhinologic Society (ARS), c/o Frank Lucente, Long Island College Hospital, Brooklyn, NY 11201
T: (718) 780-1281; Fax: (718) 802-1036
Founded: 1954; Members: 604
Focus: Otorhinolaryngology
Periodicals
Journal of International Rhinology (1-4 times annually)
Membership Directory (bi-annually)
Newsletter (4-5 times annually) 13357

American Risk and Insurance Association (ARIA), c/o Chase Communications, POB 9001, Mount Vernon, NY 10552
T: (914) 699-2020; E-Mail: aria@pipeline.com; Fax: (914) 699-2025
Founded: 1932; Members: 2000
Gen Secr: Carole H. Acunto
Focus: Insurance
Periodical
The Journal of Risk and Insurance (quarterly) 13358

American Rock Art Research Association (ARARA), POB 65, San Miguel, CA 93451
T: (805) 467-3704; Fax: (805) 467-2532
Focus: Archeol 13359

American Roentgen Ray Society (ARRS), 1891 Preston White Dr, Reston, VA 22091
T: (703) 648-8992; Fax: (703) 264-8863
Founded: 1900; Members: 12400
Gen Secr: Paul R. Fullagar
Focus: X-Ray Tech
Periodicals
American Journal of Roentgenology (monthly)
Membership Directory (annually) 13360

American School Health Association (ASHA), 7263 State Rte 43, POB 708, Kent, OH 44240
T: (216) 678-1601; Fax: (216) 678-4526
Founded: 1927; Members: 4000
Focus: Public Health
Periodical
Journal of School Health (10 times annually) 13361

American Schools Association (ASA), 3069 Amwiler Rd, Ste 4, Atlanta, GA 30360
T: (404) 449-7141
Founded: 1914
Focus: Educ 13362

American Schools of Oriental Research, 3301 N Charles St, Baltimore, MD 21218
T: (410) 516-3498; Fax: (410) 516-3499
Gen Secr: Rudolph H. Dornemann
Focus: Ethnology 13363

American Security Council (ASC), 5545 Security Cir, Boston, VA 22713
T: (703) 547-1750; Fax: (703) 547-9737
Founded: 1955; Members: 325700
Gen Secr: Greg Hilton
Focus: Safety
Periodical
National Security Report (monthly) 13364

American Security Council Foundation (ASCF), 5545 Security Cir, Boston, VA 22713
T: (703) 547-1776; Fax: (703) 547-9737
Founded: 1958
Pres: John M. Fisher
Focus: Safety 13365

American Social Health Association (ASHA), POB 13827, Research Triangle Park, NC 27709
T: (919) 361-8400; Fax: (919) 361-8425
Founded: 1914; Members: 14000
Focus: Public Health
Periodical
Helper (quarterly) 13366

American Society for Adolescent Psychiatry (ASAP), 4330 East West Hwy, Ste 1117, Bethesda, MD 20814
T: (301) 718-6502; Fax: (301) 656-0989
Founded: 1967; Members: 1500
Focus: Psychiatry
Periodicals
Annals of Adolescent Psychiatry (annually)
Newsletter (3 times annually) 13367

American Society for Advancement of Anesthesia in Dentistry (ASAAD), c/o Dr. Louis L. Zall, 11245 W Atlantic Blvd, Apt 301, Coral Springs, FL 33071-5112
T: (305) 584-5600; Fax: (305) 584-5601
Founded: 1929; Members: 400
Gen Secr: Dr. Louis L. Zall
Focus: Anesthetics 13368

American Society for Aesthetic Plastic Surgery (ASAPS), 3922 Atlantic Av, Long Beach, CA 90807
T: (310) 595-4275; Fax: (310) 427-2234
Founded: 1967; Members: 1052
Focus: Surgery
Periodical
Aesthetic Surgery (3 times annually) 13369

American Society for Biochemistry and Molecular Biology (ASBMC), 9650 Rockville Pike, Bethesda, MD 20814
T: (301) 530-7145; Fax: (301) 571-1824
Founded: 1906; Members: 9200
Gen Secr: Charles C. Hancock
Focus: Biochem
Periodical
Journal of Biological Chemistry (weekly) . 13370

American Society for Bone and Mineral Research (ASBMR), 1200 19 St NW, Ste 300, Washington, DC 20036
T: (202) 857-1161; Fax: (202) 223-4579
Founded: 1977; Members: 2300
Gen Secr: William E. Kelley
Focus: Biochem
Periodicals
Membership Roster (annually)
Newsletter (3 times annually) 13371

American Society for Cell Biology (ASCB), 9650 Rockville Pike, Bethesda, MD 20814
T: (301) 530-7153; Fax: (301) 530-7139
Founded: 1960; Members: 7100
Focus: Cell Biol & Cancer Res
Periodicals
Journal of Cell Biology (monthly)
Newsletter (quarterly) 13372

American Society for Clinical Investigation (ASCI), 6900 Grove Rd, Thorofare, NJ 08086
T: (609) 848-1000; Fax: (609) 848-5247
Founded: 1909; Members: 2400
Focus: Med
Periodical
Journal of Clinical Investigation (monthly) 13373

American Society for Clinical Laboratory Science (ASCLS), 7910 Woodmont Av, Ste 1301, Bethesda, MD 20814
T: (301) 657-2768; Fax: (301) 657-2909
Founded: 1932; Members: 20000
Gen Secr: Elissa Passiment
Focus: Med; Eng
Periodical
Clinical Laboratory Science (bi-monthly) . 13374

American Society for Clinical Nutrition (ASCN), 9650 Rockville Pike, Bethesda, MD 20814-3998
T: (301) 530-7110; Fax: (301) 571-1892
Founded: 1959; Members: 1200
Focus: Food
Periodical
The American Journal of Clinical Nutrition (monthly) 13375

American Society for Colposcopy and Cervical Pathology (ASCCP), 409 12 St SW, Washington, DC 20024-2188
Fax: (202) 863-2453 (202) 554-0453
Founded: 1964; Members: 3100
Gen Secr: Kathleen Poole
Focus: Gynecology
Periodical
The Colposcopist (quarterly) 13376

American Society for Conservation Archaeology (ASCA), c/o Anthony Lutonski, 435 Montano Rd NE, Albuquerque, NM 87107
T: (505) 761-8792; Fax: (505) 761-8911
Founded: 1974; Members: 300
Focus: Archeol 13377

American Society for Cybernetics (ASC), c/o Dept of Decision Sciences, George Mason University, Fairfax, VA 22030
T: (800) 422-2319; Fax: (800) 422-2319
Founded: 1964; Members: 250
Focus: Cybernetics
Periodicals
Conference Proceedings (annually)
Cybernetic (quarterly)
Newsletter (monthly) 13378

American Society for Cytotechnology (ASCT), 920 Paverstone Dr, Raleigh, NC 27614
T: (919) 848-9911; Fax: (919) 848-9853
Founded: 1979; Members: 1500
Focus: Cell Biol & Cancer Res
Periodical
Newsletter (monthly) 13379

American Society for Dental Aesthetics (ASDA), 635 Madison Av, New York, NY 10022
T: (212) 751-3263; Fax: (212) 308-5182
Founded: 1978; Members: 109
Focus: Dent
Periodical
Newsletter (semi-annually) 13380

American Society for Dermatologic Surgery (ASDS), POB 4014, Schaumburg, IL 60204
T: (708) 330-0230; Fax: (708) 869-4382
Founded: 1970; Members: 2157
Focus: Derm; Surgery
Periodicals
Journal of Dermatologic Surgery and Oncology (monthly)
Roster (annually) 13381

American Society for Eighteenth-Century Studies (ASECS), c/o Utah State University, 108 Computer Center, Logan, UT 84322-3730
T: (801) 750-4065; Fax: (801) 750-4065
Founded: 1970; Members: 3921
Gen Secr: Jeffrey Smitten
Focus: Hist; Lit; Sci; Poli Sci; Philos
Periodicals
Eighteenth-Century Studies (quarterly)
Studies in Eighteenth-Century Culture (annually) 13382

American Society for Engineering Education (ASEE), 1818 N St NW, Ste 600, Washington, DC 20036
T: (202) 331-3545; E-Mail: f.huband@asee.org; Fax: (202) 265-8504
Gen Secr: Dr. Frank L. Huband
Focus: Eng; Educ 13383

American Society for Engineering Management (ASEM), POB 867, Annapolis, MD 21401
T: (410) 263-7065
Founded: 1979; Members: 800
Focus: Eng
Periodicals
Engineering Management International (quarterly)
Newsletter (quarterly)
Proceedings of Annual Meeting 13384

American Society for Ethnohistory (ASE), c/o Dept of Anthropology, Cornell University, McGraw Hall, Ithaca, NY 14853
T: (607) 277-0109
Founded: 1954; Members: 1300
Gen Secr: Frederic W. Gleach
Focus: Hist; Ethnology; Cultur Hist
Periodical
Ethnohistory (quarterly) 13385

American Society for Gastrointestinal Endoscopy (ASGE), 13 Elm St, POB 1565, Manchester, MA 01944
T: (508) 526-8330; Fax: (508) 526-4018
Founded: 1941; Members: 5000
Focus: Gastroenter
Periodical
Gastrointestinal Endoscopy (bi-monthly) . 13386

American Society for Geriatric Dentistry (ASGD), 211 E Chicago Av, Chicago, IL 60611
T: (312) 440-2661
Founded: 1965; Members: 450
Focus: Dent; Geriatrics
Periodical
Newsletter (quarterly) 13387

American Society for Head and Neck Surgery (ASHNS), c/o Dept of Otolaryngology, 203 Lothrop St, Ste 519, Pittsburgh, PA 15213
T: (412) 647-2227; E-Mail: rlwa@med.pitt.edu; Fax: (412) 647-8944
Founded: 1959; Members: 800
Gen Secr: Dr. Jonas T. Johnson
Focus: Surgery; Otorhinolaryngology
Periodical
Archives and Otolaryngology (annually) . 13388

American Society for Healthcare Education and Training of the American Hospital Association (ASHET), 1 N Franklin, Chicago, IL 60606
T: (312) 422-3721; Fax: (312) 422-4575
Founded: 1970; Members: 1500
Gen Secr: Linda N. Brooks
Focus: Educ; Public Health
Periodicals
Healthcare Education Dataline (3 times annually)
Journal of Healthcare Education and Training 13389

American Society for Healthcare Human Resources Administration (ASHHRA), c/o American Hospital Association, 1 N Franklin, Chicago, IL 60606
T: (312) 280-6722; Fax: (312) 280-4152
Founded: 1964; Members: 2900
Gen Secr: Linda Brooks
Focus: Med
Periodicals
Hospital (bi-weekly)
Human Resources Administration (quarterly) 13390

American Society for Horticultural Science (ASHS), 600 Cameron St, Alexandria, VA 22314-2562
T: (703) 836-4606; Fax: (703) 836-2024
Founded: 1903; Members: 5000
Pres: Donald N. Maynard; Gen Secr: Charles H. Emely
Focus: Hort
Periodicals
HortScience (monthly)
HortTechnology (quarterly)
Journal of the American Society for Horticultural Science (bi-monthly) 13391

American Society for Hospital Engineering (ASHE), c/o American Hospital Association, 1 N Franklin, Ste 2700, Chicago, IL 60606
T: (312) 422-3800; Fax: (312) 422-4571
Founded: 1962; Members: 5500
Gen Secr: Joseph J. Martori
Focus: Med; Eng
Periodicals
Hospital Codes and Standards Update Letters (4-6 times annually)
Hospital Engineering Bulletin (monthly)
Technical Documents (monthly) 13392

American Society for Information Science (ASIS), 8720 Georgia Av, Ste 501, Silver Spring, MD 20910
T: (301) 495-0900; Fax: (301) 495-0810
Founded: 1937; Members: 4700
Pres: Debora Shaw; Gen Secr: Richard B. Hill
Focus: Computer & Info Sci
Periodicals
Bulletin (bi-monthly)
Jobline (monthly)
Journal (bi-monthly) 13393

American Society for Investigative Pathology (ASIP), 9650 Rockville Pike, Bethesda, MD 20814-3993
T: (301) 530-7130; Fax: (301) 571-1879
Founded: 1976; Members: 2300
Gen Secr: Frances A. Pitlick
Focus: Pathology
Periodicals
AAP Newsletter (quarterly)
American Journal of Pathology (monthly) 13394

American Society for Laser Medicine and Surgery (ASLMS), 2404 Stewart Sq, Wausau, WI 54401
T: (715) 845-9283; Fax: (715) 848-2493
Founded: 1980; Members: 1728
Focus: Radiology; Surgery
Periodicals
Lasers in Surgery and Medicine (bi-monthly)
Official ASLMS Newsletter (bi-monthly) . 13395

American Society for Legal History (ASLH), c/o Prof. M. de Landon, Dept of History, University of Mississippi, University, MS 38677
T: (601) 232-7148; Fax: (601) 232-5918
Founded: 1956; Members: 1100
Focus: Law 13396

American Society for Mass Spectrometry (ASMS), 1201 Don Diego, Santa Fe, NM 82505
T: (505) 989-4517
Founded: 1969; Members: 3500
Gen Secr: Judith A. Sjoberg
Focus: Astronomy 13397

American Society for Microbiology (ASM), 1325 Massachusetts Av NW, Washington, DC 20006
T: (202) 737-3600; Fax: (202) 887-0327
Founded: 1899; Members: 37000
Gen Secr: Michael I. Goldberg
Focus: Microbio
Periodicals
ASM News (monthly)
International Journal of Systematic Bacteriology (quarterly)
Journal of Bacteriology, Applied and Environmental Microbiology (bi-weekly)
Journal of Clinical Microbiology (monthly)
Journal of Virology, Infection and Immunity (monthly)
Microbiological Review (quarterly) 13398

American Society for Neurochemistry (ASN), 200 University Blvd, Ste 519, Galveston, TX 77555-0843
T: (409) 772-2108; Fax: (409) 762-9382
Founded: 1969; Members: 1018
Gen Secr: Dr. Bernard Haber
Focus: Chem; Neurology
Periodicals
Membership Directory (annually)
Newsletter (semi-annually)
Transactions (annually) 13399

American Society for Nondestructive Testing (ASNT), 1711 Arlingate Ln, POB 28518, Columbus, OH 43228-0518
T: (614) 274-6003; Fax: (614) 274-6899
Founded: 1941; Members: 11000
Focus: Materials Sci
Periodicals
Materials Evaluation (monthly)
Research in Nondestructive Evaluation (quarterly) 13400

American Society for Parenteral and Enteral Nutrition (ASPEN), 8630 Fenton St, Ste 412, Silver Spring, MD 20910-3805
T: (301) 587-6315; Fax: (301) 587-2365
Founded: 1975; Members: 7200
Focus: Hematology
Periodicals
Journal of Parenteral and Enteral Nutrition (bi-monthly)
Nutrition in Clinical Practice (bi-monthly) . 13401

American Society for Pharmacology and Experimental Therapeutics (ASPET), 9650 Rockville Pike, Bethesda, MD 20814-3995
T: (301) 530-7060
Founded: 1908; Members: 4120
Pres: Charles O. Rutledge; Gen Secr: Kay A. Croker
Focus: Pharmacol
Periodicals
Drug Metabolism and Disposition (bi-monthly)
Journal of Pharmacology and Experimental Therapeutics (monthly)
Molecular Pharmacology (monthly)
Pharmacological Reviews (quarterly)
The Pharmacologist (quarterly) 13402

American Society for Pharmacy Law (ASPL), c/o Donald A. Dee, POB 2184, Vienna, VA 22183
T: (701) 281-0107
Founded: 1974; Members: 800
Focus: Law; Pharmacol
Periodicals
ASPL Membership Directory (annually)
RX Ipsa Loquitur (monthly) 13403

American Society for Photobiology (ASP), Biotech Park, 1021 15 St, Ste 9, Augusta, GA 30901
T: (706) 722-7511; Fax: (706) 722-7515
Founded: 1972; Members: 1400
Gen Secr: Dr. Sherwood M. Reichard
Focus: Bio
Periodicals
Newsletter (monthly)
Photochemistry and Photobiology (monthly) 13404

American Society for Photogrammetry and Remote Sensing, 5410 Grosvenor Ln, Ste 210, Bethesda, MD 20814-2160
T: (301) 493-0290; Fax: (301) 493-0208
Founded: 1934; Members: 7000
Pres: Tina K. Carey; Gen Secr: William D. French
Focus: Surveying
Periodical
Photogrametric Engineering and Remote Sensing (monthly) 13405

American Society for Political and Legal Philosophy (ASPLP), c/o Philosophy Dept, Wheaton College, Knapton Hall, Norton, MA 02766
T: (508) 285-7722
Founded: 1955; Members: 500
Pres: Martha Nussbaum; Gen Secr: Prof. Kenneth I. Winston
Focus: Philos; Poli Sci 13406

American Society for Psychical Research (ASPR), 5 W 73 St, New York, NY 10023
T: (212) 799-5050; Fax: (212) 496-2497
Founded: 1885; Members: 2000
Gen Secr: Patrice Keane
Focus: Psych
Periodicals
ASPR Newsletter (quarterly)
Journal of the American Society for Psychical Research (quarterly) 13407

American Society for Psychoprophylaxis in Obstetrics (ASPO/Lamaze), 1200 19 St NW, Rm 300, Washington, DC 20036-1128
T: (202) 857-1128; E-Mail: aspo@sba.com; Fax: (202) 223-4579
Founded: 1960; Members: 5000
Gen Secr: Linda Harmon
Focus: Gynecology
Periodicals
Annual Directory (annually)
Genesis (bi-monthly) 13408

American Society for Public Administration (ASPA), 1120 G St NW, Ste 700, Washington, DC 20005
T: (202) 393-7878; Fax: (202) 638-4952
Founded: 1939; Members: 13000
Gen Secr: John P. Thomas
Focus: Public Admin
Periodicals
Public Administration Review (bi-monthly)
Public Administration Times (bi-weekly) . 13409

American Society for Quality Control (ASQC), 611 E Wisconsin Av, Milwaukee, WI 53201-3005
T: (414) 272-8575; Fax: (414) 272-1734
Founded: 1946; Members: 68500
Focus: Materials Sci
Periodicals
Journal of Quality Technology (quarterly)
Quality Engineering (quarterly)
Quality Progress (monthly)
The Quality Review (quarterly)
Technometrics (quarterly) 13410

American Society for Reproductive Medicine (ASRM), 1209 Montgomery Hwy, Birmingham, AL 35216-2809
T: (205) 978-5000; Fax: (205) 978-5005
Founded: 1944; Members: 10500
Gen Secr: Nancy C. Hayley
Focus: Gynecology; Urology; Vet Med
Periodicals
Fertility and Sterility (monthly)
Fertility News (quarterly) 13411

American Society for Stereotactic and Functional Neurosurgery (ASSFN), c/o Philip L. Gildenberg, 6624 Fannin, Ste 1620, Houston, TX 77030
T: (713) 790-0795; Fax: (713) 669-0388
Founded: 1968; Members: 300
Gen Secr: Philip L. Gildenberg
Focus: Neurology
Periodical
Applied Neurophysiology (bi-monthly) . . 13412

American Society for Surgery of the Hand (ASSH), 6060 Greenwood Plaza Blvd, Englewood, CO 80111-4801
T: (303) 771-9236; Fax: (303) 771-9269
Founded: 1946; Members: 1415
Gen Secr: Gail M. Gorman
Focus: Surgery
Periodical
Journal of Hand Surgery (bi-monthly) . . 13413

American Society for Technion-Israel Institute of Technology (ASTITT), 810 Seventh Av, New York, NY 10019
T: (212) 262-6200; Fax: (212) 262-6155
Founded: 1940; Members: 24000
Focus: Eng

Periodicals
Technion Magazine (semi-annually)
Technion USA Magazine (semi-annually)
Update Newsletter (quarterly) 13414

American Society for Testing and Materials (ASTM), 1916 Race St, Philadelphia, PA 19103
T: (215) 299-5400; Fax: (215) 977-9679
Founded: 1902; Members: 35000
Pres: James A. Thomas
Focus: Standards
Periodical
Annual Book of ASTM Standards (annually) 13415

American Society for Theatre Research (ASTR), c/o Dept of Theatre, Brown University, Providence, RI 02912
T: (401) 521-6293
Founded: 1956; Members: 806
Gen Secr: Prof. Don Wilmeth
Focus: Perf Arts
Periodicals
Newsletter (semi-annually)
Theatre Survey (semi-annually) 13416

American Society for Therapeutic Radiology and Oncology (ASTRO), 1891 Preston White Dr, Reston, VA 22091
T: (703) 716-7588; Fax: (703) 476-8167
Founded: 1955; Members: 4200
Gen Secr: Gregg Robinson
Focus: Radiology; Cell Biol & Cancer Res
Periodicals
ASTRO Newsletter
The International Journal of Radiation Oncology, Biology and Physics 13417

American Society for Training and Development (ASTD), 1640 King St, Box 1443, Alexandria, VA 22313
T: (703) 683-8100; Fax: (703) 683-8103
Founded: 1944; Members: 55000
Focus: Educ; Econ
Periodicals
Journal (monthly)
National Report on Human Resources (monthly) 13418

American Society for Value Inquiry (ASVI), c/o Div of Arts and Humanities, Bergen Community College, 400 Paramus Rd, Paramus, NJ 07652-1595
T: (201) 447-9282
Founded: 1970; Members: 200
Pres: Martha Nussbaum
Focus: Philos
Periodicals
Journal of Value Inquiry (quarterly)
Newsletter (semi-annually) 13419

American Society of Abdominal Surgeons (ASAS), 675 Main St, Melrose, MA 02176
T: (617) 665-6102; Fax: (617) 665-4127
Founded: 1959; Members: 9300
Gen Secr: Louis F. Alfano
Focus: Surgery
Periodicals
Abdominal Surgery (monthly)
The Surgeon 13420

American Society of Addiction Medicine (ASAM), 4601 N Park Av, Arcade, Ste 101, Chevy Chase, MD 20815
T: (301) 656-3920; E-Mail: usamoffice@aol.com; Fax: (301) 656-3815
Founded: 1954; Members: 3000
Gen Secr: James F. Callahan
Focus: Med
Periodical
Journal of Addictive Diseases (quarterly) 13421

American Society of Agricultural Engineers (ASAE), 2950 Niles Rd, Saint Joseph, MI 49085
T: (616) 429-0300; Fax: (616) 429-3852
Founded: 1907; Members: 9000
Gen Secr: Roger R. Castenson
Focus: Agri; Eng
Periodicals
Resource Magazine (monthly)
Standards (annually)
Transactions of the ASAE (bi-monthly) . 13422

American Society of Agronomy (ASA), 677 S Segoe Rd, Madison, WI 53711
T: (608) 273-8080; Fax: (608) 273-2021
Founded: 1907; Members: 12600
Gen Secr: Robert F. Barnes
Focus: Agri
Periodicals
Agronomy Abstracts (annually)
Agronomy Journal (bi-monthly)
Agronomy News (monthly)
Journal of Agronomic Education (semi-annually)
Journal of Environmental Quality (quarterly)
Journal of Production Agriculture (quarterly) 13423

American Society of Anesthesiologists (ASA), 520 N Northwest Hwy, Park Ridge, IL 60068-2573
T: (708) 825-5586; Fax: (708) 825-1682
Founded: 1905; Members: 28000
Focus: Anesthetics
Periodicals
Anesthesiology (monthly)
ASA Newsletter (monthly) 13424

American Society of Animal Science (ASAS), c/o Carl D. Johnson, 309 W Clark St, Campaign, IL 61820
T: (217) 356-3182; Fax: (217) 3984119
Founded: 1908; Members: 4500
Pres: Elton D. Aberle; Gen Secr: Barbara Glenn
Focus: Zoology
Periodical
Journal of Animal Science (monthly) . . 13425

American Society of Bakery Engineers (ASBE), 2 N Riverside Plaza, Rm 1733, Chicago, IL 60606
T: (312) 332-2246
Founded: 1924; Members: 2700
Focus: Food 13426

American Society of Body and Design Engineers (ASBDE), Wilshire Office Center, Stes 30-31, 24634 Five Mile, Redford, MI 48239
T: (313) 532-6100
Founded: 1946; Members: 1500
Gen Secr: H. Eby Jr.
Focus: Eng
Periodicals
Body Engineering Journal (semi-annually)
Directory (annually)
Newsletter (7 times annually)
Proceedings (annually) 13427

American Society of Breast Disease, POB 140186, Dallas, TX 75214
T: (214) 368-6836; Fax: (214) 368-5719
Founded: 1976; Members: 560
Pres: Melvin J. Silverstein
Focus: Intern Med 13428

American Society of Brewing Chemists (ASBC), 3340 Pilot Knob Rd, Saint Paul, MN 55121-2097
T: (612) 454-7250; Fax: (612) 454-0766
Founded: 1934; Members: 600
Focus: Chem
Periodical
Journal of the ASBC (quarterly) 13429

American Society of Cardiovascular Professionals/Society for Cardiovascular Management (ASCP/SCM), 120 Falcon Dr, Fredericksburg, VA 22408
T: (703) 891-0079; E-Mail: scanmce@aol.com; Fax: (703) 898-2393
Founded: 1967; Members: 3200
Gen Secr: Peggy McElgunn
Focus: Cardiol 13430

American Society of Cataract and Refractive Surgery (ASCRS), 4000 Lugato Rd, Ste 850, Fairfax, VA 22033
T: (703) 591-2220; Fax: (703) 591-0614
Founded: 1974; Members: 4500
Focus: Surgery
Periodical
Journal of Cataract and Refractive Surgery (bi-monthly) 13431

American Society of Certified Engineering Technicians (ASCET), POB 1348, Flowery Branch, GA 30542-1348
T: (770) 967-9173; Fax: (770) 967-8049
Founded: 1964; Members: 3000
Gen Secr: Kurt H. Schuler
Focus: Eng
Periodicals
Annual Report (annually)
Certified Engineering Technician Magazine (bi-monthly)
President's Message (bi-monthly) 13432

American Society of Church History (ASCH), POB 8517, Red Bank, NJ 07701
Founded: 1888; Members: 1500
Gen Secr: Henry W. Bowden
Focus: Hist
Periodical
Church History (quarterly) 13433

American Society of Civil Engineers (ASCE), 1801 Alexander Bell Dr, Reston, VA 20191-4400
T: (202) 705-7406
Founded: 1852; Members: 105000
Gen Secr: James E. Davis
Focus: Civil Eng
Periodicals
ASCE News (monthly)
Civil Engineering (monthly)
Construction Journal (quarterly)
Energy Journal (irregularly)
Energy Mechnics Journal (monthly)
Environment Journal (bi-monthly)
Geotechnical Journal (monthly)
Hydraulic Journal (monthly)
Irrigation/Drainage Journal (bi-monthly)
Professional Journal (quarterly)
Structural Journal (monthly)
Surveying Journal (quarterly)
Transportation/Pipeline Journal (bi-monthly)
Urban Planning Journal (irregularly)
Water Resources Journal (bi-monthly)
Waterway/Port/Coastal Journal (bi-monthly) 13434

American Society of Clinical Hypnosis (ASCH), 2200 E Devon Av, Ste 291, Des Plaines, IL 60018
T: (708) 297-3317; Fax: (708) 297-7309
Founded: 1957; Members: 4200
Pres: Dr. Richard P. Kluft; Gen Secr: Dr Moshe S. Torem
Focus: Med; Psych
Periodicals
American Journal of Clinical Hypnosis (quarterly)
Directory (annually)
News Letter (8 times annually) 13435

American Society of Clinical Oncology (ASCO), 435 N Michigan Av, Ste 1717, Chicago, IL 60611-4067
T: (312) 644-0828; Fax: (312) 644-8557
Founded: 1964; Members: 8744
Focus: Cell Biol & Cancer Res
Periodicals
Directory (bi-annually)
Journal of Clinical Oncology (monthly) . 13436

American Society of Clinical Pathologists (ASCP), 2100 W Harrison St, Chicago, IL 60612
T: (312) 738-1336; Fax: (312) 738-1619
Founded: 1922; Members: 68340
Pres: Dr. M. Desmond Burke; Gen Secr: Dr. Anna R. Graham
Focus: Pathology
Periodicals
American Journal of Clinical Pathology (monthly)
Laboratory Medicine (monthly) 13437

American Society of Colon and Rectal Surgeons (ASCRS), 85 W Algonquin Rd, Ste 550, Arlington Heights, IL 60005
T: (708) 290-9184; Fax: (708) 290-9203
Founded: 1899; Members: 1600
Gen Secr: James R. Slawny
Focus: Surgery
Periodical
Diseases of the Colon and Rectum (monthly) 13438

American Society of Comparative Law (ASCL), c/o Harvard Law School, Cambridge, MA 02138
T: (617) 495-3193; E-Mail: vonmehre@hulawl.harvard.edu; Fax: (617) 495-1110
Founded: 1951; Members: 81
Pres: Dr. Arthur T. von Mehren
Focus: Law 13439

American Society of Consultant Pharmacists (ASCP), 1321 Duke St, Alexandria, VA 22314-3563
T: (703) 739-1300; Fax: (703) 739-1321
Founded: 1969; Members: 5000
Focus: Pharmacol
Periodicals
Clinical Consult Newsletter (quarterly)
The Consultant Pharmacist Journal (monthly)
Update Newsletter (monthly) 13440

American Society of Contemporary Ophthalmology (ASCO), 4711 W Golf Rd, Ste 408, Skokie, IL 60076
T: (708) 568-1500
Founded: 1966; Members: 6000
Focus: Ophthal
Periodicals
Annals of Ophthalmology (monthly)
Glancoma (bi-monthly) 13441

American Society of Criminology (ASC), 1314 Kinnear Rd, Ste 212, Columbus, OH 43212
T: (614) 292-9207
Founded: 1941; Members: 2150
Focus: Criminology
Periodicals
The Criminologist Newsletter (bi-monthly)
Criminology (quarterly) 13442

American Society of Cytopathology (ASC), 400 W Ninth St, Ste 201, Wilmington, DE 19801
T: (302) 429-8802; Fax: (302) 429-8807
Founded: 1951; Members: 3500
Gen Secr: Y.S. Erozan
Focus: Cell Biol & Cancer Res
Periodicals
Acta Cytologica (bi-monthly)
The Cytotechnologist's Bulletin (bi-monthly) 13443

American Society of Danish Engineers (ASDE), c/o T.H. Storm, POB 606, Larchmont, NY 10538
T: (914) 632-7632; Fax: (914) 632-7631
Founded: 1930; Members: 200
Focus: Eng 13444

American Society of Dentistry for Children (ASDC), 875 N Michigan Av, Ste 4040, Chicago, IL 60611-1901
T: (312) 943-1244; Fax: (312) 943-3541
Founded: 1927; Members: 5000
Gen Secr: Carol Teuscher
Focus: Dent
Periodicals
ASDC Newsletter
Journal of Dentistry for Children 13445

American Society of Dermatopathology (ASD), 3601 Fourth St, Ste 4A-118, Lubbock, TX 79430
T: (806) 743-1106; Fax: (806) 743-1106
Founded: 1962; Members: 965
Gen Secr: Carol Daugherty
Focus: Derm; Pathology 13446

American Society of Echocardiography (ASE), 4101 Lake Boone Trail, Ste 201, Raleigh, NC 27607
T: (919) 787-5181; Fax: (919) 787-4916
Founded: 1976; Members: 5000
Focus: Cardiol
Periodical
Journal of the American Society of Echocardiography 13447

American Society of Extra-Corporeal Technology (AmSECT), 11480 Sunset Hills Rd, Ste 210E, Reston, VA 22090
T: (703) 435-8556; Fax: (703) 435-0056
Founded: 1964; Members: 3000
Gen Secr: George M. Cate
Focus: Cardiol
Periodicals
Journal of Extra-Corporal Technology (quarterly)
Perfusion Life (11 times annually) . . . 13448

American Society of Forensic Odontology (ASFO), c/o Dr. E. Steven Smith, Northwestern University Dental School, 240 E Huron, Chicago, IL 60611
T: (312) 503-0900; Fax: (312) 503-9898
Founded: 1966; Members: 450
Gen Secr: Dr. E. Steven Smith
Focus: Dent; Forensic Med
Periodicals
Membership Directory (annually)
Newsletter (quarterly) 13449

American Society of Gas Engineers (ASGE), POB 66001, Anaheim, CA 92816
T: (714) 666-0411; Fax: (714) 666-0411
Founded: 1954; Members: 550
Gen Secr: Daryl Hosler
Focus: Energy 13450

American Society of Genealogists (ASG), 1732 Ridgedale Dr, Tuscaloosa, AL 35406
T: (205) 752-4031; Fax: (205) 752-5979
Founded: 1940; Members: 50
Gen Secr: Elizabeth Shown Mills
Focus: Genealogy 13451

American Society of Geolinguistics (ASG), c/o Dr. Jesse Levitt, 485 Brooklawn Av, Fairfield, CT 06432
T: (203) 333-8920
Founded: 1964; Members: 120
Focus: Ling
Periodical
Geolinguistics (annually) 13452

American Society of Golf Course Architects (ASGCA), 221 N LaSalle St, Chicago, IL 60601
T: (312) 372-7090; Fax: (312) 372-6160
Members: 115
Focus: Archit
Periodical
ASGCA Newsletter (monthly) 13453

American Society of Group Psychotherapy and Psychodrama (ASGP&P), 6728 Old McLean Village Dr, McLean, VA 22101
T: (703) 556-9222
Founded: 1942; Members: 800
Focus: Therapeutics
Periodical
Group Psychodrama (annually) 13454

American Society of Hand Therapists (ASHT), 401 N Michigan Av, Chicago, IL 60611
T: (312) 321-6866; Fax: (312) 527-6636
Founded: 1977; Members: 1950
Gen Secr: Ruth Easterling
Focus: Physical Therapy
Periodical
Newsletter (bi-monthly) 13455

American Society of Heating, Refrigerating and Air-Conditioning Engineers (ASHRAE), 1791 Tullie Circle NE, Atlanta, GA 30329
T: (404) 636-8400; Fax: (404) 321-5478
Founded: 1959; Members: 50000
Gen Secr: Frank M. Coda
Focus: Air Cond
Periodicals
Handbook (annually)
Journal (monthly)
Transactions (semi-annually) 13456

American Society of Hematology (ASH), 1200 19 St NW, Ste 300, Washington, DC 20036-2412
T: (202) 857-1118; Fax: (202) 857-1164
Founded: 1958; Members: 7900
Gen Secr: Michael L. Payne
Focus: Hematology
Periodicals
Blood (monthly)
Directory of Members
Meeting Program (annually) 13457

American Society of Hospital Pharmacists (ASHP), 7272 Wisconsin Av, Bethesda, MD 20814
T: (301) 657-3000; Fax: (301) 652-8278
Founded: 1942; Members: 30000
Gen Secr: Joseph A. Oddis
Focus: Pharmacol
Periodicals
American Hospital Formulary Service (annually)
American Journal of Hospital Pharmacy (monthly)
Clinical Pharmacy (monthly)
International Pharmaceutical Abstracts (bi-weekly) 13458

American Society of Human Genetics (ASHG), 9650 Rockville Pike, Bethesda, MD 20814
T: (301) 571-1825; Fax: (301) 530-7079
Founded: 1948; Members: 6000
Pres: Charles J. Epstein; Gen Secr: Elaine Strass
Focus: Genetics
Periodical
American Journal of Human Genetics (monthly) 13459

American Society of Ichthyologists and Herpetologists (ASIH), c/o Texas Natural History Collection, University of Texas, Austin, TX 78712-1100
T: (512) 471-0998; Fax: (512) 471-9775
Founded: 1913; Members: 3600
Gen Secr: Dean A. Henrickson
Focus: Nat Sci; Zoology
Periodical
Copeia (quarterly) 13460

American Society of Indexers (ASI), POB 48267, Seattle, WA 98148-0267
T: (206) 241-9196; E-Mail: asi@well.com;
Fax: (206) 727-6430
Founded: 1968; Members: 1200
Pres: Ann Blum
Focus: Libraries & Bk Sci
Periodicals
ASI Newsletter (5 times annually)
The Indexer (semi-annually)
Register of Indexers (annually) 13461

American Society of Internal Medicine (ASIM), 2011 Pennsylvania Av NW, Ste 800, Washington, DC 20006-1808
T: (202) 835-2746; Fax: (202) 835-0443
Founded: 1956; Members: 26000
Focus: Intern Med
Periodicals
The Internist: Health Policy in Practice (monthly)
Internist's Intercom (monthly) 13462

American Society of International Law (ASIL), 2223 Massachusetts Av NW, Washington, DC 20008
T: (202) 265-4313; Fax: (202) 797-7133
Founded: 1906; Members: 8000
Pres: Charles N. Brower; Gen Secr: Charlotte Ka
Focus: Law
Periodicals
American Journal of International Law (quarterly)
Newsletter (bi-monthly) 13463

American Society of Irrigation Consultants (ASIC), 425A Oak St, POB 426, Byron, CA 94514-0426
T: (510) 516-1124; Fax: (510) 516-1301
Founded: 1970; Members: 185
Gen Secr: Wanda M. Sarsfield
Focus: Agri
Periodicals
ASIC Newsletter (quarterly)
Bulletin (monthly)
Membership Roster (annually) 13464

American Society of Landscape Architects (ASLA), 4401 Connecticut Av NW, Washington, DC 20008-2302
T: (202) 686-2752; Fax: (202) 686-1001
Founded: 1899; Members: 10500
Focus: Archit
Periodicals
Land: Landscape Architectural News Digest (monthly)
Landscape Architecture (bi-monthly)
LATIS: Landscape Architecture Technical Information Series (quarterly) 13465

American Society of Law, Medicine and Ethics (ASLME), 765 Commonwealth Av, Boston, MA 02215
T: (617) 262-4990; E-Mail: aslme@bu.edu;
Fax: (617) 437-7596
Founded: 1972; Members: 4500
Gen Secr: Michael Vasko
Focus: Med; Law; Forensic Med
Periodicals
American Journal of Law and Medicine (quarterly)
Law, Medicine and Health Care (bi-monthly)
. . . . 13466

American Society of Limnology and Oceanography (ASLO), c/o Virginia Institute of Marine Science, College of William and Mary, Rte 1208, Gloucester Point, VA 23062
T: (804) 642-7242; Fax: (804) 357-0422
Founded: 1936; Members: 3500
Focus: Hydrology; Oceanography
Periodical
Limnology and Oceanography (bi-monthly)   13467

American Society of Mammalogists (ASM), c/o Monte L. Bean Life Science Museum, Brigham Young University, 501 Widtsoe Bldg, Provo, UT 84602
T: (801) 378-2492
Founded: 1920; Members: 3600
Gen Secr: Dr. H. Duane Smith
Focus: Zoology
Periodicals
Journal of Mammalogy (quarterly)
Mammalian Species (annually) 13468

American Society of Master Dental Technologists (ASMDT), POB 248, Oakland Gardens, NY 11364
T: (718) 428-0075
Founded: 1976; Members: 125
Focus: Dent 13469

American Society of Maxillofacial Surgeons (ASMS), 444 E Algonquin Rd, Arlington Heights, IL 6005
T: (708) 228-8375; Fax: (708) 228-6509
Founded: 1947; Members: 385
Pres: Paul N. Manson
Focus: Surgery 13470

American Society of Mechanical Engineers (ASME), 345 E 47 St, New York, NY 10017
T: (212) 705-7722; Fax: (212) 705-7674
Founded: 1880; Members: 122000
Pres: J.A. Falcon Jr.; Gen Secr: Dr. David L. Belden
Focus: Eng
Periodicals
Applied Mechanics (quarterly)
Applied Mechanics Review (monthly)
Biomechanical Engineering (quarterly)
Dynamic Systems, Measurement and Control (quarterly)
Energy Resources Technology (quarterly)
Engineering for Gas Turbines and Power (quarterly)
Engineering for Industry (quarterly)
Engineering Materials and Technology (quarterly)
Fluids Engineering (quarterly)
Heat Transfer (quarterly)
The Journal of Electronic Packaging (quarterly)
Manufacturing Review (quarterly)
Mechanical Design (quarterly)
Mechanical Engineering (monthly)
Offshore Mechanics and Arctic Engineering (quarterly)
Pressure Vessel Technology (quarterly)
Solar Energy Engineering (quarterly)
Tribology (quarterly)
Turbomachinery (quarterly)
Vibration and Acoustics (quarterly) . . . 13471

American Society of Naturalists (ASN), c/o Dept of Ecology and Evolutionary Biology, University of California, Irvine, CA 92717
T: (714) 856-8130
Founded: 1883; Members: 1835
Pres: Montgomery Slatkin; Gen Secr: Nancy T. Burley
Focus: Bio
Periodical
The American Naturalist (monthly) . . . 13472

American Society of Naval Engineers (ASNE), 1452 Duke St, Alexandria, VA 22314-3458
T: (703) 836-6727; Fax: (703) 836-7491
Founded: 1888; Members: 8000
Pres: Robert J. Scott; Gen Secr: Dennis Kruse
Focus: Navig; Eng
Periodical
Naval Engineers Journal (bi-monthly) . . 13473

American Society of Nephrology (ASN), 1200 19 St NW, Ste 300, Washington, DC 20036
T: (202) 857-1190; E-Mail: asn@sba.com;
Fax: (202) 223-4579
Founded: 1966; Members: 6200
Gen Secr: Judith Thomas
Focus: Med; Geriatrics
Periodicals
Abstracts and Program (annually)
Kidney International (monthly)
Membership Directory 13474

American Society of Neuroradiology (ASNR), 2210 Midwest Rd, Ste 207, Oak Brook, IL 60521
T: (708) 574-0220; Fax: (708) 574-0661
Founded: 1962; Members: 2028
Focus: Radiology
Periodicals
American Journal of Neuroradiology (bi-monthly)
Membership Roster (annually) 13475

American Society of Notaries (ASN), POB 5707, Tallahassee, FL 32314-5707
T: (904) 671-5164; Fax: (904) 671-5165
Founded: 1965; Members: 20000
Gen Secr: Nancy Dell Lawhorn
Focus: Law
Periodical
American Notary (bi-monthly) 13476

American Society of Papyrologists (ASP), c/o Dept of Classics, Saint Joseph's University, Philadelphia, PA 19131
Founded: 1961; Members: 175
Pres: Prof. Jennifer Sheridan
Focus: Hist 13477

American Society of Parasitologists (ASP), POB 1897, Lawrence, KS 66044
Founded: 1924; Members: 1800
Focus: Microbio
Periodicals
The Journal of Parasitology (bi-monthly)
Newsletter (quarterly) 13478

American Society of Pharmacognosy (ASP), c/o Dr. William J. Keller, School of Pharmacy, Northeast Louisiana University, Monroe, LA 71209
T: (318) 342-1692; Fax: (318) 342-1600
Founded: 1959; Members: 1000
Gen Secr: Dr. William J. Keller
Focus: Pharmacol
Periodicals
Journal of Natural Products (bi-monthly)
Newsletter (quarterly) 13479

American Society of Plant Physiologists (ASPP), 15501 Monona Dr, Rockville, MD 20855-2768
T: (301) 251-0560; Fax: (301) 279-2996
Founded: 1924; Members: 5200
Focus: Botany 13480

American Society of Plant Taxonomists (ASPT), c/o Dept of Biology, Saint Mary's College, Notre Dame, IN 46556

T: (219) 284-4674; Fax: (219) 284-4716
Founded: 1937; Members: 1200
Gen Secr: Dr. Richard Jensen
Focus: Botany
Periodicals
Systematic Botany (quarterly)
Systematic Botany Monographs 13481

American Society of Plastic and Reconstructive Surgeons (ASPRS), 444 E Algonquin Rd, Arlington Heights, IL 60006
T: (312) 228-9900; Fax: (312) 228-9131
Founded: 1931; Members: 5000
Focus: Surgery
Periodicals
Journal of Plastic and Reconstructive Surgery (monthly)
Plastic and Reconstructive Surgeons combined Roster (annually)
Plastic Surgery News (monthly) 13482

American Society of Plumbing Engineers (ASPE), 3617 Thousand Oaks Blvd, Westlake, CA 91362
T: (805) 495-7120; Fax: (805) 495-4861
Founded: 1964; Members: 6400
Focus: Eng 13483

American Society of Podiatric Dermatology (ASPD), c/o Dr. Steven Berlin, POB 7378, Baltimore, MD 21227-0378
T: (410) 247-4770; Fax: (410) 247-7329
Founded: 1914; Members: 260
Pres: Dr. Steven Berlin
Focus: Derm
Periodical
Newsletter (semi-annually) 13484

American Society of Primatologists (ASP), c/o Dept OB/GYN, Rush-Presbyterian Saint Lukes Medical Center, 1653 W Congress Pkwy, Chicago, IL 60612
T: (312) 942-2152
Founded: 1976; Members: 600
Focus: Anthro 13485

American Society of Psychopathology of Expression (ASPE), 74 Lawton St, Brookline, MA 02146
T: (617) 738-9821
Founded: 1964; Members: 137
Focus: Pathology; Psych
Periodicals
Annual Proceedings (annually)
Psychiatry and Art 13486

American Society of Questioned Document Examiners (ASQDE), 11420 SW 88 St, Ste 206, Miami, FL 33176
T: (703) 285-2482; Fax: (703) 596-2618
Founded: 1942; Members: 110
Pres: Gideon Epstein
Focus: Law 13487

American Society of Radiologic Technologists (ASRT), 15000 Central Av SE, Albuquerque, NM 87123-3909
T: (505) 298-4500; Fax: (505) 298-5063
Founded: 1920; Members: 18000
Focus: Radiology
Periodicals
Journal
Scanner 13488

American Society of Regional Anesthesia (ASRA), 1910 Byrd Av, POB 11086, Richmond, VA 23230-1086
T: (804) 282-0010; Fax: (804) 282-0090
Founded: 1974; Members: 6000
Focus: Anesthetics
Periodical
Regional Anesthesia (quarterly) 13489

American Society of Safety Engineers (ASSE), 1800 E Oakton St, Des Plaines, IL 60018-2187
T: (847) 699-2929; Fax: (847) 296-3769
Founded: 1911; Members: 32000
Gen Secr: Judy T. Neel
Focus: Safety
Periodicals
Conference Proceedings (annually)
Professional Safety (monthly) 13490

American Society of Sanitary Engineering (ASSE), 28901 Clemens Rd, Ste 100, Cleveland, OH 44145-1166
T: (216) 835-3040; Fax: (216) 835-3488
Founded: 1906; Members: 2700
Gen Secr: Gael H. Dunn
Focus: Eng; Hygiene
Periodicals
A.S.S.E. Year Book (annually)
Standards Report (annually) 13491

American Society of Sephardic Studies (ASOSS), 500 W 185 St, New York, NY 10033
T: (212) 960-5236; Fax: (212) 960-0288
Founded: 1963; Members: 117
Focus: Hist 13492

American Society of Sugar Beet Technologists (ASSBT), 800 Grant St, Ste 900, Denver, CO 80203
T: (303) 832-4460; Fax: (303) 832-4468
Founded: 1937; Members: 600
Gen Secr: Thomas K. Schwartz
Focus: Food
Periodical
Journal of Sugar Beet Research (quarterly)
. . . . 13493

American Society of Swedish Engineers (ASSE), c/o Swedish Seamen's Church, 5 E 48 St, New York, NY 10017
T: (203) 380-4840
Founded: 1888; Members: 150
Pres: Dr. Gunnar Hovstadius
Focus: Eng
Periodical
Membership Directory (annually) 13494

American Society of Trial Consultants, c/o Dept of Speech and Mass Communication, Towson State University, Towson, MD 21204
T: (410) 830-2448
Founded: 1982; Members: 225
Focus: Behav Sci; Law
Periodicals
Court Call (quarterly)
Directory (annually) 13495

American Society of Tropical Medicine and Hygiene (ASTMH), 60 Revere Dr, Ste 500, Northbrook, IL 60062
T: (847) 480-9592; Fax: (847) 480-9282
Founded: 1951; Members: 3000
Gen Secr: Joyce L. Paschall
Focus: Hygiene; Trop Med
Periodicals
American Journal of Tropical Medicine and Hygiene (bi-monthly)
Tropical Medicine and Hygiene News (bi-monthly)
. . . . 13496

American Society of Veterinary Ophthalmology (ASVO), 1416 W Liberty Av, Stillwater, OK 74075
T: (405) 377-4388
Founded: 1957; Members: 250
Gen Secr: V.A. Schultz
Focus: Vet Med; Ophthal
Periodical
Newsletter 13497

American Society of Zoologists (ASZ), 401 N Michigan Av, Chicago, IL 60651-4267
T: (312) 527-6697
Founded: 1890; Members: 3700
Focus: Zoology
Periodical
American Zoologist (quarterly) 13498

American Sociological Association (ASA), 1722 N St NW, Washington, DC 20036
T: (202) 833-3410
Founded: 1905; Members: 13000
Pres: A. Etzioni; Gen Secr: Felice J. Levine
Focus: Sociology
Periodicals
American Sociological Review (bi-monthly)
Contemporary Sociology: A Journal of Reviews (bi-monthly)
Directory of Departments (annually)
Directory of Members (annually)
Footnotes (9 times annually)
Guide to Graduate Departments of Sociology (annually)
Journal of Health and Social Behavior (quarterly)
Social Psychology (quarterly)
Sociological Theory (quarterly)
Sociology of Education (quarterly)
Teaching Sociology (quarterly) 13499

American Software Users Group (ASUG), 401 N Michigan, Chicago, IL 60611
T: (312) 644-6610; Fax: (312) 245-1084
Founded: 1980; Members: 300
Focus: Computer & Info Sci 13500

American Solar Energy Association (ASEA), c/o John Lillard, 124 South St, Annapolis, MD 21401
T: (410) 268-1900; Fax: (410) 268-5544
Founded: 1977; Members: 2000
Gen Secr: John Lillard
Focus: Energy
Periodical
Solar Today (bi-monthly) 13501

American Speech-Language-Hearing Association (ASHA), 10801 Rockville Pike, Rockville, MD 20852
T: (301) 897-5700; Fax: (301) 571-0457
Founded: 1925; Members: 84000
Gen Secr: Frederick T. Spahr
Focus: Logopedy
Periodicals
ASHA (monthly)
ASHA Monograph (irregularly)
ASHA Report (irregularly)
Journal of Speech and Hearing Disorders (quarterly)
Journal of Speech and Hearing Research (quarterly)
Language, Speech and Hearing Services in Schools (quarterly) 13502

American Spelean History Association (ASHA), 711 E Atlantic Av, Altoona, PA 16602
T: (814) 946-3155
Founded: 1968; Members: 150
Focus: Geology; Hist
Periodical
Journal of Spelean History (quarterly) . . 13503

American Spinal Injury Association (ASIA), 345 E Superior, Rm 1436, Chicago, IL 60611
T: (312) 908-6207; Fax: (312) 503-0869
Founded: 1973; Members: 500
Gen Secr: Marianne G. Kaplan
Focus: Pathology; Physiology

Periodical
ASIA Bulletin (semi-annually) 13504

American Sports Education Institute (ASEI), 200 Castlewood Dr, North Palm Beach, FL 33408
T: (407) 842-4100; E-Mail: mmsgma@aol.com; Fax: (407) 863-8984
Founded: 1977; Members: 20000
Gen Secr: Michael May
Focus: Sports
Periodical
Booster (bi-monthly) 13505

American Statistical Association (ASA), 1429 Duke St, Alexandria, VA 22314
T: (703) 684-1221; Fax: (703) 684-7037
Founded: 1839; Members: 18200
Gen Secr: Ray A. Waller
Focus: Stats
Periodicals
The American Statistician (quarterly)
AMSTAT News (10 times annually)
Current Index to Statistics: Applications, Methods and Theory (annually)
Journal of ASA (quarterly)
Journal of Business & Economic Statistics (quarterly)
Journal of Educational Statistics (quarterly)
Proceedings (annually)
Technometrics (quarterly) 13506

American String Teachers Association (ASTA), 1806 Robert Fulton Dr, Ste 300, Reston, VA 22091
Founded: 1946; Members: 9600
Gen Secr: G. Wixson
Focus: Music; Educ
Periodical
American String Teacher (3 times annually) 13507

American Student Dental Association (ASDA), 211 E Chicago Av, Ste 840, Chicago, IL 60611
T: (312) 440-2795; Fax: (312) 440-2820
Founded: 1971; Members: 13500
Focus: Dent
Periodicals
Dental Student Handbook (annually)
Dentistry (quarterly)
News (monthly) 13508

American Studies Association (ASA), 1120 19 St NW, Ste 301, Washington, DC 20036
T: (202) 467-4783; E-Mail: pp001366@interramp.com; Fax: (202) 467-4786
Founded: 1951; Members: 5000
Gen Secr: John F. Stephens
Focus: Hist; Lit; Arts
Periodicals
American Quarterly (quarterly)
American Studies Association Newsletter (quarterly) 13509

American Surgical Association (ASA), c/o PR/RI, 13 Elm St, Manchester, MA 01944
T: (508) 526-8330
Founded: 1880; Members: 949
Focus: Surgery
Periodicals
Annals of Surgery (monthly)
Transactions (annually) 13510

American Swedish Institute (ASI), 2600 Park Av, Minneapolis, MN 55407
T: (612) 871-4907; Fax: (612) 871-8682
Founded: 1929; Members: 6700
Focus: Ethnology 13511

American Technical Education Association (ATEA), c/o North Dakota State College of Science, Wahpeton, ND 58076
T: (701) 671-2240; Fax: (701) 671-2145
Founded: 1928; Members: 2500
Focus: Adult Educ; Eng
Periodical
ATEA Journal (quarterly) 13512

American Teilhard Association (ATA), 40 Hillside Ln, Syosset, NY 11791
T: (516) 921-8655
Founded: 1964
Focus: Rel & Theol; Futurology
Periodicals
Teilhard Perspective (semi-annually)
Teilhard Studies (semi-annually) 13513

American Theatre Critics Association (ATCA), c/o Clara Hieronymus, The Tennessean, 2200 Hemingway Dr, Nashville, TN 37215
T: (615) 665-0595; Fax: (615) 259-8057
Founded: 1974; Members: 275
Focus: Perf Arts 13514

American Theatre Organ Society (ATOS), POB 551081, Indianapolis, IN 46205-1081
T: (317) 251-6441; E-Mail: felenxer@in.net; Fax: (317) 251-6443
Founded: 1955; Members: 6000
Gen Secr: Richard J. Sklenar
Focus: Music
Periodical
Theatre Organ (bi-monthly) 13515

American Theological Library Association (ATLA), 820 Church St, Ste 400, Evanston, IL 60201
T: (847) 869-7788; Fax: (847) 869-8513
Founded: 1947; Members: 750
Pres: M. Patrick Graham; Gen Secr: Dennis A. Norlin
Focus: Libraries & Bk Sci; Rel & Theol
Periodicals
Index to Book Reviews in Religion: (IBRR) (annually)
Newsletter (quarterly)
Religion Index One: Periodicals (semi-annually)
Religion Index Two: Multi-Author Works: (RIT) (annually)
Research in Ministry: (RIM) (annually)
Summary of Proceedings of the Annual Conference (annually) 13516

American Theological Society – Midwest Division, c/o North Park Theological Seminary, 3225 W Foster Av, Chicago, IL 60625
T: (312) 244-6231; Fax: (312) 244-6244
Founded: 1927; Members: 102
Gen Secr: Dr. John Weborg
Focus: Rel & Theol
Periodical
Membership Directory 13517

American Thoracic Society (ATS), 1740 Broadway, New York, NY 10019-4374
T: (212) 315-8778; Fax: (212) 315-6498
Founded: 1905; Members: 11000
Gen Secr: Marilyn Hansen
Focus: Intern Med
Periodicals
American Journal of Respiratory Cell and Molecular Biology
American Review of Respiratory Disease (monthly) 13518

American Tinnitus Association (ATA), POB 5, Portland, OR 97207
T: (503) 248-9985
Founded: 1971; Members: 150000
Focus: Otorhinolaryngology
Periodical
Tinnitus Today (quarterly) 13519

American Tolkien Society (ATS), c/o Phil Helms, POB 373, Highland, MI 48357-0373
T: (813) 585-0985
Founded: 1975; Members: 475
Focus: Lit
Periodical
Minas Tirith Evening Star (quarterly) . . 13520

American Trauma Society (ATS), 8903 Presidential Pkwy, Ste 512, Upper Marlboro, MD 20772
T: (301) 420-4189; Fax: (301) 420-0617
Founded: 1968; Members: 2500
Focus: Traumatology
Periodicals
ATS Hotline (monthly)
Directory of Specialty Referral Centers
EMS News (quarterly) 13521

American Type Culture Collection (ATCC), 12301 Parklawn Dr, Rockville, MD 20852
T: (301) 881-2600; Fax: (301) 231-5826
Founded: 1925
Focus: Bio
Periodical
Newsletter (quarterly) 13522

American Underground-Construction Association (AUA), 511 11 Av S, Ste 248, Minneapolis, MN 55415
T: (612) 339-5403; Fax: (612) 339-3207
Founded: 1975; Members: 500
Gen Secr: Susan R. Nelson
Focus: Archit; Eng
Periodical
AVA News (quarterly) 13523

American Urological Association (AUA), 1120 N Charles St, Baltimore, MD 21201
T: (410) 727-1100; Fax: (410) 223-4370
Founded: 1902; Members: 11300
Pres: Dr. Jack W. McAninch; Gen Secr: Dr. William R. Turner
Focus: Urology
Periodicals
AUA News (bi-monthly)
Journal of Urology (monthly)
Membership Roster (bi-annually) 13524

American Vacuum Society (AVS), 120 Wall St, New York, NY 10005
T: (212) 248-0200; E-Mail: avsnyc@vacuum.org; Fax: (212) 248-0245
Founded: 1953; Members: 5500
Gen Secr: Yvonne Towse
Focus: Physics
Periodical
Journal of Vacuum Science and Technology (JVST) (monthly) 13525

American Veterinary Medical Association (AVMA), 1931 N Meacham Rd, Schaumburg, IL 60173-4360
T: (847) 915-8070; Fax: (847) 925-1329
Founded: 1863; Members: 46000
Gen Secr: Dr. Bruce Little
Focus: Vet Med
Periodicals
American Journal of Veterinary Research (monthly)
Journal (bi-weekly) 13526

American Veterinary Society of Animal Behavior (AVSAB), c/o Dr. Debra Horwitz, 253 S Graeser, Saint Louis, MO 63141
T: (314) 567-3864; Fax: (314) 567-3864
Founded: 1975; Members: 425
Gen Secr: Dr. Debra Horwitz
Focus: Vet Med 13527

American Vocational Association (AVA), 1410 King St, Alexandria, VA 22314
T: (703) 683-3111; Fax: (703) 683-7424
Founded: 1925; Members: 40000
Gen Secr: Charles H. Buzzell
Focus: Adult Educ
Periodical
Vocational Education Journal (8 times annually) 13528

American Vocational Education Personnel Development Association (AVEPDA), c/o Dept of Vocational-Technical Education, 1500 W Seventh Av, Stillwater, OK 74074
T: (405) 743-5535; Fax: (405) 743-5541
Founded: 1972; Members: 250
Focus: Educ 13529

American Vocational Education Research Association (AVERA), c/o Michael K. Swan, Teacher Education, North Dakota State University, 155 E. Morrow Lebedeff Hall, Fargo, ND 55108-6197
T: (701) 231-7439; E-Mail: swan@plains.nodak.edu; Fax: (701) 231-9685
Founded: 1966; Members: 500
Gen Secr: Michael K. Swan
Focus: Adult Educ
Periodicals
The Beacon (quarterly)
Journal of Vocational Education Research (quarterly) 13530

American Water Resources Association (AWRA), 950 Herndon Pky, Ste 300, Herdon, VA 22070-5528
T: (703) 904-1225; E-Mail: awrahQ@aol.com; Fax: (703) 904-1228
Founded: 1964; Members: 3800
Gen Secr: Kenneth D. Reid
Focus: Water Res
Periodicals
Hydata News and Views (bi-monthly)
Proceedings (annually)
Water Resources Bulletin (bi-monthly) . . 13531

American Welding Society (AWS), 550 NW LeJeune Rd, Miami, FL 33126
T: (305) 443-9353; Fax: (305) 443-7559
Founded: 1919; Members: 46000
Gen Secr: Dr. Frank G. DeLaurier
Focus: Metallurgy
Periodical
Welding Journal (monthly) 13532

American Wind Energy Association (AWEA), 122 C St NW, Washington, DC 20001
T: (202) 383-2500; Fax: (202) 383-2505
Founded: 1974
Gen Secr: Randall Swisher
Focus: Energy
Periodicals
AWEA Wind Energy (weekly)
Windletter (8 times annually) 13533

American Wood-Preservers' Association (AWPA), POB 286, Woodstock, MD 21163-0286
T: (410) 465-3169; Fax: (410) 465-3195
Founded: 1904; Members: 1700
Focus: Forestry 13534

American Wood Preservers Institute (AWPI), 1945 Old Gallows Rd, Ste 550, Vienna, VA 22182
T: (703) 893-4005; Fax: (703) 893-8942
Founded: 1921; Members: 150
Focus: Ecology
Periodicals
Environmental Report (monthly)
Wood Preserving Statistics (annually) . . 13535

Americas Association of Cooperative / Mutual Insurance Societies (AAC/MIS), c/o Nationwide Insurance Companies, 1 Nationwide Plaza, 1-35-05, Columbus, OH 43215-2220
T: (614) 249-6344; Fax: (614) 249-3090
Gen Secr: Patrick S. Roberts
Focus: Insurance 13536

Amerika Katolika Esperanto-Societo (AKES), c/o Mubarak Anwar Amar, Saint Patrick's Roman Catholic Church, 213 S Bogardus, POB 19, Elkhart, IL 62634
Founded: 1967; Members: 75
Gen Secr: Mubarak Anwar Amar
Focus: Ling
Periodical
Annual Report of the Representative (annually) 13537

Amerind Foundation (AF), POB 248, Dragoon, AZ 85609
T: (602) 586-3666; Fax: (602) 586-3667
Founded: 1937
Focus: Ethnology; Archeol 13538

Ancient Astronaut Society (AAS), 1921 Saint Johns Av, Highland Park, IL 60035
T: (708) 295-8899
Founded: 1973; Members: 6000
Focus: Aero
Periodical
Ancient Skies (bi-monthly) 13539

Animal Behavior Society (ABS), c/o Susan A. Foster, Dept of Biology, Clark University, 950 Main St, Worcester, MA 01610
T: (508) 793-7204; Fax: (508) 793-8861
Founded: 1964; Members: 3000
Gen Secr: Susan A. Foster
Focus: Zoology; Behav Sci
Periodicals
Animal Behavior (quarterly)
Newsletter (quarterly) 13540

Animal Medical Center (AMC), 510 E 62 St, New York, NY 10021
T: (212) 838-8100; Fax: (212) 832-9630
Founded: 1910
Focus: Vet Med 13541

Animal Nutrition Research Council (ANRD), c/o Roger L. Garrett, Diversified Laboratories Inc, 3810 Concorde Pkwy, Chantilly, VA 22030
T: (703) 222-8700
Founded: 1939; Members: 421
Focus: Vet Med
Periodical
Annual Proceedings (annually) 13542

Animal Protection Institute of America (API), 2831 Fruitridge Rd, Sacramento, CA 95820
T: (916) 731-5521; E-Mail: onlineAPI@aol.com; Fax: (916) 731-5521
Founded: 1968; Members: 65000
Gen Secr: Alan H. Berger
Focus: Ecology
Periodical
Mainstream Magazine (quarterly) 13543

Annual Reviews (AR), 4139 El Camino Way, POB 10139, Palo Alto, CA 94303-0897
T: (415) 493-4400; Fax: (415) 855-9815
Focus: Nat Sci
Periodicals
Annual Review of Anthropology (annually)
Annual Review of Astronomy & Astrophysics (annually)
Annual Review of Biochemistry (annually)
Annual Review of Biophysics & Biophysical Chemistry (annually)
Annual Review of Cell Biology (annually)
Annual Review of Computer Science (annually)
Annual Review of Earth & Planetary Sciences (annually)
Annual Review of Ecology & Systematics (annually)
Annual Review of Energy (annually)
Annual Review of Entomology (annually)
Annual Review of Fluid Mechanics (annually)
Annual Review of Genetics (annually)
Annual Review of Immunology (annually)
Annual Review of Materials Science (annually)
Annual Review of Medicine (annually)
Annual Review of Microbiology (annually)
Annual Review of Neuroscience (annually)
Annual Review of Nuclear & Particle Science (annually)
Annual Review of Nutrition (annually)
Annual Review of Pharmacology & Toxicology (annually)
Annual Review of Physical Chemistry (annually)
Annual Review of Physiology (annually)
Annual Review of Phytopathology (annually)
Annual Review of Plant Physiology & Plant Molecular Biology (annually)
Annual Review of Psychology (annually)
Annual Review of Public Health (annually)
Annual Review of Sociology (annually) . 13544

Anonymous Arts Recovery Society (AARS), 380 W Broadway, New York, NY 10012
T: (212) 431-3600
Founded: 1960
Focus: Arts 13545

Anonymous Families History Project (AFHP), c/o Prof. Tamara K. Hareven, Dept of Individual and Family Studies, University of Delaware, 101 Alison Hall, Newark, DE 19716
T: (302) 831-6500; Fax: (302) 831-8776
Founded: 1971
Gen Secr: Prof. Tamara K. Hareven
Focus: Hist 13546

Antarctica and Southern Ocean Coalition (ASOC), 424 C St NE, Washington, DC 20002
T: (202) 544-0236; E-Mail: Econet:antarctica@igc.org; Fax: (202) 544-8483
Founded: 1978; Members: 230
Gen Secr: Beth Marks
Focus: Geography 13547

Antenna Measurement Techniques Association (AMTA), 6065 Roswell Rd, Ste 2252, Atlanta, GA 30328
T: (707) 427-2410; Fax: (707) 427-0823
Founded: 1979; Members: 400
Gen Secr: Sally Vogliano
Focus: Electric Eng
Periodicals
Call for Papers (semi-annually)
Newsletter (quarterly) 13548

Anthology Film Archives (AFA), 32-34 Second Av, New York, NY 10003
T: (212) 505-5181; Fax: (212) 477-2714
Founded: 1970; Members: 600
Focus: Cinema
Periodical
Film Culture 13549

Anthropology Film Center Foundation (AFCF), POB 493, Santa Fe, NM 87501
T: (505) 983-4127
Founded: 1965
Focus: Anthro 13550

AOAC International (AOAC), 2200 Wilson Blvd, Ste 400, Arlington, VA 22201-3301
T: (703) 522-3032; Fax: (703) 522-5468
Founded: 1884; Members: 3700
Focus: Chem
Periodicals
Journal of the AOAC (bi-monthly)
The Referee (monthly) 13551

AOIP, 231 W 29 St, Ste 1205, New York, NY 10001
T: (212) 967-4008; Fax: (212) 971-4682
Founded: 1980; Members: 94
Focus: Lit 13552

APEC, Miami Valley Tower, Ste 2100, 40 W Fourth St, Dayton, OH 45402
T: (513) 228-2602
Founded: 1966; Members: 200
Focus: Eng
Periodical
Journal (quarterly) 13553

APPA: The Association of Higher Education Facilities Officers, 1643 Prince St, Alexandria, VA 22314-2818
T: (703) 684-1446; E-Mail: infi@appa.org; Fax: (703) 549-2772
Founded: 1914; Members: 4500
Gen Secr: Wayne E. Leroy
Focus: Sports
Periodicals
APPA Newsletter (monthly)
Facilities Management Magazine (quarterly) 13554

Applied Research and Development Institute International (ARDI), 2121 S Oneida St, Ste 633, Denver, CO 80224
T: (303) 691-6076; E-Mail: ardiintl@aol.com; Fax: (303) 691-6077
Gen Secr: Ann Werner
Focus: Develop Areas 13555

Applied Technology Council (ATC), 555 Twin Dolphin Dr, Ste 550, Redwood City, CA 94065
T: (415) 595-1542; Fax: (415) 593-2320
Founded: 1971; Members: 12
Focus: Nat Sci 13556

Appropriate Technology International (ATI), 1828 L St NW, Ste 1000, Washington, DC 20036
T: (202) 293-4600; E-Mail: info@ati.org; Fax: (202) 293-4598
Gen Secr: Andrew Maguire
Focus: Eng 13557

Aquatic Plant Management Society (APMS), POB 2695, Washington, DC 20013
T: (202) 547-5437; Fax: (202) 547-5645
Founded: 1961; Members: 600
Gen Secr: William N. Rushing
Focus: Botany
Periodicals
Directory of Membership APMS
Journal of Aquatic Plant Management (semi-annually)
Newsletter 13558

Aquatic Research Institute (ARI), 2242 Davis Ct, Hayward, CA 94545
T: (510) 785-2216; Fax: (510) 784-0945
Founded: 1962
Focus: Oceanography
Periodicals
Aquariculture (quarterly)
Aquatica 13559

Arab Management Society (AMS), c/o Canisius College, 2001 Main St, Buffalo, NY 14208
Gen Secr: Dr. Edward Gress
Focus: Business Admin 13560

Archaeological Conservancy (AC), 5301 Central Av NE, Ste 1218, Albuquerque, NM 87108
T: (505) 266-1540
Founded: 1979; Members: 13000
Pres: Mark Michel
Focus: Archeol
Periodical
Newsletter (quarterly) 13561

Archaeological Institute of America (AIA), 656 Beacon St, Boston, MA 02215
T: (617) 353-9361; Fax: (617) 353-6550
Founded: 1879; Members: 11000
Pres: Stephen Dyson; Gen Secr: Mark J. Meister
Focus: Archeol
Periodicals
American Journal of Archaeology (quarterly)
Archaeology (bi-monthly) 13562

Archeology Section (AS), c/o American Anthropological Association, 4350 N Fairfax Dr, Ste 640, Arlington, VA 22203
T: (703) 528-1902; Fax: (703) 528-3546
Founded: 1984; Members: 1984
Pres: David Grove
Focus: Archeol 13563

Architectural League of New York (ALNY), 457 Madison Av, New York, NY 10022
T: (212) 753-1722
Founded: 1881; Members: 1000
Focus: Archit 13564

Archives of American Art (AAA), c/o Smithsonian Institution, Rm 331, Eighth and G Sts NW, Washington, DC 20560
T: (202) 357-2781; Fax: (202) 786-2608
Founded: 1954; Members: 1900
Gen Secr: Richard J. Wattenmaker
Focus: Arts
Periodical
Archives of American Art Journal (quarterly)
. . . . 13565

Arctic Ocean Science Board (AOSB), c/o Directorate for Geosciences, National Science Foundation, Division of Ocean Sciences, 4201 Wilson Blvd, Rm 1070, Arlington, VA 22230
T: (703) 306-1516; E-Mail: lbrown@nsf.gov; Fax: (703) 306-0091
Focus: Oceanography 13566

Arica Institute (AI), 145 Palisade St, Ste 401, Dobbs Ferry, NY 10522-1617
T: (914) 674-4091
Founded: 1971; Members: 800
Focus: Psych 13567

Ark-La-Tex Genealogical Association (ALTGA), POB 4462, Shreveport, LA 71134-0462
T: (318) 868-2807
Founded: 1955; Members: 300
Pres: Charles Pratt
Focus: Genealogy
Periodical
The Genie (quarterly) 13568

Armed Forces Institute of Pathology (AFIP), 6825 16 St NW, Washington, DC 20306-6000
T: (202) 782-2100; Fax: (202) 782-7164
Founded: 1862
Gen Secr: Michael J. Dickerson
Focus: Pathology
Periodical
Letter (bi-monthly) 13569

Armenian Centre for National and International Studies, POB 57666, Sherman Oaks, CA 91403
Focus: Poli Sci; Sociology 13570

Armenian Educational Foundation (AEF), 600 W Broadway, Ste 130, Glendale, CA 91204
T: (818) 242-4154
Founded: 1950; Members: 100
Focus: Educ 13571

Armenian Literary Society (ALS), 77 Everett Rd, Demarest, NJ 07627
T: (201) 767-1494
Founded: 1956; Members: 300
Focus: Lit
Periodical
Kir ou Kirk (irregularly) 13572

Art Institute of Light (AIL), POB 429, Gap, PA 17527-0429
T: (717) 768-8255
Founded: 1930
Focus: Arts 13573

Art Libraries Society of North America (ARLIS/NA), 4101 Lake Boone Trail, Ste 201, Raleigh, NC 27607-7509
T: (919) 787-5181; Fax: (919) 787-4916
Founded: 1972; Members: 1365
Pres: Jack Robertson; Gen Secr: Penney Depas
Focus: Libraries & Bk Sci
Periodical
Art Documentation (quarterly) 13574

Arts International, c/o IIE, 809 United Nations Plaza, New York, NY 10017-3580
T: (212) 984-5370; E-Mail: ainternational@iie.org; Fax: (212) 984-5574
Founded: 1981; Members: 250
Gen Secr: Noreen Tomassi
Focus: Arts; Educ 13575

Asia-Pacific Council of Optometry (APCO), c/o College of Optometry, Pacific University, 2043 College Way, Forest Grove, OR 97116
T: (503) 359-2170; Fax: (503) 359-2929
Gen Secr: Prof. Willard Bleything
Focus: Ophthal 13576

Asia Pacific Public Health Nutrition Association, c/o Public Health Nutrition Program, University of California, 421 Warren Hall, Berkeley, CA 94720-7360
T: (510) 642-3852; E-Mail: zaksabry@uclink.berkeley.edu; Fax: (510) 643-6981
Gen Secr: Prof. Zak Sabry
Focus: Public Health; Nutrition 13577

Asia Society (AS), 725 Park Av, New York, NY 10021
T: (212) 288-6400; E-Mail: mirzab@asiasoc.org; Fax: (212) 517-8315
Founded: 1956; Members: 5600
Focus: Ethnology; Poli Sci 13578

Asian Literature Division (of MLA) (ALD), c/o Dept of East Asian Languages and Culture, Indiana University, Bloomington, IN 47405
T: (812) 855-5339; Fax: (812) 855-6402
Founded: 1953
Focus: Lit 13579

Asian Studies Center, Michigan, c/o Michigan State University, 110 Center for International Programs, East Lansing, MI 48824-1035
T: (517) 353-1680; Fax: (517) 432-2659
Focus: Ethnology 13580

ASM International, 9639 Kinsman, Materials Park, OH 44073
T: (216) 338-5151; Fax: (216) 338-4634
Founded: 1913; Members: 54000
Gen Secr: Edward L. Langer
Focus: Metallurgy
Periodicals
Advanced Materials and Processes (monthly)
ASM News (monthly)
Bulletin of Alloy Phase Diagrams (bi-monthly)
International Materials Reviews (bi-monthly)
Journal of Heat Treating (semi-annually)
Journal of Materials Engineering (quarterly)
Journal of Materials Shaping Technology (quarterly)
Metallurgical Transactions A (monthly)
Metallurgical Transactions B (bi-monthly) . 13581

ASME International Gas Turbine Institute (IGTI), POB 422029, Atlanta, GA 30342
T: (404) 847-0072 Ext 237; E-Mail: grossw@asme.org; Fax: (404) 847-0151, 843-2517
Gen Secr: Wayne H. Gross
Focus: Mach Eng 13582

Aspen Institute (TAI), Wye River Conference Center, 2010 Carmichael Rd, POB 222, Queenstown, MD 21658
T: (410) 827-7168; Fax: (410) 827-9182
Founded: 1949
Pres: David T. McLaughlin
Focus: Sociology 13583

Assembly of the World's Religions, 4 W 43 St, New York, NY 10036
T: (212) 869-6023; Fax: (212) 869-6424
Gen Secr: Thomas G. Walsh
Focus: Rel & Theol 13584

Associated Business Writers of America (ABWA), 1450 S Havana, Ste 424, Aurora, CO 80012
T: (303) 751-7844; Fax: (303) 751-8593
Founded: 1945; Members: 150
Gen Secr: Sandy Whelchel
Focus: Lit
Periodicals
Authorship (bi-monthly)
Flash Market News (monthly) 13585

Associated Colleges of the Midwest (ACM), 205 W Wacker Dr, Ste 1300, Chicago, IL 60606
T: (312) 263-5000; Fax: (312) 263-5879
Founded: 1958; Members: 14
Pres: Elizabeth R. Hayford
Focus: Educ 13586

Associated Laboratories (AL), POB 1037, Wrightsville Beach, NC 28480
T: (910) 256-3934
Founded: 1958; Members: 23
Pres: Johnnie C. Baker
Focus: Water Res 13587

Associated Schools of Construction (ASC), POB 834, Peoria, IL 61652
T: (309) 677-2943
Founded: 1965; Members: 89
Focus: Civil Eng; Adult Educ
Periodicals
Annual Report (annually)
Proceedings of the Annual Meeting (annually)
. . . . 13588

Associated Universities (AUI), 1400 16 St NW, Ste 730, Washington, DC 20036
T: (202) 462-1676
Founded: 1946
Focus: Sci 13589

Associates for World Action in Rehabilitation and Education (AWARE), 3383 Lakeshore Dr, Mohegan Lake, NY 10547
T: (914) 528-0567; Fax: (914) 528-0567
Gen Secr: Anne Yeadon
Focus: Educ; Rehabil 13590

Association for Academic Surgery (AAS), 420 Delaware St SE, Box 242 UMHC, Minneapolis, MN 55455
T: (612) 626-1999; Fax: (612) 625-8496
Founded: 1966; Members: 2400
Focus: Surgery
Periodical
Journal of Surgical Research (monthly) . 13591

Association for Advancement of Behavior Therapy (AABT), 305 Seventh Av, New York, NY 10001-6008
T: (212) 647-1890; Fax: (212) 647-1865
Founded: 1966; Members: 4300
Gen Secr: Mary Jane Eimer
Focus: Psychiatry; Behav Sci
Periodicals
The Behavior Therapist (10 times annually)
Behavior Therapy (quarterly)
Membership Directory (bi-annually) . . . 13592

Association for Advancement of Psychoanalysis (AAP), 329 E 62 St, New York, NY 10021
T: (212) 838-8044
Founded: 1941; Members: 80
Focus: Psychoan
Periodical
The American Journal of Psychoanalysis (quarterly) 13593

Association for Advancement of Psychology (AAP), POB 38129, Colorado Springs, 80937
T: (719) 520-0688; Fax: (719) 520-0375
Founded: 1974; Members: 6000
Focus: Psych
Periodical
Advance (quarterly) 13594

Association for American Schools in South America (AASSA), 14750 NW 77 Court, Ste 210, Miami Lakes, FL 33016
T: (305) 821-0345; Fax: (305) 821-4244
Gen Secr: Jim Morris
Focus: Educ 13595

Association for Applied Psychophysiology and Biofeedback (AAPB), 10200 W 44 Av, Ste 304, Wheat Ridge, CO 80033
T: (303) 422-8436; Fax: (303) 422-8894
Founded: 1969; Members: 2100
Focus: Physiology 13596

Association for Arid Lands Studies (AALS), c/o International Center Arid and Semi-Arid Land Studies, Texas Technical University, Box 41036, Lubbock, TX 79409-1036
T: (806) 742-2218; Fax: (806) 742-1954
Founded: 1977; Members: 250
Focus: Ecology 13597

Association for Asian Studies (AAS), c/o University of Michigan, 1 Lane Hall, Ann Arbor, MI 48109
T: (313) 665-2490; Fax: (313) 665-3801
Founded: 1941; Members: 7500
Gen Secr: John Campbell
Focus: Ethnology
Periodicals
Asian Studies Newsletter (5 times annually)
Bibliography of Asian Studies (annually)
Doctoral Dissertations on Asia (annually)
Journal of Asian Studies (quarterly)
Monograph Series (irregularly) 13598

Association for Assessment in Counseling (AAC), c/o American Counseling Association, 5999 Stevenson Av, Alexandria, VA 22304
T: (703) 823-9800; Fax: (703) 823-0252
Founded: 1965; Members: 1684
Focus: Law
Periodicals
Measurement and Evaluation in Counseling and Development (quarterly)
Newsnotes (quarterly) 13599

Association for Astrological Psychology (AAP), 360 Quietwood Dr, San Rafael, CA 94903
T: (415) 499-1553; Fax: (415) 499-1553
Founded: 1987; Members: 300
Pres: Glenn Perry
Focus: Psych 13600

Association for Behavior Analysis International (ABA), c/o Western Michigan University, 213 West Hall, Kalamazoo, MI 49008-5052
T: (616) 387-8341; Fax: (616) 387-8342
Founded: 1974; Members: 2000
Gen Secr: Maria E. Malott
Focus: Psychoan
Periodicals
Membership Directory (bi-annually)
Newsletter (3 times annually)
Program Book (annually) 13601

Association for Birth Psychology (ABP), 444 E 82 St, New York, NY 10028
T: (212) 988-6617
Founded: 1978; Members: 352
Focus: Psych
Periodical
Birth Psychology Bulletin (semi-annually) . 13602

Association for Bridge Construction and Design (ABCD), POB 23264, Pittsburgh, PA 15222
T: (412) 281-9900; Fax: (412) 281-2056
Founded: 1976; Members: 300
Focus: Archit 13603

Association for Business Communication, c/o Dept of Management, College of Business, University of North Texas, Denton, TX 76203
T: (817) 565-4423; Fax: (817) 565-4930
Founded: 1935; Members: 2500
Focus: Econ
Periodicals
The Bulletin of the Association for Business Communication (quarterly)
The Journal of Business Communication (quarterly)
. . . . 13604

Association for Canadian Studies in the United States (ACSUS), 1 Dupont Circle, Ste 620, Washington, DC 20036
T: (202) 887-6375; Fax: (202) 296-8379
Founded: 1971; Members: 1300
Focus: Educ
Periodical
American Review of Canadian Studies (3 times annually) 13605

Association for Central Asian Studies (ACAS), c/o Univ. of Wisconsin, 3211 Humanities Bldg, 455 N Park St, Madison, NY 53706
T: (608) 263-1825; Fax: (608) 262-2150

Gen Secr: Prof. Kemal H. Karpat
Focus: Ethnology 13606

Association for Chemoreception Sciences (AChemS), c/o Panacea Associates, 229 Westridge Dr, Tallahassee, FL 32304
T: (904) 576-5530; Fax: (215) 898-2084
Founded: 1979; Members: 649
Focus: Chem 13607

Association for Child Psychoanalysis (ACP), POB 253, Ramsey, NJ 07446
T: (201) 825-3138; Fax: (201) 825-3138
Founded: 1965; Members: 500
Gen Secr: Nancy Hall
Focus: Psychoan
Periodicals
Membership Roster (bi-annually)
Newsletter (annually) 13608

Association for Childbirth at Home, International (ACHI), POB 430, Glendale, CA 91209
T: (818) 545-7128; Fax: (818) 409-1728
Founded: 1972; Members: 30000
Pres: Tonya Brooks
Focus: Gynecology
Periodicals
Birth Notes (quarterly)
Founders Letter (bi-monthly) 13609

Association for Childhood Education International (ACEI), 11501 Georgia Av, Ste 312, Wheaton, MD 20902
T: (301) 942-2443; Fax: (301) 942-3012
Founded: 1931; Members: 17000
Gen Secr: Gerald Odland
Focus: Educ
Periodicals
ACEI Exchange (monthly)
Childhood Education (5 times annually)
Journal of Research in Childhood Education (bi-annually) 13610

Association for Communication Administration (ACA), 5105 Backlick Rd, Annandale, VA 22003
T: (703) 750-0533; Fax: (703) 914-9471
Founded: 1971; Members: 325
Gen Secr: James L. Gaudino
Focus: Comm Sci
Periodical
Journal (quarterly) 13611

Association for Comparative Economic Studies (ACES), c/o Michael R. Dohan, Dept of Economics, Queens College, CUNY, 65-30 Kissena Blvd, Flushing, NY 11367
T: (718) 997-5461; Fax: (718) 997-5535
Founded: 1972; Members: 600
Gen Secr: Michael R. Dohan
Focus: Econ
Periodical
ACES Bulletin (3-4 times annually) . . . 13612

Association for Computational Linguistics (ACL), POB 6090, Somerset, NJ 08875
T: (908) 873-3898; E-Mail: acl@bbellcore.com; Fax: (908) 873-0014
Founded: 1962; Members: 2000
Gen Secr: Priscilla Rasmussen
Focus: Ling
Periodicals
Computational Linguistics (quarterly)
The Finite String (quarterly) 13613

Association for Computers and the Humanities (ACH), c/o Randall Jones, Brigham Young University, 2054 JKHB, Provo, UT 84602
T: (801) 378-2779; Fax: (801) 378-4649
Founded: 1978; Members: 350
Gen Secr: Randall Jones
Focus: Computer & Info Sci
Periodical
Newsletter (quarterly) 13614

Association for Computing Machinery (ACM), 1515 Broadway, New York, NY 10036
T: (212) 869-7440; Fax: (212) 944-1318
Founded: 1947; Members: 75000
Focus: Computer & Info Sci
Periodicals
ACM Guide to Computing Literature (Guide) (annually)
ACM Transactions on Computer Systems (TOCS) (quarterly)
ACM Transactions on Database Systems (TODS) (quarterly)
ACM Transactions on Graphics (TOG) (quarterly)
ACM Transactions on Mathematical Software (TOMS) (quarterly)
ACM Transactions on Office Information Systems (TOOIS) (quarterly)
ACM Transactions on Programming Languages & Systems (TOPLAS) (quarterly)
Communications of the ACM (monthly)
Computing Reviews (quarterly)
Computing Surveys (quarterly)
Journal of the ACM (quarterly) 13615

Association for Continuing Higher Education (ACHE), c/o Dr. Wayne Whelan, Trident Technical College, POB 118067, CE-P, Charleston, SC 29423-8067
T: (803) 722-5546; Fax: (803) 722-5520
Founded: 1939; Members: 1400
Gen Secr: Dr. Wayne Whelan
Focus: Adult Educ
Periodicals
5 Minutes with ACHE (9 times annually)
Journal of Continuing Higher Education (quarterly) 13616

Association for Counselling, Organization, Research and Development (ACORD), 279 E 44 St, Apt 16-F, New York, NY 10017
T: (212) 867-3607
Focus: Sci 13617

Association for Counselor Education and Supervision (ACES), c/o American Counseling Association, 5999 Stevenson Av, Alexandria, VA 22304
T: (703) 823-9800; Fax: (703)823-0252
Founded: 1964; Members: 2940
Focus: Educ
Periodicals
Counselor Education and Supervision (quarterly)
Newsletter (quarterly) 13618

Association for Documentary Editing (ADE), c/o Sharon Ritenour Stevens, George C. Marshall Fund, POB 1600, Lexington, VA 24450
T: (540) 463-7103; Fax: (540) 464-5229
Founded: 1978; Members: 500
Gen Secr: Sharon Ritenour Stevens
Focus: Libraries & Bk Sci
Periodicals
Directory (annually)
Documentary Editing (quarterly) 13619

Association for Education and Rehabilitation of the Blind and Visually Impaired (AER), 206 N Washington St, Ste 320, Alexandria, VA 22314
T: (703) 548-1884
Founded: 1984; Members: 5500
Focus: Educ Handic
Periodicals
AER Report (monthly)
Education of the Visually Handicapped (quarterly)
Job Exchange (monthly) 13620

Association for Education in Journalism and Mass Communication (AEJMC), c/o College of Journalism, University of South Carolina, 1621 College St, Columbia, SC 29208
T: (803) 777-2005; Fax: (803) 777-4728
Founded: 1912; Members: 2800
Focus: Adult Educ; Journalism
Periodicals
Journalism Educator (quarterly)
Journalism Monographs (quarterly)
Newsletter (bi-monthly) 13621

Association for Educational Communications and Technology (AECT), 1025 Vermont Av NW, Ste 820, Washington, DC 20005
T: (202) 347-7834; Fax: (202) 347-7834
Founded: 1923; Members: 5000
Focus: Educ
Periodicals
Educational Communication & Technology Journal (quarterly)
Instructional Innovator Magazine (8 times annually)
Journal of Instructional Development (quarterly) 13622

Association for Equine Sports Medicine (AESM), c/o Veterinary Practice Publishing Company, POB 4457, Santa Barbara, CA 93160-4457
T: (805) 965-1028; Fax: (805) 965-0722
Founded: 1982; Members: 400
Focus: Vet Med 13623

Association for Evolutionary Economics (AFEE), c/o Dept of Economics, College of Business Administration, University of Nebraska, Lincoln, NE 68588
T: (402) 472-3967
Founded: 1963; Members: 2000
Focus: Econ; Sociology
Periodical
Journal of Economic Issues (quarterly) . 13624

Association for Faculty in the Medical Humanities (AFMH), 6728 Old McLean Village Dr, McLean, VA 22101
T: (703) 556-9222
Founded: 1983; Members: 350
Focus: Med 13625

Association for Finishing Processes of the Society of Manufacturing Engineers (AFP/SME), 1 SME Dr, POB 930, Dearborn, MI 48121-0930
T: (313) 271-1500; Fax: (313) 271-2861
Founded: 1975; Members: 3000
Focus: Eng
Periodical
The Finishing Line (quarterly) 13626

Association for General and Liberal Studies (AGLS), 1601 N Benton Av, Helena, MT 59625-0002
Founded: 1961; Members: 539
Gen Secr: Dr. Bruce Busby
Focus: Educ
Periodicals
Directory of Members (annually)
Newsletter (bi-monthly)
Perspectives (3 times annually) 13627

Association for Gerontology in Higher Education (AGHE), 1001 Connecticut Av NW, Ste 410, Washington, DC 20036
T: (202) 429-9277
Founded: 1974; Members: 320
Focus: Geriatrics
Periodicals
AGHE Exchange Newsletter (quarterly)
Brief Bibliography Series (3-4 times annually)
National Directory of Educational Programs in Gerontology (4-5 times annually) 13628

Association for Gnotobiotics (AG), 65 Brooklea Dr, East Aurora, NY 14062-1917
T: (716) 655-1680
Founded: 1961; Members: 415
Focus: Vet Med
Periodicals
Membership Directory (annually)
Newsletter (annually) 13629

Association for Group Psychoanalysis and Process (AGPP), c/o Dr. Milton M. Berger, 501 E 79 St, New York, NY 10021
T: (212) 288-2297
Founded: 1957; Members: 25
Focus: Psychoan; Psych 13630

Association for Hospital Medical Education (AHME), 1200 19 St NW, Washington, DC 20036-2401
T: (202) 857-1196; Fax: (202) 223-4579
Founded: 1954; Members: 700
Gen Secr: Michael S. Hamm
Focus: Adult Educ; Med
Periodicals
Membership Directory (bi-annually)
Newsletter (monthly) 13631

Association for Humanistic Education (AHE), c/o University of Wyoming, Box 3374, Laramie, WY 82071-3374
T: (307) 766-5329
Founded: 1976; Members: 400
Focus: Humanities; Educ
Periodicals
Celebrations (quarterly)
Journal of Humanistic Education (annually) 13632

Association for Humanistic Education and Development (AHEAD), c/o American Counseling Association, 5999 Stevenson Av, Alexandria, VA 22304
T: (703) 823-9800
Founded: 1951; Members: 2272
Focus: Educ
Periodicals
Infochange (6-8 times annually)
Journal of Humanistic Education and Development (quarterly) 13633

Association for Humanistic Psychology (AHP), 45 Franklin St, Ste 315, San Francisco, CA 94192
T: (415) 864-8850; E-Mail: ahpoffice@aol.com; Fax: (415) 864-8853
Founded: 1962; Members: 3500
Gen Secr: M.A. Bjarkman
Focus: Psych
Periodicals
AHP Perspective (monthly)
Journal of Humanistic Psychology (quarterly) 13634

Association for Institutional Research (AIR), c/o Florida State University, 114 Stone Bldg, Tallahassee, FL 32306-3038
T: (904) 644-4470; E-Mail: air@mailer.fsu.edu; Fax: (904) 644-8824
Founded: 1965; Members: 2500
Gen Secr: Terrence R. Russell
Focus: Educ
Periodicals
Directory (annually)
Journal (8 times annually)
Newsletter (quarterly)
Professional File (quarterly)
Research Monograph (quarterly) 13635

Association for Intelligent Systems Technology (AIST), 2-212 Center for Science and Technology, Syracuse, NY 13244-4100
T: (315) 443-5324; Fax: (315) 443-1865
Founded: 1986; Members: 110
Pres: Ronald Kalinoski
Focus: Electronic Eng 13636

Association for International Practical Training (AIPT), 10400 Little Patuxent Pkwy, Ste 250, Columbia, MD 21044-3510
T: (410) 997-2200; E-Mail: aipt@aipt.org; Fax: (410) 992-3924
Founded: 1950
Gen Secr: Robert M. Sprinkle
Focus: Educ
Periodical
International IAESTE Annual Report (annually) 13637

Association for Investment Management and Research (AIMR), 5 Boar's Head Ln, POB 3668, Charlottesville, VA 22903
T: (804) 980-3668; Fax: (804) 980-3685
Founded: 1947; Members: 22500
Gen Secr: Wendi E. Ruschmann
Focus: Finance 13638

Association for Jewish Demography and Statistics - American Branch, 4320 Cedarhurst Circle, Los Angeles, CA 90027
T: (213) 469-4976
Founded: 1957; Members: 50
Focus: Ethnology; Stats 13639

Association for Jewish Studies (AJS), c/o Brandeis University, POB 9110, Waltham, MA 02254-9110
T: (617) 736-2981; Fax: (617) 736-2982
Founded: 1969; Members: 1400
Gen Secr: Aaron L. Katchen
Focus: Rel & Theol
Periodicals
AJS Newsletter (semi-annually)
AJS Review (semi-annually) 13640

Association for Korean Studies (AKS), 30104 Av Tranquila, Rancho Palos Verdes, CA 91754
T: (213) 544-1267
Founded: 1974; Members: 35
Focus: Ethnology 13641

Association for Library and Information Science Education (ALISE), c/o UM School of Information, 550 E University Av, Rm 304, West Hall, Ann Arbor, MI 48109-1092
T: (313) 936-9812; Fax: (313) 764-2475
Founded: 1915; Members: 733
Gen Secr: Emily Lenhart
Focus: Adult Educ; Libraries & Bk Sci
Periodicals
Journal of Education for Library and Information Science (5 times annually)
Library and Information Science Education Statistical Report (annually) 13642

Association for Library Collections and Technical Services (ALCTS), c/o American Library Association, 50 E Huron St, Chicago, IL 60611
T: (312) 280-5305; Fax: (312) 280-3257
Founded: 1957; Members: 6000
Focus: Libraries & Bk Sci
Periodicals
ALCTS Newsletter (8 times annually)
Library Resources and Technical Services (quarterly) 13643

Association for Library Service to Children (ALSC), 50 E Huron St, Chicago, IL 60611
T: (312) 280-2163
Founded: 1901; Members: 3665
Focus: Libraries & Bk Sci
Periodicals
Journal of Youth Services in Libraries (quarterly)
Newsletter (semi-annually) 13644

Association for Living Historical Farms and Agricultural Museums (ALHFAM), 8774 Rte 45 NW, North Bloomfield, OH 44450-9701
T: (216) 685-4410; Fax: (216) 685-4410
Founded: 1970; Members: 1000
Gen Secr: Judith M. Sheridan
Focus: Agri
Periodicals
Convention Proceedings (annually)
Living Historical Farms Bulletin (bi-monthly)
Membership List (annually) 13645

Association for Macular Diseases (AMD), 210 E 64 St, New York, NY 10021
T: (212) 605-3719
Founded: 1977; Members: 4000
Focus: Ophthal 13646

Association for Mexican Cave Studies (AMCS), POB 7037, Austin, TX 78712
T: (512) 452-5709
Founded: 1963
Focus: Geology 13647

Association for Politics and the Life Sciences (APLS), c/o Dept of Political Science, Northern Illinois University, DeKalb, IL 60115-2854
T: (815) 753-9675; Fax: (815) 753-3202
Gen Secr: James N. Schubert
Focus: Poli Sci; Soc Sci 13648

Association for Population/Family Planning Libraries and Information Centers International (APLIC), c/o AVSC International Library, 79 Madison Av, New York, NY 10016
T: (212) 561-8040; E-Mail: rmccann@coss.fsu.edu; Fax: (212) 779-9439
Founded: 1968; Members: 115
Gen Secr: William Record
Focus: Libraries & Bk Sci
Periodicals
APLIC Communicator (quarterly)
Proceedings of Annual Conference (annually) 13649

Association for Practical Theology (APT), c/o George S. Worcester, Eden Theological Seminary, 475 E Lodgewood, Saint Louis, MO 63119
T: (314) 961-3627; Fax: (314) 961-5738
Founded: 1950; Members: 75
Focus: Rel & Theol 13650

Association for Practitioners in Infection Control (APIC), 1016 16 St NW, Washington, DC 20036
T: (202) 296-2742; Fax: (202) 296-5645
Founded: 1972; Members: 9000
Gen Secr: Richard Dorman
Focus: Med
Periodical
American Journal of Infection Control (bi-monthly) 13651

Association for Pre- and Perinatal Psychology and Health (APPPAH), 1600 Prince St, Ste 500, Alexandria, VA 22314-2838
T: (703) 548-2808; Fax: (703) 548-2802
Focus: Psych; Public Health 13652

Association for Preservation Technology International, POB 3511, Fredericksburg, VA 23187
T: (703) 373-1621; Fax: (703) 373-7787
Gen Secr: Susan Ford Johnson
Focus: Eng 13653

Association for Progressive Communications (APC), c/o IGC, Presidio Bldg, Torney Av, San Francisco, CA 94129, POB 29904
T: (415) 561-6100; E-Mail: efarwell@igc.apc.org; Fax: (415) 561-6101
Members: 8000
Focus: Comm Sci 13654

Association for Psychoanalytic Medicine (APM), 4560 Delafield Av, New York, NY 10471
T: (212) 548-6088; Fax: (212) 548-8302
Founded: 1945; Members: 241
Focus: Psychoan
Periodicals
Bulletin (quarterly)
Roster (bi-annually) 13655

Association for Quality and Participation (AQP), 801B W Eighth St, Ste 501, Cincinnati, OH 45203-1601
T: (513) 381-1959; Fax: (513) 381-0070
Founded: 1977; Members: 10000
Gen Secr: Cathy Kramer
Focus: Materials Sci
Periodicals
Circle Report (bi-monthly)
Conference Proceedings (annually)
Quality Circle (quarterly)
Quality Circles Journal (quarterly) . . . 13656

Association for Recorded Sound Collections (ARSC), POB 543, Annapolis, MD 21404-0543
T: (410) 757-0488; E-Mail: peters@umd5.umd.edu; Fax: (410) 349-0175
Founded: 1966; Members: 1000
Gen Secr: Peter Shambarger
Focus: Libraries & Bk Sci; Archives
Periodicals
Journal (semi-annually)
Membership Directory (bi-annually)
Newsletter (quarterly)
Recorded Sound 13657

Association for Research and Enlightenment (ARE), c/o Edgar Cayce Foundation, 67 St and Atlantic Av, POB 595, Virginia Beach, VA 23451-0595
T: (804) 428-3588; Fax: (804) 422-4631
Founded: 1931; Members: 70000
Pres: Dr. Charles Thomas Cayce
Focus: Parapsych
Periodicals
Magazine Venture Inward (bi-monthly)
Perspective on Consciousness and Psi Research (monthly) 13658

Association for Research in Nervous and Mental Disease (ARNMD), c/o Dr. James E. Goldman, 630 W 168 St, New York, NY 10032
T: (212) 740-7608; Fax: (212) 305-4548
Founded: 1920; Members: 850
Gen Secr: Dr. James E. Goldman
Focus: Psychiatry; Neurology
Periodical
Proceedings (annually) 13659

Association for Research in Vision and Ophthalmology (ARVO), 9650 Rockville Pike, Bethesda, MD 20814-3998
T: (301) 571-1844; Fax: (301) 571-8311
Founded: 1928; Members: 9840
Gen Secr: Dr. Janice M. Burke
Focus: Ophthal
Periodical
Investigative Ophthalmology and Vision Science (monthly) 13660

Association for Research of Childhood Cancer (AROCC), POB 251, Buffalo, NY 14225-0251
T: (716) 681-4433
Founded: 1970; Members: 1000
Focus: Cell Biol & Cancer Res; Pediatrics
Periodical
Newsletter (bi-monthly) 13661

Association for Research on Nonprofit Organization and Voluntary Action (ARNOVA), c/o Dept of Economics, 516 Cavanaugh Hall, IUPUI, Indianapolis, IN 46202-5140
T: (317) 274-8671; E-Mail: rsteinbe@indycms.iupui.edu; Fax: (317) 274-2347
Gen Secr: Rich Steinberg
Focus: Sci 13662

Association for Science, Technology and Innovation (ASTI), POB 1242, Arlington, VA 22210
T: (703) 352-2850; Fax: (703) 241-2850
Founded: 1978; Members: 100
Pres: Elizabeth Robertson
Focus: Nat Sci; Eng 13663

Association for Social Anthropology in Oceania (ASAO), c/o Suzanne Falgout, University of Hawaii-West Oahu, 96-043 Ala Ike, Pearl City, HI 96782
T: (808) 456-4718; Fax: (518) 276-4092
Founded: 1967; Members: 300
Gen Secr: Dr. Tamar Gordon
Focus: Anthro
Periodical
Newsletter (quarterly) 13664

Association for Social Economics (ASE), c/o Louisiana Technical University, Box 10318, Ruston, LA 71272
T: (318) 257-3701; Fax: (318) 257-4253
Founded: 1941; Members: 500
Focus: Econ
Periodicals
Forum (semi-annually)
Review of Social Economy (quarterly) . . 13665

Association for Specialists in Group Work (ASGW), c/o American Counseling Assoiation, 5999 Stevenson Av, Alexandria, VA 22304-3300
T: (703) 823-9800; Fax: (703) 823-0252
Founded: 1974; Members: 5393
Focus: Educ
Periodicals
Journal of Specialists in Group Work (quarterly)
Newsletter (3 times annually) 13666

Association for Spiritual, Ethical and Religious Values in Counseling, c/o American Counseling Association, 5999 Stevenson Av, Alexandria, VA 22304
T: (703) 823-9800; Fax: (703) 823-0252
Founded: 1955; Members: 4665
Gen Secr: John L. Jaco
Focus: Educ 13667

Association for Supervision and Curriculum Development (ASCD), 1250 N Pitt St, Alexandria, VA 22314-1403
T: (703) 549-9110; Fax: (703) 549-3891
Founded: 1943; Members: 150000
Focus: Educ
Periodicals
ASCD Update (8 times annually)
ASCD Yearbook (annually)
Educational Leadership (8 times annually) 13668

Association for Surgical Education (ASE), c/o Merrill T. Dayton, University Medical Center, 50 N Medical Dr, Rm 3B 312, Salt Lake City, UT 84132
T: (801) 581-7124
Founded: 1980; Members: 700
Pres: Merrill T. Dayton
Focus: Educ; Surgery 13669

Association for Symbolic Logic (ASL), c/o Dept of Mathematics, University of Illinois, 1409 W Green St, Urbana, IL 61801
T: (217) 244-7902; E-Mail: asl@symcom.math.uiuc.edu; Fax: (217) 333-9576
Founded: 1936; Members: 1550
Gen Secr: C. Ward Henson
Focus: Logic
Periodical
Journal of Symbolic Logic (quarterly) . . 13670

Association for Systems Management (ASM), 1433 W Bagley Rd, POB 38370, Cleveland, OH 44138-0370
T: (216) 243-6900; Fax: (216) 234-2930
Founded: 1947; Members: 7000
Focus: Business Admin 13671

Association for Technology in Music Instruction (ATMI), c/o Peter Webster, School of Music, Northwestern University, Evanston, IL 60208
T: (847) 491-5740; Fax: (847) 491-5260
Founded: 1975; Members: 300
Gen Secr: Gary Karpinski
Focus: Music 13672

Association for the Advancement of Baltic Studies (AABS), 111 Knob Hill Rd, Hackettstown, NJ 07840
T: (908) 852-5258; Fax: (908) 852-3233
Founded: 1968; Members: 1000
Focus: Ethnology
Periodicals
AABS Newsletter (quarterly)
Journal of Baltic Studies (quarterly) . . 13673

Association for the Advancement of Central Asian Research (AACAR), c/o History Dept, Univ. of Massachussetts, POB 33930, Amherst, MA 01003
T: (413) 545-1330
Gen Secr: Audrey L. Altstadt
Focus: Ethnology 13674

Association for the Advancement of Health Education (AAHE), 1900 Association Dr, Reston, VA 22091
T: (703) 476-3437
Founded: 1937; Members: 11000
Focus: Public Health; Educ
Periodicals
HE-XTRA (3-4 times annually)
Health Education (bi-monthly) 13675

Association for the Advancement of International Education (AAIE), c/o Westminster College, Thompson House, New Wilmington, PA 16172
T: (412) 946-7192; E-Mail: grel-lla@westminster.edu; Fax: (412) 946-7194
Founded: 1966; Members: 500
Gen Secr: Dr. Lewis A. Grell
Focus: Educ 13676

Association for the Advancement of Policy, Research and Development in the Third World, POB 70257, Washington, DC 20024-0257
T: (202) 723-7010; Fax: (202) 723-7010
Founded: 1981
Gen Secr: Dr. Mekki Mtewa
Focus: Poli Sci; Develop Areas
Periodical
Journal for Inter-Regional Cooperation and Development (annually) 13677

Association for the Advancement of Psychotherapy (AAP), c/o T. Byram Karasu, Albert Einstein College of Medicine, 1300 Morris Park Av, Bronx, NY 10461-1602
T: (718) 430-3503; Fax: (718) 430-8907
Founded: 1939; Members: 400
Gen Secr: T. Byram Karasu
Focus: Therapeutics
Periodical
American Journal of Psychotherapy (quarterly) 13678

Association for the Behavioral Sciences and Medical Education (ABSAME), 3900 E Camelback, Phoenix, AZ 85018
T: (602) 912-5300; Fax: (602) 957-4828
Founded: 1970; Members: 117
Gen Secr: Pauline Wampler
Focus: Behav Sci; Educ 13679

Association for the Bibliography of History (ABH), c/o Charles A. d'Aniello, Lockwood Memorial Library, State University of New York at Buffalo, Amherst, NY 14260
T: (716) 636-2817; Fax: (716) 636-3859
Founded: 1978; Members: 400
Focus: Hist
Periodicals
ABH Bulletin (quarterly)
Membership Directory (annually) 13680

Association for the Care of Children's Health (ACCH), 7910 Woodmont Av, Ste 300, Bethesda, MD 20814
T: (301) 654-6549; Fax: (301) 986-4553
Founded: 1965; Members: 4300
Focus: Pediatrics
Periodicals
ACCH Network (quarterly)
ACCH News (bi-monthly)
Children's Health Care (quarterly)
Directory of Psychosocial Policy and Programs 13681

Association for the Development of Human Potential (ADHP), 2328 W Pacific Av, Spokane, WA 99204
T: (509) 838-6652; Fax: (509) 838-6652
Founded: 1970; Members: 25
Focus: Educ; Psych 13682

Association for the Development of Religious Information Systems, c/o Dept of Social and Cultural Sciences, Marquette University, Milwaukee, WI 53201-1881
T: (414) 357-7247; E-Mail: adris@telalink.net; Fax: (615) 662-5251
Founded: 1971
Gen Secr: Dr. David O. Moberg
Focus: Comm Sci 13683

Association for the Education of Teachers in Science (AETS), c/o Dept of Elementary Education, University of West Florida, 11000 University Pky, Pensacola, FL 32514-5753
T: (904) 474-2860; E-Mail: jpeters@uwf.cc.uwf.edu; Fax: (904) 474-3205
Founded: 1930; Members: 850
Gen Secr: Joe Peters
Focus: Educ; Sci 13684

Association for the Management of Information Technology in Higher Education (CAUSE), 4840 Pearl E Circle, Ste 302E, Boulder, CO 80301
T: (303) 449-4430; E-Mail: info@cause.org; Fax: (303) 440-0461
Gen Secr: Jane S. Ryland
Focus: Educ; Business Admin; Computer & Info Sci 13685

Association for the Preservation of Virginia Antiquities (APVA), 204 W Franklin St, Richmond, VA 23220
T: (804) 648-1889; E-Mail: apva@200.net; Fax: (804) 775-0802
Founded: 1889; Members: 6000
Gen Secr: Peter D. Grover
Focus: Preserv Hist Monuments
Periodicals
Discovery (annually)
Newsletter – APVA News (3 times annually) 13686

Association for the Social Scientific Study of Jewry (ASSJ), c/o J. Winter, Dept of Sociology, Box 5302, New London, CT 06320
T: (203) 439-2241; E-Mail: jAwin@counncoill.edu; Fax: (203) 439-5223
Founded: 1971; Members: 300
Gen Secr: J. Winter
Focus: Sociology
Periodicals
Journal (annually)
Newsletter (3 times annually) 13687

Association for the Sociology of Religion (ASR), 401 N Ridge St, Cambridge, IL 61238-1154
T: (309) 937-5696; Fax: (309) 937-5692
Founded: 1938; Members: 724
Gen Secr: Dr. William H. Swatos Jr.
Focus: Sociology; Rel & Theol; Anthro
Periodical
Sociological Analysis (quarterly) 13688

Association for the Study of Afro-American Life and History (ASALH), 1407 14 St NW, Washington, DC 20005
T: (202) 667-2822; Fax: (202) 387-9802
Founded: 1915; Members: 2200
Focus: Ethnology; Hist
Periodicals
Black History Kit (annually)
Journal of Negro History (annually)
Negro History Bulletin (annually) 13689

Association for the Study of Dada and Surrealism (ASDS), c/o George H. Bauer, Dept of French and Italian, University of Southern California, Taper 126, University Park, Los Angeles, CA 90089
T: (310) 546-1438; Fax: (213) 746-7297
Founded: 1964; Members: 150
Focus: Arts; Lit
Periodical
Dada-Surrealism (annually) 13690

Association for the Study of Higher Education (ASHE), c/o D. Stanley Carpenter, Dept of Educational Administration, Texas A & M University, College Station, TX 77843
T: (409) 845-0393; Fax: (409) 845-6129
Founded: 1972; Members: 800
Focus: Educ
Periodical
Review of Higher Education (quarterly) . 13691

Association for the Study of Jewish Languages, 67-07 215 St, Oakland Garden, NY 11364-2523
Founded: 1979
Focus: Ling 13692

Association for the Treatment of Sexual Abusers (ABTSA), 10700 SW Beaverton Hillsdale Hwy, Beaverton, OR 97005-3035
T: (503) 233-2312; Fax: (503) 494-6152
Founded: 1985; Members: 400
Gen Secr: Dianne Price
Focus: Behav Sci 13693

Association for the World University (AWU), 847 N 28 St, Allentown, PA 18164
T: (215) 432-3124
Founded: 1959; Members: 80
Focus: Adult Educ 13694

Association for Theatre in Higher Education (ATHE), 158 W 15 St, New York, NY 10011
T: (212) 620-0855
Founded: 1968; Members: 70
Gen Secr: Anthony Mannino
Focus: Educ 13695

Association for Transpersonal Psychology (ATP), POB 3049, Stanford, CA 94309
T: (415) 327-2066; Fax: (415) 327-2066
Founded: 1971; Members: 2600
Gen Secr: Miles A. Vich
Focus: Psych 13696

Association for Tropical Biology (ATB), c/o J.S. Denslow, Dept of Plant Biology, Louisiana State University, Baton Rouge, LA 70803
T: (504) 388-8411; Fax: (504) 388-8459
Founded: 1963; Members: 1350
Gen Secr: J.S. Denslow
Focus: Bio 13697

Association for University Business and Economic Research (AUBER), c/o Terry Creeth, IBRC, 801 W Michigan, Indianapolis, IN 46202-5151
T: (317) 274-2204
Founded: 1947; Members: 170
Focus: Business Admin; Econ
Periodicals
Bibliography of Publications (annually)
Membership Directory (annually)
Newsletter (quarterly) 13698

Association for Women Geoscientists (AWG), 4779 126 St N, White Bear Lake, MN 55110-5910
T: (612) 426-3316; E-Mail: leete@mmacalstr.edu; Fax: (612) 426-5449
Founded: 1977; Members: 1100
Gen Secr: Dr. Jeanette H. Leete
Focus: Geology
Periodical
Gaea (bi-monthly) 13699

Association for Women in Computing (AWC), 41 Sutter St, Ste 1006, San Francisco, CA 94104
T: (415) 905-4663
Founded: 1978; Members: 650
Focus: Computer & Info Sci
Periodicals
Conference Proceedings (annually)
Directory (annually)
Newsletter (bi-monthly) 13700

Association for Women in Mathematics (AWM), c/o University of Maryland, 4114 Computer and Space Science Bldg, College Park, MD 20742-2461
T: (301) 405-7892
Founded: 1971; Members: 4000
Focus: Math
Periodical
Newsletter (bi-monthly) 13701

Association for Women in Psychology (AWP), c/o Sharon Siegel, 8235 Santa Monica Blvd, Ste 303, Los Angeles, CA 90046
T: (310) 455-3232; Fax: (310) 455-3832
Founded: 1969; Members: 2400
Gen Secr: Sharon Siegel
Focus: Psych
Periodical
Newsletter (quarterly) 13702

Association for Women in Science (AWIS), 1522 K St NW, Ste 820, Washington, DC 20005
T: (202) 408-0742; Fax: (202) 408-8321
Founded: 1971; Members: 3700
Focus: Sci
Periodicals
AWIS Legislative Update (bi-monthly)
Newsletter (bi-monthly)
Resources for Women in Science Series (annually) 13703

Association for Women Veterinarians (AWV), c/o Chris Stone Payne, 32205 Allison Dr, Union City, CA 94587
T: (510) 471-8379
Founded: 1947; Members: 625
Focus: Vet Med
Periodical
AWV Bulletin (quarterly) 13704

Association for World Education (AWE), POB 3777, Omaha, NE 68103-0777
Gen Secr: Dr. J. Richard Gilliand
Focus: Educ 13705

Association Henri Capitant (AHC), c/o Lousiana State University Law Center, Baton Rouge, LA 70903
T: (504) 388-1126; Fax: (504) 388-3677
Founded: 1935; Members: 200
Focus: Law 13706

Association of Academic Health Centers (AAHC), 1400 16 St NW, Ste 410, Washington, DC 20036
T: (202) 265-9600
Founded: 1969; Members: 102
Focus: Public Health 13707

Association of Academic Health Sciences Library Directors (AAHSLD), c/o Houston Academy of Medicine, Texas Medical Center Library, 1133 M.D. Anderson Blvd, Houston, TX 77030
T: (713) 790-7060; Fax: (713) 790-7052
Founded: 1978; Members: 125
Pres: Judith Wilson, Sandra Messerle
Focus: Libraries & Bk Sci 13708

Association of Academic Physiatrists (AAP), 5987 E 71 St, Ste 112, Indianapolis, IN 46220
T: (317) 845-4200; Fax: (317) 845-4299
Founded: 1967; Members: 1000
Focus: Rehabil 13709

Association of Advanced Rabbinical and Talmudic Schools (AARTS), 175 Fifth Av, New York, NY 10010
T: (212) 477-0950; Fax: (212) 533-5335
Founded: 1971; Members: 54
Focus: Educ; Rel & Theol
Periodical
Annual Handbook 13710

Association of African Studies Programs (AASP), c/o Africana Studies Programme, New York University, 269 Mercer St, New York, NY 10003
T: (212) 988-3972
Gen Secr: François Manchvelle
Focus: Ethnology 13711

Association of Air Medical Services (AAMS), 35 S Raymond Av, Ste 205, Pasadena, CA 91105
T: (818) 793-1232; Fax: (818) 793-1039
Founded: 1980; Members: 300
Focus: Med
Periodicals
Aeromedical Journal (bi-monthly)
Membership Directory (annually) 13712

Association of American Colleges and Universities, 1818 R St NW, Washington, DC 20009
T: (202) 387-3760; Fax: (202) 265-9532
Founded: 1915; Members: 650
Pres: Paula P. Brownlee
Focus: Educ
Periodicals
Liberal Education (quarterly)
On Campus with Women (bi-monthly) . . 13713

Association of American Geographers (AAG), 1710 16 St NW, Washington, DC 20009-3198
T: (202) 234-1450; Fax: (202) 234-2744
Founded: 1904; Members: 7300
Gen Secr: Ronald F. Abler
Focus: Geography
Periodicals
Annals (quarterly)
Newsletter (10 times annually)
The Professional Geographer (quarterly) . 13714

Association of American Indian Physicians (AAIP), 1235 Sovereign Row, Ste C-7, Oklahoma City, OK 73108
T: (405) 946-7072; Fax: (405) 946-7651
Founded: 1971; Members: 220
Gen Secr: Margaret Knight
Focus: Physiology
Periodical
Newsletter (quarterly) 13715

Association of American Jurists (AAJ), POB 673, Berkeley, CA 94701
T: (510) 848-0599; Fax: (510) 848-6008
Founded: 1974
Focus: Law; Prom Peace
Periodical
Association of American Jurists Newsletter (quarterly) 13716

Association of American Law Schools (AALS), 1201 Connecticut Av NW, Ste 800, Washington, DC 20036
T: (202) 296-8851; Fax: (202) 296-8869
Founded: 1900; Members: 160
Gen Secr: Carl C. Monk
Focus: Adult Educ; Law
Periodicals
Journal of Legal Education (quarterly)
Newsletter (quarterly)
Placement Bulletin (bi-monthly) 13717

Association of American Medical Colleges (AAMC), 2450 N St NW, Washington, DC 20037-1126
T: (202) 828-0400; Fax: (202) 828-1125
Founded: 1876; Members: 630
Pres: Dr. Jordan J. Cohen
Focus: Adult Educ; Med
Periodicals
Curriculum Directory (annually)
Journal of Medical Education (monthly)
Weekly Report (weekly) 13718

Association of American Physicians (AAP), c/o Krannert Institute of Cardiology, Indiana University School of Medicine, 1111 W Tenth St, Indianapolis, IN 46202-4800
T: (317) 630-6468
Founded: 1886; Members: 1200
Focus: Physiology
Periodical
Transactions on the Association of American Physicians (annually) 13719

Association of American Physicians and Surgeons (AAPS), 1601 N Tucson Blvd, Ste 9, Tucson, AZ 85716
T: (602) 327-4885; Fax: (602) 290-9674
Founded: 1943
Focus: Surgery; Physiology
Periodical
AAPS News (monthly) 13720

Association of American Schools in Central America, Colombian-Caribbean and Mexico (Tri-Association), c/o US Embassy Quito Unit5372, POB 004, Miami, FL 34039
T: (593) 2477-534, 2242-996; Fax: 2434-985
Gen Secr: Mary V. Sanchez
Focus: Ethnology 13721

Association of American Schools in South America (AASSA), 6972 NW 50 St, Miami, FL 33166
T: (305) 594-3936; Fax: (305) 940-5772
Founded: 1961; Members: 28
Focus: Educ 13722

Association of American Seed Control Officials (AASCO), c/o Malcolm Sarna, 50 Harry S. Truman Pkwy, Annapolis, MD 21401
T: (410) 841-5960; Fax: (410) 841-5969
Founded: 1956; Members: 53
Pres: Malcolm Sarna
Focus: Agri 13723

Association of American State Geologists (AASG), c/o Earl Bennett, Idaho Geological Survey, 332 Morrill Hall, Moscow, ID 83843
T: (717) 787-2169; Fax: (717) 783-7267
Founded: 1908; Members: 51
Gen Secr: Walter Schmidt
Focus: Geology
Periodical
Journal (annually) 13724

Association of American Universities (AAU), 1 Dupont Circle NW, Ste 730, Washington, DC 20036
T: (202) 466-5030
Founded: 1900; Members: 60
Pres: Cornelius C.J. Pings
Focus: Sci 13725

Association of American Veterinary Medical Colleges (AAVMC), 1101 Vermont Av, Ste 710, Washington, DC 20005
T: (202) 371-9195; Fax: (202) 842-4360
Founded: 1966; Members: 41
Focus: Adult Educ; Vet Med
Periodical
Journal of Veterinary Medical Education (semi-annually) 13726

Association of Analytical Chemists (ANACHEM), 2017 Hyde Park Rd, Detroit, MI 48207
T: (313) 393-3685
Founded: 1941; Members: 250
Focus: Chem 13727

Association of Ancient Historians (AAH), c/o Prof. Carol Thomas, Dept of History, University of Washington, Seattle, WA 98195
T: (206) 543-5790; E-Mail: Carolt@u.washington.edu; Fax: (206) 543-9451
Founded: 1974; Members: 750
Pres: Prof. Carol Thomas
Focus: Hist
Periodical
Newsletter (3 times annually) 13728

Association of Applied Insect Ecologists (AAIE), 1008 Tenth St, Ste 549, Sacramento, CA 95814
T: (916) 444-5224
Founded: 1967; Members: 300
Focus: Entomology; Ecology
Periodical
AAIE Bulletin (quarterly) 13729

Association of Arab-American University Graduates (AAUG), 2121 Wisconsin Av NW, Ste 310, Washington, DC 20007
E-Mail: aaug@igc.apc.org
Founded: 1967
Gen Secr: Ziad J. Asali
Focus: Adult Educ; Poli Sci; Ethnology
Periodicals
Arab Studies (quarterly)
Newsletter (bi-monthly) 13730

Association of Asphalt Paving Technologists (AAPT), 400 Selby Av, Ste 1, Saint Paul, MN 55102
T: (612) 293-9188; Fax: (612) 293-9193
Founded: 1924; Members: 825
Gen Secr: Eugene L. Skok
Focus: Civil Eng
Periodical
Asphalt Paving Technology (annually) . . 13731

Association of Avian Veterinarians (AAV), POB 811720, Boca Raton, FL 33481-1720
T: (407) 393-8901; Fax: (407) 393-8902
Gen Secr: Adina Rae Freedman
Focus: Vet Med 13732

Association of Avian Veterinarias (AAV), POB 811720, Boca Raton, FL 33481
T: (407) 393-8901; Fax: (407) 393-8902
Founded: 1980; Members: 3000
Focus: Vet Med 13733

Association of Aviation Psychologists (AAP), c/o Dr. Kathleen Mosier, NASA Aims Research Center, MS-262-4, Moffett Field, CA 94035
T: (415) 604-0007
Founded: 1964; Members: 350
Gen Secr: Dr. Kathleen Mosier
Focus: Psych 13734

Association of Balloon and Airship Constructors (ABAC), POB 90864, San Diego, CA 92169
T: (619) 270-4049; Fax: (619) 270-4049
Founded: 1974; Members: 250
Focus: Aero 13735

Association of Biological Collections Appraisers (ABCA), 3493 Greenfield Pl, Carmel, CA 93923
T: (408) 624-5677
Founded: 1980; Members: 34
Focus: Bio 13736

Association of Biomedical Communication Directors (ABCD), c/o Richard A. McNeely, Biomedical Communications, University of Arizona, Tucson, AZ 85724
T: (602) 626-7343; Fax: (602) 626-2145
Founded: 1972; Members: 87
Gen Secr: Richard A. McNeely
Focus: Comm Sci 13737

Association of Black Anthropologists (ABA), c/o American Anthropological Association, 4350 N Fairfax Dr, Ste 640, Arlington, VA 22203-1620
T: (703) 528-1902; E-Mail: (name)@aaa.mhs.compuserve.com; Fax: (703) 528-3546
Founded: 1970; Members: 130
Pres: H. Page
Focus: Anthro 13738

Association of Black Psychologists (ABP), POB 55999, Washington, DC 20040-5999
T: (202) 722-0808; Fax: (202) 722-5941
Founded: 1968; Members: 650
Focus: Psych
Periodicals
Journal of Black Psycholoy (semi-annually)
NIA (bi-monthly)
Psych Discourse (bi-monthly) 13739

Association of Black Sociologists (ABS), c/o Robert G. Newby, Dept of Sociology, Central Michigan University, Mount Pleasant, MI 48859
T: (517) 774-3160; E-Mail: ABSLST-L@CMUVM.CSV.CMICH.EDU; Fax: (517) 774-7106
Founded: 1968; Members: 400
Gen Secr: Robert G. Newby
Focus: Sociology 13740

Association of Black Women in Higher Education (ABWHE), c/o Delores V. Smalls, 234 Hudson Av, Albany, NY 12210
T: (518) 572-7141; Fax: (518) 572-7646
Founded: 1979; Members: 350
Pres: Delores V. Smalls
Focus: Educ 13741

Association of Bone and Joint Surgeons (ABJS), 6300 N River Rd, Ste 727, Rosemont, IL 60018-4226
T: (708) 698-1636; Fax: (708) 823-0536
Founded: 1947; Members: 185
Gen Secr: Arlene Napolilli
Focus: Surgery; Orthopedics
Periodical
Clinical Orthopedics and Related Research (8 times annually) 13742

Association of Business Officers of Preparatory Schools (ABOPS), c/o Aubrey K. Loomis, Loomis Chaffee School, Windsor, CT 06095
T: (203) 688-4937
Founded: 1924; Members: 36
Focus: Econ 13743

Association of Caribbean Studies (ACS), POB 22202, Lexington, KY 40522
T: (606) 257-6966; Fax: (606) 257-1074
Founded: 1978; Members: 1200
Focus: Ethnology 13744

Association of Catholic Colleges and Universities (ACCU), 1 Dupont Circle, Ste 650, Washington, DC 20036
T: (202) 457-0650; Fax: (202) 728-0977
Founded: 1899; Members: 206
Focus: Educ 13745

Association of Catholic Diocesan Archivists (ACDA), c/o Archdiocese of Chicago Archives and Records Center, 5150 Northwest Hwy, Chicago, IL 60630
T: (312) 736-5150; Fax: (312) 736-0488
Founded: 1981; Members: 180
Pres: Francis Weber
Focus: Archives 13746

Association of Chairmen of Departments of Mechanics (ACDM), c/o Prof. James T. Jenkins, Dept of Theoretical and Applied Mechanics, Cornell University, Ithaca, NY 14853
T: (607) 255-7185; E-Mail: jtjz@cornell.edu; Fax: (607) 255-2011
Founded: 1969; Members: 103
Gen Secr: Prof. James T. Jenkins
Focus: Eng
Periodical
Newsletter (semi-annually) 13747

Association of Chiropractic Colleges (ACC), 2005 Via Barrett, POB 367, San Lorenzo, CA 94580
T: (310) 902-3330; Fax: (310) 947-7863
Founded: 1977; Members: 18
Pres: Reed B. Phillips
Focus: Educ; Med 13748

Association of Christian Librarians (ACL), POB 4, Cedarville, OH 45314
T: (513) 766-7842; Fax: (513) 766-2337
Founded: 1957; Members: 300
Focus: Libraries & Bk Sci
Periodical
Christian Librarian (quarterly) 13749

Association of Clinical Scientists (ACS), POB 1292, Farmington, CT 06034
T: (203) 679-2154; Fax: (203) 679-2154
Founded: 1949; Members: 658
Focus: Med
Periodical
Annals of Clinical Laboratory Science (bi-monthly) 13750

Association of College and Research Libraries (ACRL), 50 E Huron St, Chicago, IL 60611-2795
T: (312) 280-3248; E-Mail: ajenkins@ala.org; Fax: (312) 280-2516
Founded: 1889; Members: 10800
Gen Secr: Altea Jenkins
Focus: Libraries & Bk Sci
Periodicals
Choice (11 times annually)
College and Research Libraries (bi-monthly)
College and Research Libraries News (11 times annually)
Fast Job Listing Service (monthly)
Publications in Librarianship
Rare Books and Manuscripts Librarianship (semi-annually) 13751

Association of College and University Telecommunications Administrators (ACUTA), 152 W Zandale Dr, Ste 200, Lexington, KY 40503
T: (606) 278-3338; E-Mail: jsemer@acuta.org; Fax: (606) 278-3268
Founded: 1971; Members: 1200
Gen Secr: Jeri A. Semer
Focus: Comm
Periodicals
ACUTA News (monthly)
Membership Directory (annually) 13752

Association of College Unions – International (ACU-I), 400 E Seventh St, Bloomington, IN 47405
T: (812) 332-8017; Fax: (812) 333-8050
Gen Secr: Richard Blackburn
Focus: Educ 13753

Association of Collegiate Schools of Architecture (ACSA), 1735 New York Av NW, Washington, DC 20006
T: (202) 785-2324; Fax: (202) 626-7421
Founded: 1912
Focus: Archit; Adult Educ
Periodicals
ACSA News (monthly)
Journal of Architectural Education (quarterly) 13754

Association of Collegiate Schools of Planning (ACSP), c/o Hunter College, CUNY, 695 Park Av, New York, NY 10021
T: (212) 772-4150; Fax: (212) 650-3655
Founded: 1959; Members: 1517

Pres: Eugenie L. Birch
Focus: Urban Plan
Periodicals
Directory (bi-annually)
Journal of Planning Education and Research (quarterly) 13755

Association of Community Cancer Centers (ACCC), 11600 Nebel St, Ste 201, Rockville, MD 20852
T: (301) 984-9496; Fax: (301) 770-1949
Founded: 1974; Members: 715
Focus: Cell Biol & Cancer Res 13756

Association of Community College Trustees (ACCT), 1740 N St NW, Washington, DC 20036
T: (202) 775-4667; Fax: (202) 223-1297
Founded: 1969; Members: 780
Focus: Educ
Periodicals
ACCT-O-Line (bi-weekly)
Advisor (monthly) 13757

Association of Community Tribal Schools (ACTS), c/o Dr. Roger Bordeaux, 616 Fourth Av W, Sisseton, SD 57262-1349
T: (605) 698-3112; Fax: (605) 658-7686
Founded: 1982; Members: 30
Focus: Educ 13758

Association of Consulting Chemists and Chemical Engineers (ACC&CE), 44 W 45 St, New York, NY 10036
T: (212) 983-3160; Fax: (212) 983-3161
Founded: 1928; Members: 160
Gen Secr: Elizabeth K. Jones
Focus: Chem
Periodical
Consulting Services Directory (quarterly) . 13759

Association of Continuing Legal Education Administrators (ACLEA), c/o Texas Institute of Continuing Legal Education, POB 4646, Austin, TX 78765
T: (512) 451-6960; Fax: (512) 451-2911
Founded: 1965; Members: 400
Gen Secr: Donna J. Passons
Focus: Educ; Law 13760

Association of Defense Trial Attorneys (ADTA), 600 Bank One Bldg, Peoria, IL 61602
T: (309) 676-0400
Founded: 1937; Members: 700
Focus: Insurance 13761

Association of Departments of English (ADE), 10 Astor Pl, New York, NY 10003
T: (212) 614-6317
Founded: 1962; Members: 840
Focus: Ling
Periodicals
ADE Bulletin (3 times annually)
MLA/ADE Job Information List (5 times annually) 13762

Association of Departments of Foreign Languages (ADFL), 10 Astor Pl, New York, NY 10003
T: (212) 614-6319
Founded: 1969; Members: 1050
Focus: Ling; Adult Educ
Periodicals
ADFL Bulletin (3 times annually)
MLA/ADFL Job Information List (5 times annually) 13763

Association of Earth Science Editors (AESE), c/o Katherine Lessing, 781 Northwest Dr, Morgantown, WV 26505
T: (304) 599-2865; Fax: (304) 599-8904
Founded: 1967; Members: 350
Gen Secr: Katherine Lessing
Focus: Geology
Periodicals
Blueline (quarterly)
Membership Directory (annually) 13764

Association of Energy Engineers (AEE), 4025 Pleasantdale Rd, Ste 420, Atlanta, GA 30340
T: (404) 447-5083; Fax: (404) 446-3969
Founded: 1977; Members: 8000
Focus: Energy 13765

Association of Engineering Geologists (AEG), 323 Boston Post Rd, Ste 2D, Sudbury, MA 01776
T: (508) 443-4639
Founded: 1957; Members: 3200
Focus: Geology
Periodical
Bulletin of the Association of Engineering Geologists (quarterly) 13766

Association of Environmental Engineering Professors (AEEP), 2101 Winchester Dr, Champaign, IL 61821
T: (217) 398-6969; Fax: (217) 333-9576
Founded: 1963; Members: 600
Gen Secr: Joanne Fetzner
Focus: Eng
Periodicals
Membership List (annually)
Newsletter (3 times annually) 13767

Association of Episcopal Colleges (AEC), 815 Second Av, New York, NY 10017-4594
T: (212) 986-0989; Fax: (212) 986-5039
Founded: 1962; Members: 12
Focus: Educ; Rel & Theol
Periodicals
President's Report (annually)
Views and Views (semi-annually) . . . 13768

Association of Exploration Geochemists (AEG), c/o US Geological Survey, Federal Center, MS 973, POB 25046, Denver, CO 80225
T: (303) 236-5521; Fax: (303) 236-3200
Gen Secr: Dr. S. P. Marsh
Focus: Chem 13769

Association of Federal Communications Consulting Engineers (AFCCE), POB 19333, 20 St Station, Washington, DC 20036
T: (202) 898-0111
Founded: 1948; Members: 200
Gen Secr: Sid Khanna
Focus: Electric Eng 13770

Association of Field Ornithologists (AFO), c/o Elissa Landre, Broadmoor Wildlife Sanctuary, Massachusetts Audubon Society, 280 Eliot St, South Natick, MA 01760
T: (508) 655-2296
Founded: 1924; Members: 1400
Focus: Ornithology
Periodical
Journal of Field Ornithology (quarterly) . 13771

Association of Firearm and Tool Mark Examiners (AFTE), 7857 Esterel Dr, La Jolla, CA 92037
T: (619) 453-0847
Founded: 1969; Members: 500
Focus: Eng 13772

Association of Food and Drug Officials (AFDO), POB 3425, York, PA 17402
T: (717) 757-2888; Fax: (717) 755-8089
Founded: 1897; Members: 600
Focus: Food
Periodicals
Bulletin (5 times annually)
Journal of the Association of Food and Drug Officials (5 times annually)
News and Views (quarterly) 13773

Association of Forensic Document Examiners (AFDE), 3813 Sheridan Av S, Minneapolis, MN 55410
T: (612) 922-3060
Founded: 1985; Members: 20
Focus: Graphology; Forensic Med; Criminology 13774

Association of Graduate Liberal Studies Programs (AGLSP), c/o Diane Sasson, Duke University, POB 90095, Durham, NC 27708
T: (919) 684-3222; E-Mail: aqspeacpub@duke.edu; Fax: (919) 684-8905
Founded: 1975; Members: 112
Gen Secr: Dr. Diane Sasson
Focus: Educ; Adult Educ
Periodical
Newsletter 13775

Association of Graduate Schools in Association of American Universities (AGS), 1 Dupont Circle NW, Ste 730, Washington, DC 20036
T: (202) 466-5030
Founded: 1948; Members: 56
Focus: Educ
Periodical
Newsletter 13776

Association of Information and Dissemination Centers (ASIDIC), POB 8105, Athens, GA 30603
T: (706) 542-6820
Founded: 1968; Members: 85
Focus: Computer & Info Sci 13777

Association of Internal Management Consultants (AIMC), c/o Margaret M. Custer, POB 304, East Bloomfield, NY 14443
T: (716) 657-7878
Founded: 1971; Members: 280
Focus: Business Admin 13778

Association of International Colleges and Universities (AICU), 1301 S Noland Rd, Independence, MO 64055
T: (816) 461-3633; Fax: (816) 461-3634
Founded: 1973; Members: 4011
Focus: Sci
Periodical
Directory (annually) 13779

Association of International Education Administrators (AIEA), c/o Capstone International Programme Centre, Univ. of Alabama at Tuscaloosa, POB 870254, Tuscaloosa, AL 35487-0254
T: (205) 348-5256; E-Mail: emoseley@ualvm.ua.edu; Fax: (205) 348-5298
Gen Secr: Edward H. Moseley
Focus: Educ 13780

Association of International Health Researchers (AIHR), 2665 Pleasant Valley Rd, Mobile, AL 36606
T: (205) 473-3946
Founded: 1982; Members: 123
Focus: Public Health 13781

Association of Iron and Steel Engineers (AISE), 3 Gateway Center, Ste 2350, Pittsburgh, PA 15222
T: (412) 281-6323; Fax: (412) 281-4657
Founded: 1907; Members: 10000
Focus: Eng; Metallurgy
Periodicals
Directory Iron and Steel Plants (annually)
Iron and Steel Engineer (monthly) . . . 13782

Association of Jesuit Colleges and Universities (AJCU), 1 Dupont Circle, Ste 405, Washington, DC 20036
T: (202) 862-9893; Fax: (202) 862-8523
Founded: 1970; Members: 28
Pres: Paul S. Tipton
Focus: Educ; Rel & Theol; Sci
Periodical
Higher Education Report (10 times annually) 13783

Association of Jewish Genealogical Societies, POB 50245, Palo Alto, CA 94303
T: (415) 424-1622
Gen Secr: Robert Weiss
Focus: Genealogy 13784

Association of Jewish Libraries (AJL), 15 E 26 St, Rm 1034, New York, NY 10010-1579
T: (212) 678-8092; Fax: (212) 678-8998
Founded: 1965; Members: 1000
Pres: Esther Nussbaum
Focus: Libraries & Bk Sci
Periodicals
AJL Newsletter (quarterly)
Judaica Librarianship (bi-annually) . . . 13785

Association of Laban Movement Analysts (AALMA), c/o Laban/Bartenieff Institute for Movement Studies, 11 E Fourth St, New York, NY 10003
T: (212) 477-4299; Fax: (212) 477-3702
Founded: 1976; Members: 400
Pres: Lucy Rumark
Focus: Sports; Psych
Periodicals
Directory (annually)
Newsletter (3 times annually) 13786

Association of Latin American and Caribbean Economists (AEALC), c/o Dept of Economics, Fordham Univ., Bronx, NY 10458
T: (718) 817-4064
Gen Secr: Prof. Darryl McLeod
Focus: Econ 13787

Association of Legal Administrators (ALA), 175 E Hawthorn Pkwy, Ste 325, Vernon Hills, IL 60061-1428
T: (708) 816-1212
Founded: 1971; Members: 8800
Focus: Law 13788

Association of Life Insurance Counsel (ALIC), c/o Michael Keefer, 200 E Berry St, Fort Wayne, IN 46802
T: (219) 455-5582; Fax: (219) 455-5403
Founded: 1913; Members: 950
Gen Secr: J. Michael Keefer
Focus: Insurance 13789

Association of Lutheran Secondary Schools (ALSS), c/o Lutheran High School, 3201 W Arizona Av, Denver, CO 80219
T: (303) 934-2345
Founded: 1944; Members: 64
Gen Secr: Dr. Kenneth Palmreuter
Focus: Educ 13790

Association of Management (AM), Rte 17, POB 1301, Grafton, VA 23692-1301
T: (804) 479-5363; Fax: (804) 479-0656
Founded: 1975; Members: 2800
Focus: Psych
Periodicals
HRMOB News (quarterly)
Journal of Information Resources Management Systems (quarterly)
Journal of Management in Practice (quarterly) 13791

Association of Maternal and Child Health Programs (AMCHP), 1350 Connecticut Av NW, Ste 803, Washington, DC 20036
T: (202) 775-0436; Fax: (202) 775-0061
Founded: 1944; Members: 300
Focus: Public Health 13792

Association of Medical Education and Research in Substance Abuse (AMERSA), c/o Center for Alcohol and Addiction Studies, Brown University, Box G-BH, Providence, RI 02912
T: (401) 863-7791; Fax: (401) 863-3510
Founded: 1976; Members: 500
Focus: Educ; Med 13793

Association of Medical School Pediatric Department Chairmen (AMSPDC), c/o Jean Bartholomew, 111 Silver Cedar Ct, Chapel Hill, NC 27514-1651
T: (919) 942-1993; Fax: (919) 929-9255
Founded: 1961; Members: 144
Gen Secr: Jean Bartholomew
Focus: Pediatrics
Periodical
AMSPDC Membership List (annually) . . 13794

Association of Mental Health Administrators (AMHA), 60 Revere Dr, Ste 500, Northbrook, IL 60062
T: (708) 480-9626; Fax: (708) 480-9282
Founded: 1959; Members: 1450
Focus: Psychiatry
Periodicals
Journal (semi-annually)
Newsletter (monthly) 13795

Association of Mercy Colleges (AMC), c/o Dr. Grace Ann Geibel, Carlow College, 3333 Fifth Av, Pittsburgh, PA 15213
T: (412) 578-6123; Fax: (412) 578-6358
Founded: 1982; Members: 19
Pres: Dr. Grace Ann Geibel
Focus: Educ 13796

Association of Military Colleges and Schools of the United States (AMCS), 9115 Mc Nair Dr, Alexandria, VA 22309
T: (703) 360-1678
Founded: 1914; Members: 45
Focus: Adult Educ; Military Sci
Periodicals
Membership List (annually)
Newsletter (8 times annually) 13797

Association of Military Surgeons of the U.S. (AMSUS), 9320 Old Georgetown Rd, Bethesda, MD 20814
T: (301) 897-8800; Fax: (301) 530-5446
Founded: 1891; Members: 15000
Focus: Surgery
Periodical
Military Medicine (monthly) 13798

Association of Minicomputers Users (AMU), 363 E Central St, Franklin, MA 02038
T: (617) 520-1555; Fax: (617) 520-1558
Founded: 1978; Members: 1000
Focus: Computer & Info Sci
Periodicals
Mini-Beacon (bi-monthly)
Minicomputer Software Quarterly (quarterly) 13799

Association of Minority Health Professions Schools (AMHPS), 507 Capitol Court, Ste 200, Washington, DC 20002
T: (202) 544-7499; Fax: (202) 546-7105
Founded: 1978; Members: 11
Gen Secr: Dale P. Dirks
Focus: Educ; Public Health 13800

Association of Muslim Scientists and Engineers (AMSE), POB 38, Plainfield, IN 46168
T: (317) 839-8157
Founded: 1969; Members: 640
Focus: Eng; Sci
Periodicals
ASME Membership Directory (bi-monthly)
International Journal of Science and Technology (quarterly)
Newsletter (quarterly)
Proceedings of Conference (annually) . . 13801

Association of Muslim Social Scientists (AMSS), POB 669, Herndon, VA 22070
T: (703) 471-1745; Fax: (703) 471-3922
Founded: 1972; Members: 580
Focus: Sociology 13802

Association of Naval R.O.T.C. Colleges and Universities, c/o Keith Kurz, University of Rochester, Administrative Office Box 41, Rochester, NY 14607
T: (716) 275-4111; Fax: (716) 275-8531
Founded: 1946; Members: 63
Gen Secr: Keith Kurz
Focus: Educ; Navig 13803

Association of North American Operations Research Societies within IFORS (NORAM), 940-A Elkridge Landing Rd, Linthicum, MD 21090-2909
Fax: (410) 684-2963
Gen Secr: Ellen Duncan
Focus: Business Admin 13804

Association of Official Racing Chemists (AORC), POB 19232, Portland, OR 97280
T: (503) 644-9224; Fax: (503) 626-7039
Founded: 1947; Members: 140
Focus: Chem 13805

Association of Official Seed Analysts (AOSA), POB 81152, Lincoln, NE 68501-1152
T: (402) 476-3852; Fax: (402) 476-6547
Founded: 1908; Members: 141
Pres: Deborah Meyer
Focus: Agri
Periodicals
Journal of Seed Technology (semi-annually)
Newsletter (3 times annually) 13806

Association of Old Crows (AOC), 1000 N Payne St, Alexandria, VA 22314
T: (703) 549-1600
Founded: 1964; Members: 23000
Focus: Electronic Eng 13807

Association of Optometric Educators (AOE), c/o Dr. Debra Bezan, NSU College of Optometry, 1001 N Grand Av, Tahlequah, OK 74464-7017
T: (918) 456-5511; Fax: (918) 458-2104
Founded: 1972; Members: 100
Pres: Dr. Debra Bezan
Focus: Adult Educ; Ophthal 13808

Association of Orthodox Jewish Scientists (AOJS), 27-33 W 23 St, New York, NY 10010
T: (212) 229-2340; Fax: (212) 229-2319
Founded: 1948; Members: 1500
Gen Secr: Joel Schwartz
Focus: Rel & Theol; Sci
Periodicals
Intercom (quarterly)
Membership Directory
Newsletter (5 times annually)
Proceedings (annually) 13809

Association of Orthodox Jewish Teachers (AOJT), 1577 Coney Island Av, Brooklyn, NY 11230
T: (718) 258-3585; Fax: (718) 258-3586
Founded: 1964; Members: 5000
Focus: Educ
Periodical
Newspaper 13810

Association of Osteopathic State Executive Directors (AOSED), 455 Capitol Mall, Ste 225, Sacramento, CA 95814
T: (916) 447-2004
Founded: 1918; Members: 112
Focus: Pathology
Periodicals
Directory of Osteopathic Publications (bi-annually)
Newsletter (monthly) 13811

Association of Pacific Systematists (APS), c/o Botanical Research Institute of Texas, 509 Pecan St, Fort Worth, TX 76102-4060
Founded: 1982
Gen Secr: S.H. Sohmer
Focus: Botany
Periodical
Association of Pacific Systematists Newsletter 13812

Association of Pathology Chairs (APC), c/o Dr. Frances A. Pitlick, 9650 Rockville Pike, Bethesda, MD 20814-3993
T: (301) 571-1880; E-Mail: apc@pathol.faseb.org; Fax: (301) 571-1879
Founded: 1967; Members: 152
Gen Secr: Dr. Frances A. Pitlick
Focus: Pathology 13813

Association of Philippine Physicians in America (APPA), 2717 W Olive Av, Ste 200, Burbank, CA 91505
T: (818) 843-8616
Founded: 1972; Members: 3000
Focus: Physiology
Periodicals
APPA Quarterly (quarterly)
Leadership Roster of Officers (annually)
Newsletter (quarterly) 13814

Association of Physician Assistant Programs (APAP), 950 N Washington St, Alexandria, VA 22314
T: (703) 548-5538
Founded: 1972; Members: 53
Pres: Ron Garcia
Focus: Physiology
Periodicals
Conference Proceedings (annually)
National Directory of Physician Assistant Programs (semi-annually)
Newsletter (bi-weekly) 13815

Association of Physician Assistants in Cardiovascular Surgery (APACVS), 11250 Rodger Bacon Dr, Ste 8, Reston, VA 22090
T: (703) 707-0476; Fax: (703) 435-4390
Founded: 1981; Members: 675
Gen Secr: Richard A. Guggok
Focus: Cardiol; Surgery 13816

Association of Presbyterian Colleges and Universities (APCU), 100 Witherspoon St, Rm M040, Louisville, KY 40202-1396
T: (502) 569-5606
Founded: 1983; Members: 68
Pres: William D. Peterson
Focus: Educ 13817

Association of Professional Baseball Physicians (APBP), c/o Dr. Leonard J. Michienzi, 6515 Barrie Rd, Edina, MN 55435
T: (612) 920-5663; Fax: (612) 924-1659
Founded: 1970; Members: 36
Pres: Dr. Leonard J. Michienzi
Focus: Physical Therapy; Physiology . . 13818

Association of Professional Genealogists (APG), 3421 M St NW, Ste 236, Washington, DC 20007-3552
T: (703) 920-2385
Founded: 1979; Members: 600
Focus: Genealogy
Periodical
APG Quarterly (quarterly) 13819

Association of Professional Material Handling Consultants (APMHC), 8720 Red Oak Blvd, Ste 224, Charlotte, NC 28217
T: (704) 558-4749; Fax: (704) 558-4753
Founded: 1960; Members: 40
Gen Secr: Hal Vandiver
Focus: Materials Sci 13820

Association of Professional Schools of International Affairs (APSIA), 2400 N St NW, Washington, DC 20037
T: (202) 862-7989; E-Mail: apsia@erols.com; Fax: (202) 862-3750
Gen Secr: Kay King
Focus: Educ 13821

Association of Professors of Gynecology and Obstetrics (APGO), 409 12 St SW, Washington, DC 20024
T: (202) 863-2507; Fax: (202) 863-2514
Founded: 1962; Members: 156
Focus: Gynecology
Periodicals
Academic Position Report (quarterly)
Membership Directory (annually)
Newsletter (quarterly) 13822

Association of Professors of Medicine (APM), 1200 19 St NW, Ste 300, Washington, DC 20036
T: (202) 857-1158; Fax: (202) 223-4579
Founded: 1954; Members: 125
Gen Secr: James Terwilliger
Focus: Med 13823

Association of Research Directors (ARD), c/o R. Keith Darlington, Elf Atochem N.A., POB 61516, King of Prussia, PA 19406
T: (610) 337-6540; Fax: (610) 337-6784
Founded: 1945; Members: 50
Gen Secr: R. Keith Darlington
Focus: Business Admin 13824

Association of Research Libraries (ARL), 21 Dupont Circle, Ste 800, Washington, DC 20036
T: (202) 296-2296
Founded: 1932; Members: 119
Gen Secr: Duane A. Webster
Focus: Libraries & Bk Sci
Periodicals
ARL Newsletter (5 times annually)
ARL Salary Survey (annually)
ARL Statistics (annually)
Minutes of the Art Meetings (semi-annually) 13825

Association of Safety Council Executives (ASCE), c/o Larry Schenck, 3710 NW 51 St, Ste A, Gainesville, FL 32606
T: (904) 377-2566; Fax: (904) 377-7544
Founded: 1936; Members: 250
Focus: Safety 13826

Association of School Business Officials International (ASBO), 11401 N Shore Dr, Reston, VA 22090
T: (703) 478-0405; Fax: (703) 478-0205
Founded: 1910; Members: 6900
Focus: Educ
Periodicals
ASBO Accents (monthly)
School Business Affairs (monthly) . . . 13827

Association of Schools and Colleges of Optometry (ASCO), 6110 Executive Blvd, Ste 690, Rockville, MD 20852
T: (301) 231-5944; Fax: (301) 770-1828
Founded: 1941; Members: 19
Focus: Adult Educ; Ophthal
Periodicals
Information for Applicants to Schools and Colleges of Optometry (annually)
Journal of Optometric Education (quarterly)
Proceedings (annually) 13828

Association of Schools of Journalism and Mass Communication (ASJMC), c/o Jennifer H. McGill, University of South Carolina, LeConte College, Rm 121, Columbia, SC 29208-0251
T: (803) 777-2005; Fax: (803) 777-4728
Founded: 1917; Members: 206
Gen Secr: Jennifer H. McGill
Focus: Journalism
Periodicals
JMC Administrator (quarterly)
Journalism Educator (quarterly) 13829

Association of Schools of Public Health (ASPH), 1660 L St NW, Ste 204, Washington, DC 20036
T: (202) 296-1099; Fax: (202) 296-1252
Founded: 1941; Members: 27
Gen Secr: Michael K. Gemmell
Focus: Adult Educ; Public Health
Periodical
Graduate Education for Public Health (bi-annually) 13830

Association of Science Museum Directors (ASMD), c/o Chicago Academy of Sciences, 2001 N Clark St, Chicago, IL 60614
T: (312) 549-0606
Founded: 1960; Members: 92
Focus: Sci
Periodical
Science Museum News 13831

Association of Science-Technology Centers (ASTC), 1025 Vermont Av NW, Ste 500, Washington, DC 20005
T: (202) 783-7200
Founded: 1973; Members: 417
Focus: Eng; Sci
Periodical
ASTC Newsletter (bi-monthly) 13832

Association of Social and Behavioral Scientists (ASBS), c/o Dr. Jacqueline Rovse, Dept of History, American University, 4400 Massachusetts Av, Washington, DC 20016-8038
T: (202) 885-2461
Founded: 1935; Members: 200
Focus: Sociology; Behav Sci
Periodical
Journal of Social and Behavioral Sciences (annually) 13833

Association of Southern Baptist Colleges and Schools (ASBCS), 901 Commerce, Ste 600, Nashville, TN 37203
T: (615) 244-2362; Fax: (615) 242-2153
Founded: 1915; Members: 140
Focus: Educ
Periodicals
Directory of Southern Baptist Colleges and Schools (bi-annually)
The Southern Baptist Educator (monthly) 13834

Association of Space Explorers (ASE), 800 Connecticut AV NW, Ste 111, Washington, DC 20006-2709
T: (202) 331-3885; Fax: (202) 331-3886
Founded: 1985; Members: 210
Focus: Astrophys 13835

Association of Specialized and Cooperative Library Agencies (ASCLA), c/o American Library Association, 50 E Huron St, Chicago, IL 60611
T: (312) 280-4399; Fax: (312) 280-3257
Founded: 1978; Members: 1432
Focus: Libraries & Bk Sci 13836

Association of State and Interstate Water Pollution Control Administrators (ASIWPCA), 750 First St NE, Ste 910, Washington, DC 20002
T: (202) 898-0905
Founded: 1960; Members: 57
Focus: Ecology 13837

Association of State and Territorial Dental Directors (ASTDD), c/o Minnesota Dept of Health, 717 Delaware St SE, Minneapolis, MN 55440
T: (616) 623-5441; Fax: (616) 623-5775
Members: 53
Gen Secr: Dr. Robert Isman
Focus: Dent 13838

Association of State and Territorial Directors of Public Health Education (ASTDPHE), c/o Lydia Pendley, Health Promotion Bureau, New Mexico Dept of Health, 1190 Saint Francis Dr, POB 26110, Santa Fe, NM 87502-6110
T: (505) 827-2380; Fax: (505) 827-0021
Founded: 1946; Members: 76
Pres: Lydia Pendley
Focus: Public Health
Periodicals
Conference Call (quarterly)
Proceedings (bi-annually) 13839

Association of State and Territorial Health Officials (ASTHO), 415 Second St NE, Ste 200, Washington, DC 20002
T: (202) 546-5400
Founded: 1942; Members: 55
Focus: Public Health
Periodicals
Conference Proceedings (annually)
Membership Directory (bi-annually)
Newsletter (irregularly) 13840

Association of State Supervisors of Mathematics (ASSM), c/o Charles Watson, Dept of Education, 4 Capitol Mall, Little Rock, AR 72201
T: (501) 682-4474; Fax: (501) 682-4618
Founded: 1959; Members: 200
Focus: Math 13841

Association of Surgical Technologists (AST), 7108C S Alton Way, Englewood, CO 80112
T: (303) 694-9130; Fax: (303) 694-9169
Founded: 1969; Members: 14600
Focus: Surgery; Eng
Periodical
The Surgical Technologist (bi-monthly) . 13842

Association of Systematics Collections (ASC), 1725 K St NW, Ste 601, Washington, DC 20006-1401
T: (202) 835-9050; Fax: (202) 347-0072
Founded: 1972; Members: 100
Gen Secr: Dr. K. Elaine Hoagland
Focus: Bio 13843

Association of Teacher Educators (ATE), 1900 Association Dr, Ste ATE, Reston, VA 22091
T: (703) 620-3110; Fax: (703) 620-3110
Founded: 1920; Members: 4000
Focus: Adult Educ; Educ 13844

Association of Teachers of Japanese (ATJ), c/o Japanese Program, Middlebury College, Middlebury, VT 05753
T: (802) 388-3711
Founded: 1962; Members: 550
Focus: Ling; Educ
Periodicals
ATJ Newsletter (3 times annually)
Journal of the Association of Teachers of Japanese (semi-annually) 13845

Association of Teachers of Latin American Studies (ATLAS), Harding Station, POB 620754, Flushing, NY 11362-0754
T: (718) 428-1237
Gen Secr: Daniel J. Mugan
Focus: Educ; Ethnology 13846

Association of Teachers of Maternal and Child Health (ATMCH), 2000 15 St N, Ste 701, Arlington, VA 22201-2617
T: (703) 524-7802; E-Mail: ncemchol@gumedlib.dml.georgetown.edu; Fax: (703) 524-9335
Founded: 1968; Members: 200
Pres: Jonathan Kotch
Focus: Public Health 13847

Association of Teachers of Preventive Medicine (ATPM), 1660 L St NW, Ste 208, Washington, DC 20036
T: (202) 463-0550; Fax: (202) 463-0555
Founded: 1942; Members: 700
Gen Secr: Barbara J. Calgins
Focus: Adult Educ; Hygiene
Periodicals
American Journal of Preventive Medicine (bi-monthly)
Newsletter (quarterly)
Perspectives on Prevention (quarterly) . . 13848

Association of Teachers of Technical Writing (ATTW), c/o Madelyn Flammia, Dept of English, University of Central Florida, POB 25000, Orlando, FL 32816
T: (407) 823-2212
Founded: 1973; Members: 1200
Pres: Sherry Burgus Little
Focus: Educ 13849

Association of the German Nobility in North America (DAGNA) / Deutsche Adels-Gesellschaft in Nord-Amerika, 1101 W Second St, Benicia, CA 94510
T: (707) 745-1605
Founded: 1980; Members: 48
Focus: Genealogy
Periodicals
Der Adelsbote
Review (annually) 13850

Association of the Health Occupations Teacher Educators (AHOTE), c/o School of Education, University of Louisville, Louisville, KY 40292
T: (502) 852-0608
Founded: 1978; Members: 28
Pres: Dr. Patricia K. Leitsch
Focus: Educ; Public Health 13851

Association of the Institute for Certification of Computer Professionals (AICCP), 2200 E Devon Av, Ste 268, Des Plaines, IL 60018
T: (312) 299-4227; Fax: (312) 299-4280
Founded: 1982; Members: 45000
Focus: Computer & Info Sci 13852

Association of Theological Schools (ATS), 10 Summit Park Dr, Pittsburgh, PA 15275-1103
T: (412) 788-6505
Founded: 1918; Members: 211
Focus: Educ; Rel & Theol
Periodical
Theological Education (semi-annually) . . 13853

Association of Third World Affairs (ATWA), 1629 K St NW, Ste 802, Washington, DC 20006
T: (202) 331-8455; Fax: (202) 785-3607
Founded: 1967; Members: 1000
Focus: Develop Areas
Periodicals
Monographs
Third World Forum (bi-monthly) 13854

Association of Third World Studies (ATWS), POB 1232, Americus, GA 31709
T: (601) 957-0282
Gen Secr: Donald Simmons
Focus: Develop Areas 13855

Association of Trial Lawyers of America (ATLA), 1050 31 St NW, Washington, DC 20007
T: (202) 965-3500; Fax: (202) 337-0977
Founded: 1946; Members: 56000
Focus: Law 13856

Association of United States Members of the International Institute of Space Law (AUSMIISL), c/o Patricia Sterns, Sterns & Tennen, 849 N Third Av, Phoenix, AZ 85003
T: (602) 254-5197; Fax: (602) 253-7767
Members: 110
Gen Secr: Patricia Sterns
Focus: Law 13857

Association of Universities for Research in Astronomy (AURA), 1625 Massachusetts Av NW, Ste 550, Washington, DC 20036
T: (202) 483-2101; Fax: (202) 483-2106
Founded: 1957; Members: 22
Pres: Dr. Goetz K. Oertel
Focus: Astronomy 13858

Association of University Anesthesiologists (AUA), c/o Michael J. Bishop, 2033 Sixth Av, Seattle, WA 98121
T: (206) 441-6020
Founded: 1953; Members: 600
Focus: Anesthetics
Periodical
Directory 13859

Association of University Architects (AUA), c/o Facility Planning, Florida Gulf Coast University, 17595 Tamiami Tri, Ste 200, Fort Myers, FL 33908-4500
T: (813) 590-1010
Founded: 1955; Members: 130
Gen Secr: Jack Fenwick
Focus: Archit 13860

Association of University Professors of Ophthalmology (AUPO), POB 420369, San Francisco, CA 94142-0369
T: (415) 561-8548
Founded: 1966; Members: 205
Focus: Ophthal
Periodicals
Bulletin (quarterly)
Membership Directory 13861

Association of University Programs in Health Administration (AUPHA), 1911 N Fort Myer Dr, Ste 503, Arlington, VA 22209
T: (703) 524-5500
Founded: 1948; Members: 1200
Focus: Public Health

Periodicals
Health Services Administration Education Directory (bi-annually)
Journal of Health Administration Education (quarterly)
Staff Report (bi-monthly) 13862

Association of University Radiologists (AUR), 1891 Preston White Dr, Reston, VA 22091
T: (703) 716-7597; Fax: (703) 476-8167
Founded: 1953; Members: 1600
Gen Secr: Gregg Robinson
Focus: Radiology
Periodical
Investigative Radiology (monthly) 13863

Association of University Related Research Parks (AURRP), 4500 S Lakeshore Dr, Ste 405, Tempe, AZ 85282-7056
T: (602) 752-2002; E-Mail: aurrp@goodnet.com; Fax: (602) 752-2003
Founded: 1986; Members: 285
Focus: Sci 13864

Association of University Summer Sessions (AUSS), c/o Dr. Leslie J. Coyne, Summer Sessions/Special Programs, Indiana University, 254 Maxwell Hall, Bloomington, IN 47405
T: (812) 335-5048; Fax: (812)855-3815
Founded: 1925; Members: 50
Focus: Adult Educ; Sci 13865

Association of Visual Science Librarians (AVSL), c/o Illinois College of Optometry, 3241 S Michigan Av, Chicago, IL 60616
Founded: 1968; Members: 75
Pres: Gerald Dujsik
Focus: Libraries & Bk Sci 13866

Association of Waldorf Schools of North America (AWSNA), 3911 Bannister Rd, Fair Oaks, CA 95628
T: (916) 961-0927
Gen Secr: David Alsop
Focus: Educ 13867

Association of Youth Museums (AYM), 1775 K St NW, Ste 595, Washington, DC 20006
T: (202) 466-4144; E-Mail: aymdc@aol.com; Fax: (202) 466-4233
Founded: 1962; Members: 340
Gen Secr: Janet Rice Elman
Focus: Arts
Periodical
Hand to Hand (quarterly) 13868

Association on Boarding Schools (ABS), c/o NAIS, 1620 L St NW, Washington, DC 20036
T: (202) 973-9700; E-Mail: SteveRuz@cais.com; Fax: (202) 973-9790
Founded: 1976; Members: 277
Gen Secr: Steven D. Ruzicka
Focus: Educ
Periodicals
Boarding School Life (annually)
Boarding Schools Directory (annually) . . 13869

Association to Advance Ethical Hypnosis (AAEH), 2675 Oakwood Dr, Cuyahoga Falls, OH 44221
T: (216) 923-8880; Fax: (216) 923-8880
Founded: 1955; Members: 1500
Focus: Psychoan
Periodical
Suggestion (quarterly) 13870

Asthma and Allergy Foundation of America (AAFA), 1125 15 St NW, Ste 502, Washington, DC 20005
T: (202) 466-7643; Fax: (202) 466-8940
Founded: 1953
Focus: Med 13871

Astro-Psychology Institute (API), 2640 Greenwich, Ste 403, San Francisco, CA 94123
T: (415) 921-1192
Founded: 1979
Focus: Psych 13872

Astrologers' Guild of America (AGA), 5 Fair Meadow Dr, Brewster, NY 10509
T: (914) 279-4935
Founded: 1927
Focus: Astronomy
Periodical
Astrological Review (quarterly) 13873

Astronomical League (AL), c/o Berton Stevens, 2112 E Kingfisher Ln, Rolling Meadows, IL 60008
T: (708) 398-0562
Founded: 1946; Members: 11100
Focus: Astronomy
Periodicals
Convention Proceedings (annually)
The Reflector (quarterly) 13874

Astronomical Society of the Pacific (ASP), 390 Ashton Av, San Francisco, CA 94112
T: (415) 337-1100; Fax: (415) 337-5205
Founded: 1889; Members: 7000
Focus: Astronomy
Periodicals
Information Pockets on Astronomy (irregularly)
Mercury (bi-monthly)
Universe in the Classroom (quarterly) . . 13875

Astronomical Society of the Pacific (ASP), 390 Ashton Av, San Francisco, CA 94112
T: (415) 337-1100; Fax: (415) 337-5205
Gen Secr: Robert Havlen
Focus: Astronomy 13876

Atex Newspaper Users Group (ANUG), c/o Audrey Novak, City News Bureau of Chicago, 35 E Walker Dr, Ste 792, Chicago, IL 60601
T: (215) 854-4607; Fax: (215) 854-4737
Founded: 1975; Members: 223
Focus: Computer & Info Sci
Periodicals
Membership Directory (annually)
Weekly Wire (weekly) 13877

Athenaeum of Philadelphia (PAT), 219 S Sixth St, E Washington Sq, Philadelphia, PA 19106
T: (215) 925-2688; Fax: (215) 925-3755
Founded: 1814; Members: 1200
Focus: Arts; Lit; Archit
Periodicals
Athenaeum Annotations
Athenaeum Architectural Archives
Book List (monthly) 13878

Atlantic Council of the United States (ACUS), 910 17 St NW, Ste 1000, Washington, DC 20006
Founded: 1961
Pres: David C. Acheson
Focus: Poli Sci
Periodical
Bulletin (quarterly) 13879

Atlantic Economic Society (AES), c/o Southern Illinois University at Edwardsville, Box 1101, Edwardsville, IL 62026-1101
T: (618) 692-2291; Fax: (618) 692-3400
Founded: 1973; Members: 1000
Gen Secr: Dr. John M. Virgo
Focus: Econ
Periodical
Atlantic Economic Journal (quarterly) . . 13880

Atlantic Gas Research Exchange (AGRE), c/o Gas Research Institute, 8600 W Bryn Mawr Av, Chicago, IL 60631-3562
T: (312) 399-8272; Fax: (312) 399-8170
Gen Secr: Steve Gauthier
Focus: Energy 13881

Audio Engineering Society (AES), 60 E 42 St, Rm 2520, New York, NY 10065
T: (212) 661-8528; Fax: (212) 682-0477
Founded: 1948; Members: 10100
Focus: Eng
Periodical
Journal of the AES (10 times annually) . 13882

Audubon Naturalist Society of the Central Atlantic States (ANS), 8940 Jones Mill Rd, Chevy Chase, MD 20815
T: (301) 652-9188
Founded: 1897; Members: 14000
Focus: Nat Sci; Educ
Periodical
Audubon Naturalist News (10 times annually)
. . . . 13883

August Derleth Society (ADS), POB 481, Sauk City, WI 53583
T: (608) 643-3242
Founded: 1978; Members: 450
Gen Secr: Kay Price
Focus: Lit 13884

Augustan Reprint Society (ARS), 56 E 13 St, New York, NY 10003
T: (212) 777-4700
Founded: 1946; Members: 700
Focus: Lit 13885

Augustan Society (AS), POB P, Torrance, CA 90508-0210
T: (213) 320-7766; Fax: (213) 530-7530
Founded: 1957; Members: 4195
Focus: Genealogy
Periodicals
The Augustan (quarterly)
Roll of Arms 13886

Augustana Historical Society (AHS), c/o Augustana College Library, 3435 Ninth 1/2 Av, Rock Island, IL 61201
T: (309) 794-7317
Founded: 1930; Members: 225
Focus: Hist
Periodical
Newsletter (semi-annually) 13887

Australasian Association of Clinical Biochemists, POB 278, Mt Lawley, WA 6929
T: (619) 370-5224; Fax: (619) 370-4409
Gen Secr: D. C. Sampson
Focus: Chem 13888

Authors Guild (AG), 330 W 42 St, New York, NY 10036
T: (212) 563-5904; Fax: (212) 564-8363
Founded: 1912; Members: 6500
Focus: Lit
Periodical
The Authors Guild Bulletin (quarterly) . . 13889

Authors League of America (ALA), 330 W 42 St, New York, NY 10036
T: (212) 564-8350
Founded: 1912; Members: 14700
Focus: Lit
Periodicals
The Authors Guild Bulletin (quarterly)
The Dramatist Guild Quarterly (quarterly) 13890

Autism Services Center (ASC), 605 Ninth St, POB 507, Huntington, WV 25710-0507
T: (304) 525-8014; Fax: (304) 525-8026
Founded: 1979
Focus: Psych 13891

Autism Society of America (ASA), 7910 Woodmont Av, Ste 650, Bethesda, MD 20814
T: (301) 657-0881; Fax: (301) 657-0869
Founded: 1965; Members: 18000
Pres: Sandra H. Kownacki
Focus: Psych 13892

Automotive Market Research Council (AMRC), 10 Laboratory Dr, POB 13966, Research Triangle Park, NC 27709-3966
T: (919) 549-4800; Fax: (919) 549-4824
Founded: 1966; Members: 100
Pres: Charles Ruth
Focus: Marketing
Periodicals
Automotive Data Bibliography (bi-annually)
Newsletter (quarterly)
Semiannual Vehicle Forecasts (semi-annually)
. . . . 13893

Auxiliary to the American Osteopathic Association (AAOA), 142 E Ontario St, Chicago, IL 60611
T: (312) 266-5640; Fax: (312) 280-3860
Founded: 1940; Members: 5000
Gen Secr: Bridget Price
Focus: Pathology
Periodicals
Annual Report (annually)
Newsletter (monthly)
Record (quarterly)
Roster of Affiliates (annually) 13894

Auxiliary to the American Pharmaceutical Association, 7327 Danburyway, Clearwater, FL 34624
T: (813) 531-1729
Founded: 1936; Members: 400
Pres: Nan Tower
Focus: Pharmacol
Periodicals
APHA Auxiliary Newsletter (semi-annually)
Journal (2-4 times annually) 13895

Aviation Maintenance Foundation International (AMFI), POB 2826, Redmond, WA 98073
T: (206) 827-2295; Fax: (206) 827-2320
Founded: 1971; Members: 6000
Pres: Richard S. Kost
Focus: Aero
Periodicals
AMFI Industry News (bi-monthly)
AMFI Industry Survey Report (annually)
Professionalism (irregularly)
World of Aviation Maintenance (annually) 13896

Aviation Safety Institute (ASI), 6797 N High St, Ste 316, Worthington, OH 43085
T: (614) 885-4242; Fax: (614) 885-5891
Founded: 1973; Members: 500
Gen Secr: Edward Wachs
Focus: Safety; Aero
Periodical
Monitor (bi-weekly) 13897

Aviation/Space Writers Association (AWA), 6540 50 St N, Oakdale, MN 55128
T: (612) 779-9390
Founded: 1938; Members: 650
Gen Secr: Madeline Mohanco Field
Focus: Lit
Periodicals
Newsletter (quarterly)
Yearbook and Directory (annually) . . . 13898

Aviation Technician Education Council (ATEC), 2090 Wexford Ct, Harrisburg, PA 17112-1579
T: (717) 540-7121
Founded: 1961; Members: 167
Focus: Aero; Adult Educ
Periodical
Newsletter (5 times annually) 13899

Avicultural Society of America (ASA), c/o Joe Krader, 29831 Weatherwood, Laguna Niguel, CA 92677-1945
T: (714) 996-5538
Founded: 1927; Members: 1000
Pres: Joe Krader
Focus: Ornithology
Periodical
Avicultural Bulletin (monthly) 13900

AVKO Educational Research Foundation (AVKOERF), 3084 W Willard Rd, Birch Run, MI 48415
T: (313) 686-9283; Fax: (313) 686-1101
Founded: 1974; Members: 500
Focus: Educ 13901

Baker Street Irregulars (BSI), 34 Pierson Av, Norwood, NJ 07648
T: (201) 768-2241
Founded: 1934; Members: 275
Focus: Lit
Periodical
The Baker Street Journal (quarterly) . . 13902

Basque Educational Organization (BEO), POB 640037, San Francisco, CA 94164-0037
T: (415) 583-4035; Fax: (415) 753-0298
Founded: 1983; Members: 7
Focus: Ling; Educ 13903

Bay Area Physicians for Human Rights (BAPHR), POB 14188, San Francisco, CA 94114-0188
T: (415) 558-9353
Founded: 1977; Members: 350
Focus: Law; Physiology 13904

Beef Improvement Federation (BIF), c/o Northwest Research Extension, Kansas State University, 105 Experiment Farm Rd, Colby, KS 67701
T: (913) 462-7575; E-Mail: rbolze@oznet.ksu.edu; Fax: (913) 462-2315
Founded: 1967; Members: 82
Gen Secr: Dr. Ron Bolze
Focus: Vet Med
Periodical
Update (monthly) 13905

Behavior Genetics Association (BGA), c/o George Vogler, Div of Biostatistics, Washington University School of Medicine, 660 S Euclid, Saint Louis, MO 63110
T: (316) 362-3642; Fax: (316) 362-2994
Founded: 1971; Members: 330
Focus: Genetics
Periodical
Behavior Genetics (quarterly) 13906

Behavioral Pharmacology Society (BPS), c/o Larry D. Byrd, Div of Behavioral Biology, Yerkes Regional Primate Research Center, Emory University, Atlanta, GA 30322
T: (404) 727-7730; Fax: (404) 727-7845
Founded: 1957; Members: 200
Focus: Pharmacol 13907

Belgian American Educational Foundation (BAEF), 195 Church St, New Haven, CT 06510
T: (203) 777-5765
Founded: 1920; Members: 250
Focus: Educ 13908

The Bernard Shaw Society (BSS), POB 1159, Madison Square Station, New York, NY 10159-1159
T: (212) 982-9885
Founded: 1962; Members: 300
Focus: Lit
Periodical
The Independent Shavian (3 times annually)
. . . . 13909

Bertrand Russell Society (BRS), c/o John R. Lenz, 38-B Loantaka Way, Madison, NJ 07940
T: (201) 408-3275; Fax: (201) 408-3768
Founded: 1974; Members: 300
Pres: Johnh R. Lenz
Focus: Lit; Philos
Periodical
Russell Society News (quarterly) 13910

Bet Nahrain (BN), POB 4116, Modesto, CA 95352
T: (209) 522-3229; Fax: (209) 538-2795
Founded: 1974; Members: 5000
Focus: Ling; Ethnology
Periodical
Bet-Nahrain Journal (monthly) 13911

Beta Phi Mu – International Library and Information Science Honor Society, c/o School of Library and Information Science, Univ. of Pittsburgh, Pittsburgh, PA 15260
T: (412) 624-9435
Gen Secr: Blanche Woolls
Focus: Libraries & Bk Sci; Computer & Info Sci
. . . . 13912

Better Education thru Simplified Spelling (BETSS), 300 Riverfront, Ste 2608, Detroit, MI 48226-4524
T: (313) 393-5850; Fax: (313) 393-5850
Founded: 1978; Members: 50
Pres: Charles F. Kleber
Focus: Ling; Educ 13913

Better Hearing Institute (BHI), POB 1840, Washington, DC 20013
T: (703) 642-0580; Fax: (703) 750-9302
Founded: 1973
Focus: Otorhinolaryngology 13914

Better Vision Institute (BVI), 1800 N Kent St, Ste 904, Rosslyn, VA 22209
T: (703) 243-1528; Fax: (703) 243-1537
Founded: 1929
Gen Secr: Susan Burton
Focus: Ophthal
Periodical
Newsletter (annually) 13915

Bibliographical Society of America (BSA), POB 397, Grand Central Station, New York, NY 10163
T: (212) 647-9171
Founded: 1927; Members: 1250
Gen Secr: Marjory Zaik
Focus: Libraries & Bk Sci
Periodical
Papers (quarterly) 13916

Bibliographical Society of the University of Virginia (BSUV), c/o University of Virginia Library, Charlottesville, VA 22903
Founded: 1947; Members: 600
Gen Secr: Penelope Weiss
Focus: Libraries & Bk Sci
Periodical
Studies in Bibliography (annually) . . . *13917*

Bio-Integral Resource Center (BIRC), POB 7414, Berkeley, CA 94707
T: (415) 524-2567; Fax: (415) 524-1758
Founded: 1978; Members: 4000
Focus: Agri; Nat Sci
Periodicals
Common Sense Pest Control (quarterly)
IPM Practitioner (10 times annually) . . *13918*

Bioelectromagnetics Society (BEMS), 7519 Ridge Rd, Frederick, MD 21702
T: (301) 663-4252; Fax: (301) 371-8955
Founded: 1978; Members: 700
Gen Secr: Dr. William D. Wisecup
Focus: Electronic Eng *13919*

Biological Anthropological Section (BIO), c/o Dr. David Frayer, Dept of Anthropology, University of Kansas, 622 Fraser, Lawrence, KS 66045-2110
T: (913) 864-4103; Fax: (913) 864-5224
Founded: 1984; Members: 512
Focus: Anthro *13920*

Biological Photographic Association (BPA), 1819 Peachtree Rd NE, Ste 620, Atlanta, GA 30309-1849
T: (404) 351-6300; Fax: (404) 351-3348
Founded: 1931; Members: 920
Gen Secr: Thomas P. Hurtgen
Focus: Bio; Photo
Periodical
Journal (quarterly) *13921*

Biological Stain Commission (BSC), POB 626, Rochester, NY 14642
T: (716) 275-2751; Fax: (716) 273-1027
Founded: 1922; Members: 75
Gen Secr: James M. Powers
Focus: Bio
Periodical
Stain Technology (bi-monthly) *13922*

Biomass Energy Research Association (BERA), c/o Dr. Donald L. Klass, Entech International Inc, 25543 W Scott Rd, Barrington, IL 60010
T: (800) 247-1755; Fax: (847) 382-5595
Founded: 1982; Members: 200
Pres: Dr. Donald L. Klass
Focus: Energy
Periodicals
BioEnergy Update (monthly)
Biologue (monthly) *13923*

Biomedical Engineering Society (BMES), POB 2399, Culver City, CA 90231
T: (310) 618-9322
Founded: 1968; Members: 1700
Focus: Med; Eng; Bio
Periodicals
Annals of Biomedical Engineering (bi-monthly)
Bulletin (quarterly) *13924*

Biometric Society, 808 17 St NW, Ste 200, Washington, DC 20006-3910
T: (202) 223-9669; E-Mail: 75703-1470@compuserve.com; Fax: (202) 223-9569
Founded: 1947; Members: 6500
Gen Secr: Charles McGrath
Focus: Bio
Periodical
Biometrics (quarterly) *13925*

Biometric Society, Western North American Region, c/o Robert Cochran, Dept of Statistics, University of Wyoming, Laramie, WY 82071
T: (307) 766-3341; Fax: (307) 766-3927
Founded: 1948; Members: 650
Focus: Bio
Periodicals
Biometric Bulletin (10 times annually)
Biometrics (quarterly) *13926*

Biophysical Society (BPS), 9650 Rockville Pike, Rm L-0512, Bethesda, MD 20814
T: (301) 530-7114; Fax: (301) 530-7133
Founded: 1957; Members: 4500
Pres: Lila Gierasch; Gen Secr: Sarah Hitchcock-Degregori
Focus: Biophys
Periodical
Biophysical Journal *13927*

Black Filmmakers Hall of Fame (BFHFI), 405 14 St, Ste 515, Oakland, CA 94612
T: (510) 465-0804; Fax: (510) 839-9858
Founded: 1973; Members: 500
Focus: Cinema *13928*

Black Lung Association (BLA), c/o Bill Bailey, Box 872, Crab Orchard, WV 25827
T: (304) 252-9654
Founded: 1968; Members: 73000
Focus: Pulmon Dis *13929*

Black Psychiatrists of America (BPA), c/o Dr. Isaac Slaughter, 2730 Adeline St, Oakland, CA 94607
T: (510) 465-1800
Founded: 1968; Members: 550
Focus: Psychiatry

Periodical
BPA Quarterly (quarterly) *13930*

Black Resources Information Coordinating Services (BRICS), 614 Howard Av, Tallahassee, FL 32304
T: (904) 576-7522
Founded: 1972; Members: 670
Focus: Genealogy
Periodicals
Brics Bracs (quarterly)
Media Showcase (annually)
Newsletter (bi-monthly) *13931*

Black Women's Educational Alliance (BWEA), 6625 Greene St, Philadelphia, PA 19119
Founded: 1976; Members: 300
Focus: Educ *13932*

Bloomsday Club (BC), c/o Old York Books, 122 French St, New Brunswick, NJ 08901
T: (201) 249-0430
Founded: 1975; Members: 150
Focus: Lit *13933*

B'Nai B'Rith International Commission on Continuing Jewish Education (BBICCJE), 1640 Rhode Island Av NW, Washington, DC 20036
T: (202) 857-6580; Fax: (202) 857-0980
Founded: 1959
Focus: Educ *13934*

Board on Science and Technology for International Development (BOSTID), c/o National Research Council, 2101 Constitution Av NW, Washington, DC 20418
T: (202) 334-2633; E-Mail: mdow@nas.edu; Fax: (202) 334-2660
Gen Secr: Dr. Michael McD Dow
Focus: Eng; Develop Areas *13935*

Bockus International Society of Gastroenterology, 16 Cedric Rd, Summit, NJ 07901
T: (908) 273-2648; E-Mail: drdkaufman@aol.com; Fax: (908) 353-7974
Founded: 1958
Gen Secr: Dr. David Kaufman
Focus: Gastroenter *13936*

Bolivarian Society of the United States, 7 E 51 St, New York, NY 10022
T: (212) 826-1660
Founded: 1941; Members: 60
Focus: Hist *13937*

Book Industry Study Group (BISG), 160 Fifth Av, New York, NY 10010
T: (212) 929-1393; Fax: (212) 989-7542
Founded: 1976; Members: 220
Focus: Lit *13938*

Boston Theological Institute (BTI), 210 Herrick Rd, Newton Centre, MA 02159
T: (617) 527-4880; Fax: (617) 527-1073
Founded: 1967
Focus: Rel & Theol
Periodicals
Catalog (annually)
Faculty Directory (annually)
Journal (annually)
Newsletter (weekly) *13939*

Bostonian Society (BS), 206 Washington St, Old State House, Boston, MA 02109
T: (617) 720-1713; Fax: (617) 720-3289
Founded: 1881; Members: 1200
Focus: Hist
Periodical
Proceedings *13940*

Botanical Society of America (BSA), c/o Dept of Botany and Plant Sciences, University of California, Riverside, CA 92521-0124
Founded: 1906; Members: 3000
Gen Secr: Darleen Demason
Focus: Botany
Periodicals
American Journal of Botany (monthly)
Plant Science Bulletin (bi-monthly) . . . *13941*

Brain Information Service (BIS), c/o School of Medicine, UCLA, Los Angeles, CA 90095-1746
T: (310) 825-3417; Fax: (310) 206-3499
Founded: 1964
Gen Secr: Dr. Michael H. Chase
Focus: Neurology *13942*

Bram Stoker Memorial Association (BSMA), 29 Washington Sq W, New York, NY 10011
T: (212) 982-6754
Founded: 1985; Members: 336
Focus: Lit *13943*

Brandeis-Bardin Institute (BBI), 1101 Peppertree Ln, Brandeis, CA 93064
T: (805) 582-4450; Fax: (805) 526-1398
Founded: 1941; Members: 1000
Focus: Educ
Periodical
News (bi-monthly) *13944*

The Bridge, 248 W 108 St, New York, NY 10025
T: (212) 663-3000; Fax: (212) 663-3181
Founded: 1954; Members: 350
Focus: Therapeutics *13945*

British Schools and Universities Foundation (BSUF), 575 Madison Av, Ste 1006, New York, NY 10022-2511
T: (212) 662-5576
Founded: 1961; Members: 350
Focus: Educ *13946*

Broadcast Education Association (BEA), 1771 N St NW, Washington, DC 20036-2891
T: (202) 429-5354; Fax: (202) 429-5343
Founded: 1955; Members: 1250
Gen Secr: Louisa A. Nielsen
Focus: Adult Educ; Journalism
Periodicals
Feedback (quarterly)
Journal of Broadcasting & Electronic Media (quarterly) *13947*

Browning Institute (BI), POB 2983, Grand Central Station, New York, NY 10163-2983
T: (316) 221-2779
Founded: 1971; Members: 350
Focus: Lit *13948*

Bruckner Society of America (BSA), 2150 Dubuque Rd, Iowa City, IA 52240
T: (319) 351-5758
Founded: 1932
Focus: Music
Periodical
Chord and Discord *13949*

Buffalo Bill Memorial Association (BBHC), POB 1000, Cody, WY 82414
T: (307) 587-4771
Founded: 1927
Focus: Cultur Hist
Periodical
Newsletter (quarterly) *13950*

Building Officials and Code Administrators International (BOCA), 4051 W Flossmoor Rd, Country Club Hills, IL 60478-5795
T: (708) 799-2300; Fax: (708) 799-4981
Founded: 1915; Members: 12000
Focus: Civil Eng
Periodical
BOCA Magazine *13951*

Bureau of Professional Education of the American Osteopathic Association (BPEAOA), c/o Douglas Ward, American Osteopathic Association, 142 E Ontario St, Chicago, IL 60611
T: (312) 280-5800; Fax: (312) 280-5803
Focus: Pathology *13952*

Burlesque Historical Society (BHS), c/o Exotic World, 29053 Wild Rd, Helendale, CA 92342
T: (619) 243-5261
Founded: 1963; Members: 500
Focus: Perf Arts
Periodical
The Legend of Jennie Lee *13953*

Business Association of Latin American Studies (BALAS), c/o School of Business Administration, University of San Diego, Alcala Park, San Diego, CA 92110
T: (619) 260-4836; Fax: (619) 260-4891
Gen Secr: Dr. Denise Dimon
Focus: Econ *13954*

Business-Higher Education Forum (B-HEF), 1 Dupont Circle NW, Ste 800, Washington, DC 20036
T: (202) 939-9345; Fax: (202) 833-4723
Founded: 1978; Members: 90
Focus: Educ; Econ *13955*

Business History Conference (BHC), c/o William J. Hausman, Dept of Economics, College of William and Mary, Williamsburg, VA 23187-8795
T: (804) 221-2381; Fax: (804) 221-2390
Founded: 1954; Members: 450
Focus: Econ
Periodicals
Conference Newsletter (semi-annually)
Economic and Business History (annually)
List of Members (bi-annually) *13956*

Business Professionals of America (BPA), 5454 Cleveland Av, Columbus, OH 43231
T: (614) 895-7277
Founded: 1966; Members: 54000
Focus: Educ; Business Admin *13957*

Byron Society (BS), c/o Dept of English, University of Delaware, Newark, DE 19716
T: (302) 831-3654; Fax: (302) 831-1586
Founded: 1971; Members: 2000
Gen Secr: Marsha M. Manns
Focus: Lit *13958*

Cajal Club (CC), c/o Dr. David Whitlock, Dept of Cellular and Structural Biology, University of Colorado Health Sciences Center, 4200 E Ninth Av, Denver, CO 80262
T: (303) 270-8201; Fax: (303) 270-5969
Founded: 1947; Members: 450
Focus: Neurology
Periodicals
History of Cajal Club
Proceedings (irregularly) *13959*

California Institute of International Studies (CIIS), c/o Hoover Institution, Stanford University, Stanford, CA 94305-6010
T: (415) 322-2026; E-Mail: Hilton@stanford.edu; Fax: (415) 723-1687

Gen Secr: Ronald Hilton
Focus: Poli Sci *13960*

California Institute of Pan African Studies (CIPAS), c/o UCLA Center for Afro-American Studies Library, 44 Haines Hall, 405 Hilgard Av, Los Angeles, CA 90024-1545
T: (310) 825-6060; E-Mail: idh7lib@mvs.oac.ucla.edu; Fax: (310) 206-3421
Gen Secr: Itibari M. Zulu
Focus: Ethnology *13961*

Calorimetry Conference (CC), c/o College of Pharmacy, Florida A & M University, Tallahassee, FL 32307
T: (904) 561-2672; Fax: (904) 599-3731
Founded: 1947; Members: 250
Gen Secr: R. Renee Reams
Focus: Energy *13962*

Cambodian Buddhist Society (CBS), 13800 New Hampshire Av, Silver Spring, MD 20904
T: (301) 622-6544
Founded: 1978; Members: 1000
Focus: Rel & Theol *13963*

Canal Society of New York State (CSNYS), 311 Montgomery St, Syracuse, NY 13202
T: (315) 428-1862
Founded: 1956; Members: 235
Focus: Hist *13964*

Cancer Care (CC), 1180 Av of the Americas, New York, NY 10036
T: (212) 221-3300; Fax: (212) 719-0263
Founded: 1944; Members: 20000
Focus: Cell Biol & Cancer Res *13965*

Cancer Control Society (CCS), 2043 N Berendo St, Los Angeles, CA 90027
T: (213) 663-7801
Founded: 1973; Members: 5500
Focus: Cell Biol & Cancer Res
Periodicals
Cancer Book House List (bi-annually)
Doctor and Clinic Directory (bi-monthly)
Patient Directory (bi-monthly) *13966*

Cancer Federation, POB 1298, Banning, CA 92220-0009
Founded: 1977; Members: 1500
Gen Secr: John Steinbacher
Focus: Cell Biol & Cancer Res
Periodicals
Challenge (quarterly)
Newsletter (irregularly)
Proceedings of Annual Riverside Conference on Stress, Emotions and Cancer (annually) . *13967*

Candlelighters Childhood Cancer Foundation (CCCF), 7910 Woodmont Av, Ste 460, Bethesda, MD 20814
T: (301) 657-8401; Fax: (301) 657-8319
Founded: 1976; Members: 33000
Focus: Cell Biol & Cancer Res *13968*

Canon Law Society of America (CLDA), c/o Catholic University, 431 Caldwell Hall, Washington, DC 20064
T: (202) 269-3491; Fax: (202) 319-5719
Founded: 1939; Members: 1900
Focus: Rel & Theol; Law
Periodicals
Convention Proceedings (annually)
Membership Directory
Newsletter (quarterly) *13969*

Cardiovascular Credentialing International (CCI), 4456 Corporation Ln, Ste 120, Virginia Beach, VA 23462
T: (804) 497-3380; Fax: (804) 497-3491
Founded: 1988; Members: 15000
Gen Secr: Julia Dow
Focus: Cardiol *13970*

Cardiovascular System Dynamics Society, c/o Likoff Cardiovascular Institute, Hahnemann University, Broad and Vine Sts, Mail Stop 110, Philadelphia, PA 19102-1192
T: (215) 448-1703
Founded: 1976
Gen Secr: Prof. J. Yasha Kresh
Focus: Cardiol *13971*

Career College Association (CCA), 750 First St NE, Ste 900, Washington, DC 20002
T: (202) 336-6700; Fax: (202) 336-6828
Founded: 1991; Members: 1900
Focus: Adult Educ; Business Admin; Eng
Periodicals
Career Training (quarterly)
CCA News (weekly)
Washington Update (weekly) *13972*

Caribbean Sea and Gulf of Mexico Regional Hydrographic Commission (CGMHC), c/o Coast Survey, National Ocean Service, SSMC Building 3, 1315 E-West Hwy, Silver Spring, MD 20910-2133
Gen Secr: F. W. Maloney
Focus: Water Res *13973*

Carnegie Foundation for the Advancement of Teaching (CFAT), 5 Ivy Ln, Princeton, NJ 08540
T: (609) 452-1780
Founded: 1905
Focus: Educ *13974*

Carnegie Institution of Washington (CIW), 1530 P St NW, Washington, DC 20005
T: (202) 387-6400; Fax: (202) 387-8092
Founded: 1902
Focus: Physics; Astronomy; Botany; Bio; Geology
Periodical
Year Book (annually) 13975

Catalysis Society (North America), c/o Dr. Michael B. D'Amore, Dupont Co. Experimental Station, POB 80262, Wilmington, DE 19880-0262
T: (302) 695-2488; E-Mail: damore@esvax.dnet.dupont.com; Fax: (302) 695-8347
Founded: 1956; Members: 2200
Gen Secr: Dr. Michael B. D'Amore
Focus: Chem
Periodical
Newsletter (quarterly) 13976

Catecholamine Club (CC), c/o Walter R. Dixon, Dept of Pharmacology and Toxicology, School of Pharmacy, University of Kansas, Lawrence, KS 66045
T: (913) 864-3951
Founded: 1969; Members: 350
Focus: Chem 13977

Catgut Acoustical Society (CAS), c/o Carleen Maley Hutchins, 112 Essex Av, Montclair, NJ 07042
T: (201) 744-4029; E-Mail: CATGUTAS@MSN.COM; Fax: (201) 744-9197
Founded: 1963; Members: 800
Gen Secr: Carleen Maley Hutchins
Focus: Music
Periodical
Journal of the Catgut Acoustical Society (semi-annually) 13978

Catholic Audio-Visual Educators Association (CAVE), c/o John Manear, POB 9257, Pittsburgh, PA 15224
T: (412) 561-3583
Founded: 1948; Members: 2000
Focus: Educ
Periodicals
CAVE Evaluation
Newsletter (quarterly) 13979

Catholic Biblical Association of America (CBA), c/o Catholic University, 620 Michigan Av NE, Washington, DC 20064
T: (202) 319-5519; Fax: (202) 319-4479
Founded: 1936; Members: 1200
Focus: Educ; Rel & Theol
Periodicals
The Catholic Biblical Quarterly (quarterly)
Old Testament Abstracts (3 times annually)
. . . . 13980

Catholic Commission on Intellectual and Cultural Affairs (CCICA), c/o La Salle University, 1900 W Olney Av, POB 673, Philadelphia, PA 19141-1199
T: (215) 951-1221; Fax: (215) 951-1488
Founded: 1946; Members: 300
Gen Secr: Daniel Burke
Focus: Humanities 13981

Catholic Fine Arts Society (CFAS), c/o Jean Dominici de Maria, Molloy College, 1000 Hampstead Av, Rockville Centre, NY 11570
T: (516) 678-5460; Fax: (516) 678-7295
Founded: 1955; Members: 200
Focus: Fine Arts
Periodicals
Membership List (annually)
Newsletter (quarterly) 13982

Catholic Health Association of the United States (CHA), 4455 Woodson Rd, Saint Louis, MO 63134-0889
T: (314) 427-2500; Fax: (314) 427-0029
Founded: 1915; Members: 1200
Focus: Public Health
Periodicals
Catholic Health World: Official Assoc. Newspaper (bi-monthly)
Guidebook of Catholic Healthcare Facilities (annually)
Health Progress: Official Journal (10 times annually) 13983

Catholic Library Association (CLA), c/o Library, Saint Joseph Central High School, 22 Maplewood Av, Pittsfield, MA 01201-4780
T: (413) 443-2252
Founded: 1921; Members: 3100
Pres: Jean R. Bostley; Gen Secr: Anthony Prete
Focus: Libraries & Bk Sci
Periodicals
Catholic Library World (bi-monthly)
Catholic Periodical and Literature Index (bi-monthly)
Handbook and Membership Directory (annually)
. . . . 13984

Catholic Medical Mission Board (CMMB), 10 W 17 St, New York, NY 10011-5765
T: (212) 242-7757; Fax: (212) 807-9161
Founded: 1928
Focus: Med 13985

Catholic Theological Society of America (CTSA), c/o Creighton University, 2500 California Plaza, Omaha, NE 68178-0116
T: (402) 280-2505; Fax: (402) 280-2502
Founded: 1946; Members: 1400
Gen Secr: Joan Mueller
Focus: Rel & Theol
Periodical
Proceedings (annually) 13986

Caucus for a New Political Science (CNPS), c/o Government Dept, Suffolk University, Boston, MA 02108-2770
T: (617) 573-8126
Founded: 1967; Members: 350
Focus: Soc Sci
Periodical
New Political Science (quarterly) 13987

CDS International (CDSI), 330 Seventh Av, New York, NY 10001
T: (212) 760-1400; Fax: (212) 268-1288
Founded: 1968
Focus: Econ 13988

Cecchetti Council of America (CCA), POB 74, Manchester, MI 48158
T: (313) 428-7782
Founded: 1939; Members: 500
Pres: Lee Ann King
Focus: Perf Arts
Periodical
CCA Newsletter (semi-annually) 13989

CEDAM International, 1 Fox Rd, Croton on Hudson, NY 10520
T: (914) 271-5365; Fax: (914) 271-4723
Founded: 1967; Members: 1000
Focus: Archeol
Periodicals
Bulletin (quarterly)
Reef Report (quarterly) 13990

Center for Advanced Study in the Behavioral Sciences (CASBS), 202 Junipero Serra Blvd, Stanford, CA 94305
T: (415) 321-2052; Fax: (415) 321-1192
Founded: 1954; Members: 50
Focus: Sci; Humanities; Stats; Med; Behav Sci
Periodical
Annual Report (annually) 13991

Center for American Archaeology (CAA), POB 366, Kampsville, IL 62053
T: (618) 653-4316
Founded: 1953; Members: 545
Focus: Archeol
Periodicals
Center for American Archaeology Annual Report (annually)
Center for American Archaeology Newsletter (semi-annually)
Kampsville Archaeological Center Research Series
Kampsville Archaeological Center Technical Report
. . . . 13992

Center for Applied Linguistics (CAL), 1118 22 St NW, Washington, DC 20037
T: (202) 429-9292; Fax: (202) 429-9766
Founded: 1959; Members: 80
Focus: Ling 13993

Center for Applied Research in the Apostolate (CARA), c/o Georgetown University, POB 1601, Washington, DC 20057
T: (202) 687-8080; Fax: (202) 687-8083
Founded: 1945; Members: 8
Focus: Rel & Theol
Periodicals
Cara Seminary Directory (annually)
Cara Seminary Forum (quarterly) . . . 13994

Center for Arab-Islamic Studies (CAIS), POB 678, Brattleboro, VT 05301
T: (802) 257-0872
Founded: 1980
Focus: Ling 13995

Center for Attitudinal Healing (CAH), 33 Buchanan Dr, Sausalito, CA 94965
T: (415) 331-6161; Fax: (415) 331-4545
Founded: 1975
Gen Secr: Don Goewey
Focus: Public Health 13996

Center for Austrian Studies (CAS), c/o University of Minnesota, 314 Social Sciences, 267 19 Av S, Minneapolis, MN 55455
T: (612) 624-9811; Fax: (612) 626-2242
Founded: 1977
Focus: Ethnology 13997

Center for Auto Safety (CAS), 2001 S St NW, Ste 410, Washington, DC 20009-1160
T: (202) 328-7700
Founded: 1970; Members: 12000
Focus: Safety 13998

Center for Chinese Research Materials (CCRM), POB 3090, Oakton, VA 22124
T: (703) 281-7731
Founded: 1967
Focus: Ethnology; Libraries & Bk Sci
Periodical
Newsletter 13999

Center for Community Change (CCC), 1000 Wisconsin Av NW, Washington, DC 20007
T: (202) 342-0519
Founded: 1968
Focus: Public Health; Sociology
Periodicals
Friday Report (weekly)
Monitor (4-5 times annually) 14000

Center for Computer-Assisted Legal Instruction (CALI), 229 19 Av S, Minneapolis, MN 55455
T: (612) 625-3419
Founded: 1982
Focus: Educ; Law; Computer & Info Sci 14001

Center for Cuban Studies (CCS), 124 W 23 St, New York, NY 10011
T: (212) 242-0559
Founded: 1972; Members: 2000
Focus: Adult Educ
Periodical
Cuba Update (bi-monthly) 14002

Center for Death Education and Research (CDER), c/o University of Minnesota, 1167 Social Science Bldg, 267 19 Av S, Minneapolis, MN 55455
T: (612) 624-1895
Founded: 1969
Focus: Educ 14003

Center for Design Planning (CDP), 2300 E Mallory St, Pemsacola, FL 32503
T: (904) 432-8478; Fax: (904) 438-1662
Founded: 1973
Focus: Urban Plan 14004

Center for Early Adolescence (CEA), c/o University of North Carolina at Chapel Hill, D-2 Carr Mill Town Center, Carrboro, NC 27510
T: (919) 966-1148; Fax: (919) 966-7657
Founded: 1978; Members: 6000
Focus: Educ
Periodical
Common Focus (irregularly) 14005

Center for Economic Conversion (CEC), 222 View St, Ste C, Mountain View, CA 94041
T: (415) 968-8798; Fax: (415) 968-1126
Founded: 1975; Members: 2400
Focus: Econ
Periodicals
Plowshare Press (quarterly)
Positive Alternatives (quarterly) 14006

Center for Energy Policy and Research (CEPR), c/o New York Institute of Technology, Old Westbury, NY 11568
T: (516) 686-7578
Founded: 1975
Focus: Energy 14007

Center for Field Research (CFR), POB 9104, Watertown, MA 02272
T: (617) 926-8200; E-Mail: cfr@earthwatch.org; Fax: (617) 926-8532
Founded: 1971
Gen Secr: Dr. Andrew Hudson
Focus: Sci 14008

Center for Global Education (CGE), c/o Augsburg College, 731 21 Av S, Minneapolis, MN 55454
T: (612) 330-1159; Fax: (612) 330-1695
Founded: 1982
Focus: Educ 14009

Center for Marine Conservation (CMC), 1725 DeSales NW, Ste 500, Washington, 20036
T: (202) 429-5609; Fax: (202) 872-0619
Founded: 1972
Focus: Ecology
Periodicals
Directory of Environmental Education Resources
Report (quarterly) 14010

Center for Medical Consumers and Health Care Information (CMC), 237 Thompson St, New York, NY 10012
T: (212) 674-7105; Fax: (212) 674-7100
Founded: 1976; Members: 1500
Focus: Public Health
Periodical
Health Facts (monthly) 14011

Center for Medieval and Early Renaissance Studies (CEMERS), c/o State University of New York at Binghamton, POB 6000, Binghamton, NY 13902-6000
T: (607) 777-2730
Founded: 1966; Members: 75
Focus: Hist
Periodicals
Acta (annually)
Mediaevalia (annually)
Old English Newsletter (semi-annually)
Proceedings of Conference (annually) . . 14012

Center for Medieval and Renaissance Studies (CMRS), c/o Ohio State University, 256 Cunz Hall, 1841 Millikiu Rd, Columbus, OH 43210
T: (614) 292-7495; E-Mail: howe.23@osu.edu; Fax: (614) 292-1599
Founded: 1965; Members: 100
Gen Secr: Nicholas Howe
Focus: Hist
Periodical
Nouvelles (quarterly) 14013

Center for Migration Studies of New York (CMS), 209 Flagg Pl, Staten Island, NY 10304
T: (718) 351-8800; Fax: (718) 667-4598
Founded: 1964
Focus: Ethnology
Periodicals
International Migration Review (quarterly)
Migration World (bi-monthly)
Newsletter (semi-annually) 14014

Center for Neo-Hellenic Studies (CNHS), 1010 W 22 St, Austin, TX 78705
T: (512) 477-5526
Founded: 1965; Members: 150
Focus: Hist
Periodicals
Bulletin (annually)
Neo-Hellenika (annually) 14015

Center for Oceans Law and Policy, c/o School of Law, University of Virginia, 580 Nancy Rd, Charlottesville, VA 22901
T: (804) 924-7441
Founded: 1976
Focus: Oceanography; Law 14016

Center for Peace Education, 118A E Main St, Carrboro, NC 27510
T: (919) 929-9821; Fax: (919) 929-7465
Gen Secr: Marion O'Malley
Focus: Prom Peace; Educ 14017

Center for Philosophy, Law, Citizenship (CPLC), 15 Knapp Hall, SUNY, Farmingdale, NY 11735
T: (516) 420-2047; Fax: (516) 420-2698
Founded: 1972; Members: 800
Focus: Philos; Law; Poli Sci
Periodicals
AITIA Magazine (3 times annually)
Perspective in Philosophy 14018

Center for Process Studies (CPS), 1325 College Av, Claremont, CA 91711-3154
T: (909) 621-5330; E-Mail: process@ctr4process.org; Fax: (909) 626-7062
Founded: 1974; Members: 400
Gen Secr: Prof. David Griffin
Focus: Philos 14019

Center for Public Justice (CPJ), POB 48368, Washington, DC 20002-0368
T: (410) 263-5909; Fax: (410) 263-3857
Founded: 1973
Gen Secr: James W. Skillen
Focus: Poli Sci
Periodical
Public Justice Report (10 times annually) 14020

Center for Research in Ambulatory Health Care Administration (CRAHCA), 104 Inverness Terrace E, Englewood, CO 80112-5306
T: (303) 397-7879; Fax: (303) 799-1683
Founded: 1973
Focus: Public Health; Med 14021

Center for Research Libraries (CRL), 6050 S Kenwood Av, Chicago, IL 60637
T: (312) 955-4545; Fax: (312) 955-4339
Founded: 1949; Members: 135
Focus: Libraries & Bk Sci
Periodicals
Annual Report (annually)
Center for Reseach Libraries Directory (annually)
Focus (bi-monthly)
Handbook (bi-annually) 14022

Center for Responsive Psychology (CRP), 2900 Bedford Av, Brooklyn, NY 11210
T: (718) 951-5000; Fax: (718) 951-4810
Founded: 1972; Members: 37
Gen Secr: Justin Anderson
Focus: Psych
Periodical
Social Action and the Law (quarterly) . 14023

Center for Safety in the Arts (CSA), 5 Beekman St, New York, NY 10038
T: (212) 227-6220
Founded: 1977; Members: 45000
Focus: Safety
Periodical
Newsletter (10 times annually) 14024

Center for Science in the Public Interest (CSPI), 1875 Connecticut Av NW, Washington, DC 20009
T: (202) 332-9110; Fax: (202) 265-4954
Founded: 1971; Members: 250000
Focus: Materials Sci; Sci
Periodical
Nutrition Action Healthletter (10 times annually)
. . . . 14025

Center for Short Lived Phenomena (CSLP), POB 199, Harvard Square Station, Cambridge, MA 02238
T: (617) 492-3310
Founded: 1968
Focus: Physics
Periodical
Oil Spill Intelligence Report (weekly) . . 14026

Center for Social Research and Education (CSRE), 1095 Market St, Ste 618, San Francisco, CA 94103
T: (415) 255-2296; Fax: (415) 255-2298
Founded: 1980; Members: 30
Gen Secr: L.A. Kauffman
Focus: Sociology
Periodicals
Public Sphere (quarterly)
Socialist Review (quarterly) 14027

Center for Socialist History (CSH), 2633 Etna St, Berkeley, CA 94704
T: (510) 843-4658
Founded: 1981
Focus: Socialism
Periodical
Journal of Socialist History 14028

Center for Studies in Criminal Justice (CSCJ), c/o University of Chicago Law School, 1111 E 60 St, Chicago, IL 60637
T: (312) 702-9493; Fax: (312) 702-0730
Founded: 1965
Focus: Law 14029

Center for Sustainable Agriculture (CSA), 232 B St, Davis, CA 95616
T: (916) 756-7177; E-Mail: agaccess@davis.com; Fax: (916) 756-7188
Founded: 1977; Members: 275000
Gen Secr: David Katz
Focus: Agri
Periodical
Washington Newsletter (monthly) 14030

Center for Sutton Movement Writing, POB 7344, Newport Beach, CA 92660
T: (610) 551-0365
Founded: 1973; Members: 300
Gen Secr: Valerie J. Sutton
Focus: Educ
Periodical
The Sign Writer (2-4 times annually) . . 14031

Center for the Study of Human Rights (CSHR), c/o Columbia University, 1108 International Affairs Bldg, New York, NY 10027
T: (212) 854-2479; Fax: (212) 864-4847
Founded: 1977; Members: 34
Focus: Poli Sci; Prom Peace
Periodicals
Annual Report (annually)
Newsletter (quarterly) 14032

Center for the Study of Parent Involvement (CSPI), c/o JFK University, 12 Altarinda Rd, Orinda, CA 94563
T: (510) 254-0110; E-Mail: DSAERANI@JFKU.edu; Fax: (510) 254-4870
Founded: 1973
Pres: Daniel Safran
Focus: Educ 14033

Center for the Study of the Presidency (CSP), 208 E 75 St, New York, NY 10021
T: (212) 249-1200; Fax: (212) 628-9503
Founded: 1965; Members: 5000
Focus: Poli Sci
Periodicals
Center House Bulletin (quarterly)
Presidential Studies Quarterly
Proceedings (annually) 14034

Center for Urban and Regional Studies (CURS), c/o University of North Carolina at Chapel Hill, Hickerson House, Campus Box 3410, Chapel Hill, NC 27599-3410
T: (919) 962-3074; Fax: (919) 962-2518
Founded: 1957; Members: 6
Focus: Urban Plan 14035

Center for War, Peace and the News Media (CWPNM), c/o New York University, 10 Washington Pl, New York, NY 10003
T: (212) 998-7960; Fax: (212) 995-4143
Founded: 1985
Focus: Poli Sci 14036

Center for War/Peace Studies (CW/PS), 218 E 18 St, New York, NY 10003
T: (212) 475-1077; Fax: (212) 260-6384
Founded: 1966; Members: 2000
Gen Secr: Richard Hudson
Focus: Military Sci; Prom Peace
Periodicals
Global Report: Newsletter (quarterly)
Special Studies (irregularly) 14037

Center on Education and Training for Employment (CETE), c/o Ohio State University, 1900 Kenny Rd, Columbus, OH 43210
T: (614) 292-4353; Fax: (614) 292-1260
Founded: 1965
Focus: Adult Educ
Periodicals
Centergram (monthly)
Vocational Educator (quarterly) 14038

Centers and Regional Associations (CARA), c/o Mediaeval Academy of America, 1430 Massachusetts Av, Cambridge, MA 02138
T: (617) 491-1622
Founded: 1968; Members: 87
Focus: Hist 14039

Central Organization for Jewish Education (COJE), 770 Eastern Pkwy, Brooklyn, NY 11213
T: (718) 774-4000
Founded: 1943; Members: 600000
Focus: Educ 14040

Central Society for Clinical Research (CSCR), c/o Dr. Morton Arusdorf, 1228 W Nelson St, Chicago, IL 60657
T: (312) 871-1618; Fax: (312) 871-0525
Founded: 1928; Members: 1294
Gen Secr: Dr. Morton Arusdorf
Focus: Med
Periodical
The Journal of Laboratory and Clinical Medicine (monthly) 14041

Central States Anthropological Society (CSAS), c/o Robert Kegerleis, Dayton Museum of Natural History, 2600 Dewese Pkwy, Dayton, OH 45414
T: (513) 275-7431
Founded: 1921; Members: 500
Focus: Anthro
Periodicals
Central States Anthropology Society Bulletin
Current Issues in Anthropology Newsletter (semi-annually) 14042

Centre for Development of International Law, Grand Central Station, POB 2022, New York, NY 10163
T: (212) 599-2542; E-Mail: cdil@igc.apc.org; Fax: (212) 599-1332
Focus: Law 14043

Centre for UN Reform Education (CURE), 139 E McClellan Av, Livingston, NJ 07039-1397
T: (201) 994-1826; Fax: (201) 994-3903
Gen Secr: Walter Hoffmann
Focus: Educ 14044

Cephalopod International Advisory Council (CIAC), c/o Univ. of Texas Medical Branch, Marine Biomedical Institute, 301 Univ. Blvd, Galveston, TX 77555-1163
T: (409) 772-3661, 772-2133; E-Mail: budelmann@mbian.utmb.edu; Fax: (409) 772-6993
Gen Secr: Dr. Bernd-Ulrich Budelmann
Focus: Med 14045

Ceramic Educational Council (CEC), 735 Ceramic Pl, Westerville, OH 43081
T: (614) 890-4700; Fax: (614) 899-6109
Founded: 1938; Members: 360
Focus: Educ 14046

C.G. Jung Foundation for Analytical Psychology, 28 E 39 St, New York, NY 10016
T: (212) 697-6430; Fax: (212) 953-3989
Founded: 1963; Members: 2500
Focus: Psychoan; Psych; Anthro
Periodicals
Annual Report (annually)
Quadrant (semi-annually) 14047

Character Education Institute (CEI), 8918 Tesoro Dr, Ste 220, San Antonio, TX 78217-6253
T: (210) 829-1727; Fax: (210) 829-1729
Founded: 1942
Focus: Educ 14048

Charles Ives Society, c/o School of Music, Indiana University, Bloomington, IN 47405
T: (812) 855-7097; Fax: (812) 855-4936
Founded: 1973
Pres: J. Peter Burkholder
Focus: Music 14049

Charles S. Peirce Society (CPS), c/o Mark Migotti, Dept of Philosophy, Hamilton College, 198 College Hill Rd, Clinton, NY 13323
T: (315) 859-4628; Fax: (315) 859-4185
Founded: 1946; Members: 590
Gen Secr: Mark Migotti
Focus: Philos
Periodical
Transactions (quarterly) 14050

Chautauqua Literary and Scientific Circle (CLSC), c/o Chautauqua Institution, 1 Ames Av, Chautauqua, NY 14722
T: (716) 357-6232; Fax: (716) 357-9014
Founded: 1878; Members: 2000
Gen Secr: Norman Pederson
Focus: Lit 14051

CHEIRON – The International Society for the History of Behavioral and Social Sciences, c/o Dept of Psychology, Univ. of Wisconsin-Parkside, Kenosha, WI 53141
T: (414) 595-2112
Gen Secr: Prof. Bejamin Harris
Focus: Hist; Sociology 14052

Chemical Industry Institute of Toxicology (CIIT), POB 12137, Research Triangle Park, NC 27709
T: (919) 558-1200; E-Mail: ciitinfo@ciit.org; Fax: (919) 558-1300
Founded: 1974; Members: 37
Pres: Dr. Roger O. McClellan
Focus: Toxicology
Periodical
CIIT Activities (monthly) 14053

Chemical Management and Resources Association (CMRA), 60 Gay St, Ste 702, Staten Island, NY 10301
T: (718) 876-8800
Founded: 1940; Members: 900
Focus: Marketing
Periodical
Chemical Marketing and Management (quarterly) 14054

Chemists' Club, 295 Madison Av, New York, NY 10017
T: (212) 532-7649; Fax: (212) 532-7649
Founded: 1898; Members: 2500
Focus: Chem
Periodical
Newsletter (monthly) 14055

Cherokee National Historical Society (CNHS), POB 515, Tahlequah, OK 74465
T: (918) 456-6007
Founded: 1963; Members: 900
Focus: Hist
Periodical
The Columns (quarterly) 14056

Chesapeake and Ohio Historical Society (COHS), POB 79, Clifton Forge, VA 24422
T: (703) 862-2210
Founded: 1969; Members: 2500
Focus: Hist
Periodical
Chesapeake and Ohio Historical Magazine (monthly) 14057

Chief Officers of State Library Agencies (COSLA), 167 W Main St, Ste 600, Lexington, KY 40507
T: (606) 231-1925; E-Mail: acrouch@iglou.com; Fax: (606) 231-1928
Founded: 1973; Members: 50
Pres: Maurice Travillian
Focus: Libraries & Bk Sci 14058

Child Neurology Society (CNS), 3900 Northwoods Dr, Ste 175, Saint Paul, MN 55112-6966
T: (612) 486-9447; Fax: (612) 486-9436
Founded: 1971; Members: 1000
Gen Secr: Mary Currey
Focus: Neurology; Pediatrics 14059

Childbirth without Pain Education Association (CWPEA), 20134 Snowden, Detroit, MI 48235
T: (313) 341-3816
Founded: 1958; Members: 2000
Gen Secr: Flora Hommel
Focus: Gynecology
Periodical
Memo (bi-monthly) 14060

Children's Leukemia Research Association, 585 Stewart Av, Ste 536, Garden City, NY 11530
T: (516) 222-1944; Fax: (516) 222-0457
Founded: 1965
Gen Secr: Allan D. Weinberg
Focus: Cell Biol & Cancer Res 14061

Children's Literature Association (ChLA), POB 138, Battle Creek, MI 49016
T: (616) 965-8180
Founded: 1972; Members: 700
Focus: Lit 14062

China Institute in America (CIA), 125 E 65 St, New York, NY 10021
T: (212) 744-8181; Fax: (212) 628-4159
Founded: 1926; Members: 1100
Focus: Ethnology
Periodicals
Annual Report (annually)
Art Exhibition Catalogs (semi-annually)
Bulletin (quarterly)
Journal of Inner Asian Studies (annually)
School Catalog (semi-annually) 14063

China Medical Board of New York (CMBNY), 750 Third Av, New York, NY 10017
T: (212) 682-8000; Fax: (212) 949-8726
Founded: 1928; Members: 11
Focus: Med
Periodical
Annual Report (semi-annually) 14064

Chinese-American Librarians Association (CALA), c/o Sheila Lai, CSU at Sacramento, 2000 Jed Smith Dr, Sacramento, CA 95819-6039
T: (916) 278-6201; Fax: (916) 363-0868
Founded: 1973; Members: 500
Focus: Libraries & Bk Sci 14065

Chinese Culture Association (CCA), POB 1272, Palo Alto, CA 94302-1272
T: (415) 948-2251
Founded: 1966; Members: 2000
Focus: Humanities 14066

Chinese Historical Society of America (CHSA), 650 Commercial St, San Francisco, CA 94111
T: (415) 391-1188
Founded: 1963; Members: 500
Focus: Ethnology; Hist
Periodicals
Bulletin (monthly)
Chinese America: History and Perspectives 14067

Chinese Language Teachers Association (CLTA), c/o Dept of Foreign Languages, Kalamazoo College, 1200 Academy St, Kalamazoo, MI 49006
T: (616) 337-7001; Fax: (616) 337-7251
Founded: 1963; Members: 700
Focus: Ling; Educ
Periodical
Journal (3 times annually) 14068

Chinese Music Society of North America (CMSNA), 22W381 75 St, Naperville, IL 60565-9245
T: (630) 910-1551; Fax: (630) 910-1561
Founded: 1976; Members: 900
Pres: Sin-Yan Shen
Focus: Music; Acoustics
Periodical
Chinese Music (quarterly) 14069

Chinese Musical and Theatrical Association (CMTA), 24 Pell St, New York, NY 10013
T: (212) 385-3531
Founded: 1934; Members: 150
Focus: Music; Perf Arts 14070

Christian Association for Psychological Studies (CAPS), c/o Dr. Randolph K. Sanders, POB 310400, New Braunfels, TX 78131-0400
T: (210) 629-2277; Fax: (210) 629-2342
Founded: 1956; Members: 2400
Gen Secr: Dr. Randolph K. Sanders
Focus: Psych
Periodical
Journal of Psychology and Christianity (quarterly) 14071

Christian Dental Society (CDS), c/o Richard Haw, POB 177, Sumner, IA 50674
T: (319) 578-8843
Founded: 1962; Members: 800
Gen Secr: Richard Haw
Focus: Dent 14072

Christian Educators Association International, POB 41300, Pasadena, CA 91114
T: (818) 798-1124; E-Mail: Educa@aol.com; Fax: (818) 798-2346
Gen Secr: Forrest L. Turpen
Focus: Educ 14073

Christian Literacy Associates (CLA), 541 Perry Hwy, Pittsburgh, PA 15229
T: (412) 364-3777
Founded: 1977; Members: 3200
Focus: Lit 14074

Christian Research Institute International (CRI), POB 500, San Juan Capistrano, CA 92693-0500
Founded: 1960
Focus: Rel & Theol 14075

Christian Research Institute International (CRI), POB 500, San Juan Capistrano, CA 92693-0500
Gen Secr: Hendrik Hanegraaff
Focus: Rel & Theol 14076

Christian Schools International (CSI), 3350 E Paris Av SE, POB 8709, Grand Rapids, MI 49512
T: (616) 957-1070; Fax: (616) 957-5022
Founded: 1920; Members: 450
Focus: Educ
Periodicals
Christian Home and School (8 times annually)
Directory (annually)
Intercom (5 times annually) 14077

Christopher Morley Knothole Association (CMKA), c/o Bryant Library, Paper Mill Rd, Roslyn, NY 11576
T: (516) 621-2240
Founded: 1961; Members: 180
Focus: Lit 14078

Church and Synagogue Library Association (CSLA), POB 19357, Portland, OR 97280
T: (503) 244-6919
Founded: 1967; Members: 1900
Focus: Libraries & Bk Sci
Periodical
Church and Synagogue Libraries (bi-monthly) 14079

CIANS – International Association for Integrative Nervous Functions – Neurobiology of Behaviour and Psychosomatics (CIANS), c/o New Jersey Medical School, 88 Ross St, East Orange, NJ 07018
Gen Secr: Prof. B. H. Natelson
Focus: Neurology 14080

Circus Historical Society (CHS), 3477 Vienna Court, Westerville, OH 43081
Founded: 1939; Members: 1400
Focus: Hist 14081

Cities in Schools (CIS), 1199 N Fairfax, Alexandria, VA 22314
T: (703) 519-8999; Fax: (703) 519-7213
Founded: 1977
Pres: William E. Milliken
Focus: Educ 14082

City of Hope (CH), 1500 E Duarte Rd, Duarte, CA 91010
T: (818) 359-8111; Fax: (818) 301-8115
Founded: 1913
Focus: Med 14083

Civil Aviation Medical Association (CAMA), POB 23864, Oklahoma City, OK 73123-3864
T: (405) 840-0199; Fax: (405) 848-1053
Gen Secr: James L. Harris
Focus: Med 14084

Civil War Press Corps (CWPC), 7674 Heriot Dr, Fayetteville, NC 28311
T: (910) 464-1344
Founded: 1958; Members: 500
Gen Secr: Joseph A. Malcom
Focus: Hist
Periodical
Civil War Byline (8 times annually) . . 14085

Civil War Round Table Associates (CWRTA), POB 7388, Little Rock, AR 72217
T: (501) 225-3996; Fax: (501) 225-5167
Founded: 1968; Members: 1500
Focus: Hist 14086

Classical America (CA), 227 E 50 St, New York, NY 10022
T: (212) 753-4376
Founded: 1968; Members: 700
Focus: Arts 14087

Classification Society of North America, c/o Univ. of Illinois, Psychology and Statistics, 603 E Daniel St, Champaign, IL 61820
T: (217) 333-3325; Fax: (217) 244-5876
Gen Secr: Stanley Wasserman
Focus: Standards 14088

Clay Minerals Society (CMS), POB 4417, Boulder, CO 80306
T: (303) 444-6505
Founded: 1963; Members: 950
Focus: Mineralogy
Periodicals
Clays and Clay Minerals (bi-monthly)
Newsletter (bi-monthly) 14089

Clinical Orthopedic Society (COS), 2416 W Washington St, Ste D-3, Bloomington, IL 61704
T: (309) 662-0545
Founded: 1912; Members: 700
Gen Secr: Barbara Dehority
Focus: Orthopedics
Periodical
Directory (annually) 14090

Coalition for Christian Colleges and Universities (CCC), 329 Eighth St NE, Washington, DC 20002
T: (202) 546-8713; Fax: (202) 546-8913
Founded: 1976; Members: 90
Pres: Dr. Robert C. Andringa
Focus: Educ
Periodicals
Christian College News (monthly)
Guide to Christian Colleges (annually) . 14091

Coalition for International Cooperation and Peace (CICP), 301 E 45 St, New York, NY 10017
T: (212) 983-3353
Founded: 1975; Members: 500
Focus: Prom Peace
Periodicals
Conference Reports (annually)
Lifelines (irregularly)
Newsletter (quarterly) 14092

Coalition for the Advancement in Jewish Education (CAJE), 261 W 35 St, Flat 12A, New York, NY 10001
T: (212) 268-4210; Fax: (212) 268-4214
Founded: 1976; Members: 3800
Focus: Educ 14093

Coastal Engineering Research Council (CERC), c/o Edge & Associates Inc., 4911 Bay Oaks Ct, College Station, TX 77845
T: (409) 690-0306; Fax: (409) 690-6505
Founded: 1950
Gen Secr: Billy L. Edge
Focus: Oceanography; Eng
Periodical
Proceedings (bi-annually) 14094

Coastal Society (TCS), POB 25408, Alexandria, VA 22313-5408
T: (703) 768-1599; Fax: (703) 768-1598
Founded: 1975; Members: 300
Focus: Ecology
Periodicals
Bulletin (quarterly)
Directory 14095

Coblentz Society (CS), c/o David W. Schiering, Perkin-Elmer Corp., 761 Main Av, Norwalk, CT 06859-0240
T: (203) 761-2915; Fax: (203) 761-2842
Founded: 1954; Members: 600
Gen Secr: David W. Schiering
Focus: Physics
Periodical
Coblentz Society Mailings (quarterly) . 14096

Cognitive Science Society (CSS), c/o Alan M. Lesgold, Learning Research and Development Center, University of Pittsburgh, Pittsburgh, PA 15260
T: (412) 624-7046; Fax: (412) 624-9149
Members: 800
Focus: Psych 14097

College Art Association (CAA), 275 Seventh Av, New York, NY 10001
T: (212) 691-1051; Fax: (212) 627-2381
Founded: 1911; Members: 14465
Gen Secr: Susan Ball
Focus: Arts
Periodicals
Art Bulletin (quarterly)
The Art Bulletin (quarterly)
Art Journal (quarterly)
Newsletter (quarterly) 14098

The College Board (TCB), 45 Columbus Av, New York, NY 10023
T: (212) 713-8000; Fax: (212) 713-8255
Founded: 1900; Members: 2800
Focus: Educ
Periodicals
College Board News (quarterly)
College Board Review (quarterly)
College Times (annually)
Going Right on (annually)
Membership Directory (annually)
Proceedings (annually) 14099

College English Association (CEA), c/o Earl J. Wilcox, English Dept, Winthrop University, Rock Hill, SC 29733
T: (803) 323-4633; Fax: (803) 323-4837
Founded: 1939; Members: 1500
Gen Secr: Earl J. Wilcox
Focus: Ling
Periodicals
The CEA Critic (quarterly)
The CEA Forum (quarterly) 14100

College Language Association (CLA), c/o Lucy C. Grigsby, Clark Atlanta University, James P. Brawley Dr at Fair St SW, Atlanta, GA 30314
T: (404) 808-8524; Fax: (404) 880-8222
Founded: 1937; Members: 350
Focus: Ling 14101

College Music Society (CMS), 202 W Spruce, Missoula, MT 59802
T: (406) 721-9616
Founded: 1947; Members: 4500
Focus: Music
Periodicals
Bibliographies in American Music (annually)
Directory of Music Faculties in Colleges and Universities, U.S. and Canada
Symposium 14102

College of American Pathologists (CAP), 325 Waukegan Rd, Northfield, IL 60093-2750
T: (708) 446-8800; Fax: (708) 446-8807
Founded: 1947; Members: 13500
Focus: Pathology
Periodicals
CAP Today (monthly)
Directory (semi-annually)
Job Placement Bulletin
Newsletter 14103

College of Optometrists in Vision Development (COVD), POB 285, Chula Vista, CA 92012
T: (714) 425-6191
Founded: 1970; Members: 1400
Focus: Ophthal
Periodicals
Fellow Directory (annually)
Journal of Optometric Vision Development (quarterly)
Newsletter (quarterly) 14104

College Reading and Learning Association (CRLA), c/o Jo-Ann Mullen, University of North Colorado, 213 McKee, Greeley, CO 80639
T: (303) 351-2189; Fax: (303) 351-2312
Founded: 1967; Members: 1000
Gen Secr: Jo-Ann Mullen
Focus: Educ
Periodicals
Journal of College Reading and Learning (annually)
WCRLA Newsletter (quarterly) 14105

College Theology Society (CTS), c/o Dept of Theology, University of San Diego, Alcala Park, San Diego, CA 92110
T: (619) 260-4053; Fax: (619) 260-2660
Founded: 1954; Members: 960
Pres: Dr. Brennan Hill
Focus: Rel & Theol
Periodical
Horizons (semi-annually) 14106

College-University Resource Institute (CURI), 1001 Connecticut Av, Ste 901, Washington, DC 20036
T: (202) 659-2104; Fax: (202) 835-1159
Founded: 1982
Focus: Educ 14107

Collegium Internationale Chirurgiae Digestivae (CICD), c/o Dept of Surgery, Medical College of Wisconsin, 9200 W Wisconsin Av, Milwaukee, WI 53226
T: (414) 454-5705; Fax: (414) 259-9225
Founded: 1969; Members: 2600
Gen Secr: Robert E. Condon
Focus: Surgery
Periodical
World Journal of Surgery (bi-monthly) . . 14108

Colonial Society of Massachusetts (CSM), 87 Mount Vernon St, Boston, MA 02108
T: (617) 227-2782
Founded: 1892; Members: 240
Focus: Hist
Periodical
New England (quarterly) 14109

Commission of Studies for Latin American Church History (CEHILA), 3001 S Congress Av, POB 949, Austin, TX 78704-6489
Gen Secr: José Oscar Beozzo
Focus: Rel & Theol; Hist 14110

Commission on Accreditation of Allied Health Education Programs (CAAHEP), 515 N State St, Ste 7530, Chicago, IL 60610-4377
T: (312) 464-4622; E-Mail: 75767,1444@compuserve.com; Fax: (312) 464-5830
Founded: 1994; Members: 70
Gen Secr: L.M. Detmer
Focus: Educ; Public Health 14111

Commission on Accreditation of Rehabilitation Facilities (CARF), 1835 Rohlwing Rd, Ste E, Rolling Meadows, IL 60008
T: (847) 394-1785; Fax: (847) 394-2108
Founded: 1972; Members: 29
Gen Secr: Jeanne Boland Patterson
Focus: Rehabil
Periodical
Report (semi-annually) 14112

Commission on Gay/Lesbian Issues in Social Work Education, c/o Council on Social Work Education, 1600 Duke St, Alexandria, VA 22314
T: (703) 683-8080; Fax: (703) 683-8099

Founded: 1980; Members: 9
Focus: Educ; Soc Sci 14113

Commission on Mental and Physical Disability Law (CMPDL), c/o American Bar Association, 1800 M St NW, Washington, DC 20036
T: (202) 331-2240; Fax: (202) 331-2220
Founded: 1976
Focus: Law 14114

Commission on Pastoral Research (COMMISS), 7135 Minstrel Way, Ste 101, Columbia, MD 21045
T: (410) 312-7620; Fax: (410) 312-7644
Founded: 1972; Members: 8
Pres: Dr. Reginald Burgess
Focus: Law
Periodical
Abstracts of Research in Pastoral Care and Counseling (annually) 14115

Commission on Professional and Hospital Activities (CPHA), 1 N Franklin St, Chicago, IL 60606-3421
Founded: 1953
Pres: Dr. William Jessee
Focus: Med
Periodical
Length of Stay, by Diagnosis, by Operation (annually) 14116

Commission on Professionals in Science and Technology (CPST), 1200 New York Av, Ste 390, Washington, DC 20005
T: (202) 326-7080; Fax: (202) 842-1603
Founded: 1953; Members: 525
Gen Secr: Catherine D. Gaddy
Focus: Eng
Periodicals
Professional Women and Minorities: A Manpower Data Resource Service (annually)
Salaries of Scientists, Engineers and Technicians (bi-annually)
Scientific, Engineering, Technical Manpower Comments (monthly)
Supply and Demand for Scientists and Engineers (irregularly) 14117

Commission on the Study of Peace (CSP), c/o Dept of Anthropology, Syracuse University, Syracuse, NY 13244-1090
T: (315) 443-2367; Fax: (315) 443-3818
Gen Secr: Dr. Robert A. Rubinstein
Focus: Prom Peace 14118

Commission on World Standards of the world Association of Societies of Pathology – Anatomic and Clinical (COWS), c/o College of American Pathologists, 325 Waukegan Rd, Northfield, IL 60093-2750
T: (847) 446-8800; Fax: (847) 446-8807
Gen Secr: Dr. Kenneth D. McClatchey
Focus: Pathology 14119

Commission to Study the Organization of Peace (CSOP), c/o School of Law, George Washington University, 720 20 St NW, Washington, DC 20052
T: (202) 994-7390; Fax: (202) 994-9446
Founded: 1939; Members: 90
Pres: Prof. Louis B. Sohn
Focus: Prom Peace 14120

Committee for Better Transit (CBT), POB 3106, Long Island City, NY 11103
T: (718) 278-0650
Founded: 1962; Members: 350
Focus: Transport
Periodical
Notes from Unterground (monthly) . . . 14121

Committee for Economic Development (CED), 2000 L St NW, Ste 700, Washington, DC 20036
T: (202) 296-5860; Fax: (202) 223-0776
Founded: 1942; Members: 225
Focus: Econ 14122

Committee for Freedom of Choice in Medicine (CFCM), 1180 Walnut Av, Chula Vista, CA 92011
T: (619) 429-8200; Fax: (619) 429-8004
Founded: 1972; Members: 30000
Focus: Cell Biol & Cancer Res 14123

Committee for Hispanic Arts and Research (CHAR), POB 12865, Austin, TX 78711
T: (512) 479-6397
Founded: 1980; Members: 250
Focus: Arts
Periodical
Arriba (monthly) 14124

Committee for the Implementation of the Standardized Yiddish Orthography (CISYO), 200 W 72 St, Ste 40, New York, NY 10023
T: (212) 787-6675
Founded: 1958
Focus: Ling 14125

Committee for the Promotion of Medical Research, 191 Hayward St, Yonkers, NY 10704
T: (914) 968-0262
Founded: 1944
Focus: Med 14126

Committee for the Scientific Investigation of Claims of the Paranormal (CSICOP), POB 703, Amherst, NY 14226-0703
T: (716) 636-1425; E-Mail: SKEPTINY@aol.com; Fax: (716) 636-1733

Gen Secr: Barry Karr
Focus: Parapsych 14127

Committee for the Scientific Investigation of Claims of the Paranormal (CSICOP), POB 703, Buffalo, NY 14226
T: (716) 636-1425; Fax: (716) 636-1733
Founded: 1976; Members: 150
Focus: Psych
Periodicals
Skeptical Briefs (quarterly)
The Skeptical Inquirer (quarterly) 14128

Committee on Capacity Building in Science (CCBS), c/o FERMILAB, POB 500, Batavia, IL 60510-0500
Fax: (708) 840-8752
Gen Secr: Leon Lederman
Focus: Sci 14129

Committee on Changing International Realities (CIR), c/o National Planning Association, 1424 16 St NW, Ste 700, Washington, DC 20036
T: (202) 265-7685
Founded: 1975; Members: 60
Focus: Int'l Relat 14130

Committee on Continuing Education for School Personnel (CCESP), c/o Dr. George Sisko, Academic Services, Kean College of New Jersey, Union, NJ 07083
T: (201) 527-2161
Founded: 1922; Members: 42
Focus: Educ 14131

Committee on Institutional Cooperation (CIC), 302 E John St, Ste 1705, Champaign, IL 61820
T: (217) 333-8475; Fax: (217) 244-7127
Founded: 1958; Members: 12
Focus: Educ
Periodicals
Biennial Report (bi-annually)
CIC Directory of Minority Ph.D. Candidates and Recipients (annually)
President's Newsletter 14132

Committee on Political Education, AFL-CIO (COPE), 815 16 St NW, Washington, DC 20006
T: (202) 637-5101
Founded: 1955; Members: 50
Focus: Poli Sci 14133

Committee on Research Materials on Southeast Asia (CORMOSEA), c/o Echols Collection, Icroch Library, Cornell University, Ithaca, NY 14853
T: (607) 255-8889; E-Mail: ajr2@cornell.edu; Fax: (607) 255-8438
Founded: 1969; Members: 12
Gen Secr: Allen Riedy
Focus: Libraries & Bk Sci
Periodical
CORMOSEA Bulletin (semi-annually) . . 14134

Committee on the Role and Status of Women in Educational Research and Development, c/o Dannelle Stevens, School of Education, Portland State University, POB 751, Portland, OR 97207
T: (503) 725-4679; E-Mail: dannelle@ed.pdx.edu; Fax: (503) 725-4679
Founded: 1972; Members: 7
Pres: Dannelle Stevens
Focus: Educ 14135

Committee on Women in Asian Studies (CWAS), c/o S Asian Studies, Univ. of Hawaii, Honolulu, HI 96820
T: (409) 845-2576; Fax: (409) 845-4727
Gen Secr: Dr. Miriam Sharma
Focus: Ethnology 14136

Common Market of Scientific and Technological Knowledge (MERCOCYT Programm), 1889 F St 200 K NW, Washington, DC 20006
T: (202) 458-3323; Fax: (202) 458-6263
Focus: Sci; Eng 14137

Community Associations Institute (CAI), 1630 Duke St, Alexandria, VA 22314
T: (703) 548-8600; Fax: (703) 684-1581
Founded: 1973; Members: 13000
Focus: Urban Plan
Periodicals
Common Ground (bi-monthly)
Law Reporter (monthly)
News (monthly)
Report (quarterly) 14138

Community College Association for Instruction and Technology (CCAIT), c/o Cedar Valley College, Lancaster, TX 75134
T: (214) 372-8243; Fax: (214) 372-8207
Founded: 1971; Members: 350
Pres: Dr. James Butzek
Focus: Educ 14139

Community Colleges for International Development (CCID), 800 Main St, Pewaukee, WI 53072
T: (414) 6915106; Fax: (414) 691-5593
Gen Secr: Thomas L. Millard
Focus: Develop Areas 14140

Community Development Society (CDS), 1123 N Water St, Milwaukee, WI 53202
T: (414) 276-7106; Fax: (414) 276-7704
Founded: 1969; Members: 1100
Gen Secr: John Gulick
Focus: Sociology 14141

Community Environmental Council (CEC), 930 Miramonte Dr, Santa Barbara, CA 93109
T: (805) 963-0583; Fax: (805) 962-9080
Founded: 1970; Members: 750
Focus: Ecology 14142

Community for Religious Research and Education (CRRE), c/o Michael McKale, Religious Studies Dept, Saint Francis College, Loretto, PA 15940
T: (814) 472-3396
Founded: 1973; Members: 1000
Focus: Rel & Theol; Poli Sci; Sociology
Periodical
Radical Religion (quarterly) 14143

Community Guidance Service (CGS), 133 E 73 St, New York, NY 10021
T: (212) 988-4800
Founded: 1953
Focus: Therapeutics 14144

Community Nutrition Institute (CNI), 2001 S St NW, Ste 530, Washington, DC 20009
T: (202) 462-4700
Founded: 1970
Focus: Hematology
Periodical
Nutrition Week (weekly) 14145

Company of Military Historians (CMH), N Main St, Westbrook, CT 06498
T: (203) 399-9460; Fax: (203) 399-9320
Founded: 1951; Members: 2500
Focus: Military Sci
Periodicals
Military Collector and Historian (quarterly)
Military Uniforms in America (quarterly) . 14146

Comparative and International Education Society (CIES), c/o Institute of International Education, 1400 K St NW, Washington, DC 20005-2403
T: (202) 326-7759; Fax: (202) 326-7709
Founded: 1956; Members: 2500
Gen Secr: Page Baldwin
Focus: Educ
Periodicals
Comparative Education Review (quarterly)
Directory (annually)
Newsletter (quarterly) 14147

Computer Aided Manufacturing International (CAM-I), 1250 E Copeland Rd, Ste 500, Arlington, TX 76011
T: (817) 860-1654; Fax: (817) 275-6450
Founded: 1972; Members: 100
Focus: Computer & Info Sci 14148

Computer Law Association (CLA), 3028 Javier Rd, Ste 402, Fairfax, VA 22031
T: (703) 560-7747; Fax: (703) 207-7028
Founded: 1971; Members: 1600
Gen Secr: Barbara G. Fieser
Focus: Law
Periodicals
Computer Law Association Newsletter (quarterly)
International Update Newsletter (quarterly)
Membership Directory (annually) 14149

Conduit, c/o University of Iowa, 100 Oakdale Campus, M-306, Iowa City, IA 52242-5000
T: (319) 335-4100; E-Mail: conduit@uiowa.edu; Fax: (319) 335-4077
Founded: 1971
Gen Secr: P. Trotter
Focus: Educ 14150

Confederate Memorial Literary Society (CMLS), c/o The Museum of the Confederacy, 1201 E Clay St, Richmond, VA 23219
T: (804) 649-1861; Fax: (804) 644-7150
Founded: 1890; Members: 3000
Focus: Lit
Periodicals
Interpretative Catalogue (semi-annually)
Journal (semi-annually) 14151

Conference Board of Associated Research Councils (CBARC), c/o American Council of Learned Societies, 228 E 45 St, New York, NY 10017
T: (202) 697-1505; Fax: (202) 949-5058
Focus: Sci 14152

Conference Board of the Mathematical Sciences (CBMS), 1529 18 St NW, Washington, DC 20036
T: (202) 293-1170; Fax: (202) 265-2384
Founded: 1960; Members: 15
Focus: Math 14153

Conference for Chinese Oral and Performing Literature (CHINOPERL), c/o Susan Blader, Asian Studies Program, Dartmouth College, 6191 Bartlett Hall, Hanover, NH 03755
T: (603) 646-3478
Founded: 1969; Members: 200
Focus: Lit
Periodical
CHINOPERL Papers (annually) 14154

Conference Group on French Politics and Society (CGFPS), c/o Center for European Studies, Harvard University, 27 Kirkland St, Cambridge, MA 02138
T: (617) 495-4303; Fax: (617) 495-4303
Founded: 1974; Members: 300
Focus: Poli Sci
Periodicals
French Politics and Society (quarterly)
Research and Teaching Register 14155

Conference Group on German Politics (CGGP), POB 345, Durham, NH 03824
T: (603) 862-1778
Founded: 1968; Members: 250
Focus: Poli Sci
Periodicals
Directory of Current Research
Newsletter 14156

Conference of Chief Justices (CCJ), c/o National Center for State Courts, 300 Newport Av, Williamsburg, VA 23187
T: (804) 253-2000
Founded: 1949; Members: 58
Focus: Law 14157

Conference of Consulting Actuaries (CCA), 1110 W Lake Cook Rd, Ste 235, Buffalo Grove, IL 60089-1968
T: (847) 419-9090; Fax: (847) 419-9091
Founded: 1950; Members: 1030
Gen Secr: Rita K. DeGraaf
Focus: Insurance
Periodical
Proceedings (annually) 14158

Conference of Educational Administrators Serving the Deaf (CEASD), c/o Dr. Susanna Lee, Sterck Scholl, 620 E Chestnut Hill Rd, Newark, DE 19713
T: (302) 454-2303; Fax: (302) 454-3493
Founded: 1868; Members: 355
Pres: Dr. Oscar Cohen
Focus: Educ Handic
Periodicals
Advocate for Education of the Deaf (quarterly)
American Annals of the Deaf (5 times annually)
Newsletter (bi-monthly) 14159

Conference of Latin Americanist Geographers (CLAG), c/o University of Texas, POB 7819, Austin, TX 78712
Focus: Geography 14160

Conference of Podiatry Executives (COPE), 5310 McKitrick Blvd, Columbus, OH 43235
T: (614) 457-6269; Fax: (614) 457-3375
Founded: 1960; Members: 22
Focus: Orthopedics 14161

Conference of Research Workers in Animal Diseases (CRWAD), c/o Dr. Robert Ellis, Dept of Microbiology, Colorado State University, Fort Collins, CO 80523
T: (303) 491-5740; Fax: (303) 491-1815
Founded: 1919; Members: 700
Focus: Vet Med 14162

Conference on Asian History (CAH), c/o Prof. George M. Wilson, East Asian Studies Center, Indiana University, Bloomington, IN 47405
T: (812) 855-3765; Fax: (812) 855-7765
Founded: 1953; Members: 100
Focus: Hist 14163

Conference on Christianity and Literature (CCL), c/o Prof. Jewel Spears Brooker, Eckerd College, 501 68 Av S, Saint Petersburg, FL 33705
T: (813) 867-6533; Fax: (813) 866-2304
Founded: 1956; Members: 1400
Gen Secr: Prof. Jewel Spears Brooker
Focus: Lit; Educ; Rel & Theol
Periodical
Christianity and Literature (quarterly) . . 14164

Conference on College Composition and Communication (CCCC), 1111 W Kenyon Rd, Urbana, IL 61801
T: (217) 328-3870; Fax: (217) 328-9645
Founded: 1949; Members: 7000
Focus: Educ
Periodical
College Composition and Communication (quarterly) 14165

Conference on Consumer Finance Law (CCFL), c/o Lawrence X. Pusateri, Peterson & Ross, 200 E Randolph Dr, Ste 7300, Chicago, IL 60601
T: (312) 861-1400; Fax: (312) 565-0832
Founded: 1927; Members: 584
Focus: Law 14166

Conference on English Education (CEE), 1111 Kenyon Rd, Urbana, IL 61801
T: (217) 328-3870; Fax: (217) 328-9645
Founded: 1963; Members: 2000
Focus: Ling; Educ 14167

Conference on Latin American History (CLAH), c/o Auburn University, 320A Tchach Hall, Auburn, AL 36849-5258
T: (205) 844-4161; Fax: (205) 844-6673
Founded: 1926; Members: 850
Gen Secr: Michael Conniff
Focus: Hist
Periodical
CLAH Newsletter (semi-annually) 14168

Congress of Lung Association Staff (CLAS), 1726 M St NW, Ste 902, Washington, DC 20036
T: (202) 785-3355; Fax: (202) 452-1805
Founded: 1912; Members: 800
Focus: Pulmon Dis
Periodicals
Membership Directory (annually)
Newsletter (quarterly) 14169

Congress of Neurological Surgeons (CNS), c/o Daniel L. Barrow, Emory Clinic, 1365 Clifton Rd NE, Atlanta, GA 30322
T: (404) 248-4369; Fax: (404) 248-3791
Founded: 1951; Members: 3500
Gen Secr: Daniel L. Barrow
Focus: Neurology; Surgery
Periodicals
Clinical Neurosurgery (annually)
Neurosurgery (monthly)
Newsletter (quarterly) 14170

Congress on Research in Dance (CORD), c/o Dept of Dance, SUNY at Brockport, Brockport, NY 14420
T: (716) 395-2590; Fax: (716) 395-5397
Founded: 1965; Members: 900
Focus: Perf Arts
Periodical
Dance Research Journal (bi-annually) . . 14171

Conseil International d'Etudes Francophones (CIEF), c/o Dept of French, Montclair State College, Upper Montclair, NJ 07043
T: (201) 655-5143; Fax: (201) 666-3715
Members: 300
Gen Secr: Maurice Cagnon
Focus: Ling 14172

Conservation International (CI), 1015 18 St NW, Washington, DC 20036
T: (202) 429-5660; Fax: (202) 887-5188
Founded: 1987
Focus: Ecology 14173

Consortium for Graduate Study in Management (CGSM), 200 S Hanley Rd, Ste 1102, Saint Louis, MO 63105-3415
T: (314) 935-6324; Fax: (314) 935-5014
Founded: 1967; Members: 9
Gen Secr: Wallace L. Jones
Focus: Business Admin 14174

Consortium for International Earth Science Information Network (CIESIN), 2250 Pierce Rd, University Center, MI 48710
T: (517) 797-2700; E-Mail: elaine.brown@ciesin.org
Gen Secr: Roberta Balstad Miller
Focus: Geology 14175

Consortium for International Pacific Education and Communication Experiments by Satellite (PEACESAT), c/o Univ. of Hawaii, Old Engineering Quad, Building 31, Honolulu, HI 96822
T: (808) 956-7794; E-Mail: peacesat@uhccux.uhcc.hawaii.edu; Fax: (808) 956-2512
Gen Secr: Don Topping
Focus: Educ 14176

Consortium for International Studies Education (CISE), 1501 Neil Av, Columbus, OH 43201-2602
T: (614) 292-1681; Fax: (614) 292-2407
Founded: 1972; Members: 20
Gen Secr: Dr. Charles Hermann
Focus: Educ 14177

Consortium of College and University Media Centers, c/o Media Resources Center, Iowa State University, 121 Pearson Hall, Ames, IA 50011-2203
T: (515) 294-1811; E-Mail: ccumc@ccumnc.org; Fax: (515) 294-8089
Founded: 1971; Members: 400
Gen Secr: Don Rieck
Focus: Cinema
Periodicals
CUFC Leader (semi-annually)
Educational Film Locator 14178

Consortium of Latin American Studies Programs (CLASP), c/o Univ of Connecticut, 843 Bolton Rd, U-161, Storrs, CT 06269-1161
T: (860) 486-4964; E-Mail: Lamsadm@uconnvm.uconn.edu; Fax: (860) 486-2963
Gen Secr: Dr. Elizabeth Mahan
Focus: Ethnology 14179

Consortium on Peace Research, Education and Development (COPRED), c/o Institute for Conflict Analysis and Resolution, George Mason University, 4103 Chain Bridge Rd, Ste 315, Fairfax, VA 22030
T: (703) 273-4485; E-Mail: bwien@gmu.edu; Fax: (703) 273-4486
Founded: 1970; Members: 800
Gen Secr: Barbara Wien
Focus: Poli Sci 14180

Constantine Porphyrogenetus / Planning and Regional Development Studies Association, 168 N Michigan Av, Ste 300, Chicago, IL 60611
T: (0312) 3465050
Pres: Prof. John Karkazis
Focus: Urban Plan 14181

Construction Specifications Institute (CSI), 601 Madison St, Alexandria, VA 22314-1791
T: (703) 684-0300; Fax: (703) 684-0465
Founded: 1948; Members: 17000
Focus: Civil Eng
Periodical
The Construction Specifier (monthly) . . 14182

Construction Writers Association (CWA), c/o Sheila Wertz, POB 5586, Buffalo Grove, IL 60089-5586
T: (847) 398-7756; Fax: (847) 590-5241
Founded: 1957; Members: 150
Gen Secr: Sheila Wertz
Focus: Lit
Periodical
Newsletter (quarterly) 14183

Consultative Group on International Agricultural Research (CGIAR), 701 18 St NW, Rm J-4073, Washington, DC DC 20433
T: (202) 473-8918; E-Mail: Avonderostensack@worldbank.org; Fax: (202) 473-8110
Founded: 1971; Members: 26
Gen Secr: Alexander von der Osten
Focus: Agri 14184

Consumer Education Research Center (CERC), 350 Scotland Rd, Orange, NJ 07050
T: (201) 676-6663; Fax: (201) 676-3241
Founded: 1969; Members: 18169
Focus: Educ; Econ 14185

Consumer Energy Council of America Research Foundation (CECA/RF), 2000 L St NW, Ste 802, Washington, DC 20036
T: (202) 659-0404; Fax: (202) 659-0407
Founded: 1973; Members: 70
Focus: Energy 14186

Contact Literacy Center (CLC), POB 81826, Linoln, NE 86501
T: (402) 464-0602; Fax: (402) 464-5931
Founded: 1978
Pres: Gary Hill
Focus: Lit 14187

Continuing Library Education Network and Exchange Round Table (CLENERT), c/o American Library Association, 50 E Huron St, Chicago, IL 60611
T: (312) 280-4278; Fax: (312) 280-3256
Founded: 1984; Members: 378
Focus: Libraries & Bk Sci 14188

Convention of American Instructors of the Deaf (CAID), POB 377, Bedford, TX 76095-0377
T: (817) 354-8414
Founded: 1850; Members: 1200
Pres: Carl Kirchner
Focus: Educ Handic
Periodicals
American Annals of the Deaf (5 times annually)
Newsletter (quarterly)
Proceedings of the Convention of American Instructors of the Deaf 14189

Cooling Tower Institute (CTI), POB 73383, Houston, TX 77273
T: (713) 583-4087; Fax: (713) 537-1721
Founded: 1950; Members: 400
Focus: Eng
Periodicals
CTI News (quarterly)
Journal of the CTI (semi-annually) . . . 14190

Cooper Ornithological Society (COS), c/o Martin L. Morton, Biology Dept, Occidental College, Los Angeles, CA 90041
T: (310) 259-2674
Founded: 1893; Members: 2200
Focus: Ornithology
Periodicals
Condor (quarterly)
The Flock (every 2-3 years) 14191

Cooperative Marine Science Programme for the Black Sea (COMSBlack), WHOI, Woods Hole, MA 02543
T: (508) 289-2852; E-Mail: aubrey@mud.whoi.edu; Fax: (508) 457-2187
Gen Secr: Dr. D. Aubrey
Focus: Oceanography 14192

Coordinating Committee for Intercontinental Research Networking (CCIRN), DynCorp-Meridan, 4001 N Fairfax Dr, Ste 200, Arlington, VA 22203-1614
T: (703) 522-6410; E-Mail: behnke@arpa.mil; Fax: (703) 522-7161
Gen Secr: Lynn Behnke
Focus: Sci 14193

Coordinating Committee for Women in History, c/o Peggy Renner, 1500 N Verdugo Rd, Glendale, CA 91208
T: (818) 240-1000; Fax: (818) 549-9436
Founded: 1969; Members: 800
Gen Secr: Peggy Renner
Focus: Hist
Periodical
CCWHP/CGWH Newsletter (bi-monthly) . 14194

Coordinating Research Council (CRC), 219 Perimeter Center Pkwy, Ste 400, Atlanta, GA 30346
T: (770) 396-7900
Founded: 1942; Members: 1000
Gen Secr: A.E. Zengel
Focus: Eng 14195

Copyright Society of the U.S.A. (CSUSA), 1133 Av of the Americas, New York, NY 10036
T: (212) 354-6401; Fax: (212) 354-2847
Founded: 1953; Members: 850
Pres: Eugene L. Girden
Focus: Law
Periodical
Journal (quarterly) 14196

Coronary Club (CC), 9500 Euclid Av, Cleveland, OH 44106
T: (216) 444-3690; Fax: (216) 444-9385
Founded: 1969; Members: 9000
Gen Secr: Kathryn E. Ryan-Muldoon
Focus: Cardiol 14197

Corporate Data Exchange (CDE), 255 Broadway, Ste 2625, New York, NY 10007
T: (212) 962-2980
Founded: 1975
Focus: Econ 14198

Correctional Education Association (CEA), 4380 Forbes Blvd, Lanham, MD 20706
T: (301) 918-1915; Fax: (301) 918-1900
Founded: 1945; Members: 3200
Gen Secr: Dr. Stephen J. Steurer
Focus: Educ
Periodicals
Journal of Correctional Education (quarterly)
Newsletter (quarterly) 14199

Costume Society of America (CSA), 55 Edgewater Dr, POB 73, Earleville, MD 21919-0073
T: (410) 275-2329; Fax: (410) 275-8936
Founded: 1973; Members: 1605
Focus: Textiles 14200

Council for Advancement and Support of Education (CASE), 11 Dupont Circle NW, Ste 400, Washington, DC 20036
T: (202) 328-5900; Fax: (202) 387-4973
Founded: 1974; Members: 2800
Focus: Educ 14201

Council for Agricultural Science and Technology (CAST), 4420 W Lincoln Way, Ames, IA 50014-3447
T: (515) 292-2125
Founded: 1972; Members: 4000
Pres: Dr. Victor L. Lechtenberg; Gen Secr: Dr. Richard E. Stuckey
Focus: Agri
Periodicals
Comments
News from CAST (irregularly)
Papers
Reports
Science of Food and Agriculture (quarterly)
Special Publications 14202

Council for American Private Education (CAPE), 1726 M St NW, Ste 1102, Washington, DC 20036
T: (202) 659-0016; Fax: (202) 659-0018
Founded: 1971; Members: 14
Focus: Educ
Periodicals
Directory of Private Schools
Outlook (monthly) 14203

Council for Basic Education (CBE), 1319 F St NW,Ste 900, Washington, DC 20004-1152
T: (202) 347-4171; Fax: (202) 347-5047
Founded: 1956; Members: 7500
Pres: Christopher Cross
Focus: Educ
Periodicals
Basic Education (monthly)
Perspectives (quarterly) 14204

Council for Biomedical Communications Associations, c/o Stewart White, Biomedical Communications, University of Michigan, 1327 Jones Dr, Ste 104, Ann Arbor, MI 48105
T: (313) 998-6140; Fax: (313) 998-6150
Founded: 1970; Members: 5
Focus: Comm Sci 14205

Council for Children with Behavioral Disorders (CCBD), c/o Council for Exceptional Children, 1920 Association Dr, Reston, VA 22091-1589
T: (703) 620-3660; Fax: (703) 264-9494
Founded: 1962; Members: 8500
Focus: Educ Handic; Behav Sci
Periodicals
Behavioral Disorders (quarterly)
CCBD Newsletter (quarterly) 14206

Council for Educational Development and Research (CEDaR), 200 L St NW, Ste 601, Washington, DC 20036
T: (202) 223-1593
Founded: 1971; Members: 14
Focus: Educ
Periodicals
Directory (annually)
Newsletter (monthly)
R & D Preview (bi-monthly) 14207

Council for Elementary Science International (CESI), 212 Townsend Hall, Columbia, MO 65211
T: (314) 882-4831
Founded: 1920; Members: 1600
Pres: Eileen Bingtson
Focus: Sci
Periodicals
CESI Directory (annually)
CESI News (quarterly)
CESI Source Books (1-2 times annually)
Monograph (annually) 14208

Council for European Studies (CES), 807-807a International Affairs Bldg, Columbia University, New York, NY 10027
T: (212) 854-4172; Fax: (212) 854-8808
Founded: 1970; Members: 934
Gen Secr: Dr. Ioannis Sinanoglou
Focus: Soc Sci; Hist 14209

Council for Indian Education (CIE), 2032 Woody Dr, Billings, MT 59102
T: (406) 652-7398
Founded: 1970; Members: 100
Pres: Dr. Hap Gilliland
Focus: Educ 14210

Council for Jewish Education (CJE), 730 Broadway, New York, NY 10003
T: (212) 529-2000; Fax: (212) 529-2009
Founded: 1926; Members: 275
Gen Secr: Dr. Solomon Goldman
Focus: Educ
Periodicals
Jewish Education (quarterly)
Membership Directory (bi-annually)
Sheviley Hahinuch (quarterly) 14211

Council for Medical Affairs (CFMA), POB 10944, Chicago, IL 60610
T: (312) 464-4655; Fax: (312) 464-5830
Founded: 1980; Members: 15
Focus: Med 14212

Council for Museum Anthropology (CMA), c/o Enid Schildkrout, Dept of Anthropology, American Museum of Natural History, Central Parl W at 79 St, New York, NY 10024-5192
T: (212) 769-5432; Fax: (212) 769-5334
Founded: 1975; Members: 600
Pres: Enid Schildkrout
Focus: Anthro
Periodical
Museum Anthropology (quarterly) 14213

Council for Philosophical Studies (CPS), c/o Jules Coleman, Yale Law School, 127 Wall, New Haven, CT 06520
T: (203) 432-4842; Fax: (203) 432-8260
Founded: 1965; Members: 15
Focus: Philos 14214

Council for Religion in Independent Schools (CRIS), 4405 East-West Hwy, Bethesda, MD 20814-4536
T: (301) 657-0912; Fax: (301) 657-0915
Founded: 1898; Members: 345
Gen Secr: Robert J. Rokusek
Focus: Educ; Rel & Theol
Periodical
Newsletter (monthly) 14215

Council for Research in Music Education (CRME), c/o School of Music, University of Illinois, 1114 W Nevada, Urbana, IL 61801
T: (217) 333-1027
Founded: 1963; Members: 150
Focus: Music; Educ
Periodical
Bulletin (quarterly) 14216

Council for Research in Values and Philosophy (RVP), POB 261, Cardinal Station, Washington, DC 20064
T: (202) 319-5636; Fax: (202) 319-6089
Founded: 1983
Gen Secr: Prof. George F. McLean
Focus: Philos 14217

Council for Sex Information and Education (CSIE), 2272 Colorado Blvd, Los Angeles, CA 90041
Founded: 1977
Focus: Public Health 14218

Council for the Advancement of Science Writing (CASW), POB 404, Greenlawn, NY 11740
T: (516) 757-5664; Fax: (516) 757-0069
Founded: 1959; Members: 26
Focus: Sci 14219

Council for Tobacco Research – U.S.A. (CTR-USA), 900 Third Av, New York, NY 10022
T: (212) 421-8885
Founded: 1954
Focus: Agri
Periodical
Report (annually) 14220

Council of 1890 College Presidents (CCP), c/o Southern University and A&M College System, Baton Rouge, LA 70813
T: (504) 771-4680; Fax: (504) 771-5522
Founded: 1913; Members: 18
Pres: Dr. Dolores Spikes
Focus: Educ 14221

Council of Academies of Engineering and Technological Sciences (CAETS), 2101 Constitution Av NW, Rm 306, Washington, DC 20418
T: (202) 334-3603; E-Mail: sanastas@nas.edu.; Fax: (202) 334-2290
Gen Secr: Steven N. Anastasion
Focus: Eng 14222

Council of Administrators of Special Education (CASE), 615 16 St NW, Albuquerque, NM 87104
T: (505) 243-7622; Fax: (505) 247-4822
Founded: 1951; Members: 4700
Focus: Educ
Periodicals
CASE in Point (3 times annually)
Newsletter (5 times annually) 14223

Council of American Overseas Research Centres (CAORC), c/o Smithsonian Institution, 1100 Jefferson Dr SW, IC 3123, MRC 750, Washington, DC 20560
T: (202) 842-8636; E-Mail: caorc102@sivm.si.edu.; Fax: (202) 786-2430
Gen Secr: Mary Ellen Lane
Focus: Sci 14224

Council of Biology Editors (CBE), 60 Revere Dr, Ste 500, Northbrook, IL 60062
T: (847) 480-6349; Fax: (847) 480-9282
Founded: 1957; Members: 1000
Focus: Bio
Periodical
CBE Views (bi-monthly) 14225

Council of Chief State School Officers (CCSSO), 1 Massachusetts Av NW, Ste 700, Washington, DC 20001
T: (202) 408-5505; Fax: (202) 393-1228
Founded: 1927; Members: 57
Focus: Educ
Periodicals
Directory of State Education Agencies (annually)
Membership List (monthly)
State Education Indicators Report (annually)
. . . . 14226

Council of Colleges of Arts and Sciences (CCAS), c/o College of Liberal Arts and Sciences, Arizona State University, 100 Social Sciences, POB 873901, Tempe, AZ 85287-6064
T: (602) 727-6064; E-Mail: RHOPKIN@ASU.EDU; Fax: (602) 727-6078
Founded: 1965; Members: 430
Gen Secr: Richard J. Hopkins
Focus: Arts; Sci
Periodicals
CCAS Newsletter (bi-monthly)
Membership Directory (annually) 14227

Council of Community Blood Centers (CCBC), 725 15 St NW, Ste 700, Washington, DC 20005
T: (202) 393-5725; Fax: (202) 393-1282
Founded: 1962; Members: 51
Focus: Med
Periodical
CCBC Newsletter (weekly) 14228

Council of Consulting Organizations (IMC), 521 Fifth Av, New York, NY 10175
T: (212) 697-9693
Founded: 1968; Members: 2200
Focus: Business Admin 14229

Council of Engineering and Scientific Society Executives (CESSE), 400 Commonwealth Dr, Warrendale, PA 15096-0001
T: (412) 776-4841; Fax: (412) 776-5944
Founded: 1949; Members: 600
Gen Secr: Max E. Rumbaugh Jr.
Focus: Eng; Sci
Periodicals
The Quill (3 times annually)
Yearbook (annually) 14230

Council of Graduate Schools (CGS), 1 Dupont Circle NW, Ste 430, Washington, DC 20036
T: (202) 223-3791
Founded: 1960; Members: 400
Focus: Educ 14231

Council of International Programs (CIP), c/o Cleveland International Program, 1700 E 13 St, Ste 4 SE, Cleveland, OH 44114-3213
E-Mail: 74143.43@compuserve.com
Founded: 1956; Members: 7000
Gen Secr: Dorothy A. Faller
Focus: Sociology 14232

Council of Landscape Architectural Registration Boards (CLARB), 12700 Fair Lakes Cir, Ste 110, Fairfax, VA 22033
T: (703) 818-1300; Fax: (703) 818-1309
Founded: 1961; Members: 40
Focus: Archit 14233

Council of Mennonite Colleges (CMC), c/o L. Belzer, Tabor College, 400 S Jefferson, Hillsboro, KS 67063
T: (316) 947-3121; Fax: (316) 947-2607
Founded: 1942; Members: 11
Pres: Dr. David Brandt
Focus: Educ 14234

Council of National Library and Information Associations (CNLIA), 1700 18 St NW, Ste B-1, Washington, DC 20009
Founded: 1942; Members: 19
Pres: Madeleine Taylor; Gen Secr: Marie F. Melton
Focus: Libraries & Bk Sci
Periodicals
Roster (annually)
Update (quarterly) 14235

Council of Scientific Society Presidents (CSSP), 1155 16 St NW, Ste 100, Washington, DC 20036
T: (202) 872-4452; Fax: (202) 872-4615
Founded: 1973; Members: 58
Focus: Sci; Educ 14236

Council of Societies for the Study of Religion (CSSR), c/o Valparaiso University, Valparaiso, IN 46383
T: (219) 464-5515; Fax: (219) 464-6714
Founded: 1969
Focus: Rel & Theol
Periodicals
CSSR Bulletin (quarterly)
Religious Studies Review (quarterly) . . 14237

Council of Teaching Hospitals (COTH), c/o Association of American Medical Colleges, 2450 N St NW, Washington, DC 20037-1127
T: (202) 828-4792
Founded: 1965; Members: 400
Gen Secr: Robert M. Dickler
Focus: Med; Adult Educ
Periodicals
COTH Report (monthly)
Directory of Educational Services and Programs (annually) 14238

Council of the Great City Schools (CGCS), 1301 Pennsylvania Av NW, Ste 702, Washington, DC 20004
T: (202) 393-2427; Fax: (202) 393-2400
Founded: 1961; Members: 47
Gen Secr: Michael D. Casserly
Focus: Educ 14239

Council of Undergraduate Research (CUR), c/o John Stevens, University of North Carolina, Asheville, NC 28804
T: (704) 251-6006
Founded: 1978; Members: 1800
Focus: Educ 14240

Council on Accreditation of Nurse Anesthesia Educational Programs/Schools, 222 Prespect Av, Park Ridge, IL 60068-4010
T: (847) 692-7050; Fax: (847) 692-7137
Founded: 1975; Members: 100
Gen Secr: Betty Horton
Focus: Educ; Anesthetics 14241

Council on Anthropology and Education (CAE), c/o American Anthropological Association, 4350 N Fairfax Dr, Ste 640, Arlington, VA 22203-1620
T: (703) 528-1902; Fax: (703) 528-3546
Founded: 1968; Members: 921
Gen Secr: Susan Florio-Ruane
Focus: Anthro; Educ
Periodical
Anthropology and Education (quarterly) . 14242

Council on Arteriosclerosis of the American Heart Association (CAAHA), 7320 Greenville Av, Dallas, TX 75231
T: (214) 706-1293; Fax: (214) 706-1341
Founded: 1946; Members: 1014
Focus: Cardiol
Periodicals
Arteriosclerosis (bi-monthly)
Newsletter (semi-annually) 14243

Council on Chiropractic Education (CCE), 7595 N Hayden Rd, No A-210, Scottsdale, AZ 85258-3246
T: (602) 443-8877; Fax: (602) 483-7333
Founded: 1971; Members: 23
Gen Secr: Dr. Paul D. Walker
Focus: Educ; Med 14244

Council on Chiropractic Physiological Therapeutics (CCPT), c/o Dr. Carol Krol, 4760 W Atlantic Av, Delray Beach, FL 33445
Founded: 1920; Members: 200
Pres: Brandstetter Delray
Focus: Therapeutics 14245

Council on Diagnostic Imaging, POB 25, Palatine, IL 60078-0025
T: (847) 705-1177; Fax: (847) 705-1178
Founded: 1936; Members: 2000
Gen Secr: Dr. Lawrence Pyzik
Focus: X-Ray Tech
Periodical
Roentgenological Briefs (monthly) 14246

Council on Education for Public Health (CEPH), 1015 15 St NW, Washington, DC 20005
T: (202) 789-1050
Founded: 1974; Members: 42
Focus: Public Health 14247

Council on Education of the Deaf (CED), 800 Florida Av NE, Washington, DC 20002
T: (202) 651-5020; Fax: (202) 351-5708
Founded: 1960; Members: 12
Gen Secr: D. Hicks
Focus: Educ Handic
Periodicals
CED Approved Programs (annually)
Newsletter (semi-annually)
Standards for the Certification of Teachers of the Hearing Impaired
Standards for the Evaluation of Programs for the Preparation of Teachers for the Hearing Impaired
. . . . 14248

Council on Electrolysis Education (CEE), 2026 Park Av, Hot Springs, AR 71901
T: (901) 458-1431
Founded: 1972
Pres: Dorothy Graves
Focus: Educ 14249

Council on Governmental Relations (COGR), 1 Dupont Circle NW, Ste 425, Washington, DC 20036
T: (202) 331-1803; Fax: (202) 331-8483
Founded: 1948; Members: 135
Focus: Poli Sci 14250

Council on Health Information and Education (CHIE), 2272 Colorado Blvd, Los Angeles, CA 90041
Founded: 1978
Focus: Public Health 14251

Council on International Educational Exchange, 205 E 42nd St, New York, NY 10017
T: (212) 661-1414; E-Mail: strooboff@ciee.org; Fax: (212) 972-3231

Gen Secr: Stevan Trooboff
Focus: Educ 14252

Council on Legal Education Opportunity (CLEO), 1420 N St NW, Washington, DC 20005
T: (202) 785-4840; Fax: (202) 223-5633
Founded: 1968
Gen Secr: Irshad Abdal-Haqq
Focus: Adult Educ; Law 14253

Council on Library-Media Technical Assistants (COLT), c/o Margaret Barron, Library-Media Technology Dept, Cyahoga Community College, 2900 Community College Av, Cleveland, OH 44115
T: (216) 987-4296; Fax: (216) 987-4404
Founded: 1965; Members: 700
Focus: Libraries & Bk Sci
Periodicals
Membership Directory and Data Book (bi-annually)
Newsletter (monthly) 14254

Council on Library Resources (CLR), 1400 16 St NW, Ste 510, Washington, DC 20036-2217
T: (202) 483-7474; Fax: (202) 483-6410
Founded: 1956; Members: 11
Pres: W. David Penniman
Focus: Libraries & Bk Sci
Periodicals
CLR Report (irregularly)
Recent Developments (irregularly) . . . 14255

Council on Medical Education of the American Medical Association (CME-AMA), 515 N State St, Chicago, IL 60610
T: (312) 464-4804; Fax: (312) 464-5830
Founded: 1847; Members: 12
Focus: Adult Educ; Med
Periodicals
Allied Health Education Directory (annually)
Directory of Residency Training Programs (annually) 14256

Council on National Literatures (CNL), POB 81, Whitestone, NY 11357
T: (212) 767-8380; Fax: (212) 767-8380
Founded: 1974; Members: 1200
Focus: Lit
Periodicals
CNL/Review of Books (bi-monthly)
CNL/World Report (annually) 14257

Council on Nutritional Anthropology (CNA), c/o American Anthropological Association, 4350 N Fairfax Dr, Ste 640, Arlington, VA 22203-1620
T: (703) 528-1902; Fax: (703) 528-3546
Founded: 1973; Members: 328
Pres: Rebecca Huss-Ashmore
Focus: Anthro 14258

Council on Ocean Law, 1600 H St NW, Washington, DC 20006
T: (202) 347-3766; Fax: (202) 842-0030
Gen Secr: Charles Higginson
Focus: Law 14259

Council on Podiatric Medical Education (CPME), 9312 Old Georgetown Rd, Bethesda, MD 20814-1621
T: (301) 571-9200; Fax: (301) 530-2752
Founded: 1918; Members: 11
Focus: Adult Educ 14260

Council on Resident Education in Obstetrics and Gynecology (CREOG), 409 12 St SW, Washington, DC 20024
T: (202) 863-2554; Fax: (202) 484-5107
Founded: 1967; Members: 450
Focus: Gynecology 14261

Council on Social Work Education (CSWE), 1600 Duke St, Ste 300, Alexandria, VA 22314
T: (703) 683-8080; Fax: (703) 683-8099
Founded: 1952; Members: 5000
Focus: Adult Educ; Sociology
Periodicals
Journal of Education for Social Work (3 times annually)
Social Work Education Reporter (3 times annually)
Statistics on Social Work Education in the United States (annually)
Summary Information on Master of Social Work Programs (annually) 14262

Council on Standards for International Educational Travel (CSIET), 3 Loudoun St SE, Ste 3, Leesburg, VA 20175
T: (703) 771-2040; Fax: (703) 771-2046
Gen Secr: Maureen Gavaghan
Focus: Educ 14263

Council on Tall Buildings and Urban Habitat (CTBUH), c/o Lehigh University, 13 E Packer Av, Bethlehem, PA 18015-3191
T: (610) 758-3515; E-Mail: inctbuh@lehigh.edu; Fax: (215) 758-4522
Founded: 1969; Members: 1200
Gen Secr: Dr. Lynn S. Beedle
Focus: Archit
Periodicals
Brochure (annually)
The Times (3-4 times annually) 14264

Council on Technology Teacher Education (CTTE), c/o Everett N. Israel, College of Technology, Eastern Michigan University, Ypsilanti, MI 48197
T: (313) 487-2040; Fax: (313) 487-8755
Founded: 1950; Members: 900
Pres: Everett N. Israel
Focus: Adult Educ; Arts 14265

Country Day School Headmasters Association of the U.S. (CDSHA), c/o Charlotte Country Day School, 1440 Carmel Rd, Charlotte, NC 28226
T: (704) 366-1241; Fax: (704) 364-4110
Founded: 1912; Members: 100
Focus: Educ 14266

Cousteau Society (TCS), 777 Uited Nations Plaza, New York, NY 10017
T: (212) 949-6290; Fax: (212) 949-6296
Founded: 1973; Members: 300000
Gen Secr: Jacques-Yves Cousteau
Focus: Ecology 14267

Cranial Academy (CA), 8606 Allisonville Rd, Ste 130, Indianapolis, IN 46250-3585
T: (317) 879-0713; Fax: (317) 879-0718
Founded: 1946; Members: 900
Gen Secr: Patricia Crampton
Focus: Med
Periodicals
Directory (annually)
News Letter (quarterly) 14268

Creation Research Society (CRS), POB 8263, Saint Joseph, MO 64508-8263
E-Mail: CRSnetwork@aol.com
Founded: 1963; Members: 1800
Pres: E. Williams
Focus: Sci
Periodical
Creation Research Society Quarterly (quarterly) 14269

Creek Indian Memorial Association (CIMA), c/o Creek Council House Museum, Town Sq, Okmulgee, OK 74447
T: (918) 756-2324
Founded: 1923; Members: 113
Focus: Hist 14270

Critical Mass Energy Project of Public Citizen (CMEPPC), 215 Pennsylvania Av SE, Washington, DC 20003
T: (202) 546-4996; Fax: (202) 547-7392
Founded: 1974
Focus: Energy 14271

Crop Science Society of America (CSSA), 677 S Segoe Rd, Madison, WI 53711
T: (608) 273-8080; Fax: (608) 273-2021
Founded: 1955; Members: 5500
Focus: Agri; Ecology
Periodicals
Agronomy Journal (bi-monthly)
Crop Science (bi-monthly)
Journal of Agronomic Education (semi-annually)
Journal of Environmental Quality (quarterly)
Journal of Production Agriculture (quarterly)
Soil Science Society of America Journal (bi-monthly) 14272

Cross-Examination Debate Association (CEDA), c/o Pacific Lutheran University, Tacoma, WA 98447
Founded: 1971; Members: 320
Gen Secr: Mike Bartanen
Focus: Ling 14273

Cryogenic Engineering Conference (CEC), c/o Dr. P. Kittel, MS 244-10, NASA/AMES, Moffet Field, CA 94035
T: (415) 604-4297
Founded: 1954; Members: 4000
Focus: Eng
Periodical
Advances in Cryogenic Engineering (bi-annually) 14274

Cryogenic Society of America (CSA), c/o Laurie Huget, Huget Advertising, 1033 South Blvd, Oak Park, IL 60302
T: (708) 383-6220; Fax: (708) 383-9337
Founded: 1964; Members: 400
Focus: Physics 14275

Customs and International Trade Bar Association (CITBA), 475 Park Av S, New York, NY 10016
T: (212) 725-0200; Fax: (212) 889-4135
Gen Secr: Rufus E. Jarman
Focus: Law 14276

Czechoslovak Society of Arts and Sciences (CSAS), c/o F. Marlow, 4064 Woodcliff Rd, Sherman Oaks, CA 91403
T: (818) 784-0970; Fax: (818) 788-7063
Founded: 1958; Members: 1500
Focus: Arts; Sci
Periodicals
Bulletin (3 times annually)
Kosmas (semi-annually)
Promeny (semi-annually)
Zpravy (bi-monthly) 14277

Dairy Research Foundation (DRINC), 95 King St, Oak Grove Village, IL 60007
T: (708) 228-7742
Founded: 1969; Members: 350000
Focus: Dairy Sci 14278

Dairy Society International (DSI), 7185 Ruritan Dr, Chambersburg, PA 17201
T: (717) 375-4392
Founded: 1946; Members: 500
Gen Secr: George W. Weigold
Focus: Dairy Sci 14279

Dalcroze Society of America (DSA), c/o Anne Farber, 161 W 86 St, New York, NY 10024
T: (212) 724-5009
Founded: 1967; Members: 300
Pres: Anne Farber
Focus: Music 14280

Damien Dutton Society for Leprosy Aid (DDSLA), 616 Bedford Av, Bellmore, NY 11710
T: (516) 221-5829; Fax: (516) 221-5909
Founded: 1944; Members: 30000
Pres: Howard E. Crouch
Focus: Derm
Periodical
Damien-Dutton Call (quarterly) 14281

Dana Center for Preventive Ophthalmology (DCPO), c/o Wilmer Eye Institute, Rm 120, Johns Hopkins University, 600 N Wolfe St, Baltimore, MD 21205
T: (301) 955-2777; Fax: (301) 955-2542
Founded: 1979
Gen Secr: Dr. Harry A. Quigley
Focus: Ophthal 14282

Dance Films Association (DFA), 31 W 21 St, New York, NY 10010
T: (212) 727-0764
Founded: 1956
Gen Secr: Victor Lipari
Focus: Cinema
Periodical
Dance on Camera News (bi-monthly) . . 14283

Dannemiller Memorial Educational Foundation (DMEF), 12500 Network Blvd, Ste 101, San Antonio, TX 78249-3302
T: (210) 641-8311
Founded: 1971; Members: 30
Focus: Anesthetics
Periodical
Anesthesia File (monthly) 14284

Dante Society of America (DSA), 61 Kirkland St, Cambridge, MA 02138
T: (617) 495-0738; Fax: (617) 495-0730
Founded: 1881; Members: 450
Focus: Lit
Periodical
Dante Studies (annually) 14285

David M Kennedy Center for International Studies, c/o Brigham Young University, 237 Harald R Clark Building, Provo, UT 84602
T: (801) 378-3377
Focus: Poli Sci 14286

David Rockefeller Centre for Latin American Studies, c/o Harvard University, Cambridge, MA 02138
Focus: Ethnology 14287

Deafness Research Foundation (DRF), 9 E 38 St, New York, NY 10016
T: (212) 684-6556; Fax: (212) 779-2125
Founded: 1958; Members: 2400
Focus: Otorhinolaryngology 14288

Decision Sciences Institute (DSI), University Plaza, Atlanta, GA 30303
T: (404) 651-4000
Founded: 1969; Members: 5500
Focus: Econ 14289

Delta Dental Plans Association (DDPA), 1515 W 22 St, No 1200, Oak Brook, IL 60521
T: (312) 337-4707
Founded: 1965; Members: 37
Pres: Carl Zimmerman
Focus: Dent
Periodicals
Delta Dictum (quarterly)
Dozzle (quarterly)
Newsletter (bi-monthly) 14290

Deltiologists of America (D. of A.), POB 8, Norwood, PA 19074
T: (215) 485-8572
Founded: 1966; Members: 800
Focus: Hist; Arts
Periodical
Postcard Classics (bi-monthly) 14291

Dental Assisting National Board (DANB), 216 E Ontario St, Chicago, IL 60611
T: (312) 642-3368
Founded: 1948
Focus: Dent 14292

Dental Health International (DHI), 847 S Milledge Av, Athens, GA 30605
T: (404) 546-1715
Founded: 1973
Focus: Dent 14293

Dermatology Foundation (DF), 1566 Sherman Av, Ste 302, Evanston, IL 60201-4802
T: (312) 328-2256
Founded: 1964; Members: 3300
Focus: Derm 14294

DES Action International, 1615 Broadway, Ste 510, Oakland, CA 94612
T: (510) 465-4011; Fax: (510) 465-4815
Founded: 1977
Focus: Cell Biol & Cancer Res
Periodical
DES Action Voice (quarterly) 14295

Desert Botanical Garden (DBG), 1201 N Galvin Pkwy, Phoenix, AZ 85008
T: (602) 941-1225; Fax: (602) 991-8933
Founded: 1937; Members: 5500
Focus: Botany; Ecology
Periodicals
Agave (quarterly)
Saguaroland Bulletin (quarterly) 14296

Desert Fishes Council, POB 337, Bishop, CA 93515
T: (619) 872-8751; Fax: (619) 872-8751
Founded: 1970; Members: 500
Focus: Ecology
Periodical
Proceedings of the Desert Fishes Council (annually) 14297

Desert Protective Council (DPC), POB 2312, Valley Center, CA 92082
T: (619) 749-3485
Founded: 1954; Members: 400
Gen Secr: Opal Maletta
Focus: Agri; Ecology
Periodical
El Paisano (quarterly) 14298

Desert Tortoise Preserve Committee (DTPC), POB 2910, San Bernardino, CA 92406
T: (909) 884-9700; Fax: (909) 525-2443
Founded: 1974; Members: 1500
Gen Secr: Tom Dodson
Focus: Ecology
Periodical
Proceedings of Symposium (annually) . . 14299

Design-Build Institute of America, 1010 Massachusetts Av NW, Ste 350, Washington, DC 20001
T: (202) 682-0110; Fax: (202) 682-5877
Founded: 1983; Members: 200
Gen Secr: Jeffrey L. Beard
Focus: Archit
Periodical
Design/Build Digest 14300

Designs for Change (DFC), 6 N Michigan, No 1600, Chicago, IL 60602
T: (312) 857-9292; Fax: (312) 857-9299
Founded: 1977
Gen Secr: Dr. Donald Moore
Focus: Educ 14301

D.H. Lawrence Society of North America, c/o Charles Rossman, Dept of English, University of Texas, Austin, TX 78712-1164
T: (512) 245-2163; Fax: (512) 471-8766
Founded: 1975; Members: 200
Pres: Charles Rossman
Focus: Lit 14302

Dickens Society (DS), c/o Dept of Humanities, Worcester Polytechnic Institute, Worcester, MA 01609-2280
T: (508) 831-5572; Fax: (508) 831-5483
Founded: 1970; Members: 500
Focus: Lit
Periodical
Dickens Quarterly (quarterly) 14303

Dictionary Society of North America (DSNA), 1983 E 24 St, Cleveland, OH 44115-2403
T: (216) 687-4830
Founded: 1975; Members: 550
Gen Secr: Prof. Louis T. Milic
Focus: Libraries & Bk Sci 14304

Dietary Managers Association (DMA), 1 Pierce Pl, No 1220W, Itasca, IL 60143
T: (708) 775-9200; Fax: (708) 775-9250
Founded: 1960; Members: 14000
Gen Secr: William S. Saint John
Focus: Nutrition; Educ
Periodicals
Flyer (bi-monthly)
Issues (bi-monthly) 14305

Direct Marketing Educational Foundation (DMEF), 1120 Av of the Americas, New York, NY 10036-6700
T: (212) 768-7277; E-Mail: craiglis@the_dma.org; Fax: (212) 790-1561
Founded: 1965; Members: 500
Pres: Dr. Richard L. Montesi
Focus: Educ; Business Admin 14306

Disability Insurance Training Council (DITC), 1000 Connecticut Av NW, Ste 1111, Washington, DC 20036
T: (202) 223-5533; Fax: (202) 785-2274
Founded: 1951; Members: 11000
Focus: Adult Educ 14307

Disability Rights Center (DRC), 2500 Q St NW, Ste 121, Washington, DC 20007
T: (301) 324-0112
Founded: 1976
Gen Secr: Carmen Jones
Focus: Rehabil 14308

Distillers Feed Research Council (DFRC), 1885 Dixie, No 270, Covington, KY 41011-2624
T: (606) 344-8008; Fax: (606) 344-8008
Founded: 1947; Members: 19
Gen Secr: Robert H. Hatch
Focus: Food
Periodical
Proceedings (annually) 14309

Distributive Education Clubs of America (DECA), 1908 Association Dr, Reston, VA 22091
T: (703) 860-5000
Founded: 1946; Members: 180000
Focus: Educ
Periodicals
Guide (annually)
New Dimensions (bi-monthly)
Newsletter (bi-monthly) 14310

Division for Early Childhood, c/o Council for Exceptional Children, 1920 Association Dr, Reston, VA 22091
T: (703) 620-3660; Fax: (703) 264-9494
Founded: 1973; Members: 7000
Focus: Educ Handic
Periodicals
The DEC Communicator (quarterly)
Journal of Early Intervention (quarterly) . 14311

Division of Applied Experimental and Engineering Psychologists (DAEEP), c/o Pacific Science & Engineering, 6310 Greenwich Dr, Ste 200, San Diego, CA 92122
T: (619) 535-1661; Fax: (619) 535-1665
Founded: 1957; Members: 600
Pres: Dr. Arthur T. Fisk
Focus: Psych
Periodicals
Applied Experimental and Engineering Psychology (quarterly)
Newsletter (quarterly) 14312

Division on Mental Retardation and Developmental Disabilities of the Council for Exceptional Children, c/o Tom Smith, Arkansas University Affiliated Facility, 1120 Marshall St, Ste 120, Little Rock, AR 72202
Founded: 1963; Members: 8120
Gen Secr: Dr. Dana M. Anderson
Focus: Educ Handic
Periodicals
CEC-M Report (bi-annually)
Education and Training in Mental Retardation (quarterly) 14313

Django Reinhardt Society (DRS), 10 W Jackson Av, Middletown, NY 10940
T: (914) 342-1696
Founded: 1985; Members: 200
Focus: Music 14314

Dozenal Society of America (DSA), c/o Dept of Mathematics, Nassau Community College, Garden City, NY 11530
T: (516) 669-0273
Founded: 1944; Members: 144
Pres: Prof. Jay Schiffman
Focus: Math; Standards
Periodical
Duodecimal Bulletin (semi-annually) . . . 14315

Drama Tree (DT), 158 W 15 St, New York, NY 10011
T: (212) 620-0855
Founded: 1968; Members: 70
Focus: Perf Arts 14316

Drawing Society, 15 Penn Plaza, 415 Seventh Av, New York, NY 10001
T: (212) 563-4822; Fax: (212) 563-4829
Founded: 1959; Members: 1226
Focus: Fine Arts
Periodical
Drawing (bi-monthly) 14317

Drug and Alcohol Nursing Association (DANA), 660 Lonely Cottage Dr, Upper Black Eddy, PA 18972-9313
T: (610) 847-5396; Fax: (610) 847-5063
Founded: 1979; Members: 340
Gen Secr: Paul Piscator
Focus: Med 14318

Drug Information Association (DIA), POB 3113, Maple Glen, PA 19002
T: (215) 628-2288
Founded: 1965; Members: 6000
Focus: Pharmacol
Periodicals
Journal (quarterly)
Membership Directory (annually) 14319

Ductile Iron Pipe Research Association (DIPRA), 245 Riverchase Pkwy E, Ste O, Birmingham, AL 35244
T: (205) 988-9870; Fax: (205) 988-9822
Founded: 1915; Members: 7
Focus: Eng 14320

Ductile Iron Society (DIS), 28938 Lorain Rd, Ste 202, North Olmsted, OH 44070
T: (216) 734-8040
Founded: 1958; Members: 80
Focus: Metallurgy
Periodical
Ductile Iron News (3 times annually) . . 14321

Dyleague, 5900 Canoga Av, Ste 100, Woodland Hills, CA 91367
T: (818) 716-1616
Founded: 1992; Members: 600
Focus: Computer & Info Sci
Periodical
Proceedings (annually) 14322

Dynamics International Gardening Association (DIGA), Drawer 1165, Asheboro, NC 27204-1165
T: (919) 625-4790
Founded: 1950; Members: 18230
Gen Secr: William A. Barnes
Focus: Hort
Periodicals
Garden Today News (quarterly)
Tips 14323

Dystonia Medical Research Foundation (DMRF), 1 E Wacker Dr, Ste 2430, Chicago, IL 60601-2001
T: (312) 755-0198; E-Mail: dystfndt@aol.com; Fax: (312) 803-0138
Founded: 1977; Members: 25000
Gen Secr: Valerie F. Levitin
Focus: Neurology
Periodical
Newsletter (quarterly) 14324

Dystrophic Epidermolysis Bullosa Research Association of America (DEBRA), 40 Rector St, New York, NY 10006
T: (212) 693-6610
Founded: 1979
Gen Secr: Miram Fedar
Focus: Derm 14325

EAA Aviation Foundation (EAAAF), POB 3065, Oshkosh, WI 54903-3065
T: (414) 426-4800
Founded: 1962
Focus: Aero 14326

Earl Warren Legal Training Program (EWLTP), 99 Hudson St, Ste 1600, New York, NY 10013
T: (212) 219-1900
Founded: 1972
Focus: Law 14327

Early Settlers Association of the Western Reserve (ESAWR), 24740 Antler Dr, North Olmsted, OH 44070
T: (216) 777-7088
Founded: 1879; Members: 500
Focus: Hist
Periodicals
Annals
The Pioneer (quarterly)
Roster 14328

Early Sites Research Society (ESRS), Long Hill, Rowley, MA 01969
T: (508) 948-2410; Fax: (508) 948-7270
Founded: 1973; Members: 225
Gen Secr: James Whittall
Focus: Archeol 14329

Earthmind, POB 743, Mariposa, CA 95338
T: (408) 336-5026
Founded: 1972
Focus: Ecology 14330

Earthquake Engineering Research Institute (EERI), 499 14 St, Ste 320, Oakland, CA 94612-1902
T: (510) 451-0905; Fax: (510) 451-5411
Founded: 1949; Members: 2250
Focus: Eng; Geophys
Periodicals
Earthquake Spectra (quarterly)
EERI Newsletter (monthly) 14331

Earthrise, c/o John Danner, 20 Rubio Rd, Santa Barbara, CA 93103
T: (805) 966-5156; Fax: (805) 966-9457
Founded: 1972; Members: 300
Gen Secr: John Danner
Focus: Futurology 14332

East Asia Regional Council of Overseas Schools (EARCOS), c/o Virginia Tech Graduate Centre, 2990 Telestar Crt, Rm 315, Falls Church, VA 22042
T: (703) 280-4690; Fax: (703) 280-4890
Gen Secr: Dr. Fred J. Brieve
Focus: Educ 14333

East Asian Studies Centre, Bloomington, c/o Indiana Univ., Bloomington, IN 47405
T: (812) 855-4848
Gen Secr: George M. Wilson
Focus: Ethnology 14334

East-West Center (EWC), 1601 East-West Rd, Honolulu, HI 96848-1601
T: (808) 944-7111; E-Mail: ewcinfo@ewc.hawaii.edu; Fax: (808) 944-7376
Founded: 1960; Members: 2003
Focus: Poli Sci; Econ 14335

East-West Management Institute (EWMI), c/o Soros Business and Management Foundation, 520 Madison Av, New York, NY 10022
T: (212) 843-7660; E-Mail: bpattison@sorosny.org.; Fax: (212) 843-1485
Gen Secr: Herta Lande Seidman
Focus: Business Admin 14336

Eastern Bird Banding Association (EBBA), 4 View Point Dr, Hopewell, NJ 08525
T: (609) 466-1871
Founded: 1923; Members: 800
Gen Secr: Hannah B. Suthers
Focus: Ornithology
Periodical
North American Bird Bander (quarterly) . 14337

Eastern Finance Association (EFA), c/o Prof. Dr. Donald A. Nast, Dept of Finance, Florida State University, Tallahassee, FL 32306-1042
T: (904) 644-4220
Founded: 1965; Members: 1950
Gen Secr: Prof. Dr. Donald A. Nast
Focus: Finance 14338

Ecological and Toxicological Association of Dyes and Organic Pigments Manufacturers (ETAD), 1100 New York Av NW, Ste 1090, Washington, DC 20005
T: (202) 414-4100; Fax: (202) 289-8584
Focus: Ecology; Toxicology 14339

Ecological Society of America (ESA), 2010 Massachusetts Av NW, Ste 400, Washington, DC 20036
T: (202) 833-8773; E-Mail: esahq@esa.org; Fax: (202) 833-8775
Founded: 1915; Members: 7000
Gen Secr: Brian Keller
Focus: Ecology 14340

EcoNet, c/o IGC, 1012 Presidio Bldg, Torney Av, San Francisco, CA 94129-0904, POB 29904
T: (415) 442-0220; E-Mail: info@igc.org
Focus: Ecology 14341

Econometric Society (ES), c/o Dept of Economics, Northwestern University, Evanston, IL 60208-2600
T: (847) 491-3615
Founded: 1930; Members: 7000
Gen Secr: Dr. Julie P. Gordon
Focus: Stats; Math
Periodical
Econometrica (bi-monthly) 14342

Economic History Association (EHA), c/o Dept of Economics, University of Kansas, 213 Summerfield Hall, Lawrence, KS 66045
Founded: 1940; Members: 2210
Gen Secr: Thomas Weiss
Focus: Hist; Econ
Periodical
Journal of Economic History (quarterly) . 14343

ECRI, 5200 Butler Pike, Plymouth Meeting, PA 19462
T: (215) 825-6000; Fax: (215) 834-1275
Founded: 1955; Members: 2500
Focus: Med
Periodicals
Health Device Alerts (weekly)
Health Devices (monthly)
Health Devices Sourcebook (annually)
Issues in Health Care Technology (bi-monthly) 14344

Edgar Allan Poe Society of Baltimore (EAPSB), c/o University of Baltimore, 1420 N Charles St, Baltimore, MD 21201
T: (410) 661-1180
Founded: 1923; Members: 350
Pres: Carol Peirce
Focus: Lit 14345

Edison Birthplace Association (EBA), c/o Edison Birthplace Museum, 9 Edison Dr, POB 451, Milan, OH 44846
T: (419) 499-2135
Founded: 1951; Members: 250
Focus: Preserv Hist Monuments 14346

Edison Electric Institute (EEI), 701 Pennsylvania Av NW, Washington, DC 20004-2696
T: (202) 508-5000; Fax: (202) 508-5360
Founded: 1933; Members: 190
Pres: Thomas R. Kuhn
Focus: Electric Eng
Periodicals
Electrical Report (weekly)
Rate Book (annually)
Statistical Report (weekly)
Statistical Yearbook (annually) 14347

Editorial Projects in Education (EPE), 4301 Connecticut Av NW, Ste 250, Washington, DC 20008
T: (202) 364-4114; Fax: (202) 364-1039
Founded: 1959
Focus: Journalism
Periodical
Education Week (40 times annually) . . 14348

Education Commission of the States (ECS), 707 17 St, Ste 2700, Denver, CO 80202-3427
T: (303) 299-3600; Fax: (303) 296-8332
Founded: 1966; Members: 60
Focus: Educ
Periodical
State Education Leader (quarterly) . . . 14349

Education Development Center (EDC), 55 Chapel St, Newton, MA 02160
T: (617) 969-7100; Fax: (617) 244-3436
Founded: 1958
Pres: Janet Whitla
Focus: Educ
Periodical
Annual Report (annually) 14350

Education Turnkey Systems, 256 N Washington St, Falls Church, VA 22046
T: (703) 536-2313; Fax: (703) 536-3225
Founded: 1979
Focus: Computer & Info Sci 14351

Education Writers Association (EWA), 1001 Connecticut Av NW, Ste 310, Washington, DC 20036
T: (202) 429-9680; Fax: (202) 872-4016
Founded: 1947; Members: 550
Focus: Lit; Educ
Periodicals
The Education Reporter (bi-monthly)
Membership Directory (annually) 14352

Educational Center for Applied Ekistics (ECAE), 1900 DeKalb Av NE, Atlanta, GA 30307
T: (404) 378-2219
Founded: 1977
Focus: Educ
Periodical
Ekistical Education (quarterly) 14353

Educational Commission for Foreign Medical Graduates (ECFMG), 3624 Market St, Philadelphia, PA 19104
T: (215) 386-5900; E-Mail: ecfmg@ecfmg.org; Fax: (215) 387-9963
Founded: 1956; Members: 20
Gen Secr: Nancy E. Gary
Focus: Med; Adult Educ
Periodicals
ECFMG Annual Report (annually)
ECFMG Information Booklet (semi-annually) 14354

Educational Foundation for the Fashion Industries (EFFI), 227 W 27 St, New York, NY 10001
T: (212) 760-7641
Founded: 1944
Focus: Educ; Textiles 14355

Educational Leadership Institute (ELI), POB 11411, Shorewood, WI 53211
T: (414) 289-0706
Founded: 1980
Focus: Educ 14356

Educational Planning Institute (EPI), 161 W 12 St, New York, NY 10011
T: (212) 807-7877; Fax: (212) 807-7884
Founded: 1971
Focus: Educ 14357

Educational Records Bureau (ERB), 345 E 47 St, New York, NY 10017
T: (212) 705-8888; Fax: (212) 705-8870
Founded: 1927; Members: 1150
Pres: Dr. Otto R. Norwood
Focus: Educ
Periodicals
Catalog of Programs and Services (annually)
Newsletter (quarterly)
Prospectus (annually) 14358

Educational Research Analysts (EdReAn), POB 7518, Longview, TX 75607-7518
T: (903) 753-5993
Founded: 1961
Focus: Educ 14359

Educational Research Service (ERS), 2000 Clarendon Blvd, Arlington, VA 22201
T: (703) 243-2100; Fax: (703) 243-1985
Founded: 1973; Members: 2600
Focus: Educ
Periodical
Bulletin (10 times annually) 14360

Educational Testing Service (ETS), Rosedale Rd, Princeton, NJ 08541
T: (609) 921-9000; Fax: (609) 734-5410
Founded: 1947
Focus: Educ 14361

Educational Theatre Association (ETA), 3368 Central Pkwy, Cincinnati, OH 45225-2392
T: (513) 599-1996; E-Mail: info@etassoc.org; Fax: (513) 559-0012
Gen Secr: Ronald L. Longstreth
Focus: Educ; Perf Arts 14362

Electric Auto Association (EAA), 2710 SE Giles Ln, Mountain View, CA 94040
T: (415) 591-6698; Fax: (415) 537-2882
Founded: 1967; Members: 1500
Pres: Stan Stokan
Focus: Transport; Auto Eng
Periodical
News (monthly) 14363

Electric Vehicle Association (EVA), 601 California St, Ste 502, San Francisco, CA 94108
T: (415) 249-2690; Fax: (415) 249-2699
Founded: 1990; Members: 50
Gen Secr: Robert Hayden
Focus: Electric Eng 14364

Electricity Consumers Resource Council (ELCON), 1333 H St NW, Washington, DC 20005
T: (202) 682-1390
Founded: 1976; Members: 21
Focus: Electric Eng
Periodical
Report (quarterly) 14365

Electrochemical Society (ECS), 10 S Main St, Pennington, NJ 08534
T: (609) 737-1902
Founded: 1902; Members: 7000
Gen Secr: R.J. Calvo
Focus: Electrochem
Periodicals
Interface (quarterly)
Journal (monthly) 14366

Electronic Music Consortium (EMC), c/o Dr. Thomas Wells, School of Music, Ohio State University, Columbus, OH 43210
T: (614) 292-1102
Founded: 1977; Members: 56
Pres: Dr. Thomas Wells
Focus: Music 14367

Elizabeth Linington Society (ELS), 1223 Glen Terrace, Glassboro, NJ 08028-1315
T: (609) 589-1571
Founded: 1983; Members: 150
Focus: Lit *14368*

Elm Research Institute (ERI), Elm St, POB 805, Harrisville, NH 03450
T: (603) 827-3048; Fax: (603) 827-3794
Founded: 1967; Members: 2000
Gen Secr: John P. Hansel
Focus: Ecology
Periodical
Press Release (monthly) *14369*

Employee Benefit Research Institute (EBRI), 2121 K St NW, Ste 600, Washington, DC 20037
T: (202) 659-0670; Fax: (202) 775-6312
Founded: 1978
Focus: Sociology
Periodical
Proceedings (bi-annually) *14370*

Emulsion Polymers Institute (EPI), c/o Lehigh University, 111 Research Dr, Bethlehem, PA 18015
T: (215) 758-3590; Fax: (215) 758-5880
Founded: 1975
Focus: Chem; Eng; Materials Sci . . . *14371*

Endocrine Society (ES), 4350 East West Hwy, Ste 500, Bethesda, MD 20814-4410
T: (301) 941-0200; Fax: (301) 941-0259
Founded: 1915; Members: 8000
Gen Secr: Scott Hunt
Focus: Endocrinology
Periodicals
Endocrine Review (quarterly)
Endocrinology (monthly)
Journal of Clinical Endocrinology and Metabolism (monthly)
Molecular Endocrinology (monthly)
Newsletter *14372*

Endometriosis Association (EA), 8585 N 76 Pl, Milwaukee, WI 53223
T: (414) 355-2200; Fax: (414) 355-6065
Founded: 1980
Gen Secr: Mary Lou Ballweg
Focus: Gynecology
Periodical
Newsletter (bi-monthly) *14373*

Energy Research Institute (ERI), 6850 Rattlesnake Hammock Rd, Hwy 951, Naples, FL 33962
T: (813) 793-1922; Fax: (813) 793-1260
Founded: 1980; Members: 4500
Focus: Energy
Periodicals
Directory
Report *14374*

Energy Strategies for Sustainable Development, 3128 NW Cascade Dr, Portland, OR 97201
T: (503) 228-5388; E-Mail: jlebens@aol.com; Fax: (503) 228-5388
Gen Secr: John Lebens
Focus: Energy *14375*

Engineered Wood Research Foundation, POB 11700, Tacoma, WA 98411
T: (206) 565-6600; Fax: (206) 565-7265
Founded: 1944; Members: 178
Gen Secr: Bob Potter
Focus: Materials Sci *14376*

Engineering Workforce Commission (EMC), 1111 19 St NW, Ste 608, Washington, DC 20036-3690
T: (202) 296-2237; E-Mail: aaes@; Fax: (202) 296-1151
Founded: 1950; Members: 40
Pres: Jack Doyle
Focus: Eng
Periodical
Engineering and Technology Degrees (annually)
. . . . *14377*

English Institute (EI), c/o Center for Literary and Cultural Studies, Harvard University, 61 Kirkland St, Cambridge, MA 02138
T: (617) 496-1006
Founded: 1938; Members: 5000
Focus: Lit
Periodical
Selected Essays (annually) *14378*

Entomological Society of America (ESA), 9301 Annapolis Rd, Ste 300, Lanham, MD 20706-3115
T: (301) 731-4535
Founded: 1889; Members: 9000
Gen Secr: Harry A. Bradley
Focus: Entomology
Periodicals
Annals (bi-monthly)
Annual Review of Entomology (annually)
Bulletin (quarterly)
Environmental Entomology (bi-monthly)
ESA Newsletter (monthly)
Journal of Economic Entomology (bi-monthly)
Journal of Medical Entomology (bi-monthly)
. . . . *14379*

Environic Foundation International, 916 Saint Vincent St, South Bend, IN 46617
T: (219) 233-3357; Fax: (219) 289-6716
Founded: 1970

Pres: Patrick Horsbrugh
Focus: Eng *14380*

Environmental Design Research Association (EDRA), POB 7146, Edmond, OK 73083-7146
T: (405) 330-4863; Fax: (405) 330-4150
Founded: 1968; Members: 800
Gen Secr: Janet Singer
Focus: Anthro; Archit; Econ; Eng; Geography; Urban Plan
Periodical
Design Research News (quarterly) . . . *14381*

Environmental Law Alliance Worldwide (E-LAW), 1877 Garden Av, Eugene, OR 97403
T: (514) 687-8454; E-Mail: elawus@igc.apc.org.; Fax: (514) 687-0535
Focus: Law *14382*

Environmental Law Institute (ELI), 1616 P St NW, Ste 200, Washington, DC 20036
T: (202) 328-5150
Founded: 1969
Focus: Ecology; Law *14383*

Environmental Mutagen Society (EMS), c/o Drohan Management Group, 1730 N Lynn St, Ste 502, Arlington, VA 22209
T: (703) 525-1191; Fax: (703) 276-8196
Founded: 1969; Members: 1150
Pres: J.T. McGregor; Gen Secr: Richard A. Guggolz
Focus: Bio
Periodical
Environmental and Molecular Mutagenesis (8 times annually) *14384*

Environmental Technology Seminar (ETS), 620 Fayette Dr N, Safety Harbor, FL 34695-4304
Founded: 1969
Pres: Jean Wood
Focus: Ecology
Periodical
The Environmentalist *14385*

EPA Futures Studies Group, c/o US Environmental Protection Agency, 401 M St SW, Washington, DC 20460
T: (202) 260-6523, 260-6514; Fax: (202) 260-4903
Focus: Futurology *14386*

Epigraphic Society (ES), 2443 Filmore St, Ste 328, San Francisco, CA 94115
T: (619) 571-1344; Fax: (619) 571-1124
Founded: 1974; Members: 800
Pres: Dr. Barry Fell
Focus: Archeol
Periodical
ESOP Annual (annually) *14387*

Esalen Institute (EI), Hwy 1, Big Sur, CA 93920
T: (408) 667-3000; E-Mail: friends@esalen.org; Fax: (408) 667-2724
Founded: 1962
Pres: Sharon Thom
Focus: Psych *14388*

Esperantic Studies Foundation (ESF), 3900 Northampton St NW, Washington, DC 20015
T: (202) 362-3963; E-Mail: ejl@wis2.circ.gwu.edu; Fax: (202) 363-6899
Founded: 1968
Gen Secr: Dr. E. James Lieberman
Focus: Ling *14389*

Esperanto League for North America (ELNA), POB 1129, El Cerrito, CA 94530
T: (415) 653-0998
Founded: 1952; Members: 1080
Focus: Ling
Periodicals
Catalog (annually)
ELNA-Adresaro (annually)
ELNA Newsletter (bi-monthly) *14390*

Estonian Learned Society of America (ELSA), c/o Estonian Educational Society, Estonian House, 243 E 34 St, New York, NY 10016
T: (416) 485-5559
Founded: 1950; Members: 200
Focus: Ethnology *14391*

Estuarine Research Federation (ERF), c/o Joy Bartholomew, 490 Chippingwood Dr, No 2, Port Republic, MD 20676
T: (410) 586-0997; Fax: (410) 586-9226
Founded: 1949; Members: 2900
Gen Secr: Joy Bartholomew
Focus: Oceanography
Periodicals
Estuaries (quarterly)
Newsletter (quarterly) *14392*

Ethnic Materials and Information Exchange Round Table (EMIERT), c/o American Library Association, 50 E Huron St, Chicago, IL 60611
T: (312) 280-4295; Fax: (312) 280-3256
Founded: 1971; Members: 700
Focus: Libraries & Bk Sci
Periodical
EMIERT Bulletin (quarterly) *14393*

Etruscan Foundation (EF), 377 Ficher Rd, Ste D2, Grosse Pointe, MI 48230
T: (313) 882-2462; Fax: (313) 882-2462
Founded: 1959; Members: 425
Pres: Count Ferdinand Cinelli
Focus: Archeol

Periodicals
Etruscans (annually)
Friends of Spannocchia (quarterly)
Newsletter *14394*

Eugene O'Neill Society (EOS), c/o Dept of English, Suffolk University, 41 Temple St, Boston, MA 02114
T: (617) 573-8271; Fax: (617) 722-9440
Founded: 1978; Members: 225
Gen Secr: Thomas F. Connolly
Focus: Lit *14395*

European Community Studies Association (ECSA), c/o University of Pittsburgh, 405 Bellefield Hall, Pittsburgh, PA 15260
T: (412) 648-7635; E-Mail: ecsa@pitt.edu; Fax: (412) 648-1168
Founded: 1988
Gen Secr: Valerie Staats
Focus: Poli Sci *14396*

European School of Oncology (ESO), c/o American Italian Cancer Foundation, 872 Madison Av, New York, NY 10021
T: (212) 628-9090; Fax: (212) 517-6089
Focus: Educ; Cell Biol & Cancer Res . *14397*

European Space Agency (ESA), 955 L'Enfant Plaza, Ste 7800, Washington, DC 20024
T: (202) 488-4158; Fax: (202) 488-4930
Focus: Aero *14398*

European Union Studies Centre, New York (EUSC), 25 W 43 St, Ste 418, New York, NY 10036
E-Mail: kaufmann@qcvaxa.acc.qc.edu
Gen Secr: Prof. Hugo M. Kaufmann
Focus: Poli Sci *14399*

Evangelical Lutheran Education Association (ELEA), 6020 Radford Av, North Hollywood, CA 91606
T: (818) 752-1019
Founded: 1961; Members: 351
Focus: Educ
Periodical
Views and Vision (9 times annually) . . *14400*

Evelyn Waugh Society (EWS), c/o English Dept, Nassau Community College, State University of New York, Garden City, NY 11530
T: (516) 572-7792
Founded: 1967; Members: 187
Pres: Dr. Paul A. Doyle
Focus: Lit
Periodical
Evelyn Waugh Newsletter (3 times annually) *14401*

Executive Council on Foreign Diplomacy (ECFD), 818 Connecticut Av NW, Washington, DC 20006-2702
T: (914) 273-9100; Fax: (914) 273-6884
Gen Secr: James Stoutenberg
Focus: Poli Sci *14402*

Exodus Trust (ET), 1523 Franklin St, San Francisco, CA 94109
T: (415) 928-1133
Founded: 1968
Focus: Educ *14403*

Expanded Shale Clay and Slate Institute (ESCSI), 2225 E Murray Holladay Rd, Salt Lake City, UT 84117
T: (801) 272-7070; Fax: (801) 272-3377
Founded: 1952; Members: 27
Focus: Civil Eng
Periodicals
Information Sheet
Special Bulletin *14404*

Experimental Aircraft Association (EAA), EAA Aircraft Center, POB 3086, Oshkosh, WI 54903-3086
T: (414) 426-4800; Fax: (414) 426-4828
Members: 128000
Focus: Aero
Periodicals
Chapter Bulletin (monthly)
The EAA Experimenter (monthly)
Sport Aerobatics (monthly)
Sport Aviation (monthly)
The Vintage Airplane (monthly) *14405*

Experiments in Art and Technology (EAT), 69 Apple Tree Rd, Berkeley Heights, NJ 07922
T: (212) 285-1690
Founded: 1966
Pres: Billie Kluver
Focus: Arts; Eng *14406*

The Explorers Club (EC), 46 E 70 St, New York, NY 10021
T: (212) 628-8383; Fax: (212) 288-4449
Founded: 1904; Members: 3000
Focus: Geography
Periodicals
Explorers Journal (quarterly)
Newsletter (quarterly) *14407*

Extractive Metallurgy Institute (EMI), 1550 E Missouri Av, No 302, Phoenix, AZ 85014-2457
T: (602) 234-8908; E-Mail: dremco@syspac.com; Fax: (602) 234-8909
Founded: 1981
Pres: Dr. Douglas J. Robinson
Focus: Metallurgy *14408*

Ezra Pound Society (EPS), c/o University of Maine, 302 Neville Hall, Orono, ME 04469
T: (207) 581-3814
Founded: 1978
Focus: Lit
Periodicals
Paideuma (3 times annually)
Sagetrieb (3 times annually) *14409*

F. Marion Crawford Memorial Sociey (FMCMS), 2148 Av de los Flores, Santa Clara, CA 95054
Founded: 1975; Members: 35
Gen Secr: Jesse Knight
Focus: Lit *14410*

Family Health International (FHI), POB 13950, Research Triangle Park, NC 27709
T: (919) 544-7040; Fax: (919) 544-7261
Founded: 1971; Members: 230
Gen Secr: Dr. Theodore M. King
Focus: Family Plan; Pediatrics; Public Health
Periodical
network (quarterly) *14411*

Family Planning International Assistance (FPIA), 810 Seventh Av, New York, NY 10019
T: (212) 541-7800; E-Mail: fpiafax@ppfa.org.; Fax: (212) 247-6274
Gen Secr: Dr. Daniel R. Weintraub
Focus: Family Plan *14412*

Farm Foundation (FF), 1211 W 22 St, Ste 216, Oak Brook, IL 60521
T: (708) 571-9393; Fax: (708) 571-9580
Founded: 1933
Focus: Agri *14413*

FDI World Dental Federation, 2155 Webster St, San Francisco, CA 94115
Gen Secr: Dr. Arthur A. Dugoni
Focus: Dent *14414*

Federal Bar Association (FBA), 1815 H St NW, Ste 408, Washington, DC 20006
T: (202) 638-0252; Fax: (202) 775-0295
Founded: 1920; Members: 15000
Gen Secr: John G. Blanche
Focus: Law
Periodicals
Federal Bar News and Journal (10 times annually)
Membership Directory *14415*

Federal Education Association (FEA), 1201 16 St NW, Washington, DC 20036
T: (202) 822-7850; Fax: (202) 822-7816
Founded: 1956; Members: 6700
Gen Secr: Ronald R. Austin
Focus: Educ
Periodicals
Journal (monthly)
OEA Leader
OEA News *14416*

Federated Council of Beth Jacob Schools (FCBJS), 142 Broome St, New York, NY 10002
T: (212) 473-4500
Founded: 1940; Members: 100
Focus: Educ *14417*

Federation for Unified Science Education (FUSE), c/o Capital University, 231 Battele Hall of Science, Columbus, OH 43209
T: (614) 236-6816
Founded: 1966; Members: 450
Focus: Educ
Periodicals
Prism II (quarterly)
Proceedings of Annual Conference (bi-annually)
. . . . *14418*

Federation of American Scientists (FAS), 307 Massachusetts Av NE, Washington, DC 20002
T: (202) 546-3300
Founded: 1945; Members: 4000
Focus: Sci
Periodical
FAS Public Incerest Report (10 times annually)
. . . . *14419*

Federation of American Societies for Experimental Biology (FASEB), 9650 Rockville Pike, Bethesda, MD 20814
T: (301) 530-7090; Fax: (301) 530-7049
Founded: 1912; Members: 8
Gen Secr: Michael J. Jackson
Focus: Bio
Periodical
The FASEB Journal (monthly) *14420*

Federation of Analytical Chemistry and Spectroscopy Societies (FACSS), 201-B Broadway St, Frederick, MD 21701
T: (301) 846-4797; Fax: (301) 694-6860
Founded: 1972; Members: 7
Pres: Rachael Barbour
Focus: Chem; Physics *14421*

Federation of Behavioral, Psychological and Cognitive Sciences (FBPCS), 750 First NW, Ste 5004, Washington, DC 20002-5004
T: (202) 336-5920; Fax: (202) 336-5920
Founded: 1980; Members: 16
Gen Secr: David H. Johnson
Focus: Psych
Periodicals
Annual Report (annually)
Federation News (monthly) *14422*

Federation of Government Information Processing Councils (FGIPC), c/o U.S. General Services Administration, 4KTH-A, 401 W Peachtre St, Atlanta, GA 30365-2550
T: (404) 331-5106
Founded: 1978; Members: 12000
Gen Secr: Virginia McCormick
Focus: Public Admin; Computer & Info Sci
Periodicals
Directory (annually)
FedFacts (quarterly) 14423

Federation of Insurance and Corporate Counsel (FICC), POB 111, Walpole, MA 02081
T: (508) 668-6859; Fax: (508) 668-6892
Founded: 1935; Members: 1300
Gen Secr: Joseph R. Olshan
Focus: Insurance 14424

Federation of International Poetry Associations (FIPA), POB 579, Santa Claus, IN 47579-0579
Gen Secr: Dr. Carol L. Abell
Focus: Lit 14425

Federation of Materials Societies (FMS), 1899 L St NW, Ste 500, Washington, DC 20036
T: (202) 296-9282; Fax: (202) 833-3014
Founded: 1972; Members: 14
Gen Secr: Betsy Houston
Focus: Materials Sci 14426

Federation of Orthodontic Associations (FOA), c/o Dr. Robert C. Webber, 711 Giddings Av, Cheyboygan Falls, WI 53085
T: (414) 467-4070
Founded: 1969
Gen Secr: Dr. Robert Weber
Focus: Dent 14427

Federation of Prosthodontic Organizations (FPO), 211 E Chicago Av, Ste 948, Chicago, IL 60611
T: (312) 642-7538
Founded: 1965; Members: 16
Focus: Dent
Periodicals
Directory (annually)
Newsletter (quarterly) 14428

Federation of Societies for Coatings Technology (FSCT), 492 Norristown Rd, Blue Bell, PA 18422
T: (215) 940-0777; Fax: (215) 940-0292
Founded: 1922; Members: 7300
Focus: Eng; Civil Eng
Periodical
Journal of Coatings Technology (monthly) 14429

Federation of State Medical Boards of the United States (FSMB), 6000 Western Pl, Ste 707, Fort Worth, TX 76107
T: (817) 735-8445
Founded: 1912; Members: 67
Focus: Med
Periodicals
Federation Bulletin (monthly)
FSMB Newsletter (quarterly)
Handbook (annually) 14430

Fiber Society (FS), c/o School of Textiles, Clemson University, 161 Sirrine Hall, Clemson, SC 29634-1307
T: (803) 656-5957; E-Mail: gbhuven@demson.edu; Fax: (803) 656-5973
Founded: 1941; Members: 400
Gen Secr: Dr. B. Goswami
Focus: Chem; Physics; Eng
Periodical
Membership Directory (annually) 14431

Financial Management Association (FMA), c/o School of Business, University of South Florida, Tampa, FL 33620-5500
T: (813) 974-2084; Fax: (813) 974-3318
Founded: 1970; Members: 12600
Focus: Econ
Periodical
Financial Management (quarterly) 14432

Finnish-American Historical Society of the West (FAHSW), POB 5522, Portland, OR 97208
T: (503) 654-0448
Founded: 1962; Members: 400
Focus: Hist
Periodical
FINNAM Newsletter (quarterly) 14433

Firearms Research and Identification Association (FRIA), 21465 E Fort Bowie Dr, Walnut, CA 91789
T: (909) 598-8919; Fax: (714) 598-5666
Founded: 1978; Members: 16
Pres: John Armand Caudron
Focus: Military Sci 14434

Five College Programs in Peace and World Security Studies (PAWSS), Hampshire College, Prescott Center, Ste D, Amherst, MA 01002
T: (413) 549-4600
Gen Secr: Michael Klare
Focus: Prom Peace 14435

Flag Research Center (FRC), POB 580, Winchester, MA 01890
T: (617) 729-9410; Fax: (617) 721-4817
Founded: 1962; Members: 1160
Focus: Hist
Periodicals
The Flag Bulletin (bi-monthly)
National Flags (quarterly) 14436

Flat Earth Research Society International (FERSI), POB 2533, Lancaster, CA 93539
T: (805) 727-1635
Founded: 1800; Members: 2800
Focus: Geology
Periodical
Flat Earth News (quarterly) 14437

Fleischner Society, c/o Dept of Radiology, University of California, San Francisco, CA 94143-0628
Gen Secr: Dr. W. Richard Webb
Focus: Radiology 14438

Flight Safety Foundation, 601 Madison St, Ste 300, Alexandria, VA 22314
T: (703) 739-6700; Fax: (703) 739-6705
Founded: 1945; Members: 540
Pres: John H. Enders
Focus: Safety; Aero 14439

Flower Essence Society (FES), POB 459, Nevada City, CA 95959
T: (916) 265-9163; Fax: (916) 265-6467
Founded: 1979; Members: 25000
Focus: Med
Periodicals
Directory
The Flower Essence Society Newsletter (quarterly) 14440

Fluid Power Society (FPS), 2433 N Mayfair Rd, Ste 111, Milwaukee, WI 53226
T: (414) 257-0910; Fax: (414) 257-4092
Founded: 1957; Members: 2440
Focus: Energy
Periodical
Newsletter (10 times annually) 14441

Flying Chiropractors Association (FCA), 7301 Hasbrook Av, Philadelphia, PA 19111
T: (215) 722-7200
Founded: 1968; Members: 300
Focus: Med 14442

Flying Dentists Association (FDA), 4700 Chamblee-Dunwoody Rd, Dunwoody, GA 30338
T: (404) 457-1351; Fax: (404) 458-0890
Founded: 1960; Members: 500
Focus: Dent
Periodical
Flight Watch (quarterly) 14443

Flying Physicians Association (FPA), POB 677427, Orlando, FL 32867
T: (407) 359-1423; Fax: (407) 359-1167
Founded: 1954; Members: 1200
Gen Secr: Patricia A. Nodecker
Focus: Physiology 14444

Flying Veterinarians Association (FVA), POB 1081, Columbia, MO 65205
T: (314) 882-7228; Fax: (314) 882-2950
Founded: 1966; Members: 328
Focus: Vet Med
Periodicals
Directory (annually)
Newsletter 14445

Food and Nutrition Board (FNB), c/o Institute of Medicine, 2101 Constitution Av NW, Washington, DC 20418
T: (202) 334-1732
Founded: 1940; Members: 17
Focus: Food; Nutrition; Biochem
Periodicals
Activities Report
Directory (annually) 14446

Food Distribution Research Society (FDRS), c/o Food and Fiber Center, POB 9642, Jackson, MS 39762
T: (601) 325-2160; E-Mail: virgilc@mces.msstate.com; Fax: (601) 325-7844
Founded: 1967; Members: 150
Gen Secr: V.P. Culver
Focus: Food 14447

Foreign Policy Association (FPA), 470 Park Av S, New York, NY 10016
T: (212) 481-8100; Fax: (212) 481-9275
Founded: 1918
Focus: Poli Sci
Periodicals
Great Decisions (annually)
Headline Series (quarterly) 14448

Foreign Services Research Institute (FSRI), POB 6317, Washington, DC 20015-0317
Founded: 1974
Focus: Hist; Philos; Sociology; Poli Sci 14449

Forest History Society (FHS), 701 Vickers Av, Durham, NC 27701
T: (919) 682-9319
Founded: 1946; Members: 1750
Focus: Forestry; Cultur Hist
Periodicals
Forest & Conservation History (quarterly)
Forest History Cruiser (quarterly)
Guides to Forest and Conservation History of North America (irregularly) 14450

Forest Products Society (FPS), 2801 Marshall Court, Madison, WI 53705
T: (608) 231-1361; Fax: (608) 231-2152
Founded: 1947; Members: 3000
Pres: Arthur B. Brauner
Focus: Forestry
Periodicals
Forest Products Journal (monthly)
FPRS Technical Newsletter (quarterly) 14451

Foresta Institute for Ocean and Mountain Studies, 3400 E Speedway Ste 118-293, Tucson, AZ 85716
Gen Secr: Dr. Richard Gordon Miller
Focus: Oceanography; Geology 14452

The Forum, POB 5915, Santa Fe, NM 87502
T: (505) 983-7077
Founded: 1970; Members: 100
Gen Secr: Carol Bell Knight
Focus: Psych
Periodical
The Torch (quarterly) 14453

Forum for Medical Affairs (FMA), c/o Medical Society of the State of New York, 420 Lakeville Rd, Lake Success, NY 11042
T: (516) 488-6100
Founded: 1944; Members: 800
Focus: Med 14454

Forum International: International Ecosystems University (IEU), 91 Gregory Ln, Pleasant Hill, CA 94523
T: (510) 671-2900; Fax: (510) 946-1500
Founded: 1965; Members: 32000
Focus: Ecology 14455

Fostoria Glass Society of America (FGSA), POB 826, Moundsville, WV 26041-0826
T: (304) 845-9188
Founded: 1981; Members: 800
Pres: James Davis
Focus: Graphic & Dec Arts, Design
Periodical
Facets of Fostoria (bi-monthly) 14456

Foundation for Accounting Education (FAE), 530 Fifth Av, New York, NY 10036
T: (212) 719-8300; Fax: (212) 719-3365
Founded: 1972
Gen Secr: Robert L. Gray
Focus: Business Admin; Educ 14457

Foundation for Advancement in Cancer Therapy (FACT), POB 1242, Old Chelsea Station, New York, NY 10113
T: (212) 741-2790
Founded: 1971
Focus: Cell Biol & Cancer Res; Therapeutics 14458

Foundation for Biomedical Research (FBR), 818 Connecticut Av NW, Ste 303, Washington, DC 20006
T: (202) 457-0654
Founded: 1981
Focus: Vet Med 14459

Foundation for Chiropractic Education and Research (FCER), 1701 Clarendon Blvd, Arlington, VA 22209
T: (703) 276-7445; Fax: (703) 276-8178
Founded: 1944; Members: 6000
Focus: Orthopedics
Periodicals
Advance (bi-monthly)
Spinal Manipulation (quarterly)
Staying Well (bi-monthly) 14460

Foundation for Educational Futures (FEF), POB 2463, Charlotte, NC 28226
T: (704) 541-6256
Founded: 1983
Focus: Educ 14461

Foundation for Enterprise Development (FED), POB 2149, La Jolla, CA 92038-2149
T: (619) 459-4662; E-Mail: info@fed.org.; Fax: (619) 459-6921
Focus: Business Admin 14462

Foundation for Exceptional Children (FEC), 1920 Association Dr, Reston, VA 22091
T: (703) 620-1054
Founded: 1971; Members: 1000
Focus: Educ Handic 14463

Foundation for Interior Design Education Research (FIDER), 60 Monroe Center NW, Grand Rapids, MI 49503
T: (616) 458-0400; Fax: (616) 458-0460
Founded: 1971
Focus: Educ; Graphic & Dec Arts, Design 14464

Foundation for International Cooperation (FIC), 1237 S Western Av, Park Ridge, IL 60068
T: (708) 518-0934
Founded: 1960
Focus: Educ 14465

Foundation for International Dermatologic Education, 4647 W 103 St, Oak Lawn, IL 60453
Gen Secr: Marshall L. Blankenship
Focus: Derm; Educ 14466

Foundation for International Exchange of Scientific and Cultural Information by Telecommunications (FISCIT), c/o University of Pennsylvania, 225 Van Pelt 34 TH and Walnut St, Philadelphia, PA 19104-6206
Gen Secr: Dr. Martin Meyerson
Focus: Comm Sci 14467

Foundation for Latin American Anthropological Research (FLAAR), c/o Brevard Community College, 1519 Clearlake Rd, Cocoa, FL 32922
T: (407) 632-1111; Fax: (407) 633-4565
Founded: 1969
Pres: Dr. Nicholas M. Hellmuth
Focus: Anthro 14468

Foundation for Microbiology (FFM), 300 E 54 St, Ste 5K, New York, NY 10022
T: (212) 759-8729
Founded: 1951; Members: 9
Pres: Byron H. Waksman
Focus: Microbio
Periodical
Report (annually) 14469

Foundation for Mideast Communication (FMC), POB 5264, Beverly Hills, CA 90210
T: (310) 450-5386; Fax: (213) 450-9279
Founded: 1983
Gen Secr: Michael Lame
Focus: Ethnology 14470

Foundation for Research in the Afro-American Creative Arts (FRAACA), PO Drawer 1, Cambria Heights, NY 11411
Founded: 1971; Members: 1000
Focus: Arts 14471

Foundation for Science and Disability (FSD), 236 Grand St, Morgantown, WV 26505-7509
T: (304) 293-5201; E-Mail: u0072@wvnvm.wvnet.edu; Fax: (304) 293-6363
Founded: 1978; Members: 252
Gen Secr: E.C. Keller
Focus: Educ Handic
Periodical
Newsletter (bi-monthly) 14472

Foundation for the Advancement of Chiropractic Tenets and Science (FACTS), c/o International Chiropractors Association, 1110 N Glebe Rd, Ste 1000, Arlington, VA 22201
T: (703) 528-5000
Founded: 1972
Focus: Med 14473

Foundation for the Support of International Medical Training (FSIMT), 417 Center St, Lewiston, NY 14092
T: (716) 754-4883; Fax: (716) 754-4883
Founded: 1960; Members: 6000000
Focus: Med; Nucl Med
Periodicals
Brochures (annually)
Directory (annually)
Immunization Chart (annually)
Malaria Risk Chart (annually)
Traveller Clinical Chart (annually) 14474

Francis Bacon Foundation (FBF), 655 N Dartmouth Av, Claremont, CA 91711
T: (714) 624-6305
Founded: 1938
Focus: Lit 14475

Frank Lloyd Wright Association (FLWF), Taliesin W, Scottsdale, AZ 85261
T: (602) 860-2700; Fax: (602) 451-8989
Founded: 1990; Members: 2600
Gen Secr: Richard Carney
Focus: Archit
Periodical
Friends of Taliesin (3 times annually) 14476

Franklin and Eleanor Roosevelt Institute, 511 Albany Post Rd, Hyde Park, NY 12538
T: (914) 229-5321; Fax: (914) 229-9046
Founded: 1987
Focus: Hist 14477

Frederick Douglass Memorial and Historical Association (FDMHA), 10594 Twin Rivers Rd, Apt E-1, Columbia, MD 21044
T: (410) 854-2938
Founded: 1900
Pres: Mary E.C. Gregory
Focus: Hist 14478

Friars Club (FC), 57 E 55 St, New York, NY 10022
T: (212) 751-7272; Fax: (212) 355-0217
Founded: 1904; Members: 1400
Focus: Perf Arts 14479

Friends Historical Association (FHA), c/o Quaker Collection, Haverford College Library, Haverford, PA 19041
T: (215) 896-1161
Founded: 1873; Members: 800
Focus: Hist; Rel & Theol
Periodical
Quaker History (semi-annually) 14480

Friends of American Art in Religion (FAAR), 143 E 43 St, New York, NY 10017
T: (212) 682-5722
Founded: 1970; Members: 100
Gen Secr: E.V. Clark
Focus: Arts 14481

Friends of Cast Iron Architecture (FCIA), 235 E 87 St, Rm 6C, New York, NY 10128
T: (212) 369-6004
Founded: 1970; Members: 1000
Focus: Preserv Hist Monuments 14482

Friends of George Sand (FGS), c/o Hofstra Cultural Center, Hofstra University, Hempstead, NY 11550
T: (516) 463-5669; Fax: (516) 564-4297
Founded: 1976; Members: 319
Focus: Lit 14483

Friends of the Sea Lion Marine Mammal Center (FSLMMC), 20612 Laguna Canyon Rd, Laguna Beach, CA 92651
T: (714) 494-3050
Founded: 1971; Members: 2500
Focus: Zoology 14484

Galactic Society International (TGS), Box 326, Rock Hill, SC 29731
T: (803) 328-0705; Fax: (803) 329-9798
Founded: 1989
Pres: J.G. Bowman III
Focus: Aero 14485

Gas Research Institute (GRI), 8600 W Bryn Mawr Av, Chicago, IL 60631
T: (312) 399-8100; Fax: (312) 399-8170
Founded: 1976; Members: 319
Focus: Energy
Periodical
Gas Research Institute Digest (quarterly) 14486

General Anthropology Division (GAD), c/o American Anthropological Association, 4350 N Fairfax Dr, Ste 640, Arlington, VA 22203-1620
T: (703) 528-1902; Fax: (703) 528-3546
Founded: 1984; Members: 4877
Pres: David McCurdy
Focus: Anthro
Periodical
American Anthropologist 14487

General Society of Mechanics and Tradesmen (GSMT), 20 W 44 St, New York, NY 10036
T: (212) 840-1840
Founded: 1785
Focus: Eng 14488

Genetics of Industrial Microorganisms – International Commission (GIM-IC), c/o Lilly Research Laboratories, Lilly Corporate Center, Indianapolis, IN 46285
Gen Secr: Dr. R. H. Baltz
Focus: Genetics 14489

Genetics Society of America (GSA), 9650 Rockville Pike, Bethesda, MD 20814
T: (301) 571-1825; Fax: (301) 530-7079
Founded: 1932; Members: 4400
Pres: Rochelle E. Esposito; Gen Secr: Elaine Strass
Focus: Genetics 14490

Geochemical Society (GS), c/o Dept of Terrestrial Magnetism, Carnegie Institute of Washington, 5241 Broad Branch Rd NW, Washington, DC 20015
T: (202) 686-4370
Founded: 1955; Members: 1800
Pres: A. Lasaga; Gen Secr: Dr. S.B. Shirey
Focus: Geology; Chem; Geophys; Mineralogy
Periodical
Geochimica et Cosmochimica Acta (monthly) 14491

Geological Society of America (GSA), 3300 Penrose Pl, POB 9140, Boulder, CO 80301
T: (303) 447-2020; Fax: (303) 447-1133
Founded: 1888; Members: 14400
Gen Secr: Donald M. Davidson
Focus: Geology
Periodicals
The Geological Society of America Bulletin (monthly)
Geology (monthly)
GSA News & Information (monthly) . . 14492

George C. Marshall Foundation (GCMF), Drawer 1600, Lexington, VA 24450
T: (703) 463-7103; Fax: (703) 464-5229
Founded: 1953
Focus: Hist; Military Sci
Periodical
The Papers of George Catlett Marshall . 14493

Geothermal Resources Council (GRC), POB 1350, Davis, CA 95617
T: (916) 758-2360; Fax: (916) 758-2839
Founded: 1972; Members: 1048
Focus: Geology 14494

German-American Information and Education Association (GIEA), POB 492, Vienna, VA 22183-0492
T: (703) 425-0707
Founded: 1986
Pres: Stanley Rittenhouse
Focus: Educ; Ling 14495

German American World Society (GAWS), 529A Central Av, Jersey City, NJ 07307
T: (201) 420-0159; Fax: (201) 420-0469
Founded: 1980
Focus: Hist 14496

The Gerontological Society of America, 1275 K St NW, Ste 350, Washington, DC 20005-4006
T: (202) 842-1275; Fax: (202) 842-1150
Founded: 1945; Members: 7100
Gen Secr: Carol A. Schutz
Focus: Geriatrics
Periodicals
The Gerontologist (bi-monthly)
Journal of Gerontology (bi-monthly) . . . 14497

Gerson Institute (GI), POB 430, Bonita, CA 91908-0430
T: (619) 585-7600; E-Mail: GERSON@AOL.com; Fax: (619) 585-7610
Founded: 1977; Members: 3000
Pres: Charlotte Gerson
Focus: Med 14498

Gilbert and Sullivan Society (GSS), 1351 65 St, Brooklym, NY 11219
T: (718) 259-6431
Founded: 1936; Members: 400
Gen Secr: Frances Yasperica
Focus: Music
Periodical
The Palace Peeper (10 times annually) . 14499

Glass Art Society (GAS), 1305 Fourth Av, Ste 711, Seattle, WA 98101-2401
T: (206) 382-1305; Fax: (206) 382-2630
Founded: 1971; Members: 1300
Focus: Graphic & Dec Arts, Design
Periodicals
Journal (annually)
Resource Directory (annually) 14500

Glazounov Society (GS), 17320 Park Av, Sonoma, CA 95476
T: (707) 996-1653
Founded: 1985; Members: 48
Focus: Music 14501

Global Alliance for Women's Health, 777 UN Plaza, New York, NY 10017
T: (212) 286-0424; Fax: (212) 286-9561
Focus: Public Health 14502

Global Art Project (GAP), POB 40445, Tucson, AZ 85717
T: (602) 628-8353; Fax: (602) 624-6284
Gen Secr: Katherine Josten
Focus: Arts 14503

Global Change System for Analysis, Research and Training (START), c/o START Secretariat, 2000 Florida Av NW, Ste 200, Washington, DC 20009-1277
T: (202) 462-2213; E-Mail: rfuchs@kosmos.org; Fax: (202) 457-5859
Gen Secr: Roland Fuchs
Focus: Sociology 14504

Global Climate Coalition, 1331 Pennsylvania Av NW, Ste 1500 – N Tower, Washington, DC 20004-1703
T: (202) 637-3158
Focus: Geophys 14505

Global Education Associates (GEA), 475 Riverside Dr, Ste 1848, New York, NY 10115
T: (212) 870-3290; E-Mail: gea475@igc.apc.org; Fax: (212) 870-2729
Founded: 1973; Members: 8000
Focus: Educ 14506

Global Education Motivators, c/o Chestnut Hill College, Germantown and NW Av, Chestnut Hill, PA 19118
T: (215) 248-1150; E-Mail: gem@netaxs.com; Fax: (215) 248-7056
Gen Secr: Wayne Jacoby
Focus: Educ 14507

Global Energy and Water Cycle Experiment (GEWEX), c/o WCRP, Int GEWEX Project Office, Ste 1210, 1100 Wayne Av, Silver Spring, MD 20910
T: (301) 427-2089 Ext 521; E-Mail: gewex@cais.com; Fax: (301) 427-2222
Focus: Energy; Water Res 14508

Global Learning (GL), 1018 Stuyvesant Av, Union, NJ 07083
T: (908) 964-1114; Fax: (908) 964-6335
Founded: 1974
Gen Secr: Jeffrey L. Brown
Focus: Educ
Periodical
Global Learning Teacher Education Manual 14509

Global Mapping International, POB 25399, Colorado Springs, CO 80936-5399
T: (719) 531-3599; E-Mail: info@gmi.org
Focus: Cart 14510

Global Options (GO), POB 40601, San Francisco, CA 94140
T: (415) 550-1703
Founded: 1977; Members: 53
Focus: Socialism; Sociology; Poli Sci; Econ
Periodicals
Central America Education Project (quarterly)
Contra Watch (monthly)
Crime and Social Justice (quarterly) . . 14511

Global Population Information Network (POPIN), c/o Population Division, Dept Economic ans Social Information and Policy Analysis, United National, 2 United National Plaza, New York, NY 10017
T: (212) 963-3203; E-Mail: popin@undp.org; Fax: (212) 963-2147
Gen Secr: Dr. Susan Pasquariella
Focus: Sociology 14512

Global Rivers Environmental Education Network (GREEN), 206 S Fifth Av, Ste 150, An Arbor, MI 48104
T: (313) 761-8142; E-Mail: green@green.org; Fax: (313) 761-4951
Focus: Ecology; Educ 14513

Global Volcanism Network, c/o Museum of Natural History, MRC 129, Smithsonian Institution, 1000 Jefferson Dr SW, Washington, DC 20560
T: (202) 357-1511; Fax: (202) 786-2557
Gen Secr: R. Wunderman
Focus: Geology 14514

Global Warming International Centre (GWIC), One Heritage Plaza, POB 5275, Woodridge, IL 60517-0275
T: (630) 910-1551; Fax: (630) 910-1561
Gen Secr: Dr. Sinyan Shen
Focus: Geophys 14515

Goethe Society of North America (GSNA), c/o German Dept, University of California, Irvine, CA 92717
T: (714) 856-6406
Founded: 1979; Members: 200
Focus: Lit 14516

Goudy Society (GS), 408 Eighth Av, New York, NY 10001
T: (212) 629-3232; Fax: (212) 465-2012
Founded: 1965; Members: 100
Pres: Steven J. Kennedy
Focus: Eng 14517

Governmental Research Association (GRA), c/o Samford University, 402 Samford Hall, Birmingham, AL 35229-7017
T: (205) 870-2482
Founded: 1914; Members: 150
Pres: James W. Williams
Focus: Poli Sci; Public Admin
Periodicals
Bibliography of Governmental Research Directory (bi-annually)
Reporter (quarterly) 14518

Grace Contrino Abrams Peace Education Foundation, 2627 Biscayne Blvd, Miami, FL 33137-3854
T: (305) 576-5075; Fax: (305) 576-3106
Gen Secr: John R. Mazzarella
Focus: Prom Peace; Educ 14519

Graduate Management Admission Council (GMAC), 2400 Broadway, Ste 230, Santa Monica, CA 90404
T: (310) 998-9299; Fax: (310) 998-9238
Founded: 1970; Members: 113
Pres: William Broesamle
Focus: Business Admin 14520

Graduate Record Examinations Board (GRE BOARD), c/o Educational Testing Service 33-V, Princeton, NJ 08541
T: (609) 951-6506; Fax: (609) 951-1090
Founded: 1966
Focus: Adult Educ
Periodicals
Board Newsletter (quarterly)
General Test Practice Book (annually)
GRE Information Bulletin (annually)
Guide to the Graduate Record Examinations Program (annually) 14521

Graphic Communications Association (GCA), 100 Daingerfield Rd, Alexandria, VA 22314
T: (703) 519-8160; Fax: (703) 548-2867
Founded: 1966; Members: 350
Focus: Computer & Info Sci; Eng
Periodicals
Newsletter (irregularly)
Spectrum Proceedings (irregularly) . . . 14522

Gravure Association of America (GAA), 1200A Scottsville Rd, Rochester, NY 14624
T: (716) 436-2150; Fax: (716) 463-7689
Founded: 1987; Members: 250
Gen Secr: Cheryl Kasunich
Focus: Eng 14523

Great Lakes Colleges Association (GLCA), 2929 Plymouth Rd, Ste 207, Ann Arbor, MI 48105-3206
T: (313) 761-4833; Fax: (313) 761-3939
Founded: 1961; Members: 12
Focus: Educ
Periodical
Faculty Newsletter (5 times annually) . . 14524

Great Lakes Commission (GLC), 400 Fourth St, Ann Arbor, MI 48103-4816
T: (313) 665-9135; Fax: (313) 665-4370
Founded: 1955; Members: 36
Focus: Water Res; Navig
Periodicals
Great Lakes Research Checklist (semi-annually)
Minutes of Regular Meeting (semi-annually) 14525

Great Lakes Historical Society (GLHS), c/o Great Lakes Historical Society Museum, 480 Main St, Vermilion, OH 44089
T: (216) 967-3467; Fax: (216) 967-1519
Founded: 1944; Members: 3000
Focus: Hist
Periodicals
Chadburn (quarterly)
Inland Seas (quarterly) 14526

Great Lakes Maritime Institute (GLMI), 100 Strand Dr, 1 Belle Isle, Detroit, MI 48207
T: (313) 267-6440
Founded: 1948; Members: 1700
Focus: Navig
Periodical
Telescope (bi-monthly) 14527

Great Plains Agricultural Council (GPAC), c/o Dept of Agricultural and Resource Economics, Colorado State University, Fort Collins, CO 80523-0002
T: (303) 491-7370
Founded: 1946; Members: 27
Focus: Agri 14528

Group for the Advancement of Psychiatry (GAP), POB 28218, Dallas, TX 75228
T: (214) 613-3044; Fax: (214) 613-5532
Founded: 1946; Members: 300
Gen Secr: Frances Roton
Focus: Psychiatry 14529

Group for the Use of Psychology in History (GUPH), c/o University of Illinois at Springfield, 440 Brookens, Springfield, IL 62794-9243
T: (217) 786-6778; Fax: (217) 786-7188
Founded: 1972; Members: 600
Gen Secr: Larry Shiner
Focus: Hist; Psych
Periodical
The Psychohistory Review (3 times annually) 14530

Group Health Association of America (GHAA), 1129 20 St NW, Ste 600, Washington, DC 20036
T: (202) 778-3200
Founded: 1959; Members: 1000
Focus: Public Health
Periodicals
Group Health News (monthly)
Journal (semi-annually)
Medical Directors Conference Proceedings (semi-annually) 14531

Groupe de Recherches sur l'Afrique Francophone (GRAF), c/o African Studies Center, Boston University, 270 Bay State Rd, Boston, MA 02215
T: (617) 353-7307; E-Mail: ebustin@acs.bu.edu; Fax: (617) 353-4975
Gen Secr: Edouard Bustin
Focus: Sociology 14532

Groupement des allergologistes et immunologistes de langues latines (GAILL), 9 Hillbrook Dr, Portola Valley, CA 94028
T: (415) 851-4916
Gen Secr: Georges M. Halpern
Focus: Derm; Immunology 14533

Gulf and Caribbean Fisheries Institute (GCFI), 266 Meeting St, Charleston, SC 29401
T: (803) 723-1050
Founded: 1948; Members: 950
Gen Secr: Melvin Goodwin
Focus: Fisheries
Periodical
Proceedings (annually) 14534

Gustav E von Grunebaum Centre for Near Eastern Studies, 405 Hilgard Av, POB 951480, Los Angeles, CA 90024-1480
T: (310) 825-1181; Fax: (310) 206-2406
Gen Secr: Irene Bierman
Focus: Geography 14535

Gypsy Lore Society (GLS), 5607 Greenleaf Rd, Cheverly, MD 20785
T: (301) 341-1261
Founded: 1977; Members: 250
Focus: Ethnology
Periodicals
Membership Directory (annually)
Newsletter (quarterly) 14536

Hagop Kevorkian Centre for Near Eastern Studies, New York, c/o New York University, 50 Washington Square S, Rm 400, New York, NY 10012
T: (212) 998-8877; Fax: (212) 995-4144
Focus: Geography 14537

Haiku Society of America (HSA), c/o Japan Society, Japan House, 333 E 47 St, New York, NY 10017
T: (212) 348-8614
Founded: 1968; Members: 600
Pres: Bruce Ross
Focus: Lit 14538

Haitian Coalition on Aids (HCA), 50 Court St, Ste 605, Brooklyn, NY 11201
T: (718) 855-0972; Fax: (718) 855-0972
Founded: 1983; Members: 70
Focus: Immunology 14539

Handwriting Analysts – International (HAI), 1504 W 29 ST, Davenport, IA 52804
T: (319) 391-7350
Founded: 1964; Members: 80
Focus: Graphology 14540

Harry S. Truman Library Institute for National and International Affairs, US 24 Hwy and Delaware St, Independence, MO 64050-1798
T: (816) 833-1400; Fax: (816) 833-4368
Founded: 1957; Members: 2000
Gen Secr: Larry J. Hackman
Focus: Int'l Relat; Poli Sci
Periodical
Newsletter (quarterly) 14541

Harvard Environmental Law Society (ELS), c/o Harvard Law School, 201 Austin, Cambridge, MA 02138
T: (617) 495-3125
Founded: 1945; Members: 250
Focus: Ecology 14542

Harvey Society (HS), c/o Dept of Cell Biology and Anatomy, Mount Sinai School of Medicine, 1 Gusgaze Levy Pl, New York, NY 10029
T: (212) 241-1505; Fax: (212) 860-1174
Founded: 1905; Members: 1600
Gen Secr: Dr. Paul Lazerow
Focus: Lit; Med
Periodical
Harvey Lectures (annually) 14543

Haunt Hunters (HH), c/o Philip Goodwilling, 509 Big Horn Basin Ct, Saint Louis, MO 63011
T: (314) 458-3739; Fax: (314) 458-2779
Founded: 1965; Members: 300
Gen Secr: Gordon J. Hoener
Focus: Psych 14544

Hazardous Materials Advisory Council (HMAC), 1101 Vermont Av NW, Ste 301, Washington, DC 20005
T: (202) 289-4550; Fax: (202) 289-4074
Gen Secr: Jonathan Collom
Focus: Ecology 14545

Headmasters Association (HA), c/o Agnes Underwood, National Cathedral School, Mount Saint Alban, Washington, DC 20016
T: (202) 537-6353; Fax: (202) 537-5625
Founded: 1893; Members: 263
Gen Secr: Agnes Underwood
Focus: Educ
Periodical
Membership List (annually) 14546

Health Industry Business Communications Council (HIBCC), 5110 N 40 St, Ste 250, Phoenix, AZ 85018
T: (602) 381-1091; Fax: (602) 381-1093
Founded: 1984; Members: 1000
Focus: Computer & Info Sci 14547

Health Optimizing Institute (HOI), POB 1233, Del Mar, CA 92014
T: (619) 481-7751
Founded: 1978
Focus: Public Health 14548

Health Physics Society (HPS), 1313 Dolley Madison Blvd, Ste 402, McLean, VA 22101-3926
T: (703) 790-1745; Fax: (703) 790-9063
Founded: 1956; Members: 6890
Gen Secr: Richard J. Burk Jr.
Focus: Public Health; Physics
Periodicals
Health Physics Journal (monthly)
Membership Handbook (annually)
Newsletter (monthly) 14549

Health Sciences Communications Association (HESCA), c/o Eastern Brothers Service, 1 Wedgewood Dr, Jewitt City, CT 06351
T: (203) 376-5915; Fax: (203) 376-6621
Founded: 1956; Members: 400
Focus: Public Health
Periodicals
Feedback (bi-monthly)
Journal of Biocommunications (quarterly) . 14550

Health Sciences Consortium (HSC), 201 Silver Cedar Ct, Chapel Hill, NC 27514
T: (919) 942-8731; Fax: (919) 942-3689
Founded: 1971; Members: 1000
Focus: Public Health 14551

Hear Center, 301 E Del Mar Blvd, Pasadena, CA 91101
T: (818) 796-2016; Fax: (818) 796-2320
Founded: 1954
Gen Secr: Josephine F. Wilson
Focus: Otorhinolaryngology
Periodical
The Listener (bi-monthly) 14552

Hearing International, c/o Dept of Audiology – MSU, 101 Wilson Rd, Rm 115, East Lansing, MI 48824-1220
T: (517) 432-1264; E-Mail: kapur@msu.edu; Fax: (517) 353-3176
Gen Secr: Y. P. Kapur
Focus: Otorhinolaryngology 14553

Heart Disease Research Foundation (HDRF), 50 Court St, Rm 306, Brooklyn, NY 11201
T: (718) 649-6210
Founded: 1962
Focus: Cardiol 14554

Hegel Society of America (HSA), c/o Dept of Philosophy, Loyola University of Chicago, Chicago, IL 60626
T: (312) 508-3477; E-Mail: acollins@wpo.it.luc.edu
Founded: 1969; Members: 500
Gen Secr: Ardis B. Collins
Focus: Philos
Periodical
The Owl of Minerva (semi-annually) . . 14555

Helen Kollegg Institute for International Studies, c/o University of Notre Dame, 216 Hesburgh Center of Int Studies, Notre Dame, IN 46556-5677
T: (219) 631-6580; Fax: (219) 631-6717
Focus: Poli Sci 14556

Hemingway Society (HS), c/o Prof. Linda Wagner-Martin, Dept of English, University of North Carolina, CB No 3520, Chapel Hill, NC 27599-3520
T: (919) 962-8765
Founded: 1980; Members: 600
Pres: Prof. Linda Wagner-Martin
Focus: Lit 14557

Henry A. Wallace Institute for Alternative Agriculture (IAA), 9200 Edmonston Rd, Ste 117, Greenbelt, MD 20770
T: (301) 441-8777; E-Mail: Hawiaa@access.digex.net
Founded: 1983; Members: 2000
Gen Secr: I. Garth Youngberg
Focus: Agri 14558

Herbert Hoover Presidential Library Association (HHPLA), POB 696, West Branch, IA 52358
T: (319) 643-5327
Founded: 1954
Focus: Libraries & Bk Sci
Periodical
Newsletter (quarterly) 14559

Herpes Resource Center – American Social Health Association, POB 13827, Research Triangle Park, NC 27709
T: (919) 361-8488; Fax: (919) 361-8425
Founded: 1979; Members: 28000
Gen Secr: Melissa Peacock
Focus: Med 14560

Herpetologists' League, c/o Dept of Biological Sciences, East Tennessee State University, POB 70726, Johnson City, TN 37614-0726
T: (615) 929-6929; E-Mail: PylesR@etsuarts.East-Tenn-St.edu; Fax: (615) 929-5958
Founded: 1936; Members: 2000
Gen Secr: Dr. Rebecca A. Pyles
Focus: Zoology
Periodicals
Herpetologica (quarterly)
Herpetological Monographs 14561

High Frontier (HF), 2800 Shirlington Rd, Ste 405A, Arlington, VA 22206
T: (703) 671-4111; Fax: (703) 931-6432
Founded: 1982
Focus: Aero 14562

Higher Education Consortium for Urban Affairs (HECUA), c/o Hamline University, 1536 Hewitt Av, Saint Paul, MN 55104
T: (612) 646-8832; E-Mail: hecuae@alex.stkate.edu; Fax: (612) 659-9421
Founded: 1971; Members: 19
Gen Secr: Amy Sunderland
Focus: Educ 14563

Higher Education Panel (HEP), c/o Elaine El-Khawas, American Council on Education, 1 Dupont Circle, Washington, DC 20036
T: (202) 939-9450; Fax: (202) 833-4760
Founded: 1971; Members: 666
Gen Secr: Elaine El-Khawas
Focus: Educ 14564

Higher Education Resource Services/New England (HERS), c/o Wellesley College, Waban House, Wellesley, MA 02181-8259
T: (617) 283-2529; E-Mail: Sknawles@Wellesley.ed; Fax: (617) 283-3645
Founded: 1972
Gen Secr: Susan Knowles
Focus: Educ 14565

Highway Users Federation for Safety and Mobility (HUF), 1776 Massachussets Av NW, Washington, DC 20036
T: (202) 857-1200; Fax: (202) 857-1220
Founded: 1970; Members: 400
Focus: Safety 14566

Himalayan International Institute of Yoga Science and Philosophy of the U.S.A., RR 1, Box 400, Honesdale, PA 18431
T: (717) 253-5551; Fax: (717) 253-9078
Founded: 1971; Members: 2500
Focus: Philos; Psych
Periodicals
Dawn (quarterly)
Himalayan Institute Quarterly (quarterly)
Research Bulletin (irregularly) 14567

Hispanic Association of Colleges and Universities (HACU), 4204 Gardenale St, Ste 216, San Antonio, TX 78229
T: (210) 692-3805; Fax: (210) 692-0823
Gen Secr: Diana Marin
Focus: Educ 14568

Hispanic Institute (HI), 612 W 116 St, New York, NY 10027
T: (212) 854-4187
Founded: 1920; Members: 189
Focus: Ethnology
Periodical
Revista Hispánica Moderna (semi-annually) 14569

Hispanic Society of America (HSA), 613 W 155 St, New York, NY 10032
T: (212) 926-2234
Founded: 1904; Members: 400
Gen Secr: Mitchell A, Codding
Focus: Hist; Arts; Lit; Ling
Periodical
Hispanic Review (quarterly) 14570

Histadruth Ivrith of America (HIA), 47 W 34 St, New York, NY 10001
T: (212) 629-9443
Founded: 1916; Members: 10000
Focus: Ling
Periodicals
Hadoar (weekly)
Lamishpacha (monthly) 14571

Histochemical Society (HCS), 4 Barlows Landing Rd, Ste 8, Pocasset, MA 02559
T: (508) 563-1155; Fax: (508) 563-1211
Founded: 1950; Members: 550
Gen Secr: Lawrence M. Maser
Focus: Chem
Periodicals
The Journal of Histochemistry and Cytochemistry (monthly)
Membership Roster (annually) 14572

Historical Committee of the Mennonite Church (MHC), 1700 S Main St, Goshen, IN 46526
T: (219) 535-7477; Fax: (219) 535-7660
Members: 8
Focus: Hist; Rel & Theol
Periodical
Mennonite Historical Bulletin (quarterly) . 14573

Historical Society of Washington, DC (HSWDC), 1307 New Hampshire Av NW, Washington, DC 20036
T: (202) 785-2068
Founded: 1894; Members: 1800
Focus: Hist
Periodicals
Calendar of Events (quarterly)
Newsletter (3 times annually)
Records of Columbia Historical Society (semi-annually) 14574

History of Dermatology Society (HDS), 1819 J.F. Kennedy Blvd, Ste 465, Philadelphia, PA 19103
T: (215) 563-8333
Founded: 1973; Members: 120
Focus: Derm 14575

History of Economics Society (HES), c/o Dept of Economics, University of Richmond, Richmond, VA 23173
T: (804) 289-8566
Founded: 1973; Members: 750
Gen Secr: Prof. J. Patrick Raines
Focus: Econ
Periodical
Bulletin (semi-annually) 14576

History of Education Society (HES), c/o College of Education, University of Oregon, Eugene, OR 97403
T: (503) 346-1367; Fax: (503) 346-5174
Founded: 1960; Members: 450
Gen Secr: C.H. Edson
Focus: Hist; Educ
Periodical
History of Education (quarterly) 14577

History of Science Society (HSS), c/o University of Washington, POB 351330, Seattle, WA 98195-1330
T: (206) 543-9366; Fax: (206) 685-9544
Founded: 1924; Members: 3000
Pres: Frederick Gregory; Gen Secr: Keith R. Benson
Focus: Hist; Sci
Periodicals
HSS Newsletter (quarterly)
Isis (quarterly)
Osiris (annually)
Resource Letters 14578

Hohenzollern Society (HS), 82 Atlantic St, Keyport, NJ 07735
T: (908) 739-1799
Founded: 1983
Focus: Hist 14579

Holistic Dental Association (HDA), 4801 Richmond Sq, Oklahoma City, OK 73118
T: (405) 840-5600
Founded: 1980; Members: 200
Pres: Dr. Paul Plowman
Focus: Dent 14580

Holistic Health Havens (HHH), 5020 Spring Mountain Rd, No 2, Las Vegas, NV 89102-8704
T: (702) 873-4542
Founded: 1980
Pres: Dr. Joseph M. Kadans
Focus: Public Health 14581

Home Study International, c/o Griggs University, 12501 Old Columbia Pike, Silver Springs, MD 20904
T: (301) 680-6570; Fax: (301) 680-5157
Gen Secr: Joseph E. Gurubatham
Focus: Home Econ 14582

Homeopathic Council for Research and Education (HCRE), 50 Park Av, New York, NY 10016
T: (212) 684-2290
Founded: 1965; Members: 5
Gen Secr: William Bergman
Focus: Homeopathy 14583

Horace Mann League of the U.S.A. (HML), POB 252, Summit, NJ 07902
T: (402) 554-3443; E-Mail: McKay@coe.unomaha.edu; Fax: (402) 554-2722
Founded: 1922; Members: 500
Gen Secr: Dr. Jack McKay
Focus: Educ
Periodical
Newsletter 14584

Horatio Alger Society (HAS), 585 E Saint Andrews Dr, Media, PA 19063
T: (610) 566-5917
Founded: 1961; Members: 273
Gen Secr: Robert E. Kasper
Focus: Lit
Periodical
The Newsboy (bi-monthly) 14585

Horticultural Research Institute (HRI), 1250 I St NW, Ste 500, Washington, DC 20005
T: (202) 789-2900; Fax: (202) 789-1893
Founded: 1962; Members: 300
Focus: Hort 14586

Hospital Research and Educational Trust (HRET), 1 N Franklin, Chicago, IL 60606
T: (312) 422-2600
Founded: 1944
Gen Secr: Deborah Bohr
Focus: Med
Periodicals
Economic Trends (5 times annually)
Health Services Research (bi-monthly) . 14587

House Ear Institute (HEI), 2100 W Third St, Los Angeles, CA 90057
T: (213) 483-4431; Fax: (213) 413-6739
Founded: 1946
Focus: Otorhinolaryngology
Periodicals
Oto Review (quarterly)
Research Bulletin (semi-annually) 14588

Human Biology Association (HBA), c/o Dr. Lynnette E. Leidy, Dept of Anthropology, University of Massachusetts at Amherst, Machmer Hall, Amherst, MA 01003-4805
T: (413) 545-1379; E-Mail: leidy@anthro.umas.edu; Fax: (413) 545-9494
Founded: 1974
Gen Secr: Lynnette E. Leidy
Focus: Bio 14589

Human Factors and Ergonomics Society (HFES), POB 1369, Santa Monica, CA 90406-1369
T: (310) 394-1811; E-Mail: 72133.1474@comouserve.com; Fax: (310) 394-2410
Founded: 1957; Members: 5200
Gen Secr: Lynn Strother
Focus: Physiology; Eng; Psych
Periodicals
Bulletin (monthly)
Directory & Yearbook (annually)
Human Factors (bi-monthly)
Proceedings of The Human Factors Society (annually) 14590

Human Lactation Center (HLC), 666 Sturges Hwy, Westport, CT 06880
T: (203) 259-5995; Fax: (203) 259-7667
Founded: 1975; Members: 1000
Focus: Public Health
Periodical
The Lactation Review 14591

Human Relations Area Files (HRAF), 755 Prospect St, New Haven, CT 06511
T: (203) 764-9401; E-Mail: hrafmem@minerva.cis.yale.edu; Fax: (203) 764-9404
Founded: 1949; Members: 300
Pres: Melvin Ember
Focus: Anthro; Geography; Sociology; Psych
Periodical
Behavior Science Research: HRAF Journal ot Comparative Studies (annually) 14592

Human Resource Certification Institute, 606 N Washington St, Alexandria, VA 22314
T: (703) 548-3440; Fax: (703) 836-0367
Founded: 1975; Members: 7500
Focus: Business Admin 14593

Human Resource Planning Society (HRPS), 317 Madison Av, Ste 1509, New York, NY 10017
T: (212) 490-6387; Fax: (212) 682-6851
Founded: 1977; Members: 2500
Gen Secr: Noel P. Innocenti
Focus: Business Admin 14594

Human Resources Research Organization (HumRRO), 66 Canal Center Pl, Ste 400, Alexandria, VA 22314
T: (703) 549-3611; Fax: (703) 549-9025
Founded: 1951
Focus: Sociology
Periodical
Bibliography 14595

Huntington's Disease Society of America (HDSA), 140 W 22 St, New York, NY 10011-2420
T: (212) 242-1968; Fax: (212) 243-2443
Founded: 1986; Members: 45000
Focus: Neurology
Periodical
The Matter (quarterly) 14596

Hydroponic Society of America (HSA), POB 3075, San Ramon, CA 94583
T: (510) 743-9605; Fax: (510) 743-9302
Founded: 1978; Members: 600
Gen Secr: Patty Bates
Focus: Hort
Periodicals
Directory of Suppliers (irregularly)
The Hydroponic/Soilless Grower (bi-monthly)
Proceedings (annually) 14597

IAHS International Commission on Continental Erosion (ICCE), USDA-ARS, Southern Plains Area Office, 7607 Eastmark Dr, Ste 230, College Station, TX 77840
T: (409) 260-9346; Fax: (409) 260-9415
Gen Secr: Dr. C. A. Onstad
Focus: Geology 14598

IAHS International Commission on Groundwater (ICGW), c/o Dept of Applied Earth Sciences, Stanford University, Stanford, CA 94305-2225
T: (415) 725-2950; E-Mail: gorelick@danube.stanford.edu; Fax: (415) 725-0979

Gen Secr: Dr. Steven M. Gorelick
Focus: Water Res 14599

IAHS International Commission on Snow and Ice (ICSI), c/o US Geological Survey, POB 25046, ms-412 Denver, CO 80225
T: (360) 696-7582; E-Mail: andrew@usgs.gov; Fax: (360) 696-7866
Gen Secr: Andrew G. Fountain
Focus: Geophys 14600

IAHS International Commission on Water Quality (ICWQ), c/o US Geological Survey, Water Resources Division, Peachtree Business Center, 3039 Amwiler Rd, Ste 130, Atlanta, GA 30360-2824
T: (404) 903-9145; Fax: (404) 903-9199
Gen Secr: Dr. Norman E. Peters
Focus: Water Res 14601

IAHS International Committee on Atmosphere – Soil – Vegetation Relations (ICASVR), c/o University of New Hampshire, Institute for the Study of the Earth, Oceans and Space, Durham, NH 03824
T: (603) 862-1792; Fax: (603) 862-0188
Gen Secr: Dr. Ch. Vorosmarty
Focus: Geology; Geophys 14602

IAHS International Committee on Remote Sensing and Data Transmission (ICRSDT), c/o USDA ARS Hydrology Lab, BARC-W Bldg 007, Beltsville, MD 20705
T: (301) 504-7490; Fax: (301) 504-8931
Gen Secr: Jerry C. Ritchie
Focus: Geology 14603

IASPEI Commission on Controlled Source Seismology (CSS), c/o US Geological Survey, Mail Stop 977, 345 Middlefield Rd, Menlo Park, CA 94025
T: (415) 329-4765; E-Mail: mooney@andreas.wr.usgs.gov; Fax: (415) 329-5163
Gen Secr: Dr. W.D. Mooney
Focus: Geology 14604

IASPEI Commission on Earthquake Hazard and Prediction, c/o Geophysical Institut, University of Alaska, Fairbanks, AK 99775-0800
T: (907) 474-5529; E-Mail: max@gaia.gi.alaska.edu; Fax: (907) 474-7290
Gen Secr: Prof. M. Wyss
Focus: Geology 14605

IASPEI Commission on Practice, c/o US Geological Survey, MS 967, POB 25046, DFC, Denver, CO 80225
T: (303) 273-8415; E-Mail: sipkin@gldfs.cr.usgs.gov; Fax: (303) 273-8450
Gen Secr: Dr. S.A. Sipkin
Focus: Geology 14606

IASPEI Commission on the International Decade of Natural Disaster Reduction (IDNDR), c/o Dept of Geology and Geophysics, Univ. ov California, Berkeley, CA 94720
T: (510) 642-7030; Fax: (510) 845-4816
Gen Secr: Prof. B.A. Bolt
Focus: Geology 14607

IASPEI Committee on Education, c/o US Geological Survey, Mail Stop 977, 345 Middlefield Rd, Menlo Park, CA 94025
T: (415) 329-4754; E-Mail: whklee@ix.netcom.com; Fax: (415) 329-5163
Gen Secr: Dr. W.H.K. Lee
Focus: Educ 14608

IASPEI/IACVEI Committee on Volcano Seismology, c/o US Geological Survey, 345 Middlefield Rd, Mail Stop 977, Menlo Park, CA 94025
E-Mail: chouet@andreas.wr.usgs.gov
Gen Secr: Dr. B. Chouet
Focus: Geology 14609

IASPEI-IAVCEI Inter-Association Commission on Physical and Chemical Properties of Materials of the Earth's Interior, c/o Dept of Geosciences, Deike Building, Pennsylvania State University, University Park, PA 16802
T: (814) 865-2310; E-Mail: mack@geosc.psu.edu; Fax: (814) 863-7823
Gen Secr: Prof. Stephen J. Mackwell
Focus: Geology 14610

IAU Commission on Atomic and Molecular Data, c/o Center for Astrophysics, 60 Garden Str, Cambridge, MA 02138
T: (617) 495-4865; E-Mail: wparkinson@cfa.harvard.edu; Fax: (617) 495-7455
Gen Secr: Dr. W.H. Parkinson
Focus: Physics 14611

IAU Commission on Bioastronomy, c/o NASA Ames Research Centre, Seti Project, MS 244-11, Moffett Field, CA 94035-1000
T: (415) 604-5727; E-Mail: tarter@bkyast@berkeley.edu; Fax: (415) 968-5830
Gen Secr: Dr. J. C. Tarter
Focus: Astronomy 14612

IAU Commission on Double and Multiple Stars, c/o Astrometry Dept, US Naval Observatory, 3450 Massachusetts Av NW, Washington, DC 20392-5420
Gen Secr: Charles E. Worley
Focus: Astronomy 14613

IAU Commission on Exchange of Astronomers, NRAO, Edgemont Rd, Charlottesville, VA 22903
T: (804) 296-0233; E-Mail: mroberts@nrao.edu; Fax: (804) 296-0278
Gen Secr: Dr. M.S. Roberts
Focus: Astronomy 14614

IAU Commission on Galaxies, c/o Department of Physics, Univ. of California, Irvine, CA 92717
T: (714) 856-6948; E-Mail: vtrimble@uci.edu – astro.umd.edu; Fax: (714) 725-2174
Gen Secr: Dr. V.L. Trimble
Focus: Astronomy 14615

IAU Commission on Identificationand Protection of Observatory Sites, c/o University of Washington, Seattle, WA
Gen Secr: Dr. W. Sullivan
Focus: Astronomy 14616

IAU Commission on Physical Study of Comets, Minor Planets and Meteorites, c/o Dept of Astronomy, University of Maryland, College Park, MD 20742
T: (301) 405-6076
Gen Secr: M.F. A'Hearn
Focus: Astronomy 14617

IAU Commission on Positional Astronomy, c/o Astrometry Department, US Naval Observatory, 3450 Massachusetts Av NW, Washington, DC 20392-5420
T: (202) 762-1423; E-Mail: tec@sicon.usno.navy.mil
Gen Secr: Dr. Thomas E. Corbin
Focus: Astronomy 14618

IAU Commission on Positions and Motions of Minor Planets, Comets, Satellites, JPL, MS 301-150G, 4800 Oak Grove Dr, Pasadena, CA 91109
T: (818) 354-2127; E-Mail: donald.k.yeomans@jpl.nasa.gov; Fax: (818) 393-1159
Gen Secr: Dr. D.K. Yeomans
Focus: Astronomy 14619

IAU Commission on Space and High Energy Astrophysics, c/o Smithonian Astrophysical Observatory, Cambridge, MA
Gen Secr: Dr. Giovanni Fazio
Focus: Astrophys 14620

IAU Commission on Time, El Moreno Av, POB 8682, La Crescenta, CA 91214
T: (213) 648-7452; Fax: (213) 336-5076
Gen Secr: Dr. H.F. Fliegel
Focus: Physics 14621

IAVCEI Commission on Granites, c/o Department of Geology, Univ. of Maryland, College Park, MD 20742-4211
T: (301) 405-2783; E-Mail: candela@earthsun.umd.edu; Fax: (301) 314-9662
Gen Secr: P. A. Candela
Focus: Geology 14622

IAVCEI Commission on Large-Volume Basaltic Provinces, c/o Institute for Geophysics, Univ. of Texas at Austin, 8701 N Mopac Expressway, Austin, TX 78759-8397
T: (512) 471-0429; E-Mail: mikec@coffin.ig.utexas.edu; Fax: (512) 471-8844
Gen Secr: M. Coffin
Focus: Geology 14623

IAVCEI Commission on Remote Sensing, c/o Hawaii Institute of Geophysics and Planetology, Univ. of Hawaii, 2525 Correa Rd, Honolulu, HI 96822
T: (808) 956-3147; E-Mail: pmm@kahana.pgd.hawaii.edu; Fax: (808) 956-6322
Gen Secr: P.J. Mouginis-Mark
Focus: Geology 14624

IAVCEI Commission on Volcanism and the Earth's Atmosphere, c/o Department of Geology and Geophysics, University of Hawaii at Manoa, Honolulu, HI 96822
T: (808) 956-5996; E-Mail: self@soest.hawaii.edu; Fax: (808) 956-2538
Gen Secr: S. Self
Focus: Geology 14625

Iberian Latin American Society of Neuroradiology, c/o Massachusetts General Hospital, Boston, MA 02114-2696
T: (617) 726-8344; Fax: (617) 726-1037
Gen Secr: Dr. J.M. Taveras
Focus: Radiology 14626

ICOM International Committee for Documentation (CIDOC), c/o Getty Information Institute, Ste 1100, 401 Wilshire Blvd, Santa Monica, CA 90401-1455
T: (310) 451-6332; Fax: (310) 451-5570
Gen Secr: Patricia Young
Focus: Doc 14627

ICOM International Committee for Egyptology (CIPEG), c/o Dept of Ancient Egyptian, Nubian and Near Eastern Art, Museum of Fine Arts – Boston, 465 Huntington Av, Boston, MA 02115
T: (617) 267-9300; Fax: (617) 267-0280
Gen Secr: Rita E. Freed
Focus: Cultur Hist 14628

ICOM International Committee for Management (INTERCOM), c/o The Getty Conservation Institut, 1200 Getty Center Dr, Los Angeles, CA 90049-1694
T: (310) 440-7325; E-Mail: mtorre@getty.edu; Fax: (310) 440-7702
Gen Secr: Marta de la Torre
Focus: Arts 14629

ICOM International Committee for Museum Security (ICMS), c/o Official of Protection Services, Smithsonian Institution, 955 L'Enfant Plaza, Ste 7200, Washington, DC 20560
T: (202) 287-2585; E-Mail: ops1.liston@ic.si.edu; Fax: (202) 287-2589
Gen Secr: David Liston
Focus: Arts 14630

ICOM International Committee for Museums and Collections of Glass, c/o The Corning Museum of Glass, One Museum Way, Corning, NY 14830-2253
T: (607) 937-5371; Fax: (607) 937-3352
Gen Secr: Dr. Jutta Annette Bruhn
Focus: Arts 14631

ICOM International Committee on Exhibition Exchange (ICEE), c/o The Humanities Exchange, POB 1608, Largo, FL 34649
T: (813) 581-7328; Fax: (813) 585-6398
Gen Secr: Shirley Reiff Howarth
Focus: Arts 14632

ICSU Advisory Committee on the Environment (ACE), c/o Museum of Comparative Zoology, Harvard University, 26 Oxford St, Cambridge, MA 02138
T: (617) 495-2330; E-Mail: james_j_mccarthy@harvard.edu; Fax: (617) 495-0506
Gen Secr: Prof. James McCarthy
Focus: Ecology 14633

IEEE Control Systems Society, c/o Institute of Electrical and Electronics Engineers, 345 E 47 St, New York, NY 10017
T: (212) 705-7900; Fax: (212) 705-4929
Members: 9820
Focus: Electric Eng
Periodicals
Control Systems Magazine (bi-monthly)
Transactions on Automatic Control (monthly)
. . . . 14634

IEEE Ultrasonics, Ferroelectrics and Frequency Control Society (UFFCS), c/o Gary K. Montress, Raytheon Research Div, 131 Spring St, Lexington, MA 02173
T: (617) 860-3053; Fax: (617) 860-3194
Members: 2352
Pres: Harry L. Salvo Jr.
Focus: Electric Eng
Periodical
Transactions on Ultrasonics, Ferroelecrics and Frequency Control (bi-monthly) 14635

IGU Commission on Natural Hazards Studies, c/o Department of Geosciences, Oregon State University, Corvallis, OR 97331-5506
T: (503) 737-1208; E-Mail: rosenfec@bcc.orst.edu; Fax: (503) 737-1200
Gen Secr: Dr. Charles Rosenfeld
Focus: Geophys 14636

Illuminating Engineering Society of North America (IESNA), 120 Wall St, New York, NY 10005
Founded: 1906; Members: 10000
Gen Secr: William Hanley
Focus: Eng; Electric Eng
Periodicals
Journal of the I.E.S. (semi-annually)
Lighting Design + Application Magazine (monthly)
. . . . 14637

Immigration History Society (IHS), c/o Roger Daniels, Dept of History, University of Cincinnati, Cincinnati, OH 45221
T: (513) 556-2144; E-Mail: alexanje@uebeh.san.uc.edu; Fax: (513) 556-7901
Founded: 1965; Members: 830
Pres: Roger Daniels
Focus: Hist
Periodicals
Immigration History Newsletter (semi-annually)
Journal of American Ethnic History (semi-annually)
. . . . 14638

Independent Association of Questioned Document Examiners (IAQDE), 403 W Washington, Red Oak, IA 51566
T: (712) 623-9130
Founded: 1969; Members: 175
Focus: Law 14639

Independent Citizens Research Foundation for the Study of Degenerative Diseases (ICRFSDD), POB 97, Ardsley, NY 10502
T: (914) 478-1862
Founded: 1957
Focus: Med 14640

Independent Computer Consultants Association (ICCA), 11131 S Towne Sq, Ste F, Saint Louis, MO 63123
T: (314) 892-1675; Fax: (314) 487-1345
Founded: 1976; Members: 1700
Focus: Computer & Info Sci
Periodical
The Independent (bi-monthly) 14641

Independent Educational Services (IES), 353 Nassau St, Princeton, NJ 08542
T: (609) 921-6195
Founded: 1968
Focus: Educ
Periodicals
Ideas Newsletter (quarterly)
TREE (5 times annually) 14642

Independent Research Libraries Association (IRLA), c/o Glen Porter, Hagley Museum and Library, POB 3630, Wilmington, DE 19807
T: (302) 658-2400; Fax: (302) 658-5021
Founded: 1972; Members: 15
Pres: Werner Gundersheimer
Focus: Libraries & Bk Sci 14643

Independent Scholars of Asia (ISA), 2321 Russell, Berkeley, CA 94705
T: (510) 849-3791
Founded: 1977; Members: 186
Focus: Ethnology
Periodicals
Newsletter (3 times annually)
Proceedings (annually)
Trance and Healing in Southeast Asia Today
. . . . 14644

Indian Dental Association U.S.A. (IDA), 146-02 89 Av, Jamaica, NY 11435
T: (718) 523-8438
Founded: 1983; Members: 345
Focus: Dent 14645

Indian Educators Federation (IEF), POB 2020, Farmington, NM 87499
T: (505) 327-7733; Fax: (505) 327-9558
Founded: 1967; Members: 400
Gen Secr: Patrick Baxstrom
Focus: Educ 14646

Indian Law Resource Center, 602 N Ewing St, Helena, MT 59601
T: (406) 449-2006; Fax: (406) 449-2031
Gen Secr: Robert T. Coulter
Focus: Law 14647

Indians Into Medicine (INMED), c/o School of Medicine, University of North Dakota, 501 N Columbia Rd, Grand Forks, ND 58203
T: (701) 777-3037; Fax: (701) 777-3277
Founded: 1973
Focus: Med 14648

Industrial Mathematics Society (IMS), POB 159, Roseville, MI 48066
T: (313) 771-0403
Founded: 1949; Members: 100
Pres: Leonard G. Johnson; Gen Secr: Leo S. Parry
Focus: Math
Periodical
Industrial Mathematics (semi-annually) . . 14649

Industrial Relations Research Association (IRRA), c/o University of Wisconsin, 4233 Social Science Bldg, 1180 Observatory Dr, Madison, WI 53706
T: (608) 262-2762; E-Mail: kbhutchi@facstaff.wisc.edu; Fax: (608) 265-4591
Founded: 1947; Members: 4200
Gen Secr: Kay B. Hutchinson
Focus: Business Admin; Poli Sci; Sociology; Econ
Periodicals
Annual Research Volume (annually)
Newsletter (quarterly)
Proceedings of IRRA Annual Meeting (annually)
Proceedings of IRRA Spring Meeting (annually)
. . . . 14650

Industrial Research Institute (IRI), 1550 M St NW, Ste 1100, Washington, DC 20005-1708
T: (202) 296-8811; Fax: (202) 776-0756
Founded: 1938; Members: 270
Gen Secr: Charles F. Larson
Focus: Eng
Periodicals
Annual Report (annually)
Research Management (bi-monthly) . . . 14651

Infectious Diseases Society of America (IDSA), 1200 19 St NW, Ste 300, Washington, DC 20036-2401
T: (202) 857-1139; Fax: (202) 223-4579
Founded: 1963; Members: 4500
Gen Secr: Vincent T. Andriole
Focus: Immunology
Periodicals
Journal of Infectious Diseases (monthly)
Membership Roster (semi-annually)
Reviews of Infectious Diseases (bi-monthly)
. . . . 14652

Inland Bird Banding Association (IBBA), Rte 2, Box 26, Wisner, NE 68791
T: (402) 529-6679
Founded: 1922; Members: 1000
Focus: Ornithology
Periodicals
Inland Bird Banding Newsletter (quarterly)
North American Bird Bander (quarterly) . 14653

Inroads, 10 S Broadway, Saint Louis, MO 63102
T: (314) 241-7488; Fax: (314) 241-9325
Founded: 1970
Pres: Charles I. Story
Focus: Econ 14654

Institute Control Theory, Reality Therapy and Quality Management (ICTRTQM), 22024 Lassen St, No 118, Chatsworth, CA 91311
T: (818) 700-8000; Fax: (818) 700-0555
Founded: 1967
Pres: William Glasser
Focus: Psych
Periodicals
Journal of Reality Therapy (semi-annually)
Newsletter (quarterly) 14655

Institute for Advanced Research in Asian Science and Medicine (IARASM), POB 67336, Chestnut Hill, MA 02167
T: (617) 739-1182; Fax: (617) 739-1183
Founded: 1972
Gen Secr: Dr. John J. Kao
Focus: Med; Sci 14656

Institute for Advanced Studies in the Theatre Arts (IASTA), c/o John D. Mitchell, 311 W 57 St, POB 399, New York, NY 10019-3101
T: (212) 581-3133; Fax: (212) 581-3133
Founded: 1958; Members: 200
Pres: John D. Mitchell
Focus: Perf Arts 14657

Institute for Advanced Studies of World Religions (IASWR), RD 2, Rte 301, Carmel, NY 10512
T: (914) 225-1445; Fax: (914) 225-1485
Founded: 1970
Focus: Rel & Theol
Periodicals
Asian Religious Studies Information
Buddhist Text Information
IASWR Conference Proceedings 14658

Institute for American Indian Studies (IAIS), 38 Curtis St, POB 1260, Washington, CT 06793-0260
T: (203) 868-0518; Fax: (203) 868-1649
Founded: 1971; Members: 1350
Focus: Archeol
Periodicals
Artifacts (5 times annually)
Research Report (annually) 14659

Institute for Biblical Research (IBR), c/o Dr. Bastiaan Van Elderen, 8203 Radcliffe Circle Dr SE, Grand Rapids, MI 49546
T: (616) 957-0876
Founded: 1973; Members: 350
Pres: Dr. Bastiaan Van Elderen
Focus: Rel & Theol 14660

Institute for Certification of Computer Professionals (ICCP), 2200 E Devon Av, Ste 268, Des Plaines, IL 60018
T: (312) 299-4227; Fax: (312) 299-4280
Founded: 1973; Members: 14
Focus: Computer & Info Sci 14661

Institute for Childhood Resources (INICR), 220 Montgomery St, San Francisco, CA 94104
T: (415) 864-1169
Founded: 1975
Gen Secr: Dr. Stevanne Auerbach
Focus: Educ 14662

Institute for Community Design Analysis (ICDA), 66 Clover Dr, Great Neck, NY 11021
T: (516) 773-4727; Fax: (516) 482-5254
Founded: 1974
Focus: Archit 14663

Institute for Defense Analyses (IDA), 1801 N Beauregard, Alexandria, VA 22311
T: (703) 845-2300; Fax: (703) 845-2588
Founded: 1956
Focus: Military Sci 14664

Institute for Development of Educational Activities (IDEA), 259 Regency Ridge, Dayton, OH 45459
T: (513) 434-6969; Fax: (513) 434-5203
Founded: 1965
Focus: Educ 14665

Institute for Econometric Research (IER), 3471 N Federal Hwy, Fort Lauderdale, FL 33306
T: (305) 563-9000; Fax: (305) 563-9003
Founded: 1971; Members: 1500
Focus: Stats; Econ
Periodicals
Income and Safety (monthly)
The Insiders (bi-weekly)
Market Logic (bi-weekly)
Mutual Fund Forecaster (monthly)
New Issues (monthly) 14666

Institute for Economic Analysis (IEA), 508 Thayer Av, Silver Springs, MD 20910
T: (301) 588-4569
Founded: 1974
Focus: Econ
Periodical
Pocket Charts (monthly) 14667

Institute for Educational Leadership (IEL), 1001 Connecticut Av NW, Ste 310, Washington, DC 20036
T: (202) 822-8405
Founded: 1971
Focus: Educ 14668

Institute for Expressive Analysis (IEA), c/o Robert Wolf, 27 W 96 St, No 1A, New York, NY 10036
T: (212) 362-5085; Fax: (212) 760-0287
Founded: 1976; Members: 64
Gen Secr: Robert Wolf
Focus: Therapeutics
Periodical
Journal (annually) 14669

Institute for Fluitronics Education, POB 106, Elm Grove, WI 53122-0106
T: (414) 782-0410; Fax: (414) 786-0419
Founded: 1971
Focus: Educ 14670

Institute for Food and Development Policy (IFDP), 398 60 St, Oakland, CA 94618-1212
T: (510) 654-4400; E-Mail: foodfirst@igc.apc.org;
Fax: (510) 654-4551
Founded: 1975; Members: 17000
Gen Secr: Peter Rosset
Focus: Sociology; Econ; Nutrition . . . 14671

Institute for Gravitational Strain Pathology (IGSP), POB 526, Rangeley, ME 04970
T: (207) 864-5511
Founded: 1957
Focus: Pathology 14672

Institute for Hospital Clinical Nursing Education (IHCNE), c/o American Hospital Association Center for Nursing, 840 N Lake Shore Dr, Chicago, IL 60611
T: (312) 280-6432; Fax: (312) 280-5995
Founded: 1967; Members: 165
Focus: Adult Educ; Med
Periodical
The Assembly Communique (quarterly) . 14673

Institute for Intercultural Studies (IIS), 165 E 72 St, Ste 1B, New York, NY 10021
T: (212) 737-1011
Founded: 1943; Members: 6
Focus: Hist 14674

Institute for Labor and Mental Health (ILMH), 3137 Telegraph Av, Oakland, CA 94609
T: (510) 653-6166
Founded: 1977; Members: 50
Focus: Psychiatry
Periodicals
Directory
Occupational Stress (bi-monthly) . . . 14675

Institute for Mediterranean Affairs (IMA), 1420 Walnut St, Ste 200, Philadelphia, PA 19102
T: (215) 545-4800; Fax: (215) 545-4810
Founded: 1957; Members: 250
Gen Secr: Jack Yampolsky
Focus: Poli Sci
Periodical
Mediterranean Survey (irregularly) . . . 14676

Institute for Palestine Studies (IPS), 3501 M St NW, Washington, DC 20007
T: (202) 342-3990; Fax: (202) 342-3927
Founded: 1963; Members: 40
Focus: Hist; Poli Sci
Periodicals
Journal of Palestine Studies (quarterly)
Revue d'Etudes Palestiniennes (quarterly) 14677

Institute for Philosophy and Public Policy (IPPP), c/o University of Maryland, College Park, MD 20742
T: (301) 405-4753; Fax: (301) 314-9346
Founded: 1976
Gen Secr: William Galston
Focus: Poli Sci; Philos
Periodical
Report from the Institute for Philosophy and Public Policy (quarterly) 14678

Institute for Policy Studies (IPS), 1601 Connecticut Av NW, Washington, DC 20009
T: (202) 234-9382; Fax: (202) 387-7915
Founded: 1963
Gen Secr: Robert L. Borosage
Focus: Sociology; Philos; Sci; Hist; Soc Sci
. . . . 14679

Institute for Psychohistory (IP), 140 Riverside Dr, New York, NY 10024
T: (212) 799-2294; Fax: (212) 799-2294
Founded: 1976; Members: 50
Gen Secr: Lloyd deMause
Focus: Hist; Psych 14680

Institute for Public Relations Research and Education (IPRRE), c/o University of Florida, POB 118400, Gainesville, FL 32611-8400
T: (352) 392-0280; E-Mail: iprre@grove.ufl.edu;
Fax: (352) 846-1122
Founded: 1956
Pres: John W. Felton
Focus: Educ 14681

Institute for Rational-Emotive Therapy (IRET), 45 E 65 St, New York, NY 10021
T: (212) 535-0822
Founded: 1968
Focus: Therapeutics; Psych
Periodical
Journal of Rational-Emotive Therapy (semi-annually) 14682

Institute for Research in Hypnosis and Psychotherapy (IRHP), 1991 Broadway, Apt 188, New York, NY 10023
T: (212) 874-5290; Fax: (212) 238-1422
Founded: 1954
Focus: Psych
Periodical
Morton Prince Digest of Hypnotherapy and Hypnoanalysis (annually) 14683

Institute for Responsive Education (IRE), 605 Commonwealth Av, Boston, MA 02215
T: (617) 353-3309; Fax: (617) 353-8444
Founded: 1973
Focus: Educ
Periodical
Equity and Choice (3 times annually) . 14684

Institute for Social Research (ISR), c/o Robert B. Zajoni, University of Michigan, POB 1248, Ann Arbor, MI 48106
T: (313) 764-8363; Fax: (313) 764-2377
Founded: 1948
Gen Secr: Marlene Smith
Focus: Poli Sci; Sociology; Econ; Psych 14685

Institute for Southern Studies (ISS), POB 531, Durham, NC 27702
T: (919) 419-8311; Fax: (919) 419-8315
Founded: 1970; Members: 8000
Focus: Hist 14686

Institute for Studies in American Music (ISAM), c/o Conservatory of Music, Brooklyn College, Brooklyn, NY 11210
T: (718) 780-5655; Fax: (718) 951-6140
Founded: 1971; Members: 3900
Focus: Music
Periodical
ISAM Newsletter (semi-annually) 14687

Institute for the Development of Emotional and Life Skills (IDEALS), 4400 East-West Hwy, Ste 28, Bethesda, MD 20814
T: (301) 986-1479; Fax: (301) 699-8835
Founded: 1972; Members: 12
Gen Secr: Dr. William Nordling
Focus: Public Health 14688

Institute for the Development of Indian Law (IDIL), c/o School of Law, Oklahoma City University, 2501 N Blackwelder, Oklahoma City, OK 73106
T: (405) 521-5188
Founded: 1971
Gen Secr: K.K. Kickingbird
Focus: Law
Periodical
American Indian Journal (quarterly) . . . 14689

Institute for the Future (IF), 2744 Sand Hill Rd, Menlo Park, CA 94025-7020
T: (415) 854-6322; Fax: (415) 854-7850
Founded: 1968
Focus: Futurology 14690

Institute for the Study of Human Knowledge (ISHK), POB 176, Los Altos, CA 94023
T: (415) 948-9428
Founded: 1969
Focus: Sci 14691

Institute for the Study of Man (ISM), 1133 13 St NW, No C-2, Washington, DC 20005
T: (202) 371-2700; Fax: (202) 371-1523
Founded: 1975
Gen Secr: Roger Pearson
Focus: Anthro
Periodical
Journal of Indo-European Studies (quarterly)
. . . . 14692

Institute for Theological Encounter with Science and Technology (ITEST), 221 N Grand Blvd, Saint Louis, MO 63103
T: (314) 658-2703
Founded: 1968; Members: 575
Focus: Rel & Theol
Periodical
Bulletin (quarterly) 14693

Institute for Urban Design (IUD), 454 W 46 St, No 3CN, New York, NY 10036
T: (212) 581-5178; Fax: (212) 581-5178
Founded: 1979; Members: 500
Gen Secr: Ann Ferebee
Focus: Archit
Periodicals
Project Monograph: Urban Design Case Studies (quarterly)
Urban Design International (annually)
Urban Design Update (bi-monthly) . . . 14694

Institute of American Indian Arts (IAIA), POB 20007, Santa Fe, NM 87504
T: (505) 988-6463; Fax: (505) 988-6446
Founded: 1962
Focus: Arts 14695

Institute of Andean Research (IAR), c/o Dept of Anthropology, American Museum of Natural History, Central Park W at 79 St, New York, NY 10024
T: (212) 769-5883; Fax: (212)769-5334
Founded: 1937; Members: 25
Gen Secr: Craig Morris
Focus: Anthro 14696

Institute of Andean Studies (IAS), POB 9307, Berkeley, CA 94709
T: (510) 525-7816
Founded: 1960; Members: 181
Focus: Archeol
Periodical
Nawpa Pacha (annually) 14697

Institute of Certified Financial Planners (ICFP), 3801 E Florida Av, Ste 708, Denver, CO 80210-2571
T: (303) 759-4900; Fax: (303) 759-0749
Founded: 1973; Members: 9500
Gen Secr: David Brand
Focus: Finance 14698

Institute of Chinese Culture (ICC), 86 Riverside Dr, New York, NY 10024
T: (212) 787-6969
Founded: 1944; Members: 100
Focus: Ethnology 14699

Institute of Civil War Studies (ICWS), c/o Dept of History, Meramec College, 11333 Big Bend, Saint Louis, MO 63122
T: (601) 966-7687
Founded: 1974
Focus: Hist 14700

Institute of Cultural Affairs (ICA), 4750 N Sheridan Rd, Chicago, IL 60640
T: (312) 769-6363; Fax: (312) 769-1144
Founded: 1973; Members: 1500
Focus: Sociology; Psych 14701

Institute of Early American History and Culture (IEAHC), POB 8781, Williamsburg, VA 23187
T: (804) 221-1110
Founded: 1943
Gen Secr: Ronald Hoffman
Focus: Cultur Hist; Hist
Periodicals
Newsletter
William and Mary Quarterly (quarterly) . 14702

Institute of Electrical and Electronics Engineers (IEEE), 345 E 47 St, New York, NY 10017
T: (212) 705-7900; Fax: (212) 752-4929
Founded: 1884; Members: 320000
Gen Secr: John H. Powers
Focus: Electronic Eng; Electric Eng . . 14703

Institute of Environmental Sciences (IES), 940 E Northwest Hwy, Mount Prospect, IL 60056
T: (312) 255-1561
Founded: 1959; Members: 4200
Focus: Nat Sci
Periodicals
Journal of Environmental Sciences (bi-monthly)
Newsletter (quarterly) 14704

Institute of Financial Education (IFE), 111 E Wacker Dr, Chicago, IL 60601-4680
T: (312) 946-8801; Fax: (312) 946-8802
Founded: 1922; Members: 50000
Pres: Gail Rafter Meneley
Focus: Adult Educ; Finance
Periodical
Membership Newsletter (bi-monthly) . . . 14705

Institute of Food Technologists (IFT), 221 N LaSalle St, Ste 300, Chicago, IL 60601
T: (312) 782-8424; Fax: (312) 782-8348
Founded: 1939; Members: 28000
Pres: Robert E. Smith; Gen Secr: Daniel E. Weber
Focus: Food
Periodicals
Food Technology (monthly)
Journal of Food Science (bi-monthly)
Membership Directory (annually) 14706

Institute of Gas Technology (IGT), 1700 S Mount Prospect Rd, Des Plaines, IL 60018-1804
T: (847) 768-0500; E-Mail: feingold@igt.org;
Fax: (847) 768-0501
Founded: 1941; Members: 170
Gen Secr: Bonnie Feingold
Focus: Eng; Energy
Periodicals
Energy Statistics (quarterly)
Gas Abstracts (monthly)
International Gas Technology Highlights (bi-weekly)
. . . . 14707

Institute of General Semantics (IGS), 163 Engle St, Englewood, NJ 07631
T: (201) 568-0051; Fax: (201) 569-1793
Founded: 1938; Members: 500
Gen Secr: Marjorie S. Zelner
Focus: Ling 14708

Institute of Global Education, POB 20728, Portland, OR 97294
T: (503) 252-3639; Fax: (503) 255-5216
Gen Secr: Dr. F. Richard Schneider
Focus: Educ 14709

Institute of Industrial Engineers (IIE), 25 Technology Park, Norcross, GA 30092
T: (404) 449-0460; Fax: (404) 263-8532
Founded: 1948; Members: 30000
Gen Secr: Dr. Woodrow Leake
Focus: Eng
Periodicals
The Engineering Economist (quarterly)
Industrial Engineering (monthly)
Industrial Management (bi-monthly)
Transactions (quarterly) 14710

Institute of International Education (IIE), 809 United Nations Plaza, New York, NY 10017
T: (212) 883-8200; Fax: (212) 984-5452
Founded: 1919; Members: 350
Pres: Richard Krasno
Focus: Educ 14711

Institute of International Education (IIE), 1400 K St NW, Ste 650, Washington, DC 2005
T: (202) 326-7725; Fax: (202) 326-7763
Focus: Educ 14712

Institute of Judicial Administration (IJA), c/o New York School of Law, 40 Washington Sq S, New York, NY 10012
T: (212) 998-6196; Fax: (212) 995-4036
Founded: 1952; Members: 1000
Gen Secr: Prof. Samuel Estreicher
Focus: Law 14713

Institute of Laboratory Animal Resources (ILAR), c/o National Research Council, 2101 Constitution Av NW, Washington, DC 20418
T: (202) 334-2590; Fax: (202) 334-1639
Founded: 1952
Focus: Vet Med
Periodical
ILAR News (quarterly) *14714*

Institute of Lithuanian Studies (ILS), c/o Dept of Slavic and Baltic Studies, University of Illinois at Chicago, 601 S Morgan, Chicago, IL 60607-7110
T: (312) 996-4412; Fax: (312) 996-0953
Founded: 1951; Members: 135
Pres: Dr. Violeta Kelertas
Focus: Ethnology
Periodicals
Lithuanian Studies
Proceedings of Conferences of the Institute of Lithuanian Studies: Lituanistikos Instituto Suvaziavimo Darbai (bi-annually) . . . *14715*

The Institute of Management Sciences (TIMS), 290 Westminster St, Providence, RI 02903
T: (401) 274-2525; Fax: (401) 274-3189
Founded: 1953; Members: 8000
Pres: Gary Lilien
Focus: Business Admin
Periodicals
Information Systems Research (quarterly)
Interfaces (bi-monthly)
Management Science (monthly)
Marketing Science (quarterly)
Mathematics of Operations Research (quarterly)
Organization Science (quarterly) *14716*

Institute of Mathematical Statistics (IMS), 3401 Investment Blvd, Ste 7, Hayward, CA 94545-3819
T: (510) 783-8141; E-Mail: ims@stat.berkeley.edu; Fax: (510) 783-4131
Founded: 1935; Members: 1000000
Gen Secr: Hari G. Mukerjee
Focus: Stats
Periodicals
The Annals of Probability (quarterly)
The Annals of Statistics (quarterly)
The IMS Bulletin (bi-monthly)
Statistical Science (quarterly) *14717*

Institute of Medicine (IOM), 2101 Constitution Av NW, Washington, DC 20418
T: (202) 334-2138
Founded: 1970; Members: 500
Pres: Dr. Kenneth I. Shine; Gen Secr: Dr. Karen Hein
Focus: Med
Periodical
IOM News (quarterly) *14718*

Institute of Nautical Archaeology (INA), PO Drawer HG, College Station, TX 77841
T: (409) 845-6694; Fax: (409) 845-6399
Founded: 1973; Members: 900
Focus: Archeol *14719*

Institute of Navigation (ION), 1800 Diagonal Rd, Ste 480, Alexandria, VA 22314
T: (703) 683-7101; Fax: (703) 683-7105
Founded: 1945; Members: 4000
Focus: Navig
Periodical
Navigation (quarterly) *14720*

Institute of Noise Control Engineering (INCE), POB 3206, Arlington Branch, Poughkeepsie, NY 12603
T: (914) 462-4006; E-Mail: inceus@aol.com; Fax: (914) 463-0201
Founded: 1971; Members: 500
Gen Secr: George C. Maling
Focus: Public Health
Periodicals
Noise Control Engineering Journal (bi-monthly)
Noise/News (bi-monthly) *14721*

Institute of Nuclear Materials Management (INMM), 60 Revere Dr, Ste 500, Northbrook, IL 60062
T: (312) 480-9573; Fax: (312) 480-9282
Founded: 1958; Members: 800
Gen Secr: Barbara Scott
Focus: Nucl Res
Periodicals
Journal of Nuclear Materials Management (quarterly)
Proceedings of Annual Meeting *14722*

Institute of Outdoor Drama (IOD), c/o University of North Carolina, CB 3240 Nations Bank Plaza, Chapel Hill, NC 27599-3240
T: (919) 962-1328
Founded: 1963
Focus: Perf Arts
Periodical
Newsletter (quarterly) *14723*

Institute of Public Administration (IPA), 55 W 44 St, New York, NY 10036
T: (212) 730-5480; E-Mail: ipa@delphi.com; Fax: (212) 768-9071
Founded: 1906
Pres: David Mammen
Focus: Poli Sci; Public Admin *14724*

Institute of the American Musical (IAM), 121 N Detroit St, Los Angeles, CA 90036
T: (213) 934-1221
Founded: 1972
Focus: Music *14725*

Institute of the Great Plains (IGP), c/o Museum of the Great Plains, Steve Wilson Dr, POB 68, Lawton, OK 73502
T: (405) 581-3460
Founded: 1960; Members: 814
Focus: Hist
Periodicals
Great Plains Journal (annually)
Museum of the Great Plains Newsletter . *14726*

Institute of Transportation Engineers (ITE), 525 School St SW, Ste 410, Washington, DC 20024-2797
T: (202) 554-8050; Fax: (202) 863-5486
Founded: 1930; Members: 11000
Focus: Transport
Periodicals
Directory (annually)
Journal (monthly) *14727*

Institute of World Affairs (IWA), 1321 Pennsylvania Av SE, Washington, DC 20003
T: (202) 544-4141; E-Mail: info@iwa.org; Fax: (202) 544-5115
Founded: 1924
Gen Secr: Bradford P. Johnson
Focus: Sci *14728*

Institute on Psychiatric Services/American Psychiatric Association, 1400 K St NW, Washington, 20005
T: (202) 682-6314; E-Mail: JGruber@psych.org; Fax: (202) 682-6345
Founded: 1949
Gen Secr: Jill L. Gruber
Focus: Psychiatry *14729*

Instrument Society of America (ISA), 67 Alexander Dr, POB 12277, Research Triangle Park, NC 27709
T: (919) 549-8411; Fax: (919) 549-8288
Gen Secr: Glenn F. Harvey
Focus: Eng *14730*

Insulated Cable Engineers Association (ICEA), POB 440, South Yarmouth, MA 02664
T: (508) 394-4424; Fax: (508) 394-1194
Founded: 1925; Members: 100
Gen Secr: Edward E. McIlveen
Focus: Electronic Eng; Eng *14731*

Insurance Information Institute (III), 110 William St, New York, NY 10038
T: (212) 669-9200; Fax: (212) 732-1916
Founded: 1959; Members: 250
Focus: Insurance
Periodicals
Data Base Reports (monthly)
Insurance Facts (annually)
Insurance Review (monthly) *14732*

Intelligent Buildings Institute (IBI), 2101 L St NW, Ste 300, Washington, DC 20037
T: (202) 457-1988; Fax: (202) 457-1989
Founded: 1986; Members: 300
Focus: Archit
Periodicals
Directory (annually)
IBI News (quarterly) *14733*

Inter-American Bar Foundation, 1819 H St NW, Rm 320A, Washington, DC 20006
T: (202) 293-1455; Fax: (202) 828-0157
Gen Secr: Judd L. Kessler
Focus: Law *14734*

Inter-American College Association (IACA), 1832 Stratford Pl, Pomona, CA 91768
T: (714) 629-1460
Founded: 1962; Members: 25
Focus: Educ
Periodicals
Listing of Inter-American Graduate Programs (bi-annually)
Progress Bulletin (monthly) *14735*

Inter-American College of Physicians and Surgeons (ICPS), 915 Broadway, Ste 1105, New York, NY 10010
T: (212) 777-3642; Fax: (202) 505-7984
Gen Secr: Dr. René F. Rodriguez
Focus: Med; Surgery *14736*

Inter-American College of Radiology (IACR), 45-42 N Federal Hwy, Fort Lauderdale, FL 33308
Gen Secr: Gaston Mendez
Focus: Radiology *14737*

Inter-American Commercial Arbitration Commission (I-ACAC), OAS Administrative Bldg, 19 and Constitution Av NW, Rm 211, Washington, DC 20006
T: (202) 458-3249; Fax: (202) 828-0157
Founded: 1934
Focus: Law *14738*

Inter-American Council for Education, Science and Culture (CIECC), c/o Organization of American States, 1889 F St NW, Washington, DC 20006
T: (202) 458-3783
Founded: 1948; Members: 32
Focus: Educ *14739*

Inter-American Distance Education Consortium (CREAD), c/o CREAD Executive Office, Pennsylvania State University, 211 Mitchell Building, University Park, PA 16802-3601
T: (814) 863-0488; E-Mail: axv4@cde.psu.edu; Fax: (814) 865-3290
Gen Secr: Dr. Armando Villarroel
Focus: Educ *14740*

Inter American Heart Foundation, 7272 Greenville Av, Dallas, TX 75231-4596
T: (214) 706-1218; E-Mail: Beatrizc@amhrt.org; Fax: (214) 562-3807, 373-0268
Gen Secr: Dr. Beatriz Marcet Champagne
Focus: Cardiol *14741*

Inter-American Investigative Journalism Institute, 2911 NW 39 St, Miami, FL 33142
T: (305) 634-2465
Focus: Journalism *14742*

Inter-American Music Council (IAM), 2511 P St NW, Washington, DC 20007
Founded: 1956; Members: 32
Gen Secr: Prof. Efrain Paesky
Focus: Music *14743*

Inter-American Nuclear Energy Commission (IANEC), c/o OAS, 1889 F St NW, Washington, DC 20006
T: (202) 458-3368; Fax: (202) 458-3167
Focus: Energy *14744*

Inter-American Safety Council (IASC), 33 Park Pl, Englewood, NJ 07631
T: (201) 871-0004; Fax: (201) 871-2074
Founded: 1938; Members: 3200
Gen Secr: Glen E. Mickey
Focus: Safety
Periodicals
Noticias de Seguridad (monthly)
El Supervisor (monthly) *14745*

Inter-American Society of Hypertension (IASH), c/o Medical University of South Carolina, Dept Biometry and Epidemiology, 171 Ashley Av, Charleston, SC 29425-2503
T: (803) 792-4081; Fax: (803) 792-3180
Gen Secr: Dr. J.B. Dunbar
Focus: Med *14746*

Inter-American Tropical Tuna Comission, c/o Scripps Institution of Oceanography, 8604 La Jolla Shores Dr, La Jolla, CA 92037-1508
T: (619) 546-7100; Fax: (619) 546-7133
Founded: 1950
Gen Secr: James Joseph
Focus: Fisheries; Zoology
Periodicals
Annual Report (annually)
Bulletin (irregularly)
Special Report (irregularly) *14747*

Inter-American University Council for Economic and Social Development (CUIDES), c/o University of Houston System, 1600 Smith, Ste 3400, Houston, TX 77002
T: (713) 754-7505; Fax: (713) 754-7409
Gen Secr: Dr. Alexander F. Schilt
Focus: Econ; Soc Sci *14748*

Inter-Society Color Council (ISCC), c/o Data Color International, 5 Princess Rd, Lawrenceville, NJ 08648
T: (609) 895-7427; Fax: (609) 895-7461
Founded: 1931; Members: 900
Gen Secr: Dr. Danny C. Rich
Focus: Chem
Periodical
Newsletter (bi-monthly) *14749*

Inter-University Communications Network (BITNET), c/o Computing and Information Technology, Princeton Univ., 220 Nassau Hall, Princeton, NJ 08544
T: (609) 258-5601; Fax: (609) 258-1495
Gen Secr: Ira Fuchs
Focus: Educ *14750*

Inter-University Consortium for Political and Social Research (ICPSR), c/o School of Social Work, San José State University, Washington Square Hall, San José, CA 95192
T: (408) 924-5839; E-Mail: pclee@sjsu.edu; Fax: (408) 924-5892
Founded: 1962; Members: 340
Gen Secr: Dr. Peter C.Y. Lee
Focus: Poli Sci; Sociology
Periodicals
Annual Report (annually)
Bulletin (quarterly)
Guide to Resources and Services (annually) *14751*

Intercollegiate Broadcasting System (IBS), 367 Windsor Hwy, New Windsor, NY 12553
T: (914) 565-6710; Fax: (914) 565-7446
Founded: 1940; Members: 650
Gen Secr: Fritz Kass
Focus: Educ *14752*

Intercultural Development Research Association (IDRA), 5835 Callaghan Rd, Ste 350, San Antonio, TX 78228
T: (210) 684-8180; Fax: (210) 684-5389
Founded: 1974
Focus: Ling *14753*

Interfaith Forum on Religion, Art and Architecture (IFRAA), c/o American Institute of Architects, 1735 New York Av NW, Washington, DC 20006
T: (202) 626-7305
Founded: 1978; Members: 900
Pres: Richard Bergemann
Focus: Archit; Rel & Theol; Arts
Periodicals
Faith and Forum (semi-annually)
Newsletter (quarterly) *14754*

Intergalactic Spacecraft – UFO – Intercontinental Research and Analytic Network (ICUFON), 35-40 75 St, Ste 4G, Flushing, NY 11372-4465
T: (718) 672-7948
Gen Secr: Colman S. VonKeviczky
Focus: Parapsych *14755*

Intergovernmental Commission for Chagas Disease, c/o PAHO, 525 Twenty-Third St NW, Washington, DC 20037
T: (202) 861-3200; Fax: (202) 223-5971
Focus: Med *14756*

Interior Design Educators Council (IDEC), 14252 Culver Dr, Ste A-311, Irvine, CA 92714
T: (714) 551-1622
Founded: 1962; Members: 350
Focus: Adult Educ; Graphic & Dec Arts, Design
Periodicals
Journal of Interior Design Education and Research (semi-annually)
Record (quarterly) *14757*

International Academy at Santa Barbara (IASB), 800 Garden, Ste D, Santa Barbara, CA 93101-1552
T: (805) 965-5010; Fax: (805) 965-6071
Founded: 1960
Focus: Sci
Periodicals
Current World Leaders (8 times annually)
Energy Review (bi-monthly)
Environmental Periodicals Bibliography (bi-monthly) *14758*

International Academy for Quality (IAQ), 16080 Camino del Cerro, Los Gatos, CA 95032
Gen Secr: Dr. James Harrington
Focus: Econ *14759*

International Academy for Research in Learning Disabilities (IARLD), Northwestern University, Evanston, IL 60208
Gen Secr: Dr. Doris Johnson
Focus: Educ *14760*

International Academy for the Study of Tourism, University of Wisconsin-Stout, Menomonie, WI 54751
T: (715) 232-2339; E-Mail: JAFARI@uwstout.edu; Fax: (715) 232-3200
Gen Secr: Jafar Jafari
Focus: Educ *14761*

International Academy of Chest Physicians and Surgeons (IACPS), c/o American College of Chest Physicians, 3300 Dundee Rd, Northbrook, IL 60062
T: (708) 498-1400; Fax: (708) 698-1791
Founded: 1941; Members: 15000
Focus: Surgery
Periodicals
Journal (monthly)
Member Bulletin
Membership Directory (annually) *14762*

International Academy of Chiropractic Occupational Health Consultants (IACOHC), c/o Northwestern Chiropractic College, 2501 W 84 St, Bloomington, MN 55431
Gen Secr: Dr. Joseph Sweere
Focus: Public Health *14763*

International Academy of Culture and Political Science, Mastin Lake Station, POB 3282, Huntsville, AL 35810-0282
T: (205) 534-5501; Fax: (205) 536-1018
Gen Secr: Dr.Charles Mercieca
Focus: Cultur Hist; Poli Sci *14764*

International Academy of Matrimonial Lawyers, 10 S LaSalle St, Ste 2424, Chicago, IL 60603
Gen Secr: Arthur M. Berman
Focus: Law *14765*

International Academy of Myodontics (IAM), 800 Airport Blvd, Doylestown, PA 18901
T: (215) 345-1149; Fax: (215) 609-2588
Founded: 1970; Members: 1100
Pres: Harry N. Cooperman
Focus: Dent *14766*

International Academy of Nutrition and Preventive Medicine, POB 18433, Asheville, NC 28814-0433
T: (704) 258-3243
Founded: 1971; Members: 400
Focus: Med; Hygiene; Public Health
Periodicals
Conference Proceedings (annually)
Directory (annually)
Journal (semi-annually)
Lay Newsletter (10 times annually)
Professional Newsletter (monthly) . . . *14767*

International Academy of Pathology (IAP), c/o Center for Advanced Pathology, Armed Forces Institute of Pathology, 14 St and Alaska Av NW, Washington, DC 20306-6000
T: (202) 782-2503; E-Mail: MULLICK@email.afip.osd.mil; Fax: (202) 782-7166
Founded: 1906; Members: 8300
Gen Secr: Dr. Florabel G. Mullick
Focus: Pathology
Periodical
International Pathology (quarterly) . . . 14768

International Academy of Periodontology, c/o Dept of Periodontics, School of Dental Medicine, State Univ., Stony Brook, NY
Gen Secr: Dr. Vincent J. Iacono
Focus: Dent 14769

International Academy of Sex Research (IASR), c/o Kinsey Inst for Research in Sex, Gender and Reproduction, Morrison Hall, Indiana University, Bloomington, IN 47405
T: (812) 855-8277; E-Mail: jbancroft@indiana.edu; Fax: (812) 855-8277
Gen Secr: John Bancroft
Focus: Soc Sci; Venereology 14770

International Academy of Trial Lawyers (IATL), 4 N Second St, Ste 175, San Jose, CA 95113
T: (408) 275-6767; Fax: (408) 275-6767
Founded: 1954; Members: 554
Focus: Law 14771

International Academy of Wood Science (IAWS), c/o Forest Products Laboratory, University of California, 1301 S 46 St, Richmond, CA 94804
T: (510) 215-4233; E-Mail: Frank.Beall@ucop.edu; Fax: (510) 215-4299
Gen Secr: Prof. Frank C. Beall
Focus: Forestry 14772

International Aerosol Research Assembly (IARA), c/o Environmental Protection Agency, MD-52, Research Triangle Park, NC 27711
T: (919) 541-2551; Fax: (919) 541-0245
Gen Secr: Dr. William E. Wilson
Focus: Physics 14773

International Alban Berg Society (IABS), 33 W 42 St, New York, NY 10036
T: (212) 642-2389; Fax: (212) 642-2642
Founded: 1966; Members: 300
Gen Secr: John Frisch
Focus: Music 14774

International Alliance for Sustainable Agriculture (IASA), c/o Newman Center, University of Minnesota, 1701 University Av SE, Rm 202, Minneapolis, MN 55414
T: (612) 331-1099; Fax: (612) 379-1527
Gen Secr: Terry Gips
Focus: Agri 14775

International Alliance of Women in Music (IAWM), c/o George Washington University, Dept of Music, B-144 Academic Center, Washington, DC 20052
T: (202) 994-6338; E-Mail: sasha@gwis2.circ.gwu.edu
Gen Secr: Sasha Kennison
Focus: Music 14776

International Aloe Science Council (IASC), 1033 La Posada Dr, Ste 220, Austin, TX 78752-3824
T: (817) 338-1315; Fax: (817) 338-1319
Founded: 1981; Members: 120
Gen Secr: Gene Hale
Focus: Pharmacol 14777

International Anesthesia Research Society (IARS), 2 Summit Park Dr, Ste 140, Cleveland, OH 44131-2553
T: (216) 642-1124; Fax: (216) 642-1127
Founded: 1922; Members: 15000
Focus: Anesthetics
Periodical
Anesthesia and Analgesia (monthly) . . 14778

International Animated Film Society (ASIFA), 725 S Victory, Burbank, CA 91502
T: (818) 842-8330
Gen Secr: Antran Manoogian
Focus: Cinema 14779

International Arthur Schnitzler Research Association (IASRA), c/o Dept of Foreign Languages, California State University, San Bernardino, CA 92407
T: (714) 880-5851
Founded: 1961; Members: 700
Focus: Lit; Cultur Hist
Periodical
Modern Austrian Literature (quarterly) . . 14780

International Arthurian Society (SIA), c/o Dept of Modern Languages, University of Oklahoma, Norman, OK 73019
T: (405) 325-5088
Gen Secr: Prof. Keith Busby
Focus: Lit 14781

International Association for Aquatic Animal Medicine (IAAAM), POB 96, Baltimore, MD 21203
T: (410) 467-5056
Founded: 1969; Members: 450
Gen Secr: Sarah Poynton
Focus: Vet Med
Periodicals
IAAAM Conference Abstract (annually)
Newsletter (quarterly) 14782

International Association for Child and Adolescent Psychiatry and Allied Professions (IACAPAP), c/o Child Study Centre, POB 207900, New Haven, CT 06520-7900
T: (203) 785-5759; Fax: (203) 785-7402
Gen Secr: Donald J. Cohen
Focus: Psychiatry 14783

International Association for Comparative Research on Leukemia and Related Diseases (IACRLRD), c/o Dept of Cancer Biology, Harvard School of Public Health, Boston, MA 02115
T: (617) 432-1023; Fax: (617) 739-8348
Founded: 1963; Members: 500
Gen Secr: Dr. Myron Essex
Focus: Hematology
Periodical
Symposium Proceedings (bi-annually) . . 14784

International Association for Computer Information Systems (IACIS), c/o Dr. G. Daryl Nord, College of Business Administration, Oklahoma State University, Stillwater, OK 74078
T: (405) 744-8632; E-Mail: dnord@okway.okstate.edu; Fax: (405) 744-5180
Founded: 1960; Members: 700
Gen Secr: Dr. G. Daryl Nord
Focus: Computer & Info Sci; Educ
Periodical
The Journal of Computer Information Systems (quarterly) 14785

International Association for Computer Methods and Advances in Geomechanics (IACMAG), c/o Dept of Civil Engineering and Engineering Mechanics, University of Arizona, Tucson, AZ 85721
T: (602) 621-2260; Fax: (602) 621-2550
Gen Secr: Prof. C.S. Desai
Focus: Computer & Info Sci 14786

International Association for Conflict Management (IACM), c/o University of Minnesota, Conflict and Change Center, Hubert H. Humphrey Institute, 301 19 Av S, Minneapolis, MN 55455
T: (612) 625-0362; E-Mail: iacm@gold.tc.umn.edu; Fax: (612) 625-3513
Gen Secr: Dr. Thomas Fiutak
Focus: Prom Peace 14787

International Association for Conservation of Natural Resources and Energy (IACNRE), POB 487, Jackson Heights, Queens, NY 11372
T: (718) 639-7709; Fax: (718) 639-7709
Gen Secr: Prof. Dr. George Preda
Focus: Ecology; Energy 14788

International Association for Cross-Cultural Psychology (IACCP), c/o Department of Psychology, California State University, Chico, CA 95929-0234
T: (916) 898-5363; E-Mail: tsingelis@oavax.csuchico.edu; Fax: (916) 898-4740
Gen Secr: Ted Singelis
Focus: Psych 14789

International Association for Dental Research (IADR), 1619 Duke St, Alexandria, VA 22314-3406
T: (703) 548-0066; E-Mail: research@iadr.com; Fax: (703) 548-1883
Founded: 1920; Members: 9500
Gen Secr: Dr. John J. Clarkson
Focus: Dent
Periodicals
IADR Newsletter (quarterly)
Journal of Dental Research (monthly) . . 14790

International Association for Ecology (INTECOL), c/o Savannah River Ecology Laboratory, Drawer E, Aiken, SC 29802
T: (803) 725-2472; E-Mail: intecol@srel.edu; Fax: (803) 725-3309
Founded: 1967; Members: 1300
Gen Secr: Dr. Rebecca R. Sharitz
Focus: Ecology
Periodicals
Ecology International (1-2 times annually)
INTECOL Newsletter (bi-monthly) 14791

International Association for Educational Assessment (IAEA), POB 6665, Princeton, NJ 08541-6665
T: (609) 951-1633; Fax: (609) 734-5410
Gen Secr: Frances M. Ottobre
Focus: Educ 14792

International Association for Energy Economics (IAEE), 28790 Chagrin Blvd, Ste 210, Cleveland, OH 44122
T: (216) 464-5365; E-Mail: iaee@iaee.org; Fax: (216) 464-2737
Founded: 1977; Members: 3000
Gen Secr: David Williams
Focus: Energy
Periodicals
The Energy Journal (quarterly)
The LAEE Membership Directory (annually) 14793

International Association for Fire Safety Science (IAFSS), c/o Dept of Fire Protection Engineering, Univ. of Maryland, College Park, MD 20742
T: (301) 405-3993; E-Mail: jimg@GLue.umd.edu; Fax: (301) 405-9383
Gen Secr: Prof. J.G. Quintiere
Focus: Eng 14794

International Association for Great Lakes Research (IAGLR), 2200 Bonisteel Blvd, Ann Arbor, MI 48109-2099
T: (313) 747-1673; Fax: (313) 747-2748
Founded: 1967; Members: 1000
Focus: Geography
Periodicals
Journal of Great Lakes Research (quarterly)
Lakes Letter (semi-annually) 14795

International Association for Healthcare Security and Safety (IAHS2), POB 637, Lombard, IL 60148
T: (708) 953-0990; Fax: (708) 957-1786
Founded: 1968; Members: 1500
Focus: Med
Periodicals
Healthcare Protection Management (semi-annually)
Membership Directory (annually)
Newsletter (quarterly)
Training Bulletin 14796

International Association for Housing Science (IAHS), POB 340254, Coral Gables, FL 33134
T: (305) 348-3171; Fax: (305) 348-3171
Founded: 1972; Members: 600
Pres: Prof. Oktay Ural
Focus: Archit
Periodical
International Journal for Housing Science (quarterly) 14797

International Association for Hydrogen Energy (IAHE), POB 248294, Coral Gables, FL 33124
T: (305) 284-4666; Fax: (305) 284-4792
Founded: 1974; Members: 2500
Pres: T. Nejat Veziroglu
Focus: Energy
Periodical
International Journal of Hydrogen Energy (monthly) 14798

International Association for Identification (IAI), POB 2423, Alameda, CA 94501
T: (510) 865-2174
Gen Secr: A.R. Crooker
Focus: Standards 14799

International Association for Learning Laboratories (IALL), c/o Tom Browne, Humanities Learning Center, Macalester College, 1600 Grand Av, Saint Paul, MN 55105
T: (612) 696-6336; Fax: (612) 696-6435
Founded: 1965; Members: 700
Gen Secr: Tom Browne
Focus: Ling; Educ; Adult Educ; Eng
Periodical
The Journal of Educational Techniques and Technologies (quarterly) 14800

International Association for Management of Technology (IAMOT), c/o Graduale School, Univ. of Miami, POB 248125, Coral Gables, FL 33124-4220
T: (305) 284-4154; Fax: (305) 284-5441
Focus: Business Admin; Eng 14801

International Association for Mathematical and Computer Modelling and Scientific Computing (IAMCM), POB 31670, Saint Louis, MO 63131
T: (314) 341-4585; Fax: (314) 445-1015
Gen Secr: Prof. Xavier J.R. Avula
Focus: Math; Computer & Info Sci . . . 14802

International Association for Mathematical Geology (IAMG), c/o Kansas Geological Survey, 1930 Constant Av, Lawrence, KS 66047
T: (913) 964-4991; E-Mail: olea@kgs.ukans.edu; Fax: (913) 964-5317
Founded: 1968; Members: 600
Pres: Dr. Ricardo A. Olea
Focus: Geology
Periodicals
Computer & Geosciences (quarterly)
Mathematical Geology (bi-monthly) . . . 14803

International Association for Mathematics and Computers in Simulation (IMACS), c/o Dept of Computer Science, Rutgers University, Piscataway, NJ 08854
E-Mail: imacs@cs.rutgers.edu; Fax: (908) 932-0537
Focus: Math; Computer & Info Sci . . . 14804

International Association for Media and Communication Research (IAMCR), c/o School of International Service, American University, 4400 Massachusetts Av NW, Washington, DC 20016-8071
T: (202) 885-1628; E-Mail: mowlana@american.edu; Fax: (202) 885-2494
Gen Secr: Prof. Hamid Mowlana
Focus: Mass Media; Comm Sci 14805

International Association for Near-Death Studies (IANDS), POB 502, East Windsor Hill, CT 06028
T: (203) 528-5144; Fax: (203) 528-9169
Founded: 1981; Members: 1200
Pres: Nancy Evans Bush
Focus: Parapsych
Periodicals
Journal of Near-Death Studies (quarterly)
Revitalized Signs Newsletter (quarterly) . 14806

International Association for Obsidian Studies (IAOS), c/o Univ. of Missouri, 223 Research Reactor, Columbia, MO 65211
E-Mail: glascock@reactor.murr.missouri.edu
Gen Secr: Michael D. Glascock
Focus: Mineralogy 14807

International Association for Orthodontics (IAO), 1100 W Lake Dr, Ste 240, Oak Park, IL 60301
T: (708) 445-0320; Fax: (708) 445-0321
Founded: 1961; Members: 1800
Gen Secr: Joanna Carey
Focus: Dent 14808

International Association for Philosophy of Law and Social Philosophy – American Section (AMINTAPHIL), c/o Coillege of Law, University of Florida, Gainesville, FL 32611-2038
T: (904) 392-2211; Fax: (904) 392-8727
Founded: 1963; Members: 350
Gen Secr: Robert Moffat
Focus: Philos 14809

International Association for Research in Income and Wealth (IARIW), c/o Dept of Economics, New York Univerity, 269 Mercer St, Rm 700, New York, NY 10003
T: (212) 924-4386; Fax: (212) 366-5067
Founded: 1947; Members: 400
Gen Secr: Jane Forman
Focus: Econ
Periodicals
Membership Directory
The Review of Income and Wealth (quarterly) 14810

International Association for Research in Vietnamese Music (IARVM), POB 16, Kent, OH 44240
T: (216) 677-9703; E-Mail: IARVM@aol.com
Gen Secr: Tuyen T. Tonnu
Focus: Music 14811

International Association for Shell and Spatial Structures (IASS), 111 New Montgomery St, San Francisco, CA 94105
T: (415) 392-8760; Fax: (415) 543-3906
Gen Secr: Dr. S.J. Medwadowski
Focus: Nat Sci 14812

International Association for Stability and Handling of Liquid Fuels (IASH), c/o US Dept of Energy, FE-422, 3G-063, Forrestal Bldg, 1000 Intependence Av SW, Washington, DC 20585-0340
T: (202) 586-4731; E-Mail: harry.giles@hg.doe.gov; Fax: (202) 586-7919
Gen Secr: Harry N. Giles
Focus: Energy 14813

International Association for Suicide Prevention and Crisis Intervention (IASP), c/o Central Administrative Office-IASP, Center for Suicide Research and Prevention, 1725 W Harrison St, Ste 955, Chicago, IL 60612
T: (312) 942-7208; E-Mail: iasp@aol.com
Gen Secr: Mary Kelly Campos
Focus: Psych 14814

International Association for Technology Assessment and Forecasting Institutions (IATAFI), c/o Argonne National Laboratory, Ste 702, 901 D St SW, Washington, DC 20024
T: (202) 488-2418; E-Mail: Williams@smtplink.eid.anl.gov; Fax: (202) 488-2413
Gen Secr: Dr. Gary Williams
Focus: Eng 14815

International Association for the Advancement of Earth and Environmental Sciences (IAAEES), c/o Geography and Environmental Studies Dept, Northeastern Illinois University, 5500 N Saint Louis Av, Chicago, IL 60625
T: (312) 794-2628; Fax: (708) 824-8436
Founded: 1972; Members: 10000
Pres: Dr. Musa Qutub
Focus: Ecology
Periodical
Environmental Resource Magazine (quarterly) 14816

International Association for the Advancement of High Pressure Science and Technology (AIRAPT), c/o Los Alamos National Laboratory, P-DO Physics MS D408, POB 1663, Los Alamos, NM 87545
Gen Secr: Dr. John W. Shaner
Focus: Eng 14817

International Association for the History of Crime and Criminal Justice (IAHCCJ), c/o City University of New York, John Jay College of Criminal Justice, Dept of History, 445 W 59 St, New York, NY 10019
T: (212) 237-8818; Fax: (212) 237-8742
Gen Secr: Mary Gibson
Focus: Law; Hist 14818

International Association for the Physical Sciences of the Oceans (IAPSO), POB 820440, Vicksburg, MS 39182-0440
T: (601) 636-1363; E-Mail: camfield@vicksburg.com; Fax: (601) 629-9640
Founded: 1919; Members: 6000
Gen Secr: Dr. Fred E. Camfield
Focus: Oceanography
Periodicals
Procès-Verbaux (every two years)
Publication Scientifique (annually) 14819

International Association for the Properties of Water and Steam (IAPWS), POB, Palo Alto, CA 94303
T: (415) 855-2458
Founded: 1971; Members: 9
Gen Secr: Dr. Barry Dooley
Focus: Standards; Physics
Periodical
Releases and Guidelines 14820

International Association for the Study of Common Property (IASCP), c/o Indiana University, 513 N Park Av, Bloomington, IN 47408
T: (812) 855-8082; E-Mail: iascp@indiana.edu; Fax: (812) 855-3150
Gen Secr: Michelle Curtain
Focus: Econ 14821

International Association for the Study of Cooperation in Education (IASCE), POB 1582, Santa Cruz, CA 95061-1582
T: (408) 426-7926; Fax: (408) 426-3360
Founded: 1979; Members: 3500
Gen Secr: Liana Forest
Focus: Educ 14822

International Association for the Study of Obesity (IASO), c/o Pennington Biomedical Research Center, 6400 Perkins Rd, Baton Rouge, LA 70808-4124
Fax: (504) 763-0935
Gen Secr: Dr. George A. Bray
Focus: Med 14823

International Association for the Study of Organized Crime (IASOC), c/o Univ. of Illinois at Chicago, OICJ (M/C 777), 1033 W Van Buren St, Chicago, IL 60607-2919
Gen Secr: Jeffrey Builta
Focus: Criminology 14824

International Association for the Study of Pain (IASP), 909 NE 43 St, Rm 306, Seattle, WA 98105-6020
T: (206) 547-6409; E-Mail: IASP@locke.hs.washington.edu; Fax: (206) 547-1703
Gen Secr: Louisa E. Jones
Focus: Med 14825

International Association for the Study of Traditional Environments (IASTE), c/o Center for Environmental Design Research, Univ. of California, 390 Wurster Hall, Berkeley, CA 94720
T: (510) 642-2896; E-Mail: wicak@ced.berkeley.edu; Fax: (510) 643-5571
Gen Secr: Ananya Roy
Focus: Preserv Hist Monuments 14826

International Association for the Study of Traumatic Brain Injury (IASTBI), c/o Rusk Rehabilitation Center, 1 Hospital Dr 2R01, Columbia, MO 66212
Gen Secr: Dr. Henry H. Stonnington
Focus: Traumatology 14827

International Association of Agricultural Economists (IAAE), c/o Farm Foundation, 1211 W 22 St, Ste 216, Oak Brook, IL 60521-2197
T: (708) 571-9393; E-Mail: farmfnd@interaccess.com; Fax: (708) 571-9580
Founded: 1929; Members: 1850
Gen Secr: Dr. Walter J. Armbruster
Focus: Agri 14828

International Association of Allergology and Clinical Immunology (IAACI), c/o Health Sciences Centre, State University of New York at Stony Brook, Stony Brook, NY11794
Founded: 1945; Members: 17000
Gen Secr: Allen Kaplan
Focus: Immunology
Periodical
Allergy & Clinical Immunology News (bi-monthly) 14829

International Association of Applied Linguistics (AILA), c/o Dept of English, Second Language, Univ. of Minnesota, 320 16 Av SE, Minneapolis, MN 55455
E-Mail: adcohen@waroon.tc.umn.edu; Fax: (612) 624-4579
Gen Secr: Dr. Andrew D. Cohen
Focus: Ling 14830

International Association of Aquatic and Marine Science Libraries and Information Centers (IAMSLIC), c/o Harbor Branch, Oceanographic Institution, Library, 5600 US 1 N, Fort Pierce, FL 34946
T: (800) 333-4264 Ext 201; Fax: (407) 465-2446
Focus: Oceanography; Libraries & Bk Sci 14831

International Association of Boards of Examiners in Optometry (IAB), 4330 East West Hwy, Ste 1117, Bethesda, MD 20814
T: (301) 718-6506; Fax: (301) 656-0989
Founded: 1919; Members: 54
Focus: Adult Educ; Ophthal
Periodical
State Board Forum (3 times annually) . 14832

International Association of Boundary Element Methods (IABEM), c/o Dept of Mechanical Engineering, Vanderbilt University, POB 1592, Station B, Nashville, TN 37235
Gen Secr: Dr. Thomas A. Cruse
Focus: Eng 14833

International Association of Buddhist Studies (IABS), c/o Dept of Religious Studies, Amherst College, Amherst, MA
Founded: 1976; Members: 500
Gen Secr: Prof. Janet Gyatso
Focus: Rel & Theol
Periodical
Journal of the International Association of Buddhist Studies (semi-annually) 14834

International Association of Campus Law Enforcement Administrators (IACLEA), c/o Peter J. Berry, 638 Prospect Av, Hartford, CT 06105-4298
T: (860) 586-7517; Fax: (860-586-7550
Founded: 1958; Members: 1200
Gen Secr: Peter J. Berry
Focus: Law
Periodicals
Campus Law Enforcement Journal (bi-monthly)
Conference Proceedings (annually)
Membership Directory (annually) 14835

International Association of Career Consulting Firms (IACCF), 11250 Roger Bacon Dr, Ste 8, Reston, VA 22090-5202
T: (703) 525-1191; Fax: (703) 276-8146
Founded: 1987; Members: 35
Gen Secr: Brian J. Goodman
Focus: Business Admin 14836

International Association of Clinical Laser Acupuncturists, 14300 Conway Meadows Ct E, Ste 301, Chesterfield, MO 63017
T: (314) 843-8520; Fax: (314) 434-3539
Gen Secr: Laureda J. Edstrom
Focus: Med 14837

International Association of Coroners and Medical Examiners (IACME), 6913 W Plank Rd, Peoria, IL 61604
T: (309) 697-8100
Founded: 1938; Members: 335
Focus: Med
Periodical
Newsletter (bi-annually) 14838

International Association of Counseling Services (IACS), 101 S Whiting St, Ste 211, Alexandria, VA 22304
T: (703) 823-9840; Fax: (703) 823-9843
Members: 250
Focus: Educ
Periodicals
Counseling Services
Directory of Counseling Services 14839

International Association of Defense Counsel (IADC), 1 N Franklin St, No 2400, Chicago, IL 60606-3401
T: (312) 368-1494
Founded: 1920; Members: 2500
Gen Secr: Richard J. Hayes
Focus: Law; Insurance
Periodical
Insurance Counsel Journal (quarterly) . . 14840

International Association of Dento-Maxillo-Facial Radiology (IADMFR), c/o Dental Diagnostic Sc, UTHSC Dental School, 7703 Curt Floyd Dr, San Antonio, TX 78284
T: (512) 567-3347
Gen Secr: Prof. Robert P. Langlais
Focus: Radiology 14841

International Association of Educational Peace Officers (IAEPO), c/o Alan Bragg, Spring I.S.D. Police Dept, 15330-A Kuykendahl, Houston, TX 77090
T: (713) 586-2101; Fax: (713) 586-2110
Founded: 1977; Members: 127
Gen Secr: Alan Bragg
Focus: Educ 14842

International Association of Educators for World Peace (IAEWP), POB 3282, Mastin Lake Station, Huntsville, AL 35810-0282
T: (205) 534-5501; E-Mail: mercieca@hiwaay.net; Fax: (205) 536-1018
Founded: 1969; Members: 18500
Gen Secr: Dr. Charles Mercieca
Focus: Educ; Poli Sci; Prom Peace
Periodicals
Circulation Newsletter (quarterly)
Directory (annually)
Peace Progress (annually) 14843

International Association of Electoral Science, 3921 Wilshire Blvd, Ste 303, Los Angeles, CA 90010
Focus: Poli Sci 14844

International Association of Endocrine Surgeons (IAES), c/o Mount Zion Medical Centre of UCSF, 1600 Divisadero, San Francisco, CA 94120
T: (415) 885-7616; Fax: (415) 885-7617
Gen Secr: Prof. Orlo H. Clark
Focus: Surgery 14845

International Association of Environmental Mutagen Societies (IAEMS), c/o Dept of environmental and Occupational Health, University of Pittsburgh, 130 DeSoto St, GSPH – Rm A731, Pittsburgh, PA 15261
Gen Secr: Prof. H.S. Rosenkranz
Focus: Ecology 14846

International Association of Family Sociology (IAFS), c/o Dept of Sociology, Northern Illinois Univ., De Kalb, IL 60115-2854
T: (815) 753-6423
Gen Secr: Man Singh Das
Focus: Sociology 14847

International Association of Forensic Toxicologists, c/o Vina Spiehler, 422 Tustin, Newport Beach, CA 92663
T: (714) 642-0574; E-Mail: spiehluaa@aol.com; Fax: (714) 642-2852
Founded: 1965; Members: 1200
Gen Secr: Vina Spiehler
Focus: Toxicology
Periodical
Bulletin (quarterly) 14848

International Association of Gandhian Studies (IAGS), 2942 Valley Dr, Doylestown, PA 18901
Gen Secr: Henry O. Thompson
Focus: Prom Peace 14849

International Association of Geomagnetism ans Aeronomy (IAGA), NOAA R/E/SE, 325 Broadway, Boulder, CO 80303-3328
T: (303) 497-5147; E-Mail: jjoselyn@sec.noaa.gov; Fax: (303) 497-3645
Gen Secr: Dr. J.A. Joselyn
Focus: Geophys 14850

International Association of Gerontology (IAG), c/o University of Rochester, Medical School, Monroe Community Hospital, 435 E Henrietta Rd, Rochester, NY 14620
Gen Secr: Dr. T. Franklin Williams
Focus: Geriatrics; Med 14851

International Association of Hispanists (AIH), c/o Spanish and Portuguese HB 6072, Dartmouth College, Hanover, NH 03755-3511
Gen Secr: Lía Schwartz
Focus: Ling; Lit 14852

International Association of Human-Animal Interaction Organizations (IAHAIO), c/o Delta Society, 289 Perimeter Rd E, Renton, WA 98055-1329
T: (206) 226-7357; Fax: (206) 235-1076
Founded: 1974
Gen Secr: Linda M. Hines
Focus: Behav Sci 14853

International Association of Humanist Educators, Counsellors and Leaders (IAHECL), 435 Kirkwood Lane, Plymouth, MN 55441
Gen Secr: Carol Wintermute
Focus: Educ 14854

International Association of Hydrogeologists (IAH), 1730 Grape St, Denver, CO 80220
Gen Secr: Dr. John E. Moore
Focus: Geology; Hydrology 14855

International Association of Institutes of Navigation (IAIN), 7897 Wellington Dr, Warrenton, VA 20186-9719
T: (540) 349-9310; E-Mail: 74245.535@compuserve.com; Fax: (540) 349-4337
Gen Secr: David C. Scull
Focus: Transport 14856

International Association of Jazz Educators (IAJE), POB 724, Manhattan, KS 66502
T: (913) 776-8744
Founded: 1968; Members: 6800
Focus: Music; Educ
Periodical
Jazz Educators Journal (quarterly) . . . 14857

International Association of Knowledge Engineers (IAKE), 973D Russell Av, Gaithersburg, MD 20879
T: (301) 948-5390; Fax: (301) 926-4243
Founded: 1987; Members: 2500
Gen Secr: Julie Walker
Focus: Electronic Eng 14858

International Association of Laryngectomees (IAL), c/o American Cancer Society, 1599 Clifton Rd NE, Atlanta, GA 30329
T: (404) 320-3333
Founded: 1952; Members: 30000
Focus: Otorhinolaryngology
Periodicals
Directory (annually)
News (quarterly) 14859

International Association of Law Libraries (IALL), c/o Arthur J. Morris Law Library, University of Virginia, 580 Massie Rd, Charlottesville, VA 22903-1789
Fax: (804) 982-2232, 924-7239
Gen Secr: Prof. Larry B. Wenger
Focus: Libraries & Bk Sci 14860

International Association of Mathematical Physics (IAMP), c/o Lyman Laboratory of Physics, Harvard University, Cambridge, MA 02138
T: (617) 495-4320; E-Mail: iamp@physics.harvard.edu; Fax: (617) 495-0416
Gen Secr: Prof. A.M. Jaffe
Focus: Physics 14861

International Association of Music Libraries – United States Branch (IAML-US), c/o Music Library, University of Arizona, Tucson, AZ 85721
Founded: 1955; Members: 415
Pres: Ruth Henderson
Focus: Libraries & Bk Sci 14862

International Association of Ocular Surgeons (IAOS), 4711 W Golf Rd, Ste 408, Skokie, IL 60076
T: (708) 568-1500; Fax: (708) 568-1527
Founded: 1981; Members: 900
Gen Secr: Randall Bellows
Focus: Surgery; Ophthal
Periodical
Journal of Ocular Therapy and Surgery (bi-monthly) 14863

International Association of Optometric Executives (IAOE), 100 S University Av, Ste 311, Little Rock, AR 72205-5216
T: (501) 661-7675; Fax: (501) 661-1039
Members: 75
Gen Secr: Betty Valachovic
Focus: Ophthal 14864

International Association of Oral and Maxillofacial Surgeons (IAOMS), c/o Dept of Oral and Maxillofacial Surgery, Medical College of Virginia, MCV Station, POB 980410, Richmond, VA 23298-0410
T: (804) 828-8515; Fax: (804) 828-1753
Gen Secr: Prof. Daniel M. Laskin
Focus: Surgery 14865

International Association of Orientalist Librarians (IAOL), c/o East Asian College, Univ. of California at Irvine, POB 19557, Irvine, CA 92623
T: (714) 824-8147
Gen Secr: William Wong
Focus: Libraries & Bk Sci 14866

International Association of Pancreatology (IAP), c/o Massachusetts General Hospital, 15 Parkman St, WAC 336, Boston, MA 02114-3139
T: (617) 726-8254; Fax: (617) 726-7593
Gen Secr: Dr. Andrew L. Warshaw
Focus: Intern Med 14867

International Association of Pediatric Laboratory Medicine (IAPLM), 6728 Old McLean Village Dr, McLean, VA 22101
T: (703) 556-9222; E-Mail: degnon@aol.com; Fax: (703) 556-8729
Gen Secr: George Degnon
Focus: Pediatrics 14868

International Association of Penal Law (IAPL), c/o DePaul Univ., College of Law, 25 E Jackson Blvd, Chicago, IL 60604
T: (312) 362-8332; Fax: (312) 362-5642
Gen Secr: Prof. M. Cherif Bassiouni
Focus: Law 14869

International Association of Physical Education and Sports for Girls and Women (IAPESGW), c/o Barbara J. Kelly, University of Delaware, Carpenter Sports Bldg, Newark, DE 19716
T: (302) 831-2644; E-Mail: barbara.kelly@mvs.vdel.edu; Fax: (302) 831-4261
Founded: 1949; Members: 400
Gen Secr: Barbara J. Kelly
Focus: Sports
Periodical
Report Following Congresses 14870

International Association of Radiopharmacology, c/o Dept of Nuclear Medicine, University of Massachusetts Medical Center, 55 Lake Av N, Worcester, MA 01655
T: (508) 856-4256; Fax: (508) 856-4572
Gen Secr: Dr. D. J. Hnatowich
Focus: Pharmacol 14871

International Association of School Librarianship (IASL), POB 34069, Dept 300, Seattle, WA 98124-1069
Founded: 1971; Members: 875
Gen Secr: Ken Haycock
Focus: Libraries & Bk Sci
Periodicals
Annual Conference Proceedings (annually)
Newsletter (quarterly) 14872

International Association of Seismology and Physics of the Earth's Interior (IASPEI), c/o US Geological Survey, Denver Federal Center, Mail Stop 967, POB 25046, Denver, CO 80225
T: (303) 273-8422; E-Mail: engdahl@gldfs.cr.usgs.gov; Fax: (303) 273-8450
Gen Secr: Dr. E.R. Engdahl
Focus: Geophys 14873

International Association of Severe Weather Specialists (IASWS), POB 31808, Tucson, AZ 85751
T: (520) 751-9964; E-Mail: storm5@internet.com; Fax: (520) 751-1185
Gen Secr: Warren Faidley
Focus: Geophys 14874

International Association of Theoretical and Applied Limnology (IATAL), c/o Dept of Biology, University of Alabama, Tuscaloosa, AL 35487-0344
T: (205) 438-1793; Fax: (205) 348-1403
Founded: 1922; Members: 3000
Gen Secr: Prof. Robert G. Wetzel
Focus: Water Res 14875

International Association of University Presidents (IAUP), 428 Bella, Corte Mountain View, CA 94043
T: (415) 964-6041; E-Mail: 76453.3372@compuserve.com; Fax: (415) 964-5030
Gen Secr: Dr. Maurice Harari

Focus: Educ 14876

International Association of Young Lawyers (AIJA), 136 Waverly Place, New York, NY 10014
T: (212) 741-3389; Fax: (212) 741-3389
Gen Secr: Humphrey Uddoh
Focus: Law 14877

International Association of Zoo Educators (IZE), c/o San Diego Zoo, San Diego, CA 92161
Gen Secr: Dr. Peggy Harvey
Focus: Educ; Zoology 14878

International Atherosclerosis Society (IAS), 6565 Fannin St, Ste 1423, Houston, TX 77030
T: (713) 790-4226; Fax: (713) 793-1080
Founded: 1979; Members: 7000
Gen Secr: Barbara Gordin
Focus: Cardiol 14879

International Azerbaijan Research and Development Institute (IARDI), c/o ILI, 1615 New Hampshire Avenue NW, Washington, DC 20009
T: (202) 483-3036; Fax: (202) 483-3029
Focus: Ethnology; Develop Areas . . . 14880

International Banking Security Association (ISBA), 175 Fifth Av, Ste 2566, New York, NY 10010
Focus: Eng 14881

International Benchmark Sites Network for Agrotechnology Transfer (IBSNAT), c/o IBSNAT Network, 2500 Dole St, Kraus Hall 22, Honolulu, HI 96822
T: (808) 956-8858; E-Mail: ibsnat@hawaii.edu; Fax: (808) 956-3421
Focus: Agri; Eng 14882

International Bible Society (IBS), 1820 Jet Stream Dr, Colorado Springs, CO 80921-3696
T: (719) 488-9200; E-Mail: ibs@gospelcom.net; Fax: (719) 488-0912
Gen Secr: Dr. Lars B. Dunberg
Focus: Rel & Theol 14883

International Bio-Environmental Foundation (IBEF), 15300 Ventura Blvd, Ste 405, Sherman Oaks, CA 91403
T: (818) 907-5483
Founded: 1978; Members: 400
Gen Secr: Steven A. Ross
Focus: Ecology 14884

International Biometric Society, c/o BOSTROM, 808 17 St NW, Ste 200, Washington, DC 2006-3910
T: (202) 223-9669; E-Mail: 75703.1470@compuserve.com; Fax: (202) 223-9569
Gen Secr: Charles McGrath
Focus: Bio 14885

International Bird Rescue Research Center (IBRRC), 699 Potter St, Berkeley, CA 94710
T: (510) 841-9086; Fax: (510) 841-9089
Founded: 1971; Members: 800
Focus: Ecology; Ornithology 14886

International Bone Marrow Transplant Group (IBMTG), c/o IBMTR Statistical Centre, Medical College ofWisconsin, POB 26509, Milwaukee, WI 53226
Gen Secr: Dr. Mary M. Horowitz
Focus: Surgery 14887

International Botanical Congress (IBC), Missouri Botanical Garden, POB 299, Saint Louis, MO 63166-0299
Gen Secr: Peter Hoch
Focus: Botany 14888

International Brecht Society (IBS), c/o Dept of Germanic and Slavic Languages, University of Georgia, Athens, GA 30602
T: (706) 542-3663
Founded: 1968; Members: 300
Gen Secr: Prof. Ward B. Lewis
Focus: Lit
Periodicals
Brecht Yearbook (annually)
Communications (semi-annually) 14889

International Bridge, Tunnel and Turnpike Association (IBTTA), 2120 L St NW, Ste 305, Washington, DC 20037
T: (202) 659-4620; Fax: (202) 659-0500
Founded: 1932; Members: 260
Gen Secr: Neil D. Schuster
Focus: Civil Eng
Periodical
Tollways (monthly) 14890

International Bronchoesophagological Society (IBES), c/o Mayo Clinic Scottsdale, 13400 E Shea Blvd, Scottsdale, AZ 85259
T: (602) 301-8265; Fax: (602) 301-8610
Members: 400
Gen Secr: David R. Sanderson
Focus: Otorhinolaryngology 14891

International Bulb Society (IBS), POB 4928, Culver City, CA 90230-4928
T: (310) 827-3229; Fax: (714) 856-8511
Founded: 1933; Members: 500
Gen Secr: Marilynn Howe
Focus: Botany
Periodicals
Herbertia (semi-annually)
Newsletter of APLS (quarterly) 14892

International Bundle Branch Block Association (IBBBA), 6631 W 83 St, Los Angeles, CA 90045-2899
T: (310) 670-9132
Founded: 1979
Gen Secr: Rita Kurtz Lewis
Focus: Med
Periodical
Heartbeat (quarterly) 14893

International Cancer Information Center (ICIC), c/o National Cancer Institute, Building 82, Bethesda, MD 20892
T: (301) 496-4907
Focus: Cell Biol & Cancer Res 14894

International Cardiology Foundation (ICF), c/o American Heart Association, 7272 Greenville Av, Dallas, TX 75231-4599
T: (214) 373-6300
Founded: 1957; Members: 2500
Focus: Cardiol 14895

International Catholic Esperanto Association, c/o Mubarak Anwar Amar, 213 S Bogardus St, POB 19, Elkhart, IL 62634-0019
T: (217) 947-2714
Founded: 1910; Members: 1300
Gen Secr: Mubarak Anwar Amar
Focus: Ling
Periodicals
Espero Katolika (monthly)
Jarliboro (annually) 14896

International Center for Law in Development (ICLD), 777 United Nations Plaza, New York, NY 10017
T: (212) 687-0036; Fax: (212) 972-9878
Founded: 1978
Focus: Law 14897

International Center for Medicine and Law, Staten Island (ICML), 170 Forest Green, Staten Island, NY 10312
T: (212) 747-1755
Gen Secr: A. Berkowitz
Focus: Med; Law 14898

International Center for Research on Women (ICRW), 1717 Massachusetts Av NW, Ste 302, Washington, DC 20036
T: (202) 797-0007; E-Mail: icrw@igc.apc.org; Fax: (202) 797-0020
Founded: 1976
Focus: Sociology; Econ
Periodical
Series of Occasional Papers (irregularly) 14899

International Center for the Solution of Environmental Problems (ICSEP), 535 Lovett Blvd, Houston, TX 77006
T: (713) 527-8711; Fax: (713) 527-8025
Founded: 1976
Focus: Ecology 14900

International Center of Medieval Art (ICMA), The Cloisters, Fort Tryon Park, New York, NY 10040
T: (212) 928-1146
Founded: 1956; Members: 1200
Focus: Arts
Periodicals
Gesta (semi-annually)
Newsletter (3 times annually) 14901

International Center of Photography (ICP), 1130 Fifth Av, New York, NY 10128
T: (212) 860-1777; Fax: (212) 360-6490
Founded: 1974; Members: 6800
Focus: Photo 14902

International Centre for Gas Technology Information (ICGTI), 1331 Pennsylvania Av NW, Ste 730 N, Washington, DC 20004
T: (202) 662-8991; E-Mail: icgti@gasinfo.gri.org; Fax: (202) 393-6092
Gen Secr: William F. Hederman
Focus: Eng; Energy 14903

International Centre for Textile Research and Development, c/o Texas Tech Univ., POB 4349, Lubbock, TX 79409
T: (806) 742-2011
Gen Secr: Dean Ethridge
Focus: Textiles 14904

International Cerebral Hemodynamics Society (IAPM), 701 16 Av, Seattle, WA 98122
T: (206) 553-7330; Fax: (206) 553-1717
Gen Secr: Dr. M.P. Spencer
Focus: Med 14905

International Child Health Foundation (ICHF), 10630 Little Patuxent Pkwy, Century Plaza, Ste 325, Columbia, MD 21044
T: (301) 596-4514; Fax: (301) 992-5641
Gen Secr: Charlene B. Dale
Focus: Pediatrics 14906

International Child Safety and Health Centre, National Safety Town Centre, POB 39312, Cleveland, OH 44139
Gen Secr: Dr. Dorothy Chlad
Focus: Pediatrics 14907

International Childbirth Education Association (ICEA), POB 20048, Minneapolis, MN 55420-0048
T: (612) 854-8660
Founded: 1960; Members: 12000
Gen Secr: Doris Olson
Focus: Gynecology
Periodicals
ICEA Bookmarks (3 times annually)
International Journal of Childbirth Education (quarterly)
Membership Directory (annually) 14908

International Chinese Statistical Association (ICSA), 2575 Ardath Rd, La Jolla, CA 92037
T: (619) 546-7123; E-Mail: nlo@ucsd.edu; Fax: (619) 546-5656
Gen Secr: Dr. Nancy Lo
Focus: Stats 14909

International Chiropractors Association (ICA), 1110 N Glebe Rd, Ste 1000, Arlington, VA 22201
T: (703) 528-5000; Fax: (703) 528-5023
Founded: 1926; Members: 6000
Gen Secr: Ronald Hendrickson
Focus: Orthopedics
Periodicals
ICA Today: Newsletter (bi-monthly)
International Review of Chiropractic (bi-monthly)
Membership Directory (annually) 14910

International Christian Esperanto Association (ICEA), c/o Cornelius J. McKown, 460 Orlando Av, State College, PA 16803
Founded: 1911; Members: 1300
Gen Secr: Cornelius J. McKown
Focus: Ling 14911

International Christian Leprosy Mission (ICLM), POB 23353, Portland, OR 97281-3353
T: (503) 244-5935
Founded: 1943; Members: 12
Focus: Hygiene
Periodical
Global Missions (quarterly) 14912

International Christian Media Commission (ICMC), POB 70632, Seattle, WA 98107
T: (206) 781-0461; E-Mail: icmc@igc.apc.org; Fax: (206) 781-0571
Gen Secr: William L. Thatcher
Focus: Mass Media 14913

International Christian Studies Association (ICSA), 2828 3 St, Ste 11, Santa Monica, CA 90405
T: (310) 396-0517
Gen Secr: Dr. Oskar Gruenwald
Focus: Rel & Theol 14914

International Churchill Society (ICS), 1847 Stonewood Dr, Baton Rouge, LA 70816
T: (603) 746-4433; Fax: (603) 746-4260
Gen Secr: Richard M. Langworth
Focus: Poli Sci; Hist 14915

International Clinical Epidemiology Network (INCLEN), 3600 Market St, Ste 380, Philadelphia, PA 19104
T: (215) 222-7700; E-Mail: inclen@mcimail.com; Fax: (215) 222-7741
Gen Secr: Shelly Kessler
Focus: Med 14916

International Clinical Hyperthermia Society (ICHS), c/o Univ. Heights Cancer Center, 1502 E County Line Rd S, Indianapolis, IN 46227
T: (317) 887-7651; Fax: (317) 887-7650
Gen Secr: Dr. Homayoon Shidnia
Focus: Cell Biol & Cancer Res 14917

International Clinical Phonetics and Linguistics Association (ICPLA), c/o Louisiana State Univ. Medical Centre, 1900 Gravier St, New Orleans, LA 70112
E-Mail: tpowel@lsumc.edu
Gen Secr: Dr. Thomas Powell
Focus: Logopedy 14918

International College of Angiology (ICA), 5 Daremy Court, Nesconset, NY 11767
Gen Secr: Denise M. Rossignol
Focus: Hematology 14919

International College of Dentists (ICD), 51 Monroe St, Ste 1501, Rockville, MD 20850
T: (301) 251-8861; Fax: (301) 738-9143
Founded: 1928; Members: 7200
Gen Secr: Richard G. Shaffer
Focus: Dent
Periodicals
Annual News Letter (annually)
Roster 14920

International College of Surgeons (ICS), 1516 N Lake Shore Dr, Chicago, IL 60610-1694
T: (312) 642-3555; Fax: (312) 787-1624
Founded: 1935; Members: 14000
Gen Secr: Max C. Downham
Focus: Surgery
Periodical
International Surgery (quarterly) 14921

International Commission for Protection Against Environmental Mutagens and Carcinogens (ICPEMC), Hazleton Washington, 9200 Leesburg Pike, Vienna, VA 22182
T: (703) 893-5400; Fax: (703) 759-6947
Gen Secr: T. Berndt
Focus: Ecology 14922

International Commission for the Prevention of Alcoholism and Drug Dependency (ICPADD), 12501 Old Columbia Pike, Silver Spring, MD 20904
T: (301) 680-6719; E-Mail: 74617.1663@compuserve.com; Fax: (301) 680-6090
Founded: 1952; Members: 250
Gen Secr: Thomas R. Neslund
Focus: Public Health
Periodical
Quarterly Bulletin (quarterly) 14923

International Commission of Jurists (ICJ), c/o American Association for ICJ, 777 UN Plaza, New York, NY 10017
T: (212) 972-0883
Gen Secr: William J. Butler
Focus: Law 14924

International Commission on Antifungal Susceptibility Testing (ICAS), c/o Medical College of Virginia/VCU, MCV POB 49, Richmond, VA 23298
T: (804) 828-9711; Fax: (804) 828-3097
Gen Secr: Dr. A. Espinel-Ingroff
Focus: Med 14925

International Commission on Antigens and Molecular Diagnostics (ICAMD), c/o National Center for Infectious Diseases, Div. of Bacterial and Mycotic Diseases, Emerging Bacterial and Mycotic Diseases Branch, 1600 Clifton Rd NE, Atlanta, GA 30333
T: (404) 639-3374; E-Mail: ERR2@ciddbd2.em.cdc.gov; Fax: (404) 639-3333
Gen Secr: Dr. Errol Reiss
Focus: Med 14926

International Commission on Atmospheric Electricity (ICAE), c/o Univ. of Arizona, Inst. of Atmospheric Physics, Tucson, AZ 85721
T: (602) 621-6831; Fax: (602) 621-6833
Gen Secr: Prof. Dr. E.P. Krider
Focus: Geophys 14927

International Commission on Climate (ICCL), c/o US Global Change Research Program, Code YS-1, 300 E St SW, Washington, DC 20546
T: (202) 358-0421; E-Mail: mmaccrac@usgcrp.gov; Fax: (202) 358-4103
Gen Secr: Michael MacCracken
Focus: Geophys 14928

International Commission on Computational Physics, c/o Computational Science, Computers Science and Mathematics Center, Sandia National Laboratories, Albuquerque, NM 87185-5800
E-Mail: (505) 845-7442
Gen Secr: W.J. Camp
Focus: Computer & Info Sci 14929

International Commission on Cosmic Rays, c/o Bartol Research Institute, University of Delaware, Newark, DE 19716
T: (302) 831-8113; E-Mail: gaisser@bartol.udel.edu; Fax: (302) 831-1843
Gen Secr: T.K. Gaisser
Focus: Aero; Physics 14930

International Commission on English in the Liturgy (ICEL), 1522 K St NW, Ste 1000, Washington, DC 20005-1202
T: (202) 347-0800; Fax: (202) 347-1839
Gen Secr: John R. Page
Focus: Rel & Theol; Ling 14931

International Commission on Particles and Fields, c/o California Institute of Technology, Lauritsen Laboratory HEP 256-48, Pasadena, CA 91125
T: (818) 395-6684; E-Mail: barish@ligo.caltech.edu; Fax: (818) 795-3951
Gen Secr: B.C. Barish
Focus: Eng 14932

International Commission on Penicillium and Aspergillus (ICPA), c/o USDA Agric Res Service, Southern Regional Research Center, POB 19687, New Orleans, LA 70179
T: (504) 286-4361; E-Mail: mklich@nola.srrc.usda.gov; Fax: (504) 286-4419
Gen Secr: Dr. M.A. Klich
Focus: Pharmacol 14933

International Commission on Radiation Units and Measurements (ICRU), 7910 Woodmont Av, Ste 800, Bethesda, MD 20814-3095
T: (301) 657-2652; Fax: (301) 907-8768
Founded: 1925; Members: 101
Gen Secr: W. Roger Ney
Focus: Radiology
Periodical
ICRU Report 14934

International Commission on Radiological Education and Information (ICRE), c/o Dept of Radiology, University of Utah, Medical Center, 50 N Medical Dr, Salt Lake City, UT 84132
Fax: (801) 581-2414
Gen Secr: Prof. Ann G. Osborne
Focus: Educ; Radiology 14935

International Commission on Statistical Physics, c/o Office of the Provost, Yale University, POB 20836, New Haven, CT 06520-8239
Fax: (203) 432-7107
Gen Secr: Prof. P.C. Hohenberg
Focus: Physics; Stats 14936

International Commission on the History of the Geological Sciences, c/o Harvard-Smithsonian Center for Astrophysics, 60 Garden St, Cambridge, MA 02138
T: (617) 495-7270; Fax: (617) 495-7001
Founded: 1967; Members: 119
Focus: Hist; Geology
Periodical
INHIGEO Newsletter (annually) 14937

International Commission on Yeasts (ICY), c/o Dept of Biology, Georgia State University, Atlanta, GA 3032-4010
Gen Secr: Dr. Sally Ann Meyer
Focus: Food 14938

International Committee Against Mental Illness, c/o Dept of Psychiatry, NY University Medical Center, 550 1st Av, New York, NY 10016
T: (212) 340-6214
Gen Secr: Robert Cancro
Focus: Psychiatry 14939

International Committee for Adlerian Summer Schools and Institutes (ICASSI), 1116 Saint Louis St, Edwardsville, IL 62025
Gen Secr: Prof. Dr. Eva Dreikurs Ferguson
Focus: Educ 14940

International Committee for Coal and Organic Petrology (ICCP), c/o Pennsylvania State Univ., Coal and Organic Petrology Laboratories,, 105 Academic Projects, University Park, PA 16802
T: (814) 865-6544; Fax: (814) 865-3573
Gen Secr: Prof. Dr. Alan Davis
Focus: Energy 14941

International Committee for Pre-Ottoman and Ottoman Studies (CIEPO), c/o Middle Eastern and Islamic History Dept, Univ. of Minnesota, 614 Social Science Tower, 267 19 Av S, Minneapolis, MN 55455
Gen Secr: Prof. Caesar E. Farah
Focus: Cultur Hist 14942

International Committee of Lawyers for Tibet (ICLT), 2288 Fulton St, Ste 312, Berkeley, CA 94704
T: (510) 486-0588; E-Mail: iclt@igc.apc.org; Fax: (510) 548-3785
Gen Secr: Glen C. Gilbert
Focus: Law 14943

International Committee on Avian Anatomical Nomenclature (ICAAN), c/o University of Washington, Burke Museum, POB 353010, Seattle, WA 98195-3010
T: (206) 685-9866
Gen Secr: Prof. Dr. Julian J. Baumel
Focus: Ornithology 14944

International Committee on Computational Linguistics (ICCL), Xerox Parc, 3333 Coyote Hill Rd, Palox Alto, CA 94304
Gen Secr: Martin Kay
Focus: Ling; Computer & Info Sci . . . 14945

International Committee on Education in Mycology (ICEM), 1463 La Chona Court, Atlanta, GA 30329
Gen Secr: Dr. H. Jean Shadomy
Focus: Educ; Botany 14946

International Committee on Mechanics in Medicine and Biology, c/o Int Conference on Mechanics in Medicine and Biology, 2150 GG Brown Building, Univ. of Michigan, Ann Arbor, MI 48109
T: (317) 764-9910
Gen Secr: Wen-Jei Yang
Focus: Eng; Med; Bio 14947

International Committee on Microbial Ecology (ICOME), c/o Center for Microbial Ecology, Michigan State University, Plant and Soil Science Bldg, East Lansing, MI 48824-1325
T: (517) 353-9021; Fax: (517) 353-2917
Gen Secr: Prof. James M. Tiedje
Focus: Ecology 14948

International Committee on Systematic Bacteriology (ICSB), c/o National Center for Agricultural Ultilization Research, 1815 N University St, Peoria, IL 61604
T: (309) 681-6397; E-Mail: dlabeda@ncaur.gov; Fax: (309) 681-6672
Gen Secr: David P. Labeda
Focus: Microbio 14949

International Committee on Veterinary Embryological Nomenclature (ICVEN), c/o Dept of Veterinary Anatomy, Cornell University, Ithaca, NY 14853
Gen Secr: Prof. W.O. Sack
Focus: Vet Med 14950

International Committee on Veterinary Histological Nomenclature (ICVHN), c/o Purdue University, Lynn Hall, West Lafayette, IN 47907
Fax: (317) 494-1772
Gen Secr: Prof. R. Hullinger
Focus: Vet Med 14951

International Communication Association (ICA), 8140 Burnet Rd, POB 9589, Austin, TX 78757-7799
T: (512) 454-8299; Fax: (512) 454-4221
Founded: 1950; Members: 2800
Pres: Charles R. Berger; Gen Secr: Robert L. Cox
Focus: Journalism; Comm Sci
Periodicals
Communication Theory (quarterly)
Communication Yearbook
Human Communication Research (quarterly)
Membership Directory (bi-annually)
Newsletter (quarterly) 14952

International Community Education Association (ICEA), c/o Center for Community School Development and Field Services, 250 Reid Hall, Montana State University, Bozeman, MT 59717
Gen Secr: Dr. Gloria Gregg
Focus: Educ 14953

International Comparative Literature Association (ICLA), c/o Comparative Literature, Catholic University of America, Washington, DC 20064
T: (202) 319-5488
Gen Secr: Dr. Prof. Virgil Nemoianu
Focus: Lit 14954

International Confederation of Architectural Museums (ICAM), c/o Avery Architectural and Fine Arts Library, Columbia University, 116 St and Broadway, New York, NY 10027
T: (212) 854-3068; Fax: (212) 854-8904
Gen Secr: Angela Giral
Focus: Archit 14955

International Conference of Building Officials (ICBO), 5360 S Workman Mill Rd, Whittier, CA 90601-2298
T: (310) 699-0541; Fax: (310) 692-3853
Founded: 1922; Members: 15000
Gen Secr: J. Traw
Focus: Civil Eng 14956

International Conference on Mechanics in Medicine and Biology (ICMMB), c/o University of Michigan, 2150 G.G. Brown Bldg, Ann Arbor, MI 48109
T: (313) 764-9910; Fax: (313) 747-3170
Founded: 1977
Focus: Eng; Med; Bio
Periodicals
Digest (bi-annually)
Directory of Conference Participants (bi-annually) 14957

International Conference on the Unity of the Sciences, 147 Goodrich Av, Lexington, KY 40503
T: (606) 277-3743; Fax: (606) 278-4000
Focus: Sci 14958

International Congress of Oral Implantologists (ICOI), 248 Lorraine Av, Upper Montclair, NJ 07043
T: (201) 783-6300; Fax: (201) 783-1175
Founded: 1975; Members: 3000
Gen Secr: R. Craig Johnson
Focus: Dent
Periodicals
Bulletin
Implantologist: The International Journal of Oral Implantology (semi-annually)
Membership Directory (annually) 14959

International Congress of Systematic and Evolutionary Biology (ICSEB), c/o Maryland Biotechnology Institute, 4321 Hartwick Rd, Ste 550, College Park, MD 20740
T: (301) 403-0501; E-Mail: colwellr@umbi.umd.edu; Fax: (301) 454-8123
Gen Secr: Prof. Rita R. Colwell
Focus: Bio 14960

International Congress on High-Speed Photography and Photonics (ICHSPP), Bellingham, WA 98227
T: (360) 676-3250; E-Mail: june@spie-org; Fax: (360) 647-1445
Founded: POB 10 1952; Members: 31
Gen Secr: William G. Hyzer
Focus: Optics; Photo
Periodical
Proceedings (bi-annually) 14961

International Consortium for Agricultural Systems Applications (ICASA), c/o IBSNAT Network, 2500 Dole St, Krauss Hall 22, Honolulu, HI 96822
T: (808) 956-8858; E-Mail: gordont@hawaii.edu; Fax: (808) 956-3421
Gen Secr: Gordon Y. Tsuji
Focus: Agri 14962

International Consular Academy, 2330 S Brentwood Blvd, Saint Louis, MO 63144-2096
T: (304) 961-2300
Gen Secr: George G. White
Focus: Poli Sci 14963

International Coordinating Committee on Solid State Transducers Research, c/o Berkeley Sensor and Actuator Center, Dept of EECS, Univ. of California, Berkeley, CA 94720
T: (510) 642-0614; E-Mail: muller@eecs.berkeley.edu; Fax: (510) 643-6637
Gen Secr: Richard S. Muller
Focus: Eng 14964

International Coordination Office of Pediatric Endocrine Societies (COPES), c/o Baylor College of Medicine, One Baylor Plaza, Houston, TX 77030-2399
T: (713) 770-3780; E-Mail: kcopeland@msmail.his.tch.tmc.edu; Fax: (713) 770-3903
Gen Secr: Prof. Dr. Kenneth C. Copeland
Focus: Pediatrics 14965

International Copper Association (ICA), 260 Madison Av, New York, NY 10016
T: (212) 251-7240; Fax: (212) 251-7245
Founded: 1960; Members: 42
Focus: Metallurgy
Periodical
Report (semi-annually) 14966

International Correspondence Society of Allergists (ICSA), 5811 Outlook Dr, Shawnee Mission, KS 66202
T: (913) 432-0625; Fax: (913) 432-5833
Founded: 1936; Members: 415
Gen Secr: Jeremy E. Baptist
Focus: Immunology
Periodical
The Allergy Letters (monthly) 14967

International Cost Engineering Council (ICEC), 23 Hidden Lake Dr, Granite Falls, NC 28630-9200
T: (704) 728-5287; Fax: (704) 728-0048
Founded: 1956; Members: 15
Gen Secr: Kenneth K. Humphreys
Focus: Public Admin 14968

International Council for Computer Communication (ICCC), POB 9745, Washington, DC 20016-9745
T: (703) 836-7787; Fax: (703) 836-7787
Gen Secr: Dr. Ronald P. Uhlig
Focus: Computer & Info Sci 14969

International Council for Health, Physical Education, Recreation, Sport and Dance, 1900 Association Dr, Reston, VA 22091
T: (703) 476-3462; Fax: (703) 476-9527
Founded: 1958; Members: 600
Gen Secr: Dr. Dong Ja Yang
Focus: Public Health; Physical Therapy; Sports
Periodicals
Congress Proceedings (bi-annually)
International Journal of Physical Education (quarterly) 14970

International Council for Laboratory Animal Science (ICLAS), c/o Division of Comparative Medicine, Univ. of Texas, Southwestern Medical Centre, 5323 Harry Hines Blvd, Dallas, TX 75235-9037
T: (214) 648-3340; E-Mail: spakes@mednet.swmed.edu; Fax: (214) 648-2659
Gen Secr: S.P. Pakes
Focus: Vet Med 14971

International Council for Pressure Vessel Technology, c/o Marquette University, 1515 W Wisconsin Av, Milwaukee, WI 53233
T: (414) 288-7259; Fax: (414) 288-1647
Founded: 1969; Members: 2500
Pres: Prof. G.E.O. Widera
Focus: Eng 14972

International Council for Science Policy Studies (ICSPS), c/o Harvard University, Dept of History of Science, Science Center 235, 1 Oxford St, Cambridge, MA 02138
Gen Secr: Prof. E. Mendelsohn
Focus: Poli Sci 14973

International Council for Traditional Music (ICTM), c/o Dept of Music, Columbia University, 417 Dodge, New York, NY 10027-7294
T: (212) 678-0332; E-Mail: ICTM@woof.music.columbia.edu
Founded: 1947; Members: 1300
Focus: Music
Periodicals
Bulletin ICTM (semi-annually)
Yearbook for Traditional Music (annually) 14974

International Council – National Academy of Television Arts and Sciences (IC/NATAS), 142 W 57 St, New York, NY 10019
T: (212) 489-6969; Fax: (212) 489-6557
Founded: 1968; Members: 75
Focus: Cinema 14975

International Council of Chemical Associations (ICCA), c/o CMA, 2501 M St NW, Washington, DC 20037
Gen Secr: Fred L. Webber
Focus: Chem 14976

International Council of Fine Arts Deans (ICFAD), POB 1772, San Marcos, TX 78667-1772
T: (512) 245-3387; Fax: (512) 245-8181
Focus: Arts 14977

International Council of Kinetography Laban (ICKL), 554 S Sixth St, Columbus, OH 43206
T: (614) 469-9984; E-Mail: venable.1@osu.edu; Fax: (614) 292-0939
Gen Secr: Lucy Venable
Focus: Cinema 14978

International Council of Library Association Executives (ICLAE), c/o California Library Association, 717 K St, Ste 300, Sacramento, CA 95814
T: (916) 447-8541
Founded: 1970; Members: 29
Pres: Mary Sue Ferrell
Focus: Libraries & Bk Sci 14979

International Council of Museums – Committee of the American Association of Museums (AAM/ICOM), 1225 Eye St NW, Washington, DC 20005
T: (202) 289-1818; Fax: (202) 289-6578
Founded: 1946; Members: 800
Focus: Arts 14980

International Council of Ophthalmology (ICO), c/o Northwestern Healthcare Network, 980 N Michigan Av, Ste 1500, Chicago, IL 60611
T: (312) 335-6035; Fax: (312) 335-6030
Gen Secr: Dr. Bruce E. Spicey
Focus: Ophthal 14981

International Council of Psychologists (ICP), c/o Dept of Psychology, Southwest Texas State University, San Marcos, TX 78666-4616
T: (512) 245-2526; E-Mail: JD04@academia.swt.edu; Fax: (512) 245-3153
Founded: 1942; Members: 1700
Gen Secr: Prof. John M. Davis
Focus: Psych
Periodicals
Directory (bi-annually)
International Psychologist (quarterly) . . . 14982

International Council of Societies of Pathology (ICSP), 7001 Georgia St, Chevy Chase, MD 20815
T: (202) 782-2759; Fax: (202) 782-3056
Gen Secr: Dr. F.K. Mostofi
Focus: Pathology 14983

International Council of the Museum of Modern Art, 11 W 53 St, New York, NY 10019
T: (212) 708-9474
Founded: 1953; Members: 155
Gen Secr: Elizabeth Streibert
Focus: Arts 14984

International Council on Education for Teaching (ICET), 2009 N 14 St, Ste 609, Arlington, VA 22201
T: (703) 525-5253; Fax: (703) 351-9381
Founded: 1953
Focus: Adult Educ; Educ
Periodicals
International Yearbook on Teacher Education
Newsletter (quarterly)
Proceedings (annually) 14985

International Council on Women's Health Issues (ICOWHI), c/o Indiana University School of Nursing, 1111 Middle Dr, Indianapolis, IN 46202
T: (317) 274-0032; E-Mail: PSTERN@INDYVAX.IUPUI.EDU; Fax: (317) 274-4928
Gen Secr: Phyllis Stern
Focus: Public Health 14986

International Courtly Literature Society (ICLS), 1920 S First St, Minneapolis, MN 55454
T: (612) 338-8020; Fax: (612) 626-7735
Founded: 1973; Members: 700
Gen Secr: Prof. Stephanie Cain Van Delden
Focus: Lit 14987

International Crane Foundation (ICF), E-11376 Shady Lane Rd, Baraboo, WI 53913
T: (608) 356-9462; Fax: (608) 356-9465
Founded: 1973; Members: 5000
Gen Secr: George W. Archibald
Focus: Agri
Periodical
ICF Bugle (quarterly) 14988

International Criminal Law Commission (ICLC), 825 Woodland Dr, Montecito, CA 93108
T: (805) 565-1949; Fax: (805) 565-1536
Founded: 1965; Members: 35
Gen Secr: A. Ballester
Focus: Law
Periodical
The Establishment of an International Criminal Court (annually) 14989

International Cryogenic Engineering Committee (ICEC), c/o International Cryogenic Materials Conference, POB 3345, Boulder, CO 80307
Focus: Eng 14990

International Dark-Sky Association (IDSA), 3545 N Stewart, Tucson, AZ 85716
T: (602) 795-1381
Founded: 1988; Members: 1100
Focus: Astronomy 14991

International Dental Health Foundation (IDHF), 1111-60F S Lakes Dr, Ste 345, Reston, VA 22091
T: (703) 860-9244; Fax: (703) 860-9245
Founded: 1981; Members: 450
Gen Secr: Patricia L. Cartwright
Focus: Dent 14992

International Design Conference in Aspen (IDCA), POB 664, Aspen, CO 81612
T: (303) 925-2257; Fax: (303) 925-2257
Founded: 1950
Focus: Graphic & Dec Arts, Design . . 14993

International Development Research Council (IDRC), 35 Technology Park Atlanta, Ste 150, Norcross, GA 30092
T: (770) 446-8955; Fax: (770) 662-8950
Founded: 1961; Members: 2000
Gen Secr: Prentice Knight
Focus: Business Admin; Econ
Periodicals
IDRC Communicator (monthly)
Industrial Development (bi-monthly) . . . 14994

International Development Research Council (IDRC), 35 Technology Park/Atlanta, Ste 150, Norcross, GA 30092-9934
T: (404) 446-8955; E-Mail: idrc@conway.com; Fax: (404) 662-8950
Gen Secr: Prentice Knight
Focus: Eng 14995

International Diabetes Federation (IDF), c/o American Diabetes Association, 1660 Duke St, Alexandria, VA 22314
T: (703) 549-1500; Fax: (703) 683-1839
Gen Secr: Linda Cann
Focus: Diabetes 14996

International Documentary Association (IDA), 1551 S Robertson Blvd, Ste 201, Los Angeles, CA 90035
T: (310) 284-8422; E-Mail: IDF@netcom.com; Fax: (310) 785-9334
Gen Secr: Dr. Betsy A. McLane
Focus: Doc 14997

International Dostoevsky Society (IDS), 3707 Emily St, Kensington, MD 20895
T: (301) 933-2945
Founded: 1971; Members: 250
Gen Secr: Prof. Nadine Natov
Focus: Lit
Periodicals
Dostoevsky Studies (annually)
Newsletter (semi-annually)
Proceedings of the International Symposia (every 3-4 years) 14998

International Education Research Foundation (IERF), POB 66940, Los Angeles, CA 90066
T: (310) 397-3655; Fax: (310) 397-7686
Founded: 1969
Focus: Educ 14999

International Educational Development – Humanitarian Law Project, 8124 W Third St, Ste 105, Los Angeles, CA 90048
T: (213) 653-6583
Gen Secr: Lydia Brazon
Focus: Educ; Law 15000

International Educators Cooperative, 212 Alcott Rd, East Falmouth, MA 02536
T: (508) 540-8173; Fax: (508) 540-8173
Gen Secr: Louis J. Fuccillo
Focus: Educ 15001

International Electrology Educators (IEE), c/o SCME, 132 Great Rd, No 200, Stow, MA 01775
Founded: 1979; Members: 55
Pres: Ann O'Brien
Focus: Educ; Med 15002

International Electronics Packaging Society (IEPS), 114 N Hale St, Wheaton, IL 60187-5113
T: (708) 260-1044; Fax: (708) 260-0867
Founded: 1977; Members: 1500
Focus: Electronic Eng
Periodicals
News (monthly)
Newsletter (quarterly) 15003

International Embryo Transfer Society (IETS), 309 W Clark St, Champaign, IL 61820
T: (217) 356-3182; Fax: (217) 398-4119
Founded: 1974; Members: 850
Gen Secr: Carl D. Johnson
Focus: Vet Med 15004

International Environmetrics Society (TIES), c/o Dept of Statistics, Virginia Tech, Blacksburgh, VA 24061-0439
E-Mail: epsmith@vt.edu; Fax: (703) 231-3863
Gen Secr: Dr. Eric P. Smith
Focus: Ecology 15005

International Erosion Control Association (IECA), Box 4904, Steamboat Springs, CO 80477
T: (303) 879-3010; Fax: (303) 879-8563
Founded: 1972; Members: 400
Focus: Geomorph; Agri
Periodicals
Membership Directory (annually)
Newsletter (bi-monthly) 15006

International Estuarine Research Federation, 490 Chippingswood Dr, Ste 2, Port Republic, MD 20676
T: (410) 586-0997
Gen Secr: Jon Bartholomew
Focus: Hydrology 15007

International Eye Foundation (IEF), 7801 Norfolk Av, Bethesda, MD 20814
T: (301) 986-1830; E-Mail: vsheffield@ief.permanet.org; Fax: (301) 986-1876
Gen Secr: Victoria M. Sheffield
Focus: Ophthal 15008

International Federation for Family Health (IFFH), 6100 N E Mineral Springs Rd, Carlton, OR 97111
Gen Secr: Elton Kessel
Focus: Public Health 15009

International Federation for Home Economics (IFHE), c/o Family and Consumer Sciences, 305 History Bldg, Texas A and M University, College Station
T: (409) 845-3850, 845-1953; E-Mail: n-granovsky@tamu.edu; Fax: (409) 845-6496
Gen Secr: Prof. Nancy L. Granovsky
Focus: Home Econ 15010

International Federation for Tropical Medicine, c/o Div. of Gastroenterology, Medical College of Ohio, Dept of Medicine, POB 10008, Toledo, OH 43699-0008
Gen Secr: Dr. William A. Sodeman
Focus: Trop Med 15011

International Federation of Cell Biology (IFCB), c/o Univ. of Texas Health Sciences, Centr at San Antonio, San Antonio, TX 78284-7762
Gen Secr: Prof. Ivan L. Cameron
Focus: Cell Biol & Cancer Res 15012

International Federation of Classification Societies (IFCS), c/o Graduate School of Management, Rutgers University, 92 New St, Newark, NJ 07102-1895
T: (201) 648-5814; E-Mail: dcarroll@gandalf.rutgers.edu; Fax: (201) 648-1459
Gen Secr: Prof. J. Douglas Carroll
Focus: Standards 15013

International Federation of Dental Education Associations (IFDEA), c/o American Association of Dental Schools, 1625 Massachusetts Av NW, Washington, DC 20036
T: (202) 667-9433
Focus: Educ; Dent 15014

International Federation of Eye Banks (IFEB), 815 Park Av, Baltimore, MD 21201
T: (301) 752-3800; Fax: (301) 454-4457
Focus: Ophthal 15015

International Federation of Marfan Syndrome Organizations (IFMSO), 382 Main St, Port Washington, NY 11050
T: (516) 883-8712
Gen Secr: Priscilla Ciccariello
Focus: Med 15016

International Federation of Ophthalmological Societies (IFOS), c/o Northwestern Healthcare Network, 980 N Michigan Av, Ste 1500, Chicago, IL 60611
T: (312) 335-6035; Fax: (312) 335-6030
Gen Secr: Dr. Bruce E. Spivey
Focus: Ophthal 15017

International Federation of Ophthalmological Societies / International Council of Ophthalmology, 980 N Michigan Av, Ste 1500, Chicago, IL 60611
T: (312) 335-6035; Fax: (312) 335-6030
Founded: 1857; Members: 75
Pres: Prof. A. Nakajiama; Gen Secr: Prof. B.E. Spivey
Focus: Ophthal 15018

International Federation of Organizations for School Correspondence and Exchanges (FIOCES), c/o Student Letter Exchange, RR Suite 4, Waseca, MN 56093
T: (507) 835-3691
Gen Secr: Wayne J. Dankert
Focus: Educ 15019

International Federation of Oto-Rhino-Laryngological Societies (IFOS), c/o American Academy of ORL, Head and Neck Surgery, 1 Prince St, Alexandria, VA 22314-3357
T: (703) 836-4444; Fax: (703) 683-5100
Gen Secr: Dr. Jerome G. Goldstein
Focus: Otorhinolaryngology 15020

International Federation of Palynological Societies (IFPS), c/o Centr for Environmental Sciences and Education, Northern Arizona Univ., POB 5694, Flagstaff, AZ 86011-5694
T: (502) 523-5821; E-Mail: sa@nauvax.ucc.nau.edu; Fax: (502) 523-7423
Gen Secr: Dr. R. Scott Anderson
Focus: Botany 15021

International Federation of Placental Associations (IFPA), c/o Dept Obstetrics and Gynecology, University of Rochester Medical Center, 601 Elmwood Av, Rochester, NY 14642-8668
T: (716) 275-3638; E-Mail: IFPA@obgyn.rochester.edu; Fax: (716) 244-2209
Gen Secr: Dr. Richard K. Miller
Focus: Gynecology 15022

International Federation of Psoriasis Associations (IFPA), 6600 SW 92 Av, Ste 300, Portland, OR 97223-7195
T: (503) 244-7404; E-Mail: 76135.2746@compuserve.com; Fax: (503) 245-0626
Gen Secr: Gail M. Zimmerman
Focus: Derm 15023

International Federation of Scoliosis Associations (IFOSA), 9908 Cape Scott Ct, Raleigh, NC 27614-9025
T: (919) 846-2204; E-Mail: ifosausa@aol.com; Fax: (919) 846-6782
Gen Secr: Howard M. Shulman
Focus: Med 15024

International Federation of Societies for Electron Microscopy (IFSEM), c/o Dept of Materials Science and Engineering, University of California, 280 Hearst Mining Bldg, Berkeley, CA 94720
T: (510) 642-3813; Fax: (510) 486-5933
Founded: 1962; Members: 42
Pres: Gareth Thomas
Focus: Optics 15025

International Federation of Societies of Endoscopic Surgeons (IFSES), c/o Thomas Jefferson Univ., MOB, 1100 Walnut St, Ste 700, Philadelphia, PA 19107
T: (215) 955-5875; Fax: (215) 955-5874
Gen Secr: Louisa Ward-Smith
Focus: Surgery 15026

International Federation of Societies of Toxicologic Pathologists (IFSTP), c/o Labpath Management Inc, Six Bruce Court, Suffern, NY 10901
T: (914) 357-6377; Fax: (914) 357-6711
Gen Secr: Dr. Michael J. Iatropoulos
Focus: Pathology; Toxicology 15027

International Federation of Sports Chiropractic (FICS), 695 NE 126th, North Miami, FL 33161
T: (305) 893-3892; Fax: (305) 895-5867
Gen Secr: Dr. Thomas Hyde
Focus: Med 15028

International Federation of Sports Medicine (FIMS), c/o Center for Sports Medicine, Pennsylvania State University, 146 REC Building, University Park, PA 16802-5700
T: (814) 865-7107, 238-1314; E-Mail: hgk2@psu.edu; Fax: (814) 865-7077
Gen Secr: Prof. Howard G. Knuttgen
Focus: Med 15029

International Federation of Surgical Colleges (IFSC), c/o Dept of Surgery, Univ. of Philadelphia Hospital, 4 Silverstein, 3400 Spruce St, Philadelphia, PA 19104
Focus: Educ; Surgery 15030

International Federation of Training and Development Organizations (IFTDO), POB 33213, Washington, DC 20033-0213
T: (202) 333-1811; E-Mail: ngvb09b@prodigy.com; Fax: (202) 342-6055
Gen Secr: Dr. David Waugh
Focus: Educ 15031

International Federation of Vexillological Associations (FIAV), POB 580, Winchester, MA 01890
T: (617) 729-9410; Fax: (617) 721-4817
Founded: 1967; Members: 25
Gen Secr: Dr. Whitney Smith
Focus: Hist
Periodical
Report of the International Congresses of Vexillology (bi-annually) 15032

International Federation of Women Lawyers (FIDA), 140 W 86 St, New York, NY 10024
T: (212) 362-8844; Fax: (212) 362-7952
Gen Secr: Eleanor A. Brown
Focus: Law 15033

International Fertilizer Development Center (IFDC), POB 2040, Muscle Shoals, AL 35662
T: (205) 381-6600; E-Mail: General@hiwaay.net; Fax: (205) 381-7408
Founded: 1974
Pres: Dr. Amit H. Roy
Focus: Agri 15034

International Field Emission Society, c/o Oak Ridge National Lab, POB 2008, Oak Ridge, TN 37831-6376
T: (423) 574-4719; E-Mail: xkm@cosmail1.ctd.ornl.gov; Fax: (423) 574-0641
Gen Secr: Dr. M.K. Miller
Focus: Ecology 15035

International Film Seminars (IFS), 305 W 21 St, New York, NY 10011
T: (212) 727-7262; Fax: (212) 691-9565
Founded: 1960
Focus: Cinema 15036

International Food Policy Research Institute (IFPRI), 1200 17 St NW, Washington, DC 20036-3006
T: (202) 862-5600; E-Mail: ifpri@cgnet.com; Fax: (202) 467-4439
Gen Secr: Per Pinstrup-Andersen
Focus: Food 15037

International Forum on Globalization (IFG), POB 12218, San Francisco, CA 94112-0218
T: (415) 771-3394; E-Mail: ifg@igc.org; Fax: (415) 771-1121
Focus: Poli Sci 15038

International Foundation for Art Research (IFAR), 46 E 70 St, New York, NY 10021
T: (212) 879-1780; Fax: (212) 734-4174
Founded: 1968
Gen Secr: Dr. Constance Lowenthal
Focus: Arts
Periodical
IFAR Reports (monthly) 15039

International Foundation for Dermatology (IFD), c/o Skin and Cancer Unit, 350 Fifth Av, Ste 7805, New York, NY 10118-0189
T: (212) 263-5260; Fax: (516) 741-3806
Gen Secr: Dr. Alfred W. Kopf
Focus: Derm 15040

International Foundation for Earth Construction (IFEC), 3282 Theresa Lane, Lafayette, CA 94549
T: (510) 933-2412
Gen Secr: Dr. Richard Ferm
Focus: Civil Eng 15041

International Foundation for Electoral Systems (IFES), 1101 15 St NW, Washington, DC 20005
T: (202) 828-8507; Fax: (202) 452-0804
Gen Secr: Charles T. Manatt
Focus: Poli Sci 15042

International Foundation for Homeopathy (IFH), 2366 Eastlake Av E, Seattle, WA 98102
T: (206) 324-8230
Founded: 1978; Members: 2000
Gen Secr: Fred Bishop
Focus: Homeopathy
Periodical
Resonance (bi-monthly) 15043

International Foundation for Production Research (IFPR), c/o Department of ISE, Virginia Polytechnical Inst and State Univ, Blacksburg, VA 24061-0118
T: (703) 231-6053; Fax: (703) 953-1887
Gen Secr: Dr. James M. Moore
Focus: Econ 15044

International Foundation for Studies in Reproduction (USIF), c/o WFFH, 405 Main St, Port Washington, NY 11050
T: (516) 944-8655; Fax: (516) 944-8663
Focus: Eng 15045

International Galdos Association (IGA), c/o Dept of Spanish, University of California at Davis, Davis, CA 95616
T: (916) 752-0837
Founded: 1979; Members: 205
Pres: G. Gullon
Focus: Lit 15046

International Geosynthetics Society (IGS), 226 Sitton Rd, Easley, SC 29642
T: (803) 855-0504; Fax: (803) 859-1698
Focus: Geophys 15047

International Geotechnical Engineering Committee (IGEC), c/o Univ. of Southern Illinois, Carbondale, IL 62901
Fax: (618) 453-7455
Gen Secr: Prof. Braja M. Das
Focus: Eng 15048

International Geranium Society (IGS), POB 92734, Pasadena, CA 91109-2734
T: (619) 727-0309
Gen Secr: Frederica Sedgwick
Focus: Botany 15049

International Global Atmospheric Chemistry Project (IGAC), c/o Core Project Office, Massachusetts Inst. of Technology, Bldg 24-409, Cambridge, MA 02139
T: (617) 253-9887; E-Mail: pszenny@mit.edu; Fax: (617) 253-9886
Gen Secr: Dr. Alex Pszenny
Focus: Chem 15050

International Glutamate Technical Committee (IGTC), POB 76181, Atlanta, GA 30358
Gen Secr: Dr. A.G. Ebert
Focus: Eng 15051

International GPS Service for Geodynamics (IGS), c/o Jet Propulsion Laboratory, California Institute of Technology, 4800 Oak Grove Dr, Pasadena, CA 91109-8099
T: (818) 354-4321; E-Mail: igscb@igscb.ipl.nasa.gov; Fax: (818) 393-8330
Gen Secr: Ruth E. Neilan
Focus: Geophys 15052

International Graphic Arts Education Association (IGAEA), 4615 Forbes Av, Pittsburgh, PA 15213
T: (412) 682-5170
Founded: 1923; Members: 700
Focus: Adult Educ; Graphic & Dec Arts, Design
Periodicals
The Communicator (7 times annually)
Membership Directory (annually)
Visual Communications Journal (annually) 15053

International Graphoanalysis Society (IGAS), 111 N Canal St, Chicago, IL 60606
T: (312) 930-9446
Founded: 1929; Members: 50000
Focus: Graphology
Periodical
The Journal of Graphoanalysis (monthly) 15054

International Group of Research Reactors (IGORR), c/o Oak Ridge National Laboratory, FEDC Bldg, POB 2009, Oak Ridge, TN 37831-8218
T: (423) 574-0558; E-Mail: kfr@ornl.gov; Fax: (423) 576-3041
Gen Secr: Kathy Rosenbalm
Focus: Energy 15055

International Guild of Advanced Sciences (IGAS), POB 2917, Palm Springs, CA 92263
T: (619) 327-7355; E-Mail: Asgard@ix.netcom.com; Fax: (619) 327-7355
Focus: Sci 15056

International Guild of Occult Sciences (IGOS), 255 N El Cielo Rd, Ste 565, Palm Springs, CA 92262
T: (619) 327-7355; Fax: (619) 327-7355
Focus: Parapsych 15057

International Gynecologic Cancer Society (IGCS), c/o University of Louisville, POB 3086, Louisville, KY 40201
Gen Secr: Robert D. Hilgers
Focus: Cell Biol & Cancer Res 15058

International Health and Temperance Association (IHTA), 12501 Old Columbia Pike, Silver Spring, MD 20904
T: (301) 680-6719; Fax: (301) 680-6090
Gen Secr: Tom Neslund
Focus: Physics 15059

International Health Evaluation Association (IHEA), 90 W Montgomery Av, Ste 340, Rockville, MD 20850
T: (301) 762-6050; Fax: (301) 762-7127
Founded: 1971; Members: 300
Gen Secr: Harold A. Timken
Focus: Public Health
Periodical
Newsletter (quarterly) 15060

International Health Futures Network (IHFN), Care Forum, 830 Market St, San Francisco, CA 94102
T: (415) 421-8810; Fax: (415) 421-8837
Gen Secr: Kathryn Johnson
Focus: Public Health 15061

International Health Society (IHS), 1001 E Oxford Ln, Englewood, CO 80110
T: (303) 789-3003
Founded: 1944; Members: 500
Gen Secr: Franklin L. Bowling
Focus: Adult Educ; Public Health
Periodicals
Bulletin (quarterly)
Directory 15062

International Hepato-Pancreato-Biliary Association (IHPBA), c/o Brigham and Women's Hospital, Div of Gastroenterology, 75 Francis St, Boston, MA 02115
T: (617) 732-7414
Gen Secr: David Carr-Locke
Focus: Gastroenter 15063

International Hospital Federation (IHF), c/o American Hospital Association, 1 N Franklin, Chicago, IL 60611
T: (312) 422-3000; Fax: (312) 422-4796
Founded: 1947; Members: 1788
Gen Secr: Jose Gonzalez
Focus: Med
Periodicals
Membership List (annually)
Official Yearbook (annually)
World Hospitals (quarterly) 15064

International Human Powered Vehicle Association (IHPVA), POB 51255, Indianapolis, IN 46251
T: (317) 876-9478; Fax: (317) 876-9478
Founded: 1975; Members: 2000
Focus: Physiology 15065

International Hurricane Centre, c/o FIU, Dept of Sociology, Miami, FL 33199
T: (305) 348-2242; E-Mail: peacock@servax.fiu.edu; Fax: (305) 348-3605
Gen Secr: Walter G. Peacock
Focus: Geophys 15066

International Husserl and Phenomenological Research Society (IHPRS), 348 Payson Rd, Belmont, MA 02178
T: (617) 489-3696
Gen Secr: Prof. Anna-Teresa Tymieniecka
Focus: Parapsych 15067

International Imagery Association (IIA), POB 1046, Bronx, NY 10471
Founded: 1979
Focus: Psych; Lit
Periodicals
Imagery Today: Newsletter (semi-annually)
International Imagery Bulletin (quarterly)
Journal of Mental Imagery (quarterly) . . 15068

International Institute for Bioenergetic Analysis (IIBA), 144 E 36 St, New York, NY 10016
T: (212) 532-7742; Fax: (212) 532-5331
Founded: 1956; Members: 1000
Focus: Psychiatry 15069

International Institute for Christian Studies, POB 12147, Overland Park, KS 66282-2147
T: (913) 642-1166; E-Mail: 73754.1132@compuserve.com; Fax: (913) 642-1280
Gen Secr: Dr. Daryl McCarthy
Focus: Rel & Theol 15070

International Institute for Energy Conservation (IIEC), 750 First St NE, Ste 940, Washington, DC 20002
T: (202) 842-3388; E-Mail: iiec@solstice.crest.org
Gen Secr: Deborah Bleviss
Focus: Energy 15071

International Institute for Human Evolutionary Research (IIHER), c/o Oregon State University Library, Corvallis, OR 97331-4501
T: (503) 383-7215; E-Mail: NBOAZ@oregon.uoregon.edu; Fax: (503) 383-7506
Focus: Bio 15072

International Institute for Suburban and Regional Studies, POB 28060, Baltimore, MD 21239-8060
Fax: (410) 426-6062
Focus: Urban Plan 15073

International Institute for Theoretical and Applied Physics (IITAP), 123 Office and Laboratory, Iowa State University, Ames, IA 50011-3022
T: (515) 294-3555; E-Mail: iitap@iastate.edu; Fax: (515) 294-9933
Gen Secr: Dr. James Vary
Focus: Physics 15074

International Institute for Vital Registration and Statistics (IIVRS), 9650 Rockville Pike, Bethesda, MD 20014
Gen Secr: Iwao M. Moriyama
Focus: Stats 15075

International Institute of Ibero-American Literature (IILI), 1312 CL, University of Pittsburgh, Pittsburgh, PA 15260
T: (412) 624-3359
Gen Secr: Prof. Keith McDuffie
Focus: Lit 15076

International Institute of Islamic Medicine (IIIM), c/o IBN SINA Professional Bldg, 1936 W Martin Luther King Blvd, Ste 201, Tampa, FL 33607-6530
T: (813) 661-6161; Fax: (813) 681-3606
Gen Secr: Dr. Husain F. Nagamia
Focus: Med 15077

International Institute of Islamic Thought (IIIT), 555 Grove St, POB 669, Herndo, VA 22070
T: (703) 471-1133; E-Mail: iiit@iiit.dgsys.com; Fax: (703) 471-3922
Gen Secr: Dr. Mohammad Jaghlit
Focus: Rel & Theol 15078

International Institute of Projectiology (IIP), 20 E 49th St, 2F, New York, NY 10017
T: (718) 721-6257; E-Mail: iipnyusa@aol.com; Fax: (718) 721-6257
Gen Secr: Simone de La Tour
Focus: Sci 15079

International Institute of Rural Reconstruction - U.S. Chapter (IIRR), 475 Riverside Dr, Rm 1270, New York, NY 10015
T: (212) 870-2992; Fax: (212) 870-2981
Founded: 1960
Focus: Sociology; Poli Sci; Public Health; Develop Areas; Educ
Periodicals
IIRR Report (semi-annually)
International Sharing (3 times annually)
Rural Reconstruction Review (annually) . 15080

International Institute of Sociology (IIS), c/o Gerontology Centre, University of Kansas, 4089 Dole Human Development Centre, Lawrence, KS 66045
T: (913) 864-4130; Fax: (913) 864-5063
Gen Secr: Dr. Rhonda Montgomery
Focus: Sociology 15081

International Institute of Tourism Studies (IITS), c/o Georg Washington Univ, School of Business and Public Management, 817 23rd St NW, Washington, DC 20052
T: (202) 994-6281; Fax: (202) 994-1420
Gen Secr: Dr. Donald E. Hawkins
Focus: Business Admin 15082

International Institute of Tropical Agriculture (IITA), POB 025443, Miami, FL 33102
Focus: Agri 15083

International Institute on Peace Education (IIPE), c/o Peace Education Program, Teachers College, Columbia University, 525 W 120 St, New York, NY 10027
T: (212) 678-3972; Fax: (212) 678-4048
Gen Secr: Betty A. Reardon
Focus: Educ; Prom Peace 15084

International Institution of Entreprenology, POB 3609, Winchester, VA 22604-2520
Focus: Econ 15085

International Insurance Society (IIS), POB 870223, Tuscaloosa, AL 35487
T: (205) 348-8974; Fax: (205) 348-8973
Founded: 1965; Members: 1200
Gen Secr: Nancy J. Allen
Focus: Insurance 15086

International Intraocular Implant Club, c/o Cullen Eye Institute, 6501 Fannin, NC-200, Houston, TX 77030
T: (713) 798-6443; Fax: (713) 798-3027
Gen Secr: Douglas D. Koch
Focus: Ophthal 15087

International Isotope Society (IIS), c/o Dr. Dale W. Blackburn, 144 Ramblewood Rd, Moorestown, NJ 08057
T: (609) 235-1360; Fax: (609) 235-1360
Founded: 1986; Members: 500
Gen Secr: Dr. Dale W. Blackburn
Focus: Biochem 15088

International Joint Conferences on Artificial Intelligence (IJCAII), c/o AT & T Labs, 600 Mountain Av 2B-403, Murray Hill, NJ 07974
T: (908) 582-2269; E-Mail: rjb@research.att.com; Fax: (908) 582-7550
Gen Secr: Dr. R. J. Brachman
Focus: Computer & Info Sci 15089

International Joseph Diseases Foundation (IJDF), POB 2550, Livermore, CA 94551-2550
T: (510) 371-1287; Fax: (510) 371-1288
Founded: 1977; Members: 1800
Focus: Med
Periodical
Newsletter (quarterly) 15090

International Kirlian Research Association (IKRA), 2202 Quentin Rd, Brooklyn, NY 11229
T: (718) 339-3888
Founded: 1975; Members: 200
Focus: Electric Eng
Periodical
Communications and Acta Electrografica (quarterly) 15091

International Kundalini Yoga Teachers Association (IKYTA), Rte 2, Shady Lane, POB 4, Espanola, NM 87532
Gen Secr: Nam Kaur
Focus: Educ 15092

International Labor Rights Fund, 110 Maryland Av NE, POB 74, Washington, DC 20002
T: (202) 544-7198; E-Mail: laborrights@igc.apc.org; Fax: (202) 543-5999
Gen Secr: Pharis J. Harvey
Focus: Law 15093

International Landslide Research Group (ILRG), 3262 Ross Rd, Palo alto, CA 94303
Gen Secr: Earl E. Brabb
Focus: Geology 15094

International Laser Display Association (ILDA), 4301 32 St W, Ste E-8, Bradenton, FL 34205
T: (941) 758-6881; E-Mail: ildadirect@aol.com; Fax: (941) 758-1605
Gen Secr: Linda Hare
Focus: Electric Eng 15095

International Law Commission (ILC), c/o United Nations, Rm S-3460A, New York, NY 10017
T: (212) 963-8469; Fax: (212) 965-0159
Gen Secr: Dr. Roy S. Lee
Focus: Law 15096

International Law Institute (ILI), 1615 New Hampshire Av NW, Washington, DC 20009
T: (202) 483-3036; E-Mail: training@ili.org; Fax: (202) 483-3029
Founded: 1955
Gen Secr: Stuart Kerr
Focus: Law 15097

International Lead Zinc Research Organization (ILZRO), 2525 Meridian Pkwy, Ste 100, POB 12036, Research Triangle Park, NC 27709
T: (919) 361-4647; Fax: (919) 361-1957
Founded: 1958; Members: 77
Pres: Dr. Jerome F. Cole
Focus: Metallurgy
Periodicals
Environmental Bulletin (quarterly)
R & D Focus (quarterly) 15098

International League Against Epilepsy (ILAE), c/o Dept of Neurology, Reed Neurological Research Center, UCLA School of Medicine, 710 Westwood Plaza, Los Angeles, CA 90024-1769
T: (310) 825-5745; Fax: (310) 206-8461
Gen Secr: Prof. Jerome Engel
Focus: Neurology 15099

International League of Associations for Rheumatology (ILAR), c/o Vanderbilt University, Chief Medical Office, 3810A TVC, Nashville, TN 37232-5545
T: (615) 343-9324; Fax: (615) 343-6478
Gen Secr: Dr. John S. Sergent
Focus: Rheuma 15100

International League of Dermatological Societies (ILDS), c/o Dept of Dermatology, University of Iowa Hospitals and Clinics, 200 Hawkins Dr BT2045, Iowa City, IA 52242-1090
T: (319) 356-2274; E-Mail: jstrauss@blue.weeg.uiowa.edu; Fax: (319) 356-8317
Gen Secr: Prof. John S. Strauss
Focus: Derm 15101

International Life Sciences Institute (ILSI), 1126 Sixteenth St NW, Washington, DC 20036-4810
T: (202) 659-0074; E-Mail: ilsi@dc.ilsi.org; Fax: (202) 659-3859
Gen Secr: Dr. Alex Malaspina
Focus: Bio 15102

International Linguistic Association, c/o Hispanic Society of America, 613 W 155th St, New York, NY 10032
Gen Secr: Dr. Theodore S. Beardsley
Focus: Ling 15103

International Literacy Institute (ILI), c/o Univ. of Pennsylvania, 3910 Chestnut St, Philadelphia, PA 19104-3111
T: (215) 898-2100; E-Mail: ILI@literacy.upenn.edu; Fax: (215) 898-9804
Gen Secr: Daniel A. Wagner
Focus: Lit 15104

International Magnesium Association (IMA), 1303 Vincent Pl, Ste 1, McLean, VA 22101
T: (703) 442-8888; Fax: (703) 821-1824
Founded: 1943; Members: 91
Gen Secr: Byron B. Clow
Focus: Metallurgy
Periodicals
Magnesium (9 times annually)
Proceedings (annually) 15105

International Maledicta Society (IMS), POB 14123, Santa Rosa, CA 95402-6123
T: (707) 523-4761
Founded: 1975; Members: 3000
Pres: Reinhold A. Aman
Focus: Ling
Periodical
Maledicta: The International Journal of Verbal Aggression (semi-annually) 15106

International Management Development Association (IMDA), 1201 Stonegate Rd, POB 216, Hummelstown, PA 17036
T: (717) 566-3054; Fax: (717) 566-1191
Gen Secr: Dr. Erdener Kaynak
Focus: Business Admin 15107

International Marine Simulator Forum (IMSF), 1 Maritime Plaza, Toledo, OH 43604
E-Mail: IMSF@aol.com
Gen Secr: Harry J. Crooks
Focus: Oceanography 15108

International Medical Corps (IMC), 12233 W Olympic Blvd, Ste 280, Los Angeles, CA 90064-1052
T: (310) 826-7800; E-Mail: imc@imc-la.com; Fax: (310) 442-6622
Gen Secr: Nancy A. Aossey
Focus: Med 15109

International Medical Informatics Association (IMIA), c/o Information Service, University of Maryland at Baltimore, 100 N Greene St, Baltimore, MD 21201-1503
T: (410) 706-2004; E-Mail: mjb@umab.umd.edu; Fax: (410) 706-8459
Gen Secr: Dr. Marion J. Ball
Focus: Computer & Info Sci 15110

International Medical Services for Health (INMED), 45449 Severn Way, Ste 161, Sterling, VA 20166-8918
T: (703) 444-4477; E-Mail: ricer@iia.org; Fax: (703) 444-4471
Gen Secr: Linda Pfeiffer
Focus: Med; Public Health 15111

International Meniere's Disease Research Institute (IMDRI), 300 E Hampden Av, Ste 401, Englewood, CO 80110-2776
T: (303) 781-7223, 788-4235; Fax: (303) 788-4234
Gen Secr: Lance M. Olson
Focus: Med 15112

International Microwave Power Institute (IMPI), 10210 Leatherleaf Ct, Manassas, VA 22111
T: (703) 257-1415; Fax: (703) 257-0213
Founded: 1966; Members: 8000
Gen Secr: Robert C. Lagasse
Focus: Eng; Energy
Periodicals
Journal of Microwave Power
Microwave World 15113

International Mycological Association (IMA), c/o Dept of Plant Biology, Louisiana State University, Baton Rouge, LA 70803
T: (504) 3888485; E-Mail: BTBLAC@unix1.sncc.lsu.edu
Gen Secr: Prof. Meredith Blackwell
Focus: Botany 15114

International Naval Research Organization (INRO), 1st St Station, POB 3249, Radford, VA 24143
Gen Secr: George F. Dale
Focus: Transport 15115

International Navigation Association (INA), POB 2324, Arlington, VA 22202-0324
T: (604) 276-4626; Fax: (604) 274-8156
Founded: 1975; Members: 200
Pres: Ian S. Anderson
Focus: Navig
Periodical
Proceedings (annually) 15116

International Network for Adult Learners with Disabilities, c/o Centre for Lifelong Learning for Peoples with Disabilities, 2020 Pennsylvania Av NW, Ste 210, Washington, DC 20006
T: (202) 298-9570; Fax: (202) 429-2852
Focus: Adult Educ 15117

International Network for Global Education (INGE), 45 John St, Ste 908, New York, NY 10038
T: (212) 732-8606
Gen Secr: Andrew F. Smith
Focus: Educ 15118

International Network for Social Network Analysis (INSNA), c/o Dept of Sociology, Univ. of South Carolina, Columbia, SC 29208
T: (803) 777-3140; Fax: (803) 777-5251
Gen Secr: Steve Borgatti
Focus: Soc Sci 15119

International Network for Sustainable Energy (INFORSE), c/o Environmental Action, Energy Conservation Coalition, 6930 Carroll Av 600, Takoma Park, MD 20912
T: (301) 891-1100; E-Mail: eaf@igc.apc.org; Fax: (301) 891-2218
Focus: Energy 15120

International Neural Network Society (INNS), 875 King's Hwy, Ste 200, Woodbury, NJ 08096-3172
T: (609) 845-9094; E-Mail: 74577.504@compuserve.com; Fax: (609) 853-0411
Gen Secr: Shun-ichi Amari
Focus: Neurology 15121

International Neuromodulation Society (INS), 1015 Chestnut St, Ste 1400, Philadelphia, PA 19107
T: (215) 955-2364; Fax: (215) 923-4939
Gen Secr: Sherri Kae Calkins
Focus: Neurology 15122

International New Thought Alliance (INTA), 5003 E Broadway Rd, Mesa, AZ 85206
T: (602) 830-2461; Fax: (602) 830-2461
Founded: 1914
Focus: Philos
Periodical
New Thought Quarterly (quarterly) . . . 15123

International Numismatic Society Authentication Bureau (INSAB), POB 33134, Philadelphia, PA 19142
T: (215) 365-0752; Fax: (215) 365-0752
Founded: 1976; Members: 500
Focus: Numismatics
Periodicals
Insight (quarterly)
Newsletter 15124

International Ocean Drilling Program (ODP), c/o Division of Ocean Sciences, National Science Foundation, 4201 Wilson Blvd, Arlington, VA 22230
Focus: Eng 15125

International Oculoplastic Society, 630 Park Av, New York, NY 10021
T: (212) 734-1010; Fax: (212) 871-8474
Gen Secr: Pierre Guibor
Focus: Ophthal 15126

International Offshore Mechanics and Arctic Engineering Association, c/o US Army Cold Regions Research and Engineering Laboratory, CECRL-PP, 72 Lyme Rd, Hanover, NH 03755-1290
T: (603) 646-4289; E-Mail: femi@crre141.crrel.usace.army.mil; Fax: (603) 646-4448
Gen Secr: Dr. Olufemi A. Ayorinde
Focus: Eng 15127

International Organization for Chemical Sciences in Development (IOCD), POB 8156, Falls Church, VA 22041
T: (703) 845-9078; E-Mail: iocd@igc.apc.org; Fax: (703) 845-9078
Gen Secr: Dr. Robert Maybury
Focus: Chem 15128

International Organization for Medical Physics (IOMP), c/o Gershenson Radiation Oncology Center, Harper-Grace Hospitals, 3990 John R, Detroit, MI 48201
T: (313) 745-2489; E-Mail: colino@rocdec.roc.wayne.edu; Fax: (313) 745-2314
Gen Secr: Prof. Colin Orton
Focus: Physics 15129

International Organization for Mycoplasmology (IOM), c/o Dept of Medical Microbiology and Immunology, Ohio State University, 333 W 10 Av, Columbus, OH 43210-1239
Founded: 1974; Members: 450
Gen Secr: Dr. J. Dennis Pollack
Focus: Microbio
Periodicals
Congress Abstracts (bi-annually)
Congress Proceedings (bi-annually)
Newsletter (quarterly) 15130

International Organization for Septuagint and Cognate Studies (IOSCS), c/o Creighton University, 2500 California Plaza, Omaha, NE 68179
Gen Secr: Leonard Greenspoon
Focus: Rel & Theol 15131

International Organization for Succulent Plant Study (IOS), c/o Desert Botanical Garden, 1201 N Galvin Pkwy, Phoenix, AZ 85008
Gen Secr: Dr. E.F. Anderson
Focus: Botany 15132

International Organization for the Education of the Hearing Impaired (IOEHI), c/o Alexander Graham Bell Association for the Deaf, 3417 Volta Pl NW, Washington, DC 20007-2778
T: (202) 337-5220
Founded: 1967; Members: 450
Gen Secr: Susan Coffman
Focus: Educ 15133

International Organization for the Study of Group Tensions (IOSGT), 240 E 76 St, Apt 1-B, New York, NY 10021
T: (212) 628-1797
Founded: 1970; Members: 150
Pres: Dr. Benjamin B. Wolman
Focus: Psych
Periodical
International Journal of Group Tensions (quarterly) 15134

International Organization of Citrus Virologists (IOCV), c/o Univ. of Florida, CREC, 700 Experiment Station Rd, Lake Alfred, FL 33850
T: (813) 956-1151; Fax: (813) 956-4631
Gen Secr: Dr. L.W. Timmer
Focus: Agri 15135

International Organization of Crystal Growth (IOCG), c/o Dept Material Sciences, 304 EMRO, University of Utah, Salt Lake City, UT 84112
Fax: (801) 581-4816
Gen Secr: Prof. G. B. Stringfellow
Focus: Mineralogy 15136

International Organization of Plant Biosystematists (IOBP), c/o Missouri Botanical Garden, POB 299, St. Louis MO
T: (314) 577-5110; Fax: (314) 577-9595
Gen Secr: Dr. Peter Houch
Focus: Botany 15137

International Ornithological Committee (IOC), c/o Dept of Biological Sciences, Columbia University, Schermerhorn Hall, POB 37, New York, NY 10027
T: (212) 854-4487; Fax: (212) 865-8246
Gen Secr: Prof. Walter J. Bock
Focus: Ornithology 15138

International Ornithological Congress (IOC), c/o Dept of Biological Sciences, Colombia University, 1200 Amsterdam Av, POB 37, New York, NY 10027-5521
E-Mail: wb4@columbia.edu
Gen Secr: Prof. Walter J. Bock
Focus: Ornithology 15139

International Ozone Association (IOA), 31 Strawberry Hill Av, Stamford, CT 06902-2608
T: (203) 348-3542; Fax: (203) 967-4845
Gen Secr: Margit Istok
Focus: Ecology 15140

International Paediatric Pathology Association (IPPA), c/o Dept of Pathology, Women and Infants Hosp of Rhode Island, 50 Maude St, Providence, RI 02908
Gen Secr: Dr. Don Singer
Focus: Pathology; Pediatrics 15141

International Peace Academy (IPA), 777 UN Plaza, New York, NY 10017-3521
T: (212) 949-8480; E-Mail: ipa@ipapost.ipacademy.org; Fax: (212) 983-8246
Gen Secr: Olara A. Otunnu
Focus: Prom Peace 15142

International Peace Research Association (IPRA), c/o ICAR, George Mason University, Fairfax, VA 22030-4444
T: (703) 993-1300; E-Mail: kclement@gmu.edu; Fax: (703) 993-1302
Gen Secr: Kevin Clements
Focus: Prom Peace 15143

International Pediatric Association (IPA), c/o University of Rochester School of Medicine and Dentistry, Rm 4-8104, 601 Elmwood Av, Rochester, NY 14642-8777
T: (716) 275-0225, 275-7242; Fax: (716) 273-1038
Gen Secr: Dr. Robert J. Haggerty
Focus: Pediatrics 15144

International Pediatric Nephrology Association (IPNA), c/o Dept of Paediatrics, Albert Einstein College of Medicine, 1825 Eastchester Rd, Bronx, NY 10461
T: (718) 904-2857; Fax: (718) 409-1048
Gen Secr: Prof. Ira Greifer
Focus: Pediatrics 15145

International Percy Grainger Society (IPGS), 7 Cromwell Pl, White Plains, NY 10601-5005
T: (212) 877-8953
Founded: 1964; Members: 400
Focus: Music 15146

International Perimetric Society (IPS), University of Iowa, College of Medicine, Dept Neurology, Iowa City, IA 52242
T: (319) 356-8758
Gen Secr: Michael Wall
Focus: Neurology 15147

International Personnel Management Association (IPMA), 1617 Duke St, Alexandria, VA 22314
T: (703) 549-7100; Fax: (703) 684-0948
Founded: 1973; Members: 6500
Focus: Business Admin
Periodicals
Agency Issues (bi-weekly)
IPMA News (monthly)
Membership Directory (annually)
Public Personnel Management (quarterly) 15148

International Pharmaceutical Excipients Council (IPEC), 1361 Alps Rd, Bldg 3, Wayne, NJ 07470
T: (201) 628-3231; Fax: (201) 628-3794
Gen Secr: Louis Blecher
Focus: Pharmacol 15149

International Phenomenological Society (IPS), c/o Philosophy and Phenomenological Research, Brown University, POB 1947, Providence, RI 02912
T: (401) 863-2718; Fax: (401) 863-2719
Founded: 1939
Pres: Prof. Ernest Sosa
Focus: Philos
Periodical
Philosophy and Phenomenological Research (quarterly) 15150

International Photobiology Association (AIP), c/o Dept Chemistry, Univ Nebraska, Lincoln, NE 68588-0304
T: (402) 472-2749; E-Mail: pssong@unlinfo.nnl.edu; Fax: (402) 472-2044
Gen Secr: Prof. Dr. Pill-Sonn Song
Focus: Bio 15151

International Phycological Society (IPS), c/o Harbor Branch, Oceanographic Institute, 5600 Old Dixie Hwy, Fort Pierce, FL 34946
Gen Secr: Dr. M.D. Hanisak
Focus: Oceanography 15152

International Plan of Action on Ageing, c/o UN Program on Ageing, Rm DC2-1358, 2 UN Plaza, New York, NY 10017
Fax: (212) 963-0500
Focus: Geriatrics 15153

International Planetarium Society (IPS), c/o Storer Planetarium, 600 Dares Beach Rd, Prince Frederick, MD 20678
T: (410) 535-7339; E-Mail: 102424.1032@compuserve.com
Founded: 1970; Members: 400
Gen Secr: Shawn Laatsch
Focus: Astronomy; Aero
Periodicals
Directory of Planetaria and Planetarians (annually)
Planetarian (quarterly) 15154

International Plant Propagators Society (IPPS), c/o Washington Park Arboretum, University of Washington, POB 358010, Seattle, WA 98195
T: (206) 543-8602; Fax: (206) 325-8893
Founded: 1950; Members: 3200
Gen Secr: John A. Wott
Focus: Botany 15155

International Policy Council on Agriculture and Trade (IPC), 1616 P St NW, Ste 100, Washington, DC 20036
T: (202) 328-5056; E-Mail: lacy@rff.org; Fax: (202) 328-5133
Gen Secr: Peter G. Lacy
Focus: Poli Sci; Agri; Commerce . . . 15156

International Polio Network (IPN), 4207 Lindell Blvd, Ste 110, Saint Louis, MO 63108-2915
T: (314) 534-0475; E-Mail: gini-intl@msn.com; Fax: (314) 534-5070
Gen Secr: Joan Headley
Focus: Med 15157

International Polychaetology Association, c/o Invertebrate Zoology, Smithsonian Institute of Natural History, Washington, DC 20560
Gen Secr: Dr. Krishan Fauchald
Focus: Zoology 15158

International Precious Metals Institute (IPMI), 4905 Tilghman St, Ste 160, Allentown, PA 18104
T: (215) 395-9700; Fax: (215) 395-5855
Founded: 1976; Members: 1000
Focus: Metallurgy
Periodicals
Membership Directory (annually)
Precious Metals News amd Reviews (monthly) 15159

International Primatological Society (IPS), c/o University of California, Davis, CA 95616
Gen Secr: Sally Mendoza
Focus: Zoology 15160

International Professional Surrogates Association (IPSA), POB 3016, Venice, CA 90294
T: (213) 469-4720; Fax: (213) 581-9903
Founded: 1973; Members: 50
Pres: Larry Villarin
Focus: Med
Periodical
Newsletter (monthly) 15161

International Program for Technology Research in Irrigation and Drainage (IPTRID), c/o Agriculture and Natural Resources Dept, Rm N-7015 Th World Bank, 1818 H St NW, Washington, DC 20433
T: (202) 473-5571; E-Mail: RPURCELL@worldbank.org; Fax: (202) 334-8748
Focus: Eng 15162

International Psycho-Oncology Society (IPOS), 1275 York Av, POB 421, New York, NY 10021
T: (212) 639-7051; Fax: (212) 717-3087
Focus: Psych; Cell Biol & Cancer Res . 15163

International Psychogeriatric Association (IPA), 3127 Greenleaf Av, Wilmette, IL 60091
T: (847) 251-5516; E-Mail: orgipahq@aol.com; Fax: (847) 251-9692
Gen Secr: Fern F. Finkel
Focus: Psych; Geriatrics 15164

International Psychohistorical Association (IPA), POB 314, New York, NY 10024
T: (201) 891-4980
Founded: 1976; Members: 200
Focus: Hist; Psych
Periodical
Psychohistory News (semi-annually) . . . 15165

International Public Policy Institute, 1038 E Lester St, Tucson, AZ 85719
T: (602) 792-9610; Fax: (602) 795-6998
Gen Secr: Robert Manley
Focus: Poli Sci 15166

International Quantum Structures Association (IQSA), c/o Dept of Mathematics and Statistics, Louisiana Tech University, Ruston, LA 71272
E-Mail: Greechie@math.latech.edu
Gen Secr: Richard Greechie
Focus: Physics 15167

International Reading Association (IRA), 800 Barksdale Rd, POB 8139, Newark, DE 19714
T: (302) 731-1600 ext 220; E-Mail: 75141.2005@compuserve.com; Fax: (302) 731-1057
Founded: 1956; Members: 93000
Gen Secr: Alan E. Farstrup
Focus: Educ
Periodicals
Journal of Reading (8 times annually)
Lectura Vida (quarterly)
Reading Research Quarterly (quarterly)
Reading Teacher (9 times annually) . . 15168

International Reference Organization in Forensic Medicine and Sciences (INFORM), POB 8282, Wichita, KS 67208
T: (316) 685-7612
Founded: 1966; Members: 1200
Gen Secr: Dr. William G. Eckert
Focus: Forensic Med
Periodicals
Conference Proceeding (semi-annually)
Criminalist's Sourcebook (annually)
Letter (quarterly) 15169

International Rehabilitation Medicine Association (IRMA), c/o Dept of Physical Medicine, 1333 Moursund Av, Rm A-221, Houston, TX 77030
T: (713) 799-5086; Fax: (713) 799-5058
Gen Secr: Donna Jones
Focus: Rehabil 15170

International Repertory of Musical Iconography (RIdIM), c/o RCMI, City University of New York, 33 W 42 St, New York, NY 10036
T: (212) 642-2709; E-Mail: zdr@cunyvms1.gc.cuny.edu; Fax: (212) 642-1973
Gen Secr: Zdravko Blazeković
Focus: Music 15171

International Repertory of Musical Literature (RILM), c/o City Univ of New York, 33 W 42 St, New York, NY 10036
T: (212) 642-2844; Fax: (212) 642-1973
Gen Secr: Dr. Barbara Dubbs Mackenzie
Focus: Lit 15172

International Reproductive Rights Research Action Group (IRRRAG), c/o Hunter College, 695 Park Av, New York, NY 10021
T: (212) 772-5682; Fax: (212) 772-4268
Gen Secr: Dr. Rosalind Petchesky
Focus: Law 15173

International Research and Exchanges Board (IREX), 1616 H St NW, Washington, DC 20006
T: (202) 628-8188; E-Mail: irex@info.irex.org; Fax: (202) 628-8189
Gen Secr: Herbert Ellison
Focus: Sci 15174

International Research Center for Energy and Economic Development (ICEED), 909 14 St, Ste 201, Boulder, CO 80302
T: (303) 492-7667, 442-4014, 541-9504; Fax: (303) 442-5042
Gen Secr: Dorothea El Mallakh
Focus: Energy; Develop Areas 15175

International Research/Study Team on Nonviolent Large Systems Change, c/o RODC, The O. D. Institute, 11234 Walnut Ridge Rd, Chesterland, OH 44026
T: (216) 461-4333; Fax: (216) 729-9319
Gen Secr: Dr. Donald W. Cole
Focus: Sci 15176

International Rett Syndrome Association (IRSA), 9121 Piscataway Rd, Clinton, MD 20735
T: (301) 856-3334
Gen Secr: Kathy Hunter
Focus: Med 15177

International Road Educational Foundation (IREF), c/o IRF, 2600 Virginia Av NW, Washington, DC 20037
T: (202) 338-4641; Fax: (202) 338-8104
Gen Secr: Richard B. Robertson
Focus: Educ 15178

International Rural Sociological Association (IRSA), c/o Dept of Agricultural Economics and Rural Sociology, 111 Armsby Building, University Park, PA 16802-5600
Gen Secr: Prof. Dr. Al Luloff
Focus: Sociology 15179

International Satellite Land-Surface Climatology Project (ISLSCP), c/o International GEWEX Project Office, 1100 Wayne Av, Ste 1210, Silver Spring, MD 20910
T: (301) 427-2089; E-Mail: gewex@cais.com; Fax: (301) 427-2222
Gen Secr: Paul D. Try
Focus: Geophys 15180

International School-to-School Experience (ISSE), 4873 Millerstown Rd, Urbana, OH 43078
T: (513) 652-3345; Fax: (513) 652-1564
Gen Secr: Lillian Coon
Focus: Educ 15181

International Schools Services (ISS), 15 Roszel Rd, POB 5910, Princeton, NJ 08543
T: (609) 452-0990; Fax: (609) 452-2690
Founded: 1955
Pres: William P. Davison
Focus: Educ

Periodicals
ISS Directory of Overseas Schools (annually)
NewsLinks (monthly) 15182

International Science Foundation (ISF), 455 First Av, New York, NY 10016
T: (212) 576-8451; E-Mail: isf@phri.nyu.edu; Fax: (212) 576-8457
Gen Secr: Gregory Johnson
Focus: Sci 15183

International Science Writers Association (ISWA), 7310 Broxburn Ct, Bethesda, MD 20817
T: (301) 229-6770; Fax: (301) 229-8764
Gen Secr: Howard J. Lewis
Focus: Lit 15184

International Skeletal Society, c/o V. A. Medical Center, Dept of Radiology, 3350 La Jolla Village Dr, San Diego, CA 92161
T: (619) 552-8585 Ext 3343; Fax: (619) 552-7452
Gen Secr: Dr. Donald Resnick
Focus: Anat 15185

International Sled Dog Veterinar Medical Association (ISDVMA), POB 543, Sylvania, OH 43560
T: (419) 531-5589; Fax: (419) 531-5404
Gen Secr: Thomas D. Young
Focus: Vet Med 15186

International Society for Adolescent Psychiatry (ISAP), 610 Timber Lane, Nashville, TN 37215
T: (615) 297-7738; Fax: (615) 385-2069
Gen Secr: Mary D. Staples
Focus: Psychiatry 15187

International Society for Analytical Cytology (ISAC), POB 7849, Breckenridge, CO 80424
T: (970) 453-2058, 453-1894; Fax: (970) 453-2636
Gen Secr: Justine J. Parker
Focus: Cell Biol & Cancer Res 15188

International Society for Animal Genetics (ISAG), c/o Univ of Wisconsin, 1675 Observatory Dr, Madison, WI 53706
T: (608) 263-4323; E-Mail: kirkpat@calshp.cals.wisc.edu; Fax: (608) 262-5157
Gen Secr: Dr. B. Kirkpatrick
Focus: Vet Med 15189

International Society for Anthrozoology (ISAZ), c/o Tufts Center for Animals and Public, 200 Westboro Rd, North Grafton, MA 01536
T: (508) 839-7991; E-Mail: arowan@opal.tufts.edu; Fax: (508) 839-2953
Gen Secr: Dr. Andrew N. Rowan
Focus: Zoology 15190

International Society for Artificial Organs (ISAO), 8937 Euclid Av, Cleveland, OH 44106
T: (216) 421-0757; Fax: (216) 421-1652
Founded: 1977; Members: 1000
Focus: Med 15191

International Society for Asphalt Pavements (ISAP), 2602 Dellana Lane, Austin, TX 78746
T: (512) 327-4211; Fax: (512) 328-7246
Gen Secr: Morris Reinhardt
Focus: Materials Sci 15192

International Society for Astrological Research (ISAR), 19622 Telegraph Rd, Santa Paula, CA 93060-9637
T: (805) 525-0461; Fax: (805) 933-0301
Members: 600
Gen Secr: Marguerite da Boggia
Focus: Parapsych
Periodicals
Kosmos (quarterly)
Newsletter (annually) 15193

International Society for British Genealogy and Family History (ISBGFH), POB 3115, Salt Lake City, UT 84110-3115
T: (801) 240-2089
Founded: 1979; Members: 1000
Gen Secr: Anne Wuehler
Focus: Genealogy
Periodical
Newsletter (quarterly) 15194

International Society for Burn Injuries (ISBI), 2322 Harney Rd, Houston, TX 78234-6315
T: (210) 224-9553; Fax: (210) 237-8502
Founded: 1965; Members: 1300
Gen Secr: Basil A. Pruitt
Focus: Hygiene
Periodicals
Bulletin and Clinical Review of Burn Injuries (quarterly)
Journal Burns (bi-monthly)
Membership Directory of ISBI (annually) . 15195

International Society for Business Education - United States Chapter (ISBE), 1914 Association Dr, Reston, VA 22091
T: (703) 860-8300; Fax: (703) 620-8300
Members: 750
Focus: Adult Educ; Econ 15196

International Society for Cardiovascular Surgery (ICVS), 13 Elm St, Manchester, MA 01944-1314
T: (508) 526-8330; Fax: (508) 526-4018
Founded: 1951; Members: 2500
Gen Secr: William T. Maloney
Focus: Cardiol; Surgery 15197

International Society for Chronobiology (ISC), c/o Div of Biological Sciences, SUNY Stony Brook, Life Sciences Bldg, Rm 370, Stony Brook, NY 11794
Founded: 1937; Members: 680
Gen Secr: Prof. Leland N. Edmunds
Focus: Bio
Periodicals
Chronobiologia (quarterly)
International Journal of Chronobiology (quarterly)
. . . . 15198

International Society for Clinical Enzymology (ISCE), c/o Wadsworth Laboratories, New York State Dept of Health, Empire State Plaza, Albany, NY 12201-0509
T: (518) 474-1166; Fax: (518) 473-7130
Gen Secr: Dr. Robert Rej
Focus: Med 15199

International Society for Clinical Laboratory Technology (ISCLT), 818 Olive St, Ste 918, Saint Louis, MO 63101-1598
T: (314) 241-1445; Fax: (314) 241-1449
Founded: 1962; Members: 7500
Focus: Med; Eng
Periodical
ISCLT Newsletter (bi-monthly) 15200

International Society for Dermatologic Surgery (ISDS), POB 4014, Schaumburg, IL 60168-4014
T: (708) 330-9830; Fax: (708) 330-0050
Founded: 1976; Members: 1100
Gen Secr: Lawrence F. Rosenthal
Focus: Derm; Surgery 15201

International Society for Dermatologic Surgery (ISDS), POB 4014, Schaumburg, IL 60204
T: (847) 330-9830; Fax: (847) 330-0050
Gen Secr: Cheryl K. Nordstedt
Focus: Surgery; Derm 15202

International Society for Development Neuroscience (ISDN), c/o Univ of Texas Medical Branch, 301 Univ Blvd, 436 Gail Borden F52, Galveston, TX 77555-0652
T: (409) 772-3667; Fax: (409) 772-8028
Gen Secr: J. Regino Perez-Polo
Focus: Neurology 15203

International Society for Development Psychobiology (ISDP), c/o Virginia Tech, Blacksburg, VA 27061
T: (703) 231-5346; Fax: (703) 231-3652
Gen Secr: Dr. Robert Lickliter
Focus: Bio 15204

International Society for Ecological Econimics (ISEE), POB 1589, Solomons, MD 20688
T: (410) 326-0794; E-Mail: hinrichs@cbl.cees.edu; Fax: (410) 326-7354
Gen Secr: Douglas Hinrichs
Focus: Ecology; Econ 15205

International Society for Educational Planning (ISEP), c/o Robert H. Beach, Memphis State University, South Campus Bldg 48, Rm 102, Memphis, TN 38152
T: (901) 678-2652; Fax: (901) 678-4778
Founded: 1970; Members: 350
Gen Secr: Robert H. Beach
Focus: Educ
Periodicals
Directory (annually)
Educational Planning (quarterly) 15206

International Society for Educational Planning (ISEP), c/o University of Memphis, S Campus Bldg 48, Rm 102, Memphis, TN 38152
T: (901) 678-2363; Fax: (901) 678-4778
Gen Secr: Robert H. Beach
Focus: Educ 15207

International Society for Evolutionary Protistology (ISEP), c/o Ecosystems Science, NASA,, Ames Research Centre, Mail Stop 239-12, Moffitt Field, CA 94035
T: (415) 604-6525; E-Mail: Lrothschild@mail.arc.nasa.gov
Gen Secr: Lynn J. Rothschild
Focus: Bio 15208

International Society for Experimental Hematology (ISEH), c/o UT College of Veterinary Medicine, POB 1071, Knoxville, TN 37901
T: (615) 546-9230
Gen Secr: Dr. T.P. McDonald
Focus: Hematology 15209

International Society for Fat Research (ISF), 1608 Broadmoor Dr, POB 3489, Champaign, IL 61826-3489
T: (217) 359-2344; Fax: (217) 351-8091
Focus: Materials Sci 15210

International Society for General Semantics (ISGS), POB 728, Concord, CA 94522
T: (510) 798-0311; E-Mail: isgs@crl.com; Fax: (510) 798-0312
Founded: 1943; Members: 2400
Gen Secr: Paul Johnston
Focus: Ling 15211

International Society for Heart and Lung Transplantation (ISHLT), 14673 Midway Rd, Ste 108, Dallas, TX 75244
T: (214) 490-9495; Fax: (214) 490-9499
Gen Secr: Amanda W. Rowe
Focus: Surgery; Cardiol 15212

International Society for Heart Research (ISHR), c/o Dept of Physiology and Biophysics, University of Illinois at Chicago, 835 S Walcott Av, Chicago, IL 60612-7342
T: (312) 996-1645; Fax: (312) 996-1414
Gen Secr: Dr. R. John Solaro
Focus: Cardiol 15213

International Society for Historical Linguistics (ISHL), c/o Linguistics Program, University of South Carolina, Columbia, SC 29208
Gen Secr: Dorothy Disterheft
Focus: Ling 15214

International Society for HIV/AIDS Education and Prevention (ISHEP), c/o Pediatric/Adolescent HIV/AIDS Program, 341 Ponce de Leon Av, Ste 201, Atlanta, GA 30308
T: (404) 616-9791; Fax: (404) 616-9898
Focus: Educ 15215

International Society for Human Ethology (ISHE), c/o Dept of Psychology, Wayne State University, Detroit, MI 48202
T: (313) 577-2835; Fax: (313) 577-7636
Founded: 1973; Members: 400
Gen Secr: Dr. Glenn E. Weisfeld
Focus: Behav Sci 15216

International Society for Humor Studies (ISHS), c/o English Dept, Arizona State University, Tempe, AZ 85287-0302
T: (602) 965-7952; E-Mail: don.nilsen@asu.edu; Fax: (602) 965-3451
Founded: 1980; Members: 400
Gen Secr: Don L.F. Nilsen
Focus: Ling; Lit
Periodical
Humor: International Journal of Humor Research (quarterly) 15217

International Society for Hybrid Microelectronics (ISHM), 1850 Centennial Park Dr, Reston, VA 22091
T: (703) 758-1060; Fax: (703) 471-1066
Founded: 1967; Members: 7000
Gen Secr: Richard Breck
Focus: Electronic Eng
Periodical
International Journal for Hybrid Microelectronics (quarterly) 15218

International Society for Infectious Diseases (ISID), 180 Longwood Av, Boston, MA 02115
T: (617) 227-0551; Fax: (617) 731-1541
Focus: Med 15219

International Society for Infectious Diseases in Obstetrics and Gynaecology (ISIDOG), c/o Department of OB/GYN, New York Hospital, Cornell Medical Center, 525 E 68th St 3010, New York, NY 10021-8085
Gen Secr: Prof. William J. Ledger
Focus: Gynecology 15220

International Society for Intercommunications of New Ideas (ISINI), 145 Moss Hill Rd, Jamaica Plain, MA 02130
T: (617) 524-4580
Gen Secr: Prof. Anghel N. Rugina
Focus: Comm Sci 15221

International Society for Intercultural Education, Training and Research, 808 17 St NW, Washington, DC 20006
T: (202) 466-7883; Fax: (202) 223-9569
Founded: 1974; Members: 2200
Focus: Educ 15222

International Society for Interferon and Cytokine Research (ISICR), c/o Dept of Molecular Genetics and Microbiology, UMDNJ-Robert Wood Johnson Medical School, 675 Hoes Lane, Piscataway, NJ 08854-5635
T: (908) 235-5116; E-Mail: ISICR%MBCL.bitnet@mitvma.mit.edu; Fax: (908) 235-5223
Gen Secr: Dr. Sidney Pestka
Focus: Med; Microbio 15223

International Society for Labour Law and Social Security (ISLLSS), c/o Law School, University of Pennsylvania, 3400 Chestnut St, Philadelphia, PA 19104
Founded: 1961; Members: 245
Gen Secr: Prof. Clyde Summers
Focus: Law
Periodicals
Comparative Labor Law Journal (quarterly)
Proceedings of the Congress 15224

International Society for Magnetic Resonance in Medicine (ISMRM), 2118 Milvia St, Ste 201, Berkeley, CA 94704
T: (510) 841-1899; Fax: (510) 841-2340
Focus: Physics; Med 15225

International Society for Measurement and Control, c/o ISA, 67 Alexander Dr, POB 12277, Research Triangle Park, NC 27709
T: (919) 549-8411; Fax: (919) 549-8288
Gen Secr: Glenn F. Harvey
Focus: Eng 15226

International Society for Medical and Applied Malacology, POB 2715, Ann Arbor, MI 48106
Gen Secr: J. B. Burch
Focus: Zoology 15227

International Society for Medical and Psychological Hypnosis (ISMPH), 1991 Broadway, Ste 18B, New York, NY 10023
T: (212) 874-5290; Fax: (914) 238-1422
Gen Secr: Dr. Milton V. Kline
Focus: Psych 15228

International Society for Metaphysics, c/o Dept of Philosophy, Catholic Univ of America, Washington, DC 20064
T: (202) 319-5636; Fax: (202) 319-6089
Gen Secr: Prof. George F. McLean
Focus: Philos 15229

International Society for Neoplatonic Studies (ISNS), c/o Dept of Philosophy, Old Dominion University, Norfolk, VA 23529-0082
T: (804) 440-3879; Fax: (804) 683-5345
Founded: 1973; Members: 600
Gen Secr: R. Baine Harris
Focus: Philos 15230

International Society for Neurochemistry (ISN), c/o UCLA Mental Retardation Research Center, 760 Westwood Plaza, Rm 68-225, NPI, Los Angeles, CA
T: (310) 825-9395; E-Mail: jdevellis@npimain.medsch.ucla.edu; Fax: (310) 206-5061
Gen Secr: Jean de Vellis
Focus: Chem; Neurology 15231

International Society for Neuroimmunomodulation (ISNIM), c/o National Institutes of Health, 10 Center Dr (MSC-1284) , Bldg 10, 2D46, Bethesda, MD 20892-1284
T: (301) 496-4561; E-Mail: ccs@codon.nih.gov; Fax: (301) 402-1561
Gen Secr: Craig C. Smith
Focus: Neurology; Immunology 15232

International Society for Optical Engineering (SPIE), POB 10, Bellingham, WA 98227-0010
T: (206) 676-3290; E-Mail: spie@mom.spie.org; Fax: (206) 647-1445
Gen Secr: James E. Pearson
Focus: Eng; Optics 15233

International Society for Pediatric and Adolescent Diabetes (ISPAD), c/o New England Diabetes and Endocrinology Center, 40 Second Av, Ste 170, Waltham, MA 02154-1132
T: (617) 890-3610; E-Mail: sbrink@opal.tufts.edu; Fax: (617) 890-3612
Gen Secr: Dr. Stuart Brink
Focus: Diabetes 15234

International Society for Peritoneal Dialysis, c/o Nephrology Div, Georgetown Univ Hospital, Washington, DC 20007
T: (202) 784-3662; E-Mail: jwinch@ix.netcom.com; Fax: (202) 687-2808
Gen Secr: Dr. James Winchester
Focus: Hematology 15235

International Society for Pharmaceutical Engineering (ISPE), 3816 W Linebaugh Av, No 412, Tampa, FL 33624
T: (813) 960-2105; E-Mail: ispehq@ispe.org; Fax: (813) 264-2816
Gen Secr: Robert P. Best
Focus: Eng; Pharmacol 15236

International Society for Pharmacoepidemiology, c/o University of Kansas Medical Centre, Dept of Preventative Medicine, 3901 Rainbow Blvd, Robinson 4004, Kansas City, KS 66160-7313
T: (913) 588-2790; E-Mail: ispe@kumc.edu; Fax: (913) 588-2791
Gen Secr: Prof. Stanley A. Edlavitch
Focus: Med 15237

International Society for Phenomenology and Literature (ISPL), c/o WPI, 348 Payson Rd, Belmont, MA 02178
T: (617) 489-3696
Gen Secr: Prof. Anna-Teresa Tymieniecka
Focus: Parapsych; Lit 15238

International Society for Philosophical Enquiry (ISPE), POB 34304, Omaha, NE 68134
T: (901) 372-1203; Fax: (901) 377-4952
Founded: 1974; Members: 530
Gen Secr: Harry Callahan
Focus: Philos 15239

International Society for Philosophy of Life and the Sciences of Life, c/o WPI, 348 Payson Rd, Belmont, MA 02178
T: (617) 489-3696
Gen Secr: Prof. Anna-Teresa Tymieniecka
Focus: Philos 15240

International Society for Plant Molecular Biology (ISPMB), c/o Biochemistry Dept, University of Georgia, Athens, GA 30602-7229
T: (706) 542-3239; Fax: (706) 542-2090
Founded: 1982; Members: 1850
Focus: Bio
Periodicals
Directory of Members (bi-annually)
Plant Molecular Biology (monthly)
Plant Molecular Biology Reporter (quarterly)
. . . . 15241

International Society for Plastination, c/o Mercer Univ School of Medicine, Dept of Pathology, 1550 College St, Macon, GA 31207
T: (912) 752-4071
Gen Secr: Harmon Bickley
Focus: Pathology 15242

International Society for Polycyclic Aromatic Compounds (ISPAC), c/o Organic Analytical Research Division, National Inst of Standards and Technology, Chemistry Bldg, Rm B158, Gaithersburg, MD 20899
T: (301) 975-3108; Fax: (301) 926-8671
Gen Secr: Dr. Willie E. May
Focus: Chem 15243

International Society for Preventive Oncology (ISPO), 217 E 85 St, Ste 303, New York, NY 10028
T: (212) 534-4991, 856-1822; E-Mail: cancer@banyan.ummed.edu; Fax: (212) 856-1824
Gen Secr: Dr. Herbert E. Nieburgs
Focus: Cell Biol & Cancer Res 15244

International Society for Reef Studies (ISRS), c/o Florida Institute for Oceanography, 830 First St S, St Petersburg, FL 33701
T: (813) 893-9100; Fax: (813) 893-9109
Gen Secr: John C. Ogden
Focus: Oceanography 15245

International Society for Research on Aggression (ISRA), c/o Research Center for Group Dynamics, Institute for Social Research, University of Michigan, Ann Arbor, MI 48106
T: (313) 747-3662; E-Mail: Huesmann@umich.edu; Fax: (313) 936-0200
Founded: 1970; Members: 450
Gen Secr: Prof. L. Rowell Huesmann
Focus: Psych; Behav Sci
Periodicals
Agressive Behavior (quarterly)
Bulletin (3 times annually) 15246

International Society for Rheumatic Therapeutics (ISRT), c/o Div of Rheumatology, Beth Israel Hospital and Health Care, 330 Brookline Av, Boston, MA 02215
T: (617) 667-2560; Fax: (617) 667-7805
Gen Secr: Dr. David E. Trentham
Focus: Rheuma; Therapeutics 15247

International Society for Sexually Transmitted Diseases Research (ISSTDR), c/o School of Medicine, Louisiana State University, Medical Centre, Section of Infectious Diseases, 1542 Tulane Av, New Orleans, LA 70112-2822
T: (504) 568-5031; Fax: (504) 568-6752
Gen Secr: Dr. David H. Martin
Focus: Venereology 15248

International Society for Systems Sciences (ISSS), c/o Elsevier Science Publication Comp, 655 Av of the Americas, New York, NY 10010
Gen Secr: Dr. Harold A. Linstone
Focus: Computer & Info Sci 15249

International Society for Technology in Education (ISTE), c/o University of Oregon, 1787 Agate St, Eugene, OR 97403
T: (503) 346-4414; Fax: (503) 346-5890
Founded: 1989; Members: 10000
Gen Secr: Maia S. Howes
Focus: Computer & Info Sci; Educ
Periodicals
Handbook and Directory
Journal (quarterly)
Newsletter 15250

International Society for Technology in Education (ISTE), c/o University of Oregon, 1787 Agate St, Eugene, OR 97403-1923
T: (541) 346-4414; E-Mail: iste@oregon.uoregon.edu; Fax: (541) 346-5890
Gen Secr: Maia Howes
Focus: Educ; Eng 15251

International Society for Terrain-Vehicle Systems (ISTVS), 72 Lyme Rd, Hanover, NH 03755-1290
T: (603) 646-4362
Founded: 1962; Members: 350
Gen Secr: Dr. Ronald A. Liston
Focus: Eng
Periodicals
Journal of Terramechanics (quarterly)
Newsletter (quarterly) 15252

International Society for the Arts, Sciences and Technology (ISAST), 508 Connecticut St, San Francisco, CA 94107
Gen Secr: Roger Malina
Focus: Arts; Nat Sci; Eng 15253

International Society for the History of Medicine (ISHM), c/o Medical Branch, University of Texas, Galveston, TX 75555-1311
Gen Secr: Dr. Chester R. Burns
Focus: Med; Hist 15254

International Society for the History of Rhetoric, c/o Dept of English, Texas A and M University, College Station, TX 77843
Gen Secr: Prof. Craig Kallendorf
Focus: Ling; Hist 15255

International Society for the Performing Arts, 2920 Fuller Av NW, Ste 205, Grand Rapids, MI 49505
T: (616) 364-3000; Fax: (616) 364-9010
Founded: 1948; Members: 600
Gen Secr: Dr. Michael C. Hardy
Focus: Perf Arts
Periodical
Forum Newsletter (monthly) 15256

International Society for the Study of Dissociation (ISSD), 7700 W Lake Av, Glenview, IL 60025-1485
T: (708) 375-4718; Fax: (708) 375-4777
Gen Secr: Jeffrey W. Engle
Focus: Eng 15257

International Society for the Study of Expressionism (ISSE-ETMS) / Ernst Toller Memorial Society, POB 20183, Cincinnati, OH 45220-0183
Founded: 1979
Focus: Lit 15258

International Society for the Study of Personal Relationships (ISSPR), c/o Kent School of Social Work, Univ of Louisville, Louisville, KY 40292
Gen Secr: Dr. Anita Barbee
Focus: Soc Sci 15259

International Society for the Study of Subtle Energies and Energy Medicine (ISSSEEM), 356 Goldco Circle, Golden, CO 80401
T: (303) 278-2228; Fax: (303) 279-3530
Gen Secr: C.P. Hiernu
Focus: Med 15260

International Society for the Study of Time (ISST), POB 67, Westerville, OH 43081
Gen Secr: Mark H. Aultman
Focus: Physics 15261

International Society for the Study of Vulvovaginal Disease (ISSVD), 930 N Meacham Rd, Schaumburg, IL 60176-6016
T: (708) 330-9830; Fax: (708) 330-0050
Gen Secr: Marilynne McKay
Focus: Venereology 15262

International Society for Third-Sector Research (ISTR), c/o Johns Hopkins Univ, 551 Wyman Park Bldg, 3400 N Charles St, Baltimore, MD 21218
T: (410) 516-4678; E-Mail: istrmbd@jhunix.hcf.jhu.edu; Fax: (410) 516-4870
Gen Secr: Margery B. Daniels
Focus: Sci 15263

International Society for Traumatic Stress Studies (ISTSS), 60 Revere Dr, Ste 500, Northbrook, IL 60062
T: (847) 480-9028; E-Mail: istss@istss.com; Fax: (847) 480-9282
Gen Secr: Greg Schultz
Focus: Traumatology 15264

International Society for Tropical Root Crops (ISTRC), c/o G. W. Carver Agriculture Experimental Station, School of Agriculture and Home Economics, 100 Campbell Building, Tuskegee Univ, Tuskegee, AL 36088
T: (334) 727-8333; Fax: (334) 724-4451
Gen Secr: Prof. Conrad K. Bonsi
Focus: Agri 15265

International Society of Aesthetic Plastic Surgery (ISAPS), 339 Govermor Rd, Hershey, PA 17033
T: (717) 533-2099; Fax: (717) 534-1071
Gen Secr: Dr. Thomas S. Davis
Focus: Surgery 15266

International Society of African Scientists (ISAS), POB 9209, Wilmington, DE 19809
T: (302) 366-5429
Gen Secr: Dr. Kwaku Temeng
Focus: Sci 15267

International Society of Air Breathing Engines (ISOABE), c/o Purdue University, 1003 Chaffee Hall, West Lafayette, IN 47907-1003
Gen Secr: Dr. S.N.B. Murthy
Focus: Mach Eng 15268

International Society of Air Safety Investigators (ISASI), Technology Trading Park, 5 Export Dr, Sterling, VA 20174-4421
T: (703) 430-9668; Fax: (703) 450-1745
Founded: 1964; Members: 1190
Gen Secr: Richard Stone
Focus: Safety
Periodicals
The Forum (quarterly)
Membership Roster (bi-annually) 15269

International Society of Animal Clinical Biochemistry (ISACB), c/o Dept of Pathology, Microbiology and Immunology, School of Veterinary Medicine, Univ. of California, Davis, CA 95616
Fax: (916) 752-3349
Gen Secr: Dr. J.J. Kaneko
Focus: Vet Med 15270

International Society of Applied Intelligence (ISAI), c/o Southwest Texas State Univ, Dept of Computer Science, 601 University Dr, San Marcos, TX 78666-4616
T: (512) 245-3409; E-Mail: ma04@swt.edu; Fax: (512) 245-8750
Gen Secr: Dr. Moonis Ali
Focus: Computer & Info Sci 15271

International Society of Arboriculture (ISA), 6 Dunlap Ct, POB GG, Savoy, IL 61874-9902
T: (217) 355-9411; Fax: (217) 355-9516
Founded: 1924; Members: 6500
Gen Secr: William P. Kruidenier
Focus: Bio
Periodicals
Journal of Arboriculture (monthly)
Membership Roster
Yearbook (annually) 15272

International Society of Arterial Chemoreception (ISAC), c/o Dept of Physiology, School of Medicine, 410 Chiheta Way, Rm 156, Research Park, Salt Lake City, UT 84108
Gen Secr: Dr. S. Fidone
Focus: Physiology 15273

International Society of Arthroscopy, Knee Surgery and Orthopaedic Sports Medicine (ISAKOS), 6300 N River Rd, Ste 727, Rosemont, IL 60018-4238
T: (708) 698-1632; Fax: (708) 823-0536
Focus: Surgery; Orthopedics; Med . . . 15274

International Society of Behavioral Medicine (ISBM), c/o University of Miami, School of Medicine, 1611 NW 12 Av, Institute Bldg, Rm 105B, Miami, FL 33136
T: (305) 585-6115; Fax: (305) 585-0092
Gen Secr: Prof. Stephen M. Weiss
Focus: Med 15275

International Society of Biorheology (ISB), c/o School of Chemical Engineering and Materials Science, University of Oklahoma, Energy Center, 100 E Boyd, Norman, OK 73019-0628
T: (405) 325-5811; Fax: (405) 325-5813
Gen Secr: Prof. Edgar A. O'Rear
Focus: Eng 15276

International Society of Blood Purification, c/o Univ of Arkansas for Medical Sciences, Div of Nephrology, 4301 W Markham, Slot 501, Little Rock, AR 72205
T: (501) 686-7878
Gen Secr: Prof. Thomas A. Golper
Focus: Hematology 15277

International Society of Business, Economics and Ethics (ISBEE), c/o Dept of Philosophy, Univ of Kansas, Lawrence, KS 66045
T: (913) 864-3976; E-Mail: degeorge@kuhub.cc.ukans.edu; Fax: (913) 864-4298
Gen Secr: Prof. Richard T. De George
Focus: Commerce; Econ; Philos 15278

International Society of Cardiovascular Ultrasound (ISCU), c/o Univ of Alabama, Heart Station SW/S102, Birmingham, AL 35233
T: (205) 934-8256; Fax: (205) 934-6747
Gen Secr: Dr. Ming C. Hsiung
Focus: Cardiol 15279

International Society of Chemical Ecology (ISCE), c/o Dept of Biology, University of South Florida, Tampa, FL 33620
T: (813) 974-3250; E-Mail: Romeo@chuma.cas.usf.edu; Fax: (813) 974-3263
Founded: 1983; Members: 750
Gen Secr: Dr. John T. Romeo
Focus: Ecology
Periodicals
ISCE Newsletter
Journal of Chemical Ecology (monthly)
Proceedings of the Annual Meeting . . 15280

International Society of Citriculture (ISC), c/o Botany and Plant Sciences, University of California, Riverside, CA 92521
T: (909) 787-4412; E-Mail: charles.coggins@ucr.edu; Fax: (909) 787-4437
Gen Secr: Charles W. Jr. Coggins
Focus: Agri 15281

International Society of Classical Bibliography, c/o Dept of Classics, Univ of North Carolina, Chapel Hill, NC 27514
Focus: Libraries & Bk Sci 15282

International Society of Cryptozoology (ISC), POB 43070, Tucson, AZ 85733
T: (602) 884-8369; Fax: (602) 884-8369
Founded: 1982; Members: 800
Focus: Zoology
Periodicals
Cryptozoology (annually)
The ISC Newsletter (quarterly) 15283

International Society of Dermatology: Tropical, Geographic and Ecologic (ISD), 200 First St SW, Rochester, MN 55905
T: (507) 284-3736
Founded: 1957; Members: 3000
Focus: Derm 15284

International Society of Development Biologists (ISDB), c/o Dept of Biology 0357, University of California, San Diego, 9500 Gilman Dr, La Jolla, CA 92093-0357
T: (619) 822-0458; Fax: (619) 822-0460
Gen Secr: Dr. William McGinnis
Focus: Bio 15285

International Society of Differentiation (ISD), POB 131854, Saint Paul, MN 55113-1318
T: (612) 659-9493; Fax: (612) 659-9493
Founded: 1970; Members: 300
Gen Secr: Robert G. McKinnell
Focus: Bio
Periodicals
Conference Proceedings
Differentation (bi-monthly)
Newsletter 15286

International Society of Educators of Physical Therapy (ISEPT), c/o Health Sciences Dept, Kapiolani Community College, Univ of Hawaii, 4303 Diamond Head Rd, Honolulu, HI 96816
T: (808) 734-9270; E-Mail: marilynm@uhunix.uhcc.hawaii.edu; Fax: (808) 734-9126
Gen Secr: Dr. Marilyn Miller
Focus: Educ; Therapeutics 15287

International Society of Environmental Epidemiology (ISEE), c/o Harvard School of Public Health, 665 Huntington Av, Boston, MA 02115
E-Mail: dockery@sparc6a.harvard.edu; Fax: (617) 277-2382
Gen Secr: Dr. Douglas Dockery
Focus: Med 15288

International Society of Exposure Analysis, Seven Bouvant Dr, Princeton, NJ 08540
T: (601) 683-4750; Fax: (601) 683-0838
Gen Secr: Myron A. Mehlman
Focus: Med 15289

International Society of Family Law (ISFL), 518 JRCB, Brigham Young University, POB 28000, Provo, UT 84602-8000
T: (801) 378-2617; E-Mail: Wardle@lawgate.byu.edu; Fax: (801) 378-3595
Gen Secr: Lynn D. Wardle
Focus: Law 15290

International Society of Financial Analysts (ISFA), POB 3668, Charlottesville, VA 22903
T: (804) 980-3682; Fax: (804) 980-3685
Gen Secr: Wendi Ruschmann
Focus: Finance 15291

International Society of Fire Service Instructors (ISFSI), c/o Industrial Risk Insurers, 85 Woodland St, Hartford, CT 06102
T: (203) 520-7391
Gen Secr: Larry Davis
Focus: Educ 15292

International Society of Geographic Ophthalmology (ISGO), c/o LSU Shreveport, LA Medical Center, 1501 Kings Hwy, Shreveport, LA 71130-3932
Gen Secr: Dr. James Ganley
Focus: Ophthal 15293

International Society of Gynaecological Pathologists (ISGP), c/o Thomas Jefferson University, Jefferson Medical College, Dept of Pathology, 11 and Walnut St, Main Bldg, Rm 263A, Philadelphia, PA 19107-5244
T: (215) 955-2433, 955-2434; Fax: (215) 955-8703
Gen Secr: A. Talerman
Focus: Gynecology; Pathology 15294

International Society of Hematology, c/o Mayo Clinic, 920 Hilton Bldg, Rochester, NY 55905
T: (507) 284-3937; Fax: (507) 284-0043
Founded: 1948; Members: 2600
Gen Secr: Prof. Robert A. Kyle
Focus: Hematology
Periodical
Newsletter (semi-annually) 15295

International Society of Invertebrate Reproduction (ISIR), c/o Dept of Zoology, Washington State Univ, Pullman, WA 99164-4236
Fax: (509) 335-3517
Gen Secr: Prof. Paul Schroeder
Focus: Zoology 15296

International Society of Lymphology (ISL), c/o Dept of Surgery, University of Arizona, Rm 4406, 1501 N Campbell Av, Tucson, AZ 85724
T: (602) 626-6118; Fax: (602) 626-0822
Gen Secr: Dr. Marlys H. Witte
Focus: Med 15297

International Society of Mediterranean Ecology (ISOMED), c/o Dept of Biology, San Diego State University, San Diego, CA 91935
Gen Secr: Dr. W.C. Oechel
Focus: Ecology 15298

International Society of Nuclear Air Treatment Technology (ISNATT), c/o Ellis and Watts, 4400 Glen Willow Lake Lane, Batavia, OH 45103
T: (513) 752-9000; E-Mail: ISNAIT@aol.com; Fax: (513) 752-4545
Gen Secr: Richard D. Porco
Focus: Eng 15299

International Society of Nutrition and Metabolism in Renal Disease, c/o Emory Univ School of Medicine, Dept of Medicine, 1364 Clifton Rd NE, Atlanta, GA 30322
T: (404) 727-3425; Fax: (404) 727-2525
Gen Secr: William E. Mitch
Focus: Food 15300

International Society of Offshore and Polar Engineers (ISOPE), POB 1107, Golden, CO 80402-1107
T: (303) 420-8114, 273-3673; Fax: (303) 420-3760
Gen Secr: Prof. Jin S. Chung
Focus: Eng 15301

International Society of Oxygen Transport to Tissue, c/o Dept of Biochem and Biophys, School of Medicine, Univ of Pennsylvania, Philadelphia, PA 19104
Gen Secr: Dr. David F. Wilson
Focus: Biophys 15302

International Society of Parametric Analysts (ISPA), POB 6402, Town Country Branch, Chesterfield, MO 63006-6402
T: (314) 527-2955; Fax: (314) 256-8358
Founded: 1979; Members: 800
Gen Secr: Marilee Wheaton
Focus: Finance
Periodicals
Journal of Parametrics (quarterly)
Parametric World (bi-monthly) 15303

International Society of Phenomenology, Aesthetics and the Fine Arts (ISPAFA), c/o Michigan State Univ, Romance and Classical Languages, 313 Old Horticulture Bldg, East Lansing, MI 48824-1112
Gen Secr: Prof. Marlies Kronegger
Focus: Parapsych; Arts 15304

International Society of Photosynthesis Research, c/o USDA/ARS and Dept of Plant Biology, University of Illinois, 148 PABL, 1201 W Gregory Av, Urbana, IL 61801
Gen Secr: Prof. Donald Ort
Focus: Botany 15305

International Society of Plant Molecular Biology (ISPMB), c/o Biochemistry Department, Univ of Georgia, Athens, GA 30602-7229
T: (706) 542-2086, 542-3239; E-Mail: dtyner@uga.cc.uga.edu; Fax: (706) 542-2090
Gen Secr: Dianne Tyner
Focus: Botany 15306

International Society of Political Psychology (ISPP), c/o Dept of Political Science, Williams College, Williamstown, MA 01267
T: (413) 597-2538; E-Mail: George.E.Marcus@williams.edu; Fax: (413) 597-4200
Gen Secr: George E. Marcus
Focus: Psych 15307

International Society of Refractive Surgery (ISRS), c/o Phillips Eye Institute, 2215 Park Av, Minneapolis, MN 55404
T: (612) 336-7575; Fax: (612) 336-5530
Gen Secr: Michelle M. Quade
Focus: Surgery 15308

International Society of Regulatory Toxicology and Pharmacology (ISRTP), 6546 Belleview Dr, Columbia, MD 21046-1054
T: (410) 992-9083; Fax: (410) 740-9181
Gen Secr: Sallie W. Carr
Focus: Toxicology; Pharmacol 15309

International Society of Reproductive Medicine (ISRM), 11 Furman Ct, Rancho Mirage, CA 92270
T: (619) 340-5080; Fax: (619) 340-6920
Members: 300
Gen Secr: Donald C. McEwen
Focus: Med 15310

International Society of Statistical Science in Economics (IS-SSE), 536 Oasis Dr, Santa Rosa, CA 95407
T: (707) 575-3529
Gen Secr: Vladislav V. Shvyrkov
Focus: Stats; Econ 15311

International Society of the Knee (ISK), 6300 N River Rd, Ste 727, Rosemont, IL 60018-4238
T: (708) 698-1632; Fax: (708) 823-0536
Gen Secr: Priscilla Wessell
Focus: Med 15312

International Society of Travel Medicine (ISTM), POB 871089, Stone Mountain, GA 30087-0028
T: (770) 736-7060; E-Mail: bcbistm@aol.com; Fax: (770) 736-6732
Focus: Med 15313

International Society of University Colon and Rectal Surgeons (ISUCRS), c/o Dept of Colon and Rectal Surgery, 1514 Jefferson Hwy, New Orleans, LA 70121
Gen Secr: Dr. J.B. Gathright
Focus: Surgery 15314

International Society of Vertebrate Morphologists (ISVM), c/o Department of Orthodontics, Univ of Washington, POB 357446, Seattle, WA 98195-7446
T: (206) 543-3203; E-Mail: herring@u.washington.edu; Fax: (206) 685-8163
Gen Secr: Prof. S.W. Herring
Focus: Zoology 15315

International Society on Immunopharmacology (ISIP), c/o Harvard Medical School, Brigham and Women's Hospital, 250 Longwood Av, Seeley G. Mudd Bldg, Rm 604, Boston, MA 02115
Gen Secr: K. Frank Austen
Focus: Pharmacol 15316

International Society on Metabolic Eye Diseases (ISMED), 1125 Park Av, New York, NY 10128
T: (212) 427-1246
Founded: 1971; Members: 600
Gen Secr: Dr. Heskel M. Haddad
Focus: Ophthal
Periodical
Metabolic, Pediatric and Systemic Ophthalmology (quarterly) 15317

International Society on Thrombosis and Hemostasis (ISTH), c/o Medical School, University of North Carolina, Chapel Hill, NC 27599-7035
T: (919) 929-3807; Fax: (919) 929-3935
Founded: 1969; Members: 1400
Focus: Hematology
Periodical
Thrombosis and Hemostasis Journal . . 15318

International Society on Toxinology (IST), c/o Dept Anatomy, Pathology and Pharmacology, Oklahoma State Univ, Stillwater, OK 74078
Gen Secr: Prof. Charlotte Ownby
Focus: Toxicology 15319

International Sociological and Legal Research Centre (INTERLEGAL), 165 E 72 St, Ste 1B, New York, NY 10021
Gen Secr: Harvey Dale
Focus: Sociology; Law 15320

International Soil Conservation Organization (ISCO), c/o WASWC, 317 Marvin Av, Volga, SD 57071
Focus: Geology 15321

International Soil Tillage Research Organization (ISTRO), c/o Ohio State University, School of Natural Resources, 1680 Madison Av, Wooster, OH 44691-4096
T: (330) 263-3877; E-Mail: dick.5@osu.edu; Fax: (330) 263-3658
Gen Secr: Warren A. Dick
Focus: Geology 15322

International Solar Energy Society (ISES), c/o Innovative Design, 850 W Morgan St, Raleigh, NC 27603
T: (919) 832-6303; Fax: (919) 832-3339
Gen Secr: Michael Niklas
Focus: Energy 15323

International Species Information System (ISIS), 12101 Johnny Cake Ridge Rd, Bldg A, Rm 6, Apple Valley, MN 55124-8151
T: (612) 431-9295; E-Mail: isis@isis.worldzoo.org; Fax: (612) 432-2757
Focus: Zoology 15324

International Spinal Development and Research Foundation, 500 S Rancho Dr, Ste 8A, Las Vegas, NV 89106-4806
E-Mail: isdrf@vegas.infi.net; Fax: (702) 259-1026
Gen Secr: James M. Giuffre
Focus: Med 15325

International Statistical Programs Center (ISPC), c/o US Bureau of the Census, Washington Plaza, Washington, DC 20233-0001
T: (301) 763-2860; Fax: (301) 763-7589
Gen Secr: J. Howard Bryant
Focus: Stats 15326

International Stereoscopic Union (ISU), 241 Sycamore Place, Decatur, GA 30030
T: (404) 373-0773; Fax: (404) 373-0773
Gen Secr: Marilyn Morton
Focus: Med 15327

International Stereotactic Radiosurgery Society (ISRS), c/o Univ of Pittsburgh, School of Medicine, Dept of Neurological Surgery, B-400 Presbyterian University Hospital, Pittsburgh, PA 15213
T: (412) 647-6781; Fax: (412) 647-5559
Gen Secr: L. Dade Lunsford
Focus: Surgery 15328

International Strabismological Association (ISA), c/o Pediatric Ophtalmology, Indiana University School of Medicine, 702 Rotary Circle, Indianapolis, IN 46202-5175
T: (317) 274-1214; Fax: (317) 274-1111
Gen Secr: Dr. Eugene M. Helveston
Focus: Ophthal 15329

International Stress Management Association (ISMA), c/o US International Univ, Inst for Stress Management, 10455 Pomerado Rd, San Diego, CA 92131
T: (619) 635-4698; Fax: (619) 693-4669
Gen Secr: Dr. F.J. McGuigan
Focus: Psych 15330

International Studies Association (ISA), c/o University of Arizona, 324 Social Sciences Bldg, Tucson, AZ 85721
T: (520) 621-7715; E-Mail: Isa@arizona.edu; Fax: (520) 621-5780
Founded: 1959; Members: 2900
Gen Secr: Thomas J. Volgy
Focus: Sci
Periodicals
International Studies Newsletter (10 times annually)
International Studies Notes (3 times annually)
International Studies Quarterly (quarterly)
New Dimensions in International Studies (annually) 15331

International Survey Library Association (ISLA), c/o Roper Center, University of Connecticut, POB 440, Storrs, CT 06268
T: (203) 486-4440
Founded: 1964; Members: 57
Focus: Libraries & Bk Sci
Periodical
Data Acquisitions Catalog (semi-annually) 15332

International Systems Institute (ISI), 25781 Morse Dr, Carmel, CA 93923
T: (408) 625-3178; E-Mail: belasr@aol.com; Fax: (408) 625-3178
Gen Secr: Prof. Bela H. Banathy
Focus: Computer & Info Sci 15333

International Technology Education Association (ITEA), 1914 Association Dr, Reston, VA 20191-1539
T: (703) 860-0353; E-Mail: itea@tmn.com
Founded: 1939; Members: 6700
Gen Secr: Dr. Kendall Starkweather
Focus: Arts
Periodicals
Journal of Technology Education (semi-annually)
Teacher Education Newsletter
Technology Teacher (8 times annually) . 15334

International Technology Education Association - Council for Supervisors (ITEA-CS), c/o Virginia Dept of Education, POB 2120, Richmond, VA 23216-2120
T: (804) 225-2020; Fax: (804) 371-0249
Founded: 1951; Members: 300
Gen Secr: George R. Willcox
Focus: Arts
Periodical
Super Link (3 times annually) 15335

International Tele-Education (INTEL-ED), 4619 Larchwood Av, Philadelphia, PA 19143-2107
T: (215) 898-8918
Founded: 1977
Focus: Educ 15336

International Telecommunications Society (ITS), c/o University of Colorado, ITP OT-3-37, Engineering Center, Campus POB 530, Boulder, CO 80309-0530
T: (303) 492-8717; E-Mail: houstong@spot.colorado.edu; Fax: (303) 492-1112
Gen Secr: Prof. James Alleman
Focus: Electric Eng 15337

International Test and Evaluation Association (ITEA), 4400 Fair Lakes Ct, Fairfax, VA 22033-3899
T: (703) 631-6220; Fax: (703) 631-6221
Founded: 1980; Members: 2000
Focus: Eng
Periodicals
Journal of Test and Evaluation (quarterly)
Symposia Proceedings (annually) 15338

International Textile and Apparel Association (ITAA), POB 1360, Monument, CO 80132
T: (719) 488-3716
Founded: 1944; Members: 950
Gen Secr: Dr. Sandra S. Hutton
Focus: Educ; Textiles 15339

International Thermoelectric Society (ITS), c/o Jet Propulsion Laboratory, California Institute of Technology, M/S 277-212, 4800 Oak Grove Dr, Pasadena, CA 91109-8099
T: (818) 354-4144; Fax: (818) 393-6951
Gen Secr: Dr. Jean Pierre Fleurial
Focus: Physics 15340

International Thespian Society (ITS), 3368 Central Pkwy, Cincinnati, OH 45225-2392
T: (513) 559-1996; E-Mail: info@etassoc.org; Fax: (513) 559-0012
Founded: 1929; Members: 28000
Gen Secr: Ronald L. Longstreth
Focus: Perf Arts
Periodicals
Dramatics Magazine (9 times annually)
ITS Today (3-4 times annually)
State Directors' Newsletter (quarterly)
Super Trouper (3-4 times annually) . . 15341

International Third World Legal Studies Association (INTWORLSA), c/o Int Center for Law in Development, 777 United Nations Plaza, New York, NY 10017
T: (212) 687-0036; Fax: (212) 370-9844
Gen Secr: James Paul
Focus: Law 15342

International Thorstein Veblen Association, c/o Department of Public Administration, Univ of Nevada, Las Vegas, NV 89154
Gen Secr: Rick Tilman
Focus: Public Admin 15343

International Tourism Education and Resources Network (INTERN), 250 Summer St, Boston, MA 02210
T: (617) 345-0880; Fax: (617) 330-1732
Focus: Educ 15344

International Training in Communication (ITC), 2519 Woodland Dr, Anaheim, CA 92801
T: (714) 995-3660; Fax: (714) 995-6974
Gen Secr: Muriel Bryant
Focus: Educ; Comm Sci 15345

International Training Network for Water and Waste Management (ITN), c/o INUWS-World Bank, Piers Cross, 1818 H St NW, Washington, DC 20433
T: (202) 473-3475; Fax: (202) 477-0164
Focus: Educ; Water Res; Ecology . . . 15346

International Transactional Analysis Association (ITAA), 450 Pacific Av, Ste 250, San Francisco, CA 94133-4640
T: (415) 989-5640; Fax: (415) 989-9343
Founded: 1958; Members: 7000
Gen Secr: Susan D. Sevilla
Focus: Psychiatry
Periodicals
Script Newsletter (9 times annually)
Transactional Analysis Journal (quarterly) 15347

International Trauma Anesthesia and Critical Care Society (ITACCS), POB 4826, Baltimore, MD 21211
T: (410) 235-7697; Fax: (410) 235-8084
Gen Secr: Christopher M. Grande
Focus: Anesthetics 15348

International Tree Crops Institute U.S.A. (ITCI), POB 4460, Davis, CA 95617
T: (916) 753-4535; Fax: (916) 753-4535
Founded: 1977
Focus: Forestry
Periodical
Technical Papers 15349

International Tsunami Information Centre (ITIC), POB 50027, Honolulu, HI 96850-4993
T: (808) 541-1657; Fax: (808) 541-1678
Founded: 1965; Members: 750
Gen Secr: Dr. Charles S. McCreery
Focus: Oceanography
Periodicals
Newsletter (3 times annually)
Report (annually) 15350

International Turfgrass Society (ITS), c/o EREC, University of Florida, POB 8003, Belle Glade, FL 33430
T: (407) 996-3062; E-Mail: ghs@gnv.ufl.edu; Fax: (407) 996-0339
Founded: 1969; Members: 350
Gen Secr: John R. Hall
Focus: Agri
Periodical
Proceedings of Conference 15351

International Union Against Cancer (UICC), c/o The Pacific NW Cancer Foundation, 120 Northgate Plaza, Ste 205, Seattle, WA 98125
Gen Secr: Dr. Gerald P. Murphy
Focus: Cell Biol & Cancer Res 15352

International Union for Health Promotion and Education (IUHPE), c/o Association for the Advancement of Health Education, 1900 Association Dr, Reston, VA 22091
T: (703) 476-3437; Fax: (703) 476-6638
Gen Secr: Dr. Becky Smith
Focus: Public Health; Educ 15353

International Union for Quaternary Research (INQUA), c/o Quaternary Research Center, Univ of Washington, Seattle, WA 98195
T: (206) 543-1166; E-Mail: scporter@u.washington.edu; Fax: (206) 543-3836
Gen Secr: Prof. Stephen C. Porter
Focus: Nat Sci 15354

International Union of Architects (IUA), c/o Loebl, Schlossman and Hackl, 130 E Randolph Dr, Ste 3400, Chicago, IL 60601-6313
T: (312) 565-4500; Fax: (312) 565-5912
Gen Secr: Donald J. Hackl
Focus: Archit 15355

International Union of Biological Sciences (IUBS), c/o Department of Integrative Biology, Univ of California, Berkeley, CA 94720
T: (510) 642-4743; Fax: (510) 643-6264
Gen Secr: Prof. Marvalee H. Wake
Focus: Bio 15356

International Union of Esthetics Medicine, 2063 Vista Alcedo, Camarillo, CA 93012
Gen Secr: Dr. Delune
Focus: Med 15357

International Union of Materials Research Societies (IUMRS), 9800 Mc Knight Rd, Pittsburgh, PA 15237
T: (412) 367-3003
Focus: Materials Sci 15358

International Union of Physiological Sciences (IUPS), c/o IUPS Executive Office, Dept of Physiology, Michigan State University, 240 Gittner Hall, East Lansing, MI 48824-1101
Gen Secr: Prof. Harvey Sparks
Focus: Physiology 15359

International Union of Pure and Applied Chemistry (IUPAC), c/o Dept of Chemistry, University of Kansas, Malott Hall, Lawrence, KS 66045
T: (913) 864-5172; E-Mail: busch@kuhub.cc.ukans.edu; Fax: (913) 749-7393
Gen Secr: Prof. D. H. Busch
Focus: Chem 15360

International Union of the History and Philosophy of Science (IUHPS), c/o Dept of Philosophy, Univ of Wisconsin, 5185 Helen C White Hall, Madison, WI 53706
T: (608) 263-5718; E-Mail: esober@macc.wisc.edu; Fax: (608) 265-3701
Gen Secr: Elliott Sober
Focus: Hist; Philos; Sci 15361

International University Consortium (IUC), c/o Univ of Maryland, Univ College, College Park, MD 20742-1612
T: (301) 985-7811; Fax: (301) 985-7845
Gen Secr: Dr. Eugene Rubin
Focus: Educ 15362

International University Foundation (IUF), 1301 S Noland Rd, Independence, MO 64055
T: (816) 461-3633; Fax: (816) 461-3634
Gen Secr: Dr. John Wayne Johnston
Focus: Educ 15363

International Urogynaecological Association (IUGA), c/o Dept of Obstetrics and Gynacology, Evanston Hospital, Evanston Continence Center, 1000 Central St, Evanston, IL 60201-1797
T: (847) 570-2750; Fax: (847) 570-1386
Gen Secr: Dr. Peter K. Sand
Focus: Gynecology 15364

International Veterinary Acupuncture Society (IVAS), 268 W Third St, Ste 2, POB 2074, Nederland, CO 80466-2074
T: (303) 449-7936; E-Mail: IVASJAGG@msn.com; Fax: (303) 449-8312
Founded: 1974; Members: 900
Gen Secr: David H. Jaggar
Focus: Vet Med
Periodical
Newsletter (quarterly) 15365

International Veterinary Auxiliary (IVA), 4813 Bardstown Rd, Louisville, KY 40291
T: (502) 499-1457; Fax: (502) 231-2325
Gen Secr: Carolyn S. Sims
Focus: Vet Med 15366

International Visual Literacy Association (IVLA), c/o Dr. Barbara I. Clark, Gonzaga University, E 502 Boone AD25, Spokane, WA 99258-0001
T: (509) 328-4220; E-Mail: bclark@soe.gonzaga.edu
Founded: 1968; Members: 200
Pres: Nancy Knüpfer
Focus: Lit 15367

International Vitamin A Consultative Group (IVACG), c/o ILSI Human Nutrition Institute, 1126 16 St NW, Washington, DC 20036-4810
T: (202) 659-9024; E-Mail: omni@dc.ilsi.org; Fax: (202) 659-3617
Gen Secr: Dr. A. Horwitz
Focus: Food 15368

International Vocational Education and Training Association (IVETA), 676B Enterprise Dr, Lewiscenter, OH 43035
T: (614) 847-9550; Fax: (614) 847-9844
Gen Secr: Dr. Valija M. Axelrod
Focus: Educ 15369

International Water Resources Association (IWRA), c/o University of Illinois, 1101 W Peabody Dr, Urbana, IL 61801-2352
T: (217) 333-6275; E-Mail: g-stout@uiuc.edu; Fax: (217) 244-6633
Founded: 1972; Members: 1400
Gen Secr: Glenn E. Stout
Focus: Water Res
Periodical
Water International (quarterly) 15370

International Weed Science Society (IWSS), c/o IPPC, Oregon State University, Cordley Hall, Corvallis, OR 97331-2915
T: (503) 731-3541; Fax: (503) 737-3080
Founded: 1976; Members: 630
Gen Secr: Susan Larson
Focus: Agri 15371

International Wheat Gluten Association (IWGA), 4510 W 89th St, Ste 100, Prairie Village, KS 66207
T: (913) 341-1155; Fax: (913) 341-3625
Gen Secr: J.M. Hesser
Focus: Agri 15372

International Wizard of Oz Club (IWOC), 1438 N Ullman St, Appleton, WI 54911-3930
Founded: 1957; Members: 2500
Gen Secr: Fred M. Meyer
Focus: Lit
Periodicals
The Baum Bugle (3 times annually)
Membership Directory (annually)
Oz Trading Post (quarterly) 15373

International Women's Anthropology Conference (IWAC), 1010 Spruce St, Philadelphia, PA 19107
T: (205) 440-0758
Founded: 1978; Members: 450
Gen Secr: Anne Okongwu
Focus: Anthro
Periodicals
Bulletin
IWAC Newsletter (semi-annually) 15374

International Women's Health Coalition (IWHC), 24 E 21 St, New York, NY 10010
T: (212) 979-8500; E-Mail: iwhc@igc.apc.org; Fax: (212) 979-9009
Founded: 1980
Pres: Joan B. Dunlop
Focus: Public Health 15375

International Working Group of Legume Virologists (IWGLV), c/o Department of Plant Pathology, Physiology and Weed Science, VPI and State University, Blacksburg, VA 24061-0330
Gen Secr: Dr. Sue E. Tolin
Focus: Microbio 15376

International Working Group on Citrus Bacterial Canker, c/o USDA AMS National Program Staff, BARC-West, Bldg 005, Rm 230, Beltsville, MD 20705
Gen Secr: Dr. E.L. Civerolo
Focus: Microbio 15377

International Zeolite Association (IZA), c/o Chemical Catalyst RandD, Engelhard Corporation, 23800 Mercantile Rd, Beachwood, OH 44122-5945
T: (216) 360-5013; Fax: (216) 464-5780
Gen Secr: Dr. Roland von Ballmoos
Focus: Mineralogy 15378

Internet Engineering Task Force (IETF), c/o Corporation for National Research Initiatives, 1895 Preston White Dr, Ste 100, Reston, VA 20191-5434
T: (703) 620-8990; E-Mail: ietf-info@ietf.org; Fax: (703) 758-5913
Focus: Eng 15379

Intersociety Committee on Pathology Information (ICPI), 4733 Bethesda Av, Ste 700, Bethesda, MD 20814
T: (301) 656-2944; Fax: (301) 656-3179
Founded: 1957; Members: 5
Focus: Pathology
Periodical
Directory of Pathology Training Programs (annually) 15380

Interstate Postgraduate Medical Association of North America (IPMANA), POB 5474, Madison, WI 53705
T: (608) 257-1401; Fax: (608) 257-1401
Founded: 1916
Focus: Adult Educ; Med 15381

Intertel, POB 1083, Tulsa, OK 74101-1083
T: (918) 583-2928
Founded: 1966; Members: 1700
Focus: Philos
Periodical
Integra (monthly) 15382

IOC Committee for the Global Investigation of Pollution in the Marine Environment (GIPME), c/o Chemical Oceanography Programme, National Science Foundation, 1800 G St NW, Washington, DC 20550
T: (202) 957-7910; Fax: (202) 357-7621
Gen Secr: Dr. Neil R. Andersen
Focus: Ecology; Oceanography 15383

IOC Sub-Commission for the Caribbean and Adjacent Regions (IOCARIBE), c/o NOAA Southeast Fisheries Science Center, 75 Virginia Beach Dr, Miami, FL 33149
T: (305) 361-4284; E-Mail: Brown@Semi3.Sefsc.NOAA.Gov; Fax: (305) 361-4219
Gen Secr: Dr. Bradford E. Brown
Focus: Oceanography 15384

IRI Research Institute, 169 Greenwich Av, POB 1276, Stamford, CT 06904-1276
T: (203) 327-5985; Fax: (203) 359-1595
Founded: 1950
Focus: Agri 15385

Irish American Cultural Institute (IACI), 19 Pine St, Morristown, NJ 07960
T: (201) 605-1991; Fax: (201) 605-8875
Founded: 1962
Pres: John P. Walsh
Focus: Hist; Lit
Periodical
Eire-Ireland (quarterly) 15386

Iron Overload Diseases Association (IOD), 433 Westwind Dr, North Palm Beach, FL 33408
T: (407) 840-8512; Fax: (407) 842-9881
Founded: 1981; Members: 2000
Focus: Hematology
Periodical
Ironic Blood: Newsletter (bi-monthly) . . 15387

Islamic Medical Association of North America (IMA), 4121 Fairview, Ste 203, Downers Grove, IL 60515
T: (708) 852-2122; E-Mail: imana@aol.com; Fax: (708) 852-2151
Gen Secr: Dr. Khursheed Mallick
Focus: Med 15388

Italian American Librarians Caucus (IALC), 6 Peter Cooper Rd, Apt 11G, New York, NY 10010
T: (212) 228-8438
Founded: 1974; Members: 200
Focus: Libraries & Bk Sci 15389

Italian Historical Society of America (IHS), 111 Columbia Heights, Brooklyn, NY 11201
T: (718) 852-2929; Fax: (718) 855-3925
Founded: 1949; Members: 1900
Focus: Hist
Periodicals
Italian-American Newsletter
Italian-American Review (quarterly) . . . 15390

IUAES Commission for the Anthropological and Ethnological Study of Peace, c/o Dept of Anthropology, Northwestern University, Evanston, IL 60201
T: (312) 491-5402
Gen Secr: Dr. Robert A. Rubinstein
Focus: Anthro; Prom Peace; Ethnology . 15391

IUAES Commission on Anthropology in Policy and Practice, c/o Dept of Anthropology, Wayne State University, College of Liberal Arts, Detroit, MI 48202
Fax: (313) 577-5958
Gen Secr: Prof. Marietta L. Baba
Focus: Anthro; Poli Sci 15392

IUAES Commission on Anthropology of Women, c/o Dept of Anthropology, Univ of Tennessee, 252 S Stadium Hall, Knoxville, TN 37996-0720
T: (423) 974-4408; E-Mail: fharriso@utk.edu; Fax: (423) 974-2686
Gen Secr: Dr. Faye Harrison
Focus: Anthro 15393

IUAES Commission on Cultural Dimensions of Global Change, c/o Dept of Anthopology, College of William and Mary, POB 8795, Williamsburg, VA 23187
Gen Secr: Prof. Tomoko Hamada
Focus: Ethnology 15394

IUAES Commission on Documentation (CoD), c/o Dept of Anthropology, University of Florida, Gainesville, FL 32611
T: (904) 392-2031; E-Mail: ufruss@earn.nervm
Gen Secr: Dr. H. Russell Bernard
Focus: Doc 15395

IUAES Commission on Ethnic Relations (COER), c/o Anthropology/SAC Dept, Eastern Michigan University, Ypsilanti, MI 48197
T: (313) 572-9843; Fax: (313) 487-7010
Gen Secr: Prof. Dr. E.L. Cerroni-Long
Focus: Ethnology 15396

IUAES Commission on the Anthropology of Tourism, c/o Dept of Anthropology, Southern Methodist University, Dallas, TX 75275-0336
T: (214) 768-2926; Fax: (214) 768-4289
Gen Secr: Prof. Robert V. Kemper
Focus: Anthro 15397

IUBS-IUPS-IUPAB Commission on Comparative Physiology, c/o Dept of Biology, University of California, 405 Hilgard Av, Los Angeles, CA 90024-1606
T: (310) 825-4579; Fax: (310) 206-3987
Gen Secr: Malcolm Gordon
Focus: Physiology 15398

IUCN Primate Specialist Group, c/o Conservation International, 1015 18 St NW, Ste 1000, Washington, DC 20036
T: (202) 429-5660; Fax: (202) 887-5188
Gen Secr: Russell A. Mittermeier
Focus: Zoology 15399

IUDZG – International Union of Directors of Zoological Gardens – World Zoo Organization, c/o ISIS, 12101 Johnny Cake Ridge Rd, Bldg A, Rm 6, Apple Valley, MN 55124-8151
T: (612) 431-9295; E-Mail: iudzg-wzo@worldzoo.org; Fax: (612) 432-2757
Focus: Zoology 15400

IUGS Commission on Comparative Planetology (CCP), c/o Geomechanics-Rock Fracture Group, Dept of Geological Sciences, Mackay School of Mines, Univ of Nevada, Reno, NV 89557-0138
T: (702) 784-4318; E-Mail: schultz@mines.unr.edu; Fax: (702) 784-1833
Gen Secr: Dr. Richard A. Schultz
Focus: Geology 15401

IUGS Commission on Global Sedimentary Geology (CSG), c/o Geomechanics-Rock Fracture Group, Dept of Geological Sciences, Mackay School of Mines, Univ of Nevada, Reno, NV 89557-0138
T: (702) 784-4318; E-Mail: schultz@mines.unr.edu; Fax: (702) 784-1833
Gen Secr: Dr. Richard A. Schultz
Focus: Geology 15402

IUGS Commission on Management and Application of Geoscience Information (COGEOINFO), c/o US Geological Survey, 801 National Center, Reston, VA 22092
T: (703) 648-7108; Fax: (703) 648-7069
Gen Secr: Dr. James E. Biesecker
Focus: Geology 15403

IUMS Division of Virology, c/o Dept of Microbiology and Immunology, Emory University, 3001 Rollins Research Centre, Atlanta, GA 30322
Gen Secr: Richard W. Compans
Focus: Microbio 15404

IUPAB Special Commission on Cell and Membrane Biophysics, c/o Dept of Biochemistry, University of Virginia, Health Sciences Center, Charlottesville, VA 22908
T: (804) 924-2651; E-Mail: tet@virginia.edu; Fax: (804) 924-5069
Gen Secr: Prof. T.E. Thompson
Focus: Biophys 15405

IUPAB Special Commission on Education and Development in Biophysics, c/o Dept of Biochemistry, University of Minnesota, 1479 Gortner Av, St Paul, MN 55108-1022
Gen Secr: Prof. N.M. Allewell
Focus: Educ; Biophys 15406

IUPAB Special Commission on NMR in Biology and Medicine, c/o Bringham and Women's Hospital, NMR Laboratory of Physiological Chemistry, Dept of Medicine, 75 Francis St, Boston, MA 02115
T: (617) 732-6994; Fax: (617) 732-6990
Gen Secr: Prof. J.S. Ingwall
Focus: Bio; Med 15407

IUPS Commission on Bioengineering in Physiology, c/o University of Washington, Center for Bioengineering, Seattle, WA 98195-7962
T: (206) 685-2005; Fax: (206) 685-2651
Gen Secr: Prof. James B. Bassingthwaighte
Focus: Eng; Physiology 15408

IUPS Commission on Chronophysiology, c/o Dept of Neurology and Physiology, Northwestern Univ, 2153 N Campus Dr, Evanston, IL 60208-3520
T: (708) 491-5521; Fax: (708) 491-5211
Gen Secr: Prof. F.W. Turek
Focus: Physiology 15409

IUPS Commission on Endocrinology, c/o Dept Neurobiology and Behavior, The Rockefeller University, 1230 York Av, New York, NY 10021-6399
Gen Secr: Prof. Donald Pfaff
Focus: Endocrinology 15410

IUPS Commission on Environmental Physiology, c/o Dept of Biological Sciences, University of Nevada, Las Vegas, NV 89154
T: (702) 739-3399
Gen Secr: Prof. M.K. Yousef
Focus: Physiology 15411

IUPS Commission on Food and Fluid Intake, c/o University of Pittsburgh, 479 Crawford Hall, Pittsburgh, PA 15260
T: (412) 624-4569; Fax: (412) 624-9198
Gen Secr: Prof. Edward M. Stricker
Focus: Food 15412

IUPS Commission on Memory and Learning, c/o Center for Neurobiology and Behaviour, College of Physicians and Surgeons, Columbia Univ, New York, NY 10032
Gen Secr: Prof. E.R. Kandel
Focus: Educ 15413

IUPS Commission on Respiratory Physiology, c/o UCSD, Section of Physiology 0623 A, Dept of Medicine, 9500 Gilman Dr, La Jolla, CA 92093-0623
T: (619) 534-4190; Fax: (619) 534-4812
Gen Secr: Prof. John B. West
Focus: Physiology 15414

IUPS Commission on the Teaching of Physiology, c/o Duke University Medical Center, POB 3709, Durham, NC 27710-0001
T: (919) 681-8404; E-Mail: g.somjen@cellbio.duke.edu; Fax: (919) 684-5481
Gen Secr: George G. Somjen
Focus: Educ; Physiology 15415

IUPS Commission on Undersea Physiology and Medicine, c/o Medical College of Wisconsin, 9200 W Wisconsin Av, Milwaukee, WI 53226
T: (414) 454-5060
Gen Secr: Dr. Eric P. Kindwall
Focus: Physiology; Med 15416

Jack London Research Center (JLRC), 14300 Arnold Dr, POB 337, Glen Ellen, CA 95442
T: (707) 996-2888
Founded: 1971
Focus: Lit 15417

Jack Point Preservation Society (JPPS), POB 179, New Ellenton, SC 29809
T: 803) 652-3492
Founded: 1985; Members: 26
Focus: Music 15418

James Joyce Society (JJS), 41 W 47 St, New York, NY 10036
T: (212) 719-4448
Founded: 1947; Members: 250
Focus: Lit
Periodical
James Joyce Journal (annually) 15419

James S Coleman African Studies Center, Los Angeles (JSCASC), c/o University of California, 405 Hilgard Av, 10244 Bunche Hall, Los Angeles, CA 90024-1310
T: (310) 825-3686; Fax: (310) 206-2250
Gen Secr: Prof. Edmond J. Keller
Focus: Ethnology 15420

Japanese American Society for Legal Studies (JASLS), c/o University of Washington Law School, 110 NE Campus Pkwy, Seattle, WA 98105
T: (206) 685-1897; Fax: (206) 543-5671
Founded: 1964; Members: 1250
Gen Secr: Prof. Daniel H. Foote
Focus: Law
Periodical
Law in Japan (annually) 15421

Jargon Society (JS), 8 W Third St, Ste 400, Winston-Salem, NC 27101
T: (919) 724-7619; Fax: (919) 727-0919
Founded: 1951; Members: 100
Pres: Jonathan Williams
Focus: Ling 15422

Jean Piaget Society (JPSSKD) / Society for the Study of Knowledge and Development, c/o Dept of Human Development, Harvard GS Education, 703 Larsen, Cambridge, MA 02138
T: (617) 495-3614; Fax: (617) 495-3626
Founded: 1970; Members: 500
Focus: Psych
Periodicals
The Genetic Epistemologist (quarterly)
Symposium Proceedings (annually) . . . 15423

Jefferson Davis Association (JDA), c/o Rice University, 6100 Main St, Houston, TX 77005-1892
T: (713) 527-4990
Founded: 1963
Pres: Frank E. Vandiver
Focus: Hist
Periodical
The Papers of Jefferson Davis (bi-annually) . . . 15424

Jesse Stuart Foundation (JSF), POB 391, Ashland, KY 41114
T: (606) 329-5232; E-Mail: j.giffor@msuacad.morehead-st.edu
Founded: 1979; Members: 7000
Gen Secr: Dr. James M. Gifford
Focus: Lit . . . 15425

Jesuit Philosophical Association (JPA), c/o Dept of Philosophy, Boston College, Chestnut Hill, MA 02167
T: (617) 552-3872; Fax: (617) 552-2977
Founded: 1935; Members: 120
Gen Secr: Gary Gurtler
Focus: Philos
Periodical
Proceedings of the Jesuit Philosophical Association (annually) . . . 15426

Jesuit Secondary Education Association (JSEA), 1616 P St NW, Ste 400, Washington, DC 20036-1405
T: (202) 667-3888; Fax: (202) 328-9212
Founded: 1970; Members: 45
Pres: Carl E. Meirose
Focus: Educ
Periodicals
Annual Directory of Jesuit High Schools and Universities (annually)
News Bulletin (monthly) . . . 15427

Jesuit Seismological Association (JSA), c/o Weston Observatory, Boston College, 381 Concord Rd, Weston, MA 02193-1340
T: (617) 552-8325; Fax: (617) 552-8388
Founded: 1925; Members: 12
Gen Secr: James McCaffrey
Focus: Geology . . . 15428

Jewish Braille Institute of America (JBI), 110 E 30 St, New York, NY 10016
T: (212) 889-2525; Fax: (212) 689-3692
Founded: 1931
Focus: Rehabil . . . 15429

Jewish Education Service of North America (JESNA), 730 Broadway, New York, NY 10003-9540
T: (212) 529-2000
Founded: 1939; Members: 1000
Focus: Educ
Periodicals
Jewish Education Directory (tri-annually)
Pedagogic Reporter (quarterly)
Trends (quarterly) . . . 15430

Jewish Educators Assembly (JEA), 106-06 Queens Blvd, Flushing, NY 11375-4248
T: (718) 268-9452; Fax: (718) 520-4369
Founded: 1951; Members: 450
Gen Secr: Bernard D. Troy
Focus: Educ
Periodicals
Observer (quarterly)
Yearbook (annually) . . . 15431

Jewish Lawyers Guild (JLG), 299 Broadway, New York, NY 10007
T: (212) 227-8075; Fax: (212) 227-8075
Founded: 1962; Members: 750
Focus: Law
Periodical
Confrontation . . . 15432

Jewish Teachers Association – Morim (JTA-M), 45 E 33 St, Ste 604, New York, NY 10016
T: (212) 684-0556
Founded: 1924; Members: 8000
Focus: Educ
Periodical
Morim Bulletin (quarterly) . . . 15433

Joan B Kroc Institute for International Peace Studies, c/o University of Notre Dame, POB 639, Notre Dame, IN 46556-0639
T: (219) 631-5665; E-Mail: RAIMO.V.VAYRYNEN@nd.edu; Fax: (219) 631-6973
Gen Secr: Raimo Väyrynen
Focus: Prom Peace . . . 15434

John Burroughs Association (JBA), c/o American Museum of Natural History, Central Park W at 79 St, New York, NY 10024
T: (212) 769-5169; Fax: (212) 769-5233
Founded: 1921; Members: 429
Focus: Nat Sci
Periodicals
Bulletin
Wakerobin (semi-annually) . . . 15435

John Dewey Society (JDS), c/o Dr. Robert C. Morris, West Georgia College, Carrollton, GA 30118
T: (404) 836-6564; E-Mail: rmorris@westga.edu; Fax: (404) 836-6729
Founded: 1935; Members: 450
Gen Secr: Dr. Robert C. Morris
Focus: Educ
Periodicals
Current Issues (annually)
Insights (bi-annually)
John Dewey Lectures (annually) . . . 15436

John E Fogarty International Center for Advanced Study in the Health Sciences, c/o National Institutes of Health, Bldg 31, Rm B2002, 31 Center Dr, MSC 2220, Bethesda, MD 20892-2220
T: (301) 496-2075; Fax: (301) 594-1211
Gen Secr: Dr. Philip E. Schambra
Focus: Public Health . . . 15437

John Ericsson Society (JES), c/o Church of Sweden, 5 E 48 St, New York, NY 10017
T: (212) 980-9655; Fax: (212) 755-7953
Founded: 1907; Members: 140
Pres: Kjell Lagerstrom
Focus: Hist . . . 15438

The Johnsonians, c/o Stuart Sherman, Dept of English, University of Chicago, 1050 E 59 St, Chicago, IL 60637
T: (312) 477-8015; Fax: (312) 477-6176
Founded: 1946; Members: 50
Gen Secr: Stuart Sherman
Focus: Lit . . . 15439

Joint Center for Political and Economic Studies (JCPES), 1090 Vermont Av NW, Ste 1100, Washington, DC 20005
T: (202) 789-3500; Fax: (202) 789-6390
Founded: 1970
Focus: Poli Sci; Econ
Periodicals
Focus (monthly)
National Roster of Black Elected Officials (annually) . . . 15440

Joint Commission of History and Philosophy of Science, c/o Dept of Philosophy, University of Wisconsin, 5185 Helen C White Hall, Madison, WI 53706
E-Mail: esober@wiscmacc.bitnet; Fax: (608) 265-3701
Gen Secr: Elliott Sober
Focus: Hist; Philos; Sci . . . 15441

Joint Commission on Accreditation of Healthcare Organizations (JCAHO), 1 Renaissance Blvd, Oakbrook Terrace, IL 60181
T: (630) 792-5000; Fax: (630) 792-5001
Founded: 1951
Pres: Dennis S. O'Leary
Focus: Med
Periodicals
Clinical Standards Digest
Joint Commission Perspectives
PTSM Series
Quality Review Bulletin . . . 15442

Joint Commission on Allied Health Personnel in Ophthalmology (JCAHPO), 2025 Woodlane Dr, St Paul, MN 55125-2995
T: (612) 731-2944; Fax: (612) 284-3937
Gen Secr: Prof. Peter Y. Evans
Focus: Ophthal . . . 15443

Joint Committee of the States to Study Alcoholic Beverage Laws, c/o National Alcoholic Beverage Control Association, 4216 King St W, Alexandria, VA 22302
T: (703) 578-4200; Fax: (703) 820-3551
Focus: Law . . . 15444

Joint Council of Allergy, Asthma and Immunology (JCAAI), 50 N Brockway, No 3-3, Palatine, IL 60067
T: (708) 934-1918; E-Mail: jcaai@aol.com
Founded: 1975; Members: 2850
Gen Secr: Joseph J. Lotharius
Focus: Immunology . . . 15445

Joint Global Ocean Flux Study (JGOFS), c/o SCOR, Dept of Earth and Planetary Sciences, Johns Hopkins University, Baltimore, MD 21218
T: (410) 516-4070; E-Mail: scor@jhu.edu; Fax: (410) 516-4019
Gen Secr: Elizabeth Gross
Focus: Oceanography . . . 15446

Joint Industry Council (JIC), c/o IACUB, 702 Bloomington Rd, Champaign, IL 61820
T: (217) 359-2469
Founded: 1978; Members: 10
Focus: Standards . . . 15447

Joint IUBMB-IUPAB Bioenergetics Group, c/o School of Chemical Sciences, University of Illinois, 505 S Matthews Av, Urbana, IL 61801
Gen Secr: Prof. R.B. Gennis
Focus: Energy . . . 15448

Joint Review Committee for Respiratory Therapy Education (JRCRTE), 1701 W Euless Blvd, Ste 200, Euless, TX 76040
T: (817) 283-2835
Founded: 1963; Members: 13
Focus: Therapeutics . . . 15449

Joint Review Committee for the Ophthalmic Medical Personnel (JRCOMP), 2025 Woodlane Dr, Saint Paul, MN 55125-2995
T: (612) 731-2944
Members: 5
Focus: Ophthal . . . 15450

Joint Review Committee on Education in Diagnostic Medical Sonography (JRCDMS), 7108C S Alton Way, Englewood, CO 80112
T: (303) 741-3533; Fax: (303) 741-3655
Founded: 1979; Members: 8
Gen Secr: Annamarie Dubies-Appel
Focus: Educ; Med . . . 15451

Joint Review Committee on Education in Radiologic Technology (JRCERT), 20 E Wacker Dr, Ste 900, Chicago, IL 60606
T: (312) 704-5300; Fax: (312) 704-5304
Founded: 1969
Focus: Educ; Radiology . . . 15452

Joint Review Committee on Educational Programs for the EMT-Paramedic (JRCEMT-P), 1701 W Euless Blvd, Ste 200, Euless, TX 76040
T: (817) 283-2836
Founded: 1979
Focus: Educ; Med . . . 15453

Joseph H Lauder Institute of Management and International Studies, c/o Univ of Pennsylvania, 256 S 37 St, Philadelphia, PA 19104-6330
T: (215) 898-1215; Fax: (215) 898-2067
Gen Secr: Dr. Stephen J. Kobrin
Focus: Business Admin; Poli Sci . . . 15454

Joslin Diabetes Center (JDC), 1 Joslin Pl, Boston, MA 02215
T: (617) 732-2400; Fax: (617) 732-2562
Founded: 1968
Focus: Diabetes . . . 15455

Journalism Association of Community Colleges (JACC), c/o Michael Cornner, Los Angeles Pierce College, 6201 Winnetka Av, Woodland Hills, CA 91371
T: (818) 719-6427; Fax: (818) 710-9844
Founded: 1957; Members: 70
Gen Secr: Michael Cornner
Focus: Adult Educ; Journalism
Periodicals
Directory (annually)
Idea Exchange (semi-annually)
Newsletter (bi-monthly) . . . 15456

Journalism Education Association (JEA), c/o Kansas State University, Kedzie Hall 103, Manhattan, KS 66506-1505
T: (913) 532-5532; Fax: (913) 532-7309
Founded: 1924; Members: 1700
Focus: Adult Educ; Journalism
Periodical
Communication: Journalism Education Today (quarterly) . . . 15457

Jozef Pilsudski Institute of America for Research in the Modern History of Poland, 180 Second Av, New York, NY 10003-5778
T: (212) 505-9077; Fax: (212) 505-9052
Founded: 1943; Members: 1000
Pres: Dr. Janusz Cisek
Focus: Hist
Periodical
Wiadomosci Instytutu J. Pilsudskiego (quarterly) . . . 15458

Judaica Society, 16 Hausman Court, Maplewood, NJ 07040
T: (201) 763-8880
Gen Secr: Hy Kusnetz
Focus: Rel & Theol; Cultur Hist . . . 15459

Jugoslavia Study Group (JSG), 1514 N Third Av, Wausau, WI 54401
T: (715) 675-2833
Founded: 1974; Members: 40
Focus: Hist; Ethnology
Periodical
The Trumpeter (quarterly) . . . 15460

Junior Achievement (JA), 1 Education Way, Colorado Springs, CO 80906
T: (719) 540-8000; Fax: (719) 540-9150
Founded: 1919; Members: 1200000
Focus: Adult Educ; Econ . . . 15461

Junior Classical League (JCL), c/o Miami University, Oxford, OH 45056
T: (513) 529-7741; Fax: (513) 529-7741
Founded: 1936; Members: 50000
Focus: Ling . . . 15462

Juvenile Diabetes Foundation International (JDFI), 120 Wall St, New York, NY 10005-3904
T: (212) 889-7575; E-Mail: jbroch@jdf.usa.com; Fax: (212) 725-7259
Founded: 1970; Members: 115
Gen Secr: Javier Broch
Focus: Diabetes . . . 15463

Kafka Society of America (KSA), c/o Prof. Maria Luise Caputo-Mayr, Dept of French, German, Italian and Slavic Languages, Temple University, Philadelphia, PA 19122
T: (215) 204-8282
Founded: 1975; Members: 500
Gen Secr: Prof. Maria Luise Caputo-Mayr
Focus: Lit
Periodical
Journal of the Kafka Society . . . 15464

Kate Greenaway Society (KGS), POB 8, Norwood, PA 19074
T: (215) 485-8572
Founded: 1971; Members: 450
Focus: Lit
Periodical
Under the Window (quarterly) . . . 15465

Keats-Shelley Association of America (KSAA), c/o New York Public Library, Rm 226, Fifth Av and 42 St, New York, NY 10018
T: (212) 764-0655
Founded: 1948; Members: 1000
Focus: Lit
Periodical
Keats-Shelley Journal (annually) . . . 15466

Keyboard Teachers Association International (KTAI), 361 Pin Oak Ln, Westbury, NY 11590-1941
T: (516) 333-3236
Founded: 1963
Pres: Dr. Albert DeVito
Focus: Music; Educ
Periodical
Keyboard Teacher (quarterly) . . . 15467

Kipling Society of North America (KS), c/o Dept of English, Rockford College, Rockford, IL 61101
T: (815) 226-4183; Fax: (815) 226-4119
Founded: 1986; Members: 200
Gen Secr: Dr. E. Karim
Focus: Lit
Periodical
Kipling Journal (quarterly) . . . 15468

Kosciuszko Foundation (KF), 15 E 65 ST, New York, NY 10021
T: (212) 734-2130; Fax: (212) 628-4552
Founded: 1925; Members: 4000
Focus: Hist . . . 15469

Kroeber Anthropological Society (KAS), c/o Dept of Anthropology, University of California, Kroeber Hall 232, Berkeley, CA 94720
T: (415) 642-6932
Founded: 1949; Members: 500
Focus: Anthro
Periodical
Papers (annually) . . . 15470

Kurt Weill Foundation for Music (KWFM), 7 E 20 St, New York, NY 10003-1106
T: (212) 505-5240
Founded: 1962
Focus: Music . . . 15471

Laban/Bartenieff Institute of Movement Studies (LBIMS), 11 E Fourth St, New York, NY 10003
T: (212) 477-4299; Fax: (212) 477-3702
Founded: 1978; Members: 500
Focus: Sports; Psych
Periodicals
Membership Directory (annually)
Newsletter (quarterly) . . . 15472

Labor Policy Association (LPA), 1015 15 St NW, Washington, DC 20005
T: (202) 789-8670; Fax: (202) 789-0064
Members: 180
Focus: Poli Sci . . . 15473

Labor Research Association (LRA), 145 E 28 St, New York, NY 10001-6191
T: (212) 714-1677; Fax: (212) 714-1674
Founded: 1927; Members: 3000
Focus: Econ
Periodicals
Economic Notes (monthly)
Trade Union Adviser (bi-weekly) . . . 15474

Laboratory Animal Management Association (LAMA), POB 1744, Silver Spring, MD 20915
T: (317) 494-7592; Fax: (317) 494-0781
Founded: 1984; Members: 435
Pres: Fred Douglas
Focus: Vet Med . . . 15475

Landscape Architecture Foundation (LAF), 4401 Connecticut Av NW, Washington, DC 20008
T: (202) 686-0068; Fax: (202) 686-1001
Founded: 1966
Focus: Archit
Periodical
Agora . . . 15476

Laser Institute of America (LIA), 12424 Research Pkwy, Ste 130, Orlando, FL 32826
T: (407) 380-1553; Fax: (407) 380-5588
Founded: 1968; Members: 1700
Focus: Eng
Periodical
Journal of Laser Applications (quarterly) . 15477

Latin American Council for Experimental Biology and Medicine (CLABE), c/o Univ of California, School of Microbiology and Immunology, Tupper Hall, Rm 3134, Davis, CA 95616
T: (916) 752-3157; E-Mail: jvtorres@ucdavis.edu; Fax: (916) 752-6763, 752-8692
Gen Secr: Dr. Jose V. Torres
Focus: Bio; Med . . . 15478

Latin American Management Association (LAMA), 419 New Jersey Av SE, Washington, DC 20003
T: (202) 546-3803; Fax: (202) 546-3807
Gen Secr: Marina Morales Laverdy
Focus: Business Admin . . . 15479

Latin American Studies Association (LASA), c/o University of Pittsburgh, 946 William Pitt Union, Pittsburgh, PA 15260
T: (412) 648-7929; E-Mail: LASA@vms.cis.pitt.edu; Fax: (412) 624-7145

Founded: 1966; Members: 3000
Gen Secr: Reid Reading
Focus: Anthro; Poli Sci; Hist; Econ; Humanities
Periodicals
Lasa Forum/Newsletter (quarterly)
Latin American Research Review (3 times annually)
Professional Journal (3 times annually) . 15480

Laubach Literacy International (LLI), 1320 Jamesville Av, Box 131, Syracuse, NY 13210
T: (315) 422-9121; Fax: (315) 422-6369
Founded: 1955; Members: 80000
Focus: Lit 15481

Laubach Literacy International, 1320 Jamesville Av, Box 131, Syracuse, NY 13210
T: (315) 422-9121; Fax: (315) 422-6369
Founded: 1968; Members: 55000
Gen Secr: Robert F. Caswell
Focus: Lit
Periodicals
Directory (annually)
Literacy Advance (quarterly) 15482

Laughter Therapy (LT), 2359 Nichols Canyon Rd, Los Angeles, CA 90046
T: (213) 851-3394
Founded: 1981
Focus: Psych; Psychiatry 15483

Laura Ingalls Wilder Memorial Society (LIWMS), POB 269, Peplin, WI 54759
T: (715) 442-3161
Founded: 1974; Members: 425
Focus: Lit 15484

Law and Society Association (LSA), c/o University of Massachusetts, Hampshire House, POB 33615, Amherst, MA 01003-3615
T: (413) 545-4617; Fax: (413) 545-1640
Founded: 1964; Members: 1400
Gen Secr: Ronald Pipkin
Focus: Law; Sociology
Periodical
Law & Society Review (quarterly) . . . 15485

Law of the Sea Institute (LSI), c/o Richardson School of Law, University of Hawaii, 2515 Dole St, Rm 208, Honolulu, HI 96822
T: (808) 956-6750; Fax: (808) 956-6402
Founded: 1965; Members: 300
Focus: Law
Periodicals
Occasional Papers
Proceedings 15486

Law School Admission Council – Law School Admission Services (LSAC/LSAS), POB 40, Newtown, PA 18940
T: (215) 968-1101
Founded: 1948; Members: 190
Focus: Law
Periodicals
Annual Report (annually)
Law School Admission Bulletin (quarterly)
Prelaw Handbook (annually) 15487

Lawyers' Committee for Civil Rights under Law (LCCRUL), 1450 G St NW, Ste 400, Washington, DC 20005
T: (202) 662-8600; Fax: (202) 783-0857
Founded: 1963; Members: 185
Gen Secr: Barbara R. Arnwine
Focus: Law 15488

League for Industrial Democracy (LID), 815 15 St NW, Ste 511, Washington, DC 20005
T: (202) 638-1515; Fax: (202) 347-5585
Founded: 1905; Members: 1500
Focus: Poli Sci; Econ 15489

Lentz Peace Research Laboratory (LPRL), c/o University of Missouri, 8001 Natural Bridge Rd, Saint Louis, 63121
T: (314) 516-6040
Founded: 1945; Members: 100
Gen Secr: Miranda Duncan
Focus: Poli Sci; Psych; Soc Sci; Prom Peace
Periodical
Peace Research (3 times annually) . . 15490

Leo Baeck Institute (LBI), 129 E 73 St, New York, NY 10021
T: (212) 744-6400; Fax: (212) 988-1305
Founded: 1955
Focus: Hist 15491

Leonard Wood Memorial – American Leprosy Foundation (LWM), 11600 Nebel St, Ste 210, Rockville, MD 20852
T: (301) 984-1336
Founded: 1928
Focus: Derm 15492

Leonardo – The International Society for the Arts, Sciences and Technology, 236 W Portland Av, No 781, San Francisco, CA 94127
T: (415) 338-1444; E-Mail: isast@sfsu.edu;
Fax: (415) 338-0915
Founded: 1968; Members: 700
Pres: Roger Malina
Focus: Arts; Sci; Eng 15493

Leschetizky Association (LA), c/o Maria Waldman, 884 West End Av, No 105, New York, NY 10025-3517
T: (212) 222-2733; E-Mail: 74640.2646@ compuserve.com; Fax: (212) 222-2733
Founded: 1942; Members: 140
Pres: Maria Waldman
Focus: Music

Periodical
News Bulletin (annually) 15494

Lessing Society (LS), c/o German Dept, University of Cincinnati, Cincinnati, OH 45221-0372
T: (513) 556-2744
Founded: 1966; Members: 350
Focus: Lit
Periodical
Lessing Yearbook (annually) 15495

Leukemia Society of America (LSA), 600 Third Av, New York, NY 10016
T: (212) 573-8484; Fax: (212) 972-5776
Founded: 1949
Focus: Hematology
Periodical
Society News (bi-monthly) 15496

Lewis Carroll Society of North America (LCNA), 1655 34 St NW, Washington, DC 20007
E-Mail: joel.birenbaum@att.com
Founded: 1974; Members: 380
Pres: Joel Birenbaum
Focus: Lit
Periodical
Knight Letter (quarterly) 15497

Lexington Group in Transportation History (LGTH), c/o Dept of History, Saint Cloud State University, Saint Cloud University, MN 56301
T: (612) 255-4906; Fax: (612) 654-5198
Founded: 1942; Members: 460
Focus: Cultur Hist; Transport
Periodical
Lexington Quarterly (quarterly) 15498

Liaison Committee on Medical Education (LCME), c/o American Medical Association, 515 N State St, Chicago, IL 60610
T: (312) 464-4657; E-Mail: Harry_Jonas@ama-assn.org; Fax: (312) 464-5830
Founded: 1942; Members: 18
Gen Secr: Harry S. Jonas
Focus: Adult Educ; Med 15499

Library Administration and Management Association (LAMA), 50 E Huron St, Chicago, IL 60611
T: (312) 944-6780; Fax: (312) 280-3257
Founded: 1957; Members: 5223
Focus: Libraries & Bk Sci
Periodical
Library Administration and Management (quarterly) 15500

Library and Information Technology Association (LITA), 50 E Huron St, Chicago, IL 60611-2795
T: (312) 280-4270; Fax: (312) 280-3257
Founded: 1966; Members: 5000
Focus: Libraries & Bk Sci 15501

Library Public Relations Council (LPRC), 2 Jean Walling Civic Center, East Brunswick NJ 08816
T: (908) 390-6761
Founded: 1939; Members: 300
Focus: Libraries & Bk Sci 15502

Life Education International (LEC), POB 1454, Elmhurst, IL 60126-2127
T: (708) 530-8999; E-Mail: lifed@aol.com;
Fax: (708) 530-7241
Gen Secr: David Noffs
Focus: Educ 15503

LIMRA, Box 208, Hartford, CT 06141
T: (203) 688-3358; Fax: (203) 298-9555
Founded: 1916; Members: 600
Pres: John C. Scully
Focus: Insurance
Periodical
Proceedings 15504

Lincoln Center for the Performing Arts (LCPA), 70 Lincoln Center Plaza, New York, NY 10023-6583
T: (212) 875-5000
Founded: 1956; Members: 2500
Focus: Perf Arts 15505

Lincoln Institute for Research and Education (LIRE), 1001 Connecticut Av NW, Ste 1135, Washington, DC 20036
T: (202) 223-5112
Founded: 1978
Focus: Educ; Poli Sci 15506

Linguistic Society of America (LSA), 1325 18 St NW, Ste 211, Washington, DC 20035-6501
T: (202) 835-1714
Founded: 1924; Members: 7000
Pres: Janet Dean Fodor; Gen Secr: Elizabeth C. Traugott
Focus: Ling
Periodical
Bulletin (quarterly) 15507

Literacy and Evangelism International (LEI), 1800 S Jackson, Tulsa, OK 74107-1897
T: (918) 585-3826; E-Mail: 75313.2613@ compuserve.com; Fax: (918) 585-3224
Founded: 1967
Gen Secr: John C. Taylor
Focus: Lit; Rel & Theol 15508

Literacy Training and Development Programme for Africa (LTDPA), c/o Literacy Research Center, University of Pennsylvania, 3910 Chestnut St, Philadelphia, PA 19104-3111
Gen Secr: Laurie Puchner
Focus: Educ; Develop Areas 15509

Literacy Volunteers of America (LVA), 5795 S Widewaters Pkwy, Syracuse, NY 13214
T: (315) 445-8000; Fax: (315) 445-8006
Founded: 1962; Members: 100000
Focus: Lit 15510

Louisa May Alcott Memorial Association (LMAMA), POB 343, Concord, MA 01742
T: (508) 369-4118
Founded: 1911; Members: 57
Focus: Lit 15511

Luso-American Education Foundation (LAEF), POB 2967, Dublin, CA 94568
T: (510) 828-3883; Fax: (510) 828-3883
Founded: 1963; Members: 275
Pres: Manuel Barroca
Focus: Educ 15512

Lutheran Church Library Association (LCLA), 122 W Franklin Av, Minneapolis, MN 55404
T: (612) 870-3623
Founded: 1958; Members: 1750
Focus: Libraries & Bk Sci
Periodical
Lutheran Libraries (quarterly) 15513

Lutheran Education Association (LEA), 7400 Augusta Blvd, River Forest, IL 60305
T: (708) 209-3343; Fax: (708) 209-3458
Founded: 1942; Members: 3850
Gen Secr: Perry A. Bresemann
Focus: Educ 15514

Lutheran Educational Conference of North America (LECNA), 1001 Connecticut Av NW, Ste 504, Washington, DC 20036
T: (202) 463-6486; E-Mail: donald_stoike.parti@ ecunet.org; Fax: (202) 463-6609
Founded: 1910; Members: 43
Gen Secr: Don Stoike
Focus: Educ
Periodicals
Lutheran Higher Education Directory (annually)
Papers and Proceedings (annually) . . . 15515

Lutheran Historical Conference (LHC), c/o James W. Albers, Dept of Theology, Valparaiso University, Valparaiso, IN 46383
T: (219) 464-5313; Fax: (219) 462-4640
Founded: 1962; Members: 150
Pres: James L. Schaaf
Focus: Hist; Rel & Theol 15516

Lyman L Lemnitzer Center for NATO and European Union Studies, c/o Kent State University, 124 Bowman Hall, POB 5190, Kent, OH 44242-0001
T: (330) 672-7980; E-Mail: spapacos@Kent.edu;
Fax: (330) 672-4025
Gen Secr: Dr. S. Victor Papacosma
Focus: Poli Sci 15517

Lynchburg Peace Education Centre, POB 3143, Lynchburg, VA 24503
T: (804) 847-5477; Fax: (804) 384-6561
Focus: Prom Peace; Educ 15518

The Madison Project (TMP), c/o Robert B. Davis, Graduate School of Education, Rutgers University, 10 Seminary Pl, New Brunswick, NJ 08903
T: (908) 932-7971; Fax: (908) 932-7939
Founded: 1957
Gen Secr: Robert B. Davis
Focus: Math 15519

Magnolia Society, c/o Roberta Davids Hagen, 6616 81 St, Cabin John, MD 20818
T: (301) 320-4296; Fax: (301) 320-4296
Founded: 1961; Members: 600
Gen Secr: Roberta Davids Hagen
Focus: Botany 15520

Management Association for Private Photogrammetric Surveyors (MAPPS), 12020 Sunrise Valley Dr, Ste 100, Reston, VA 22091
T: (703) 391-2739; Fax: (703) 476-2217
Founded: 1982; Members: 120
Gen Secr: John M. Palatiello
Focus: Surveying
Periodicals
Flightline (bi-monthly)
MAPPS Capability Survey (annually) . . 15521

Manchester College Peace Studies Institute, c/o Manchester College, 604 College, POB 27, North Manchester, IN 46962
T: (219) 982-5343; E-Mail: klbrown@ manchester.edu; Fax: (219) 982-6868
Gen Secr: Dr. Kenneth L. Brown
Focus: Prom Peace 15522

Mandala Society (MS), POB 1233, Del Mar, CA 92014
T: (619) 481-7751
Founded: 1972
Focus: Philos 15523

Manufacturers Standardization Society of the Valve and Fittings Industry (MSS), 127 Park St NE, Vienna, VA 22180
T: (703) 281-6613
Founded: 1924; Members: 75
Focus: Standards 15524

Maria Mitchell Association (MMA), 2 Vestal St, Nantucket, MA 02554
T: (508) 228-9198
Founded: 1903; Members: 1700
Focus: Astronomy 15525

Marine Environment Research Institute (MERI), 772 west End Av, New York, NY 10025
Gen Secr: Susan D. Shaw
Focus: Ecology 15526

Marine Technology Society (MTS), 1828 L St NW, Ste 900, Washington, DC 20036-5104
T: (202) 775-5966; Fax: (202) 429-9417
Founded: 1963; Members: 3000
Focus: Oceanography; Eng
Periodicals
Marine Technology Society Journal (quarterly)
Membership Directory
Newsletter (monthly) 15527

Mark Twain Association (MTA), 245 W 25 St, Apt 6C, New York, NY 10001
T: (212) 255-9640
Founded: 1926; Members: 200
Focus: Lit 15528

Mark Twain Research Foundation (MTRF), Rte 1, Box 54, Stoutsville, MO 65283
T: (314) 565-3449
Founded: 1939; Members: 400
Pres: Catherine Allen
Focus: Lit
Periodical
The Twainian (bi-monthly) 15529

Marketing Research Association (MRA), 2189 Silas Deane Hwy, Ste 5, Rocky Hill, CT 06067
T: (203) 257-4008; Fax: (203) 257-3990
Founded: 1954; Members: 2300
Focus: Marketing 15530

Marketing Science Institute (MSI), 1000 Massachusetts Av, Cambridge, MA 02138
T: (617) 491-2060; Fax: (617) 491-2065
Founded: 1961; Members: 64
Focus: Marketing 15531

Marlowe Society of America (MSA), c/o Dept of English, Texas Technical University, Lubbock, TX 79409
T: (806) 742-2501
Founded: 1976; Members: 150
Gen Secr: Dr. Constance Brown Kuriyama
Focus: Lit 15532

Marquandia Society (MS), 5125 N Pennsylvania St, Indianapolis, IN 46205
T: (317) 253-4767; Fax: (317) 253-4974
Founded: 1971; Members: 15
Gen Secr: John R. Thelin
Focus: Hist; Lit
Periodical
Newsletter 15533

Marymount International Schools, 50 Wilson Park Dr, Tarrytown, NY 10591
Focus: Educ 15534

Masonry Society, 3970 Broadway, Ste 201-D, Boulder, CO 80304-1135
T: (303) 939-9700; Fax: (303) 541-9215
Founded: 1977; Members: 1000
Gen Secr: William D. Palmer
Focus: Civil Eng
Periodical
Journal (semi-annually) 15535

Massenet Society (MS), 9 Drury Ln, Fort Lee, NJ 07024
T: (201) 224-4526
Founded: 1977; Members: 75
Pres: Robert A. Frone
Focus: Music
Periodical
Massenet Newsletter (annually) 15536

Material Handling and Management Society (MHMS), 8720 Red Oak Blvd, Ste 224, Charlotte, NC 28217
T: (704) 525-4667; E-Mail: 102512.1772@ compuserve.com; Fax: (704) 558-4753
Founded: 1949; Members: 1500
Gen Secr: F. Hal Vandiver
Focus: Materials Sci 15537

Materials Properties Council (MPC), 345 E 47 St, New York, NY 10017
T: (212) 705-7693; Fax: (212) 752-4929
Founded: 1966; Members: 800
Focus: Metallurgy
Periodical
Annual Report (annually) 15538

Maternity Center Association (MCA), 48 E 92 St, New York, NY 10128
T: (212) 369-7300; Fax: (212) 369-8747
Founded: 1918; Members: 600
Focus: Gynecology
Periodical
Special Delivery (quarterly) 15539

Math/Science Network, c/o Mills College, 5000 MacArthur Blvd, Oakland, CA 94613
T: (510) 430-2222; E-Mail: MSNeyh@mills.edu;
Fax: (510) 430-2090
Founded: 1975; Members: 275
Gen Secr: Betty Levitin
Focus: Math
Periodical
Broadcast (quarterly) 15540

Mathematical Association of America (MAA), 1529 18 St NW, Washington, DC 20036
T: (202) 387-5200; Fax: (202) 265-2384
Founded: 1915; Members: 30000
Pres: Donald L. Kreider; Gen Secr: Dr. Marcia P. Sward
Focus: Math

Periodicals
American Mathematical (10 times annually)
College Mathematics Journal (3 times annually)
Mathematics Magazine (5 times annually) 15541

Matthew B. Ridgway Center for International Security Studies, c/o University of Pittsburgh, 4G40 Forbes Quadrangle, Pittsburgh, PA 15260
T: (412) 648-7392; Fax: (412) 648-2199
Focus: Military Sci 15542

Maximilian Numismatic and Historical Society (Max Society), c/o Don Bailey, POB 98, Homer, MI 49245-0098
T: (517) 568-4014
Founded: 1967; Members: 60
Gen Secr: Don Bailey
Focus: Numismatics; Hist 15543

The Media Institute (TMI), 1000 Potomac St NW, Ste 301, Washington, DC 20007
T: (202) 298-7512; Fax: (202) 337-7092
Founded: 1976; Members: 350
Pres: Patrick D. Maines
Focus: Comm Sci; Mass Media 15544

Medical Letter (ML), 1000 Main St, New Rochelle, NY 10801
T: (914) 235-0500; Fax: (914) 576-3377
Founded: 1959
Focus: Pharmacol
Periodical
Medical Letter on Drugs and Therapeutics (bi-weekly) 15545

Medical Library Association (MLA), 6 N Michigan Av, Ste 300, Chicago, IL 60602
T: (312) 419-9094; Fax: (312) 419-8950
Founded: 1898; Members: 5000
Gen Secr: Carla J. Funk
Focus: Libraries & Bk Sci
Periodicals
Bulletin (quarterly)
Current Catalog Proof Sheets (weekly)
MLA News (monthly) 15546

Medical Mycological Society of the Americas (MMSA), c/o Dept of Pathology, Johns Hopkins Hospital, Baltimore, MD 21287-7093
T: (410) 955-5077; Fax: (410) 955-0767
Founded: 1966; Members: 408
Gen Secr: Dr. William G. Merz
Focus: Botany, Specific
Periodicals
Bulletin (quarterly)
Directory 15547

Medical Society of the United States and Mexico (MSUSM), c/o Arizona Medical Association, 810 W Bethany Home Rd, Phoenix, AZ 85013
T: (602) 246-8901
Founded: 1954; Members: 400
Focus: Med
Periodical
Directory (annually) 15548

Médicins du monde (MDM), 625 Broedway, New York, NY 10012
T: (212) 529-1556; E-Mail: DOW@igc.apc.org; Fax: (212) 529-1571
Focus: Med 15549

Medieval Academy of America (MAA), 1430 Massachusetts Av, Cambridge, MA 02138
T: (617) 491-1622; Fax: (617) 492-3303
Founded: 1925; Members: 4100
Pres: John Baldwin; Gen Secr: Luke H. Wenger
Focus: Hist; Lit; Arts; Philos
Periodical
Speculum: A Journal of Medieval Studies (quarterly) 15550

Melanesian Studies Resource Center, c/o 0175-R, University Library, Univ of California, San Diego, La Jolla, CA 92093-0175
T: (619) 534-2029; E-Mail: kcreely@ucsd.edu; Fax: (619) 534-7548
Gen Secr: Kathryn Creely
Focus: Ethnology 15551

Melville Society (MS), c/o Sanford E. Marovitz, English Dept, Kent State University, Kent, OH 44242
T: (216) 672-7884; E-Mail: Engib@vaxc.hofsta.edu; Fax: (216) 672-3152
Founded: 1945; Members: 750
Gen Secr: Sanford E. Marovitz
Focus: Lit
Periodical
Melville Society Extracts (quarterly) 15552

Mencken Society (MS), POB 16218, Baltimore, MD 21210
T: (410) 377-2333
Founded: 1976; Members: 375
Pres: Arthur Gutman
Focus: Lit 15553

Mended Hearts (MH), 7272 Greenville Av, Dallas, TX 75231
T: (214) 706-1442
Founded: 1951; Members: 24000
Focus: Cardiol
Periodical
Heartbeat (quarterly) 15554

Mental Health Materials Center (MHMC), POB 304, Bronxville, NY 10708
T: (914) 337-6596
Founded: 1953
Focus: Psychiatry 15555

Mental Research Institute (MRI), 555 Middlefield Rd, Palo Alto, CA 94301
T: (415) 321-3055; Fax: (415) 321-3785
Founded: 1959
Focus: Med; Physiology
Periodical
Newsletter (quarterly) 15556

Mershon Center for Education in National Security, c/o Ohio State University, 1501 Neil Av, Columbus, OH 43201-2602
Gen Secr: Chadwick Alger
Focus: Educ; Military Sci 15557

Metal Treating Institute (MTI), 1550 Roberts Dr, Jacksonville Beach, FL 32250
T: (904) 249-0448; E-Mail: metaltreat@aol.com; Fax: (904) 249-0459
Founded: 1933; Members: 400
Gen Secr: M. Lance Miller
Focus: Metallurgy 15558

Metaphysical Society of America (MSA), c/o Dept of Philosophy, University of Alabama at Huntsville, Huntsville, AL 35899
T: (205) 895-6555
Founded: 1950; Members: 700
Pres: Mary Clark; Gen Secr: Brian J. Martine
Focus: Philos 15559

Meteoritical Society (MS), c/o Joseph I. Goldstein, College of Engineering, University of Massachusetts, 125 Marston Hall, Amherst, MA 01003
T: (413) 545-0300; Fax: (413) 545-0724
Founded: 1933; Members: 900
Pres: Harry Y. McSween
Focus: Geophys
Periodicals
Geochimica et Cosmochimica Acta (monthly)
Meteoritics (quarterly) 15560

Michael E. Debakey International Surgical Society (MEDISS), c/o Dept of Surgery, 1 Baylor Plaza, Houston, TX 77030
T: (713) 798-4557
Founded: 1976; Members: 540
Gen Secr: Kenneth L. Mattox
Focus: Cardiol 15561

Michael Fund – International Foundation for Genetic Research (MF-IFGR), 500A Garden City Dr, Monroeville, PA 15146-1128
T: (412) 823-6380
Gen Secr: Randy Engel
Focus: Genetics 15562

Microalgae International Union (MIU), 910 Harmon Gulch, POB 644, Boulder Creek, CA 95006
T: (408) 338-2544
Gen Secr: Dr. Christopher Hills
Focus: Microbio 15563

Microbeam Analysis Society (MAS), c/o VCH Publishers, 303 NW 12 Av, Deerfield Beach, FL 33442-1788
T: (800) 367-8249; Fax: (800) 428-8201
Founded: 1967; Members: 1000
Focus: Physics; Med
Periodical
Micronews (quarterly) 15564

Microneurography Society (MNS), c/o Cardiovascular Physiology, V.A. Medical Center, Richmond, VA 23249
T: (804) 230-0001
Founded: 1981; Members: 60
Focus: Neurology
Periodical
Directory (annually) 15565

Microscopy Society of America (MSA), 4 Barlows Landing Rd, Ste 8, Pocasset, MA 02559
T: (508) 5631155; Fax: (508) 508-1211
Founded: 1942; Members: 4800
Gen Secr: Barbara Reine
Focus: Electronic Eng; Optics
Periodicals
Directory (bi-annually)
Journal (bi-monthly)
Proceedings of Annual Meeting (annually) 15566

Mid-Continent Railway Historical Society (MCRHS), POB 358, North Freedom, WI 53951-4261
T: (608) 522-4490
Founded: 1959; Members: 625
Gen Secr: Don Meyer
Focus: Cultur Hist
Periodicals
Membership Roster
Railway Gazette (bi-monthly) 15567

Middle Atlantic Council of Latin American Studies (MACLAS), 5 Pueblo Court, Gaithersgurg, MD 20878
Gen Secr: Danusia Meson-Sesnowski
Focus: Ethnology 15568

Middle Atlantic Planetarium Society (MAPS), c/o Fred Stutz, 302 Beechgrove Ct, Millersville, MD 21108
T: (410) 987-8436; E-Mail: stutzstar@aol.com
Founded: 1965; Members: 200
Gen Secr: Fred Stutz
Focus: Astronomy
Periodical
Constellation (quarterly) 15569

Middle East Institute (MEI), 1761 N St NW, Washington, DC 20036
T: (202) 785-1141; E-Mail: mej@mideasti.org; Fax: (202) 331-8861
Founded: 1946; Members: 1500
Gen Secr: Roscoe S. Suddarth
Focus: Educ
Periodical
The Middle East Journal (quarterly) 15570

Middle East Librarians' Association (MELA), c/o Andras Riedlmayer, Fine Arts Library, Harvard University, Cambridge, MA 02138
T: (617) 495-3372; E-Mail: MELANET-L@cornell.edu; Fax: (617) 496-4889
Founded: 1972; Members: 300
Gen Secr: Andras Riedlmayer
Focus: Libraries & Bk Sci
Periodical
Notes (3 times annually) 15571

Middle East Policy Council, 1730 M St NW, Ste 512, Washington, DC 20036
T: (202) 296-6767; E-Mail: arj@capitol.net; Fax: (202) 296-5791
Gen Secr: George McGovern
Focus: Poli Sci 15572

Middle East Research and Information Project (MERIP), 1500 Massachusetts Av NW, Ste 119, Washington, DC 20005
T: (202) 223-3677; E-Mail: merip@igc.apc.org; Fax: (202) 223-3604
Founded: 1971; Members: 15
Gen Secr: Peggy Hutchison
Focus: Ethnology; Poli Sci
Periodical
Middle East Report (9 times annually) 15573

Middle East Studies Association of North America (MESA), 1232 N Cherry Av, Tucson, AZ 85721
T: (602) 621-5850; Fax: (602) 321-7752
Founded: 1966; Members: 2300
Gen Secr: Anne H. Betteridge
Focus: Educ; Int'l Relat
Periodicals
Abstracts of Papers Delivered at Annual Meeting (annually)
Bulletin (semi-annually)
Directory of Graduate and Undergraduate Programs and Courses in Middle East Studies in the U.S., Canada and Abroad
International Journal of Middle East Studies (quarterly)
Newsletter
Roster of MESA Fellows (annually) 15574

Middle East Water Information Network (MEWIN), c/o Univ of Pennsylvania, 847 Williams Hall, Philadelphia, PA 19104-6305
T: (215) 471-0167; E-Mail: tnaff@sas.upenn.edu; Fax: (215) 747-6211
Gen Secr: Prof. Thomas Naff
Focus: Water Res 15575

Middle States Association of Colleges and Schools (MSA), 3624 Market St, Philadelphia, PA 19104
T: (215) 662-5600; Fax: (215) 662-5950
Founded: 1887; Members: 3500
Focus: Educ 15576

Midwest Archives Conference (MAC), c/o Kraft General Foods Archives, 6350 Kirk St, Morton Grove, IL 60053
T: (708) 998-2981
Founded: 1972; Members: 1100
Focus: Archives 15577

Midwest Association for Latin American Studies (MALAS), c/o University of Missouri, Dept of History, Columbia, MO 65211
Gen Secr: Winfield Burggraaf
Focus: Ethnology 15578

Midwest Railway Historical Society (MRHS), 533 W Glencoe, Palatine, IL 60067
Founded: 1968
Focus: Hist 15579

Midwest Universities Consortium for International Activities (MUCIA), c/o Ohio State University, 110 Enarson Hall, 154 W 12th Av, Colombus, OH 43210-1390
T: (614) 292-2992; Fax: (614) 292-2124
Gen Secr: Prof. Dr. Edward Jennings
Focus: Educ 15580

Military Operations Research Society (MORS), Landmark Towers, 101 S Whiting St, Ste 202, Alexandria, VA 22304
T: (703) 751-7290; Fax: (703) 751-8171
Founded: 1957; Members: 2700
Focus: Military Sci
Periodical
Phalanx (quarterly) 15581

Milton H. Erickson Foundation (MHEF), 3606 N 24 St, Phoenix, AZ 85016
T: (602) 956-6196; Fax: (602) 956-0519
Founded: 1979
Focus: Psych; Psychiatry
Periodicals
The Ericksonian Monographs (3 times annually)
Newsletter (3 times annually) 15582

Milton Helpern Institute of Forensic Medicine (MHIFM), 520 First Av, New York, NY 10016
T: (212) 447-2030; Fax: (212) 447-2716
Founded: 1968; Members: 405
Gen Secr: Dr. Charles S. Hirsch
Focus: Forensic Med
Periodical
The International Microform Journal of Legal Medicine and Forensic Sciences (quarterly) 15583

Milton Society of America (MSA), c/o Duquesne University, Pittsburgh, PA 15282
T: (412) 434-6420
Founded: 1948; Members: 500
Focus: Lit
Periodical
Bulletin (annually) 15584

Mineralogical Society of America (MSA), 1015 18 St NW, Ste 601, Washington, DC 20036-5203
T: (202) 775-4344; Fax: (202) 775-0018
Founded: 1919; Members: 2200
Focus: Mineralogy
Periodicals
The American Mineralogist (bi-monthly)
Lattice (quarterly)
Mineralogical Abstracts (quarterly) 15585

Minerals, Metals and Materials Society, 420 Commonwealth Dr, Warrendale, PA 15086
T: (412) 776-9000; Fax: (412) 776-3770
Founded: 1957; Members: 12000
Focus: Metallurgy; Mineralogy; Materials Sci
Periodicals
Journal of Electronic Materials (bi-monthly)
Journal of Metals (monthly)
Membership Directory (annually)
Transactions A (monthly)
Transactions B (quarterly) 15586

Mining and Metallurgical Society of America (MMSA), 9 Escalle Ln, Larkspur, CA 94939
T: (415) 924-7441; Fax: (415) 924-7463
Founded: 1908; Members: 315
Focus: Mining; Metallurgy
Periodicals
Bulletin
News-Letter (bi-monthly) 15587

Missile, Space and Range Pioneers (MSRP), POB 255227, Patrick Air Force Base, FL 32925
T: (305) 494-4001
Founded: 1966; Members: 1500
Gen Secr: Wayne Penley
Focus: Hist; Eng 15588

Mission Doctors Association (MDA), 1531 W Ninth St, Los Angeles, CA 90015
T: (818) 285-8868; Fax: (818) 309-1716
Founded: 1957
Focus: Med 15589

Moby Dick Academy (MDA), POB 589, Ocean Park, WA 98640
T: (206) 665-4577
Founded: 1981
Gen Secr: Mary Tufts
Focus: Educ
Periodicals
Com-line (quarterly)
FCLA Teachers and their Areas of Expertise (annually)
Touchstone (monthly) 15590

Model Secondary School for the Deaf (MSSD), c/o Gallaudet University, 800 Florida Av NE, Washington, DC 20002
T: (202) 651-5346; Fax: (202) 651-5109
Founded: 1969
Gen Secr: Vivian Rice
Focus: Educ Handic 15591

Modern Greek Studies Association (MGSA), c/o Dept of Political Sc, Southern Connecticut State College, New Haven, CT 06515
Gen Secr: Prof. John Iatrides
Focus: Ling 15592

Modern Language Association of America (MLAA), 10 Astor Pl, New York, NY 10003
T: (212) 475-9500; Fax: (212) 477-9863
Founded: 1883; Members: 32000
Gen Secr: Prof. Phyllis Franklin
Focus: Ling
Periodicals
MLA Directory of Periodicals (bi-annually)
MLA International Bibliography (annually)
PMLA (bi-monthly) 15593

Modern Poetry Association (MPA), 60 W Walton St, Chicago, IL 60610
T: (312) 255-3703
Founded: 1941
Gen Secr: Joseph Parisi
Focus: Lit
Periodical
Poetry Magazine (monthly) 15594

Mongolia Society, c/o Indiana University, 322 Goodbody Hall, Bloomington, IN 47405
T: (812) 855-4078; E-Mail: Monsoc@indiana.edu; Fax: (812) 855-7500
Founded: 1961; Members: 475
Gen Secr: Susie Drost
Focus: Ethnology

Periodicals
The Mongolia Society Bulletin
The Mongolia Society Newsletter
Mongolian Studies: Journal of the Mongolia Society *15595*

The Monroe Institute (TMI), Rte 1, Box 175, Faber, VA 22938
T: (804) 361-1252
Founded: 1971; Members: 1500
Focus: Educ
Periodical
Breakthrough (quarterly) *15596*

Monterey Institute of International Studies, 425 Van Buren St, Monterey, CA 93940
T: (408) 647-4154; Fax: (408) 647-3519
Focus: Poli Sci *15597*

Moody Institute of Science (MIS), 820 N LaSalle Dr, Chicago, IL 60610-3284
T: (312) 329-2190; Fax: (312) 329-4496
Founded: 1945
Focus: Sci *15598*

Mormon History Association (MHA), 2470 N 1000 W, Layton, UT 84041
T: (801) 773-4620; E-Mail: VALH15A@Prodigy.com
Founded: 1965; Members: 1000
Gen Secr: Craig L. Foster
Focus: Hist; Rel & Theol
Periodical
Journal of Mormon History (annually) . . *15599*

Motorcycle Safety Foundation (MSF), 2 Jenner St, Ste 150, Irvine, CA 92718-3899
T: (714) 727-3227; Fax: (714) 727-4217
Founded: 1973; Members: 5
Focus: Safety
Periodicals
Annual Report (annually)
Safe Cycling (quarterly) *15600*

MTM Association for Standards and Research, 1111 E Touly Av, Des Plaines, IL 60018
T: (847) 299-1111; E-Mail: mtmASSOC@AOL.com; Fax: (847) 299-3509
Founded: 1951; Members: 1000
Gen Secr: Dirk J. Rauglas
Focus: Physiology
Periodical
MTM Journal (annually) *15601*

Multinational Project on Basic Education (MULTIPROBE), c/o Dept of Educational Affairs, OAS, 1889 F St NW, Washington, DC 20006
T: (202) 458-3325; E-Mail: leonel_zuniga@umail.umd.edu; Fax: (202) 458-3149
Gen Secr: Leonel Zúñiga
Focus: Educ *15602*

Musculo-Skeletal Tumor Society of North America, 1601 E 19 Av, Denver, CO 80218
T: (303) 839-5383; Fax: (303) 839-7800
Gen Secr: Dr. Ross M. Wilkins
Focus: Cell Biol & Cancer Res *15603*

Museum Association of the American Frontier (MAAF), 6321 Hwy 20, Chadron, NE 69337
T: (308) 432-3843
Founded: 1949; Members: 3000
Gen Secr: Charles E. Hanson
Focus: Hist
Periodical
Museum of the Fur Trade Quarterly (quarterly) *15604*

Museum Computer Network (MCN), 8720 Georgia Av, Ste 501, Silver Spring, MD 20910
T: (301) 585-4413; Fax: (301) 495-0810
Founded: 1967; Members: 500
Gen Secr: Leslie Johnston
Focus: Computer & Info Sci
Periodical
Spectra (quarterly) *15605*

Museum Education Roundtable (MER), 3000 Connecticut Av NW, Ste 237D, Washington, DC 20008
T: (202) 232-6084; Fax: (202) 232-8726
Founded: 1969; Members: 900
Gen Secr: A.T. Stephens
Focus: Educ *15606*

Museum Services International (MSI), Washington, DC 20036
E-Mail: guenther.dembski@telecom.at; Fax: (202) 462-2380
Gen Secr: Roger Wulff
Focus: Arts *15607*

Music Critics Association (MCA), 7 Pine Ct, Westfield, NJ 07090
T: (908) 233-8468; Fax: (908) 233-8468
Founded: 1957; Members: 254
Focus: Music; Journalism
Periodicals
Membership List (annually)
Newsletter (3 times annually) *15608*

Music Educators National Conference (MENC), 1806 Robert Fulton Dr, Reston, VA 22091
T: (703) 860-4000; E-Mail: mbmenc@aol.com; Fax: (703) 860-1531
Founded: 1907; Members: 65000
Gen Secr: John J. Mahlmann
Focus: Music; Educ
Periodicals
General Music Today (3 times annually)
Journal of Research in Music Education (quarterly)
Music Educators Journal (9 times annually)
Newsletter (quarterly) *15609*

Music Library Association (MLA), POB 487, Canton, MA 02021
T: (617) 828-8450; Fax: (617) 828-8915
Founded: 1931; Members: 2900
Gen Secr: Richard Griscom
Focus: Libraries & Bk Sci
Periodicals
Index Series (irregularly)
Music Cataloging Bulletin (monthly)
Newsletter (quarterly)
Notes (quarterly)
Technical Reports *15610*

Music Teachers National Association (MTNA), 441 Vine St, Ste 505, Cincinnati, OH 45202-2814
T: (513) 421-1420; Fax: (513) 421-2503
Founded: 1876; Members: 24000
Gen Secr: Shirley A. Raut
Focus: Music; Educ
Periodicals
American Music Teacher Magazine (bi-monthly)
Directory of Nationally Certified Teachers (annually) *15611*

Mystic Seaport Museum (MSM), 75 Greenmanville Av, Mystic, CT 06355-0990
T: (203) 572-0711; Fax: (203) 572-5328
Founded: 1929; Members: 22000
Gen Secr: J. Revell Carr
Focus: Hist; Navig
Periodical
The LOG (quarterly) *15612*

Mythopoeic Society (MS), POB 6707, Altadena, CA 91003
T: (818) 571-7727
Founded: 1967; Members: 650
Focus: Lit
Periodicals
Mythic Circle (quarterly)
Mythlore (quarterly)
Mythprint (monthly) *15613*

NACE International, POB 218340, Houston, TX 77218
T: (713) 492-0535; Fax: (713) 492-8254
Founded: 1943; Members: 15000
Gen Secr: G.M. Shankel
Focus: Metallurgy
Periodicals
Corrosion (monthly)
Corrosion Abstracts (bi-monthly)
Materials Performance (monthly) *15614*

NAFSA – Association of International Educators, 1875 Connecticut Av NW, Ste 1000, Washington, DC 20009
T: (202) 462-4811; E-Mail: inbox@nafsa.org; Fax: (202) 667-3419
Gen Secr: Naomi F. Collins
Focus: Educ *15615*

Nathaniel Hawthorne Society (NHS), c/o Leland S. Person, College of Liberal Arts, South Illinois University, Carbondale, IL 62901-4522
T: (618) 453-2466; Fax: (618) 453-3253
Founded: 1974; Members: 500
Gen Secr: Leland S. Person
Focus: Lit *15616*

National Academic Advising Association (NACADA), c/o Kansas State University, 2323 Anderson Av, Ste 225, Manhattan, KS 66502
T: (913) 532-5717; E-Mail: nacada@ksu.ksu.edu; Fax: (913) 532-7732
Founded: 1979; Members: 4500
Gen Secr: Roberta Flaherty
Focus: Sci
Periodicals
NACADA Journal (semi-annually)
NACADA Newsletter (quarterly)
Proceedings of Annual Conference . . . *15617*

National Academy of Design (NAD), 1083 Fifth Av, New York, NY 10128
T: (212) 369-4880; Fax: (212) 360-6795
Founded: 1825; Members: 450
Pres: William King; Gen Secr: Edward P. Gallagher
Focus: Graphic & Dec Arts, Design
Periodicals
Academy Bulletin (quarterly)
Academy Calendar (bi-monthly) *15618*

National Academy of Education (NAE), c/o School of Education, Stanford University, 108 CERAS, Stanford, CA 94305-3084
T: (415) 725-1003; Fax: (415) 723-7235
Founded: 1965; Members: 138
Pres: Carl Kaestle; Gen Secr: Charles Bidwell
Focus: Educ *15619*

National Academy of Engineering (NAE), 2101 Constitution Av NW, Washington, DC 20418
T: (202) 334-3200; Fax: (202) 334-1684
Founded: 1964; Members: 1620
Pres: Robert M. White; Gen Secr: Simon Ostrach; Gerald P. Dinneen
Focus: Eng *15620*

National Academy of Opticianry (NAO), 10111 Martin Luther King jr. Hwy, Ste 112, Bowie, MD 20720
T: (301) 577-4828; Fax: (301) 577-3880
Founded: 1973; Members: 6000
Focus: Optics
Periodical
Academy Newsletter (quarterly) *15621*

National Academy of Public Administration (NAPA), 1120 G St NW, Ste 850, Washington, DC 20005
T: (202) 347-3190; Fax: (202) 393-0993
Founded: 1967; Members: 400
Focus: Public Admin *15622*

National Academy of Recording Arts and Sciences (NARAS), 3402 Pico Blvd, Santa Monica, CA 90405
T: (310) 392-3777
Founded: 1957; Members: 9000
Pres: C. Michael Greene
Focus: Music; Eng
Periodicals
Grammy Pulse (quarterly)
Program Book (annually) *15623*

National Academy of Western Art (NAWA), 1700 NE 63 St, Oklahoma City, OK 73111
T: (405) 478-2250; Fax: (405) 478-4714
Founded: 1973; Members: 57
Focus: Arts *15624*

National Accrediting Agency for Clinical Laboratory Sciences (NAACLS), 8410 W Bryn Mawr Av, Ste 670, Chicago, IL 60631
T: (312) 714-8880
Founded: 1973; Members: 734
Focus: Med; Eng
Periodical
Newsletter (2-4 times annually) *15625*

National Accrediting Commission of Cosmetology Arts and Sciences (NACCAS), 901 N State St, Arlington, VA 22203
T: (703) 527-7600; Fax: (703) 527-8811
Founded: 1969; Members: 32
Focus: Adult Educ
Periodicals
Directory of Accredited Cosmetology Schools (annually)
NACCAS Review (bi-monthly) *15626*

National Adult Vocational Education Association (NAVEA), c/o Jackie Jacobus EHOVE Career Center, 316 W Mason Rd, Milan, OH 44846
T: (419) 499-4663; Fax: (419) 499-4076
Founded: 1978; Members: 500
Gen Secr: Jackie Jacobus
Focus: Adult Educ *15627*

National Alliance for Safe Schools (NASS), 9344 Lanham Severn Rd, No 104, Lanham, MD 20706
T: (301) 306-0200; E-Mail: nass@allware.com; Fax: (301) 306-0711
Founded: 1977
Pres: Peter D. Blauvelt
Focus: Educ *15628*

National Alliance of Black School Educators (NABSE), 2816 Georgia Av NW, Washington, DC 20001
T: (202) 483-1549; Fax: (202) 483-8323
Founded: 1970; Members: 5000
Focus: Educ
Periodical
Membership Roster (annually) *15629*

National Alliance of Media Arts and Culture (NAMAC), 655 13 St, Ste 201, Oakland, CA 94612
T: (510) 451-2717; E-Mail: namac@aol.com; Fax: (510) 451-2715
Founded: 1978; Members: 300
Gen Secr: Julian Low
Focus: Arts *15630*

National Alopecia Areata Foundation (NAAF), POB 150760, San Rafael, CA 94915-0760
T: (415) 456-4644; Fax: (415) 456-4274
Founded: 1981; Members: 5000
Focus: Med
Periodical
National Alopecia Areata Foundation Newsletter (bi-monthly) *15631*

National Architectural Accrediting Board (NAAB), 1735 New York Av NW, Washington, DC 20006
T: (202) 783-2007; Fax: (202) 626-7421
Founded: 1940; Members: 11
Focus: Archit
Periodicals
Criteria and Procedures (bi-annually)
List of Accredited Programs in Architecture (annually) *15632*

National Archives and Records Administration Volunteer Association (NARAVA), c/o N.E. Office of Public Programs, National Archives, Eighth at Pennsylvania Av NW, Washington, DC 20408
T: (202) 501-5205
Founded: 1976; Members: 170
Focus: Archives *15633*

National Art Education Association (NAEA), 1916 Association Dr, Reston, VA 22091-1590
T: (703) 860-8000; Fax: (703) 860-2960
Founded: 1947; Members: 13000
Focus: Arts; Educ
Periodicals
Art Education (bi-monthly)
Newsletter (bi-monthly)
Studies in Art Education (bi-monthly) . . *15634*

National Association for Ambulatory Care Medicine, 18870 Rutledge Rd, Wayzata, MN 55391
T: (612) 476-0015; Fax: (612) 476-0646
Founded: 1981; Members: 600
Pres: William H. Wenmark
Focus: Med *15635*

National Association for Applied Arts, Science and Education (NAAASE), POB 100410, Milwaukee, WI 53210
T: (414) 264-2455
Founded: 1956; Members: 250
Gen Secr: R.A. Kurth
Focus: Arts; Lit *15636*

National Association for Armenian Studies and Research (NAASR), 395 Concord Av, Belmont, MA 02178-3049
T: (617) 489-1610
Founded: 1955; Members: 1200
Focus: Ethnology
Periodicals
AICS Bulletin (monthly)
NAASR Newsletter (quarterly) *15637*

National Association for Bilingual Education (NABE), 1220 L St NW, Ste 605, Washington, DC 20005-4018
T: (202) 898-1829; E-Mail: nabe@nabe.org; Fax: (202) 789-2866
Founded: 1975; Members: 3000
Gen Secr: James J. Lyons
Focus: Ling; Educ
Periodicals
Journal (3 times annually)
Newsletter (10 times annually) *15638*

National Association for Biomedical Research (NABR), 818 Connecticut Av NW, Ste 303, Washington, DC 20006
T: (202) 857-0540; Fax: (202) 659-1902
Founded: 1979; Members: 350
Pres: Frankie L. Trull; Gen Secr: Barbara Rich
Focus: Med
Periodicals
NABR Alert (bi-weekly)
NABR Update (bi-weekly)
Report (annually) *15639*

National Association for Business Teacher Education (NABTE), 1914 Association Dr, Reston, VA 22091
T: (703) 860-8300; Fax: (703) 620-4483
Founded: 1927; Members: 210
Focus: Adult Educ
Periodical
NABTE Review (annually) *15640*

National Association for Core Curriculum (NACC), 1100 E Summit St, Ste 5, Kent, OH 44240-4094
T: (330) 677-5008; Fax: (330) 677-5008
Founded: 1953; Members: 200
Gen Secr: Gordon F. Vars
Focus: Educ
Periodical
The Core Teacher (quarterly) *15641*

National Association for Equal Opportunity in Higher Education (NAFEO), 420 12 St NE, Washington, DC 20002
T: (202) 543-9111; Fax: (202) 543-9113
Founded: 1969; Members: 117
Focus: Educ *15642*

National Association for Ethnic Studies (NAES), c/o Dept of English, Arizona State University, Tempe, AZ 85287
T: (602) 965-2197; Fax: (602) 965-2012
Founded: 1975; Members: 300
Focus: Ethnology
Periodicals
The Ethnic Reporter (semi-annually)
Explorations in Ethnic Studies (semi-annually)
Explorations in Sights and Sounds (annually) *15643*

National Association for Family and Community Education, POB 835, Burlington, KY 41005-0835
T: (606) 586-8333; Fax: (606) 586-8348
Founded: 1936; Members: 40000
Pres: Oarlene Wingate
Focus: Home Econ
Periodicals
Handbook (annually)
The Homemaker Update (bi-monthly) . . *15644*

National Association for Hearing and Speech Action (NAHSA), 10801 Rockville Pike, Rockville, MD 20852
T: (301) 897-8682
Founded: 1919; Members: 2000
Focus: Logopedy *15645*

National Association for Human Development (NAHD), 1424 16 St NW, Ste 102, Washington, DC 20036
T: (202) 328-2191

Founded: 1974
Focus: Geriatrics *15646*

National Association for Humane and Environmental Education (NAHEE), POB 362, East Haddam, CT 06423-0362
T: (203) 434-8666; Fax: (203) 434-9579
Founded: 1974; Members: 2000
Focus: Educ
Periodicals
Children and Animals (quarterly)
Kind News (5 times annually) *15647*

National Association for Humanities Education (NAHE), c/o Dr. Darrell Bourque, Dept of English, University of Southwestern Louisiana, POB 44691, Lafayette, LA 70504-4961
T: (318) 482-6906; Fax: (318) 482-6195
Founded: 1967; Members: 400
Pres: James Mebl
Focus: Humanities; Educ
Periodical
Humanities Education (quarterly) *15648*

National Association for Industry-Education Cooperation (NAIEC), 235 Hendricks Blvd, Buffalo, NY 14226-3304
T: (716) 834-7047; Fax: (716) 834-7047
Founded: 1948; Members: 1180
Focus: Adult Educ; Econ
Periodicals
Journal
Newsletter (bi-monthly) *15649*

National Association for Interpretation (NAI), POB 1892, Fort Collins, CO 80522
T: (970) 484-8283; Fax: (970) 484-8179
Founded: 1988; Members: 3000
Gen Secr: Tim Merriman
Focus: Nat Sci
Periodicals
Journal of Interpretation (bi-monthly)
National Workshop Proceedings (annually) *15650*

National Association for Legal Support of Alternative Schools (NALSAS), POB 2823, Santa Fe, NM 87501
T: (505) 471-6928
Founded: 1973; Members: 6000
Focus: Educ
Periodical
Tidbits (semi-annually) *15651*

National Association for Outlaw and Lawman History (NOLA), c/o Richard J. Miller, 1201 Holly Ct, Harker Heights, TX 76548
T: (817) 698-6518
Founded: 1974; Members: 400
Gen Secr: Richard J. Miller
Focus: Cultur Hist; Hist
Periodicals
Index to NOLA Publications (bi-annually)
Newsletter (quarterly)
Quarterly (quarterly) *15652*

National Association for Physical Education in Higher Education (NAPEHE), c/o Dept of HUP, San Jose State University, San Jose, CA 95192
T: (408) 924-3029; Fax: (408) 924-3053
Founded: 1978; Members: 500
Focus: Sports
Periodicals
Newsletter (quarterly)
Quest (semi-annually) *15653*

National Association for Poetry Therapy (NAPT), c/o Alicia Seeger, POB 551, Port Washington, NY 11050
T: (516) 944-9791; Fax: (516) 944-5818
Founded: 1981; Members: 380
Pres: George Bell
Focus: Therapeutics
Periodicals
The Journal of Poetry Therapy
NAPT News Letter *15654*

National Association for Practical Nurse Education and Service (NAPNES), 1400 Spring St, Ste 310, Silver Spring, MD 20910
T: (301) 588-2491; Fax: (301) 588-2839
Founded: 1941; Members: 30000
Focus: Adult Educ; Med
Periodicals
Career Directory
Journal of Practical Nursing (quarterly) . *15655*

National Association for Research in Science Teaching (NARST), c/o Arthur L. White, Ohio State University, 219 Bluemont Hall, Rm 200E, 1929 Kenny Rd, Columbus, OH 43210
T: (614) 292-3339; E-Mail: TS0002@ohstmvsa.acs.ohio_state.edu; Fax: (614) 292-1595
Founded: 1928; Members: 1500
Gen Secr: Dr. Arthur L. White
Focus: Educ
Periodicals
Abstracts of Papers Presented to Annual Meeting (annually)
Journal of Research in Science Teaching (bi-monthly)
Membership Directory (semi-annually)
Newsletter (quarterly) *15656*

National Association for Rural Mental Health (ARMH), POB 570, Wood River, IL 62095
T: (618) 251-0589; Fax: (618) 251-6246
Founded: 1977; Members: 350
Pres: Ed Calahan
Focus: Psychiatry

Periodical
Rural Community Health Newsletter (quarterly)
 . . . . *15657*

National Association for Search and Rescue (NASAR), 4500 Southgate Pl, Ste 100, Chantilly, VA 22021
T: (703) 222-6277; E-Mail: nasar@nasar.org; Fax: (703) 222-6283
Founded: 1974; Members: 3500
Gen Secr: Lawrence Jacobson
Focus: Med
Periodicals
Response (bi-monthly)
Update (quarterly) *15658*

National Association for Sport and Physical Education (NASPE), 1900 Association Dr, Reston, VA 22091
T: (703) 476-3410; Fax: (703) 476-9527
Founded: 1974; Members: 30000
Focus: Sports *15659*

National Association for the Advancement of Black Americans in Vocational Education (NAABAVE), c/o Dr. Ethel O. Washington, POB 04437, Detroit, MI 48204
T: (313) 494-1660; Fax: (313) 494-1132
Founded: 1977; Members: 900
Pres: Dr. Ethel O. Washington
Focus: Educ *15660*

National Association for the Advancement of Psychoanalysis and The American Board for Accreditation in Psychoanalysis (NAAPABAP), 80 Eighth Av, Ste 1501, New York, NY 10011-1501
T: (212) 741-0515; E-Mail: NAAP95@AOL.COM; Fax: (212) 741-0515
Founded: 1972; Members: 1670
Gen Secr: Margery Quackenbush
Focus: Psychoan *15661*

National Association for the Education of Young Children (NAEYC), 1509 16 St NW, Washington, DC 20036
T: (202) 232-8777; Fax: (202) 328-1846
Founded: 1926; Members: 95000
Gen Secr: Dr. Marilyn M. Smith
Focus: Educ
Periodical
Young Children (bi-monthly) *15662*

National Association for the Exchange of Industrial Resources (NAEIR), 560 McClure St, POB 8076, Galesburg, IL 61402
T: (309) 343-0704; Fax: (309) 343-0862
Founded: 1977; Members: 7000
Focus: Educ; Econ
Periodical
NAEIR News (monthly) *15663*

National Association for the Practice of Anthropology (NAPA), c/o American Anthropological Association, 4350 N Fairfax Dr, Ste 640, Arlington, VA 22203-1620
T: (703) 528-1902; Fax: (703) 528-3546
Founded: 1983; Members: 887
Pres: Elizabeth K. Briody
Focus: Anthro
Periodicals
Bulletin Series
Cultural Experts Directory *15664*

National Association for Trade and Industrial Education (NATIE), POB 1665, Leesburg, VA 22075
T: (703) 777-1740
Founded: 1974; Members: 1400
Focus: Adult Educ *15665*

National Association for Veterinary Acupuncture (NAVA), 951 W Bastan Chury Rd, Fullerton, CA 92635
T: (714) 871-3000
Founded: 1973; Members: 60
Focus: Vet Med *15666*

National Association for Women in Education (NAWE), 1325 18 St NW, Ste 210, Washington, DC 20036-6511
T: (202) 659-9330; Fax: (202) 457-0946
Founded: 1916; Members: 1900
Focus: Educ *15667*

National Association for Year-Round Education (NCYRE), POB 711386, San Diego, CA 92171-1386
T: (619) 276-5296; Fax: (619) 571-5754
Founded: 1972; Members: 1250
Gen Secr: Dr. Charles Ballinger
Focus: Educ
Periodicals
Directory of Year-Round Schools (annually)
The Year-Rounder (quarterly) *15668*

National Association of Academic Advisors for Athletics, 8402 Westover Dr, Prospect, KY 40059
T: (502) 228-4053; Fax: (502) 228-5638
Founded: 1975; Members: 400
Gen Secr: Susan Gibbs
Focus: Sports; Educ
Periodical
Academic Athletic Journal (semi-annually) *15669*

National Association of Academies of Science (NAAS), c/o Dept of Mathematical Sciences, University of South Carolina, 133 Willard Bldg, Columbia, SC 29208
T: (803) 777-7007; Fax: (402) 399-2686

Founded: 1926; Members: 45
Focus: Sci
Periodicals
Directory and Proceedings (annually)
Newsletter (quarterly) *15670*

National Association of Advisors for the Health Professions (NAAHP), POB 1518, Champaign, IL 61825-1518
T: (217) 355-0063; Fax: (217) 355-1287
Founded: 1974; Members: 1275
Gen Secr: Julian M. Frankenberg
Focus: Educ; Med *15671*

National Association of Alcoholism and Drug Abuse Counselors (NAADAC), 1911 Fort Myer Dr, Ste 900, Arlington, VA 22209
T: (703) 920-4644; Fax: (703) 920-4672
Founded: 1972; Members: 18000
Gen Secr: Linda Kaplan
Focus: Soc Sci *15672*

National Association of Baptist Professors of Religion (NABPR), c/o Mercer University, Macon, GA 31207
T: (912) 752-2755
Founded: 1927; Members: 650
Gen Secr: Richard F. Wilson
Focus: Rel & Theol
Periodicals
Bibliographic Series (irregularly)
Dissertation Series (irregularly)
Monograph/Special Studies Series (irregularly)
Perspectives in Religious Studies (quarterly)
 . . . . *15673*

National Association of Bar Executives (NABE), c/o Div for Bar Services, 541 N Fairbanks, Chicago, IL 60611-3314
T: (312) 988-5346; Fax: (312) 988-5492
Founded: 1941; Members: 550
Focus: Law *15674*

National Association of Biology Teachers (NABT), 11250 Roger Bacon Dr, Reston, VA 22090
T: (703) 471-1134
Founded: 1938; Members: 7000
Focus: Bio; Educ
Periodicals
The American Biology Teacher (8 times annually)
News + Views (5 times annually) . . . *15675*

National Association of Black Professors (NABP), POB 526, Chrisfield, MD 21817
T: (410) 968-2393
Founded: 1974; Members: 135
Focus: Adult Educ *15676*

National Association of Blind Teachers (NABT), c/o American Council of the Blind, 1155 15 St NW, Ste 720, Washington, DC 20005
T: (202) 467-5081; Fax: (202) 476-5085
Founded: 1971; Members: 190
Focus: Educ *15677*

National Association of Boards of Pharmacy (NABP), 700 Busse Hwy, Park Ridge, IL 60068
T: (708) 698-6227
Founded: 1904; Members: 56
Focus: Pharmacol
Periodicals
Newsletter (monthly)
State Board Newsletter (quarterly) . . . *15678*

National Association of Bond Lawyers (NABL), POB 397, Hinsdale, IL 60522
T: (708) 920-0160
Founded: 1979; Members: 2750
Focus: Law *15679*

National Association of Business Education State Supervisors (NABESS), c/o Arizona Dept of Education, 1535 W Jefferson, Phoenix, AZ 85007
T: (602) 542-5350; Fax: (602) 542-1849
Founded: 1965; Members: 125
Gen Secr: Janet Gandy
Focus: Educ; Econ *15680*

National Association of Children's Hospitals and Related Institutions (NACHRI), 401 Wythe St, Alexandria, VA 22314
T: (703) 684-1355; Fax: (703) 684-1589
Founded: 1968; Members: 110
Focus: Pediatrics
Periodicals
Guide to Children's Hospitals (annually)
Newsletter (quarterly) *15681*

National Association of Classroom Educators in Business Education (NACEBE), c/o Watauga High School, Hwy 105 S, Boone, NC 28607
T: (704) 264-2407; Fax: (704) 264-9030
Founded: 1968; Members: 700
Pres: Janet H. Auten
Focus: Educ; Econ *15682*

National Association of College and University Attorneys (NACUA), 1 Dupont Circle, Ste 620, Washington, DC 20036
T: (202) 833-8390; Fax: (202) 296-8379
Founded: 1961; Members: 2500
Focus: Law *15683*

National Association of College and University Business Officers (NACUBO), 1 Dupont Circle NW, Ste 500, Washington, DC 20036
T: (202) 861-2500; Fax: (202) 861-2583
Founded: 1950; Members: 2100
Focus: Econ

Periodicals
Annual Report (annually)
Business Officer *15684*

National Association of College Deans, Registrars and Admissions Officers (NACDRAO), 917 Dorsett St, Albany, GA 31701
T: (912) 435-4945
Founded: 1925; Members: 325
Focus: Educ *15685*

National Association of College Wind and Percussion Instructors (NACWPI), c/o Div of Fine Arts, Northeast Missouri State University, Kirksville, MO 63501
T: (816) 785-4442; Fax: (816) 785-4181
Founded: 1952; Members: 1200
Focus: Music
Periodical
Journal (quarterly) *15686*

National Association of Colleges and Teachers of Agriculture (NACTA), c/o Murry A. Brown, Sam Houston State University, POB 2088, Huntsville, TX 73341
T: (409) 294-1226
Founded: 1955; Members: 1500
Gen Secr: Dr. Jack C. Everly
Focus: Educ; Agri
Periodical
NACTA Journal (quarterly) *15687*

National Association of Community Health Centers (NACHC), 1330 New Hampshire Av NW, Ste 122, Washington, DC 20036
T: (202) 659-8008; Fax: (202) 659-8519
Founded: 1970; Members: 950
Focus: Public Health
Periodicals
Community Health Guides (bi-monthly)
Community Health Listing (annually)
Washington Update (bi-weekly) . . . *15688*

National Association of County Engineers (NACE), 440 First St NW, Washington, DC 20001
T: (202) 393-5041; Fax: (202) 393-2630
Founded: 1956; Members: 1800
Gen Secr: A.R. Giancola
Focus: Eng
Periodical
Newsletter (quarterly) *15689*

National Association of County Planners (NACP), c/o National Association of Counties, 440 First St NW, Washington, DC 20001
T: (202) 393-6226; Fax: (202) 393-2630
Founded: 1965; Members: 500
Focus: Urban Plan *15690*

National Association of Dental Assistants (NADA), 900 S Washington St, Falls Church, VA 22046
T: (703) 237-8616
Founded: 1974; Members: 4000
Focus: Dent *15691*

National Association of Dental Laboratories (NADL), 555 E Braddock Rd, Alexandria, VA 22314-2106
T: (703) 683-5263; Fax: (703) 549-4788
Founded: 1951; Members: 2900
Gen Secr: Robert W. Stanley
Focus: Dent
Periodicals
Executive Information Series
Trends and Techniques (10 times annually)
Who's Who in the Dental Laboratory Industry (annually) *15692*

National Association of Disability Examiners (NADE), POB 4188, Frankfort, KY 40603
T: (502) 875-8388
Founded: 1963; Members: 2373
Focus: Med *15693*

National Association of Dramatic and Speech Arts (NADSA), 208 Cherokee Dr, Blacksburg, VA 24060
T: (540) 552-6862
Founded: 1936; Members: 1000
Gen Secr: Dr. H.D. Flowers
Focus: Perf Arts
Periodicals
Encore (bi-annually)
NADSA Conference Directory (annually)
NADSA Update (semi-annually)
Newsletter (quarterly) *15694*

National Association of Educational Buyers (NAEB), 450 Wireless Blvd, Hauppauge, NY 11788
T: (516) 273-2600; Fax: (516) 273-2305
Founded: 1920; Members: 2200
Focus: Educ *15695*

National Association of Elementary School Principals (NAESP), 1615 Duke St, Alexandria, VA 22314
T: (703) 684-3345; Fax: (703) 548-6021
Founded: 1921; Members: 26000
Focus: Educ
Periodicals
Communicator (10 times annually)
Principal (5 times annually) *15696*

National Association of Emergency Medical Technicians (NAEMT), 102 W Leake St, Clinton, MS 39056
T: (601) 924-7744; Fax: (601) 924-7325
Founded: 1975; Members: 5000

Gen Secr: Barbara Sanders
Focus: Med
Periodicals
Newsletter (bi-monthly)
Perspective (quarterly) 15697

National Association of Environmental Professionals (NAEP), 5165 MacArthur Blvd NW, POB 9400, Washington, DC 20016-3315
T: (202) 966-1500; Fax: (202) 966-1977
Founded: 1975; Members: 3000
Focus: Ecology
Periodical
Newsletter (monthly) 15698

National Association of Episcopal Schools (NAES), 815 Second Av, New York, NY 10017-4594
T: (212) 922-5173; Fax: (212) 949-6781
Founded: 1954; Members: 360
Focus: Educ
Periodicals
Directory of Episcopal Church Schools
NAES Journal (annually)
Newsletter (quarterly) 15699

National Association of Extension 4-H Agents (NAE4-HA), c/o University of Georgia, Hoke Smith Annex, Athens, GA 30602
T: (706) 978-8171; Fax: (404) 978-8171
Founded: 1946; Members: 3452
Gen Secr: Peggy M. Adkins
Focus: Educ; Agri
Periodicals
Journal of Extension (bi-monthly)
Membership Report (annually)
NAE4-HA Membership Directory (annually)
News and Views (quarterly) 15700

National Association of Federal Veterinarians (NAFV), 1101 Vermont Av NW, Ste 710, Washington, DC 20005-3521
T: (202) 289-6334
Founded: 1918; Members: 1600
Focus: Vet Med
Periodical
The Federal Veterinarian (monthly) . . . 15701

National Association of Flight Instructors (NAFI), Ohio State University Airport, POB 793, Columbus, OH 43017
T: (614) 889-6148; Fax: (614) 889-2610
Founded: 1966; Members: 2000
Focus: Aero
Periodical
Newsletter (bi-monthly) 15702

National Association of Health Career Schools (NAHCS), 750 First St NE, Ste 940, Washington, DC 20002
T: (202) 842-1592; Fax: (202) 842-1565
Founded: 1980; Members: 180
Gen Secr: Jeanne Russell
Focus: Adult Educ; Public Health
Periodical
Bulletin (weekly) 15703

National Association of Health Services Executives (NAHSE), 10320 Little Patuxent Pkwy, Ste 1106, Columbia, MD 21044
T: (202) 628-3953; Fax: (202) 628-3958
Founded: 1968; Members: 500
Focus: Public Health
Periodical
Notes (bi-monthly) 15704

National Association of Hebrew Day School Administrators (NAHDSA), 1114 J Av, Brooklyn, NY 11230
T: (718) 258-7767
Members: 400
Focus: Educ
Periodical
Directory 15705

National Association of Hebrew Day School PTA'S, 160 Broadway, New York, NY 10038
T: (212) 227-1000; Fax: (212) 406-6934
Founded: 1947; Members: 300
Focus: Educ
Periodical
National PTA Bulletin (3 times annually) 15706

National Association of Home and Workshop Writers (NAHWW), c/o David A. Warren, 400 E Randolph, No 3306, Chicago, IL 60601-7304
T: (815) 459-6255; Fax: (815) 459-6258
Founded: 1973; Members: 90
Pres: David A. Warren
Focus: Lit
Periodical
NAH & WW Newsletter (bi-monthly) . . 15707

National Association of Independent Colleges and Universities (NAICU), 1025 Connecticut Av, Ste 700, Washington, DC 20036
T: (202) 785-8866; Fax: (202) 835-0003
Founded: 1976; Members: 830
Pres: David L. Warren
Focus: Sci 15708

National Association of Independent Schools (NAIS), 1620 L St NW, Washington, DC 20036-5605
T: (202) 973-9700; Fax: (202) 973-9790
Founded: 1962; Members: 1130
Pres: Peter Relic
Focus: Educ
Periodical
Independent School (3 times annually) . 15709

National Association of Industrial and Technical Teacher Educators (NAITTE), c/o Dept of Technological and Adult Education, University of Tennessee, 402 Claxton Addition, Knoxville, TN 37996-3400
T: (615) 974-2574; Fax: (615) 974-2048
Founded: 1937; Members: 850
Focus: Adult Educ; Eng
Periodicals
Directory (annually)
Journal of Industrial Teacher Education (quarterly)
News and Views (3 times annually) . . 15710

National Association of Legal Assistants (NALA), 1516 S Boston, Ste 200, Tulsa, OK 74119
T: (918) 587-6828; Fax: (918) 582-6772
Founded: 1975; Members: 6000
Gen Secr: Marge Dover
Focus: Law
Periodical
Facts & Findings (bi-monthly) 15711

National Association of Marine Surveyors (NAMS), POB 9306, Chesapeake, VA 23321-9306
T: (800) 822-6267
Founded: 1960; Members: 400
Focus: Surveying; Navig
Periodical
NAMS Newsletter (quarterly) 15712

National Association of Medical Examiners (NAME), 1402 S Grand Blvd, Saint Louis, MO 63104
T: (314) 577-8298; Fax: (314) 772-1307
Founded: 1966
Focus: Med
Periodical
American Journal of Forensic Medicine and Pathology (quarterly) 15713

National Association of Music Executives in State Universities (NAMESU), c/o School of Music, University of Arizona, Tucson, AZ 85721
T: (602) 621-7023; Fax: (602) 621-8118
Founded: 1935; Members: 50
Gen Secr: Dr. Dorothy Payne
Focus: Music 15714

National Association of Nutrition and Aging Services Programs (NANASP), 2675 44 St NW, Ste 305, Grand Rapids, MI 49509
T: (616) 531-9909; Fax: (616) 531-3103
Founded: 1977; Members: 1000
Gen Secr: Connie Benton Wolfe
Focus: Nutrition; Geriatrics
Periodicals
Annual Report (annually)
Monthly Membership Updates (monthly)
NANASP News (quarterly)
Special Bulletin (monthly) 15715

National Association of Optometrists and Opticians (NAOO), 18903 S Miles Rd, Cleveland, OH 44128
T: (216) 475-8925
Founded: 1960; Members: 13225
Focus: Ophthal; Optics 15716

National Association of Pastoral Musicians (NPM), 225 Sheridan St NW, Washington, DC 20011-1492
T: (202) 723-5800; Fax: (202) 723-2262
Founded: 1976; Members: 8500
Focus: Music
Periodicals
Pastoral Music Magazine (bi-monthly)
Pastoral Musician's Notebook (bi-monthly) 15717

National Association of Power Engineers (NAPE), 1 Springfield St, Chicopee, MA 01013
T: (413) 592-6273; Fax: (413) 592-1998
Founded: 1882; Members: 3500
Gen Secr: William Judd
Focus: Energy
Periodical
National Engineer (monthly) 15718

National Association of Principals of Schools for Girls (NAPSG), 41 Van Brunt Manor Rd, East Setauket, NY 11733
T: (516) 751-0850; Fax: (516) 689-7311
Founded: 1920; Members: 600
Gen Secr: Carol M. Lane
Focus: Educ
Periodical
Proceedings (annually) 15719

National Association of Private Schools for Exceptional Children (NAPSEC), 1525 K St NW, Ste 1032, Washington, DC 20005
T: (202) 408-3338; Fax: (202) 408-3340
Founded: 1971; Members: 200
Focus: Educ
Periodicals
Directory (bi-annually)
Newsbriefs (3 times annually)
Newsletter (3 times annually) 15720

National Association of Professional Educators (NAPE), 412 First St SE, Washington, DC 20003
T: (202) 484-8969
Founded: 1972
Focus: Educ 15721

National Association of Professors of Hebrew (NAPH), c/o University of Wisconsin, 1346 Van Hise Hall, 1220 Linden Dr, Madison, WI 53706-1558
T: (608) 262-2968; Fax: (608) 262-9417
Founded: 1950; Members: 450
Gen Secr: G. Moragh
Focus: Ling; Lit
Periodicals
Hebrew Studies Journal (annually)
Iggeret (semi-annually) 15722

National Association of School Psychologists (NASP), 4340 East-West Hwy, Str 402, Bethesda, MD 20814-4411
T: (301) 657-0270; E-Mail: SPCONVNASP@aol.com; Fax: (301) 657-0275
Founded: 1969; Members: 18980
Gen Secr: Susan Gorin
Focus: Psych
Periodicals
Directory (bi-annually)
Journal Review (quarterly)
Newsletter (8 times annually) 15723

National Association of Schools and Colleges of the United Methodist Church (NASCUMC), POB 871, Nashville, TN 37202-0871
T: (615) 340-7399; Fax: (615) 340-7048
Founded: 1940; Members: 128
Focus: Educ 15724

National Association of Schools of Art and Design (NASAD), 11250 Roger Bacon Dr, Reston, VA 22090
T: (703) 437-0700
Founded: 1944; Members: 172
Focus: Graphic & Dec Arts, Design; Educ
Periodicals
Directory (annually)
Handbook 15725

National Association of Schools of Music (NASM), 11250 Roger Bacon Dr, Reston, VA 22090
T: (703) 437-0700
Founded: 1924; Members: 550
Focus: Music; Educ
Periodicals
Directory (annually)
Handbook (bi-annually)
Proceedings (annually) 15726

National Association of Schools of Public Affairs and Administration (NASPAA), 1120 G St NW, Ste 730, Washington, DC 20005
T: (202) 628-8965; Fax: (202) 626-4978
Founded: 1970; Members: 223
Focus: Public Admin 15727

National Association of Schools of Theatre (NAST), 11250 Roger Bacon Dr, Reston, VA 22090
T: (703) 437-0700
Founded: 1969; Members: 83
Focus: Educ 15728

National Association of Science Writers (NASW), POB 294, Greenlawn, NY 11740
T: (516) 757-5664; Fax: (516) 757-0069
Founded: 1934; Members: 1715
Focus: Sci; Journalism
Periodical
NASW Newsletter (quarterly) 15729

National Association of Secondary School Principals (NASSP), 1904 Association Dr, Reston, VA 22091
T: (703) 860-0200; Fax: (703) 476-5432
Founded: 1916; Members: 43000
Focus: Educ
Periodicals
Bulletin (9 times annually)
Curriculum Report (5 times annually)
Legal Memorandum (5 times annually)
Newsleader (9 times annually)
Practitioner (quarterly)
School Technology News (bi-monthly)
Schools in the Middle (quarterly)
Student Acitivities Magazine (monthly)
Tips for Principals 15730

National Association of State Archeologists (NASA), c/o Brona Simon, Massachusetts Historical Commission, 220 Morrissey Blvd, Boston, MA 02125
T: (617) 272-8470; Fax: (617) 272-5128
Founded: 1979; Members: 53
Gen Secr: Robert L. Brooks
Focus: Archeol
Periodicals
Directory (annually)
Newsletter (quarterly) 15731

National Association of State Boards of Education (NASBE), 1012 Cameron St, Alexandria, VA 22314
T: (703) 684-4000; Fax: (703) 836-2313
Founded: 1958; Members: 590
Focus: Educ 15732

National Association of State Development Agencies (NASDA), 750 First St NE, Ste 710, Washington, DC 20002
T: (202) 898-1302
Founded: 1946; Members: 250
Focus: Econ
Periodical
NASDA Letter (every 6-8 weeks) . . . 15733

National Association of State Directors of Special Education (NASDSE), 1800 Diagonal Rd, Ste 320, Alexandria, VA 22314
T: (703) 519-3800; Fax: (703) 519-3808
Founded: 1938; Members: 2100
Focus: Educ
Periodicals
Counterpoint (quarterly)
Liaison Bulletin (bi-weekly) 15734

National Association of State Directors of Teacher Education and Certification (NASDTEC), 3600 Whitman Av N, Ste 105, Seattle, WA 98103
T: (206) 547-0437; Fax: (206) 548-0116
Founded: 1922; Members: 100
Gen Secr: Dr. Donald Hair
Focus: Adult Educ; Educ
Periodical
Roster (annually) 15735

National Association of State Directors of Vocational Technical Education Consortium (NASDVTE), 444 N Capitol St NW, Ste 830, Washington, DC 20001
T: (202) 737-0303; Fax: (202) 737-1106
Founded: 1920; Members: 220
Pres: Dr. Anne L. Matthews
Focus: Adult Educ 15736

National Association of State Educational Media Professionals (NASTEMP), c/o Janie Walters, Tennessee Dept of Education, 710 James Robertson Pkwy, Nashville, TN 37243-0375
T: (615) 741-2731; Fax: (615) 741-6236
Founded: 1976; Members: 110
Focus: Educ 15737

National Association of State Mental Health Program Directors (NASMHPD), 66 Canal Center Plaza, Ste 302, Alexandria, VA 22314
T: (703) 739-9333; Fax: (703) 548-9517
Founded: 1963; Members: 55
Focus: Psychiatry 15738

National Association of State Mental Retardation Program Directors, 113 Oronoco St, Alexandria, VA 22314
T: (703) 683-4202
Founded: 1963; Members: 53
Focus: Psychiatry
Periodicals
Community Management Initiative Reports
Federal Funding Inquiry Reports
New Directions (monthly) 15739

National Association of State Park Directors (NASPD), 126 Mill Branch Rd, Tallahassee, FL 32312
T: (904) 893-4959
Founded: 1982; Members: 50
Focus: Astrophys 15740

National Association of State Public Health Veterinarians (NASPHV), c/o Ohio Dept of Health, POB 118, Columbus, OH 43266-0118
T: (614) 466-0283; Fax: (614) 644-7740
Founded: 1953; Members: 50
Focus: Vet Med
Periodical
Annual National Compendium of Animal Rabies Control (annually) 15741

National Association of State Supervisors of Vocational Home Economics (NASSVHE), c/o Gay Nell McGinnas, Texas Education Agency, 1701 N Congress Av, Austin, TX 78701
T: (512) 463-9454; Fax: (512) 475-3575
Members: 175
Pres: Judith Heatherly
Focus: Home Econ; Educ
Periodicals
Directory (annually)
Newsletter (2-3 times annually) 15742

National Association of State Units on Aging (NASUA), 1225 Eye St NW, Ste 725, Washington, DC 20005
T: (202) 898-2578; E-Mail: staff@nasua.org; Fax: (202) 898-2583
Founded: 1964; Members: 57
Gen Secr: Daniel A. Quirk
Focus: Geriatrics 15743

National Association of State Universities and Land-Grant Colleges (NASULGC), 1 Dupont Circle NW, Ste 710, Washington, DC 20036-1191
T: (202) 778-0818; Fax: (202) 296-6456
Founded: 1962; Members: 160
Focus: Educ; Sci
Periodicals
Annual Report (annually)
The Green Sheet (10 times annually)
Washington Gleanings (bi-weekly) . . . 15744

National Association of Supervisors of Agricultural Education (NASAE), c/o Dr. Gene Eulinger, Dept of Elementary and Secondary Education, POB 480, Jefferson City, MO 65102-0480
T: (573) 751-8468; Fax: (573) 526-4261
Founded: 1962; Members: 152
Pres: Dr. Gene Eulinger
Focus: Adult Educ; Agri 15745

National Association of Supervisors of Business Education (NASBE), c/o Fort Worth Independent School District, 3210 W Lancaster, Fort Worth, TX 76107
T: (817) 878-3741
Founded: 1955; Members: 300
Pres: Jean Lane
Focus: Business Admin; Adult Educ . . 15746

National Association of Teacher Educators for Business Education (NATEBE), c/o Business Education Dept, University of Missouri at Columbia, 303 Hill Hall, Columbia, MO 65211
T: (314) 882-2377
Founded: 1970; Members: 350
Pres: Dr. Lonnie Echpernacht
Focus: Educ; Econ 15747

National Association of Teachers of Singing (NATS), 2800 University Blvd N, Jacksonville, FL 32211
T: (904) 744-9022; Fax: (904) 744-9022
Founded: 1944; Members: 5000
Focus: Music; Educ
Periodicals
Inter NOS (3 times annually)
Journal (5 times annually)
Membership Directory (bi-annually) . . . 15748

National Association of Test Directors (NATD), c/o H. Guy Glidden, Wichita Public Schools, 217 N Water St, Wichita, KS 67202
T: (316) 833-4180; Fax: (316) 833-4726
Founded: 1985; Members: 250
Gen Secr: H. Guy Glidden
Focus: Educ 15749

National Association of University Women (NAUW), c/o Phyllis Eggleston, 1501 11 St NW, Washington, DC 20001
Founded: 1923; Members: 4000
Pres: Phyllis Eggleston
Focus: Educ
Periodicals
Bulletin (bi-annually)
Directory of Branch Presidents and Members (annually)
Journal of the National Association of University Women (bi-annually) 15750

National Association of Vocational Education Special Needs Personnel (NAVESNP), c/o Pennsylvania State University, 101 Ostermayer, McKeesport, PA 15132
T: (412) 675-9065; Fax: (412) 675-9067
Founded: 1973; Members: 2200
Focus: Educ 15751

National Association of Women Lawyers (NAWL), c/o American Bar Center, 750 N Lake Shore Dr, Chicago, IL 60611
T: (312) 988-6186; Fax: (312) 988-6281
Founded: 1911; Members: 1200
Gen Secr: Peggy L. Golden
Focus: Law
Periodical
Women Lawyers Journal (quarterly) . . . 15752

National Association on Drug Abuse Problems (PACT/NADAP), 335 Lexington Av, New York, NY 10017
T: (212) 986-1170; Fax: (212) 697-2939
Founded: 1971; Members: 27
Focus: Public Health; Rehabil 15753

National Assoiation of Self-Instructional Language Programs (NASILP), c/o Critical Languages Center, Temple University, 022-38 Anderson Hall, Philadelphia, PA 19122
T: (215) 787-1715; Fax: (215) 787-3731
Founded: 1971; Members: 145
Focus: Ling 15754

National Audubon Society, c/o Human Population and Resource Use Dept, 4150 Darley Av, Ste 5, Boulder, CO 80303
Focus: Soc Sci 15755

National Bar Association, 1226 11th St NW, Washington, DC 20001-4217
Gen Secr: Paulette Brown
Focus: Law 15756

National Black MBA Association (NBMBAA), 180 N Michigan Av, Ste 1820, Chicago, IL 60601
T: (312) 236-2622; Fax: (312) 236-4131
Founded: 1871; Members: 2000
Focus: Educ
Periodical
National Black MBA Association Newsletter (quarterly) 15757

National Black Music Caucus of the Music Educators National Conference (NBMC), c/o University of Michigan, Ann Arbor, MI 48109
T: (313) 764-0586
Founded: 1972
Gen Secr: Dr. Willis Patterson
Focus: Music 15758

National Black Women's Health Project (NBWHP), 1237 Ralph David Abernathy Blvd SW, Atlanta, GA 30310
T: (404) 758-9590; Fax: (404) 752-6756
Founded: 1981; Members: 2000
Focus: Public Health 15759

National Board for Certification in Dental Technology, 555 E Braddock Rd, Alexandria, VA 22314-2106
T: (703) 683-5310; Fax: (703) 549-4788
Founded: 1958; Members: 10000
Gen Secr: Sandra Stewart
Focus: Dent 15760

National Board for Certification of Dental Laboratories (NBCDL), 555 E Braddock Rd, Alexandria, VA 22314-2106
T: (703) 683-5310; Fax: (703) 549-4788
Founded: 1979; Members: 600
Gen Secr: Robert W. Stanley
Focus: Dent 15761

National Board for Respiratory Care (NBRC), 8310 Nieman Rd, Lenexa, KS 66214
T: (913) 599-4200
Founded: 1960; Members: 90000
Focus: Therapeutics
Periodicals
Annual Directory (annually)
Newsletter (monthly) 15762

National Board of Examiners in Optometry (NBEO), 4340 East West Hwy, Ste 1010, Bethesda, MD 20814
T: (301) 652-5192; E-Mail: NBEO@OPTOMETRY.ORG; Fax: (301) 907-0013
Founded: 1951
Gen Secr: Dr. Norman E. Wallis
Focus: Optics
Periodicals
Cardichte's Guide (annually)
Newsletter (quarterly)
Report & Boara Activities (bi-annually)
Report & Examinations (semi-annually) . 15763

National Board of Medical Examiners (NBME), 3750 Market St, Philadelphia, PA 19104
T: (215) 590-9500; Fax: (215) 590-9555
Founded: 1915; Members: 75
Pres: L. Thompson Bowles
Focus: Med
Periodicals
Annual Report (annually)
The National Board Examiner (quarterly) 15764

National Bureau of Economic Research (NBER), 1050 Massachusetts Av, Cambridge, MA 02138
T: (617) 868-3900; Fax: (617) 868-2742
Founded: 1920
Focus: Econ 15765

National Burn Victim Foundation (NBVF), 32-34 Scotland Rd, Orange, NJ 07050
T: (201) 676-7700; Fax: (201) 673-6353
Founded: 1974; Members: 26
Focus: Derm 15766

National Business Education Association (NBEA), 1914 Association Dr, Reston, VA 22091
T: (703) 860-8300
Founded: 1892; Members: 18000
Focus: Adult Educ; Business Admin
Periodical
Business Education Forum (8 times annually) 15767

National Cancer Center (NCC), 88 Sunnyside Blvd, Plainview, NY 11803
T: (516) 349-0610
Founded: 1953
Focus: Cell Biol & Cancer Res 15768

National Cancer Registrars Association (NCRA), 505 E Hawley St, Mundelein, IL 60060
T: (708) 566-0833; Fax: (708) 566-7282
Founded: 1974; Members: 1700
Gen Secr: Robert B. Willis
Focus: Cell Biol & Cancer Res
Periodicals
Abstract (bi-monthly)
Membership Roster (annually)
Proceedings/Annual Report 15769

National Captioning Institute (NCI), 1900 Gallows Rd, Ste 3000, Vienna, VA 22182
T: (703) 917-7600; Fax: (703) 917-9878
Founded: 1979
Gen Secr: Philip W. Bravin
Focus: Educ Handic 15770

National Catholic Business Education Association (NCBEA), c/o Richard F. Reichterer, POB 4527, Topeka, KS 66604-0527
T: (316) 343-8463; Fax: (316) 234-4601
Founded: 1945; Members: 1000
Gen Secr: Richard F. Reicherter
Focus: Adult Educ 15771

National Catholic Conference for Interracial Justice (NCCIJ), 3033 Fourth St NE, Washington, DC 20017-1102
T: (202) 529-6480
Founded: 1969; Members: 1151
Focus: Law 15772

National Catholic Educational Association (NCEA), 1077 30 St NW, Ste 100, Washington, 20007
T: (202) 337-6232; Fax: (202) 333-6706
Founded: 1904; Members: 20000
Focus: Educ
Periodicals
Notes (5 times annually)
Private School Law Digest (5 times annually)
Update (bi-monthly) 15773

National Catholic Forensic League (NCFL), 21 Nancy Rd, Milford, MA 01757
T: (617) 473-0438
Founded: 1952; Members: 775
Gen Secr: Richard Gaudette
Focus: Law
Periodical
NCFL Newsletter (3 times annually) . . 15774

National Catholic Pharmacists Guild of the United States (NCPG), 1012 Surrey Hills Dr, Saint Louis, MO 63117-1438
T: (314) 645-0085
Founded: 1962; Members: 400
Focus: Pharmacol
Periodical
The Catholic Pharmacist (quarterly) . . . 15775

National Center for Appropriate Technology (NCAT), POB 3838, Butte, MT 59702
T: (406) 494-4572; Fax: (406) 494-2905
Founded: 1976
Focus: Energy 15776

National Center for Automated Information Research (NCAIR), 165 E 72 St, Ste 1B, New York, NY 10021
T: (212) 249-0760
Founded: 1966; Members: 25
Focus: Law; Computer & Info Sci . . . 15777

National Center for Business and Economic Communication (NCBEC), c/o The American University, 4400 Massachusetts Av, Washington, DC 20016
T: (202) 885-6167
Founded: 1979
Focus: Econ 15778

National Center for Computer Crime Data (NCCCD), 1222 17 Av, Ste B, Santa Cruz, CA 95062
T: (408) 475-4457; Fax: (408) 475-5336
Founded: 1978
Focus: Criminology; Computer & Info Sci
Periodicals
Annual Statistical Report (annually)
Computer Crime Chronicles
Computer Crime Law Reporter (annually) 15779

National Center for Disability Services (NCDS), 201 I.U. Willets Rd W, Albertson, NY 11507
T: (516) 747-5400; Fax: (516) 747-5378
Founded: 1952
Focus: Educ; Rehabil 15780

National Center for Fair and Open Testing, 342 Broadway, Cambridge, MA 02139
T: (617) 864-4810; Fax: (617) 497-2224
Founded: 1985
Focus: Educ 15781

National Center for Homeopathy (NCH), 801 N Fairfax St, Ste 306, Alexandria, VA 22314
T: (703) 548-7790
Founded: 1974; Members: 3500
Focus: Homeopathy
Periodicals
Directory of Homeopathic Physicians in the U.S. (bi-annually)
Homeopathy Today (monthly) 15782

National Center for Housing Management (NCHM), 1275 K St NW, Ste 700, Washington, DC 20005-4006
T: (202) 872-1717
Founded: 1972
Focus: Business Admin 15783

National Center for Law and Deafness (NCLD), 8000 Florida Av NE, Washington, DC 20002
T: (202) 651-5373; Fax: (202) 651-5381
Founded: 1975
Focus: Law; Otorhinolaryngology 15784

National Center for State Courts (NCSC), 300 Newport Av, Williamsburg, VA 23187
T: (804) 253-2000; Fax: (804) 220-0449
Founded: 1971
Focus: Law
Periodicals
Report and Master Calendar (monthly)
State Court Journal (quarterly)
Survey of Judicial Salaries (semi-annually) 15785

National Center for Youth Law (NCYL), 114 Sansome St, Ste 900, San Francisco, CA 94104
T: (415) 543-3307; Fax: (415) 956-9024
Founded: 1978
Focus: Law 15786

National Center on Arts and the Aging (NCAA), c/o National Council on the Aging, 409 Third St SW, Washington, DC 20024
T: (202) 479-1200; Fax: (202) 424-9046
Founded: 1973
Focus: Geriatrics 15787

National Center on Institutions and Alternatives (NCIA), 635 Slaters Ln, Ste G-100, Alexandria, VA 22314
T: (703) 684-0373; Fax: (703) 684-6037
Founded: 1979
Focus: Sociology; Law 15788

National Certification Agency for Medical Lab Personnel (NCA), POB 15945-289, Lenexa, KS 654-1622
T: (301) 654-1622; Fax: (301) 657-2909
Founded: 1977; Members: 65000
Gen Secr: Kathleen M. Greenberg
Focus: Med; Eng 15789

National Character Laboratory (NCL), 4635 Leeds Av, El Paso, TX 79903
T: (915) 562-5046; Fax: (915) 562-5046
Founded: 1971; Members: 75
Pres: A.J. Stuart
Focus: Anthro; Psych
Periodical
Newsletter (quarterly) 15790

National Coalition for Literacy (NCL), 50 E Huron, Chicago, IL 60611
T: (312) 280-3217; Fax: (312) 280-3224
Founded: 1981; Members: 37
Pres: Lennox McLendon
Focus: Lit 15791

National Coalition for Women and Girls in Education (NCWGE), c/o National Women's Law Center, 11 Dupont Circle NW, Ste 800, Washington, DC 20032
T: (202) 588-5180; Fax: (202) 588-5185
Founded: 1975; Members: 50
Pres: Verna Williams
Focus: Educ 15792

National Coalition of Alternative Community Schools (NCACS), POB 15036, Santa Fe, NM 87506
T: (505) 474-4312; E-Mail: djjv663@prodigy.com
Founded: 1976; Members: 1500
Gen Secr: Ed Nagel
Focus: Educ
Periodicals
Newsletter (bi-monthly)
There Ought to be Free Choice 15793

National College of District Attorneys (NCDA), c/o Law Center, University of Houston, Houston, TX 77204-6380
T: (713) 747-6232
Founded: 1969
Focus: Law 15794

National College of Foot Surgeons (NCFS), c/o Dr. Albert Apkarian, POB 264, Woodland Hills, CA 31365
T: (818) 340-0616
Founded: 1960
Gen Secr: Dr. Albert Apkarian
Focus: Surgery; Orthopedics
Periodical
Journal (annually) 15795

National Collegiate Conference Association (NCCA), c/o Raymond J. Freda, 21 N Main St, Apt 5, Albany, NY 12203
T: (518) 438-4935
Founded: 1947; Members: 2140
Gen Secr: Raymond J. Freda
Focus: Educ 15796

National Commission for Cooperative Education (NCCE), 360 Huntington Av, Boston, MA 02115-5096
T: (617) 373-3770; Fax: (617) 373-3463
Founded: 1962; Members: 265
Pres: Dr. Paul J. Stonely
Focus: Educ
Periodical
Co-op Education Undergraduate Program Directory (annually) 15797

National Committee for Latin and Greek (NCLG), c/o Virginia Barrett, 6669 Vinahaven, Cypress, CA 90630
T: (714) 373-0588
Founded: 1978; Members: 15
Pres: Virginia Barrett
Focus: Ling 15798

National Committee for Quality Health Care (NCQHC), 1500 K St NW, Ste 360, Washington, DC 20005
T: (202) 347-5731; Fax: (202) 347-5836
Founded: 1978; Members: 151
Focus: Public Health
Periodicals
Capital Outlock (4-8 times annually)
Quality Outlook (monthly) 15799

National Committee for the Furtherance of Jewish Education (NCFJE), 824 Eastern Pkwy, Brooklyn, NY 11213
T: (718) 735-0200; Fax: (718) 735-4455
Founded: 1940; Members: 400
Focus: Educ 15800

National Committee on American Foreign Policy (NCAFP), 320 Park Av, New York, NY 10022
T: (212) 224-1120; Fax: (212) 224-2524
Gen Secr: Dr. George D. Schwab
Focus: Poli Sci 15801

National Committee on the Treatment of Intractable Pain (NCTIP), 1333 New Hampshire Av NW, Washington, DC 20036
T: (202) 452-4836; Fax: (202) 293-4827
Founded: 1977; Members: 3500
Pres: Wayne Coy
Focus: Med; Anesthetics
Periodical
Newsletter (2-3 times annually) 15802

National Community Education Association (NCEA), 3929 Old Lee Hwy, Ste 91A, Fairfax, VA 22030
T: (703) 359-9873; E-Mail: ncea@ids2.idsonline.com; Fax: (703) 359-0972
Founded: 1966; Members: 1500

Gen Secr: Starla Jewell-Kelly
Focus: Educ
Periodicals
Community Education Journal (quarterly)
Community Education Today (monthly)
Membership Directory (annually) *15803*

National Conference of Bankruptcy Judges (NCBJ), c/o Christine J. Molick, 235 Secret Cove Dr, Lexington, SC 29072
T: (803) 957-6225
Founded: 1926; Members: 320
Gen Secr: Christine J. Molick
Focus: Law *15804*

National Conference of Black Lawyers (NCBL), 2 W 125 St, New York, NY 10027
T: (212) 864-4000
Founded: 1968; Members: 1000
Focus: Law *15805*

National Conference of Commissioners on Uniform State Laws (NCCUSL), 676 N Saint Clair, Ste 1700, Chicago, IL 60611
T: (312) 915-0195; Fax: (312) 915-0187
Founded: 1892; Members: 307
Focus: Law *15806*

National Conference of Regulatory Utility Commission Engineers (NCRUCE), c/o Tennessee Public Service Commission, 460 James Robertson Pkwy, Nashville, TN 37219
T: (615) 741-2844
Founded: 1923; Members: 150
Gen Secr: Glynn Blanton
Focus: Standards *15807*

National Conference of Standards Laboratories (NCSL), 1800 30 St, Ste 305B, Boulder, CO 80301
T: (303) 440-3339; Fax: (303) 440-3384
Founded: 1961; Members: 1200
Focus: Standards
Periodicals
Conference Proceedings (annually)
Newsletter (quarterly)
Training Information Directory (annually) . *15808*

National Conference of States on Building Codes and Standards (NCSBCS), 505 Huntmar Park Dr, Ste 210, Herndon, VA 22070
T: (703) 437-0100; Fax: (703) 481-3596
Founded: 1967; Members: 250
Focus: Civil Eng; Standards *15809*

National Conference of Yeshiva Principals (NCYP), 160 Broadway, New York, NY 10038
T: (212) 227-1000; Fax: (212) 406-6934
Founded: 1947; Members: 1000
Focus: Educ
Periodicals
Machberes Hamenahel (monthly)
Newsletter (monthly) *15810*

National Conference on Fluid Power (NCFP), 3333 N Mayfair Rd, Milwaukee, WI 53222
T: (414) 778-3368; Fax: (414) 778-3361
Founded: 1945
Focus: Energy
Periodical
National Conference on Fluid Power (annually)
. . . . *15811*

National Conference on Research in Language and Literacy (NCRLL), c/o Rudine Sims Bishop, College of Education, Ohio State University, 29 W Woodruff, Columbus, OH 43210
T: (614) 292-6968; Fax: (614) 292-4260
Founded: 1937; Members: 625
Pres: Rudine Sims Bishop
Focus: Ling; Educ
Periodicals
Directory (bi-annually)
Newsletter (semi-annually) *15812*

National Conference on the Advancement of Research (NCAR), c/o Southwest Research Institute, PO Drawer 28510, San Antonio, TX 78228
T: (210) 522-2202; Fax: (210) 520-5505
Founded: 1947; Members: 260
Gen Secr: A.W. Betts
Focus: Sci
Periodical
Proceedings (annually) *15813*

National Conference on Weights and Measures (NCWM), POB 4025, Gaithersburg, MD 20885
T: (301) 975-4004; Fax: (301) 926-0647
Founded: 1905; Members: 3000
Gen Secr: C.S. Brickenkamp
Focus: Standards
Periodicals
NBS Handbook (annually)
Report (annually) *15814*

National Congress for Community Economic Development (NCCED), 1875 Connecticut Av NW, Ste 524, Washington, DC 20009
T: (202) 234-5009
Founded: 1970; Members: 320
Focus: Sociology; Econ
Periodical
Resources for Community-Based Economic Development (monthly) *15815*

National Congress of Inventors Organizations (NCIO), c/o Intervention Services International Corporation, POB 93669, Los Angeles, CA 90093-6690

T: (213) 878-6959; Fax: (213) 962-8588
Founded: 1982; Members: 63
Gen Secr: Cordell Lundahl
Focus: Sci *15816*

National Consortium for Child Mental Health Services (NCCMHS), 601 13 St NW, Ste 400 North, Washington, DC 20005
T: (202) 347-8600; Fax: (202) 393-6137
Founded: 1971; Members: 5000
Gen Secr: Virginia Q. Anthony
Focus: Psychiatry *15817*

National Consortium of Arts and Letters for Historically Black Colleges and Universities (NCALHBCU), c/o Dr. Walter Anderson, 2555 Pennsylvania Av NW, Ste 818, Washington, DC 20037
T: (202) 833-1327
Founded: 1984; Members: 38
Gen Secr: Dr. Walter F. Anderson
Focus: Educ *15818*

National Consumer Law Center (NCLC), 18 Tremont St, Ste 400, Boston, MA 02108
T: (617) 523-8010; E-Mail: hn0639@handsnet.org; Fax: (617) 523-7398
Founded: 1969
Gen Secr: Willard Ogburn
Focus: Law *15819*

National Council for Accreditation of Teacher Education (NCATE), 2010 Massachusetts Av NW, Ste 500, Washington, DC 20036-1023
T: (202) 466-7496; Fax: (202) 296-6620
Founded: 1954; Members: 500
Pres: Arthur E. Wise
Focus: Adult Educ; Educ
Periodical
Annual List of Accredited Institutions (annually)
. . . . *15820*

National Council for Black Studies (NCBS), c/o Ohio State University, 208 Mount Hall, 1050 Carmack Rd, Columbus, OH 43210
T: (614) 292-1035; Fax: (614) 292-7363
Founded: 1975; Members: 500
Gen Secr: Jacqueline E. Wade
Focus: Educ *15821*

National Council for Culture and Art (NCCA), 1600 Broadway, Ste 611C, New York, NY 10019
T: (212) 757-7933
Founded: 1980; Members: 1500
Focus: Arts *15822*

National Council for Geographic Education (NCGE), c/o Indiana University of Pennsylvania, 16A Leonard Hall, Indiana, PA 15705
T: (412) 357-6290; E-Mail: clmccard@ grove.iup.edu; Fax: (412) 357-7708
Founded: 1915; Members: 3900
Gen Secr: Ruth I. Shirey
Focus: Geography; Educ
Periodicals
Journal of Geography (bi-monthly)
Perspective (5 times annually) *15823*

National Council for International Health (NCIH), 1701 K St NW, Ste 600, Washington, DC 20006-1503
T: (202) 833-5900; E-Mail: ncih@igc.org; Fax: (202) 833-0075
Gen Secr: Frank Lostumbo
Focus: Public Health *15824*

National Council for Research and Planning (NCRP), c/o Radford University, POB 6924, Radford, VA 24142
T: (703) 639-1263
Founded: 1977; Members: 256
Pres: Dr. Edith Carter
Focus: Educ
Periodicals
Community College Journal for Research and Planning (semi-annually)
New Directors for Two-Year Colleges (bi-annually)
Newsletter (quarterly) *15825*

National Council for Textile Education (NCTE), c/o Georgia Institute of Technology, School of Textile and Fiber Engineering, Atlanta, GA 30332-0295
T: (404) 894-2490; E-Mail: fred.cook@ tfl.gatech.edu; Fax: (404) 894-8780
Founded: 1933; Members: 30
Pres: Fred Cook
Focus: Adult Educ; Textiles *15826*

National Council for the Social Studies (NCSS), 3501 Newark St NW, Washington, DC 20016
T: (202) 966-7840; Fax: (202) 966-2061
Founded: 1921; Members: 26000
Focus: Sociology
Periodicals
Bulletin (3 times annually)
Social Education (7 times annually)
Social Studies Professionals (5 times annually)
. . . . *15827*

National Council for the Traditional Arts (NCTA), 1320 Fenwick Ln, Ste 200, Silver Spring, MD 20910
T: (301) 565-0654; Fax: (301) 565-0472
Founded: 1934
Focus: Arts *15828*

National Council for Torah Education (NCTE), c/o Religious Zionists of America, 25 W 26 St, New York, NY 10010
T: (212) 689-1414
Founded: 1939
Focus: Educ; Rel & Theol *15829*

National Council for Urban Economic Development (CUED), 1730 K St NW, Ste 915, Washington, DC 20006
T: (202) 223-4735; Fax: (202) 223-4745
Founded: 1967; Members: 1200
Focus: Urban Plan; Econ
Periodicals
Commentary (quarterly)
Legislative Report
Urban Economic Developments: Newsletter (monthly) *15830*

National Council of Athletic Training, c/o National Association for Sport and Physical Education, 1900 Association Dr, Reston, VA 22091
T: (703) 476-3410; Fax: (703) 476-9527
Founded: 1976; Members: 2000
Focus: Sports
Periodicals
Directory (annually)
Newsletter *15831*

National Council of Examiners for Engineering and Surveying (NCEE), POB 1686, Clemson, SC 29633
T: (803) 654-6824; Fax: (803) 654-6033
Founded: 1920; Members: 68
Focus: Eng *15832*

National Council of Forestry Association Executives (NCFAE), c/o MFPC, 146 State St, Augusta, ME 04330
T: (207) 287-2793
Founded: 1949; Members: 400
Gen Secr: William J. Vail
Focus: Forestry *15833*

National Council of Guilds for Infant Survival (NCIS), 8178 Nadine River Cir, Fountain Valley, CA 92708
T: (800) 247-4370
Founded: 1964; Members: 200
Pres: Chris Elliot
Focus: Pediatrics
Periodical
Newsletter (quarterly) *15834*

National Council of Juvenile and Family Court Judges (NCJFCJ), c/o University of Nevada, POB 8970, Reno, NV 89507
T: (702) 784-6012; Fax: (702) 784-6628
Founded: 1937; Members: 2500
Gen Secr: Louis W. McHardy
Focus: Law
Periodicals
Juvenile and Family Court Journal (quarterly)
Juvenile and Family Court Newsletter (8 times annually)
Juvenile and Family Law Digest (monthly) *15835*

National Council of State Directors of Community Colleges, c/o American Association of Community Colleges, 1 Dupont Cir, Ste 410, Washington, DC 20036-1176
T: (202) 728-0200; Fax: (202) 833-2467
Members: 38
Gen Secr: Florence Guyer
Focus: Educ *15836*

National Council of State Education Associations (NCSEA), 1201 NW 16 St, Washington, DC 20036
T: (202) 822-7745
Founded: 1966; Members: 130
Focus: Educ *15837*

National Council of State Pharmacy Association Executives (NCSPAE), c/o Al Melbane, POB 151, Chapel Hill, NC 27514-0151
T: (800) 852-7343; Fax: (919) 968-9430
Founded: 1927; Members: 52
Gen Secr: Al Melbane
Focus: Pharmacol *15838*

National Council of State Supervisors of Foreign Languages (NCSSFL), c/o Dept of Education, 4 Capitol Mall, Little Rock, AR 72201-1071
T: (501) 682-4398; Fax: (501) 682-4618
Founded: 1960; Members: 67
Focus: Ling; Educ *15839*

National Council of State Supervisors of Music (NCSSM), c/o June Hinckley, Dept of Education, 325 W Gaines St, Tallahassee, FL 32399
T: (904) 488-6047; Fax: (904) 487-0716
Founded: 1938; Members: 31
Gen Secr: June Hinckley
Focus: Music; Educ *15840*

National Council of Teachers of English (NCTE), 1111 Kenyon Rd, Urbana, IL 61801
T: (217) 328-3870; Fax: (217) 328-9645
Founded: 1911; Members: 120000
Focus: Ling; Educ
Periodicals
College English (8 times annually)
English Journal (8 times annually)
Language Arts (8 times annually) . . . *15841*

National Council of Teachers of Mathematics (NCTM), 1906 Association Dr, Reston, VA 22091-1593
T: (703) 620-9840; Fax: (703) 476-2970
Founded: 1920; Members: 98000
Focus: Math; Educ
Periodicals
Arithmetic Teacher (9 times annually)
Mathematics Teacher (9 times annually)
News Bulletin (9 times annually) *15842*

National Council of the Paper Industry for Air and Stream Improvement (NCASI), POB 13318, Research Triangle Park, NC 27709-3318
T: (919) 558-1999; Fax: (919) 558-1998
Founded: 1943; Members: 100
Pres: Dr. Isaiah Gellman
Focus: Eng
Periodical
Technical Bulletin (20 times annually) . . *15843*

National Council of University Research Administrators (NCURA), 1 Dupont Circle NW, Ste 220, Washington, DC 20036
T: (202) 466-3894
Founded: 1960; Members: 1900
Focus: Sci
Periodicals
Newsletter (bi-monthly)
Research Management Review (semi-annually)
. . . . *15844*

National Council of Urban Education Associations (NCUEA), c/o National Education Association, 1201 16 St NW, Washington, DC 20036
T: (202) 822-7137
Founded: 1964; Members: 201
Focus: Educ *15845*

National Council of World Affairs Organizations (NCWAO), 1726 M St NW, Ste 800, Washington, DC 20036
T: (202) 785-4703; Fax: (202) 833-2369
Gen Secr: G. Philip Hughes
Focus: Poli Sci *15846*

National Council on Agricultural Life and Labor Research Fund (NCALL), 20 E Division St, POB 1092, Dover, DE 19903
T: (302) 678-9400; Fax: (302) 678-9058
Founded: 1976; Members: 1200
Focus: Archit *15847*

National Council on Alcoholism and Drug Dependence (NCADD), 12 W 21 St, New York, NY 10010
T: (212) 206-6770; Fax: (212) 645-1690
Founded: 1944
Focus: Public Health *15848*

National Council on Crime and Delinquency (NCCD), 685 Market St, San Francisco, CA 94105
T: (415) 896-6223; Fax: (415) 956-1559
Founded: 1907; Members: 11000
Focus: Criminology
Periodicals
Crime and Delinquency (quarterly)
Criminal Justice Newsletter (bi-weekly)
Journal of Research in Crime and Delinquency (semi-annually) *15849*

National Council on Economic Education (NCEE), 1140 Av of the Americas, New York, NY 10036
T: (212) 730-7007; Fax: (212) 730-1793
Founded: 1949
Pres: Robert F. Duvall
Focus: Educ; Econ
Periodicals
Annual Report (annually)
Directory of Affiliated Councils and Centers (annually)
Economic Education Update (semi-annually)
. . . . *15850*

National Council on Employment Policy (NCEP), 1717 K St NW, Ste 1200, Washington, DC 20006
T: (202) 833-2530
Founded: 1964; Members: 7
Focus: Poli Sci; Econ *15851*

National Council on Family Relations (NCFR), 3989 Central Av NE, Ste 550, Minneapolis, MN 55421
T: (612) 781-9331; Fax: (612) 781-9348
Founded: 1938; Members: 3900
Focus: Sociology; Family Plan *15852*

National Council on Gene Resources (NCGR), 1738 Thousand Oaks Blvd, Berkeley, CA 94707
T: (510) 524-8973
Founded: 1980
Focus: Genetics *15853*

National Council on Measurement in Education (NCME), 1230 17 St NW, Washington, DC 20036
T: (202) 223-9318; Fax: (202) 775-1824
Founded: 1938; Members: 2100
Focus: Educ
Periodicals
Educational Measurement: Issues and Practice (quarterly)
Journal of Educational Measurement (quarterly)
. . . . *15854*

National Council on Public History (NCPH), c/o David G. Vanderstel, Indiana University-Purdue University at Indiana, 327 Cavanaugh, 425 University Blvd, Indianapolis, IN 46202
T: (317) 274-2716; E-Mail: ncph@iupui.edu; Fax: (317) 274-2347
Founded: 1979; Members: 1500
Gen Secr: David G. Vanderstel
Focus: Hist; Sociology 15855

National Council on Radiation Protection and Measurements (NCRPM), 7910 Woodmont Av, Ste 800, Bethesda, MD 20814
T: (301) 657-2652; Fax: (301) 907-8768
Founded: 1929; Members: 75
Focus: Radiology
Periodicals
Lauriston S. Taylor Lectures (annually)
NCRP Commentaries
NCRP Reports
Proceedings of the Annual Meeting (annually) 15856

National Council on Religion and Public Education (NCRPE), c/o Iowa State University, N155 Lagomarcino Hall, Ames, IA 50011
T: (515) 294-2881; Fax: (515) 294-6206
Founded: 1971; Members: 550
Focus: Rel & Theol; Educ 15857

National Council on the Aging, 409 3rd St SW, Washington, DC 20024
T: (202) 479-1200; Fax: (202) 479-0735
Focus: Geriatrics 15858

National Crime Prevention Institute (NCPI), c/o University of Louisville, Brigman Hall, Louisville, KY 40292-0001
T: (502) 852-6987; Fax: (502) 852-6990
Founded: 1971
Gen Secr: Wilbur Rykert
Focus: Criminology 15859

National Criminal Defense College (NCDC), c/o Mercer Law School, Macon, GA 31207
T: (912) 746-4151; Fax: (912) 743-0160
Founded: 1985
Focus: Law; Criminology 15860

National Dairy Council (NDC), 10255 Higgins, Rosemont, IL 60018
T: (708) 803-2000
Founded: 1915; Members: 24
Focus: Dairy Sci 15861

National Democratic Institute for International Affairs (NDIIA), 1717 Massachussets Av NW, Ste 503, Washington, DC 20036
T: (202) 328-3136; Fax: (202) 939-3166
Gen Secr: Kenneth D. Wollack
Focus: Poli Sci 15862

National Dental Assistants Association (NDAA), c/o Dr. Robert Johns, 5506 Connecticut Av NW, Ste 24, Washington, DC 20015
T: (202) 244-7555; Fax: (202) 244-5992
Founded: 1964; Members: 500
Gen Secr: Dr. Robert Johns
Focus: Dent 15863

National Dental Association (NDA), 5506 Connecticut Av NW, Ste 24, Washington, DC 20015
T: (202) 244-7555; Fax: (202) 244-5992
Founded: 1913; Members: 2500
Focus: Dent
Periodicals
Journal (quarterly)
Newsletter (bi-monthly) 15864

National Dental Hygienists' Association (NDHA), 28315 Kalong Cir W, Southfield, MI 48034-5658
T: (810) 358-0432; Fax: (313) 446-1839
Founded: 1932; Members: 80
Pres: Dr. Barbara Purifoy-Seldon
Focus: Dent; Hygiene 15865

National Denturist Association (NDA), POB 40307, Portland, OR 97240-0307
T: (503) 292-7994
Founded: 1975; Members: 350
Gen Secr: Dr. James Davis
Focus: Dent 15866

National Digestive Diseases Information Clearinghouse (NDDIC), 2 Information Way, Bethesda, MD 20892-3570
T: (301) 654-3810; Fax: (301) 907-8906
Founded: 1980
Gen Secr: Kathy Kranzfelder
Focus: Gastroenter
Periodical
Directory of Digestive Diseases Organizations (annually) 15867

National District Attorneys Association (NDAA), 99 Canal CN Plaza, Ste 510, Alexandria, VA 22314
T: (703) 549-9222; Fax: (703) 836-3195
Founded: 1950; Members: 7000
Gen Secr: N. Flanagan
Focus: Law
Periodical
The Prosecutor (bi-monthly) 15868

National Dry Bean Council (NDBC), 1101 Connecticut Av NW, Ste 700, Washington, DC 20036
T: (202) 857-1169
Founded: 1950; Members: 12
Focus: Food 15869

National Earth Science Teachers Association (NESTA), 2000 Florida Av NW, Washington, DC 20009
T: (202) 462-6900; E-Mail: fireton@kosmos.agu.org; Fax: (202) 328-0566
Founded: 1983; Members: 1000
Focus: Geology; Educ 15870

National Economic Association (NEA), c/o School of Business, University of Michigan, Ann Arbor, MI 48109-1234
T: (313) 763-0121
Founded: 1969
Gen Secr: Alfred L. Edwards
Focus: Finance 15871

National Education Association of the United States, 1201 16 St NW, Washington, DC 20036
T: (202) 833-4000
Founded: 1857; Members: 2000000
Gen Secr: Don Cameron
Focus: Educ
Periodicals
NEA Now (weekly)
NEA Today (9 times annually)
Today's Education (annually) 15872

National Energy Management Institute, 601 N Fairfax St, Ste 160, Alexandria, VA 22314
T: (703) 739-7100; Fax: (703) 683-7615
Founded: 1981
Focus: Energy
Periodical
News from EMI (monthly) 15873

National Energy Resources Organization (NERO), 919 18 St NW, Ste 450, Washington, DC 20006
T: (202) 466-6535; Fax: (703) 739-9248
Founded: 1975; Members: 450
Focus: Energy 15874

National Environmental Health Association (NEHA), 720 S Colorado Blvd, Ste 970, Denver, CO 80222
T: (303) 756-9090; Fax: (303) 691-9490
Founded: 1930; Members: 5700
Focus: Public Health
Periodical
Journal of Environmental Health (bi-monthly) 15875

National Federation Interscholastic Music Association (NFIMA), 11724 NW Plaza Cir, POB 20626, Kansas City, MO 64195-0626
T: (816) 464-5400; Fax: (816) 464-5571
Founded: 1983; Members: 605
Focus: Music 15876

National Federation of Abstracting and Information Services (NFAIS), 1518 Walnut St, Ste 307, Philadelphia, PA 19102
T: (215) 893-1561; Fax: (215) 893-1564
Founded: 1958; Members: 70
Pres: Taissa Kusma; Gen Secr: Richard T. Kaser
Focus: Educ
Periodicals
Membership Directory (annually)
NFAIS Newsletter (monthly)
Report Series (quarterly) 15877

National Federation of Catholic Physicians Guilds (NFCPG), 850 Elm Grove Rd, Elm Grove, WI 53122
T: (414) 784-3435; Fax: (414) 782-8788
Founded: 1932; Members: 3500
Focus: Physiology
Periodical
The Linacre (quarterly) 15878

National Federation of Modern Language Teachers Associations (NFMLTA), c/o Dr. Gerard Ervin, Slavic Dept, Ohio State University, 232 Cunz Hall, Columbus, OH 43210
T: (614) 451-7894; E-Mail: 76703.2063@compuserve.com; Fax: (614) 451-7924
Founded: 1916; Members: 15
Gen Secr: Dr. Gerard Ervin
Focus: Ling; Educ
Periodical
The Modern Language Journal (quarterly) 15879

National Federation of Societies for Clinical Social Work (NFSCSW), POB 3740, Arlington, VA 22203
T: (703) 522-3866; Fax: (703) 522-3866
Founded: 1971
Focus: Sociology
Periodical
Clinical Social Work Journal (quarterly) . 15880

National Federation of State Poetry Societies (NFSPS), c/o Ralph Hammond, POB 486, Arab, AL 35016
T: (205) 586-4151
Founded: 1959; Members: 6600
Pres: Ralph Hammond
Focus: Lit
Periodical
Strophes (quarterly) 15881

National FFA Organization (NFFAO), 5632 Mount Vernon Memorial Hwy, POB 15160, Alexandria, VA 22309-0160
T: (703) 360-3600; Fax: (703) 360-5524
Founded: 1928; Members: 385376
Focus: Adult Educ; Agri 15882

National Fire Protection Association (NFPA), 1 Batterymarch Park, Quincy, MA 02269-9101
T: (617) 770-3000; Fax: (617) 770-0700
Founded: 1896; Members: 57000
Focus: Safety
Periodical
Fire Journal (bi-monthly) 15883

National Forensic Association (NFA), c/o Dept of Speech Communication, Otterbein College, Westerville, OH 43081
T: (614) 898-1753; Fax: (614) 898-1200
Founded: 1974; Members: 300
Pres: Dr. Christina Reynolds
Focus: Ling 15884

National Forensic League (NFL), POB 38, Ripon, WI 54971
T: (414) 748-6206
Founded: 1925; Members: 798000
Focus: Law
Periodical
Rostrum (monthly) 15885

National Foundation for Advancement in the Arts (NFAA), 800 Brickell Av, Ste 500, Miami, FL 33131
T: (305) 377-1140; E-Mail: NFAA@ARTBANK.com; Fax: (305) 377-1149
Founded: 1981; Members: 750
Pres: Dr. William H. Banchs
Focus: Arts 15886

National Foundation for Brain Research (NFBR), 1250 24 St NW, St 300, Washington, DC 20037
T: (202) 293-5453; Fax: (202) 466-2888
Founded: 1953; Members: 230
Focus: Pathology
Periodicals
Annual Report (annually)
Newsletter 15887

National Foundation for Non-Invasive Diagnostics (NFNID), 103 Carnegie Center, Ste 311, Princeton, NJ 08540
T: (609) 520-1300; Fax: (609) 452-8544
Founded: 1977
Focus: Med 15888

National Foundation of Dentistry for the Handicapped (NFDH), 1800 Glenarm Pl, Ste 500, Denver, CO 80202
T: (303) 298-9650; Fax: (303) 573-0267
Founded: 1974
Gen Secr: Larry Coffee
Focus: Dent 15889

National Genealogical Society (NGS), 4527 17 St N, Arlington, VA 22207-2399
T: (703) 525-0050; Fax: (703) 525-0052
Founded: 1903; Members: 13000
Focus: Genealogy 15890

National Geographic Society (NGS), 17 and M Sts NW, Washington, DC 20036
T: (202) 857-7000
Founded: 1888
Pres: Reg Murphy
Focus: Geography
Periodicals
National Geographic (monthly)
National Geographic World (monthly) . . 15891

National Grants Management Association (NGMA), POB 5333, Rockville, MD 20848-5333
T: (301) 871-0730; Fax: (301) 253-8809
Founded: 1978; Members: 400
Pres: Cynthia J. Schwimer
Focus: Finance 15892

National Guild of Catholic Psychiatrists (NGCP), c/o Taylor Manor Hospital, 4100 College Av, Ellicott City, MD 21041-0396
T: (410) 465-3322; Fax: (410) 461-7075
Founded: 1949; Members: 75
Focus: Psychiatry
Periodical
Bulletin (annually) 15893

National Guild of Community Schools of the Arts (NGCSA), POB 8018, Englewood, NJ 07631
T: (201) 871-3337; Fax: (201) 871-7639
Founded: 1937; Members: 300
Focus: Arts; Music; Educ
Periodical
Guildletter (bi-monthly) 15894

National Guild of Piano Teachers (NGPT), 808 Rio Grande, POB 1807, Austin, TX 78767
T: (512) 478-5775
Founded: 1929; Members: 11868
Focus: Music; Educ 15895

National Hardwood Lumber Association (NHLA), POB 34518, Memphis, TN 38184-0518
T: (901) 377-1818; Fax: (901) 382-6419
Founded: 1898; Members: 1300
Gen Secr: Ernest J. Stebbins
Focus: Forestry
Periodical
Proceedings: Annual Hardwood Symposium 15896

National Health Council (NHC), 1730 M St NW, Ste 500, Washington, DC 20036
T: (202) 785-3910; Fax: (202) 785-5923
Founded: 1920; Members: 130
Pres: Joseph C. Isaacs
Focus: Public Health 15897

National Health Federation (NHF), POB 688, Monrovia, CA 91016
T: (818) 357-2181; Fax: (818) 303-0642
Founded: 1955; Members: 20000
Focus: Public Health
Periodical
Health Freedom News (11 times annually) 15898

National Health Law Program (NHeLP), 2639 S La Cienega Blvd, Los Angeles, CA 90034
T: (310) 204-6010; Fax: (310) 204-0891
Members: 8
Focus: Public Health
Periodical
Health Advocate (quarterly) 15899

National Health Lawyers Association (NHLA), 1120 Connecticut Av NW, Ste 950, Washington, DC 20036
T: (202) 833-1100; Fax: (202) 833-1105
Founded: 1971; Members: 7000
Focus: Law; Public Health
Periodicals
Health Law Digest (monthly)
Health Lawyers News Report (monthly) . 15900

National Hearing Conservation Association (NHCA), 611 E Wells St, Milwaukee, WI 53202
T: (414) 276-6045; Fax: (414) 276-3349
Founded: 1977; Members: 700
Gen Secr: Lee-Ann Wiensch
Focus: Otorhinolaryngology 15901

National Heart Council (NHC), 306 W Joppa Rd, Baltimore, MD 21204
T: (410) 494-0300; Fax: (410) 494-0725
Founded: 1982
Pres: Howard H. Farrington
Focus: Cardiol 15902

National Home Study Council (NHSC), 1601 18 St NW, Ste 2, Washington, DC 20009
T: (202) 234-5100
Founded: 1926; Members: 92
Focus: Educ 15903

National Hormone and Pituitary Program (NHPP), 685 Lofstrand Dr, Rockville, MD 20850
T: (301) 309-3667; Fax: (301) 340-9245
Founded: 1963
Gen Secr: Dr. Philip Smith
Focus: Med; Microbio 15904

National Housing Conference (NHC), 815 15 St NW, Ste 711, Washington, DC 20005
T: (202) 393-5772; E-Mail: nhc@nhcdbase; Fax: (202) 393-5656
Founded: 1931; Members: 500
Gen Secr: Robert J. Reid
Focus: Archit
Periodicals
Newsletter (monthly)
NHC Policy and Resolutions (annually) . 15905

National Humane Education Society (NHES), 521A E Market St, Leesburg, VA 22075
T: (703) 777-8319; Fax: (703) 771-4048
Founded: 1948; Members: 200000
Pres: Anna Briggs
Focus: Educ
Periodical
NHES Quarterly Journal (quarterly) . . . 15906

National Humanities Center (NHC), 7 Alexander Dr, POB 12256, Research Triangle Park, NC 27709
T: (919) 549-0661
Founded: 1976; Members: 40
Focus: Humanities
Periodical
Newsletter (3 times annually) 15907

National Hydropower Association (NHA), 122 C St NW, Washington, DC 20001
T: (202) 383-2530; E-Mail: hydroinfo@aol.com; Fax: (202) 383-2531
Founded: 1983; Members: 150
Gen Secr: Linda Church Ciocci
Focus: Energy; Water Res
Periodicals
Hydro Regulatory Report (monthly)
NHA News from Washington (monthly) . 15908

National Identification Program for the Advancement of Women in Higher Education Administration (NIP), c/o Office of Women in Higher Education, American Council on Education, 1 Dupont Circle NW, Washington, DC 20036
T: (202) 939-9390; Fax: (202) 833-4760
Founded: 1977
Focus: Educ 15909

National Immigration Law Center (NILC), 1102 Crenshaw Blvd, Ste 101, Los Angeles, CA 90019
T: (213) 487-2531; Fax: (213) 964-7940
Founded: 1977
Gen Secr: Charles Wheeler
Focus: Law
Periodical
Legalization Update (monthly) 15910

National Indian Education Association (NIEA), 121 Oronoco St, Alexandria, VA 22314
T: (703) 838-2870; Fax: (703) 838-1620
Founded: 1970; Members: 2000
Gen Secr: Lorraine P. Edmo
Focus: Educ
Periodical
Indian Education Newsletter (quarterly) . 15911

National Industrial Zoning Committee (NIZC), 1858 Chatfield Rd, Columbus, OH 43221
T: (614) 488-9001
Founded: 1948; Members: 8
Focus: Econ 15912

National Information Center for Educational Media (NICEM), POB 8640, Albuquerque, NM 87198
T: (505) 265-3591; E-Mail: nicem@nicem.com; Fax: (505) 256-1080
Founded: 1967
Pres: Marjorie M.K. Hlava
Focus: Educ 15913

National Information Service for Earthquake Engineering (NISEE), c/o Earthquake Engineering Research Center, University of California, 1301 S 46 St, Richmond, CA 94804-4698
T: (510) 231-9403; E-Mail: eerclib@eerc.berkeley.edu; Fax: (510) 231-9461
Founded: 1971
Gen Secr: Katherine A. Frohmberg
Focus: Eng; Geophys
Periodicals
Abstract Journal in Earthquake Engineering (semi-annually)
Computer Applications Program Catalog (irregularly)
Current Abstract Update Service (quarterly)
Customized Current Information Service (quarterly)
Earthquake Engineering Research Center Reports (irregularly)
Library Acquisitions Alert (irregularly) . . 15914

National Institute for Burn Medicine (NIBM), POB 15138, Ann Arbor, MI 48106-5138
T: (313) 769-9000; Fax: (313) 769-9009
Founded: 1968
Gen Secr: Claudella A. Jones
Focus: Med
Periodical
National Burn Information Exchange Newsletter (2-3 times annually) 15915

National Institute for Certification in Engineering Technologies (NICET), 1420 King St, Alexandria, VA 22314-2794
T: (703) 684-2835
Founded: 1981
Focus: Eng
Periodical
Newsletter 15916

National Institute for Farm Safety (NIFS), 2-70 Agriculture Engineering, Columbia, MO 65211
T: (573) 882-6385; E-Mail: david_e_baker@muccmail.missouri.edu; Fax: (573) 884-7993
Founded: 1962; Members: 204
Gen Secr: David E. Baker
Focus: Safety 15917

National Institute for Public Policy (NIPP), 3031 Javier Rd, Fairfax, VA 22031
T: (703) 698-0563
Founded: 1981
Focus: Poli Sci 15918

National Institute for Rehabilitation Engineering (NIRE), POB T, Hewitt, NJ 07421
T: (201) 853-6585
Founded: 1967
Focus: Rehabil; Eng 15919

National Institute of Ceramic Engineers (NICE), c/o Diane C. Folz, Dept of Materials Science and Engineering, University of Florida, POB 116400, Gainesville, FL 32611-6400
T: (352) 392-3163; E-Mail: dfolz@mse.ufl.edu; Fax: (352) 846-2033
Founded: 1937; Members: 750
Gen Secr: Diane Folz
Focus: Eng 15920

National Institute of Management Counsellors (NIMC), POB 193, Great Neck, NY 11022
T: (516) 482-5683
Founded: 1954; Members: 250
Focus: Business Admin 15921

National Institute of Science (NIS), c/o Dr. Arthur C. Washington, Tennessee State University, 3500 John Merritt Blvd, Nashville, TN 37209-1561
T: (615) 963-5332; Fax: (615) 963-5326
Founded: 1942; Members: 843
Gen Secr: Dr. Arthur C. Washington
Focus: Sci
Periodicals
Newsletter (semi-annually)
Transactions (annually) 15922

National Institute of Social Sciences (NISS), 150 Amsterdam Av, New York, NY 10023
Founded: 1899; Members: 900
Pres: J. Sinclair Armstrong; Gen Secr: Bruce E. Balding
Focus: Sociology 15923

National Institute of Steel Detailing (NISD), c/o Don Pope, POB 121484, Arlington, VA 76012
T: (817) 860-9890; Fax: (817) 860-9891
Founded: 1969; Members: 141
Pres: Don Pope
Focus: Metallurgy 15924

National Jewish Center for Immunology and Respiratory Medicine (NJCIRM), 1400 Jackson St, Denver, CO 80206
T: (303) 388-4461
Founded: 1978; Members: 1200
Focus: Med 15925

National Judicial College (NJC), c/o Judicial College, University of Nevada, Reno, NV 89557
T: (702) 784-6747; Fax: (702) 784-4234
Founded: 1963
Focus: Law 15926

National League of American PEN Women (NLAPW), 1300 17 St NW, Washington, DC 20036
T: (202) 785-1997
Founded: 1897; Members: 5000
Focus: Arts; Music; Lit
Periodicals
The PEN Woman (9 times annually)
Roster (bi-annually) 15927

National Librarians Association (NLA), POB 486, Alma, MI 48801
T: (517) 463-7227; Fax: (517) 463-8694
Founded: 1975; Members: 150
Gen Secr: Peter Dollard
Focus: Libraries & Bk Sci
Periodical
The National Librarian (quarterly) . . . 15928

National Marine Educators Association (NMEA), POB 512515, Pacific Grove, CA 93950
T: (408) 648-4841; Fax: (408) 372-8471
Founded: 1976; Members: 1200
Focus: Adult Educ
Periodicals
Current: The Journal of Marine Education (quarterly)
NMEA News (quarterly) 15929

National Mastitis Council (NMC), 1840 Wilson Blvd, Ste 400, Arlington, VA 22201
T: (703) 243-8268; Fax: (703) 931-4520
Founded: 1961; Members: 1900
Gen Secr: Anne Saeman
Focus: Vet Med
Periodical
Annual Meeting Proceedings 15930

National Materials Advisory Board (NMAB), 2101 Constitution Av NW, Washington, DC 20418
T: (202) 334-3505
Founded: 1951; Members: 16
Focus: Materials Sci
Periodical
Newsletter (quarterly) 15931

National Medical and Dental Association (NMDA), 72-41 Grand Av, Maspeth, NY 11378
T: (718) 478-3333
Founded: 1910; Members: 400
Focus: Med; Dent
Periodical
Bulletin (annually) 15932

National Medical Association (NMA), 1012 Tenth St NW, Washington, DC 20001
T: (202) 347-1895; Fax: (202) 842-3293
Founded: 1895; Members: 14500
Focus: Med
Periodicals
Journal of the National Medical Association (monthly)
National Medical Association Newsletter (quarterly) 15933

National Medical Fellowships (NMF), 254 W 31 St, New York, NY 10001
T: (212) 714-0933; Fax: (212) 239-9718
Founded: 1946
Focus: Educ; Med 15934

National Mental Health Association (NMHA), 1021 Prince St, Alexandria, VA 22314-2971
T: (703) 684-7722; Fax: (703) 684-5968
Founded: 1950; Members: 440
Pres: Michael M. Faenza
Focus: Psychiatry
Periodical
Focus (quarterly) 15935

National Middle School Association (NMSA), 2600 Corporate Exchange Dr, Ste 370, Columbus, OH 43231
T: (614) 895-4730; Fax: (614) 895-4750
Founded: 1973; Members: 20000
Gen Secr: Sue Swaim
Focus: Educ
Periodicals
Middle Ground (semi-annually)
Middle School Journal (quarterly)
Target (semi-annually) 15936

National Multiple Sclerosis Society (NMSS), 733 Third Av, New York, NY 10017
T: (212) 986-3240; Fax: (212) 986-7981
Founded: 1946; Members: 470000
Focus: Med; Pathology
Periodical
Inside MS (quarterly) 15937

National Music Council (NMC), c/o Dept of Music, Kingsborough College, 2001 Oriental Blvd, Brooklyn, NY 11235
T: (718) 368-5179
Founded: 1940; Members: 50
Gen Secr: Dr. David Sanders
Focus: Music
Periodical
NMC News 15938

National Old Timers' Association of the Energy Industry (NOTAEI), POB 168, Mineola, NY 11501
T: (516) 431-4668; Fax: (516) 431-9850
Founded: 1926; Members: 1000
Focus: Energy 15939

National Opera Association (NOA), c/o Arvio Knutsen, 6805 Tenneyson Dr, McLean, VA 22101
T: (703) 790-3393
Founded: 1955; Members: 600
Pres: Robert Hansen
Focus: Music
Periodicals
NOA Newsletter (quarterly)
Opera Journal (quarterly) 15940

National Optometric Association (NOA), 1489 E Livingston Av, Columbus, OH 43205
T: (614) 253-5593
Founded: 1969; Members: 350
Focus: Ophthal
Periodical
Newsletter (quarterly) 15941

National Orchestral Association (NOA), 575 Lexington Av, New York, NY 10022
T: (212) 350-4676; Fax: (212) 350-1440
Founded: 1930; Members: 75
Pres: Frances J. Kennedy
Focus: Music
Periodicals
Fact Sheet (annually)
NOA News (semi-annually) 15942

National Organization for Continuing Education of Roman Catholic Clergy (NOCERCC), 1337 W Ohio St, Chicago, IL 60622
T: (312) 226-1890
Founded: 1973; Members: 425
Focus: Educ 15943

National Organization for Rare Disorders (NORD), POB 8923, New Fairfield, CT 06812-1783
T: (203) 746-6518; Fax: (203) 746-6481
Founded: 1983; Members: 40000
Focus: Med 15944

National Organization of Minority Architects (NOMA), c/o School of Architecture and Planning, Howard University, 2366 Sixth St, Washington, DC 20059
T: (804) 788-0338; Fax: (804) 649-8502
Founded: 1971; Members: 250
Focus: Archit
Periodicals
Newsletter (quarterly)
Roster of Minority Firms 15945

National Organization on Legal Problems of Education (NOLPE), 3601 W 29 St, Ste 223, Topeka, KS 66614
T: (913) 273-3550
Founded: 1954; Members: 1800
Focus: Law; Educ 15946

National Orthotic and Prosthetic Research Institute (NOPRI), POB 491, Lenox Hill, NY 10021
T: (212) 755-3366
Founded: 1969; Members: 10
Focus: Rehabil 15947

National Osteopathic Guild Association (NOGA), c/o Auxiliary to the American Osteopathic Association, 142 E Ontario St, Chicago, IL 60611
T: (312) 266-5640; Fax: (312) 280-3860
Founded: 1955; Members: 1800
Pres: Laverne Furlong
Focus: Pathology
Periodical
Newsletter (quarterly) 15948

National Perinatal Association (NPA), 3500 E Fletcher Av, Ste 209, Tampa, FL 33613
T: (813) 971-1008; E-Mail: npaonline@aol.com; Fax: (813) 971-9306
Founded: 1976; Members: 1500
Gen Secr: Julie A. Leachman
Focus: Gynecology
Periodicals
Newsletter (bi-monthly)
Proceedings (annually) 15949

National Pest Control Association (NPCA), 8100 Oak St, Dunn Loring, VA 22027
T: (703) 573-8330; Fax: (703) 573-4116
Founded: 1933; Members: 2300
Focus: Microbio 15950

National Pharmaceutical Association (NPhA), c/o College of Pharmacy and Pharmacological Sciences, Howard University, POB 835332, Richardson, TX 75083
T: (214) 806-6530; Fax: (214) 235-4211
Founded: 1947; Members: 325
Pres: Dr. Billie McMiller
Focus: Pharmacol
Periodical
Journal (quarterly) 15951

National Photography Instructors Association (NPIA), 1255 Hill Dr, Eagle Rock, CA 90041
T: (213) 254-1549; Fax: (213) 254-1549
Focus: Photo 15952

National Piano Foundation (NPF), c/o Brenda Dillon, 4020 McEwen St, Ste 105, Dallas, TX 75244
T: (214) 233-9107; Fax: (214) 490-4219
Founded: 1962
Gen Secr: Donald W. Dillon
Focus: Music
Periodical
NPF Piano News (quarterly) 15953

National Plant Board (NPB), c/o Div of Plant Industries, North Carolina Dept of Agriculture, POB 27647, Raleigh, NC 27611
T: (919) 733-3933; Fax: (919) 733-1041
Founded: 1925; Members: 51
Pres: Howard Singletary Jr.
Focus: Agri 15954

National Podriatic Medical Association (NPMA), c/o Raymond E. Lee, 1706 E 87 St, Chicago, IL 60617
T: (312) 374-1616; Fax: (312) 374-5860
Founded: 1971; Members: 200
Gen Secr: Raymond E. Lee
Focus: Orthopedics
Periodicals
Annual Seminar Ad Book
Newsletter (annually) 15955

National Psoriasis Foundation (NPF), 6600 SW 92 St, Ste 300, Portland, OR 97223-7195
T: (503) 244-7404; E-Mail: 76135.2746@compuserve.com; Fax: (503) 245-0626
Founded: 1968; Members: 35000
Gen Secr: Gail M. Zimmerman
Focus: Derm 15956

National Psychological Association for Psychoanalysis (NPAP), 150 W 13 St, New York, NY 10011
T: (212) 924-7440; Fax: (212) 989-7543
Founded: 1946; Members: 355
Focus: Psychoan
Periodicals
Bulletin (bi-annually)
News & Reviews (quarterly)
The Psychoanalytic Review (quarterly) . . 15957

National Ramah Commission (NRC), 3080 Broadway, New York, NY 10027
T: (212) 678-8881; Fax: (212) 749-8251
Founded: 1953; Members: 45
Focus: Rel & Theol 15958

National Reading Conference (NRC), 200 N Michigan Av, Ste 300, Chicago, IL 60601
T: (312) 541-1272; Fax: (312) 541-1271
Founded: 1950; Members: 1000
Gen Secr: Judith Burnison
Focus: Educ
Periodicals
Journal of Reading Behavior (quarterly)
Yearbook (annually) 15959

National Records Management Council (NAREMCO), 60 E 42 St, New York, NY 10165
T: (212) 697-0290
Founded: 1948
Focus: Public Admin; Business Admin
Periodicals
Information Alert (monthly)
NAREMCO Report (quarterly) 15960

National Registry in Clinical Chemistry (NRCC), POB 27848, Washington, DC 20038-7848
T: (202) 393-7140; Fax: (202) 393-4059
Founded: 1967; Members: 700
Gen Secr: Gilbert E. Smith
Focus: Chem
Periodical
Directory (annually) 15961

National Rehabilitation Association (NRA), 633 S Washington St, Alexandria, VA 22314
T: (703) 836-0850; Fax: (703) 836-0848
Founded: 1925; Members: 17000
Focus: Rehabil
Periodicals
Journal of Rehabilitation (quarterly)
Newsletter (8 times annually) 15962

National Research Council (NRC), 2101 Constitution Av NW, Washington, DC 20418
T: (202) 334-2000; Fax: (202) 334-2158
Founded: 1916; Members: 9500
Focus: Sci; Eng
Periodical
News Report (10 times annually) . . . 15963

National Resident Matching Program (NRMP), 2450 N St NW, Ste 201, Washington, DC 20037-1141
T: (202) 828-0676
Founded: 1951; Members: 30000
Gen Secr: Edward Stemmler
Focus: Educ; Med 15964

National Resource Center for Consumers of Legal Services (NRCCLS), POB 340, Gloucester, VA 23061
T: (804) 693-9330; Fax: (804) 693-7363
Founded: 1977
Focus: Law
Periodical
Legal Plan Letter (bi-weekly) 15965

National Rural Education Association (NREA), c/o Colorado State University, 230 Education Bldg, Fort Collins, CO 80523
T: (303) 491-7022; Fax: (303) 491-1317
Founded: 1907; Members: 1000
Gen Secr: Joseph T. Newlin
Focus: Educ 15966

National Safety Council (NSC), 1121 Spring Lake Dr, Itasca, IL 60143
T: (708) 285-1121; Fax: (708) 285-1315
Founded: 1913; Members: 12000
Pres: T.C. Gilchrest
Focus: Safety
Periodicals
Fleet Safety Newsletter (bi-monthly)
Forest Industries Newsletter (bi-monthly)
Glass and Ceramics Newsletter (bi-monthly)
Health Care Newsletter (bi-monthly)
Metals Newsletter (monthly)
Mining Newsletter (bi-monthly)
Petroleum Newsletter (bi-monthly)
Power Press and Forging Newsletter (bi-monthly)
Printing and Publishing Newsletter (bi-monthly)
Public Employee Newsletter (bi-monthly)
Public Utilities Newsletter (bi-monthly)
Railroad Newsletter (bi-monthly) 15967

National Safety Management Society (NSMS), 12 Pickens Ln, Weaverville, NC 28787
T: (704) 645-5229; Fax: (704) 645-5229
Founded: 1968; Members: 750
Focus: Safety
Periodical
Update Newsletter (10 times annually) . 15968

National School Boards Association (NSBA), 1680 Duke St, Alexandria, VA 22314
T: (703) 838-6722; Fax: (703) 683-7590
Founded: 1940; Members: 53
Focus: Educ
Periodicals
The American School Board Journal (monthly)
Beliefs and Policies (annually)
The Executive Educator (monthly)
Inquiry and Analysis (bi-monthly)
Leadership Reports (quarterly)
School Board News (bi-weekly)
Updating School Board Policies (monthly) 15969

National School Public Relations Association (NSPRA), 1501 Lee Hwy, Ste 201, Arlington, VA 22209
T: (703) 528-5840; Fax: (703) 528-7017
Founded: 1935; Members: 2000
Focus: Educ
Periodicals
Education USA (weekly)
Paragraphs (monthly)
Starts in the Classroom (monthly) . . . 15970

National Schools Committee for Economic Education (NSCEE), 86 Valley Rd, POB 295, Cos Cob, CT 06807
T: (203) 869-1706
Founded: 1953; Members: 465
Focus: Educ; Econ 15971

National Science Teachers Association (NSTA), 1840 Wilson Blvd, Arlington, VA 22201-3000
Founded: 1895; Members: 53000
Pres: Shelley A. Fisher Jr.; Gen Secr: Bill G. Aldridge
Focus: Educ
Periodicals
Journal of College Science Teaching (bi-monthly)
Science and Children (8 times annually)
Science Scope (8 times annually)
The Science Teacher (9 times annually) 15972

National Sculpture Society (NSS), 1177 Av of the Americas, New York, NY 10036
T: (212) 764-5645; Fax: (212) 764-5651
Founded: 1893; Members: 4820
Gen Secr: Gwen Pier
Focus: Fine Arts
Periodicals
Newsletter (monthly)
Sculpture Review (quarterly) 15973

National Society for Experiential Education (NSEE), 3509 Haworth Dr, Ste 207, Raleigh, NC 27609-7229
T: (919) 787-3263
Founded: 1978; Members: 1300
Focus: Educ 15974

National Society for the Preservation of Covered Bridges (NSPCB), 44 Cleveland Av, Worcester, MA 01603
T: (617) 756-4516
Founded: 1948; Members: 1004
Focus: Preserv Hist Monuments
Periodicals
Bulletin (bi-monthly)
Covered Bridge Topics (quarterly)
Notices (monthly) 15975

National Society for the Study of Education (NSSE), 5835 Kimbark Av, Chicago, IL 60637
T: (312) 702-1582; Fax: (312) 702-0248
Founded: 1901; Members: 1500
Gen Secr: Kenneth J. Rehage
Focus: Educ
Periodical
Yearbook (annually) 15976

National Society of Professional Engineers (NSPE), 1420 King St, Alexandria, VA 22314
T: (703) 684-2800; Fax: (703) 836-4875
Founded: 1934; Members: 69000
Gen Secr: Russell C. Jones
Focus: Eng
Periodicals
Directory of Professional Engineers in Private Practice (bi-annually)
Engineering Times (monthly) 15977

National Space Club (NSC), 655 15 St NW, Washington, DC 20005
Founded: 1957; Members: 1700
Focus: Astrophys
Periodical
Newsletter (monthly) 15978

National Space Society (NSS), c/o David Brandt, 922 Pennsylvania Av SE, Washington, DC 20003
T: (202) 543-1900; E-Mail: nsshq@nss.org; Fax: (202) 546-4189
Founded: 1974; Members: 30000
Gen Secr: Lori B. Garver
Focus: Astrophys
Periodical
Space World (monthly) 15979

National Speleological Society (NSS), 2813 Cave Av, Huntsville, AL 35810-4431
T: (205) 852-1300; Fax: (205) 851-9241
Founded: 1941; Members: 11300
Gen Secr: Dave Luckins
Focus: Speleology
Periodicals
Membership List (annually)
Monthly News (monthly)
NSS Bulletin (semi-annually) 15980

National Standard Plumbing Code Committee (NSPCC), 180 S Washington St, POB 6808, Falls Church, VA 22040
T: (703) 237-8100; Fax: (703) 237-7442
Founded: 1970; Members: 12
Focus: Standards 15981

National Student Nurses' Association (NSNA), 555 W 57 St, Ste 1327, New York, NY 10019
T: (212) 581-2211; Fax: (212) 581-2368
Founded: 1953; Members: 35000
Focus: Adult Educ; Med
Periodical
Imprint (5 times annually) 15982

National Student Speech Language Hearing Association (NSSLHA), 10801 Rockville Pike, Rockville, MD 20852
T: (301) 897-5700; Fax: (301) 571-0457
Founded: 1972; Members: 12500
Focus: Logopedy
Periodicals
Clinical Series (bi-annually)
Journal (annually) 15983

National Study of School Evaluation (NSSE), c/o Dr. Kathleen Fitzpatrick, 1699 E Woodfield Rd, Ste 406, Schaumburg, IL 60173
T: (708) 995-9080; Fax: (708) 995-9088
Founded: 1933; Members: 6
Gen Secr: Dr. Kathleen Fitzpatrick
Focus: Educ 15984

National Tax Association – Tax Institute of America (NTA-TIA), 5310 E Main St, Ste 104, Columbus, OH 43213
T: (614) 864-1221
Founded: 1973; Members: 1800
Focus: Finance; Law; Econ
Periodical
National Tax Journal (quarterly) 15985

National Technical Association (NTA), POB 7045, Washington, DC 20032-0145
T: (202) 829-6100; Fax: (202) 684-3952
Founded: 1926; Members: 1500
Focus: Eng
Periodicals
Journal (semi-annually)
Newsletter (quarterly) 15986

National Technical Services Association (NTSA), 325 S Patrick St, Ste 104, Alexandria, VA 22314-3501
T: (703) 684-4722; Fax: (703) 684-7627
Founded: 1961; Members: 150
Focus: Eng
Periodicals
Membership Roster (annually)
Reporter (quarterly) 15987

National Telemedia Council (NTC), 120 E Wilson St, Madison, WI 53703
T: (608) 257-7712; Fax: (608) 257-7714
Founded: 1953
Focus: Mass Media
Periodicals
Look-Listen Project Report (annually)
Notable Programs (monthly)
Telemedium (4-6 times annually) . . . 15988

National Theatre Institute (NTI), 305 Great Neck Rd, Waterford, CT 06385
T: (203) 443-7139; Fax: (203) 443-9653
Founded: 1970
Focus: Perf Arts
Periodical
Alumnae Newsletter (semi-annually) . . . 15989

National Therapeutic Recreation Society (NTRS), 2775 S Quincy St, Ste 300, Arlington, VA 22206
T: (703) 578-5548; Fax: (703) 671-6772
Founded: 1966; Members: 2700
Gen Secr: Rikki S. Epstein
Focus: Therapeutics
Periodicals
Journal of Leisure Research (quarterly)
NTRS Newsletter (quarterly)
Parks and Recreation (monthly)
Therapeutic Recreation Journal (quarterly) 15990

National University Continuing Education Association (NUCEA), 1 Dupont Circle, Ste 615, Washington, DC 20036
T: (202) 659-3130; Fax: (202) 785-0374
Founded: 1915; Members: 2170
Focus: Adult Educ 15991

National Urban League (NUL), 500 E 62 St, New York, NY 10021
T: (212) 310-9000; Fax: (212) 593-8250
Founded: 1910; Members: 50000
Focus: Law
Periodical
The Urban League News (quarterly) . . 15992

National Vocational Agricultural Teachers' Association (NVATA), POB 15450, Alexandria, VA 22309
T: (703) 780-1862
Founded: 1948; Members: 9000
Focus: Adult Educ; Agri
Periodical
News and Views of NVATA (monthly) . 15993

National Vocational Technical Educational Foundation (NVTEF), 444 N Capitol St NW, No 830, Washington, DC 20001
T: (202) 737-0303; Fax: (202) 737-1106
Founded: 1979
Gen Secr: Madeleine B. Hemmings
Focus: Educ 15994

National Water Resources Association (NWRA), 3800 N Fairfax Dr, Ste 4, Arlington, VA 22203
T: (703) 524-1544; Fax: (703) 524-1548
Founded: 1932; Members: 4800
Focus: Water Res
Periodicals
National Water Resources Association Directory (bi-annually)
National Waterline (monthly) 15995

National Wildlife Federation (NWF), 8925 Leesburg Pike, Vienna, VA 22184
T: (703) 790-4000; Fax: (703) 790-4075
Founded: 1936; Members: 4000000
Pres: Mary Van Putten
Focus: Ecology 15996

National Women's Health Network (NWHN), 514 Tenth St NW, Ste 400, Washington, DC 20004
T: (202) 347-1140; Fax: (202) 347-1162
Founded: 1976; Members: 15000
Gen Secr: Beverly Baker
Focus: Public Health
Periodicals
Network News (bi-monthly)
Newsalerts 15997

National Women's Studies Association (NWSA), c/o Loretta Younger, 7100 Baltimore Av, Ste 301, College Park, MD 20740
T: (301) 405-0525; Fax: (301) 403-4137
Founded: 1977; Members: 3100
Gen Secr: Loretta Younger
Focus: Adult Educ
Periodicals
NWSA Action (quarterly)
NWSA Journal (quarterly)
Women's Studies Program Directory (bi-annually)
. . . . 15998

National Writers Association (NWA), 1450 S Havana St, Ste 424, Aurora, CO 80012
T: (303) 751-7844; Fax: (303) 751-8593
Founded: 1937; Members: 4000
Gen Secr: Sandy Whelchel
Focus: Lit
Periodicals
Authorship (bi-monthly)
Flash Market News (monthly)
Market Update (bi-monthly)
NWC Newsletter (10 times annually)
Professional Freelance Directory (annually) 15999

National Writing Project (NWP), c/o University of California, 5511 Tolman Hall, No 1670, Berkeley, CA 94720-1670
T: (510) 642-0963; E-Mail: nwp@garnet.berkeley.edu; Fax: (510) 642-4545
Founded: 1974; Members: 166
Gen Secr: Richard Sterling
Focus: Educ
Periodical
The Quarterly (quarterly) 16000

Nation's Report Card – National Assessment of Educational Progress (NRC), Rosedale Rd, Mail Stop 30E, Princeton, NJ 08541
T: (800) 223-0267; Fax: (609) 734-1878
Founded: 1964
Gen Secr: Paul Williams
Focus: Educ 16001

Native Seeds/Search (NS/S), 2509 N Campbell Av, Tucson, AZ 85719
T: (602) 327-9123
Founded: 1982; Members: 3200
Focus: Agri
Periodicals
Fall Harvest Catalog (annually)
Seedhead News (quarterly)
Seedlisting (annually) 16002

Natural Resources Defense Council (NRDC), 40 W 20 St, New York, NY 10011
T: (212) 727-2700; Fax: (212) 727-1773
Founded: 1970; Members: 170000
Focus: Ecology 16003

The Nature Conservancy (TNC), 1815 N Lynn St, Arlington, VA 22209
T: (703) 841-5300; Fax: (703) 841-1283
Founded: 1951; Members: 800000
Gen Secr: John C. Sawhill
Focus: Ecology
Periodical
The Nature Conservancy Magazine (bi-monthly)
. . . . 16004

NCCLS – The Clinical Laboratory Standards Organization (CLSO), 940 W Valley Rd, Ste 1400, Wayne, PA 19087-1898
T: (610) 688-0100
Founded: 1968; Members: 2000
Gen Secr: John V. Bergen
Focus: Med 16005

Near East Archaeological Society (NEAS), c/o Bill Berry, 701 Main St, Evanston, IL 60202
T: (708) 869-1573; Fax: (708) 869-4825
Founded: 1960; Members: 200
Pres: Dr. Keith N. Schoville
Focus: Archeol
Periodicals
NEAS Bulletin (semi-annually)
NEAS Newsletter (semi-annually) 16006

Near East College Association (NECA), 850 Third Av, New York, NY 10022
T: (212) 319-2453; Fax: (212) 752-6971
Founded: 1919; Members: 6
Focus: Educ 16007

Nepal Studies Association (NSA), c/o Dept of Anthropology, California State University, 1811 Nordhoff St, Northridge, CA 91330-8244
T: (818) 677-3331; E-Mail: nbishop@csun.edu; Fax: (818) 677-2873
Founded: 1972; Members: 400
Pres: Dr. Naomi Bishop
Focus: Ethnology
Periodical
Himalayan Research Bulletin (3 times annually)
. . . . 16008

Network, 801 Pennsylvania Av SE, Ste 460, Washington, DC 20003-2167
T: (202) 547-5556; E-Mail: network@igc.apc.org; Fax: (202) 547-5510
Founded: 1971; Members: 10000
Gen Secr: Kathy Thornton
Focus: Energy 16009

Network of Arab Scientists and Technologists Abroad (ASTA), 402 Willard St, Urbana, IL 61801
Focus: Sci; Eng 16010

Neurosurgical Society of America (NSA), c/o Dr. Russell W. Hardy, 11100 Euclid Av, Cleveland, OH 44106-5042
T: (216) 844-5949; Fax: (216) 844-3014
Founded: 1948; Members: 162
Gen Secr: Dr. Russell W. Hardy
Focus: Surgery; Neurology 16011

New Ecumenical Research Association (New ERA), 4 West 43rd St, New York, NY 10036
T: (212) 997-0050; Fax: (212) 869-6424
Gen Secr: Dr. Thomas G. Walsh
Focus: Rel & Theol 16012

New England Antiquities Research Association (NEARA), 10 Loring Av, Kingston, MA 02364
T: (617) 585-4666
Founded: 1964; Members: 350
Gen Secr: Ann Humphrey
Focus: Antique
Periodical
Journal (quarterly) 16013

New England Association of Schools and Colleges (NEASC), 209 Burlington Rd, Bedford, MA 01730-1406
T: (617) 271-0022; Fax: (617) 271-0950
Founded: 1885; Members: 1700
Gen Secr: Vincent L. Ferrandino
Focus: Educ
Periodicals
Membership Directory (annually)
Newsletter (3 times annually) 16014

New England Council of Latin American Studies (NECLAS), c/o Dept of Government, Smith College, Seelye Hall, Rm 210, Northampton, MA 01063
T: (413) 585-3591; E-Mail: Kgauger@smith.edu; Fax: (413) 585-3593
Gen Secr: Susan C. Bourque
Focus: Ethnology 16015

New England Historic Genealogical Society (NEHGS), 101 Newbury St, Boston, MA 02116-3007
T: (617) 536-5740; Fax: (617) 536-7307
Founded: 1845; Members: 16500
Gen Secr: Ralph J. Crandall
Focus: Genealogy
Periodical
New England Historical and Genealogical Register (quarterly) 16016

New World Educational Foundation, POB 42206, Washington, DC 20015
Focus: Educ 16017

New York Academy of Sciences (NYAS), 2 E 63 St, New York, NY 10021
T: (212) 838-0230; Fax: (212) 888-2894
Founded: 1817; Members: 40000
Pres: Rodney W. Nichols
Focus: Sci 16018

New York African Studies Association (NYASA), 301 Old Man Building, New Paltz, New York, NY 12561
T: (914) 257-2303
Focus: Ethnology 16019

New York Browning Society (NYBS), POB 2911, New York, NY 10185
T: (215) 667-5941
Founded: 1907; Members: 65
Focus: Lit
Periodicals
Bulletin (monthly)
Directory (bi-annually) 16020

New York C.S. Lewis Society (NYCSLS), c/o York College, Jamaica, NY 11451
T: (718) 262-2400
Founded: 1969; Members: 600
Gen Secr: James Como
Focus: Lit 16021

New York Drama Critics Circle (NYDCC), c/o Associated Press, 50 Rockefeller Plaza, New York, NY 10163
T: (212) 621-1841
Founded: 1935; Members: 23
Gen Secr: Michael Kuchwara
Focus: Perf Arts; Journalism 16022

New York Financial Writers' Association (NYFWA), POB 21, Syosset, NY 11791
T: (800) 533-7551; Fax: (800) 533-7560
Founded: 1938; Members: 350
Gen Secr: Joyce Spartonos
Focus: Journalism; Finance
Periodical
Directory (annually) 16023

New York Genealogical and Biographical Society (NYGBS), 122 E 58 St, New York, NY 10022-1939
T: (212) 755-8532
Founded: 1869; Members: 1500
Focus: Genealogy
Periodical
New York Genealogical and Biographical Record (quarterly) 16024

New York Pigment Club (NYPC), c/o BASF Corporation, C & C Div., 3000 Continental Dr N, Mount Olive, NJ 07828
T: (201) 426-2600
Founded: 1953; Members: 100
Focus: Chem
Periodical
Membership Roster (bi-annually) 16025

Newcomen Society of the United States (NSUS), 412 Newcomen Rd, Exton, PA 19341
T: (215) 363-6600; Fax: (215) 363-0612
Founded: 1923; Members: 15000
Focus: Hist
Periodical
Monographs of Corporate and Institutional Histories (bi-weekly) 16026

Nickel Producers Environmental Research Association (NiPERA), 2605 Meridian Pkwy, Ste 200, Durham, NC 27713
T: (919) 544-7722; Fax: (919) 544-7724
Focus: Ecology 16027

Nieman Foundation (NF), c/o Walter Lippmann House, Harvard University, 1 Francis Av, Cambridge, MA 02138
T: (617) 495-2237
Founded: 1938; Members: 910
Focus: Ling 16028

Nockian Society (NS), 42 Leathers St, Fort Mitchell, KY 41017
T: (606) 341-4841
Founded: 1963; Members: 750
Focus: Lit 16029

North America Society for Trenchless Technology (NASTT), 435 N Michigan Av, Ste 1717, Chicago, IL 60611-4067
T: (312) 644-0828; Fax: (312) 644-8557
Gen Secr: W.W.S. Gray
Focus: Eng 16030

North American Academy of Ecumenists (NAAE), 1818 Coal Pl SE, Albuquerque, NM 87106-4095
T: (505) 242-3462; Fax: (505) 256-0071
Founded: 1967; Members: 375
Pres: Ernest R. Falardeau
Focus: Rel & Theol 16031

North American Association for Environmental Education (NAEE), 1255 23 St NW, Ste 400, Washington, DC 20037-1199
T: (202) 884-8912; Fax: (202) 884-8701
Founded: 1971; Members: 1600
Gen Secr: Edward McCrea
Focus: Educ 16032

North American Association of Professors of Christian Education (NAPCE), 850 N Grove Av, Ste C, Elgin, IL 60120
T: (708) 741-2400; Fax: (708) 741-0595
Founded: 1947; Members: 250
Focus: Educ 16033

North American Association of Summer Sessions (NAASS), 11728 Summerhaven Dr, Saint Louis, MO 63146
T: (314) 872-8406
Founded: 1964; Members: 425
Gen Secr: Michael U. Nelson
Focus: Educ 16034

North American Clinical Dermatologic Society (NACDS), c/o John W. White Jr., Mayo Clinic, 4500 San Pablo Rd, Jacksonville, FL 32224
T: (904) 953-2219; Fax: (904) 953-2005
Founded: 1959; Members: 210
Gen Secr: John W. White Jr.
Focus: Derm
Periodicals
Cutis (annually)
Program (annually) 16035

North American Committee (CAC), c/o National Planning Association, 1424 16 St NW, Ste 700, Washington, DC 20036
T: (202) 265-7685; Fax: (202) 797-5516
Founded: 1957; Members: 110
Gen Secr: Dahlia Stein
Focus: Poli Sci 16036

North American Conference on British Studies, c/o Prof. David Harris Sacks, Reed College, Portland, OR 97202
T: (503) 771-1112; Fax: (503) 777-7769
Founded: 1951; Members: 1000
Gen Secr: Prof. David Harris Sacks
Focus: Ethnology; Hist
Periodicals
Albion (quarterly)
Journal of British Studies (quarterly) . . 16037

North American Dostoevsky Society (NADS), c/o Dept of Russian and Eastern Studies, University of Kentucky, 1055 Patterson Office Tower, Lexington, KY 40506-0027
T: (606) 257-3761
Founded: 1970; Members: 120
Pres: Roger Andersen
Focus: Lit 16038

North American Electric Reliability Council (NERC), 116-390 Village Blvd, Princeton, NJ 08540-5731
T: (609) 452-8060; E-Mail: info@nercl.nerc.com; Fax: (609) 452-9550
Founded: 1968; Members: 9
Pres: Michael R. Gent
Focus: Electric Eng
Periodicals
Annual Report (annually)
Electricity Supply and Demand (annually)
Reliability Assessment (annually) 16039

North American Federation of the International College of Surgeons, c/o Dept of Gynecology and Obstetrics, LSU Medical Center, 1501 Kings Highway, Shreveport, LA 71130-3932
Gen Secr: Dr. Harvey Huddleston
Focus: Surgery 16040

North American Medical/Dental Association (NAMDA), POB 1982, Newport Beach, CA 92663
T: (714) 642-7689
Founded: 1968; Members: 10000
Focus: Med; Dent 16041

North American Mycological Association (NAMA), 3556 Oakwood St, Ann Arbor, MI 48104-5213
T: (313) 971-2552
Founded: 1959; Members: 1700
Focus: Botany, Specific
Periodicals
McIlvainea (annually)
The Mycophile (bi-monthly) 16042

North American Primary Care Research Group (NAPCRG), c/o Medical College of Virginia, POB 251, Richmond, VA 23298
T: (804) 786-9625; Fax: (804) 786-5856
Founded: 1972; Members: 500
Focus: Med 16043

North American Region of the World Federation for Mental Health (NAC/WFMH), 4930 N Lake Dr, Milwaukee, WI 53217
Gen Secr: L. Patt Franciosi
Focus: Psychiatry 16044

North American Regional Association of Schools of Social Work, c/o University of Connecticut, School of Social Work, 1798 Asylum Av, West Hartford, CT 06117-2648
Focus: Educ; Soc Sci 16045

North American Simulation and Gaming Association (NASAGA), c/o Jay Schindler, University of Wisconsin, 203 Mitchell Hall, La Crosse, WI 54601
T: (608) 785-8162
Founded: 1974; Members: 200
Gen Secr: Jay Schindler
Focus: Educ 16046

North American Society for Pediatric Gastroenterology and Nutrition (NASPGN), c/o John T. Boyle, Rainbow Babies and Children's Hospital, 2074 Abington Rd, Cleveland, OH 44106
T: (216) 844-1767; Fax: (216) 844-3757
Founded: 1970; Members: 350
Gen Secr: John T. Boyle
Focus: Pediatrics; Gastroenter
Periodicals
NASPG Membership Directory (annually)
Newsletter of the NASPG (4-6 times annually) 16047

North American Society for Social Philosophy (NASSP), c/o Univ of Colorado, Boulder, CO 80309
Gen Secr: Alison Jaggar
Focus: Philos 16048

North American Society for Sport History (NASSH), c/o Ronald A. Smith, Pennsylvania State University, 101 White Bldg, University Park, PA 16802-3903
T: (814) 238-1288
Founded: 1972; Members: 950
Gen Secr: Ronald A. Smith
Focus: Sports; Cultur Hist
Periodicals
Journal of Sport History (3 times annually)
Newsletter (irregularly)
Proceedings (annually) 16049

North American Society for Sport Psychology and Physical Activity (NASPSPA), c/o Dept of ESS, UNCG, Geensboro, NC 27412
Gen Secr: Kathleen Williams
Focus: Psych; Sports 16050

North American Society of Adlerian Psychology (NASAP), 65 E Wacker Pl, No 400, Chicago, IL 60601
T: (312) 629-8801
Founded: 1951; Members: 1200
Gen Secr: Neva L. Hefner
Focus: Psych
Periodicals
Calendar-Newsletter (monthly)
Individual Psychology: The Journal of Adlerian Theory, Research & Practice (quarterly)
Membership List (bi-annually) 16051

North American Society of Pacing and Electrophysiology (NASPE), 2 Vision Dr, Natick, MA 01760-2059
T: (508) 647-0100; Fax: (508) 647-0124
Founded: 1979; Members: 1900
Gen Secr: Carol J. McGlinchey
Focus: Physiology; Electric Eng
Periodicals
NASPE News (quarterly)
PACE (monthly) 16052

North American Thermal Analysis Society (NATAS), c/o LRSM, University of Pennsylvania, 3231 Walnut St, Philadelphia, PA 19104-6202
Founded: 1968; Members: 750
Gen Secr: Dr. A.R. McGhie
Focus: Energy
Periodicals
Conference Proceedings (annually)
Membership Directory (annually)
Notes (quarterly) 16053

North American Vexillological Association (NAVA), 1977 N Olden Av, Ste 225, Trenton, NJ 08618-2193
T: (609) 381-7684
Founded: 1967; Members: 340
Pres: Nicholas A. Artimovich II
Focus: Hist
Periodical
NAVA News (bi-monthly) 16054

North and Central America and Caribbean Ostomy Association, 841 N Ottawa, Park Ridge, IL 60068
T: (847) 823-6312; Fax: (847) 823-6313
Gen Secr: Marilyn A. Mau
Focus: Med 16055

North Central Association of Colleges and Schools (NCACS), c/o Commission on Schools, Arizona State University, Tempe, AZ 85287-3011
T: (602) 965-8700; Fax: (602) 965-9423
Founded: 1895; Members: 8200
Focus: Educ 16056

North Central Conference on Summer Schools (NCCSS), c/o Dr. Roger Swanson, Summer Sessions, University of Wisconsin at River Falls, River Falls, WI 54022
T: (715) 425-3851
Founded: 1949; Members: 150
Gen Secr: Dr. Roger Swanson
Focus: Educ 16057

North Pacific Marine Science Organization (PICES), c/o Univ of Washington, School of Marine Affairs, 3707 Brooklyn Av, Seattle, WA 98105-6715
T: (206) 685-2497; E-Mail: wooster@u.washington.edu; Fax: (206) 543-1417
Gen Secr: Dr. Warren S. Wooster
Focus: Oceanography 16058

Northeast Conference on the Teaching of Foreign Languages (NEC), c/o Dickinson College, POB 1773, Carlisle, PA 17013-2896
T: (717) 245-1977; Fax: (717) 245-1976
Founded: 1954; Members: 13000
Gen Secr: Rebecca R. Kline
Focus: Ling; Educ
Periodicals
Conference Program (annually)
Newsletter (semi-annually)
Reports (annually) 16059

Northern Libraries Colloquy (NLC), c/o Barbara Sokolov, University of Alaska at Anchorage Library, 3211 Providence Dr, Anchorage, AK 99508
T: (907) 786-1877; Fax: (907) 786-6050
Founded: 1970
Gen Secr: Barbara Sokolov
Focus: Libraries & Bk Sci
Periodicals
Directory of Polar and Regions Library Resources
Northern Libraries Bulletin 16060

Northwest Association of Schools and Colleges (NASC), c/o Boise State University, 1910 University Dr, Boise, ID 83725
T: (208) 334-3226; E-Mail: sclemens@rarney.idbsu.edu; Fax: (208) 334-3228
Founded: 1917; Members: 1385
Gen Secr: David Steadman
Focus: Educ
Periodicals
Directory of Accredited and Affiliated Institutions (annually)
Newsletter (semi-annually) 16061

Northwest Medical Teams International (NMTI), POB 10, Portland, OR 97207
T: (503) 644-6000; E-Mail: nmti@nwmti.org; Fax: (503) 644-9000
Gen Secr: Ron Post
Focus: Med 16062

Northwest Regional Consortium for Southeast Asian Studies (NWRCSEAS), c/o Southeast Asian Studies, University of Washington, 303 Thomson DR-05, Seattle, WA 98195-0001
T: (206) 543-9606; Fax: (206) 685-0668
Gen Secr: Maureen Jackson
Focus: Ethnology 16063

Norwegian-American Historical Association (NAHA), c/o Saint Olaf College, 1510 Saint Olaf Av, Northfield, MN 55057-1097
T: (507) 646-3221
Founded: 1925; Members: 1700
Focus: Hist
Periodicals
Norwegian-American Studies (irregularly)
Travel and Description Series (irregularly) 16064

NTL Institute for Applied Behavioral Science, 1240 N Pitt St, Ste 100, Alexandria, VA 22314-1403
T: (703) 548-1500; Fax: (703) 684-1256
Founded: 1947; Members: 450
Focus: Behav Sci
Periodical
The Journal of Applied Behavioral Science 16065

Nuclear Energy Institute, 1776 I St NW, Ste 400, Washington, DC 20006
T: (202) 739-8000; Fax: (202) 785-1898
Founded: 1987; Members: 300
Pres: J. Philip Bayne
Focus: Nucl Res
Periodicals
INFO (monthly)
Nuclear Industry (quarterly) 16066

Numismatic Literary Guild (NLG), 12 Abbington Terrace, Glen Rock, NJ 07452
T: (201) 612-0482; Fax: (201) 612-9581
Founded: 1968; Members: 360
Focus: Numismatics
Periodical
Newsletter (bi-monthly) 16067

Nutrition Institute of America (NIA), 200 W 86 St, Ste 17B, New York, NY 10024
T: (212) 721-6044; Fax: (212) 875-8066
Founded: 1974; Members: 6
Pres: Gary Null
Focus: Nutrition 16068

Nuttall Ornithological Club (NOC), c/o Museum of Comparative Zoology, Harvard University, Cambridge, MA 02138
T: (617) 495-2471
Founded: 1873; Members: 130
Focus: Ornithology 16069

Oak Ridge Associated Universities (ORAU), POB 117, Oak Ridge, TN 37831-0117
T: (615) 576-3000; Fax: (615) 576-3643
Founded: 1946; Members: 88
Pres: Dr. J.M. Veigel
Focus: Energy

Periodical
Annual Report (annually) 16070

Oceanic Educational Foundation (OEF), 3710 Whispering Ln, Falls Church, VA 22041
T: (703) 256-0279
Founded: 1970; Members: 6000
Focus: Educ 16071

Oceanic Federation of Coloproctology (OFCP), 600 Broadway, Ste 40, Seattle, WA 98122
Gen Secr: Richard P. Billingham
Focus: Oceanography 16072

Oceanic Society Expeditions (OSE), Fort Mason Center, Bldg E, San Francisco, CA 94123
T: (415) 441-1106; Fax: (415) 474-3395
Founded: 1972; Members: 70000
Focus: Oceanography
Periodicals
Oceanic Expeditions Brochure (semi-annually)
Oceans Magazine (bi-monthly) 16073

Odyssey Institute Corporation (OCI), 5 Hedley Farms Rd, Westport, CT 06880
T: (203) 255-4198; Fax: (203) 255-3006
Founded: 1975
Focus: Rehabil 16074

Office for Advancement of Public Black Colleges of the National Association of State Universities and Land Grant Colleges (OAPBC), 1 Dupont Circle NW, Ste 710, Washington, DC 20036-1191
T: (202) 778-0818
Founded: 1968; Members: 35
Focus: Educ 16075

Office of International Education of the American Council on Education, 1 Dupont Circle NW, Ste 800, Washington, DC 20036
T: (202) 939-9313; Fax: (202) 833-4760
Founded: 1979
Focus: Educ 16076

Office of Management Services (OMS), c/o Association of Research Libraries, 21 Dupont Cir, Washington, DC 20036
T: (202) 296-8656; Fax: (202) 872-0884
Founded: 1970; Members: 119
Gen Secr: Susan Jurow
Focus: Libraries & Bk Sci
Periodical
SPEC Kit (10 times annually) 16077

Office Systems Research Association (OSRA), c/o Computer Information Systems, Southwest Missouri State University, 901 S National Av, Springfield, MO 65804-0089
T: (417) 836-6319; E-Mail: hrp262f@wpgate.smsu.edu; Fax: (417) 836-6337
Founded: 1980; Members: 350
Gen Secr: Heidi Perreault
Focus: Business Admin 16078

Offshore Mechanics and Polar Engineering Council (OMPEC), c/o ISOPE, POB 1107, Golden, CO 80402-1107
T: (303) 420-8114; Fax: (303) 420-3760
Focus: Eng 16079

Oncology Nursing Society (ONS), 501 Holiday Dr, Pittsburgh, PA 15220
T: (412) 921-7373; Fax: (412) 921-6565
Founded: 1975; Members: 22000
Focus: Cell Biol & Cancer Res
Periodicals
Oncology Nursing Forum (bi-monthly)
Proceedings of Annual Congress 16080

Open Space Institute (OSI), 666 Broadway, New York, NY 10012
T: (212) 505-7480; Fax: (212) 353-2052
Founded: 1973
Pres: Christopher J. Elliman
Focus: Ecology 16081

Opera America, 777 14 St NW, Ste 520, Washington, DC 20005
T: (202) 347-9262; Fax: (202) 393-0735
Founded: 1970; Members: 800
Focus: Music
Periodicals
Bulletin (quarterly)
Intercompany Announcements (10 times annually)
Membership Directory (semi-annually)
Repertoire Survey (annually) 16082

Operation Enterprise (OE), c/o American Management Association, POB 88, Hamilton, NY 13346
T: (315) 824-2000; Fax: (315) 824-2000
Founded: 1963
Focus: Business Admin
Periodical
Operation Enterprise Newsletter (semi-annually)
. . . . 16083

Operations Research Society of America (ORSA), 1314 Guilford Av, Baltimore, MD 21202
T: (410) 528-4146; Fax: (410) 528-8556
Founded: 1952; Members: 8300
Focus: Business Admin
Periodicals
Interfaces (bi-monthly)
Mathematics of Operations Research (quarterly)
Operations Research (bi-monthly)
ORSA Journal on Computing (quarterly) . 16084

Ophthalmic Research Institute (ORI), 433 East West Hwy, Ste 1117, Bethesda, MD 20814-4408
T: (301) 718-6524; Fax: (301) 656-0989
Founded: 1972
Gen Secr: James S. Vrac
Focus: Ophthal 16085

Optical Society of America (OSA), 2010 Massachusetts Av NW, Washington, DC 20036
T: (202) 223-8130; Fax: (202) 223-1096
Founded: 1916; Members: 10250
Pres: Duncan Moore; Gen Secr: David Hennage
Focus: Optics
Periodicals
Applied Optics (36 times annually)
Atmospheric Optics (monthly)
Journal of Lightwave Technology (monthly)
Journal of the Optical Society of America A (monthly)
Journal of the Optical Society of America B (monthly)
Optics and Spectroscpy (monthly)
Optics Letters (bi-weekly)
Optics News (monthly) 16086

Opticians Association of America (OAA), 10341 Democracy Ln, Fairfax, VA 22030
T: (703) 691-8355; Fax: (703) 691-3929
Founded: 1926; Members: 700
Focus: Optics
Periodicals
Guild Quarterly (quarterly)
OAA News (8 times annually)
State Leadership Bulletin (quarterly) . . 16087

Optometric Historical Society (OHS), 243 N Lindbergh Blvd, Saint Louis, MO 63141
T: (314) 991-4100; Fax: (314) 991-4101
Founded: 1969
Focus: Ophthal
Periodical
Newsletter (quarterly) 16088

Oral History Association (OHA), POB 97234, Waco, TX 76798-7234
T: (817) 755-2764; E-Mail: oha_support@baylor.edu; Fax: (817) 755-1571
Founded: 1966; Members: 1400
Gen Secr: Rebecca Sharpless
Focus: Hist
Periodicals
Annual Report and Membership Directory (annually)
Newsletter (quarterly)
Oral History Review (annually) 16089

Order of the Indian Wars (OIW), POB 7401, Little Rock, AR 72217
T: (501) 225-3996; Fax: (501) 225-5167
Founded: 1979; Members: 750
Focus: Hist
Periodicals
Communique (monthly)
Journal of the Order of Indian Wars (quarterly)
. . . . 16090

Organ Historical Society (OHS), POB 26811, Richmond, VA 23261
T: (804) 353-9226; Fax: (804) 353-9266
Founded: 1956; Members: 2900
Focus: Music
Periodicals
Organ Handbook (annually)
The Tracker (quarterly) 16091

Organization Development Institute (ODI), 11234 Walnut Ridge Rd, Chesterland, OH 44026
T: (216) 461-4333; Fax: (216) 729-9319
Founded: 1968; Members: 488
Focus: Business Admin
Periodicals
The Organization Development Journal (quarterly)
Organizations and Change (monthly) . . 16092

Organization for Flora Neotropica (OFN), c/o New York Botanical Garden, Bronx, NY 10458-5126
T: (718) 817-8625; E-Mail: wthomas@nybg.org; Fax: (718) 562-6780
Founded: 1964; Members: 150
Gen Secr: W.W. Thomas
Focus: Botany
Periodical
Flora Neotropica (5 times annually) . . 16093

Organization for Tropical Studies (OTS), c/o North American Office, POB 90630, Durham, NC 27708-0630
T: (919) 684-5774; E-Mail: nao@acpub.duke.edu; Fax: (919) 684-5661
Founded: 1963; Members: 50
Gen Secr: Donald E. Stone
Focus: Bio 16094

Organization for Tropical Studies, POB 90630, Durham, NC 27708
T: (919) 684-5774; Fax: (919) 684-5661
Gen Secr: Donald E. Stone
Focus: Geography 16095

Organization of American Historians (OAH), 112 N Bryan St, Bloomington, IN 47408
T: (812) 855-7311
Founded: 1907; Members: 12100
Pres: Michael Kammen; Gen Secr: Arnita A. Jones
Focus: Hist
Periodical
Magazine of History 16096

Organization of American Kodaly Educators (OAKE), c/o Glenys Wignes, 1457 S 23 St, Fargo, ND 58103-3708
T: (701) 235-0366; Fax: (701) 241-7051
Founded: 1974; Members: 1500
Gen Secr: Glenys Wignes
Focus: Music; Educ
Periodical
The Kodaly Envoy (quarterly) 16097

Organization of Professional Acting Coaches and Teachers (OPACT), 3968 Eureka Dr, Studio City, CA 91604
T: (213) 877-4988; Fax: (213) 877-4988
Founded: 1980; Members: 12
Focus: Educ 16098

Organizational Behavior Teaching Society (OBTS), c/o College of Business Administration, University of Oklahoma, 4 Adams Hall, Norman, OK 73019
T: (405) 325-2931; Fax: (405) 325-7688
Founded: 1973
Focus: Psych; Educ 16099

Oriental Numismatic Society (ONS), POB 356, Now Hope, PA 18938
Gen Secr: W.B. Warden
Focus: Numismatics 16100

Orthodontic Education and Research Foundation (OERF), 3556 Caroline St, Saint Louis, MO 63104
T: (314) 577-8189
Founded: 1957; Members: 500
Focus: Dent; Educ 16101

Orthodox Theological Society in America (OTSA), c/o Holy Cross School of Theology, 50 Goddard Av, Brookline, MA 02146
T: (617) 731-3500
Founded: 1968; Members: 95
Pres: Thomas Fitzgerald
Focus: Rel & Theol
Periodicals
Bulletin (monthly)
Membership Directory
Presidents Report (annually) 16102

Orthopedic Foundation for Animals (OFA), 2300 Nifong Blvd, Columbia, MO 65201
T: (314) 442-0418
Founded: 1967
Focus: Vet Med 16103

Orthopedic Research Society (ORS), 6300 N River Rd, Ste 727, Rosemont, IL 60018-4238
T: (708) 698-1625; Fax: (708) 823-0536
Founded: 1954; Members: 1500
Focus: Orthopedics
Periodicals
Journal of Orthopedic Research (quarterly)
Proceedings of Annual Meeting 16104

Orton Dyslexia Society (ODS), 8600 LaSalle Rd, Ste 382, Baltimore, MD 21286-2044
T: (410) 296-0232
Founded: 1949; Members: 9000
Focus: Med 16105

Osteopathic Colleges of Ophthalmology and Otolaryngology, Head and Neck Surgery, c/o Dayton District Academy of Osteopathic Medicine, 3 Mac Koil Av, Dayton, OH 45403
T: (513) 252-0868; Fax: (513) 252-0968
Founded: 1916; Members: 580
Gen Secr: Sharon D. Alexiades
Focus: Otorhinolaryngology; Ophthal
Periodicals
Newsletter (quarterly)
Photo Roster 16106

Outdoor Education Association (OEA), 143 Fox Hill Rd, Denville, NJ 07834
T: (201) 627-7214
Founded: 1940; Members: 200
Pres: Dr. Edward J. Ambry
Focus: Educ
Periodical
Extending Education 16107

Outdoor Ethics Guild (OEG), General Delivery, Bucks Harbor, ME 04618
Founded: 1967
Pres: Bruce Bandurski
Focus: Ecology 16108

Outer Critics Circle (OCC), 101 W 57 St, New York, NY 10019
T: (212) 765-8557
Founded: 1950; Members: 70
Pres: Marjorie Gunner
Focus: Lit; Perf Arts; Journalism 16109

Overseas Council for Theological Education and Missions (OCTE), POB 751, Greenwood, IN 46142
T: (317) 882-4174; Fax: (317) 882-4195
Focus: Rel & Theol; Educ 16110

Overseas Ministries Study Centre (OMSC), 490 Prospect St, New haven, CT 06511-2196
T: (203) 624-6672; E-Mail: studyprogram@omsc.org; Fax: (203) 865-2857
Focus: Rel & Theol 16111

Pacific Arts Association (PAA), 900 S Beretania St, Honolulu, HI 96814
T: (808) 538-3693; Fax: (808) 521-6591
Founded: 1974; Members: 300
Focus: Arts 16112

Pacific Association of Pediatric Surgeons, c/o Childrens Hospital, Dept of Surgery, 111 Michigan Av NW, Washington, DC 20010
T: (202) 884-2151; Fax: (202) 884-4174
Gen Secr: Marshall Z. Schwartz
Focus: Surgery; Pediatrics 16113

Pacific Basin Consortium for Hazardous Waste Research, c/o East-West Center, 1777 E-W Rd, Honolulu, HI 96848
T: (808) 944-7555; Fax: (808) 944-7970
Gen Secr: Richard R. Cirillo
Focus: Ecology 16114

Pacific Council on International Policy, c/o School of International Relations, University of Southern California, Los Angeles, CA 90089-0043
T: (213) 740-2139; Fax: (213) 742-0281
Focus: Poli Sci 16115

Pacific Dermatological Association (PDA), 930 N Meacham Rd, Schaumburg, IL 60173-6016
Founded: 1948; Members: 1200
Focus: Derm
Periodical
Transactions (annually) 16116

Pacific Forum Center for Security and International Studies (Pacific Forum/CSIS), c/o Pacific Forum, 1001 Bishop St, Pauahi Tower, Ste 1150, Honolulu, HI 96813
T: (808) 521-6745; Fax: (808) 599-8690
Gen Secr: Ralph A. Cossa
Focus: Military Sci; Poli Sci 16117

Pacific Institute for Studies in Development, Environment and Security, 1204 Preservation Park Way, Oakland, CA 94612
T: (510) 251-1600; Fax: (510) 251-2203
Gen Secr: Dr. Peter H. Gleick
Focus: Develop Areas; Ecology; Military Sci
. . . . 16118

Pacific Mathematics and Science Regional Consortium, c/o PREL, 828 Fort St Mall, Ste 500, Honolulu, HI 96813-4321
T: (808) 533-6000; E-Mail: askmathsci@prel.hawaii.edu; Fax: (808) 533-7599
Focus: Math; Sci 16119

Pacific Planetarium Association (PPA), c/o Lane ESD Planetarium, 2300 Leo Harris Pkwy, Eugene, OR 97401
T: (451) 461-8227; E-Mail: planetarium@edlane.lane.edu; Fax: (451) 687-6459
Gen Secr: Jon Elvert
Focus: Astronomy 16120

Pacific Region Educational Laboratory (PREL), 828 Fort St Mall, Suite 500, Honolulu, HI 96813-4321
T: (808) 533-6000; E-Mail: askprel@prel.hawaii.edu; Fax: (808) 533-7599
Gen Secr: Dr. John W. Kofel
Focus: Educ 16121

Pacific Rim Council on Urban Development (PRCUD), 2215 Fifth St, Berkeley, CA 94710
T: (510) 540-7331; Fax: (510) 540-7344
Gen Secr: Sheila Brady
Focus: Urban Plan 16122

Pacific Rocket Society (PRS), 1825 N Oxnard Blvd, Ste 24, Oxnard, CA 93030
T: (805) 983-1947
Founded: 1946; Members: 100
Focus: Eng 16123

Pacific Science Association (PSA), POB 17801, Honolulu, HI 96817-0801
T: (808) 848-4139; E-Mail: psa@bishop.bishop.hawaii.org; Fax: (808) 847-8252
Founded: 1920; Members: 1500
Gen Secr: Dr. L.G. Eldredge
Focus: Sci
Periodical
Information Bulletin (quarterly) 16124

Pacific Seabird Group (PSG), c/o Savannah River Ecology Laboratory, PO Drawer E, Aiken, SC 29801
T: (803) 725-2475
Founded: 1972; Members: 450
Focus: Ornithology
Periodicals
Bulletin (semi-annually)
Membership Directory 16125

Pacific Studies Center (PSC), 222B View St, Mountain View, CA 94041
T: (415) 969-1545; Fax: (415) 968-1126
Founded: 1969
Focus: Poli Sci
Periodicals
California Military Monitor (bi-monthly)
Global Electronics (monthly) 16126

Packaging Education Foundation (PEF), 481 Carlisle Dr, Herndon, VA 22070
T: (703) 318-8975; Fax: (703) 318-0310
Founded: 1957
Focus: Materials Sci
Periodicals
Leader Newsletter (quarterly)
PEF Leader (semi-annually) 16127

Paleontological Research Institution (PRI), 1259 Trumansburg Rd, Ithaca, NY 14850
T: (607) 273-6623; Fax: (607) 273-6620
Founded: 1932; Members: 1000
Gen Secr: Dr. Warren D. Allmon
Focus: Paleontology

Periodicals
Bulletin of American Paleontology (semi-annually)
Paleontographica Americana 16128

Paleontological Society (PS), 7621 Granite Hill Dr, Riverside, CA 92509
T: (714) 685-5818
Founded: 1908; Members: 1710
Gen Secr: Donald L. Wolberg
Focus: Paleontology
Periodicals
Journal of Paleontology (6 times annually)
Memoirs in Paleontology (irregularly)
Paleobiology (quarterly) 16129

Paleopathology Association, 18655 Parkside, Detroit, MI 48221-2208
T: (313) 864-7944; Fax: (313) 864-7944
Gen Secr: Eve Cockburn
Focus: Pathology 16130

Pan American Allergy Society, POB 947, Fredericksburg, TX 78624
T: (210) 997-9853; Fax: (210) 997-8625
Gen Secr: Ann Brey
Focus: Derm 16131

Pan American Association for Biochemistry and Molecular Biology (PABMB), c/o School of Biological Sciences, Univ of Missouri-Kansas City, 109 Biological Science Bldg, Kansas City, MO 64110-2499
T: (816) 235-5246
Gen Secr: Dr. Marino Martinez-Carrion
Focus: Biochem; Microbio 16132

Pan-American Association of Biochemistry and Molecular Biology, c/o Dr. Marino Martinez-Carrion, School of Biological Sciences, University of Missouri at Kansas City, 109 Biological Sciences Bldg, Kansas City, MO 64110
T: (816) 235-2249; Fax: (816) 235-5158
Founded: 1969; Members: 12
Gen Secr: Dr. Marino Martinez-Carrion
Focus: Biochem 16133

Pan-American Association of Ophthalmology (PAAO), 1301 S Bowen Rd, Ste 365, Arlington, TX 76013
T: (817) 265-2831; Fax: (817) 275-3961
Founded: 1939; Members: 8000
Gen Secr: Teresa J. Bradshaw
Focus: Ophthal
Periodical
Insights (quarterly) 16134

Pan American Association of Oto-Rhino-Laryngology - Head and Neck Surgery, c/o Univ Hospitals of Cleveland, 11100 Euclid Av, Cleveland, OH 44106-5045
Gen Secr: Dr. Anthony J. Maniglia
Focus: Otorhinolaryngology 16135

Pan-American Biodeterioration Society (PABS), c/o Dept of Forensic Sciences, George Washington University, Washington, DC 20052
T: (202) 994-7319; Fax: (202) 994-0458
Founded: 1985; Members: 100
Gen Secr: Charles O'Rear
Focus: Bio
Periodicals
Conference Proceedings
Newsletter (quarterly) 16136

Pan American Federation of Engineering Economics and Costs (FEPIEC), c/o Project Management Associates, 226 West Liberty St, Ann Arbor, MI 48104
T: (313) 769-0530
Gen Secr: Gui Ponce de León
Focus: Eng; Econ 16137

Pan American Health and Education Foundation (PAHEF), c/o PAHO, 525 23 St NW, Washington, DC 20037-2895
T: (202) 974-3416; E-Mail: marksric@paho.org; Fax: (202) 974-3658
Focus: Public Health; Educ 16138

Pan American Health Organization (PAHO), 525 23 St NW, Washington, DC 20037
T: (202) 861-3200; E-Mail: info@paho.org; Fax: (202) 861-3143
Founded: 1902; Members: 38
Gen Secr: Dr. George A. Alleyne
Focus: Public Health
Periodicals
Bulletin of the Pan American Health Organization (quarterly)
Disaster Preparedness in the Americas (quarterly)
EPI Newsletter (monthly)
Epidemiological Bulletin (bi-monthly) . . . 16139

Pan American Infectious Diseases Association (PAIDA), POB 5206-86, Miami, FL 33152-0686
E-Mail: api@netcolombia.com; Fax: (571) 611-5768
Gen Secr: Dr. Guillermo Prada
Focus: Med 16140

Pan American League of Associations for Rheumatology (PANLAR), c/o Division of Rheumatology, MS509, University of Arkansas for Medical Sciences, 4301 West Markham, Little Rock, AR 72205
T: (501) 686-6770; Fax: (501) 686-8188
Gen Secr: Dr. Hugo E. Jasin
Focus: Rheuma 16141

Pan-American Medical Association (PAMA), 745 Fifth Av, Ste 403, New York, NY 10151
T: (212) 753-6033
Founded: 1925; Members: 6000
Gen Secr: F.C. Fenig
Focus: Med 16142

Pan Pacific Consortium of Maritime Museums (PANPAC), 151 E Pacific Coast Highway, Newport Beach, CA 92660
Gen Secr: Dr. Sheli Smith
Focus: Oceanography 16143

Pan-Pacific Surgical Association (PPSA), 1360 S Beretania, Ste 304, Honolulu, HI 96814
T: (808) 528-1180; Fax: (808) 528-1188
Founded: 1929; Members: 2716
Gen Secr: Gayle Yoshida
Focus: Surgery
Periodical
Newsletter (quarterly) 16144

Panamerican Cultural Circle (PCC), 16 Malvern Pl, Verona, NJ 07044
T: (201) 239-3125
Founded: 1963; Members: 800
Focus: Hist; Lit
Periodicals
Circulo Poético (annually)
Circulo: Revista de Cultura (annually) . . 16145

Parapsychological Association (PA), POB 797, Fairhaven, MA 02719-0700
Founded: 1957; Members: 280
Gen Secr: Dr. Emily Williams
Focus: Parapsych
Periodical
Proceedings (annually) 16146

Parker Chiropractic Resource Foundation (PCRF), POB 40444, Fort Worth, TX 76140
T: (817) 293-6444; Fax: (817) 293-0776
Founded: 1951; Members: 30000
Focus: Med 16147

Passaic River Coalition (PRC), 246 Madisonville Rd, Basking Ridge, NJ 07920
T: (201) 766-7550; Fax: (201) 766-7550
Founded: 1971; Members: 2500
Focus: Ecology
Periodicals
Goals & Strategies (semi-annually)
Groundwater News (quarterly)
Vibes from the Libe (annually) 16148

Pattern Recognition Society (PRS), c/o National Biomedical Research Foundation, Georgetown University Medical Center, 3900 Reservoir Rd NW, Washington, DC 20007
T: (202) 687-2121
Founded: 1966; Members: 550
Focus: Sci
Periodical
Pattern Recognition (bi-monthly) 16149

Peace Action Education Fund, 866 United Nations Plaza, Rm 4053, New York, NY 10017-1822
T: (212) 750-5795; E-Mail: paintl@igc.apc.org; Fax: (212) 750-5849
Focus: Educ 16150

Peace History Society (PHS), c/o History Dept, Miami University, Oxford, OH 45056
T: (513) 529-5125; E-Mail: jkimball@miamiu.acs.muohio.edu; Fax: (513) 529-3841
Gen Secr: Jeffrey Kimball
Focus: Hist; Prom Peace 16151

Peace Research Society (PRS), c/o Jeffrey Kimball, Dept of History, Miami University, Oxford, OH 45056
T: (513) 545-2150; Fax: (513) 530-5646
Founded: 1963; Members: 250
Pres: G. Smith
Focus: Hist; Prom Peace 16152

Peace Science Society International (PSSI), c/o Dept of Political Science, Binghamton University, POB 6000, Binghamton, NY 13902-6000
T: (607) 777-2946; Fax: (607) 777-2562
Founded: 1963; Members: 500
Gen Secr: Prof. Stuart A. Bremer
Focus: Prom Peace
Periodical
Conflict Management and Peace Science (semi-annually) 16153

Peace Studies Association (PSA), c/o Peace and Global Studies, Earlham College, Drawer 105, Richmond, IN 47374-4095
T: (317) 983-1386; E-Mail: psa@earlham.edu; Fax: (317) 983-1229
Gen Secr: Anthony Bing
Focus: Prom Peace 16154

PEN American Center (PENAC), 568 Broadway, New York, NY 10012
T: (212) 334-1660; Fax: (212) 334-2181
Founded: 1921; Members: 2500
Focus: Lit
Periodicals
Grants and Awards Available to American Writers (bi-annually)
Newsletter (quarterly) 16155

People United for Rural Education (PURE), Box 14, Alden, IA 50006-0014
T: (515) 855-4332
Founded: 1977; Members: 3500
Pres: Fred Erickson
Focus: Educ 16156

People's Decade of Human Rights Education (PDHRE-International), 536 W 111 St, Ste 4E, New York, NY 10025
T: (212) 749-3156; E-Mail: pdhr@igc.apc.org; Fax: (212) 666-6325
Gen Secr: Shulamith Koenig
Focus: Educ; Law 16157

Percussive Arts Society (PAS), POB 25, Lawton, OK 73502
T: (405) 353-1455; Fax: (405) 353-1456
Founded: 1960; Members: 5500
Focus: Music
Periodicals
Percussion News (monthly)
Percussive Notes (5 times annually)
Research Edit (annually) 16158

Performing and Visual Arts Society (PAVAS), c/o Saint Francis High School, 4129 Lake Shore Rd, Athol Springs, NY 14010-0400
T: (716) 627-2386; Fax: (716) 627-4610
Founded: 1967; Members: 400
Pres: David Nease
Focus: Arts 16159

Perlite Institute (PI), 88 New Dorp Plaza, Staten Island, NY 10306
T: (718) 351-5723; Fax: (718) 351-5725
Founded: 1949; Members: 65
Focus: Mining 16160

Permanent International Association of Navigation Congresses - United States Section (PIANC), 7701 Telegraph Rd, Alexandria, VA 22315-3868
T: (703) 355-0286; Fax: (703) 355-3171
Founded: 1902; Members: 600
Gen Secr: Thomas M. Ballentine
Focus: Navig
Periodical
Newsletter (quarterly) 16161

Peruvian Heart Association (PHA), 100 S Greenleaf Av, Gurnee, IL 60031-3378
T: (708) 249-2111; Fax: (708) 249-2772
Founded: 1967; Members: 400
Gen Secr: Luis Vasquez
Focus: Cardiol 16162

Philip C. Jessup International Law Moot Court Competition (PCJILMCC), c/o International Law Students Association, 2223 Massachusetts Av NW, Washington, DC 20008
T: (202) 939-6033; Fax: (202) 265-0386
Founded: 1959; Members: 1500
Focus: Law 16163

Philip Jose Farmer Society (PJFS), 310 S Prospect Av, Champaign, IL 61820-4715
T: (217) 355-1937; E-Mail: scheetz@prairienet.org
Founded: 1978; Members: 150
Gen Secr: George H. Scheetz
Focus: Lit 16164

Philosophic Society for the Study of Sport (PSSS), c/o Dept of Physical Education, Recreation and Health, 130 D'Angola Gymnasium, Kean College of New Jersey, Union, NJ 07083-7131
T: (908) 527-2549; Fax: (908) 527-1808
Founded: 1972; Members: 150
Gen Secr: Prof. Janet M. Oussaty
Focus: Philos; Sports
Periodical
Journal of the Philosophy of Sport (annually) 16165

Philosophical Research Society (PRS), 3910 Los Feliz Blvd, Los Angeles, CA 90027
T: (213) 663-2167; Fax: (213) 663-9443
Founded: 1934
Focus: Philos
Periodical
Journal (quarterly) 16166

Philosophy of Science Association (PSA), c/o Dept of Philosophy, Michigan State University, 503 S Kedzie Hall, East Lansing, MI 48824
T: (517) 353-9392
Founded: 1934; Members: 1000
Pres: Abner Shimony; Gen Secr: Prof. Peter D. Asquith
Focus: Philos
Periodical
Philosophy of Science (quarterly) . . . 16167

Phoenix Society for Burn Survivors (PSBS), 11 Rust Hill Rd, Levittown, PA 19056
T: (215) 946-2876; Fax: (215) 946-4788
Founded: 1977; Members: 7500
Gen Secr: Alan J. Breslau
Focus: Rehabil 16168

Photographic Art and Science Foundation (PASF), 111 Stratford, Des Plaines, IL 60016-2105
T: (708) 824-6855
Founded: 1965; Members: 375
Focus: Photo 16169

Physicians Forum (PF), 1507 53 St, Ste 155, Chicago, IL 60615
T: (312) 922-1968; Fax: (312) 633-6442
Founded: 1939; Members: 1000
Focus: Physiology
Periodicals
Newsletter (quarterly)
Physicians Forum Bulletin (quarterly) . . 16170

Pierre Fauchard Academy (PFA), 8021 W 79 St, Justice, IL 60458-1607
T: (708) 594-5884; Fax: (708) 496-1066
Founded: 1936; Members: 5000
Gen Secr: Dr. Richard Kozal
Focus: Dent
Periodicals
Dental World (quarterly)
Membership Roster 16171

Pilgrim Society (PS), 75 Court St, Plymouth, MA 02360
T: (508) 746-1620
Founded: 1820; Members: 850
Gen Secr: Peggy M. Baker
Focus: Hist
Periodical
Pilgrim Society Notes (irregularly) . . . 16172

Pioneer America Society (PAS), c/o Charles F. Calkins, Dept of Geography, UW Center-Waukesha, Waukesha, WI 53188
T: (415) 524-5498
Founded: 1967; Members: 500
Gen Secr: Charles F. Calkins
Focus: Hist; Folklore
Periodicals
Material Culture (3 times annually)
Newsletter (irregularly)
P.A.S.T.: Pioneer America Society Transactions (annually) 16173

Pirandello Society of America (PSA), c/o Dept of English, Saint John's University, Jamaica, NY 11439
T: (718) 767-8380; Fax: (718) 767-8380
Founded: 1958; Members: 500
Pres: Dr. Anne Paolucci
Focus: Lit
Periodical
PSA (3-4 times annually) 16174

Planetary Society (PS), 65 N Catalina Av, Pasadena, CA 91106-2301
T: (818) 793-5100; E-Mail: tps@mars.planetary.org; Fax: (818) 793-5528
Founded: 1980; Members: 100000
Focus: Astronomy
Periodical
Planetary Report (bi-monthly) 16175

Planned Parenthood Federation of America (PPFA), 810 Seventh Av, New York, NY 10019
T: (212) 541-7800; Fax: (212) 245-1845
Founded: 1916; Members: 169
Focus: Med; Sociology; Family Plan . . 16176

Plastic Surgery Research Council (PSRC), c/o Peter Johnson, University of Pittsburgh, 676 Scaife Hall, Pittsburgh, PA 15261
T: (412) 648-8100
Founded: 1955; Members: 232
Gen Secr: Peter Johnson
Focus: Surgery
Periodical
Meeting Abstracts (annually) 16177

Plastics Institute of America (PIA), 277 Fairfield Rd, Ste 100, Fairfield, NJ 07004-1932
T: (201) 808-5950; Fax: (201) 808-5953
Founded: 1961; Members: 50
Focus: Eng
Periodicals
Institute Report (semi-annually)
Pipeline (quarterly) 16178

Play Schools Association (PSA), POB 573, New York, NY 10156-0573
T: (212) 725-6540; Fax: (212) 532-9674
Founded: 1917
Gen Secr: Joseph Corrado
Focus: Educ 16179

Poe Foundation (PF), 1914-1916 Main St, Richmond, VA 23223
T: (804) 648-5523
Founded: 1921
Focus: Lit 16180

Poe Studies Association (PSA), c/o Roberta Sharp, 1010 Rosemary Ln, La Verne, CA 91750
Founded: 1971; Members: 206
Gen Secr: Roberta Sharp
Focus: Lit 16181

Poetry Society of America (PSA), 15 Gramercy Park, New York, NY 10003
T: (212) 254-9628
Founded: 1910; Members: 2000
Pres: John Barr; Gen Secr: Elise Paschen
Focus: Lit
Periodical
Journal (semi-annually) 16182

Policy Studies Organization (PSO), c/o University of Illinois, 361 Lincoln Hall, 702 S Wright St, Urbana, IL 61801
T: (217) 359-8541; Fax: (217) 244-5712
Founded: 1971; Members: 2200
Focus: Poli Sci
Periodicals
Policy Studies Journal (quarterly)
Policy Studies Review (quarterly) . . . 16183

Polish American Historical Association (PAHA), 984 N Milwaukee Av, Chicago, IL 60622
T: (313) 384-3352
Founded: 1941; Members: 600
Focus: Hist

Periodicals
Newsletter (quarterly)
Polish American Studies (semi-annually) . 16184

Polish Genealogical Society (PGS), 984 N Milwaukee Av, Chicago, IL 60622
T: (312) 384-3352
Founded: 1978; Members: 760
Focus: Genealogy
Periodical
PGS Newsletter (semi-annually) 16185

Polish Institute of Arts and Sciences in America (PIASA), 208 E 30 St, New York, NY 10016
T: (212) 686-4164; Fax: (212) 545-1130
Founded: 1942; Members: 1500
Focus: Arts; Sci
Periodical
Polish Review (quarterly) 16186

Popular Culture Association (PCA), Popular Culture Center, Bowling Green State University, Bowling Green, OH 43403
T: (419) 372-7861; Fax: (419) 372-8095
Founded: 1969; Members: 2500
Focus: Hist
Periodical
Journal of Popular Culture (quarterly) . . 16187

Population Action International, 1120 NW 19 St, Ste 550, Washington, DC 20036
T: (202) 659-1833; Fax: (202) 293-1795
Founded: 1965; Members: 1500
Pres: J. Joseph Speidel
Focus: Sociology 16188

Population Association of America (PAA), 1722 N St NW, Washington, DC 20036
T: (202) 429-0891; Fax: (202) 785-0146
Founded: 1931; Members: 2700
Pres: L. Waite
Focus: Sociology 16189

Population Council (PC), 1 Dag Hammarskjold Plaza, New York, NY 10017
T: (212) 339-0500; Fax: (212) 755-6052
Founded: 1952
Pres: Margaret Catley-Carlson
Focus: Sociology 16190

Population Reference Bureau (PRB), 1875 Connecticut Av NW, Ste 520, Washington, DC 20009
T: (202) 483-1100; Fax: (202) 328-3937
Founded: 1929; Members: 4200
Focus: Sociology
Periodicals
Interchange (quarterly)
Intercom (bi-monthly)
Population Bulletin (quarterly)
US Population Data Sheet (annually) . . 16191

Postal History Society (PHS), 8207 Daren Ct, Pikesville, MD 21208
T: (410) 653-0665
Founded: 1951; Members: 600
Focus: Cultur Hist
Periodical
Postal History Journal (3 times annually) 16192

Postgraduate Center for Mental Health (PCMH), 124 E 28 St, New York, NY 10016
T: (212) 689-7700; Fax: (212) 576-4194
Founded: 1945
Focus: Psychiatry
Periodicals
Dynamic Psychotherapy Journal (semi-annually)
New Outlook (monthly)
Pathways (semi-annually) 16193

Potash and Phosphate Institute (PPI), 655 Engineering Dr, No 110, Norcross, GA 30092
T: (770) 447-0335; Fax: (770) 448-0439
Founded: 1935; Members: 13
Pres: D.W. Dibb
Focus: Agri 16194

Potato Association of America (PAA), c/o John Ojala, University of Idaho, 1776 Science Center Dr, Idaho Falls, ID 83402
T: (208) 529-8376; Fax: (208) 522-2954
Founded: 1913; Members: 1100
Gen Secr: John Ojala
Focus: Food; Agri 16195

Poultry Science Association (PSA), 309 W Clark St, Champaign, IL 61820
T: (217) 356-3182; Fax: (217) 398-4119
Founded: 1908; Members: 1800
Pres: Henry Marks; Gen Secr: Carl D. Johnson
Focus: Zoology
Periodical
Poultry Science (monthly) 16196

Powys Society of North America (PSNA), c/o English Dept, Valparaiso University, Valparaiso, IN 46383
T: (219) 464-5069
Founded: 1983; Members: 150
Focus: Lit 16197

Practical Allergy Research Foundation (PARF), POB 60, Buffalo, NY 14223
T: (716) 875-5578; Fax: (716) 877-8475
Focus: Med 16198

Practising Law Institute (PLI), 810 Seventh Av, New York, NY 10019
T: (212) 765-5700; Fax: (212) 265-4742
Founded: 1933; Members: 50000
Focus: Law 16199

Precision Chiropractic Research Society (PCRS), 1412 Alta Mesa Way, Brea, CA 92621
T: (213) 694-4181
Founded: 1976; Members: 200
Focus: Orthopedics 16200

Precision Measurements Association (PMA), 3685 Motor Av, Ste 240, Los Angeles, CA 90034
T: (310) 287-0941; Fax: (310) 287-1851
Founded: 1959; Members: 600
Focus: Eng
Periodical
Newsnotes (quarterly) 16201

Presbyterian Historical Society (PHS), 425 Lombard St, Philadelphia, PA 19147
T: (215) 627-1852; Fax: (215) 627-0509
Founded: 1852; Members: 1100
Gen Secr: Frederick J. Heuser Jr.
Focus: Hist
Periodical
American Presbyterians (quarterly) . . . 16202

Price-Pottenger Nutrition Foundation (PPNF), POB 2614, La Mesa, CA 91943-2614
T: (619) 574-7763; E-Mail: PPNF@aol.com; Fax: (619) 574-1314
Founded: 1952; Members: 800
Gen Secr: Marion Patricia Connolly
Focus: Food
Periodical
Membership Journal (quarterly) 16203

Primitive Art Society of Chicago (PAS), POB 1840, Chicago, IL 60690
T: (312) 280-0208
Founded: 1977; Members: 100
Focus: Arts 16204

Print Council of America (PCA), c/o Dept of Prints, Drawings and Photographs, Yale University Art Gallery, 2006 Yale Station, New Haven, CT 06520
T: (203) 432-0628; Fax: (203) 432-8150
Founded: 1956; Members: 150
Pres: Richard S. Field
Focus: Eng 16205

Probe Ministries International (PMI), 1900 Firman Dr, Ste 100, Richardson, TX 75081-6796
T: (214) 480-0240; Fax: (214) 644-9664
Founded: 1973
Focus: Educ 16206

Professional Football Researches Association (PFRA), 12870 Rte 30, North Huntington, PA 15642
T: (412) 863-6345
Founded: 1979; Members: 220
Focus: Sports
Periodicals
Coffin Corner (bi-monthly)
End of Year Journal (annually)
Membership Directory (annually) 16207

Professional Numismatists Guild (PNG), c/o Robert Brueggeman, 3950 Concordia Ln, Fallbrook, CA 92028
T: (619) 728-1300; Fax: (619) 728-8507
Founded: 1954; Members: 250
Gen Secr: Robert Brueggeman
Focus: Numismatics 16208

Professional Psychics United (PPU), 7115 W North Av, Oak Park, IL 60302
T: (312) 877-2662; Fax: (312) 693-6737
Founded: 1977; Members: 350
Pres: Phyllis Allen
Focus: Parapsych 16209

Professors of Curriculum (PC), c/o Peter Hlebowitsh, University of Iowa, N259 Linquist Center, Iowa City, IA 52242
T: (713) 743-4956
Members: 100
Gen Secr: Peter Hlebowitsh
Focus: Educ
Periodical
Directory 16210

Professors World Peace Academy (PWPA), 2700 University Av W, Ste 47, Saint Paul, MN 55114
T: (612) 644-2809; Fax: (612) 644-0997
Gen Secr: Dr. Gordon L. Anderson
Focus: Prom Peace 16211

Program for Appropriate Technology in Health (PATH), 4 Nickerson St, Ste 300, Seattle, WA 98109-1699
T: (206) 285-3500; E-Mail: info@path.org; Fax: (206) 285-6619
Founded: 1981
Pres: Dr. Gordon W. Perkin
Focus: Public Health; Eng 16212

Program of Joint Studies on Latin American Economic Integration (ECIEL), c/o Editor Ensayos Eciel, Brookings Institution, 1775 Massachusetts Av NW, Washington, DC 20036
Focus: Develop Areas 16213

Program on the Analysis and Resolution of Conflicts (PARC), c/o Syracuse University, 410 Maxwell Hall, Syracuse, NY 13244
T: (315) 443-2367; Fax: (315) 443-3818
Gen Secr: Robert A. Rubinstein
Focus: Military Sci 16214

Project Magic (PM), c/o Kansas Rehabilitation Hospital, 1504 SW Eighth St, Topeka, KS 66606
T: (913) 235-6600
Founded: 1982
Focus: Rehabil 16215

Project Management Institute (PMI), 130 S State Rd, Upper Darby, PA 19082
T: (610) 734-3330; E-Mail: pmieo@ix.netcom.com; Fax: (610) 734-3266
Founded: 1969; Members: 18000
Gen Secr: Deborah Bigelow
Focus: Business Admin
Periodical
Project Management Journal (5 times annually) 16216

Protein Society, 9650 Rockville Pike, Bethesda, MD 20814
T: (301) 571-0662; E-Mail: Newburgh@protein.faseb.org; Fax: (301) 571-0666
Founded: 1986; Members: 2800
Gen Secr: Robert W. Newburgh
Focus: Biochem 16217

Proust Research Association (PRA), c/o Dept of French and Italian, University of Kansas, Lawrence, KS 66045
T: (913) 864-3388
Founded: 1967; Members: 250
Gen Secr: J. Theodore Johnson
Focus: Lit
Periodical
Newsletter (annually) 16218

Psi Chi – National Honor Society in Psychology, 407 E Fifth St, Ste B, Chattanooga, TN 37403
T: (423) 756-2044; Fax: (423) 265-1529
Founded: 1929; Members: 260000
Gen Secr: Kay Wilson
Focus: Psych
Periodicals
Handbook (bi-annually)
Newsletter (quarterly) 16219

Psoriasis Research Association (PRA), 107 Vista del Grande, San Carlos, CA 94070
T: (415) 593-1394
Founded: 1952
Focus: Derm
Periodicals
Abstracts (quarterly)
Bulletin 16220

Psoriasis Research Institute (PRI), 600 Town and Country Village, Palo Alto, CA 94301
T: (415) 326-1848; Fax: (415) 326-1262
Founded: 1979
Focus: Derm 16221

Psychic Science International Special Interest Group (PSISIG), 7514 Belleplain Dr, Huber Heights, OH 45424-3229
T: (513) 236-0361; Fax: (513) 236-0361
Founded: 1976; Members: 130
Focus: Psych 16222

Psychology of Religion, c/o Siang-Yang Tan, Fuller Theological Seminary, 180 N Oakland Av, Pasadena, CA 91101-1792
T: (818) 584-5532
Founded: 1948; Members: 1350
Gen Secr: Dr. Siang-Yang Tan
Focus: Rel & Theol; Psych
Periodical
Newsletter (quarterly) 16223

Psychology Society (PS), 100 Beekman St, New York, NY 10038-1810
T: (212) 285-1872
Founded: 1960; Members: 3200
Focus: Psych
Periodicals
Membership List (bi-annually)
PS Quarterly (quarterly) 16224

Psychometric Society (PS), c/o University of Illinois, 260 Education Bldg, 1310 S Sixth St, Champaign, IL 61820
T: (217) 244-3361; Fax: (217) 244-7620
Founded: 1935; Members: 750
Gen Secr: Dr. Terry Ackerman
Focus: Psych
Periodical
Psychometrika (quarterly) 16225

Psychonomic Society (PS), c/o Dr. Randi C. Martin, Psychology Dept, Rice University, 6100 S Main St, Houston, TX 77005
T: (713) 527-8101; Fax: (713) 258-5221
Founded: 1959; Members: 2400
Gen Secr: Dr. Randi C. Martin
Focus: Psych
Periodicals
Animal Learning and Behavior (quarterly)
Behavior Research Methods (bi-monthly)
Bulletin (monthly)
Memory & Cognition (bi-monthly)
Perception and Psychophysics (monthly)
Psychobiology (quarterly) 16226

Public Citizen Health Research Group (PCHRG), 2000 P St NW, Washington, DC 20036
T: (202) 833-3000
Founded: 1971
Focus: Public Health
Periodical
Health Letter (bi-monthly) 16227

Public Law Education Institute (PLEI), 454 New Jersey Av SE, Washington, DC 20003
T: (202) 544-8646
Founded: 1968
Pres: Thomas P. Alder
Focus: Law 16228

Public Leadership Education Network (PLEN), 1001 Connecticut Av NW, Ste 925, Washington, DC 20036
T: (202) 872-1585
Founded: 1978; Members: 17
Focus: Educ 16229

Public Library Association (PLA), c/o American Library Association, 50 E Huron St, Chicago, IL 60611
T: (312) 280-5752; Fax: (312) 280-5029
Founded: 1944; Members: 7300
Focus: Libraries & Bk Sci
Periodicals
Public Libraries (quarterly)
Public Library Reporter (irregularly) . . . 16230

Public Relations Society of America (PRSA), 33 Irving Pl, New York, NY 10003-2376
T: (212) 995-2230; Fax: (212) 995-0757
Founded: 1947; Members: 15462
Focus: Public Health
Periodical
Health Academy News (quarterly) . . . 16231

Public Responsibility in Medicine and Research (PRIM&R), 132 Boylston St, Boston, MA 02116
T: (617) 423-4112; Fax: (617) 423-1185
Founded: 1974; Members: 65
Focus: Med
Periodical
Conference Report (semi-annually) . . . 16232

Public Service Research Council (PSRC), 527 Maple Av, Vienna, VA 22180
T: (703) 242-3575; Fax: (703) 242-3579
Founded: 1973; Members: 15000
Pres: David Y. Denholm
Focus: Public Admin
Periodicals
The Government Union Critique (bi-weekly)
Government Union Review (quarterly) . . 16233

Public Works Historical Society (PWHS), 1801 Maple, Evanton, IL 60637
T: (708) 491-5829; Fax: (312) 667-2304
Founded: 1975; Members: 1900
Focus: Hist 16234

R.A. Bloch Cancer Foundation, 4410 Main, Kansas City, MO 64111
T: (816) 932-8453; Fax: (816) 753-5346
Founded: 1980
Focus: Cell Biol & Cancer Res 16235

Rabbinic Center for Research and Counseling (RCRC), 128 E Dudley Av, Westfield, NJ 07090
T: (908) 233-0419
Founded: 1970
Focus: Therapeutics 16236

The Radiance Technique Association International (TRTAI), POB 40570, Saint Petersburg, FL 33743-0570
T: (813) 347-3421
Founded: 1980
Focus: Med
Periodical
The Radiance Technique Journal . . . 16237

Radiation Research Society (RRS), 2021 Spring Rd, Ste 600, Oak Brook, IL 60521
T: (708) 571-2881; Fax: (708) 571-7837
Founded: 1952; Members: 1970
Pres: J. Martin Browne; Gen Secr: Mark Watson
Focus: Radiology
Periodicals
Radiation Research (annually)
RRS News (quarterly) 16238

Radiation Therapy Oncology Group (RTOG), c/o American College of Radiology, 1101 Market St, Philadelphia, PA 19107
T: (215) 574-3150
Founded: 1971; Members: 120
Focus: Cell Biol & Cancer Res; Radiology; Therapeutics 16239

Radio and Television Research Council (RTRC), 245 Fifth Av, Ste 2103, New York, NY 10016
T: (212) 481-3038; Fax: (212) 481-3071
Founded: 1941; Members: 200
Focus: Mass Media 16240

Radiological Society of North America (RSNA), 2021 Spring Rd, Ste 600, Oak Brook, IL 60521
T: (708) 571-2670; Fax: (708) 571-7837
Founded: 1915; Members: 30000
Pres: Dr. Ernest Ferris; Gen Secr: C. Douglas Maynard
Focus: Radiology
Periodicals
Radio Graphics (bi-monthly)
Radiology (monthly)
RSNA Today (quarterly) 16241

Radix Institute (RI), 6300 Ridglea Pl, No 1212, Fort Worth, TX 76116-5738
T: (817) 738-3638; E-Mail: Steprad@aol.com
Founded: 1960; Members: 96
Gen Secr: Dale Cummings

Focus: Psych 16242

Railroad Station Historical Society (RSHS), 430 Ivy Av, Crete, NE 68333
T: (402) 826-3356
Founded: 1967; Members: 400
Focus: Hist
Periodicals
The Bulletin (bi-monthly)
Monograph (annually) 16243

Ralph Waldo Emerson Memorial Association (RWEMA), 79 Milk St, Boston, MA 02109
T: (617) 423-5705
Founded: 1930; Members: 15
Gen Secr: Roger L. Gregg
Focus: Lit 16244

RAND Center for Russian and Eurasian Studies, 1700 Main St, POB 2138, Santa Monica, CA 90407-2138
T: (310) 393-0411; Fax: (310) 451-7036
Focus: Ethnology 16245

Rare Earth Research Conference (RERC), c/o Dept of Chemistry, University of Minnesota, Duluth, MN 55812
T: (218) 726-8716
Founded: 1960; Members: 325
Gen Secr: Dr. Larry C. Thompson
Focus: Sci
Periodical
Proceedings of Conference (bi-annually) . 16246

Read Natural Childbirth Foundation (RNCF), POB 150956, San Rafael, CA 94915
T: (415) 456-3143; Fax: (415) 456-3143
Founded: 1978; Members: 30
Pres: Margaret B. Farley
Focus: Gynecology 16247

Reading is Fundamental (RIF), 600 Maryland Av SW, Ste 500, Washington, DC 20024
T: (202) 287-3220; Fax: (202) 287-3196
Founded: 1966; Members: 3559
Focus: Ling 16248

Reading Reform Foundation (RRF), POB 98785, Tacoma, WA 98498-0785
T: (206) 588-3436; Fax: (206) 582-7877
Founded: 1961; Members: 258
Focus: Ling
Periodical
The Reading Informator (quarterly) . . . 16249

Reference and Adult Services Division (of ALA) (RASD), c/o American Library Association, 50 E Huron St, Chicago, IL 60611
T: (312) 280-4398; Fax: (312) 545-2433
Founded: 1972; Members: 5500
Focus: Libraries & Bk Sci
Periodicals
RASD Update (quarterly)
RQ (quarterly) 16250

Reforma: National Association to Promote Library Services to the Spanish-Speaking, c/o Mario M. Gonzalez, Office of Programs and Services, New York Public Library, 455 Fifth Av, New York, NY 10016
T: (212) 340-0924; Fax: (212) 340-0988
Founded: 1971; Members: 700
Pres: Mario M. Gonzalez
Focus: Libraries & Bk Sci
Periodical
Reforma (quarterly) 16251

Refugee Policy Group (RPG), 1424 16 St NW, Ste 401, Washington, DC 20036
T: (202) 387-3015; Fax: (202) 667-5034
Gen Secr: Dennis Gallagher
Focus: Poli Sci 16252

Regional Education Board of the Christian Brothers, c/o Christian Brothers Conference, 4351 Garden City Dr, Ste 200, Landover, MD 20785
T: (301) 459-9410; E-Mail: dehrmantra@aol.com;
Fax: (301) 459-8056
Founded: 1970; Members: 9
Gen Secr: Theodore Drahmann
Focus: Educ 16253

Regional Institute of Social Welfare Research (RISWR), POB 152, Athens, GA 30603
T: (404) 546-0798
Founded: 1970
Focus: Sociology
Periodical
Annual Report (annually) 16254

Regional Network for Research on Economic Policy, c/o IDB, Div of Research in Development Policies, 1300 New York Av, Washington, DC 20577
T: (202) 623-1000; Fax: (202) 789-2835
Focus: Poli Sci 16255

Regional Program for Educational Development (PREDE/OEA), c/o OAS, 17 St and Constitution Av NW, Washington, DC 20006
T: (202) 458-3000
Focus: Educ 16256

Regional Science Association International (RSA), c/o Observatory, University of Illinois, 901 S Matthews, Urbana, IL 61801
T: (217) 333-8904; Fax: (217) 333-3065
Founded: 1954; Members: 2500
Gen Secr: Dr. G. Hewings
Focus: Urban Plan 16257

Registered Medical Assistants of American Medical Technologists (RMAAMT), 710 Higgins Rd, Park Ridge, IL 60068-5765
T: (708) 823-5169; Fax: (708) 823-0458
Founded: 1976; Members: 9000
Focus: Med
Periodicals
AMT Directory (annually)
Vital Signs (quarterly) 16258

Rehabilitation Information Round Table (RIRT), c/o American Physical Therapy Association, 1111 N Fairfax St, Alexandria, VA 22314
T: (703) 706-3210
Founded: 1979; Members: 60
Gen Secr: Phyllis Quinn
Focus: Rehabil
Periodical
Newsletter (semi-annually) 16259

Rehabilitation International (RI), 25 E 21 St, New York, NY 10010
T: (212) 420-1500; Fax: (212) 505-0871
Founded: 1992; Members: 145
Gen Secr: Susan B. Parker
Focus: Rehabil
Periodicals
International Journal of Rehabilitation Research (quarterly)
International Rehabilitation Review
One-in-Ten (quarterly)
Rehabilitation (semi-annually) 16260

Reinforced Concrete Research Council (RCRC), c/o Ferguson Laboratory, 10100 Burnet Rd, Austin, TX 78758
T: (512) 471-7298
Founded: 1948; Members: 40
Gen Secr: Sharon L. Wood
Focus: Civil Eng 16261

Religious Research Association (RRA), c/o Catholic University of America, 108 Marist Hall, Washington, DC 20064
T: (202) 319-5447
Founded: 1959; Members: 400
Gen Secr: W. Swatos
Focus: Sociology; Rel & Theol
Periodical
Review of Religious Research (quarterly) . 16262

Religious Speech Communication Association (RSCA), c/o Roxane S. Lulufs, Azusa Pacific University, Azusa, CA 91702-7000
T: (818) 969-3434; E-Mail: rlulofs@class.org;
Fax: (818) 969-7180
Founded: 1973; Members: 265
Gen Secr: Roxane S. Lulofs
Focus: Ling 16263

Renaissance English Text Society (RETS), c/o Arthur F. Kinney, Dept of English, University of Massachusetts, Amherst, MA 01003
T: (413) 545-2332; Fax: (413) 545-3880
Founded: 1959; Members: 250
Pres: Arthur F. Kinney
Focus: Lit 16264

Renaissance Society of America (RSA), 24 W 12 St, New York, NY 10011
T: (212) 998-3797; Fax: (212) 995-4205
Founded: 1954; Members: 3500
Gen Secr: John Monfasani
Focus: Hist
Periodical
Renaissance Quarterly (quarterly) 16265

Research and Engineering Council of the Graphic Arts Industry (RECGAI), Marshallton Bldg, POB 639, Chadds Ford, PA 19317
T: (215) 388-7394; Fax: (215) 388-2708
Founded: 1950; Members: 325
Focus: Eng
Periodical
The Review: Recent Patents of Interest to the Graphic Arts Industry (quarterly) 16266

Research Association of Minority Professors (RAMP), PO Drawer 67, Prairie View, TX 77446
T: (800) 434-5650; E-Mail: hfrank@ipa.pvamu.edu;
Fax: (800) 857-2019
Founded: 1982; Members: 111
Pres: Bennie Adams
Focus: Educ 16267

Research Council on Structural Connections (RCSC), c/o Sagent & Lyndy, 55 E Monroe St, Chicago, IL 60603
T: (312) 269-2424
Founded: 1946; Members: 56
Focus: Eng 16268

Research Libraries Group (RLG), 1200 Villa St, Mountain View, CA 94041-1100
T: (415) 962-9951; Fax: (415) 964-0943
Founded: 1974; Members: 120
Focus: Libraries & Bk Sci 16269

Research Society for Victorian Periodicals (RSVP), c/o Dept of English, Southern Illinois University, Edwardsville, IL 62026-1436
T: (618) 692-2326
Founded: 1969; Members: 600
Gen Secr: Prof. B.Q. Schmidt
Focus: Lit; Journalism
Periodical
Victorian Periodicals Review (quarterly) . 16270

Research Society on Alcoholism (RSA), 4314 Medical Pkwy, Austin, TX 78756
T: (512) 454-0022; Fax: (512) 454-0022
Founded: 1976; Members: 870
Focus: Soc Sci 16271

Research to Prevent Blindness (RPB), 645 Madison Av, New York, NY 10022-1010
T: (212) 752-4333; Fax: (212) 688-6231
Founded: 1960
Pres: David F. Weeks
Focus: Ophthal 16272

Rhetoric Society of America (RSA), c/o Kathleen Welch, Dept of English, University of Oklahoma, Norman, OK 73019
T: (405) 325-4661; Fax: (405) 325-0831
Founded: 1968; Members: 1200
Gen Secr: Kathleen Welch
Focus: Humanities
Periodical
Rhetoric Society Quarterly (quarterly) . . 16273

Richard III Society, POB 13786, New Orleans, LA 70185
T: (504) 827-0161; Fax: (504) 822-7599
Founded: 1924; Members: 750
Focus: Hist
Periodicals
The Ricardian (quarterly)
The Ricardian Register (quarterly) . . . 16274

Robinson Jeffers Committee (RJC), c/o Dept of English, California State University, 1250 Bellflower Blvd, Long Beach, CA 90840-2403
T: (310) 985-4235; Fax: (310) 985-2269
Founded: 1962; Members: 3
Gen Secr: Robert J. Brophy
Focus: Lit 16275

Robotics International of the Society of Manufacturing Engineers (RI/SME), 1 SME Dr, POB 930, Dearborn, MI 48121
T: (313) 271-1500; Fax: (313) 271-2861
Founded: 1980; Members: 7800
Focus: Electronic Eng; Computer & Info Sci
Periodical
Robotics Today Magazine (bi-monthly) . 16276

Rodale International (RI), 222 Main St, Emmaus, PA 18049
T: (215) 967-5171; Fax: (215) 967-8963
Founded: 1982; Members: 75000
Pres: John Haberern
Focus: Agri 16277

Rodeo Historical Society (RHS), 1700 NE 63 St, Oklahoma City, OK 73111
T: (405) 478-2250; Fax: (405) 478-4714
Founded: 1968; Members: 1200
Focus: Hist 16278

Rogers Group (RG), 4932 Prince George Av, Beltsville, MD 20705
T: (301) 937-7899
Founded: 1970; Members: 110
Focus: Arts 16279

Rolf Institute (RI), POB 1868, Boulder, CO 80306
T: (303) 449-5903; Fax: (303) 449-5978
Founded: 1971; Members: 745
Focus: Physical Therapy
Periodicals
Bulletin of Structural Integration (quarterly)
Directory of Certified Rolfers and Movement Teachers (semi-annually)
National Listing of Rolfers (quarterly) . . 16280

Rose Kushner Breast Cancer Advisory Center (RKBCAC), POB 224, Kensington, MD 20895
T: (301) 897-3445; Fax: (301) 897-3444
Founded: 1975
Gen Secr: Harvey D. Kushner
Focus: Cell Biol & Cancer Res 16281

RTCA, 1140 Connecticut Av NW, Ste 1020, Washington, DC 20036
T: (202) 833-9339; Fax: (202) 833-9434
Founded: 1935; Members: 185
Gen Secr: David S. Watrous
Focus: Electric Eng; Aero
Periodical
RTCA Digest (quarterly) 16282

Rural Community Assistance Program (RCAP), 602 S King St, Ste 402, Leesburg, VA 22075
T: (703) 771-8636
Founded: 1973; Members: 13
Focus: Water Res
Periodicals
Directory of Network Organizations (semi-annually)
Rural Water News (bi-monthly) 16283

Rural Sociological Society (RSS), c/o Dept of Sociology, Western Washington University, 510 Arntzen Hall, Bellingham, WA 98225
T: (360) 650-7571; E-Mail: rural-soc@cc.wwu.edu;
Fax: (360) 650-7295
Founded: 1937; Members: 1050
Gen Secr: R.J. Burdge
Focus: Sociology
Periodicals
The Rural Sociologist (quarterly)
Rural Sociology (quarterly) 16284

Rushlight Club (RC), 1657 The Fairway, Ste 196, Jenkintown, PA 19046
T: (215) 797-3637; Fax: (215) 263-5746
Founded: 1932
Pres: William Righter
Focus: Hist
Periodical
The Rushlight (quarterly) 16285

SAE International, 400 Commonwealth Dr, Warrendale, PA 15096-0001
T: (412) 776-4841; Fax: (412) 776-5760
Founded: 1905; Members: 60000
Focus: Eng
Periodicals
Aerospace Engineering (monthly)
Automotive Engineering (monthly)
Handbook (annually)
SAE Update (monthly) 16286

Safe Association, 107 Music City Cir, Ste 112, Nashville, TN 37214
T: (615) 902-0056; Fax: (615) 902-0077
Founded: 1960; Members: 900
Gen Secr: Jean Benton
Focus: Eng; Transport
Periodical
Safe Journal (quarterly) 16287

Safety Equipment Institute (SEI), 1901 N Moore St, Ste 808, Arlington, VA 22209
T: (703) 525-3354; Fax: (703) 528-2148
Focus: Safety
Periodical
SEI Certified Product List (semi-annually)   16288

Salt Institute (SI), 700 N Fairfax, Ste 600, Alexandria, VA 22314-2040
T: (703) 549-4648; Fax: (703) 548-2194
Founded: 1914; Members: 25
Focus: Mineralogy
Periodicals
Agriculture Digest (semi-annually)
Highway Digest (semi-annually) 16289

Salzburg Seminar (SS), c/o Marble Works, POB 886, Middlebury, VT 05753
T: (802) 388-0007; Fax: (802) 388-1030
Founded: 1947
Focus: Hist 16290

San Martin Society of Washington, DC, POB 33, McLean, VA 22101
T: (703) 883-0950; Fax: (703) 243-1020
Founded: 1977; Members: 305
Focus: Hist 16291

Saving and Preserving Arts and Cultural Environments (SPACES), 1804 N Van Ness, Los Angeles, CA 90028
T: (213) 463-1629
Founded: 1978; Members: 250
Focus: Arts 16292

Scandinavian Seminar College (SS), 24 Dickinson St, Amherst, MA 01002
T: (413) 253-9736; Fax: (413) 253-5282
Founded: 1949
Gen Secr: Wegard D. Holby
Focus: Ethnology 16293

School Management Study Group (SMSG), 860 18 Av, Salt Lake City, UT 84103
T: (801) 532-5340; Fax: (801) 484-2089
Founded: 1969; Members: 400
Focus: Educ 16294

School Science and Mathematics Association (SSMA), 400 E Second St, Bloomsburg, PA 17815
T: (717) 389-4915; E-Mail: pratt@ bf486.bloomu.edu; Fax: (717) 389-3894
Founded: 1903; Members: 1100
Gen Secr: Donald L. Pratt
Focus: Math; Educ
Periodicals
Convention Program (annually)
Newsletter (quarterly)
School Science and Mathematics (8 times annually) 16295

Science Fiction Research Association (SFRA), c/o Joe Sanders, 6345 Brooks Blvd, Mentor, OH 44060
T: (216) 257-3646; E-Mail: jsanders@ Lcc2.lakeland.cc.oh.us; Fax: (216) 953-9710
Founded: 1970; Members: 325
Gen Secr: Joe Sanders
Focus: Lit
Periodical
Book Review Journal (10 times annually)   16296

Science Service (SS), 1719 N St NW, Washington, DC 20036
T: (202) 785-2255; Fax: (202) 785-1243
Founded: 1921
Focus: Educ 16297

Scientific Committee on Oceanic Research, c/o Dept of Earth and Planetary Sciences, Johns Hopkins University, Baltimore, MD 21218
T: (410) 516-4070 (410) 516-4070; E-Mail: scor@ jhu.edu; Fax: (410) 516-4019
Founded: 1957
Gen Secr: Elizabeth Gross
Focus: Oceanography 16298

Scientific Committee on Solar-Terrestrial Physics (SCOSTEP), c/o NOAA/NGDC, 325 Broadway, Boulder, CO 80303
T: (303) 497-7284; E-Mail: jallen@ngdc.noaa.gov;
Fax: (303) 497-6513

Gen Secr: J.H. Allen
Focus: Physics 16299

Scientific Committee on Water Research (SCOWAR), c/o World Bank, 1818 H St NW, Rm H-7007, Washington, DC 20433
T: (202) 473-2253; E-Mail: jkindler@worldbank.org;
Fax: (202) 477-1981
Gen Secr: J. Kindler
Focus: Hydrology 16300

Scientists and Engineers for Secure Energy (SE2), 570 Seventh Av, Ste 1007, New York, NY 10018
T: (212) 840-6595; Fax: (212) 840-6597
Founded: 1976; Members: 1200
Focus: Energy 16301

Scoliosis Research Society (SRSO), 6300 N River Rd, Ste 727, Rosemont, IL 60018-4226
T: (847) 698-1627; Fax: (847) 823-0536
Founded: 1966; Members: 620
Gen Secr: Tressa Goulding
Focus: Orthopedics 16302

Scribes, c/o School of Law, Wake Forest University, POB 7206, Reynolds Station, Winston-Salem, NC 27109
T: (919) 759-5440; Fax: (919) 759-4301
Founded: 1952; Members: 1004
Gen Secr: Thomas M. Steele
Focus: Lit; Law 16303

Sea Education Association (SEA), POB 6, Woods Hole, MA 02543
T: (508) 540-3954; Fax: (508) 457-4673
Founded: 1971
Focus: Adult Educ
Periodicals
Annual Report (annually)
Following Sea (semi-annually) 16304

Sea Grant Association (SGA), c/o Dr. Anders W. Andren, Wisconsin Sea Grant Institute, University of Wisconsin, 1800 University Av, Madison, WI 53705-4094
T: (608) 262-0905; Fax: (608) 263-2063
Founded: 1970; Members: 39
Pres: Dr. Anders W. Andren
Focus: Oceanography 16305

Search Foundation, POB 380757, Birmingham, AL 35238-0757
T: (205) 991-9516; Fax: (205) 991-2807
Founded: 1969
Pres: John M. Bradley
Focus: Archeol 16306

Search Group (SGI), 7311 Greenhaven Dr, Ste 145, Sacramento, CA 95831
T: (916) 392-2550; Fax: (916) 392-8440
Founded: 1969; Members: 60
Focus: Law
Periodicals
Interface (quarterly)
Report (annually) 16307

Secondary School Admission Test Board (SSATB), 12 Stockton St, Princeton, NJ 08540
T: (609) 683-4440
Founded: 1957; Members: 650
Focus: Educ
Periodicals
Bulletin of Information (annually)
Newsletter (quarterly)
SSATB Network Directory (annually) . . 16308

Section for Rehabilitation Hospitals and Programs (SRHP), c/o American Hospital Association, 1 N Franklin St, Chicago, IL 60606
T: (312) 422-3000
Founded: 1984; Members: 890
Gen Secr: Susanne Sonik
Focus: Rehabil 16309

Section on Women in Legal Education of the AALS, c/o Association of American Law Schools, 1201 Connecticut Av NW, Ste 800, Washington, DC 20036
T: (202) 296-8851
Focus: Law
Periodical
Newsletter (semi-annually) 16310

Seingalt Society (SS), 555 13 Av, Salt Lake City, UT 84103
T: (801) 532-2204
Founded: 1985; Members: 45
Focus: Lit 16311

Seismological Society of America (SSA), 201 El Cerrito Plaza Professional Bldg, El Cerrito, CA 94530
T: (510) 525-5474; Fax: (510) 525-7204
Founded: 1906; Members: 1900
Gen Secr: Joe J. Litehiser
Focus: Geology; Geophys
Periodical
Bulletin (bi-monthly) 16312

Seminar on the Acquisition of Latin American Library Materials (SALALM), c/o Benson Latin American Collection, University of Texas at Austin, 1-109 Sid Richardson Hall, Austin, TX 78713
T: (512) 495-4471; Fax: (512) 495-4488
Founded: 1956; Members: 500
Gen Secr: Laura Gutiérrez-Witt
Focus: Libraries & Bk Sci

Periodicals
Bibliography of Latin American and Caribbean Bibliographies (annually)
Microfilming Projects Newsletter (annually)
Papers of the Seminar on the Acquisition of Latin American Library Materials (annually)
SALALM Bibliography and Reference Series (3 times annually)
SALALM Newsletter (quarterly) 16313

Semiotic Society of America (SSA), c/o University of West Florida, 11000 University Dr, POB 32086, Pensacola, FL 32514
T: (904) 474-2186; Fax: (904) 474-3131
Founded: 1975; Members: 600
Gen Secr: Terry J. Prewitt
Focus: Ling
Periodical
American Journal of Semiotics (quarterly) 16314

Senior Scholars (SS), c/o Office of Continuing Education, Case Western Reserve University, 10900 Euclid Av, Cleveland, OH 44106-7116
T: (216) 368-2090; Fax: (216) 368-2091
Founded: 1972; Members: 130
Gen Secr: Kathy Manos
Focus: Adult Educ 16315

Serendipity Association for Research and Implementation of Holistic Health and World Peace, 4614 Edgeware Rd, San Diego, CA 92116-4760
T: (619) 284-2468
Gen Secr: Dr. Doug Hemstreet
Focus: Public Health; Prom Peace . . . 16316

Sex Information and Education Council of the U.S. (SIECUS), 130 W 42 St, Ste 2500, New York, NY 10036
T: (212) 819-9770; Fax: (212) 819-9776
Founded: 1964; Members: 3600
Focus: Educ
Periodical
SIECUS Report (bi-monthly) 16317

SFI Foundation, 15708 Pomerado Rd, Poway, CA 92064
T: (619) 451-8868; Fax: (619) 451-9268
Founded: 1978
Focus: Eng 16318

Shakespeare Association of America (SAA), c/o Dept of English, Southern Methodist University, Dallas, TX 75275
Founded: 1972; Members: 800
Focus: Lit
Periodicals
Bulletin (semi-annually)
Directory of Members (annually) 16319

Shakespeare Data Bank (SDB), 1217 Ashland Av, Evanston, IL 60202
T: (708) 475-7550; Fax: (708) 475-2415
Founded: 1984; Members: 160
Focus: Lit 16320

Shakespeare Society of America (SSA), 1107 N Kings Rd, West Hollywood, CA 90069
T: (213) 654-5623
Founded: 1967; Members: 1500
Pres: R. Thad Taylor
Focus: Lit 16321

Shaybani Society of International Law (SSIL), c/o ILI, 1615 New Hampshire Av NW, Washington, DC 20009
T: (202) 483-3036; Fax: (202) 483-3029
Gen Secr: Prof. Majid Khadduri
Focus: Law 16322

Sherwood Anderson Society (SAS), c/o Dept of English, Virginia Tech, 200 William Hall, Blacksburg, VA 24061-0112
T: (540) 231-6501; Fax: (540) 231-5692
Founded: 1975; Members: 150
Gen Secr: Charles E. Modlin
Focus: Lit
Periodicals
Bibliography (annually)
Winesburg Eagle (semi-annually) 16323

Shevchenko Scientific Society (SSS), 63 Fourth Av, New York, NY 10003
T: (212) 254-5130; Fax: (212) 254-5139
Founded: 1873; Members: 600
Focus: Sci
Periodicals
Memoirs
Nationalities Papers (semi-annually)
Newsletter (quarterly)
Proceedings
Ukrainian Bibliographical Quarterly
Ukrainska Knyha: Ukrainian Book (quarterly)
. . . . 16324

Sierra Club (SC), 730 Polk St, San Francisco, CA 94109
T: (415) 776-2211; Fax: (415) 776-0350
Founded: 1892; Members: 650000
Focus: Ecology 16325

Sigma Xi – The Scientific Research Society, 99 Alexander Dr, POB 13975, Research Triangle Park, NC 27708
T: (919) 549-4691; Fax: (919) 549-0090
Founded: 1886; Members: 90000
Pres: Robert A. Frosch; Gen Secr: Peter D. Blair
Focus: Humanities; Nat Sci
Periodical
American Scientist (bi-monthly) 16326

Sigmund Freud Archives (SFA), 23 The Hemlocks, Roslyn, NY 11576
T: (516) 621-6850; Fax: (516) 621-3014
Founded: 1951; Members: 18
Gen Secr: Harold P. Blum
Focus: Archives; Psych 16327

Signal Processing Society, c/o Institute of Electrical and Electronics Engineers, 345 E 47 St, New York, NY 10017
T: (212) 705-7900; Fax: (212) 705-4929
Members: 13383
Focus: Electric Eng 16328

Simian Society of America (SSA), 3625 Watson Rd, Saint Louis, MO 63109
T: (314) 647-6218
Founded: 1957; Members: 400
Focus: Zoology
Periodicals
Membership Roster (annually)
The Simian (monthly) 16329

Sir Thomas Beecham Society, 664 S Irena Av, Redondo Beach, CA 90277
T: (213) 540-7265
Founded: 1964; Members: 720
Gen Secr: Charles Niss
Focus: Music 16330

Sister Kenny Institute (SKI), 800 E 28 St, Minneapolis, MN 55407
T: (612) 863-4457
Founded: 1942
Focus: Rehabil
Periodical
The Independent (semi-annually) 16331

Skin Cancer Foundation (SCF), 245 Fifth Av, Ste 2402, New York, NY 10016
T: (212) 725-5176; Fax: (212) 725-5751
Founded: 1977
Focus: Cell Biol & Cancer Res 16332

Slavic Gospel Association (SGA), 6151 Commonwealth Dr, Loves Park, IL 61111
T: (815) 282-8900; E-Mail: sga@sga.org;
Fax: (815) 282-8901
Gen Secr: Dr. Robert W. Provost
Focus: Music 16333

Sleep Research Society (SRS), c/o Wallace Mendelson, Dept of Neurology, Cleveland Clinic, 9500 Euclid Av, Cleveland, OH 44195
T: (216) 444-8275; Fax: (216) 445-7471
Founded: 1961; Members: 600
Pres: Dr. Adrian Morrison
Focus: Psychiatry
Periodicals
Sleep (quarterly)
Sleep Research (annually) 16334

Small Enterprise Education and Promotion Network (SEEP), c/o PACT, 777 United Nations Plaza, New York, NY 10017
T: (212) 808-0084; E-Mail: seepny@undp.org;
Fax: (212) 682-2949
Gen Secr: Elaine L. Edgcomb
Focus: Educ; Business Admin 16335

Small Towns Institute (STI), Third amd Poplar St, POB 517, Ellensburg, WA 98926
T: (509) 925-1830
Founded: 1969; Members: 1850
Focus: Urban Plan
Periodical
Small Town (bi-monthly) 16336

Smithsonian Institution (S.I.), 1000 Jefferson Dr SW, Washington, DC 20560
T: (202) 357-2700
Founded: 1846
Gen Secr: Ira Michael Heyman
Focus: Humanities; Nat Sci; Educ
Periodicals
Smithsonian Contributions to Anthropology (irregularly)
Smithsonian Contributions to Botany (irregularly)
Smithsonian Contributions to Paleobiology (irregularly)
Smithsonian Contributions to the Earth Sciences (irregularly)
Smithsonian Contributions to the Marine Sciences (irregularly)
Smithsonian Contributions to Zoology (irregularly)
Smithsonian Folklife Studies (irregularly)
Smithsonian Studies in History and Technology (irregularly)
Smithsonian Studies to Air and Space (irregularly)
. . . . 16337

Social Psychiatry Research Institute (SPRI), 150 E 69 St, Ste 2H, New York, NY 10021
T: (212) 628-4800; Fax: (212) 249-8546
Founded: 1970
Focus: Psychiatry 16338

Social Responsibilities Round Table (SRRT), c/o American Library Association, 50 E Huron St, Chicago, IL 60611
T: (312) 280-4294
Founded: 1969; Members: 1500
Focus: Libraries & Bk Sci 16339

Social Science Education Consortium (SSEC), POB 21270, Boulder, CO 80308-4270
T: (303) 492-8154; Fax: (303) 449-3925
Founded: 1963; Members: 130
Gen Secr: James R. Giese
Focus: Educ; Sociology; Soc Sci . . . 16340

Social Science Research Council (SSRC), 810 Seventh Av, New York, NY 10019
T: (212) 377-2700; Fax: (212) 377-2727
Founded: 1923
Pres: Ken Prewitt
Focus: Soc Sci
Periodicals
Annual Report (annually)
Items (quarterly) 16341

Social Sciences Services and Resources (SSSR), POB 153, Wasco, IL 60183-0153
T: (708) 897-5345
Founded: 1973
Focus: Econ; Sociology; Public Admin; Business Admin; Develop Areas
Periodicals
American Communities Tomorrow (annually)
Best Books in the Social Sciences (semi-annually)
. . . . 16342

Social Welfare History Group (SWHG), c/o School of Social Work, Michigan State University, 212 Baker Hall, East Lansing, MI 48824
T: (517) 353-8620
Founded: 1956; Members: 250
Pres: John Herrick
Focus: Sociology; Hist
Periodical
Newsletter 16343

Société des Professeurs Français et Francophones en Amérique (SPFFA), 140 E 95 St, New York, NY 10128
T: (212) 996-2376; Fax: (212) 996-2367
Founded: 1904; Members: 500
Pres: Gerard Roubichou
Focus: Ling; Educ
Periodical
Bulletin (annually) 16344

Société internationale de recherche orthopédique et traumatologique (SIROT), c/o UCSD Medical Centre, Dept of Orthopaedics, 200 West Arbor Dr, San Diego, CA 92103-8894
T: (619) 543-5944; Fax: (619) 543-2540
Gen Secr: Prof. Wayne Akeson
Focus: Orthopedics; Traumatology . . . 16345

Society for Academic Emergency Medicine (SAEM), 901 N Washington Av, Lansing, MI 48906
T: (517) 485-5484; Fax: (517) 485-0801
Founded: 1989; Members: 3400
Gen Secr: Mary Ann Schroop
Focus: Adult Educ; Med
Periodicals
Annals of Emergency Medicine (monthly)
Directory (annually)
Status Report (bi-monthly) 16346

Society for Adolescent Medicine (SAM), 1916 NW Copper Oaks Cir, Blue Springs, MO 64014
T: (816) 795-8336
Founded: 1968; Members: 1250
Gen Secr: John W. Kulig
Focus: Pediatrics
Periodical
Journal of Adolescent Health Care (bi-monthly)
. . . . 16347

Society for Advancement of Management (SAM), Box 889, Vinton, VA 24179
T: (703) 342-5563; Fax: (703) 342-6413
Founded: 1912; Members: 11000
Gen Secr: Joseph L. Bush Jr.
Focus: Business Admin 16348

Society for American Archaeology (SAA), 900 Second St NE, No 12, Washington, DC 20002
T: (202) 789-8200; E-Mail: headquarters@saa.org;
Fax: (202) 789-0284
Founded: 1934; Members: 5600
Gen Secr: Tolbi A. Brimsek
Focus: Archeol
Periodicals
American Antiquity (quarterly)
Bulletin (bi-monthly) 16349

Society for Ancient Greek Philosophy (SAGP), c/o Dept of Philosophy, Binghamton University, Binghamton, NY 13902-6000
T: (607) 777-2886; Fax: (607) 777-4000
Founded: 1953; Members: 500
Gen Secr: Anthony Preus
Focus: Philos
Periodical
Essays in Ancient Greek Philosophy (irregularly)
. . . . 16350

Society for Applied Anthropology (SAA), POB 24083, Oklahoma City, OK 73124-0083
T: (405) 843-5113
Founded: 1941; Members: 2500
Pres: Jean J. Schensul
Focus: Anthro
Periodicals
Human Organization (quarterly)
Practicing Anthropology (quarterly) . . . 16351

Society for Applied Learning Technology (SALT), 50 Culpeper St, Warrenton, VA 22186
T: (703) 347-0055; Fax: (703) 349-3169
Founded: 1972; Members: 875
Focus: Educ 16352

Society for Applied Spectroscopy (SAS), 2018 Broadway St, Frederick, MD 21701
T: (301) 694-8122; Fax: (301) 694-6860
Founded: 1958; Members: 6500
Gen Secr: Frederick Holcombe
Focus: Physics
Periodicals
Applied Spectroscopy (8 times annually)
Newsletter (quarterly) 16353

Society for Armenian Studies (SAS), c/o Armenian Research Center, University of Michigan, 4901 Evergreen Rd, Dearborn, MI 48128-1491
T: (313) 593-5181; Fax: (313) 593-5452
Founded: 1974; Members: 172
Focus: Anthro 16354

Society for Asian and Comparative Philosophy (SACP), c/o Roger T. Ames, Dept of Philosophy, University of Hawaii, 2530 Dole St, Honolulu, HI 96822
T: (808) 956-7288; E-Mail: RTAmes@Hawaii.Edu; Fax: (808) 956-9228
Founded: 1968; Members: 400
Gen Secr: Roger T. Ames
Focus: Philos 16355

Society for Asian Art (SAA), c/o Asian Art Museum, Golden Gate Park, San Francisco, CA 94118
T: (415) 379-8805; Fax: (415) 387-5737
Founded: 1958 Deming, Willis; Members: 1200
Focus: Arts
Periodical
The Society for Asian Art Newsletter (quarterly) 16356

Society for Asian Music (SAM), c/o Dept of Asian Studies, Cornell University, 388 Rockefeller Hall, Ithaca, NY 14853
T: (607) 255-4097; Fax: (607) 255-1454
Founded: 1959; Members: 500
Focus: Music
Periodical
Asian Music (semi-annually) 16357

Society for Austrian and Habsburg History (SAHH), c/o Lawrence Sondhaus, Dept of History, University of Indianapolis, 1400 E Hanna Av, Indianapolis, IN 46227
T: (317) 788-3463; E-Mail: sondhaus@gandlf.uindy.edu; Fax: (317) 788-3569
Founded: 1957; Members: 450
Gen Secr: Lawrence Sondhaus
Focus: Hist
Periodical
Austrian History Yearbook (annually) . . 16358

Society for Biomaterials (SB), 6518 Walker St, Ste 215, Minneapolis, MN 55426
T: (612) 927-8108; Fax: (612) 927-8127
Founded: 1974; Members: 1700
Gen Secr: Rosalee M. Lee
Focus: Med; Eng
Periodicals
Journal of Biomedical Materials Research (monthly)
The Torch (2-3 times annually) 16359

Society for Business Ethics (SBE), c/o American College, 270 S Bryn Mawr Av, Bryn Mawr, PA 19010
T: (610) 526-1387; E-Mail: DUSKA@aol.com; Fax: (610) 526-1359
Founded: 1979; Members: 800
Gen Secr: Ronald Duska
Focus: Econ 16360

Society for Calligraphy (SC), POB 64174, Los Angeles, CA 90064
T: (310) 306-2326
Founded: 1974; Members: 1194
Focus: Graphic & Dec Arts, Design
Periodical
Newsletter (4-6 times annually) 16361

Society for Cardiac Angiography and Interventions (SCA&I), 4101 Lake Boone Tr, No 201, Raleigh, NC 27607
T: (919) 787-5181; Fax: (919) 787-4916
Founded: 1978; Members: 1100
Gen Secr: Mary Alice Dilday
Focus: Cardiol 16362

Society for Ch'ing Studies (SCS), c/o Johns Hopkins University Press, 2715 N Charles St, Baltimore, MD 21218-4319
T: (410) 516-6944; Fax: (410) 516-6968
Founded: 1965; Members: 500
Gen Secr: William T. Rowe
Focus: Hist 16363

Society for Cinema Studies (SCS), c/o Charles Maland, English Dept, University of Tennessee, 313 McClung Tower, Knoxville, TN 37916
Founded: 1959; Members: 1000
Gen Secr: Marcia Landy
Focus: Cinema
Periodical
Cinema Journal (quarterly) 16364

Society for Clinical and Experimental Hypnosis (SCEH), 128A Kings Park Dr, Liverpool, NY 13090
T: (315) 652-7299
Founded: 1949; Members: 1100
Gen Secr: Marion Kenn
Focus: Med; Psych; Therapeutics
Periodicals
International Journal of Clinical and Experimental Hypnosis (quarterly)
SCEH Newsletter (quarterly) 16365

Society for Clinical Trials (SCT), 600 Wyndhurst Av, Baltimore, MD 21210
T: (410) 433-4722; Fax: (410) 435-8631
Founded: 1978; Members: 1450
Focus: Med 16366

Society for College and University Planning (SCUP), c/o University of Michigan, 2026M School of Education Bldg, 610 E University Av, Ann Arbor, MI 48109
T: (313) 998-7832; Fax: (313) 998-6532
Founded: 1965; Members: 3000
Gen Secr: Mary Ann Armour
Focus: Adult Educ
Periodicals
Membership Roster (annually)
News (quarterly)
Planning for Higher Education (quarterly) 16367

Society for Commercial Archeology (SCA), c/o National Museum of American History, Rm 5010, Washington, DC 20560
T: (202) 882-5424
Founded: 1977; Members: 800
Focus: Archeol 16368

Society for Computer Simulation International (SCSI), POB 17900, San Diego, CA 92117-7900
T: (619) 277-3888; E-Mail: scs@sdsc.edu; Fax: (619) 277-3930
Founded: 1952; Members: 2000
Focus: Computer & Info Sci
Periodicals
Simulation (monthly)
Transactions (quarterly) 16369

Society for Conceptual and Contents Analysis by Computer (SCCAC), Bowling Green State, Bowling Green, OH 43403
Gen Secr: Dr. Klaus M. Schmidt
Focus: Computer & Info Sci 16370

Society for Conservation Biology, c/o Univ of Washington, POB 351800, Seattle, WA 98195-1800
E-Mail: conbio@u.washington.edu
Gen Secr: Alice Blandin
Focus: Bio 16371

Society for Creative Anachronism (SCA), 1526 Pacific Av, Santa Cruz, CA 95060
T: (408) 429-9009
Founded: 1966; Members: 22000
Gen Secr: K. Joe Gossett
Focus: Cultur Hist
Periodicals
Compleat Anachronist (bi-monthly)
Tournaments Illuminated (quarterly) . . . 16372

Society for Cryobiology (SC), c/o Dept of Mechanical Engineering, University of Texas, Austin, TX 78712
T: (512) 471-7167; Fax: (301) 530-7001
Founded: 1964; Members: 450
Pres: Kenneth Diller
Focus: Bio
Periodical
Cryobiology: International Journal of Low Temperature Biology and Medicine (bi-monthly) 16373

Society for Cultural Anthropology (SCA), 1703 New Hampshire Av NW, Washington, DC 20009
T: (202) 232-8800; Fax: (202) 667-5345
Founded: 1983; Members: 764
Focus: Anthro
Periodical
Cultural Anthropology (quarterly) 16374

Society for Developmental Biology (SDB), 9650 Rockville Pike, Bethesda, MD 20814-3998
Founded: 1939; Members: 1400
Focus: Bio
Periodical
Developmental Biology (monthly) 16375

Society for Economic Botany (SEB), c/o Dept of Anthropology, University of Missouri, Columbia, MO 65211
T: (314) 882-3038; Fax: (314) 882-9410
Founded: 1959; Members: 700
Pres: Dr. Douglas Kinghorn; Gen Secr: Dr. Deborah Pearsall
Focus: Botany
Periodicals
Economic Botany (quarterly)
SEB Newsletter (semi-annually) 16376

Society for Educational Reconstruction (SER), c/o Dr. Darrol Bussler, Mankato State University, Mankato, MN 56002-8400
T: (507) 389-6222; Fax: (507) 389-5854
Founded: 1969; Members: 100
Pres: Dr. Darrol Bussler
Focus: Educ
Periodical
SER in Action Newsletter (irregularly) . . 16377

Society for Environmental Geochemistry and Health (SEGH), c/o Life Sciences Dept, Univ of Missouri-Rolla, Rolla, MO 65401
T: (314) 341-4819; E-Mail: plutz@umy.edu; Fax: (314) 341-4821
Gen Secr: Paula M. Lutz
Focus: Chem; Public Health 16378

Society for Epidemiologic Research (SER), c/o Joseph L. Lyon, Dept of Family and Preventine Medicine, 50 N Medical Dr, Salt Lake City, UT 84132
T: (801) 581-7234; Fax: (801) 581-2759
Founded: 1967; Members: 3000
Gen Secr: Dr. Joseph L. Lyon
Focus: Immunology
Periodicals
Abstracts (annually)
Newsletter (semi-annually) 16379

Society for Ethnomusicology (SEM), c/o Indiana University, 005 Morrison Hall, Bloomington, IN 47405-2501
T: (812) 855-6672; Fax: (812) 855-6673
Founded: 1955; Members: 2300
Pres: Ruth Stone; Gen Secr: Judith Gray
Focus: Music; Ethnology
Periodicals
Ethnomusicology (3 times annually)
Newsletter (3 times annually) 16380

Society for Experimental and Descriptive Malacology (SEDM), POB 3037, Ann Arbor, MI 48106
T: (313) 764-0470
Founded: 1967; Members: 600
Focus: Zoology
Periodicals
Malacological Review (annually)
Walkerana-Proceedings 16381

Society for Experimental Biology and Medicine (SEBM), 162 W 56 St, Ste 203, New York, NY 10019
Founded: 1903; Members: 1500
Gen Secr: Felice O'Grady
Focus: Bio; Med
Periodical
Proceedings of the Society for Experimental Biology and Medicine (11 times annually) 16382

Society for Experimental Mechanics (SEM), 7 School St, Bethel, CT 06801
T: (203) 790-6373; Fax: (203) 790-4472
Founded: 1943; Members: 2607
Focus: Eng
Periodicals
Experimental Mechanics (quarterly)
Experimental Techniques (bi-monthly)
International Journal of Experimental and Analytical Modal Analysis (quarterly) 16383

Society for French American Cultural Services and Educational Aid (FACSEA), 972 Fifth Av, New York, NY 10021
T: (212) 439-1439; Fax: (212) 439-1455
Founded: 1955
Focus: Educ 16384

Society for French Historical Studies (SFHS), c/o Dept of History, University of Iowa, Iowa City, IA 52242
T: (319) 335-2330
Founded: 1955; Members: 1450
Focus: Hist 16385

Society for General Music (SGM), c/o Music Educators National Conference, 1806 Robert Fulton Dr, Reston, VA 22091
T: (703) 860-4000; Fax: (703) 860-4826
Founded: 1982; Members: 3100
Gen Secr: John J. Mahlmann
Focus: Music
Periodical
Soundings (quarterly) 16386

Society for German-American Studies (SGAS), c/o Dr Don Heinrich Tolzmann, Blegen Library, University of Cincinnati, POB 210113, Cincinnati, OH 45221
T: (513) 556-1955
Founded: 1968; Members: 24000
Pres: Dr. Don Heinrich Tolzmann
Focus: Hist
Periodicals
Newsletter (quarterly)
Yearbook (annually) 16387

Society for Gynecologic Investigation (SGI), 409 12 St SW, Washington, DC 20024
T: (202) 863-2544; Fax: (202) 544-0453
Founded: 1953; Members: 600
Focus: Gynecology
Periodical
Gynecologic Investigation (semi-annually) . 16388

Society for Historians of American Foreign Relations (SHAFR), c/o Dept of History, Wright State University, Dayton, OH 45435
T: (513) 873-3110
Founded: 1967; Members: 1200
Gen Secr: Allan Spetter
Focus: Hist
Periodicals
Diplomatic History (quarterly)
Newsletter (quarterly)
Roster and Research List (bi-annually) . 16389

Society for Historical Archaeology (SHA), POB 30446, Tucson, AZ 85751-0446
T: (602) 886-8006; Fax: (602) 886-0182
Founded: 1967; Members: 2000
Focus: Archeol
Periodicals
Historical Archaeology (annually)
Newsletter (quarterly) 16390

Society for History Education (SHE), c/o California State University at Long Beach, Long Beach, CA 90840
T: (310) 985-1653; Fax: (310) 985-5431
Founded: 1972; Members: 2000
Focus: Hist; Educ
Periodicals
The History Teacher (quarterly)
Network News Exchange (semi-annually) . 16391

Society for Human Resource Management (SHRM), 606 N Washington St, Alexandria, VA 22314
T: (703) 548-3440; Fax: (703) 836-0367
Founded: 1948; Members: 50000
Focus: Business Admin
Periodicals
HR Magazine (monthly)
Personnel Administrator (monthly)
Resource (monthly) 16392

Society for Humanistic Anthropology (SHA), c/o Jeanne Simonelli, Dept of Anthropology, SUNY-Oneonta, Oneonta, NY 13820
T: (607) 436-3226; Fax: (607) 436-3103
Founded: 1971; Members: 300
Pres: Barbara Babcock
Focus: Anthro
Periodical
Quarterly of Humanistic Anthropology (quarterly) 16393

Society for Humanistic Judaism (SHJ), 28611 W 12 Mile Rd, Farmington Hills, MI 48334
T: (313) 478-7610; Fax: (313) 477-9014
Founded: 1970; Members: 2000
Focus: Rel & Theol
Periodicals
Humanistic Judaism (quarterly)
Newsletter (3-4 times annually) 16394

Society for Iberian and Latin American Thought (SILAT), c/o American Univ, Language and Foreign Studies, 4400 Massachusetts Av NW, Washington, DC 20016-8045
T: (202) 885-2140
Gen Secr: Amy A. Oliver
Focus: Ling; Lit 16395

Society for Industrial and Applied Mathematics (SIAM), 3600 University City Science Center, Philadelphia, PA 19104-2688
T: (215) 382-9800; Fax: (215) 386-7999
Founded: 1952; Members: 7500
Focus: Math
Periodicals
Journal of Scientific and Statistical Computing (bi-monthly)
Journal on Applied Mathematics (bi-monthly)
Journal on Computing (bi-monthly)
Journal on Control (bi-monthly)
Journal on Mathematical Analysis (bi-monthly)
Journal on Numerical Analysis (bi-monthly)
News (bi-monthly)
SIAM Journal on Discrete Mathematics (quarterly)
SIAM Journal on Matrix Analysis (quarterly) 16396

Society for Industrial Archaeology (SIA), c/o Withum, Smith & Brown, 100 Overlook Ctr, Princeton, NJ 08540
T: (609) 520-1188; Fax: (609) 520-9882
Founded: 1971; Members: 1650
Pres: Duncan Hay
Focus: Archeol
Periodicals
Bibliography
Journal (annually)
Newsletter (quarterly) 16397

Society for Industrial Microbiology (SIM), 3929 Old Lee Hwy, No 92A, Fairfax, VA 22030-2421
T: (703) 941-5373; Fax: (703) 941-8790
Founded: 1948; Members: 2122
Gen Secr: Ann Kulback
Focus: Microbio
Periodicals
Developments in Industrial Microbiology (annually)
Journal of Industrial Microbiology (bi-monthly) 16398

Society for Information Display (SID), 1526 Brookhollow Dr, Ste 82, Santa Ana, CA 92705-5421
T: (714) 545-1526; E-Mail: socforinfodisplay@mcimail.com; Fax: (714) 545-1547
Founded: 1962; Members: 4000
Gen Secr: Lauren K. Kinsey
Focus: Computer & Info Sci
Periodicals
Proceedings (irregularly)
Quarterly Proceedings (quarterly) 16399

Society for Information Management (SIM), 401 N Michigan Av, Chicago, IL 60611-4267
T: (312) 644-6610; Fax: (312) 321-6869
Founded: 1968; Members: 2500
Focus: Business Admin
Periodicals
Member Forum (bi-monthly)
Proceedings (annually) 16400

Society for International Numismatics (SIN), POB 943, Santa Monica, CA 90406
T: (213) 399-1085
Founded: 1955; Members: 450
Focus: Numismatics

Periodical
SINformation (bi-monthly) 16401

Society for Invertebrate Pathology (SIP), c/o FASEB, 9650 Rockville Pike, Bethesda, MD 20814
T: (301) 530-7120; Fax: (301) 530-7120
Founded: 1967; Members: 723
Gen Secr: Dr. Wendy Gelernter
Focus: Vet Med
Periodicals
Abstracts of Symposia (annually)
Directory for Invertebrate Pathology
Newsletter (bi-monthly) 16402

Society for Investigative Dermatology (SID), c/o David R. Bickers, 11001 Cedar Av, Ste 500A, Cleveland, OH 44106
T: (216) 844-6859; E-Mail: sid@halcyon.com; Fax: (216) 844-6810
Founded: 1937; Members: 2300
Gen Secr: Angela Welsh
Focus: Derm
Periodical
The Journal of Investigative Dermatology 16403

Society for Iranian Studies (SIS), c/o Middle East Center, University of Washington, 225 Thomson Hall, POB 353650, Seattle, WA 98195
T: (206) 543-4227; E-Mail: calbrigh@u.washington.edu; Fax: (206) 685-0668
Founded: 1967; Members: 450
Gen Secr: Charlotte Albrigh
Focus: Ethnology 16404

Society for Italian Historical Studies (SIHS), c/o Boston College, Chestnut Hill, MA 02167
T: (617) 552-3814
Founded: 1955; Members: 350
Focus: Hist
Periodicals
Membership List (annually)
Newsletter (annually) 16405

Society for Latin American Anthropology (SLAA), c/o American Anthropological Association, 4350 N Fairfax Dr, Ste 640, Arlington, VA 22203-1620
T: (703) 528-1902; Fax: (703) 528-3546
Founded: 1969; Members: 610
Pres: Michael Kearney
Focus: Anthro
Periodical
Proceedings (annually) 16406

Society for Leukocyte Biology, c/o Debbie Stoutamire, 9650 Rockville Pike, Bethesda, MD 20814
T: (301) 530-7120; Fax: (301) 530-7049
Founded: 1954; Members: 1025
Gen Secr: Debbie Stoutamire
Focus: Pathology; Physiology
Periodicals
Directory and Constitution (annually)
RES (monthly) 16407

Society for Life History Research (SLHR), c/o Temple University, Philadelphia, PA 19122
T: (215) 204-8080
Founded: 1970; Members: 700
Gen Secr: Joan McCord
Focus: Psychiatry 16408

Society for Linguistic Anthropology (SLA), 1703 New Hampshire Av NW, Washington, DC 20009
T: (202) 232-8800; Fax: (202) 667-5345
Founded: 1983; Members: 512
Focus: Anthro 16409

Society for Literature and Science (SLS), c/o Worchester Polytechnic Institute, Dept of Chemistry, Worchester, MA 01609
Gen Secr: Prof. S. Weiniger
Focus: Lit; Sci 16410

Society for Medical Anthropology (SMA), c/o American Anthropological Association, 4350 N Fairfax Dr, Ste 640, Arlington, VA 22203
T: (703) 528-1902; Fax: (703) 528-3546
Founded: 1971; Members: 1700
Pres: Carole Browner
Focus: Anthro
Periodical
Medical Anthropology Quarterly (quarterly) 16411

Society for Mining, Metallurgy and Exploration, POB 625002, Littleton, CO 80162-5002
T: (303) 973-9550; Fax: (303) 973-3845
Founded: 1871; Members: 20000
Focus: Mining
Periodicals
Minerals and Metallurgical Processing
Mining Engineering (quarterly) 16412

Society for Music Teacher Education (SMTE), c/o Music Educators National Conference, 1806 Robert Fulton Dr, Reston, VA 22091
T: (703) 860-4000; Fax: (703) 860-4826
Founded: 1983
Gen Secr: John J. Mahlmann
Focus: Educ; Music 16413

Society for Natural Philosophy (SNP), c/o Prof. Donald E. Carlson, Dept of Theoretical and Applied Mechanics, University of Illinois at Urbana-Champaign, Urbana, IL 61801-2935
T: (217) 333-3846; Fax: (217) 244-5707
Founded: 1963; Members: 300
Gen Secr: Prof. Donald E. Carlson
Focus: Philos
Periodical
List of Members and Officers (annually) . 16414

Society for Neuroscience (SN), 11 Dupont Circle, Ste 500, Washington, DC 20036
T: (202) 462-6688
Founded: 1969; Members: 18000
Gen Secr: Nancy Beang
Focus: Neurology
Periodicals
Directory (annually)
The Journal of Neuroscience (monthly)
Neuroscience Newsletter (bi-monthly)
Neuroscience Training Programs in North America (bi-annually) 16415

Society for New Language Study (SNLS), POB 10596, Denver, CO 80210
T: (303) 777-6115
Founded: 1972; Members: 12
Focus: Ling 16416

Society for Nutrition Education (SNE), 2850 Metro Dr, Ste 416, Minneapolis, MN 55425-1412
T: (612) 854-6721; E-Mail: labat004@tc.umn.edu; Fax: (612) 854-7869
Founded: 1967; Members: 2500
Gen Secr: Faye Labatt
Focus: Nutrition
Periodicals
Journal of Nutrition Education (bi-monthly)
SNE Exchange (quarterly) 16417

Society for Obstetric Anesthesia and Perinatology (SOAP), 1910 Byrd Av, Ste 100, POB 11086, Richmond, VA 23230-1086
T: (804) 282-5051; E-Mail: 75112.2053@compuserve.com; Fax: (804) 282-0090
Founded: 1969; Members: 1000
Gen Secr: John A. Hinckley
Focus: Anesthetics; Gynecology
Periodical
Newsletter (quarterly) 16418

Society for Occlusal Studies (SOS), 1010 Carondelet Dr, Kansas City, MO 64114
T: (816) 941-0509
Founded: 1964; Members: 800
Pres: Dr. Bernard Williams
Focus: Dent
Periodicals
Newsletter (quarterly)
Roster (annually) 16419

Society for Occupational and Environmental Health (SOEH), 6728 Old McLean Village Dr, McLean, VA 22101
T: (703) 556-9222
Founded: 1972; Members: 350
Focus: Pathology
Periodical
Letter (quarterly) 16420

Society for Pediatric Dermatology (SPD), c/o James E. Rasmussen, University of Michigan Hospitals, 1910 Taubman Health Care Center, Ann Arbor, MI 48109-0314
T: (312) 880-4697; Fax: (312) 880-3025
Founded: 1975; Members: 450
Gen Secr: Amy S. Paller
Focus: Derm; Pediatrics
Periodical
Newsletter (quarterly) 16421

Society for Pediatric Pathology (SPP), 6728 Old McLean Village Dr, McLean, VA 22101
T: (703) 556-9222; E-Mail: socpedpath@aol.com; Fax: (703) 556-8729
Gen Secr: Marge Degnon
Focus: Pediatrics; Pathology 16422

Society for Pediatric Psychology (SPP), c/o Conway Saylor, Dept of Psychiatry, The Citadel, Charleston, SC 29409
T: (803) 953-5320; Fax: (803) 724-1747
Founded: 1968; Members: 995
Gen Secr: Conway Saylor
Focus: Psych
Periodical
Journal of Pediatric Psychology (quarterly) 16423

Society for Pediatric Radiology (SPR), 2021 Spring Rd, Ste 600, Oak Brook, IL 60521
T: (708) 571-2197; Fax: (708) 571-7837
Founded: 1958; Members: 800
Focus: Pediatrics; Radiology
Periodical
Membership Directory (annually) 16424

Society for Pediatric Research (SPR), 141 Northwest Point Blvd, POB 675, Elk Grove Village, IL 60009-0675
T: (708) 427-0205; Fax: (708) 427-1305
Founded: 1929; Members: 2000
Gen Secr: Dr. Gail Demmler
Focus: Pediatrics
Periodical
Pediatric Research-Program Issue (annually) 16425

Society for Pediatric Urology (SPU), c/o Children's Hospital and Medical Center, POB 5371, Seattle, WA 98105
T: (206) 527-3950; Fax: (206) 527-3966
Founded: 1941; Members: 300
Focus: Pediatrics; Urology
Periodicals
Breakthroughs (monthly)
For a Change (monthly) 16426

Society for Personality Assessment (SPA), 750 First St SE, Washington, DC 20002
T: (202) 336-6192; Fax: (202) 336-6158
Founded: 1938; Members: 3000
Focus: Psych
Periodical
Journal of Personality Assessment (quarterly) 16427

Society for Phenomenology and Existential Philosophy (SPEP), c/o Debra Bergoffen, Dept of Philosophy and Religious Studies, George Mason University, Fairfax, VA 22030
T: (703) 993-1294
Founded: 1962; Members: 1600
Gen Secr: Debra Bergoffen
Focus: Philos
Periodicals
Newsletter (semi-annually)
Volume of Essays (semi-annually) . . . 16428

Society for Philosophy and Public Affairs (SPPA), c/o Prof. Carol C. Gould, Dept of Humanities and Liberal Arts, Stevens Institute of Technology, Hoboken, NJ 07030
T: (201) 216-5405; E-Mail: cgould@stevens.tech.edu; Fax: (201) 216-8245
Founded: 1969; Members: 300
Gen Secr: Prof. Carol C. Gould
Focus: Philos; Poli Sci
Periodicals
Having Children
Philosophy and Political Action
Philosophy, Morality and International Affairs
The Sporadical (quarterly) 16429

Society for Philosophy of Religion (SPR), c/o Dept of Philosophy, University of Georgia, Peabody Hall, Athens, GA 30602
T: (706) 542-2823
Founded: 1940; Members: 125
Gen Secr: Frank R. Harrison
Focus: Philos; Rel & Theol 16430

Society for Photographic Education (SPE), POB 222116, Dallas, TX 75222-2116
T: (817) 272-2845; Fax: (817) 272-2846
Founded: 1963; Members: 1600
Gen Secr: M.L. Hutchins
Focus: Photo; Adult Educ
Periodicals
Exposure (quarterly)
Membership Directory (annually)
Newsletter (5 times annually) 16431

Society for Psychological Anthropology (SPA), c/o American Anthropological Association, 4350 N Fairfax Dr, Ste 640, Arlington, VA 22203-1620
T: (703) 528-1902; Fax: (703) 528-3546
Founded: 1976; Members: 1400
Pres: Robert L. Munroe
Focus: Anthro
Periodical
Ethos (quarterly) 16432

Society for Psychological Study of Social Issues (SPSSI), POB 1248, Ann Arbor, MI 48106-1248
T: (313) 662-9130; E-Mail: spssi@umich.edu; Fax: (313) 662-5607
Focus: Soc Sci 16433

Society for Psychophysiological Research (SPR), c/o Robert J. Gatchel, Psychology Dept, University of Texas Southwestern Medical Center, 5323 Harry Hines Blvd, Dallas, TX 75235-9044
T: (214) 648-5277
Founded: 1960; Members: 906
Gen Secr: Robert J. Gatchel
Focus: Psych; Physiology; Psychiatry; Med
Periodical
Psychophysiology (bi-monthly) 16434

Society for Public Health Education (SOPHE), 2001 Addison St, Ste 220, Berkeley, CA 94704
T: (510) 644-9242; Fax: (510) 644-9319
Founded: 1950; Members: 1200
Focus: Public Health
Periodicals
Health Education Quarterly (quarterly)
SOPHE News and Views (quarterly) . . 16435

Society for Range Management (SRM), 1839 York St, Denver, CO 80206
T: (303) 355-7070
Founded: 1948; Members: 5700
Focus: Business Admin 16436

Society for Reformation Research (SRR), c/o Center for Reformation Research, 6477 San Benito Av, Saint Louis, MO 63105
T: (314) 727-6655
Founded: 1947; Members: 400
Focus: Hist 16437

Society for Research in Child Development (SRCD), c/o University of Michigan, 300 N Ingalls, Ann Arbor, MI 48109-0406
T: (313) 998-6578; Fax: (313) 998-6569
Founded: 1933; Members: 490
Gen Secr: John W. Hagen
Focus: Educ
Periodicals
Child Development (bi-monthly)
Child Development Abstracts & Bibliography (3 times annually)
Monographs (irregularly) 16438

Society for Risk Analysis International, 1313 Dolley Madison Blvd, Ste 402, McLean, VA 22101
T: (703) 790-1745; Fax: (703) 790-9063
Founded: 1981; Members: 2000
Gen Secr: Richard J. Burk
Focus: Math
Periodicals
Newsletter (quarterly)
Risk Analysis Journal (quarterly) 16439

Society for Sedimentary Geology, 1731 E 71 St, Tulsa, OK 74136-5108
T: (918) 493-3361; Fax: (918) 493-2093
Founded: 1926; Members: 5260
Pres: John M. Armentrout
Focus: Mineralogy; Paleontology; Econ
Periodicals
Journal of Sedimentary Paleontology (bi-monthly)
Palaios (bi-monthly)
SEPM Newsletter (3 times annually) . . 16440

Society for Slovene Studies (SSS), c/o Dept of Slavic Languages and Literatures, Indiana University, Bloomington, IN 47405
T: (812) 855-2608; Fax: (812) 855-2107
Founded: 1973; Members: 300
Pres: Dr. Tom Priestly
Focus: Lit; Ling; Hist; Anthro; Ethnology
Periodicals
Journal of Slovene Studies (annually)
Letter (bi-annually) 16441

Society for Social Studies of Science (SSSS), c/o Dept of Sociology, Louisiana State University, Baton Rouge, LA 70803
T: (504) 388-1645
Founded: 1975; Members: 500
Gen Secr: Wesley Shrum
Focus: Soc Sci
Periodical
Science and Technology Studies (quarterly) 16442

Society for Spanish and Portuguese Historical Studies (SSPHS), c/o William D. Phillips Jr., Dept of History, University of Minnesota, Minneapolis, MN 55455
T: (612) 624-6813; Fax: (612) 624-7096
Founded: 1969; Members: 450
Gen Secr: William D. Phillips Jr.
Focus: Hist
Periodicals
Membership Directory (bi-annually)
Society for Spanish and Portuguese Historical Studies Bulletin (3 times annually) . . . 16443

Society for Technical Communication (STC), 901 N Stuart St, Ste 904, Arlington, VA 22203
T: (703) 522-4114; E-Mail: stc@tmn.com; Fax: (703) 522-2075
Founded: 1953; Members: 21000
Gen Secr: William C. Stolgitis
Focus: Eng 16444

Society for the Advancement of American Philosophy (SAAP), c/o Dept of Philosophy, Seattle University, Seattle, WA 98122
T: (206) 296-5467; Fax: (206) 296-5997
Founded: 1972; Members: 900
Focus: Philos 16445

Society for the Advancement of Behavior Analysis (SABA), c/o Western Michigan University, 260 Wood Hall, Kalamazoo, MI 49008-5052
T: (616) 387-4584; Fax: (616) 387-4457
Founded: 1980; Members: 150
Gen Secr: Maria Malott
Focus: Psychoan
Periodical
The Behavior Analyst (semi-annually) . . 16446

Society for the Advancement of Education (SAE), 99 W Hawthorne Av, Valley Stream, NY 11580
T: (516) 568-9191
Founded: 1939; Members: 3000
Focus: Educ
Periodical
USA Today (monthly) 16447

Society for the Advancement of Material and Process Engineering (SAMPE), POB 2459, Covina, CA 91722
T: (818) 331-0616; Fax: (818) 332-8929
Founded: 1944; Members: 11000
Focus: Materials Sci
Periodicals
National SAMPE Technical Conference Series (annually)
SAMPE Journal (bi-monthly)
SAMPE Quarterly (quarterly)
The Science of Advaneed Materials + Process Engineering (annually) 16448

Society for the Advancement of Scandinavian Study (SASS), c/o Brigham Young University, POB 236118, Provo, UT 84602-6118
T: (801) 378-5598; E-Mail: scandst2@jkhbhrc.byu.edu; Fax: (801) 378-4649
Founded: 1911; Members: 800
Gen Secr: Steven P. Sondrap
Focus: Ethnology
Periodical
Scandinavian Studies (quarterly) 16449

Society for the Anthropology of Europe (SAE), c/o American Anthropological Association, 4350 N Fairfax Dr, Ste 640, Arlington, VA 22203-1620
T: (703) 528-1902; Fax: (703) 528-3546
Founded: 1986; Members: 530
Pres: David Kertzer
Focus: Anthro 16450

Society for the Arts, Religion and Contemporary Culture (ARC), c/o N. Vos, Muhlenberg College, 24 Chew St, Allentown, PA 18104
T: (610) 821-3454
Founded: 1961; Members: 160
Pres: N. Vos
Focus: Arts; Rel & Theol
Periodical
SEEDBED (bi-annually) 16451

Society for the Comparative Study of Society and History (CSSH), c/o University of Michigan, 102 Rackham Bldg, Ann Arbor, MI 48109-1070
T: (313) 764-6362; Fax: (313) 763-2447
Founded: 1958
Focus: Hist; Sociology; Anthro
Periodical
Comparative Studies in Society and History (quarterly) 16452

Society for the Conservation of Bighorn Sheep (SCBS), POB 801, La Canada Flintridge, CA 91012
T: (805) 259-9828; Fax: (805) 257-8259
Founded: 1963; Members: 250
Pres: Steven Hill
Focus: Animal Husb
Periodical
Sheepherder (bi-monthly) 16453

Society for the Furtherance and Study of Fantasy and Science Fiction, POB 1624, Madison, WI 53701-1624
T: (608) 233-5640
Founded: 1977; Members: 75
Focus: Cinema; Lit
Periodicals
Cube (bi-monthly)
New Moon
SF3 Locater List (annually) 16454

Society for the History of Authorship, Reading and Publishing (SHARP), c/o Drew University, History Dept, Madison, NJ 07940
T: (201) 408-3545; E-Mail: jerose@drew.drew.edu; Fax: (201) 408-3768
Gen Secr: Jonathan Rose
Focus: Lit; Journalism; Libraries & Bk Sci 16455

Society for the History of Czechoslovak Jews (SHCJ), 760 Pompton Av, Cedar Grove, NJ 07009
T: (201) 239-2333; Fax: (201) 239-7935
Founded: 1961; Members: 200
Pres: Norman Patz
Focus: Hist 16456

Society for the History of Discoveries (SHD), 6300 Waterway Dr, Falls Church, VA 22044-1316
T: (703) 256-9217
Founded: 1960; Members: 375
Focus: Hist
Periodical
Terrae Incognitae (annually) 16457

Society for the History of Technology (SHOT), c/o Dept of History, Auburn University, Auburn, AL 36849-5207
T: (334) 844-6645; Fax: (334) 844-6673
Founded: 1958; Members: 2600
Pres: Dr. Alex Roland; Gen Secr: Dr. Lindy Biggs
Focus: Cultur Hist; Eng
Periodicals
SHOT Newsletter (quarterly)
Technology and Culture (quarterly) . . . 16458

Society for the History of the Germans in Maryland (SHGM), POB 22585, Baltimore, MD 21203
T: (410) 685-0450
Founded: 1886; Members: 350
Pres: Gerard W. Wittstadt
Focus: Hist
Periodical
The Report: A Journal of German American History (bi-annually) 16459

Society for the Humanities (SH), c/o Andrew White House, Cornell University, 27 East Av, Ithaca, NY 14853
T: (607) 255-9274; E-Mail: as63@cornell.edu
Founded: 1966
Gen Secr: Dominick LaCapra
Focus: Humanities 16460

Society for the Investigation of Recurring Events (SIRE), c/o Peter G. Constable, POB 274, Iselin, NJ 08830
T: (800) 906-9000
Founded: 1957; Members: 300
Pres: Peter G. Constable
Focus: Hist
Periodical
Abstract (monthly) 16461

Society for the Philosophical Study of Marxism (SPSM), c/o Prof. James Lawler, Dept of Philosophy, University of New York at Buffalo, Buffalo, NY 14260
T: (716) 645-2444; E-Mail: phijiml@ubrms.cc.buffalo.edu
Founded: 1962; Members: 50
Pres: Prof. Howard L. Parsons
Focus: Philos
Periodical
SPSM Newsletter (bi-annually) 16462

Society for the Preservation of American Business History (SPABH), Drawer JH, Williamsburg, VA 23187-3632
T: (804) 220-3838
Founded: 1981; Members: 100
Focus: Econ; Business Admin 16463

Society for the Preservation of English Language and Literature (SPELL), POB 118, Waleska, GA 30183
T: (706) 479-8685; E-Mail: YAUU49A@PRODIGY.COM; Fax: (706) 479-2350
Founded: 1984; Members: 1800
Pres: Richard Dowis
Focus: Ling; Lit
Periodical
Spell/Binder (quarterly) 16464

Society for the Preservation of New England Antiquities (SPNEA), 141 Cambridge St, Boston, MA 02114
T: (617) 227-3956
Founded: 1910; Members: 3000
Focus: Preserv Hist Monuments
Periodicals
House Guide (annually)
Newsletter 16465

Society for the Promotion of Science and Scholarship (SPOSS), 4139 El Camino Way, POB 10139, Palo Alto, CA 94303-0897
T: (415) 321-7964
Founded: 1975
Gen Secr: Dr. Janet Gardiner
Focus: Nat Sci 16466

Society for the Protection of Old Fishes (SPOOF), c/o School of Fisheries, University of Washington, Seattle, WA 98195
T: (206) 778-7397; Fax: (206) 685-7471
Founded: 1967; Members: 200
Focus: Fisheries
Periodicals
Membership List (annually)
Newsletter 16467

Society for the Psychological Study of Social Issues (SPSSI), POB 1248, Ann Arbor, MI 48106-1248
T: (313) 662-9130; Fax: (313) 662-5607
Founded: 1936; Members: 3000
Focus: Psych; Sociology
Periodicals
Journal of Social Issues (quarterly)
Newsletter (3 times annually) 16468

Society for the Scientific Study of Religion (SSSR), c/o Sociology Dept, Purdue University, 1365 Stone Hall, West Lafayette, IN 47907-1365
T: (317) 494-6286
Founded: 1949; Members: 1500
Pres: N. Jay Demerath; Gen Secr: M. Cornwall
Focus: Rel & Theol; Philos; Behav Sci
Periodical
Journal for the Scientific Study of Religion (quarterly) 16469

Society for the Scientific Study of Sex (SSSS), POB 208, Mount Vernon, IA 52314
T: (319) 895-8407; Fax: (319) 895-6203
Founded: 1957; Members: 1100
Gen Secr: Howard J. Ruppel
Focus: Bio
Periodical
The Journal of Sex Research (quarterly) 16470

Society for the Study of Amphibians and Reptiles (SSAR), c/o Karen Toepfer, POB 626, Hays, KS 67601-0626
T: (913) 623-4258; Fax: (913) 625-8890
Founded: 1958; Members: 2700
Gen Secr: Karen Toepfer
Focus: Zoology
Periodicals
Herpetological Circulars
Herpetological Review (quarterly)
Journal of Herpetology (quarterly) . . . 16471

Society for the Study of Blood (SSB), c/o Brooklyn VA Medical Center, 800 Poly Pl, Brooklyn, NY 11209
T: (718) 836-6600
Founded: 1945; Members: 200
Gen Secr: Dr. Ian Yudelman
Focus: Hematology 16472

Society for the Study of Early China (SSEC), c/o Institute of East Asian Studies, University of California, Berkeley, CA 94720
T: (510) 643-6325; Fax: (510) 643-7062
Founded: 1975; Members: 350
Focus: Hist
Periodical
Early China (annually) 16473

Society for the Study of Evolution (SSE), POB 1897, Lawrence, KS 66044
Fax: (608) 262-7509
Founded: 1946; Members: 2500
Gen Secr: Kent Holsinger
Focus: Bio
Periodicals
Evolution (bi-monthly)
Membership Directory 16474

Society for the Study of Male Psychology and Physiology (SSMPP), 321 Iuka, Montpellier, OH 43543
T: (419) 485-3602
Founded: 1975; Members: 180
Gen Secr: Jerry Bergman
Focus: Psych 16475

Society for the Study of Process Philosophies (SSPP), c/o Dept of Philosophy, University of Southern Maine, 96 Falmouth St, Portland, ME 04103
T: (207) 780-4259
Founded: 1966; Members: 350
Gen Secr: Dr. Joseph Grange
Focus: Philos 16476

Society for the Study of Reproduction (SSR), 1506 Jefferson, Madison, WI 53711-2106
T: (608) 256-2777; E-Mail: ssr@ssr.org; Fax: (217) 256-4610
Founded: 1967; Members: 2400
Gen Secr: Judith Janson
Focus: Med
Periodical
Biology of Reproduction (10 times annually) 16477

Society for the Study of Social Biology (SSSB), c/o Jacci L. Rodgers, Meinders School of Business, Oklahoma City University, Oklahoma City, OK 73106
T: (405) 521-5824
Founded: 1926; Members: 300
Pres: Joseph Lee Rodgers
Focus: Bio
Periodical
Social Biology (quarterly) 16478

Society for the Study of Social Problems (SSSP), c/o Dept of Sociology, University of Tennessee, 906 McClung Tower, Knoxville, TN 37996-0490
T: (423) 974-3620; E-Mail: Tomhood@UTK.edu.423; Fax: (423) 974-7013
Founded: 1951; Members: 1625
Gen Secr: Thomas C. Hood
Focus: Sociology 16479

Society for the Study of Southern Literature (SSSL), c/o Dept of English, Loyola University, New Orleans, LA 70118
T: (504) 865-2476
Founded: 1968; Members: 425
Gen Secr: David C. Estes
Focus: Lit
Periodical
News-Letter (semi-annually) 16480

Society for the Study of Symbolic Interaction (SSSI), c/o Tennessee Tech University, Cookeville, TN 38505
T: (615) 372-3437
Founded: 1975; Members: 600
Gen Secr: Donna Kelleher Darden
Focus: Sociology
Periodicals
Journal (semi-annually)
Newsletter (quarterly) 16481

Society for the Study of the Indigenous Languages of the Americas (SSILA), c/o Dept of Anthropology, Univ of Iowa, Iowa City, IA 52242
T: (319) 335-0533; Fax: (319) 335-0653
Gen Secr: N. England
Focus: Lit 16482

Society for Theriogenology (ST), POB 2118, Hastings, NE 68902
T: (402) 463-0392; Fax: (402) 461-4103
Founded: 1954; Members: 2508
Focus: Vet Med
Periodicals
Newsletter (bi-monthly)
Proceedings of Annual Meeting 16483

Society for Values in Higher Education (SVHE), c/o Georgetown University, Washington, DC 20057
T: (202) 687-3653; E-Mail: svhe@gunet.georgetown.edu; Fax: (202) 687-5094
Founded: 1923; Members: 1375
Gen Secr: Kathleen McGrory
Focus: Educ
Periodical
Soundings: An Interdisciplinary Journal (quarterly) 16484

Society for Vascular Surgery (SVS), 13 Elm St, POB 1565, Manchester, MA 01944
T: (508) 526-8330; Fax: (508) 526-4018
Founded: 1945; Members: 500
Focus: Surgery
Periodical
Journal of Vascular Surgery (monthly) . 16485

Society for Vector Ecology (SVE), POB 87, Santa Ana, CA 92702
T: (714) 971-2421; Fax: (714) 971-3940
Founded: 1968; Members: 820
Focus: Ecology 16486

Society for Visual Anthropology (SVA), c/o Smithsonian Institution, Natural Science Bldg, Rm 85, Washington, DC 20560
T: (202) 357-1861; Fax: (202) 357-2801
Founded: 1968; Members: 525
Pres: Joanna C. Scherer
Focus: Anthro
Periodicals
Directory of Visual Anthropologists
Newsletter (quarterly) 16487

Society for Women in Philosophy – Pacific Division (SWIP), c/o Dept of Philosophy, San Jose State University, San Jose, CA 95192
T: (408) 924-4501
Founded: 1975; Members: 140
Gen Secr: Rita Manning
Focus: Philos
Periodical
Newsletter (semi-annually) 16488

Society of Actuaries (SOA), 475 N Martingale Rd, Ste 800, Schaumburg, IL 60173
T: (708) 706-3500; Fax: (708) 706-3599
Founded: 1949; Members: 16300
Gen Secr: Linda M. Delgadillo
Focus: Insurance
Periodicals
The Actuary (10 times annually)
The Record (quarterly)
Transactions (annually) 16489

Society of Africanist Archaeologists (SAfA), 1350 Turlington Hall, Gainesville, FL 32611
Gen Secr: Dr. Steven Brandt
Focus: Archeol 16490

Society of Allied Weight Engineers (SAWE), 5530 Aztec Dr, La Mesa, CA 91942-2110
T: (619) 465-1367; Fax: (619) 465-2561
Founded: 1939; Members: 950
Gen Secr: Robert E. Johnston
Focus: Eng
Periodicals
Newsletter (quarterly)
Weight Engineering Journal (3 times annually) 16491

Society of American Archivists (SAA), 600 S Federal St, Ste 504, Chicago, IL 60605
T: (312) 922-0140; Fax: (312) 347-1452
Founded: 1936; Members: 3800
Pres: Nicholas Burckel; Gen Secr: Susan E. Fox
Focus: Archives
Periodicals
The American Archivist (quarterly)
Archival Outlook (bi-monthly)
Membership Directory (semi-annually) . . 16492

Society of American Foresters (SAF), 5400 Grosvenor Ln, Washington, DC 20814-2198
T: (301) 897-8720; Fax: (301) 897-3690
Founded: 1900; Members: 180000
Pres: John W. Moser Jr.; Gen Secr: William H. Banzhaf
Focus: Forestry
Periodicals
Forest Science (quarterly)
Journal of Forestry (monthly)
Northern Journal of Applied Forestry (quarterly)
Southern Journal of Applied Forestry (quarterly)
Western Journal of Applied Forestry (quarterly) 16493

Society of American Historians (SAH), c/o Butler Library, Columbia University, New York, NY 10027
T: (212) 854-2221; Fax: (212) 932-0602
Founded: 1939; Members: 350
Pres: David McCullough; Gen Secr: Mark C. Carnes
Focus: Hist 16494

Society of American Law Teachers (SALT), c/o Law School, New York University, 40 Washington Sq S, New York, NY 10012
T: (212) 998-6265; Fax: (212) 995-3156
Founded: 1974; Members: 500
Gen Secr: Sylvia A. Law
Focus: Educ; Law 16495

Society of American Registered Architects (SARA), 1245 S Highland Av, Lombard, IL 60148
T: (708) 932-4622
Founded: 1956; Members: 800
Focus: Archit 16496

Society of American Value Engineers (SAVE), 60 Revere Dr, Ste 500, Northbrook, IL 60062
T: (847) 480-1730; Fax: (847) 480-9282
Founded: 1959; Members: 1200
Gen Secr: Barbara Scott
Focus: Standards
Periodicals
Interactions (monthly)
Value World (quarterly) 16497

Society of Architectural Historians (SAH), 1365 N Astor St, Chicago, IL 60610-2144
T: (312) 573-1365; Fax: (312) 573-1141
Founded: 1940; Members: 4000
Pres: Patricia Waddy; Gen Secr: Dennis McFadden

Focus: Archit; Hist
Periodicals
Journal of the SAH (quarterly)
Newsletter (bi-monthly)
Preservation Forum (semi-annually) . . . 16498

Society of Automotive Engineers International (SAE International), 400 Commonwealth Dr, Warrendale, PA 15096-0001
T: (412) 776-4841; Fax: (412) 776-5760
Gen Secr: Max E. Rumbaugh
Focus: Auto Eng 16499

Society of Basque Studies in America (SBSA), 19 Colonial Gardens, Brooklyn, NY 11209
T: (718) 745-1141
Founded: 1978; Members: 1000
Gen Secr: Ignacio R. Galbis
Focus: Ling 16500

Society of Behavioral Medicine (SBM), 103 S Adams St, Rockville, MD 20850
T: (301) 251-2790; Fax: (301) 279-6749
Founded: 1978; Members: 2500
Focus: Behav Sci
Periodicals
Annals of Behavioral Medicine (quarterly)
Behavioral Medicine Abstracts (quarterly) . 16501

Society of Biblical Literature (SBL), 1201 Clairmont Rd, Ste 300, Decatur, GA 30033-4635
T: (404) 636-4744; Fax: (404) 248-0815
Founded: 1880; Members: 7000
Gen Secr: Kent Richards
Focus: Lit; Rel & Theol
Periodicals
Journal of Biblical Literature (quarterly)
Semeia (quarterly) 16502

Society of Biological Psychiatry (SBP), c/o Dept of Psychiatry and Pharmacology, Mayo Clinic of Jacksonville, 4500 San Pablo Rd, Jacksonville, FL 32224
T: (904) 953-2842; E-Mail: maggie@mayo.edu; Fax: (904) 953-7117
Founded: 1945; Members: 950
Gen Secr: Elliott Richelson
Focus: Psychiatry
Periodical
Biological Psychiatry (bi-monthly) 16503

Society of Broadcast Engineers (SBE), 8445 Keystone Crossing, Ste 140, Indianapolis, IN 46240
T: (317) 253-1640; Fax: (317) 253-0418
Founded: 1963; Members: 5000
Gen Secr: John L. Poray
Focus: Electric Eng 16504

Society of Cable Telecommunications Engineers (SCTE), 140 Philips Rd, Exton, PA 19341-1316
T: (610) 363-6888; Fax: (610) 363-5898
Founded: 1969; Members: 14000
Pres: William M. Riker
Focus: Eng; Mass Media
Periodical
The Interval (monthly) 16505

Society of Carbide and Tool Engineers (SCTE), c/o American Society for Metals, Metals Park, OH 44073
T: (216) 388-5151
Founded: 1947; Members: 1500
Focus: Eng
Periodical
Carbide and Tool Journal (bi-monthly) . 16506

Society of Cardiovascular and Interventional Radiology (SCVIR), 10201 Lee Hwy, Ste 160, Fairfax, VA 22030
T: (703) 691-1805; Fax: (703) 691-1855
Founded: 1973; Members: 2000
Focus: Radiology
Periodical
SCVIR Newsletter (quarterly) 16507

Society of Cardiovascular Anesthesiologists (SCA), 1910 Byrd Av, POB 11086, Richmond, VA 23230-1086
T: (804) 282-0084; Fax: (804) 282-0090
Members: 4000
Focus: Anesthetics
Periodical
SCA Newsletter (quarterly) 16508

Society of Christian Ethics (SCE), c/o School of Theology, Boston University, 745 Commonwealth Av, Boston, MA 02215
T: (617) 353-7322
Founded: 1959; Members: 950
Focus: Philos 16509

Society of Cosmetic Chemists (SCC), 120 Wall St, Ste 2400, New York, NY 10005
T: (212) 668-1500; Fax: (212) 668-1504
Founded: 1945; Members: 3250
Gen Secr: Theresa Cesario
Focus: Chem
Periodicals
Journal (bi-monthly)
Newsletter (quarterly) 16510

Society of Cost Estimating and Analysis (SCEA), 101 S Whiting St, Ste 201, Alexandria, VA 22304
T: (703) 751-8069; Fax: (703) 461-7328
Founded: 1990; Members: 4000
Focus: Finance
Periodicals
Journal of Cost Analysis (semi-annually)
Newsletter (quarterly) 16511

Society of Critical Care Medicine (SCCM), 8101 E Kaiser Bldv, Anaheim, CA 92808
T: (714) 282-6000; Fax: (714) 870-5243
Founded: 1970; Members: 4000
Focus: Med
Periodicals
Critical Care Medicine (monthly)
Critical Care: State of the Art (annually)
Newsmagazine Concern (quarterly) . . . 16512

Society of Diagnostic Medical Sonographers (SDMS), 12770 Coit Rd, Ste 508, Dallas, TX 75251
T: (214) 239-7367; Fax: (214) 239-7378
Founded: 1970; Members: 12000
Gen Secr: Gwen Grim
Focus: Med
Periodicals
Journal of Diagnostic Medical Sonography (bi-monthly)
Newsletter (bi-monthly) 16513

Society of Economic Geologists (SEG), 185 Estes St, Lakewood, CO 80226
Founded: 1920; Members: 1500
Gen Secr: A.L. Brokaw
Focus: Geology; Econ
Periodicals
Economic Geology (8 times annually)
Membership List (bi-annually) 16514

Society of Engineering Science (SES), c/o Prof. J. Mark Duva, Dept of Applied Mathematics, University of Virginia, 111G Olsson Hall, Charlottesville, VA 22903-2442
T: (804) 924-1029; Fax: (804) 924-6270
Founded: 1963; Members: 300
Gen Secr: Prof. J. Mark Duva
Focus: Eng 16515

Society of Ethnic and Special Studies (SESS), c/o Southern Illinois University at Edwardsville, POB 1652, Edwardsville, IL 62026
T: (618) 692-2042
Founded: 1973; Members: 400
Focus: Ethnology; Educ
Periodical
Journal (semi-annually) 16516

Society of Ethnobiology (SE), c/o Gayle Fritz, Dept of Anthropology, Washington University, Campus Box 1114, Saint Louis, MO 63130
T: (314) 935-8588; E-Mail: gjfritz@artsci.wush.edu; Fax: (314) 935-8535
Founded: 1978; Members: 450
Gen Secr: Gayle Fritz
Focus: Bio
Periodical
Journal of Ethnobiology (semi-annually) . 16517

Society of Experimental Psychologists (SEP), c/o Dr. Byron A. Campbell, Dept of Psychology, Princeton University, Princeton, NJ 08544-1010
T: (609) 258-0906; Fax: (609) 258-1113
Founded: 1929; Members: 180
Gen Secr: Dr. Byron A. Campbell
Focus: Psych
Periodical
Annual Report (annually) 16518

Society of Experimental Test Pilots, POB 986, Lancaster, CA 93534
T: (805) 942-9574; Fax: (805) 940-0398
Members: 1900
Focus: Aero 16519

Society of Exploration Geophysicists (SEG), POB 702740, Tulsa, OK 74170
T: (918) 493-3516; Fax: (918) 493-2074
Founded: 1930; Members: 15000
Gen Secr: John Hyden
Focus: Geophys
Periodicals
Geophysics (monthly)
Roster (annually) 16520

Society of Federal Linguists (SFL), POB 7765, Washington, DC 20044
T: (202) 707-5397
Founded: 1930; Members: 150
Pres: Dr. Everette E. Larson
Focus: Ling 16521

Society of Fire Protection Engineers (SFPE), 1 Liberty Sq, Boston, MA 02109-9825
T: (617) 482-0686; Fax: (617) 482-8184
Founded: 1950; Members: 3250
Focus: Safety 16522

Society of Flavor Chemists (SFC), c/o Richard F. Heinze, Griffith Laboratories, 1 Griffith Center, Alsip, IL 60658-3495
T: (708) 371-0900; Fax: (708) 371-9945
Founded: 1959; Members: 300
Gen Secr: Richard F. Heinze
Focus: Chem 16523

Society of Flight Test Engineers (SFTE), POB 4047, Lancaster, CA 93539
T: (805) 538-9715; Fax: (805) 538-9715
Founded: 1968; Members: 1100
Focus: Eng
Periodicals
Flight Test News (monthly)
Membership Directory (bi-annually) . . . 16524

Society of Freight Car Historians (SFCH), POB 2480, Monrovia, CA 91017
Founded: 1980; Members: 1000
Focus: Transport
Periodicals
Freight Cars Journal (quarterly)
Freight Cars Journal Monograph (6-10 times annually) 16525

Society of Gastroenterology Nurses and Associates (SGNA), 1070 Sibley Tower, Rochester, NY 14604
T: (716) 546-7241; Fax: (716) 546-5141
Founded: 1974; Members: 6000
Focus: Gastroenter
Periodical
Journal (quarterly) 16526

Society of General Physiologists (SGP), POB 257, Woods Hole, MA 02543
T: (508) 540-6719; Fax: (508) 540-0155
Founded: 1946; Members: 1000
Focus: Physiology
Periodical
Journal of General Physiology (monthly) . 16527

Society of Head and Neck Surgeons (SHNS), 4900B S 31 St, Arlington, VA 22206
T: (703) 820-7400; Fax: (703) 931-4520
Founded: 1954; Members: 700
Focus: Surgery 16528

Society of Imaging Science and Technology (SPSE), 7003 Kilworth Ln, Springfield, VA 22151
T: (703) 642-9090; Fax: (703) 642-9094
Founded: 1947; Members: 3000
Focus: Photo
Periodicals
Journal of Imaging Technology (bi-monthly)
Photographic Imaging Science (bi-monthly) 16529

Society of Independent Professional Earth Scientists (SIPES), 4925 Greenville Av, Ste 170, Dallas, TX 75206
T: (214) 363-1780; Fax: (214) 363-8195
Founded: 1963; Members: 1400
Focus: Geology
Periodical
Newsletter (quarterly) 16530

Society of Insurance Research (SIR), 691 Crossfire Ridge, Marietta, GA 30064
T: (770) 426-9270; Fax: (770) 426-9298
Founded: 1970; Members: 500
Gen Secr: Stanley M. Hopp
Focus: Insurance
Periodical
Research Review (bi-monthly) 16531

Society of Jewish Science (SJS), 109 E 39 St, New York, NY 10016
T: (212) 682-2626
Founded: 1922; Members: 250
Gen Secr: David Goldstein
Focus: Sci
Periodical
Jewish Science Interpreter (8 times annually) 16532

Society of Logistics Engineers (SOLE), 8100 Professional Pl, Ste 211, New Carrollton, MD 20785
T: (301) 459-8446; Fax: (301) 459-1522
Members: 9000
Focus: Business Admin
Periodicals
Annals (semi-annually)
Member's Handbook and Membership Directory (annually)
Soletter (monthly)
Spectrum (quarterly) 16533

Society of Manufacturing Engineers (SME), POB 930, Dearborn, MI 48121-0930
T: (313) 271-1500; Fax: (313) 271-2861
Founded: 1932; Members: 75000
Gen Secr: Philip Trimble
Focus: Eng 16534

Society of Medical Consultants to the Armed Forces (SMCAF), POB 2700, Kensington, MD 20891-2700
T: (301) 295-3903; Fax: (301) 728-3616
Founded: 1945; Members: 1000
Gen Secr: Anne Hufman
Focus: Med
Periodicals
Newsletter (3 times annually)
Roster 16535

Society of Medical Jurisprudence (SMJ), POB 20678, New York, NY 10021-0073
Founded: 1883; Members: 250
Focus: Law; Med
Periodical
Proceedings (monthly) 16536

Society of Motion Picture and Television Art Directors (SMPTAD), 11365 Ventura Blvd, Ste 315, Studio City, CA 91604
T: (818) 762-9995
Founded: 1960; Members: 400
Focus: Cinema 16537

Society of Motion Picture and Television Engineers (SMPTE), 595 W Hartsdale Av, White Plains, NY 10607
T: (914) 761-1100; Fax: (914) 761-3115
Founded: 1916; Members: 9000
Gen Secr: Frederick C. Motts
Focus: Cinema
Periodicals
Directory (annually)
Journal (monthly)
News and Notes (monthly) 16538

Society of Multivariate Experimental Psychology (SMEP), c/o Dept of Psychology, University of Virginia, 102 Gilmer Hall, Charlottesville, VA 22903
T: (804) 924-3374
Founded: 1960; Members: 65
Gen Secr: Dr. Jack McArdle
Focus: Psych
Periodical
Multivariate Behavioral Research (quarterly) 16539

Society of Naval Architects and Marine Engineers (SNAME), 601 Pavonia Av, Ste 400, Jersey City, NJ 07306
T: (201) 798-4800; Fax: (201) 798-4975
Founded: 1893; Members: 10000
Gen Secr: Francis M. Cagliari
Focus: Eng; Archit
Periodicals
Journal of Ship Production (quarterly)
Journal of Ship Research (quarterly)
Marine Technology (quarterly)
Transactions (annually) 16540

Society of Nematologists (SON), Bldg 011A, Rm 153, BARC.West, Beetsville, MD 20705
T: (301) 344-3081; Fax: (301) 344-2016
Founded: 1961; Members: 860
Gen Secr: Dr. David Chitwood
Focus: Zoology
Periodicals
Annual Meeting Presentations Abstracts (annually)
Journal of Nematology (quarterly)
Nematology Newsletter (quarterly) . . . 16541

Society of Neurological Surgeons (SNS), 750 Washington St, POB 178, Boston, MA 02111
T: (617) 956-5858
Founded: 1920; Members: 215
Focus: Surgery; Neurology 16542

Society of Neurosurgical Anesthesia and Critical Care (SNACC), POB 1502, Midlothian, VA 23113-1502
T: (804) 379-5513; Fax: (804) 379-1386
Founded: 1973; Members: 500
Gen Secr: Kimberly R. Roberts
Focus: Neurology
Periodicals
Comprehensive Bibliography in Neuroanesthesia (semi-annually)
Newsletter (3-4 times annually) 16543

Society of Nuclear Medicine (SNM), 1850 Samuel Morse Dr, Reston, VA 22090
T: (703) 708-9000; Fax: (703) 708-9015
Founded: 1954; Members: 14000
Gen Secr: Torry Mark Sansone
Focus: Nucl Med 16544

Society of Pelvic Surgeons (SPS), c/o Dept of OB-GYN, Mount Sinai School of Medicine, 1176 Fifth Av, New York, NY 10029
T: (212) 241-6554; Fax: (212) 360-6917
Founded: 1952; Members: 125
Gen Secr: Dr. Carmel Cohen
Focus: Surgery 16545

Society of Petroleum Engineers (SPE), POB 833836, Richardson, TX 75083-3836
T: (214) 952-9393; Fax: (214) 952-9435
Founded: 1922; Members: 53000
Focus: Petrochem
Periodicals
Enhanced Oil-Recovery Field Reports (quarterly)
Journal of Petroleum Technology (monthly)
SPE Drilling Engineering (quarterly)
SPE Formation Evaluation (quarterly)
SPE Production Engineering (quarterly)
SPE Reservoir Engineering (quarterly) . . 16546

Society of Philatelists and Numismatists (SPAN), 1929 Millis St, Montebello, CA 90640
T: (213) 724-1595
Members: 300
Focus: Numismatics
Periodical
Expansion (bi-monthly) 16547

Society of Plastics Engineers (SPE), 14 Fairfield Dr, Brookfield, CT 06804-0403
T: (203) 775-0471; Fax: (203) 775-8490
Founded: 1942; Members: 37000
Focus: Eng
Periodicals
Journal of Vinyl Technology (quarterly)
Plastics Engineering (monthly)
Polymer Composites (quarterly)
Polymer Engineering (18 times annually) 16548

Society of Professional Archaeologists (SOPA), c/o A.L. Novick, Planning and Environmental Branch, North Carolina Dept of Transportation, Raleigh, NC 27611
T: (913) 733-3141; Fax: (913) 733-9794
Founded: 1976; Members: 800
Pres: William B. Lees
Focus: Archeol
Periodicals
Directory of Professional Archaeoloists (annually)
Newsletter (monthly) 16549

Society of Professional Well Log Analysts (SPWLA), 8866 Gulf Freeway, Ste 320, Houston, TX 77017
T: (713) 947-8727; Fax: (713) 947-7181
Founded: 1959; Members: 4000
Gen Secr: Vicki J. King
Focus: Geology; Eng; Energy
Periodicals
Annual Transactions (annually)
The Log Analyst (bi-monthly) 16550

Society of Professors of Child and Adolescent Psychiatry (SPCAP), 3615 Wisconsin Av NW, Washington, DC 20016-3007
T: (202) 966-7300
Founded: 1969; Members: 160
Focus: Psychiatry 16551

Society of Professors of Education (SPE), c/o Dalton Curtis, College of Education, Southeast Missouri State University, 1 University Plaza, Cape Girardeau, MO 63701
T: (615) 974-2201; Fax: (615) 974-8718
Founded: 1902; Members: 274
Gen Secr: Dalton Curtis
Focus: Educ
Periodicals
DeGarmo Lectures (annually)
Membership Directory
Monograph Series (annually) 16552

Society of Prospective Medicine (SPM), 4417 Anchor Mill Dr, Omaha, NE 68123
T: (402) 291-3297; Fax: (317) 549-3670
Founded: 1972; Members: 250
Gen Secr: Jan Foerster
Focus: Med
Periodicals
Membership Directory (annually)
An Ounce of Prevention (quarterly) . . . 16553

Society of Protozoologists (SP), c/o Baruch College, 17 Lexington, New York, NY 10010
T: (212) 387-1230; Fax: (212) 387-1258
Founded: 1947; Members: 1125
Pres: Lea K. Bleyman
Focus: Zoology 16554

Society of Research Administrators (SRA), 1200 19 St NW, Washington, DC 20002
T: (202) 857-1141; Fax: (202) 223-4579
Founded: 1967; Members: 3000
Gen Secr: Carolyn M. Freeland
Focus: Sci
Periodicals
Journal (quarterly)
Membership Directory (annually)
Newsletter (bi-monthly) 16555

Society of Rheology (SOR), 500 Sunnyside Blvd, Woodbury, NY 11797
Founded: 1929; Members: 1200
Pres: R.C. Armstrong; Gen Secr: A.M. Kraynik
Focus: Bio; Chem; Physics
Periodicals
Journal of Rheology (8 times annually)
Rheology Bulletin (semi-annually) 16556

Society of Spanish and Spanish-American Studies (SSSAS), c/o Dept of Spanish and Portuguese, McKenna Language Building, University of Colorado, Campus POB 278, Boulder, CO 80309-0278
T: (303) 492-7308; E-Mail: spanish@ cubldr.colorado.edu; Fax: (303) 492-3699
Gen Secr: Luis T. Gonzáles-del-Valle
Focus: Ethnology; Ling; Lit 16557

Society of State Directors of Health, Physical Education and Recreation (SSDHPER), 9805 Hillridge Dr, Kensington, MD 20895
T: (301) 949-0709
Founded: 1926; Members: 180
Focus: Sports
Periodicals
Directory (annually)
Newsletter 16558

Society of Surgical Oncology (SSO), c/o James R. Slawny, 85 W Algonquin Rd, Ste 550, Arlington Heights, IL 60005
T: (708) 427-1400; Fax: (708) 427-1294
Founded: 1940; Members: 1350
Gen Secr: James R. Slawny
Focus: Cell Biol & Cancer Res 16559

Society of Systematic Biologists (SSB), c/o National Museum of Natural History, Washington, DC 20560
T: (202) 357-2964
Founded: 1948; Members: 1550
Focus: Bio
Periodical
Systematic Zoology (quarterly) 16560

Society of Teachers in Education of Professional Photography (STEPP), 371 Greenport Dr, West Carrollton, OH 45449
T: (513) 859-0180
Founded: 1978; Members: 75
Focus: Educ; Photo
Periodicals
Journal (quarterly)
Membership Directory (annually) 16561

Society of Teachers of Family Medicine (STFM), 8880 Ward Pkwy, POB 8729, Kansas City, MO 64114
T: (816) 333-9700; Fax: (816) 333-3884

Founded: 1968; Members: 3200
Focus: Family Plan; Med
Periodical
Family Medicine: Journal (bi-monthly) . . 16562

Society of Thoracic Surgeons (STS), 401 N Michigan Av, Chicago, IL 60611-4267
T: (312) 644-6610; Fax: (312) 527-6635
Founded: 1964; Members: 3228
Focus: Surgery
Periodical
Annals of Thoracic Surgery (monthly) . . 16563

Society of Toxicology (SOT), 1767 Business Center Dr, Ste 302, Reston, VA 22090-5332
T: (703) 438-3115; E-Mail: sothq@toxicology.org; Fax: (703) 438-3113
Founded: 1961; Members: 3700
Gen Secr: Shawn Douglas Lamb
Focus: Toxicology
Periodicals
Fundamental and Applied Toxicology (bi-monthly)
Newsletter (bi-monthly)
Toxicology and Applied Pharmacology (15 times annually) 16564

Society of Turkish Architects, Engineers and Scientists in America (STAESA), 821 U.N. Plaza, New York, NY 10017
T: (212) 682-7688; Fax: (609) 275-5357
Founded: 1970; Members: 500
Focus: Eng; Archit
Periodicals
MIM Membership Directory
MIM News Bulletin (monthly) 16565

Society of United States Air Force Flight Surgeons, POB 35387, Brooks Air Force Base, TX 78235
T: (210) 536-2844; Fax: (210) 536-2017
Founded: 1960; Members: 15000
Gen Secr: George Johnson
Focus: Surgery
Periodical
Society of USAF Flight Surgeons Newsletter
. . . . 16566

Society of University Surgeons (SUS), c/o Keith D. Lillemoe, POB 16549, West Haven, CT 06516
T: (203) 932-0541; E-Mail: Samolar@_2000.com; Fax: (203) 937-7716
Founded: 1938; Members: 1280
Gen Secr: Keith D. Lillemoe
Focus: Surgery 16567

Society of Vertebrate Paleontology (SVP), 401 N Michigan Av, Chicago, IL 60611-4267
T: (312) 321-3708; Fax: (312) 245-1085
Founded: 1941; Members: 1700
Pres: David Krause; Gen Secr: John Flynn
Focus: Paleontology
Periodicals
Bibliography of Fossil Vertebrates (annually)
Journal of Vertebrate Paleontology (quarterly)
News Bulletin (3 times annually) 16568

Society of Women Engineers (SWE), 120 Wall St, New York, NY 10005
T: (212) 509-9577; Fax: (212) 509-0224
Founded: 1950; Members: 16000
Gen Secr: Elaine Osterman
Focus: Eng
Periodical
U.S. Woman Engineer (bi-monthly) . . . 16569

Society of Wood Science and Technology (SWST), 1 Gifford Pinchot Dr, Madison, WI 53705
T: (608) 231-9347; Fax: (608) 231-9592
Founded: 1958; Members: 400
Focus: Forestry
Periodicals
Newsletter (bi-monthly)
Wood and Fiber Science (quarterly) . . 16570

Soiety for Northwestern Vertebrate Biology (SNVB), c/o Wildlife Management Div, Washington State Department of Wildlife, 600 Capitol Way N, Olympia, WA 98501-1091
T: (206) 753-2868
Founded: 1920; Members: 400
Gen Secr: John Pierce
Focus: Ornithology; Zoology
Periodical
Northwestern Naturalist (3 times annually) 16571

Soil and Water Conservation Society (SWCS), 7515 NE Ankeny Rd, Ankeny, IA 50021
T: (515) 289-2331; Fax: (515) 289-1227
Founded: 1945; Members: 13000
Focus: Agri; Ecology
Periodical
Journal of Soil and Water Conservation (bi-monthly) 16572

Soil Science Society of America (SSSA), 677 S Segoe Rd, Madison, WI 53711
T: (608) 273-8080; Fax: (608) 273-2021
Founded: 1936; Members: 6300
Gen Secr: Robert F. Barnes
Focus: Agri
Periodicals
Journal of Environmental Quality (quarterly)
Journal of Production Agriculture (quarterly)
. . . . 16573

Solar Energy International (SEI), POB 715, Carbondale, CO 81623-0715
T: (970) 963-8855; E-Mail: sei@solarenergy.org; Fax: (970) 963-8866
Focus: Energy 16574

Solartherm, 1315 Apple Av, Silver Spring, MD 20910
T: (301) 587-8686
Founded: 1977; Members: 600
Focus: Energy 16575

SOLE – The International Society of Logistics Engineers, 8100 Professional Place, Ste 211, Hyatsville, MD 20785
T: (301) 459-8446; E-Mail: solehq@aol.com; Fax: (301) 459-1522
Gen Secr: Paul D. Wisniewski
Focus: Eng 16576

Solid Waste Association of North America (SWANA), 1100 Wayne Av, Ste 700, POB 7219, Silver Spring, MD 20907
T: (301) 585-2898; Fax: (301) 589-7068
Founded: 1961; Members: 7000
Gen Secr: H.L. Hickman Jr.
Focus: Ecology
Periodical
Municipal Solid Waste News (monthly) . 16577

Solomon Schecher Day School Association (SSDSA), 155 Fifth Av, New York, NY 10010
T: (212) 260-8450
Founded: 1964; Members: 63
Focus: Educ 16578

Sonneck Society (SS), POB 476, Canton, MA 02021
T: (617) 828-8450; Fax: (617) 828-8915
Founded: 1974; Members: 960
Focus: Music 16579

South American Explorers Club (SAEC), 126 Indian Creek Rd, Ithaca, NY 14850
T: (607) 277-0488
Founded: 1977; Members: 6500
Focus: Bio; Anthro; Archeol; Geography
Periodical
South American Explorer (quarterly) . . 16580

Southeast Asia Council Association for Asian Studies, c/o Dept of History, University of Wisconsin, Madison, WI 53706
Gen Secr: Prof. Thongchui Winichakul
Focus: Ethnology 16581

Southern Association of Colleges and Schools (SACS), 1866 Southern Ln, Decatur, GA 30033
T: (404) 679-4500; Fax: (404) 329-6598
Founded: 1895; Members: 11811
Focus: Educ
Periodicals
Membership List
Newsletter (7 times annually)
Proceedings 16582

Southern Building Code Congress – International (SBCCI), 900 Montclair Rd, Birmingham, AL 35213
T: (205) 591-1853; Fax: (205) 592-7001
Founded: 1940; Members: 7300
Focus: Civil Eng 16583

Southern Historical Association (SHA), c/o Dept of History, University of Georgia, Athens, GA 30602
T: (706) 542-8848; Fax: (706) 542-2455
Founded: 1934; Members: 4500
Focus: Hist
Periodical
The Journal of Southern History (quarterly)
. . . . 16584

Southern Humanities Conference (SHC), c/o Dr. John Phillips, University of Tennessee at Chattanooga, Chattanooga, TN 37403
T: (615) 755-4153; Fax: (615) 755-4279
Founded: 1947; Members: 200
Gen Secr: Dr. John Phillips
Focus: Humanities
Periodicals
Humanities in the South (semi-annually)
Southern Humanities Review (quarterly) . 16585

Southern Regional Council (SRC), 133 Carnegie Way, Ste 900, Atlanta, GA 30303-1024
T: (404) 522-8764; E-Mail: 73251.2024@ compuserve.com; Fax: (404) 522-8791
Founded: 1944; Members: 120
Gen Secr: Wendy Johnson
Focus: Sociology
Periodical
Southern Changes (bi-monthly) 16586

Southern Society of Genealogists (SSG), RFD 5, Box 109, Piedmont, AL 36272
T: (205) 447-2939
Founded: 1962; Members: 50
Pres: F. Stewart
Focus: Genealogy
Periodicals
Bulletin
Directory (annually) 16587

Southern States Communication Association (SSCA), c/o Dr. Richard R. Ranta, College of Communication and Fine Arts, University of Memphis, Memphis, TN 38152
T: (901) 678-2350; Fax: (901) 678-5118
Founded: 1930; Members: 1500
Gen Secr: Dr. Richard R. Ranta

Focus: Ling
Periodical
Southern Speech Communication Journal (quarterly) 16588

Southwest Parks and Monuments Association (SPMA), 221 N Court Av, Tucson, AZ 85701
T: (602) 622-1999; Fax: (602) 623-9519
Founded: 1937; Members: 259
Focus: Travel 16589

Southwestern Legal Foundation (SWLF), POB 830707, Richardson, TX 75083-0707
T: (214) 690-2370; Fax: (214) 690-2458
Founded: 1947; Members: 700
Focus: Law
Periodicals
Labor Law Developments (annually)
Oil and Gas Reporter (monthly)
Patent Law Annual (annually)
Private Investors Abroad: Problems and Solutions in International Business (annually) . . . 16590

Space Settlement Studies Program (SSSP), c/o Niagara University, Niagara Institute, NY 14109
T: (716) 286-8094; E-Mail: swhitney@ eagle.niagara.edu; Fax: (716) 286-8061
Founded: 1977; Members: 1000
Gen Secr: Stewart B. Whitney
Focus: Aero 16591

Space Studies Institute (SSI), POB 82, Princeton, NJ 08542
T: (609) 921-0377; Fax: (609) 921-0389
Founded: 1977; Members: 5000
Focus: Astrophys
Periodical
Update (bi-monthly) 16592

Special Interest Group for Computer Personnel Research (SIGCPR), c/o Thomas W. Ferratt, Dept of MIS Decision Sciences, College of Business, University of Dayton, Dayton, OH 45469-2130
T: (513) 229-2728; Fax: (513) 229-4000
Founded: 1962; Members: 200
Pres: Thomas W. Ferratt
Focus: Computer & Info Sci
Periodical
Newsletter (quarterly) 16593

Special Interest Group for Computer Uses in Education (SIGCUE), c/o John Lawson, Center for Electronic Studying, 5265 University of Oregon, Eugene, OR 97403-5265
T: (714) 449-4191; Fax: (714) 449-7101
Members: 1699
Pres: John Lawson
Focus: Computer & Info Sci; Educ . . . 16594

Special Interest Group for Symbolic and Algebraic Manipulation (SIGSAM), c/o ACM, 1515 Broadway, New York, NY 10036-5701
T: (212) 869-7440; Fax: (212) 302-5826
Founded: 1967; Members: 2000
Pres: Stephen Watt
Focus: Math
Periodicals
Bulletin (quarterly)
Proceedings of Symposia (bi-annually) . 16595

Special Interest Group on Artificial Intelligence (SIGART), c/o Association for Computing Machinery, 1515 Broadway, New York, NY 10036
T: (212) 869-7440; Fax: (212) 302-5826
Members: 8255
Focus: Computer & Info Sci
Periodical
SIGART Newsletter 16596

Special Interest Group on Biomedical Computing (SIGBIO), c/o Duke University Medical Center, POB 2914, Durham, NC 27710
T: (919) 684-6421; Fax: (919) 684-8675
Founded: 1967; Members: 1006
Pres: William E. Hammond
Focus: Computer & Info Sci
Periodical
Newsletter (quarterly) 16597

Special Interest Group on Information Retrieval (SIGIR), c/o Dept of Computer Science, Virginia Polytechnic Institute, Blackburg, VA 24061-0106
T: (703) 231-5113; Fax: (703) 545-1249
Founded: 1966; Members: 1845
Focus: Computer & Info Sci 16598

Special Libraries Association (SLA), 1700 18 St NW, Washington, DC 20009
T: (202) 234-4700; Fax: (202) 265-9317
Founded: 1909; Members: 14000
Gen Secr: David R. Bender
Focus: Libraries & Bk Sci
Periodicals
Special Libraries (quarterly)
SpeciaList (monthly)
Who's Who in Special Libraries (annually) 16599

Special Programme for African Agricultural Research (SPAAR), c/o World Bank, 1818 H St NW, Washington, DC 20433
T: (202) 473-9008; Fax: (202) 676-0007
Gen Secr: Mohammood Abdi Noor
Focus: Agri 16600

Speech Communication Association (SCA), 5105 Backlick Rd, Bldg E, Annandale, VA 22003
T: (703) 750-0533; Fax: (703) 914-9471
Founded: 1914; Members: 7000
Gen Secr: James L. Gaudino
Focus: Ling
Periodicals
Communication Education (quarterly)
Communication Monographs (quarterly)
Critical Studies In Mass Communication (quarterly)
Journal of Speech (quarterly)
Spectra (11 times annually) 16601

Spenser Society (SS), c/o John Webster, Dept of English, University of Washington, Seattle, WA 98195
T: (206) 543-6203; Fax: (206) 685-2673
Members: 200
Gen Secr: John Webster
Focus: Lit 16602

Spirit and Breath Association (SBA), 1409 Gordon Terrace, Deerfield, IL 60015-4738
T: (708) 948-0370; Fax: (708) 948-0371
Founded: 1979; Members: 250
Pres: Morton Liebling
Focus: Cell Biol & Cancer Res 16603

Standards Engineering Society (SES), 1704 Darst Av, Dayton, OH 45403-3104
Founded: 1947; Members: 750
Focus: Standards
Periodicals
Membership Directory (annually)
Proceedings (annually)
Standards Engineering (bi-monthly) . . . 16604

Steel Structures Painting Council (SSPC), 40 24 St, Pittsburgh, PA 15222-4643
T: (412) 281-2331; Fax: (412) 281-9992
Founded: 1950; Members: 8600
Gen Secr: Dr. Bernard R. Appleman
Focus: Chem; Metallurgy 16605

Stonehenge Study Group (SSG), 2261 Las Positas Rd, Santa Barbara, CA 93105-4116
T: (805) 687-9350
Founded: 1970
Focus: Astronomy; Geology; Archeol
Periodical
Stonehenge Viewpoint (bi-monthly) . . . 16606

Strategic Management Society (SMS), c/o Krannert Graduate School of Mgt, Purdue University, West Lafayette, IN 47907
Gen Secr: Prof. Dan Schendel
Focus: Business Admin 16607

Structural Stability Research Council (SSRC), c/o Fritz Engineering Laboratory, Lehigh University, 13 E Packer Av, Bethlehem, PA 18015
T: (215) 758-3522; Fax: (215) 758-4522
Founded: 1944; Members: 400
Focus: Eng
Periodical
SSRC Annual Technical Session Proceedings (annually) 16608

Student National Medical Association (SNMA), 1012 Tenth St NW, Washington, DC 20001
T: (202) 371-1616
Founded: 1964; Members: 2600
Focus: Educ; Med 16609

Study Group for Mathematical Learning (SGML), 501 S First Av, Highland Park, NJ 08904
T: (908) 545-4960; Fax: (908) 932-8206
Founded: 1956
Pres: Robert B. Davis
Focus: Math 16610

Subterranean Sociological Association (SSA), c/o Dept of Sociology, Eastern Michigan University, Ypsilanti, MI 48197
T: (517) 522-3551
Founded: 1975; Members: 200
Focus: Sociology
Periodical
The Subterranean Sociology Newsletter . 16611

Sulphur Institute (SI), 1140 Connecticut Av NW, Ste 612, Washington, DC 20036-4002
T: (202) 331-9660; E-Mail: sulphur@access.digex.net; Fax: (202) 293-2940
Founded: 1960; Members: 35
Pres: Robert J. Morris
Focus: Agri; Chem; Eng
Periodical
Sulphur in Agriculture (1-2 times annually) 16612

Sumi-E Society of America (SSA), 7614 Arnet Ln, Bethesda, VA 20817
T: (301) 229-3184; Fax: (301) 320-9029
Founded: 1962; Members: 450
Gen Secr: Cecil Yeharar
Focus: Arts
Periodicals
Catalogue (annually)
Membership List
Sumi-E (quarterly) 16613

SUNSAT Energy Council, 6 Nowell Place, Hopewell, NJ 08525
T: (609) 466-9698; E-Mail: maryniak@ocean.rutgers.edu
Gen Secr: Gregg Maryniak
Focus: Energy 16614

Superstition Mountain Historical Society (SMHS), POB 3845, Apache Junction, AZ 85217-3845
T: (602) 983-4888
Founded: 1980; Members: 270
Focus: Hist 16615

Supreme Court Historical Society (SCHS), 111 Second St NE, Washington, DC 20002
T: (202) 543-0400
Founded: 1974; Members: 4200
Focus: Hist 16616

Surgical Eye Expeditions International, 27 E De la Guerra St C-2, Santa Barbara, CA 93101-2202
T: (805) 963-3303; Fax: (805) 965-3564
Gen Secr: Baillie R. Brown
Focus: Surgery 16617

Surveyors Historical Society (SHS), 300 W High St, Ste 2, Lawrenceburg, IN 47025-1912
T: (812) 537-2000; Fax: (812) 537-2000
Founded: 1977; Members: 400
Gen Secr: Roger Woodfill
Focus: Surveying
Periodicals
Backsight (semi-annually)
Membership Directory (bi-annually) . . . 16618

Suzuki Association of the Americas (SAA), POB 17310, Boulder, CO 80308
T: (303) 444-0948; Fax: (303) 444-0984
Founded: 1972; Members: 5000
Gen Secr: Pamela Brasch
Focus: Music 16619

Swedish-American Historical Society (SAHS), 5125 N Spaulding Av, Chicago, IL 60625
T: (312) 583-5722
Founded: 1948; Members: 1200
Focus: Hist
Periodical
The Swedish-American Historical Quarterly (quarterly) 16620

Swedish Colonial Society (SCS), c/o Gloria Dei Church, 916 Swanson St, Philadelphia, PA 19147
T: (215) 688-1766
Founded: 1908; Members: 400
Pres: John C. Cameron
Focus: Hist
Periodical
Directory 16621

Swedish Women's Educational Association International (SWEA), 7414 Herschel Av, POB 2585, La Jolla, CA 92038-2585
T: (619) 459-8435
Founded: 1979; Members: 4500
Focus: Educ
Periodical
SWEA Forum (3 times annually) . . . 16622

Swiss-American Historical Society (SAHS), c/o Prof. Erdmann Schmocker, 6440 N Bosworth Av, Chicago, IL 60626
T: (312) 262-8336
Founded: 1927; Members: 375
Pres: Prof. E. Schmocker
Focus: Hist
Periodical
Review (3 times annually) 16623

Tamarind Institute (TI), 108 Cornell Dr SE, Albuquerque, NM 87106
T: (505) 277-3901; Fax: (505) 277-3920
Founded: 1970
Gen Secr: Marjorie Devon
Focus: Arts
Periodical
The Tamarind Papers (semi-annually) . . 16624

Tarlton Institute for Marine Education (TIME), 50 Francisco, Ste 103, San Francisco, CA 94133
T: (415) 433-3163; Fax: (415) 989-7867
Founded: 1991
Gen Secr: Julie Begley
Focus: Zoology
Periodicals
Whale Center Newsletter (quarterly)
Whales Tales (quarterly) 16625

Tax Analysts (TA), 6830 N Fairfax Dr, Arlington, VA 22213
T: (703) 533-4400; Fax: (703) 533-4444
Founded: 1970
Focus: Law; Stats
Periodicals
Highlights and Documents
Microfiche Tax Data Base (weekly)
The Tax Directory (quarterly)
Tax Notes 16626

TDES – Celebrating the Music of Duke Ellington, POB 31, Church St Station, New York, NY 10008
T: (908) 878-7746
Founded: 1958; Members: 400
Pres: Lynne Maeller
Focus: Music
Periodical
TDES Newsletter (10 times annually) . . 16627

Teachers' Educational Council – Association of Accredited Cosmetology Schools (TEC/AACS), 901 N Washington St, Ste 206, Alexandria, VA 22314-1535
T: (703) 683-1700; Fax: (703) 683-2376
Founded: 1956; Members: 600
Pres: Ronald E. Smith
Focus: Adult Educ
Periodicals
Date (annually)
NAACS News (monthly)
Washington Update (monthly) 16628

Teachers of English to Speakers of Other Languages (TESOL), 1600 Cameron St, Ste 300, Alexandria, VA 22314
T: (703) 836-0774; Fax: (703) 836-6447
Founded: 1966; Members: 23000
Gen Secr: Susan Bayley
Focus: Ling; Educ
Periodicals
TESOL Newsletter (bi-monthly)
TESOL Quarterly (quarterly) 16629

Technical Association of the Graphic Arts (TAGA), 68 Lomb Memorial Dr, Rochester, NY 14623-5604
T: (716) 475-7470; E-Mail: tagaofc@aol.com; Fax: (716) 475-2250
Founded: 1948; Members: 1300
Gen Secr: Karen Lawrence
Focus: Eng; Graphic & Dec Arts, Design
Periodical
Proceedings (annually) 16630

Technical Association of the Pulp and Paper Industry (TAPPI), POB 105113, Atlanta, GA 30348-5113
T: (404) 446-1400; Fax: (404) 446-6947
Focus: Eng 16631

Technology Transfer Society (TTS), 23 N Main St, Ste C, Franklin, IN 46131-2335
T: (317) 738-3908; E-Mail: t2s@iquest.net; Fax: (317) 738-3980
Founded: 1975; Members: 750
Gen Secr: F. Timothy Janis
Focus: Eng
Periodicals
Journal of Technology Transfer (quarterly)
TSQUARED (monthly) 16632

Tennessee Folklore Society (TFS), c/o Middle Tennessee State University, POB 529, Murfreesboro, TN 37132
T: (615) 898-2576
Founded: 1934; Members: 500
Focus: Cultur Hist 16633

Teratology Society (TS), 9650 Rockville Pike, Bethesda, MD 20814
T: (301) 571-1841; Fax: (301) 571-1852
Founded: 1960; Members: 750
Focus: Toxicology
Periodical
Teratology: The International Journal of Abnormal Development (bi-monthly) 16634

Theatre Guild (TG), 226 W 47 St, New York, NY 10036
T: (212) 869-5470; Fax: (212) 869-5463
Founded: 1919; Members: 105000
Focus: Perf Arts 16635

Theatre Historical Society of America (THSA), 152 N York Rd, Ste 200, Elmhurst, IL 60126-2806
T: (708) 782-1800; Fax: (708) 782-1802
Founded: 1969; Members: 1000
Gen Secr: Richard J. Sklenar
Focus: Hist; Perf Arts
Periodicals
Directory
Marquee (quarterly) 16636

Theatre Library Association (TLA), 111 Amsterdam Av, Rm 513, New York, NY 10023
T: (212) 870-1670
Founded: 1937; Members: 500
Pres: Geraldine Duclow; Gen Secr: Richard M. Buck
Focus: Libraries & Bk Sci; Perf Arts
Periodicals
Broadside: Newsletter of the TLA (quarterly)
Performing Arts Resources (annually) . . 16637

Theodor Herzl Institute (THI), 110 E 59 St, New York, NY 10022
T: (212) 339-6038; Fax: (212) 318-6175
Founded: 1955; Members: 1000
Focus: Educ
Periodicals
Annual Season Preview (annually)
Herzl Institute Bulletin (bi-weekly) . . . 16638

Theodore Roosevelt Association (TRA), POB 719, Oyster Bay, NY 11771
T: (516) 921-6319; Fax: (516) 921-6481
Founded: 1919; Members: 2200
Gen Secr: John A. Gable
Focus: Hist
Periodical
Journal (quarterly) 16639

Therapy Dogs International (TDI), 6 Hilltop Rd, Mendham, NJ 07945
T: (201) 543-0888; E-Mail: tdi@gti.net; Fax: (201) 543-0989
Gen Secr: Ursula Kempe
Focus: Therapeutics 16640

Thomas Wolfe Society (TWS), c/o Joseph M. Flora, Dept of English, UNC, Chapel Hill, NC 27599
T: (919) 942-4902; Fax: (919) 962-3520
Founded: 1979; Members: 600
Pres: Joseph M. Flora
Focus: Lit
Periodical
The Thomas Wolfe Review (semi-annually) 16641

Thoreau Society (TS), 44 Baker Farm, Lincoln, MA 01773-3004
T: (617) 259-4112; Fax: (617) 259-1470
Founded: 1941; Members: 1500
Gen Secr: B. Dean
Focus: Lit
Periodicals
Bulletin (quarterly)
The Concord Saunterer (annually) . . . 16642

Thorne Ecological Institute (TEI), 5398 Manhattan Circle, Boulder, CO 80303
T: (303) 499-3647
Founded: 1954
Focus: Ecology 16643

Tibet Society (TS), POB 1968, Bloomington, IN 47402
T: (812) 335-8222
Founded: 1966; Members: 450
Focus: Ethnology
Periodicals
Journal of the Tibet Society (annually)
Tibet Society Bulletin (annually) 16644

Torrey Botanical Club (TBC), c/o Dana Floris, POB 1897, Lawrence, KS 66044
Founded: 1860
Pres: Dr. H.D. Hammond
Focus: Botany 16645

Touch for Health Association, 6955 Fernhill Dr, Ste 5A, Malibu, CA 90265-4238
T: (310) 457-8342; E-Mail: tch4hlth@aol.com; Fax: (310) 457-9267
Founded: 1974; Members: 1500
Pres: Robert Abdulache
Focus: Med
Periodicals
In Touch for Health (bi-monthly)
Touch for Health Directory (annually)
Touch for Health Journal (annually)
Touch for Health Times (quarterly) . . . 16646

Tourette Syndrome Association (TSA), 40-42 Bell Blvd, Bayside, NY 11361
T: (718) 224-2999; Fax: (718) 279-9596
Founded: 1972; Members: 30000
Focus: Neurology; Psychiatry
Periodical
TSA Newsletter (quarterly) 16647

Transplantation Society (TS), c/o Dr. Felix Rapaport, Dept of Surgery, SUNY at Stony Brook, Health Science Center, Stony Brook, NY 11794-8192
T: (516) 444-2209; E-Mail: rapaport@surg.som.sunysh.edu; Fax: (516) 444-3831
Founded: 1966; Members: 1400
Gen Secr: Dr. Felix Rapaport
Focus: Med
Periodicals
Transplantation (monthly)
Transplantation Proceedings (bi-monthly) . 16648

Transportation Alternatives (TA), 92 Saint Marks Pl, New York, NY 10009
T: (212) 475-4600
Founded: 1973; Members: 1500
Focus: Transport 16649

Transportation Research Board (TRB), 2101 Constitution Av NW, Washington, DC 20418
T: (202) 334-2934; Fax: (202) 334-2003
Founded: 1920; Members: 5600
Focus: Transport
Periodicals
National Cooperative Highway Research Program Report
National Cooperative Transit Research and Development Program Reports (semi-annually)
NCHRP Synthesis of Highway Practice
NCTRP Research Result Digest (irregularly)
NCTRP Synthesis of Transit Practice (semi-annually)
Special Report
Transportation Research Circular
Transportation Research Record 16650

Tree-Ring Society (TRS), c/o Tree-Ring Research Laboratory, University of Arizona, Tucson, AZ 85721
T: (602) 621-1608; Fax: (602) 621-8229
Founded: 1934; Members: 320
Gen Secr: Jeffrey S. Dean
Focus: Forestry
Periodical
Tree-Ring Bulletin (annually) 16651

Tripoli Rocketry Association (TRA), POB 339, Kenner, LA 70065-0339
T: (504) 467-1967
Founded: 1985; Members: 1892
Focus: Educ; Eng
Periodical
Tripolitan (bi-monthly) 16652

Trout Unlimited (TU), 1500 Wilson Blvd, Ste 310, Arlington, VA 22209-2310
T: (703) 522-0200; E-Mail: troutu@aol.com; Fax: (703) 284-9400
Founded: 1959; Members: 85000
Gen Secr: Charles F. Gauvin
Focus: Fisheries; Water Res

Periodicals
Chapter and Council Handbook (annually)
Lines to Leaders (quarterly)
Trout Magazine (quarterly) *16653*

The Trumpeter Swan Society (TTSS), 3800 County Rd 24, Maple Plain, MN 55359
T: (612) 476-4663; Fax: (612) 476-1514
Founded: 1968; Members: 500
Focus: Zoology
Periodicals
Conference Proceedings and Papers (bi-annually)
Newsletter (quarterly) *16654*

Turkish American Physicians Association (TAPA), 222 Middle Country Rd, Smithtown, NY 11787
T: (516) 724-0777
Founded: 1969; Members: 1260
Gen Secr: Dr. Cemil Bikmen
Focus: Physiology
Periodical
Membership Roster (bi-annually) *16655*

Ukrainian Academy of Arts and Sciences in the U.S. (UAAS), 206 W 100 St, New York, NY 10025
T: (212) 222-1866
Founded: 1950; Members: 223
Focus: Arts; Sci *16656*

Ukrainian Engineers' Society of America (UESA), c/o Ukrainian Institute, 2 E 79 St, New York, NY 10021
T: (212) 288-8660
Founded: 1948; Members: 900
Pres: Gregory Kuzma
Focus: Eng
Periodicals
Bulletin (quarterly)
Ukrainian Engineers News (quarterly) . . *16657*

Ukrainian Institute of America (UIA), 2 E 79 St, New York, NY 10021
T: (212) 288-8660
Founded: 1948; Members: 450
Focus: Ethnology *16658*

Ukrainian Medical Asociation of North America (UMANA), 2247 W Chicago Av, Chicago, IL 60622
T: (312) 278-6262
Founded: 1950; Members: 1000
Focus: Med
Periodicals
Medical Journal (quarterly)
Newsletter to Membership (quarterly) . . *16659*

Ukrainian Political Science Association in the United States (UPSA), POB 12963, Philadelphia, PA 19108
Founded: 1970; Members: 104
Focus: Poli Sci
Periodical
Newsletter (semi-annually) *16660*

ULI – Urban Land Institute, 625 Indiana Av NW, Ste 400, Washington, DC 20004
T: (202) 624-7000; Fax: (202) 624-7140
Founded: 1936; Members: 13000
Pres: Joseph C. Canizaro
Focus: Urban Plan *16661*

Undersea and Hyperbaric Medical Society (UHMS), 10531 Metropolitan Av, Kensington, MD 20895
T: (301) 942-2980; E-Mail: uhms@radix.nez; Fax: (301) 942-7804
Founded: 1967; Members: 2500
Gen Secr: Leon J. Greenbaum Jr.
Focus: Med
Periodicals
Journal of Hyperbaric Medicine (quarterly)
Pressure: Newsletter (bi-monthly)
Undersea Biomedical Research: Journal (bi-monthly)
Undersea & Hyperbaric Medicine: Abstracts from the Literature Abstract Journal (bi-monthly) *16662*

Union of Concerned Scientists (UCS), 2 Brattle Square, Cambridge, MA 02238-9105
T: (617) 547-5552; E-Mail: hris@ucsusa.org; Fax: (617) 864-9405
Gen Secr: Howard Ris
Focus: Sci *16663*

Union of Writers of the African Peoples (UWAP), c/o Dept of Africana Studies, Univ of Pittsburgh, Forbes Quad 3T, Pittsburgh, PA 15260
T: (412) 648-7540, 648-7556; Fax: (412) 648-7214
Gen Secr: Dennis Brutus
Focus: Lit *16664*

Unitarian Universalist Historical Society (UUHS), c/o Conrad E. Wright, Massachusetts Historical Society, 1154 Boylston St, Boston, MA 02215
T: (617) 536-1608; E-Mail: M9_Masshist@nelinet.org; Fax: (617) 859-0074
Founded: 1978; Members: 350
Pres: Conrad E. Wright
Focus: Hist *16665*

Unitas Malacologica, c/o Field Mus Nat Hist, Div of Vertebrates, Roosevelt Rd, Chicago, IL 60605-2496
Gen Secr: Dr. Rüdiger Bieler
Focus: Zoology *16666*

United Board for Christian Higher Education in Asia (UBCHEA), 475 Riverside Dr, Rm 1221, New York, NY 10115
T: (212) 870-2609; E-Mail: staff@ubchea.org; Fax: (212) 870-2322
Founded: 1932; Members: 45
Pres: Dr. David W. Vikner
Focus: Educ
Periodicals
Annual Report (annually)
New Horizons (3 times annually) . . . *16667*

United Cerebral Palsy Associations (UPCA), 1522 K St NW, Ste 1112, Washington, DC 20005
T: (202) 842-1266; Fax: (202) 842-3519
Founded: 1948; Members: 155
Focus: Med *16668*

United Cerebral Palsy Research and Educational Foundation (UCPREF), 1660 L St NW, Ste 700, Washington, DC 20036-5602
T: (202) 973-7140; Fax: (212) 776-0414
Founded: 1955
Gen Secr: Murray Goldstein
Focus: Med; Educ *16669*

United Engineering Trustees (UET), 345 E 47 St, New York, NY 10017
T: (212) 705-7828; Fax: (212) 705-7441
Founded: 1904
Focus: Eng *16670*

United Nations Bibliographic Information System (UNBIS), c/o United Nations, Head Librarian, Dag Hammarskjöld Library, New York, NY 10017
T: (212) 963-7443; Fax: (212) 963-0077
Focus: Libraries & Bk Sci *16671*

United Nations Commission on Population and Development, c/o Division for Policy and Coordination and ECOSOC Affairs, Dept for Policy Coordination and Sustainable Development, United Nations Headquarters, Rm 2963, New York, NY 10017
T: (212) 963-1234; Fax: (212) 963-5935
Focus: Soc Sci *16672*

United Nations Commission on Science and Technology for Development, United Nations, New York, NY 10017
T: (212) 963-1234; Fax: (212) 758-2718
Focus: Sci; Eng *16673*

United Nations Committee on New and Renewable Sources of Energy and Energy for Development, c/o Energy and Natural Resources Branch, Sustainable Development Div, Dept of Policy Coordination and Sustainable Development, 2 UN Plaza, United Nations, DC 2-2220, New York, NY 10017
T: (212) 963-4515; Fax: (212) 963-1795
Focus: Energy *16674*

United Nations Educational, Scientific and Cultural Organization (UNESCO), 2 UN Plaza, United Nations, DC 2-9000, New York, NY 10017
T: (212) 963-5995; E-Mail: UHNYO@unesco.org; Fax: (212) 963-8014
Focus: Educ; Sci; Ethnology *16675*

United Nations Group of Experts on Geographical Names (UNGEGN), c/o Div for Environment Management and Social Development, Dept for Development Support and Management Services, 2 UN Plaza, United Nations, New York, NY 10017
T: (212) 963-8568; Fax: (212) 963-8270
Focus: Geography *16676*

United Nations Statistical Commission, c/o Division for Policy and Coordination and ECOSOC Affairs, Dept for Policy Coordination and Sustainable Development, United Nations Headquarters, Rm 2963, New York, NY 10017
T: (212) 963-1234; Fax: (212) 963-5935
Focus: Stats *16677*

United New Conservationists (UNC), POB 362, Campbell, CA 95009
T: (408) 241-5769
Founded: 1969; Members: 58
Focus: Ecology *16678*

United Ostomy Association (UOA), 36 Executive Park, Ste 120, Irvine, CA 92714
T: (714) 660-8624; Fax: (714) 660-9262
Founded: 1962; Members: 50000
Focus: Gastroenter
Periodicals
Ostomy Quarterly (quarterly)
The Phoenix (monthly) *16679*

United Planetary Federation (UPF), POB 17470, Chicago, IL 60617-0470
E-Mail: upf@upf.org
Focus: Astronomy *16680*

United Poets Laureate International, 2226 Pheasant Dr, Hercules, CA 94547
Gen Secr: Dr. Benjamin R. Yuzon
Focus: Lit *16681*

United States Antarctic Research Program (USARP), c/o Guy G. Guthridge, Polar Information Program, National Science Foundation, 4201 Wilson Blvd, Rm 755, Arlington, VA 22230
T: (703) 306-1031; E-Mail: dfriscic@nsf.gov; Fax: (703) 306-0139
Founded: 1959
Gen Secr: Guy G. Guthridge
Focus: Geography; Bio; Oceanography; Astronomy
Periodical
Antarctic Journal of the United States (quarterly) *16682*

United States Branch of the International Committee for the Defense of the Breton Language (US ICDBL), 169 Greenwood Av, Jenkintown, PA 19046
T: (215) 886-6361
Founded: 1981; Members: 150
Gen Secr: L. Kuter
Focus: Ling *16683*

United States Capitol Historical Society (USCHS), 200 Maryland Av NE, Washington, DC 20002
T: (202) 543-8919
Founded: 1962; Members: 12000
Focus: Hist
Periodicals
The Capitol Dome (quarterly)
Congress and the Presidency (semi-annually) *16684*

United States Committee of the International Association of Art (USCIAA), POB 28068, Central Station, Washington, DC 20038-8068
T: (202) 628-9633
Founded: 1952; Members: 12
Focus: Arts *16685*

United States Committee on Irrigation and Drainage (USCID), 1616 17 St, Denver, CO 80202
T: (303) 628-5430; Fax: (303) 628-5451
Founded: 1952; Members: 700
Focus: Water Res
Periodical
ICID Bulletin (quarterly) *16686*

United States Committee on Large Dams (USCOLD), 1616 17 St, Denver, CO 80202
T: (303) 628-5430; Fax: (303) 628-5431
Founded: 1928; Members: 1150
Focus: Civil Eng *16687*

United States Energy Association (USEA), 1620 Eye St, Ste 1000, Washington, DC 20006
T: (202) 331-0415; Fax: (202) 331-0418
Founded: 1924; Members: 186
Gen Secr: Barry K. Worthington
Focus: Energy *16688*

United States Federation for Culture Collections (USFCC), c/o Dept 47P, AP9A, Abbott Laboratories, Abbott Park, IL 60064
T: (708) 937-8764; Fax: (708) 938-6603
Founded: 1970; Members: 260
Gen Secr: Marianna Jackson
Focus: Bio
Periodicals
Directory (semi-annually)
Newsletter (quarterly) *16689*

United States Federation of Scholars and Scientists (USFSS), c/o Dept of Physics, California State University at Fullerton, Fullerton, CA 92634
T: (714) 773-3421; Fax: (714) 449-5810
Founded: 1938
Gen Secr: Prof. Roger Dittmann
Focus: Sci
Periodical
Scientific World (quarterly) *16690*

United States Institute for Theatre Technology (USITT), 10 W 19 St, Ste 5A, New York, NY 10011
T: (212) 924-9088; Fax: (212) 924-9343
Founded: 1960; Members: 3500
Focus: Eng; Perf Arts; Educ
Periodicals
Theatre Design and Technology (quarterly)
USITT Newsletter (monthly) *16691*

United States Metric Association (USMA), 10245 Andasol Av, Los Angeles, CA 91325-1504
T: (818) 363-5606; Fax: (818) 368-7443
Founded: 1915; Members: 1500
Focus: Sci; Math
Periodical
USMA Newsletter (bi-monthly) *16692*

United States-Mexico Border Health Association (USMBHA), 6006 N Mesa, Ste 600, El Paso, TX 79912
T: (915) 581-6645; Fax: (915) 833-4768
Founded: 1943; Members: 2300
Focus: Public Health
Periodicals
Border Health Journal (quarterly)
Epidemiological Bulletin (bi-monthly) . . . *16693*

United States National Committee for Byzantine Studies (USNCBS), c/o Dept of History, University of Wisconsin, Madison, WI 53706
T: (608) 263-1800
Founded: 1962; Members: 140
Gen Secr: John Barker
Focus: Hist *16694*

United States National Committee of the International Union of Radio Science (USNC-URSI), c/o Board on Physics and Astronomy, National Research Council, 2101 Constitution Av NW, Washington, DC 20418
T: (202) 334-3520; E-Mail: bpa@nas.edu; Fax: (202) 334-2791
Founded: 1919; Members: 30
Gen Secr: Dr. Robert L. Riemer
Focus: Electric Eng
Periodical
Program and Abstract of Meetings (annually) *16695*

United States National Committee on Theoretical and Applied Mechanics (USNC/TAM), c/o National Research Council, 2101 Constitution Av NW, Washington, DC 20418
T: (202) 334-3142; Fax: (202) 334-2571
Founded: 1947; Members: 29
Focus: Eng; Physics
Periodical
Proceedings *16696*

United States National Society for the International Society of Soil Mechanics and Foundation Engineering (USNSISSMMFE), c/o Civil Engineering Dept, North Carolina State University, Box 7908, Raleigh, NC 27695
T: (919) 515-7344; Fax: (919) 515-7908
Founded: 1947; Members: 4500
Gen Secr: Prof. Harvey E. Wahls
Focus: Eng
Periodical
Geotechnical News (quarterly) *16697*

United States Pharmacopeial Convention (USP), 12601 Twinbrook Pkwy, Rockville, MD 20852
T: (301) 881-0666; Fax: (301) 816-8247
Founded: 1820; Members: 391
Focus: Pharmacol
Periodicals
About your Medicines (bi-annually)
Advice for the Patient (annually)
Drug Information for the Health Care Professional (annually)
Pharmacopeial Forum (bi-monthly)
USP DI Review (bi-monthly)
U.S.P. Dispensing Information (annually) . *16698*

United States Physical Therapy Association (USPTA), 1803 Avon Ln, Arlington Heights, IL 60004
Founded: 1970; Members: 12700
Focus: Physical Therapy
Periodical
Journal *16699*

United States Space Education Association (USSEA), c/o Global Operations Center, 231 School Ln, POB 249, Rheems, PA 17570-0249
T: (717) 367-5196; Fax: (717) 367-5196
Founded: 1973; Members: 1000
Pres: Stephen M. Cobaugh
Focus: Aero
Periodicals
Space Age Times: The Internntional Publication of Space News, Benefits and Education (monthly)
Update (monthly) *16700*

United States Sports Academy (USSA), 1 Academy Dr, Daphne, AL 36526
T: (205) 626-3303; Fax: (205) 626-3874
Founded: 1972
Focus: Sports *16701*

United Synagogue of Conservative Judaism Commission on Jewish Education (USCJCOJE), 155 Fifth Av, New York, NY 10010
T: (212) 260-8450; Fax: (212) 353-9439
Members: 39
Gen Secr: Dr. Robert Abramson
Focus: Educ
Periodicals
In Your Hands (quarterly)
Your Child (quarterly) *16702*

Universities Council on Water Resources (UCOWR), c/o Southern Illinois University, 4543 Faner Hall, Carbondale, IL 62901
T: (618) 536-7571; Fax: (618) 453-2671
Founded: 1962; Members: 97
Focus: Water Res
Periodicals
Newsletter (quarterly)
Proceedings of Annual Meetings *16703*

Universities Research Association (URA), 1111 19 St NW, Ste 400, Washington, DC 20036
T: (202) 293-1382; Fax: (202) 293-5012
Founded: 1965; Members: 78
Focus: Physics *16704*

Universities Space Research Association (USRA), American City Bldg, Ste 212, Columbia, MD 21044
T: (410) 730-2656; Fax: (410) 730-3496
Founded: 1969; Members: 75
Focus: Astronomy
Periodicals
Lunar and Planetary Information Bulletin (quarterly)
News and Notes (quarterly) *16705*

University and College Designers Association (UCDA), 209 Commerce St, Alexandria, VA 22314
T: (703) 548-1770; E-Mail: ucdadirect@aol.com; Fax: (703) 548-1936
Founded: 1971; Members: 1000
Gen Secr: Jennifer Jackson Salopek
Focus: Adult Educ; Graphic & Dec Arts, Design *16706*

University and College Labor Education Association (UCLEA), c/o Labor Education Dept, Rutgers State University, Ryders Ln and Clifton Av, New Brunswick, NJ 08903

T: (812) 855-9082; Fax: (812) 855-9779
Founded: 1959; Members: 373
Focus: Educ *16707*

University Aviation Association (UAA), 3410 Skyway Dr, Opelika, AL 36801
T: (205) 844-2434
Founded: 1948; Members: 540
Focus: Aero
Periodicals
Newsletter (bi-monthly)
Proceedings (annually) *16708*

University Consortium for Instructional Development and Technology (UCIDT), c/o Dept of Instructional Technology, University of Georgia, 607 Aderhold Hall, Athens, GA 30602
T: (706) 542-3810; Fax: (706) 542-2321
Founded: 1967; Members: 12
Gen Secr: Dr. Kent L. Gustafson
Focus: Educ; Adult Educ *16709*

University Corporation for Atmospheric Research (UCAR), POB 3000, Boulder, CO 80307-3000
T: (303) 497-1673
Founded: 1960; Members: 59
Focus: Geophys
Periodicals
Annual Report (annually)
Newsletter (bi-monthly) *16710*

University Council for Educational Administration (UCEA), c/o Pennsylvania State University, 212 Rackley Bldg, University Park, PA 16802-3200
T: (814) 863-7916; E-Mail: pbf2@psu.edu;
Fax: (814) 863-7918
Founded: 1959; Members: 51
Gen Secr: Patrick B. Forsyth
Focus: Educ
Periodicals
Educational Administration Abstracts (quarterly)
Journal of Educational Equity and Leadership (quarterly)
Review (4-5 times annually) *16711*

University Film and Video Association (UFVA), c/o Donald J. Zirpola, Communication Arts Dept, Loyola Marymount University, Loyola Blvd W & 80 St, Los Angeles, CA 90045
T: (310) 338-3033; Fax: (310) 338-3030
Founded: 1947; Members: 800
Pres: Donald J. Zirpola
Focus: Cinema
Periodicals
Digest (bi-monthly)
Journal of Film and Video (quarterly)
Membership Directory (bi-annually) . . . *16712*

University Photographers Association of America (UPAA), c/o Neil Rankin, News Services, Western Michigan University, Kalamazoo, MI 49008
T: (616) 387-4111; Fax: (616) 387-4124
Founded: 1961; Members: 300
Pres: Neil Rankin
Focus: Photo
Periodical
Newsletter (quarterly) *16713*

University Professors for Academic Order (UPAO), 724 Walnut Av, Redlands, CA 92373
T: (909) 792-1264
Founded: 1970; Members: 300
Gen Secr: Helen Law
Focus: Adult Educ
Periodical
Universitas (monthly) *16714*

Urban Affairs Association (UAA),
c/o University of Delaware, Newark, DE 19716
T: (302) 831-1681
Founded: 1969; Members: 355
Gen Secr: Mary Helen Callahan
Focus: Urban Plan
Periodicals
Communication (bi-monthly)
Directory of University Urban Programs
Journal of Urban Affairs (quarterly) . . . *16715*

Urban Agricultural Network, 1711 Lamont St NW, Washington, DC 20010
T: (202) 483-8130; Fax: (202) 986-6732
Gen Secr: Jae Smit
Focus: Agri *16716*

Urban and Regional Information Systems Association (URISA), 900 Second St NE, Ste 304, Washington, DC 20002
T: (202) 289-1685; Fax: (202) 842-1850
Founded: 1963; Members: 3800
Focus: Computer & Info Sci
Periodical
Annual Conference Proceedings *16717*

Urban Libraries Council (ULC), 1603 Orrington Av, Ste 1080, Evanston, IL 60201-5000
T: (708) 866-9999; Fax: (708) 866-9989
Founded: 1971; Members: 100
Pres: Eleanor Jo Rodger
Focus: Libraries & Bk Sci
Periodical
Urban Libraries Exchange (monthly) . . *16718*

URSI Commission on Electromagnetic Metrology, Electromagnetic Measurements and Standards, c/o Electromagnetic Fields Div, National Inst of Standards and Tech, 325 Broadway, Boulder, CO 80303-3328

T: (303) 497-5320; E-Mail: mkanda@ boulder.nist.gov; Fax: (303) 497-6665
Gen Secr: Dr. M. Kanda
Focus: Physics *16719*

URSI Commission on Fields and Waves, Electromagnetic Theory and Applications, c/o Dept of Electrical and Computer Engineering, Riggs Hall, Clemson, SC 29634-0915
T: (864) 656-5922; E-Mail: cbutler@ eng.clemson.edu; Fax: (864) 656-5910
Gen Secr: Prof. C.M. Butler
Focus: Physics *16720*

URSI Commission on Ionospheric Radio and Propagation, c/o University of Massachusetts Lowell, Center for Atmospheric Research, 1 University Av, Lowell, MA 01854
T: (508) 458-2504; E-Mail: reinisch@cae.uml.edu; Fax: (508) 453-6586
Gen Secr: Prof. B.W. Reinisch
Focus: Astrophys *16721*

Vachel Lindsay Association (VLA), 603 S Fifth St, POB 9356, Springfield, IL 62791-9356
T: (217) 528-9254
Founded: 1946; Members: 500
Pres: Susan U. Hammond
Focus: Lit *16722*

Valley Forge Historical Society (VFHS), POB 122, Valley Forge, PA 19481
T: (215) 783-0535
Founded: 1918; Members: 900
Focus: Hist *16723*

Vergilian Society (VS), POB 817, Oxford, OH 45056
T: (513) 529-1482; Fax: (513) 529-1516
Founded: 1937; Members: 1200
Gen Secr: John A. Dutra
Focus: Hist
Periodicals
The Augustan Age (annually)
Newsletter (semi-annually)
Vergilius (annually) *16724*

Vernacular Architecture Forum (VAF), c/o Gabrielle Lanier, POB 962, Newark, DE 19715-0962
E-Mail: gabriell@strauss.udel.edu
Founded: 1980; Members: 750
Gen Secr: Gabrielle Lanier
Focus: Archit *16725*

Vesterheim Genealogical Center and NAESETH Library, 415 W Main St, Madison, WI 53703
T: (608) 255-2224; Fax: (608) 255-6842
Founded: 1975; Members: 1900
Gen Secr: Blaine Hedberg
Focus: Genealogy
Periodical
Norwegian Tracks: Newsletter (quarterly) . *16726*

Veterinary Cancer Society (VCS), c/o Dr. Robert Rosenthal, 2816 Monroe Av, Rochester, NY 14618
T: (716) 271-5454; Fax: (716) 271-7815
Founded: 1974; Members: 500
Gen Secr: Dr. Robert Rosenthal
Focus: Vet Med *16727*

Veterinary Orthopaedic Society (VOS), POB 9491, Salt Lake City, UT 84109-0491
T: (801) 484-8912
Founded: 1972; Members: 500
Focus: Vet Med *16728*

Victorian Society in America (VSA), 219 S Sixth St, Philadelphia, PA 19106
T: (215) 627-4252
Founded: 1966; Members: 2800
Focus: Hist
Periodicals
Classic America (quarterly)
The Victorian (quarterly) *16729*

Virginia Woolf Society (VWS), c/o Denise Marshall, 14549 W Bay Rd, Sterling, NY 13156
T: (315) 947-6603
Founded: 1975; Members: 400
Pres: Prof. Melba Cuddy-Keane
Focus: Lit
Periodical
Virginia Woolf Miscellany (semi-annually) . *16730*

Visual Arts Resource and Research Centre Relating to the Caribbean, c/o Caribbean Cultural Centre, 408 W 58 St, New York, NY 10019
T: (212) 307-7420; Fax: (212) 315-1086
Gen Secr: Marta Moreno
Focus: Arts *16731*

Vladimir Nabokov Society (VNS), c/o Slavic Languages and Literatures, University of Kansas, Lawrence, KS 66045
T: (913) 864-3313
Founded: 1978; Members: 280
Focus: Lit *16732*

Vocational Industrial Clubs of America (VICA), POB 3000, Leesburg, VA 22075
T: (703) 777-8810; Fax: (703) 777-8999
Founded: 1965; Members: 272000
Focus: Adult Educ *16733*

Vocational Instructional Materials Section (VIM), c/o University of Missouri, 10 London Hall, Columbia, MO 65211
T: (314) 882-2884
Founded: 1969; Members: 85

Pres: Harley Schlichting
Focus: Educ *16734*

Volunteer Committees of Art Museums of Canada and the United States (VCAMCUS), c/o Anne Burlingame, Philbrook Museum of Art, 2727 S Rockford Rd, Tulsa, OK 74114
T: (918) 749-5279; Fax: (918) 743-4230
Founded: 1952; Members: 119
Pres: Anne Burlingame
Focus: Arts
Periodicals
Conference Report
Directory
News (quarterly) *16735*

Von Braun Astronomical Society (VBAS), POB 1142, Huntsville, AL 35807
T: (205) 539-0316
Founded: 1954; Members: 150
Focus: Astronomy
Periodical
Via Stellaris (bi-monthly) *16736*

Wagner Society of New York (WSNY), POB 949, Ansonia Station, New York, NY 10023
T: (212) 749-4561
Founded: 1977; Members: 1000
Focus: Music *16737*

Walter Bagehot Research Council on National Sovereignty (WBRC), POB 81, Whitestone, NY 11357
T: (718) 767-5364
Founded: 1972; Members: 800
Pres: Henry Paolucci
Focus: Poli Sci
Periodical
State of the Nation *16738*

Washington Foundation for European Studies (WFES), c/o John Hopkins University, School of Advanced International Studies, 1619 Massachusetts Av NW, Ste 624, Washington, DC 20036
T: (202) 663-5600, 663-5796; Fax: (202) 663-5784
Gen Secr: David Calleo
Focus: Ethnology *16739*

Washington Institute of Foreign Affairs, 2121 Massachusetts Av NW, Washington, DC 20006
T: (301) 469-7223; Fax: (301) 365-0859
Gen Secr: Geneviève L. Weiler
Focus: Poli Sci *16740*

Washington Journalism Center (WJC), 1282 National Press Bldg, Washington, DC 20045
T: (202) 662-7352; Fax: (202) 662-1232
Founded: 1965
Gen Secr: Bob Meyers
Focus: Journalism *16741*

Water Environment Federation (WEF), 601 Wythe St, Alexandria, VA 22314-1994
T: (703) 684-2400; Fax: (703) 684-2492
Founded: 1928; Members: 38000
Focus: Eng; Ecology
Periodicals
Highlights (monthly)
Journal of the Water Pollution Federation (monthly)
Operations Forum (monthly) *16742*

Water Quality Association, 4151 Naperville Rd, Lisle, IL 60532
T: (708) 505-0160; Fax: (708) 505-9637
Founded: 1950; Members: 2300
Gen Secr: Peter J. Censky
Focus: Water Res; Hygiene *16743*

Water Resources Congress (WRC), 8133 Lessburg Pike, No 760, Vienna, VA 22182
T: (703) 556-4447; Fax: (703) 556-4449
Founded: 1971; Members: 300
Gen Secr: Kathleen A. Phelps
Focus: Water Res
Periodicals
Hotline
Platform (annually)
Washington Report (monthly) *16744*

W.E. Upjohn Institute for Employment Research, 300 S Westnedge Av, Kalamazoo, MI 49007-4686
T: (616) 343-5541; Fax: (616) 343-3308
Founded: 1945
Focus: Rehabil *16745*

Weather Modification Association (WMA), POB 26926, Fresno, CA 93729-6926
T: (209) 434-3486; Fax: (209) 434-3486
Founded: 1951; Members: 200
Gen Secr: Hilda Duckering
Focus: Geophys
Periodicals
Journal of Weather Modification (annually)
Newsletter (quarterly) *16746*

Weed Science Society of America (WSSA), 1508 W University Av, Champaign, IL 61821-3133
Founded: 1950; Members: 2300
Focus: Agri
Periodicals
Abstracts (annually)
Newsletter (quarterly)
Weed Science (bi-monthly)
Weeds Technology (quarterly) *16747*

Welding Research Council (WRC), 345 E 47 St, New York, NY 10017
T: (212) 705-7956; Fax: (212) 371-9622
Founded: 1935; Members: 400
Pres: Dr. Martin Prager
Focus: Eng
Periodicals
Bulletin (monthly)
Progress Reports (monthly)
Welding Research Abroad (monthly)
Welding Research News (quarterly)
Yearbook (annually) *16748*

Wenner-Gren Centre Foundation for Scientific Research, 14 E 71st St, New York, NY 10021
T: (212) 737-2900
Gen Secr: Lita Osmundson
Focus: Sci *16749*

Wenner-Gren Foundation for Anthropological Research (WGFAR), 220 Fifth Av, New York, NY 10001-7708
T: (212) 683-5000
Founded: 1941
Focus: Anthro
Periodicals
Annual Report (annually)
Current Anthropology (bi-monthly) . . . *16750*

Western Association of Map Libraries (WAML), c/o Dorothy McGarry, POB 931119, Los Angeles, CA 90093-1119
T: (310) 825-3438; Fax: (310) 206-3908
Founded: 1967; Members: 204
Gen Secr: Dorothy McGarry
Focus: Libraries & Bk Sci; Cart *16751*

Western College Association (WCA), c/o Mills College, POB 9990, Oakland, CA 94613
T: (510) 632-5000; Fax: (510) 632-8361
Founded: 1924; Members: 181
Focus: Educ
Periodical
Addresses and Proceedings (annually) . *16752*

Western History Association (WHA), c/o University of New Mexico, 1080 Mesa Vista Hall, Albuquerque, NM 87131-1181
T: (505) 277-5234; Fax: (505) 277-6023
Founded: 1962; Members: 2000
Focus: Hist
Periodicals
Montana (bi-monthly)
Western Historical Quarterly (quarterly) . *16753*

Western Literature Association (WLA), c/o English Dept, Utah State University, Logan, UT 84322-3200
T: (801) 750-1603
Founded: 1966; Members: 500
Focus: Lit
Periodical
Western American Literature (quarterly) . *16754*

Western Society of Malacologists (WSM), c/o George Metz, 121 Wild Horse Valley Dr, Novato, CA 94947
T: (415) 892-4960
Founded: 1968; Members: 300
Gen Secr: George Metz
Focus: Zoology
Periodical
Annual Report (annually) *16755*

Western Society of Naturalists (WSN), c/o Moss Landing Marine Laboratories, POB 450, Moss Landing, CA 95039
T: (408) 755-8650; Fax: (408) 753-2826
Founded: 1911; Members: 2100
Gen Secr: Dr. Michael Foster
Focus: Nat Sci
Periodicals
Abstracts of Contributed Papers (annually)
Newsletter (semi-annually) *16756*

Western Surgical Association (WSA), c/o Dept of Surgery, University of Louisville, 530 S Jackson St, Louisville, KY 40292
T: (502) 852-1704; Fax: (502) 852-8915
Founded: 1891; Members: 600
Gen Secr: Dr. David Richardson
Focus: Surgery
Periodicals
Newsletter (quarterly)
Program (annually)
Transactions (annually) *16757*

Western Veterinary Conference (WVC), 2425 E Oquendo Rd, Las Vegas, NV 89120
T: (702) 739-6698
Founded: 1928; Members: 3800
Focus: Vet Med
Periodical
Directory (annually) *16758*

Whaling Museum Society (WMS), Main St, POB 25, Cold Spring Harbor, NY 11724
T: (516) 367-3418
Founded: 1936; Members: 1000
Focus: Hist; Navig
Periodicals
Annual Report (annually)
Newsletter (quarterly) *16759*

White House Historical Association (WHHA), 740 Jackson Pl NW, Washington, DC 20503
T: (202) 737-8292; Fax: (202) 789-0440
Founded: 1961
Focus: Hist *16760*

Wilbur Hot Springs Health Sanctuary (WHSHS), 3375 Wilbur Springs Rd, Williams-9709, CA 95987
T: (916) 473-2306
Founded: 1972
Gen Secr: Dr. Richard Louis Miller
Focus: Psych 16761

Wilderness Education Association (WEA), c/o Dept of Natural Resource, Recreation and Tourism, Colorado Sate University, Fort Collins, CO 80523
T: (970) 223-6252; E-Mail: wea@lamar.colostate.edu; Fax: (970) 223-6252
Founded: 1977; Members: 900
Gen Secr: Kent Clement
Focus: Educ
Periodical
Newsletter (semi-annually) 16762

Wilderness Medical Society (WMS), POB 2463, Indianapolis, IN 46206
T: (317) 631-1745; Fax: (317) 634-7817
Founded: 1983; Members: 2800
Focus: Med
Periodical
Wilderness Medicine (quarterly) 16763

The Wilderness Society (TWS), 900 17 St NW, Washington, DC 20006-2596
T: (202) 833-2300; Fax: (202) 429-3958
Founded: 1935; Members: 310000
Focus: Ecology
Periodical
Wilderness (quarterly) 16764

Wildlife Management Institute (WMI), 1101 14 St NW, Ste 801, Washington, DC 20005
T: (202) 371-1808; Fax: (202) 408-5059
Founded: 1946
Pres: Rollin D. Sparrowe; Gen Secr: Richard E. McCabe
Focus: Ecology
Periodical
Outdoor News Bulletin (monthly) 16765

Wildlife Preservation Trust International (WPTI), 3400 W Girard Av, Philadelphia, PA 19104
T: (215) 222-3636; Fax: (215) 222-2191
Founded: 1971; Members: 3000
Focus: Ecology 16766

The Wildlife Society (TWS), 5410 Grosvenor Ln, Bethesda, MD 20814
T: (301) 897-9770; Fax: (301) 530-2471
Founded: 1937; Members: 9700
Gen Secr: Harry E. Hodgdon
Focus: Ecology
Periodicals
Wildlife Monographs (irregularly)
Wildlife Society Bulletin (quarterly) . . . 16767

Willem Mengelberg Society (WMS), 1408A Marshall St, Manitowoc, WI 54220-5140
Founded: 1970
Focus: Music
Periodical
Newsletter (quarterly) 16768

William Morris Society in the United States (WMS/US), c/o Mark Samuels Lasner, 1870 Wyoming Av NW, Apt 101, Washington, DC 20009
T: (202) 745-1927; E-Mail: biblio@aol.com
Founded: 1956; Members: 525
Gen Secr: Mark Samuels Lasner
Focus: Lit 16769

Wilson Ornithological Society (WOS), c/o Museum of Zoology, University of Michigan, Ann Arbor, MI 48109-1079
T: (313) 764-0457
Founded: 1888; Members: 1592
Focus: Ornithology
Periodical
The Wilson Bulletin (quarterly) 16770

Wilson's Disease Association (WDA), POB 75324, Washington, DC 20013
T: (203) 775-4664
Founded: 1979; Members: 150
Pres: H. Ascher Sellner
Focus: Intern Med
Periodical
Newsletter (quarterly) 16771

Winrock International Institute for Agricultural Development (WIIAD), Petit Jean Mountain, Rte 3, Box 376, Morrilton, AR 72110-9543
T: (501) 727-5435; Fax: (501) 727-5242
Founded: 1985
Focus: Agri
Periodical
Annual Report (annually) 16772

Women and Mathematics Education (WME), c/o Mount Holyoke College, 302 Shattuck Hall, South Hadley, MA 01075
T: (413) 538-2608
Founded: 1978; Members: 500
Gen Secr: Charlene Morrow
Focus: Math; Educ
Periodicals
Newsletter (3 times annually)
WME Directory (annually)
Women and Mathematics Education of Girls and Women 16773

Women Educators (WE), c/o College of Education, University of Toledo, Toledo, OH 43636-3390
T: (419) 537-4337; Fax: (419) 267-1052
Founded: 1973; Members: 300
Pres: Renee Martin
Focus: Educ
Periodicals
Annual Awards Report (annually)
Newsletter (quarterly) 16774

Women in Aerospace (WIA), 922 Pennsylvania Av SE, Washington, DC 20003
T: (202) 547-9451; Fax: (202) 546-4189
Founded: 1985; Members: 300
Pres: Lori Garver
Focus: Aero 16775

Women's Auxiliary of the ICA (WAICA), 1110 N Glebe Rd, Ste 1000, Arlington, VA 22201
T: (703) 528-5000; Fax: (703) 528-5023
Founded: 1951; Members: 500
Pres: Joni Ressmeyer
Focus: Med 16776

Women's Caucus for Art (WCA), c/o Moore College of Art, 20 and The Parkway, Philadelphia, PA 19103
T: (215) 854-0922
Founded: 1972; Members: 3500
Focus: Arts 16777

Women's Caucus for Political Science (WCPS), c/o Judith Stiehm, Dept of Political Science, Florida International University, Miami, FL 33199
T: (305) 348-2226; E-Mail: stiehmj@servax.fiu.edu; Fax: (305) 348-3765
Founded: 1969; Members: 900
Pres: Judith Stiehm
Focus: Poli Sci
Periodicals
Membership Directory (annually)
WCPS Quarterly (quarterly) 16778

Women's Caucus for the Modern Languages (WCML), c/o Ruth Salvaggio, Dept of American Studies, University of New Mexico, 305 Ortega Hall, Albuquerque, NM 87131
T: (505) 277-3929; Fax: (505) 277-0351
Founded: 1970; Members: 800
Gen Secr: Ruth Salvaggio
Focus: Ling
Periodical
Concerns (3 times annually) 16779

Women's Caucus of the Endocrine Society (WCES), c/o Dept of Physiology, School of Medicine, University of Marylamd, 655 W Baltimore St, Baltimore, MD 21201
T: (410) 328-3851
Founded: 1975; Members: 850
Focus: Endocrinology 16780

Women's Classical Caucus (WCC), 5 Chester Dr, Rye, NY 10580
T: (914) 698-8798
Founded: 1972; Members: 500
Gen Secr: Prof. Barbara McManus
Focus: Humanities
Periodical
Newsletter (semi-annually) 16781

Women's College Coalition (WCC), 125 Michigan Av NE, Washington, DC 20017
T: (202) 234-0443; Fax: (202) 234-0445
Founded: 1972; Members: 70
Gen Secr: Jadwiga S. Sebrechts
Focus: Educ 16782

Wordsworth-Coleridge Association, c/o Dept of English, University of Michigan, Ann Arbor, MI 48109
Founded: 1970; Members: 300
Pres: Marlon Ross
Focus: Lit
Periodical
The Wordsworth Circle (quarterly) . . . 16783

World Academy of Art and Science, c/o Univ of Minnesota, 161 Hubert H Humphrey Center, 301 19 Av S, Minneapolis, MN 55455
T: (612) 625-6062; Fax: (612) 625-6351
Gen Secr: Prof. Harlan Cleveland
Focus: Arts; Sci 16784

World Academy of Productivity Science (WAPS), c/o Centre for Organizational Performance Improvement, 1900 Draft Dr, Ste 200, Blacksbury, VA 24061-0617
Focus: Business Admin 16785

World Alliance of Organizations for the Prevention of Birth Defects, c/o March of Dimes, 1275 Mamaroneck Av, White Plains, NY 10605
T: (914) 428-7100
Focus: Gynecology 16786

World Apheresis Association (WAA), c/o University Medical Center, Transfution Service, 2500 N State St, Jackson, MS 39216
T: (601) 984-5775; Fax: (601) 984-5608
Gen Secr: Francis S. Morrison
Focus: Hematology 16787

World Aquaculture Society (WAS), c/o Louisiana State University, 143 J.M. Parker Coliseum, Baton Rouge, LA 70803
T: (504) 388-3137; Fax: (504) 388-3493
Founded: 1970; Members: 2300
Focus: Bio; Oceanography
Periodicals
Abstracts (annually)
Directory (annually)
Journal of the World Aquaculture Society (quarterly)
World Aquaculture (quarterly) 16788

World Archaeological Society (WAS), 120 Lakewood Dr, Hollister, MO 65672
T: (417) 334-2377
Founded: 1971
Gen Secr: Ron Miller
Focus: Archeol
Periodicals
Special Publications (irregularly)
WAS Newsletter (irregularly) 16789

World Association for Case Method Research and Application – Americas (WACRA Americas), 23 Mackintosh Av, Needham, MA 02192
Focus: Philos 16790

World Association for Cooperative Education, 360 Hungtington Av, Ste 384, Boston, MA 02115-5096
T: (617) 373-8885; E-Mail: pfranks@lynx.neu.edu; Fax: (617) 373-3463
Gen Secr: Peter J. Franks
Focus: Educ 16791

World Association for Disaster and Emergency Medicine (WADEM), c/o Safar Center for Rescusitation Research, University of Pittsburgh, 3434 Fifth Av, Ste 243, Pittsburgh, PA 15260
T: (412) 383-1904; Fax: (412) 614-0943
Gen Secr: Dr. Ernesto Pretto
Focus: Med 16792

World Association for Infant Mental Health (WAIMH), c/o Inst of Children, Youth and Families, Dept of Psychiatry, Michigan State Univ, 27 Kellogg Center 27, East Lansing, MI 48824
T: (517) 432-3793; E-Mail: 10983HEF%MSU.EDU@mitvma.mit.edu; Fax: (517) 432-3694, 432-2476
Gen Secr: Dr. Yvon Gauthier
Focus: Psychiatry 16793

World Association for Public Opinion Research (WAPOR), c/o School of Journalism and Mass Communication, Univ of North Carolina at Chapel Hill, CB-3365, Howell Hall, Chapel Hill, NC 27599-3365
T: (919) 962-6396; E-Mail: kcole@unc.edu; Fax: (919) 962-4079
Gen Secr: Katherine Cole
Focus: Soc Sci 16794

World Association for Sexology (WAS), c/o Program in Human Sexuality, Dept of Family Practice and Community Health, Univ of Minnesota, Medical School, 1300 S Second St, Ste 180, Minneapolis, MN 55414
T: (612) 625-1500; Fax: (612) 626-8311
Gen Secr: Prof. Dr. Eli Coleman
Focus: Soc Sci 16795

World Association for Social Psychiatry (WASP), 656 Romero Canyon Rd, Santa Barbara, CA 93108-1527
T: (805) 969-1376
Focus: Psychiatry 16796

World Association for the Advancement of Veterinary Parasitology (WAAVP), c/o Merck AgVet Division, POB 2000, Rahway, NY 07065-0912
T: (908) 855-3750; Fax: (908) 855-3647
Gen Secr: Dr. Mark D. Soll
Focus: Vet Med 16797

World Association of Energy Lawyers (WAEL), c/o WJA, 1000 Connecticut Av NW, Ste 202, Washington, DC 20036
T: (202) 466-5428; Fax: (202) 452-8540
Focus: Law 16798

World Association of Law Professors (WALP), 1000 Connecticut Av NW, Ste 202, Washington, DC 20036
T: (202) 466-5426; Fax: (202) 452-8540
Gen Secr: Serafin V. Guingona
Focus: Law 16799

World Association of Lawyers (WAL), 1000 Connecticut Av NW, Ste 202, Washington, DC 20036
T: (202) 466-5428; Fax: (202) 452-8540
Gen Secr: Jack Streeter
Focus: Law 16800

World Association of Universities and Colleges (WAUC), 6655 W Sahara B-200, Las Vegas, NV 89102
T: (702) 221-2004
Gen Secr: Dr. Maxine Asher
Focus: Educ 16801

World Association of Veterinary Anatomists (WAVA), c/o Dept of Veterinary Anatomy, Purdue University, West Lafayette, IN 47907
T: (317) 494-7882
Founded: 1957; Members: 350
Focus: Vet Med
Periodical
Anatomia, Histologia, Embryologia (quarterly) 16802

World Association of Veterinary Educators (WAVE), c/o School of Veterinary Medicine, Tuskegee Univ, Tuskegee, AL 36088
T: (334) 727-8478, 826-2994; E-Mail: isidd@acd.tusk.edu; Fax: (334) 727-8177
Gen Secr: Prof. Irtaza H. Siddique
Focus: Educ; Vet Med 16803

World Association of Veterinary Laboratory Diagnosticians (WAVLD), POB 3040, College Station, TX 77841
T: (409) 845-9000; Fax: (409) 845-1794
Gen Secr: Dr. A.K. Eugster
Focus: Vet Med 16804

World Business Academy (WBA), POB 191210, San Francisco, CA 94119-1210
T: (415) 393-8251; E-Mail: wba@well.com; Fax: (415) 393-8369
Focus: Econ 16805

World Communication Association (WCA), c/o Sharon A. Ratliffe, Golden West College, 15744 Golden West St, Huntington Beach, CA 92647
T: (714) 895-8180; E-Mail: sratliffe@cccd.edu; Fax: (714) 895-8253
Founded: 1968; Members: 200
Pres: Judy C. Pearson
Focus: Comm Sci 16806

World Congress of Herpetology (WCH), c/o Dept Integrative Biology, Univ of California at Berkeley, Berkeley, CA 94720
T: (510) 643-6264; E-Mail: mhwake@garnet.berkeley.edu; Fax: (510) 642-4743
Gen Secr: Marvalee H. Wake
Focus: Zoology 16807

World Council for Curriculum and Instruction (WCCI), c/o College of Education, University of Cincinnati, POB 210002, Cincinnati, OH 45221-0002
T: (513) 556-3573; Fax: (513) 556-2483
Gen Secr: Estela C. Matriano
Focus: Educ 16808

World Council of Comparative Education Societies (WCCES), c/o Institute for International Studies in Education, Univ of Pittsburgh, SK01 Forbes Quadrangle, Pittsburgh, PA 15260
Fax: (412) 648-5911
Gen Secr: Mark Ginsburg
Focus: Educ 16809

World Education (WE), 210 Lincoln St, Boston, MA 02111
T: (617) 482-9485; Fax: (617) 482-0617
Gen Secr: David W. Kahler
Focus: Educ 16810

World Education Fellowship, United States Section (WEF), c/o Dr. Joan Brogan, College of New Rochelle, 29 Castle Pl, New Rochelle, NY 10805
T: (914) 769-8317
Founded: 1921; Members: 75
Pres: Dr. Joan Brogan
Focus: Educ
Periodical
The New Era (quarterly) 16811

World Federation of Associations of Pediatric Surgeons, c/o Children's Mercy Hospital, 24 and Gillham Rd, Kansas City, MO 64108
Gen Secr: Prof. Keith W. Ashcraft
Focus: Surgery; Pediatrics 16812

World Federation of Neurosurgical Societies (WFNS), c/o Univ of Virginia, HSC, Dept of Neurosurgery, POB 212, Charlottesville, VA 22908
T: (804) 924-2650; Fax: (804) 924-5894
Gen Secr: Edward R. Laws
Focus: Surgery 16813

World Federation of Personnel Management Associations (WFPMA), c/o SHRM Institute for Human Resource Management, 606 N Washington St, Alexandria, VA 22314
T: (703) 548-3440 Ext 2101; E-Mail: intldiv@shrm.org; Fax: (703) 836-0367
Gen Secr: Michael R. Losey
Focus: Business Admin 16814

World Federation of Public Health Associations (WFPHA), c/o American Public Health Association, 1015 15 St NW, Washington, DC 20005
T: (202) 789-5696; Fax: (202) 789-5681
Founded: 1967; Members: 45
Focus: Public Health
Periodicals
Annual Report (annually)
Salubritas (quarterly) 16815

World Federation of Public Health Associations (WFPHA), c/o APHA, 1015 15 St NW, Ste 300, Washington, DC 20005
E-Mail: diane.kuntz@msmail.apha.org; Fax: (202) 789-5661
Gen Secr: Dr. Fernando M. Treviño
Focus: Public Health 16816

World Federation of Sleep Research Societies (WFSRS), c/o Department of Animal Biology, School of Veterinary Medicine, Univ of Pennsylvania, 3800 Spruce St, Philadelphia, PA 19104-6045
T: (215) 898-8891; E-Mail: aamsleep@pobox.upenn.edu; Fax: (215) 573-2004
Gen Secr: Adrian R. Morrison
Focus: Bio 16817

World Federation of Societies of Intensive and Critical Care Medicine, c/o Dept of Anesthesiology, Montefiore Medical Center, 111 E 210 St, New York, NY 10467-2490
T: (718) 920-4175; Fax: (718) 881-2245
Gen Secr: Dr. Christopher W. Bryan-Brown
Focus: Med 16818

World Federation of Therapeutic Communities (WFTC), 54 W 40 St, New York, NY 10018
T: (212) 354-6000; Fax: (212) 840-3008
Gen Secr: Patricia A. Zingale
Focus: Therapeutics 16819

World Foundation for Medical Studies in Female Health (WFFH), 405 Main St, Port Washington, NY 11050
T: (516) 944-8655; Fax: (516) 944-8663
Focus: Gynecology 16820

World Future Society (WFS), 7910 Woodmont Av, Ste 450, Bethesda, MD 20814
T: (301) 656-8274; Fax: (301) 951-0394
Founded: 1966; Members: 30000
Pres: Edward S. Cornish
Focus: Futurology
Periodicals
Future Survey: A Monthly Abstract of Books, Articles and Reports concerning Forecasts, Trends and Ideas about the Future (monthly)
Futures Research Quarterly (quarterly)
The Futurist: A Journal of Forecasts, Trends and Ideas about the Future (bi-monthly) . . 16821

World Hemophilia Aids Center (WHAC), 10 Congress St, Ste 340, Pasadena, CA 91105
T: (818) 577-4366; Fax: (818) 796-2875
Founded: 1983
Focus: Hematology
Periodical
Hemophilia World (quarterly) 16822

World Hypertension League (WHL), c/o Medical College of Ohio, Dept of Medicine, 3000 Arlington Av, POB 10008, Toledo, OH 43699-0008
T: (419) 381-6016; E-Mail: WHLSEC@magnum.mco.edu; Fax: (419) 381-5360
Gen Secr: Dr. Patrick J. Mulrow
Focus: Hematology 16823

World Institute for Advanced Phenomenological Research and Learning (WPI), 348 Payson Rd, Belmont, MA 02178
T: (617) 480-3696
Gen Secr: Anna-Teresa Tymieniecka
Focus: Parapsych 16824

World Institute for Safety Education and Research (WISER), c/o WSO, 305 E Market St, POB 518, Warrensburg, MO 64093
T: (972) 404-8202; E-Mail: wiserwso@aol.com
Focus: Educ; Eng 16825

World Jurist Association (WJA), 1000 Connecticut Av NW, Ste 202, Washington, DC 20036
T: (202) 466-5428; E-Mail: WJA@geocities.com; Fax: (202) 452-8540
Gen Secr: Margaret M. Henneberry
Focus: Law 16826

World Learning, 1015 15 St NW, Ste 750, Washington, DC 20005
E-Mail: sam.mariam@worldlearning.org; Fax: (202) 408-5397
Focus: Educ 16827

World Life Research Institute (WLRI), 23000 Grand Terrace Rd, Grand Terrace, CA 92313
T: (909) 825-4773; Fax: (909) 783-3477
Gen Secr: Dr. Bruce W. Halstead
Focus: Bio 16828

World Methodist Historical Society (WMHS), POB 127, Madison, NJ 07940
T: (201) 408-3189
Gen Secr: Dr. Charles Yrigoyen
Focus: Hist; Rel & Theol 16829

World Monuments Fund (WMF), 949 Park Av, New York, NY 10028
Gen Secr: John Stubbs
Focus: Preserv Hist Monuments 16830

World Organization for Human Potential (WOHP), 8801 Stenton Av, Philadelphia, PA 19118
T: (215) 233-2050; Fax: (215) 233-3940
Founded: 1968
Focus: Rehabil
Periodical
The IN-Report (bi-monthly) 16831

World Organization for Rights, Literature and Development, 532 W 111 St, Ste 75, New York, NY 10025
T: (212) 932-0678; Fax: (212) 932-0678
Focus: Law; Lit 16832

World Population Society (WPS), 1333 H St NW, Ste 106, Washington, DC 20005
T: (202) 898-1303; Fax: (202) 861-0621
Founded: 1973; Members: 1100
Focus: Sociology 16833

World Proof Numismatic Association (WPNA), POB 4094, Pittsburgh, PA 15201-0094
T: (412) 782-4477; Fax: (412) 782-0227
Gen Secr: Gail P. Gray
Focus: Numismatics 16834

World Rehabilitation Fund (WRF), 386 Park Av, Ste 500, New York, NY 10016
T: (212) 725-7875; Fax: (212) 725-8402
Founded: 1970; Members: 27
Focus: Rehabil 16835

World Research Foundation, 20501 Ventura Blvd, Ste 100, Wooland Hills, CA 91364
T: (818) 907-5483; Fax: (818) 907-6044
Focus: Sci 16836

World Society for Mushroom Biology and Mushroom Products (WSMBMP), c/o Dept of Biological Sciences, State Univ of New York at Buffalo, Cooke Hall, Buffalo, New York, NY 14260
T: (716) 636-2363; Fax: (716) 645-2975
Gen Secr: Prof. P.G. Miles
Focus: Botany; Food; Agri 16837

World Society for Stereotactic and Functional Neurosurgery (WSSFN), 6624 Fannin, Ste 1620, Houston, TX 12030
T: (713) 790-0795; Fax: (713) 669-0388
Founded: 1963; Members: 600
Gen Secr: Dr. Philip L. Gildenberg
Focus: Surgery; Neurology
Periodicals
Applied Neurophysiology (quarterly)
Studies in Stereoencephalotomy 16838

World Society of Magnetic Resonance, 2118 Milvia St, Ste 201, Berkeley, CA 94704
T: (510) 841-1899; E-Mail: info@smr.org; Fax: (510) 841-2340
Gen Secr: Jane Tiemann
Focus: Physics 16839

World Space Foundation, POB Y, South Pasadena, CA 91031-1000
T: (818) 357-2878
Founded: 1979
Focus: Aero 16840

World Union of Catholic Philosophical Societies, c/o School of Philosophy, Catholic Univ of America, Washington, DC 20064
T: (202) 319-5636; Fax: (202) 319-6089
Gen Secr: Prof. George F. McLean
Focus: Philos 16841

World University Network (PWPA), 2700 University Av West, Ste 47, Saint Paul, MN 55114
T: (612) 644-2809; Fax: (612) 644-0997
Focus: Educ 16842

World University Roundtable, POB 2470, Benson, AZ 85602
T: (602) 586-2985; E-Mail: afessler@nrl.nursing.arizona.edu; Fax: (602) 686-4764
Founded: 1920; Members: 60
Gen Secr: Prof. Dr. Howard John Zitko
Focus: Adult Educ 16843

World War Two Studies Association (WWTSA), c/o Prof. Mark Parillo, Dept of History, Kansas State University, Eisenhower Hall, Manhattan, KS 66506-1002
T: (913) 532-0374; Fax: (913) 532-7004
Founded: 1967; Members: 368
Gen Secr: Prof. Mark Parilli
Focus: Hist
Periodical
Newsletter of the American Committee on the History of the Second World War (semi-annually) 16844

World's Poultry Science Association – U.S.A. Branch (WPSA), c/o Dr. Michael D. Ruff, U.S. Dept of Agriculture, Bldg 003, BARC-W, Beltsville, MD 20705
T: (301) 504-6428; Fax: (301) 504-5863
Founded: 1965; Members: 660
Gen Secr: Dr. Michael D. Ruff
Focus: Ornithology
Periodical
Journal (3 times annually) 16845

Wound, Ostomy and Continence Nurses – An Association of E.T. Nurses, 2755 Bristol St, Ste 110, Costa Mesa, CA 92626
T: (714) 476-0268
Founded: 1969; Members: 2400
Focus: Med 16846

W.T. Bandy Center for Baudelaire Studies (CBS), c/o Vanderbilt University, POB 6325, Station B, Nashville, TN 37235
T: (615) 343-0372
Founded: 1968; Members: 450
Gen Secr: Claude Pichois
Focus: Lit
Periodical
Bulletin Baudelairien (semi-annually) . . 16847

XPLOR International, 2550 Via Tejon, Ste 3L, POB 1501, Palos Verdes Estates, CA 90274
T: (310) 373-3633; Fax: (310) 375-4240
Members: 1400
Focus: Nat Sci
Periodicals
Proceedings of European Conference (annually)
Proceedings of Worldwide Conference (annually) 16848

Yellowstone-Bighorn Research Association (YBRA), 7314 Charolais St, Billings, MT 59106
T: (406) 652-1760
Founded: 1931; Members: 350
Focus: Geology 16849

YIVO Institute for Jewish Research, 555 W 57 St, New York, NY 10019
T: (212) 246-6080; Fax: (212) 292-1892
Founded: 1925
Gen Secr: Lawrence H. Rubinstein
Focus: Ethnology 16850

Yosemite Association (YA), POB 545, Yosemite National Park, CA 95389
T: (209) 379-2646; Fax: (209) 379-2486
Founded: 1920; Members: 6000
Focus: Nat Sci
Periodical
Newsletter 16851

Yuki Teikei Haiku Society of the United States and Canada, POB 90456, San Jose, CA 95109-3456
T: (408) 297-0692
Founded: 1975; Members: 145
Gen Secr: Kiyoko Tokutomi
Focus: Lit 16852

Zane Grey's West Society (ZGWS), 708 Warwick Av, Fort Wayne, IN 46825
T: (219) 484-2904
Founded: 1983; Members: 300
Gen Secr: Carolym Timmerman
Focus: Lit 16853

Uzbekistan

Scientific Industrial Association „Biology", Ul Khodzhaeva 28, 700125 Tashkent
T: 625821
Focus: Bio 16854

Scientific Industrial Association „Solar Physics", Ul Timiryazeva 2b, 700084 Tashkent
T: 331271
Focus: Physics 16855

Uzbek Academy of Sciences, Ul Gogolya 70, 700000 Tashkent
T: (03712) 333802; Fax: 334901
Members: 144
Pres: M.S. Salokhitdinov
Focus: Sci
Periodicals
Doklady: Bulletin
Fan va Turmush: Life and Science
Geliozekhnika: Helio Engineering
Izvestiya AN Uzbekistana-Tekhnicheskie Nauki: Journal of the Uzbek Academy of Sciences: Engineering Sciences
Khimiya Prirodnykh Soedinenii: Chemistry of Natural Compounds
Nauki v Uzbekistane: Social Sciences in Uzbekistan
Uzbek Tili va Adabieti: Uzbek Language and Literature
Uzbekskii Geologicheskii Zhurnal: Uzbek Geological Journal
Uzbekskii Khimicheskii Zhurnal: Uzbek Chemical Journal
Zapiski Uzbekskogo Otdelenia Vsesoyuznogo Mineralohicheskogo Obshchestva: Notes of the Uzbek Division of the All-Union Mineralogy Society 16856

Vatican City

Accademia Romana di S. Tommaso d'Aquino e di Religione Cattolica, Piazza della Cancelleria 1, 00186 Città del Vaticano
Founded: 1879; Members: 70
Pres: Cardinal Mario Luigi Ciappi; Gen Secr: Luigi Bogliolo
Focus: Rel & Theol 16857

Collegium Cultorum Martyrum, Via Napoleone III 1, 00185 Città del Vaticano
Founded: 1879; Members: 750
Gen Secr: Pietro Pozzi
Focus: Hist; Rel & Theol 16858

Commission Théologique Internationale / International Theological Commission, Palazzo del S. Uffizio, 00120 Città del Vaticano
T: Palazzo del (06) 6984753
Founded: 1969
Gen Secr: Georges Cottier
Focus: Rel & Theol 16859

Pontificia Academia Mariana Internationalis (PAMI), Via Merulana 124, 00185 Città del Vaticano
T: (06) 70373235; E-Mail: pami@ofm.org; Fax: 70373234
Founded: 1946; Members: 400
Pres: Gaspar Calvo Moralejo; Gen Secr: Stefano Cecchin
Focus: Rel & Theol 16860

Pontificia Academia Scientiarum / Pontifical Academy of Sciences, Casina Pio IV, 00120 Città del Vaticano
T: (06) 69883451, 69883195; Fax: 69885218
Founded: 1936; Members: 80
Pres: Prof. Nicola Cabibbo; Gen Secr: Mons. Renato Dardozzi
Focus: Sci 16861

Pontificia Accademia dell'Immacolata (PAJ), Via del Serafico 1, 00142 Città del Vaticano
Founded: 1835; Members: 8
Pres: Cardinal Andrea M. Deskur; Gen Secr: Prof. Dr. Lorenzo Di Fonzo
Focus: Rel & Theol 16862

Pontificia Accademia Romana di Archeologia, Palazzo della Cancelleria Apostolica, 00186 Città del Vaticano
Founded: 1810; Members: 113
Pres: Victor Saxer; Gen Secr: Silvio Panciera
Focus: Archeol
Periodicals
Memorie
Rendiconti 16863

Pontificia Accademia Teologica Romana, Piazza S. Giovanni in Laterano 4, 00184 Città del Vaticano
Founded: 1718; Members: 74
Pres: Cardinal William W. Baum; Gen Secr: Antonio Piolanti
Focus: Rel & Theol 16864

Pontificia Insigne Accademia Artistica dei Virtuosi al Pantheon, Palazzo della Canceleria Apostolica, 00186 Città del Vaticano
Founded: 1543; Members: 132
Pres: Prof. Vitaliano Tiberia; Gen Secr: Ernesto Lamagna
Focus: Arts 16865

Venezuela

Academia de Ciencias Físicas, Matemáticas y Naturales, Av Universidad-Bolsa a San Francisco, Apdo 1421, Caracas 1010
T: (02) 4834133; Fax: 4846611
Founded: 1917; Members: 80
Pres: Paul Lustgarten; Gen Secr: José M. Carrillo
Focus: Math; Nat Sci; Physics
Periodical
Boletín de la Academia de Ciencias Fı1sicas, Matemáticas y Naturales (3 times annually) 16866

Academia de Ciencias Políticas y Sociales, Palacio de las Academias, Bolsa a San Francisco, Caracas 1010
T: (02) 4832674
Founded: 1917; Members: 33
Pres: Dr. G. Parra Aranguren; Gen Secr: Dr. José G. Sarmiento Nuñez
Focus: Poli Sci; Sociology
Periodical
Boletín 16867

Academia de Historia del Zulia, c/o Academia de Bellas Artes, Maracaibo
Founded: 1940; Members: 12
Pres: Abrahán Belloso; Gen Secr: Aniceto Ramirez y Astier
Focus: Hist
Periodical
Boletín 16868

Academia Nacional de la Historia, Palacio de las Academias, Bolsa a San Franciso, Caracas 1010
Founded: 1888
Pres: Dr. Rafael Fernandez Heres; Gen Secr: Marianela Ponce
Focus: Hist
Periodicals
Anuario
Boletín
Memorias 16869

Academia Nacional de Medicina, Bolsa a San Franciso, Caracas, 1010
T: (02) 421868
Founded: 1904; Members: 120
Pres: Dr. Augusto León; Gen Secr: Dr. J. Morales Rocha
Focus: Med
Periodical
Gaceta Medica de Caracas (quarterly) . 16870

Academia Venezolana, Bolsa a San Franciso, Caracas 1010
T: (02) 4818716
Founded: 1883; Members: 24
Focus: Ling
Periodicals
Boletín (quarterly)
Clásicos Venezolanos 16871

Action Committee for the Establishment of a Latin American Network of Technological Information (RITLA), c/o SELA, Torre Europa, Av Francisco de Miranda, Caracas 1010A
T: (02) 9514233
Founded: 1979; Members: 4
Focus: Computer & Info Sci 16872

Action for National Information Systems, c/o Ministerio de Información y Turismo, Altamira 68644, Caracas
Focus: Computer & Info Sci 16873

Asociación Cultural Humboldt, Av Leonardo da Vinci, Colinas de Bello Monte, Apdo 60501, Chacao, Caracas
Founded: 1949; Members: 450
Focus: Hist; Lit; Poli Sci; Ethnology; Geography
Periodical
Boletín (annually) 16874

Asociación de Agrimensores de Venezuela, c/o Colegio de Ingenieros de Venezuela, Caracas
Focus: Agri 16875

Asociación de Linguistica y Filologia de América Latina (ALFAL), Av Rio Orinoco 12-41, Cumbres de Curumo, Caracas 108
Founded: 1962; Members: 500
Focus: Ling; Lit 16876

Asociación Nacional de Escritores Venezolanos, Velázquez a Miseria 22, Apdo 429, Caracas
Founded: 1935
Focus: Lit 16877

Asociación Psiquiátrica de la América Latina (APAL), Apdo 3380, Caracas
Founded: 1951; Members: 500
Focus: Psychiatry 16878

Asociación Venezolana Amigos del Arte Colonial Caracas, Quinta de Anauco, Av Panteon San Bernardino, Caracas
T: (02) 518650
Founded: 1942; Members: 242
Focus: Arts 16879

Asociación Venezolana de Facultades de Medicina (AVEFAM), Av Las Ciencias, Los Chaguaramos, Apdo 50681, Caracas
T: 6614585
Focus: Med 16880

Asociación Venezolana de Geología, Minería y Petróleo, Apdo Este 4000, Caracas
Founded: 1948
Focus: Mining; Geology 16881

Asociación Venezolana de Ingeniería Eléctrica y Mecánica (AVIEM), c/o Colegio de Ingenieros de Venezuela, Apdo 6255, Caracas 1050
T: 5713657
Founded: 1956; Members: 3500
Focus: Electric Eng; Eng 16882

Asociación Venezolana de Ingeniería Sanitaria y Ambiental Caracas, c/o Colegio de Ingenieros de Venezuela, Apdo 6255, Caracas
Focus: Eng 16883

Asociación Venezolana para el Avance de la Ciencia (ASOVAC), Apdo del Este 61843, Caracas
Founded: 1950; Members: 3000
Focus: Sci
Periodical
Acta Científica Venezolana: Multidisciplinary Scientific Journal (bi-monthly) 16884

Ateneo Venezolano de Morfología, El Rosal 1060, Caracas
Founded: 1963
Focus: Bio 16885

Biosciences Information Network for Latin America and the Caribbean (BINLAC), Apdo 21827, Caracas 1020
T: (02) 749543; Fax: 691957
Founded: 1987
Focus: Bio 16886

Caribbean Institute for Social Formation (CARISFORM), c/o UTAL, CLAT'S Headquarter, POB 6681, Caracas 1010
Members: 30
Focus: Soc Sci; Educ 16887

Center for OPEC Studies, Torre Oeste, Piso 16, Parque Central, Caracas 1010
T: (02) 5076657; Fax: 5754386
Founded: 1981
Focus: Energy 16888

Centro de Estudios Venezolanos Indigenas, Apdo 261, Caracas
Founded: 1943; Members: 50
Focus: Ethnology 16889

Centro de Historia del Táchira, Carrera 4, No 13-68, San Cristóbal, Táchira
T: 433079
Founded: 1942; Members: 25
Focus: Hist
Periodical
Boletín del Centro de Historia del Táchira (irregularly) 16890

Centro de Historia Larense, Calle 22, Diagonal a Plaza Lara, Apdo 406, Barquisimeto, Distr. Iribarren
Founded: 1941; Members: 12
Focus: Hist 16891

Centro Histórico del Zulia, c/o Academia de Bellas Artes, Maracaibo
Founded: 1940
Focus: Hist 16892

Centro Histórico Sucrense, Cumana
Founded: 1945
Focus: Hist 16893

Centro Interamericano de Desarrollo e Investigación Ambiental y Territorial (CIDIAT), Parque La Isla, Apdo 219, Mérida
T: (074) 445477, 442647, 449511; E-Mail: cidiat@dino.conicit.ve; Fax: 441461
Founded: 1965; Members: 14
Pres: Tomás A. Bandes; Gen Secr: Luis R. Rázuri Ramirez
Focus: Ecology 16894

Centro Interamericano para el Desarrollo Regional (CINDER), Calle 69, No 15D-32, Apdo 1304, Maracaibo 4001
T: (061) 516953, 517336; E-Mail: CINDER; Fax: 523554
Founded: 1976; Members: 14
Focus: Econ; Public Admin
Periodical
Boletín Informativo (annually) 16895

Centro Latinoamericano de Adminstración para el Desarrollo (CLAD) / Latinamerican Centre for Development Administration, Calle Herrera Toro, Qta Clad, Sector Los Naranjos, Las Mercedes, Apdo 4181, Caracas 1010
T: (02) 924064, 923297, 925953; Fax: 918427
Founded: 1974; Members: 24
Focus: Public Admin
Periodicals
Boletín de Resumenes (quarterly)
Boletín Informativo del CLAD (semi-annually)
Reforma y Democracia: Revista del CLAD (semi-annually)
Servicio de Información al Dia en Gestión Pública (monthly) 16896

Centro Latinoamericano de Creación e Investigación Teatral (CELCIT), Av Juan Germán Rocio 9, Quinta Marisela, San Bernadino, Caracas 101
T: (02) 511675
Founded: 1977
Focus: Perf Arts 16897

Centro Nacional de Investigaciones Agropecuarias (CENIAP) / National Centre of Agricultural Research, Zona Universitaria, Via El Limon, Apdo 4653, Maracay 2101
T: (043) 452491; Fax: 454320
Founded: 1937; Members: 2239
Focus: Agri
Periodicals
Agronomica Tropical
Veterinaria Tropical (semi-annually) . . . 16898

Colegio de Abogados del Distrito Federal, Apdo 347, Caracas
Founded: 1788; Members: 2000
Focus: Law 16899

Colegio de Economistas del Distrito Federal y Estado Miranda, Calle Vicuña, Urb. Valle Arriba, Caracas
T: 918787
Founded: 1958
Focus: Econ 16900

Colegio de Farmacéuticos del Distrito Federal y Estado Miranda, Urbanización Las Mercedes, Caracas 1060
Founded: 1949; Members: 1200
Focus: Pharmacol
Periodical
Colfar 16901

Colegio de Médicos del Distrito Federal, Pl de Bellas Artes, Caracas
Founded: 1942; Members: 2800
Focus: Med 16902

Colegio de Médicos del Estado Anzoátegui, Apdo 84, Barcelona
Focus: Med 16903

Colegio de Médicos del Estado Mérida, Mérida
Focus: Med 16904

Colegio de Médicos del Estado Miranda, Av El Golf, Qta. La Setentiseis, El Bosque, Caracas
Founded: 1944; Members: 3100
Focus: Med 16905

Comité para la Defensa de las Lenguas Indígenas de América Latina y el Caribe, Urbanización California Norte, Av La Haya, Quinta Lilibeth, Caracas
T: (02) 214829; Fax: 6622245
Founded: 1987
Pres: Dr. Esteban Emilio Mosonyi
Focus: Ling 16906

Consejo de Desarrollo Científico y Humanístico, c/o Universidad Central de Venezuela, Caracas
Fax: (02) 2851104
Founded: 1958
Focus: Sci; Humanities 16907

Consejo Nacional de Investigaciones Científicas y Tecnológicas (CONICIT), Los Ruices, Apdo 70617, Caracas
T: 349621
Founded: 1967
Focus: Sci; Eng 16908

Consejo Nacional de la Cultura (CONAC), Av Principal de Chuao, Edificio Los Roques, Apdo 50 995, Caracas
Founded: 1975
Focus: Hist 16909

Consejo Venezolano del Niño, Av San Martín, Apdo 1209, Caracas
Founded: 1951
Focus: Educ 16910

Consejo Zuliano de Planificación y Coordinación (CONZUPLAN), Av 5 de Julio, Edificio Las Laras, Apdo 1053, Maracaibo
T: 80754/55
Founded: 1964; Members: 100
Focus: Business Admin; Urban Plan . . 16911

Federación Médica Venezolana, Av El Golf, El Bosque
Founded: 1954
Focus: Med 16912

Federación Panamericana de Asociaciones de Facultades y Escuelas de Medicina (FEPAFEM) / Panamerican Federation of Associations of Medical Schools, Apdo 60411, Caracas 1060
T: 936271, 930875; Fax: 936346
Founded: 1962; Members: 353
Focus: Med
Periodicals
Boletín FEPAFEM: PAFAMS Bulletin (quarterly)
FEPAFEM Informa: PAFAMS Newsletter (monthly) 16913

Federación Venezolana de Camaras y Asociaciones de Comercio y Producción, Av El Empalme, El Bosque, Apdo 2568, Caracas
T: 719742
Founded: 1973
Focus: Econ 16914

Sociedad Amigos del Museo de Bellas Artes, c/o Museo de Bellas Artes, Parque los Caobos, Caracas
Founded: 1957; Members: 250
Focus: Fine Arts 16915

Sociedad Bolivariana de Venezuela, Apdo 874, Caracas
Founded: 1938; Members: 180
Focus: Hist 16916

Sociedad de Ciencias Naturales La Salle, Av Boyacá 3, Apdo 1930, Caracas 101
Founded: 1940
Focus: Nat Sci 16917

Sociedad de Obstetricia y Ginecología de Venezuela, Maternidad Concepción Palacios, Av San Martín, Apdo 20081, Caracas 1020
Focus: Gynecology
Periodical
Revista de Obstetricia y Ginecología de Venezuela 16918

Sociedad de Tisiología y Neumonología de Venezuela, c/o Instituto Nacional de Tuberculosis, El Algodonal, Antimano
Founded: 1937
Focus: Pulmon Dis 16919

Sociedad Latinoamericana de Farmacología, Apdo 2455, Caracas
Founded: 1964; Members: 250
Focus: Pharmacol 16920

Sociedad Médica, Ciudad Bolivar, Bolivar
Focus: Med 16921

Sociedad Odontológica Zuliana de Prótesis Maracaibo, Edificio Cruz Roja, Local 1, Av 11, Maracaibo
Founded: 1964
Focus: Dent 16922

Sociedad Venezolana de Angiologia, c/o Colegio de Médicos del DF, Pl de Bellas Artes, Los Chaguaramos, Caracas
Focus: Hematology 16923

Sociedad Venezolana de Cardiología (SVC), Urb. Santa Fé, Av José María Vargas, Torre del Colegio, Apdo 80917, Caracas 1080
Members: 196
Focus: Cardiol 16924

Sociedad Venezolana de Ciencias Naturales, Calle Cumaco con Arichuna El Marqués, Apdo 1521, Caracas 1070
T: 217653, 217780, 217579
Founded: 1931; Members: 980
Focus: Nat Sci
Periodicals
Boletín (semi-annually)
Newsletter (quarterly) 16925

Sociedad Venezolana de Cirugía, Torre del Colegio, Av José María Vargas, Urb. Santa Fé, Caracas 1080
Founded: 1945
Focus: Surgery 16926

Sociedad Venezolana de Cirugía Plástica y Reconstrucción, Edificio Bucaral, Av La Salle, Caracas
Focus: Surgery 16927

Sociedad Venezolana de Cirurgía Ortopédica y Traumatología, c/o Colegio de Médicos del DF, Pl Las Tres Gracías, Los Ghaguaramós, Caracas
Founded: 1949; Members: 197
Focus: Surgery; Orthopedics; Traumatology 16928

Sociedad Venezolana de Entomología, Apdo 4579-A, Maracay 2101
T: (043) 450153; E-Mail: vsavini@reacciun.ve; Fax: 454175
Founded: 1964; Members: 320
Pres: Gustavo Yépez
Focus: Entomology
Periodical
Boletin de Entomologia Venezolana (semi-annually) 16929

Sociedad Venezolana de Hematología, c/o Hospital Vargas, San José, Caracas
Focus: Hematology 16930

Sociedad Venezolana de Historia de la Medicina, Palacio de las Academias, Bolsa a San Francisco, Caracas 101
Focus: Med; Cultur Hist 16931

Sociedad Venezolana de Ingenieros de Minas y Metalúrgicos, Apdo 18223, Caracas 1010
Founded: 1958; Members: 400
Focus: Mining
Periodical
Fusión (bi-monthly) 16932

Sociedad Venezolana de Medicina del Trabajo y Deportes, c/o Clínica Luis Razetti, Los Caobos, Caracas
Focus: Med; Hygiene 16933

Sociedad Venezolana de Oftalmología, Apdo Este 50150A, Caracas 1050
Founded: 1953; Members: 600
Focus: Ophthal
Periodical
Revista Oftalmológica Venezolana (quarterly) 16934

Sociedad Venezolana de Otorinolaringología, Av Cajigal, San Bernardino, Apdo 40174, Caracas 1011
Focus: Otorhinolaryngology
Periodical
Acta Venezolana de ORL (annually) . . 16935

Sociedad Venezolana de Psiquiatría y Neurología, Apdo 3380, Caracas
Focus: Neurology; Psychiatry 16936

Sociedad Venezolana de Puericultura y Pediatría, Av Libertador, Edificio La Linea, Caracas 105
Focus: Pediatrics 16937

Sociedad Venezolana de Radiología, c/o Policlínica Méndez Gimón, Av Andrés Bello, Caracas
Focus: Radiology 16938

Sociedad Venezolana de Tisiología y Neumonología, c/o Sanatorio Simón Bolívar, Carretera de Antímano, Caracas
Founded: 1937
Focus: Pulmon Dis 16939

Sociedad Venezolana de Urología, Apdo 75988, Caracas 1071
Founded: 1940; Members: 200
Focus: Urology
Periodical
Revista Venezolana de Urología 16940

Vietnam

Vietnam Union of Sientific and Technical Associations, 53 Nguyen Du, Hanoi
T: 57785
Founded: 1983
Focus: Sci; Eng 16941

Vietnamese Association of Acupuncture, c/o General Association of Medicine, 68 Ba Trieu St, Hanoi
T: 52323
Founded: 1968
Focus: Pathology 16942

Vietnamese Association of Agriculture, c/o Vietnam Union of Scientific and Technical Associations, 53 Nguyen Du, Hanoi
T: 57785
Focus: Agri 16943

Vietnamese Association of Anaesthesiology, c/o General Association of Medicine, 68 Ba Trieu St, Hanoi
T: 52323
Founded: 1978
Focus: Anesthetics 16944

Vietnamese Association of Anti-Contagious Diseases, c/o General Association of Medicine, 68 Ba Trieu St, Hanoi
T: 52323
Founded: 1978
Focus: Immunology 16945

Vietnamese Association of Anti-Tuberculosis and Lung Diseases, c/o General Association of Medicine, 68 Ba Trieu St, Hanoi
T: 52323
Founded: 1961
Focus: Pulmon Dis 16946

Vietnamese Association of Architects, c/o Vietnam Union of Scientific and Technical Associations, 53 Nguyen Du, Hanoi
T: 57785
Focus: Archit 16947

Vietnamese Association of Biology, c/o Vietnam Union of Scientific and Technical Associations, 53 Nguyen Du, Hanoi
T: 57785
Focus: Bio 16948

Vietnamese Association of Cast and Metallurgy, c/o Vietnam Union of Scientific and Technical Associations, 53 Nguyen Du, Hanoi
T: 57785
Focus: Metallurgy 16949

Vietnamese Association of Chemistry, c/o Vietnam Union of Scientific and Technical Associations, 53 Nguyen Du, Hanoi
T: 57785
Focus: Chem 16950

Vietnamese Association of Dermatology, c/o General Association of Medicine, 68 Ba Trieu St, Hanoi
T: 52323
Founded: 1961
Focus: Derm 16951

Vietnamese Association of Engineering, c/o Vietnam Union of Scientific and Technical Associations, 53 Nguyen Du, Hanoi
T: 57785
Focus: Eng 16952

Vietnamese Association of Forensic Scientists, c/o General Association of Medicine, 68 Ba Trieu St, Hanoi
T: 52323
Founded: 1978
Focus: Forensic Med; Law 16953

Vietnamese Association of Forestry, c/o Vietnam Union of Scientific and Technical Associations, 53 Nguyen Du, Hanoi
T: 57785
Focus: Forestry 16954

Vietnamese Association of Geography, c/o Vietnam Union of Scientific and Technical Associations, 53 Nguyen Du, Hanoi
T: 57785
Focus: Geography 16955

Vietnamese Association of Geology, c/o Vietnam Union of Scientific and Technical Associations, 53 Nguyen Du, Hanoi
T: 57785
Focus: Geology 16956

Vietnamese Association of Internal Medicine, c/o General Association of Medicine, 68 Ba Trieu St, Hanoi
T: 52323
Founded: 1960
Focus: Intern Med 16957

Vietnamese Association of Mathematics, c/o Vietnam Union of Scientific and Technical Associations, 53 Nguyen Du, Hanoi
T: 57785
Focus: Math 16958

Vietnamese Association of Medical Biochemistry, c/o General Association of Medicine, 68 Ba Trieu St, Hanoi
T: 52323
Founded: 1963
Focus: Biochem 16959

Vietnamese Association of Morphology, c/o General Association of Medicine, 68 Ba Trieu St, Hanoi
T: 52323
Founded: 1967
Focus: Pathology 16960

Vietnamese Association of Neurology, Psychiatry and Neurosurgery, c/o General Association of Medicine, 68 Ba Trieu St, Hanoi
T: 52323
Founded: 1962
Focus: Neurology; Psychiatry; Surgery . . 16961

Vietnamese Association of Obstetrics, Gynaecology and Family Planning, c/o General Association of Medicine, 68 Ba Trieu St, Hanoi
T: 52323
Founded: 1961
Focus: Gynecology; Family Plan 16962

Vietnamese Association of Odonto-Maxillo-Facial Medicine, c/o General Association of Medicine, 68 Ba Trieu St, Hanoi
T: 52323
Founded: 1960
Focus: Dent 16963

Vietnamese Association of Ophthalmology, c/o General Association of Medicine, 68 Ba Trieu St, Hanoi
T: 52323
Founded: 1960
Focus: Ophthal 16964

Vietnamese Association of Oto-Rhino-Laryngology, c/o National ENT Institute of Vietnam, Bach Mai, Hanoi
T: 52323
Focus: Otorhinolaryngology 16965

Vietnamese Association of Paediatrics, c/o General Association of Medicine, 68 Ba Trieu St, Hanoi
T: 52323
Founded: 1961
Focus: Pediatrics 16966

Vietnamese Association of Pharmacy, c/o General Association of Medicine, 68 Ba Trieu St., Hanoi
T: 52323
Founded: 1960
Focus: Pharmacol 16967

Vietnamese Association of Physics, c/o Vietnam Union of Scientific and Technical Associations, 53 Nguyen Du, Hanoi
T: 57785
Focus: Physics 16968

Vietnamese Association of Physiology, c/o General Association of Medicine, 68 Ba Trieu St, Hanoi
T: 52323
Founded: 1969; Members: 231
Focus: Physiology
Periodical
Sinh-Ly-Hoc (annually) 16969

Vietnamese Association of Prophylactic Hygiene, c/o General Association of Medicine, 68 Ba Trieu St, Hanoi
T: 52323
Founded: 1961
Focus: Hygiene 16970

Vietnamese Association of Radio-Electronics, c/o Vietnam Union of Scientific and Technical Associations, 53 Nguyen Du, Hanoi
T: 57785
Focus: Electronic Eng 16971

Vietnamese Association of Radiology, c/o General Association of Medicine, 68 Ba Trieu St, Hanoi
T: 52323
Founded: 1961
Focus: Radiology 16972

Vietnamese Association of Serum and Blood Transfusion, c/o General Association of Medicine, 68 Ba Trieu St, Hanoi
T: 52323
Founded: 1978
Focus: Intern Med 16973

Vietnamese Association of Surgery, c/o General Association of Medicine, 68 Ba Trieu St, Hanoi
T: 52323
Founded: 1961
Focus: Surgery 16974

Vietnamese Fine Arts Association, c/o Writers and Artists Union, 51 Tran Hung Dao St, Hanoi
T: 52694
Focus: Fine Arts 16975

Vietnamese Photographers Association, c/o Writers and Artists Union, 51 Tran Hung Dao St, Hanoi
T: 52694
Focus: Photo 16976

Vietnamese Writers' Association, c/o Writers and Artists Union, 51 Tran Hung Dao St, Hanoi
T: 52694
Focus: Lit 16977

Writers and Artists Union, 51 Tran Hung Dao St, Hanoi
T: 52694
Founded: 1957
Focus: Lit; Arts 16978

Virgin Islands (U.S.)

Caribbean Food Crops Society (CFCS), c/o University of the Virgin Islands, POB 10000, Saint Croix, VI 00850
T: (809) 778-0246; Fax: 778-6570
Founded: 1962
Focus: Crop Husb
Periodical
CFCS Newsletter (3 times annually) . . 16979

Caribbean Natural Resources Institute (CANARI), 1104 Strand St, Christiansted, Saint Croix, VI 00820
T: (809) 773-9854; Fax: 773-5770
Founded: 1977; Members: 18
Focus: Geology 16980

Consortium of Caribbean Universities for Resource Management, c/o University of the Virgin Islands, VI 00802, Saint Thomas
T: (809) 776-0200 ext 1343
Founded: 1988; Members: 15
Focus: Educ; Business Admin 16981

Yugoslavia

Akademia e Shkencave dhe e Arteve e Kosovës / Akademija Nauka i Umetnosti Kosova / Academy of Sciences and Arts of Kosovo, Milladin Popoviqi 10, 38000 Priština
Founded: 1976
Pres: Dr. Vukasin Filipović; Gen Secr: Osman Imami
Focus: Ling; Lit; Arts; Soc Sci; Nat Sci
Periodicals
Acta Biologiae et Medicinae Experimentalis
Bibliografia/Bibliografija
Botime të Veçanta/Posebna Izdanja: Monographs
Kërkime/Istraživanja: Research
Libërshënuesi/Spomenica: Diary
Studime/Studije: Studies
Vjetari/Godisnjak: Annual Report 16982

Association of Jurists of Serbia, Proleterskih Brigada 74, 11000 Beograd
Founded: 1946
Focus: Law
Periodical
Pravni Život 16983

Association of Pharmacists of Serbia, Terazije 12, 11000 Beograd
Founded: 1946
Focus: Pharmacol
Periodicals
Arhiv za Farmaciju
Bilten 16984

Association of the Mathematicians', Physicists' and Astronomers' Societies of Yugoslavia, c/o Akademija Nauka SAP Kosovo, POB 194, 38000 Priština
Founded: 1950
Focus: Math; Physics; Astronomy
Periodicals
Bilten: Astronomy
Fizika, Matematičko-Fizički List za Učenike Srednjih Škola
Matematica Balkanica
Matematički List za Učenike Osnovnih Škola
Topologija 16985

Crnogorska Akademija Nauka i Umjetnosti (CANU) / Montenegrin Academy of Sciences and Arts, Rista Stijovića 5, 81000 Podgorica
T: (081) 31095
Members: 34
Pres: D. Vukotić; Gen Secr: M. Saranovič
Focus: Arts; Sci
Periodicals
Glasnik: Review
Godišnjak CANU (annually) 16986

Društvo Arhitekata Srbije, Kneza Miloša 7, 11000 Beograd
T: (011) 330059
Focus: Archit 16987

Društvo Arhivskih Radnika Srbije, Karnegijeva 2, 11000 Beograd
T: (011) 323132
Focus: Archives 16988

Društvo Bibliotekara Vojvodine, c/o Bibliothèque Centrale de la Faculté des Lettres et de Sciences, Université, 21000 Novi Sad
Focus: Libraries & Bk Sci 16989

Društvo Istoričara Srbije / Historical Society of Serbia, Cika Ljubina 18-20, 11000 Beograd
Founded: 1948; Members: 1500
Focus: Hist
Periodical
Istoriski glasnik (semi-annually) 16990

Društvo Lekara Vojvodine, Vase Stajica 9, 21000 Novi Sad
Focus: Med
Periodical
Medicinski pregled: Journal for General Medicine (bi-monthly) 16991

Društvo Ljekara Crne Gore, Krusevac bb, 81000 Podgorica
T: 41620
Focus: Med 16992

Društvo Matematičara Srbije / Society of Mathematicians of Serbia, Knez Mihailova 35, 11000 Beograd
T: (011) 638263
Founded: 1948
Focus: Math
Periodical
Matematički Vesnik (quarterly) 16993

Društvo Psihologa Srbije, Drusvina 7, 11000 Beograd
T: (011) 339685
Focus: Psych 16994

Društvo Veterinara Srbije, Bulevar JNA 18, 11000 Beograd
T: (011) 684597
Focus: Vet Med 16995

Društvo za Srpski Jezik i Književnost / Society of Serbian Language and Literature, c/o Belgrade University, 11000 Beograd
Founded: 1910
Focus: Ling; Lit
Periodical
Pritozi za Knjizevnost, Jezik, Istorija i Folklor 16996

Društvo za Srpskohrvatski Jezik i Književnost, Knez Mihailova 35, 11000 Beograd
T: (011) 630089
Focus: Ling; Lit 16997

Economists' Society of Serbia, Nusićeva 6, 11000 Beograd
Founded: 1944
Focus: Econ
Periodical
Ekonomika preduzeća (monthly) 16998

Filozofsko Društvo Srbije, Studentski Trg 1, 11000 Beograd
Focus: Philos 16999

Jugoslovenski Centar za Tehničku i Naučnu Dokumentaciju / Yugoslav Centre for Technical and Scientific Documentation, S. Penezića-Krcuna 29-31, POB 724, 11000 Beograd
T: (011) 644250
Founded: 1952
Focus: Doc; Eng
Periodicals
Bulletin of Documentation
Informatika
Scientific and Professional Meetings in Yugoslavia and Foreign Countries 17000

Jugoslovenski Savez za Zavarivanje (JSZ) / Yugoslav Welding Association, Svetozara Markovića 56, 11000 Beograd
T: (011) 687221, 682963
Founded: 1953; Members: 6
Focus: Eng
Periodicals
Varilna tehnika (quarterly)
Zavarivač (quarterly)
Zavarivanje (bi-monthly) 17001

Jugoslovenski Zavod za Produktivnost Rada, Uzun Mirkova 1, 11000 Beograd
T: (011) 637978
Focus: Business Admin 17002

Jugoslovenski Zavod za Standardizaciju, Slobodana Penezića-Krcuna 35, POB 933, 11000 Beograd
T: (011) 643557
Focus: Standards 17003

Jugoslovensko Društvo za Fiziologiju, c/o Zavod za Biohemiju, Medicinski Fakultet, 21000 Novi Sad
Focus: Physiology 17004

Jugoslovensko Društvo za Mehaniku, Kneza Milosa 9-13, 11000 Beograd
T: (011) 342273
Focus: Eng 17005

Jugoslovensko Društvo za Proučavanje Zemljišta, Nemanjina 6, 11080 Zemun
Founded: 1953
Focus: Agri
Periodicals
Agrohemija (bi-monthly)
Zemljišste i biljka (3 times annually) . . 17006

Jugoslovensko Naučno Voársko Društvo, Vojvode Stepe 5, 32000 Cačak
T: (032) 47411 ext 13
Founded: 1954
Focus: Hort
Periodical
Jugoslovensko Voćarstvo: Journal of Yugoslav Pomology (quarterly) 17007

Jugoslovensko Udruženje za Filozofiju, Studebtski Trg 1, 11000 Beograd
T: (011) 638104
Focus: Philos 17008

Jugoslovensko Udruženje za Sociologiju, Studentski Trg 1, 11000 Beograd
Founded: 1954
Focus: Sociology
Periodical
Sociology (quarterly) 17009

Matica Srpska / Serbian Society, Ul Matice Srpske 1, 21000 Novi Sad
Founded: 1826
Gen Secr: Dr. Dušan Popv
Focus: Ling; Lit
Periodicals
Letopis Matice Srpske
Proceedings 17010

Nikola Tesla Association of Societies for Promotion of Technical Sciences in Yugoslavia, POB 359, 11000 Beograd
Focus: Eng 17011

Pedagogical Society of Yugoslavia, Moše Pijade 12, 11000 Beograd
Founded: 1952
Focus: Educ
Periodicals
Pedagogícja
Predškolsko Dete 17012

Savez Arheološki Društava Jugoslavije, Cara Urosa 20, 11000 Beograd
Members: 300
Focus: Archeol 17013

Savez Astronautičkih i Raketnih Organizacija Jugoslavije (SAROJ), Bulevar Revolucije 44, 11000 Beograd
T: (011) 33404
Founded: 1953; Members: 475
Focus: Aero 17014

Savez Bibliotečkih Radnika Srbije / Union of Serbian Library Workers, Skerlićeva 1, 11000 Beograd
Founded: 1947
Focus: Libraries & Bk Sci
Periodical
Bibliotekar (semi-annually) 17015

Savez Društava Arhiviskih Radnika Jugoslavije (SDAR), Karnegijeva 2, 11000 Beograd
Founded: 1953; Members: 950
Focus: Archives 17016

Savez Društava Istoričara Jugoslavije, Karnegijeva 2, 11000 Beograd
T: (011) 338431
Founded: 1951
Focus: Hist 17017

Savez Društava Matematičara, Fizičara i Astronoma Jugoslavije (SDMFAJ), c/o Institut za Matematiku, Dr. Ilije Djuricica 4, 21000 Novi Sad
Founded: 1950; Members: 2007
Focus: Math; Physics; Astronomy . . . *17018*

Savez Društava Veterinara Jugoslavije, Bulevar JNA 18, 11000 Beograd
T: (011) 684597
Focus: Vet Med *17019*

Savez Društava za Strane Jezike i Knjizevnosti Jugoslavije, Knez Mihajlova 35, 11000 Beograd
Focus: Ling; Lit; Educ *17020*

Savez Društava Zubarskih Radnika Jugoslavije, Mose Pijade 12, 11000 Beograd
T: (011) 339928
Focus: Dent *17021*

Savez Ekonomista Jugoslavije / Yugoslav Economists' Association, Nusiceva 6, 11000 Beograd
T: (011) 334417
Founded: 1945
Focus: Econ
Periodical
Ekonomist (quarterly) *17022*

Savez Lekarskih Društava Jugoslavije (SLD), Zeleni Venac 1, 11000 Beograd
T: (011) 320992
Founded: 1946
Focus: Med *17023*

Savez Muzejskih Društava Jugoslavije / Federation of Museums Associations, c/o Istorijski Muzej Srbije, Nemanjina 24, 11000 Beograd
Focus: Archives
Periodical
Muzeji *17024*

Savez Pedagoških Društava Jugoslavije, Mose Pijade 12, 11000 Beograd
T: (011) 339381
Founded: 1950
Focus: Educ *17025*

Savez Pedagoških Društava Srbije / Federation of Pedagogical Societies of Serbia, Terazije 26, 11000 Beograd
T: (011) 325569
Founded: 1923; Members: 800
Focus: Educ
Periodicals
Nastava i va spitanje (5 times annually)
Pedagoška Biblioteka *17026*

Savez Udruženja Pravnika Jugoslavije, Proleterskih Brigada 74, 11000 Beograd
T: (011) 441910
Founded: 1947; Members: 10000
Focus: Law *17027*

Savez Udruženja za Krivično Pravo i Kriminolgiju Jugoslavije (SUKKJ), Gracanicka 18, 11000 Beograd
T: (011) 626322
Founded: 1958; Members: 2500
Focus: Law; Criminology *17028*

Serbian Association against Cancer, Knez Mihailova 2, 11000 Beograd
Founded: 1967
Focus: Cell Biol & Cancer Res *17029*

Sindikat Radnicka Drustvenih Delatnosti Jugoslavije, Trg Marksa i Engelsa 5, 11000 Beograd
T: (011) 332953
Members: 30000
Focus: Educ *17030*

Srpska Akademija Nauka i Umetnosti (SANU) / Serbian Academy of Sciences and Arts, Knez Mihailova ul 35, POB 366, 11000 Beograd
T: (011) 187144; Fax: 182825
Founded: 1886; Members: 158
Pres: A. Despič; Gen Secr: Miroslav Pantič
Focus: Sci; Arts
Periodicals
Glas: Review
Godišnjak: Yearbook (annually)
Posebna izdanja: Monographs
Spomenik: Monument
Srpski etnografski zbornik: Serbian Ethnographic Collection *17031*

Srpsko Biološko Društvo / Serbian Biological Society, Kneza Miloša 101, 11000 Beograd
T: (011) 682966 ext 303
Founded: 1947; Members: 700
Focus: Bio
Periodicals
Archive of Biological Science
Contemporary Biology (semi-annually) . . *17032*

Srpsko Geografsko Društvo / Serbian Geographical Society, Studentski trg 3, 11000 Beograd
Founded: 1910; Members: 1350
Focus: Geography
Periodicals
Bulletin (semi-annually)
Globus (annually)
Terre et Hommes (annually) *17033*

Srpsko Geološko Društvo / Serbian Geological Society, Kamenicka 6, POB 227, 11000 Beograd
Founded: 1891; Members: 602
Focus: Geology
Periodical
Zapisnici Srpskog Geološkog Društva (annually)
. . . . *17034*

Srpsko Hemijsko Društvo / Serbian Chemical Society, Karnegijeva 4, POB 462, 11000 Beograd
T: (011) 328583
Founded: 1897; Members: 2200
Focus: Chem
Periodicals
Chemical Review (bi-monthly)
Journal of the Serbian Chemical Society (monthly)
. . . . *17035*

Srpsko Lekarsko Društvo, Zeleni Venac 1, 11000 Beograd
T: (011) 327181
Founded: 1872
Focus: Med
Periodicals
Gastroenterohepatološki Arhiv (quarterly)
Kardiologija (quarterly)
List Lekar (quarterly)
Srpski arhiv za celokupno lekarstvo (monthly)
Stomatološki glasnik Srbije (bi-monthly) . *17036*

Udruženje Univerzitetskih Nastavnika i Van-Univerzitetskih Naučnik Radnika, Safarikova 7, 11000 Beograd
T: (011) 324939
Focus: Educ; Adult Educ *17037*

Unija Bioloških Naučnih Društava Jugoslavije, Nemanjina 6, POB 127, 11080 Zemun
Focus: Bio *17038*

Union of Engineers and Technicians of Serbia, Kneza Miloša 7a, 11000 Beograd
T: (011) 330067
Founded: 1945; Members: 8014
Focus: Eng
Periodical
Tehnika (monthly) *17039*

Union of Engineers and Technicians of Yugoslavia, Kneza Miloša 9-11, POB 187, 11000 Beograd
T: (011) 335816
Founded: 1841
Focus: Eng
Periodicals
It Novine (monthly)
Tehnika (monthly) *17040*

Union of Jurists' Associations of Yugoslavia, Proleterskih Brigade 74, 11000 Beograd
Founded: 1947; Members: 30000
Focus: Law
Periodical
The New Yugoslav Law *17041*

Urbanisticki Savez Jugoslavije, Bul Avnoj 3, 21000 Novi Sad
Focus: Urban Plan *17042*

Yugoslav Economists' Association, Nušićva 6, 11000 Beograd
Founded: 1945
Focus: Econ
Periodical
Ekonomist (quarterly) *17043*

Zajednica Universitéta Jugoslavije / Association of Yugoslav Universities, Palmotićeva 22, 11000 Beograd
T: (011) 334524
Founded: 1957
Focus: Educ; Adult Educ
Periodical
University Today (quarterly) *17044*

Zambia

Africa Association for Liturgy, Music and Arts (AFALMA), c/o United Church of Zambia, POB 50122, Lusaka
Focus: Rel & Theol; Arts; Music . . . *17045*

Africa Literature Centre (ALC), POB 21319, Kitwe
Founded: 1959
Focus: Lit *17046*

Agricultural Research Council of Zambia, POB 2218, Lusaka
Founded: 1967
Focus: Agri *17047*

Association of Medical Schools in Africa (AMSA), c/o Faculty of Medicine, University of Zambia, POB 50110, Lusaka
T: (01) 252641
Founded: 1964
Focus: Educ; Med *17048*

The Engineering Institution of Zambia, POB 34730, Lusaka
Founded: 1955; Members: 1500
Focus: Eng
Periodical
Journal (quarterly) *17049*

International Red Locust Control Organisation for Central and Southern Africa (IRLCO-CSA), POB 240252, Ndola
T: 612433
Founded: 1970; Members: 10
Focus: Entomology
Periodicals
Annual Report (annually)
Quarterly Report (quarterly)
Scientific Papers *17050*

National Council for Scientific Research, Chelston, POB CH 158, Lusaka
T: (01) 281081
Founded: 1967; Members: 20
Focus: Sci
Periodicals
Zambia Journal of Science and Technology (irregularly)
Zambia Science Abstracts (annually) . . *17051*

National Food and Nutrition Commission (N.F.N.C.), POB 32669, Lusaka
T: (01) 211724; E-Mail: Fonutcom, Lusaka
Founded: 1967; Members: 5
Focus: Nutrition
Periodical
Nutrition News (3 times annually) . . . *17052*

National Monuments Commission, POB 60124, Livingstone
T: (03) 320481
Founded: 1948
Focus: Ecology; Preserv Hist Monuments
Periodicals
Annual Report (annually)
Archaeologia Zambiana Newsletter (irregularly)
Research Publications *17053*

Wildlife Conservation Society of Zambia (WCSZ), POB 30255, Lusaka
T: (01) 254226; Fax: 222906
Founded: 1953; Members: 1000
Pres: Prof. A.A. Siwela; Gen Secr: M. Sichilongo
Focus: Ecology
Periodical
Black Lechwe (irregularly) *17054*

Zambia Library Association, POB 32839, Lusaka
Pres: C. Zulu; Gen Secr: W.C. Mulalami
Focus: Libraries & Bk Sci
Periodicals
Journal (quarterly)
Newsletter (bi-monthly) *17055*

Zambia Medical Association, POB 148, Lusaka
Pres: Dr. S. Sikaneta; Gen Secr: Dr. D. Leviti
Focus: Med *17056*

Zimbabwe

African Organization for Research and Training in Cancer (AORTIC), c/o Dept of Medicine, University of Zimbabwe, POB A178, Avondale, Harare
Founded: 1982
Focus: Intern Med
Periodical
AORTIC Bulletin (quarterly) *17057*

African Regional Computer Confederation (ARCC), POB 8385, Causeway, Harare
T: (04) 752657
Focus: Computer & Info Sci *17058*

African Rehabilitation Institute (ARI), POB 4056, Harare
T: (04) 731083
Founded: 1985; Members: 12
Focus: Rehabil
Periodical
African Rehabilitation Journal (quarterly) . *17059*

Agricultural Research Council of Zimbabwe, POB 8108, Causeway, Harare
Founded: 1970; Members: 12
Focus: Agri
Periodicals
Annual Report (annually)
Technical Report *17060*

Arts Association Harare, POB 4011, Harare
Founded: 1968
Focus: Arts *17061*

Botanical Society of Zimbabwe, POB 461, Harare
Founded: 1934
Focus: Botany *17062*

Commonwealth Association for the Education and Training of Adults (CAETA), c/o Dept of Adult Education, University of Zimbabwe, POB MP 167, Mount Pleasant, Harare
T: (04) 303211 ext 1528; Fax: 732828
Founded: 1985; Members: 660
Focus: Adult Educ
Periodical
CAETA Newsletter (quarterly) *17063*

Conference of African Theological Institutions (CATI), POB MP 36, Mount Pleasant, Harare
T: (04) 303211
Founded: 1980
Focus: Rel & Theol *17064*

Crop Science Society of Zimbabwe, Union Av, POB UA 409, Harare
Focus: Agri *17065*

Dental Association of Zimbabwe, POB 3303, Harare
Focus: Dent *17066*

Ecumenical Documentation and Information Centre for Eastern and Southern Africa (EDICESA), POB H 94, Harare
T: (04) 50311
Founded: 1987
Focus: Rel & Theol *17067*

Geographical Association of Zimbabwe, c/o Dept of Geography, University of Zimbabwe, POB MP 167, Mount Pleasant, Harare
T: (04) 303211
Members: 200
Focus: Geography
Periodicals
Geographical Education Magazine
Proceedings *17068*

Geological Society of Zimbabwe, POB 8427, Causeway, Harare
Focus: Geology *17069*

Joint Health Systems Research Programme for Eastern and Southern Africa, POB CY 348, Harare 611=
T: (04) 728991/7; E-Mail: mwaluko@healthnet.zw; Fax: 728998
Founded: 1987; Members: 21 Countries
Pres: Ministries of Health of Participating countries
Focus: Public Health *17070*

Kirk Biological Society, c/o Div of Biological Sciences, Univeristy of Zimbabwe, POB MP 167, Mount Pleasant, Harare
Focus: Bio *17071*

The Literature Bureau, Zimbabwe, POB 8137, Causeway, Harare
Founded: 1954
Focus: Lit
Periodical
Bureau Bulletin (quarterly) *17072*

Lowveld Natural History Branch, Wildlife Society of Zimbabwe, POB 81, Chiredzi
Founded: 1968
Focus: Hist; Nat Sci
Periodicals
The Hartebeest (annually)
Newsletter (monthly) *17073*

Mennel Society, c/o Dept of Geology, University of Zimbabwe, POB MP 167, Mount Pleasant, Harare
Founded: 1964; Members: 30
Focus: Geology
Periodical
Detritus *17074*

Ornithological Association of Zimbabwe, POB 8382, Causeway, Harare
T: (04) 48347
Focus: Ornithology
Periodical
Honeyguide (quarterly) *17075*

PEN Centre of Zimbabwe, POB 1900, Harare
Focus: Lit *17076*

Pharmaceutical Society of Zimbabwe, POB 8520, Causeway, Harare
Focus: Pharmacol *17077*

Pre-History Society of Zimbabwe, POB 876, Harare
Founded: 1958
Focus: Hist; Anthro
Periodical
Zimbabwe Prehistory *17078*

Scientific Council of Zimbabwe, POB 8510, Causeway, Harare
Founded: 1964
Focus: Sci *17079*

Standards Association of Central Africa, 17 Coventry Rd, Workington, POB 2259, Harare
T: (04) 760258; E-Mail: SACA
Founded: 1957; Members: 322
Focus: Standards
Periodicals
Annual Report (annually)
Central African Specifications and Codes of Practice *17080*

Survey Institute of Zimbabwe, POB 3869, Harare
Founded: 1967; Members: 150
Focus: Surveying *17081*

Wildlife Society of Zimbabwe, POB 3497, Harare
Founded: 1927; Members: 1500
Focus: Ecology
Periodical
Zimbabwe Wildlife (quarterly) *17082*

Zimbabwe Agricultural Society, POB 442,
Harare
Focus: Agri *17083*

**Zimbabwe Association for Science
Education**, 16 Dirriemuur Dr, Marlborough,
Harare
T: (04) 32867
Members: 210
Focus: Sci; Educ *17084*

Zimbabwe Library Association, POB 3133,

Harare
Founded: 1959; Members: 254
Pres: Driden Kunaka; Gen Secr: Angela
Muchabaiwa
Focus: Libraries & Bk Sci
Periodical
Zimbabwe Librarian *17085*

Zimbabwe Medical Association, POB 3671,
Harare
T: (04) 720731

Focus: Med *17086*

Zimbabwe Scientific Association, POB 978,
Harare
Founded: 1899; Members: 350
Pres: Dr. L. Mhlanga; Gen Secr: Prof. B.E.
Marshall
Focus: Sci
Periodicals
Transactions of the Zimbabwe Sientific Association
(5 times annually)

Zimbabwe Science News (bi-monthly)   . . *17087*

Zimbabwe Veterinary Association, POB 8387,
Causeway, Harare
Focus: Vet Med
Periodical
Zimbabwe Veterinary Journal (quarterly)   . *17088*

Zimbabwe Writers Union, POB MP 167, Mount
Pleasant, Harare
Members: 250
Focus: Lit *17089*

Alphabetical Index to Association Names

Alphabetisches Verzeichnis
der Gesellschaftsnamen

Alphabetical Index: American 314

American Association of Plastic Surgeons, Bryn Mawr *12920*
American Association of Poison Control Centers, Washington *12921*
American Association of Presidents of Independent Colleges and Universities, Provo *12922*
American Association of Pro Life Obstetricians and Gynecologists, Elm Grove *12923*
American Association of Professional Hypnotherapists, Boones Mill *12924*
American Association of Professors of Yiddish, Flushing *12925*
American Association of Psychiatric Administrators, Atlanta *12926*
American Association of Psychiatric Services for Children, Rochester *12927*
American Association of Public Health Dentistry, Richmond *12928*
American Association of Public Health Physicians, Madison *12929*
American Association of School Librarians, Chicago *12930*
American Association of School Personnel Administrators, Sacramento *12931*
American Association of Sex Educators, Counselors and Therapists, Chicago *12932*
American Association of Small Ruminant Practitioners, Ithaca *12933*
American Association of State Colleges and Universities, Washington *12934*
American Association of Suicidology, Washington *12935*
American Association of Teachers of Arabic, Provo *12936*
American Association of Teachers of Esperanto, Santa Barbara *12937*
American Association of Teachers of French, Champaign *12938*
American Association of Teachers of German, Cherry Hill *12939*
American Association of Teachers of Spanish and Portuguese, Greeley *12940*
American Association of Teachers of Turkic Languages, Princeton *12941*
American Association of Textile Chemists and Colorists, Research Triangle Park *12942*
American Association of Tissue Banks, McLean *12943*
American Association of University Professors, Washington *12944*
American Association of University Women, Washington *12945*
American Association of University Women Educational Foundation, Washington *12946*
American Association of Variable Star Observers, Cambridge *12947*
American Association of Veterinary Anatomists, Auburn *12948*
American Association of Veterinary Laboratory Diagnosticians, Columbia *12949*
American Association of Veterinary Parasitologists, Mundelein *12950*
American Association of Veterinary State Boards, Jefferson City *12951*
American Association of Wildlife Veterinarians, Athens *12952*
American Association of Women Dentists, Chicago *12953*
American Association of Zoo Keepers, Topeka *12954*
American Association of Zoo Veterinarians, Philadelphia *12955*
American Association of Zoological Parks and Aquariums, Wheeling *12956*
American Association on Mental Retardation, Washington *12957*
American Astronautical Society, Springfield *12958*
American Astronomical Society, Baton Rouge *12959*
American Auditory Society, Phoenix *12960*
American Automatic Control Council, Evanston *12961*
American Aviation Historical Society, Santa Ana *12962*
American Bamboo Society, La Jolla *12963*
American Baptist Historical Society, Valley Forge *12964*
American Bar Association, Chicago *12965*
American Beethoven Society, San Jose *12966*
American Biblical Encyclopedia Society, Monsey *12967*
American Birding Association, Colorado Springs *12968*
American Board for Certification in Orthotics and Prosthetics, Alexandria *12969*
American Board of Abdominal Surgery, Melrose *12970*
American Board of Allergy and Immunology, Philadelphia *12971*
American Board of Anesthesiology, Raleight *12972*
American Board of Bioanalysis, Saint Louis *12973*
American Board of Colon and Rectal Surgery, Taylor *12974*
American Board of Dental Public Health, Gainesville *12975*
American Board of Dermatology, Detroit *12976*
American Board of Endodontics, Chicago *12977*
American Board of Funeral Service Education, Brunswick *12978*
American Board of Health Physics, McLean *12979*
American Board of Internal Medicine, Philadelphia *12980*
American Board of Master Educators, Nashville *12981*
American Board of Neurological Surgery, Houston *12982*
American Board of Nuclear Medicine, Los Angeles *12983*
American Board of Nutrition, Birmingham *12984*
American Board of Obstetrics and Gynecology, Dallas *12985*
American Board of Ophthalmology, Bala Cynwyd *12986*
American Board of Opticianry, Fairfax *12987*
American Board of Oral and Maxillofacial Pathology, Tampa *12988*
American Board of Orthodontics, Saint Louis *12989*
American Board of Orthopedic Surgery, Chapel Hill *12990*
American Board of Otolaryngology, Houston *12991*
American Board of Pathology, Tampa *12992*
American Board of Pediatric Dentistry, Carmel *12993*
American Board of Pediatrics, Chapel Hill *12994*
American Board of Periodontology, Baltimore *12995*
American Board of Physical Medicine and Rehabilitation, Rochester *12996*
American Board of Plastic Surgery, Philadelphia *12997*
American Board of Podiatric Orthopedics and Primary Medicine, Chicago *12998*
American Board of Podiatric Surgery, San Francisco *12999*
American Board of Preventive Medicine, Schiller Park *13000*
American Board of Professional Psychology, Columbia *13001*
American Board of Prosthodontics, Atlanta *13002*
American Board of Psychiatry and Neurology, Deerfield *13003*
American Board of Psychological Hypnosis, Beverly *13004*
American Board of Radiology, Tucson *13005*
American Board of Surgery, Philadelphia *13006*
American Board of Thoracic Surgery, Evanston *13007*
American Board of Urology, Bingham Farms *13008*
American Board of Vocational Experts, Glenview *13009*
American Boccaccio Association, Saint Louis *13010*
American Boxwood Society, Boyce *13011*
American Brain Tumor Association, Des Plaines *13012*
American Broncho-Esophagological Association, Saint Louis *13013*
American Bryological and Lichenological Society, Lewiston *13014*
American Bureau for Medical Advancement in China, New York *13015*
American Burn Association, New York *13016*
American-Canadian Genealogical Society, Manchester *13017*
American Canal Society, York *13018*
American Cancer Society, New York *13019*
American Carbon Society, Saint Marys *13020*
American Cartographic Association, Bethesda *13021*
American Catholic Historical Association, Washington *13022*
American Catholic Philosophical Association, Washington *13023*
American Celiac Society, West Orange *13024*
American Center for Design, Chicago *13025*
American Center for the Alexander Technique, New York *13026*
American Ceramic Society, Westerville *13027*
American Cetacean Society, San Pedro *13028*
American Chemical Society, Washington *13029*
American Chestnut Foundation, Bennington *13030*
American Chiropractic Association, Arlington *13031*
American Civil War Historical Re-Enactment Society, Downsview *01652*
American Civil War Round Table, United Kingdom, Weybridge *10768*
American Classical League, Oxford *13032*
American Cleft Palate-Craniofacial Association, Pittsburgh *13033*
American Clinical and Climatological Association, Rochester *13034*
American Cocoa Research Institute, McLean *13035*
American College Health Association, Baltimore *13036*
American College of Allergy and Immunology, Arlington Heights *13037*
American College of Apothecaries, Memphis *13038*
American College of Cardiology, Bethesda *13039*
American College of Chest Physicians, Northbrook *13040*
American College of Chiropractic Orthopedists, El Centro *13041*
American College of Clinical Pharmacology, New Hartford *13042*
American College of Cryosurgery, Schaumburg *13043*
American College of Dentists, Gaithersburg *13044*
American College of Emergency Physicians, Dallas *13045*
American College of Foot and Ankle Orthopedics and Medicine, Cocolla *13046*
American College of Foot and Ankle Pediatrics, Philadelphia *13047*
American College of Foot and Ankle Surgeons, Park Ridge *13048*
American College of Gastroenterology, Arlington *13049*
American College of Healthcare Executives, Chicago *13050*
American College of Heraldry, Tuscaloosa *13051*
American College of International Physicians, Washington *13052*
American College of Medical Practice Executives, Englewood *13053*
American College of Medical Toxicology, Harrisburg *13054*
American College of MOHS Micrographic Surgery and Cutaneous Oncology, Schaumburg *13055*
American College of Musicians, Austin *13056*
American College of Neuropsychiatrists, Farmington Hills *13057*
American College of Neuropsychopharmacology, Nashville *13058*
American College of Nuclear Physicians, Washington *13059*
American College of Nurse-Midwives, Washington *13060*
American College of Nutrition, New York *13061*
American College of Obstetricians and Gynecologists, Washington *13062*
American College of Oral and Maxillofacial Surgeons, San Antonio *13063*
American College of Orgonomy, Princeton *13064*
American College of Osteopathic Family Physicians, Arlington Heights *13065*
American College of Osteopathic Internists, Washington *13066*
American College of Osteopathic Obstetricians and Gynecologists, Pontiac *13067*
American College of Osteopathic Pediatricians, Washington *13068*
American College of Osteopathic Surgeons, Alexandria *13069*
American College of Physicians, Philadelphia *13070*
American College of Preventive Medicine, Washington *13071*
American College of Prosthodontists, Chicago *13072*
American College of Psychiatrists, Greenbelt *13073*
American College of Psychoanalysts, Benicia *13074*
American College of Rheumatology, Atlanta *13075*
American College of Sports Medicine, Indianapolis *13076*
American College of Surgeons, Chicago *13077*
American College of Veterinary Internal Medicine, Lakewood *13078*
American College of Veterinary Pathologists, West Deptford *13079*
American College of Veterinary Radiology, Glencoe *13080*
American College Testing, Iowa City *13081*
American Collegiate Retailing Association, New Orleans *13082*
American Committee for International Conservation, Washington *13083*
American Committee for the Weizmann Institute of Science, New York *13084*
American Committee to Advance the Study of Petroglyphs and Pictographs, Shepherdstown *13085*
American Comparative Literature Association, Eugene *13086*
American Concrete Institute, Detroit *13087*
American Conference for Irish Studies, Syracuse *13088*
American Conference of Academic Deans, Washington *13089*
American Conference of Governmental Industrial Hygienists, Cincinnati *13090*
American Congress of Rehabilitation Medicine, Glenview *13091*
American Congress on Surveying and Mapping, Bethesda *13092*
American Conservation Association, New York *13093*
American Consulting Engineers Council, Washington *13094*
American Correctional Association, Lanham *13095*
American Correctional Health Services Association, Dayton *13096*
American Coucil for an Energy Efficient Economy, Washington *13097*
American Council for Construction Education, Monroe *13098*
American Council for International Studies, Boston *13099*
American Council for the Arts, New York *13100*
American Council of Applied Clinical Nutrition, Florissant *13101*
American Council of Independent Laboratories, Washington *13102*
American Council of Learned Societies, New York *13103*
American Council of the International Institute of Welding, Miami *13104*
American Council on Consumer Interests, Columbia *13105*
American Council on Education, Washington *13106*
American Council on Pharmaceutical Education, Chicago *13107*
American Council on Schools and Colleges, Tampa *13108*
American Council on the Teaching of Foreign Languages, Yonkers *13109*
American Counseling Association, Alexandria *13110*
American Criminal Justice Association – Lambda Alpha Epsilon, Sacramento *13111*
American Cryonics Society, Cupertino *13112*
American Crystallographic Association, Buffalo *13113*
American Dairy Science Association, Savoy *13114*
American Dance Therapy Association, Columbia *13115*
American Deafness and Rehabilitation Association, Little Rock *13116*
American Dental Assistants Association, Chicago *13117*
American Dental Association, Chicago *13118*
American Dental Hygienists' Association, Chicago *13119*
American Dental Society of Anesthesiology, Chicago *13120*
American Dental Society of Europe, London *10769*
American Dermatologic Society of Allergy and Immunology, Rochester *13121*
American Dermatological Association, Augusta *13122*
American Design Drafting Association, Rockville *13123*
American Diabetes Association, Alexandria *13124*
American Dialect Society, Jacksonville *13125*
American Dietetic Association, Chicago *13126*
American Diopter and Decibel Society, Pittsburgh *13127*
American Economic Association, Nashville *13128*
American Economic Development Council, Rosemont *13129*
American Education Association, Center Moriches *13130*
American Educational Research Association, Washington *13131*
American Educational Studies Association, Hiram *13132*
American Electroencephalographic Society, Bloomfield *13133*
American Electrology Association, Trumbull *13134*
American Electronics Association, Santa Clara *13135*
American Electroplaters and Surface Finishers Society, Orlando *13136*
American Endodontic Society, Fullerton *13137*
American Entomological Society, Philadelphia *13138*
American Epilepsy Society, Hartford *13139*
American Equilibration Society, Morton Grove *13140*
American Ethnological Society, Durham *13141*
American Family Therapy Association, Washington *13142*
American Farm Bureau Research Foundation, Park Ridge *13143*
American Federation for Clinical Research, Thorofare *13144*
American Federation of Arts, New York *13145*
American Federation of Astrologers, Tempe *13146*
American Federation of Mineralogical Societies, Oklahoma City *13147*
American Fern Society, Washington *13148*
American Film Institute, Washington *13149*
American Finance Association, New York *13150*
American Fine Arts Society, New York *13151*
American Fisheries Society, Bethesda *13152*
American Folklore Society, Arlington *13153*
American Foreign Law Association, New York *13154*
American Forensic Association, River Falls *13155*
American Forests, Washington *13156*
American Forum for Global Education, New York *13157*
American Foundation for Aids Research, New York *13158*
American Foundation for Vision Awareness, Saint Louis *13159*
American Foundrymen's Society, Des Plaines *13160*
American Fracture Association, Bloomington *13161*
American-French Genealogical Society, Pawtucket *13162*
American Friends of Cambridge University, New York *13163*
American Friends of Lafayette, Easton *13164*
American Gastroenterological Association, Bethesda *13165*
American Genetic Association, Buckeystown *13166*
American Geographical Society, New York *13167*
American Geological Institute, Alexandria *13168*
American Geophysical Union, Washington *13169*
American Geriatrics Society, New York *13170*
American Group Practice Association, Alexandria *13171*
American Group Psychotherapy Association, New York *13172*
American Guild of Hypnotherapists, Kenner *13173*
American Gynecological and Obstetrical Society, Charlottesville *13174*
American Harp Society, Teaneck *13175*
American Health Information Management Association, Chicago *13176*
American Health Planning Association, Falls Church *13177*
American Hearing Research Foundation, Chicago *13178*
American Heart Association, Dallas *13179*
American Herb Association, Nevada City *13180*
American Historical Association, Washington *13181*
American Historical Society of Germans from Russia, Calgary *01653*
American Historical Society of Germans from Russia, Lincoln *13182*
American Hobbit Association, Mason *13183*
American Holistic Medical Association, Raleigh *13184*
American Holistic Medical Foundation, Raleigh *13185*
American Horticultural Society, Alexandria *13186*
American Horticultural Therapy Association, Gaithersburg *13187*
American Hospital Association, Chicago *13188*
American Hungarian Educators' Association, Silver Spring *13189*
American Hungarian Library and Historical Society, New York *13190*
American Indian Culture Research Center, Marvin *13191*
American Indian Lore Association, Logan *13192*
American Indian Science and Engineering Society, Boulder *13193*
American Industrial Health Council, Washington *13194*
American Industrial Hygiene Association, Fairfax *13195*
American Institute for Conservation of Historic and Artistic Works, Washington *13196*
American Institute for Contemporary German Studies, Washington *13197*
American Institute for CPCU, Malvern *13198*
American Institute for Economic Research, Great Barrington *13199*
American Institute for Foreign Study, Greenwich *13200*
American Institute for Maghreb Studies, Washington *13201*

Alphabetical Index: American 316

American Society of Plumbing Engineers, Westlake 13483
American Society of Podiatric Dermatology, Baltimore 13484
American Society of Primatologists, Chicago 13485
American Society of Psychopathology of Expression, Brookline 13486
American Society of Questioned Document Examiners, Miami 13487
American Society of Radiologic Technologists, Albuquerque 13488
American Society of Regional Anesthesia, Richmond 13489
American Society of Safety Engineers, Des Plaines 13490
American Society of Sanitary Engineering, Cleveland 13491
American Society of Sephardic Studies, New York 13492
American Society of Sugar Beet Technologists, Denver 13493
American Society of Swedish Engineers, New York 13494
American Society of Trial Consultants, Towson 13495
American Society of Tropical Medicine and Hygiene, Northbrook 13496
American Society of Veterinary Ophthalmology, Stillwater 13497
American Society of Zoologists, Chicago 13498
American Sociological Association, Washington 13499
American Software Users Group, Chicago 13500
American Solar Energy Association, Annapolis 13501
American Speech-Language-Hearing Association, Rockville 13502
American Spelean History Association, Altoona 13503
American Spinal Injury Association, Chicago 13504
American Sports Education Institute, North Palm Beach 13505
American Statistical Association, Alexandria 13506
American String Teachers Association, Reston 13507
American Student Dental Association, Chicago 13508
American Studies Association, Washington 13509
American Surgical Association, Manchester 13510
American Swedish Institute, Minneapolis 13511
American Technical Education Association, Wahpeton 13512
American Teilhard Association, Syosset 13513
American Theatre Critics Association, Nashville 13514
American Theatre Organ Society, Indianapolis 13515
American Theological Library Association, Evanston 13516
American Theological Society – Midwest Division, Chicago 13517
American Thoracic Society, New York 13518
American Tinnitus Association, Portland 13519
American Tolkien Society, Highland 13520
American Trauma Society, Upper Marlboro 13521
American Type Culture Collection, Rockville 13522
American Underground-Construction Association, Minneapolis 13523
American Urological Association, Baltimore 13524
American Vacuum Society, New York 13525
American Veterinary Medical Association, Schaumburg 13526
American Veterinary Society of Animal Behavior, Saint Louis 13527
American Vocational Association, Alexandria 13528
American Vocational Education Personnel Development Association, Stillwater 13529
American Vocational Education Research Association, Fargo 13530
American Water Resources Association, Herdon 13531
American Welding Society, Miami 13532
American Wind Energy Association, Washington 13533
American Wood-Preservers' Association, Woodstock 13534
American Wood Preservers Institute, Vienna 13535
Americas Association of Cooperative / Mutual Insurance Societies, Columbus 13536
Amerika Katolika Esperanto-Societo, Elkhart 13537
Amerind Foundation, Dragoon 13538
AMERSA, Providence 13793
AMES, Liverpool 10898
AMEWPR, Kuala Lumpur 08220
AmFAR, New York 13158
AMFFA, Lock Haven 13266
AMFI, Redmond 13896
AMG, Mülheim a.d. Ruhr 04369
AMHA, Northbrook 13795
Amherst Township Historical Society, Amherst 01656
AMHPS, Washington 13800
AMIA, Bethesda 13267
Amici Thomae Mori, Angers 03500
AMINTAPHIL, Gainesville 14809
AMIS, Tarzana 13280
Amis de Guy de Maupassant, Paris 03501
Amis de Rimbaud, Paris 03502
A.M.I.S.I., Milano 06995
AMJ, Barnet 10899
AMM, Winnipeg 01719
AMMLA, New York 13272
A.M.O.R., Roma 06847
AMP, Cambrai 03634
AMPAS, Beverly Hills 12664
AMPF, Wienhausen 04495
AMPT, Ickenham 10815
AMQUA, Amherst 13348
AMR, Wien 00414
AMRA, Dakar 09510
AMRC, Research Triangle Park 13893
AMREF, Nairobi 08068
AMREF, New York 12708
AMRO, Hopton 10886
AMS, Boston 13274
AMS, Buffalo 13560
AMS, Cairo 03261
AMS, Chestertown 13276
AMS, Coral Gables 12663
AMS, Geneseo 13273
A.M.S., Hobart 00212
AMS, London 10773, 10938
AMS, New York 13277
AMS, Philadelphia 13281
AMS, Princeton 13275
AMS, Providence 13259
AMSA, Chicago 13261
AMSA, Lusaka 17048
A.M.S.E., Gent 00977
AMSE, Plainfield 13801
AmSECT, Reston 13448
AMSPDC, Chapel Hill 13794
AMSS, Herndon 13802
AMSUS, Bethesda 13798
AMT, Belconnen 00213
AMT, Park Ridge 13268
AMTA, Atlanta 13548
AMTA, Evanston 13257
AMTIESA, Arusha 10592
AMU, Franklin 13799
AMU, Ibadan 08760
AMU, Kingston 13254
A.M.V.M.I., Maisons Alfort 03613
AMWA, Alexandria 13269
AMWA, Bethesda 13270
Amyotrophic Lateral Sclerosis Society of Canada, Toronto 01657
An Comunn Gaidhealach, Inverness 10770
ANA, Bologna 06851
ANA, Chicago 13283
ANA, Colorado Springs 13289
ANA, Minneapolis 13287
ANABAD, Madrid 09730
ANACHEM, Detroit 13727
Anaesthetic Research Society, Leeds 10771
ANAI, Roma 06998
ANAI, Tangiers 08377
ANAIC, Perth 00126
Anatomical Society of Great Britain and Ireland, London 10772
Anatomische Gesellschaft, Lübeck 04416
ANC, Guilden Morden 10904
ANCEFN, Buenos Aires 00028
Ancient Astronaut Society, Highland Park 13539
Ancient Iran Cultural Society, Teheran 06562
Ancient Monuments Society, London 10773
ANCOLD, Brisbane 00215
Andean Commission of Jurists, Lima 08975
Andean Institute for Population Studies and Development, Lima 08976
Andean Institute of Social Studies, Lima 08977
Andean Instiute of Popular Arts, Quito 03233
Andean Technological Information System, Lima 08978
ANDIS, Roma 07005
ANEA, Lima 08985
ANEJ, Paris 03618
ANENA, Grenoble 03624
ANET, Roma 07008
ANFFAS, Roma 07009
Anglo-Continental Dental Society, London 10774
Anglo-European College of Chiropractic, Bournemouth 10775
Anglo-Norman Text Society, London 10776
ANGOC, Manila 09034
ANGOS, Birmingham 12721
ANHS, Tampa 13285
ANHSO, Oxford 10797
ANIAI, Roma 07012
ANID, Dakar 09500
ANID, Napoli 07014
ANIEST, Roma 07015
A.N.I.M., Roma 07013
A.N.I.M.A., Milano 07011
Animal Behavior Society, Worcester 13540
Animal Breeding Research Organization, Edinburgh 10777
Animal Diseases Research Association, Edinburgh 10778
Animal Health Trust, Newmarket 10779
Animal Medical Center, New York 13541
Animal Nutrition Research Council, Chantilly 13542
Animal Protection Institute of America, Sacramento 13543
ANIPLA, Milano 07016
Anjuman-i-Islam Islamic Research Association, Mumbai 06399
ANL, Laufen 04529
ANL, Montevideo 12606
Anna-Seghers-Gesellschaft Berlin und Mainz e.V., Berlin 04417
Annette von Droste-Gesellschaft e.V., Münster 04418
Annual Reviews, Palo Alto 13544
Anonymous Arts Recovery Society, New York 13545
Anonymous Families History Project, Newark 13546
ANP, Berlin 04514
ANPGP, Milano 07002
ANPI, Louvain-La-Neuve 00978
ANPO, Kendal 10903
ANPUR, Roma 07021
ANRD, Chantilly 13542
A.N.R.T, Paris 03614
ANS, Chevy Chase 13883
ANS, La Grange Park 13288
ANS, New York 13282, 13290
ANS, Sydney 00217
ANSI, New York 13284
ANSI, Roma 07019
ANSP, Philadelphia 12665
ANSS, Homer 13286
ANSTI, Nairobi 08069
ANSTO, Menai 00216
Antarctica and Southern Ocean Coalition, Washington 13547
Antenna Measurement Techniques Association, Atlanta 13548
Anthology Film Archives, New York 13549
Anthropological Society of Mumbai, Mumbai 06400
Anthropological Society of New South Wales, Sydney 00118
Anthropological Society of Nippon, Tokyo 07912
Anthropological Survey of India, Calcutta 06401
Anthropologische Gesellschaft in Wien, Wien 00400
Anthropology Film Center Foundation, Santa Fe 13550
Anthropos Institut, Sankt Augustin 04419
Anthroposophical Society in Canada, Toronto 01658
Anthroposophical Society in Great Britain, London 10780
Anthroposophische Gesellschaft in Deutschland, Stuttgart 04420
Antiquarian and Numismatic Society of Montréal, Montréal 02371
Antiquarian Horological Society, Wadhurst 10781
Antiquarische Gesellschaft in Zürich, Zürich 10025
Anton Bruckner Institut Linz, Linz 00401
ANTS, London 10776
ANUG, Chicago 13877
A.N.V.W., Tilburg 08395
ANZAAS, Canberra 00159
AOA, Chicago 13308
AOA, London 10906
AOA, New York 13302
AOA, Rosemont 13299
AOA, Saint Louis 13294
AOAC, Arlington 13551
AOAC International, Arlington 13551
AOAS, Wilmington 13306
AOASM, Middleton 13307
AOC, Alexandria 13807
AOC, Madison 13303
AOCA, Independence 13310
AOCAI, Scottsdale 13309
AOCD, Kirksville 13311
AOCP, Pembroke Pines 13312
AOCPr, Union 13313
AOCR, Milan 13314
AOCRM, Des Plaines 13315
AOCS, Champaign 13292
AOD, Manassas 12667
AOD, Menomonie 12666
AOE, Tahlequah 13808
AÖG, Wien 00409
AOFAS, Seattle 13300
AOFOG, Singapore 09523
AOI, Firenze 07023
AOIP, New York 13552
AOJS, New York 13809
AOJT, Brooklyn 13810
AOOI, Roma 07022
AOPA, Alexandria 13304
AORC, Portland 13805
AORTIC, Harare 17057
AOS, Ann Arbor 13296
AOS, Bucuresti 09271
AOS, Dallas 13298
AOS, Durham 13293
AOS, Maywood 13316
AOS, West Palm Beach 13295
AOSA, Lincoln 13806
AOSB, Arlington 13566
Aosdana, Dublin 06582
AOSED, Sacramento 13811
AOSSM, Rosemont 13301
A.O.T., Cambridge 10927
AOTA, Bethesda 13291
AOTA, Hiroshima 07711
AOTA, Yaoundé 01607
AOU, Washington 13297
AP-LS, Philadelphia 13345
APA, Buenos Aires 00059
A.P.A., Lima 08987
A.P.A., London 10913
APA, McLean 12736
APA, Newark 13325
APA, Sepulveda 13317
APA, Washington 13342, 13344
APA, Worcester 13324
APAC, Dakar 09508
APACM, Pittsford 13329
APACVS, Reston 13816
APADI, Jakarta 06553
APAL, Caracas 16878
APALMS, Singapore 09524
APANF, Cotonou 01325
APAP, Alexandria 13815
APASWE, Bundoora 00123
APB, Bonn 04376
APB, São Paulo 01416
APBB, Nürnberg 04433
APBD, Thy-le-Château 00985
APBP, Edina 13818
APC, Bethesda 13813
APC, Broxborn 10909
APC, Lisburn 10910
APC, San Francisco 13654
APCAS, Bangkok 10619
APCC, Sydney 00128
APCChE, Barton 00127
APCO, Forest Grove 13576
APCO, Tokyo 07712
APCP, México 08278
A.P.C.T., Saint Leonards-on-Sea 10907
APCTT, New Delhi 06403
APCU, Jakarta 06547
APCU, Louisville 13817
APDA, Staten Island 13318
APDF, Singapore 09525
A.P.D.P., Lisboa 09187
APE, Lisboa 09179
APEA, Huntington 10816
APEA, Sydney 00220
APEC, Dayton 13553
APED, Bangkok 10621
APEE, Lisboa 09189
APESS, Strassen 08168
APF, Brookline 13330
APF, Porto 09182
APFA, Khartoum 09843
APFAN, Canberra 00122
APFC, Bangkok 10623
APFCB, Adelaide 00129
APFHRM, Hong Kong 02540
APFTC, Bangkok 10632
APG, Berlin 04480
APG, Washington 13819
APGO, Washington 13822
APHA, New York 13340
APhA, Washington 13323
APHA, Washington 13347
APHS, Morgantown 13338
API, Reston 13339
API, Sacramento 13543
API, San Francisco 13872
API, Washington 13322, 13333
APIC, Washington 13651
APIMO, Roma 07036
Apimondia, Roma 06889
APINESS, Bangkok 10624
APINMAP, Bangkok 10626
APJT, Edinburgh 10912
APL, São Paulo 01384
APLA, Halifax 01738
APLAR, Semarang 06549
Aplastic Anemia Association of Canada, Etobicoke 01659
APLIC, New York 13649
APLIC, Ottawa 01721
APLS, DeKalb 13648
APLV, Paris 03517
APM, Chicago 12669
APM, Lisboa 09183
APM, New York 13655
APM, Washington 13823
APMA, Bethesda 13334
APMHC, Charlotte 13820
APMS, Washington 13558
APO, Tokyo 07713
APOAC, Taipei 02666
APÖ, Wien 00407
Apothecaries' Hall, Dublin 06583
APPA, Burbank 13814
APPA, Paris 03635
APPA, Saint Louis 13346
APPA: The Association of Higher Education Facilities Officers, Alexandria 13554
APPEAL, Bangkok 10625
APPEN, Penang 08216
Appita, Carlton 00119
Applied Research and Development Institute International, Denver 13555
Applied Scientific Research Corporation of Thailand, Bangkok 10613
Applied Technology Council, Redwood City 13556
APPPAH, Alexandria 13652
APPPC, Bangkok 10620
Appropriate Health Resources and Technologies Action Group, London 10782
Appropriate Technology International, Washington 13557
APPROTECH ASIA, Manila 09027
A.P.P.S., Bruxelles 00980
APPS, Toowoomba 00149
APPSA, Singapore 09526
APPSGAN, East Perth 00130
APPTEA, Manila 09025
APQO, Quezon City 09026
A.P.R., Bucuresti 09272
APRES, Stillwater 13320
APRI, Lagos 08761
A.P.R.S., Edinburgh 10828
APS, Bethesda 13331
APS, Chicago 13341
APS, College Park 13327
APS, Fort Worth 13812
APS, New York 12668
APS, Philadelphia 13326
APS, Reedsport 13335
APS, Saint Louis 13321
APS, Saint Paul 13332
APS, University Park 13337
APS, Washington 13319
APSA, Armidale 00150
APSA, Edinburgh 10817
APSA, Sydney 00148
APSA, Washington 13336
APsaA, New York 13343
APSC, Seoul 08122
APSGB, Harrogate 10908
APSIA, Washington 13821
A.P.S.M., Monaco 08372
APSSEAR, Manila 09042
APT, Saint Louis 13650
APTA, Alexandria 13328
APTI, Baghdad 06574
APTIRC, Singapore 09528
APVA, Richmond 13686
APWLD, Kuala Lumpur 08215
APWSS, Laguna 09035
AQP, Cincinnati 13656
AQSG, San Francisco 13349
Aquatic Plant Management Society, Washington 13558
Aquatic Research Institute, Hayward 13559
Aquatic Sciences and Fisheries Information System, Roma 06890
AR, Palo Alto 13544
ARA, Bedford 10762
ARA, Camarines Sur 09036
ARA, Minneapolis 12670
ARAB, Bruxelles 00986
Arab Academy of Damascus, Damascus 10582
Arab Academy of Music, Baghdad 06568
Arab Aerospace Educational Organization, Cairo 03255
Arab Agronomists Union, Damascus 10583
Arab Atomic Energy Agency, Tunis 10674
Arab Biosciences Network, Jubaiha 08052
Arab Bureau of Education for the Gulf States, Riyadh 09486
Arab Center for Energy Studies, Cairo 03256
Arab Center for Medical Literature, Safat 08143
Arab Center for the Studies of Arid Zones and Dry Lands, Damascus 10584
Arab Centre for Information Studies on Population, Development and Construction, Damascus 10585
Arab Commission for International Law, Cairo 03257
Arab Committee for Ottoman Studies, Zaghouan 10675
Arab Council for Childhood and Development, Cairo 03258
Arab Council for Medical Specialization, Damascus 10586
Arab Dental Federation, Baghdad 06569
Arab Federation for Technical Education, Baghdad 06570
Arab Federation for the Organs of the Deaf, Damascus 10587
Arab Federation of Sports Medicine, Tunis 10676
Arab Higher Committee for Pharmacological Affairs, Cairo 03259
Arab Historians Association, Baghdad 06571
Arab Industrial Development and Mining Organization, Baghdad 06572
Arab Information Network for Terminology, Tunis 10677
Arab Institute for Forestry and Ranges, Lattakia 10588
Arab Institute of Navigation, Alexandria 03260
Arab League Educational, Cultural and Scientific Organization, Tunis 10678
Arab Literacy and Adult Education Organization, Baghdad 06573
Arab Management Society, Buffalo 13560
Arab Management Society, Cairo 03261
Arab Medical Union, Tunis 10679

317 Alphabetical Index: ASEAN

Arab Music Rostrum, Paris 03503
Arab Organization for Standardization and Metrology, Cairo 03262
Arab Petroleum Training Institute, Baghdad 06574
Arab Planning Institute Kuwait, Safat 08144
Arab Regional Branch of the International Council on Archives, Riyadh 09487
Arab Regional Branch of the International Council on Archives, Tunis 10680
Arab Research Centre, London 10783
Arab Scientific Advisory Committee for Blood Transfer, Cairo 03263
Arab Security Studies and Training Center, Riyadh 09488
Arab States Regional Broadcasting Training Centre, Damascus 10589
Arab States Regional Centre for Functional Literacy in Rural Areas, Menoufia 03264
Arab Union for Cement and Building Materials, Damascus 10590
Arab Union of Veterinary Surgeons, Baghdad 06575
Arab Urban Development Institute, Riyadh 09489
Arab World Institute, Paris 03504
ARABN, Jubaiha 08052
ARABTERM, Tunis 10677
Arachnological Society of Japan, Osaka 07944
ARAHE, Seoul 08123
ARAN, London 10829
ARARA, San Miguel 13359
ARB, Pôrto Alegre 01420
Arbeit und Leben, Düsseldorf 04421
Arbeitsausschuß Wälzlager im DIN Deutsches Institut für Normung e.V., Köln 04422
Arbeitsgemeinschaft Allensbach e.V., Allensbach 04423
Arbeitsgemeinschaft audiovisueller Archive Österreichs, Graz 00402
Arbeitsgemeinschaft außeruniversitärer historischer Forschungseinrichtungen in der Bundesrepublik Deutschland e.V., München 04424
Arbeitsgemeinschaft Berufliche Bildung der deutschen Zeitungsverlage, Bonn 04425
Arbeitsgemeinschaft Demokratischer Bildungswerke e.V., Bonn 04426
Arbeitsgemeinschaft der Archive und Bibliotheken in der evangelischen Kirche, Nürnberg 04427
Arbeitsgemeinschaft der Deutschen Werkkunstschulen, Bremen 04428
Arbeitsgemeinschaft der Hauswirtschaftslehrerinnen-Seminarien der Schweiz, Chur 10026
Arbeitsgemeinschaft der kirchlichen Büchereiverbände, Bonn 04429
Arbeitsgemeinschaft der Leiter musikpädagogischer Studiengänge in der Bundesrepublik Deutschland, Berlin 04430
Arbeitsgemeinschaft der Musikakademien, Konservatorien und Hochschulinstitute, Darmstadt 04431
Arbeitsgemeinschaft der Musikerzieher Österreichs, Wien 00403
Arbeitsgemeinschaft der Ordenshochschulen, Vallendar 04432
Arbeitsgemeinschaft der Parlaments- und Behördenbibliotheken, Nürnberg 04433
Arbeitsgemeinschaft der Regionalbibliotheken, Saarbrücken 04434
Arbeitsgemeinschaft der Sozialdemokraten im Gesundheitswesen, Bonn 04435
Arbeitsgemeinschaft der Spezialbibliotheken e.V., Leverkusen 04436
Arbeitsgemeinschaft der Wirtschaft für Produktdesign und Produktplanung e.V., Essen 04516
Arbeitsgemeinschaft der wissenschaftlichen Institute des Handwerks der EG-Länder, München 04437
Arbeitsgemeinschaft Deutsche Lateinamerika-Forschung, Eichstätt 04438
Arbeitsgemeinschaft Deutscher Chorverbände e.V., Wolfenbüttel 04439
Arbeitsgemeinschaft Deutscher Tumorzentren e.V., München 04440
Arbeitsgemeinschaft deutscher wirtschaftswissenschaftlicher Forschungsinstitute e.V., Berlin 04441
Arbeitsgemeinschaft deutschsprachiger Autoren, Fulda 04442
Arbeitsgemeinschaft Evangelischer Schulbünde e.V., Siegen 04443
Arbeitsgemeinschaft Fernwärme e.V., Frankfurt 04444
Arbeitsgemeinschaft Freier Schulen, Vereinigungen und Verbände gemeinnütziger Schulen in freier Trägerschaft, Berlin 04445
Arbeitsgemeinschaft Friedensforschung und Europäische Sicherheitspolitik e.V., Mosbach 04446
Arbeitsgemeinschaft Friedhof und Denkmal e.V., Kassel 04447
Arbeitsgemeinschaft für betriebliche Altersversorgung e.V., Heidelberg 04448
Arbeitsgemeinschaft für Deutschdidaktik, Klagenfurt 00404
Arbeitsgemeinschaft für elementare Bildung, Zürich 10027
Arbeitsgemeinschaft für Jugendhilfe, Bonn 04449
Arbeitsgemeinschaft für juristisches Bibliotheks- und Dokumentationswesen, Würzburg 04450
Arbeitsgemeinschaft für Kieferchirurgie innerhalb der Deutschen Gesellschaft für Zahn-, Mund- und Kieferheilkunde, Kiel 04451
Arbeitsgemeinschaft für klinische Ernährung (AKE), Wien 00405
Arbeitsgemeinschaft für Krebsbekämpfung des Landes Niedersachsen e.V., Hannover 04452
Arbeitsgemeinschaft für Landschaftsentwicklung, Bonn 04453
Arbeitsgemeinschaft für medizinisches Bibliothekswesen, Mannheim 04454
Arbeitsgemeinschaft für Osteuropaforschung, Tübingen 04455
Arbeitsgemeinschaft für Präventivpsychologie, Wien 00406
Arbeitsgemeinschaft für Psychotechnik in Österreich, Wien 00407
Arbeitsgemeinschaft für Umweltfragen e.V., Bonn 04456
Arbeitsgemeinschaft für wirtschaftliche Verwaltung e.V., Eschborn 04457
Arbeitsgemeinschaft für Wissenschaft und Politik, Innsbruck 00408
Arbeitsgemeinschaft für zeitgemässes Bauen e.V., Kiel 04458
Arbeitsgemeinschaft Getreideforschung e.V., Detmold 04459
Arbeitsgemeinschaft Grünland und Futterbau in der Gesellschaft für Pflanzenbauwissenschaften, Aulendorf 04460
Arbeitsgemeinschaft Hauswirtschaft e.V., Bonn 04461
Arbeitsgemeinschaft Historischer Kommissionen und Landesgeschichtlicher Institute e.V., Marburg 04462
Arbeitsgemeinschaft industrieller Forschungsvereinigungen „Otto von Guericke" e.V., Köln 04463
Arbeitsgemeinschaft Kartoffelforschung e.V., Detmold 04464
Arbeitsgemeinschaft kath.-sozialer Bildungswerke in der Bundesrepublik Deutschland, Bonn 04465
Arbeitsgemeinschaft katholisch-theologischer Bibliotheken, Paderborn 04466
Arbeitsgemeinschaft Katholischer Fachkrankenhäuser für Suchtkranke, Freiburg 04467
Arbeitsgemeinschaft Kirchlicher Museen und Schatzkammern, Trier 04468
Arbeitsgemeinschaft Korrosion e.V., Frankfurt 04469
Arbeitsgemeinschaft Literarischer Gesellschaften e.V., Berlin 04470
Arbeitsgemeinschaft Literatur im Deutschen Kulturrat, Bonn 04471
Arbeitsgemeinschaft Media-Analyse e.V., Frankfurt 04472
Arbeitsgemeinschaft Österreichischer Entomologen, Wien 00409
Arbeitsgemeinschaft Personenzentrierte Psychotherapie und Gesprächsführung, Wien 00410
Arbeitsgemeinschaft Rosalia Chladek in Deutschland e.V., Berlin 04473
Arbeitsgemeinschaft Solar 91, Zürich 10028, 10029
Arbeitsgemeinschaft Sozialwissenschaftlicher Institute e.V., Bonn 04474
Arbeitsgemeinschaft Spina bifida und Hydrocephalus e.V., Dortmund 04475
Arbeitsgemeinschaft staatlich anerkannter evangelischer Ausbildungsstätten für Altenpflege im DEVA, Hannover 04476
Arbeitsgemeinschaft Verstärkte Kunststoffe e. V., Frankfurt 04477
Arbeitsgemeinschaft Versuchsreaktor, Düsseldorf 04478
Arbeitsgemeinschaft wildbiologischer und jagdkundlicher Forschungsstätten, Bonn 04479
Arbeitsgemeinschaft Wirtschaft und Gesellschaft, Sankt Gallen 10030
Arbeitsgemeinschaft zur Erforschung der Ärztlichen Allgemeinpraxis, Brunn 00411
Arbeitsgemeinschaft zur Preußischen Geschichte e.V., Berlin 04480
Arbeitsgemeinschaft der Kunst- und Museumsbibliotheken, Roma 06891
Arbeitsgruppe für strukturelle Molekularbiologie in der Max-Planck-Gesellschaft, Hamburg 04481
Arbeitskreis Bildung und Politik Rheinland, Remagen 04482
Arbeitskreis Chemische Industrie, Köln 04483
Arbeitskreis der Musikbildungsstätten in der Bundesrepublik Deutschland, Wolfenbüttel 04484
Arbeitskreis der Wiener Altgermanisten, Wien 00412
Arbeitskreis der Wiener Skandinavisten, Wien 00413
Arbeitskreis Deutsch als Fremdsprache in der Schweiz, Zürich 10031
Arbeitskreis deutscher Bildungsstätten e.V., Bonn 04485
Arbeitskreis Entwicklungspolitik e.V., Vlotho 04486
Arbeitskreis Ethnomedizin, Hamburg 04487
Arbeitskreis für Betriebsführung München, Thaining 04488
Arbeitskreis für die Bundesrepublik Deutschland e.V., Düsseldorf 04421
Arbeitskreis für Hochschuldidaktik, Hamburg 04489
Arbeitskreis für Jugendliteratur e.V., München 04490
Arbeitskreis für neue Methoden in der Regionalforschung, Wien 00414
Arbeitskreis für Schulmusik und allgemeine Musikpädagogik e.V., Würzburg 04491
Arbeitskreis für Tibetische und Buddhistische Studien, Wien 00415
Arbeitskreis Gesundheitskunde e.V., Sankt Georgen 04492
Arbeitskreis Hauptschule e.V., Dortmund 04493
Arbeitskreis katholischer Schulen in freier Trägerschaft in der Bundesrepublik Deutschland, Bonn 04494
Arbeitskreis Musikpädagogische Forschung e.V., Wienhausen 04495
Arbeitskreis Rhetorik in Wirtschaft, Politik und Verwaltung, Bonn-Ippendorf 04496
Arbeitskreis Studium populärer Musik e.V., Halstenbek 04497
Arbeitskreis Verkehr und Umwelt e.V., Berlin 04498
Arbeitswissenschaft im Landbau e.V., Stuttgart 04499
Arbeo-Gesellschaft e.V., Bachenhausen 04500
ARBICA, Riyadh 09487
ARBICA, Tunis 10680
Arboricultural Association, Romsey 10784
ARC, Allentown 16451
ARC, Brighton 10940
ARC, Chesterfield 10792
ARC, Dearborn 12641
ARC-D, Berlin 04473
ARCA, Alexandria 13354
ARCASIA, Karachi 08892
ARCC, Harare 17058
ARCEDEM, Ibadan 08762
Archaeological and Anthropological Society of Victoria, Melbourne 00120
Archaeological Conservancy, Albuquerque 13561
Archaeological Foundation, Bruxelles 01173
Archaeological Institute of America, Boston 13562
Archaeological Society of Athens, Athinai 06212
Archaeological Society of Macedonia, Skopje 08205
Archaeological Society of Sri Lanka, Colombo 09827
Archaeologiki Hetairia, Athinai 06212
Archäologische Gesellschaft zu Berlin, Berlin 04501
Archaeoloische Gesellschaft Steiermark, Graz 00416
Archeology Section, Arlington 13563
Archief- en Biblioteekwezen in Belgie, Bruxelles 00938
Architects and Surveyors Institute, Chippenham 10785
Architects Council of Europe, Bruxelles 00937
Architects Regional Council Asia, Karachi 08892
Architectural and Archaeological Society of Durham and Northumberland, Durham City 10786
Architectural Association, London 10787
Architectural Association of Ireland, Dublin 06584
Architectural Intitute of British Columbia, Vancouver 01660
Architectural League of New York, New York 13564
Architectural Society of China, Beijing 02539
Archival Association, Helsinki 03340
Archives Association of British Columbia, Vancouver 01661
Archives Association of Ontario, Toronto 01662
Archives Council of Prince Edward Island, Charlottetown 01663
Archives et Bibliothèques de Belgique, Bruxelles 00938
Archives of American Art, Washington 13565
Archives Society of Alberta, Calgary 01664
ARCIS, Ibadan 08754
ARCT, Dakar 09501
Arctic Institute, København 02966
Arctic Institute of North America, Calgary 01665
Arctic Ocean Science Board, Arlington 13566
ARD, King of Prussia 13824
ARDE, Roma 07038
ARDI, Bruxelles 00988
ARDI, Denver 13555
ARE, Cumnor Hill 10820
ARE, Sheffield 10819
ARE, Virginia Beach 13658
AREA, Camberwell 00225
ARELS, London 10914
AREUEA, Bloomington 13351
ARF, New York 12696
Argentine Association of Geophysicists and Geodesists, Buenos Aires 00045
Argentine Centre of Engineering, Buenos Aires 00064
Argentine Entomological Society, La Plata 00109
Argentine Society of Endocrinology and Metabolism, Buenos Aires 00090
Argentine Society of Geographical Studies, Buenos Aires 00091
Argentine Society of Physiological Sciences, Buenos Aires 00088
Argentinian Geological Association, Buenos Aires 00055
Arhivsko Društvo Slovenije, Ljubljana 09583
ARI, Harare 17059
ARI, Hayward 13559
ARI, Monterey Park 12690
ARIA, Mount Vernon 13358
ARIC, Saint-Denis 03638
Arica Institute, Dobbs Ferry 13567
ARIPS, Molinetto di Mazzano 06912
The Aristotelian Society, London 10788
ARIT, Philadelphia 13355
Ark-La-Tex Genealogical Association, Shreveport 13568
Arkistoyhdistys, Helsinki 03340
Arkitektafélag Islands, Reykjavik 06361
Arktisk Institut, København 02966
ARL, Hannover 04396
ARL, Washington 13825
ARLIS/NA, Raleigh 13574
ARLIS UK and Ireland- Art Libraries Society of the United Kingdom and Ireland, Bromsgrove 10789
ARLO, Baghdad 06573
A.R.L.T., Woking 10830
ARMB, Bruxelles 00932
Armed Forces Institute of Pathology, Washington 13569
Armenian Artistic Union, Cairo 03265
Armenian Centre for National and International Studies, Sherman Oaks 13570
Armenian Educational Foundation, Glendale 13571
Armenian Literary Society, Demarest 13572
Armenian National Academy of Sciences, Yerevan 00113
ARMH, Wood River 15657
ARMS, London 10916
Arms and Armour Society of Great Britain, London 10790
ARNM, Okigwi 08763
ARNMD, New York 13659
Arnold Bennett Literary Society, Stoke-on-Trent 10791
Arnold-Bergstraesser-Institut für kulturwissenschaftliche Forschung e.V., Freiburg 04502
ARNOVA, Indianapolis 13662
AROCC, Buffalo 13661
A.R.O.E.V.E.N., Paris 03654
A.R.P., Roma 06808
ARPLA, Bangkok 10627
A.R.P.L.O.E.V., Paris 03639
ARPR, Bloomfield 12671
ARR, Northwood 10818
ARRG, Witham 10822
ARRS, Reston 13360
ARRT, Flushing 13356
ARRT, Mendota Heights 13352
ARS, Brooklyn 13357
ARS, New York 13885
ARS, Philadelphia 13350
ARS, Remscheid 04401
ARSC, Annapolis 13657
ARSO, Nairobi 08070
Art Institute of Light, Gap 13573
Art Libraries Society of North America, Raleigh 13574
Art Society of India, Bombay 06402
ARTC, Brooklyn 12691
ARTDO, Manila 09037
The Arthritis and Rheumatism Council, Chesterfield 10792
Arthritis Society, Toronto 01666
Arthur Rubinstein International Music Society, Tel Aviv 06677
Arthur Schnitzler-Institut, Wien 00417
Artists' Association of the 18th of November, København 03154
Arts Association, London 10793
Arts Association Harare, Harare 17061
The Arts Council, Dublin 06585
Arts Council, Reykjavik 06375
Arts Council of Australia, Sydney 00121
Arts Council of England, London 10794
Arts Council of Ghana, Accra 06191
Arts Council of Northern Ireland, Belfast 10795
Arts Council of Pakistan, Karachi 08893
Arts Council of Sri Lanka, Battaramulla 09828
Arts Council of Wales, Cardiff 10796
Arts International, New York 13575
ARVAC, Wivenhoe 10821
ARVO, Bethesda 13660
Arxiu Històric de la Ciutat de Barcelona, Barcelona 09727
Arzneimittelkommission der Deutschen Ärzteschaft, Köln 04503
Arzneimittelkommission der Schweizer Apotheker, Bern 10032
AS, Arlington 13563
A.S., Ascot 10943
AS, Blacksburg 12692
AS, Kidlington 10766
AS, New York 13578
AS, Torrance 13886
ASA, Alexandria 13506
ASA, Atlanta 12709, 13362
ASA, Bethesda 13892
ASA, Laguna Niguel 13900
ASA, London 10921
ASA, Madison 13423
ASA, Manchester 13510
ASA, Omaha 12701
ASA, Paddington 00236
ASA, Park Ridge 13424
A.S.A., Strawberry Hills 00237
ASA, Sydney 00133
ASA, Washington 13499, 13509
ASA, Woodbury 12687
ASAAD, Coral Springs 13368
ASAB, Saint Andrews 10831
ASAE, Saint Joseph 13422
ASAIHL, Bangkok 10635
ASALH, Washington 13689
ASAM, Chevy Chase 13421
ASANAL, Kuala Lumpur 08217
ASAO, Newark 10920
ASAO, Pearl City 13664
ASAP, Bethesda 13367
ASAPS, Long Beach 13369
ASAS, Campaign 13425
ASAS, Melrose 13420
ASAUK, London 10756
ASB Management-Zentrum-Heidelberg e.V., Heidelberg 04504
ASBAD, Dakar 09511
ASBAH, Peterborough 10825
ASBC, Saint Paul 13429
ASBCS, Nashville 13834
ASBDE, Redford 13427
ASBE, Chicago 13426
ASbH, Dortmund 04475
ASBMC, Bethesda 13370
ASBMR, Washington 13371
ASBO, Reston 13827
ASBS, Washington 13833
ASC, Boston 13364
ASC, Columbus 13442
ASC, Fairfax 13378
ASC, Huntington 13891
ASC, Peoria 13588
ASC, Washington 13843
ASC, Wilmington 13443
ASCA, Albuquerque 13377
ASCA, Taipei 02668
ASCB, Bethesda 13372
ASCCP, Washington 13376
ASCD, Alexandria 13668
ASCE, Gainesville 13826
ASCE, Reston 13434
ASCET, Flowery Branch 13432
ASCF, Boston 13365
ASCH, Des Plaines 13435
ASCH, Red Bank 13433
ASCHB, London 10826
ASCI, Thorofare 13373
ASCL, Cambridge 13439
ASCLA, Chicago 13836
ASCLS, Bethesda 13374
ASCN, Bethesda 13375
ASCO, Chicago 13436
ASCO, Rockville 13828
ASCO, Skokie 13441
ASCOBIC, Dakar 09502
ASCOLBI, Bogotá 02769
ASCP, Alexandria 13440
ASCP, Chicago 13437
ASCP/SCM, Fredericksburg 13430
ASCRS, Arlington Heights 13438
ASCRS, Fairfax 13431
ASCT, Raleigh 13379
ASCUN, Bogotá 02773
ASD, Lubbock 13446
ASDA, Chicago 13508
ASDA, Genève 10047
ASDA, New York 13380
ASDC, Chicago 13445
ASDE, Larchmont 13444
ASDS, Los Angeles 13690
ASDS, Schaumburg 13381
A.S.E., Adelaide 00240
A.S.E., Edinburgh 10939
A.S.E., Hatfield 10823
ASE, Ithaca 13385
ASE, Raleigh 13447
ASE, Ruston 13665
ASE, Salt Lake City 13669
ASE, Washington 12730, 13835
ASEA, Annapolis 13501
ASEAN Association for Planning and Housing, Manila 09022
ASEAN Council of Teachers, Jakarta 06543

Alphabetical Index: ASEAN 318

ASEAN Energy Management and Research Training Centre, Jakarta *06544*
ASEAN Federation of Endocrine Societies, Jakarta *06545*
ASEAN Federation of Engineering Organizations, Bangkok *10614*
ASEAN Federation of Plastic Surgeons, Bangkok *10615*
ASEAN Institute for Health Development, Nakhon Pathom *10616*
ASEAN Law Association, Jakarta *06546*
ASEAN Neurological Society, Manila *09023*
ASEAN Otorhinolaryngological Head and Neck Federation, Bangkok *10617*
ASEAN Plant Quarantine Centre and Training Institute, Serdang *08214*
ASEAN Population Coordination Unit, Jakarta *06547*
ASEAN Population Information Network, Jakarta *06548*
ASEAN Sub Committee on Non-Conventional Energy Research, Bangkok *10618*
ASEAN Training Centre for Preventive Drug Education, Manila *09024*
ASEANPOPIN, Jakarta *06548*
ASECS, Logan *13382*
ASEE, Washington *13383*
ASEI, North Palm Beach *13505*
ASEM, Annapolis *13384*
ASEM, Quito *03235*
ASEP, Bangkok *10633*
ASESP, Nairobi *08071*
ASET, Berryville *12674*
ASFEC, Menoufia *03264*
ASFFHF, Los Angeles *12672*
ASFIS, Roma *06890*
ASFO, Chicago *13449*
ASG, Bonn *04435*
ASG, Fairfield *13452*
ASG, Göttingen *04370*
ASG, Tuscaloosa *13451*
ASGCA, Chicago *13453*
ASGD, Chicago *13387*
ASGE, Anaheim *13450*
ASGE, Manchester *13386*
ASGP, Sheffield *10832*
ASGP&P, McLean *13454*
ASGW, Alexandria *13666*
ASH, San Diego *12673*
ASH, Washington *13457*
ASHA, Altoona *13503*
ASHA, Kent *13361*
ASHA, Research Triangle Park *13366*
ASHA, Rockville *13502*
ASHE, Chicago *13392*
ASHE, College Station *13691*
ASHET, Chicago *13389*
ASHG, Bethesda *13459*
ASHHRA, Chicago *13390*
Ashmolean Natural History Society of Oxfordshire, Oxford *10797*
ASHNS, Pittsburgh *13388*
ASHP, Bethesda *13458*
ASHRAE, Atlanta *13456*
ASHS, Alexandria *13391*
ASHT, Chicago *13455*
ASI, Bonn *04474*
ASI, Chippenham *10785*
A.S.I., Milano *07043*
ASI, Minneapolis *13511*
ASI, Paris *03658*
ASI, Seattle *13461*
ASI, Worthington *13897*
ASIA, Chicago *13504*
Asia and Oceania Federation of Obstetrics and Gynecology, Singapore *09523*
Asia and Pacific Commission on Agricultural Statistics, Bangkok *10619*
Asia and Pacific Plant Protection Commission, Bangkok *10620*
Asia and Pacific Programme of Educational Innovation for Development, Bangkok *10621*
Asia Crime Prevention Foundation, Tokyo *07710*
Asia Foundation, Bangkok *10622*
Asia Foundation, Islamabad *08894*
Asia Foundation, Seoul *08118*
Asia-Pacific Council of Optometry, Forest Grove *13576*
Asia Pacific Food Analysis Network, Canberra *00122*
Asia-Pacific Forestry Commission, Bangkok *10623*
Asia Pacific Forum on Women, Law and Development, Kuala Lumpur *08215*
Asia-Pacific Information Network in Social Sciences, Bangkok *10624*
Asia-Pacific Lawyers Association, Seoul *08119*
Asia Pacific League against Rheumatism, Semarang *06549*
Asia-Pacific Office Automation Council, Taipei *02666*
Asia-Pacific People's Environment Network, Penang *08216*
Asia Pacific Physics Teachers and Educators Association, Manila *09025*
Asia-Pacific Programme of Education for All, Bangkok *10625*
Asia Pacific Public Health Nutrition Association, Berkeley *13577*
Asia Pacific Quality Organization, Quezon City *09026*
Asia Society, New York *13578*
Asia Soil Conservation Network for the Humid Tropics, Jakarta *06550*
Asian Alliance of Appropriate Technology Practitioners, Manila *09027*
Asian and Oceanian Thyroid Association, Hiroshima *07711*
Asian and Pacific Association for Social Work Education, Bundoora *00123*
Asian and Pacific Centre for Transfer of Technology, New Delhi *06403*
Asian and Pacific Information Network on Medicinal and Aromatic Plants, Bangkok *10626*
Asian and Pacific Project for Labour Administration, Bangkok *10627*
Asian Association for Biology Education, Manila *09028*
Asian Association of Agricultural Colleges and Universities, Laguna *09029*
Asian Association of National Languages, Kuala Lumpur *08217*
Asian Association of Occupational Health, Bangkok *10628*
Asian Association of Open Universities, Seoul *08120*
Asian-Australasian Society of Neurological Surgeons, Brisbane *00124*
Asian-Australian Association of Animal Production Societies, Miaoli *02667*
Asian Center for Organization, Research and Development, New Delhi *06404*
Asian Centre of Educational Innovation for Development, Bangkok *10629*
Asian Confederation of Teachers, Manila *09030*
Asian Coordinating Group for Chemistry, Darwin *00125*
Asian Crystallographic Association, Taipei *02668*
Asian Disaster Preparedness Center, Bangkok *10630*
Asian Ecological Society, Taichung *02669*
Asian Fisheries Society, Manila *09031*
Asian Food Council, Taipei *02670*
Asian Institute for Development Communication, Kuala Lumpur *08218*
Asian Institute of Management, Manila *09032*
Asian Institute of Technology Library and Regional Documentation Centre, Bangkok *10631*
Asian Institute of Tourism, Manila *09033*
Asian Literature Division (of MLA), Bloomington *13579*
Asian Music Rostrum, Paris *03505*
Asian Network for Analytical and Inorganic Chemistry, Perth *00126*
Asian NGO Coalition for Agrarian Reform and Rural Development, Manila *09034*
Asian-Pacific Association for Laser Medicine and Surgery, Singapore *09524*
Asian Pacific Association for the Study of the Liver, Seoul *08121*
Asian Pacific Confederation of Chemical Engineering, Barton *00127*
Asian-Pacific Corrosion Control Organization, Sydney *00128*
Asian Pacific Dental Federation, Singapore *09525*
Asian Pacific Federation of Clinical Biochemistry, Adelaide *00129*
Asian Pacific Federation of Human Resource Management, Hong Kong *02540*
Asian-Pacific Federation of Therapeutic Communities, Bangkok *10632*
Asian-Pacific Political Science Association, Singapore *09526*
Asian Pacific Section of the International Confederation for Plastic and Reconstructive Surgery, Singapore *09527*
Asian-Pacific Society of Cardiology, Seoul *08122*
Asian-Pacific Tax and Investment Research Centre, Singapore *09528*
Asian-Pacific Weed Science Society, Laguna *09035*
Asian Pan-Pacific Society for Paediatric Gastroenterology and Nutrition, East Perth *00130*
Asian Parasite Control Organization, Tokyo *07712*
Asian Physics Education Network, Jakarta *06551*
Asian Productivity Organization, Tokyo *07713*
Asian Recycling Association, Camarines Sur *09036*
Asian Regional Association for Home Economics, Seoul *08123*
Asian Regional Cooperative Project on Food Irradiation, Wien *00418*
Asian Regional Training and Development Organization, Manila *09037*
Asian Rice Farming Network, Manila *09038*
Asian Securities Analysts Federation, Sydney *00131*
Asian Society for Environmental Protection, Bangkok *10633*
Asian Society of Agricultural Economists, Seoul *08124*
Asian Society of Oto-Rhino-Laryngology, Jakarta *06552*
Asian Studies Center, Michigan, East Lansing *13580*
Asian Vegetable Research and Development Center, Tainan *02671*
Asian Wetland Bureau, Kuala Lumpur *08219*
Asian Women's Research and Action Network, Manila *09039*
Asiatic Society, Calcutta *06405*
Asiatic Society of Bangladesh, Dhaka *00910*
Asiatic Society of Mumbai, Mumbai *06406*
ASIC, Byron *13464*
ASIDIC, Athens *13777*
ASIFA, Burbank *14779*
ASIH, Austin *13460*
ASIL, Washington *13463*
ASIM, Washington *13462*
ASIO, Zürich *10251*
ASIP, Bethesda *13394*
A.S.I.P., Roma *07033*
ASIS, Silver Spring *13393*
ASISTI, Balagué *03506*
ASIWPCA, Washington *13837*
ASJMC, Columbia *13829*
ASL, Urbana *13670*
A.S.L.A., Palermo *07040*
ASLA, Washington *13465*
ASLH, University *13396*
ASLIB, London *10808*
Aslib – Association for Information Management, London *10798*
ASLME, Boston *13466*
ASLMS, Wausau *13395*
ASLO, Gloucester Point *13467*
ASLP, Manila *09043*
ASLS, Aberdeen *10824*
A.S.M., Bucuresti *09265*
ASM, Cleveland *13671*
A.S.M., Melbourne *00232*
ASM, Provo *13468*
ASM, Tübingen *04409*
ASM, Washington *13398*
ASM International, Materials Park *13581*
ASM International-European Council, Bruxelles *00939*
AsMA, Alexandria *12700*
A.S.M.A.F., Paris *03656*
ASMB, Nicosia *02896*
ASMD, Chicago *13831*
ASMDT, Oakland Gardens *13469*
ASME, Dundee *10833*
ASME, New York *13471*
ASME International Gas Turbine Institute, Atlanta *13582*
ASMECCANICA, Milano *07006*
ASMER, Montevideo *12615*
ASMR, Paris *03505*
ASMS, Arlington Heights *13470*
ASMS, Santa Fe *13397*
ASN, Galveston *13399*
ASN, Irvine *13472*
ASN, Tallahassee *13476*
ASN, Washington *13474*
ASNE, Alexandria *13473*
ASNEMGE, London *10902*
ASNHS, Lancing *10917*
ASNR, Oak Brook *13475*
ASNT, Columbus *13400*
ASOC, Washington *13547*
Asociace Hudebních Umělcu a Vedcu, Praha *02910*
Asociácia pre Výskum Slovenskej a Svetovej Ekonomiky, Bratislava *09545*
Asociación Amics del Museus de Catalunya, Barcelona *09728*
Asociación Archivística Argentina, Buenos Aires *00035*
Asociación Argentina Amigos de la Astronomía, Buenos Aires *00036*
Asociación Argentina de Astronomía, La Plata *00037*
Asociación Argentina de Bibliotecas y Centros de Información Científicos y Técnicos, Buenos Aires *00038*
Asociación Argentina de Biología y Medicina Nuclear, Buenos Aires *00039*
Asociación Argentina de Ciencias Naturales, Buenos Aires *00040*
Asociación Argentina de Cirugía, Buenos Aires *00041*
Asociación Argentina de Ecología, Córdoba *00042*
Asociación Argentina de Estudios Americanos, Buenos Aires *00043*
Asociación Argentina de Farmacia y Bioquímica Industrial, Buenos Aires *00044*
Asociación Argentina de Geofísicos y Geodestas, Buenos Aires *00045*
Asociación Argentina de la Ciencia del Suelo, Buenos Aires *00046*
Asociación Argentina de Micología, Buenos Aires *00047*
Asociación Argentina de Ortopedía y Traumatología, Buenos Aires *00048*
Asociación Argentina del Frío, Buenos Aires *00049*
Asociación Argentina para el Progreso de las Ciencias, Buenos Aires *00050*
Asociación Bernardino Rivadavia, Bahía Blanca *00051*
Asociación Bibliotecológica Guatemalteca, Guatemala City *06262*
Asociación Bioquímica Argentina, Buenos Aires *00052*
Asociación Centroamericana de Sociología, Panamá City *08940*
Asociación Chilena de Astronomía y Astronáutica, Santiago *02447*
Asociación Chilena de Informatica y Computación en Educación, Santiago *02448*
Asociación Chilena de Microbiología, Santiago *02449*
Asociación Chilena de Sismología e Ingeniería Antisísmica, Santiago *02450*
Asociación Científica y Técnica de Chile, Santiago *02451*
Asociación Colombiana de Bibliotecarios, Bogotá *02769*
Asociación Colombiana de Facultades de Medicina, Bogotá *02770*
Asociación Colombiana de Fisioterapía, Bogotá *02771*
Asociación Colombiana de Sociedades Científicas, Bogotá *02772*
Asociación Colombiana de Universidades, Bogotá *02773*
Asociación Colombiana de Usarios de Computadores, Bogotá *02774*
Asociación Costarricense de Bibliotecarios, San José *02844*
Asociación Costarricense de Cirurgíca, San José *02845*
Asociación Costarricense de Pediatría, San José *02846*
Asociación Cultural Humboldt, Caracas *16874*
Asociación de Agrimensores de Venezuela, Caracas *16875*
Asociación de Artistas Aficionados, Lima *08979*
Asociación de Bibliotecarios de El Salvador, San Salvador *03310*
Asociación de Bibliotecarios del Paraguay, Asunción *08958*
Asociación de Bibliotecarios Graduados de la República Argentina, Buenos Aires *00053*
Asociación de Bibliotecarios Graduados del Istmo de Panamá, Panamá City *08941*
Asociación de Bibliotecarios Universitarios del Paraguay, Asunción *08959*
Asociación de Bibliotecarios y Archiveros de Honduras, Tegucigalpa *06282*
Asociación de Bibliotecarios y Documentalistas Agrícolas del Perú, Lima *08980*
Asociación de Bibliotecólogos del Uruguay, Montevideo *12609*
Asociación de Cardiología, San José *02847*
Asociación de Escritores y Artistas Españoles, Madrid *09729*
Asociación de Ingenieros Civiles del Perú, Lima *08981*
Asociación de Ingenieros del Uruguay, Montevideo *12610*
Asociación de Ingenieros y Arquitectos de México, México *08263*
Asociación de Ingenieros y Geólogos de Yacimientos Petrolíferos Fiscales Bolivianos, La Paz *01338*
Asociación de Linguistica y Filologia de América Latina, Caracas *16876*
Asociación de Médicas Mexicanas, México *08264*
Asociación de Medicina Interna, San José *02848*
Asociación de Obstetricia y Ginecología, San José *02849*
Asociación de Ortodoncistas de Guatemala, Guatemala City *06263*
Asociación de Psicólogos Infanto-Juveniles, Santiago *02452*
Asociación de Química y Farmacia del Uruguay, Montevideo *12611*
Asociación de Radiólogos de América Central y Panamá, San Salvador *03311*
Asociación de Universidades Confiadas a la Compañía de Jesús en América Latina, Bogotá *02775*
Asociación Dominicana de Bibliotecarios, Santo Domingo *03222*
Asociación Dominicana de Rectores de Universidades, Santo Domingo *03223*
Asociación Dominicana pro Bienestar de la Familia, Santo Domingo *03224*
Asociación Ecuatoriana de Bibliotecarios, Quito *03234*
Asociación Ecuatoriana de Museos, Quito *03235*
Asociación Electrotécnica Argentina, Buenos Aires *00054*
Asociación Electrotécnica Peruana, Lima *08982*
Asociación Española de Archiveros, Bibliotecarios, Museólogos y Documentalistas, Madrid *09730*
Asociación Española de Entomología, Burjasot *09731*
Asociación Española de Logopedia, Foniatria y Audiología, Barcelona *09732*
Asociación Española de Pediatría, Madrid *09733*
Asociación Española de Pintores y Escultores, Madrid *09734*
Asociación Geológica Argentina, Buenos Aires *00055*
Asociación Guatemalteca de Historia Natural, Guatemala City *06264*
Asociación Iberoamericana de Educación Superior a Distancia, Madrid *09735*
Asociación Interamericana de Gastroentereología, México *08265*
Asociación Interamericana de Ingeniería Sanitaria y Ambiental, Santiago *02453*
Asociación Interamericana de Ingenieria Sanitaria y Ambiental, Saõ Paulo *01388*
Asociación Internacional de Pediatría, Paris *03572*
Asociación Judicial de Chile, Santiago *02454*
Asociación Latinoamericana Científico de Plantas, Lima *08983*
Asociación Latinoamericana de Centros de Educación, Rosario *00056*
Asociación Latinoamericana de Ecodesarrollo, Mexicali *08266*
Asociación Latinoamericana de Educación Radiofónica, Quito *03236*
Asociacion Latinoamericana de Escuelas de Cirurgía Dental, Guatemala City *06265*
Asociación Latinoamericana de Escuelas de Trabajo Social, Saõ Luís *01389*
Asociación Latinoamericana de Escuelas y Facultades de Enfermería, Quito *03237*
Asociación Latinoamericana de Micología, La Habana *02879*
Asociación Latinoamericana de Paleobotánica y Palinología, Porto Alegre *01390*
Asociación Latinoamericana de Sociología, México *08267*
Asociación Latinoamericana para la Producción Animal, Porto Alegre *01391*
Asociación Médica Argentina, Buenos Aires *00057*
Asociación Médica de Santiago, Santiago de los Caballeros *03225*
Asociación Médica del Hospital Beistegui, México *08268*
Asociación Médica Dominicana, Santo Domingo *03226*
Asociación Médica Franco-Mexicana, México *08269*
Asociación Médica Peruana Daniel A. Carrión, Lima *08984*
Asociación Mexicana de Administración Científica, México *08270*
Asociación Mexicana de Bibliotecarios, AC, México *08271*
Asociación Mexicana de Facultades y Escuelas de Medicina, San Luis de Potosí *08272*
Asociación Mexicana de Géologos Petroleros, México *08273*
Asociación Mexicana de Ginecologia y Obstetricia, México *08274*
Asociación Mexicana de Profesores de Microbiología y Parasitología en Escuelas de Medicina, Guadalajara *08275*
Asociación Musical Manuel M. Ponce, México *08276*
Asociación Nacional de Escritores Venezolanos, Caracas *16877*
Asociación Nacional de Escritores y Artistas, Lima *08985*
Asociación Nacional de Químicos de España, Madrid *09736*
Asociación Nacional de Universidades e Institutos de Educación Superior, México *08277*
Asociación Nicaragüense de Bibliotecarios y Profesionales afines, Managua *08748*
Asociación Odontológica Argentina, Buenos Aires *00058*
Asociación Ondontológica Uruguaya, Montevideo *12612*
Asociación Paleontológica Argentina, Buenos Aires *00059*
Asociación Panameña de Bibliotecarios, Panamá City *08942*
Asociación Panamericana de Cirurgía Pediátrica, México *08278*
Asociación Panamericana de Oftalmología, Panamá City *08943*
Asociación para la Lucha contra la Parálisis Infantil, Buenos Aires *00060*
Asociación Pediátrica de Guatemala, Guatemala City *06266*
Asociación Peruana de Archiveros, Lima *08986*
Asociación Peruana de Astronomía, Lima *08987*
Asociación Peruana de Bibliotecarios, Lima *08988*
Asociación Plástica Latina Internacional de Chile, Santiago *02455*
Asociación Psiquiátrica de la América Latina, Caracas *16878*
Asociación Química Argentina, Buenos Aires *00061*
Asociación Rural del Uruguay, Montevideo *12613*

321 Alphabetical Index: Association

Association Française pour l'Etude du Sol, Ardon 03559
Association Française pour l'Information en Economie Ménagère, Paris 03560
Association Francophone de Spectrométrie des Masses Solides, Lannion 03561
Association Francophone d'Education Comparée, Sèvres 03562
Association Francophone Internationale des Directeurs d'Etablissements Scolaires, Montréal 01699
Association Francophone Internationale des Groupes d'Animation de la Paraplégie, Coubert 03563
Association Générale des Conservateurs des Collections Publiques de France, Paris 03564
Association Générale des Hygiénistes et Techniciens Municipaux, Paris 03565
Association Générale des Médecins de France, Paris 03566
Association Géologique du Canada, Saint John's 02116
Association Guillaume Budé, Paris 03567
Association Henri Capitant, Baton Rouge 13706
Association Historique Internationale de l'Océan Indien, Sainte-Clotilde 09263
Association in Scotland to Research into Astronautics, Wishaw 10837
Association Internationale de Cybernétique, Namur 00964
Association Internationale de Droit Economique, Louvain-la-Neuve 00965
Association Internationale de Droit Pénal, Pau 03568
Association Internationale de la Securité Sociale, Genève 10041
Association Internationale de l'Inspection du Travail, Paris 03569
Association Internationale de Littérature Comparée, Paris 03570
Association Internationale de Médecine et de Biologie de l'Environnement, Paris 03571
Association Internationale de Pédiatrie, Paris 03572
Association Internationale de Psychologie du Travail de Langue Française, Motn Saint-Aignan 03573
Association Internationale de Recherche en Informatique Toxicologique, Paris 03574
Association Internationale d'Epigraphie Grecque et Latine, Paris 03575
Association Internationale des Amis de Vasile Stanciu, Paris 03576
Association Internationale des Archives Francophones, Tunis 10682
Association Internationale des Arts Plastiques, Paris 03577
Association Internationale des Critiques de Théâtre, Paris 03578
Association Internationale des Critiques Littéraires, Paris 03579
Association Internationale des Démographes de Langue Française, Paris 03580
Association Internationale des Directeurs d'Ecoles Hôtelières, Lausanne 10042
Association Internationale des Docteurs en Economie du Tourisme, Aix-en-Provence 03581
Association Internationale des Ecoles des Sciences de l'Information, Paris 03582
Association Internationale des Ecoles Supérieures d'Education Physique, Liège 00966
Association Internationale des Educateurs de Jeunes Inadaptés, Pau 03583
Association Internationale des Etudes Arméniennes, Jerusalem 06680
Association Internationale des Etudes Coptes, Louvain-la-Neuve 00967
Association Internationale des Etudes de l'Asie du Sud-Est, Paris 03584
Association Internationale des Etudes Françaises, Paris 03585
Association Internationale des Juristes Démocrates, Bruxelles 00968
Association Internationale des Laboratoires Textiles Lainiers, Bruxelles 00969
Association Internationale des Mathématiques et Calculateurs en Simulation, Liège 00970
Association Internationale des Métiers et Enseignements d'Art, Bruxelles 00971
Association Internationale des Ponts et Charpentes (AIPC), Zürich 10186
Association Internationale des Professeurs de Philosophie, Minden 04506
Association Internationale des Professeurs et Maîtres de Conférences des Universités, Nancy 03586
Association Internationale des Sciences Juridiques, Paris 03587
Association Internationale des Sociologues de Langue Française, Toulouse 03588
Association Internationale des Statisticiens d'Enquêtes, Paris 03589
Association Internationale des Techniciens Biologistes de Langue Française, Le Perreux 03590
Association Internationale des Travaux en Souterrain, Bron 03591
Association Internationale d'Essais de Semences, Zürich 10189
Association Internationale d'Etudes Occitanes, Wien 08397
Association Internationale d'Histoire Economique, Paris 03592
Association Internationale d'Information Scolaire, Universitaire et Professionnelle, Paris 03593
Association Internationale d'Irradiation Industrielle, Charbonnières-les-Bains 03594
Association Internationale d'Océanographie Médicale, Nice 03595
Association Internationale Données pour le Développement, Marseille 03596
Association Internationale du Théâtre pour l'Enfance et la Jeunesse, Wien 00419
Association Internationale Francophone de Recherche Odontologique, Rennes 03597
Association Internationale pour la Coopération et le Développement en Afrique Australe, Winksele 00972
Association Internationale pour la Protection de la Propriété Industrielle, Zürich 10187
Association Internationale pour le Développement de l'Odonto-Stomatologie Tropicale, Bordeaux 03598
Association Internationale pour le Développement des Gommes Naturelles, Neuilly-sur-Seine 03599
Association Internationale pour le Développement des Universités Internationales et Mondiales, Aulnay-sous-Bois 03600
Association Internationale pour le Management du Sport, Saint-Michel 03601
Association Internationale pour le Progrès Social, Bruxelles 00973
Association Internationale pour l'Etude de la Paléontologie Humaine, Paris 03602
Association Internationale pour l'Histoire Contemporaine de l'Europe, Genève 10043
Association Internationale pour l'Histoire du Verre, Lochem 08398
Association Internationale pour l'Utilisation des Langues Régionales à l'Ecole, Liège 00974
Association Interprofessionnelle de France, Seclin 03603
Association Interprofessionnelle des Centres Médicaux et Sociaux de la Région Parisienne, Paris 03604
Association Interprofessionnelle pour la Formation Permanente dans le Commerce Textile, Paris 03605
Association Laïque pour l'Education et la Formation Professionnelle des Adolescents en Europe, Bruxelles 00975
Association Les Amis de Gustave Courbet, Ornans 03606
Association Libanaise des Sciences Juridiques, Beirut 08152
Association Linguistique Franco-Européenne, Paris 03607
Association Littéraire et Artistique Internationale, Paris 03608
Association Lyonnaise de Criminologie et Anthropologie Sociale, Lyon 03609
Association Maghrébine des Etudes de la Population, Tunis 10683
Association Marc Bloch, Paris 03610
Association Maria Montessori, Paris 03611
Association Mathématique du Québec, Montréal 01700
Association Mauritanienne des Bibliothécaires, Archivistes et Documentalistes, Nouakchott 08253
Association Médicale Canadienne, Ottawa 01925
Association Médicale du Québec, Montréal 01701
Association Médicale Européenne, Bruxelles 00976
Association Médico-Sociale Protestante de Langue Française, Alfortville 03612
Association Mondiale des Sciences de l'Education, Gent 00977
Association Mondiale des Vétérinaires Microbiologistes, Immunologistes et Spécialistes des Maladies Infectieuses, Maisons Alfort 03613
Association Monégasque de Préhistoire, Monaco 08372
Association Montessori Internationale, Amsterdam 08399
Association Museums New Brunswick, Fredericton 01702
Association Nationale d'Art Photographique, Clearbrook 02218
Association Nationale de la Recherche Technique, Paris 03614
Association Nationale des Bibliothécaires, Paris 03615
Association Nationale des Cours Professionnels pour les Préparateurs en Pharmacie, Paris 03616
Association Nationale des Docteurs en Droit, Paris 03617
Association Nationale des Educateurs de Jeunes Inadaptés, Paris 03618
Association Nationale des Géographes Marocains, Rabat 08380
Association Nationale des Informatistes, Rabat 08381
Association Nationale des Professeurs en Economie Sociale et Familiale, Paris 03619
Association Nationale pour la Formation et la Promotion Professionnelle dans l'Industrie et le Commerce de la Chaussure et des Cuirs et Peaux, Paris 03620
Association Nationale pour la Protection contre l'Incendie et l'Intrusion, Louvain-La-Neuve 00978
Association Nationale pour la Protection des Eaux, Paris 03621
Association Nationale pour la Protection des Villes d'Art, Paris 03622
Association Nationale pour la Réhabilitation Professionelle par le Travail Protégé, Paris 03623
Association Nationale pour l'Etude de la Neige et des Avalanches, Grenoble 03624
Association Nucléaire Canadienne, Toronto 01932
Association Oecuménique des Théologiens Africains, Yaoundé 01607
Association of Academic Agronomists, Helsinki 03339
Association of Academic Health Centers, Washington 13707
Association of Academic Health Sciences Library Directors, Houston 13708
Association of Academic Physiatrists, Indianapolis 13709
Association of Advanced Rabbinical and Talmudic Schools, New York 13710
Association of Advisers in Design and Technical Studies, Camberley 10838
Association of Advisers on Education in International Religious Congregations, Roma 06892
Association of African Geological Surveys, Orléans 03625
Association of African Maritime Training Institutes, Alexandria 03267
Association of African Studies Programs, New York 13711
Association of African Universities, Accra 06192
Association of African Women for Research and Development, Dakar 09509
Association of Agricultural Education Staffs, Mogerhanger 10839
Association of Agricultural Research Institutions in the Near East and North Africa, Cairo 03268
Association of Air Medical Services, Pasadena 13712
Association of all Medical Faculties in the Federal Republic of Germany, Erlangen 05750
Association of Amazonian Universities, Belém 01423
Association of American Colleges and Universities, Washington 13713
Association of American Geographers, Washington 13714
Association of American Indian Physicians, Oklahoma City 13715
Association of American Jurists, Berkeley 13716
Association of American Law Schools, Washington 13717
Association of American Medical Colleges, Washington 13718
Association of American Physicians, Indianapolis 13719
Association of American Physicians and Surgeons, Tucson 13720
Association of American Schools in Central America, Colombian-Caribbean and Mexico (Tri-Association), Miami 13721
Association of American Schools in South America, Miami 13722
Association of American Seed Control Officials, Annapolis 13723
Association of American State Geologists, Moscow 13724
Association of American Universities, Washington 13725
Association of American Veterinary Medical Colleges, Washington 13726
Association of Anaesthetists of Great Britain and Ireland, London 10840
Association of Analytical Chemists, Detroit 13727
Association of Ancient Historians, Seattle 13728
The Association of Applied Biologists, Warwick 10841
Association of Applied Insect Ecologists, Sacramento 13729
Association of Arab-American University Graduates, Washington 13730
Association of Arab Geologists, Baghdad 06576
Association of Arab Institutes and Centres for Economic and Social Research, Tunis 10684
Association of Arab Universities, Amman 08053
Association of Art Historians in Poland, Warszawa 09148
Association of Art Institutions, Hereford 10842
Association of Arts Centres in Scotland, Aberdeen 10843
Association of Asphalt Paving Technologists, Saint Paul 13731
Association of Australasian and Pacific Area Police Medical Officers, Melbourne 00132
Association of Avian Veterinarians, Boca Raton 13732
Association of Avian Veterinarias, Boca Raton 13733
Association of Aviation Psychologists, Moffett Field 13734
Association of Balloon and Airship Constructors, San Diego 13735
Association of Basic Science Teachers in Dentistry, Glasgow 10844
Association of Beauty Teachers, Southampton 10845
Association of Belgian Actuaries, Leuven 00979
Association of Biological Collections Appraisers, Carmel 13736
Association of Biomedical Communication Directors, Tucson 13737
Association of Black Anthropologists, Arlington 13738
Association of Black Psychologists, Washington 13739
Association of Black Sociologists, Mount Pleasant 13740
Association of Black Women in Higher Education, Albany 13741
Association of Blind and Partially-Sights Teachers and Students, London 10846
Association of Bone and Joint Surgeons, Rosemont 13742
Association of British Climatologists, London 10847
Association of British Columbia Teachers of English as an Additional Language, Burnaby 01703
Association of British Correspondence Colleges, London 10848
Association of British Dispensing Opticians, London 10849
Association of British Forensic Specialists, Moseley 10850
Association of British Geodesists, Dagenham 10851
Association of British Neurologists, London 10852
Association of British Paediatric Nurses, London 10853
Association of British Science Writers, London 10854
Association of British Spectroscopists, Kent 10855
Association of British Theological and Philosophical Libraries, Cambridge 10856
The Association of Building Engineers, Northampton 10857
Association of Business Officers of Preparatory Schools, Windsor 13743
Association of Canadian Archivists, Ottawa 01704
Association of Canadian Bible Colleges, Three Hills 01705
Association of Canadian College and University Teachers of English, Halifax 01706
Association of Canadian Community Colleges, Ottawa 01707
Association of Canadian Faculties of Dentistry, Ottawa 01708
Association of Canadian Map Libraries and Archives, Ottawa 01709
Association of Canadian Medical Colleges, Ottawa 01710
Association of Canadian Universities for Northern Studies, Ottawa 01711
Association of Canadian University Planning Programs, Winnipeg 01712
Association of Caribbean Economists, Kingston 07687
Association of Caribbean Studies, Lexington 13744
Association of Catholic Colleges and Universities, Washington 13745
Association of Catholic Diocesan Archivists, Chicago 13746
Association of Cereal Research, Detmold 04459
Association of Chairmen of Departments of Mechanics, Ithaca 13747
Association of Chartered Engineers in Iceland, Reykjavik 06386
Association of Chief Architects of Scottish Local Authorities, Lanark 10858
Association of Child Education of the Republic of China, Taipei 02672
Association of Child Psychotherapists, London 10859
Association of Chiropractic Colleges, San Lorenzo 13748
Association of Christian Librarians, Cedarville 13749
The Association of Clinical Biochemists, London 10860
Association of Clinical Pathologists, Hove 10861
Association of Clinical Scientists, Farmington 13750
Association of College and Research Libraries, Chicago 13751
Association of College and University Telecommunications Administrators, Lexington 13752
Association of College Unions – International, Bloomington 13753
Association of Colleges for Further and Higher Education, Swindon 10862
Association of Collegiate Schools of Architecture, Washington 13754
Association of Collegiate Schools of Planning, New York 13755
Association of Commonwealth Archivists and Records Managers, London 10863
Association of Commonwealth Teachers, London 10864
Association of Commonwealth Universities, London 10865
Association of Community Cancer Centers, Rockville 13756
Association of Community College Trustees, Washington 13757
Association of Community Health Councils for England and Wales, London 10866
Association of Community Tribal Schools, Sisseton 13758
Association of Concern for Ultimate Reality and Meaning, Toronto 01713
Association of Consulting Actuaries, London 10867
Association of Consulting Chemists and Chemical Engineers, New York 13759
Association of Continuing Legal Education Administrators, Austin 13760
Association of County Public Health Officers, Malmesbury 10868
Association of Crematorium Medical Referees, Westcliff-on-Sea 10869
The Association of Danish Biologists, Birkerød 03116
Association of Danish Graduates in Forestry, Klampenborg 03089
Association of Danish Graduates in Landscape Architecture, Klampenborg 03158
Association of Danish Music Libraries, København 03036
Association of Danish Pharmacists, København 02998
Association of Danish Physiotherapists, København 03090
Association of Deans of Pharmacy of Canada, Montréal 01714
Association of Deans of Southeast Asian Graduate Schools of Management, Makati City 09041
Association of Defense Trial Attorneys, Peoria 13761
Association of Dental Hospitals of Great Britain and Northern Ireland, Birmingham 10870
Association of Departments of English, New York 13762
Association of Departments of Foreign Languages, New York 13763
Association of Development Research and Training Institutes of Asia and the Pacific, Kuala Lumpur 08221
Association of Directors of Education in Scotland, Dundee 10871
Association of Directors of Journalism Programs in Canadian Universities, Ottawa 01715
Association of Directors of Social Services, Stockport 10872
Association of Directors of Social Work, Melrose 10873
Association of Disabled Professionals, Horbury 10874
Association of District Medical Officers, Bath 10875
Association of Earth Science Editors, Morgantown 13764
Association of Economic Jurisprudence, Tokyo 07754
Association of Economic Scientific Institutions, Moskva 09331
Association of Educational Psychologists, Durham 10876
Association of Educators of Gifted, Talented and Creative Children, Vancouver 01716
Association of Energy Engineers, Atlanta 13765
Association of Engineering Geologists, Sudbury 13766
Association of Engineers, Lisboa 09201
Association of Engineers and Architects in Israel, Tel Aviv 06681
Association of Engineers and Technicians of Slovenia, Ljubljana 09584
Association of Environmental Engineering Professors, Champaign 13767
Association of Episcopal Colleges, New York 13768
Association of European Cancer Leagues, København 02967

Alphabetical Index: Association 322

Association of European Conjuncture Institutes, Louvain-la-Neuve *00954*
Association of European Federations of Agro-Engineers, Bad Honnef *04507*
Association of European Geological Societies, Essen *04508*
Association of European Latin Americanist Historians, Liverpool *10877*
Association of European Open Air Museums, Chichester *10878*
Association of European Operational Research Societies, Bologna *06893*
Association of European Paediatric Cardiologists, Nijmegen *08400*
Association of European Psychiatrists, Luxembourg *08169*
Association of European Schools and Colleges of Optometry, Bures-sur-Yvette *03626*
Association of European Universities, Genève *10044*
Association of Exploration Geochemists, Denver *13769*
Association of Exploration Geochemists, Nepean *01717*
Association of Faculties of Pharmacy of Canada, Sakatoon *01718*
Association of Faculties of Science in African Universities, Nairobi *08077*
Association of Federal Communications Consulting Engineers, Washington *13770*
Association of Field Ornithologists, South Natick *13771*
Association of Finnish Authors, Helsinki *03413*
Association of Finnish Chemical Societies, Helsinki *03411*
Association of Firearm and Tool Mark Examiners, La Jolla *13772*
Association of Folklorists of Macedonia, Skopje *08206*
Association of Food and Drug Officials, York *13773*
Association of Forensic Document Examiners, Minneapolis *13774*
Association of French-Speaking Planetariums, Strasbourg *03627*
Association of French Teachers in Africa, Khartoum *09843*
Association of Genealogists and Record Agents, Horsham *10879*
Association of General Practitioner Hospitals, Lichfield *10880*
Association of Geoscientists for International Development, Bangkok *10634*
Association of German Engineers, Düsseldorf *06080*
Association of Governing Bodies of Girls Public Schools, Petersfield *10881*
Association of Governing Bodies of Public Schools (Boys), Petersfield *10882*
Association of Graduate Liberal Studies Programs, Durham *13775*
Association of Graduate Schools in Association of American Universities, Washington *13776*
Association of Greek Chemists, Athinai *06231*
Association of Hairdressing Teachers in Colleges of Further Education, Balby *10883*
Association of Head and Neck Oncologists of Great Britain, London *10884*
Association of Heads of Independent Schools, Windor *10885*
Association of Health Care Information and Medical Records Officers, Hopton *10886*
Association of Health Service Treasurers, Warwick *10887*
Association of Higher Education Libraries in French-Speaking West Africa, Dakar *09505*
Association of Hispanists of Great Britain and Ireland, London *10888*
Association of Historic Councils and Regional History Institutes, Marburg *04462*
Association of Hungarian Librarians, Budapest *06324*
Association of Icelandic Visual Artists, Reykjavik *06365*
Association of Independent Libraries, Birmingham *10889*
Association of Independent Research and Technology Organisations, Cambridge *10890*
Association of Indian Universities, New Delhi *06407*
Association of Information and Dissemination Centers, Athens *13777*
Association of Institute and School of Education In-Service Tutors, Durham *10891*
Association of Institutes of European Studies, Genève *10035*
Association of Internal Management Consultants, East Bloomfield *13778*
Association of International Accountants, Gateshead *10892*
Association of International Colleges and Universities, Independence *13779*
Association of International Consultants on Human Rights, Genève *10045*
Association of International Development of Natural Gums, Neuilly-sur-Seine *03599*
Association of International Education, Tokyo *07820*
Association of International Education Administrators, Tuscaloosa *13780*
Association of International Health Researchers, Mobile *13781*
Association of International Industrial Irradiation, Charbonnières-les-Bains *03594*
Association of International Law, Moskva *09332*
Association of International Law, Tokyo *07762*
Association of International Libraries, Genève *10033*
Association of International Schools in Africa, Nairobi *08078*
Association of Irish Jurists, Dublin *06586*
Association of Iron and Steel Engineers, Pittsburgh *13782*
Association of Jesuit Colleges and Universities, Washington *13783*
Association of Jewish Genealogical Societies, Palo Alto *13784*
Association of Jewish Libraries, New York *13785*
Association of Jurists of Serbia, Beograd *16983*
Association of Laban Movement Analysts, New York *13786*
Association of Latin American and Caribbean Economists, Bronx *13787*
Association of Latin American Lawyers for the Defense of Human Rights, São Paulo *01424*
The Association of Law Teachers, Leicester *10893*
Association of Lecturers in Accountancy, Edinburgh *10894*
Association of Lecturers in Colleges of Education in Scotland, Beech Grove *10895*
Association of Legal Administrators, Vernon Hills *13788*
Association of Life Insurance Counsel, Fort Wayne *13789*
Association of Life Insurance Medicine of Japan, Tokyo *07795*
Association of London Chief Librarians, Barking *10896*
Association of Lutheran Secondary Schools, Denver *13790*
Association of Maize Researchers in Africa, Dakar *09510*
Association of Management, Grafton *13791*
Association of Management Training Institutions of Eastern and Southern Africa, Arusha *10592*
Association of Manitoba Museums, Winnipeg *01719*
Association of Manufacturing Chemists, London *10897*
Association of Marine Engineering Schools, Liverpool *10898*
Association of Maternal and Child Health Programs, Washington *13792*
Association of Mathematicians, Physicists and Astronomers of Slovenia, Ljubljana *09585*
Association of Meat Inspectors, Barnet *10899*
Association of Medical Advisers to the Pharmaceutical Industry, London *10900*
Association of Medical Doctors of Asia, Okayama *07714*
Association of Medical Education and Research in Substance Abuse, Providence *13793*
Association of Medical Physicists of India, Mumbai *06408*
Association of Medical School Pediatric Department Chairmen, Chapel Hill *13794*
Association of Medical Schools in Africa, Lusaka *17048*
Association of Mental Health Administrators, Northbrook *13795*
Association of Mercy Colleges, Pittsburgh *13796*
Association of Microbiologists of India, New Delhi *06409*
Association of Military Colleges and Schools of the United States, Alexandria *13797*
Association of Military Surgeons of the U.S., Bethesda *13798*
Association of Minicomputers Users, Franklin *13799*
Association of Minority Health Professions Schools, Washington *13800*
Association of Municipal Engineers, London *10901*
Association of Muslim Scientists and Engineers, Plainfield *13801*
Association of Muslim Social Scientists, Herndon *13802*
Association of National European and Mediterranean Societies of Gastroenterology, London *10902*
Association of National Park Officers, Kendal *10903*
Association of Naval R.O.T.C. Colleges and Universities, Rochester *13803*
Association of Noise Consultants, Guilden Morden *10904*
Association of Nordic Paper Historians, Stockholm *09856*
Association of North American Operations Research Societies within IFORS, Linthicum *13804*
Association of Northumberland Local History Societies, Newcastle-upon-Tyne *10905*
The Association of Norwegian Visual Artists, Oslo *08851*
The Association of Obstetrics and Gynecology of the Republic of China, Taipei *02673*
Association of Occupational Therapists of Manitoba, Winnipeg *01720*
Association of Official Architects, London *10906*
Association of Official Racing Chemists, Portland *13805*
Association of Official Seed Analysts, Lincoln *13806*
Association of Old Crows, Alexandria *13807*
Association of Optometric Educators, Tahlequah *13808*
Association of Orientalists, Moskva *09333*
Association of Orthodox Jewish Scientists, New York *13809*
Association of Orthodox Jewish Teachers, Brooklyn *13810*
Association of Osteopathic State Executive Directors, Sacramento *13811*
Association of Pacific Systematists, Fort Worth *13812*
Association of Paediatric Education in Europe, Lisboa *09189*
Association of Painting Craft Teachers, Saint Leonards-on-Sea *10907*
Association of Parliamentary Librarians in Canada, Ottawa *01721*
Association of Pathology Chairs, Bethesda *13813*
Association of Pediatric Societies of the Southeast Asian Region, Manila *09042*
Association of Pharmacists of Serbia, Beograd *16984*
Association of Philippine Physicians in America, Burbank *13814*
Association of Physician Assistant Programs, Alexandria *13815*
Association of Physician Assistants in Cardiovascular Surgery, Reston *13816*
Association of Police Surgeons, Harrogate *10908*
Association of Political Sciences, Moskva *09334*
Association of Presbyterian Colleges and Universities, Louisville *13817*
Association of Principals of Colleges, Broxborn *10909*
Association of Principals of Colleges (Northern Ireland Branch), Lisburn *10910*
Association of Private Universities of Japan, Tokyo *07853*
Association of Professional Baseball Physicians, Edina *13818*
Association of Professional Genealogists, Washington *13819*
Association of Professional Material Handling Consultants, Charlotte *13820*
Association of Professional Schools of International Affairs, Washington *13821*
Association of Professional Scientists and Technologists, London *10911*
Association of Professors of Gynecology and Obstetrics, Washington *13822*
Association of Professors of Medicine, Washington *13823*
Association of Psychiatrists in Training, Edinburgh *10912*
Association of Psychologists of Nova Scotia, Halifax *01722*
Association of Public Analysts, London *10913*
Association of Recognised English Language Services, London *10914*
Association of Registrars of the Universities and Colleges of Canada, Lennoxville *01723*
Association of Religious in Education, London *10915*
Association of Religious Writers, Jerusalem *06682*
Association of Research Directors, King of Prussia *13824*
Association of Research Libraries, Washington *13825*
Association of Researchers in Medicine and Science, London *10916*
Association of Safety Council Executives, Gainesville *13826*
Association of School Business Officials International, Reston *13827*
Association of School Natural History Societies, Lancing *10917*
Association of Schools and Colleges of Optometry, Rockville *13828*
Association of Schools of Journalism and Mass Communication, Columbia *13829*
Association of Schools of Public Health, Washington *13830*
Association of Schools of Public Health in the European Region, Bristol *10918*
Association of Science Museum Directors, Chicago *13831*
Association of Science-Technology Centers, Washington *13832*
Association of Sciences and Art, Bitola *08187*
Association of Scientific, Technical and Managerial Staffs, London *10919*
Association of Secondary Teachers, Ireland, Dublin *06587*
Association of Show and Agricultural Organisations, Newark *10920*
Association of Sinologists, Moskva *09335*
Association of Slovak Mathematicians and Physicists, Bratislava *09546*
Association of Small Public Libraries of Ontario, Saint Marys *01724*
Association of Social and Behavioral Scientists, Washington *13833*
Association of Social Anthropologists of the Commonwealth, London *10921*
Association of Southeast Asian Institutions of Higher Learning, Bangkok *10635*
Association of Southeast Asian Marine Scientists, Bangkok *10636*
Association of Southern Baptist Colleges and Schools, Nashville *13834*
Association of Space Explorers, Washington *13835*
Association of Spanish Artists and Sculptors, Madrid *09734*
Association of Special Libraries of the Philippines, Manila *09043*
Association of Specialized and Cooperative Library Agencies, Chicago *13836*
Association of Sports Medicine of the Balkan, Nicosia *02896*
Association of State and Interstate Water Pollution Control Administrators, Washington *13837*
Association of State and Territorial Dental Directors, Minneapolis *13838*
Association of State and Territorial Directors of Public Health Education, Santa Fe *13839*
Association of State and Territorial Health Officials, Washington *13840*
Association of State Supervisors of Mathematics, Little Rock *13841*
Association of Surgeons of East Africa, Nairobi *08079*
Association of Surgeons of Great Britain and Ireland, London *10922*
Association of Surgeons of India, Madras *06410*
Association of Surgeons of South Africa, Johannesburg *09610*
Association of Surgical Technologists, Englewood *13842*
Association of Swimming Therapy, Shrewsbury *10923*
Association of Systematics Collections, Washington *13843*
Association of Teacher Educators, Reston *13844*
Association of Teachers of Japanese, Middlebury *13845*
Association of Teachers of Latin American Studies, Flushing *13846*
Association of Teachers of Management, London *10924*
Association of Teachers of Maternal and Child Health, Arlington *13847*
Association of Teachers of Mathematics, Derby *10925*
Association of Teachers of Preventive Medicine, Washington *13848*
Association of Teachers of Technical Writing, Orlando *13849*
Association of the Geographical Societies of Slovenia, Ljubljana *09601*
Association of the German Nobility in North America, Benicia *13850*
Association of the Health Occupations Teacher Educators, Louisville *13851*
Association of the Institute for Certification of Computer Professionals, Des Plaines *13852*
Association of the Mathematicians', Physicists' and Astronomers' Societies of Yugoslavia, Priština *16985*
Association of the Slovak Librarians and Information Workers, Bratislava *09582*
Association of Theological Institutes in the Middle East, Beirut *08153*
Association of Theological Institutions of Eastern Africa, Nairobi *08080*
Association of Theological Schools, Pittsburgh *13853*
Association of Third World Affairs, Washington *13854*
Association of Third World Studies, Americus *13855*
Association of Track and Field Statisticians, Salisbury *10926*
Association of Trial Lawyers of America, Washington *13856*
Association of Tutors, Cambridge *10927*
Association of Tutors in Adult Education, Nottingham *10928*
Association of United States Members of the International Institute of Space Law, Phoenix *13857*
Association of Universities and Colleges of Canada, Ottawa *01725*
Association of Universities for Research in Astronomy, Washington *13858*
Association of Universities of Bangladesh, Dhaka *00911*
Association of University Anesthesiologists, Seattle *13859*
Association of University Architects, Fort Myers *13860*
Association of University Forestry Schools of Canada, Sainte-Foy *01726*
Association of University of New Brunswick Teachers, Fredericton *01727*
Association of University Professors of Ophthalmology, San Francisco *13861*
Association of University Programs in Health Administration, Arlington *13862*
Association of University Radiation Protection Officers, Cardiff *10929*
Association of University Radiologists, Reston *13863*
Association of University Related Research Parks, Tempe *13864*
Association of University Summer Sessions, Bloomington *13865*
Association of University Teachers, London *10930*
Association of University Teachers in Accounting, Sheffield *10931*
Association of University Teachers (Scotland), Glasgow *10932*
Association of Veterinary Anaesthetists of Great Britain and Ireland, Bury Saint Edmunds *10933*
Association of Veterinary Teachers and Research Workers, Edinburgh *10934*
Association of Visual Science Librarians, Chicago *13866*
Association of Voluntary Aided Secondary Schools, Beckenham *10935*
Association of Waldorf Schools of North America, Fair Oaks *13867*
Association of Workers' Compensation Boards of Canada, Edmonton *01728*
Association of Young Irish Archaeologists, Belfast *10936*
Association of Youth Museums, Washington *13868*
Association of Yugoslav Universities, Beograd *17044*
Association Olympique Internationale pour la Recherche Médico-Sportive, Lausanne *10046*
Association on Boarding Schools, Washington *13869*
Association on Marginal Literature and Art, Leuven *01182*
Association Paritaire de Prévention pour la Santé et la Securité du Travail, Anjou *01729*
Association Pharmaceutique Canadienne, Ottawa *01945*
Association Philotechnique, Paris *03628*
Association pour la Fondation Internationale du Cinéma et de la Communication Audiovisuelle, Paris *03629*
Association pour la Formation aux Professions Immobilières, Paris *03630*
Association pour la Formation des Cadres de l'Industrie et du Commerce, Paris *03631*
Association pour la Formation Professionnelle dans les Industries Céréalières, Paris *03632*
Association pour la Formation Professionnelle dans les Industries de l'Ameublement, Paris *03633*
Association pour la Médiathèque Public, Cambrai *03634*
Association pour la Prévention de la Pollution Atmosphérique, Paris *03635*
Association pour la Promotion de la Pédagogie Nouvelle, Paris *03636*
Association pour la Promotion des Publications Scientifiques, Bruxelles *00980*
Association pour la Recherche dans l'Industrie Sidérurgique Canadienne, Ottawa *02012*
Association pour la Recherche et le Développement en Informatique Chimique, Paris *03637*
Association pour la Recherche Interculturelle, Saint-Denis *03638*
Association pour la Rééducation de la Parole et du Langage Oral et Ecrit et de la Voix, Paris *03639*
Association pour l'Avancement des Sciences et des Techniques de la Documentation, Montréal *01730*
Association pour le Développement de la Formation Professionnelle Continue dans les Industries Lourdes du Bois, Paris *03640*
Association pour le Développement de la Formation Professionnelle dans les Transports, Paris *03641*
Association pour le Développement de la Recherche en Toxicologie Expérimentale, Paris *03642*
Association pour le Développement de la Stomatologie, Paris *03643*

323 Alphabetical Index: Ateneo

Association pour le Développement de la Traduction Automatique et de Linguistique Appliqué, Paris 03644
Association pour le Développement de l'Enseignement et des Recherches Scientifiques auprès des Universités de la Région Parisienne, Paris 03645
Association pour le Développement des Etudes Biologiques en Psychiatrie, Paris 03646
Association pour le Développement des Relations Médicales entre la France et les Pays Etrangers, Paris 03647
Association pour le Développement des Techniques de Transport, d'Environnement et de Circulation, Paris 03648
Association pour le Développement du Droit Mondial, Paris 03649
Association pour l'Education Permanente dans les Universités du Canada, Ottawa 01808
Association pour l'Enseignement de l'Assurance, Paris 03650
Association pour les Etudes et Recherches de Zoologie Appliquée et de Phytopathologie, Sint-Truiden 00981
Association pour les Etudes sur la Radio-Télévision Canadienne, Montréal 01697
Association pour l'Etude et l'Evaluation Epidémiologiques des Désastres dans les Pays en Voie de Développement, Bruxelles 00982
Association pour l'Etude Taxonomique de la Flore d'Afrique Tropicale, Rosières 00983
Association pour l'Innovation Scientifique, Paris 03651
Association Professionnelle Belge des Pédiatres, Bruxelles 00984
Association Professionnelle des Bibliothécaires et Documentalistes, Thy-le-Château 00985
Association Professionnelle des Gégraphes du Québec, Saint-Rédempteur-de-Lévis 01731
Association Provinciale des Enseignants Protestants du Québec, Kirkland 02330
Association Psychoanalytique de France, Paris 03652
Association Pulmonaire du Nouveau-Brunswick, Fredericton 02230
Association Pulmonaire du Québec, Montréal 01732
Association Québécoise des Archivistes Médicales, Rock-Forest 01733
Association Québécoise des Techniques de l'Eau, Montréal 01734
Association Régionale d'Education Permanente, Paris 03653
Association Régionale des Oeuvres Educatives et des Vacances de l'Education Nationale, Paris 03654
Association Régionale d'Informations Sociales, Paris 03655
Association Royale des Actuaires Belges, Bruxelles 00986
Association Royale des Demeures Historiques de Belgique, Bruxelles 00987
Association Scientifique des Médecins Acupuncteurs de France, Paris 03656
Association Scientifique et Technique pour l'Exploitation des Océans, Paris-La Défense 03657
Association Sénégalaise de Bibliothécaires, Archivistes et Documentalistes, Dakar 09511
Association Stomatologique Internationale, Paris 03658
Association Suisse de Droit Aérien et Spatial, Genève 10047
Association Suisse de Géographie, Basel 10530
Association Suisse de l'Arbitrage, ZZürich 10414
Association Suisse de Politique Sociale, Zürich 10415
Association Suisse des Ecoles Hôtelières, Glion-sur-Montreux 10048
Association Suisse des Ingénieurs Agronomes et des Ingénieurs en Technologie Alimentaire, Zollikofen 10465
Association Suisse des Médecins Assistants et Chefs de Clinique, Bern 10537
Association Suisse des Professeurs de Français, Kehrsatz 10049
Association Suisse pour l'Etude de l'Antiquité, Basel 10399
Association Technique de la Fonderie, Paris 03659
Association Technique de la Réfrigération et de l'Equipement Ménager, Paris 03660
Association Technique de la Sidérurgie Française, Paris la Défense 03661
Association Technique de l'Industrie du Gaz en France, Paris 03662
Association Technique de l'Industrie Papetière, Paris 03663
Association Technique Maritime et Aéronautique, Paris 03664
Association Technique pour l'Etude de la Gestion des Institutions Publiques et des Entreprises Privées, Paris 03665
Association to Advance Ethical Hypnosis, Cuyahoga Falls 13870
Association to Combat Huntington's Chorea, Hinckley 10937
Association Togolaise pour le Développement de la Documentation, des Bibliothèques, Archives et Musées, Lomé 10650
Association Tunisienne des Bibliothécaires, Documentalistes et Archivistes, Tunis 10685
Association Universitaire Canadienne d'Etudes Nordiques, Ottawa 01711
Association Universitaire pour le Développement de l'Enseignement et de la Culture en Afrique et à Madagascar, Paris 03666
Association Zaïroise des Archivistes, Bibliothécaires et Documentalistes, Kinshasa 02832
Associazione Alessandro Scarlatti, Napoli 06894
Associazione Anestesisti Rianimatori Ospedalieri Italiani, Napoli 06895
Associazione Archaeologica Romana, Roma 06896
Associazione Archeologica Allumiere Adolfo Klitsche de la Grange, Allumiere 06897
Associazione Archeologica Centumcellae, Civitavecchia 06898
Associazione Archeologica Romana, Roma 06899
Associazione Archivistica Ecclesiastica, Roma 06900
Associazione Astrofili Bolognesi, Bologna 06901
Associazione Bresciana di Ricerche Economiche, Brescia 06902
Associazione Campana degli Insegnanti di Scienze Naturali, Napoli 06903
Associazione Centri di Orientamento Scolastico Professionale e Sociale, Roma 06904
Associazione Criogenica Italiana, Genova 06905
Associazione degli Africanisti Italiani, Pavia 06906
Associazione degli Statistici, Udine 06907
Associazione dei Critici Letterari Italiani, Roma 06908
Associazione dei Geografi Italiani, Roma 06909
Associazione di Cultura Lao Silesu, Iglesias 06910
Associazione di Cultura Romana Te Roma Sequor, Roma 06911
Associazione di Ricerca e Interventi Psicosociali e Psicoterapeutici, Molinetto di Mazzano 06912
Associazione Educatrice Italiana, Roma 06913
Associazione Elettrotecnica ed Elettronica Italiana, Milano 06914
Associazione Forense Italiana, Roma 06915
Associazione Forestale Italiana, Roma 06916
Associazione Genetica Italiana, Padova 06917
Associazione Geo-Archeologica Italiana, Roma 06918
Associazione Geofisica Italiana, Roma 06919
Associazione Geotecnica Italiana, Roma 06920
Associazione Giacomo Boni per la Difesa dei Monumenti di Roma Antica, Roma 06921
Associazione Grafologica Italiana, Ancona 06922
Associazione Idrotecnica Italiana, Roma 06923
Associazione Internazionale Centro Studi di Storia e Documentazione delle Regioni, Reggio Emilia 06924
Associazione Internazionale di Archeologia Classica, Roma 06925
Associazione Internazionale di Diritto Nucleare, Roma 06926
Associazione Internazionale di Poesia, Roma 06927
Associazione Internazionale Giuristi Italia-USA, Roma 06928
Associazione Internazionale per lo Studio del Diritto Canonico, Roma 06929
Associazione Italiana Biblioteche, Roma 06930
Associazione Italiana Condizionamento dell'Aria, Riscaldamento e Refrigerazione, Milano 06931
Associazione Italiana degli Insegnanti di Geografia, Trieste 06932
Associazione Italiana degli Slavisti, Pisa 06933
Associazione Italiana dei Chimici del Cuoio, Torino 06934
Associazione Italiana dei Giuristi Europei, Roma 06935
Associazione Italiana di Aeronautica e Astronautica, Roma 06936
Associazione Italiana di Anestesia Odontostomatologica, Bologna 06937
Associazione Italiana di Anglistica, Pisa 06938
Associazione Italiana di Cardiostimolazione, Pisa 06939
Associazione Italiana di Cartografia, Napoli 06940
Associazione Italiana di Chimica Tessile e Coloristica, Milano 06941
Associazione Italiana di Cinematografia Scientifica, Roma 06942
Associazione Italiana di Cultura Classica, Firenze 06943
Associazione Italiana di Dietetica e Nutrizione Clinica, Roma 06944
Associazione Italiana di Diritto Marittimo, Roma 06945
Associazione Italiana di Documentazione e di Informazione, Roma 06946
Associazione Italiana di Fisica Sanitaria e di Protezione contro le Radiazioni, Torino 06947
Associazione Italiana di Genio Rurale, Padova 06948
Associazione Italiana di Immuno-Oncologia Clinico-Pratica, Mantova 06949
Associazione Italiana di Ingegneria Chimica, Milano 06950
Associazione Italiana di Ingegneria Medica e Biologica, Napoli 06951
Associazione Italiana di Medicina Aeronautica e Spaziale, Roma 06952
Associazione Italiana di Medicina dell'Assicurazione Vita, Roma 06953
Associazione Italiana di Metallurgia, Milano 06954
Associazione Italiana di Microbiologia Applicata, Milano 06955
Associazione Italiana di Oncologia Medica, Milano 06956
Associazione Italiana di Protezione contro le Radiazione, Bologna 06957
Associazione Italiana di Psicologia dello Sport, Ferrara 06958
Associazione Italiana di Radiobiologia Medica e Medicina Nucleare, Roma 06959
Associazione Italiana di Radiologia e Medicina Nucleare, Roma 06960
Associazione Italiana di Ricerca Operativa, Genova 06961
Associazione Italiana di Robotica, Cinisello Balsamo 06962
Associazione Italiana di Scienze Politiche e Sociali, Roma 06963
Associazione Italiana di Sociologia, Roma 06964
Associazione Italiana di Strumentisti, Milano 06965
Associazione Italiana di Studi Semiotici, Torino 06966
Associazione Italiana di Studio delle Relazioni Industriali, Roma 06967
Associazione Italiana di Tecnica Navale, Genova 06968
Associazione Italiana di Tecnologia Alimentare, Milano 06969
Associazione Italiana di Terapia Occupazionale, Roma 06970
Associazione Italiana Giuristi Democratici, Roma 06971
Associazione Italiana per gli Studi di Marketing, Milano 06972
Associazione Italiana per la Difesa degli Interessi di Diabetici, Roma 06973
Associazione Italiana per la Promozione degli Studi e delle Ricerche per l'Edifizia, Milano 06974
Associazione Italiana per la Psicologia Umanistica e Transpersonale, Roma 06975
Associazione Italiana per la Qualità, Milano 06976
Associazione Italiana per la Ricerca Industriale, Roma 06977
Associazione Italiana per la Ricerca nell'Impiego degli Elastomeri, Milano 06978
Associazione Italiana per l'Analisi delle Sollecitazioni, Trieste 06979
Associazione Italiana per le Ricerche di Storia del Cinema, Roma 06980
Associazione Italiana per L'Educazione Sanitaria, Perugia 06981
Associazione Italiana per l'Informatica et il Calcolo Automatico, Milano 06982
Associazione Italiana per lo Studio del Dolore, Firenze 06983
Associazione Italiana per lo Studio della Psicologia Analitica, Roma 06984
Associazione Italiana per lo Sviluppo Internazionale, Roma 06985
Associazione Italiana Santa Cecilia per la Musica Sacra, Roma 06986
Associazione Italiana Scientifica di Metapsichica, Milano 06987
Associazione Italiana Sclerosi Multipla, Roma 06988
Associazione Italiana Socioanalisi Individuale, Milano 06989
Associazione Italiana Studi Americanisti, Genova 06990
Associazione Italiana Tecnico-Economica del Cemento, Roma 06991
Associazione Italiana tra Foniatri e Logopedisti, Padova 06992
Associazione La Nostra Famiglia, Ponte Lambro 06993
Associazione Ligure per lo Studio e la Divulgazione dell'Astronomia e dell'Astronautica, Genova 07048
Associazione Medica Italiana di Idroclimatologia, Talassologia e Terapia Fisica, Roma 06994
Associazione Medica Italiana per lo Studio della Ipnosi, Milano 06995
Associazione Medici Dentisti Italiani, Roma 06996
Associazione Micologica ed Ecologica Romana, Roma 06997
Associazione Nazionale Archivistica Italiana, Roma 06998
Associazione Nazionale Assistenti Sociali, Roma 06999
Associazione Nazionale degli Urbanisti, Treviso 07000
Associazione Nazionale dei Musei Italiani, Roma 07001
Associazione Nazionale dei Periti Grafici a Base Psicologica, Milano 07002
Associazione Nazionale del Libero Pensiero Giordano Bruno, Roma-Prati 07003
Associazione Nazionale di Ingegneria Nucleare, Roma 07004
Associazione Nazionale di Ingegneria Sanitaria, Roma 07005
Associazione Nazionale di Meccanica, Milano 07006
Associazione Nazionale Disegno di Macchine, Palermo 07007
Associazione Nazionale Esercenti Teatri, Roma 07008
Associazione Nazionale Famiglie di Fanciulli e Adulti Subnormali, Roma 07009
Associazione Nazionale Filosofia Arti Scienze, Bologna 07010
Associazione Nazionale Industria Meccanica Varia ed Affine, Milano 07011
Associazione Nazionale Ingegneri ed Architetti Italiani, Roma 07012
Associazione Nazionale Ingegneri Minerari, Roma 07013
Associazione Nazionale Insegnanti di Disegno, Napoli 07014
Associazione Nazionale Italiana Esperti Scientifici del Turismo, Roma 07015
Associazione Nazionale Italiana per l'Automazione, Milano 07016
Associazione Nazionale per i Centri Storico-Artistici, Gubbio 07017
Associazione Nazionale per il Progresso della Scuola Italiana, Roma 07018
Associazione Nazionale per la Scuola Italiana, Roma 07019
Associazione Nazionale per lo Studio dei Problemi del Credito, Roma 07020
Associazione Nazionale Professori Universitari di Ruolo, Roma 07021
Associazione Otologica Ospedaliera Italiano, Roma 07022
Associazione Ottica Italiana, Firenze 07023
Associazione Pedagogica Italiana, Bologna 07024
Associazione per il Diabete Infantile e Giovanile, Roma 07025
Associazione per il Superamento delle Barriere Linguistiche in Europa, Verona 07245
Associazione per Imola Storico-Artistica, Imola 07026
Associazione per la Conservazione delle Tradizioni Popolari, Palermo 07027
Associazione per l'Agricoltura Biodinamica, Milano 07028
Associazione per le Previsioni Econometriche, Bologna 07029
Associazione per lo Studio del Problema Mondiale dei Rifugiati, Sezione Italiana, Roma 07030
Associazione per lo Sviluppo degli Studi di Banca e Borsa, Milano 07031
Associazione per lo Sviluppo delle Scienze Religiose in Italia, Bologna 07032
Associazione per lo Sviluppo dell'Istruzione e della Formazione Professionale, Roma 07033
Associazione per lo Sviluppo di Studi e Ricerche nell'Industria Tessile Laniera Oreste Rivetti, Biella 07034
Associazione Piemontese di Studi Filosofici, Biella 07035
Associazione Professionale Italiana Medici Oculisti, Roma 07036
Associazione Psicanalitica Italiana, Milano 07037
Associazione Romana di Entomologia, Roma 07038
Associazione Scientifica di Produzione Animale, Napoli 07039
Associazione Siciliana per le Lettere e le Arti, Palermo 07040
Associazione Sociologi Lucani, Lauria Inferiore 07041
Associazione Sole Italico, Sulmona 07042
Associazione Studi sull'Informazione, Milano 07043
Associazione Tecnica Italiana per la Cellulosa e la Carta, Milano 07044
Associazione Tecnica Italiana per la Cinematografia, Roma 07045
Associazione Teologica Italiana per lo Studio della Morale, Novara 07046
Associazione Termotecnica Italiana, Milano 07047
Associazione Urania, Genova 07048
Associção dos Arquitectos Portugueses, Lisboa 09190
(A.S.S.P.), Bucuresti 09266
ASSS, Cairo 03252
ASSSI, Saint Lucia 00246
ASSTC, Riyadh 09488
Assurance Medical Society, London 10938
ASSURBANISTI, Treviso 07000
AST, Englewood 13842
AST, Shrewsbury 10923
ASTA, Reston 13507
ASTA, Urbana 16010
A.S.T.A., Warradale 00228
ASTC, Washington 13832
ASTD, Alexandria 13418
ASTDD, Minneapolis 13838
ASTDPHE, Santa Fe 13839
ASTED, Montréal 01730
ASTEJ, Zürich 10468
A.St.G., Wien 00392
ASTHEOL-CENTRAL, Yaoundé 01606
ASTHEOL-WEST, Kinshasa 02831
Asthma and Allergy Foundation of America, Washington 13871
Asthma Society of Canada, Toronto 01735
ASTHO, Washington 13840
ASTI, Arlington 13663
ASTIN, Philadelphia 12689
ASTITT, New York 13414
ASTM, Philadelphia 13415
ASTMH, Northbrook 13496
ASTR, Providence 13416
ASTRA, Wishaw 10837
ASTRO, Reston 13417
Astro-Psychology Institute, San Francisco 13872
Astrologers' Guild of America, Brewster 13873
Astronautical Society of the Republic of China, Taipei 02674
Astronomical and Geodesical Society, Moskva 09336
Astronomical Association of Indonesia, Jakarta 06554
Astronomical Data Centre, Strasbourg 03667
Astronomical League, Rolling Meadows 13874
Astronomical Society of Australia, Sydney 00133
Astronomical Society of Bermuda, Hamilton 01327
Astronomical Society of Edinburgh, Edinburgh 10939
Astronomical Society of India, Hyderabad 06411
Astronomical Society of Japan, Tokyo 07860
Astronomical Society of Queensland, Boondall 00134
Astronomical Society of South Australia, Adelaide 00135
Astronomical Society of Southern Africa, Observatory 09611
Astronomical Society of Spain and America, Barcelona 09808
Astronomical Society of Tasmania, Hobart 00136
Astronomical Society of the Pacific, San Francisco 13875, 13876
Astronomical Society of the Republic of China, Taipei 02675
Astronomical Society of Victoria, Melbourne 00137
Astronomische Gesellschaft e.V., Jena 04509
ASTS, Johannesburg 09609
ASUE, Hamburg 04510
ASUE (Arbeitsgemeinschaft für sparsamen und umweltfreundlichen Energieverbrauch e.V.), Hamburg 04510
ASUG, Chicago 13500
ASV, Melbourne 00137
ASVI, Paramus 13419
ASVO, Stillwater 13497
ASZ, Chicago 13498
ATA, Portland 13519
ATA, Syosset 13513
ATAE, Nottingham 10928
ATAS, North Hollywood 12675
ATB, Baton Rouge 13697
ATC, Redwood City 13556
ATCA, Nashville 13514
ATCC, Rockville 13522
ATE, Reston 13844
ATEA, Wahpeton 13512
ATEC, Harrisburg 13899
ATEC, Paris 03648
ATEE, Bruxelles 00963
ATEGIPE, Paris 03665
Atelier, Alexandria 03269
ATENA, Genova 06968
Ateneo Científico, Literario y Artístico, Madrid 09738
Ateneo Científico, Literario y Artístico, Mahón 09739
Ateneo de Ciencias y Artes de Chiapas, Tuxtla Gutiérrez 08279

327 Alphabetical Index: Campaign

British Trolleybus Society, Reading *11206*
British Trust for Ornithology, Thetford *11207*
British Tunnelling Society, London *11208*
British Universities Association of Slavists, Reading *11209*
British Universities Film and Video Council, London *11210*
British Universities Industrial Relations Association, Manchester *11211*
British Urban and Regional Information System Association, Winchester *11212*
British Veterinary Association, London *11213*
British Veterinary Radiology Association, Hatfield *11214*
British Veterinary Zoological Society, London *11215*
British Vexillological Society, Beckenham *11216*
British Watercolour Society, Ilkley *11217*
British Wind Energy Association, Milton Keynes *11218*
British Wood Preserving and Damp-proofing Association, London *11219*
British Zeolite Association, London *11220*
Brittle Bone Society, Dundee *11221*
Broadcast Education Association, Washington *13947*
Broadcast Educators Association of Canada, Brantford *01761*
Broadcast Research Council of Canada, Toronto *01762*
Brodie Club, Belleville *01763*
The Brontë Society, Keighley *11222*
Brothers Waga Lomza Scientific Society, Lomza *09078*
Browning Institute, New York *13948*
Browning Society of London, London *11223*
BRPS, Buckingham *11155*
BRS, Madison *13910*
Bruce Law Association, Walkerton *01764*
Bruckner Society of America, Iowa City *13949*
Brüder Grimm-Gesellschaft e.V., Kassel *04603*
Brunel Society, Bristol *11224*
BS, Boston *13940*
BS, Newark *13958*
BSA, Durham *11201*
BSA, Iowa City *13949*
BSA, Llanfairfeuhan *10982*
BSA, New York *13916*
BSA, Nottingham *11189*
B.S.A., Reading *11191*
BSA, Riverside *13941*
BSA, Zürich *10055*
BSAC, Birmingham *11165*
BSACI, Manchester *11164*
BSALS, Reading *11163*
BSAVA, Cheltenham *11161*
B.S.B.C., London *11162*
B.S.B.I, London *10989*
BSC, London *11157*
BSC, Rochester *13922*
B.S.C.B., Cambridge *11166*
BSCC, Manchester *11167*
BSCC, New Maldon *11160*
B.S.D., Ashford *11192*
BSDB, Aberdeen *11168*
BSE, Essen *04672*
BSECS, Aberdeen *11169*
BSEM, London *11170*
BSES, London *11158*
BSF, Haverhill *11193*
BSFA, Daventry *11159*
B.S.G., London *11194*
B.S.H., London *11171*
BSH, London *11195*
BSHP, Edinburgh *11183*
BSHS, Faringdon *11184*
BSI, London *11202*
BSI, Norwood *13902*
BSMA, New York *13943*
BSMT, East Barnet *11173*
BSN, Sofia *01569*
BSPP, Cambridge *11175*
BSPS, Oxford *11185*
BSRA, Manchester *11176*
B.S.R.D., London *11177*
BSRIA, Bracknell *11227*
BSS, Dublin *06590*
B.S.S., Edinburgh *10988*
BSS, New York *13909*
BSSG, Dunstable *11199*
BSSO, London *11188*
BSSRS, London *11179*
BSSS, Aberdeen *11200*
BSUF, New York *13946*
BSUV, Charlottesville *13917*
bsw, Dresden *04593*
B.T.A., London *11203*
BTA, London *11205*
BTHG, Folkestone *10976*
BTI, London *11204*
BTI, Newton Centre *13939*
BTN, Bydgoszcz *09071*
BTO, Thetford *11207*
BTRA, Mumbai *06508*
BTS, Reading *11206*
BUAS, Kelso *10986*
BUAS, Reading *11209*
Buckinghamshire Archaeological Society, Aylesbury *11225*
Budapest Union for the International Recognition of the Deposit of Microorganisms for the Purposes of Patent Procedure, Genève *10053*
Buddhist Academy of Ceylon, Colombo *09829*
The Buddhist Society, London *11226*
Buffalo Bill Memorial Association, Cody *13950*
BUFVC, London *11210*
Building Centre, Hørsholm *02970*
Building Officials and Code Administrators International, Country Club Hills *13951*
Building Services Research and Information Association, Bracknell *11227*
BUIRA, Manchester *11211*
Bulgarian Academy of Sciences, Sofia *01546*
Bulgarian Association of Criminology, Sofia *01547*
Bulgarian Association of International Law, Sofia *01548*
Bulgarian Association of Penal Law, Sofia *01549*
Bulgarian Astronautical Society, Sofia *01550*
Bulgarian Biochemical and Biophysical Society, Sofia *01551*
Bulgarian Botanical Society, Sofia *01552*
Bulgarian Dermatological Society, Sofia *01553*
Bulgarian Geographical Society, Sofia *01554*
Bulgarian Geological Society, Sofia *01555*
The Bulgarian Gynecological and Obstetrical Society, Sofia *01556*
Bulgarian Historical Society, Sofia *01557*
Bulgarian Nutrition Society, Sofia *01558*
Bulgarian Philologists' Society, Sofia *01559*
Bulgarian Philosophical Society, Sofia *01560*
Bulgarian Psychological Association, Sofia *01561*
Bulgarian Scientific Pharmaceutical Association, Sofia *01562*
Bulgarian Society for Microbiology, Sofia *01563*
Bulgarian Society of Anaesthesiology and Resuscitation, Sofia *01564*
Bulgarian Society of Cardiology, Sofia *01565*
Bulgarian Society of Electroencephalography, Electromyography and Clinical Neurophysiology, Sofia *01566*
Bulgarian Society of Natural History, Sofia *01567*
Bulgarian Society of Neuroscience, Sofia *01568*
Bulgarian Society of Neurosurgery, Sofia *01569*
Bulgarian Society of Parasitology, Sofia *01570*
Bulgarian Society of Physiological Sciences, Sofia *01571*
Bulgarian Society of Sports Medicine and Kinesitherapy, Sofia *01572*
Bulgarian Sociological Society, Sofia *01573*
Bulgarian Soil Society, Sofia *01574*
Bulgarian Translators' Union, Sofia *01575*
Bulgarian Union of Public Libraries, Sofia *01576*
BUND, Bonn *04614*
Bund demokratischer Wissenschaftlerinnen und Wissenschaftler e.V., Marburg *04604*
Bund der Freien Waldorfschulen e.V., Stuttgart *04605*
Bund Deutscher Architekten, Bonn *04606*
Bund Deutscher Baumeister, Architekten und Ingenieure, Bonn *04607*
Bund Deutscher Kunsterzieher e.V., Hannover *04608*
Bund deutscher Volksbühnen e.V., Essen *04609*
Bund Freiheit der Wissenschaft e.V., Bonn *04610*
Bund für Deutsche Schrift und Sprache, Ahlhorn *04611*
Bund für freie und angewandte Kunst e.V., Darmstadt *04612*
Bund für Lebensmittelrecht und Lebensmittelkunde e.V., Bonn *04613*
Bund für Umwelt und Naturschutz Deutschland e.V., Bonn *04614*
Bund für Umwelt und Naturschutz Deutschland, Landesverband Hessen e.V., Mörfelden-Walldorf *04615*
Bund für vereinfachte rechtschreibung, Zürich *10054*
Bund katholischer Erzieher Deutschlands, Essen *04616*
Bund Naturschutz in Bayern e.V., Regensburg *04617*
Bund Schweizer Architekten, Zürich *10055*
Bund Technischer Experten e.V., Bremen *04618*
Bundes-Arbeitsgemeinschaft Akademischer Räte in der Bundesrepublik, München *04619*
Bundesärztekammer, Köln *04620*
Bundesakademie für musikalische Jugendbildung Trossingen, Trossingen *04621*
Bundesakademie für öffentliche Verwaltung, Bonn *04622*
Bundesarbeitsgemeinschaft der Musikinitiativen e.V., Hannover *04623*
Bundesarbeitsgemeinschaft der Träger psychiatrischer Krankenhäuser, Köln *04624*
Bundesarbeitsgemeinschaft Evangelischer Familien-Bildungsstätten e.V., Stein *04625*
Bundesarbeitsgemeinschaft für Darstellendes Spiel in der Schule e.V., Frankfurt/Main *04626*
Bundesarbeitsgemeinschaft für Rehabilitation, Frankfurt *04627*
Bundesarbeitsgemeinschaft katholischer Familienbildungsstätten, Düsseldorf *04628*
Bundesarbeitsgemeinschaft Schule-Wirtschaft, Köln *04629*
Bundesarbeitsgemeinschaft Spiel und Theater e.V., Hannover *04630*
Bundesarbeitsgemeinschaft von Familienbildung und Beratung e.V., Elmshorn *04631*
Bundesarbeitsgemeinschaft zur Förderung haltungsgefährdeter Kinder und Jugendlicher e.V., Mainz *04632*
Bundesarbeitskreis der Seminar- und Fachleiter e.V., Ubstadt-Weiher *04633*
Bundesarchitektenkammer, Bonn *04634*
Bundesausschuß Betriebswirtschaft, Eschborn *04635*
Bundesausschuß der Ärzte und Krankenkassen, Köln *04636*
Bundeselternvereinigung für anthroposophische Heilpädagogik und Sozialtherapie e.V., Echzell *04637*
Bundesfachgruppe Musikpädagogik e.V., Köln *04638*
Bundesgeschäftsstelle, Bonn *04641*
Bundeskammer der Tierärzte Österreichs, Wien *00425*
Bundestierärztekammer e.V., Bonn *04639*
Bundesverband beruflicher Naturschutz, Bonn *04640*
Bundesverband Bildender Künstlerinnen und Künstler, Bonn *04641*
Bundesverband der Apotheker im öffentlichen Dienst e.V., Alsbach *04642*
Bundesverband der beamteten Tierärzte, Lichtenfels *04643*
Bundesverband der Bibliotheken und Museen für Darstellende Künste e.V., München *04644*
Bundesverband der Diplom-Ingenieure Gartenbau und Landespflege e.V., Bonn *04645*
Bundesverband der freiberuflichen und unabhängigen Sachverständigen für das Kraftfahrzeugwesen e.V., Königswinter *04646*
Bundesverband der Friedrich-Bödecker-Kreise e.V., Mainz *04647*
Bundesverband der Jugendkunstschulen und Kulturpädagogischen Einrichtungen e.V., Unna *04648*
Bundesverband der Lebensmittelchemiker/innen im öffentlichen Dienst e.V., Moers *04649*
Bundesverband der Lehrkräfte der russischen Sprache e.V., Kaarst *04650*
Bundesverband der öffentlichen angestellten und vereidigten Chemiker e.V., Hamburg *04651*
Bundesverband der Pneumologen, Mülheim *04652*
Bundesverband der Vertrauens- und Rentenversicherungsärzte, Aurich *04653*
Bundesverband der Zahnärzte des öffentlichen Gesundheitsdienstes e.V., Berlin *04654*
Bundesverband Deutscher Ärzte für Mund-Kiefer-Gesichtschirurgie e.V., Hamburg *04655*
Bundesverband Deutscher Autoren e.V., Berlin *04656*
Bundesverband Deutscher Gesangspädagogen, Hannover *04657*
Bundesverband Deutscher Privatkrankenanstalten e.V., Bonn *04658*
Bundesverband Deutscher Privatschulen (VDP), Frankfurt am Main *04659*
Bundesverband Deutscher Verwaltungs- und Wirtschafts-Akademien e.V., Frankfurt/Main *04660*
Bundesverband evangelischer Einrichtungen und Dienste, Hannover *05198*
Bundesverband Evangelischer Erzieherinnen und Sozialpädagoginnen e.V., Kassel *04661*
Bundesverband Freier Theater e.V., Rastatt *04662*
Bundesverband für den Selbstschutz, Bonn *04663*
Bundesverband für Gesundheitsförderung, Bad Wörishofen *05670*
Bundesverband für Tanztherapie Deutschland e.V., Monheim *04664*
Bundesverband Hilfe für das autistische Kind e.V., Hamburg *04665*
Bundesverband junger Autoren und Autorinnen e.V., Meckenheim *04666*
Bundesverband Katholischer Ingenieure und Wirtschaftler Deutschlands, Bonn *04667*
Bundesverband Legasthenie e.V., Hannover *04668*
Bundesverband Museumspädagogik e.V., Hannover *04669*
Bundesverband Neue Erziehung e.V., Bonn *04670*
Bundesverband Rhythmische Erziehung e.V., Remscheid *04671*
Bundesverband Solarenergie e.V., Essen *04672*
Bundesverband Theaterpädagogik e.V., Köln *04673*
Bundesverband unabhängiger deutscher Sicherheitsberater und -Ingenieure e.V., Berlin *04674*
Bundesverband wissenschaftlicher Vogelschutz e.V., Kiel *04675*
Bundesverein der Bibliotheks-Assistenten/innen und anderer Mitarbeiter/innen an Bibliotheken e.V., Offenbach *04676*
Bundesvereinigung der Oberstudiendirektoren, Bundes-Direktoren-Konferenz, Gundelfingen *04677*
Bundesvereinigung Deutscher Bibliotheksverbände e.V., Hamburg *04678*
Bundesvereinigung Deutscher Blas- und Volksmusikverbände e.V., Stuttgart *04679*
Bundesvereinigung für Gesundheit e.V., Bonn *04680*
Bundesvereinigung Kulturelle Jugendbildung e.V., Remscheid *04681*
Bundesvereinigung Lebenshilfe für geistig Behinderte e.V., Marburg *04682*
Bundesvereinigung Logistik e.V., Bremen *04683*
Bundeszahnärztekammer, Köln *04684*
Bureau Canadien de l'Education Internationale, Ottawa *01839*
Bureau Canadien de Soudage, Mississauga *02024*
Bureau Canadien pour l'Avancement de Musique, Toronto *01840*
Bureau Européen des Langues moins Répandues, Bruxelles *01112*
Bureau International d'Audiophonologie, Bruxelles *00999*
Bureau International de Documentation, Paris *03669*
Bureau International de la Paix, Genève *10056*
Bureau International de la Récupération et du Recyclage, Bruxelles *01000*
Bureau International de Liaison et de Documentation, Paris *03670*
Bureau International d'Education – International Bureau of Education, Genève *10057*
Bureau International des Poids et Mesures, Sèvres *03671*
Bureau International Technique de l'ABS, Bruxelles *01001*
Bureau International Technique des Polyesters Insaturés, Bruxelles *01002*
Bureau International Technique du Spathfluor, Bruxelles *01003*
Bureau of Professional Education of the American Osteopathic Association, Chicago *13952*
BURISA, Winchester *11212*
Burlesque Historical Society, Helendale *13953*
The Burns Federation, Kilmarnock *11228*
Business Association of Latin American Studies, San Diego *13954*
Business-Higher Education Forum, Washington *13955*
Business History Conference, Williamsburg *13956*
Business Professionals of America, Columbus *13957*
BUT, Köln *04673*
Buteshire Natural History Society, Bute *11229*
Butsuri Tansa Gakkai, Tokyo *07717*
BVA, Düsseldorf *04560*
BVA, London *11213*
BVDN, Frankfurt *04567*
BVFI, Reykjavik *06363*
BVI, Rosslyn *13915*
BVjA, Meckenheim *04666*
BVL, Bremen *04683*
BVÖ, Leoben *00801*
BVRA, Hatfield *11214*
BVS, Beckenham *11216*
BVS, Peacehaven *10953*
BVSK, Königswinter *04646*
BVT, Monheim *04664*
BWA, Wiesbaden *04574*
B.W.A.S., Birmingham *10972*
BWEA, Philadelphia *13932*
BWG, Braunschweig *04599*
BWG, Wien *00579*
BWHW, Frankfurt/Main *04588*
BWPA, London *11219*
BWR, Bremen *04596*
BWRP, Mainz *04592*
BWTW, Erfurt *04594*
BWV, Kiel *04675*
BWV, München *04556*
Bydgoskie Towarzystwo Naukowe, Bydgoszcz *09071*
Byggecentrum, Hørsholm *02970*
Byron Society, London *11230*
Byron Society, Newark *13958*
BZA, London *11220*
BZÖG, Berlin *04654*

CA, Indianapolis *14268*
CA, New York *14087*
CAA, Kampsville *13992*
CAA, New York *14098*
CAA, Thames Ditton *11288*
CAAHA, Dallas *14243*
CAAHEP, Chicago *14111*
CAAS, Guelph *01791*
CAB International, Wallingford *11231*
CAB International Bureau of Crop Protection, Wallingford *11232*
CAB International Bureau of Horticulture and Plantation Crops, Wallingford *11233*
CAB International Bureau of Plant Breeding and Genetics, Wallingford *11234*
CAB International Department of Dairy Science and Technology, Wallingford *11235*
CAB International Department of Soils, Wallingford *11236*
CAB International Division of Animal Health and Medical Parasitology, Wallingford *11237*
CAB International Division of Animal Production, Wallingford *11238*
CAB International Forestry Department, Wallingford *11239*
CAB International Institute of Entomology, London *11240*
CAC, Washington *16036*
CACC, London *11357*
CACYT, Lima *08997*
CAD, London *11314*
CADAS, Coventry *11367*
CADEICA, Bruxelles *01051*
Cadmium Pigments Association, Bruxelles *01004*
CAE, Arlington *14242*
CAEJC, London *02062*
CAEMC, Bruxelles *01031*
Caernarvonshire Historical Society, Caernarfon *11241*
CAETA, Harare *17063*
CAETS, Washington *14222*
CAFRA, Tunapuna *10655*
CAFS, Nairobi *08082*
CAG, Montréal *01814*
CAGRIS, Saint Augustine *10662*
CAGS, Beijing *02558*
CAH, Bloomington *14163*
CAH, Sausalito *13996*
C.A.H.S., North York *01836*
CAI, Alexandria *14138*
CAI, Buenos Aires *00064*
CAICYT, Buenos Aires *00063*
CAID, Bedford *14189*
Cairo Odontological Society, Cairo *03270*
CAIS, Brattleboro *13995*
Cajal Club, Denver *13959*
CAJE, New York *14093*
CAL, Washington *13993*
CALA, Sacramento *14065*
Calcutta Mathematical Society, Calcutta *06419*
Calgary Zoological Society, Calgary *01765*
CALI, Minneapolis *14001*
California Institute of International Studies, Stanford *13960*
California Institute of Pan African Studies, Los Angeles *13961*
CALL, Kingston *01816*
Calorimetry Conference, Tallahassee *13962*
CAM, Calgary *02063*
CAM, Mons *01023*
CAM-I, Arlington *14148*
CAMA, Oklahoma City *14084*
CAMAS, Dar es Salaam *10593*
Cambodian Buddhist Society, Silver Spring *13963*
Cambrian Archaeological Association, Newport *11242*
Cambridge Bibliographical Society, Cambridge *11243*
Cambridge Philosophical Society, Cambridge *11244*
Cambridge Refrigeration Technology, Cambridge *11245*
Cambridge Society for Industrial Archaeology, Cambridge *11246*
CAMHDD, Sheffield *11315*
CAML, Ottawa *01819*
Campagne d'Education Civique Européenne, Genève *10058*
Campaign for the Advancement of State Education, London *11247*
Campaign for the Protection of Rural Wales, Welshpool *11248*

333 Alphabetical Index: Conference

Comité d'Etudes Fiscales et Contentieuses, Paris *03711*
Comité d'Etudes pour un Nouveau Contrat Social, Paris *03712*
Comité du Film Ethnographique, Paris *03713*
Comité Economique et Social des Communautés Européennes, Bruxelles *01036*
Comité Euro-International du Béton, Lausanne *10089*
Comité Européen de Recherche et de Développement, Bruxelles *01037*
Comité Européen Permanent de Recherches pour la Protection des Populations contre les Risques d'Intoxication à Long Terme, Paris *03714*
Comité Européen pour l'Education des Enfants et Adolescents Précoces, Doués, Talentueux, Nîmes *03715*
Comité Français de l'Electricité, Paris-La Défense *03716*
Comité Français d'Education et d'Assistance de l'Enfance Déficiente, Paris *03717*
Comité Historique du Centre-Est, Lyon *03718*
Comité International de l'AISS pour la Prévention des Risques Professionnels du Bâtiment et des Travaux Publics, Boulogne-Billancourt *03719*
Comité International de Médecine Militaire, Liège *01038*
Comité International de Paléographie Latine, Paris *03720*
Comité International de Recherche et d'Etude de Facteurs de l'Ambiance, Bruxelles *01039*
Comité International des Sciences Historiques, Paris *03721*
Comité International d'Etudes Morisques, Zaghouan *10686*
Comité International d'Histoire de l'Art, Utrecht *08412*
Comité International Permanent des Etudes Mycéniennes, Vitoria *09747*
Comité International pour l'Information et la Documentation en Sciences Sociales, Paris *03722*
Comité Nacional del Consejo Internacional de Museos, Bogotá *02781*
Comité Nacional Español del Consejo Internacional de la Música, Madrid *09748*
Comité National Belge de l'Organisation Scientifique, Bruxelles *01040*
Comité National contre les Maladies Respiratoires et la Tuberculose, Paris *03723*
Comité National de Géographie du Maroc, Rabat *08383*
Comité National de l'Enseignement Libre, Paris *03724*
Comité National des Conseillers de l'Enseignement Technique, Paris *03725*
Comité National des Ecoles Françaises de Service Social, Paris *03726*
Comité National des Musées, Tunis *10687*
Comité National Français de Géodesie et Géophysique, Paris *03727*
Comité National Français de Géographie, Paris *03728*
Comité National Français de Mathématiciens, Orsay *03729*
Comité National Français des Recherches Antarctiques, saint Etienne *03730*
Comité National pour l'Etude et la Prévention de l'Alcoolisme et des Autres Toxicomanies, Bruxelles *01041*
Comité Oceanográfico Nacional, Valparaíso *02462*
Comité para la Defensa de las Lenguas Indígenas de América Latina y el Caribe, Caracas *16906*
Comité pour les Données Scientifiques et Technologiques, Paris *03731*
Comité Scientifique du Club Alpin Français, Paris *03732*
Comité Scientifique Inter-Africain Post-Récolte, Dakar *09513*
Comité Universitaire d'Information Pédagogique, Paris *03733*
Comitetul National al Geologilor din Romania, Bucuresti *09276*
COMLA, Mandeville *07695*
Commemorative Collectors Society, Newark *11309*
COMMISS, Columbia *14115*
Commission Belge de Bibliographie, Bruxelles *01042*
Commission de la Carte Géologique du Monde, Paris *03734*
Commission de l'Enseignement Supérieur en Biologie, Paris *03735*
Commission Electrotechnique Internationale, Genève *10067*
Commission for Archaeology, Khartoum *09844*
Commission for Controlling the Desert Locust in the Eastern Region of its Distribution Area in South West Asia, Roma *07205*
Commission for Controlling the Desert Locust in the Near East, Jeddah *09491*
Commission for Scientific and Technical Co-operation of the Academy of Sciences and Organizations of Moscow Oblast, Moskva *09343*
Commission for the Conservation of Antarctic Marine Living Resources, Hobart *00259*
Commission for the European (Vienna) Centre for Co-ordination of Research and Documentation in Social Sciences, Moskva *09344*
Commission for the Geological Map of the World, Paris *03734*
Commission for the Study of Production Forces and Natural Resources, Tbilisi *04332*
Commission Grand-Ducale d'Instruction, Luxembourg *08171*
Commission Interaméricaine d'Arbitrage Commercial (Section Canadienne), Ottawa *02145*
Commission Internationale de Bibliographie, Paris *03736*
Commission Internationale de l'Eclairage, Wien *00427*
Commission Internationale de Marketing, Brixham *11310*
Commission Internationale des Grands Barrages, Paris *03737*
Commission Internationale d'Etudes Historiques Latinoaméricaines et des Caraïbes, Paris *03738*
Commission Internationale d'Histoire des Mouvements Sociaux et des Structures Sociales, Paris *03739*
Commission Internationale d'Histoire du Sel, Innsbruck *00428*
Commission Internationale pour l'Exploration Scientifique de la Mer Méditerranée, Monaco *08373*
Commission Médicale Chrétienne, Genève *10068*
Commission Océanographique Intergouvernementale, Paris *03740*
Commission of Socialist Teachers of the European Community, Zutphen *08413*
Commission of Studies for Latin American Church History, Austin *14110*
Commission of Studies for Latin American Church History, México *08300*
Commission of the European Communities Liaison Committee of Historians, Louvain-la-Neuve *01043*
Commission on Accreditation of Allied Health Education Programs, Chicago *14111*
Commission on Accreditation of Rehabilitation Facilities, Rolling Meadows *14112*
Commission on Biosphere and Ecology Research, Tbilisi *04333*
Commission on Gay/Lesbian Issues in Social Work Education, Alexandria *14113*
Commission on Livestock Development in Latin America and the Caribbean, Santiago *02463*
Commission on Mental and Physical Disability Law, Washington *14114*
Commission on Pastoral Research, Columbia *14115*
Commission on Professional and Hospital Activities, Chicago *14116*
Commission on Professionals in Science and Technology, Washington *14117*
Commission on Terminology, Bishkek *09345*
Commission on the Study of Peace, Syracuse *14118*
Commission on World Standards of the world Association of Societies of Pathology – Anatomic and Clinical, Northfield *14119*
Commission Royale d'Histoire, Bruxelles *01044*
Commission Théologique Internationale, Città del Vaticano *16859*
Commission to Study the Organization of Peace, Washington *14120*
Commissione di Studio dei Fenomeni di Corrosione Elettrolitica, Bologna *07206*
Committee for Better Transit, Long Island City *14121*
Committee for Co-ordination of Investigations of the Lower Mekong Basin, Bangkok *10637*
Committee for Economic Development, Washington *14122*
Committee for Economic Development of Australia, Melbourne *00260*
Committee for European Marine Biology Symposia, Brest *03741*
Committee for Freedom of Choice in Medicine, Chula Vista *14123*
Committee for Hispanic Arts and Research, Austin *14124*
Committee for International Cooperation in National Research in Demography, Paris *03742*
Committee for the European Development of Science and Technology, Roma *07207*
Committee for the Implementation of the Standardized Yiddish Orthography, New York *14125*
Committee for the Promotion of Medical Research, Yonkers *14126*
Committee for the Scientific Investigation of Claims of the Paranormal, Amherst *14127*
Committee for the Scientific Investigation of Claims of the Paranormal, Buffalo *14128*
Committee of Directors of Polytechnics, London *11311*
Committee of International Development Institutions on the Environment, Nairobi *08085*
Committee of Vice-Chancellors and Principals of the Universities of the United Kingdom, London *11312*
Committee on Atlantic Studies, Ottawa *02061*
Committee on Capacity Building in Science, Batavia *14129*
Committee on Changing International Realities, Washington *14130*
Committee on Conceptual and Terminological Analysis, Oslo *08788*
Committee on Continuing Education for School Personnel, Union *14131*
Committee on Data for Science and Technology, Paris *03731, 03743*
Committee on Family Research, Uppsala *09865*
Committee on Forest Development in the Tropics, Roma *07208*
Committee on Higher Education in the European Community, Bruxelles *01045*
Committee on Institutional Cooperation, Champaign *14132*
Committee on Political Education, AFL-CIO, Washington *14133*
Committee on Research Materials on Southeast Asia, Ithaca *14134*
Committee on Space Research, Paris *03744*
Committee on the Challenges of Modern Society, Bruxelles *01046*
Committee on the Promotion of the Peaceful Uses of Atomic Energy, Taipei *02716*
Committee on the Role and Status of Women in Educational Research and Development, Portland *14135*
Committee on Women in Asian Studies, Honolulu *14136*
Common Market of Scientific and Technological Knowledge, Washington *14137*
Common Office for European Training, Mons *01047*
Commons, Open Spaces and Footpaths Preservation Society, Henley-on-Thames *11313*
Commonwealth Association for Development, London *11314*
Commonwealth Association for Education in Journalism and Communication, London *02062*
Commonwealth Association for Mental Handicap and Developmental Disabilities, Sheffield *11315*
Commonwealth Association for Public Administration and Management, London *11316*
Commonwealth Association for the Education and Training of Adults, Harare *17063*
Commonwealth Association of Architects – Education Committee, London *11317*
Commonwealth Association of Museums, Calgary *02063*
Commonwealth Association of Planners, Kingston *07693*
Commonwealth Association of Polytechnics in Africa, Nairobi *08086*
Commonwealth Association of Science and Mathematics Educators, London *11318*
Commonwealth Association of Scientific Agricultural Societies, Kuala Lumpur *08222*
Commonwealth Association on Surveying and Land Economy, London *11319*
Commonwealth Caribbean Medical Research Council, Kingston *07694*
Commonwealth Commercial Crime Unit, London *11320*
Commonwealth Council for Educational Administration and Management, Lincoln *11321*
Commonwealth Defence Science Organisation, London *11322*
Commonwealth Dental Association, London *11323*
Commonwealth Education Liaison Committee, London *11324*
Commonwealth Education Programme, London *11325*
Commonwealth Forestry Association, Oxford *11326*
Commonwealth Heraldry Board, Auckland *08670*
Commonwealth Industrial Training and Experience Programme, London *11327*
Commonwealth Institute of Valuers, Sydney *00261*
Commonwealth Lawyers' Association, London *11328*
Commonwealth Legal Education Association, London *11329*
Commonwealth Library Association, Mandeville *07695*
Commonwealth Medical Association, London *11330*
Commonwealth Music Association, London *11331*
Commonwealth of Learning, Vancouver *02064*
Commonwealth Partnership for Technology Management, London *11332*
Commonwealth Pharmaceutical Association, London *11333*
Commonwealth Scientific and Industrial Research Organisation, Parkville *00262*
Commonwealth Secretariat, Education Programme, Human Resource, Development Group, London *11334*
Commonwealth Trust, London *11335*
Commonwealth Veterinary Association, Bangalore *06421*
Community Associations Institute, Alexandria *14138*
Community College Association for Instruction and Technology, Lancaster *14139*
Community Colleges for International Development, Pewaukee *14140*
Community Development Society, Milwaukee *14141*
Community Environmental Council, Santa Barbara *14142*
Community for Religious Research and Education, Loretto *14143*
Community Guidance Service, New York *14144*
Community Network for European Education and Training, Liège *01048*
Community Nutrition Institute, Washington *14145*
Community of European Management Schools, Jouy-en-Josas *03745*
Community of Mediterranean Universities, Bari *07209*
Community Planning Association of Alberta, Calgary *02065*
Community Planning Association of Canada, Regina *02066*
COMNET, Liège *01048*
Compagnie des Experts-Architectes près la Cour d'Appel de Paris, Paris *03746*
The Company Chemists' Association, Nottingham *11336*
Company of Military Historians, Westbrook *14146*
Comparative and International Education Society, Washington *14147*
Comparative Education Society in Europe, Bruxelles *01049*
Comparative Literature Society of Japan, Tokyo *07899*
Composers' Guild of Great Britain, London *11337*
Computer Aided Manufacturing International, Arlington *14148*
Computer Arts Society, London *11338*
Computer Communications Institute, North York *02067*
Computer Law Association, Fairfax *14149*
COMSBlack, Woods Hole *14192*
CONAC, Caracas *16909*
CONACYT, México *08304*
CONAE-CENID, Montevideo *12622*
CONAMOH, Panamá City *08947*
Conchological Society of Great Britain and Ireland, Ilford *11339*
Concorde, Bruxelles *01050*
Conduit, Iowa City *14150*
Confederación Centroamericana de Medicina del Deporte, Heredía *02856*
Confederación de Educadores Americanos, México *08301*
Confederación Interamericana de Educación Católica, Bogotá *02782*
Confederación Latinoamericana de Sociedades de Anestesiología, Bogotá *02783*
Confederación Panamericana de Medicina Deportiva, Porto Alegre *01452*
Confederate Historical Society, Leigh-on-Sea *11340*
Confederate Memorial Literary Society, Richmond *14151*
Confédération d'Associations d'Ecoles Indépendantes de la Communauté Européenne, Bruxelles *01051*
Confédération des Sociétés Scientifiques Françaises, Paris *03747*
Confédération des Syndicats Médicaux Français, Paris *03748*
Confédération Européenne des Syndicats Nationaux et Associations Professionnelles de Pédiatres, Bruxelles *01052*
Confédération Européenne pour la Thérapie Physique, Paris *03749*
Confédération Internationale des Associations de Médecines Alternatives Naturelles, Pierrelatte *03750*
Confédération Internationale des Sociétés d'Auteurs et Compositeurs, Paris *03751*
Confédération Nationale des Syndicats Dentaires, Paris *03752*
Confederation of African Medical Associations and Societies, Dar es Salaam *10593*
Confederation of Alberta Faculty Associations, Edmonton *02068*
Confederation of British Industry, London *11341*
Confederation of European Laryngectomees, Bebra *04696*
Confederation of European Specialists in Paediatrics, Bruxelles *01053*
Confederation of Medical Associations in Asia and Oceania, Manila *09046*
Conference Board of Associated Research Councils, New York *14152*
Conference Board of Canada, Ottawa *02069*
Conference Board of the Mathematical Sciences, Washington *14153*
Conférence Canadienne des Arts, Ottawa *01856*
Conférence des Facultés et Ecoles de Médecine d'Afrique d'Expression Française, Dakar *09514*
Conférence des Présidents d'Université, Paris *03753*
Conférence des Recteurs des Universités Belges, Bruxelles *01054*
Conférence des Recteurs des Universités Francophones d'Afrique, Kinshasa *02836*
Conférence des Recteurs Français, Paris *03754*
Conférence des Regions de l'Europe du Nord-Ouest, Brugge *01057*
Conférence Diplomatique de Droit Maritime International, Bruxelles *01055*
Conference for Chinese Oral and Performing Literature, Hanover *14154*
Conference Group on French Politics and Society, Cambridge *14155*
Conference Group on German Politics, Durham *14156*
Conférence intercantonale des chefs des départements de l'instruction publique de la Suisse romande et du Tessin, Lausanne *10069*
Conférence Internationale des Doyens des Facultés de Médecine d'Expression Française, Tours *03755*
Conférence Internationale des Facultés de Droit ayant en Commun l'Usage du Français, Aix-en-Provence *03756*
Conférence Internationale des Facultés, Instituts et Ecoles de Pharmacie d'Expression Française, Paris *03757*
Conférence Internationale des Formations d'Ingénieurs et Techniciens d'Expression Française, Villeurbanne *03758*
Conférence Internationale des Grands Réseaux Electriques à Haute Tension, Paris *03759*
Conférence Internationale des Responsables des Universités et Instituts à Dominante Scientifique et Technique d'Expression Française, Talence *03760*
Conférence Internationale Permanente de Directeurs d'Instituts Universitaires pour la Formation de Traducteurs et d'Interprètes, Antwerpen *01056*
Conference of African Theological Institutions, Harare *17064*
Conference of Asian-Pacific Pastoral Institutes, Manila *09047*
Conference of Baltic Oceanographers, Kiel *04697*
Conference of Chief Justices, Williamsburg *14157*
Conference of Consulting Actuaries, Buffalo Grove *14158*
Conference of Defence Associations Institute, Ottawa *02070*
Conference of Educational Administrators Serving the Deaf, Newark *14159*
Conference of European Computer User Associations, Bussum *08414*
Conference of European Statisticians, Genève *10070*
Conference of Latin Americanist Geographers, Austin *14160*
Conference of Podiatry Executives, Columbus *14161*
Conference of Regions of North-West-Europe, Brugge *01057*
Conference of Research Workers in Animal Diseases, Fort Collins *14162*
Conference of the Baltic Oceanographers, Norrköping *09866*
Conference on Asian History, Bloomington *14163*
Conference on Christianity and Literature, Saint Petersburg *14164*
Conference on College Composition and Communication, Urbana *14165*
Conference on Consumer Finance Law, Chicago *14166*
Conference on English Education, Urbana *14167*
Conference on Latin American History, Auburn *14168*

Dansk Selskab for Akupunktur, København 03055
Dansk Selskab for Allergologi og Immunologi, København 03056
Dansk Selskab for Bygningsstatik, Lyngby 03057
Dansk Selskab for Cancerforskning, København 03058
Dansk Selskab for Europaforskning, København 03059
Dansk Selskab for Fotogrammetri og Landmåling, Ålborg 03060
Dansk Selskab for Intern Medicin, Gentofte 03061
Dansk Selskab for Materialprøvning og -forskning, København 03062
Dansk Selskab for Musikforskning, København 03063
Dansk Selskab for Obstetrik og Gynaekologi, Aarhus 03064
Dansk Selskab for Oldtids- og Middelalderforskning, København 03065
Dansk Selskab for Oligofreniforskning, København 03066
Dansk Selskab for Optometri, Vedbaek 03067
Dansk Selskab for Opvarmnings- og Ventilationsteknik, København 03068
Dansk Selskab for Patologi, København 03069
Dansk Selskab for Rumfartsforskning, København 03070
Dansk Selskab for Social Medicin, Odense 03071
Dansk Selskab for Teoretisk Statistik, København 03072
Dansk Skattevidenskabelig Forening, København 03073
Dansk Skovforening, Frederiksberg 03074
Dansk Socialradgiverforening, København 03075
Dansk Sociologisk Selskab, København 03076
Dansk Sprogvaern, Vaerløse 03077
Dansk Svejseteknisk Landsforening, Taastrup 03078
Dansk Tandlaegeforening, København 03079
Dansk Teknisk Laererforening, København 03080
Dansk Vandteknisk Forening, Viby 03081
Dansk Veterinaerhistorisk Samfund, Thisted 03082
Det Danske Afrika Selskab, Hellerup 03083
Den Danske Aktuarforening, København 03084
Danske Arkitekters Landsforbund, København 03085
Danske Bibelselskab, København 03086
Danske Dermato-Venerologers Organisation, Alborg 03087
Den Danske Dyrlaegeforening, Vanlöse 03088
Danske Forstkandidaters Forening, Klampenborg 03089
Danske Fysioterapeuter, København 03090
Det Danske Hedeselskab, Viborg 03091
Den Danske Historiske Forening, København 03092
Danske Interne Medicineres Organisation, Ballerup 03093
Danske Komité for Historikernes Internationale Samarbejde, København 03094
Danske Lunglaegers Organisation, Holbaek 03095
Danske Nervelaegers Organisation, Odense 03096
Det Danske Orgelselskab, Vanløse 03097
Danske Radiologers Organisation, Sønderborg 03098
Det Danske Shakespeare Selskab, København 03099
Danske Sprog- og Litteraturselskab, København 03100
Danske Veterinårhygiejnikeres Organisation, Slagense 03101
Dante Society of America, Cambridge 14285
danvak VVS Teknisk Forening, Lyngby 03102
DARL, Hannover 04723
Dartmoor Pony Society, Newton Abbot 11377
Dartmoor Preservation Association, Plymouth 11378
DAS, Exeter 11386
D.A.S., Uttoxeter 11381
DASA, Houghton 09621
DAS, Arhus 02983
DASt, Köln 04994
Data for Development International Association, Marseille 03596
DAtF, Bonn 05073
DAu, København 02984
Dauthendey-Gesellschaft, Gerbrunn 04702
DAV, Hannover 04995
David Davis Memorial Institut of International Studies, London 11379
David M Kennedy Center for International Studies, Provo 14286
David Rockefeller Centre for Latin American Studies, Cambridge 14287
DAW, Cardiff 11401
DB, Ballerup 02974
DBFT, Essen 04999
DBG, Frankfurt 04719
DBG, Phoenix 14296
dbi, Berlin 05074
DBS, Essen 04998
DBS, Ljubljana 09597
DBT, Remscheid 05003
DBV, Berlin 05001
DBV, Braubach 04720
DBV, Köln 05002
DBV, Wiesbaden 05000
DCF, Lyngby 02992
DCPO, Baltimore 14282
DCS, Herlev 02991
DCWAB, London 11389
DDA, Essen 05004
DdD, Vanlöse 03088
DDG, Magdeburg 04722
DDH, Viborg 03091
DDPA, Oak Brook 14290
DDS, København 02995
DDSLA, Bellmore 14281
DE, Berlin 04730
DEAE, Karlsruhe 04731
Deafness Research Foundation, New York 14288
DEBRA, New York 14325
DECA, Reston 14310
DECHEMA, Frankfurt 04763
Decision Sciences Institute, Atlanta 14289
Decus Europe, Genève 10079
Dedicated Road Infrastructure for Vehicle Safety in Europe, Bruxelles 01067
Defence Science and Technolohy Organisation, Canberra 00266
DeGePo, Bremerhaven 04846
Delphinium Society, Farnham 11380
Delta Dental Plans Association, Oak Brook 14290
Deltiologists of America, Norwood 14291
Demeure Historique, Paris 03778
Demographic Society of Finland, Statistics Finland 03441
Denki Gakkai, Tokyo 07721
Denshi Joho Tsushin Gakkai, Tokyo 07722
Dental Assisting National Board, Chicago 14292
Dental Association of Prince Edward Island, Charlottetown 02083
Dental Association of South Africa, Houghton 09621
Dental Association of Zimbabwe, Harare 17066
Dental Council, Dublin 06596
Dental Health International, Athens 14293
Dentist's Liaison Committee for the EEC, Bruxelles 01068
Denturist Association of Canada, Winnipeg 02084
Departamento de Antropología e Historia de Nayarit, Tepic 08305
Departamento de Educación Audiovisual, México 08306
Departamento de Estudios Etnográficos y Coloniales, Santa Fé 00072
Departamento de Historia del Arte Diego Velázquez, Madrid 09753
Dept of Ethnographical and Colonial Studies, Santa Fé 00072
Deputazione di Storia Patria per gli Abruzzi, L'Aquila 07216
Deputazione di Storia Patria per il Friuli, Udine 07217
Deputazione di Storia Patria per la Calabria, Reggio Calabria 07218
Deputazione di Storia Patria per la Lucania, Potenza 07219
Deputazione di Storia Patria per la Sardegna, Cagliari 07220
Deputazione di Storia Patria per la Toscana, Firenze 07221
Deputazione di Storia Patria per le Antiche Province Modenesi, Modena 07222
Deputazione di Storia Patria per le Marche, Ancona 07223
Deputazione di Storia Patria per le Province di Romagna, Bologna 07224
Deputazione di Storia Patria per le Province Parmensi, Parma 07225
Deputazione di Storia Patria per le Venezie, Venezia 07226
Deputazione di Storia Patria per l'Umbria, Perugia 07227
Deputazione Provinciale Ferrarese di Storia Patria, Ferrara 07228
Deputazione Reggiana di Storia Patria, Reggio Emilia 07229
Deputazione Subalpina di Storia Patria, Torino 07230
Derbyshire Archaeological Society, Uttoxeter 11381
Dermatology Foundation, Evanston 14294
DES Action International, Oakland 14295
Desert Botanical Garden, Phoenix 14296
Desert Fishes Council, Bishop 14297
Desert Locust Control Organization for Eastern Africa, Addis Ababa 03332
Desert Locust Control Organization for Eastern Africa, Nairobi 08087
Desert Protective Council, Valley Center 14298
Desert Tortoise Preserve Committee, San Bernardino 14299
Design and Industries Association, London 11382
Design-Build Institute of America, Washington 14300
Design Council, London 11383
Design Zentrum Nordrhein-Westfalen e.V., Essen 04703
Designers and Art Directors Association of London, London 11384
Designs for Change, Chicago 14301
DESY, Hamburg 05075
Deuqua, Hannover 04947
Deutsch-Pazifische Gesellschaft e.V. (DPG)/German Pacific Society (GPS), München 04704
Deutsche Adels-Gesellschaft in Nord-Amerika, Benicia 13850
Deutsche Akademie der Darstellenden Künste e.V., Frankfurt/Main 04705
Deutsche Akademie der Naturforscher Leopoldina, Halle 04706
Deutsche Akademie des Tanzes e.V., Nürnberg 04707
Deutsche Akademie für Kinder- und Jugendliteratur e.V., Würzburg 04708
Deutsche Akademie für Landeskunde e.V., Frankfurt/Main 04709
Deutsche Akademie für medizinische Fortbildung, Kassel 04710
Deutsche Akademie für Nuklearmedizin, Hannover 04711
Deutsche Akademie für Sprache und Dichtung e.V., Darmstadt 04712
Deutsche Akademie für Städtebau und Landesplanung, Berlin 04713
Deutsche Akademie Villa Massimo, Roma 06881
Deutsche Alzheimer Gesellschaft e.V., Stuttgart 04714
Deutsche Anwalt-Akademie, Bonn 04715
Deutsche Arbeitsgemeinschaft für Paradontologie, Goslar 04716
Deutsche Arbeitsgemeinschaft Genealogischer Verbände e.V., Brühl 04717
Deutsche Botanische Gesellschaft e.V., Göttingen 04718
Deutsche Bunsen-Gesellschaft für Physikalische Chemie e.V., Frankfurt 04719
Deutsche Burgenvereinigung e.V., Braubach 04720
Deutsche Chopin-Gesellschaft e.V., Cottbus 04721
Deutsche Dante-Gesellschaft e.V., Magdeburg 04722
Deutsche Dekane- und Abteilungsleiterkonferenz für Architektur, Raumplanung und Landschaftsarchitektur, Hannover 04723
Deutsche Dendrologische Gesellschaft, Waake 04724
Deutsche Dermatologische Gesellschaft, Kiel 04725
Deutsche Diabetes-Gesellschaft, Bad Oeynhausen 04726
Deutsche Dostojewskij-Gesellschaft e.V., Hamburg 04727
Deutsche EEG-Gesellschaft, Berlin 04728
Deutsche Elektrotechnische Kommission im DIN und VDE, Frankfurt 04729
Deutsche Epilepsievereinigung e.V., Berlin 04730
Deutsche Evangelische Arbeitsgemeinschaft für Erwachsenenbildung e.V., Karlsruhe 04731
Deutsche Exlibris Gesellschaft e.V., Koblenz 04732
Deutsche farbwissenschaftliche Gesellschaft e.V., Berlin 04733
Deutsche Film- und Fernsehakademie Berlin, Berlin 04734
Deutsche Forschungs- und Versuchsanstalt für Luft- und Raumfahrt e.V., Köln 04735
Deutsche Forschungsgemeinschaft, Bonn 04736
Deutsche Forschungsgesellschaft für Oberflächenbehandlung e.V., Düsseldorf 04737
Deutsche Ganghofer-Gesellschaft e.V., Kaufbeuren 04738
Deutsche Gartenbauwissenschaftliche Gesellschaft e.V., Hannover 04739
Deutsche Gemmologische Gesellschaft e.V., Idar-Oberstein 04740
Deutsche Geodätische Kommission, München 04741
Deutsche Geologische Gesellschaft, Hannover 04742
Deutsche Geophysikalische Gesellschaft e.V., Münster 04743
Deutsche Gesellschaft für Aesthetische Medizin, Berlin 04744
Deutsche Gesellschaft für Agrarrecht, Bonn 04745
Deutsche Gesellschaft für Allergie- und Immunitätsforschung, Bochum 04746
Deutsche Gesellschaft für Allergieforschung, Tübingen 04747
Deutsche Gesellschaft für allgemeine und angewandte Entomologie e.V., Dossenheim 04748
Deutsche Gesellschaft für Alternative Medizin e.V., Seelze 04749
Deutsche Gesellschaft für Amerikastudien e.V., Halle/Saale 04750
Deutsche Gesellschaft für Anästhesiologie und Intensivmedizin, Nürnberg 04751
Deutsche Gesellschaft für Analytische Psychologie e.V., Berlin 04752
Deutsche Gesellschaft für angewandte Optik e.V., Oberkochen 04753
Deutsche Gesellschaft für Angiologie, Esslingen 04754
Deutsche Gesellschaft für Arbeitsmedizin e.V., München 04755
Deutsche Gesellschaft für Asienkunde e.V., Hamburg 04756
Deutsche Gesellschaft für Auswärtige Politik e.V., Bonn 04757
Deutsche Gesellschaft für Baukybernetik e.V, Holzminden 04758
Deutsche Gesellschaft für Baurecht e.V., Frankfurt/Main 04759
Deutsche Gesellschaft für Betriebswirtschaft e.V., Berlin 05943
Deutsche Gesellschaft für Biomedizinische Technik e.V., Berlin 04760
Deutsche Gesellschaft für Biophysik, Garching 04761
Deutsche Gesellschaft für Bluttransfusion und Immunhämatologie e.V., Frankfurt 04762
Deutsche Gesellschaft für Chemisches Apparatewesen, Chemische Technik und Biotechnologie e.V., Frankfurt 04763
Deutsche Gesellschaft für Christliche Kunst e.V., München 04764
Deutsche Gesellschaft für Chronometrie e.V., Ditzingen 04765
Deutsche Gesellschaft für das Badewesen e.V., Essen 04766
Deutsche Gesellschaft für die Bekämpfung der Muskelkrankheiten e.V., Freiburg 04767
Deutsche Gesellschaft für die Erforschung des 18. Jahrhunderts, Wolfenbüttel 04768
Deutsche Gesellschaft für die Vereinten Nationen e.V., Bonn 04769
Deutsche Gesellschaft für Dokumentation e.V., Frankfurt/Main 04770
Deutsche Gesellschaft für Dynamische Psychiatrie, München 04771
Deutsche Gesellschaft für Edelsteinkunde, Idar-Oberstein 04740
Deutsche Gesellschaft für Eisenbahngeschichte e.V., Werl 04772
Deutsche Gesellschaft für Elektroakustische Musik e.V., Berlin 04773
Deutsche Gesellschaft für Elektronenmikroskopie e.V., Berlin 04774
Deutsche Gesellschaft für Endokrinologie, Berlin 04775
Deutsche Gesellschaft für Erd- und Grundbau e.V., Essen 04776
Deutsche Gesellschaft für Ernährung e.V., Frankfurt 04777
Deutsche Gesellschaft für Erziehungswissenschaft, Berlin 04778
Deutsche Gesellschaft für Familienplanung, Sexualpädagogik und Sexualberatung e.V., Frankfurt/Main 05890
Deutsche Gesellschaft für Fettwissenschaft e.V., Münster 04779
Deutsche Gesellschaft für Film- und Fernsehforschung, München 04780
Deutsche Gesellschaft für Filmdokumentation, Wiesbaden 04781
Deutsche Gesellschaft für Forschung im Graphischen Gewerbe, München 04782
Deutsche Gesellschaft für Galvano- und Oberflächentechnik e.V., Düsseldorf 04783
Deutsche Gesellschaft für Gartenkunst und Landschaftspflege e.V., Berlin 04784
Deutsche Gesellschaft für Geographie (DGfG), Duisburg 04785
Deutsche Gesellschaft für Gerontologie und Geriatrie, Lübeck 04786
Deutsche Gesellschaft für Geschichte der Medizin, Naturwissenschaft und Technik e.V., Regensburg 04787
Deutsche Gesellschaft für Geschlechtserziehung e.V., Kiel 04788
Deutsche Gesellschaft für Gesetzgebung e.V., Hamburg 04789
Deutsche Gesellschaft für Gesundheitsvorsorge e.V., Leverkusen 04790
Deutsche Gesellschaft für Gynäkologie und Geburtshilfe, Amberg 04791
Deutsche Gesellschaft für Hämatologie und Onkologie e.V., München 04792
Deutsche Gesellschaft für Hals-Nasen-Ohren-Heilkunde, Kopf- und Hals-Chirurgie, Bonn 04793
Deutsche Gesellschaft für Heereskunde e.V., Baden-Baden 04794
Deutsche Gesellschaft für Herpetologie und Terrarienkunde e.V., Rheinbach 04795
Deutsche Gesellschaft für Holzforschung e.V., München 04796
Deutsche Gesellschaft für Hopfenforschung e.V., Wolnzach 04797
Deutsche Gesellschaft für Hydrokultur e.V., Herten 04798
Deutsche Gesellschaft für Hygiene und Mikrobiologie e.V., Heidelberg 04799
Deutsche Gesellschaft für Immunologie e.V., Marburg 04800
Deutsche Gesellschaft für Innere Medizin, Wiesbaden 04801
Deutsche Gesellschaft für Internistische Intensivmedizin, Hamburg 04802
Deutsche Gesellschaft für Kardiologie – Herz- und Kreislaufforschung, Düsseldorf 04803
Deutsche Gesellschaft für Kartographie, München 04804
Deutsche Gesellschaft für Kieferorthopädie e.V., Heidelberg 04805
Deutsche Gesellschaft für Kinder- und Jugendpsychiatrie und Psychotherapie e.V., Marburg 04806
Deutsche Gesellschaft für Kinderheilkunde, Hannover 04807
Deutsche Gesellschaft für Kommunikationsforschung, München 04808
Deutsche Gesellschaft für Laboratoriumsmedizin e.V., Düsseldorf 04809
Deutsche Gesellschaft für Lichtforschung, Hanau 04810
Deutsche Gesellschaft für Logistik e.V., Dortmund 04811
Deutsche Gesellschaft für Luft- und Raumfahrt e.V., Bonn 04812
Deutsche Gesellschaft für Luft- und Raumfahrtmedizin e.V., Ulm 04813
Deutsche Gesellschaft für Lungenkrankheiten und Tuberkulose, Freiburg 04814
Deutsche Gesellschaft für Manuelle Medizin e.V., Boppard 04815
Deutsche Gesellschaft für Materialkunde e.V., Frankfurt 04816
Deutsche Gesellschaft für Medizinische Informatik, Biometrie und Epidemiologie, Köln 04817
Deutsche Gesellschaft für Medizinische Soziologie, Ulm 04818
Deutsche Gesellschaft für Missionswissenschaft, Heidelberg 04819
Deutsche Gesellschaft für Moor- und Torfkunde e.V., Hannover 04820
Deutsche Gesellschaft für Mund-, Kiefer- und Gesichtschirurgie, Bonn 04821
Deutsche Gesellschaft für Musik des Orients e.V., Berlin 04822
Deutsche Gesellschaft für Musiktherapie e.V., Berlin 04823
Deutsche Gesellschaft für Neurochirurgie, Essen 04824
Deutsche Gesellschaft für Neurologie, Würzburg 04825
Deutsche Gesellschaft für Neuropathologie und Neuroanatomie e.V., München 04826
Deutsche Gesellschaft für Neuroradiologie, Würzburg 04827
Deutsche Gesellschaft für Nuklearmedizin, Freiburg 04828
Deutsche Gesellschaft für Orthopädie und Traumatologie e.V., Frankfurt/Main 04829
Deutsche Gesellschaft für Ortung und Navigation e.V., Düsseldorf 04830
Deutsche Gesellschaft für Osteuropakunde e.V., Berlin 04831
Deutsche Gesellschaft für Parasitologie e.V., Marburg 04832
Deutsche Gesellschaft für Parodontologie, Hamburg 04833
Deutsche Gesellschaft für Pathologie, Frankfurt 04834
Deutsche Gesellschaft für Perinatale Medizin, Berlin 04835
Deutsche Gesellschaft für Personalführung e.V., Düsseldorf 04836
Deutsche Gesellschaft für Pharmakologie und Toxikologie, Darmstadt 04837
Deutsche Gesellschaft für Phlebologie, Norderney 04838
Deutsche Gesellschaft für Photogrammetrie und Fernerkundung e.V., Berlin 04839
Deutsche Gesellschaft für Photographie e.V., Köln 04840
Deutsche Gesellschaft für Physikalische Medizin und Rehabilitation, Hannover 04841
Deutsche Gesellschaft für Pilzkunde, Karlsruhe 04842
Deutsche Gesellschaft für Plastische und Wiederherstellende Chirurgie e.V., Rotenburg 04843
Deutsche Gesellschaft für Pneumologie, Greifenstein 04844
Deutsche Gesellschaft für Poesie- und Bibliotherapie e.V., Köln 04845
Deutsche Gesellschaft für Polarforschung, Bremerhaven 04846

349 Alphabetical Index: Institution

Institut „Finanzen und Steuern" e.V., Bonn 05516
Institut Forestier du Canada, Ottawa 01909
Institut Français d'Analyse de Groupe et de Psychodrame, Paris 03883
Institut Français de l'Energie, Paris 03884
Institut Français des Relations Internationales, Paris 03885
Institut Français d'Etudes Byzantines, Paris 03886
Institut Français d'Histoire Sociale, Paris 03887
Institut für angewandte Arbeitswissenschaft e.V., Köln 05517
Institut für Angewandte Geodäsie, Frankfurt 05518
Institut für angewandte Verbraucherforschung e.V., Köln 05519
Institut für Angewandte Wirtschaftsforschung, Tübingen 05520
Institut für Auslandsbeziehungen, Stuttgart 05521
Institut für Bauforschung e.V., Hannover 05522
Institut für Chemiefasern, Denkendorf 05523
Institut für den Wissenschaftlichen Film, Göttingen 05524
Institut für Energie- und Umweltforschung Heidelberg e.V., Heidelberg 05525
Institut für Europäische Umweltpolitik, Bonn 05526
Institut für Film und Bild in Wissenschaft und Unterricht, Grünwald 05527
Institut für Gesellschaftswissenschaften Walberberg e.V., Bonn 05528
Institut für gewerbliche Wasserwirtschaft und Luftreinhaltung e.V., Köln 05529
Institut für Grenzgebiete der Wissenschaft, Innsbruck 00504
Institut für Handwerkswirtschaft München, München 05530
Institut für Kunststoffverarbeitung, -anwendung und -prüfung, Würzburg 05976
Institut für Länderkunde e.V., Leipzig 05531
Institut für nationale und internationale Fleisch- und Ernährungswirtschaft, Heidelberg 05532
Institut für Neue Musik und Musikerziehung e.V., Darmstadt 05533
Institut für Neue Technische Form e.V., Darmstadt 05534
Institut für ökologische Forschung und Bildung e.V., Münster 05535
Institut für Österreichische Musikdokumentation, Wien 00505
Institut für Österreichkunde, Wien 00506
Institut für religiöse Volkskunde e.V., Münster 05536
Institut für Schadenverhütung und Schadenforschung der öffentlich-rechtlichen Versicherer e.V., Kiel 05537
Institut für Sozial- und Wirtschaftspolitische Ausbildung e.V., Köln 05538
Institut für Sozialarbeit und Sozialpädagogik e.V., Frankfurt/Main 05539
Institut für Sozialdienste, gemeinnützige GmbH, Bregenz 00507
Institut für Soziales Design – Entwicklung und Forschung, Wien 00508
Institut für Sozialforschung und Sozialwirtschaft e.V., Saarbrücken 05540
Institut für Technik der Betriebsführung im Handwerk, Karlsruhe 05541
Institut für technische Weiterbildung Berlin e.V., Berlin 05542
Institut für Textil- und Faserforschung Stuttgart, Denkendorf 05543
Institut für Wirtschaft und Gesellschaft Bonn e.V., Bonn 05544
Institut für Wissenschaft und Kunst, Wien 00509
Institut für Wissenschaftliche Zusammenarbeit, Tübingen 05545
Institut für Zeitungsforschung, Dortmund 05546
Institut für Ziegelforschung Essen e.V., Essen 05547
Institut Géographique National, Bruxelles 01195
Institut Géographique National, Paris 03888
Institut Historique Belge de Rome, Bruxelles 01196
Institut International d'Administration Publique, Paris 03889
Institut International de Droit d'Expression et d'Inspiration Françaises, Paris 03890
Institut International de Planification de l'Education, Paris 03891
Institut International de Psychologie et de Psychothérapie Charles Baudouin, Coppet 10161
Institut International de Recherches Betteravières, Bruxelles 01197
Institut International des Droits de l'Homme, Strasbourg 03892
Institut International des Sciences Administratives, Bruxelles 01198
Institut International du Froid, Paris 03893
Institut International du Théâtre, Paris 03894
Institut Militaire de Québec, Québec 02135
Institut National d'Archéologie et d'Art, Tunis 10689
Institut National de Cinématographie Scientifique de Belgique, Bruxelles 01199
Institut National Genevois, Genève 10162
Institut Neue Wirtschaft e.V., Hamburg 05548
Institut of Actuaries, London 11651
Institut of Biomedical Science, London 11652
Institut Royal Belge du Pétrole, Bruxelles 01200
Institut Royal d'Architecture du Canada, Ottawa 02337
Institut Royal des Relations Internationales, Bruxelles 01201
Institut Suisse de Recherches Expérimentales sur le Cancer, Epalinges 10163
Institut Suisse pour l'Etude de l'Art, Zürich 10489
Institut zur Förderung publizistischen Nachwuchses e.V., München 05549
Institute Control Theory, Reality Therapy and Quality Management, Chatsworth 14655
Institute for Advanced Research in Asian Science and Medicine, Chestnut Hill 14656
Institute for Advanced Studies in the Theatre Arts, New York 14657
Institute for Advanced Studies of World Religions, Carmel 14658
Institute for Aerospace Studies, North York 02136
Institute for American Indian Studies, Washington 14659
Institute for Animal Health, Newbury 11653
Institute for Animal Health Pirbright, Pirbright Woking 11654
Institute for Applied Social Sciences, Nijmegen 08473
Institute for Biblical Research, Grand Rapids 14660
Institute for Canadian Studies, Winnipeg 02137
Institute for Certification of Computer Professionals, Des Plaines 14661
Institute for Childhood Resources, San Francisco 14662
Institute for Community Design Analysis, Great Neck 14663
Institute for Consumer Ergonomics, Loughborough 11655
Institute for Cultural Research, Tunbridge Wells 11656
Institute for Defense Analyses, Alexandria 14664
Institute for Development of Educational Activities, Dayton 14665
Institute for Econometric Research, Fort Lauderdale 14666
Institute for Economic Analysis, Silver Springs 14667
Institute for Educational Leadership, Washington 14668
Institute for Esperanto in Commerce and Industry, Valkenswaard 08470
Institute for Expressive Analysis, New York 14669
The Institute for Fiscal Studies, London 11657
Institute for Fluitronics Education, Elm Grove 14670
Institute for Food and Development Policy, Oakland 14671
Institute for Gravitational Strain Pathology, Rangeley 14672
Institute for Hospital Clinical Nursing Education, Chicago 14673
Institute for Intercultural Studies, New York 14674
Institute for International Economic Cooperation and Development, Roma 07368
Institute for Jewish Policy Research, London 11658
Institute for Labor and Mental Health, Oakland 14675
Institute for Mediterranean Affairs, Philadelphia 14676
Institute for Palestine Studies, Washington 14677
Institute for Perception Research, Eindhoven 08498
Institute for Philosophy and Public Policy, College Park 14678
Institute for Policy Studies, Washington 14679
Institute for Psychohistory, New York 14680
Institute for Public Relations Research and Education, Gainesville 14681
Institute for Rational-Emotive Therapy, New York 14682
Institute for Research in Hypnosis and Psychotherapy, New York 14683
Institute for Research on Public Policy, Montréal 02138
Institute for Responsive Education, Boston 14684
Institute for Sex Education and Research, Birmingham 11659
Institute for Social Research, Ann Arbor 14685
Institute for Southern Studies, Durham 14686
Institute for Standardization, Moskva 09363
Institute for Studies in American Music, Brooklyn 14687
Institute for Supervision and Management, Lichfield 11660
Institute for the Development of Emotional and Life Skills, Bethesda 14688
Institute for the Development of Indian Law, Oklahoma City 14689
Institute for the Future, Menlo Park 14690
Institute for the Protection of Cultural Monuments of Macedonia, Skopje 08193
Institute for the Study of Human Knowledge, Los Altos 14691
Institute for the Study of Man, Washington 14692
Institute for Theological Encounter with Science and Technology, Saint Louis 14693
Institute for Urban Design, New York 14694
Institute of Actuaries, London 11661
Institute of Administrative Management, Orpington 11662
Institute of Agricultural Engineering, Wageningen 08471
Institute of American Indian Arts, Santa Fe 14695
Institute of Andean Research, New York 14696
Institute of Andean Studies, Berkeley 14697
Institute of Arab Music, Alexandria 03296
Institute of Arab Music, Cairo 03297
Institute of Asturian Studies, Oviedo 09796
Institute of Bankers in Scotland, Edinburgh 11663
Institute of Bankers in South Africa, Marshalltown 09635
Institute of Biology, London 11664
Institute of Biomedical Science, London 11665
Institute of Business Administration, Wigan 11666
Institute of Canadian Advertising, Toronto 02139
Institute of Catalan Studies, Barcelona 09762
Institute of Ceramics, Stoke-on-Trent 11667
Institute of Certified Financial Planners, Denver 14698
The Institute of Chartered Accountants in England and Wales, London 11668
Institute of Chartered Accountants in Ireland, Dublin 06609
Institute of Chartered Accountants of India, New Delhi 06493
Institute of Chartered Accountants of Ontario, Toronto 02140
Institute of Chartered Accountants of Scotland, Edinburgh 11669
Institute of Chartered Foresters, Edinburgh 11670
Institute of Chartered Secretaries and Administrators, London 11671
Institute of Chemistry of Ireland, Dublin 06610
Institute of Chinese Culture, New York 14699
Institute of Civil War Studies, Saint Louis 14700
Institute of Clay Technology, Ripley 11672
Institute of Community Studies, London 11673
The Institute of Concrete Technology, Beaconsfield 11674
Institute of Construction Management, London 11675
Institute of Contemporary Arts, London 11676
Institute of Contemporary History and Wiener Library, London 11677
Institute of Corrosion, Leighton Buzzard 11678
Institute of Cost and Management Accountants of Pakistan, Karachi 08899
Institute of Credit Management, Stamford 11679
Institute of Cultural Affairs, Chicago 14701
Institute of Data Processing Management, London 11680
Institute of Directors, London 11681
Institute of Early American History and Culture, Williamsburg 14702
Institute of Eastern Culture, Tokyo 08039
Institute of Economic Affairs, London 11682
Institute of Electrical and Electronics Engineers, New York 14703
Institute of Electrical and Electronics Engineers Canada, Dundas 02141
Institute of Electrical Engineers of Japan, Tokyo 07721
Institute of Electrolysis, Manchester 11683
Institute of Electronics, Information and Communication Engineers of Japan, Tokyo 07722
Institute of Energy, London 11684
Institute of Energy (New Zealand Section), Wellington 08675
Institute of Engineers and Technicians, London 11685
Institute of Environmental Sciences, Mount Prospect 14704
Institute of Financial Education, Chicago 14705
Institute of Fisheries Management, Holmer 11686
Institute of Food Research, Reading 11687
Institute of Food Science and Technology of The United Kingdom, London 11688
Institute of Food Technologists, Chicago 14706
Institute of Gas Technology, Des Plaines 14707
Institute of General Semantics, Englewood 14708
Institute of Geological and Nuclear Sciences, Lower Hutt 08676
Institute of Global Education, Portland 14709
The Institute of Group-Analysis, London 11689
Institute of Health Education, Manchester 11690
Institute of Heraldic and Genealogical Studies, Canterbury 11691
Institute of Housing, Coventry 11692
Institute of Industrial Engineers, Dublin 06611
Institute of Industrial Engineers, Norcross 14710
Institute of Industrial Science, Tokyo 08015
Institute of Information Scientists, London 11693
Institute of International Education, New York 14711
Institute of International Education, Washington 14712
Institute of International Sociology, Gorizia, Gorizia 07336
Institute of Inventors, London 11694
Institute of Investment Management and Research, London 11695
Institute of Islamic Culture, Lahore 08900
Institute of Jamaica, Kingston 07697
Institute of Judicial Administration, New York 14713
Institute of Laboratory Animal Resources, Washington 14714
Institute of Leisure and Amenity Management, Reading 11696
Institute of Linguists, London 11697
Institute of Lithuanian Studies, Chicago 14715
Institute of Logistics, Corby 11698
Institute of Management, London 11699
Institute of Management Consultants in Ireland, Dublin 06612
The Institute of Management Sciences, Providence 14716
Institute of Management Services, Enfield 11700
Institute of Marine Engineers, London 11701
Institute of Materials, London 11702
Institute of Materials Handling, South Melbourne 00291
Institute of Mathematical Statistics, Hayward 14717
The Institute of Mathematics and its Applications, Southend-on-Sea 11703
Institute of Measurement and Control, London 11704
Institute of Medicine, Washington 14718
Institute of Mental Health Research and Postgraduate Training, Parkville 00292
The Institute of Metals, London 11705
Institute of Metals and Materials Australasia, North Melbourne 00293
Institute of Moralogy, Chiba 07769
Institute of Municipal Building Management, Colwyn Bay 11706
Institute of Municipal Management, South Melbourne 00294
Institute of Nautical Archaeology, College Station 14719
Institute of Navigation, Alexandria 14720
Institute of Noise Control Engineering, Poughkeepsie 14721
Institute of Nuclear Materials Management, Northbrook 14722
Institute of Occupational Medicine, Edinburgh 11707
Institute of Outdoor Drama, Chapel Hill 14723
Institute of Packaging, Melton Mowbray 11708
Institute of Personnel and Development, London 11709
Institute of Petroleum, London 11710
Institute of Photographic Technology, Melbourne 00295
Institute of Physics, London 11711
Institute of Physics – Singapore, Singapore 09534
Institute of Plasmaphysics Rijnhuizen, Nieuwegein 08457
Institute of Printing, Tunbridge Wells 11712
Institute of Professional Investigators, Blackburn 11713
Institute of Psycho-Analysis, London 11714
Institute of Psycho-Sexual Medicine, London 11715
Institute of Public Administration, Dublin 06613
Institute of Public Administration, New York 14724
Institute of Public Administration of Canada, Toronto 02142
Institute of Public Affairs, Jolimont 00296
Institute of Quarrying, Nottingham 11716
Institute of Race Relations, London 11717
Institute of Refrigeration, Carshalton 11718
Institute of Sales and Marketing Management, Royal Leamington Spa 11719
Institute of Science Technology, Lichfield 11720
Institute of Scientific and Technical Communicators, London 11721
Institute of Sheet Metal Engineering, Birmingham 11722
Institute of Small Business, London 11723
Institute of South African Architects, Houghton 09636
Institute of Southeast Asian Studies, Singapore 09535
Institute of Sports Medicine, London 11724
Institute of Statisticians, Preston 11725
Institute of Technicians in Venereology, Orsett 11726
Institute of Textile Science, Sainte-Anne-de-Bellevue 02143
Institute of the American Musical, Los Angeles 14725
Institute of the Great Plains, Lawton 14726
Institute of Translation and Interpreting, London 11727
Institute of Transport, Beverly Hills 00297
Institute of Transport Economics, Oslo 08792
Institute of Transportation Economics, Tokyo 08047
Institute of Transportation Engineers, Washington 14727
Institute of Trichologists, London 11728
Institute of Value Management, Buxton 11729
Institute of Water Resources Management and Air Pollution Control, Köln 05529
Institute of Wood Science, High Wycombe 11730
Institute of World Affairs, Washington 14728
Institute on Psychiatric Services/American Psychiatric Association, Washington 14729
Institute os Hispanic Art, Barcelona 09760
Institutio Santoriana, Milano 07307
Institution of Agricultural Engineers, Bedford 11731
Institution of British Telecom Engineers, London 11732
The Institution of Chemical Engineers, Rugby 11733
The Institution of Civil Engineers, London 11734
Institution of Civil Engineers (Republic of Ireland), Bray 06614
Institution of Corrosion Science and Technology, Leighton Buzzard 11735
Institution of Electrical Engineers, Lahore 08901
Institution of Electrical Engineers, London 11736
Institution of Electrical Engineers (Irish Centre), Dublin 06615
Institution of Electronics, Rochdale 11737
Institution of Electronics and Electrical Incorporated Engineers, London 11738
Institution of Electronics and Telecommunication Engineers, New Dehli 06494
Institution of Engineering Designers, Westbury 11739
Institution of Engineers amd Shipbuilders in Scotland, Glasgow 11740
Institution of Engineers – Australia, Barton 00298
Institution of Engineers – Bangladesh, Dhaka 00918
Institution of Engineers (India), Calcutta 06495
Institution of Engineers of Ireland, Dublin 06616

351 Alphabetical Index: International

International Association of Agricultural Information Specialists, Montpellier 03897
International Association of Agricultural Museums, Reading 11764
International Association of Allergology and Clinical Immunology, Stony Brook 14829
International Association of Applied Linguistics, Edinburgh 11765
International Association of Applied Linguistics, Minneapolis 14830
International Association of Applied Psychology, Nijmegen 08480
International Association of Aquatic and Marine Science Libraries and Information Centers, Fort Pierce 14831
International Association of Biblicists and Orientalists, Ravenna 07311
International Association of Biological Standardization, Hassocks 11766
International Association of Boards of Examiners in Optometry, Bethesda 14832
International Association of Boundary Element Methods, Nashville 14833
International Association of Buddhist Studies, Amherst 14834
International Association of Campus Law Enforcement Administrators, Hartford 14835
International Association of Career Consulting Firms, Reston 14836
International Association of Clinical Laser Acupuncturists, Chesterfield 14837
International Association of Coroners and Medical Examiners, Peoria 14838
International Association of Counseling Services, Alexandria 14839
International Association of Defense Counsel, Chicago 14840
International Association of Democratic Lawyers, Bruxelles 00968
International Association of Dento-Maxillo-Facial Radiology, San Antonio 14841
International Association of Educational Peace Officers, Houston 14842
International Association of Educators for World Peace, Huntsville 14843
International Association of Electoral Science, Los Angeles 14844
International Association of Endocrine Surgeons, San Francisco 14845
International Association of Engineering Geology, Paris 03898
International Association of Engineering Geology, Sezione Italiana, Bari 07312
International Association of Environmental Coordinators, Chalfont Saint Gills 11767
International Association of Environmental Mutagen Societies, Adelaide 00301
International Association of Environmental Mutagen Societies, Pittsburgh 14846
International Association of Family Sociology, De Kalb 14847
International Association of Forensic Toxicologists, Newport Beach 14848
International Association of French-Language Demographers, Paris 03580
International Association of French-Speaking Directors of Educational Institutions, Montréal 01699
International Association of French-Speaking Psychologists of the Working Environment, Motn Saint-Aignan 03573
International Association of Gandhian Studies, Doylestown 14849
International Association of Geochemistry and Cosmochemistry, Pinawa 02147
International Association of Geodesy, København 03131
International Association of Geomagnetism ans Aeronomy, Boulder 14850
International Association of Gerontology, México 08316
International Association of Gerontology, Rochester 14851
International Association of Hispanists, Hanover 14852
International Association of Historians of Asia, Manila 09053
International Association of Human-Animal Interaction Organizations, Renton 14853
International Association of Humanist Educators, Counsellors and Leaders, Plymouth 14854
International Association of Hydrogeologists, Denver 14855
International Association of Institutes of Navigation, London 11768
International Association of Institutes of Navigation, Warrenton 14856
International Association of Jazz Educators, Manhattan 14857
International Association of Jewish Lawyers and Jurists, Tel Aviv 06691
International Association of Knowledge Engineers, Gaithersburg 14858
International Association of Labour Inspections, Paris 03569
International Association of Laryngectomees, Atlanta 14859
International Association of Law Libraries, Charlottesville 14860
International Association of Legal Science, Paris 03587
International Association of Master Penmen and Teachers of Handwriting, Ottawa 02148
International Association of Mathematical Physics, Cambridge 14861
International Association of Medical Laboratory Technologists, Stockholm 09890
International Association of Medical Oceanography, Nice 03595
International Association of Music Libraries, Archives and Documentation Centres, Ottawa 02149
International Association of Music Libraries, Archives and Documentation Centres (United Kingdom Branch), Aylesbury 11769
International Association of Music Libraries - United States Branch, Tucson 14862
International Association of Ocular Surgeons, Skokie 14863
International Association of Optometric Executives, Little Rock 14864
International Association of Oral and Maxillofacial Surgeons, Richmond 14865
International Association of Orientalist Librarians, Irvine 14866
International Association of Paediatric Dentistry, London 11770
International Association of Pancreatology, Boston 14867
International Association of Pediatric Laboratory Medicine, McLean 14868
International Association of Penal Law, Chicago 14869
International Association of Physical Education and Sports for Girls and Women, Newark 14870
International Association of Physical Education and Sports for Girls and Women, Viborg 03132
International Association of Radiopharmacology, Worcester 14871
International Association of Sanskrit Studies, Paris 03899
International Association of School Librarianship, Seattle 14872
International Association of Schools of Social Work, Wien 00510
International Association of Seismology and Physics of the Earth's Interior, Denver 14873
International Association of Severe Weather Specialists, Tucson 14874
International Association of Sound and Audiovisual Archives, Stockholm 09891
International Association of South-East European Studies, Bucuresti 09280
International Association of Survey Statisticians, Paris 03589
International Association of Teachers of English as a Foreign Language, Whitstable 11771
International Association of Teachers of Philosophy, Minden 04506
International Association of Technological University Libraries, Espoo 03352
International Association of Theoretical and Applied Limnology, Tuscaloosa 14875
International Association of Trichologists, Sydney 00302
International Association of Universities, Paris 03900
International Association of University Presidents, Corte Mountain View 14876
International Association of University Professors of English, Marazion 11772
International Association of Volcanology and Chemistry of the Earth's Interior, Leeds 11773
International Association of Wood Anatomists, Utrecht 08481
International Association of Young Lawyers, New York 14877
International Association of Zoo Educators, San Diego 14878
International Association on Mechanization of Field Experiments, Uppsala 09892
International Association on Water Quality, London 11774
International Astronautical Association, Paris 03901
International Astronomical Union, Paris 04297
International Atherosclerosis Society, Houston 14879
International Atomic Energy Agency, Wien 00511
International Azerbaijan Research and Development Institute, Washington 14880
International Banking Research Institute, København 03133
International Banking Security Association, New York 14881
International Bar Association, London 11775
International Bee Research Association, Cardiff 11776
International Benchmark Sites Network for Agrotechnology Transfer, Honolulu 14882
International Bible Society, Colorado Springs 14883
International Bibliographic Commission, Paris 03736
International Bio-Environmental Foundation, Sherman Oaks 14884
International Biometric Society, Washington 14885
International Bird Rescue Research Center, Berkeley 14886
International Board for Plant Genetic Resources, Roma 07313
International Board on Books for Young People, Basel 10167
International Bone Marrow Transplant Group, Milwaukee 14887
International Botanical Congress, Saint Louis 14888
International Brecht Society, Athens 14889
International Bridge, Tunnel and Turnpike Association, Washington 14890
International Bronchoesophagological Society, Scottsdale 14891
International Bulb Society, Culver City 14892
International Bundle Branch Block Association, Los Angeles 14893
International Bureau of Education, Genève 10057
International Bureau of Fiscal Documentation, Amsterdam 08482
International Cancer Information Center, Bethesda 14894
International Cardiology Foundation, Dallas 14895
International Catholic Esperanto Association, Elkhart 14896
International Catholic Movement for Intellectual and Cultural Affairs/ICMICA-Pax Romana, Genève 10209
International Center for Law in Development, New York 14897
International Center for Medicine and Law, Staten Island, Staten Island 14898
International Center for Research on Women, Washington 14899
International Center for the Solution of Environmental Problems, Houston 14900
International Center of Medical and Psychological Hypnosis, Milano 07066
International Center of Medieval Art, New York 14901
International Center of Photography, New York 14902
International Centre for Advanced Technical and Vocational Training, Torino 07314
International Centre for Gas Technology Information, Washington 14903
International Centre for Mechanical Sciences, Udine 07068, 07315
International Centre for Studies in Religious Education, Bruxelles 01018
International Centre for Textile Research and Development, Lubbock 14904
International Centre for the Study of Medieval Painting in the Schelde and the Meuse Valleys, Bruxelles 01017
International Centre for Theoretical Physics, Trieste 07316
International Centre of Films for Children and Young People, Paris 03692
International Cerebral Hemodynamics Society, Seattle 14905
International Cerebral Palsy Society, London 11777
International Child Health Foundation, Columbia 14906
International Child Safety and Health Centre, Cleveland 14907
International Childbirth Education Association, Minneapolis 14908
International Chinese Statistical Association, La Jolla 14909
International Chiropractors Association, Arlington 14910
International Christian Esperanto Association, Alphen a/d Rijn 08523
International Christian Esperanto Association, State College 14911
International Christian Leprosy Mission, Portland 14912
International Christian Media Commission, Seattle 14913
International Christian Studies Association, Santa Monica 14914
International Churchill Society, Baton Rouge 14915
International Civil Defence Organization, Petit-Lancy 10220
International Clinical Epidemiology Network, Philadelphia 14916
International Clinical Hyperthermia Society, Indianapolis 14917
International Clinical Phonetics and Linguistics Association, New Orleans 14918
International College of Angiology, Nesconset 14919
International College of Dentists, Rockville 14920
International College of Surgeons, Chicago 14921
International Colour Association, Eindhoven 08483
International Commission for Plant-Bee Relationships, Lusignan 03902
International Commission for Protection Against Environmental Mutagens and Carcinogens, Vienna 14922
International Commission for The History of Representative and Parliamentary Institutions, Brighton 11778
International Commission for the Nomenclature of Cultivated Plants, Wageningen 08484
International Commission for the Prevention of Alcoholism and Drug Dependency, Silver Spring 14923
International Commission for the Protection of the Rhine against Pollution, Koblenz 05575
International Commission for Uniform Methods of Sugar Analysis, North Ryde 00303
International Commission for Uniform Methods of Sugar Analysis, North Ryde, Australia 05553
International Commission of Jurists, New York 14924
International Commission of Sugar Technology, Rain 05554
International Commission on Antifungal Susceptibility Testing, Richmond 14925
International Commission on Antigens and Molecular Diagnostics, Atlanta 14926
International Commission on Atmospheric Electricity, Tucson 14927
International Commission on Climate, Washington 14928
International Commission on Computational Physics, Albuquerque 14929
International Commission on Cosmic Rays, Newark 14930
International Commission on English in the Liturgy, Washington 14931
International Commission on Illumination, Wien 00427
International Commission on Large Dams, Paris 03737
International Commission on Particles and Fields, Pasadena 14932
International Commission on Penicillium and Aspergillus, New Orleans 14933
International Commission on Polar Meteorology, Cambridge 11779
International Commission on Radiation Units and Measurements, Bethesda 14934
International Commission on Radiological Education and Information, Salt Lake City 14935
International Commission on Statistical Physics, New Haven 14936
International Commission on the History of the Geological Sciences, Cambridge 14937
International Commission on Yeasts, Atlanta 14938
International Commission on Zoological Nomenclature, London 11780
International Commitee for Histochemistry and Cytochemistry, Leiden 08485
International Committee Against Mental Illness, New York 14939
International Committee for Adlerian Summer Schools and Institutes, Edwardsville 14940
International Committee for Coal and Organic Petrology, University Park 14941
International Committee for Pre-Ottoman and Ottoman Studies, Minneapolis 14942
International Committee for Recording the Productivity of Milk Animals, Roma 07317
International Committee of Dialectologists, Leuven 01202
International Committee of Lawyers for Tibet, Berkeley 14943
International Committee of Military Medicine, Liège 01038
International Committee on Avian Anatomical Nomenclature, Seattle 14944
International Committee on Computational Linguistics, Palox Alto 14945
International Committee on Education in Mycology, Atlanta 14946
International Committee on Mechanics in Medicine and Biology, Ann Arbor 14947
International Committee on Microbial Ecology, East Lansing 14948
International Committee on Systematic Bacteriology, Peoria 14949
International Committee on Veterinary Anatomical Nomenclature, Zürich 10193
International Committee on Veterinary Embryological Nomenclature, Ithaca 14950
International Committee on Veterinary Histological Nomenclature, West Lafayette 14951
International Communication Agency, Guadalajara 08317
International Communication Agency, México 08318
International Communication Agency, Monterrey 08319
International Communication Agency, São Paulo 01496
International Communication Association, Austin 14952
International Community Education Association, Bozeman 14953
International Comparative Literature Association, Paris 03570
International Comparative Literature Association, Washington 14954
International Computing Centre, Genève 10168
International Confederation of Architectural Museums, New York 14955
International Confederation of Theatre, Moskva 09364
International Conference of Building Officials, Whittier 14956
International Conference on Large High Voltage Electric Systems, Paris 03759
International Conference on Mechanics in Medicine and Biology, Ann Arbor 14957
International Conference on Social Science and Medicine, Brighton 11781
International Conference on the Unity of the Sciences, Lexington 14958
International Congress of Oral Implantologists, Upper Montclair 14959
International Congress of Systematic and Evolutionary Biology, College Park 14960
International Congress of University Adult Education, Fredericton 02150
International Congress on High-Speed Photography and Photonics, Bellingham 14961
International Consortium for Agricultural Systems Applications, Honolulu 14962
International Consular Academy, Saint Louis 14963
International Coordinating Committee on Solid State Transducers Research, Berkeley 14964
International Coordination Office of Pediatric Endocrine Societies, Houston 14965
International Copper Association, New York 14966
International Copyright Society, München 05555
International Correspondence Society of Allergists, Shawnee Mission 14967
International Cost Engineering Council, Granite Falls 14968
International Council for Adult Education, Toronto 02151
International Council for Computer Communication, Washington 14969
International Council for Educational Media, Paris 03771
International Council for Health, Physical Education, Recreation, Sport and Dance, Reston 14970
International Council for Laboratory Animal Science, Dallas 14971
International Council for Pressure Vessel Technology, Milwaukee 14972
International Council for Science Policy Studies, Cambridge 14973
International Council for Scientific and Technical Information, Paris 03774
International Council for the Exploration of the Sea, København 03134
International Council for Traditional Music, New York 14974
International Council - National Academy of Television Arts and Sciences, New York 14975
International Council of Chemical Associations, Washington 14976
International Council of Environmental Law, Bonn 05556
International Council of Fine Arts Deans, San Marcos 14977
International Council of Kinetography, London 11782
International Council of Kinetography Laban, Columbus 14978
International Council of Library Association Executives, Sacramento 14979
International Council of Museums, Milano 07318
International Council of Museums, Paris 03903
International Council of Museums, Andorran National Committee, Aixovall 00016
International Council of Museums - Committee of the American Association of Museums, Washington 14980
International Council of Onomastic Sciences, Leuven 01203
International Council of Ophthalmology, Chicago 14981, 15018
International Council of Psychologists, San Marcos 14982
International Council of Scientific Unions, Paris 03773

Alphabetical Index: National 362

National Council on Radiation Protection and Measurements, Bethesda *15856*
National Council on Religion and Public Education, Ames *15857*
National Council on the Aging, Washington *15858*
National Crime Prevention Institute, Louisville *15859*
National Criminal Defense College, Macon *15860*
National Culture Commission, Bangkok *10642*
National Dairy Council, Rosemont *15861*
National Democratic Institute for International Affairs, Washington *15862*
National Dental Assistants Association, Washington *15863*
National Dental Association, Washington *15864*
National Dental Examining Board of Canada, Ottawa *02220*
National Dental Hygienists' Association, Southfield *15865*
National Denturist Association, Portland *15866*
National Digestive Diseases Information Clearinghouse, Bethesda *15867*
National District Attorneys Association, Alexandria *15868*
National Dry Bean Council, Washington *15869*
National Earth Science Teachers Association, Washington *15870*
National Economic Association, Ann Arbor *15871*
National Eczema Society, London *12002*
National Education Association, Tewin Wood *12003*
National Education Association of the United States, Washington *15872*
National Education Society of Ceylon, Colombo *09837*
National Educational Information System, Santiago *02474*
National Energy Management Institute, Alexandria *15873*
National Energy Resources Organization, Washington *15874*
National Environmental Health Association, Denver *15875*
National Federation Interscholastic Music Association, Kansas City *15876*
National Federation of Abstracting and Information Services, Philadelphia *15877*
National Federation of Catholic Physicians Guilds, Elm Grove *15878*
National Federation of Continuative Teachers' Associations, Bexley *12004*
National Federation of Modern Language Teachers Associations, Columbus *15879*
National Federation of Sailing Schools, Lymington *12005*
National Federation of Societies for Clinical Social Work, Arlington *15880*
National Federation of State Poetry Societies, Arab *15881*
National Federation of Voluntary Literacy Schemes, London *12006*
National FFA Organization, Alexandria *15882*
National Fire Protection Association, Quincy *15883*
National Food and Nutrition Commission, Lusaka *17052*
National Forensic Association, Westerville *15884*
National Forensic League, Ripon *15885*
National Foundation for Advancement in the Arts, Miami *15886*
National Foundation for Brain Research, Washington *15887*
National Foundation for Educational Research in England and Wales, Slough *12007*
National Foundation for Non-Invasive Diagnostics, Princeton *15888*
National Foundation of Dentistry for the Handicapped, Denver *15889*
National Foundry and Engineering Training Association, Glasgow *12008*
National Genealogical Society, Arlington *15890*
National Geographic Society, Washington *15891*
National Geographical Society of India, Varanasi *06518*
National Grants Management Association, Rockville *15892*
National Guild of Catholic Psychiatrists, Ellicott City *15893*
National Guild of Community Schools of the Arts, Englewood *15894*
National Guild of Piano Teachers, Austin *15895*
National Hardwood Lumber Association, Memphis *15896*
National Health and Medical Research Council, Camberra *00313*
National Health Council, Washington *15897*
National Health Federation, Monrovia *15898*
National Health Law Program, Los Angeles *15899*
National Health Lawyers Association, Washington *15900*
National Hearing Conservation Association, Milwaukee *15901*
National Heart Council, Baltimore *15902*
National Home Study Council, Washington *15903*
National Hormone and Pituitary Program, Rockville *15904*
National Housing and Town Planning Council, London *12009*
National Housing Conference, Washington *15905*
National Humane Education Society, Leesburg *15906*
National Humanities Center, Research Triangle Park *15907*
National Hungarian Cecilia Society, Budapest *06353*
National Hydropower Association, Washington *15908*
National Identification Program for the Advancement of Women in Higher Education Administration, Washington *15909*
National Immigration Law Center, Los Angeles *15910*
National Immunological Society, Moskva *09396*
National Indian Education Association, Alexandria *15911*
National Industrial Zoning Committee, Columbus *15912*
National Information and Documentation Centre, Cairo *03299*
National Information Center for Educational Media, Albuquerque *15913*
National Information Service for Earthquake Engineering, Richmond *15914*
National Institut of Public Administration, Madrid *09768*
National Institute for Burn Medicine, Ann Arbor *15915*
National Institute for Certification in Engineering Technologies, Alexandria *15916*
National Institute for Compilation and Translation, Taipei *02738*
National Institute for Educational Research, Brasília *01488*
National Institute for Farm Safety, Columbia *15917*
National Institute for Medical Research, London *12010*
National Institute for Public Policy, Fairfax *15918*
National Institute for Rehabilitation Engineering, Hewitt *15919*
National Institute for Social Work, London *12011*
National Institute of Adult Continuing Education (England and Wales), Leicester *12012*
National Institute of Agricultural Botany, Cambridge *12013*
National Institute of Ceramic Engineers, Gainesville *15920*
National Institute of Economic and Social Research, London *12014*
National Institute of Folk and Traditional Heritage, Islamabad *08906*
National Institute of Industrial Psychology, Slough *12015*
National Institute of Management Counsellors, Great Neck *15921*
National Institute of Medical Herbalists, Exeter *12016*
National Institute of Science, Nashville *15922*
National Institute of Social Sciences, New York *15923*
National Institute of Steel Detailing, Arlington *15924*
National Institute of Technology, Rio de Janeiro *01491*
National Jewish Center for Immunology and Respiratory Medicine, Denver *15925*
National Judicial College, Reno *15926*
National League of American PEN Women, Washington *15927*
National Librarians Association, Alma *15928*
National Marine Educators Association, Pacific Grove *15929*
National Mastitis Council, Arlington *15930*
National Materials Advisory Board, Washington *15931*
National Materials Handling Centre, Bedford *12017*
National Medical and Dental Association, Maspeth *15932*
National Medical and Technical Scientific Society, Moskva *09397*
National Medical Association, Washington *15933*
National Medical Fellowships, New York *15934*
National Mental Health Association, Alexandria *15935*
National Middle School Association, Columbus *15936*
National Monuments Commission, Livingstone *17053*
National Multiple Sclerosis Society, New York *15937*
National Music Council, Brooklyn *15938*
National Music Council of China, Taipei *02739*
National Office for Research and Special Libraries, Oslo *08877*
National Old Timers' Association of the Energy Industry, Mineola *15939*
National Opera Association, McLean *15940*
National Operatic and Dramatic Association, London *12018*
National Ophthalmological Society, Moskva *09398*
National Optometric Association, Columbus *15941*
National Orchestral Association, New York *15942*
National Organization for Continuing Education of Roman Catholic Clergy, Chicago *15943*
National Organization for Rare Disorders, New Fairfield *15944*
National Organization of Minority Architects, Washington *15945*
National Organization on Legal Problems of Education, Topeka *15946*
National Orthotic and Prosthetic Research Institute, Lenox Hill *15947*
National Osteopathic Guild Association, Chicago *15948*
National Perinatal Association, Tampa *15949*
National Pest Control Association, Dunn Loring *15950*
National Pharmaceutical Association, Richardson *15951*
National Pharmaceutical Society, Moskva *09399*
National Photography Instructors Association, Eagle Rock *15952*
National Piano Foundation, Dallas *15953*
National Plant Board, Raleigh *15954*
National Podriatic Medical Association, Chicago *15955*
National Productivity Council, New Delhi *06519*
National Psoriasis Foundation, Portland *15956*
National Psychological Association for Psychoanalysis, New York *15957*
National Ramah Commission, New York *15958*
National Reading Conference, Chicago *15959*
National Records Management Council, New York *15960*
National Registry in Clinical Chemistry, Washington *15961*
National Rehabilitation Association, Alexandria *15962*
National Research Centre, Cairo *03300*
National Research Council, Reykjavik *06376*
National Research Council, Washington *15963*
National Research Council of the Philippines, Manila *09054*
National Resident Matching Program, Washington *15964*
National Resource Center for Consumers of Legal Services, Gloucester *15965*
National Romanian Society for Soil Science, Bucuresti *09319*
National Rural Education Association, Fort Collins *15966*
National Safety Council, Dublin *06653*
National Safety Council, Itasca *15967*
National Safety Management Society, Weaverville *15968*
National School Boards Association, Alexandria *15969*
National School Public Relations Association, Arlington *15970*
National Schools Committee for Economic Education, Cos Cob *15971*
National Science Council, Taipei *02740*
National Science Council of Pakistan, Islamabad *08909*
National Science Teachers Association, Arlington *15972*
National Scientific Medical Society of Anatomists, Histologists and Embryologists, Moskva *09400*
National Scientific Medical Society of Endocrinologists, Moskva *09401*
National Scientific Medical Society of Gastroenterologists, Moskva *09402*
National Scientific Medical Society of Haematologists and Transfusiologists, Moskva *09403*
National Scientific Medical Society of History of Medicine, Moskva *09404*
National Scientific Medical Society of Hygienists, Moskva *09405*
National Scientific Medical Society of Infectionists, Moskva *09406*
National Scientific Medical Society of Medical Geneticists, Moskva *09407*
National Scientific Medical Society of Nephrologists, Moskva *09408*
National Scientific Medical Society of Neuropathologists and Psychiatrists, Moskva *09409*
National Scientific Medical Society of Neurosurgeons, Moskva *09410*
National Scientific Medical Society of Obstetricians and Gynaecologists, Moskva *09411*
National Scientific Medical Society of Oncologists, St. Petersburg *09412*
National Scientific Medical Society of Oto-Rhino-Laryngologists, Moskva *09413*
National Scientific Medical Society of Paediatriciams, Moskva *09414*
National Scientific Medical Society of Phtisiologists, Moskva *09415*
National Scientific Medical Society of Physical Therapists and Health-Resort Physicians, Moskva *09416*
National Scientific Medical Society of Physicians-Analysts, Moskva *09417*
National Scientific Medical Society of Physicians in Curative Physical Culture and Sports Medicine, Moskva *09418*
National Scientific Medical Society of Rheumatologists, Moskva *09419*
National Scientific Medical Society of Roentgenologists and Radiologists, Moskva *09420*
National Scientific Medical Society of Stomatologists, Moskva *09421*
National Scientific Medical Society of Surgeons, Moskva *09422*
National Scientific Medical Society of Therapists, Moskva *09423*
National Scientific Medical Society of Toxicologists, St. Petersburg *09424*
National Scientific Medical Society of Traumatic Surgeons and Orthopaedists, Moskva *09425*
National Scientific Medical Society of Venereologists and Dermatologists, Moskva *09426*
National Scientific Society of Urological Surgeons, Moskva *09427*
National Sculpture Society, New York *15973*
National Secular Society, London *12019*
National Society (Church of England) for Promoting Religious Education, London *12020*
National Society for Clean Air and Environmental Protection, Brighton *12021*
National Society for Education in Art and Design, Corsham *12022*
National Society for Epilepsy, Gerrards Cross *12023*
National Society for Experiential Education, Raleigh *15974*
National Society for Research into Allergy, Hinckley *12024*
National Society for the Preservation of Covered Bridges, Worcester *15975*
National Society for the Study of Education, Chicago *15976*
National Society for Transplant Surgery, Cardiff *12025*
National Society of Fine Arts, Lisboa *09224*
National Society of General Practice of Romania, Bucuresti *09318*
National Society of Professional Engineers, Alexandria *15977*
National Space Club, Washington *15978*
National Space Society, Washington *15979*
National Speleological Society, Huntsville *15980*
National Standard Plumbing Code Committee, Falls Church *15981*
National Strict Baptist Sunday School Association, Bishops Stortford *12026*
National Student Nurses' Association, New York *15982*
National Student Speech Language Hearing Association, Rockville *15983*
National Study of School Evaluation, Schaumburg *15984*
National Tax Association – Tax Institute of America, Columbus *15985*
National Tax Research Association of China, Taipei *02741*
National Technical Association, Washington *15986*
National Technical Services Association, Alexandria *15987*
National Telemedia Council, Madison *15988*
National Theatre Institute, Waterford *15989*
National Therapeutic Recreation Society, Arlington *15990*
National Trolleybus Association, Bedford *12027*
National Trust for Places of Historic Interest or Natural Beauty, London *12028*
National Trust for Scotland, Edinburgh *12029*
National Union of Teachers, London *12030*
National University Continuing Education Association, Washington *15991*
National Urban League, New York *15992*
National Vocational Agricultural Teachers' Association, Alexandria *15993*
National Vocational Technical Educational Foundation, Washington *15994*
National Water Resources Association, Arlington *15995*
National Wildlife Federation, Vienna *15996*
National Women's Health Network, Washington *15997*
National Women's Studies Association, College Park *15998*
National Writers Association, Aurora *15999*
National Writing Project, Berkeley *16000*
National Young Writers Association of China, Taipei *02742*
Nationale Vereniging voor Economisch Onderwijs, Bergen *08531*
Nationalekonomiska Föreningen, Stockholm *09922*
Nationalkomitee der Bundesrepublik Deutschland im International Council for Traditional Music, Bamberg *05761*
Nationalökonomische Gesellschaft, Wien *00561*
Nationaløkonomisk Forening, København *03166*
Nation's Report Card – National Assessment of Educational Progress, Princeton *16001*
Native Plants Preservation Society of Victoria, Toorak *00314*
Native Seeds/Search, Tucson *16002*
NATMH, Aylesbury *11989*
NATS, Jacksonville *15748*
Natur und Medizin e.V., Fördergemeinschaft für Erfahrungsheilkunde, Bonn *05762*
Natural Environment Research Council, Swindon *12031*
The Natural History Society of Northumbria, Newcastle-upon-Tyne *12032*
Natural History Society of Prince Edward Island, Charlottetown *02221*
Natural Products Chemistry Research Group, Johannesburg *09644*
Natural Resources Conservation League of Victoria, Springvale South *00315*
Natural Resources Defense Council, New York *16003*
The Natural Resources Research Organization, Jerusalem *06742*
Les Naturalistes Belges, Bruxelles *01229*
Naturalistes Parisiens, Paris *03922*
The Nature Conservancy, Arlington *16004*
Naturforschende Gesellschaft Bamberg e.V., Viereth-Trunstadt *05763*
Naturforschende Gesellschaft des Kantons Glarus, Glarus *10210*
Naturforschende Gesellschaft Freiburg, Freiburg *05764*
Naturforschende Gesellschaft in Basel, Basel *10211*
Naturforschende Gesellschaft in Bern, Bern *10212*
Naturforschende Gesellschaft in Zürich, Grüt *10213*
Naturforschende Gesellschaft Luzern, Luzern *10214*
Naturforschende Gesellschaft Schaffhausen, Schaffhausen *10215*
Naturforschende Gesellschaft Solothurn, Bugglen *10216*
Naturhistorische Gesellschaft Hannover, Hannover *05765*
Naturhistorische Gesellschaft Nürnberg e.V., Nürnberg *05766*
Naturhistorischer Verein der Rheinlande und Westfalens, Bonn *05767*
Naturhistorisk Forening for Jylland, Arhus *03167*
Naturhistorisk Forening for Nordsjaelland, Hillerød *03168*
Naturvetenskapliga Forskningsrådet, Stockholm *09923*
Naturwissenschaftlich-Medizinische Vereinigung in Salzburg, Salzburg *00562*
Naturwissenschaftlich-medizinischer Verein in Innsbruck, Innsbruck *00563*
Naturwissenschaftliche Gesellschaft Winterthur, Wiesendangen *10217*
Naturwissenschaftlicher und Historischer Verein für das Land Lippe e.V., Detmold *05768*
Naturwissenschaftlicher Verein für das Fürstentum Lüneburg von 1851 e.V., Lüneburg *05769*
Naturwissenschaftlicher Verein für Kärnten, Klagenfurt *00564*
Naturwissenschaftlicher Verein für Steiermark, Graz *00565*
Naturwissenschaftlicher Verein in Hamburg, Hamburg *05770*
Naturwissenschaftlicher Verein zu Bremen, Bremen *05771*
Natuurhistorisch Genootschap in Limburg, Maastricht *08532*
The Nautical Institute, London *12033*
NAUW, Washington *15750*
NAV, Köln *05772, 05851*
NAV-Virchowbund, Köln *05772*
NAVA, Fullerton *15666*
NAVA, Trenton *16054*
NAVEA, Milan *15627*
NAVESNP, McKeesport *15751*
NAVp, Berlin *05852*
NAVS, London *11973*
Navy Records Society, London *12034*
NAW, Berlin *05855*
NAWA, Oklahoma City *15624*
NAWE, Washington *15667*

RASD, Chicago *16250*
RASE, Stoneleigh Park *12168*
R.A.S.N.Z., Wellington *08741*
Rat für Baukultur im Deutschen Kulturrat, Essen *05898*
Rat für Darstellende Künste im Deutschen Kulturrat, Köln *05899*
Rat für Formgebung, Frankfurt *05900*
Rat für Soziokultur im Deutschen Kulturrat, Bonn *05901*
Rat von Sachverständigen für Umweltfragen, Wiesbaden *05902*
Raten Amerika Kyokai Kenkyubu, Tokyo *08010*
Rationalisierungs-Gemeinschaft Bauwesen im RKW, Eschborn *05903*
Rationalisierungs-Gemeinschaft Verpackung im RKW, Eschborn *05904*
Rationalisierungs-Kuratorium der Deutschen Wirtschaft e.V., Eschborn *05905*
Rationalisierungs-Kuratorium der Deutschen Wirtschaft e.V., Landesgruppe Baden-Württemberg, Stuttgart *05906*
Rationalisierungs-Kuratorium der Deutschen Wirtschaft e.V., Landesgruppe Berlin, Berlin *05907*
Rationalisierungs-Kuratorium der Deutschen Wirtschaft e.V., Landesgruppe Bremen, Bremen *05908*
Rationalisierungs-Kuratorium der Deutschen Wirtschaft e.V., Landesgruppe Hamburg, Hamburg *05909*
Rationalisierungs-Kuratorium der Deutschen Wirtschaft e.V., Landesgruppe Hessen, Eschborn *05910*
Rationalisierungs-Kuratorium der Deutschen Wirtschaft e.V., Landesgruppe Niedersachsen, Hannover *05911*
Rationalisierungs-Kuratorium der Deutschen Wirtschaft e.V., Landesgruppe Nord-Ost, Kiel *05912*
Rationalisierungs-Kuratorium der Deutschen Wirtschaft e.V., Landesgruppe Nordrhein-Westfalen, Düsseldorf *05913*
Rationalisierungs-Kuratorium der Deutschen Wirtschaft e.V., Landesgruppe Rheinland-Pfalz, Mainz *05914*
Rationalisierungs-Kuratorium für Landwirtschaft e.V., Osterrönfeld *05915*
The Ray Society, London *12147*
Raziskovalna Skupnost Slovenije, Ljubljana *09590*
RC, Jenkintown *16285*
R.C.A., Conwy *12176*
RCAA, Wadebridge *12200*
RCAP, Leesburg *16283*
R.C.G.P., London *12180*
RCHS, Edinburgh *12175*
RCM, London *12181*
R.C.M., London *12182*
RCN, London *12183*
RCO, London *12186*
R.C.O.G., London *12184*
RCP, London *12189*
R.C.P.E., Edinburgh *12191*
RCPSC, Ottawa *02344*
RCR, London *12193*
RCRC, Austin *16261*
RCRC, Westfield *16236*
RCS, London *12178*
RCSC, Chicago *16268*
R.C.S.E., London *12195*
RCSI, Dublin *06659*
R.C.T.S., London *12143*
R.C.V.S., London *12196*
RDA, Purley *12144*
R.D.S., Dublin *06660*
RDS, London *12154, 12201*
Read Natural Childbirth Foundation, San Rafael *16247*
Reading is Fundamental, Washington *16248*
Reading Reform Foundation, Tacoma *16249*
Real Academia de Bellas Artes de la Purísima Concepción, Valladolid *09773*
Real Academia de Bellas Artes de San Fernando, Madrid *09774*
Real Academia de Bellas Artes de San Telmo, Málaga *09775*
Real Academia de Bellas Artes de Santa Isabel de Hungría, Sevilla *09776*
Real Academia de Bellas Artes y Ciencias Históricas de Toledo, Toledo *09777*
Real Acadèmia de Bones Letres, Barcelona *09778*
Real Academia de Ciencias Exactas, Físicas y Naturales, Madrid *09779*
Real Academia de Ciencias Morales y Políticas, Madrid *09780*
Real Academia de Ciencias Veterinarias de España, Madrid *09781*
Real Academia de Ciencias y Artes de Barcelona, Barcelona *09782*
Real Academia de Córdoba de Ciencias, Bellas Letras y Nobles Artes, Córdoba *09783*
Real Academia de Doctores, Madrid *09784*
Real Academia de Farmacia, Madrid *09785*
Real Academia de Jurisprudencia y Legislación, Madrid *09786*
Real Academia de la Historia, Madrid *09787*
Real Academia de la Lengua Vasca – Euskaltzaindia, Bilbao *09788*
Real Academia de Medicina y Cirugía de Palma de Mallorca, Palma de Mallorca *09789*
Real Academia de Nobles y Bellas Artes de San Luis, Zaragoza *09790*
Real Academia Española, Madrid *09791*
Real Academia Gallega, La Coruña *09792*
Real Academia Hispano-Americana, Cádiz *09793*
Real Academia Nacional de Medicina, Madrid *09794*
Real Academia Sevillana de Buenas Letras, Sevilla *09795*
Real Instituto Arqueológico de Portugal, Lisboa *09204*
Real Institutode Estudios Asturianos, Oviedo *09796*
Real Sociedad Arqueológica Tarraconense, Tarragona *09797*
Real Sociedad Bascongada de los Amigos del País, San Sebastián *09798*
Real Sociedad Económica de Amigos del País de Tenerife, Tenerife *09799*
Real Sociedad Española de Historia Natural, Madrid *09800*
Real Sociedad Española de Química, Madrid *09801*
Real Sociedad Fotográfica Española, Madrid *09802*
Real Sociedad Geográfica, Madrid *09803*
Real Sociedad Matemática Española, Madrid *09804*
Real Sociedade Arqueológica Lusitana, Santiago do Cacém *09205*
RECGAI, Chadds Ford *16266*
Rechts- und Staatswissenschaftliche Vereinigung Düsseldorf e.V., Düsseldorf *05916*
Rectoren College, Utrecht *08618*
Rectors' Conference, Bangkok *10643*
REFA-Verband für Arbeitsstudien und Betriebsorganisation e.V., Darmstadt *05917*
Reference and Adult Services Division (of ALA), Chicago *16250*
Reforma: National Association to Promote Library Services to the Spanish-Speaking, New York *16251*
Refugee Policy Group, Washington *16252*
Regency Society of Brighton and Hove, Brighton *12148*
Regional Education Board of the Christian Brothers, Landover *16253*
Regional Institute of Social Welfare Research, Athens *16254*
Regional Maritime Academy, Abidjan, Abidjan *07682*
Regional Network for Research on Economic Policy, Washington *16255*
Regional Program for Educational Development, Washington *16256*
Regional Science Association International, Urbana *16257*
Regional Studies Association, London *12149*
Regionale Organisation der FDI für Europa (ERO), Köln *05918*
Registered Medical Assistants of American Medical Technologists, Park Ridge *16258*
Regroupement pour la Surveillance du Nucléaire, Montréal *01852*
Rehabilitation Information Round Table, Alexandria *16259*
Rehabilitation International, New York *16260*
Reial Acadèmia Catalana de Belles Arts de Sant Jordi, Barcelona *09805*
Reinforced Concrete Research Council, Austin *16261*
Reinforcing Steel Institute of Canada, Richmond Hill *02334*
Reinhold-Schneider-Gesellschaft e.V., Paderborn *05919*
Reinsurance Research Council, Toronto *02335*
Rektorkollegiet, København *03189*
The Religious Drama Society of Great Britain, London *12141*
Religious Research Association, Washington *16262*
Religious Society of Friends, London *12150*
Religious Speech Communication Association, Azusa *16263*
Remote Sensing Society, Nottingham *12151*
REMP, Den Haag *08619*
Renaissance English Text Society, Amherst *16264*
Renaissance, Schweizerischer Verband katholischer Akademiker-Gesellschaften, Luzern *10229*
Renaissance Society of America, New York *16265*
The Renal Association, London *12152*
Republic of China Society of Cardiology, Taipei *02750*
Republički Zavod za Zaštita na Spomenicite na Kulturata, Skopje *08193*
RERC, Duluth *16246*
Rersearch Council for Applied Mathematics, Moskva *09437*
R.E.S., London *12202*
RES, London *12203*
Research and Development Society, London *12153*
Research and Engineering Council of the Graphic Arts Industry, Chadds Ford *16266*
Research Association of Minority Professors, Prairie View *16267*
Research Association of Statistical Sciences, Fukuoka *08040*
Research Community of Slovenia, Ljubljana *09590*
The Research Council of Norway, Oslo *08793*
Research Council of Norway, Oslo *08876*
Research Council on Structural Connections, Chicago *16268*
Research Defence Society, London *12154*
Research Designs and Standards Organization, Lucknow *06525*
Research Group for European Migration Problems, Den Haag *08619*
Research Group for Lung Metabolism, Tygerberg *09655*
Research Group for Neurochemistry, Tygerberg *09656*
Research Institute for Foreign travellers in Italy, Genova *07152*
Research into Lost Knowledge Organisation, Orpington *12155*
Research Libraries Group, Mountain View *16269*
Research Society for Natural Therapeutics, Bournemouth *12156*
Research Society for Victorian Periodicals, Edwardsville *16270*
Research Society of Pakistan, Lahore *08931*
Research Society on Alcoholism, Austin *16271*
Research to Prevent Blindness, New York *16272*
RETS, Amherst *16264*
Réunion Internationale des Laboratoires d'Essais et de Recherche sur les Matériaux et les Constructions, Cachan *03943*
R.F.S., Tring *12207*
RFSU, Twickenham *12276*
RG, Beltsville *16279*
R.G.S., London *12208*
R.G.S.A., Fortitude Valley *00341*
R.H.A.S.S., Edinburgh *12209*
Rheinaubund, Schweizerische Arbeitsgemeinschaft für Natur und Heimat, Schaffhausen *10230*
Rheinisch-Westfälische Akademie der Wissenschaften, Düsseldorf *05920*
Rheinisch-Westfälische Vereinigung für Lungen- und Bronchialheilkunde, Essen *05921*
Rheinisch-Westfälisches Institut für Wirtschaftsforschung, Essen *05922*
Rheinische Adalbert-Stifter-Gemeinschaft, Leverkusen *05923*
Rheinische Naturforschende Gesellschaft, Mainz *05924*
Rheinische Vereinigung für Volkskunde, Bonn *05925*
Rhetoric Society of America, Norman *16273*
RHS, London *12211*
RHS, Oklahoma City *16278*
R.H.S.Q., Brisbane North Quay *00342*
RHSV, Melbourne *00343*
RI, Boulder *16280*
RI, Emmaus *16277*
RI, Fort Worth *16242*
RI, New York *16260*
RI/SME, Dearborn *16276*
R.I.A., Dublin *06664*
RIAI, Dublin *06663*
RIAM, Dublin *06665*
RIBA, London *12213*
RIC, Truro *12222*
Richard III Society, London *12157*
Richard III Society, New Orleans *16274*
Richard Ivey Foundation, London *02336*
Richard Jefferies Society, Swindon *12158*
Richard-Strauss-Gesellschaft e.V., München *05926*
Richard-Wagner-Verband Bayreuth e.V., Bayreuth *05927*
RIdIM, New York *15171*
RIF, Washington *16248*
R.I.G.B., London *12223*
Right to a Comprehensive Education, London *12159*
RIIA, London *12214*
Rijksbureau voor Kunsthistorische Documentatie, Den Haag *08620*
RIK, Zürich *10575*
Riksbibliotektjenesten, Oslo *08877*
Riksföreningen för Lärarna i Moderna Språk, Hisings Kärra *09934*
RILEM, Cachan *03943*
RILKO, Orpington *12155*
RILM, New York *15172*
RIN, London *12215*
RIPA, London *12219*
Riron Keiryo Keizai Gakkai, Tokyo *08011*
RIRT, Alexandria *16259*
Rissho Koseikai, Tokyo *08012*
Rissho Koseikai Fuzoku Kosei Toshokan, Tokyo *08012*
RISW, Swansea *12225*
RISWR, Athens *16254*
Rithöfundasamband Islands, Reykjavik *06378*
RITLA, Caracas *16872*
River Thames Society, Richmond *12160*
RJC, Long Beach *16275*
RKBCAC, Kensington *16281*
R.K.D., Den Haag *08620*
RKW, Eschborn *05905*
RLAS, London *12230*
RLAS, Preston *12228*
RLG, Mountain View *16269*
R.M.A., London *12234*
RMAAMT, Park Ridge *16258*
RMS, Oxford *12233*
RNAA, Norwich *12236*
RNBWS, Southsea *12235*
RNCF, San Rafael *16247*
RNSHS, Dartmouth *02345*
Robert Schumann-Gesellschaft e.V., Düsseldorf *05928*
Robert Schumann-Gesellschaft Zwickau e.V., Zwickau *05929*
Robinson Jeffers Committee, Long Beach *16275*
Robotics International of the Society of Manufacturing Engineers, Dearborn *16276*
ROCSOC, Taipei *02750*
Rodale International, Emmaus *16277*
Rodeo Historical Society, Oklahoma City *16278*
Rogers Group, Beltsville *16279*
Roland Eötvös Physical Society, Budapest *06287*
Rolf-Dieter-Brinkmann-Gesellschaft e.V., Vechta *05930*
Rolf Institute, Boulder *16280*
Romanian Association of Political Sciences, Bucuresti *09274*
Romanian General Association of Economists, Bucuresti *09269*
Romanian Medical Association, Bucuresti *09283*
Romanian Psychiatric Association, Bucuresti *09272*
Romanian Society for Orthopaedics and Traumatology, Bucuresti *09323*
Romanian Society of Neurosurgery, Bucuresti *09322*
Romanian Support Society for People Suffering of Alzheimer Type Diseases, Bucuresti *09324*
ROREP, Bern *10390*
Rose Kushner Breast Cancer Advisory Center, Kensington *16281*
ROSPA, Birmingham *12250*
Royal Academy for Islamic Civilization Research, Amman *08056*
Royal Academy of Arts in London, London *12161*
Royal Academy of Belles Lettres, Barcelona *09778*
Royal Academy of Dancing, London *12162*
Royal Academy of Dramatic Art, London *12163*
Royal Academy of Engineering, London *12164*
The Royal Academy of Letters, History and Antiquities, Stockholm *09912*
Royal Academy of Medicine, Dublin *06657*
Royal Academy of Music, London *12165*
Royal Academy of Veterinary Sciences of Spain, Madrid *09781*
Royal Aeronautical Society, London *12166*
The Royal Aeronautical Society (Australian Division), Mascot *00324*
Royal Aeronautical Society, New Zealand Division, Wellington *08739*
Royal Aeronautical Society, Southern Africa Division, Bryanston *09657*
The Royal African Society, London *12167*
Royal Agricultural and Horticultural Society of South Australia, Wayville *00325*
Royal Agricultural Society of England, Stoneleigh Park *12168*
Royal Agricultural Society of New Zealand, Wellington *08740*
Royal Agricultural Society of Tasmania, Glenorchy *00326*
The Royal Agricultural Society of Western Australia, Claremont *00327*
Royal Anthropological Institute of Great Britain and Ireland, London *12169*
Royal Archaeological Institute, London *12170*
Royal Architectural Institute of Canada, Ottawa *02337*
Royal Art Society of New South Wales, North Sydney *00328*
Royal Asiatic Society, Hong Kong Branch, Hong Kong *02658*
Royal Asiatic Society, Korea Branch, Seoul *08142*
Royal Asiatic Society, Malaysian Branch, Kuala Lumpur *08238*
Royal Asiatic Society of Great Britain and Ireland, London *12171*
Royal Asiatic Society of Sri Lanka, Colombo *09838*
Royal Association for Disability and Rehabilitation, London *12172*
Royal Astronomical Society, London *12173*
Royal Astronomical Society of Canada, Toronto *02338*
Royal Astronomical Society of New Zealand, Wellington *08741*
Royal Australasian College of Dental Surgeons, Sydney *00329*
The Royal Australasian College of Physicians, Sydney *00330*
The Royal Australasian College of Radiologists, Sydney *00331*
Royal Australasian College of Surgeons, Melbourne *00332*
Royal Australasian Ornithologists Union, Hawthorn East *00333*
Royal Australian and New-Zealand College of Psychiatrists, Melbourne *00334*
Royal Australian Chemical Institute, North Melbourne *00335*
Royal Australian College of Ophthalmologists, Sydney *00336*
Royal Australian Historical Society, Sydney *00337*
Royal Australian Planning Institute, Hawthorn *00338*
Royal Bath and West of England Society, Shepton Mallet *12174*
Royal Belgian Society of Surgery, Bruxelles *01278*
Royal Caledonian Horticultural Society, Edinburgh *12175*
Royal Cambrian Academy of Art, Conwy *12176*
Royal Canadian Academy of Arts, Toronto *02339*
Royal Canadian Geographical Society, Vanier *02340*
Royal Canadian Institute, Toronto *02341*
Royal Canadian Military Institute, Toronto *02342*
Royal Celtic Society, Edinburgh *12177*
Royal Choral Society, London *12178*
The Royal College of Anaesthetists, London *12179*
Royal College of Dental Surgeons of Ontario, Toronto *02343*
Royal College of General Practitioners, London *12180*
Royal College of Midwives, London *12181*
Royal College of Music, London *12182*
Royal College of Nursing – Australia, Deakin *00339*
Royal College of Nursing of The United Kingdom, London *12183*
Royal College of Obstetricians and Gynaecologists, London *12184*
Royal College of Ophthalmologists, London *12185*
The Royal College of Organists, London *12186*
Royal College of Paediatrics and Child Health, London *12187*
Royal College of Pathologists, London *12188*
Royal College of Pathologists of Australasia, Surrey Hills *00340*
Royal College of Physicians, London *12189*
Royal College of Physicians and Surgeons of Canada, Ottawa *02344*
Royal College of Physicians and Surgeons of Glasgow, Glasgow *12190*
Royal College of Physicians of Edinburgh, Edinburgh *12191*
Royal College of Physicians of Ireland, Dublin *06658*
The Royal College of Psychiatrists, London *12192*
Royal College of Radiologists, London *12193*
Royal College of Surgeons in Ireland, Dublin *06659*
The Royal College of Surgeons of Edinburgh, Edinburgh *12194*
Royal College of Surgeons of England, London *12195*
Royal College of Veterinary Surgeons, London *12196*
Royal Commission for The Exhibition of 1851, London *12197*
Royal Commission on Historical Manuscripts, London *12198*
Royal Commonwealth Society, London *12199*
The Royal Cornwall Agricultural Association, Wadebridge *12200*
The Royal Danish Academy of Sciences and Letters, København *03150*
Royal Danish Agricultural Society, Frederiksberg *03148*
Royal Drawing Society, London *12201*
Royal Dublin Society, Dublin *06660*

371 Alphabetical Index: SATRA

Royal Dutch Geographical Society, Utrecht 08502
Royal Economic Society, London 12202
Royal Economic Society of Friends of Tenerife, Tenerife 09799
Royal Entomological Society of London, London 12203
The Royal Faculty of Procurators in Glasgow, Glasgow 12204
Royal Fine Art Commission, London 12205
Royal Fine Art Commission for Scotland, Edinburgh 12206
Royal Forestry Society of England, Wales and Northern Ireland, Tring 12207
Royal Geographical Society, London 12208
Royal Geographical Society of Queensland, Fortitude Valley 00341
Royal Geological and Mining Society of the Netherlands, Haarlem 08503
Royal Hibernian Academy of Arts, Dublin 06661
Royal Highland and Agricultural Society of Scotland, Edinburgh 12209
Royal Historical Society, London 12210
The Royal Historical Society of Queensland, Brisbane North Quay 00342
Royal Historical Society of Victoria, Melbourne 00343
Royal Horticultural Society, London 12211
Royal Horticultural Society of Ireland, Dublin 06662
Royal Horticultural Society of New South Wales, Sydney 00344
Royal Incorporation of Architects in Scotland, Edinburgh 12212
Royal Institute, Bangkok 10644
Royal Institute of Architects of Ireland, Dublin 06663
Royal Institute of British Architects, London 12213
Royal Institute of International Affairs, London 12214
Royal Institute of Linguistics and Anthropology, Leiden 08501
Royal Institute of Navigation, London 12215
Royal Institute of Oil Painters, London 12216
Royal Institute of Painters in Water Colours, London 12217
Royal Institute of Philosophy, London 12218
Royal Institute of Public Administration, London 12219
The Royal Institute of Public Health and Hygiene, London 12220
Royal Institution of Chartered Surveyors, London 12221
Royal Institution of Cornwall, Truro 12222
Royal Institution of Great Britain, London 12223
The Royal Institution of Naval Architects, London 12224
Royal Institution of South Wales, Swansea 12225
Royal Irish Academy, Dublin 06664
Royal Irish Academy of Music, Dublin 06665
Royal Isle of Wight Agricultural Society, Newport 12226
Royal Jersey Agricultural and Horticultural Society, Trinity 12227
Royal Lancashire Agricultural Society, Preston 12228
Royal Liverpool Philharmonic Society, Liverpool 12229
Royal London Aid Society, London 12230
Royal Medical Society, Edinburgh 12231
Royal Melbourne Institute of Technology, Melbourne 00345
Royal Meteorological Society, Reading 12232
Royal Microscopical Society, Oxford 12233
Royal Musical Association, London 12234
Royal Naval Bird Watching Society, Southsea 12235
Royal Nepal Academy, Kathmandu 08392
Royal Nepal Academy of Science and Technology, Kathmandu 08393
Royal Netherlands Association for Advancement of Pharmacy, Den Haag 08517
Royal Netherlands Association of Musicians, Amsterdam 08520
Royal Norfolk Agricultural Association, Norwich 12236
Royal Norwegian Council for Scientific and Industrial Research, Oslo 08809
Royal Nova Scotia Historical Society, Dartmouth 02345
Royal Numismatic Society, London 12237
Royal Pharmaceutical Society of Great Britain, London 12238
The Royal Philharmonic Society, London 12239
Royal Philosophical Society of Glasgow, Glasgow 12240
Royal Photographic Society of Great Britain, Bath 12241
Royal Physical Society of Edinburgh, Edinburgh 12242
Royal Queensland Art Society, Brisbane 00346
Royal Scientific Society, Amman 08057
Royal Scottish Academy, Edinburgh 12243
Royal Scottish Forestry Society, Dalkeith 12244
Royal Scottish Geographical Society, Glasgow 12245
The Royal Society, London 12246
Royal Society for Asian Affairs, London 12247
Royal Society for Nature Conservation, Lincoln 12248
Royal Society for the Encouragement of Arts, Manufactures and Commerce, London 12249
Royal Society for The Prevention of Accidents, Birmingham 12250
Royal Society for the Protection of Birds, Sandy 12251
The Royal Society of Antiquaries of Ireland, Dublin 06666
Royal Society of Arts, London 12252
Royal Society of Arts and Science of Göteborg, Göteborg 09909
Royal Society of Arts and Sciences of Mauritius, Réduit 08254
Royal Society of British Artists, London 12253
Royal Society of British Sculptors, London 12254
Royal Society of Canada, Ottawa 02346
The Royal Society of Chemistry, London 12255
The Royal Society of Edinburgh, Edinburgh 12256
The Royal Society of Health, London 12257
Royal Society of Literature of the United Kingdom, London 12258
Royal Society of Marine Artists, London 12259
Royal Society of Medicine, London 12260
Royal Society of New South Wales, North Ryde 00347
Royal Society of New Zealand, Wellington 08742
Royal Society of Portrait Painters, London 12261
Royal Society of Queensland, Saint Lucia 00348
Royal Society of South Africa, Cape Town 09658
Royal Society of South Australia, Adelaide 00349
Royal Society of Tasmania, Hobart 00350
Royal Society of the Humanities at Uppsala, Uppsala 09904
The Royal Society of Tropical Medicine and Hygiene, London 12262
Royal Society of Ulster Architects, Belfast 12263
Royal Society of Victoria, Melbourne 00351
Royal Society of Western Australia, Perth 00352
Royal South Australian Society of Arts, Adelaide 00353
Royal Statistical Society, London 12264
Royal Stuart Society, Huntingdon 12265
Royal Swaziland Society of Science and Technology, Kwaluseni 09852
Royal Swedish Academy of Military Sciences, Stockholm 09905
Royal Swedish Academy of Sciences, Stockholm 09911
Royal Television Society, London 12266
Royal Town Planning Institute, London 12267
Royal Ulster Academy, Lurgan 12268
Royal Ulster Academy Association, Lambeg 12269
Royal Ulster Agricultural Society, Belfast 12270
Royal Watercolour Society, London 12271
Royal Welsh Agricultural Society, Powys 12272
Royal West of England Academy, Bristol 12273
Royal Western Australian Historical Society, Nedlands 00354
Royal Zoological Society, Amsterdam 08625
Royal Zoological Society of Antwerp, Antwerpen 01223
Royal Zoological Society of New South Wales, Mosman 00355
The Royal Zoological Society of Scotland, Edinburgh 12274
Royal Zoological Society of South Australia, Adelaide 00356
RPA, Liverpool 11863
RPB, New York 16272
RPFI, Wien 00418
RPG, Washington 16252
R.P.S., Great Glenn 12146
RRA, Washington 16262
RRF, Tacoma 16249
RRS, Oak Brook 16238
RSA, Austin 16271
R.S.A., Edinburgh 12243
RSA, London 12149, 12252
RSA, New York 16265
RSA, Norman 16273
RSA, Urbana 16257
R.S.A.I., Dublin 06666
R.S.A.T., Tarragona 09797
RSC, London 12255
RSCA, Azusa 16263
R.S.E., Edinburgh 12256
RSF, Madrid 09802
RSG, Düsseldorf 05928
RSG, Paderborn 05919
R.S.G.B., Potters Bar 12140
R.S.G.S., Glasgow 12245
R.S.H., London 12257
RSHS, Crete 16243
RSM, London 12260
R.S.M.E., Madrid 09804
RSNA, Oak Brook 16241
RSNC, Lincoln 12248
RSNC Wildlife Trusts Partnership, Lincoln 12275
RSNZ, Wellington 08742
RSP, Quezon City 09066
R.S.P.B., Sandy 12251
R.S.S., Amman 08057
RSS, Bellingham 16284
RSS, Nottingham 12151
R.S.S.P.S.A.D., Bucuresti 09324
RSUA, Belfast 12263
RSVP, Edwardsville 16270
RTCA, Washington 16282
RTCE, London 12159
RTOG, Philadelphia 16239
RTPI, London 12267
RTRC, New York 16240
RTS, London 12266
RTS, Richmond 12160
RUA, Lurgan 12268
R.U.A.A., Lambeg 12269
RUAS, Belfast 12270
Rudolf Borchardt-Gesellschaft e.V., Ebersberg 05931
Rudolf Kassner-Gesellschaft, Wien 00787
Rückert-Gesellschaft e.V., Schweinfurt 05932
Rugby Football Schools Union, Twickenham 12276
Rural Community Assistance Program, Leesburg 16283
Rural Education and Development Association, Edmonton 02347
Rural Sociological Society, Bellingham 16284
Rushlight Club, Jenkintown 16285
Russian Academy of Agricultural Sciences, Moskva 09438
Russian Academy of Arts, Moskva 09439
Russian Academy of Medical Sciences, Moskva 09440
Russian Academy of Pedagogical Sciences, Moskva 09441
Russian Academy of Sciences, Moskva 09442
Russian Association for Comparative Literature, Moskva 09443
Russian Botanical Society, St. Petersburg 09444
Russian Geographical Society, St. Petersburg 09445
Russian Linguistics Society, Moskva 09446
Russian Literary Society in Japan, Tokyo 07963
Russian Mineralogical Society, St. Petersburg 09447
Russian Palaeontological Society, St. Petersburg 09448
Russian Palestine Society, Moskva 09449
Russian PEN Centre, Moskva 09450
Russian Pharmacological Society, Moskva 09451
Russian Pugwash Committee, Moskva 09452
Russian Society of Genetics and Breeders, Moskva 09453
Russian Union of Composers, Moskva 09454
Rutland Agricultural Society, Rutland 12277
Ruusbroecgenootschap, Antwerpen 01235
RVP, Washington 14217
RWEMA, Boston 16244
R.Z.S.I., Dublin 06674

SA, Helsinki 03386
SA, London 12410
S.A., Paris 03952
SA, Zürich 10256
SAA, Boulder 16619
SAA, Chicago 16492
SAA, Dallas 16319
SAA, Hull 12341
SAA, Ipswich 12479
SAA, Oklahoma City 16351
SAA, San Francisco 16356
SAA, Washington 16349
SAAD, London 12382
SAAFoST, Edenvale 09667
SAAI, Buenos Aires 00083
SAAP, Seattle 16445
Saarländisch-Pfälzische Internistengesellschaft e.V., Ludwigshafen 05933
Saarländische Gesellschaft für zahnärztliche Fortbildung, Saarbrücken 05934
Saarländischer Gymnasiallehrerverband e.V., Losheim 05935
S.A.A.S., Vlaeberg 09666
S.A.A.T.V.E, Arcadia 09668
SAB, Newton Abbot 12348
SAB, Stockholm 10002
SAB, Winchester 12461
SABA, Kalamazoo 16446
SABAM, Bruxelles 01254
SABET, Paisley 12291
S.A.B.L., Bayeux 04045
SAC, Edinburgh 12290
SAC, Paris 03947
S.A.C.A.C., Pretoria 09675
SACF, Buenos Aires 00088
Sachverständigenrat für die Konzertierte Aktion im Gesundheitswesen, Bonn 05936
S.A.C.I., Yeoville 09674
SACO Sveriges Akademikers Centralorganisation, Stockholm 09935
SACP, Honolulu 16355
SACS, Decatur 16582
SAD, Paris 04025
SADAIC, Buenos Aires 00085
SADAS, Athinai 06254
SAE, Arlington 16450
SAE, Valley Stream 16447
SAE International, Warrendale 16286, 16499
SAEC, Ithaca 16580
Sächsische Akademie der Wissenschaften zu Leipzig, Leipzig 05937
Sächsischer Volkshochschulverband e.V., Chemnitz 05938
SAEE, Bern 10268
SAEM, Lansing 16346
Säteilyturvakeskus, Helsinki 03370
S.A.F., Paris 03954
SAF, Paris 04017
SAF, Washington 16493
SAfA, FL 32611 16490
Safe Association, Nashville 16287
Safe Water Association of New South Wales, Sydney 00357
Safety Equipment Institute, Arlington 16288
SAFI, Linköping 09951
SAFJL, Hillcrest 09678
SAFR, Luzern 10252
SAG, Bern 10238
SAG, Neukirch 10496
SAG, Zürich 10255
SAGA, Genève 10243
SAGB, Bangor 12283
SAGHOM, Adliswil 10236
SAGP, Binghamton 16350
S.A.G.S., Wits 09663
SAGSET, Ryton 12360
SAGT, Hamilton 12294
SAGUF, Zürich 10244
SAH, Buenos Aires 00096
SAH, Chicago 16498
SAH, New York 16494
SAH, Rorschach 10247
SAHAAS, Saint Albans 12278
SAHGB, Farnham 12408
SAHH, Indianapolis 16358
Sahitya Akademi, New Dehli 06526
SAHS, Chicago 16620, 16623
SAIAeE, Sunnyside 09682
SAIF, Pretoria 09712
Saint Albans and Hertfordshire Architectural and Archaeological Society, Saint Albans 12278
Saint George's Historical Society, Saint George's 01334
Saint John's Hospital Dermatological Society, London 12279
Saintpaulia and Houseplant Society, Ilford 12280
S.A.I.P., Cape Town 09688
S.A.I.P., Faure 09687
SAJBJ, Pretoria 09680
SAJM, Landquart 10250
S.A.K., Stockholm 10003
SAL, Liège 01238
S.A.L., London 12404
S.A.L., Palma de Mallorca 09825
SALALM, Austin 16313
Salomon Ludwig Steinheim-Institut für deutsch-jüdische Geschichte e.V., Duisburg 05939
SALT, New York 16495
SALT, Warrenton 16352
Salt Institute, Alexandria 16289
Saltire Society, Edinburgh 12281
SALV, Ebikon 10428
Salzburg Seminar, Middlebury 16290
Salzburger Ärztegesellschaft, Salzburg 00788
Salzburger Arbeitskreis für Psychoanalyse, Salzburg 00789
Salzburger Institut für juristische Information und Fortbildung, Salzburg 00790
Salzburger Juristische Gesellschaft, Salzburg 00791
Salzburger Kulturvereinigung, Salzburg 00792
SAM, Blue Springs 16347
SAM, Ithaca 16357
SAM, Vinton 16348
SAMA, Sunnyside 09713
Samenwerkingsverband van de Universiteitsbibliotheken, de Koninklijke Bibliotheek en de Bibliotheek van de Koninklijke Nederlandse Akademie van Wetenschappen, Amsterdam 08621
Samfundet De Nio, Stockholm 09936
Samfundet for Dansk Genealogi og Personalhistorie, Virum 03190
Samfundet til Udgivelse af Dansk Musik, København 03191
Sammenslutningen af Danmarks Forskningsbiblioteker, Lyngby 03192
Sammenslutningen af Danske Kunstforeninger, København 03193
Sammenslutningen af Lokalarkiver, Vejle 03194
Sammenslutningen af Medieforskere i Danmark, Alborg 03195
Sammenslutningen af Praktiserende Dyrlaeger, Vanløse 03196
SAMPE, Covina 16448
SAMRA, Johannesburg 09691
SAMS, Oban 12292
SAMS, Pretoria 09692
SAMW, Basel 10239
San Martin Society of Washington, DC, McLean 16291
San-yo Gijutsu Shinkokai, Okayama-ken 08013
SANCI, Pretoria 09694
Sandford Fleming Foundation, Waterloo 02348
Sangeet Natak Akademi, New Delhi 06527
S.A.N.G.O.R.M., Marshalltown 09695
S.A.N.H.S., Taunton 12452
Sankt Ingberter Literaturforum, Sankt Ingbert 05940
Sanskrita Academy, Madras 06528
SANTA, Johannesburg 09697
SANU, Beograd 17031
Sanyo Association for Advancement of Science and Technology, Okayama-ken 08013
S.A.O.A., Adelaide 00365
SAP, Coímbra 09211
S.A.P., Paris 03959
SAPD, Vanløse 03196
Sapporo Norin Gakkai, Sapporo 08014
Sapporo Society of Agriculture and Fisheries, Sapporo 08014
SAPUZ, Zürich 10434
SAR, Stockholm 09961
SARA, Lombard 16496
SAROC, Taipei 02752
SAROJ, Beograd 17014
Sartre-Gesellschaft, Berlin 05941
SAS, Blacksburg 16323
SAS, Dearborn 16354
SAS, Frederick 16353
SAS, Göteborg 09959
S.A.S., Guildford 12484
S.A.S., Lewes 12486
SAS, Much Wenlock 12337
SAS, Trieste 07389
SASA, Rosebank 09704
Saskatchewan Association of Library Technicians, Saskatoon 02349
Saskatchewan Association of Medical Radiation Technologists, Saskatoon 02350
Saskatchewan Association of Teachers of French, Saskatoon 01686
Saskatchewan Dietetic Association, Regina 02351
Saskatchewan Genealogical Society, Regina 02352
Saskatchewan Geological Society, Regina 02353
Saskatchewan Horticultural Association, Parkside 02354
Saskatchewan Institute of Agrologists, Saskatoon 02355
Saskatchewan Library Association, Regina 02356
Saskatchewan Lung Association, Sakatoon 02357
Saskatchewan Medical Association, Saskatoon 02358
Saskatchewan Pharmaceutical Association, Regina 02359
Saskatchewan Psychiatric Association, Saskatoon 02360
Saskatchewan Safety Council, Regina 02361
Saskatchewan Society of Medical Laboratory Technologists, Regina 02362
Saskatchewan Society of Occupational Therapists, Saskatoon 02363
Saskatchewan Teachers' Federation, Saskatoon 02364
Saskatchewan Veterinary Medical Association, Saskatoon 02365
SASMI, Roma 07385
SASMIRA, Mumbai 06529
SASS, Provo 16449
SASSA, Luzern 10246
SAT, Tours 03950
SAT-AMIKARO, Paris 04303
S.A.T.F, Paris 04024
SATIPS, Altrincham 12411
SATL, Helsinki 03390
SATRA Technology Centre, Kettering 12282

SG, London 12427
SGA, Lenzburg 10279
SGA, Loves Park 16333
SGA, Madison 16305
SGA, Zürich 10280
SGAB, Zürich 10276
SGAE, Madrid 09821
SGAG, Winterthur 10277
SGAM, Lichtensteig 10274
SGAS, Cincinnati 16387
S.G.B., Liège 01267
SGB, São Paulo 01529
SGBF, Aarau 10283
SGE, Basel 10291
SGEAJ, Zürich 10287
SGF, Linköping 09977
SGF, Norrköping 09976
SGF, Paris 04195
SGFF, Thun 10292
SGFT, Zürich 10293
SGG, Bern 10296
SGG, Bienne 10270
SGGP, Muri 10299
SGH, Renens 10301
S.G.I, Roma 07434
S.G.I., Roma 07435
SGI, Sacramento 16307
SGI, Washington 16388
SGK, Bern 10271
SGKGS, Fribourg 10309
SGKM, Bern 10308
SGKV, Frankfurt 05966
SGL, Bern 10311
SGLWT, Wädenswil 10310
SGM, Reston 16386
SGMB, Rennes 04196
SGMK, Zürich 10317
SGML, Highland Park 16610
SGNA, Rochester 16526
SGNM, Lausanne 10232
SGO, Bern 10321
SGP, Bern 10326
SGP, Lima 09010
SGP, Woods Hole 16527
SGP, Zürich 10324
SGS, Hässelby 09978
SGSG, Basel 10289
SGSS, Zürich 10334
S.G.T., Sheffield 12428
SGTK, Basel 10338
SGTS, Aberdeen 12304
SGU, Uppsala 10008
SGU, Zürich 10341
SGVW, Bern 10347
SH, Ithaca 16460
SHA, Athens 16584
SHA, London 12344
SHA, Moncton 02378
SHA, Oneonta 16393
SHA, Tucson 16390
S.H.A.A., South Croydon 12430
SHAFR, Dayton 16389
Shah Waliullah Academy, Hyderabad 08933
Shakai Keizaishi Gakkai, Tokyo 08021
Shakai Seisaku Gakkai, Tokyo 08022
Shakespeare Association of America, Dallas 16319
Shakespeare Birthplace Trust, Stratford-upon-Avon 12331
Shakespeare Data Bank, Evanston 16320
Shakespeare Institue, Stratford-upon-Avon 12332
Shakespeare Reading Society, London 12333
Shakespeare Society of America, West Hollywood 16321
SHAL, Saint Julien les Metz 04088
SHARP, Madison 16455
Shaybani Society of International Law, Washington 16322
SHC, Chattanooga 16585
SHCJ, Cedar Grove 16456
SHD, Falls Church 16457
S.H.D., Paris 04084
SHE, London 12384
SHE, Long Beach 16391
Sheffield Metallurgical and Engineering Association, Rotherham 12334
Sherlock Holmes Society of London, Orpington 12335
Sherwood Anderson Society, Blacksburg 16323
Shetland Council of Social Service, Lerwick 12336
Shevchenko Scientific Society, New York 16324
SHG, Zürich 10355
SHG/SGKH, Adliswil 10360
SHGM, Baltimore 16459
Shigaku-kai, Tokyo 08023
Shigaku Kenkyukai, Kyoto 08024
Shika Kiso Igakkai, Tokyo 08025
Shinto Gakkai, Tokyo 08026
Shinto Shukyo Gakkai, Tokyo 08027
Shipbuilding Engineering Society, St. Petersburg 09457
Shipowners Refrigerated Cargo Research Association, Cambridge 11245
SHJ, Farmington Hills 16394
SHK, Bern 10358
SHNS, Arlington 16528
Shokubai Gakkai, Tokyo 08028
Shokubutsu Bunrui Chiri Gakkai, Kyoto 08029
Shoqata e Gjeologeve te Shqiperise, Tirana 00005
SHOT, Auburn 16458
S.H.P., Paris 04083
SHRM, Alexandria 16392
Shropshire Archaeological and Parish Register Society, Much Wenlock 12337
SHS, Helsinki 03405
SHS, Lancaster 12340
SHS, Lawrenceburg 16618
SHS, Warszawa 09148
SI, Alexandria 16289
S.I., Washington 16337
SI, Washington 16612
SIA, Bologna 07453
SIA, Norman 14781
S.I.A., Pisa 07457
SIA, Princeton 16397
SIA, Roma 07461
SIA, Singapore 09539
SIA, Zürich 10450
SIAE, Firenze 07592
SIAM, Philadelphia 16396
Siam Society, Bangkok 10646
SIANS, Milano 07444
S.I.A.R., Siena 07459
SIAS, Brighton 12487
S.I.A.S.A., Napoli 07593
S.I.A.S.O., Viareggio 07587
S.I.A.S.P., Trieste 07442
S.I.A.T., Roma 07510
SIB, Firenze 07468
S.I.B., Siena 07465
SIBC, Paris 04202
S.I.B.M., Livorno 07466
S.I.B.S., Napoli 07467
SIC, Genève 10502
SIC, Paris 04204
SIC, Pavia 07472
SIC, Reinach 10505
SICOT, Bruxelles 01268
S.I.C.R.E.O., Roma 07445
SID, Cleveland 16403
SID, Roma 07655
SID, Santa Ana 16399
S.I.D.E.A., Reggio Emilia 07487
S.I.De.S., Milano 07602
SIDES, Roma 07484
SIDM, Roma 07532
S.I.E., Milano 07492
SIE, Roma 07491
SIECCAN, East York 02369
SIECUS, New York 16317
SIEDS, Roma 07488
S.I.E.M., Milano 07595
S.I.E.P.M., Louvain-la-Neuve 01271
Sierra Club, San Francisco 16325
Sierra Leone Association of Archivists, Librarians and Information Scientists, Freetown 09519
Sierra Leone Medical and Dental Assication, Freetown 09520
Sierra Leone Science Association, Freetown 09521
S.I.E.S., Milano 07493
SIFET, Milano 07403
S.I.F.E.T., Milano 07501
S.I.G., Pisa 07508
SIGA, Foggia 07503
SIGART, New York 16596
SIGBIO, Durham 16597
SIGCPR, Dayton 16593
SIGCUE, Eugene 16594
SIGE, Bologna 07502
SIGIR, Blackburg 16598
SIGM, Milano 07507
SIGMA - Salzburger Gesellschaft für Semiologie, Salzburg 00793
Sigma Xi - The Scientific Research Society, Research Triangle Park 16326
Sigmund Freud Archives, Roslyn 16327
Sigmund Freud-Gesellschaft, Wien 00794
Signal Processing Society, New York 16328
SIGSAM, New York 16595
SIHS, Chestnut Hill 16405
SIIA, Singapore 09540
S.I.I.I., Bari 07509
SIJIF, Salzburg 00790
SIK, Zürich 10489
SILAT, Washington 16395
Silk and Art Silk Mills' Research Association, Mumbai 06529
SIM, Chicago 16400
SIM, Fairfax 16398
S.I.M., Milano 07514
SIMA, Milano 06955
S.I.M.A., Roma 07528
S.I.M.F.E.R., Moncalieri 07519
SIMI, Roma 07520
Simian Society of America, Saint Louis 16329
S.I.M.L.A., Padova 07521
SIMP, Milano 07531
SIMP, Roma 07523
Simplified Speeling Society, Beckenham 12338
S.I.M.P.S., Genova 07522
SIMS, Torino 07524
S.I.M.S.I., Napoli 07525
SIMT, Roma 07516
S.I.M.T.A., Bologna 07582
SIMTI, Roma 07526
SIN, Ancona 07533
SIN, Santa Monica 16401
Sind Library Association, Hyderabad 08934
Sindacato Autonomo Scuola Media Italiana, Roma 07385
Sindacato Nazionale Autori Drammatici, Roma 07386
Sindacato Nazionale Istruzione Artistica, Roma 07387
Sindacato Nazionale Scrittori, Roma 07388
Sindhi Adabi Board, Tamshoro 08935
Sindicato Nacional dos Odontologistas Portuguesas, Lisboa 09206
Sindicato Nacional dos Professionais de Serviço Social, Lisboa 09207
Sindicato Nacional dos Professores, Lisboa 09208
Sindicato Nacional dos Protésicos Dentários, Lisboa 09209
Sindikat Radnicka Drustvenih Delatnosti Jugoslavije, Beograd 17030
Singapore Art Society, Singapore 09537
Singapore Association for the Advancement of Science, Singapore 09538
Singapore Institute of Architects, Singapore 09539
Singapore Institute of International Affairs, Singapore 09540
Singapore Mathematical Society, Singapore 09541
Singapore Medical Association, Singapore 09542
Singapore National Academy of Science, Singapore 09543
Singapore Society of Asian Studies, Singapore 09544
SINIE, Santiago 02474
The Sinological Society, Tokyo 08038
SINPI, Napoli 07536
S.I.N.S., Bologna 07538
SINTEF, Trondheim 08886
S.I.O.C.M.F., L'Aquila 07542
S.I.O.e Ch.C.-F., Roma 07547
S.I.O.G., Roma 07545
SIOI, Roma 07541
S.I.O.I., Roma 07591
S.I.O.P., Roma 07548
S.I.O.T., Roma 07544
SIP, Bethesda 16402
SIP, Milano 07557
S.I.P., Roma 07555
S.I.P., Valencia 09807
S.I.P.A., Perugia 07551
S.I.P.A.I., Cremona 07563
S.I.P.A.O.C., Catania 07552
SIPE, Paris 04207
SIPES, Dallas 16530
S.I.P.I., Milano 07560
S.I.P.S., Milano 07438
SIPS, Palermo 07561
S.I.Ps., Roma 07559
S.I.P.T., Firenze 07562
S.I.P.V., Roma 07554
SIR, Marietta 16531
Sir Joseph Flavelle Foundation, Toronto 02370
Sir Thomas Beecham Society, Redondo Beach 16330
Sira, Chislehurst 12339
SIRE, Iselin 16461
S.I.R.I., Cinisello Balsamo 06962
SIRMCE, Bruxelles 01270
SIROT, San Diego 16345
SIS, Roma 07574
SIS, Seattle 16404
SIS, Stockholm 09941
S.I.S.A., Bari 07598
S.I.S.A., Milano 07594
S.I.S.C.A., Genova 07596
SISF, Milano 07567
S.I.S.MED., Bologna 07575
S.I.S.S., Firenze 07449
Sistema Nacional de Información en Educación, Santiago 02474
Sister Kenny Institute, Minneapolis 16331
SIT, Arundel 02398
SIT, Middlesbrough 12433
S.I.T.H., Castellamare di Stabia 07441
SITS, Les Ulis 04209
SIU, Paris 04211
S.I.U., Roma 07581
SIWA, Edinburgh 12308
SJFR, Stockholm 09939
SJS, New York 16532
SKAF, Luzern 10362
Skandinavisk Museumsforbund, Danish Section, København 03211
SKDL, Chur 10363
SKF, Uppsala 09954
SKHF, Zürich 10366
SKHS, Helsingin Yliopisto 03415
SKI, Minneapolis 16331
SKIF, Stockholm 10017
Skin Cancer Foundation, New York 16332
SKJP, Solothurn 10568
Skogbrukets og Skogindustrienes Forskningsforening, Aas 08881
Skógraektarfélag Islands, Reykjavik 06379
Skogs- och Jordbrukets Forskningsråd, Stockholm 09939
Skolledarna, Stockholm 09940
SKS, Hamburg 05959
SKS, Helsinki 03384, 03385
SKV, Salzburg 00792
SKZ, Würzburg 05976
SLA, Washington 16409, 16599
SLAA, Arlington 16406
SLANT, Darwin 00358
Slavic Gospel Association, Loves Park 16333
Slavistično Društvo Slovenije, Ljubljana 09591
SLD, Beograd 17023
Sleep Research Society, Cleveland 16334
SLF, Stockholm 09940
SLG, Bern 10369
SLgE, Zürich 10371
S.L.H.A., Lincoln 12363
SLHR, Philadelphia 16408
S.L.I., Roma 07405
Slovak Academy of Sciences, Bratislava 09549
Slovak Anthropological Society, Bratislava 09550
Slovak Archaeological Society, Nitra 09551
Slovak Architects Society, Bratislava 09581
Slovak Association of Classical Philologists, Bratislava 09564
Slovak Astronomical Society, Tatranská Lomnica 09552
Slovak Biochemical Society, Bratislava 09553
Slovak Bioclimatology Society, Bratislava 09554
Slovak Biological Soiety, Bratislava 09555
Slovak Botanical Society, Bratislava 09556
Slovak Chemical Society, Bratislava 09557
Slovak Demographic and Statistical Society, Bratislava 09558
Slovak Education Society, Prešov 09571
Slovak Entomology Society, Bratislava 09559
Slovak Ethnography Society, Bratislava 09568
Slovak Geographical Society, Bratislava 09560
Slovak Geological Society, Bratislava 09561
Slovak Historical Society, Bratislava 09562
Slovak Linguistics Society, Bratislava 09563
Slovak Literary Society, Bratislava 09566
Slovak Medical Society, Bratislava 09565
Slovak Meteorological Society, Bratislava 09567
The Slovak Philosophical Association, Bratislava 09580
Slovak Psychological Society, Bratislava 09573
Slovak Society for Agriculture, Forestry and Food, Ivanka pri Dunaji 09578
Slovak Society for Cybernetics and Informatics, Bratislava 09576
Slovak Society for History of Science and Technology, Bratislava 09575
Slovak Society for International Law, Bratislava 09574
Slovak Society for Mechanics, Bratislava 09577
Slovak Society for Oriental Studies, Bratislava 09569
Slovak Society for Parasitology, Košice 09570
Slovak Society of Pneumology and Phtisiology, Bratislava 09572
Slovak Zoological Society, Bratislava 09579
Slovenian Academy of Sciencesand Art, Ljubljana 09592
Slovenian Historical Association, Ljubljana 09603
Slovenian Society, Ljubljana 09593
Slovenian Society of Historians of Art, Ljubljana 09594
Slovenská Akadémia Vied, Bratislava 09549
Slovenska Akademija Znanosti in Umetnosti, Ljubljana 09592
Slovenská Antropologická Spoločnost, Bratislava 09550
Slovenská Archeologická Spoločnost, Nitra 09551
Slovenská Astronomická Spoločnost, Tatranská Lomnica 09552
Slovenská Biochemiká Spoločnost, Bratislava 09553
Slovenská Bioklimatologická Spoločnost, Bratislava 09554
Slovenská Biologická Spoločnost, Bratislava 09555
Slovenská Botanická Spoločnost, Bratislava 09556
Slovenská Chemická Spoločnost, Bratislava 09557
Slovenská Demografická a Štatistická Spoločnost, Bratislava 09558
Slovenská Entonologická Spoločnost, Bratislava 09559
Slovenská Geografická Spoločnost, Bratislava 09560
Slovenská Geologická Spoločnost, Bratislava 09561
Slovenská Historická Spoločnost, Bratislava 09562
Slovenská Jazykovedná Spoločnost, Bratislava 09563
Slovenská Jednota Klassických Filológov, Bratislava 09564
Slovenská Lekárska Spoločnost, Bratislava 09565
Slovenská Literárnovedná Spoločnost, Bratislava 09566
Slovenska Matica, Ljubljana 09593
Slovenská Meteorologická Spoločnost, Bratislava 09567
Slovenská Národopisná Spoločnost, Bratislava 09568
Slovenská Orientalistická Spoločnost, Bratislava 09569
Slovenská Parazitologická Spoločnost, Košice 09570
Slovenská Pedagogická Spoločnost, Prešov 09571
Slovenská Pneumologická a Ftizeologická Spoločnost, Bratislava 09572
Slovenská Psychologická Spoločnost, Bratislava 09573
Slovenská Spoločnost Medzinárodné Právo, Bratislava 09574
Slovenská Spoločnost pre Dejiny Vied a Techniky pri SAV, Bratislava 09575
Slovenská Spoločnost pre Kybernetiku a Informatiku, Bratislava 09576
Slovenská Spoločnost pre Mechaniku, Bratislava 09577
Slovenská Spoločnost pre Vedy Polnohospodarske, Lesnické a Potravinárské, Ivanka pri Dunaji 09578
Slovenská Zoologická Spoločnost, Bratislava 09579
Slovenské Filozofické Združenie, Bratislava 09580
Slovensko Umetnostno Zgodovinsko Društvo, Ljubljana 09594
SLRS, London 12330
SLS, Bratislava 09565
SLS, Helsinki 03444
SLS, London 12476
SLS, Rickmansworth 12454
SLS, Stockholm 09985
SLS, Worchester 16410
SLTB, London 12364
SMA, Arlington 16411
S.M.A., México 08333
SMA, Shrewsbury 12366
SMA, Singapore 09542
Small Enterprise Education and Promotion Network, New York 16335
Small Towns Institute, Ellensburg 16336
SMC, México 08335
SMCAF, Kensington 16535
SME, Dearborn 16534
SMEA, Rotherham 12334
SMEP, Charlottesville 16539
SMF, Boulogne-Billancourt 04223
SMF, Montecillo 08340
S.M.F., Paris 04217
SMG, Genève 10373
SMG, Zürich 10372
SMHS, Apache Junction 16615
SMIER, Paris 04219
Smithsonian Institution, Washington 16337
SMJ, New York 16536
SML, Helsinki 03426
SMM, México 08330
SMPTAD, Studio City 16537
SMPTE, White Plains 16538
SMS, Hergiswil 10539
S.M.S., Roma 07160
SMS, West Lafayette 16607
SMSG, Salt Lake City 16294
SMSG, Zürich 10374
SMSR, México 08350
SMTE, Reston 16413
SMY, Helsinki 03425
SN, Washington 16415
SNAC, Paris 04265
SNACC, Midlothian 16543
SNAD, Roma 07386
SNALC, Paris 04273
SNAME, Jersey City 16540
SNAS, Singapore 09543
S.N.B.A., Paris 04229
SNCF, Paris 04267
S.N.E., Luxembourg 08177
SNE, Minneapolis 16417
S.N.E.S., Paris 04271
SNF, Stockholm 09993
SNFGE, Vandoeuvre 04232
SNG, Bern 10240
SNG, Frankfurt 05947
SNG, Zürich 10376
SNHF, Paris 04231
S.N.I., Firenze 07621
S.N.I.A., Roma 07387
SNL, Luxembourg 08175
SNLS, Denver 16416
SNM, Reston 16544
SNMA, Washington 16609
SNMG, Bucuresti 09318
SNMOF, Nancy 04283
S.N.M.S., Paris 04279
SNP, Urbana 16414
S.N.P.A.M., Paris 04292
SNPDES, Paris 04291
SNPEN, Paris 04293
SNPF, Clermont-Ferrand 04290
SNPMT, Toulouse 04296
SNPN, Paris 04226
SNR, Bucuresti 09320
SNR, London 12368

375 Alphabetical Index: Sociedade

S.N.R.S.S., Bucuresti *09319*
SNS, Boston *16542*
SNS, Roma *07388*
SNS, Stockholm *09947*
SNSS, Gillingham *12284*
SNTS, Paris *04227*
SNV, Zürich *10377*
SNV Studiengesellschaft Verkehr, Hamburg *05948*
SNVB, Olympia *16571*
SOA, Schaumburg *16489*
SOAP, Richmond *16418*
SOC, Concepción *02536*
SOC, Edinburgh *12313*
SOCEPTA, Dar-es-Salaam *10605*
SOCHIL, Santiago *02495*
Social Affairs Federation, Montréal *02096*
Social History Society of the United Kingdom, Lancaster *12340*
Social Policy Association, Hull *12341*
Social Psychiatry Research Institute, New York *16338*
Social Research Association, London *12342*
Social Responsibilities Round Table, Chicago *16339*
Social Science Education Consortium, Boulder *16340*
Social Science Research Council, New York *16341*
Social Sciences Services and Resources, Wasco *16342*
Social Welfare History Group, East Lansing *16343*
Socialist Educational Association, Stockport *12343*
Socialist Health Association, London *12344*
Socialpaedagogernes Landsforbund, København *03212*
Sociedad Agronómica de Chile, Santiago *02475*
Sociedad Agronómica Mexicana, México *08321*
Sociedad Amantes de la Luz, Santiago de los Caballeros *03229*
Sociedad Americana de Oftalmologia y Optometria, Bogotá *02807*
Sociedad Amigos del Museo de Bellas Artes, Caracas *16915*
Sociedad Antioqueña de Ingenieros y Architectos, Medellín *02808*
Sociedad Argentina de Alergia e Inmunopatología, Buenos Aires *00083*
Sociedad Argentina de Antropología, Buenos Aires *00084*
Sociedad Argentina de Autores y Compositores de Música, Buenos Aires *00085*
Sociedad Argentina de Biología, Buenos Aires *00086*
Sociedad Argentina de Botánica, Buenos Aires *00087*
Sociedad Argentina de Ciencias Fisiológicas, Buenos Aires *00088*
Sociedad Argentina de Ciencias Neurológicas, Psiquiátricas y Neuroquirúrgicas, Buenos Aires *00089*
Sociedad Argentina de Endocrinología y Metabolismo, Buenos Aires *00090*
Sociedad Argentina de Estudios Geográficos, Buenos Aires *00091*
Sociedad Argentina de Farmacología y Terapéutica, Buenos Aires *00092*
Sociedad Argentina de Fisiología Vegetal, Bahía Blanca *00093*
Sociedad Argentina de Gastroenterología, Buenos Aires *00094*
Sociedad Argentina de Gerontología y Geriatría, Buenos Aires *00095*
Sociedad Argentina de Hematología, Buenos Aires *00096*
Sociedad Argentina de Investigación Clínica, Buenos Aires *00097*
Sociedad Argentina de Leprología, Buenos Aires *00098*
Sociedad Argentina de Oftalmología, Buenos Aires *00099*
Sociedad Argentina de Patología, Buenos Aires *00100*
Sociedad Argentina de Pediatría, Buenos Aires *00101*
Sociedad Argentina de Psicología, Buenos Aires *00102*
Sociedad Argentina de Sociología, Córdoba *00103*
Sociedad Arqueológica de la Serena, La Serena *02476*
Sociedad Astronómica de España y América, Barcelona *09808*
Sociedad Astronómica de México, México *08322*
Sociedad Bolivariana de Colombia, Bogotá *02809*
Sociedad Bolivariana de Venezuela, Caracas *16916*
Sociedad Central de Arquitectos, Buenos Aires *00104*
Sociedad Centroamericana de Dermatologia, Guatemala City *06272*
Sociedad Chilena de Alergia e Immunología, Santiago *02477*
Sociedad Chilena de Cancerología, Santiago *02478*
Sociedad Chilena de Cardiología y Cirugía Cardiovascular, Santiago *02479*
Sociedad Chilena de Cirugía Plástica y Reparadora, Santiago *02480*
Sociedad Chilena de Citología, Santiago *02481*
Sociedad Chilena de Dermatología y Venereología, Santiago *02482*
Sociedad Chilena de Endocrinología y Metabolismo, Santiago *02483*
Sociedad Chilena de Enfermedades Respiratorias, Santiago *02484*
Sociedad Chilena de Entomología, Santiago *02485*
Sociedad Chilena de Física, Santiago *02486*
Sociedad Chilena de Fotogrametría y Percepción Remota, Santiago *02487*
Sociedad Chilena de Gastroenterología, Santiago *02488*
Sociedad Chilena de Gerontología, Santiago *02489*
Sociedad Chilena de Hematología, Santiago *02490*
Sociedad Chilena de Historia Natural, Santiago *02491*
Sociedad Chilena de Historia y Geografía, Santiago *02492*
Sociedad Chilena de Immunología, Santiago *02493*
Sociedad Chilena de la Ciencia del Suelo, Santiago *02494*
Sociedad Chilena de Lingüística, Santiago *02495*
Sociedad Chilena de Neurocirugía, Santiago *02496*
Sociedad Chilena de Obstetricia y Ginecología, Santiago *02497*
Sociedad Chilena de Oftalmología, Santiago *02498*
Sociedad Chilena de Ortopedía y Traumatología, Santiago *02499*
Sociedad Chilena de Otorrinolaringología, Santiago *02500*
Sociedad Chilena de Parasitología, Santiago *02501*
Sociedad Chilena de Patología de la Adaptación y del Mesenquima, Santiago *02502*
Sociedad Chilena de Pediatría, Santiago *02503*
Sociedad Chilena de Producción Animal, Santiago *02504*
Sociedad Chilena de Química, Concepción *02505*
Sociedad Chilena de Reumatología, Santiago *02506*
Sociedad Chilena de Sanidad, Santiago *02507*
Sociedad Chilena de Tecnología de Alimentos, Santiago *02508*
Sociedad Chilena de Tisiología y Enfermedades Broncopulmonares, Santiago *02509*
Sociedad Chilena de Urología, Santiago *02510*
Sociedad Científica Argentina, Buenos Aires *00105*
Sociedad Científica Chilena Claudio Gay, Santiago *02511*
Sociedad Científica de Chile, Santiago *02512*
Sociedad Científica del Paraguay, Asunción *08966*
Sociedad Colombiana de Biologí, Bogotá *02810*
Sociedad Colombiana de Cardiología, Bogotá *02811*
Sociedad Colombiana de Cirugía, Bogotá *02812*
Sociedad Colombiana de Cirugía Ortopedica y Traumatología, Bogotá *02813*
Sociedad Colombiana de Economistas, Bogotá *02814*
Sociedad Colombiana de Ingenieros, Bogotá *02815*
Sociedad Colombiana de la Ciencia del Suelo, Bogotá *02816*
Sociedad Colombiana de Matemáticas, Bogotá *02817*
Sociedad Colombiana de Obstetricia y Ginecologia, Bogotá *02818*
Sociedad Colombiana de Patología, Cali *02819*
Sociedad Colombiana de Pediatría, Cali *02820*
Sociedad Colombiana de Psiquiatría, Bogotá *02821*
Sociedad Colombiana de Químicos e Ingenieros Químicos, Bogotá *02822*
Sociedad Colombiana de Radiología, Bogotá *02823*
Sociedad Cubana de Hipnosis, La Habana *02889*
Sociedad Cubana de Historia de la Ciencia y de la Técnica, La Habana *02890*
Sociedad Cubana de Historia de la Medicina, La Habana *02891*
Sociedad Cubana de Ingenieros, La Habana *02892*
Sociedad Cubana de Radiología, La Habana *02893*
Sociedad de Amigos de Arqueología, Montevideo *12631*
Sociedad de Anatomía Normal y Patológica de Chile, Santiago *02513*
Sociedad de Anestesiología de Chile, Santiago *02514*
Sociedad de Anestiología de El Salvador, San Salvador *03321*
Sociedad de Antropología de Antioquía, Medellín *02824*
Sociedad de Bibliófilos Chilenos, Santiago *02515*
Sociedad de Bibliotecarios de Puerto Rico, San Juan *09260*
Sociedad de Biología de Chile, Santiago *02516*
Sociedad de Biología de Concepción, Concepción *02517*
Sociedad de Biología de Montevideo, Montevideo *12632*
Sociedad de Bioquímica de Concepción, Concepción *02518*
Sociedad de Bioquímica y Biología Molecular de Chile, Santiago *02519*
Sociedad de Ciencias Aranzadi Zientzi Elkartea, San Sebastián *09809*
Sociedad de Ciencias, Letras y Artes, Las Palmas *09810*
Sociedad de Ciencias Naturales Caldas, Medellín *02825*
Sociedad de Ciencias Naturales La Salle, Caracas *16917*
Sociedad de Cirugía de Buenos Aires, Buenos Aires *00106*
Sociedad de Cirugía del Uruguay, Montevideo *12633*
Sociedad de Cirujanos de Chile, Santiago *02520*
Sociedad de Educación, México *08323*
Sociedad de Estadística e Investigación Operativa, Madrid *09811*
Sociedad de Estudios Biológicos, México *08324*
Sociedad de Estudios Geográficos e Históricos, Santa Cruz de la Sierra *01343*
Sociedad de Farmacología de Chile, Santiago *02521*
Sociedad de Genética de Chile, Santiago *02522*
Sociedad de Ginecología y Obstetricia de El Salvador, San Salvador *03322*
Sociedad de Ingenieros del Perú, Lima *09007*
Sociedad de Matemática de Chile, Santiago *02523*
Sociedad de Medicina Legal y Toxicologia, Buenos Aires *00107*
Sociedad de Medicina Veterinaria de Chile, Santiago *02524*
Sociedad de Neurología, Psiquiatría y Neurocirugía de Chile, Santiago *02525*
Sociedad de Obstetricia y Ginecología de Venezuela, Caracas *16918*
Sociedad de Oftalmología del Hospital de Oftalmológico de Nuestra Señora de la Luz, México *08325*
Sociedad de Oftalmología Nicaragüense, Managua *08749*
Sociedad de Ortodoncía de Chile, Santiago *02526*
Sociedad de Otorinolaringología de Valparaíso, Valparaíso *02527*
Sociedad de Pediatría de Cochabamba, Cochabamba *01344*
Sociedad de Pediatría de Madrid y Castilla La Mancha, Madrid *09812*
Sociedad de Pediatría de Valparaíso, Valparaíso *02528*
Sociedad de Pediatría y Puericultura del Atlántico, Barranquilla *02826*
Sociedad de Pediatría y Puericultura del Paraguay, Asunción *08967*
Sociedad de Psicología Médica, Psicoanálisis y Medicina Psicosomática, Buenos Aires *00108*
Sociedad de Radiología del Uruguay, Montevideo *12634*
Sociedad de Tisiología y Neumonología de Venezuela, Antimano *16919*
Sociedad de Vida Silvestre de Chile, Temuco *02529*
Sociedad Económica de Amigos del País, La Habana *02894*
Sociedad Ecuatoriana de Alergía y Ciencias Afinas, Quito *03245*
Sociedad Ecuatoriana de Astronomía, Quito *03246*
Sociedad Ecuatoriana de Pediatría, Guayaquil *03247*
Sociedad Entomológica Argentina, La Plata *00109*
Sociedad Entomológica del Perú, Lima *09008*
Sociedad Española de Bioquímica y Biología Molecular, Madrid *09813*
Sociedad Española de Cerámica y Vidrio, Madrid *09814*
Sociedad Española de Cirugía Plástica, Reparadora y Estética, Madrid *09815*
Sociedad Española de Diabetes, Madrid *09816*
Sociedad Española de Etología, Barcelona *09817*
Sociedad Española de Mecánica del Suelo y Cimentaciones, Madrid *09818*
Sociedad Española de Patología Digestiva y de la Nutrición, Madrid *09819*
Sociedad Española de Radiología Medica, Madrid *09820*
Sociedad Forestal Mexicana, México *08326*
Sociedad General de Autores de España, Madrid *09821*
Sociedad General de Autores de la Argentina, Buenos Aires *00110*
Sociedad Geográfica de Colombia, Bogotá *02827*
Sociedad Geográfica de La Paz, La Paz *01345*
Sociedad Geográfica de Lima, Lima *09009*
Sociedad Geográfica y de Historia Potosí, Potosí *01346*
Sociedad Geográfica y de Historia Sucre, Sucre *01347*
Sociedad Geológica Boliviana, La Paz *01348*
Sociedad Geológica de Chile, Santiago *02530*
Sociedad Geológica de España, Madrid *09822*
Sociedad Geológica del Perú, Lima *09010*
Sociedad Geológica Mexicana, México *08327*
Sociedad Ibero-Americana de Estudios Numismáticos, Madrid *09823*
Sociedad Interamericana de Cardiología, México *08328*
Sociedad Jurídica de la Universidad Nacional, Bogotá *02828*
Sociedad Latinoamericana de Alergología, México *08329*
Sociedad Latinoamericana de Farmacología, Caracas *16920*
Sociedad Latinoamericana de Farmacología, Quito *03248*
Sociedad Latinoamericana de Investigación Pediátrica, Lima *09011*
Sociedad Malacológica del Uruguay, Montevideo *12635*
Sociedad Matemática Mexicana, México *08330*
Sociedad Mayagüezana por Bellas Artes, Mayaguez *09261*
Sociedad Médica, Bolivar *16921*
Sociedad Médica de Concepción, Concepción *02531*
Sociedad Médica de Salud Pública, San Salvador *03323*
Sociedad Médica de Santiago, Santiago *02532*
Sociedad Médica de Valparaíso, Valparaíso *02533*
Sociedad Médica del Hospital General, México *08331*
Sociedad Médica del Hospital Oftalmológico de Nuestra Señora de la Luz, México *08332*
Sociedad Mexicana de Antropología, México *08333*
Sociedad Mexicana de Bibliografía, México *08334*
Sociedad Mexicana de Cardiología, México *08335*
Sociedad Mexicana de Entomología, Veracruz *08336*
Sociedad Mexicana de Estudios Psico-Pedagógicos, México *08337*
Sociedad Mexicana de Eugenesia, México *08338*
Sociedad Mexicana de Fitogenética, México *08339*
Sociedad Mexicana de Fitopatología, Montecillo *08340*
Sociedad Mexicana de Geografía y Estadística, México *08341*
Sociedad Mexicana de Historia de la Ciencia y la Tecnología, México *08342*
Sociedad Mexicana de Historia Natural, México *08343*
Sociedad Mexicana de Historia y Filosofia de la Medicina, México *08344*
Sociedad Mexicana de Neurologia y Psiquiatria, México *08345*
Sociedad Mexicana de Nutrición y Endocrinología, México *08346*
Sociedad Mexicana de Parasitología, México *08347*
Sociedad Mexicana de Pediatría, México *08348*
Sociedad Mexicana de Salud Pública, México *08349*
Sociedad Mexicana de Seguridad Radiologica, México *08350*
Sociedad Mexicana de Tisiología, México *08351*
Sociedad Nacional Agraria, Lima *09012*
Sociedad Nacional de Agricultura, Santiago *02534*
Sociedad Nacional de Minería, Lima *09013*
Sociedad Nacional de Minería, Santiago *02535*
Sociedad Nicaragüense de Psiquiatría y Psicología, Managua *08750*
Sociedad Nuclear Mexicana, México *08352*
Sociedad Nuevoleonesa de Historia, Geografía y Estadística, Monterrey *08353*
Sociedad Odontológica de Concepción, Concepción *02536*
Sociedad Odontológica Zuliana de Prótesis Maracaibo, Maracaibo *16922*
Sociedad Peruana de Espeleología, Lima *09014*
Sociedad Peruana de Eugenesia, Lima *09015*
Sociedad Peruana de Historia de la Medicina, Lima *09016*
Sociedad Peruana de Ortopedia y Traumatología, Lima *09017*
Sociedad Peruana de Tisiología y Enfermedades Respiratorias, Lima *09018*
Sociedad Pro-Arte Musical, Guatemala City *06273*
Sociedad Química de México, México *08354*
Sociedad Química del Perú, Lima *09019*
Sociedad Rural Argentina, Buenos Aires *00111*
Sociedad Rural Boliviana, La Paz *01349*
Sociedad Uruguaya de Patología Clínica, Montevideo *12636*
Sociedad Uruguaya de Pediatría, Montevideo *12637*
Sociedad Venezolana de Angiologia, Caracas *16923*
Sociedad Venezolana de Cardiología, Caracas *16924*
Sociedad Venezolana de Ciencias Naturales, Caracas *16925*
Sociedad Venezolana de Cirugía, Caracas *16926*
Sociedad Venezolana de Cirugía Plástica y Reconstrucción, Caracas *16927*
Sociedad Venezolana de Cirurgía Ortopédica y Traumatología, Caracas *16928*
Sociedad Venezolana de Entomología, Maracay *16929*
Sociedad Venezolana de Hematología, Caracas *16930*
Sociedad Venezolana de Historia de la Medicina, Caracas *16931*
Sociedad Venezolana de Ingenieros de Minas y Metalúrgicos, Caracas *16932*
Sociedad Venezolana de Medicina del Trabajo y Deportes, Caracas *16933*
Sociedad Venezolana de Oftalmología, Caracas *16934*
Sociedad Venezolana de Otorinolaringología, Caracas *16935*
Sociedad Venezolana de Psiquiatría y Neurología, Caracas *16936*
Sociedad Venezolana de Puericultura y Pediatría, Caracas *16937*
Sociedad Venezolana de Radiología, Caracas *16938*
Sociedad Venezolana de Tisiología y Neumonología, Caracas *16939*
Sociedad Venezolana de Urología, Caracas *16940*
Sociedad Veterinaria de Zootecnica de España, Madrid *09824*
Sociedad Zoológica del Uruguay, Montevideo *12638*
Sociedade Anatómica Luso-Hispano-Americana, Lisboa *09210*
Sociedade Anatómica Portuguesa, Coimbra *09211*
Sociedade Astronómica de Portugal, Lisboa *09212*
Sociedade Botânica do Brasil, Brasília *01504*
Sociedade Brasileira de Autores Teatrais, Rio de Janeiro *01505*
Sociedade Brasileira de Belas Artes, Rio de Janeiro *01506*
Sociedade Brasileira de Cartografia, Rio de Janeiro *01507*
Sociedade Brasileira de Cultura, São Paulo *01508*
Sociedade Brasileira de Dermatologia, Rio de Janeiro *01509*
Sociedade Brasileira de Entomologia, São Paulo *01510*
Sociedade Brasileira de Filosofia, Rio de Janeiro *01511*
Sociedade Brasileira de Genética, Ribeirão Preto *01512*
Sociedade Brasileira de Geografia, Rio de Janeiro *01513*
Sociedade Brasileira de Geologia, São Paulo *01514*
Sociedade Brasileira de Instrução, Botafogo *01515*
Sociedade Brasileira de Microbiologia, Rio de Janeiro *01516*
Sociedade Brasileira de Romanistas, Rio de Janeiro *01517*
Sociedade Brasileira para o Progresso da Ciência, São Paulo *01518*
Sociedade Broteriana, Coimbra *09213*
Sociedade Científica da Universidade Católica Portuguesa, Lisboa *09214*
Sociedade Científica de São Paulo, São Paulo *01519*
Sociedade Civil de Educação São Marcos, São Paulo *01520*
Sociedade das Ciências Médicas de Lisboa, Lisboa *09215*
Sociedade de Biologia do Brasil, Rio de Janeiro *01521*
Sociedade de Biologia do Rio Grande do Sul, Pôrto Alegre *01522*
Sociedade de Ciências Agrárias de Portugal, Lisboa *09216*
Sociedade de Cultura e Educação do Litoral Sul, Registro *01523*

Alphabetical Index: Sociedade 376

Sociedade de Engenharia do Rio Grande do Sul, Pôrto Alegre 01524
Sociedade de Ensino Piratininga, São Paulo 01525
Sociedade de Estudos Açoreanos Afonso Chaves, Ponta Delgada 09217
Sociedade de Estudos Técnicos SARL-SETEC, Lisboa 09218
Sociedade de Farmácia e Química de São Paulo, São Paulo 01526
Sociedade de Geografia de Lisboa, Lisboa 09219
Sociedade de Lingua Portuguesa, Lisboa 09220
Sociedade de Medicina de Alagoas, Maceió 01527
Sociedade de Pediatria da Bahia, Salvador 01528
Sociedade Geográfica Brasileira, São Paulo 01529
Sociedade Geológica de Portugal, Lisboa 09221
Sociedade Histórica da Independência de Portugal, Lisboa 09222
Sociedade Martins Sarmento, Guimarães 09223
Sociedade Nacional de Agricultura, Rio de Janeiro 01530
Sociedade Nacional de Belas Artes, Lisboa 09224
Sociedade Paranaense de Matemática, Curitiba 01531
Sociedade Portuguesa de Alergologia e Imunologia Clínica, Lisboa 09225
Sociedade Portuguesa de Anestesiologia, Lisboa 09226
Sociedade Portuguesa de Antropologia e Etnologia, Porto 09227
Sociedade Portuguesa de Autores, Lisboa 09228
Sociedade Portuguesa de Bioquímica, Lisboa 09229
Sociedade Portuguesa de Cardiologia, Lisboa 09230
Sociedade Portuguesa de Ciências Naturais, Lisboa 09231
Sociedade Portuguesa de Ciências Veterinárias, Lisboa 09232
Sociedade Portuguesa de Dermatologia e Venereologia, Lisboa 09233
Sociedade Portuguesa de Educação Médica, Lisboa 09234
Sociedade Portuguesa de Especialistas de Pequenos Animales, Lisboa 09235
Sociedade Portuguesa de Espeleologia, Lisboa 09236
Sociedade Portuguesa de Gastroenterologia, Lisboa 09237
Sociedade Portuguesa de Hemorreologia e Microcirculaçã0, Lisboa 09238
Sociedade Portuguesa de Higiene Alimentar, Lisboa 09239
Sociedade Portuguesa de Medicina Fisica e Reabilitação, Lisboa 09240
Sociedade Portuguesa de Neurologia e Psiquiatria, Lisboa 09241
Sociedade Portuguesa de Numismática, Porto 09242
Sociedade Portuguesa de Nutrição e Alimentação Animal, Lisboa 09243
Sociedade Portuguesa de Oftalmologia, Lisboa 09244
Sociedade Portuguesa de Ortopedia e Traumatologia, Lisboa 09245
Sociedade Portuguesa de Patologia, Lisboa 09246
Sociedade Portuguesa de Pediatria, Lisboa 09247
Sociedade Portuguesa de Química, Lisboa 09248
Sociedade Portuguesa de Reprodução Animal, Lisboa 09249
Sociedade Portuguesa de Reumatologia, Lisboa 09250
Sociedade Portuguesa Veterinária de Anatomia Comparativa, Lisboa 09251
Sociedade Portuguesa Veterinária de Estudos Sociológicos, Lisboa 09252
Sociedade Portuguese de Estomatologia, Lisboa 09253
Sociedade Propagadora Esdeva, Juiz de Fora 01532
Sociedade Visconde de São Leopoldo, Santos 01533
Società Adriatica di Scienze, Trieste 07389
Società Archeologica Comense, Como 07390
Società Archeologica Viterbese Pro Ferento, Viterbo 07391
Società Astronomica Italiana, Firenze 07392
Società Botanica Italiana, Firenze 07393
Società Chimica Italiana, Roma 07394
Società Consortile per Azioni per lo Sviluppo della Ricerca Farmaceutica, Pomezia 07662
Società Dalmata di Storia Patria, Roma 07395
Società Dante Alighieri, Roma 07396
Società Dantesca Italiana, Firenze 07397
Società Dauna di Cultura, Foggia 07398
Società degli Amici del Museo Civico di Storia Naturale Giacomo Doria, Genova 07399
Società degli Ingegneri e degli Architetti in Torino, Torino 07400
Società dei Naturalisti in Napoli, Napoli 07401
Società di Etnografia Italiana, Roma 07402
Società di Fotogrammetria e Topografia, Milano 07403
Società di Letture e Conversazioni Scientifiche, Genova 07404
Società di Linguistica Italiana, Roma 07405
Società di Medicina Legale e delle Assicurazioni, Roma 07406
Società di Minerva, Trieste 07407
Società di Ortopedia e Traumatologia dell'Istituto Meridionale ed Insulare, Napoli 07408
Società di Scienze Farmacologiche Applicate, Milano 07409
Società di Scienze Naturali del Trentino, Trento 07410
Società di Storia Patria di Terra di Lavoro, Caserta 07411
Società di Storia Patria per la Puglia, Bari 07412
Società di Storia Patria per la Sicilia Orientale, Catania 07413
Società di Studi Celestiniani, Isernia 07414
Società di Studi Geografici, Firenze 07415
Società di Studi Romagnoli, Cesena 07416
Società di Studi Trentini di Scienze Storiche, Trento 07417
Società di Studi Valdesi, Torre Pellice 07418
Società d'Incoraggiamento d'Arti e Mestieri, Milano 07419
Società Ecologica Friulana, Campoformido 07420
Società Economica di Chiavari, Chiavari 07421
Società Emiliana Pro Montibus et Silvis, Bologna 07422
Società Entomologica Italiana, Genova 07423
Società Europea di Cultura, Venezia 07424
Società Europea di Patologia, Milano 07425
Società Farmaceutica del Mediterraneo Latino, Messina 07426
Società Filarmonica di Trento, Trento 07427
Società Filologica Friulana G.I. Ascoli, Udine 07428
Società Filologica Romana, Roma 07429
Società Filosofica Calabrese, Palmi 07430
Società Filosofica Italiana, Roma 07431
Società Filosofica Romana, Roma 07432
Società Gallaratese per gli Studi Patri, Gallarate 07433
Società Generale per Progettazioni, Consulenze e Partecipazioni, Roma 07376
Società Geografica Italiana, Roma 07434
Società Geologica Italiana, Roma 07435
Società Incoraggiamento Arti e Mestieri, Milano 07436
Società Internazionale di Diritto Penale Militare e di Diritto della Guerra, Gruppo Italiano, Roma 07437
Società Internazionale di Psicologia della Scrittura, Milano 07438
Società Internazionale di Studi Francescani, Assisi 07439
Società Internazionale di Studi Gemellari, Roma 07440
Società Internazionale di Tecnica Idrotermale, Castellamare di Stabia 07441
Società Istriana di Archeologia e Storia Patria, Trieste 07442
Società Italiana Amici dei Fiori, Firenze 07443
Società Italiana Attività Nervosa Superiore, Milano 07444
Società Italiana Calcolo Ricerca Economica Operativa, Roma 07445
Società Italiana degli Autori e Editori, Roma 07446
Società Italiana degli Economisti, Ancona 07447
Società Italiana della Continenza, Roma 07448
Società Italiana della Scienza del Suolo, Firenze 07449
Società Italiana della Trasfusione del Sangue, Torino 07450
Società Italiana delle Scienze Veterinarie, Brescia 07451
Società Italiana di Agopuntura, Torino 07452
Società Italiana di Agronomia, Bologna 07453
Società Italiana di Allergologia e Immunologia Clinica, Roma 07454
Società Italiana di Anatomia, Firenze 07455
Società Italiana di Anatomia Patologica, Messina 07456
Società Italiana di Andrologia, Pisa 07457
Società Italiana di Anestesia, Analgesia, Rianimazione e Terapia Intensiva, Firenze 07458
Società Italiana di Anestesiologia e Rianimazione, Siena 07459
Società Italiana di Antropologia e Etnologia, Firenze 07460
Società Italiana di Audiologia e Foniatria, Roma 07461
Società Italiana di Aziendologia, Milano 07462
Società Italiana di Biochimica, Perugia 07463
Società Italiana di Biochimica Clinica e Biologia Molecolare Clinica, Milano 07464
Società Italiana di Biogeografia, Siena 07465
Società Italiana di Biologia Marina, Livorno 07466
Società Italiana di Biologia Sperimentale, Napoli 07467
Società Italiana di Biometria, Firenze 07468
Società Italiana di Buiatria, Torino 07469
Società Italiana di Cancerologia, Napoli 07470
Società Italiana di Cardiologia, Roma 07471
Società Italiana di Chemioterapia, Pavia 07472
Società Italiana di Chirurgia, Roma 07473
Società Italiana di Chirurgia Cardiaca e Vascolare, Roma 07474
Società Italiana di Chirurgia Clinica, Roma 07475
Società Italiana di Chirurgia della Mano, Firenze 07476
Società Italiana di Chirurgia d'Urgenza, di Pronto Soccorso e di Terapia Intensiva Chirurgica, Milano 07477
Società Italiana di Chirurgia Estetica, Roma 07478
Società Italiana di Chirurgia Pediatrica, Roma 07479
Società Italiana di Chirurgia Plastica, Verona 07480
Società Italiana di Chirurgia Toracica, Roma 07481
Società Italiana di Citologia Clinica e Sociale, Roma 07482
Società Italiana di Criminologia, Roma 07483
Società Italiana di Dermatologia e Sifilografia, Roma 07484
Società Italiana di Diabetologia, Torino 07485
Società Italiana di Diabetologia e Endocrinologia Pediatrica, Milano 07486
Società Italiana di Economia Agraria, Reggio Emilia 07487
Società Italiana di Economia, Demografia e Statistica, Roma 07488
Società Italiana di Elettroencefalografia e Neurofisiologia, Bologna 07489
Società Italiana di Ematologia, Milano 07490
Società Italiana di Endocrinologia, Roma 07491
Società Italiana di Ergonomia, Milano 07492
Società Italiana di Ergonomia Stomatologica, Milano 07493
Società Italiana di Farmacologia, Milano 07494
Società Italiana di Farmacologia Clinica, Pisa 07495
Società Italiana di Filosofia Giuridica e Politica, Roma 07496
Società Italiana di Fisica, Bologna 07497
Società Italiana di Fisiologia, Firenze 07498
Società Italiana di Foniatria, Catania 07499
Società Italiana di Fotobiologia, S. Maria di Galeria 07500
Società Italiana di Fotogrammetria e Topografia, Milano 07501
Società Italiana di Gastroenterologia, Bologna 07502
Società Italiana di Genetica Agraria, Foggia 07503
Società Italiana di Geofisica e Meteorologia, Genova 07504
Società Italiana di Gerontologia e Geriatria, Firenze 07505
Società Italiana di Ginecologia ed Ostetricia, Roma 07506
Società Italiana di Ginnastica Medica, Medicina Fisica e Riabilitazione, Milano 07507
Società Italiana di Glottologia, Pisa 07508
Società Italiana di Immunologia e di Immunopatologia, Bari 07509
Società Italiana di Ingegneria, Aerofotogrammetria e Topografia, Roma 07510
Società Italiana di Ippologia, Roma 07511
Società Italiana di Laringologia, Otologia, Rinologia e Patologia Cervico-Facciale, Roma 07512
Società Italiana di Liposcultura, Roma 07513
Società Italiana di Malacologia, Milano 07514
Società Italiana di Medicina del Lavoro e di Igiene Industriale, Pavia 07515
Società Italiana di Medicina del Traffico, Roma 07516
Società Italiana di Medicina e Igiene della Scuola, Milano 07517
Società Italiana di Medicina Estetica, Roma 07518
Società Italiana di Medicina Fisica e Riabilitazione, Moncalieri 07519
Società Italiana di Medicina Interna, Roma 07520
Società Italiana di Medicina Legale e delle Assicurazioni, Padova 07521
Società Italiana di Medicina Preventiva e Sociale, Genova 07522
Società Italiana di Medicina Psicosomatica, Roma 07523
Società Italiana di Medicina Sociale, Torino 07524
Società Italiana di Medicina Subacquea ed Iperbarica, Napoli 07525
Società Italiana di Medicina Trasfusionale e di Immunoematologia, Roma 07526
Società Italiana di Mesoterapia, Roma 07527
Società Italiana di Meteorologia Applicata, Roma 07528
Società Italiana di Microangiologia e Microcorcolazione, Pisa 07529
Società Italiana di Microbiologia, Catania 07530
Società Italiana di Mineralogia e Petrologia, Milano 07531
Società Italiana di Musicologia, Roma 07532
Società Italiana di Neurochirurgia, Ancona 07533
Società Italiana di Neurologia, Roma 07534
Società Italiana di Neuropediatria, Siena 07535
Società Italiana di Neuropsichiatria Infantile, Napoli 07536
Società Italiana di Neuroradiologia, Napoli 07537
Società Italiana di Neurosonologia, Bologna 07538
Società Italiana di Nipiologia, Roma 07539
Società Italiana di Nutrizione Umana, Roma 07540
Società Italiana di Odontoiatria Infantile, Roma 07541
Società Italiana di Odontostomatologia e Chirurgia Maxillo-Facciale, L'Aquila 07542
Società Italiana di Oncologia Ginecologica, Roma 07543
Società Italiana di Ortopedia e Traumatologia, Roma 07544
Società Italiana di Ostetricia e Ginecologia, Roma 07545
Società Italiana di Oto-Neuro-Oftalmologia, Bologna 07546
Società Italiana di Otorinolaringologia e Chirurgia Cervico Facciale, Roma 07547
Società Italiana di Otorinolaringologia Pediatrica, Roma 07548
Società Italiana di Parassitologia, Roma 07549
Società Italiana di Patologia, Milano 07550
Società Italiana di Patologia Aviare, Perugia 07551
Società Italiana di Patologia e di Allevamento degli Ovini e dei Caprini, Catania 07552
Società Italiana di Patologia ed Allevamento dei Suini, Parma 07553
Società Italiana di Patologia Vascolare, Roma 07554
Società Italiana di Pediatria, Roma 07555
Società Italiana di Pneumologia, Torino 07556
Società Italiana di Psichiatria, Milano 07557
Società Italiana di Psichiatria Biologica, Napoli 07558
Società Italiana di Psicologia, Roma 07559
Società Italiana di Psicologia Individuale, Milano 07560
Società Italiana di Psicologia Scientifica, Palermo 07561
Società Italiana di Psicosintesi Terapeutica, Firenze 07562
Società Italiana di Psicoterapia Analitica Immaginativa, Cremona 07563
Società Italiana di Radiologia Medica e di Medicina Nucleare, Milano 07564
Società Italiana di Reologia, Napoli 07565
Società Italiana di Reumatologia, Parma 07566
Società Italiana di Scienze Farmaceutiche, Milano 07567
Società Italiana di Scienze Fisiche e Matematiche Mathesis, Roma 07568
Società Italiana di Scienze Naturali, Milano 07569
Società Italiana di Senologia, Roma 07570
Società Italiana di Sessuologia Clinica, Roma 07571
Società Italiana di Sessuologia Medica, Roma 07572
Società Italiana di Sociologà, Roma 07573
Società Italiana di Statistica, Roma 07574
Società Italiana di Storia della Medicina, Bologna 07575
Società Italiana di Studi sul Secolo XVIII, Roma 07576
Società Italiana di Terapia Familiare, Roma 07577
Società Italiana di Tossicologia, Milano 07578
Società Italiana di Traumatologia della Strada, Roma 07579
Società Italiana di Urodinamica, Bologna 07580
Società Italiana di Urologia, Roma 07581
Società Italiana Medica del Training Autogeno, Bologna 07582
Società Italiana Medici e Operatori Geriatrici, Firenze 07583
Società Italiana Medico-Chirurgica di Pronto Soccorso, Bologna 07584
Società Italiana Musica Contemporanea, Roma 07585
Società Italiana Organi Artificiali, Roma 07586
Società Italiana per gli Archivi Sanitari Ospedalieri, Viareggio 07587
Società Italiana per gli Studi Filosofici e Religiosi, Milano 07588
Società Italiana per il Progresso della Zootecnia, Milano 07589
Società Italiana per il Progresso delle Scienze, Roma 07590
Società Italiana per la Organizzazione Internazionale, Roma 07591
Società Italiana per l'Antropologia e la Etnologia, Firenze 07592
Società Italiana per l'Archeologia e la Storia delle Arti, Napoli 07593
Società Italiana per le Scienze Ambientali: Biometeorologia, Bioclimatologia ed Ecologia, Milano 07594
Società Italiana per l'Educazione Musicale, Milano 07595
Società Italiana per lo Studio della Cancerogenesi Ambientale ed Epidemiologia dei Tumori, Genova 07596
Società Italiana per lo Studio della Fertilità e della Sterilità, Roma 07597
Società Italiana per lo Studio dell'Arteriosclerosi, Bari 07598
Società Italiana per lo Studio delle Sostanze Grasse, Milano 07599
Società Italiana per lo Studio e l'Applicazione del Pirodiserbo, Piacenza 07600
Società Italiana per l'Organizzazione Internazionale, Roma 07601
Società Italiana pro Deontologia Sanitaria, Milano 07602
Società Italiana Sistemi Informativi Elettronici, Roma 07378
Società Jonico-Salentina di Medicina e Chirurgia, Taranto 07603
Società Laziale Abruzzese di Medicina del Lavoro, Roma 07604
Società Laziale – Abruzzese Marchigiana Molisana di Ostetricia e Ginecologia, Roma 07605
Società Letteraria, Verona 07606
Società Ligure di Storia Patria, Genova 07607
Società Lombarda di Criminologia, Milano 07608
Società Mazziniana Pensiero e Azione, Roma 07609
Società Medica Chirurgica di Bologna, Bologna 07610
Società Medico-Chirugica, Bari 07611
Società Medico-Chirurgica di Ferrara, Ferrara 07612
Società Medico-Chirurgica di Modena, Modena 07613
Società Medico-Psicologica, Milano 07614
Società Messinese di Storia Patria, Messina 07615
Società Napoletana di Chirurgia, Napoli 07616
Società Napoletana di Storia Patria, Napoli 07617
Società Naturalisti Veronesi F. Zorzi, Verona 07618
Società Nazionale di Informatica delle Camere di Commercio per la Gestione dei Centri Elettronici Reteconnessi Valutazione Elaborazione Dati, Roma 07619
Società Nazionale di Scienze, Lettere ed Arti, Napoli 07620
Società Nucleare Italiana, Firenze 07621
Società Oftalmologica Italiana, Bologna 07622
Società Ornitologica Italiana, Ravenna 07623

Société des Peintres, Sculpteurs et Architectes Suisses, Muttenz 10145
Société des Physiciens des Hôpitaux d'Expression Française, Liège 01264
Société des Poètes Français, Paris 04043
Société des Professeurs d'Allemand en Suisse Romande et Italienne, Genève 10499
Société des Professeurs de Dessin et d'Arts Plastiques de l'Enseignement Secondaire, Paris 04044
Société des Professeurs Français et Francophones en Amérique, New York 16344
Société des Sciences, Arts et Belles-Lettres de Bayeux, Bayeux 04045
Société des Sciences Historiques et Naturelles de la Corse, Bastia 04046
Société des Sciences Naturelles de Bourgogne, Dijon 04047
Société des Sciences Naturelles et Physiques du Maroc, Rabat 08384
Société des Sciences Physiques et Naturelles de Bordeaux, Talence 04048
Société des Sculpteurs du Canada, Toronto 02367
Société d'Ethnographie de Paris, Paris 04049
Société d'Ethnologie Française, Paris 04050
Société d'Ethnozoologie et d'Ethnobotanique, Paris 04051
Société d'Etude de Psychodrame Pratique et Théorique, Paris 04052
Société d'Etude du Dix-Septième Siècle, Paris 04053
Société d'Etudes Ardennaises, Charleville-Mézières 04054
Société d'Etudes Dantesques, Nice 04055
Société d'Etudes Economiques et Comptables, Paris 04056
Société d'Etudes Economiques, Sociales et Statistiques du Maroc, Rabat 08385
Société d'Etudes et de Contrôles Juridiques, Paris 04057
Société d'Etudes et de Documentation Economiques, Industrielles et Sociales, Rueil-Malmaison 04058
Société d'Etudes et de Recherches Biologiques, Paris 04059
Société d'Etudes et de Recherches en Sciences Sociales, Paris 04060
Société d'Etudes et de Recherches pour la Connaissance de l'Homme, Paris 04061
Société d'Etudes et de Soins pour les Enfants Paralysés, Paris 04062
Société d'Etudes Ferroviaires, Paris 04063
Société d'Etudes Financières et Meunières, Paris 04064
Société d'Etudes Folkloriques du Centre-Ouest, Saint-Jean d'Angely 04065
Société d'Etudes Hispaniques et de Diffusion de la Culture Française à l'Etranger, Périgueux 04066
Société d'Etudes Historiques, Paris 04067
Société d'Etudes Italiennes, Paris 04068
Société d'Etudes Jaurésiennes, Paris 04069
Société d'Etudes Juives, Paris 04070
Société d'Etudes Juridiques, Economiques et Fiscales, Paris 04071
Société d'Etudes Latines de Bruxelles, Tournai 01265
Société d'Etudes Linguistiques et Anthropologiques de France, Paris 04072
Société d'Etudes Minières, Industrielles et Financières, Paris 04073
Société d'Etudes Ornithologiques des France, Paris 04074
Société d'Etudes pour le Développement Economique et Social, Paris 04075
Société d'Etudes Psychiques, Nancy 04076
Société d'Etudes Robespierristes, Paris 04077
Société d'Etudes Romantiques, Clermont-Ferrand 04078
Société d'Etudes Scientifiques et de Recherches, Herblay 04079
Société d'Etudes Techniques, Paris 04080
Société d'Histoire de Bordeaux, Bordeaux 04081
Société d'Histoire de la Médecine Hébraïque, Paris 04082
Société d'Histoire de la Pharmacie, Paris 04083
Société d'Histoire de la Suisse Romande, Lausanne 10500
Société d'Histoire du Droit, Paris 04084
Société d'Histoire du Droit Normand, Caen 04085
Société d'Histoire du Théâtre, Paris 04086
Société d'Histoire et d'Archéologie de Bretagne, Rennes 04087
Société d'Histoire et d'Archéologie de Genève, Genève 10501
Société d'Histoire et d'Archéologie de la Lorraine, Saint Julien les Metz 04088
Société d'Histoire et d'Archéologie Le Vieux Montmartre, Paris 04089
Société d'Histoire Générale et d'Histoire Diplomatique, Paris 04090
Société d'Histoire Littéraire de la France, Paris 04091
Société d'Histoire Moderne et Contemporaine, Paris 04092
Société d'Histoire Religieuse de la France, Paris 04093
Société d'Hygiène International, Paris 04094
Société d'Obstétrique et de Gynécologie de Marseille, Marseille 04095
Société d'Obstétrique et de Gynécologie de Toulouse, Toulouse 04096
Société d'Océanographie de France, Paris 04097
Société d'Ophtalmologie de l'Est de la France, Nancy 04098
Société d'Ophtalmologie de Lyon, Lyon 04099
Société d'Ophtalmologie de Paris, Paris 04100
Société d'Oto-Neuro-Ophthalmologie du Sud-Est de la France, Marseille 04101
Société du Salon d'Automne, Paris 04102
Société Entomologique de France, Paris 04103
Société Entomologique d'Egypte, Cairo 03303
Société Entomologique Suisse, Neuchâtel 10265
Société et Fédération Internationale de Cardiologie, Genève 10502
Société Européenne de Cardiologie, Rotterdam 08453
Société Européenne de Culture, Venezia 07424
Société Européenne de Radiologie Cardio-Vasculaire et de Radiologie d'Intervention, Lyon 04104
Société Européenne de Radiologie Pédiatrique, Paris 04105
Société Européenne pour la Formation des Ingénieurs, Bruxelles 01266
Société Financière Européenne, Paris 04106
Société Finno-Ougrienne, Helsinki 03383
Société Française d'Acoustique, Paris 04107
Société Française d'Allergologie et d'Immuno-Allergie Clinique, Paris 04108
Société Française d'Anesthésie et de Réanimation, Paris 04109
Société Française d'Angéiologie, Lyon 04110
Société Française d'Archéocivilisation et de Folklore, Paris 04111
Société Française d'Archéologie, Paris 04112
Société Française d'Art Contemporain, Paris 04113
Société Française de Biochimie et Biologie Moléculaire, Paris 04114
Société Française de Biologie Clinique, Paris 04115
Société Française de Cardiologie, Paris 04116
Société Française de Céramique, Paris 04117
Société Française de Chimie, Paris 04118
Société Française de Chirurgie Orthopédique et Traumatologique, Paris 04119
Société Française de Chirurgie Pédiatrique, Lyon 04120
Société Française de Chirurgie Plastique et Reconstructive, Paris 04121
Société Française de Chronométrie et de Microtechnique, Besançon 04122
Société Française de Composition, Paris 04123
Société Française de Dermatologie et de Syphiligraphie, Paris 04124
Société Française de Droit Aérien et Spatial, Paris 04125
Société Française de Génétique, Orléans 04126
Société Française de Géographie Economique, Paris 04127
Société Française de Graphologie, Paris 04128
Société Française de Gynécologie, Paris 04129
Société Française de Malacologie, Paris 04130
Société Française de Médecine Aérospatiale, Bretigny 04131
Société Française de Médecine du Sport, Paris 04132
Société Française de Médecine du Trafic, Paris 04133
Société Française de Médecine Esthétique, Courbevoie 04134
Société Française de Médecine Générale, Issy les Moulineaux 04135
Société Française de Médecine Orthopédique et Thérapeutique Manuelle, Paris 04136
Société Française de Médecine Préventive et Sociale, Paris 04137
Société Française de Médecine Psychosomatique, Paris 04138
Société Française de Mesothérapie, Paris 04139
Société Française de Métallurgie et de Matériaux, Nanterre 04140
Société Française de Microbiologie, Paris 04141
Société Française de Microscopie Electronique, Paris 04142
Société Française de Minéralogie et de Cristallographie, Paris 04143
Société Française de Musicologie, Paris 04144
Société Française de Mycologie Médicale, Paris 04145
Société Française de Néonatologie, Paris 04146
Société Française de Neurologie, Paris 04147
Société Française de Numismatique, Paris 04148
Société Française de Pathologie Respiratoire, Paris 04149
Société Française de Pédagogie, Paris 04150
Société Française de Pédiatrie, Paris 04151
Société Française de Philosophie, Paris 04152
Société Française de Phlébologie, Paris 04153
Société Française de Phoniatrie, Paris 04154
Société Française de Photogrammétrie et de Télédétection, Saint-Mandé 04155
Société Française de Photographie, Paris 04156
Société Française de Physiologie Végétale, Paris 04157
Société Française de Physique, Paris 04158
Société Française de Phytiatrie et de Phytopharmacie, Versailles 04159
Société Française de Psychologie, Paris 04160
Société Française de Radiologie et d'Imagerie Médicale, Paris 04161
Société Française de Santé Publique, Vandoeuvre lès Nancy 04162
Société Française de Sciences et Techniques Pharmaceutiques, Paris 04163
Société Française de Sexologie Clinique, Paris 04164
Société Française de Sociologie, Paris 04165
Société Française de Thérapeutique et de Pharmacologe Clinique, Paris 04166
Société Française de Toxicologie, Paris 04167
Société Française d'Ecologie, Brunoy 04168
Société Française d'Economie Rurale, Paris 04169
Société Française d'Egyptologie, Paris 04170
Société Française d'Endocrinologie, Paris 04171
Société Française d'Energie Nucléaire, Paris 04172
Société Française des Architectes, Paris 04173
Société Française des Physiciens d'Hôpital, Paris 04174
Société Française des Thermiciens, Paris 04175
Société Française des Urbanistes, Paris 04176
Société Française d'Etude du Dix-Huitième Siècle, Nantes 04177
Société Française d'Etudes des Phénomènes Psychiques, Paris 04178
Société Française d'Etudes et de Réalisations Cartographiques, Paris 04179
Société Française d'Etudes Juridiques, Paris 04180
Société Française d'Hématologie, Paris 04181
Société Française d'Héraldique et de Sigillographie, Paris 04182
Société Française d'Histoire de la Médecine, Reims 04183
Société Française d'Histoire d'Outre-Mer, Saint-Denis 04184
Société Française d'Hydrologie et de Climatologie Médicales, Paris 04185
Société Française d'Ichtyologie, Paris 04186
Société Française d'Ophthalmologie, Paris 04187
Société Française d'Optique Physiologique, Paris 04188
Société Française d'Orthopédie, Paris 04189
Société Française d'Oto-Rhino-Laryngologie et de Pathologie Cervico-Faciale, Paris 04190
Société Française du Cancer, Paris 04191
Société Française du Vide, Paris 04192
Société Française d'Urologie, Paris 04193
Société Française pour le Droit International, Nanterre 04194
Société Fribourgeoise des Sciences Naturelles, Fribourg 10503
Société Généalogique Canadienne-Française, Montréal 02377
Société Géographique Royale du Canada, Vanier 02340
Société Géologique de Belgique, Liège 01267
Société Géologique de France, Paris 04195
Société Géologique et Minéralogique de Bretagne, Rennes 04196
Société Géologique Suisse, Genève 10504
La Société Guernesiaise, Saint Peter Port 12345
Société Héraldique du Canada, Gloucester 02122
Société Historique Acadienne, Moncton 02378
Société Historique Algérienne, Alger 00009
Société Historique, Archéologique et Littéraire de Lyon, Lyon 04197
Société Historique de la Province de Maine, Le Mans 04198
Société Historique de Québec, Québec 02379
Société Historique du Bas-Limousin, Tulle 04199
Société Historique du Saguenay, Chicoutimi 02380
Société Historique et Archéologique du Périgord, Périgueux 04200
Société Huntington du Canada, Cambridge 02127
Société Hydrotechnique de France, Paris 04201
Société Internationale de Bibliographie Classique, Paris 04202
Société Internationale de Biologie Mathématique, Antony 04203
Société Internationale de Chirurgie, Reinach 10505
Société Internationale de Chirurgie Orthopédique et de Traumatologie, Bruxelles 01268
Société Internationale de Criminologie, Paris 04204
Société Internationale de Droit Pénal Militaire et de Droit de la Guerre, Bruxelles 01269
Société Internationale de Droit Penal Militaire et de Droit de la Guerre; Groupe Italienne, Roma 07437
Societé Internationale de Musicologie, Basel 10183
Société Internationale de Podologie Médico-Chirurgicale, Cannes-la-Bocca 04205
Société Internationale de Psycho-Prophylaxie Obstétricale, Paris 04206
Société Internationale de Psychopathologie de l'Expression, Paris 04207
Société internationale de recherche orthopédique et traumatologique, San Diego 16345
Société Internationale de Recherches pour l'Environnement et la Santé, Paris 04208
Société Internationale de Transfusion Sanguine, Les Ulis 04209
Société Internationale des Amis de Montaigne, Paris 04210
Société Internationale d'Urologie, Paris 04211
Société Internationale pour la Lutte contre le Cancer du Sein, Paris 04212
Société Internationale pour la Recherche sur les Maladies de Civilisation et sur l'Environnement, Bruxelles 01270
Société Internationale pour l'Enseignement Commercial, Odense 03214
Société Internationale pour l'Etude de la Philosophie Médiévale, Louvain-la-Neuve 01271
Société J. S. Bach, Paris 04213
Société Jean-Jacques Rousseau, Genève 10506
Société Jersiaise, Saint Helier 12346
Société Juridique et Fiscale de France, Levallois Perret 04214
Société Linnéenne de Provence, Marseille 04215
Société Longuédocienne de Géographie, Montpellier 04216
Société Luxembourgeoise de Radiologie, Luxembourg 08176
Société Mathématique de Belgique, Bruxelles 01272
Société Mathématique de France, Paris 04217
Société Mathématique du Canada, Ottawa 01923
Société Mathématique Suisse, Genève 10373
Société Médicale de la Suisse Romande, Sion 10507
Société Médicale des Hôpitaux de Paris, Paris 04218
Société Médicale d'Imagerie, Enseignement et Recherche, Paris 04219
Société Médicale du Nouveau-Brunswick, Fredericton 02231
Société Médico-Chirurgicale des Hôpitaux et Formations Sanitaires des Armées, Paris 04220
Société Médico-Chirurgicale des Hôpitaux Libres, Paris 04221
Société Médico-Psychologique, Boulogne 04222
Société Météorologique de France, Boulogne-Billancourt 04223
Société Mycologique de France, Paris 04224
Société Nationale Académique de Cherbourg, Cherbourg 04225
Société Nationale de Laiterie, Bruxelles 01273
Société Nationale de Protection de la Nature, Paris 04226
Société Nationale de Transfusion Sanguine, Paris 04227
Société Nationale des Architectes de France, Paris 04228
Société Nationale des Beaux-Arts, Paris 04229
Société Nationale des Sciences Naturelles et Mathématiques de Cherbourg, Cherbourg 04230
Société Nationale d'Horticulture de France, Paris 04231
Société Nationale Française de Gastro-Entérologie, Vandoeuvre 04232
Société Nationale Française de Rééducation et Réadaption Fonctionnelles, Paris 04233
Société Neuchâteloise des Sciences Naturelles, Neuchâtel 10508
Société Odontologique de Paris, Paris 04234
Société Parisienne d'Etudes et de Recherches Foncières, Paris 04235
Société Parisienne d'Etudes Spéciales, Paris 04236
Société Pédagogique de la Suisse Romande, Carouge 10509
Société Philosophique de Bruxelles, Bruxelles 01274
Société Philosophique de Louvain, Louvain-la-Neuve 01275
Société Phycologique de France, Paris 04237
Société pour la Protection des Paysages, Sites et Monuments, Paris 04238
Société pour le Développement Minier de la Côte d'Ivoire, Abidjan 07685
Société pour l'Etude de l'Architecture au Canada, Ottawa 02383
Société Professionnelle de Recherche en Marketing, Toronto 02328
Société Provençale de Pédiatrie, Marseille 04239
Société Psychoanalytique de Paris, Paris 04240
Société Québécoise d'Assainissement des Eaux, Montréal 02381
Société Racinienne, Neuilly-sur-Seine 04241
Société Romande d'Audiophonologie et de Pathologie du Langage, Delémont 10510
Société Royale Belge d'Anthropologie et de Préhistoire, Bruxelles 01276
Société Royale Belge d'Astronomie, de Météorologie et de Physique du Globe, Bruxelles 01277
Société Royale Belge de Chirurgie, Bruxelles 01278
Société Royale Belge de Dermatologie et de Vénérologie, Gent 01222
Société Royale Belge de Géographie, Bruxelles 01279
Société Royale Belge de Gynécologie et d'Obstétrique, Bruxelles 01280
Société Royale Belge de Médecine Physique et de Réhabilitation, Bruxelles 01281
Société Royale Belge de Rheumatologie, Bruxelles 01282
Société Royale Belge de Stomatologie et Chirurgie Maxillo-Faciale, Gent 01283
Société Royale Belge d'Entomologie, Bruxelles 01284
Société Royale Belge des Electriciens, Bruxelles 01285
Société Royale Belge des Ingénieurs et Industriels, Bruxelles 01286
Société Royale d'Archéologie de Bruxelles, Bruxelles 01287
Société Royale d'Astronomie du Canada, Toronto 02338
Société Royale de Chimie, Bruxelles 01288
Société Royale de Médecine Mentale de Belgique, Bruxelles 01289
Société Royale de Numismatique de Belgique, Bruxelles 01290
Société Royale d'Economie Politique de Belgique, Charleroi 01291
Société Royale des Amis du Musée Royal de l'Armée et d'Histoire Militaire, Bruxelles 01292
Société Royale des Beaux-Arts, Bruxelles 01293
Société Royale des Bibliophiles et Iconophiles de Belgique, Bruxelles 01294
Société Royale des Sciences de Liège, Liège 01295

379 Alphabetical Index: Society

Société Royale des Sciences Médicales et Naturelles de Bruxelles, Bruxelles *01296*
Société Royale du Canada, Ottawa *02346*
Société Royale Zoologique de Belgique, Bruxelles *01297*
Société Saint-Simon, Sceaux *04242*
Société Savoisienne d'Histoire et d'Archéologie, Chambéry *04243*
Société Scientifique de Bretagne, Rennes *04244*
Société Scientifique de Bruxelles, Namur *01298*
Société Scientifique d'Hygiène Alimentaire, Paris *04245*
Société Statistique du Canada, London *02397*
Société Suisse de Cardiologie, Bern *10303*
Société Suisse de Chirurgie, Lausanne *10511*
Société Suisse de Droit Pénal, Zürich *10368*
Société Suisse de Juristes, Lausanne *10512*
Société Suisse de Numismatique, Bern *10378*
Société Suisse de Pédagogie Musicale, Bassersdorf *10454*
Société Suisse de Pharmacie, Bern-Liebefeld *10432*
Société Suisse de Philosophie, Basel *10381*
Société Suisse de Physique, Neuchâtel *10382*
Société Suisse de Sociologie, Zürich *10335*
Société Suisse de Statistique et d'Economie Politique, Bern *10337*
Société Suisse des Américanistes, Genève *10513*
Société Suisse des Auteurs, Lausanne *10514*
Société Suisse des Professeurs de Français, La Chaux-de-Fonds *10515*
Société Suisse des Professeurs de Musique de l'Enseignement Secondaire, Emmenbrücke *10516*
Société Suisse des Professeurs de Sciences Commerciales, Sankt Gallen *10449*
Société Suisse d'Ethnologie, Bern *10267*
Société Suisse d'Etudes Africaines, Bern *10238*
Société Suisse d'Etudes Anglaises, Genève *10243*
Société Suisse d'Histoire de la Médicine et des Sciences Naturelles, Bern *10297*
Société Suisse d'Oto-Rhino-Laryngologie et de Chirurgie Cervico-Faciale, Sankt Gallen *10322*
Société Suisse pour la Recherche en Education, Carouge *10517*
Société Technique d'Etudes Mécaniques et d'Outillage, Paris *04246*
Société Technique et Chimique de Sucrerie de Belgique, Bruxelles *01299*
Société Théosophique de France, Paris *04247*
Société Universitaire Européenne de Recherches Financières, Amsterdam *08622*
Société Vaudoise des Sciences Naturelles, Lausanne *10518*
Société Vaudoise d'Histoire et d'Archéologie, Chavannes-près-Renens *10519*
Société Vétérinaire Pratique de France, Paris *04248*
Société Zoologique de France, Paris *04249*
Sociétés de Statistique de Paris et de France, Paris *04250*
Society for Academic Emergency Medicine, Lansing *16346*
Society for Adolescent Medicine, Blue Springs *16347*
Society for Advancement of Management, Vinton *16348*
Society for African Church History, Aberdeen *12347*
Society for American Archaeology, Washington *16349*
Society for Ancient Greek Philosophy, Binghamton *16350*
Society for Applied Anthropology, Oklahoma City *16351*
Society for Applied Bacteriology, Newton Abbot *12348*
Society for Applied Learning Technology, Warrenton *16352*
Society for Applied Spectroscopy, Frederick *16353*
Society for Armenian Studies, Dearborn *16354*
The Society for Army Historical Research, London *12349*
Society for Asian and Comparative Philosophy, Honolulu *16355*
Society for Asian Art, San Francisco *16356*
Society for Asian Music, Ithaca *16357*
Society for Asian Political and Economic Studies, Tokyo *07709*
Society for Austrian and Habsburg History, Indianapolis *16358*
Society for Back Pain Research, London *12350*
Society for Biomaterials, Minneapolis *16359*
Society for Business Ethics, Bryn Mawr *16360*
Society for Byzantine Studies, Athinai *06235*
Society for Calligraphy, Los Angeles *16361*
Society for Cardiac Angiography and Interventions, Raleigh *16362*
Society for Ch'ing Studies, Baltimore *16363*
Society for Cinema Studies, Knoxville *16364*
Society for Clinical and Experimental Hypnosis, Liverpool *16365*
Society for Clinical and Experimental Pharmacology in SADC/COMESSA/PTA Countries, Dar-es-Salaam *10605*
Society for Clinical Trials, Baltimore *16366*
Society for College and University Planning, Ann Arbor *16367*
Society for Commercial Archeology, Washington *16368*
Society for Computer Simulation International, San Diego *16369*
Society for Computers and Law, Bristol *12351*
Society for Conceptual and Contents Analysis by Computer, Bowling Green *16370*
Society for Conservation Biology, Seattle *16371*
Society for Contemorary Music, Baku *00896*
Society for Cooperation in Russian and Soviet Studies, London *12352*
Society for Coptic Archaeology, Cairo *03304*
Society for Creative Anachronism, Santa Cruz *16372*
Society for Cryobiology, Austin *16373*
Society for Cultural Anthropology, Washington *16374*
Society for Developmental Biology, Bethesda *16375*
Society for Dissemination of Sciences, Budapest *06360*
Society for Earthquake and Civil Engineering Dynamics, London *12353*
Society for Economic Botany, Columbia *16376*
Society for Education in Film and Television, London *12354*
Society for Educational Reconstruction, Mankato *16377*
Society for Endocrinology, Bristol *12355*
Society for Endocrinology, Metabolism and Diabetes of Southern Africa, Sandton *09660*
Society for Environmental Geochemistry and Health, Rolla *16378*
Society for Environmental Therapy, Manchester *12356*
Society for Epidemiologic Research, Salt Lake City *16379*
Society for Ethnomusicology, Bloomington *16380*
Society for Experimental and Descriptive Malacology, Ann Arbor *16381*
Society for Experimental Biology, Johannesburg *09661*
The Society for Experimental Biology, London *12357*
Society for Experimental Biology and Medicine, New York *16382*
Society for Experimental Mechanics, Bethel *16383*
Society for Fermentation and Bioengineering Japan, Osaka *07845*
Society for Folk Life Studies, Hollywood *12358*
Society for French American Cultural Services and Educational Aid, New York *16384*
Society for French Historical Studies, Iowa City *16385*
Society for General Microbiology, Reading *12359*
Society for General Music, Reston *16386*
Society for German-American Studies, Cincinnati *16387*
Society for Gynecologic Investigation, Washington *16388*
Society for Historians of American Foreign Relations, Dayton *16389*
Society for Historical Archaeology, Tucson *16390*
Society for History Education, Long Beach *16391*
Society for Human Resource Management, Alexandria *16392*
Society for Humanistic Anthropology, Oneonta *16393*
Society for Humanistic Judaism, Farmington Hills *16394*
Society for Iberian and Latin American Thought, Washington *16395*
Society for Indian and Northern Education, Saskatoon *02382*
Society for Industrial and Applied Mathematics, Philadelphia *16396*
Society for Industrial Archaeology, Princeton *16397*
Society for Industrial Microbiology, Fairfax *16398*
Society for Information Display, Santa Ana *16399*
Society for Information Management, Chicago *16400*
Society for Interactive Learning, Ryton *12360*
Society for International Development, Roma *07655*
Society for International Numismatics, Santa Monica *16401*
Society for Invertebrate Pathology, Bethesda *16402*
Society for Investigative Dermatology, Cleveland *16403*
Society for Iranian Studies, Seattle *16404*
Society for Italian Historical Studies, Chestnut Hill *16405*
Society for Italic Handwriting, London *12361*
Society for Latin American Anthropology, Arlington *16406*
Society for Leukocyte Biology, Bethesda *16407*
Society for Libyan Studies, London *12362*
Society for Life History Research, Philadelphia *16408*
Society for Lincolnshire History and Archaeology, Lincoln *12363*
Society for Linguistic Anthropology, Washington *16409*
Society for Literature and Science, Worchester *16410*
Society for Low Temperature Biology, London *12364*
Society for Macedonian Studies, Thessaloniki *06236*
Society for Manyo Studies, Osaka *07766*
Society for Medical Anthropology, Arlington *16411*
Society for Medicinal Plant Research, Kleinrinderfeld *05349*
Society for Medicine and Law in Israel, Haifa *06745*
Society for Medicine Research, London *12365*
Society for Medieval Archaeology, Shrewsbury *12366*
Society for Metal Science, Brno *02963*
Society for Mining, Metallurgy and Exploration, Littleton *16412*
Society for Multivariate Experimental Psychology, Upton Park *12367*
Society for Music Teacher Education, Reston *16413*
Society for National Art, København *03124*
Society for Natural Philosophy, Urbana *16414*
Society for Natural Sciences of Slovenia, Ljubljana *09595*
Society for Nautical Research, London *12368*
Society for Near Eastern Studies in Japan, Tokyo *07957*
Society for Neuroscience, Washington *16415*
Society for New Language Study, Denver *16416*
Society for New Testament Study, Lancaster *12369*
Society for Nutrition Education, Minneapolis *16417*
Society for Obstetric Anesthesia and Perinatology, Richmond *16418*
Society for Occlusal Studies, Kansas City *16419*
Society for Occupational and Environmental Health, McLean *16420*
Society for Organization and Management Science, Budapest *06357*
Society for Pediatric Dermatology, Ann Arbor *16421*
Society for Pediatric Pathology, McLean *16422*
Society for Pediatric Psychology, Charleston *16423*
Society for Pediatric Radiology, Oak Brook *16424*
Society for Pediatric Research, Elk Grove Village *16425*
Society for Pediatric Urology, Seattle *16426*
Society for Personality Assessment, Washington *16427*
Society for Phenomenology and Existential Philosophy, Fairfax *16428*
Society for Philosophy and Public Affairs, Hoboken *16429*
Society for Philosophy of Religion, Athens *16430*
Society for Philosophy, Sociology and Politics of Macedonia, Skopje *08186*
Society for Photographic Education, Dallas *16431*
Society for Popular Astronomy, Nottingham *12370*
Society for Post-Medieval Archaeology, London *12371*
Society for Promoting Christian Knowledge, London *12372*
Society for Promotion of Educational Reform through Teacher Training, London *12373*
Society for Psychical Research, London *12374*
Society for Psychological Anthropology, Arlington *16432*
Society for Psychological Study of Social Issues, Ann Arbor *16433*
Society for Psychophysiological Research, Dallas *16434*
Society for Psychosomatic Research, London *12375*
Society for Public Health Education, Berkeley *16435*
Society for Radiological Protection, Didcot *12376*
Society for Railway Transport, Moskva *09458*
Society for Range Management, Denver *16436*
Society for Reformation Research, Saint Louis *16437*
Society for Renaissance Studies, Bristol *12377*
Society for Research and Promotion of Maritime Sciences, Rijeka *02869*
The Society for Research in Asiatic Music, Tokyo *08045*
Society for Research in Child Development, Ann Arbor *16438*
Society for Research in The Psychology of Music and Music Education, Dagenham *12378*
Society for Research into Higher Education, London *12379*
Society for Research into Hydrocephalus and Spina Bifida, Darlington *12380*
Society for Research on the Azores, Ponta Delgada *09217*
Society for Risk Analysis International, McLean *16439*
Society for Sedimentary Geology, Tulsa *16440*
Society for Slavonic Studies in Slovenia, Ljubljana *09591*
Society for Slovene Studies, Bloomington *16441*
Society for Social Responsibility in Science (A.C.T.), Canberra *00361*
Society for Social Studies of Science, Baton Rouge *16442*
Society for South Asian Studies, London *12381*
Society for Spanish and Portuguese Historical Studies, Minneapolis *16443*
Society for Technical Communication, Arlington *16444*
Society for the Advancement of American Philosophy, Seattle *16445*
Society for the Advancement of Anaesthesia in Dentistry, London *12382*
Society for the Advancement of Behavior Analysis, Kalamazoo *16446*
Society for the Advancement of Education, Valley Stream *16447*
Society for the Advancement of Material and Process Engineering, Covina *16448*
Society for the Advancement of Research, Laguna *09067*
Society for the Advancement of Scandinavian Study, Provo *16449*
Society for the Advancement of Science, Bergen *08880*
Society for the Advancement of the Vegetable Industry, Laguna *09068*
Society for the Anthropology of Europe, Arlington *16450*
Society for the Arts, Religion and Contemporary Culture, Allentown *16451*
Society for the Comparative Study of Society and History, Ann Arbor *16452*
Society for the Conservation of Bighorn Sheep, La Canada Flintridge *16453*
Society for The Development of Techniques in Industrial Marketing, Nuneaton *12383*
Society for the Furtherance and Study of Fantasy and Science Fiction, Madison *16454*
Society for The Health Education, London *12384*
Society for The History of Alchemy and Chemistry, London *12385*
Society for the History of Authorship, Reading and Publishing, Madison *16455*
Society for the History of Czechoslovak Jews, Cedar Grove *16456*
Society for the History of Discoveries, Falls Church *16457*
Society for The History of Natural History, London *12386*
Society for the History of Technology, Auburn *16458*
Society for the History of the Germans in Maryland, Baltimore *16459*
Society for the Humanities, Ithaca *16460*
Society for the Investigation of Recurring Events, Iselin *16461*
Society for the Philosophical Study of Marxism, Buffalo *16462*
Society for the Preservation of American Business History, Williamsburg *16463*
Society for the Preservation of Ancient Monuments in Norway, Oslo *08789*
Society for the Preservation of English Language and Literature, Waleska *16464*
Society for the Preservation of New England Antiquities, Boston *16465*
Society for the Promotion and Improvement of Libraries, Karachi *08936*
Society for the Promotion of Greek Education, Athinai *06255*
Society for the Promotion of Hellenic Studies, London *12387*
Society for the Promotion of New Music, London *12388*
Society for The Promotion of Principles, Birmingham *12389*
Society for the Promotion of Roman Studies, London *12390*
Society for the Promotion of Science and Scholarship, Palo Alto *16466*
Society for The Promotion of Vocational Training and Education, Bristol *12391*
Society for the Propagation of Knowledge, Warszawa *09166*
The Society for the Protection of Ancient Buildings, London *12392*
Society for the Protection of Nature in Israel, Tel Aviv *06746*
Society for the Protection of Old Fishes, Seattle *16467*
Society for The Protection of Science and Learning, London *12393*
Society for the Psychological Study of Social Issues, Ann Arbor *16468*
Society for the Scientific Study of Religion, West Lafayette *16469*
Society for the Scientific Study of Sex, Mount Vernon *16470*
Society for The Social History of Medicine, Manchester *12394*
Society for the Study and Conservation of Nature, Valletta *08252*
Society for The Study of Addiction, Horsham *12395*
Society for the Study of Amphibians and Reptiles, Hays *16471*
Society for the Study of Architecture in Canada, Ottawa *02383*
Society for the Study of Blood, Brooklyn *16472*
Society for the Study of Early China, Berkeley *16473*
Society for the Study of Egyptian Antiquities, Toronto *02384*
Society for the Study of Evolution, Lawrence *16474*
Society for the Study of Human Biology, Oxford *12396*
Society for The Study of Inborn Errors of Metabolism, Manchester *12397*
Society for The Study of Information Transfer, Beckenham *12398*
Society for the Study of Japanese Language, Tokyo *07761*
Society for the Study of Knowledge and Development, Cambridge *15423*
Society for The Study of Labour History, London *12399*
Society for the Study of Male Psychology and Physiology, Montpellier *16475*
Society for the Study of Medieval Languages and Literature, Oxford *12400*
Society for The Study of Normal Psychology, London *12401*
Society for the Study of Process Philosophies, Portland *16476*
Society for the Study of Reproduction, Madison *16477*
Society for the Study of Social Biology, Oklahoma City *16478*
Society for the Study of Social Problems, Knoxville *16479*
Society for the Study of Southern Literature, New Orleans *16480*
Society for the Study of Symbolic Interaction, Cookeville *16481*
Society for the Study of the Indigenous Languages of the Americas, Iowa City *16482*
The Society for Theatre Research, London *12402*
Society for Theriogenology, Hastings *16483*
Society for Trade and Commerce, Moskva *09459*
Society for Underwater Technology, London *12403*
Society for Values in Higher Education, Washington *16484*
Society for Vascular Surgery, Manchester *16485*
Society for Vector Ecology, Santa Ana *16486*
Society for Visual Anthropology, Washington *16487*
Society for Women in Philosophy – Pacific Division, San Jose *16488*
Society of Actuaries, Schaumburg *16489*
Society of Aesthetes and Art and Literary Critics, Sofia *01590*
Society of Africanist Archaeologists, FL 32611 *16490*
Society of Agricultural Machinery, Saitama *08007*
Society of Agricultural Meteorology of Japan, Tokyo *07952*

Alphabetical Index: Vereinigung 386

Vereinigung deutscher Wirtschaftsarchivare e.V., Bochum 06121
Vereinigung für Agrar- und Umweltrecht e.V., Bonn 04745
Vereinigung für angewandte Botanik, Göttingen 06122
Vereinigung für Angewandte Lagerstättenforschung, Leoben 00851
Vereinigung für Bankbetriebsorganisation e.V., Frankfurt 06123
Vereinigung für die physiotherapeutischen Berufe e.V., Hamburg 06069
Vereinigung für Hydrogeologische Forschungen in Graz, Graz 00852
Vereinigung für Rechsstaat und Individualrechte, Solothurn 10562
Vereinigung für Schweizerische Kirchengeschichte, Rain 10563
Vereinigung für Stadt-, Regional- und Landesplanung e.V., Berlin 06124
Vereinigung für Walsertum, Brig 10564
Vereinigung für Wirtschaftsforschung Schweiz-Europa/Asien, Genève 10565
Vereinigung für wissenschaftliche Grundlagenforschung, Graz 00853
Vereinigung Getreide-, Markt- und Ernährungsforschung e.V., Bonn 06125
Vereinigung katholischer Schulen in Ordenstradition, Lingen 06126
Vereinigung Österreichischer Ärzte, Wien 00854
Vereinigung Österreichischer Bibliothekarinnen und Bibliothekare, Innsbruck 00855
Vereinigung Schweizerischer Archivare, Bern 10566
Vereinigung Schweizerischer Hochschuldozenten, Bremgarten 10567
Vereinigung Schweizerischer Kinder- und Jugendpsychologen, Solothurn 10568
Vereinigung Schweizerischer Naturwissenschaftslehrer, Neerach 10569
Vereinigung Schweizerischer Petroleumgeologen und -Ingenieure, Gelterkinden 10570
Vereinigung Süddeutscher Orthopäden e.V., Baden-Baden 06127
Vereinigung Südwestdeutscher Dermatologen, Freiburg 06128
Vereinigung Südwestdeutscher HNO-Ärzte, Köln 06129
Vereinigung Südwestdeutscher Radiologen und Nuklearmediziner (VSRN), Sindelfingen 06130
Vereinigung Umwelt und Bevölkerung, Zollikofen 10571
Vereinigung Westdeutscher Hals-, Nasen- und Ohrenärzte, Köln 06131
Vereinigung zur Erforschung der Neueren Geschichte e.V., Bonn 06132
Vereinigung zur Förderung der technischen Optik e.V., Wetzlar 06133
Vereinigung zur Förderung des Deutschen Brandschutzes e.V., Altenberge 06134
Vereinigung zur Förderung des Instituts für Kunststoffverarbeitung in Industrie und Handwerk an der Rhein.-Westf. Technischen Hochschule Aachen e.V., Aachen 06135
Vereinigung zur Förderung des Straßen- und Verkehrswesen, Bonn 04964
Vereinigung zur Reform der Versorgung psychisch Kranker e.V., Bonn 04407
Vereniging der Antwerpsche Bibliophielen, Antwerpen 01313
Vereniging Glere, Arnhem 08636
Vereniging Het Nederlandsch Economisch-Historisch Archief, Amsterdam 08637
Vereniging Leraars Aardrijkskunde, Heverlee 01314
Vereniging Natuurmonumenten, 's-Graveland 08638
Vereniging NBLC, Den Haag 08639
Vereniging Sint Lucas, Amsterdam 08640
Vereniging tot Beoefening van Gelderse Geschiedenis, Oudheidkunde en Recht, Arnhem 08460
Vereniging tot Bevordering der Homoeopathie in Nederland, Den Haag 08641
Vereniging van Archivarissen in Nederland, Leeuwarden 08642
Vereniging van Docenten in Geschiedenis en Staatsrichting in Nederland, Dordrecht 08643
Vereniging van Homoeopathische Artsen in Nederland, Utrecht 08644
Vereniging van Katholieke Leraren Sint-Bonaventura, Hengelo 08645
Vereniging van Nederlandse Kunsthistorici, Groningen 08646
Vereniging van Religieus-Wetenschappelijke Bibliothecarissen, Sint Truiden 01315
Vereniging van Samenwerkende Nederlandse Universiteiten, Utrecht 08647
Vereniging voor Agrarisch Recht, Wageningen 08648
Vereniging voor Arbeidsrecht, Woerden 08649
Vereniging voor Bouwrecht, Den Haag 08650
Vereniging voor Calvinistische Wijsbegeerte, Amersfoort 08651
Vereniging voor de Staathuishoudkunde, Amsterdam 08652
Vereniging voor Filosofie-Onderwijs, Nijmegen 08653
Vereniging voor het Invoeren van Nieuwe Biologische Nomenklatuur, Kalmthout 00940
Vereniging voor het Theologisch Bibliothecariaat, Nijmegen 08654
Vereniging voor Hoger Beroepsonderwijs, Amsterdam 08655
Vereniging voor Nederlandse Muziekgeschiedenis, Utrecht 08656
Vereniging voor Penningkunst, Alkmaar 08657
Vereniging voor Statistiek, Barendrecht 08658
Vereniging voor Studie en Onderzoek over Fytopathologie en Toegepaste Zoologie, Sint-Truiden 00981
Vereniging voor Wijsbegeerte des Rechts, Amsterdam 08659
Vereniging voor Wijsbegeerte te s'-Gravenhage, Den Haag 08660
Vereniging voor Zuivelindustrie en Melkhygiëne, Den Haag 08661
Vergilian Society, Oxford 16724
Verkfraedingafélag Islands, Reykjavik 06386
Vernacular Architecture Forum, Newark 16725
Vernacular Architecture Group, Tamworth 12548
Versicherungswissenschaftlicher Verein in Hamburg e.V., Hamburg 06136
Versuchsgrubengesellschaft, Dortmund 06137
Verulam Institute, Chichester 12549
Vesterheim Genealogical Center and NAESETH Library, Madison 16726
Veterinärmedizinischer Fakultätentag, Hannover 06138
Veterinary Cancer Society, Rochester 16727
Veterinary Council, Dublin 06673
Veterinary History Society, London 12550
Veterinary Orthopaedic Society, Salt Lake City 16728
Veterinary Services Council, Wellington 08744
VFA, Bonn 06063
VFDB, Altenberge 06134
VFG, Wien 00830
VFHS, Valley Forge 16723
VFMG, Heidelberg 06112
VfW, Brig 10564
VFWL, Zürich 10556
VfZ, Darmstadt 06099
VGB, Essen 05984
VGB-Forschungsstiftung, Essen 06139
VGCT, München 06089
VGDH, Duisburg 06023
VGDH, München 06022
VGN, Dordrecht 08643
VGS, Zürich 10572
VGStW, Wien 00833
VHpA, Luzern 10525
VHW, Bonn 06067
VICA, Leesburg 16733
Victoria Foundation, Victoria 02411
The Victoria Institute or Philosophical Society of Great Britain, Welling 12551
Victoria Librarians Association, Victoria 02412
Victoria Natural History Society, Victoria 02413
Victorian Artists' Society, East Melbourne 00380
Victorian Military Society, Northampton 12552
Victorian Public Interest Research Group, Fitzroy 00381
Victorian Society, London 12553
Victorian Society in America, Philadelphia 16729
Vieilles Maisons Françaises, Paris 04326
Vienna Institute for Development and Cooperation, Wien 00867
Vietnam Union of Sientific and Technical Associations, Hanoi 16941
Vietnamese Association of Acupuncture, Hanoi 16942
Vietnamese Association of Agriculture, Hanoi 16943
Vietnamese Association of Anaesthesiology, Hanoi 16944
Vietnamese Association of Anti-Contagious Diseases, Hanoi 16945
Vietnamese Association of Anti-Tuberculosis and Lung Diseases, Hanoi 16946
Vietnamese Association of Architects, Hanoi 16947
Vietnamese Association of Biology, Hanoi 16948
Vietnamese Association of Cast and Metallurgy, Hanoi 16949
Vietnamese Association of Chemistry, Hanoi 16950
Vietnamese Association of Dermatology, Hanoi 16951
Vietnamese Association of Engineering, Hanoi 16952
Vietnamese Association of Forensic Scientists, Hanoi 16953
Vietnamese Association of Forestry, Hanoi 16954
Vietnamese Association of Geography, Hanoi 16955
Vietnamese Association of Geology, Hanoi 16956
Vietnamese Association of Internal Medicine, Hanoi 16957
Vietnamese Association of Mathematics, Hanoi 16958
Vietnamese Association of Medical Biochemistry, Hanoi 16959
Vietnamese Association of Morphology, Hanoi 16960
Vietnamese Association of Neurology, Psychiatry and Neurosurgery, Hanoi 16961
Vietnamese Association of Obstetrics, Gynaecology and Family Planning, Hanoi 16962
Vietnamese Association of Odonto-Maxillo-Facial Medicine, Hanoi 16963
Vietnamese Association of Ophthalmology, Hanoi 16964
Vietnamese Association of Oto-Rhino-Laryngology, Hanoi 16965
Vietnamese Association of Paediatrics, Hanoi 16966
Vietnamese Association of Pharmacy, Hanoi 16967
Vietnamese Association of Physics, Hanoi 16968
Vietnamese Association of Physiology, Hanoi 16969
Vietnamese Association of Prophylactic Hygiene, Hanoi 16970
Vietnamese Association of Radio-Electronics, Hanoi 16971
Vietnamese Association of Radiology, Hanoi 16972
Vietnamese Association of Serum and Blood Transfusion, Hanoi 16973
Vietnamese Association of Surgery, Hanoi 16974
Vietnamese Fine Arts Association, Hanoi 16975
Vietnamese Photographers Association, Hanoi 16976
Vietnamese Writers' Association, Hanoi 16977
Viking Society for Northern Research, London 12554
VIM, Columbia 16734
Vintage Light Music Society, West Wickham 12555
Viola da Gamba Society, London 12556
Virgil Society, London 12557
Virginia Woolf Society, Sterling 16730
Visible Record and Minicomputer Society, Croydon 12558
Vísindafélag Islendinga, Reykjavik 06387
Visual Arts Manitoba, Winnipeg 02414
Visual Arts Nova Scotia, Halifax 02415
Visual Arts Ontario, Toronto 02416
Visual Arts Resource and Research Centre Relating to the Caribbean, New York 16731
Vitamin Society of Japan, Kyoto 07873
Vivaldi Society, London 12559
VkdL, Essen 06100
V.K.L., Hengelo 08645
VKV, Poperinge 01316
VLA, Springfield 16722
Vlaams Kinesitherapeuten Verbond, Poperinge 01316
Vlaamse Chemische Vereniging, Gent 01317
Vlaamse Interuniversitaire Raad, Bruxelles 01318
Vlaamse Museumvereniging, Dendermonde 01319
Vlaamse Vereniging voor Familiekunde, Merksen 01320
Vladimir Nabokov Society, Lawrence 16732
VLMB, Thun 10527
VLMS, West Wickham 12555
VLMV, Bregenz 00858
VLP, Bern 10410
VMF, Paris 04326
VMÖ, Wien 00809
VMPA, Berlin 06029
VMS, Northampton 12552
VMSÖ, Wien 00814
VNK, Groningen 08646
VNM, Utrecht 08656
VNS, Lawrence 16732
Vocational Industrial Clubs of America, Leesburg 16733
Vocational Instructional Materials Section, Columbia 16734
VÖA, Wien 00816
VÖÄ, Wien 00854
VÖBB, Innsbruck 00855
VÖCH, Wien 00485
V.Ö.L.B., Wien 00840
VÖLT, Wien 00841
VÖN, Wien 00811
VÖTC, Dornbirn 00842
VÖWA, Wien 00825
Volcanological Society of Japan, Tokyo 07924
Volkenrechtelijk Instituut, Utrecht 08662
Volks- und Betriebswirtschaftliche Vereinigung im Rheinisch-Westfälischen Industriegebiet e.V., Duisburg 06140
Volksgesundheit Schweiz, Zürich 10572
Volkshochschulverband Baden-Württemberg e.V., Leinfelden-Echterdingen 06141
Volkshochschulverband Mecklenburg-Vorpommern e.V., Schwerin 06142
Volkskundliche Kommission für Westfalen, Münster 06143
Volkswirtschaftliche Gesellschaft Österreich, Wien 00856
Volkswirtschaftliche Gesellschaft Wien, Wien 00857
Volunteer Committees of Art Museums of Canada and the United States, Tulsa 16735
Von Braun Astronomical Society, Huntsville 16736
Von Karman Institute for Fluid Dynamics, Rhode-Saint-Genese 01321
Von Recklinghausen-Gesellschaft e.V., Hamburg 06144
Vorarlberger Landesmuseumsverein, Bregenz 00858
VOS, Salt Lake City 16728
VRA, Groningen 08570
V.R.B., Sint Truiden 01315
VRG, Potsdam 06094
VRÖ, Wien 00812
VRS, Cape Town 09718
VS, Oxford 16724
VS, Stuttgart 06050
VSA, Bern 10566
VSA, Philadelphia 16729
VSA, Zürich 10536
VSAO, Bern 10537
VSB, Bern 10050
VSB, Brig 10421
VSG, Bern 10547
VSGg, Wohlen 10551
VSH, Wabern 10538
VSJDB, Fribourg 10549
VSMT, Bellach 10561
VSN, Neerach 10569
VSP, Bern 10540
VSRN, Sindelfingen 06130
VSVM, Zürich 10245
VSVT, Burgdorf 10541
VTB, Nijmegen 08654
VTCC, Heidelberg 06073
VTS, Chez-le-Bart 10542
VVB, Köln 06116
V.v.C.W., Amersfoort 08651
V.V.S., Barendrecht 08658
VVZM, Den Haag 08661
VWA, Frankfurt/Main 04660
VWGÖ, Wien 00813
VWS, Sterling 16730

WAA, Jackson 16787
WAAVP, Rahway 16797
WACRA Americas, Needham 16790
WADEM, Pittsburgh 16792
WAEC, Accra 06207
WAEL, Washington 16798
Wagner Society, Amsterdam 08663
Wagner Society, Wickford 12560
Wagner Society of New York, New York 16737
Wagnervereeniging, Amsterdam 08663
WAICA, Arlington 16776
Waikato Geological and Lapidary Society, Hamilton 08745
WAIMH, East Lansing 16793
Waka Bungakkai, Tokyo 08048
WAL, Washington 16800
Waldviertler Heimatbund, Wissenschaftliche Sektion, Horn 00859
Waldwirtschaft Verband Schweiz, Solothurn 10573
Wallaceburg and District Historical Society, Wallaceburg 02417
WALP, Washington 16799
The Walpole Society, London 12561
Walter Bagehot Research Council on National Sovereignty, Whitestone 16738
WAML, Los Angeles 16751
W.A.N.H.S., Devizes 12577
WAPOR, Chapel Hill 16794
WAPS, Blacksbury 16785
Warsaw Scientific Society, Warszawa 09161
WAS, Baton Rouge 16788
WAS, Hollister 16789
WAS, Minneapolis 16795
W.A.S.C., Perth 00388
Washington Foundation for European Studies, Washington 16739
Washington Institute of Foreign Affairs, Washington 16740
Washington Journalism Center, Washington 16741
WASP, Santa Barbara 16796
WASP, Tokyo 08049
Water Authorities Association of Victoria, Melbourne 00382
Water Environment Federation, Alexandria 16742
Water Management Society, Moskva 09480
Water Quality Association, Lisle 16743
Water Research Centre, Marlow 12562
Water Research Commission, Pretoria 09719
Water Research Foundation of Australia, Canberra 00383
Water Resources Congress, Vienna 16744
Water Systems Research Group, Johannesburg 09720
Waterloo Centre for Groundwater Research, Waterloo 02418
Waterloo Historical Society, Kitchener 02419
Waterloo Regional Arts Council, Kitchener 02420
WAUC, Las Vegas 16801
WAVA, West Lafayette 16802
WAVE, Tuskegee 16803
WAVLD, College Station 16804
WBA, San Francisco 16805
WBG, Wien 00861, 00862
WBL, Bonn 06165
WBRC, Whitestone 16738
WCA, Huntington Beach 16806
WCA, Oakland 16752
WCA, Philadelphia 16777
WCC, Rye 16781
WCC, Washington 16782
WCCES, Pittsburgh 16809
WCCI, Cincinnati 16808
WCES, Baltimore 16780
WCH, Berkeley 16807
WCML, Albuquerque 16779
WCPS, Miami 16778
WCSZ, Lusaka 17054
WDA, Washington 16771
WE, Boston 16810
WE, Toledo 16774
W.E. Upjohn Institute for Employment Research, Kalamazoo 16745
WEA, Fort Collins 16762
WEA, London 12583
Weather Modification Association, Fresno 16746
Webb Society, London 12563
Wedgwood Society, Fordingbridge 12564
WEE, Heidelberg 06145
Weed Science Society of America, Champaign 16747
Weed Science Society of New South Wales, Haymarket 00384
Weed Science Society of South Australia, Glenside 00385
WEF, Alexandria 16742
WEF, Chigwell 12586
WEF, New Rochelle 16811
Welding Research Council, New York 16748
Welland Historical Society, Welland 02421
Wellesbourne Vegetable Research Association, Warwick 12565
Wellington Medical Research Foundation, Wellington 08746
Welsh Academy, Cardiff 10742
Welsh Arts Council, Cardiff 12566
Welsh Baptist Historical Society, LLnlli 12567
Welsh Federation of Head Teachers' Associations, Swansea 12568
Welsh Folk Dance Society, Llanfair Caereinion 12569
Welsh Folk Song Society, Aberystwyth 12570
Welsh Library Association, Aberystwyth 12571
Weltbund für Erneuerung der Erziehung, Deutschsprachige Sektion, Heidelberg 06145
Welwyn Hall Research Association, Hatfield 12572
Wenner-Gren Centre Foundation for Scientific Research, New York 16749
Wenner-Gren Foundation for Anthropological Research, New York 16750
Werkgemeinschaft Musik e.V., Düsseldorf 06146
WES, Taipei 02760
Wesley Historical Society, Birmingham 12573
West African Association of Agricultural Economists, Ibadan 08787
West African Examinations Council, Accra 06207
West African Science Association, Accra 06208
West Coast Environmental Law Research Foundation, Vancouver 02422
West- und Süddeutscher Verband für Altertumsforschung, Mainz 06147
Westdeutsche Gesellschaft für Familienkunde e.V., Köln 06148
Westdeutscher Medizinischer Fakultätentag, Erlangen 06149
Western Association of Map Libraries, Los Angeles 16751
Western Australian Mental Health Association, Subiaco 00386
The Western Australian Naturalists' Club, Nedlands 00387
Western Australian Shell Club, Perth 00388
Western Board of Music, Edmonton 02423
Western Canada Water and Wastewater Association, Calgary 02424
Western College Association, Oakland 16752
Western Communities Arts Council, Victoria 02425

387 Alphabetical Index: Zambia

Western History Association, Albuquerque 16753
Western Literature Association, Logan 16754
Western Society of Malacologists, Novato 16755
Western Society of Naturalists, Moss Landing 16756
Western Surgical Association, Louisville 16757
Western Veterinary Conference, Las Vegas 16758
Westfälische Gesellschaft für Zahn-, Mund- und Kieferheilkunde, Münster 06150
WFES, Washington 16739
WFFH, Port Washington 16820
WFNS, Charlottesville 16813
WFNS, Nijmegen 08665
WFPHA, Washington 16815, 16816
WFPMA, Alexandria 16814
WFS, Bethesda 16821
WFSA, Cardiff 12588
WFSF, Roma 07681
WFSRS, Philadelphia 16817
WFSS, Aberystwyth 12570
WFTC, New York 16819
W.G., Delft 08664
WGFAR, New York 16750
WGfF, Köln 06148
WGGB, London 12594
WHA, Albuquerque 16753
WHAC, Pasadena 16822
Whaling Museum Society, Cold Spring Harbor 16759
WHHA, Washington 16760
White House Historical Association, Washington 16760
WHL, Toledo 16823
WHO, Genève 10578
W.H.R.A., Hatfield 12572
WHS, Birmingham 12573
WHSHS, Williams-9709 16761
WIA, Washington 16775
Wiener Arbeitskreis für Psychoanalyse, Wien 00860
Wiener Beethoven-Gesellschaft, Wien 00861
Wiener Bibliophilen-Gesellschaft, Wien 00862
Wiener Gesellschaft für Innere Medizin, Wien 00863
Wiener Gesellschaft für Theaterforschung, Wien 00864
Wiener Goethe-Verein, Wien 00865
Wiener Humanistische Gesellschaft, Wien 00866
Wiener Institut für Entwicklungsfragen und Zusammenarbeit, Wien 00867
Wiener Institut für Internationale Wirtschaftsvergleiche, Wien 00868
Wiener Juristische Gesellschaft, Wien 00869
Wiener Katholische Akademie, Wien 00870
Wiener Konzerthausgesellschaft, Wien 00871
Wiener Kulturkreis, Wien 00872
Wiener Medizinische Akademie für Ärztliche Fortbildung und Forschung, Wien 00873
Wiener Psychoanalytische Vereinigung, Wien 00874
Wiener Rechtsgeschichtliche Gesellschaft, Wien 00875
Wiener Schubertbund, Wien 00876
Wiener Secession, Wien 00847, 00877
Wiener Sprachgesellschaft, Wien 00878
WIFIS, Hamburg 06162
WIIAD, Morrilton 16772
Wilbur Hot Springs Health Sanctuary, Williams-9709 16761
Wilderness Education Association, Fort Collins 16762
Wilderness Medical Society, Indiamapolis 16763
The Wilderness Society, Washington 16764
Wildlife Conservation Society, Lavington 00389
Wildlife Conservation Society of Zambia, Lusaka 17054
Wildlife Management Institute, Washington 16765
Wildlife Preservation Society of Australia, Sydney 00390
Wildlife Preservation Trust International, Philadelphia 16766
The Wildlife Society, Bethesda 16767
Wildlife Society of Southern Africa, Linden 09721
Wildlife Society of Zimbabwe, Harare 17082
Wildlife Sound Recording Society, Farnham 12574
Wilhelm-Busch-Gesellschaft e.V., Hannover 06151
Wilhelm Furtwängler Society, London 12575
Willem Mengelberg Society, Manitowoc 16768
William Morris Society, London 12576
William Morris Society in the United States, Washington 16769
William-Stern-Gesellschaft für Begabungsförderung Begabtenförderung e.V., Hamburg 06152
Willibald Pirckheimer Gesellschaft zur Erforschung von Renaissance und Humanismus e.V., Mainz 06153
Wilson Ornithological Society, Ann Arbor 16770
Wilson's Disease Association, Washington 16771
Wiltshire Archaeological and Natural History Society, Devizes 12577
Wiltshire Record Society, Trowbridge 12578
Winnipeg Film Group, Winnipeg 02426
Winnipeg Jewish School Teachers Association, Winnipeg 02427
Winrock International Institute for Agricultural Development, Morrilton 16772
WIPO, Genève 10579
Wireless Preservation Society, Shanklin 12579
Wirtschafts- und Sozialwissenschaftlicher Fakultätentag, Mannheim 06154
Wirtschaftsakademie für Lehrer e.V., Bad Harzburg 06155
Wirtschaftspolitische Gesellschaft von 1947 e.V., Frankfurt/Main 06156
Wirtschaftsverband für Geodäsie und Kartographie e.V., Oberkochen 05316
WISER, Warrensburg 16825
Wiskundig Genootschap, Delft 08664
WISOFT, Mannheim 06154
Wissenschaftliche Ärztegesellschaft Innsbruck, Innsbruck 00879
Wissenschaftliche Arbeitsgemeinschaft für Leibeserziehung und Sportmedizin in Innsbruck, Innsbruck 00880
Wissenschaftliche Gesellschaft an der Johann Wolfgang Goethe-Universität Frankfurt am Main, Frankfurt 06157
Wissenschaftliche Gesellschaft der Ärzte in der Steiermark, Graz 00881
Wissenschaftliche Gesellschaft für Europarecht, Trier 06158
Wissenschaftliche Gesellschaft für Sport und Leibeserziehung am Institut für Sportwissenschaften der Universität Salzburg, Salzburg 00882
Wissenschaftliche Gesellschaft für Theologie e.V., Tübingen 06159
Wissenschaftliche Vereinigung deutscher, österreichischer und schweizerischer Kriminologen, Tübingen 05777
Wissenschaftliche Vereinigung für Augenoptik und Optometrie e.V., Mainz 06160
Wissenschaftliche Vereinigung zur Pflege des Wirtschafts- und Konsumentenschutzrechts, Zürich 10574
Wissenschaftliche Vereinigung zur Pflege von Rhtorik, Informationsverarbeitung und Kommunikation, Zürich 10575
Wissenschaftlicher Verein – Arbeitsgemeinschaft für Reibungs- und Verschleissfragen, Wien 00739
Wissenschaftlicher Verein für Verkehrswesen e.V., Dortmund 06161
Wissenschaftliches Forum für internationale Sicherheit e.V., Hamburg 06162
Wissenschaftsförderung der Sparkassenorganisation e.V., Bonn 06163
Wissenschaftsforum Berlin, Berlin 06164
Wissenschaftsgemeinschaft Blaue Liste e.V., Bonn 06165
Wissenschaftskolleg zu Berlin e.V., Berlin 06166
Wissenschaftsrat, Köln 06167
Wissenschaftszentrum, Bonn 05372
Wissenschaftszentrum – Gemeinsame Dienste e.V., Bonn 06168
Wissenschaftszentrum Nordrhein-Westfalen, Düsseldorf 06169
Wittheit zu Bremen e.V., Bremen 06170
WJA, Washington 16826
WJC, Washington 16741
WJG, Wien 00869
WLA, Logan 16754
Wloclawek Scientific Society, Wloclawek 09168
Wloclawskie Towarzystwo Naukowe, Wloclawek 09168
W.L.P.S. of A., Sydney 00390
WLRI, Grand Terrace 16828
WMA, Ferney-Voltaire 04328
WMA, Fresno 16746
WMA, London 12584
WME, South Hadley 16773
WMF, New York 16830
WMFT, Erlangen 06149
WMHS, Madison 16829
WMI, Washington 16765
WMS, Cold Spring Harbor 16759
WMS, Indiamapolis 16763
WMS, Manitowoc 16768
WMS/US, Washington 16769
WOHP, Philadelphia 16831
Wolfram von Eschenbach-Gesellschaft e.V., Eichstätt 06171
Wolverton and District Archaeological Society, Milton Keynes 12580
Women and Mathematics Education, South Hadley 16773
Women Educators, Toledo 16774
Women in Aerospace, Washington 16775
Women's Auxiliary of the ICA, Arlington 16776
Women's Caucus for Art, Philadelphia 16777
Women's Caucus for Political Science, Miami 16778
Women's Caucus for the Modern Languages, Albuquerque 16779
Women's Caucus of the Endocrine Society, Baltimore 16780
Women's Classical Caucus, Rye 16781
Women's College Coalition, Washington 16782
Woodworkers' Accident Prevention Association, Cambridge 02428
Woolhope Naturalists' Field Club, Hereford 12581
Worcestershire Archaeological Society, Malvern 12582
Wordsworth-Coleridge Association, Ann Arbor 16783
Work Efficiency Institute, Helsinki 03459
Workers' Educational Association, London 12583
Workers' Educational Association of Canada, Toronto 02429
Workers' Music Association, London 12584
Working Committee of the Scientific Institutes for Crafts in the EEC Countries, München 04437
World Academy of Art and Science, Minneapolis 16784
World Academy of Productivity Science, Blacksbury 16785
World Aerospace Education Organization, Cairo 03306
World Alliance of Organizations for the Prevention of Birth Defects, White Plains 16786
World Apheresis Association, Jackson 16787
World Aquaculture Society, Baton Rouge 16788
World Archaeological Society, Hollister 16789
World Association for Animal Production, Roma 07680
World Association for Case Method Research and Application – Americas, Needham 16790
World Association for Cooperative Education, Boston 16791
World Association for Disaster and Emergency Medicine, Pittsburgh 16792
World Association for Educational Research, Gent 00977
World Association for Infant Mental Health, East Lansing 16793
World Association for Public Opinion Research, Chapel Hill 16794
World Association for Sexology, Minneapolis 16795
World Association for Social Psychiatry, Santa Barbara 16796
World Association for the Advancement of Veterinary Parasitology, Rahway 16797
World Association for the School as an Instrument of Peace, Genève 10576
World Association of Energy Lawyers, Washington 16798
World Association of Law Professors, Washington 16799
World Association of Lawyers, Washington 16800
World Association of Societies of Pathology (Anatomic and Clinical), Tokyo 08049
World Association of Universities and Colleges, Las Vegas 16801
World Association of Veterinary Anatomists, West Lafayette 16802
World Association of Veterinary Educators, Tuskegee 16803
World Association of Veterinary Laboratory Diagnosticians, College Station 16804
World Bureau of Metal Statistics, London 12585
World Business Academy, San Francisco 16805
World Communication Association, Huntington Beach 16806
World Confederation of Organizations of the Teaching Profession, Morges 10577
World Congress of Herpetology, Berkeley 16807
World Conservation Union, Gland 10180
World Council for Curriculum and Instruction, Cincinnati 16808
World Council of Comparative Education Societies, Pittsburgh 16809
World Education, Boston 16810
World Education Fellowship, Chigwell 12586
World Education Fellowship, United States Section, New Rochelle 16811
World Federation for Medical Education, Edinburgh 12587
World Federation of Associations of Pediatric Surgeons, Kansas City 16812
World Federation of Neurosurgical Societies, Charlottesville 16813
World Federation of Neurosurgical Societies, Nijmegen 08665
World Federation of Personnel Management Associations, Alexandria 16814
World Federation of Public Health Associations, Washington 16815, 16816
World Federation of Scientific Workers, Montreuil 04327
World Federation of Sleep Research Societies, Philadelphia 16817
World Federation of Societies of Anaesthesiologists, Cardiff 12588
World Federation of Societies of Intensive and Critical Care Medicine, New York 16818
World Federation of Therapeutic Communities, New York 16819
World Foundation for Medical Studies in Female Health, Port Washington 16820
World Future Society, Bethesda 16821
World Future Studies Federation, Roma 07681
World Health Organization, Genève 10578
World Hemophilia Aids Center, Pasadena 16822
World Hypertension League, Toledo 16823
World Institute for Advanced Phenomenological Research and Learning, Belmont 16824
World Institute for Safety Education and Research, Warrensburg 16825
World Intellectual Property Organization, Genève 10579
World Jurist Association, Washington 16826
World Learning, Washington 16827
World Life Research Institute, Grand Terrace 16828
World Medical Association, Ferney-Voltaire 04328
World Medical Tennis Association, Poole 12589
World Meteorological Organization, Genève 10221
World Methodist Historical Society, Madison 16829
World Monuments Fund, New York 16830
World Organization for Human Potential, Philadelphia 16831
World Organization for Rights, Literature and Development, New York 16832
World Population Society, Washington 16833
World Proof Numismatic Association, Pittsburgh 16834
World Psychiatric Association, Prilly 10580
World Rabbit Science Association, Cheltenham 12590
World Rehabilitation Fund, New York 16835
World Research Foundation, Wooland Hills 16836
World Society for Ekistics, Athinai 06256
World Society for Mushroom Biology and Mushroom Products, New York 16837
World Society for Stereotactic and Functional Neurosurgery, Houston 16838
World Society of Magnetic Resonance, Berkeley 16839
World Space Foundation, South Pasadena 16840
World Union of Catholic Philosophical Societies, Washington 16841
World Union of Catholic Teachers, Roma 07666
World Union of Pythagorean Organizations, Lutton 12591
World University Network, Saint Paul 16842
World University Roundtable, Benson 16843
World Veterinary Poultry Association, Giessen 06172
World War Two Studies Association, Manhattan 16844
World-wide Education Service of The Bell Educational Trust, London 12592
World Wide Ethical Society, Taipei 02760
World's Poultry Science Association – U.S.A. Branch, Beltsville 16845
Worshipful Society of Apothecaries of London, London 12593
WOS, Ann Arbor 16770
WOTRO, Den Haag 08630
Wound, Ostomy and Continence Nurses – An Association of E.T. Nurses, Costa Mesa 16846
WPI, Belmont 16824
WPNA, Pittsburgh 16834
WPS, Shanklin 12579
WPS, Washington 16833
WPSA, Beltsville 16845
WPTI, Philadelphia 16766
WRC, Marlow 12562
WRC, New York 16748
WRC, Vienna 16744
WRF, New York 16835
Writers and Artists Union, Hanoi 16978
Writers Association for Romance and Mainstream, Longueuil 02430
Writers' Guild of Great Britain, London 12594
Writers' Union of the SRR, Bucuresti 09328
Wroclaw Scientific Society, Wroclaw 09169
Wroclawskie Towarzystwo Naukowe, Wroclaw 09169
W.R.S., Trowbridge 12578
W.R.S.A., Cheltenham 12590
WSA, Louisville 16757
W.S.E., Athinai 06256
WSG, Hamburg 06152
WSG, Wien 00878
WSM, Novato 16755
WSMBMP, New York 16837
WSN, Moss Landing 16756
WSNY, New York 16737
WSRS, Farnham 12574
WSSA, Champaign 16747
WSSFN, Houston 16838
W.T. Bandy Center for Baudelaire Studies, Nashville 16847
WTN, Wloclawek 09168
Württembergische Bibliotheksgesellschaft, Vereinigung der Freunde der Landesbibliothek, Stuttgart 06173
WUPO, Lutton 12591
Wuppertaler Kreis e.V., Köln 06174
WVAO, Mainz 06160
WVC, Las Vegas 16758
W.V.P.A., Giessen 06172
WVV, Dortmund 06161
WWTSA, Manhattan 16844

XPLOR International, Palos Verdes Estates 16848

YA, Yosemite National Park 16851
Yad Izhak Ben-Zvi, Jerusalem 06753
Y.A.S., Leeds 12596
YBRA, Billings 16849
Y.D.S., Leeds 12598
Yellowstone-Bighorn Research Association, Billings 16849
Yeni Felsefe Cemiyeti, Istanbul 10725
Yeni Musiqi, Baku 00896
Yerevan Academy of National Economy, Yerevan 00114
Yeshivat Dvar Yerushalayim, Jerusalem 06754
Y.G.S., Cottingham 12599
YIVO Institute for Jewish Research, New York 16850
York Technology Association, Aurora 02431
Yorkshire Agricultural Society, Harrogate 12595
Yorkshire Archaeological Society, Leeds 12596
Yorkshire Arts Association, Bradford 12597
Yorkshire Dialect Society, Leeds 12598
Yorkshire Geological Society, Cottingham 12599
Yorkshire Philosophical Society, York 12600
Yorkton Natural History Society, Yorkton 02432
Yosemite Association, Yosemite National Park 16851
Yosetsu Gakkai, Tokyo 08050
Youth Science Foundation, Ottawa 02433
Y.P.S., York 12600
Yugoslav Centre for Technical and Scientific Documentation, Beograd 17000
Yugoslav Economists' Association, Beograd 17022, 17043
Yugoslav Welding Association, Beograd 17001
Yuki Teikei Haiku Society of the United States and Canada, San Jose 16852
Yukon Historical and Museums Association, Whitehorse 02434
Yukon Medical Association, Whitehorse 02435
Yukon Teacher-Librarians' Association, Whitehorse 02436
Yukon Teachers' Association, Whitehorse 02437

ZADI, Bonn 06184
Zahnärztekammer Berlin, Berlin 06175
Zahnärztekammer Bremen, Bremen 06176
Zahnärztekammer Hamburg, Hamburg 06177
Zahnärztekammer Niedersachsen, Hannover 06178
Zahnärztekammer Nordrhein, Düsseldorf 06179
Zahnärztekammer Schleswig-Holstein, Kiel 06180
Zahnärztekammer Westfalen-Lippe, Münster 06181
Zajednica Universitéta Jugoslavije, Beograd 17044
Zambia Library Association, Lusaka 17055
Zambia Medical Association, Lusaka 17056

Subject Index

Register nach Fachgebieten

German-English Concordance to Areas of Specialization
Deutsch-Englische Konkordanz der Fachgebiete

Akustik s. Acoustics
Anästhesiologie s. Anesthetics
Anatomie s. Anatomy
Anthropologie s. Anthropology
Antiquitäten s. Antiquities
Archäologie s. Archeology
Architektur s. Architecture
Archivwesen s. Archives
Astronomie s. Astronomy
Astrophysik s. Astrophysics
Augenheilkunde s. Ophthalmology
Bautechnik s. Civil Engineering
Behindertenpädagogik s. Education of the
  Handicapped
Bergbau s. Mining
Bibliotheks- und Buchwesen s. Librarianship
  and Book Science
Biochemie s. Biochemistry
Biologie s. Biology
Biophysik s. Biophysics
Botanik s. Botany
Botanik, Systematische s. Botany, Specific
Chemie s. Chemistry
Chirurgie s. Surgery
Darstellende Künste, Theater s. Performing
  Arts, Theater
Denkmalschutz, Restaurierung s. Preservation
  of Historical Monuments, Restoration
Dermatologie s. Dermatology
Diabetes s. Diabetes
Dokumentation s. Documentation
Elektrochemie s. Electrochemistry
Elektronik s. Electronic Engineering
Elektrotechnik s. Electrical Engineering
Endokrinologie s. Endocrinology
Energiewesen s. Energy
Entwicklungshilfe s. Developing Areas
Ernährung s. Nutrition
Erwachsenenbildung s. Adult Education
Erziehung und Ausbildung s. Education
Familienplanung s. Family Planning
Filmkunst s. Cinematography
Finanzen s. Finance
Fischerei s. Fisheries
Forstwirtschaft s. Forestry
Friedensforschung s. Promotion of Peace
Futurologie s. Futurology
Gartenbau s. Horticulture
Gastroenterologie s. Gastroenterology
Geisteswissenschaften, allgemeine s.
  Humanities, general
Genealogie, Heraldik s. Genealogy, Heraldry

Genetik s. Genetics
Geographie s. Geography
Geologie s. Geology
Geomorphologie s. Geomorphology
Geophysik s. Geophysics
Geriatrie s. Geriatrics
Gerichtsmedizin s. Forensic Medicine
Geschichte s. History
Gesundheitswesen s. Public Health
Graphische und Dekorative Künste, Design s.
  Graphic and Decorative Arts, Design
Graphologie s. Graphology
Gynäkologie s. Gynecology
Hämatologie s. Hematology
Hals-Nasen-Ohrenheilkunde s. Otorhinolaryngo-
  logy
Handel s. Commerce
Hauswirtschaft s. Home Economics
Höhlenkunde s. Speleology
Homöopathie s. Homeopathy
Hydrologie s. Hydrology
Hygiene s. Hygiene
Immunologie s. Immunology
Informatik, Datenverarbeitung s. Computer and
  Information Science, Data Processing
Ingenieurwesen s. Engineering
Innere Medizin s. Internal Medicine
Insektenkunde s. Entomology
Internationale Beziehungen s. International
  Relations
Kaffee, Tee, Kakao s. Coffee, Tea, Cocoa
Kardiologie s. Cardiology
Kartographie s. Cartography
Kernforschung s. Nuclear Research
Klimatechnik s. Air Conditioning
Kommunikationswissenschaft s. Communication
  Science
Kraftfahrzeugbau s. Automotive Engineering
Kriminologie s. Criminology
Kulturgeschichte s. Cultural History, History of
  Civilization
Kunst s. Arts
Kybernetik s. Cybernetics
Landvermessung, Photogrammetrie s.
  Surveying, Photogrammetry
Landwirtschaft s. Agriculture
Linguistik s. Linguistics
Literatur s. Literature
Logik s. Logic
Logopädie s. Logopedy
Luftfahrt, Raumfahrttechnik s. Aeronautics,
  Aviation, Space Technology

Malerei, Bildhauerei s. Fine Arts
Marktforschung s. Marketing
Maschinenbau s. Machine Engineering
Massenmedien s. Mass Media
Mathematik s. Mathematics
Medizin s. Medicine
Meereskunde s. Oceanography, Marine
  Sciences
Metallurgie s. Metallurgy
Mikrobiologie s. Microbiology
Milchwirtschaft s. Dairy Science
Militärwissenschaft s. Military Science
Mineralogie s. Mineralogy
Musikwissenschaft s. Musicology
Nachrichtentechnik s. Communications
Nahrungsmittel s. Food
Naturwissenschaften, allgemeine s. Natural
  Sciences, general
Navigation s. Navigation
Neurologie s. Neurology
Normung s. Standardization
Nuklearmedizin s. Nuclear Medicine
Numismatik s. Numismatics
Nutzpflanzenzüchtung s. Crop Husbandry
Ökologie s. Ecology
Optik s. Optics
Ornithologie s. Ornithology
Orthopädie s. Orthopedics
Pädiatrie s. Pediatrics
Paläontologie s. Paleontology
Parapsychologie s. Parapsychology
Pathologie s. Pathology
Petrochemie s. Petrochemistry
Pharmakologie s. Pharmacology
Philosophie s. Philosophy
Photographie s. Photography
Physik s. Physics
Physiologie s. Physiology
Physiotherapie s. Physical Therapy
Politologie s. Political Science
Psychiatrie s. Psychiatry
Psychoanalyse s. Psychoanalysis
Psychologie s. Psychology
Publizistik s. Journalism
Pulmologie s. Pulmonary Disease
Radiologie s. Radiology

Recht s. Law
Rehabilitation s. Rehabilitation
Reisen und Tourismus s. Travel and Tourism
Religionsphilosophie, Theologie s. Religions
  and Theology
Rheumatologie s. Rheumatology
Roentgenologie s. X-Ray Technology
Rohstoffe s. Natural Resources
Sozialismus s. Socialism
Sozialwissenschaften s. Social Sciences
Soziologie s. Sociology
Sport s. Sports
Stadt- und Regionalplanung s. Urban and
  Regional Planning
Statistik s. Statistics
Stomatologie s. Stomatology
Tabak s. Tobacco
Textilien s. Textiles
Therapeutik s. Therapeutics
Tiefenpsychologie s. Depth Psychology
Tierzüchtung s. Animal Husbandry
Toxikologie s. Toxicology
Traumatologie s. Traumatology
Tropenmedizin s. Tropical Medicine
Unfallverhütung, Sicherheitstechnik s. Safety
  and Protection, Safety Engineering
Unternehmensführung, Betriebswirtschaft s.
  Business Administration, Management
Urologie s. Urology
Venerologie s. Venereology
Verhaltensforschung s. Behavioral Sciences
Verkehrswesen s. Transport and Traffic
Versicherung s. Insurance
Verwaltung s. Public Administration
Veterinärmedizin s. Veterinary Medicine
Völkerkunde s. Ethnology
Volkskunde s. Folklore
Wasserversorung s. Water Resources
Wein und Weinbau s. Wines and Wine Making
Werbung s. Advertising
Werkstoffkunde s. Materials Science
Wirtschaft s. Economics
Wissenschaft, allgemeine s. Science, general
Zahnheilkunde s. Dentistry
Zellbiologie, Krebsforschung s. Cell Biology,
  Cancer Research
Zoologie s. Zoology

393 Subject Index: Adult Education

Accident Prevention s. Safety and Protection, Safety Engineering

Acoustics

Australia
Australian Acoustical Society, Darlinghurst *00155*

Canada
Canadian Acoustical Association, Toronto *01780*

China, People's Republic
Acoustical Society of China, Beijing *02538*

Denmark
Nordisk Akustik Selskab, Lyngby *03172*

France
Société Française d'Acoustique, Paris *04107*

Germany
Deutsches High-Fidelity Institut e.V., Frankfurt *05080*

Japan
Nippon Onkyo Gakkai, Tokyo *07955*

Sweden
Svenska Akustiska Sällskapet, Göteborg *09959*

U.S.A.
Acoustical Society of America, Woodbury *12687*
Chinese Music Society of North America, Naperville *14069*

Adult Education

Australia
Australian Association of Adult and Community Education, Jamison Centre *00163*
Australian Postgraduate Federation in Medicine, Camperdown *00223*
Council of Adult Education, Melbourne *00265*

Austria
European Association for Catholic Adult Education, Linz *00437*
Evangelische Akademie in Wien, Wien *00442*
International Association of Schools of Social Work, Wien *00510*
Verband niederösterreichischer Volkshochschulen, Wien *00815*
Verband Österreichischer Volkshochschulen, Wien *00824*
Wiener Medizinische Akademie für Ärztliche Fortbildung und Forschung, Wien *00873*

Belgium
Association Laïque pour l'Education et la Formation Professionnelle des Adolescents en Europe, Bruxelles *00975*
Conseil Interuniversitaire de la Communauté Française, Bruxelles *01060*
European International Business Academy, Bruxelles *01159*
Vlaamse Interuniversitaire Raad, Bruxelles *01318*

Canada
Canadian Association for Adult Education, Toronto *01790*
Canadian Association for the Study of Adult Education, Vancouver *01807*
Institut Canadien d'Education des Adultes, Montréal *02133*
International Congress of University Adult Education, Fredericton *02150*
International Council for Adult Education, Toronto *02151*
Workers' Educational Association of Canada, Toronto *02429*

Colombia
Instituto Colombiano para el Fomento de la Educación Superior, Bogotá *02798*

Costa Rica
Consejo Superior Universitario Centroemericano, San José *02857*

Denmark
Foreningen for Danske Lanbrugsskoler, Greve *03123*
Nordic Federation for Medical Education, København *03170*
Société Internationale pour l'Enseignement Commercial, Odense *03214*

Egypt
Arab States Regional Centre for Functional Literacy in Rural Areas, Menoufia *03264*

Finland
Suomen Kansanopistoyhdistys, Helsinki *03409*
Teknillisten Oppilaitosten Opettajainliitto, Helsinki *03451*

France
Association Française de Formation, Paris *03524*
Association Française de Formation, Coopération, Promotion et Animation d'Entreprises, Paris *03525*
Association Interprofessionnelle pour la Formation Permanente dans le Commerce Textile, Paris *03605*
Association Nationale des Cours Professionnels pour les Préparateurs en Pharmacie, Paris *03616*
Association Nationale pour la Formation et la Promotion Professionnelle dans l'Industrie et le Commerce de la Chaussure et des Cuirs et Peaux, Paris *03620*
Association pour la Formation aux Professions Immobilières, Paris *03630*
Association pour la Formation des Cadres de l'Industrie et du Commerce, Paris *03631*
Association pour la Formation Professionnelle dans les Industries Céréalières, Paris *03632*
Association pour la Formation Professionnelle dans les Industries de l'Ameublement, Paris *03633*
Association pour le Développement de la Formation Professionnelle Continue dans les Industries Lourdes du Bois, Paris *03640*
Association pour le Développement de la Formation Professionnelle dans les Transports, Paris *03641*
Association Universitaire pour le Développement de l'Enseignement et de la Culture en Afrique et à Madagascar, Paris *03666*
Comité d'Education Sanitaire et Sociale de la Pharmacie Française, Paris *03705*
Comité d'Etudes et de Liaison Interprofessionnel de la Haute-Marne, Saint-Dizier *03709*
Comité d'Etudes et de Liaison Interprofessionnel du Département de l'Aisne, Saint-Quentin *03710*
Comité Européen pour l'Education des Enfants et Adolescents Précoces, Doués, Talentueux, Nîmes *03715*
Comité National des Conseillers de l'Enseignement Technique, Paris *03725*
Comité Universitaire d'Information Pédagogique, Paris *03733*
Conférence des Présidents d'Université, Paris *03753*
Fédération Internationale pour l'Education des Parents, Sèvres *03854*
Ligue Française de l'Enseignement et de l'Education Permanente, Paris *03913*
Office National d'Information sur les Enseignements et les Professions, Marne la Vallée *03926*
Syndicat National de l'Enseignement Technique, Paris *04260*
Union Professionnelle des Professeurs, Cadres et Techniciens du Secrétariat et de la Comptabilité, Paris *04321*

Germany
Akademikergesellschaft für Erwachsenenfortbildung mbH, Stuttgart *04404*
Arbeitskreis deutscher Bildungsstätten e.V., Bonn *04485*
Arbeitskreis für Hochschuldidaktik, Hamburg *04489*
Bayerischer Volkshochschulverband e.V., München *04542*
Berliner Institut für Lehrerfort- und -weiterbildung und Schulentwicklung, Berlin *04549*
Berufliche Fortbildungszentren der Bayerischen Arbeitgeberverbände e.V., München *04555*
Bildungswerk der Bayerischen Wirtschaft e.V., München *04587*
Bildungswerk der Hessischen Wirtschaft e.V., Frankfurt/Main *04588*
Bildungswerk der Nordrhein-Westfälischen Wirtschaft e.V., Schwelm *04591*
Brandenburgischer Volkshochschulverband e.V., Brandenburg *04598*
Bundesakademie für öffentliche Verwaltung, Bonn *04622*
Bundesarbeitsgemeinschaft Evangelischer Familien-Bildungsstätten e.V., Stein *04625*
Bundesarbeitsgemeinschaft katholischer Familienbildungsstätten, Düsseldorf *04628*
Bundesarbeitsgemeinschaft von Familienbildung und Beratung e.V., Elmshorn *04631*
Carl-Cranz-Gesellschaft e.V., Weßling *04685*
Deutsche Akademie für medizinische Fortbildung, Kassel *04710*
Deutsche Evangelische Arbeitsgemeinschaft für Erwachsenenbildung e.V., Karlsruhe *04731*
Deutsche Kommission für Ingenieurausbildung, Düsseldorf *04908*
Deutsche Sekretärinnen-Akademie e.V., Lübeck *04956*
Deutscher Berufsverband der Sozialarbeiter und Sozialpädagogen e.V., Essen *04998*
Deutscher Stenografielehrerverband e.V., Hamburg *05046*
Deutscher Volkshochschul-Verband e.V., Bonn *05066*
Deutsches Institut für Erwachsenenbildung/Pädagogische Arbeitsstelle des Deutschen Volkshochschul-Verbandes e.V., Frankfurt *05084*
ESTA-Bildungswerk e.V., Bad Oeynhausen *05129*
Europäische Staatsbürger-Akademie e.V., Bocholt *05148*
Evangelische Akademie Bad Boll, Bad Boll *05173*
Evangelische Akademie Baden (Bad Herrenalb), Karlsruhe *05174*
Evangelische Akademie Hofgeismar, Hofgeismar *05179*
Evangelische Akademie Loccum, Rehburg-Loccum *05183*
Evangelische Akademie Tutzing, Tutzing *05190*
Evangelische Akademien in Deutschland e.V., Bad Boll *05191*
Fördergemeinschaft für das Süddeutsche Kunststoff-Zentrum e.V., Würzburg *05221*
Forschungsinstitut für Arbeiterbildung e.V., Recklinghausen *05250*
Friedrich-Ebert-Stiftung e.V., Bonn *05298*
Hessische Akademie für Bürowirtschaft e.V., Frankfurt *05473*
Hessischer Volkshochschulverband e.V., Frankfurt/Main *05477*
Institut der Hessischen Volkshochschulen, Frankfurt *05515*
Institut für Sozialarbeit und Sozialpädagogik e.V., Frankfurt/Main *05539*
Institut für technische Weiterbildung Berlin e.V., Berlin *05542*
Katholische Akademie in Bayern, München *05647*
Katholische Akademie Trier, Trier *05651*
Katholische Bundesarbeitsgemeinschaft für Erwachsenenbildung, Bonn *05654*
Katholische Erwachsenenbildung im Lande Niedersachsen e.V., Hannover *05655*
Kongreßgesellschaft für ärztliche Fortbildung e.V., Berlin *05686*
Kuratorium der Deutschen Wirtschaft für Berufsbildung, Bonn *05696*
Ländliche Erwachsenenbildung in Niedersachsen e.V., Hannover *05701*
Landesausschuß der Volkshochschulen des Landes Bremen, Bremen *05708*
Landesverband der Volkshochschulen Niedersachsens e.V., Hannover *05709*
Landesverband der Volkshochschulen Sachsen-Anhalt e.V., Magdeburg *05710*
Landesverband der Volkshochschulen Schleswig-Holsteins e.V., Kiel *05711*
Landesverband der Volkshochschulen von Nordrhein-Westfalen e.V., Dortmund *05712*
Leiterkreis der Katholischen Akademien, Stuttgart *05716*
Management Akademie München, München *05735*
Mathematisch-Naturwissenschaftlicher Fakultätentag, Halle/Saale *05741*
Niedersächsischer Bund für freie Erwachsenenbildung e.V., Hannover *05779*
Niedersächsischer Landesverband der Heimvolkshochschulen e.V., Hannover *05780*
Nordwestdeutsche Gesellschaft für ärztliche Fortbildung e.V., Steinburg *05784*
Postakademie, Kleinheubach *05889*
Sächsischer Volkshochschulverband e.V., Chemnitz *05938*
Süddeutsches Kunststoff-Zentrum, Würzburg *05976*
Thomas-Morus-Akademie Bensberg, Bergisch Gladbach *05988*
Thüringer Volkshochschulverband e.V., Jena *05989*
Verband Bildung und Erziehung e.V., Bonn *06014*
Verband der Dozenten an Deutschen Ingenieurschulen, Mainz *06019*
Verband der Volkshochschulen des Landes Bremen, Bremen *06032*
Verband der Volkshochschulen des Saarlandes e.V., Saarbrücken *06033*
Verband der Volkshochschulen von Rheinland-Pfalz e.V., Mainz *06034*
Verband Hochschule und Wissenschaft im Deutschen Beamtenbund, Bonn *06067*
Verband Katholischer Landvolkshochschulen Deutschlands, Bad Honnef *06068*
Vereinigung der Hochschullehrer für Zahn-, Mund- und Kieferheilkunde, Frankfurt *06113*
Volkshochschulverband Baden-Württemberg e.V., Leinfelden-Echterdingen *06141*
Volkshochschulverband Mecklenburg-Vorpommern e.V., Schwerin *06142*
Westdeutscher Medizinischer Fakultätentag, Erlangen *06149*
Wuppertaler Kreis e.V., Köln *06174*

Greece
Hellenic Association of University Women, Athinai *06241*

Guyana
Adult Education Association of Guyana, Georgetown *06275*

India
Indian Adult Education Association, New Delhi *06438*

Italy
Accademia Culturale di Rapallo, Rapallo *06771*
Accademia degli Abruzzi per le Scienze e le Arti, Chieti *06772*
Associazione Nazionale Insegnanti di Disegno, Napoli *07014*
Associazione Nazionale Professori Universitari di Ruolo, Roma *07021*
Ente Istruzione Professionale Artigiana, Milano *07238*
International Centre for Advanced Technical and Vocational Training, Torino *07314*
Istituto per la Cooperazione Universitaria, Roma *07369*

Kenya
African Association for Literacy and Adult Education, Nairobi *08060*
African Training Centre for Literacy and Adult Education, Nairobi *08072*

Mexico
Center of Regional Cooperation in Adult Education for Latin America, Patzcuaro *08285*
Centro Regional de Educación de Adultos y Alfabetización Funcional para América Latina, Pátzcuaro *08296*

Netherlands
European Association for the Education of Adults, Amersfoort *08429*
Vereniging van Docenten in Geschiedenis en Staatsrichting in Nederland, Dordrecht *08643*
Vereniging voor Hoger Beroepsonderwijs, Amsterdam *08655*

Norway
Norsk Faglaererlag, Oslo *08817*

Paraguay
Federación Universitaria del Paraguay, Asunción *08962*

South Africa
South African Association for Technical and Vocational Education, Arcadia *09668*

Switzerland
Association Internationale des Directeurs d'Ecoles Hôtelières, Lausanne *10042*
Association Suisse des Ecoles Hôtelières, Glion-sur-Montreux *10048*
Europäisches Zentrum für die Bildung im Versicherungswesen, Sankt Gallen *10092*
Katholische Arbeitsgemeinschaft für Erwachsenenbildung der Schweiz und Liechtensteins, Luzern *10198*
Konferenz Schweizerischer Handelsschulrektoren, Chur *10204*
Schweizerische Direktoren-Konferenz gewerblicher Berufs- und Fachschulen, Bern *10263*
Schweizerische Gesellschaft für kaufmännisches Bildungswesen, Zürich *10305*
Schweizerische Hochschulkonferenz, Bern *10358*
Schweizerische Konferenz der Rektoren kaufmännischer Berufsschulen, Zürich *10365*
Schweizerische Vereinigung für Erwachsenenbildung, Zürich *10405*
Schweizerischer Bund für Elternbildung, Zürich *10439*
Schweizerischer Handelslehrerverein, Sankt Gallen *10449*
Schweizerischer Verband der Lehrerinnen und Lehrer an kaufmännischen Berufsschulen, Schaffhausen *10466*
Verband der Lehrerinnen und Lehrer für Bürofächer, Thun *10527*
Verband der Schweizerischen Volkshochschulen, Bern *10531*
Vereinigung der Gymnastiklehrer, Zürich *10558*

United Kingdom
Agricultural Education Association, York *10760*
Association for Adult and Continuing Education, London *10799*
Association for the Study of Medical Education, Dundee *10833*
Association of Agricultural Education Staffs, Mogerhanger *10839*
Association of Blind and Partially-Sights Teachers and Students, London *10846*
Association of Colleges for Further and Higher Education, Swindon *10862*
Association of Hairdressing Teachers in Colleges of Further Education, Balby *10883*
Association of Lecturers in Accountancy, Edinburgh *10894*
Association of Marine Engineering Schools, Liverpool *10898*
Association of Painting Craft Teachers, Saint Leonards-on-Sea *10907*
Association of Tutors, Cambridge *10927*
Association of Tutors in Adult Education, Nottingham *10928*
Association of University Teachers, London *10930*
Careers Research and Advisory Centre, Cambridge *11252*
Distributive Trades Education and Training Council, London *11393*
Institute of Bankers in Scotland, Edinburgh *11663*
Institute of Professional Investigators, Blackburn *11713*
International Association of University Professors of English, Marazion *11772*
International Federation on Aging – European Office, London *11793*
National Adult School Organisation, Birmingham *11972*
National Association of Careers and Guidance Teachers, Townbridge *11982*
National Association of Principal Agricultural Education Officers, Beverley *11986*
National Association of Teachers in Further and Higher Education, London *11988*
National Federation of Continuative Teachers' Associations, Bexley *12004*
National Federation of Voluntary Literacy Schemes, London *12006*
National Foundation for Educational Research in England and Wales, Slough *12007*
National Foundry and Engineering Training Association, Glasgow *12008*
National Institute of Adult Continuing Education (England and Wales), Leicester *12012*
Scottish Association for Building Education and Training, Paisley *12291*
Scottish Business Education Council, Edinburgh *12296*
Society for Interactive Learning, Ryton *12360*
Society for The Promotion of Vocational Training and Education, Bristol *12391*
Society of Industrial Tutors, Middlesbrough *12433*

Uruguay
Centro Interamericano de Investigación y Documentación sobre Formación Profesional, Montevideo *12620*

U.S.A.
Accrediting Bureau of Health Education Schools, Elkhart *12681*
Accrediting Council for Continuing Education and Training, Arlington *12683*
Accrediting Council on Education in Journalism and Mass Communications, Lawrence *12684*
Adult Christian Education Foundation, Madison *12694*
American Academy of Sanitarians, Miami *12797*
American Assembly of Collegiate Schools of Business, Saint Louis *12818*
American Association for Adult and Continuing Education, Washington *12820*

Advertising
s. a. Marketing

Austria

Canada

Germany

Ireland

Switzerland

United Kingdom

U.S.A.

Aeronautics, Aviation, Space Technology

Argentina

Australia

Belgium

Bulgaria

Canada

Chile

China, People's Republic

China, Republic

Cyprus

Egypt

France

Germany

Greece

India

Israel

Italy

Netherlands

New Zealand

Norway

Poland

Russia

Senegal

South Africa

Sweden

Switzerland

United Kingdom

U.S.A.

Yugoslavia

Agriculture
s. a. Dairy Science; Wines and Wine Making; Crop Husbandry; Animal Husbandry

Argentina

Australia

Subject Index: Agriculture 396

Senegal
Association of Maize Researchers in Africa, Dakar 09510

Slovakia
Slovenská Spoločnost pre Vedy Polnohospodarske, Lesnické a Potravinárské, Ivanka pri Dunaji 09578

South Africa
Organic Soil Association of South Africa, Parklands 09647
Soil Science Society of Southern Africa, Pretoria 09664

Spain
Institut Agrícola Català de Sant Isidre, Barcelona 09759

Suriname
Centre for Agricultural Research in Suriname, Paramaribo 09849

Sweden
International Association on Mechanization of Field Experiments, Uppsala 09892
Kungliga Skogs- och Lantbruksakademien, Stockholm 09908
Skogs- och Jordbrukets Forskningsråd, Stockholm 09939

Switzerland
Collaborative International Pesticides Analytical Council, Wädenswil 10065
Direktorenkonferenz der landwirtschaftlichen Ingenieurschulen, Bern 10084
Fédération des Sociétés d'Agriculture de la Suisse Romande, Lausanne 10122
Internationale Vereinigung für Saatgutprüfung, Zürich 10189
Internationales Kali-Institut, Basel 10194
Schweizerische Bodenkundliche Gesellschaft, Zürich 10259
Schweizerische Gesellschaft für Agrarwirtschaft, Zürich 10272
Schweizerischer Verband der Ingenieur-Agronomen und der Lebensmittel-Ingenieure, Zollikofen 10465
Schweizerischer Verband für Landtechnik, Riniken 10474
Union Internationale pour la Protection des Obtentions Végétales, Genève 10523

Syria
Arab Agronomists Union, Damascus 10583

Tanzania
East African Agriculture and Forestry Research Organization, Arusha 10596

Thailand
Agricultural Science Society of Thailand, Bangkok 10612
Asia and Pacific Commission on Agricultural Statistics, Bangkok 10619
Asia and Pacific Plant Protection Commission, Bangkok 10620
ESCAP/FAO/UNIDO Fertilizer, Development and Information Network for Asia and the Pacific, Bangkok 10639

Trinidad and Tobago
Agricultural Society of Trinidad and Tobago, Port of Spain 10652
Caribbean Agricultural Research and Development Institute, Saint Augustine 10653
Caribbean Agro-Economic Society, Saint Augustine 10654
Caribbean Information System for the Agricultural Sciences, Saint Augustine 10662
Eastern Caribbean Institute of Agriculture and Forestry, Arima 10667
Tobago District Agricultural Society, Scarborough 10672

Turkey
Türkiye Ziraat Odalari Birligi, Ankara 10724

Uganda
East African Agricultural Economics Society, Kampala 10728

Ukraine
Ukrainian Academy of Agrarian Sciences, Kiev 10737

United Kingdom
Abergavenny and Border Counties Agricultural Society, Abergavenny 10740
Agricultural and Food Research Council, Swindon 10758
Agricultural Economics Society, Belfast 10759
Agricultural Education Association, York 10760
Agricultural Research Institute of Northern Ireland, Hillsborough 10761
Association of Agricultural Education Staffs, Mogerhanger 10839
Association of Show and Agricultural Organisations, Newark 10920
Ayrshire Agricultural Association, Ayr 10944
Bio-dynamic Agricultural Association, Stourbridge 10964
Border Union Agricultural Society, Kelso 10986
British Agricultural History Society, Exeter 10999
British Association of Seed Analysts, London 11042
British Society for Agricultural Labour Science, Reading 11163
British Society for Plant Pathology, Cambridge 11175
British Society of Animal Science, Penicuik 11190
British Society of Soil Science, Aberdeen 11200
CAB International, Wallingford 11231
CAB International Bureau of Crop Protection, Wallingford 11232
CAB International Bureau of Horticulture and Plantation Crops, Wallingford 11233
CAB International Bureau of Plant Breeding and Genetics, Wallingford 11234
CAB International Department of Dairy Science and Technology, Wallingford 11235
CAB International Department of Soils, Wallingford 11236
Collaborative International Pesticides Analytic Council, London 11302
Commonwealth Association on Surveying and Land Economy, London 11319
East of England Agricultural Society, Peterborough 11413
English Guernsey Cattle Society, Chesham 11453
Essex Agricultural Society, Chelmsford 11465
Farm and Food Society, London 11520
Farm Buildings Association, Oxford 11521
Glasgow Agricultural Society, Ayr 11574
Henry Doubleday Research Association, Coventry 11612
Institute for Animal Health, Newbury 11653
Institute of Food Research, Reading 11687
Institution of Agricultural Engineers, Bedford 11731
International Association of Agricultural Museums, Reading 11764
Kent County Agricultural Society, Maidstone 11854
Merioneth Agricultural Society, Dolgellau 11941
National Association of Principal Agricultural Education Officers, Beverley 11986
Newark and Nottinghamshire Agricultural Society, Newark 12037
North Somerset Agricultural Society, Bristol 12045
North Tyne and Redesdale Agricultural Society, Morpeth 12047
North Wales Agricultural Society, Portdinorwic 12048
Pembrokeshire Agricultural Society, Haverfordwest 12093
Royal Agricultural Society of England, Stoneleigh Park 12168
Royal Bath and West of England Society, Shepton Mallet 12174
The Royal Cornwall Agricultural Association, Wadebridge 12200
Royal Highland and Agricultural Society of Scotland, Edinburgh 12209
Royal Isle of Wight Agricultural Society, Newport 12226
Royal Jersey Agricultural and Horticultural Society, Trinity 12227
Royal Lancashire Agricultural Society, Preston 12228
Royal Norfolk Agricultural Association, Norwich 12236
Royal Ulster Agricultural Society, Belfast 12270
Royal Welsh Agricultural Society, Powys 12272
Rutland Agricultural Society, Rutland 12277
Scottish Society for Crop Research, Dundee 12318
Society of Feed Technologists, Reading 12426
Soil Association, Bristol 12451
South of England Agricultural Society, Haywards Heath 12457
Staffordshire Agricultural Society, Stafford 12465
Suffolk Agricultural Association, Ipswich 12479
Three Counties Agricultural Society, Malvern 12504
Tobacco Research Council, London 12506
Yorkshire Agricultural Society, Harrogate 12595

Uruguay
Asociación Rural del Uruguay, Montevideo 12613
Centro de Investigaciones Agrícolas Alberto Boerger, La Estanzuela 12617

U.S.A.
Agricultural Communicators in Education, Gainesville 12714
Agricultural History Society, Washington 12715
Agriservices Foundation, Clovis 12716
Alternative Energy Resources Organization, Helena 12732
American Agricultural Economics Association, Ames 12804
American Agricultural Law Association, Fayetteville 12805
American Association for Agricultural Education, University Park 12822
American Farm Bureau Research Foundation, Park Ridge 13143
American Poultry Historical Society, Morgantown 13338
American Society of Agricultural Engineers, Saint Joseph 13422
American Society of Agronomy, Madison 13423
American Society of Irrigation Consultants, Byron 13464
Association for Living Historical Farms and Agricultural Museums, North Bloomfield 13645
Association of American Seed Control Officials, Annapolis 13723
Association of Official Seed Analysts, Lincoln 13806
Bio-Integral Resource Center, Berkeley 13918
Center for Sustainable Agriculture, Davis 14030
Consultative Group on International Agricultural Research, Washington 14184
Council for Agricultural Science and Technology, Ames 14202
Council for Tobacco Research – U.S.A., New York 14220
Crop Science Society of America, Madison 14272
Desert Protective Council, Valley Center 14298
Farm Foundation, Oak Brook 14413
Great Plains Agricultural Council, Fort Collins 14528
Henry A. Wallace Institute for Alternative Agriculture, Greenbelt 14558
International Alliance for Sustainable Agriculture, Minneapolis 14775
International Association of Agricultural Economists, Oak Brook 14828
International Benchmark Sites Network for Agrotechnology Transfer, Honolulu 14882
International Consortium for Agricultural Systems Applications, Honolulu 14962
International Crane Foundation, Baraboo 14988
International Erosion Control Association, Steamboat Springs 15006
International Fertilizer Development Center, Muscle Shoals 15034
International Institute of Tropical Agriculture, Miami 15083
International Organization of Citrus Virologists, Lake Alfred 15135
International Policy Council on Agriculture and Trade, Washington 15156
International Society for Tropical Root Crops, Tuskegee 15265
International Society of Citriculture, Riverside 15281
International Turfgrass Society, Belle Glade 15351
International Weed Science Society, Corvallis 15371
International Wheat Gluten Association, Prairie Village 15372
IRI Research Institute, Stamford 15385
National Association of Colleges and Teachers of Agriculture, Huntsville 15687
National Association of Extension 4-H Agents, Athens 15700
National Association of Supervisors of Agricultural Education, Jefferson City 15745
National FFA Organization, Alexandria 15882
National Plant Board, Raleigh 15954
National Vocational Agricultural Teachers' Association, Alexandria 15993
Native Seeds/Search, Tucson 16002
Potash and Phosphate Institute, Norcross 16194
Potato Association of America, Idaho Falls 16195
Rodale International, Emmaus 16277
Soil and Water Conservation Society, Ankeny 16572
Soil Science Society of America, Madison 16573
Special Programme for African Agricultural Research, Washington 16600
Sulphur Institute, Washington 16612
Urban Agricultural Network, Washington 16716
Weed Science Society of America, Champaign 16747
Winrock International Institute for Agricultural Development, Morrilton 16772
World Society for Mushroom Biology and Mushroom Products, New York 16837

Venezuela
Asociación de Agrimensores de Venezuela, Caracas 16875
Centro Nacional de Investigaciones Agropecuarias, Maracay 16898

Vietnam
Vietnamese Association of Agriculture, Hanoi 16943

Yugoslavia
Jugoslovensko Društvo za Proučavanje Zemljišta, Zemun 17006

Zambia
Agricultural Research Council of Zambia, Lusaka 17047

Zimbabwe
Agricultural Research Council of Zimbabwe, Harare 17060
Crop Science Society of Zimbabwe, Harare 17065
Zimbabwe Agricultural Society, Harare 17083

Air Conditioning

Argentina
Asociación Argentina del Frío, Buenos Aires 00049

Denmark
Dansk Selskab for Opvarmnings- og Ventilationsteknik, København 03068

France
Association Française du Froid, Paris 03550
Association Technique de la Réfrigération et de l'Equipement Ménager, Paris 03660
Institut International du Froid, Paris 03893

Germany
Arbeitsgemeinschaft Fernwärme e.V., Frankfurt 04444
Deutscher Kälte- und Klimatechnischer Verein e.V., Stuttgart 05020
Forschungsrat Kältetechnik e.V., Frankfurt 05256
Forschungsvereinigung für Luft- und Trocknungstechnik e.V., Frankfurt 05270
Gaswärme-Institut e.V., Essen 05306

Italy
Associazione Criogenica Italiana, Genova 06905
Associazione Italiana Condizionamento dell'Aria, Riscaldamento e Refrigerazione, Milano 06931
Associazione Termotecnica Italiana, Milano 07047
Comitato Termotecnico Italiano, Milano 07204

Japan
Kuki-Chowa Eisei Kogakkai, Tokyo 07764

U.S.A.
American Society of Heating, Refrigerating and Air-Conditioning Engineers, Atlanta 13456

Allergology s. Immunology

Anatomy

Canada
Canadian Association for Anatomy, Neurobiology and Cell Biology, Winnipeg 01792

Chile
Sociedad de Anatomía Normal y Patológica de Chile, Santiago 02513

China, People's Republic
Chinese Society for Anatomical Sciences, Beijing 02607

Czech Republic
Czech Anatomical Society, Praha 02948

France
Société Anatomique de Paris, Paris 03949
Syndicat National des Médecins Anatomo-Cyto-Pathologistes Français, Paris 04275

Georgia
Georgian Society of Patho-Anatomists, Tbilisi 04349

Germany
Anatomische Gesellschaft, Lübeck 04416
Gesellschaft für Wirbelsäulenforschung, Frankfurt 05416
Vereinigung Deutscher Neuropathologen und Neuroanatomen, Giessen 06120

Hungary
Magyar Anatómus Társaság, Budapest 06297

Italy
Accademia Anatomico-Chirurgica, Perugia 06765
Società Italiana di Anatomia, Firenze 07455
Società Italiana di Anatomia Patologica, Messina 07456

Japan
Nippon Kaibo Gakkai, Tokyo 07918

Netherlands
Nederlandse Anatomen Vereniging, Amsterdam 08551
Nederlandse Patholoog Anatomen Vereniging, Maastricht 08566

Poland
Polskie Towarzystwo Anatomiczne, Warszawa 09086

Portugal
Sociedade Anatómica Luso-Hispano-Americana, Lisboa 09210
Sociedade Anatómica Portuguesa, Coímbra 09211
Sociedade Portuguesa Veterinária de Anatomia Comparativa, Lisboa 09251

Russia
National Scientific Medical Society of Anatomists, Histologists and Embryologists, Moskva 09400
Scientific Medical Society of Anatomists-Pathologists, Moskva 09455

Sweden
Svensk Förening för Anatomi, Umeå 09950

United Kingdom
Anatomical Society of Great Britain and Ireland, London 10772
British Association of Clinical Anatomists, Manchester 11025
Ergonomics Society, Loughborough 11462
International Anatomical Nomenclature Committee, London 11760

U.S.A.
American Association of Anatomists, New Orleans 12859
American Association of Veterinary Anatomists, Auburn 12948
International Skeletal Society, San Diego 15185

Anesthetics

Argentina
Federación Argentina de Asociaciones de Anestesiología, Buenos Aires 00073

Australia
Australian Society of Anaesthesists, Paddington 00236

Animal Husbandry

Anthropology

399 Subject Index: Archives

Society of Antiquaries of Newcastle-upon-Tyne, Newcastle-upon-Tyne 12405
Society of Antiquaries of Scotland, Edinburgh 12406
Society of Archer Antiquaries, Bridlington 12407
Somerset Archaeological and Natural History Society, Taunton 12452
South Bedfordshire Archaeological Society, Great Yarmouth 12455
South Staffordshire Archaeological and Historical Society, Walsall 12459
Suffolk Institute of Archaeology and History, Ipswich 12480
Surrey Archaeological Society, Guildford 12484
Sussex Archaeological Society, Lewes 12486
Sussex Industrial Archaeology Society, Brighton 12487
The Thoroton Society of Nottinghamshire, Nottingham 12503
Ulster Archaeological Society, Belfast 12519
Ulster Archery Association, Belfast 12520
University of Bristol Spelaeological Society, Bristol 12545
Wiltshire Archaeological and Natural History Society, Devizes 12577
Wolverton and District Archaeological Society, Milton Keynes 12580
Woolhope Naturalists' Field Club, Hereford 12581
Worcestershire Archaeological Society, Malvern 12582
Yorkshire Archaeological Society, Leeds 12596

Uruguay

Sociedad de Amigos de Arqueología, Montevideo 12631

U.S.A.

American Committee to Advance the Study of Petroglyphs and Pictographs, Shepherdstown 13085
American Oriental Society, Ann Arbor 13296
American Philosophical Society, Philadelphia 13326
American Rock Art Research Association, San Miguel 13359
American Society for Conservation Archaeology, Albuquerque 13377
Amerind Foundation, Dragoon 13538
Archaeological Conservancy, Albuquerque 13561
Archaeological Institute of America, Boston 13562
Archeology Section, Arlington 13563
CEDAM International, Croton on Hudson 13990
Center for American Archaeology, Kampsville 13992
Early Sites Research Society, Rowley 14329
Epigraphic Society, San Francisco 14387
Etruscan Foundation, Grosse Pointe 14394
Institute for American Indian Studies, Washington 14659
Institute of Andean Studies, Berkeley 14697
Institute of Nautical Archaeology, College Station 14719
National Association of State Archeologists, Boston 15731
Near East Archaeological Society, Evanston 16006
Search Foundation, Birmingham 16306
Society for American Archaeology, Washington 16349
Society for Commercial Archeology, Washington 16368
Society for Historical Archaeology, Tucson 16390
Society for Industrial Archaeology, Princeton 16397
Society of Africanist Archaeologists, FL 32611 16490
Society of Professional Archaeologists, Raleigh 16549
South American Explorers Club, Ithaca 16580
Stonehenge Study Group, Santa Barbara 16606
World Archaeological Society, Hollister 16789

Vatican City

Pontificia Accademia Romana di Archeologia, Città del Vaticano 16863

Yugoslavia

Savez Arheološki Društava Jugoslavije, Beograd 17013

Architecture s. a. Civil Engineering; Urban and Regional Planning

Argentina

Sociedad Central de Arquitectos, Buenos Aires 00104

Austria

European Architectural Endoscopy Association, Wien 00436
Österreichische Gesellschaft für Architektur, Wien 00612
Österreichischer Ingenieur- und Architektenverein, Wien 00757
Zentralvereinigung der Architekten Österreichs, Wien 00883

Belgium

Architects Council of Europe, Bruxelles 00937
Comité de Liaison des Architectes de l'Europe Unie, Bruxelles 01032
European Association of Architectural Education, Louvain-la-Neuve 01096
Fédération Royale des Sociétés d'Architectes de Belgique, Bruxelles 01172
Ordre des Architectes, Bruxelles 01233
Société Belge des Urbanistes et Architectes Modernistes, Bruxelles 01255
Société Centrale d'Architecture de Belgique, Bruxelles 01260

Bolivia

Colegio de Arquitectos de Bolivia, La Paz 01341

Bulgaria

Union of Architects in Bulgaria, Sofia 01591

Canada

Architectural Intitute of British Columbia, Vancouver 01660
Canadian Centre for Architecture, Montréal 01847
Canadian Society of Landscape Architects, Okotoks 01996
Ontario Association of Architects, North York 02267
Royal Architectural Institute of Canada, Ottawa 02337
Society for the Study of Architecture in Canada, Ottawa 02383

Chile

Colegio de Arquitectos de Chile, Santiago 02456

China, People's Republic

Architectural Society of China, Beijing 02539

Colombia

Sociedad Antioqueña de Ingenieros y Architectos, Medellín 02808

Cyprus

Cyprus Civil Engineers and Architects Association, Nicosia 02899

Czech Republic

Obec Architektů, Praha 02957

Denmark

Byggecentrum, Hørsholm 02970
Danske Arkitekters Landsforbund, København 03085
Landskabsarkitekternes Fagforening, Klampenborg 03158

France

Académie d'Architecture, Paris 03463
Cercle d'Etudes Architecturales, Paris 03699
Compagnie des Experts-Architectes près la Cour d'Appel de Paris, Paris 03746
Conseil National de l'Ordre des Architectes, Paris 03776
Ordre des Architectes, Paris 03927
Société Française des Architectes, Paris 04173
Société Nationale des Architectes de France, Paris 04228
Union Internationale des Architectes, Paris 04311
Union Internationale des Femmes Architectes, Paris 04313
Vieilles Maisons Françaises, Paris 04326

Germany

Association Européenne pour l'Enseignement de l'Architecture, Kassel 04505
Bund Deutscher Architekten, Bonn 04606
Bund Deutscher Baumeister, Architekten und Ingenieure, Bonn 04607
Bundesarchitektenkammer, Bonn 04634
Deutsche Burgenvereinigung e.V., Braubach 04720
Deutsche Dekane- und Abteilungsleiterkonferenz für Architektur, Raumplanung und Landschaftsarchitektur, Hannover 04723
Rat für Baukultur im Deutschen Kulturrat, Essen 05898
Verein für Grüne Solararchitektur zur Förderung der Wohn- und Umweltqualität e.V., Tübingen 06092

Ghana

Ghana Institute of Architects, Accra 06200

Greece

Syllogos Architktonon Diplomatouchon Anotaton Scholon, Athinai 06254
World Society for Ekistics, Athinai 06256

Hungary

Epitéstudományi Egyesület, Budapest 06288

India

Academy of Architecture, Mumbai 06388
Indian Institute of Architects, Mumbai 06460

Ireland

Architectural Association of Ireland, Dublin 06584
Irish Georgian Society, Dublin 06628
Royal Hibernian Academy of Arts, Dublin 06661
Royal Institute of Architects of Ireland, Dublin 06663

Israel

Association of Engineers and Architects in Israel, Tel Aviv 06681

Italy

Associazione Nazionale Ingegneri ed Architetti Italiani, Roma 07012
Centro Internazionale di Studi di Architettura Andrea Palladio, Vicenza 07070
Consiglio Nazionale degli Architetti, Roma 07210
Ente Autonomo La Biennale de Venezia, Venezia 07233
Istituto Cooperativo per l'Innovazione, Roma 07333
Istituto di Diritto Romano e dei Diritti dell'Oriente Mediterraneo, Roma 07335
Istituto Nazionale di Architettura, Roma 07361
Società degli Ingegneri e degli Architetti in Torino, Torino 07400

Jamaica

Jamaican Institute of Architects, Kingston 07705

Japan

Nihon Zoen Gakkai, Tokyo 07870

Malaysia

Malaysian Institute of Architects, Kuala Lumpur 08231

Malta

Chamber of Architects and Civil Engineers, Saint Andrews 08242

Mexico

Asociación de Ingenieros y Arquitectos de México, México 08263

Namibia

Namibia Institute of Architects, Windhoek 08389

Netherlands

Bond Heemschut, Amsterdam 08403
College van Toezicht, Amsterdam 08411
Genootschap Architectura et Amicitia, Amsterdam 08462
Koninklijke Maatschappij tot Bevordering der Bouwkunst, Bond van Nederlandse Architekten, Amsterdam 08508
Stichting Centrale Raad voor de Academies van Bouwkunst, Amsterdam 08623

New Zealand

New Zealand Institute of Architects, Wellington 08702

Norway

Norske Arkitekters Landsforbund, Oslo 08850

Pakistan

Architects Regional Council Asia, Karachi 08892
Pakistan Council of Architects and Town Planners, Karachi 08916

Peru

Colegio de Arquitectos del Perú, Lima 08996

Philippines

Philippine Institute of Architects, Manila 09058

Portugal

Associção dos Arquitectos Portugueses, Lisboa 09190

Romania

Uniunea Arhitectilor din Romania, Bucuresti 09325

Russia

Union of Russian Architects, Moskva 09476

Singapore

Singapore Institute of Architects, Singapore 09539

Slovakia

Spolok Architektov Slovenska, Bratislava 09581

Slovenia

Zveza Društev Arhitektov Slovenije, Ljubljana 09598

South Africa

Institute of South African Architects, Houghton 09636

Spain

Collegi d'Arquitectes de Cataluñya, Barcelona 09746

Sweden

Statens Råd för Byggnadsforskning, Stockholm 09943
Svenska Arkitekters Riksförbund, Stockholm 09961
Svenska Fornminnesföreningen, Stockholm 09973

Switzerland

Bund Schweizer Architekten, Zürich 10055
Fachgruppe für Arbeiten im Ausland des SIA, Zürich 10110
Fachgruppe für Architektur des SIA, Zürich 10111
Gesellschaft Schweizerischer Maler, Bildhauer und Architekten, Muttenz 10145
Internationale Architekten-Union, Sektion Schweiz, Zürich 10181
Schweizerischer Ingenieur- und Architekten-Verein, Zürich 10450
Schweizerischer Werkbund, Zürich 10485
Verband freierwerbender Schweizer Architekten, Lachen 10533

Turkey

Türk Mühendis ve Mimar Odalari Birligi, Ankara 10709

United Kingdom

Architects and Surveyors Institute, Chippenham 10785
Architectural and Archaeological Society of Durham and Northumberland, Durham City 10786
Architectural Association, London 10787
Association of Chief Architects of Scottish Local Authorities, Lanark 10858
Association of Official Architects, London 10906
The British Institute of Persian Studies, London 11102
Buckinghamshire Archaeological Society, Aylesbury 11225
Charles Rennie Mackintosh Society, Glasgow 11266
Cinema Theatre Association, Teddington 11294
Commonwealth Association of Architects – Education Committee, London 11317
Council of Professors of Building, Birmingham 11362
County, City and Borough Architects' Association, Harrow 11363
Edinburgh Architectural Association, Edinburgh 11423
Education in CAAD in Europe, Glasgow 11432
Farm Buildings Association, Oxford 11521
Incorporated Association of Architects, Weston Favell 11643
Men of The Stones, Stamford 11939
Oxfordshire Architectural and Historical Society, Oxford 12079
Regency Society of Brighton and Hove, Brighton 12148
Research into Lost Knowledge Organisation, Orpington 12155
Royal Incorporation of Architects in Scotland, Edinburgh 12212
Royal Institute of British Architects, London 12213
Royal Society of Ulster Architects, Belfast 12263
Saint Albans and Hertfordshire Architectural and Archaeological Society, Saint Albans 12278
Society of Architectural Historians of Great Britain, Farnham 12408
Society of Chief Architects of Local Authorities, Wirral 12417
Ulster Architectural Heritage Society, Belfast 12521
Vernacular Architecture Group, Tamworth 12548
Victorian Society, London 12553
Welwyn Hall Research Association, Hatfield 12572

U.S.A.

American Architectural Foundation, Washington 12815
American Institute of Architects, Washington 13205
American Institute of Building Design, Westport 13208
American Society of Golf Course Architects, Chicago 13453
American Society of Landscape Architects, Washington 13465
American Underground-Construction Association, Minneapolis 13523
Architectural League of New York, New York 13564
Association for Bridge Construction and Design, Pittsburgh 13603
Association of Collegiate Schools of Architecture, Washington 13754
Association of University Architects, Fort Myers 13860
Athenaeum of Philadelphia, Philadelphia 13878
Council of Landscape Architectural Registration Boards, Fairfax 14233
Council on Tall Buildings and Urban Habitat, Bethlehem 14264
Design-Build Institute of America, Washington 14300
Environmental Design Research Association, Edmond 14381
Frank Lloyd Wright Association, Scottsdale 14476
Institute for Community Design Analysis, Great Neck 14663
Institute for Urban Design, New York 14694
Intelligent Buildings Institute, Washington 14733
Interfaith Forum on Religion, Art and Architecture, Washington 14754
International Association for Housing Science, Coral Gables 14797
International Confederation of Architectural Museums, New York 14955
International Union of Architects, Chicago 15355
Landscape Architecture Foundation, Washington 15476
National Architectural Accrediting Board, Washington 15632
National Council on Agricultural Life and Labor Research Fund, Dover 15847
National Housing Conference, Washington 15905
National Organization of Minority Architects, Washington 15945
Society of American Registered Architects, Lombard 16496
Society of Architectural Historians, Chicago 16498
Society of Naval Architects and Marine Engineers, Jersey City 16540
Society of Turkish Architects, Engineers and Scientists in America, New York 16565
Vernacular Architecture Forum, Newark 16725

Vietnam

Vietnamese Association of Architects, Hanoi 16947

Yugoslavia

Društvo Arhitekata Srbije, Beograd 16987

Archives

Argentina

Asociación Archivística Argentina, Buenos Aires 00035

Association Les Amis de Gustave Courbet, Ornans 03606
Association Littéraire et Artistique Internationale, Paris 03608
European Association for American Studies, Lyon 03794
Fédération Française des Sociétés d'Amis de Musées, Paris 03840
International Association of Sanskrit Studies, Paris 03899
International Council of Museums, Paris 03903
Le Pays Bas-Normand, Flers 03939
Société Académique des Arts Libéraux de Paris, La Varenne Saint-Hilaire 03946
Société de l'Histoire de l'Art Français, Paris 03981
Société d'Emulation du Bourbonnais, Moulins 04013
Société des Amis d'Eugène Delacroix, Paris 04021
Société des Artistes Décorateurs, Paris 04025
Société des Artistes Français, Paris 04026
Société des Artistes Indépendants, Paris 04027
Société des Professeurs de Dessin et d'Arts Plastiques de l'Enseignement Secondaire, Paris 04044
Société des Sciences, Arts et Belles-Lettres de Bayeux, Bayeux 04045
Société d'Etude du Dix-Septième Siècle, Paris 04053
Société d'Etudes Juives, Paris 04070
Société d'Histoire et d'Archéologie Le Vieux Montmartre, Paris 04089
Société du Salon d'Automne, Paris 04102
Société Française d'Art Contemporain, Paris 04113
Société Française de Céramique, Paris 04117
Société Nationale des Beaux-Arts, Paris 04229
Union Centrale des Arts Décoratifs, Paris 04298

Germany

Akademie der Künste, Berlin 04375
Akademie Remscheid für musische Bildung und Medienerziehung e.V., Remscheid 04401
Arbeitsgemeinschaft der Deutschen Werkkunstschulen, Bremen 04428
Arbeitsgemeinschaft Kirchlicher Museen und Schatzkammern, Trier 04468
Bayerische Akademie der Schönen Künste, München 04524
Bund Deutscher Kunsterzieher e.V., Hannover 04608
Bund für freie und angewandte Kunst e.V., Darmstadt 04612
Bundesverband der Jugendkunstschulen und Kulturpädagogischen Einrichtungen e.V., Unna 04648
Bundesverband Museumspädagogik e.V., Hannover 04669
Deutsche Gesellschaft für Asienkunde e.V., Hamburg 04756
Deutsche Gesellschaft für Christliche Kunst e.V., München 04764
Deutsche Morgenländische Gesellschaft e.V., Heidelberg 04925
Deutscher Künstlerbund e.V., Berlin 05024
Deutscher Museumsbund e.V., Dresden 05030
Deutscher Verein für Kunstwissenschaft e.V., Berlin 05062
Ernst Barlach Gesellschaft e.V., Wedel 05125
Forschungsgemeinschaft Hönn-Wolf, Römhild 05233
Freie Akademie der Künste in Hamburg e.V., Hamburg 05289
Freie Akademie der Künste Mannheim, Mannheim 05290
Gesellschaft der Musik- und Kunstfreunde Heidelberg e.V., Gaiberg 05340
Gesellschaft für Goldschmiedekunst, Hanau 05370
Gesellschaft für pommersche Geschichte, Altertumskunde und Kunst e.V., Marburg 05394
Humboldt-Gesellschaft für Wissenschaft, Kunst und Bildung e.V., Mannheim 05500
ICOM-Deutschland, Deutsches Nationalkomitee des Internationalen Museumsrates, München 05502
Internationale Arbeitsgemeinschaft der Archiv-, Bibliotheks- und Graphikrestauratoren, Göttingen 05566
Internationale Gesellschaft der Bildenden Künste, Sektion der Bundesrepublik Deutschland, Bonn 05570
Internationaler Kunstkritikerverband, Sektion der Bundesrepublik Deutschland e.V., Köln 05589
Kestner-Gesellschaft, Hannover 05663
Kunstrat im Deutschen Kulturrat, Bonn 05694
Kunstwissenschaftler- und Kunstkritiker-Verband e.V, Berlin 05695
Mainzer Altertumsverein e.V., Mainz 05734
Normenausschuss Bühnentechnik in Theatern und Mehrzweckhallen im DIN Deutsches Institut für Normung e.V., Berlin 05794
Peter-Schwingen-Gesellschaft e.V., Bonn 05879
Südosteuropa-Gesellschaft e.V., München 05978
Verband der Gemeinschaften der Künstlerinnen und Kunstfreunde e.V., Wuppertal 06021
Verband Deutscher Kunsthistoriker e.V., München 06042

Ghana

Arts Council of Ghana, Accra 06191
Ghana Academy of Arts and Sciences, Accra 06196

Greece

Kallitechnikon Epimelitirion Ellados, Athinai 06248

Hungary

Széchenyi Irodalmi és Müvészeti Akadémia, Budapest 06356

Iceland

Arkitektafélag Islands, Reykjavik 06361
Bandalag Islenzkra Listamanna, Reykjavik 06362
Félag Islenzkra Myndlistarmanna, Reykjavik 06365
Menntamálaráð, Reykjavik 06375

India

All-India Fine Arts and Crafts Society, New Delhi 06395
Art Society of India, Bombay 06402
Crafts Council of Western India, Mumbai 06423
Indian Society of Oriental Art, Calcutta 06487
Jammu and Kashmir Academy of Art, Culture and Languages, Srinagar 06499
Mumbai Art Society, Mumbai 06505
Museums Association of India, Lucknow 06509
National Academy of Art, New Dehli 06511
South India Society of Painters, Madras 06532

Iraq

Society of Iraqi Artists, Baghdad 06581

Ireland

Aosdana, Dublin 06582
The Arts Council, Dublin 06585
Irish Society for Design and Craftwork, Dublin 06641
Irish Society of Arts and Commerce, Dublin 06642
Royal Hibernian Academy of Arts, Dublin 06661

Israel

Israel Painters and Sculptors Association, Tel Aviv 06710
Museums Association of Israel, Jerusalem 06740

Italy

Academia Española de Bellas Artes en Roma, Roma 06758
Academia Petrarca di Lettere, Arti e Scienze, Arezzo 06760
Accademia Albertina di Belle Arti, Torino 06762
Accademia Biella Cultura, Biella 06767
Accademia degli Euteleti, San Miniato 06773
Accademia degli Incamminati, Modigliana 06774
Accademia degli Sbalzati, Sansepolcro 06777
Accademia dei Filodrammatici, Milano 06779
Accademia dei Filopatridi (Rubiconia), Savignano sul Rubicone 06780
Accademia dei Gelati, Scanno 06781
Accademia di Belle Arti, Bologna 06792
Accademia di Belle Arti, Firenze 06793
Accademia di Belle Arti, Lecce 06794
Accademia di Belle Arti, Milano 06795
Accademia di Belle Arti, Napoli 06796
Accademia di Belle Arti, Palermo 06797
Accademia di Belle Arti, Perugia 06798
Accademia di Belle Arti, Ravenna 06799
Accademia di Belle Arti, Roma 06800
Accademia di Belle Arti, Venezia 06801
Accademia di Belle Arti e Liceo Artistico, Carrara 06802
Accademia di Paestum Eremo Italico, Mercato San Severino 06807
Accademia di Scienze, Lettere e Arti, Udine 06811
Accademia di Scienze, Lettere e Belle Arti degli Zelanti e dei Dafnici, Acireale 06812
Accademia di Scienze, Lettere ed Arti, Palermo 06813
Accademia Fulginia di Arti, Lettere, Scienze, Foligno 06820
Accademia Il Tetradramma, Roma 06824
Accademia Internazionale d'Arte Moderna, Roma 06825
Accademia Internazionale della Tavola Rotonda, Milano 06826
Accademia Ligustica de Belle Arti, Genova 06838
Accademia Nazionale di Belle Arti di Parma, Parma 06853
Accademia Nazionale di San Luca, Roma 06857
Accademia Nazionale di Scienze, Lettere e Arti, Modena 06859
Accademia Nazionale di Scienze, Lettere ed Arti, Palermo 06860
Accademia Nazionale Virgiliana di Scienze, Lettere e Arti di Mantova, Mantova 06862
Accademia Olimpica, Vicenza 06863
Accademia Petrarca di Lettere, Arti e Scienze, Arezzo 06864
Accademia Pomposiana, Codigoro 06866
Accademia Pontaniana, Napoli 06867
Accademia Prenestina del Cimento di Musica, Lettere, Scienze, Arti Visive e Figurative, Palestrina 06869
Accademia Romana di Cultura, Roma 06872
Accademia Salentina di Lettere ed Arti, Lecce 06875
Accademia Scientifica, Letteraria, Artistica del Frignano Lo Scoltenna, Pievepelago 06876
Accademia Senese degli Intronati, Siena 06877
Accademia Spagnola di Belle Arti, Roma 06879
Accademia Spoletina, Spoleto 06880
Accademia Tedesca Villa Massimo, Roma 06881
Accademia Universale Citta' Eterna, Roma 06884
Accademia Universale Guglielmo Marconi, Roma 06885
Associazione di Cultura Lao Silesu, Iglesias 06910
Associazione Nazionale dei Musei Italiani, Roma 07001
Associazione per Imola Storico-Artistica, Imola 07026
Associazione Siciliana per le Lettere e le Arti, Palermo 07040
Associazione Sole Italico, Sulmona 07042
Centro Camuno di Studi Preistorici, Capo di Ponte 07054
Centro Internazionale per l'Educazione Artistica della Fondazione Giorgio Cini, Venezia 07079
Centro Studi e Documentazione della Cultura Armena, Milano 07150
Comitato per Bologna Storica-Artistica, Bologna 07203
Ente Autonomo La Biennale de Venezia, Venezia 07233
Istituto Nazionale di Archeologia e Storia dell'Arte, Roma 07360
Istituto Veneto di Scienze, Lettere ed Arti, Venezia 07375
Sindacato Nazionale Istruzione Artistica, Roma 07387
Società Dauna di Cultura, Foggia 07398
Società d'Incoraggiamento d'Arti e Mestieri, Milano 07419
Società Europea di Cultura, Venezia 07424
Società Incoraggiamento Arti e Mestieri, Milano 07436
Società Italiana per l'Archeologia e la Storia delle Arti, Napoli 07593
Società Nazionale di Scienze, Lettere ed Arti, Napoli 07620
Società per gli Studi Storici, Archeologici ed Artistici della Provincia di Cuneo, Cuneo 07627
Società Tarquiniense d'Arte e Storia, Tarquinia 07648
Società Tiburtina di Storia e d'Arte, Tivoli 07650

Japan

Bijutsu-shi Gakkai, Tokyo 07716

Kenya

Kenya National Academy of Sciences, Nairobi 08103

Korea, Republic

National Academy of Arts, Seoul 08140
Royal Asiatic Society, Korea Branch, Seoul 08142

Kuwait

National Council for Culture, Arts and Literature, Safat 08145

Liberia

Liberia Arts and Crafts Association, Monrovia 08157

Libya

Union of Libyan Authors, Writers and Artists, Tripoli 08160

Macedonia

Društvo na Istoričarite na Umetnosta od Makedonija, Skopje 08180
Makedonska Akademija na Naukite i Umetnostite, Skopje 08190

Madagascar

Association des Bibliothécaires, Documentalistes, Archivistes et Muséographes de Madagascar, Antananarivo 08208

Malta

Malta Society of Arts, Manufactures and Commerce, Valletta 08248

Mauritius

Royal Society of Arts and Sciences of Mauritius, Réduit 08254

Mexico

Ateneo de Ciencias y Artes de Chiapas, Tuxtla Gutiérrez 08279
Ateneo Nacional de Ciencias y Artes de México, México 08280
Equipe 7 des Arts Visuels, México 08308
Instituto Nacional de Bellas Artes, México 08312

Netherlands

Comité International d'Histoire de l'Art, Utrecht 08412
Koninklijk Oudheidkundig Genootschap Amsterdam, Amsterdam 08506
Maatschappij Arti et Amicitiae, Amsterdam 08526
Nederlandse Museumvereniging, Amsterdam 08559
Rijksbureau voor Kunsthistorische Documentatie, Den Haag 08620
Vereniging Sint Lucas, Amsterdam 08640
Vereniging van Nederlandse Kunsthistorici, Groningen 08646

New Zealand

Creative New Zealand, Wellington 08671
Museums Association of Aotearoa New Zealand Te Ropu Hanga Kaupapa, Wellington 08681
New Zealand Academy of Fine Arts, Wellington 08682
New Zealand Maori Arts and Crafts Institute, Rotorua 08714

Norway

Norges Kunstnerråd, Oslo 08806
Norske Kunst- og Kulturhistoriske Museer, Oslo 08859
Norwegian Council of Cultural Affairs, Oslo 08872

Pakistan

Arts Council of Pakistan, Karachi 08893
Pakistan Museum Association, Karachi 08923

Peru

Asociación de Artistas Aficionados, Lima 08979

Poland

Poznánskie Towarzystwo Przyjaciól Nauk, Poznan 09144
Stowarzyszenie Historyków Sztuki, Warszawa 09148

Portugal

Academia Nacional de Belas-Artes, Lisboa 09174
Real Sociedade Arqueológica Lusitana, Santiago do Cacém 09205
Sociedade Científica da Universidade Católica Portuguesa, Lisboa 09214
Sociedade Nacional de Belas Artes, Lisboa 09224

Puerto Rico

Ateneo de Ponce, Ponce 09256
Ateneo Puertorriqueño, San Juan 09257
Sociedad Mayagüezana por Bellas Artes, Mayaguez 09261

Romania

Uniunea Artistilor Plastici din Romania, Bucuresti 09326

Russia

Museum Council, Moskva 09376
Russian Academy of Arts, Moskva 09439
Union of Arts of the Russian Federation, Moskva 09475

Saudi Arabia

King Abdul Aziz Research Centre, Riyadh 09492

Singapore

Indian Fine Arts Society, Singapore 09533
Singapore Art Society, Singapore 09537

South Africa

Human Sciences Research Council, Pretoria 09634
South African Academy of Science and Arts, Pretoria 09665
South African Association of Arts, Pretoria 09669
Southern African Museums Association, Sunnyside 09713

Spain

Asociación Española de Pintores y Escultores, Madrid 09734
Ateneo Científico, Literario y Artístico, Madrid 09738
Ateneo Científico, Literario y Artístico, Mahón 09739
Ateneu Barcelonés, Barcelona 09740
Departamento de Historia del Arte Diego Velázquez, Madrid 09753
Institución Fernando el Católico, Zaragoza 09758
Institut Amatller d'Art Hispànic, Barcelona 09760
Real Academia de Bellas Artes de la Purísima Concepción, Valladolid 09773
Real Academia de Bellas Artes de San Fernando, Madrid 09774
Real Academia de Bellas Artes de San Telmo, Málaga 09775
Real Academia de Bellas Artes de Santa Isabel de Hungria, Sevilla 09776
Real Academia de Bellas Artes y Ciencias Históricas de Toledo, Toledo 09777
Real Academia de Ciencias y Artes de Barcelona, Barcelona 09782
Real Academia de Córdoba de Ciencias, Bellas Letras y Nobles Artes, Córdoba 09783
Real Academia de Nobles y Bellas Artes de San Luis, Zaragoza 09790
Real Sociedad Fotográfica Española, Madrid 09802
Sociedad de Ciencias, Letras y Artes, Las Palmas 09810

Sri Lanka

Arts Council of Sri Lanka, Battaramulla 09828
Ceylon Society of Arts, Colombo 09833
Royal Asiatic Society of Sri Lanka, Colombo 09838

Suriname

Stichting Cultureel Centrum Suriname, Paramaribo 09851

Swaziland

Swaziland Art Society, Mbabane 09853

Sweden

Konsthistoriska Sällskapet, Stockholm 09900
Kungliga Akademien för de fria Konsterna, Stockholm 09901
Kungliga Vetenskaps- och Vitterhets-Samhället i Göteborg, Göteborg 09909
Svenska Museiföreningen, Stockholm 09990
Sveriges Allmänna Konstförening, Stockholm 10003
Sveriges Museimannaförbund, Nacka 10009

Switzerland

Förderverein Schweizerisches Institut für Kunstwissenschaft, Zürich 10127
Gesellschaft für das Schweizerische Landesmuseum, Zürich 10135
Gesellschaft für Schweizerische Kunstgeschichte, Bern 10140
Gesellschaft Schweizerischer bildender Künstlerinnen, Basel 10144
Gesellschaft Schweizerischer Zeichenlehrerinnen und Zeichenlehrer, Heidem 10147
ICOM – Conseil International des Musées, Comité National Suisse, Solothurn 10157
Kunstverein Sankt Gallen, Sankt Gallen 10206
Opera Svizzera dei Monumenti d'Arte/Inventario Beni Culturali, Bellinzona 10219
Pro Helvetia, Zürich 10226
Schweizerischer Kunstverein, Zürich 10453
Schweizerisches Institut für Kunstwissenschaft, Zürich 10489
Verband der Museen der Schweiz, Solothurn 10529
Vereinigung der Freunde antiker Kunst, Basel 10557

Vereinigung der Kunsthistorikerinnen und Kunsthistoriker in der Schweiz, Zürich 10559

Thailand
Royal Institute, Bangkok 10644

Togo
Association Togolaise pour le Développement de la Documentation, des Bibliothèques, Archives et Musées, Lomé 10650

Tunisia
Comité National des Musées, Tunis 10687

United Kingdom
Arts Association, London 10793
Arts Council of England, London 10794
Arts Council of Northern Ireland, Belfast 10795
Arts Council of Wales, Cardiff 10796
Association of Art Institutions, Hereford 10842
Association of Arts Centres in Scotland, Aberdeen 10843
Association of Principals of Colleges (Northern Ireland Branch), Lisburn 10910
Birmingham and Midland Institute, Birmingham 10971
British Archaeological Association, Lomdon 11005
British Arts, London 11006
British Association of Friends of Museums, Manchester 11029
The British Institute of Persian Studies, London 11102
British Museum Society, London 11129
British Watercolour Society, Ilkley 11217
Chester Society of Natural Science, Literatur and Art, Chester 11283
Chippendale Society, Leeds 11287
Contemporary Art Society, London 11344
County Museum Society, Kidderminster 11365
Designers and Art Directors Association of London, London 11384
The Devonshire Association for the Advancement of Science, Literature and Art, Exeter 11387
East Midlands Arts Board, Loughborough 11412
Federation of British Artists, London 11526
Hesketh Hubbard Art Society, London 11618
Honourable Society of Cymmrodorion, London 11631
Institute of Contemporary Arts, London 11676
London Medieval Society, London 11886
Museum Attendants Association, Old Portsmouth 11962
Museum Training Institute, Bradford 11963
Museums and Galleries Commission, London 11964
The Museums Association, London 11965
National Art-Collections Fund, London 11974
National Society for Education in Art and Design, Corsham 12022
New English Art Club, London 12036
North Wales Arts Association, Bangor 12049
The Oriental Ceramic Society, London 12071
Pastel Society, London 12089
The Plymouth Athenaeum, Plymouth 12112
Royal Academy of Arts in London, London 12161
Royal Cambrian Academy of Art, Conwy 12176
Royal Drawing Society, London 12201
Royal Fine Art Commission, London 12205
Royal Institute of Painters in Water Colours, London 12217
Royal Society for the Encouragement of Arts, Manufactures and Commerce, London 12249
Royal Society of Arts, London 12252
Royal Society of British Artists, London 12253
Royal Society of Portrait Painters, London 12261
Royal West of England Academy, Bristol 12273
Saltire Society, Edinburgh 12281
Scottish Arts Council, Edinburgh 12290
Society of County Museum Directors, West Malling 12421
Society of Wildlife Artists, London 12448
Society of Women Artists, London 12449
Southern Arts Board, Winchester 12461
Standing Conference of Arts and Social Sciences, Cardiff 12470
United Kingdom Institute for Conservation of Historic and Artistic Works, London 12537
The Walpole Society, London 12561
Wedgwood Society, Fordingbridge 12564
Welsh Arts Council, Cardiff 12566
William Morris Society, London 12576
Yorkshire Arts Association, Bradford 12597

U.S.A.
Academy of Arts and Sciences of the Americas, Miami 12653
American Academy of Arts and Letters, New York 12743
American Academy of Arts and Sciences, Cambridge 12744
American Association of Museums, Washington 12908
American Council for the Arts, New York 13100
American Federation of Arts, New York 13145
American Fine Arts Society, New York 13151
American Institute for Conservation of Historic and Artistic Works, Washington 13196
American Oriental Society, Ann Arbor 13296
American Studies Association, Washington 13509
Anonymous Arts Recovery Society, New York 13545
Archives of American Art, Washington 13565
Art Institute of Light, Gap 13573
Arts International, New York 13575
Association for the Study of Dada and Surrealism, Los Angeles 13690
Association of Youth Museums, Washington 13868
Athenaeum of Philadelphia, Philadelphia 13878
Classical America, New York 14087
College Art Association, New York 14098
Committee for Hispanic Arts and Research, Austin 14124
Council of Colleges of Arts and Sciences, Tempe 14227
Council on Technology Teacher Education, Ypsilanti 14265
Czechoslovak Society of Arts and Sciences, Sherman Oaks 14277
Deltiologists of America, Norwood 14291
Experiments in Art and Technology, Berkeley Heights 14406
Foundation for Research in the Afro-American Creative Arts, Cambria Heights 14471
Friends of American Art in Religion, New York 14481
Global Art Project, Tucson 14503
Hispanic Society of America, New York 14570
ICOM International Committee for Management, Los Angeles 14629
ICOM International Committee for Museum Security, Washington 14630
ICOM International Committee for Museums and Collections of Glass, Corning 14631
ICOM International Committee on Exhibition Exchange, Largo 14632
Institute of American Indian Arts, Santa Fe 14695
Interfaith Forum on Religion, Art and Architecture, Washington 14754
International Center of Medieval Art, New York 14901
International Council of Fine Arts Deans, San Marcos 14977
International Council of Museums – Committee of the American Association of Museums, Washington 14980
International Council of the Museum of Modern Art, New York 14984
International Foundation for Art Research, New York 15039
International Society for the Arts, Sciences and Technology, San Francisco 15253
International Society of Phenomenology, Aesthetics and the Fine Arts, East Lansing 15304
International Technology Education Association, Reston 15334
International Technology Education Association – Council for Supervisors, Richmond 15335
Leonardo – The International Society for the Arts, Sciences and Technology, San Francisco 15493
Medieval Academy of America, Cambridge 15550
Museum Services International, Washington 15607
National Academy of Western Art, Oklahoma City 15624
National Alliance of Media Arts and Culture, Oakland 15630
National Art Education Association, Reston 15634
National Association for Applied Arts, Science and Education, Milwaukee 15636
National Council for Culture and Art, New York 15822
National Council for the Traditional Arts, Silver Spring 15828
National Foundation for Advancement in the Arts, Miami 15886
National Guild of Community Schools of the Arts, Englewood 15894
National League of American PEN Women, Washington 15927
Pacific Arts Association, Honolulu 16112
Performing and Visual Arts Society, Athol Springs 16159
Polish Institute of Arts and Sciences in America, New York 16186
Primitive Art Society of Chicago, Chicago 16204
Rogers Group, Beltsville 16279
Saving and Preserving Arts and Cultural Environments, Los Angeles 16292
Society for Asian Art, San Francisco 16356
Society for the Arts, Religion and Contemporary Culture, Allentown 16451
Sumi-E Society of America, Bethesda 16613
Tamarind Institute, Albuquerque 16624
Ukrainian Academy of Arts and Sciences in the U.S., New York 16656
United States Committee of the International Association of Art, Washington 16685
Visual Arts Resource and Research Centre Relating to the Caribbean, New York 16731
Volunteer Committees of Art Museums of Canada and the United States, Tulsa 16735
Women's Caucus for Art, Philadelphia 16777
World Academy of Art and Science, Minneapolis 16784

Vatican City
Pontificia Insigne Accademia Artistica dei Virtuosi al Pantheon, Città del Vaticano 16865

Venezuela
Asociación Venezolana Amigos del Arte Colonial Caracas, Caracas 16879

Vietnam
Writers and Artists Union, Hanoi 16978

Yugoslavia
Akademia e Shkencave dhe e Arteve e Kosovës, Priština 16982
Crnogorska Akademija Nauka i Umjetnosti, Podgorica 16986
Srpska Akademija Nauka i Umetnosti, Beograd 17031

Zambia
Africa Association for Liturgy, Music and Arts, Lusaka 17045

Zimbabwe
Arts Association Harare, Harare 17061

Astronomy

Argentina
Asociación Argentina Amigos de la Astronomía, Buenos Aires 00036
Asociación Argentina de Astronomía, La Plata 00037

Australia
Astronomical Society of Australia, Sydney 00133
Astronomical Society of Queensland, Boondall 00134
Astronomical Society of South Australia, Adelaide 00135
Astronomical Society of Tasmania, Hobart 00136
Astronomical Society of Victoria, Melbourne 00137
Inter-Union Commission on Frequency Allocations for Radio Astronomy and Space Science, Epping 00300

Austria
Österreichische Gesellschaft für Weltraumforschung, Innsbruck 00697
Österreichischer Astronomischer Verein, Wien 00752

Belgium
Koninklijk Sterrenkundige Genootschap van Antwerpen, Antwerpen 01217
Société Astronomique de Liège, Liège 01238
Société Royale Belge d'Astronomie, de Météorologie et de Physique du Globe, Bruxelles 01277

Bermuda
Astronomical Society of Bermuda, Hamilton 01327

Bosnia and Hercegovina
Društvo Matematičara, Fizičara i Astronoma BiH, Sarajevo 01353

Brazil
Associação Internacional de Lunologia, São Paulo 01412

Canada
Canadian Astronomical Society, Montréal 01833
Royal Astronomical Society of Canada, Toronto 02338

Chile
Asociación Chilena de Astronomía y Astronáutica, Santiago 02447

China, People's Republic
Chinese Astronomical Society, Nanjing 02578

China, Republic
Astronomical Society of the Republic of China, Taipei 02675

Czech Republic
Česká Astronomická Společnost, Praha 02914

Ecuador
Sociedad Ecuatoriana de Astronomía, Quito 03246

Finland
Tähtitieteellinen Yhdistys Ursa, Helsinki 03446

France
Association Française d'Astronomie, Paris 03522
Association Française d'Observateurs d'Etoiles Variables, Strasbourg 03549
Association of French-Speaking Planetariums, Strasbourg 03627
Astronomical Data Centre, Strasbourg 03667
Committee on Space Research, Paris 03744
Société Astronomique de Bordeaux, Bordeaux 03953
Société Astronomique de France, Paris 03954
Société Astronomique de Lyon, Saint-Genis-Laval 03955
Union Astronomique Internationale, Paris 04297

Germany
Astronomische Gesellschaft e.V., Jena 04509
Deutsche Gesellschaft für Chronometrie e.V., Ditzingen 04765

Greece
Greek National Committee for Astronomy, Athinai 06239
Greek National Committee for Space Research, Athinai 06240

India
Astronomical Society of India, Hyderabad 06411
Indian Space Research Organization, Bangalore 06489

Indonesia
Astronomical Association of Indonesia, Jakarta 06554

Ireland
Irish Astronomical Society, Dublin 06622

Israel
Tel Aviv Astronomical Association, Tel Aviv 06751

Italy
Associazione Astrofili Bolognesi, Bologna 06901
Associazione Urania, Genova 07048
Gruppo Nazionale per l'Astronomia, Roma 07303
Società Astronomica Italiana, Firenze 07392

Japan
Ikomasan Tenmon Kyokai, Nara Ken 07734
Nihon Tenmon Gakkai, Tokyo 07860

Mexico
Sociedad Astronómica de México, México 08322

Netherlands
Nederlandse Astronomenclub, Leiden 08552

New Zealand
Royal Astronomical Society of New Zealand, Wellington 08741

Peru
Asociación Peruana de Astronomía, Lima 08987

Poland
Polskie Towarzystwo Astronomiczne, Warszawa 09089
Polskie Towarzystwo Milosników Astronomii, Kraków 09122

Portugal
Sociedade Astronómica de Portugal, Lisboa 09212

Russia
Astronomical and Geodesical Society, Moskva 09336

Slovakia
Slovenská Astronomická Spoločnosť, Tatranská Lomnica 09552

Slovenia
Društvo Matematikov, Fizikov i Astronomov Slovenije, Ljubljana 09585

South Africa
Astronomical Society of Southern Africa, Observatory 09611

Spain
Sociedad Astronómica de España y América, Barcelona 09808

Sweden
Svenska Astronomiska Sällskapet, Saltsjöbaden 09963

Switzerland
Schweizerische Astronomische Gesellschaft, Neukirch-Egnach 10257
Schweizerische Gesellschaft für Astrophysik und Astronomie, Binningen 10278
Société Astronomique Suisse, Neukirch 10496

United Kingdom
Association in Scotland to Research into Astronautics, Wishaw 10837
Astronomical Society of Edinburgh, Edinburgh 10939
British Astronomical Association, London 11050
British Interplanetary Society, London 11111
British National Committee on Space Research, London 11132
European Space Association, Stevenston 11506
Interplanetary Space Travel Research Association, London 11835
Northamptonshire Natural History Society and Field Club, Northampton 12054
Royal Astronomical Society, London 12173
Science and Engineering Research Council, Swindon 12285
Society for Popular Astronomy, Nottingham 12370
Webb Society, London 12563

U.S.A.
American Association of Variable Star Observers, Cambridge 12947
American Astronomical Society, Baton Rouge 12959
American Lunar Society, East Pittsburgh 13252
American Society for Mass Spectrometry, Santa Fe 13397
Association of Universities for Research in Astronomy, Washington 13858
Astrologers' Guild of America, Brewster 13873
Astronomical League, Rolling Meadows 13874
Astronomical Society of the Pacific, San Francisco 13875, 13876
Carnegie Institution of Washington, Washington 13975
IAU Commission on Bioastronomy, Moffett Field 14612
IAU Commission on Double and Multiple Stars, Washington 14613
IAU Commission on Exchange of Astronomers, Charlottesville 14614
IAU Commission on Galaxies, Irvine 14615
IAU Commission on Identificationand Protection of Observatory Sites, Seattle 14616
IAU Commission on Physical Study of Comets, Minor Planets and Meteorites, College Park 14617
IAU Commission on Positional Astronomy, Washington 14618

IAU Commission on Positions and Motions of Minor Planets, Comets, Satellites, Pasadena 14619
International Dark-Sky Association, Tucson 14991
International Planetarium Society, Prince Frederick 15154
Maria Mitchell Association, Nantucket 15525
Middle Atlantic Planetarium Society, Millersville 15569
Pacific Planetarium Association, Eugene 16120
Planetary Society, Pasadena 16175
Stonehenge Study Group, Santa Barbara 16606
United Planetary Federation, Chicago 16680
United States Antarctic Research Program, Arlington 16682
Universities Space Research Association, Columbia 16705
Von Braun Astronomical Society, Huntsville 16736

Yugoslavia

Association of the Mathematicians', Physicists' and Astronomers' Societies of Yugoslavia, Priština 16985
Savez Društava Matematičara, Fizičara i Astronoma Jugoslavije, Novi Sad 17018

Astrophysics

Australia

Astronomical Society of Australia, Sydney 00133

Italy

Gruppo Italiano di Fisica Cosmica, Roma 07293

Slovakia

Slovenská Meteorologická Spoločnost, Bratislava 09567

Switzerland

Schweizerische Gesellschaft für Astrophysik und Astronomie, Binningen 10278

U.S.A.

Association of Space Explorers, Washington 13835
IAU Commission on Space and High Energy Astrophysics, Cambridge 14620
National Association of State Park Directors, Tallahassee 15740
National Space Club, Washington 15978
National Space Society, Washington 15979
Space Studies Institute, Princeton 16592
URSI Commission on Ionospheric Radio and Propagation, Lowell 16721

Automotive Engineering
s. a. Machine Engineering

Canada

Electric Vehicle Association of Canada, Nepean 02087

Finland

Suomen Autoteknillinen Liitto, Helsinki 03390

France

Union Technique de l'Automobile, du Motocycle et du Cycle, Paris 04323

Germany

Bundesverband der freiberuflichen und unabhängigen Sachverständigen für das Kraftfahrzeugwesen e.V., Königswinter 04646
Forschungsvereinigung Automobiltechnik e.V., Frankfurt 05263
Forschungsvereinigung Verbrennungskraftmaschinen e.V., Frankfurt 05275
Normenausschuss Kraftfahrzeuge im DIN Deutsches Institut für Normung e.V., Frankfurt 05824
TÜV-Akademie Rheinland, Köln 05992
TÜV Akademie Westfalen, Bochum 05993
VDI-Gesellschaft Fahrzeug- und Verkehrstechnik, Düsseldorf 06006

India

Automotive Research Association of India, Pune 06412

Ireland

Society of the Irish Motor Industry, Dublin 06669

Italy

Centro Sviluppo Impiego Diesel, Trieste 07181
Federazione Italiana delle Scienze e delle Attività Motorie, Roma 07276

Russia

Automobile and Road Building Society, Moskva 09337

Switzerland

Fachgruppe Carosserie- und Fahrzeugtechnik des STV, Sissach 10109
International Solarcar Federation, Zürich 10178

United Kingdom

Motor Industry Research Association, Nuneaton 11959

U.S.A.

Electric Auto Association, Mountain View 14363
Society of Automotive Engineers International, Warrendale 16499

Aviation
s. Aeronautics, Aviation, Space Technology

Bacteriology
s. Microbiology

Banking
s. Finance

Behavioral Sciences
s. a. Psychology

Italy

International Society for Twin Studies, Roma 07327

South Africa

Primate Behaviour Research Group, Johannesburg 09652

United Kingdom

Association for the Study of Animal Behaviour, Saint Andrews 10831
Group-Analytic Society (London), London 11586
Institute for Sex Education and Research, Birmingham 11659
The Institute of Group-Analysis, London 11689

U.S.A.

American Institutes for Research in the Behavioral Sciences, Washington 13230
American Society of Trial Consultants, Towson 13495
Animal Behavior Society, Worcester 13540
Association for Advancement of Behavior Therapy, New York 13592
Association for the Behavioral Sciences and Medical Education, Phoenix 13679
Association for the Treatment of Sexual Abusers, Beaverton 13693
Association of Social and Behavioral Scientists, Washington 13833
Center for Advanced Study in the Behavioral Sciences, Stanford 13991
Council for Children with Behavioral Disorders, Reston 14206
International Association of Human-Animal Interaction Organizations, Renton 14853
International Society for Human Ethology, Detroit 15216
International Society for Research on Aggression, Ann Arbor 15246
NTL Institute for Applied Behavioral Science, Alexandria 16065
Society for the Scientific Study of Religion, West Lafayette 16469
Society of Behavioral Medicine, Rockville 16501

Biochemistry

Argentina

Asociación Argentina de Farmacia y Bioquímica Industrial, Buenos Aires 00044
Asociación Bioquímica Argentina, Buenos Aires 00052

Australia

Australasian Association of Clinical Biochemists, Mount Lawley 00140
Australian Biochemical Society, Canberra 00168

Austria

Internationale Gesellschaft für Getreidewissenschaft und -technologie, Schwechat 00522
Österreichische Biochemische Gesellschaft, Salzburg 00581

Azerbaijan

Azerbaijan Biochemical Society, Baku 00886

Belgium

Société Belge de Biochimie et de Biologie Moléculaire, Bruxelles 01241

Bulgaria

Bulgarian Biochemical and Biophysical Society, Sofia 01551

Chile

Sociedad de Bioquímica de Concepción, Concepción 02518
Sociedad de Bioquímica y Biología Molecular de Chile, Santiago 02519

China, People's Republic

The Chinese Society of Biochemistry and Molecular Biology, Beijing 02622

Czech Republic

Česká Parazitologická Společnost, Praha 02926

Finland

Societas Biochemica, Biophysica et Microbiologica Fenniae, Helsingin Yliopisto 03373

France

Société de Chimie Biologique, Paris 03965
Société Française de Biochimie et Biologie Moléculaire, Paris 04114
Société Française de Biologie Clinique, Paris 04115

Georgia

Georgian Society of Biochemists, Tbilisi 04346

Germany

Gesellschaft für Biochemie und Molekularbiologie e.V., Frankfurt am Main 05352

Hungary

Magyar Biokemiai Társaság, Budapest 06300

India

Society of Biological Chemists, India, Bangalore 06530

Israel

Biochemical Society of Israel, Rehovot 06683

Italy

Bioelectrochemical Society, Bologna 07050
Società Italiana di Biochimica, Perugia 07463
Società Italiana di Biochimica Clinica e Biologia Molecolare Clinica, Milano 07464
Società Italiana di Patologia Vascolare, Roma 07554

Malaysia

Malaysian Biochemical Society, Kuala Lumpur 08228

Mexico

Centro de Investigación y de Estudios Avanzados del Instituto Politécnico Nacional, México 08293

Netherlands

Het Nederlands Kanker Instituut, Amsterdam 08543

New Zealand

Australian Association of Clinical Biochemists – New Zealand Branch, Hamilton 08669
New Zealand Association of Clinical Biochemists, Wellington 08684
New Zealand Society for Biochemistry and Molecular Biology, Hamilton 08722

Poland

Polskie Towarzystwo Biochemiczne, Warszawa 09091

Portugal

Sociedade Portuguesa de Bioquímica, Lisboa 09229

Russia

Biochemical Society, Moskva 09338
National Committee of Biochemists, Moskva 09379

Slovakia

Slovenská Biochemiká Spoločnost, Bratislava 09553

South Africa

Physiological and Biochemical Society of Southern Africa, Pretoria 09648
Society of Physiologists, Biochemists and Pharmacologists, Pretoria 09662

Spain

Sociedad Española de Bioquímica y Biología Molecular, Madrid 09813

United Kingdom

The Association of Clinical Biochemists, London 10860
Biochemical Society, London 10965
Institute for Animal Health Pirbright, Pirbright Woking 11654
Phytochemical Society of Europe, Oxford 12105

U.S.A.

American Crystallographic Association, Buffalo 13113
American Society for Biochemistry and Molecular Biology, Bethesda 13370
American Society for Bone and Mineral Research, Washington 13371
Food and Nutrition Board, Washington 14446
International Isotope Society, Moorestown 15088
Pan American Association for Biochemistry and Molecular Biology, Kansas City 16132
Pan-American Association of Biochemistry and Molecular Biology, Kansas City 16133
Protein Society, Bethesda 16217

Vietnam

Vietnamese Association of Medical Biochemistry, Hanoi 16959

Biology

Algeria

Unité de Recherches sur les Resources Biologiques Terrestres, Alger 00011

Argentina

Asociación Argentina de Biología y Medicina Nuclear, Buenos Aires 00039
Sociedad Argentina de Biología, Buenos Aires 00086

Australia

Australian Federation for Medical and Biological Engineering, Parkville 00188
Australian Society for Limnology, Abbotsford 00230
Australian Society for Reproductive Biology, Newcastle 00235
Bio-Rhythm Research and Information Centre, Brisbane 00253
International Association of Environmental Mutagen Societies, Adelaide 00301

Austria

Gesellschaft der Freunde der Biologischen Station Wilhelminenberg, Wien 00456
Haus des Meeres Vivarium Wien, Wien 00495
Wiener Katholische Akademie, Wien 00870

Belgium

Asocio por la Enkonduko de Nova Biologia Nomenklaturo, Kalmthout 00940
European Community Biologists Association, Namur 01134
European Society for Radiation Biology, Liège 01161

Brazil

Centro de Biomédica de Campina Grande, Campina Grande 01431
Instituto Nacional de Pesquisas da Amazonia, Manaus 01489
International Seaweed Association, São Paulo 01498

Sociedade de Biologia do Brasil, Rio de Janeiro 01521
Sociedade de Biologia do Rio Grande do Sul, Pôrto Alegre 01522
Sociedade de Farmácia e Química de São Paulo, São Paulo 01526

Canada

Alberta Society of Professional Biologists, Edmonton 01642
Association des Biologistes du Québec, Montréal 01673
Canadian Association for Anatomy, Neurobiology and Cell Biology, Winnipeg 01792
Canadian Council of University Biology Chairs, Guelph 01862
Canadian Federation of Biological Societies, Ottawa 01879
Canadian Medical and Biological Engineering Society, Ottawa 01924
Canadian Quaternary Association, Fredericton 01958
Canadian Society of Environmental Biologists, Toronto 01995
Pulp and Paper Research Institute of Canada, Pointe Claire 02332

Chile

Sociedad de Biología de Chile, Santiago 02516
Sociedad de Biología de Concepción, Concepción 02517

China, People's Republic

The Chinese Society of Biochemistry and Molecular Biology, Beijing 02622

China, Republic

Biological Society of China, Taipei 02677

Colombia

Sociedad Colombiana de Biologí, Bogotá 02810

Cuba

Centro Nacional de Investigaciones Científicas, La Habana 02885

Czech Republic

Česká Biologicka Společnost, Brno 02915
Česká Společnost Bioklimatologická, Praha 02931
Česká Společnost pro Biomechaniku, Praha 02937

Denmark

Biologisk Selskab, København 02969
Dansk Biologisk Selskab, København 02988
Foreningen af Danske Biologer., Birkerød 03116

Egypt

Egyptian Organization for Biological Products and Vaccines, Giza 03281

Finland

Societas Biologica Fennica Vanamo, Helsingin Yliopisto 03374
Societas Entomologica Fennica, Helsinki 03375

France

Association Internationale de Médecine et de Biologie de l'Environnement, Paris 03571
Association pour le Développement des Etudes Biologiques en Psychiatrie, Paris 03646
Commission de l'Enseignement Supérieur en Biologie, Paris 03844
Fédération Générale des Syndicats de Biologistes, Paris 03844
International Commission for Plant-Bee Relationships, Lusignan 03902
Société Centrale d'Apiculture, Paris 03958
Société de Biologie, Paris 03963
Société de Biométrie Humaine, Paris 03964
Société d'Etudes et de Recherches Biologiques, Paris 04059
Société Internationale de Biologie Mathématique, Antony 04203
Syndicat National des Médecins Biologistes, Paris 04276
Union des Biologistes de France, Paris 04299
Union Internationale des Sciences Biologiques, Paris 04314
Union Nationale des Techniciens Biologistes, Le Perreux 04319

Germany

Arbeitsgemeinschaft wildbiologischer und jagdkundlicher Forschungsstätten, Bonn 04479

405 Subject Index: Business Administration, Management

France

International Commission for Plant-Bee Relationships, Lusignan 03902
Société Botanique de France, Paris 03956
Société des Lettres, Sciences et Arts La Haute-Auvergne, Aurillac 04040
Société d'Ethnozoologie et d'Ethnobotanique, Paris 04051
Société Française de Physiologie Végétale, Paris 04157
Société Française de Phytiatrie et de Phytopharmacie, Versailles 04159
Société Phycologique de France, Paris 04237

Germany

Bayerische Botanische Gesellschaft, München 04530
Deutsche Botanische Gesellschaft e.V., Göttingen 04718
Deutsche Gesellschaft für Qualitätsforschung (Pflanzliche Nahrungsmittel) e.V., Freising 04852
Deutsche Orchideen-Gesellschaft, Schloß Holte-Stukenbrock 04933
European Weed Research Society, Leverkusen 05170
Internationale Vereinigung für Vegetationskunde, Göttingen 05584
Vereinigung für angewandte Botanik, Göttingen 06122

Gibraltar

Gibraltar Ornithological and Natural History Society, Gibraltar 06209

India

Botanical Survey of India, Calcutta 06418
Indian Botanical Society, Madras 06446
Indian Phytopathological Society, New Dehli 06472
Indian Society of Genetics and Plant Breeding, New Dehli 06485
International Society of Plant Morphologists, Dehli 06497
Palynological Society of India, Thiruvananthapuram 06521

Israel

Botanical Society of Israel, Haifa 06684

Italy

Ente Fauna Siciliana, Noto 07236
Gruppo di Ricerca per i Virus e Virosi delle Piante, Sassari 07288
Gruppo di Ricerca per la Patologia delle Piante Ortensi, Torino 07289
Società Botanica Italiana, Firenze 07393
Società degli Amici del Museo Civico di Storia Naturale Giacomo Doria, Genova 07399
Società Italiana Amici dei Fiori, Firenze 07443
Società Italiana di Biogeografia, Siena 07465

Ivory Coast

African Oil Palm Development Association, Abidjan 07684

Japan

Nippon Shokubutsu Gakkai, Tokyo 07990
Nippon Shokubutsu Seiri Gakkai, Kyoto 07991
Shokubutsu Bunrui Chiri Gakkai, Kyoto 08029

Malta

Society for the Study and Conservation of Nature, Valletta 08252

Mexico

Sociedad Mexicana de Fitogenética, México 08339
Sociedad Mexicana de Fitopatología, Montecillo 08340

Moldova, Republic of

Society of Botanists of Moldova, Chişinău 08368
Society of Plant Physiologists of Moldova, Chişinău 08370

Netherlands

European Association for Research on Plant Breeding, Wageningen 08428
International Commission for the Nomenclature of Cultivated Plants, Wageningen 08484
Koninklijke Maatschappij Tuinbouw en Plantkunde, Den Haag 08509
Koninklijke Nederlandse Botanische Vereniging, Amsterdam 08515

New Zealand

New Zealand Society of Plant Physiologists, Levinj 08727
Systematics Association of New Zealand, Dunedin 08743

Norway

Norsk Botanisk Forening, Oslo 08816

Peru

Asociación Latinoamericana Científico de Plantas, Lima 08983

Philippines

Asian-Pacific Weed Science Society, Laguna 09035

Poland

Polskie Towarzystwo Botaniczne, Warszawa 09092

Portugal

Sociedade Broteriana, Coimbra 09213

Russia

Russian Botanical Society, St. Petersburg 09444

Slovakia

Slovenská Botanická Spoločnosť, Bratislava 09556

South Africa

The Botanical Society of South Africa, Claremont 09613
The South African Association of Botanists, Alice 09670
Succulent Society of South Africa, Pretoria 09716

Sweden

Bergianska Stiftelsen, Stockholm 09858
Lunds Botaniska Förening, Lund 09917
Svenska Botaniska Föreningen, Stockholm 09966
Svenska Växtgeografiska Sällskapet, Uppsala 10000

Switzerland

Bernische Botanische Gesellschaft, Bern 10051
Interessengemeinschaft der botanischen Gärten der Schweiz, Neuchâtel 10164
Schweizerische Botanische Gesellschaft, Zürich 10260
Schweizerische Dendrologische Gesellschaft, Andeer 10261

Thailand

Asian and Pacific Information Network on Medicinal and Aromatic Plants, Bangkok 10626

United Kingdom

Biodeterioration Society, Kew 10966
The Botanical Society of Scotland, Edinburgh 10988
Botanical Society of the British Isles, London 10989
British and European Geranium Society, Higher Poynton 11001
British Bryological Society, Cardiff 11055
British Lichen Society, London 11120
British Phycological Society, London 11148
British Society for Plant Pathology, Cambridge 11175
British Society of Flavourists, Haverhill 11193
CAB International, Wallingford 11231
CAB International Bureau of Plant Breeding and Genetics, Wallingford 11234
Flora Europaea Organization, Liverpool 11541
Institution of Plant Engineers, London 11753
International Organization of Palaeobotany, London 11809
National Institute of Agricultural Botany, Cambridge 12013
Northamptonshire Natural History Society and Field Club, Northampton 12054
Phytochemical Society of Europe, Oxford 12105
The Ray Society, London 12147

U.S.A.

American Association of Botanical Gardens and Arboreta, Wayne 12864
American Bamboo Society, La Jolla 12963
American Bryological and Lichenological Society, Lewiston 13014
American Chestnut Foundation, Bennington 13030
American Fern Society, Washington 13148
American Herb Association, Nevada City 13180
American Orchid Society, West Palm Beach 13295
American Phytopathological Society, Saint Paul 13332
American Society of Plant Physiologists, Rockville 13480
American Society of Plant Taxonomists, Notre Dame 13481
Aquatic Plant Management Society, Washington 13558
Association of Pacific Systematists, Fort Worth 13812
Botanical Society of America, Riverside 13941
Carnegie Institution of Washington, Washington 13975
Desert Botanical Garden, Phoenix 14296
International Botanical Congress, Saint Louis 14888
International Bulb Society, Culver City 14892
International Committee on Education in Mycology, Atlanta 14946
International Federation of Palynological Societies, Flagstaff 15021
International Geranium Society, Pasadena 15049
International Mycological Association, Baton Rouge 15114
International Organization for Succulent Plant Study, Phoenix 15132
International Organization of Plant Biosystematists, St. Louis MO 15137
International Plant Propagators Society, Seattle 15155
International Society of Photosynthesis Research, Urbana 15305
International Society of Plant Molecular Biology, Athens 15306
Magnolia Society, Cabin John 15520
Organization for Flora Neotropica, Bronx 16093
Society for Economic Botany, Columbia 16376
Torrey Botanical Club, Lawrence 16645
World Society for Mushroom Biology and Mushroom Products, New York 16837

Zimbabwe

Botanical Society of Zimbabwe, Harare 17062

Botany, Specific

Argentina

Asociación Argentina de Micología, Buenos Aires 00047

Czech Republic

Česká Vědecká Společnost pro Mykologii, Praha 02943

France

Société Française de Mycologie Médicale, Paris 04145
Société Mycologique de France, Paris 04224

Georgia

Georgian Botanical Society, Tbilisi 04338

Germany

Deutsche Gesellschaft für Pilzkunde, Karlsruhe 04842
Zentralstelle für Pilzforschung und Pilzverwertung, Waghäusel 06186

Italy

Associazione Micologica ed Ecologica Romana, Roma 06997
Unione Micologica Italiana, Bologna 07678

Japan

Nihon Ishinkin Gakkai, Tokyo 07801
Nihon Kin Gakkai, Tokyo 07812

Malaysia

ASEAN Plant Quarantine Centre and Training Institute, Serdang 08214

Netherlands

Nederlandse Mycologische Vereniging, Wyster 08560

United Kingdom

British Association Representing Breeders, Norfolk 11049
British Iris Society, Great Bookham 11112
Heather Society, Ipswich 11610
International Mycological Institute, Egham 11807

U.S.A.

Medical Mycological Society of the Americas, Baltimore 15547
North American Mycological Association, Ann Arbor 16042

Building and Construction s. Civil Engineering

Business Administration, Management

Australia

Accounting Association of Australia and New Zealand, Melbourne 00116
Australian Institute of Management, Saint Kilda 00200
Institute of Public Affairs, Jolimont 00296

Austria

Gesellschaft für Strategische Unternehmensführung, Innsbruck 00482
Österreichische Gesellschaft für Operations Research, Wien 00669
Österreichische Gesellschaft für Warenkunde und Technologie, Wien 00696
Österreichische Verwaltungswissenschaftliche Gesellschaft, Wien 00743
Österreichisches Produktivitäts- und Wirtschaftlichkeits-Zentrum, Wien 00778

Belgium

China-Europe Management Institute, Bruxelles 01028
Euro-China Research Association in Management, Bruxelles 01071
Euro-China Research Centre for Business Cooperation, Bruxelles 01072
European Accounting Association, Bruxelles 01078
European Association for Research in Industrial Economics, Bruxelles 01088
European Federation of Energy Management Associations, Antwerpen 01157
Institut Belge des Sciences Administratives, Bruxelles 01191
International Institute for Organizational and Social Development, Leuven 01206

Brazil

Associação Prudentina de Educação e Cultura, Presidente Prudente 01419

Canada

Canadian Academic Accounting Association, Hamilton 01767
Canadian Institute for Organization Management, Ottawa 01903
Canadian Institute of Chartered Accountants, Toronto 01905
Canadian Institute of Management, North York 01912
Canadian Operational Research Society, Ottawa 01934
Canadian Research Management Association, Ottawa 01961
Canadian Society for Engineering Management, North York 01974
Conference Board of Canada, Ottawa 02069
Society of Management Accountants of Canada, Hamilton 02388

China, People's Republic

Asian Pacific Federation of Human Resource Management, Hong Kong 02540
Chinese Research Society for the Modernization of Management, Beijing 02605
Hong Kong Management Association, Hong Kong 02652

China, Republic

Asia-Pacific Office Automation Council, Taipei 02666
China Association of the Five Principles of Administrative Authority, Taipei 02679
Cooperative League of the Republic of China, Taipei 02718
Public Administration Society of China, Taipei 02748

Costa Rica

Central American Institute for Business Administration, Alajuela 02850

Denmark

Foreningen af Danske Civiløkonomer, København 03117

Egypt

Arab Management Society, Cairo 03261

Finland

Työtehoseura, Helsinki 03459

France

Association Française de Management, Paris 03530
Association Internationale de l'Inspection du Travail, Paris 03569
Association Internationale des Docteurs en Economie du Tourisme, Aix-en-Provence 03581
Association Internationale pour le Management du Sport, Saint-Michel 03601
Association Technique pour l'Etude de la Gestion des Institutions Publiques et des Entreprises Privées, Paris 03665
Centre de Rencontres et d'Etudes des Dirigeants des Administrations Fiscales, Paris 03677
Community of European Management Schools, Jouy-en-Josas 03745

Germany

Akademie Führung und Organisation, Bonn 04382
Akademie für Führungskräfte der Wirtschaft e.V., Bad Harzburg 04387
Akademie für Organisation, Bonn 04393
Arbeitsgemeinschaft für wirtschaftliche Verwaltung e.V., Eschborn 04457
Arbeitskreis für Betriebsführung München, Thaining 04488
ASB Management-Zentrum-Heidelberg e.V., Heidelberg 04504
Betriebswirtschafts-Akademie e.V., Wiesbaden 04574
Bildungswerk der Rheinland-Pfälzischen Wirtschaft e.V., Mainz 04592
Bildungswerk der Sächsischen Wirtschaft e.V., Dresden 04593
Bildungswerk der Thüringer Wirtschaft e.V., Erfurt 04594
Bildungszentrum Tannenfelde, Studien- und Fördergesellschaft der Schleswig-Holsteinischen Wirtschaft e.V., Aukrug 04597
Bundesausschuß Betriebswirtschaft, Eschborn 04635
Deutsche Gesellschaft für Personalführung e.V., Düsseldorf 04836
Deutsche Management Akademie Niedersachsen, Celle 04917
Deutscher Juristinnenbund, Vereinigung der Juristinnen, Volkswirtinnen und Betriebswirtinnen e.V., Bonn 05019
Deutsches Institut für Betriebswirtschaft e.V. (CIB), Frankfurt 05083
Deutsches Institut für Wertanalyse e.V., Frankfurt/Main 05091
Euro-Handelsinstitut e.V., Köln 05131
Europäischer Verband für Produktivitätsförderung, Hamburg 05151
European Council of Management, Eschborn 05160
Forschungsinstitut für Rationalisierung e.V., Aachen 05252
Fortbildungsakademie der Wirtschaft, Köln 05279
Gesellschaft für Arbeitswissenschaft e.V., Dortmund 05348
Gesellschaft für Informationsvermittlung und Technologieberatung, München 05374
Institut für Technik der Betriebsführung im Handwerk, Karlsruhe 05541
Normenausschuss Bürowesen im DIN Deutsches Institut für Normung e.V., Berlin 05795
Rationalisierungs-Gemeinschaft Bauwesen im RKW, Eschborn 05903
Rationalisierungs-Gemeinschaft Verpackung im RKW, Eschborn 05904
Rationalisierungs-Kuratorium der Deutschen Wirtschaft e.V., Eschborn 05905
Rationalisierungs-Kuratorium der Deutschen Wirtschaft e.V., Landesgruppe Baden-Württemberg, Stuttgart 05906
Rationalisierungs-Kuratorium der Deutschen Wirtschaft e.V., Landesgruppe Berlin, Berlin 05907
Rationalisierungs-Kuratorium der Deutschen Wirtschaft e.V., Landesgruppe Bremen, Bremen 05908
Rationalisierungs-Kuratorium der Deutschen Wirtschaft e.V., Landesgruppe Hamburg, Hamburg 05909
Rationalisierungs-Kuratorium der Deutschen Wirtschaft e.V., Landesgruppe Hessen, Eschborn 05910
Rationalisierungs-Kuratorium der Deutschen Wirtschaft e.V., Landesgruppe Niedersachsen, Hannover 05911
Rationalisierungs-Kuratorium der Deutschen Wirtschaft e.V., Landesgruppe Nord-Ost, Kiel 05912
Rationalisierungs-Kuratorium der Deutschen Wirtschaft e.V., Landesgruppe Nordrhein-Westfalen, Düsseldorf 05913
Rationalisierungs-Kuratorium der Deutschen Wirtschaft e.V., Landesgruppe Rheinland-Pfalz, Mainz 05914

Subject Index: Business Administration, Management 406

REFA-Verband für Arbeitsstudien und Betriebsorganisation e.V., Darmstadt 05917
Schmalenbach-Gesellschaft, Berlin 05943
Südwestdeutsche Akademie für Marketing und Kommunikation e.V., Stuttgart 05979
Vereinigung der Versicherungs-Betriebswirte e.V., Köln 06116
Volks- und Betriebswirtschaftliche Vereinigung im Rheinisch-Westfälischen Industriegebiet e.V., Duisburg 06140
Wuppertaler Kreis e.V., Köln 06174

Greece
Ellinikon Kentron Paragogikotitos, Athinai 06228

Hungary
Szervezési és Vezetési Tudományos Társaság, Budapest 06357

India
Asian Center for Organization, Research and Development, New Delhi 06404
Institute of Chartered Accountants of India, New Delhi 06493
National Productivity Council, New Delhi 06519

Indonesia
ASEAN Energy Management and Research Training Centre, Jakarta 06544

Iran
Iran Management Association, Teheran 06563

Ireland
Institute of Management Consultants in Ireland, Dublin 06612
Irish Management Institute, Dublin 06631
Irish Productivity Centre, Dublin 06638

Israel
Israel Institute of Productivity, Tel Aviv 06704

Italy
Accademia degli Incamminati, Modigliana 06774
Associazione Italiana di Ricerca Operativa, Genova 06961
Associazione Italiana di Studio delle Relazioni Industriali, Roma 06967
Comitato Nazionale Italiana per l'Organizzazione Scientifica, Roma 07201
Societá Italiana di Aziendologia, Milano 07462
Società Italiana per la Organizzazione Internazionale, Roma 07591
Società Italiana per l'Organizzazione Internazionale, Roma 07601
Società per la Formazione la Ricerca e l'Addestramento per le Aziende e le Organizzazioni, Milano 07628

Japan
Asian Productivity Organization, Tokyo 07713
Japan Techno-Economics Society, Tokyo 07740
Nippon Gyosei Gakkai, Tokyo 07897
Nippon Keiei Gakkai, Tokyo 07925
Nippon Noritsu Kyokai Shiryoshitsu, Tokyo 07953
Nippon Shogyo Gakkai, Tokyo 07987
Seisan Gijutsu Kenkyusho, Tokyo 08015

Kenya
Church Organization Research and Advisory Trust of Africa, Nairobi 08083

Netherlands
International Academy of Management, Den Haag 08475
Nederlandse Vereniging voor Management, Den Haag 08591
Nederlandse Vereniging voor Personeelbeleid, Utrecht 08601
Nederlandse Vereniging voor Produktieleiding, Den Haag 08602

New Zealand
The New Zealand Institute of Management, Wellington 08707

Nigeria
Nigerian Institute of Management, Lagos 08780

Norway
Høyokoleutdannedes Forbund, Oslo 08791
Den Polytekniske Forening, Oslo 08875

Pakistan
Institute of Cost and Management Accountants of Pakistan, Karachi 08899
Pakistan Council of Scientific and Industrial Research, Karachi 08917

Philippines
Asian Institute of Management, Manila 09032
Association of Deans of Southeast Asian Graduate Schools of Management, Makati City 09041

Poland
Towarzystwo Naukowe Organizacji i Kierownictwa, Warszawa 09158

Portugal
Associação Portuguesa de Management, Lisboa 09183

Russia
Council for the Study of Productive Forces, Moskva 09349

Senegal
Centre Africain d'Etudes Supérieures en Gestion, Dakar 09512

South Africa
The South African Institute of Organization and Methods, Pretoria 09686

Sweden
Akademikerförbundet SSR, Stockholm 09855
European Federation of Productivity Services, Stockholm 09874
Företagsekonomiska Föreningen, Stockholm 09880
Sveriges Rationaliseringsförbund, Stockholm 10011

Switzerland
Europäische Organisation für Qualität, Bern 10091
Fachgruppe für das Management im Bauwesen des SIA, Zürich 10114
Gesellschaft für Führungspraxis und Personalentwicklung, Feldmeilen 10139
International Industrial Relations Association, Genève 10171
International Institute for Management Development, Lausanne 10172
Schweizerische Gesellschaft für Personalfragen, Zürich 10324
Schweizerische Management-Gesellschaft, Zürich 10372
Schweizerische Zentralstelle für Baurationalisierung, Zürich 10424
Schweizerischer Verband für Betriebsorganisation und Fertigungstechnik, Winterthur 10469

Tanzania
Association of Management Training Institutions of Eastern and Southern Africa, Arusha 10592
Eastern and Southern African Management Institute, Arusha 10601

Thailand
Asian and Pacific Project for Labour Administration, Bangkok 10627

Trinidad and Tobago
Caribbean Industrial Research Institute, Tunapuna 10660

United Kingdom
Association for Information Management, London 10808
Association of Principals of Colleges (Northern Ireland Branch), Lisburn 10910
Association of Scientific, Technical and Managerial Staffs, London 10919
Association of Teachers of Management, London 10924
Association of University Teachers in Accounting, Sheffield 10931
Chartered Institute of Public Finance and Accountancy, London 11274
Commonwealth Association for Public Administration and Management, London 11316
Commonwealth Partnership for Technology Management, London 11332
European Council for Industrial Marketing, Brixham 11489
European Group for Organization Studies, Plymouth 11497
Institute of Administrative Management, Orpington 11662
Institute of Business Administration, Wigan 11666
Institute of Directors, London 11681
Institute of Management, London 11699
Institute of Management Services, Enfield 11700
Institute of Personnel and Development, London 11709
International Management Centre from Buckingham, Buckingham 11804
Management Research Groups, Corby 11902
Manpower Society, London 11909
Production Mangagement Action Group, Henley-on-Thames 12130
Society of Business Economists, Watford 12414

U.S.A.
Academy of Management, Briarcliff Manor 12662
Academy of Marketing Science, Coral Gables 12663
AMA International, New York 12735
American Accounting Association, Sarasota 12802
American Collegiate Retailing Association, New Orleans 13082
American Institute of Management, Quincy 13218
American Management Association International, New York 13255
Arab Management Society, Buffalo 13560
Association for Systems Management, Cleveland 13671
Association for the Management of Information Technology in Higher Education, Boulder 13685
Association for University Business and Economic Research, Indianapolis 13698
Association of Internal Management Consultants, East Bloomfield 13778
Association of North American Operations Research Societies within IFORS, Linthicum 13804
Association of Research Directors, King of Prussia 13824
Business Professionals of America, Columbus 13957
Career College Association, Washington 13972
Consortium for Graduate Study in Management, Saint Louis 14174
Council of Consulting Organizations, New York 14229
Direct Marketing Educational Foundation, New York 14306
East-West Management Institute, New York 14336
Foundation for Accounting Education, New York 14457
Foundation for Enterprise Development, La Jolla 14462
Graduate Management Admission Council, Santa Monica 14520
Human Resource Certification Institute, Alexandria 14593
Human Resource Planning Society, New York 14594
Industrial Relations Research Association, Madison 14650
The Institute of Management Sciences, Providence 14716
International Association for Management of Technology, Coral Gables 14801
International Association of Career Consulting Firms, Reston 14836
International Development Research Council, Norcross 14994
International Institute of Tourism Studies, Washington 15082
International Management Development Association, Hummelstown 15107
International Personnel Management Association, Alexandria 15148
Joseph H Lauder Institute of Management and International Studies, Philadelphia 15454
Latin American Management Association, Washington 15479
National Association of Supervisors of Business Education, Fort Worth 15746
National Business Education Association, Reston 15767
National Center for Housing Management, Washington 15783
National Institute of Management Counsellors, Great Neck 15921
National Records Management Council, New York 15960
Office Systems Research Association, Springfield 16078
Operation Enterprise, Hamilton 16083
Operations Research Society of America, Baltimore 16084
Organization Development Institute, Chesterland 16092
Project Management Institute, Upper Darby 16216
Small Enterprise Education and Promotion Network, New York 16335
Social Sciences Services and Resources, Wasco 16342
Society for Advancement of Management, Vinton 16348
Society for Human Resource Management, Alexandria 16392
Society for Information Management, Chicago 16400
Society for Range Management, Denver 16436
Society for the Preservation of American Business History, Williamsburg 16463
Society of Logistics Engineers, New Carrollton 16533
Strategic Management Society, West Lafayette 16607
World Academy of Productivity Science, Blacksbury 16785
World Federation of Personnel Management Associations, Alexandria 16814

Venezuela
Consejo Zuliano de Planificación y Coordinación, Maracaibo 16911

Virgin Islands (U.S.)
Consortium of Caribbean Universities for Resource Management, Saint Thomas 16981

Yugoslavia
Jugoslovenski Zavod za Produktivnost Rada, Beograd 17002

Cancer Research s. Cell Biology, Cancer Research

Cardiology

Australia
The Cardiac Society of Australia and New Zealand, Sydney 00256

Austria
Österreichische Kardiologische Gesellschaft, Wien 00713

Belgium
Société Belge de Cardiologie, Bruxelles 01242

Bulgaria
Bulgarian Society of Cardiology, Sofia 01565

Canada
Canadian Cardiovascular Society, Westmount 01843
Canadian Diabetes Association, Toronto 01869
Canadian Society of Cardiology Technologists, Winnipeg 01990
Cardiology Technologists Association of British Columbia, Vancouver 02028
Cardiology Technologists Association of Ontario, London 02029
Heart and Stroke Foundation of Alberta, Calgary 02121

Chile
Sociedad Chilena de Cardiología y Cirugía Cardiovascular, Santiago 02479

China, Republic
International Academy of Chest Physicians and Surgeons of the American College of Chest Physicians, Republic of China Chapter, Taipei 02727
Republic of China Society of Cardiology, Taipei 02750

Colombia
Sociedad Colombiana de Cardiología, Bogotá 02811

Costa Rica
Asociación de Cardiología, San José 02847

Denmark
Dansk Cardiologisk Selskab, Herlev 02991

France
Société Française de Cardiologie, Paris 04116
Syndicat National des Médecins Français Spécialistes des Maladies du Coeur et des Vaisseaux, Paris 04281

Germany
Deutsche Gesellschaft für Kardiologie – Herz- und Kreislaufforschung, Düsseldorf 04803

Greece
Elliniki Kardiologiki Etairia, Athinai 06219

Hungary
Magyar Kardiologusok Társasága, Budapest 06320

Italy
Associazione Italiana di Cardiostimolazione, Pisa 06939
Società Italiana di Cardiologia, Roma 07471

Japan
Japanese Circulation Society, Kyoto 07742

Korea, Republic
Asian-Pacific Society of Cardiology, Seoul 08122

Mexico
Sociedad Interamericana de Cardiología, México 08328
Sociedad Mexicana de Cardiología, México 08335

Netherlands
Association of European Paediatric Cardiologists, Nijmegen 08400
European Society of Cardiology, Rotterdam 08453
Nederlandse Vereniging voor Cardiologie, Nieuwegein 08582

Poland
Polskie Towarzystwo Kardiologiczne, Warszawa 09114

Portugal
Sociedade Portuguesa de Cardiologia, Lisboa 09230

Romania
Societatea de Cardiologie, Bucuresti 09286

Russia
Society of Cardiology, Moskva 09460

South Africa
Southern Africa Cardiac Society, Durban 09710

Switzerland
Schweizerische Gesellschaft für Kardiologie, Bern 10303
Société et Fédération Internationale de Cardiologie, Genève 10502

Turkey
Türk Kardiyoloji Derneği, Istanbul 10706

United Kingdom
British Cardiac Society, London 11057
Northern Ireland Chest, Heart and Stroke Association, Belfast 12058
Society of Thoracic and Cardiovascular Surgeons of Great Britain and Ireland, Conventry 12446

U.S.A.
Academy of Veterinary Cardiology, Floral Park 12676
American Association of Cardiovascular and Pulmonary Rehabilitation, Middleton 12866
American College of Cardiology, Bethesda 13039
American College of Chest Physicians, Northbrook 13040
American Heart Association, Dallas 13179
American Society of Cardiovascular Professionals/Society for Cardiovascular Management, Fredericksburg 13430
American Society of Echocardiography, Raleigh 13447
American Society of Extra-Corporeal Technology, Reston 13448
Association of Physician Assistants in Cardiovascular Surgery, Reston 13816
Cardiovascular Credentialing International, Virginia Beach 13970
Cardiovascular System Dynamics Society, Philadelphia 13971
Coronary Club, Cleveland 14197
Council on Arteriosclerosis of the American Heart Association, Dallas 14243
Heart Disease Research Foundation, Brooklyn 14554
Inter American Heart Foundation, Dallas 14741
International Atherosclerosis Society, Houston 14879
International Cardiology Foundation, Dallas 14895
International Society for Cardiovascular Surgery, Manchester 15197
International Society for Heart and Lung Transplantation, Dallas 15212

409 Subject Index: Communications

U.S.A.
Academy of Motion Picture Arts and Sciences, Beverly Hills *12664*
Academy of Science Fiction, Fantasy and Horror Films, Los Angeles *12672*
American Film Institute, Washington *13149*
Anthology Film Archives, New York *13549*
Black Filmmakers Hall of Fame, Oakland *13928*
Consortium of College and University Media Centers, Ames *14178*
Dance Films Association, New York *14283*
International Animated Film Society, Burbank *14779*
International Council – National Academy of Television Arts and Sciences, New York *14975*
International Council of Kinetography Laban, Columbus *14978*
International Film Seminars, New York *15036*
Society for Cinema Studies, Knoxville *16364*
Society for the Furtherance and Study of Fantasy and Science Fiction, Madison *16454*
Society of Motion Picture and Television Art Directors, Studio City *16537*
Society of Motion Picture and Television Engineers, White Plains *16538*
University Film and Video Association, Los Angeles *16712*

Civil Engineering s. a. Architecture; Urban and Regional Planning

Argentina
Grupo Latinoamericano de R.I.L.E.M., Buenos Aires *00078*

Australia
Australian National Committee on Large Dams, Brisbane *00215*
Eastern Dredging Association, Brisbane *00268*
Water Authorities Association of Victoria, Melbourne *00382*

Austria
Forschungsgesellschaft für das Verkehrs- und Straßenwesen im ÖIAV, Wien *00445*
Forschungsgesellschaft für Wohnen, Bauen und Planen, Wien *00447*
Österreichischer Stahlbauverband, Wien *00766*

Belgium
European Convention for Constructional Steelwork, Bruxelles *01140*
Union Belge des Géomètres-Experts Immobiliers, Bruxelles *01303*

Bulgaria
Scientific and Technical Union of Civil Engineering, Sofia *01580*
Scientific and Technical Union of Water Works, Sofia *01589*

Canada
Alberta Construction Association, Edmonton *01624*
Canadian Construction Association, Ottawa *01857*
Canadian Sheet Steel Building Institute, Cambridge *01965*
Canadian Society for Civil Engineering, Montréal *01967*

Chile
Colegio de Arquitectos de Chile, Santiago *02456*

China, Republic
Chinese Institute of Civil and Hydraulic Engineering, Taipei *02697*

Denmark
Dansk Geoteknisk Forening, Lyngby *03010*
Dansk Selskab for Bygningsstatik, Lyngby *03057*

Egypt
General Organization for Housing and Building Research, Cairo *03291*

France
Association Française de Recherches d'Essais sur les Matériaux et les Constructions, Paris *03534*
Association Internationale des Travaux en Souterrain, Bron *03591*
Commission Internationale des Grands Barrages, Paris *03737*
European Committee of Construction Economists, Paris *03812*
Office Général du Bâtiment et des Travaux Publics, Paris *03923*
Organisation Scientifique des Industries du Bâtiment, Paris *03937*
Réunion Internationale des Laboratoires d'Essais et de Recherche sur les Matériaux et les Constructions, Cachan *03943*

Germany
Arbeitsgemeinschaft für zeitgemässes Bauen e.V., Kiel *04458*
Deutsche Gesellschaft für Baukybernetik e.V, Holzminden *04758*
Deutsche Gesellschaft für Erd- und Grundbau e.V., Essen *04776*
Deutscher Ausschuss für Stahlbau, Köln *04994*
Deutscher Stahlbau-Verband, Köln *05045*
Fakultätentag für Bauingenieur- und Vermessungswesen, Dresden *05212*
Forschungsgesellschaft für Strassen- und Verkehrswesen e.V., Köln *05242*
Forschungsinstitut für Wärmeschutz e.V. München (FIW), Gräfelfing *05253*
Fraunhofer-Gesellschaft zur Förderung der angewandten Forschung e.V., München *05288*
Gesellschaft des Bauwesens e.V., Eschborn *05341*
Hafenbautechnische Gesellschaft e.V., Hamburg *05451*
Institut für Bauforschung e.V., Hannover *05522*
Intitut für Baustoffprüfung und Fußbodenforschung, Troisdorf *05594*
Kuratorium für Technik und Bauwesen in der Landwirtschaft e.V., Darmstadt *05698*
Normenausschuss Akustik, Lärmminderung und Schwingungstechnik im DIN Deutsches Institut für Normung e.V., Berlin *05787*
Normenausschuss Bauwesen im DIN Deutsches Institut für Normung e.V., Berlin *05790*
Rationalisierungs-Gemeinschaft Bauwesen im RKW, Eschborn *05903*
Studiengemeinschaft für Fertigbau e.V., Wiesbaden *05964*
Studiengemeinschaft Holzleimbau e.V., Düsseldorf *05965*
VDI-Gesellschaft Bautechnik, Düsseldorf *06003*

Hungary
Epitéstudományi Egyesület, Budapest *06288*

Italy
Associazione Italiana di Genio Rurale, Padova *06948*
Associazione Italiana per la Promozione degli Studi e delle Ricerche per l'Edifizia, Milano *06974*
Associazione Italiana Tecnico-Economica del Cemento, Roma *06991*
Tecnocasa, L'Aquila *07660*

Japan
Doboku-Gakkai, Tokyo *07723*
Doshitsu Kogakkai, Tokyo *07724*
Nihon Kensetsu Kikaika Kyokai, Tokyo *07809*

Malta
Chamber of Architects and Civil Engineers, Saint Andrews *08242*

Netherlands
European Asphalt Pavement Association, Breukelen *08418*
International Federation for Housing and Planning, Den Haag *08486*
Stichting Economisch Instituut voor de Bouwnijverheid, Amsterdam *08624*

New Zealand
The New Zealand National Society for Earthquake Engineering, Wellington *08719*

Norway
Norske Sivilingeniørers Forening, Oslo *08867*

Pakistan
Pakistan Concrete Institute, Karachi *08915*

Peru
Asociación de Ingenieros Civiles del Perú, Lima *08981*

Russia
Automobile and Road Building Society, Moskva *09337*

South Africa
The South African Institution of Civil Engineering, Yeoville *09690*
South African National Group of the International Society for Rock Mechanics, Marshalltown *09695*

Spain
International Association for Shell and Spatial Structures, Madrid *09771*
Sociedad Española de Mecánica del Suelo y Cimentaciones, Madrid *09818*

Sweden
Sveriges Civilingenjörsförbund, Stockholm *10005*

Switzerland
EUROPAN SUISSE – Verein zur Förderung des exemplarischen Wohnungsbaus, Lausanne *10093*
Fachgruppe für Brückenbau und Hochbau des SIA, Zürich *10113*
Fachgruppe für industrielles Bauen des SIA, Zürich *10116*
Fachgruppe für Untertagbau des SIA, Zürich *10118*
Internationale Vereinigung für Brückenbau und Hochbau (IVBH), Zürich *10186*
Schweizerische Vereinigung der Baufachlehrer, Luzern *10394*
Schweizerische Zentralstelle für Baurationalisierung, Zürich *10424*
Schweizerischer Ingenieur- und Architekten-Verein, Zürich *10450*

United Kingdom
The Association of Building Engineers, Northampton *10857*
British Tunnelling Society, London *11208*
Building Services Research and Information Association, Bracknell *11227*
The Chartered Institute of Building, Ascot *11270*
Chartered Institution of Building Services Engineers, London *11276*
Construction Industry Research and Information Association, London *11343*
Dry Stone Walling Association, Oswestry *11403*
The Institute of Concrete Technology, Beaconsfield *11674*
Institute of Construction Management, London *11675*
The Institution of Civil Engineers, London *11734*
Institution of Highways and Transportation, London *11745*
Scottish Association for Building Education and Training, Paisley *12291*
Society for Earthquake and Civil Engineering Dynamics, London *12353*
Structural Fire Protection Association, London *12478*
Timber Research and Development Association, High Wycombe *12505*

U.S.A.
American Concrete Institute, Detroit *13087*
American Institute of Building Design, Westport *13208*
American Institute of Constructors, Saint Petersburg *13211*
American Institute of Steel Construction, Chicago *13226*
American Society of Civil Engineers, Reston *13434*
Associated Schools of Construction, Peoria *13588*
Association of Asphalt Paving Technologists, Saint Paul *13731*
Building Officials and Code Administrators International, Country Club Hills *13951*
Construction Specifications Institute, Alexandria *14182*
Expanded Shale Clay and Slate Institute, Salt Lake City *14404*
Federation of Societies for Coatings Technology, Blue Bell *14429*
International Bridge, Tunnel and Turnpike Association, Washington *14890*
International Conference of Building Officials, Whittier *14956*
International Foundation for Earth Construction, Lafayette *15041*
Masonry Society, Boulder *15535*
National Conference of States on Building Codes and Standards, Herndon *15809*
Reinforced Concrete Research Council, Austin *16261*
Southern Building Code Congress – International, Birmingham *16583*
United States Committee on Large Dams, Denver *16687*

Cocoa s. Coffee, Tea, Cocoa

Coffee, Tea, Cocoa

Italy
Centro Luigi Lavazza per gli Studi e Ricerche sul Caffe', Torino *07098*

U.S.A.
American Cocoa Research Institute, McLean *13035*

Commerce

Germany
Forschungsstelle für den Handel Berlin (FfH) e.V., Berlin *05259*
Forschungsverband für den Handelsvertreter- und Handelsmaklerberuf, Köln *05261*
HWWA – Institut für Wirtschaftsforschung – Hamburg, Hamburg *05501*
Zentralstelle für Berufsbildung im Einzelhandel e.V., Köln *06185*

Ireland
Irish Institute of Purchasing and Materials Management, Dublin *06630*

Italy
Centro per gli Studi sui Sistemi Distributivi e il Turismo, Milano *07104*
Società d'Incoraggiamento d'Arti e Mestieri, Milano *07419*

Malta
Malta Society of Arts, Manufactures and Commerce, Valletta *08248*

Russia
Society for Trade and Commerce, Moskva *09459*

Switzerland
Schweizerische Vereinigung für die Vereinfachung der Verfahren im internationalen Handel, Bern *10402*
Verband Schweizerischer Handelsschulen, Wabern *10538*

United Kingdom
Institute for Supervision and Management, Lichfield *11660*
Institute of Small Business, London *11723*
Royal Society for the Encouragement of Arts, Manufactures and Commerce, London *12249*

U.S.A.
International Policy Council on Agriculture and Trade, Washington *15156*
International Society of Business, Economics and Ethics, Lawrence *15278*

Communication Science

Austria
Kontext – Institut für Kommunikations- und Textanalysen, Wien *00545*
Mediacult – Internationales Forschungsinstitut für Medien, Kommunikation und kulturelle Entwicklung, Wien *00555*
Österreichische Gesellschaft für Filmwissenschaft, Kommunikations- und Medienforschung, Wien *00630*
Österreichische Gesellschaft für Kommunikationsfragen, Salzburg *00655*

Canada
Commonwealth Association for Education in Journalism and Communication, London *02062*

France
Association pour la Fondation Internationale du Cinéma et de la Communication Audiovisuelle, Paris *03629*

Germany
Akademie für Kommunikation Baden-Württemberg e.V., Stuttgart *04389*
Bildungswerk des Instituts für angewandte Kommunikationsforschung in der außerschulischen Bildung e.V., Bonn *04595*
Deutsche Gesellschaft für Kommunikationsforschung, München *04808*
Deutsche Gesellschaft für Publizistik- und Kommunikationswissenschaft e.V., Leipzig *04850*
Deutsches Institut für angewandte Kommunikation und Projektförderung e.V., Bonn *05082*
Münchner Kreis, München *05758*
Südwestdeutsche Akademie für Marketing und Kommunikation e.V., Stuttgart *05979*

Italy
Accademia di Relazioni Pubbliche, Roma *06808*
Accademia Prenestina del Cimento di Musica, Lettere, Scienze, Arti Visive e Figurative, Palestrina *06869*
Centro Internazionale di Documentazione e Comunicazione, Roma *07065*
Istituto Italiano di Pubblicismo, Roma *07350*

Jamaica
Caribbean Institute of Mass Communications, Mona *07691*

Japan
Denshi Joho Tsushin Gakkai, Tokyo *07722*

Kenya
African Council for Communication Education, Nairobi *08064*

Malaysia
Asian Institute for Development Communication, Kuala Lumpur *08218*

Senegal
Association des Professionnelles Africaines de la Communication, Dakar *09508*

Switzerland
Schweizerische Gesellschaft für Kommunikations- und Medienwissenschaft, Bern *10308*
Schweizerische Studiengesellschaft für Kommunikation und Administration, Bern *10389*
Wissenschaftliche Vereinigung zur Pflege von Rhtorik, Informationsverarbeitung und Kommunikation, Zürich *10575*

United Kingdom
Industrial Society, London *11650*

U.S.A.
Association for Communication Administration, Annandale *13611*
Association for Progressive Communications, San Francisco *13654*
Association for the Development of Religious Information Systems, Milwaukee *13683*
Association of Biomedical Communication Directors, Tucson *13737*
Council for Biomedical Communications Associations, Ann Arbor *14205*
Foundation for International Exchange of Scientific and Cultural Information by Telecommunications, Philadelphia *14467*
International Association for Media and Communication Research, Washington *14805*
International Communication Association, Austin *14952*
International Society for Intercommunications of New Ideas, Jamaica Plain *15221*
International Training in Communication, Anaheim *15345*
The Media Institute, Washington *15544*
World Communication Association, Huntington Beach *16806*

Communications

Australia
Inter-Union Commission on Frequency Allocations for Radio Astronomy and Space Science, Epping *00300*

Belgium
Union Radio-Scientifique Internationale, Gent *01309*

Bulgaria
Scientific and Technical Union of Energetics, Sofia *01581*

Canada
Alberta Educational Communications Corporation, Edmonton *01627*

Germany
Informationstechnische Gesellschaft im VDE, Frankfurt *05512*

Italy
Associazione Studi sull'Informazione, Milano *07043*
Istituto Internazionale delle Comunicazioni, Genova *07340*

411 Subject Index: Dairy Science

Saudi Arabia
Arab Security Studies and Training Center, Riyadh *09488*

Sweden
Svenska Kriminalistföreningen, Stockholm *09982*

United Kingdom
Citizens Protection Society, London *11296*

U.S.A.
American Correctional Association, Lanham *13095*
American Criminal Justice Association – Lambda Alpha Epsilon, Sacramento *13111*
American Society of Criminology, Columbus *13442*
Association of Forensic Document Examiners, Minneapolis *13774*
International Association for the Study of Organized Crime, Chicago *14824*
National Center for Computer Crime Data, Santa Cruz *15779*
National Council on Crime and Delinquency, San Francisco *15849*
National Crime Prevention Institute, Louisville *15859*
National Criminal Defense College, Macon *15860*

Yugoslavia
Savez Udruženja za Krivično Pravo i Kriminolgiju Jugoslavije, Beograd *17028*

Crop Husbandry

Belgium
European Crop Protection Association, Bruxelles *01144*

Costa Rica
Central American, Mexican and Caribbean Network for Bean Research, San José *02853*

Germany
Gemeinschaft zur Förderung der privaten deutschen Pflanzenzüchtung e.V., Bonn *05310*

Japan
Nihon Sakumotsu Gakkai, Tokyo *07840*
Nippon Shokubutsu-Byori Gakkai, Tokyo *07989*

Mexico
Comisión Latinoamericana de Investigadores en Sorgo, México *08299*

Netherlands
Centrum voor Plantenveredelings- en Reproduktieonderzoek, Wageningen *08409*
European Association for Research on Plant Breeding, Wageningen *08428*

Peru
CIAT Andean Zone Network for Bean Research, Lima *08995*

United Kingdom
Scottish Society for Crop Research, Dundee *12318*

Virgin Islands (U.S.)
Caribbean Food Crops Society, Saint Croix *16979*

Cultural History, History of Civilization

Algeria
El-Djazairia El-Mossilia, Alger *00006*

Andorra
Associació Cultural i Artística Els Esquirols, La Massana *00012*

Austria
Commission Internationale d'Histoire du Sel, Innsbruck *00428*
Österreichische Byzantinische Gesellschaft, Wien *00584*
Österreichische Gesellschaft für Amerikastudien, Salzburg *00603*
Österreichisches Ost- und Südosteuropa-Institut, Wien *00777*

Barbados
Caribbean Conservation Association, Saint Michael *00925*

Belgium
Association des Diplomés en Histoire de l'Art et Archéologie de l'Université Catholique de Louvain, Louvain-la-Neuve *00950*
European Association for Burgundy Studies, Bruxelles *01084*

Brazil
Instituto Brasileiro de Educácão, Ciencia e Cultura, Rio de Janeiro *01464*
Instituto Nami Jafet para o Progreso da Ciência e Cultura, São Paulo *01495*
Sociedade Brasileira de Cultura, São Paulo *01508*

Canada
Canadian Association for the Advancement of Netherlandic Studies, Wolfville *01805*
Canadian Committee of Byzantinists, Waterloo *01855*
Canadian Railroad Historical Association, Saint Constant *01959*
Canadian Rodeo Historical Association, Calgary *01962*
Canadian Science and Technology Historical Association, Ottawa *01964*
Canadian Society for the History and Philosophy of Science, Burnaby *01982*
Micmac Association for Cultural Studies, Sydney *02207*
Ontario Electric Railway Historical Association, Milton *02278*
Postal History Society of Canada, Carleton Place *02314*
Society for the Study of Egyptian Antiquities, Toronto *02384*

China, People's Republic
Royal Asiatic Society, Hong Kong Branch, Hong Kong *02658*

Cuba
Casa de las Américas, La Habana *02881*
Sociedad Cubana de Historia de la Medicina, La Habana *02891*

Czech Republic
Česká Komise pro UNESCO, Praha *02922*

Denmark
Dansk Medicinsk-Historisk Selskab, København *03030*
Skandinavisk Museumsforbund, Danish Section, København *03211*

Egypt
The Egyptian Society for the Dissemination of Universal Culture and Knowledge, Cairo *03284*

France
Arab World Institute, Paris *03504*
Association pour la Recherche Interculturelle, Saint-Denis *03638*
Commission Internationale d'Etudes Historiques Latinoaméricaines et des Caraïbes, Paris *03738*
European Association for Chinese Studies, Paris *03795*
Institut Français d'Etudes Byzantines, Paris *03886*
International Association of Sanskrit Studies, Paris *03899*
Société de l'Histoire de l'Art Français, Paris *03981*
Société Française d'Histoire de la Médecine, Reims *04183*

Germany
Baltische Gesellschaft in Deutschland e. V., München *04521*
Deutsche Gesellschaft für Geschichte der Medizin, Naturwissenschaft und Technik e.V., Regensburg *04787*
Deutscher Kulturrat, Bonn *05025*
European Association for Japanese Studies, Duisburg *05152*
Frobenius-Gesellschaft e.V., Frankfurt *05303*
Gesellschaft für Theatergeschichte, Berlin *05410*
Herder-Institut e.V., Marburg *05470*
Kulturkreis der deutschen Wirtschaft im Bundesverband der Deutschen Industrie e.V., Köln *05691*
Kulturwerk für Südtirol e.V., München *05693*
Leiterkreis der Katholischen Akademien, Stuttgart *05716*
Moses Mendelssohn Zentrum für europäisch-jüdische Studien, Potsdam *05753*
Nordfriisk Institut, Bräist *05781*
Ost-Akademie e.V., Lüneburg *05866*
Peter-Schwingen-Gesellschaft e.V., Bonn *05879*
Rat für Soziokultur im Deutschen Kulturrat, Bonn *05901*
Verband Deutscher Kunsthistoriker e.V., München *06042*
Verein von Altertumsfreunden im Rheinlande, Bonn *06103*
Zentralinstitut für Kunstgeschichte, München *06183*

Greece
Etaireia Byzantinon Spoudon, Athinai *06235*

Hungary
Magyar Müvelódési Intézet, Budapest *06328*

India
All-India Oriental Conference, Pune *06397*
International Tamil People Promotive Organization, Chennai *06498*

Israel
Yad Izhak Ben-Zvi, Jerusalem *06753*

Italy
Accademia delle Scienze e delle Arti degli Ardenti di Viterbo, Viterbo *06788*
Accademia di Scienze, Lettere e Arti, Lucca *06810*
Accademia Raffaello, Urbino *06871*
Accademia Spoletina, Spoleto *06880*
Associazione Nazionale per i Centri Storico-Artistici, Gubbio *07017*
Centro di Studi e Ricerche di Museologia Agraria, Milano *07061*
Centro per la Storia della Tradizione Aristotelica Nel Veneto, Padova *07109*
Centro Ricerche di Storia e Arte Bitontina, Bitonto *07119*
Centro Studi Storici di Mestre, Mestre *07175*
Consiglio Nazionale per i Beni Culturali e Ambientali, Roma *07214*
Istituto di Diritto Romano e dei Diritti dell'Oriente Mediterraneo, Roma *07335*
Istituto Italiano di Storia della Chimica, Roma *07351*
Istituto Nazionale di Studi Etruschi ed Italici, Firenze *07363*
Società Italiana di Storia della Medicina, Bologna *07575*
Società Italiana per l'Archeologia e la Storia delle Arti, Napoli *07593*
Società Tarquiniense d'Arte e Storia, Tarquinia *07648*
Società Tiburtina di Storia e d'Arte, Tivoli *07650*

Japan
Suifumeitokukai Shokokan, Ibaraki-ken *08032*

Jordan
Royal Academy for Islamic Civilization Research, Amman *08056*

Korea, Republic
Academy of Korean Studies, Kyonggi-do *08117*
Royal Asiatic Society, Korea Branch, Seoul *08142*

Kuwait
National Council for Culture, Arts and Literature, Safat *08145*

Macedonia
Društvo na Istoričarite na Umetnosta od Makedonija, Skopje *08180*

Netherlands
Comité International d'Histoire de l'Art, Utrecht *08412*
Koninklijk Oudheidkundig Genootschap Amsterdam, Amsterdam *08506*
Raad Cultuur, Den Haag *08617*

New Zealand
Commonwealth Heraldry Board, Auckland *08670*

Pakistan
Lok Virsa, Islamabad *08906*
Research Society of Pakistan, Lahore *08931*

Peru
Sociedad Peruana de Historia de la Medicina, Lima *09016*

Poland
Katowickie Towarzystwo Spoleczno-Kulturalne, Katowice *09075*
Polskie Towarzystwo Historii Medycyny i Farmacji, Warszawa *09110*
Stowarzyszenie Historyków Sztuki, Warszawa *09148*

Portugal
Academia Internacional da Cultura Portuguesa, Lisboa *09173*

Singapore
Singapore Society of Asian Studies, Singapore *09544*

Slovakia
Slovenská Spoločnost pre Dejiny Vied a Techniky pri SAV, Bratislava *09575*

Slovenia
Slovensko Umetnostno Zgodovinsko Društvo, Ljubljana *09594*

Spain
Comité International Permanent des Etudes Mycéniennes, Vitoria *09747*
Real Institutode Estudios Asturianos, Oviedo *09796*

Sweden
Statens Kulturråd, Stockholm *09942*

Switzerland
Association des Instituts d'Etudes Européennes, Genève *10035*
Interessengemeinschaft für die Volkskultur in der Schweiz und dem Fürstentum Liechtenstein, Jona *10165*
Schweizerische Gesellschaft für Altertumswissenschaft, Fribourg *10275*
Schweizerische Gesellschaft für Geschichte der Medizin und der Naturwissenschaften, Bern *10297*
Schweizerische Gesellschaft Pro Technorama, Winterthur *10351*

United Kingdom
Association of European Open Air Museums, Chichester *10878*
British Archaeological Association, London *11005*
British Association for American Studies, Leicester *11008*
British Postmark Society, Chorley *11150*
British Vexillological Society, Beckenham *11216*
Centre for Iberian Studies, Keele *11261*
The Costume Society, Bristol *11350*
Disinfected Mail Study Circle, London *11392*
The Ephemera Society, London *11460*
Furniture History Society, London *11554*
Hertfordshire Local History Council, Hitchin *11616*
Institute for Cultural Research, Tunbridge Wells *11656*
Local Population Studies Society, London *11881*
Printing Historical Society, London *12125*
Scottish Society for The Preservation of Historical Machinery, Glasgow *12320*
Scottish Society of The History of Medicine, Aberdeen *12321*
Society for South Asian Studies, London *12381*

U.S.A.
American Association for the History of Medicine, Boston *12852*
American Institute for Patristic and Byzantine Studies, Kingston *13202*
American Institute of the History of Pharmacy, Madison *13227*
American Society for Ethnohistory, Ithaca *13385*
Buffalo Bill Memorial Association, Cody *13950*
Forest History Society, Durham *14450*
ICOM International Committee for Egyptology, Boston *14628*
Institute of Early American History and Culture, Williamsburg *14702*
International Academy of Culture and Political Science, Huntsville *14764*
International Arthur Schnitzler Research Association, San Bernardino *14780*
International Committee for Pre-Ottoman and Ottoman Studies, Minneapolis *14942*
Judaica Society, Maplewood *15459*
Lexington Group in Transportation History, Saint Cloud University *15498*
Mid-Continent Railway Historical Society, North Freedom *15567*
National Association for Outlaw and Lawman History, Harker Heights *15652*
North American Society for Sport History, University Park *16049*
Postal History Society, Pikesville *16192*
Society for Creative Anachronism, Santa Cruz *16372*
Society for the History of Technology, Auburn *16458*
Tennessee Folklore Society, Murfreesboro *16633*

Venezuela
Sociedad Venezolana de Historia de la Medicina, Caracas *16931*

Cybernetics

Austria
Forschungsgesellschaft für Psycho-Elektronik und Kybernetik, Wien *00446*
Österreichische Studiengesellschaft für Kybernetik, Wien *00738*

Belgium
Association Internationale de Cybernétique, Namur *00964*

France
Association Française pour la Cybernetique Economique et Technique, Paris *03553*
Centre International de Cyto-Cybernétique, Paris *03685*

Germany
Deutsche Gesellschaft für Baukybernetik e.V, Holzminden *04758*

Greece
European Institute of Environmental Cybernetics, Athinai *06238*

Japan
Tokei Kagaku Kenkyukai, Fukuoka *08040*

Slovakia
Slovenská Spoločnost pre Kybernetiku a Informatiku, Bratislava *09576*

U.S.A.
American Society for Cybernetics, Fairfax *13378*

Dairy Science

Belgium
Société Nationale de Laiterie, Bruxelles *01273*

Denmark
Dansk Mejeringeniør Forening, Odense *03033*

Egypt
Egyptian Society of Dairy Science, Cairo *03285*

France
Centre Technique et de Promotion des Laitiers Sidérurgiques, Paris La Défense *03698*

Italy
Centro Lattiero Caseario di Assistenza e Sperimentazione Antonio Bizzozero, Parma *07096*

Norway
Norske Meierifolks Landsforening, Oslo *08862*

United Kingdom
British Goat Society, Bovey Tracey *11087*
Society of Dairy Technology, Huntingdon *12422*

U.S.A.
Dairy Research Foundation, Oak Grove Village *14278*
Dairy Society International, Chambersburg *14279*
National Dairy Council, Rosemont *15861*

Data Processing s. Computer and Information Science, Data Processing

Decorative Arts s. Graphic and Decorative Arts, Design

United Kingdom
British Diabetic Association, London *11071*

U.S.A.
American Association of Diabetes Educators, Chicago *12883*
American Diabetes Association, Alexandria *13124*
International Diabetes Federation, Alexandria *14996*
International Society for Pediatric and Adolescent Diabetes, Waltham *15234*
Joslin Diabetes Center, Boston *15455*
Juvenile Diabetes Foundation International, New York *15463*

Dietetics s. Nutrition

Documentation

Argentina
Centro Argentino de Información Científica y Tecnológica, Buenos Aires *00063*

Austria
Österreichische Gesellschaft für Dokumentation und Information, Wien *00625*

Belgium
Association Belge de Documentation, Bruxelles *00942*
Association Professionnelle des Bibliothécaires et Documentalistes, Thy-le-Château *00985*
INBEL, Institut Belge d'Information et de Documentation, Bruxelles *01183*

Brazil
Comissão Brasileira de Documentâcão Agricola, Brasília *01449*

Canada
Association pour l'Avancement des Sciences et des Techniques de la Documentation, Montréal *01730*
Canadian Institute for Historical Microreproductions, Ottawa *01902*
International Association of Music Libraries, Archives and Documentation Centres, Ottawa *02149*
Société des Auteurs, Recherchistes, Documentalistes et Compositeurs, Montréal *02375*

Congo, Democratic Republic
Association Zaïroise des Archivistes, Bibliothécaires et Documentalistes, Kinshasa *02832*

Costa Rica
Inter-American Association of Agricultural Librarians and Documentalists, Turrialba *02862*

Dominican Republic
Servicio de Documentación y Biblioteca, Santo Domingo *03228*

Egypt
National Information and Documentation Centre, Cairo *03299*

France
Association des Professionnels de l'Information et de la Documentation, Paris *03518*
Association pour la Médiathèque Public, Cambrai *03634*
Bureau International de Documentation, Paris *03669*
Centre d'Etudes, de Documentation, d'Information et d'Action Sociales, Paris *03678*
Comité International pour l'Information et la Documentation en Sciences Sociales, Paris *03722*
International Association of Agricultural Information Specialists, Montpellier *03897*
Société d'Etudes et de Documentation Economiques, Industrielles et Sociales, Rueil-Malmaison *04058*
Union Française des Organismes de Documentation, Paris *04305*

Germany
Arbeitsgemeinschaft für juristisches Bibliotheks- und Dokumentationswesen, Würzburg *04450*
AWV-Fachausschuss Mikrofilm/Optische Informationssysteme, Eschborn *04517*
Berliner Arbeitskreis Information, Berlin *04547*
Deutsche Gesellschaft für Dokumentation e.V., Frankfurt/Main *04770*
Deutsche Gesellschaft für Filmdokumentation, Wiesbaden *04781*
Deutsche Gesellschaft für Medizinische Informatik, Biometrie und Epidemiologie, Köln *04817*
Deutsches Institut für medizinische Dokumentation und Information, Köln *05087*
Gesellschaft für Bibliothekswesen und Dokumentation des Landbaues, Freising *05351*
Immuno, Heidelberg *05506*
Institut für nationale und internationale Fleisch- und Ernährungswirtschaft, Heidelberg *05532*
Normenausschuss Bibliotheks- und Dokumentationswesen im DIN Deutsches Institut für Normung e.V., Berlin *05792*
VDD-Berufsverband Dokumentation, Information, Kommunikation, Bonn *05998*
Zentralstelle für Agrardokumentation und -information, Bonn *06184*

Indonesia
Asosiasi Perpustakaan, Arsip dan Dokumentasi Indonesia, Jakarta *06553*

Italy
Associazione Internazionale Centro Studi di Storia e Documentazione delle Regioni, Reggio Emilia *06924*
Associazione Italiana di Documentazione e di Informazione, Roma *06946*
Cenacolo Triestino, Trieste *07051*
Centro di Documentazione, Pistoia *07056*
Centro Internazionale di Documentazione e Comunicazione, Roma *07065*
Centro per la Documentazione Automatica, Milano *07106*
Documentation and Research Centre, Roma *07231*
International Centre for Advanced Technical and Vocational Training, Torino *07314*
Società Italiana per gli Archivi Sanitari Ospedalieri, Viareggio *07587*
SVP Italia, Milano *07657*

Japan
Gakujutsu Bunken Fukyu-Kai, Tokyo *07726*
Kagaku Gijutsu Shinko Jigyodan, Saitama *07747*
Nippon Dokumenesyon Kyokai, Tokyo *07888*

Madagascar
Association des Bibliothécaires, Documentalistes, Archivistes et Muséographes de Madagascar, Antananarivo *08208*

Mauritania
Association Mauritanienne des Bibliothécaires, Archivistes et Documentalistes, Nouakchott *08253*

Morocco
Centre National de Documentation, Rabat *08382*

Netherlands
Federatie van Organisaties van Bibliotheek-, Informatie-, Dokumentatiewezen, Delft *08454*
Fédération Internationale d'Information et de Documentation, Den Haag *08455*
International Bureau of Fiscal Documentation, Amsterdam *08482*
Nederlandse Vereniging van Bibliothecarissen, Documentalisten en Literatuuronderzoekers, Utrecht *08571*
Rijksbureau voor Kunsthistorische Documentatie, Den Haag *08620*

Paraguay
Comisión Paraguaya de Documentación e Información, Asunción *08961*

Portugal
Associação Portuguesa de Bibliotecários, Arquivistas e Documentalistas, Lisboa *09177*
Junta Nacional de Investigação Científica e Tecnológica, Lisboa *09200*

Senegal
Association Sénégalaise de Bibliothécaires, Archivistes et Documentalistes, Dakar *09511*
Ecole de Bibliothécaires, Archivistes et Documentalistes, Dakar *09516*

Sweden
Tekniska Litteratursällskapet, Stockholm *10018*

Switzerland
Centre Suisse de Documentation en Matière d'Enseignement et d'Education, Grand-Saconnex *10061*
Institut de Recherche et de Documentation Pédagogique, Neuchâtel *10160*
Schweizerische Vereinigung für Dokumentation, Zürich *10403*

Thailand
Asian Institute of Technology Library and Regional Documentation Centre, Bangkok *10631*

Togo
Association Togolaise pour le Développement de la Documentation, des Bibliothèques, Archives et Musées, Lomé *10650*

Trinidad and Tobago
Caribbean Documentation Centre, Port of Spain *10658*

Tunisia
Association Tunisienne des Bibliothécaires, Documentalistes et Archivistes, Tunis *10685*

U.S.A.
American College of Oral and Maxillofacial Surgeons, San Antonio *13063*
ICOM International Committee for Documentation, Santa Monica *14627*
International Documentary Association, Los Angeles *14997*
IUAES Commission on Documentation, Gainesville *15395*

Yugoslavia
Jugoslovenski Centar za Tehničku i Naučnu Dokumentaciju, Beograd *17000*

Ecology

Algeria
Unité de Recherches sur les Resources Biologiques Terrestres, Alger *00011*

Andorra
Associació per la Defensa de la Natura, Andorra la Vella *00013*

Argentina
Asociación Argentina de Ecología, Córdoba *00042*

Australia
Australian Agricultural and Resource Economics Society, Canberra *00156*
Australian Conservation Foundation, Fitzroy *00176*
Australian Council of National Trusts, Civic Square *00179*
Clean Air Society of Australia and New Zealand, Eastwood *00258*
Commission for the Conservation of Antarctic Marine Living Resources, Hobart *00259*
Ecological Society of Australia, Canberra *00269*
Field Naturalists Club of Victoria, Blackburn *00277*
The Field Naturalists' Society of South Australia, Adelaide *00278*
Native Plants Preservation Society of Victoria, Toorak *00314*
Natural Resources Conservation League of Victoria, Springvale South *00315*
North Queensland Naturalists Club, Cairns *00316*
Plant Protection Society of Western Australia, Victoria Park *00321*
The Queensland Naturalists' Club, Brisbane *00323*
The Western Australian Naturalists' Club, Nedlands *00387*
Western Australian Shell Club, Perth *00388*
Wildlife Conservation Society, Lavington *00389*
Wildlife Preservation Society of Australia, Sydney *00390*

Austria
International Institute for Applied Systems Analysis, Laxenburg *00514*
Ökosoziales Forum, Wien *00568*
Österreichische Gesellschaft für Humanökologie, Wien *00643*
Österreichische Gesellschaft und Institut für Umweltschutz, Umwelttechnologie und Umweltwissenschaften, Wien *00704*
Österreichische Gesellschaft zur Föderung von Umweltschutz und Energieforschung, Wien *00708*
Österreichischer Arbeitsring für Lärmbekämpfung, Wien *00751*
Österreichischer Naturschutzbund, Salzburg *00762*
Österreichischer Verband für Strahlenschutz, Seibersdorf *00768*

Bahamas
Bahamas National Trust, Nassau *00898*

Barbados
Caribbean Conservation Association, Saint Michael *00925*

Belgium
Bureau International de la Récupération et du Recyclage, Bruxelles *01000*
Comité International de Recherche et d'Etude de Facteurs de l'Ambiance, Bruxelles *01039*
Committee on the Challenges of Modern Society, Bruxelles *01046*
European Association against Fibre Pollution, Bruxelles *01081*
European Bureau for Conservation and Development, Bruxelles *01111*
European Centre for Ecotoxicology and Toxicology of Chemicals, Bruxelles *01118*
European Centre for Plastics in the Environment, Bruxelles *01121*
European Environment Agency, Bruxelles *01149*
European Environment Information and Observation Network, Bruxelles *01150*
European Environmental Bureau, Bruxelles *01151*
Institut Européen d'Ecologie et de Cancérologie, Bruxelles *01192*
Koninklijke Vereniging voor Natuur- en Stedeschoon, Antwerpen *01224*
Société Internationale pour la Recherche sur les Maladies de Civilisation et sur l'Environnement, Bruxelles *01270*

Bermuda
Bermuda Audubon Society, Hamilton *01328*

Brazil
Associação Brasileira de Engenharia Sanitária e Ambiental, Rio de Janeiro *01394*
Instituto de Planejamento de Pernambuco, Recife *01468*
Instituto Nacional de Pesquisas da Amazonia, Manaus *01489*

Canada
Canadian Institute of Treated Wood, Ottawa *01916*
Canadian Society of Environmental Biologists, Toronto *01995*
Canadian Water Quality Association, Waterloo *02023*
Pollution Probe Foundation, Toronto *02313*

Chile
Sociedad de Vida Silvestre de Chile, Temuco *02529*

China, People's Republic
Chinese Society of Environmental Sciences, Beijing *02625*
Ecological Society of China, Beijing *02645*

China, Republic
Asian Ecological Society, Taichung *02669*

Denmark
Danmarks Naturfredningsforening, København *02979*
Dansk Økologisk Forening Oikos, København *03044*
Det Danske Hedeselskab, Viborg *03091*
Euroenviron, København *03107*

Ethiopia
African Forum for Mathematical Ecology, Asmara *03326*
Desert Locust Control Organization for Eastern Africa, Addis Ababa *03332*

Finland
International Peat Society, Jyskä *03354*

France
Association Française pour la Protection des Eaux, Paris *03554*
Association Internationale de Médecine et de Biologie de l'Environnement, Paris *03571*
Association Nationale pour la Protection des Eaux, Paris *03621*
Association pour la Prévention de la Pollution Atmosphérique, Paris *03635*
Centre Naturopa, Strasbourg *03697*
Conseil Mondial d'Ethique des Droits de l'Animal, Asnières *03775*
European and Mediterranean Plant Protection Organization, Paris *03793*
Fédération Française des Sociétés de Protection de la Nature, Paris *03841*
Fédération Française des Sociétés de Sciences Naturelles, Paris *03842*
Program on Man and the Biosphere, Paris *03942*
Scientific Committee on Problems of the Environment, Paris *03944*
Société Française d'Ecologie, Brunoy *04168*
Société Française d'Ichtyologie, Paris *04186*
Société Internationale de Recherches pour l'Environnement et la Santé, Paris *04208*
Société Nationale de Protection de la Nature, Paris *04226*
Société pour la Protection des Paysages, Sites et Monuments, Paris *04238*
Universités Unies pour l'Environnement, Paris *04325*

Georgia
Commission on Biosphere and Ecology Research, Tbilisi *04333*

Germany
Akademie für Natur- und Umweltschutz beim Ministerium für Umwelt und Verkehr Baden-Württemberg, Stuttgart *04391*
Aktionsgemeinschaft Natur- und Umweltschutz Baden-Württemberg, Stuttgart *04408*
Alfred Toepfer Akademie für Naturschutz, Schneverdingen *04412*
Arbeitsgemeinschaft für Landschaftsentwicklung, Bonn *04453*
Arbeitsgemeinschaft für Umweltfragen e.V., Bonn *04456*
Arbeitskreis Chemische Industrie, Köln *04483*
Arbeitskreis Verkehr und Umwelt e.V., Berlin *04498*
Badischer Landesverein für Naturkunde und Naturschutz e.V., Freiburg *04520*
Bayerische Akademie für Naturschutz und Landschaftspflege, Laufen *04529*
Bund für Umwelt und Naturschutz Deutschland e.V., Bonn *04614*
Bund für Umwelt und Naturschutz Deutschland, Landesverband Hessen e.V., Mörfelden-Walldorf *04615*
Bund Naturschutz in Bayern e.V., Regensburg *04617*
Bundesverband beruflicher Naturschutz, Bonn *04640*
Bundesverband der Diplom-Ingenieure Gartenbau und Landespflege e.V., Bonn *04645*
Bundesverband wissenschaftlicher Vogelschutz e.V., Kiel *04675*
Dachverband wissenschaftlicher Gesellschaften der Agrar-, Forst-, Ernährungs-, Veterinär- und Umweltforschung e.V., Frankfurt *04701*
Deutsche Gesellschaft für Gartenkunst und Landschaftspflege e.V., Berlin *04784*
Deutsche Gesellschaft für Umwelterziehung e.V., Hamburg *04870*
Deutscher Naturschutzring e.V., Dachverband der deutschen Natur- und Umweltschutzverbände, Bonn *05034*
Deutscher Rat für Landespflege, Bonn *05038*
E.-F.-Schumacher-Gesellschaft für politische Ökologie e.V., München *05116*
Energie- und Umweltzentrum am Deister e.V., Springe-Eldagsen *05121*
European Water Pollution Control Association e.V., Hennef *05169*
Forschungsgemeinschaft Eisenhüttenschlacken e.V., Duisburg *05229*
Forschungsgesellschaft Landschaftsentwicklung Landschaftsbau e.V., Bonn *05244*
Fortbildungszentrum Gesundheits- und Umweltschutz Berlin e.V., Berlin *05280*
Fraunhofer-Gesellschaft zur Förderung der angewandten Forschung e.V., München *05288*
Gesellschaft für Naturkunde in Württemberg e.V., Stuttgart *05389*
Gesellschaft für Strahlen- und Umweltforschung, Ergersheim *05407*
Gesellschaft für Technologiefolgenforschung e.V. (GTF), Berlin *05409*
Gruppe Ökologie, Hannover *05446*
Institut für angewandte Verbraucherforschung e.V., Köln *05519*
Institut für Energie- und Umweltforschung Heidelberg e.V., Heidelberg *05525*
Institut für Europäische Umweltpolitik, Bonn *05526*
Institut für gewerbliche Wasserwirtschaft und Luftreinhaltung e.V., Köln *05529*
Institut für ökologische Forschung und Bildung e.V., Münster *05535*

Economics

421 Subject Index: Education

Educational Television Association, York 11437
Esperanto Teachers Association, Leicester 11464
European Association for Special Education, Birmingham 11474
European Association of Establishments for Veterinary Education, Roslin 11477
European Council of International Schools, Petersfield 11490
European Design Education Network, Glasgow 11494
Federal Trust for Education and Research, London 11523
General Studies Association, York 11564
General Teaching Council for Scotland, Edinburgh 11565
Girl's Schools Association, Oxford 11572
Greater London Federation of Parent-Teacher Associations, London 11584
Head Teachers' Association of Scotland, Glasgow 11607
Higher Education Funding Council for England, Bristol 11621
History of Education Society, Leicester 11630
Honours Graduate Teachers' Association, Ayr 11632
Independent Schools Joint Committee, Petersfield 11647
International Association of Teachers of English as a Foreign Language, Whitstable 11771
International Study Group for Mathematics Learning, London 11823
Jersey Association of The National Association of Schoolmasters, Saint Saviour's 11843
The Joint Association of Classical Teachers, London 11848
League for the Exchange of Commonwealth Teachers, London 11867
London Association of Science Teachers, London 11884
Mathematical Instruction Subcommittee, London 11919
Medau Society of Great Britain and Northern Ireland, London 11921
The Montessori Society A.M.I. (UK), London 11955
Museum Training Institute, Bradford 11963
Music Advisers' National Association, Warwick 11966
National Association for Environmental Education (UK), Walsall 11975
National Association for Multiracial Education, Slough 11976
National Association for Outdoor Education, Sheffield 11977
National Association for Road Safety Instruction in Schools, London 11978
National Association for The Teaching of English, Sheffield 11981
National Association of Head Teachers, Haywards Heath 11984
National Association of Schoolmasters, Birmingham 11987
National Association of Teachers in Further and Higher Education, London 11988
National Associations of Teachers of Home Economics and Technology, London 11990
National Campaign for Nursery Education, London 11995
National Christian Education Council, Birmingham 11996
National Conference of University Professors, Newcastle upon Tyne 11997
National Council for Educational Technology, Coventry 11998
National Council of Jewish Religious Day Schools, London 12000
National Education Association, Tewin Wood 12003
National Foundation for Educational Research in England and Wales, Slough 12007
National Society (Church of England) for Promoting Religious Education, London 12020
National Society for Education in Art and Design, Corsham 12022
National Strict Baptist Sunday School Association, Bishops Stortford 12026
National Union of Teachers, London 12030
Open and Distance Learning Quality Council, London 12064
Organisation of Teachers of Transport Studies, Southall 12070
Philosophy of Education Society of Great Britain, Coleraine 12102
Polish Educational Society, London 12115
Professional Association of Teachers, Derby 12131
Right to a Comprehensive Education, London 12159
Royal College of Physicians, London 12189
Royal Society for the Encouragement of Arts, Manufactures and Commerce, London 12249
School Natural Science Society, Gillingham 12284
Scottish Association of Geography Teachers, Hamilton 12294
Scottish Secondary Teachers' Association, Edinburgh 12317
Socialist Educational Association, Stockport 12343
Society for Education in Film and Television, London 12354
Society for Interactive Learning, Ryton 12360
Society for Promotion of Educational Reform through Teacher Training, London 12373
Society for Research in The Psychology of Music and Music Education, Dagenham 12378
Society for Research into Higher Education, London 12379
Society for The Health Education, London 12384
Society for The Protection of Science and Learning, London 12393
Society of Assistants Teaching in Preparatory Schools, Altrincham 12411
Society of Indexers, London 12432
Society of Public Teachers of Law, Buckingham 12441
Society of Teachers in Business Education, Sheffield 12444
Sound Learning Society, Rickmansworth 12454
South Place Ethical Society, London 12458
UK Council for Graduate Education, Coventry 12518
Ulster Teachers' Union, Belfast 12529
Union of Educational Institutions, Birmingham 12531
Union of Lancashire and Cheshire Institutes, Manchester 12532
United Kingdom Reading Association, Widnes 12538
United World Colleges, London 12543
University Association for Contemporary European Studies, London 12544
Welsh Federation of Head Teachers' Associations, Swansea 12568
Workers' Educational Association, London 12583
World Education Fellowship, Chigwell 12586
World Federation for Medical Education, Edinburgh 12587
World-wide Education Service of The Bell Educational Trust, London 12592

Uruguay

Consejo Nacional de Educación, Centro Nacional de Información y Documentación, Montevideo 12622

U.S.A.

Academy for Educational Development, Washington 12644
Academy of Criminal Justice Sciences, Highland Heights 12654
Academy of Security Educators and Trainees, Berryville 12674
Accordion Teacher's Guild, Kansas City 12677
Aerospace Education Foundation, Arlington 12698
Agency for Instructional Technology, Bloomington 12712
ALI-ABA Committee on Continuing Professional Education, Philadelphia 12727
American Academy of Teachers of Singing, New York 12799
American Association for Agricultural Education, University Park 12822
American Association for Career Education, Hermosa Beach 12827
American Association for Higher Education, Washington 12837
American Association for Paralegal Education, Overland 12844
American Association for Women in Community Colleges, Amarillo 12857
American Association of Christian Schools, Independence 12871
American Association of Colleges for Teacher Education, Washington 12872
American Association of Community Colleges, Washington 12877
American Association of Diabetes Educators, Chicago 12883
American Association of Housing Educators, College Station 12896
American Association of Philosophy Teachers, Knoxville 12915
American Association of Physics Teachers, College Park 12919
American Association of Professors of Yiddish, Flushing 12925
American Association of School Personnel Administrators, Sacramento 12931
American Association of Sex Educators, Counselors and Therapists, Chicago 12932
American Association of Teachers of Arabic, Provo 12936
American Association of Teachers of Esperanto, Santa Barbara 12937
American Association of Teachers of French, Champaign 12938
American Association of Teachers of German, Cherry Hill 12939
American Association of Teachers of Spanish and Portuguese, Greeley 12940
American Association of Teachers of Turkic Languages, Princeton 12941
American Association of University Women Educational Foundation, Washington 12946
American Board of Funeral Service Education, Brunswick 12978
American Board of Master Educators, Nashville 12981
American Board of Vocational Experts, Glenview 13009
American Classical League, Oxford 13032
American College Testing, Iowa City 13081
American Correctional Association, Lanham 13095
American Council for Construction Education, Monroe 13098
American Council on Education, Washington 13106
American Council on Schools and Colleges, Tampa 13108
American Council on the Teaching of Foreign Languages, Yonkers 13109
American Counseling Association, Alexandria 13110
American Education Association, Center Moriches 13130
American Educational Research Association, Washington 13131
American Forum for Global Education, New York 13157
American Friends of Cambridge University, New York 13163
American Hungarian Educators' Association, Silver Spring 13189
American Institute for Foreign Study, Greenwich 13200
American Mathematical Association of Two Year Colleges, Memphis 13258
American Medical Association Education and Research Foundation, Chicago 13264
American Montessori Society, New York 13277
American Orthopsychiatric Association, New York 13302
American Osteopathic College of Radiology, Milan 13314
American Schools Association, Atlanta 13362
American Society for Engineering Education, Washington 13383
American Society for Healthcare Education and Training of the American Hospital Association, Chicago 13389
American Society for Training and Development, Alexandria 13418
American String Teachers Association, Reston 13507
American Vocational Education Personnel Development Association, Stillwater 13529
Armenian Educational Foundation, Glendale 13571
Arts International, New York 13575
Associated Colleges of the Midwest, Chicago 13586
Associates for World Action in Rehabilitation and Education, Mohegan Lake 13590
Association for American Schools in South America, Miami Lakes 13595
Association for Canadian Studies in the United States, Washington 13605
Association for Childhood Education International, Wheaton 13610
Association for Counselor Education and Supervision, Alexandria 13618
Association for Educational Communications and Technology, Washington 13622
Association for General and Liberal Studies, Helena 13627
Association for Humanistic Education, Laramie 13632
Association for Humanistic Education and Development, Alexandria 13633
Association for Institutional Research, Tallahassee 13635
Association for International Practical Training, Columbia 13637
Association for Specialists in Group Work, Alexandria 13666
Association for Spiritual, Ethical and Religious Values in Counseling, Alexandria 13667
Association for Supervision and Curriculum Development, Alexandria 13668
Association for Surgical Education, Salt Lake City 13669
Association for the Advancement of Health Education, Reston 13675
Association for the Advancement of International Education, New Wilmington 13676
Association for the Behavioral Sciences and Medical Education, Phoenix 13679
Association for the Development of Human Potential, Spokane 13682
Association for the Education of Teachers in Science, Pensacola 13684
Association for the Management of Information Technology in Higher Education, Boulder 13685
Association for the Study of Higher Education, College Station 13691
Association for Theatre in Higher Education, New York 13695
Association for World Education, Omaha 13705
Association of Advanced Rabbinical and Talmudic Schools, New York 13710
Association of American Colleges and Universities, Washington 13713
Association of American Schools in South America, Miami 13722
Association of Black Women in Higher Education, Albany 13741
Association of Catholic Colleges and Universities, Washington 13745
Association of Chiropractic Colleges, San Lorenzo 13748
Association of College Unions – International, Bloomington 13753
Association of Community College Trustees, Washington 13757
Association of Community Tribal Schools, Sisseton 13758
Association of Continuing Legal Education Administrators, Austin 13760
Association of Episcopal Colleges, New York 13768
Association of Graduate Liberal Studies Programs, Durham 13775
Association of Graduate Schools in Association of American Universities, Washington 13776
Association of International Education Administrators, Tuscaloosa 13780
Association of Jesuit Colleges and Universities, Washington 13783
Association of Lutheran Secondary Schools, Denver 13790
Association of Medical Education and Research in Substance Abuse, Providence 13793
Association of Mercy Colleges, Pittsburgh 13796
Association of Minority Health Professions Schools, Washington 13800
Association of Naval R.O.T.C. Colleges and Universities, Rochester 13803
Association of Orthodox Jewish Teachers, Brooklyn 13810
Association of Presbyterian Colleges and Universities, Louisville 13817
Association of Professional Schools of International Affairs, Washington 13821
Association of School Business Officials International, Reston 13827
Association of Southern Baptist Colleges and Schools, Nashville 13834
Association of Teacher Educators, Reston 13844
Association of Teachers of Japanese, Middlebury 13845
Association of Teachers of Latin American Studies, Flushing 13846
Association of Teachers of Technical Writing, Orlando 13849
Association of the Health Occupations Teacher Educators, Louisville 13851
Association of Theological Schools, Pittsburgh 13853
Association of Waldorf Schools of North America, Fair Oaks 13867
Association on Boarding Schools, Washington 13869
Audubon Naturalist Society of the Central Atlantic States, Chevy Chase 13883
AVKO Educational Research Foundation, Birch Run 13901
Basque Educational Organization, San Francisco 13903
Belgian American Educational Foundation, New Haven 13908
Better Education thru Simplified Spelling, Detroit 13913
Black Women's Educational Alliance, Philadelphia 13932
B'Nai B'Rith International Commission on Continuing Jewish Education, Washington 13934
Brandeis-Bardin Institute, Brandeis 13944
British Schools and Universities Foundation, New York 13946
Business-Higher Education Forum, Washington 13955
Business Professionals of America, Columbus 13957
Carnegie Foundation for the Advancement of Teaching, Princeton 13974
Catholic Audio-Visual Educators Association, Pittsburgh 13979
Catholic Biblical Association of America, Washington 13980
Center for Computer-Assisted Legal Instruction, Minneapolis 14001
Center for Death Education and Research, Minneapolis 14003
Center for Early Adolescence, Carrboro 14005
Center for Global Education, Minneapolis 14009
Center for Peace Education, Carrboro 14017
Center for Sutton Movement Writing, Newport Beach 14031
Center for the Study of Parent Involvement, Orinda 14033
Central Organization for Jewish Education, Brooklyn 14040
Centre for UN Reform Education, Livingston 14044
Ceramic Educational Council, Westerville 14046
Character Education Institute, San Antonio 14048
Chinese Language Teachers Association, Kalamazoo 14068
Christian Educators Association International, Pasadena 14073
Christian Schools International, Grand Rapids 14077
Cities in Schools, Alexandria 14082
Coalition for Christian Colleges and Universities, Washington 14091
Coalition for the Advancement in Jewish Education, New York 14093
The College Board, New York 14099
College Reading and Learning Association, Greeley 14105
College-University Resource Institute, Washington 14107
Commission on Accreditation of Allied Health Education Programs, Chicago 14111
Commission on Gay/Lesbian Issues in Social Work Education, Alexandria 14113
Committee on Continuing Education for School Personnel, Union 14131
Committee on Institutional Cooperation, Champaign 14132
Committee on the Role and Status of Women in Educational Research and Development, Portland 14135
Community College Association for Instruction and Technology, Lancaster 14139
Comparative and International Education Society, Washington 14147
Conduit, Iowa City 14150
Conference on Christianity and Literature, Saint Petersburg 14164
Conference on College Composition and Communication, Urbana 14165
Conference on English Education, Urbana 14167
Consortium for International Pacific Education and Communication Experiments by Satellite, Honolulu 14176
Consortium for International Studies Education, Columbus 14177
Consumer Education Research Center, Orange 14185
Correctional Education Association, Lanham 14199
Council for Advancement and Support of Education, Washington 14201
Council for American Private Education, Washington 14203
Council for Basic Education, Washington 14204
Council for Educational Development and Research, Washington 14207
Council for Indian Education, Billings 14210
Council for Jewish Education, New York 14211
Council for Religion in Independent Schools, Bethesda 14215
Council for Research in Music Education, Urbana 14216
Council of 1890 College Presidents, Baton Rouge 14221
Council of Administrators of Special Education, Albuquerque 14223
Council of Chief State School Officers, Washington 14226
Council of Graduate Schools, Washington 14231
Council of Mennonite Colleges, Hillsboro 14234
Council of Scientific Society Presidents, Washington 14236
Council of the Great City Schools, Washington 14239
Council of Undergraduate Research, Asheville 14240
Council on Accreditation of Nurse Anesthesia Educational Programs/Schools, Park Ridge 14241
Council on Anthropology and Education, Arlington 14242
Council on Chiropractic Education, Scottsdale 14244
Council on Electrolysis Education, Hot Springs 14249
Council on International Educational Exchange, New York 14252
Council on Standards for International Educational Travel, Leesburg 14263

423 Subject Index: Electronic Engineering

Overseas Council for Theological Education and Missions, Greenwood *16110*
Pacific Region Educational Laboratory, Honolulu *16121*
Pan American Health and Education Foundation, Washington *16138*
Peace Action Education Fund, New York *16150*
People United for Rural Education, Alden *16156*
People's Decade of Human Rights Education, New York *16157*
Play Schools Association, New York *16179*
Probe Ministries International, Richardson *16206*
Professors of Curriculum, Iowa City *16210*
Public Leadership Education Network, Washington *16229*
Regional Education Board of the Christian Brothers, Landover *16253*
Regional Program for Educational Development, Washington *16256*
Research Association of Minority Professors, Prairie View *16267*
School Management Study Group, Salt Lake City *16294*
School Science and Mathematics Association, BLoomsburg *16295*
Science Service, Washington *16297*
Secondary School Admission Test Board, Princeton *16308*
Sex Information and Education Council of the U.S., New York *16317*
Small Enterprise Education and Promotion Network, New York *16335*
Smithsonian Institution, Washington *16337*
Social Science Education Consortium, Boulder *16340*
Société des Professeurs Français et Francophones en Amérique, New York *16344*
Society for Applied Learning Technology, Warrenton *16352*
Society for Educational Reconstruction, Mankato *16377*
Society for French American Cultural Services and Educational Aid, New York *16384*
Society for History Education, Long Beach *16391*
Society for Music Teacher Education, Reston *16413*
Society for Research in Child Development, Ann Arbor *16438*
Society for the Advancement of Education, Valley Stream *16447*
Society for Values in Higher Education, Washington *16484*
Society of American Law Teachers, New York *16495*
Society of Ethnic and Special Studies, Edwardsville *16516*
Society of Professors of Education, Cape Girardeau *16552*
Society of Teachers in Education of Professional Photography, West Carrollton *16561*
Solomon Schecher Day School Association, New York *16578*
Southern Association of Colleges and Schools, Decatur *16582*
Special Interest Group for Computer Uses in Education, Eugene *16594*
Student National Medical Association, Washington *16609*
Swedish Women's Educational Association International, La Jolla *16622*
Teachers of English to Speakers of Other Languages, Alexandria *16629*
Theodor Herzl Institute, New York *16638*
Tripoli Rocketry Association, Kenner *16652*
United Board for Christian Higher Education in Asia, New York *16667*
United Cerebral Palsy Research and Educational Foundation, Washington *16669*
United Nations Educational, Scientific and Cultural Organization, New York *16675*
United States Institute for Theatre Technology, New York *16691*
United Synagogue of Conservative Judaism Commission on Jewish Education, New York *16702*
University and College Labor Education Association, New Brunswick *16707*
University Consortium for Instructional Development and Technology, Athens *16709*
University Council for Educational Administration, University Park *16711*
Vocational Instructional Materials Section, Columbia *16734*
Western College Association, Oakland *16752*
Wilderness Education Association, Fort Collins *16762*
Women and Mathematics Education, South Hadley *16773*
Women Educators, Toledo *16774*
Women's College Coalition, Washington *16782*
World Association for Cooperative Education, Boston *16791*
World Association of Universities and Colleges, Las Vegas *16801*
World Association of Veterinary Educators, Tuskegee *16803*
World Council for Curriculum and Instruction, Cincinnati *16808*
World Council of Comparative Education Societies, Pittsburgh *16809*
World Education, Boston *16810*
World Education Fellowship, United States Section, New Rochelle *16811*
World Institute for Safety Education and Research, Warrensburg *16825*
World Learning, Washington *16827*
World University Network, Saint Paul *16842*

Venezuela
Caribbean Institute for Social Formation, Caracas *16887*
Consejo Venezolano del Niño, Caracas *16910*

Virgin Islands (U.S.)
Consortium of Caribbean Universities for Resource Management, Saint Thomas *16981*

Yugoslavia
Pedagogical Society of Yugoslavia, Beograd *17012*
Savez Društava za Strane Jezike i Knjizevnosti Jugoslavije, Beograd *17020*
Savez Pedagoških Društava Jugoslavije, Beograd *17025*
Savez Pedagoških Društava Srbije, Beograd *17026*
Sindikat Radnicka Drustvenih Delatnosti Jugoslavije, Beograd *17030*
Udruženje Univerzitetskih Nastavnika i Van-Univerzitetskih Naučnik Radnika, Beograd *17037*
Zajednica Universitéta Jugoslavije, Beograd *17044*

Zambia
Association of Medical Schools in Africa, Lusaka *17048*

Zimbabwe
Zimbabwe Association for Science Education, Harare *17084*

Education of the Handicapped

Austria
Österreichische Gesellschaft für Sprachheilpädagogik, Wien *00684*

Belgium
Groupe Belge d'Etude de l'Arriération Mentale, Bruxelles *01177*

France
Société d'Etudes et de Soins pour les Enfants Paralysés, Paris *04062*

Germany
Berufsverband Deutscher Hörgeschädigtenpädagogen, Hamburg *04566*
Bundesverband Hilfe für das autistische Kind e.V., Hamburg *04665*
Bundesverband Legasthenie e.V., Hannover *04668*
Bundesvereinigung Lebenshilfe für geistig Behinderte e.V., Marburg *04682*
Deutsche Gesellschaft zur Förderung der Gehörlosen und Schwerhörigen e.V., München *04890*
Gesellschaft für wissenschaftliche Gesprächspsychotherapie e.V., Köln *05419*
Lernen Fördern – Bundesverband zur Förderung Lernbehinderter e.V., Köln *05718*

Italy
Associazione La Nostra Famiglia, Ponte Lambro *06993*
Associazione Nazionale Famiglie di Fanciulli e Adulti Subnormali, Roma *07009*

Spain
Centro de Documentación y Estudios SiiS, San Sebastián *09741*

United Kingdom
Association for Independent Disabled Self-Sufficiency, Bath *10806*
Association for the Education and Welfare of the Visually Handicapped, Droitwich Spa *10827*
Association of Blind and Partially-Sights Teachers and Students, London *10846*
Association of Disabled Professionals, Horbury *10874*
British Association of Teachers of the Deaf, Cheadle Hulme *11046*
The British Institute for Brain Injured Children, Bridgwater *11095*
British Institute of Learning Disabilities, Kidderminster *11100*
Disabled Living Foundation, London *11391*
Dyslexia Institute, Staines *11407*
Hyper Active Children's Support Group, Chichester *11641*
National Association of Teachers of The Mentally Handicapped, Aylesbury *11989*

U.S.A.
Alexander Graham Bell Association for the Deaf, Washington *12725*
American Association on Mental Retardation, Washington *12957*
Association for Education and Rehabilitation of the Blind and Visually Impaired, Alexandria *13620*
Conference of Educational Administrators Serving the Deaf, Newark *14159*
Convention of American Instructors of the Deaf, Bedford *14189*
Council for Children with Behavioral Disorders, Reston *14206*
Council on Education of the Deaf, Washington *14248*
Division for Early Childhood, Reston *14311*
Division on Mental Retardation and Developmental Disabilities of the Council for Exceptional Children, Little Rock *14313*
Foundation for Exceptional Children, Reston *14463*
Foundation for Science and Disability, Morgantown *14472*
Model Secondary School for the Deaf, Washington *15591*
National Captioning Institute, Vienna *15770*

Electrical Engineering

Argentina
Asociación Electrotécnica Argentina, Buenos Aires *00054*

Australia
Telecommunication Society of Australia, Melbourne *00376*

Austria
Österreichischer Verband für Elektrotechnik, Wien *00767*

Belgium
Société Royale Belge des Electriciens, Bruxelles *01285*
Union Radio-Scientifique Internationale, Gent *01309*

Bulgaria
Scientific and Technical Union of Energetics, Sofia *01581*
Union of Electronic and Electrical Engineering and Communications, Sofia *01599*

Canada
Canadian Electricity Association, Montréal *01874*
Institute of Electrical and Electronics Engineers Canada, Dundas *02141*

China, People's Republic
China Electrotechnical Society, Beijing *02549*
Chinese Society of Electrical Engineering, Beijing *02623*

Denmark
Dansk Køleforening, Lyngby *03022*
Elektroteknisk Forening, Hellerup *03105*
Lysteknisk Selskab, Stenløse *03161*

France
Association Française de l'Eclairage, Paris *03528*
Comité Français de l'Electricité, Paris-La Défense *03716*
Conférence Internationale des Grands Réseaux Electriques à Haute Tension, Paris *03759*
Société des Electriciens et des Electroniciens, Paris *04032*
Union Internationale d'Electrothermie, Paris-La Défense *04310*
Union Technique de l'Electricité, Paris-La Défense *04324*

Germany
Deutsche Elektrotechnische Kommission im DIN und VDE, Frankfurt *04729*
Deutsche Lichttechnische Gesellschaft e.V., Berlin *04914*
Deutscher Fakultätentag für Elektrotechnik, Dresden *05008*
Dokumentationsring Elektrotechnik, Erlangen *05113*
Forschungsgemeinschaft für Hochspannungs- und Hochstromtechnik e.V., Mannheim *05231*
Forschungsvereinigung Elektrotechnik beim ZVEI e.V., Frankfurt *05267*
Gesellschaft für Elektrische Hochleistungsprüfungen, Frankfurt *05358*
Gesellschaft für Informationsvermittlung und Technologieberatung, München *05374*
Informationstechnische Gesellschaft im VDE, Frankfurt *05512*
Normenausschuss Heiz-, Koch- und Wärmegeräte im DIN Deutsches Institut für Normung e.V., Frankfurt *05815*
Normenausschuss Lichttechnik im DIN Deutsches Institut für Normung e.V., Berlin *05828*
VDE Verband Deutscher Elektrotechniker e.V., Frankfurt *06001*

Hungary
Hiradástechnikai Tudományos Egyesület, Budapest *06291*
Magyar Elektrotechnikai Egyesület, Budapest *06304*

India
Institution of Electronics and Telecommunication Engineers, New Dehli *06494*

Ireland
Institution of Electrical Engineers (Irish Centre), Dublin *06615*

Italy
Associazione Elettrotecnica ed Elettronica Italiana, Milano *06914*
Comitato Elettrotecnico Italiano, Milano *07196*
Gruppo di Ricerca sulle Alte Tensioni, Roma *07290*
Gruppo di Ricerca sulle Macchine Elettriche, Roma *07291*
Istituto Elettrotecnico Nazionale Galileo Ferraris, Torino *07338*

Japan
Nihon Reito Kyokai, Tokyo *07836*

Pakistan
Institution of Electrical Engineers, Lahore *08901*

Peru
Asociación Electrotécnica Peruana, Lima *08982*

Russia
Power and Electrical Power Engineering Society, St. Petersburg *09432*
Radio Engineering, Electronics and Telecommunications Society, Moskva *09436*

South Africa
South African Council for Automation and Computation, Pretoria *09675*
The South African National Committee on Illumination, Pretoria *09694*

Sweden
Svenska Föreningen för Ljuskultur, Stockholm *09969*

Switzerland
Commission Electrotechnique Internationale, Genève *10067*
Schweizerische Lichttechnische Gesellschaft, Bern *10369*
Schweizerischer Elektrotechnischer Verein, Zürich *10443*

United Kingdom
Battery Vehicle Society, Peacehaven *10953*
ERA Technology, Leatherhead *11461*
Institution of British Telecom Engineers, London *11732*
Institution of Electrical Engineers, London *11736*
Institution of Electronics and Electrical Incorporated Engineers, London *11738*
Institution of Lighting Engineers, Rugby *11746*
International Special Committee on Radio Interference, London *11822*
Measurement and Instrumentation Centre, London *11920*
Radio Society of Great Britain, Potters Bar *12140*
Royal Television Society, London *12266*
Visible Record and Minicomputer Society, Croydon *12558*
Wireless Preservation Society, Shanklin *12579*

U.S.A.
Aerospace Electrical Society, Grand Prairie *12699*
Antenna Measurement Techniques Association, Atlanta *13548*
Association of Federal Communications Consulting Engineers, Washington *13770*
Edison Electric Institute, Washington *14347*
Electric Vehicle Association, San Francisco *14364*
Electricity Consumers Resource Council, Washington *14365*
IEEE Control Systems Society, New York *14634*
IEEE Ultrasonics, Ferroelectrics and Frequency Control Society, Lexington *14635*
Illuminating Engineering Society of North America, New York *14637*
Institute of Electrical and Electronics Engineers, New York *14703*
International Kirlian Research Association, Brooklyn *15091*
International Laser Display Association, Bradenton *15095*
International Telecommunications Society, Boulder *15337*
North American Electric Reliability Council, Princeton *16039*
North American Society of Pacing and Electrophysiology, Natick *16052*
RTCA, Washington *16282*
Signal Processing Society, New York *16328*
Society of Broadcast Engineers, Indianapolis *16504*
United States National Committee of the International Union of Radio Science, Washington *16695*

Venezuela
Asociación Venezolana de Ingeniería Eléctrica y Mecánica, Caracas *16882*

Electrochemistry

India
Electrochemical Society of India, Bangalore *06426*

Japan
Nihon Kandenchi Kogyokai, Tokyo *07807*

United Kingdom
Scottish Electrophysiological Society, Saint Andrews *12301*

U.S.A.
Electrochemical Society, Pennington *14366*

Electronic Engineering

Austria
Forschungsgesellschaft für Psycho-Elektronik und Kybernetik, Wien *00446*
Österreichische Gesellschaft für Artificial Intelligence, Wien *00613*

Belgium
European Power Electronics and Drives Association, Bruxelles *01160*
Société Belge de Microscopie Electronique, Liège *01245*

China, People's Republic
Chinese Computer Federation, Beijing *02582*

France
Organisation Européenne pour l'Equipement de l'Aviation Civile, Paris *03933*
Société Française de Microscopie Electronique, Paris *04142*

Germany
CENELEC Electronic Components Committee, Frankfurt *04690*
Deutsche Gesellschaft für Chronometrie e.V., Ditzingen *04765*
Elektrotechnischer Verein Berlin e.V., Berlin *05118*
Fraunhofer-Gesellschaft zur Förderung der angewandten Forschung e.V., München *05288*
GES-Gesellschaft für elektronische Systemforschung, Allensbach *05331*

425 Subject Index: Engineering

Institution of Surveyors – Australia, Canberra *00299*
Royal Melbourne Institute of Technology, Melbourne *00345*
Society of Leather Technologists and Chemists, Botany *00363*
Sydney University Chemical Engineering Association, Sydney *00368*
University of New South Wales Chemical Engineering Association, Kensington *00379*

Austria
Commission Internationale de l'Eclairage, Wien *00427*
International Federation of Automatic Control, Laxenburg *00513*
International Institute for Applied Systems Analysis, Laxenburg *00514*
Internationale Gesellschaft für Ingenieurpädagogik, Klagenfurt *00523*
Ludwig Boltzmann-Gesellschaft, Österreichische Vereinigung zur Förderung der wissenschaftlichen Forschung, Wien *00553*
Mikrographische Gesellschaft, Wien *00557*
Österreichische Gesellschaft für Schweisstechnik, Wien *00681*
Österreichische Gesellschaft für Vakuumtechnik, Wien *00692*
Österreichische Gesellschaft für Warenkunde und Technologie, Wien *00696*
Österreichische Gesellschaft und Institut für Umweltschutz, Umwelttechnologie und Umweltwissenschaften, Wien *00704*
Österreichische Tribologische Gesellschaft, Wien *00739*
Österreichische Vereinigung der Zellstoff- und Papierchemiker und -techniker, Wien *00740*
Verein Forschung für die graphischen Medien, Wien *00830*
Verein Österreichischer Lebensmittel- und Biotechnologen, Wien *00840*
Verein österreichischer Ledertechniker, Wien *00841*

Bahrain
Bahrain Society of Engineers, Manama *00906*

Bangladesh
Bangladesh Council of Scientific and Industrial Research, Dhaka *00915*
Institution of Engineers – Bangladesh, Dhaka *00918*

Belgium
ASM International-European Council, Bruxelles *00939*
Association Européenne Camac, Louvain-la-Neuve *00955*
Association for European Training for Employees in Technology, Bruxelles *00962*
Biotechnology Research for Innovation, Development and Growth in Europe, Bruxelles *00995*
Bureau International Technique de l'ABS, Bruxelles *01001*
Bureau International Technique des Polyesters Insaturés, Bruxelles *01002*
Bureau International Technique du Spathfluor, Bruxelles *01003*
European Association for the Study of Safety Problems in the Production and Use of Propellant Powders, Bruxelles *01093*
European Confederation for EC Agricultural Engineers, Bruxelles *01137*
European Cooperation in the Field of Scientific and Technical Research, Bruxelles *01141*
Institut Belge de la Soudure, Bruxelles *01187*
Institut Belge de Régulation et d'Automatisme, Bruxelles *01189*
Institut Européen des Armes de Chasse et de Sport, Liège *01193*
Koninklijke Academie voor Wetenschappen, Letteren en Schone Kunsten van België, Bruxelles *01221*
Koninklijke Vlaamse Ingenieursvereniging, Antwerpen *01227*
Société Belge de Vacuologie et de Vacuotechnique, Bruxelles *01252*
Société Belge d'Ergologie, Bruxelles *01253*
Société d'Ergonomie de Langue Française, Bruxelles *01262*
Société Européenne pour la Formation des Ingénieurs, Bruxelles *01266*
Société Royale Belge des Ingénieurs et Industriels, Bruxelles *01286*
Société Technique et Chimique de Sucrerie de Belgique, Bruxelles *01299*
Tantalum-Niobium International Study Center, Bruxelles *01300*
top E – European Consulting Engineering Network, Bruxelles *01301*

Bermuda
Bermuda Technical Society, Hamilton *01333*

Brazil
Asociación Interamericana de Ingenieria Sanitaria y Ambiental, Saõ Paulo *01388*
Associação Brasileira de Mecânica dos Solos e Engenharia Geotécnica, São Paulo *01398*
Associação de Engenharia Química, São Paulo *01404*
Conselho Nacional de Desenvolvimento Científico e Tecnológico, Brasília *01455*
Instituto de Engenharia de São Paulo, São Paulo *01467*
Instituto Nacional de Pesquisas da Amazonia, Manaus *01489*
Instituto Nacional de Tecnologia, Rio de Janeiro *01491*
Sociedade de Engenharia do Rio Grande do Sul, Pôrto Alegre *01524*

Bulgaria
Central Council of Scientific and Technical Unions, Sofia *01578*
Federation of Scientific and Technical Unions in Bulgaria, Sofia *01579*
Scientific and Technical Union of Energetics, Sofia *01581*
Scientific and Technical Union of Mechanical Engineering, Sofia *01583*
Scientific and Technical Union of the Food Industry, Sofia *01587*

Canada
American Society of Heating, Refrigerating and Air Conditioning Engineers – Toronto Chapter, Mississauga *01655*
Association des Diplômés de Polytechnique, Montréal *01676*
Association des Ingénieurs-Conseils du Québec, Montréal *01679*
Association des Professeurs de l'Ecole Polytechnique de Montréal, Montréal *01688*
Canadian Academy of Engineering, Ottawa *01770*
Canadian Advanced Technology Association, Ottawa *01781*
Canadian Council of Professional Engineers, Ottawa *01860*
Canadian Drilling Association, North Bay *01871*
Canadian Geotechnical Society, Etobicoke *01893*
Canadian Medical and Biological Engineering Society, Ottawa *01924*
Canadian Science and Technology Historical Association, Ottawa *01964*
Canadian Society for Engineering Management, North York *01974*
Canadian Society for Mechanical Engineering, Ottawa *01978*
Canadian Technion Society, Toronto *02014*
Centre for Engineering Research, Edmonton *02034*
Engineering Institute of Canada, Gloucester *02089*
Human Factors Association of Canada, Mississauga *02126*
Ontario Society for Cable Television Engineers, Mississauga *02295*
Prince Edward Island Society of Medical Technologists, Charlottetown *02322*
Pulp and Paper Research Institute of Canada, Pointe Claire *02332*
Toronto Society of Model Engineers, Newmarket *02402*
York Technology Association, Aurora *02431*

Chile
Asociación Científica y Técnica de Chile, Santiago *02451*
Asociación Interamericana de Ingeniería Sanitaria y Ambiental, Santiago *02453*
Colegio de Arquitectos de Chile, Santiago *02456*
Colegio de Ingenieros de Chile, Santiago *02458*
Instituto de Ingenieros de Chile, Santiago *02468*
Instituto de Ingenieros de Minas de Chile, Santiago *02469*
Sociedad Chilena de Tecnología de Alimentos, Santiago *02508*

China, People's Republic
Chemical Industry and Engineering Society of China, Beijing *02543*
China Association for Science and Technology, Beijing *02545*
China Engineering Graphics Society, Beijing *02551*
China Fire Protection Association, Beijing *02552*
Chinese Association of Automation, Beijing *02574*
Chinese Civil Engineering Society, Beijing *02581*
Chinese Light Industry Society, Beijing *02590*
Chinese Mechanical Engineering Society, Beijing *02592*
Chinese Railway Society, Beijing *02604*
Chinese Society for Rock Mechanics, Bejing *02614*
Chinese Society for Scientific and Technical Information, Beijing *02615*
Chinese Society for the Science and Technology of Labour Protection, Beijing *02616*
Chinese Society for Theoretical and Applied Mechanics, Beijing *02617*
Chinese Society of Engineering Thermophysics, Beijing *02624*
Chinese Society of the History of Science and Technology, Beijing *02636*
Chinese Society of Theoretical and Applied Mechanics, Beijing *02637*
Chinese Textile Engineering Society, Beijing *02641*
Society of Autmotive Engineering of China, Beijing *02660*
Systems Engineering Society of China, Beijing *02662*

China, Republic
Chinese Institute of Engineers, Taipei *02698*

Colombia
Instituto Colombiano de Crédito Educativo y Estudios Técnicos en el Exterior, Bogotá *02791*
Instituto Colombiano de Normas Técnicas, Bogotá *02795*
Sociedad Antioqueña de Ingenieros y Architectos, Medellín *02808*
Sociedad Colombiana de Ingenieros, Bogotá *02815*
Sociedad Colombiana de Químicos e Ingenieros Químicos, Bogotá *02822*

Congo, Republic
Union Panafricaine de la Science et de la Technologie, Brazzaville *02840*

Cuba
Sociedad Cubana de Historia de la Ciencia y de la Técnica, La Habana *02890*
Sociedad Cubana de Ingenieros, La Habana *02892*

Cyprus
Cyprus Joint Technical Council, Nicosia *02902*

Czech Republic
Český Svaz Vědeckotechnických Společností, Praha *02947*
Společnost pro Dějiny Věd a Techniky, Praha *02960*

Denmark
Akademiet for de Tekniske Videnskaber, Lyngby *02964*
Dansk Automationsselskab, København *02984*
Dansk Medikoteknisk Selskab, Holte *03032*
Dansk Mejeringeniør Forening, Odense *03033*
Dansk Selskab for Opvarmnings- og Ventilationsteknik, København *03068*
Dansk Selskab for Rumfartsforskning, København *03070*
Dansk Svejseteknisk Landsforening, Taastrup *03078*
danvak VVS Teknisk Forening, Lyngby *03102*
FORCE Institutterne, Glostrup *03115*
Ingeniør-Sammenslutningen, København *03130*
Militaerteknisk Forening, København *03165*
Polymerteknisk Selskab, København *03187*
Polyteknisk Forening, Lyngby *03188*
Selskabet for Tekniske Uddanelsespørgsmal, København *03209*
Teknisk Skoleforening, Odense *03216*

Ecuador
Centro Andino de Tecnología Rural, Loja *03239*

Egypt
Academy of Scientific Research and Technology, Cairo *03249*
Egyptian Society of Engineers, Cairo *03286*

Finland
Kemiallisteknillinen Yhdistys, Helsinki *03360*
Rakenteiden Mekaniikan Seura, Espoo *03369*
Suomen Hitsausteknillinen Yhdistys, Helsinki *03407*
Suomen Tekstiiliteknillinen Liitto, Tampere *03438*
Svenska Tekniska Vetenskapsakademien i Finland, Espoo *03445*
Tekniikan Akateemisten Liitto, Helsinki *03450*
Teknillisten Tieteiden Akatemia, Espoo *03452*
Tekniska Föreningen i Finland, Helsinki *03453*

France
Association Française des Ingénieurs, Chimistes et Techniciens des Industries du Cuir, Lyon *03542*
Association Française du Froid, Paris *03550*
Association Générale des Hygiénistes et Techniciens Municipaux, Paris *03565*
Association Internationale des Techniciens Biologistes de Langue Française, Le Perreux *03590*
Association Internationale d'Irradiation Industrielle, Charbonnières-les-Bains *03594*
Association Nationale de la Recherche Technique, Paris *03614*
Association Technique de la Réfrigération et de l'Equipement Ménager, Paris *03660*
Association Technique de l'Industrie Papetière, Paris *03663*
Association Technique Maritime et Aéronautique, Paris *03664*
Centre de Perfectionnement des Industries Textiles Rhône-Alpes, Lyon *03676*
Collège International pour l'Etude Scientifique des Techniques de Production Mécanique, Paris *03704*
Comité National des Conseillers de l'Enseignement Technique, Paris *03725*
Conférence Internationale des Formations d'Ingénieurs et Techniciens d'Expression Française, Villeurbanne *03758*
Conférence Internationale des Responsables des Universités et Instituts à Dominante Scientifique et Technique d'Expression Française, Talence *03760*
Conseil National des Ingénieurs et des Scientifiques de France, Paris *03777*
Eurocoast, Marseille *03788*
European Association of Contract Research Organizations, Plaisir *03798*
European Association of Marine Sciences and Techniques, Talence *03800*
European Consortium for Ocean Drilling, Strasbourg *03814*
France Intec, Paris *03862*
Société d'Etudes Financières et Meunières, Paris *04064*
Société d'Etudes Minières, Industrielles et Financières, Paris *04073*
Société d'Etudes Techniques, Paris *04080*
Société Française de Chronométrie et de Microtechnique, Besançon *04122*
Société Française des Thermiciens, Paris *04175*
Société Française du Vide, Paris *04192*
Société Hydrotechnique de France, Paris *04201*
Société Technique d'Etudes Mécaniques et d'Outillage, Paris *04246*

Georgia
Council on the History of Natural Sciences and Technology, Tbilisi *04335*
Scientific-Technical Council on Computer Technology, Mathematical Modelling, Automation of Scientific Research and Instrument Making, Tbilisi *04352*

Germany
Arbeitsausschuß Wälzlager im DIN Deutsches Institut für Normung e.V., Köln *04422*
Arbeitsgemeinschaft industrieller Forschungsvereinigungen „Otto von Guericke" e.V., Köln *04463*
Arbeitswissenschaft im Landbau e.V., Stuttgart *04499*
ATV (Abwassertechnische Vereinigung e.V.), Hennef *04511*
Battelle-Institut e.V., Frankfurt *04523*
Bund Technischer Experten e.V., Bremen *04618*
Bundesverband für den Selbstschutz, Bonn *04663*
Bundesverband Katholischer Ingenieure und Wirtschaftler Deutschlands, Bonn *04667*
Bundesverband unabhängiger deutscher Sicherheitsberater und -Ingenieure e.V., Berlin *04674*
Carl-Cranz-Gesellschaft e.V., Weßling *04685*
Deutsche Forschungsgesellschaft für Oberflächenbehandlung e.V., Düsseldorf *04737*
Deutsche Gesellschaft für Biomedizinische Technik e.V., Berlin *04760*
Deutsche Gesellschaft für Chemisches Apparatewesen, Chemische Technik und Biotechnologie e.V., Frankfurt *04763*
Deutsche Gesellschaft für Chronometrie e.V., Ditzingen *04765*
Deutsche Gesellschaft für Forschung im Graphischen Gewerbe, München *04782*
Deutsche Gesellschaft für Galvano- und Oberflächentechnik e.V., Düsseldorf *04783*
Deutsche Gesellschaft für Geschichte der Medizin, Naturwissenschaft und Technik e.V., Regensburg *04787*
Deutsche Gesellschaft für Technische Zusammenarbeit, Eschborn *04868*
Deutsche Gesellschaft für Zerstörungsfreie Prüfung e.V., Berlin *04886*
Deutsche Glastechnische Gesellschaft e.V., Frankfurt *04892*
Deutsche Kommission für Ingenieurausbildung, Düsseldorf *04908*
Deutsche Vereinigung für Verbrennungsforschung e.V., Essen *04977*
Deutscher Dampfkesselausschuss, Essen *05004*
Deutscher Erfinderring e.V., Nürnberg *05006*
Deutscher Ingenieurinnenbund e.V., München *05016*
Deutscher Verband für Schweisstechnik e.V., Düsseldorf *05056*
Deutscher Verband technisch-wissenschaftlicher Vereine, Düsseldorf *05058*
Deutsches Handwerksinstitut e.V., München *05079*
Deutsches Komitee Instandhaltung e.V., Düsseldorf *05095*
Europäische Föderation Biotechnologie, Frankfurt *05144*
Europäische Föderation für Chemie-Ingenieur-Wesen, Frankfurt *05145*
Europäischer Verband für Produktivitätsförderung, Hamburg *05151*
European Committee for Future Accelerators, Aachen *05159*
Fakultätentag für Maschinenbau und Verfahrenstechnik, München *05213*
Fördergemeinschaft für das Süddeutsche Kunststoff-Zentrum e.V., Würzburg *05221*
FOGRA Forschungsgesellschaft Druck e.V., München *05226*
Forschungs-Gesellschaft Verfahrenstechnik e.V., Düsseldorf *05227*
Forschungsgemeinschaft Eisenhüttenschlacken e.V., Duisburg *05229*
Forschungsgemeinschaft Industrieofenbau e.V., Frankfurt *05234*
Forschungsgemeinschaft Werkzeuge und Werkstoffe e.V., Remscheid *05238*
Forschungsgesellschaft Stahlverformung e.V., Hagen *05245*
Forschungsvereinigung Antriebstechnik e.V., Frankfurt *05262*
Forschungsvereinigung Feinmechanik und Optik e.V., Köln *05268*
Forschungsvereinigung für angewandte Schloß-, Beschlag- und präventive Sicherheitstechnik e.V., Velbert *05269*
Frauen in Naturwissenschaft und Technik e.V., Berlin *05287*
Fraunhofer-Gesellschaft zur Förderung der angewandten Forschung e.V., München *05288*
Frontinus-Gesellschaft e.V., Bergisch Gladbach *05304*
Georg-Agricola-Gesellschaft zur Förderung der Geschichte der Naturwissenschaften und der Technik e.V., Bochum *05322*
Gesellschaft für Angewandte Mathematik und Mechanik, Dresden *05345*
Gesellschaft für die Geschichte und Bibliographie des Brauwesens e.V., Berlin *05357*
Gesellschaft für Technologiefolgenforschung e.V. (GTF), Berlin *05409*
Gesellschaft für Tribologie e.V., Moers *05411*
Gesundheitstechnische Gesellschaft e.V., Berlin *05436*
GKSS-Forschungszentrum Geesthacht, Geesthacht *05438*
GVC/VDI-Gesellschaft Verfahrenstechnik und Chemieingenieurwesen, Düsseldorf *05450*
Hahn-Schickard-Gesellschaft für angewandte Forschung e.V., Stuttgart *05452*
Hannoversches Forschungsinstitut für Fertigungsfragen e.V., Hannover *05456*
Haus der Technik e.V., Essen *05462*
Hüttentechnische Vereinigung der Deutschen Glasindustrie e.V., Frankfurt *05497*
IFRA (Inca-Fiej Research Association), Darmstadt *05504*
Institut für Europäische Umweltpolitik, Bonn *05526*
Institut für technische Weiterbildung Berlin e.V., Berlin *05542*
International Commission of Sugar Technology, Rain *05554*
Kuratorium für Forschung und Technik der Zellstoff- und Papierindustrie, Bonn *05697*

Subject Index: Engineering 426

Kuratorium für Technik und Bauwesen in der Landwirtschaft e.V., Darmstadt *05698*
Normenausschuss Armaturen im DIN Deutsches Institut für Normung e.V., Köln *05789*
Normenausschuss Chemischer Apparatebau im DIN Deutsches Institut für Normung e.V., Köln *05796*
Normenausschuss Dichtungen im DIN Deutsches Institut für Normung e.V., Köln *05798*
Normenausschuss Druck- und Reproduktionstechnik im DIN Deutsches Institut für Normung e.V., Berlin *05799*
Normenausschuss Druckgasanlagen im DIN Deutsches Institut für Normung e.V., Berlin *05800*
Normenausschuss Eisen-, Blech- und Metallwaren im DIN Deutsches Institut für Normung e.V., Düsseldorf *05801*
Normenausschuss Erdöl- und Erdgasgewinnung im DIN Deutsches Institut für Normung e.V., Köln *05803*
Normenausschuss Fahrräder im DIN Deutsches Institut für Normung e.V., Köln *05805*
Normenausschuss Feinmechanik und Optik im DIN Deutsches Institut für Normung e.V., Pforzheim *05807*
Normenausschuss Feuerwehrwesen im DIN Deutsches Institut für Normung e.V., Berlin *05808*
Normenausschuss Gastechnik im DIN Deutsches Institut für Normung e.V., Eschborn *05809*
Normenausschuss Gleitlager im DIN Deutsches Insitut für Normung e.V., Köln *05812*
Normenausschuss Graphische Symbole im DIN Deutsches Institut für Normung e.V., Berlin *05813*
Normenausschuss Heiz- und Raumlufttechnik im DIN Deutsches Institut für Normung e.V., Berlin *05816*
Normenausschuss Instandhaltung im DIN Deutsches Institut für Normung e.V., Köln *05819*
Normenausschuss Kältetechnik im DIN Deutsches Institut für Normung e.V., Köln *05820*
Normenausschuss Kautschuktechnik im DIN Deutsches Institut für Normung e.V., Frankfurt *05821*
Normenausschuss Kommunale Technik im DIN Deutsches Institut für Normung e.V., Berlin *05823*
Normenausschuss Kraftfahrzeuge im DIN Deutsches Institut für Normung e.V., Frankfurt *05824*
Normenausschuss Laborgeräte und Laboreinrichtungen im DIN Deutsches Institut für Normung e.V., Frankfurt *05826*
Normenausschuss Mechanische Verbindungselemente im DIN Deutsches Institut für Normung e.V., Köln *05831*
Normenausschuss Rohre, Rohrverbindungen und Rohrleitungen im DIN Deutsches Institut für Normung e.V., Köln *05838*
Normenausschuss Rundstahlketten im DIN Deutsches Institut für Normung e.V., Köln *05839*
Normenausschuss Schienenfahrzeuge im DIN Deutsches Institut für Normung e.V., Kassel *05840*
Normenausschuss Schmiedetechnik im DIN Deutsches Institut für Normung e.V., Hagen *05841*
Normenausschuss Schweisstechnik im DIN Deutsches Institut für Normung e.V., Berlin *05842*
Normenausschuss Sport- und Freizeitgerät im DIN Deutsches Institut für Normung e.V., Köln *05843*
Normenausschuss Stahldraht und Stahldrahterzeugnisse im DIN Deutsches Institut für Normung e.V., Köln *05844*
Normenausschuss Transportkette im DIN Deutsches Institut für Normung e.V., Berlin *05848*
Normenausschuss Überwachungsbedürftige Anlagen im DIN Deutsches Institut für Normung e.V., Köln *05849*
Normenausschuss Uhren und Schmuck im DIN Deutsches Institut für Normung e.V., Pforzheim *05850*
Normenausschuss Vakuumtechnik im DIN Deutsches Institut für Normung e.V., Köln *05851*
Normenausschuss Waagenbau im DIN Deutsches Institut für Normung e.V., Berlin *05853*
Normenausschuss Wärmebehandlungstechnik metallischer Werkstoffe im DIN Deutsches Institut für Normung e.V., Köln *05854*
Normenausschuss Werkzeuge und Spannzeuge im DIN Deutsches Institut für Normung e.V., Köln *05856*
Normenausschuss Werkzeugmaschinen im DIN Deutsches Institut für Normung e.V., Frankfurt *05857*
Rheinisch-Westfälische Akademie der Wissenschaften, Düsseldorf *05920*
Schiffbautechnische Gesellschaft e.V., Hamburg *05942*
Studiengesellschaft Stahlanwendung e.V., Düsseldorf *05970*
Technikerschule für Druck und Papierverarbeitung, München *05980*
Technische Akademie Esslingen e.V., Ostfildern *05981*
Technische Akademie Wuppertal e.V., Wuppertal *05982*
VDE/VDI-Gesellschaft Mikroelektronik, Mikro- und Feinwerktechnik, Düsseldorf *06000*
VDI-Gesellschaft Entwicklung Konstruktion Vertrieb, Düsseldorf *06005*
VDI-Gesellschaft Fördertechnik Materialfluss Logistik, Düsseldorf *06007*
VDI-Gesellschaft Kunststofftechnik, Düsseldorf *06008*
VDI-Gesellschaft Produktionstechnik, Düsseldorf *06009*
VDI-Gesellschaft Technische Gebäudeausrüstung, Düsseldorf *06010*
VDI-Kommission Lärmminderung, Düsseldorf *06012*
VDI/VDE-Gesellschaft Mess- und Automatisierungstechnik, Düsseldorf *06013*
Verband der Dozenten an Deutschen Ingenieurschulen, Mainz *06019*
Verband der Technischen Überwachungs-Vereine e.V., Essen *06030*
Verein Deutscher Emailfachleute e.V., Hagen *06078*
Verein Deutscher Ingenieure, Düsseldorf *06080*
Verein für Gerberei-Chemie und -Technik e.V., München *06089*
Vereinigung zur Förderung des Deutschen Brandschutzes e.V., Altenberge *06134*
VGB-Forschungsstiftung, Essen *06139*

Ghana

Council for Scientific and Industrial Research, Accra *06193*
Ghana Institution of Engineers, Accra *06201*

Greece

Epimelitirion Ikastikon Technon Ellados, Athinai *06234*
Panellinios Enosis Technikon, Athinai *06251*

Guatemala

Center for Meso American Studies on Appropriate Technology, Guatemala City *06267*
Colegio de Ingenieros de Guatemala, Guatemala City *06269*
Instituto Centroamericano de Investigación y Tecnología, Guatemala City *06271*

Hungary

Faipari Tudományos Egyesület, Budapest *06289*
Gépipari Tudományos Egyesület, Budapest *06290*
Magyar Asztronautikai Egyesület, Budapest *06298*
Magyar Iparjogvédelmi és Szerzöi Jogi Egyesület, Budapest *06316*
Méréstechnikai és Automatizálási Tudományos Egyesület, Budapest *06348*
Müszaki és Természettudományi Egyesületek Szövetsége, Budapest *06349*
Optikai, Akusztikai, Filmtechnikai és Szinháztechnikai Tudomanyos Egyesület, Budapest *06350*
Papir- és Nyomdaipari Müszaki Egyesület, Budapest *06355*
Szilikátipari Tudományos Egyesület, Budapest *06358*
Textilipari Müszaki és Tudományos Egyesület, Budapest *06359*

Iceland

Verkfraedingafélag Islands, Reykjavik *06386*

India

Asian and Pacific Centre for Transfer of Technology, New Delhi *06403*
Council of Scientific and Industrial Research, New Delhi *06422*
India Society of Engineers, Calcutta *06436*
Indian National Academy of Engineering, New Delhi *06467*
Indian Science Congress Association, Calcutta *06477*
Indian Society of Mechanical Engineers, New Delhi *06486*
Institution of Electronics and Telecommunication Engineers, New Dehli *06494*
Institution of Engineers (India), Calcutta *06495*
Research Designs and Standards Organization, Lucknow *06525*

Indonesia

Akademi Teknologi Kulit, Jogjakarta *06542*
Persatuan Insinyur Indonesia, Jakarta *06561*

Ireland

Engineering and Scientific Association of Ireland, Mount Merrion *06598*
Institute of Industrial Engineers, Dublin *06611*
Institution of Civil Engineers (Republic of Ireland), Bray *06614*
Institution of Engineers of Ireland, Dublin *06616*
Irish Welding Association, Dublin *06643*

Israel

Society of Municipal Engineers of Israel, Tel Aviv *06748*
Technion Research and Development Foundation Ltd, Haifa *06750*

Italy

Accademia Olimpica, Vicenza *06863*
Associazione Criogenica Italiana, Genova *06905*
Associazione Italiana di Ingegneria Chimica, Milano *06950*
Associazione Italiana di Ingegneria Medica e Biologica, Napoli *06951*
Associazione Italiana di Strumentisti, Milano *06965*
Associazione Italiana per la Ricerca Industriale, Roma *06977*
Associazione Italiana per l'Analisi delle Sollecitazioni, Trieste *06979*
Associazione Nazionale di Ingegneria Sanitaria, Roma *07005*
Associazione Nazionale di Meccanica, Milano *07006*
Associazione Nazionale Industria Meccanica Varia ed Affine, Milano *07011*
Associazione Nazionale Ingegneri ed Architetti Italiani, Roma *07012*
Associazione Nazionale Italiana per l'Automazione, Milano *07016*
Associazione Tecnica Italiana per la Cellulosa e la Carta, Milano *07044*
Centro Internazionale di Scienze Meccaniche, Udine *07068*
Centro Provinciale Impiego Combinato Tecniche Agricole, Bologna *07113*
Centro Studi di Economia Applicata all'Ingegneria, Bari *07138*
Centro Studi di Economia Applicata all'Ingegneria, Napoli *07139*
Centro Studi e Applicazioni in Tecnologie Avanzate, Bari *07147*
Collegio dei Tecnici dell' Acciaio, Milano *07191*
Committee for the European Development of Science and Technology, Roma *07207*
Ente per le Nuove Tecnologie, l'Energia e l'Ambiente, Roma *07242*
European Safeguards Research and Development Association, Ispra *07266*
Federazione delle Associazioni Scientifiche e Tecniche, Milano *07271*
Gruppo Automazione Navale e Problemi delle Navi di Grande Tonnellaggio, Genova *07287*
Gruppo Nazionale di Sistemistica e di Informatica dell'Ingegneria, Napoli *07298*
International Association of Engineering Geology, Sezione Italiana, Bari *07312*
International Centre for Advanced Technical and Vocational Training, Torino *07314*
International Centre for Mechanical Sciences, Udine *07315*
Istituto di Studi Nucleari per l'Agricoltura, Roma *07337*
Istituto Italiano della Saldatura, Genova *07346*
ITALCONSULT, Roma *07376*
Società Dauna di Cultura, Foggia *07398*
Società degli Ingegneri e degli Architetti in Torino, Torino *07400*

Jamaica

Caribbean Council of Engineering Organizations, Kingston *07688*
Jamaica Institution of Engineers, Kingston *07700*

Japan

Kansai Zosen Kyokai, Osaka *07750*
Keisoku Jidouseigyo Gakkai SICE, Tokyo *07752*
Kogyo Kayaku Kyokai, Tokyo *07759*
Kuki-Chowa Eisei Kogakkai, Tokyo *07764*
Nihon Aisotopu Kyokai, Tokyo *07772*
Nihon Kikai Gakkai, Tokyo *07810*
Nihon Seibutsu-kogaku Kai, Osaka *07845*
Nihon Yosetsu Kyokai, Tokyo *07866*
Nihon Zosen Gakkai, Tokyo *07871*
Nippon Jidoseigyo Kyokai, Kyoto *07910*
Nippon Kagaku-Gijutsu Joho Sentah, Tokyo *07915*
Nippon Kogakukai, Tokyo *07936*
Nippon Koku Uchu Gakkai, Tokyo *07939*
Nippon Nensho Gakkai, Tokyo *07947*
Nippon Nensho Kenkyukai, Kyoto *07948*
Nippon Shashin Gakkai, Tokyo *07978*
Nippon Tribologi Gakkai, Tokyo *08002*
Nogyokikai Gakkai, Saitama *08007*
San-yo Gijutsu Shinkokai, Okayama-ken *08013*
Sekiyu Gijutsu Kyokai, Tokyo *08017*
Sen-i Gakkai, Tokyo *08019*
Yosetsu Gakkai, Tokyo *08050*

Kenya

African Centre for Technology Studies, Nairobi *08062*
African Institute for Higher Technical Training and Research, Nairobi *08067*
African Network of Scientific and Technological Institutions, Nairobi *08069*
East African Engineering Consultants, Nairobi *08091*
East African Industrial Research Organization, Nairobi *08092*
Institution of Engineers of Kenya, Nairobi *08099*
National Council for Science and Technology, Nairobi *08105*

Korea, Democratic People's Republic

Academy of Light Industry Science, Pyongyang *08111*
Academy of Railway Sciences, Pyongyang *08113*

Luxembourg

European Association for the Transfer of Technologies, Innovations and Industrial Information, Luxembourg *08172*

Macedonia

Sojuz na Inženeri i Tehničari na Makedonija, Skopje *08201*

Mauritius

Société de Technologie Agricole et Sucrière de l'Ile Maurice, Réduit *08256*

Mexico

Asociación de Ingenieros y Arquitectos de México, México *08263*
Centro Científico y Técnico Francés en México, México *08287*
Centro Nacional de Ciencias y Tecnologías Marinas, Veracruz *08295*
Consejo Nacional de Ciencia y Tecnología, México *08304*
Sociedad Mexicana de Historia de la Ciencia y la Tecnología, México *08342*

Nepal

National Council for Science and Technology, Kathmandu *08391*
Royal Nepal Academy of Science and Technology, Kathmandu *08393*

Netherlands

European Committee for the Advancement of Thermal Sciences and Heat Transfer, Delft *08444*
European Full-Scale Modelling Association, Wageningen *08450*
International Association for Hydraulic Research, Delft *08476*
International Technical and Scientific Organization for Soaring Flight, Wessling *08497*
Koninklijk Instituut van Ingenieurs, Den Haag *08500*
Koninklijke Nederlandse Vereniging voor Luchtvaart, Den Haag *08521*
Nederlandse Organisatie voor Wetenschappelijk Onderzoek, Den Haag *08563*

New Zealand

Institution of Professional Engineers New Zealand, Wellington *08677*
New Zealand Dairy Technology Society, Waitoa *08691*
New Zealand Institute of Food Science and Technology, Auckland *08704*
New Zealand Institute of Surveyors, Wellington *08709*
New Zealand Society of Dairy Science and Technology, Edgecumbe *08726*

Nigeria

African Regional Centre for Engineering Design and Manufacturing, Ibadan *08762*
Organization of African Unity – Scientific, Technical and Research Commission, Lagos *08785*

Norway

Norges Teknisk-Naturvitenskapelige Forskningsråd, Oslo *08809*
Norges Tekniske Vitenskapsakademi, Trondheim *08810*
Norsk Astronautisk Forening, Oslo *08814*
Norsk Geoteknisk Forening, Oslo *08827*
Den Polytekniske Forening, Oslo *08875*
Selskapet for Lyskultur, Sandvika *08879*
Stiftelsen for Industriell og Teknisk Forskning ved Norges Tekniske Høgskole, Trondheim *08886*

Pakistan

Institution of Engineers – Pakistan, Lahore *08902*
Pakistan Concrete Institute, Karachi *08915*

Paraguay

Servicio Técnico Interamericano de Cooperación Agrícola, Asunción *08965*
Unión Sudamericana de Asociaciones de Ingenieros, Asunción *08968*

Peru

Centro Latinoamericana de Estudios y Difusión de la Construcción en Tierra, Lima *08993*
Consejo Andino de Cienccia y Tecnología, Lima *08997*
Instituto Peruano de Ingenieros Mecánicos, Lima *09003*
Sociedad de Ingenieros del Perú, Lima *09007*

Philippines

Asian Alliance of Appropriate Technology Practitioners, Manila *09027*
Association for Engineering Education in Southeast Asia and the Pacific, Diliman *09040*
United Technological Organizations of the Philippines, Manila *09069*

Poland

Polski Komitet Pomiarów Automatyki, Warszawa *09084*
Polskie Towarzystwo Mechaniki Teoretycznej i Stosowanej, Warszawa *09119*

Portugal

Associação Técnica da Indústria do Cimento, Lisboa *09188*
Ordem dos Engenheiros, Lisboa *09201*
Sociedade de Estudos Técnicos SARL-SETEC, Lisboa *09218*

Russia

Biological Engineering Society, Moskva *09339*
Civil Engineering Society, Moskva *09340*
Commission for Scientific and Technical Co-operation of the Academy of Sciences and Organizations of Moscow Oblast, Moskva *09343*
Mapping and Prospecting Engineering Society, Moskva *09367*
Mechanical Engineering Society, Moskva *09369*
Medical Engineering Society, Moskva *09370*
National Committee of History and Philosophy of Natural Science and Technology, Moskva *09384*
National Medical and Technical Scientific Society, Moskva *09397*
Press and Publishing Engineering Society, Moskva *09433*
Programme Committee Surface Physics, Chemistry and Mechanics, Moskva *09434*
Russian Pugwash Committee, Moskva *09452*
Scientific-Technical Association, St. Petersburg *09456*
Shipbuilding Engineering Society, St. Petersburg *09457*

Senegal

African Regional Centre for Technology, Dakar *09501*

Slovakia

Slovenská Spoločnost pre Mechaniku, Bratislava *09577*

Slovenia

Association of Engineers and Technicians of Slovenia, Ljubljana *09584*
Društvo za Medicinsku i Biološku Tehniku, Ljubljana *09587*
Raziskovalna Skupnost Slovenije, Ljubljana *09590*
Zveza Društev za Varilno Tehniko Slovenije, Ljubljana *09599*

427 Subject Index: Engineering

South Africa

Associated Scientific and Technical Societies of South Africa, Johannesburg *09609*
Chemical Engineering Research Group, Durban *09616*
CSIR, Pretoria *09620*
Division of Energy Technology, Pretoria *09623*
Pollution Research Group, Durban *09649*
South African Filtration Society, Hillcrest *09678*
South African Institute of Aeronautical Engineers, Sunnyside *09682*
South African Institute of Assayers and Analysts, Mashalltown *09683*
South African Institute of Printing, Cape Town *09688*

Spain

Col-legi Oficial d'Enginyers Industrials de Catalunya, Barcelona *09744*

Sri Lanka

Institution of Engineers – Sri Lanka, Colombo *09835*

Swaziland

Royal Swaziland Society of Science and Technology, Kwaluseni *09852*

Sweden

Ingenjörsvetenskapsakademien, Stockholm *09888*
Kungliga Fysiografiska Sällskapet i Lund, Lund *09902*
Styrelsen för Teknisk Utveckling, Stockholm *09948*
Svenska Färgeritekniska Riksförbundet, Göteborg *09968*
Svenska Föreningen för Medicinsk Teknik och Fysik, Umea *09970*
Svenska Geotekniska Föreningen, Linköping *09977*
Svenska Kyltekniska Föreningen, Järfälla *09983*
Svenska Livsmedelstekniska Föreningen, Stockholm *09988*
Svetstekniska Föreningen, Stockholm *10015*
Teknikkonsulterna, Stockholm *10017*
Tekniska Samfundet i Göteborg, Göteborg *10019*

Switzerland

Consultative Council for Postal Studies, Bern *10074*
Direktorenkonferenz der Ingenieurschulen (Abend-HTL) der Schweiz, Lausanne *10080*
Direktorenkonferenz der Ingenieurschulen der Schweiz, Winterthur *10081, 10082*
Direktorenkonferenz der Ingenieurschulen (Tages-HTL) der Schweiz, Sion *10083*
Direktorenkonferenz der landwirtschaftlichen Ingenieurschulen, Bern *10084*
Fachgruppe Carosserie- und Fahrzeugtechnik des STV, Sissach *10109*
Fachgruppe für Arbeiten im Ausland des SIA, Zürich *10110*
Fachgruppe für Betriebstechnik des STV, Winterthur *10112*
Fachgruppe für Verfahrenstechnik des SIA, Basel *10119*
Ingenieurinnen und Ingenieure für Umweltschutz, Bern *10159*
Organisation Internationale de Protection Civile, Petit-Lancy *10220*
Schweizerische Akademie der Technischen Wissenschaften, Zürich *10242*
Schweizerische Gesellschaft für Automatik, Zürich *10280*
Schweizerische Gesellschaft für Boden- und Felsmechanik, Zürich *10284*
Schweizerische Gesellschaft für Feintechnik, Zürich *10293*
Schweizerische Gesellschaft für Lebensmittel-Wissenschaft und -Technologie, Wädenswil *10310*
Schweizerische Gesellschaft für Oberflächentechnik, Bettlach *10319*
Schweizerische Gesellschaft für Vakuum-Physik und -Technik, Zürich *10344*
Schweizerische Gesellschaft Pro Technorama, Winterthur *10351*
Schweizerische Vereinigung für Gesundheitstechnik, Zürich *10407*
Schweizerischer Fachverband der diplomierten medizinischen Laborantinnen und Laboranten, Bern *10444*
Schweizerischer Technischer Verband STV, Zürich *10458*
Schweizerischer Verband der Dozenten an Höheren Technischen Lehranstalten, Biel *10462*
Schweizerischer Verband für die Wärmebehandlung der Werkstoffe, Winterthur *10471*
Schweizerischer Verband für Landtechnik, Riniken *10474*
Schweizerischer Verein für Schweisstechnik, Basel *10481*
Schweizerischer Verein für Vermessung und Kulturtechnik, Solothurn *10483*
Verband Schweizer Abwasser- und Gewässerschutzfachleute, Zürich *10536*
Verband technischer Schulen, Chez-le-Bart *10542*

Tanzania

Tanzania Commission for Science and Technology, Dar es Salaam *10606*

Thailand

ASEAN Federation of Engineering Organizations, Bangkok *10614*
Asian Disaster Preparedness Center, Bangkok *10630*
Asian Institute of Technology Library and Regional Documentation Centre, Bangkok *10631*
Geotechnical Engineering International Resources Center, Pathumthani *10640*
Southeast Asian Society of Soil Engineering, Bangkok *10647*

Trinidad and Tobago

Caribbean Council for Science and Technology, Port of Spain *10657*
Sugar Technologist's Association of Trinidad and Tobago, Port of Spain *10670*

Turkey

Otomatik Kontrol Türk Milli Komitesi, Gümüssuyu *10694*
Türk Mühendis ve Mimar Odalari Birligi, Ankara *10709*

Ukraine

Scientific and Technical Societies National Headquarters, Kiev *10736*

United Kingdom

Antiquarian Horological Society, Wadhurst *10781*
Association for Medical Physics Technology, Ickenham *10815*
Association of Advisers in Design and Technical Studies, Camberley *10838*
Association of Independent Research and Technology Organisations, Cambridge *10890*
Association of Marine Engineering Schools, Liverpool *10898*
Association of Municipal Engineers, London *10901*
Association of Noise Consultants, Guilden Morden *10904*
Association of Principals of Colleges (Northern Ireland Branch), Lisburn *10910*
Association of Professional Scientists and Technologists, London *10911*
Association of Scientific, Technical and Managerial Staffs, London *10919*
Audio Engineering Society, British Section, Sevenoaks *10941*
Biological Engineering Society, London *10967*
Biotechnology and Biological Sciences Research Council, Swindon *10969*
BMT Cortec, Wallsend *10981*
BRF International, Nutfield *10992*
British Association for Brazing and Soldering, Cambridge *11010*
British Compressed Air Society, London *11065*
British Cryogenics Council, London *11068*
British Geotechnical Society, London *11085*
British Horological Institute, Newark *11090*
The British Institute of Cleaning Science, Northampton *11096*
Brunel Society, Bristol *11224*
Centre for Alternative Technology, Machynlleth *11260*
Confederation of British Industry, London *11341*
Design and Industries Association, London *11382*
The Educational Institute of Design, Craft and Technology, Melton Mowbray *11435*
Engineering Council, London *11447*
Ergonomics Society, Loughborough *11462*
European Committee for Civil Engineers, London *11481*
Fabric Care Research Association, Harrogate *11511*
Fire Protection Association, Borehamwood *11538*
Furniture Industry Research Association, Stevenage *11555*
HATRA, Nottingham *11603*
High Pressure Technology Association, Leeds *11620*
Institute of Engineers and Technicians, London *11685*
Institute of Food Science and Technology of The United Kingdom, London *11688*
Institute of Inventors, London *11694*
Institute of Marine Engineers, London *11701*
Institute of Measurement and Control, London *11704*
Institute of Packaging, Melton Mowbray *11708*
Institute of Refrigeration, Carshalton *11718*
Institute of Science Technology, Lichfield *11720*
Institute of Scientific and Technical Communicators, London *11721*
Institute of Sheet Metal Engineering, Birmingham *11722*
Institution of Agricultural Engineers, Bedford *11731*
The Institution of Chemical Engineers, Rugby *11733*
Institution of Engineering Designers, Westbury *11739*
Institution of Engineers amd Shipbuilders in Scotland, Glasgow *11740*
Institution of Fire Engineers, Leicester *11743*
Institution of Gas Engineers, London *11744*
Institution of Mechanical Engineers, London *11747*
Institution of Mechanical Incorporated Engineers, London *11748*
The Institution of Mining Engineers, Doncaster *11750*
Institution of Physics and Engineering in Medicine an Biology, York *11752*
Institution of Plant Engineers, London *11753*
Institution of Polish Engineers in Great Britain, London *11754*
Institution of Railway Signal Engineers, Dawlish *11755*
Institution of Structural Engineers, London *11756*
Intermediate Technology Development Group, Rugby *11758*
International Federation of Airworthiness, Ruislip *11787*
International Hydrofoil Society, London *11798*
International Society for Soil Mechanics and Foundation Engineering, Cambridge *11817*
National Foundry and Engineering Training Association, Glasgow *12008*
The Newcomen Society, London *12038*
Newcomen Society for the Study of the History of Engineering and Technology, London *12039*
Parliamentary and Scientific Committee, London *12087*
Pira International, Leatherhead *12107*
Printing Historical Society, London *12125*
Production Engineering Research Association, Melton Mowbray *12129*
Research and Development Society, London *12153*
Royal Academy of Engineering, London *12164*
The Royal Institution of Naval Architects, London *12224*
SATRA Technology Centre, Kettering *12282*
Science and Engineering Research Council, Swindon *12285*
Scottish Society for The Preservation of Historical Machinery, Glasgow *12320*
Sheffield Metallurgical and Engineering Association, Rotherham *12334*
Sira, Chislehurst *12339*
Society for Underwater Technology, London *12403*
Society of Consulting Marine Engineers and Ship Surveyors, London *12419*
Society of Engineers, Colchester *12425*
Society of Licensed Aircraft Engineers and Technologists, Kingston-upon-Thames *12435*
Society of Technical Analysts, Cambridge *12445*
South Wales Institute of Engineers, Cardiff *12460*
Spring Research and Manufacturers Association, Sheffield *12464*
Tensor Society of Great Britain, Surbiton *12492*
TWI, Cambridge *12517*
UMIST Association, Manchester *12530*

Uruguay

Academia Nacional de Ingeniería, Montevideo *12605*
Asociación de Ingenieros del Uruguay, Montevideo *12610*
Consejo Nacional de Investigaciones Científicas y Técnicas, Montevideo *12624*
Instituto Uruguayo de Normas Técnicas, Montevideo *12628*

U.S.A.

AACE International, Morgantown *12639*
Abrasive Engineering Society, Butler *12642*
Academy of Security Educators and Trainees, Berryville *12674*
Accreditation Board for Engineering and Technology, Baltimore *12679*
ACEC Research and Management Foundation, Washington *12685*
AIDIS-USA Section, Alexandria *12718*
American Academy of Environmental Engineers, Annapolis *12753*
American Academy of Mechanics, Blacksburg *12767*
American Association of Engineering Societies, Washington *12886*
American Automatic Control Council, Evanston *12961*
American Canal Society, York *13018*
American Consulting Engineers Council, Washington *13094*
American Council of the International Institute of Welding, Miami *13104*
American Indian Science and Engineering Society, Boulder *13193*
American Institute of Plant Engineers, Cincinnati *13225*
American Institute of Timber Construction, Englewood *13228*
American Society for Clinical Laboratory Science, Bethesda *13374*
American Society for Engineering Education, Washington *13383*
American Society for Engineering Management, Annapolis *13384*
American Society for Hospital Engineering, Chicago *13392*
American Society for Technion-Israel Institute of Technology, New York *13414*
American Society of Agricultural Engineers, Saint Joseph *13422*
American Society of Body and Design Engineers, Redford *13427*
American Society of Certified Engineering Technicians, Flowery Branch *13432*
American Society of Danish Engineers, Larchmont *13444*
American Society of Mechanical Engineers, New York *13471*
American Society of Naval Engineers, Alexandria *13473*
American Society of Plumbing Engineers, Westlake *13483*
American Society of Sanitary Engineering, Cleveland *13491*
American Society of Swedish Engineers, New York *13494*
American Technical Education Association, Wahpeton *13512*
American Underground-Construction Association, Minneapolis *13523*
APEC, Dayton *13553*
Appropriate Technology International, Washington *13557*
Association for Finishing Processes of the Society of Manufacturing Engineers, Dearborn *13626*
Association for Preservation Technology International, Fredericksburg *13653*
Association for Science, Technology and Innovation, Arlington *13663*
Association of Chairmen of Departments of Mechanics, Ithaca *13747*
Association of Environmental Engineering Professors, Champaign *13767*
Association of Firearm and Tool Mark Examiners, La Jolla *13772*
Association of Iron and Steel Engineers, Pittsburgh *13782*
Association of Muslim Scientists and Engineers, Plainfield *13801*
Association of Science-Technology Centers, Washington *13832*
Association of Surgical Technologists, Englewood *13842*
Audio Engineering Society, New York *13882*
Biomedical Engineering Society, Culver City *13924*
Board on Science and Technology for International Development, Washington *13935*
Career College Association, Washington *13972*
Coastal Engineering Research Council, College Station *14094*
Commission on Professionals in Science and Technology, Washington *14117*
Common Market of Scientific and Technological Knowledge, Washington *14137*
Cooling Tower Institute, Houston *14190*
Coordinating Research Council, Atlanta *14195*
Council of Academies of Engineering and Technological Sciences, Washington *14222*
Council of Engineering and Scientific Society Executives, Warrendale *14230*
Cryogenic Engineering Conference, Moffet Field *14274*
Ductile Iron Pipe Research Association, Birmingham *14320*
Earthquake Engineering Research Institute, Oakland *14331*
Emulsion Polymers Institute, Bethlehem *14371*
Engineering Workforce Commission, Washington *14377*
Environic Foundation International, South Bend *14380*
Environmental Design Research Association, Edmond *14381*
Experiments in Art and Technology, Berkeley Heights *14406*
Federation of Societies for Coatings Technology, Blue Bell *14429*
Fiber Society, Clemson *14431*
General Society of Mechanics and Tradesmen, New York *14488*
Goudy Society, New York *14517*
Graphic Communications Association, Alexandria *14522*
Gravure Association of America, Rochester *14523*
Human Factors and Ergonomics Society, Santa Monica *14590*
Illuminating Engineering Society of North America, New York *14637*
Industrial Research Institute, Washington *14651*
Institute of Gas Technology, Des Plaines *14707*
Institute of Industrial Engineers, Norcross *14710*
Instrument Society of America, Research Triangle Park *14730*
Insulated Cable Engineers Association, South Yarmouth *14731*
International Association for Fire Safety Science, College Park *14794*
International Association for Learning Laboratories, Saint Paul *14800*
International Association for Management of Technology, Coral Gables *14801*
International Association for Technology Assessment and Forecasting Institutions, Washington *14815*
International Association for the Advencement of High Pressure Science and Technology, Los Alamos *14817*
International Association of Boundary Element Methods, Nashville *14833*
International Banking Security Association, New York *14881*
International Benchmark Sites Network for Agrotechnology Transfer, Honolulu *14882*
International Centre for Gas Technology Information, Washington *14903*
International Commission on Particles and Fields, Pasadena *14932*
International Committee on Mechanics in Medicine and Biology, Ann Arbor *14947*
International Conference on Mechanics in Medicine and Biology, Ann Arbor *14957*
International Coordinating Committee on Solid State Transducers Research, Berkeley *14964*
International Council for Pressure Vessel Technology, Milwaukee *14972*
International Cryogenic Engineering Committee, Boulder *14990*
International Development Research Council, Norcross *14995*
International Foundation for Studies in Reproduction, Port Washington *15045*
International Geotechnical Engineering Committee, Carbondale *15048*
International Glutamate Technical Committee, Atlanta *15051*
International Microwave Power Institute, Manassas *15113*
International Ocean Drilling Program, Arlington *15125*
International Offshore Mechanics and Arctic Engineering Association, Hanover *15127*
International Program for Technology Research in Irrigation and Drainage, Washington *15162*
International Society for Clinical Laboratory Technology, Saint Louis *15200*
International Society for Measurement and Control, Research Triangle Park *15226*
International Society for Optical Engineering, Bellingham *15233*
International Society for Pharmaceutical Engineering, Tampa *15236*
International Society for Technology in Education, Eugene *15251*
International Society for Terrain-Vehicle Systems, Hanover *15252*
International Society for the Arts, Sciences and Technology, San Francisco *15253*
International Society for the Study of Dissociation, Glenview *15257*
International Society of Biorheology, Norman *15276*
International Society of Nuclear Air Treatment Technology, Batavia *15299*
International Society of Offshore and Polar Engineers, Golden *15301*
International Test and Evaluation Association, Fairfax *15338*
Internet Engineering Task Force, Reston *15379*
IUPS Commission on Bioengineering in Physiology, Seattle *15408*
Laser Institute of America, Orlando *15477*

Subject Index: Engineering 428

Leonardo – The International Society for the Arts, Sciences and Technology, San Francisco 15493
Marine Technology Society, Washington 15527
Missile, Space and Range Pioneers, Patrick Air Force Base 15588
National Academy of Engineering, Washington 15620
National Academy of Recording Arts and Sciences, Santa Monica 15623
National Accrediting Agency for Clinical Laboratory Sciences, Chicago 15625
National Association of County Engineers, Washington 15689
National Association of Industrial and Technical Teacher Educators, Knoxville 15710
National Certification Agency for Medical Lab Personnel, Lenexa 15789
National Council of Examiners for Engineering and Surveying, Clemson 15832
National Council of the Paper Industry for Air and Stream Improvement, Research Triangle Park 15843
National Information Service for Earthquake Engineering, Richmond 15914
National Institute for Certification in Engineering Technologies, Alexandria 15916
National Institute for Rehabilitation Engineering, Hewitt 15919
National Institute of Ceramic Engineers, Gainesville 15920
National Research Council, Washington 15963
National Society of Professional Engineers, Alexandria 15977
National Technical Association, Washington 15986
National Technical Services Association, Alexandria 15987
Network of Arab Scientists and Technologists Abroad, Urbana 16010
North America Society for Trenchless Technology, Chicago 16030
Offshore Mechanics and Polar Engineering Council, Golden 16079
Pacific Rocket Society, Oxnard 16123
Pan American Federation of Engineering Economics and Costs, Ann Arbor 16137
Plastics Institute of America, Fairfield 16178
Precision Measurements Association, Los Angeles 16201
Print Council of America, New Haven 16205
Program for Appropriate Technology in Health, Seattle 16212
Research and Engineering Council of the Graphic Arts Industry, Chadds Ford 16266
Research Council on Structural Connections, Chicago 16268
SAE International, Warrendale 16286
Safe Association, Nashville 16287
SFI Foundation, Poway 16318
Society for Biomaterials, Minneapolis 16359
Society for Experimental Mechanics, Bethel 16383
Society for Technical Communication, Arlington 16444
Society for the History of Technology, Auburn 16458
Society of Allied Weight Engineers, La Mesa 16491
Society of Cable Telecommunications Engineers, Exton 16505
Society of Carbide and Tool Engineers, Metals Park 16506
Society of Engineering Science, Charlottesville 16515
Society of Flight Test Engineers, Lancaster 16524
Society of Manufacturing Engineers, Dearborn 16534
Society of Naval Architects and Marine Engineers, Jersey City 16540
Society of Plastics Engineers, Brookfield 16548
Society of Professional Well Log Analysts, Houston 16550
Society of Turkish Architects, Engineers and Scientists in America, New York 16565
Society of Women Engineers, New York 16569
SOLE – The International Society of Logistics Engineers, Hyatsville 16576
Structural Stability Research Council, Bethlehem 16608
Sulphur Institute, Washington 16612
Technical Association of the Graphic Arts, Rochester 16630
Technical Association of the Pulp and Paper Industry, Atlanta 16631
Technology Transfer Society, Franklin 16632
Tripoli Rocketry Association, Kenner 16652
Ukrainian Engineers' Society of America, New York 16657
United Engineering Trustees, New York 16670
United Nations Commission on Science and Technology for Development, New York 16673
United States Institute for Theatre Technology, New York 16691
United States National Committee on Theoretical and Applied Mechanics, Washington 16696
United States National Society for the International Society of Soil Mechanics and Foundation Engineering, Raleigh 16697
Water Environment Federation, Alexandria 16742
Welding Research Council, New York 16748
World Institute for Safety Education and Research, Warrensburg 16825

Venezuela

Asociación Venezolana de Ingeniería Eléctrica y Mecánica, Caracas 16882
Asociación Venezolana de Ingeniería Sanitaria y Ambiental Caracas, Caracas 16883
Consejo Nacional de Investigaciones Científicas y Tecnológicas, Caracas 16908

Vietnam

Vietnam Union of Sientific and Technical Associations, Hanoi 16941
Vietnamese Association of Engineering, Hanoi 16952

Yugoslavia

Jugoslovenski Centar za Tehničku i Naučnu Dokumentaciju, Beograd 17000
Jugoslovenski Savez za Zavarivanje, Beograd 17001
Jugoslovensko Društvo za Mehaniku, Beograd 17005
Nikola Tesla Association of Societies for Promotion of Technical Sciences in Yugoslavia, Beograd 17011
Union of Engineers and Technicians of Serbia, Beograd 17039
Union of Engineers and Technicians of Yugoslavia, Beograd 17040

Zambia

The Engineering Institution of Zambia, Lusaka 17049

Entomology

Argentina

Sociedad Entomológica Argentina, La Plata 00109

Australia

The Australian Entomological Society, Burnley 00186
Council for International Congresses of Entomology, Canberra 00264
Entomological Society of New South Wales, Sydney 00272
Entomological Society of Queensland, Brisbane 00273

Austria

Arbeitsgemeinschaft Österreichischer Entomologen, Wien 00409
Österreichische Entomologische Gesellschaft, Graz 00588

Belgium

Société Royale Belge d'Entomologie, Bruxelles 01284

Brazil

Sociedade Brasileira de Entomologia, São Paulo 01510

Canada

Entomological Society of British Columbia, Saanichton 02090
Entomological Society of Canada, Ottawa 02091
Entomological Society of Manitoba, Winnipeg 02092
Entomological Society of Ontario, Sault Sainte-Marie 02093
Entomological Society of Saskatchewan, Saskatoon 02094
Societe d'Entomologie du Quebec, Saint-Jean-sur-Richelieu 02374

Chile

Sociedad Chilena de Entomología, Santiago 02485

China, People's Republic

Entomological Society of China, Beijing 02646

Czech Republic

Česká Společnost Entomologická, Praha 02934

Denmark

Entomologisk Forening, København 03106

Egypt

Société Entomologique d'Egypte, Cairo 03303

France

Société des Lépidopteristes Français, Paris 04039
Société Entomologique de France, Paris 04103

Germany

Deutsche Gesellschaft für allgemeine und angewandte Entomologie e.V., Dossenheim 04748
Münchner Entomologische Gesellschaft e.V., München 05757

Hungary

Magyar Rovartani Társaság, Budapest 06338

Italy

Accademia Nazionale di Entomologia, Firenze 06855
Accademia Nazionale Italiana di Entomologia, Firenze 06861
Apimondia, Roma 06889
Associazione Romana di Entomologia, Roma 07038
Società Entomologica Italiana, Genova 07423

Japan

Nippon Kontyu Gakkai, Tokyo 07941
Nippon Oyo-Dobutsu-Konchu Gakkai, Tokyo 07958

Kenya

African Association of Insect Scientists, Nairobi 08061

Mexico

Sociedad Mexicana de Entomología, Veracruz 08336

Netherlands

Nederlandse Entomologische Vereniging, Amsterdam 08556

New Zealand

Entomological Society of New Zealand, Upper Hutt 08672
New Zealand Society for Parasitology, Hamilton 08724

Nigeria

Entomological Society of Nigeria, Zaria 08767

Peru

Sociedad Entomológica del Perú, Lima 09008

Poland

Polskie Towarzystwo Entomologiczne, Wroclaw 09097

South Africa

Entomological Society of Southern Africa, Pretoria 09627

Switzerland

Schweizerische Entomologische Gesellschaft, Neuchâtel 10265

United Kingdom

Amateur Entomologists' Society, Feltham 10767
CAB International Institute of Entomology, London 11240
Royal Entomological Society of London, London 12203

U.S.A.

American Entomological Society, Philadelphia 13138
American Mosquito Control Association, Lake Charles 13278
Association of Applied Insect Ecologists, Sacramento 13729
Entomological Society of America, Lanham 14379

Venezuela

Sociedad Venezolana de Entomología, Maracay 16929

Zambia

International Red Locust Control Organisation for Central and Southern Africa, Ndola 17050

Environmental Protection s. Ecology

Ethnology s. a. Folklore

Argentina

Asociación Argentina de Estudios Americanos, Buenos Aires 00043
Departamento de Estudios Etnográficos y Coloniales, Santa Fé 00072

Australia

Australian Institute of Aboriginal and Torres Strait Islander Studies, Canberra 00191

Austria

Akademische Arbeitsgemeinschaft für Volkskunde, Wien 00399
Anthropologische Gesellschaft in Wien, Wien 00400
Arbeitskreis für Tibetische und Buddhistische Studien, Wien 00415
Gesellschaft für Ost- und Südostkunde, Linz 00476
Gesellschaft zur Erforschung slawischer Sprachen und Kulturen, Graz 00487
Gesellschaft zur Förderung von Nordamerika-Studien an der Universität Wien, Wien 00491
Niederösterreichisches Bildungs- und Heimatwerk, Arbeitsgemeinschaft für Volkskunde, Wien 00566
Österreichische Ethnologische Gesellschaft, Wien 00589
Österreichische Ethnomedizinische Gesellschaft, Wien 00590
Österreichische Kulturgemeinschaft, Wien 00716
Österreichische Orient-Gesellschaft Hammer-Purgstall, Wien 00726
Österreichischer Fachverband für Volkskunde, Graz 00755
Österreichisches Lateinamerika-Institut, Wien 00775
Orientalische Gesellschaft, Wien 00780
Pro Austria, Wien 00786
Salzburger Kulturvereinigung, Salzburg 00792
SIGMA – Salzburger Gesellschaft für Semiologie, Salzburg 00793
Verein Freunde der Völkerkunde, Wien 00831
Verein für Volkskunde in Wien, Wien 00837

Belgium

Association Européenne de l'Ethnie Française, Bruxelles 00956
Fondation Egyptologique Reine Elisabeth, Bruxelles 01174

Brazil

Centro de Pesquisas Folclóricas, Rio de Janeiro 01439
Comissão Nacional de Folclore, Rio de Janeiro 01451
Coordenação de Folclore e Cultura Popular, Rio de Janeiro 01458
Instituto Histórico, Geográfico e Etnográfico Paranaense, Curitiba 01487

Canada

African Studies Committee, Ottawa 01616
Canadian Association for Irish Studies, Peterborough 01799
Canadian Association for Scottish Studies, Guelph 01804
Canadian Association of African Studies, Montréal 01809
Canadian Ethnic Studies Association, Montréal 01877
Canadian Institute of Ukrainian Studies, Edmonton 01917

China, People's Republic

Chinese Association for European Studies, Beijing 02569
Royal Asiatic Society, Hong Kong Branch, Hong Kong 02658

China, Republic

China Society, Taipei 02684
Chinese Association for Folklore, Taipei 02686
Ethnological Society of China, Taipei 02721

Colombia

Comité Nacional del Consejo Internacional de Museos, Bogotá 02781
Junta Nacional de Folclore, Bogotá 02802

Cyprus

Etaireia Kypriakon Spoudon, Nicosia 02907

Czech Republic

Národopisná Společnost, Praha 02956

Denmark

Det Danske Afrika Selskab, Hellerup 03083
Orientalsk Samfund, København 03184

Egypt

The Egyptian Society for the Dissemination of Universal Culture and Knowledge, Cairo 03284
Institut d'Egypte, Cairo 03295

Finland

Kalevalaseura, Helsinki 03357
Museovirasto, Helsinki 03366
Suomen Itämainen Seura, Helsingin Yliopisto 03408
Suomen Muinaismuistoyhdistys, Helsinki 03425

France

Association des Etudes Tsiganes, Paris 03515
Association Française des Arabisants, Paris 03537
Association Française d'Etudes Américaines, Paris 03548
Association Internationale des Etudes de l'Asie du Sud-Est, Paris 03584
Société Africaine de Culture, Paris 03947
Société Asiatique, Paris 03952
Société des Africanistes, Paris 04016
Société des Américanistes, Paris 04018
Société des Amis du Musée de l'Homme, Paris 04023
Société des Océanistes, Paris 04042
Société d'Ethnographie de Paris, Paris 04049
Société d'Ethnologie Française, Paris 04050
Société d'Etudes et de Recherches pour la Connaissance de l'Homme, Paris 04061
Société d'Etudes Folkloriques du Centre-Ouest, Saint-Jean d'Angely 04065
Société d'Etudes Hispaniques et de Diffusion de la Culture Française à l'Etranger, Périgueux 04066
Société d'Etudes Italiennes, Paris 04068
Société d'Etudes Linguistiques et Anthropologiques de France, Paris 04072
Union Internationale des Etudes Orientales et Asiatiques, Saint-Maur 04312

French Polynesia

Société des Etudes Océaniennes, Papeete 04329

Germany

Arbeitskreis Ethnomedizin, Hamburg 04487
Arnold-Bergstraesser-Institut für kulturwissenschaftliche Forschung e.V., Freiburg 04502
Berliner Gesellschaft für Anthropologie, Ethnologie und Urgeschichte, Berlin 04548
Deutsche Gesellschaft für Amerikastudien e.V., Halle/Saale 04750
Deutsche Gesellschaft für Asienkunde e.V., Hamburg 04756
Deutsche Gesellschaft für Völkerkunde e.V., Frankfurt/M. 04876
Deutsche Morgenländische Gesellschaft e.V., Heidelberg 04925
Deutsches Orient-Institut, Hamburg 05102
European Association for Japanese Studies, Duisburg 05152
Frobenius-Gesellschaft e.V., Frankfurt 05303
Geographische Gesellschaft Bremen, Bremen 05318
Gesellschaft für bedrohte Völker e.V., Göttingen 05350
Gesellschaft für Erd- und Völkerkunde, Bonn 05361
Gesellschaft für Erd- und Völkerkunde zu Stuttgart e.V., Stuttgart 05362
Gesellschaft für Natur- und Völkerkunde Ostasiens e.V., Hamburg 05388
Nah- und Mittelost-Verein e.V., Hamburg 05760
Naturhistorische Gesellschaft Nürnberg e.V., Nürnberg 05766
Osteuropa-Institut München, München 05868
Sorbisches Institut e.V., Bautzen 05949
Südosteuropa-Gesellschaft e.V., München 05978
Volkskundliche Kommission für Westfalen, Münster 06143
Zentrum für Türkeistudien e.V., Essen 06188

Greece
Elliniki Laographiki Etaireia, Athinai *06221*
Istoriki kai Ethnologiki Etaireia tis Ellados, Athinai *06247*

Hungary
Magyar Néprajzi Társasag, Budapest *06329*

India
All-India Oriental Conference, Pune *06397*
Asiatic Society, Calcutta *06405*
Asiatic Society of Mumbai, Mumbai *06406*
Ethnographic and Folk Culture Society, Lucknow *06427*
Indian Society of Afro-Asian Studies, New Delhi *06480*
International Academy of Indian Culture, New Delhi *06496*
Jammu and Kashmir Academy of Art, Culture and Languages, Srinagar *06499*

Ireland
Folklore of Ireland Society, Dublin *06601*

Israel
Israel Oriental Society, Jerusalem *06709*

Italy
Accademia di Romania, Roma *06809*
Associazione degli Africanisti Italiani, Pavia *06906*
Associazione Italiana di Cultura Classica, Firenze *06943*
Associazione Italiana Studi Americanisti, Genova *06990*
Associazione per la Conservazione delle Tradizioni Popolari, Palermo *07027*
Associazione Sole Italico, Sulmona *07042*
Centro Camuno di Studi Preistorici, Capo di Ponte *07054*
Centro Internazionale di Studi Sardi, Cagliari *07073*
Centro Polesano di Studi Storici, Archeologici ed Etnografici, Rovigo *07112*
Centro Ricerche di Storia e Arte Bitontina, Bitonto *07119*
Centro Studi Zingari, Roma *07179*
International Association of Biblicists and Orientalists, Ravenna *07311*
Istituto Italiano per il Medio ed Estremo Oriente, Roma *07353*
Istituto Italiano per l'Africa e l'Oriente, Roma *07356*
Istituto Nazionale di Studi Etruschi ed Italici, Firenze *07363*
Istituto per l'Oriente, Roma *07372*
Società di Etnografia Italiana, Roma *07402*
Società Italiana di Antropologia e Etnologia, Firenze *07460*
Società Italiana per l'Antropologia e la Etnologia, Firenze *07592*
Union Generela di Ladins dla Dolomites, Ortisei-Urtijëi *07664*
Union Ladins Val Badia, Pedraces *07665*

Jamaica
Institute of Jamaica, Kingston *07697*

Japan
Nippon Afurika Gakkai, Tokyo *07872*
Nippon Dokyo Gakkai, Tokyo *07889*
Nippon Orient Gakkai, Tokyo *07957*
Todai Chugoku Gakkai, Tokyo *08038*

Korea, Republic
Korean Association of Sinology, Seoul *08127*

Malta
Ghaqda Tal Folklor, Sliema *08245*

Mexico
Instituto Indigenista Interamericano, México *08311*

Netherlands
Association Internationale d'Etudes Occitanes, Wien *08397*
Koninklijk Instituut voor Taal-, Land- en Volkenkunde, Leiden *08501*

New Caledonia
Société des Etudes Mélanésiennes, Nouméa *08666*

New Zealand
Polynesian Society, Auckland *08737*

Pakistan
Institute of Islamic Culture, Lahore *08900*
Lok Virsa, Islamabad *08906*

Poland
Polskie Towarzystwo Ludoznawcze, Wroclaw *09117*
Polskie Towarzystwo Orientalistyczne, Warszawa *09129*

Portugal
Sociedade Portuguesa de Antropologia e Etnologia, Porto *09227*

Puerto Rico
Caribbean Studies Association, Rio Piedras *09258*

Romania
International Association of South-East European Studies, Bucuresti *09280*

Russia
Association of Orientalists, Moskva *09333*
Association of Sinologists, Moskva *09335*

Singapore
The China Society, Singapore *09531*

Slovakia
Slovenská Národopisná Spoločnost, Bratislava *09568*
Slovenská Orientalistická Spoločnost, Bratislava *09569*

South Africa
Africa Institute of South Africa, Pretoria *09606*

Spain
Real Sociedad Económica de Amigos del País de Tenerife, Tenerife *09799*
Sociedad de Ciencias, Letras y Artes, Las Palmas *09810*

Sri Lanka
Royal Asiatic Society of Sri Lanka, Colombo *09838*

Sweden
Kungliga Gustav Adolfs Akademien för Svensk Folkkultur, Uppsala *09903*

Switzerland
Geographisch-Ethnologische Gesellschaft Basel, Basel *10131*
Schweizerische Afrika-Gesellschaft, Bern *10238*
Schweizerische Asiengesellschaft, Zürich *10256*
Schweizerische Ethnologische Gesellschaft, Bern *10267*
Société Suisse des Américanistes, Genève *10513*

Tanzania
Tanzania Society, Dar es Salaam *10609*

Thailand
Siam Society, Bangkok *10646*

Tunisia
Comité International d'Etudes Morisques, Zaghouan *10686*
Institut National d'Archéologie et d'Art, Tunis *10689*

United Kingdom
African Studies Association of the United Kingdom, London *10756*
An Comunn Gaidhealach, Inverness *10770*
Arab Research Centre, London *10783*
British Association for American Studies, Leicester *11008*
China Society, London *11286*
Egypt Exploration Society, London *11439*
Folklore Society, London *11543*
Hispanic and Luso-Brazilian Council, London *11622*
Institution of Polish Engineers in Great Britain, London *11754*
International African Institute, London *11759*
Maghreb Studies Association, London *11898*
National Association for Soviet and East European Studies, Milton Keynes *11979*
The Royal African Society, London *12167*
Royal Asiatic Society of Great Britain and Ireland, London *12171*
Royal Celtic Society, Edinburgh *12177*
Royal Commonwealth Society, London *12199*
Royal Society for Asian Affairs, London *12247*
Scottish Society for Northern Studies, Edinburgh *12319*
Society for Cooperation in Russian and Soviet Studies, London *12352*
Society for Folk Life Studies, Hollywood *12358*
Society for Libyan Studies, London *12362*
Society for South Asian Studies, London *12381*
Ulster Folklife Society, Holywood *12523*

U.S.A.
Aboriginal Research Club, Dearborn *12641*
Afghanistan Studies Association, Omaha *12701*
African Heritage Center for African Dance and Music, Washington *12706*
African Studies Association, Atlanta *12709*
Afro-Asian Center, Saugerties *12711*
American Academy for Jewish Research, New York *12739*
American Conference for Irish Studies, Syracuse *13088*
American Ethnological Society, Durham *13141*
American Folklore Society, Arlington *13153*
American Indian Lore Association, Logan *13192*
American Institute of Indian Studies, Chicago *13214*
American Institute of Iranian Studies, Columbus *13215*
American Institute of Islamic Studies, Denver *13216*
American Oriental Society, Ann Arbor *13296*
American Research Institute in Turkey, Philadelphia *13355*
American Schools of Oriental Research, Baltimore *13363*
American Society for Ethnohistory, Ithaca *13385*
American Swedish Institute, Minneapolis *13511*
Amerind Foundation, Dragoon *13538*
Asia Society, New York *13578*
Asian Studies Center, Michigan, East Lansing *13580*
Association for Asian Studies, Ann Arbor *13598*
Association for Central Asian Studies, Madison *13606*
Association for Jewish Demography and Statistics – American Branch, Los Angeles *13639*
Association for Korean Studies, Rancho Palos Verdes *13641*
Association for the Advancement of Baltic Studies, Hackettstown *13673*
Association for the Advancement of Central Asian Research, Amherst *13674*
Association for the Study of Afro-American Life and History, Washington *13689*
Association of African Studies Programs, New York *13711*
Association of American Schools in Central America, Colombian-Caribbean and Mexico (Tri-Association), Miami *13721*
Association of Arab-American University Graduates, Washington *13730*
Association of Caribbean Studies, Lexington *13744*
Association of Teachers of Latin American Studies, Flushing *13846*
Bet Nahrain, Modesto *13911*
California Institute of Pan African Studies, Los Angeles *13961*
Center for Austrian Studies, Minneapolis *13997*
Center for Chinese Research Materials, Oakton *13999*
Center for Migration Studies of New York, Staten Island *14014*
China Institute in America, New York *14063*
Chinese Historical Society of America, San Francisco *14067*
Committee on Women in Asian Studies, Honolulu *14136*
Consortium of Latin American Studies Programs, Storrs *14179*
David Rockefeller Centre for Latin American Studies, Cambridge *14287*
East Asian Studies Centre, Bloomington, Bloomington *14334*
Estonian Learned Society of America, New York *14391*
Foundation for Mideast Communication, Beverly Hills *14470*
Gypsy Lore Society, Cheverly *14536*
Hispanic Institute, New York *14569*
Independent Scholars of Asia, Berkeley *14644*
Institute of Chinese Culture, New York *14699*
Institute of Lithuanian Studies, Chicago *14715*
International Azerbaijan Research and Development Institute, Washington *14880*
IUAES Commission for the Anthropological and Ethnological Study of Peace, Evanston *15391*
IUAES Commission on Cultural Dimensions of Global Change, Williamsburg *15394*
IUAES Commission on Ethnic Relations, Ypsilanti *15396*
James S Coleman African Studies Center, Los Angeles, Los Angeles *15420*
Jugoslavia Study Group, Wausau *15460*
Melanesian Studies Resource Center, La Jolla *15551*
Middle Atlantic Council of Latin American Studies, Gaithersgurg *15568*
Middle East Research and Information Project, Washington *15573*
Midwest Association for Latin American Studies, Columbia *15578*
Mongolia Society, Bloomington *15595*
National Association for Armenian Studies and Research, Belmont *15637*
National Association for Ethnic Studies, Tempe *15643*
Nepal Studies Association, Northridge *16008*
New England Council of Latin American Studies, Northampton *16015*
New York African Studies Association, New York *16019*
North American Conference on British Studies, Portland *16037*
Northwest Regional Consortium for Southeast Asian Studies, Seattle *16063*
RAND Center for Russian and Eurasian Studies, Santa Monica *16245*
Scandinavian Seminar College, Amherst *16293*
Society for Ethnomusicology, Bloomington *16380*
Society for Iranian Studies, Seattle *16404*
Society for Slovene Studies, Bloomington *16441*
Society for the Advancement of Scandinavian Study, Provo *16449*
Society of Ethnic and Special Studies, Edwardsville *16516*
Society of Spanish and Spanish-American Studies, Boulder *16557*
Southeast Asia Council Association for Asian Studies, Madison *16581*
Tibet Society, Bloomington *16644*
Ukrainian Institute of America, New York *16658*
United Nations Educational, Scientific and Cultural Organization, New York *16675*
Washington Foundation for European Studies, Washington *16739*
YIVO Institute for Jewish Research, New York *16850*

Venezuela
Asociación Cultural Humboldt, Caracas *16874*
Centro de Estudios Venezolanos Indigenas, Caracas *16889*

Family Planning

Canada
Cumberland County Family Planning Association, Amherst *02082*
Fédération du Québec pour le Planning des Naissances, Montréal *02098*
Serena Canada, Ottawa *02368*

Dominican Republic
Asociación Dominicana pro Bienestar de la Familia, Santo Domingo *03224*

Germany
Bundesarbeitsgemeinschaft von Familienbildung und Beratung e.V., Elmshorn *04631*
Deutsches Institut für Vormundschaftswesen, Heidelberg *05090*
Pro Familia, Frankfurt/Main *05890*

Ireland
Irish Family Planning Association, Dublin *06626*

Italy
Centro Internazionale Studi Famiglia, Milano *07084*
Centro per la Riforma del Diritto di Famiglia, Milano *07107*
Famiglia e Libertà, Roma *07270*
Unione Consultori Italiani Prematrimoniali e Matrimoniali, Bologna *07672*

Kenya
Centre for African Family Studies, Nairobi *08082*

Switzerland
Schweizerische Gesellschaft für Fertilität, Sterilität und Familienplanung, Lausanne *10294*

United Kingdom
The Family Planning Association, London *11519*

Uruguay
Centro de Investigaciones y Estudios Familiares, Montevideo *12618*

U.S.A.
Family Health International, Research Triangle Park *14411*
Family Planning International Assistance, New York *14412*
National Council on Family Relations, Minneapolis *15852*
Planned Parenthood Federation of America, New York *16176*
Society of Teachers of Family Medicine, Kansas City *16562*

Vietnam
Vietnamese Association of Obstetrics, Gynaecology and Family Planning, Hanoi *16962*

Finance

Australia
Accounting Association of Australia and New Zealand, Melbourne *00116*
Australian Institute of Credit Management, Artarmon *00194*
Australian Institute of Valuers and Land Economists, Deakin *00209*
Commonwealth Institute of Valuers, Sydney *00261*

Austria
Österreichische Bankwissenschaftliche Gesellschaft, Wien *00579*
Österreichisches Forschungsinstitut für Sparkassenwesen, Wien *00771*

Belgium
Association Belge des Analystes Financiers, Bruxelles *00947*
European Finance Association, Bruxelles *01158*

Benin
African Union for the Management of Development Banks, Cotonou *01324*

Canada
Canadian Institute of Financial Planning, Toronto *01907*
Institute of Chartered Accountants of Ontario, Toronto *02140*

China, Republic
Chinese Society of Budgetary Management, Taipei *02710*
Finance Association of China, Taipei *02722*

Denmark
International Banking Research Institute, København *03133*

France
Centre for the Advancement and Study of the European Currency, Lyon *03683*
Institut des Actuaires Français, Paris *03881*
Société d'Etudes Financières et Meunières, Paris *04064*
Société d'Etudes Minières, Industrielles et Financières, Paris *04073*
Société Financière Européenne, Paris *04106*

Germany
Bankakademie e.V., Frankfurt/Main *04522*
Deutsche Vereinigung für Finanzanalyse und Anlageberatung e.V., Dreieich *04969*
Deutsche Vereinigung für Internationales Steuerrecht, Köln *04971*
Deutsche Vereinigung für internationales Steuerrecht im Verband der Fiscal Association, Bayerische Sektion e.V., München *04972*
Deutsches wissenschaftliches Steuerinstitut der Steuerberater e.V., Bonn *05106*
Europäische Vereinigung für Eigentumsbildung, Hermann-Lindrath-Gesellschaft e.V., Hannover *05149*
Gesellschaft für internationale Geldgeschichte, Frankfurt *05376*

Groupe Rhône-Alpes de Recherche et d'Etudes en Gestion, Lyon 03871
Institut Géographique National, Paris 03888
Société de Biogéographie, Paris 03962
Société de Géographie, Paris 03972
Société de Géographie Commerciale de Bordeaux, Bordeaux 03973
Société de Géographie Commerciale de Paris, Paris 03974
Société de Géographie de Lille, Lille 03975
Société de Géographie de Lyon, Lyon 03976
Société de Géographie de Toulouse, Toulouse 03977
Société de Géographie Humaine de Paris, Paris 03978
Société des Amis de la Revue de Géographie de Lyon, Lyon 04019
Société des Explorateurs et des Voyageurs Français, Paris 04037
Société Française de Géographie Economique, Paris 04127
Société Languedocienne de Géographie, Montpellier 04216

Georgia
Georgian Geographical Society, Tbilisi 04340

Germany
Arbeitsgemeinschaft für Osteuropaforschung, Tübingen 04455
Deutsche Akademie für Landeskunde e.V., Frankfurt/Main 04709
Deutsche Gesellschaft für Geographie (DGfG), Duisburg 04785
Deutsche Gesellschaft für Polarforschung, Bremerhaven 04846
Fränkische Geographische Gesellschaft e.V., Erlangen 05282
Frankfurter Geographische Gesellschaft e.V., Frankfurt 05285
Geographische Gesellschaft, München 05317
Geographische Gesellschaft Bremen, Bremen 05318
Geographische Gesellschaft in Hamburg e.V., Hamburg 05319
Geographische Gesellschaft zu Hannover, Hannover 05320
Gesellschaft für Erd- und Völkerkunde, Bonn 05361
Gesellschaft für Erd- und Völkerkunde zu Stuttgart e.V., Stuttgart 05362
Gesellschaft für Erdkunde zu Berlin, Berlin 05363
Gesellschaft für Erdkunde zu Köln e.V., Köln 05364
Institut für Länderkunde e.V., Leipzig 05531
International Geographical Union (IGU), Bonn 05559
Verband der Geographen an Deutschen Hochschulen, München 06022
Verband der Geographen an Deutschen Hochschulen (VGDH), Duisburg 06023
Verband Deutscher Schulgeographen e.V., Großburgwedel 06051
Zentralausschuss für Deutsche Landeskunde e.V., Frankfurt 06182

Ghana
Ghana Geographical Association, Accra 06199

Greece
Elliniki Geografiki Etaireia, Athinai 06218

Guatemala
Academia de Geografía e Historia de Guatemala, Guatemala City 06259

Honduras
Academia Hondureña de Geografía e Historia, Tegucigalpa 06281

Hungary
Magyar Földrajzi Társaság, Budapest 06310

India
Geographical Society of India, Calcutta 06429
National Geographical Society of India, Varanasi 06518

Ireland
Geographical Society of Ireland, Dublin 06604

Israel
Israel Geographical Society, Jerusalem 06701

Italy
Accademia Lunigianese di Scienze Giovanni Capellini, La Spezia 06839
Associazione dei Geografi Italiani, Roma 06909
Associazione Italiana degli Insegnanti di Geografia, Trieste 06932
Centro Studi e Ricerche per la Conoscenza della Liguria Attraverso le Testimonianze dei Viaggiatori Stranieri, Genova 07152
Centro Studi Nord e Sud, Napoli 07161
Comitato dei Geografi Italiani, Roma 07195
Istituto Geografico Militare, Firenze 07339
Società di Studi Geografici, Firenze 07415
Società di Studi Romagnoli, Cesena 07416
Società Geografica Italiana, Roma 07434
Società Istriana di Archeologia e Storia Patria, Trieste 07442

Jamaica
Jamaican Geographical Society, Kingston 07704

Japan
Keizai Chiri Gakkai, Tokyo 07753
Nippon Chiri Gakkai, Tokyo 07880
Nippon Seibutsuchiri Gakkai, Tokyo 07969
Shigaku Kenkyukai, Kyoto 08024
Tokyo Chigaku Kyokai, Tokyo 08042

Korea, Republic
Korean Geographical Society, Seoul 08131

Kyrgyzstan
Kyrgyz Geographical Society, Bishkek 08148

Macedonia
Geografsko Društvo na Makedonija, Skopje 08189

Malta
Malta Geographical Society, Gzira 08246

Mexico
Academia Nacional de Historia y Geografía, México 08261
Center of Coordination and Diffusion of Latin American Studies, México 08284
Instituto Panamericano de Geografía e Historia, México 08315
Sociedad Mexicana de Geografía y Estadística, México 08341
Sociedad Nuevoleonesa de Historia, Geografía y Estadística, Monterrey 08353

Moldova, Republic of
Geographic Society of Moldova, Chişinău 08357

Morocco
Association Nationale des Géographes Marocains, Rabat 08380
Comité National de Géographie du Maroc, Rabat 08383

Netherlands
Koninklijk Nederlands Aardrijkskundig Genootschap, Utrecht 08502

New Zealand
New Zealand Geographical Society, Hamilton 08697

Nigeria
Nigerian Geographical Association, Ibadan 08778

Norway
Norsk Samfunnsgeografisk Forening, Dragvoll 08846
Det Norske Geografiske Selskap, Oslo 08855

Peru
Instituto Geográfico Nacional, Lima 09002
Sociedad Geográfica de Lima, Lima 09009

Poland
Polskie Towarzystwo Geograficzne, Warszawa 09104

Portugal
Sociedade de Geografia de Lisboa, Lisboa 09219

Romania
Societatea de Stiinte Geografice din Romania, Bucuresti 09313

Russia
Russian Geographical Society, St. Petersburg 09445
Tropical Committee, Moskva 09474

Saudi Arabia
King Abdul Aziz Research Centre, Riyadh 09492

Slovakia
Slovenská Geografická Spoločnost, Bratislava 09560

Slovenia
Zveza Geografskih Društev Slovenije, Ljubljana 09601

South Africa
Africa Institute of South Africa, Pretoria 09606
Society of South African Geographers, Wits 09663

Spain
Instituto Geográfico Nacional, Madrid 09767
Real Sociedad Geográfica, Madrid 09803

Sri Lanka
Ceylon Geographical Society, Colombo 09830

Sweden
Geografilärarnas Riksförening, Lund 09883
Geografiska Förbundet, Stockholm 09884
Svenska Sällskapet för Antropologi och Geografi, Stockholm 09998

Switzerland
Geographisch-Ethnographische Gesellschaft Zürich, Zürich 10130
Geographisch-Ethnologische Gesellschaft Basel, Basel 10131
Geographische Gesellschaft Bern, Bern 10132
Schweizerische Gesellschaft für angewandte Geographie, Winterthur 10277
Schweizerische Stiftung für Alpine Forschungen, Zürich 10387
Société de Géographie de Genève, Genève 10497
Verband der Schweizer Geographen, Basel 10530
Verein Schweizerischer Geographielehrerinnen und Geographielehrer, Wohlen 10551

United Kingdom
British Geomorphological Research Group, London 11084
Council for British Geography, London 11352
Council of British Geography, London 11360
The Geographical Association, Sheffield 11567
The Hakluyt Society, London 11596
Hispanic and Luso-Brazilian Council, London 11622
Manchester Geographical Society, Manchester 11903
Palestine Exploration Fund, London 12084
Remote Sensing Society, Nottingham 12151
Royal Geographical Society, London 12208
Royal Scottish Geographical Society, Glasgow 12245
Scientific Committee on Antarctic Research, Cambridge 12286
Scientific Exploration Society, Marlborough 12287
Scottish Association of Geography Teachers, Hamilton 12294
Society for Libyan Studies, London 12362
Trans-Antarctic Association, Cambridge 12510

Uruguay
Instituto Histórico y Geográfico del Uruguay, Montevideo 12627

U.S.A.
American Geographical Society, New York 13167
American Institute for Maghreb Studies, Washington 13201
American Polar Society, Reedsport 13335
Antarctica and Southern Ocean Coalition, Washington 13547
Association of American Geographers, Washington 13714
Conference of Latin Americanist Geographers, Austin 14160
Environmental Design Research Association, Edmond 14381
The Explorers Club, New York 14407
Gustav E von Grunebaum Centre for Near Eastern Studies, Los Angeles 14535
Hagop Kevorkian Centre for Near Eastern Studies, New York, New York 14537
Human Relations Area Files, New Haven 14592
International Association for Great Lakes Research, Ann Arbor 14795
National Council for Geographic Education, Indiana 15823
National Geographic Society, Washington 15891
Organization for Tropical Studies, Durham 16095
South American Explorers Club, Ithaca 16580
United Nations Group of Experts on Geographical Names, New York 16676
United States Antarctic Research Program, Arlington 16682

Venezuela
Asociación Cultural Humboldt, Caracas 16874

Vietnam
Vietnamese Association of Geography, Hanoi 16955

Yugoslavia
Srpsko Geografsko Društvo, Beograd 17033

Zimbabwe
Geographical Association of Zimbabwe, Harare 17068

Geology

Albania
Shoqata e Gjeologeve te Shqiperise, Tirana 00005

Argentina
Asociación Argentina de Geofísicos y Geodestas, Buenos Aires 00045
Asociación Geológica Argentina, Buenos Aires 00055
Centro Argentino de Espeleología, Buenos Aires 00062
Fundación Miguel Lillo, San Miguel de Tucumán 00076

Australia
Australian Geological Survey Organisation, Canberra 00189
Australian Geomechanics Society, Barton 00190
Geological Society of Australia, Sydney 00284
Geological Survey of New South Wales, Saint Leonards 00285
Geological Survey of Victoria, Fitzroy 00286
Tasmanian Geological Survey, Rosny 00373

Austria
Gesellschaft der Geologie- und Bergbaustudenten in Österreich, Wien 00459
Österreichische Bodenkundliche Gesellschaft, Wien 00583
Österreichische Geologische Gesellschaft, Wien 00597
Österreichische Gesellschaft für Erdölwissenschaften, Wien 00628
Österreichische Himalaya-Gesellschaft, Wien 00711
Österreichischer Alpenverein, Wissenschaftlicher Unterausschuss, Innsbruck 00746
Vereinigung für Angewandte Lagerstättenforschung, Leoben 00851
Vereinigung für Hydrogeologische Forschungen in Graz, Graz 00852

Barbados
Barbados Museum and Historical Society, Saint Ann's Garrison 00923

Belgium
European Centre for Geodynamics and Seismology, Bruxelles 01120
Geologica Belgica, Bruxelles 01176
Société Belge de Géologie, Bruxelles 01243
Société Géologique de Belgique, Liège 01267

Bolivia
Asociación de Ingenieros y Geólogos de Yacimientos Petrolíferos Fiscales Bolivianos, La Paz 01338
Sociedad Geológica Boliviana, La Paz 01348

Brazil
Sociedade Brasileira de Geologia, São Paulo 01514

Bulgaria
Bulgarian Geological Society, Sofia 01555
Carpathian Balkan Geological Association, Sofia 01577
Scientific and Technical Union of Mining, Geology and Metallurgy, Sofia 01584

Canada
Association of Exploration Geochemists, Nepean 01717
Canadian Geoscience Council, Waterloo 01892
Canadian Quaternary Association, Fredericton 01958
Canadian Society of Petroleum Geologists, Calgary 02001
Geological Association of Canada, Saint John's 02116
International Association of Geochemistry and Cosmochemistry, Pinawa 02147
Saskatchewan Geological Society, Regina 02353

Chile
Corporación para el Desarrollo de la Ciencia, Santiago 02465
Sociedad Geológica de Chile, Santiago 02530

China, People's Republic
Chinese Academy of Geological Sciences, Beijing 02558
Geological Society of China, Beijing 02649

China, Republic
Geological Society of China, Taipei 02724

Colombia
Instituto de Ciencias Naturales, Bogotá 02799
Instituto Nacional de Investigaciones Geológico-Mineras, Bogotá 02800

Czech Republic
Česká Geologická Společnost, Praha 02919

Denmark
Dansk Geologisk Forening, København 03009

El Salvador
Centro de Estudios e Investigaciones Geotécnicas, San Salvador 03316

Ethiopia
African Mountain Association, Asmara 03327

Finland
Geologian Tutkimuskeskus, Espoo 03349
International Peat Society, Jyskä 03354
Suomen Geologinen Seura, Espoo 03402

France
Association Française pour l'Etude du Quaternaire, Caen 03558
Association of African Geological Surveys, Orléans 03625
Eurocoast, Marseille 03788
EUROLAT – European Network for Studies on Laterites and Tropical Environment, Strasbourg 03789
International Association of Engineering Geology, Paris 03898
Société des Lettres, Sciences et Arts La Haute-Auvergne, Aurillac 04040
Société Géologique de France, Paris 04195
Société Géologique et Minéralogique de Bretagne, Rennes 04196
Société Parisienne d'Etudes et de Recherches Foncières, Paris 04235
Union Géodésique et Géophysique Internationale, Toulouse 04308

Georgia
Georgian Geological Society, Tbilisi 04341
Georgian National Speleological Society, Tbilisi 04344

Germany
Association of European Geological Societies, Essen 04508
Deutsche Geologische Gesellschaft, Hannover 04742
Deutsche Gesellschaft für Moor- und Torfkunde e.V., Hannover 04820
Deutsche Gesellschaft für Polarforschung, Bremerhaven 04846

Geomorphology

Geophysics

International Urogynaecological Association, Evanston *15364*
Maternity Center Association, New York *15539*
National Perinatal Association, Tampa *15949*
Read Natural Childbirth Foundation, San Rafael *16247*
Society for Gynecologic Investigation, Washington *16388*
Society for Obstetric Anesthesia and Perinatology, Richmond *16418*
World Alliance of Organizations for the Prevention of Birth Defects, White Plains *16786*
World Foundation for Medical Studies in Female Health, Port Washington *16820*

Venezuela

Sociedad de Obstetricia y Ginecología de Venezuela, Caracas *16918*

Vietnam

Vietnamese Association of Obstetrics, Gynaecology and Family Planning, Hanoi *16962*

Heat Engineering s. Air Conditioning

Hematology

Argentina

Sociedad Argentina de Hematología, Buenos Aires *00096*

Austria

Österreichische Hämophilie-Gesellschaft, Wien *00710*

Canada

Canadian Hematology Society, Ottawa *01897*
Canadian Sickle Cell Society, Montréal *01966*

Chile

Sociedad Chilena de Hematología, Santiago *02490*

Denmark

Dansk Haematologisk Selskab, Hellerup *03013*

France

Association Française des Hémophiles, Paris *03540*
Société Française d'Angéiologie, Lyon *04110*
Société Française d'Hématologie, Paris *04181*
Société Internationale de Transfusion Sanguine, Les Ulis *04209*
Société Nationale de Transfusion Sanguine, Paris *04227*
Union Syndicale Nationale des Angiologues, Paris *04322*

Germany

Deutsche Gesellschaft für Angiologie, Esslingen *04754*
Deutsche Gesellschaft für Bluttransfusion und Immunhämatologie e.V., Frankfurt *04762*
Deutsche Gesellschaft für Hämatologie und Onkologie e.V., München *04792*
Deutsche Hämophilieberatung, Marl-Hüls *04895*
Deutsche Hämophiliegesellschaft zur Bekämpfung von Blutungskrankheiten e.V., Hamburg *04896*
Deutsche Liga zur Bekämpfung des hohen Blutdruckes e.V., Deutsche Hypertonie Gesellschaft, Heidelberg *04915*
Gesellschaft zur Förderung der Erforschung der Zuckerkrankheit e.V., Düsseldorf *05427*
KfH-Kuratorium für Dialyse und Nierentransplantation e.V., Neu-Isenburg *05664*

Israel

Israel Society for Hematology and Blood Transfusion, Jerusalem *06721*

Italy

Associazione Italiana di Dietetica e Nutrizione Clinica, Roma *06944*
European Renal Association – European Dialysis and Transplant Association, Parma *07265*
Società Italiana della Trasfusione del Sangue, Torino *07450*
Società Italiana di Ematologia, Milano *07490*
Società Italiana di Medicina Trasfusionale e di Immunoematologia, Roma *07526*

Jamaica

Medical Research Council Laboratories, Kingston *07707*

Japan

Japan Society of Blood Transfusion, Tokyo *07739*
Nippon Ketsueki Gakkai, Kyoto *07930*

Poland

Polskie Towarzystwo Hematologiczne, Wroclaw *09108*

Russia

National Scientific Medical Society of Haematologists and Transfusiologists, Moskva *09403*

South Africa

South African Dietetics and Home Economics Association, Stellenbosch *09677*

Switzerland

Schweizerische Hämophilie-Gesellschaft, Zürich *10355*

United Kingdom

British Committee for Standards in Haematology, London *11064*
British Society for Haematology, London *11171*
Haemophilia Society, London *11595*

U.S.A.

American Celiac Society, West Orange *13024*
American College of Nutrition, New York *13061*
American Council of Applied Clinical Nutrition, Florissant *13101*
American Society for Parenteral and Enteral Nutrition, Silver Spring *13401*
American Society of Hematology, Washington *13457*
Community Nutrition Institute, Washington *14145*
International Association for Comparative Research on Leukemia and Related Diseases, Boston *14784*
International College of Angiology, Nesconset *14919*
International Society for Experimental Hematology, Knoxville *15209*
International Society for Peritoneal Dialysis, Washington *15235*
International Society of Blood Purification, Little Rock *15277*
International Society of Hematology, Rochester *15295*
International Society on Thrombosis and Hemostasis, Chapel Hill *15318*
Iron Overload Diseases Association, North Palm Beach *15387*
Leukemia Society of America, New York *15496*
Society for the Study of Blood, Brooklyn *16472*
World Apheresis Association, Jackson *16787*
World Hemophilia Aids Center, Pasadena *16822*
World Hypertension League, Toledo *16823*

Venezuela

Sociedad Venezolana de Angiologia, Caracas *16923*
Sociedad Venezolana de Hematología, Caracas *16930*

Heraldry s. Genealogy, Heraldry

History

Algeria

Société Historique Algérienne, Alger *00009*

Andorra

Comité Andorrà de Ciències Històriques, Andorra la Vella *00015*

Argentina

Academia Nacional de la Historia, Buenos Aires *00033*

Australia

Australasian and Pacific Society for Eighteenth-Century Studies, Clayton *00138*
Australasian Association for the History, Philosophy and Social Studies of Science, Sydney *00139*
Australian and New Zealand Association for Medieval and Renaissance Studies, Sydney *00158*
Australian Association for the Study of Religions, Stanmore *00162*
Field Naturalists Club of Victoria, Blackburn *00277*
The Field Naturalists' Society of South Australia, Adelaide *00278*
Gosford District Historical Research and Heritage Association, Hardy's Bay *00287*
Indo-Pacific Prehistory Association, Canberra *00290*
Linnean Society of New South Wales, Milsons Point *00306*
North Queensland Naturalists Club, Cairns *00316*
Oaks Historical Society, The Oaks *00317*
The Queensland Naturalists' Club, Brisbane *00323*
Royal Australian Historical Society, Sydney *00337*
The Royal Historical Society of Queensland, Brisbane North Quay *00342*
Royal Historical Society of Victoria, Melbourne *00343*
Royal Western Australian Historical Society, Nedlands *00354*
Tasmanian Historical Research Association, Sandy Bay *00374*
The Western Australian Naturalists' Club, Nedlands *00387*

Austria

Anthropologische Gesellschaft in Wien, Wien *00400*
Deutscher Rechtshistorikertag, Graz *00429*
Dokumentationsarchiv des österreichischen Widerstandes, Wien *00431*
Eranos Vindobonensis, Wien *00433*
Geschichtsverein für Kärnten, Klagenfurt *00452*
Gesellschaft für die Geschichte des Protestantismus in Österreich, Wien *00466*
Gesellschaft für Geschichte der Neuzeit, Salzburg *00468*
Gesellschaft für österreichische Kulturgeschichte, Eisenstadt *00475*
Gesellschaft für Photographie und Geschichte, Wien *00478*
Gesellschaft für Salzburger Landeskunde, Salzburg *00480*
Historische Landeskommission für Steiermark, Graz *00497*
Historischer Verein für Steiermark, Graz *00498*
Institut für Österreichkunde, Wien *00506*
Internationale Tagung der Historikerinnen und Historiker der Arbeiterinnen- und Arbeiterbewegung (ITH), Wien *00533*
Kommission für Neuere Geschichte Österreichs, Salzburg *00544*
Kulturgeschichtliche Gesellschaft am Landesmuseum Joanneum, Graz *00548*
Kunsthistorische Gesellschaft, Wien *00549*
Kunsthistorische Gesellschaft an der Universität Graz, Graz *00550*
Montanhistorischer Verein für Österreich, Leoben-Donawitz *00558*
Österreichische Byzantinische Gesellschaft, Wien *00584*
Österreichische Gesellschaft für Amerikastudien, Salzburg *00603*
Österreichische Gesellschaft für Geschichte der Pharmazie, Wien *00636*
Österreichische Gesellschaft für Unternehmensgeschichte, Wien *00689*
Österreichische Gesellschaft für Ur- und Frühgeschichte, Wien *00690*
Österreichische Gesellschaft für Wissenschaftsgeschichte, Wien *00701*
Österreichische Gesellschaft für Zeitgeschichte, Wien *00703*
Österreichische Gesellschaft zur Erforschung des 18. Jahrhunderts, Wien *00707*
Österreichischer Arbeitskreis für Stadtgeschichtsforschung, Linz *00749*
Österreichischer Burgenlandbund, Arbeitsgemeinschaft für Burgenländische Geschichte und Persönlichkeiten-Deutschtum in Ungarn, Eisenstadt *00753*
Österreichischer Burgenverein, Wien *00754*
Österreichischer Kunsthistorikerverband, Wien *00760*
Österreichisches Ost- und Südosteuropa-Institut, Wien *00777*
SIGMA – Salzburger Gesellschaft für Semiologie, Salzburg *00793*
Theresianische Akademie, Wien *00803*
Verband der Österreicher zur Wahrung der Geschichte Österreichs, Wien *00810*
Verband Österreichischer Historiker und Geschichtsvereine, Wien *00818*
Verein der Freunde des Radwerkes IV in Vordernberg, Vordernberg *00827*
Verein für Geschichte der Arbeiterbewegung, Wien *00832*
Verein für Geschichte der Stadt Wien, Wien *00833*
Verein für Landeskunde von Niederösterreich, Wien *00834*
Verein Tiroler Landesmuseum Ferdinandeum, Innsbruck *00843*
Vorarlberger Landesmuseumsverein, Bregenz *00858*
Waldviertler Heimatbund, Wissenschaftliche Sektion, Horn *00859*
Wiener Humanistische Gesellschaft, Wien *00866*

Bahamas

Bahamas Historical Society, Nassau *00897*

Bahrain

Bahrain Historical and Archaeological Society, Manama *00904*

Barbados

Barbados Museum and Historical Society, Saint Ann's Garrison *00923*

Belgium

Association des Diplomés en Histoire de l'Art et Archéologie de l'Université Catholique de Louvain, Louvain-la-Neuve *00950*
Centre International de Recherches Glyptographiques, Braine-le-Château *01015*
Centre International des Langues, Littératures et Traditions d'Afrique au Service du Développement, Louvain-la-Neuve *01016*
Cercle Benelux d'Histoire de la Pharmacie, Kortrijk *01024*
Commission of the European Communities Liaison Committee of Historians, Louvain-la-Neuve *01043*
Commission Royale d'Histoire, Bruxelles *01044*
European Association of Historical Associations, Louvain-la-Neuve *01102*
Institut Archéologique du Luxembourg, Arlon *01184*
Institut Archéologique Liégeois, Liège *01185*
Institut Belge des Hautes Etudes Chinoises, Bruxelles *01190*
Institut Historique Belge de Rome, Bruxelles *01196*
Koninklijke Academie voor Wetenschappen, Letteren en Schone Kunsten van België, Bruxelles *01221*
Société Archéologique de Namur, Namur *01237*
Société Belge d'Etudes Byzantines, Bruxelles *01256*
Société Belge d'Histoire des Hôpitaux, Bruxelles *01257*
Société des Bollandistes, Bruxelles *01263*
Société d'Etudes Latines de Bruxelles, Tournai *01265*
Société Royale Belge d'Anthropologie et de Préhistoire, Bruxelles *01276*
Société Royale des Amis du Musée Royal de l'Armée et d'Histoire Militaire, Bruxelles *01292*
Union Internationale des Sciences Préhistoriques et Protohistoriques, Gent *01307*

Bermuda

Bermuda Historical Society, Hamilton *01329*
Saint George's Historical Society, Saint George's *01334*

Bolivia

Academia Nacional de la Historia, La Paz *01337*
Sociedad de Estudios Geográficos e Históricos, Santa Cruz de la Sierra *01343*
Sociedad Geográfica y de Historia Potosí, Potosí *01346*

Bosnia and Hercegovina

Društvo Istoričara BiH, Sarajevo *01351*

Brazil

Centro de Estudos de Demografía Histórica de América Latina, São Paulo *01433*
Fundação Joaquim Nabuco, Recife *01461*
Instituto Arqueológico, Histórico e Geográfico Pernambucano, Recife *01462*
Instituto do Ceará, Fortaleza *01469*
Instituto Geográfico e Histórico da Bahia, Salvador *01472*
Instituto Geográfico e Histórico do Amazonas, Manaus *01473*
Instituto Histórico de Alagoas, Maceio *01474*
Instituto Histórico e Geográfico Brasileiro, Rio de Janeiro *01475*
Instituto Histórico e Geográfico de Goiás, Goiânia *01476*
Instituto Histórico e Geográfico de Santa Catarina, Florianópolis *01477*
Instituto Histórico e Geográfico de Santos, Santos *01478*
Instituto Histórico e Geográfico de São Paulo, São Paulo *01479*
Instituto Histórico e Geográfico de Sergipe, Aracajú *01480*
Instituto Histórico e Geográfico do Espírito Santo, Vitória *01481*
Instituto Histórico e Geográfico do Maranhão, São Luís *01482*
Instituto Histórico e Geográfico do Pará, Belém *01483*
Instituto Histórico e Geográfico do Rio Grande do Norte, Natal *01484*
Instituto Histórico e Geográfico do Rio Grande do Sul, Porto Alegre *01485*
Instituto Histórico e Geográfico Paraíbano, João Pessoa *01486*
Instituto Histórico, Geográfico e Etnográfico Paranaense, Curitiba *01487*
Secretaria do Patrimônio Histórico e Artístico Nacional Nacional, Rio de Janeiro *01503*

Bulgaria

Bulgarian Historical Society, Sofia *01557*

Canada

Alberta Family History Society, Calgary *01628*
American Civil War Historical Re-Enactment Society, Downsview *01652*
American Historical Society of Germans from Russia, Calgary *01653*
Amherst Township Historical Society, Amherst *01656*
Association for Canadian Studies, Montréal *01695*
Association of Canadian Universities for Northern Studies, Ottawa *01711*
British Columbia Historical Federation, Grand Forks *01749*
Canadian Association for American Studies, Guelph *01791*
Canadian Aviation Historical Society, North York *01836*
Canadian Catholic Historical Association (English Section), Toronto *01845*
Canadian Chiropractic Historial Association, Toronto *01851*
Canadian Historical Association, Ottawa *01898*
Canadian Oral History Association, Ottawa *01936*
Canadian Polish Research Institute, Toronto *01949*
Canadian Railroad Historical Association, Saint Constant *01959*
Canadian Society for Eighteenth-Century Studies, Waterloo *01972*
Canadian Society for Italian Studies, Waterloo *01977*
Champlain Society, Toronto *02042*
Historical Society of Alberta, Calgary *02123*
Historical Society of Mecklenburg Upper Canada, Toronto *02124*
Historical Society of the Gatineau, Chelsea *02125*
Institut d'Histoire de l'Amérique Française, Montréal *02134*
Manitoba Historical Society, Winnipeg *02190*
Multicultural History Society of Ontario, Toronto *02214*
New Brunswick Historical Society, Saint John *02228*
Newfoundland Historical Society, Saint John's *02241*
Ontario Black History Society, Toronto *02269*
Ontario Historical Society, North York *02282*
Royal Nova Scotia Historical Society, Dartmouth *02345*
Société Historique Acadienne, Moncton *02378*
Société Historique de Québec, Québec *02379*
Société Historique du Saguenay, Chicoutimi *02380*
Vancouver Museum Association, Vancouver *02407*
Victoria Natural History Society, Victoria *02413*
Wallaceburg and District Historical Society, Wallaceburg *02417*
Waterloo Historical Society, Kitchener *02419*
Welland Historical Society, Welland *02421*
Yorkton Natural History Society, Yorkton *02432*
Yukon Historical and Museums Association, Whitehorse *02434*

Chile

Academia Chilena de la Historia, Santiago *02444*
Sociedad Chilena de Historia y Geografía, Santiago *02492*

Hydrology

Hygiene
s. a. Public Health

Immunology

Labour Movement
s. Socialism

Language and Languages
s. Linguistics

Laryngology
s. Otorhinolaryngology

Law

447 Subject Index: Linguistics

Cyprus
Etaireia Kypriakon Spoudon, Nicosia *02907*

Czech Republic
Český Esperantský Svaz, Praha *02944*

Denmark
Dansk Laererforeningen, København *03027*
Dansk Sprogvaern, Vaerløse *03077*
Danske Sprog- og Litteraturselskab, København *03100*
Filologisk-Historiske Samfund, København *03113*
Frankslaererforeningen, København *03125*
Selskab for Nordisk Filologi, København *03201*
Tysklaererforeningen for Gymnasiet og Hf., Nykøbing *03218*

Dominican Republic
Academia Dominicana de la Lengua, Santo Domingo *03221*

Egypt
Academy of the Arabic Language, Cairo *03250*

Finland
Äidinkielen Opettajain Liitto, Helsinki *03338*
Kalevalaseura, Helsinki *03357*
Kotikielen Seura, Helsingin Yliopisto *03362*
Suomalais-Ugrilainen Seura, Helsinki *03383*
Suomalaisen Kirjallisuuden Seura, Helsinki *03384*
Suomen Englanninopettajat, Helsinki *03394*
Suomen Kielen Seura, Turku *03412*
Uusfilologinen Yhdistys, Helsingin Yliopisto *03460*

France
Académie Française, Paris *03488*
Association des Professeurs de Langues Vivantes, Paris *03517*
Association Française des Arabisants, Paris *03537*
Association Française des Enseignants de Français, Paris *03538*
Association Française des Professeurs de Langues Vivantes, Paris *03544*
Association Française des Russisants, Paris *03545*
Association Internationale d'Epigraphie Grecque et Latine, Paris *03575*
Association Internationale des Etudes Françaises, Paris *03585*
Association Linguistique Franco-Européenne, Paris *03607*
Association Philotechnique, Paris *03628*
Association pour le Développement de la Traduction Automatique et de Linguistique Appliqué, Paris *03644*
Centre International d'Etudes Latines, Paris *03690*
Comité International de Paléographie Latine, Paris *03720*
Conseil International de la Langue Française, Paris *03767*
Esperanto Academy, Paris *03785*
Fédération Internationale des Professeurs de Français, Sèvres *03851*
Groupe Leibniz, Grenoble *03868*
Groupe Phonétique de Paris, Paris *03869*
International Association of Sanskrit Studies, Paris *03899*
Organisation de la Jeunesse Esperantiste Française, Paris *03932*
Société de Linguistique de Paris, Paris *03983*
Société de Linguistique Romane, Strasbourg *03984*
Société d'Etudes Folkloriques du Centre-Ouest, Saint-Jean d'Angely *04065*
Société d'Etudes Linguistiques et Anthropologiques de France, Paris *04072*
Union des Travailleurs Espérantistes des Pays de Langue Française, Paris *04303*
Union Française pour l'Espéranto, Paris *04306*

Georgia
Amateur Society of Basque Language, Tbilisi *04331*
Council on Co-ordinating Scientific Studies of the Georgian Language, Tbilisi *04334*

Germany
Arbeitskreis Rhetorik in Wirtschaft, Politik und Verwaltung, Bonn-Ippendorf *04496*
Bund für Deutsche Schrift und Sprache, Ahlhorn *04611*
Bundesverband der Lehrkräfte der russischen Sprache e.V., Kaarst *04650*
Deutsche Akademie für Sprache und Dichtung e.V., Darmstadt *04712*
Deutsche Gesellschaft für Sprachwissenschaft, Passau *04864*
Deutsche Gesellschaft für Sprechwissenschaft und Sprecherziehung e.V., Heidelberg *04865*
Deutsche Morgenländische Gesellschaft e.V., Heidelberg *04925*
Deutscher Altphilologen-Verband, Berlin *04991*
Deutscher Germanistenverband, Bonn *05012*
Deutscher Hispanistenverband, Berlin *05014*
Deutscher Romanistenverband, Münster *05039*
Deutscher Spanischlehrerverband, Nürnberg *05041*
European Association for Japanese Studies, Duisburg *05152*
Fachverband Moderne Fremdsprachen, Augsburg *05208*
Fachvereinigung Niederländisch e.V., Münster *05211*
Germana Esperanto Asocio r.a., Bonn *05328*
Gesellschaft für deutsche Sprache e.V., Wiesbaden *05356*
Gesellschaft für Interkulturelle Germanistik e.V., Bayreuth *05375*
Gesellschaft für internationale Sprache e.V., Reinbek *05377*
Hessischer Philologen-Verband, Wiesbaden *05476*
Sprachverband Deutsch für ausländische Arbeitnehmer e.V., Mainz *05957*
Ständiger Ausschuss für geographische Namen (StAGN), Frankfurt *05960*
Südosteuropa-Gesellschaft e.V., München *05978*
Verein Nordfriesisches Institut e.V., Bredstedt *06102*

Greece
Hetaireia Hellenon Philologon, Athinai *06244*

Guatemala
Academia de la Lengua Maya Quiché, Quezaltenango *06260*

Hungary
Magyar Nyelvtudományi Társaság, Budapest *06331*

India
Academy of Sanskrit Research, Melkote *06389*
International Tamil People Promotive Organization, Chennai *06498*
Jammu and Kashmir Academy of Art, Culture and Languages, Srinagar *06499*
Linguistic Society of India, Pune *06501*
Sanskrita Academy, Madras *06528*
Tamil Association, Thanjavur *06534*
Tamil Nadu Tamil Development and Research Council, Madras *06535*

Ireland
Conradh na Gaeilge, Dublin *06592*
Institiúid Teangeolaíochta Eireann, Dublin *06608*

Israel
Academy of the Hebrew Language, Jerusalem *06675*
Association Internationale des Etudes Arméniennes, Jerusalem *06680*

Italy
Accademia della Crusca, Firenze *06784*
Accademia di Agricoltura Scienze e Lettere, Verona *06791*
Accademia Ligustica de Belle Arti, Genova *06838*
Accademia Olimpica, Vicenza *06863*
Associazione Italiana degli Slavisti, Pisa *06933*
Associazione Italiana di Anglistica, Pisa *06938*
Associazione Italiana di Studi Semiotici, Torino *06966*
Centro Di, Firenze *07055*
Centro di Studi Atesini, Roma *07060*
Centro per lo Studio dei Dialetti Veneti dell'Istria, Trieste *07110*
Europa Club, Sezione Italiana, Verona *07245*
Gruppo Italiano di Linguistica Applicata, Pisa *07294*
International League of Esperantist Teachers, Massa *07322*
International Linguistic Club, Torino *07323*
Istituto Italiano di Studi Germanici, Roma *07352*
Società di Linguistica Italiana, Roma *07405*
Società Filologica Friulana G.I. Ascoli, Udine *07428*
Società Filologica Romana, Roma *07429*
Società Istriana di Archeologia e Storia Patria, Trieste *07442*
Società Italiana di Glottologia, Pisa *07508*
Union Ladins Val Badia, Pedraces *07665*

Jamaica
Association for Commonwealth Language and Literature Studies, Kingston *07686*

Japan
Kokugo Gakkai, Tokyo *07761*
Nihon Chugoku Gakkai, Tokyo *07776*
Nihon Eibungakkai, Tokyo *07782*
Nihon Esperanto Gakkai, Tokyo *07785*
Nihon Gengogakkai, Kyoto *07789*
Nippon Onsei Gakkai, Tokyo *07956*
Nippon Rosiya Bungakkai, Tokyo *07963*
Toho Gakkai, Tokyo *08039*

Malaysia
Asian Association of National Languages, Kuala Lumpur *08217*
Dewan Bahasa dan Pustaka, Kuala Lumpur *08223*
Tamil Language Society, Kuala Lumpur *08239*

Mexico
Academia Mexicana de la Lengua, México *08259*

Netherlands
Center for Research and Documentation on the World Language Problem, Rotterdam *08406*
Fryske Akademy, Leeuwarden *08459*
Institute for Esperanto in Commerce and Industry, Valkenswaard *08470*
Koninklijk Instituut voor Taal-, Land- en Volkenkunde, Leiden *08501*
Kristana Esperantista Ligo Internacia, Alphen a/d Rijn *08523*
Maatschappij der Nederlandse Letterkunde, Leiden *08527*
Nederlandse Vereniging voor Toegepaste Taalwetenschap, Utrecht *08605*
Permanent International Committee of Linguists, Leiden *08614*
Universal Esperanto Association, Rotterdam *08635*

New Zealand
Australasian Universities Language and Literature Association, Christchurch *08668*

Nicaragua
Academia Nicaragüense de la Lengua, Managua *08747*

Norway
Landslaget for Språklig Samling, Oslo *08798*
Norske Akademi for Sprog og Litteratur, Oslo *08848*

Pakistan
Baluchi Academy, Quetta *08895*
Iqbal Academy Pakistan, Lahore *08903*
Pashto Academy, Peshawar *08925*
Punjabi Adabi Academy, Lahore *08929*
Urdu Academy, Bahawalpur *08937*

Panama
Academia Panameña de la Lengua, Panamá City *08939*

Paraguay
Academia de la Lengua y Cultura Guaraní, Asunción *08956*

Poland
Polskie Towarzystwo Filologiczne, Warszawa *09099*
Polskie Towarzystwo Jezykoznawcze, Kraków *09113*
Polskie Towarzystwo Neofilologiczne, Poznan *09126*
Polskie Towarzystwo Semiotyczne, Warszawa *09138*
Towarzystwo Milosnikow Jezyka Polskiego, Kraków *09157*

Portugal
Academia Internacional da Cultura Portuguesa, Lisboa *09173*
Sociedade de Lingua Portuguesa, Lisboa *09220*

Puerto Rico
Academia Puertorriqueña de la Lengua Española, San Juan *09255*

Romania
Societatea de Stiinte Filologice din Romania, Bucuresti *09311*
Societatea Romana de Linguistica, Bucuresti *09321*

Russia
National Committee of Finno-Ugric Philologists, Moskva *09382*
National Committee of Slavonic Philologists, Moskva *09387*
National Committee of Turkish Philologists, Moskva *09392*
Russian Linguistics Society, Moskva *09446*

Singapore
Chinese Language and Research Centre, Singapore *09532*
Singapore Society of Asian Studies, Singapore *09544*

Slovakia
Kružok Moderných Filológov, Bratislava *09547*
Slovenská Jazykovedná Spoločnost, Bratislava *09563*
Slovenská Jednota Klassických Filológov, Bratislava *09564*

Slovenia
Slavistično Društvo Slovenije, Ljubljana *09591*
Slovenska Matica, Ljubljana *09593*

South Africa
Classical Association of South Africa, Cape Town *09617*
English Academy of Southern Africa, Wits *09626*
Federasie van Rapportryerskorpse, Aucklandpark *09629*

Spain
Institución Fernando el Católico, Zaragoza *09758*
Instituto de Filologia, Madrid *09765*
Real Academia de la Lengua Vasca – Euskaltzaindia, Bilbao *09788*
Real Academia Española, Madrid *09791*
Seminario de Filología Vasca Julio de Urquijo, San Sebastián *09806*

Sri Lanka
English Speaking Union of Sri Lanka, Colombo *09834*
Royal Asiatic Society of Sri Lanka, Colombo *09838*

Sudan
Association des Professeurs de Français en Afrique, Khartoum *09843*

Sweden
Riksföreningen för Lärarna i Moderna Språk, Hisings Kärra *09934*
Svenska Akademien, Stockholm *09956*
Svenska Klassikerförbundet, Stockholm *09981*

Switzerland
Association des Sociétés Suisses des Professeurs de Langues Vivantes, Luzern *10036*
Association Suisse des Professeurs de Français, Kehrsatz *10049*
Bund für vereinfachte rechtschreibung, Zürich *10054*
Collegium Romanicum, Lausanne *10066*
Deutschschweizerischer Sprachverein, Bremgarten *10076*
Fédération Internationale des Associations d'Etudes Classiques, Bellevue *10123*
Gesellschaft für deutsche Sprache und Literatur in Zürich, Zürich *10136*
Junge Esperantisten der Schweiz, Les Brenets *10196*
Präsidentenkonferenz Schweizerischer Fremdsprachenlehrerverbände, Luzern *10225*
Pro Natura, Genève *10228*
Schweizerische Akademische Gesellschaft der Anglisten, Genève *10243*
Schweizerische Esperanto-Gesellschaft, La Chaux-de-Fonds *10266*
Schweizerische Gesellschaft für Skandinavische Studien, Zürich *10334*
Schweizerische Sprachwissenschaftliche Gesellschaft, Lausanne *10386*
Schweizerischer Altphilologen-Verband, Einsiedeln *10429*
Schweizerischer Anglistenverband, Galgenen *10430*
Schweizerischer Internationaler Lyceum-Club, Bienne *10451*
Schweizerischer Übersetzer-, Terminologen- und Dolmetscher-Verband, Bern *10459*
Schweizerischer Verein für die deutsche Sprache, Luzern *10479*
Società Retorumantscha, Chur *10492*
Société des Professeurs d'Allemand en Suisse Romande et Italienne, Genève *10499*
Société Suisse des Professeurs de Français, La Chaux-de-Fonds *10515*
Verein Schweizerdeutsch, Zürich *10548*
Verein schweizerischer Deutschlehrer und Deutschlehrerinnen, Winterthur *10550*
Wissenschaftliche Vereinigung zur Pflege von Rhtorik, Informationsverarbeitung und Kommunikation, Zürich *10575*

Syria
Académie Arabe de Damas, Damascus *10582*

Tanzania
Eastern African Centre for Research on Oral Traditions and African National Languages, Zanzibar *10600*

Thailand
Thai-Bhara Cultural Lodge and Swami Satyananda Puri Foundation, Bangkok *10648*

Turkey
Türk Dil Kurumu, Ankara *10700*
Türkiyat Arastirmalari Entitüsü, Istanbul *10721*

United Kingdom
Academi Gymreig, Cardiff *10742*
An Comunn Gaidhealach, Inverness *10770*
Association for Language Learning, Rugby *10810*
Association for the Reform of the Latin Teaching, Woking *10830*
Association of Recognised English Language Services, London *10914*
British Association for Applied Linguistics, Clevedon *11009*
British Association of Academic Phoneticians, Glasgow *11021*
British Association of Blind Esperantists, Middlesborough *11024*
British Council, London *11067*
The British Institute of Persian Studies, London *11102*
British Interlingua Society, Sheffield *11108*
British Universities Association of Slavists, Reading *11209*
Cymdeithas yr Iaith Gymraeg, Aberystwyth *11375*
The English Association, Leicester *11449*
English Place-Name Society, Nottingham *11454*
English Speaking Board (International), Southport *11455*
English Spelling Association, London *11456*
Esperanto-Asocio de Britio, London *11463*
Esperanto Teachers Association, Leicester *11464*
Fellowship of British Christian Esperantists, Hornchurch *11533*
The Greek Institute, London *11585*
Institute of Linguists, London *11697*
Institute of Translation and Interpreting, London *11727*
International Association for Esperanto in Libraries, London *11761*
International Association of Applied Linguistics, Edinburgh *11765*
International Association of Teachers of English as a Foreign Language, Whitstable *11771*
International Association of University Professors of English, Marazion *11772*
International Federation for Modern Languages and Literatures, Belfast *11785*
International Language Union, Harrogate *11801*
International Phonetic Association, Leeds *11812*
Lakeland Dialect Society, Carlisle *11859*
Lancashire Dialect Society, Stockport *11861*
Linguistics Association of Great Britain, York *11876*
London Medieval Society, London *11886*
London Welsh Association, London *11895*
The Manx Gaelic Society, Douglas *11911*
Names Society, Thames Ditton *11968*
National Association for The Teaching of English, Sheffield *11981*
National Association of Language Advisers, Rugby *11985*
The Philological Society, London *12100*
Quaker Esperanto Society, Morecambe *12137*
Queen's English Society, London *12138*
Scottish Language Society, Inverness *12309*
Scottish National Dictionary Association, Edinburgh *12311*
Simplified Speeling Society, Beckenham *12338*
Society for Italic Handwriting, London *12361*
Society for the Study of Medieval Languages and Literature, Oxford *12400*
Yorkshire Dialect Society, Leeds *12598*

Uruguay

Academia Nacional de Letras, Montevideo 12606

U.S.A.

American Association for Chinese Studies, Columbus 12828
American Association of Language Specialists, Washington 12900
American Association of Phonetic Sciences, Gainesville 12916
American Association of Professors of Yiddish, Flushing 12925
American Association of Teachers of Arabic, Provo 12936
American Association of Teachers of Esperanto, Santa Barbara 12937
American Association of Teachers of French, Champaign 12938
American Association of Teachers of German, Cherry Hill 12939
American Association of Teachers of Spanish and Portuguese, Greeley 12940
American Association of Teachers of Turkic Languages, Princeton 12941
American Classical League, Oxford 13032
American Council on the Teaching of Foreign Languages, Yonkers 13109
American Dialect Society, Jacksonville 13125
American Institute for Contemporary German Studies, Washington 13197
American Name Society, New York 13282
American Oriental Society, Ann Arbor 13296
American Society of Geolinguistics, Fairfield 13452
Amerika Katolika Esperanto-Societo, Elkhart 13537
Association for Computational Linguistics, Somerset 13613
Association for the Study of Jewish Languages, Oakland Garden 13692
Association of Departments of English, New York 13762
Association of Departments of Foreign Languages, New York 13763
Association of Teachers of Japanese, Middlebury 13845
Basque Educational Organization, San Francisco 13903
Bet Nahrain, Modesto 13911
Better Education thru Simplified Spelling, Detroit 13913
Center for Applied Linguistics, Washington 13993
Center for Arab-Islamic Studies, Brattleboro 13995
Chinese Language Teachers Association, Kalamazoo 14068
College English Association, Rock Hill 14100
College Language Association, Atlanta 14101
Committee for the Implementation of the Standardized Yiddish Orthography, New York 14125
Conference on English Education, Urbana 14167
Conseil International d'Etudes Francophones, Upper Montclair 14172
Cross-Examination Debate Association, Tacoma 14273
Esperantic Studies Foundation, Washington 14389
Esperanto League for North America, El Cerrito 14390
German-American Information and Education Association, Vienna 14495
Hispanic Society of America, New York 14570
Histadruth Ivrith of America, New York 14571
Institute of General Semantics, Englewood 14708
Intercultural Development Research Association, San Antonio 14753
International Association for Learning Laboratories, Saint Paul 14800
International Association of Applied Linguistics, Minneapolis 14830
International Association of Hispanists, Hanover 14852
International Catholic Esperanto Association, Elkhart 14896
International Christian Esperanto Association, State College 14911
International Commission on English in the Liturgy, Washington 14931
International Committee on Computational Linguistics, Palox Alto 14945
International Linguistic Association, New York 15103
International Maledicta Society, Santa Rosa 15106
International Society for General Semantics, Concord 15211
International Society for Historical Linguistics, Columbia 15214
International Society for Humor Studies, Tempe 15217
International Society for the History of Rhetoric, College Station 15255
Jargon Society, Winston-Salem 15422
Junior Classical League, Oxford 15462
Linguistic Society of America, Washington 15507
Modern Greek Studies Association, New Haven 15592
Modern Language Association of America, New York 15593
National Association for Bilingual Education, Washington 15638
National Association of Professors of Hebrew, Madison 15722
National Assoiation of Self-Instructional Language Programs, Philadelphia 15754
National Committee for Latin and Greek, Cypress 15798
National Conference on Research in Language and Literacy, Columbus 15812
National Council of State Supervisors of Foreign Languages, Little Rock 15839
National Council of Teachers of English, Urbana 15841
National Federation of Modern Language Teachers Associations, Columbus 15879
National Forensic Association, Westerville 15884
Nieman Foundation, Cambridge 16028
Northeast Conference on the Teaching of Foreign Languages, Carlisle 16059
Reading is Fundamental, Washington 16248
Reading Reform Foundation, Tacoma 16249
Religious Speech Communication Association, Azusa 16263
Semiotic Society of America, Pensacola 16314
Société des Professeurs Français et Francophones en Amérique, New York 16344
Society for Iberian and Latin American Thought, Washington 16395
Society for New Language Study, Denver 16416
Society for Slovene Studies, Bloomington 16441
Society for the Preservation of English Language and Literature, Waleska 16464
Society of Basque Studies in America, Brooklyn 16500
Society of Federal Linguists, Washington 16521
Society of Spanish and Spanish-American Studies, Boulder 16557
Southern States Communication Association, Memphis 16588
Speech Communication Association, Annandale 16601
Teachers of English to Speakers of Other Languages, Alexandria 16629
United States Branch of the International Committee for the Defense of the Breton Language, Jenkintown 16683
Women's Caucus for the Modern Languages, Albuquerque 16779

Venezuela

Academia Venezolana, Caracas 16871
Asociación de Linguistica y Filologia de América Latina, Caracas 16876
Comité para la Defensa de las Lenguas Indígenas de América Latina y el Caribe, Caracas 16906

Yugoslavia

Akademia e Shkencave dhe e Arteve e Kosovës, Priština 16982
Društvo za Srpski Jezik i Književnost, Beograd 16996
Društvo za Srpskohrvatski Jezik i Književnost, Beograd 16997
Matica Srpska, Novi Sad 17010
Savez Društava za Strane Jezike i Knjizevnosti Jugoslavije, Beograd 17020

Literature
s. a. Journalism; Linguistics

Albania

Lidhja e Shkrimtareve dhe e Artisteve te Shqiperise, Tirana 00003
PEN Centre of Albania, Tirana 00004

Andorra

Cercle de les Arts i de les Lletres, Escaldes-Engordany 00014

Angola

União dos Escritores Angolanos, Luanda 00018

Argentina

Academia Argentina de Letras, Buenos Aires 00021
PEN Club Argentino, Buenos Aires 00082
Sociedad Argentina de Autores y Compositores de Música, Buenos Aires 00085
Sociedad General de Autores de la Argentina, Buenos Aires 00110

Australia

Australian and New Zealand Association for Medieval and Renaissance Studies, Sydney 00158
Australian Society of Authors, Strawberry Hills 00237
Fellowship of Australian Writers, Rezelle 00276
PEN International (Sydney Centre), Woollahra 00320

Austria

Adalbert Stifter-Gesellschaft, Wien 00392
Arbeitsgemeinschaft für Deutschdidaktik, Klagenfurt 00404
Arbeitskreis der Wiener Altgermanisten, Wien 00412
Arbeitskreis der Wiener Skandinavisten, Wien 00413
Arthur Schnitzler-Institut, Wien 00417
Autorenkreis Linz, Linz 00422
Dokumentationsstelle für neuere österreichische Literatur, Wien 00432
Eranos Vindobonensis, Wien 00433
Friedrich Hebbel-Gesellschaft, Wien 00450
Gesellschaft für Klassische Philologie in Innsbruck, Innsbruck 00471
Gesellschaft zur Förderung Slawistischer Studien, Wien 00490
Grillparzer-Gesellschaft, Wien 00494
Innsbrucker Germanistische Arbeitsgemeinschaft, Innsbruck 00501
Institut für Österreichkunde, Wien 00506
Internationale Lenau-Gesellschaft e.V., Stockerau 00528
Internationale Nestroy-Gesellschaft, Wien 00529
Internationales Institut für Jugendliteratur und Leseforschung, Wien 00538
Johann-Joseph-Fux-Gesellschaft, Graz 00540
Österreichische Exlibris-Gesellschaft, Wien 00591
Österreichische Gesellschaft für Amerikastudien, Salzburg 00603
Österreichische Gesellschaft für Literatur, Wien 00657
Österreichische Gesellschaft für Neugriechische Studien, Wien 00665
Österreichischer PEN-Club, Wien 00763
Österreichischer Schriftstellerverband, Wien 00764
Rudolf Kassner-Gesellschaft, Wien 00787
SIGMA – Salzburger Gesellschaft für Semiologie, Salzburg 00793
Verband der österreichischen Neuphilologen, Wien 00811
Verein der Mundartfreunde Österreichs, Wien 00828
Verein Wiener Frauenverlag, Wien 00844
Wiener Goethe-Verein, Wien 00865
Wiener Humanistische Gesellschaft, Wien 00866

Bahrain

Bahrain Writers and Literators Association, Manama 00908

Bangladesh

Society of Arts, Literature and Welfare, Chittagong 00920

Belgium

Académie Européenne des Ecrivains Publics, Bruxelles 00929
Académie Royale de Langue et de Littérature Françaises, Bruxelles 00931
Académie Royale des Sciences, des Lettres et des Beaux-Arts de Belgique, Bruxelles 00933
Association des Ecrivains Belges de Langue Française, Bruxelles 00951
Centre International des Langues, Littératures et Traditions d'Afrique au Service du Développement, Louvain-la-Neuve 01016
Chambre Belge des Traducteurs, Interprètes et Philologues, Bruxelles 01027
European Association for the Promotion of Poetry, Leuven 01091
Icon, Leuven 01182
International PEN Club, Flemish Centre, Dilbeek 01210
International PEN Club, French Speaking Branch, Kraainem 01211
Koninklijke Academie voor Nederlandse Taal- en Letterkunde, Gent 01220
Koninklijke Academie voor Wetenschappen, Letteren en Schone Kunsten van België, Bruxelles 01221
Société Belge des Auteurs, Compositeurs et Editeurs, Bruxelles 01254
Société de Langue et de Littérature Wallonnes, Liège 01261
Union Belge des Journalistes et Ecrivains du Tourisme, Vilvoorde 01304

Bolivia

PEN Club de Bolivia-Centro Internacional de Escritores, La Paz 01342

Bosnia and Hercegovina

Udruženje Književnika BiH, Sarajevo 01360

Brazil

Academia Alagoana de Letras, Maceió 01365
Academia Amazonense de Letras, Manaus 01366
Academia Brasileira de Letras, Rio de Janeiro 01369
Academia Cachoeirense de Letras, Cachoeira de Itapemerim 01370
Academia Campinense de Letras, Campinas 01371
Academia Catarinense de Letras, Florianópolis 01372
Academia Cearense de Letras, Fortaleza 01373
Academia de Letras, Jöao Pessoa 01374
Academia de Letras da Bahia, Salvador 01375
Academia de Letras de Piauí, Teresina 01376
Academia de Letras e Artes do Planalto, Luziânia 01377
Academia Matogrossense de Letras, Cuiabá 01379
Academia Mineira de Letras, Belo Horizonte 01380
Academia Paraibana de Letras, João Pessoa 01383
Academia Paulista de Letras, São Paulo 01384
Academia Pernambucana de Letras, Recife 01385
Academia Riograndense de Letras, Pôrto Alegre 01387
Centro de Ciências, Letras e Artes, Campinas 01432
International Communication Agency, São Paulo 01496
PEN Clube do Brasil – Associação Universal de Escritores, Rio de Janeiro 01501

Bulgaria

Bulgarian Philologists' Society, Sofia 01559
Society of Aesthetes and Art and Literary Critics, Sofia 01590
Union of Bulgarian Writers, Sofia 01596

Canada

Académie des Lettres du Québec, Montréal 01608
African Literature Association, Edmonton 01615
Association of Canadian Universities for Northern Studies, Ottawa 01711
Canadian Association for the Advancement of Netherlandic Studies, Wolfville 01805
Canadian Authors Association, Campbellford 01835
Canadian Society of Children's Authors, Illustrators and Performers, Toronto 01991
Canadian Writers' Foundation, Ottawa 02026
Jane Austen Society of North America, Sudbury 02162
Laubach Literacy Canada, Saint John 02165
League of Canadian Poets, Toronto 02172
Société des Auteurs, Recherchistes, Documentalistes et Compositeurs, Montréal 02375
Société des Ecrivains Canadiens, Montréal 02376
Society of Composers, Authors and Music Publishers of Canada, North York 02387
Writers Association for Romance and Mainstream, Longueuil 02430

China, People's Republic

Chinese Writers' Association, Beijing 02642
Hong Kong Chinese PEN Centre, Hong Kong 02650

China, Republic

China National Association of Literature and the Arts, Taipei 02682
Chinese Center, International PEN, Taipei 02690
Chinese Women Writer's Association, Taipei 02714
National Young Writers Association of China, Taipei 02742
Playwriters Association of the Republic of China, Taipei 02746

Colombia

Instituto Caro y Cuervo, Bogotá 02786
Instituto Colombiano de Cultura, Bogotá 02792
Instituto Colombiano de Cultura Hispánica, Bogotá 02793
PEN Club de Colombia, Bogotá 02804
Unión Nacional de Escritores, Bogotá 02829

Congo, Republic

PEN Centre de Congo, Brazzaville 02839

Cuba

Unión de Escritores y Artistas de Cuba, La Habana 02895

Czech Republic

Czech Centre of International PEN, Praha 02949
Literárněvědná Společnost, Praha 02953
Matice Moravská, Brno 02955
Obec Spisovatelu, Praha 02958

Denmark

Dansk Forfatterforening, København 03004
Det Danske Shakespeare Selskab, København 03099
Danske Sprog- og Litteraturselskab, København 03100
DTL – Dansk Forening for Information og Dokumentation, Lyngby 03104
Filologisk-Historiske Samfund, København 03113
Izlenzka Fraedafélag, Hillerød 03139
Selskab for Nordisk Filologi, København 03201

Ecuador

Academia Ecuatoriana de la Lengua, Quito 03230
Casa de la Cultura Ecuatoriana, Quito 03238

Egypt

Atelier, Alexandria 03269
High Council of Arts and Literature, Cairo 03293
High Council of Culture, Cairo 03294

Ethiopia

African Association of Science Editors, Addis Ababa 03325

Finland

Äidinkielen Opettajain Liitto, Helsinki 03338
Finlands Svenska Författareförening, Helsinki 03344
Klassillis-Filologinen Yhdistys, Helsingin Yliopisto 03361
Kotikielen Seura, Helsingin Yliopisto 03362
Suomalainen Tiedeakatemia, Helsinki 03382
Suomalaisen Kirjallisuuden Seura, Helsinki 03384
Suomen Kirjailijaliitto, Helsinki 03413
Svenska Litteratursällskapet i Finland, Helsinki 03444
Uusfilologinen Yhdistys, Helsingin Yliopisto 03460

France

Académie de Savoie, Chambéry 03469
Académie des Belles-Lettres, Sciences et Arts de La Rochelle, La Rochelle 03471
Académie des Inscriptions et Belles-Lettres, Paris 03472
Académie des Jeux Floraux, Toulouse 03473
Académie des Sciences, Agriculture, Arts et Belles-Lettres d'Aix, Aix-en-Provence 03475
Académie des Sciences, Arts et Belles-Lettres de Dijon, Dijon 03476
Académie des Sciences, Belles-Lettres et Arts de Clermont, Clermont-Ferrand 03477
Académie des Sciences, Belles-Lettres et Arts de Lyon, Lyon 03478
Académie des Sciences, Belles-Lettres et Arts de Rouen, Rouen 03479
Académie des Sciences et Lettres de Montpellier, Montpellier 03481
Académie des Sciences, Lettres et Arts d'Arras, Arras 03483
Académie des Sciences, Lettres et Arts de Marseille, Marseille 03484
Académie d'Orléans – Agriculture, Sciences, Belles-Lettres et Arts, Orléans 03487
Académie Française, Paris 03488
Académie Goncourt, Paris 03489
Académie Mallarmé, Paris 03491
Académie Montaigne, Sillé-le-Guillaume 03492
Académie Nationale des Sciences, Belles-Lettres et Arts de Bordeaux, Bordeaux 03497

Logic

Logopedy

Machine Engineering
s. a. Automotive Engineering

Management
s. Business Administration, Management

Marine Sciences
s. Oceanography, Marine Sciences

Marketing
s. a. Advertising

Commission Internationale de Marketing, Brixham 11310
European College of Marketing and Marketing Research, Brixham 11480
European Industrial Marketing Research Society, Nuneaton 11498
Institute of Sales and Marketing Management, Royal Leamington Spa 11719
International Wool Secretariat, London 11833

U.S.A.

Alliance for Alternatives in Healthcare, Thousand Oaks 12728
American Marketing Association, Chicago 13256
Automotive Market Research Council, Research Triangle Park 13893
Chemical Management and Resources Association, Staten Island 14054
Marketing Research Association, Rocky Hill 15530
Marketing Science Institute, Cambridge 15531

Mass Media

Austria

Mediacult – Internationales Forschungsinstitut für Medien, Kommunikation und kulturelle Entwicklung, Wien 00555
Österreichische Gesellschaft für Amerikastudien, Salzburg 00603
SYNEMA – Gesellschaft für Film und Medien, Wien 00800

Belgium

European Academy for Film and Television, Bruxelles 01077

Bulgaria

Balkanmedia Association, Sofia 01545

Canada

Academy of Canadian Cinema and Television, Toronto 01609
Association for Media and Technology in Education, Etobicoke 01696
Association for the Study of Canadian Radio and Television, Montréal 01697
Broadcast Research Council of Canada, Toronto 01762

Czech Republic

Český Filmový a Televizní Svaz, Praha 02945

Germany

Arbeitsgemeinschaft Berufliche Bildung der deutschen Zeitungsverlage, Bonn 04425
Arbeitsgemeinschaft Media-Analyse e.V., Frankfurt 04472
Bayerische Akademie für Fernsehen e.V., München 04528
Catholic Media Council, Aachen 04689
Deutsche Hörfunkakademie, Dortmund 04898
Evangelische Medienakademie im GEP e.V., Frankfurt/Main 05195
Gesellschaft für Medienpädagogik und Kommunikationskultur e.V., Bielefeld 05384
Gesellschaft für Programmierte Instruktion und Mediendidaktik e.V., Giessen 05397
Internationales Zentralinstitut für das Jugend- und Bildungsfernsehen, München 05592
Intitut für Bildungsmedien e.V., Frankfurt 05595
KIM Katholisches Institut für Medieninformation GmbH, Köln 05665
Studienkreis für Presserecht und Pressefreiheit, Stuttgart 05973

Netherlands

International Association for Media in Science, Utrecht 08477

Russia

National Committee of the International Scientific Radio Union, Moskva 09389

Switzerland

Schweizerischer Werkbund, Zürich 10485

United Kingdom

Media Studies Association, Leeds 11922

U.S.A.

International Association for Media and Communication Research, Washington 14805
International Christian Media Commission, Seattle 14913
The Media Institute, Washington 15544
National Telemedia Council, Madison 15988
Radio and Television Research Council, New York 16240
Society of Cable Telecommunications Engineers, Exton 16505

Materials Science

Argentina

Grupo Latinoamericano de R.I.L.E.M., Buenos Aires 00078

Australia

Appita, Carlton 00119
Australasian Ceramic Society, Menai 00142
Institute of Materials Handling, South Melbourne 00291

Belgium

Centre Belge pour la Gestion de la Qualité, Berchem 01007
Comité d'Etude de la Corrosion et de la Protection des Canalisations, Liège 01034
European Bitumen Association, Bruxelles 01109
European Extruded Polystyrene Insulation Board Association, Bruxelles 01152
European Technical Association for Protective Coatings, Merksem 01163
Institut Royal Belge du Pétrole, Bruxelles 01200
Union Scientifique Continentale du Verre, Charleroi 01311

Brazil

Associação Brasileira de Metalurgia e Materiais, São Paulo 01399

Canada

Canadian Association for Production and Inventory Control, Toronto 01803
Canadian Ceramic Society, North York 01848
Canadian Society for Nondestructive Testing, Mississauga 01979
Pulp and Paper Research Institute of Canada, Pointe Claire 02332

China, People's Republic

Chinese Ceramic Society, Beijing 02579

China, Republic

Chinese Society for Materials Science, Hsinchu 02709

Denmark

Dansk Betonforening, København 02985
Dansk Selskab for Materialprøvning og -forskning, København 03062
Nordisk Laederforskningsråd, Taastrup 03180

Finland

Suomen Betoniyhdistys, Helsinki 03391

France

Association Française de Recherches d'Essais sur les Matériaux et les Constructions, Paris 03534
Association Internationale pour le Développement des Gommes Naturelles, Neuilly-sur-Seine 03599
Réunion Internationale des Laboratoires d'Essais et de Recherche sur les Matériaux et les Constructions, Cachan 03943
Société Française de Métallurgie et de Matériaux, Nanterre 04140

Germany

Arbeitsgemeinschaft Verstärkte Kunststoffe e. V., Frankfurt 04477
Beton-Verein Berlin e.V., Berlin 04573
Deutsche farbwissenschaftliche Gesellschaft e.V., Berlin 04733
Deutsche Gesellschaft für Fettwissenschaft e.V., Münster 04779
Deutsche Gesellschaft für Qualität e.V., Frankfurt 04851
Deutsche Kautschuk-Gesellschaft e.V., Frankfurt 04905
Deutsche Keramische Gesellschaft e.V., Köln 04906
Deutsche Rheologische Gesellschaft e.V., Berlin 04950
Deutscher Beton-Verein e.V., Wiesbaden 05000
Deutscher Verband Farbe, Berlin 05051
Deutscher Verband für Materialforschung und -prüfung e.V., Berlin 05054
Deutsches Kunststoff-Institut, Darmstadt 05097
Deutsches Kupfer-Institut e.V., Berlin 05098
Fördergemeinschaft für das Süddeutsche Kunststoff-Zentrum e.V., Würzburg 05221
Forschungsgemeinschaft Feuerfest e.V., Bonn 05230
Forschungsgemeinschaft für technisches Glas e.V., Wertheim 05232
Forschungsgemeinschaft Kalk und Mörtel e.V., Köln 05235
Forschungsgemeinschaft Kraftpapiere und Papiersäcke, Wiesbaden 05236
Forschungsgemeinschaft Naturstein-Industrie e.V., Köln 05237
Forschungsgemeinschaft Zink e.V., Düsseldorf 05239
Forschungsgesellschaft Kunststoffe e.V., Darmstadt 05243
Forschungsgesellschaft Steinzeugindustrie e.V., Köln 05246
Forschungsinstitut für Pigmente und Lacke e.V., Stuttgart 05251
Forschungsstelle der Deutschen Ziegelindustrie e.V., Bonn 05257
Forschungsvereinigung der Deutschen Asphaltindustrie e.V., Offenbach 05264
Forschungsvereinigung der Gipsindustrie e.V., Darmstadt 05265
Forschungsvereinigung der Rheinischen Bimsindustrie e.V., Neuwied 05266
Forschungsvereinigung Kalk-Sand e.V., Hannover 05271
Forschungsvereinigung Porenbeton e.V., Wiesbaden 05272
Forschungsvereinigung Ziegelindustrie, Bonn 05276
Fraunhofer-Gesellschaft zur Förderung der angewandten Forschung e.V., München 05288
Hüttentechnische Vereinigung der Deutschen Glasindustrie e.V., Frankfurt 05497
Institut für Ziegelforschung Essen e.V., Essen 05547
Interessengemeinschaft für Lederforschung und Häuteschädenbekämpfung im Verband der deutschen Lederindustrie e.V., Frankfurt 05551
Intitut für Baustoffprüfung und Fußbodenforschung, Troisdorf 05594
Normenausschuss Anstrichstoffe und ähnliche Beschichtungsstoffe im DIN Deutsches Institut für Normung e.V., Berlin 05788
Normenausschuss Farbe im DIN Deutsches Institut für Normung e.V., Berlin 05806
Normenausschuss Kunststoffe im DIN Deutsches Institut für Normung e.V., Berlin 05825
Normenausschuss Materialprüfung im DIN Deutsches Institut für Normung e.V., Berlin 05830
Normenausschuss Papier und Pappe im DIN Deutsches Institut für Normung e.V., Berlin 05834
Normenausschuss Pigmente und Füllstoffe im DIN Deutsches Institut für Normung e.V., Berlin 05836
Normenausschuss Verpackungswesen im DIN Deutsches Institut für Normung e.V., Berlin 05852
Prüf- und Forschungsinstitut für die Schuhherstellung e.V., Pirmasens 05891
Studiengesellschaft für Holzschwellenoberbau e.V., Wiesbaden 05967
Studiengesellschaft für Stahlleitplanken e.V., Siegen 05968
Süddeutsches Kunststoff-Zentrum, Würzburg 05976
Technische Fördergemeinschaft Holzsilo, Freiburg 05983
VDI-Gesellschaft Werkstofftechnik, Düsseldorf 06011
Verband der Materialprüfungsämter e.V., Berlin 06029
Verein der Zellstoff- und Papier-Chemiker und -Ingenieure e.V., Darmstadt 06074
Verein für technische Holzfragen e.V., Braunschweig 06095
Vereinigung zur Förderung des Instituts für Kunststoffverarbeitung in Industrie und Handwerk an der Rhein.-Westf. Technischen Hochschule Aachen e.V., Aachen 06135

Hungary

Bör-, Cipö-, és Börfeldolgozóipari Tudományos Egyesület, Budapest 06284

India

The Indian Ceramic Society, Calcutta 06449
Indian Rubber Manufacturers Research Association, Thane 06476
National Council for Cement and Building Materials, New Delhi Ghosh, Dr. S.P. 06515

Ireland

Irish Institute of Purchasing and Materials Management, Dublin 06630
Irish Quality Control Association, Dublin 06640

Israel

Israel Plastics and Rubber Center, Haifa 06713
Technion Research and Development Foundation Ltd, Haifa 06750

Italy

Associazione Italiana per la Qualità, Milano 06976
Associazione Italiana per la Ricerca nell'Impiego degli Elastomeri, Milano 06978
Centro Internazionale per lo Studio dei Papiri Ercolanesi, Napoli 07081
Centro Italiano Sviluppo Impieghi Acciaio, Milano 07094
European Centre for the Validation of Alternative Methods, Ispra 07255
Gruppo Nazionale di Struttura della Materia, Roma 07299
Istituto Italiano del Marchio di Qualità, Milano 07345
Società Italiana per lo Studio delle Sostanze Grasse, Milano 07599

Japan

Nihon Gomu Kyokai, Tokyo 07791
Nihon Setchakuzai Kogyokai Toshoshitsu, Tokyo 07848
Nihon Zairyo Gakkai, Kyoto 07867
Nihon Zairyo Kyodo Gakkai, Sendai 07868
Nippon Seramikkusu Kyokai, Tokyo 07975

Malaysia

Malaysian Rubber Research and Development Board, Kuala Lumpur 08234

Netherlands

International Organisation for the Study of the Endurance of Wire Ropes, Delft 08489
Nederlands Verpakkingscentrum, Gouda 08546

New Zealand

New Zealand Leather and Shoe Research Association, Palmerston North 08711
New Zealand Pottery and Ceramics Research Association, Lower Hutt 08720

Norway

Papirindustriens Forskningsinstitutt, Oslo 08874

Philippines

Asia Pacific Quality Organization, Quezon City 09026

Portugal

Associação Portuguesa para a Qualidade Industrial, Lisboa 09186

South Africa

South African Ceramic Society, Northmead 09673

Spain

Sociedad Española de Cerámica y Vidrio, Madrid 09814

Switzerland

Euro-International Committee for Concrete, Lausanne 10089
Schweizerische Gesellschaft für Zerstörungsfreie Prüfung, Basel 10350
Schweizerischer Fachverband für Schweiss- und Schneidmaterial, Zürich 10445
Schweizerischer Verband für die Materialtechnik, Pully 10470

Syria

Arab Union for Cement and Building Materials, Damascus 10590

United Kingdom

British Cement Association, Crowthorne 11061
British Ceramic Society, Stoke-on-Trent 11062
British Ceramic Tile Council, Stoke-on-Trent 11063
British Leather Confederation, Northampton 11117
British Society of Rheology, Colney 11198
British Society of Scientific Glassblowers, Dunstable 11199
CERAM Research, Stoke-on-Trent 11263
Colour Group (Great Britain), Harrow 11307
Cutlery and Allied Trades Research Association, Sheffield 11373
European Electrostatic Discharge Association, Crowthorne 11495
Institute of Ceramics, Stoke-on-Trent 11667
Institute of Clay Technology, Ripley 11672
Institute of Materials, London 11702
International Rubber Study Group, Wembley 11814
International Tar Conference, London 11824
International Wool Study Group, London 11834
Lace Research Association, Nottingham 11858
National Materials Handling Centre, Bedford 12017
Organisation Internationale pour l'Etude de l'Endurance des Cables, Reading 12068
Paint Research Association, Teddington 12082
The Plastics and Rubber Institute, London 12110
RAPRA Technology, Shrewsbury 12145
Society of Glass Technology, Sheffield 12428
Steel Construction Institute, Ascot 12475

U.S.A.

American Ceramic Society, Westerville 13027
American Society for Nondestructive Testing, Columbus 13400
American Society for Quality Control, Milwaukee 13410
Association for Quality and Participation, Cincinnati 13656
Association of Professional Material Handling Consultants, Charlotte 13820
Center for Science in the Public Interest, Washington 14025
Emulsion Polymers Institute, Bethlehem 14371
Engineered Wood Research Foundation, Tacoma 14376
Federation of Materials Societies, Washington 14426
International Society for Asphalt Pavements, Austin 15192
International Society for Fat Research, Champaign 15210
International Union of Materials Research Societies, Pittsburgh 15358
Material Handling and Management Society, Charlotte 15537
Minerals, Metals and Materials Society, Warrendale 15586
National Materials Advisory Board, Washington 15931
Packaging Education Foundation, Herndon 16127
Society for the Advancement of Material and Process Engineering, Covina 16448

Mathematics

Argentina

Academia Nacional de Ciencias Exactas, Físicas y Naturales, Buenos Aires 00028
Unión Matemática Argentina, Cordoba 00112

Australia

The Australian Mathematical Society, Hobart 00212
Australian Mathematics Trust, Belconnen 00213

Austria

Mathematisch-Physikalische Gesellschaft in Innsbruck, Innsbruck 00554
Österreichische Gesellschaft für Operations Research, Wien 00669
Österreichische Mathematische Gesellschaft, Wien 00718

Azerbaijan

Azerbaijan Mathematics Society, Baku 00888

Belgium

Association Internationale des Mathématiques et Calculateurs en Simulation, Liège 00970
Société Mathématique de Belgique, Bruxelles 01272

Bosnia and Hercegovina

Društvo Matematičara, Fizičara i Astronoma BiH, Sarajevo 01353

Brazil

International Mathematical Union, Rio de Janeiro 01497
Sociedade Paranaense de Matemática, Curitiba 01531

Bulgaria

Union of Bulgarian Mathematicians, Sofia 01595

Canada

Association Mathématique du Québec, Montréal 01700

Medicine

Honduras
Colegio de Arquitectos de Honduras, Tegucigalpa *06283*

Hungary
Magyar Orvostudományi Társaságok és Egyesületek Szövetsége, Budapest *06332*

Iceland
Loeknafélag Islands, Reykjavik *06374*

India
Association of Medical Physicists of India, Mumbai *06408*
Indian Council of Medical Research, New Dehli *06454*
Indian Medical Association, New Dehli *06465*
Indian Science Congress Association, Calcutta *06477*
Indian Society for Medical Statistics, New Delhi *06478*
Medical Council of India, New Dehli *06503*
Mumbai Medical Union, Mumbai *06506*

Indonesia
Ikatan Dokter Indonesia, Jakarta *06557*

Iraq
Iraqi Medical Society, Baghdad *06579*

Ireland
Irish Medical Association, Dublin *06634*
Medical Council, Dublin *06647*
Medical Research Council of Ireland, Dublin *06648*
Royal Academy of Medicine, Dublin *06657*
Royal College of Physicians of Ireland, Dublin *06658*

Israel
International Society of Computerized and Quantitative EMG, Jerusalem *06692*
Israel Gerontological Society, Ramat Gan *06703*
Israel Medical Association, Ramat Gan *06707*
Israel Society for Experimental Biology and Medicine, Rehovoth *06719*
Israel Society of Clinical Neurophysiology, Jerusalem *06726*
Society for Medicine and Law in Israel, Haifa *06745*

Italy
Academia Gentium Pro Pace, Roma *06759*
Accademia delle Scienze Mediche di Palermo, Palermo *06789*
Accademia di Medicina di Torino, Torino *06806*
Accademia Internazionale di Medicina Legale e di Medicina Sociale, Roma *06827*
Accademia Medica, Genova *06840*
Accademia Medica di Roma, Roma *06841*
Accademia Medica Lombarda, Milano *06842*
Accademia Medica Pistoiese Filippo Pacini, Pistoia *06843*
Accademia Medico-Chirurgica del Piceno, Ancona *06844*
Accademia Medico-Fisica Fiorentina, Firenze *06845*
Accademia Pratese di Medicina e Scienze, Prato *06868*
Accademia Romana di Scienze Mediche e Biologiche, Roma *06873*
Associazione Italiana di Ingegneria Medica e Biologica, Napoli *06951*
Associazione Italiana di Medicina Aeronautica e Spaziale, Roma *06952*
Associazione Italiana di Medicina dell'Assicurazione Vita, Roma *06953*
Centro Internazionale di Ipnosi Medica e Psicologica, Milano *07066*
Centro Ricerche Applicazione Bioritmo, Roma *07116*
Centro Studi Problemi Medici, Milano *07171*
European Association of Perinatal Medicine, Perugia *07249*
European Association of Senior Hospital Physicians, Udine *07251*
European Association of Social Medicine, Torino *07252*
Federazione Medico-Sportiva Italiana, Roma *07278*
Federazione Nazionale degli Ordini dei Medici Chirurghi e Odontoiatri, Roma *07280*
Institutio Santoriana, Milano *07307*
International Society for Medical and Psychological Hypnosis, Milano *07325*
International Society for Twin Studies, Roma *07327*
Società Italiana di Liposcultura, Roma *07513*
Società Italiana di Medicina del Lavoro e di Igiene Industriale, Pavia *07515*
Società Italiana di Medicina e Igiene della Scuola, Milano *07517*
Società Italiana di Medicina Legale e delle Assicurazioni, Padova *07521*
Società Italiana di Parassitologia, Roma *07549*
Società Italiana di Senologia, Roma *07570*
Società Italiana di Storia della Medicina, Bologna *07575*
Società Italiana per gli Archivi Sanitari Ospedalieri, Viareggio *07587*
Società Jonico-Salentina de Medicina e Chirurgia, Taranto *07603*

Jamaica
Commonwealth Caribbean Medical Research Council, Kingston *07694*
Medical Association of Jamaica, Kingston *07706*

Japan
Asian Parasite Control Organization, Tokyo *07712*
Association of Medical Doctors of Asia, Okayama *07714*
Nihon Arerugi Gakkai, Tokyo *07773*
Nihon Hoken Igakkai, Tokyo *07795*
Nihon Ishi-Kai, Tokyo *07800*
Nihon Kakuigakukai, Tokyo *07806*
Nihon Koko Geka Gakkai, Tokyo *07816*
Nihon Kotsu Igakkai, Tokyo *07822*
Nihon Naika Gakkai, Tokyo *07831*
Nihon Nettai Igakkai, Nagasaki *07832*
Nihon Tairyoku Igakkai, Tokyo *07859*
Nihon Uirusu Gakkai, Tokyo *07864*
Nippon Bitamin Gakkai, Kyoto *07873*
Nippon Hoi Gakkai, Tokyo *07901*
Nippon Junkan-ki Gakkai, Kyoto *07913*
Nippon Junkatsu Gakkai, Tokyo *07914*
Nippon Kango Kyokai, Tokyo *07922*
Nippon Kansenshoh Gakkai, Tokyo *07923*
Nippon Uirusu Gakkai, Tokyo *08003*
Toa Igaku Kyokai, Tokyo *08035*

Kenya
African Medical and Research Foundation, Nairobi *08068*
Kenya Medical Association, Nairobi *08102*

Korea, Democratic People's Republic
Academy of Medical Sciences, Pyongyang *08112*

Korea, Republic
Korean Medical Association, Seoul *08134*

Liechtenstein
Liechtensteinischer Ärzteverein, Vaduz *08164*

Luxembourg
Association des Médecins et Médecins-Dentistes du Grand-Duché de Luxembourg, Luxembourg *08167*
Collège Mé1dical, Luxembourg *08170*

Macedonia
Makedonsko Lekarsko Društvo, Skopje *08192*

Malawi
Medical Association of Malawi, Blantyre *08211*

Malaysia
Academy of Family Physicians of Malaysia, Kuala Lumpur *08213*
Association for Medical Education in the Western Pacific Region, Kuala Lumpur *08220*
Malaysian Medical Association, Kuala Lumpur *08232*

Malta
Medical Association of Malta, Paceville *08250*

Mexico
Academia Nacional de Medicina, México *08262*
Asociación de Médicas Mexicanas, México *08264*
Asociación Médica del Hospital Beistegui, México *08268*
Asociación Médica Franco-Mexicana, México *08269*
Asociación Mexicana de Facultades y Escuelas de Medicina, San Luis de Potosí *08272*
Sociedad Médica del Hospital General, México *08331*
Sociedad Mexicana de Parasitología, México *08347*

Netherlands
Genootschap ter Bevordering von Natuur-, Genees- en Heelkunde, Amsterdam *08463*
International Huntington Association, Harfsen *08488*
Koninklijke Nederlandsche Maatschappij tot Bevordering der Geneeskunst, Utrecht *08512*
Landelijke Huisartsen Vereniging, Utrecht *08524*
Nederlands Huisartsen Genootschap, Utrecht *08540*
Nederlandse Bond voor Natuurgeneeswijze, Amsterdam *08553*
Nederlandse Organisatie voor Wetenschappelijk Onderzoek, Den Haag *08563*
Nederlandse Vereniging van biomedisch Laboratoriumsmedewerkers, Utrecht *08572*
Nederlandse Vereniging voor Medisch Onderwijs, Utrecht *08592*
Nederlandse Werkgroep van Praktizijns in de Natuurlijke Geneeskunst, Leusden *08610*
Orde van Medisch Specialisten, Utrecht *08613*

New Zealand
Hawke's Bay Medical Research Foundation, Napier *08674*
Medical Research Council of New Zealand, Auckland *08678*
New Zealand Medical Association, Wellington *08717*
Palmerston North Medical Research Foundation, Palmerston North *08734*
Wellington Medical Research Foundation, Wellington *08746*

Nigeria
The Medical and Dental Council of Nigeria, Lagos *08773*

Norway
Medicinske Selskap i Bergen, Bergen *08800*
Den Norske Laegeforening, Lysaker *08860*
Det Norske Medicinske Selskab, Oslo *08861*

Pakistan
College of Physicians and Surgeons Pakistan, Karachi *08896*
Pakistan Medical Association, Karachi *08921*
Pakistan Medical Research Council, Karachi *08922*

Peru
Academia Nacional de Medicina, Lima *08971*
Asociación Médica Peruana Daniel A. Carrión, Lima *08984*
Federación Médica Peruana, Lima *09000*
Sociedad Peruana de Historia de la Medicina, Lima *09016*

Philippines
Confederation of Medical Associations in Asia and Oceania, Manila *09046*
Philippine Medical Association, Quezon City *09060*
Philippine Society of Parasitology, Manila *09063*

Poland
Polskie Towarzystwo Historii Medycyny i Farmacji, Warszawa *09110*
Polskie Towarzystwo Lekarski, Warszawa *09115*
Polskie Towarzystwo Medycyny Pracy, Sosnowiec *09120*
Zrzeszenie Polskich Towarzystw Medycznych, Warszawa *09171*

Portugal
Ordem dos Médicos, Lisboa *09203*
Sociedade das Ciências Médicas de Lisboa, Lisboa *09215*
Sociedade Portuguesa de Hemorreologia e Microcirculaçã0, Lisboa *09238*

Romania
Academia de Stiinte Medicale, Bucuresti *09265*
Asociatia Medicala Romana, Bucuresti *09270*
Balkan Medical Union, Bucuresti *09275*
Entente Médicale Méditerranéenne, Bucuresti *09277*
Romanian Medical Association, Bucuresti *09283*
Societatea de Medici si Naturalisti, Iasi *09298*
Societatea de Medicinà Generalà, Bucuresti *09299*
Societatea Nationala de Medicina Generala din Romania, Bucuresti *09318*

Russia
Council of Scientific Medical Societies, Moskva *09350*
National Medical and Technical Scientific Society, Moskva *09397*
National Scientific Medical Society of History of Medicine, Moskva *09404*
National Scientific Medical Society of Infectionists, Moskva *09406*
National Scientific Medical Society of Nephrologists, Moskva *09408*
National Scientific Medical Society of Phtisiologists, Moskva *09415*
National Scientific Medical Society of Physical Therapists and Health-Resort Physicians, Moskva *09416*
National Scientific Medical Society of Physicians-Analysts, Moskva *09417*
National Scientific Medical Society of Physicians in Curative Physical Culture and Sports Medicine, Moskva *09418*
Russian Academy of Medical Sciences, Moskva *09440*

San Marino
European Centre for Disaster Medicine, San Marino *09485*

Senegal
Conférence des Facultés et Ecoles de Médecine d'Afrique d'Expression Française, Dakar *09514*

Sierra Leone
Sierra Leone Medical and Dental Assication, Freetown *09520*

Singapore
Academy of Medicine, Singapore, Singapore *09522*
Singapore Medical Association, Singapore *09542*

Slovakia
Slovenská Lekárska Společnost, Bratislava *09565*
Slovenská Parazitologická Spoločnost, Košice *09570*

South Africa
Carbohydrate and Lipid Metabolism Research Group, Johannesburg *09615*
The College of Medicine of South Africa, Rondebosch *09619*
The Medical Association of South Africa, Lynnwood *09638*
Medical Graduates' Association of the University of the Witwatersrand, Johannesburg *09639*
The South African Association for Food Science and Technology, Edenvale *09667*
The South African Association of Physicists in Medicine and Biology, Pretoria *09671*
The South African Institute for Medical Research, Johannesburg *09681*
The South African Medical Research Council, Tygerberg *09693*
South African National Multiple Sclerosis Society, Walmer *09696*

Spain
Academia de Ciencias Médicas de Bilbao, Bilbao *09724*
Academia Médico-Quirúrgica Española, Madrid *09726*
Organización Médica Colegial – Consejo General de Colegios Médicos de Espańa, Madrid *09772*
Real Academia de Doctores, Madrid *09784*
Real Academia de Medicina y Cirugía de Palma de Mallorca, Palma de Mallorca *09789*
Real Academia Nacional de Medicina, Madrid *09794*
Societat Catalana de Medicina Aerospacial, Subaquàtica i Ambiental, Barcelona *09826*

Sri Lanka
Sri Lanka Medical Association, Colombo *09841*

Sweden
Göteborgs Läkarförening, Göteborg *09886*
International Association of Medical Laboratory Technologists, Stockholm *09890*
Kungliga Fysiografiska Sällskapet i Lund, Lund *09902*
Medicinska Forskningsrådet, Stockholm *09920*
Svenska Föreningen för Medicinsk Teknik och Fysik, Umea *09970*
Svenska Läkaresällskapet, Stockholm *09985*
Sveriges Praktiserande Läkares Förening, Stockholm *10010*

Switzerland
Association Olympique Internationale pour la Recherche Médico-Sportive, Lausanne *10046*
Conseil des Organisations Internationales des Sciences Médicales, Genève *10072*
Gesellschaft schweizerischer Amtsärzte, Bern *10143*
Permanent Working Group of European Junior Hospital Doctors, Bern *10222*
Schweizer Olympischer Verband (SOV) /Sportmed, Bern *10234*
Schweizerische Ärztegesellschaft für Holistische Medizin, Adliswil *10236*
Schweizerische Ärztegesellschaft für Manuelle Medizin, Zürich *10237*
Schweizerische Akademie der medizinischen Wissenschaften, Basel *10239*
Schweizerische Gesellschaft für Allgemeinmedizin, Lichtensteig *10274*
Schweizerische Gesellschaft für Fertilität, Sterilität und Familienplanung, Lausanne *10294*
Schweizerische Gesellschaft für Geschichte der Medizin und der Naturwissenschaften, Bern *10297*
Schweizerische Gesellschaft für Sportmedizin, Bern *10336*
Schweizerische Zentralstelle für Heilpädagogik, Luzern *10425*
Schweizerischer Fachverband der diplomierten medizinischen Laborantinnen und Laboranten, Bern *10444*
Société Médicale de la Suisse Romande, Sion *10507*
Verband deutschschweizerischer Ärzte-Gesellschaften, Tuggen *10532*
Verband Schweizerischer Assistenz- und Oberärzte, Bern *10537*

Syria
Arab Council for Medical Specialization, Damascus *10586*
Arab Federation for the Organs of the Deaf, Damascus *10587*

Tanzania
Confederation of African Medical Associations and Societies, Dar es Salaam *10593*
East Africa Medical Research Council, Arusha *10595*
East, Central and Southern African College of Nursing, Arusha *10598*
Tanzania Medical Association, Dar es Salaam *10608*

Thailand
Medical Association of Thailand, Bangkok *10641*

Trinidad and Tobago
Caribbean Sports Medicine Association, Port of Spain *10666*

Tunisia
Arab Federation of Sports Medicine, Tunis *10676*
Arab Medical Union, Tunis *10679*

Uganda
Uganda Medical Association, Kampala *10732*

Ukraine
Ukrainian Academy of Medical Sciences, Kiev *10738*

United Kingdom
Action in International Medicine, London *10746*
Anglo-European College of Chiropractic, Bournemouth *10775*
Association for Medical Deans in Europe, Belfast *10813*
Association for Medical Education in Europe, Dundee *10814*
Association for Spina Bifida and Hydrocephalus, Peterborough *10825*
Association for the Study of Medical Education, Dundee *10833*
Association of Crematorium Medical Referees, Westcliff-on-Sea *10869*
Association of District Medical Officers, Bath *10875*
Association of Health Care Information and Medical Records Officers, Hopton *10886*
Association of Researchers in Medicine and Science, London *10916*
Association to Combat Huntington's Chorea, Hinckley *10937*
Assurance Medical Society, London *10938*
British Acupuncture Association and Register, London *10998*
British Association for Accident and Emergency Medicine, London *11007*
British Association for Immediate Care, Ipswich *11014*

Musicology

Zambia

Mycology
s. Botany, Specific

Natural History
s. Natural Sciences,
general

Natural Resources

Argentina

Australia

Canada

Natural Sciences,
general

Argentina

Australia

Austria

Azerbaijan

Belgium

Bulgaria

Canada

Chile

China, People's Republic

Colombia

Croatia

Cuba

Denmark

Ecuador

Finland

France

Germany

Guatemala

Hungary

Iceland

India

Indonesia

Italy

Japan

Kenya

Luxembourg

Malaysia

Mexico

Moldova, Republic of

463 Subject Index: Ophthalmology

Gesellschaft für Ernährungsbiologie e.V., München 05365
Gesellschaft für Ernährungsphysiologie, Frankfurt 05366
Informationskreis Mundhygiene und Ernährungsverhalten, Frankfurt/Main 05511
Institut für nationale und internationale Fleisch- und Ernährungswirtschaft, Heidelberg 05532
International Commission for Uniform Methods of Sugar Analysis, North Ryde, Australia 05553
Margarine-Institut für gesunde Ernährung, Hamburg 05739
Vereinigung Getreide-, Markt- und Ernährungsforschung e.V., Bonn 06125

Italy

Associazione Italiana di Tecnologia Alimentare, Milano 06969
Centro Nazionale di Dietobiologia ed Igiene della Alimentazione, Milano 07099
Società Italiana di Nutrizione Umana, Roma 07540

Japan

Nippon Bitamin Gakkai, Kyoto 07873

New Zealand

New Zealand Dietetic Association, Wellington 08692

Nigeria

African Council of Food and Nutrition Sciences, Harare 08757

Portugal

Sociedade Portuguesa de Higiene Alimentar, Lisboa 09239

South Africa

Organic Soil Association of South Africa, Parklands 09647

Spain

Sociedad Española de Patología Digestiva y de la Nutrición, Madrid 09819

Switzerland

Schweizerischer Verband der Ingenieur-Agronomen und der Lebensmittel-Ingenieure, Zollikofen 10465

Trinidad and Tobago

Caribbean Association of Nutritionists and Dieticians, West Moorings 10656

United Kingdom

The British Dietetic Association, Birmingham 11072
British Nutrition Foundation, London 11138
CAB International, Wallingford 11231
Gooseberry Society, Barnet 11581
Institute of Food Research, Reading 11687
International Union of Nutritional Sciences, London 11830
The Royal Institute of Public Health and Hygiene, London 12220

U.S.A.

American Celiac Society, West Orange 13024
American Dietetic Association, Chicago 13126
American Institute of Nutrition, Bethesda 13221
Asia Pacific Public Health Nutrition Association, Berkeley 13577
Dietary Managers Association, Itasca 14305
Food and Nutrition Board, Washington 14446
Institute for Food and Development Policy, Oakland 14671
National Association of Nutrition and Aging Services Programs, Grand Rapids 15715
Nutrition Institute of America, New York 16068
Society for Nutrition Education, Minneapolis 16417

Zambia

National Food and Nutrition Commission, Lusaka 17052

Occultism s. Parapsychology

Oceanography, Marine Sciences

Australia

Australian Institute of Marine Science, Townsville 00201

Austria

Haus des Meeres Vivarium Wien, Wien 00495

Canada

Canadian Meteorological and Oceanographic Society, Ottawa 01926

Chile

Comité Oceanográfico Nacional, Valparaíso 02462

China, People's Republic

Chinese Society for Oceanology and Limnology, Qingdao 02613
Chinese Society of Oceanography, Beijing 02631
Chinese Society of Oceanology and Limnology, Qingdao 02632

Croatia

Drustvo za Proučavanje i Unapredenje Pomorstva, Rijeka 02869

Denmark

International Council for the Exploration of the Sea, København 03134
Nordisk Kollegium for Fysisk Oceanografi, København 03179

Finland

Geofysiikan Seura, Espoo 03348

France

Association Internationale d'Océanographie Médicale, Nice 03595
Association Scientifique et Technique pour l'Exploitation des Océans, Paris-La Défense 03657
Commission Océanographique Intergouvernementale, Paris 03740
Committee for European Marine Biology Symposia, Brest 03741
European Association of Marine Sciences and Techniques, Talence 03800
European Marine and Polar Science (EMAPS) Boards, Strasbourg 03821
Fédération Française d'Etudes et de Sports Sous Marins, Marseille 03843
Joint Committee on Climatic Changes and the Ocean, Paris 03911
Société d'Océanographie de France, Paris 04097
Union des Océanographes de France, Paris 04300

Germany

Conference of Baltic Oceanographers, Kiel 04697
Deutsche Meteorologische Gesellschaft e.V., Traben-Trarbach 04921
Deutsche Meteorologische Gesellschaft e.V., Zweigverein Hamburg, Hamburg 04922
Deutsche Wissenschaftliche Kommission für Meeresforschung, Hamburg 04982

Italy

Società Italiana di Biologia Marina, Livorno 07466

Ivory Coast

Académie Régionale des Sciences et Techniques de la Mer d'Abidjan, Abidjan 07682

Japan

Kaiyoo Kisho Gakkai, Kboe 07749
Nippon Kaiyo Gakkai, Tokyo 07921

Kenya

East Asian Seas Action Plan, Nairobi 08095

Malta

Euro-Mediterranean Centre on Insular Coastal Dynamics, Valletta 08243

Monaco

Commission Internationale pour l'Exploration Scientifique de la Mer Méditerranée, Monaco 08373

New Zealand

New Zealand Marine Sciences Society, Wellington 08715

Norway

Norske Havforskeres Forening, Nordnes 08857

Russia

National Committee of the Pacific Ocean Research Association, Moskva 09390

Sweden

Baltic Marine Biologists, Lysekil 09857
Conference of the Baltic Oceanographers, Norrköping 09866

Thailand

Association of Southeast Asian Marine Scientists, Bangkok 10636

United Kingdom

Advisory Committee on Protection of the Sea, London 10751
British Marine Aquarist Association, Hull 11121
Challenger Society for Marine Science, Southampton 11264
International Glaciological Society, Cambridge 11796
International Hydrofoil Society, London 11798
Marine Biological Association of the United Kingdom, Plymouth 11912
Maritime Information Association, London 11914
The Scottish Association for Marine Sciemce, Oban 12292

U.S.A.

American Society of Limnology and Oceanography, Gloucester Point 13467
Aquatic Research Institute, Hayward 13559
Arctic Ocean Science Board, Arlington 13566
Center for Oceans Law and Policy, Charlottesville 14016
Coastal Engineering Research Council, College Station 14094
Cooperative Marine Science Programme for the Black Sea, Woods Hole 14192
Estuarine Research Federation, Port Republic 14392
Foresta Institute for Ocean and Mountain Studies, Tucson 14452
International Association for the Physical Sciences of the Oceans, Vicksburg 14819
International Association of Aquatic and Marine Science Libraries and Information Centers, Fort Pierce 14831
International Marine Simulator Forum, Toledo 15108
International Phycological Society, Fort Pierce 15152
International Society for Reef Studies, St Petersburg 15245
International Tsunami Information Centre, Honolulu 15350
IOC Committee for the Global Investigation of Pollution in the Marine Environment, Washington 15383
IOC Sub-Commission for the Caribbean and Adjacent Regions, Miami 15384
Joint Global Ocean Flux Study, Baltimore 15446
Marine Technology Society, Washington 15527
North Pacific Marine Science Organization, Seattle 16058
Oceanic Federation of Coloproctology, Seattle 16072
Oceanic Society Expeditions, San Francisco 16073
Pan Pacific Consortium of Maritime Museums, Newport Beach 16143
Scientific Committee on Oceanic Research, Baltimore 16298
Sea Grant Association, Madison 16305
United States Antarctic Research Program, Arlington 16682
World Aquaculture Society, Baton Rouge 16788

Ophthalmology

Argentina

Sociedad Argentina de Oftalmología, Buenos Aires 00099

Australia

The Contact Lens Society of Australia, Sydney 00263
Opticians and Optometrists Association of New South Wales, Sydney 00318
Royal Australian College of Ophthalmologists, Sydney 00336

Austria

Österreichische Ophthalmologische Gesellschaft, Wien 00724

Belgium

European Centre of Ophthalmology, Bruxelles 01123
European Community University Professors in Ophthalmology, Gent 01136
Société Belge d'Ophthalmologie, Section Francophone, Bruxelles 01258
Union Professionnelle Belge des Médécins Ophthalmologistes, Bruxelles 01308

Canada

Canadian Association of Optometrists, Ottawa 01820
Canadian Ophthalmological Society, Ottawa 01935
Canadian Orthoptic Society, Halifax 01937
Nova Scotia Association of Optometrists, Lower Sackville 02247
Operation Eyesight Universal, Calgary 02302
Société Québécoise d'Assainissement des Eaux, Montréal 02381

Chile

Sociedad Chilena de Oftalmología, Santiago 02498

China, Republic

Ophthalmological Society of the Republic of China, Taipei 02743

Colombia

Sociedad Americana de Oftalmologia y Optometria, Bogotá 02807

Cyprus

Cyprus Ophthalmological Society, Larnaca 02904

Czech Republic

Česká Oftalmologická Společnost, Praha 02925

Denmark

Dansk Oftalmologisk Selskab, København 03043

Egypt

Ophthalmological Society of Egypt, Cairo 03301

France

Association of European Schools and Colleges of Optometry, Bures-sur-Yvette 03626
Organisation Internationale contre le Trachome, Créteil 03934
Société d'Ophtalmologie de l'Est de la France, Nancy 04098
Société d'Ophtalmologie de Lyon, Lyon 04099
Société d'Ophtalmologie de Paris, Paris 04100
Société d'Oto-Neuro-Ophthalmologie du Sud-Est de la France, Marseille 04101
Société Française d'Ophthalmologie, Paris 04187

Germany

Berufsverband der Augenärzte Deutschlands e.V., Düsseldorf 04560
Deutsche Ophthalmologische Gesellschaft Heidelberg e.V., Heidelberg 04932
Vereinigung Bayerischer Augenärzte, München 06109
Wissenschaftliche Vereinigung für Augenoptik und Optometrie e.V., Mainz 06160

India

All-India Ophthalmological Society, New Delhi 06396
Indian Optometric Association, New Delhi 06469

Italy

Associazione Professionale Italiana Medici Oculisti, Roma 07036
Società Italiana di Oto-Neuro-Oftalmologia, Bologna 07546
Società Oftalmologica Italiana, Bologna 07622

Japan

Nippon Ganka Gakkai, Tokyo 07894

Kenya

Ophthalmological Society of East Africa, Nairobi 08106

Mexico

Sociedad de Oftalmología del Hospital de Oftalmológico de Nuestra Señora de la Luz, México 08325
Sociedad Médica del Hospital Oftalmológico de Nuestra Señora de la Luz, México 08332

Netherlands

Nederlands Oogheelkundig Gezelschap, Nijmegen 08544

Nicaragua

Sociedad de Oftalmología Nicaragüense, Managua 08749

Panama

Asociación Panamericana de Oftalmología, Panamá City 08943

Portugal

Sociedade Portuguesa de Oftalmologia, Lisboa 09244

Romania

Societatea de Oftalmologie, Bucuresti 09304

Russia

National Ophthalmological Society, Moskva 09398

Sweden

Svenska Ogonläkareföreningen, Stockholm 09995

Switzerland

Schweizerische Ophthalmologische Gesellschaft, Heerbrugg 10379

Turkey

Türk Oftalmoloji Derneği, Istanbul 10711

United Kingdom

British Orthoptic Society, London 11145
British Retinitis Pigmentosa Society, Buckingham 11155
College of Ophthalmologists, London 11303
European Contact Lens Society of Ophthalmologists, London 11488
Medical Contact Lens Association, London 11923
Royal College of Ophthalmologists, London 12185

U.S.A.

American Academy of Ophthalmology, San Francisco 12771
American Academy of Optometry, Bethesda 12772
American Academy of Otolaryngic Allergy, Silver Spring 12780
American Association for Pediatric Ophthalmology and Strabismus, San Francisco 12845
American Board of Ophthalmology, Bala Cynwyd 12986
American Diopter and Decibel Society, Pittsburgh 13127
American Foundation for Vision Awareness, Saint Louis 13159
American Ophthalmological Society, Durham 13293
American Optometric Association, Saint Louis 13294
American Orthoptic Council, Madison 13303
American Society of Contemporary Ophthalmology, Skokie 13441
American Society of Veterinary Ophthalmology, Stillwater 13497
Asia-Pacific Council of Optometry, Forest Grove 13576
Association for Macular Diseases, New York 13646
Association for Research in Vision and Ophthalmology, Bethesda 13660
Association of Optometric Educators, Tahlequah 13808
Association of Schools and Colleges of Optometry, Rockville 13828
Association of University Professors of Ophthalmology, San Francisco 13861
Better Vision Institute, Rosslyn 13915
College of Optometrists in Vision Development, Chula Vista 14104
Dana Center for Preventive Ophthalmology, Baltimore 14282
International Association of Boards of Examiners in Optometry, Bethesda 14832
International Association of Ocular Surgeons, Skokie 14863
International Association of Optometric Executives, Little Rock 14864
International Council of Ophthalmology, Chicago 14981
International Eye Foundation, Bethesda 15008
International Federation of Eye Banks, Baltimore 15015
International Federation of Ophthalmological Societies, Chicago 15017, 15018
International Intraocular Implant Club, Houston 15087
International Oculoplastic Society, New York 15126
International Society of Geographic Ophthalmology, Shreveport 15293

International Rhinologic Society, Bruxelles 01212

Canada
Canadian Academy of Oral Pathology, London 01772
Canadian Academy of Oral Radiology, Toronto 01773
Canadian Society of Otolaryngology, Head and Neck Surgery, Toronto 01999

Chile
Sociedad Chilena de Otorrinolaringología, Santiago 02500
Sociedad de Otorinolaringología de Valparaíso, Valparaíso 02527

China, Republic
Taiwan Otolaryngological Society, Taipei 02758

Denmark
Dansk Oto-laryngologisk Selskab, Hellerup 03047

France
European Audio Phonological Centers Association, Saint-Etienne 03805
Societas Oto-Rhino-Laryngologia Latina, Montpellier 03945
Société d'Oto-Neuro-Ophthalmologie du Sud-Est de la France, Marseille 04101
Société Française de Phoniatrie, Paris 04154
Société Française d'Oto-Rhino-Laryngologie et de Pathologie Cervico-Faciale, Paris 04190
Syndicat National des Médecins Spécialisés en Phoniatrie, Saint-Denis 04286
Syndicat National des Oto-Rhino-Laryngologistes Français, Paris 04289

Germany
Berufsverband der Berliner Hals-, Nasen-, Ohren-Ärzte, Berlin 04561
Confederation of European Laryngectomees, Bebra 04696
Deutsche Gesellschaft für Hals-Nasen-Ohren-Heilkunde, Kopf- und Hals-Chirurgie, Bonn 04793
Deutscher Berufsverband der Hals-Nasen-Ohrenärzte e.V., Neumünster 04997
Nordwestdeutsche Vereinigung der Hals-Nasen-Ohrenärzte, Kiel 05786
Vereinigung Südwestdeutscher HNO-Ärzte, Köln 06129
Vereinigung Westdeutscher Hals-, Nasen- und Ohrenärzte, Köln 06131

Indonesia
Asian Society of Oto-Rhino-Laryngology, Jakarta 06552

Israel
Oto-Laryngological Society of Israel, Tel Aviv 06743

Italy
Associazione Otologica Ospedaliera Italiano, Roma 07022
Società Italiana di Audiologia e Foniatria, Roma 07461
Società Italiana di Foniatria, Catania 07499
Società Italiana di Laringologia, Otologia, Rinologia e Patologia Cervico-Facciale, Roma 07512
Società Italiana di Oto-Neuro-Oftalmologia, Bologna 07546
Società Italiana di Otorinolaringologia e Chirurgia Cervico Facciale, Roma 07547
Società Italiana di Otorinolaringologia Pediatrica, Roma 07548

Japan
Nippon Jibi-Inkoka Gakkai, Tokyo 07909
Shika Kiso Igakkai, Tokyo 08025

Netherlands
Nederlandse Vereniging voor Mondziekten en Kaakchirurgie, Den Haag 08595

Poland
Polskie Towarzystwo Otolaryngologiczne, Warszawa 09131

Portugal
Associação Portuguesa de Otorinolaringologia e Cirurgia Cérvico-Facial, Lisboa 09185

Romania
Societatea de Oto-Rino-Laringologie, Bucuresti 09305

Russia
National Scientific Medical Society of Oto-Rhino-Laryngologists, Moskva 09413

South Africa
South African Society of Otorhinolaryngology, Bellville 09705

Spain
Asociación Española de Logopedia, Foniatria y Audiología, Barcelona 09732

Sweden
Svensk Otolaryngologisk Förening, Stockholm 09955

Switzerland
Schweizerische Arbeitsgemeinschaft für orale Implantologie, Zürich 10251
Schweizerische Gesellschaft für Otorhinolaryngologie, Hals- und Gesichtschirurgie, Sankt Gallen 10322
Société Romande d'Audiophonologie et de Pathologie du Langage, Delémont 10510

Thailand
ASEAN Otorhinolaryngological Head and Neck Federation, Bangkok 10617

Turkey
Türk Oto-Rino-Laringoloji Cemiyeti, Istanbul 10713

United Kingdom
British Association of Otorhinolaryngologists, Head and Neck Surgeons, London 11037
British Kidney Patient Association, Bordon 11114
British Society of Audiology, Reading 11191
British Tinnitus Association, London 11205
International Society of Audiology, London 11818

U.S.A.
Academy of Dispensing Audiologists, Columbia 12657
Academy of Rehabilitative Audiology, Minneapolis 12670
American Academy of Oral Medicine, Arlington 12774
American Academy of Otolaryngic Allergy, Silver Spring 12780
American Auditory Society, Phoenix 12960
American Board of Otolaryngology, Houston 12991
American Broncho-Esophagological Association, Saint Louis 13013
American Cleft Palate-Craniofacial Association, Pittsburgh 13033
American Laryngological Association, Boston 13240
American Laryngological, Rhinological and Otological Society, Saint Louis 13241
American Otological Society, Maywood 13316
American Rhinologic Society, Brooklyn 13357
American Society for Head and Neck Surgery, Pittsburgh 13388
American Tinnitus Association, Portland 13519
Better Hearing Institute, Washington 13914
Deafness Research Foundation, New York 14288
Hear Center, Pasadena 14552
Hearing International, East Lansing 14553
House Ear Institute, Los Angeles 14588
International Association of Laryngectomees, Atlanta 14859
International Bronchoesophagological Society, Scottsdale 14891
International Federation of Oto-Rhino-Laryngological Societies, Alexandria 15020
National Center for Law and Deafness, Washington 15784
National Hearing Conservation Association, Milwaukee 15901
Osteopathic Colleges of Ophthalmology and Otolaryngology, Head and Neck Surgery, Dayton 16106
Pan American Association of Oto-Rhino-Laryngology – Head and Neck Surgery, Cleveland 16135

Venezuela
Sociedad Venezolana de Otorinolaringología, Caracas 16935

Vietnam
Vietnamese Association of Oto-Rhino-Laryngology, Hanoi 16965

Paleontology

Argentina
Asociación Paleontológica Argentina, Buenos Aires 00059

Austria
Österreichische Paläontologische Gesellschaft, Wien 00728

Azerbaijan
Palaeontological Society, Baku 00893

Brazil
Asociación Latinoamericana de Paleobotánica y Palinología, Porto Alegre 01390

China, People's Republic
Palaeontological Society of China, Nanjing 02657

France
Association Internationale pour l'Etude de la Paléontologie Humaine, Paris 03602

Germany
Paläontologische Gesellschaft, Frankfurt 05872

Italy
Accademia Valdarnese del Poggio, Montevarchi 06886
Centro Studi Ricerche Ligabue, Venezia 07173
Istituto Italiano di Paleontologia Umana, Roma 07349
Società degli Amici del Museo Civico di Storia Naturale Giacomo Doria, Genova 07399
Società Italiana di Biogeografia, Siena 07465

Japan
Nippon Koseibutsu Gakkai, Tokyo 07942

Malta
Society for the Study and Conservation of Nature, Valletta 08252

Russia
Russian Palaeontological Society, St. Petersburg 09448

Switzerland
Schweizerische Paläontologische Gesellschaft, Genève 10380

United Kingdom
Moray Society, Moray 11957
Palaeontographical Society, Nottingham 12083

U.S.A.
Paleontological Research Institution, Ithaca 16128
Paleontological Society, Riverside 16129
Society for Sedimentary Geology, Tulsa 16440
Society of Vertebrate Paleontology, Chicago 16568

Parapsychology

Austria
Österreichische Gesellschaft für Parapsychologie und Grenzbereiche der Wissenschaften, Wien 00671

Canada
International Society for Research in Palmistry, Westmount 02158

France
European Association for the Study of Dreans, Ile-Saint-Denis 03797

India
Theosophical Society, Chennai 06536

Italy
Associazione Italiana Scientifica di Metapsichica, Milano 06987
Centro Ricerche Metapsichiche e Psicofoniche, Fermo 07123

Switzerland
Schweizerische Vereinigung für Parapsychologie, Bern 10412

United Kingdom
Direct Investigation Group on Aerial Phenomena, Bury 11390
Faculty of Astrological Studies, London 11514
Society for Psychical Research, London 12374

U.S.A.
American Federation of Astrologers, Tempe 13146
Association for Research and Enlightenment, Virginia Beach 13658
Committee for the Scientific Investigation of Claims of the Paranormal, Amherst 14127
Intergalactic Spacecraft – UFO – Intercontinental Research and Analytic Network, Flushing 14755
International Association for Near-Death Studies, East Windsor Hill 14806
International Guild of Occult Sciences, Palm Springs 15057
International Husserl and Phenomenological Research Society, Belmont 15067
International Society for Astrological Research, Santa Paula 15193
International Society for Phenomenology and Literature, Belmont 15238
International Society of Phenomenology, Aesthetics and the Fine Arts, East Lansing 15304
Parapsychological Association, Fairhaven 16146
Professional Psychics United, Oak Park 16209
World Institute for Advanced Phenomenological Research and Learning, Belmont 16824

Parasitology s. Microbiology

Pathology

Argentina
Sociedad Argentina de Patología, Buenos Aires 00100

Australia
Royal College of Pathologists of Australasia, Surrey Hills 00340

Austria
Österreichische Arbeitsgemeinschaft für morphologische und funktionelle Atherosklerоseforschung, Wien 00574
Österreichische Gesellschaft für Neuropathologie, Wien 00668
Österreichische Gesellschaft für Pathologie, Wien 00672
Österreichische Gesellschaft zur Bekämpfung der Cystischen Fibrose, Wien 00706

Belgium
Association pour les Etudes et Recherches de Zoologie Appliquée et de Phytopathologie, Sint-Truiden 00981
Dentist's Liaison Committee for the EEC, Bruxelles 01068
International Institute of Cellular and Molecular Pathology, Bruxelles 01207
Ligue Belge contre l'Epilepsie, Bruxelles 01228

Canada
Canadian Academy of Oral Pathology, London 01772
Canadian Association of Pathologists, Toronto 01822
Canadian Osteogenesis Imperfecta Society, Chatham 01938
Canadian Osteopathic Aid Society, London 01939
Canadian Osteopathic Association, London 01940
Canadian Paraplegic Association, Ottawa 01942
Epilepsy Canada, Montréal 02095
New Brunswick Association of Pathologists, Saint John 02222
Osteoporosis Society of Canada, Toronto 02304
Spina Bifida and Hydrocephalus Association of Ontario, Toronto 02393
Spina Bifida Association of British Columbia, Surrey 02394
Spina Bifida Association of Canada, Winnipeg 02395

Chile
Sociedad Chilena de Patología de la Adaptación y del Mesenquima, Santiago 02502
Sociedad de Anatomía Normal y Patológica de Chile, Santiago 02513

Colombia
Sociedad Colombiana de Patología, Cali 02819

Denmark
Dansk Selskab for Akupunktur, København 03055
Dansk Selskab for Patologi, København 03069
European Association for Haematopathology, Aarhus 03110

France
Ligue Française contre la Sclérose en Plaques, Paris 03912
Société de Pathologie Comparée, Paris 03995
Société de Pathologie Exotique, Paris 03996
Société Française de Néonatologie, Paris 04146
Société Française de Pathologie Respiratoire, Paris 04149
Syndicat National des Médecins Anatomo-Cyto-Pathologistes Français, Paris 04275

Germany
Deutsche Gesellschaft für die Bekämpfung der Muskelkrankheiten e.V., Freiburg 04767
Deutsche Gesellschaft für Pathologie, Frankfurt 04834
Deutsche Gesellschaft für Phlebologie, Norderney 04838
Deutsche Sektion der Internationalen Liga gegen Epilepsie, Bielefeld 04958
Internationale Akademie für Pathologie, Deutsche Abteilung e.V., Bonn 05564
Vereinigung Deutscher Neuropathologen und Neuroanatomen, Giessen 06120

Hungary
Magyar Elettani Társaság, Budapest 06306
Magyar Pathológusok Társasága, Budapest 06333

Ireland
Brainwave – Irish Epilepsy Association, Dublin 06589

Israel
Israel Society of Pathologists, Beer-Sheva 06732

Italy
Associazione Italiana per lo Studio del Dolore, Firenze 06983
Associazione Italiana Sclerosi Multipla, Roma 06988
International Study Group for Steroid Hormones, Roma 07330
Società Europea di Patologia, Milano 07425
Societá Italiana della Continenza, Roma 07448
Società Italiana di Anatomia Patologica, Messina 07456
Società Italiana di Andrologia, Pisa 07457
Società Italiana di Immunologia e di Immunopatologia, Bari 07509
Società Italiana di Patologia, Milano 07550
Società Italiana di Patologia Vascolare, Roma 07554
Società Italiana per lo Studio dell'Arteriosclerosi, Bari 07598
Società Laziale Abruzzese di Medicina del Lavoro, Roma 07604

Japan
Nihon Rinsho Byori Gakkai, Tokyo 07838
Nippon Byori Gakkai, Tokyo 07878
World Association of Societies of Pathology (Anatomic and Clinical), Tokyo 08049

Netherlands
Nederlandse Patholoog Anatomen Vereniging, Maastricht 08566
Nederlandse Vereniging voor Pathologie, Rotterdam 08600

Poland
Polskie Towarzystwo Patologów, Lódź 09133

Portugal
Sociedade Portuguesa de Patologia, Lisboa 09246

Romania
Societatea de Ftiziologie, Bucuresti 09292
Societatea de Patologie Infectioasà, Bucuresti 09306

473 Subject Index: Psychology

American Psychiatric Association, Washington *13342*
American Psychoanalytic Association, New York *13343*
American Psychopathological Association, Saint Louis *13346*
American Society for Adolescent Psychiatry, Bethesda *13367*
Association for Advancement of Behavior Therapy, New York *13592*
Association for Research in Nervous and Mental Disease, New York *13659*
Association of Mental Health Administrators, Northbrook *13795*
Black Psychiatrists of America, Oakland *13930*
Group for the Advancement of Psychiatry, Dallas *14529*
Institute for Labor and Mental Health, Oakland *14675*
Institute on Psychiatric Services/American Psychiatric Association, Washington *14729*
International Association for Child and Adolescent Psychiatry and Allied Professions, New Haven *14783*
International Committee Against Mental Illness, New York *14939*
International Institute for Bioenergetic Analysis, New York *15069*
International Society for Adolescent Psychiatry, Nashville *15187*
International Transactional Analysis Association, San Francisco *15347*
Laughter Therapy, Los Angeles *15483*
Mental Health Materials Center, Bronxville *15555*
Milton H. Erickson Foundation, Phoenix *15582*
National Association for Rural Mental Health, Wood River *15657*
National Association of State Mental Health Program Directors, Alexandria *15738*
National Association of State Mental Retardation Program Directors, Alexandria *15739*
National Consortium for Child Mental Health Services, Washington *15817*
National Guild of Catholic Psychiatrists, Ellicott City *15893*
National Mental Health Association, Alexandria *15935*
North American Region of the World Federation for Mental Health, Milwaukee *16044*
Postgraduate Center for Mental Health, New York *16193*
Sleep Research Society, Cleveland *16334*
Social Psychiatry Research Institute, New York *16338*
Society for Life History Research, Philadelphia *16408*
Society for Psychophysiological Research, Dallas *16434*
Society of Biological Psychiatry, Jacksonville *16503*
Society of Professors of Child and Adolescent Psychiatry, Washington *16551*
Tourette Syndrome Association, Bayside *16647*
World Association for Infant Mental Health, East Lansing *16793*
World Association for Social Psychiatry, Santa Barbara *16796*

Venezuela
Asociación Psiquiátrica de la América Latina, Caracas *16878*
Sociedad Venezolana de Psiquiatría y Neurología, Caracas *16936*

Vietnam
Vietnamese Association of Neurology, Psychiatry and Neurosurgery, Hanoi *16961*

Psychoanalysis

Austria
Innsbrucker Arbeitskreis für Psychoanalyse, Psychoanalytisches Forschungs- und Ausbildungsinstitut, Innsbruck *00500*
Österreichische Gesellschaft für Autogenes Training und allgemeine Psychotherapie, Wien *00615*
Österreichische Studiengesellschaft für Kinderpsychoanalyse, Salzburg *00737*
Salzburger Arbeitskreis für Psychoanalyse, Salzburg *00789*
Sigmund Freud-Gesellschaft, Wien *00794*
Wiener Arbeitskreis für Psychoanalyse, Wien *00860*
Wiener Psychoanalytische Vereinigung, Wien *00874*

Canada
Canadian Institute of Hypnotism, Montréal *01910*
Canadian Psychoanalytic Society, Montréal *01954*

Denmark
Dansk Psykoanalytisk Selskab, København *03051*

France
Association Psychoanalytique de France, Paris *03652*
Congrès des Psychoanalystes de Langues Romanes, Paris *03763*
Société Psychoanalytique de Paris, Paris *04240*

Germany
Deutsche Gesellschaft für Analytische Psychologie e.V., Berlin *04752*
Deutsche Psychoanalytische Gesellschaft e.V., München *04944*

Ireland
Irish Psychoanalytical Association, Dublin *06639*

Italy
Associazione Italiana per lo Studio della Psicologia Analitica, Roma *06984*
Associazione Medica Italiana per lo Studio della Ipnosi, Milano *06995*
Associazione Psicanalitica Italiana, Milano *07037*
International Society of Theoretical and Experimental Hypnosis, Milano *07328*

Netherlands
Nederlands Psychoanalytisch Genootschap, Utrecht *08545*

Sweden
Svenska Psykoanalytiska Föreningen, Stockholm *09997*

Switzerland
CIP International Study and Research Center in Psychosynteresis, Lausanne *10064*

United Kingdom
British Psycho-Analytical Society, London *11151*
Institute of Psycho-Analysis, London *11714*
International Psychoanalytical Association, London *11813*

U.S.A.
American Academy of Psychoanalysis, New York *12792*
American College of Psychoanalysts, Benicia *13074*
Association for Advancement of Psychoanalysis, New York *13593*
Association for Behavior Analysis International, Kalamazoo *13601*
Association for Child Psychoanalysis, Ramsey *13608*
Association for Group Psychoanalysis and Process, New York *13630*
Association for Psychoanalytic Medicine, New York *13655*
Association to Advance Ethical Hypnosis, Cuyahoga Falls *13870*
C.G. Jung Foundation for Analytical Psychology, New York *14047*
National Association for the Advancement of Psychoanalysis and The American Board for Accreditation in Psychoanalysis, New York *15661*
National Psychological Association for Psychoanalysis, New York *15957*
Society for the Advancement of Behavior Analysis, Kalamazoo *16446*

Psychology s. a. Behavioral Sciences; Depth Psychology; Psychoanalysis

Argentina
Sociedad Argentina de Psicología, Buenos Aires *00102*
Sociedad de Psicología Médica, Psicoanálisis y Medicina Psicosomática, Buenos Aires *00108*

Australia
Australian Institute of Industrial Psychology, Sydney *00198*
The Australian Psychological Society, Carlton *00224*
Sydney University Psychological Society, Sydney *00371*

Austria
Arbeitsgemeinschaft für Präventivpsychologie, Wien *00406*
Arbeitsgemeinschaft für Psychotechnik in Österreich, Wien *00407*
Arbeitsgemeinschaft Personenzentrierte Psychotherapie und Gesprächsführung, Wien *00410*
Berufsverband Österreichischer Psychologen, Wien *00424*
Gesellschaft für Kulturpsychologie, Salzburg *00472*
Internationale Vereinigung für Selbstmordprophylaxe, Wien *00534*
Österreichische Ärztegesellschaft für Psychotherapie, Wien *00569*
Österreichische Arbeitsgemeinschaft für Neuropsychiatrie und Psychologie des Kindes- und Jugendalters und verwandter Berufe, Wien *00575*
Österreichische Arbeitskreise für Tiefenpsychologie, Salzburg *00578*
Österreichische Gesellschaft für ärztliche Hypnose und autogenes Training, Wien *00599*
Österreichische Gesellschaft für Bionome Psychotherapie, Wien *00618*
Österreichischer Verein für Individualpsychologie, Wien *00769*
Sigmund Freud-Gesellschaft, Wien *00794*
Steirische Gesellschaft für Psychologie, Graz *00799*

Belgium
Association de l'Europe Occidentale pour la Psychologie Aéronautique, Bruxelles *00949*
European Association of Experimental Social Psychology, Louvain-la-Neuve *01100*
European Down's Syndrome Association, Verviers *01145*
Société Belge de Psychologie, Bruxelles *01251*
Société d'Ergonomie de Langue Française, Bruxelles *01262*

Bulgaria
Bulgarian Psychological Association, Sofia *01561*

Canada
Academy of Psychology, Ottawa *01612*
Adlerian Psychological Association of British Columbia, Vancouver *01613*
Association de Psychologie du Travail de Langue Française, Québec *01670*
Association des Psycho-Educateurs du Québec, Montréal *01689*
Association des Psychologues du Québec, Montréal *01690*
Association of Psychologists of Nova Scotia, Halifax *01722*
Canadian Group Psychotherapy Association, Whitby *01894*
Canadian Psychological Association, Ottawa *01955*
Canadian Society for Psychomotor Learning and Sport Psychology, Calgary *01981*
Human Factors Association of Canada, Mississauga *02126*
Psychological Society of Saskatchewan, Regina *02331*

Chile
Asociación de Psicólogos Infanto-Juveniles, Santiago *02452*

China, People's Republic
Chinese Association for Mental Health, Beijing *02570*
Chinese Psychological Society, Beijing *02603*

China, Republic
Chinese Association of Psychological Testing, Taipei *02688*
Chinese Psychological Association, Taipei *02707*

Cuba
Sociedad Cubana de Hipnosis, La Habana *02889*

Czech Republic
Česká Psychologická Společnost, Praha *02928*

Denmark
Dansk Psykoanalytisk Selskab, København *03051*
Dansk Psykolog Forening, København *03052*
Selskabet for Filosofi og Psykologi, København *03206*

Egypt
Egyptian Association for Mental Health, Cairo *03273*
Egyptian Association for Psychological Studies, Cairo *03274*

Finland
Suomen Psykologiliitto, Helsinki *03430*

France
Association Internationale de Psychologie du Travail de Langue Française, Motn Saint-Aignan *03573*
Conseil International des Sciences Sociales, Paris *03772*
Institut Français d'Analyse de Groupe et de Psychodrame, Paris *03883*
Société de Neuropsychologie de Langue Française, Toulouse *03993*
Société de Psychologie Médicale de Langue Française, Bron *04002*
Société d'Etude de Psychodrame Pratique et Théorique, Paris *04052*
Société Française de Psychologie, Paris *04160*
Société Française d'Etudes des Phénomènes Psychiques, Paris *04178*
Société Médico-Psychologique, Boulogne *04222*

Georgia
Georgian Society of Psychologists, Tbilisi *04351*

Germany
Berufsverband Deutscher Psychologinnen und Psychologen e.V., Bonn *04568*
Berufsverband Geprüfter Graphologen/Psychologen e.V., München *04571*
Bundesverband Legasthenie e.V., Hannover *04668*
Dachverband Psychosozialer Hilfsvereinigungen e.V., Bonn *04700*
Deutsche Gesellschaft für Analytische Psychologie e.V., Berlin *04752*
Deutsche Gesellschaft für Psychologie e.V., Münster *04848*
Deutsche Gesellschaft für Psychosomatische Medizin e.V., München *04849*
Deutsche Gesellschaft für Sexualforschung e.V., Hamburg *04856*
Deutsche Gesellschaft für Suchtforschung und Suchttherapie e.V., Hamm *04866*
Deutsche Hauptstelle gegen die Suchtgefahren e.V., Hamm *04897*
Deutsche Psychoanalytische Vereinigung e.V., Berlin *04945*
Gesellschaft für Psychotherapie, Psychosomatik und Medizinische Psychologie e.V., Leipzig *05398*
Psychobiologische Gesellschaft, Mülheim *05892*

Hungary
Magyar Pszichológiai Társaság, Budapest *06335*

Ireland
Psychological Society of Ireland, Dublin *06656*

Israel
Israel Psychological Association, Tel Aviv *06716*

Italy
Associazione di Ricerca e Interventi Psicosociali e Psicoterapeutici, Molinetto di Mazzano *06912*
Associazione Italiana di Psicologia dello Sport, Ferrara *06958*
Associazione Italiana per la Psicologia Umanistica e Transpersonale, Roma *06975*
Associazione Italiana per lo Studio della Psicologia Analitica, Roma *06984*
Associazione Italiana Socioanalisi Individuale, Milano *06989*
Associazione Nazionale dei Periti Grafici a Base Psicologica, Milano *07002*
Centro di Ricerche Biopsichiche di Padova, Padova *07059*
Centro Internazionale di Ipnosi Medica e Psicologica, Milano *07066*
Centro Internazionale Studi Umanistici Scientifici Psicologici, Roma *07086*
Centro Psico-Pedagogico Didattico, Bologna *07114*
Centro Studi di Psicologia e Sociologia Applicate ad Indirizzo Adleriano, Roma *07143*
Centro Studi Wilhelm Reich, Napoli *07178*
International Society for Medical and Psychological Hypnosis, Milano *07325*
Sezione di Training Autogeno del Centro Internazionale de Ipnosi, Milano *07384*
Società Internazionale di Psicologia della Scrittura, Milano *07438*
Società Italiana di Psicologia, Roma *07559*
Società Italiana di Psicologia Individuale, Milano *07560*
Società Italiana di Psicologia Scientifica, Palermo *07561*
Società Medico-Psicologica, Milano *07614*
Unione Italiana Lotta alla Distrofia Muscolare, Padova *07676*

Japan
Nihon Kyoiku-shinri Gakkai, Tokyo *07827*
Nihon Oyo Shinri-gakkai, Tokyo *07833*
Nihon Shakai Shinri Gakkai, Tokyo *07849*
Nihon Shinrigakkai, Tokyo *07852*
Nippon Shakai Shinri Gakkai, Tokyo *07977*

Korea, Republic
Korean Psychological Association, Seoul *08136*

Macedonia
Društvo za Nauka i Umetnost, Bitola *08187*

Mexico
Sociedad Mexicana de Estudios Psico-Pedagógicos, México *08337*

Netherlands
International Association of Applied Psychology, Nijmegen *08480*
Studievereniging voor Psychical Research, Voorburg *08631*

New Zealand
New Zealand Psychological Society, Wellington *08721*

Nicaragua
Sociedad Nicaragüense de Psiquiatría y Psicología, Managua *08750*

Poland
Polskie Towarzystwo Psychologiczne, Warszawa *09137*

Romania
Asociatia Psihologilor din Romania, Bucuresti *09273*

Russia
Society of Psychologists, Moskva *09467*

Slovakia
Slovenská Psychologická Spoločnost, Bratislava *09573*

South Africa
Psychological Society of South Africa, Lynnwood Ridge *09654*

Switzerland
Europäische Gesellschaft für Schriftpsychologie und Schriftexpertise e.V., Zürich *10090*
Institut International de Psychologie et de Psychothérapie Charles Baudouin, Coppet *10161*
International Federation for Psychotherapy, Bern *10169*
Kantonalverband der Zürcher Psychologinnen und Psycologen, Zürich *10197*
Schweizerische Gesellschaft für Lehrerinnen- und Lehrerbildung, Bern *10311*
Schweizerische Gesellschaft für Psychologie, Zürich *10331*
Schweizerische Stiftung für Angewandte Psychologie, Zürich *10388*
Schweizerischer Berufsverband für Angewandte Psychologie, Forch *10436*
Schweizerischer Feldenkrais-Verband, Affoltern a.A. *10447*
Vereinigung Schweizerischer Kinder- und Jugendpsychologen, Solothurn *10568*

United Kingdom
Association for Child Psychology and Psychiatry, London *10803*
Association for Group and Individual Psychotherapy, London *10805*
Association for the Teaching of Psychology, Leicester *10834*
Association of Educational Psychologists, Durham *10876*
Association of Social Anthropologists of the Commonwealth, London *10921*
Balint Society, London *10946*
British Association of Psychotherapists, London *11041*
British Institute of Practical Psychology, London *11103*
The British Psychological Society, Leicester *11152*
Clinical Theology Association, Oxford *11301*
Ergonomics Society, Loughborough *11462*
European Psycho-Analytical Federation, London *11503*
Experimental Psychology Society, Glasgow *11509*
Guild of Pastoral Psychology, London *11592*
National Council of Psycho-Therapists, London *12001*

Subject Index: Psychology 474

National Institute of Industrial Psychology, Slough 12015
Society for Multivariate Experimental Psychology, Upton Park 12367
Society for Research in The Psychology of Music and Music Education, Dagenham 12378
Society for The Study of Normal Psychology, London 12401
Tavistock Institute of Medical Psychology, Camberley 12490
Theosophical Society in England, London 12496

U.S.A.

Academy of Psychosomatic Medicine, Chicago 12669
Academy of Religion and Psychical Research, Bloomfield 12671
Academy of Scientific Hypnotherapy, San Diego 12673
Alfred Adler Institute, New York 12726
American Academy of Crisis Interveners, Louisville 12748
American Association for Correctional Psychology, South Charleston 12830
American Association of Mental Health Professionals in Corrections, Sacramento 12906
American Association on Mental Retardation, Washington 12957
American Board of Professional Psychology, Columbia 13001
American Board of Psychological Hypnosis, Beverly 13004
American Guild of Hypnotherapists, Kenner 13173
American Orthopsychiatric Association, New York 13302
American Psychological Association, Washington 13344
American Psychology-Law Society, Philadelphia 13345
American Society for Psychical Research, New York 13407
American Society of Clinical Hypnosis, Des Plaines 13435
American Society of Psychopathology of Expression, Brookline 13486
Arica Institute, Dobbs Ferry 13567
Association for Advancement of Psychology, Colorado Springs 13594
Association for Astrological Psychology, San Rafael 13600
Association for Birth Psychology, New York 13602
Association for Group Psychoanalysis and Process, New York 13630
Association for Humanistic Psychology, San Francisco 13634
Association for Pre- and Perinatal Psychology and Health, Alexandria 13652
Association for the Development of Human Potential, Spokane 13682
Association for Transpersonal Psychology, Stanford 13696
Association for Women in Psychology, Los Angeles 13702
Association of Aviation Psychologists, Moffett Field 13734
Association of Black Psychologists, Washington 13739
Association of Laban Movement Analysts, New York 13786
Association of Management, Grafton 13791
Astro-Psychology Institute, San Francisco 13872
Autism Services Center, Huntington 13891
Autism Society of America, Bethesda 13892
Center for Responsive Psychology, Brooklyn 14023
C.G. Jung Foundation for Analytical Psychology, New York 14047
Christian Association for Psychological Studies, New Braunfels 14071
Cognitive Science Society, Pittsburgh 14097
Committee for the Scientific Investigation of Claims of the Paranormal, Buffalo 14128
Division of Applied Experimental and Engineering Psychologists, San Diego 14312
Esalen Institute, Big Sur 14388
Federation of Behavioral, Psychological and Cognitive Sciences, Washington 14422
The Forum, Santa Fe 14453
Group for the Use of Psychology in History, Springfield 14530
Haunt Hunters, Saint Louis 14544
Himalayan International Institute of Yoga Science and Philosophy of the U.S.A., Honesdale 14567
Human Factors and Ergonomics Society, Santa Monica 14590
Human Relations Area Files, New Haven 14592
Institute Control Theory, Reality Therapy and Quality Management, Chatsworth 14655
Institute for Psychohistory, New York 14680
Institute for Rational-Emotive Therapy, New York 14682
Institute for Research in Hypnosis and Psychotherapy, New York 14683
Institute for Social Research, Ann Arbor 14685
Institute of Cultural Affairs, Chicago 14701
International Association for Cross-Cultural Psychology, Chico 14789
International Association for Suicide Prevention and Crisis Intervention, Chicago 14814
International Council of Psychologists, San Marcos 14982
International Imagery Association, Bronx 15068
International Organization for the Study of Group Tensions, New York 15134
International Psycho-Oncology Society, New York 15163
International Psychogeriatric Association, Wilmette 15164
International Psychohistorical Association, New York 15165
International Society for Medical and Psychological Hypnosis, New York 15228
International Society for Research on Aggression, Ann Arbor 15246
International Society of Political Psychology, Williamstown 15307
International Stress Management Association, San Diego 15330
Jean Piaget Society, Cambridge 15423
Laban/Bartenieff Institute of Movement Studies, New York 15472
Laughter Therapy, Los Angeles 15483
Lentz Peace Research Laboratory, Saint Louis 15490
Milton H. Erickson Foundation, Phoenix 15582
National Association of School Psychologists, Bethesda 15723
National Character Laboratory, El Paso 15790
North American Society for Sport Psychology and Physical Activity, Geensboro 16050
North American Society of Adlerian Psychology, Chicago 16051
Organizational Behavior Teaching Society, Norman 16099
Psi Chi – National Honor Society in Psychology, Chattanooga 16219
Psychic Science International Special Interest Group, Huber Heights 16222
Psychology of Religion, Pasadena 16223
Psychology Society, New York 16224
Psychometric Society, Champaign 16225
Psychonomic Society, Houston 16226
Radix Institute, Fort Worth 16242
Sigmund Freud Archives, Roslyn 16327
Society for Clinical and Experimental Hypnosis, Liverpool 16365
Society for Pediatric Psychology, Charleston 16423
Society for Personality Assessment, Washington 16427
Society for Psychophysiological Research, Dallas 16434
Society for the Psychological Study of Social Issues, Ann Arbor 16468
Society for the Study of Male Psychology and Physiology, Montpellier 16475
Society of Experimental Psychologists, Princeton 16518
Society of Multivariate Experimental Psychology, Charlottesville 16539
Wilbur Hot Springs Health Sanctuary, Williams-9709 16761

Yugoslavia

Društvo Psihologa Srbije, Beograd 16994

Psychotherapy s. Therapeutics

Public Administration

Australia

Institute of Municipal Management, South Melbourne 00294

Belgium

European Centre for Strategic Management of Universities, Bruxelles 01122
Institut International des Sciences Administratives, Bruxelles 01198

Brazil

Academia Brasileira de Ciência da Administração, Rio de Janeiro 01367
Centro de Estudos e Pesquisas em Administração, Porto Alegre 01434

Canada

Administrative Sciences Association of Canada, Montréal 01614
Canadian University and College Counselling Association, Hamilton 02018
Fédération des Commissions Scolaires du Québec, Sainte Foy 02097
Fédération Québécoise des Directeurs et Directrices d'Etablissements d'Enseignement, Anjou 02106
Institute of Public Administration of Canada, Toronto 02142
Nova Scotia School Boards Association, Halifax 02258

Costa Rica

Central American Institute of Public Administration, San José 02851
Instituto Centroamericano de Administración Pública, San José 02858

Finland

Hallinnon Tutkimuksen Seura, Tampere 03350

France

Institut International d'Administration Publique, Paris 03889

Germany

Bundes-Arbeitsgemeinschaft Akademischer Räte in der Bundesrepublik, München 04619
Bundesverband Deutscher Verwaltungs- und Wirtschafts-Akademien e.V., Frankfurt/Main 04660
Deutsche Sektion des Internationalen Instituts für Verwaltungswissenschaften, Bonn 04959
Gesellschaft für Deutsche Postgeschichte, Frankfurt 05355

Hungary

Szervezési és Vezetési Tudományos Társaság, Budapest 06357

Iran

Sazemane Pachuhesh va Barnamerizi Amuzeshi, Teheran 06567

Morocco

African Training and Research Centre in Administration for Development, Tangiers 08378

Philippines

Eastern Regional Organization for Public Administration, Manila 09050

Spain

Instituto Nacional de Administración Pública, Madrid 09768

Sudan

Sudan Academy for Administrative Sciences, Khartoum 09847

Sweden

Akademikerförbundet SSR, Stockholm 09855

Switzerland

Schweizerische Gesellschaft für Verwaltungswissenschaften, Bern 10347
Schweizerische Studiengesellschaft für Kommunikation und Administration, Bern 10389

United Kingdom

Association for Research in the Voluntary and Community Sector, Wivenhoe 10821
Commonwealth Association for Public Administration and Management, London 11316
Commonwealth Council for Educational Administration and Management, Lincoln 11321
Institute of Chartered Secretaries and Administrators, London 11671
Social Policy Association, Hull 12341

U.S.A.

American Academy of Podiatric Administration, West Hartford 12787
American Society for Public Administration, Washington 13409
Federation of Government Information Processing Councils, Atlanta 14423
Governmental Research Association, Birmingham 14518
Institute of Public Administration, New York 14724
International Cost Engineering Council, Granite Falls 14968
International Thorstein Veblen Association, Las Vegas 15343
National Academy of Public Administration, Washington 15622
National Association of Schools of Public Affairs and Administration, Washington 15727
National Records Management Council, New York 15960
Public Service Research Council, Vienna 16233
Social Sciences Services and Resources, Wasco 16342

Venezuela

Centro Interamericano para el Desarrollo Regional, Maracaibo 16895
Centro Latinoamericano de Adminstración para el Desarrollo, Caracas 16896

Public Health s. a. Hygiene

Australia

The Australian Council for Health, Physical Education and Recreation, Hindmarsh 00178
National Health and Medical Research Council, Camberra 00313

Austria

Österreichische Arbeitsgemeinschaft für Volksgesundheit, Wien 00577

Belgium

Association Belge de Santé Publique, Bruxelles 00946
Association Belge d'Hygiène et de Médecine Sociale, Bruxelles 00948
Association pour l'Etude et l'Evaluation Epidémiologiques des Désastres dans les Pays en Voie de Développement, Bruxelles 00982
Société Internationale pour la Recherche sur les Maladies de Civilisation et sur l'Environnement, Bruxelles 01270

Canada

Alberta Health Record Association, Edmonton 01631
Alberta Public Health Association, Peace River 01637
Association Paritaire de Prévention pour la Santé et la Securité du Travail, Anjou 01729
British Columbia Public Health Association, Vancouver 01755
Canadian Association for Health, Physical Education, Recreation and Dance, Gloucester 01797
Canadian Health Libraries Association, Toronto 01895
Canadian Institute of Stress, Toronto 01915
Canadian Natural Health Association, Toronto 01929
Canadian Public Health Association, Ottawa 01956
Canadian Society for International Health, Ottawa 01976
Health Libraries Association of British Columbia, Vancouver 02120
International Development Research Centre, Ottawa 02153
International Federation of Health Records Organizations, Vancouver 02154
Manitoba Health Libraries Association, Winnipeg 02188
Manitoba Health Record Association, Winnipeg 02189
New Brunswick Health Record Association, Moncton 02227

Chile

Sociedad Chilena de Sanidad, Santiago 02507

China, Republic

School Health Association of the Republic of China, Taipei 02751

Colombia

Instituto Nacional de Salud, Bogotá 02801

Congo, Republic

Association for Health Information and Libraries in Africa, Brazzaville 02838

Denmark

European Advisory Committee on Health Research, København 03109

El Salvador

Central American Public Health Council, San Salvador 03315
Sociedad Médica de Salud Pública, San Salvador 03323

France

Fédération Caribe de Santé Mentale, Fort de France 03826
Médecins sans Frontières, Paris 03919
Société Française de Santé Publique, Vandoeuvre lès Nancy 04162
Société Française de Sexologie Clinique, Paris 04164
Société Internationale de Recherches pour l'Environnement et la Santé, Paris 04208

Germany

Akademie für öffentliches Gesundheitswesen, Düsseldorf 04392
Arbeitsgemeinschaft der Sozialdemokraten im Gesundheitswesen, Bonn 04435
Arbeitskreis Gesundheitskunde e.V., Sankt Georgen 04492
Bundesvereinigung für Gesundheit e.V., Bonn 04680
Deutsche Gesellschaft für das Badewesen e.V., Essen 04766
Deutsche Gesellschaft für Gesundheitsvorsorge e.V., Leverkusen 04790
Deutsche Gesellschaft für Suchtforschung und Suchttherapie e.V., Hamm 04866
Deutsche Gesundheitshilfe e.V., Frankfurt/Main 04891
Deutsche Hauptstelle gegen die Suchtgefahren e.V., Hamm 04897
Deutsche Zentrale für Volksgesundheitspflege e.V., Frankfurt 04983
Deutscher Arbeitsring für Lärmbekämpfung e.V., Düsseldorf 04993
Deutscher Bäderverband e.V., Bonn 04996
Deutscher Medizinischer Informationsdienst e.V., Frankfurt 05029
Fortbildungszentrum Gesundheits- und Umweltschutz Berlin e.V., Berlin 05280
Fraunhofer-Gesellschaft zur Förderung der angewandten Forschung e.V., München 05288
Gesundheitstechnische Gesellschaft e.V., Berlin 05436
Hartmannbund, Bonn 05459
Kneipp-Bund e.V., Bad Wörishofen 05670
Landesärztekammer Baden-Württemberg, Stuttgart 05702
Sachverständigenrat für die Konzertierte Aktion im Gesundheitswesen, Bonn 05936

Guyana

Pan-American Health Organization – Guyana Office, Georgetown 06278

India

Indian Public Health Association, Calcutta 06475

Ireland

European Healthcare Management Association, Dublin 06599
Health Research Board, Dublin 06605

Italy

Associazione Italiana di Fisica Sanitaria e di Protezione contro le Radiazioni, Torino 06947
Centre for Human Evolution Studies, Roma 07053
Centro Studi per il Progresso della Educazione Sanitaria e del Diritto Sanitario, Roma 07164
Comitato Italiano per l'Educazione Sanitaria, Perugia 07198
European Centre for Research and Development in Primary Health Care, Perugia 07254
Società di Medicina Legale e delle Assicurazioni, Roma 07406
Società Italiana di Medicina Preventiva e Sociale, Genova 07522
Società Italiana per lo Studio della Cancerogenesi Ambientale ed Epidemiologia dei Tumori, Genova 07596

Japan

Nihon Gakko-hoken Gakkai, Tokyo 07786
Nippon Koshu-Eisei Kyokai, Tokyo 07943

Mexico

Sociedad Mexicana de Salud Pública, México 08349

Netherlands

Consortium of Institutions of Higher Education in Health and Rehabilitation in Europe, Nijmegen 08415
Genootschap ter Bevordering von Natuur-, Genees- en Heelkunde, Amsterdam 08463
Nederlandse Vereniging voor Algemene Gezondheidszorg, Rotterdam 08580

Paraguay

Servicio Cooperativo Interamericano de Salud Pública, Asunción *08964*

Romania

Societatea de Igiena si Sànàtate Publica, Bucuresti *09296*

South Africa

Organic Soil Association of South Africa, Parklands *09647*
The South African Medical Research Council, Tygerberg *09693*

Switzerland

Commission Médicale Chrétienne, Genève *10068*
Schweizerische Gesellschaft für ein Soziales Gesundheitswesen, Basel *10289*
Schweizerische Gesellschaft für Gesundheitspolitik, Muri *10299*
Schweizerische Gesellschaft für Prävention und Gesundheitswesen, Basel *10327*
Schweizerische Gesellschaft für Prävention und Gesundheitswesen, Bern *10328*
Schweizerisches Institut für das Gesundheitswesen, Aarau *10488*
Volksgesundheit Schweiz, Zürich *10572*
World Health Organization, Genève *10578*

Thailand

ASEAN Institute for Health Development, Nakhon Pathom *10616*
Asian Association of Occupational Health, Bangkok *10628*

United Kingdom

Appropriate Health Resources and Technologies Action Group, London *10782*
Association of Community Health Councils for England and Wales, London *10866*
Association of County Public Health Officers, Malmesbury *10868*
Association of General Practitioner Hospitals, Lichfield *10880*
Association of Health Care Information and Medical Records Officers, Hopton *10886*
Association of Health Service Treasurers, Warwick *10887*
Association of Schools of Public Health in the European Region, Bristol *10918*
The British Fluoridation Society, Alderley Edge *11082*
British Natural Hygiene Society, Frinton-on-Sea *11133*
British Naturopathic and Osteopathic Association, London *11135*
The British Society of Dowsers, Ashford *11192*
CAB International, Wallingford *11231*
Disinfected Mail Study Circle, London *11392*
Group and Association of County Medical Officers of Health of England and Wales, Stafford *11587*
Health Service Social Worker Group, Barnet *11608*
Hyper Active Children's Support Group, Chichester *11641*
Institute for Consumer Ergonomics, Loughborough *11655*
Institute of Health Education, Manchester *11690*
Medical Officers of Schools Association, London *11925*
National Campaign for Nursery Education, London *11995*
The Royal Institute of Public Health and Hygiene, London *12220*
The Royal Society of Health, London *12257*
The Royal Society of Tropical Medicine and Hygiene, London *12262*
Socialist Health Association, London *12344*
Society for The Health Education, London *12384*
Society of Health and Beauty Therapists, London *12429*
The Society of Public Health, Huddersfield *12440*

U.S.A.

Accrediting Commission on Education for Health Services Administration, Arlington *12682*
American Association for World Health, Washington *12858*
American Association of Blood Banks, Bethesda *12863*
American Association of Public Health Physicians, Madison *12929*
American Board of Health Physics, McLean *12979*
American College Health Association, Baltimore *13036*
American Correctional Health Services Association, Dayton *13096*
American Health Planning Association, Falls Church *13177*
American Hospital Association, Chicago *13188*
American Industrial Health Council, Washington *13194*
American Medical Associaction Auxiliary, Chicago *13262*
American Public Health Association, Washington *13347*
American School Health Association, Kent *13361*
American Social Health Association, Research Triangle Park *13366*
American Society for Healthcare Education and Training of the American Hospital Association, Chicago *13389*
Asia Pacific Public Health Nutrition Association, Berkeley *13577*
Association for Pre- and Perinatal Psychology and Health, Alexandria *13652*
Association for the Advancement of Health Education, Reston *13675*
Association of Academic Health Centers, Washington *13707*
Association of International Health Researchers, Mobile *13781*
Association of Maternal and Child Health Programs, Washington *13792*
Association of Minority Health Professions Schools, Washington *13800*
Association of Schools of Public Health, Washington *13830*
Association of State and Territorial Directors of Public Health Education, Santa Fe *13839*
Association of State and Territorial Health Officials, Washington *13840*
Association of Teachers of Maternal and Child Health, Arlington *13847*
Association of the Health Occupations Teacher Educators, Louisville *13851*
Association of University Programs in Health Administration, Arlington *13862*
Catholic Health Association of the United States, Saint Louis *13983*
Center for Attitudinal Healing, Sausalito *13996*
Center for Community Change, Washington *14000*
Center for Medical Consumers and Health Care Information, New York *14011*
Center for Research in Ambulatory Health Care Administration, Englewood *14021*
Commission on Accreditation of Allied Health Education Programs, Chicago *14111*
Council for Sex Information and Education, Los Angeles *14218*
Council on Education for Public Health, Washington *14247*
Council on Health Information and Education, Los Angeles *14251*
Family Health International, Research Triangle Park *14411*
Global Alliance for Women's Health, New York *14502*
Group Health Association of America, Washington *14531*
Health Optimizing Institute, Del Mar *14548*
Health Physics Society, McLean *14549*
Health Sciences Communications Association, Jewitt City *14550*
Health Sciences Consortium, Chapel Hill *14551*
Holistic Health Havens, Las Vegas *14581*
Human Lactation Center, Westport *14591*
Institute for the Development of Emotional and Life Skills, Bethesda *14688*
Institute of Noise Control Engineering, Poughkeepsie *14721*
International Academy of Chiropractic Occupational Health Consultants, Bloomington *14763*
International Academy of Nutrition and Preventive Medicine, Asheville *14767*
International Commission for the Prevention of Alcoholism and Drug Dependency, Silver Spring *14923*
International Council for Health, Physical Education, Recreation, Sport and Dance, Reston *14970*
International Council on Women's Health Issues, Indianapolis *14986*
International Federation for Family Health, Carlton *15009*
International Health Evaluation Association, Rockville *15060*
International Health Futures Network, San Francisco *15061*
International Health Society, Englewood *15062*
International Institute of Rural Reconstruction – U.S. Chapter, New York *15080*
International Medical Services for Health, Sterling *15111*
International Union for Health Promotion and Education, Reston *15353*
International Women's Health Coalition, New York *15375*
John E Fogarty International Center for Advanced Study in the Health Sciences, Bethesda *15437*
National Association of Community Health Centers, Washington *15688*
National Association of Health Career Schools, Washington *15703*
National Association of Health Services Executives, Columbia *15704*
National Association on Drug Abuse Problems, New York *15753*
National Black Women's Health Project, Atlanta *15759*
National Committee for Quality Health Care, Washington *15799*
National Council for International Health, Washington *15824*
National Council on Alcoholism and Drug Dependence, New York *15848*
National Environmental Health Association, Denver *15875*
National Health Council, Washington *15897*
National Health Federation, Monrovia *15898*
National Health Law Program, Los Angeles *15899*
National Health Lawyers Association, Washington *15900*
National Women's Health Network, Washington *15997*
Pan American Health and Education Foundation, Washington *16138*
Pan American Health Organization, Washington *16139*
Program for Appropriate Technology in Health, Seattle *16212*
Public Citizen Health Research Group, Washington *16227*
Public Relations Society of America, New York *16231*
Serendipity Association for Research and Implementation of Holistic Health and World Peace, San Diego *16316*
Society for Environmental Geochemistry and Health, Rolla *16378*
Society for Public Health Education, Berkeley *16435*
United States-Mexico Border Health Association, El Paso *16693*
World Federation of Public Health Associations, Washington *16815, 16816*

Zimbabwe

Joint Health Systems Research Programme for Eastern and Southern Africa, Harare 611= *17070*

Public Relations s. Advertising

Pulmonary Disease

Argentina

Liga Argentina contra la Tuberculosis, Buenos Aires *00081*

Austria

Österreichische Gesellschaft für Lungenerkrankungen und Tuberkulose, Wien *00659*

Canada

Alberta Lung Association, Edmonton *01633*
Association Pulmonaire du Québec, Montréal *01732*
Canadian Lung Association, Gloucester *01921*
Canadian Thoracic Society, Gloucester *02016*
Lung Association of Nova Scotia, Halifax *02176*
Manitoba Lung Association, Winnipeg *02195*
New Brunswick Lung Association, Fredericton *02230*
Newfoundland Lung Association, Saint John's *02242*
Ontario Lung Association, Toronto *02285*
Ontario Thoracic Society, Toronto *02300*
Prince Edward Island Lung Association, Charlottetown *02320*
Saskatchewan Lung Association, Sakatoon *02357*

Chile

Sociedad Chilena de Tisiología y Enfermedades Broncopulmonares, Santiago *02509*

China, People's Republic

Chinese Anti-Tuberculosis Society, Beijing *02567*

Cuba

Consejo Nacional de Tuberculosis Paulina Aldina, La Habana *02886*

Denmark

Dansk Pneumologisk Selskab, Allrød *03049*
Danske Lunglaegers Organisation, Holbaek *03095*

France

Comité National contre les Maladies Respiratoires et la Tuberculose, Paris *03723*

Germany

Bundesverband der Pneumologen, Mülheim *04652*
Deutsche Gesellschaft für Lungenkrankheiten und Tuberkulose, Freiburg *04814*
Deutsche Gesellschaft für Pneumologie, Greifenstein *04844*
Deutsches Zentralkomitee zur Bekämpfung der Tuberkulose, Mainz *05109*
Gesellschaft für Lungen- und Atmungsforschung e.V., Bochum *05381*
Gesellschaft zur Förderung der Lufthygiene und Silikoseforschung e.V., Düsseldorf *05429*
Rheinisch-Westfälische Vereinigung für Lungen- und Bronchialheilkunde, Essen *05921*

Italy

Federazione Italiana contro la Tubercolosi e le Malattie Polmonari Sociali, Roma *07274*
Società Italiana di Pneumologia, Torino *07556*

Japan

Nippon Kekkaku-byo Gakkai, Tokyo *07928*
Nippon Kikan-Shokudo-ka Gakkai, Tokyo *07931*

Mexico

Sociedad Mexicana de Tisiología, México *08351*

Peru

Sociedad Peruana de Tisiología y Enfermedades Respiratorias, Lima *09018*

Slovakia

Slovenská Pneumologická a Ftizeologická Spoločnosť, Bratislava *09572*

South Africa

Research Group for Lung Metabolism, Tygerberg *09655*
South African National Tuberculosis Association, Johannesburg *09697*

Switzerland

Schweizerische Gesellschaft für Pneumologie, Bern *10326*
Schweizerische Vereinigung gegen Tuberkulose und Lungenkrankheiten, Bern *10420*

United Kingdom

National Asthma Campaign, London *11991*
Northern Ireland Chest, Heart and Stroke Association, Belfast *12058*
Thoracic Society, Southampton *12501*
Tuberous Sclerosis Association, Bromsgrove *12514*

Uruguay

Liga Uruguaya contra la Tuberculosis, Montevideo *12630*

U.S.A.

American College of Chest Physicians, Northbrook *13040*
American Lung Association, New York *13253*
Black Lung Association, Crab Orchard *13929*
Congress of Lung Association Staff, Washington *14169*

Venezuela

Sociedad de Tisiología y Neumonología de Venezuela, Antimano *16919*
Sociedad Venezolana de Tisiología y Neumonología, Caracas *16939*

Vietnam

Vietnamese Association of Anti-Tuberculosis and Lung Diseases, Hanoi *16946*

Radiology s. a. X-Ray Technology; Nuclear Medicine

Australia

Australian Institute of Radiography, East Melbourne *00207*
The Royal Australasian College of Radiologists, Sydney *00331*

Austria

Österreichische Gesellschaft für Industrielle Strahltechnik, Wien *00645*
Österreichische Röntgengesellschaft – Gesellschaft für medizinische Radiologie und Nuklearmedizin, Wien *00734*
Österreichischer Verband für Strahlenschutz, Seibersdorf *00768*
Verband für medizinischen Strahlenschutz in Österreich, Wien *00814*

Belgium

Association Belge de Radioprotection, Bruxelles *00945*
European Association of Radiology, Leuven *01105*
European Society for Radiation Biology, Liège *01161*

Canada

Alberta Association of Medical Radiation Technologists, Lethbridge *01620*
Canadian Academy of Oral Radiology, Toronto *01773*
Manitoba Association of Medical Radiation Technologists, Winnipeg *02182*
Newfoundland Association of Medical Radiation Technologists, Paradise *02239*
Nova Scotia Society of Medical Radiation Technologists, Bedford *02259*
Prince Edward Island Association of Medical Radiation Technologists, Charlottetown *02316*
Saskatchewan Association of Medical Radiation Technologists, Saskatoon *02350*

China, Republic

The Radiological Society of the Republic of China, Taipei *02749*

Cuba

Grupo Nacional de Radiología, La Habana *02888*
Sociedad Cubana de Radiología, La Habana *02893*

Czech Republic

Česká Radiologická Společnost, Praha *02929*

Denmark

Dansk Radiologisk Selskab, Herlev *03053*

El Salvador

Asociación de Radiólogos de América Central y Panamá, San Salvador *03311*

Finland

Säteilyturvakeskus, Helsinki *03370*
Suomen Radiologiyhdistys, Helsinki *03431*

France

European Association of Radiology, Le Kremlin Bicêtre *03803*
Fédération Nationale des Médecins Radiologues et Spécialistes en Imagerie Diagnostique et Thérapeutique, Paris *03858*
Fédération Nationale des Syndicats Départementaux de Médecins Electro-Radiologistes Qualifiés, Paris *03859*
Société Européenne de Radiologie Cardio-Vasculaire et de Radiologie d'Intervention, Lyon *04104*
Société Européenne de Radiologie Pédiatrique, Paris *04105*
Société Française de Radiologie et d'Imagerie Médicale, Paris *04161*
Société Médicale d'Imagerie, Enseignement et Recherche, Paris *04219*
Syndicat National des Médecins Electro-Radiologistes Qualifiés, Paris *04280*

Germany

Berufsverband der Deutschen Radiologen und Nuklearmediziner e.V., München *04564*
Deutsche Gesellschaft für Neuroradiologie, Würzburg *04827*
Deutsche Röntgengesellschaft, Neu-Isenburg *04953*

Recreation
s. Travel and Tourism

Refrigeration
s. Air Conditioning

Regional Planning
s. Urban and Regional Planning

Rehabilitation

Religions and Theology

Restoration
s. Preservation of Historical Monuments, Restoration

Rheumatology

U.S.A.

American College of Rheumatology, Atlanta *13075*
International League of Associations for Rheumatology, Nashville *15100*
International Society for Rheumatic Therapeutics, Boston *15247*
Pan American League of Associations for Rheumatology, Little Rock *16141*

Rhinology s. Otorhinolaryngology

Roentgenology s. X-Ray Technology

Safety and Protection, Safety Engineering

Belgium

Association Nationale pour la Protection contre l'Incendie et l'Intrusion, Louvain-La-Neuve *00978*

Canada

Alberta Safety Council, Edmonton *01640*
Association of Workers' Compensation Boards of Canada, Edmonton *01728*
Association Paritaire de Prévention pour la Santé et la Securité du Travail, Anjou *01729*
Canada Safety Council, Ottawa *01766*
Canadian Alarm and Security Association, Markham *01785*
Canadian Fire Safety Association, North York *01884*
Canadian Society of Safety Engineering, Toronto *02004*
Ceramics and Stone Accident Prevention Association, North York *02037*
Chemical Industries Accident Prevention Association, North York *02044*
Construction Safety Association of Ontario, Toronto *02074*
Fire Prevention Canada Association, Ottawa *02107*
Food Products Accident Prevention Association, Cambridge *02110*
Grain, Feed and Fertilizer Accident Prevention Association, London *02118*
Ligue de Sécurite du Québec, Lasalle *02175*
Manitoba Safety Council, Winnipeg *02198*
New Brunswick Safety Council, Fredericton *02233*
Nova Scotia Safety Council, Halifax *02257*
Ottawa-Carleton Safety Council, Ottawa *02305*
Printing Trades Accident Prevention Association, North York *02326*
Saskatchewan Safety Council, Regina *02361*
Woodworkers' Accident Prevention Association, Cambridge *02428*

Finland

Säteilyturvakeskus, Helsinki *03370*
Suomen Palontorjuntaliitto, Helsinki *03429*

France

Association Française de Prévention des Accidents de Travail et Incendie, Paris *03532*
Association Interprofessionnelle de France, Seclin *03603*
Comité International de l'AISS pour la Prévention des Risques Professionnels du Bâtiment et des Travaux Publics, Boulogne-Billancourt *03719*

Germany

Deutsche Gesellschaft für Wirtschaftliche Fertigung und Sicherheitstechnik e.V., Kaarst *04881*
Deutscher Verkehrssicherheitsrat e.V., Bonn *05065*
Gesellschaft für Anlagen- und Reaktorsicherheit, Köln *05346*
Gesellschaft für Sicherheitswissenschaft e.V., Wuppertal *05405*
Normenausschuss Feuerwehrwesen im DIN Deutsches Institut für Normung e.V., Berlin *05808*
Normenausschuss Persönliche Schutzausrüstung und Sicherheitskennzeichnung im DIN Deutsches Insitut für Normung e.V., Berlin *05835*
Verband der Technischen Überwachungs-Vereine e.V., Essen *06030*

Ireland

National Safety Council, Dublin *06653*

Netherlands

Nederlandse Vereniging voor Veiligheidskunde, Amsterdam *08608*

Sweden

Svenska Brandförsvarsföreningen, Stockholm *09967*

United Kingdom

Association for Petroleum and Explosives Administration, Huntington *10816*
British Safety Council, London *11157*
Industrial Fire Protection Association of Great Britain, London *11649*
North West Regional Association of Industrial Safety Groups, Preston *12050*
Royal Society for The Prevention of Accidents, Birmingham *12250*

U.S.A.

American Academy of Safety Education, Warrensburg *12796*
American Security Council, Boston *13364*
American Security Council Foundation, Boston *13365*
American Society of Safety Engineers, Des Plaines *13490*
Association of Safety Council Executives, Gainesville *13826*
Aviation Safety Institute, Worthington *13897*
Center for Auto Safety, Washington *13998*
Center for Safety in the Arts, New York *14024*
Flight Safety Foundation, Alexandria *14439*
Highway Users Federation for Safety and Mobility, Washington *14566*
Inter-American Safety Council, Englewood *14745*
International Society of Air Safety Investigators, Sterling *15269*
Motorcycle Safety Foundation, Irvine *15600*
National Fire Protection Association, Quincy *15883*
National Institute for Farm Safety, Columbia *15917*
National Safety Council, Itasca *15967*
National Safety Management Society, Weaverville *15968*
Safety Equipment Institute, Arlington *16288*
Society of Fire Protection Engineers, Boston *16522*

Science, general

Afghanistan

Afghanistan Academy of Sciences, Kabul *00001*

Albania

Academy of Sciences, Tirana *00002*

Algeria

Organisme National de la Recherche Scientifique, Alger *00007*

Andorra

Societat Andorrana de Ciències, Andorra la Vella *00017*

Argentina

Academia Nacional de Ciencias de Buenos Aires, Buenos Aires *00025*
Centro Argentino de Información Científica y Tecnológica, Buenos Aires *00063*
Consejo Nacional de Investigaciones Científicas y Técnicas, Buenos Aires *00071*
Sociedad Científica Argentina, Buenos Aires *00105*

Armenia

Armenian National Academy of Sciences, Yerevan *00113*

Australia

Australian Academy of Science, Canberra *00152*
Australian and New Zealand Association for the Advancement of Science, Canberra *00159*
Australian Science Teachers Association, Warradale *00228*
Commonwealth Scientific and Industrial Research Organisation, Parkville *00262*
Federation of Australian Scientific and Technological Societies, Deakin West *00275*
Royal Society of New South Wales, North Ryde *00347*
Royal Society of Queensland, Saint Lucia *00348*
Royal Society of South Australia, Adelaide *00349*
Royal Society of Tasmania, Hobart *00350*
Royal Society of Victoria, Melbourne *00351*
Royal Society of Western Australia, Perth *00352*
Science Teachers Association of Queensland, Spring Hill *00359*
Science Teachers' Association of Victoria, Parkville *00360*
South Australian Science Teachers Association, Parkside *00366*

Austria

Arbeitsgemeinschaft für Wissenschaft und Politik, Innsbruck *00408*
Institut für Grenzgebiete der Wissenschaft, Innsbruck *00504*
Institut für Wissenschaft und Kunst, Wien *00509*
Internationales Forschungszentrum für Grundfragen der Wissenschaften, Salzburg *00536*
Österreichische Akademie der Wissenschaften, Wien *00573*
Österreichische Forschungsgemeinschaft, Wien *00592*
Verband der Akademikerinnen Österreichs, Wien *00806*
Verband der wissenschaftlichen Gesellschaften Österreichs, Wien *00813*
Vereinigung für wissenschaftliche Grundlagenforschung, Graz *00853*
Vorarlberger Landesmuseumsverein, Bregenz *00858*
Wiener Kulturkreis, Wien *00872*

Azerbaijan

Azerbaijan Academy of Sciences, Baku *00885*

Bahrain

Bahrain Centre for Studies and Research, Manama *00901*

Bangladesh

Bangla Academy, Dhaka *00912*
Bangladesh Academy of Sciences, Dhaka *00913*
Bangladesh Council of Scientific and Industrial Research, Dhaka *00915*

Belarus

Academy of Sciences of Belarus, Minsk *00928*

Belgium

Académie Royale des Sciences, des Lettres et des Beaux-Arts de Belgique, Bruxelles *00933*
Centre International de Documentation Marguerite Yourcenar, Bruxelles *01012*
Committee on the Challenges of Modern Society, Bruxelles *01046*
Conférence des Recteurs des Universités Belges, Bruxelles *01054*
Eureka, Bruxelles *01070*
European Community Network of the National Academic Recognition Information Centres, Bruxelles *01135*
European Cooperation in the Field of Scientific and Technical Research, Bruxelles *01141*
Société Royale des Sciences de Liège, Liège *01295*
Société Scientifique de Bruxelles, Namur *01298*
Union Académique Internationale, Bruxelles *01302*

Bolivia

Academia Boliviana, La Paz *01335*
Academia Nacional de Ciencias de Bolivia, La Paz *01336*

Botswana

Botswana Society, Gaborone *01364*

Brazil

Academia Brasileira de Ciências, Rio de Janeiro *01368*
Centro Académico Hugo Simas, Curitiba *01425*
Centro Brasileiro de Estudos, Campinas *01426*
Centro Cultural de Botucatu, Botucatu *01428*
Centro Nacional de Pesquisa de Seringueira, Manaus *01445*
Fundação Getulio Vargas, Rio de Janeiro *01460*
Instituto Brasileiro de Educãcão, Ciencia e Cultura, Rio de Janeiro *01464*
Instituto Nami Jafet para o Progreso da Ciência e Cultura, São Paulo *01495*
Sociedade Brasileira para o Progresso da Ciência, São Paulo *01518*
Sociedade Cientifica de São Paulo, São Paulo *01519*
Sociedade Propagadora Esdeva, Juiz de Fora *01532*
Sociedade Visconde de São Leopoldo, Santos *01533*
Unidade de Pesquisa de Ambito Estadual em Barreiras, Barreiras *01534*
Unidade de Pesquisa de Ambito Estadual em Campos, Campos *01535*
Unidade de Pesquisa de Ambito Estadual em Corumba, Corumba *01536*
Unidade de Pesquisa de Ambito Estadual em Dourados, Dourados *01537*
Unidade de Pesquisa de Ambito Estadual em Itaguai, Nova Iguaçu *01538*
Unidade de Pesquisa de Ambito Estadual em Itapirema, Goiânia *01539*
Unidade de Pesquisa de Ambito Estadual em Manaus, Manaus *01540*
Unidade de Pesquisa de Ambito Estadual em Ponta Grossa, Ponta Grossa *01541*
Unidade de Pesquisa de Ambito Estadual em Porto Velho, Porto Velho *01542*
Unidade de Pesquisa de Ambito Estadual em Teresina, Teresina *01543*

Bulgaria

Bulgarian Academy of Sciences, Sofia *01546*
Central Council of Scientific and Technical Unions, Sofia *01578*
Federation of Scientific and Technical Unions in Bulgaria, Sofia *01579*
Union of Scientists in Bulgaria, Sofia *01603*

Canada

Alberta Science Centre Society, Calgary *01641*
Association of Universities and Colleges of Canada, Ottawa *01725*
Atlantic Provinces Council on the Sciences, Sain John's *01737*
Canadian Academy International, Sudbury *01768*
Canadian Society for the Weizmann Institute of Science, North York *01985*
Charles H. Ivey Foundation, Willowdale *02043*
Confederation of Alberta Faculty Associations, Edmonton *02068*
Council of Ontario Universities, Toronto *02077*
Donner Canadian Foundation, Toronto *02085*
Federation of New Brunswick Faculty Associations, Fredericton *02104*
Fondation J. Armand Bombardier, Valcourt *02108*
Fondation Lionel Groulx, Outremont *02109*
Fraser Institute, Vancouver *02111*
Gairdner Foundation, Willowdale *02112*
Hamber Foundation, Vancouver *02119*
Nova Scotia Confederation of University Faculty Associations, Halifax *02250*
Nova Scotian Institute of Science, Halifax *02263*
Richard Ivey Foundation, London *02336*
Royal Canadian Institute, Toronto *02341*
Royal Society of Canada, Ottawa *02346*
Sandford Fleming Foundation, Waterloo *02348*
Sir Joseph Flavelle Foundation, Toronto *02370*
Sport Medicine and Science Council of Canada, Gloucester *02396*
Victoria Foundation, Victoria *02411*

Chile

Academia Chilena de Ciencias, Santiago *02441*
Asociación Científica y Técnica de Chile, Santiago *02451*
Consejo de Rectores de Universidades Chilenas, Santiago *02464*
Instituto de Chile, Santiago *02466*
Sociedad Científica Chilena Claudio Gay, Santiago *02511*
Sociedad Científica de Chile, Santiago *02512*

China, People's Republic

China Association for Science and Technology, Beijing *02545*
Chinese Academy of Sciences, Beijing *02561*
Chinese Society for Scientific and Technical Information, Beijing *02615*
Chinese Society of the History of Science and Technology, Beijing *02636*

China, Republic

Academia Sinica, Taipei *02664*
Chinese Association for the Advancement of Science, Taipei *02687*
Chinese Youth Academic Research Association, Taipei *02715*
National Science Council, Taipei *02740*
Television Academy of Arts and Sciences of the Republic of China, Taipei *02759*

Colombia

Asociación Colombiana de Sociedades Científicas, Bogotá *02772*
Asociación Colombiana de Universidades, Bogotá *02773*

Congo, Republic

Union Panafricaine de la Science et de la Technologie, Brazzaville *02840*

Costa Rica

Consejo Superior Universitario Centroemericano, San José *02857*

Croatia

Hrvatska Akademija Znanosti i Umjetnosti, Zagreb *02870*

Cuba

Academia de Ciencias de Cuba, La Habana *02878*

Czech Republic

Česká Akademie Věd, Praha *02911*
Česká Hudební Společnost, Praha *02920*
Český Svaz Vědeckotechnických Společností, Praha *02947*
Společnost pro Dějiny Věd a Techniky, Praha *02960*

Denmark

Det Kongelige Danske Videnskabernes Selskab, København *03150*
Det Laerde Selskab i Aarhus, Aarhus *03155*
Nordforsk, København *03169*

Egypt

Academy of Scientific Research and Technology, Cairo *03249*
National Research Centre, Cairo *03300*

El Salvador

Academia Salvadoreña, San Salvador *03308*

Estonia

Estonian Academy of Sciences, Tallinn *03324*

Fiji

Fiji Society, Suva *03337*

Finland

Finska Vetenskaps-Societeten, Helsinki *03347*
Societas Scientiarum Fennica, Helsinki *03378*
Suomen Akatemia, Helsinki *03386*
Tieteellisten Seurain Valtuuskunta, Helsinki *03454*
Tietohuollon Neuvottelukunta, Helsinki *03455*

France

Académie d'Arles, Arles *03464*
Académie de Nîmes, Nîmes *03467*
Académie de Savoie, Chambéry *03469*
Académie des Jeux Floraux, Toulouse *03473*
Académie des Sciences, Paris *03474*
Académie des Sciences, Agriculture, Arts et Belles-Lettres d'Aix, Aix-en-Provence *03475*
Académie des Sciences, Arts et Belles-Lettres de Dijon, Dijon *03476*
Académie des Sciences, Belles-Lettres et Arts de Clermont, Clermont-Ferrand *03477*
Académie des Sciences, Belles-Lettres et Arts de Lyon, Lyon *03478*
Académie des Sciences, Belles-Lettres et Arts de Rouen, Rouen *03479*
Académie des Sciences et Lettres de Montpellier, Montpellier *03481*
Académie des Sciences, Lettres et Arts d'Amiens, Amiens *03482*
Académie des Sciences, Lettres et Arts d'Arras, Arras *03483*
Académie des Sciences, Lettres et Arts de Marseille, Marseille *03484*
Académie d'Orléans – Agriculture, Sciences, Belles-Lettres et Arts, Orléans *03487*
Académie Nationale de Metz, Metz *03495*
Académie Nationale des Sciences, Belles-Lettres et Arts de Bordeaux, Bordeaux *03497*
Académie Polonaise des Sciences, Paris *03498*
Association Internationale des Professeurs et Maîtres de Conférences des Universités, Nancy *03586*

Association Internationale pour le Développement des Universités Internationales et Mondiales, Aulnay-sous-Bois 03600
Association pour le Développement de l'Enseignement et des Recherches Scientifiques auprès des Universités de la Région Parisienne, Paris 03645
Association pour l'Innovation Scientifique, Paris 03651
Centre International de Synthèse, Paris 03688
Chambre Syndicale des Sociétés d'Etudes et de Conseils, Paris 03701
Comité des Travaux Historiques et Scientifiques, Paris 03707
Confédération des Sociétés Scientifiques Françaises, Paris 03747
Conférence Internationale des Responsables des Universités et Instituts à Dominante Scientifique et Technique d'Expression Française, Talence 03760
Conseil International des Unions Scientifiques, Paris 03773
Conseil National des Ingénieurs et des Scientifiques de France, Paris 03777
European Academic and Research Network, Orsay 03790
Euskaltzaindia/Bayonne Académie de la Langue Basque, Bayonne 03822
Fédération Internationale des Universités Catholiques, Paris 03852
Institut de France, Paris 03880
International Academy of the History of Science, Paris 03896
Mouvement Universel de la Responsabilité Scientifique, Paris 03921
Société d'Emulation du Bourbonnais, Moulins 04013
Société des Sciences, Arts et Belles-Lettres de Bayeux, Bayeux 04045
Société d'Etudes Scientifiques et de Recherches, Herblay 04079
Société Nationale Académique de Cherbourg, Cherbourg 04225
Société Parisienne d'Etudes Spéciales, Paris 04236
Société Scientifique de Bretagne, Rennes 04244
World Federation of Scientific Workers, Montreuil 04327

Georgia
Council on the History of Natural Sciences and Technology, Tbilisi 04335
Georgian Academy of Sciences, Tbilisi 04336

Germany
Akademie der Wissenschaften in Göttingen, Göttingen 04377
Akademie der Wissenschaften und der Literatur zu Mainz, Mainz 04378
Akademie der Wissenschaften zu Berlin, Berlin 04379
Akademie Gesellschaft und Wissenschaft e.V., Goslar 04398
Arbeitsgemeinschaft Deutsche Lateinamerika-Forschung, Eichstätt 04438
Bayerische Akademie der Wissenschaften, München 04526
Berlin-Brandenburgische Akademie der Wissenschaften, Berlin 04546
Braunschweigische Wissenschaftliche Gesellschaft, Braunschweig 04599
Bund demokratischer Wissenschaftlerinnen und Wissenschaftler e.V., Marburg 04604
Bund Freiheit der Wissenschaft e.V., Bonn 04610
Carl Duisberg Gesellschaft e.V., Köln 04686
Deutsche Forschungsgemeinschaft, Bonn 04736
Deutsche MERU Gesellschaft, Bissendorf 04920
Deutscher Akademikerinnenbund e.V., Heilbronn 04987
Deutscher Akademischer Austauschdienst, Bonn 04988
Forschungsgruppe Köln, Köln 05248
Forschungsgruppe Modellprojekte e.V., Heidelberg 05249
Gemeinschaft katholischer Studierender und Akademiker, Viernheim 05309
Geschäftsführendes Sekretariat des Kuratoriums für die Tagungen der Nobelpreisträger in Lindau, Lindau 05334
Görres-Gesellschaft zur Pflege der Wissenschaft, Köln 05439
Heidelberger Akademie der Wissenschaften, Heidelberg 05465
Hermann von Helmholtzgemeinschaft Deutscher Forschungszentren (HGF), Bonn 05471
Humboldt-Gesellschaft für Wissenschaft, Kunst und Bildung e.V., Mannheim 05500
Institut für angewandte Arbeitswissenschaft e.V., Köln 05517
Institut für den Wissenschaftlichen Film, Göttingen 05524
Institut für Wissenschaftliche Zusammenarbeit, Tübingen 05545
Internationaler Arbeitskreis Sonnenberg, Braunschweig 05588
Katholische Akademikerarbeit Deutschlands, Bonn 05652
Katholischer Akademikerverband Deutschlands, Bonn 05659
Katholischer Akademischer Ausländer-Dienst, Bonn 05660
Konferenz der deutschen Akademien der Wissenschaften, Mainz 05681
Max-Planck-Gesellschaft zur Förderung der Wissenschaften e.V., München 05744
Nordrhein-Westfälische Akademie der Wissenschaften, Düsseldorf 05782
Sächsische Akademie der Wissenschaften zu Leipzig, Leipzig 05937
Stifterverband für die Deutsche Wissenschaft, Essen 05962
Urania Berlin e.V., Berlin 05997
Verband Hochschule und Wissenschaft im Deutschen Beamtenbund, Bonn 06067
Wissenschaftliche Gesellschaft an der Johann Wolfgang Goethe-Universität Frankfurt am Main, Frankfurt 06157
Wissenschaftsforum Berlin, Berlin 06164
Wissenschaftsgemeinschaft Blaue Liste e.V., Bonn 06165
Wissenschaftskolleg zu Berlin e.V., Berlin 06166
Wissenschaftsrat, Köln 06167
Wissenschaftszentrum – Gemeinsame Dienste e.V., Bonn 06168
Wissenschaftszentrum Nordrhein-Westfalen, Düsseldorf 06169
Wittheit zu Bremen e.V., Bremen 06170

Ghana
Council for Scientific and Industrial Research, Accra 06193
Ghana Academy of Arts and Sciences, Accra 06196
Ghana Science Association, Accra 06203
West African Science Association, Accra 06208

Greece
Akadimia Athinon, Athinai 06211

Guatemala
Academia Guatemalteca de la Lengua, Guatemala City 06261
Federación de Universidades Privadas de América Central, Guatemala City 06270

Haiti
Conseil National des Recherches Scientifiques, Port-au-Prince 06279

Honduras
Academia Hondureña, Tegucigalpa 06280

Hungary
Magyar Tudományos Akadémia, Budapest 06343

Iceland
Rannsóknarád Rikisins, Reykjavik 06376
Visindafélag Islendinga, Reykjavik 06387

India
Association of Indian Universities, New Delhi 06407
Council of Scientific and Industrial Research, New Delhi 06422
Indian Academy of Sciences, Bangalore 06437
Indian National Science Academy, New Delhi 06468
Indian Science Congress Association, Calcutta 06477
National Academy of Sciences, Allahabad 06512
Rajasthan Academy of Science, Pilani 06524
Society of Young Scientists, New Dehli 06531

Indonesia
Balai Pengetahuan Umum Bandung, Bandung 06555

Iraq
Federation of Arab Scientific Councils, Baghdad 06577
Iraq Academy, Baghdad 06578
Scientific Research Council, Baghdad 06580

Ireland
Engineering and Scientific Association of Ireland, Mount Merrion 06598
Royal Dublin Society, Dublin 06660
Royal Irish Academy, Dublin 06664

Israel
Association for the Advancement of Science in Israel, Ramat-Gan 06678
The Israel Academy of Sciences and Humanities, Jerusalem 06693
National Council for Research and Development, Jerusalem 06741

Italy
Academia Petrarca di Lettere, Arti e Scienze, Arezzo 06760
Accademia Americana, Roma 06764
Accademia degli Abruzzi per le Scienze e le Arti, Chieti 06772
Accademia degli Euteleti, San Miniato 06773
Accademia degli Incamminati, Modigliana 06774
Accademia dei Filedoni, Perugia 06778
Accademia dei Filopatridi (Rubiconia), Savignano sul Rubicone 06780
Accademia dei Sepolti, Volterra 06783
Accademia della Crusca, Firenze 06784
Accademia delle Scienze dell'Istituto di Bologna, Bologna 06785
Accademia delle Scienze di Ferrara, Ferrara 06786
Accademia delle Scienze di Torino, Torino 06787
Accademia di Agricoltura Scienze e Lettere, Verona 06791
Accademia di Danimarca, Roma 06804
Accademia di Francia, Roma 06805
Accademia di Paestum Eremo Italico, Mercato San Severino 06807
Accademia di Romania, Roma 06809
Accademia di Scienze, Lettere e Arti, Udine 06811
Accademia di Scienze, Lettere e Belle Arti degli Zelanti e dei Dafnici, Acireale 06812
Accademia di Scienze, Lettere ed Arti, Palermo 06813
Accademia Etrusca, Cortona-Arezzo 06814
Accademia Fulginia di Arti, Lettere, Scienze, Foligno 06820
Accademia Il Tetradramma, Roma 06824
Accademia Internazionale della Tavola Rotonda, Milano 06826
Accademia Ligure di Scienze e Lettere, Genova 06837
Accademia Lunigianese di Scienze Giovanni Capellini, La Spezia 06839
Accademia Nazionale dei Lincei, Roma 06848
Accademia Nazionale dei Sartori, Roma 06849
Accademia Nazionale di Scienze, Lettere e Arti, Modena 06859
Accademia Nazionale di Scienze, Lettere ed Arti, Palermo 06860
Accademia Nazionale Virgiliana di Scienze, Lettere e Arti di Mantova, Mantova 06862
Accademia Petrarca di Lettere, Arti e Scienze, Arezzo 06864
Accademia Pontaniana, Napoli 06867
Accademia Pratese di Medicina e Scienze, Prato 06868
Accademia Pugliese delle Scienze, Bari 06870
Accademia Romana di Cultura, Roma 06872
Accademia Roveretana degli Agiati, Rovereto 06874
Accademia Tiberina, Roma 06882
Accademia Toscana di Scienze e Lettere La Colombaria, Firenze 06883
Accademia Universale Guglielmo Marconi, Roma 06885
Associazione Nazionale Filosofia Arti Scienze, Bologna 07010
Committee for the European Development of Science and Technology, Roma 07207
Consiglio Nazionale delle Ricerche, Roma 07212
Ente per le Nuove Tecnologie, l'Energia e l'Ambiente, Roma 07242
European Network of Scientific Information Referral Centres, Frascati 07264
Federazione delle Associazioni Scientifiche e Tecniche, Milano 07271
Istituto Lombardo Accademia di Scienze e Lettere, Milano 07358
Istituto Veneto di Scienze, Lettere ed Arti, Venezia 07375
Società Adriatica di Scienze, Trieste 07389
Società di Letture e Conversazioni Scientifiche, Genova 07404
Società Italiana per il Progresso delle Scienze, Roma 07590
Società Nazionale di Scienze, Lettere ed Arti, Napoli 07620
Società Torricelliana di Scienze e Lettere, Faenza 07651
Unione della Legion d'Oro, Roma 07673

Jamaica
Scientific Research Council, Kingston 07708

Japan
Japanese College of Angiology, Tokyo 07743
Manyo Gakkai, Osaka 07766
Nihon Gakujutsu Kaigi, Tokyo 07787
Nihon Kagakushi Gakkai, Tokyo 07804
Nihon Sangyo Eisei Gakkai, Tokyo 07841
Nippon Kagaku-Gijutsu Joho Sentah, Tokyo 07915
Nippon Rodo-ho Gakkai, Tokyo 07962
Nippon Saikingakkai, Tokyo 07964
Nogyo-Doboku Gakkai, Tokyo 08005
San-yo Gijutsu Shinkokai, Okayama-ken 08013
Toa Kumo Gakkai, Osaka 08036

Jordan
Islamic Academy of Sciences, Amman 08054
Royal Scientific Society, Amman 08057

Kazakhstan
Kazakhstan Academy of Sciences, Almaty 08058

Kenya
East African Academy, Nairobi 08090
Kenya National Academy of Sciences, Nairobi 08103
National Council for Science and Technology, Nairobi 08105

Korea, Democratic People's Republic
Academy of Sciences, Pyongyang 08114

Korea, Republic
Academy of Korean Studies, Kyonggi-do 08117
National Academy of Sciences, Seoul 08141

Kyrgyzstan
Kyrgyz Academy of Sciences, Bishkek 08146

Latvia
Latvian Academy of Sciences, Riga 08151

Libya
National Academy for Scientific Research, Tripoli 08159

Lithuania
Lithuanian Academy of Sciences, Vilnius 08165

Macedonia
Makedonska Akademija na Naukite i Umetnostite, Skopje 08190

Madagascar
Académie Malgache, Antananarivo 08207

Malawi
Society of Malawi, Blantyre 08212

Malaysia
Malaysian Scientific Association, Kuala Lumpur 08235

Mauritius
Royal Society of Arts and Sciences of Mauritius, Réduit 08254

Mexico
Academia Nacional de Ciencias, México 08260
Asociación Nacional de Universidades e Institutos de Educación Superior, México 08277
Ateneo Nacional de Ciencias y Artes de México, México 08280
Sociedad Mexicana de Historia de la Ciencia y la Tecnología, México 08342
Unión de Universidades de América Latina, México 08355

Moldova, Republic of
Moldovan Academy of Sciences, Chişinău 08361

Mongolia
Academy of Sciences, Ulan Bator 08375

Morocco
Académie du Royaume du Maroc, Rabat 08376

Myanmar
Central Research Organization, Yangon 08388

Namibia
Namibia Scientific Society, Windhoek 08390

Nepal
National Council for Science and Technology, Kathmandu 08391
Royal Nepal Academy, Kathmandu 08392
Royal Nepal Academy of Science and Technology, Kathmandu 08393

Netherlands
Bataafsch Genootschap der Proefondervindelijke Wijsbegeerte, Rotterdam 08401
Hollandsche Maatschappij der Wetenschappen, Haarlem 08469
International Technical and Scientific Organization for Soaring Flight, Wessling 08497
Koninklijke Nederlandse Akademie van Wetenschappen, Amsterdam 08513
Trans European Research and Education Networking Association, Amsterdam 08633

New Zealand
New Zealand Association of Scientists, Wellington 08685
Royal Society of New Zealand, Wellington 08742

Nigeria
Nigerian Academy of Science, Akoka 08775
Organization of African Unity – Scientific, Technical and Research Commission, Lagos 08785

Norway
Kongelige Norske Videnskabers Selskab, Trondheim 08796
Det Norske Videnskaps-Akademi, Oslo 08871
Research Council of Norway, Oslo 08876
Selskapet til Vitenskapenes Fremme, Bergen 08880

Pakistan
National Science Council of Pakistan, Islamabad 08909
Pakistan Academy of Sciences, Islamabad 08911
Pakistan Council of Scientific and Industrial Research, Karachi 08917
Quaid-i-Azam Academy, Karachi 08930
Scientific Society of Pakistan, Karachi 08932

Panama
Centro para el Desarrollo de la Capacidad Nacional de Investigación, Panamá City 08946
Consejo Nacional de Ciencia, Panamá City 08949

Papua New Guinea
Papua New Guinea Scientific Society, Boroko 08954

Paraguay
Academia Paraguaya, Asunción 08957
Sociedad Científica del Paraguay, Asunción 08966

Peru
Consejo Andino de Cienccia y Tecnología, Lima 08997
Consejo Nacional de la Universidad Peruana, Lima 08998

Philippines
Academia Filipina, Manila 09020
National Research Council of the Philippines, Manila 09054

Poland
Bialostockie Towarzystwo Naukowe, Bialystok 09070
Bydgoskie Towarzystwo Naukowe, Bydgoszcz 09071
Czestochowskie Towarzystwo Naukowe, Czestochowa 09072
Gdánskie Towarzystwo Naukowe, Gdánsk 09073
Karkonoskie Towarzystwo Naukowe, Jelenia Góra 09074
Katowickie Towarzystwo Spoleczno-Kulturalne, Katowice 09075
Kieleckie Towarzystwo Naukowe, Kielce 09076
Lódzkie Towarzystwo Naukowe, Lódź 09077
Lomzynskie Towarzystwo Naukowe im. Wagow, Lomza 09078

Subject Index: Science, general 480

Lubelskie Towarzystwo Naukowe, Lublin 09079
Lubuskie Towarzystwo Naukowe, Zielona Gora 09080
Opolskie Towarzystwo Przyjaciol Nauk, Opole 09081
Polska Akademia Nauk, Warszawa 09082
Poznánskie Towarzystwo Przyjaciól Nauk, Poznan 09144
Radomskie Towarzystwo Naukowe, Radom 09145
Szczecinskie Towarzystwo Naukowe, Szczecin 09150
Towarzystwo Naukowe Plockie, Płock 09159
Towarzystwo Naukowe w Toruniu, Torun 09160
Towarzystwo Naukowe Warszawskie, Warszawa 09161
Towarzystwo Przjaciol Nauk w Miedzyrzecu Podlaskim, Warszawa 09162
Towarzystwo Przyjaciól Nauk w Przymyslu, Przemysl 09163
Towarzystwo Przyjaciól w Legnicy, Legnica 09164
Towarzystwo Wiedzy Powszechnej, Warszawa 09166
Wloclawskie Towarzystwo Naukowe, Wloclawek 09168
Wroclawskie Towarzystwo Naukowe, Wroclaw 09169
Zamojskie Towarzystwo Przyjaciól Bauk, Zamosc 09170

Portugal

Academia das Ciências de Lisboa, Lisboa 09172
Sociedade Cientifica da Universidade Católica Portuguesa, Lisboa 09214

Réunion

Académie de l'Ile de la Réunion, Saint-Denis 09262

Romania

Academia Romana, Bucuresti 09267
Asociatia Oamenilor de Stiinta din Romania, Bucuresti 09271
European Committee for Scientific and Cultural Relations with Romania, Bucuresti 09279

Russia

Co-ordination Council for Information on Achievements, Moskva 09341
Commission for Scientific and Technical Co-operation of the Academy of Sciences and Organizations of Moscow Oblast, Moskva 09343
Group of the Far Eastern Division, Moskva 09360
Moscow Science-Production Association, Moskva 09373
National Committee of the International Council of Scientific Unions, Moskva 09388
Russian Academy of Sciences, Moskva 09442
Union of Scientific and Learned Societies, Moskva 09479
Znanie, Moskva 09481

Sierra Leone

Sierra Leone Science Association, Freetown 09521

Singapore

Singapore Association for the Advancement of Science, Singapore 09538
Singapore National Academy of Science, Singapore 09543

Slovakia

Organizačné Stredisko Vedeckých Spoločností pri SAV, Bratislava 09548
Slovenská Akadémia Vied, Bratislava 09549

Slovenia

Prirodoslovno Društvo Slovenije v Ljubljani, Ljubljana 09589
Slovenska Akademija Znanosti in Umetnosti, Ljubljana 09592

South Africa

Associated Scientific and Technical Societies of South Africa, Johannesburg 09609
CSIR, Pretoria 09620
Joint Council of Scientific Societies, Yeoville 09637
The National Association of Scientists, Pretoria 09643
Royal Society of South Africa, Cape Town 09658
South African Academy of Science and Arts, Pretoria 09665
Southern African Association for the Advancement of Science, Arcadia 09711

Spain

Dirección General de Relaciones Culturales y Cientificas, Madrid 09754
Instituto de España, Madrid 09764
Real Academia de Ciencias Exactas, Físicas y Naturales, Madrid 09779
Real Academia de Ciencias y Artes de Barcelona, Barcelona 09782
Real Academia Gallega, La Coruña 09792
Real Academia Hispano-Americana, Cádiz 09793

Sri Lanka

National Academy of Sciences of Sri Lanka, Colombo 09836
Sri Lanka Association for the Advancement of Science, Colombo 09839

Sudan

National Centre for Research, Khartoum 09845

Swaziland

Royal Swaziland Society of Science and Technology, Kwaluseni 09852

Sweden

European Incoherent Scatter Scientific Association, Kiruna 09875
Forskningsrådsnämnden, Stockholm 09881
Kungliga Fysiografiska Sällskapet i Lund, Lund 09902
Kungliga Vetenskaps- och Vitterhets-Samhället i Göteborg, Göteborg 09909
Kungliga Vetenskaps-Societeten i Uppsala, Uppsala 09910
Kungliga Vetenskapsakademien, Stockholm 09911
Nobelstiftelsen, Stockholm 09924
SACO Sveriges Akademikers Centralorganisation, Stockholm 09935
Svenska Linné-Sällskapet, Uppsala 09986

Switzerland

European Association of Development Research and Training, Genève 10098
Fédération Internationale des Femmes Diplômées des Universités, Genève 10124
Forum für verantwortbare Anwendung der Wissenschaft (Basel), Flüth 10129
Institut National Genevois, Genève 10162
Kommission zur Förderung der wissenschaftlichen Forschung, Bern 10199
Mouvement International des Intellectuels Catholiques/MIIC-Pax Romana, Genève 10209
Renaissance, Schweizerischer Verband katholischer Akademiker-Gesellschaften, Luzern 10229
Schweizerischer Verband der Akademikerinnen, Chur 10460
Schweizerischer Wissenschaftsrat, Bern 10486
Société Académique, Neuchâtel 10495

Tajikistan

Tajik Academy of Sciences, Dushanbe 10591

Tanzania

Tanzania Commission for Science and Technology, Dar es Salaam 10606

Thailand

Applied Scientific Research Corporation of Thailand, Bangkok 10613
National Culture Commission, Bangkok 10642
Royal Institute, Bangkok 10644
Science Society of Thailand, Bangkok 10645

Tunisia

Arab League Educational, Cultural and Scientific Organization, Tunis 10678

Turkmenistan

Turkmen Academy of Sciences, Ashkhabad 10726

Ukraine

National Academy of Sciences of Ukraine, Kiev 10735
Scientific and Technical Societies National Headquarters, Kiev 10736

United Kingdom

Academia Europaea, London 10743
Association for Science Education, Hatfield 10823
Association of British Science Writers, London 10854
Association of Principals of Colleges (Northern Ireland Branch), Lisburn 10910
Association of Professional Scientists and Technologists, London 10911
Association of Scientific, Technical and Managerial Staffs, London 10919
British Association for the Advancement of Science, London 11018
British Association of Friends of Museums, Manchester 11029
British Federation of Women Graduates, London 11080
British Society for Middle Eastern Studies, Durham 11172
Committee of Vice-Chancellors and Principals of the Universities of the United Kingdom, London 11312
Commonwealth Association of Science and Mathematics Educators, London 11318
Commonwealth Trust, London 11335
The Devonshire Association for the Advancement of Science, Literature and Art, Exeter 11387
Institute of Scientific and Technical Communicators, London 11721
International Union of Independent Laboratories, Elstree 11829
Kilvert Society, Worcester 11855
Parliamentary and Scientific Committee, London 12087
The Plymouth Athenaeum, Plymouth 12112
Pugwash Conferences on Science and World Affairs, London 12134
Research and Development Society, London 12153
Research Defence Society, London 12154
Royal Institution of Cornwall, Truro 12222
Royal Institution of Great Britain, London 12223
Royal Institution of South Wales, Swansea 12225
Royal Microscopical Society, Oxford 12233
Royal Scottish Academy, Edinburgh 12243
The Royal Society of Edinburgh, Edinburgh 12256
Royal Ulster Academy, Lurgan 12268
Royal Ulster Academy Association, Lambeg 12269
Society for The Protection of Science and Learning, London 12393
Society for Underwater Technology, London 12403
South-Eastern Union of Scientific Societies, Shoreham-by-Sea 12456
Tensor Society of Great Britain, Surbiton 12492
Theosophical Society in England, London 12496
UMIST Association, Manchester 12530
United Kingdom Science Park Association, Birmingham 12539

Uruguay

Consejo Nacional de Investigaciones Científicas y Técnicas, Montevideo 12624

U.S.A.

Academic Council on the United Nations System, Providence 12643
Academy of Interscience Methodology, Hinsdale 12646
Academy of Applied Science, Concord 12652
Academy of Arts and Sciences of the Americas, Miami 12653
Academy of Improbable Research, Cambridge 12659
African Medical and Research Foundation, New York 12708
American Academy of Arts and Sciences, Cambridge 12744
American Association for the Advancement of Science, Washington 12850
American Association for the Advancement of Slavic Studies, Stanford 12851
American Association of Meta-Science, Huntsville 12907
American Association of Presidents of Independent Colleges and Universities, Provo 12922
American Association of State Colleges and Universities, Washington 12934
American Committee for the Weizmann Institute of Science, New York 13084
American Indian Science and Engineering Society, Boulder 13193
American Philosophical Society, Philadelphia 13326
American Society for Eighteenth-Century Studies, Logan 13382
Associated Universities, Washington 13589
Association for Counselling, Organization, Research and Development, New York 13617
Association for Research on Nonprofit Organization and Voluntary Action, Indianapolis 13662
Association for the Education of Teachers in Science, Pensacola 13684
Association for Women in Science, Washington 13703
Association of American Universities, Washington 13725
Association of International Colleges and Universities, Independence 13779
Association of Jesuit Colleges and Universities, Washington 13783
Association of Muslim Scientists and Engineers, Plainfield 13801
Association of Orthodox Jewish Scientists, New York 13809
Association of Science Museum Directors, Chicago 13831
Association of Science-Technology Centers, Washington 13832
Association of University Related Research Parks, Tempe 13864
Association of University Summer Sessions, Bloomington 13865
Center for Advanced Study in the Behavioral Sciences, Stanford 13991
Center for Field Research, Watertown 14008
Center for Science in the Public Interest, Washington 14025
Committee on Capacity Building in Science, Batavia 14129
Common Market of Scientific and Technological Knowledge, Washington 14137
Conference Board of Associated Research Councils, New York 14152
Coordinating Committee for Intercontinental Research Networking, Arlington 14193
Council for Elementary Science International, Columbia 14208
Council for the Advancement of Science Writing, Greenlawn 14219
Council of American Overseas Research Centres, Washington 14224
Council of Colleges of Arts and Sciences, Tempe 14227
Council of Engineering and Scientific Society Executives, Warrendale 14230
Council of Scientific Society Presidents, Washington 14236
Creation Research Society, Saint Joseph 14269
Czechoslovak Society of Arts and Sciences, Sherman Oaks 14277
Federation of American Scientists, Washington 14419
History of Science Society, Seattle 14578
Institute for Advanced Research in Asian Science and Medicine, Chestnut Hill 14656
Institute for Policy Studies, Washington 14679
Institute for the Study of Human Knowledge, Los Altos 14691
Institute of World Affairs, Washington 14728
International Academy at Santa Barbara, Santa Barbara 14758
International Conference on the Unity of the Sciences, Lexington 14958
International Guild of Advanced Sciences, Palm Springs 15056
International Institute of Projectiology, New York 15079
International Research and Exchanges Board, Washington 15174
International Research/Study Team on Nonviolent Large Systems Change, Chesterland 15176
International Science Foundation, New York 15183
International Society for Third-Sector Research, Baltimore 15263
International Society of African Scientists, Wilmington 15267
International Studies Association, Tucson 15331
International Union of the History and Philosophy of Science, Madison 15361
Joint Commission of History and Philosophy of Science, Medison 15441
Leonardo – The International Society for the Arts, Sciences and Technology, San Francisco 15493
Moody Institute of Science, Chicago 15598
National Academic Advising Association, Manhattan 15617
National Association of Academies of Science, Columbia 15670
National Association of Independent Colleges and Universities, Washington 15708
National Association of Science Writers, Greenlawn 15729
National Association of State Universities and Land-Grant Colleges, Washington 15744
National Conference on the Advancement of Research, San Antonio 15813
National Congress of Inventors Organizations, Los Angeles 15816
National Council of University Research Administrators, Washington 15844
National Institute of Science, Nashville 15922
National Research Council, Washington 15963
Network of Arab Scientists and Technologists Abroad, Urbana 16010
New York Academy of Sciences, New York 16018
Pacific Mathematics and Science Regional Consortium, Honolulu 16119
Pacific Science Association, Honolulu 16124
Pattern Recognition Society, Washington 16149
Polish Institute of Arts and Sciences in America, New York 16186
Rare Earth Research Conference, Duluth 16246
Shevchenko Scientific Society, New York 16324
Society for Literature and Science, Worchester 16410
Society of Jewish Science, New York 16532
Society of Research Administrators, Washington 16555
Ukrainian Academy of Arts and Sciences in the U.S., New York 16656
Union of Concerned Scientists, Cambridge 16663
United Nations Commission on Science and Technology for Development, New York 16673
United Nations Educational, Scientific and Cultural Organization, New York 16675
United States Federation of Scholars and Scientists, Fullerton 16690
United States Metric Association, Los Angeles 16692
Wenner-Gren Centre Foundation for Scientific Research, New York 16749
World Academy of Art and Science, Minneapolis 16784
World Research Foundation, Wooland Hills 16836

Uzbekistan

Uzbek Academy of Sciences, Tashkent 16856

Vatican City

Pontificia Academia Scientiarum, Città del Vaticano 16861

Venezuela

Asociación Venezolana para el Avance de la Ciencia, Caracas 16884
Consejo de Desarrollo Cientifico y Humanístico, Caracas 16907
Consejo Nacional de Investigaciones Científicas y Tecnológicas, Caracas 16908

Vietnam

Vietnam Union of Sientific and Technical Associations, Hanoi 16941

Yugoslavia

Crnogorska Akademija Nauka i Umjetnosti, Podgorica 16986
Srpska Akademija Nauka i Umetnosti, Beograd 17031

Zambia

National Council for Scientific Research, Lusaka 17051

Zimbabwe

Scientific Council of Zimbabwe, Harare 17079
Zimbabwe Association for Science Education, Harare 17084
Zimbabwe Scientific Association, Harare 17087

Social Sciences

Australia

Asian and Pacific Association for Social Work Education, Bundoora 00123

Austria

Akademie für Sozialarbeit der Stadt Wien, Wien 00398
European Centre for Social Welfare Policy and Research, Wien 00439
European Cooperation in Social Science Information and Documentation, Wien 00440
European Coordination Centre for Research and Documentation in Social Sciences, Wien 00441
Institut für Sozialdienste, gemeinnützige GmbH, Bregenz 00507
International Council on Social Welfare, Wien 00512
Internationales Institut für den Frieden, Wien 00537

Belgium

Centre for Research on European Women, Bruxelles *01010*
Institut Européen Interuniversitaire de l'Action Sociale, Marcinelle *01194*
Société d'Ergonomie de Langue Française, Bruxelles *01262*

Brazil

Asociación Latinoamericana de Escuelas de Trabajo Social, Saõ Luís *01389*

Canada

Centre for Research on Latin America and the Caribbean, North York *02035*
Fédération des Affaires Sociales, Montréal *02096*
International Development Research Centre, Ottawa *02153*

China, People's Republic

Chinese Academy of Social Sciences, Beijing *02562*

Congo, Democratic Republic

Centre for the Coordination of Research and Documentation in Social Science for Sub-Saharan Africa, Kinshasa *02835*

Costa Rica

Central American Institute of Social Studies, San José *02852*

Czech Republic

Česká Demografická Společnost, Praha *02917*

Denmark

Nordisk Institut for Asienstudier, København *03177*

Egypt

Zoological Society of Egypt, Cairo *03307*

France

Association Française des Russisants, Paris *03545*
Association Internationale des Démographes de Langue Française, Paris *03580*
Association Médico-Sociale Protestante de Langue Française, Alfortville *03612*
Center for Studies, Research and Training in International Understanding and Cooperation, Paris *03672*
Centre d'Archives et de Documentation Politiques et Sociales, Paris *03673*
Club of Rome, Paris *03703*
Committee for International Cooperation in National Research in Demography, Paris *03742*
European Association for American Studies, Lyon *03794*
Société d'Ethnographie de Paris, Paris *04049*

Germany

Arbeitsgemeinschaft für betriebliche Altersversorgung e.V., Heidelberg *04448*
Arbeitsgemeinschaft Sozialwissenschaftlicher Institute e.V., Bonn *04474*
Deutsches Zentralinstitut für soziale Fragen, Berlin *05108*
Gesellschaft für Sozial- und Wirtschaftsgeschichte, Heidelberg *05406*
Gesellschaft Sozialwissenschaftlicher Infrastruktureinrichtungen e.V., Mannheim *05424*
GFM-GETAS Gesellschaft für Marketing-, Kommunikations- und Sozialforschung, Hamburg *05437*
Thomas-Morus-Akademie Bensberg, Bergisch Gladbach *05988*

Hungary

Magyar Gerontológiai Társaság, Budapest *06312*

Indonesia

ASEAN Population Coordination Unit, Jakarta *06547*
ASEAN Population Information Network, Jakarta *06548*

Ireland

Royal Irish Academy, Dublin *06664*

Israel

Israel Gerontological Society, Ramat Gan *06703*

Italy

Accademia Internazionale per le Scienze Economiche, Sociali e Sanitarie, Roma *06828*

Accademia Polacca delle Scienze, Roma *06865*
Accademia Simba, Roma *06878*
Centre for Human Evolution Studies, Roma *07053*
Centro Internazionale per le Communicazione Sociali, Roma *07078*
Centro Studi e Ricerche sui Rapporti Umani, Roma *07153*
European Council for Social Research on Latin America, Roma *07262*
Gruppo Interdisciplinare per la Ricerca Sociale, Roma *07292*
Unione Italiana Lotta alla Distrofia Muscolare, Padova *07676*

Ivory Coast

African Institute for Economic and Social Development, Abidjan *07683*

Macao

Associação de Ciências Socias de Macau, Macau *08178*

Malaysia

Asia Pacific Forum on Women, Law and Development, Kuala Lumpur *08215*

Mexico

Center for Economic and Social Studies in the Third World, México *08283*
Center of Coordination and Diffusion of Latin American Studies, México *08284*

Netherlands

European Association for Population Studies, Den Haag *08426*
European Centre for Work and Society, Maastricht *08441*
Fryske Akademy, Leeuwarden *08459*
Instituut voor Toegepaste Sociale Wetenschapen, Nijmegen *08473*
Nederlandse Organisatie voor Wetenschappelijk Onderzoek, Den Haag *08563*

New Zealand

Population Association of New Zealand, Wellington *08738*

Nigeria

African Curriculum Organization, Ibadan *08758*

Peru

Andean Institute for Population Studies and Development, Lima *08976*
Andean Institute of Social Studies, Lima *08977*

Philippines

Asian Women's Research and Action Network, Manila *09039*

Russia

Commission for the European (Vienna) Centre for Co-ordination of Research and Documentation in Social Sciences, Moskva *09344*
Council for International Co-operation in Social Sciences, Moskva *09346*

Senegal

African Council for Social and Human Sciences, Dakar *09498*

Sri Lanka

Royal Asiatic Society of Sri Lanka, Colombo *09838*

Sweden

Akademikerförbundet SSR, Stockholm *09855*
European Association of Labour Economists, Stockholm *09870*
Humanistisk-Samhällsvetenskapliga Forskningsrådet, Stockholm *09887*

Switzerland

Alkohol- und Suchtfachleute, Schweiz. Fachverband, Oberkirch *10022*
Arbeitsgemeinschaft Wirtschaft und Gesellschaft, Sankt Gallen *10030*
Internationale Vereinigung wissenschaftlicher Fremdenverkehrsexperten, Sankt Gallen *10192*
Schweizerische Akademie der Sozial- und Geisteswissenschaften, Bern *10241*
Schweizerische Arbeitsgemeinschaft der Höheren Fachschulen für Soziale Arbeit, Luzern *10246*
Schweizerische Arbeitsgemeinschaft der Höheren Fachschulen für Sozialpädagogik, Rorschach *10247*
Schweizerische Asiengesellschaft, Zürich *10256*
Schweizerische Gesellschaft für praktische Sozialforschung, Bern *10329*

Verband Schweizerischer Marketing- und Sozialforscher, Hergiswil *10539*

Syria

Arab Centre for Information Studies on Population, Development and Construction, Damascus *10585*

Thailand

Asia-Pacific Information Network in Social Sciences, Bangkok *10624*

Trinidad and Tobago

Caribbean Association for Feminist Research and Action, Tunapuna *10655*
Caribbean Information System for Economic and Social Planning, Port of Spain *10661*

Tunisia

Association of Arab Institutes and Centres for Economic and Social Research, Tunis *10684*

United Kingdom

Association for Child Psychology and Psychiatry, London *10803*
Centre for Iberian Studies, Keele *11261*
National Institute of Economic and Social Research, London *12014*
Standing Conference of Arts and Social Sciences, Cardiff *12470*
Theosophical Society in England, London *12496*

U.S.A.

American Association on Mental Retardation, Washington *12957*
American Council of Learned Societies, New York *13103*
American Orthopsychiatric Association, New York *13302*
Association for Politics and the Life Sciences, DeKalb *13648*
Caucus for a New Political Science, Boston *13987*
Commission on Gay/Lesbian Issues in Social Work Education, Alexandria *14113*
Council for European Studies, New York *14209*
Institute for Policy Studies, Washington *14679*
Inter-American University Council for Economic and Social Development, Houston *14748*
International Academy of Sex Research, Bloomington *14770*
International Network for Social Network Analysis, Columbia *15119*
International Society for the Study of Personal Relationships, Louisville *15259*
Lentz Peace Research Laboratory, Saint Louis *15490*
National Association of Alcoholism and Drug Abuse Counselors, Arlington *15672*
National Audubon Society, Boulder *15755*
North American Regional Association of Schools of Social Work, West Hartford *16045*
Research Society on Alcoholism, Austin *16271*
Social Science Education Consortium, Boulder *16340*
Social Science Research Council, New York *16341*
Society for Psychological Study of Social Issues, Ann Arbor *16433*
Society for Social Studies of Science, Baton Rouge *16442*
United Nations Commission on Population and Development, New York *16672*
World Association for Public Opinion Research, Chapel Hill *16794*
World Association for Sexology, Minneapolis *16795*

Venezuela

Caribbean Institute for Social Formation, Caracas *16887*

Yugoslavia

Akademia e Shkencave dhe e Arteve e Kosovës, Priština *16982*

Socialism

Australia

Australian Fabian Society, Melbourne *00187*

Austria

Internationale Tagung der Historikerinnen und Historiker der Arbeiterinnen- und Arbeiterbewegung (ITH), Wien *00533*
Verein für Geschichte der Arbeiterbewegung, Wien *00832*

Belgium

European Trade Union Institute, Bruxelles *01164*

Italy

Centro Ligure di Storia Sociale, Genova *07097*

U.S.A.

Center for Socialist History, Berkeley *14028*
Global Options, San Francisco *14511*

Sociology

Argentina

Academia Nacional de Derecho y Ciencias Sociales, Buenos Aires *00030*
Academia Nacional de Derecho y Ciencias Sociales (Córdoba), Córdoba *00031*
Sociedad Argentina de Sociología, Córdoba *00103*

Australia

Academy of the Social Sciences in Australia, Canberra *00115*
Australasian Association for the History, Philosophy and Social Studies of Science, Sydney *00139*
Australian Association of Social Workers, North Richmond *00166*
Australian Sociological Association, Clayton *00247*
Society for Social Responsibility in Science (A.C.T.), Canberra *00361*
Sociological Association of Australia and New Zealand, Bathurst *00364*

Austria

Europäisches Zentrum für Wohlfahrtspolitik und Sozialforschung, Wien *00435*
Gesellschaft für Ganzheitsforschung, Wien *00467*
Gesellschaft für Soziologie an der Universität Graz, Graz *00481*
International Association of Schools of Social Work, Wien *00510*
Mediacult – Internationales Forschungsinstitut für Medien, Kommunikation und kulturelle Entwicklung, Wien *00555*
Österreichische Gesellschaft für China-Forschung, Wien *00619*
Österreichische Gesellschaft für Medizinsoziologie, Wien *00660*
Österreichische Gesellschaft für Soziologie, Wien *00683*
Österreichische Gesellschaft für Wirtschaftssoziologie, Wien *00700*
Österreichischer Arbeitskreis für Soziologie des Sports und der Leibeserziehung, Wien *00748*
Österreichisches Lateinamerika-Institut, Wien *00775*
Sozialwissenschaftliche Arbeitsgemeinschaft, Wien *00797*
Sozialwissenschaftliche Studiengesellschaft, Wien *00798*
Verein für Geschichte der Arbeiterbewegung, Wien *00832*

Bahrain

Bahrain Society of Sociologists, Manama *00907*

Belgium

Association Internationale pour le Progrès Social, Bruxelles *00973*
Comité Economique et Social des Communautés Européennes, Bruxelles *01036*
Comité National pour l'Etude et la Prévention de l'Alcoolisme et des Autres Toxicomanies, Bruxelles *01041*
Conseil Consultatif Economique et Social de l'Union Economique Benelux, Bruxelles *01058*
European Trade Union Institute, Bruxelles *01164*
Fédération Internationale des Instituts de Recherches Socio-Religieuses, Louvain-la-Neuve *01170*
Institut Européen Interuniversitaire de l'Action Sociale, Marcinelle *01194*
International Union for the Scientific Study of Population, Liège *01214*
Union des Associations d'Assistants Sociaux Francophones, Bruxelles *01305*

Brazil

Conselho Nacional Serviço Social, Rio de Janeiro *01457*
Fundação Joaquim Nabuco, Recife *01461*
Instituto de Planejamento de Pernambuco, Recife *01468*
Sociedade Brasileira de Instrução, Botafogo *01515*

Bulgaria

Bulgarian Sociological Society, Sofia *01573*

Canada

Association for Canadian Studies, Montréal *01695*
Association of Canadian Universities for Northern Studies, Ottawa *01711*
Canadian Association for the Advancement of Netherlandic Studies, Wolfville *01805*
Canadian Association for the Social Studies, Saint John's *01806*
Canadian Council on Social Development, Ottawa *01864*
Canadian Law and Society Association, Toronto *01918*
Canadian Polish Research Institute, Toronto *01949*
Canadian Research Institute for the Advancement of Women, Ottawa *01960*
Canadian Sociology and Anthropology Association, Montréal *02007*
Fédération des Affaires Sociales, Montréal *02096*
Institute for Canadian Studies, Winnipeg *02137*
Migraine Association of Canada, Toronto *02209*
Ontario Public Interest Research Group, Toronto *02289*
Youth Science Foundation, Ottawa *02433*

Chile

Academia Chilena de Ciencias Sociales, Politicas y Morales, Santiago *02443*

China, People's Republic

Chinese Sociological Research Society, Beijing *02639*

China, Republic

China Social Education Society, Taipei *02683*
Population Association of China, Taipei *02747*

Colombia

Centro Interamericano de Vivienda y Planeamiento, Bogotá *02778*
Instituto Colombiano de Bienestar Familiar, Bogotá *02790*

Cyprus

Cyprus Research Centre, Nicosia *02906*

Czech Republic

Masarykova Česká Sociologická Společnost, Praha *02954*

Denmark

Dansk Forening for Retssociologi, København *03003*
Dansk Socialrådgiverforening, København *03075*
Dansk Sociologisk Selskab, København *03076*
Nordisk Forening for Rettssociologi, København *03176*
Paedagogisk Forening, København *03186*
Scandinavian Society for Economic and Social History, Odense *03197*
Scandinavian Sociological Association, København *03198*
Selskab for Arbejdsmiljø, København *03200*
Socialpaedagogernes Landsforbund, København *03212*

Ecuador

Instituto Latinoamericano de Investigaciones Sociales, Quito *03244*

Ethiopia

African Training and Research Centre for Women, Addis Ababa *03329*

France

Association Française d'Etude des Relations Professionnelles, Fresnes *03547*
Association Internationale des Sociologues de Langue Française, Toulouse *03588*
Association Interprofessionnelle des Centres Médicaux et Sociaux de la Région Parisienne, Paris *03604*
Association Nationale des Professeurs en Economie Sociale et Familiale, Paris *03619*
Association Régionale d'Informations Sociales, Paris *03655*
Centre d'Etudes, de Documentation, d'Information et d'Action Sociales, Paris *03678*
Centre National de la Recherche Scientifique, Paris *03694*

483 Subject Index: Standardization

Austria
Internationale Sportwissenschaftliche Gesellschaft Graz, Graz-Weinitzen 00532
Österreichische Sportwissenschaftliche Gesellschaft, Salzburg 00735
Österreichischer Arbeitskreis für Soziologie des Sports und der Leibeserziehung, Wien 00748
Österreichischer Sportlehrerverband, Wien 00765
Wissenschaftliche Arbeitsgemeinschaft für Leibeserziehung und Sportmedizin in Innsbruck, Innsbruck 00880
Wissenschaftliche Gesellschaft für Sport und Leibeserziehung am Institut für Sportwissenschaften der Universität Salzburg, Salzburg 00882

Belgium
Association Internationale des Ecoles Supérieures d'Education Physique, Liège 00966
European Association for Research into Adapted Physical Activity, Bruxelles 01089
Fédération Belge d'Education Physique, Bruxelles 01166

Canada
Canadian Association for Health, Physical Education, Recreation and Dance, Gloucester 01797
Canadian Council of University Physical Education and Kinesiology Administrators, Montréal 01863

Denmark
Dansk Idraetslaererforening, Nyborg 03017
International Association of Physical Education and Sports for Girls and Women, Viborg 03132

France
Fédération de l'Education Nationale, Paris 03828
Fédération Française d'Education Physique et de Gymnastique Volontaire, Paris 03839
Fédération Internationale Catholique d'Education Physique et Sportive, Paris 03847
Syndicat National des Professeurs d'Arts Martiaux, Paris 04292
Union Fédérative des Sociétés d'Education Physique et de Préparation Militaire, Paris 04304

Germany
Deutsche Vereinigung für Sportwissenschaft, Hamburg 04976
Deutscher Skilehrerverband e.V., München 05040
Deutscher Sportbund, Frankfurt 05043
Deutscher Sportlehrerverband e.V., Wetzlar 05044
Deutscher Verband für das Skilehrwesen e.V., Oberstdorf 05053
International Council of Sport Science and Physical Education, Berlin 05557
Konferenz Sportwissenschaftlicher Hochschuleinrichtungen, Köln 05685
Normenausschuss Sport- und Freizeitgerät im DIN Deutsches Institut für Normung e.V., Köln 05843
Verband Deutscher Diplom-Trainer, Bonn 06039
Verband Deutscher Tennislehrer e.V., Essen 06056

Italy
Associazione Italiana di Psicologia dello Sport, Ferrara 06958
Centro Studi di Diritto Sportivo, Vicenza 07137
Federazione Medico-Sportiva Italiana, Roma 07278
Federazione Nazionale Insegnanti Educazione Fisica, Roma 07282

Japan
Nippon Taiiku Gakkai, Tokyo 07997

Netherlands
Koninklijke Vereniging van Leraren in de Lichamelijke Opvoeding, Zeist 08522

Romania
Societatea de Medicinà Sportiva, Bucuresti 09301

Sweden
Svenska Gymnastikläraresällskapet, Hässelby 09978

Switzerland
Schweizerischer Verband für Sport in der Schule, Bern 10475
Vereinigung der Gymnastiklehrer, Zürich 10558

United Kingdom
British Association of Advisers and Lecturers in Pysical Education, Exmouth 11022
Central Council of Physical Recreation, London 11257
English Sports Council, London 11457
Fédération Internationale d'Education Physique, Cheltenham 11525
National Federation of Sailing Schools, Lymington 12005
Rugby Football Schools Union, Twickenham 12276
Scottish Association of Advisers in Physical Education, Dumbarton 12293
Scottish Physical Education Association, Glasgow 12315

U.S.A.
American Academy of Kinesiology and Physical Education, Baton Rouge 12764
American Academy of Sports Physicians, Encino 12798
American Alliance for Health, Physical Education, Recreation and Dance, Reston 12807
American Center for the Alexander Technique, New York 13026
American Osteopathic Academy of Sports Medicine, Middleton 13307
American Sports Education Institute, North Palm Beach 13505
APPA: The Association of Higher Education Facilities Officers, Alexandria 13554
Association of Laban Movement Analysts, New York 13786
International Association of Physical Education and Sports for Girls and Women, Newark 14870
International Council for Health, Physical Education, Recreation, Sport and Dance, Reston 14970
Laban/Bartenieff Institute of Movement Studies, New York 15472
National Association for Physical Education in Higher Education, San Jose 15653
National Association for Sport and Physical Education, Reston 15659
National Association of Academic Advisors for Athletics, Prospect 15669
National Council of Athletic Training, Reston 15831
North American Society for Sport History, University Park 16049
North American Society for Sport Psychology and Physical Activity, Geensboro 16050
Philosophic Society for the Study of Sport, Union 16165
Professional Football Researches Association, North Huntington 16207
Society of State Directors of Health, Physical Education and Recreation, Kensington 16558
United States Sports Academy, Daphne 16701

Standardization

Argentina
Comisión Panamericana de Normas Técnicas, Buenos Aires 00070

Austria
Österreichisches Normungsinstitut, Wien 00776

Belgium
Asocio por la Enkonduko de Nova Biologia Nomenklaturo, Kalmthout 00940
CENELEC, Bruxelles 01005
European Association of Classification Societies, Antwerpen 01098
European Committee for Electrotechnical Standardization, Bruxelles 01128
European Committee for Iron and Steel Standardization, Bruxelles 01130
Institut Belge de Normalisation, Bruxelles 01188

Canada
Canadian General Standards Board, Ottawa 01891
Canadian Standards Association, Etobicoke 02010
Canadian Welding Bureau, Mississauga 02024
Indexing and Abstracting Society of Canada, Toronto 02130
Multiple Dwelling Standards Association, North York 02215

Colombia
Instituto Colombiano de Normas Técnicas, Bogotá 02795

Egypt
Arab Organization for Standardization and Metrology, Cairo 03262

Finland
Suomen Standardisoimisliitto, Helsinki 03433

France
Association Française de Normalisation, Paris La Défence 03531
Bureau International des Poids et Mesures, Sèvres 03671
Centre de Coopération pour les Recherches Scientifiques Relatives au Tabac, Paris 03675
Organisation Internationale de Métrologie Légale, Paris 03935

Germany
Arbeitsausschuß Wälzlager im DIN Deutsches Institut für Normung e.V., Köln 04422
Arbeitswissenschaft im Landbau e.V., Stuttgart 04499
Ausschuss Normenpraxis im DIN Deutsches Institut für Normung e.V., Berlin 04514
Deutsche Elektrotechnische Kommission im DIN und VDE, Frankfurt 04729
Deutscher Beton-Verein e.V., Wiesbaden 05000
DIN Deutsches Institut für Normung e.V., Berlin 05112
Gesellschaft für Klassifikation e.V., Karlsruhe 05378
Hannoversches Forschungsinstitut für Fertigungsfragen e.V., Hannover 05456
Institut für Neue Technische Form e.V., Darmstadt 05534
Normenausschuss Akustik, Lärmminderung und Schwingungstechnik im DIN Deutsches Institut für Normung e.V., Berlin 05787
Normenausschuss Anstrichstoffe und ähnliche Beschichtungsstoffe im DIN Deutsches Institut für Normung e.V., Berlin 05788
Normenausschuss Armaturen im DIN Deutsches Institut für Normung e.V., Köln 05789
Normenausschuss Bauwesen im DIN Deutsches Institut für Normung e.V., Berlin 05790
Normenausschuss Bergbau im DIN Deutsches Institut für Normung e.V., Essen 05791
Normenausschuss Bibliotheks- und Dokumentationswesen im DIN Deutsches Institut für Normung e.V., Berlin 05792
Normenausschuss Bild und Film im DIN Deutsches Institut für Normung e.V., Berlin 05793
Normenausschuss Bühnentechnik in Theatern und Mehrzweckhallen im DIN Deutsches Institut für Normung e.V., Berlin 05794
Normenausschuss Bürowesen im DIN Deutsches Institut für Normung e.V., Berlin 05795
Normenausschuss Chemischer Apparatebau im DIN Deutsches Institut für Normung e.V., Köln 05796
Normenausschuss Dental im DIN Deutsches Institut für Normung e.V., Pforzheim 05797
Normenausschuss Dichtungen im DIN Deutsches Institut für Normung e.V., Köln 05798
Normenausschuss Druck- und Reproduktionstechnik im DIN Deutsches Institut für Normung e.V., Berlin 05799
Normenausschuss Druckgasanlagen im DIN Deutsches Institut für Normung e.V., Berlin 05800
Normenausschuss Eisen-, Blech- und Metallwaren im DIN Deutsches Institut für Normung e.V., Düsseldorf 05801
Normenausschuß Eisen und Stahl im DIN Deutsches Institut für Normung e.V., Düsseldorf 05802
Normenausschuss Erdöl- und Erdgasgewinnung im DIN Deutsches Institut für Normung e.V., Köln 05803
Normenausschuss Ergonomie im DIN Deutsches Institut für Normung e.V., Berlin 05804
Normenausschuss Fahrräder im DIN Deutsches Institut für Normung e.V., Köln 05805
Normenausschuss Farbe im DIN Deutsches Institut für Normung e.V., Berlin 05806
Normenausschuss Feinmechanik und Optik im DIN Deutsches Institut für Normung e.V., Pforzheim 05807
Normenausschuss Feuerwehrwesen im DIN Deutsches Institut für Normung e.V., Berlin 05808
Normenausschuss Gastechnik im DIN Deutsches Institut für Normung e.V., Eschborn 05809
Normenausschuss Gebrauchstauglichkeit im DIN Deutsches Institut für Normung e.V., Berlin 05810
Normenausschuss Giessereiwesen im DIN Deutsches Institut für Normung e.V., Köln 05811
Normenausschuss Gleitlager im DIN Deutsches Insitut für Normung e.V., Köln 05812
Normenausschuss Graphische Symbole im DIN Deutsches Institut für Normung e.V., Berlin 05813
Normenausschuss Grundlagen der Normung im DIN Deutsches Institut für Normung e.V., Berlin 05814
Normenausschuss Heiz-, Koch- und Wärmegeräte im DIN Deutsches Institut für Normung e.V., Frankfurt 05815
Normenausschuss Heiz- und Raumlufttechnik im DIN Deutsches Institut für Normung e.V., Berlin 05816
Normenausschuss Holzwirtschaft und Möbel im DIN Deutsches Institut für Normung e.V., Köln 05817
Normenausschuß Informationstechnik im DIN Deutsches Institut für Normung e.V., Berlin 05818
Normenausschuss Instandhaltung im DIN Deutsches Institut für Normung e.V., Köln 05819
Normenausschuss Kältetechnik im DIN Deutsches Institut für Normung e.V., Köln 05820
Normenausschuss Kautschuktechnik im DIN Deutsches Institut für Normung e.V., Frankfurt 05821
Normenausschuss Kerntechnik im DIN Deutsches Institut für Normung e.V., Berlin 05822
Normenausschuss Kommunale Technik im DIN Deutsches Institut für Normung e.V., Berlin 05823
Normenausschuss Kraftfahrzeuge im DIN Deutsches Institut für Normung e.V., Frankfurt 05824
Normenausschuss Kunststoffe im DIN Deutsches Institut für Normung e.V., Berlin 05825
Normenausschuss Laborgeräte und Laboreinrichtungen im DIN Deutsches Institut für Normung e.V., Frankfurt 05826
Normenausschuss Lebensmittel und Landwirtschaftliche Produkte im DIN Deutsches Institut für Normung e.V., Berlin 05827
Normenausschuss Lichttechnik im DIN Deutsches Institut für Normung e.V., Berlin 05828
Normenausschuss Maschinenbau (NAM) im DIN Deutsches Institut für Normung e.V., Frankfurt 05829
Normenausschuss Materialprüfung im DIN Deutsches Institut für Normung e.V., Berlin 05830
Normenausschuss Mechanische Verbindungselemente im DIN Deutsches Institut für Normung e.V., Köln 05831
Normenausschuss Medizin im DIN Deutsches Institut für Normung e.V., Berlin 05832
Normenausschuss Nichteisenmetalle im DIN Deutsches Institut für Normung e.V., Köln 05833
Normenausschuss Papier und Pappe im DIN Deutsches Institut für Normung e.V., Berlin 05834
Normenausschuss Persönliche Schutzausrüstung und Sicherheitskennzeichnung im DIN Deutsches Institut für Normung e.V., Berlin 05835
Normenausschuss Pigmente und Füllstoffe im DIN Deutsches Institut für Normung e.V., Berlin 05836
Normenausschuss Pulvermetallurgie im DIN Deutsches Institut für Normung e.V., Köln 05837
Normenausschuss Rohre, Rohrverbindungen und Rohrleitungen im DIN Deutsches Institut für Normung e.V., Köln 05838
Normenausschuss Rundstahlketten im DIN Deutsches Institut für Normung e.V., Köln 05839
Normenausschuss Schienenfahrzeuge im DIN Deutsches Institut für Normung e.V., Kassel 05840
Normenausschuss Schmiedetechnik im DIN Deutsches Institut für Normung e.V., Hagen 05841
Normenausschuss Schweisstechnik im DIN Deutsches Institut für Normung e.V., Berlin 05842
Normenausschuss Sport- und Freizeitgerät im DIN Deutsches Institut für Normung e.V., Köln 05843
Normenausschuss Stahldraht und Stahldrahterzeugnisse im DIN Deutsches Institut für Normung e.V., Köln 05844
Normenausschuss Technische Grundlagen im DIN Deutsches Institut für Normung e.V., Berlin 05845
Normenausschuss Terminologie im DIN Deutsches Institut für Normung e.V., Berlin 05846
Normenausschuss Textil und Textilmaschinen im DIN Deutsches Institut für Normung e.V., Berlin 05847
Normenausschuss Transportkette im DIN Deutsches Institut für Normung e.V., Berlin 05848
Normenausschuss Überwachungsbedürftige Anlagen im DIN Deutsches Institut für Normung e.V., Köln 05849
Normenausschuss Uhren und Schmuck im DIN Deutsches Institut für Normung e.V., Pforzheim 05850
Normenausschuss Vakuumtechnik im DIN Deutsches Institut für Normung e.V., Köln 05851
Normenausschuss Verpackungswesen im DIN Deutsches Institut für Normung e.V., Berlin 05852
Normenausschuss Waagenbau im DIN Deutsches Institut für Normung e.V., Berlin 05853
Normenausschuss Wärmebehandlungstechnik metallischer Werkstoffe im DIN Deutsches Institut für Normung e.V., Köln 05854
Normenausschuss Wasserwesen im DIN Deutsches Institut für Normung e.V., Berlin 05855
Normenausschuss Werkzeuge und Spannzeuge im DIN Deutsches Institut für Normung e.V., Köln 05856
Normenausschuss Werkzeugmaschinen im DIN Deutsches Institut für Normung e.V., Frankfurt 05857
Normenausschuss Zeichnungswesen im DIN Deutsches Institut für Normung e.V., Berlin 05858

Greece
Elliniki Etaireia Orologias, Penteli 06217
Ellinikos Organismos Tipopoiisis, Athinai 06229

India
Indian Standards Institution, New Dehli 06490
Research Designs and Standards Organization, Lucknow 06525

Indonesia
Jajasan Dana Normalisasi Indonesia, Bandung 06559

Italy
Ente Nazionale Italiano di Unificazione, Milano 07240

Japan
Nihon Kikaku Kyokai Gaikoku Kikaku Raiburari, Tokyo 07811

Kenya
African Regional Organization for Standardization, Nairobi 08070

Norway
Norges Standardiseringsforbund, Oslo 08808
Standardiseringsforeningen, Oslo 08883

Russia
Council for Metrological Provision and Standardization, St. Petersburg 09348
Institute for Standardization, Moskva 09363

Sweden
Standardiseringskommissionen i Sverige, Stockholm 09941

Switzerland
International Organization for Standardization, Genève 10174
Schweizerische Normen-Vereinigung, Zürich 10377

Turkey
Türk Standartlari Enstitüsü, Ankara 10715

United Kingdom
British Measures Group, Teddington 11123
British Standards Institution, London 11202
The Dozenal Society of Great Britain, Moulsford 11400
International Anatomical Nomenclature Committee, London 11760
International Association of Biological Standardization, Hassocks 11766
International Commission on Zoological Nomenclature, London 11780
Society of Indexers, London 12432

Uruguay
Instituto Uruguayo de Normas Técnicas, Montevideo 12628

U.S.A.
American National Standards Institute, New York 13284
American Society for Testing and Materials, Philadelphia 13415

485

Subject Index: Surveying, Photogrammetry

Deutsche Gesellschaft für Mund-, Kiefer- und Gesichtschirurgie, Bonn *04821*
Deutsche Gesellschaft für Neurochirurgie, Essen *04824*
Deutsche Gesellschaft für Plastische und Wiederherstellende Chirurgie e.V., Rotenburg *04843*
Deutsche Gesellschaft für Thorax-, Herz- und Gefässchirurgie, Bad Nauheim *04869*
Deutsche Gesellschaft für Unfallheilkunde e.V., Frankfurt *04871*
Deutschsprachige Arbeitsgemeinschaft für Handchirurgie, Hamburg *05111*
Fachschaft Berliner Chirurgen e.V., Berlin *05205*
KfH-Kuratorium für Dialyse und Nierentransplantation e.V., Neu-Isenburg *05664*
Vereinigung der Bayerischen Chirurgen e.V., Altötting *06111*

Greece
Elliniki Cheirourgiki Etaireia, Athinai *06216*

Hungary
Magyar Sebész Társaság, Budapest *06339*

India
Association of Surgeons of India, Madras *06410*

Ireland
Royal College of Surgeons in Ireland, Dublin *06659*

Israel
Society of Orthopedic Surgeons of the Israel Medical Association, Tel Aviv *06749*

Italy
Accademia Anatomico-Chirurgica, Perugia *06765*
Accademia Medica Pistoiese Filippo Pacini, Pistoia *06843*
Accademia Medico-Chirurgica del Piceno, Ancona *06844*
European Renal Association – European Dialysis and Transplant Association, Parma *07265*
Società Italiana di Chirurgia, Roma *07473*
Società Italiana di Chirurgia Cardiaca e Vascolare, Roma *07474*
Società Italiana di Chirurgia Clinica, Roma *07475*
Società Italiana di Chirurgia della Mano, Firenze *07476*
Società Italiana di Chirurgia d'Urgenza, di Pronto Soccorso e di Terapia Intensiva Chirurgica, Milano *07477*
Società Italiana di Chirurgia Estetica, Roma *07478*
Società Italiana di Chirurgia Pediatrica, Roma *07479*
Società Italiana di Chirurgia Plastica, Verona *07480*
Società Italiana di Chirurgia Toracica, Roma *07481*
Società Italiana di Ingegneria, Aerofotogrammetria e Topografia, Roma *07510*
Società Italiana di Medicina del Traffico, Roma *07516*
Società Italiana di Neurochirurgia, Ancona *07533*
Società Italiana di Odontostomatologia e Chirurgia Maxillo-Facciale, L'Aquila *07542*
Società Italiana Medico-Chirurgica di Pronto Soccorso, Bologna *07584*
Società Italiana Organi Artificiali, Roma *07586*
Società Jonico-Salentina de Medicina e Chirurgia, Taranto *07603*
Società Medica Chirurgica di Bologna, Bologna *07610*
Società Medico-Chirugica, Bari *07611*
Società Medico-Chirurgica di Ferrara, Ferrara *07612*
Società Medico-Chirurgica di Modena, Modena *07613*
Società Napoletana di Chirurgia, Napoli *07616*
Società Romana di Chirurgia, Roma *07637*

Japan
Japanese Society for Stereotactic and Functional Neurosurgery, Tokyo *07744*
Nihon Koko Geka Gakkai, Tokyo *07816*
Nihon Kyobu Geka Gakkai, Tokyo *07824*
Nippon Geka Gakkai, Tokyo *07896*
Nippon No-Shinkei Gek Gakkai, Tokyo *07950*

Kenya
Association of Surgeons of East Africa, Nairobi *08079*

Mexico
Asociación Panamericana de Cirurgía Pediátrica, México *08278*

Netherlands
Nederlandse Vereniging van Neurochirurgen, Rotterdam *08574*
Nederlandse Vereniging voor Heelkunde, Utrecht *08586*
Nederlandse Vereniging voor Mondziekten en Kaakchirurgie, Den Haag *08595*
Nederlandse Vereniging voor Thoraxchirurgie, Groningen *08604*
World Federation of Neurosurgical Societies, Nijmegen *08665*

Norway
Norsk Kirurgisk Forening, Lysaker *08831*

Pakistan
College of Physicians and Surgeons Pakistan, Karachi *08896*

Peru
Academia Peruana de Cirurgía, Lima *08972*

Poland
Towarzystwo Chirurgów Polskich, Warszawa *09152*

Romania
Societatea de Chirurgie, Bucuresti *09287*
Societatea Romana de Neurochirurgie, Bucuresti *09322*

Russia
National Scientific Medical Society of Neurosurgeons, Moskva *09410*
National Scientific Medical Society of Surgeons, Moskva *09422*
National Scientific Medical Society of Traumatic Surgeons and Orthopaedists, Moskva *09425*
National Scientific Society of Urological Surgeons, Moskva *09427*

Singapore
Asian-Pacific Association for Laser Medicine and Surgery, Singapore *09524*
Asian Pacific Section of the International Confederation for Plastic and Reconstructive Surgery, Singapore *09527*

South Africa
Association of Surgeons of South Africa, Johannesburg *09610*

Spain
Academia Médico-Quirúrgica Española, Madrid *09726*
Real Academia de Medicina y Cirugía de Palma de Mallorca, Palma de Mallorca *09789*
Sociedad Española de Cirugía Plástica, Reparadora y Estética, Madrid *09815*

Sweden
Svensk Kirurgisk Förening, Uppsala *09954*

Switzerland
European Association for Cardio-Thoracic Surgery, Zürich *10094*
European Council of Coloproctology, Genève *10104*
International Federation of Surgical Colleges, Bogis-Bossey *10170*
Schweizerische Gesellschaft für Otorhinolaryngologie, Hals- und Gesichtschirurgie, Sankt Gallen *10322*
Société Internationale de Chirurgie, Reinach *10505*
Société Suisse de Chirurgie, Lausanne *10511*

Thailand
ASEAN Federation of Plastic Surgeons, Bangkok *10615*

Turkey
Türk Cerrahi Cemiyeti, Istanbul *10698*

United Kingdom
Association of Surgeons of Great Britain and Ireland, London *10922*
British Association for Accident and Emergency Medicine, London *11007*
British Association of Clinical Anatomists, Manchester *11025*
British Association of Cosmetic Surgeons, London *11026*
British Association of Hair Transplant Surgeons, Birmingham *11030*
British Association of Oral and Maxillofacial Surgeons, London *11035*
British Association of Otorhinolaryngologists, Head and Neck Surgeons, London *11037*
British Association of Paediatric Surgeons, Edinburgh *11038*
British Association of Plastic Surgeons, London *11040*
British Association of Surgical Oncology, London *11045*
British Association of Urological Surgeons, London *11048*
British Institute of Surgical Technologists, Sevenoaks *11106*
British Society for Surgery of the Hand, London *11180*
European Academy of Facial Plastic Surgery, London *11470*
Faculty of Dental Surgery, London *11515*
National Society for Transplant Surgery, Cardiff *12025*
Royal College of Physicians and Surgeons of Glasgow, Glasgow *12190*
The Royal College of Surgeons of Edinburgh, Edinburgh *12194*
Royal College of Surgeons of England, London *12195*
Society of British Neurological Surgeons, Manchester *12413*
Society of Thoracic and Cardiovascular Surgeons of Great Britain and Ireland, Conventry *12446*
Surgical Research Society, Glasgow *12483*
Transplantation Society, London *12511*

Uruguay
Ateneo de Clínica Quirúrgica, Montevideo *12616*
Sociedad de Cirugía del Uruguay, Montevideo *12633*

U.S.A.
Academy of Ambulatory Foot Surgery, Tuscaloosa *12648*
American Academy of Cosmetic Surgery, Chicago *12747*
American Academy of Dental Electrosurgery, New York *12749*
American Academy of Facial Plastic and Reconstructive Surgery, Washington *12755*
American Academy of Neurological Surgery, Ann Arbor *12770*
American Academy of Orthopaedic Surgeons, Rosemont *12777*
American Association for Hand Surgery, Arlington Heights *12836*
American Association for Thoracic Surgery, Manchester *12855*
American Association of Genito-Urinary Surgeons, Charlottesville *12891*
American Association of Neurological Surgeons, Park Ridge *12909*
American Association of Plastic Surgeons, Bryn Mawr *12920*
American Association of Tissue Banks, McLean *12943*
American Board of Abdominal Surgery, Melrose *12970*
American Board of Colon and Rectal Surgery, Taylor *12974*
American Board of Neurological Surgery, Houston *12982*
American Board of Orthopedic Surgery, Chapel Hill *12990*
American Board of Plastic Surgery, Philadelphia *12997*
American Board of Podiatric Surgery, San Francisco *12999*
American Board of Surgery, Philadelphia *13006*
American Board of Thoracic Surgery, Evanston *13007*
American Clinical and Climatological Association, Rochester *13034*
American College of Cryosurgery, Schaumburg *13043*
American College of Foot and Ankle Surgeons, Park Ridge *13048*
American College of MOHS Micrographic Surgery and Cutaneous Oncology, Schaumburg *13055*
American College of Osteopathic Family Physicians, Arlington Heights *13065*
American College of Osteopathic Surgeons, Alexandria *13069*
American College of Surgeons, Chicago *13077*
American Fracture Association, Bloomington *13161*
American Laryngological Association, Boston *13240*
American Society for Aesthetic Plastic Surgery, Long Beach *13369*
American Society for Dermatologic Surgery, Schaumburg *13381*
American Society for Head and Neck Surgery, Pittsburgh *13388*
American Society for Laser Medicine and Surgery, Wausau *13395*
American Society for Surgery of the Hand, Englewood *13413*
American Society of Abdominal Surgeons, Melrose *13420*
American Society of Cataract and Refractive Surgery, Fairfax *13431*
American Society of Colon and Rectal Surgeons, Arlington Heights *13438*
American Society of Maxillofacial Surgeons, Arlington Heights *13470*
American Society of Plastic and Reconstructive Surgeons, Arlington Heights *13482*
American Surgical Association, Manchester *13510*
Association for Academic Surgery, Minneapolis *13591*
Association for Surgical Education, Salt Lake City *13669*
Association of American Physicians and Surgeons, Tucson *13720*
Association of Bone and Joint Surgeons, Rosemont *13742*
Association of Military Surgeons of the U.S., Bethesda *13798*
Association of Physician Assistants in Cardiovascular Surgery, Reston *13816*
Association of Surgical Technologists, Englewood *13842*
Collegium Internationale Chirurgiae Digestivae, Milwaukee *14108*
Congress of Neurological Surgeons, Atlanta *14170*
Inter-American College of Physicians and Surgeons, New York *14736*
International Academy of Chest Physicians and Surgeons, Northbrook *14762*
International Association of Endocrine Surgeons, San Francisco *14845*
International Association of Ocular Surgeons, Skokie *14863*
International Association of Oral and Maxillofacial Surgeons, Richmond *14865*
International Bone Marrow Transplant Group, Milwaukee *14887*
International College of Surgeons, Chicago *14921*
International Federation of Societies of Endoscopic Surgeons, Philadelphia *15026*
International Federation of Surgical Colleges, Philadelphia *15030*
International Society for Cardiovascular Surgery, Manchester *15197*
International Society for Dermatologic Surgery, Schaumburg *15201, 15202*
International Society for Heart and Lung Transplantation, Dallas *15212*
International Society of Aesthetic Plastic Surgery, Hershey *15266*
International Society of Arthroscopy, Knee Surgery and Orthopaedic Sports Medicine, Rosemont *15274*
International Society of Refractive Surgery, Minneapolis *15308*
International Society of University Colon and Rectal Surgeons, New Orleans *15314*
International Stereotactic Radiosurgery Society, Pittsburgh *15328*
National College of Foot Surgeons, Woodland Hills *15795*
Neurosurgical Society of America, Cleveland *16011*
North American Federation of the International College of Surgeons, Shreveport *16040*
Pacific Association of Pediatric Surgeons, Washington *16113*
Pan-Pacific Surgical Association, Honolulu *16144*
Plastic Surgery Research Council, Pittsburgh *16177*
Society for Vascular Surgery, Manchester *16485*
Society of Head and Neck Surgeons, Arlington *16528*
Society of Neurological Surgeons, Boston *16542*
Society of Pelvic Surgeons, New York *16545*
Society of Thoracic Surgeons, Chicago *16563*
Society of United States Air Force Flight Surgeons, Brooks Air Force Base *16566*
Society of University Surgeons, West Haven *16567*
Surgical Eye Expeditions International, Santa Barbara *16617*
Western Surgical Association, Louisville *16757*
World Federation of Associations of Pediatric Surgeons, Kansas City *16812*
World Federation of Neurosurgical Societies, Charlottesville *16813*
World Society for Stereotactic and Functional Neurosurgery, Houston *16838*

Venezuela
Sociedad Venezolana de Cirugía, Caracas *16926*
Sociedad Venezolana de Cirugía Plástica y Reconstrucción, Caracas *16927*
Sociedad Venezolana de Cirugía Ortopédica y Traumatología, Caracas *16928*

Vietnam
Vietnamese Association of Neurology, Psychiatry and Neurosurgery, Hanoi *16961*
Vietnamese Association of Surgery, Hanoi *16974*

Surveying, Photogrammetry s. a. Cartography

Argentina
Asociación Argentina de Geofísicos y Geodestas, Buenos Aires *00045*

Australia
Australian Institute of Quantity Surveyors, Deakin West *00206*

Austria
Österreichische Geodätische Kommission, Wien *00594*
Österreichische Gesellschaft für Vermessung und Geoinformation, Wien *00693*

Belgium
Société Belge de Photogrammétrie, de Télédétection et de Cartographie, Bruxelles *01249*
Union Belge des Géomètres-Experts Immobiliers, Bruxelles *01303*

Bulgaria
Union of Surveyors and Land Managers, Sofia *01604*

Chile
Sociedad Chilena de Fotogrametría y Percepción Remota, Santiago *02487*

China, People's Republic
Chinese Society of Geodesy, Photogrammetry and Cartography, Beijing *02627*

Colombia
Centro Interamericano de Fotointerpretación, Bogotá *02777*
Servicio Interamericana de Geodesía, Bogotá *02805*

Cyprus
Cyprus Photogrammetric Society, Nicosia *02905*

Denmark
Dansk Selskab for Fotogrammetri og Landmåling, Ålborg *03060*
International Association of Geodesy, København *03131*

Finland
Maanmittaustieteiden Seura, Helsinki *03363*

France
Comité National Français de Géodesie et Géophysique, Paris *03727*
Ordre des Géomètres-Experts, Paris *03929*
Société Française de Photogrammétrie et de Télédétection, Saint-Mandé *04155*

Germany
Bayerische Kommission für die Internationale Erdmessung, München *04531*
Deutsche Geodätische Kommission, München *04741*
Deutsche Gesellschaft für Photogrammetrie und Fernerkundung e.V., Berlin *04839*
Deutscher Verein für Vermessungswesen e.V., Heidelberg *05063*
GEO-KART, Oberkochen *05316*
Institut für Angewandte Geodäsie, Frankfurt *05518*

Hungary
Magyar Földmérési, Térképészeti és Távérzélési Társaság, Budapest *06309*

Ireland
Society of Chartered Surveyors in the Republic of Ireland, Dublin *06667*

Italy
Società di Fotogrammetria e Topografia, Milano *07403*
Società Italiana di Fotogrammetria e Topografia, Milano *07501*

Subject Index: Surveying, Photogrammetry 486

Japan

Nippon Shashin Sokuryo Gakkai, Tokyo *07979*
Nippon Sokuchi Gakkai, Ibaraki *07992*

Malawi

Geological Survey of Malawi, Zomba *08209*

Malaysia

Geological Survey of Malaysia, Ipoh *08224*

Netherlands

Nederlandse Vereniging voor Geodesie, Apeldoorn *08585*

Portugal

Associação Portuguesa de Fotogrametria, Lisboa *09181*

South Africa

Aerial Survey, Photogrammetric and Remote Sensing Research Group, Durban *09604*

Switzerland

Fachgruppe für Vermessung und Kulturtechnik (Deutsch-Schweiz) des STV, Weiningen *10120*
Schweizerischer Verein für Vermessung und Kulturtechnik, Solothurn *10483*
Verband Schweizerischer Vermessungsfachleute, Burgdorf *10541*

United Kingdom

Architects and Surveyors Institute, Chippenham *10785*
Association of British Geodesists, Dagenham *10851*
Commonwealth Association on Surveying and Land Economy, London *11319*
London Subterranean Survey Association, London *11891*
The Photogrammetric Society, London *12103*
Royal Institution of Chartered Surveyors, London *12221*

U.S.A.

American Association for Geodetic Surveying, Bethesda *12834*
American Congress on Surveying and Mapping, Bethesda *13092*
American Society for Photogrammetry and Remote Sensing, Bethesda *13405*
Management Association for Private Photogrammetric Surveyors, Reston *15521*
National Association of Marine Surveyors, Chesapeake *15712*
Surveyors Historical Society, Lawrenceburg *16618*

Zimbabwe

Survey Institute of Zimbabwe, Harare *17081*

Tea
s. Coffee, Tea, Cocoa

Textiles

Argentina

Federación Lanera Argentina, Buenos Aires *00074*

Australia

Australian Wool Corporation, Parkville *00250*

Belgium

Association Internationale des Laboratoires Textiles Lainiers, Bruxelles *00969*
European Association for Textile Polyolefins, Bruxelles *01090*

Bulgaria

Scientific and Technical Union of Textiles, Clothing and Leather, Sofia *01586*

Canada

Institute of Textile Science, Sainte-Anne-de-Bellevue *02143*

China, People's Republic

Chinese Textile Engineering Society, Beijing *02641*

France

Association Interprofessionnelle pour la Formation Permanente dans le Commerce Textile, Paris *03605*
Centre de Perfectionnement des Industries Textiles Rhône-Alpes, Lyon *03676*
Centre International d'Etude des Textiles Anciens, Lyon *03689*

Germany

Deutsches Textilforschungszentrum Nord-West e.V., Krefeld *05104*
Deutsches Wollforschungsinstitut, Aachen *05107*
Fachinformationszentrum Technik e.V., Frankfurt *05203*
Fachverband Textilunterricht e.V., Münster *05210*
Forschungskuratorium Gesamttextil, Eschborn *05254*
Institut für Chemiefasern, Denkendorf *05523*
Institut für Textil- und Faserforschung Stuttgart, Denkendorf *05543*
Normenausschuss Textil und Textilmaschinen im DIN Deutsches Institut für Normung e.V., Berlin *05847*

Hungary

Textilipari Müszaki és Tudományos Egyesület, Budapest *06359*

India

Ahmedabad Textile Industry's Research Association, Ahmadabad *06394*
Mumbai Textile Research Association, Mumbai *06508*
Silk and Art Silk Mills' Research Association, Mumbai *06529*
South India Textile Research Association, Coimbatore *06533*

Italy

Associazione Italiana di Chimica Tessile e Coloristica, Milano *06941*
Associazione per lo Sviluppo di Studi e Ricerche nell'Industria Tessile Laniera Oreste Rivetti, Biella *07034*
Tecnotessile, Prato *07663*

Norway

Teko Teknisk Forening, Fantoft *08888*

Switzerland

Internationale Föderation der Vereine der Textilchemiker und Coloristen, Reinach *10182*

United Kingdom

International Wool Secretariat, London *11833*
The Textile Institute, Manchester *12493*

U.S.A.

American Association for Textile Technology, Gastonia *12849*
American Association of Textile Chemists and Colorists, Research Triangle Park *12942*
Costume Society of America, Earleville *14200*
Educational Foundation for the Fashion Industries, New York *14355*
International Centre for Textile Research and Development, Lubbock *14904*
International Textile and Apparel Association, Monument *15339*
National Council for Textile Education, Atlanta *15826*

Theater
s. Performing Arts, Theater

Theology
s. Religions and Theology

Therapeutics
s. a. Psychiatry; Rehabilitation; Psychology

Argentina

Sociedad Argentina de Farmacología y Terapéutica, Buenos Aires *00092*

Australia

Australian Association of Occupational Therapists, Alphington *00165*
Australian Physiotherapy Association, Concord *00222*
Australian Society of Clinical Hypnotherapists, Eastwood *00238*

Austria

Arbeitsgemeinschaft Personenzentrierte Psychotherapie und Gesprächsführung, Wien *00410*
Gesellschaft für Logotherapie und Existenzanalyse, Wien *00473*
Österreichische Ärztegesellschaft für Psychotherapie, Wien *00569*
Österreichische ärztliche Gesellschaft für medizinisches und technisches Ozon, Wien *00572*
Österreichische Gesellschaft für Autogenes Training und allgemeine Psychotherapie, Wien *00615*
Österreichische Gesellschaft für Bionome Psychotherapie, Wien *00618*
Österreichische medizinische Gesellschaft für Neuraltherapie nach Huneke-Regulationsforschung, Graz *00719*
Österreichischer Arbeitskreis für Gruppentherapie und Gruppendynamik, Wien *00747*

Belgium

European Family Therapy Association, Bruxelles *01153*
Vlaams Kinesitherapeuten Verbond, Poperinge *01316*

Bulgaria

Bulgarian Society of Sports Medicine and Kinesitherapy, Sofia *01572*

Canada

Alberta Association of Registered Occupational Therapists, Edmonton *01621*
Association of Occupational Therapists of Manitoba, Winnipeg *01720*
British Columbia Art Therapy Association, Duncan *01743*
British Columbia Society of Occupational Therapists, Vancouver *01756*
British Columbia Society of Respiratory Therapists, Vancouver *01757*
Canadian Association for Music Therapy, Waterloo *01801*
Canadian Group Psychotherapy Association, Whitby *01894*
International Phototherapy Association, Vancouver *02156*
Manitoba Society of Occupational Therapists, Winnipeg *02200*
Newfoundland and Labrador Association of Occupational Therapists, Saint John's *02237*
Nova Scotia Society of Occupational Therapists, Halifax *02260*
Ontario Society of Occupational Therapists, Toronto *02298*
Pacific Coast Family Therapy Training Association, Vancouver *02306*
Saskatchewan Society of Occupational Therapists, Saskatoon *02363*

China, Republic

China Spiritual Therapy Study Association, Taipei *02685*

Denmark

Danske Fysioterapeuter, København *03090*
Landsforeningen af Foldterapeuter, København *03156*

Finland

Suomen Fysioterapeuttiliitto, Helsinki *03398*

France

Confédération Européenne pour la Thérapie Physique, Paris *03749*
European Brachytherapy Group, Villejuif *03806*
Institut Français d'Analyse de Groupe et de Psychodrame, Paris *03883*
Société de Recherches Psychothérapiques de Langue Française, Versailles *04007*
Société Française de Médecine Orthopédique et Thérapeutique Manuelle, Paris *04136*
Société Française de Mesothérapie, Paris *04139*
Société Française de Thérapeutique et de Pharmacologe Clinique, Paris *04166*
Syndicat National des Médecins Ostéothérapeutes Français, Nancy *04283*
Union Internationale Thérapeutique, Paris *04317*

Germany

Ärztliche Gesellschaft für Physiotherapie, Kneippärztebund e.V., Bad Münstereifel *04367*
Allgemeine Ärztliche Gesellschaft für Psychotherapie, Düsseldorf *04413*
Bundeselternvereinigung für anthroposophische Heilpädagogik und Sozialtherapie e.V., Echzell *04637*
Bundesverband für Tanztherapie Deutschland e.V., Monheim *04664*
Bundesverband Hilfe für das autistische Kind e.V., Hamburg *04665*
Dachverband Psychosozialer Hilfsvereinigungen e.V., Bonn *04700*
Deutsche Gesellschaft für Musiktherapie e.V., Berlin *04823*
Deutsche Gesellschaft für Poesie- und Bibliotherapie e.V., Köln *04845*
Deutsche Gesellschaft für Verhaltenstherapie e.V., Tübingen *04874*
Deutsche Gruppenpsychotherapeutische Gesellschaft e.V., Berlin *04894*
Deutscher Verband für Physiotherapie, Köln *05055*
Gesellschaft für prä- und postoperative Tumortherapie e.V., Undenheim *05395*
Gesellschaft für Psychotherapie, Psychosomatik und Medizinische Psychologie e.V., Leipzig *05398*
Verband für anthroposophische Heilpädagogik, Sozialtherapie und soziale Arbeit e.V., Echzell *06064*
Verband Physikalische Therapie, Hamburg *06069*

Italy

Associazione Medica Italiana di Idroclimatologia, Talassologia e Terapia Fisica, Roma *06994*
Centro di Ricerche Biopsichiche di Padova, Padova *07059*
Centro Internazionale di Ipnosi Medica e Psicologica, Milano *07066*
European Society of Hypnosis in Psychotherapy and Psychosomatic Medicine-Italian Constituent Society, Verona *07269*
International Society for Medical and Psychological Hypnosis, Milano *07325*
Istituto Italiano Studi di Ipnosi Clinica e Psicoterapia, Verona *07357*
Società Italiana di Chemioterapia, Pavia *07472*
Società Italiana di Medicina Subacquea ed Iperbarica, Napoli *07525*
Società Italiana di Mesoterapia, Roma *07527*
Società Italiana di Psicosintesi Terapeutica, Firenze *07562*
Società Italiana di Psicoterapia Analitica Immaginativa, Cremona *07563*
Società Italiana di Terapia Familiare, Roma *07577*
Società Italiana Medica del Training Autogeno, Bologna *07582*

Netherlands

Nederlands Genootschap voor Fysiotherapie, Amersfoort *08538*

Norway

Norske Fysioterapeuters Forbund, Oslo *08854*

Portugal

Associação Portuguesa de Fisioterapeutas, Lisboa *09180*

Romania

Societatea de Anestezie si Terapie Intensiva, Bucuresti *09284*

Russia

National Scientific Medical Society of Therapists, Moskva *09423*

Saint Lucia

Caribbean Association for Rehabilitation Therapists, Castries *09483*

South Africa

The South African Society of Physiotherapy, Johannesburg *09706*

Sweden

Förbundet Sveriges Arbetsterapeuter, Nacka *09877*
Legitimerade Sjukgymnasters Riksförbund, Stockholm *09915*

Switzerland

ErgotherapeutInnen-Verband Schweiz, Zürich *10088*
Gesellschaft für Arzneipflanzenforschung e.V., Zürich *10134*
Institut International de Psychologie et de Psychothérapie Charles Baudouin, Coppet *10161*
International Federation for Psychotherapy, Bern *10169*
Schweizerische Gesellschaft für Schicksalsanalytische Therapie, Reichenburg *10333*
Schweizerische Gesellschaft für Verhaltenstherapie, Conthey *10345*
Schweizerischer Physiotherapeuten-Verband, Sempach-Stadt *10456*

Thailand

Asian-Pacific Federation of Therapeutic Communities, Bangkok *10632*

Turkey

Fizik Tedavi ve Rehabilitasyon Derneği, Istanbul *10691*

United Kingdom

Association for Group and Individual Psychotherapy, London *10805*
Association of Child Psychotherapists, London *10859*
Association of Swimming Therapy, Shrewsbury *10923*
British Association for Counselling, Rugby *11013*
British Association of Art Therapists, Brighton *11023*
British Association of Psychotherapists, London *11041*
British Hypnotherapy Association, London *11093*
British Institute of Industrial Therapy, Southampton *11098*
British Society for Antimicrobial Chemotherapy, Birmingham *11165*
British Society for Music Therapy, East Barnet *11173*
British Society of Hypnotherapists, London *11195*
The Chartered Society of Physiotherapy, London *11280*
European Association for Behaviour and Cognitive Therapies, Harrow *11472*
International Federation of Practitioners of Natural Therapeutics, London *11791*
National Council of Psycho-Therapists, London *12001*
Research Society for Natural Therapeutics, Bournemouth *12156*
Society of Health and Beauty Therapists, London *12429*
Society of Remedial Gymnasts and Recreational Therapies, Cardiff *12442*
World Medical Tennis Association, Poole *12589*

U.S.A.

Academy of Scientific Hypnotherapy, San Diego *12673*
Ackerman Institute for Family Therapy, New York *12686*
American Academy of Psychotherapists, Decatur *12793*
American Apitherapy Society, Red Bank *12813*
American Art Therapy Association, Mundelein *12816*
American Association for Marriage and Family Therapy, Washington *12841*
American Association for Music Therapy, Valley Forge *12843*
American Association of Behavioral Therapists, Ormond Beach *12861*
American Association of Professional Hypnotherapists, Boones Mill *12924*
American Dance Therapy Association, Columbia *13115*
American Family Therapy Association, Washington *13142*
American Group Psychotherapy Association, New York *13172*
American Horticultural Therapy Association, Gaithersburg *13187*
American Massage Therapy Association, Evanston *13257*
American Occupational Therapy Association, Bethesda *13291*
American Osteopathic Academy of Sclerotherapy, Wilmington *13306*
American Physical Therapy Association, Alexandria *13328*
American Society of Group Psychotherapy and Psychodrama, McLean *13454*
Association for the Advancement of Psychotherapy, Bronx *13678*
The Bridge, New York *13945*
Community Guidance Service, New York *14144*
Council on Chiropractic Physiological Therapeutics, Delray Beach *14245*
Foundation for Advancement in Cancer Therapy, New York *14458*
Institute for Expressive Analysis, New York *14669*
Institute for Rational-Emotive Therapy, New York *14682*
International Society for Rheumatic Therapeutics, Boston *15247*
International Society of Educators of Physical Therapy, Honolulu *15287*
Joint Review Committee for Respiratory Therapy Education, Euless *15449*
National Association for Poetry Therapy, Port Washington *15654*
National Board for Respiratory Care, Lenexa *15762*
National Therapeutic Recreation Society, Arlington *15990*

487 Subject Index: Urban and Regional Planning

Rabbinic Center for Research and Counseling, Westfield *16236*
Radiation Therapy Oncology Group, Philadelphia *16239*
Society for Clinical and Experimental Hypnosis, Liverpool *16365*
Therapy Dogs International, Mendham *16640*
World Federation of Therapeutic Communities, New York *16819*

Tobacco

France

Centre de Coopération pour les Recherches Scientifiques Relatives au Tabac, Paris *03675*

Topography s. Surveying, Photogrammetry

Tourism s. Travel and Tourism

Toxicology

Argentina

Sociedad de Medicina Legal y Toxicologia, Buenos Aires *00107*

Belgium

Association Européenne des Centres de Lutte contre les Poisons, Bruxelles *00958*
European Centre for Ecotoxicology and Toxicology of Chemicals, Bruxelles *01118*

France

Association Internationale de Recherche en Informatique Toxicologique, Paris *03574*
Association pour le Développement de la Recherche en Toxicologie Expérimentale, Paris *03642*
Comité Européen Permanent de Recherches pour la Protection des Populations contre les Risques d'Intoxication à Long Terme, Paris *03714*
Société de Médecine Légale et de Criminologie de France, Paris *03989*
Société Française de Toxicologie, Paris *04167*

Germany

Deutsche Gesellschaft für Pharmakologie und Toxikologie, Darmstadt *04837*
Gesellschaft zur Förderung der Lufthygiene und Silikoseforschung e.V., Düsseldorf *05429*

Italy

Società Italiana di Tossicologia, Milano *07578*

Russia

National Scientific Medical Society of Toxicologists, St. Petersburg *09424*

Switzerland

Conseil International sur les Problèmes de l'Alcoolisme et des Toxicomanies, Lausanne *10073*
Ecological and Toxicological Association of the Dyestuffs Manufacturing Industry, Basel *10085*

United Kingdom

Society for Environmental Therapy, Manchester *12356*

U.S.A.

American Association of Poison Control Centers, Washington *12921*
American College of Medical Toxicology, Harrisburg *13054*
Chemical Industry Institute of Toxicology, Research Triangle Park *14053*
Ecological and Toxicological Association of Dyes and Organic Pigments Manufacturers, Washington *14339*
International Association of Forensic Toxicologists, Newport Beach *14848*
International Federation of Societies of Toxicologic Pathologists, Suffern *15027*
International Society of Regulatory Toxicology and Pharmacology, Columbia *15309*
International Society on Toxinology, Stillwater *15319*
Society of Toxicology, Reston *16564*
Teratology Society, Bethesda *16634*

Trade s. Commerce

Transport and Traffic

Australia

Chartered Institute of Transport in Australia, Sydney *00257*
Institute of Transport, Beverly Hills *00297*

Austria

Forschungsgesellschaft für das Verkehrs- und Straßenwesen im ÖIAV, Wien *00445*
Kuratorium für Verkehrssicherheit, Wien *00551*
Österreichische Gesellschaft für Strassenwesen, Wien *00686*
Österreichische Verkehrswissenschaftliche Gesellschaft, Wien *00742*

Belgium

Dedicated Road Infrastructure for Vehicle Safety in Europe, Bruxelles *01067*

Bulgaria

Scientific and Technical Union of Transport, Sofia *01588*

Canada

Canadian Urban Transit Association, Toronto *02020*
Traffic Injury Research Foundation of Canada, Ottawa *02403*
Transport 2000 Canada, Ottawa *02404*

China, People's Republic

Chinese Railway Society, Beijing *02604*

Denmark

Orlogsmuseetsvenner – Marinehistorisk Selskab, København *03185*

Egypt

Arab Institute of Navigation, Alexandria *03260*

France

Association pour le Développement des Techniques de Transport, d'Environnement et de Circulation, Paris *03648*
Conference on the Development and the Planning of Urban Transport in Developing Countries, La Défense *03761*
Société d'Etudes Ferroviaires, Paris *04063*

Germany

Arbeitskreis Verkehr und Umwelt e.V., Berlin *04498*
Deutsche Straßenliga e.V., Bonn *04964*
Deutsche Verkehrswissenschaftliche Gesellschaft e.V., Bergisch Gladbach *04979*
Deutscher Verkehrssicherheitsrat e.V., Bonn *05065*
Forschungsgesellschaft für Strassen- und Verkehrswesen e.V., Köln *05242*
Freie Vereinigung von Fachleuten öffentlicher Verkehrsbetriebe, Gelsenkirchen *05291*
Gesellschaft für Ursachenforschung bei Verkehrsunfällen e.V., Köln *05414*
Normenausschuss Transportkette im DIN Deutsches Institut für Normung e.V., Berlin *05848*
SNV Studiengesellschaft Verkehr, Hamburg *05948*
Studiengesellschaft für den kombinierten Verkehr e.V., Frankfurt *05966*
Studiengesellschaft für unterirdische Verkehrsanlagen e.V., Köln *05969*
VDI-Gesellschaft Fahrzeug- und Verkehrstechnik, Düsseldorf *06006*
Verein für europäische Binnenschiffahrt und Wasserstraßen e.V., Duisburg *06085*
Wissenschaftlicher Verein für Verkehrswesen e.V., Dortmund *06161*

Hungary

Közlekedéstudományi Egyesület, Budapest *06294*

Italy

Centro Italiano Ricerche e Studi Trasporto Aereo, Roma *07090*
Centro Italiano Studi Containers, Genova *07091*
Collegio degli Ingegneri Ferroviari Italiani, Roma *07190*

Japan

Nihon Kotsu Kyokai Toshokan, Tokyo *07823*
Un-yu Chosakyoku Johobu Toshoshitsu, Tokyo *08047*

Netherlands

Nederlandse Vereniging voor Zeegeschiedenis, Leiden *08609*

Norway

Institute of Transport Economics, Oslo *08792*
Nordic Road Safety Council, Oslo *08801*

Russia

Society for Railway Transport, Moskva *09458*

Spain

Instituto de Historia y Cultura Naval, Madrid *09766*

Switzerland

Schweizerische Verkehrswirtschaftliche Gesellschaft, Sankt Gallen *10422*
Schweizerischer Ausschuss für Prüfung und Zertifizierung, Zürich *10434*
Schweizerischer Verkehrssicherheitsrat, Bern *10484*

United Kingdom

Barge and Canal Development Association, Wakefield *10951*
Birmingham Transport Historical Group, Folkestone *10976*
Branch Line Society, Huddersfield *10990*
British Trolleybus Society, Reading *11206*
Cambridge Refrigeration Technology, Cambridge *11245*
Chartered Institute of Transport, London *11275*
County Surveyors Society, Northampton *11366*
Electric Railway Society, Sutton Coldfield *11442*
Great Western Society, Didcot *11583*
London Underground Railway Society, Morden *11893*
Narrow Gauge Railway Society, Huddersfield *11971*
National Association for Road Safety Instruction in Schools, London *11978*
National Trolleybus Association, Bedford *12027*
Omnibus Society, London *12063*
Organisation of Teachers of Transport Studies, Southall *12070*
Railway Correspondence and Travel Society, London *12143*
Railway Development Association, Purley *12144*
Scottish Inland Waterways Association, Edinburgh *12308*
Scottish Tramway Museum Society, Glasgow *12324*
Stephenson Locomotive Society, London *12476*
Tramway Museum Society, Matlock *12509*
Transport Ticket Society, Tunbridge Wells *12512*

U.S.A.

Advanced Transit Association, Escondido *12695*
Committee for Better Transit, Long Island City *14121*
Electric Auto Association, Mountain View *14363*
Institute of Transportation Engineers, Washington *14727*
International Association of Institutes of Navigation, Warrenton *14856*
International Naval Research Organization, Radford *15115*
Lexington Group in Transportation History, Saint Cloud University *15498*
Safe Association, Nashville *16287*
Society of Freight Car Historians, Monrovia *16525*
Transportation Alternatives, New York *16649*
Transportation Research Board, Washington *16650*

Traumatology

Argentina

Asociación Argentina de Ortopedía y Traumatología, Buenos Aires *00048*

Belgium

Société Internationale de Chirurgie Orthopédique et de Traumatologie, Bruxelles *01268*

Chile

Sociedad Chilena de Ortopedía y Traumatología, Santiago *02499*

Colombia

Sociedad Colombiana de Cirugía Ortopedica y Traumatología, Bogotá *02813*

France

Groupement National d'Etude des Médecins du Bâtiment et des Travaux Publics, Paris *03878*
International Research Council on Biokinetics of Impacts, Bron *03906*
Société Française de Chirurgie Orthopédique et Traumatologique, Paris *04119*

Hungary

Magyar Traumatológus Társaság, Budapest *06342*

Italy

Società di Ortopedia e Traumatologia dell'Istituto Meridionale ed Insulare, Napoli *07408*
Società Italiana di Medicina del Traffico, Roma *07516*
Società Italiana di Ortopedia e Traumatologia, Roma *07544*
Società Italiana di Traumatologia della Strada, Roma *07579*
Società Piemontese, Ligure, Lombarda di Ortopedia e Traumatologia, Genova *07631*

Peru

Sociedad Peruana de Ortopedia y Traumatología, Lima *09017*

Poland

Polskie Towarzystwo Ortopedyczne i Traumatologiczne, Warszawa *09130*

Portugal

Sociedade Portuguesa de Ortopedia e Traumatologia, Lisboa *09245*

Romania

Societatea Românâ de Ortopedie şi Traumatologie, Bucuresti *09323*

Switzerland

Schweizerische Gesellschaft für Traumatologie und Versicherungsmedizin, Luzern *10339*

Turkey

Türk Ortopedi ve Travmatoloji Dernegi, Istanbul *10712*

U.S.A.

American Burn Association, New York *13016*
American Trauma Society, Upper Marlboro *13521*
International Association for the Study of Traumatic Brain Injury, Columbia *14827*
International Society for Traumatic Stress Studies, Northbrook *15264*
Société internationale de recherche orthopédique et traumatologique, San Diego *16345*

Venezuela

Sociedad Venezolana de Cirurgía Ortopédica y Traumatología, Caracas *16928*

Travel and Tourism

Italy

Accademia Euro-Afro-Asiatica del Turismo, Catania *06815*
Centro per gli Studi sui Sistemi Distributivi e il Turismo, Milano *07104*
Centro Studi e Ricerche per la Conoscenza della Liguria Attraverso le Testimonianze dei Viaggiatori Stranieri, Genova *07152*
International Centre for Advanced Technical and Vocational Training, Torino *07314*

United Kingdom

British Association of the Experiment in International Living, Malvern *11047*
Institute of Leisure and Amenity Management, Reading *11696*
Leisure Studies Association, Edinburgh *11871*

U.S.A.

Southwest Parks and Monuments Association, Tucson *16589*

Tropical Medicine

Austria

Österreichische Gesellschaft für Tropenmedizin und Parasitologie, Wien *00687*

Belgium

Association pour l'Etude et l'Evaluation Epidémiologiques des Désastres dans les Pays en Voie de Développement, Bruxelles *00982*
Belgische Vereniging voor Tropische Geneeskunde, Antwerpen *00991*
Société Belge de Médecine Tropicale, Antwerpen *01244*

Egypt

Egyptian Society of Medicine and Tropical Hygiene, Alexandria *03288*

France

Société de Pathologie Exotique, Paris *03996*

Germany

Deutsche Tropenmedizinische Gesellschaft e.V., Hamburg *04967*

Netherlands

Nederlandse Vereniging voor Tropische Geneeskunde, Driebergen-Rijsenburg *08606*

Switzerland

Schweizerische Gesellschaft für Tropenmedizin und Parasitologie, Basel *10340*

United Kingdom

The Royal Society of Tropical Medicine and Hygiene, London *12262*

U.S.A.

American Society of Tropical Medicine and Hygiene, Northbrook *13496*
International Federation for Tropical Medicine, Toledo *15011*

Tuberculosis s. Pulmonary Disease

Urban and Regional Planning s. a. Architecture; Civil Engineering

Australia

Australian Institute of Urban Studies, Canberra *00208*
Royal Australian Planning Institute, Hawthorn *00338*

Austria

Arbeitskreis für neue Methoden in der Regionalforschung, Wien *00414*
Österreichische Gesellschaft für Raumplanung, Wien *00678*
Österreichische Raumordnungskonferenz, Wien *00732*

Belgium

Association Européenne des Institutions d'Aménagement Rural, Bruxelles *00960*
Conferentie voor Regionale Ontwikkeling in Noord-West-Europa, Brugge *01057*
European Association for Country Planning Institutions, Bruxelles *01085*
Koninklijke Vereniging voor Natuur- en Stedeschoon, Antwerpen *01224*
Société Belge des Urbanistes et Architectes Modernistes, Bruxelles *01255*

Canada

Association of Canadian University Planning Programs, Winnipeg *01712*
Atlantic Planning Institute, Halifax *01736*
Canadian Institute of Planners, Ottawa *01914*
Community Planning Association of Alberta, Calgary *02065*
Community Planning Association of Canada, Regina *02066*
Planning Institute of British Columbia, Richmond *02312*
Urban Development Institute of Canada, Vancouver *02406*

China, People's Republic

Chinese Society for Urban Studies, Beijing *02618*

China, Republic
International House Association, Taipei Chapter, Taipei 02729

Colombia
Centro Interamericano de Vivienda y Planeamiento, Bogotá 02778

Denmark
Byggecentrum, Hørsholm 02970
Dansk Byplanlaboratorium, København 02990
Nordisk Byggedag, København 03173

Egypt
General Organization for Housing and Building Research, Cairo 03291

France
Société Française des Urbanistes, Paris 04176

Germany
Akademie für Raumforschung und Landesplanung, Hannover 04396
Deutsche Akademie für Städtebau und Landesplanung, Berlin 04713
Deutsche Dekane- und Abteilungsleiterkonferenz für Architektur, Raumplanung und Landschaftsarchitektur, Hannover 04723
Deutsches Institut für Urbanistik (Difu), Berlin 05089
Gesellschaft für Regionalforschung e.V., Berlin 05403
Gesellschaft für Wohnungsrecht und Wohnungswirtschaft Köln e.V., Köln 05420
Vereinigung für Stadt-, Regional- und Landesplanung e.V., Berlin 06124

Greece
Constantine Porphyrogenetus, Zografou 06213
World Society for Ekistics, Athinai 06256

Italy
Associazione Nazionale degli Urbanisti, Treviso 07000
Centro Nazionale di Studi Urbanistici, Roma 07100
Centro Ricerche Urbanistiche e di Progettazione, Milano 07125
Istituto Nazionale di Urbanistica, Roma 07365

Jamaica
Commonwealth Association of Planners, Kingston 07693
Jamaica National Trust Commission, Kingston 07702

Japan
Nippon Toshi Keikaku Gakkai, Tokyo 08000
Toshi Kaihatsu Kyokai Joho Sabisu Senta Shiryoshitsu, Tokyo 08044

Netherlands
Bond van Nederlandse Stedebouwkundigen, Amsterdam 08404
International Federation for Housing and Planning, Den Haag 08486
International Society of City and Regional Planners, Den Haag 08494
Stichting Centrale Raad voor de Academies van Bouwkunst, Amsterdam 08623

Norway
Norsk Institutt for By- og Regionforskning, Oslo 08830

Pakistan
Pakistan Council of Architects and Town Planners, Karachi 08916

Philippines
ASEAN Association for Planning and Housing, Manila 09022

Poland
Towarzystwo Urbanistów Polskich, Warszawa 09165

Saudi Arabia
Arab Urban Development Institute, Riyadh 09489

Spain
Federación de Urbanismo y de la Vivienda, Madrid 09755

Sweden
Nordiska Institutet för Samhällsplanering, Stockholm 09929

Switzerland
Fachgruppe für Raumplanung und Umwelt des SIA, Zürich 10117
Schweizerische Studiengesellschaft für Raumordnungs- und Regionalpolitik, Bern 10390
Schweizerische Vereinigung für Landesplanung, Bern 10410

Turkey
Türk Mühendis ve Mimar Odalari Birligi, Ankara 10709

United Kingdom
European Council of Town Planners, London 11492
Institute of Municipal Building Management, Colwyn Bay 11706
London Society, London 11890
National Housing and Town Planning Council, London 12009
Open Spaces Society, Henley-on-Thames 12065
Planning Officers Society, Ashton-under-Lyne 12109
Regional Studies Association, London 12149
Royal Town Planning Institute, London 12267
Scottish National Housing and Town Planning Council, Troon 12312
Society of Town Planning Technicians, London 12447
Town and Country Planning Association, London 12508

U.S.A.
Association of Collegiate Schools of Planning, New York 13755
Center for Design Planning, Pemsacola 14004
Center for Urban and Regional Studies, Chapel Hill 14035
Community Associations Institute, Alexandria 14138
Constantine Porphyrogenetus, Chicago 14181
Environmental Design Research Association, Edmond 14381
International Institute for Suburban and Regional Studies, Baltimore 15073
National Association of County Planners, Washington 15690
National Council for Urban Economic Development, Washington 15830
Pacific Rim Council on Urban Development, Berkeley 16122
Regional Science Association International, Urbana 16257
Small Towns Institute, Ellensburg 16336
ULI – Urban Land Institute, Washington 16661
Urban Affairs Association, Newark 16715

Venezuela
Consejo Zuliano de Planificación y Coordinación, Maracaibo 16911

Yugoslavia
Urbanisticki Savez Jugoslavije, Novi Sad 17042

Urology

Austria
Österreichische Gesellschaft für Urologie, Wien 00691

Canada
Association des Urologues du Québec, Montréal 01692
Canadian Academy of Urological Surgeons, Toronto 01779
Canadian Urological Association, Winnipeg 02021

Chile
Sociedad Chilena de Urología, Santiago 02510

France
Association Française d'Urologie, Paris 03551
European Association of Urology, Paris 03804
Société Française d'Urologie, Paris 04193
Société Internationale d'Urologie, Paris 04211

Germany
Berufsverband der Deutschen Fachärzte für Urologie, Hamburg 04563
Berufsverband der Deutschen Urologen e.V., Dorfen 04565
Deutsche Gesellschaft für Urologie, Hannover 04872
Nordrhein-Westfälische Gesellschaft für Urologie, Osnabrück 05783

Italy
Società Italiana di Urodinamica, Bologna 07580
Società Italiana di Urologia, Roma 07581

Japan
Nihon Hinyokika Gakkai, Tokyo 07793
Nippon Hinyoki-ka Gakkai, Tokyo 07900

Netherlands
Nederlandse Vereniging voor Urologie, Utrecht 08607

Poland
Polskie Towarzystwo Urologiczne, Katowice 09141

Russia
National Scientific Society of Urological Surgeons, Moskva 09427

Switzerland
Schweizerische Gesellschaft für Urologie, Lausanne 10343

Turkey
Türk Uroloji Dernegi, Istanbul 10719

United Kingdom
British Association of Urological Surgeons, London 11048

U.S.A.
American Association of Genito-Urinary Surgeons, Charlottesville 12891
American Board of Urology, Bingham Farms 13008
American Society for Reproductive Medicine, Birmingham 13411
American Urological Association, Baltimore 13524
Society for Pediatric Urology, Seattle 16426

Venezuela
Sociedad Venezolana de Urología, Caracas 16940

Venereology

Australia
Australasian College of Sexual Health Physicians, Sydney 00145

Belgium
Koninklijke Belgische Vereniging voor Dermatologie en Venereologie, Gent 01222

Canada
Canadian Fertility and Andrology Society, Montréal 01881

Denmark
Danske Dermato-Venerologers Organisation, Alborg 03087

France
Société Française de Dermatologie et de Syphiligraphie, Paris 04124
Syndicat National Français des Dermatologistes et Vénéréologistes, Paris 04295

Italy
Società Italiana di Dermatologia e Sifilografia, Roma 07484
Società Italiana di Sessuologia Clinica, Roma 07571
Società Italiana di Sessuologia Medica, Roma 07572
Società Italiana per lo Studio della Fertilità e della Sterilità, Roma 07597

Netherlands
Nederlandse Vereniging voor Dermatologie en Venereologie, Breda 08583

Portugal
Sociedade Portuguesa de Dermatologia e Venereologia, Lisboa 09233

Romania
Societatea de Dermato-Venerologie, Bucuresti 09288

Russia
National Scientific Medical Society of Venereologists and Dermatologists, Moskva 09426

Spain
Academia Española de Dermatología y Sifilografía, Madrid 09725

Sweden
Swedish Society for Dermatology and Venerology, Stockholm 10016

Switzerland
Schweizerische Gesellschaft für Dermatologie und Venerologie, Zürich 10286

United Kingdom
Institute of Technicians in Venereology, Orsett 11726
International Union Against The Venereal Diseases and The Treponematoses, London 11825
Medical Society for the Study of Venereal Diseases, London 11933

U.S.A.
International Academy of Sex Research, Bloomington 14770
International Society for Sexually Transmitted Diseases Research, New Orleans 15248
International Society for the Study of Vulvovaginal Disease, Schaumburg 15262

Ventilation
s. Air Conditioning

Veterinary Medicine

Argentina
Academia Nacional de Agronomía y Veterinaría, Buenos Aires 00023
Sociedad Rural Argentina, Buenos Aires 00111

Australia
Australian Veterinary Association, Artarmon 00248
Sydney University Veterinary Society, Sydney 00372

Austria
Berufsverband freiberuflich tätiger Tierärzte Österreichs, Neukirchen 00423
Bundeskammer der Tierärzte Österreichs, Wien 00425
Österreichische Gesellschaft der Tierärzte, Wien 00598

Belgium
European Association of Veterinary Anatomists, Merelbeke 01107
European Federation of Animal Health, Bruxelles 01155
Federation of Veterinarians of Europe, Bruxelles 01171
Union Syndicale Vétérinaire Belge, Bruxelles 01312

Brazil
Associação Prudentina de Educação e Cultura, Presidente Prudente 01419

Canada
Alberta Veterinary Medical Association, Edmonton 01646
Canadian Association for Laboratory Animal Science, Edmonton 01800
Canadian Veterinary Medical Association, Ottawa 02022
Manitoba Veterinary Medicine Association, Winnipeg 02203
New Brunswick Veterinary Medical Association, Moncton 02236
Newfoundland and Labrador Veterinary Medical Association, Mount Pearl 02238
Nova Scotia Veterinary Medical Association, Lower Sackville 02262
Ontario Veterinary Medical Association, Milton 02301
Prince Edward Island Veterinary Medical Association, Montague 02325
Saskatchewan Veterinary Medical Association, Saskatoon 02365

Chile
Sociedad de Medicina Veterinaria de Chile, Santiago 02524

China, People's Republic
Chinese Association of Animal Science and Veterinary Medicine, Beijing 02573

Denmark
Dansk Veterinaerhistorisk Samfund, Thisted 03082
Den Danske Dyrlaegeforening, Vanlöse 03088
Danske Veterinärhygiejnikeres Organisation, Slagense 03101

Sweden
Sammenslutningen af Praktiserende Dyrlaeger, Vanløse 03196

Finland
Suomen Eläinlääkäriliitto, Helsinki 03393

France
Académie Vétérinaire de France, Paris 03499
Association Centrale des Vétérinaires, Paris 03508
Association Mondiale des Vétérinaires Microbiologistes, Immunologistes et Spécialistes des Maladies Infectieuses, Maisons Alfort 03613
Société Vétérinaire Pratique de France, Paris 04248
Syndicat des Vétérinaires de la Région Parisienne, Paris 04256
Syndicat National des Vétérinaires Français, Paris 04294

Germany
Bundestierärztekammer e.V., Bonn 04639
Bundesverband der beamteten Tierärzte, Lichtenfels 04643
Dachverband wissenschaftlicher Gesellschaften der Agrar-, Forst-, Ernährungs-, Veterinär- und Umweltforschung e.V., Frankfurt 04701
Deutsche Gesellschaft für Parasitologie e.V., Marburg 04832
Deutsche Veterinärmedizinische Gesellschaft e.V., Giessen 04980
Münchener Tierärztliche Gesellschaft, München 05755
Verband der Gemeinde-Tierärzte Baden-Württembergs, Baden-Baden 06020
Verband der Tierheilpraktiker e.V., Meitingen 06031
Verband Deutscher Tierarztfrauen und Tierärztinnen e.V., Varel 06057
Veterinärmedizinischer Fakultätentag, Hannover 06138
World Veterinary Poultry Association, Giessen 06172

Greece
Elliniki Ktiniatriki Eteria, Athinai 06220

India
Commonwealth Veterinary Association, Bangalore 06421
Helminthological Society of India, Mathura 06433

Iraq
Arab Union of Veterinary Surgeons, Baghdad 06575

Ireland
Veterinary Council, Dublin 06673

Israel
Israel Veterinary Medical Association, Tel Aviv 06736

Italy
European Commission for the Control of Foot-and-Mouth Disease, Roma 07258
Federazione Nazionale degli Ordini dei Veterinari Italiani, Roma 07281
International Association for Veterinary Homeopathy, Milano 07309
Società Italiana delle Scienze Veterinarie, Brescia 07451
Società Italiana di Buiatria, Torino 07469
Società Italiana di Ippologia, Roma 07511
Società Italiana di Patologia Aviare, Perugia 07551
Società Italiana di Patologia e di Allevamento degli Ovini e dei Caprini, Catania 07552
Società Italiana di Patologia ed Allevamento dei Suini, Parma 07553

Japan
Nihon Dobutsu Shinri Gakkai, Tsukuba 07780
Nihon Jui Gakkai, Tokyo 07803
Nippon Eisei-Dobutsu Gakkai, Tokyo 07890

Kenya
African Trypanotolerant Livestock Network, Nairobi 08073

Macedonia
Sojuz na Društvata na Veterinarnite Lekari i Tehničari na Makedonija, Skopje 08198

Netherlands
European Association of State Veterinary Officers, Rotterdam 08435
European Association of Veterinary Pharmacology and Toxicology, Utrecht 08436

Koninklijke Nederlandse Maatschappij voor Diergeneeskunde, Utrecht *08518*

New Zealand
New Zealand Veterinary Association, Wellington *08730*
Veterinary Services Council, Wellington *08744*

Nigeria
Nigerian Veterinary Medical Association, Vom *08783*

Norway
Den Norske Veterinaerforening, Oslo *08870*

Peru
Centro Nacional de Patologia Animal, Lima *08994*

Philippines
Philippine Veterinary Medical Association, Quezon City *09064*

Poland
Polskie Towarzystwo Nauk Weterynaryjnych, Warszawa *09124*

Portugal
Sociedade Portuguesa de Ciências Veterinárias, Lisboa *09232*
Sociedade Portuguesa Veterinária de Anatomia Comparativa, Lisboa *09251*
Sociedade Portuguesa Veterinária de Estudos Sociológicos, Lisboa *09252*

Senegal
Association des Etablissements d'Enseignement Vétérinaire Totalement ou Partiellement de Langue Française, Dakar *09506*

South Africa
South African Veterinary Association, Monument Park *09709*

Spain
Real Academia de Ciencias Veterinarias de España, Madrid *09781*

Sweden
Sveriges Veterinärförbund, Stockholm *10014*

Switzerland
Gesellschaft Schweizerischer Tierärzte, Bern *10146*
Internationale Veterinäranatomische Nomenklatur-Kommission, Zürich *10193*
Schweizerische Vereinigung für Kleintiermedizin, Bern *10409*

Tanzania
Tanzania Veterinary Association, Morogoro *10610*

Turkey
Türk Veteriner Hekimleri Dernegi, Ankara *10720*

United Kingdom
Animal Diseases Research Association, Edinburgh *10778*
Animal Health Trust, Newmarket *10779*
Association for Veterinary Clinical Pharmacology and Therapeutics, Dorking *10836*
Association of Meat Inspectors, Barnet *10899*
Association of Veterinary Anaesthetists of Great Britain and Ireland, Bury Saint Edmunds *10933*
Association of Veterinary Teachers and Research Workers, Edinburgh *10934*
British Association of Homoeopathic Veterinary Surgeons, Stanford-in-the-Vale *11032*
British Laboratory Animals Veterinary Association, Salisbury *11116*
British Small Animal Veterinary Association, Cheltenham *11161*
British Veterinary Association, London *11213*
British Veterinary Radiology Association, Hatfield *11214*
British Veterinary Zoological Society, London *11215*
CAB International Division of Animal Health and Medical Parasitology, Wallingford *11237*
European Association of Establishments for Veterinary Education, Roslin *11477*
Federation of European Veterinaries in Industry and Research, Hounslow *11527*
Institute for Animal Health, Newbury *11653*
National Anti-Vivisection Society, London *11973*
Royal College of Veterinary Surgeons, London *12196*
Veterinary History Society, London *12550*

U.S.A.
Academy of Veterinary Cardiology, Floral Park *12676*
American Academy of Veterinary Dermatology, Phoenix *12801*
American Animal Hospital Association, Denver *12809*
American Association for Accreditation of Laboratory Animal Care, Rockville *12819*
American Association for Laboratory Animal Science, Cordova *12840*
American Association of Avian Pathologists, Kennett Square *12860*
American Association of Bovine Practitioners, Rome *12865*
American Association of Equine Practitioners, Lexington *12888*
American Association of Industrial Veterinarians, Columbia *12898*
American Association of Small Ruminant Practitioners, Ithaca *12933*
American Association of Veterinary Anatomists, Auburn *12948*
American Association of Veterinary Laboratory Diagnosticians, Columbia *12949*
American Association of Veterinary Parasitologists, Mundelein *12950*
American Association of Veterinary State Boards, Jefferson City *12951*
American Association of Wildlife Veterinarians, Athens *12952*
American Association of Zoo Veterinarians, Philadelphia *12955*
American College of Veterinary Internal Medicine, Lakewood *13078*
American College of Veterinary Pathologists, West Deptford *13079*
American College of Veterinary Radiology, Glencoe *13080*
American Society for Reproductive Medicine, Birmingham *13411*
American Society of Veterinary Ophthalmology, Stillwater *13497*
American Veterinary Medical Association, Schaumburg *13526*
American Veterinary Society of Animal Behavior, Saint Louis *13527*
Animal Medical Center, New York *13541*
Animal Nutrition Research Council, Chantilly *13542*
Association for Equine Sports Medicine, Santa Barbara *13623*
Association for Gnotobiotics, East Aurora *13629*
Association for Women Veterinarians, Union City *13704*
Association of American Veterinary Medical Colleges, Washington *13726*
Association of Avian Veterinarians, Boca Raton *13732*
Association of Avian Veterinarias, Boca Raton *13733*
Beef Improvement Federation, Colby *13905*
Conference of Research Workers in Animal Diseases, Fort Collins *14162*
Flying Veterinarians Association, Columbia *14445*
Foundation for Biomedical Research, Washington *14459*
Institute of Laboratory Animal Resources, Washington *14714*
International Association for Aquatic Animal Medicine, Baltimore *14782*
International Committee on Veterinary Embryological Nomenclature, Ithaca *14950*
International Committee on Veterinary Histological Nomenclature, West Lafayette *14951*
International Council for Laboratory Animal Science, Dallas *14971*
International Embryo Transfer Society, Champaign *15004*
International Sled Dog Veterinar Medical Association, Sylvania *15186*
International Society for Animal Genetics, Madison *15189*
International Society of Animal Clinical Biochemistry, Davis *15270*
International Veterinary Acupuncture Society, Nederland *15365*
International Veterinary Auxiliary, Louisville *15366*
Laboratory Animal Management Association, Silver Spring *15475*
National Association for Veterinary Acupuncture, Fullerton *15666*
National Association of Federal Veterinarians, Washington *15701*
National Association of State Public Health Veterinarians, Columbus *15741*
National Mastitis Council, Arlington *15930*
Orthopedic Foundation for Animals, Columbia *16103*
Society for Invertebrate Pathology, Bethesda *16402*
Society for Theriogenology, Hastings *16483*
Veterinary Cancer Society, Rochester *16727*
Veterinary Orthopaedic Society, Salt Lake City *16728*
Western Veterinary Conference, Las Vegas *16758*
World Association for the Advencement of Veterinary Parasitology, Rahway *16797*
World Association of Veterinary Anatomists, West Lafayette *16802*
World Association of Veterinary Educators, Tuskegee *16803*
World Association of Veterinary Laboratory Diagnosticians, College Station *16804*

Yugoslavia
Društvo Veterinara Srbije, Beograd *16995*
Savez Društava Veterinara Jugoslavije, Beograd *17019*

Zimbabwe
Zimbabwe Veterinary Association, Harare *17088*

Vocational Training s. Adult Education

Water Resources

Australia
Safe Water Association of New South Wales, Sydney *00357*
Water Research Foundation of Australia, Canberra *00383*

Brazil
Instituto Nacional de Pesquisas Hidroviarias, Rio de Janeiro *01490*

Canada
Association Québécoise des Techniques de l'Eau, Montréal *01734*
Canadian Association on Water Quality, Gloucester *01832*
Canadian Water Quality Association, Waterloo *02023*
Waterloo Centre for Groundwater Research, Waterloo *02418*
Western Canada Water and Wastewater Association, Calgary *02424*

Denmark
Dansk Vandteknisk Forening, Viby *03081*

France
Intergovernmental Council for the International Hydrological Programme, Paris *03895*
Office International de l'Eau, Limoges *03924*
Société Française d'Hydrologie et de Climatologie Médicales, Paris *04185*

Germany
Deutscher Verband für Wasserwirtschaft und Kulturbau e.V., Bonn *05057*
Deutscher Verein des Gas- und Wasserfaches e.V., Eschborn *05060*
Institut für gewerbliche Wasserwirtschaft und Luftreinhaltung e.V., Köln *05529*
Normenausschuss Wasserwesen im DIN Deutsches Institut für Normung e.V., Berlin *05855*

Hungary
Magyar Hidrológiai Társaság, Budapest *06314*

India
Indian Association of Geohydrologists, Calcutta *06441*

Italy
Associazione Idrotecnica Italiana, Roma *06923*
Centro Internazionale per gli Studi sulla Irrigazione, Verona *07076*
Società Internazionale di Tecnica Idrotermale, Castellamare di Stabia *07441*
Tecneco, Fano *07659*

Japan
Nippon Kaisui Gakkai, Tokyo *07920*

Kenya
African Water Network, Nairobi *08074*

Monaco
Organisation Hydrographique Internationale, Monte Carlo *08374*

Netherlands
Nederlandse Vereniging voor Afvalwaterbehandeling en Waterkwaliteitsbeheer, Rijswijk *08579*

New Zealand
New Zealand Hydrological Society, Wellington *08700*

Russia
Water Management Society, Moskva *09480*

South Africa
Water Systems Research Group, Johannesburg *09720*

Switzerland
Schweizerischer Verein des Gas- und Wasserfaches, Zürich *10478*

Thailand
Committee for Co-ordination of Investigations of the Lower Mekong Basin, Bangkok *10637*

United Kingdom
International Association on Water Quality, London *11774*
Water Research Centre, Marlow *12562*

U.S.A.
American Cetacean Society, San Pedro *13028*
American Water Resources Association, Herdon *13531*
Associated Laboratories, Wrightsville Beach *13587*
Caribbean Sea and Gulf of Mexico Regional Hydrographic Commission, Silver Spring *13973*
Global Energy and Water Cycle Experiment, Silver Spring *14508*
Great Lakes Commission, Ann Arbor *14525*
IAHS International Commission on Groundwater, Stanford *14599*
IAHS International Commission on Water Quality, Atlanta *14601*
International Association of Theoretical and Applied Limnology, Tuscaloosa *14875*
International Training Network for Water and Waste Management, Washington *15346*
International Water Resources Association, Urbana *15370*
Middle East Water Information Network, Philadelphia *15575*
National Hydropower Association, Washington *15908*
National Water Resources Association, Arlington *15995*
Rural Community Assistance Program, Leesburg *16283*
Trout Unlimited, Arlington *16653*
United States Committee on Irrigation and Drainage, Denver *16686*
Universities Council on Water Resources, Carbondale *16703*
Water Quality Association, Lisle *16743*
Water Resources Congress, Vienna *16744*

Wines and Wine Making

Italy
Ente per la Valorizzazione dei Vini Astigiani, Asti *07241*

X-Ray Technology s. a. Radiology

Austria
Österreichische Röntgengesellschaft – Gesellschaft für medizinische Radiologie und Nuklearmedizin, Wien *00734*

Denmark
Danske Radiologers Organisation, Sønderborg *03098*

Germany
Bayerische Röntgengesellschaft, Fürth *04535*
Deutsche Röntgengesellschaft, Neu-Isenburg *04953*
Vereinigung Südwestdeutscher Radiologen und Nuklearmediziner (VSRN), Sindelfingen *06130*

Russia
National Scientific Medical Society of Roentgenologists and Radiologists, Moskva *09420*

U.S.A.
American Roentgen Ray Society, Reston *13360*
Council on Diagnostic Imaging, Palatine *14246*

Zoology s. a. Ornithology; Entomology

Argentina
Fundación Miguel Lillo, San Miguel de Tucumán *00076*

Australia
Australian Mammal Society, Townsville *00211*
Australian Society for Fish Biology, Queenscliff *00229*
Australian Society of Herpetologists Inc., Lyneham *00241*
Malacological Society of Australia, Sydney *00307*
Royal Zoological Society of New South Wales, Mosman *00355*
Royal Zoological Society of South Australia, Adelaide *00356*
Zoological Board of Victoria, Parkville *00391*

Austria
Zoologisch-Botanische Gesellschaft in Österreich, Wien *00884*

Bangladesh
Zoological Society of Bangladesh, Dhaka *00921*

Barbados
Barbados Museum and Historical Society, Saint Ann's Garrison *00923*

Belgium
Association pour les Etudes et Recherches de Zoologie Appliquée et de Phytopathologie, Sint-Truiden *00981*
European Society of Nematologists, Merkelbeke *01162*
Koninklijke Maatschappij voor Dierkunde van Antwerpen, Antwerpen *01223*
Société Royale Zoologique de Belgique, Bruxelles *01297*

Canada
Calgary Zoological Society, Calgary *01765*
Canadian Society of Animal Science, Ottawa *01988*
Canadian Society of Zoologists, Québec *02006*
Zoological Society of Metropolitan Toronto, Scarborough *02438*
Zoological Society of Montréal, Montréal *02439*

China, People's Republic
Chinese Association of Animal Science and Veterinary Medicine, Beijing *02573*
Chinese Society of Oceanology and Limnology, Qingdao *02632*
Chinese Zoological Society, Beijing *02643*

China, Republic
Malacological Society of China, Taipei *02731*

Colombia
Instituto de Ciencias Naturales, Bogotá *02799*

Czech Republic
Česká Společnost Zoologická, Praha *02942*

Denmark
Lepidopterologisk Forening, Holte *03159*

Finland
Societas pro Fauna et Flora Fennica, Helsingin Yliopisto *03377*

France
Société d'Ethnozoologie et d'Ethnobotanique, Paris *04051*
Société Française de Malacologie, Paris *04130*
Société Française d'Ichtyologie, Paris *04186*
Société Zoologique de France, Paris *04249*

Georgia
Georgian Society of Helminthologists, Tbilisi *04348*

Publications Index

Register der periodischen Publikationen

503 Publications Index: Le

Chemistry International 11831
Chemistry Letters 07917
Chemistry of Life 02622
Chemistry of Materials 13029
Chemists' Club: Newsletter 14055
CHEMTECH 13029
ChemWorld 08128
Chesapeake and Ohio Historical Magazine 14057
Chest 13040
Chester Zoo Life 12044
Chigiana: Rivista annuale di studi musicologici 06846
Chikyu-kagaku: Earth Science 07718
Child Development 16438
Child Development Abstracts & Bibliography 16438
Child Health 01906
Childbirth without Pain Education Association: Memo 14060
Childhood Education 13610
Children and Animals 15647
Children's Book News 01849
Children's Health Care 13681
Chiltern News 11284
CHIMIA 10218
Chimia 10442
La Chimica e l'Industria: Quaderni dell'Ingegnere Chimico Italiano 07394
Chimica nella Scuola 07394
Chimie Nouvelle 01288
Chimika Chronika 06231
China Institute in America: Annual Report 14063
China Institute in America: Bulletin 14063
China Journal of TCM 02546
China Law Reporter 12965
China Medical Board of New York: Annual Report 14064
China-Report 00619
China Society: Journal 02684
The China Society: Journal 09531
Chinese Academy of Geological Sciences: Bulletin 02558
Chinese Acupuncture and Moxibustion 02544, 02547
Chinese AEC Bulletin 02676
Chinese America: History and Perspectives 14067
Chinese Chemical Letters 02580
Chinese Historical Society of America: Bulletin 14067
Chinese Journal of Acoustics 02538
Chinese Journal of Biochemistry and Molecular Biology 02622
Chinese Journal of Chemistry 02580
Chinese Journal of Materials Science 02709
Chinese Journal of Oceanology and Limnology 02613
Chinese Journal of Physics 02744
Chinese Journal of Polymer Science 02580
Chinese Journal of Psychology 02707
Chinese Journal of Radiology 02749
Chinese Journal of Space Science 02634
Chinese Language Monthly 02700
Chinese Language Teachers Association: Journal 14068
Chinese Medical Journal 02593, 02702
Chinese Music 14069
The Chinese PEN 02690
Chinese Statistical Journal 02712
Chinese Writers 02642
Chinook 01926
CHINOPERL Papers 14154
Chiribotan 07805
Chirihak 08131
Chiron 05072
Chiron: Mitteilungen der Kommission für Alte Geschichte und Epigraphik des Deutschen Archäologischen Instituts 05673
Chiropractic Advancement Association: News Bulletin 11288
Der Chirurg BDC: Informationen des Berufsverbandes der Deutschen Chirurgen 04562
Chirurgia Narządów Ruchu i Ortopedia Polska 09130
Chirurgie 03465, 09287
Chirurgie Pédiatrique 04120
Le Chirurgien-Dentiste de France 03752
Le Chirurgien-Dentiste de Paris 04251
The Chopin Society: Newsletter 11290
Chord and Discord 13949
The Choreologist 10958
Christ und Bildung 05656
Christian College News 14091
Christian Home and School 14077
Christian Librarian 13749
Christian Schools International: Directory 14077
Christianity and Literature 14164
Chronica Horticulturae 08492
Chronique d'Egypte 01174
Chronique UGGI 04308
Chronobiologia 15198
Church and King 12434
Church and Synagogue Libraries 14079
Church Education Society: Annual Report 06591
Church History 13433
Churchscape 11358
CIAT International 02779
CIAT Report 02779
CIC Directory of Minority Ph.D. Candidates and Recipients 14132
CICRED Bulletin 03742
CIE 00427
CIE Newsletter 02698
Le Ciel 01238
Ciel et Espace 03522
Ciel et Terre 01277
Ciencia del Suelo 00046
Ciencia e Investigación 00050
CIFST Journal 01908
C.I.I. Journal 11278
CIIT Activities 14053
CIJL Bulletin 10060
CILECT Newsletter 01013
CIMMYT Economics Working Paper 08294
CIMMYT hechos y tendencias mundiales relacionadas con maíz 08294
CIMMYT hechos y tendencias mundiales relacionadas con trigo 08294
CIMMYT Hoy 08294
CIMMYT IN 08294
CIMMYT Réalité et tendances-le mais dans le monde: le potentiel maisicole de l'Afrique subsaharienne 08294
CIMMYT Research Report 08294
CIMMYT Today 08294
CIMMYT Wheat Special Report 08294
CIMMYT World Maize Facts and Trends 08294
CIMMYT World Wheat Facts and Trends 08294
Cina 07353
Cinema Journal 16364
Cinema Organ 11293
Cinema Technology 11115
Cinema Theatre Association: Bulletin 11294
Cinésiologie: La Revue Internationale des Médecins du Sport 04279
CIOMS Organization and Activities/Directory of Members 10072
CIPA 11273
CIPAC Proceedings 11302
CIPRA Internationale Alpenschutzkommission: Info-Bulletin 08161
Circular Técnica 01436, 01437, 01443, 01444, 01445
Circulo Poético 16145
Circulo: Revista de Cultura 16145
CIRP Annals 03704
Cirúgia del Uruguay 12633
Cirugía Plástica Iberolatinoamericana 09815
CISCo-News: Notiziario 07091
CITIA News 00257
Cito-Notícias 02481
Citologia Informazioni 07482
Città Eterna 06884
City and Guilds: Handbook 11297
City and Guilds: Report and Accounts 11297
City of Stoke on Trent Museum Archaeological Society: Newsletter 11298
City Planning Review 08000
Civil and Hydraulic Engineering 02697
Civil Engineering 09690, 13434
Civil Engineering in Japan 07723
Civil Engineering Transactions 00298
Civil War Byline 14085
Civilingenjören 10005
Civitas Pacis 07064
CLAH Newsletter 14168
CLANews 11328
Clase: Citas Latinoamericanas en Sociología en Ciencias y Humanidades 08291
Clásicos Venezolanos 16871
Classic America 16729
Classical and Quantum Gravity 11711
The Classical Outlook 13032
Classical Quarterly 11299
Classical Review 11299
Clay Minerals 11950
Clay Minerals Society: Newsletter 14089
Clays and Clay Minerals 14089
Clean Air and Environmental Protection 12021
Clean Air Journal 09642
Clean Slate 11260
Cleft Palate Journal 13033
Clima 00049
Climatological Bulletin 01926
Clinica: Rivista Internazionale di Psichiatria 07037
La Clinica Termale 06994
Clinical Allergy 11164
Clinical and Experimental Dermatology 12279
Clinical Chemistry Journal 12829
Clinical Chemistry News 12829
Clinical Chemistry Reference Edition 12829
Clinical Consult Newsletter 13440
Clinical Diabetes 13124
Clinical EEG 13265
Clinical & Experimental Optometry 00218
Clinical Forensic Medicine 10908
Clinical Justice and Behavior 12830
Clinical Laboratory Science 13374
Clinical Neurology and Neurosurgery 08596
Clinical Neurology and Neurosurgery: CNN 08574
Clinical Neuroscience 00164
Clinical Neurosurgery 14170
Clinical Oncology 12193
Clinical Orthopedic Society: Directory 14090
Clinical Orthopedics and Related Research 13742
Clinical Pharmacy 13458
Clinical Preventive Dentistry 09646
Clinical Psychiatry Quarterly 12746
Clinical Radiology 12193
Clinical Reports of Allergy and Immunology 00083
Clinical Research 13144
Clinical Science 10965
Clinical Series 15983
Clinical Social Work Journal 15880
Clinical Staging of Lung Cancer 07770
Clinical Standards Digest 15442
Clinical Theology Association: Contact 11301
Clinics in Developmental Medicine 12288
Clio 03220
CLR Report 14255
CMA Journal: Journal de l'Association médicale canadienne 01925
CMC Contact Newsletter 10068
CMU Bulletin 07209
CNA Annual International Conference Proceedings 01932
CNL/Review of Books 14257
CNL/World Report 14257
Co-op Education Undergraduate Program Directory 15797
Coalition for International Cooperation and Peace: Conference Reports 14092
Coalition for International Cooperation and Peace: Newsletter 14092
Coastal Engineering in Japan 07723
Coastal Engineering Research Council: Proceedings 14094
Coastal Reporter 13250
Coastal Society: Bulletin 14095
Coastal Society: Directory 14095
The Coat of Arms 11615
Coating Regulations and Environmental Issues 12082
Coblentz Society Mailings 14096
COCTA News 08788
CODATA Bulletin 03731
CODATA Newsletter 03731
Code of Conduct 11560
CODESRIA Bulletin 09515
Coffin Corner 16207
COHEHRE Newsletter 08415
Coin Hoards 12237
Colegio de Abogados de la Ciudad de Buenos Aires: Revista 00065
Colegio de Arquitectos de Chile: Boletín 02456
Colfar 16901
Collection d'Etudes Latines 04034
Collection linguistique 03983
Collection of Czech Chemical Publications 02911
Collections for a History of Staffordshire 12467
Collective Bargaining Newsletter 12944
College and Research Libraries 13751
College and Research Libraries News 13751
College Art Association: Newsletter 14098
College Board News 14099
College Board Review 14099
The College Board: Membership Directory 14099
The College Board: Proceedings 14099
College Canada 01707
College Composition and Communication 14165
College English 15841
College Mathematics Journal 15541
College Music Society: Symposium 14102
College of American Pathologists: Directory 14103
College of American Pathologists: Newsletter 14103
College of Europe: Information 01030
College of Optometrists in Vision Development: Newsletter 14104
College Times 14099
Colleges and Schools of Pharmacy, Accredited Professional Degree Programs 13107
Colloquia Academica: Akademievorträge junger Wissenschaftler 04378
Colloquium Proceedings 04297
The Colposcopist 13376
The Columns 14056
Com-line 15590
Combinatorica 06285
Comecon Data 00868
Comércio Externo 09210
Comet 12082
Comisión Nacional de Museos y de Monumentos y Lugares Históricos: Boletín 00068
Comisión Nacional Protectora de Bibliotecas Populares: Boletín 00069
Comité National Français des Recherches Antarctiques: Report 03730
Comité pour les Données Scientifiques et Technologiques: Conference Proceedings 03731
COMLA Newsletter 07695
Commemorative Collectors Society: Collecting Commemorabilia 11309
Commemorative Collectors Society: Newsletter 11309
Commentarii Mathematici Helvetici 10373
Commentationes Mathematicae 09118
Commission Internationale d'Etudes Historiques Latinoaméricaines et des Caraïbes: Newsletter 03738
Commission on Accreditation of Rehabilitation Facilities: Report 14112
Committee on Institutional Cooperation: Biennial Report 14132
Common Sense Pest Control 13918
Commonwealth Education 11329
Commonwealth Education News 11325, 11334
Commonwealth Forestry Association: Review 11326
Commonwealth Heraldry Bulletin 08670
The Commonwealth Lawyer 11328
Commonwealth Trust: Newsletter 11335
Commonwealth Universities Yearbook 10865
Communication 11992, 16715
Communication Education 16601
Communication: Journalism Education Today 15457
Communication Monographs 16601
Communication Theory 14952
Communication Yearbook 14952
Communicationes 00977
Communications 03626, 08399, 14889
Communications and Acta Electrografica 15091
Communications et Mémoires 03466
Communications Law 12965
Communications of the ACM 13615
The Communicator 11721
Communicator 12751
The Communicator 15053
Communicator 15696
Community Associations Institute: Common Ground 14138
Community Associations Institute: News 14138
Community Associations Institute: Report 14138
Community College Journal for Research and Planning 15825
Community Dentistry and Oral Epidemiology 09646
Community Education Journal 15803
Community Education Today 15803
Community Health Guides 15688
Community Health Listing 15688
Community Management Initiative Reports 15739
Community, Technical and Junior College Journal 12877
Community, Technical and Junior College Times 12877
COMNET Newsletter 01048
Comp Flash 13255
Company Secretarial Practice 11671
Comparative and International Education Society: Directory 14147
Comparative and International Education Society: Newsletter 14147
Comparative Education Review 14147
Comparative Immunology Microbiology and infection disease 03613
Comparative Labor Law Journal 15224
Comparative Psychology and Behavior 13344
Comparative Studies in Society and History 16452
Compensation and Benefits Review 13255
Compleat Anachronist 16372
The Compleat Lawyer 12965
Composers' Guild of Great Britain: Compass News 11337
Comprehensive Bibliography in Neuroanesthesia 16543
Comprehensive Education 12159
Comprehensive Psychiatry 13346
Comprendre 07424
Compte rendus de la Société de Biologie 03963
Comptes rendus de l'Académie d'Agriculture de France 03462
Comptes-Rendus de l'Académie des Sciences 03474
Les comptes rendus de l'Académie des Sciences 03880
Comptes Rendus des Travaux 01291
Computational Linguistics 13613
Computer Applications Program Catalog 15914
Computer Bulletin 11066
Computer Crime Chronicles 15779
Computer Crime Law Reporter 15779
Computer & Geosciences 14803
Computer Journal 11066
Computer Law Association Newsletter 14149
Computer Law Association: Membership Directory 14149
Computer Newssheet 11342
Computers in Genealogy 12427
Computers & Law 12351
Computing, Communications, Media and Socio-Technology-Trend Monitor 10808
Computing & Control Engineering Journal 11736
Computing Reviews 13615
Computing Surveys 13615
Comunicado Técnico 01437, 01443
La Comunità Internazionale 07591
The Concord Saunterer 16642
Concrete International: Design & Construction 13087
The Concrete Yearbook 11734
Condizionamento dell'Aria 06931
Condor 14191
Confederate Memorial Literary Society: Journal 14151
Conference Group on German Politics: Directory of Current Research 14156
Conference Group on German Politics: Newsletter 14156
Conference of Consulting Actuaries: Proceedings 14158
Conference of Educational Administrators Serving the Deaf: Newsletter 14159
Conferentie voor Regionale Ontwikkeling in Noord-West-Europa: Proceedings of Seminars Organized 01057
Conflict Management and Peace Science 16153
Confrontation 15432
Confucius-Mencius Monthly 02717
La Congiuntura in Toscana 07108
Congrès Archéologique de France 04112
Congrès de Psychiatrie et de Neurologie de Langue Française: Annual Report 03762
Congress and the Presidency 16684
Congress of Lung Association Staff: Membership Directory 14169
Congress of Lung Association Staff: Newsletter 14169
Congress of Neurological Surgeons: Newsletter 14170
Connect 12517
Connection 11992
Conquest 12154
Conseil Consultatif Economique et Social de l'Union Economique Benelux: Report of Council Meetings 01058
Conseil International pour l'Information Scientifique et Technique: Forum 03774
Conservation News 12537
The Conservator 12537
The Consort 11394
Construction 01857
Construction Computing 11270
Construction Industry Computing Association: Evaluation Reports 11342
Construction Industry Software Selector 11342
Construction Journal 13434
Construction Management-Focus 11675
Construction Manager 11270
The Construction Specifier 14182
Construction Today 11734
Construction Writers Association: Newsletter 14183
Constructive Triangle 13277
The Consultant 11634
The Consultant Pharmacist Journal 13440
Consulting Services Directory 13759
Contemporary Accounting Research 01767
Contemporary Biology 17032
Contemporary Psychology 13344
Contemporary Sexuality Newsletter 12932
Contemporary Sociology: A Journal of Reviews 13499
Contemporary Southeast Asia 09535
Contemporary Trends in Education 03298
Contingencies 12740
Continuing Medical Education Journal 09638
Continuing Pharmaceutical Education, Approved Providers 13107
Contra Watch 14511
Contributi del Centro Linceo Interdisciplinare B. Segre 06848
Contributions à l'Etude des Primitifs Flamands 01017
Control Column 10752
Control Systems Magazine 14634
Convention of American Instructors of the Deaf: Newsletter 14189
Convergence 10209
Convivium: Revista de Investigação e Cultura 01508
Convorbiri literare 09328
Coolia: Journal 08560
Cooperation and Conflict: Nordic Journal of International Politics 09930
Cooperative Research Report 03134
Coordination 10160
Copeia 13460
Copyright Society of the U.S.A.: Journal 14196
The Core Teacher 15641
Corella 00169
Corhealth 13096
CORMOSEA Bulletin 14134
Cornish Archaeology 11348
Corporate Plan 10758, 11929
Le Corps Médical 08167

517 Publications Index: New

National Association of Industrial and Technical Teacher Educators: News and Views 15710
National Association of Legal Assistants: Facts & Findings 15711
National Association of Nutrition and Aging Services Programs: Annual Report 15715
National Association of Nutrition and Aging Services Programs: Monthly Membership Updates 15715
National Association of Nutrition and Aging Services Programs: Special Bulletin 15715
National Association of Principals of Schools for Girls: Proceedings 15719
National Association of Private Schools for Exceptional Children: Directory 15720
National Association of Private Schools for Exceptional Children: Newsbriefs 15720
National Association of Private Schools for Exceptional Children: Newsletter 15720
National Association of School Psychologists: Directory 15723
National Association of School Psychologists: Journal Review 15723
National Association of School Psychologists: Newsletter 15723
National Association of Schools of Art and Design: Directory 15725
National Association of Schools of Art and Design: Handbook 15725
National Association of Schools of Music: Directory 15726
National Association of Schools of Music: Handbook 15726
National Association of Schools of Music: Proceedings 15726
National Association of Secondary School Principals: Bulletin 15730
National Association of Secondary School Principals: Curriculum Report 15730
National Association of State Archeologists: Directory 15731
National Association of State Archeologists: Newsletter 15731
National Association of State Directors of Teacher Education and Certification: Roster 15735
National Association of State Supervisors of Vocational Home Economics: Directory 15742
National Association of State Supervisors of Vocational Home Economics: Newsletter 15742
National Association of State Universities and Land-Grant Colleges: Annual Report 15744
National Association of Teachers of Singing: Journal 15748
National Association of Teachers of Singing: Membership Directory 15748
National Association of University Women: Bulletin 15750
National Association of University Women: Directory of Branch Presidents and Members 15750
National Biographies 13218
National Black MBA Association Newsletter 15757
The National Board Examiner 15764
National Board for Respiratory Care: Annual Directory 15762
National Board for Respiratory Care: Newsletter 15762
National Board of Examiners in Optometry: Newsletter 15763
National Board of Examiners in Optometry: Report & Examinations 15763
National Board of Medical Examiners: Annual Report 15764
National Bulletin 12938
National Burn Information Exchange Newsletter 15915
National Cancer Center: Annual Report 07770
National Cancer Center: Collected Papers 07770
National Cancer Registrars Association: Abstract 15769
National Cancer Registrars Association: Membership Roster 15769
National Cancer Registrars Association: Proceedings/Annual Report 15769
National Catholic Educational Association: Notes 15773
National Catholic Educational Association: Update 15773
National Center for Computer Crime Data: Annual Statistical Report 15779
National Center for State Courts: Report and Master Calendar 15785
National Character Laboratory: Newsletter 15790
National Coalition of Alternative Community Schools: Newsletter 15793
National College of Foot Surgeons: Journal 15795
National Committee on the Treatment of Intractable Pain: Newsletter 15802
National Community Education Association: Membership Directory 15803
National Conference of Standards Laboratories: Conference Proceedings 15808
National Conference of Standards Laboratories: Newsletter 15808
National Conference of Yeshiva Principals: Newsletter 15810
National Conference on Fluid Power 15811
National Conference on Research in Language and Literacy: Directory 15812
National Conference on Research in Language and Literacy: Newsletter 15812
National Conference on the Advancement of Research: Proceedings 15813
National Conference on Weights and Measures: Report 15814
National Cooperative Highway Research Program Report 16650
National Cooperative Transit Research and Development Program Reports 16650
National Council for Accreditation of Teacher Education: Annual List of Accredited Institutions 15820
National Council for Geographic Education: Perspective 15823
National Council for Research and Planning: Newsletter 15825
National Council for the Social Studies: Bulletin 15827
National Council for Urban Economic Development: Commentary 15830
National Council of Athletic Training: Directory 15831
National Council of Athletic Training: Newsletter 15831
National Council of Guilds for Infant Survival: Newsletter 15834
National Council of Teachers of Mathematics: News Bulletin 15842
National Council of University Research Administrators: Newsletter 15844
National Council on Economic Education: Annual Report 15850
National Council on Economic Education: Directory of Affiliated Councils and Centers 15850
National Council on Radiation Protection and Measurements: Proceedings of the Annual Meeting 15856
National Dental Association: Journal 15864
National Dental Association: Newsletter 15864
National Directory of Educational Programs in Gerontology 13628
National Directory of Physician Assistant Programs 13815
National Directory of Vocational Experts 13009
National Eczema Society: Exchange 12002
National Engineer 15718
National Federation of Abstracting and Information Services: Membership Directory 15877
National Federation of Abstracting and Information Services: Report Series 15877
National Flags 14436
National Foundation for Brain Research: Annual Report 15887
National Foundation for Brain Research: Newsletter 15887
National Foundation for Educational Research in England and Wales: Research Reports 12007
National Geographic 15891
National Geographic World 15891
National Geographical Journal of India 06518
National Guild of Catholic Psychiatrists: Bulletin 15893
National Guild of Community Schools of the Arts: Guildletter 15894
National Hardwood Lumber Association: Proceedings: Annual Hardwood Symposium 15896
The National Health 13347
National Health and Medical Research Council: Council Session Reports 00313
National Housing Conference: Newsletter 15905
National Humanities Center: Newsletter 15907
National Information Service for Earthquake Engineering: Current Abstract Update Service 15914
National Institute Discussion Papers 12014
National Institute Economic Review 12014
National Institute for Certification in Engineering Technologies: Newsletter 15916
National Institute for Compilation and Translation: The Institute Periodical 02738
National Institute for Compilation and Translation: News Bulletin 02738
National Institute Occasional Papers 12014
National Institute of Science: Newsletter 15922
National Institute of Science: Transactions 15922
National League of American PEN Women: Roster 15927
The National Librarian 15928
National Listing of Rolfers 16280
National Marine Educators Association: Current: The Journal of Marine Education 15929
National Mastitis Council: Annual Meeting Proceedings 15930
National Materials Advisory Board: Newsletter 15931
National Medical and Dental Association: Bulletin 15932
National Medical Association Newsletter 15933
National Medical Journal of China 02593
National Mental Health Association: Focus 15935
National Monuments Commission: Annual Report 17053
National Monuments Commission: Research Publications 17053
National Optometric Association: Newsletter 15941
National Orchestral Association: Fact Sheet 15942
National Organization of Minority Architects: Newsletter 15945
National Osteopathic Guild Association: Newsletter 15948
National Perinatal Association: Newsletter 15949
National Perinatal Association: Proceedings 15949
National Pharmaceutical Association: Journal 15951
National Podriatic Medical Association: Annual Seminar Ad Book 15955
National Podriatic Medical Association: Newsletter 15955
National Psychological Association for Psychoanalysis: Bulletin 15957
National Psychological Association for Psychoanalysis: News & Reviews 15957
National PTA Bulletin 15706
National Reading Conference: Yearbook 15959
National Registry in Clinical Chemistry: Directory 15961
National Rehabilitation Association: Newsletter 15962
National Report on Human Resources 13418
National Research Centre: Bulletin 03300
National Research Council: News Report 15963
National Roster of Black Elected Officials 15440
National Safety Management Society: Update Newsletter 15968
National SAMPE Technical Conference Series 16448
National Science 02740
National Science Council: Abstracts of Research Papers 02740
National Science Council: Proceedings 02740
National Sculpture Society: Newsletter 15973
National Security Report 13364
National Society (Church of England) for Promoting Religious Education: News 12020
National Society for Clean Air and Environmental Protection: Proceedings of Annual Conferences and Seminars 12021
National Society for the Preservation of Covered Bridges: Bulletin 15975
National Society for the Preservation of Covered Bridges: Notices 15975
National Society for the Study of Education: Yearbook 15976
National Space Club: Newsletter 15978
National Speleological Society: Membership List 15980
National Speleological Society: Monthly News 15980
National Student Speech Language Hearing Association: Journal 15983
National Tax Journal 15985
National Technical Association: Journal 15986
National Technical Association: Newsletter 15986
National Technical Services Association: Membership Roster 15987
National Trust for Places of Historic Interest or Natural Beauty: Annual Report 12028
National Trust for Places of Historic Interest or Natural Beauty: Members' and Visitors' Handbook 12028
National Trust for Places of Historic Interest or Natural Beauty: Newsletter 12028
National Union of Teachers: Annual Report 12030
National Water Resources Association Directory 15995
National Waterline 15995
National Workshop Proceedings 15650
National Writing Project: The Quarterly 16000
Nationalities Papers 16324
Nationaløkonomisk Tidsskrift 03166
Natterjack 11863
Náttúrufrádingurinn 06368
Natur & Umwelt 04614
Natur und Land 00762
Natur und Mensch 05766
Natur und Mensch: Schweizerische Blätter für Natur und Heimatschutz 10230
Natur und Umwelt 04615
Natura 08519, 09231
Natura: Rivista di Scienze Naturali 07569
Natura Alpina 07410
Natura e Montagna 07670
Natura & Montagna 07422
Natura Società 07283
Natural Environment Research Council: Annual Report 12031
Natural History Bulletin 10646
The Natural History Society of Northumbria: Transactions 12032
Natural Product Updates 12255
Natural Rubber Technology 08234
Natural World: Annual Review 12248
Naturalia 09231
Les Naturalistes Belges: Bulletin 01229
Der Naturarzt 05032
The Nature Conservancy Magazine 16004
Nature Study 13286
Naturforschende Gesellschaft in Bern: Mitteilungen 10212
Naturforschende Gesellschaft in Zürich: Vierteljahrsschrift 10213
Naturforschende Gesellschaft Schaffhausen: Mitteilungen 10215
Naturopa 03697
Naturopa-Newsletter 03697
Naturschutz heute 05759
Die Naturstein-Industrie 05237
Naturvetenskapliga Forskningsrådet: Annual Report 09923
Naturvetenskapliga Forskningsrådet: Yearbook 09923
Naturwissenschaftlicher Verein in Hamburg: Abhandlungen 05770
Naturwissenschaftlicher Verein in Hamburg: Verhandlungen 05770
Natuur en Milieu 08626
Natuur- en Stedeschoon 01224
Natuurbehoud 08638
Natuurhistorisch Maandblad 08532
Natuurkundige Voordrachten, Nieuwe Reeks 08510
Nauchnoe Proborostroenie: Scientific Instrumentation 09442
Nauka v Rossii: Science in Russia 09442
Nauki v Uzbekistane: Social Sciences in Uzbekistan 16856
Naunyn-Schmiedeberg's Archive of Pharmacology 04837
Naunyn-Schmiedeberg's Archives of Pharmacology 04938
Nautica Fennica 03366
Nautologia 09125
NAVA News 16054
The Naval Architect incorporating Warship Technology 12224
Naval Architecture and Ocean Engineering 07871
Naval Engineers Journal 13473
Navigation 07937, 14720
Navigation News 12215
Navy Records Society: Annual Report 12034
Nawpa Pacha 14697
NBS Handbook 15814
NBTA News 02363
NCFL Newsletter 15774
NCHRP Synthesis of Highway Practice 16650
NCRP Commentaries 15856
NCRP Reports 15856
NCTRP Research Result Digest 16650
NCTRP Synthesis of Transit Practice 16650
NEA Now 15872
NEA Today 15872
NEAS Bulletin 16006
NEAS Newsletter 16006
Nederland's Adelsboek 08407
Nederlands Archievenblad 08642
Nederlands Bosbouw Tijdschrift 08514
Het Nederlands Kanker Instituut: Scientific Annual Report 08543
Nederland's Patriciaat 08407
Nederlands Tandartsenblad: Dutch Dental Journal 08549
Nederlands Tijdschrift voor Anesthesiologie NTVA 08581
Nederlands Tijdschrift voor Fysiotherapie 08538
Nederlands Tijdschrift voor Manuele Therapie 08538
Nederlands Tijdschrift voor Obstetrie en Gynaecologie 08597
Nederlands Tijdschrift voor Opvoeding, Vorming en Onderwijs 08575
Nederlands-Zuidafrikaanse Vereniging: Annual Report 08547
Nederlandsche Internisten Vereeniging: The Newsletter 08548
De Nederlandsche Leeuw 08505
Nederlandsche Vereniging voor Druk- en Boekkunst: Mededelingen 08550
Nederlandse Genealogieen 08505
Nederlandse Historische Bronnen 08539
Nederlandse Organisatie voor Wetenschappelijk Onderzoek: Jaarboek: Annual Report 08563
Nederlandse Vereniging voor Internationaal Recht: Mededelingen 08587
Neftekhimiya: Petrochemistry 09442
Negro History Bulletin 13689
NEHA-Bulletin 08637
Neige et Avalanches 03624
Neirofiziologiya: Neurophysiology 09442
Neirokhimiya: Neurochemistry 00113, 09442
Nematological Abstracts 11231
Nematology Newsletter 16541
Nenpo 07897
Nensho Kenkyu 07947
Nensho-Kenkyu 07948
Neo-Hellenika 14015
Neo Metaphysical Digest 12436
Neofilolog 09126
Neometaphysical Series 12436
Neometaphysics & Current Affairs Series 12436
Nephrologische Nachrichten 00664
Néprajzi Hirek 06329
NERC News 12031
Nervenarzt 04847
Nestroyana: Blätter der Internationalen Nestroy-Gesellschaft 00529
Net Worth: Valeurs nettes 01925
Netherlands Journal of Agricultural Science 08507
Netherlands Journal of Cardiology 08582
The Netherlands Journal of Medicine 08548
Netherlands Journal of Zoology 08555
Netsu Shori: Journal of the Japan Society for Heat Treatment 07949
Network 11711
network 14411
Network Exchange 12729
Network News 00126, 15997
Network News Exchange 16391
Network Newsletter 02307
Die Neue Hochschule 05492
Neue Horizonte 00721
Neue Musikzeitung 05049
Die Neue Ordnung 05528
Neue Studien zur Musikwissenschaft 04378
Neue Unterrichtspraxis 05397
Neujahrsblätter 10215
Neujahrsblatt 10213
Neuphilologische Mitteilungen 03460
Neurochirurgie 03991
Neurologia i Neurochirurgia Polska 09127
Neurologia medico-chirurgica II 07950
Neurophysiologie Clinique 03992
Neuropsychiatrie 00667
Neuroradiology 05167
Neuroscience News 07986
Neuroscience Newsletter 16415
Neuroscience Research 07986
Neuroscience Training Programs in North America 16415
Neurosurgery 14170
Neurosurgical Topics 12909
Neusprachliche Mitteilungen aus Wissenschaft und Praxis 05208
New Brunswick Institute of Agrologists: Newsletter 02229
New Civil Engineer 06614
New Dimensions 14310
New Dimensions in International Studies 15331
New Directions 15739
New Directors for Two-Year Colleges 15825
New England 14109
New England Antiquities Research Association: Journal 16013
New England Association of Schools and Colleges: Membership Directory 16014
New England Association of Schools and Colleges: Newsletter 16014
New England Historical and Genealogical Register 16016
New English Art Club: Catalogue of Annual Exhibition 12036
The New Era 16811
New Era in Education 12586
New Europe Papers 11500
New Farmer and Grower 12451
New Horizons 16667
New Invention Lists 11694
New Issues 14666
New Moon 16454
New: Notes 12388
New Outlook 16193
New Political Science 13987
The New Scholasticism 13023
New Steel Construction 12475
New Swedish Technology 09948
New Testament Studies 12369
New Thought Quarterly 15123
New West Indian Guide 08501
New Writing Scotland 10824
New York Browning Society: Bulletin 16020

525 Publications Index: SRHE

Société Internationale pour la Recherche sur les Maladies de Civilisation et sur l'Environnement: Congress Proceedings *01270*
Société Jersiaise: Bulletin *12346*
Société Mathématique de Belgique: Bulletin *01272*
Société Mycologique de France: Bulletin Trimestriel *04224*
Société Nationale Académique de Cherbourg: Mémoires *04225*
Société Nationale des Sciences Naturelles et Mathématiques de Cherbourg: Mémoires *04230*
Société Neuchâteloise des Sciences Naturelles: Bulletin *10508*
Société Royale Belge d'Entomologie: Bulletin et Annales *01284*
Société Royale Belge d'Entomologie: Mémoires *01284*
Société Royale d'Archéologie de Bruxelles: Annales *01287*
Société Royale d'Archéologie de Bruxelles: Bulletin *01287*
Société Royale de Chimie: Bulletin *01288*
Société Royale des Sciences de Liège: Bulletin *01295*
Société Suisse des Américanistes: Bulletin *10513*
Société Zoologique de France: Bulletin *04249*
Société Zoologique de France: Mémoires *04249*
Society for Academic Emergency Medicine: Directory *16346*
Society for American Archaeology: Bulletin *16349*
Society for Applied Bacteriology: Symposium Series *12348*
Society for Applied Spectroscopy: Newsletter *16353*
The Society for Army Historical Research: Journal *12349*
The Society for Asian Art Newsletter *16356*
Society for Calligraphy: Newsletter *16361*
Society for College and University Planning: Membership Roster *16367*
Society for College and University Planning: News *16367*
Society for Computer Simulation International: Transactions *16369*
Society for Cooperation in Russian and Soviet Studies: Newsletter *12352*
Society for Coptic Archaeology: Bulletin *03304*
Society for Environmental Therapy: Newsletter *12356*
Society for Epidemiologic Research: Abstracts *16379*
Society for Epidemiologic Research: Newsletter *16379*
Society for Ethnomusicology: Newsletter *16380*
The Society for Experimental Biology: Seminar Series *12357*
The Society for Experimental Biology: Symposia *12357*
Society for General Microbiology Quarterly *12359*
Society for German-American Studies: Newsletter *16387*
Society for German-American Studies: Yearbook *16387*
Society for Historians of American Foreign Relations: Newsletter *16389*
Society for Historians of American Foreign Relations: Roster and Research List *16389*
Society for Historical Archaeology: Newsletter *16390*
Society for Humanistic Judaism: Newsletter *16394*
Society for Industrial and Applied Mathematics: News *16396*
Society for Industrial Archaeology: Bibliography *16397*
Society for Industrial Archaeology: Journal *16397*
Society for Industrial Archaeology: Newsletter *16397*
Society for Information Display: Proceedings *16399*
Society for Information Display: Quarterly Proceedings *16399*
Society for Information Management: Member Forum *16400*
Society for Information Management: Proceedings *16400*
Society for International Development: Compass *07655*
Society for Invertebrate Pathology: Abstracts of Symposia *16402*
Society for Invertebrate Pathology: Newsletter *16402*
Society for Italian Historical Studies: Membership List *16405*
Society for Italian Historical Studies: Newsletter *16405*
Society for Latin American Anthropology: Proceedings *16406*
Society for Leukocyte Biology: Directory and Constitution *16407*
Society for Neuroscience: Directory *16415*
Society for Obstetric Anesthesia and Perinatology: Newsletter *16418*
Society for Occlusal Studies: Newsletter *16419*
Society for Occlusal Studies: Roster *16419*
Society for Occupational and Environmental Health: Letter *16420*
Society for Pediatric Dermatology: Newsletter *16421*
Society for Pediatric Radiology: Membership Directory *16424*
Society for Phenomenology and Existential Philosophy: Newsletter *16428*
Society for Photographic Education: Membership Directory *16431*
Society for Photographic Education: Newsletter *16431*
Society for Popular Astronomy: Circular Newsletter *12370*
Society for Post-Medieval Archaeology: Journal *12371*
Society for Post-Medieval Archaeology: Newsheet *12371*
Society for Psychical Research: Proceedings *12374*
Society for Research in Child Development: Monographs *16438*
Society for Research into Higher Education: Abstracts *12379*
Society for Research into Higher Education: International Newsletter *12379*
Society for Research into Higher Education: Proceedings *12379*
Society for Risk Analysis International: Newsletter *16439*
Society for Slovene Studies: Letter *16441*
Society for Spanish and Portuguese Historical Studies Bulletin *16443*
Society for Spanish and Portuguese Historical Studies: Membership Directory *16443*
Society for The History of Natural History: Special Publications *12386*
Society for the History of the Germans in Maryland: The Report: A Journal of German American History *16459*
Society for the Investigation of Recurring Events: Abstract *16461*
Society for the Preservation of New England Antiquities: House Guide *16465*
Society for the Preservation of New England Antiquities: Newsletter *16465*
Society for the Protection of Old Fishes: Membership List *16467*
Society for the Protection of Old Fishes: Newsletter *16467*
Society for the Psychological Study of Social Issues: Newsletter *16468*
Society for the Study of Architecture in Canada: Nouvelle: News *02383*
Society for the Study of Evolution: Membership Directory *16474*
Society for the Study of Human Biology: Symposia volumes *12396*
Society for the Study of Southern Literature: News-Letter *16480*
Society for the Study of Symbolic Interaction: Journal *16481*
Society for the Study of Symbolic Interaction: Newsletter *16481*
Society for Theriogenology: Newsletter *16483*
Society for Theriogenology: Proceedings of Annual Meeting *16483*
Society for Visual Anthropology: Newsletter *16487*
Society for Women in Philosophy – Pacific Division: Newsletter *16488*
Society of Actuaries: The Record *16489*
Society of Actuaries: Transactions *16489*
Society of Allied Weight Engineers: Newsletter *16491*
Society of American Archivists: Membership Directory *16492*
Society of Antiquaries of Scotland: Monographs *12406*
Society of Antiquaries of Scotland: Proceedings *12406*
Society of Architectural Historians of Great Britain: Newsletter *12408*
Society of Architectural Historians: Newsletter *16498*
Society of Architectural Illustrators: Newsletter *12409*
Society of Architectural Illustrators: Yearbook *12409*
Society of Archivists: Journal *12410*
Society of Archivists: Newsletter *12410*
Society of Biological Chemists, India: Proceedings: Abstract of Papers Presented at the Annual Meeting *06530*
Society of Cosmetic Chemists: Journal *16510*
Society of Cosmetic Chemists: Newsletter *16510*
Society of Cost Estimating and Analysis: Newsletter *16511*
Society of County Librarians: Information *12420*
Society of Designer Craftsmen: News-Sheet *12423*
Society of Diagnostic Medical Sonographers: Newsletter *16513*
The Society of Dyers and Colourists: Journal *12424*
Society of Economic Geologists: Membership List *16514*
Society of Ethnic and Special Studies: Journal *16516*
Society of Experimental Psychologists: Annual Report *16518*
Society of Exploration Geophysicists: Roster *16520*
Society of Fellows Journal *11278*
Society of Flight Test Engineers: Membership Directory *16524*
Society of Gastroenterology Nurses and Associates: Journal *16526*
Society of Independent Professional Earth Scientists: Newsletter *16530*
Society of Insurance Research: Research Review *16531*
Society of Logistics Engineers: Annals *16533*
Society of Logistics Engineers: Member's Handbook and Membership Directory *16533*
Society of Logistics Engineers: Spectrum *16533*
Society of Malawi: Journal *08212*
Society of Medical Consultants to the Armed Forces: Newsletter *16535*
Society of Medical Consultants to the Armed Forces: Roster *16535*
Society of Medical Jurisprudence: Proceedings *16536*
Society of Motion Picture and Television Engineers: Directory *16538*
Society of Motion Picture and Television Engineers: Journal *16538*
Society of Motion Picture and Television Engineers: News and Notes *16538*
Society of Naval Architects and Marine Engineers: Transactions *16540*
Society of Nematologists: Annual Meeting Presentations Abstracts *16541*
Society of Neurosurgical Anesthesia and Critical Care: Newsletter *16543*
Society of Obstetricians and Gynaecologists of Canada: Bulletin *02389*
Society of Professional Archaeologists: Newsletter *16549*
Society of Professional Well Log Analysts: Annual Transactions *16550*
Society of Professors of Education: Membership Directory *16552*
Society of Professors of Education: Monograph Series *16552*
Society of Prospective Medicine: Membership Directory *16553*
Society of Remedial Gymnasts and Recreational Therapies: Journal *12442*
Society of Research Administrators: Journal *16555*
Society of Research Administrators: Membership Directory *16555*
Society of Research Administrators: Newsletter *16555*
Society of Scribes and Illuminators: Journal *12443*
Society of State Directors of Health, Physical Education and Recreation: Directory *16558*
Society of State Directors of Health, Physical Education and Recreation: Newsletter *16558*
Society of Teachers in Education of Professional Photography: Journal *16561*
Society of Teachers in Education of Professional Photography: Membership Directory *16561*
Society of Toxicology: Newsletter *16564*
Society of USAF Flight Surgeons Newsletter *16566*
Society of Vertebrate Paleontology: News Bulletin *16568*
Society of Wildlife Artists: Annual Catalogue *12448*
Society of Women Artists: Annual Catalogue *12449*
Society of Wood Science and Technology: Newsletter *16570*
Socijalističko Zemjodelstvo: Socialist Agriculture *08204*
Sociolinguistique: systèmes de langues et interaction sociales et culturelles *04072*
Sociológia *09549*
Sociological Analysis *13688*
Sociological Theory *13499*
Sociology *17009*
Sociology of Education *13499*
Sociology of Law *07902*
Sociology, Work, Employment and Society *11201*
Socionomen *09855*
Sodobna pedagogika *09602*
Soemmering-Forschungen *04378*
Software Engineering Journal *11066*
Soil News *08728, 09647*
Soil Science Society of America Journal *14272*
Soil Use and Management *11200*
Soils and Fertilizers *11231, 11236*
Soils and Foundations *07724*
SOJOURN: Social Issues in Southeast Asia *09535*
Sojuz na Inženeri i Tehničari po Sumarstvo i Industrija za Prerabotka na Drvo na Makedonija: Sumarski Pregled: Forester's Review *08202*
SOK-medelingen *08532*
Solar Bulletin *12947*
Solar Energy *07329*
Solar Energy Engineering *13471*
Solar Progress *00161*
Solar Today *13501*
Soldiers of The Queen *12552*
Soldiers Small Book *12552*
Soletter *16533*
Solos e Rochas *01398*
Someni: Tanzania Library Association Journal *10607*
Sondagem Conjuntural *01468*
Sønderjysk Maanedsskrift *03128*
Sønderjyske Aarbøger *03128*
Sonderschriften des Frobenius-Instituts *05303*
Sonnblick-Verein: Jahresbericht *00796*
Sonnenberg Internationale Briefe, International Journal, Revue Internationale: Rivista Trilingue (Tedesco, Inglese, Francese) *07083*
Sonnenberg-News *05588*
Sonnenenergie *04857*
Soobshcheniya Byurakanskoi Observatorii: Report of the Byurakan Astrophysical Observatory *00113*
SOPHE News and Views *16435*
Sosialøkonomen *08882*
Sot la Nape *07428*
Sotsiologicheskie Issledovaniya: Sociological Research *09442*
Souffle de Perse *03861*
Soundings *16386*
Soundings: An Interdisciplinary Journal *16484*
Soundpost *06651*
South Africa Arts Calendar *09669*
South African Academy of Science and Arts: Jaarverslag *09665*
South African Archaeological Society: Monograph Series *09666*
The South African Association of Physicists in Medicine and Biology: Congress Brochure *09671*
The South African Banker *09635*
South African Biological Society: Journal *09672*
South African Ceramic Society: Conference Proceedings *09673*
South African Geographical Journal *09663*
South African Institute for Librarianship and Information Science: Newsletter *09680*
South African Institute of Assayers and Analysts: Bulletin *09683*
The South African Institute of International Affairs: Bibliographical Series *09684*
The South African Institute of International Affairs: Special Studies *09684*
South African Journal for Librarianship and Information Science *09680*
The South African Journal of Communication Disorders *09707*
The South African Journal of Economics *09624*
South African Journal of Geology *09631*
South African Journal of International Affairs *09684*
South African Journal of Photogrammetry, Remote Sensing and Cartography *09703*
The South African Journal of Physiotherpy: Die Soid-Afrikaanse Tydskrif Fisioterapie *09706*
South African Journal of Psychology *09654*
South African Journal of Surgery *09610*
South African Journal of Zoology *09722*
South African Landscape Series *09663*
South African Market Research Association: Report *09691*
South African Medical Journal *09638, 09646*
The South African Medical Research Council: Documentum *09693*
The South African Numismatic Society: Bulletin *09698*
South African Optometrist *09699*
South African PEN Centre: Newsletter *09701*
South African Statistical Journal *09708*
South American Explorer *16580*
South and West Asian Geoscience Newsletter *10634*
The South Australian Naturalist *00278*
South Australian Ornithological Association: Newsletter *00365*
The South Australian Ornithologist *00365*
South Wales Institute of Engineers: Proceedings *12460*
Southeast Asian Affairs *09535*
Southerly *00271*
Southern Africa Literature List *12702*
Southern African Forestry Journal *09712*
Southern African Society of Aquatic Scientists: Journal *09714*
Southern Arts Board: Newsletter *12461*
Southern Association of Colleges and Schools: Membership List *16582*
Southern Association of Colleges and Schools: Newsletter *16582*
Southern Association of Colleges and Schools: Proceedings *16582*
The Southern Baptist Educator *13834*
Southern Changes *16586*
Southern Humanities Review *16585*
Southern Journal of Applied Forestry *16493*
Southern Society of Genealogists: Bulletin *16587*
Southern Society of Genealogists: Directory *16587*
Southern Speech Communication Journal *16588*
Southern Stars *08741*
Sovetskaya Tyurkologiya: Soviet Turkology *00439*
Soyabean Abstracts *11231*
Soybean Rust Newsletter *02671*
Sozial- und Präventivmedizin *04859*
Sozial- und Präventivmedizin: Médecine Sociale et Préventive *10328*
Sozialarbeit *10437*
Sozialarbeit & Suchtprobleme *10022*
Der Sozialarbeiter *04998*
Soziale Arbeit: Deutsche Zeitschrift für soziale und sozialverwandte Gebiete *05108*
Soziale Psychiatrie *04858*
Soziale Welt: Zeitschrift für sozialwissenschaftliche Forschung und Praxis *04474*
Sozialmedizinische Schriftenreihe *00745*
Das sozialpolitische Forum *10415*
Sozialwissenschaften und Berufspraxis *04569*
Soziologie *04861*
S.P.A.B. News *12392*
Space Age Times: The Internntional Publication of Space News, Benefits and Education *16700*
Space Explorer *10837*
Space Studies Institute: Update *16592*
Space World *15979*
Spaceflight *11111*
Spacereport *10837*
Spanische Forschungen *05439*
SPE Drilling Engineering *16546*
SPE Formation Evaluation *16546*
SPE Production Engineering *16546*
SPE Reservoir Engineering *16546*
SPEC Kit *16077*
Special Care in Dentistry *12894, 13118*
Special Interest Group for Computer Personnel Research: Newsletter *16593*
Special Interest Group for Symbolic and Algebraic Manipulation: Bulletin *16595*
Special Interest Group for Symbolic and Algebraic Manipulation: Proceedings of Symposia *16595*
Special Interest Group on Biomedical Computing: Newsletter *16597*
Special Libraries *16599*
SpeciaList *16599*
Specializzazione *06832*
Spectra *15605, 16601*
Spectrum Proceedings *14522*
Speculum: A Journal of Medieval Studies *15550*
Speech Communication *10096*
Spektrum der Augenheilkunde *00724*
Spell/Binder *16464*
Spina Bifida and Hydrocephalus Association of Ontario: Current: Pamphlet *02393*
Spinal Manipulation *14460*
Spohr Journal *12463*
Spoken English *11455*
Spoletium *06880*
The Sporadical *16429*
Sport Aerobatics *14405*
Sport Aviation *14405*
Sportärzteverband Hessen – aktuell *05952*
Sportärztliche Mitteilungen *04541*
Sporterziehung in der Schule *10475*
Sports Medicine Bulletin *13076*
Sportsoziologie: Informationsschrift des Österreichischen Arbeitskreises für Soziologie des Sports und der Leibeserziehung *00748*
Spotlight *12339*
Spotlight on Children *10853*
Der Sprachdienst *05356*
Die Sprache: Zeitschrift für Sprachwissenschaft *00878*
Sprache im Technischen Zeitalter *05728*
Die Sprachheilarbeit *04863*
Der Sprachheilpädagoge *00684*
Sprachkunst: Beiträge zur Literaturwissenschaft *00573*
Sprachspiegel *10076*
Språklig Samling *08798*
Správy Slovenskej Parazitologickej Spoločnosti *09570*
Sprawozdania TNT *09160*
Sprawozdania z Czynności i Posiedzeń Naukowych /various/ *09077*
Sprawozdanie roczne, Notatki Płockie: Yearbook *09159*
Sprechstunde: Das Magazin der Ärzte für Ihre Gesundheit *10532*
Spring Newsletter *12158*
SPSM Newsletter *16462*
SRF-Information *10011*
SRHE News *12379*